FEDERAL RULES OF CIVIL PROCEDURE

Amendments received through May 1, 2020

2020–2021 Educational Edition

A. BENJAMIN SPENCER
Dean & Chancellor Professor of Law
William & Mary Law School

WEST ACADEMIC PUBLISHING

© 2014 Thomson Reuters; and LEG, Inc. d/b/a West Academic
© 2015–2019 LEG, Inc. d/b/a West Academic
© 2020 LEG, Inc. d/b/a West Academic
    444 Cedar Street, Suite 700
    St. Paul, MN 55101
    1-877-888-1330

Printed in the United States of America

ISBN: 978-1-68467-990-4

TABLE OF CONTENTS

APPENDICES

HISTORICAL INTRODUCTION

The Revolution and the Constitutional Role
of the Supreme Court of the United States

The 13 American states that won their independence in 1783 attempted to conduct foreign relations jointly through the Continental Congress, an organization that had successfully conducted the Revolution. By 1787, the ineffectiveness of this organization was apparent. Many of the deficiencies pertained to the judicial institutions of the time. Western boundaries were disputed. The states were engaged in commercial competition, creating stress among them; merchants from other states were often victims of discrimination by local courts and local law. Merchants, especially those from foreign lands, such as England, were often unable to collect debts. This was an especially serious problem, because the treaty of peace with the United Kingdom guaranteed the payment of debts by American debtors, a guarantee that the Continental Congress was impotent to perform. There was some possibility that His Majesty's Royal Navy would return to collect the debts if American courts did not.

There were other problems, the greatest being fears of larger landowners and merchants in many states that the small republics were unstable. The Revolution had been fought for the declared purpose of establishing the sovereignty of the people. Henceforth, said the Declaration of Independence, power would come up from the people, and not down from their rulers. But faith in this idea was not widely shared among persons of property, influence, and status. Their fear was that what they perceived as the ignorance, greed, and mutual distrust of "the people" would soon cause the states to disintegrate into chaos, followed by despotism.

So, in 1787, 11 of the 13 states sent representatives to a meeting in Philadelphia to organize a new national government. The meeting was contentious, but the proposed Constitution was its product. Among the issues debated at the Constitutional Convention was whether the new government should take over the judicial function. It was early agreed that there should be a Supreme Court of the United States that would have responsibility for assuring compliance with the Constitution. An important feature of that Constitution was the division of political power; the purpose of those divisions was to prevent government "by the people" from getting out of control. "The people" were pitted against one another to assure balance. Thus, limited political powers were conferred on the national government, and the rest retained by the several states. And power within the national government was divided between two independent legislative bodies and an independent executive, each selected by a different process. A Supreme Court was clearly needed to maintain these limits of power. In this feature lay the most distinctive feature of American government, the use of law and courts to limit the powers of the other political organs.

Concurrent Jurisdiction: The Establishment of the Lower Federal Courts

Should there be lower federal courts? Some argued that the national government should take over the judicial function altogether. Others argued that the state judicial systems then in place should be retained as the lower courts to resolve private disputes between citizens. It was first decided by the Convention that there should be no lower federal courts, but then a compromise was reached, leaving to the Congress the decision whether there should be lower federal courts, yet limiting the power of Congress to confer jurisdiction on any courts that it might create. The Constitutional text as ratified by the people of the 13 states is set forth in Article III. *See Appendix B: United States Constitution, this volume.*

Ratification of the Constitution containing Article III was strongly contested in all states. One of the damaging arguments against ratification was that the power of Congress to create federal courts was a menace to the sovereignty of the people. Dire threats were heard; the federal judges would become the tool of the gentry and of the merchant class and would deny protection to the people of the farm, especially poor debtors.

HISTORICAL INTRODUCTION

To secure ratification, it was necessary for those favoring the Constitution to agree to ten amendments. These came to be known as the Bill of Rights. The Fifth, Sixth, and Seventh Amendments are directed primarily at Article III and served to quiet fears of the federal judiciary. The texts of these three amendments are set forth in *Appendix B* of this volume.

Among the first acts of the first Congress of the United States was the exercise in the Judiciary Act of 1789 of the power conferred by Article III to establish lower federal courts. The purpose at that time was to protect aliens (especially English creditors) and merchants engaged in interstate commerce; its major jurisdictional provision remains, with slight modification, as part of the statutory law governing the federal courts. *See Section 1332(a), Title 28, United States Code, Judiciary and Judicial Procedure (Selected Provisions), this volume.*

As Article III contemplates, each state in the federal union maintains its own system of courts. These courts, unlike the federal courts, are not all courts of *limited* jurisdiction, but may be courts of *general* jurisdiction. That is, they may entertain any action of any kind that is not specifically directed by legislation to a specialized court. These courts therefore often exercise jurisdiction that is *concurrent* with the jurisdiction of the federal courts. That is to say that many actions could be brought in either a state or a federal court. A common tactical decision faced by American lawyers is whether to bring an action in a federal or a state court, or whether to remove to a federal court an action previously brought by an adversary in state court.

The Independence of the Federal and State Judiciaries

A serious problem faced in the text of the Constitution was the identity of the judges. English judges were selected from an elite social class that did not exist in most of America. Nor was there in America any tradition of a separate judicial profession of the kind that has since developed in Germany, Japan, and other countries. It was therefore clear that the federal judges appointed under Article III would be chosen from among the practicing lawyers, or perhaps occasionally from the judges of the courts of the several states. They would necessarily be persons qualified by standards more political then technocratic.

In requiring that the selection of judges be made by the President with the "advice and consent" of the Senate, the Constitution recognized that the federal judicial appointments would be politically divisive. The drafters of the Constitution knew that by subjecting political power to legal constraints they were necessarily politicizing the legal institutions that would impose those restraints. The American judiciary would in this respect be unlike any then known to the draftsmen of the Constitution.

Unsurprisingly, the first national political crisis centered on the federal judiciary. In 1800, Thomas Jefferson was elected President. Before he took office, his predecessor, President John Adams, and the outgoing Federalist Congress, created additional federal judgeships and President Adams appointed many judges who were hostile to Jefferson's political program. Jefferson seriously considered an effort to remove the opposition judges by impeachment, and one Supreme Court Justice, Samuel Chase, was impeached. Jefferson, there is no doubt, would have liked to have removed as soon as possible the Chief Justice appointed by President Adams, who was Jefferson's cousin, John Marshall. The Chase removal failed in the Senate of the United States and the Marshall removal was never attempted. Federal judges have since been removed only in rare instances of corruption. There is thus important meaning in the term of Article III providing that judges shall be appointed "for good behavior;" federal judicial appointments are nearly always lifetime appointments.

Especially when there is a political difference between the President and Congress, as there may often be, judicial appointments are contested. In 1988, Congress controlled by the Democratic Party refused after a bitter contest to confirm the nomination by Republican President Ronald Reagan of Robert Bork to the Supreme Court. Nevertheless, because of the important role of the federal courts, the persons appointed as federal judges, have generally been persons of substantial professional merit who not only enjoyed some political influence in the party of the President, but who also commanded some and often much respect among lawyers where they practiced. It is rare for a person less than 40 years of age to be appointed to a federal judgeship, and many are appointed who are near the age of 60.

From the beginning, the federal courts were aware of their somewhat precarious political position. They were careful to avoid unnecessary exposure to political controversy. This was reflected in two ways. First, the phrase "case or controversy" in Article III was recognized to mean that the federal courts should perform no role other than adjudication defined rather narrowly. Second, the federal courts were scrupulous in refusing to decide any case not within the limits of their jurisdiction as defined by Congress pursuant to Article III.

State courts often play a political role in state government analogous to the role played by the federal courts in the federal constitutional scheme. Although the Supreme Court of the United States retains constitutional authority to review the actions of state courts to assure their compliance with national law, state courts are otherwise independent of any federal control or influence. No officer of the government of the United States has any influence whatever in the selection of the judges of the state courts.

Many states provide for the popular, direct election of judges for fixed terms. Many of these states employ diverse means of protecting judicial elections from some of the adverse consequences of such elective judicial politics, to assure some degree of independence of their judges from the control of those who provide campaign funds or otherwise influence the electorate. Thus, in some states, judges are assured of an opportunity to run for reelection without a named opponent, the voters choosing only to retain the judge or not. In some states, the Governor has the power of initial appointment, but is required to secure the assent of a non-political commission that is expected to appraise the "merit" of judicial candidates. Despite such efforts to moderate the influence of elective politics on the judiciary, state court judges are, even more than the federal judges, generally qualified by standards that are more political than technocratic.

The Effect of Nationalization on the Dual Court System

For many years, the federal courts generally conformed their procedure to that of local state courts. That is, a federal court sitting in Virginia conformed its procedure to that of state courts of the Commonwealth of Virginia. This allowed Virginia lawyers to move comfortably from state to federal court and back. This arrangement reflected the structure of state legal profession in America, which was highly localized, each state having its own distinctive bar.

Much of the state civil procedure was initially derived from English tradition, with modifications. Many states retained the English distinction between Law and Equity; Law was the body of doctrine enforced in England by the Law Courts (*e.g.*, Court of Common Pleas or the King's Bench), while Equity was the body of doctrine enforced in England by the Chancellor sitting in Chancery. Many states also retained the English common law forms of action; all this usually meant as a practical matter was that in an action "at Law," a plaintiff was required to correctly identify the legal theory underlying his claim at the very outset of the litigation.

Much of this anachronistic procedure was swept away by the movement for procedural law reform that first surfaced in New York in 1848. The Codes of Civil Procedure enacted in most states at that time provided for state abolition of almost all traces of English law, merging Law and Equity into a single system and abolishing the forms of action.

The American Civil War was fought from 1861 to 1865. That war had many consequences, but at least two bore directly on the judiciary. First, as a conclusion of the War, the Constitution was subjected to three additional amendments. One of these, the Fourteenth, extended the Due Process Clause, making it applicable to actions of state courts and governments as well as federal. Thereafter, the civil procedure of state courts was subject to basic minimum standards of fairness established by the Supreme Court of the United States. To a minimum degree, state procedure was federalized. Secondly, the Congress of the United States was thereafter in a position to enact legislation regulating the national economy. As part of that activity, the Congress enlarged the civil jurisdiction of the federal courts in an important way; in 1875, it enacted the provision that presently appears as Section 1331 of Title 28. See *Title 28, United States Code, Judiciary and Judicial Procedure (Selected Provisions), this volume.*

This provision further enlarged the political role of the federal courts. In part, this has been a result of the Constitutional scheme to divide the political power within the government of the United States. Because it is so divided, legislative power is often exercised in a manner that expresses unclear mandates. The two houses of Congress and the President are sometimes able to agree to little more than that there is a social or economic problem requiring a federal solution; they may then leave the details of that solution to the federal courts. The antitrust laws of the United States are an excellent example of law that is left almost wholly to the federal courts to define, with almost no guidance from Congress. Other examples abound.

As a result of the growth of the federal courts' role in the national economy, the federal judiciary has been steadily enlarged. In 1891, the United States Courts of Appeals were established as intermediate courts of appeals to review decisions of the district courts. Since 1891, access to the Supreme Court has by stages been limited to cases that it chooses to review.

The federal courts played a significant role in the development of state law regulating the national economy. On a number of occasions that role was politically controversial. In the continuing struggle between railroads and shippers, who were usually small farmers, the federal courts were generally enforcing the rights of the railroads. In enforcing the law of patents against farmers making use of such ideas as barbed wire and windmills, the federal courts were again seen as a forum in which farmers were at a disadvantage.

The federal courts also became the place for railroads to go to secure favorable results on accident claims by workers, and where employers sometimes went to secure injunctions against strikes. Most of the practices that were seen as anti-labor were in due course constrained by Congressional legislation, as the labor unions acquired political power.

Lawyers practicing federal law became troubled by the differences in procedure in the different federal courts, each conforming generally to the practice of its local state court. The American Bar Association, established in 1879, led a campaign for national uniformity. In 1934, Congress authorized the Supreme Court of the United States to promulgate rules of "pleading and practice" that would be uniform among all the district courts of the United States. That authority is now set forth in §§ 2071–2077. *See Title 28, United States Code, Judiciary and Judicial Procedure (Selected Sections)*, this volume.

Such rules were promulgated in 1938 as the Federal Rules of Civil Procedure. The most notable of these rules were those bearing on discovery; private lawyers representing litigants are authorized to use the power of the court to compel adversaries and non-parties to cooperate in their efforts to secure evidence bearing on a case. Other rules have since been adopted by the Court. Since 1938, a large number of states have modified their civil procedure to conform generally to the federal practice, but significant differences remain in many.

PAUL D. CARRINGTON

AN OUTLINE OF THE PROCEDURE
IN A CIVIL ACTION

[Reprinted, with permission, from West Academic, from Friedenthal, Miller, Sexton and Hershkoff, CIVIL PROCEDURE, 12th ed., Ch. 1.B.]

Lawsuits do not begin by themselves. Someone must first decide to sue someone else. If this decision is made intelligently, the person choosing to sue must have weighed several matters, among which at least three are basic. These three considerations are, first, whether legal relief is available; second, what the probability of winning a lawsuit is; and third, whether what would be won is worth the burden of litigating.

A potential litigant obviously feels aggrieved or would not be thinking of a lawsuit, but before litigating must first consider whether the grievance is one for which the law furnishes relief. There are a great many hurts a person may feel that the law will not redress. A home owner is offended by the paint on a neighbor's house; a manufacturer has worked for weeks to persuade a distributor to buy a brand of software and sees the sale go to a competitor; a property owner has been holding a plot of ground for speculation, expecting industry to move in, and the area is zoned for residential use; a visitor slips on a spot of grease in the county courthouse but the county is immune from suit. A potential litigant often must consult an attorney before deciding whether there is a case to be litigated.

Even if she concludes that the grievance is one for which the courts will grant relief, a potential litigant secondly must consider the probability of winning a lawsuit. The answer turns on a number of factors: whether the person who has caused the injury can be found and brought into court; whether witnesses and documents will be available to support the claims being sued on; whether this proof will be believed; whether the potential adversary can justify its conduct or establish any defenses to the action; and whether an accurate assessment of the law can be made ahead of time.

Thirdly, and perhaps most importantly of all, a potential litigant must consider whether what is won will be worth the time, the effort, and the expense that litigating it will cost. Most significantly, this includes the payment of fees to an attorney who provides representation in the case. In the United States, each litigating party typically bears the full costs of these attorney's fees—this is called the American Rule. These fees are calculated in several ways: by time (at an hourly rate); fixed (the attorney sets the fee prior to providing the services); task-based (the attorney charges a fee based on the nature of the tasks provided to the client); or on contingency (the attorney is paid a portion of the ultimate judgment awarding money damages or settlement). By contrast, the more widely accepted "English Rule" requires the losing party to pay the attorney's fees of the prevailing party. Congress has enacted "fee-shifting" statutes that require the losing party to pay the attorney's fees of the prevailing party in certain kinds of cases, such as antitrust and civil rights, and many states have enacted similar provisions. The purpose of these statutes is to create incentives for individuals to initiate lawsuits in a role described as that of "private attorneys general." See Maxeiner, *Cost and Fee Allocation in Civil Procedure*, 58 Am. J. Comp. L. 195, 201 (2010). A prospective litigant must weigh the costs of a lawsuit against other possibilities, among them settlement, arbitration, self-help, and letting matters rest.

Further, attention must be given to the form that the relief will take. Most frequently it will be restricted to a judgment for damages. The potential litigant thus needs to consider whether the injury is one for which a monetary payment will be satisfactory. Assuming it is, will defendant be rich enough to pay? How difficult will a judgment be to collect? How expensive? Will the recovery be enough to pay the lawyer's fees and the other litigation expenses that undoubtedly will be incurred? Even in a context in which the court may grant specific relief—for example, an order directing the opposing party to do something or to stop doing something—will compliance by defendant be possible? Worthwhile? Sufficient? In the same vein, a potential litigant must consider whether there are risks not directly tied to the suit. Will filing a lawsuit antagonize people whose goodwill plaintiff needs? Will the action publicize an error of judgment on plaintiff's part or open private affairs to public gaze?

Only after considerable thought about the utility and expense of litigation will the prospective plaintiff be ready for the steps that must be taken to bring a lawsuit. Let us now consider these steps in the light of a relatively uncluttered hypothetical case:

Aikin, while crossing the street in front of her private home, was struck and seriously injured by an automobile driven by Beasley. On inquiry, Aikin found that the automobile was owned by Cecil and that Beasley apparently had been in Cecil's employ. Beasley was predictably without substantial assets and a judgment against him for Aikin's injuries promised little material compensation. But Cecil was wealthy, and Aikin was advised that if she could establish that Beasley had indeed been working for Cecil and had been negligent, she then could recover from Cecil. Aikin decided to sue Cecil for $500,000.

1. SELECTING A PROPER COURT

Aikin initially must determine in which court to bring the action. She might have some choice between filing her lawsuit in a state or a federal court, but her choice is not open-ended. This is because the court selected must have *jurisdiction over the subject matter* (that is, the constitution and statutes under which the court operates must have conferred upon it power to decide this type of case) and also must have *jurisdiction over the person* of Cecil (that is, Cecil must be subject or amenable to suit in the state in which the court is located so that a judgment may be entered against him).

Aikin probably will bring suit in a state court, for the subject-matter jurisdiction of the federal courts is severely limited. If the court organization of Aikin's state is typical, there will be courts of original jurisdiction in which cases are brought and tried, and one court of appellate jurisdiction that sits, with rare exceptions, only to review the decisions of lower courts. (In most states there also will be a group of intermediate courts of appellate jurisdiction.) The courts of original jurisdiction probably consist of one set of courts of general jurisdiction and several sets of courts of inferior jurisdiction. "General" in this sense refers to a court's power to decide any type of dispute that comes before it, as distinguished from jurisdiction that is limited to specific kinds of disputes.

Typically, a state's courts of general jurisdiction are organized into geographic districts comprising for the most part several counties, although the largest or most populous counties each may constitute single districts. These district courts hear cases of many kinds and are competent to grant every kind of relief, but usually are authorized to hear claims for which the relief requested exceeds a statutorily fixed dollar amount. The courts of inferior jurisdiction include municipal courts, which have jurisdiction resembling that of the district courts except that the claims are of smaller financial significance; justice-of-the-peace courts, which hear very minor matters; and specialized tribunals such as traffic courts. Since Aikin's injuries are quite serious and her claim is correspondingly large, she will, if she sues in a state court, bring the action in one of the district courts.

The federal government also operates a system of courts. The principal federal courts are the United States District Courts, courts of original jurisdiction of which there is at least one in every state; the United States Courts of Appeals, each of which reviews the decisions of federal District Courts in the several states within its circuit (with the exception of the Courts of Appeals for the District of Columbia Circuit and the Federal Circuit); and the Supreme Court of the United States, which has discretionary authority to review the decisions of federal courts and decisions of state courts that involve an issue of federal law.

The jurisdiction over the subject matter of the United States District Courts extends to many, but by no means all, cases involving federal law, and also to many cases, similar to Aikin's, that do not involve federal law; the latter are cases in which there is *diversity of citizenship* (the parties are citizens of different states or one of them is a citizen of a foreign country) and the required *amount in controversy* (currently more than $75,000) is at stake. Diversity jurisdiction, in common with jurisdiction to hear cases arising under federal law, is not exclusive to the courts of the federal system. Rather, the state courts also are competent to hear these cases and have concurrent jurisdiction with the United States District Courts, unless Congress has made jurisdiction exclusive to the federal courts. If Cecil is not a citizen of Aikin's state, Aikin may bring an action for $500,000 in a federal court even though it asserts only state law claims. Indeed, in these circumstances, if Aikin sued Cecil in a state court in Aikin's home state, Cecil could "remove" the action from the state court in which it was commenced to the federal District Court in that state.*

It is not enough for the court selected by Aikin to have jurisdiction over the subject matter. That court, whether state or federal, also must be one in which Cecil can be required to appear so that it is appropriate for the legal system to enter a judgment against him. Traditionally, a court could enter a judgment only against a defendant who resided in the state or was physically in the state, even if temporarily. However, constitutional restrictions on a court's jurisdiction over the person have diminished in recent decades. If Cecil is not present in Aikin's state but he directed Beasley to drive there, Aikin probably will be able to bring the action in that state because of Cecil's prior contact with the state and the benefits that those contacts have brought him, assuming that a statute authorizes the court to exercise personal jurisdiction in these circumstances.

Not every court that has jurisdiction over the subject matter and jurisdiction over the person of the defendant can hear the case. It also is necessary that an action be brought in a court having proper venue, which refers to where within the state or district the original proceeding is to be located. Thus, although every court in Aikin's state could assert personal jurisdiction over Cecil if he was within its boundaries, that state's statutes typically will provide that the case should be brought in a court in a district that includes the county in which either Aikin or Cecil lives. Similarly, if Aikin decides to sue in federal court based on diversity of citizenship, she must bring suit in a district that has venue as defined by federal statute (currently, the district in which Cecil resides, or in a district where a substantial part of the events giving rise to the claim occurred, or in a district where Cecil is subject to personal jurisdiction, if there is no district in which the action otherwise may be brought).

A defect in a court's jurisdiction over the subject matter cannot be waived by the parties. If Aikin and Cecil are both citizens of the same state, a federal court must refuse to hear the action even though both are anxious that it do so. By contrast, the court's jurisdiction over the person and venue essentially are protections for defendant, who may waive them if he wishes.

2. COMMENCING THE ACTION

Aikin must give Cecil notice of the commencement of the action by service of process. The process typically consists of a summons, which directs defendant to appear and defend under penalty of default; that is, unless defendant answers the summons, a judgment will be entered against that party. Service refers to the delivery of the process. Service of process generally is achieved by personal service, meaning, the summons is physically delivered to defendant or is left at defendant's home, sometimes by plaintiff or her attorney, sometimes by a public official such as a sheriff or a United States marshal. If Cecil lives in another state, but the circumstances are such that a court in Aikin's state may assert personal jurisdiction over Cecil, the summons may be personally delivered to him, or some form of substituted service, such as sending the papers by registered mail or delivering the summons to Cecil's agent within Aikin's state, may be employed. Even if Cecil cannot be located, service in yet another form, usually by publication in a newspaper for a certain length of time, may be allowed, although the validity of this kind of service in the type of case Aikin is bringing against Cecil is unlikely to be upheld. The Supreme Court repeatedly has emphasized that service must be of a kind reasonably calculated to bring the action to defendant's notice.

---

* If Cecil is not a citizen of Aikin's state but Beasley is, then one of the considerations Aikin will have in deciding to join Beasley as a defendant is the effect on the availability of subject-matter jurisdiction in the federal courts. If Aikin wants to be in the federal court, she should not join Beasley; if Aikin wants the lawsuit to begin and stay in a state court, she should join him. In the latter case, there will not be complete diversity of citizenship between plaintiff on the one side and defendants on the other.

3. PLEADING AND PARTIES

With the summons, Aikin usually will serve on Cecil the first of the pleadings, commonly called the complaint. This is a written statement that will contain Aikin's claim against Cecil. What should be required of such a statement? Obviously it may vary from a simple assertion that Cecil owes her $500,000, to a second-by-second narration of the accident, closely describing the scene and the conduct of each party, followed by a gruesome recital of Aikin's medical treatment and her prognosis for recovery. No procedural system insists upon either of these extremes, but systems do vary greatly in the detail required in the pleadings. The degree of detail required largely reflects the purposes that the pleadings are expected to serve. Three objectives are particularly relevant, and to the extent that a procedural system regards one rather than another as crucial, we may expect to find differing amounts of detail required.

First, the system may desire the pleadings to furnish a basis for identifying and separating the legal and factual contentions involved so that the legal issues—and hopefully through them the entire case—may be disposed of at an early stage. Thus, suppose that Cecil's liability for Beasley's driving depends upon the degree of independence with which Beasley was working at the time of the accident. A dispute on this issue might exist on either or both of two elements. The parties might disagree as to what Beasley's duties were, and they might disagree as to whether those duties put Beasley so much under the control of Cecil that the law will impose liability on Cecil for Beasley's actions. The first disagreement would be a question of fact, and there would be no alternative to trying the suit and letting the finder of fact (usually the jury) decide the truth. But if there was agreement on that first element, a question of law would be presented by the second issue, which could be determined by the judge without a trial. The objective of identifying the legal questions is served in such a case only if the pleadings set forth exactly what Beasley's job required him to do. It would be served very inadequately if the complaint stated only that "Beasley was driving the car on Cecil's business."

Second, the pleadings may be intended to establish in advance what a party proposes to prove at trial so that the opponent will know the factual contentions and prepare to meet them. If this objective is regarded as very important it will not be enough for the complaint to state that Beasley was negligent, or that Aikin suffered serious bodily injuries. It must be more specific and say that Beasley was speeding, or was not keeping a proper look-out, or had inadequate brakes, or describe some other act of negligence and say that Aikin suffered a concussion, or a broken neck, or fractures of three ribs, or other injuries.

Third, the pleadings may be intended to give each party only a general notice of the opponent's contentions, in which event the system would rely upon subsequent stages of the lawsuit to identify the legal and factual contentions of the parties and to enable each to prepare to meet the opponent's case. If notice is the goal, then in a suit involving a car accident, it would be sufficient for the pleading to state the date and place of the incident; to describe the incident generally (for example, "defendant negligently drove a car into plaintiff"); and, to allege injury and a demand for relief.

It seems that each of the first two objectives is desirable. It is a waste of everybody's time to try lawsuits when the underlying legal claim is inadequate to support a judgment, and it is only fair that a person called upon to defend a judicial proceeding should know what the defendant is alleged to have done. But to achieve the first objective fully may require pleading after pleading in order to expose and sharpen the issues; if detail is insisted upon, a long time may be consumed in producing it. Moreover, a single pleading oversight may eliminate a contention necessary to one party's case that easily could have been proven, but that will be held to have been waived. To achieve the second objective through the pleadings will mean that the parties must take rigid positions as to their factual contentions at the very beginning of the case when they may not know what they will learn by the time trial begins. It also assumes that plaintiff knows most if not all of the important facts pertinent to the claim at the time of filing the complaint, which is not always the case or even possible. Either the first or second objective, if fully pursued, requires that the parties adhere to the positions taken in the pleadings. They could not be permitted to introduce evidence in conflict with the pleadings or to change them. To the extent that variances between pleading and proof or amendments to the pleadings are permitted, the objectives will be lost. The court frequently will find itself forced either to depart from these objectives or to tolerate lawsuits turning on the skill of the lawyers rather than on the merits of the controversy.

The third objective, insofar as it allows the parties to use the later stages of the lawsuit to identify and flesh out the issues in the case, avoids the problems created by trying to decide the case based only on the pleadings. However, simple notice pleading potentially may be used to harass defendant when plaintiff has no real claim. More often, though, plaintiff will use notice pleading to subject defendant to pretrial discovery (discussed more fully below), and in the process to reveal information so that plaintiff can determine whether a bona fide claim actually exists. Lawyers often refer to such use of the pleadings as a "fishing expedition," or alternatively as a "springboard into litigation." However, if defendant controls access to the information that plaintiff needs to establish the claim, discovery may be essential for a meritorious complaint to be drafted and to avoid dismissal. One way that courts have dealt with these problems is to sanction parties and lawyers who bring baseless claims.

4. THE RESPONSE

Following the service of Aikin's complaint, Cecil must respond. He may challenge the complaint by a *motion to dismiss*. This motion may challenge the court's jurisdiction over the subject matter or Cecil's person, the service of process, or venue. It also may be a *motion to dismiss for failure to state a claim or cause of action* (the older term for this motion is a demurrer). For the purpose of this motion, the facts alleged in the complaint are accepted as true, and the court considers whether, on this assumption, plaintiff has shown that she is entitled to legal relief.

There are three general situations in which such a motion might be granted. First, the complaint may clearly show that the injury is one for which the law furnishes no redress (for example, when plaintiff simply alleges that "defendant has made faces at me"). Second, plaintiff may have failed to include an allegation necessary to a part of the case (for example, Aikin might have alleged the accident, her injuries, and Beasley's negligence, and have forgotten to allege that Beasley was Cecil's servant). Third, the complaint may be so general or confusing that the court finds that it does not give adequate notice of what plaintiff's claim is (for example, a complaint in which Aikin merely alleged, "Cecil injured me and owes me $500,000," although complaints far more specific have fallen on this ground). The extent to which motions to dismiss will be granted on the second and third grounds will vary with the degree of detail that the particular system requires of its pleadings. A court generally has power to allow the plaintiff an opportunity to amend the pleading to cure certain kinds of defects.

If the motion to dismiss is denied, or if none is made, Cecil must file an *answer*. In this pleading, he must admit or deny Aikin's factual allegations in the complaint. Moreover, if Cecil wishes to rely on certain legal contentions called *affirmative defenses*, he must plead them in the answer. Thus, if he wishes to contend that Aikin was negligent in the manner in which she tried to cross the street and that this negligence was also a cause of the accident, he must in many states plead this in the answer; if the answer only denied the allegations in Aikin's complaint, Cecil may not advance at trial the contention that Aikin's negligence caused the accident.

There may be further pleadings, particularly a *reply* by Aikin. But the tendency today is to close the pleadings after the answer, and if Cecil has raised new matters in his answer, they automatically are taken as denied by Aikin. There is one major exception: if Cecil has a claim against Aikin, particularly one that arises out of the same occurrence being sued upon by Aikin, Cecil may plead this claim as a *counterclaim* as part of the answer. This is in essence a complaint by Cecil, and Aikin will have to respond to it just as Cecil had to respond to the original complaint.

The original action between Aikin and Cecil may expand in terms of the number of parties, and this frequently will occur at the pleading stage. For example, although Aikin decided not to sue Beasley, Cecil might *implead* Beasley, asking that Beasley be held liable to him for whatever amount he may be found liable to Aikin, since his liability depends upon Beasley having been at fault. Cecil will decide whether to do this in light of a number of practical concerns, including the effect Beasley's presence will have on the jury in Aikin's suit against Cecil.

5. OBTAINING INFORMATION PRIOR TO TRIAL

Pretrial discovery is the procedure currently designed to allow the parties to exchange information about their claims and defenses and to prepare for trial. At earlier periods, the pleadings served this purpose.

Currently, the federal system requires the parties, without a court order or a request from the opponent, to exchange certain types of information. The parties also then may initiate requests for information from the opponent and, in some situations, from persons who are not parties to the litigation. The chief method is to take *depositions* of parties and witnesses. In this procedure, the person whose deposition is to be taken is questioned by lawyers for each side through direct and cross-examination; the *deponent's* statements are taken down and transcribed. The device is useful in finding information that is relevant to the case, including unearthing leads as to other witnesses or documents; it also is useful in laying a basis for impeaching a witness who attempts to change his or her story at trial. The two parties almost certainly will want depositions taken of each other, as well as of Beasley; the depositions of Aikin and Cecil will be particularly important because they are treated as admissions and can be used by their adversaries as evidence at trial. In some circumstances, even the deposition of a nonparty witness who will be unavailable at trial may be used in place of live testimony.

Another device especially adapted to probing the content of an opponent's case is the written *interrogatory*, which usually may be addressed only to a party to the suit. (The availability of interrogatories may be one reason Aikin might wish to join Beasley as a defendant with Cecil or Cecil might wish to implead Beasley.) These interrogatories are answered by the party, presumably with counsel's aid, and the answers will not be as spontaneous as they would be on a deposition; on the other hand, interrogatories will require Cecil to supply some information that he does not carry in his head but can obtain, and may be even more valuable than the deposition in finding out what he will try to prove. Thus, information regarding Beasley's employment that Cecil cannot be expected to remember may best be exposed in this way.

Other discovery devices include the *production of documents*, such as the service record of Cecil's automobile, and requests for admissions, which will remove uncontested issues from the case. A particularly useful device for Cecil will be a court order directing Aikin to submit to a *physical examination* by a physician of Cecil's choice to determine the real extent of Aikin's alleged injuries.

The availability of discovery enables the parties to prepare for trial better than the pleadings ever did. Moreover, if a legal system permits broad discovery, the role of the pleadings will change. In particular, it may be senseless to make parties take rigid positions with respect to the issues at the very beginning of the lawsuit before they have had the chance to utilize these very useful devices for obtaining information. In addition, the availability of discovery does much to make summary judgment, which is discussed below, a viable and fair procedure, since it enables a party to ascertain those issues on which the opposing party has no evidence, while giving the opponent a chance to develop such evidence. On the other hand, if the costs of discovery are excessive, a defendant may be motivated to settle a lawsuit that satisfies a weak pleading standard yet would lack sufficient proof to prevail at trial.

6. SUMMARY JUDGMENT

One of the basic difficulties with attempting to resolve cases at the pleading stage is that the allegations of the parties must be accepted as true for the purpose of ruling on a motion to dismiss. Thus, if the plaintiff tells a highly unlikely but plausible story in the complaint, the court cannot dismiss the action even though it does not believe the allegations or think that the plaintiff will be able to prove the tale. The pleading stage is not the time to resolve questions of fact.

However, in some cases it will be possible to supplement the pleadings with additional documents to show that an apparently decisive issue is spurious. This is done by a motion for *summary judgment*. This motion can be supported by demonstrating that the crucial issue will have to be resolved in the movant's favor at trial, because the opposing party will be unable to produce sufficient admissible evidence in support of her position on the issue. For example, suppose that it is Cecil's position that prior to the accident he had fired Beasley, but that Beasley had secretly acquired keys to Cecil's automobile and taken the car without permission shortly before the accident. On the face of the pleadings, we have only an allegation that Beasley was Cecil's employee and a denial of that allegation; thus, the pleadings seem to present a question of credibility that cannot be resolved at this stage. Cecil now moves for summary judgment, alleging that this issue is not a genuine one. He accompanies his motion with affidavits of his own and two other witnesses that he had fired Beasley; a deposition of the garage attendant indicating that he had been instructed not to allow Beasley to have the car, and that it was taken without Cecil's knowledge; and a deposition of Beasley to the effect that he had been fired, but wanted to use the car once more for his own purposes. It is now incumbent upon Aikin to show that the issue is genuine; Aikin cannot rely simply upon her own assertion that all this is not so; after all, she has no personal knowledge of the facts. Aikin must convince the court that she has admissible evidence that Beasley still was acting as Cecil's employee in driving the car at the time of the accident. If Aikin fails to do so, summary judgment will be entered against her.

It should be noted that in ruling on a summary judgment motion the judge does not decide which side is telling the truth. If Aikin presents an affidavit of a witness who claims to have been present when Cecil allegedly fired Beasley, and says that Cecil told Beasley that this was only a subterfuge and that he wanted him to continue to work for him but to pretend to steal the car, summary judgment will not be appropriate even though the judge is firmly convinced that Aikin's affiant is lying.

7. SETTING THE CASE FOR TRIAL

After discovery is completed, and if the case has not been terminated by dismissal, summary judgment, or settlement, it must be set for trial. Most cases already will have been disposed of prior to trial. If Aikin's lawsuit has not yet been resolved, typically either party may file a note of issue, at which time the case will be given a number and placed on a *trial calendar*. These calendars have become extremely long in many courts, and the case may have to wait a year, three years, or more before it is called for trial, especially if a jury trial has been requested.

8. THE JURY AND ITS SELECTION

In most actions for damages, the parties have a right to have the facts tried by a jury. This right is assured in the federal courts by the Seventh Amendment to the United States Constitution, and is protected in the courts of most states by similar state constitutional provisions. If there is a right to a trial by jury, either party may assert it, but if neither wishes to do so, a judge will try the facts as well as the law. Largely for historical reasons growing out of a division of authority in the English court structure, there are many civil actions in which neither party has a right to a jury trial; these include most cases in which plaintiff wants an order directing or prohibiting specific action by defendant rather than a judgment for damages—a so-called equitable remedy.

If a jury has been demanded, the first order of business at trial will be to impanel the jurors. A large number of people, selected in an impartial manner from various lists, tax rolls, or street directories, will have been ordered to report to the courthouse for jury duty at a given term of court. The prospective jurors will be questioned—usually by the judge but sometimes by the lawyers—as to their possible biases. If one of the persons called has prior knowledge of the case or is a personal friend of one of the parties, he or she probably will be successfully challenged for cause and excused. But suppose Aikin is an architect and her lawyer finds that one of the jury panel has recently constructed a house and believes that he was greatly overcharged for its design and construction; this will likely not be enough to persuade the judge to excuse him. However, fearing the juror might be prejudiced against her client, Aikin's lawyer probably will exercise one of the small number of peremptory challenges allowed for which no reason need be given. Ultimately, a panel of between six and 12 hopefully unbiased jurors will be selected.

9.   THE TRIAL

After the jurors have been sworn, plaintiff's lawyer will make an *opening statement*, describing for the jury what the case is about, what contentions will be made, and how plaintiff plans to prove them. Defendant's lawyer also may make an opening statement at this time, but may reserve the right to do so until later when it is time to present defendant's case. Following the opening statement, plaintiff's lawyer calls her witnesses one by one. Each witness is first questioned by the lawyer who has called that witness—this is the *direct examination*; then the lawyer for the other side has the opportunity to *cross-examine* the same witness; this may be followed by *re-direct* and *re-cross* examination, and even further stages. The judge maintains some control over the length and tenor of the examination, and in particular will see to it that the stages beyond cross-examination are not prolonged.

Just as the primary responsibility for introducing evidence is on the lawyers, so too is the responsibility for objecting to evidence that is thought to be inadmissible under the rules of evidence. Suppose that Aikin's lawyer asks: "What happened while you were lying on the ground after the accident?" To which Aikin replies: "The driver of the car came over and said that he had been going too fast and he was sorry." Aikin's answer is objectionable because it contains hearsay evidence; that is, it repeats what someone else has said for the purpose of proving the truth of what was said. It is up to Cecil's counsel to object, and then the judge must rule on the objection. This particular issue is not an easy one, for Aikin's answer may well come within one of the exceptions to the rule excluding hearsay evidence. This kind of issue will recur continually throughout the trial and the judge must be prepared to make instantaneous rulings if the trial is to proceed with dispatch. Evidentiary rulings form a major source of the errors raised on appeal, but at the same time appellate courts are very reluctant to disturb the trial judge's ruling on the point. If the judge rules that Aikin's answer is inadmissible, the judge will instruct the jury to disregard the testimony. Can a juror who has heard such an important confession totally put it to the side?

Documents, pictures, and other tangible items may be put into evidence, but unless their admissibility has been stipulated to in advance, they will be introduced through witnesses. For example, if Aikin's lawyer has had pictures taken of the accident scene and wishes to get them to the jury, she will call the photographer as a witness, have him testify that he took pictures of the scene, and then show them to the photographer who will identify them as the pictures he took. At this point they may be formally introduced into evidence.

When plaintiff's lawyer has called all of her witnesses and their examinations are over, plaintiff will *rest*. At this point, defendant's lawyer may ask for a *directed verdict* (in federal practice now called a judgment as a matter of law) for defendant on the ground that plaintiff has not established a prima facie case. The thrust of the motion is that plaintiff has not introduced enough evidence to permit the jury to find in plaintiff's favor. If the motion is denied, defendant may rest and choose to rely on the jury's agreeing with him, but in almost all cases he will proceed to present witnesses of his own and these witnesses will be exposed to the same process of direct and cross-examination. When defendant has rested, plaintiff may present additional evidence to meet any new matter raised by defendant's witnesses. In turn, defendant, after plaintiff rests, may meet any new matter presented by plaintiff. This procedure will continue until both parties rest. Again, the trial judge will maintain considerable control to prevent the protraction of these latter stages.

When both parties have rested, either or both may move for a directed verdict, asking the trial judge to rule that under the evidence presented, viewed most favorably to the nonmoving party, there is no basis for a reasonable jury to find for that party with respect to that issue. If these motions are denied, the case must be submitted to the jury.

10.   SUBMITTING THE CASE TO THE JURY

At this stage the judge and the lawyers will confer out of the jury's hearing with regard to the content of the judge's *instructions* or *charge* to the jury. Each lawyer may submit proposed instructions, which the trial judge will grant or deny, but the judge is under a duty to charge the jury on the basic aspects of the case in any event. If a party's lawyer has neither requested a particular instruction nor objected to the judge's charge, a later argument that the charge was erroneous generally will not be upheld on appeal.

Ordinarily the lawyers will make their final arguments to the jury before the judge delivers the charge. The lawyers will review the evidence from their own points of view, and may suggest how the jury should weigh certain items and resolve specific issues, but it is improper for the lawyers to discuss a matter that has been excluded or has never been introduced. In other words, they are arguing, not testifying.

In the instructions the judge will summarize the facts and issues, tell the jury about the substantive law to be applied on each issue, give general information on determining the credibility of witnesses, and state who has the *burden of persuasion* on each issue of fact. The burden of persuasion in a civil case ordinarily requires that one party prove its contention on a given issue by a preponderance of the evidence. On most issues Aikin will carry this burden, but on an affirmative defense such as contributory negligence, the burden probably will be on Cecil. The burden means that if a juror is unable to resolve an issue, then a finding on that issue should be made against the party who has the burden. In the federal courts and in some states, the judge may comment on the evidence, as it is clear that the judge's opinions are not binding on the jurors. However, judicial comment is rare, and in many states it is not permitted at all.

Following the charge, the jury retires to reach its decision, called a *verdict*. The verdict will be of a type chosen by the judge. There are three types, of which by far the most common is the general verdict. This verdict permits the jurors to determine the facts and apply the law on which they have been charged to those facts; it is simple in form in that only the conclusion as to who prevails, and the amount of damages, if that party is a claimant, is stated. A second type is the *general verdict with interrogatories*, which combines the form of the general verdict with several key questions that are designed to test the jury's understanding of the issues. Suppose that the accident occurred five miles away from Beasley's appointed route. Aikin's evidence is that Beasley detoured to have the vehicle's brakes fixed; Cecil's is that Beasley was going to visit his friend. The judge might charge the jury that in the former event, but not in the latter, Beasley was acting within the scope of his employment and Cecil would be liable for his negligence, and she might direct the jury, in addition to rendering a verdict for Aikin or for Cecil, to answer the question, "Why did Beasley depart from his route?" If the general verdict was for Aikin, but the jury's answer was that Beasley was driving to his friend's home, the judge would order judgment for Cecil, for if the answer is inconsistent with the verdict, the answer controls. The third type of verdict is the *special verdict*, in which all of the factual issues in the case are submitted to the jury as questions without instructions as to their legal effect; the judge applies the law to the jury's answers and determines which party prevails.

Traditionally, only a unanimous jury verdict has been effective. However, in many states, and by consent of the parties in the federal courts, a nonunanimous verdict by the jurors may stand in a civil action. If the minimum number of jurors required for a verdict cannot reach agreement, the jury is said to be hung, and a new trial before a different jury is necessary.

11. POST-TRIAL MOTIONS

After the jury has returned its verdict, judgment will be entered thereon, but the losing party will have an opportunity to make certain post-trial motions. There may be a motion for a *judgment notwithstanding the verdict* (commonly called a motion for a *judgment n.o.v.*, from the Latin *non obstante veredicto*, but in federal practice now called a renewed motion for judgment as a matter of law). This motion raises the same question as a motion for a directed verdict. The losing party also may move for a *new trial*; the grounds for this motion are many, and may include assertions that the judge erred in admitting (or excluding) certain evidence, that the charge was defective, that attorneys, parties, or jurors have been guilty of misconduct, that the damages awarded are excessive, or that the jury's verdict is against the clear weight of the evidence. Should these motions fail, it is sometimes possible to reopen a judgment, even several months after the trial, on the grounds of clerical mistake, newly discovered evidence, or fraud, but the occasions on which such relief is granted are very rare.

12. THE JUDGMENT AND ITS ENFORCEMENT

The *judgment* is the final determination of the lawsuit, absent an appeal. Judgment may be rendered by default when the defendant does not appear; or following the granting of a demurrer, a motion to dismiss, or a motion for summary judgment; or based on a settlement agreement of the parties; or upon the jury's verdict, or the findings of fact and conclusions of law of the trial judge in a non-jury case. The judgment may be in the form of an award of money to plaintiff, a declaration of rights between the parties, specific recovery of property, or an order requiring or prohibiting some future activity. When defendant has prevailed, the judgment generally will not be "for" anything or order anything; it simply will provide that plaintiff takes nothing by her complaint.

In most cases a judgment for plaintiff will not order defendant to do anything; typically it will simply state that plaintiff shall recover a sum of money from defendant. This does not necessarily mean that defendant will pay. It is up to plaintiff to collect the money. Execution is the common method of forcing the losing party to satisfy a money judgment, if the loser does not do so voluntarily. A *writ of execution* is issued by the court commanding an officer—usually the sheriff—to seize property of the losing party and, if necessary, to sell it publicly and use the proceeds to satisfy plaintiff's judgment.

When plaintiff's recovery takes the form of an injunction requiring defendant to do something or to stop doing something, the judgment (in this context typically called a *decree*) is said to operate against defendant's person (in personam). Its sanction is direct, and if defendant fails to obey, he may be held in *contempt of court* and punished by fine or imprisonment.

Costs provided by statute and certain out-of-pocket disbursements are awarded to the prevailing party and included in the judgment. Usually these costs are nominal in relation to the total expense of litigation and include only such items as the clerk's fee and witnesses' mileage. As previously mentioned, in the United States attorney's fees are not recoverable as costs in ordinary litigation.

13. APPEAL

Every judicial system provides for review of a trial court's decisions by an appellate court. Generally a party has the right to appeal any judgment to at least one higher court. When the system contains two levels of appellate courts, appeal usually lies initially to one of the intermediate courts; review at the highest level is only at the discretion of that court except in certain classes of cases. Under current practice in the federal courts, District Court decisions are reviewed by the appropriate Circuit Court of Appeals, but review in the Supreme Court generally is discretionary and sought by a *petition for a writ of certiorari* (in a few cases, a direct appeal lies from the District Court to the Supreme Court). The discretion of a higher-level appellate court generally is exercised so that only cases with legal issues of broad importance are taken.

The record on appeal will contain the pleadings, at least a portion of the *transcript of the trial* (the court reporter's verbatim record of the trial), and the orders and rulings relevant to the appeal. The parties present their contentions to the appellate court by *written briefs* and, in most cases, also by *oral argument*. The appellate court may review any ruling of law by the trial judge, although frequently it will limit the scope of its review by holding that particular matters were within the trial judge's discretion or that the error if any was not prejudicial, that is, it did not substantially affect the outcome of the case. There are constitutional limits to the review of a jury's verdict, but even when these limits do not apply—for example, when the judge has tried the case without a jury—it is unusual for an appellate court to re-examine a question of fact, because a cold record does not convey the nuances of what the trier observed, notably the demeanor of the witnesses.

The appellate court has the power to *affirm, reverse, or modify* the judgment of the trial court. If it reverses, it may order that judgment be entered or it may *remand* the case to the trial court for a new trial or other proceedings not inconsistent with its decision. The decision of an appellate court usually is accompanied by a written opinion, signed by one of the judges hearing the appeal; there is always more than one judge deciding an appeal. Concurring and dissenting opinions also may be filed.

The opinions of a court are designed to set forth the reasons for a decision and to furnish guidance to lower courts, lawyers, and the public.

Keep in mind an important distinction between the *reviewability* of a particular ruling of a trial judge and its *appealability*. For example, a trial judge's ruling excluding certain evidence at trial as hearsay is reviewable; that is, when the judgment is appealed, that ruling may be assigned as error and the appellate court will consider whether it was correct. But trial would become excessively protracted if an appeal could be taken from every ruling at the time it is made. Thus, appeals lie only from judgments and from certain orders made in the course of litigation when immediate review is deemed so important that a delay in the action during appeal can be tolerated. Judicial systems differ in the extent to which interlocutory orders can be appealed. In the federal system, very little other than a final judgment can be taken to the courts of appeals; however, in some state systems, many kinds of interlocutory orders can be appealed before a final judgment is entered.

A good example of the contrast between the two approaches can be seen by looking at the consequences of an order denying a motion to dismiss. Suppose that Cecil moves to dismiss Aikin's complaint on the ground that even on Aikin's view of the facts Cecil is not responsible for the conduct of Beasley, and this motion is denied. In the federal courts such an order would not be appealable since it does not terminate the lawsuit. Indeed, the disposition of the motion means that the action will continue. In some states, however, this question could be taken immediately to a higher court for a ruling, while the other stages of the litigation wait.

The question of which system is better is not easy to answer. One may argue in favor of the federal practice that everything should be done at one level before going to the next, that too much time is taken in waiting for appellate courts to decide these questions serially, and that no appeal may ever be necessary, since Cecil may prevail anyway. But on the other hand, if the appellate court holds at this early stage that Aikin has no claim against Cecil, the time necessary for discovery and trial will be saved.

One point worth noting is that the resolution of the question of the appealability of interlocutory orders has an important bearing on the procedural developments within a given system. In the case of motions to dismiss, for example, if denials are not appealable, the law on this subject will be made largely in the trial courts. A trial judge who is in doubt may tend to deny such motions rather than to grant them, and the decision generally will not be disturbed. Although the ruling theoretically is reviewable after final judgment, by that time the significance of the ruling on the pleadings may have been displaced by more substantive questions. If the denial is appealable, a tactical consideration is added and such motions will be resorted to more frequently, inasmuch as they will afford defendant an additional opportunity to delay trial and thus to wear down the opponent. With respect to other procedural rulings—as in the discovery area—the absence of an interlocutory appeal will strengthen the hand of the trial judge, who will in fact if not in theory exercise a wider range of discretion because fewer rulings will come before the appellate courts and when they do they will be enmeshed in a final judgment, making it easier to conclude that any error was not prejudicial.

14. THE CONCLUSIVENESS OF JUDGMENTS

Generally, a judgment becomes final after the appeal and whatever further proceedings may take place, or, if no appeal is taken, when the time for appeal expires. With very rare exceptions, the judgment cannot be challenged in another proceeding. It is res judicata, a thing decided, and now the matter is at rest. The concept of res judicata includes claim preclusion and issue preclusion, the latter traditionally known as collateral estoppel. Defining the scope and effect of this finality principle is one of the most complex tasks in the entire law of procedure.

FEDERAL RULES OF CIVIL PROCEDURE

FOR THE

UNITED STATES DISTRICT COURTS

Amendments received through April 27, 2020*

TABLE OF RULES

TITLE I. SCOPE OF RULES; FORM OF ACTION

TITLE II. COMMENCING AN ACTION; SERVICE OF PROCESS, PLEADINGS, MOTIONS, AND ORDERS

TITLE III. PLEADINGS AND MOTIONS

---

* [The version of the rules that appears herein reflects a pending amendment to Rule 30 that has been approved by the Supreme Court and forwarded to Congress for its consideration. The pending changes are reflected with underlining and ~~strikethroughs~~. Absent congressional action, these changes will take effect on December 1, 2020. Ed.]

RULES OF CIVIL PROCEDURE

RULES OF CIVIL PROCEDURE

RULES OF CIVIL PROCEDURE

TIMETABLE FOR LAWYERS IN FEDERAL CIVIL CASES

This Timetable, prepared by the Publisher's editorial staff as a guide to the user, indicates the time for each of the steps of a civil action as provided by the Federal Rules of Civil Procedure and the Federal Rules of Appellate Procedure. Certain steps governed by statute and by the Rules of the Supreme Court are also listed. *The user should always consult the actual text of the applicable rule or statute.* In some instances, the periods permitted for each of these steps may be modified by the court in its discretion. Citations to supporting authority are in the form "Civ.R. ———" for the Rules of Civil Procedure; "App.R. ———" for the Rules of Appellate Procedure; "28 U.S.C. § ———" for statutes; and "Supreme Court Rule ———".

ADMISSIONS

Requests for admissions, service of	A party may serve on any other party a written request to admit after the parties have conferred as required by Civ.R. 26(f); if no Rule 26(f) conference is required because it is a proceeding exempted from initial disclosure under Civ.R. 26(a)(1)(B) or because the court has ordered that there need not be such a conference, then this waiting period does not apply. Civ.R. 26(d), 36(a)(1).
Response to requested admissions	Written answers or objections must be served within 30 days after service of the request, or a shorter or longer time as may be stipulated to under Civ.R. 29 or ordered by the court. Civ.R. 36(a)(3).

AMENDING pleadings   See "Pleadings" in this Table.

ANSWER   See, also, "Responsive Pleadings" in this Table.

To complaint	An answer must be served within 21 days after being served with the summons and complaint, unless another time is specified by Civ.R. 12 or a federal statute. Civ.R. 12(a)(1)(A)(i).
	An answer must be served within 60 days after the date the request for waiver of service of summons was sent or within 90 days after that date if it was sent to the defendant outside any judicial district of the United States, unless another time is specified by Civ.R. 12 or a federal statute. Civ.R. 4(d)(3), 12(a)(1)(A)(ii).
	An answer must be served within 60 days after service on the United States Attorney in an action against the United States, a United States agency, or a United States officer or employee sued only in an official capacity. Civ.R. 12(a)(2).
	In an action against a United States officer or employee sued in an individual capacity in connection with duties performed on the United States' behalf, an answer must be served within 60 days after service on the officer or employee or service on the United States attorney, whichever is later. Civ.R. 12(a)(3).
	The time for an answer to a complaint is altered by service of Civ.R. 12 motions. If the court denies the motion, the answer must be served within 14 days after notice of the court's action. Civ.R. 12(a)(4)(A). If the court grants a motion for a more definite statement, the responsive pleading must be served within 14 days after the more definite statement is served. Civ.R.

12(a)(4)(B). If the court grants a motion under Rule 12(b), the claim will be dismissed, either with or without prejudice, eliminating the need for a responsive pleading.* See "Responsive Pleadings" in this Table.

To counterclaim or crossclaim

A party must serve an answer to a counterclaim or crossclaim within 21 days after being served with the pleading that states the counterclaim or crossclaim. Civ.R. 12(a)(1)(B).

In an action against the United States, a United States agency, or a United States officer or employee, the answer to a counterclaim or crossclaim must be served within 60 days after service of the pleading that states the counterclaim or crossclaim. Civ.R. 12(a)(2), (3).

The time for an answer to a counterclaim or crossclaim is altered by service of Civ.R. 12 motions. Civ.R. 12(a)(4). See "Responsive Pleadings" in this Table.

To amended pleading

Any required response to an amended pleading must be made within the time remaining to respond to the original pleading or within 14 days after service of the amended pleading, whichever is later. Civ.R. 15(a)(3).

To notice of condemnation

In an action to condemn property, a defendant having an objection or defense to the taking must serve an answer to the complaint within 21 days after being served with the notice. Civ.R. 71.1(e)(2).

Removed actions

If the defendant did not answer before removal, the defendant must answer or present other defenses or objections within 21 days after receipt of a copy of the initial pleading stating the claim for relief, 21 days after service of summons for an initial pleading on file at time of service, or 7 days after the notice of removal is filed, whichever is longest. Civ.R. 81(c)(2).

ANSWERS (and objections) to interrogatories to party

The responding party must serve its answers and any objections within 30 days after being served with the interrogatories. A shorter or longer time may be stipulated to under Civ.R. 29 or ordered by the court. Civ.R. 33(b)(2).

APPEAL

As of right

In civil cases where no United States governmental entities or officials are parties, a notice of appeal must

---

* Civil Rule 12(a)(4) does not address the impact of a court's grant of a motion to strike on the time for serving a responsive pleading. Thus, the ordinarily operative response time of 21 days after service—or 60 (or 90) days after the sending of a waiver of service request—presumably remains applicable. However, if a defendant's motion to strike is denied, then under 12(a)(4)(A) the defendant would have 14 days after notice of the court's denial to serve the responsive pleading. The rule does not address whether this 14-day deadline supercedes the original deadline if the remaining time in the original deadline exceeds 14 days. For example, a defendant may have 60 days to respond because of a waiver of service but files a motion to strike on day 20. If the court denies the motion to strike on day 30, there would be 30 days remaining in the defendant's original response period but, under Rule 12(a)(4)(A), the defendant would have only 14 days to respond. It is possible in such a situation that the court would be amenable to setting a different time—pursuant to its authority under Rule 12(a)(4)—for serving a responsive pleading to give the defendant the benefit of the remaining time under the original deadline.

be filed with the district clerk within 30 days after entry of the judgment or order appealed from. App.R. 4(a)(1)(A), 28 U.S.C. § 2107(a).

A notice of appeal may be filed by any party within 60 days after entry of the judgment or order appealed from in cases in which the United States or its officers, employees, or agencies are parties. App.R. 4(a)(1)(B), 28 U.S.C. § 2107(b).

Entry of a judgment or order in the civil docket under Civ.R. 79(a) is entry for purposes of App.R. 4, unless Civ.R. 58(a) requires a separate document, in which case entry occurs when the judgment or order is entered under Civ.R. 79(a) and when the earlier of either the judgment or order is set forth on a separate document, or 150 days have run from entry of the judgment or order in the civil docket. App.R. 4(a)(7)(A).

If a party timely files in the district court any of the following motions under the Federal Rules of Civil Procedure, the time to file an appeal runs for all parties from the entry of the order disposing of the last such remaining motion:

(i)   for judgment under Civ.R. 50(b);

(ii) to amend or make additional factual findings under Civ.R. 52(b), whether or not granting the motion would alter the judgement;

(iii) for attorney's fees under Civ.R. 54 if the district court extends the time to appeal under Civ.R. 58;

(iv) to alter or amend the judgment under Civ.R. 59;

(v)   for a new trial under Civ.R. 59;

(vi) for relief under Civ.R. 60 if the motion is filed no later than 28 days after the judgment is entered.

App.R. 4(a)(4).

The district court may extend the time for filing a notice of appeal for excusable neglect or good cause upon motion filed no later than 30 days after the time prescribed by App.R. 4(a) expires; no extension may exceed 30 days after the prescribed time or 14 days after the date when the order granting the motion is entered, whichever is later. App.R. 4(a)(5).

If one party timely files a notice of appeal, any other party may file a notice of appeal within 14 days after the date when the first notice of appeal was filed, or within the time otherwise prescribed by App.R. 4(a), whichever period ends later. App.R. 4(a)(3).

By permission

A petition for permission to appeal must be filed with the circuit clerk within the time specified by statute or rule authorizing the appeal, or, if no such time is specified, within the time provided by App.R. 4(a) for filing a notice of appeal. App.R. 5(a).

RULES OF CIVIL PROCEDURE

Bankruptcy

If a motion for rehearing under Bankruptcy Rule 8022 is filed in a district court or in a bankruptcy appellate panel, the time for appeal to the court of appeals runs from entry of the order disposing of motion. App.R. 6(b)(2)(A).

Class action certifications

A petition for permission to appeal an order granting or denying class-action certification must be filed with the circuit clerk within 14 days after the order is entered, or within 45 days after the order is entered if any party is the United States, a United States agency, or a United States officer or employee sued for an act or omission occurring in connection with the duties performed on the United States' behalf. Civ.R. 23(f).

Inmates

A notice of appeal filed by an inmate is timely filed if deposited in the institution's internal mail system on or before the last day for filing. App.R. 4(c), 25(a)(2)(A)(iii).

Representation statement

Within 14 days after filing notice of appeal unless court of appeals designates another time, the attorney who filed the notice of appeal must file with the circuit clerk a statement naming the parties represented on appeal by that attorney. App.R. 12(b).

Entry of judgment or order, notice of

Lack of notice of entry of judgment by the clerk does not affect the time for appeal or relieve or authorize court to relieve party for failure to appeal within time allowed, except as allowed by App.R. 4(a). Civ.R. 77(d)(2).

Record (Appellant)

Within 14 days after filing a notice of appeal or entry of an order disposing of last timely remaining motion specified in App.R. 4(a)(4)(A), whichever is later: Appellant to place written order for transcript and file copy of order with clerk; if none to be ordered, file a certificate to that effect. Unless entire transcript to be included, within the 14 days provided in App.R. 10(b)(1) appellant must file a statement of issues and serve appellee a copy of the order or certificate and of the statement. App.R. 10(b).

Record (Appellee)

Within 14 days after service of the appellant's order or certificate and statement of issues, appellee to file and serve on appellant a designation of additional parts of the transcript to be ordered. Unless within 14 days after service of that designation the appellant has ordered all such parts and so notified appellee, the appellee may within the following 14 days either order the parts or move in the district court for an order requiring appellant to do so. App.R. 10(b).

Record (costs)

At the time of ordering, the party must make satisfactory arrangements with the reporter for paying the cost of the transcript. App.R. 10(b)(4).

Record (Reporter)

If the transcript cannot be completed within 30 days of receipt of order, the reporter may request an extension of time from circuit clerk. App.R. 11(b)(1).

RULES OF CIVIL PROCEDURE

Stay of proceedings to enforce judgment	Effective when bond or other security is approved by the court. Civ.R. 62(b).
	A party may obtain a stay by providing a bond or other security any time after judgment is entered. Civ.R. 62(b).
Briefs	Appellant must serve and file a brief within 40 days after the record is filed. Appellee must serve and file a brief within 30 days after service of the appellant's brief. A reply brief may be served and filed within 21 days after service of appellee's brief but, except for good cause, reply brief must be filed at least 7 days before argument. A court of appeals may shorten the time to serve and file briefs, either by local rule or by order for a particular case. App.R. 28.1(f), 31(a)(1).
Transcripts	See "Record", ante, this heading.
Tax Court decisions	Review is commenced by filing a notice of appeal with the Tax Court clerk within 90 days after entry of decision. If a timely notice of appeal is filed by one party, any other party may file a notice of appeal within 120 days after entry of decision by the Tax Court. If timely motion to vacate or revise decision is made, time to file notice of appeal runs from entry of order disposing of motion or from entry of new decision, whichever is later. App.R. 13(a)(1)(A).

APPEAL from magistrate judge to court of appeals

Appeal from judgment entered at a magistrate judge's direction may be taken to the court of appeals as would any other appeal from a district court judgment. 28 U.S.C. § 636(c)(3).

APPEAL to Supreme Court

Direct appeals from three-judge courts	Any party may appeal directly to the Supreme Court an order granting or denying an interlocutory or permanent injunction in any civil action required by Congress to be heard and determined by a district court of three judges. 28 U.S.C. § 1253. A direct appeal of any decision of a three-judge district court declaring any Act of Congress unconstitutional in whole or in part must be taken within 30 days of entry of the order, judgment or decree. 28 U.S.C. § 2101(a).
	Any other direct appeal to the Supreme Court authorized by law from a decision of a district court must be taken within 30 days from the judgment, order, or decree appealed from if interlocutory, and within 60 days if final. 28 U.S.C. § 2101(b).
Other appeals and certiorari	Within 90 days after entry of judgment or decree; a Justice of the Supreme Court for good cause shown may extend the time for applying for a writ of certiorari for a period not exceeding 60 days. 28 U.S.C. § 2101(c).

Brief opposing certiorari*	A brief opposing certiorari must be filed within 30 days after the case is placed on the docket unless time is extended by the Court or a Justice or by the Clerk; See Supreme Court Rule 15.3.
Brief on merits on appeal or certiorari	A brief on the merits must be filed by the petitioner or appellant within 45 days of the order granting the writ of certiorari or the order noting probable jurisdiction or postponing consideration of jurisdiction; see Supreme Court Rule 25.1.
	The respondent or appellee must file a brief on the merits within 30 days after the brief for the petitioner or appellant is filed; see Supreme Court Rule 25.2.
	The petitioner or appellant must file a reply brief, if any, within 30 days after the brief for respondent or appellee is filed, but any reply brief must actually be received by Clerk not later than 2 p.m. one week before the date of oral argument. See Supreme Court Rule 25.3.
Stay of mandate pending petition for certiorari	A stay of mandate pending filing a petition to the Supreme Court for certiorari must not exceed 90 days unless the period is extended for good cause or unless, within the period of stay, the party who obtained the stay notifies the circuit clerk in writing: (1) that the time for filing a petition has been extended, in which case the stay continues for the extended period, or (2) that the petition has been filed, in which case the stay will continue until final disposition by the Supreme Court. The court of appeals must issue the mandate immediately when a copy of the Supreme Court order denying the petition for writ of certiorari is received. App.R. 41(d).
ATTORNEY'S fees	See "Class actions" and "Costs" in this Table.
CLASS actions	
Certification	At an early practicable time after a person sues or is sued as a class representative, the court must determine by order whether to certify the action as a class action. Civ.R. 23(c)(1)(A).
Certification appeals	A petition for permission to appeal an order granting or denying class-action certification must be filed with the circuit clerk within 14 days after the order is entered, or within 45 days after the order is entered if any party is the United States, a United States agency, or a United States officer or employee sued for an act or omission occurring in connection with the duties performed on the United States' behalf. Civ.R. 23(f).
Attorney's fees	A claim for an award of attorney's fees and nontaxable costs must be made by motion under Civ.R. 54(d)(2) subject to Civ.R. 23(h) at a time the court sets. Notice of the motion must be served on all parties and, for

---

* No separate brief *supporting* a petition for certiorari may be filed. *See* Supreme Court Rule 14.2.

motions by class counsel, directed to class members in a reasonable manner. Civ.R. 23(h)(1).

COMPLAINT

Filing a complaint commences an action; a copy must be served with a summons. Civ.R. 3, 4(c)(1).*

Service of summons and complaint must be within 90 days after filing the complaint.** The court must extend the time for service for good cause shown. This deadline does not apply to service in a foreign country under Rule 4(f), 4(h)(2), 4(j)(1), or to service of a notice under Rule 71.1(d)(3)(A). Civ.R. 4(m).

COMPUTATION of time

When the time period is stated in days or a longer unit of time: (1) exclude day of the event that triggers the period; (2) count every day, including intermediate Saturdays, Sundays, and legal holidays; and (3) include the last day of the period, but if the last day is a Saturday, Sunday, or legal holiday, the period continues to run until the end of the next day that is not a Saturday, Sunday, or legal holiday. Civ.R. 6(a); App.R. 26(a).

When the time period is stated in hours: (1) begin counting immediately on the occurrence of the event that triggers the period; (2) count every hour, including hours during intermediate Saturdays, Sundays, and legal holidays; and (3) if the period would end on a Saturday, Sunday, or legal holiday, the period continues to run until the same time on the next day that is not a Saturday, Sunday, or legal holiday. Civ.R. 6(a).

If clerk's office is inaccessible: (1) on the last day for filing under Civ.R. (6)(a)(1), then the time for filing is extended to the first accessible day that is not a Saturday, Sunday, or legal holiday; or (2) during the last hour for filing under Civ.R. (6)(a)(2), then the time for filing is extended to the same time on the first accessible day that is not a Saturday, Sunday, or legal holiday. Civ.R. 6(a).

When a party in a proceeding before a United States District Court may or must act within a specified time after service and service is made under Civ.R. 5(b)(2)(C), (D), or (F), 3 days are added after the period would otherwise expire under Civ.R. 6(a). Civ.R. 6(d).

When a party in a proceeding before a United States Court of Appeals may or must act within a specified time after being served, and the paper is not served electronically on the party or delivered to the party on the date stated in the proof of service, 3 days are added

---

* The deadline for filing a complaint is tied to the various statutes of limitations periods that apply to the claims asserted in the complaint. Filing the complaint does not necessarily satisfy a statute of limitations deadline, as some of these statutes require both filing *and* service of process to be achieved within a certain period of time. *See Walker v. Armco Steel Corp.*, 446 U.S. 740 (1980).

** Prior to December 1, 2015, the time to achieve service was 120 days.

after the period would otherwise expire under App.R. 26(a). App.R. 26(c).

Legal holidays are defined by Civ.R. 6(a)(6) and App.R. 26(a)(6).

Supreme Court matters—See Supreme Court Rule 30.

CONDEMNATION of property

Answer to notice of condemnation

A defendant that has an objection or defense to the condemnation must serve an answer within 21 days after being served with the notice. Civ.R. 71.1(e).

CORPORATE DISCLOSURE

A nongovernmental corporate party must file, with its first appearance, pleading, petition, motion, response, or other request addressed to the court, a statement identifying any parent corporation and any publicly held corporation owning 10% or more of its stock or stating that there is no such corporation. A party must promptly file supplemental statement if any required information changes. Civ.R. 7.1.

CORRECTIONS based on clerical mistakes, oversights, or omissions in judgments, orders, or the record

The court may make such corrections whenever found, on motion or on its own, with or without notice; but after an appeal has been docketed and while pending, the court may make such corrections only with the appellate court's leave. Civ.R. 60(a).

COSTS

Costs other than attorney's fees

The clerk may tax costs on 14 days' notice. The court may review taxation of costs on motion served within the next 7 days. Civ.R. 54(d)(1).

Attorney's fees and related nontaxable expenses

Unless a statute or court order provides otherwise, a motion for attorney's fees must be filed no later than 14 days after entry of judgement. Civ.R. 54(d)(2)(B).

CROSS-APPEAL

Multiple appeals

If one party files a notice of appeal, any other party may file a notice of appeal within 14 days after the filing of first notice of appeal or within the time otherwise prescribed by App.R. 4(a), whichever period ends later. App.R. 4(a)(3).

First notice of appeal by an inmate

If an inmate files the first notice of appeal under App.R. 4(c), the 14-day period provided in App.R. 4(a)(3) for another party to file a notice of appeal runs from date the district court dockets the first notice of appeal. App.R. 4(a)(3), 4(c).

DEFAULT & DEFAULT JUDGMENT

Entry of default

When it appears that a party against whom a judgment for affirmative relief is sought has failed to plead or otherwise defend, and that failure is shown by affidavit

Notice of application to the court
for default judgment

or otherwise, the clerk must enter the party's default. Civ.R. 55(b).*

If the party against whom a default judgment is sought has appeared personally or by representative, that party or its representative must be served with written notice of application for default judgment at least 7 days before the hearing on such application. Civ.R. 55(b).

DEFENSES and objections, presentation of

By pleading

See "Answer" in this Table.

By motion

Motion asserting defenses under Rule 12(b) must be made before pleading if a responsive pleading is allowed. Civ.R. 12(b). See "Answer", this Table, for deadlines applicable to responsive pleadings.

At trial

Opposing party may assert at trial any defense to claim for relief to which such party is not required to serve responsive pleading. Civ.R. 12(b).

Motion affects time for
responsive pleading

Service of motion under Civ.R. 12 alters times for responsive pleading. Civ.R. 12(a)(4). See "Responsive Pleadings", this Table.

DEPOSITIONS

See, also, "Interrogatories to parties" and "Depositions on written questions" in this Table.

Notice of filing

A party who files the deposition must promptly notify all other parties of the filing. Civ.R. 30(f)(4) and Civ.R. 31(c)(2).

Notice of taking

A party who wants to depose a person by oral questions must give reasonable written notice to every other party. Civ.R. 30(b)(1).

Objections

As to the admissibility of deposition testimony, an objection may be made at the hearing or trial, but subject to Civ.R. 28(b) and 32(d)(3). Civ.R. 32(b).

As to errors or irregularities in the notice, objections must be promptly served on the party giving the notice. Civ.R. 32(d)(1).

As to disqualification of the officer before whom a deposition is to be taken, objection must be made before deposition begins or promptly after the basis for disqualification becomes known or could have been known with reasonable diligence. Civ.R. 32(d)(2).

Objections to the competence of the deponent or to the competence, relevance, or materiality of testimony are

---

* Determining whether a party has failed to plead or otherwise defend requires reference to the applicable deadline for acting under the Rules. For example, if one is determining whether a defendant has defaulted in response to an action filed in federal court, one must know the deadline that applies to their responsive pleading—which will be either 21 days from service of the complaint if formal service was achieved, or 60 (or 90) days from the date of a waiver request if formal service was waived. A default has occurred once the defendant has failed to serve an answer or a pre-answer motion within the applicable deadline.

not waived by failure to make the objection before or during deposition, unless the ground might have been corrected at that time. Civ.R. 32(d)(3)(A).

Errors and irregularities at oral examination in the manner of taking deposition, in the form of questions or answers, in the oath or affirmation, in the conduct of parties, or with respect to other matters that might have been corrected at that time, an objection must be timely made during the deposition or it is waived. Civ.R. 32(d)(3)(B).

As to form of written questions under Civ.R. 31, objections must be served within the time allowed for serving responsive questions or, if recross-question, within 7 days after being served with it. Civ.R. 32(d)(3)(C).

An objection to how the officer transcribed the testimony—or prepared, signed, certified, sealed, endorsed, sent, or otherwise dealt with the deposition—is waived unless a motion to suppress is made promptly after error or irregularity becomes known or, with reasonable diligence, could have been known. Civ.R. 32(d)(4).

Motion for a protective order	Subsequent to certification that movant has in good faith conferred or attempted to confer with other affected parties to resolve dispute without court action. Civ.R. 26(c)(1).
Motion to terminate or limit examination	Any time during a deposition. Civ.R. 30(d)(3).
Motion to perpetuate testimony pending appeal	Motion in court where judgment was rendered on same notice and service as if action was pending in district court. Civ.R. 27(b)(2).
Notice of a petition to perpetuate testimony before an action	The petitioner must serve notice and a copy of the verified petition at least 21 days before date of hearing. Civ.R. 27(a)(2).
Review of transcript or recording	On request by the deponent or a party before completion of the deposition, the deponent has 30 days after notice of availability of transcript or recording to review and to sign statement listing changes and reasons for making them. Civ.R. 30(e).
When taken	After parties have conferred as required by Civ.R. 26(f), except in proceeding exempted from initial disclosure under Civ.R. 26(a)(1)(B), or when authorized by rules, stipulation, or court order. Civ.R. 26(d)(1).
DEPOSITIONS on written questions	See, also, "Depositions" or "Interrogatories to parties" in this Table.
When taken	After parties have conferred as required by Civ.R. 26(f), except in proceeding exempted from initial disclosure under Civ.R. 26(a)(1)(B), or when authorized by rules, stipulation, or court order. Civ.R. 26(d)(1).

Cross-questions	Service within 14 days after being served with the notice and direct questions. Court may extend or shorten time. Civ.R. 31(a)(5).
Redirect questions	Service within 7 days after being served with cross-questions. Court may extend or shorten time. Civ.R. 31(a)(5).
Recross-questions	Service within 7 days after being served with redirect questions. Court may extend or shorten time. Civ.R. 31(a)(5).
Notice of filing	A party who files the deposition must promptly notify all other parties of the filing. Civ.R. 31(c).
Objections to form	Objections must be served within the time for serving responsive questions or, if the question is a recross-question, within 7 days after being served with it. Civ.R. 32(d)(3)(C).

DISCOVERY

See, also, "Admissions", "Depositions", "Depositions on written questions", or "Interrogatories to parties", "Production of documents" in this Table.

Discovery conference	Except in proceedings exempted from initial disclosure under Civ.R. 26(a)(1)(B) or when the court otherwise orders, as soon as practicable and at least 21 days before a scheduling conference is to be held or a scheduling order is due under Civ.R. 16(b), the parties must confer to consider the nature and basis of their claims, defenses, and possibility for settling or resolving the case, to make or arrange for disclosures required by Civ.R. 26(a)(1), to discuss any issues about preserving discoverable information, and to develop a proposed discovery plan. A written report outlining the plan is to be submitted to the court within 14 days after the conference. Civ.R. 26(f).
Initial disclosures	Except in those proceedings that are exempt from initial disclosure under Civ.R. 26(a)(1)(B), without awaiting a discovery request and at or within 14 days after the parties' Civ.R. 26(f) conference, a party must provide the information specified in Civ.R. 26(a)(1)(A), unless a different time is set by stipulation or court order, or unless a party objects during the conference. Civ.R. 26(a)(1)(C). A party that is first served or otherwise joined after the Rule 26(f) conference must make the initial disclosures within 30 days after being served or joined, unless a different time is set by stipulation or court order. Civ.R. 26(a)(2)(D).
Disclosure of expert testimony	Disclosure of expert testimony under Civ.R. 26(a)(2), in the absence of a court order or stipulation, is to be made at least 90 days before trial date or date case is to be ready for trial; if the evidence is intended solely to contradict or rebut evidence on same subject matter identified by another party under Civ.R. 26(a)(2)(B) or (C), within 30 days after the other party's disclosure. Civ.R. 26(a)(2)(D).

Pretrial disclosures; objections	A party must provide the following information at least 30 days before trial unless otherwise ordered by the court: The identity of witnesses the party expects to present or call if the need arises; an identification of documents and exhibits the party expects to offer; and the designation of witnesses whose testimony is expected to be presented by deposition, with a transcript of pertinent testimony if the deposition was not taken stenographically. Within 14 days thereafter, unless court sets different time, a party must serve and promptly file any objections. Civ.R. 26(a)(3).
DISMISSAL for lack of subject-matter jurisdiction	If the court determines at any time that it lacks subject-matter jurisdiction, the court must dismiss the action. Civ.R. 12(h)(3).
DISMISSAL by plaintiff voluntarily without court order	A plaintiff may dismiss an action without a court order by filing a notice of dismissal before service of an answer or motion for summary judgment or by filing a stipulation of dismissal signed by all parties who have appeared.* Civ.R. 41(a)(1).
DISMISSAL of counterclaim, crossclaim or third-party claim, voluntary	Before service of responsive pleading, or if none, before introduction of evidence at trial or hearing. Civ.R. 41(c).
DOCUMENTS, Production of	See "Production of documents", this Table.
ENLARGEMENT of time generally	
Act may or must be done within specified time	Court may for good cause extend time (1) with or without motion or notice if court acts, or if request is made, before the original time or its extension expires, or (2) on motion made after the time has expired if party failed to act because of excusable neglect; but court must not extend time to act under Civ.R. 50(b) and (d), 52(b), 59(b), (d) and (e), and 60(b). Civ.R. 6(b).
Service under Civil Rule 4	If the plaintiff shows good cause for the failure to serve a defendant within 90 days after the complaint is filed, the court must extend the time for service for an appropriate period. Civ.R. 4(m).
Service under Civil Rule 5(b)(2)(C), (D), or (F)	When a party may or must act within a specified time after being served and service is made under Civ.R. 5(b)(2)(C), (D), or (F), three days are added after the period would otherwise expire under Civ.R. 6(a). Civ.R. 6(d).**

---

* If the court treats a motion to dismiss under Rule 12(b)(6) or a motion for judgment on the pleadings under Rule 12(c) as a motion for summary judgment pursuant to Rule 12(d), then the motion will preclude a voluntary dismissal of the claim without the court's leave.

** Prior to December 1, 2016, Civil Rule 6(d) also added three days after electronic service under Civil Rule 5(b)(2)(E). Three days are no longer added under such circumstances.

RULES OF CIVIL PROCEDURE

Service under Appellate Rule 26(c)	When a party may or must act within a specified time after service of a paper upon that party, and the paper is not served electronically on the party or delivered to the party on the date stated in the proof of service, 3 days are added after the period would otherwise expire under Civ.R. 26(a). App.R. 26(c).
Response to request for admissions	A matter is admitted unless, within 30 days after being served, the party to whom the request for admissions is directed serves on the requesting party a written answer or objection. The time to respond may be lengthened or shortened by court or as the parties may stipulate under Civ.R. 29. Civ.R. 36(a).
Renewed motion for judgment as a matter of law	A court may not extend the 28-day period for renewing a motion for judgment as a matter of law under Civ.R. 50(b). Civ.R. 6(b).
Findings by the court, amendment of or make additional findings	A court may not extend the 28-day period for moving to amend a court's findings under Civ.R. 52(b). Civ.R. 6(b).
Motion for new trial	A court may not extend the 28-day period for seeking a new trial under Civ.R. 50(d) or 59(b), or for ordering a new trial under Civ.R. 59(d). Civ.R. 6(b).
Motion to alter or amend	A court may not extend the 28-day period for moving to alter or amend a judgment under Civ.R. 59(e). Civ.R. 6(b).
Motion for relief from judgment or order	A court may not extend the time to make a motion for relief from judgment under Civ.R. 60(b). Civ.R. 6(b).
Appellate rules	The appeals court, for good cause, may extend the time prescribed by the appellate rules or by its order to perform any act or may permit act to be done after expiration of such time; but the court may not extend time for filing notice of appeal (except as authorized in App.R. 4), or petition for permission to appeal, or a notice of appeal from or a petition to enjoin, set aside, suspend, modify, enforce or otherwise review an order of an administrative agency, board, commission, or officer of the United States, unless specifically authorized by law. App.R. 26(b).
Supreme Court matters, depositions	See Supreme Court Rule 30.

EXECUTION

Stay	Automatically: Except as provided in Civ.R. 62(c) and (d), execution on a judgment or proceedings to enforce it are stayed for 30 days after its entry, unless the court orders otherwise. Civ.R. 62(a).
	When judgment is a lien on property under the law of the state where court is located, the judgment debtor is entitled to the same stay of execution the state court would give. Civ.R. 62(f).

When there are multiple claims or multiple parties, a court may stay the enforcement of a final judgment entered under Civ.R. 54(b) until it enters a later judgment or judgments. Civ.R. 62(h).

FILING papers

Any paper after a complaint that is required to be served must be filed no later than a reasonable time after service. Civ.R. 5(d).

A party that files a pleading, written motion, or other paper questioning the constitutionality of a federal or state statute must promptly file a notice of constitutional question and serve the notice and paper on the U.S. Attorney General or relevant state attorney general. Civ.R. 5.1(a).

FINDINGS

Motion to amend

A party may move to amend a court's findings within 28 days after entry of judgment. Civ.R. 52(b). This time period may not be enlarged by the court. Civ.R. 6(b).

HEARING of motions

A district court may establish regular times and places for oral hearings on motions; by rule or order, court may provide for submitting and determining motions on briefs, without oral hearings. Civ.R. 78.

A written motion and notice of the hearing must be served at least 14 days before the time specified for the hearing unless motion may be heard ex parte, or otherwise these rules set or a court order sets a different time. Civ.R. 6(c).

If a party so moves, any defense under Civil Rule 12(b) and motion under Civil Rule 12(c) must be heard and decided before trial unless the court orders deferral until trial. Civ.R. 12(i).

HOLIDAYS

New Year's Day, Martin Luther King, Jr.'s Birthday, Washington's Birthday, Memorial Day, Independence Day, Labor Day, Columbus Day, Veterans' Day, Thanksgiving Day, Christmas Day, and any other day declared a holiday by the President or Congress and, for periods that are measured after an event, any other day declared a holiday by the state where the district court is located. Civ.R. 6(a)(6); App.R. 26(a)(6).

Holidays are included in time computations, unless the time period ends on a legal holiday, in which case the holiday is excluded from the computation. Civ.R. 6(a)(1); App.R. 26(a)(1).

INSTRUCTIONS

Requests

At the close of evidence or at any earlier reasonable time that the court orders, a party may file and furnish to every other party written requests for the jury instructions it wants the court to give. For issues that could not reasonably have been anticipated by an earlier time that the court set for requests, such requests may be made after the close of evidence.

Untimely requests for instructions on any issue may be filed with the court's permission. Civ.R. 51(a).

Proposed

The court must inform the parties of its proposed instructions before instructing the jury and before final jury arguments, and must give the parties the opportunity to object before the instructions and arguments are delivered. Civ.R. 51(b)(1), (2).

Timing of

The court may instruct the jury at any time before jury is discharged. Civ.R. 51(b)(3).

Objections

For parties informed of instructions or actions on requests before the jury is instructed and before final jury arguments, at the opportunity provided for objection under Civ.R. 51(b)(2). For parties not informed of instructions or actions on requests before time for objection under Civ.R. 51(b)(2), promptly after learning that instruction or request will be, or has been, given or refused. Civ.R. 51(c).

INTERROGATORIES to parties

See, also, "Depositions" or "Depositions on written questions" in this Table.

Except in proceedings exempted from initial disclosure under Civ.R. 26(a)(1)(B) or when the court otherwise orders or the parties stipulate, service of interrogatories may only occur after the parties have conferred pursuant to Civ.R. 26(f). Civ.R. 26(d).

Answers or objections

Answers or objections to interrogatories must be served within 30 days after service of the interrogatories. A shorter or longer time may be stipulated to or ordered by the court. Civ.R. 33(b)(2).

INTERVENTION

On timely motion. Civ.R. 24(a), (b).

Motion to intervene must be served on the parties as provided in Civ.R. 5. Civ.R. 24(c).

An attorney general notified of a constitutional question may intervene within 60 days after the notice is filed or after the court certifies the challenge, whichever is earlier. Civ.R. 5.1(c).

JUDGMENT or order

Correction of clerical mistakes, oversights, or omissions in judgment

May be corrected whenever found; but after an appeal has been docketed in appellate court and while appeal is pending, may be corrected only with leave of the appellate court. Civ.R. 60(a).

Default judgment

See "Default & Default Judgment" in this Table.

Entry of judgment

Without the court's direction—Subject to Civ.R. 54(b) and unless ordered otherwise, the clerk must promptly enter judgment when the jury returns general verdict, the court awards only costs or a sum certain, or the court denies all relief. Civ.R.58(a).

Court's approval required—Subject to Civ.R. 54(b), the court must promptly approve the form of judgment, which the clerk must promptly enter, when jury returns special verdict or general verdict with answers to written questions or when the court grants other relief not described in Civ.R. 58(b). Civ.R. 58(b).

Entry may not be delayed in order to tax costs or to award fees. Civ.R. 58(e).

The time of entry is when judgment is entered in the civil docket under Civ.R. 79(a) if a separate document is not required. If a separate document is required, the time of entry is when the judgment is entered in the civil docket under Civ.R. 79(a) and either the judgment is set out in a separate document or 150 days have run from entry of the judgment in the civil docket, whichever is earlier. Civ.R. 58(c).

When there is a certified constitutional challenge, the court may not enter a final judgment holding the statute unconstitutional prior to the expiration of the 60-day deadline for the attorney general to intervene. Civ.R. 5.1(c).

Motion for judgment as a matter of law	At any time before the case is submitted to the jury but after a party has been fully heard on the issue in question. Civ.R.50(a).
Motion for judgment on the pleadings	After pleadings are closed but early enough not to delay the trial. Civ.R. 12(c).
Motion to alter or amend judgment	Must be filed no later than 28 days after entry of judgment. Civ.R. 59(e). This time period may not be enlarged by the court. Civ.R. 6(b).
Notice of entry of judgment	Immediately after entry of judgment, the clerk must serve notice thereof as provided in Civ.R. 5(b) and record service on the docket. A party may also serve notice of entry as provided in Civ.R. 5(b). Civ.R. 77(d).
	Lack of notice of entry of judgment by the clerk does not affect the time for appeal or relieve or authorize the court to relieve a party for failing to appeal within the time allowed, except as allowed by App.R. 4(a). Civ.R. 77(d).
Offer of judgment	See "Offer of judgment" in this Table.
Relief from judgment, on grounds stated in Rule 60(b)	Motion within a reasonable time and no more than 1 year after entry of judgment or order or the date of the proceeding, for following grounds: (1) mistake, inadvertence, surprise, or excusable neglect; (2) newly discovered evidence; (3) fraud, misrepresentation, or misconduct by an opposing party. Civ.R. 60(b), (c). This time period may not be enlarged by the court. Civ.R. 6(b).
	Motion within a reasonable time, for following grounds: (1) judgment void, (2) judgment satisfied, released, or discharged, (3) prior underlying judgment reversed or vacated, (4) no longer equitable that judgment have prospective application, (5) any other reason justifying

relief. Civ.R. 60(b). This time period may not be enlarged by the court. Civ.R. 6(b).

Renewed motion for judgment as a matter of law after trial	Not later than 28 days after entry of judgment. Civ. R. 50(b). This time period may not be enlarged by the court. Civ.R. 6(b).
Stay	See "Execution" in this Table.
Summary judgment	See "Summary Judgment" in this Table.

JURY trial

Demand	A jury demand may be served any time after commencement of the action and no later than 14 days after service of last pleading directed to the triable issue. Civ.R. 38(b).
	If a party has demanded a jury trial only on some issues, any other party may serve demand for jury trial on any other or all factual issues within 14 days after service of first demand or within a shorter time ordered by the court. Civ.R. 38(c).
Removed actions	If at the time of removal all necessary pleadings have been served, a demand for a jury trial may be served:
	By removing party, 14 days after it files a notice of removal;
	By another party, within 14 days after being served with a notice of removal. Civ.R. 81(c)(3)(B).
	A jury demand after removal is not necessary in either of two instances: (1) before removal, party has made express demand in accordance with state law; (2) state law does not require express demands and the court does not order otherwise. Civ.R. 81(c)(3)(A).

LEGAL HOLIDAYS See "Holidays" in this Table.

MAGISTRATE JUDGES

Pretrial matters	Objections of the parties to an order disposing of a matter not dispositive of claim or defense to be served and filed within 14 days after being served with a copy of order. Civ.R. 72(a).
	Clerk must promptly mail copies to all parties of recommendation of magistrate judge for disposition of matter dispositive of a claim or defense of a party or prisoner petition. Specific written objections to recommended disposition may be served and filed within 14 days after being served with a copy. Response to objections may be made within 14 days after being served with a copy of the objections. Civ.R. 72(b).
MAIL	Service under Civ.R. 5(b)(2)(C), (D), or (F) adds 3 days after a prescribed period after service would otherwise expire under Civ.R. 6(a). Civ.R. 6(d).*

---

* Prior to December 1, 2016, Civil Rule 6(d) also added 3 days when service was made electronically under Civil Rule 5(b)(2)(E). Three days are no longer added under such circumstances.

When a party may or must act within a specified time after service of a paper upon that party, and the paper is not served electronically on the party or delivered to the party on the date stated in the proof of service, 3 days are added after the period would otherwise expire under Civ.R. 26(a). App.R. 26(c).

A paper filed electronically is timely filed if filed by midnight in the time zone of the circuit clerk's principal office on the last day for filing. App.R. 26(a)(4). A brief or appendix not filed electronically is timely filed if on or before the last day for filing it is mailed to the clerk by first-class mail, or other class of mail that is at least as expeditious, postage prepaid; or dispatched to a third-party commercial carrier for delivery to the clerk within three days. App.R. 25(a)(2)(A)(ii).

MASTERS

Order appointing master

A court may issue an order appointing a master only after the master files an affidavit disclosing whether there is any ground for disqualification under 28 U.S.C. § 455 and, if a ground is disclosed, the parties with court's approval waive the disqualification. Civ.R. 53(b)(3).

Amendment of order appointing

An order appointing a master may be amended at any time after notice to parties and an opportunity to be heard. Civ.R. 53(b)(4).

Order of master

A master who issues an order must file the order and promptly serve a copy on each party. The clerk must enter the order on the docket. Civ.R. 53(d).

Report of master

Master must report to court as required by appointing order. The master must file the report and promptly serve a copy on each party unless the court orders otherwise. Civ.R. 53(e).

Action on master's order, report or recommendations

In acting on the master's order, report, or recommendations the court must give the parties notice and an opportunity to be heard. Civ.R. 53(f)(1).

A party may file objections or a motion to adopt or modify no later than 21 days after the master's order, report, or recommendations is served, unless the court sets a different time. Civ.R. 53(f)(2).

Compensation of master

The court must fix the master's compensation before or after judgment on the basis and terms stated in the appointing order but the court may set a new basis and terms after notice and opportunity to be heard. Civ.R. 53(g)(1).

MORE DEFINITE STATEMENT

Motion for a more definite statement

Must be made before a responsive pleading is filed. Civ.R. 12(e).

Submitting a more definite statement

If the court orders a more definite statement and the order is not obeyed within 14 days after notice of the order or the time the court sets, the court may strike pleading or issue any other appropriate order. Civ.R. 12(e).

MOTIONS, notices, and affidavits

See, also, specific headings, this Table.

    In general

A written motion, supporting affidavits, and notice of hearing thereof—Service at least 14 days before time specified for hearing unless motion may be heard ex parte, or a different time is set by Rules of Civil Procedure or by order of court. Civ.R. 6(c).

    Hearing of Rule 12 motions and defenses

Heard and decided before trial unless the court orders deferral until trial. Civ.R. 12(i).

    Service of affidavits in opposition

Any affidavit opposing a motion must be served at least 7 days before the hearing on the motion, unless the court permits service at another time, except as Civ.R. 59(c) otherwise provides. Civ.R. 6(c)(2).

NEW TRIAL

    Motion and affidavits

A motion for new trial must be filed no later than 28 days after entry of judgment. Civ.R. 59(b). This time period may not be enlarged by the court. Civ.R. 6(b). If the motion is based on affidavits, they must be filed with the motion. Civ.R. 59(c).

    Opposing affidavits

Opposing party has 14 days after being served to file opposing affidavits in response to a motion for a new trial. Civ.R. 59(c).

    Initiative of court

Not later than 28 days after entry of judgment, a court may order a new trial for any reason that would justify granting one on a party's motion. Civ.R. 59(d). After giving parties notice and opportunity to be heard, a court may grant a timely motion for new trial, for a reason not stated in the motion. Civ.R. 59(d). This time period may not be enlarged by the court. Civ.R. 6(b).

    After entry of judgment as a matter of law

Party against whom judgment as a matter of law is rendered must file a motion for a new trial under Civ.R. 59 no later than 28 days after entry of the judgment. Civ.R. 50(d).

OBJECTIONS to orders or rulings of court

Made at the time that the ruling or order of court is requested or made; if a party had no opportunity to object to the ruling or order at time it was made, failing to object does not prejudice the party. Civ.R. 46.

OFFER of judgment

Must be served at least 14 days before the date set for trial, or 14 days before a separate hearing to determine the extent of liability. Civ.R. 68(a).

Acceptance must be served within 14 days after service of the offer. Civ.R. 68(a).

ORDERS

See "Judgment or order" in this Table.

RULES OF CIVIL PROCEDURE

PLEADINGS

    Amendment of

Once as matter of course within 21 days after serving its pleading, or if pleading is one to which a responsive pleading is required, 21 days after service of a responsive pleading or 21 days after service of a motion under Civ.R. 12(b), (e), or (f), whichever is earlier. Civ.R. 15(a). In all other cases, only with leave of the court or written consent of the opposing party. Civ.R. 15(a).

A party may move, at any time—even after judgment— to amend the pleadings to conform them to the evidence and to raise an unpleaded issue. Civ.R. 15(b).

    Supplemental

On motion and reasonable notice, a court may, on just terms, permit service of a supplemental pleading setting out transactions, etc., that happened after the date of pleading to be supplemented. Civ.R. 15(d).

The court may order the opposing party to plead in response to the supplemental pleading within a specified time. Civ.R. 15(d).

    Motion for judgment on the pleadings

After pleadings are closed, but early enough not to delay trial. Civ.R. 12(c).

    Striking of matter from

On motion made before responding to a pleading or, if no responsive pleading allowed, within 21 days after service of pleading. Civ.R. 12(f). On court's own initiative at any time. Civ.R. 12(f).

PRETRIAL conferences

Scheduling order to issue as soon as practicable but in any event within the earlier of 90 days after complaint served on defendant or 60 days after appearance of any defendant. Civ.R. 16(b).*

PROCESS

See "Summons" in this Table.

PRODUCTION of documents

    Request for, service of

More than 21 days after the summons and complaint are served on a party. Civ.R. 26(d)(2)(A).

    Response to request

Within 30 days after the parties' first Rule 26(f) conference if the request was delivered prior to the conference under Rule 26(d)(2). Otherwise, within 30 days after service of the request. A shorter or longer time may be stipulated to under Civ.R. 29 or ordered by court. Civ.R. 34(b).

    Time of inspection

The request must specify a reasonable time. Civ.R. 34(b).

    Subpoena

See "Subpoena" in this Table.

---

* Prior to December 1, 2015 these time periods were 120 and 90 days, respectively.

REHEARING

Petition for panel rehearing*	Petitions for panel rehearings may be filed within 14 days after entry of judgement unless the time is shortened or extended by order or local rule. In all civil cases in which the United States or its officer, employee, or agency is a party, the time within which any party may seek rehearing is 45 days after entry of judgment unless the time is shortened or extended by order. App.R. 40(a).
Issuance of mandate	The mandate of the court must issue 7 days after the time to file a petition for rehearing expires, or 7 days after entry of an order denying a timely petition for panel rehearing, petition for rehearing en banc, or motion for stay of mandate, whichever is later. The court may shorten or extend the time by order. App.R. 41(b).

REMOVED actions

Answers, defenses, or objections	Within 21 days after receiving, through service or otherwise, a copy of the initial pleading stating the claim for relief upon which the action or proceeding is based, or within 21 days after being served with the summons for an initial pleading on file at the time of service, or within 7 days after the notice for removal is filed, whichever period is the longest. Civ.R. 81(c).
Demand for jury trial	See "Jury trial; Removed actions" in this Table.
Notice of removal	Must be filed within 30 days after receipt through service or otherwise of a copy of the initial pleading setting forth the claim for relief upon which the action or proceeding is based, or within 30 days after service of summons if such initial pleading has then been filed in court and is not required to be served on defendant, whichever period is shorter. 28 U.S.C. § 1446(b)(1).
	If the case stated by the initial pleading is not removable, a notice of removal may be filed within 30 days after receipt by the defendant, through service or otherwise, of a copy of an amended pleading, motion, order or other paper from which it may first be ascertained that the case is one which is or has become removable. 28 U.S.C. § 1446(b)(3).
	A case may not be removed on the basis of jurisdiction conferred by 28 U.S.C. § 1332 more than one year after commencement of the action, unless the court finds that the plaintiff has acted in bad faith in order to prevent a defendant from removing the action. 28 U.S.C. § 1446(c)(1).
Remand motions	A motion to remand the case on the basis of any defect other than lack of subject matter jurisdiction must be made within 30 days after the filing of the notice of removal under section 1446(a). 28 U.S.C. § 1447(c).

---

*   Unless the court requests, no response to a petition for panel rehearing is permitted. *See* App.R. 40(a)(3).

REPLY

See, also, "Responsive pleadings" in this Table.

To answer

If ordered by court. Civ.R. 7(a). Must be served within 21 days after being served with an order to reply, unless the order specifies a different time. Civ.R. 12(a).

Alteration of time by service of Civ.R. 12 motion

See "Responsive pleadings" in this Table.

RESPONSIVE PLEADINGS

See, also, "Answer" or "Reply" in this Table.

To amended pleading

Within time remaining to respond to original pleading, or within 14 days after service of amended pleading, whichever is later, unless court orders otherwise. Civ.R. 15(a)(3).

To supplemental pleading

Within the time specified by the court. Civ.R. 15(d).

Alteration of time by service of Civ.R. 12 motion

Service of a motion permitted under Civ.R. 12 alters times for responsive pleadings as follows unless different time set by court:

(1) if the court denies the motion or postpones its disposition until trial, service of a responsive pleading is due within 14 days after notice of the court's action;

(2) if the court grants the motion for more definite statement, service of a responsive pleading is due within 14 days after service of the more definite statement. Civ.R. 12(a)(4).

SANCTIONS

On motion

A motion for sanctions must be served under Civ.R. 5, but it must not be filed or presented to the court if the challenged paper, claim, defense, contention, or denial is withdrawn or appropriately corrected within 21 days after service or within another time the court sets. Civ.R. 11(c)(2).

On court's own initiative

After notice and a reasonable opportunity to respond—afforded through an order to show cause—a court may impose an appropriate sanction on any attorney, law firm, or party that violated Civ.R. 11. Civ.R. 11(c)(1), (c)(3).

SATURDAYS AND SUNDAYS, LEGAL HOLIDAYS

See "Computation of time" in this Table.

STAY or supersedeas

See "Appeal" or "Execution" in this Table.

SUBPOENA

Objection

Before the earlier of the time specified for compliance or 14 days after service of the subpoena, service on the party or attorney designated in the subpoena of written objection to inspecting, copying, testing or sampling of any or all of the materials, or to inspecting the premises, or to producing electronically stored information in the form or forms requested. Civ.R. 45(d)(2)(B).

RULES OF CIVIL PROCEDURE

Motion to compel production	If objection has been made, the party serving the subpoena may, on notice to the person commanded, move at any time (in the district where compliance is required) for an order compelling production or inspection. Civ.R. 45(d)(2)(B).
Motion to quash	A motion to quash or modify a subpoena must be filed with the court for the district where compliance is required in a "timely" fashion. Civ.R. 45(d)(3)(A).

SUBSTITUTION of parties

In cases of death, incompetency, or transfer of interest, a motion to substitute—together with notice of hearing—must be served on parties as provided in Civ.R. 5 and on nonparties as provided in Civ.R. 4. Civ.R. 25(a), (b), (c).

If a motion to substitute a proper party in the wake of the death of a party is not made within 90 days after service of a statement noting the death, the action by or against the decedent must be dismissed. Civ.R. 25(a).

Successor of public officer substituted automatically. Court may order substitution at any time, but absence of order does not affect substitution. Civ.R. 25(d).

SUMMARY JUDGMENT

Motion for — Any time until 30 days after the close of all discovery. Civ.R. 56(b).

SUMMONS — Served with a copy of the complaint. Civ.R. 4(c)(1). If not served within 90 days after filing complaint, court must dismiss the action without prejudice, order service be made within a specified time, or for good cause shown extend the time for service for an appropriate period. Civ.R. 4(m).*

SUPPLEMENTAL pleadings — See "Pleadings", this Table.

SUPERSEDEAS or stay — See "Appeal" or "Execution" in this Table.

TEMPORARY RESTRAINING ORDER — Order must state date and hour of issuance, be promptly filed in clerk's office, and entered in the record. Civ.R. 65(b).

Expires at the time after entry, not to exceed 14 days, that court sets, unless before that time the court for good cause extends the order for like period or, with consent of party against whom order is directed, for a longer period. Civ.R. 65(b)(2).

Motion for dissolution or modification on 2 days' notice, or shorter notice set by the court; the court must then hear and decide motion as promptly as justice requires. Civ.R. 65(b)(4).

---

* Prior to December 1, 2015, this time period was 120 days.

RULES OF CIVIL PROCEDURE

TERM of court

District courts do not hold formal terms. 28 U.S.C. § 138. Every district court is considered always open. Civ.R. 77(a).

THIRD-PARTY practice

Third-party plaintiff must by motion, obtain the court's leave if it files the third-party complaint more than 14 days after serving its original answer. Civ.R. 14(a).

VERDICT

Renewal of motion for judgment after trial

Movant may renew motion for judgment as a matter of law by filing a motion no later than 28 days after the entry of judgment or—if the motion addresses a jury issue not decided by a verdict—no later than 28 days after the jury was discharged. Civ.R. 50(b). This time period may not be enlarged by the court. Civ.R. 6(b).

New trial where judgment as a matter of law rendered

Party against whom judgment as a matter of law is rendered must file a motion for a new trial under Civ.R. 59 no later than 28 days after entry of the judgment. Civ.R. 50(d). This time period may not be enlarged by the court. Civ.R. 6(b).

RULES OF CIVIL PROCEDURE

EQUITY RULES REFERENCE TABLE

Once they took effect in 1938, the Federal Rules of Civil Procedure supplanted the Federal Equity Rules. This table shows the Equity Rules to which references are made in the notes to the Federal Rules of Civil Procedure.

Equity Rules	Federal Rules of Civil Procedure
1	77
2	77
3	79
4	77
5	77
6	78
7	4, 70
8	6, 70
9	70
10	18, 54
11	71
12	3, 4, 5, 12, 55
13	4
14	4
15	4, 45
16	6, 55
17	55
18	7, 8
19	1, 15, 61
20	12
21	11, 12
22	1
23	1, 39
24	11
25	8, 9, 10, 19
26	18, 20, 82
27	23
28	15
29	7, 12, 42, 55
30	8, 13, 82
31	7, 8, 12, 55
32	15
33	7, 12
34	5
35	15
36	11

RULES OF CIVIL PROCEDURE

Equity Rules	Federal Rules of Civil Procedure
37	17, 19, 20, 24
38	23
39	19
40	20
41	17
42	19, 20
43	12, 21
44	12, 21
45	25
46	43, 61
47	26
48	43
49	53
50	30, 80
51	30, 53
52	45, 53
53	53
54	26
55	30
56	40
57	40
58	26, 33, 34, 36
59	53
60	53
61	53
61½	3
62	53
63	53
64	26
65	53
66	53
67	53
68	53
69	59
70	17
70½	52
71	54
72	60, 61
73	65

RULES OF CIVIL PROCEDURE

ORDERS OF THE SUPREME COURT OF THE UNITED STATES ADOPTING AND AMENDING RULES

ORDER OF DECEMBER 20, 1937 [302 U.S. 783]

It is ordered that Rules of Procedure for the District Courts of the United States be adopted pursuant to Section 2 of the Act of June 19, 1934, Chapter 651 (48 Stat. 1064), and the Chief Justice is authorized and directed to transmit the Rules as adopted to the Attorney General and to request him, as provided in that section, to report these Rules to the Congress at the beginning of the regular session in January next. MR. JUSTICE BRANDEIS states that he does not approve of the adoption of the Rules.

ORDER OF DECEMBER 28, 1939 [308 U.S. 641, 642]

1.   That the first sentence of Rule 81(a)(6) of the Rules of Civil Procedure be amended so as to read as follows:

"**(6)** These rules do not apply to proceedings under the Act of September 13, 1888, c. 1015, § 13 (25 Stat. 479) as amended, U.S.C., Title 8, § 282, 8 U.S.C.A. § 282, relating to deportation of Chinese; they apply to proceedings for enforcement or review of compensation orders under the Longshoremen's and Harbor Workers' Compensation Act, Act of March 4, 1927, c. 509, §§ 18, 21 (44 Stat. 1434, 1436), U.S.C., Title 33, §§ 918, 921, 33 U.S.C.A. §§ 918, 921, except to the extent that matters of procedure are provided for in that Act".

2.   Effective Date. That the foregoing amendment take effect on the day which is three months subsequent to the adjournment of the second regular session of the 76th Congress, but if that day is prior to September 1, 1940, then this amendment shall take effect on September 1, 1940. This amendment governs all proceedings in actions brought after it takes effect and also all further proceedings in actions then pending, except to the extent that in the opinion of the Court its application in a particular action pending when the amendment takes effect would not be feasible or would work injustice, in which event the former procedure applies.

3.   That THE CHIEF JUSTICE be authorized to transmit this amendment to the Attorney General with the request that he report it to the Congress at the beginning of the regular session in January, 1940.

MR. JUSTICE BLACK does not approve of the adoption of this amendment.

ORDER OF DECEMBER 27, 1946 [329 U.S. 843]

1.   That subdivisions (a) and (b) of Rule 80 of the Rules of Civil Procedure be, and they hereby are, abrogated.

2.   That Rules 6, 7, 12, 13, 14, 17, 24, 26, 27, 28, 33, 34, 36, 41, 45, 52, 54, 56, 58, 59, 60, 62, 65, 66, 68, 73, 75, 77, 79, 81, 84, and 86 of the Rules of Civil Procedure and Forms Nos. 17, 20, 22, and 25, be, and they hereby are, amended as hereinafter set forth.

[See the amendments made thereby under the respective rules and forms, post.]

RULES OF CIVIL PROCEDURE

3. That THE CHIEF JUSTICE be authorized to transmit these amendments to the Attorney General with the request that he report them to the Congress at the beginning of the regular session in January, 1947.

MR. JUSTICE FRANKFURTER joins in approval of the proposed amendments essentially because of his confidence in the informed judgment of the Advisory Committee on Rules of Civil Procedure.

ORDER OF DECEMBER 29, 1948 [335 U.S. 923]

1. That the title "Rules of Civil Procedure for the District Courts of the United States" be amended to read "Rules of Civil Procedure for the United States District Courts".

2. That Rules 1, 17, 22, 24, 25, 27, 37, 45, 57, 60, 62, 65, 66, 67, 69, 72, 73, 74, 75, 76, 79, 81, 82, and 86 of the Rules of Civil Procedure and Forms Nos. 1, 19, 22, 23, and 27, be, and they hereby are, amended as hereinafter set forth.

[See the amendments made thereby under the respective rules and forms, post.]

3. That THE CHIEF JUSTICE be authorized to transmit these amendments to the Attorney General with the request that he report them to the Congress at the beginning of the regular session in January, 1949.

ORDER OF APRIL 30, 1951 [341 U.S. 962]

1. That paragraph (7) of Rule 81(a) of the Rules of Civil Procedure, be, and it hereby is, abrogated.

2. That the Rules of Civil Procedure be, and they hereby are, amended by including therein a rule to govern condemnation cases in the United States District Courts, numbered 71A, as follows:

[See text of Rule 71A, post.]

3. Effective Date. That this Rule 71A and the amendment to Rule 81(a) will take effect on August 1, 1951. Rule 71A governs all proceedings in actions brought after it takes effect and also all further proceedings in actions then pending, except to the extent that in the opinion of the court its application in a particular action pending when the rule takes effect would not be feasible or would work injustice, in which event the former procedure applies.

4. That Forms Nos. 28 and 29 be, and they hereby are, approved and added to the Appendix of Forms to the Rules of Civil Procedure. The forms read respectively as follows:

[See text of Forms 28 and 29, post.]

5. That THE CHIEF JUSTICE be authorized to transmit these amendments to the Congress on or before May 1, 1951.

ORDER OF APRIL 17, 1961 [368 U.S. 1012]

1. That Rules 25, 54, 62 and 86 of the Rules of Civil Procedure and Forms Nos. 2 and 19, be, and they hereby are, amended as hereinafter set forth:

[See the amendments made thereby under the respective rules and forms, post.]

2. That THE CHIEF JUSTICE be authorized to transmit these amendments to Congress in accordance with the provisions of Title 28, U.S.C., Sec. 2072.

3. MR. JUSTICE BLACK does not join in approval of the Rules because he believes that it would be better for Congress to act directly by legislation on the matters treated by the Rules.

4. MR. JUSTICE DOUGLAS filed the following statement:

Most of the proposed changes in the *Rules of Civil Procedure* are picayune and harmless, yet hardly worth making apart from any overall revision of the Rules. The change in Rule 25 of the *Rules of Civil Procedure* is, however, a major one; and it seems to me unwise. The policy that a cabinet officer under one administration pursues is often not the policy of the next administration. I would not make the contrary assumption, as does the proposed change. I think the ends served by *Snyder v. Buck,* 340 U.S. 15, 71 S.Ct. 93, 95 L.Ed. 15, are proper ones. The Rule in its present form leaves the burden on the claimant who challenges a particular government policy to re-establish that the controversy he had with a predecessor is a live one as respects the successor. The burden should rest there, not with the newcomer to office.

The critical language in Rule 25(d) that is changed by the proposed amendment derived from 28 U.S.C. § 780 which the Revised Code dropped in 1949 because it had been incorporated in Rule 25(d). See 28 U.S.C., p. XXIX. The history of § 780 is reviewed in *Snyder v. Buck*, supra, pp. 18–19.

Congress dealt with the matter beginning with the Act of February 8, 1899, 30 Stat. 822. The care with which it approached the problem is shown in H.R.Rep. No. 960, 55th Cong., 2d Sess., p. 2, where it is said:

> "A mandamus proceeding against an officer is based upon the claim that he is personally refusing to perform some duty which the law requires of him in his official character, and if decided against him he is properly liable, personally, for all cost of the proceeding, but if he vacates the office before a decision, it might seem harsh to compel his successor to become a party to the suit and to the costs already accrued without having been guilty of any personal neglect of the official duty involved in the proceeding; but to provide against this seeming harshness your committee propose to amend the bill so as to give the succeeding official an opportunity to perform the official act involved in the proceeding and thereby prevent the survival of the action against himself, and if he fails to do so, he can not then complain of being mulct in costs accruing against his predecessor."

The provision of § 780 that the action might be continued against the successor in office on the requisite showing within the stated period was added by § 11 of the Judiciary Act of 1925. 43 Stat. 936, 941. The last word Congress spoke on the matter reflected the views in a Report submitted by Chief Justice Taft dated March 11, 1922, which explained § 11 in the following words:

> "It will be noted . . . that the provision is not mandatory, but leaves it to the sound discretion of the court to determine whether there is a substantial need for continuing the cause and obtaining an adjudication of the questions involved. This will tend to restrict the exercise of the right to cases which have a sound basis."

This language was repeated in the Senate Committee Print, 68th Cong., 1st Sess., of A General Review of H.R. 10479, 67th Cong., p. 16. The language so carefully tailored by Congress is now rejected by the professional group who constitute our advisors in these matters. I do not think we should allow a known and established congressional policy to be so readily abrogated.

We said in *Snyder v. Buck,* supra, p. 20, that if Rule 25(d) is to be amended in the manner then urged and now adopted 'the amending process is available.' Where we have a matter so heavily encrusted with legislative policy, I think any change should be left to Congress.

I, therefore, dissent from the submission to Congress of the proposed amendments to Rule 25 of the *Rules of Civil Procedure* under 28 U.S.C. § 2072. For under that Act the Rules submitted become effective at the expiration of a 90-day period, unless Congress takes contrary action. This machinery seems therefore, inappropriate to me for effecting such a basic change in congressional policy as the proposed Rule 25(d) achieves."

ORDER OF JANUARY 21, 1963 [374 U.S. 865]

1. That the Rules of Civil Procedure be, and they hereby are, amended by including therein Forms Number 30, 31 and 32, and the amendments to Rules 4, 5, 6, 7, 12, 13, 14, 15, 24, 25, 26, 28, 30, 41, 49, 50, 52, 56, 58, 71A, 77, 79, 81, and 86 and to Forms Number 3, 4, 5, 6, 7, 8, 9, 10, 11, 12, 13, 16, 18, 21, 22-A and 22-B, as hereinafter set forth:

[See additions and amendments made thereby under the respective rules and forms, post.]

2. That THE CHIEF JUSTICE be authorized to transmit these amendments to Congress in accordance with the provisions of Title 28, U.S.C., Sec. 2072.

MR. JUSTICE BLACK and MR. JUSTICE DOUGLAS are opposed to the submission of these rules[1] to the Congress under a statute which permits them to "take effect" and to repeal "all laws in conflict with such rules" without requiring any affirmative consideration, action, or approval of the rules by Congress or

---

[1] See our earlier statements in 368 U.S. §§ 1012–1014 and 346 U.S. §§ 946–947.

by the President.[2] We believe that while some of the Rules of Civil Procedure are simply housekeeping details,[3] many determine matters so substantially affecting the rights of litigants in law suits that in practical effect they are the equivalent of new legislation which, in our judgment, the Constitution requires to be initiated in and enacted by the Congress[4] and approved by the President.[5] The Constitution, as we read it, provides that all laws shall be enacted by the House, the Senate, and the President, not by the mere failure of Congress to reject proposals of an outside agency. Even were there not this constitutional limitation, the authorizing statute itself qualifies this Court's power by imposing upon it a solemn responsibility not to submit rules that "abridge, enlarge or modify any substantive right" and by specifically charging the Court with the duty to "preserve the right to trial by jury as at common law and as declared by the Seventh Amendment to the Constitution."[6] Our chief objections to the rules relate essentially to the fact that many of their provisions do "abridge, enlarge or modify" substantive rights and do not "preserve the right to trial by jury" but actually encroach upon it.

(1)(a) Rule 50(a) is amended by making the order of a judge granting a motion for a directed verdict effective without submitting the question to the jury at all. It was pointed out in *Galloway v. United States,* 319 U.S. 372, 396, 401–407, 63 S.Ct. 1077, 87 L.Ed. 1458 (dissenting opinion), how judges have whittled away or denied the right of trial by jury through the devices of directed verdicts and judgments notwithstanding verdicts. Although the amendment here is not itself a momentous one, it gives formal sanction to the process by which the courts have been wresting from juries the power to render verdicts. Since we do not approve of this sapping of the Seventh Amendment's guarantee of a jury trial, we cannot join even this technical *coup de grace.*

(b) The proposed amendment to 50(c) in practical effect vests appellate courts with more power than they have had to grant or deny new trials. The Court in *Cone v. West Virginia Pulp & Paper Co.,* 330 U.S. 212, 217–218, 67 S.Ct. 752, 91 L.Ed. 849, and *Globe Liquor Co. v. San Roman,* 332 U.S. 571, 68 S.Ct. 246, 92 L.Ed. 177, refused to construe the federal rules then existing to allow Courts of Appeals to interfere with trial judges' discretion to grant new trials. To the extent that jury verdicts are to be set aside and new trials granted, we believe that those who hear the evidence, the trial judges, are the ones who should primarily exercise such discretion.

(c) The proposed amendment to Rule 56(e) imposes additional burdens upon litigants to protect against summary judgments rendered without hearing evidence on the part of witnesses who are confronted by the persons against whom they testify so that these persons can subject the witnesses to cross-examination. The summary judgment procedure, while justified in some cases, is made a handy instrument to let judges rather than juries try law suits and to let those judges try cases not on evidence of witnesses subjected to cross-examination but on ex parte affidavits obtained by parties. Most trial lawyers would agree, we think, that a litigant can frequently obtain in an actual trial favorable testimony which could not have been secured by affidavits or even by depositions.

(d) If there are to be amendments, Rule 49 should be repealed. That rule authorizes judges to require juries to return "only a special verdict in the form of a special written finding upon each issue of fact" or to answer "written interrogatories upon one or more issues of fact the decision of which is necessary to a verdict" in addition to rendering the general verdict. Such devices are used to impair or wholly take away the power of a jury to render a general verdict. One of the ancient, fundamental reasons for having general jury verdicts was to preserve the right of trial by jury as an indispensable part of a free government. Many of the most famous constitutional controversies in England revolved around litigants' insistence,

---

[2]   28 U.S.C. § 2072 gives this Court the power to prescribe rules of practice and procedure for Federal District Courts and further provides that such rules

"shall not take effect until they have been reported to Congress by THE CHIEF JUSTICE at or after the beginning of a regular session thereof but not later than the first day of May, and until the expiration of ninety days after they have been thus reported."

"All laws in conflict with such rules shall be of no further force or effect after such rules have taken effect."

[3]   See 368 U.S. 1012.

[4]   "All legislative Powers herein granted shall be vested in a Congress of the United States, which shall consist of a Senate and House of Representatives." U.S. Const., Art. I, § 1.

[5]   Every Bill which shall have passed the House of Representatives and the Senate, shall, before it becomes a Law, be presented to the President of the United States; . . . " U.S. Const., Art. I, § 7.

[6]   28 U.S.C. § 2072.

particularly in seditious libel cases, that a jury had the right to render a general verdict without being compelled to return a number of subsidiary findings to support its general verdict. Some English jurors had to go to jail because they insisted upon their right to render general verdicts over the repeated commands of tyrannical judges not to do so. Rule 49 is but another means utilized by courts to weaken the constitutional power of juries and to vest judges with more power to decide cases according to their own judgments. A scrutiny of the special verdict and written interrogatory cases in appellate courts will show the confusion that necessarily results from the employment of these devices and the ease with which judges can use them to take away the right to trial by jury. We believe that Rule 49 should be repealed, not amplified.

(2) There is a proposal to amend Rule 41, which provides for dismissal of actions. We believe that, if the Rules are to be changed, a major amendment to this rule is required in the interest of justice. Before dismissing a plaintiff's action for failure of his lawyer to prosecute, the trial judge should be required to have notice served on the plaintiff himself. The hardship that can result from the absence of such requirement is shown by *Link v. Wabash R. Co.,* 370 U.S. 626, 82 S.Ct. 1386, 8 L.Ed.2d 734. Link's lawyer failed to appear in response to a judge's order for a pre-trial conference, and the judge dismissed the case. As pointed out in the dissent, plaintiff had been severely injured, and a fair system of justice should not have penalized him because his lawyer, through neglect or any other reason, failed to appear when ordered. It would do a defendant no injury for the court to refuse to dismiss any apparently bona fide case until the plaintiff has actually had notice that some failure of his lawyer has irked the judge.

(3) MR. JUSTICE BLACK and MR. JUSTICE DOUGLAS object to the changes in Rule 4, which for the first time permit a Federal District Court to obtain jurisdiction over a defendant by service of process outside the state or over his property by garnishment or attachment, under the circumstances and in the manner prescribed by state law. Those changes will apparently have little effect insofar as "federal question" litigation is concerned, since 28 U.S.C. § 1391(b) requires such suits to be brought "only in the judicial district where all defendants reside. . . ." Diversity actions, however, may be greatly increased, for the effect of proposed 4(e) is not limited to suits authorized by such statutes as the Federal Interpleader Act, 28 U.S.C. § 1335. See Advisory Committee Rept., 5–8; 28 U.S.C. § 1391(a); Fed.Rules Civ.Proc. 1. We see no justification for an increase in the number of diversity cases. We also see no reason why the extent of a Federal District Court's personal jurisdiction should depend upon the existence or nonexistence of a state "long-arm" statute. Moreover, at present a state court action commenced by attachment or garnishment can get into a District Court only if a nonresident defendant chooses to appear and remove the case, see 28 U.S.C. § 1441, and there is no good reason, absent a congressional finding, why this should be changed.

Instead of recommending changes to the present Rules, we recommend that the statute authorizing this Court to prescribe Rules of Civil Procedure, if it is to remain a law, be amended to place the responsibility upon the Judicial Conference rather than upon this Court. Since the statute was first enacted in 1934, 48 Stat. 1064, the Judicial Conference has been enlarged and improved and is now very active in its surveillance of the work of the federal courts and in recommending appropriate legislation to Congress. The present Rules produced under 28 U.S.C. § 2072 are not prepared by us but by Committees of the Judicial Conference designated by the Chief Justice, and before coming to us they are approved by the Judicial Conference pursuant to 28 U.S.C. § 331.[7] The Committees and the Conference are composed of able and distinguished members and they render a high public service. It is they, however, who do the work, not we, and the rules have only our imprimatur. The only contribution that we actually make is an occasional exercise of a veto power. If the rule-making for Federal District Courts is to continue under the present plan, we believe that the Supreme Court should not have any part in the task; rather, the statute should be amended to substitute the Judicial Conference. The Judicial Conference can participate more actively in fashioning the rules and affirmatively contribute to their content and design better than we can. Transfer of the function to the Judicial Conference would relieve us of the embarrassment of having to sit in judgment on the constitutionality of rules which we have approved and which as applied in given situations might have to be declared invalid.

---

7 "The Conference shall also carry on a continuous study of the operation and effect of the general rules of practice and procedure now or hereafter in use as prescribed by the Supreme Court for the other courts of the United States pursuant to law. Such changes in and additions to those rules as the Conference may deem desirable to promote simplicity in procedure, fairness in administration, the just determination of litigation, and the elimination of unjustifiable expense and delay shall be recommended by the Conference from time to time to the Supreme Court for its consideration and adoption, modification or rejection, in accordance with law."

RULES OF CIVIL PROCEDURE

ORDER OF FEBRUARY 28, 1966 [383 U.S. 1031]

1.   That the Rules of Civil Procedure for the United States District Courts be, and they hereby are, amended by including therein Rules 23.1, 23.2, 44.1 and 65.1, Supplemental Rules A, B, C, D, E and F for Certain Admiralty and Maritime Claims, and amendments to Rules 1, 4, 8, 9, 12, 13, 14, 15, 17, 18, 19, 20, 23, 24, 26, 38, 41, 42, 43, 44, 47, 53, 59, 65, 68, 73, 74, 75, 81 and 82, and to Forms 2 and 15, as hereinafter set forth:

[See added, amended and supplemental Rules and Forms, post.]

2.   That the foregoing amendments and additions to the Rules of Civil Procedure shall take effect on July 1, 1966, and shall govern all proceedings in actions brought thereafter and also in all further proceedings in actions then pending, except to the extent that in the opinion of the court their application in a particular action then pending would not be feasible or would work injustice, in which event the former procedure applies.

3.   That THE CHIEF JUSTICE be, and he hereby is, authorized to transmit to the Congress the foregoing amendments and additions to the Rules of Civil Procedure in accordance with the provisions of Title 28, U.S.C., §§ 2072 and 2073.

4.   That: (a) subdivision (c) of Rule 6 of the Rules of Civil Procedure for the United States District Courts promulgated by this court on December 20, 1937, effective September 16, 1938; (b) Rule 2 of the Rules for Practice and Procedure under section 25 of An Act to amend and consolidate the Acts respecting copyright, approved March 4, 1909, promulgated by this court on June 1, 1909, effective July 1, 1909; and (c) the Rules of Practice in Admiralty and Maritime Cases, promulgated by this court on December 6, 1920, effective March 7, 1921, as revised, amended and supplemented, be, and they hereby are, rescinded, effective July 1, 1966.

MR. JUSTICE BLACK, dissenting.

The Amendments to the Federal Rules of Civil and Criminal Procedure today transmitted to the Congress are the work of very capable advisory committees. Those committees, not the Court, wrote the rules. Whether by this transmittal the individual members of the Court who voted to transmit the rules intended to express approval of the varied policy decisions the rules embody I am not sure. I am reasonably certain, however, that the Court's transmittal does not carry with it a decision that the amended rules are all constitutional. For such a decision would be the equivalent of an advisory opinion which, I assume the Court would unanimously agree, we are without constitutional power to give. And I agree with my Brother DOUGLAS that some of the proposed criminal rules go to the very border line if they do not actually transgress the constitutional right of a defendant not to be compelled to be a witness against himself. This phase of the criminal rules in itself so infects the whole collection of proposals that, without mentioning other objections, I am opposed to transmittal of the proposed amendments to the criminal rules.

I am likewise opposed to transmittal of the proposed revision of the civil rules. In the first place I think the provisions of 28 U.S.C. § 2072 (1964 ed.), under which these rules are transmitted and the corresponding section, 18 U.S.C. § 3771 (1964 ed.), relating to the criminal rules, both of which provide for giving transmitted rules the effect of law as though they had been properly enacted by Congress are unconstitutional for reasons I have previously stated.[1] And in prior dissents I have stated some of the basic reasons for my objections to repeated rules revisions[2] that tend to upset established meanings and need not repeat those grounds of objection here. The confusion created by the adoption of the present rules, over my objection, has been partially dispelled by judicial interpretations of them by this Court and others. New

---

[1]   In a statement accompanying a previous transmittal of the civil rules, MR. JUSTICE DOUGLAS and I said:

"MR. JUSTICE BLACK and MR. JUSTICE DOUGLAS are opposed to the submission of these rules to the Congress under a statute which permits them to 'take effect' and to repeal 'all laws in conflict with such rules' without requiring any affirmative consideration, action, or approval of the rules by Congress or by the President. We believe that while some of the Rules of Civil Procedure are simply housekeeping details, many determine matters so substantially affecting the rights of litigants in lawsuits that in practical effect they are the equivalent of new legislation which, in our judgment, the Constitution requires to be initiated in and enacted by the Congress and approved by the President. The Constitution, as we read it, provides that all laws shall be enacted by the House, the Senate, and the President, not by the mere failure of Congress to reject proposals of an outside agency. * * * " (Footnotes omitted.) 374 U.S. 865–866.

[2]   346 U.S. 946, 374 U.S. 865. And see 368 U.S. 1011 and 1012.

rules and extensive amendments to present rules will mean renewed confusion resulting in new challenges and new reversals and prejudicial "pretrial" dismissals of cases before a trial on the merits for failure of lawyers to understand and comply with new rules of uncertain meaning. Despite my continuing objection to the old rules, it seems to me that since they have at least gained some degree of certainty it would be wiser to "bear those ills we have than fly to others we know not of," unless, of course, we are reasonably sure that the proposed reforms of the old rules are badly needed. But I am not. The new proposals, at least some of them, have, as I view them, objectionable possibilities that cause me to believe our judicial system could get along much better without them.

The momentum given the proposed revision of the old rules by this Court's transmittal makes it practically certain that Congress, just as has this Court, will permit the rules to take effect exactly as they were written by the Advisory Committee on Rules. Nevertheless, I am including here a memorandum I submitted to the Court expressing objections to the Committee's proposals and suggesting changes should they be transmitted. These suggestions chiefly center around rules that grant broad discretion to trial judges with reference to class suits, pretrial procedures, and dismissal of cases with prejudice. Cases coming before the federal courts over the years now filling nearly 40 volumes of Federal Rules Decisions show an accumulation of grievances by lawyers and litigants about the way many trial judges exercise their almost unlimited discretionary powers to use pretrial procedures to dismiss cases without trials. In fact, many of these cases indicate a belief of many judges and legal commentators that the cause of justice is best served in the long run not by trials on the merits but by summary dismissals based on out of court affidavits, pretrial depositions, and other pretrial techniques. My belief is that open court trials on the merits where litigants have the right to prove their case or defense best comports with due process of law.

The proposed rules revisions, instead of introducing changes designed to prevent the continued abuse of pretrial power to dismiss cases summarily without trials, move in the opposite direction. Of course, each such dismissal results in removal of one more case from our congested court dockets, but that factor should not weigh more heavily in our system of justice than assuring a full-fledged due process trial of every bona fide lawsuit brought to vindicate an honest, substantial claim. It is to protect this ancient right of a person to have his case tried rather than summarily thrown out of court that I suggested to the Court that it recommend changes in the Committee's proposals of the nature set out in the following memorandum.

"Dear Brethren:

"I have gone over all the proposed amendments carefully and while there are probably some good suggestions, it is my belief that the bad results that can come from the adoption of these amendments predominate over any good they can bring about. I particularly think that every member of the Court should examine with great care the amendments relating to class suits. It seems to me that they place too much power in the hands of the trial judges and that the rules might almost as well simply provide that 'class suits can be maintained either for or against particular groups whenever in the discretion of a judge he thinks it is wise.' The power given to the judge to dismiss such suits or to divide them up into groups at will subjects members of classes to dangers that could not follow from carefully prescribed legal standards enacted to control class suits.

"In addition, the rules as amended, in my judgment, greatly aggravate the evil of vesting judges with practically uncontrolled power to dismiss with prejudice cases brought by plaintiffs or defenses interposed by defendants. The power to dismiss a plaintiff's case or to render judgments by default against defendants can work great harm to both parties. There are many inherent urges in existence which may subconsciously incline a judge towards disposing of the cases before him without having to go through the burden of a trial. Mr. Chief Justice White, before he became Chief Justice, wrote an opinion in the case of *Hovey v. Elliott*, 167 U.S. 409 [17 S.Ct. 841, 42 L.Ed. 215], which pointed out grave constitutional questions raised by attempting to punish the parties by depriving them of the right to try their law suits or to defend against law suits brought against them by others.

"Rule 41 entitled 'Dismissal of Actions' points up the great power of judges to dismiss actions and provides an automatic method under which a dismissal must be construed as a dismissal 'with prejudice' unless the judge specifically states otherwise. For that reason I suggest to the Conference that if the Rules are accepted, including that one, the last sentence of Rule 41(b) be amended so as to provide that a simple order of dismissal by a judge instead of operating 'as an adjudication upon the merits,' as the amended rule reads, shall provide that such a dismissal 'does not operate as an adjudication upon the merits.'

RULES OF CIVIL PROCEDURE

"As a further guarantee against oppressive dismissals I suggest the addition of the following as subdivision (c) of Rule 41.

" 'No plaintiff's case shall be dismissed or defendant's right to defend be cut off because of the neglect, misfeasance, malfeasance, or failure of their counsel to obey any order of the court, until and unless such plaintiff or defendant shall have been personally served with notice of their counsel's delinquency, and not then unless the parties themselves do or fail to do something on their own part that can legally justify dismissal of the plaintiff's case or of the defendant's defense.'

"This proposed amendment is suggested in order to protect litigants, both plaintiffs and defendants, against being thrown out of court as a penalty for their lawyer's neglect or misconduct. The necessity for such a rule is shown, I think, by the dismissal in the plaintiff's case in *Link v. Wabash R. Co.,* 370 U.S. 626 [82 S.Ct. 1386, 8 L.Ed.2d 734]. The usual argument against this suggestion is that a party to a law suit hires his lawyer and should therefore be responsible for everything his lawyer does in the conduct of his case. This may be a good argument with reference to affluent litigants who not only know the best lawyers but are able to hire them. It is a wholly unrealistic argument, however, to make with reference to individual persons who do not know the ability of various lawyers or who are not financially able to hire those at the top of the bar and who are compelled to rely on the assumption that a lawyer licensed by the State is competent. It seems to me to be an uncivilized practice to punish clients by throwing their cases out of court because of their lawyers' conduct. It may be supportable by good, sound, formal logic but I think has no support whatever in a procedural system supposed to work as far as humanly possible to the end of obtaining equal and exact justice."

"H.L.B."

For all the reasons stated above and in my previous objections to the transmittals of rules I dissent from the transmittals here.

ORDER OF DECEMBER 4, 1967 [389 U.S. 1065]

1. That the following rules, to be known as the Federal Rules of Appellate Procedure, be, and they hereby are, prescribed, pursuant to sections 3771 and 3772 of Title 18, United States Code, and sections 2072 and 2075 of Title 28, United States Code, to govern the procedure in appeals to United States courts of appeals from the United States district courts, in the review by United States courts of appeals of decisions of the Tax Court of the United States, in proceedings in the United States courts of appeals for the review or enforcement of orders of administrative agencies, boards, commissions and officers, and in applications for writs or other relief which a United States court of appeals or judge thereof is competent to give:

[See text of Rules of Appellate Procedure, post.]

2. That the foregoing rules shall take effect on July 1, 1968, and shall govern all proceedings in appeals and petitions for review or enforcement of orders thereafter brought and in all such proceedings then pending, except to the extent that in the opinion of the court of appeals their application in a particular proceeding then pending would not be feasible or would work injustice, in which case the former procedure may be followed.

3. That Rules 6, 9, 41, 77 and 81 of the Rules of Civil Procedure for the United States District Courts be, and they hereby are, amended, effective July 1, 1968, as hereinafter set forth:

[See the amendments made thereby under the respective rules, post.]

4. That the chapter heading "IX. APPEALS", all of Rules 72, 73, 74, 75 and 76 of the Rules of Civil Procedure for the United States District Courts, and Form 27 annexed to the said rules, be, and they hereby are, abrogated, effective July 1, 1968.

[Paragraphs 5 and 6 of the order pertain to certain Rules of Criminal Procedure for the United States District Courts and to certain Forms annexed to the said rules. For text, see Pamphlet containing Federal Rules of Criminal Procedure.]

7. That THE CHIEF JUSTICE be, and he hereby is, authorized to transmit to the Congress the foregoing new rules and amendments to and abrogation of existing rules, in accordance with the provisions of Title 18, U.S.C., § 3771, and Title 28, U.S.C., §§ 2072 and 2075.

RULES OF CIVIL PROCEDURE

ORDER OF MARCH 30, 1970 [398 U.S. 979]

1.   That subdivision (a) of Rule 5, subdivision (h) of Rule 9 and Rules 26, 29, 30, 31, 32, 33, 34, 35, 36 and 37, and subdivision (d) of Rule 45, subdivision (a) of Rule 69, and Form 24 of the Rules of Civil Procedure for the United States District Courts be, and they hereby are, amended to read as follows:

[See the amendments made thereby under the respective rules and forms, post.]

2.   That the foregoing amendments to the Rules of Civil Procedure shall take effect on July 1, 1970, and shall govern all proceedings in actions brought thereafter and also in all further proceedings in actions then pending, except to the extent that in the opinion of the court their application in a particular action then pending would not be feasible or would work injustice, in which event the former procedure applies.

3.   That THE CHIEF JUSTICE be, and he hereby is, authorized to transmit to the Congress the foregoing amendments to the Rules of Civil Procedure in accordance with the provisions of Title 28, U.S.C. § 2072.

MR. JUSTICE BLACK and MR. JUSTICE DOUGLAS disapprove of the Amendments to the Federal Rules of Civil Procedure relating to Discovery, and dissent from the action of the Court in transmitting them to the Congress.

ORDER OF MARCH 1, 1971 [401 U.S. 1019]

1.   That subdivision (a) of Rule 6, paragraph (4) of subdivision (a) of Rule 27, paragraph (6) of subdivision (b) of Rule 30, subdivision (c) of Rule 77, and paragraph (2) of subdivision (a) of Rule 81 of the Federal Rules of Civil Procedure be, and they hereby are, amended, effective July 1, 1971, to read as follows:

[See amendments made thereby under the respective rules, post.]

2.   *[Certain Rules of Criminal Procedure for the United States District Courts amended].*

3.   That subdivision (a) of Rule 26 and subdivision (a) of Rule 45 of the Federal Rules of Appellate Procedure be, and they hereby are, amended, effective July 1, 1971, to read as follows:

[See amendments made thereby under the respective Rules of Appellate Procedure, post.]

4.   That THE CHIEF JUSTICE be, and he hereby is, authorized to transmit to the Congress the foregoing amendments to the Rules of Civil, Criminal and Appellate Procedure, in accordance with the provisions of Title 18 U.S.C. § 3771, and Title 28 U.S.C. §§ 2072 and 2075.

MR. JUSTICE BLACK and MR. JUSTICE DOUGLAS dissent from the order entered by the Court today amending the Federal Rules of Civil Procedure, the Federal Rules of Criminal Procedure, and the Federal Rules of Appellate Procedure.

ORDER OF NOVEMBER 20, 1972 [reprinted in H.R. Doc. No. 93–46]

1.   That the rules hereinafter set forth, to be known as the Federal Rules of Evidence, be, and they hereby are, prescribed pursuant to Sections 3402, 3771, and 3772, Title 18, United States Code, and Sections 2072 and 2075, Title 28, United States Code, to govern procedure, in the proceedings and to the extent set forth therein, in the United States courts of appeals, the United States district courts, the District Court for the District of the Canal Zone and the district courts of Guam and the Virgin Islands, and before United States magistrates.

2.   That the aforementioned Federal Rules of Evidence shall take effect on July 1, 1973, and shall be applicable to actions and proceedings brought thereafter and also to further procedure in actions and proceedings then pending, except to the extent that in the opinion of the court their application in a particular action or proceeding then pending would not be feasible or would work injustice in which event the former procedure applies.

3.   That subdivision (c) of Rule 30 and Rules 43 and 44.1 of the Federal Rules of Civil Procedure be, and they hereby are, amended, effective July 1, 1973, to read as hereinafter set forth. . . .

[See amendments made thereby under the respective rules, post.]

4.   That subdivision (c) of Rule 32 of the Federal Rules of Civil Procedure be, and it hereby is, abrogated, effective July 1, 1973.

RULES OF CIVIL PROCEDURE

5. *[Certain Rules of Criminal Procedure for the United States District Courts amended].*

6. That THE CHIEF JUSTICE be, and he hereby is, authorized to transmit the foregoing new rules and amendments to and abrogation of existing rules to the Congress at the beginning of its next regular session, in accordance with the provisions of Title 18 U.S.C. § 3771 and Title 28 U.S.C. §§ 2072 and 2075.

MR. JUSTICE DOUGLAS, dissenting. [409 U.S. 1132]

There are those who think that fashioning of rules of evidence is a task for the legislature, not for the judiciary. Wigmore thought the task was essentially a judicial one, 1 J. Wigmore, Evidence 251 *et seq.* (3d ed. 1940); and I share that view, leaving the problem for case-by-case development by the courts or by Congress.

But my concern with these Rules of Evidence is twofold. First, I doubt if rules of evidence are within the purview of the statute under which we are authorized to submit proposed Rules to Congress. The Act provides that the Supreme Court shall have the power "to prescribe by general rules, the forms of process, writs, pleadings, and motions, and the practice and procedure of the district courts and courts of appeals of the United States in civil actions, including admiralty and maritime cases, and appeals therein, and the practice and procedure in proceedings for the review by the courts of appeals of decisions of the Tax Court of the United States and for the judicial review or enforcement of orders of administrative agencies, boards, commissions, and officers." 28 U.S.C. § 2072.

I can find no legislative history that rules of evidence were to be included in "practice and procedure" as used in § 2072. The Committee Reports on the original Act throw no light on the question. H. R. Rep. No. 1829, 73d Cong., 2d Sess.; S. Rep. No. 1049, 73d Cong., 2d Sess. The words "practice and procedure" in the setting of the Act seem to me to exclude rules of evidence. They seem to me to be words of art that describe pretrial procedures, pleadings, and procedures for preserving objections and taking appeals.

Second, this Court does not write the Rules, nor supervise their writing, nor appraise them on their merits, weighing the pros and cons. The Court concededly is a mere conduit. Those who write the Rules are members of a Committee named by the Judicial Conference. The members are eminent; but they are the sole judges of the merits of the proposed Rules, our approval being merely perfunctory. In other words, we are merely the conduit to Congress. Yet the public assumes that our imprimatur is on the Rules, as of course it is.

We are so far removed from the trial arena that we have no special insight, no meaningful oversight to contribute. The Rules of Evidence—if there are to be some—should be channeled through the Judicial Conference whose members are much more qualified than we to appraise their merits when applied in actual practice.

I also dissent, for reasons set forth by Mr. Justice Black and me on prior occasions, from the amendments to the Federal Rules of Civil Procedure and the Federal Rules of Criminal Procedure. 374 U.S. 865; 368 U.S. 1012; 346 U.S. 946.

William O. Douglas.

ORDER OF DECEMBER 18, 1972 [reprinted in H.R. Doc. No. 93–46]

1. That Rule 43 of the Federal Rules of Civil Procedure, as amended by Order of this Court entered November 20, 1972, be, and it hereby is, further amended, effective July 1, 1973, to read as follows:

[See amendment made thereby under Rule 43 post.]

2. That THE CHIEF JUSTICE be, and he hereby is, authorized to transmit the foregoing amendment of Rule 43 of the Federal Rules of Civil Procedure to the Congress at the beginning of its next regular session in accordance with the provisions of Title 28, U.S.C. § 2072.

CONGRESSIONAL ACTION ON PROPOSED RULES OF EVIDENCE AND 1972 AMENDMENTS TO FEDERAL RULES OF CIVIL PROCEDURE AND FEDERAL RULES OF CRIMINAL PROCEDURE

Pub.L. 93–12, Mar. 30, 1973, 87 Stat. 9, provided: "That notwithstanding any other provisions of law, the Rules of Evidence for United States Courts and Magistrates, the Amendments to the Federal Rules of Civil Procedure, and the Amendments to the Federal Rules of Criminal Procedure, which are embraced by

RULES OF CIVIL PROCEDURE

the orders entered by the Supreme Court of the United States on Monday, November 20, 1972, and Monday, December 18, 1972, shall have no force or effect except to the extent, and with such amendments, as they may be expressly approved by Act of Congress."

Pub.L. 93–595, § 3, Jan. 2, 1975, 88 Stat. 1926, provided that: "The Congress expressly approves the amendments to the Federal Rules of Civil Procedure, and the amendments to the Federal Rules of Criminal Procedure, which are embraced by the orders entered by the Supreme Court of the United States on November 20, 1972, and December 18, 1972, and such amendments shall take effect on the one hundred and eightieth day beginning after the date of the enactment of this Act [Jan. 2, 1975]."

ORDER OF APRIL 26, 1976 [45 U.S. 1169]

1. That the rules and forms governing proceedings in the United States District Courts under Section 2254 and Section 2255 of Title 28, United States Code, as approved by the Judicial Conference of the United States be, and they hereby are, prescribed pursuant to Section 2072 of Title 28, United States Code and Sections 3771 and 3772 of Title 18, United States Code.

2. That the aforementioned rules and forms shall take effect August 1, 1976, and shall be applicable to all proceedings then pending except to the extent that in the opinion of the court their application in a particular proceeding would not be feasible or would work injustice.

3. That THE CHIEF JUSTICE be, and he hereby is, authorized to transmit the aforementioned rules and forms governing Section 2254 and Section 2255 proceedings to the Congress in accordance with the provisions of Section 2072 of Title 28 and Sections 3771 and 3772 of Title 18, United States Code.

ORDER OF APRIL 29, 1980 [446 U.S. 997]

1. That the Federal Rules of Civil Procedure be, and they hereby are, amended by including therein amendments to Rules 4, 5, 26, 28, 30, 32, 33, 34, 37 and 45 as hereinafter set forth:

[See amendments made thereby under respective rules, post.]

2. That the foregoing amendments to the Federal Rules of Civil Procedure shall take effect on August 1, 1980, and shall govern all civil proceedings thereafter commenced and, insofar as just and practicable, all proceedings then pending.

3. That subsection (e) of Rule 37 of the Federal Rules of Civil Procedure is hereby abrogated, effective August 1, 1980.

4. That THE CHIEF JUSTICE be, and he hereby is, authorized to transmit to the Congress the foregoing amendments to the Federal Rules of Civil Procedure in accordance with the provisions of Section 2072 of Title 28, United States Code.

MR. JUSTICE POWELL, with whom MR. JUSTICE STEWART and MR. JUSTICE REHNQUIST join, filed a dissenting statement.

I dissent from the Court's adoption of the amendments to Federal Rules of Civil Procedure 26, 33, 34, and 37—the cluster of Rules authorizing and regulating discovery generally, interrogatories, production of documents, and sanctions for failure to make discovery. These amendments are not inherently objectionable. Indeed, they represent the culmination of several years' work by the Judicial Conference's distinguished and conscientious Standing Committee on Rules of Practice and Procedure and Advisory Committee on Civil Rules.[1] But the changes embodied in the amendments fall short of those needed to accomplish reforms in civil litigation that are long overdue.

---

[1] This Court's role in the rulemaking process is largely formalistic. Standing and advisory committees of the Judicial Conference make the initial studies, invite comments on their drafts, and prepare the Rules. Both the Judicial Conference and this Court necessarily rely upon the careful work of these committees. Congress should bear in mind that our approval of proposed Rules is more a certification that they are the products of proper procedures than a considered judgment on the merits of the proposals themselves. See generally 409 U.S. 1132, 1133 (1973) (DOUGLAS, J., dissenting from adoption of Federal Rules of Evidence); 383 U.S. 1032 (1966) (BLACK, J., dissenting from adoption of amendment to civil rules); 374 U.S. 865, 869–870 (1963) (statement of BLACK and DOUGLAS, JJ., upon adoption of amendments to Federal Rules of Civil Procedure).

RULES OF CIVIL PROCEDURE

The American Bar Association proposed significant and substantial reforms.[2] Although the Standing Committee initially favored most of these proposals, it ultimately rejected them in large part. The ABA now accedes to the Standing Committee's amendments because they make some improvements, but the most recent report of the ABA Section of Litigation makes clear that the "serious and widespread abuse of discovery" will remain largely uncontrolled.[3] There are wide differences of opinion within the profession as to the need for reform. The bench and the bar are familiar with the existing Rules, and it often is said that the bar has a vested interest in maintaining the status quo. I imply no criticism of the bar or the Standing Committee when I suggest that the present recommendations reflect a compromise as well as the difficulty of framing satisfactory discovery Rules. But whatever considerations may have prompted the Committee's final decision, I doubt that many judges or lawyers familiar with the proposed amendments believe they will have an appreciable effect on the acute problems associated with discovery. The Court's adoption of these inadequate changes could postpone effective reform for another decade.

When the Federal Rules first appeared in 1938, the discovery provisions properly were viewed as a constructive improvement. But experience under the discovery Rules demonstrates that "not infrequently [they have been] exploited to the disadvantage of justice." *Herbert v. Lando,* 441 U.S. 153, 179 (1979) (POWELL, J., concurring). Properly limited and controlled discovery is necessary in most civil litigation. The present Rules, however, invite discovery of such scope and duration that district judges often cannot keep the practice within reasonable bounds.[4] Even in a relatively simple case, discovery through depositions, interrogatories, and demands for documents may take weeks. In complex litigation, discovery can continue for years. One must doubt whether empirical evidence would demonstrate that untrammeled discovery actually contributes to the just resolution of disputes. If there is disagreement about that, there is none whatever about the effect of discovery practices upon the average citizen's ability to afford legal remedies.

Delay and excessive expense now characterize a large percentage of all civil litigation. The problems arise in significant part, as every judge and litigator knows, from abuse of the discovery procedures available under the Rules.[5] Indeed, the National Conference on the Causes of Popular Dissatisfaction with the Administration of Justice, led by THE CHIEF JUSTICE,[6] identified "Abuse in the use of discovery [as] a major concern" within our legal system.[7] Lawyers devote an enormous number of "chargeable hours" to the practice of discovery. We may assume that discovery usually is conducted in good faith. Yet all too often discovery practices enable the party with greater financial resources to prevail by exhausting the resources of a weaker opponent. The mere threat of delay or unbearable expense denies justice to many actual or prospective litigants. Persons or businesses of comparatively limited means settle unjust claims and

---

[2]   American Bar Association, Report of the Section of Litigation Special Committee for the Study of Discovery Abuse (App.Draft 1977).

[3]   ABA Section of Litigation, Second Report of the Special Committee for the Study of Discovery Abuse, 5 (1980).

[4]   MR. JUSTICE WHITE, writing for the Court, recently reminded the federal courts that "the discovery provisions . . . are subject to the injunction of Rule 1 that they be 'construed to secure the just, *speedy,* and *inexpensive* determination of every action.'" *Herbert v. Lando,* 441 U.S. 153, 177 (1979).

In his most recent Annual Report on the State of the Judiciary, THE CHIEF JUSTICE declared that "[t]he responsibility for control [of pretrial process] rests on both judges and lawyers. Where existing rules and statutes permit abuse, they must be changed. Where the power lies with judges to prevent or correct abuse and misuse of the system, judges must act." Address to American Bar Association Mid-year Meeting, 6 (Feb. 3, 1980).

[5]   Writing from his wide experience as a judge, practicing lawyer, and Attorney General, Griffin B. Bell advised the Standing Committee that "the scope of discovery is far too broad and that excessive discovery has significantly contributed to the delays, complexity and high cost of civil litigation in the federal courts." Letter to The Honorable Roszel C. Thomsen, Chairman of the Committee on Rules of Practice and Procedure of the Judicial Conference, 1 (June 27, 1978).

[6]   THE CHIEF JUSTICE'S keynote address to this distinguished assembly, popularly known as the Pound Conference, recognized that discovery processes "are being misused and abused." See Burger, Agenda for 2000 A.D.—A Need for Systematic Anticipation, 70 F.R.D. 83, 95–96 (1976).

[7]   See Erickson, The Pound Conference Recommendations: A Blueprint for the Justice System in the Twenty-first Century, 76 F.R.D. 277, 288 (1978); ABA, Report of Pound Conference Follow-up Task Force, 74 F.R.D. 159, 171–192 (1976).

relinquish just claims simply because they cannot afford to litigate.[8] Litigation costs have become intolerable, and they cast a lengthening shadow over the basic fairness of our legal system.

I reiterate that I do not dissent because the modest amendments recommended by the Judicial Conference are undesirable. I simply believe that Congress' acceptance of these tinkering changes will delay for years the adoption of genuinely effective reforms. The process of change, as experience teaches, is tortuous and contentious. Favorable congressional action on these amendments will create complacency and encourage inertia. Meanwhile, the discovery Rules will continue to deny justice to those least able to bear the burdens of delay, escalating legal fees, and rising court costs.

The amendments to Rules 26, 33, 34, and 37 recommended by the Judicial Conference should be rejected, and the Conference should be directed to initiate a thorough re-examination of the discovery Rules that have become so central to the conduct of modern civil litigation.

ORDER OF APRIL 28, 1983 [1982 J. Sup. Ct. U.S. 575]

1.   That the Federal Rules of Civil Procedure be, and they hereby are, amended by including therein new Rules 26(g), 53(f), 72 through 76 and new Official Forms 33 and 34, and amendments to Rules 6(b), 7(b), 11, 16, 26(a) and (b), 52(a), 53(a), (b) and (c) and 67, as hereinafter set forth:

[See additions and amendments made thereby under respective rules and forms, post.]

2.   That the foregoing additions and amendments to the Federal Rules of Civil Procedure shall take effect on August 1, 1983 and shall govern all civil proceedings thereafter commenced and, insofar as just and practicable, in proceedings then pending.

3.   That THE CHIEF JUSTICE be, and he hereby is, authorized to transmit to the Congress the foregoing additions to and changes in the Federal Rules of Civil Procedure in accordance with the provisions of Section 2072 of Title 28, United States Code.

ORDER OF APRIL 29, 1985 [471 U.S. 1155]

1.   That the Federal Rules of Civil Procedure for the United States District Courts be, and they hereby are, amended by including therein a new Rule E(4)(f) to the Supplemental Rules for Certain Admiralty and Maritime Claims; amendments to Rules 6(a), 45(d)(2), 52(a), 71A(h) and 83; amendments to Supplemental Admiralty Rules B(1) and C(3); and amendments to Official Form 18-A, as hereinafter set forth:

[See additions and amendments made thereby under respective rules and forms, post.]

2.   That the foregoing additions to and changes in the Federal Rules of Civil Procedure, the Supplemental Rules for Certain Admiralty and Maritime Claims, and the Official Form shall take effect on August 1, 1985 and shall govern all proceedings in civil actions thereafter commenced and, insofar as just and practicable, all proceedings in civil actions then pending.

3.   That THE CHIEF JUSTICE be, and he hereby is, authorized to transmit to the Congress the foregoing addition to and changes in the rules of civil procedure in accordance with the provisions of Section 2072 of Title 28, United States Code.

ORDER OF MARCH 2, 1987 [480 U.S. 955]

1.   That the Federal Rules of Civil Procedure and the Supplemental Rules for Certain Admiralty and Maritime Claims be, and they hereby are, amended by including therein amendments to Civil Rules 4, 5, 6, 8, 9, 11, 12, 13, 14, 15, 16, 17, 18, 19, 20, 22, 23, 23.1, 24, 25, 26, 27, 28, 30, 31, 32, 34, 35, 36, 37 38, 41, 43, 44, 44.1, 45, 46, 49, 50, 51, 53, 54, 55, 56, 60, 62, 63, 65, 65.1, 68, 69, 71, 71A, 73, 75, 77, 78, 81, and to the Supplemental Rules for Certain Admiralty and Maritime Claims, Rules B, C, E, and F, as hereinafter set forth:

[See amendments made thereby under respective rules, post.]

---

8   "The principal function of procedural rules," as MR. JUSTICE BLACK observed in another context, "should be to serve as useful guides to help, not hinder, persons who have a legal right to bring their problems before the courts." 346 U.S. 946 (1954) (separate statement upon adoption of revised Supreme Court Rules).

2. That the foregoing amendments to the Federal Rules of Civil Procedure and the Supplemental Rules for Certain Admiralty and Maritime Claims shall take effect on August 1, 1987.

3. That THE CHIEF JUSTICE be, and he hereby is, authorized to transmit to the Congress the foregoing amendments in accordance with the provisions of Section 2072 of Title 28, United States Code.

ORDER OF APRIL 25, 1988 [485 U.S. 1045]

1. That the Federal Rules of Civil Procedure be, and they hereby are, amended by including therein amendments to Civil Rules 17 and 71A, as hereinafter set forth:

[See amendments made thereby under respective rules, post.]

2. That the foregoing amendments to the Federal Rules of Civil Procedure shall take effect on August 1, 1988.

3. That THE CHIEF JUSTICE be, and he hereby is, authorized to transmit to the Congress the foregoing amendments in accordance with the provisions of Section 2072 of Title 28, United States Code.

ORDER OF APRIL 30, 1991* [500 U.S. 965]

1. That the Federal Rules of Civil Procedure for the United States District Courts be, and they hereby are, amended by including therein new chapter headings VIII and IX, amendments to Rules C and E of the Supplemental Rules for Certain Admiralty and Maritime Claims, new Forms 1A and 1B to the Appendix of Forms, the abrogation of Form 18A, and amendments to Civil Rules 5, 15, 24, 34, 35, 41, 44, 45, 47, 48, 50, 52, 53, 63, 72, and 77, as hereinafter set forth.

[See additions and amendments made thereby under respective rules and forms, post.]

2. That the foregoing additions to and changes in the Federal Rules of Civil Procedure, the Supplemental Rules for Certain Admiralty and Maritime Claims, and the Civil Forms shall take effect on December 1, 1991, and shall govern all proceedings in civil actions thereafter commenced and, insofar as just and practicable, all proceedings in civil actions then pending.

3. That THE CHIEF JUSTICE be, and hereby is, authorized to transmit to the Congress the foregoing addition to and changes in the Rules of Civil Procedure in accordance with the provisions of Section 2072 of Title 28, United States Code.

ORDER OF APRIL 22, 1993 [507 U.S. 1091]

1. That the Federal Rules of Civil Procedure for the United States District Courts be, and they hereby are, amended by including therein amendments to Civil Rules 1, 4, 5, 11, 12, 15, 16, 26, 28, 29, 30, 31, 32, 33, 34, 36, 37, 38, 50, 52, 53, 54, 58, 71A, 72, 73, 74, 75, and 76, and new Rule 4.1, and abrogation of Form 18-A [*sic*], and amendments to Forms 2, 33, 34, and 34A, and new Forms 1A, 1B, and 35.

[See amendments made thereby under respective rules and forms, post.]

2. That the foregoing amendments to the Federal Rules of Civil Procedure shall take effect on December 1, 1993, and shall govern all proceedings in civil cases thereafter commenced and, insofar as just and practicable, all proceedings in civil cases then pending.

3. That THE CHIEF JUSTICE be, and he hereby is, authorized to transmit to the Congress the foregoing amendments to the Federal Rules of Civil Procedure in accordance with the provisions of Section 2072 of Title 23, United States Code.

JUSTICE WHITE filed a statement.

Title 28 U.S.C. § 2072 empowers the Supreme Court to prescribe general rules of practice and procedure and rules of evidence for cases in the federal courts, including proceedings before magistrates and courts of appeals.[1] But the Court does not itself draft and initially propose these rules. Section 2073 directs

---

* [In his letter of transmittal accompanying this order, Chief Justice Rehnquist noted, "The amendments proposed by the Judicial Conference to Rules 4, 4.1, 12, 26, 28, 30, and 71A are not transmitted at the present time pending further consideration by the Court." C.J. William H. Rehnquist, Letter Transmitting Proposed Amendments to the Federal Rules of Civil Procedure, 500 U.S. 694 (April 30, 1991). Ed.]

[1] Section 2075 vests a similar power in the Court with respect to rules for the bankruptcy courts.

the Judicial Conference to prescribe the procedures for proposing the rules mentioned in § 2072. The Conference is authorized to appoint committees to propose such rules. These rules advisory committees are to be made up of members of the professional bar and trial and appellate judges. The Conference is also to appoint a standing committee on rules of practice and evidence to review the recommendations of the advisory committees and to recommend to the Conference such rules and amendments to those rules "as may be necessary to maintain consistency and otherwise promote the interest of justice." § 2073(b). Any rules approved by the Conference are transmitted to the Supreme Court, which in turn transmits any rules "prescribed" pursuant to § 2072 to the Congress. Except as provided in § 2074(b), such rules become effective at a specified time unless Congress otherwise provides.

The members of the advisory and standing committees are carefully named by THE CHIEF JUSTICE, and I am quite sure that these experienced judges and lawyers take their work very seriously. It is also quite evident that neither the standing committee nor the Judicial Conference merely rubber stamps the proposals recommended to it. It is not at all rare that advisory committee proposals are returned to the originating committee for further study.

During my 31 years on the Court, the number of advisory committees has grown as necessitated by statutory changes. During that time, by my count at least, on some 64 occasions we have "prescribed" and transmitted to Congress a new set of rules or amendments to certain rules. Some of the transmissions have been minor, but many of them have been extensive. Over this time, Justices Black and Douglas, either together or separately, dissented 13 times on the ground that it was inappropriate for the Court to pass on the merits of the rules before it.[2] Aside from those two Justices, Justices Powell, Stewart and then-Justice REHNQUIST dissented on one occasion and JUSTICE O'CONNOR on another as to the substance of proposed rules. 446 U. S. 995, 997 (1980) (Powell, J., dissenting); 461 U. S. 1117, 1119 (1983) (O'CONNOR, J., dissenting). Only once in my memory did the Court refuse to transmit some of the rule changes proposed by the Judicial Conference. 500 U. S. 964 (1991).

That the Justices have hardly ever refused to transmit the rules submitted by the Judicial Conference and the fact that, aside from Justices Black and Douglas, it has been quite rare for any Justice to dissent from transmitting any such rule, suggest that a sizable majority of the 21 Justices who sat during this period concluded that Congress intended them to have a rather limited role in the rulemaking process. The vast majority (including myself) obviously have not explicitly subscribed to the Black-Douglas view that many of the rules proposed dealt with substantive matters that the Constitution reserved to Congress and that in any event were prohibited by § 2072's injunction against abridging, enlarging or modifying substantive rights.

Some of us, however, have silently shared Justice Black's and Justice Douglas' suggestion that the enabling statutes be amended

"to place the responsibility upon the Judicial Conference rather than upon this Court. Since the statute was first enacted in 1934, 48 Stat. 1064, the Judicial Conference has been enlarged and improved and is now very active in its surveillance of the work of the federal courts and in recommending appropriate legislation to Congress. The present rules produced under 28 U. S. C. § 2072 are not prepared by us but by Committees of the Judicial Conference designated by THE CHIEF JUSTICE, and before coming to us they are approved by the Judicial Conference pursuant to 28 U.S.C. § 331. The Committees and the Conference are composed of able and distinguished members and they render a high public service. It is they, however, who do the work, not we, and the rules have only our imprimatur. The only contribution that we actually make is an occasional exercise of a veto power. If the rule-making for Federal District Courts is to continue under the present plan, we believe that the Supreme Court should not have any part in the task; rather, the statute should be amended to substitute the Judicial Conference. The Judicial Conference can participate more actively in fashioning the rules and affirmatively contribute to their content and design better than we can. Transfer of the function to the

---

[2]   421 U. S. 1019, 1022 (1975) (Douglas, J., dissenting); 416 U. S. 1001, 1003 (1974) (Douglas, J., dissenting); 411 U. S. 989, 992 (1973) (Douglas, J., dissenting); 409 U. S. 1132 (1972) (Douglas, J., dissenting); 406 U. S. 979, 981 (1972) (Douglas, J., dissenting); 401 U. S. 1017, 1019 (1971) (Black and Douglas, JJ., dissenting); 400 U. S. 1029, 1031 (1971) (Black, J., with whom Douglas, J., joins, dissenting); 398 U. S. 977, 979 (1970) (Black and Douglas, JJ., dissenting); 395 U. S. 989, 990 (1969) (Black, J., not voting); 383 U. S. 1087, 1089 (1966) (Black, J., dissenting); ibid. (Douglas, J., dissenting); 383 U. S. 1029, 1032 (1966) (Black, J., dissenting); 374 U. S. 861, 865 (1963) (Black and Douglas, JJ., dissenting).

Judicial Conference would relieve us of the embarrassment of having to sit in judgment on the constitutionality of rules which we have approved and which as applied in given situations might have to be declared invalid." 374 U.S. 865, 869–870 (1963) (footnote omitted).

Despite the repeated protestations of both or one of those Justices, Congress did not eliminate our participation in the rulemaking process. Indeed, our statutory role was continued as the coverage of § 2072 was extended to the rules of evidence and to proceedings before magistrates. Congress clearly continued to direct us to "prescribe" specified rules. But most of us concluded that for at least two reasons Congress could not have intended us to provide another layer of review equivalent to that of the standing committee and the Judicial Conference. First, to perform such a function would take an inordinate amount of time, the expenditure of which would be inconsistent with the demands of a growing caseload. Second, some us, and I remain of this view, were quite sure that the Judicial Conference and its committees, "being in large part judges of the lower courts and attorneys who are using the Rules day in and day out, are in a far better position to make a practical judgment upon their utility or inutility than we." 383 U.S. 1089, 1090 (1966) (Douglas, J., dissenting in part).

I did my share of litigating when in practice and once served on the Advisory Committee for the Civil Rules, but the trial practice is a dynamic profession, and the longer one is away from it the less likely it is that he or she should presume to second-guess the careful work of the active professionals manning the rulemaking committees, work that the Judicial Conference has approved. At the very least, we should not perform a de novo review and should defer to the Judicial Conference and its committees as long as they have some rational basis for their proposed amendments.

Hence, as I have seen the Court's role over the years, it is to transmit the Judicial Conference's recommendations without change and without careful study, as long as there is no suggestion that the committee system has not operated with integrity. If it has not, such a fact, or even such a claim, about a body so open to public inspection would inevitably surface. This has been my practice, even though on several occasions, based perhaps on out-of-date conceptions, I had serious questions about the wisdom of particular proposals to amend certain rules.

In connection with the proposed rule changes now before us, there is no suggestion that the rulemaking process has failed to function properly. No doubt the proposed changes do not please everyone, as letters I have received indicate. But I assume that such opposing views have been before the committees and have been rejected on the merits. That is enough for me.

Justice Douglas thought that the Court should be taken out of the rulemaking process entirely, but as long as Congress insisted on our "prescribing" rules, he refused to be a mere conduit and would dissent to forwarding rule changes with which he disagreed. I note that JUSTICE SCALIA seems to follow that example. But I also note that as time went on, Justice Douglas confessed to insufficient familiarity with the context in which new rules would operate to pass judgment on their merits.[3]

In conclusion, I suggest that it would be a mistake for the bench, the bar, or the Congress to assume that we are duplicating the function performed by the standing committee or the Judicial Conference with respect to changes in the various rules which come to us for transmittal. As I have said, over the years our role has been a much more limited one.

JUSTICE SCALIA, with whom JUSTICE THOMAS joins, and with whom JUSTICE SOUTER joins as to Part II, filed a dissenting statement.

I dissent from the Court's adoption of the amendments to Federal Rules of Civil Procedure 11 (relating to sanctions for frivolous litigation), and 26, 30, 31, 33, and 37 (relating to discovery). In my view, the

---

[3] In dissenting from the order transmitting the Chapter XIII Bankruptcy Rules, Justice Douglas, among other things said: "Forty years ago I had perhaps some expertise in the field; and I know enough about history, our Constitution, and our decisions to oppose the adoption of Rule 920. But for most of these Rules I do not have sufficient insight and experience to know whether they are desirable or undesirable. I must, therefore, disassociate myself from them." 411 U. S. 992, 994 (1973).

With respect to Amendments to the Rules of Criminal Procedure forwarded by the Court a year later, the following statement was appended to the Court's order, 416 U. S. 1003 (1974): "MR. JUSTICE DOUGLAS is opposed to the Court's being a mere conduit of Rules to Congress since the Court has had no hand in drafting them and has no competence to design them in keeping with the titles and spirit of the Constitution."

sanctions proposal will eliminate a significant and necessary deterrent to frivolous litigation; and the discovery proposal will increase litigation costs, burden the district courts, and, perhaps worst of all, introduce into the trial process an element that is contrary to the nature of our adversary system.

I

Rule 11

It is undeniably important to the Rules' goal of "the just, speedy, and inexpensive determination of every action," Fed. Rule Civ. Proc. 1, that frivolous pleadings and motions be deterred. The current Rule 11 achieves that objective by requiring sanctions when its standards are violated (though leaving the court broad discretion as to the manner of sanction), and by allowing compensation for the moving party's expenses and attorney's fees. The proposed revision would render the Rule toothless, by allowing judges to dispense with sanction, by disfavoring compensation for litigation expenses, and by providing a 21-day "safe harbor" within which, if the party accused of a frivolous filing withdraws the filing, he is entitled to escape with no sanction at all.

To take the last first: In my view, those who file frivolous suits and pleadings should have no "safe harbor." The Rules should be solicitous of the abused (the courts and the opposing party), and not of the abuser. Under the revised Rule, parties will be able to file thoughtless, reckless, and harassing pleadings, secure in the knowledge that they have nothing to lose: If objection is raised, they can retreat without penalty. The proposed revision contradicts what this Court said only three years ago: "Baseless filing puts the machinery of justice in motion, burdening courts and individuals alike with needless expense and delay. Even if the careless litigant quickly dismisses the action, the harm triggering Rule 11's concerns has already occurred. Therefore, a litigant who violates Rule 11 merits sanctions even after a dismissal." *Cooter & Gell v. Hartmarx Corp.*, 496 U. S. 384, 398 (1990). The advisory committee itself was formerly of the same view. *Ibid.* (quoting Letter from Chairman, Advisory Committee on Civil Rules).

The proposed Rule also decreases both the likelihood and the severity of punishment for those foolish enough not to seek refuge in the safe harbor after an objection is raised. Proposed subsection (c) makes the issuance of any sanction discretionary, whereas currently it is *required*. Judges, like other human beings, do not like imposing punishment when their duty does not require it, especially upon their own acquaintances and members of their own profession. They do not immediately see, moreover, the system-wide benefits of serious Rule 11 sanctions, though they are intensely aware of the amount of their own time it would take to consider and apply sanctions in the case before them. For these reasons, I think it important to the effectiveness of the scheme that the sanctions remain mandatory.

Finally, the likelihood that frivolousness will even be *challenged* is diminished by the proposed Rule, which restricts the award of compensation to "unusual circumstances," with monetary sanctions "ordinarily" to be payable to the court. Advisory Committee Notes to Proposed Rule 11, pp. 53–54. Under Proposed Rule 11(c)(2), a court may order payment for "some or all of the reasonable attorneys' fees and other expenses incurred as a direct result of the violation" only when that is "warranted for effective deterrence." Since the deterrent effect of a fine is rarely increased by altering the identity of the payee, it takes imagination to conceive of instances in which this provision will ever apply. And the commentary makes it clear that even when compensation is granted it should be granted stingily—only for costs "directly and unavoidably caused by the violation." *Id.*, at 54. As seen from the viewpoint of the victim of an abusive litigator, these revisions convert Rule 11 from a means of obtaining compensation to an invitation to throw good money after bad. The net effect is to decrease the incentive on the part of the person best situated to alert the court to perversion of our civil justice system.

I would not have registered this dissent if there were convincing indication that the current Rule 11 regime is ineffective, or encourages excessive satellite litigation. But there appears to be general agreement, reflected in a recent report of the advisory committee itself, that Rule 11, as written, basically works. According to that report, a Federal Judicial Center survey showed that 80% of district judges believe Rule 11 has had an overall positive effect and should be retained in its present form, 95% believed the Rule had not impeded development of the law, and about 75% said the benefits justify the expenditure of judicial time. See Interim Report on Rule 11, Advisory Committee on Civil Rules, reprinted in G. Vairo, Rule 11 Sanctions: Case Law Perspectives and Preventive Measures, App. I-8-I-10 (2d ed. 1991). True, many lawyers do not like Rule 11. It may cause them financial liability, it may damage their professional reputation in front of important clients, and the cost-of-litigation savings it produces are savings not to lawyers but to litigants. But the overwhelming approval of the Rule by the federal district judges who daily grapple with the problem of litigation abuse is enough to persuade me that it should not be gutted as the proposed revision suggests.[1]

II

Discovery Rules

The proposed radical reforms to the discovery process are potentially disastrous and certainly premature—particularly the imposition on litigants of a continuing duty to disclose to opposing counsel, without awaiting any request, various information "relevant to disputed facts alleged with particularity." See Proposed Rule 26(a)(1)(A), (a)(1)(B), (e)(1). This proposal is promoted as a means of reducing the unnecessary expense and delay that occur in the present discovery regime. But the duty-to-disclose regime does not replace the current, much-criticized discovery process; rather, it *adds a further layer of discovery.* It will likely *increase* the discovery burdens on district judges, as parties litigate about what is "relevant" to "disputed facts," whether those facts have been alleged with sufficient particularity, whether the opposing side has adequately disclosed the required information, and whether it has fulfilled its continuing obligation to supplement the initial disclosure. Documents will be produced that turn out to be irrelevant to the litigation, because of the early inception of the duty to disclose and the severe penalties on a party who fails to disgorge in a manner consistent with the duty. See Proposed Rule 37(c) (prohibiting, in some circumstances, use of witnesses or information not voluntarily disclosed pursuant to the disclosure duty, and authorizing divulgement to the jury of the failure to disclose).

The proposed new regime does not fit comfortably within the American judicial system, which relies on adversarial litigation to develop the facts before a neutral decisionmaker. By placing upon lawyers the obligation to disclose information damaging to their clients—on their own initiative, and in a context where the lines between what must be disclosed and what need not be disclosed are not clear but require the exercise of considerable judgment—the new Rule would place intolerable strain upon lawyers' ethical duty to represent their clients and not to assist the opposing side. Requiring a lawyer to make a judgment as to what information is "relevant to disputed facts" plainly requires him to use his professional skills in the service of the adversary. See Advisory Committee Notes to Proposed Rule 26, p. 96.

It seems to me most imprudent to embrace such a radical alteration that has not, as the advisory committee notes, see id., at 94, been subjected to any significant testing on a local level. Two early proponents of the duty-to-disclose regime (both of whom had substantial roles in the development of the proposed rule—one as Director of the Federal Judicial Center and one as a member of the advisory committee) at one time noted the need for such study prior to adoption of a national rule. Schwarzer, The Federal Rules, the Adversary Process, and Discovery Reform, 50 U. Pitt. L. Rev. 703, 723 (1989); Brazil, The Adversary Character of Civil Discovery: A Critique and Proposals for Change, 31 Vand. L. Rev. 1295, 1361 (1978). More importantly, Congress itself reached the same conclusion that local experiments to reduce discovery costs and abuse are essential *before* major revision, and in the Civil Justice Reform Act of 1990, Pub. L. 101–650, §§ 104, 105, 104 Stat. 5097–5098, mandated an extensive pilot program for district courts. See also 28 U. S. C. §§ 471, 473(a)(2)(C). Under that legislation, short-term experiments relating to discovery and case management are to last at least three years, and the Judicial Conference is to report the results of these experiments to Congress, along with recommendations, by the end of 1995. Pub. L. 101–650, § 105, 104 Stat. 5097–5098. Apparently, the advisory committee considered this timetable schedule too prolonged, see Advisory Committee Notes to Proposed Rule 26, p. 95, preferring instead to subject the entire federal judicial system at once to an extreme, costly, and essentially untested revision of a major component of civil litigation. That seems to me unwise. Any major reform of the discovery rules should await completion of the

---

[1] I do not disagree with the proposal to make law firms liable for an attorney's misconduct under the Rule, see Proposed Rule 11(c), or with the proposal that Rule 11 sanctions be applied when claims in pleadings that at one time were not in violation of the rule are pursued after it is evident that they lack support, see Proposed Rule 11(b); Advisory Committee Notes to Proposed Rule 11, p. 51. It is curious that the proposed rule regarding sanctions for discovery abuses *requires* sanctions, and specifically recommends financial sanctions and compensation to the moving party. See Proposed Rule 37(a)(4)(A), (c)(1). No explanation for the inconsistency is given.

pilot programs authorized by Congress, especially since courts already have substantial discretion to control discovery.[2] See Fed. Rule Civ. Proc. 26.

I am also concerned that this revision has been recommended in the face of nearly universal criticism from every conceivable sector of our judicial system, including judges, practitioners, litigants, academics, public interest groups, and national, state and local bar and professional associations. See generally Bell, Varner, & Gottschalk, Automatic Disclosure in Discovery—The Rush to Reform, 27 Ga. L. Rev. 1, 28–32, and nn. 107–121 (1992). Indeed, after the proposed rule in essentially its present form was published to comply with the notice-and-comment requirement of 28 U. S. C. § 2071(b), public criticism was so severe that the advisory committee announced abandonment of its duty-to-disclose regime (in favor of limited pilot experiments), but then, without further public comment or explanation, decided six weeks later to recommend the rule. 27 Ga. L. Rev., at 35.

* * *

Constant reform of the federal rules to correct emerging problems is essential. JUSTICE WHITE observes that Justice Douglas, who in earlier years on the Court had been wont to note his disagreements with proposed changes, generally abstained from doing so later on, acknowledging that his expertise had grown stale. *Ante*, at 1095–1096, and n.3. Never having specialized in trial practice, I began at the level of expertise (and of acquiescence in others' proposals) with which Justice Douglas ended. Both categories of revision on which I remark today, however, seem to me not matters of expert detail, but rise to the level of principle and purpose that even Justice Douglas in his later years continued to address. It takes no expert to know that a measure which eliminates rather than strengthens a deterrent to frivolous litigation is not what the times demand; and that a breathtakingly novel revision of discovery practice should not be adopted nationwide without a trial run.

In the respects described, I dissent from the Court's order.

ORDER OF APRIL 27, 1995 [514 U.S. 1153]

1. That the Federal Rules of Civil Procedure for the United States District Courts be, and they hereby are, amended by including therein amendments to Civil Rules 50, 52, 59, and 83.

[See amendments made thereby under respective rules, post.]

2. That the foregoing amendments to the Federal Rules of Civil Procedure shall take effect on December 1, 1995, and shall govern all proceedings in civil cases thereafter commenced and, insofar as just and practicable, all proceedings in civil cases then pending.

3. That THE CHIEF JUSTICE be, and hereby is, authorized to transmit to the Congress the foregoing amendments to the Federal Rules of Civil Procedure in accordance with the provisions of Section 2072 of Title 28, United States Code.

ORDER OF APRIL 23, 1996 [517 U.S. 1279]

1. That the Federal Rules of Civil Procedure for the United States District Courts be, and they hereby are, amended by including therein amendments to Civil Rules 5 and 43.

[See amendments made thereby under respective rules, post]

2. That the foregoing amendments to the Federal Rules of Civil Procedure shall take effect on December 1, 1996, and shall govern all proceedings in civil cases thereafter commenced and, insofar as just and practicable, all proceedings in civil cases then pending.

3. That THE CHIEF JUSTICE be, and hereby is, authorized to transmit to the Congress the foregoing amendments to the Federal Rules of Civil Procedure in accordance with the provisions of Section 2072 of Title 28, United States Code.

---

[2] For the same reason, the proposed presumptive limits on depositions and interrogatories, see Proposed Rules 30, 31, and 33, should not be implemented.

RULES OF CIVIL PROCEDURE

ORDER OF APRIL 11, 1997 [520 U.S. 1307]

1.   That the Federal Rules of Civil Procedure for the United States District Courts be, and they hereby are, amended by including therein amendments to Civil Rules 9 and 73, and abrogation of Rules 74, 75, and 76, and amendments to Forms 33 and 34.

[See amendments made thereby under respective rules, post]

2.   That the foregoing amendments to the Federal Rules of Civil Procedure shall take effect on December 1, 1997, and shall govern all proceedings in civil cases thereafter commenced and, insofar as just and practicable, all proceedings in civil cases then pending.

3.   That THE CHIEF JUSTICE be, and hereby is, authorized to transmit to the Congress the foregoing amendments to the Federal Rules of Civil Procedure in accordance with the provisions of Section 2072 of Title 28, United States Code.

ORDER OF APRIL 24, 1998 [523 U.S. 1223]

1.   That the Federal Rules of Civil Procedure for the United States District Courts be, and they hereby are, amended by including therein a new Civil Rule 23(f).

[See amendments made thereby under respective rules, post]

2.   That the foregoing amendments to the Federal Rules of Civil Procedure shall take effect on December 1, 1998, and shall govern all proceedings in civil cases thereafter commenced and, insofar as just and practicable, all proceedings in civil cases then pending.

3.   That THE CHIEF JUSTICE be, and hereby is, authorized to transmit to the Congress the foregoing amendments to the Federal Rules of Civil Procedure in accordance with the provisions of Section 2072 of Title 28, United States Code.

ORDER OF APRIL 26, 1999 [526 U.S. 1185]

1.   That the Federal Rules of Civil Procedure for the United States District Courts be, and they hereby are, amended by including therein amendments to Civil Rule 6(b) and Form 2.

[See amendments made thereby under respective rules, post.]

2.   That the foregoing amendments to the Federal Rules of Civil Procedure shall take effect on December 1, 1999, and shall govern all proceedings in civil cases thereafter commenced and, insofar as just and practicable, all proceedings in civil cases then pending.

3.   That THE CHIEF JUSTICE be, and hereby is, authorized to transmit to the Congress the foregoing amendments to the Federal Rules of Civil Procedure in accordance with the provisions of Section 2072 of Title 28, United States Code.

ORDER OF APRIL 17, 2000 [529 U.S. 1157]

1.   That the Federal Rules of Civil Procedure for the United States District Courts be, and they hereby are, amended by including therein amendments to Civil Rules 4, 5, 12, 14, 26, 30, and 37 and to Rules B, C, and E of the Supplemental Rules for Certain Admiralty and Maritime Claims.

[See amendments made thereby under respective rules, post.]

2.   That the foregoing amendments to the Federal Rules of Civil Procedure and the Supplemental Rules for Certain Admiralty and Maritime Claims shall take effect on December 1, 2000, and shall govern all proceedings in civil cases thereafter commenced and, insofar as just and practicable, all proceedings in civil cases then pending.

3.   That THE CHIEF JUSTICE be, and hereby is, authorized to transmit to the Congress the foregoing amendments to the Federal Rules of Civil Procedure in accordance with the provisions of Section 2072 of Title 28, United States Code.

ORDER OF APRIL 23, 2001 [532 U.S. 1087]

1.   That the Federal Rules of Civil Procedure be, and they hereby are, amended by including therein amendments to Civil Rules 5, 6, 65, 77, 81, and 82.

RULES OF CIVIL PROCEDURE

[See amendments made thereby under respective rules, post.]

2.   That the foregoing amendments to the Federal Rules of Civil Procedure shall take effect on December 1, 2001, and shall govern in all proceedings in civil cases thereafter commenced and, insofar as just and practicable, all proceedings then pending.

3.   That THE CHIEF JUSTICE be, and hereby is, authorized to transmit to the Congress the foregoing amendments to the Federal Rules of Civil Procedure in accordance with the provisions of Section 2072 of Title 28, United States Code.

4.   That the Rules for Practice and Procedure under section 25 of An Act To Amend and Consolidate the Acts Respecting Copyright, approved March 4, 1909, promulgated by this Court on June 1, 1909, effective July 1, 1909, as revised, be, and they hereby are, abrogated, effective December 1, 2001.

ORDER OF APRIL 29, 2002 [535 U.S. 1149]

1.   That the Federal Rules of Civil Procedure be, and they hereby are, amended by including therein amendments to Civil Rules 54, 58, and 81, and a new Rule 7.1, and Rule C of Supplemental Rules for Certain Admiralty and Maritime Claims.

[See amendments made thereby under respective rules, post.]

2.   That the foregoing amendments to the Federal Rules of Civil Procedure shall take effect on December 1, 2002, and shall govern in all proceedings in civil cases thereafter commenced and, insofar as just and practicable, all proceedings then pending.

3.   That the CHIEF JUSTICE be, and hereby is, authorized to transmit to the Congress the foregoing amendments to the Federal Rules of Civil Procedure in accordance with the provisions of Section 2072 of Title 28, United States Code.

ORDER OF MARCH 27, 2003 [538 U.S. 1085]

1.   That the Federal Rules of Civil Procedure be, and they hereby are, amended by including therein amendments to Civil Rules 23, 51, 53, 54, and 71A.

[See amendments made thereby under respective rules and forms, post.]

2.   That Forms 19, 31, and 32 in the Appendix to the Federal Rules of Civil Procedure be, and they hereby are, amended by replacing all references to "19__" with references to "20__."

3.   That the foregoing amendments to the Federal Rules of Civil Procedure shall take effect on December 1, 2003, and shall govern in all proceedings in civil cases thereafter commenced and, insofar as just and practicable, all proceedings then pending.

4.   That the CHIEF JUSTICE be, and hereby is, authorized to transmit to the Congress the foregoing amendments to the Federal Rules of Civil Procedure in accordance with the provisions of Section 2072 of Title 28, United States Code.

ORDER OF APRIL 25, 2005 [544 U.S. 1175]

1.   That the Federal Rules of Civil Procedure be, and they hereby are, amended by including therein the amendments to Civil Rules 6, 27, and 45, and to Rules B and C of the Supplemental Rules for Certain Admiralty and Maritime Claims.

[See amendments made thereby under respective rules and forms, post.]

2.   That the foregoing amendments to the Federal Rules of Civil Procedure and the Supplemental Rules for Certain Admiralty and Maritime Claims shall take effect on December 1, 2005, and shall govern in all proceedings thereafter commenced and, insofar as just and practicable, all proceedings then pending.

3.   That the CHIEF JUSTICE be, and hereby is, authorized to transmit to the Congress the foregoing amendments to the Federal Rules of Civil Procedure in accordance with the provisions of Section 2072 of Title 28, United States Code.

RULES OF CIVIL PROCEDURE

ORDER OF APRIL 12, 2006 [547 U.S. 1221]

1. That the Federal Rules of Civil Procedure be, and they hereby are, amended by including therein the amendments to Civil Rules 5, 9, 14, 16, 24, 26, 33, 34, 37, 45, 50, and 65.1; Form 35; and new Rule 5.1.

2. That the Supplemental Rules for Admiralty or Maritime Claims and Asset Forfeiture Actions be, and they hereby are, amended by including therein the amendments to Rules A, C, and E, and new Rule G.

[See amendments made thereby under respective rules and forms, post.]

3. That the foregoing amendments to the Federal Rules of Civil Procedure and the Supplemental Rules for Admiralty or Maritime Claims and Asset Forfeiture Actions shall take effect on December 1, 2006, and shall govern in all proceedings thereafter commenced and, insofar as just and practicable, all proceedings then pending.

4. That THE CHIEF JUSTICE be, and hereby is, authorized to transmit to the Congress the foregoing amendments to the Federal Rules of Civil Procedure in accordance with the provisions of Section 2072 of Title 28, United States Code.

ORDER OF APRIL 30, 2007 [550 U.S. 1005]

1. That the Federal Rules of Civil Procedure be, and they hereby are, amended by including therein the amendments to Civil Rules 1 through 86 and new Rule 5.2.

2. That Forms 1 through 35 in the Appendix to the Federal Rules of Civil Procedure be, and they hereby are, amended to become restyled Forms 1 through 82.

[See amendments made thereby under respective rules and forms, post.]

3. That the foregoing amendments to the Federal Rules of Civil Procedure shall take effect on December 1, 2007, and shall govern in all proceedings thereafter commenced and, insofar as just and practicable, all proceedings then pending.

4. That THE CHIEF JUSTICE be, and hereby is, authorized to transmit to the Congress the foregoing amendments to the Federal Rules of Civil Procedure in accordance with the provisions of Section 2072 of Title 28, United States Code.

ORDER OF APRIL 23, 2008 [553 U.S. 1151]

1. That the Supplemental Rules for Admiralty or Maritime Claims and Asset Forfeiture Actions be, and they hereby are, amended by including therein the amendment to Rule C.

[See amendment made thereby under Rule C post.]

2. That the foregoing amendment to the Supplemental Rules for Admiralty or Maritime Claims and Asset Forfeiture Actions shall take effect on December 1, 2008, and shall govern in all proceedings thereafter commenced and, insofar as just and practicable, all proceedings then pending.

3. That THE CHIEF JUSTICE be, and hereby is, authorized to transmit to the Congress the foregoing amendment to the Supplemental Rules for Admiralty or Maritime Claims and Asset Forfeiture Actions in accordance with the provisions of Section 2072 of Title 28, United States Code.

ORDER OF MARCH 26, 2009 [2008 J. Sup. Ct. U.S. 681]

1. That the Federal Rules of Civil Procedure be, and they hereby are, amended by including therein amendments to Civil Rules 6, 12, 13, 14, 15, 23, 27, 32, 38, 48, 50, 52, 53, 54, 55, 56, 59, 62, 65, 68, 71.1, 72, and 81, and new Rule 62.1, and Supplemental Rules B, C, and G, and Illustrative Civil Forms 3, 4, and 60.

[See amendments made thereby under respective rules and forms, post.]

2. That the foregoing amendments to the Federal Rules of Civil Procedure shall take effect on December 1, 2009, and shall govern in all proceedings thereafter commenced and, insofar as just and practicable, all proceedings then pending.

3. That The Chief Justice be, and hereby is, authorized to transmit to the Congress the foregoing amendments to the Federal Rules of Civil Procedure in accordance with the provisions of Section 2072 of Title 28, United States Code.

RULES OF CIVIL PROCEDURE

ORDER OF APRIL 28, 2010 [559 U.S. 1141]

1.   That the Federal Rules of Civil Procedure be, and they hereby are, amended by including therein amendments to Civil Rules 8, 26, and 56, and Illustrative Civil Form 52.

[See amendments made thereby under respective rules and forms, post.]

2.   That the foregoing amendments to the Federal Rules of Civil Procedure shall take effect on December 1, 2010, and shall govern in all proceedings thereafter commenced and, insofar as just and practicable, all proceedings then pending.

3.   That THE CHIEF JUSTICE be, and hereby is, authorized to transmit to the Congress the foregoing amendments to the Federal Rules of Civil Procedure in accordance with the provisions of Section 2072 of Title 28, United States Code.

ORDER OF APRIL 16, 2013 [2012–2013 J. Sup. Ct. U.S. 780]

1.   That the Federal Rules of Civil Procedure be, and they hereby are, amended by including therein amendments to Civil Rules 37 and 45.

[See amendments made thereby under respective rules, post.]

2.   That the foregoing amendments to the Federal Rules of Civil Procedure shall take effect on December 1, 2013, and shall govern in all proceedings in civil cases thereafter commenced and, insofar as just and practicable, all proceedings then pending.

3.   That The Chief Justice be, and hereby is, authorized to transmit to the Congress the foregoing amendments to the Federal Rules of Civil Procedure in accordance with the provisions of Section 2072 of Title 28, United States Code.

ORDER OF APRIL 25, 2014 [2013 J. Sup. Ct. U.S. 771]

1.   That the Federal Rules of Civil Procedure be, and they hereby are, amended by including therein amendments to Civil Rule 77.

[See amendments made thereby under Rule 77, post.]

2.   That the foregoing amendments to the Federal Rules of Civil Procedure shall take effect on December 1, 2014, and shall govern in all proceedings in civil cases thereafter commenced and, insofar as just and practicable, all proceedings then pending.

3.   That The Chief Justice be, and hereby is, authorized to transmit to the Congress the foregoing amendments to the Federal Rules of Civil Procedure in accordance with the provisions of Section 2072 of Title 28, United States Code.

ORDER OF APRIL 29, 2015 [2014 J. Sup. Ct. U.S. 759]

1.   That the Federal Rules of Civil Procedure be, and they hereby are, amended by including therein amendments to Civil Rules 1, 4, 16, 26, 30, 31, 33, 34, 37, 55, and 84, and the Appendix of Forms.

[See amendments made thereby, under respective rules and forms, post.]

2.   That the foregoing amendments to the Federal Rules of Civil Procedure shall take effect on December 1, 2015, and shall govern in all proceedings in civil cases thereafter commenced and, insofar as just and practicable, all proceedings then pending.

3.   That The Chief Justice be, and hereby is, authorized to transmit to the Congress the foregoing amendments to the Federal Rules of Civil Procedure in accordance with the provisions of Section 2072 of Title 28, United States Code.

ORDER OF APRIL 28, 2016 [2015 J. Sup. Ct. U.S. 763]

1.   That the Federal Rules of Civil Procedure be, and they hereby are, amended by including therein amendments to Civil Rules 4, 6, and 82.

[See amendments made thereby, under respective rules and forms, post.]

RULES OF CIVIL PROCEDURE

2.   That the foregoing amendments to the Federal Rules of Civil Procedure shall take effect on December 1, 2016, and shall govern in all proceedings in civil cases thereafter commenced and, insofar as just and practicable, all proceedings then pending.

3.   That The Chief Justice be, and hereby is, authorized to transmit to the Congress the foregoing amendments to the Federal Rules of Civil Procedure in accordance with the provisions of Section 2072 of Title 28, United States Code.

ORDER OF APRIL 27, 2017 [2016 J. Sup. Ct. U.S. 701]

1.   That the Federal Rules of Civil Procedure be, and they hereby are, amended by including therein an amendment to Civil Rule 4.

[See amendments made thereby, under respective rules and forms, post.]

2.   That the foregoing amendment to the Federal Rules of Civil Procedure shall take effect on December 1, 2017, and shall govern in all proceedings in civil cases thereafter commenced and, insofar as just and practicable, all proceedings then pending.

3.   That The Chief Justice be, and hereby is, authorized to transmit to the Congress the foregoing amendment to the Federal Rules of Civil Procedure in accordance with the provisions of Section 2074 of Title 28, United States Code.

ORDER OF APRIL 26, 2018 [2017 J. Sup. Ct. U.S. 700]

1.   That the Federal Rules of Civil Procedure be, and they hereby are, amended by including therein amendments to Civil Rules 5, 23, 62, and 65.1.

[See amendments made thereby, under Rules 5, 23, 62, and 65.1, post.]

2.   That the foregoing amendment to the Federal Rules of Civil Procedure shall take effect on December 1, 2018, and shall govern in all proceedings in civil cases thereafter commenced and, insofar as just and practicable, all proceedings then pending.

3.   That The Chief Justice be, and hereby is, authorized to transmit to the Congress the foregoing amendments to the Federal Rules of Civil Procedure in accordance with the provisions of Section 2074 of Title 28, United States Code.

ORDER OF APRIL 27, 2020

1.   That the Federal Rules of Civil Procedure are amended to include an amendment to Civil Rule 30.

[See amendment made thereby, under Rule 30, post.]

2.   That the foregoing amendment to the Federal Rules of Civil Procedure shall take effect on December 1, 2020, and shall govern in all proceedings in civil cases thereafter commenced and, insofar as just and practicable, all proceedings then pending.

3.   THE CHIEF JUSTICE is authorized to transmit to the Congress the foregoing amendment to the Federal Rules of Civil Procedure in accordance with the provisions of Section 2074 of Title 28, United States Code.

HISTORICAL NOTES

The original Rules of Civil Procedure for the District Courts were adopted by order of the Supreme Court on Dec. 20, 1937, transmitted to Congress by the Attorney General on Jan. 3, 1938, and became effective on Sept. 16, 1938.

The Rules have been amended Dec. 28, 1939, eff. Apr. 3, 1941; Dec. 27, 1946, eff. Mar. 19, 1948; Dec. 29, 1948, eff. Oct. 20, 1949; Apr. 30, 1951, eff. Aug. 1, 1951; Apr. 17, 1961, eff. July 19, 1961; Jan. 21, 1963, eff. July 1, 1963; Feb. 28, 1966, eff. July 1, 1966; Dec. 4, 1967, eff. July 1, 1968; Mar. 30, 1970, eff. July 1, 1970; Mar. 1, 1971, eff. July 1, 1971; Nov. 20, 1972, and Dec. 18, 1972, eff. July 1, 1975; Apr. 29, 1980, eff. Aug. 1, 1980; Oct. 21, 1980, Pub.L. 96–481, Title II, § 205(a), (b), 94 Stat. 2330; Jan. 12, 1983, Pub.L. 97–462, §§ 2–4, 96 Stat. 2527–2530, eff. Feb. 26, 1983; Apr. 28, 1983, eff. Aug. 1, 1983; Apr. 29, 1985, eff. Aug. 1, 1985; Mar. 2, 1987, eff. Aug. 1, 1987; Apr. 25, 1988, eff. Aug. 1, 1988; Nov. 18, 1988, Pub.L. 100–690, Title

VII, §§ 7047(b), 7049, 7050, 102 Stat. 4401; Apr. 30, 1991, eff. Dec. 1, 1991; Apr. 22, 1993, eff. Dec. 1, 1993; Apr. 27, 1995, eff. Dec. 1, 1995; Apr. 23, 1996, eff. Dec. 1, 1996; Apr. 11, 1997, eff. Dec. 1, 1997 Apr. 24, 1998, eff. Dec. 1, 1998; Apr. 26, 1999, eff. Dec. 1, 1999; Apr. 17, 2000, eff. Dec. 1, 2000; Apr. 23, 2001, eff. Dec. 1, 2001; Apr. 29, 2002, eff. Dec. 1, 2002; Mar. 27, 2003, eff. Dec. 1, 2003; Apr. 25, 2005, eff. Dec. 1, 2005; Apr. 12, 2006, eff. Dec. 1, 2006; Apr. 30, 2007, eff. Dec. 1, 2007; Apr. 23, 2008, eff. Dec. 1, 2008; Mar. 26, 2009, eff. Dec. 1, 2009; Apr. 28, 2010, eff. Dec. 1, 2010; Apr. 16, 2013, eff. Dec. 1, 2013; Apr. 25, 2014, eff. Dec. 1, 2014; Apr. 29, 2015, eff. Dec. 1, 2015; Apr. 28, 2016, eff. Dec. 1, 2016; Apr. 27, 2017, eff. Dec. 1, 2017; Apr. 26, 2018, eff. Dec. 1, 2018; Apr. 27, 2020, eff. Dec. 1, 2020.

TITLE I. SCOPE OF RULES; FORM OF ACTION

Rule 1.   Scope and Purpose

These rules govern the procedure in all civil actions and proceedings in the United States district courts, except as stated in Rule 81. They should be construed, administered, and employed by the court and the parties to secure the just, speedy, and inexpensive determination of every action and proceeding.

(Amended December 29, 1948, effective October 20, 1949; February 28, 1966, effective July 1, 1966; April 22, 1993, effective December 1, 1993; April 30, 2007, effective December 1, 2007; April 29, 2015, effective December 1, 2015.)

ADVISORY COMMITTEE NOTES

1937 Adoption

1.   Rule 81 states certain limitations in the application of these rules to enumerated special proceedings.

2.   The expression "district courts of the United States" appearing in the statute authorizing the Supreme Court of the United States to promulgate rules of civil procedure does not include the district courts held in the territories and insular possessions. See *Mookini et al. v. United States,* 1938, 58 S. Ct. 543, 303 U.S. 201, 82 L.Ed. 748.*

3.   These rules are drawn under the authority of the Act of June 19, 1934, U.S.C., Title 28, § 723b [see 2072] (Rules in actions at law; Supreme Court authorized to make), and § 723c [see 2072] (Union of equity and action at law rules; power of Supreme Court) and also other grants of rule making power to the Court. See Clark and Moore, *A New Federal Civil Procedure—I. The Background,* 44 Yale L.J. 387, 391 (1935). Under § 723b after the rules have taken effect all laws in conflict therewith are of no further force or effect. In accordance with § 723c the Court has united the general rules prescribed for cases in equity with those in actions at law so as to secure one form of civil action and procedure for both. See Rule 2 (One Form of Action). For the former practice in equity and at law see U.S.C.A., Title 28, §§ 723 and 730 [see 2071 et seq.] (conferring power on the Supreme Court to make rules of practice in equity) and the [former] Equity Rules promulgated thereunder; U.S.C., Title 28, [former] § 724 (Conformity act); [former] Equity Rule 22 (Action at Law Erroneously Begun as Suit in Equity—Transfer); [former] Equity Rule 23 (Matters Ordinarily Determinable at Law When Arising in Suit in Equity to be Disposed of Therein); U.S.C., Title 28, [former] §§ 397 (Amendments to pleadings when case brought to wrong side of court), and 398 (Equitable defenses and equitable relief in actions at law).

4.   With the second sentence compare U.S.C., Title 28, [former] §§ 777 (Defects of form; amendments), [former] 767 (Amendment of process); [former] Equity Rule 19 (Amendments Generally).

1948 Amendment

The amendment effective Oct. 20, 1949, substituted the words "United States district courts" for the words "district courts of the United States."

---

*   [Congress has made the Federal Rules of Civil Procedure applicable to proceedings in the district courts in the U.S. Virgin Islands, *see* 48 U.S.C. § 1614(b) (2012), in Guam, *see* 48 U.S.C. § 1424–4 (2012), and in the Northern Mariana Islands, *see* 48 U.S.C. § 1821(c) (2012). Ed.]

1966 Amendment

This is the fundamental change necessary to effect unification of the civil and admiralty procedure. Just as the 1938 rules abolished the distinction between actions at law and suits in equity, this change would abolish the distinction between civil actions and suits in admiralty. See also Rule 81.

1993 Amendments

The purpose of this revision, adding the words "and administered" to the second sentence, is to recognize the affirmative duty of the court to exercise the authority conferred by these rules to ensure that civil litigation is resolved not only fairly, but also without undue cost or delay. As officers of the court, attorneys share this responsibility with the judge to whom the case is assigned.

2007 Amendment

The language of Rule 1 has been amended as part of the general restyling of the Civil Rules to make them more easily understood and to make style and terminology consistent throughout the rules. These changes are intended to be stylistic only.

The merger of law, equity, and admiralty practice is complete. There is no need to carry forward the phrases that initially accomplished the merger.

The former reference to "suits of a civil nature" is changed to the more modern "civil actions and proceedings." This change does not affect such questions as whether the Civil Rules apply to summary proceedings created by statute. *See SEC v. McCarthy*, 322 F.3d 650 (9th Cir. 2003); *see also New Hampshire Fire Ins. Co. v. Scanlon*, 362 U.S. 404 (1960).

The Style Project

The Civil Rules are the third set of the rules to be restyled. The restyled Rules of Appellate Procedure took effect in 1998. The restyled Rules of Criminal Procedure took effect in 2002. The restyled Rules of Civil Procedure apply the same general drafting guidelines and principles used in restyling the Appellate and Criminal Rules.

1.　*General Guidelines*

Guidance in drafting, usage, and style was provided by Bryan Garner, Guidelines for Drafting and Editing Court Rules, Administrative Office of the United States Courts (1996) and Bryan Garner, Dictionary of Modern Legal Usage (2d ed. 1995). See also Joseph Kimble, Guiding Principles for Restyling the Civil Rules, in Preliminary Draft of Proposed Style Revision of the Federal Rules of Civil Procedure, at x (Feb. 2005) (available at http://www.uscourts.gov/rules/Prelim_draft_proposed_pt1.pdf) [This link is no longer active. Readers may find a reproduction of this memo at www.michbar.org/file/generalinfo/plainenglish/PDFs/05_sept.pdf. Ed.].

2.　*Formatting Changes*

Many of the changes in the restyled Civil Rules result from using format to achieve clearer presentation. The rules are broken down into constituent parts, using progressively indented subparagraphs with headings and substituting vertical for horizontal lists. "Hanging indents" are used throughout. These formatting changes make the structure of the rules graphic and make the restyled rules easier to read and understand even when the words are not changed. Rule 14(a) illustrates the benefits of formatting changes.

3.　*Changes to Reduce Inconsistent, Ambiguous, Redundant, Repetitive, or Archaic Words*

The restyled rules reduce the use of inconsistent terms that say the same thing in different ways. Because different words are presumed to have different meanings, such inconsistencies can result in confusion. The restyled rules reduce inconsistencies by using the same words to express the same meaning. For example, consistent expression is achieved without affecting meaning by the changes from "infant" in many rules to "minor" in all rules; from "upon motion or on its own initiative" in Rule 4(m) and variations in many other rules to "on motion or on its own"; and from "deemed" to "considered" in Rules 5(c), 12(e), and elsewhere. Some variations of expression have been carried forward when the context made that appropriate. As an example, "stipulate," "agree," and "consent" appear throughout the rules, and "written" qualifies these words in some places but not others. The number of variations has been reduced, but at times the former words were carried forward. None of the changes, when made, alters the rule's meaning.

The restyled rules minimize the use of inherently ambiguous words. For example, the word "shall" can mean "must," "may," or something else, depending on context. The potential for confusion is exacerbated by the fact that "shall" is no longer generally used in spoken or clearly written English. The restyled rules replace "shall" with "must," "may," or "should," depending on which one the context and established interpretation make correct in each rule.

The restyled rules minimize the use of redundant "intensifiers." These are expressions that attempt to add emphasis, but instead state the obvious and create negative implications for other rules. "The court in its discretion may" becomes "the court may"; "unless the order expressly directs otherwise" becomes "unless the court orders otherwise." The absence of intensifiers in the restyled rules does not change their substantive meaning. For example, the absence of the word "reasonable" to describe the written notice of foreign law required in Rule 44.1 does not mean that "unreasonable" notice is permitted.

The restyled rules also remove words and concepts that are outdated or redundant. The reference to "at law or in equity" in Rule 1 has become redundant with the merger of law and equity. Outdated words and concepts include the reference to "demurrers, pleas, and exceptions" in Rule 7(c); the reference to "mesne" process in Rule 77(c); and the reference in Rule 81(f) to a now-abolished official position.

The restyled rules remove a number of redundant cross-references. For example, Rule 8(b) states that a general denial is subject to the obligations of Rule 11, but all pleadings are subject to Rule 11. Removing such cross-references does not defeat application of the formerly cross-referenced rule.

4.   Rule Numbers

The restyled rules keep the same rule numbers to minimize the effect on research. Subdivisions have been rearranged within some rules to achieve greater clarity and simplicity. The only change that moves one part of a rule to another is the transfer of former Rule 25(d)(2) to Rule 17(d). The restyled rules include a comparison chart to make it easy to identify transfers of provisions between subdivisions and redesignations of some subdivisions.

5.   Other Changes

The style changes to the rules are intended to make no changes in substantive meaning. A very small number of minor technical amendments that arguably do change meaning were approved separately from the restyled rules, but become effective at the same time. An example is adding "e-mail address" to the information that must be included in pleadings. These minor changes occur in Rules 4(k), 9(h), 11(a), 14(b), 16(c)(1), 26(g)(1), 30(b), 31, 40, 71.1, and 78.

2015 Amendment

Rule 1 is amended to emphasize that just as the court should construe and administer these rules to secure the just, speedy, and inexpensive determination of every action, so the parties share the responsibility to employ the rules in the same way. Most lawyers and parties cooperate to achieve these ends. But discussions of ways to improve the administration of civil justice regularly include pleas to discourage over-use, misuse, and abuse of procedural tools that increase cost and result in delay. Effective advocacy is consistent with—and indeed depends upon—cooperative and proportional use of procedure.

This amendment does not create a new or independent source of sanctions. Neither does it abridge the scope of any other of these rules.

Gap Report

No changes were made in the rule text or Committee Note as published.*

Rule 2.   One Form of Action

There is one form of action—the civil action.

(Amended April 30, 2007, effective December 1, 2007.)

---

*   [The final sentence of the committee note was added after and in response to public comment. Ed.]

ADVISORY COMMITTEE NOTES
1937 Adoption

1.   This rule modifies U.S.C., Title 28, [former] § 384 (Suits in equity, when not sustainable). U.S.C., Title 28, §§ 723 and 730 [sec. 2071, et seq.] (conferring power on the Supreme Court to make rules of practice in equity), are unaffected in so far as they relate to the rule making power in admiralty. These sections, together with § 723b [sec. 2072] (Rules in actions at law; Supreme Court authorized to make) are continued in so far as they are not inconsistent with § 2072, formerly § 723c (Union of equity and action at law rules; power of Supreme Court). See Note 3 to Rule 1. U.S.C., Title 28, [former] §§ 724 (Conformity act), 397 (Amendments to pleadings when case brought to wrong side of court) and 398 (Equitable defenses and equitable relief in actions at law) are superseded.

2.   Reference to actions at law or suits in equity in all statutes should now be treated as referring to the civil action prescribed in these rules.

3.   This rule follows in substance the usual introductory statements to code practices which provide for a single action and mode of procedure, with abolition of forms of action and procedural distinctions. Representative statutes are N.Y. Code 1848 (Laws 1848, ch. 379) § 62; N.Y.C.P.A. (1937) § 8; Calif.Code Civ.Proc. (Deering, 1937) § 307; 2 Minn.Stat.Ann.1945 § 540.01; 2 Wash.Rev.Stat.Ann. (Remington, 1932) §§ 153, 255.

2007 Amendment

The language of Rule 2 has been amended as part of the general restyling of the Civil Rules to make them more easily understood and to make style and terminology consistent throughout the rules. These changes are intended to be stylistic only.

TITLE II. COMMENCING AN ACTION; SERVICE OF PROCESS, PLEADINGS, MOTIONS, AND ORDERS

Rule 3.   Commencing an Action

A civil action is commenced by filing a complaint with the court.

(Amended April 30, 2007, effective December 1, 2007.)

ADVISORY COMMITTEE NOTES
1937 Adoption

1.   Rule 5(e) defines what constitutes filing with the court.

2.   This rule governs the commencement of all actions, including those brought by or against the United States or an officer or agency thereof, regardless of whether service is to be made personally pursuant to Rule 4(d), or otherwise pursuant to Rule 4(e).

3.   With this rule compare [former] Equity Rule 12 (Issue of Subpoena—Time for Answer) and the following statutes (and other similar statutes) which provide a similar method for commencing an action:

U.S.C., Title 28:

> § 45 [former] (District courts; practice and procedure in certain cases under interstate commerce laws).

> § 762 [see 1402] (Petition in suit against United States).

> § 766 [see 2409] (Partition suits where United States is tenant in common or joint tenant).

4.   This rule provides that the first step in an action is the filing of the complaint. Under Rule 4(a) this is to be followed forthwith by issuance of a summons and its delivery to an officer for service. Other rules providing for dismissal for failure to prosecute suggest a method available to attack unreasonable delay in prosecuting an action after it has been commenced. When a Federal or State statute of limitations is pleaded as a defense, a question may arise under this rule whether the mere filing of the complaint stops the running of the statute, or whether any further step is required, such as, service of the summons and complaint or their delivery to the marshal for service. The answer to this question may depend on whether it is competent for the Supreme Court, exercising the power to make rules of procedure without affecting substantive rights, to vary the operation of statutes of limitations. The requirement of rule 4(a) that the clerk shall forthwith issue the summons and deliver it to the marshal for service will reduce the chances of such a question arising.

2007 Amendments

The caption of Rule 3 has been amended as part of the general restyling of the Civil Rules to make them more easily understood and to make style and terminology consistent throughout the rules. These changes are intended to be stylistic only.

Rule 4.   Summons

(a) Contents; Amendments.

   (1) *Contents.* A summons must:

   (A) name the court and the parties;

   (B) be directed to the defendant;

   (C) state the name and address of the plaintiff's attorney or—if unrepresented—of the plaintiff;

   (D) state the time within which the defendant must appear and defend;

   (E) notify the defendant that a failure to appear and defend will result in a default judgment against the defendant for the relief demanded in the complaint;

   (F) be signed by the clerk; and

   (G) bear the court's seal.

   (2) *Amendments.* The court may permit a summons to be amended.

(b) Issuance. On or after filing the complaint, the plaintiff may present a summons to the clerk for signature and seal. If the summons is properly completed, the clerk must sign, seal, and issue it to the plaintiff for service on the defendant. A summons—or a copy of a summons that is addressed to multiple defendants—must be issued for each defendant to be served.

(c) Service.

   (1) *In General.* A summons must be served with a copy of the complaint. The plaintiff is responsible for having the summons and complaint served within the time allowed by Rule 4(m) and must furnish the necessary copies to the person who makes service.

   (2) *By Whom.* Any person who is at least 18 years old and not a party may serve a summons and complaint.

   (3) *By a Marshal or Someone Specially Appointed.* At the plaintiff's request, the court may order that service be made by a United States marshal or deputy marshal or by a person specially appointed by the court. The court must so order if the plaintiff is authorized to proceed in forma pauperis under 28 U.S.C. § 1915 or as a seaman under 28 U.S.C. § 1916.

(d) Waiving Service.

   (1) *Requesting a Waiver.* An individual, corporation, or association that is subject to service under Rule 4(e), (f), or (h) has a duty to avoid unnecessary expenses of serving the summons. The plaintiff may notify such a defendant that an action has been commenced and request that the defendant waive service of a summons. The notice and request must:

   (A) be in writing and be addressed:

   (i) to the individual defendant; or

> > **(ii)** for a defendant subject to service under Rule 4(h), to an officer, a managing or general agent, or any other agent authorized by appointment or by law to receive service of process;

> **(B)** name the court where the complaint was filed;

> **(C)** be accompanied by a copy of the complaint, two copies of the waiver form appended to this Rule 4, and a prepaid means for returning the form;

> **(D)** inform the defendant, using the form appended to this Rule 4, of the consequences of waiving and not waiving service;

> **(E)** state the date when the request is sent;

> **(F)** give the defendant a reasonable time of at least 30 days after the request was sent—or at least 60 days if sent to the defendant outside any judicial district of the United States—to return the waiver; and

> **(G)** be sent by first-class mail or other reliable means.

(2) *Failure to Waive.* If a defendant located within the United States fails, without good cause, to sign and return a waiver requested by a plaintiff located within the United States, the court must impose on the defendant:

> **(A)** the expenses later incurred in making service; and

> **(B)** the reasonable expenses, including attorney's fees, of any motion required to collect those service expenses.

(3) *Time to Answer After a Waiver.* A defendant who, before being served with process, timely returns a waiver need not serve an answer to the complaint until 60 days after the request was sent—or until 90 days after it was sent to the defendant outside any judicial district of the United States.

(4) *Results of Filing a Waiver.* When the plaintiff files a waiver, proof of service is not required and these rules apply as if a summons and complaint had been served at the time of filing the waiver.

(5) *Jurisdiction and Venue Not Waived.* Waiving service of a summons does not waive any objection to personal jurisdiction or to venue.

(e) **Serving an Individual Within a Judicial District of the United States.** Unless federal law provides otherwise, an individual—other than a minor, an incompetent person, or a person whose waiver has been filed—may be served in a judicial district of the United States by:

(1) following state law for serving a summons in an action brought in courts of general jurisdiction in the state where the district court is located or where service is made; or

(2) doing any of the following:

> **(A)** delivering a copy of the summons and of the complaint to the individual personally;

> **(B)** leaving a copy of each at the individual's dwelling or usual place of abode with someone of suitable age and discretion who resides there; or

> **(C)** delivering a copy of each to an agent authorized by appointment or by law to receive service of process.

(f) **Serving an Individual in a Foreign Country.** Unless federal law provides otherwise, an individual—other than a minor, an incompetent person, or a person whose waiver has been filed—may be served at a place not within any judicial district of the United States:

(1) by any internationally agreed means of service that is reasonably calculated to give notice, such as those authorized by the Hague Convention on the Service Abroad of Judicial and Extrajudicial Documents;

(2) if there is no internationally agreed means, or if an international agreement allows but does not specify other means, by a method that is reasonably calculated to give notice:

> **(A)** as prescribed by the foreign country's law for service in that country in an action in its courts of general jurisdiction;

> **(B)** as the foreign authority directs in response to a letter rogatory or letter of request; or

> **(C)** unless prohibited by the foreign country's law, by:

>> **(i)** delivering a copy of the summons and of the complaint to the individual personally; or

>> **(ii)** using any form of mail that the clerk addresses and sends to the individual and that requires a signed receipt; or

(3) by other means not prohibited by international agreement, as the court orders.

(g) **Serving a Minor or an Incompetent Person.** A minor or an incompetent person in a judicial district of the United States must be served by following state law for serving a summons or like process on such a defendant in an action brought in the courts of general jurisdiction of the state where service is made. A minor or an incompetent person who is not within any judicial district of the United States must be served in the manner prescribed by Rule 4(f)(2)(A), (f)(2)(B), or (f)(3).

(h) **Serving a Corporation, Partnership, or Association.** Unless federal law provides otherwise or the defendant's waiver has been filed, a domestic or foreign corporation, or a partnership or other unincorporated association that is subject to suit under a common name, must be served:

(1) in a judicial district of the United States:

> **(A)** in the manner prescribed by Rule 4(e)(1) for serving an individual; or

> **(B)** by delivering a copy of the summons and of the complaint to an officer, a managing or general agent, or any other agent authorized by appointment or by law to receive service of process and—if the agent is one authorized by statute and the statute so requires—by also mailing a copy of each to the defendant; or

(2) at a place not within any judicial district of the United States, in any manner prescribed by Rule 4(f) for serving an individual, except personal delivery under (f)(2)(C)(i).

(i) **Serving the United States and Its Agencies, Corporations, Officers, or Employees.**

(1) *United States.* To serve the United States, a party must:

> **(A)(i)**   deliver a copy of the summons and of the complaint to the United States attorney for the district where the action is brought—or to an assistant United States attorney or clerical employee whom the United States attorney designates in a writing filed with the court clerk—or

>> **(ii)** send a copy of each by registered or certified mail to the civil-process clerk at the United States attorney's office;

> **(B)** send a copy of each by registered or certified mail to the Attorney General of the United States at Washington, D.C.; and

> **(C)** if the action challenges an order of a nonparty agency or officer of the United States, send a copy of each by registered or certified mail to the agency or officer.

(2) *Agency; Corporation; Officer or Employee Sued in an Official Capacity.* To serve a United States agency or corporation, or a United States officer or employee sued only in an official capacity, a party must serve the United States and also send a copy of the summons and of the complaint by registered or certified mail to the agency, corporation, officer, or employee.

(3) *Officer or Employee Sued Individually.* To serve a United States officer or employee sued in an individual capacity for an act or omission occurring in connection with duties performed on the United States' behalf (whether or not the officer or employee is also sued in an official capacity), a party must serve the United States and also serve the officer or employee under Rule 4(e), (f), or (g).

(4) *Extending Time.* The court must allow a party a reasonable time to cure its failure to:

    (A) serve a person required to be served under Rule 4(i)(2), if the party has served either the United States attorney or the Attorney General of the United States; or

    (B) serve the United States under Rule 4(i)(3), if the party has served the United States officer or employee.

(j) Serving a Foreign, State, or Local Government.

(1) *Foreign State.* A foreign state or its political subdivision, agency, or instrumentality must be served in accordance with 28 U.S.C. § 1608.

(2) *State or Local Government.* A state, a municipal corporation, or any other state-created governmental organization that is subject to suit must be served by:

    (A) delivering a copy of the summons and of the complaint to its chief executive officer; or

    (B) serving a copy of each in the manner prescribed by that state's law for serving a summons or like process on such a defendant.

(k) Territorial Limits of Effective Service.

(1) *In General.* Serving a summons or filing a waiver of service establishes personal jurisdiction over a defendant:

    (A) who is subject to the jurisdiction of a court of general jurisdiction in the state where the district court is located;

    (B) who is a party joined under Rule 14 or 19 and is served within a judicial district of the United States and not more than 100 miles from where the summons was issued; or

    (C) when authorized by a federal statute.

(2) *Federal Claim Outside State-Court Jurisdiction.* For a claim that arises under federal law, serving a summons or filing a waiver of service establishes personal jurisdiction over a defendant if:

    (A) the defendant is not subject to jurisdiction in any state's courts of general jurisdiction; and

    (B) exercising jurisdiction is consistent with the United States Constitution and laws.

(*l*) Proving Service.

(1) *Affidavit Required.* Unless service is waived, proof of service must be made to the court. Except for service by a United States marshal or deputy marshal, proof must be by the server's affidavit.

(2) *Service Outside the United States.* Service not within any judicial district of the United States must be proved as follows:

    (A) if made under Rule 4(f)(1), as provided in the applicable treaty or convention; or

    (B) if made under Rule 4(f)(2) or (f)(3), by a receipt signed by the addressee, or by other evidence satisfying the court that the summons and complaint were delivered to the addressee.

   (3) *Validity of Service; Amending Proof.* Failure to prove service does not affect the validity of service. The court may permit proof of service to be amended.

(m) Time Limit for Service. If a defendant is not served within 90 days after the complaint is filed, the court—on motion or on its own after notice to the plaintiff—must dismiss the action without prejudice against that defendant or order that service be made within a specified time. But if the plaintiff shows good cause for the failure, the court must extend the time for service for an appropriate period. This subdivision (m) does not apply to service in a foreign country under Rule 4(f), 4(h)(2), or 4(j)(1), or to service of a notice under Rule 71.1(d)(3)(A).

(n) Asserting Jurisdiction over Property or Assets.

   (1) *Federal Law.* The court may assert jurisdiction over property if authorized by a federal statute. Notice to claimants of the property must be given as provided in the statute or by serving a summons under this rule.

   (2) *State Law.* On a showing that personal jurisdiction over a defendant cannot be obtained in the district where the action is brought by reasonable efforts to serve a summons under this rule, the court may assert jurisdiction over the defendant's assets found in the district. Jurisdiction is acquired by seizing the assets under the circumstances and in the manner provided by state law in that district.

(Amended January 21, 1963, effective July 1, 1963; February 28, 1966, effective July 1, 1966; April 29, 1980, effective August 1, 1980; amended by Pub.L. 97–462, § 2, January 12, 1983, 96 Stat. 2527, effective 45 days after January 12, 1983; amended March 2, 1987, effective August 1, 1987; April 22, 1993, effective December 1, 1993; April 17, 2000, effective December 1, 2000; April 30, 2007, effective December 1, 2007; April 29, 2015, effective December 1, 2015; April 28, 2016, effective December 1, 2016; April 27, 2017, effective December 1, 2017.)

Rule 4 Notice of a Lawsuit and Request to Waive Service of Summons.

(Caption)

To (*name the defendant or—if the defendant is a corporation, partnership, or association—name an officer or agent authorized to receive service*):

Why are you getting this?

A lawsuit has been filed against you, or the entity you represent, in this court under the number shown above. A copy of the complaint is attached.

This is not a summons, or an official notice from the court. It is a request that, to avoid expenses, you waive formal service of a summons by signing and returning the enclosed waiver. To avoid these expenses, you must return the signed waiver within (*give at least 30 days or at least 60 days if the defendant is outside any judicial district of the United States*) from the date shown below, which is the date this notice was sent. Two copies of the waiver form are enclosed, along with a stamped, self-addressed envelope or other prepaid means for returning one copy. You may keep the other copy.

What happens next?

If you return the signed waiver, I will file it with the court. The action will then proceed as if you had been served on the date the waiver is filed, but no summons will be served on you and you will have 60 days from the date this notice is sent (see the date below) to answer the complaint (or 90 days if this notice is sent to you outside any judicial district of the United States).

If you do not return the signed waiver within the time indicated, I will arrange to have the summons and complaint served on you. And I will ask the court to require you, or the entity you represent, to pay the expenses of making service.

Please read the enclosed statement about the duty to avoid unnecessary expenses.

I certify that this request is being sent to you on the date below.

Date: _____

_____
(Signature of the attorney or unrepresented party)

_____
(Printed name)

_____
(Address)

_____
(E-mail address)

_____
(Telephone number)

Rule 4 Waiver of the Service of Summons.

(Caption)

To (*name the plaintiff's attorney or the unrepresented plaintiff*):

I have received your request to waive service of a summons in this action along with a copy of the complaint, two copies of this waiver form, and a prepaid means of returning one signed copy of the form to you.

I, or the entity I represent, agree to save the expense of serving a summons and complaint in this case.

I understand that I, or the entity I represent, will keep all defenses or objections to the lawsuit, the court's jurisdiction, and the venue of the action, but that I waive any objections to the absence of a summons or of service.

I also understand that I, or the entity I represent, must file and serve an answer or a motion under Rule 12 within 60 days from _____, the date when this request was sent (or 90 days if it was sent outside the United States). If I fail to do so, a default judgment will be entered against me or the entity I represent.

Date: _____

_____
(Signature of the attorney or unrepresented party)

_____
(Printed name)

_____
(Address)

_____
(E-mail address)

_____
(Telephone number)

(Attach the following)

Duty to Avoid Unnecessary Expenses of Serving a Summons

Rule 4 of the Federal Rules of Civil Procedure requires certain defendants to cooperate in saving unnecessary expenses of serving a summons and complaint. A defendant who is located in the United States and who fails to return a signed waiver of service requested by a plaintiff located in the United States will be required to pay the expenses of service, unless the defendant shows good cause for the failure.

"Good cause" does not include a belief that the lawsuit is groundless, or that it has been brought in an improper venue, or that the court has no jurisdiction over this matter or over the defendant or the defendant's property.

If the waiver is signed and returned, you can still make these and all other defenses and objections, but you cannot object to the absence of a summons or of service.

If you waive service, then you must, within the time specified on the waiver form, serve an answer or a motion under Rule 12 on the plaintiff and file a copy with the court. By signing and returning the waiver form, you are allowed more time to respond than if a summons had been served.

ADVISORY COMMITTEE NOTES

1937 Adoption

Note to Subdivision (a). With the provision permitting additional summons upon request of the plaintiff, compare former Equity Rule 14 (Alias Subpoena) and the last sentence of former Equity Rule 12 (Issue of Subpoena—Time for Answer).

Note to Subdivision (b). This rule prescribes a form of summons which follows substantially the requirements stated in former Equity Rules 12 (Issue of Subpoena—Time for Answer) and 7 (Process, Mesne and Final).

U.S.C., Title 28, § 721 [now 1691] (Sealing and testing of writs) is substantially continued insofar as it applies to a summons, but its requirements as to teste of process are superseded. U.S.C., Title 28, [former] § 722 (Teste of process, day of) is superseded.

See Rule 12(a) for a statement of the time within which the defendant is required to appear and defend.

Note to Subdivision (c). This rule does not affect U.S.C., Title 28, § 503 [see 566], as amended June 15, 1935 (Marshals; duties) and such statutes as the following insofar as they provide for service of process by a marshal, but modifies them in so far as they may imply service by a marshal only:

U.S.C., Title 15:

§ 5 (Bringing in additional parties) (Sherman Act)

§ 10 (Bringing in additional parties)

§ 25 (Restraining violations; procedure)

U.S.C., Title 28:

§ 45 [former] (Practice and procedure in certain cases under the interstate commerce laws)

Compare [former] Equity Rule 15 (Process, by Whom Served).

Note to Subdivision (d). Under this rule the complaint must always be served with the summons.

Paragraph (1). For an example of a statute providing for service upon an agent of an individual see U.S.C., Title 28, § 109 [now 1400, 1694] (Patent cases).

Paragraph (3). This enumerates the officers and agents of a corporation or of a partnership or other unincorporated association upon whom service of process may be made, and permits service of process only upon the officers, managing or general agents, or agents authorized by appointment or by law, of the corporation, partnership or unincorporated association against which the action is brought. See *Christian v. International Ass'n of Machinists,* 7 F.(2d) 481 (D.C.Ky.1925) and *Singleton v. Order of Railway*

Conductors of America, 9 F.Supp. 417 (D.C.Ill.1935). Compare *Operative Plasterers' and Cement Finishers' International Ass'n of the United States and Canada v. Case,* 93 F.(2d) 56 (App.D.C.1937).

For a statute authorizing service upon a specified agent and requiring mailing to the defendant, see U.S.C., Title 6, § 7 (Surety companies as sureties; appointment of agents; service of process).

Paragraphs (4) and (5) provide a uniform and comprehensive method of service for all actions against the United States or an officer or agency thereof. For statutes providing for such service, see U.S.C., Title 7, §§ 217 (Proceedings for suspension of orders) 499k (Injunctions; application of injunction laws governing orders of Interstate Commerce Commission), 608c(15)(B) (Court review of ruling of Secretary of Agriculture), and 855 (making § 608c(15)(B) applicable to orders of the Secretary of Agriculture as to handlers of anti-hog-cholera serum and hog-cholera virus); U.S.C., Title 26, § 3679, (Bill in chancery to clear title to realty on which the United States has a lien for taxes); U.S.C., Title 28, former §§ 45, (District Courts; practice and procedure in certain cases under the interstate commerce laws), [former] 763 (Petition in suit against the United States; service; appearance by district attorney), 766 [now 2409] (Partition suits where United States is tenant in common or joint tenant), 902 [now 2410] (Foreclosure of mortgages or other liens on property in which the United States has an interest). These and similar statutes are modified in so far as they prescribe a different method of service or dispense with the service of a summons.

For the [former] Equity Rule on service, see [former] Equity Rule 13, Manner of Serving Subpoena.

Note to Subdivision (e). The provisions for the service of a summons or of notice or of an order in lieu of summons contained in U.S.C., Title 8, § 405 (Cancellation of certificates of citizenship fraudulently or illegally procured) (service by publication in accordance with State law); U.S.C., Title 28, § 118 [now 1655] (Absent defendants in suits to enforce liens); U.S.C., Title 35, § 72a [now 146, 291] (Jurisdiction of District Court of United States for the District of Columbia in certain equity suits where adverse parties reside elsewhere) (service by publication against parties residing in foreign countries); U.S.C., Title 38, § 445 [now 784] (Action against the United States on a veteran's contract of insurance) (parties not inhabitants of or not found within the district may be served with an order of the court, personally or by publication) and similar statutes are continued by this rule. Title 24, § 378 [now title 13, § 336] of the Code of the District of Columbia (Publication against non-resident; those absent for six months; unknown heirs or devisees; for divorce or in rem; actual service beyond District) is continued by this rule.

Note to Subdivision (f). This rule enlarges to some extent the present rule as to where service may be made. It does not, however, enlarge the jurisdiction of the district courts.

U.S.C., Title 28, §§ 113 [now 1392] (Suits in States containing more than one district) (where there are two or more defendants residing in different districts), [former] 115 (Suits of a local nature), 116 [now 1392] (Property in different districts in same state), [former] 838 (Executions run in all districts of state); U.S.C., Title 47, § 13 (Action for damages against a railroad or telegraph company whose officer or agent in control of a telegraph line refuses or fails to operate such line in a certain manner—"upon any agent of the company found in such state"); U.S.C., Title 49, § 321(c) [now 10330(b)] (Requiring designation of a process agent by interstate motor carriers and in case of failure so to do, service may be made upon any agent in the state) and similar statutes, allowing the running of process throughout a state, are substantially continued.

U.S.C., Title 15, §§ 5 (Bringing in additional parties) (Sherman Act), 25 (Restraining violations; procedure); U.S.C., Title 28, §§ 44 [now 2321] (Procedure in certain cases under interstate commerce laws; service of processes of court), 117 [now 754, 1692] (Property in different states in same circuit; jurisdiction of receiver), 839 [now 2413] (Executions; run in every State and Territory) and similar statutes, providing for the running of process beyond the territorial limits of a State, are expressly continued.

Note to Subdivision (g). With the second sentence compare [former] Equity Rule 15, (Process, by Whom Served).

Note to Subdivision (h). This rule substantially continues U.S.C., Title 28, [former] § 767 (Amendment of process).

1963 Amendment

Subdivision (b). Under amended subdivision (e) of this rule, an action may be commenced against a nonresident of the State in which the district court is held by complying with State procedures. Frequently the form of the summons or notice required in these cases by State law differs from the Federal form of summons described in present subdivision (b) and exemplified in Form 1. To avoid confusion, the amendment of subdivision (b) states that a form of summons or notice, corresponding "as nearly as may be" to the State form, shall be employed. See also a corresponding amendment of Rule 12(a) with regard to the time to answer.

Subdivision (d)(4). This paragraph, governing service upon the United States, is amended to allow the use of certified mail as an alternative to registered mail for sending copies of the papers to the Attorney General or to a United States officer or agency. Cf. N.J. Rule 4:5–2. See also the amendment of Rule 30(f)(1).

Subdivision (d)(7). Formerly a question was raised whether this paragraph, in the context of the rule as a whole, authorized service in original Federal actions pursuant to State statutes permitting service on a State official as a means of bringing a nonresident motorist defendant into court. It was argued in *McCoy v. Siler,* 205 F.2d 498, 501–2 (3d Cir.) (concurring opinion), cert. denied, 346 U.S. 872, 74 S.Ct. 120, 98 L.Ed. 380 (1953), that the effective service in those cases occurred not when the State official was served but when notice was given to the defendant outside the State, and that subdivision (f) (Territorial limits of effective service), as then worded, did not authorize out-of-State service. This contention found little support. A considerable number of cases held the service to be good, either by fixing upon the service on the official within the State as the effective service, thus satisfying the wording of subdivision (f) as it then stood, see *Holbrook v. Cafiero,* 18 F.R.D. 218 (D.Md.1955); *Pasternack v. Dalo,* 17 F.R.D. 420 (W.D.Pa.1955); *Super Prods. Corp. v. Parkin,* 20 F.R.D. 377 (S.D.N.Y.1957), or by reading paragraph (7) as not limited by subdivision (f). See *Giffin v. Ensign,* 234 F.2d 307 (3d Cir. 1956); 2 Moore's *Federal Practice,* ¶ 4.19 (2d ed. 1948); 1 Barron & Holtzoff, *Federal Practice & Procedure* § 182.1 (Wright ed. 1960); Comment, 27 U. of Chi.L.Rev. 751 (1960). See also *Olberding v. Illinois Central R.R.,* 201 F.2d 582 (6th Cir.), rev'd on other grounds, 346 U.S. 338, 74 S.Ct. 83, 98 L.Ed. 39 (1953); *Feinsinger v. Bard,* 195 F.2d 45 (7th Cir. 1952).

An important and growing class of State statutes base personal jurisdiction over nonresidents on the doing of acts or on other contacts within the State, and permit notice to be given the defendant outside the State without any requirement of service on a local State official. See, e.g., Ill.Ann.Stat., c. 110, §§ 16, 17 (Smith-Hurd 1956); Wis.Stat. § 262.06 (1959). This service, employed in original Federal actions pursuant to paragraph (7), has also been held proper. See *Farr & Co. v. Cia. Intercontinental de Nav. de Cuba,* 243 F.2d 342 (2d Cir. 1957); *Kappus v. Western Hills Oil, Inc.,* 24 F.R.D. 123 (E.D.Wis.1959); *Star v. Rogalny,* 162 F.Supp. 181 (E.D.Ill.1957). It has also been held that the clause of paragraph (7) which permits service "in the manner prescribed by the law of the state," etc., is not limited by subdivision (c) requiring that service of all process be made by certain designated persons. See *Farr & Co. v. Cia. Intercontinental de Nav. de Cuba, supra.* But *cf. Sappia v. Lauro Lines,* 130 F.Supp. 810 (S.D.N.Y.1955).

The salutary results of these cases are intended to be preserved. See paragraph (7), with a clarified reference to State law, and amended subdivisions (e) and (f).

Subdivision (e). For the general relation between subdivisions (d) and (e), see 2 Moore, supra, ¶ 4.32.

The amendment of the first sentence inserting the word "thereunder" supports the original intention that the "order of court" must be authorized by a specific United States statute. See 1 Barron & Holtzoff, supra, at 731. The clause added at the end of the first sentence expressly adopts the view taken by commentators that, if no manner of service is prescribed in the statute or order, the service may be made in a manner stated in Rule 4. See 2 Moore, supra, ¶ 4.32, at 1004; Smit, *International Aspects of Federal Civil Procedure,* 61 Colum.L.Rev. 1031, 1036–39 (1961). But see Commentary, 5 Fed. Rules Serv. 791 (1942).

Examples of the statutes to which the first sentence relates are 28 U.S.C. § 2361 (Interpleader; process and procedure); 28 U.S.C. § 1655 (Lien enforcement; absent defendants).

The second sentence, added by amendment, expressly allows resort in original Federal actions to the procedures provided by State law for effecting service on nonresident parties (as well as on domiciliaries not found within the State). See, as illustrative, the discussion under amended subdivision (d)(7) of service pursuant to State nonresident motorist statutes and other comparable State statutes. Of particular interest is the change brought about by the reference in this sentence to State procedures for commencing actions against nonresidents by attachment and the like, accompanied by notice. Although an action commenced in a State court by attachment may be removed to the Federal court if ordinary conditions for removal are satisfied, see 28 U.S.C. § 1450; *Rorick v. Devon Syndicate, Ltd.,* 307 U.S. 299, 59 S.Ct. 877, 83 L.Ed. 1303 (1939); *Clark v. Wells,* 203 U.S. 164, 27 S.Ct. 43, 51 L.Ed. 138 (1906), there has heretofore been no provision recognized by the courts for commencing an original Federal civil action by attachment. See Currie, *Attachment and Garnishment in the Federal Courts,* 59 Mich.L.Rev. 337 (1961), arguing that this result came about through historical anomaly. Rule 64, which refers to attachment, garnishment, and similar procedures under State law, furnishes only provisional remedies in actions otherwise validly commenced. See *Big Vein Coal Co. v. Read,* 229 U.S. 31, 33 S.Ct. 694, 57 L.Ed. 1053 (1913); *Davis v. Ensign-Bickford Co.,* 139 F.2d 624 (8th Cir. 1944); 7 Moore's *Federal Practice* ¶ 64.05 (2d ed. 1954); 3 Barron & Holtzoff, *Federal Practice & Procedure* § 1423 (Wright ed. 1958); but cf. Note, 13 So.Calif.L.Rev. 361 (1940). The amendment will now permit the institution of original Federal actions against nonresidents through the use of familiar State procedures by which property of these defendants is brought within the custody of the court and some appropriate service is made upon them.

The necessity of satisfying subject-matter jurisdictional requirements and requirements of venue will limit the practical utilization of these methods of effecting service. Within those limits, however, there appears to be no reason for denying plaintiffs means of commencing actions in Federal courts which are generally available in the State courts. See 1 Barron & Holtzoff, supra, at 374–80; Nordbye, *Comments on Proposed Amendments to Rules of Civil Procedure for the United States District Courts,* 18 F.R.D. 105, 106 (1956); Note, 34 Corn.L.Q. 103 (1948); Note, 13 So.Calif.L.Rev. 361 (1940).

If the circumstances of a particular case satisfy the applicable Federal law (first sentence of Rule 4(e), as amended) and the applicable State law (second sentence), the party seeking to make the service may proceed under the Federal or the State law, at his option.

See also amended Rule 13(a), and the Advisory Committee's Note thereto.

Subdivision (f). The first sentence is amended to assure the effectiveness of service outside the territorial limits of the State in all the cases in which any of the rules authorize service beyond those boundaries. Besides the preceding provisions of Rule 4, see Rule 71A(d)(3). In addition, the new second sentence of the subdivision permits effective service within a limited area outside the State in certain special situations, namely, to bring in additional parties to a counterclaim or cross-claim (Rule 13 (h)), impleaded parties (Rule 14), and indispensable or conditionally necessary parties to a pending action (Rule 19); and to secure compliance with an order of commitment for civil contempt. In those situations effective service can be made at points not more than 100 miles distant from the courthouse in which the action is commenced, or to which it is assigned or transferred for trial.

The bringing in of parties under the 100-mile provision in the limited situations enumerated is designed to promote the objective of enabling the court to determine entire controversies. In the light of present-day facilities for communication and travel, the territorial range of the service allowed, analogous to that which applies to the service of a subpoena under Rule 45(e)(1), can hardly work hardship on the parties summoned. The provision will be especially useful in metropolitan areas spanning more than one State. Any requirements of subject-matter jurisdiction and venue will still have to be satisfied as to the parties brought in, although these requirements will be eased in some instances when the parties can be regarded as "ancillary." See *Pennsylvania R.R. v. Erie Avenue Warehouse Co.,* 5 F.R.Serv.2d 14a.62, Case 2 (3d Cir.1962); *Dery v. Wyer,* 265 F.2d 804 (2d Cir.1959); *United Artists Corp. v. Masterpiece Productions, Inc.,* 221 F.2d 213 (2d Cir.1955); *Lesnik v. Public Industrials Corp.,* 144 F.2d 968 (2d Cir.1944); *Vaughn v. Terminal Transp. Co.,* 162 F.Supp. 647 (E.D.Tenn.1957); and compare the fifth paragraph of the Advisory Committee's Note to Rule 4(e), as amended. The amendment is but a moderate extension of the territorial reach of Federal process and has ample practical justification. See 2 Moore, supra, § 4.01[13] (Supp.1960); 1 Barron & Holtzoff, supra, § 184; Note, 51 Nw.U.L.Rev. 354 (1956). But cf. Nordbye, *Comments on Proposed Amendments to Rules of Civil Procedure for the United States District Courts,* 18 F.R.D. 105, 106 (1956).

As to the need for enlarging the territorial area in which orders of commitment for civil contempt may be served, see *Graber v. Graber,* 93 F.Supp. 281 (D.D.C.1950); *Teele Soap Mfg. Co. v. Pine Tree Products Co., Inc.,* 8 F.Supp. 546 (D.N.H.1934); *Mitchell v. Dexter,* 244 Fed. 926 (1st Cir.1917); *In re Graves,* 29 Fed. 60 (N.D.Iowa 1886).

As to the Court's power to amend subdivisions (e) and (f) as here set forth, see *Mississippi Pub. Corp. v. Murphree,* 326 U.S. 438, 66 S.Ct. 242, 90 L.Ed. 185 (1946).

Subdivision (i). The continual increase of civil litigation having international elements makes it advisable to consolidate, amplify, and clarify the provisions governing service upon parties in foreign countries. See generally Jones, *International Judicial Assistance: Procedural Chaos and a Program for Reform,* 62 Yale L.J. 515 (1953); Longley, *Serving Process, Subpoenas and Other Documents in Foreign Territory,* Proc.A.B.A., Sec.Int'l & Comp.L. 34 (1959); Smit, *International Aspects of Federal Civil Procedure,* 61 Colum.L.Rev. 1031 (1961).

As indicated in the opening lines of new subdivision (i), referring to the provisions of subdivision (e), the authority for effecting foreign service must be found in a statute of the United States or a statute or rule of court of the State in which the district court is held providing in terms or upon proper interpretation for service abroad upon persons not inhabitants of or found within the State. See the Advisory Committee's Note to amended Rule 4(d)(7) and Rule 4(e). For examples of Federal and State statutes expressly authorizing such service, see 8 U.S.C. § 1451(b); 35 U.S.C. §§ 146, 293; Me.Rev.Stat., ch. 22, § 70 (Supp.1961); Minn.Stat.Ann. § 303.13 (1947); N.Y.Veh. & Tfc.Law § 253. Several decisions have construed statutes to permit service in foreign countries, although the matter is not expressly mentioned in the statutes. See, e.g., *Chapman v. Superior Court,* 162 Cal.App.2d 421, 328 P.2d 23 (Dist.Ct.App.1958); *Sperry v. Fliegers,* 194 Misc. 438, 86 N.Y.S.2d 830 (Sup.Ct.1949); *Ewing v. Thompson,* 233 N.C. 564, 65 S.E.2d 17 (1951); *Rushing v. Bush,* 260 S.W.2d 900 (Tex.Ct.Civ.App.1953). Federal and State statutes authorizing service on nonresidents in such terms as to warrant the interpretation that service abroad is permissible include 15 U.S.C. §§ 77v(a), 78aa, 79y; 28 U.S.C. § 1655; 38 U.S.C. § 784(a); Ill.Ann.Stat., c. 110, §§ 16, 17 (Smith-Hurd 1956); Wis.Stat. § 262.06 (1959).

Under subdivisions (e) and (i), when authority to make foreign service is found in a Federal statute or statute or rule of court of a State, it is always sufficient to carry out the service in the manner indicated therein. Subdivision (i) introduces considerable further flexibility by permitting the foreign service and return thereof to be carried out in any of a number of other alternative ways that are also declared to be sufficient. Other aspects of foreign service continue to be governed by the other provisions of Rule 4. Thus, for example, subdivision (i) effects no change in the form of the summons, or the issuance of separate or additional summons, or the amendment of service.

Service of process beyond the territorial limits of the United States may involve difficulties not encountered in the case of domestic service. Service abroad may be considered by a foreign country to require the performance of judicial, and therefore, "sovereign," acts within its territory, which that country may conceive to be offensive to its policy or contrary to its law. See Jones, supra, at 537. For example, a person not qualified to serve process according to the law of the foreign country may find himself subject to sanctions if he attempts service therein. See Inter-American Juridical Committee, *Report on Uniformity of Legislation on International Cooperation in Judicial Procedures* 20 (1952). The enforcement of a judgment in the foreign country in which the service was made may be embarrassed or prevented if the service did not comport with the law of that country. See ibid.

One of the purposes of subdivision (i) is to allow accommodation to the policies and procedures of the foreign country. It is emphasized, however, that the attitudes of foreign countries vary considerably and that the question of recognition of United States judgments abroad is complex. Accordingly, if enforcement is to be sought in the country of service, the foreign law should be examined before a choice is made among the methods of service allowed by subdivision (i).

Subdivision (i)(1). Subparagraph (a) of paragraph (1), permitting service by the method prescribed by the law of the foreign country for service on a person in that country in a civil action in any of its courts of general jurisdiction, provides an alternative that is likely to create least objection in the place of service and also is likely to enhance the possibilities of securing ultimate enforcement of the judgment abroad. See *Report on Uniformity of Legislation on International Cooperation in Judicial Procedures,* supra.

In certain foreign countries service in aid of litigation pending in other countries can lawfully be accomplished only upon request to the foreign courts, which in turn directs the service to be made. In many countries this has long been a customary way of accomplishing the service. See *In re Letters Rogatory out of First Civil Court of City of Mexico,* 261 Fed. 652 (S.D.N.Y.1919); Jones, supra, at 543; Comment, 44 Colum.L.Rev. 72 (1944); Note 58 Yale L.J. 1193 (1949). Subparagraph (B) of paragraph (1), referring to a letter rogatory, validates this method. A proviso, applicable to this subparagraph and the preceding one, requires, as a safeguard, that the service made shall be reasonably calculated to give actual notice of the proceedings to the party. See *Milliken v. Meyer,* 311 U.S. 457, 61 S.Ct. 339, 85 L.Ed. 278 (1940).

Subparagraph (C) of paragraph (1), permitting foreign service by personal delivery on individuals and corporations, partnerships, and associations, provides for a manner of service that is not only traditionally preferred, but also is most likely to lead to actual notice. Explicit provision for this manner of service was thought desirable because a number of Federal and State statutes permitting foreign service do not specifically provide for service by personal delivery abroad, see e.g., 35 U.S.C. §§ 146, 293; 46 U.S.C. § 1292; Calif.Ins.Code § 1612; N.Y.Veh. & Tfc. Law § 253, and it also may be unavailable under the law of the country in which the service is made.

Subparagraph (D) of paragraph (1), permitting service by certain types of mail, affords a manner of service that is inexpensive and expeditious, and requires a minimum of activity within the foreign country. Several statutes specifically provide for service in a foreign country by mail, e.g., Hawaii Rev.Laws §§ 230–31, 230–32 (1955); Minn.Stat.Ann. § 303.13 (1947); N.Y.Civ.Prac.Act, § 229–b; N.Y.Veh. & Tfc.Law § 253, and it has been sanctioned by the courts even in the absence of statutory provision specifying that form of service. *Zurini v. United States,* 189 F.2d 722 (8th Cir.1951); *United States v. Cardillo,* 135 F.Supp. 798 (W.D.Pa.1955); *Autogiro Co. v. Kay Gyroplanes, Ltd.,* 55 F.Supp. 919 (D.D.C.1944). Since the reliability of postal service may vary from country to country, service by mail is proper only when it is addressed to the party to be served and a form of mail requiring a signed receipt is used. An additional safeguard is provided by the requirement that the mailing be attended to by the clerk of the court. See also the provisions of paragraph (2) of this subdivision (i) regarding proof of service by mail.

Under the applicable law it may be necessary, when the defendant is an infant or incompetent person, to deliver the summons and complaint to a guardian, committee, or similar fiduciary. In such a case it would be advisable to make service under subparagraph (A), (B), or (E).

Subparagraph (E) of paragraph (1) adds flexibility by permitting the court by order to tailor the manner of service to fit the necessities of a particular case or the peculiar requirements of the law of the country in which the service is to be made. A similar provision appears in a number of statutes, e.g., 35 U.S.C. §§ 146, 293; 38 U.S.C. § 784(a); 46 U.S.C. § 1292.

The next-to-last sentence of paragraph (1) permits service under (C) and (E) to be made by any person who is not a party and is not less than 18 years of age or who is designated by court order or by the foreign court. Cf. Rule 45(c); N.Y.Civ.Prac.Act §§ 233, 235. This alternative increases the possibility that the plaintiff will be able to find a process server who can proceed unimpeded in the foreign country; it also may improve the changes of enforcing the judgment in the country of service. Especially is this alternative valuable when authority for the foreign service is found in a statute or rule of court that limits the group of eligible process servers to designated officials or special appointees who, because directly connected with another "sovereign," may be particularly offensive to the foreign country. See generally Smit, supra, at 1040–41. When recourse is had to subparagraph (A) or (B) the identity of the process server always will be determined by the law of the foreign country in which the service is made.

The last sentence of paragraph (1) sets forth an alternative manner for the issuance and transmission of the summons for service. After obtaining the summons from the clerk, the plaintiff must ascertain the best manner of delivering the summons and complaint to the person, court, or officer who will make the service. Thus the clerk is not burdened with the task of determining who is permitted to serve process under the law of a particular country or the appropriate governmental or nongovernmental channel for forwarding a letter rogatory. Under (D), however, the papers must always be posted by the clerk.

Subdivision (i)(2). When service is made in a foreign country, paragraph (2) permits methods for proof of service in addition to those prescribed by subdivision (g). Proof of service in accordance with the law of the foreign country is permitted because foreign process servers, unaccustomed to the form or the requirement of return of service prevalent in the United States, have on occasion been unwilling to execute the affidavit required by Rule 4(g). See Jones, supra, at 537; Longley, supra, at 35. As a corollary of the alternate manner of service in subdivision (i)(1)(E), proof of service as directed by order of the court is permitted. The special provision for proof of service by mail is intended as an additional safeguard when that method is used. On the type of evidence of delivery that may be satisfactory to a court in lieu of a signed receipt, see *Aero Associates, Inc. v. La Metropolitana,* 183 F.Supp. 357 (S.D.N.Y. 1960).

1966 Amendment

The wording of Rule 4(f) is changed to accord with the amendment of Rule 13(h) referring to Rule 19 as amended.

1980 Amendment

Subdivision (a). This is a technical amendment to conform this subdivision with the amendment of subdivision (c).

Subdivision (c). The purpose of this amendment is to authorize service of process to be made by any person who is authorized to make service in actions in the courts of general jurisdiction of the state in which the district court is held or in which service is made.

There is a troublesome ambiguity in Rule 4. Rule 4(c) directs that all process is to be served by the marshal, by his deputy, or by a person specially appointed by the court. But Rule 4(d)(7) authorizes service in certain cases "in the manner prescribed by the law of the state in which the district court is held. . . ." And Rule 4(e), which authorizes service beyond the state and service in quasi in rem cases when state law permits such service, directs that "service may be made . . . under the circumstances and in the manner prescribed in the [state] statute or rule." State statutes and rules of the kind referred to in Rule 4(d)(7) and Rule 4(e) commonly designate the persons who are to make the service provided for, e.g., a sheriff or a plaintiff. When that is so, may the persons so designated by state law make service, or is service in all cases to be made by a marshal or by one specially appointed under present Rule 4(c)? The commentators have noted the ambiguity and have suggested the desirability of an amendment. See 2 Moore's *Federal Practice* ¶ 4.08 (1974); Wright & Miller, *Federal Practice and Procedure:* Civil § 1092 (1969). And the ambiguity has given rise to unfortunate results. See *United States for the use of Tanos v. St. Paul Mercury Ins. Co.,* 361 F.2d 838 (5th Cir. 1966); *Veeck v. Commodity Enterprises, Inc.,* 487 F.2d 423 (9th Cir. 1973).

The ambiguity can be resolved by specific amendments to Rules 4(d)(7) and 4(e), but the Committee is of the view that there is no reason why Rule 4(c) should not generally authorize service of process in all cases by anyone authorized to make service in the courts of general jurisdiction of the state in which the district court is held or in which service is made. The marshal continues to be the obvious, always effective officer for service of process.

1987 Amendment

The amendments are technical. No substantive change is intended.

1993 Amendments

SPECIAL NOTE: Mindful of the constraints of the Rules Enabling Act, the Committee calls the attention of the Supreme Court and Congress to new subdivision (k)(2). Should this limited extension of service be disapproved, the Committee nevertheless recommends adoption of the balance of the rule, with subdivision (k)(1) becoming simply subdivision (k). The Committee Notes would be revised to eliminate references to subdivision (k)(2).

Purposes of Revision. The general purpose of this revision is to facilitate the service of the summons and complaint. The revised rule explicitly authorizes a means for service of the summons and complaint on any defendant. While the methods of service so authorized always provide appropriate notice to persons against whom claims are made, effective service under this rule does not assure that personal jurisdiction has been established over the defendant served.

First, the revised rule authorizes the use of any means of service provided by the law not only of the forum state, but also of the state in which a defendant is served, unless the defendant is a minor or incompetent.

Second, the revised rule clarifies and enhances the cost-saving practice of securing the assent of the defendant to dispense with actual service of the summons and complaint. This practice was introduced to the rule in 1983 by an act of Congress authorizing "service-by-mail," a procedure that effects economic service with cooperation of the defendant. Defendants that magnify costs of service by requiring expensive service not necessary to achieve full notice of an action brought against them are required to bear the wasteful costs. This provision is made available in actions against defendants who cannot be served in the districts in which the actions are brought.

Third, the revision reduces the hazard of commencing an action against the United States or its officers, agencies, and corporations. A party failing to effect service on all the offices of the United States as required by the rule is assured adequate time to cure defects in service.

Fourth, the revision calls attention to the important effect of the Hague Convention and other treaties bearing on service of documents in foreign countries and favors the use of internationally agreed means of service. In some respects, these treaties have facilitated service in foreign countries but are not fully known to the bar.

Finally, the revised rule extends the reach of federal courts to impose jurisdiction over the person of all defendants against whom federal law claims are made and who can be constitutionally subjected to the jurisdiction of the courts of the United States. The present territorial limits on the effectiveness of service to subject a defendant to the jurisdiction of the court over the defendant's person are retained for all actions in which there is a state in which personal jurisdiction can be asserted consistently with state law and the Fourteenth Amendment. A new provision enables district courts to exercise jurisdiction, if permissible under the Constitution and not precluded by statute, when a federal claim is made against a defendant not subject to the jurisdiction of any single state.

The revised rule is reorganized to make its provisions more accessible to those not familiar with all of them. Additional subdivisions in this rule allow for more captions; several overlaps among subdivisions are eliminated; and several disconnected provisions are removed, to be relocated in a new Rule 4.1.

The Caption of the Rule. Prior to this revision, Rule 4 was entitled "Process" and applied to the service of not only the summons but also other process as well, although these are not covered by the revised rule. Service of process in eminent domain proceedings is governed by Rule 71A. Service of a subpoena is governed by Rule 45, and service of papers such as orders, motions, notices, pleadings, and other documents is governed by Rule 5.

The revised rule is entitled "Summons" and applies only to that form of legal process. Unless service of the summons is waived, a summons must be served whenever a person is joined as a party against whom a claim is made. Those few provisions of the former rule which relate specifically to service of process other than a summons are relocated in Rule 4.1 in order to simplify the text of this rule.

Subdivision (a). Revised subdivision (a) contains most of the language of the former subdivision (b). The second sentence of the former subdivision (b) has been stricken, so that the federal court summons will be the same in all cases. Few states now employ distinctive requirements of form for a summons and the applicability of such a requirement in federal court can only serve as a trap for an unwary party or attorney. A sentence is added to this subdivision authorizing an amendment of a summons. This sentence replaces the rarely used former subdivision 4(h). See 4A Wright & Miller, Federal Practice and Procedure § 1131 (2d ed. 1987).

Subdivision (b). Revised subdivision (b) replaces the former subdivision (a). The revised text makes clear that the responsibility for filling in the summons falls on the plaintiff, not the clerk of the court. If there are multiple defendants, the plaintiff may secure issuance of a summons for each defendant, or may serve copies of a single original bearing the names of multiple defendants if the addressee of the summons is effectively identified.

Subdivision (c). Paragraph (1) of revised subdivision (c) retains language from the former subdivision (d)(1). Paragraph (2) retains language from the former subdivision (a), and adds an appropriate caution regarding the time limit for service set forth in subdivision (m).

The 1983 revision of Rule 4 relieved the marshals' offices of much of the burden of serving the summons. Subdivision (c) eliminates the requirement for service by the marshal's office in actions in which the party seeking service is the United States. The United States, like other civil litigants, is now permitted to designate any person who is 18 years of age and not a party to serve its summons.

The court remains obligated to appoint a marshal, a deputy, or some other person to effect service of a summons in two classes of cases specified by statute: actions brought in forma pauperis or by a seaman. 28 U.S.C. §§ 1915, 1916. The court also retains discretion to appoint a process server on motion of a party. If a law enforcement presence appears to be necessary or advisable to keep the peace, the court should appoint a marshal or deputy or other official person to make the service. The Department of Justice may also call upon the Marshals Service to perform services in actions brought by the United States. 28 U.S.C. § 651.

Subdivision (d). This text is new, but is substantially derived from the former subdivisions (c)(2)(C) and (D), added to the rule by Congress in 1983. The aims of the provision are to eliminate the costs of service of a summons on many parties and to foster cooperation among adversaries and counsel. The rule operates to impose upon the defendant those costs that could have been avoided if the defendant had cooperated reasonably in the manner prescribed. This device is useful in dealing with defendants who are furtive, who reside in places not easily reached by process servers, or who are outside the United States and can be served only at substantial and unnecessary expense. Illustratively, there is no useful purpose achieved by requiring a plaintiff to comply with all the formalities of service in a foreign country, including costs of translation, when suing a defendant manufacturer, fluent in English, whose products are widely distributed in the United States. See Bankston v. Toyota Motor Corp., 889 F.2d 172 (8th Cir. 1989).

The former text described this process as service-by-mail. This language misled some plaintiffs into thinking that service could be effected by mail without the affirmative cooperation of the defendant. E.g., Gulley v. Mayo Foundation, 886 F.2d 161 (8th Cir. 1989). It is more accurate to describe the communication sent to the defendant as a request for a waiver of formal service.

The request for waiver of service may be sent only to defendants subject to service under subdivision (e), (f), or (h). The United States is not expected to waive service for the reason that its mail receiving facilities are inadequate to assure that the notice is actually received by the correct person in the Department of Justice. The same principle is applied to agencies, corporations, and officers of the United States and to other governments and entities subject to service under subdivision (j). Moreover, there are policy reasons why governmental entities should not be confronted with the potential for bearing costs of service in cases in which they ultimately prevail. Infants or incompetent persons likewise are not called upon to waive service because, due to their presumed inability to understand the request and its consequences, they must generally be served through fiduciaries.

It was unclear whether the former rule authorized, mailing of a request for "acknowledgement of service" to defendants outside the forum state. See 1 R. Casad, Jurisdiction in Civil Actions (2d Ed.) 5–29, 30 (1991) and cases cited. But, as Professor Casad observed, there was no reason not to employ this device in an effort to obtain service outside the state, and there are many instances in which it was in fact so used, with respect both to defendants within the United States and to defendants in other countries.

The opportunity for waiver has distinct advantages to a foreign defendant. By waiving service, the defendant can reduce the costs that may ultimately be taxed against it if unsuccessful in the lawsuit, including the sometimes substantial expense of translation that may be wholly unnecessary for defendants fluent in English. Moreover, a foreign defendant that waives service is afforded substantially more time to defend against the action than if it had been formally served: under Rule 12, a defendant ordinarily has only 20 days after service in which to file its answer or raise objections by motion, but by signing a waiver it is allowed 90 days after the date the request for waiver was mailed in which to submit its defenses. Because of the additional time needed for mailing and the unreliability of some foreign mail services, a period of 60 days (rather than the 30 days required for domestic transmissions) is provided for a return of a waiver sent to a foreign country.

It is hoped that, since transmission of the notice and waiver forms is a private nonjudicial act, does not purport to effect service, and is not accompanied by any summons or directive from a court, use of the procedure will not offend foreign sovereignties, even those that have withheld their assent to formal service by mail or have objected to the "service-by-mail" provisions of the former rule. Unless the addressee consents, receipt of the request under the revised rule does not give rise to any obligation to answer the lawsuit, does not provide a basis for default judgment, and does not suspend the statute of limitations in those states where the period continues to run until service. Nor are there any adverse consequences to a foreign defendant, since the provisions for shifting the expense of service to a defendant that declines to waive service apply only if the plaintiff and defendant are both located in the United States.

With respect to a defendant located in a foreign country like the United Kingdom, which accepts documents in English, whose Central Authority acts promptly in effecting service, and whose policies discourage its residents from waiving formal service, there will be little reason for a plaintiff to send the notice and request under subdivision (d) rather than use convention methods. On the other hand, the procedure offers significant potential benefits to a plaintiff when suing a defendant that, though fluent in English, is located in a country where, as a condition to formal service under a convention, documents must be translated into another language or where formal service will be otherwise costly or time-consuming.

Paragraph (1) is explicit that a timely waiver of service of a summons does not prejudice the right of a defendant to object by means of a motion authorized by Rule 12(b)(2) to the absence of jurisdiction over the defendant's person, or to assert other defenses that may be available. The only issues eliminated are those involving the sufficiency of the summons or the sufficiency of the method by which it is served.

Paragraph (2) states what the present rule implies: the defendant has a duty to avoid costs associated with the service of a summons not needed to inform the defendant regarding the commencement of an action. The text of the rule also sets forth the requirements for a Notice and Request for Waiver sufficient to put the cost-shifting provision in place. These requirements are illustrated in Forms 1A and 1B, which replace the former Form 18-A.

Paragraph (2)(A) is explicit that a request for waiver of service by a corporate defendant must be addressed to a person qualified to receive service. The general mail rooms of large organizations cannot be required to identify the appropriate individual recipient for an institutional summons.

Paragraph (2)(B) permits the use of alternatives to the United States mails in sending the Notice and Request. While private messenger services or electronic communications may be more expensive than the mail, they may be equally reliable and on occasion more convenient to the parties. Especially with respect to transmissions to foreign countries, alternative means may be desirable, for in some countries facsimile transmission is the most efficient and economical means of communication. If electronic means such as facsimile transmission are employed, the sender should maintain a record of the transmission to assure proof of transmission if receipt is denied, but a party receiving such a transmission has a duty to cooperate and cannot avoid liability for the resulting cost of formal service if the transmission is prevented at the point of receipt.

A defendant failing to comply with a request for waiver shall be given an opportunity to show good cause for the failure, but sufficient cause should be rare. It is not a good cause for failure to waive service that the claim is unjust or that the court lacks jurisdiction. Sufficient cause not to shift the cost of service would exist, however, if the defendant did not receive the request or was insufficiently literate in English to understand it. It should be noted that the provisions for shifting the cost of service apply only if the plaintiff and the defendant are both located in the United States, and accordingly a foreign defendant need not show "good cause" for its failure to waive service.

Paragraph (3) extends the time for answer if, before being served with process, the defendant waives formal service. The extension is intended to serve as an inducement to waive service and to assure that a defendant will not gain any delay be declining to waive service and thereby causing the additional time needed to effect service. By waiving service, a defendant is not called upon to respond to the complaint until 60 days from the date the notice was sent to it—90 days if the notice was sent to a foreign country—rather than within the 20 day period from date of service specified in Rule 12.

Paragraph (4) clarifies the effective date of service when service is waived; the provision is needed to resolve an issue arising when applicable law requires service of process to toll the statute of limitations. E.g., Morse v. Elmira Country Club, 752 F.2d 35 (2d Cir.1984). Cf. Walker v. Armco Steel Corp., 446 U.S. 740 (1980).

The provisions in former subdivision (c)(2)(C)(ii) of this rule may have been misleading to some parties. Some plaintiffs, not reading the rule carefully, supposed that receipt by the defendant of the mailed complaint had the effect both of establishing the jurisdiction of the court over the defendant's person and of tolling the statute of limitations in actions in which service of the summons is required to toll the limitations period. The revised rule is clear that, if the waiver is not returned and filed, the limitations period under such a law is not tolled and the action will not otherwise proceed until formal service of process is effected.

Some state limitations laws may toll an otherwise applicable statute at the time when the defendant receives notice of the action. Nevertheless, the device of requested waiver of service is not suitable if a limitations period which is about to expire is not tolled by filing the action. Unless there is ample time, the plaintiff should proceed directly to the formal methods for service identified in subdivisions (e), (f), or (h).

The procedure of requesting waiver of service should also not be used if the time for service under subdivision (m) will expire before the date on which the waiver must be returned. While a plaintiff has been allowed additional time for service in that situation, e.g., Prather v. Raymond Constr. Co., 570 F.Supp. 278 (N.D.Ga.1983), the court could refuse a request for additional time unless the defendant appears to have evaded service pursuant to subdivision (e) or (h). It may be noted that the presumptive time limit for service under subdivision (m) does not apply to service in a foreign country.

Paragraph (5) is a cost-shifting provision retained from the former rule. The costs that may be imposed on the defendant could include, for example, the cost of the time of a process server required to make contact with a defendant residing in a guarded apartment house or residential development. The paragraph is explicit that the costs of enforcing the cost-shifting provision are themselves recoverable from a defendant who fails to return the waiver. In the absence of such a provision, the purpose of the rule would be frustrated by the cost of its enforcement, which is likely to be high in relation to the small benefit secured by the plaintiff.

Some plaintiffs may send a notice and request for waiver and, without waiting for return of the waiver, also proceed with efforts to effect formal service on the defendant. To discourage this practice, the cost-shifting provisions in paragraphs (2) and (5) are limited to costs of effecting service incurred after the time expires for the defendant to return the waiver. Moreover, by returning the waiver within the time allowed and before being served with process, a defendant receives the benefit of the longer period for responding to the complaint afforded for waivers under paragraph (3).

Subdivision (e). This subdivision replaces former subdivisions (c)(2)(C)(i) and (d)(1). It provides a means for service of summons on individuals within a judicial district of the United States. Together with subdivision (f), it provides for service on persons anywhere, subject to constitutional and statutory constraints.

Service of the summons under this subdivision does not conclusively establish the jurisdiction of the court over the person of the defendant. A defendant may assert the territorial limits of the court's reach set forth in subdivision (k), including the constitutional limitations that may be imposed by the Due Process Clause of the Fifth Amendment.

Paragraph (1) authorizes service in any judicial district in conformity with state law. This paragraph sets forth the language of former subdivision (c)(2)(C)(i), which authorized the use of the law of the state in which the district court sits, but adds as an alternative the use of the law of the state in which the service is effected.

Paragraph (2) retains the text of the former subdivision (d)(1) and authorizes the use of the familiar methods of personal or abode service or service on an authorized agent in any judicial district.

To conform to these provisions, the former subdivision (e) bearing on proceedings against parties not found within the state is stricken. Likewise stricken is the first sentence of the former subdivision (f), which had restricted the authority of the federal process server to the state in which the district court sits.

Subdivision (f). This subdivision provides for service on individuals who are in a foreign country, replacing the former subdivision (i) that was added to Rule 4 in 1963. Reflecting the pattern of Rule 4 in incorporating state law limitations on the exercise of jurisdiction over persons, the former subdivision (i) limited service outside the United States to cases in which extraterritorial service was authorized by state or federal law. The new rule eliminates the requirement of explicit authorization. On occasion, service in a foreign country was held to be improper for lack of statutory authority. E.g., Martens v. Winder, 341 F.2d 197 (9th Cir.), cert. denied, 382 U.S. 937 (1965). This authority, however, was found to exist by implication. E.g., SEC v. VTR, Inc., 39 F.R.D. 19 (S.D.N.Y.1966). Given the substantial increase in the number of international transactions and events that are the subject of litigation in federal courts, it is appropriate to infer a general legislative authority to effect service on defendants in a foreign country.

A secondary effect of this provision for foreign service of a federal summons is to facilitate the use of federal long-arm law in actions brought to enforce the federal law against defendants who cannot be served under any state law but who can be constitutionally subjected to the jurisdiction of the federal court. Such a provision is set forth in paragraph (2) of subdivision (k) of this rule, applicable only to persons not subject to the territorial jurisdiction of any particular state.

Paragraph (1) gives effect to the Hague Convention on the Service Abroad of Judicial and Extrajudicial Documents, which entered into force for the United States on February 10, 1969. See 28 U.S.C.A., Fed.R.Civ.P. 4 (Supp.1986). This Convention is an important means of dealing with problems of service in a foreign country. See generally 1 B. Ristau, International Judicial Assistance §§ 4–1–1 to 4–5–2 (1990). Use of the Convention procedures, when available, is mandatory if documents must be transmitted abroad to effect service. See Volkswagenwerk Aktiengesellschaft v. Schlunk, 486 U.S. 694 (1988) (noting that voluntary use of these procedures may be desirable even when service could constitutionally be effected in another manner); J. Weis, The Federal Rules and the Hague Conventions: Concerns of Conformity and Comity, 50 U.Pitt.L.Rev. 903 (1989). Therefore, this paragraph provides that, when service is to be effected outside a judicial district of the United States, the methods of service appropriate under an applicable treaty shall be employed if available and if the treaty so requires.

The Hague Convention furnishes safeguards against the abridgment of rights of parties through inadequate notice. Article 15 provides for verification of actual notice or a demonstration that process was served by a method prescribed by the internal laws of the foreign state before a default judgment may be entered. Article 16 of the Convention also enables the judge to extend the time for appeal after judgment if the defendant shows a lack of adequate notice either to defend or to appeal the judgment, or has disclosed a prima facie case on the merits.

The Hague Convention does not specify a time within which a foreign country's Central Authority must effect service, but Article 15 does provide that alternate methods may be used if a Central Authority does not respond within six months. Generally, a Central Authority can be expected to respond much more quickly than that limit might permit, but there have been occasions when the signatory state was dilatory or refused to cooperate for substantive reasons. In such cases, resort may be had to the provision set forth in subdivision (f)(3).

Two minor changes in the text reflect the Hague Convention. First, the term "letter of request" has been added. Although these words are synonymous with "letter rogatory," "letter of request" is preferred in modern usage. The provision should not be interpreted to authorize use of a letter of request when there is in fact no treaty obligation on the receiving country to honor such a request from this country or when the United States does not extend diplomatic recognition to the foreign nation. Second, the passage formerly found in subdivision (i)(1)(B), "when service in either case is reasonably calculated to give actual notice," has been relocated.

Paragraph (2) provides alternative methods for use when internationally agreed methods are not intended to be exclusive, or where there is no international agreement applicable. It contains most of the language formerly set forth in subdivision (i) of the rule. Service by methods that would violate foreign law is not generally authorized. Subparagraphs (A) and (B) prescribe the more appropriate methods for conforming to local practice or using a local authority. Subparagraph (C) prescribes other methods authorized by the former rule.

Paragraph (3) authorizes the court to approve other methods of service not prohibited by international agreements. The Hague Convention, for example, authorizes special forms of service in cases of urgency if convention methods will not permit service within the time required by the circumstances. Other circumstances that might justify the use of additional methods include the failure of the foreign country's Central Authority to effect service within the six-month period provided by the Convention, or the refusal of the Central Authority to serve a complaint seeking punitive damages or to enforce the antitrust laws of the United States. In such cases, the court may direct a special method of service not explicitly authorized by international agreement if not prohibited by the agreement. Inasmuch as our Constitution requires that reasonable notice be given, an earnest effort should be made to devise a method of communication that is consistent with due process and minimizes offense to foreign law. A court may in some instances specially authorize use of ordinary mail. Cf. Levin v. Ruby Trading Corp., 248 F.Supp. 537 (S.D.N.Y.1965).

Subdivision (g). This subdivision retains the text of former subdivision (d)(2). Provision is made for service upon an infant or incompetent person in a foreign country.

Subdivision (h). This subdivision retains the text of former subdivision (d)(3), with changes reflecting those made in subdivision (e). It also contains the provisions for service on a corporation or association in a foreign country, as formerly found in subdivision (i).

Frequent use should be made of the Notice and Request procedure set forth in subdivision (d) in actions against corporations. Care must be taken, however, to address the request to an individual officer or authorized agent of the corporation. It is not effective use of the Notice and Request procedure if the mail is sent undirected to the mail room of the organization.

Subdivision (i). This subdivision retains much of the text of former subdivisions (d)(4) and (d)(5). Paragraph (1) provides for service of a summons on the United States; it amends former subdivision (d)(4) to permit the United States attorney to be served by registered or certified mail. The rule does not authorize the use of the Notice and Request procedure of revised subdivision (d) when the United States is the defendant. To assure proper handling of mail in the United States attorney's office, the authorized mail service must be specifically addressed to the civil process clerk of the office of the United States attorney.

Paragraph (2) replaces former subdivision (d)(5). Paragraph (3) saves the plaintiff from the hazard of losing a substantive right because of failure to comply with the complex requirements of multiple service under this subdivision. That risk has proved to be more than nominal. E.g., Whale v. United States, 792 F.2d 951 (9th Cir.1986). This provision should be read in connection with the provisions of subdivision (c) of Rule 15 to preclude the loss of substantive rights against the United States or its agencies, corporations, or officers resulting from a plaintiff's failure to correctly identify and serve all the persons who should be named or served.

Subdivision (j). This subdivision retains the text of former subdivision (d)(6) without material change. The waiver-of-service provision is also inapplicable to actions against governments subject to service pursuant to this subdivision.

The revision adds a new paragraph (1) referring to the statute governing service of a summons on a foreign state and its political subdivisions, agencies, and instrumentalities, the Foreign Sovereign Immunities Act of 1976, 28 U.S.C. § 1608. The caption of the subdivision reflects that change.

Subdivision (k). This subdivision replaces the former subdivision (f), with no change in the title. Paragraph (1) retains the substance of the former rule in explicitly authorizing the exercise of personal jurisdiction over persons who can be reached under state long-arm law, the "100-mile bulge" provision added in 1963, or the federal interpleader act. Paragraph (1)(D) is new, but merely calls attention to federal legislation that may provide for nationwide or even world-wide service of process in cases arising under particular federal laws. Congress has provided for nationwide service of process and full exercise of territorial jurisdiction by all district courts with respect to specified federal actions. See 1 R. Casad, Jurisdiction in Civil Actions (2d Ed.) chap. 5 (1991).

Paragraph (2) is new. It authorizes the exercise of territorial jurisdiction over the person of any defendant against whom is made a claim arising under any federal law if that person is subject to personal jurisdiction in no state. This addition is a companion to the amendments made in revised subdivisions (e) and (f).

This paragraph corrects a gap in the enforcement of federal law. Under the former rule, a problem was presented when the defendant was a non-resident of the United States having contacts with the United States sufficient to justify the application of United States law and to satisfy federal standards of forum selection, but having insufficient contact with any single state to support jurisdiction under state long-arm legislation or meet the requirements of the Fourteenth Amendment limitation on state court territorial jurisdiction. In such cases, the defendant was shielded from the enforcement of federal law by the fortuity of a favorable limitation on the power of state courts, which was incorporated into the federal practice by the former rule. In this respect, the revision responds to the suggestion of the Supreme Court made in Omni Capital Int'l. v. Rudolf Wolff & Co., Ltd., 484 U.S. 97, 111 (1987).

There remain constitutional limitations on the exercise of territorial jurisdiction by federal courts over persons outside the United States. These restrictions arise from the Fifth Amendment rather than from the Fourteenth Amendment, which limits state-court reach and which was incorporated into federal practice by the reference to state law in the text of the former subdivision (e) that is deleted by this revision. The Fifth Amendment requires that any defendant have affiliating contacts with the United States sufficient to justify the exercise of personal jurisdiction over that party. Cf. Wells Fargo & Co. v. Wells Fargo Express Co., 556 F.2d 406, 418 (9th Cir.1977). There also may be a further Fifth Amendment constraint in that a plaintiff's forum selection might be so inconvenient to a defendant that it would be a denial of "fair play and substantial justice" required by the due process clause, even though the defendant had significant affiliating contacts with the United States. See DeJames v. Magnificent Carriers, 654 F.2d 280, 286 n. 3 (3rd Cir.), cert. denied, 454 U.S. 1085 (1981). Compare World-Wide Volkswagen Corp. v. Woodson, 444 U.S. 286, 293–294 (1980); Insurance Corp. of Ireland v. Compagnie des Bauxites de Guinee, 456 U.S. 694, 702–03 (1982); Burger King Corp. v. Rudzewicz, 471 U.S. 462, 476–78 (1985); Asahi Metal Indus. v. Superior Court of Cal., Solano County, 480 U.S. 102, 108–13 (1987). See generally R. Lusardi, Nationwide Service of Process: Due Process Limitations on the Power of the Sovereign, 33 Vill.L.Rev. 1 (1988).

This provision does not affect the operation of federal venue legislation. See generally 28 U.S.C. § 1391. Nor does it affect the operation of federal law providing for the change of venue. 28 U.S.C. §§ 1404, 1406. The availability of transfer for fairness and convenience under § 1404 should preclude most conflicts between the full exercise of territorial jurisdiction permitted by this rule and the Fifth Amendment requirement of "fair play and substantial justice."

The district court should be especially scrupulous to protect aliens who reside in a foreign country from forum selections so onerous that injustice could result. "[G]reat care and reserve should be exercised when extending our notions of personal jurisdiction into the international field." Asahi Metal Indus. v. Superior Court of Cal., Solano County, 480 U.S. 102, 115 (1987), quoting United States v. First Nat'l City Bank, 379 U.S. 378, 404 (1965) (Harlan, J., dissenting).

This narrow extension of the federal reach applies only if a claim is made against the defendant under federal law. It does not establish personal jurisdiction if the only claims are those arising under state law or the law of another country, even though there might be diversity or alienage subject matter jurisdiction as to such claims. If, however, personal jurisdiction is established under this paragraph with respect to a federal claim, then 28 U.S.C. § 1367(a) provides supplemental jurisdiction over related claims against that defendant, subject to the court's discretion to decline exercise of that jurisdiction under 28 U.S.C. § 1367(c).

Subdivision (*l*). This subdivision assembles in one place all the provisions of the present rule bearing on proof of service. No material change in the rule is effected. The provision that proof of service can be amended by leave of court is retained from the former subdivision (h). See generally 4A Wright & Miller, Federal Practice and Procedure § 1132 (2d ed. 1987).

Subdivision (m). This subdivision retains much of the language of the present subdivision (j).

The new subdivision explicitly provides that the court shall allow additional time if there is good cause for the plaintiff's failure to effect service in the prescribed 120 days, and authorizes the court to relieve a plaintiff of the consequences of an application of this subdivision even if there is no good cause shown. Such relief formerly was afforded in some cases, partly in reliance on Rule 6(b). Relief may be justified, for example, if the applicable statute of limitations would bar the refiled action, or if the defendant is evading service or conceals a defect in attempted service. E.g., Ditkof v. Owens-Illinois, Inc., 114 F.R.D. 104 (E.D.Mich.1987). A specific instance of good cause is set forth in paragraph (3) of this rule, which provides for extensions if necessary to correct oversights in compliance with the requirements of multiple service in actions against the United States or its officers, agencies, and corporations. The district court should also take care to protect pro se plaintiffs from consequences of confusion or delay attending the resolution of an in forma pauperis petition. Robinson v. America's Best Contacts & Eyeglasses, 876 F.2d 596 (7th Cir.1989).

The 1983 revision of this subdivision referred to the "party on whose behalf such service was required," rather than to the "plaintiff," a term used generically elsewhere in this rule to refer to any party initiating a claim against a person who is not a party to the action. To simplify the text, the revision returns to the usual practice in the rule of referring simply to the plaintiff even though its principles apply with equal force to defendants who may assert claims against non-parties under Rules 13(h), 14, 19, 20, or 21.

Subdivision (n). This subdivision provides for in rem and quasi-in-rem jurisdiction. Paragraph (1) incorporates any requirements of 28 U.S.C. § 1655 or similar provisions bearing on seizures or liens.

Paragraph (2) provides for other uses of quasi-in-rem jurisdiction but limits its use to exigent circumstances. Provisional remedies may be employed as a means to secure jurisdiction over the property of a defendant whose person is not within reach of the court, but occasions for the use of this provision should be rare, as where the defendant is a fugitive or assets are in imminent danger of disappearing. Until 1963, it was not possible under Rule 4 to assert jurisdiction in a federal court over the property of a defendant not personally served. The 1963 amendment to subdivision (e) authorized the use of state law procedures authorizing seizures of assets as a basis for jurisdiction. Given the liberal availability of long-arm jurisdiction, the exercise of power quasi-in-rem has become almost an anachronism. Circumstances too spare to affiliate the defendant to the forum state sufficiently to support long-arm jurisdiction over the defendant's person are also inadequate to support seizure of the defendant's assets fortuitously found within the state. Shaffer v. Heitner, 433 U.S. 186 (1977).

2000 Amendment

Paragraph (2)(B) is added to Rule 4(i) to require service on the United States when a United States officer or employee is sued in an individual capacity for acts or omissions occurring in connection with duties performed on behalf of the United States. Decided cases provide uncertain guidance on the question whether the United States must be served in such actions. *See Vaccaro v. Dobre*, 81 F.3d 854, 856–857 (9th Cir.1996); *Armstrong v. Sears*, 33 F.3d 182, 185–187 (2d Cir.1994); *Ecclesiastical Order of the Ism of Am v. Chasin*, 845 F.2d 113, 116 (6th Cir.1988); *Light v. Wolf*, 816 F.2d 746 (D.C.Cir.1987); *see also Simpkins v. District of Columbia*, 108 F.3d 366, 368–369 (D.C.Cir.1997). Service on the United States will help to protect the interest of the individual defendant in securing representation by the United States, and will expedite the process of determining whether the United States will provide representation. It has been understood that the individual defendant must be served as an individual defendant, a requirement that is made explicit. Invocation of the individual service provisions of subdivisions (e), (f), and (g) invokes also the waiver-of-service provisions of subdivision (d).

Paragraph 2(B) reaches service when an officer or employee of the United States is sued in an individual capacity "for acts or omissions occurring in connection with the performance of duties on behalf of the United States." This phrase has been chosen as a functional phrase that can be applied without the occasionally distracting associations of such phrases as "scope of employment," "color of office," or "arising out of the employment." Many actions are brought against individual federal officers or employees of the United States for acts or omissions that have no connection whatever to their governmental roles. There is no reason to require service on the United States in these actions. The connection to federal employment that requires service on the United States must be determined as a practical matter, considering whether the individual defendant has reasonable grounds to look to the United States for assistance and whether the United States has reasonable grounds for demanding formal notice of the action.

An action against a former officer or employee of the United States is covered by paragraph (2)(B) in the same way as an action against a present officer or employee. Termination of the relationship between the individual defendant and the United States does not reduce the need to serve the United States.

Paragraph (3) is amended to ensure that failure to serve the United States in an action governed by paragraph 2(B) does not defeat an action. This protection is adopted because there will be cases in which the plaintiff reasonably fails to appreciate the need to serve the United States . There is no requirement, however, that the plaintiff show that the failure to serve the United States was reasonable. A reasonable time to effect service on the United States must be allowed after the failure is pointed out. An additional change ensures that if the United States or United States attorney is served in an action governed by paragraph 2(A), additional time is to be allowed even though no officer, employee, agency, or corporation of the United States was served.

GAP Report

The most important changes were made to ensure that no one would read the seemingly independent provisions of paragraphs 2(A) and 2(B) to mean that service must be made twice both on the United States and on the United States employee when the employee is sued in both official and individual capacities. The word "only" was added in subparagraph (A) and the new phrase "whether or not the officer or employee is sued also in an individual capacity" was inserted in subparagraph (B).

Minor changes were made to include "Employees" in the catch-line for subdivision (i), and to add "or employee" in paragraph 2(A). Although it may seem awkward to think of suit against an employee in an official capacity, there is no clear definition that separates "officers" from "employees" for this purpose. The published proposal to amend Rule 12(a)(3) referred to actions against an employee sued in an official capacity, and it seemed better to make the rules parallel by adding "employee" to Rule 4(i)(2)(A) than by deleting it from Rule 12(a)(3)(A).

2007 Amendment

The language of Rule 4 has been amended as part of the general restyling of the Civil Rules to make them more easily understood and to make style and terminology consistent throughout the rules. These changes are intended to be stylistic only.

Rule 4(d)(1)(C) corrects an inadvertent error in former Rule 4(d)(2)(G). The defendant needs two copies of the waiver form, not an extra copy of the notice and request.

Rule 4(g) changes "infant" to "minor." "Infant" in the present rule means "minor." Modern word usage suggests that "minor" will better maintain the intended meaning. The same change from "infant" to "minor" is made throughout the rules. In addition, subdivision (f)(3) is added to the description of methods of service that the court may order; the addition ensures the evident intent that the court not order service by means prohibited by international agreement.

Rule 4(i)(4) corrects a misleading reference to "the plaintiff" in former Rule 4(i)(3). A party other than a plaintiff may need a reasonable time to effect service. Rule 4(i)(4) properly covers any party.

Former Rule 4(j)(2) refers to service upon an "other governmental organization subject to suit." This is changed to "any other state-created governmental organization that is subject to suit." The change entrenches the meaning indicated by the caption ("Serving a Foreign, State, or Local Government"), and the invocation of state law. It excludes any risk that this rule might be read to govern service on a federal agency, or other entities not created by state law.

The former provision describing service on interpleader claimants [former (k)(1)(C)] is deleted as redundant in light of the general provision in (k)(1)(C) recognizing personal jurisdiction authorized by a federal statute.

2015 Amendment

Subdivision (d). Abrogation of Rule 84 and the other official forms requires that former Forms 5 and 6 be directly incorporated into Rule 4.

Subdivision (m). The presumptive time for serving a defendant is reduced from 120 days to 90 days. This change, together with the shortened times for issuing a scheduling order set by amended Rule 16(b)(2), will reduce delay at the beginning of litigation.

Shortening the presumptive time for service will increase the frequency of occasions to extend the time. More time may be needed, for example, when a request to waive service fails, a defendant is difficult to serve, or a marshal is to make service in an in forma pauperis action.

The final sentence is amended to make it clear that the reference to Rule 4 in Rule 71.1(d)(3)(A) does not include Rule 4(m). Dismissal under Rule 4(m) for failure to make timely service would be inconsistent with the limits on dismissal established by Rule 71.1(i)(1)(C).

Shortening the time to serve under Rule 4(m) means that the time of the notice required by Rule 15(c)(1)(C) for relation back is also shortened.

2016 Amendment

Rule 4(m) is amended to correct a possible ambiguity that appears to have generated some confusion in practice. Service in a foreign country often is accomplished by means that require more than the time set by Rule 4(m). This problem is recognized by the two clear exceptions for service on an individual in a foreign country under Rule 4(f) and for service on a foreign state under Rule 4(j)(1). The potential ambiguity arises from the lack of any explicit reference to service on a corporation, partnership, or other unincorporated association. Rule 4(h)(2) provides for service on such defendants at a place outside any judicial district of the United States "in any manner prescribed by Rule 4(f) for serving an individual, except personal delivery under (f)(2)(C)(i)." Invoking service "in the manner prescribed by Rule 4(f)" could easily be read to mean that service under Rule 4(h)(2) is also service "under" Rule 4(f). That interpretation is in keeping with the purpose to recognize the delays that often occur in effecting service in a foreign country. But it also is possible to read the words for what they seem to say—service is under Rule 4(h)(2), albeit in a manner borrowed from almost all, but not quite all, of Rule 4(f).

The amendment resolves this possible ambiguity.

Gap Report

The time to serve was set at 60 days in the published proposal. It has been changed to 90 days. Text was added to the Committee Note to address occasions to extend the time, and to call attention to the relationship between Rule 4(m) and Rule 15(c)(1)(C).

2017 Amendment

This is a technical amendment that integrates the intended effect of the amendments adopted in 2015 and 2016.

HISTORICAL NOTES

Effective and Applicability Provisions

1983 Acts. Amendment by Pub.L. 97–462 effective 45 days after Jan. 12, 1983, see section 4 of Pub.L. 97–462, set out as a note under section 2071 of this title.

LEGISLATIVE STATEMENT [Omitted]*

TREATIES AND CONVENTIONS

CONVENTION ON THE SERVICE ABROAD OF JUDICIAL AND
EXTRAJUDICIAL DOCUMENTS IN CIVIL OR COMMERCIAL MATTERS

The States signatory to the present Convention,

Desiring to create appropriate means to ensure that judicial and extrajudicial documents to be served abroad shall be brought to the notice of the addressee in sufficient time,

Desiring to improve the organisation of mutual judicial assistance for that purpose by simplifying and expediting the procedure,

Have resolved to conclude a Convention to this effect and have agreed upon the following provisions:

Article 1

The present Convention shall apply in all cases, in civil or commercial matters, where there is occasion to transmit a judicial or extrajudicial document for service abroad.

This Convention shall not apply where the address of the person to be served with the document is not known.

CHAPTER I—JUDICIAL DOCUMENTS

Article 2

Each contracting State shall designate a Central Authority which will undertake to receive requests for service coming from other contracting States and to proceed in conformity with the provisions of articles 3 to 6.

Each State shall organise the Central Authority in conformity with its own law.

Article 3

The authority or judicial officer competent under the law of the State in which the documents originate shall forward to the Central Authority of the State addressed a request conforming to the model annexed to the present Convention, without any requirement of legalisation or other equivalent formality.

The document to be served or a copy thereof shall be annexed to the request. The request and the document shall both be furnished in duplicate.

Article 4

If the Central Authority considers that the request does not comply with the provisions of the present Convention it shall promptly inform the applicant and specify its objections to the request.

---

*   [This legislative statement, which pertained exclusively to the 1983 amendment to Rule 4, is omitted. Ed.]

Article 5

The Central Authority of the State addressed shall itself serve the document or shall arrange to have it served by an appropriate agency, either—

a)   by a method prescribed by its internal law for the service of documents in domestic actions upon persons who are within its territory, or

b)   by a particular method requested by the applicant, unless such a method is incompatible with the law of the State addressed.

Subject to sub-paragraph *(b)* of the first paragraph of this article, the document may always be served by delivery to an addressee who accepts it voluntarily.

If the document is to be served under the first paragraph above, the Central Authority may require the document to be written in, or translated into, the official language or one of the official languages of the State addressed.

That part of the request, in the form attached to the present Convention, which contains a summary of the document to be served, shall be served with the document.

Article 6

The Central Authority of the State addressed or any authority which it may have designated for that purpose, shall complete a certificate in the form of the model annexed to the present Convention.

The certificate shall state that the document has been served and shall include the method, the place and the date of service and the person to whom the document was delivered. If the document has not been served, the certificate shall set out the reasons which have prevented service.

The applicant may require that a certificate not completed by a Central Authority or by a judicial authority shall be countersigned by one of these authorities.

The certificate shall be forwarded directly to the applicant.

Article 7

The standard terms in the model annexed to the present Convention shall in all cases be written either in French or in English. They may also be written in the official language, or in one of the official languages, of the State in which the documents originate.

The corresponding blanks shall be completed either in the language of the State addressed or in French or in English.

Article 8

Each contracting State shall be free to effect service of judicial documents upon persons abroad, without application of any compulsion, directly through its diplomatic or consular agents.

Any State may declare that it is opposed to such service within its territory, unless the document is to be served upon a national of the State in which the documents originate.

Article 9

Each contracting State shall be free, in addition, to use consular channels to forward documents, for the purpose of service, to those authorities of another contracting State which are designated by the latter for this purpose.

Each contracting State may, if exceptional circumstances so require, use diplomatic channels for the same purpose.

Article 10

Provided the State of destination does not object, the present Convention shall not interfere with—

a)   the freedom to send judicial documents, by postal channels, directly to persons abroad, *b)* the freedom of judicial officers, officials or other competent persons of the State of origin to effect service of judicial documents directly through the judicial officers, officials or other competent persons of the State of destination,

c) the freedom of any person interested in a judicial proceeding to effect service of judicial documents directly through the judicial officers, officials or other competent persons of the State of destination.

Article 11

The present Convention shall not prevent two or more contracting States from agreeing to permit, for the purpose of service of judicial documents, channels of transmission other than those provided for in the preceding articles and, in particular, direct communication between their respective authorities.

Article 12

The service of judicial documents coming from a contracting State shall not give rise to any payment or reimbursement of taxes or costs for the services rendered by the State addressed.

The applicant shall pay or reimburse the costs occasioned by—

a) the employment of a judicial officer or of a person competent under the law of the State of destination,

b) the use of a particular method of service.

Article 13

Where a request for service complies with the terms of the present Convention, the State addressed may refuse to comply therewith only if it deems that compliance would infringe its sovereignty or security.

It may not refuse to comply solely on the ground that, under its internal law, it claims exclusive jurisdiction over the subject-matter of the action or that its internal law would not permit the action upon which the application is based.

The Central Authority shall, in case of refusal, promptly inform the applicant and state the reasons for the refusal.

Article 14

Difficulties which may arise in connection with the transmission of judicial documents for service shall be settled through diplomatic channels.

Article 15

Where a writ of summons or an equivalent document had to be transmitted abroad for the purpose of service, under the provisions of the present Convention, and the defendant has not appeared, judgment shall not be given until it is established that—

a) the document was served by a method prescribed by the internal law of the State addressed for the service of documents in domestic actions upon persons who are within its territory, or

b) the document was actually delivered to the defendant or to his residence by another method provided for by this Convention,

and that in either of these cases the service or the delivery was effected in sufficient time to enable the defendant to defend.

Each contracting State shall be free to declare that the judge, notwithstanding the provisions of the first paragraph of this article, may give judgment even if no certificate of service or delivery has been received, if all the following conditions are fulfilled—

a) the document was transmitted by one of the methods provided for in this Convention,

b) a period of time of not less than six months, considered adequate by the judge in the particular case, has elapsed since the date of the transmission of the document,

c) no certificate of any kind has been received, even though every reasonable effort has been made to obtain it through the competent authorities of the State addressed.

Notwithstanding the provisions of the preceding paragraphs the judge may order, in case of urgency, any provisional or protective measures.

Article 16

When a writ of summons or an equivalent document had to be transmitted abroad for the purpose of service, under the provisions of the present Convention, and a judgment has been entered against a defendant who has not appeared, the judge shall have the power to relieve the defendant from the effects of the expiration of the time for appeal from the judgment if the following conditions are fulfilled—

a)   the defendant, without any fault on his part, did not have knowledge of the document in sufficient time to defend, or knowledge of the judgment in sufficient time to appeal, and

b)   the defendant has disclosed a *prima facie* defense to the action on the merits.

An application for relief may be filed only within a reasonable time after the defendant has knowledge of the judgment.

Each contracting State may declare that the application will not be entertained if it is filed after the expiration of a time to be stated in the declaration, but which shall in no case be less than one year following the date of the judgment.

This article shall not apply to judgments concerning status or capacity of persons.

CHAPTER II—EXTRAJUDICIAL DOCUMENTS

Article 17

Extrajudicial documents emanating from authorities and judicial officers of a contracting State may be transmitted for the purpose of service in another contracting State by the methods and under the provisions of the present Convention.

CHAPTER III—GENERAL CLAUSES

Article 18

Each contracting State may designate other authorities in addition to the Central Authority and shall determine the extent of their competence.

The applicant shall, however, in all cases, have the right to address a request directly to the Central Authority.

Federal States shall be free to designate more than one Central Authority.

Article 19

To the extent that the internal law of a contracting State permits methods of transmission, other than those provided for in the preceding articles, of documents coming from abroad, for service within its territory, the present Convention shall not affect such provisions.

Article 20

The present Convention shall not prevent an agreement between any two or more contracting States to dispense with—

a)   the necessity for duplicate copies of transmitted documents as required by the second paragraph of article 3,

b)   the language requirements of the third paragraph of article 5 and article 7,

c)   the provisions of the fourth paragraph of article 5,

d)   the provisions of the second paragraph of article 12.

Article 21

Each contracting State shall, at the time of the deposit of its instrument of ratification or accession, or at a later date, inform the Ministry of Foreign Affairs of the Netherlands of the following—

a)   the designation of authorities, pursuant to articles 2 and 18, *b)*   the designation of the authority competent to complete the certificate pursuant to article 6,

c)   the designation of the authority competent to receive documents transmitted by consular channels, pursuant to article 9.

Each contracting State shall similarly inform the Ministry, where appropriate, of—

a)   opposition to the use of methods of transmission pursuant to articles 8 and 10,

b)   declarations pursuant to the second paragraph of article 15 and the third paragraph of article 16,

c)   all modifications of the above designations, oppositions and declarations.

Article 22

Where Parties to the present Convention are also Parties to one or both of the Conventions on civil procedure signed at The Hague on 17th July 1905 [99 B.F.S.P. 990], and on 1st March 1954 [286 U.N.T.S. 265], this Convention shall replace as between them articles 1 to 7 of the earlier Conventions.

Article 23

The present Convention shall not affect the application of article 23 of the Convention on civil procedure signed at The Hague on 17th July 1905, or of article 24 of the Convention on civil procedure signed at The Hague on 1st March 1954.

These articles shall, however, apply only if methods of communication, identical to those provided for in these Conventions, are used.

Article 24

Supplementary agreements between parties to the Conventions of 1905 and 1954 shall be considered as equally applicable to the present Convention, unless the Parties have otherwise agreed.

Article 25

Without prejudice to the provisions of articles 22 and 24, the present Convention shall not derogate from Conventions containing provisions on the matters governed by this Convention to which the contracting States are, or shall become, Parties.

Article 26

The present Convention shall be open for signature by the States represented at the Tenth Session of the Hague Conference on Private International Law.

It shall be ratified, and the instruments of ratification shall be deposited with the Ministry of Foreign Affairs of the Netherlands.

Article 27

The present Convention shall enter into force on the sixtieth day after the deposit of the third instrument of ratification referred to in the second paragraph of article 26.

The Convention shall enter into force for each signatory State which ratifies subsequently on the sixtieth day after the deposit of its instrument of ratification.

Article 28

Any State not represented at the Tenth Session of the Hague Conference on Private International Law may accede to the present Convention after it has entered into force in accordance with the first paragraph of article 27. The instrument of accession shall be deposited with the Ministry of Foreign Affairs of the Netherlands.

The Convention shall enter into force for such a State in the absence of any objection from a State, which has ratified the Convention before such deposit, notified to the Ministry of Foreign Affairs of the Netherlands within a period of six months after the date on which the said Ministry has notified it of such accession.

In the absence of any such objection, the Convention shall enter into force for the acceding State on the first day of the month following the expiration of the last of the periods referred to in the preceding paragraph.

Article 29

Any State may, at the time of signature, ratification or accession, declare that the present Convention shall extend to all the territories for the international relations of which it is responsible, or to one or more of them. Such a declaration shall take effect on the date of entry into force of the Convention for the State concerned.

At any time thereafter, such extensions shall be notified to the Ministry of Foreign Affairs of the Netherlands.

The Convention shall enter into force for the territories mentioned in such an extension on the sixtieth day after the notification referred to in the preceding paragraph.

Article 30

The present Convention shall remain in force for five years from the date of its entry into force in accordance with the first paragraph of article 27, even for States which have ratified it or acceded to it subsequently.

If there has been no denunciation, it shall be renewed tacitly every five years.

Any denunciation shall be notified to the Ministry of Foreign Affairs of the Netherlands at least six months before the end of the five year period.

It may be limited to certain of the territories to which the Convention applies.

The denunciation shall have effect only as regards the State which has notified it. The Convention shall remain in force for the other contracting States.

Article 31

The Ministry of Foreign Affairs of the Netherlands shall give notice to the States referred to in article 26, and to the States which have acceded in accordance with article 28, of the following—

a) the signatures and ratifications referred to in article 26;

b) the date on which the present Convention enters into force in accordance with the first paragraph of article 27;

c) the accessions referred to in article 28 and the dates on which they take effect;

d) the extensions referred to in article 29 and the dates on which they take effect;

e) the designations, oppositions and declarations referred to in article 21;

f) the denunciations referred to in the third paragraph of article 30.

IN WITNESS WHEREOF the undersigned, being duly authorised thereto, have signed the present Convention.

DONE at The Hague, on the 15th day of November, 1965, in the English and French languages, both texts being equally authentic, in a single copy which shall be deposited in the archives of the Government of the Netherlands, and of which a certified copy shall be sent, through the diplomatic channel, to each of The States represented at the Tenth Session of the Hague Conference on Private International Law.

[Signatures omitted.]

RULES OF CIVIL PROCEDURE

Service of Documents Convention
ANNEX TO THE CONVENTION
Forms
REQUEST
FOR SERVICE ABROAD OF JUDICIAL OR EXTRAJUDICIAL DOCUMENTS*
Convention on the service abroad of judicial and extrajudicial documents in civil or commercial matters, signed at The Hague, November 15, 1965.

Identity and address of the applicant   Address of receiving authority

The undersigned applicant has the honour to transmit—in duplicate—the documents listed below and, in conformity with article 5 of the above-mentioned Convention, requests prompt service of one copy thereof on the addressee, i.e.,

(identity and address) ....

....

(a)   in accordance with the provisions of sub-paragraph (a) of the first paragraph of article 5 of the Convention.

(b)   in accordance with the following particular method (sub-paragraph (b) of the first paragraph of article 5):

....

....

....

(c)   by delivery to the addressee, if he accepts it voluntarily (second paragraph of article 5).

The authority is requested to return or to have returned to the applicant a copy of the documents—and of the annexes—with a certificate as provided on the reverse side.

List of documents

....

....

....

Done at .... , the ....

Signature and/or stamp...

Reverse of the request
CERTIFICATE

The undersigned authority has the honour to certify, in conformity with article 6 of the Convention,

1)   that the document has been served

—   the (date)

—   at (place, street, number)

—   in one of the following methods authorized by article 5—

---

*   [This form may be obtained from the U.S. Marshals Service, at www.usmarshals.gov/forms/usm94.pdf. Ed.]

(*a*)   in accordance with the provisions of sub-paragraph (*a*) of the first paragraph of article 5 of the Convention.*

(*b*)   in accordance with the following particular method ....

....

(*c*)   by delivery to the addressee, who accepted it voluntarily.*

The documents referred to in the request have been delivered to:

—   (identity and description of person)...

....

....

—   relationship to the addressee (family, business or other)...

2)   that the document has not been served, by reason of the following facts:

....

....

In conformity with the second paragraph of article 12 of the Convention, the applicant is requested to pay or reimburse the expenses detailed in the attached statement.

Annexes

Documents returned: ....

....

....

In appropriate cases, documents establishing the service:

....

....

....

Done at .... , the ....

Signature and/or stamp...

SUMMARY OF THE DOCUMENT TO BE SERVED

———————

Convention on the service abroad of judicial and extrajudicial documents in civil or commercial matters, signed at The Hague, the 15th of November 1965.

(article 5, fourth paragraph)

Name and address of the requesting authority: ....

....

....

Particulars of the parties:...

....

....

---

*   Delete if inappropriate

JUDICIAL DOCUMENT

Nature and purpose of the document:..

....

....

Nature and purpose of the proceedings and, where appropriate, the amount in dispute:...............................

....

Date and place for entering appearance: ....

Court which has given judgment: ....

Date of judgment: ....

Time limits stated in the document:...

....

EXTRAJUDICIAL DOCUMENT

Nature and purpose of the document:..

....

....

Time limits stated in the document:...

....

————————

Convention on the service abroad of judicial and extrajudicial documents in civil or commercial matters. Done at The Hague November 15, 1965; entered into force for the United States February 10, 1969. 20 U.S.T. 361; T.I.A.S. 6638; 658 U.N.T.S. 163.

————————

Notes and Annotations to the Convention

Litigants wishing to serve a person in one of the Convention countries should request copies in duplicate of the three forms prescribed by the Convention: the "Request", the "Certificate" and the "Summary." These forms may be obtained from the offices of the United States Marshals. Upon completion of these forms, the litigants must then transmit them, together with the documents to be served—all in duplicate—to the local process server.

The local process server thereupon mails all these documents to the "Central Authority" abroad. After service has been effected, one copy of the documents served and an executed "Certificate" all be returned to the local process server, who will transmit these documents to the litigant who initiated the request.

—— **Annotations**

"The Effect of the Hague Convention on Service Abroad of Judicial and Extrajudicial Documents in Civil or Commercial Matters", 2 Cornell Int'l L.J. 125 (1969).

Julen v. Larson, 25 Cal.App.3d 325, 101 Cal. 796 (1972).

Shoei Kako Co., Ltd. v. Superior Court, 33 Cal.App.3d 808, 109 Cal. 402 (1973).

Rule 4.1. Serving Other Process

(a) In General. Process—other than a summons under Rule 4 or a subpoena under Rule 45—must be served by a United States marshal or deputy marshal or by a person specially appointed for that purpose. It may be served anywhere within the territorial limits of the state where the district court is located and, if authorized by a federal statute, beyond those limits. Proof of service must be made under Rule 4(*l*).

(b) Enforcing Orders: Committing for Civil Contempt. An order committing a person for civil contempt of a decree or injunction issued to enforce federal law may be served and enforced in any district. Any other order in a civil-contempt proceeding may be served only in the state where the issuing court is located or elsewhere in the United States within 100 miles from where the order was issued.

(Adopted April 22, 1993, effective December 1, 1993; amended April 30, 2007, effective December 1, 2007.)

ADVISORY COMMITTEE NOTES

1993 Adoption

This is a new rule. Its purpose is to separate those few provisions of the former Rule 4 bearing on matters other than service of a summons to allow greater textual clarity in Rule 4. Subdivision (a) contains no new language.

Subdivision (b) replaces the final clause of the penultimate sentence of the former subdivision 4(f), a clause added to the rule in 1963. The new rule provides for nationwide service of orders of civil commitment enforcing decrees of injunctions issued to compel compliance with federal law. The rule makes no change in the practice with respect to the enforcement of injunctions or decrees not involving the enforcement of federally-created rights.

Service of process is not required to notify a party of a decree or injunction, or of an order that the party show cause why that party should not be held in contempt of such an order. With respect to a party who has once been served with a summons, the service of the decree or injunction itself or of an order to show cause can be made pursuant to Rule 5. Thus, for example, an injunction may be served on a party through that person's attorney. *Chagas v. United States,* 369 F.2d 643 (5th Cir. 1966). The same is true for service of an order to show cause. *Waffenschmidt v. Mackay,* 763 F.2d 711 (5th Cir. 1985).

The new rule does not affect the reach of the court to impose criminal contempt sanctions. Nationwide enforcement of federal decrees and injunctions is already available with respect to criminal contempt: a federal court may effect the arrest of a criminal contemnor anywhere in the United States, 28 U.S.C. § 3041, and a contemnor when arrested may be subject to removal to the district in which punishment may be imposed. Fed.R.Crim.P. 40. Thus, the present law permits criminal contempt enforcement against a contemnor wherever that person may be found.

The effect of the revision is to provide a choice of civil or criminal contempt sanctions in those situations to which it applies. Contempt proceedings, whether civil or criminal, must be brought in the court that was allegedly defied by a contumacious act. *Ex parte Bradley,* 74 U.S. 366 (1869). This is so even if the offensive conduct or inaction occurred outside the district of the court in which the enforcement proceeding must be conducted. *E.g., McCourtney v. United States,* 291 Fed. 497 (8th Cir.), *cert. denied,* 263 U.S. 714 (1923). For this purpose, the rule as before does not distinguish between parties and other persons subject to contempt sanctions by reason of their relation or connection to parties.

2007 Amendment

The language of Rule 4.1 has been amended as part of the general restyling of the Civil Rules to make them more easily understood and to make style and terminology consistent throughout the rules. These changes are intended to be stylistic only.

Rule 5.   Serving and Filing Pleadings and Other Papers

(a) Service: When Required.

    (1) *In General.* Unless these rules provide otherwise, each of the following papers must be served on every party:

        (A) an order stating that service is required;

     (B) a pleading filed after the original complaint, unless the court orders otherwise under Rule 5(c) because there are numerous defendants;

     (C) a discovery paper required to be served on a party, unless the court orders otherwise;

     (D) a written motion, except one that may be heard ex parte; and

     (E) a written notice, appearance, demand, or offer of judgment, or any similar paper.

  (2) *If a Party Fails to Appear.* No service is required on a party who is in default for failing to appear. But a pleading that asserts a new claim for relief against such a party must be served on that party under Rule 4.

  (3) *Seizing Property.* If an action is begun by seizing property and no person is or need be named as a defendant, any service required before the filing of an appearance, answer, or claim must be made on the person who had custody or possession of the property when it was seized.

(b) Service: How Made.

  (1) *Serving an Attorney.* If a party is represented by an attorney, service under this rule must be made on the attorney unless the court orders service on the party.

  (2) *Service in General.* A paper is served under this rule by:

     (A) handing it to the person;

     (B) leaving it:

        (i) at the person's office with a clerk or other person in charge or, if no one is in charge, in a conspicuous place in the office; or

        (ii) if the person has no office or the office is closed, at the person's dwelling or usual place of abode with someone of suitable age and discretion who resides there;

     (C) mailing it to the person's last known address—in which event service is complete upon mailing;

     (D) leaving it with the court clerk if the person has no known address;

     (E) sending it to a registered user by filing it with the court's electronic-filing system or sending it by other electronic means that the person consented to in writing—in either of which events service is complete upon filing or sending, but is not effective if the filer or sender learns that it did not reach the person to be served; or

     (F) delivering it by any other means that the person consented to in writing—in which event service is complete when the person making service delivers it to the agency designated to make delivery.

  (3) *Using Court Facilities.* [Abrogated (Apr. 26, 2018, eff. Dec. 1, 2018.)]

(c) Serving Numerous Defendants.

  (1) *In General.* If an action involves an unusually large number of defendants, the court may, on motion or on its own, order that:

     (A) defendants' pleadings and replies to them need not be served on other defendants;

     (B) any crossclaim, counterclaim, avoidance, or affirmative defense in those pleadings and replies to them will be treated as denied or avoided by all other parties; and

     (C) filing any such pleading and serving it on the plaintiff constitutes notice of the pleading to all parties.

  (2) *Notifying Parties.* A copy of every such order must be served on the parties as the court directs.

(d) Filing.

  (1) *Required Filings; Certificate of Service.*

    (A) *Papers after the Complaint.* Any paper after the complaint that is required to be served must be filed no later than a reasonable time after service. But disclosures under Rule 26(a)(1) or (2) and the following discovery requests and responses must not be filed until they are used in the proceeding or the court orders filing: depositions, interrogatories, requests for documents or tangible things or to permit entry onto land, and requests for admission.

    (B) *Certificate of Service.* No certificate of service is required when a paper is served by filing it with the court's electronic-filing system. When a paper that is required to be served is served by other means:

      (i) if the paper is filed, a certificate of service must be filed with it or within a reasonable time after service; and

      (ii) if the paper is not filed, a certificate of service need not be filed unless filing is required by a court order or by local rule.

  (2) *Nonelectronic Filing.* A paper not filed electronically is filed by delivering it:

    (A) to the clerk; or

    (B) to a judge who agrees to accept it for filing, and who must then note the filing date on the paper and promptly send it to the clerk.

  (3) *Electronic Filing and Signing.*

    (A) *By a Represented Person—Generally Required; Exceptions.* A person represented by an attorney must file electronically, unless nonelectronic filing is allowed by the court for good cause or is allowed or required by local rule.

    (B) *By an Unrepresented Person—When Allowed or* Required. A person not represented by an attorney:

      (i) may file electronically only if allowed by court order or by local rule; and

      (ii) may be required to file electronically only by court order, or by local rule that includes reasonable exceptions.

    (C) *Signing.* A filing made through a person's electronic-filing account and authorized by that person, together with that person's name on a signature block, constitutes the person's signature.

    (D) *Same as a Written Paper.* A paper filed electronically is a written paper for purposes of these rules.

  (4) *Acceptance by the Clerk.* The clerk must not refuse to file a paper solely because it is not in the form prescribed by these rules or by a local rule or practice.

(Amended January 21, 1963, effective July 1, 1963; March 30, 1970, effective July 1, 1970; April 29, 1980, effective August 1, 1980; March 2, 1987, effective August 1, 1987; April 30, 1991, effective December 1, 1991; April 22, 1993, effective December 1, 1993; April 23, 1996, effective December 1, 1996; April 17, 2000, effective December 1, 2000; April 23, 2001, effective December 1, 2001; April 12, 2006, effective December 1, 2006; April 30, 2007, effective December 1, 2007; April 26, 2018, effective December 1, 2018.)

ADVISORY COMMITTEE NOTES

1937 Adoption

    Note to Subdivisions (a) and (b). Compare 2 Minn.Stat. (1927) §§ 9240, 9241, 9242; N.Y.C.P.A. (1937) §§ 163, 164 and N.Y.R.C.P. (1937) Rules 20, 21; 2 Wash.Rev.Stat.Ann. (Remington, 1932) §§ 244 to 249.

Note to Subdivision (d). Compare the present practice under former Equity Rule 12 (Issue of Subpoena—Time for Answer).

1963 Amendment

The words "affected thereby," stricken out by the amendment, introduced a problem of interpretation. See 1 Barron & Holtzoff, *Federal Practice & Procedure* 760–61 (Wright ed. 1960). The amendment eliminates this difficulty and promotes full exchange of information among the parties by requiring service of papers on all the parties to the action, except as otherwise provided in the rules. See also subdivision (c) of Rule 5. So, for example, a third-party defendant is required to serve his answer to the third-party complaint not only upon the defendant but also upon the plaintiff. See amended Form 22-A and the Advisory Committee's Note thereto.

As to the method of serving papers upon a party whose address is unknown, see Rule 5(b).

1970 Amendment

The amendment makes clear that all papers relating to discovery which are required to be served on any party must be served on all parties, unless the court orders otherwise. The present language expressly includes notices and demands, but it is not explicit as to answers or responses as provided in Rules 33, 34, and 36. Discovery papers may be voluminous or the parties numerous, and the court is empowered to vary the requirement if in a given case it proves needlessly onerous.

In actions begun by seizure of property, service will at times have to be made before the absent owner of the property has filed an appearance. For example, a prompt deposition may be needed in a maritime action in rem. See Rules 30(a) and 30(b)(2) and the related notes. A provision is added authorizing service on the person having custody or possession of the property at the time of its seizure.

1980 Amendment

Subdivision (d). By the terms of this rule and Rule 30(f)(1) discovery materials must be promptly filed, although it often happens that no use is made of the materials after they are filed. Because the copies required for filing are an added expense and the large volume of discovery filings presents serious problems of storage in some districts, the Committee in 1978 first proposed that discovery materials not be filed unless on order of the court or for use in the proceedings. But such materials are sometimes of interest to those who may have no access to them except by a requirement of filing, such as members of a class, litigants similarly situated, or the public generally. Accordingly, this amendment and a change in Rule 30(f)(1) continue the requirement of filing but make it subject to an order of the court that discovery materials not be filed unless filing is requested by the court or is effected by parties who wish to use the materials in the proceeding.

1987 Amendment

The amendments are technical. No substantive change is intended.

1991 Amendment

Subdivision (d). This subdivision is amended to require that the person making service under the rule certify that service has been effected. Such a requirement has generally been imposed by local rule.

Having such information on file may be useful for many purposes, including proof of service if an issue arises concerning the effectiveness of the service. The certificate will generally specify the date as well as the manner of service, but parties employing private delivery services may sometimes be unable to specify the date of delivery. In the latter circumstance, a specification of the date of transmission of the paper to the delivery service may be sufficient for the purposes of this rule.

Subdivision (e). The words *"pleading and other "* are stricken as unnecessary. Pleadings are papers within the meaning of the rule. The revision also accommodates the development of the use of facsimile transmission for filing.

Several local district rules have directed the office of the clerk to refuse to accept for filing papers not conforming to certain requirements of form imposed by local rules or practice. This is not a suitable role for the office of the clerk, and the practice exposes litigants to the hazards of time bars; for these reasons, such rules are proscribed by this revision. The enforcement of these rules and of the local rules is a role for a judicial officer. A clerk may of course advise a party or counsel that a particular instrument is not in proper form, and may be directed to so inform the court.

1993 Amendments

This is a technical amendment, using the broader language of Rule 25 of the Federal Rules of Appellate Procedure. The district court—and the bankruptcy court by virtue of a cross-reference in Bankruptcy Rule 7005—can, by local rule, permit filing not only by facsimile transmissions but also by other electronic means, subject to standards approved by the Judicial Conference.

1996 Amendments

The present Rule 5(e) has authorized filing by facsimile or other electronic means on two conditions. The filing must be authorized by local rule. Use of this means of filing must be authorized by the Judicial Conference of the United States and must be consistent with standards established by the Judicial Conference. Attempts to develop Judicial Conference standards have demonstrated the value of several adjustments in the rule.

The most significant change discards the requirement that the Judicial Conference authorize local electronic filing rules. As before, each district may decide for itself whether it has the equipment and personnel required to establish electronic filing, but a district that wishes to establish electronic filing need no longer await Judicial Conference action.

The role of Judicial Conference standards is clarified by specifying that the standards are to govern technical matters. Technical standards can provide nationwide uniformity, enabling ready use of electronic filing without pausing to adjust for the otherwise inevitable variations among local rules. Judicial Conference adoption of technical standards should prove superior to specification in these rules. Electronic technology has advanced with great speed. The process of adopting Judicial Conference standards should prove speedier and more flexible in determining the time for the first uniform standards, in adjusting standards at appropriate intervals, and in sparing the Supreme Court and Congress the need to consider technological details. Until Judicial Conference standards are adopted, however, uniformity will occur only to the extent that local rules deliberately seek to copy other local rules.

It is anticipated that Judicial Conference standards will govern such technical specifications as data formatting, speed of transmission, means to transmit copies of supporting documents, and security of communication. Perhaps more important, standards must be established to assure proper maintenance and integrity of the record and to provide appropriate access and retrieval mechanisms. Local rules must address these issues until Judicial Conference standards are adopted.

The amended rule also makes clear the equality of filing by electronic means with written filings. An electronic filing that complies with the local rule satisfies all requirements for filing on paper, signature, or verification. An electronic filing that otherwise satisfies the requirements of 28 U.S.C. § 1746 need not be separately made in writing. Public access to electronic filings is governed by the same rules as govern written filings.

The separate reference to filing by facsimile transmission is deleted. Facsimile transmission continues to be included as an electronic means.

2000 Amendment

Subdivision (d). Rule 5(d) is amended to provide that disclosures under Rule 26(a)(1) and (2), and discovery requests and responses under Rules 30, 31, 33, 34, and 36 must not be filed until they are used in the action. "Discovery requests" includes deposition notices and "discovery responses" includes objections. The rule supersedes and invalidates local rules that forbid, permit, or require filing of these materials before they are used in the action. The former Rule 26(a)(4) requirement that disclosures under Rule 26(a)(1) and (2) be filed has been removed. Disclosures under Rule 26(a)(3), however, must be promptly filed as provided in Rule 26(a)(3). Filings in connection with Rule 35 examinations, which involve a motion proceeding when the parties do not agree, are unaffected by these amendments.

Recognizing the costs imposed on parties and courts by required filing of discovery materials that are never used in an action, Rule 5(d) was amended in 1980 to authorize court orders that excuse filing. Since then, many districts have adopted local rules that excuse or forbid filing. In 1989 the Judicial Conference

Local Rules Project concluded that these local rules were inconsistent with Rule 5(d), but urged the Advisory Committee to consider amending the rule. *Local Rules Project* at 92 (1989). The Judicial Conference of the Ninth Circuit gave the Committee similar advice in 1997. The reality of nonfiling reflected in these local rules has even been assumed in drafting the national rules. In 1993, Rule 30(f)(1) was amended to direct that the officer presiding at a deposition file it with the court or send it to the attorney who arranged for the transcript or recording. The Committee Note explained that this alternative to filing was designed for "courts which direct that depositions not be automatically filed." Rule 30(f)(1) has been amended to conform to this change in Rule 5(d).

Although this amendment is based on widespread experience with local rules, and confirms the results directed by these local rules, it is designed to supersede and invalidate local rules. There is no apparent reason to have different filing rules in different districts. Even if districts vary in present capacities to store filed materials that are not used in an action, there is little reason to continue expending court resources for this purpose. These costs and burdens would likely change as parties make increased use of audio- and videotaped depositions. Equipment to facilitate review and reproduction of such discovery materials may prove costly to acquire, maintain, and operate.

The amended rule provides that discovery materials and disclosures under Rule 26(a)(1) and (a)(2) must not be filed until they are "used in the proceeding." This phrase is meant to refer to proceedings in court. This filing requirement is not triggered by "use" of discovery materials in other discovery activities, such as depositions. In connection with proceedings in court, however, the rule is to be interpreted broadly; any use of discovery materials in court in connection with a motion, a pretrial conference under Rule 16, or otherwise, should be interpreted as use in the proceeding.

Once discovery or disclosure materials are used in the proceeding, the filing requirements of Rule 5(d) should apply to them. But because the filing requirement applies only with regard to materials that are used, only those parts of voluminous materials that are actually used need be filed. Any party would be free to file other pertinent portions of materials that are so used. *See* Fed. R. Evid. 106; *cf.* Rule 32(a)(4). If the parties are unduly sparing in their submissions, the court may order further filings. By local rule, a court could provide appropriate direction regarding the filing of discovery materials, such as depositions, that are used in proceedings.

"Shall" is replaced by "must" under the program to conform amended rules to current style conventions when there is no ambiguity.

GAP Report

The Advisory Committee recommends no changes to either the amendments to Rule 5(d) or the Committee Note as published.

2001 Amendments

Rule 5(b) is restyled.

Rule 5(b)(1) makes it clear that the provision for service on a party's attorney applies only to service made under Rules 5(a) and 77(d). Service under Rules 4, 4.1, 45(b), and 71A(d)(3)—as well as rules that invoke those rules—must be made as provided in those rules.

Subparagraphs (A), (B), and (C) of Rule 5(b)(2) carry forward the method-of-service provisions of former Rule 5(b).

Subparagraph (D) of Rule 5(b)(2) is new. It authorizes service by electronic means or any other means, but only if consent is obtained from the person served. The consent must be express, and cannot be implied from conduct. Early experience with electronic filing as authorized by Rule 5(d) is positive, supporting service by electronic means as well. Consent is required, however, because it is not yet possible to assume universal entry into the world of electronic communication. Subparagraph (D) also authorizes service by nonelectronic means. The Rule 5(b)(2)(B) provision making mail service complete on mailing is extended in subparagraph (D) to make service by electronic means complete on transmission; transmission is effected when the sender does the last act that must be performed by the sender. Service by other agencies is complete on delivery to the designated agency.

Finally, subparagraph (D) authorizes adoption of local rules providing for service through the court. Electronic case filing systems will come to include the capacity to make service by using the court's facilities to transmit all documents filed in the case. It may prove most efficient to establish an environment in which a party can file with the court, making use of the court's transmission facilities to serve the filed paper on all other parties. Transmission might be by such means as direct transmission of the paper, or by transmission of a notice of filing that includes an electronic link for direct access to the paper. Because service is under subparagraph (D), consent must be obtained from the persons served.

Consent to service under Rule 5(b)(2)(D) must be in writing, which can be provided by electronic means. Parties are encouraged to specify the scope and duration of the consent. The specification should include at least the persons to whom service should be made, the appropriate address or location for such service— such as the e-mail address or facsimile machine number, and the format to be used for attachments. A district court may establish a registry or other facility that allows advance consent to service by specified means for future actions.

Rule 6(e) is amended to allow additional time to respond when service is made under Rule 5(b)(2)(D). The additional time does not relieve a party who consents to service under Rule 5(b)(2)(D) of the responsibilities to monitor the facility designated for receiving service and to provide prompt notice of any address change.

Paragraph (3) addresses a question that may arise from a literal reading of the provision that service by electronic means is complete on transmission. Electronic communication is rapidly improving, but lawyers report continuing failures of transmission, particularly with respect to attachments. Ordinarily the risk of non-receipt falls on the person being served, who has consented to this form of service. But the risk should not extend to situations in which the person attempting service learns that the attempted service in fact did not reach the person to be served. Given actual knowledge that the attempt failed, service is not effected. The person attempting service must either try again or show circumstances that justify dispensing with service.

Paragraph (3) does not address the similar questions that may arise when a person attempting service learns that service by means other than electronic means in fact did not reach the person to be served. Case law provides few illustrations of circumstances in which a person attempting service actually knows that the attempt failed but seeks to act as if service had been made. This negative history suggests there is no need to address these problems in Rule 5(b)(3). This silence does not imply any view on these issues, nor on the circumstances that justify various forms of judicial action even though service has not been made.

Changes Made After Publication and Comments

Rule 5(b)(2)(D) was changed to require that consent be "in writing."

Rule 5(b)(3) is new. The published proposal did not address the question of failed service in the text of the rule. Instead, the Committee Note included this statement: "As with other modes of service, however, actual notice that the transmission was not received defeats the presumption of receipt that arises from the provision that service is complete on transmission. The sender must take additional steps to effect service. Service by other agencies is complete on delivery to the designated agency." The addition of paragraph (3) was prompted by consideration of the draft Appellate Rule 25(c) that was prepared for the meeting of the Appellate Rules Advisory Committee. This draft provided: "Service by electronic means is complete on transmission, unless the party making service is notified that the paper was not received." Although Appellate Rule 25(c) is being prepared for publication and comment, while Civil Rule 5(b) has been published and otherwise is ready to recommend for adoption, it seemed desirable to achieve some parallel between the two rules.

The draft Rule 5(b)(3) submitted for consideration by the Advisory Committee covered all means of service except for leaving a copy with the clerk of the court when the person to be served has no known address. It was not limited to electronic service for fear that a provision limited to electronic service might generate unintended negative implications as to service by other means, particularly mail. This concern was strengthened by a small number of opinions that say that service by mail is effective, because complete on mailing, even when the person making service has prompt actual notice that the mail was not delivered. The Advisory Committee voted to limit Rule 5(b)(3) to service by electronic means because this means of service is relatively new, and seems likely to miscarry more frequently than service by post. It was suggested during the Advisory Committee meeting that the question of negative implication could be addressed in the Committee Note. There was little discussion of this possibility. The Committee Note submitted above includes a "no negative implications" paragraph prepared by the Reporter for consideration by the Standing Committee.

The Advisory Committee did not consider at all a question that was framed during the later meeting of the Appellate Rules Advisory Committee. As approved by the Advisory Committee, Rule 5(b)(3) defeats service by electronic means "if the party making service learns that the attempted service did not reach the person to be served." It says nothing about the time relevant to learning of the failure. The omission may seem glaring. Curing the omission, however, requires selection of a time. As revised, proposed Appellate Rule 25(c) requires that the party making service learn of the failure within three calendar days. The Appellate Rules Advisory Committee will have the luxury of public comment and another year to consider the desirability of this short period. If Civil Rule 5(b) is to be recommended for adoption now, no such luxury is available. This issue deserves careful consideration by the Standing Committee.

Several changes are made in the Committee Note. (1) It requires that consent "be express, and cannot be implied from conduct." This addition reflects a more general concern stimulated by a reported ruling that an e-mail address on a firm's letterhead implied consent to e-mail service. (2) The paragraph discussing service through the court's facilities is expanded by describing alternative methods, including an "electronic link." (3) There is a new paragraph that states that the requirement of written consent can be satisfied by electronic means, and that suggests matters that should be addressed by the consent. (4) A paragraph is added to note the additional response time provided by amended Rule 6(e). (5) The final two paragraphs address newly added Rule 5(b)(3). The first explains the rule that electronic service is not effective if the person making service learns that it did not reach the person to be served. The second paragraph seeks to defeat any negative implications that might arise from limiting Rule 5(b)(3) to electronic service, not mail, not other means consented to such as commercial express service, and not service on another person on behalf of the person to be served.

Rule 6(e)

The Advisory Committee recommended that no change be made in Civil Rule 6(e) to reflect the provisions of Civil Rule 5(b)(2)(D) that, with the consent of the person to be served, would allow service by electronic or other means. Absent change, service by these means would not affect the time for acting in response to the paper served. Comment was requested, however, on the alternative that would allow an additional 3 days to respond. The alternative Rule 6(e) amendments are cast in a form that permits ready incorporation in the Bankruptcy Rules. Several of the comments suggest that the added three days should be provided. Electronic transmission is not always instantaneous, and may fail for any of a number of reasons. It may take three days to arrange for transmission in readable form. Providing added time to respond will not discourage people from asking for consent to electronic transmission, and may encourage people to give consent. The more who consent, the quicker will come the improvements that will make electronic service ever more attractive. Consistency with the Bankruptcy Rules will be a good thing, and the Bankruptcy Rules Advisory Committee believes the additional three days should be allowed.

2006 Amendment

Amended Rule 5(e) acknowledges that many courts have required electronic filing by means of a standing order, procedures manual, or local rule. These local practices reflect the advantages that courts and most litigants realize from electronic filing. Courts that mandate electronic filing recognize the need to make exceptions when requiring electronic filing imposes a hardship on a party. Under amended Rule 5(e), a local rule that requires electronic filing must include reasonable exceptions, but Rule 5(e) does not define the scope of those exceptions. Experience with the local rules that have been adopted and that will emerge will aid in drafting new local rules and will facilitate gradual convergence on uniform exceptions, whether in local rules or in an amended Rule 5(e).

2007 Amendment

The language of Rule 5 has been amended as part of the general restyling of the Civil Rules to make them more easily understood and to make style and terminology consistent throughout the rules. These changes are intended to be stylistic only.

Rule 5(a)(1)(E) omits the former reference to a designation of record on appeal. Appellate Rule 10 is a self-contained provision for the record on appeal, and provides for service.

Former Rule 5(b)(2)(D) literally provided that a local rule may authorize use of the court's transmission facilities to make service by non-electronic means agreed to by the parties. That was not intended. Rule 5(b)(3) restores the intended meaning—court transmission facilities can be used only for service by electronic means.

Rule 5(d)(2)(B) provides that "a" judge may accept a paper for filing, replacing the reference in former Rule 5(e) to "the" judge. Some courts do not assign a designated judge to each case, and it may be important to have another judge accept a paper for filing even when a case is on the individual docket of a particular judge. The ministerial acts of accepting the paper, noting the time, and transmitting the paper to the court clerk do not interfere with the assigned judge's authority over the action.

2018 Amendment

Subdivision (b). Rule 5(b) is amended to revise the provisions for electronic service. Provision for electronic service was first made when electronic communication was not as widespread or as fully reliable as it is now. Consent of the person served to receive service by electronic means was required as a safeguard. Those concerns have substantially diminished, but have not disappeared entirely, particularly as to persons proceeding without an attorney.

The amended rule recognizes electronic service through the court's transmission facilities as to any registered user. A court may choose to allow registration only with the court's permission. But a party who registers will be subject to service through the court's facilities unless the court provides otherwise. With the consent of the person served, electronic service also may be made by means that do not utilize the court's facilities. Consent can be limited to service at a prescribed address or in a specified form, and may be limited by other conditions.

Service is complete when a person files the paper with the court's electronic-filing system for transmission to a registered user, or when one person sends it to another person by other electronic means that the other person has consented to in writing. But service is not effective if the person who filed with the court or the person who sent by other agreed-upon electronic means learns that the paper did not reach the person to be served. The rule does not make the court responsible for notifying a person who filed the paper with the court's electronic-filing system that an attempted transmission by the court's system failed. But a filer who learns that the transmission failed is responsible for making effective service.

Because Rule 5(b)(2)(E) now authorizes service through the court's facilities as a uniform national practice, Rule 5(b)(3) is abrogated. It is no longer necessary to rely on local rules to authorize such service.

Subdivision (d). Rule 5(d)(1) has provided that any paper after the complaint that is required to be served "must be filed within a reasonable time after service." Because "within" might be read as barring filing before the paper is served, "no later than" is substituted to ensure that it is proper to file a paper before it is served.

Under amended Rule 5(d)(1)(B), a certificate of service is not required when a paper is served by filing it with the court's electronic-filing system. When service is not made by filing with the court's electronic-filing system, a certificate of service must be filed with the paper or within a reasonable time after service, and should specify the date as well as the manner of service. For papers that are required to be served but must not be filed until they are used in the proceeding or the court orders filing, the certificate need not be filed until the paper is filed, unless filing is required by local rule or court order.

Amended Rule 5(d)(3) recognizes increased reliance on electronic filing. Most districts have adopted local rules that require electronic filing, and allow reasonable exceptions as required by the former rule. The time has come to seize the advantages of electronic filing by making it generally mandatory in all districts for a person represented by an attorney. But exceptions continue to be available. Nonelectronic filing must be allowed for good cause. And a local rule may allow or require nonelectronic filing for other reasons.

Filings by a person proceeding without an attorney are treated separately. It is not yet possible to rely on an assumption that pro se litigants are generally able to seize the advantages of electronic filing. Encounters with the court's system may prove overwhelming to some. Attempts to work within the system may generate substantial burdens on a pro se party, on other parties, and on the court. Rather than mandate electronic filing, filing by pro se litigants is left for governing by local rules or court order. Efficiently handled electronic filing works to the advantage of all parties and the court. Many courts now allow electronic filing by pro se litigants with the court's permission. Such approaches may expand with growing experience in the courts, along with the greater availability of the systems required for electronic filing and the increasing familiarity of most people with electronic communication. Room is also left for a court to require electronic filing by a pro se litigant by court order or by local rule. Care should be taken to ensure that an order to file electronically does not impede access to the court, and reasonable exceptions must be included in a local rule that requires electronic filing by a pro se litigant. In the beginning, this authority is likely to be exercised only to support special programs, such as one requiring e-filing in collateral proceedings by state prisoners.

A filing made through a person's electronic-filing account and authorized by that person, together with that person's name on a signature block, constitutes the person's signature.

Gap Report

Published Rule 5(d)(1)(B) carried forward the requirement in present Rule 5(d)(1) that any paper after the complaint that is required to be served "must be filed within a reasonable time after service." That language does not clearly allow a paper to be filed before it is served. It is changed to direct filing "no later than" a reasonable time after service.

The certificate of service provisions in proposed Rule 5(d)(1)(B) are changed. First, the provision that a notice of electronic filing constitutes a certificate of service on any person served by the court's electronic-filing service is replaced by a provision that no certificate of service is required when a paper is served by filing it with the court's electronic-filing system. Next, the provision that when a paper is served by other means a certificate of service must be filed within a reasonable time after service is replaced by a two-part direction: If the paper is filed, a certificate of service must be filed with it or within a reasonable time after service, and if the paper is not filed, a certificate of service need not be filed unless filing is required by local rule or court order. The provision recognizing that a paper that has been served may not be filed reflects the direction in proposed Rule 5(d)(1)(A), carried over from present Rule 5(d)(1), that many disclosures and discovery papers must not be filed until the court orders filing or they are used in the action.

The Committee Note has been changed to reflect these changes.

Rule 5.1. Constitutional Challenge to a Statute—Notice, Certification, and Intervention

(a) Notice by a Party. A party that files a pleading, written motion, or other paper drawing into question the constitutionality of a federal or state statute must promptly:

   (1) file a notice of constitutional question stating the question and identifying the paper that raises it, if:

       (A) a federal statute is questioned and the parties do not include the United States, one of its agencies, or one of its officers or employees in an official capacity; or

       (B) a state statute is questioned and the parties do not include the state, one of its agencies, or one of its officers or employees in an official capacity; and

   (2) serve the notice and paper on the Attorney General of the United States if a federal statute is questioned—or on the state attorney general if a state statute is questioned—either by certified or registered mail or by sending it to an electronic address designated by the attorney general for this purpose.

(b) Certification by the Court. The court must, under 28 U.S.C. § 2403, certify to the appropriate attorney general that a statute has been questioned.

(c) Intervention; Final Decision on the Merits. Unless the court sets a later time, the attorney general may intervene within 60 days after the notice is filed or after the court certifies the challenge, whichever is earlier. Before the time to intervene expires, the court may reject the constitutional challenge, but may not enter a final judgment holding the statute unconstitutional.

(d) No Forfeiture. A party's failure to file and serve the notice, or the court's failure to certify, does not forfeit a constitutional claim or defense that is otherwise timely asserted.

(Adopted April 12, 2006, effective December 1, 2006; amended April 30, 2007, effective December 1, 2007.)

ADVISORY COMMITTEE NOTES

2006 Adoption

Rule 5.1 implements 28 U.S.C. § 2403, replacing the final three sentences of Rule 24(c). New Rule 5.1 requires a party that files a pleading, written motion, or other paper drawing in question the constitutionality of a federal or state statute to file a notice of constitutional question and serve it on the United States Attorney General or state attorney general. The party must promptly file and serve the notice of constitutional question. This notice requirement supplements the court's duty to certify a constitutional challenge to the United States Attorney General or state attorney general. The notice of constitutional question will ensure that the attorney general is notified of constitutional challenges and has an opportunity to exercise the statutory right to intervene at the earliest possible point in the litigation. The court's certification obligation remains, and is the only notice when the constitutionality of a federal or state statute is drawn in question by means other than a party's pleading, written motion, or other paper.

Moving the notice and certification provisions from Rule 24(c) to a new rule is designed to attract the parties' attention to these provisions by locating them in the vicinity of the rules that require notice by service and pleading.

Rule 5.1 goes beyond the requirements of § 2403 and the former Rule 24(c) provisions by requiring notice and certification of a constitutional challenge to any federal or state statute, not only those "affecting the public interest." It is better to assure, through notice, that the attorney general is able to determine whether to seek intervention on the ground that the act or statute affects a public interest. Rule 5.1 refers to a "federal statute," rather than the § 2403 reference to an "Act of Congress," to maintain consistency in the Civil Rules vocabulary. In Rule 5.1 "statute" means any congressional enactment that would qualify as an "Act of Congress."

Unless the court sets a later time, the 60-day period for intervention runs from the time a party files a notice of constitutional question or from the time the court certifies a constitutional challenge, whichever is earlier. Rule 5.1(a) directs that a party promptly serve the notice of constitutional question. The court may extend the 60–[day] period on its own or on motion. One occasion for extension may arise if the court certifies a challenge under § 2403 after a party files a notice of constitutional question. Pretrial activities may continue without interruption during the intervention period, and the court retains authority to grant interlocutory relief. The court may reject a constitutional challenge to a statute at any time. But the court may not enter a final judgment holding a statute unconstitutional before the attorney general has responded or the intervention period has expired without response. This rule does not displace any of the statutory or rule procedures that permit dismissal of all or part of an action—including a constitutional challenge—at any time, even before service of process.

2007 Amendment

The language of Rule 5.1 has been amended as part of the general restyling of the Civil Rules to make them more easily understood and to make style and terminology consistent throughout the rules. These changes are intended to be stylistic only.

Rule 5.2. Privacy Protection For Filings Made with the Court

(a) Redacted Filings. Unless the court orders otherwise, in an electronic or paper filing with the court that contains an individual's social-security number, taxpayer-identification number, or birth date, the name of an individual known to be a minor, or a financial-account number, a party or nonparty making the filing may include only:

    (1) the last four digits of the social-security number and taxpayer-identification number;

    (2) the year of the individual's birth;

    (3) the minor's initials; and

    (4) the last four digits of the financial-account number.

(b) Exemptions from the Redaction Requirement. The redaction requirement does not apply to the following:

    (1) a financial-account number that identifies the property allegedly subject to forfeiture in a forfeiture proceeding;

    (2) the record of an administrative or agency proceeding;

    (3) the official record of a state-court proceeding;

    (4) the record of a court or tribunal, if that record was not subject to the redaction requirement when originally filed;

    (5) a filing covered by Rule 5.2(c) or (d); and

    (6) a pro se filing in an action brought under 28 U.S.C. §§ 2241, 2254, or 2255.

(c) Limitations on Remote Access to Electronic Files; Social-Security Appeals and Immigration Cases. Unless the court orders otherwise, in an action for benefits under the Social Security Act, and in an action or proceeding relating to an order of removal, to relief from removal, or to immigration benefits or detention, access to an electronic file is authorized as follows:

    (1) the parties and their attorneys may have remote electronic access to any part of the case file, including the administrative record;

    (2) any other person may have electronic access to the full record at the courthouse, but may have remote electronic access only to:

        (A) the docket maintained by the court; and

        (B) an opinion, order, judgment, or other disposition of the court, but not any other part of the case file or the administrative record.

(d) Filings Made Under Seal. The court may order that a filing be made under seal without redaction. The court may later unseal the filing or order the person who made the filing to file a redacted version for the public record.

(e) Protective Orders. For good cause, the court may by order in a case:

    (1) require redaction of additional information; or

    (2) limit or prohibit a nonparty's remote electronic access to a document filed with the court.

(f) Option for Additional Unredacted Filing Under Seal. A person making a redacted filing may also file an unredacted copy under seal. The court must retain the unredacted copy as part of the record.

(g) Option for Filing a Reference List. A filing that contains redacted information may be filed together with a reference list that identifies each item of redacted information and specifies an appropriate identifier that uniquely corresponds to each item listed. The list must be filed under seal and may be amended as of right. Any reference in the case to a listed identifier will be construed to refer to the corresponding item of information.

(h) Waiver of Protection of Identifiers. A person waives the protection of Rule 5.2(a) as to the person's own information by filing it without redaction and not under seal.

(Adopted April 30, 2007, effective December 1, 2007.)

ADVISORY COMMITTEE NOTES

2007 Adoption

    The rule is adopted in compliance with section 205(c)(3) of the E-Government Act of 2002, Public Law 107–347. Section 205(c)(3) requires the Supreme Court to prescribe rules "to protect privacy and security concerns relating to electronic filing of documents and the public availability . . . of documents filed electronically." The rule goes further than the E-Government Act in regulating paper filings even when they are not converted to electronic form. But the number of filings that remain in paper form is certain to diminish over time. Most districts scan paper filings into the electronic case file, where they become available to the public in the same way as documents initially filed in electronic form. It is electronic availability, not the form of the initial filing, that raises the privacy and security concerns addressed in the E-Government Act.

The rule is derived from and implements the policy adopted by the Judicial Conference in September 2001 to address the privacy concerns resulting from public access to electronic case files. See http://www. privacy.uscourts.gov/Policy.htm. The Judicial Conference policy is that documents in case files generally should be made available electronically to the same extent they are available at the courthouse, provided that certain "personal data identifiers" are not included in the public file.

While providing for the public filing of some information, such as the last four digits of an account number, the rule does not intend to establish a presumption that this information never could or should be protected. For example, it may well be necessary in individual cases to prevent remote access by nonparties to any part of an account number or social security number. It may also be necessary to protect information not covered by the redaction requirement—such as driver's license numbers and alien registration numbers—in a particular case. In such cases, protection may be sought under subdivision (d) or (e). Moreover, the Rule does not affect the protection available under other rules, such as Civil Rules 16 and 26(c), or under other sources of protective authority.

Parties must remember that any personal information not otherwise protected by sealing or redaction will be made available over the internet. Counsel should notify clients of this fact so that an informed decision may be made on what information is to be included in a document filed with the court.

The clerk is not required to review documents filed with the court for compliance with this rule. The responsibility to redact filings rests with counsel and the party or non-party making the filing.

Subdivision (c) provides for limited public access in Social Security cases and immigration cases. Those actions are entitled to special treatment due to the prevalence of sensitive information and the volume of filings. Remote electronic access by nonparties is limited to the docket and the written dispositions of the court unless the court orders otherwise. The rule contemplates, however, that nonparties can obtain full access to the case file at the courthouse, including access through the court's public computer terminal.

Subdivision (d) reflects the interplay between redaction and filing under seal. It does not limit or expand the judicially developed rules that govern sealing. But it does reflect the possibility that redaction may provide an alternative to sealing.

Subdivision (e) provides that the court can by order in a particular case for good cause require more extensive redaction than otherwise required by the Rule. Nothing in this subdivision is intended to affect the limitations on sealing that are otherwise applicable to the court.

Subdivision (f) allows a person who makes a redacted filing to file an unredacted document under seal. This provision is derived from section 205(c)(3)(iv) of the E-Government Act.

Subdivision (g) allows the option to file a register of redacted information. This provision is derived from section 205(c)(3)(v) of the E-Government Act, as amended in 2004. In accordance with the E-Government Act, subdivision (g) refers to "redacted" information. The term "redacted" is intended to govern a filing that is prepared with abbreviated identifiers in the first instance, as well as a filing in which a personal identifier is edited after its preparation.

Subdivision (h) allows a person to waive the protections of the rule as to that person's own personal information by filing it unsealed and in unredacted form. One may wish to waive the protection if it is determined that the costs of redaction outweigh the benefits to privacy. If a person files an unredacted identifier by mistake, that person may seek relief from the court.

Trial exhibits are subject to the redaction requirements of Rule 5.2 to the extent they are filed with the court. Trial exhibits that are not initially filed with the court must be redacted in accordance with the rule if and when they are filed as part of an appeal or for other reasons.

Rule 6.   Computing and Extending Time; Time for Motion Papers

(a) **Computing Time.** The following rules apply in computing any time period specified in these rules, in any local rule or court order, or in any statute that does not specify a method of computing time.

(1) *Period Stated in Days or a Longer Unit.* When the period is stated in days or a longer unit of time:

   (A) exclude the day of the event that triggers the period;

   (B) count every day, including intermediate Saturdays, Sundays, and legal holidays; and

   (C) include the last day of the period, but if the last day is a Saturday, Sunday, or legal holiday, the period continues to run until the end of the next day that is not a Saturday, Sunday, or legal holiday.

(2) *Period Stated in Hours.* When the period is stated in hours:

   (A) begin counting immediately on the occurrence of the event that triggers the period;

   (B) count every hour, including hours during intermediate Saturdays, Sundays, and legal holidays; and

   (C) if the period would end on a Saturday, Sunday, or legal holiday, the period continues to run until the same time on the next day that is not a Saturday, Sunday, or legal holiday.

(3) *Inaccessibility of the Clerk's Office.* Unless the court orders otherwise, if the clerk's office is inaccessible:

   (A) on the last day for filing under Rule 6(a)(1), then the time for filing is extended to the first accessible day that is not a Saturday, Sunday, or legal holiday; or

   (B) during the last hour for filing under Rule 6(a)(2), then the time for filing is extended to the same time on the first accessible day that is not a Saturday, Sunday, or legal holiday.

(4) *"Last Day" Defined.* Unless a different time is set by a statute, local rule, or court order, the last day ends:

   (A) for electronic filing, at midnight in the court's time zone; and

   (B) for filing by other means, when the clerk's office is scheduled to close.

(5) *"Next Day" Defined.* The "next day" is determined by continuing to count forward when the period is measured after an event and backward when measured before an event.

(6) *"Legal Holiday" Defined.* "Legal holiday" means:

   (A) the day set aside by statute for observing New Year's Day, Martin Luther King Jr.'s Birthday, Washington's Birthday, Memorial Day, Independence Day, Labor Day, Columbus Day, Veterans' Day, Thanksgiving Day, or Christmas Day;

   (B) any day declared a holiday by the President or Congress; and

   (C) for periods that are measured after an event, any other day declared a holiday by the state where the district court is located.

(b) **Extending Time.**

(1) *In General.* When an act may or must be done within a specified time, the court may, for good cause, extend the time:

   (A) with or without motion or notice if the court acts, or if a request is made, before the original time or its extension expires; or

   (B) on motion made after the time has expired if the party failed to act because of excusable neglect.

  (2) *Exceptions.* A court must not extend the time to act under Rules 50(b) and (d), 52(b), 59(b), (d), and (e), and 60(b).

(c) **Motions, Notices of Hearing, and Affidavits.**

  (1) *In General.* A written motion and notice of the hearing must be served at least 14 days before the time specified for the hearing, with the following exceptions:

    (A) when the motion may be heard ex parte;

    (B) when these rules set a different time; or

    (C) when a court order—which a party may, for good cause, apply for ex parte—sets a different time.

  (2) *Supporting Affidavit.* Any affidavit supporting a motion must be served with the motion. Except as Rule 59(c) provides otherwise, any opposing affidavit must be served at least 7 days before the hearing, unless the court permits service at another time.

(d) **Additional Time After Certain Kinds of Service.** When a party may or must act within a specified time after being served and service is made under Rule 5(b)(2)(C) (mail), (D) (leaving with the clerk), or (F) (other means consented to), 3 days are added after the period would otherwise expire under Rule 6(a).

(Amended December 27, 1946, effective March 19, 1948; January 21, 1963, effective July 1, 1963; February 28, 1966, effective July 1, 1966; December 4, 1967, effective July 1, 1968; March 1, 1971, effective July 1, 1971; April 28, 1983, effective August 1, 1983; April 29, 1985, effective August 1, 1985; March 2, 1987, effective August 1, 1987; April 29, 1999, effective December 1, 1999; April 23, 2001, effective December 1, 2001; April 25, 2005, effective December 1, 2005; April 30, 2007, effective December 1, 2007; March 26, 2009, effective December 1, 2009; April 28, 2016, effective December 1, 2016.)

ADVISORY COMMITTEE NOTES

1937 Adoption

Note to Subdivisions (a) and (b). These are amplifications along lines common in state practices, of [former] Equity Rule 80 (Computation of Time—Sundays and Holidays) and of the provisions for enlargement of time found in [former] Equity Rules 8 (Enforcement of Final Decrees) and 16 (Defendant to Answer—Default—Decree Pro Confesso). See also Rule XIII, Rules and Forms in Criminal Cases, 1934, 292 U.S. 661, 666. Compare Ala.Code Ann. (Michie, 1928) § 13 and former Law Rule 8 of the Rules of the Supreme Court of the District of Columbia (1924), superseded in 1929 by Law Rule 8, Rules of the District Court of the United States for the District of Columbia (1937).

Note to Subdivision (c). This eliminates the difficulties caused by the expiration of terms of court. Such statutes as U.S.C., Title 28, [former] § 12 (Trials not discontinued by new term) are not affected. Compare Rules of the United States District Court of Minnesota, Rule 25 (Minn.Stat. (Mason, Supp.1936), p. 1089).

Note to Subdivision (d). Compare 2 Minn.Stat. (Mason, 1927) § 9246; N.Y.R.C.P. (1937) Rules 60 and 64.

1946 Amendment

Note to Subdivision (b). The purpose of the amendment is to clarify the finality of judgments. Prior to the advent of the Federal Rules of Civil Procedure, the general rule that a court loses jurisdiction to disturb its judgments, upon the expiration of the term at which they were entered, had long been the classic device which (together with the statutory limits on the time for appeal) gave finality to judgments. See note to rule 73(a). Rule 6(c) abrogates that limit on judicial power. That limit was open to many objections, one of them being inequality of operation because, under it, the time for vacating a judgment rendered early in a term was much longer than for a judgment rendered near the end of the term.

The question to be met under rule 6(b) is: how far should the desire to allow correction of judgments be allowed to postpone their finality? The rules contain a number of provisions permitting the vacation or modification of judgments on various grounds. Each of these rules contains express time limits on the motions for granting of relief. Rule 6(b) is a rule of general application giving wide discretion to the court to enlarge these time limits or revive them after they have expired, the only exceptions stated in the original rule being a prohibition against enlarging the time specified in Rule 59(b) and (d) for making motions for or granting new trials, and a prohibition against enlarging the time fixed by law for taking an appeal. It should also be noted that Rule 6(b) itself contains no limitation of time within which the court may exercise its discretion, and since the expiration of the term does not end its power, there is now no time limit on the exercise of its discretion under Rule 6(b).

Decisions of lower federal courts suggest that some of the rules containing time limits which may be set aside under Rule 6(b) are Rules 25, 50(b), 52(b), 60(b), and 73(g).

In a number of cases the effect of Rule 6(b) on the time limitations of these rules has been considered. Certainly the rule is susceptible of the interpretation that the court is given the power in its discretion to relieve a party from failure to act within the times specified in any of these other rules, with only the exceptions stated in Rule 6(b), and in some cases the rule has been so construed.

With regard to Rule 25(a) for substitution, it was held in *Anderson v. Brady,* Ky.1941, 1 F.R.D. 589, 4 Fed.Rules Service 25a.1, Case 1, and in *Anderson v. Yungkau,* C.C.A.6, 1946, 153 F.2d 685, certiorari granted 66 S.Ct. 1025, 328 U.S. 829, 90 L.Ed. 1606, that under Rule 6(b) the court had no authority to allow substitution of parties after the expiration of the limit fixed in Rule 25(a).

As to Rules 50(b) for judgments notwithstanding the verdict and 52(b) for amendment of findings and vacation of judgment, it was recognized in *Leishman v. Associated Wholesale Electric Co.,* 1943, 63 S.Ct. 543, 318 U.S. 203, 87 L.Ed. 714, that Rule 6(b) allowed the district court to enlarge the time to make a motion for amended findings and judgment beyond the limit expressly fixed in Rule 52(b). See *Coca-Cola v. Busch,* E.D.Pa.1943, 7 Fed.Rules Service, 59b.2, Case 4. Obviously, if the time limit in Rule 52(b) could be set aside under Rule 6(b), the time limit in Rule 50(b) for granting judgment notwithstanding the verdict (and thus vacating the judgment entered "forthwith" on the verdict) likewise could be set aside.

As to Rule 59 on motions for a new trial, it has been settled that the time limits in Rule 59(b) and (d) for making motions for or granting new trial could not be set aside under Rule 6(b), because Rule 6(b) expressly refers to Rule 59, and forbids it. See *Safeway Stores, Inc. v. Coe,* App.D.C.1943, 136 F.2d 771, 78 U.S.App.D.C. 19; *Jusino v. Morales & Tio,* C.C.A.1, 1944, 139 F.2d 946; *Coca-Cola Co. v. Busch,* E.D.Pa.1943, 7 Fed.Rules Service 59b.2, Case 4; *Peterson v. Chicago Great Western Ry. Co.,* D.Neb.1943, 3 F.R.D. 346, 7 Fed.Rules Service 59b.2, Case 1; *Leishman v. Associated Wholesale Electric Co.,* 1943, 63 S.Ct. 543, 318 U.S. 203, 87 L.Ed. 714.

As to Rule 60(b) for relief from a judgment, it was held in *Schram v. O'Connor,* Mich.1941, 5 Fed.Rules Serv. 6b.31, Case 1, 2 F.R.D. 192, s.c. 5 Fed.Rules Serv. 6b.31, Case 2, 2 F.R.D. 192, that the six-months time limit in original rule 60(b) for making a motion for relief from a judgment for surprise, mistake, or excusable neglect could be set aside under Rule 6(b). The contrary result was reached in *Wallace v. United States,* C.C.A.2, 1944, 142 F.2d 240, certiorari denied 65 S.Ct. 37, 323 U.S. 712, 89 L.Ed. 573; *Reed v. South Atlantic Steamship Co. of Del.,* Del.1942, 2 F.R.D. 475, 6 Fed.Rules Serv. 60b.31, Case 1.

As to Rule 73(g), fixing the time for docketing an appeal, it was held in *Ainsworth v. Gill Glass & Fixture Co.,* C.C.A.3, 1939, 104 F.2d 83, that under Rule 6(b) the district court, upon motion made after the expiration of the forty-day period, stated in Rule 73(g), but before the expiration of the ninety-day period therein specified, could permit the docketing of the appeal on a showing of excusable neglect. The contrary was held in *Mutual Benefit Health & Accident Ass'n v. Snyder,* C.C.A.6, 1940, 109 F.2d 469 and in *Burke v. Canfield,* 1940, 111 F.2d 526, 72 App.D.C. 127.

The amendment of Rule 6(b) now proposed is based on the view that there should be a definite point where it can be said a judgment is final; that the right method of dealing with the problem is to list in Rule 6(b) the various other rules whose time limits may not be set aside, and then, if the time limit in any of those other rules is too short, to amend that other rule to give a longer time. The further argument is that Rule 6(c) abolished the long standing device to produce finality in judgments through expiration of the term, and since that limitation on the jurisdiction of courts to set aside their own judgments has been removed by Rule 6(c), some other limitation must be substituted or judgments never can be said to be final.

In this connection reference is made to the established rule that if a motion for new trial is seasonably made, the mere making or pendency of the motion destroys the finality of the judgment, and even though the motion is ultimately denied, the full time for appeal starts anew from the date of denial. Also, a motion to amend the findings under Rule 52(b) has the same effect on the time for appeal. *Leishman v. Associated Wholesale Electric Co.,* 1943, 63 S.Ct. 543, 318 U.S. 203, 87 L.Ed. 714. By the same reasoning a motion for judgment under Rule 50(b), involving as it does the vacation of a judgment entered "forthwith" on the verdict (Rule 58), operates to postpone, until an order is made, the running of the time for appeal. The Committee believes that the abolition by Rule 6(c) of the old rule that a court's power over its judgments ends with the term, requires a substitute limitation, and that unless Rule 6(b) is amended to prevent enlargement of the times specified in Rules 50(b), 52(b) and 60(b), and the limitation as to Rule 59(b) and (d) is retained, no one can say when a judgment is final. This is also true with regard to proposed Rule 59(e), which authorizes a motion to alter or amend a judgment, hence that rule is also included in the enumeration in amended Rule 6(b). In consideration of the amendment, however, it should be noted that Rule 60(b) is also to be amended so as to lengthen the six-months period originally prescribed in that rule to one year.

As to Rule 25 on substitution, while finality is not involved, the limit there fixed should be controlling. That rule, as amended, gives the court power, upon showing of a reasonable excuse, to permit substitution after the expiration of the two-year period.

As to Rule 73(g), it is believed that the conflict in decisions should be resolved and not left to further litigation, and that the rule should be listed as one whose limitation may not be set aside under Rule 6(b).

As to Rule 59(c), fixing the time for serving affidavits on motion for new trial, it is believed that the court should have authority under Rule 6(b) to enlarge the time, because, once the motion for new trial is made, the judgment no longer has finality, and the extension of time for affidavits thus does not of itself disturb finality.

Other changes proposed in Rule 6(b) are merely clarifying and conforming. Thus "request" is substituted for "application" in clause (1) because an application is defined as a motion under Rule 7(b). The phrase "extend the time" is substituted for "enlarge the period" because the former is a more suitable expression and relates more clearly to both clauses (1) and (2). The final phrase in Rule 6(b), "or the period for taking an appeal as provided by law", is deleted and a reference to Rule 73(a) inserted, since it is proposed to state in that rule the time for appeal to a circuit court of appeals, which is the only appeal governed by the Federal Rules, and allows an extension of time. See Rule 72.

Subdivision (c). The purpose of this amendment is to prevent reliance upon the continued existence of a term as a source of power to disturb the finality of a judgment upon grounds other than those stated in these rules. See *Hill v. Hawes,* 1944, 64 S.Ct. 334, 320 U.S. 520, 88 L.Ed. 283; *Boaz v. Mutual Life Ins. Co. of New York,* C.C.A.8, 1944, 146 F.2d 321; *Bucy v. Nevada Construction Co.,* C.C.A.9, 1942, 125 F.2d 213.

1963 Amendment

Subdivision (a). This amendment is related to the amendment of Rule 77(c) changing the regulation of the days on which the clerk's office shall be open.

The wording of the first sentence of Rule 6(a) is clarified and the subdivision is made expressly applicable to computing periods of time set forth in local rules.

Saturday is to be treated in the same way as Sunday or a "legal holiday" in that it is not to be included when it falls on the last day of a computed period, nor counted as an intermediate day when the period is less than 7 days. "Legal holiday" is defined for purposes of this subdivision and amended Rule 77(c). Compare the definition of "holiday" in 11 U.S.C. § 1(18); also 5 U.S.C. § 86a; Executive Order No. 10358, *"Observance of Holidays,"* June 9, 1952, 17 Fed.Reg. 5269. In the light of these changes the last sentence of the present subdivision, dealing with half holidays, is eliminated.

With Saturdays and State holidays made "dies non" in certain cases by the amended subdivision, computation of the usual 5-day notice of motion or the 2-day notice to dissolve or modify a temporary restraining order may work out so as to cause embarrassing delay in urgent cases. The delay can be obviated by applying to the court to shorten the time, see Rules 6(d) and 65(b).

Subdivision (b). The prohibition against extending the time for taking action under Rule 25 (Substitution of parties) is eliminated. The only limitation of time provided for in amended Rule 25 is the 90-day period following a suggestion upon the record of the death of a party within which to make a motion to substitute the proper parties for the deceased party. See Rule 25(a)(1), as amended, and the Advisory Committee's Note thereto. It is intended that the court shall have discretion to enlarge that period.

1966 Amendment

P.L. 88–139, § 1, 77 Stat. 248, approved on October 16, 1963, amended 28 U.S.C. § 138 to read as follows: "The district court shall not hold formal terms." Thus Rule 6(c) is rendered unnecessary, and it is rescinded.

1967 Amendment

The amendment eliminates the references to Rule 73, which is to be abrogated.

1971 Amendment

The amendment adds Columbus Day to the list of legal holidays to conform the subdivision to the Act of June 28, 1968, 82 Stat. 250, which constituted Columbus Day a legal holiday effective after January 1, 1971.

The Act, which amended Title 5, U.S.C. § 6103(a), changes the day on which certain holidays are to be observed. Washington's Birthday, Memorial Day and Veterans Day are to be observed on the third Monday in February, the last Monday in May and the fourth Monday in October, respectively, rather than, as heretofore, on February 22, May 30, and November 11, respectively, Columbus Day is to be observed on the second Monday in October. New Year's Day, Independence Day, Thanksgiving Day and Christmas continue to be observed on the traditional days.

1983 Amendment

Subdivision (b). The amendment confers finality upon the judgments of magistrates by foreclosing enlargement of the time for appeal except as provided in new Rule 74(a) (20-day period for demonstration of excusable neglect).

1985 Amendment

Rule 6(a) is amended to acknowledge that weather conditions or other events may render the clerk's office inaccessible one or more days. Parties who are obliged to file something with the court during that period should not be penalized if they cannot do so. The amendment conforms to changes made in Federal Rule of Criminal Procedure 45(a), effective August 1, 1982.

The Rule also is amended to extend the exclusion of intermediate Saturdays, Sundays, and legal holidays to the computation of time periods less than 11 days. Under the current version of the Rule, parties bringing motions under rules with 10-day periods could have as few as 5 working days to prepare their motions. This hardship would be especially acute in the case of Rules 50(b) and (c)(2), 52(b), and 59(b), (d), and (e), which may not be enlarged at the discretion of the court. See Rule 6(b). If the exclusion of Saturdays, Sundays, and legal holidays will operate to cause excessive delay in urgent cases, the delay can be obviated by applying to the court to shorten the time. See Rule 6(b).

The Birthday of Martin Luther King, Jr., which becomes a legal holiday effective in 1986, has been added to the list of legal holidays enumerated in the Rule.

1987 Amendment

The amendments are technical. No substantive change is intended.

1999 Amendment

The reference to Rule 74(a) is stricken from the catalogue of time periods that cannot be extended by the district court. The change reflects the 1997 abrogation of Rule 74(a).

2001 Amendments

The additional three days provided by Rule 6(e) is extended to the means of service authorized by the new paragraph (D) added to Rule 5(b), including—with the consent of the person served—service by electronic or other means. The three-day addition is provided as well for service on a person with no known address by leaving a copy with the clerk of the court.

Changes Made After Publication and Comments

Proposed Rule 6(e) is the same as the "alternative proposal" that was published in August 1999.

2005 Amendments

Rule 6(e) is amended to remove any doubt as to the method for extending the time to respond after service by mail, leaving with the clerk of court, electronic means, or other means consented to by the party served. Three days are added after the prescribed period otherwise expires under Rule 6(a). Intermediate Saturdays, Sundays, and legal holidays are included in counting these added three days. If the third day is a Saturday, Sunday, or legal holiday, the last day to act is the next day that is not a Saturday, Sunday, or legal holiday. The effect of invoking the day when the prescribed period would otherwise expire under Rule 6(a) can be illustrated by assuming that the thirtieth day of a thirty-day period is a Saturday. Under Rule 6(a) the period expires on the next day that is not a Sunday or legal holiday. If the following Monday is a legal holiday, under Rule 6(a) the period expires on Tuesday. Three days are then added—Wednesday, Thursday, and Friday as the third and final day to act. If the period prescribed expires on a Friday, the three added days are Saturday, Sunday, and Monday, which is the third and final day to act unless it is a legal holiday. If Monday is a legal holiday, the next day that is not a legal holiday is the third and final day to act.

Application of Rule 6(e) to a period that is less than eleven days can be illustrated by a paper that is served by mailing on a Friday. If ten days are allowed to respond, intermediate Saturdays, Sundays, and legal holidays are excluded in determining when the period expires under Rule 6(a). If there is no legal holiday, the period expires on the Friday two weeks after the paper was mailed. The three added Rule 6(e) days are Saturday, Sunday, and Monday, which is the third and final day to act unless it is a legal holiday. If Monday is a legal holiday, the next day that is not a legal holiday is the final day to act.

2007 Amendment

The language of Rule 6 has been amended as part of the general restyling of the Civil Rules to make them more easily understood and to make style and terminology consistent throughout the rules. These changes are intended to be stylistic only.

2009 Amendments

Subdivision (a). Subdivision (a) has been amended to simplify and clarify the provisions that describe how deadlines are computed. Subdivision (a) governs the computation of any time period found in these rules, in any local rule or court order, or in any statute that does not specify a method of computing time. In accordance with Rule 83(a)(1), a local rule may not direct that a deadline be computed in a manner inconsistent with subdivision (a).

The time-computation provisions of subdivision (a) apply only when a time period must be computed. They do not apply when a fixed time to act is set. The amendments thus carry forward the approach taken in *Violette v. P.A. Days, Inc.*, 427 F.3d 1015, 1016 (6th Cir. 2005) (holding that Civil Rule 6(a) "does not apply to situations where the court has established a specific calendar day as a deadline"), and reject the contrary holding of *In re American Healthcare Management, Inc.*, 900 F.2d 827, 832 (5th Cir. 1990) (holding that Bankruptcy Rule 9006(a) governs treatment of date-certain deadline set by court order). If, for example, the date for filing is "no later than November 1, 2007," subdivision (a) does not govern. But if a filing is required to be made "within 10 days" or "within 72 hours," subdivision (a) describes how that deadline is computed.

Subdivision (a) does not apply when computing a time period set by a statute if the statute specifies a method of computing time. *See, e.g.*, 2 U.S.C. § 394 (specifying method for computing time periods prescribed by certain statutory provisions relating to contested elections to the House of Representatives).

Subdivision (a)(1). New subdivision (a)(1) addresses the computation of time periods that are stated in days. It also applies to time periods that are stated in weeks, months, or years. *See, e.g.*, Rule 60(c)(1). Subdivision (a)(1)(B)'s directive to "count every day" is relevant only if the period is stated in days (not weeks, months or years).

Under former Rule 6(a), a period of 11 days or more was computed differently than a period of less than 11 days. Intermediate Saturdays, Sundays, and legal holidays were included in computing the longer periods, but excluded in computing the shorter periods. Former Rule 6(a) thus made computing deadlines unnecessarily complicated and led to counterintuitive results. For example, a 10-day period and a 14-day period that started on the same day usually ended on the same day—and the 10-day period not infrequently ended later than the 14-day period. *See Miltimore Sales, Inc. v. Int'l Rectifier, Inc.*, 412 F.3d 685, 686 (6th Cir. 2005).

Under new subdivision (a)(1), all deadlines stated in days (no matter the length) are computed in the same way. The day of the event that triggers the deadline is not counted. All other days—including intermediate Saturdays, Sundays, and legal holidays—are counted, with only one exception: If the period ends on a Saturday, Sunday, or legal holiday, then the deadline falls on the next day that is not a Saturday, Sunday, or legal holiday. An illustration is provided below in the discussion of subdivision (a)(5). Subdivision (a)(3) addresses filing deadlines that expire on a day when the clerk's office is inaccessible.

Where subdivision (a) formerly referred to the "act, event, or default" that triggers the deadline, new subdivision (a) refers simply to the "event" that triggers the deadline; this change in terminology is adopted for brevity and simplicity, and is not intended to change meaning.

Periods previously expressed as less than 11 days will be shortened as a practical matter by the decision to count intermediate Saturdays, Sundays, and legal holidays in computing all periods. Many of those periods have been lengthened to compensate for the change. *See, e.g.*, Rule 14(a)(1).

Most of the 10-day periods were adjusted to meet the change in computation method by setting 14 days as the new period. A 14-day period corresponds to the most frequent result of a 10-day period under the former computation method—two Saturdays and two Sundays were excluded, giving 14 days in all. A 14-day period has an additional advantage. The final day falls on the same day of the week as the event that triggered the period—the 14th day after a Monday, for example, is a Monday. This advantage of using week-long periods led to adopting 7-day periods to replace some of the periods set at less than 10 days, and 21-day periods to replace 20-day periods. Thirty-day and longer periods, however, were generally retained without change.

Subdivision (a)(2). New subdivision (a)(2) addresses the computation of time periods that are stated in hours. No such deadline currently appears in the Federal Rules of Civil Procedure. But some statutes contain deadlines stated in hours, as do some court orders issued in expedited proceedings.

Under subdivision (a)(2), a deadline stated in hours starts to run immediately on the occurrence of the event that triggers the deadline. The deadline generally ends when the time expires. If, however, the time period expires at a specific time (say, 2:17 p.m.) on a Saturday, Sunday, or legal holiday, then the deadline is extended to the same time (2:17 p.m.) on the next day that is not a Saturday, Sunday, or legal holiday. Periods stated in hours are not to be "rounded up" to the next whole hour. Subdivision (a)(3) addresses situations when the clerk's office is inaccessible during the last hour before a filing deadline expires.

Subdivision (a)(2)(B) directs that every hour be counted. Thus, for example, a 72-hour period that commences at 10:23 a.m. on Friday, November 2, 2007, will run until 9:23 a.m. on Monday, November 5; the discrepancy in start and end times in this example results from the intervening shift from daylight saving time to standard time.

Subdivision (a)(3). When determining the last day of a filing period stated in days or a longer unit of time, a day on which the clerk's office is not accessible because of the weather or another reason is treated like a Saturday, Sunday, or legal holiday. When determining the end of a filing period stated in hours, if the clerk's office is inaccessible during the last hour of the filing period computed under subdivision (a)(2) then the period is extended to the same time on the next day that is not a weekend, holiday, or day when the clerk's office is inaccessible.

Subdivision (a)(3)'s extensions apply "[u]nless the court orders otherwise." In some circumstances, the court might not wish a period of inaccessibility to trigger a full 24-hour extension; in those instances, the court can specify a briefer extension.

The text of the rule no longer refers to "weather or other conditions" as the reason for the inaccessibility of the clerk's office. The reference to "weather" was deleted from the text to underscore that inaccessibility can occur for reasons unrelated to weather, such as an outage of the electronic filing system. Weather can still be a reason for inaccessibility of the clerk's office. The rule does not attempt to define inaccessibility. Rather, the concept will continue to develop through caselaw, *see, e.g.*, William G. Phelps, *When Is Office of Clerk of Court Inaccessible Due to Weather or Other Conditions for Purpose of Computing Time Period for Filing Papers under Rule 6(a) of Federal Rules of Civil Procedure*, 135 A.L.R. Fed. 259 (1996) (collecting cases). In addition, many local provisions address inaccessibility for purposes of electronic filing, *see, e.g.*, D. Kan. Rule 5.4.11 ("A Filing User whose filing is made untimely as the result of a technical failure may seek appropriate relief from the court.").

Subdivision (a)(4). New subdivision (a)(4) defines the end of the last day of a period for purposes of subdivision (a)(1). Subdivision (a)(4) does not apply in computing periods stated in hours under subdivision (a)(2), and does not apply if a different time is set by a statute, local rule, or order in the case. A local rule may, for example, address the problems that might arise if a single district has clerk's offices in different time zones, or provide that papers filed in a drop box after the normal hours of the clerk's office are filed as of the day that is date-stamped on the papers by a device in the drop box.

28 U.S.C. § 452 provides that "[a]ll courts of the United States shall be deemed always open for the purpose of filing proper papers, issuing and returning process, and making motions and orders." A corresponding provision exists in Rule 77(a). Some courts have held that these provisions permit an after-hours filing by handing the papers to an appropriate official. *See, e.g., Casalduc v. Diaz*, 117 F.2d 915, 917 (1st Cir. 1941). Subdivision (a)(4) does not address the effect of the statute on the question of after-hours filing; instead, the rule is designed to deal with filings in the ordinary course without regard to Section 452.

Subdivision (a)(5). New subdivision (a)(5) defines the "next" day for purposes of subdivisions (a)(1)(C) and (a)(2)(C). The Federal Rules of Civil Procedure contain both forward-looking time periods and backward-looking time periods. A forward-looking time period requires something to be done within a period of time *after* an event. *See, e.g.*, Rule 59(b) (motion for new trial "must be filed no later than 28 days after entry of the judgment"). A backward-looking time period requires something to be done within a period of time *before* an event. *See, e.g.*, Rule 26(f) (parties must hold Rule 26(f) conference "as soon as practicable and in any event at least 21 days before a scheduling conference is held or a scheduling order is due under Rule 16(b)"). In determining what is the "next" day for purposes of subdivisions (a)(1)(C) and (a)(2)(C), one should continue counting in the same direction—that is, forward when computing a forward-looking period and backward when computing a backward-looking period. If, for example, a filing is due within 30 days *after* an event, and the thirtieth day falls on Saturday, September 1, 2007, then the filing is due on Tuesday, September 4, 2007 (Monday, September 3, is Labor Day). But if a filing is due 21 days *before* an event, and the twenty-first day falls on Saturday, September 1, then the filing is due on Friday, August 31. If the clerk's office is inaccessible on August 31, then subdivision (a)(3) extends the filing deadline forward to the next accessible day that is not a Saturday, Sunday, or legal holiday—no later than Tuesday, September 4.

Subdivision (a)(6). New subdivision (a)(6) defines "legal holiday" for purposes of the Federal Rules of Civil Procedure, including the time-computation provisions of subdivision (a). Subdivision (a)(6) continues to include within the definition of "legal holiday" days that are declared a holiday by the President or Congress.

For forward-counted periods—*i.e.*, periods that are measured after an event—subdivision (a)(6)(C) includes certain state holidays within the definition of legal holidays. However, state legal holidays are not recognized in computing backward-counted periods. For both forward- and backward-counted periods, the rule thus protects those who may be unsure of the effect of state holidays. For forward-counted deadlines, treating state holidays the same as federal holidays extends the deadline. Thus, someone who thought that the federal courts might be closed on a state holiday would be safeguarded against an inadvertent late filing. In contrast, for backward-counted deadlines, not giving state holidays the treatment of federal holidays allows filing on the state holiday itself rather than the day before. Take, for example, Monday, April 21, 2008 (Patriot's Day, a legal holiday in the relevant state). If a filing is due 14 days after an event, and the fourteenth day is April 21, then the filing is due on Tuesday, April 22 because Monday, April 21 counts as a legal holiday. But if a filing is due 14 days before an event, and the fourteenth day is April 21, the filing is due on Monday, April 21; the fact that April 21 is a state holiday does not make April 21 a legal holiday for purposes of computing this backward-counted deadline. But note that if the clerk's office is inaccessible on Monday, April 21, then subdivision (a)(3) extends the April 21 filing deadline forward to the next accessible day that is not a Saturday, Sunday or legal holiday—no earlier than Tuesday, April 22.

[Subdivision (b)(2), (c)] The times set in the former rule at 1 or 5 days have been revised to 7 or 14 days. See the Note to Rule 6.

2016 Amendments

Rule 6(d) is amended to remove service by electronic means under Rule 5(b)(2)(E) from the modes of service that allow 3 added days to act after being served.

Rule 5(b)(2) was amended in 2001 to provide for service by electronic means. Although electronic transmission seemed virtually instantaneous even then, electronic service was included in the modes of service that allow 3 added days to act after being served. There were concerns that the transmission might be delayed for some time, and particular concerns that incompatible systems might make it difficult or impossible to open attachments. Those concerns have been substantially alleviated by advances in technology and in widespread skill in using electronic transmission.

A parallel reason for allowing the 3 added days was that electronic service was authorized only with the consent of the person to be served. Concerns about the reliability of electronic transmission might have led to refusals of consent; the 3 added days were calculated to alleviate these concerns.

Diminution of the concerns that prompted the decision to allow the 3 added days for electronic transmission is not the only reason for discarding this indulgence. Many rules have been changed to ease the task of computing time by adopting 7-, 14-, 21-, and 28-day periods that allow "day-of-the-week" counting. Adding 3 days at the end complicated the counting, and increased the occasions for further complication by invoking the provisions that apply when the last day is a Saturday, Sunday, or legal holiday.

Electronic service after business hours, or just before or during a weekend or holiday, may result in a practical reduction in the time available to respond. Extensions of time may be warranted to prevent prejudice.

Eliminating Rule 5(b) subparagraph (2)(E) from the modes of service that allow 3 added days means that the 3 added days cannot be retained by consenting to service by electronic means. Consent to electronic service in registering for electronic case filing, for example, does not count as consent to service "by any other means" of delivery under subparagraph (F).

What is now Rule 6(d) was amended in 2005 "to remove any doubt as to the method for calculating the time to respond after service by mail, leaving with the clerk of court, electronic means, or by other means consented to by the party served." A potential ambiguity was created by substituting "after service" for the earlier references to acting after service "upon the party" if a paper or notice "is served upon the party" by the specified means. "[A]fter service" could be read to refer not only to a party that has been served but also to a party that has made service. That reading would mean that a party who is allowed a specified time to act after making service can extend the time by choosing one of the means of service specified in the rule, something that was never intended by the original rule or the amendment. Rules setting a time to act after making service include Rules 14(a)(1), 15(a)(1)(A), and 38(b)(1). "[A]fter being served" is substituted for "after service" to dispel any possible misreading.

HISTORICAL NOTES

Effective and Applicability Provisions

1946 Amendments. Effective date of amendment to this rule, see rule 86(b).

TITLE III. PLEADINGS AND MOTIONS

Rule 7.   Pleadings Allowed; Form of Motions and Other Papers

(a) Pleadings. Only these pleadings are allowed:

    (1)   a complaint;

    (2)   an answer to a complaint;

    (3)   an answer to a counterclaim designated as a counterclaim;

    (4)   an answer to a crossclaim;

(5)   a third-party complaint;

(6)   an answer to a third-party complaint; and

(7)   if the court orders one, a reply to an answer.

(b) Motions and Other Papers.

    (1) *In General.* A request for a court order must be made by motion. The motion must:

        (A) be in writing unless made during a hearing or trial;

        (B) state with particularity the grounds for seeking the order; and

        (C) state the relief sought.

    (2) *Form.* The rules governing captions and other matters of form in pleadings apply to motions and other papers.

(Amended December 27, 1946, effective March 19, 1948; January 21, 1963, effective July 1, 1963; April 28, 1983, effective August 1, 1983; April 30, 2007, effective December 1, 2007.)

ADVISORY COMMITTEE NOTES

1937 Adoption

1.   A provision designating pleadings and defining a motion is common in the state practice acts. See Smith-Hurd Ill.Stats. ch. 110, § 156 (Designation and order of pleadings); 2 Minn.Stat. (Mason, 1927) § 9246 (Definition of motion); and N.Y.C.P.A. (1937) § 113 (Definition of motion). Former Equity Rules 18 (Pleadings—Technical Forms Abrogated), 29 (Defenses—How Presented), and 33 (Testing Sufficiency of Defense) abolished technical forms of pleading, demurrers and pleas, and exceptions for insufficiency of an answer.

2.   **Note to Subdivision (a).** This preserves the substance of [former] Equity Rule 31 (Reply—When Required—When Cause at Issue). Compare the English practice, *English Rules under the Judicature Act* (The Annual Practice, 1937) O. 23, r.r. 1, 2 (Reply to counterclaim; amended, 1933, to be subject to the rules applicable to defenses, O. 21). See O. 21, r.r. 1–14; O. 27, r. 13 (When pleadings deemed denied and put in issue). Under the codes the pleadings are generally limited. A reply is sometimes required to an affirmative defense in the answer. 1 Colo.Stat.Ann. (1935) § 66; Ore.Code Ann. (1930) §§ 1–614, 1–616. In other jurisdictions no reply is necessary to an affirmative defense in the answer, but a reply may be ordered by the court. N.C.Code Ann. (1935) § 525; 1 S.D.Comp.Laws (1929) § 2357. A reply to a counterclaim is usually required. Ark.Civ.Code (Crawford, 1934) §§ 123 to 125; Wis.Stat. (1935) §§ 263.20, 263.21. U.S.C. Title 28, [former] § 45 (District courts; practice and procedure in certain cases) is modified insofar as it may dispense with a reply to a counterclaim.

For amendment of pleadings, see Rule 15 dealing with amended and supplemental pleadings.

3.   All statutes which use the words "petition", "bill of complaint", "plea", "demurrer", and other such terminology are modified in form by this rule.

1946 Amendment

Note. This amendment eliminates any question as to whether the compulsory reply, where a counterclaim is pleaded, is a reply only to the counterclaim or is a general reply to the answer containing the counterclaim. The Commentary, *Scope of Reply where Defendant Has Pleaded Counterclaim,* 1939, 1 Fed.Rules Serv. 672; *Fort Chartres and Ivy Landing Drainage and Levee District No. Five v. Thompson,* Ill.1945, 8 Fed.Rules Serv. 13.32, Case 1.

1963 Amendment

Certain redundant words are eliminated and the subdivision is modified to reflect the amendment of Rule 14(a) which in certain cases eliminates the requirement of obtaining leave to bring in a third-party defendant.

1983 Amendment

One of the reasons sanctions against improper motion practice have been employed infrequently is the lack of clarity of Rule 7. That rule has stated only generally that the pleading requirements relating to captions, signing, and other matters of form also apply to motions and other papers. The addition of Rule 7(b)(3) makes explicit the applicability of the signing requirement and the sanctions of Rule 11, which have been amplified.

2007 Amendment

The language of Rule 7 has been amended as part of the general restyling of the Civil Rules to make them more easily understood and to make style and terminology consistent throughout the rules. These changes are intended to be stylistic only.

Former Rule 7(a) stated that "there shall be * * * an answer to a cross-claim, if the answer contains a cross-claim * * * ." Former Rule 12(a)(2) provided more generally that "[a] party served with a pleading stating a cross-claim against that party shall serve an answer thereto * * * ." New Rule 7(a) corrects this inconsistency by providing for an answer to a crossclaim.

For the first time, Rule 7(a)(7) expressly authorizes the court to order a reply to a counterclaim answer. A reply may be as useful in this setting as a reply to an answer, a third-party answer, or a crossclaim answer.

Former Rule 7(b)(1) stated that the writing requirement is fulfilled if the motion is stated in a written notice of hearing. This statement was deleted as redundant because a single written document can satisfy the writing requirements both for a motion and for a Rule 6(c)(1) notice.

The cross-reference to Rule 11 in former Rule 7(b)(3) is deleted as redundant. Rule 11 applies by its own terms. The force and application of Rule 11 are not diminished by the deletion.

Former Rule 7(c) is deleted because it has done its work. If a motion or pleading is described as a demurrer, plea, or exception for insufficiency, the court will treat the paper as if properly captioned.

HISTORICAL NOTES

Effective and Applicability Provisions

1946 Amendments. Effective date of amendment to this rule, see rule 86(b).

Rule 7.1.   Disclosure Statement

(a) Who Must File; Contents. A nongovernmental corporate party must file two copies of a disclosure statement that:

    (1) identifies any parent corporation and any publicly held corporation owning 10% or more of its stock; or

    (2) states that there is no such corporation.

(b) Time to File; Supplemental Filing. A party must:

    (1) file the disclosure statement with its first appearance, pleading, petition, motion, response, or other request addressed to the court; and

    (2) promptly file a supplemental statement if any required information changes.

(Adopted April 29, 2002, effective December 1, 2002; April 30, 2007, effective December 1, 2007.)

ADVISORY COMMITTEE NOTES

2002 Adoption

Rule 7.1 is drawn from Rule 26.1 of the Federal Rules of Appellate Procedure, with changes to adapt to the circumstances of district courts that dictate different provisions for the time of filing, number of copies, and the like. The information required by Rule 7.1(a) reflects the "financial interest" standard of Canon 3C(1)(c) of the Code of Conduct for United States Judges. This information will support properly informed disqualification decisions in situations that call for automatic disqualification under Canon 3C(1)(c). It does not cover all of the circumstances that may call for disqualification under the financial interest standard, and does not deal at all with other circumstances that may call for disqualification.

Although the disclosures required by Rule 7.1(a) may seem limited, they are calculated to reach a majority of the circumstances that are likely to call for disqualification on the basis of financial information that a judge may not know or recollect. Framing a rule that calls for more detailed disclosure will be difficult. Unnecessary disclosure requirements place a burden on the parties and on courts. Unnecessary disclosure of volumes of information may create a risk that a judge will overlook the one bit of information that might require disqualification, and also may create a risk that unnecessary disqualifications will be made rather than attempt to unravel a potentially difficult question. It has not been feasible to dictate more detailed disclosure requirements in Rule 7.1(a).

Rule 7.1 does not prohibit local rules that require disclosures in addition to those required by Rule 7.1. Developing experience with local disclosure practices and advances in electronic technology may provide a foundation for adopting more detailed disclosure requirements by future amendments of Rule 7.1.

Changes Made After Publication and Comment. The provisions that would require disclosure of additional information that may be required by the Judicial Conference have been deleted.

2007 Amendment

The language of Rule 7.1 has been amended as part of the general restyling of the Civil Rules to make them more easily understood and to make style and terminology consistent throughout the rules. These changes are intended to be stylistic only.

Rule 8.   General Rules of Pleading

(a) Claim for Relief. A pleading that states a claim for relief must contain:

  (1) a short and plain statement of the grounds for the court's jurisdiction, unless the court already has jurisdiction and the claim needs no new jurisdictional support;

  (2) a short and plain statement of the claim showing that the pleader is entitled to relief; and

  (3) a demand for the relief sought, which may include relief in the alternative or different types of relief.

(b) Defenses; Admissions and Denials.

  (1) *In General.* In responding to a pleading, a party must:

   (A) state in short and plain terms its defenses to each claim asserted against it; and

   (B) admit or deny the allegations asserted against it by an opposing party.

  (2) *Denials—Responding to the Substance.* A denial must fairly respond to the substance of the allegation.

  (3) *General and Specific Denials.* A party that intends in good faith to deny all the allegations of a pleading—including the jurisdictional grounds—may do so by a general denial. A party that does not intend to deny all the allegations must either specifically deny designated allegations or generally deny all except those specifically admitted.

  (4) *Denying Part of an Allegation.* A party that intends in good faith to deny only part of an allegation must admit the part that is true and deny the rest.

  (5) *Lacking Knowledge or Information.* A party that lacks knowledge or information sufficient to form a belief about the truth of an allegation must so state, and the statement has the effect of a denial. David v. Crompton

  (6) *Effect of Failing to Deny.* An allegation—other than one relating to the amount of damages—is admitted if a responsive pleading is required and the allegation is not denied. If a responsive pleading is not required, an allegation is considered denied or avoided.

(c) Affirmative Defenses.

    (1) *In General.* In responding to a pleading, a party must affirmatively state any avoidance or affirmative defense, including:

- accord and satisfaction;
- arbitration and award;
- assumption of risk;
- contributory negligence;
- duress;
- estoppel;
- failure of consideration;
- fraud;
- illegality;
- injury by fellow servant;
- laches;
- license;
- payment;
- release;
- res judicata;
- statute of frauds;
- statute of limitations; and
- waiver.

    (2) *Mistaken Designation.* If a party mistakenly designates a defense as a counterclaim, or a counterclaim as a defense, the court must, if justice requires, treat the pleading as though it were correctly designated, and may impose terms for doing so.

(d) Pleading to Be Concise and Direct; Alternative Statements; Inconsistency.

    (1) *In General.* Each allegation must be simple, concise, and direct. No technical form is required.

    (2) *Alternative Statements of a Claim or Defense.* A party may set out 2 or more statements of a claim or defense alternatively or hypothetically, either in a single count or defense or in separate ones. If a party makes alternative statements, the pleading is sufficient if any one of them is sufficient.

    (3) *Inconsistent Claims or Defenses.* A party may state as many separate claims or defenses as it has, regardless of consistency.

(e) Construing Pleadings. Pleadings must be construed so as to do justice.

(Amended February 28, 1966, effective July 1, 1966; March 2, 1987, effective August 1, 1987; April 30, 2007, effective December 1, 2007; April 28, 2010, effective December 1, 2010.)

<h3 style="text-align:center">ADVISORY COMMITTEE NOTES</h3>

<h4 style="text-align:center">1937 Adoption</h4>

Note to Subdivision (a). See [former] Equity Rules 25 (Bill of Complaint—Contents), and 30 (Answer—Contents—Counterclaim). Compare 2 Ind.Stat.Ann. (Burns, 1933) §§ 2–1004, 2–1015; 2 Ohio Gen.Code Ann. (Page, 1926) §§ 11305, 11314; Utah Rev.Stat.Ann. (1933) §§ 104–7–2, 104–9–1.

See Rule 19(c) for the requirement of a statement in a claim for relief of the names of persons who ought to be parties and the reason for their omission.

See Rule 23(b) for particular requirements as to the complaint in a secondary action by shareholders.

Note to Subdivision (b). 1. This rule supersedes the methods of pleading prescribed in U.S.C., Title 19, § 508 (Persons making seizures pleading general issue and proving special matter); U.S.C. Title 35, [former] §§ 40d (Proving under general issue, upon notice, that a statement in application for an extended patent is not true), 69 [now 282] (Pleading and proof in actions for infringement) and similar statutes.

2.   This rule is, in part, [former] Equity Rule 30 (Answer—Contents—Counterclaim), with the matter on denials largely from the Connecticut practice. See Conn. Practice Book (1934) §§ 107, 108, and 122; Conn.Gen.Stat. (1930) §§ 5508 to 5514. Compare the English practice, *English Rules Under the Judicature Act* (The Annual Practice, 1937) O. 19, r.r. 17–20.

Note to Subdivision (c). This follows substantially *English Rules Under the Judicature Act* (The Annual Practice, 1937) O. 19, r. 15 and N.Y.C.P.A. (1937) § 242, with "surprise" omitted in this rule.

Note to Subdivision (d). The first sentence is similar to former Equity Rule 30 (Answer—Contents—Counterclaim). For the second sentence see former Equity Rule 31 (Reply—When Required—When Cause at Issue). This is similar to *English Rules Under the Judicature Act* (The Annual Practice, 1937) O. 19, r.r. 13, 18; and to the practice of the States.

Note to Subdivision (e). This rule is an elaboration upon [former] Equity Rule 30 (Answer—Contents—Counterclaim), plus a statement of the actual practice under some codes. Compare also [former] Equity Rule 18 (Pleadings—Technical Forms Abrogated). See Clark, *Code Pleading* (1928), pp. 171–4, 432–5; Hankin, *Alternative and Hypothetical Pleading* (1924), 33 Yale L.J. 365.

Note to Subdivision (f). A provision of like import is of frequent occurrence in the codes. Smith-Hurd Ill.Stats. ch. 110, § 157(3); 2 Minn.Stat. (Mason, 1927) § 9266; N.Y.C.P.A. (1937) § 275; 2 N.D.Comp.Laws Ann. (1913) § 7458.

1966 Amendment

The change here is consistent with the broad purposes of unification.

1987 Amendment

The amendments are technical. No substantive change is intended.

2007 Amendment

The language of Rule 8 has been amended as part of the general restyling of the Civil Rules to make them more easily understood and to make style and terminology consistent throughout the rules. These changes are intended to be stylistic only.

The former Rule 8(b) and 8(e) cross-references to Rule 11 are deleted as redundant. Rule 11 applies by its own terms. The force and application of Rule 11 are not diminished by the deletion.

Former Rule 8(b) required a pleader denying part of an averment to "specify so much of it as is true and material and * * * deny only the remainder." "[A]nd material" is deleted to avoid the implication that it is proper to deny something that the pleader believes to be true but not material.

Deletion of former Rule 8(e)(2)'s "whether based on legal, equitable, or maritime grounds" reflects the parallel deletions in Rule 1 and elsewhere. Merger is now successfully accomplished.

2010 Amendments

Subdivision (c)(1). "[D]ischarge in bankruptcy" is deleted from the list of affirmative defenses. Under 11 U.S.C. § 524(a)(1) and (2) a discharge voids a judgment to the extent that it determines a personal liability of the debtor with respect to a discharged debt. The discharge also operates as an injunction against commencement or continuation of an action to collect, recover, or offset a discharged debt. For these reasons it is confusing to describe discharge as an affirmative defense. But § 524(a) applies only to a claim that was actually discharged. Several categories of debt set out in 11 U.S.C. § 523(a) are excepted from discharge.

The issue whether a claim was excepted from discharge may be determined either in the court that entered the discharge or—in most instances—in another court with jurisdiction over the creditor's claim.

Rule 9.   Pleading Special Matters

(a) Capacity or Authority to Sue; Legal Existence.

(1) *In General.* Except when required to show that the court has jurisdiction, a pleading need not allege:

(A) a party's capacity to sue or be sued;

(B) a party's authority to sue or be sued in a representative capacity; or

(C) the legal existence of an organized association of persons that is made a party.

(2) *Raising Those Issues.* To raise any of those issues, a party must do so by a specific denial, which must state any supporting facts that are peculiarly within the party's knowledge.

(b) Fraud or Mistake; Conditions of Mind. In alleging fraud or mistake, a party must state with particularity the circumstances constituting fraud or mistake. Malice, intent, knowledge, and other conditions of a person's mind may be alleged generally.

(c) Conditions Precedent. In pleading conditions precedent, it suffices to allege generally that all conditions precedent have occurred or been performed. But when denying that a condition precedent has occurred or been performed, a party must do so with particularity.

(d) Official Document or Act. In pleading an official document or official act, it suffices to allege that the document was legally issued or the act legally done.

(e) Judgment. In pleading a judgment or decision of a domestic or foreign court, a judicial or quasi-judicial tribunal, or a board or officer, it suffices to plead the judgment or decision without showing jurisdiction to render it.

(f) Time and Place. An allegation of time or place is material when testing the sufficiency of a pleading.

(g) Special Damages. If an item of special damage is claimed, it must be specifically stated.

(h) Admiralty or Maritime Claim.

(1) *How Designated.* If a claim for relief is within the admiralty or maritime jurisdiction and also within the court's subject-matter jurisdiction on some other ground, the pleading may designate the claim as an admiralty or maritime claim for purposes of Rules 14(c), 38(e), and 82 and the Supplemental Rules for Admiralty or Maritime Claims and Asset Forfeiture Actions. A claim cognizable only in the admiralty or maritime jurisdiction is an admiralty or maritime claim for those purposes, whether or not so designated.

(2) *Designation for Appeal.* A case that includes an admiralty or maritime claim within this subdivision (h) is an admiralty case within 28 U.S.C. § 1292(a)(3).

(Amended February 28, 1966, effective July 1, 1966; December 4, 1967, effective July 1, 1968; March 30, 1970, effective July 1, 1970; March 2, 1987, effective August 1, 1987; April 11, 1997, effective December 1, 1997; April 12, 2006, effective December 1, 2006; April 30, 2007, effective December 1, 2007.)

ADVISORY COMMITTEE NOTES

1937 Adoption

Note to Subdivision (a). Compare [former] Equity Rule 25 (Bill of Complaint—Contents) requiring disability to be stated; Utah Rev.Stat.Ann. (1933) § 104–13–15, enumerating a number of situations where a general averment of capacity is sufficient. For provisions governing averment of incorporation, see 2 Minn.Stat. (Mason, 1927) § 9271; N.Y.R.C.P. (1937) Rule 93; 2 N.D.Comp.Laws Ann. (1913) § 7981 et seq.

Note to Subdivision (b). See *English Rules Under the Judicature Act* (The Annual Practice, 1937) O. 19, r. 22.

Note to Subdivision (c). The codes generally have this or a similar provision. See *English Rules Under the Judicature Act* (The Annual Practice, 1937) O. 19, r. 14; 2 Minn.Stat. (Mason, 1927) § 9273; N.Y.R.C.P. (1937) Rule 92; 2 N.D.Comp.Laws Ann. (1913) § 7461; 2 Wash.Rev.Stat.Ann. (Remington, 1932) § 288.

Note to Subdivision (e). The rule expands the usual code provisions on pleading a judgment by including judgments or decisions of administrative tribunals and foreign courts. Compare Ark.Civ.Code (Crawford, 1934) § 141; 2 Minn.Stat. (Mason, 1927) § 9269; N.Y.R.C.P. (1937) Rule 95; 2 Wash.Rev.Stat.Ann. (Remington, 1932) § 287.

1966 Amendment

Certain distinctive features of the admiralty practice must be preserved for what are now suits in admiralty. This raises the question: After unification, when a single form of action is established, how will the counterpart of the present suit in admiralty be identifiable? In part the question is easily answered. Some claims for relief can only be suits in admiralty, either because the admiralty jurisdiction is exclusive or because no nonmaritime ground of federal jurisdiction exists. Many claims, however, are cognizable by the district courts whether asserted in admiralty or in a civil action, assuming the existence of a nonmaritime ground of jurisdiction. Thus at present the pleader has power to determine procedural consequences by the way in which he exercises the classic privilege given by the saving-to-suitors clause (28 U.S.C. § 1333) or by equivalent statutory provisions. For example, a longshoreman's claim for personal injuries suffered by reason of the unseaworthiness of a vessel may be asserted in a suit in admiralty or, if diversity of citizenship exists, in a civil action. One of the important procedural consequences is that in the civil action either party may demand a jury trial, while in the suit in admiralty there is no right to jury trial except as provided by statute.

It is no part of the purpose of unification to inject a right to jury trial into those admiralty cases in which that right is not provided by statute. Similarly as will be more specifically noted below, there is no disposition to change the present law as to interlocutory appeals in admiralty, or as to the venue of suits in admiralty; and, of course, there is no disposition to inject into the civil practice as it now is the distinctively maritime remedies (maritime attachment and garnishment, actions in rem, possessory, petitory and partition actions and limitation of liability). The unified rules must therefore provide some device for preserving the present power of the pleader to determine whether these historically maritime procedures shall be applicable to his claim or not; the pleader must be afforded some means of designating his claim as the counterpart of the present suit in admiralty, where its character as such is not clear.

The problem is different from the similar one concerning the identification of claims that were formerly suits in equity. While that problem is not free from complexities, it is broadly true that the modern counterpart of the suit in equity is distinguishable from the former action at law by the character of the relief sought. This mode of identification is possible in only a limited category of admiralty cases. In large numbers of cases the relief sought in admiralty is simple money damages, indistinguishable from the remedy afforded by the common law. This is true, for example, in the case of the longshoreman's action for personal injuries stated above. After unification has abolished the distinction between civil actions and suits in admiralty, the complaint in such an action would be almost completely ambiguous as to the pleader's intentions regarding the procedure invoked. The allegation of diversity of citizenship might be regarded as a clue indicating an intention to proceed as at present under the saving-to-suitors clause; but this, too, would be ambiguous if there were also reference to the admiralty jurisdiction, and the pleader ought not be required to forego mention of all available jurisdictional grounds.

Other methods of solving the problem were carefully explored, but the Advisory Committee concluded that the preferable solution is to allow the pleader who now has power to determine procedural consequences by filing a suit in admiralty to exercise that power under unification, for the limited instances in which procedural differences will remain, by a simple statement in his pleading to the effect that the claim is an admiralty or maritime claim.

The choice made by the pleader in identifying or in failing to identify his claim as an admiralty or maritime claim is not an irrevocable election. The rule provides that the amendment of a pleading to add or withdraw an identifying statement is subject to the principles of Rule 15.

1968 Amendment

The amendment eliminates the reference to Rule 73 which is to be abrogated and transfers to Rule 9(h) the substance of Subsection (h) of Rule 73 which preserved the right to an interlocutory appeal in admiralty cases which is provided by 28 U.S.C. § 1292(a)(3).

1970 Amendment

The reference to Rule 26(a) is deleted, in light of the transfer of that subdivision to Rule 30(a) and the elimination of the de bene esse procedure therefrom. See the Advisory Committee's note to Rule 30(a).

1987 Amendment

The amendment is technical. No substantive change is intended.

1997 Amendment

Section 1292(a)(3) of the Judicial Code provides for appeal from "[i]nterlocutory decrees of * * * district courts * * * determining the rights and liabilities of the parties to admiralty cases in which appeals from final decrees are allowed."

Rule 9(h) was added in 1966 with the unification of civil and admiralty procedure. Civil Rule 73(h) was amended at the same time to provide that the § 1292(a)(3) reference "to admiralty cases shall be construed to mean admiralty and maritime claims within the meaning of Rule 9(h)." This provision was transferred to Rule 9(h) when the Appellate Rules were adopted.

A single case can include both admiralty or maritime claims and nonadmiralty claims or parties. This combination reveals an ambiguity in the statement in present Rule 9(h) that an admiralty "claim" is an admiralty "case." An order "determining the rights and liabilities of the parties" within the meaning of § 1292(a)(3) may resolve only a nonadmiralty claim, or may simultaneously resolve interdependent admiralty and non-admiralty claims. Can appeal be taken as to the nonadmiralty matter, because it is part of a case that includes an admiralty claim, or is appeal limited to the admiralty claim?

The courts of appeals have not achieved full uniformity in applying the § 1292(a)(3) requirement that an order "determin[e] the rights and liabilities of the parties." It is common to assert that the statute should be construed narrowly, under the general policy that exceptions to the final judgment rule should be construed narrowly. This policy would suggest that the ambiguity should be resolved by limiting the interlocutory appeal right to orders that determine the rights and liabilities of the parties to an admiralty claim.

A broader view is chosen by this amendment for two reasons. The statute applies to admiralty "cases," and may itself provide for appeal from an order that disposes of a nonadmiralty claim that is joined in a single case with an admiralty claim. Although a rule of court may help to clarify and implement a statutory grant of jurisdiction, the line is not always clear between permissible implementation and impermissible withdrawal of jurisdiction. In addition, so long as an order truly disposes of the rights and liabilities of the parties within the meaning of § 1292(a)(3), it may prove important to permit appeal as to the non-admiralty claim. Disposition of the non-admiralty claim, for example, may make it unnecessary to consider the admiralty claim and have the same effect on the case and parties as disposition of the admiralty claim. Or the admiralty and non-admiralty claims may be interdependent. An illustration is provided by Roco Carriers, Ltd. v. M/V Nurnberg Express, 899 F.2d 1292 (2d Cir.1990). Claims for losses of ocean shipments were made against two defendants, one subject to admiralty jurisdiction and the other not. Summary judgment was granted in favor of the admiralty defendant and against the nonadmiralty defendant. The nonadmiralty defendant's appeal was accepted, with the explanation that the determination of its liability was "integrally linked with the determination of non-liability" of the admiralty defendant, and that "section 1292(a)(3) is not limited to admiralty claims; instead, it refers to admiralty cases." 899 F.2d at 1297. The advantages of permitting appeal by the nonadmiralty defendant would be particularly clear if the plaintiff had appealed the summary judgment in favor of the admiralty defendant.

It must be emphasized that this amendment does not rest on any particular assumptions as to the meaning of the § 1292(a)(3) provision that limits interlocutory appeal to orders that determine the rights and liabilities of the parties. It simply reflects the conclusion that so long as the case involves an admiralty claim and an order otherwise meets statutory requirements, the opportunity to appeal should not turn on the circumstance that the order does—or does not—dispose of an admiralty claim. No attempt is made to invoke the authority conferred by 28 U.S.C. § 1292(e) to provide by rule for appeal of an interlocutory decision that is not otherwise provided for by other subsections of § 1292.

GAP Report on Rule 9(h). No changes have been made in the published proposal.

2006 Amendment

Rule 9(h) is amended to conform to the changed title of the Supplemental Rules.

2007 Amendment

The language of Rule 9 has been amended as part of the general restyling of the Civil Rules to make them more easily understood and to make style and terminology consistent throughout the rules. These changes are intended to be stylistic only.

Rule 15 governs pleading amendments of its own force. The former redundant statement that Rule 15 governs an amendment that adds or withdraws a Rule 9(h) designation as an admiralty or maritime claim is deleted. The elimination of paragraph (2) means that "(3)" will be redesignated as "(2)" in Style Rule 9(h).

Rule 10. Form of Pleadings

(a) **Caption; Names of Parties.** Every pleading must have a caption with the court's name, a title, a file number, and a Rule 7(a) designation. The title of the complaint must name all the parties; the title of other pleadings, after naming the first party on each side, may refer generally to other parties.

(b) **Paragraphs; Separate Statements.** A party must state its claims or defenses in numbered paragraphs, each limited as far as practicable to a single set of circumstances. A later pleading may refer by number to a paragraph in an earlier pleading. If doing so would promote clarity, each claim founded on a separate transaction or occurrence—and each defense other than a denial—must be stated in a separate count or defense.

(c) **Adoption by Reference; Exhibits.** A statement in a pleading may be adopted by reference elsewhere in the same pleading or in any other pleading or motion. A copy of a written instrument that is an exhibit to a pleading is a part of the pleading for all purposes.

(Amended April 30, 2007, effective December 1, 2007.)

ADVISORY COMMITTEE NOTES

1937 Adoption

The first sentence is derived in part from the opening statement of former Equity Rule 25 (Bill of Complaint—Contents). The remainder of the rule is an expansion in conformity with usual state provisions. For numbered paragraphs and separate statements, see Conn.Gen.Stat., 1930, § 5513; Smith-Hurd Ill.Stats. ch. 110, § 157(2); N.Y.R.C.P., (1937) Rule 90. For incorporation by reference, see N.Y.R.C.P., (1937) Rule 90. For written instruments as exhibits, see Smith-Hurd Ill.Stats. ch. 110, § 160.

2007 Amendment

The language of Rule 10 has been amended as part of the general restyling of the Civil Rules to make them more easily understood and to make style and terminology consistent throughout the rules. These changes are intended to be stylistic only.

Rule 11. Signing Pleadings, Motions, and Other Papers; Representations to the Court; Sanctions

(a) **Signature.** Every pleading, written motion, and other paper must be signed by at least one attorney of record in the attorney's name—or by a party personally if the party is unrepresented.

The paper must state the signer's address, e-mail address, and telephone number. Unless a rule or statute specifically states otherwise, a pleading need not be verified or accompanied by an affidavit. The court must strike an unsigned paper unless the omission is promptly corrected after being called to the attorney's or party's attention.

(b) **Representations to the Court.** By presenting to the court a pleading, written motion, or other paper—whether by signing, filing, submitting, or later advocating it—an attorney or unrepresented party certifies that to the best of the person's knowledge, information, and belief, formed after an inquiry reasonable under the circumstances:

    (1) it is not being presented for any improper purpose, such as to harass, cause unnecessary delay, or needlessly increase the cost of litigation;

    (2) the claims, defenses, and other legal contentions are warranted by existing law or by a nonfrivolous argument for extending, modifying, or reversing existing law or for establishing new law;

    (3) the factual contentions have evidentiary support or, if specifically so identified, will likely have evidentiary support after a reasonable opportunity for further investigation or discovery; and

    (4) the denials of factual contentions are warranted on the evidence or, if specifically so identified, are reasonably based on belief or a lack of information.

(c) **Sanctions.**

    (1) *In General.* If, after notice and a reasonable opportunity to respond, the court determines that Rule 11(b) has been violated, the court may impose an appropriate sanction on any attorney, law firm, or party that violated the rule or is responsible for the violation. Absent exceptional circumstances, a law firm must be held jointly responsible for a violation committed by its partner, associate, or employee.

    (2) *Motion for Sanctions.* A motion for sanctions must be made separately from any other motion and must describe the specific conduct that allegedly violates Rule 11(b). The motion must be served under Rule 5, but it must not be filed or be presented to the court if the challenged paper, claim, defense, contention, or denial is withdrawn or appropriately corrected within 21 days after service or within another time the court sets. If warranted, the court may award to the prevailing party the reasonable expenses, including attorney's fees, incurred for the motion.

    (3) *On the Court's Initiative.* On its own, the court may order an attorney, law firm, or party to show cause why conduct specifically described in the order has not violated Rule 11(b).

    (4) *Nature of a Sanction.* A sanction imposed under this rule must be limited to what suffices to deter repetition of the conduct or comparable conduct by others similarly situated. The sanction may include nonmonetary directives; an order to pay a penalty into court; or, if imposed on motion and warranted for effective deterrence, an order directing payment to the movant of part or all of the reasonable attorney's fees and other expenses directly resulting from the violation.

    (5) *Limitations on Monetary Sanctions.* The court must not impose a monetary sanction:

        (A) against a represented party for violating Rule 11(b)(2); or

        (B) on its own, unless it issued the show-cause order under Rule 11(c)(3) before voluntary dismissal or settlement of the claims made by or against the party that is, or whose attorneys are, to be sanctioned.

    (6) *Requirements for an Order.* An order imposing a sanction must describe the sanctioned conduct and explain the basis for the sanction.

(d) Inapplicability to Discovery. This rule does not apply to disclosures and discovery requests, responses, objections, and motions under Rules 26 through 37.

(Amended April 28, 1983, effective August 1, 1983; March 2, 1987, effective August 1, 1987; April 22, 1993, effective December 1, 1993; April 30, 2007, effective December 1, 2007.)

ADVISORY COMMITTEE NOTES

1937 Adoption

This is substantially the content of [former] Equity Rules 24 (Signature of Counsel) and 21 (Scandal and Impertinence) consolidated and unified. Compare former Equity Rule 36 (Officers Before Whom Pleadings Verified). Compare to similar purposes, *English Rules Under the Judicature Act* (The Annual Practice, 1937) O. 19, r. 4, and *Great Australian Gold Mining Co. v. Martin,* L.R. 5 Ch.Div. 1, 10 (1877). Subscription of pleadings is required in many codes. 2 Minn.Stat. (Mason, 1927) § 9265; N.Y.R.C.P. (1937) Rule 91; 2 N.D.Comp.Laws Ann. (1913) § 7455.

This rule expressly continues any statute which requires a pleading to be verified or accompanied by an affidavit, such as: U.S.C., Title 28:

§ 381 [former] (Preliminary injunctions and temporary restraining orders)

§ 762 [now 1402] (Suit against the United States)

U.S.C., Title 28, § 829 [now 1927] (Costs; attorney liable for, when) is unaffected by this rule.

For complaints which must be verified under these rules, see Rules 23(b) (Secondary Action by Shareholders) and 65 (Injunctions).

For abolition of former rule in equity that the averments of an answer under oath must be overcome by the testimony of two witnesses or of one witness sustained by corroborating circumstances, see 12 P.S.Pa. § 1222; for the rule in equity itself, see *Greenfield v. Blumenthal,* C.C.A.3, 1934, 69 F.2d 294.

1983 Amendment

Since its original promulgation, Rule 11 has provided for the striking of pleadings and the imposition of disciplinary sanctions to check abuses in the signing of pleadings. Its provisions have always applied to motions and other papers by virtue of incorporation by reference in Rule 7(b)(2). The amendment and the addition of Rule 7(b)(3) expressly confirms this applicability.

Experience shows that in practice Rule 11 has not been effective in deterring abuses. See 6 Wright & Miller, *Federal Practice and Procedure: Civil* § 1334 (1971). There has been considerable confusion as to (1) the circumstances that should trigger striking a pleading or motion or taking disciplinary action, (2) the standard of conduct expected of attorneys who sign pleadings and motions, and (3) the range of available and appropriate sanctions. See Rodes, Ripple & Mooney, *Sanctions Imposable for Violations of the Federal Rules of Civil Procedure* 64–65, Federal Judicial Center (1981). The new language is intended to reduce the reluctance of courts to impose sanctions, see Moore, *Federal Practice* ¶ 7.05, at 1547, by emphasizing the responsibilities of the attorney and reenforcing those obligations by the imposition of sanctions.

The amended rule attempts to deal with the problem by building upon and expanding the equitable doctrine permitting the court to award expenses, including attorney's fees, to a litigant whose opponent acts in bad faith in instituting or conducting litigation. See, e.g., *Roadway Express, Inc. v. Piper,* 447 U.S. 752 (1980); *Hall v. Cole,* 412 U.S. 1, 5 (1973). Greater attention by the district courts to pleading and motion abuses and the imposition of sanctions when appropriate, should discourage dilatory or abusive tactics and help to streamline the litigation process by lessening frivolous claims or defenses.

The expanded nature of the lawyer's certification in the fifth sentence of amended Rule 11 recognizes that the litigation process may be abused for purposes other than delay. See, e.g., *Browning Debenture Holders' Committee v. DASA Corp.,* 560 F.2d 1078 (2d Cir.1977).

The words "good ground to support" the pleading in the original rule were interpreted to have both factual and legal elements. See, e.g., *Heart Disease Research Foundation v. General Motors Corp.,* 15 Fed.R.Serv.2d 1517, 1519 (S.D.N.Y.1972). They have been replaced by a standard of conduct that is more focused.

The new language stresses the need for some prefiling inquiry into both the facts and the law to satisfy the affirmative duty imposed by the rule. The standard is one of reasonableness under the circumstances. See *Kinee v. Abraham Lincoln Fed. Sav. & Loan Ass'n*, 365 F.Supp. 975 (E.D.Pa.1973). This standard is more stringent than the original good-faith formula and thus it is expected that a greater range of circumstances will trigger its violation. See *Nemeroff v. Abelson*, 620 F.2d 339 (2d Cir.1980).

The rule is not intended to chill an attorney's enthusiasm or creativity in pursuing factual or legal theories. The court is expected to avoid using the wisdom of hindsight and should test the signer's conduct by inquiring what was reasonable to believe at the time the pleading, motion, or other paper was submitted. Thus, what constitutes a reasonable inquiry may depend on such factors as how much time for investigation was available to the signer; whether he had to rely on a client for information as to the facts underlying the pleading, motion, or other paper; whether the pleading, motion, or other paper was based on a plausible view of the law; or whether he depended on forwarding counsel or another member of the bar.

The rule does not require a party or an attorney to disclose privileged communications or work product in order to show that the signing of the pleading, motion, or other paper is substantially justified. The provisions of Rule 26(c), including appropriate orders after *in camera* inspection by the court, remain available to protect a party claiming privilege or work product protection.

Amended Rule 11 continues to apply to anyone who signs a pleading, motion, or other paper. Although the standard is the same for unrepresented parties, who are obliged themselves to sign the pleadings, the court has sufficient discretion to take account of the special circumstances that often arise in *pro se* situations. See *Haines v. Kerner*, 404 U.S. 519 (1972).

The provision in the original rule for striking pleadings and motions as sham and false has been deleted. The passage has rarely been utilized, and decisions thereunder have tended to confuse the issue of attorney honesty with the merits of the action. See generally Risinger, *Honesty in Pleading and its Enforcement: Some "Striking" Problems with Fed.R.Civ.P. 11*, 61 Minn.L.Rev. 1 (1976). Motions under this provision generally present issues better dealt with under Rules 8, 12, or 56. See *Murchison v. Kirby*, 27 F.R.D. 14 (S.D.N.Y. 1961); 5 Wright & Miller, *Federal Practice and Procedure: Civil* § 1334 (1969).

The former reference to the inclusion of scandalous or indecent matter, which is itself strong indication that an improper purpose underlies the pleading, motion, or other paper, also has been deleted as unnecessary. Such matter may be stricken under Rule 12(f) as well as dealt with under the more general language of amended Rule 11.

The text of the amended rule seeks to dispel apprehensions that efforts to obtain enforcement will be fruitless by insuring that the rule will be applied when properly invoked. The word "sanctions" in the caption, for example, stresses a deterrent orientation in dealing with improper pleadings, motions or other papers. This corresponds to the approach in imposing sanctions for discovery abuses. See *National Hockey League v. Metropolitan Hockey Club,* 427 U.S. 639 (1976) (per curiam). And the words "shall impose" in the last sentence focus the court's attention on the need to impose sanctions for pleading and motion abuses. The court, however, retains the necessary flexibility to deal appropriately with violations of the rule. It has discretion to tailor sanctions to the particular facts of the case, with which it should be well acquainted.

The references in the former text to wilfulness as a prerequisite to disciplinary action has been deleted. However, in considering the nature and severity of the sanctions to be imposed, the court should take account of the state of the attorney's or party's actual or presumed knowledge when the pleading or other paper was signed. Thus, for example, when a party is not represented by counsel, the absence of legal advice is an appropriate factor to be considered.

Courts currently appear to believe they may impose sanctions on their own motion. See *North American Trading Corp. v. Zale Corp.,* 73 F.R.D. 293 (S.D.N.Y. 1979). Authority to do so has been made explicit in order to overcome the traditional reluctance of courts to intervene unless requested by one of the parties. The detection and punishment of a violation of the signing requirement, encouraged by the amended rule, is part of the court's responsibility for securing the system's effective operation.

If the duty imposed by the rule is violated, the court should have the discretion to impose sanctions on either the attorney, the party the signing attorney represents, or both, or on an unrepresented party who signed the pleading, and the new rule so provides. Although Rule 11 has been silent on the point, courts have claimed the power to impose sanctions on an attorney personally, either by imposing costs or employing the contempt technique. See 5 Wright & Miller, *Federal Practice and Procedure: Civil* § 1334 (1969); 2A Moore, *Federal Practice* ¶ 11.02, at 2104 n. 8. This power has been used infrequently. The amended rule should eliminate any doubt as to the propriety of assessing sanctions against the attorney.

Even though it is the attorney whose signature violates the rule, it may be appropriate under the circumstances of the case to impose a sanction on the client. See *Browning Debenture Holders' Committee v. DASA Corp.,* supra. This modification brings Rule 11 in line with practice under Rule 37, which allows sanctions for abuses during discovery to be imposed upon the party, the attorney, or both.

A party seeking sanctions should give notice to the court and the offending party promptly upon discovering a basis for doing so. The time when sanctions are to be imposed rests in the discretion of the trial judge. However, it is anticipated that in the case of pleadings the sanctions issue under Rule 11 normally will be determined at the end of the litigation, and in the case of motions at the time when the motion is decided or shortly thereafter. The procedure obviously must comport with due process requirements. The particular format to be followed should depend on the circumstances of the situation and the severity of the sanction under consideration. In many situations the judge's participation in the proceedings provides him with full knowledge of the relevant facts and little further inquiry will be necessary.

To assure that the efficiencies achieved through more effective operation of the pleading regimen will not be offset by the cost of satellite litigation over the imposition of sanctions, the court must to the extent possible limit the scope of sanction proceedings to the record. Thus, discovery should be conducted only by leave of the court, and then only in extraordinary circumstances.

Although the encompassing reference to "other papers" in new Rule 11 literally includes discovery papers, the certification requirement in that context is governed by proposed new Rule 26(g). Discovery motions, however, fall within the ambit of Rule 11.

1987 Amendment

The amendments are technical. No substantive change is intended.

1993 Amendments

Purpose of revision. This revision is intended to remedy problems that have arisen in the interpretation and application of the 1983 revision of the rule. For empirical examination of experience under the 1983 rule, see, *e.g.,* New York State Bar Committee on Federal Courts, *Sanctions and Attorneys' Fees* (1987); T. Willging, *The Rule 11 Sanctioning Process* (1989); American Judicature Society, *Report of the Third Circuit Task Force on Federal Rule of Civil Procedure 11* (S. Burbank ed., 1989); E. Wiggins, T. Willging, and D. Stienstra, *Report on Rule 11* (Federal Judicial Center 1991). For book-length analyses of the case law, see G. Joseph, *Sanctions: The Federal Law of Litigation Abuse* (1989); J. Solovy, *The Federal Law of Sanctions* (1991); G. Vairo, *Rule 11 Sanctions: Case Law Perspectives and Preventive Measures* (1991).

The rule retains the principle that attorneys and pro se litigants have an obligation to the court to refrain from conduct that frustrates the aims of Rule 1. The revision broadens the scope of this obligation, but places greater constraints on the imposition of sanctions and should reduce the number of motions for sanctions presented to the court. New subdivision (d) removes from the ambit of this rule all discovery requests, responses, objections, and motions subject to the provisions of Rule 26 through 37.

Subdivision (a). Retained in this subdivision are the provisions requiring signatures on pleadings, written motions, and other papers. Unsigned papers are to be received by the Clerk, but then are to be stricken if the omission of the signature is not corrected promptly after being called to the attention of the attorney or pro se litigant. Correction can be made by signing the paper on file or by submitting a duplicate that contains the signature. A court may require by local rule that papers contain additional identifying information regarding the parties or attorneys, such as telephone numbers to facilitate facsimile transmissions, though, as for omission of a signature, the paper should not be rejected for failure to provide such information.

The sentence in the former rule relating to the effect of answers under oath is no longer needed and has been eliminated. The provision in the former rule that signing a paper constitutes a certificate that it has been read by the signer also has been eliminated as unnecessary. The obligations imposed under subdivision (b) obviously require that a pleading, written motion, or other paper be read before it is filed or submitted to the court.

Subdivisions (b) and (c). These subdivisions restate the provisions requiring attorneys and pro se litigants to conduct a reasonable inquiry into the law and facts before signing pleadings, written motions, and other documents, and prescribing sanctions for violation of these obligations. The revision in part expands the responsibilities of litigants to the court, while providing greater constraints and flexibility in dealing with infractions of the rule. The rule continues to require litigants to "stop-and-think" before initially making legal or factual contentions. It also, however, emphasizes the duty of candor by subjecting litigants to potential sanctions for insisting upon a position after it is no longer tenable and by generally providing protection against sanctions if they withdraw or correct contentions after a potential violation is called to their attention.

The rule applies only to assertions contained in papers filed with or submitted to the court. It does not cover matters arising for the first time during oral presentations to the court, when counsel may make statements that would not have been made if there had been more time for study and reflection. However, a litigant's obligations with respect to the contents of these papers are not measured solely as of the time they are filed with or submitted to the court, but include reaffirming to the court and advocating positions contained in those pleadings and motions after learning that they cease to have any merit. For example, an attorney who during a pretrial conference insists on a claim or defense should be viewed as "presenting to the court" that contention and would be subject to the obligations of subdivision (b) measured as of that time. Similarly, if after a notice of removal is filed, a party urges in federal court the allegations of a pleading filed in state court (whether as claims, defenses, or in disputes regarding removal or remand), it would be viewed as "presenting"—and hence certifying to the district court under Rule 11—those allegations.

The certification with respect to allegations and other factual contentions is revised in recognition that sometimes a litigant may have good reason to believe that a fact is true or false but may need discovery, formal or informal, from opposing parties or third persons to gather and confirm the evidentiary basis for the allegation. Tolerance of factual contentions in initial pleadings by plaintiffs or defendants when specifically identified as made on information and belief does not relieve litigants from the obligation to conduct an appropriate investigation into the facts that is reasonable under the circumstances; it is not a license to join parties, make claims, or present defenses without any factual basis or justification. Moreover, if evidentiary support is not obtained after a reasonable opportunity for further investigation or discovery, the party has a duty under the rule not to persist with that contention. Subdivision (b) does not require a formal amendment to pleadings for which evidentiary support is not obtained, but rather calls upon a litigant not thereafter to advocate such claims or defenses.

The certification is that there is (or likely will be) "evidentiary support" for the allegation, not that the party will prevail with respect to its contention regarding the fact. That summary judgment is rendered against a party does not necessarily mean, for purposes of this certification, that it had no evidentiary support for its position. On the other hand, if a party has evidence with respect to a contention that would suffice to defeat a motion for summary judgment based thereon, it would have sufficient "evidentiary support" for purposes of Rule 11.

Denials of factual contentions involve somewhat different considerations. Often, of course, a denial is premised upon the existence of evidence contradicting the alleged fact. At other times a denial is permissible because, after an appropriate investigation, a party has no information concerning the matter or, indeed, has a reasonable basis for doubting the credibility of the only evidence relevant to the matter. A party should not deny an allegation it knows to be true; but it is not required, simply because it lacks contradictory evidence, to admit an allegation that it believes is not true.

The changes in subdivisions (b)(3) and (b)(4) will serve to equalize the burden of the rule upon plaintiffs and defendants, who under Rule 8(b) are in effect allowed to deny allegations by stating that from their initial investigation they lack sufficient information to form a belief as to the truth of the allegation. If, after further investigation or discovery, a denial is no longer warranted, the defendant should not continue to insist on that denial. While sometimes helpful, formal amendment of the pleadings to withdraw an allegation or denial is not required by subdivision (b).

Arguments for extensions, modifications, or reversals of existing law or for creation of new law do not violate subdivision (b)(2) provided they are "nonfrivolous." This establishes an objective standard, intended to eliminate any "empty-head pure-heart" justification for patently frivolous arguments. However, the extent to which a litigant has researched the issues and found some support for its theories even in minority opinions, in law review articles, or through consultation with other attorneys should certainly be taken into account in determining whether paragraph (2) has been violated. Although arguments for a change of law are not required to be specifically so identified, a contention that is so identified should be viewed with greater tolerance under the rule.

The court has available a variety of possible sanctions to impose for violations, such as striking the offending paper; issuing an admonition, reprimand, or censure; requiring participation in seminars or other educational programs; ordering a fine payable to the court; referring the matter to disciplinary authorities (or, in the case of government attorneys, to the Attorney General, Inspector General, or agency head), etc. *See Manual for Complex Litigation, Second,* § 42.3. The rule does not attempt to enumerate the factors a court should consider in deciding whether to impose a sanction or what sanctions would be appropriate in the circumstances; but, for emphasis, it does specifically note that a sanction may be nonmonetary as well as monetary. Whether the improper conduct was willful, or negligent; whether it was part of a pattern of activity, or an isolated event; whether it infected the entire pleading, or only one particular count or defense; whether the person has engaged in similar conduct in other litigation; whether it was intended to injure; what effect it had on the litigation process in time or expense; whether the responsible person is trained in the law; what amount, given the financial resources of the responsible person, is needed to deter that person from repetition in the same case; what amount is needed to deter similar activity by other litigants: all of these may in a particular case be proper considerations. The court has significant discretion in determining what sanctions, if any, should be imposed for a violation, subject to the principle that the sanctions should not be more severe than reasonably necessary to deter repetition of the conduct by the offending person or comparable conduct by similarly situated persons.

Since the purpose of Rule 11 sanctions is to deter rather than to compensate, the rule provides that, if a monetary sanction is imposed, it should ordinarily be paid into court as a penalty. However, under unusual circumstances, particularly for (b)(1) violations, deterrence may be ineffective unless the sanction not only requires the person violating the rule to make a monetary payment, but also directs that some or all of this payment be made to those injured by the violation. Accordingly, the rule authorizes the court, if requested in a motion and if so warranted, to award attorney's fees to another party. Any such award to another party, however, should not exceed the expenses and attorneys' fees for the services directly and unavoidably caused by the violation of the certification requirement. If, for example, a wholly unsupportable count were included in a multi-count complaint or counterclaim for the purpose of needlessly increasing the cost of litigation to an impecunious adversary, any award of expenses should be limited to those directly caused by inclusion of the improper count, and not those resulting from the filing of the complaint or answer itself. The award should not provide compensation for services that could have been avoided by an earlier disclosure of evidence or an earlier challenge to the groundless claims or defenses. Moreover, partial reimbursement of fees may constitute a sufficient deterrent with respect to violations by persons having modest financial resources. In cases brought under statutes providing for fees to be awarded to prevailing parties, the court should not employ cost-shifting under this rule in a manner that would be inconsistent with the standards that govern the statutory award of fees, such as stated in *Christiansburg Garment Co. v. EEOC,* 434 U.S. 412 (1978).

The sanction should be imposed on the persons—whether attorneys, law firms, or parties—who have violated the rule or who may be determined to be responsible for the violation. The person signing, filing, submitting, or advocating a document has a nondelegable responsibility to the court, and in most situations is the person to be sanctioned for a violation. Absent exceptional circumstances, a law firm is to be held also responsible when, as a result of a motion under subdivision (c)(1)(A), one of its partners, associates, or employees is determined to have violated the rule. Since such a motion may be filed only if the offending paper is not withdrawn or corrected within 21 days after service of the motion, it is appropriate that the law firm ordinarily be viewed as jointly responsible under established principles of agency. This provision is designed to remove the restrictions of the former rule. *Cf. Pavelic & LeFlore v. Marvel Entertainment Group,* 493 U.S. 120 (1989) (1983 version of Rule 11 does not permit sanctions against law firm of attorney signing groundless complaint).

The revision permits the court to consider whether other attorneys in the firm, co-counsel, other law firms, or the party itself should be held accountable for their part in causing a violation. When appropriate,

125

the court can make an additional inquiry in order to determine whether the sanction should be imposed on such persons, firms, or parties either in addition to or, in unusual circumstances, instead of the person actually making the presentation to the court. For example, such an inquiry may be appropriate in cases involving governmental agencies or other institutional parties that frequently impose substantial restrictions on the discretion of individual attorneys employed by it.

Sanctions that involve monetary awards (such as a fine or an award of attorney's fees) may not be imposed on a represented party for causing a violation of subdivision (b)(2), involving frivolous contentions of law. Monetary responsibility for such violations is more properly placed solely on the party's attorneys. With this limitation, the rule should not be subject to attack under the Rules Enabling Act. See *Willy v. Coastal Corp.,* 503 U.S. 131 (1992); *Business Guides, Inc. v. Chromatic Communications Enter. Inc.,* 498 U.S. 533 (1991). This restriction does not limit the court's power to impose sanctions or remedial orders that may have collateral financial consequences upon a party, such as dismissal of a claim, preclusion of a defense, or preparation of amended pleadings.

Explicit provision is made for litigants to be provided notice of the alleged violation and an opportunity to respond before sanctions are imposed. Whether the matter should be decided solely on the basis of written submissions or should be scheduled for oral argument (or, indeed, for evidentiary presentation) will depend on the circumstances. If the court imposes a sanction, it must, unless waived, indicate its reasons in a written order or on the record; the court should not ordinarily have to explain its denial of a motion for sanctions. Whether a violation has occurred and what sanctions, if any, to impose for a violation are matters committed to the discretion of the trial court; accordingly, as under current law, the standard for appellate review of these decisions will be for abuse of discretion. *See Cooter & Gell v. Hartmarx Corp.,* 496 U.S. 384 (1990) (noting, however, that an abuse would be established if the court based its ruling on an erroneous view of the law or on a clearly erroneous assessment of the evidence).

The revision leaves for resolution on a case-by-case basis, considering the particular circumstances involved, the question as to when a motion for violation of Rule 11 should be served and when, if filed, it should be decided. Ordinarily the motion should be served promptly after the inappropriate paper is filed, and, if delayed too long, may be viewed as untimely. In other circumstances, it should not be served until the other party has had a reasonable opportunity for discovery. Given the "safe harbor" provisions discussed below, a party cannot delay serving its Rule 11 motion until conclusion of the case (or judicial rejection of the offending contention).

Rule 11 motions should not be made or threatened for minor, inconsequential violations of the standards prescribed by subdivision (b). They should not be employed as a discovery device or to test the legal sufficiency or efficacy of allegations in the pleadings; other motions are available for those purposes. Nor should Rule 11 motions be prepared to emphasize the merits of a party's position, to exact an unjust settlement, to intimidate an adversary into withdrawing contentions that are fairly debatable, to increase the costs of litigation, to create a conflict of interest between attorney and client, or to seek disclosure of matters otherwise protected by the attorney-client privilege or the work-product doctrine. As under the prior rule, the court may defer its ruling (or its decision as to the identity of the persons to be sanctioned) until final resolution of the case in order to avoid immediate conflicts of interest and to reduce the disruption created if a disclosure of attorney-client communications is needed to determine whether a violation occurred or to identify the person responsible for the violation.

The rule provides that requests for sanctions must be made as a separate motion, *i.e.,* not simply included as an additional prayer for relief contained in another motion. The motion for sanctions is not, however, to be filed until at least 21 days (or such other period as the court may set) after being served. If, during this period, the alleged violation is corrected, as by withdrawing (whether formally or informally) some allegation or contention, the motion should not be filed with the court. These provisions are intended to provide a type of "safe harbor" against motions under Rule 11 in that a party will not be subject to sanctions on the basis of another party's motion unless, after receiving the motion, it refuses to withdraw that position or to acknowledge candidly that it does not currently have evidence to support a specified allegation. Under the former rule, parties were sometimes reluctant to abandon a questionable contention lest that be viewed as evidence of a violation of Rule 11; under the revision, the timely withdrawal of a contention will protect a party against a motion for sanctions.

To stress the seriousness of a motion for sanctions and to define precisely the conduct claimed to violate the rule, the revision provides that the "safe harbor" period begins to run only upon service of the motion. In most cases, however, counsel should be expected to give informal notice to the other party, whether in person or by a telephone call or letter, of a potential violation before proceeding to prepare and serve a Rule 11 motion.

As under former Rule 11, the filing of a motion for sanctions is itself subject to the requirements of the rule and can lead to sanctions. However, service of a cross motion under Rule 11 should rarely be needed since under the revision the court may award to the person who prevails on a motion under Rule 11— whether the movant or the target of the motion—reasonable expenses, including attorney's fees, incurred in presenting or opposing the motion.

The power of the court to act on its own initiative is retained, but with the condition that this be done through a show cause order. This procedure provides the person with notice and an opportunity to respond. The revision provides that a monetary sanction imposed after a court-initiated show cause order be limited to a penalty payable to the court and that it be imposed only if the show cause order is issued before any voluntary dismissal or an agreement of the parties to settle the claims made by or against the litigant. Parties settling a case should not be subsequently faced with an unexpected order from the court leading to monetary sanctions that might have affected their willingness to settle or voluntarily dismiss a case. Since show cause orders will ordinarily be issued only in situations that are akin to a contempt of court, the rule does not provide a "safe harbor" to a litigant for withdrawing a claim, defense, etc., after a show cause order has been issued on the court's own initiative. Such corrective action, however, should be taken into account in deciding what—if any—sanction to impose if, after consideration of the litigant's response, the court concludes that a violation has occurred.

Subdivision (d). Rules 26(g) and 37 establish certification standards and sanctions that apply to discovery disclosures, requests, responses, objections, and motions. It is appropriate that Rules 26 through 37, which are specially designed for the discovery process, govern such documents and conduct rather than the more general provisions of Rule 11. Subdivision (d) has been added to accomplish this result.

Rule 11 is not the exclusive source for control of improper presentations of claims, defenses, or contentions. It does not supplant statutes permitting awards of attorney's fees to prevailing parties or alter the principles governing such awards. It does not inhibit the court in punishing for contempt, in exercising its inherent powers, or in imposing sanctions, awarding expenses, or directing remedial action authorized under other rules or under 28 U.S.C. § 1927. *See Chambers v. NASCO,* 501 U.S. 32 (1991). Chambers cautions, however, against reliance upon inherent powers if appropriate sanctions can be imposed under provisions such as Rule 11, and the procedures specified in Rule 11—notice, opportunity to respond, and findings—should ordinarily be employed when imposing a sanction under the court's inherent powers. Finally, it should be noted that Rule 11 does not preclude a party from initiating an independent action for malicious prosecution or abuse of process.

2007 Amendment

The language of Rule 11 has been amended as part of the general restyling of the Civil Rules to make them more easily understood and to make style and terminology consistent throughout the rules. These changes are intended to be stylistic only.

Providing an e-mail address is useful, but does not of itself signify consent to filing or service by e-mail.

Rule 12.   Defenses and Objections: When and How Presented; Motion for Judgment on the Pleadings; Consolidating Motions; Waiving Defenses; Pretrial Hearing

(a)   Time to Serve a Responsive Pleading.

    (1)   *In General.* Unless another time is specified by this rule or a federal statute, the time for serving a responsive pleading is as follows:

        (A) A defendant must serve an answer:

            (i) within 21 days after being served with the summons and complaint; or

> (ii) if it has timely waived service under Rule 4(d), within 60 days after the request for a waiver was sent, or within 90 days after it was sent to the defendant outside any judicial district of the United States.

> **(B)** A party must serve an answer to a counterclaim or crossclaim within 21 days after being served with the pleading that states the counterclaim or crossclaim.

> **(C)** A party must serve a reply to an answer within 21 days after being served with an order to reply, unless the order specifies a different time.

(2) *United States and Its Agencies, Officers, or Employees Sued in an Official Capacity.* The United States, a United States agency, or a United States officer or employee sued only in an official capacity must serve an answer to a complaint, counterclaim, or crossclaim within 60 days after service on the United States attorney.

(3) *United States Officers or Employees Sued in an Individual Capacity.* A United States officer or employee sued in an individual capacity for an act or omission occurring in connection with duties performed on the United States' behalf must serve an answer to a complaint, counterclaim, or crossclaim within 60 days after service on the officer or employee or service on the United States attorney, whichever is later.

(4) *Effect of a Motion.* Unless the court sets a different time, serving a motion under this rule alters these periods as follows:

> **(A)** if the court denies the motion or postpones its disposition until trial, the responsive pleading must be served within 14 days after notice of the court's action; or

> **(B)** if the court grants a motion for a more definite statement, the responsive pleading must be served within 14 days after the more definite statement is served.

(b) **How to Present Defenses.** Every defense to a claim for relief in any pleading must be asserted in the responsive pleading if one is required. But a party may assert the following defenses by motion:

(1) lack of subject-matter jurisdiction;

(2) lack of personal jurisdiction;

(3) improper venue;

(4) insufficient process;

(5) insufficient service of process;

(6) failure to state a claim upon which relief can be granted; and

(7) failure to join a party under Rule 19.

A motion asserting any of these defenses must be made before pleading if a responsive pleading is allowed. If a pleading sets out a claim for relief that does not require a responsive pleading, an opposing party may assert at trial any defense to that claim. No defense or objection is waived by joining it with one or more other defenses or objections in a responsive pleading or in a motion.

(c) **Motion for Judgment on the Pleadings.** After the pleadings are closed—but early enough not to delay trial—a party may move for judgment on the pleadings.

(d) **Result of Presenting Matters Outside the Pleadings.** If, on a motion under Rule 12(b)(6) or 12(c), matters outside the pleadings are presented to and not excluded by the court, the motion must be treated as one for summary judgment under Rule 56. All parties must be given a reasonable opportunity to present all the material that is pertinent to the motion.

(e) **Motion for a More Definite Statement.** A party may move for a more definite statement of a pleading to which a responsive pleading is allowed but which is so vague or ambiguous that the party cannot reasonably prepare a response. The motion must be made before filing a responsive pleading and must point out the defects complained of and the details desired. If the court orders a more definite statement and the order is not obeyed within 14 days after notice of the order or within the time the court sets, the court may strike the pleading or issue any other appropriate order.

(f) Motion to Strike. The court may strike from a pleading an insufficient defense or any redundant, immaterial, impertinent, or scandalous matter. The court may act:

(1) on its own; or

(2) on motion made by a party either before responding to the pleading or, if a response is not allowed, within 21 days after being served with the pleading.

(g) Joining Motions.

(1) *Right to Join.* A motion under this rule may be joined with any other motion allowed by this rule.

(2) *Limitation on Further Motions.* Except as provided in Rule 12(h)(2) or (3), a party that makes a motion under this rule must not make another motion under this rule raising a defense or objection that was available to the party but omitted from its earlier motion.

(h) Waiving and Preserving Certain Defenses.

(1) *When Some Are Waived.* A party waives any defense listed in Rule 12(b)(2)–(5) by:

(A) omitting it from a motion in the circumstances described in Rule 12(g)(2); or

(B) failing to either:

(i) make it by motion under this rule; or

(ii) include it in a responsive pleading or in an amendment allowed by Rule 15(a)(1) as a matter of course.

(2) *When to Raise Others.* Failure to state a claim upon which relief can be granted, to join a person required by Rule 19(b), or to state a legal defense to a claim may be raised:

(A) in any pleading allowed or ordered under Rule 7(a);

(B) by a motion under Rule 12(c); or

(C) at trial.

(3) *Lack of Subject-Matter Jurisdiction.* If the court determines at any time that it lacks subject-matter jurisdiction, the court must dismiss the action.

(i) Hearing Before Trial. If a party so moves, any defense listed in Rule 12(b)(1)–(7)—whether made in a pleading or by motion—and a motion under Rule 12(c) must be heard and decided before trial unless the court orders a deferral until trial.

(Amended December 27, 1946, effective March 19, 1948; January 21, 1963, effective July 1, 1963; February 28, 1966, effective July 1, 1966; March 2, 1987, effective August 1, 1987; April 22, 1993, effective December 1, 1993; April 17, 2000, effective December 1, 2000; April 30, 2007, effective December 1, 2007; March 26, 2009, effective December 1, 2009.)

ADVISORY COMMITTEE NOTES

1937 Adoption

Note to Subdivision (a). 1. Compare [former] Equity Rules 12 (Issue of Subpoena—Time for Answer) and 31 (Reply—When Required—When Cause at Issue); 4 Mont.Rev.Codes Ann. (1935) §§ 9107, 9158; N.Y.C. P.A. (1937) § 263; N.Y.R.C.P. (1937) Rules 109–111.

2.   U.S.C., Title 28, § 763 (now § 547) (Petition in action against United States; service; appearance by district attorney) provides that the United States as a defendant shall have 60 days within which to answer or otherwise defend. This and other statutes which provide 60 days for the United States or an officer or agency thereof to answer or otherwise defend are continued by this rule. In so far as any statutes not excepted in rule 81 provide a different time for a defendant to defend, such statutes are modified. See U.S.C., Title 28, [former] § 45 (District courts; practice and procedure in certain cases under the interstate commerce laws) (30 days).

3.   Compare the last sentence of [former] Equity Rule 29 (Defenses—How Presented) and N.Y.C.P.A. (1937) § 283. See Rule 15(a) for time within which to plead to an amended pleading.

Note to Subdivisions (b) and (d). 1. See generally [former] Equity Rules 29 (Defenses—How Presented), 33 (Testing Sufficiency of Defense), 43 (Defect of Parties—Resisting Objection), and 44 (Defect of Parties—Tardy Objection); N.Y.C.P.A. (1937) §§ 277–280; N.Y.R.C.P. (1937) Rules 106–112; *English Rules Under the Judicature Act* (The Annual Practice, 1937) O. 25, r.r. 1–4; Clark, *Code Pleading,* 1928, pp. 371–381.

2.   For provisions authorizing defenses to be made in the answer or reply see *English Rules Under the Judicature Act,* (The Annual Practice, 1937) O. 25, r.r. 1–4; 1 Miss.Code Ann. (1930) §§ 378, 379. Compare Equity Rule 29 (Defenses—How Presented); U.S.C.A., Title 28, [former] § 45 (District Courts; practice and procedure in certain cases under the interstate commerce laws). U.S.C., Title 28, [former] § 45, substantially continued by this rule, provides: "No replication need be filed to the answer, and objections to the sufficiency of the petition or answer as not setting forth a cause of action or defense must be taken at the final hearing or by motion to dismiss the petition based on said grounds, which motion may be made at any time before answer is filed." Compare Calif.Code Civ.Proc., (Deering, 1937) § 433; 4 Nev.Comp.Laws (Hillyer, 1929) § 8600. For provisions that the defendant may demur and answer at the same time, see Calif.Code Civ.Proc. (Deering, 1937) § 431; 4 Nev.Comp.Laws (Hillyer, 1929) § 8598.

3.   [Former] Equity Rule 29 (Defenses—How Presented) abolished demurrers and provided that defenses in point of law arising on the face of the bill should be made by motion to dismiss or in the answer, with further provision that every such point of law going to the whole or material part of the cause or causes stated might be called up and disposed of before final hearing "at the discretion of the court." Likewise many state practices have abolished the demurrer, or retain it only to attack substantial and not formal defects. See 6 Tenn.Code Ann. (Williams, 1934) § 8784; Ala.Code Ann. (Michie, 1928) § 9479; 2 Mass.Gen.Laws (Ter.Ed., 1932) ch. 231, §§ 15–18; Kansas Gen.Stat.Ann. (1935) §§ 60–705, 60–706.

Note to Subdivision (c). Compare [former] Equity Rule 33 (Testing Sufficiency of Defense); N.Y.R.C.P. (1937) Rules 111 and 112.

Note to Subdivisions (e) and (f). Compare [former] Equity Rules 20 (Further and Particular Statement in Pleading May be Required) and 21 (Scandal and Impertinence); *English Rules Under the Judicature Act* (The Annual Practice, 1937) O. 19, r.r. 7, 7a, 7b, 8; 4 Mont.Rev.Codes Ann. (1935) §§ 9166, 9167; N.Y.C.P.A. (1937) § 247; N.Y.C.P.A. (1937) Rules 103, 115, 116, 117; Wyo.Rev.Stat.Ann. (Courtright, 1931) §§ 89–1033, 89–1034.

Note to Subdivision (g). Compare Rules of the District Court of the United States for the District of Columbia (1937) Equity Rule 11; N.M. Rules of Pleading, Practice and Procedure, 38 N.M.Rep. vii. [105–408] (1934); Wash.Gen.Rules of the Superior Courts, 1 Wash.Rev.Stat.Ann. (Remington, 1932) p. 160, Rule VI(e) and (f).

Note to Subdivision (h). Compare Calif.Code Civ.Proc. (Deering, 1937) § 434; 2 Minn.Stat. (Mason, 1927) § 9252; N.Y.C.P.A. (1937) §§ 278 and 279; Wash.Gen.Rules of the Superior Courts, 1 Wash.Rev.Stat.Ann. (Remington, 1932) p. 160, Rule VI(e). This rule continues U.S.C.A., Title 28, former § 80 [now 1359, 1447, 1919] (Dismissal or remand) (of action over which district court lacks jurisdiction), while U.S.C.A., Title 28, § 399 (Amendments to show diverse citizenship) is continued by Rule 15.

1946 Amendment

Note. Subdivision (a). Various minor alterations in language have been made to improve the statement of the rule. All references to bills of particulars have been stricken in accordance with changes made in subdivision (e).

Subdivision (b). The addition of defense (7), "failure to join an indispensable party", cures an omission in the rules which are silent as to the mode of raising such failure. See Commentary, *Manner of Raising Objection of Non-Joinder of Indispensable Party,* 1940, 2 Fed.Rules Serv. 658, and, 1942, 5 Fed.Rules Serv.

820. In one case, *United States v. Metropolitan Life Ins. Co.*, E.D.Pa.1941, 36 F.Supp. 399, the failure to join an indispensable party was raised under Rule 12(c).

Rule 12(b)(6), permitting a motion to dismiss for failure of the complaint to state a claim on which relief can be granted, is substantially the same as the old demurrer for failure of a pleading to state a cause of action. Some courts have held that as the rule by its terms refers to statements in the complaint, extraneous matter on affidavits, depositions or otherwise, may not be introduced in support of the motion, or to resist it. On the other hand, in many cases the district courts have permitted the introduction of such material. When these cases have reached circuit courts of appeals in situations where the extraneous material so received shows that there is no genuine issue as to any material question of fact and that on the undisputed facts as disclosed by the affidavits or depositions, one party or the other is entitled to judgment as a matter of law, the circuit courts, properly enough, have been reluctant to dispose of the case merely on the face of the pleading, and in the interest of prompt disposition of the action have made a final disposition of it. In dealing with such situations the Second Circuit has made the sound suggestion that whatever its label or original basis, the motion may be treated as a motion for summary judgment and disposed of as such. *Samara v. United States*, C.C.A.2, 1942, 129 F.2d 594, certiorari denied 63 S.Ct. 258, 317 U.S. 686, 87 L.Ed. 549; *Boro Hall Corp. v. General Motors Corp.*, C.C.A.2, 1942, 124 F.2d 822, certiorari denied 63 S.Ct. 436, 317 U.S. 695, 87 L.Ed. 556. See, also, *Kithcart v. Metropolitan Life Ins. Co.*, C.C.A.8, 1945, 150 F.2d 997.

It has also been suggested that this practice could be justified on the ground that the federal rules permit "speaking" motions. The Committee entertains the view that on motion under Rule 12(b)(6) to dismiss for failure of the complaint to state a good claim, the trial court should have authority to permit the introduction of extraneous matter, such as may be offered on a motion for summary judgment, and if it does not exclude such matter the motion should then be treated as a motion for summary judgment and disposed of in the manner and on the conditions stated in Rule 56 relating to summary judgments, and, of course, in such a situation, when the case reaches the circuit court of appeals, that court should treat the motion in the same way. The Committee believes that such practice, however, should be tied to the summary judgment rule. The term "speaking motion" is not mentioned in the rules, and if there is such a thing its limitations are undefined. Where extraneous matter is received, by tying further proceedings to the summary judgment rule the courts have a definite basis in the rules for disposing of the motion.

The Committee emphasizes particularly the fact that the summary judgment rule does not permit a case to be disposed of by judgment on the merits on affidavits, which disclose a conflict on a material issue of fact, and unless this practice is tied to the summary judgment, rule, the extent to which a court, on the introduction of such extraneous matter, may resolve questions of fact on conflicting proof would be left uncertain.

The decisions dealing with this general situation may be generally grouped as follows: (1) cases dealing with the use of affidavits and other extraneous material on motions; (2) cases reversing judgments to prevent final determination on mere pleading allegations alone.

Under group (1) are: *Boro Hall Corp. v. General Motors Corp.*, C.C.A.2, 1942, 124 F.2d 822, certiorari denied 1943, 63 S.Ct. 436, 317 U.S. 695, 87 L.Ed. 556; *Gallup v. Caldwell,* C.C.A.3, 1941, 120 F.2d 90; *Central Mexico Light & Power Co. v. Munch,* C.C.A.2, 1940, 116 F.2d 85; *National Labor Relations Board v. Montgomery Ward & Co.*, 1944, 144 F.2d 528, 79 U.S.App.D.C. 200, certiorari denied 1944, 65 S.Ct. 134, 323 U.S. 774, 89 L.Ed. 619; *Urquhart v. American-La France Foamite Corp.*, 1944, 144 F.2d 542, 79 U.S.App.D.C. 219; *Samara v. United States*, C.C.A.2, 1942, 129 F.2d 594; *Cohen v. American Window Glass Co.*, C.C.A.2, 1942, 126 F.2d 111; *Sperry Products Inc. v. Association of American Railroads*, C.C.A.2, 1942, 132 F.2d 408; *Joint Council Dining Car Employees Local 370 v. Delaware, Lackawanna and Western R. Co.*, C.C.A.2, 1946, 157 F.2d 417; *Weeks v. Bareco Oil Co.*, C.C.A.7, 1941, 125 F.2d 84; *Carroll v. Morrison Hotel Corp.*, C.C.A.7, 1945, 149 F.2d 404; *Victory v. Manning*, C.C.A.3, 1942, 128 F.2d 415; *Locals No. 1470, No. 1469, and No. 1512 of International Longshoremen's Association v. Southern Pacific Co.*, C.C.A.5, 1942, 131 F.2d 605; *Lucking v. Delano*, C.C.A.6, 1942, 129 F.2d 283; *San Francisco Lodge No. 68 of International Association of Machinists v. Forrestal*, Cal.1944, 58 F.Supp. 466; *Benson v. Export Equipment Corp.*, 1945, 164 P.2d 380, 49 N.M. 356, construing New Mexico rule identical with Rule 12(b)(6); *F. E. Myers & Bros. Co. v. Gould Pumps, Inc.*, W.D.N.Y.1946, 9 Fed.Rules Serv. 12b.33, Case 2, 5 F.R.D. 132. Cf. *Kohler v. Jacobs*, C.C.A.5, 1943, 138 F.2d 440; *Cohen v. United States*, C.C.A.8, 1942, 129 F.2d 733.

Under group (2) are: *Sparks v. England,* C.C.A.8, 1940, 113 F.2d 579; *Continental Collieries, Inc. v. Shober,* C.C.A.3, 1942, 130 F.2d 631; *Downey v. Palmer,* C.C.A.2, 1940, 114 F.2d 116; *DeLoach v. Crowley's Inc.,* C.C.A.5, 1942, 128 F.2d 378; *Leimer v. State Mutual Life Assurance Co. of Worcester, Mass.,* C.C.A.8, 1940, 108 F.2d 302; *Rossiter v. Vogel,* C.C.A.2, 1943, 134 F.2d 908, compare s.c., C.C.A.2, 1945, 148 F.2d 292; *Karl Kiefer Machine Co. v. United States Bottlers Machinery Co.,* C.C.A.7, 1940, 113 F.2d 356; *Chicago Metallic Mfg. Co. v. Edward Katzinger Co.,* C.C.A.7, 1941, 123 F.2d 518; *Louisiana Farmers' Protective Union, Inc. v. Great Atlantic & Pacific Tea Co. of America, Inc.,* C.C.A.8, 1942, 131 F.2d 419; *Publicity Bldg. Realty Corp. v. Hannegan,* C.C.A.8, 1943, 139 F.2d 583; *Dioguardi v. Durning,* C.C.A.2, 1944, 139 F.2d 774; *Package Closure Corp. v. Sealright Co., Inc.,* C.C.A.2, 1944, 141 F.2d 972; *Tahir Erk v. Glenn L. Martin Co.,* C.C.A.4, 1941, 116 F.2d 865; *Bell v. Preferred Life Assurance Society of Montgomery, Ala.,* 1943, 64 S.Ct. 5, 320 U.S. 238, 88 L.Ed. 15.

The addition at the end of subdivision (b) makes it clear that on a motion under Rule 12(b)(6) extraneous material may not be considered if the court excludes it, but that if the court does not exclude such material the motion shall be treated as a motion for summary judgment and disposed of as provided in Rule 56. It will also be observed that if a motion under Rule 12(b)(6) is thus converted into a summary judgment motion, the amendment insures that both parties shall be given a reasonable opportunity to submit affidavits and extraneous proofs to avoid taking a party by surprise through the conversion of the motion into a motion for summary judgment. In this manner and to this extent the amendment regularizes the practice above described. As the courts are already dealing with cases in this way, the effect of this amendment is really only to define the practice carefully and apply the requirements of the summary judgment rule in the disposition of the motion.

Subdivision (c). The sentence appended to subdivision (c) performs the same function and is grounded on the same reasons as the corresponding sentence added in subdivision (b).

Subdivision (d). The change here was made necessary because of the addition of defense (7) in subdivision (b).

Subdivision (e). References in this subdivision to a bill of particulars have been deleted, and the motion provided for is confined to one for more definite statement to be obtained only in cases where the movant cannot reasonably be required to frame an answer or other responsive pleading to the pleading in question. With respect to preparations for trial, the party is properly relegated to the various methods of examination and discovery provided in the rules for that purpose. *Slusher v. Jones,* E.D.Ky.1943, 7 Fed.Rules Serv. 12e.231, Case 5, 3 F.R.D. 168; *Best Foods, Inc. v. General Mills, Inc.,* D.Del.1943, 7 Fed.Rules Serv. 12e.231, Case 7, 3 F.R.D. 275; *Braden v. Callaway,* E.D.Tenn.1943, 8 Fed.Rules Serv. 12e.231, Case 1 ("... most courts ... conclude that the definiteness required is only such as will be sufficient for the party to prepare responsive pleadings"). Accordingly, the reference to the 20 day time limit has also been eliminated, since the purpose of this present provision is to state a time period where the motion for a bill is made for the purpose of preparing for trial.

Rule 12(e) as originally drawn has been the subject of more judicial rulings than any other part of the rules, and has been much criticized by commentators, judges and members of the bar. See general discussion and cases cited in 1 Moore's *Federal Practice,* 1938, Cum.Supplement, § 12.07, under "Page 657"; also, Holtzoff, *New Federal Procedure and the Courts,* 1940, 35–41. And compare vote of Second Circuit Conference of Circuit and District Judges, June 1940, recommending the abolition of the bill of particulars; *Sun Valley Mfg. Co. v. Mylish,* E.D.Pa.1944, 8 Fed.Rules Serv. 12e.231, Case 6 ("Our experience ... has demonstrated not only that 'the office of the bill of particulars is fast becoming obsolete' ... but that in view of the adequate discovery procedure available under the Rules, motions for bills of particulars should be abolished altogether."); *Walling v. American Steamship Co.,* W.D.N.Y.1945, 4 F.R.D. 355, 8 Fed.Rules Serv. 12e.244, Case 8 ("... the adoption of the rule was ill advised. It has led to confusion, duplication and delay.") The tendency of some courts freely to grant extended bills of particulars has served to neutralize any helpful benefits derived from rule 8, and has overlooked the intended use of the rules on depositions and discovery. The words "or to prepare for trial"—eliminated by the proposed amendment—have sometimes been seized upon as grounds for compulsory statement in the opposing pleading of all the details which the movant would have to meet at the trial. On the other hand, many courts have in effect read these words out of the rule. See *Walling v. Alabama Pipe Co.,* W.D.Mo.1942, 3 F.R.D. 159, 6 Fed.Rules Serv. 12e.244, Case 7; *Fleming v. Mason & Dixon Lines, Inc.,* E.D.Tenn.1941, 42 F.Supp. 230; *Kellogg Co. v. National Biscuit Co.,* D.N.J.1941, 38 F.Supp. 643; *Brown v. H. L. Green Co.,* S.D.N.Y.1943, 7 Fed.Rules Serv. 12e.231, Case 6;

Pedersen v. Standard Accident Ins. Co., W.D.Mo.1945, 8 Fed.Rules Serv. 12e.231, Case 8; *Bowles v. Ohse,* D.Neb.1945, 4 F.R.D. 403, 9 Fed.Rules Serv. 12e.231, Case 1; *Klages v. Cohen,* E.D.N.Y.1945, 9 Fed.Rules Serv. 8a.25, Case 4; *Bowles v. Lawrence,* D.Mass.1945, 8 Fed.Rules Serv. 12e.231, Case 19; *McKinney Tool & Mfg. Co. v. Hoyt,* N.D.Ohio 1945, 9 Fed.Rules Serv. 12e.235, Case 1; *Bowles v. Jack,* D.Minn.1945, 5 F.R.D. 1, 9 Fed.Rules Serv. 12e.244, Case 9. And it has been urged from the bench that the phrase be stricken, *Poole v. White,* N.D.W.Va.1941, 5 Fed.Rules Serv. 12e.231, Case 4, 2 F.R.D. 40. See also *Bowles v. Gabel,* W.D.Mo.1946, 9 Fed.Rules Serv. 12e.244, Case 10. ("The courts have never favored that portion of the rules which undertook to justify a motion of this kind for the purpose of aiding counsel in preparing his case for trial.").

Subdivision (f). This amendment affords a specific method of raising the insufficiency of a defense, a matter which has troubled some courts, although attack has been permitted in one way or another. See *Dysart v. Remington-Rand, Inc.,* D.Conn.1939, 31 F.Supp. 296; *Eastman Kodak Co. v. McAuley,* S.D.N.Y.1941, 4 Fed.Rules Serv., 12f.21, Case 8, 2 F.R.D. 21; *Schenley Distillers Corp. v. Renken,* E.D.S.C.1940, 34 F.Supp. 678; *Yale Transport Corp. v. Yellow Truck & Coach Mfg. Co.,* S.D.N.Y.1944, 3 F.R.D. 440; *United States v. Turner Milk Co.,* N.D.Ill.1941, 4 Fed.Rules Serv. 12b.51, Case 3, 1 F.R.D. 643; *Teiger v. Stephan Oderwald, Inc.,* S.D.N.Y.1940, 31 F.Supp. 626; *Teplitsky v. Pennsylvania R. Co.,* N.D.Ill.1941, 38 F.Supp. 535; *Callagher v. Carroll,* E.D.N.Y.1939, 27 F.Supp. 568; *United States v. Palmer,* S.D.N.Y.1939, 28 F.Supp. 936. And see *Indemnity Ins. Co. of North America v. Pan American Airways, Inc.,* S.D.N.Y.1944, 58 F.Supp. 338; Commentary, *Modes of Attacking Insufficient Defenses in the Answer,* 901, 1939, 1 Fed.Rules Serv. 669, 1940, 2 Fed.Rules Serv. 640.

Subdivision (g). The change in title conforms with the companion provision in subdivision (h).

The alteration of the "except" clause requires that other than provided in subdivision (h) a party who resorts to a motion to raise defenses specified in the rule, must include in one motion all that are then available to him. Under the original rule defenses which could be raised by motion were divided into two groups which could be the subjects of two successive motions.

Subdivision (h). The addition of the phrase relating to indispensable parties is one of necessity.

1963 Amendment

This amendment conforms to the amendment of Rule 4(e). See also the Advisory Committee's Note to amended Rule 4(b).

1966 Amendment

Subdivision (b)(7). The terminology of this subdivision is changed to accord with the amendment of Rule 19. See the Advisory Committee's Note to Rule 19, as amended, especially the third paragraph therein before the caption "Subdivision (c)."

Subdivision (g). Subdivision (g) has forbidden a defendant who makes a preanswer motion under this rule from making a further motion presenting any defense or objection which was available to him at the time he made the first motion and which he could have included, but did not in fact include therein. Thus if the defendant moves before answer to dismiss the complaint for failure to state a claim, he is barred from making a further motion presenting the defense of improper venue, if that defense was available to him when he made his original motion. Amended subdivision (g) is to the same effect. This required consolidation of defenses and objections in a Rule 12 motion is salutary in that it works against piecemeal consideration of a case. For exceptions to the requirement of consolidation, see the last clause of subdivision (g), referring to new subdivision (h)(2).

Subdivision (h). The question has arisen whether an omitted defense which cannot be made the basis of a second motion may nevertheless be pleaded in the answer. Subdivision (h) called for waiver of "* * * defenses and objections which he [defendant] does not present * * * by motion * * * or, if he has made no motion, in his answer * * * ." If the clause "if he has made no motion," was read literally, it seemed that the omitted defense was waived and could not be pleaded in the answer. On the other hand, the clause might be read as adding nothing of substance to the preceding words; in that event it appeared that a defense was not waived by reason of being omitted from the motion and might be set up in the answer. The decisions were divided. Favoring waiver, see *Keef v. Derounian,* 6 F.R.D. 11 (N.D.Ill.1946); *Elbinger v. Precision Metal Workers Corp.,* 18 F.R.D. 467 (E.D.Wis.1956); see also *Rensing v. Turner Aviation Corp.,* 166 F.Supp. 790

(N.D.Ill.1958); *P. Beiersdorf & Co. v. Duke Laboratories, Inc.,* 10 F.R.D. 282 (S.D.N.Y.1950); *Neset v. Christensen,* 92 F.Supp. 78 (E.D.N.Y.1950). Opposing waiver, see *Phillips v. Baker,* 121 F.2d 752 (9th Cir.1941); *Crum v. Graham,* 32 F.R.D. 173 (D.Mont.1963) (regretfully following the Phillips case); see also *Birnbaum v. Birrell,* 9 F.R.D. 72 (S.D.N.Y.1948); *Johnson v. Joseph Schlitz Brewing Co.,* 33 F.Supp. 176 (E.D.Tenn.1940); cf. *Carter v. American Bus Lines, Inc.,* 22 F.R.D. 323 (D.Neb.1958).

Amended subdivision (h)(1)(A) eliminates the ambiguity and states that certain specified defenses which were available to a party when he made a preanswer motion, but which he omitted from the motion, are waived. The specified defenses are lack of jurisdiction over the person, improper venue, insufficiency of process, and insufficiency of service of process (see Rule 12(b)(2)–(5)). A party who by motion invites the court to pass upon a threshold defense should bring forward all the specified defenses he then has and thus allow the court to do a reasonably complete job. The waiver reinforces the policy of subdivision (g) forbidding successive motions.

By amended subdivision (h)(1)(B), the specified defenses, even if not waived by the operation of (A), are waived by the failure to raise them by a motion under Rule 12 or in the responsive pleading or any amendment thereof to which the party is entitled as a matter of course. The specified defenses are of such a character that they should not be delayed and brought up for the first time by means of an application to the court to amend the responsive pleading.

Since the language of the subdivisions is made clear, the party is put on fair notice of the effect of his actions and omissions and can guard himself against unintended waiver. It is to be noted that while the defenses specified in subdivision (h)(1) are subject to waiver as there provided, the more substantial defenses of failure to state a claim upon which relief can be granted, failure to join a party indispensable under Rule 19, and failure to state a legal defense to a claim (see Rule 12(b)(6), (7), (f)), as well as the defense of lack of jurisdiction over the subject matter (see Rule 12(b)(1)), are expressly preserved against waiver by amended subdivision (h)(2) and (3).

1987 Amendment

The amendments are technical. No substantive change is intended.

1993 Amendment

Subdivision (a) is divided into paragraphs for greater clarity, and paragraph (1)(B) is added to reflect amendments to Rule 4. Consistent with Rule 4(d)(3), a defendant that timely waives service is allowed 60 days from the date the request was mailed in which to respond to the complaint, with an additional 30 days afforded if the request was sent out of the country. Service is timely waived if the waiver is returned within the time specified in the request (30 days after the request was mailed, or 60 days if mailed out of the country) and before being formally served with process. Sometimes a plaintiff may attempt to serve a defendant with process while also sending the defendant a request for waiver of service; if the defendant executes the waiver of service within the time specified and before being served with process, it should have the longer time to respond afforded by waiving service.

The date of sending the request is to be inserted by the plaintiff on the face of the request for waiver and on the waiver itself. This date is used to measure the return day for the waiver form, so that the plaintiff can know on a day certain whether formal service of process will be necessary; it is also a useful date to measure the time for answer when service is waived. The defendant who returns the waiver is given additional time for answer in order to assure that it loses nothing by waiving service of process.

2000 Amendment

Rule 12(a)(3)(B) is added to complement the addition of Rule 4(i)(2)(B). The purposes that underlie the requirement that service be made on the United States in an action that asserts individual liability of a United States officer or employee for acts occurring in connection with the performance of duties on behalf of the United States also require that the time to answer be extended to 60 days. Time is needed for the United States to determine whether to provide representation to the defendant officer or employee. If the United States provides representation, the need for an extended answer period is the same as in actions against the United States, a United States agency, or a United States officer sued in an official capacity.

An action against a former officer or employee of the United States is covered by subparagraph (3)(B) in the same way as an action against a present officer or employee. Termination of the relationship between the individual defendant and the United States does not reduce the need for additional time to answer.

2007 Amendment

The language of Rule 12 has been amended as part of the general restyling of the Civil Rules to make them more easily understood and to make style and terminology consistent throughout the rules. These changes are intended to be stylistic only.

Former Rule 12(a)(4)(A) referred to an order that postpones disposition of a motion "until the trial on the merits." Rule 12(a)(4) now refers to postponing disposition "until trial." The new expression avoids the ambiguity that inheres in "trial on the merits," which may become confusing when there is a separate trial of a single issue or another event different from a single all-encompassing trial.

2009 Amendments

The times set in the former rule at 10 or 20 days have been revised to 14 or 21 days. See the Note to Rule 6.

Rule 13.   Counterclaim and Crossclaim

(a) Compulsory Counterclaim.

    (1) *In General.* A pleading must state as a counterclaim any claim that—at the time of its service—the pleader has against an opposing party if the claim:

        (A) arises out of the transaction or occurrence that is the subject matter of the opposing party's claim; and

        (B) does not require adding another party over whom the court cannot acquire jurisdiction.

    (2) *Exceptions.* The pleader need not state the claim if:

        (A) when the action was commenced, the claim was the subject of another pending action; or

        (B) the opposing party sued on its claim by attachment or other process that did not establish personal jurisdiction over the pleader on that claim, and the pleader does not assert any counterclaim under this rule.

(b) Permissive Counterclaim. A pleading may state as a counterclaim against an opposing party any claim that is not compulsory.

(c) Relief Sought in a Counterclaim. A counterclaim need not diminish or defeat the recovery sought by the opposing party. It may request relief that exceeds in amount or differs in kind from the relief sought by the opposing party.

(d) Counterclaim Against the United States. These rules do not expand the right to assert a counterclaim—or to claim a credit—against the United States or a United States officer or agency.

(e) Counterclaim Maturing or Acquired After Pleading. The court may permit a party to file a supplemental pleading asserting a counterclaim that matured or was acquired by the party after serving an earlier pleading.

(f) [Abrogated]

(g) Crossclaim Against a Coparty. A pleading may state as a crossclaim any claim by one party against a coparty if the claim arises out of the transaction or occurrence that is the subject matter of the original action or of a counterclaim, or if the claim relates to any property that is the subject matter of the original action. The crossclaim may include a claim that the coparty is or may be liable to the cross-claimant for all or part of a claim asserted in the action against the cross-claimant.

(h) Joining Additional Parties. Rules 19 and 20 govern the addition of a person as a party to a counterclaim or crossclaim.

(i) Separate Trials; Separate Judgments. If the court orders separate trials under Rule 42(b), it may enter judgment on a counterclaim or crossclaim under Rule 54(b) when it has jurisdiction to do so, even if the opposing party's claims have been dismissed or otherwise resolved.

(Amended December 27, 1946, effective March 19, 1948; January 21, 1963, effective July 1, 1963; February 28, 1966, effective July 1, 1966; March 2, 1987, effective August 1, 1987; April 30, 2007, effective December 1, 2007; March 26, 2009, effective December 1, 2009.)

ADVISORY COMMITTEE NOTES

1937 Adoption

1.   This is substantially [former] Equity Rule 30 (Answer—Contents—Counterclaim), broadened to include legal as well as equitable counterclaims.

2.   Compare the English practice, *English Rules Under the Judicature Act* (The Annual Practice, 1937) O. 19, r.r. 2 and 3, and O. 21, r.r. 10–17; *Beddall v. Maitland,* L.R. 17 Ch.Div. 174, 181, 182 (1881).

3.   Certain States have also adopted almost unrestricted provisions concerning both the subject matter of and the parties to a counterclaim. This seems to be the modern tendency. Ark.Civ.Code (Crawford, 1934) §§ 117 (as amended) and 118; N.J.Comp.Stat. (2 Cum.Supp. 1911–1924); N.Y.C.P.A. (1937) §§ 262, 266, 267 (all as amended, Laws of 1936, ch. 324), 268, 269, and 271; Wis.Stat. (1935) § 263.14(1)(c).

4.   Most codes do not expressly provide for a counterclaim in the reply. Clark, *Code Pleading* (1928), p. 486. Ky.Codes (Carroll, 1932) Civ.Pract. § 98 does provide, however, for such counterclaim.

5.   The provisions of this rule respecting counterclaims are subject to Rule 82 (Jurisdiction and Venue Unaffected). For a discussion of Federal jurisdiction and venue in regard to counterclaims and cross-claims, see Shulman and Jaegerman, *Some Jurisdictional Limitations in Federal Procedure* (1936), 45 Yale L.J. 393, 410 et seq.

6.   This rule does not affect such statutes of the United States as U.S.C., Title 28, § 41(1) (now §§ 1332, 1345, 1359) (United States as plaintiff; civil suits at common law and in equity), relating to assigned claims in actions based on diversity of citizenship.

7.   If the action proceeds to judgment without the interposition of a counterclaim as required by subdivision (a) of this rule, the counterclaim is barred. See *American Mills Co. v. American Surety Co.*, 260 U.S. 360, 43 S.Ct. 149, 67 L.Ed. 306 (1922); *Marconi Wireless Telegraph Co. v. National Electric Signalling Co.*, 206 Fed. 295 (E.D.N.Y., 1913); Hopkins, *Federal Equity Rules* (8th ed., 1933), p. 213; Simkins, *Federal Practice* (1934), p. 663.

8.   For allowance of credits against the United States see U.S.C., Title 26, §§ 1672–1673 [sec. 7442] (Suits for refunds of internal revenue taxes—limitations); U.S.C., Title 28, § 774 (now § 2406) (Suits by United States against individuals; credits), [former] § 775 (Suits under postal laws; credits); U.S.C., Title 31, § 227 [now 3728] (Offsets against judgments and claims against United States).

1946 Amendment

Note. Subdivision (a). The use of the word "filing" was inadvertent. The word "serving" conforms with subdivision (e) and with usage generally throughout the rules.

The removal of the phrase "not the subject of a pending action" and the addition of the new clause at the end of the subdivision is designed to eliminate the ambiguity noted in *Prudential Insurance Co. of America v. Saxe,* App.D.C.1943, 77 U.S.App.D.C. 144, 134 F.2d 16, 33–34, cert. den., 1943, 319 U.S. 745, 63 S.Ct. 1033. The rewording of the subdivision in this respect insures against an undesirable possibility presented under the original rule whereby a party having a claim which would be the subject of a compulsory counterclaim could avoid stating it as such by bringing an independent action in another court after the commencement of the federal action but before serving his pleading in the federal action.

Subdivision (g). The amendment is to care for a situation such as where a second mortgagee is made defendant in a foreclosure proceeding and wishes to file a cross-complaint against the mortgagor in order to secure a personal judgment for the indebtedness and foreclose his lien. A claim of this sort by the second mortgagee may not necessarily arise out of the transaction or occurrence that is the subject matter of the original action under the terms of Rule 13(g).

Subdivision (h). The change clarifies the interdependence of Rules 13(i) and 54(b).

1963 Amendment

When a defendant, if he desires to defend his interest in property, is obliged to come in and litigate in a court to whose jurisdiction he could not ordinarily be subjected, fairness suggests that he should not be required to assert counterclaims, but should rather be permitted to do so at his election. If, however, he does elect to assert a counterclaim, it seems fair to require him to assert any other which is compulsory within the meaning of Rule 13(a). Clause (2), added by amendment to Rule 13(a), carries out this idea. It will apply to various cases described in Rule 4(e), as amended, where service is effected through attachment or other process by which the court does not acquire jurisdiction to render a personal judgment against the defendant. Clause (2) will also apply to actions commenced in State courts jurisdictionally grounded on attachment or the like, and removed to the Federal courts.

1966 Amendment

Rule 13(h), dealing with the joinder of additional parties to a counterclaim or cross-claim, has partaken of some of the textual difficulties of Rule 19 on necessary joinder of parties. See Advisory Committee's Note to Rule 19, as amended; cf. 3 *Moore's Federal Practice,* par. 13.39 (2d ed. 1963), and Supp. thereto; 1A Barron & Holtzoff, *Federal Practice and Procedure* § 399 (Wright ed. 1960). Rule 13(h) has also been inadequate in failing to call attention to the fact that a party pleading a counterclaim or cross-claim may join additional persons when the conditions for permissive joinder of parties under Rule 20 are satisfied.

The amendment of Rule 13(h) supplies the latter omission by expressly referring to Rule 20, as amended, and also incorporates by direct reference the revised criteria and procedures of Rule 19, as amended. Hereafter, for the purpose of determining who must or may be joined as additional parties to a counterclaim or cross-claim, the party pleading the claim is to be regarded as a plaintiff and the additional parties as plaintiffs or defendants as the case may be, and amended Rules 19 and 20 are to be applied in the usual fashion. See also Rules 13(a) (compulsory counterclaims) and 22 (interpleader).

The amendment of Rule 13(h), like the amendment of Rule 19, does not attempt to regulate Federal jurisdiction or venue. See Rule 82. It should be noted, however, that in some situations the decisional law has recognized "ancillary" Federal jurisdiction over counterclaims and cross-claims and "ancillary" venue as to parties to these claims.

1987 Amendment

The amendments are technical. No substantive change is intended.

2007 Amendment

The language of Rule 13 has been amended as part of the general restyling of the Civil Rules to make them more easily understood and to make style and terminology consistent throughout the rules. These changes are intended to be stylistic only.

The meaning of former Rule 13(b) is better expressed by deleting "not arising out of the transaction or occurrence that is the subject matter of the opposing party's claim." Both as a matter of intended meaning and current practice, a party may state as a permissive counterclaim a claim that does grow out of the same transaction or occurrence as an opposing party's claim even though one of the exceptions in Rule 13(a) means the claim is not a compulsory counterclaim.

2009 Amendments

Rule 13(f) is deleted as largely redundant and potentially misleading. An amendment to add a counterclaim will be governed by Rule 15. Rule 15(a)(1) permits some amendments to be made as a matter of course or with the opposing party's written consent. When the court's leave is required, the reasons described in Rule 13(f) for permitting amendment of a pleading to add an omitted counterclaim sound different from the general amendment standard in Rule 15(a)(2), but seem to be administered—as they should be—according to the same standard directing that leave should be freely given when justice so requires. The independent existence of Rule 13(f) has, however, created some uncertainty as to the availability of relation back of the amendment under Rule 15(c). *See 6 C. Wright, A. Miller & M. Kane, Federal Practice & Procedure: Civil 2d, § 1430 (1990).* Deletion of Rule 13(f) ensures that relation back is governed by the tests that apply to all other pleading amendments.

Rule 14.   Third-Party Practice

(a) When a Defending Party May Bring in a Third Party.

(1) ***Timing of the Summons and Complaint.*** A defending party may, as third-party plaintiff, serve a summons and complaint on a nonparty who is or may be liable to it for all or part of the claim against it. But the third-party plaintiff must, by motion, obtain the court's leave if it files the third-party complaint more than 14 days after serving its original answer.

(2) ***Third-Party Defendant's Claims and Defenses.*** The person served with the summons and third-party complaint—the "third-party defendant":

(A) must assert any defense against the third-party plaintiff's claim under Rule 12;

(B) must assert any counterclaim against the third-party plaintiff under Rule 13(a), and may assert any counterclaim against the third-party plaintiff under Rule 13(b) or any crossclaim against another third-party defendant under Rule 13(g);

(C) may assert against the plaintiff any defense that the third-party plaintiff has to the plaintiff's claim; and

(D) may also assert against the plaintiff any claim arising out of the transaction or occurrence that is the subject matter of the plaintiff's claim against the third-party plaintiff.

(3) ***Plaintiff's Claims Against a Third-Party Defendant.*** The plaintiff may assert against the third-party defendant any claim arising out of the transaction or occurrence that is the subject matter of the plaintiff's claim against the third-party plaintiff. The third-party defendant must then assert any defense under Rule 12 and any counterclaim under Rule 13(a), and may assert any counterclaim under Rule 13(b) or any crossclaim under Rule 13(g).

(4) ***Motion to Strike, Sever, or Try Separately.*** Any party may move to strike the third-party claim, to sever it, or to try it separately.

(5) ***Third-Party Defendant's Claim Against a Nonparty.*** A third-party defendant may proceed under this rule against a nonparty who is or may be liable to the third-party defendant for all or part of any claim against it.

(6) ***Third-Party Complaint In Rem.*** If it is within the admiralty or maritime jurisdiction, a third-party complaint may be in rem. In that event, a reference in this rule to the "summons" includes the warrant of arrest, and a reference to the defendant or third-party plaintiff includes, when appropriate, a person who asserts a right under Supplemental Rule C(6)(a)(i) in the property arrested.

(b) When a Plaintiff May Bring in a Third Party. When a claim is asserted against a plaintiff, the plaintiff may bring in a third party if this rule would allow a defendant to do so.

(c) Admiralty or Maritime Claim.

(1) ***Scope of Impleader.*** If a plaintiff asserts an admiralty or maritime claim under Rule 9(h), the defendant or a person who asserts a right under Supplemental Rule C(6)(a)(i) may, as a third-party plaintiff, bring in a third-party defendant who may be wholly or partly liable—either to the plaintiff or to the third-party plaintiff—for remedy over, contribution, or otherwise on account of the same transaction, occurrence, or series of transactions or occurrences.

(2) *Defending Against a Demand for Judgment for the Plaintiff.* The third-party plaintiff may demand judgment in the plaintiff's favor against the third-party defendant. In that event, the third-party defendant must defend under Rule 12 against the plaintiff's claim as well as the third-party plaintiff's claim; and the action proceeds as if the plaintiff had sued both the third-party defendant and the third-party plaintiff.

(Amended December 27, 1946, effective March 19, 1948; January 21, 1963, effective July 1, 1963; February 28, 1966, effective July 1, 1966; March 2, 1987, effective August 1, 1987; April 17, 2000, effective December 1, 2000; April 12, 2006, effective December 1, 2006; April 30, 2007, effective December 1, 2007; March 26, 2009, effective December 1, 2009.)

ADVISORY COMMITTEE NOTES

1937 Adoption

Third-party impleader is in some aspects a modern innovation in law and equity although well known in admiralty. Because of its many advantages a liberal procedure with respect to it has developed in England, in the federal admiralty courts, and in some American state jurisdictions. See *English Rules Under the Judicature Act* (The Annual Practice, 1937) O. 16A, r.r. 1–13; United States Supreme Court Admiralty Rules (1920), Rule 56 (Right to Bring in Party Jointly Liable); 12 P.S.Pa. § 141; Wis.Stat. (1935) §§ 260.19, 260.20; N.Y.C.P.A. (1937) §§ 193(2), 211(a). Compare La.Code Pract. (Dart, 1932) §§ 378–388. For the practice in Texas as developed by judicial decision, see *Lottman v. Cuilla,* Tex.1926, 288 S.W. 123, 126. For a treatment of this subject see Gregory, *Legislative Loss Distribution in Negligence Actions* (1936); *Shulman and Jaegerman, Some Jurisdictional Limitations on Federal Procedure (1936),* 45 Yale L.J. 393, 417 et seq.

Third-party impleader under the conformity act has been applied in actions at law in the Federal courts. *Lowry and Co., Inc. v. National City Bank of New York,* N.Y.1928, 28 F.2d 895; *Yellow Cab Co. of Philadelphia v. Rodgers,* C.C.A.3, 1932, 61 F.2d 729.

1946 Amendment

Note. The provisions in Rule 14(a) which relate to the impleading of a third party who is or may be liable to the plaintiff have been deleted by the proposed amendment. It has been held that under Rule 14(a) the plaintiff need not amend his complaint to state a claim against such third party if he does not wish to do so. *Satink v. Holland Township,* D.N.J.1940, 31 F.Supp. 229, noted, 1940, 88 U.Pa.L.Rev. 751; *Connelly v. Bender,* E.D.Mich.1941, 36 F.Supp. 368; *Whitmire v. Partin (Milton),* E.D.Tenn.1941, 2 F.R.D. 83, 5 Fed.Rules Serv. 14a.513, Case 2; *Crim v. Lumbermen's Mutual Casualty Co.,* D.D.C.1939, 26 F.Supp. 715; *Carbola Chemical Co., Inc. v. Trundle,* S.D.N.Y.1943, 3 F.R.D. 502, 7 Fed.Rules Serv. 14a.224, Case 1; *Roadway Express, Inc. v. Automobile Ins. Co. of Hartford, Conn., (Providence Washington Ins. Co.)* N.D.Ohio 1945, 8 Fed.Rules Serv. 14a.513, Case 3. In *Delano v. Ives,* E.D.Pa.1941, 40 F.Supp. 672, the court said: ". . . the weight of authority is to the effect that a defendant cannot compel the plaintiff, who has sued him, to sue also a third party whom he does not wish to sue, by tendering in a third party complaint the third party as an additional defendant directly liable to the plaintiff." Thus impleader here amounts to no more than a mere offer of a party to the plaintiff, and if he rejects it, the attempt is a time-consuming futility. See *Satink v. Holland Township, supra; Malkin v. Arundel Corp.,* D.Md.1941, 36 F.Supp. 948; also Koenigsberger, *Suggestions for Changes in the Federal Rules of Civil Procedure,* 1941, 4 Fed.Rules Serv. 1010. But cf. *Atlantic Coast Line R. Co. v. United States Fidelity & Guaranty Co.,* Ga.1943, 52 F.Supp. 177. Moreover, in any case where the plaintiff could not have joined the third party originally because of jurisdictional limitations such as lack of diversity of citizenship, the majority view is that any attempt by the plaintiff to amend his complaint and assert a claim against the impleaded third party would be unavailing. *Hoskie v. Prudential Ins. Co. of America, (Lorrac Real Estate Corp.),* E.D.N.Y.1941, 39 F.Supp. 305; *Johnson v. G. J. Sherrard Co., (New England Telephone & Telegraph Co.),* D.Mass.1941, 5 Fed.Rules Serv. 14a.511, Case 1, 2 F.R.D. 164; *Thompson v. Cranston,* W.D.N.Y.1942, 6 Fed.Rules Serv. 14a.511, Case 1, 2 F.R.D. 270, affirmed CCA2d, 1942, 132 F.2d 631, certiorari denied 1945, 63 S.Ct. 1028, 319 U.S. 741, 87 L.Ed. 1698; *Friend v. Middle Atlantic Transportation Co.,* C.C.A.2, 1946, 153 F.2d 778, certiorari denied 1946, 66 S.Ct. 1370, 328 U.S. 865, 90 L.Ed. 1635; *Herrington v. Jones,* E.D.La.1941, 5 Fed.Rules Serv. 14a.511, Case 2, 2 F.R.D. 108; *Banks v. Employers' Liability Assurance Corp., (Central Surety & Ins. Corp.)* W.D.Mo.1943, 7 Fed.Rules Serv. 14a.11, Case 2; *Saunders v. Baltimore & Ohio R. Co.,* S.D.W.Va.1945, 9 Fed.Rules Serv. 14a.62, Case 2; *Hull v. United States Rubber Co. (Johnson Larsen and Co.),* E.D.Mich.1945, 9 Fed.Rules

Serv. 14a.62, Case 3. See also concurring opinion of Circuit Judge Minton in *People of State of Illinois for Use of Trust Co. of Chicago v. Maryland Casualty Co.,* C.C.A.7, 1942, 132 F.2d 850, 853. Contra: *Sklar v. Hayes (Singer),* E.D.Pa.1941, 4 Fed.Rules Serv. 14a.511, Case 2, 1 F.R.D. 594. Discussion of the problem will be found in Commentary, *Amendment of Plaintiff's Pleading to Assert Claim Against Third-Party Defendant,* 1942, 5 Fed.Rules Serv. 811; Commentary, *Federal Jurisdiction in Third-Party Practice,* 1943, 6 Fed.Rules Serv. 766; Holtzoff, *Some Problems Under Federal Third-Party Practice,* 1941, 3 La.L.Rev. 408, 419–420; 1 Moore's *Federal Practice,* 1938, Cum.Supplement § 14.08. For these reasons therefore, the words "or to the plaintiff" in the first sentence of subdivision (a) have been removed by the amendment; and in conformance therewith the words "the plaintiff" in the second sentence of the subdivision, and the words "or to the third-party plaintiff" in the concluding sentence thereof have likewise been eliminated.

The third sentence of rule 14(a) has been expanded to clarify the right of the third-party defendant to assert any defenses which the third-party plaintiff may have to the plaintiff's claim. This protects the impleaded third-party defendant where the third-party plaintiff fails or neglects to assert a proper defense to the plaintiff's action. A new sentence has also been inserted giving the third-party defendant the right to assert directly against the original plaintiff any claim arising out of the transaction or occurrence that is the subject matter of the plaintiff's claim against the third-party plaintiff. This permits all claims arising out of the same transaction or occurrence to be heard and determined in the same action. See *Atlantic Coast Line R. Co. v. United States Fidelity & Guaranty Co.,* Ga.1943, 52 F.Supp. 177. Accordingly, the next to the last sentence of subdivision (a) has also been revised to make clear that the plaintiff may, if he desires, assert directly against the third-party defendant either by amendment or by a new pleading any claim he may have against him arising out of the transaction or occurrence that is the subject matter of the plaintiff's claim against the third-party plaintiff. In such a case, the third-party defendant then is entitled to assert the defenses, counter-claims and cross-claims provided in Rules 12 and 13.

The sentence reading "The third-party defendant is bound by the adjudication of the third-party plaintiff's liability to the plaintiff, as well as of his own to the plaintiff, or to the third-party plaintiff" has been stricken from Rule 14(a), not to change the law, but because the sentence states a rule of substantive law which is not within the scope of a procedural rule. It is not the purpose of the rules to state the effect of a judgment.

The elimination of the words "the third-party plaintiff, or any other party" from the second sentence of rule 14(a), together with the insertion of the new phrases therein, are not changes of substance but are merely for the purpose of clarification.

1963 Amendment

Under the amendment of the initial sentences of the subdivision, a defendant as a third-party plaintiff may freely and without leave of court bring in a third-party defendant if he files the third-party complaint not later than 10 days after he serves his original answer. When the impleader comes so early in the case, there is little value in requiring a preliminary ruling by the court on the propriety of the impleader.

After the third-party defendant is brought in, the court has discretion to strike the third-party claim if it is obviously unmeritorious and can only delay or prejudice the disposition of the plaintiff's claim, or to sever the third-party claim or accord it separate trial if confusion or prejudice would otherwise result. This discretion, applicable not merely to the cases covered by the amendment where the third-party defendant is brought in without leave, but to all impleaders under the rule, is emphasized in the next-to-last sentence of the subdivision, added by amendment.

In dispensing with leave of court for an impleader filed not later than 10 days after serving the answer, but retaining the leave requirement for impleaders sought to be effected thereafter, the amended subdivision takes a moderate position on the lines urged by some commentators, see Note, 43 Minn.L.Rev. 115 (1958); cf. Pa.R.Civ.P. 2252–53 (60 days after service on the defendant; Minn.R.Civ.P. 14.01 (45 days). Other commentators would dispense with the requirement of leave regardless of the time when impleader is effected, and would rely on subsequent action by the court to dismiss the impleader if it would unduly delay or complicate the litigation or would be otherwise objectionable. See 1A Barron & Holtzoff, *Federal Practice & Procedure* 649–50 (Wright ed. 1960); Comment, 58 Colum.L.Rev. 532, 546 (1958); cf. N.Y.Civ.Prac.Act § 193–a; Me.R.Civ.P. 14. The amended subdivision preserves the value of a preliminary screening, through the leave procedure, of impleaders attempted after the 10-day period.

The amendment applies also when an impleader is initiated by a third-party defendant against a person who may be liable to him, as provided in the last sentence of the subdivision.

1966 Amendment

Rule 14 was modeled on Admiralty Rule 56. An important feature of Admiralty Rule 56 was that it allowed impleader not only of a person who might be liable to the defendant by way of remedy over, but also of any person who might be liable to the plaintiff. The importance of this provision was that the defendant was entitled to insist that the plaintiff proceed to judgment against the third-party defendant. In certain cases this was a valuable implementation of a substantive right. For example, in a case of ship collision where a finding of mutual fault is possible, one shipowner, if sued alone, faces the prospect of an absolute judgment for the full amount of the damage suffered by an innocent third party; but if he can implead the owner of the other vessel, and if mutual fault is found, the judgment against the original defendant will be in the first instance only for a moiety of the damages; liability for the remainder will be conditioned on the plaintiff's inability to collect from the third-party defendant.

This feature was originally incorporated in Rule 14, but was eliminated by the amendment of 1946, so that under the amended rule a third party could not be impleaded on the basis that he might be liable to the plaintiff. One of the reasons for the amendment was that the Civil Rule, unlike the Admiralty Rule, did not require the plaintiff to go to judgment against the third-party defendant. Another reason was that where jurisdiction depended on diversity of citizenship the impleader of an adversary having the same citizenship as the plaintiff was not considered possible.

Retention of the admiralty practice in those cases that will be counterparts of a suit in admiralty is clearly desirable.

1987 Amendment

The amendments are technical. No substantive change is intended.

2000 Amendment

Subdivisions (a) and (c) are amended to reflect revisions in Supplemental Rule C(6).

2006 Amendment

Rule 14 is amended to conform to changes in designating the paragraphs of Supplemental Rule C(6).

2007 Amendment

The language of Rule 14 has been amended as part of the general restyling of the Civil Rules to make them more easily understood and to make style and terminology consistent throughout the rules. These changes are intended to be stylistic only.

Former Rule 14 twice refers to counterclaims under Rule 13. In each case, the operation of Rule 13(a) depends on the state of the action at the time the pleading is filed. If plaintiff and third-party defendant have become opposing parties because one has made a claim for relief against the other, Rule 13(a) requires assertion of any counterclaim that grows out of the transaction or occurrence that is the subject matter of that claim. Rules 14(a)(2)(B) and (a)(3) reflect the distinction between compulsory and permissive counterclaims.

A plaintiff should be on equal footing with the defendant in making third-party claims, whether the claim against the plaintiff is asserted as a counterclaim or as another form of claim. The limit imposed by the former reference to "counterclaim" is deleted.

2009 Amendments

The time set in the former rule at 10 days has been revised to 14 days. See the Note to Rule 6.

Rule 15.   Amended and Supplemental Pleadings

(a) Amendments Before Trial.

    (1) *Amending as a Matter of Course.* A party may amend its pleading once as a matter of course within:

     (A) 21 days after serving it, or

     (B) if the pleading is one to which a responsive pleading is required, 21 days after service of a responsive pleading or 21 days after service of a motion under Rule 12(b), (e), or (f), whichever is earlier.

(2) **_Other Amendments._** In all other cases, a party may amend its pleading only with the opposing party's written consent or the court's leave. The court should freely give leave when justice so requires.

(3) **_Time to Respond._** Unless the court orders otherwise, any required response to an amended pleading must be made within the time remaining to respond to the original pleading or within 14 days after service of the amended pleading, whichever is later.

(b) **Amendments During and After Trial.**

  (1) **_Based on an Objection at Trial._** If, at trial, a party objects that evidence is not within the issues raised in the pleadings, the court may permit the pleadings to be amended. The court should freely permit an amendment when doing so will aid in presenting the merits and the objecting party fails to satisfy the court that the evidence would prejudice that party's action or defense on the merits. The court may grant a continuance to enable the objecting party to meet the evidence.

  (2) **_For Issues Tried by Consent._** When an issue not raised by the pleadings is tried by the parties' express or implied consent, it must be treated in all respects as if raised in the pleadings. A party may move—at any time, even after judgment—to amend the pleadings to conform them to the evidence and to raise an unpleaded issue. But failure to amend does not affect the result of the trial of that issue.

(c) **Relation Back of Amendments.**

  (1) **_When an Amendment Relates Back._** An amendment to a pleading relates back to the date of the original pleading when:

     (A) the law that provides the applicable statute of limitations allows relation back;

     (B) the amendment asserts a claim or defense that arose out of the conduct, transaction, or occurrence set out—or attempted to be set out—in the original pleading; or

     (C) the amendment changes the party or the naming of the party against whom a claim is asserted, if Rule 15(c)(1)(B) is satisfied and if, within the period provided by Rule 4(m)* for serving the summons and complaint, the party to be brought in by amendment:

       (i) received such notice of the action that it will not be prejudiced in defending on the merits; and

       (ii) knew or should have known that the action would have been brought against it, but for a mistake concerning the proper party's identity.

  (2) **_Notice to the United States._** When the United States or a United States officer or agency is added as a defendant by amendment, the notice requirements of Rule 15(c)(1)(C)(i) and (ii) are satisfied if, during the stated period, process was delivered or mailed to the United States attorney or the United States attorney's designee, to the Attorney General of the United States, or to the officer or agency.

(d) **Supplemental Pleadings.** On motion and reasonable notice, the court may, on just terms, permit a party to serve a supplemental pleading setting out any transaction, occurrence, or event that happened after the date of the pleading to be supplemented. The court may permit supplementation even though the original pleading is defective in stating a claim or defense. The

---

*   [Under Rule 4(m), this period is currently 90 days from the filing of the complaint. Ed.]

court may order that the opposing party plead to the supplemental pleading within a specified time.

(Amended January 21, 1963, effective July 1, 1963; February 28, 1966, effective July 1, 1966; March 2, 1987, effective August 1, 1987; April 30, 1991, effective December 1, 1991; amended by Pub.L. 102–198, § 11, December 9, 1991, 105 Stat. 1626; amended April 22, 1993, effective December 1, 1993; April 30, 2007, effective December 1, 2007; March 26, 2009, effective December 1, 2009.)

ADVISORY COMMITTEE NOTES

1937 Adoption

See generally for the present federal practice, [former] Equity Rules 19 (Amendments Generally), 28 (Amendment of Bill as of Course), 32 (Answer to Amended Bill), 34 (Supplemental Pleading), and 35 (Bills of Revivor and Supplemental Bills—Form); U.S.C. Title 28, § 399 [now 1653] (Amendments to show diverse citizenship) and [former] 777 (Defects of form; amendments). See *English Rules Under the Judicature Act* (The Annual Practice, 1937) O. 28, r. r. 1–13; O. 20, r. 4; O. 24, r. r. 1–3.

Note to Subdivision (a). The right to serve an amended pleading once as of course is common. 4 Mont.Rev.Codes Ann. (1935) § 9186; 1 Ore.Code Ann. (1930) § 1–904; 1 S.C.Code (Michie, 1932) § 493; *English Rules Under the Judicature Act* (The Annual Practice, 1937) O. 28, r. 2. Provision for amendment of pleading before trial, by leave of court, is in almost every code. If there is no statute the power of the court to grant leave is said to be inherent. Clark, *Code Pleading* (1928), pp. 498, 509.

Note to Subdivision (b). Compare [former] Equity Rule 19 (Amendments Generally) and code provisions which allow an amendment "at any time in furtherance of justice," (e.g., Ark.Civ.Code (Crawford, 1934) § 155) and which allow an amendment of pleadings to conform to the evidence, where the adverse party has not been misled and prejudiced (e.g., N.M.Stat.Ann. (Courtright, 1929) §§ 105–601, 105–602).

Note to Subdivision (c). "Relation back" is a well recognized doctrine of recent and now more frequent application. Compare Ala.Code Ann. (Michie, 1928) § 9513; Smith-Hurd Ill.Stats. ch. 110, § 170(2); 2 Wash.Rev.Stat.Ann. (Remington, 1932) § 308–3(4). See U.S.C., Title 28, § 399 [now 1653] (Amendments to show diverse citizenship) for a provision for "relation back".

Note to Subdivision (d). This is an adaptation of former Equity Rule 34 (Supplemental Pleading).

1963 Amendment

Rule 15(d) is intended to give the court broad discretion in allowing a supplemental pleading. However, some cases, opposed by other cases and criticized by the commentators, have taken the rigid and formalistic view that where the original complaint fails to state a claim upon which relief can be granted, leave to serve a supplemental complaint must be denied. See *Bonner v. Elizabeth Arden, Inc.,* 177 F.2d 703 (2d Cir. 1949); *Bowles v. Senderowitz,* 65 F.Supp. 548 (E.D.Pa.), rev'd on other grounds, 158 F.2d 435 (3d Cir. 1946), cert. denied, *Senderowitz v. Fleming,* 330 U.S. 848, 67 S.Ct. 1091, 91 L.Ed. 1292 (1947); cf. *LaSalle Nat. Bank v. 222 East Chestnut St. Corp.,* 267 F.2d 247 (7th Cir.), cert. denied, 361 U.S. 836, 80 S.Ct. 88, 4 L.Ed.2d 77 (1959). But see *Camilla Cotton Oil Co. v. Spencer Kellogg & Sons,* 257 F.2d 162 (5th Cir. 1958); *Genuth v. National Biscuit Co.,* 81 F.Supp. 213 (S.D.N.Y.1948), app. dism., 177 F.2d 962 (2d Cir. 1949); 3 Moore's *Federal Practice* ¶ 15.01[5] (Supp.1960); 1A Barron & Holtzoff, *Federal Practice & Procedure* 820–21 (Wright ed. 1960). Thus plaintiffs have sometimes been needlessly remitted to the difficulties of commencing a new action even though events occurring after the commencement of the original action have made clear the right to relief.

Under the amendment the court has discretion to permit a supplemental pleading despite the fact that the original pleading is defective. As in other situations where a supplemental pleading is offered, the court is to determine in the light of the particular circumstances whether filing should be permitted, and if so, upon what terms. The amendment does not attempt to deal with such questions as the relation of the statute of limitations to supplemental pleadings, the operation of the doctrine of laches, or the availability of other defenses. All these questions are for decision in accordance with the principles applicable to supplemental pleadings generally. Cf. *Blau v. Lamb,* 191 F.Supp. 906 (S.D.N.Y.1961); *Lendonsol Amusement Corp. v. B. & Q. Assoc., Inc.,* 23 F.R.Serv. 15d.3, Case 1 (D.Mass.1957).

1966 Amendment

Rule 15(c) is amplified to state more clearly when an amendment of a pleading changing the party against whom a claim is asserted (including an amendment to correct a misnomer or misdescription of a defendant) shall "relate back" to the date of the original pleading.

The problem has arisen most acutely in certain actions by private parties against officers or agencies of the United States. Thus an individual denied social security benefits by the Secretary of Health, Education, and Welfare may secure review of the decision by bringing a civil action against that officer within sixty days. 42 U.S.C. § 405(g) (Supp. III, 1962). In several recent cases the claimants instituted timely action but mistakenly named as defendant the United States, the Department of HEW, the "Federal Security Administration" (a nonexistent agency), and a Secretary who had retired from the office nineteen days before. Discovering their mistakes, the claimants moved to amend their complaints to name the proper defendant; by this time the statutory sixty-day period had expired. The motions were denied on the ground that the amendment "would amount to the commencement of a new proceeding and would not relate back in time so as to avoid the statutory provision * * * that suit be brought within sixty days * * *" *Cohn v. Federal Security Adm.,* 199 F.Supp. 884, 885 (W.D.N.Y.1961); see also *Cunningham v. United States,* 199 F.Supp. 541 (W.D.Mo.1958); *Hall v. Department of HEW,* 199 F.Supp. 833 (S.D.Tex.1960); *Sandridge v. Folsom, Secretary of HEW,* 200 F.Supp. 25 (M.D.Tenn.1959). [The Secretary of Health, Education, and Welfare has approved certain ameliorative regulations under 42 U.S.C. § 405(g). See 29 Fed.Reg. 8209 (June 30, 1964); Jacoby, *The Effect of Recent Changes in the Law of "Nonstatutory" Judicial Review,* 53 Geo.L.J. 19, 42–43 (1964); see also *Simmons v. United States Dept. HEW,* 328 F.2d 86 (3d Cir. 1964).]

Analysis in terms of "new proceeding" is traceable to *Davis v. L. L. Cohen & Co.,* 268 U.S. 638 (1925), and *Mellon v. Arkansas Land & Lumber Co.,* 275 U.S. 460 (1928), but those cases antedate the adoption of the Rules which import different criteria for determining when an amendment is to "relate back". As lower courts have continued to rely on the *Davis* and *Mellon* cases despite the contrary intent of the Rules, clarification of Rule 15(c) is considered advisable.

Relation back is intimately connected with the policy of the statute of limitations. The policy of the statute limiting the time for suit against the Secretary of HEW would not have been offended by allowing relation back in the situations described above. For the government was put on notice of the claim within the stated period—in the particular instances, by means of the initial delivery of process to a responsible government official (see Rule 4(d)(4) and (5)). In these circumstances, characterization of the amendment as a new proceeding is not responsive to the realty [sic], but is merely question-begging; and to deny relation back is to defeat unjustly the claimant's opportunity to prove his case. See the full discussion by Byse, *Suing the "Wrong" Defendant in Judicial Review of Federal Administrative Action: Proposals for Reform,* 77 Harv.L.Rev. 40 (1963); see also Ill.Civ.P. Act § 46(4).

Much the same question arises in other types of actions against the government (see *Byse,* supra, at 45 n. 15). In actions between private parties, the problem of relation back of amendments changing defendants has generally been better handled by the courts, but incorrect criteria have sometimes been applied, leading sporadically to doubtful results. See 1A Barron & Holtzoff, *Federal Practice & Procedure* § 451 (Wright ed. 1960); 1 id. § 186 (1960); 2 id. § 543 (1961); 3 *Moore's Federal Practice,* par. 15.15 (Cum.Supp.1962); Annot., *Change in Party After Statute of Limitations Has Run,* 8 A.L.R.2d 6 (1949). Rule 15(c) has been amplified to provide a general solution. An amendment changing the party against whom a claim is asserted relates back if the amendment satisfies the usual condition of Rule 15(c) of "arising out of the conduct * * * set forth * * * in the original pleading," and if, within the applicable limitations period, the party brought in by amendment, first, received such notice of the institution of the action—the notice need not be formal—that he would not be prejudiced in defending the action, and, second, knew or should have known that the action would have been brought against him initially had there not been a mistake concerning the identity of the proper party. Revised Rule 15(c) goes on to provide specifically in the government cases that the first and second requirements are satisfied when the government has been notified in the manner there described (see Rule 4(d)(4) and (5)). As applied to the government cases, revised Rule 15(c) further advances the objectives of the 1961 amendment of Rule 25(d) (substitution of public officers).

The relation back of amendments changing plaintiffs is not expressly treated in revised Rule 15(c) since the problem is generally easier. Again the chief consideration of policy is that of the statute of limitations, and the attitude taken in revised Rule 15(c) toward change of defendants extends by analogy to amendments changing plaintiffs. Also relevant is the amendment of Rule 17(a) (real party in interest). To avoid forfeitures of just claims, revised Rule 17(a) would provide that no action shall be dismissed on the ground that it is not prosecuted in the name of the real party in interest until a reasonable time has been allowed for correction of the defect in the manner there stated.

1987 Amendment

The amendments are technical. No substantive change is intended.

1991 Amendment

The rule has been revised to prevent parties against whom claims are made from taking unjust advantage of otherwise inconsequential pleading errors to sustain a limitations defense.

Paragraph (c)(1). This provision is new. It is intended to make it clear that the rule does not apply to preclude any relation back that may be permitted under the applicable limitations law. Generally, the applicable limitations law will be state law. If federal jurisdiction is based on the citizenship of the parties, the primary reference is the law of the state in which the district court sits. *Walker v. Armco Steel Corp.,* 446 U.S. 740 (1980). If federal jurisdiction is based on a federal question, the reference may be to the law of the state governing relations between the parties. *E.g., Board of Regents v. Tomanio,* 446 U.S. 478 (1980). In some circumstances, the controlling limitations law may be federal law. *E.g., West v. Conrail, Inc.,* 107 S.Ct. 1538 (1987). Cf. *Burlington Northern R. Co. v. Woods,* 480 U.S. 1 (1987); *Stewart Organization v. Ricoh,* 108 S.Ct. 2239 (1988). Whatever may be the controlling body of limitations law, if that law affords a more forgiving principle of relation back than the one provided in this rule, it should be available to save the claim. Accord, *Marshall v. Mulrenin,* 508 F.2d 39 (1st Cir.1974). If *Schiavone v. Fortune,* 106 S.Ct. 2379 (1986) implies the contrary, this paragraph is intended to make a material change in the rule.

Paragraph (c)(3). This paragraph has been revised to change the result in *Schiavone v. Fortune, supra,* with respect to the problem of a misnamed defendant. An intended defendant who is notified of an action within the period allowed by Rule 4(m) [subdivision (m) in Rule 4 was a proposed subdivision which was withdrawn by the Supreme Court] for service of a summons and complaint may not under the revised rule defeat the action on account of a defect in the pleading with respect to the defendant's name, provided that the requirements of clauses (A) and (B) have been met. If the notice requirement is met within the Rule 4(m) [subdivision (m) in Rule 4 was a proposed subdivision which was withdrawn by the Supreme Court] period, a complaint may be amended at any time to correct a formal defect such as a misnomer or misidentification. On the basis of the text of the former rule, the Court reached a result in *Schiavone v. Fortune* that was inconsistent with the liberal pleading practices secured by Rule 8. See Bauer, Schiavone: *An Un-Fortune-ate Illustration of the Supreme Court's Role as Interpreter of the Federal Rules of Civil Procedure,* 63 Notre Dame L.Rev. 720 (1988); Brussack, *Outrageous Fortune: The Case for Amending Rule 15(c) Again,* 61 S.Cal.L.Rev. 671 (1988); Lewis, *The Excessive History of Federal Rule 15(c) and Its Lessons for Civil Rules Revision,* 86 Mich.L.Rev. 1507 (1987).

In allowing a name-correcting amendment within the time allowed by Rule 4(m), this rule allows not only the 120 days specified in that rule, but also any additional time resulting from any extension ordered by the court pursuant to that rule, as may be granted, for example, if the defendant is a fugitive from service of the summons.

This revision, together with the revision of Rule 4(i) with respect to the failure of a plaintiff in an action against the United States to effect timely service on all the appropriate officials, is intended to produce results contrary to those reached in *Gardner v. Gartman,* 880 F.2d 797 (4th Cir. 1989), *Rys v. U.S. Postal Service,* 886 F.2d 443 (1st Cir. 1989), *Martin's Food & Liquor, Inc. v. U.S. Dept. of Agriculture,* 14 F.R.D.3d 86 (N.D.Ill.1988). *But cf. Montgomery v. United States Postal Service,* 867 F.2d 900 (5th Cir. 1989), *Warren v. Department of the Army,* 867 F.2d 1156 (8th Cir. 1989); *Miles v. Department of the Army,* 881 F.2d 777 (9th Cir. 1989), *Barsten v. Department of the Interior,* 896 F.2d 422 (9th Cir. 1990); *Brown v. Georgia Dept. of Revenue,* 881 F.2d 1018 (11th Cir. 1989).

1993 Amendments

The amendment conforms the cross reference to Rule 4 to the revision of that rule.

2007 Amendment

The language of Rule 15 has been amended as part of the general restyling of the Civil Rules to make them more easily understood and to make style and terminology consistent throughout the rules. These changes are intended to be stylistic only.

Former Rule 15(c)(3)(A) called for notice of the "institution" of the action. Rule 15(c)(1)(C)(i) omits the reference to "institution" as potentially confusing. What counts is that the party to be brought in have notice of the existence of the action, whether or not the notice includes details as to its "institution."

2009 Amendments

Rule 15(a)(1) is amended to make three changes in the time allowed to make one amendment as a matter of course.

Former Rule 15(a) addressed amendment of a pleading to which a responsive pleading is required by distinguishing between the means used to challenge the pleading. Serving a responsive pleading terminated the right to amend. Serving a motion attacking the pleading did not terminate the right to amend, because a motion is not a "pleading" as defined in Rule 7. The right to amend survived beyond decision of the motion unless the decision expressly cut off the right to amend.

The distinction drawn in former Rule 15(a) is changed in two ways. First, the right to amend once as a matter of course terminates 21 days after service of a motion under Rule 12(b), (e), or (f). This provision will force the pleader to consider carefully and promptly the wisdom of amending to meet the arguments in the motion. A responsive amendment may avoid the need to decide the motion or reduce the number of issues to be decided, and will expedite determination of issues that otherwise might be raised seriatim. It also should advance other pretrial proceedings.

Second, the right to amend once as a matter of course is no longer terminated by service of a responsive pleading. The responsive pleading may point out issues that the original pleader had not considered and persuade the pleader that amendment is wise. Just as amendment was permitted by former Rule 15(a) in response to a motion, so the amended rule permits one amendment as a matter of course in response to a responsive pleading. The right is subject to the same 21-day limit as the right to amend in response to a motion.

The 21-day periods to amend once as a matter of course after service of a responsive pleading or after service of a designated motion are not cumulative. If a responsive pleading is served after one of the designated motions is served, for example, there is no new 21-day period.

Finally, amended Rule 15(a)(1) extends from 20 to 21 days the period to amend a pleading to which no responsive pleading is allowed and omits the provision that cuts off the right if the action is on the trial calendar. Rule 40 no longer refers to a trial calendar, and many courts have abandoned formal trial calendars. It is more effective to rely on scheduling orders or other pretrial directions to establish time limits for amendment in the few situations that otherwise might allow one amendment as a matter of course at a time that would disrupt trial preparations. Leave to amend still can be sought under Rule 15(a)(2), or at and after trial under Rule 15(b). Amended Rule 15(a)(3) extends from 10 to 14 days the period to respond to an amended pleading.

Abrogation of Rule 13(f) establishes Rule 15 as the sole rule governing amendment of a pleading to add a counterclaim.

The times set in the former rule at 10 or 20 days have been revised to 14 or 21 days. See the Note to Rule 6.

HISTORICAL NOTES

Effective and Applicability Provisions

1991 Acts. Section 11(a) of Pub.L. 102–198 amended subd. (c)(3) of this rule, as transmitted to the Congress by the Supreme Court pursuant to section 2074 of title 28, United States Code, to become effective on December 1, 1991.

Rule 16.   Pretrial Conferences; Scheduling; Management

(a) Purposes of a Pretrial Conference. In any action, the court may order the attorneys and any unrepresented parties to appear for one or more pretrial conferences for such purposes as:

   (1) expediting disposition of the action;

   (2) establishing early and continuing control so that the case will not be protracted because of lack of management;

   (3) discouraging wasteful pretrial activities;

   (4) improving the quality of the trial through more thorough preparation; and

   (5) facilitating settlement.

(b) Scheduling.

   (1) *Scheduling Order.* Except in categories of actions exempted by local rule, the district judge—or a magistrate judge when authorized by local rule—must issue a scheduling order:

   (A) after receiving the parties' report under Rule 26(f); or

   (B) after consulting with the parties' attorneys and any unrepresented parties at a scheduling conference.

   (2) *Time to Issue.* The judge must issue the scheduling order as soon as practicable, but unless the judge finds good cause for delay, the judge must issue it within the earlier of 90 days after any defendant has been served with the complaint or 60 days after any defendant has appeared.

   (3) *Contents of the Order.*

   (A) *Required Contents.* The scheduling order must limit the time to join other parties, amend the pleadings, complete discovery, and file motions.

   (B) *Permitted Contents.* The scheduling order may:

   (i) modify the timing of disclosures under Rules 26(a) and 26(e)(1);

   (ii) modify the extent of discovery;

   (iii) provide for disclosure, discovery, or preservation of electronically stored information;

   (iv) include any agreements the parties reach for asserting claims of privilege or of protection as trial-preparation material after information is produced, including agreements reached under Federal Rule of Evidence 502;

   (v) direct that before moving for an order relating to discovery, the movant must request a conference with the court;

   (vi) set dates for pretrial conferences and for trial; and

   (vii) include other appropriate matters.

   (4) *Modifying a Schedule.* A schedule may be modified only for good cause and with the judge's consent.

(c) Attendance and Matters for Consideration at a Pretrial Conference.

   (1) *Attendance.* A represented party must authorize at least one of its attorneys to make stipulations and admissions about all matters that can reasonably be anticipated for discussion at a pretrial conference. If appropriate, the court may require that a party or its representative be present or reasonably available by other means to consider possible settlement.

   (2) **Matters for Consideration.** At any pretrial conference, the court may consider and take appropriate action on the following matters:

     (A) formulating and simplifying the issues, and eliminating frivolous claims or defenses;

     (B) amending the pleadings if necessary or desirable;

     (C) obtaining admissions and stipulations about facts and documents to avoid unnecessary proof, and ruling in advance on the admissibility of evidence;

     (D) avoiding unnecessary proof and cumulative evidence, and limiting the use of testimony under Federal Rule of Evidence 702;

     (E) determining the appropriateness and timing of summary adjudication under Rule 56;

     (F) controlling and scheduling discovery, including orders affecting disclosures and discovery under Rule 26 and Rules 29 through 37;

     (G) identifying witnesses and documents, scheduling the filing and exchange of any pretrial briefs, and setting dates for further conferences and for trial;

     (H) referring matters to a magistrate judge or a master;

     (I) settling the case and using special procedures to assist in resolving the dispute when authorized by statute or local rule;

     (J) determining the form and content of the pretrial order;

     (K) disposing of pending motions;

     (L) adopting special procedures for managing potentially difficult or protracted actions that may involve complex issues, multiple parties, difficult legal questions, or unusual proof problems;

     (M) ordering a separate trial under Rule 42(b) of a claim, counterclaim, crossclaim, third-party claim, or particular issue;

     (N) ordering the presentation of evidence early in the trial on a manageable issue that might, on the evidence, be the basis for a judgment as a matter of law under Rule 50(a) or a judgment on partial findings under Rule 52(c);

     (O) establishing a reasonable limit on the time allowed to present evidence; and

     (P) facilitating in other ways the just, speedy, and inexpensive disposition of the action.

(d) Pretrial Orders. After any conference under this rule, the court should issue an order reciting the action taken. This order controls the course of the action unless the court modifies it.

(e) Final Pretrial Conference and Orders. The court may hold a final pretrial conference to formulate a trial plan, including a plan to facilitate the admission of evidence. The conference must be held as close to the start of trial as is reasonable, and must be attended by at least one attorney who will conduct the trial for each party and by any unrepresented party. The court may modify the order issued after a final pretrial conference only to prevent manifest injustice.

(f) Sanctions.

   (1) **In General.** On motion or on its own, the court may issue any just orders, including those authorized by Rule 37(b)(2)(A)(ii)–(vii), if a party or its attorney:

     (A) fails to appear at a scheduling or other pretrial conference;

     (B) is substantially unprepared to participate—or does not participate in good faith—in the conference; or

     (C) fails to obey a scheduling or other pretrial order.

(2) ***Imposing Fees and Costs.*** Instead of or in addition to any other sanction, the court must order the party, its attorney, or both to pay the reasonable expenses—including attorney's fees—incurred because of any noncompliance with this rule, unless the noncompliance was substantially justified or other circumstances make an award of expenses unjust.

(Amended April 28, 1983, effective August 1, 1983; March 2, 1987, effective August 1, 1987; April 22, 1993, effective December 1, 1993; April 12, 2006, effective December 1, 2006; April 30, 2007, effective December 1, 2007; April 29, 2015, effective December 1, 2015.)

ADVISORY COMMITTEE NOTES

1937 Adoption

1.   Similar rules of pre-trial procedure are now in force in Boston, Cleveland, Detroit, and Los Angeles, and a rule substantially like this one has been proposed for the urban centers of New York state. For a discussion of the successful operation of pre-trial procedure in relieving the congested condition of trial calendars of the courts in such cities and for the proposed New York plan, see *A Proposal for Minimizing Calendar Delay in Jury Cases* (Dec. 1936—published by the New York Law Society); *Pre-Trial Procedure and Administration,* Third Annual Report of the Judicial Council of the State of New York (1937), pages 207–243; *Report of the Commission on the Administration of Justice in New York State* (1934), pp. (288) to (290). See also *Pre-Trial Procedure in the Wayne Circuit Court,* Detroit, Michigan, Sixth Annual Report of the Judicial Council of Michigan (1936), pp. 63 to 75; and Sunderland, *The Theory and Practice of Pre-trial Procedure* (Dec. 1937) 36 Mich.L.Rev. 215–226, 21 J.Am.Jud.Soc. 125. Compare the English procedure known as the "summons for directions", *English Rules Under the Judicature Act* (The Annual Practice, 1937) O. 38a; and a similar procedure in New Jersey, N.J.S.A. 2:27–135, 2:27–136, 2:27–160; N.J. Supreme Court Rules, 2 N.J.Misc.Rep. (1924) 1230, Rules 94, 92, 93, 95 (the last three as amended 1933, 11 N.J.Misc.Rep. (1933) 955).

2.   Compare the similar procedure under Rule 56(d) (Summary Judgment—Case Not Fully Adjudicated on Motion). Rule 12(g) (Consolidation of Motions), by requiring to some extent the consolidation of motions dealing with matters preliminary to trial, is a step in the same direction. In connection with clause (5) of this rule, see Rules 53(b) (Masters; Reference) and 53(e)(3) (Master's Report; In Jury Actions).

1983 Amendment

Introduction

Rule 16 has not been amended since the Federal Rules were promulgated in 1938. In many respects, the rule has been a success. For example, there is evidence that pretrial conferences may improve the quality of justice rendered in the federal courts by sharpening the preparation and presentation of cases, tending to eliminate trial surprise, and improving, as well as facilitating, the settlement process. See 6 Wright & Miller, *Federal Practice and Procedure:* Civil § 1522 (1971). However, in other respects particularly with regard to case management, the rule has not always been as helpful as it might have been. Thus there has been a widespread feeling that amendment is necessary to encourage pretrial management that meets the needs of modern litigation. See *Report of the National Commission for the Review of Antitrust Laws and Procedures* (1979).

Major criticism of Rule 16 has centered on the fact that its application can result in over-regulation of some cases and under-regulation of others. In simple, run-of-the-mill cases, attorneys have found pretrial requirements burdensome. It is claimed that over-administration leads to a series of mini-trials that result in a waste of an attorney's time and needless expense to a client. Pollack, *Pretrial Procedures More Effectively Handled,* 65 F.R.D. 475 (1974). This is especially likely to be true when pretrial proceedings occur long before trial. At the other end of the spectrum, the discretionary character of Rule 16 and its orientation toward a single conference late in the pretrial process has led to under-administration of complex or protracted cases. Without judicial guidance beginning shortly after institution, these cases often become mired in discovery.

Four sources of criticism of pretrial have been identified. First, conferences often are seen as a mere exchange of legalistic contentions without any real analysis of the particular case. Second, the result frequently is nothing but a formal agreement on minutiae. Third, the conferences are seen as unnecessary and time-consuming in cases that will be settled before trial. Fourth, the meetings can be ceremonial and ritualistic, having little effect on the trial and being of minimal value, particularly when the attorneys attending the sessions are not the ones who will try the case or lack authority to enter into binding stipulations. See generally *McCargo v. Hedrick,* 545 F.2d 393 (4th Cir.1976); Pollack, *Pretrial Procedures More Effectively Handled,* 65 F.R.D. 475 (1974); Rosenberg, *The Pretrial Conference and Effective Justice* 45 (1964).

There also have been difficulties with the pretrial orders that issue following Rule 16 conferences. When an order is entered far in advance of trial, some issues may not be properly formulated. Counsel naturally are cautious and often try to preserve as many options as possible. If the judge who tries the case did not conduct the conference, he could find it difficult to determine exactly what was agreed to at the conference. But any insistence on a detailed order may be too burdensome, depending on the nature or posture of the case.

Given the significant changes in federal civil litigation since 1938 that are not reflected in Rule 16, it has been extensively rewritten and expanded to meet the challenges of modern litigation. Empirical studies reveal that when a trial judge intervenes personally at an early stage to assume judicial control over a case and to schedule dates for completion by the parties of the principal pretrial steps, the case is disposed of by settlement or trial more efficiently and with less cost and delay than when the parties are left to their own devices. Flanders, *Case Management and Court Management in United States District Courts* 17, Federal Judicial Center (1977). Thus, the rule mandates a pretrial scheduling order. However, although scheduling and pretrial conferences are encouraged in appropriate cases, they are not mandated.

Discussion

Subdivision (a); Pretrial Conferences; Objectives. The amended rule makes scheduling and case management an express goal of pretrial procedure. This is done in Rule 16(a) by shifting the emphasis away from a conference focused solely on the trial and toward a process of judicial management that embraces the entire pretrial phase, especially motions and discovery. In addition, the amendment explicitly recognizes some of the objectives of pretrial conferences and the powers that many courts already have assumed. Rule 16 thus will be a more accurate reflection of actual practice.

Subdivision (b); Scheduling and Planning. The most significant change in Rule 16 is the mandatory scheduling order described in Rule 16(b), which is based in part on Wisconsin Civil Procedure Rule 802.10. The idea of scheduling orders is not new. It has been used by many federal courts. See, *e.g.,* Southern District of Indiana, Local Rule 19.

Although a mandatory scheduling order encourages the court to become involved in case management early in the litigation, it represents a degree of judicial involvement that is not warranted in many cases. Thus, subdivision (b) permits each district court to promulgate a local rule under Rule 83 exempting certain categories of cases in which the burdens of scheduling orders exceed the administrative efficiencies that would be gained. See Eastern District of Virginia, Local Rule 12(1). Logical candidates for this treatment include social security disability matters, habeas corpus petitions, forfeitures, and reviews of certain administrative actions.

A scheduling conference may be requested either by the judge, a magistrate when authorized by district court rule, or a party within 120 days after the summons and complaint are filed. If a scheduling conference is not arranged within that time and the case is not exempted by local rule, a scheduling order must be issued under Rule 16(b), after some communication with the parties, which may be by telephone or mail rather than in person. The use of the term "judge" in subdivision (b) reflects the Advisory Committee's judgment that it is preferable that this task should be handled by a district judge rather than a magistrate, except when the magistrate is acting under 28 U.S.C. § 636(c). While personal supervision by the trial judge is preferred, the rule, in recognition of the impracticality or difficulty of complying with such a requirement in some districts, authorizes a district by local rule to delegate the duties to a magistrate. In order to formulate a practicable scheduling order, the judge, or a magistrate when authorized by district court rule, and attorneys are required to develop a timetable for the matters listed in Rule 16(b)(1)–(3). As indicated in Rule 16(b)(4)–(5), the order may also deal with a wide range of other matters. The rule is phrased permissively as to clauses (4) and (5), however, because scheduling these items at an early point may not be feasible or appropriate. Even though subdivision (b) relates only to scheduling, there is no reason why some of the procedural matters listed in Rule 16(c) cannot be addressed at the same time, at least when a scheduling conference is held.

Item (1) assures that at some point both the parties and the pleadings will be fixed, by setting a time within which joinder of parties shall be completed and the pleadings amended.

Item (2) requires setting time limits for interposing various motions that otherwise might be used as stalling techniques.

Item (3) deals with the problem of procrastination and delay by attorneys in a context in which scheduling is especially important-discovery. Scheduling the completion of discovery can serve some of the same functions as the conference described in Rule 26(f).

Item (4) refers to setting dates for conferences and for trial. Scheduling multiple pretrial conferences may well be desirable if the case is complex and the court believes that a more elaborate pretrial structure, such as that described in the *Manual for Complex Litigation,* should be employed. On the other hand, only one pretrial conference may be necessary in an uncomplicated case.

As long as the case is not exempted by local rule, the court must issue a written scheduling order even if no scheduling conference is called. The order, like pretrial orders under the former rule and those under new Rule 16(c), normally will "control the subsequent course of the action." See Rule 16(e). After consultation with the attorneys for the parties and any unrepresented parties-a formal motion is not necessary-the court may modify the schedule on a showing of good cause if it cannot reasonably be met despite the diligence of the party seeking the extension. Since the scheduling order is entered early in the litigation, this standard seems more appropriate than a "manifest injustice" or "substantial hardship" test. Otherwise, a fear that extensions will not be granted may encourage counsel to request the longest possible periods for completing pleading, joinder, and discovery. Moreover, changes in the court's calendar sometimes will oblige the judge or magistrate when authorized by district court rule to modify the scheduling order.

The district courts undoubtedly will develop several prototype scheduling orders for different types of cases. In addition, when no formal conference is held, the court may obtain scheduling information by telephone, mail, or otherwise. In many instances this will result in a scheduling order better suited to the individual case than a standard order, without taking the time that would be required by a formal conference.

Rule 16(b) assures that the judge will take some early control over the litigation, even when its character does not warrant holding a scheduling conference. Despite the fact that the process of preparing a scheduling order does not always bring the attorneys and judge together, the fixing of time limits serves

to stimulate litigants to narrow the areas of inquiry and advocacy to those they believe are truly relevant and material. Time limits not only compress the amount of time for litigation, they should also reduce the amount of resources invested in litigation. Litigants are forced to establish discovery priorities and thus to do the most important work first.

Report of the National Commission for the Review of Antitrust Laws and Procedures 28 (1979).

Thus, except in exempted cases, the judge or a magistrate when authorized by district court rule will have taken some action in every case within 120 days after the complaint is filed that notifies the attorneys that the case will be moving toward trial. Subdivision (b) is reenforced by subdivision (f), which makes it clear that the sanctions for violating a scheduling order are the same as those for violating a pretrial order.

Subdivision (c); Subjects to be Discussed at Pretrial Conferences. This subdivision expands upon the list of things that may be discussed at a pretrial conference that appeared in original Rule 16. The intention is to encourage better planning and management of litigation. Increased judicial control during the pretrial process accelerates the processing and termination of cases. Flanders, *Case Management and Court Management in United States District Courts,* 39 Federal Judicial Center (1977). See also *Report of the National Commission for the Review of Antitrust Laws and Procedures* (1979).

The reference in Rule 16(c)(1) to "formulation" is intended to clarify and confirm the court's power to identify the litigable issues. It has been added in the hope of promoting efficiency and conserving judicial resources by identifying the real issues prior to trial, thereby saving time and expense for everyone. See generally *Meadow Gold Prods. Co. v. Wright,* 278 F.2d 867 (D.C.Cir.1960). The notion is emphasized by expressly authorizing the elimination of frivolous claims or defenses at a pretrial conference. There is no reason to require that this await a formal motion for summary judgment. Nor is there any reason for the court to wait for the parties to initiate the process called for in Rule 16(c)(1).

The timing of any attempt at issue formulation is a matter of judicial discretion. In relatively simple cases it may not be necessary or may take the form of a stipulation between counsel or a request by the court that counsel work together to draft a proposed order.

Counsel bear a substantial responsibility for assisting the court in identifying the factual issues worthy of trial. If counsel fail to identify an issue for the court, the right to have the issue tried is waived. Although an order specifying the issues is intended to be binding, it may be amended at trial to avoid manifest injustice. See Rule 16(e). However, the rule's effectiveness depends on the court employing its discretion sparingly.

Clause (6) acknowledges the widespread availability and use of magistrates. The corresponding provision in the original rule referred only to masters and limited the function of the reference to the making of "findings to be used as evidence" in a case to be tried to a jury. The new text is not limited and broadens the potential use of a magistrate to that permitted by the Magistrate's Act.

Clause (7) explicitly recognizes that it has become commonplace to discuss settlement at pretrial conferences. Since it obviously eases crowded court dockets and results in savings to the litigants and the judicial system, settlement should be facilitated at as early a stage of the litigation as possible. Although it is not the purpose of Rule 16(b)(7) to impose settlement negotiations on unwilling litigants, it is believed that providing a neutral forum for discussing the subject might foster it. See Moore's *Federal Practice* ¶ 16.17; 6 Wright & Miller, *Federal Practice and Procedure: Civil* § 1522 (1971). For instance, a judge to whom a case has been assigned may arrange, on his own motion or at a party's request, to have settlement conferences handled by another member of the court or by a magistrate. The rule does not make settlement conferences mandatory because they would be a waste of time in many cases. See Flanders, *Case Management and Court Management in the United States District Courts,* 39 Federal Judicial Center (1977). Requests for a conference from a party indicating a willingness to talk settlement normally should be honored, unless thought to be frivolous or dilatory.

A settlement conference is appropriate at any time. It may be held in conjunction with a pretrial or discovery conference, although various objectives of pretrial management, such as moving the case toward trial, may not always be compatible with settlement negotiations, and thus a separate settlement conference may be desirable. See 6 Wright & Miller, *Federal Practice and Procedure: Civil* § 1522, at p. 571 (1971).

In addition to settlement, Rule 16(c)(7) refers to exploring the use of procedures other than litigation to resolve the dispute. This includes urging the litigants to employ adjudicatory techniques outside the courthouse. See, for example, the experiment described in *Green, Marks & Olson, Settling Large Case Litigation: An Alternative Approach,* 11 Loyola of L.A.L.Rev. 493 (1978).

Rule 16(c)(10) authorizes the use of special pretrial procedures to expedite the adjudication of potentially difficult or protracted cases. Some district courts obviously have done so for many years. See Rubin, *The Managed Calendar: Some Pragmatic Suggestions About Achieving the Just, Speedy and Inexpensive Determination of Civil Cases in Federal Courts,* 4 Just.Sys.J. 135 (1976). Clause 10 provides an explicit authorization for such procedures and encourages their use. No particular techniques have been described; the Committee felt that flexibility and experience are the keys to efficient management of complex cases. Extensive guidance is offered in such documents as the *Manual for Complex Litigation.*

The rule simply identifies characteristics that make a case a strong candidate for special treatment. The four mentioned are illustrative, not exhaustive, and overlap to some degree. But experience has shown that one or more of them will be present in every protracted or difficult case and it seems desirable to set them out. See Kendig, *Procedures for Management of Non-Routine Cases,* 3 Hofstra L.Rev. 701 (1975).

The last sentence of subdivision (c) is new. See Wisconsin Civil Procedure Rule 802.11(2). It has been added to meet one of the criticisms of the present practice described earlier and insure proper preconference preparation so that the meeting is more than a ceremonial or ritualistic event. The reference to "authority" is not intended to insist upon the ability to settle the litigation. Nor should the rule be read to encourage the judge conducting the conference to compel attorneys to enter into stipulations or to make admissions that they consider to be unreasonable, that touch on matters that could not normally have been anticipated to arise at the conference, or on subjects of a dimension that normally require prior consultation with and approval from the client.

Subdivision (d); Final Pretrial Conference. This provision has been added to make it clear that the time between any final pretrial conference (which in a simple case may be the **only** pretrial conference) and trial should be as short as possible to be certain that the litigants make substantial progress with the case and avoid the inefficiency of having that preparation repeated when there is a delay between the last pretrial conference and trial. An optimum time of 10 days to two weeks has been suggested by one federal judge. Rubin, *The Managed Calendar: Some Pragmatic Suggestions About Achieving the Just, Speedy and Inexpensive Determination of Civil Cases in Federal Courts,* 4 Just.Sys.J. 135, 141 (1976). The Committee, however, concluded that it would be inappropriate to fix a precise time in the rule, given the numerous variables that could bear on the matter. Thus the timing has been left to the court's discretion.

At least one of the attorneys who will conduct the trial for each party must be present at the final pretrial conference. At this late date there should be no doubt as to which attorney or attorneys this will be. Since the agreements and stipulations made at this final conference will control the trial, the presence of lawyers who will be involved in it is especially useful to assist the judge in structuring the case, and to lead to a more effective trial.

Subdivision (e); Pretrial Orders. Rule 16(e) does not substantially change the portion of the original rule dealing with pretrial orders. The purpose of an order is to guide the course of the litigation and the language of the original rule making that clear has been retained. No compelling reason has been found for major revision, especially since this portion of the rule has been interpreted and clarified by over forty years of judicial decisions with comparatively little difficulty. See 6 Wright & Miller, *Federal Practice and Procedure: Civil* §§ 1521–30 (1971). Changes in language therefore have been kept to a minimum to avoid confusion.

Since the amended rule encourages more extensive pretrial management than did the original, two or more conferences may be held in many cases. The language of Rule 16(e) recognizes this possibility and the corresponding need to issue more than one pretrial order in a single case.

Once formulated, pretrial orders should not be changed lightly; but total inflexibility is undesirable. See, *e.g., Clark v. Pennsylvania R.R. Co.,* 328 F.2d 591 (2d Cir.1964). The exact words used to describe the standard for amending the pretrial order probably are less important than the meaning given them in practice. By not imposing any limitation on the ability to modify a pretrial order, the rule reflects the reality that in any process of continuous management, what is done at one conference may have to be altered at the next. In the case of the final pretrial order, however, a more stringent standard is called for and the words "to prevent manifest injustice," which appeared in the original rule, have been retained. They have the virtue of familiarity and adequately describe the restraint the trial judge should exercise.

Many local rules make the plaintiff's attorney responsible for drafting a proposed pretrial order, either before or after the conference. Others allow the court to appoint any of the attorneys to perform the task, and others leave it to the court. See Note, *Pretrial Conference: A Critical Examination of Local Rules Adopted by Federal District Courts,* 64 Va.L.Rev. 467 (1978). Rule 16 has never addressed this matter. Since there is no consensus about which method of drafting the order works best and there is no reason to believe that nationwide uniformity is needed, the rule has been left silent on the point. See *Handbook for Effective Pretrial Procedure,* 37 F.R.D. 225 (1964).

Subdivision (f); Sanctions. Original Rule 16 did not mention the sanctions that might be imposed for failing to comply with the rule. However, courts have not hesitated to enforce it by appropriate measures. See, e.g., *Link v. Wabash R. Co.,* 370 U.S. 628 (1962) (district court's dismissal under Rule 41(b) after plaintiff's attorney failed to appear at a pretrial conference upheld); *Admiral Theatre Corp. v. Douglas Theatre,* 585 F.2d 877 (8th Cir.1978) (district court has discretion to exclude exhibits or refuse to permit the testimony of a witness not listed prior to trial in contravention of its pretrial order).

To reflect that existing practice, and to obviate dependence upon Rule 41(b) or the court's inherent power to regulate litigation, *cf. Societe Internationale Pour Participations Industrielles et Commerciales, S.A. v. Rogers,* 357 U.S. 197 (1958), Rule 16(f) expressly provides for imposing sanctions on disobedient or recalcitrant parties, their attorneys, or both in four types of situations. Rodes, Ripple & Mooney, *Sanctions Imposable for Violations of the Federal Rules of Civil Procedure* 65–67, 80–84, Federal Judicial Center (1981). Furthermore, explicit reference to sanctions reenforces the rule's intention to encourage forceful judicial management.

Rule 16(f) incorporates portions of Rule 37(b)(2), which prescribes sanctions for failing to make discovery. This should facilitate application of Rule 16(f), since courts and lawyers already are familiar with the Rule 37 standards. Among the sanctions authorized by the new subdivision are: preclusion order, striking a pleading, staying the proceeding, default judgment, contempt, and charging a party, his attorney, or both with the expenses, including attorney's fees, caused by noncompliance. The contempt sanction, however, is only available for a violation of a court order. The references in Rule 16(f) are not exhaustive.

As is true under Rule 37(b)(2), the imposition of sanctions may be sought by either the court or a party. In addition, the court has discretion to impose whichever sanction it feels is appropriate under the circumstances. Its action is reviewable under the abuse-of-discretion standard. See *National Hockey League v. Metropolitan Hockey Club, Inc.,* 427 U.S. 639 (1976).

1987 Amendment

The amendments are technical. No substantive change is intended.

1993 Amendments

Subdivision (b). One purpose of this amendment is to provide a more appropriate deadline for the initial scheduling order required by the rule. The former rule directed that the order be entered within 120 days from the filing of the complaint. This requirement has created problems because Rule 4(m) allows 120 days for service and ordinarily at least one defendant should be available to participate in the process of formulating the scheduling order. The revision provides that the order is to be entered within 90 days after the date a defendant first appears (whether by answer or by a motion under Rule 12) or, if earlier (as may occur in some actions against the United States or if service is waived under Rule 4), within 120 days after service of the complaint on a defendant. The longer time provided by the revision is not intended to encourage unnecessary delays in entering the scheduling order. Indeed, in most cases the order can and should be entered at a much earlier date. Rather, the additional time is intended to alleviate problems in multi-defendant cases and should ordinarily be adequate to enable participation by all defendants initially named in the action.

In many cases the scheduling order can and should be entered before this deadline. However, when setting a scheduling conference, the court should take into account the effect this setting will have in establishing deadlines for the parties to meet under revised Rule 26(f) and to exchange information under revised Rule 26(a)(1). While the parties are expected to stipulate to additional time for making their disclosures when warranted by the circumstances, a scheduling conference held before defendants have had time to learn much about the case may result in diminishing the value of the Rule 26(f) meeting, the parties' proposed discovery plan, and indeed the conference itself.

New paragraph (4) has been added to highlight that it will frequently be desirable for the scheduling order to include provisions relating to the timing of disclosures under Rule 26(a). While the initial disclosures required by Rule 26(a)(1) will ordinarily have been made before entry of the scheduling order, the timing and sequence for disclosure of expert testimony and of the witnesses and exhibits to be used at trial should be tailored to the circumstances of the case and is a matter that should be considered at the initial scheduling conference. Similarly, the scheduling order might contain provisions modifying the extent of discovery (*e.g.,* number and length of depositions) otherwise permitted under these rules or by a local rule.

The report from the attorneys concerning their meeting and proposed discovery plan, as required by revised Rule 26(f), should be submitted to the court before the scheduling order is entered. Their proposals, particularly regarding matters on which they agree, should be of substantial value to the court in setting the timing and limitations on discovery and should reduce the time of the court needed to conduct a meaningful conference under Rule 16(b). As under the prior rule, while a scheduling order is mandated, a scheduling conference is not. However, in view of the benefits to be derived from the litigants and a judicial officer meeting in person, a Rule 16(b) conference should, to the extent practicable, be held in all cases that will involve discovery.

This subdivision, as well as subdivision (c)(8), also is revised to reflect the new title of United States Magistrate Judges pursuant to the Judicial Improvements Act of 1990.

Subdivision (c). The primary purposes of the changes in subdivision (c) are to call attention to the opportunities for structuring of trial under Rules 42, 50, and 52 and to eliminate questions that have occasionally been raised regarding the authority of the court to make appropriate orders designed either to facilitate settlement or to provide for an efficient and economical trial. The prefatory language of this subdivision is revised to clarify the court's power to enter appropriate orders at a conference notwithstanding the objection of a party. Of course settlement is dependent upon agreement by the parties and, indeed, a conference is most effective and productive when the parties participate in a spirit of cooperation and mindful of their responsibilities under Rule 1.

Paragraph (4) is revised to clarify that in advance of trial the court may address the need for, and possible limitations on, the use of expert testimony under Rule 702 of the Federal Rules of Evidence. Even when proposed expert testimony might be admissible under the standards of Rules 403 and 702 of the evidence rules, the court may preclude or limit such testimony if the cost to the litigants—which may include the cost to adversaries of securing testimony on the same subjects by other experts—would be unduly expensive given the needs of the case and the other evidence available at trial.

Paragraph (5) is added (and the remaining paragraphs renumbered) in recognition that use of Rule 56 to avoid or reduce the scope of trial is a topic that can, and often should, be considered at a pretrial conference. Renumbered paragraph (11) enables the court to rule on pending motions for summary adjudication that are ripe for decision at the time of the conference. Often, however, the potential use of Rule 56 is a matter that arises from discussions during a conference. The court may then call for motions to be filed.

Paragraph (6) is added to emphasize that a major objective of pretrial conferences should be to consider appropriate controls on the extent and timing of discovery. In many cases the court should also specify the times and sequence for disclosure of written reports from experts under revised Rule 26(a)(2)(B) and perhaps direct changes in the types of experts from whom written reports are required. Consideration should also be given to possible changes in the timing or form of the disclosure of trial witnesses and documents under Rule 26(a)(3).

Paragraph (9) is revised to describe more accurately the various procedures that, in addition to traditional settlement conferences, may be helpful in settling litigation. Even if a case cannot immediately be settled, the judge and attorneys can explore possible use of alternative procedures such as mini-trials, summary jury trials, mediation, neutral evaluation, and nonbinding arbitration that can lead to consensual resolution of the dispute without a full trial on the merits. The rule acknowledges the presence of statutes and local rules or plans that may authorize use of some of these procedures even when not agreed to by the parties. See 28 U.S.C. §§ 473(a)(6), 473(b)(4), 651–58; Section 104(b)(2), Pub.L. 101–650. The rule does not attempt to resolve questions as to the extent a court would be authorized to require such proceedings as an exercise of its inherent powers.

The amendment of paragraph (9) should be read in conjunction with the sentence added to the end of subdivision (c), authorizing the court to direct that, in appropriate cases, a responsible representative of the parties be present or available by telephone during a conference in order to discuss possible settlement of the case. The sentence refers to participation by a party or its representative. Whether this would be the individual party, an officer of a corporate party, a representative from an insurance carrier, or someone else would depend on the circumstances. Particularly in litigation in which governmental agencies or large amounts of money are involved, there may be no one with on-the-spot settlement authority, and the most that should be expected is access to a person who would have a major role in submitting a recommendation to the body or board with ultimate decision-making responsibility. The selection of the appropriate representative should ordinarily be left to the party and its counsel. Finally, it should be noted that the unwillingness of a party to be available, even by telephone, for a settlement conference may be a clear signal that the time and expense involved in pursuing settlement is likely to be unproductive and that personal participation by the parties should not be required.

The explicit authorization in the rule to require personal participation in the manner stated is not intended to limit the reasonable exercise of the court's inherent powers, *e.g., G. Heileman Brewing Co. v. Joseph Oat Corp.*, 871 F.2d 648 (7th Cir.1989), or its power to require party participation under the Civil Justice Reform Act of 1990. See 28 U.S.C. § 473(b)(5) (civil justice expense and delay reduction plans adopted by district courts may include requirement that representatives "with authority to bind [parties] in settlement discussions" be available during settlement conferences).

New paragraphs (13) and (14) are added to call attention to the opportunities for structuring of trial under Rule 42 and under revised Rules 50 and 52.

Paragraph (15) is also new. It supplements the power of the court to limit the extent of evidence under Rules 403 and 611(a) of the Federal Rules of Evidence, which typically would be invoked as a result of developments during trial. Limits on the length of trial established at a conference in advance of trial can provide the parties with a better opportunity to determine priorities and exercise selectivity in presenting evidence than when limits are imposed during trial. Any such limits must be reasonable under the circumstances, and ordinarily the court should impose them only after receiving appropriate submissions from the parties outlining the nature of the testimony expected to be presented through various witnesses, and the expected duration of direct and cross-examination.

2006 Amendment

The amendment to Rule 16(b) is designed to alert the court to the possible need to address the handling of discovery of electronically stored information early in the litigation if such discovery is expected to occur. Rule 26(f) is amended to direct the parties to discuss discovery of electronically stored information if such discovery is contemplated in the action. Form 35 is amended to call for a report to the court about the results of this discussion. In many instances, the court's involvement early in the litigation will help avoid difficulties that might otherwise arise.

Rule 16(b) is also amended to include among the topics that may be addressed in the scheduling order any agreements that the parties reach to facilitate discovery by minimizing the risk of waiver of privilege or work-product protection. Rule 26(f) is amended to add to the discovery plan the parties' proposal for the court to enter a case-management or other order adopting such an agreement. The parties may agree to various arrangements. For example, they may agree to initial provision of requested materials without waiver of privilege or protection to enable the party seeking production to designate the materials desired or protection for actual production, with the privilege review of only those materials to follow. Alternatively, they may agree that if privileged or protected information is inadvertently produced, the producing party may by timely notice assert the privilege or protection and obtain return of the materials without waiver. Other arrangements are possible. In most circumstances, a party who receives information under such an arrangement cannot assert that production of the information waived a claim of privilege or of protection as trial-preparation material.

An order that includes the parties' agreement may be helpful in avoiding delay and excessive cost in discovery. *See Manual for Complex Litigation* (4th) § 11.446. Rule 16(b)(6) recognizes the propriety of including such agreements in the court's order. The rule does not provide the court with authority to enter such a case-management or other order without party agreement, or limit the court's authority to act on motion.

2007 Amendment

The language of Rule 16 has been amended as part of the general restyling of the Civil Rules to make them more easily understood and to make style and terminology consistent throughout the rules. These changes are intended to be stylistic only.

When a party or its representative is not present, it is enough to be reasonably available by any suitable means, whether telephone or other communication device.

2015 Amendment

The provision for consulting at a scheduling conference by "telephone, mail, or other means" is deleted. A scheduling conference is more effective if the court and parties engage in direct simultaneous communication. The conference may be held in person, by telephone, or by more sophisticated electronic means.

The time to issue the scheduling order is reduced to the earlier of 90 days (not 120 days) after any defendant has been served, or 60 days (not 90 days) after any defendant has appeared. This change, together with the shortened time for making service under Rule 4(m), will reduce delay at the beginning of litigation. At the same time, a new provision recognizes that the court may find good cause to extend the time to issue the scheduling order. In some cases it may be that the parties cannot prepare adequately for a meaningful Rule 26(f) conference and then a scheduling conference in the time allowed. Litigation involving complex issues, multiple parties, and large organizations, public or private, may be more likely to need extra time to establish meaningful collaboration between counsel and the people who can supply the information needed to participate in a useful way. Because the time for the Rule 26(f) conference is geared to the time for the scheduling conference or order, an order extending the time for the scheduling conference will also extend the time for the Rule 26(f) conference. But in most cases it will be desirable to hold at least a first scheduling conference in the time set by the rule.

Three items are added to the list of permitted contents in Rule 16(b)(3)(B).

The order may provide for preservation of electronically stored information, a topic also added to the provisions of a discovery plan under Rule 26(f)(3)(C). Parallel amendments of Rule 37(e) recognize that a duty to preserve discoverable information may arise before an action is filed.

The order also may include agreements incorporated in a court order under Evidence Rule 502 controlling the effects of disclosure of information covered by attorney-client privilege or work-product protection, a topic also added to the provisions of a discovery plan under Rule 26(f)(3)(D).

Finally, the order may direct that before filing a motion for an order relating to discovery the movant must request a conference with the court. Many judges who hold such conferences find them an efficient way to resolve most discovery disputes without the delay and burdens attending a formal motion, but the decision whether to require such conferences is left to the discretion of the judge in each case.

Gap Report

No changes were made in the published rule text. Language was added to the Committee Note to address examples of circumstances that may establish good cause to delay issuing the scheduling order.

TITLE IV. PARTIES

Rule 17.   Plaintiff and Defendant; Capacity; Public Officers

(a) Real Party in Interest.

    (1) *Designation in General.* An action must be prosecuted in the name of the real party in interest. The following may sue in their own names without joining the person for whose benefit the action is brought:

        (A) an executor;

        (B) an administrator;

        (C) a guardian;

        (D) a bailee;

        (E) a trustee of an express trust;

        (F) a party with whom or in whose name a contract has been made for another's benefit; and

        (G) a party authorized by statute.

    (2) *Action in the Name of the United States for Another's Use or Benefit.* When a federal statute so provides, an action for another's use or benefit must be brought in the name of the United States.

    (3) *Joinder of the Real Party in Interest.* The court may not dismiss an action for failure to prosecute in the name of the real party in interest until, after an objection, a reasonable time has been allowed for the real party in interest to ratify, join, or be substituted into the action. After ratification, joinder, or substitution, the action proceeds as if it had been originally commenced by the real party in interest.

(b) Capacity to Sue or Be Sued. Capacity to sue or be sued is determined as follows:

(1) for an individual who is not acting in a representative capacity, by the law of the individual's domicile;

(2) for a corporation, by the law under which it was organized; and

(3) for all other parties, by the law of the state where the court is located, except that:

  (A) a partnership or other unincorporated association with no such capacity under that state's law may sue or be sued in its common name to enforce a substantive right existing under the United States Constitution or laws; and

  (B) 28 U.S.C. §§ 754 and 959(a) govern the capacity of a receiver appointed by a United States court to sue or be sued in a United States court.

(c) Minor or Incompetent Person.

  (1) *With a Representative.* The following representatives may sue or defend on behalf of a minor or an incompetent person:

  (A) a general guardian;

  (B) a committee;

  (C) a conservator; or

  (D) a like fiduciary.

  (2) *Without a Representative.* A minor or an incompetent person who does not have a duly appointed representative may sue by a next friend or by a guardian ad litem. The court must appoint a guardian ad litem—or issue another appropriate order—to protect a minor or incompetent person who is unrepresented in an action.

(d) Public Officer's Title and Name. A public officer who sues or is sued in an official capacity may be designated by official title rather than by name, but the court may order that the officer's name be added.

(Amended December 27, 1946, effective March 19, 1948; December 29, 1948, effective October 20, 1949; February 28, 1966, effective July 1, 1966; March 2, 1987, effective August 1, 1987; April 25, 1988, effective August 1, 1988; amended by Pub.L. 100–690, Title VII, § 7049, November 18, 1988, 102 Stat. 4401 (although amendment by Pub.L. 100–690 could not be executed due to prior amendment by Court order which made the same change effective August 1, 1988); April 30, 2007, effective December 1, 2007.)

ADVISORY COMMITTEE NOTES

1937 Adoption

Note to Subdivision (a). The real party in interest provision, except for the last clause which is new, is taken verbatim from [former] Equity Rule 37 (Parties Generally—Intervention), except that the word "expressly" has been omitted. For similar provisions see N.Y.C.P.A., (1937) § 210; Wyo.Rev.Stat.Ann. (1931) §§ 89–501, 89–502, 89–503; *English Rules Under the Judicature Act* (The Annual Practice, 1937) O. 16, r. 8. See, also Equity Rule 41 (Suit to Execute Trusts of Will—Heir as Party). For examples of statutes of the United States providing particularly for an action for the use or benefit of another in the name of the United States, see U.S.C., Title 40, § 270b [see now 40 U.S.C.A. § 3133(b)] (Suit by persons furnishing labor and material for work on public building contracts * * * may sue on a payment bond, "in the name of the United States for the use of the person suing"); and U.S.C., Title 25, § 201 (Penalties under laws relating to Indians—how recovered). Compare U.S.C., Title 26, Int.Rev.Code [1939], § 3745(c) [former § 1645(c)] (Suits for penalties, fines, and forfeitures, under this title, where not otherwise provided for, to be in name of United States).

Note to Subdivision (b). For capacity see generally Clark and Moore, *New Federal Civil Procedure—* II. Pleadings and Parties, 44 Yale L.J. 1291, 1312–1317 (1935) and specifically *Coppedge v. Clinton,* 72 F.2d 531 (C.C.A.10th, 1934) (natural person); *David Lupton's Sons Co. v. Automobile Club of America,* 225 U.S. 489, 32 S.Ct. 711, 56 L.Ed. 1177, Ann.Cas.1914A, 699 (1912) (corporation); *Puerto Rico v. Russell & Co.,* 288 U.S. 476, 53 S.Ct. 447, 77 L.Ed. 903 (1933) (unincorporated assn.); *United Mine Workers of America v.*

Coronado Coal Co., 259 U.S. 344, 42 S.Ct. 570, 66 L.Ed. 975, 27 A.L.R. 762 (1922) (federal substantive right enforced against unincorporated association by suit against the association in its common name without naming all its members as parties). This rule follows the existing law as to such associations, as declared in the case last cited above. Compare *Moffat Tunnel League v. United States,* 289 U.S. 113, 53 S.Ct. 543, 77 L.Ed. 1069 (1933). See note to Rule 23, clause (1).

Note to Subdivision (c). The provision for infants and incompetent persons is substantially former Equity Rule 70 (Suits by or Against Incompetents) with slight additions. Compare the more detailed English provisions, *English Rules Under the Judicature Act* (The Annual Practice, 1937) O. 16, r.r. 16–21.

1946 Amendment

Note. The new matter [in subdivision (b)] makes clear the controlling character of Rule 66 regarding suits by or against a federal receiver in a federal court.

1948 Amendment

The amendment effective October 20, 1949, deleted the words "Rule 66" at the end of subdivision (b) and substituted the words "Title 28, U.S.C., §§ 754 and 959(a)".

1966 Amendment

The minor change in the text of the rule is designed to make it clear that the specific instances enumerated are not exceptions to, but illustrations of, the rule. These illustrations, of course, carry no negative implication to the effect that there are not other instances of recognition as the real party in interest of one whose standing as such may be in doubt. The enumeration is simply of cases in which there might be substantial doubt as to the issue but for the specific enumeration. There are other potentially arguable cases that are not excluded by the enumeration. For example, the enumeration states that the promisee in a contract for the benefit of a third party may sue as real party in interest; it does not say, because it is obvious, that the third-party beneficiary may sue (when the applicable law gives him that right.)

The rule adds to the illustrative list of real parties in interest a bailee—meaning, of course, a bailee suing on behalf of the bailor with respect to the property bailed. (When the possessor of property other than the owner sues for an invasion of the possessory interest he is the real party in interest.) The word "bailee" is added primarily to preserve the admiralty practice whereby the owner of a vessel as bailee of the cargo, or the master of the vessel as bailee of both vessel and cargo, sues for damage to either property interest or both. But there is no reason to limit such a provision to maritime situations. The owner of a warehouse in which household furniture is stored is equally entitled to sue on behalf of the numerous owners of the furniture stored. Cf. *Gulf Oil Corp. v. Gilbert*, 330 U.S. 501 (1947).

The provision that no action shall be dismissed on the ground that it is not prosecuted in the name of the real party in interest until a reasonable time has been allowed, after the objection has been raised, for ratification, substitution, etc., is added simply in the interests of justice. In its origin the rule concerning the real party in interest was permissive in purpose: it was designed to allow an assignee to sue in his own name. That having been accomplished, the modern function of the rule in its negative aspect is simply to protect the defendant against a subsequent action by the party actually entitled to recover, and to insure generally that the judgment will have its proper effect as res judicata.

This provision keeps pace with the law as it is actually developing. Modern decisions are inclined to be lenient when an honest mistake has been made in choosing the party in whose name the action is to be filed—in both maritime and nonmaritime cases. See *Levinson v. Deupree*, 345 U.S. 648 (1953); *Link Aviation, Inc. v. Downs*, 325 F.2d 613 (D.C.Cir. 1963). The provision should not be misunderstood or distorted. It is intended to prevent forfeiture when determination of the proper party to sue is difficult or when an understandable mistake has been made. It does not mean, for example, that, following an airplane crash in which all aboard were killed, an action may be filed in the name of John Doe (a fictitious person), as personal representative of Richard Roe (another fictitious person), in the hope that at a later time the attorney filing the action may substitute the real name of the real personal representative of a real victim, and have the benefit of suspension of the limitation period. It does not even mean, when an action is filed by the personal representative of John Smith, of Buffalo, in the good faith belief that he was aboard the flight, that upon discovery that Smith is alive and well, having missed the fatal flight, the representative of James Brown, of

San Francisco, an actual victim, can be substituted to take advantage of the suspension of the limitation period. It is, in cases of this sort, intended to insure against forfeiture and injustice—in short, to codify in broad terms the salutary principle of *Levinson v. Deupree*, 345 U.S. 648 (1953), and *Link Aviation, Inc. v. Downs*, 325 F.2d 613 (D.C.Cir. 1963).

1987 Amendment

The amendments are technical. No substantive change is intended.

1988 Amendment

The amendment is technical. No substantive change is intended.

2007 Amendment

The language of Rule 17 has been amended as part of the general restyling of the Civil Rules to make them more easily understood and to make style and terminology consistent throughout the rules. These changes are intended to be stylistic only.

Rule 17(d) incorporates the provisions of former Rule 25(d)(2), which fit better with Rule 17.

Rule 18.   Joinder of Claims

(a) In General. A party asserting a claim, counterclaim, crossclaim, or third-party claim may join, as independent or alternative claims, as many claims as it has against an opposing party.

(b) Joinder of Contingent Claims. A party may join two claims even though one of them is contingent on the disposition of the other; but the court may grant relief only in accordance with the parties' relative substantive rights. In particular, a plaintiff may state a claim for money and a claim to set aside a conveyance that is fraudulent as to that plaintiff, without first obtaining a judgment for the money.

(Amended February 28, 1966, effective July 1, 1966; March 2, 1987, effective August 1, 1987; April 30, 2007, effective December 1, 2007.)

ADVISORY COMMITTEE NOTES

1937 Adoption

Note to Subdivision (a). 1. Recent development, both in code and common law states, has been toward unlimited joinder of actions. See Ill.Rev.Stat. (1937) ch. 110, § 168; N.J.S.A. 2:27–37, as modified by N.J.Sup.Ct.Rules, Rule 21, 2 N.J.Misc. 1208 (1924); N.Y.C.P.A. (1937) § 258 as amended by Laws of 1935, ch. 339.

2.   This provision for joinder of actions has been patterned upon [former] Equity Rule 26 (Joinder of Causes of Action) and broadened to include multiple parties. Compare the English practice, *English Rules Under the Judicature Act* (The Annual Practice, 1937) O. 18, r.r. 1–9 (noting rules 1 and 6). The earlier American codes set forth classes of joinder, following the now abandoned New York rule. See N.Y.C.P.A. § 258 before amended in 1935; Compare Kan.Gen.Stat.Ann. (1935) § 60–601; Wis.Stat.(1935) § 263.04 for the more liberal practice.

3.   The provisions of this rule for the joinder of claims are subject to Rule 82 (Jurisdiction and Venue Unaffected). For the jurisdictional aspects of joinder of claims, see Shulman and Jaegerman, *Some Jurisdictional Limitations on Federal Procedure* (1936), 45 Yale L.J. 393, 397–410. For separate trials of joined claims, see Rule 42(b).

Note to Subdivision (b). This rule is inserted to make it clear that in a single action a party should be accorded all the relief to which he is entitled regardless of whether it is legal or equitable or both. This necessarily includes a deficiency judgment in foreclosure actions formerly provided for in [former] Equity Rule 10 (Decree for Deficiency in Foreclosures, Etc.). In respect to fraudulent conveyances the rule changes the former rule requiring a prior judgment against the owner (*Braun v. American Laundry Mach. Co.*, 56 F.2d 197 (S.D.N.Y. 1932)) to conform to the provisions of the Uniform Fraudulent Conveyance Act, §§ 9 and 10. See McLaughlin, *Application of the Uniform Fraudulent Conveyance Act,* 46 Harv.L.Rev. 404, 444 (1933).

1966 Amendment

The Rules "proceed upon the theory that no inconvenience can result from the joinder of any two or more matters in the pleadings, but only from trying two or more matters together which have little or nothing in common." Sunderland, *The New Federal Rules*, 45 W.Va.L.Q. 5, 13 (1938); see Clark, Code Pleading 58 (2d ed. 1947). Accordingly, Rule 18(a) has permitted a party to plead multiple claims of all types against an opposing party, subject to the court's power to direct an appropriate procedure for trying the claims. See Rules 42(b), 20(b), 21.

The liberal policy regarding joinder of claims in the pleadings extends to cases with multiple parties. However, the language used in the second sentence of Rule 18(a)—"if the requirements of Rules 19 [necessary joinder of parties], 20 [permissive joinder of parties], and 22 [interpleader] are satisfied"—has led some courts to infer that the rules regulating joinder of parties are intended to carry back to Rule 18(a) and to impose some special limits on joinder of claims in multiparty cases. In particular, Rule 20(a) has been read as restricting the operation of Rule 18(a) in certain situations in which a number of parties have been permissively joined in an action. In *Federal Housing Admr. v. Christianson*, 26 F.Supp. 419 (D.Conn.1939), the indorsee of two notes sued the three comakers of one note, and sought to join in the action a count on a second note which had been made by two of the three defendants. There was no doubt about the propriety of the joinder of the three parties defendant, for a right to relief was being asserted against all three defendants which arose out of a single "transaction" (the first note) and a question of fact or law "common" to all three defendants would arise in the action. See the text of Rule 20(a). The court, however, refused to allow the joinder of the count on the second note, on the ground that this right to relief, assumed to arise from a distinct transaction, did not involve a question common to all the defendants but only two of them. For analysis of the *Christianson* case and other authorities, see 2 Barron & Holtzoff, *Federal Practice & Procedure*, § 533.1 (Wright ed. 1961); 3 Moore's *Federal Practice*, par. 18.04[3] (2d ed. 1963).

If the court's view is followed, it becomes necessary to enter at the pleading stage into speculations about the exact relation between the claim sought to be joined against fewer than all the defendants properly joined in the action, and the claims asserted against all the defendants. Cf. Wright, *Joinder of Claims and Parties Under Modern Pleading Rules*, 36 Minn.L.Rev. 580, 605–06 (1952). Thus if it could be found in the Christianson situation that the claim on the second note arose out of the same transaction as the claim on the first or out of a transaction forming part of a "series," and that any question of fact or law with respect to the second note also arose with regard to the first, it would be held that the claim on the second note could be joined in the complaint. See 2 Barron & Holtzoff, supra, at 109; see also id. at 198 n. 60.4; cf. 3 Moore's *Federal Practice*, supra, at 1811. Such pleading niceties provide a basis for delaying and wasteful maneuver. It is more compatible with the design of the Rules to allow the claim to be joined in the pleading, leaving the question of possible separate trial of that claim to be later decided. See 2 Barron & Holtzoff, supra, § 533.1; Wright, supra, 36 Minn.L.Rev. at 604–11; *Developments in the Law—Multiparty Litigation in the Federal Courts*, 71 Harv.[L.Rev.] 874, 970–71 (1958); Commentary, *Relation Between Joinder of Parties and Joinder of Claims*, 5 F.R.Serv. 822 (1942). It is instructive to note that the court in the *Christianson* case, while holding that the claim on the second note could not be joined as a matter of pleading, held open the possibility that both claims would later be consolidated for trial under Rule 42(a). See 26 F.Supp. 419.

Rule 18(a) is now amended not only to overcome the *Christianson* decision and similar authority, but also to state clearly as a comprehensive proposition, that a party asserting a claim (an original claim, counterclaim, cross-claim, or third-party claim) may join as many claims as he has against an opposing party. See *Noland Co., Inc. v. Graver Tank & Mfg. Co.*, 301 F.2d 43, 49–51 (4th Cir.1962); but cf. *C. W. Humphrey Co. v. Security Alum. Co.*, 31 F.R.D. 41 (E.D.Mich.1962). This permitted joinder of claims is not affected by the fact that there are multiple parties in the action. The joinder of parties is governed by other rules operating independently.

It is emphasized that amended Rule 18(a) deals only with pleading. As already indicated, a claim properly joined as a matter of pleading need not be proceeded with together with the other claims if fairness or convenience justifies separate treatment.

Amended Rule 18(a), like the rule prior to amendment, does not purport to deal with questions of jurisdiction or venue which may arise with respect to claims properly joined as a matter of pleading. See Rule 82.

See also the amendment of Rule 20(a) and the Advisory Committee's Note thereto.

Free joinder of claims and remedies is one of the basic purposes of unification of the admiralty and civil procedure. The amendment accordingly provides for the inclusion in the rule of maritime claims as well as those which are legal and equitable in character.

1987 Amendment

The amendments are technical. No substantive change is intended.

2007 Amendment

The language of Rule 18 has been amended as part of the general restyling of the Civil Rules to make them more easily understood and to make style and terminology consistent throughout the rules. These changes are intended to be stylistic only.

Modification of the obscure former reference to a claim "heretofore cognizable only after another claim has been prosecuted to a conclusion" avoids any uncertainty whether Rule 18(b)'s meaning is fixed by retrospective inquiry from some particular date.

Rule 19.   Required Joinder of Parties

(a) Persons Required to Be Joined if Feasible.

    (1) *Required Party.* A person who is subject to service of process and whose joinder will not deprive the court of subject-matter jurisdiction must be joined as a party if:

        (A) in that person's absence, the court cannot accord complete relief among existing parties; or

        (B) that person claims an interest relating to the subject of the action and is so situated that disposing of the action in the person's absence may:

            (i) as a practical matter impair or impede the person's ability to protect the interest; or

            (ii) leave an existing party subject to a substantial risk of incurring double, multiple, or otherwise inconsistent obligations because of the interest.

    (2) *Joinder by Court Order.* If a person has not been joined as required, the court must order that the person be made a party. A person who refuses to join as a plaintiff may be made either a defendant or, in a proper case, an involuntary plaintiff.

    (3) *Venue.* If a joined party objects to venue and the joinder would make venue improper, the court must dismiss that party.

(b) When Joinder Is Not Feasible. If a person who is required to be joined if feasible cannot be joined, the court must determine whether, in equity and good conscience, the action should proceed among the existing parties or should be dismissed. The factors for the court to consider include:

    (1) the extent to which a judgment rendered in the person's absence might prejudice that person or the existing parties;

    (2) the extent to which any prejudice could be lessened or avoided by:

        (A) protective provisions in the judgment;

        (B) shaping the relief; or

        (C) other measures;

    (3) whether a judgment rendered in the person's absence would be adequate; and

    (4) whether the plaintiff would have an adequate remedy if the action were dismissed for nonjoinder.

(c) **Pleading the Reasons for Nonjoinder.** When asserting a claim for relief, a party must state:

(1) the name, if known, of any person who is required to be joined if feasible but is not joined; and

(2) the reasons for not joining that person.

(d) **Exception for Class Actions.** This rule is subject to Rule 23.

(Amended February 28, 1966, effective July 1, 1966; March 2, 1987, effective August 1, 1987; April 30, 2007, effective December 1, 2007.)

ADVISORY COMMITTEE NOTES

1937 Adoption

Note to Subdivision (a). The first sentence with verbal differences (e.g., "united" interest for "joint" interest) is to be found in [former] Equity Rule 37 (Parties Generally—Intervention). Such compulsory joinder provisions are common. Compare Alaska Comp.Laws (1933) § 3392 (containing in same sentence a "class suit" provision); Wyo.Rev.Stat.Ann. (Courtright, 1931) § 89–515 (immediately followed by "class suit" provisions, § 89–516). See also former Equity Rule 42 (Joint and Several Demands). For example of a proper case for involuntary plaintiff, see *Independent Wireless Telegraph Co. v. Radio Corp. of America,* 269 U.S. 459, 46 S.Ct. 166, 70 L.Ed. 357 (1926).

The joinder provisions of this rule are subject to Rule 82 (Jurisdiction and Venue Unaffected).

Note to Subdivision (b). For the substance of this rule see [former] Equity Rule 39 (Absence of Persons Who Would be Proper Parties) and U.S.C., Title 28, § 111 [now § 1391] (When part of several defendants cannot be served); *Camp v. Gress,* 250 U.S. 308, 39 S.Ct. 478, 63 L.Ed. 997 (1919). See also the second and third sentences of [former] Equity Rule 37 (Parties Generally—Intervention).

Note to Subdivision (c). For the substance of this rule see the fourth subdivision of [former] Equity Rule 25 (Bill of Complaint—Contents).

1966 Amendment

General Considerations

Whenever feasible, the persons materially interested in the subject of an action—see the more detailed description of these persons in the discussion of new subdivision (a) below—should be joined as parties so that they may be heard and a complete disposition made. When this comprehensive joinder cannot be accomplished—a situation which may be encountered in Federal courts because of limitations on service of process, subject matter jurisdiction, and venue—the case should be examined pragmatically and a choice made between the alternatives of proceeding with the action in the absence of particular interested persons, and dismissing the action.

Even if the court is mistaken in its decision to proceed in the absence of an interested person, it does not by that token deprive itself of the power to adjudicate as between the parties already before it through proper service of process. But the court can make a legally binding adjudication only between the parties actually joined in the action. It is true that an adjudication between the parties before the court may on occasion adversely affect the absent person as a practical matter, or leave a party exposed to a later inconsistent recovery by the absent person. These are factors which should be considered in deciding whether the action should proceed, or should rather be dismissed; but they do not themselves negate the court's power to adjudicate as between the parties who have been joined.

Defects in the Original Rule

The foregoing propositions were well understood in the older equity practice, see Hazard, *Indispensable Party: The Historical Origin of a Procedural Phantom,* 61 Colum.L.Rev. 1254 (1961), and Rule 19 could be and often was applied in consonance with them. But experience showed that the rule was defective in its phrasing and did not point clearly to the proper basis of decision.

Textual defects.—(1) The expression "persons * * * who ought to be parties if complete relief is to be accorded between those already parties," appearing in original subdivision (b), was apparently intended as a description of the persons whom it would be desirable to join in the action, all questions of feasibility of joinder being put to one side; but it was not adequately descriptive of those persons.

(2)   The word "indispensable," appearing in original subdivision (b), was apparently intended as an inclusive reference to the interested persons in whose absence it would be advisable, all factors having been considered, to dismiss the action. Yet the sentence implied that there might be interested persons, not "indispensable," in whose absence the action ought also to be dismissed. Further, it seemed at least superficially plausible to equate the word "indispensable" with the expression "having a joint interest," appearing in subdivision (a). See *United States v. Washington Inst. of Tech., Inc.,* 138 F.2d 25, 26 (3d Cir. 1943); cf. *Chidester v. City of Newark,* 162 F.2d 598 (3d Cir. 1947). But persons holding an interest technically "joint" are not always so related to an action that it would be unwise to proceed without joining all of them, whereas persons holding an interest not technically "joint" may have this relation to an action. See Reed, *Compulsory Joinder of Parties in Civil Actions,* 55 Mich.L.Rev. 327, 356 ff., 483 (1957).

(3)   The use of "indispensable" and "joint interest" in the context of original Rule 19 directed attention to the technical or abstract character of the rights or obligations of the persons whose joinder was in question, and correspondingly distracted attention from the pragmatic considerations which should be controlling.

(4)   The original rule, in dealing with the feasibility of joining a person as a party to the action, besides referring to whether the person was "subject to the jurisdiction of the court as to both service of process and venue," spoke of whether the person could be made a party "without depriving the court of jurisdiction of the parties before it." The second quoted expression used "jurisdiction" in the sense of the competence of the court over the subject matter of the action, and in this sense the expression was apt. However, by a familiar confusion, the expression seems to have suggested to some that the absence from the lawsuit of a person who was "indispensable" or "who ought to be [a] part[y]" itself deprived the court of the power to adjudicate as between the parties already joined. See *Samuel Goldwyn, Inc. v. United Artists Corp.,* 113 F.2d 703, 707 (3d Cir. 1940); *McArthur v. Rosenbaum Co. of Pittsburgh,* 180 F.2d 617, 621 (3d Cir. 1949); cf. *Calcote v. Texas Pac. Coal & Oil Co.,* 157 F.2d 216 (5th Cir. 1946), cert. denied, 329 U.S. 782 (1946), noted in 56 Yale L.J. 1088 (1947); Reed, supra, 55 Mich.L.Rev. at 332–34.

Failure to point to correct basis of decision. The original rule did not state affirmatively what factors were relevant in deciding whether the action should proceed or be dismissed when joinder of interested persons was infeasible. In some instances courts did not undertake the relevant inquiry or were misled by the "jurisdiction" fallacy. In other instances there was undue preoccupation with abstract classifications of rights or obligations, as against consideration of the particular consequences of proceeding with the action and the ways by which these consequences might be ameliorated by the shaping of final relief or other precautions.

Although these difficulties cannot be said to have been general analysis of the cases showed that there was good reason for attempting to strengthen the rule. The literature also indicated how the rule should be reformed. See Reed, supra (discussion of the important case of *Shields v. Barrow,* 17 How. (58 U.S.) 130 (1854), appears at 55 Mich.L.Rev., p. 340 ff.); Hazard, supra; N.Y. Temporary Comm. on Courts, First Preliminary Report, Legis.Doc.1957, No. 6(b), pp. 28, 233; N.Y. Judicial Council, Twelfth Ann.Rep., Legis.Doc.1946, No. 17, p. 163; Joint Comm. on Michigan Procedural Revision, Final Report, Pt. III, p. 69 (1960); Note, *Indispensable Parties in the Federal Courts,* 65 Harv.L.Rev. 1050 (1952); *Developments in the Law—Multiparty Litigation in the Federal Courts,* 71 Harv.L.Rev. 874, 879 (1958); Mich.Gen.Court Rules, R. 205 (effective Jan. 1, 1963); N.Y.Civ.Prac.Law & Rules, § 1001 (effective Sept. 1, 1963).

The Amended Rule

New subdivision (a) defines the persons whose joinder in the action is desirable. Clause (1) stresses the desirability of joining those persons in whose absence the court would be obliged to grant partial or "hollow" rather than complete relief to the parties before the court. The interests that are being furthered here are not only those of the parties, but also that of the public in avoiding repeated lawsuits on the same essential subject matter. Clause (2)(i) recognizes the importance of protecting the person whose joinder is in question against the practical prejudice to him which may arise through a disposition of the action in his absence. Clause (2)(ii) recognizes the need for considering whether a party may be left, after the adjudication, in a position where a person not joined can subject him to a double or otherwise inconsistent liability. See Reed, supra, 55 Mich.L.Rev. at 330, 338; Note, supra, 65 Harv.L.Rev. at 1052–57; *Developments in the Law,* supra, 71 Harv.L.Rev. at 881–85.

The subdivision (a) definition of persons to be joined is not couched in terms of the abstract nature of their interests—"joint," "united," "separable," or the like. See N.Y. Temporary Comm. on Courts, First Preliminary Report, supra; Developments in the Law, supra, at 880. It should be noted particularly, however, that the description is not at variance with the settled authorities holding that a tortfeasor with the usual "joint-and-several" liability is merely a permissive party to an action against another with like liability. See 3 Moore's *Federal Practice* 2153 (2d ed. 1963); 2 Barron & Holtzoff, *Federal Practice & Procedure* § 513.8 (Wright ed. 1961). Joinder of these tortfeasors continues to be regulated by Rule 20; compare Rule 14 on third-party practice.

If a person as described in subdivision (a)(1)(2) is amenable to service of process and his joinder would not deprive the court of jurisdiction in the sense of competence over the action, he should be joined as a party; and if he has not been joined, the court should order him to be brought into the action. If a party joined has a valid objection to the venue and chooses to assert it, he will be dismissed from the action.

Subdivision (b).—When a person as described in subdivision (a)(1)–(2) cannot be made a party, the court is to determine whether in equity and good conscience the action should proceed among the parties already before it, or should be dismissed. That this decision is to be made in the light of pragmatic considerations has often been acknowledged by the courts. See *Roos v. Texas Co.,* 23 F.2d 171 (2d Cir. 1927), cert. denied 277 U.S. 587 (1928); *Niles-Bement-Pond Co. v. Iron Moulders' Union,* 254 U.S. 77, 80 (1920). The subdivision sets out four relevant considerations drawn from the experience revealed in the decided cases. The factors are to a certain extent overlapping, and they are not intended to exclude other considerations which may be applicable in particular situations.

The first factor brings in a consideration of what a judgment in the action would mean to the absentee. Would the absentee be adversely affected in a practical sense, and if so, would the prejudice be immediate and serious, or remote and minor? The possible collateral consequences of the judgment upon the parties already joined are also to be appraised. Would any party be exposed to a fresh action by the absentee, and if so, how serious is the threat? See the elaborate discussion in Reed, supra; cf. *A. L. Smith Iron Co. v. Dickson,* 141 F.2d 3 (2d Cir. 1944); *Caldwell Mfg. Co. v. Unique Balance Co.,* 18 F.R.D. 258 (S.D.N.Y.1955).

The second factor calls attention to the measures by which prejudice may be averted or lessened. The "shaping of relief" is a familiar expedient to this end. See, e.g., the award of money damages in lieu of specific relief where the latter might affect an absentee adversely. *Ward v. Deavers,* 203 F.2d 72 (D.C.Cir.1953); *Miller & Lux, Inc. v. Nickel,* 141 F.Supp. 41 (N.D.Calif.1956). On the use of "protective provisions," see *Roos v. Texas Co.,* supra; *Atwood v. Rhode Island Hosp. Trust Co.,* 275 Fed. 513, 519 (1st Cir. 1921), cert. denied, 257 U.S. 661 (1922); cf. *Stumpf v. Fidelity Gas Co.,* 294 F.2d 886 (9th Cir. 1961); and the general statement in *National Licorice Co. v. Labor Board,* 309 U.S. 350, 363 (1940).

Sometimes the party is himself able to take measures to avoid prejudice. Thus a defendant faced with a prospect of a second suit by an absentee may be in a position to bring the latter into the action by defensive interpleader. See *Hudson v. Newell,* 172 F.2d 848, 852 mod., 176 F.2d 546 (5th Cir. 1949); *Gauss v. Kirk,* 198 F.2d 83, 86 (D.C.Cir. 1952); *Abel v. Brayton Flying Service, Inc.,* 248 F.2d 713, 716 (5th Cir. 1957) (suggestion of possibility of counter-claim under Rule 13(h)); cf. *Parker Rust-Proof Co. v. Western Union Tel. Co.,* 105 F.2d 976 (2d Cir. 1939), cert. denied, 308 U.S. 597 (1939). So also the absentee may sometimes be able to avert prejudice to himself by voluntarily appearing in the action or intervening on an ancillary basis. See *Developments in the Law,* supra, 71 Harv.L.Rev. at 882; Annot., *Intervention or Subsequent Joinder of Parties as Affecting Jurisdiction of Federal Court Based on Diversity of Citizenship,* 134 A.L.R. 335 (1941); *Johnson v. Middleton,* 175 F.2d 535 (7th Cir. 1949); *Kentucky Nat. Gas Corp. v. Duggins,* 165 F.2d 1011 (6th Cir. 1948); *McComb v. McCormack,* 159 F.2d 219 (5th Cir. 1947). The court should consider whether this, in turn, would impose undue hardship on the absentee. (For the possibility of the court's informing an absentee of the pendency of the action, see comment under subdivision (c) below.)

The third factor—whether an "adequate" judgment can be rendered in the absence of a given person— calls attention to the extent of the relief that can be accorded among the parties joined. It meshes with the other factors, especially the "shaping of relief" mentioned under the second factor. Cf. *Kroese v. General Steel Castings Corp.,* 179 F.2d 760 (3d Cir. 1949), cert. denied, 339 U.S. 983 (1950).

The fourth factor, looking to the practical effects of a dismissal, indicates that the court should consider whether there is any assurance that the plaintiff, if dismissed, could sue effectively in another forum where better joinder would be possible. See *Fitzgerald v. Haynes,* 241 F.2d 417, 420 (3d Cir. 1957); *Fouke v. Schenewerk,* 197 F.2d 234, 236 (5th Cir. 1952); cf. *Warfield v. Marks,* 190 F.2d 178 (5th Cir. 1951).

The subdivision uses the word "indispensable" only in a conclusory sense, that is, a person is "regarded as indispensable" when he cannot be made a party and, upon consideration of the factors above mentioned, it is determined that in his absence it would be preferable to dismiss the action, rather than to retain it.

A person may be added as a party at any stage of the action on motion or on the court's initiative (see Rule 21); and a motion to dismiss, on the ground that a person has not been joined and justice requires that the action should not proceed in his absence, may be made as late as the trial on the merits (see Rule 12(h)(2), as amended; cf. Rule 12(b)(7), as amended). However, when the moving party is seeking dismissal in order to protect himself against a later suit by the absent person (subdivision (a)(2)(ii)), and is not seeking vicariously to protect the absent person against a prejudicial judgment (subdivision (a)(2)(i)), his undue delay in making the motion can properly be counted against him as a reason for denying the motion. A joinder question should be decided with reasonable promptness, but decision may properly be deferred if adequate information is not available at the time. Thus the relationship of an absent person to the action, and the practical effects of an adjudication upon him and others, may not be sufficiently revealed at the pleading stage; in such a case it would be appropriate to defer decision until the action was further advanced. Cf. Rule 12(d).

The amended rule makes no special provision for the problem arising in suits against subordinate Federal officials where it has often been set up as a defense that some superior officer must be joined. Frequently this defense has been accompanied by or intermingled with defenses of sovereign community or lack of consent of the United States to suit. So far as the issue of joinder can be isolated from the rest, the new subdivision seems better adapted to handle it than the predecessor provision. See the discussion in *Johnson v. Kirkland,* 290 F.2d 440, 446–47 (5th Cir. 1961) (stressing the practical orientation of the decisions); *Shaughnessy v. Pedreiro,* 349 U.S. 48, 54 (1955). Recent legislation, P.L. 87–748, 76 Stat. 744, approved October 5, 1962, adding §§ 1361, 1391(e) to Title 28, U.S.C., vests original jurisdiction in the District Courts over actions in the nature of mandamus to compel officials of the United States to perform their legal duties, and extends the range of service of process and liberalizes venue in these actions. If, then, it is found that a particular official should be joined in the action, the legislation will make it easy to bring him in.

Subdivision (c) parallels the predecessor subdivision (c) of Rule 19. In some situations it may be desirable to advise a person who has not been joined of the fact that the action is pending, and in particular cases the court in its discretion may itself convey this information by directing a letter or other informal notice to the absentee.

Subdivision (d) repeats the exception contained in the first clause of the predecessor subdivision (a).

1987 Amendment

The amendments are technical. No substantive change is intended.

2007 Amendment

The language of Rule 19 has been amended as part of the general restyling of the Civil Rules to make them more easily understood and to make style and terminology consistent throughout the rules. These changes are intended to be stylistic only.

Former Rule 19(b) described the conclusion that an action should be dismissed for inability to join a Rule 19(a) party by carrying forward traditional terminology: "the absent person being thus regarded as indispensable." "Indispensable" was used only to express a conclusion reached by applying the tests of Rule 19(b). It has been discarded as redundant.

Rule 20. Permissive Joinder of Parties

(a) Persons Who May Join or Be Joined.

    (1) *Plaintiffs.* Persons may join in one action as plaintiffs if:

(A) they assert any right to relief jointly, severally, or in the alternative with respect to or arising out of the same transaction, occurrence, or series of transactions or occurrences; and

(B) any question of law or fact common to all plaintiffs will arise in the action.

(2) *Defendants.* Persons—as well as a vessel, cargo, or other property subject to admiralty process in rem—may be joined in one action as defendants if:

(A) any right to relief is asserted against them jointly, severally, or in the alternative with respect to or arising out of the same transaction, occurrence, or series of transactions or occurrences; and

(B) any question of law or fact common to all defendants will arise in the action.

(3) *Extent of Relief.* Neither a plaintiff nor a defendant need be interested in obtaining or defending against all the relief demanded. The court may grant judgment to one or more plaintiffs according to their rights, and against one or more defendants according to their liabilities.

(b) **Protective Measures.** The court may issue orders—including an order for separate trials—to protect a party against embarrassment, delay, expense, or other prejudice that arises from including a person against whom the party asserts no claim and who asserts no claim against the party.

(Amended February 28, 1966, effective July 1, 1966; March 2, 1987, effective August 1, 1987; April 30, 2007, effective December 1, 2007.)

ADVISORY COMMITTEE NOTES

1937 Adoption

The provisions for joinder here stated are in substance the provisions found in England, California, Illinois, New Jersey, and New York. They represent only a moderate expansion of the present federal equity practice to cover both law and equity actions.

With this rule compare also [former] Equity Rules 26 (Joinder of Causes of Action), 37 (Parties Generally—Intervention), 40 (Nominal Parties), and 42 (Joint and Several Demands).

The provisions of this rule for the joinder of parties are subject to Rule 82 (Jurisdiction and Venue Unaffected).

Note to Subdivision (a). The first sentence is derived from *English Rules Under the Judicature Act* (The Annual Practice, 1937) O. 16, r. 1. Compare Calif.Code Civ.Proc. (Deering, 1937) §§ 378, 379a; Ill.Rev.Stat. (1937) ch. 110, § 147–148; N.J.Comp.Stat. (2 Cum.Supp., 1911–1924), N.Y.C.P.A. (1937) §§ 209, 211. The second sentence is derived from *English Rules Under the Judicature Act* (The Annual Practice, 1937) O. 16, r. 4. The third sentence is derived from O. 16, r. 5, and the fourth from O. 16, r.r. 1 and 4.

Note to Subdivision (b). This is derived from *English Rules Under the Judicature Act* (The Annual Practice, 1937) O. 16, r.r. 1 and 5.

1966 Amendment

See the amendment of Rule 18(a) and the Advisory Committee's Note thereto. It has been thought that a lack of clarity in the antecedent of the word "them," as it appeared in two places in Rule 20(a), contributed to the view, taken by some courts, that this rule limited the joinder of claims in certain situations of permissive party joinder. Although the amendment of Rule 18(a) should make clear that this view is untenable, it has been considered advisable to amend Rule 20(a) to eliminate any ambiguity. See 2 Barron & Holtzoff, *Federal Practice & Procedure* 202 (Wright Ed. 1961).

A basic purpose of unification of admiralty and civil procedure is to reduce barriers to joinder; hence the reference to "any vessel," etc.

1987 Amendment

The amendments are technical. No substantive change is intended.

2007 Amendment

The language of Rule 20 has been amended as part of the general restyling of the Civil Rules to make them more easily understood and to make style and terminology consistent throughout the rules. These changes are intended to be stylistic only.

Rule 21.   Misjoinder and Nonjoinder of Parties

Misjoinder of parties is not a ground for dismissing an action. On motion or on its own, the court may at any time, on just terms, add or drop a party. The court may also sever any claim against a party.

(Amended April 30, 2007, effective December 1, 2007.)

ADVISORY COMMITTEE NOTES

1937 Adoption

See *English Rules Under the Judicature Act* (The Annual Practice, 1937) O. 16, r. 11. See also [former] Equity Rules 43 (Defect of Parties—Resisting Objection) and 44 (Defect of Parties—Tardy Objection).

For separate trials see Rules 13(i) (Counterclaims and Cross-Claims: Separate Trials; Separate Judgments), 20(b) (Permissive Joinder of Parties: Separate Trials), and 42(b) (Separate Trials, generally) and the note to the latter rule.

2007 Amendment

The language of Rule 21 has been amended as part of the general restyling of the Civil Rules to make them more easily understood and to make style and terminology consistent throughout the rules. These changes are intended to be stylistic only.

Rule 22.   Interpleader

(a) Grounds.

    (1) *By a Plaintiff.* Persons with claims that may expose a plaintiff to double or multiple liability may be joined as defendants and required to interplead. Joinder for interpleader is proper even though:

        (A) the claims of the several claimants, or the titles on which their claims depend, lack a common origin or are adverse and independent rather than identical; or

        (B) the plaintiff denies liability in whole or in part to any or all of the claimants.

    (2) *By a Defendant.* A defendant exposed to similar liability may seek interpleader through a crossclaim or counterclaim.

(b) Relation to Other Rules and Statutes. This rule supplements—and does not limit—the joinder of parties allowed by Rule 20. The remedy this rule provides is in addition to—and does not supersede or limit—the remedy provided by 28 U.S.C. §§ 1335, 1397, and 2361. An action under those statutes must be conducted under these rules.

(Amended December 29, 1948, effective October 20, 1949; March 2, 1987, effective August 1, 1987; April 30, 2007, effective December 1, 2007.)

ADVISORY COMMITTEE NOTES

1937 Adoption

The first paragraph provides for interpleader relief along the newer and more liberal lines of joinder in the alternative. It avoids the confusion and restrictions that developed around actions of strict interpleader and actions in the nature of interpleader. Compare *John Hancock Mutual Life Insurance Co.*

v. Kegan et al., 22 F.Supp. 326 (D.C.Md.1938). It does not change the rules on service of process, jurisdiction, and venue, as established by judicial decision.

The second paragraph allows an action to be brought under the recent interpleader statute when applicable. By this paragraph all remedies under the statute are continued, but the manner of obtaining them is in accordance with these rules. For temporary restraining orders and preliminary injunctions under this statute, see Rule 65(e).

This rule substantially continues such statutory provisions as U.S.C., Title 38, § 445 [now 784] (Actions on claims; jurisdiction; parties; procedure; limitation; witnesses; definitions) (actions upon veterans' contracts of insurance with the United States), providing for interpleader by the United States where it acknowledges indebtedness under a contract of insurance with the United States; U.S.C., Title 49, § 97 (Interpleader of conflicting claimants) (by carrier which has issued bill of lading). See Chaffee, *The Federal Interpleader Act of 1936: I and II* (1936), 45 Yale L.J. 963, 1161.

1948 Amendment

The amendment effective October 20, 1949, substituted the reference to "Title 28, U.S.C., §§ 1335, 1397, and 2361," at the end of the first sentence of paragraph (2), for the reference to "Section 24(26) of the Judicial Code, as amended, U.S.C., Title 28, § 41(26)." The amendment also substituted the words "those provisions" in the second sentence of paragraph (2) for the words "that section."

1987 Amendment

The amendment is technical. No substantive change is intended.

2007 Amendment

The language of Rule 22 has been amended as part of the general restyling of the Civil Rules to make them more easily understood and to make style and terminology consistent throughout the rules. These changes are intended to be stylistic only.

Rule 23.   Class Actions

(a) **Prerequisites.** One or more members of a class may sue or be sued as representative parties on behalf of all members only if:

  (1) the class is so numerous that joinder of all members is impracticable;

  (2) there are questions of law or fact common to the class;

  (3) the claims or defenses of the representative parties are typical of the claims or defenses of the class; and

  (4) the representative parties will fairly and adequately protect the interests of the class.

(b) **Types of Class Actions.** A class action may be maintained if Rule 23(a) is satisfied and if:

  (1) prosecuting separate actions by or against individual class members would create a risk of:

   (A) inconsistent or varying adjudications with respect to individual class members that would establish incompatible standards of conduct for the party opposing the class; or

   (B) adjudications with respect to individual class members that, as a practical matter, would be dispositive of the interests of the other members not parties to the individual adjudications or would substantially impair or impede their ability to protect their interests;

  (2) the party opposing the class has acted or refused to act on grounds that apply generally to the class, so that final injunctive relief or corresponding declaratory relief is appropriate respecting the class as a whole; or

  (3) the court finds that the questions of law or fact common to class members predominate over any questions affecting only individual members, and that a class action is superior to other

available methods for fairly and efficiently adjudicating the controversy. The matters pertinent to these findings include:

    (A) the class members' interests in individually controlling the prosecution or defense of separate actions;

    (B) the extent and nature of any litigation concerning the controversy already begun by or against class members;

    (C) the desirability or undesirability of concentrating the litigation of the claims in the particular forum; and

    (D) the likely difficulties in managing a class action.

(c) **Certification Order; Notice to Class Members; Judgment; Issues Classes; Subclasses.**

  (1) *Certification Order.*

    (A) *Time to Issue.* At an early practicable time after a person sues or is sued as a class representative, the court must determine by order whether to certify the action as a class action.

    (B) *Defining the Class; Appointing Class Counsel.* An order that certifies a class action must define the class and the class claims, issues, or defenses, and must appoint class counsel under Rule 23(g).

    (C) *Altering or Amending the Order.* An order that grants or denies class certification may be altered or amended before final judgment.

  (2) *Notice.*

    (A) *For (b)(1) or (b)(2) Classes.* For any class certified under Rule 23(b)(1) or (b)(2), the court may direct appropriate notice to the class.

    (B) *For (b)(3) Classes.* For any class certified under Rule 23(b)(3)—or upon ordering notice under Rule 23(e)(1) to a class proposed to be certified for purposes of settlement under Rule 23(b)(3)—the court must direct to class members the best notice that is practicable under the circumstances, including individual notice to all members who can be identified through reasonable effort. The notice may be by one or more of the following: United States mail, electronic means, or other appropriate means. The notice must clearly and concisely state in plain, easily understood language:

      (i) the nature of the action;

      (ii) the definition of the class certified;

      (iii) the class claims, issues, or defenses;

      (iv) that a class member may enter an appearance through an attorney if the member so desires;

      (v) that the court will exclude from the class any member who requests exclusion;

      (vi) the time and manner for requesting exclusion; and

      (vii) the binding effect of a class judgment on members under Rule 23(c)(3).

  (3) *Judgment.* Whether or not favorable to the class, the judgment in a class action must:

    (A) for any class certified under Rule 23(b)(1) or (b)(2), include and describe those whom the court finds to be class members; and

    (B) for any class certified under Rule 23(b)(3), include and specify or describe those to whom the Rule 23(c)(2) notice was directed, who have not requested exclusion, and whom the court finds to be class members.

(4) *Particular Issues.* When appropriate, an action may be brought or maintained as a class action with respect to particular issues.

(5) *Subclasses.* When appropriate, a class may be divided into subclasses that are each treated as a class under this rule.

(d) Conducting the Action.

(1) *In General.* In conducting an action under this rule, the court may issue orders that:

(A) determine the course of proceedings or prescribe measures to prevent undue repetition or complication in presenting evidence or argument;

(B) require—to protect class members and fairly conduct the action—giving appropriate notice to some or all class members of:

(i) any step in the action;

(ii) the proposed extent of the judgment; or

(iii) the members' opportunity to signify whether they consider the representation fair and adequate, to intervene and present claims or defenses, or to otherwise come into the action;

(C) impose conditions on the representative parties or on intervenors;

(D) require that the pleadings be amended to eliminate allegations about representation of absent persons and that the action proceed accordingly; or

(E) deal with similar procedural matters.

(2) *Combining and Amending Orders.* An order under Rule 23(d)(1) may be altered or amended from time to time and may be combined with an order under Rule 16.

(e) Settlement, Voluntary Dismissal, or Compromise. The claims, issues, or defenses of a certified class—or a class proposed to be certified for purposes of settlement—may be settled, voluntarily dismissed, or compromised only with the court's approval. The following procedures apply to a proposed settlement, voluntary dismissal, or compromise:

(1) *Notice to the Class.*

(A) *Information That Parties Must Provide to the Court.* The parties must provide the court with information sufficient to enable it to determine whether to give notice of the proposal to the class.

(B) *Grounds for a Decision to Give Notice.* The court must direct notice in a reasonable manner to all class members who would be bound by the proposal if giving notice is justified by the parties' showing that the court will likely be able to:

(i) approve the proposal under Rule 23(e)(2); and

(ii) certify the class for purposes of judgment on the proposal.

(2) *Approval of the Proposal.* If the proposal would bind class members, the court may approve it only after a hearing and only on finding that it is fair, reasonable, and adequate after considering whether:

(A) the class representatives and class counsel have adequately represented the class;

(B) the proposal was negotiated at arm's length;

(C) the relief provided for the class is adequate, taking into account:

(i) the costs, risks, and delay of trial and appeal;

(ii) the effectiveness of any proposed method of distributing relief to the class, including the method of processing class-member claims;

      (iii) the terms of any proposed award of attorney's fees, including timing of payment; and

      (iv) any agreement required to be identified under Rule 23(e)(3); and

  (D) the proposal treats class members equitably relative to each other.

(3) *Identifying Agreements.* The parties seeking approval must file a statement identifying any agreement made in connection with the proposal.

(4) *New Opportunity to Be Excluded.* If the class action was previously certified under Rule 23(b)(3), the court may refuse to approve a settlement unless it affords a new opportunity to request exclusion to individual class members who had an earlier opportunity to request exclusion but did not do so.

(5) *Class-Member Objections.*

  (A) *In General.* Any class member may object to the proposal if it requires court approval under this subdivision (e). The objection must state whether it applies only to the objector, to a specific subset of the class, or to the entire class, and also state with specificity the grounds for the objection.

  (B) *Court Approval Required for Payment in Connection with an Objection.* Unless approved by the court after a hearing, no payment or other consideration may be provided in connection with:

      (i) forgoing or withdrawing an objection, or

      (ii) forgoing, dismissing, or abandoning an appeal from a judgment approving the proposal.

  (C) *Procedure for Approval After an Appeal.* If approval under Rule 23(e)(5)(B) has not been obtained before an appeal is docketed in the court of appeals, the procedure of Rule 62.1 applies while the appeal remains pending.

(f) **Appeals.** A court of appeals may permit an appeal from an order granting or denying class-action certification under this rule, but not from an order under Rule 23(e)(1). A party must file a petition for permission to appeal with the circuit clerk within 14 days after the order is entered, or within 45 days after the order is entered if any party is the United States, a United States agency, or a United States officer or employee sued for an act or omission occurring in connection with the duties performed on the United States' behalf. An appeal does not stay proceedings in the district court unless the district judge or the court of appeals so orders.

(g) **Class Counsel.**

(1) *Appointing Class Counsel.* Unless a statute provides otherwise, a court that certifies a class must appoint class counsel. In appointing class counsel, the court:

  (A) must consider:

      (i) the work counsel has done in identifying or investigating potential claims in the action;

      (ii) counsel's experience in handling class actions, other complex litigation, and the types of claims asserted in the action;

      (iii) counsel's knowledge of the applicable law; and

      (iv) the resources that counsel will commit to representing the class;

  (B) may consider any other matter pertinent to counsel's ability to fairly and adequately represent the interests of the class;

(C) may order potential class counsel to provide information on any subject pertinent to the appointment and to propose terms for attorney's fees and nontaxable costs;

(D) may include in the appointing order provisions about the award of attorney's fees or nontaxable costs under Rule 23(h); and

(E) may make further orders in connection with the appointment.

(2) *Standard for Appointing Class Counsel.* When one applicant seeks appointment as class counsel, the court may appoint that applicant only if the applicant is adequate under Rule 23(g)(1) and (4). If more than one adequate applicant seeks appointment, the court must appoint the applicant best able to represent the interests of the class.

(3) *Interim Counsel.* The court may designate interim counsel to act on behalf of a putative class before determining whether to certify the action as a class action.

(4) *Duty of Class Counsel.* Class counsel must fairly and adequately represent the interests of the class.

(h) **Attorney's Fees and Nontaxable Costs.** In a certified class action, the court may award reasonable attorney's fees and nontaxable costs that are authorized by law or by the parties' agreement. The following procedures apply:

(1) A claim for an award must be made by motion under Rule 54(d)(2), subject to the provisions of this subdivision (h), at a time the court sets. Notice of the motion must be served on all parties and, for motions by class counsel, directed to class members in a reasonable manner.

(2) A class member, or a party from whom payment is sought, may object to the motion.

(3) The court may hold a hearing and must find the facts and state its legal conclusions under Rule 52(a).

(4) The court may refer issues related to the amount of the award to a special master or a magistrate judge, as provided in Rule 54(d)(2)(D).

(Amended February 28, 1966, effective July 1, 1966; March 2, 1987, effective August 1, 1987; April 24, 1998, effective December 1, 1998; March 27, 2003, effective December 1, 2003; April 30, 2007, effective December 1, 2007; March 26, 2009, effective December 1, 2009; April 26, 2018, effective December 1, 2018.)

ADVISORY COMMITTEE NOTES

1937 Adoption

Note to Subdivision (a). This is a substantial restatement of [former] Equity Rule 38 (Representatives of Class) as that rule has been construed. It applies to all actions, whether formerly denominated legal or equitable. For a general analysis of class actions, effect of judgment, and requisites of jurisdiction see Moore, *Federal Rules of Civil Procedure: Some Problems Raised by the Preliminary Draft,* 25 Georgetown L.J. 551, 570 et seq. (1937); Moore and Cohn, *Federal Class Actions,* 32 Ill.L.Rev. 307 (1937); Moore and Cohn, *Federal Class Actions—Jurisdiction and Effect of Judgment,* 32 Ill.L.Rev. 555–567 (1938); Lesar, *Class Suits and the Federal Rules,* 22 Minn.L.Rev. 34 (1937); cf. Arnold and James, *Cases on Trials, Judgments and Appeals* (1936) 175; and see Blume, *Jurisdictional Amount in Representative Suits,* 15 Minn.L.Rev. 501 (1931).

The general test of [former] Equity Rule 38 (Representatives of Class) that the question should be "one of common or general interest to many persons constituting a class so numerous as to make it impracticable to bring them all before the court," is a common test. For states which require the two elements of a common or general interest and numerous persons, as provided for in [former] Equity Rule 38, see Del.Ch. Rule 113; Fla.Comp.Gen.Laws Ann. (Supp., 1936) § 4918(7); Georgia Code (1933) § 37–1002, and see *English Rules Under the Judicature Act* (The Annual Practice, 1937) O. 16, r. 9. For statutory provisions providing for class actions when the question is one of common or general interest or when the parties are numerous, see Ala.Code Ann. (Michie, 1928) § 5701; 2 Ind.Stat.Ann. (Burns, 1933) § 2–220; N.Y.C.P.A. (1937) 195; Wis.Stat. (1935) § 260.12. These statutes have, however, been uniformly construed as though phrased in the conjunctive. See *Garfein v. Stiglitz,* 260 Ky. 430, 86 S.W.2d 155 (1935). The rule adopts the test of [former] Equity Rule 38, but defines what constitutes a "common or general interest". Compare with code provisions which make the action dependent upon the propriety of joinder of the parties. See Blume, *The "Common Questions" Principle in the Code Provision for Representative Suits,* 30 Mich.L.Rev. 878 (1932). For discussion of what constitutes "numerous persons" see Wheaton, *Representative Suits Involving Numerous Litigants,* 19 Corn.L.Q. 399 (1934); Note, 36 Harv.L.Rev. 89 (1922).

Clause (1), Joint, Common, or Secondary Right. This clause is illustrated in actions brought by or against representatives of an unincorporated association. See *Oster v. Brotherhood of Locomotive Firemen and Enginemen,* 271 Pa. 419, 114 Atl. 377 (1921); *Pickett v. Walsh,* 192 Mass. 572, 78 N.E. 753, 6 L.R.A., N.S., 1067 (1906); *Colt v. Hicks,* 97 Ind.App. 177, 179 N.E. 335 (1932). Compare Rule 17(b) as to when an unincorporated association has capacity to sue or be sued in its common name; *United Mine Workers of America v. Coronado Coal Co.,* 42 S.Ct. 570, 259 U.S. 344, 66 L.Ed. 975, 27 A.L.R. 762 (1922) (an unincorporated association was sued as an entity for the purpose of enforcing against it a federal substantive right); Moore, *Federal Rules of Civil Procedure: Some Problems Raised by the Preliminary Draft,* 25 Georgetown L.J. 551, 566 (for discussion of jurisdictional requisites when an unincorporated association sues or is sued in its common name and jurisdiction is founded upon diversity of citizenship). For an action brought by representatives of one group against representatives of another group for distribution of a fund held by an unincorporated association, see *Smith v. Swormstedt,* 16 How. 288, 14 L.Ed. 942 (U.S. 1853). Compare *Christopher, et al. v. Brusselback,* 1938, 58 S.Ct. 350, 302 U.S. 500, 82 L.Ed. 388.

For an action to enforce rights held in common by policyholders against the corporate issuer of the policies, see *Supreme Tribe of Ben Hur v. Cauble,* 255 U.S. 356, 41 S.Ct. 338, 65 L.Ed. 673 (1921). See also *Terry v. Little,* 101 U.S. 216, 25 L.Ed. 864 (1880); *John A. Roebling's Sons Co. v. Kinnicutt,* 248 Fed. 596 (D.C.N.Y., 1917) dealing with the right held in common by creditors to enforce the statutory liability of stockholders.

Typical of a secondary action is a suit by stockholders to enforce a corporate right. For discussion of the general nature of these actions see *Ashwander v. Tennessee Valley Authority,* 297 U.S. 288, 56 S.Ct. 466, 80 L.Ed. 688 (1936); Glenn, *The Stockholder's Suit—Corporate and Individual Grievances,* 33 Yale L.J. 580 (1924); McLaughlin, *Capacity of Plaintiff-Stockholder to Terminate a Stockholder's Suit,* 46 Yale L.J. 421 (1937). See also Subdivision (b) of this rule which deals with Shareholder's Action; Note, 15 Minn.L.Rev. 453 (1931).

Clause (2). A creditor's action for liquidation or reorganization of a corporation is illustrative of this clause. An action by a stockholder against certain named defendants as representatives of numerous claimants presents a situation converse to the creditor's action.

Clause (3). See *Everglades Drainage League v. Napoleon Broward Drainage Dist.,* 253 Fed. 246 (D.C.Fla., 1918); *Gramling v. Maxwell,* 52 F.2d 256 (D.C.N.C., 1931), approved in 30 Mich.L.Rev. 624 (1932); *Skinner v. Mitchell,* 108 Kan. 861, 197 Pac. 569 (1921); *Duke of Bedford v. Ellis* (1901) A.C. 1, for class actions when there were numerous persons and there was only a question of law or fact common to them; and see Blume, *The "Common Questions" Principle in the Code Provision for Representative Suits,* 30 Mich.L.Rev. 878 (1932).

Note to Subdivision (b). This is [former] Equity Rule 27 (Stockholder's Bill) with verbal changes. See also *Hawes v. Oakland,* 104 U.S. 450, 26 L.Ed. 827 (1882) and former Equity Rule 94, promulgated January 23, 1882, 104 U.S. IX.

Note to Subdivision (c). See McLaughlin, Capacity of Plaintiff-Stockholder to Terminate a Stockholder's Suit, 46 Yale L.J. 421 (1937).

Supplementary Note

Note. Subdivision (b), relating to secondary actions by shareholders, provides among other things, that in such an action the complainant "shall aver (1) that the plaintiff was a shareholder at the time of the transaction of which he complains or that his share thereafter devolved on him by operation of law * * * ".

As a result of the decision in *Erie R. Co. v. Tompkins,* 1938, 304 U.S. 64, 58 S.Ct. 817 (decided April 25, 1938, after this rule was promulgated by the Supreme Court, though before it took effect) a question has arisen as to whether the provision above quoted deals with a matter of substantive right or is a matter of procedure. If it is a matter of substantive law or right, then under *Erie R. Co. v. Tompkins* clause (1) may not be validly applied in cases pending in states whose local law permits a shareholder to maintain such actions, although not a shareholder at the time of the transactions complained of. The Advisory Committee, believing the question should be settled in the courts, proposes no change in Rule 23 but thinks rather that the situation should be explained in an appropriate note.

The rule has a long history. In *Hawes v. Oakland,* 1882, 104 U.S. 450, the Court held that a shareholder could not maintain such an action unless he owned shares at the time of the transactions complained of, or unless they devolved on him by operation of law. At that time the decision in *Swift v. Tyson,* 1842, 16 Peters 1, was the law, and the federal courts considered themselves free to establish their own principles of equity jurisprudence, so the Court was not in 1882 and has not been, until *Erie R. Co. v. Tompkins* in 1938, concerned with the question whether *Hawes v. Oakland* dealt with substantive right or procedure.

Following the decision in *Hawes v. Oakland,* and at the same term, the Court, to implement its decision, adopted [former] Equity Rule 94, which contained the same provision above quoted from Rule 23 F.R.C.P. The provision in [former] Equity Rule 94 was later embodied in [former] Equity Rule 27, of which the present Rule 23 is substantially a copy.

In *City of Quincy v. Steel,* 1887, 120 U.S. 241, 245, 7 S.Ct. 520, the Court referring to *Hawes v. Oakland* said: "In order to give effect to the principles there laid down, this Court at that term adopted Rule 94 of the rules of practice for courts of equity of the United States."

Some other cases dealing with [former] Equity Rules 94 or 27 prior to the decision in *Erie R. Co. v. Tompkins* are *Dimpfel v. Ohio & Miss. R.R.*, 1884, 3 S.Ct. 573, 110 U.S. 209, 28 L.Ed. 121; *Illinois Central R. Co. v. Adams*, 1901, 21 S.Ct. 251, 180 U.S. 28, 34, 45 L.Ed. 410; *Venner v. Great Northern Ry.,* 1908, 28 S.Ct. 328, 209 U.S. 24, 30, 52 L.Ed. 666; *Jacobson v. General Motors Corp.*, S.D.N.Y.1938, 22 F.Supp. 255, 257. These cases generally treat *Hawes v. Oakland* as establishing a "principle" of equity, or as dealing not with jurisdiction but with the "right" to maintain an action, or have said that the defense under the equity rule is analogous to the defense that the plaintiff has no "title" and results in a dismissal "for want of equity."

Those state decisions which held that a shareholder acquiring stock after the event may maintain a derivative action are founded on the view that it is a right belonging to the shareholder at the time of the transaction and which passes as a right to the subsequent purchaser. See *Pollitz v. Gould*, 1911, 202 N.Y. 11, 94 N.E. 1088.

The first case arising after the decision in *Erie R. Co. v. Tompkins,* in which this problem was involved, was *Summers v. Hearst,* S.D.N.Y.1938, 23 F.Supp. 986. It concerned [former] Equity Rule 27, as Federal Rule 23 was not then in effect. In a well considered opinion Judge Leibell reviewed the decisions and said: "The federal cases that discuss this section of [former] Rule 27 support the view that it states a principle of substantive law." He quoted *Pollitz v. Gould,* 1911, 202 N.Y. 11, 94 N.E. 1088, as saying that the United States Supreme Court "seems to have been more concerned with establishing this rule as one of practice than of substantive law" but that "whether it be regarded as establishing a principle of law or a rule of practice, this authority has been subsequently followed in the United States courts."

He then concluded that, although the federal decisions treat the equity rule as "stating a principle of substantive law", if "[former] Equity Rule 27 is to be modified or revoked in view of *Erie R. Co. v. Tompkins,* it is not the province of this Court to suggest it, much less impliedly to follow that course by disregarding the mandatory provisions of the Rule."

In *Piccard v. Sperry Corporation,* S.D.N.Y.1941, 36 F.Supp. 1006, 1009–10, affirmed without opinion, C.C.A.2d 1941, 120 F.2d 328, a shareholder, not such at the time of the transactions complained of, sought to intervene. The court held an intervenor was as much subject to Rule 23 as an original plaintiff; and that the requirement of Rule 23(b) was "a matter of practice," not substance, and applied in New York where the state law was otherwise, despite *Erie R. Co. v. Tompkins*. In *New York v. Guaranty Trust Co. of New York,* C.C.A.2, 1944, 143 F.2d 503, rev'd on other grounds, 1945, 65 S.Ct. 1464, the court said: "Restrictions on the bringing of stockholders' actions, such as those imposed by F.R.C.P. 23(b) or other state statutes are procedural," citing the *Piccard* and other cases.

Some other federal decisions since 1938 touch the question.

In *Gallup v. Caldwell,* C.C.A.3, 1941, 120 F.2d 90, 95 arising in New Jersey, the point was raised but not decided, the court saying that it was not satisfied that the then New Jersey rule differed from Rule 23(b), and that "under the circumstances the proper course was to follow Rule 23(b)."

In *Mullins v. DeSoto Securities Co.,* W.D.La.1942, 45 F.Supp. 871, 878, the point was not decided, because the court found the Louisiana rule to be the same as that stated in Rule 23(b).

In *Toebelman v. Missouri-Kansas Pipe Line Co.,* D.Del.1941, 41 F.Supp. 334, 340, the court dealt only with another part of Rule 23(b), relating to prior demands on the stockholders and did not discuss *Erie R. Co. v. Tompkins,* or its effect on the rule.

In *Perrott v. United States Banking Corp.,* D.Del.1944, 53 F.Supp. 953, it appeared that the Delaware law does not require the plaintiff to have owned shares at the time of the transaction complained of. The court sustained Rule 23(b), after discussion of the authorities, saying:

"It seems to me the rule does not go beyond procedure. * * * Simply because a particular plaintiff cannot qualify as a proper party to maintain such an action does not destroy or even whittle at the cause of action. The cause of action exists until a qualified plaintiff can get it started in a federal court."

In *Bankers Nat. Corp. v. Barr,* S.D.N.Y.1945, 9 Fed.Rules Serv. 23b.11, Case 1, the court held Rule 23(b) to be one of procedure, but that whether the plaintiff was a stockholder was a substantive question to be settled by state law.

The New York rule, as stated in *Pollitz v. Gould,* supra, has been altered by an act of the New York Legislature, Chapter 667, Laws of 1944, effective April 9, 1944, General Corporation Law, § 61, which provides that "in any action brought by a shareholder in the right of a * * * corporation, it must appear that the plaintiff was a stockholder at the time of the transaction of which he complains, or that his stock thereafter devolved upon him by operation of law." At the same time a further and separate provision was enacted, requiring under certain circumstances the giving of security for reasonable expenses and attorney's fees, to which security the corporation in whose right the action is brought and the defendants therein may have recourse. (Chapter 668, Laws of 1944, effective April 9, 1944, General Corporation Law, § 61–b.) These provisions are aimed at so-called "strike" stockholders' suits and their attendant abuses. *Shielcrawt v. Moffett,* Ct.App.1945, 294 N.Y. 180, 61 N.E.2d 435, rev'g 51 N.Y.S.2d 188, aff'g 49 N.Y.S.2d 64; *Noel Associates, Inc. v. Merrill,* Sup.Ct.1944, 184 Misc. 646, 63 N.Y.S.2d 143.

Insofar as § 61 is concerned, it has been held that the section is procedural in nature. *Klum v. Clinton Trust Co.,* Sup.Ct.1944, 183 Misc. 340, 48 N.Y.S.2d 267; *Noel Associates, Inc. v. Merrill,* supra. In the latter case the court pointed out that "The 1944 amendment to Section 61 rejected the rule laid down in the Pollitz case and substituted, in place thereof, in its precise language, the rule which has long prevailed in the Federal Courts and which is now Rule 23(b) * * *". There is, nevertheless, a difference of opinion regarding the application of the statute to pending actions. See *Klum v. Clinton Trust Co.,* supra (applicable); *Noel Associates, Inc. v. Merrill,* supra (inapplicable).

With respect to § 61–b, which may be regarded as a separate problem, *Noel Associates, Inc. v. Merrill,* supra, it has been held that even though the statute is procedural in nature—a matter not definitely decided—the Legislature evinced no intent that the provisions should apply to actions pending when it became effective. *Shielcrawt v. Moffett,* supra. As to actions instituted after the effective date of the legislation, the constitutionality of § 61–b is in dispute. See *Wolf v. Atkinson,* Sup.Ct.1944, 182 Misc. 675, 49 N.Y.S.2d 703 (constitutional); *Citron v. Mangel Stores Corp.,* Sup.Ct.1944, 50 N.Y.S.2d 416 (unconstitutional); Zlinkoff, *The American Investor and the Constitutionality of § 61–b of the New York General Corporation Law,* 1945, 54 Yale L.J. 352.

New Jersey also enacted a statute, similar to Chapters 667 and 668 of the New York law. See P.L.1945, Ch. 131, R.S.Cum.Supp. 14:3–15. The New Jersey provision similar to Chapter 668, § 61–b, differs, however, in that it specifically applies retroactively. It has been held that this provision is procedural and hence will not govern a pending action brought against a New Jersey corporation in the New York courts. *Shielcrawt v. Moffett,* Sup.Ct.N.Y.1945, 184 Misc. 1074, 56 N.Y.S.2d 134.

See, also generally, 2 Moore's *Federal Practice,* 1938, 2250–2253, and Cum.Supplement § 23.05.

The decisions here discussed show that the question is a debatable one, and that there is respectable authority for either view, with a recent trend towards the view that Rule 23(b)(1) is procedural. There is reason to say that the question is one which should not be decided by the Supreme Court ex parte, but left to await a judicial decision in a litigated case, and that in the light of the material in this note, the only inference to be drawn from a failure to amend Rule 23(b) would be that the question is postponed to await a litigated case.

The Advisory Committee is unanimously of the opinion that this course should be followed.

If, however, the final conclusion is that the rule deals with a matter of substantive right, then the rule should be amended by adding a provision that Rule 23(b)(1) does not apply in jurisdictions where state law permits a shareholder to maintain a secondary action, although he was not a shareholder at the time of the transactions of which he complains.

1966 Amendment

Difficulties with the original rule. The categories of class actions in the original rule were defined in terms of the abstract nature of the rights involved: the so-called "true" category was defined as involving "joint, common, or secondary rights"; the "hybrid" category, as involving "several" rights related to "specific property"; the "spurious" category, as involving "several" rights affected by a common question and related to common relief. It was thought that the definitions accurately described the situations amenable to the class-suit device, and also would indicate the proper extent of the judgment in each category, which would in turn help to determine the res judicata effect of the judgment if questioned in a later action. Thus the judgments in "true" and "hybrid" class actions would extend to the class (although in somewhat different ways); the judgment in a "spurious" class action would extend only to the parties including intervenors. See Moore, *Federal Rules of Civil Procedure: Some Problems Raised by the Preliminary Draft,* 25 Geo.L.J. 551, 570–76 (1937).

In practice the terms "joint," "common," etc., which were used as the basis of the Rule 23 classification proved obscure and uncertain. See Chafee, *Some Problems of Equity* 245–46, 256–57 (1950); Kalven & Rosenfield, *The Contemporary Function of the Class Suit,* 8 U. of Chi.L.Rev. 684, 707 & n. 73 (1941); Keeffe, Levy & Donovan, *Lee Defeats Ben Hur,* 33 Corn.L.Q. 327, 329–36 (1948); *Developments in the Law: Multiparty Litigation in the Federal Courts,* 71 Harv. L.Rev. 874, 931 (1958); Advisory Committee's Note to Rule 19, as amended. The courts had considerable difficulty with these terms. See, e.g., *Gullo v. Veterans' Coop. H. Assn.,* 13 F.R.D. 11 (D.D.C.1952); *Shipley v. Pittsburgh & L.E.R. Co.,* 70 F.Supp. 870 (W.D.Pa.1947); *Deckert v. Independence Shares Corp.,* 27 F.Supp. 763 (E.D.Pa.1939), rev'd 108 F.2d 51 (3d Cir. 1939), rev'd, 311 U.S. 282 (1940), on remand, 39 F.Supp. 592 (E.D.Pa.1941), rev'd sub nom. *Pennsylvania Co. for Ins. on Lives v. Deckert,* 123 F.2d 979 (3d Cir.1941) (see Chafee, supra, at 264–65).

Nor did the rule provide an adequate guide to the proper extent of the judgments in class actions. First, we find instances of the courts classifying actions as "true" or intimating that the judgments would be decisive for the class where these results seemed appropriate but were reached by dint of depriving the word "several" of coherent meaning. See, e.g., *System Federation No. 91 v. Reed,* 180 F.2d 991 (6th Cir.1950); *Wilson v. City of Paducah,* 100 F.Supp. 116 (W.D.Ky.1951); *Citizens Banking Co. v. Monticello State Bank,* 143 F.2d 261 (8th Cir.1944); *Redmond v. Commerce Trust Co.,* 144 F.2d 140 (8th Cir.1944), cert. denied, 323 U.S. 776 (1944); *United States v. American Optical Co.,* 97 F.Supp. 66 (N.D.Ill.1951); *National Hairdressers' & C. Assn. v. Philad Co.,* 34 F.Supp. 264 (D.Del.1940); 41 F.Supp. 701 (D.Del.1940), aff'd mem., 129 F.2d 1020 (3d Cir.1942). Second, we find cases classified by the courts as "spurious" in which, on a realistic view, it would seem fitting for the judgments to extend to the class. See, e.g., *Knapp v. Bankers Sec. Corp.,* 17 F.R.D. 245 (E.D.Pa.1954), aff'd 230 F.2d 717 (3d Cir.1956); *Giesecke v. Denver Tramway Corp.,* 81 F.Supp. 957 (D.Del.1949); *York v. Guaranty Trust Co.,* 143 F.2d 503 (2d Cir.1944), rev'd on grounds not here relevant, 326 U.S. 99 (1945) (see Chafee, supra, at 208); cf. *Webster Eisenlohr, Inc. v. Kalodner,* 145 F.2d 316, 320 (3d Cir.1944), cert. denied, 325 U.S. 867 (1945). But cf. the early decisions, *Duke of Bedford v. Ellis,* [1901] A.C. 1; *Sheffield Waterworks v. Yeomans,* L.R. 2 Ch.App. 8 (1866); *Brown v. Vermuden,* 1 Ch.Cas. 272, 22 Eng.Rep. 796 (1676).

The "spurious" action envisaged by original Rule 23 was in any event an anomaly because, although denominated a "class" action and pleaded as such, it was supposed not to adjudicate the rights or liabilities of any person not a party. It was believed to be an advantage of the "spurious" category that it would invite decisions that a member of the "class" could, like a member of the class in a "true" or "hybrid" action, intervene on an ancillary basis without being required to show an independent basis of Federal jurisdiction, and have the benefit of the date of the commencement of the action for purposes of the statute of limitations.

See 3 Moore's *Federal Practice,* pars. 23.10[1], 23.12 (2d ed.1963). These results were attained in some instances but not in others. On the statute of limitations, see *Union Carbide & Carbon Corp. v. Nisley,* 300 F.2d 561 (10th Cir.1961), pet. cert. dism., 371 U.S. 801 (1963); but cf. *P. W. Husserl, Inc. v. Newman,* 25 F.R.D. 264 (S.D.N.Y.1960); *Athas v. Day,* 161 F.Supp. 916 (D.Colo.1958). On ancillary intervention, see *Amen v. Black,* 234 F.2d 12 (10th Cir.1956), cert. granted, 352 U.S. 888 (1956), dism. on stip., 355 U.S. 600 (1958); but cf. *Wagner v. Kemper,* 13 F.R.D. 128 (W.D.Mo.1952). The results, however, can hardly depend upon the mere appearance of a "spurious" category in the rule; they should turn on more basic considerations. See discussion of subdivision (c)(1) below.

Finally, the original rule did not squarely address itself to the question of the measures that might be taken during the course of the action to assure procedural fairness, particularly giving notice to members of the class, which may in turn be related in some instances to the extension of the judgment to the class. See Chafee, supra, at 230–31; Keeffe, Levy & Donovan, supra; *Developments in the law,* supra, 71 Harv.L.Rev. at 937–38; Note, *Binding Effect of Class Actions,* 67 Harv.L.Rev. 1059, 1062–65 (1954); Note, *Federal Class Actions: A Suggested Revision of Rule 23,* 46 Colum.L.Rev. 818, 833–36 (1946); Mich.Gen.Court R. 208.4 (effective Jan. 1, 1963); Idaho R.Civ.P. 23(d); Minn.R.Civ.P. 23.04; N.Dak.R.Civ.P. 23(d).

The amended rule describes in more practical terms the occasions for maintaining class actions; provides that all class actions maintained to the end as such will result in judgments including those whom the court finds to be members of the class, whether or not the judgment is favorable to the class; and refers to the measures which can be taken to assure the fair conduct of these actions.

Subdivision (a) states the prerequisites for maintaining any class action in terms of the numerousness of the class making joinder of the members impracticable, the existence of questions common to the class, and the desired qualifications of the representative parties. See Weinstein, *Revision of Procedure: Some Problems in Class Actions,* 9 Buffalo L.Rev. 433, 458–59 (1960); 2 Barron & Holtzoff, *Federal Practice & Procedure* § 562, at 265, § 572, at 351–52 (Wright ed. 1961). These are necessary but not sufficient conditions for a class action. See, e.g., *Giordano v. Radio Corp. of Am.,* 183 F.2d 558, 560 (3d Cir.1950); *Zachman v. Erwin,* 186 F.Supp. 681 (S.D.Tex.1959); *Baim & Blank, Inc. v. Warren-Connelly Co., Inc.,* 19 F.R.D. 108 (S.D.N.Y.1956). Subdivision (b) describes the additional elements which in varying situations justify the use of a class action.

Subdivision (b)(1). The difficulties which would be likely to arise if resort were had to separate actions by or against the individual members of the class here furnish the reasons for, and the principal key to, the propriety and value of utilizing the class-action device. The considerations stated under clauses (A) and (B) are comparable to certain of the elements which define the persons whose joinder in an action is desirable as stated in Rule 19(a), as amended. See amended Rule 19(a)(2)(i) and (ii), and the Advisory Committee's Note thereto; Hazard, *Indispensable Party: The Historical Origin of a Procedural Phantom,* 61 Colum.L.Rev. 1254, 1259–60 (1961); cf. 3 Moore, supra, par. 23.08, at 3435.

Clause (A): One person may have rights against, or be under duties toward, numerous persons constituting a class, and be so positioned that conflicting or varying adjudications in lawsuits with individual members of the class might establish incompatible standards to govern his conduct. The class action device can be used effectively to obviate the actual or virtual dilemma which would thus confront the party opposing the class. The matter has been stated thus: "The felt necessity for a class action is greatest when the courts are called upon to order or sanction the alteration of the status quo in circumstances such that a large number of persons are in a position to call on a single person to alter the status quo, or to complain if it is altered, and the possibility exists that [the] actor might be called upon to act in inconsistent ways." Louisell & Hazard, *Pleading and Procedure: State and Federal* 719 (1962); see *Supreme Tribe of Ben-Hur v. Cauble,* 255 U.S. 356, 366–67 (1921). To illustrate: Separate actions by individuals against a municipality to declare a bond issue invalid or condition or limit it, to prevent or limit the making of a particular appropriation or to compel or invalidate an assessment, might create a risk of inconsistent or varying determinations. In the same way, individual litigations of the rights and duties of riparian owners, or of landowners' rights and duties respecting a claimed nuisance, could create a possibility of incompatible adjudications. Actions by or against a class provide a ready and fair means of achieving unitary adjudication. See *Maricopa County Mun. Water Con. Dist. v. Looney,* 219 F.2d 529 (9th Cir.1955); *Rank v. Krug,* 142 F.Supp. 1, 154–59 (S.D.Calif.1956), on app., *State of California v. Rank,* 293 F.2d 340, 348 (9th Cir.1961); *Gart v. Cole,* 263 F.2d 244 (2d Cir.1959), cert. denied 359 U.S. 978 (1959); cf. *Martinez v. Maverick Cty. Water Con. & Imp. Dist.,* 219 F.2d 666 (5th Cir.1955); 3 Moore, supra, par. 23.11[2], at 3458–59.

Clause (B): This clause takes in situations where the judgment in a nonclass action by or against an individual member of the class, while not technically concluding the other members, might do so as a practical matter. The vice of an individual action would lie in the fact that the other members of the class, thus practically concluded, would have had no representation in the lawsuit. In an action by policy holders against a fraternal benefit association attacking a financial reorganization of the society, it would hardly have been practical, if indeed it would have been possible, to confine the effects of a validation of the reorganization to the individual plaintiffs. Consequently a class action was called for with adequate representation of all members of the class. See *Supreme Tribe of Ben-Hur v. Cauble,* 255 U.S. 356 (1921); *Waybright v. Columbian Mut. Life Ins. Co.,* 30 F.Supp. 885 (W.D.Tenn.1939); cf. *Smith v. Swormstedt,* 16 How. (57 U.S.) 288 (1853). For much the same reason actions by shareholders to compel the declaration of a dividend[,] the proper recognition and handling of redemption or pre-emption rights, or the like (or actions by the corporation for corresponding declarations of rights), should ordinarily be conducted as class actions, although the matter has been much obscured by the insistence that each shareholder has an individual claim. See *Knapp v. Bankers Securities Corp.,* 17 F.R.D. 245 (E.D.Pa.1954), aff'd, 230 F.2d 717 (3d Cir.1956); *Giesecke v. Denver Tramway Corp.,* 81 F.Supp. 957 (D.Del.1949); *Zahn v. Transamerica Corp.,* 162 F.2d 36 (3d Cir.1947); *Speed v. Transamerica Corp.,* 100 F.Supp. 461 (D.Del.1951); *Sobel v. Whittier Corp.,* 95 F.Supp. 643 (E.D.Mich.1951), app. dism., 195 F.2d 361 (6th Cir.1952); *Goldberg v. Whittier Corp.,* 111 F.Supp. 382 (E.D.Mich.1953); *Dann v. Studebaker-Packard Corp.,* 288 F.2d 201 (6th Cir.1961); *Edgerton v. Armour & Co.,* 94 F.Supp. 549 (S.D.Calif.1950); *Ames v. Mengel Co.,* 190 F.2d 344 (2d Cir.1951). (These shareholders' actions are to be distinguished from derivative actions by shareholders dealt with in new Rule 23.1). The same reasoning applies to an action which charges a breach of trust by an indenture trustee or other fiduciary similarly affecting the members of a large class of security holders or other beneficiaries, and which requires an accounting or like measures to restore the subject of the trust. See *Boesenberg v. Chicago T. & T. Co.,* 128 F.2d 245 (7th Cir.1942); *Citizens Banking Co. v. Monticello State Bank,* 143 F.2d 261 (8th Cir.1944); *Redmond v. Commerce Trust Co.,* 144 F.2d 140 (8th Cir.1944), cert. denied, 323 U.S. 776 (1944); cf. *York v. Guaranty Trust Co.,* 143 F.2d 503 (2d Cir.1944), rev'd on grounds not here relevant, 326 U.S. 99 (1945).

In various situations an adjudication as to one or more members of the class will necessarily or probably have an adverse practical effect on the interests of other members who should therefore be represented in the lawsuit. This is plainly the case when claims are made by numerous persons against a fund insufficient to satisfy all claims. A class action by or against representative members to settle the validity of the claims as a whole, or in groups, followed by separate proof of the amount of each valid claim and proportionate distribution of the fund, meets the problem. Cf. *Dickinson v. Burnham,* 197 F.2d 973 (2d Cir.1952), cert. denied, 344 U.S. 875 (1952); 3 Moore, supra, at par. 23.09. The same reasoning applies to an action by a creditor to set aside a fraudulent conveyance by the debtor and to appropriate the property to his claim, when the debtor's assets are insufficient to pay all creditors' claims. See *Heffernan v. Bennett & Armour,* 110 Cal.App.2d 564, 243 P.2d 846 (1952); cf. *City & County of San Francisco v. Market Street Ry.,* 95 Cal.App.2d 648, 213 P.2d 780 (1950). Similar problems, however, can arise in the absence of a fund either present or potential. A negative or mandatory injunction secured by one of a numerous class may disable the opposing party from performing claimed duties toward the other members of the class or materially affect his ability to do so. An adjudication as to movie "clearances and runs" nominally affecting only one exhibitor would often have practical effects on all the exhibitors in the same territorial area. Cf. *United States v. Paramount Pictures, Inc.,* 66 F.Supp. 323, 341–46 (S.D.N.Y.1946); 334 U.S. 131, 144–48 (1948). Assuming a sufficiently numerous class of exhibitors, a class action would be advisable. (Here representation of subclasses of exhibitors could become necessary; see subdivision (c)(3)(B).)

Subdivision (b)(2). This subdivision is intended to reach situations where a party has taken action or refused to take action with respect to a class, and final relief of an injunctive nature or of a corresponding declaratory nature, settling the legality of the behavior with respect to the class as a whole, is appropriate. Declaratory relief "corresponds" to injunctive relief when as a practical matter it affords injunctive relief or serves as a basis for later injunctive relief. The subdivision does not extend to cases in which the appropriate final relief relates exclusively or predominantly to money damages. Action or inaction is directed to a class within the meaning of this subdivision even if it has taken effect or is threatened only as to one or a few members of the class, provided it is based on grounds which have general application to the class.

Illustrative are various actions in the civil-rights field where a party is charged with discriminating unlawfully against a class, usually one whose members are incapable of specific enumeration. See *Potts v.*

Flax, 313 F.2d 284 (5th Cir. 1963); *Bailey v. Patterson,* 323 F.2d 201 (5th Cir. 1963), cert. denied, 376 U.S. 910, (1964); *Brunson v. Board of Trustees of School District No. 1, Clarendon Cty., S.C.,* 311 F.2d 107 (4th Cir. 1962), cert. denied, 373 U.S. 933 (1963); *Green v. School Bd. of Roanoke, Va.,* 304 F.2d 118 (4th Cir. 1962); *Orleans Parish School Bd. v. Bush,* 242 F.2d 156 (5th Cir. 1957), cert. denied, 354 U.S. 921 (1957); *Mannings v. Board of Public Inst. of Hillsborough County, Fla.,* 277 F.2d 370 (5th Cir. 1960); *Northcross v. Board of Ed. of City of Memphis,* 302 F.2d 818 (6th Cir. 1962), cert. denied, 370 U.S. 944 (1962); *Frasier v. Board of Trustees of Univ. of N.C.,* 134 F.Supp. 589 (M.D.N.C.1955, 3-judge court), aff'd 350 U.S. 979 (1956). Subdivision (b)(2) is not limited to civil-rights cases. Thus an action looking to specific or declaratory relief could be brought by a numerous class of purchasers, say retailers of a given description, against a seller alleged to have undertaken to sell to that class at prices higher than those set for other purchasers, say retailers of another description, when the applicable law forbids such a pricing differential. So also a patentee of a machine, charged with selling or licensing the machine on condition that purchasers or licensees also purchase or obtain licenses to use an ancillary unpatented machine, could be sued on a class basis by a numerous group of purchasers or licensees, or by a numerous group of competing sellers or licensors of the unpatented machine, to test the legality of the "tying" condition.

Subdivision (b)(3). In the situations to which this subdivision relates, class-action treatment is not as clearly called for as in those described above, but it may nevertheless be convenient and desirable depending upon the particular facts. Subdivision (b)(3) encompasses those cases in which a class action would achieve economies of time, effort, and expense, and promote uniformity of decision as to persons similarly situated, without sacrificing procedural fairness or bringing about other undesirable results. Cf. Chafee, supra, at 201.

The court is required to find, as a condition of holding that a class action may be maintained under this subdivision, that the questions common to the class predominate over the questions affecting individual members. It is only where this predominance exists that economies can be achieved by means of the class-action device. In this view, a fraud perpetrated on numerous persons by the use of similar misrepresentations may be an appealing situation for a class action, and it may remain so despite the need, if liability is found, for separate determination of the damages suffered by individuals within the class. On the other hand, although having some common core, a fraud case may be unsuited for treatment as a class action if there was material variation in the representations made or in the kinds or degrees of reliance by the persons to whom they were addressed. See *Oppenheimer v. F. J. Young & Co., Inc.,* 144 F.2d 387 (2d Cir. 1944); *Miller v. National City Bank of N.Y.,* 166 F.2d 723 (2d Cir. 1948); and for like problems in other contexts, see *Hughes v. Encyclopaedia Britannica,* 199 F.2d 295 (7th Cir. 1952); *Sturgeon v. Great Lakes Steel Corp.,* 143 F.2d 819 (6th Cir. 1944). A "mass accident" resulting in injuries to numerous persons is ordinarily not appropriate for a class action because of the likelihood that significant questions, not only of damages but of liability and defenses of liability, would be present, affecting the individuals in different ways. In these circumstances an action conducted nominally as a class action would degenerate in practice into multiple lawsuits separately tried. See *Pennsylvania R.R. v. United States,* 111 F.Supp. 80 (D.N.J.1953); cf. Weinstein, supra, 9 Buffalo L.Rev. at 469. Private damage claims by numerous individuals arising out of concerted antitrust violations may or may not involve predominating common questions. See *Union Carbide & Carbon Corp. v. Nisley,* 300 F.2d 561 (10th Cir. 1961), pet. cert. dism., 371 U.S. 801 (1963); cf. *Weeks v. Bareco Oil Co.,* 125 F.2d 84 (7th Cir. 1941); *Kainz v. Anheuser-Busch, Inc.,* 194 F.2d 737 (7th Cir. 1952); *Hess v. Anderson, Clayton & Co.,* 20 F.R.D. 466 (S.D.Calif.1957).

That common questions predominate is not itself sufficient to justify a class action under subdivision (b)(3), for another method of handling the litigious situation may be available which has greater practical advantages. Thus one or more actions agreed to by the parties as test or model actions may be preferable to a class action; or it may prove feasible and preferable to consolidate actions. Cf. Weinstein, supra, 9 Buffalo L.Rev. at 438–54. Even when a number of separate actions are proceeding simultaneously, experience shows that the burdens on the parties and the courts can sometimes be reduced by arrangements for avoiding repetitious discovery or the like. Currently the Coordinating Committee on Multiple Litigation in the United States District Courts (a subcommittee of the Committee on Trial Practice and Technique of the Judicial Conference of the United States) is charged with developing methods for expediting such massive litigation. To reinforce the point that the court with the aid of the parties ought to assess the relative advantages of alternative procedures for handling the total controversy, subdivision (b)(3) requires, as a further condition of maintaining the class action, that the court shall find that that procedure is "superior" to the others in the particular circumstances.

Factors (A)–(D) are listed, non-exhaustively, as pertinent to the findings. The court is to consider the interests of individual members of the class in controlling their own litigations and carrying them on as they see fit. See *Weeks v. Bareco Oil Co.,* 125 F.2d 84, 88–90, 93–94 (7th Cir. 1941) (anti-trust action); see also *Pentland v. Dravo Corp.,* 152 F.2d 851 (3d Cir. 1945), and Chafee, supra, at 273–75, regarding policy of Fair Labor Standards Act of 1938, § 16(b), 29 U.S.C. § 216(b), prior to amendment by Portal-to-Portal Act of 1947, § 5(a). [The present provisions of 29 U.S.C. § 216(b) are not intended to be affected by Rule 23, as amended.]

In this connection the court should inform itself of any litigation actually pending by or against the individuals. The interests of individuals in conducting separate lawsuits may be so strong as to call for denial of a class action. On the other hand, these interests may be theoretic rather than practical; the class may have a high degree of cohesion and prosecution of the action through representatives would be quite unobjectionable, or the amounts at stake for individuals may be so small that separate suits would be impracticable. The burden that separate suits would impose on the party opposing the class, or upon the court calendars, may also fairly be considered. (See the discussion, under subdivision (c)(2) below, of the right of members to be excluded from the class upon their request.)

Also pertinent is the question of the desirability of concentrating the trial of the claims in the particular forum by means of a class action, in contrast to allowing the claims to be litigated separately in forums to which they would ordinarily be brought. Finally, the court should consider the problems of management which are likely to arise in the conduct of a class action.

Subdivision (c)(1). In order to give clear definition to the action, this provision requires the court to determine, as early in the proceedings as may be practicable, whether an action brought as a class action is to be so maintained. The determination depends in each case on satisfaction of the terms of subdivision (a) and the relevant provisions of subdivision (b).

An order embodying a determination can be conditional; the court may rule, for example, that a class action may be maintained only if the representation is improved through intervention of additional parties of a stated type. A determination once made can be altered or amended before the decision on the merits if, upon fuller development of the facts, the original determination appears unsound. A negative determination means that the action should be stripped of its character as a class action. See subdivision (d)(4). Although an action thus becomes a nonclass action, the court may still be receptive to interventions before the decision on the merits so that the litigation may cover as many interests as can be conveniently handled; the questions whether the intervenors in the nonclass action shall be permitted to claim "ancillary" jurisdiction or the benefit of the date of the commencement of the action for purposes of the statute of limitations are to be decided by reference to the laws governing jurisdiction and limitations as they apply in particular contexts.

Whether the court should require notice to be given to members of the class of its intention to make a determination, or of the order embodying it, is left to the court's discretion under subdivision (d)(2).

Subdivision (c)(2) makes special provision for class actions maintained under subdivision (b)(3). As noted in the discussion of the latter subdivision, the interests of the individuals in pursing their own litigations may be so strong here as to warrant denial of a class action altogether. Even when a class action is maintained under subdivision (b)(3), this individual interest is respected. Thus the court is required to direct notice to the members of the class of the right of each member to be excluded from the class upon his request. A member who does not request exclusion may, if he wishes, enter an appearance in the action through his counsel; whether or not he does so, the judgment in the action will embrace him.

The notice[,] setting forth the alternatives open to the members of the class, is to be the best practicable under the circumstances, and shall include individual notice to the members who can be identified through reasonable effort. (For further discussion of this notice, see the statement under subdivision (d)(2) below.)

Subdivision (c)(3). The judgment in a class action maintained as such to the end will embrace the class, that is, in a class action under subdivision (b)(1) or (b)(2), those found by the court to be class members; in a class action under subdivision (b)(3), those to whom the notice prescribed by subdivision (c)(2) was directed, excepting those who requested exclusion or who are ultimately found by the court not to be members of the class. The judgment has this scope whether it is favorable or unfavorable to the class. In a (b)(1) or (b)(2) action the judgment "describes" the members of the class, but need not specify the individual members; in a (b)(3) action the judgment "specifies" the individual members who have been identified and described the others.

Compare subdivision (c)(4) as to actions conducted as class actions only with respect to particular issues. Where the class-action character of the lawsuit is based solely on the existence of a "limited fund," the judgment, while extending to all claims of class members against the fund, has ordinarily left unaffected the personal claims of nonappearing members against the debtor. See 3 Moore, supra, par. 23.11[4].

Hitherto, in a few actions conducted as "spurious" class actions and thus nominally designed to extend only to parties and others intervening before the determination of liability, courts have held or intimated that class members might be permitted to intervene after a decision on the merits favorable to their interests, in order to secure the benefits of the decision for themselves, although they would presumably be unaffected by an unfavorable decision. See, as to the propriety of this so-called "one-way" intervention in "spurious" actions, the conflicting views expressed in *Union Carbide & Carbon Corp. v. Nisley,* 300 F.2d 561 (10th Cir. 1961), pet. cert. dism., 371 U.S. 801 (1963); *York v. Guaranty Trust Co.,* 143 F.2d 503, 529 (2d Cir. 1944), rev'd on grounds not here relevant, 326 U.S. 99 (1945); *Pentland v. Dravo Corp.,* 152 F.2d 851, 856 (3d Cir. 1945); *Speed v. Transamerica Corp.,* 100 F.Supp. 461, 463 (D.Del.1951); *State Wholesale Grocers v. Great Atl. & Pac. Tea Co.,* 24 F.R.D. 510 (N.D.Ill.1959); *Alabama Ind. Serv. Stat. Assn. v. Shell Pet. Corp.,* 28 F.Supp. 386, 390 (N.D.Ala.1939); *Tolliver v. Cudahy Packing Co.,* 39 F.Supp. 337, 339 (E.D.Tenn.1941); Kalven & Rosenfield, supra, 8 U. of Chi.L.Rev. 684 (1941); Comment, 53 Nw.U.L.Rev. 627, 632–33 (1958); *Developments in the Law,* supra, 71 Harv.L.Rev. at 935; 2 Barron & Holtzoff, supra, § 568; but cf. *Lockwood v. Hercules Powder Co.,* 7 F.R.D. 24, 28–29 (W.D.Mo.1947); *Abram v. San Joaquin Cotton Oil Co.,* 46 F.Supp. 969, 976–77 (S.D.Calif.1942); Chafee, supra, at 280, 285; 3 Moore, supra, par. 23.12, at 3476. Under proposed subdivision (c)(3), one-way intervention is excluded; the action will have been early determined to be a class or nonclass action, and in the former case the judgment, whether or not favorable, will include the class, as above stated.

Although thus declaring that the judgment in a class action includes the class, as defined, subdivision (c)(3) does not disturb the recognized principle that the court conducting the action cannot predetermine the *res judicata* effect of the judgment; this can be tested only in a subsequent action. See Restatement, Judgments § 86, comment (h), § 116 (1942). The court, however, in framing the judgment in any suit brought as a class action, must decide what its extent or coverage shall be, and if the matter is carefully considered, questions of *res judicata* are less likely to be raised at a later time and if raised will be more satisfactorily answered. See Chafee, supra, at 294; Weinstein, supra, 9 Buffalo L.Rev. at 460.

Subdivision (c)(4). This provision recognizes that an action may be maintained as a class action as to particular issues only. For example, in a fraud or similar case the action may retain its "class" character only through the adjudication of liability to the class; the members of the class may thereafter be required to come in individually and prove the amounts of their respective claims.

Two or more classes may be represented in a single action. Where a class is found to include subclasses divergent in interest, the class may be divided correspondingly, and each subclass treated as a class.

Subdivision (d) is concerned with the fair and efficient conduct of the action and lists some types of orders which may be appropriate.

The court should consider how the proceedings are to be arranged in sequence, and what measures should be taken to simplify the proof and argument. See subdivision (d)(1). The orders resulting from this consideration, like the others referred to in subdivision (d), may be combined with a pretrial order under Rule 16, and are subject to modification as the case proceeds.

Subdivision (d)(2) sets out a non-exhaustive list of possible occasions for orders requiring notice to the class. Such notice is not a novel conception. For example, in "limited fund" cases, members of the class have been notified to present individual claims after the basic class decision. Notice has gone to members of a class so that they might express any opposition to the representation, see *United States v. American Optical Co.,* 97 F.Supp. 66 (N.D.Ill.1951), and 1950–51 CCH Trade Cases 64573–74 (par. 62869); cf. *Weeks v. Bareco Oil Co.,* 125 F.2d 84, 94 (7th Cir. 1941), and notice may encourage interventions to improve the representation of the class. Cf. *Oppenheimer v. F. J. Young & Co.,* 144 F.2d 387 (2d Cir. 1944). Notice has been used to poll members on a proposed modification of a consent decree. See record in *Sam Fox Publishing Co. v. United States,* 366 U.S. 683 (1961).

Subdivision (d)(2) does not require notice at any stage, but rather calls attention to its availability and invokes the court's discretion. In the degree that there is cohesiveness or unity in the class and the representation is effective, the need for notice to the class will tend toward a minimum. These indicators suggest that notice under subdivision (d)(2) may be particularly useful and advisable in certain class actions maintained under subdivision (b)(3), for example, to permit members of the class to object to the representation. Indeed, under subdivision (c)(2), notice must be ordered, and is not merely discretionary, to give the members in a subdivision (b)(3) class action an opportunity to secure exclusion from the class. This mandatory notice pursuant to subdivision (c)(2), together with any discretionary notice which the court may find it advisable to give under subdivision (d)(2), is designed to fulfill requirements of due process to which the class action procedure is of course subject. See *Hansberry v. Lee,* 311 U.S. 32 (1940); *Mullane v. Central Hanover Bank & Trust Co.,* 339 U.S. 306 (1950); cf. *Dickinson v. Burnham,* 197 F.2d 973, 979 (2d Cir. 1952), and studies cited at 979 in 4; see also *All American Airways, Inc. v. Elderd,* 209 F.2d 247, 249 (2d Cir. 1954); *Gart v. Cole,* 263 F.2d 244, 248–49 (2d Cir. 1959), cert. denied, 359 U.S. 978 (1959).

Notice to members of the class, whenever employed under amended Rule 23, should be accommodated to the particular purpose but need not comply with the formalities for service of process. See Chafee, supra, at 230–31; *Brendle v. Smith,* 7 F.R.D. 119 (S.D.N.Y.1946). The fact that notice is given at one stage of the action does not mean that it must be given at subsequent stages. Notice is available fundamentally "for the protection of the members of the class or otherwise for the fair conduct of the action" and should not be used merely as a device for the undesirable solicitation of claims. See the discussion in *Cherner v. Transitron Electronic Corp.,* 201 F.Supp. 934 (D.Mass.1962); *Hormel v. United States,* 17 F.R.D. 303 (S.D.N.Y.1955).

In appropriate cases the court should notify interested government agencies of the pendency of the action or of particular steps therein.

Subdivision (d)(3) reflects the possibility of conditioning the maintenance of a class action, e.g., on the strengthening of the representation, see subdivision (c)(1) above; and recognizes that the imposition of conditions on intervenors may be required for the proper and efficient conduct of the action.

As to orders under subdivision (d)(4), see subdivision (c)(1) above.

Subdivision (e) requires approval of the court, after notice, for the dismissal or compromise of any class action.

1987 Amendment

The amendments are technical. No substantive change is intended.

1998 Amendments

Subdivision (f). This permissive interlocutory appeal provision is adopted under the power conferred by 28 U.S.C. § 1292(e). Appeal from an order granting or denying class certification is permitted in the sole discretion of the court of appeals. No other type of Rule 23 order is covered by this provision. The court of appeals is given unfettered discretion whether to permit the appeal, akin to the discretion exercised by the Supreme Court in acting on a petition for certiorari. This discretion suggests an analogy to the provision in 28 U.S.C. § 1292(b) for permissive appeal on certification by a district court. Subdivision (f), however, departs from the § 1291(b) model in two significant ways. It does not require that the district court certify the certification ruling for appeal, although the district court often can assist the parties and court of appeals by offering advice on the desirability of appeal. And it does not include the potentially limiting requirements of § 1292(b) that the district court order "involve[ ] a controlling question of law as to which there is substantial ground for difference of opinion and that an immediate appeal from the order may materially advance the ultimate termination of the litigation.

The courts of appeals will develop standards for granting review that reflect the changing areas of uncertainty in class litigation. The Federal Judicial Center study supports the view that many suits with class-action allegations present familiar and almost routine issues that are no more worthy of immediate appeal than many other interlocutory rulings. Yet several concerns justify expansion of present opportunities to appeal. An order denying certification may confront the plaintiff with a situation in which the only sure path to appellate review is by proceeding to final judgment on the merits of an individual claim that, standing alone, is far smaller than the costs of litigation. An order granting certification, on the other hand, may force a defendant to settle rather than incur the costs of defending a class action and run the risk of potentially ruinous liability. These concerns can be met at low cost by establishing in the court of appeals a discretionary power to grant interlocutory review in cases that show appeal-worthy certification issues.

Permission to appeal may be granted or denied on the basis of any consideration that the court of appeals finds persuasive. Permission is most likely to be granted when the certification decision turns on a novel or unsettled question of law, or when, as a practical matter, the decision on certification is likely dispositive of the litigation.

The district court, having worked through the certification decision, often will be able to provide cogent advice on the factors that bear on the decision whether to permit appeal. This advice can be particularly valuable if the certification decision is tentative. Even as to a firm certification decision, a statement of reasons bearing on the probably benefits and costs of immediate appeal can help focus the court of appeals decision, and may persuade the disappointed party that an attempt to appeal would be fruitless.

The 10-day period for seeking permission to appeal is designed to reduce the risk that attempted appeals will disrupt continuing proceedings. It is expected that the courts of appeals will act quickly in making the preliminary determination whether to permit appeal. Permission to appeal does not stay trial court proceedings. A stay should be sought first from the trial court. If the trial court refuses a stay, its action and any explanation of its views should weigh heavily with the court of appeals.

Appellate Rule 5 has been modified to establish the procedure for petitioning for leave to appeal under subdivision (f).

2003 Amendments

Subdivision (c). Subdivision (c) is amended in several respects. The requirement that the court determine whether to certify a class "as soon as practicable after commencement of an action" is replaced by requiring determination "at an early practicable time." The notice provisions are substantially revised.

Paragraph (1). Subdivision (c)(1)(A) is changed to require that the determination whether to certify a class be made "at an early practicable time." The "as soon as practicable" exaction neither reflects prevailing practice nor captures the many valid reasons that may justify deferring the initial certification decision. See Willging, Hooper & Niemic, *Empirical Study of Class Actions in Four Federal District Courts: Final Report to the Advisory Committee on Civil Rules 26–36* (Federal Judicial Center 1996).

Time may be needed to gather information necessary to make the certification decision. Although an evaluation of the probable outcome on the merits is not properly part of the certification decision, discovery in aid of the certification decision often includes information required to identify the nature of the issues that actually will be presented at trial. In this sense it is appropriate to conduct controlled discovery into the "merits," limited to those aspects relevant to making the certification decision on an informed basis. Active judicial supervision may be required to achieve the most effective balance that expedites an informed certification determination without forcing an artificial and ultimately wasteful division between "certification discovery" and "merits discovery." A critical need is to determine how the case will be tried. An increasing number of courts require a party requesting class certification to present a "trial plan" that describes the issues likely to be presented at trial and tests whether they are susceptible of class-wide proof. See Manual For Complex Litigation Third, § 21.213, p. 44; § 30.11, p. 214; § 30.12, p. 215.

Other considerations may affect the timing of the certification decision. The party opposing the class may prefer to win dismissal or summary judgment as to the individual plaintiffs without certification and without binding the class that might have been certified. Time may be needed to explore designation of class counsel under Rule 23(g), recognizing that in many cases the need to progress toward the certification determination may require designation of interim counsel under Rule 23(g)(2)(A).

Although many circumstances may justify deferring the certification decision, active management may be necessary to ensure that the certification decision is not unjustifiably delayed.

Subdivision (c)(1)(C) reflects two amendments. The provision that a class certification "may be conditional" is deleted. A court that is not satisfied that the requirements of Rule 23 have been met should refuse certification until they have been met. The provision that permits alteration or amendment of an order granting or denying class certification is amended to set the cut-off point at final judgment rather than "the decision on the merits." This change avoids the possible ambiguity in referring to "the decision on the merits." Following a determination of liability, for example, proceedings to define the remedy may demonstrate the need to amend the class definition or subdivide the class. In this setting the final judgment concept is pragmatic. It is not the same as the concept used for appeal purposes, but it should be flexible, particularly in protracted litigation.

The authority to amend an order under Rule 23(c)(1) before final judgment does not restore the practice of "one-way intervention" that was rejected by the 1966 revision of Rule 23. A determination of liability after certification, however, may show a need to amend the class definition. Decertification may be warranted after further proceedings.

If the definition of a class certified under Rule 23(b)(3) is altered to include members who have not been afforded notice and an opportunity to request exclusion, notice—including an opportunity to request exclusion—must be directed to the new class members under Rule 23(c)(2)(B).

Paragraph (2). The first change made in Rule 23(c)(2) is to call attention to the court's authority—already established in part by Rule 23(d)(2)—to direct notice of certification to a Rule 23(b)(1) or (b)(2) class. The present rule expressly requires notice only in actions certified under Rule 23(b)(3). Members of classes certified under Rules 23(b)(1) or (b)(2) have interests that may deserve protection by notice.

The authority to direct notice to class members in a (b)(1) or (b)(2) class action should be exercised with care. For several reasons, there may be less need for notice than in a (b)(3) class action. There is no right to request exclusion from a (b)(1) or (b)(2) class. The characteristics of the class may reduce the need for formal notice. The cost of providing notice, moreover, could easily cripple actions that do not seek damages. The court may decide not to direct notice after balancing the risk that notice costs may deter the pursuit of class relief against the benefits of notice.

When the court does direct certification notice in a (b)(1) or (b)(2) class action, the discretion and flexibility established by subdivision (c)(2)(A) extend to the method of giving notice. Notice facilitates the opportunity to participate. Notice calculated to reach a significant number of class members often will protect the interests of all. Informal methods may prove effective. A simple posting in a place visited by many class members, directing attention to a source of more detailed information, may suffice. The court should consider the costs of notice in relation to the probable reach of inexpensive methods.

If a Rule 23(b)(3) class is certified in conjunction with a (b)(2) class, the (c)(2)(B) notice requirements must be satisfied as to the (b)(3) class.

The direction that class-certification notice be couched in plain, easily understood language is a reminder of the need to work unremittingly at the difficult task of communicating with class members. It is difficult to provide information about most class actions that is both accurate and easily understood by class members who are not themselves lawyers. Factual uncertainty, legal complexity, and the complication of class-action procedure raise the barriers high. The Federal Judicial Center has created illustrative clear-notice forms that provide a helpful starting point for actions similar to those described in the forms.

Subdivision (e). Subdivision (e) is amended to strengthen the process of reviewing proposed class-action settlements. Settlement may be a desirable means of resolving a class action. But court review and approval are essential to assure adequate representation of class members who have not participated in shaping the settlement.

Paragraph (1). Subdivision (e)(1)(A) expressly recognizes the power of a class representative to settle class claims, issues, or defenses.

Rule 23(e)(1)(A) resolves the ambiguity in former Rule 23(e)'s reference to dismissal or compromise of "a class action." That language could be—and at times was—read to require court approval of settlements with putative class representatives that resolved only individual claims. See Manual for Complex Litigation Third, § 30.41. The new rule requires approval only if the claims, issues, or defenses of a certified class are resolved by a settlement, voluntary dismissal, or compromise.

Subdivision (e)(1)(B) carries forward the notice requirement of present Rule 23(e) when the settlement binds the class through claim or issue preclusion; notice is not required when the settlement binds only the individual class representatives. Notice of a settlement binding on the class is required either when the settlement follows class certification or when the decisions on certification and settlement proceed simultaneously.

Reasonable settlement notice may require individual notice in the manner required by Rule 23(c)(2)(B) for certification notice to a Rule 23(b)(3) class. Individual notice is appropriate, for example, if class members are required to take action—such as filing claims—to participate in the judgment, or if the court orders a settlement opt-out opportunity under Rule 23(e)(3).

Subdivision (e)(1)(C) confirms and mandates the already common practice of holding hearings as part of the process of approving settlement, voluntary dismissal, or compromise that would bind members of a class.

Subdivision (e)(1)(C) states the standard for approving a proposed settlement that would bind class members. The settlement must be fair, reasonable, and adequate. A helpful review of many factors that may deserve consideration is provided by *In re: Prudential Ins. Co. America Sales Practice Litigation Agent Actions,* 148 F.3d 283, 316–324 (3d Cir. 1998). Further guidance can be found in the Manual for Complex Litigation.

The court must make findings that support the conclusion that the settlement is fair, reasonable, and adequate. The findings must be set out in sufficient detail to explain to class members and the appellate court the factors that bear on applying the standard.

Settlement review also may provide an occasion to review the cogency of the initial class definition. The terms of the settlement themselves, or objections, may reveal divergent interests of class members and demonstrate the need to redefine the class or to designate subclasses. Redefinition of a class certified under Rule 23(b)(3) may require notice to new class members under Rule 23(c)(2)(B). See Rule 23(c)(1)(C).

Paragraph (2). Subdivision (e)(2) requires parties seeking approval of a settlement, voluntary dismissal, or compromise under Rule 23(e)(1) to file a statement identifying any agreement made in connection with the settlement. This provision does not change the basic requirement that the parties disclose all terms of the settlement or compromise that the court must approve under Rule 23(e)(1). It aims instead at related undertakings that, although seemingly separate, may have influenced the terms of the settlement by trading away possible advantages for the class in return for advantages for others. Doubts should be resolved in favor of identification.

Further inquiry into the agreements identified by the parties should not become the occasion for discovery by the parties or objectors. The court may direct the parties to provide to the court or other parties a summary or copy of the full terms of any agreement identified by the parties. The court also may direct the parties to provide a summary or copy of any agreement not identified by the parties that the court considers relevant to its review of a proposed settlement. In exercising discretion under this rule, the court may act in steps, calling first for a summary of any agreement that may have affected the settlement and then for a complete version if the summary does not provide an adequate basis for review. A direction to disclose a summary or copy of an agreement may raise concerns of confidentiality. Some agreements may include information that merits protection against general disclosure. And the court must provide an opportunity to claim work-product or other protections.

Paragraph (3). Subdivision (e)(3) authorizes the court to refuse to approve a settlement unless the settlement affords class members a new opportunity to request exclusion from a class certified under Rule 23(b)(3) after settlement terms are known. An agreement by the parties themselves to permit class members to elect exclusion at this point by the settlement agreement may be one factor supporting approval of the settlement. Often there is an opportunity to opt out at this point because the class is certified and settlement is reached in circumstances that lead to simultaneous notice of certification and notice of settlement. In these cases, the basic opportunity to elect exclusion applies without further complication. In some cases, particularly if settlement appears imminent at the time of certification, it may be possible to achieve equivalent protection by deferring notice and the opportunity to elect exclusion until actual settlement terms are known. This approach avoids the cost and potential confusion of providing two notices and makes the single notice more meaningful. But notice should not be delayed unduly after certification in the hope of settlement.

Rule 23(e)(3) authorizes the court to refuse to approve a settlement unless the settlement affords a new opportunity to elect exclusion in a case that settles after a certification decision if the earlier opportunity to elect exclusion provided with the certification notice has expired by the time of the settlement notice. A decision to remain in the class is likely to be more carefully considered and is better informed when settlement terms are known.

The opportunity to request exclusion from a proposed settlement is limited to members of a (b)(3) class. Exclusion may be requested only by individual class members; no class member may purport to opt out other class members by way of another class action.

The decision whether to approve a settlement that does not allow a new opportunity to elect exclusion is confided to the court's discretion. The court may make this decision before directing notice to the class under Rule 23(e)(1)(B) or after the Rule 23(e)(1)(C) hearing. Many factors may influence the court's decision. Among these are changes in the information available to class members since expiration of the first opportunity to request exclusion, and the nature of the individual class members' claims.

The terms set for permitting a new opportunity to elect exclusion from the proposed settlement of a Rule 23(b)(3) class action may address concerns of potential misuse. The court might direct, for example, that class members who elect exclusion are bound by rulings on the merits made before the settlement was proposed for approval. Still other terms or conditions may be appropriate.

Paragraph (4). Subdivision (e)(4) confirms the right of class members to object to a proposed settlement, voluntary dismissal, or compromise. The right is defined in relation to a disposition that, because it would bind the class, requires court approval under subdivision (e)(1)(C).

Subdivision (e)(4)(B) requires court approval for withdrawal of objections made under subdivision (e)(4)(A). Review follows automatically if the objections are withdrawn on terms that lead to modification of the settlement with the class. Review also is required if the objector formally withdraws the objections. If the objector simply abandons pursuit of the objection, the court may inquire into the circumstances.

Approval under paragraph (4)(B) may be given or denied with little need for further inquiry if the objection and the disposition go only to a protest that the individual treatment afforded the objector under the proposed settlement is unfair because of factors that distinguish the objector from other class members. Different considerations may apply if the objector has protested that the proposed settlement is not fair, reasonable, or adequate on grounds that apply generally to a class or subclass. Such objections, which purport to represent class-wide interests, may augment the opportunity for obstruction or delay. If such objections are surrendered on terms that do not affect the class settlement or the objector's participation in the class settlement, the court often can approve withdrawal of the objections without elaborate inquiry.

Once an objector appeals, control of the proceeding lies in the court of appeals. The court of appeals may undertake review and approval of a settlement with the objector, perhaps as part of appeal settlement procedures, or may remand to the district court to take advantage of the district court's familiarity with the action and settlement.

Subdivision (g). Subdivision (g) is new. It responds to the reality that the selection and activity of class counsel are often critically important to the successful handling of a class action. Until now, courts have scrutinized proposed class counsel as well as the class representative under Rule 23(a)(4). This experience has recognized the importance of judicial evaluation of the proposed lawyer for the class, and this new subdivision builds on that experience rather than introducing an entirely new element into the class certification process. Rule 23(a)(4) will continue to call for scrutiny of the proposed class representative, while this subdivision will guide the court in assessing proposed class counsel as part of the certification decision. This subdivision recognizes the importance of class counsel, states the obligation to represent the interests of the class, and provides a framework for selection of class counsel. The procedure and standards for appointment vary depending on whether there are multiple applicants to be class counsel. The new subdivision also provides a method by which the court may make directions from the outset about the potential fee award to class counsel in the event the action is successful.

Paragraph (1) sets out the basic requirement that class counsel be appointed if a class is certified and articulates the obligation of class counsel to represent the interests of the class, as opposed to the potentially conflicting interests of individual class members. It also sets out the factors the court should consider in assessing proposed class counsel.

Paragraph (1)(A) requires that the court appoint class counsel to represent the class. Class counsel must be appointed for all classes, including each subclass that the court certifies to represent divergent interests.

Paragraph (1)(A) does not apply if "a statute provides otherwise." This recognizes that provisions of the Private Securities Litigation Reform Act of 1995, Pub. L. No. 104–67, 109 Stat. 737 (1995) (codified in various sections of 15 U.S.C.), contain directives that bear on selection of a lead plaintiff and the retention of counsel. This subdivision does not purport to supersede or to affect the interpretation of those provisions, or any similar provisions of other legislation.

Paragraph 1(B) recognizes that the primary responsibility of class counsel, resulting from appointment as class counsel, is to represent the best interests of the class. The rule thus establishes the obligation of class counsel, an obligation that may be different from the customary obligations of counsel to individual clients. Appointment as class counsel means that the primary obligation of counsel is to the class rather than to any individual members of it. The class representatives do not have an unfettered right to "fire" class counsel. In the same vein, the class representatives cannot command class counsel to accept or reject a settlement proposal. To the contrary, class counsel must determine whether seeking the court's approval of a settlement would be in the best interests of the class as a whole.

Paragraph (1)(C) articulates the basic responsibility of the court to appoint class counsel who will provide the adequate representation called for by paragraph (1)(B). It identifies criteria that must be considered and invites the court to consider any other pertinent matters. Although couched in terms of the court's duty, the listing also informs counsel seeking appointment about the topics that should be addressed in an application for appointment or in the motion for class certification.

The court may direct potential class counsel to provide additional information about the topics mentioned in paragraph (1)(C) or about any other relevant topic. For example, the court may direct applicants to inform the court concerning any agreements about a prospective award of attorney fees or nontaxable costs, as such agreements may sometimes be significant in the selection of class counsel. The court might also direct that potential class counsel indicate how parallel litigation might be coordinated or consolidated with the action before the court.

The court may also direct counsel to propose terms for a potential award of attorney fees and nontaxable costs. Attorney fee awards are an important feature of class action practice, and attention to this subject from the outset may often be a productive technique. Paragraph (2)(C) therefore authorizes the court to provide directions about attorney fees and costs when appointing class counsel. Because there will be numerous class actions in which this information is not likely to be useful, the court need not consider it in all class actions.

Some information relevant to class counsel appointment may involve matters that include adversary preparation in a way that should be shielded from disclosure to other parties. An appropriate protective order may be necessary to preserve confidentiality.

In evaluating prospective class counsel, the court should weigh all pertinent factors. No single factor should necessarily be determinative in a given case. For example, the resources counsel will commit to the case must be appropriate to its needs, but the court should be careful not to limit consideration to lawyers with the greatest resources.

If, after review of all applicants, the court concludes that none would be satisfactory class counsel, it may deny class certification, reject all applications, recommend that an application be modified, invite new applications, or make any other appropriate order regarding selection and appointment of class counsel.

Paragraph (2). This paragraph sets out the procedure that should be followed in appointing class counsel. Although it affords substantial flexibility, it provides the framework for appointment of class counsel in all class actions. For counsel who filed the action, the materials submitted in support of the motion for class certification may suffice to justify appointment so long as the information described in paragraph (g)(1)(C) is included. If there are other applicants, they ordinarily would file a formal application detailing their suitability for the position.

In a plaintiff class action the court usually would appoint as class counsel only an attorney or attorneys who have sought appointment. Different considerations may apply in defendant class actions.

The rule states that the court should appoint "class counsel." In many instances, the applicant will be an individual attorney. In other cases, however, an entire firm, or perhaps numerous attorneys who are not otherwise affiliated but are collaborating on the action will apply. No rule of thumb exists to determine when such arrangements are appropriate; the court should be alert to the need for adequate staffing of the case, but also to the risk of overstaffing or an ungainly counsel structure.

Paragraph (2)(A) authorizes the court to designate interim counsel during the pre-certification period if necessary to protect the interests of the putative class. Rule 23(c)(1)(B) directs that the order certifying the class include appointment of class counsel. Before class certification, however, it will usually be important for an attorney to take action to prepare for the certification decision. The amendment to Rule 23(c)(1) recognizes that some discovery is often necessary for that determination. It also may be important to make or respond to motions before certification. Settlement may be discussed before certification. Ordinarily, such work is handled by the lawyer who filed the action. In some cases, however, there may be rivalry or uncertainty that makes formal designation of interim counsel appropriate. Rule 23(g)(2)(A) authorizes the court to designate interim counsel to act on behalf of the putative class before the certification decision is made. Failure to make the formal designation does not prevent the attorney who filed the action from proceeding in it. Whether or not formally designated interim counsel, an attorney who acts on behalf of the class before certification must act in the best interests of the class as a whole. For example, an attorney who negotiates a pre-certification settlement must seek a settlement that is fair, reasonable, and adequate for the class.

Rule 23(c)(1) provides that the court should decide whether to certify the class "at an early practicable time," and directs that class counsel should be appointed in the order certifying the class. In some cases, it may be appropriate for the court to allow a reasonable period after commencement of the action for filing applications to serve as class counsel. The primary ground for deferring appointment would be that there is reason to anticipate competing applications to serve as class counsel. Examples might include instances in which more than one class action has been filed, or in which other attorneys have filed individual actions on behalf of putative class members. The purpose of facilitating competing applications in such a case is to afford the best possible representation for the class. Another possible reason for deferring appointment would be that the initial applicant was found inadequate, but it seems appropriate to permit additional applications rather than deny class certification.

Paragraph (2)(B) states the basic standard the court should use in deciding whether to certify the class and appoint class counsel in the single applicant situation—that the applicant be able to provide the representation called for by paragraph (1)(B) in light of the factors identified in paragraph (1)(C).

If there are multiple adequate applicants, paragraph (2)(B) directs the court to select the class counsel best able to represent the interests of the class. This decision should also be made using the factors outlined in paragraph (1)(C), but in the multiple applicant situation the court is to go beyond scrutinizing the adequacy of counsel and make a comparison of the strengths of the various applicants. As with the decision whether to appoint the sole applicant for the position, no single factor should be dispositive in selecting class counsel in cases in which there are multiple applicants. The fact that a given attorney filed the instant action, for example, might not weigh heavily in the decision if that lawyer had not done significant work identifying or investigating claims. Depending on the nature of the case, one important consideration might be the applicant's existing attorney-client relationship with the proposed class representative.

Paragraph (2)(C) builds on the appointment process by authorizing the court to include provisions regarding attorney fees in the order appointing class counsel. Courts may find it desirable to adopt guidelines for fees or nontaxable costs, or to direct class counsel to report to the court at regular intervals on the efforts undertaken in the action, to facilitate the court's later determination of a reasonable attorney fee.

Subdivision (h). Subdivision (h) is new. Fee awards are a powerful influence on the way attorneys initiate, develop, and conclude class actions. Class action attorney fee awards have heretofore been handled, along with all other attorney fee awards, under Rule 54(d)(2), but that rule is not addressed to the particular concerns of class actions. This subdivision is designed to work in tandem with new subdivision (g) on appointment of class counsel, which may afford an opportunity for the court to provide an early framework for an eventual fee award, or for monitoring the work of class counsel during the pendency of the action.

Subdivision (h) applies to "an action certified as a class action." This includes cases in which there is a simultaneous proposal for class certification and settlement even though technically the class may not be certified unless the court approves the settlement pursuant to review under Rule 23(e). When a settlement is proposed for Rule 23(e) approval, either after certification or with a request for certification, notice to class members about class counsel's fee motion would ordinarily accompany the notice to the class about the settlement proposal itself.

This subdivision does not undertake to create new grounds for an award of attorney fees or nontaxable costs. Instead, it applies when such awards are authorized by law or by agreement of the parties. Against that background, it provides a format for all awards of attorney fees and nontaxable costs in connection with a class action, not only the award to class counsel. In some situations, there may be a basis for making an award to other counsel whose work produced a beneficial result for the class, such as attorneys who acted for the class before certification but were not appointed class counsel, or attorneys who represented objectors to a proposed settlement under Rule 23(e) or to the fee motion of class counsel. Other situations in which fee awards are authorized by law or by agreement of the parties may exist.

This subdivision authorizes an award of "reasonable" attorney fees and nontaxable costs. This is the customary term for measurement of fee awards in cases in which counsel may obtain an award of fees under the "common fund" theory that applies in many class actions, and is used in many fee-shifting statutes. Depending on the circumstances, courts have approached the determination of what is reasonable in different ways. In particular, there is some variation among courts about whether in "common fund" cases the court should use the lodestar or a percentage method of determining what fee is reasonable. The rule does not attempt to resolve the question whether the lodestar or percentage approach should be viewed as preferable.

Active judicial involvement in measuring fee awards is singularly important to the proper operation of the class-action process. Continued reliance on caselaw development of fee-award measures does not diminish the court's responsibility. In a class action, the district court must ensure that the amount and mode of payment of attorney fees are fair and proper whether the fees come from a common fund or are otherwise paid. Even in the absence of objections, the court bears this responsibility.

Courts discharging this responsibility have looked to a variety of factors. One fundamental focus is the result actually achieved for class members, a basic consideration in any case in which fees are sought on the basis of a benefit achieved for class members. The Private Securities Litigation Reform Act of 1995 explicitly makes this factor a cap for a fee award in actions to which it applies. See 15 U.S.C. §§ 77z–1(a)(6); 78u–4(a)(6) (fee award should not exceed a "reasonable percentage of the amount of any damages and prejudgment interest actually paid to the class"). For a percentage approach to fee measurement, results achieved is the basic starting point.

In many instances, the court may need to proceed with care in assessing the value conferred on class members. Settlement regimes that provide for future payments, for example, may not result in significant actual payments to class members. In this connection, the court may need to scrutinize the manner and operation of any applicable claims procedure. In some cases, it may be appropriate to defer some portion of the fee award until actual payouts to class members are known. Settlements involving nonmonetary provisions for class members also deserve careful scrutiny to ensure that these provisions have actual value to the class. On occasion the court's Rule 23(e) review will provide a solid basis for this sort of evaluation, but in any event it is also important to assessing the fee award for the class.

At the same time, it is important to recognize that in some class actions the monetary relief obtained is not the sole determinant of an appropriate attorney fees award. Cf. *Blanchard v. Bergeron*, 489 U.S. 87, 95 (1989) (cautioning in an individual case against an "undesirable emphasis" on "the importance of the recovery of damages in civil rights litigation" that might "shortchange efforts to seek effective injunctive or declaratory relief").

Any directions or orders made by the court in connection with appointing class counsel under Rule 23(g) should weigh heavily in making a fee award under this subdivision.

Courts have also given weight to agreements among the parties regarding the fee motion, and to agreements between class counsel and others about the fees claimed by the motion. Rule 54(d)(2)(B) provides: "If directed by the court, the motion shall also disclose the terms of any agreement with respect to fees to be paid for the services for which claim is made." The agreement by a settling party not to oppose a fee application up to a certain amount, for example, is worthy of consideration, but the court remains responsible to determine a reasonable fee. "Side agreements" regarding fees provide at least perspective pertinent to an appropriate fee award.

In addition, courts may take account of the fees charged by class counsel or other attorneys for representing individual claimants or objectors in the case. In determining a fee for class counsel, the court's objective is to ensure an overall fee that is fair for counsel and equitable within the class. In some circumstances individual fee agreements between class counsel and class members might have provisions inconsistent with those goals, and the court might determine that adjustments in the class fee award were necessary as a result.

Finally, it is important to scrutinize separately the application for an award covering nontaxable costs. If costs were addressed in the order appointing class counsel, those directives should be a presumptive starting point in determining what is an appropriate award.

Paragraph (1). Any claim for an award of attorney fees must be sought by motion under Rule 54(d)(2), which invokes the provisions for timing of appeal in Rule 58 and Appellate Rule 4. Owing to the distinctive features of class action fee motions, however, the provisions of this subdivision control disposition of fee motions in class actions, while Rule 54(d)(2) applies to matters not addressed in this subdivision.

The court should direct when the fee motion must be filed. For motions by class counsel in cases subject to court review of a proposed settlement under Rule 23(e), it would be important to require the filing of at least the initial motion in time for inclusion of information about the motion in the notice to the class about the proposed settlement that is required by Rule 23(e). In cases litigated to judgment, the court might also order class counsel's motion to be filed promptly so that notice to the class under this subdivision (h) can be given.

Besides service of the motion on all parties, notice of class counsel's motion for attorney fees must be "directed to the class in a reasonable manner." Because members of the class have an interest in the arrangements for payment of class counsel whether that payment comes from the class fund or is made directly by another party, notice is required in all instances. In cases in which settlement approval is contemplated under Rule 23(e), notice of class counsel's fee motion should be combined with notice of the proposed settlement, and the provision regarding notice to the class is parallel to the requirements for notice under Rule 23(e). In adjudicated class actions, the court may calibrate the notice to avoid undue expense.

Paragraph (2). A class member and any party from whom payment is sought may object to the fee motion. Other parties—for example, nonsettling defendants—may not object because they lack a sufficient interest in the amount the court awards. The rule does not specify a time limit for making an objection. In setting the date objections are due, the court should provide sufficient time after the full fee motion is on file to enable potential objectors to examine the motion.

The court may allow an objector discovery relevant to the objections. In determining whether to allow discovery, the court should weigh the need for the information against the cost and delay that would attend discovery. See Rule 26(b)(2). One factor in determining whether to authorize discovery is the completeness of the material submitted in support of the fee motion, which depends in part on the fee measurement standard applicable to the case. If the motion provides thorough information, the burden should be on the objector to justify discovery to obtain further information.

Paragraph (3). Whether or not there are formal objections, the court must determine whether a fee award is justified and, if so, set a reasonable fee. The rule does not require a formal hearing in all cases. The form and extent of a hearing depend on the circumstances of the case. The rule does require findings and conclusions under Rule 52(a).

Paragraph (4). By incorporating Rule 54(d)(2), this provision gives the court broad authority to obtain assistance in determining the appropriate amount to award. In deciding whether to direct submission of such questions to a special master or magistrate judge, the court should give appropriate consideration to the cost and delay that such a process might entail.

2007 Amendment

The language of Rule 23 has been amended as part of the general restyling of the Civil Rules to make them more easily understood and to make style and terminology consistent throughout the rules. These changes are intended to be stylistic only.

Amended Rule 23(d)(2) carries forward the provisions of former Rule 23(d) that recognize two separate propositions. First, a Rule 23(d) order may be combined with a pretrial order under Rule 16. Second, the standard for amending the Rule 23(d) order continues to be the more open-ended standard for amending Rule 23(d) orders, not the more exacting standard for amending Rule 16 orders.

As part of the general restyling, intensifiers that provide emphasis but add no meaning are consistently deleted. Amended Rule 23(f) omits as redundant the explicit reference to court of appeals discretion in deciding whether to permit an interlocutory appeal. The omission does not in any way limit the unfettered discretion established by the original rule.

2009 Amendment

The time set in the former rule at 10 days has been revised to 14 days. See the Note to Rule 6.

2018 Amendments

Rule 23 is amended mainly to address issues related to settlement, and also to take account of issues that have emerged since the rule was last amended in 2003.

Subdivision (c)(2). As amended, Rule 23(e)(1) provides that the court must direct notice to the class regarding a proposed class-action settlement only after determining that the prospect of class certification and approval of the proposed settlement justifies giving notice. This decision has been called "preliminary approval" of the proposed class certification in Rule 23(b)(3) actions. It is common to send notice to the class simultaneously under both Rule 23(e)(1) and Rule 23(c)(2)(B), including a provision for class members to decide by a certain date whether to opt out. This amendment recognizes the propriety of this combined notice practice.

Subdivision (c)(2) is also amended to recognize contemporary methods of giving notice to class members. Since *Eisen v. Carlisle & Jacquelin*, 417 U.S. 156 (1974), interpreted the individual notice requirement for class members in Rule 23(b)(3) class actions, many courts have read the rule to require notice by first class mail in every case. But technological change since 1974 has introduced other means of communication that may sometimes provide a reliable additional or alternative method for giving notice. Although first class mail may often be the preferred primary method of giving notice, courts and counsel have begun to employ new technology to make notice more effective. Because there is no reason to expect that technological change will cease, when selecting a method or methods of giving notice courts should consider the capacity and limits of current technology, including class members' likely access to such technology.

Rule 23(c)(2)(B) is amended to take account of these changes. The rule continues to call for giving class members "the best notice that is practicable." It does not specify any particular means as preferred. Although it may sometimes be true that electronic methods of notice, for example email, are the most promising, it is important to keep in mind that a significant portion of class members in certain cases may have limited or no access to email or the Internet.

Instead of preferring any one means of notice, therefore, the amended rule relies on courts and counsel to focus on the means or combination of means most likely to be effective in the case before the court. The court should exercise its discretion to select appropriate means of giving notice. In providing the court with sufficient information to enable it to decide whether to give notice to the class of a proposed class-action settlement under Rule 23(e)(1), it would ordinarily be important to include details about the proposed method of giving notice and to provide the court with a copy of each notice the parties propose to use.

In determining whether the proposed means of giving notice is appropriate, the court should also give careful attention to the content and format of the notice and, if notice is given under both Rule 23(e)(1) and Rule 23(c)(2)(B), any claim form class members must submit to obtain relief.

Counsel should consider which method or methods of giving notice will be most effective; simply assuming that the "traditional" methods are best may disregard contemporary communication realities. The ultimate goal of giving notice is to enable class members to make informed decisions about whether to opt out or, in instances where a proposed settlement is involved, to object or to make claims. Rule 23(c)(2)(B) directs that the notice be "in plain, easily understood language." Means, format, and content that would be appropriate for class members likely to be sophisticated, for example in a securities fraud class action, might not be appropriate for a class having many members likely to be less sophisticated. The court and counsel may wish to consider the use of class notice experts or professional claims administrators.

Attention should focus also on the method of opting out provided in the notice. The proposed method should be as convenient as possible, while protecting against unauthorized opt-out notices.

Subdivision (e). The introductory paragraph of Rule 23(e) is amended to make explicit that its procedural requirements apply in instances in which the court has not certified a class at the time that a proposed settlement is presented to the court. The notice required under Rule 23(e)(1) then should also satisfy the notice requirements of amended Rule 23(c)(2)(B) for a class to be certified under Rule 23(b)(3), and trigger the class members' time to request exclusion. Information about the opt-out rate could then be available to the court when it considers final approval of the proposed settlement.

Subdivision (e)(1). The decision to give notice of a proposed settlement to the class is an important event. It should be based on a solid record supporting the conclusion that the proposed settlement will likely earn final approval after notice and an opportunity to object. The parties must provide the court with information sufficient to determine whether notice should be sent. At the time they seek notice to the class, the proponents of the settlement should ordinarily provide the court with all available materials they intend to submit to support approval under Rule 23(e)(2) and that they intend to make available to class members. The amended rule also specifies the standard the court should use in deciding whether to send notice—that it likely will be able both to approve the settlement proposal under Rule 23(e)(2) and, if it has not previously certified a class, to certify the class for purposes of judgment on the proposal.

The subjects to be addressed depend on the specifics of the particular class action and proposed settlement. But some general observations can be made.

One key element is class certification. If the court has already certified a class, the only information ordinarily necessary is whether the proposed settlement calls for any change in the class certified, or of the claims, defenses, or issues regarding which certification was granted. But if a class has not been certified, the parties must ensure that the court has a basis for concluding that it likely will be able, after the final hearing, to certify the class. Although the standards for certification differ for settlement and litigation purposes, the court cannot make the decision regarding the prospects for certification without a suitable basis in the record. The ultimate decision to certify the class for purposes of settlement cannot be made until the hearing on final approval of the proposed settlement. If the settlement is not approved, the parties' positions regarding certification for settlement should not be considered if certification is later sought for purposes of litigation.

Regarding the proposed settlement, many types of information might appropriately be provided to the court. A basic focus is the extent and type of benefits that the settlement will confer on the members of the class. Depending on the nature of the proposed relief, that showing may include details of the contemplated claims process and the anticipated rate of claims by class members. Because some funds are frequently left unclaimed, the settlement agreement ordinarily should address the distribution of those funds.

The parties should also supply the court with information about the likely range of litigated outcomes, and about the risks that might attend full litigation. Information about the extent of discovery completed in the litigation or in parallel actions may often be important. In addition, as suggested by Rule 23(b)(3)(B), the parties should provide information about the existence of other pending or anticipated litigation on behalf of class members involving claims that would be released under the proposal.

The proposed handling of an award of attorney's fees under Rule 23(h) ordinarily should be addressed in the parties' submission to the court. In some cases, it will be important to relate the amount of an award of attorney's fees to the expected benefits to the class. One way to address this issue is to defer some or all of the award of attorney's fees until the court is advised of the actual claims rate and results.

Another topic that normally should be considered is any agreement that must be identified under Rule 23(e)(3).

The parties may supply information to the court on any other topic that they regard as pertinent to the determination whether the proposal is fair, reasonable, and adequate. The court may direct the parties to supply further information about the topics they do address, or to supply information on topics they do not address. The court should not direct notice to the class until the parties' submissions show it is likely that the court will be able to approve the proposal after notice to the class and a final approval hearing.

Subdivision (e)(2). The central concern in reviewing a proposed class-action settlement is that it be fair, reasonable, and adequate. Courts have generated lists of factors to shed light on this concern. Overall, these factors focus on comparable considerations, but each circuit has developed its own vocabulary for expressing these concerns. In some circuits, these lists have remained essentially unchanged for thirty or forty years. The goal of this amendment is not to displace any factor, but rather to focus the court and the lawyers on the core concerns of procedure and substance that should guide the decision whether to approve the proposal.

A lengthy list of factors can take on an independent life, potentially distracting attention from the central concerns that inform the settlement-review process. A circuit's list might include a dozen or more separately articulated factors. Some of those factors—perhaps many—may not be relevant to a particular case or settlement proposal. Those that are relevant may be more or less important to the particular case. Yet counsel and courts may feel it necessary to address every factor on a given circuit's list in every case. The sheer number of factors can distract both the court and the parties from the central concerns that bear on review under Rule 23(e)(2).

This amendment therefore directs the parties to present the settlement to the court in terms of a shorter list of core concerns, by focusing on the primary procedural considerations and substantive qualities that should always matter to the decision whether to approve the proposal.

Approval under Rule 23(e)(2) is required only when class members would be bound under Rule 23(c)(3). Accordingly, in addition to evaluating the proposal itself, the court must determine whether it can certify the class under the standards of Rule 23(a) and (b) for purposes of judgment based on the proposal.

Paragraphs (A) and (B). These paragraphs identify matters that might be described as "procedural" concerns, looking to the conduct of the litigation and of the negotiations leading up to the proposed settlement. Attention to these matters is an important foundation for scrutinizing the substance of the proposed settlement. If the court has appointed class counsel or interim class counsel, it will have made an initial evaluation of counsel's capacities and experience. But the focus at this point is on the actual performance of counsel acting on behalf of the class.

The information submitted under Rule 23(e)(1) may provide a useful starting point in assessing these topics. For example, the nature and amount of discovery in this or other cases, or the actual outcomes of other cases, may indicate whether counsel negotiating on behalf of the class had an adequate information base. The pendency of other litigation about the same general subject on behalf of class members may also be pertinent. The conduct of the negotiations may be important as well. For example, the involvement of a neutral or court-affiliated mediator or facilitator in those negotiations may bear on whether they were conducted in a manner that would protect and further the class interests. Particular attention might focus on the treatment of any award of attorney's fees, with respect to both the manner of negotiating the fee award and its terms.

Paragraphs (C) and (D). These paragraphs focus on what might be called a "substantive" review of the terms of the proposed settlement. The relief that the settlement is expected to provide to class members is a central concern. Measuring the proposed relief may require evaluation of any proposed claims process; directing that the parties report back to the court about actual claims experience may be important. The contents of any agreement identified under Rule 23(e)(3) may also bear on the adequacy of the proposed relief, particularly regarding the equitable treatment of all members of the class.

Another central concern will relate to the cost and risk involved in pursuing a litigated outcome. Often, courts may need to forecast the likely range of possible classwide recoveries and the likelihood of success in obtaining such results. That forecast cannot be done with arithmetic accuracy, but it can provide a benchmark for comparison with the settlement figure.

If the class has not yet been certified for trial, the court may consider whether certification for litigation would be granted were the settlement not approved.

Examination of the attorney-fee provisions may also be valuable in assessing the fairness of the proposed settlement. Ultimately, any award of attorney's fees must be evaluated under Rule 23(h), and no rigid limits exist for such awards. Nonetheless, the relief actually delivered to the class can be a significant factor in determining the appropriate fee award.

Often it will be important for the court to scrutinize the method of claims processing to ensure that it facilitates filing legitimate claims. A claims processing method should deter or defeat unjustified claims, but the court should be alert to whether the claims process is unduly demanding.

Paragraph (D) calls attention to a concern that may apply to some class action settlements—inequitable treatment of some class members vis-a-vis others. Matters of concern could include whether the apportionment of relief among class members takes appropriate account of differences among their claims, and whether the scope of the release may affect class members in different ways that bear on the apportionment of relief.

Subdivisions (e)(3) and (e)(4). Headings are added to subdivisions (e)(3) and (e)(4) in accord with style conventions. These additions are intended to be stylistic only.

Subdivision (e)(5). The submissions required by Rule 23(e)(1) may provide information critical to decisions whether to object or opt out. Objections by class members can provide the court with important information bearing on its determination under Rule 23(e)(2) whether to approve the proposal.

Subdivision (e)(5)(A). The rule is amended to remove the requirement of court approval for every withdrawal of an objection. An objector should be free to withdraw on concluding that an objection is not justified. But Rule 23(e)(5)(B)(i) requires court approval of any payment or other consideration in connection with withdrawing the objection.

The rule is also amended to clarify that objections must provide sufficient specifics to enable the parties to respond to them and the court to evaluate them. One feature required of objections is specification whether the objection asserts interests of only the objector, or of some subset of the class, or of all class members. Beyond that, the rule directs that the objection state its grounds "with specificity." Failure to provide needed specificity may be a basis for rejecting an objection. Courts should take care, however, to avoid unduly burdening class members who wish to object, and to recognize that a class member who is not represented by counsel may present objections that do not adhere to technical legal standards.

Subdivision (e)(5)(B). Good-faith objections can assist the court in evaluating a proposal under Rule 23(e)(2). It is legitimate for an objector to seek payment for providing such assistance under Rule 23(h).

But some objectors may be seeking only personal gain, and using objections to obtain benefits for themselves rather than assisting in the settlement-review process. At least in some instances, it seems that objectors—or their counsel—have sought to obtain consideration for withdrawing their objections or dismissing appeals from judgments approving class settlements. And class counsel sometimes may feel that avoiding the delay produced by an appeal justifies providing payment or other consideration to these objectors. Although the payment may advance class interests in a particular case, allowing payment perpetuates a system that can encourage objections advanced for improper purposes.

The court-approval requirement currently in Rule 23(e)(5) partly addresses this concern. Because the concern only applies when consideration is given in connection with withdrawal of an objection, however, the amendment requires approval under Rule 23(e)(5)(B)(i) only when consideration is involved. Although such payment is usually made to objectors or their counsel, the rule also requires court approval if a payment in connection with forgoing or withdrawing an objection or appeal is instead to another recipient. The term "consideration" should be broadly interpreted, particularly when the withdrawal includes some arrangements beneficial to objector counsel. If the consideration involves a payment to counsel for an objector, the proper procedure is by motion under Rule 23(h) for an award of fees.

Rule 23(e)(5)(B)(ii) applies to consideration in connection with forgoing, dismissing, or abandoning an appeal from a judgment approving the proposal. Because an appeal by a class-action objector may produce much longer delay than an objection before the district court, it is important to extend the court-approval requirement to apply in the appellate context. The district court is best positioned to determine whether to approve such arrangements; hence, the rule requires that the motion seeking approval be made to the district court.

Until the appeal is docketed by the circuit clerk, the district court may dismiss the appeal on stipulation of the parties or on the appellant's motion. See Fed. R. App. P. 42(a). Thereafter, the court of appeals has authority to decide whether to dismiss the appeal. This rule's requirement of district court approval of any consideration in connection with such dismissal by the court of appeals has no effect on the authority of the court of appeals to decide whether to dismiss the appeal. It is, instead, a requirement that applies only to providing consideration in connection with forgoing, dismissing, or abandoning an appeal.

Subdivision (e)(5)(C). Because the court of appeals has jurisdiction over an objector's appeal from the time that it is docketed in the court of appeals, the procedure of Rule 62.1 applies. That procedure does not apply after the court of appeals' mandate returns the case to the district court.

Subdivision (f). As amended, Rule 23(e)(1) provides that the court must direct notice to the class regarding a proposed class-action settlement only after determining that the prospect of eventual class certification justifies giving notice. But this decision does not grant or deny class certification, and review under Rule 23(f) would be premature. This amendment makes it clear that an appeal under this rule is not permitted until the district court decides whether to certify the class.

The rule is also amended to extend the time to file a petition for review of a class-action certification order to 45 days whenever a party is the United States, one of its agencies, or a United States officer or employee sued for an act or omission occurring in connection with duties performed on the United States' behalf. In such a case, the extension applies to a petition for permission to appeal by any party. The extension recognizes—as under Rules 4(i) and 12(a) and Appellate Rules 4(a)(1)(B) and 40(a)(1)—that the United States has a special need for additional time in regard to these matters. It applies whether the officer or employee is sued in an official capacity or an individual capacity. An action against a former officer or employee of the United States is covered by this provision in the same way as an action against a present officer or employee. Termination of the relationship between the individual defendant and the United States does not reduce the need for additional time.

Gap Report

At several points, the rule language was revised to shorten it or to shift to active voice. In Rule 23(c)(2)(B), the amendment proposal was revised to state that individual notice in Rule 23(b)(3) class actions be sent by "one or more of the following" before inviting use of United States mail, electronic means, or other appropriate means. In Rule 23(e)(2), the phrase "under Rule 23(c)(3)," originally proposed to be added, was removed from the proposed amendment in light of concerns that it might prove misleading in practice. The language of Rule 23(e)(2)(C)(ii) was adjusted to better parallel that of the following subsections. Rule 23(e)(5)(B) was modified to require court approval of any payments or other consideration provided in connection with forgoing, withdrawing or abandoning an objection to a class-action settlement or an appeal from rejection of such an objection. The Committee Note was revised to take account of these modifications in the rule language, to respond to some concerns raised during the public comment period, and to shorten the Note.

HISTORICAL NOTES

Amendments to Civil Rules Proposed March 27, 2003

Pub.L. 109–2, § 7, Feb. 18, 2005, 119 Stat. 13, provided that amendments to rule 23 of the Federal Rules of Civil Procedure, which are set forth in the order entered by the Supreme Court of the United States on March 27, 2003, shall take effect on the date of enactment of that Act [Feb. 18, 2005] or on December 1, 2003 (as specified in that order), whichever occurred first, see Pub.L. 109–2, § 7, set out as a note under 28 U.S.C.A. § 2074.

Rule 23.1.   Derivative Actions

(a) Prerequisites. This rule applies when one or more shareholders or members of a corporation or an unincorporated association bring a derivative action to enforce a right that the corporation or association may properly assert but has failed to enforce. The derivative action may not be maintained if it appears that the plaintiff does not fairly and adequately represent the interests of shareholders or members who are similarly situated in enforcing the right of the corporation or association.

(b) Pleading Requirements. The complaint must be verified and must:

(1) allege that the plaintiff was a shareholder or member at the time of the transaction complained of, or that the plaintiff's share or membership later devolved on it by operation of law;

(2) allege that the action is not a collusive one to confer jurisdiction that the court would otherwise lack; and

(3) state with particularity:

(A) any effort by the plaintiff to obtain the desired action from the directors or comparable authority and, if necessary, from the shareholders or members; and

(B) the reasons for not obtaining the action or not making the effort.

(c) Settlement, Dismissal, and Compromise. A derivative action may be settled, voluntarily dismissed, or compromised only with the court's approval. Notice of a proposed settlement, voluntary dismissal, or compromise must be given to shareholders or members in the manner that the court orders.

(Adopted February 28, 1966, effective July 1, 1966; amended March 2, 1987, effective August 1, 1987; April 30, 2007, effective December 1, 2007.)

ADVISORY COMMITTEE NOTES

1966 Addition

A derivative action by a shareholder of a corporation or by a member of an unincorporated association has distinctive aspects which require the special provisions set forth in the new rule. The next-to-the-last sentence recognizes that the question of adequacy of representation may arise when the plaintiff is one of a group of shareholders or members. Cf. 3 Moore's *Federal Practice*, par. 23.08 (2d ed. 1963).

The court has inherent power to provide for the conduct of the proceedings in a derivative action, including the power to determine the course of the proceedings and require that any appropriate notice be given to shareholders or members.

1987 Amendment

The amendments are technical. No substantive change is intended.

2007 Amendment

The language of Rule 23.1 has been amended as part of the general restyling of the Civil Rules to make them more easily understood and to make style and terminology consistent throughout the rules. These changes are intended to be stylistic only.

Rule 23.2.   Actions Relating to Unincorporated Associations

This rule applies to an action brought by or against the members of an unincorporated association as a class by naming certain members as representative parties. The action may be maintained only if it appears that those parties will fairly and adequately protect the interests of the association and its members. In conducting the action, the court may issue any appropriate orders corresponding with those in Rule 23(d), and the procedure for settlement, voluntary dismissal, or compromise must correspond with the procedure in Rule 23(e).

(Adopted February 28, 1966, effective July 1, 1966; amended April 30, 2007, effective December 1, 2007.)

ADVISORY COMMITTEE NOTES

1966 Addition

Although an action by or against representatives of the membership of an unincorporated association has often been viewed as a class action, the real or main purpose of this characterization has been to give "entity treatment" to the association when for formal reasons it cannot sue or be sued as a jural person under Rule 17(b). See Louisell & Hazard, *Pleading and Procedure: State and Federal* 718 (1962); 3 Moore's

Federal Practice, par. 23.08 (2d ed. 1963); Story, J. in *West v. Randall,* 29 Fed.Cas. 718, 722–23, No. 17,424 (C.C.D.R.I.1820); and, for examples, *Gibbs v. Buck,* 307 U.S. 66 (1939); *Tunstall v. Brotherhood of Locomotive F. & E.,* 148 F.2d 403 (4th Cir. 1945); *Oskoian v. Canuel,* 269 F.2d 311 (1st Cir. 1959). Rule 23.2 deals separately with these actions, referring where appropriate to Rule 23.

2007 Amendment

The language of Rule 23.2 has been amended as part of the general restyling of the Civil Rules to make them more easily understood and to make style and terminology consistent throughout the rules. These changes are intended to be stylistic only.

Rule 24.   Intervention

(a) Intervention of Right. On timely motion, the court must permit anyone to intervene who:

   (1) is given an unconditional right to intervene by a federal statute; or

   (2) claims an interest relating to the property or transaction that is the subject of the action, and is so situated that disposing of the action may as a practical matter impair or impede the movant's ability to protect its interest, unless existing parties adequately represent that interest.

(b) Permissive Intervention.

   (1) *In General.* On timely motion, the court may permit anyone to intervene who:

      (A) is given a conditional right to intervene by a federal statute; or

      (B) has a claim or defense that shares with the main action a common question of law or fact.

   (2) *By a Government Officer or Agency.* On timely motion, the court may permit a federal or state governmental officer or agency to intervene if a party's claim or defense is based on:

      (A) a statute or executive order administered by the officer or agency; or

      (B) any regulation, order, requirement, or agreement issued or made under the statute or executive order.

   (3) *Delay or Prejudice.* In exercising its discretion, the court must consider whether the intervention will unduly delay or prejudice the adjudication of the original parties' rights.

(c) Notice and Pleading Required. A motion to intervene must be served on the parties as provided in Rule 5. The motion must state the grounds for intervention and be accompanied by a pleading that sets out the claim or defense for which intervention is sought.

(Amended December 27, 1946, effective March 19, 1948; December 29, 1948, effective October 20, 1949; January 21, 1963, effective July 1, 1963; February 28, 1966, effective July 1, 1966; March 2, 1987, effective August 1, 1987; April 30, 1991, effective December 1, 1991; April 12, 2006, effective December 1, 2006; April 30, 2007, effective December 1, 2007.)

ADVISORY COMMITTEE NOTES

1937 Adoption

The right to intervene given by the following and similar statutes is preserved, but the procedure for its assertion is governed by this rule:

U.S.C., Title 28 former sections:

   45a [now 2323] (Special attorneys; participation by Interstate Commerce Commission; intervention) (in certain cases under interstate commerce laws)

   48 [now 2322] (Suits to be against United States; intervention by United States)

   401 [now 2403] (Intervention by United States; constitutionality of Federal statute)

U.S.C., Title 40:

> 276a–2(b) [now 3162(a)(2)] (Bonds of contractors for public buildings or works; rights of persons furnishing labor and materials).

Compare with the last sentence of [former] Equity Rule 37 (Parties Generally—Intervention). This rule amplifies and restates the present federal practice at law and in equity. For the practice in admiralty see Admiralty Rules 34 (How Third Party May Intervene) and 42 (Claims Against Proceeds in Registry). See generally Moore and Levi, *Federal Intervention: I The Right to Intervene and Reorganization* (1936), 45 Yale L.J. 565. Under the codes two types of intervention are provided, one for the recovery of specific real or personal property (2 Ohio Gen.Code Ann. (Page, 1926) § 11263; Wyo.Rev.Stat.Ann. (Courtright, 1931) § 89–522), and the other allowing intervention generally when the applicant has an interest in the matter in litigation (1 Colo.Stat.Ann. (1935) Code Civ.Proc. § 22; La.Code Pract. (Dart, 1932) Arts. 389–394; Utah Rev.Stat.Ann. (1933) § 104–3–24). The English intervention practice is based upon various rules and decisions and falls into the two categories of absolute right and discretionary right. For the absolute right see *English Rules Under the Judicature Act* (The Annual Practice, 1937) O. 12, r. 24 (admiralty), r. 25 (land), r. 23 (probate); O. 57, r. 12 (execution); J.A. (1925) §§ 181, 182, 183(2) (divorce); *In re Metropolitan Amalgamated Estates, Ltd.,* (1912) 2 Ch. 497 (receivership); *Wilson v. Church,* 9 Ch.D. 552 (1878) (representative action). For the discretionary right see O. 16, r. 11 (non-joinder) and *Re Fowler,* 142 L.T.Jo. 94 (Ch.1916), *Vavasseur v. Krupp,* 9 Ch.D. 351 (1878) (persons out of the jurisdiction).

1946 Amendment

Note. Subdivision (a). The addition to subdivision (a)(3) covers the situation where property may be in the actual custody of some other officer or agency—such as the Secretary of the Treasury—but the control and disposition of the property is lodged in the court wherein the action is pending.

Subdivision (b). The addition in subdivision (b) permits the intervention of governmental officers or agencies in proper cases and thus avoids exclusionary constructions of the rule. For an example of the latter, see *Matter of Bender Body Co.,* Ref. Ohio 1941, 47 F.Supp. 224, holding that the Administra4tor of the Office of Price Administration, then acting under the authority of an Executive Order of the President, could not intervene in a bankruptcy proceeding to protest the sale of assets above ceiling prices. Compare, however, *Securities and Exchange Commission v. United States Realty & Improvement Co.,* 1940, 310 U.S. 434, 60 S.Ct. 1044, where permissive intervention of the Commission to protect the public interest in an arrangement proceeding under Chapter XI of the Bankruptcy Act was upheld. See also dissenting opinion in *Securities and Exchange Commission v. Long Island Lighting Co.,* C.C.A.2d 1945, 148 F.2d 252, judgment vacated as moot and case remanded with direction to dismiss complaint, 1945, 325 U.S. 833, 65 S.Ct. 1085. For discussion see Commentary, *Nature of Permissive Intervention Under Rule 24b,* 1940, 3 Fed.Rules Serv. 704; Berger, *Intervention by Public Agencies in Private Litigation in the Federal Courts,* 1940, 50 Yale L.J. 65.

Regarding the construction of subdivision (b)(2), see *Allen Calculators, Inc. v. National Cash Register Co.,* 1944, 64 S.Ct. 905, 322 U.S. 137, 88 L.Ed. 1188.

1948 Amendment

The amendment effective Oct. 20, 1949, substituted the reference to "Title 28, U.S.C.A. § 2403" at the end of subdivision (c) for the reference to "the Act of August 24, 1937, c. 754, § 1."

1963 Amendment

This amendment conforms to the amendment of Rule 5(a). See the Advisory Committee's Note to that amendment.

1966 Amendment

In attempting to overcome certain difficulties which have arisen in the application of present Rule 24(a)(2) and (3), this amendment draws upon the revision of the related Rules 19 (joinder of persons needed for just adjudication) and 23 (class actions), and the reasoning underlying that revision.

Rule 24(a)(3) as amended in 1948 provided for intervention of right where the applicant established that he would be adversely affected by the distribution or disposition of property involved in an action to which he had not been made a party. Significantly, some decided cases virtually disregarded the language of this provision. Thus Professor Moore states: "The concept of a fund has been applied so loosely that it is possible for a court to find a fund in almost any in personam action." 4 Moore's *Federal Practice,* par. 24.09[3], at 55 (2d ed. 1962), and see, e.g., *Formulabs, Inc. v. Hartley Pen Co.,* 275 F.2d 52 (9th Cir.1960). This development was quite natural, for Rule 24(a)(3) was unduly restricted. If an absentee would be substantially affected by the determination made in an action, he should, as a general rule, be entitled to intervene, and his right to do so should not depend on whether there is a fund to be distributed or otherwise disposed of. Intervention of right is here seen to be a kind of counterpart to Rule 19(a)(2)(i) on joinder of persons needed for a just adjudication: where, upon motion of a party in an action, an absentee should be joined so that he may protect his interest which as a practical matter may be substantially impaired by the disposition of the action, he ought to have a right to intervene in the action on his own motion. See Louisell & Hazard, *Pleading and Procedure: State and Federal* 749–50 (1962).

The general purpose of original Rule 24(a)(2) was to entitle an absentee, purportedly represented by a party, to intervene in the action if he could establish with fair probability that the representation was inadequate. Thus, where an action is being prosecuted or defended by a trustee, a beneficiary of the trust should have a right to intervene if he can show that the trustee's representation of his interest probably is inadequate; similarly a member of a class should have the right to intervene in a class action if he can show the inadequacy of the representation of his interest by the representative parties before the court.

Original Rule 24(a)(2), however, made it a condition of intervention that "the applicant is or may be bound by a judgment in the action," and this created difficulties with intervention in class actions. If the "bound" language was read literally in the sense of res judicata, it could defeat intervention in some meritorious cases. A member of a class to whom a judgment in a class action extended by its terms (see Rule 23(c)(3), as amended) might be entitled to show in a later action, when the judgment in the class action was claimed to operate as res judicata against him, that the "representative" in the class action had not in fact adequately represented him. If he could make this showing, the class-action judgment might be held not to bind him. See *Hansberry v. Lee,* 311 U.S. 32 (1940). If a class member sought to intervene in the class action proper, while it was still pending, on grounds of inadequacy of representation, he could be met with the argument: if the representation was in fact inadequate, he would not be "bound" by the judgment when it was subsequently asserted against him as res judicata, hence he was not entitled to intervene; if the representation was in fact adequate, there was no occasion or ground for intervention. See *Sam Fox Publishing Co. v. United States,* 366 U.S. 683 (1961); cf. *Sutphen Estates, Inc. v. United States,* 342 U.S. 19 (1951). This reasoning might be linguistically justified by original Rule 24(a)(2); but it could lead to poor results. Compare the discussion in *International M. & I. Corp. v. Von Clemm,* 301 F.2d 857 (2d Cir.1962); *Atlantic Refining Co. v. Standard Oil Co.,* 304 F.2d 387 (D.C.Cir.1962). A class member who claims that his "representative" does not adequately represent him, and is able to establish that proposition with sufficient probability, should not be put to the risk of having a judgment entered in the action which by its terms extends to him, and be obliged to test the validity of the judgment as applied to his interest by a later collateral attack. Rather he should, as a general rule, be entitled to intervene in the action.

The amendment provides that an applicant is entitled to intervene in an action when his position is comparable to that of a person under Rule 19(a)(2)(i), as amended, unless his interest is already adequately represented in the action by existing parties. The Rule 19(a)(2)(i) criterion imports practical considerations, and the deletion of the "bound" language similarly frees the rule from undue preoccupation with strict considerations of res judicata.

The representation whose adequacy comes into question under the amended rule is not confined to formal representation like that provided by a trustee for his beneficiary or a representative party in a class action for a member of the class. A party to an action may provide practical representation to the absentee seeking intervention although no such formal relationship exists between them, and the adequacy of this practical representation will then have to be weighed. See *International M. & I. Crop. v. Von Clemm,* and *Atlantic Refining Co. v. Standard Oil Co.,* both supra; *Wolpe v. Poretsky,* 144 F.2d 505 (D.C.Cir.1944), cert. denied, 323 U.S. 777 (1944); cf. *Ford Motor Co. v. Bisanz Bros.,* 249 F.2d 22 (8th Cir.1957); and generally, Annot., 84 A.L.R.2d 1412 (1961).

An intervention of right under the amended rule may be subject to appropriate conditions or restrictions responsive among other things to the requirements of efficient conduct of the proceedings.

1987 Amendment

The amendments are technical. No substantive change is intended.

1991 Amendment

Language is added to bring Rule 24(c) into conformity with the statute cited, resolving some confusion reflected in district court rules. As the text provides, counsel challenging the constitutionality of legislation in an action in which the appropriate government is not a party should call the attention of the court to its duty to notify the appropriate governmental officers. The statute imposes the burden of notification on the court, not the party making the constitutional challenge, partly in order to protect against any possible waiver of constitutional rights by parties inattentive to the need for notice. For this reason, the failure of a party to call the court's attention to the matter cannot be treated as a waiver.

2006 Amendment

New Rule 5.1 replaces the final three sentences of Rule 24(c), implementing the provisions of 28 U.S.C. § 2403. Section 2403 requires notification to the Attorney General of the United States when the constitutionality of an Act of Congress is called in question, and to the state attorney general when the constitutionality of a state statute is drawn into question.

2007 Amendment

The language of Rule 24 has been amended as part of the general restyling of the Civil Rules to make them more easily understood and to make style and terminology consistent throughout the rules. These changes are intended to be stylistic only.

The former rule stated that the same procedure is followed when a United States statute gives a right to intervene. This statement is deleted because it added nothing.

Rule 25. Substitution of Parties

(a) Death.

    (1) *Substitution if the Claim Is Not Extinguished.* If a party dies and the claim is not extinguished, the court may order substitution of the proper party. A motion for substitution may be made by any party or by the decedent's successor or representative. If the motion is not made within 90 days after service of a statement noting the death, the action by or against the decedent must be dismissed.

    (2) *Continuation Among the Remaining Parties.* After a party's death, if the right sought to be enforced survives only to or against the remaining parties, the action does not abate, but proceeds in favor of or against the remaining parties. The death should be noted on the record.

    (3) *Service.* A motion to substitute, together with a notice of hearing, must be served on the parties as provided in Rule 5 and on nonparties as provided in Rule 4. A statement noting death must be served in the same manner. Service may be made in any judicial district.

(b) Incompetency. If a party becomes incompetent, the court may, on motion, permit the action to be continued by or against the party's representative. The motion must be served as provided in Rule 25(a)(3).

(c) Transfer of Interest. If an interest is transferred, the action may be continued by or against the original party unless the court, on motion, orders the transferee to be substituted in the action or joined with the original party. The motion must be served as provided in Rule 25(a)(3).

(d) Public Officers; Death or Separation from Office. An action does not abate when a public officer who is a party in an official capacity dies, resigns, or otherwise ceases to hold office while the action is pending. The officer's successor is automatically substituted as a party. Later proceedings should be in the substituted party's name, but any misnomer not affecting the parties' substantial rights must be disregarded. The court may order substitution at any time, but the absence of such an order does not affect the substitution.

(Amended December 29, 1948, effective October 20, 1949; April 17, 1961, effective July 19, 1961; January 21, 1963, effective July 1, 1963; March 2, 1987, effective August 1, 1987; April 30, 2007, effective December 1, 2007.)

ADVISORY COMMITTEE NOTES

1937 Adoption

Note to Subdivision (a). 1. The first paragraph of this rule is based upon [former] Equity Rule 45 (Death of Party—Revivor) and U.S.C., Title 28, former § 778 (Death of parties; substitution of executor or administrator). The *scire facias* procedure provided for in the statute cited is superseded and the writ is abolished by Rule 81(b). Paragraph two states the content of U.S.C., Title 28, former § 779 (Death of one of several plaintiffs or defendants). With these two paragraphs compare generally *English Rules Under the Judicature Act* (The Annual Practice, 1937) O. 17, r.r. 1–10.

2. This rule modifies U.S.C., Title 28, [former] §§ 778 (Death of parties; substitution of executor or administrator), 779 (Death of one of several plaintiffs or defendants), and 780 (Survival of actions, suits, or proceedings, etc.), in so far as they differ from it.

Note to Subdivisions (b) and (c). These are a combination and adaptation of N.Y.C.P.A. (1937) § 83 and Calif.Code Civ.Proc. (1937) § 385; see also 4 Nev.Comp.Laws (Hillyer, 1929) § 8561.

Note to Subdivision (d). With the first and last sentences compare U.S.C.A., Title 28, former § 780 (Survival of actions, suits, or proceedings, etc.). With the second sentence of this subdivision compare *Ex parte La Prade,* 1933, 53 S.Ct. 682, 289 U.S. 444, 77 L.Ed. 1311.

1948 Amendment

The amendment effective October 19, 1949, inserted the words, "the Canal Zone, a territory, an insular possession," in the first sentence of subdivision (d), and, in the same sentence, after the phrase "or other governmental agency," deleted the words, "or any other officer specified in the Act of February 13, 1925, c. 229, § 11 (43 Stat. 941), formerly section 780 of this title."

1961 Amendment

Subdivision (d)(1). Present Rule 25(d) is generally considered to be unsatisfactory. 4 Moore's *Federal Practice* ¶ 25.01[7] (2d ed. 1950); Wright, *Amendments to the Federal Rules: The Function of a Continuing Rules Committee,* 7 Vand.L.Rev. 521, 529 (1954); *Developments in the Law—Remedies Against the United States and Its Officials,* 70 Harv.L.Rev. 827, 931–34 (1957). To require, as a condition of substituting a successor public officer as a party to a pending action, that an application be made with a showing that there is substantial need for continuing the litigation, can rarely serve any useful purpose and fosters a burdensome formality. And to prescribe a short, fixed time period for substitution which cannot be extended even by agreement, see *Snyder v. Buck,* 340 U.S. 15, 19 (1950), with the penalty of dismissal of the action, "makes a trap for unsuspecting litigants which seems unworthy of a great government." *Vibra Brush Corp. v. Schaffer,* 256 F.2d 681, 684 (2d Cir.1958). Although courts have on occasion found means of undercutting the rule, e.g. *Acheson v. Furusho,* 212 F.2d 284 (9th Cir.1954) (substitution of defendant officer unnecessary on theory that only a declaration of status was sought), it has operated harshly in many instances, e.g. *Snyder v. Buck,* supra; *Poindexter v. Folsom,* 242 F.2d 516 (3d Cir.1957).

Under the amendment, the successor is automatically substituted as a party without an application or showing of need to continue the action. An order of substitution is not required, but may be entered at any time if a party desires or the court thinks fit.

The general term "public officer" is used in preference to the enumeration which appears in the present rule. It comprises Federal, State, and local officers.

The expression "in his official capacity" is to be interpreted in its context as part of a simple procedural rule for substitution; care should be taken not to distort its meaning by mistaken analogies to the doctrine of sovereign immunity from suit or the Eleventh Amendment. The amended rule will apply to all actions brought by public officers for the government, and to any action brought in form against a named officer, but intrinsically against the government or the office or the incumbent thereof whoever he may be from time to time during the action. Thus the amended rule will apply to actions against officers to compel performance of official duties or to obtain judicial review of their orders. It will also apply to actions to prevent officers from acting in excess of their authority or under authority not validly conferred, cf. *Philadelphia Co. v. Stimson,* 223 U.S. 605 (1912), or from enforcing unconstitutional enactments, cf. *Ex parte Young,* 209 U.S. 123 (1908); *Ex parte La Prade,* 289 U.S. 444 (1933). In general it will apply whenever effective relief would call for corrective behavior by the one then having official status and power, rather than one who has lost that status and power through ceasing to hold office. Cf. *Land v. Dollar,* 330 U.S. 731 (1947); *Larson v. Domestic & Foreign Commerce Corp.,* 337 U.S. 682 (1949). Excluded from the operation of the amended rule will be the relatively infrequent actions which are directed to securing money judgments against the named officers enforceable against their personal assets; in these cases Rule 25(a)(1), not Rule 25(d), applies to the question of substitution. Examples are actions against officers seeking to make them pay damages out of their own pockets for defamatory utterances or other misconduct in some way related to the office, see *Barr v. Matteo,* 360 U.S. 564 (1959); *Howard v. Lyons,* 360 U.S. 593 (1959); *Gregoire v. Biddle,* 177 F.2d 579 (2d Cir.1949), cert. denied, 339 U.S. 949 (1950). Another example is the anomalous action for a tax refund against a collector of internal revenue, see *Ignelzi v. Granger,* 16 F.R.D. 517 (W.D.Pa.1955), 28 U.S.C. § 2006, 4 Moore, supra, ¶ 25.05, p. 531; but see 28 U.S.C. § 1346(a)(1), authorizing the bringing of such suits against the United States rather than the officer.

Automatic substitution under the amended rule, being merely a procedural device for substituting a successor for a past officeholder as a party, is distinct from and does not affect any substantive issues which may be involved in the action. Thus a defense of immunity from suit will remain in the case despite a substitution.

Where the successor does not intend to pursue the policy of his predecessor which gave rise to the lawsuit, it will be open to him, after substitution, as plaintiff to seek voluntary dismissal of the action, or as defendant to seek to have the action dismissed as moot or to take other appropriate steps to avert a judgment or decree. Contrast *Ex parte La Prade,* supra; *Allen v. Regents of the University System,* 304 U.S. 439 (1938); *McGrath v. National Assn. of Mfgrs.,* 344 U.S. 804 (1952); *Danenberg v. Cohen,* 213 F.2d 944 (7th Cir.1954).

As the present amendment of Rule 25(d)(1) eliminates a specified time period to secure substitution of public officers, the reference in Rule 6(b) (regarding enlargement of time) to Rule 25 will no longer apply to these public-officer substitutions.

As to substitution on appeal, the rules of the appellate courts should be consulted.

Subdivision (d)(2). This provision, applicable in "official capacity" cases as described above, will encourage the use of the official title without any mention of the officer individually, thereby recognizing the intrinsic character of the action and helping to eliminate concern with the problem of substitution. If for any reason it seems desirable to add the individual's name, this may be done upon motion or on the court's initiative; thereafter the procedure of amended Rule 25(d)(1) will apply if the individual named ceases to hold office.

For examples of naming the officer or title rather than the officeholder, see *Annot.,* 102 A.L.R. 943, 948–52; *Comment,* 50 Mich.L.Rev. 443, 450 (1952); cf. 26 U.S.C. § 7484. Where an action is brought by or against a board or agency with continuity of existence, it has been often decided that there is no need to name the individual members and substitution is unnecessary when the personnel changes. 4 Moore, supra, ¶ 25.09, p. 536. The practice encouraged by amended Rule 25(d)(2) is similar.

1963 Amendment

Present Rule 25(a)(1), together with present Rule 6(b), results in an inflexible requirement that an action be dismissed as to a deceased party if substitution is not carried out within a fixed period measured from the time of the death. The hardships and inequities of this unyielding requirement plainly appear from the cases. See, e.g., *Anderson v. Yungkau,* 329 U.S. 482, 67 S.Ct. 428, 91 L.Ed. 436 (1947); *Iovino v. Waterson,* 274 F.2d 41 (1959), cert. denied, *Carlin v. Sovino,* 362 U.S. 949, 80 S.Ct. 860, 4 L.Ed.2d 867 (1960); *Perry v. Allen,* 239 F.2d 107 (5th Cir.1956); *Starnes v. Pennsylvania R.R.,* 26 F.R.D. 625 (E.D.N.Y.), aff'd per curiam, 295 F.2d 704 (2d Cir.1961), cert. denied, 369 U.S. 813, 82 S.Ct. 688, 7 L.Ed.2d 612 (1962); *Zdanok v. Glidden Co.,* 28 F.R.D. 346 (S.D.N.Y.1961). See also 4 Moore's *Federal Practice* ¶ 25.01[9] (Supp.1960); 2 Barron & Holtzoff, *Federal Practice & Procedure* § 621, at 420–21 (Wright ed.1961).

The amended rule establishes a time limit for the motion to substitute based not upon the time of the death, but rather upon the time information of the death is provided by means of a suggestion of death upon the record, i.e. service of a statement of the fact of the death. Cf. Ill.Ann.Stat., c. 110, § 54(2) (Smith-Hurd

1956). The motion may not be made later than 90 days after the service of the statement unless the period is extended pursuant to Rule 6(b), as amended. See the Advisory Committee's Note to amended Rule 6(b). See also the new Official Form 30.

A motion to substitute may be made by any party or by the representative of the deceased party without awaiting the suggestion of death. Indeed, the motion will usually be so made. If a party or the representative of the deceased party desires to limit the time within which another may make the motion, he may do so by suggesting the death upon the record.

A motion to substitute made within the prescribed time will ordinarily be granted, but under the permissive language of the first sentence of the amended rule ("the court may order") it may be denied by the court in the exercise of a sound discretion if made long after the death—as can occur if the suggestion of death is not made or is delayed—and circumstances have arisen rendering it unfair to allow substitution. Cf. *Anderson v. Yungkau,* supra, 329 U.S. at 485, 486, 67 S.Ct. at 430, 431, 91 L.Ed. 436, where it was noted under the present rule that settlement and distribution of the estate of a deceased defendant might be so far advanced as to warrant denial of a motion for substitution even though made within the time limit prescribed by that rule. Accordingly, a party interested in securing substitution under the amended rule should not assume that he can rest indefinitely awaiting the suggestion of death before he makes his motion to substitute.

1987 Amendment

The amendments are technical. No substantive change is intended.

2007 Amendment

The language of Rule 25 has been amended as part of the general restyling of the Civil Rules to make them more easily understood and to make style and terminology consistent throughout the rules. These changes are intended to be stylistic only.

Former Rule 25(d)(2) is transferred to become Rule 17(d) because it deals with designation of a public officer, not substitution.

HISTORICAL NOTES

Effective and Applicability Provisions

1961 Amendments. Amendment adopted on Apr. 17, 1961, effective July 19, 1961, see rule 86(d).

TITLE V. DISCLOSURES AND DISCOVERY

ADVISORY COMMITTEE'S EXPLANATORY STATEMENT
CONCERNING 1970 AMENDMENTS TO DISCOVERY RULES

This statement is intended to serve as a general introduction to the amendments of Rules 26–37, concerning discovery, as well as related amendments of other rules. A separate note of customary scope is appended to amendments proposed for each rule. This statement provides a framework for the consideration of individual rule changes.

Changes in the Discovery Rules

The discovery rules, as adopted in 1938, were a striking and imaginative departure from tradition. It was expected from the outset that they would be important, but experience has shown them to play an even larger role than was initially foreseen. Although the discovery rules have been amended since 1938, the changes were relatively few and narrowly focused, made in order to remedy specific defects. The amendments now proposed reflect the first comprehensive review of the discovery rules undertaken since 1938. These amendments make substantial changes in the discovery rules. Those summarized here are among the more important changes.

Scope of Discovery. New provisions are made and existing provisions changed affecting the scope of discovery: (1) The contents of insurance policies are made discoverable (Rule 26(b)(2)). (2) A showing of good cause is no longer required for discovery of documents and things and entry upon land (Rule 34). However, a showing of need is required for discovery of "trial preparation" materials other than a party's discovery of his own statement and a witness' discovery of his own statement; and protection is afforded against disclosure in such documents of mental impressions, conclusions, opinions, or legal theories concerning the litigation. (Rule 26(b)(3)). (3) Provision is made for discovery with respect to experts retained for trial preparation, and particularly those experts who will be called to testify at trial (Rule 26(b)(4)). (4) It is provided that interrogatories and requests for admission are not objectionable simply because they relate to matters of opinion or contention, subject of course to the supervisory power of the court (Rules 33(b), 36(a)). (5) Medical examination is made available as to certain nonparties. (Rule 35(a)).

Mechanics of Discovery. A variety of changes are made in the mechanics of the discovery process, affecting the sequence and timing of discovery, the respective obligations of the parties with respect to requests, responses, and motions for court orders, and the related powers of the court to enforce discovery requests and to protect against their abusive use. A new provision eliminates the automatic grant of priority in discovery to one side (Rule 26(d)). Another provides that a party is not under a duty to supplement his responses to requests for discovery, except as specified (Rule 26(e)).

Other changes in the mechanics of discovery are designed to encourage extrajudicial discovery with a minimum of court intervention. Among these are the following: (1) The requirement that a plaintiff seek leave of court for early discovery requests is eliminated or reduced, and motions for a court order under Rule 34 are made unnecessary. Motions under Rule 35 are continued. (2) Answers and objections are to be served together and an enlargement of the time for response is provided. (3) The party seeking discovery, rather than the objecting party, is made responsible for invoking judicial determination of discovery disputes not resolved by the parties. (4) Judicial sanctions are tightened with respect to unjustified insistence upon or objection to discovery. These changes bring Rules 33, 34, and 36 substantially into line with the procedure now provided for depositions.

Failure to amend Rule 35 in the same way is based upon two considerations. First, the Columbia Survey (described below) finds that only about 5 percent of medical examinations require court motions, of which about half result in court orders. Second and of greater importance, the interest of the person to be examined in the privacy of his person was recently stressed by the Supreme Court in *Schlagenhauf v. Holder*, 379 U.S. 104 (1964). The court emphasized the trial judge's responsibility to assure that the medical examination was justified, particularly as to its scope.

Rearrangement of Rules. A limited rearrangement of the discovery rules has been made, whereby certain provisions are transferred from one rule to another. The reasons for this rearrangement are discussed below in a separate section of this statement and the details are set out in a table at the end of this statement.

Optional Procedures. In two instances, new optional procedures have been made available. A new procedure is provided to a party seeking to take the deposition of a corporation or other organization (Rule 30(b)(6)). A party on whom interrogatories have been served requesting information derivable from his business records may under specified circumstances produce the records rather than give answers (Rule 33(c)).

Other Changes. This summary of changes is by no means exhaustive. Various changes have been made in order to improve, tighten, or clarify particular provisions, to resolve conflicts in the case law, and to improve language. All changes, whether mentioned here or not, are discussed in the appropriate note for each rule.

A Field Survey of Discovery Practice

Despite widespread acceptance of discovery as an essential part of litigation, disputes have inevitably arisen concerning the values claimed for discovery and abuses alleged to exist. Many disputes about discovery relate to particular rule provisions or court decisions and can be studied in traditional fashion with a view to specific amendment. Since discovery is in large measure extra-judicial, however, even these disputes may be enlightened by a study of discovery "in the field." And some of the larger questions concerning discovery can be pursued only by a study of its operation at the law office level and in unreported cases.

The Committee, therefore, invited the Project for Effective Justice of Columbia Law School to conduct a field survey of discovery. Funds were obtained from the Ford Foundation and the Walter E. Meyer Research Institute of Law, Inc. The survey was carried on under the direction of Prof. Maurice Rosenberg of Columbia Law School. The Project for Effective Justice has submitted a report to the Committee entitled "Field Survey of Federal Pretrial Discovery" (hereafter referred to as the Columbia Survey). The Committee is deeply grateful for the benefit of this extensive undertaking and is most appreciative of the cooperation of the Project and the funding organizations. The Committee is particularly grateful to Professor Rosenberg who not only directed the survey but has given much time in order to assist the Committee in assessing the results.

The Columbia Survey concludes, in general, that there is no empirical evidence to warrant a fundamental change in the philosophy of the discovery rules. No widespread or profound failings are disclosed in the scope or availability of discovery. The costs of discovery do not appear to be oppressive, as a general matter, either in relation to ability to pay or to the stakes of the litigation. Discovery frequently provides evidence that would not otherwise be available to the parties and thereby makes for a fairer trial or settlement. On the other hand, no positive evidence is found that discovery promotes settlement.

More specific findings of the Columbia Survey are described in other Committee notes, in relation to particular rule provisions and amendments. Those interested in more detailed information may obtain it from the Project for Effective Justice.

Rearrangement of the Discovery Rules

The present discovery rules are structured entirely in terms of individual discovery devices, except for Rule 27 which deals with perpetuation of testimony, and Rule 37 which provides sanctions to enforce discovery. Thus, Rules 26 and 28 to 32 are in terms addressed only to the taking of a deposition of a party or third person. Rules 33 to 36 then deal in succession with four additional discovery devices: Written interrogatories to parties, production for inspection of documents and things, physical or mental examination and requests for admission.

Under the rules as promulgated in 1938, therefore, each of the discovery devices was separate and self-contained. A defect of this arrangement is that there is no natural location in the discovery rules for provisions generally applicable to all discovery or to several discovery devices. From 1938 until the present, a few amendments have applied a discovery provision to several rules. For example, in 1948, the scope of deposition discovery in Rule 26(b) and the provision for protective orders in Rule 30(b) were incorporated by reference in Rules 33 and 34. The arrangement was adequate so long as there were few provisions governing discovery generally and these provisions were relatively simple.

As will be seen, however, a series of amendments are now proposed which govern most or all of the discovery devices. Proposals of a similar nature will probably be made in the future. Under these circumstances, it is very desirable, even necessary, that the discovery rules contain one rule addressing itself to discovery generally.

Rule 26 is obviously the most appropriate rule for this purpose. One of its subdivisions, Rule 26(b), in terms governs only scope of deposition discovery, but it has been expressly incorporated by reference in Rules 33 and 34 and is treated by courts as setting a general standard. By means of a transfer to Rule 26 of the provisions for protective orders now contained in Rule 30(b), and a transfer from Rule 26 of provisions addressed exclusively to depositions, Rule 26 is converted into a rule concerned with discovery generally. It becomes a convenient vehicle for the inclusion of new provisions dealing with the scope, timing, and regulation of discovery. Few additional transfers are needed. See table showing rearrangement of rules, set out following this statement.

There are, to be sure, disadvantages in transferring any provision from one rule to another. Familiarity with the present pattern, reinforced by the references made by prior court decisions and the various secondary writings about the rules, is not lightly to be sacrificed. Revision of treatises and other reference works is burdensome and costly. Moreover, many States have adopted the existing pattern as a model for their rules.

On the other hand, the amendments now proposed will in any event require revision of texts and reference works as well as reconsideration by States following the Federal model. If these amendments are to be incorporated in an understandable way, a rule with general discovery provisions is needed. As will be seen, the proposed rearrangement produces a more coherent and intelligible pattern for the discovery rules taken as a whole. The difficulties described are those encountered whenever statutes are reexamined and revised. Failure to rearrange the discovery rules now would freeze the present scheme, making future change even more difficult.

Table Showing Rearrangement of Rules

Existing Rule No.	New Rule No.
26(a)	30(a), 31(a)
26(c)	30(c)
26(d)	32(a)
26(e)	32(b)
26(f)	32(c)
30(a)	30(b)
30(b)	26(c)
32	32(d)

Rule 26.   Duty to Disclose; General Provisions Governing Discovery

(a) Required Disclosures.

(1) *Initial Disclosure.*

(A) *In General.* Except as exempted by Rule 26(a)(1)(B) or as otherwise stipulated or ordered by the court, a party must, without awaiting a discovery request, provide to the other parties:

(i) the name and, if known, the address and telephone number of each individual likely to have discoverable information—along with the subjects of that information—that the disclosing party may use to support its claims or defenses, unless the use would be solely for impeachment;

(ii) a copy—or a description by category and location—of all documents, electronically stored information, and tangible things that the disclosing party has in its possession, custody, or control and may use to support its claims or defenses, unless the use would be solely for impeachment;

(iii) a computation of each category of damages claimed by the disclosing party—who must also make available for inspection and copying as under Rule 34 the documents or other evidentiary material, unless privileged or protected from disclosure, on which each computation is based, including materials bearing on the nature and extent of injuries suffered; and

(iv) for inspection and copying as under Rule 34, any insurance agreement under which an insurance business may be liable to satisfy all or part of a possible judgment in the action or to indemnify or reimburse for payments made to satisfy the judgment.

(B) *Proceedings Exempt from Initial Disclosure.* The following proceedings are exempt from initial disclosure:

(i) an action for review on an administrative record;

(ii) a forfeiture action in rem arising from a federal statute;

(iii) a petition for habeas corpus or any other proceeding to challenge a criminal conviction or sentence;

(iv) an action brought without an attorney by a person in the custody of the United States, a state, or a state subdivision;

    (v)   an action to enforce or quash an administrative summons or subpoena;

    (vi)   an action by the United States to recover benefit payments;

    (vii)   an action by the United States to collect on a student loan guaranteed by the United States;

    (viii) a proceeding ancillary to a proceeding in another court; and

    (ix)   an action to enforce an arbitration award.

  (C) *Time for Initial Disclosures—In General.* A party must make the initial disclosures at or within 14 days after the parties' Rule 26(f) conference unless a different time is set by stipulation or court order, or unless a party objects during the conference that initial disclosures are not appropriate in this action and states the objection in the proposed discovery plan. In ruling on the objection, the court must determine what disclosures, if any, are to be made and must set the time for disclosure.

  (D) *Time for Initial Disclosures—For Parties Served or Joined Later.* A party that is first served or otherwise joined after the Rule 26(f) conference must make the initial disclosures within 30 days after being served or joined, unless a different time is set by stipulation or court order.

  (E) *Basis for Initial Disclosure; Unacceptable Excuses.* A party must make its initial disclosures based on the information then reasonably available to it. A party is not excused from making its disclosures because it has not fully investigated the case or because it challenges the sufficiency of another party's disclosures or because another party has not made its disclosures.

(2) ***Disclosure of Expert Testimony.***

  (A) *In General.* In addition to the disclosures required by Rule 26(a)(1), a party must disclose to the other parties the identity of any witness it may use at trial to present evidence under Federal Rule of Evidence 702, 703, or 705.

  (B) *Witnesses Who Must Provide a Written Report.* Unless otherwise stipulated or ordered by the court, this disclosure must be accompanied by a written report—prepared and signed by the witness—if the witness is one retained or specially employed to provide expert testimony in the case or one whose duties as the party's employee regularly involve giving expert testimony. The report must contain:

    (i)   a complete statement of all opinions the witness will express and the basis and reasons for them;

    (ii)   the facts or data considered by the witness in forming them;

    (iii) any exhibits that will be used to summarize or support them;

    (iv) the witness's qualifications, including a list of all publications authored in the previous 10 years;

    (v)   a list of all other cases in which, during the previous 4 years, the witness testified as an expert at trial or by deposition; and

    (vi) a statement of the compensation to be paid for the study and testimony in the case.

  (C) *Witnesses Who Do Not Provide a Written Report.* Unless otherwise stipulated or ordered by the court, if the witness is not required to provide a written report, this disclosure must state:

    (i)   the subject matter on which the witness is expected to present evidence under Federal Rule of Evidence 702, 703, or 705; and

    (ii)   a summary of the facts and opinions to which the witness is expected to testify.

(D) *Time to Disclose Expert Testimony.* A party must make these disclosures at the times and in the sequence that the court orders. Absent a stipulation or a court order, the disclosures must be made:

    (i) at least 90 days before the date set for trial or for the case to be ready for trial; or

    (ii) if the evidence is intended solely to contradict or rebut evidence on the same subject matter identified by another party under Rule 26(a)(2)(B) or (C), within 30 days after the other party's disclosure.

(E) *Supplementing the Disclosure.* The parties must supplement these disclosures when required under Rule 26(e).

(3) *Pretrial Disclosures.*

  (A) *In General.* In addition to the disclosures required by Rule 26(a)(1) and (2), a party must provide to the other parties and promptly file the following information about the evidence that it may present at trial other than solely for impeachment:

    (i) the name and, if not previously provided, the address and telephone number of each witness—separately identifying those the party expects to present and those it may call if the need arises;

    (ii) the designation of those witnesses whose testimony the party expects to present by deposition and, if not taken stenographically, a transcript of the pertinent parts of the deposition; and

    (iii) an identification of each document or other exhibit, including summaries of other evidence—separately identifying those items the party expects to offer and those it may offer if the need arises.

  (B) *Time for Pretrial Disclosures; Objections.* Unless the court orders otherwise, these disclosures must be made at least 30 days before trial. Within 14 days after they are made, unless the court sets a different time, a party may serve and promptly file a list of the following objections: any objections to the use under Rule 32(a) of a deposition designated by another party under Rule 26(a)(3)(A)(ii); and any objection, together with the grounds for it, that may be made to the admissibility of materials identified under Rule 26(a)(3)(A)(iii). An objection not so made—except for one under Federal Rule of Evidence 402 or 403—is waived unless excused by the court for good cause.

(4) *Form of Disclosures.* Unless the court orders otherwise, all disclosures under Rule 26(a) must be in writing, signed, and served.

(b) **Discovery Scope and Limits.**

(1) *Scope in General.* Unless otherwise limited by court order, the scope of discovery is as follows: Parties may obtain discovery regarding any nonprivileged matter that is relevant to any party's claim or defense and proportional to the needs of the case, considering the importance of the issues at stake in the action, the amount in controversy, the parties' relative access to relevant information, the parties' resources, the importance of the discovery in resolving the issues, and whether the burden or expense of the proposed discovery outweighs its likely benefit. Information within this scope of discovery need not be admissible in evidence to be discoverable.

(2) *Limitations on Frequency and Extent.*

  (A) *When Permitted.* By order, the court may alter the limits in these rules on the number of depositions and interrogatories or on the length of depositions under Rule 30. By order or local rule, the court may also limit the number of requests under Rule 36.

  (B) *Specific Limitations on Electronically Stored Information.* A party need not provide discovery of electronically stored information from sources that the party identifies as not reasonably accessible because of undue burden or cost. On motion to compel discovery or for a protective order, the party from whom discovery is sought must show that the information is not reasonably accessible because of undue burden or cost. If that showing is made, the court may nonetheless order discovery from such sources if the requesting party shows good cause, considering the limitations of Rule 26(b)(2)(C). The court may specify conditions for the discovery.

(C) *When Required.* On motion or on its own, the court must limit the frequency or extent of discovery otherwise allowed by these rules or by local rule if it determines that:

   (i) the discovery sought is unreasonably cumulative or duplicative, or can be obtained from some other source that is more convenient, less burdensome, or less expensive;

   (ii) the party seeking discovery has had ample opportunity to obtain the information by discovery in the action; or

   (iii) the proposed discovery is outside the scope permitted by Rule 26(b)(1).

(3) *Trial Preparation: Materials.*

   (A) *Documents and Tangible Things.* Ordinarily, a party may not discover documents and tangible things that are prepared in anticipation of litigation or for trial by or for another party or its representative (including the other party's attorney, consultant, surety, indemnitor, insurer, or agent). But, subject to Rule 26(b)(4), those materials may be discovered if:

      (i) they are otherwise discoverable under Rule 26(b)(1); and

      (ii) the party shows that it has substantial need for the materials to prepare its case and cannot, without undue hardship, obtain their substantial equivalent by other means.

   (B) *Protection Against Disclosure.* If the court orders discovery of those materials, it must protect against disclosure of the mental impressions, conclusions, opinions, or legal theories of a party's attorney or other representative concerning the litigation.

   (C) *Previous Statement.* Any party or other person may, on request and without the required showing, obtain the person's own previous statement about the action or its subject matter. If the request is refused, the person may move for a court order, and Rule 37(a)(5) applies to the award of expenses. A previous statement is either:

      (i) a written statement that the person has signed or otherwise adopted or approved; or

      (ii) a contemporaneous stenographic, mechanical, electrical, or other recording—or a transcription of it—that recites substantially verbatim the person's oral statement.

(4) *Trial Preparation: Experts.*

   (A) *Deposition of an Expert Who May Testify.* A party may depose any person who has been identified as an expert whose opinions may be presented at trial. If Rule 26(a)(2)(B) requires a report from the expert, the deposition may be conducted only after the report is provided.

   (B) *Trial-Preparation Protection for Draft Reports or Disclosures.* Rules 26(b)(3)(A) and (B) protect drafts of any report or disclosure required under Rule 26(a)(2), regardless of the form in which the draft is recorded.

   (C) *Trial-Preparation Protection for Communications Between a Party's Attorney and Expert Witnesses.* Rules 26(b)(3)(A) and (B) protect communications between the party's attorney and any witness required to provide a report under Rule 26(a)(2)(B), regardless of the form of the communications, except to the extent that the communications:

(i)   relate to compensation for the expert's study or testimony;

(ii)   identify facts or data that the party's attorney provided and that the expert considered in forming the opinions to be expressed; or

(iii) identify assumptions that the party's attorney provided and that the expert relied on in forming the opinions to be expressed.

(D) *Expert Employed Only for Trial Preparation.* Ordinarily, a party may not, by interrogatories or deposition, discover facts known or opinions held by an expert who has been retained or specially employed by another party in anticipation of litigation or to prepare for trial and who is not expected to be called as a witness at trial. But a party may do so only:

(i)   as provided in Rule 35(b); or

(ii)   on showing exceptional circumstances under which it is impracticable for the party to obtain facts or opinions on the same subject by other means.

(E) *Payment.* Unless manifest injustice would result, the court must require that the party seeking discovery:

(i)   pay the expert a reasonable fee for time spent in responding to discovery under Rule 26(b)(4)(A) or (D); and

(ii)   for discovery under (D), also pay the other party a fair portion of the fees and expenses it reasonably incurred in obtaining the expert's facts and opinions.

(5) ***Claiming Privilege or Protecting Trial-Preparation Materials.***

(A) *Information Withheld.* When a party withholds information otherwise discoverable by claiming that the information is privileged or subject to protection as trial-preparation material, the party must:

(i)   expressly make the claim; and

(ii)   describe the nature of the documents, communications, or tangible things not produced or disclosed—and do so in a manner that, without revealing information itself privileged or protected, will enable other parties to assess the claim.

(B) *Information Produced.* If information produced in discovery is subject to a claim of privilege or of protection as trial-preparation material, the party making the claim may notify any party that received the information of the claim and the basis for it. After being notified, a party must promptly return, sequester, or destroy the specified information and any copies it has; must not use or disclose the information until the claim is resolved; must take reasonable steps to retrieve the information if the party disclosed it before being notified; and may promptly present the information to the court under seal for a determination of the claim. The producing party must preserve the information until the claim is resolved.

(c) Protective Orders.

(1) ***In General.*** A party or any person from whom discovery is sought may move for a protective order in the court where the action is pending—or as an alternative on matters relating to a deposition, in the court for the district where the deposition will be taken. The motion must include a certification that the movant has in good faith conferred or attempted to confer with other affected parties in an effort to resolve the dispute without court action. The court may, for good cause, issue an order to protect a party or person from annoyance, embarrassment, oppression, or undue burden or expense, including one or more of the following:

(A) forbidding the disclosure or discovery;

(B) specifying terms, including time and place or the allocation of expenses, for the disclosure or discovery;

(C) prescribing a discovery method other than the one selected by the party seeking discovery;

(D) forbidding inquiry into certain matters, or limiting the scope of disclosure or discovery to certain matters;

(E) designating the persons who may be present while the discovery is conducted;

(F) requiring that a deposition be sealed and opened only on court order;

(G) requiring that a trade secret or other confidential research, development, or commercial information not be revealed or be revealed only in a specified way; and

(H) requiring that the parties simultaneously file specified documents or information in sealed envelopes, to be opened as the court directs.

(2) *Ordering Discovery.* If a motion for a protective order is wholly or partly denied, the court may, on just terms, order that any party or person provide or permit discovery.

(3) *Awarding Expenses.* Rule 37(a)(5) applies to the award of expenses.

(d) **Timing and Sequence of Discovery.**

(1) *Timing.* A party may not seek discovery from any source before the parties have conferred as required by Rule 26(f), except in a proceeding exempted from initial disclosure under Rule 26(a)(1)(B), or when authorized by these rules, by stipulation, or by court order.

(2) *Early Rule 34 Requests.*

(A) *Time to Deliver.* More than 21 days after the summons and complaint are served on a party, a request under Rule 34 may be delivered:

(i) to that party by any other party, and

(ii) by that party to any plaintiff or to any other party that has been served.

(B) *When Considered Served.* The request is considered to have been served at the first Rule 26(f) conference.

(3) *Sequence.* Unless the parties stipulate or the court orders otherwise for the parties' and witnesses' convenience and in the interests of justice:

(A) methods of discovery may be used in any sequence; and

(B) discovery by one party does not require any other party to delay its discovery.

(e) **Supplementing Disclosures and Responses.**

(1) *In General.* A party who has made a disclosure under Rule 26(a)—or who has responded to an interrogatory, request for production, or request for admission—must supplement or correct its disclosure or response:

(A) in a timely manner if the party learns that in some material respect the disclosure or response is incomplete or incorrect, and if the additional or corrective information has not otherwise been made known to the other parties during the discovery process or in writing; or

(B) as ordered by the court.

(2) *Expert Witness.* For an expert whose report must be disclosed under Rule 26(a)(2)(B), the party's duty to supplement extends both to information included in the report and to information given during the expert's deposition. Any additions or changes to this information must be disclosed by the time the party's pretrial disclosures under Rule 26(a)(3) are due.

(f) Conference of the Parties; Planning for Discovery.

(1) *Conference Timing.* Except in a proceeding exempted from initial disclosure under Rule 26(a)(1)(B) or when the court orders otherwise, the parties must confer as soon as practicable—and in any event at least 21 days before a scheduling conference is to be held or a scheduling order is due under Rule 16(b).

(2) *Conference Content; Parties' Responsibilities.* In conferring, the parties must consider the nature and basis of their claims and defenses and the possibilities for promptly settling or resolving the case; make or arrange for the disclosures required by Rule 26(a)(1); discuss any issues about preserving discoverable information; and develop a proposed discovery plan. The attorneys of record and all unrepresented parties that have appeared in the case are jointly responsible for arranging the conference, for attempting in good faith to agree on the proposed discovery plan, and for submitting to the court within 14 days after the conference a written report outlining the plan. The court may order the parties or attorneys to attend the conference in person.

(3) *Discovery Plan.* A discovery plan must state the parties' views and proposals on:

(A) what changes should be made in the timing, form, or requirement for disclosures under Rule 26(a), including a statement of when initial disclosures were made or will be made;

(B) the subjects on which discovery may be needed, when discovery should be completed, and whether discovery should be conducted in phases or be limited to or focused on particular issues;

(C) any issues about disclosure, discovery, or preservation of electronically stored information, including the form or forms in which it should be produced;

(D) any issues about claims of privilege or of protection as trial-preparation materials, including—if the parties agree on a procedure to assert these claims after production—whether to ask the court to include their agreement in an order under Federal Rule of Evidence 502;

(E) what changes should be made in the limitations on discovery imposed under these rules or by local rule, and what other limitations should be imposed; and

(F) any other orders that the court should issue under Rule 26(c) or under Rule 16(b) and (c).

(4) *Expedited Schedule.* If necessary to comply with its expedited schedule for Rule 16(b) conferences, a court may by local rule:

(A) require the parties' conference to occur less than 21 days before the scheduling conference is held or a scheduling order is due under Rule 16(b); and

(B) require the written report outlining the discovery plan to be filed less than 14 days after the parties' conference, or excuse the parties from submitting a written report and permit them to report orally on their discovery plan at the Rule 16(b) conference.

(g) Signing Disclosures and Discovery Requests, Responses, and Objections.

(1) *Signature Required; Effect of Signature.* Every disclosure under Rule 26(a)(1) or (a)(3) and every discovery request, response, or objection must be signed by at least one attorney of record in the attorney's own name—or by the party personally, if unrepresented—and must state the signer's address, e-mail address, and telephone number. By signing, an attorney or party certifies that to the best of the person's knowledge, information, and belief formed after a reasonable inquiry:

(A) with respect to a disclosure, it is complete and correct as of the time it is made; and

(B) with respect to a discovery request, response, or objection, it is:

    (i) consistent with these rules and warranted by existing law or by a nonfrivolous argument for extending, modifying, or reversing existing law, or for establishing new law;

    (ii) not interposed for any improper purpose, such as to harass, cause unnecessary delay, or needlessly increase the cost of litigation; and

    (iii) neither unreasonable nor unduly burdensome or expensive, considering the needs of the case, prior discovery in the case, the amount in controversy, and the importance of the issues at stake in the action.

(2) *Failure to Sign.* Other parties have no duty to act on an unsigned disclosure, request, response, or objection until it is signed, and the court must strike it unless a signature is promptly supplied after the omission is called to the attorney's or party's attention.

(3) *Sanction for Improper Certification.* If a certification violates this rule without substantial justification, the court, on motion or on its own, must impose an appropriate sanction on the signer, the party on whose behalf the signer was acting, or both. The sanction may include an order to pay the reasonable expenses, including attorney's fees, caused by the violation.

(Amended December 27, 1946, effective March 19, 1948; January 21, 1963, effective July 1, 1963; February 28, 1966, effective July 1, 1966; March 30, 1970, effective July 1, 1970; April 29, 1980, effective August 1, 1980; April 28, 1983, effective August 1, 1983; March 2, 1987, effective August 1, 1987; April 22, 1993, effective December 1, 1993; April 17, 2000, effective December 1, 2000; April 12, 2006, effective December 1, 2006; April 30, 2007, effective December 1, 2007; April 28, 2010, effective December 1, 2010; April 29, 2015, effective December 1, 2015.)

ADVISORY COMMITTEE NOTES

1937 Adoption

Note to Subdivision (a). This rule freely authorizes the taking of depositions under the same circumstances and by the same methods whether for the purpose of discovery or for the purpose of obtaining evidence. Many states have adopted this practice on account of its simplicity and effectiveness, safeguarding it by imposing such restrictions upon the subsequent use of the deposition at the trial or hearing as are deemed advisable. See Ark.Civ.Code (Crawford, 1934) §§ 606 to 607; Calif.Code Civ.Proc. (Deering, 1937) § 2021; 1 Colo.Stat.Ann. (1935) Code Civ.Proc. § 376; Idaho Code Ann. (1932) § 16–906; Ill.Rules of Pract.Rule 19 (Smith-Hurd Ill.Stats. c. 110, § 259.19); Smith-Hurd Ill.Stats. c. 51, § 24; 2 Ind.Stat.Ann. (Burns, 1933) §§ 2–1501, 2–1506; Ky.Codes (Carroll, 1932) Civ.Pract. § 557; 1 Mo.Rev.Stat. (1929) § 1753; 4 Mont.Rev.Codes Ann. (1935) § 10645; Neb.Comp.Stat. (1929) ch. 20, §§ 1246–7; 4 Nev.Comp.Laws (Hillyer, 1929) § 9001; 2 N.H.Pub.Laws (1926) ch. 337, § 1; N.C.Code Ann. (1935) § 1809; 2 N.D.Comp.Laws Ann. (1913) §§ 7889 to 7897; 2 Ohio Gen.Code Ann. (Page, 1926) §§ 11525–6; 1 Ore.Code Ann. (1930) Tit. 9, § 1503; 1 S.D.Comp.Laws (1929) §§ 2713–16; Vernon's Ann.Civ.Stats.Tex. arts. 3738, 3752, 3769; Utah Rev.Stat.Ann. (1933) § 104–51–7; Wash.Rules of Practice adopted by the Supreme Ct., Rule 8, 2 Wash.Rev.Stat.Ann. (Remington, 1932) § 308–8; W.Va.Code (1931) ch. 57, art. 4, § 1. Compare [former] Equity Rules 47 (Depositions—To be Taken in Exceptional Instances); 54 (Depositions Under Revised Statutes, §§ 863, 865, 866, 867—Cross Examination); 58 (Discovery—Interrogatories—Inspection and Production of Documents—Admission of Execution or Genuineness).

This and subsequent rules incorporate, modify, and broaden the provisions for depositions under U.S.C., Title 28, [former] §§ 639 (Depositions *de bene esse;* when and where taken; notice), 640 (Same; mode of taking), 641 (Same; transmission to court), 644 (Depositions under *dedimus potestatem* and *in perpetuam*), 646 (Deposition under *dedimus potestatem;* how taken). These statutes are superseded in so far as they differ from this and subsequent rules. U.S.C. Title 28, [former] § 643 (Depositions; taken in mode prescribed by State laws) is superseded by the third sentence of Subdivision (a).

While a number of states permit discovery only from parties or their agents, others either make no distinction between parties or agents of parties and ordinary witnesses, or authorize the taking of ordinary depositions, without restriction, from any persons who have knowledge of relevant facts. See Ark.Civ.Code (Crawford, 1934) §§ 606 to 607; 1 Idaho Code Ann. (1932) § 16–906; Ill.Rules of Pract., Rule 19 (Smith-Hurd Ill.Stats. c. 110, § 259.19); Smith-Hurd Ill.Stats. c. 51, § 24; 2 Ind.Stat.Ann. (Burns, 1933) § 2–1501; Ky.Codes (Carroll, 1932) Civ.Pract. §§ 554 to 558; 2 Md.Ann.Code (Bagby, 1924) Art. 35, § 21; 2 Minn.Stat. (Mason, 1927) § 9820; Mo.St.Ann. §§ 1753, 1759, pp. 4023, 4026; Neb.Comp.Stat. (1929) ch. 20, §§ 1246–7; 2 N.H.Pub.Laws (1926) ch. 337, § 1; 2 N.D.Comp.Laws Ann. (1913) § 7897; 2 Ohio Gen.Code Ann. (Page, 1926) §§ 11525–6; 1 S.D.Comp.Laws (1929) §§ 2713–16; Vernon's Ann.Civil Stats.Tex. arts. 3738, 3752, 3769; Utah Rev.Stat.Ann. (1933) § 104–51–7; Wash.Rules of Practice adopted by Supreme Ct., Rule 8, 2 Wash.Rev.Stat.Ann. (Remington, 1932) § 308–8; W.Va.Code (1931) ch. 57, art. 4, § 1.

The more common practice in the United States is to take depositions on notice by the party desiring them, without any order from the court, and this has been followed in these rules. See Calif.Code Civ.Proc. (Deering, 1937) § 2031; 2 Fla.Comp.Gen.Laws Ann. (1927) §§ 4405–7; 1 Idaho Code Ann. (1932) § 16–902; Ill.Rules of Pract., Rule 19 (Smith-Hurd Ill.Stats. c. 110, § 259.19); Smith-Hurd Ill.Stats. c. 51, § 24; 2 Ind.Stat.Ann. (Burns, 1933) § 2–1502; Kan.Gen.Stat.Ann. (1935) § 60–2827; Ky.Codes (Carroll, 1932) Civ.Pract. § 565; 2 Minn.Stat. (Mason, 1927) § 9820; Mo.St.Ann. § 1761, p. 4029; 4 Mont.Rev.Codes Ann. (1935) § 10651; Nev.Comp.Laws (Hillyer, 1929) § 9002; N.C.Code Ann. (1935) § 1809; 2 N.D.Comp.Laws Ann. (1913) § 7895; Utah Rev.Stat.Ann. (1933) § 104–51–8.

Note to Subdivision (b). While the old chancery practice limited discovery to facts supporting the case of the party seeking it, this limitation has been largely abandoned by modern legislation. See Ala.Code Ann. (Michie, 1928) §§ 7764 to 7773; 2 Ind.Stat.Ann. (Burns, 1933) §§ 2–1028, 2–1506, 2–1728–2–1732; Iowa Code (1935) § 11185; Ky.Codes (Carroll, 1932) Civ.Pract. §§ 557, 606(8); La.Code Pract. (Dart, 1932) arts. 347–356; 2 Mass.Gen.Laws (Ter.Ed., 1932) ch. 231, §§ 61 to 67; Mo.St.Ann. §§ 1753, 1759, pp. 4023, 4026; Neb.Comp.Stat. (1929) §§ 20–1246, 20–1247; 2 N.H.Pub.Laws (1926) ch. 337, § 1; 2 Ohio Gen.Code Ann. (Page, 1926) §§ 11497, 11526; Vernon's Ann.Civ.Stats.Tex. arts. 3738, 3753, 3769; Wis.Stat. (1935) § 326.12; Ontario Consol.Rules of Pract. (1928) Rules 237–347; Quebec Code of Civ.Proc. (Curran, 1922) §§ 286 to 290.

Note to Subdivisions (d), (e), and (f). The restrictions here placed upon the use of depositions at the trial or hearing are substantially the same as those provided in U.S.C., Title 28, [former] § 641, for depositions taken, *de bene esse,* with the additional provision that any deposition may be used when the court finds the existence of exceptional circumstances. Compare English Rules Under the Judicature Act (The Annual Practice, 1937) O. 37, r. 18 (with additional provision permitting use of deposition by consent of the parties). See also [former] Equity Rule 64 (Former Depositions, Etc. May be Used Before Master); and 2 Minn.Stat. (Mason, 1927) § 9835 (Use in a subsequent action of a deposition filed in a previously dismissed action between the same parties and involving the same subject matter).

1946 Amendment

Note. Subdivision (a). The amendment eliminates the requirement of leave of court for the taking of a deposition except where a plaintiff seeks to take a deposition within 20 days after the commencement of the action. The retention of the requirement where a deposition is sought by a plaintiff within 20 days of the commencement of the action protects a defendant who has not had an opportunity to retain counsel and inform himself as to the nature of the suit; the plaintiff, of course, needs no such protection. The present rule forbids the plaintiff to take a deposition, without leave of court, before the answer is served. Sometimes the defendant delays the serving of an answer for more than 20 days, but as 20 days are sufficient time for him to obtain a lawyer, there is no reason to forbid the plaintiff to take a deposition without leave merely because the answer has not been served. In all cases, Rule 30(a) empowers the court, for cause shown, to alter the time of the taking of a deposition, and Rule 30(b) contains provisions giving ample protection to persons who are unreasonably pressed. The modified practice here adopted is along the line of that followed in various states. See e.g., 8 Mo.Rev.Stat.Ann.1939, § 1917; 2 Burns' Ind.Stat.Ann.1933, § 2–1506.

Subdivision (b). The amendments to subdivision (b) make clear the broad scope of examination and that it may cover not only evidence for use at the trial but also inquiry into matters in themselves inadmissible as evidence but which will lead to the discovery of such evidence. The purpose of discovery is to allow a broad search for facts, the names of witnesses, or any other matters which may aid a party in the preparation or presentation of his case. *Engl v. Aetna Life Ins. Co.*, C.C.A.2, 1943, 139 F.2d 469; *Mahler v. Pennsylvania R. Co.*, E.D.N.Y.1945, 8 Fed.Rules Serv. 33.351, Case 1. In such a preliminary inquiry admissibility at trial should not be the test as to whether the information sought is within the scope of proper examination. Such a standard unnecessarily curtails the utility of discovery practice. Of course, matters entirely without bearing either as direct evidence or as leads to evidence are not within the scope of inquiry, but to the extent that the examination develops useful information, it functions successfully as an instrument of discovery, even if it produces no testimony directly admissible. *Lewis v. United Air Lines Transportation Corp.*, D.Conn.1939, 27 F.Supp. 946; *Engl v. Aetna Life Ins. Co.*, supra; *Mahler v. Pennsylvania R. Co.*, supra; *Bloomer v. Sirian Lamp Co.*, D.Del.1944, 8 Fed.Rules Serv. 26b.31, Case 3; *Rosseau v. Langley*, N.Y.1945, 9 Fed.Rules Serv. 34.41, Case 1 (Rule 26 contemplates "examinations not merely for the narrow purpose of adducing testimony which may be offered in evidence but also for the broad discovery of information which may be useful in preparation for trial."); *Olson Transportation Co. v. Socony-Vacuum Co.*, E.D.Wis.1944, 8 Fed.Rules Serv. 34.41, Case 2 (". . . the Rules . . . permit 'fishing' for evidence as they should."); Note, 1945, 45 Col.L.Rev. 482. Thus hearsay, while inadmissible itself, may suggest testimony which properly may be proved. Under Rule 26(b) several cases, however, have erroneously limited discovery on the basis of admissibility, holding that the word "relevant" in effect meant "material and competent under the rules of evidence". *Poppino v. Jones Store Co.*, W.D.Mo.1940, 1 F.R.D. 215, 3 Fed.Rules Serv. 26b.5, Case 1; *Benevento v. A. & P. Food Stores, Inc.*, E.D.N.Y.1939, 26 F.Supp. 424. Thus it has been said that inquiry might not be made into statements or other matters which, when disclosed, amounted only to hearsay. See *Maryland for use of Montvila v. Pan-American Bus Lines, Inc.*, D.Md.1940, 1 F.R.D. 213, 3 Fed.Rules Serv. 26b.211, Case 3; *Gitto v. "Italia," Societa Anonima Di Navigazione*, E.D.N.Y.1940, 31 F.Supp. 567; *Rose Silk Mills, Inc. v. Insurance Co. of North America*, S.D.N.Y.1939, 29 F.Supp. 504; *Colpak v. Hetterick*, E.D.N.Y.1941, 40 F.Supp. 350; *Matthies v. Peter F. Connolly Co.*, E.D.N.Y.1941, 6 Fed.Rules Serv. 30a.22, Case 1, 2 F.R.D. 277; *Matter of Examination of Citizens Casualty Co. of New York*, S.D.N.Y.1942, 3 F.R.D. 171, 7 Fed.Rules Serv. 26b.211, Case 1; *United States v. Silliman*, D.C.N.J.1944, 8 Fed.Rules Serv. 26b.52, Case 1. The contrary and better view, however, has often been stated. See, e.g., *Engl v. Aetna Life Ins. Co.*, supra; *Stevenson v. Melady*, S.D.N.Y.1940, 3 Fed.Rules Serv. 26b.31, Case 1, 1 F.R.D. 329; *Lewis v. United Air Lines Transport Corp.*, supra; *Application of Zenith Radio Corp.*, E.D.Pa.1941, 4 Fed.Rules Serv. 30b.21, Case 1, 1 F.R.D. 627; *Steingut v. Guaranty Trust Co. of New York*, S.D.N.Y.1941, 1 F.R.D. 723, 4 Fed.Rules Serv. 26b.5, Case 2; *DeSeversky v. Republic Aviation Corp.*, E.D.N.Y.1941, 2 F.R.D. 183, 5 Fed.Rules Serv. 26b.31, Case 5; *Moore v. George A. Hormel & Co.*, S.D.N.Y.1942, 6 Fed.Rules Serv. 30b.41, Case 1, 2 F.R.D. 340; *Hercules Powder Co. v. Rohm & Haas Co.*, D.Del.1943, 7 Fed.Rules Serv. 45b.311, Case 2, 3 F.R.D. 302; *Bloomer v. Sirian Lamp Co.*, supra; *Crosby Steam Gage & Valve Co. v. Manning, Maxwell & Moore, Inc.*, D.Mass.1944, 8 Fed.Rules Serv. 26b.31, Case 1; *Patterson Oil Terminals, Inc. v. Charles Kurz & Co., Inc.*, E.D.Pa.1945, 9 Fed.Rules Serv. 33.321, Case 2; *Pueblo Trading Co. v. Reclamation Dist. No. 1500*, N.D.Cal.1945, 9 Fed.Rules Serv. 33.321, Case 4, 4 F.R.D. 471. See also discussion as to the broad scope of discovery in *Hoffman v. Palmer*, C.C.A.2, 1942, 129 F.2d 976, 995–997; affirmed 63 S.Ct. 477, 318 U.S. 109, 87 L.Ed. 645; Note, 1945, 45 Col.L.Rev. 482.

1963 Amendment

This amendment conforms to the amendment of Rule 28(b). See the next-to-last paragraph of the Advisory Committee's Note to that amendment.

1966 Amendment

The requirement that the plaintiff obtain leave of court in order to serve notice of taking of a deposition within 20 days after commencement of the action gives rise to difficulties when the prospective deponent is about to become unavailable for examination. The problem is not confined to admiralty, but has been of special concern in that context because of the mobility of vessels and their personnel. When Rule 26 was adopted as Admiralty Rule 30A in 1961, the problem was alleviated by permitting depositions *de bene esse,* for which leave of court is not required. See Advisory Committee's Note to Admiralty Rule 30A (1961).

A continuing study is being made in the effort to devise a modification of the 20-day rule appropriate to both the civil and admiralty practice to the end that Rule 26(a) shall state a uniform rule applicable alike to what are now civil actions and suits in admiralty. Meanwhile, the exigencies of maritime litigation require preservation, for the time being at least, of the traditional *de bene esse* procedure for the post-unification counterpart of the present suit in admiralty. Accordingly, the amendment provides for continued availability of that procedure in admiralty and maritime claims within the meaning of Rule 9(h).

1970 Amendment

A limited rearrangement of the discovery rules is made, whereby certain rule provisions are transferred, as follows: Existing Rule 26(a) is transferred to Rules 30(a) and 31(a). Existing Rule 26(c) is transferred to Rule 30(c). Existing Rules 26(d), (e), and (f) are transferred to Rule 32. Revisions of the transferred provisions, if any, are discussed in the notes appended to Rules 30, 31, and 32. In addition, Rule 30(b) is transferred to Rule 26(c). The purpose of this rearrangement is to establish Rule 26 as a rule governing discovery in general. (The reasons are set out in the Advisory Committee's explanatory statement.)

Subdivision (a)—Discovery Devices. This is a new subdivision listing all of the discovery devices provided in the discovery rules and establishing the relationship between the general provisions of Rule 26 and the specific rules for particular discovery devices. The provision that the frequency of use of these methods is not limited confirms existing law. It incorporates in general form a provision now found in Rule 33.

Subdivision (b)—Scope of Discovery. This subdivision is recast to cover the scope of discovery generally. It regulates the discovery obtainable through any of the discovery devices listed in Rule 26(a).

All provisions as to scope of discovery are subject to the initial qualification that the court may limit discovery in accordance with these rules. Rule 26(c) (transferred from 30(b)) confers broad powers on the courts to regulate or prevent discovery even though the materials sought are within the scope of 26(b), and these powers have always been freely exercised. For example, a party's income tax return is generally held not privileged, 2A Barron & Holtzoff, *Federal Practice and Procedure,* § 651.2 (Wright ed. 1961), and yet courts have recognized that interests in privacy may call for a measure of extra protection. E.g., *Wiesenberger v. W. E. Hutton & Co.,* 35 F.R.D. 556 (S.D.N.Y.1964). Similarly, the courts have in appropriate circumstances protected materials that are primarily of an impeaching character. These two types of materials merely illustrate the many situations, not capable of governance by precise rule, in which courts must exercise judgment. The new subsections in Rule 26(b) do not change existing law with respect to such situations.

Subdivision (b)(1)—In General. The language is changed to provide for the scope of discovery in general terms. The existing subdivision, although in terms applicable only to depositions, is incorporated by reference in existing Rules 33 and 34. Since decisions as to relevance to the subject matter of the action are made for discovery purposes well in advance of trial, a flexible treatment of relevance is required and the making of discovery, whether voluntary or under court order, is not a concession or determination of relevance for purposes of trial. *Cf. 4 Moore's Federal Practice* ¶ 26–16[1] (2d ed. 1966).

Subdivision (b)(2)—Insurance Policies. Both the cases and commentators are sharply in conflict on the question whether defendant's liability insurance coverage is subject to discovery in the usual situation when the insurance coverage is not itself admissible and does not bear on another issue in the case. Examples of Federal cases requiring disclosure and supporting comments: *Cook v. Welty,* 253 F.Supp. 875 (D.D.C.1966) (cases cited); *Johanek v. Aberle,* 27 F.R.D. 272 (D.Mont.1961); Williams, *Discovery of Dollar Limits in Liability Policies in Automobile Tort Cases,* 10 Ala.L.Rev. 355 (1958); Thode, *Some Reflections on the 1957 Amendments to the Texas Rules,* 37 Tex.L.Rev. 33, 40–42 (1958). Examples of Federal cases refusing disclosure and supporting comments: *Bisserier v. Manning,* 207 F.Supp. 476 (D.N.J.1962); *Cooper v. Stender,* 30 F.R.D. 389 (E.D.Tenn.1962); Frank, *Discovery and Insurance, Coverage,* 1959 Ins.L.J. 281; Fournier, *Pre-trial Discovery of Insurance Coverage and Limits,* 28 Ford.L.Rev. 215 (1959).

The division in reported cases is close. State decisions based on provisions similar to the federal rules are similarly divided. See cases collected in 2A Barron & Holtzoff, *Federal Practice and Procedure* § 647.1, nn. 45.5, 45.6 (Wright ed. 1961). It appears to be difficult if not impossible to obtain appellate review of the issue. Resolution by rule amendment is indicated. The question is essentially procedural in that it bears upon preparation for trial and settlement before trial, and courts confronting the question, however they have decided it, have generally treated it as procedural and governed by the rules.

The amendment resolves this issue in favor of disclosure. Most of the decisions denying discovery, some explicitly, reason from the text of Rule 26(b) that it permits discovery only of matters which will be admissible in evidence or appear reasonably calculated to lead to such evidence; they avoid considerations of policy, regarding them as foreclosed. See *Bisserier v. Manning, supra.* Some note also that facts about a defendant's financial status are not discoverable as such, prior to judgment with execution unsatisfied, and fear that, if courts hold insurance coverage discoverable, they must extend the principle to other aspects of the defendant's financial status. The cases favoring disclosure rely heavily on the practical significance of insurance in the decisions lawyers make about settlement and trial preparation. In *Clauss v. Danker,* 264 F.Supp. 246 (S.D.N.Y.1967), the court held that the rules forbid disclosure but called for an amendment to permit it.

Disclosure of insurance coverage will enable counsel for both sides to make the same realistic appraisal of the case, so that settlement and litigation strategy are based on knowledge and not speculation. It will conduce to settlement and avoid protracted litigation in some cases, though in others it may have an opposite effect. The amendment is limited to insurance coverage, which should be distinguished from any other facts concerning defendant's financial status (1) because insurance is an asset created specifically to satisfy the claim; (2) because the insurance company ordinarily controls the litigation; (3) because information about coverage is available only from defendant or his insurer; and (4) because disclosure does not involve a significant invasion of privacy.

Disclosure is required when the insurer "may be liable" on part or all of the judgment. Thus, an insurance company must disclose even when it contests liability under the policy, and such disclosure does not constitute a waiver of its claim. It is immaterial whether the liability is to satisfy the judgment directly or merely to indemnify or reimburse another after he pays the judgment.

The provision applies only to persons "carrying on an insurance business" and thus covers insurance companies and not the ordinary business concern that enters into a contract of indemnification. *Cf.* N.Y.Ins.Law § 41. Thus, the provision makes no change in existing law on discovery of indemnity agreements other than insurance agreements by persons carrying on an insurance business. Similarly, the provision does not cover the business concern that creates a reserve fund for purposes of self-insurance.

For some purposes other than discovery, an application for insurance is treated as a part of the insurance agreement. The provision makes clear that, for discovery purposes, the application is not to be so treated. The insurance application may contain personal and financial information concerning the insured, discovery of which is beyond the purpose of this provision.

In no instance does disclosure make the facts concerning insurance coverage admissible in evidence.

Subdivision (b)(3)—Trial Preparation: Materials. Some of the most controversial and vexing problems to emerge from the discovery rules have arisen out of requests for the production of documents or things prepared in anticipation of litigation or for trial. The existing rules make no explicit provision for such materials. Yet, two verbally distinct doctrines have developed, each conferring a qualified immunity on these materials—the "good cause" requirement in Rule 34 (now generally held applicable to discovery of documents via deposition under Rule 45 and interrogatories under Rule 33) and the work-product doctrine of *Hickman v. Taylor,* 329 U.S. 495 (1947). Both demand a showing of justification before production can be had, the one of "good cause" and the other variously described in the *Hickman* case: "necessity or justification," "denial * * * would unduly prejudice the preparation of petitioner's case," or "cause hardship or injustice" 329 U.S. at 509–510.

In deciding the *Hickman* case, the Supreme Court appears to have expressed a preference in 1947 for an approach to the problem of trial preparation materials by judicial decision rather than by rule. Sufficient experience has accumulated, however, with lower court applications of the *Hickman* decision to warrant a reappraisal.

The major difficulties visible in the existing case law are (1) confusion and disagreement as to whether "good cause" is made out by a showing of relevance and lack of privilege, or requires an additional showing of necessity, (2) confusion and disagreement as to the scope of the *Hickman* work-product doctrine, particularly whether it extends beyond work actually performed by lawyers, and (3) the resulting difficulty of relating the "good cause" required by Rule 34 and the "necessity or justification" of the work-product doctrine, so that their respective roles and the distinctions between them are understood.

Basic Standard.—Since Rule 34 in terms requires a showing of "good cause" for the production of all documents and things, whether or not trial preparation is involved, courts have felt that a single formula is called for and have differed over whether a showing of relevance and lack of privilege is enough or whether more must be shown. When the facts of the cases are studied, however, a distinction emerges based upon the type of materials. With respect to documents not obtained or prepared with an eye to litigation, the decisions, while not uniform, reflect a strong and increasing tendency to relate "good cause" to a showing that the documents are relevant to the subject matter of the action. *E.g., Connecticut Mutual Life Ins. Co. v. Shields,* 17 F.R.D. 273 (S.D.N.Y.1959), with cases cited; *Houdry Process Corp. v. Commonwealth Oil Refining Co.,* 24 F.R.D. 58 (S.D.N.Y.1955); see *Bell v. Commercial Ins. Co.,* 280 F.2d 514, 517 (3d Cir. 1960). When the party whose documents are sought shows that the request for production is unduly burdensome or oppressive, courts have denied discovery for lack of "good cause", although they might just as easily have based their decision on the protective provisions of existing Rule 30(b) (new Rule 26(c)). *E.g., Lauer v. Tankrederi,* 39 F.R.D. 334 (E.D.Pa.1966).

As to trial-preparation materials, however, the courts are increasingly interpreting "good cause" as requiring more than relevance. When lawyers have prepared or obtained the materials for trial, all courts require more than relevance; so much is clearly commanded by *Hickman.* But even as to the preparatory work of nonlawyers, while some courts ignore work-product and equate "good cause" with relevance, *e.g., Brown v. New York, N.H. & H.R.R.,* 17 F.R.D. 324 (S.D.N.Y.1955), the more recent trend is to read "good cause" as requiring inquiry into the importance of and need for the materials as well as into alternative sources for securing the same information. In *Guilford Nat'l Bank v. Southern Ry.,* 297 F.2d 921 (4th Cir. 1962), statements of witnesses obtained by claim agents were held not discoverable because both parties had had equal access to the witnesses at about the same time, shortly after the collision in question. The decision was based solely on Rule 34 and "good cause"; the court declined to rule on whether the statements were work-products. The court's treatment of "good cause" is quoted at length and with approval in *Schlagenhauf v. Holder,* 379 U.S. 104, 117–118 (1964). See also *Mitchell v. Bass,* 252 F.2d 513 (8th Cir. 1958); *Hauger v. Chicago, R.I. & Pac. R.R.,* 216 F.2d 501 (7th Cir. 1954); *Burke v. United States,* 32 F.R.D. 213 (E.D.N.Y.1963). While the opinions dealing with "good cause" do not often draw an explicit distinction between trial preparation materials and other materials, in fact an overwhelming proportion of the cases in which a special showing is required are cases involving trial preparation materials.

The rules are amended by eliminating the general requirement of "good cause" from Rule 34 but retaining a requirement of a special showing for trial preparation materials in this subdivision. The required showing is expressed, not in terms of "good cause" whose generality has tended to encourage confusion and controversy, but in terms of the elements of the special showing to be made: substantial need of the materials in the preparation of the case and inability without undue hardship to obtain the substantial equivalent of the materials by other means.

These changes conform to the holdings of the cases, when viewed in light of their facts. Apart from trial preparation, the fact that the materials sought are documentary does not in and of itself require a special showing beyond relevance and absence of privilege. The protective provisions are of course available, and if the party from whom production is sought raises a special issue of privacy (as with respect to income tax returns or grand jury minutes) or points to evidence primarily impeaching, or can show serious burden or expense, the court will exercise its traditional power to decide whether to issue a protective order. On the other hand, the requirement of a special showing for discovery of trial preparation materials reflects the view that each side's informal evaluation of its case should be protected, that each side should be encouraged to prepare independently, and that one side should not automatically have the benefit of the detailed preparatory work of the other side. See Field and McKusick, *Maine Civil Practice* 264 (1959).

Elimination of a "good cause" requirement from Rule 34 and the establishment of a requirement of a special showing in this subdivision will eliminate the confusion caused by having two verbally distinct requirements of justification that the courts have been unable to distinguish clearly. Moreover, the language of the subdivision suggests the factors which the courts should consider in determining whether the requisite showing has been made. The importance of the materials sought to the party seeking them in preparation of his case and the difficulty he will have obtaining them by other means are factors noted in the *Hickman* case. The courts should also consider the likelihood that the party, even if he obtains the information by independent means, will not have the substantial equivalent of the documents the production of which he seeks.

Consideration of these factors may well lead the court to distinguish between witness statements taken by an investigator, on the one hand, and other parts of the investigative file, on the other. The court in

Southern Ry. v. Lanham, 403 F.2d 119 (5th Cir. 1968), while it naturally addressed itself to the "good cause" requirements of Rule 34, set forth as controlling considerations the factors contained in the language of this subdivision. The analysis of the court suggests circumstances under which witness statements will be discoverable. The witness may have given a fresh and contemporaneous account in a written statement while he is available to the party seeking discovery only a substantial time thereafter. *Lanham, supra* at 127–128; *Guilford, supra* at 926. Or he may be reluctant or hostile. *Lanham, supra* at 128–129; *Brookshire v. Pennsylvania RR,* 14 F.R.D. 154 (N.D.Ohio 1953); *Diamond v. Mohawk Rubber Co.,* 33 F.R.D. 264 (D.Colo.1963). Or he may have a lapse of memory. *Tannenbaum v. Walker,* 16 F.R.D. 570 (E.D.Pa.1954). Or he may probably be deviating from his prior statement. *Cf. Hauger v. Chicago, R.I. & Pac. RR,* 216 F.2d 501 (7th Cir. 1954). On the other hand, a much stronger showing is needed to obtain evaluative materials in an investigator's reports. *Lanham, supra* at 131–133; *Pickett v. L. R. Ryan, Inc.,* 237 F.Supp. 198 (E.D.S.C.1965).

Materials assembled in the ordinary course of business, or pursuant to public requirements unrelated to litigation, or for other nonlitigation purposes are not under the qualified immunity provided by this subdivision. *Goosman v. A. Duie Pyle, Inc.,* 320 F.2d 45 (4th Cir. 1963); cf. *United States v. New York Foreign Trade Zone Operators, Inc.,* 304 F.2d 792 (2d Cir. 1962). No change is made in the existing doctrine, noted in the *Hickman* case, that one party may discover relevant facts known or available to the other party, even though such facts are contained in a document which is not itself discoverable.

Treatment of Lawyers; Special Protection of Mental Impressions, Conclusions, Opinions, and Legal Theories Concerning the Litigation.—The courts are divided as to whether the work-product doctrine extends to the preparatory work only of lawyers. The *Hickman* case left this issue open since the statements in that case were taken by a lawyer. As to courts of appeals compare *Alltmont v. United States,* 177 F.2d 971, 976 (3d Cir. 1949), cert. denied, 339 U.S. 967 (1950) (*Hickman* applied to statements obtained by FBI agents on theory it should apply to "all statements of prospective witnesses which a party has obtained for his trial counsel's use"), with *Southern Ry. v. Campbell,* 309 F.2d 569 (5th Cir. 1962) (Statements taken by claim agents not work-product), and *Guilford Nat'l Bank v. Southern Ry.,* 297 F.2d 921 (4th Cir. 1962) (avoiding issue of work-product as to claim agents, deciding case instead under Rule 34 "good cause"). Similarly, the district courts are divided on statements obtained by claim agents, compare, e.g., *Brown v. New York, N.H. & H.R.R.,* 17 F.R.D. 324 (S.D.N.Y.1955) with *Hanke v. Milwaukee Electric Ry. & Transp. Co.,* 7 F.R.D. 540 (E.D.Wis.1947); investigators, compare *Burke v. United States,* 32 F.R.D. 213 (E.D.N.Y.1963) with *Snyder v. United States,* 20 F.R.D. 7 (E.D.N.Y.1956); and insurers, compare *Gottlieb v. Bresler,* 24 F.R.D. 371 (D.D.C.1959) with *Burns v. Mulder,* 20 F.R.D. 605 (E.D.Pa.1957). See 4 Moore's *Federal Practice* ¶ 26.23[8.1] (2d ed. 1966); 2A Barron & Holtzoff, *Federal Practice and Procedure* § 652.2 (Wright ed. 1961).

A complication is introduced by the use made by courts of the "good cause" requirement of Rule 34, as described above. A court may conclude that trial preparation materials are not work-product because not the result of lawyer's work and yet hold that they are not producible because "good cause" has not been shown. *Cf. Guilford Nat'l Bank v. Southern Ry.,* 297 F.2d 921 (4th Cir. 1962), cited and described above. When the decisions on "good cause" are taken into account, the weight of authority affords protection of the preparatory work of both lawyers and nonlawyers (though not necessarily to the same extent) by requiring more than a showing of relevance to secure production.

Subdivision (b)(3) reflects the trend of the cases by requiring a special showing, not merely as to materials prepared by an attorney, but also as to materials prepared in anticipation of litigation or preparation for trial by or for a party or any representative acting on his behalf. The subdivision then goes on to protect against disclosure the mental impressions, conclusions, opinions, or legal theories concerning the litigation of an attorney or other representative of a party. The *Hickman* opinion drew special attention to the need for protecting an attorney against discovery of memoranda prepared from recollection of oral interviews. The courts have steadfastly safeguarded against disclosure of lawyers' mental impressions and legal theories, as well as mental impressions and subjective evaluations of investigators and claim-agents. In enforcing this provision of the subdivision, the courts will sometimes find it necessary to order disclosure of a document but with portions deleted.

Rules 33 and 36 have been revised in order to permit discovery calling for opinions, contentions, and admissions relating not only to fact but also to the application of law to fact. Under those rules, a party and his attorney or other representative may be required to disclose, to some extent, mental impressions, opinions, or conclusions. But documents or parts of documents containing these matters are protected against discovery by this subdivision. Even though a party may ultimately have to disclose in response to interrogatories or requests to admit, he is entitled to keep confidential documents containing such matters prepared for internal use.

Party's Right to Own Statement.—An exception to the requirement of this subdivision enables a party to secure production of his own statement without any special showing. The cases are divided. Compare, *e.g., Safeway Stores, Inc. v. Reynolds,* 176 F.2d 476 (D.C. Cir.1949); *Shupe v. Pennsylvania R.R.,* 19 F.R.D. 144 (W.D.Pa.1956); with *e.g., New York Central R.R. v. Carr,* 251 F.2d 433 (4th Cir. 1957); *Belback v. Wilson Freight Forwarding Co.,* 40 F.R.D. 16 (W.D.Pa.1966).

Courts which treat a party's statement as though it were that of any witness overlook the fact that the party's statement is, without more, admissible in evidence. Ordinarily, a party gives a statement without insisting on a copy because he does not yet have a lawyer and does not understand the legal consequences of his actions. Thus, the statement is given at a time when he functions at a disadvantage. Discrepancies between his trial testimony and earlier statement may result from lapse of memory or ordinary inaccuracy; a written statement produced for the first time at trial may give such discrepancies a prominence which they do not deserve. In appropriate cases the court may order a party to be deposed before his statement is produced. *E.g., Smith v. Central Linen Service Co.,* 39 F.R.D. 15 (D.Md.1966); *McCoy v. General Motors Corp.,* 33 F.R.D. 354 (W.D.Pa.1963).

Commentators strongly support the view that a party be able to secure his statement without a showing. 4 *Moore's Federal Practice* ¶ 26.23[8.4] (2d ed. 1966); 2A Barron & Holtzoff, *Federal Practice and Procedure* § 652.3 (Wright ed. 1961); see also Note, *Developments in the Law—Discovery,* 74 Harv.L.Rev. 940, 1039 (1961). The following states have by statute or rule taken the same position: *Statutes:* Fla.Stat.Ann. § 92.33; Ga.Code Ann. § 38–2109(b); La.Stat.Ann.R.S. 13:3732; Mass.Gen.Laws Ann. c. 271, § 44; Minn.Stat.Ann. § 602.01; N.Y.C.P.L.R. § 3101(e); *Rules:* Mo.R.C.P. 56.01(a); N.Dak.R.C.P. 34(b); Wyo.R.C.P. 34(b); *cf.* Mich.G.C.R. 306.2.

In order to clarify and tighten the provision on statements by a party, the term "statement" is defined. The definition is adapted from 18 U.S.C. § 3500(e) (Jencks Act). The statement of a party may of course be that of plaintiff or defendant, and it may be that of an individual or of a corporation or other organization.

Witness' Right to Own Statement.—A second exception to the requirement of this subdivision permits a non-party witness to obtain a copy of his own statement without any special showing. Many, though not all, of the considerations supporting a party's right to obtain his statement apply also to the non-party witness. Insurance companies are increasingly recognizing that a witness is entitled to a copy of his statement and are modifying their regular practice accordingly.

Subdivision (b)(4)—Trial Preparation: Experts. This is a new provision dealing with discovery of information (including facts and opinions) obtained by a party from an expert retained by that party in relation to litigation or obtained by the expert and not yet transmitted to the party. The subdivision deals separately with those experts whom the party expects to call as trial witnesses and with those experts who have been retained or specially employed by the party but who are not expected to be witnesses. It should be noted that the subdivision does not address itself to the expert whose information was not acquired in preparation for trial but rather because he was an actor or viewer with respect to transactions or occurrences that are part of the subject matter of the lawsuit. Such an expert should be treated as an ordinary witness.

Subsection (b)(4)(A) deals with discovery of information obtained by or through experts who will be called as witnesses at trial. The provision is responsive to problems suggested by a relatively recent line of authorities. Many of these cases present intricate and difficult issues as to which expert testimony is likely to be determinative. Prominent among them are food and drug, patent, and condemnation cases. See, *e.g., United States v. Nysco Laboratories, Inc.,* 26 F.R.D. 159, 162 (E.D.N.Y.1960) (food and drug); *E. I. du Pont de Nemours & Co. v. Phillips Petroleum Co.,* 24 F.R.D. 416, 421 (D.Del.1959) (patent); *Cold Metal Process Co. v. Aluminum Co. of America,* 7 F.R.D. 425 (N.D.Ohio 1947), aff'd, *Sachs v. Aluminum Co. of America,* 167 F.2d 570 (6th Cir. 1948) (same); *United States v. 50.34 Acres of Land,* 13 F.R.D. 19 (E.D.N.Y.1952) (condemnation).

In cases of this character, a prohibition against discovery of information held by expert witnesses produces in acute form the very evils that discovery has been created to prevent. Effective cross-examination of an expert witness requires advance preparation. The lawyer even with the help of his own experts frequently cannot anticipate the particular approach his adversary's expert will take or the data on which he will base his judgment on the stand. McGlothlin, *Some Practical Problems in Proof of Economic, Scientific, and Technical Facts,* 23 F.R.D. 467, 478 (1958). A California study of discovery and pretrial in condemnation cases notes that the only substitute for discovery of experts' valuation materials is "lengthy— and often fruitless—cross-examination during trial," and recommends pretrial exchange of such material. Calif.Law Rev.Comm'n, Discovery in Eminent Domain Proceedings 707–710 (Jan. 1963). Similarly, effective rebuttal requires advance knowledge of the line of testimony of the other side. If the latter is foreclosed by a rule against discovery, then the narrowing of issues and elimination of surprise which discovery normally produces are frustrated.

These considerations appear to account for the broadening of discovery against experts in the cases cited where expert testimony was central to the case. In some instances, the opinions are explicit in relating expanded discovery to improved cross-examination and rebuttal at trial. *Franks v. National Dairy Products Corp.,* 41 F.R.D. 234 (W.D.Tex.1966); *United States v. 23.76 Acres,* 32 F.R.D. 593 (D.Md.1963); see also an unpublished opinion of Judge Hincks, quoted in *United States v. 48 Jars, etc.,* 23 F.R.D. 192, 198 (D.D.C.1958). On the other hand, the need for a new provision is shown by the many cases in which discovery of expert trial witnesses is needed for effective cross-examination and rebuttal, and yet courts apply the traditional doctrine and refuse disclosure. *E.g., United States v. Certain Parcels of Land,* 25 F.R.D. 192 (N.D.Cal.1959); *United States v. Certain Acres,* 18 F.R.D. 98 (M.D.Ga.1955).

Although the trial problems flowing from lack of discovery of expert witnesses are most acute and noteworthy when the case turns largely on experts, the same problems are encountered when a single expert testifies. Thus, subdivision (b)(4)(A) draws no line between complex and simple cases, or between cases with many experts and those with but one. It establishes by rule substantially the procedure adopted by decision of the court in *Knighton v. Villian & Fassio,* 39 F.R.D. 11 (D.Md.1965). For a full analysis of the problem and strong recommendations to the same effect, see Friedenthal, *Discovery and Use of an Adverse Party's Expert Information,* 14 Stan.L.Rev. 455, 485–488 (1962); Long, *Discovery and Experts under the Federal Rules of Civil Procedure,* 38 F.R.D. 111 (1965).

Past judicial restrictions on discovery of an adversary's expert, particularly as to his opinions, reflect the fear that one side will benefit unduly from the other's better preparation. The procedure established in subsection (b)(4)(A) holds the risk to a minimum. Discovery is limited to trial witnesses, and may be obtained only at a time when the parties know who their expert witnesses will be. A party must as a practical matter prepare his own case in advance of that time, for he can hardly hope to build his case out of his opponent's experts.

Subdivision (b)(4)(A) provides for discovery of an expert who is to testify at the trial. A party can require one who intends to use the expert to state the substance of the testimony that the expert is expected to give. The court may order further discovery, and it has ample power to regulate its timing and scope and to prevent abuse. Ordinarily, the order for further discovery shall compensate the expert for his time, and may compensate the party who intends to use the expert for past expenses reasonably incurred in obtaining facts or opinions from the expert. Those provisions are likely to discourage abusive practices.

Subdivision (b)(4)(B) deals with an expert who has been retained or specially employed by the party in anticipation of litigation or preparation for trial (thus excluding an expert who is simply a general employee of the party not specially employed on the case), but who is not expected to be called as a witness. Under its provisions, a party may discover facts known or opinions held by such an expert only on a showing of exceptional circumstances under which it is impracticable for the party seeking discovery to obtain facts or opinions on the same subject by other means.

Subdivision (b)(4)(B) is concerned only with experts retained or specially consulted in relation to trial preparation. Thus the subdivision precludes discovery against experts who were informally consulted in preparation for trial, but not retained or specially employed. As an ancillary procedure, a party may on a proper showing require the other party to name experts retained or specially employed, but not those informally consulted.

These new provisions of subdivision (b)(4) repudiate the few decisions that have held an expert's information privileged simply because of his status as an expert, *e.g., American Oil Co. v. Pennsylvania Petroleum Products Co.,* 23 F.R.D. 680, 685–686 (D.R.I.1959). See *Louisell, Modern California Discovery*

315–316 (1963). They also reject as ill-considered the decisions which have sought to bring expert information within the work-product doctrine. See *United States v. McKay,* 372 F.2d 174, 176–177 (5th Cir. 1967). The provisions adopt a form of the more recently developed doctrine of "unfairness". See *e.g., United States v. 23.76 Acres of Land,* 32 F.R.D. 593, 597 (D.Md.1963); Louisell, *supra,* at 317–318; 4 *Moore's Federal Practice* 26.24 (2d ed. 1966).

Under subdivision (b)(4)(C), the court is directed or authorized to issue protective orders, including an order that the expert be paid a reasonable fee for time spent in responding to discovery, and that the party whose expert is made subject to discovery be paid a fair portion of the fees and expenses that the party incurred in obtaining information from the expert. The court may issue the latter order as a condition of discovery, or it may delay the order until after discovery is completed. These provisions for fees and expenses meet the objection that it is unfair to permit one side to obtain without cost the benefit of an expert's work for which the other side has paid, often a substantial sum. E.g., *Lewis v. United Air Lines Transp. Corp.,* 32 F.Supp. 21 (W.D.Pa.1940); *Walsh v. Reynolds Metal Co.,* 15 F.R.D. 376 (D.N.J.1954). On the other hand, a party may not obtain discovery simply by offering to pay fees and expenses. Cf. *Boynton v. R. J. Reynolds Tobacco Co.,* 36 F.Supp. 593 (D.Mass.1941).

In instances of discovery under subdivision (b)(4)(B), the court is directed to award fees and expenses to the other party, since the information is of direct value to the discovering party's preparation of his case. In ordering discovery under (b)(4)(A)(ii), the court has discretion whether to award fees and expenses to the other party; its decision should depend upon whether the discovering party is simply learning about the other party's case or is going beyond this to develop his own case. Even in cases where the court is directed to issue a protective order, it may decline to do so if it finds that manifest injustice would result. Thus, the court can protect, when necessary and appropriate, the interests of an indigent party.

Subdivision (c)—Protective Orders. The provisions of existing Rule 30(b) are transferred to this subdivision (c), as part of the rearrangement of Rule 26. The language has been changed to give it application to discovery generally. The subdivision recognizes the power of the court in the district where a deposition is being taken to make protective orders. Such power is needed when the deposition is being taken far from the court where the action is pending. The court in the district where the deposition is being taken may, and frequently will, remit the deponent or party to the court where the action is pending.

In addition, drafting changes are made to carry out and clarify the sense of the rule. Insertions are made to avoid any possible implication that a protective order does not extend to "time" as well as to "place" or may not safeguard against "undue burden or expense."

The new reference to trade secrets and other confidential commercial information reflects existing law. The courts have not given trade secrets automatic and complete immunity against disclosure, but have in each case weighed their claim to privacy against the need for disclosure. Frequently, they have been afforded a limited protection. See, *e.g., Covey Oil Co. v. Continental Oil Co.,* 340 F.2d 993 (10th Cir. 1965); *Julius M. Ames Co. v. Bostitch, Inc.,* 235 F.Supp. 856 (S.D.N.Y.1964).

The subdivision contains new matter relating to sanctions. When a motion for a protective order is made and the court is disposed to deny it, the court may go a step further and issue an order to provide or permit discovery. This will bring the sanctions of Rule 37(b) directly into play. Since the court has heard the contentions of all interested persons, an affirmative order is justified. See *Rosenberg, Sanctions to Effectuate Pretrial Discovery,* 58 Col.L.Rev. 480, 492–493 (1958). In addition, the court may require the payment of expenses incurred in relation to the motion.

Subdivision (d)—Sequence and Priority. This new provision is concerned with the sequence in which parties may proceed with discovery and with related problems of timing. The principal effects of the new provision are first, to eliminate any fixed priority in the sequence of discovery, and second, to make clear and explicit the court's power to establish priority by an order issued in a particular case.

A priority rule developed by some courts, which confers priority on the party who first serves notice of taking a deposition, is unsatisfactory in several important respects:

First, this priority rule permits a party to establish a priority running to all depositions as to which he has given earlier notice. Since he can on a given day serve notice of taking many depositions he is in a position to delay his adversary's taking of depositions for an inordinate time. Some courts have ruled that deposition priority also permits a party to delay his answers to interrogatories and production of documents.

E.g., E. I. du Pont de Nemours & Co. v. Phillips Petroleum Co., 23 F.R.D. 237 (D.Del.1959); *but cf. Sturdevant v. Sears, Roebuck & Co.,* 32 F.R.D. 426 (W.D.Mo.1963).

Second, since notice is the key to priority, if both parties wish to take depositions first a race results. See *Caldwell-Clements, Inc. v. McGraw-Hill Pub. Co.,* 11 F.R.D. 156 (S.D.N.Y.1951) (description of tactics used by parties). But the existing rules on notice of deposition create a race with runners starting from different positions. The plaintiff may not give notice without leave of court until 20 days after commencement of the action, whereas the defendant may serve notice at any time after commencement. Thus, a careful and prompt defendant can almost always secure priority. This advantage of defendants is fortuitous, because the purpose of requiring plaintiff to wait 20 days is to afford defendant an opportunity to obtain counsel, not to confer priority.

Third, although courts have ordered a change in the normal sequence of discovery on a number of occasions, *e.g., Kaeppler v. James H. Matthews & Co.,* 200 F.Supp. 229 (E.D.Pa.1961); *Park & Tilford Distillers Corp. v. Distillers Co.,* 19 F.R.D. 169 (S.D.N.Y.1956), and have at all times avowed discretion to vary the usual priority, most commentators are agreed that courts in fact grant relief only for "the most obviously compelling reasons." 2A Barron & Holtzoff, *Federal Practice and Procedure* 44–47 (Wright ed. 1961); see also Younger, *Priority of Pretrial Examination in the Federal Courts—A Comment,* 34 N.Y.U.L.Rev. 1271 (1959); Freund, *The Pleading and Pretrial of an Antitrust Claim,* 46 Corn.L.Q. 555, 564 (1964). Discontent with the fairness of actual practice has been evinced by other observers. Comments, 59 Yale L.J. 117, 134–136 (1949); Yudkin, *Some Refinements in Federal Discovery Procedure,* 11 Fed.B.J. 289, 296–297 (1951); *Developments in the Law-Discovery,* 74 Harv.L.Rev. 940, 954–958 (1961).

Despite these difficulties, some courts have adhered to the priority rule, presumably because it provides a test which is easily understood and applied by the parties without much court intervention. It thus permits deposition discovery to function extrajudicially, which the rules provide for and the courts desire. For these same reasons, courts are reluctant to make numerous exceptions to the rule.

The Columbia Survey makes clear that the problem of priority does not affect litigants generally. It found that most litigants do not move quickly to obtain discovery. In over half of the cases, both parties waited at least 50 days. During the first 20 days after commencement of the action—the period when defendant might assure his priority by noticing depositions—16 percent of the defendants acted to obtain discovery. A race could not have occurred in more than 16 percent of the cases and it undoubtedly occurred in fewer. On the other hand, five times as many defendants as plaintiffs served notice of deposition during the first 19 days. To the same effect, see Comment, *Tactical Use and Abuse of Depositions Under the Federal Rules,* 59 Yale L.J. 117, 134 (1949).

These findings do not mean, however, that the priority rule is satisfactory or that a problem of priority does not exist. The court decisions show that parties do battle on this issue and carry their disputes to court. The statistics show that these court cases are not typical. By the same token, they reveal that more extensive exercise of judicial discretion to vary the priority will not bring a flood of litigation, and that a change in the priority rule will in fact affect only a small fraction of the cases.

It is contended by some that there is no need to alter the existing priority practice. In support, it is urged that there is no evidence that injustices in fact result from present practice and that, in any event, the courts can and do promulgate local rules, as in New York, to deal with local situations and issue orders to avoid possible injustice in particular cases.

Subdivision (d) is based on the contrary view that the rule of priority based on notice is unsatisfactory and unfair in its operation. Subdivision (d) follows an approach adapted from Civil Rule 4 of the District Court for the Southern District of New York. That rule provides that starting 40 days after commencement of the action, unless otherwise ordered by the court, the fact that one party is taking a deposition shall not prevent another party from doing so "concurrently." In practice, the depositions are not usually taken simultaneously; rather, the parties work out arrangements for alternation in the taking of depositions. One party may take a complete deposition and then the other, or, if the depositions are extensive, one party deposes for a set time, and then the other. See *Caldwell-Clements, Inc. v. McCraw-Hill Pub. Co.,* 11 F.R.D. 156 (S.D.N.Y.1951).

In principle, one party's initiation of discovery should not wait upon the other's completion, unless delay is dictated by special considerations. Clearly the principle is feasible with respect to all methods of discovery other than depositions. And the experience of the Southern District of New York shows that the principle can be applied to depositions as well. The courts have not had an increase in motion business on this matter. Once it is clear to lawyers that they bargain on an equal footing, they are usually able to arrange for an orderly succession of depositions without judicial intervention. Professor Moore has called attention to Civil Rule 4 and suggested that it may usefully be extended to other areas. 4 *Moore's Federal Practice* 1154 (2d ed. 1966).

The court may upon motion and by order grant priority in a particular case. But a local court rule purporting to confer priority in certain classes of cases would be inconsistent with this subdivision and thus void.

Subdivision (e)—Supplementation of Responses. The rules do not now state whether interrogatories (and questions at deposition as well as requests for inspection and admissions) impose a "continuing burden" on the responding party to supplement his answers if he obtains new information. The issue is acute when new information renders substantially incomplete or inaccurate an answer which was complete and accurate when made. It is essential that the rules provide an answer to this question. The parties can adjust to a rule either way, once they know what it is. See 4 *Moore's Federal Practice* ¶ 33.25[4] (2d ed. 1966).

Arguments can be made both ways. Imposition of a continuing burden reduces the proliferation of additional sets of interrogatories. Some courts have adopted local rules establishing such a burden. *E.g.,* E.D.Pa.R. 20(f), quoted in *Taggart v. Vermont Transp. Co.,* 32 F.R.D. 587 (E.D.Pa.1963); D.Me.R. 15(c). Others have imposed the burden by decision. *E.g., Chenault v. Nebraska Farm Products, Inc.,* 9 F.R.D. 529, 533 (D.Nebr.1949). On the other hand, there are serious objections to the burden, especially in protracted cases. Although the party signs the answers, it is his lawyer who understands their significance and bears the responsibility to bring answers up to date. In a complex case all sorts of information reaches the party, who little understands its bearing on answers previously given to interrogatories. In practice, therefore, the lawyer under a continuing burden must periodically recheck all interrogatories and canvass all new information. But a full set of new answers may no longer be needed by the interrogating party. Some issues will have been dropped from the case, some questions are now seen as unimportant, and other questions must in any event be reformulated. See *Novick v. Pennsylvania R.R.,* 18 F.R.D. 296, 298 (W.D.Pa.1955).

Subdivision (e) provides that a party is not under a continuing burden except as expressly provided. Cf. Note, 68 Harv.L.Rev. 673, 677 (1955). An exception is made as to the identity of persons having knowledge of discoverable matters, because of the obvious importance to each side of knowing all witnesses and because information about witnesses routinely comes to each lawyer's attention. Many of the decisions on the issue of a continuing burden have in fact concerned the identity of witnesses. An exception is also made as to expert trial witnesses in order to carry out the provisions of Rule 26(b)(4). See *Diversified Products Corp. v. Sports Center Co.,* 42 F.R.D. 3 (D.Md.1967).

Another exception is made for the situation in which a party, or more frequently his lawyer, obtains actual knowledge that a prior response is incorrect. This exception does not impose a duty to check the accuracy of prior responses, but it prevents knowing concealment by a party or attorney. Finally, a duty to supplement may be imposed by order of the court in a particular case (including an order resulting from a pretrial conference) or by agreement of the parties. A party may of course make a new discovery request which requires supplementation of prior responses.

The duty will normally be enforced, in those limited instances where it is imposed, through sanctions imposed by the trial court, including exclusion of evidence, continuance, or other action, as the court may deem appropriate.

1980 Amendment

Subdivision (f). This subdivision is new. There has been widespread criticism of abuse of discovery. The Committee has considered a number of proposals to eliminate abuse, including a change in Rule 26(b)(1) with respect to the scope of discovery and a change in Rule 33(a) to limit the number of questions that can be asked by interrogatories to parties.

The Committee believes that abuse of discovery, while very serious in certain cases, is not so general as to require such basic changes in the rules that govern discovery in all cases. A very recent study of discovery in selected metropolitan districts tends to support its belief. P. Connolly, E. Holleman, & M.

Kuhlman, *Judicial Controls and the Civil Litigative Process: Discovery* (Federal Judicial Center, 1978). In the judgment of the Committee abuse can best be prevented by intervention by the court as soon as abuse is threatened.

To this end this subdivision provides that counsel who has attempted without success to effect with opposing counsel a reasonable program or plan for discovery is entitled to the assistance of the court.

It is not contemplated that requests for discovery conferences will be made routinely. A relatively narrow discovery dispute should be resolved by resort to Rules 26(c) or 37(a), and if it appears that a request for a conference is in fact grounded in such a dispute, the court may refer counsel to those rules. If the court is persuaded that a request is frivolous or vexatious, it can strike it. See Rules 11 and 7(b)(2).

A number of courts routinely consider discovery matters in preliminary pretrial conferences held shortly after the pleadings are closed. This subdivision does not interfere with such a practice. It authorizes the court to combine a discovery conference with a pretrial conference under Rule 16 if a pretrial conference is held sufficiently early to prevent or curb abuse.

1983 Amendment

Excessive discovery and evasion or resistance to reasonable discovery requests pose significant problems. Recent studies have made some attempt to determine the sources and extent of the difficulties. See Brazil, *Civil Discovery: Lawyers' Views of its Effectiveness, Principal Problems and Abuses,* American Bar Foundation (1980); Connolly, Holleman & Kuhlman, *Judicial Controls and the Civil Litigative Process: Discovery,* Federal Judicial Center (1978); Ellington, *A Study of Sanctions for Discovery Abuse,* Department of Justice (1979); Schroeder & Frank, *The Proposed Changes in the Discovery Rules,* 1978 Ariz.St.L.J. 475.

The purpose of discovery is to provide a mechanism for making relevant information available to the litigants. "Mutual knowledge of all the relevant facts gathered by both parties is essential to proper litigation." *Hickman v. Taylor,* 329 U.S. 495, 507 (1947). Thus the spirit of the rules is violated when advocates attempt to use discovery tools as tactical weapons rather than to expose the facts and illuminate the issues by overuse of discovery or unnecessary use of defensive weapons or evasive responses. All of this results in excessively costly and time-consuming activities that are disproportionate to the nature of the case, the amount involved, or the issues or values at stake.

Given our adversary tradition and the current discovery rules, it is not surprising that there are many opportunities, if not incentives, for attorneys to engage in discovery that, although authorized by the broad, permissive terms of the rules, nevertheless results in delay. See Brazil, *The Adversary Character of Civil Discovery: A Critique and Proposals for Change,* 31 Vand.L.Rev. 1259 (1978). As a result, it has been said that the rules have "not infrequently [been] exploited to the disadvantage of justice." *Herbert v. Lando,* 441 U.S. 153, 179 (1979) (Powell, J., concurring). These practices impose costs on an already overburdened system and impede the fundamental goal of the "just, speedy, and inexpensive determination of every action." Fed.R.Civ.P. 1.

Subdivision (a); Discovery Methods. The deletion of the last sentence of Rule 26(a)(1), which provided that unless the court ordered otherwise under Rule 26(c) "the frequency of use" of the various discovery methods was not to be limited, is an attempt to address the problem of duplicative, redundant, and excessive discovery and to reduce it. The amendment, in conjunction with the changes in Rule 26(b)(1), is designed to encourage district judges to identify instances of needless discovery and to limit the use of the various discovery devices accordingly. The question may be raised by one of the parties, typically on a motion for a protective order, or by the court on its own initiative. It is entirely appropriate to consider a limitation on the frequency of use of discovery at a discovery conference under Rule 26(f) or at any other pretrial conference authorized by these rules. In considering the discovery needs of a particular case, the court should consider the factors described in Rule 26(b)(1).

Subdivision (b); Discovery Scope and Limits. Rule 26(b)(1) has been amended to add a sentence to deal with the problem of over-discovery. The objective is to guard against redundant or disproportionate discovery by giving the court authority to reduce the amount of discovery that may be directed to matters that are otherwise proper subjects of inquiry. The new sentence is intended to encourage judges to be more aggressive in identifying and discouraging discovery overuse. The grounds mentioned in the amended rule for limiting discovery reflect the existing practice of many courts in issuing protective orders under Rule 26(c). See, e.g., *Carlson Cos. v. Sperry & Hutchinson Co.,* 374 F.Supp. 1080 (D.Minn.1974); *Dolgow v.*

Anderson, 53 F.R.D. 661 (E.D.N.Y.1971); *Mitchell v. American Tobacco Co.,* 33 F.R.D. 262 (M.D.Pa.1963); *Welty v. Clute,* 1 F.R.D. 446 (W.D.N.Y.1941). On the whole, however, district judges have been reluctant to limit the use of the discovery devices. See, *e.g., Apco Oil Co. v. Certified Transp., Inc.,* 46 F.R.D. 428 (W.D.Mo.1969). See generally 8 Wright & Miller, *Federal Practice and Procedure: Civil* §§ 2036, 2037, 2039, 2040 (1970).

The first element of the standard, Rule 26(b)(1)(i), is designed to minimize redundancy in discovery and encourage attorneys to be sensitive to the comparative costs of different methods of securing information. Subdivision (b)(1)(ii) also seeks to reduce repetitiveness and to oblige lawyers to think through their discovery activities in advance so that full utilization is made of each deposition, document request, or set of interrogatories. The elements of Rule 26(b)(1)(iii) address the problem of discovery that is disproportionate to the individual lawsuit as measured by such matters as its nature and complexity, the importance of the issues at stake in a case seeking damages, the limitations on a financially weak litigant to withstand extensive opposition to a discovery program or to respond to discovery requests, and the significance of the substantive issues, as measured in philosophic, social, or institutional terms. Thus the rule recognizes that many cases in public policy spheres, such as employment practices, free speech, and other matters, may have importance far beyond the monetary amount involved. The court must apply the standards in an even-handed manner that will prevent use of discovery to wage a war of attrition or as a device to coerce a party, whether financially weak or affluent.

The rule contemplates greater judicial involvement in the discovery process and thus acknowledges the reality that it cannot always operate on a self-regulating basis. See Connolly, Holleman & Kuhlman, *Judicial Controls and the Civil Litigative Process: Discovery* 77, Federal Judicial Center (1978). In an appropriate case the court could restrict the number of depositions, interrogatories, or the scope of a production request. But the court must be careful not to deprive a party of discovery that is reasonably necessary to afford a fair opportunity to develop and prepare the case.

The court may act on motion, or its own initiative. It is entirely appropriate to resort to the amended rule in conjunction with a discovery conference under Rule 26(f) or one of the other pretrial conferences authorized by the rules.

Subdivision (g); Signing of Discovery Requests, Responses, and Objections. Rule 26(g) imposes an affirmative duty to engage in pretrial discovery in a responsible manner that is consistent with the spirit and purposes of Rules 26 through 37. In addition, Rule 26(g) is designed to curb discovery abuse by explicitly encouraging the imposition of sanctions. The subdivision provides a deterrent to both excessive discovery and evasion by imposing a certification requirement that obliges each attorney to stop and think about the legitimacy of a discovery request, a response thereto, or an objection. The term "response" includes answers to interrogatories and to requests to admit as well as responses to production requests.

If primary responsibility for conducting discovery is to continue to rest with the litigants, they must be obliged to act responsibly and avoid abuse. With this in mind, Rule 26(g), which parallels the amendments to Rule 11, requires an attorney or unrepresented party to sign each discovery request, response, or objection. Motions relating to discovery are governed by Rule 11. However, since a discovery request, response, or objection usually deals with more specific subject matter than motions or papers, the elements that must be certified in connection with the former are spelled out more completely. The signature is a certification of the elements set forth in Rule 26(g).

Although the certification duty requires the lawyer to pause and consider the reasonableness of his request, response, or objection, it is not meant to discourage or restrict necessary and legitimate discovery. The rule simply requires that the attorney make a reasonable inquiry into the factual basis of his response, request, or objection.

The duty to make a "reasonable inquiry" is satisfied if the investigation undertaken by the attorney and the conclusions drawn therefrom are reasonable under the circumstances. It is an objective standard similar to the one imposed by Rule 11. See the Advisory Committee Note to Rule 11. See also *Kinee v. Abraham Lincoln Fed. Sav. & Loan Ass'n,* 365 F.Supp. 975 (E.D.Pa.1973). In making the inquiry, the attorney may rely on assertions by the client and on communications with other counsel in the case as long as that reliance is appropriate under the circumstances. Ultimately, what is reasonable is a matter for the court to decide on the totality of the circumstances.

Rule 26(g) does not require the signing attorney to certify the truthfulness of the client's factual responses to a discovery request. Rather, the signature certifies that the lawyer has made a reasonable effort to assure that the client has provided all the information and documents available to him that are responsive to the discovery demand. Thus, the lawyer's certification under Rule 26(g) should be distinguished from other signature requirements in the rules, such as those in Rules 30(e) and 33.

Nor does the rule require a party or an attorney to disclose privileged communications or work product in order to show that a discovery request, response, or objection is substantially justified. The provisions of Rule 26(c), including appropriate orders after *in camera* inspection by the court, remain available to protect a party claiming privilege or work product protection.

The signing requirement means that every discovery request, response, or objection should be grounded on a theory that is reasonable under the precedents or a good faith belief as to what should be the law. This standard is heavily dependent on the circumstances of each case. The certification speaks as of the time it is made. The duty to supplement discovery responses continues to be governed by Rule 26(e).

Concern about discovery abuse has led to widespread recognition that there is a need for more aggressive judicial control and supervision. *ACF Industries, Inc. v. EEOC,* 439 U.S. 1081 (1979) (certiorari denied) (Powell, J., dissenting). Sanctions to deter discovery abuse would be more effective if they were diligently applied "not merely to penalize those whose conduct may be deemed to warrant such a sanction, but to deter those who might be tempted to such conduct in the absence of such a deterrent." *National Hockey League v. Metropolitan Hockey Club,* 427 U.S. 639, 643 (1976). See also Note, *The Emerging Deterrence Orientation in the Imposition of Discovery Sanctions,* 91 Harv.L.Rev. 1033 (1978). Thus the premise of Rule 26(g) is that imposing sanctions on attorneys who fail to meet the rule's standards will significantly reduce abuse by imposing disadvantages therefor.

Because of the asserted reluctance to impose sanctions on attorneys who abuse the discovery rules, see Brazil, *Civil Discovery: Lawyers' Views of its Effectiveness, Principal Problems and Abuses,* American Bar Foundation (1980); Ellington, *A Study of Sanctions for Discovery Abuse,* Department of Justice (1979), Rule 26(g) makes explicit the authority judges now have to impose appropriate sanctions and requires them to use it. This authority derives from Rule 37, 28 U.S.C. § 1927, and the court's inherent power. See *Roadway Express, Inc. v. Piper,* 447 U.S. 752 (1980); *Martin v. Bell Helicopter Co.,* 85 F.R.D. 654, 661–62 (D.Col.1980); Note, *Sanctions Imposed by Courts on Attorneys Who Abuse the Judicial Process,* 44 U.Chi.L.Rev. 619 (1977). The new rule mandates that sanctions be imposed on attorneys who fail to meet the standards established in the first portion of Rule 26(g). The nature of the sanction is a matter of judicial discretion to be exercised in light of the particular circumstances. The court may take into account any failure by the party seeking sanctions to invoke protection under Rule 26(c) at an early stage in the litigation.

The sanctioning process must comport with due process requirements. The kind of notice and hearing required will depend on the facts of the case and the severity of the sanction being considered. To prevent the proliferation of the sanction procedure and to avoid multiple hearings, discovery in any sanction proceeding normally should be permitted only when it is clearly required by the interests of justice. In most cases the court will be aware of the circumstances and only a brief hearing should be necessary.

1987 Amendment

The amendments are technical. No substantive change is intended.

1993 Amendments

Subdivision (a). Through the addition of paragraphs (1)–(4), this subdivision imposes on parties a duty to disclose, without awaiting formal discovery requests, certain basic information that is needed in most cases to prepare for trial or make an informed decision about settlement. The rule requires all parties (1) early in the case to exchange information regarding potential witnesses, documentary evidence, damages, and insurance, (2) at an appropriate time during the discovery period to identify expert witnesses and provide a detailed written statement of the testimony that may be offered at trial through specially retained experts, and (3) as the trial date approaches to identify the particular evidence that may be offered at trial. The enumeration in Rule 26(a) of items to be disclosed does not prevent a court from requiring by order or local rule that the parties disclose additional information without a discovery request. Nor are parties precluded from using traditional discovery methods to obtain further information regarding these matters, as for example asking an expert during a deposition about testimony given in other litigation beyond the four-year period specified in Rule 26(a)(2)(B).

A major purpose of the revision is to accelerate the exchange of basic information about the case and to eliminate the paper work involved in requesting such information, and the rule should be applied in a manner to achieve those objectives. The concepts of imposing a duty of disclosure were set forth in Brazil, *The Adversary Character of Civil Discovery: A Critique and Proposals for Change*, 31 *Vand.L.Rev.* 1348 (1978), and Schwarzer, *The Federal Rules, the Adversary Process, and Discovery Reform*, 50 *U.Pitt.L.Rev. 703, 721–23 (1989)*.

The rule is based upon the experience of district courts that have required disclosure of some of this information through local rules, court-approved standard interrogatories, and standing orders. Most have required pretrial disclosure of the kind of information described in Rule 26(a)(3). Many have required written reports from experts containing information like that specified in Rule 26(a)(2)(B). While far more limited, the experience of the few state and federal courts that have required pre-discovery exchange of core information such as is contemplated in Rule 26(a)(1) indicates that savings in time and expense can be achieved, particularly if the litigants meet and discuss the issues in the case as a predicate for this exchange and if a judge supports the process, as by using the results to guide further proceedings in the case. Courts in Canada and the United Kingdom have for many years required disclosure of certain information without awaiting a request from an adversary.

Paragraph (1). As the functional equivalent of court-ordered interrogatories, this paragraph requires early disclosure, without need for any request, of four types of information that have been customarily secured early in litigation through formal discovery. The introductory clause permits the court, by local rule, to exempt all or particular types of cases from these disclosure requirement *[sic]* or to modify the nature of the information to be disclosed. It is expected that courts would, for example, exempt cases like Social Security reviews and government collection cases in which discovery would not be appropriate or would be unlikely. By order the court may eliminate or modify the disclosure requirements in a particular case, and similarly the parties, unless precluded by order or local rule, can stipulate to elimination or modification of the requirements for that case. The disclosure obligations specified in paragraph (1) will not be appropriate for all cases, and it is expected that changes in these obligations will be made by the court or parties when the circumstances warrant.

Authorization of these local variations is, in large measure, included in order to accommodate the Civil Justice Reform Act of 1990, which implicitly directs districts to experiment during the study period with differing procedures to reduce the time and expense of civil litigation. The civil justice delay and expense reduction plans adopted by the courts under the Act differ as to the type, form, and timing of disclosures required. Section 105(c)(1) of the Act calls for a report by the Judicial Conference to Congress by December 31, 1995, comparing experience in twenty of these courts; and section 105(c)(2)(B) contemplates that some changes in the Rules may then be needed. While these studies may indicate the desirability of further changes in Rule 26(a)(1), these changes probably could not become effective before December 1998 at the earliest. In the meantime, the present revision puts in place a series of disclosure obligations that, unless a court acts affirmatively to impose other requirements or indeed to reject all such requirements for the present, are designed to eliminate certain discovery, help focus the discovery that is needed, and facilitate preparation for trial or settlement.

Subparagraph (A) requires identification of all persons who, based on the investigation conducted thus far, are likely to have discoverable information relevant to the factual disputes between the parties. All persons with such information should be disclosed, whether or not their testimony will be supportive of the position of the disclosing party. As officers of the court, counsel are expected to disclose the identity of those persons who may be used by them as witnesses or who, if their potential testimony were known, might reasonably be expected to be deposed or called as a witness by any of the other parties. Indicating briefly the general topics on which such persons have information should not be burdensome, and will assist other parties in deciding which depositions will actually be needed.

Subparagraph (B) is included as a substitute for the inquiries routinely made about the existence and location of documents and other tangible things in the possession, custody, or control of the disclosing party. Although, unlike subdivision (a)(3)(C), an itemized listing of each exhibit is not required, the disclosure should describe and categorize, to the extent identified during the initial investigation, the nature and location of potentially relevant documents and records, including computerized data and other electronically-recorded information, sufficiently to enable opposing parties (1) to make an informed decision concerning which documents might need to be examined, at least initially, and (2) to frame their document requests in a manner likely to avoid squabbles resulting from the wording of the requests. As with potential witnesses, the requirement for disclosure of documents applies to all potentially relevant items then known to the party, whether or not supportive of its contentions in the case.

Unlike subparagraphs (C) and (D), subparagraph (B) does not require production of any documents. Of course, in cases involving few documents a disclosing party may prefer to provide copies of the documents rather than describe them, and the rule is written to afford this option to the disclosing party. If, as will be more typical, only the description is provided, the other parties are expected to obtain the documents desired by proceeding under Rule 34 or through informal requests. The disclosing party does not, by describing documents under subparagraph (B), waive its right to object to production on the basis of privilege or work product protection, or to assert that the documents are not sufficiently relevant to justify the burden or expense of production.

The initial disclosure requirements of subparagraphs (A) and (B) are limited to identification of potential evidence "relevant to disputed facts alleged with particularity in the pleadings." There is no need for a party to identify potential evidence with respect to allegations that are admitted. Broad, vague, and conclusory allegations sometimes tolerated in notice pleading—for example, the assertion that a product with many component parts is defective in some unspecified manner—should not impose upon responding parties the obligation at that point to search for and identify all persons possibly involved in, or all documents affecting, the design, manufacture, and assembly of the product. The greater the specificity and clarity of the allegations in the pleadings, the more complete should be the listing of potential witnesses and types of documentary evidence. Although paragraphs (1)(A) and (1)(B) by their terms refer to the factual disputes defined in the pleadings, the rule contemplates that these issues would be informally refined and clarified during the meeting of the parties under subdivision (f) and that the disclosure obligations would be adjusted in the light of these discussions. The disclosure requirements should, in short, be applied with common sense in light of the principles of Rule 1, keeping in mind the salutary purposes that the rule is intended to accomplish. The litigants should not indulge in gamesmanship with respect to the disclosure obligations.

Subparagraph (C) imposes a burden of disclosure that includes the functional equivalent of a standing Request for Production under Rule 34. A party claiming damages or other monetary relief must, in addition to disclosing the calculation of such damages, make available the supporting documents for inspection and copying as if a request for such materials had been made under Rule 34. This obligation applies only with respect to documents then reasonably available to it and not privileged or protected as work product. Likewise, a party would not be expected to provide a calculation of damages which, as in many patent infringement actions, depends on information in the possession of another party or person.

Subparagraph (D) replaces subdivision (b)(2) of Rule 26, and provides that liability insurance policies be made available for inspection and copying. The last two sentences of that subdivision have been omitted as unnecessary, not to signify any change of law. The disclosure of insurance information does not thereby render such information admissible in evidence. See Rule 411, Federal Rules of Evidence. Nor does subparagraph (D) require disclosure of applications for insurance, though in particular cases such information may be discoverable in accordance with revised subdivision (a)(5).

Unless the court directs a different time, the disclosures required by subdivision (a)(1) are to be made at or within 10 days after the meeting of the parties under subdivision (f). One of the purposes of this meeting is to refine the factual disputes with respect to which disclosures should be made under paragraphs (1)(A) and (1)(B), particularly if an answer has not been filed by a defendant, or, indeed, to afford the parties an opportunity to modify by stipulation the timing or scope of these obligations. The time of this meeting is generally left to the parties provided it is held at least 14 days before a scheduling conference is held or before a scheduling order is due under Rule 16(b). In cases in which no scheduling conference is held, this will mean that the meeting must ordinarily be held within 75 days after a defendant has first appeared in the case and hence that the initial disclosures would be due no later than 85 days after the first appearance of a defendant.

Before making its disclosures, a party has the obligation under subdivision (g)(1) to make a reasonable inquiry into the facts of the case. The rule does not demand an exhaustive investigation at this stage of the case, but one that is reasonable under the circumstances, focusing on the facts that are alleged with particularity in the pleadings. The type of investigation that can be expected at this point will vary based upon such factors as the number and complexity of the issues; the location, nature, number, and availability of potentially relevant witnesses and documents; the extent of past working relationships between the attorney and the client, particularly in handling related or similar litigation; and of course how long the party has to conduct an investigation, either before or after filing of the case. As provided in the last sentence of subdivision (a)(1), a party is not excused from the duty of disclosure merely because its investigation is incomplete. The party should make its initial disclosures based on the pleadings and the information then reasonably available to it. As its investigation continues and as the issues in the pleadings are clarified, it should supplement its disclosures as required by subdivision (e)(1). A party is not relieved from its obligation of disclosure merely because another party has not made its disclosures or has made an inadequate disclosure.

It will often be desirable, particularly if the claims made in the complaint are broadly stated, for the parties to have their Rule 26(f) meeting early in the case, perhaps before a defendant has answered the complaint or had time to conduct other than a cursory investigation. In such circumstances, in order to facilitate more meaningful and useful initial disclosures, they can and should stipulate to a period of more than 10 days after the meeting in which to make these disclosures, at least for defendants who had no advance notice of the potential litigation. A stipulation at an early meeting affording such a defendant at least 60 days after receiving the complaint in which to make its disclosures under subdivision (a)(1)—a period that is two weeks longer than the time formerly specified for responding to interrogatories served with a complaint—should be adequate and appropriate in most cases.

Paragraph (2). This paragraph imposes an additional duty to disclose information regarding expert testimony sufficiently in advance of trial that opposing parties have a reasonable opportunity to prepare for effective cross examination and perhaps arrange for expert testimony from other witnesses. Normally the court should prescribe a time for these disclosures in a scheduling order under Rule 16(b), and in most cases the party with the burden of proof on an issue should disclose its expert testimony on that issue before other parties are required to make their disclosures with respect to that issue. In the absence of such a direction, the disclosures are to be made by all parties at least 90 days before the trial date or the date by which the case is to be ready for trial, except that an additional 30 days is allowed (unless the court specifies another time) for disclosure of expert testimony to be used solely to contradict or rebut the testimony that may be presented by another party's expert. For a discussion of procedures that have been used to enhance the reliability of expert testimony, see M. Graham, *Expert Witness Testimony and the Federal Rules of Evidence: Insuring Adequate Assurance of Trustworthiness,* 1986 U.Ill.L.Rev. 90.

Paragraph (2)(B) requires that persons retained or specially employed to provide expert testimony, or whose duties as an employee of the party regularly involve the giving of expert testimony, must prepare a detailed and complete written report, stating the testimony the witness is expected to present during direct examination, together with the reasons therefor. The information disclosed under the former rule in answering interrogatories about the "substance" of expert testimony was frequently so sketchy and vague that it rarely dispensed with the need to depose the expert and often was even of little help in preparing for a deposition of the witness. Revised Rule 37(c)(1) provides an incentive for full disclosure; namely, that a party will not ordinarily be permitted to use on direct examination any expert testimony not so disclosed. Rule 26(a)(2)(B) does not preclude counsel from providing assistance to experts in preparing the reports, and indeed, with experts such as automobile mechanics, this assistance may be needed. Nevertheless, the report, which is intended to set forth the substance of the direct examination, should be written in a manner that reflects the testimony to be given by the witness and it must be signed by the witness.

The report is to disclose the data and other information considered by the expert and any exhibits or charts that summarize or support the expert's opinions. Given this obligation of disclosure, litigants should no longer be able to argue that materials furnished to their experts to be used in forming their opinions— whether or not ultimately relied upon by the expert—are privileged or otherwise protected from disclosure when such persons are testifying or being deposed.

Revised subdivision (b)(4)(A) authorizes the deposition of expert witnesses. Since depositions of experts required to prepare a written report may be taken only after the report has been served, the length of the deposition of such experts should be reduced, and in many cases the report may eliminate the need for a deposition. Revised subdivision (e)(1) requires disclosure of any material changes made in the opinions of an expert from whom a report is required, whether the changes are in the written report or in testimony given at a deposition.

For convenience, this rule and revised Rule 30 continue to use the term "expert" to refer to those persons who will testify under Rule 702 of the Federal Rules of Evidence with respect to scientific, technical, and other specialized matters. The requirement of a written report in paragraph (2)(B), however, applies only to those experts who are retained or specially employed to provide such testimony in the case or whose duties as an employee of a party regularly involve the giving of such testimony. A treating physician, for example, can be deposed or called to testify at trial without any requirement for a written report. By local rule, order, or written stipulation, the requirement of a written report may be waived for particular experts or imposed upon additional persons who will provide opinions under Rule 702.

Paragraph (3). This paragraph imposes an additional duty to disclose, without any request, information customarily needed in final preparation for trial. These disclosures are to be made in accordance with schedules adopted by the court under Rule 16(b) or by special order. If no such schedule is directed by the court, the disclosures are to be made at least 30 days before commencement of the trial. By its terms, rule 26(a)(3) does not require disclosure of evidence to be used solely for impeachment purposes; however, disclosure of such evidence—as well as other items relating to conduct of trial—may be required by local rule or a pretrial order.

Subparagraph (A) requires the parties to designate the persons whose testimony they may present as substantive evidence at trial, whether in person or by deposition. Those who will probably be called as witnesses should be listed separately from those who are not likely to be called but who are being listed in order to preserve the right to do so if needed because of developments during trial. Revised Rule 37(c)(1) provides that only persons so listed may be used at trial to present substantive evidence. This restriction does not apply unless the omission was "without substantial justification" and hence would not bar an unlisted witness if the need for such testimony is based upon developments during trial that could not reasonably have been anticipated—*e.g.,* a change of testimony.

Listing a witness does not obligate the party to secure the attendance of the person at trial, but should preclude the party from objecting if the person is called to testify by another party who did not list the person as a witness.

Subparagraph (B) requires the party to indicate which of these potential witnesses will be presented by deposition at trial. A party expecting to use at trial a deposition not recorded by stenographic means is required by revised Rule 32 to provide the court with a transcript of the pertinent portions of such depositions. This rule requires that copies of the transcript of a nonstenographic deposition be provided to other parties in advance of trial for verification, an obvious concern since counsel often utilize their own personnel to prepare transcripts from audio or video tapes. By order or local rule, the court may require that parties designate the particular portions of stenographic depositions to be used at trial.

Subparagraph (C) requires disclosure of exhibits, including summaries (whether to be offered in lieu of other documentary evidence or to be used as an aid in understanding such evidence), that may be offered as substantive evidence. The rule requires a separate listing of each such exhibit, though it should permit voluminous items of a similar or standardized character to be described by meaningful categories. For example, unless the court has otherwise directed, a series of vouchers might be shown collectively as a single exhibit with their starting and ending dates. As with witnesses, the exhibits that will probably be offered are to be listed separately from those which are unlikely to be offered but which are listed in order to preserve the right to do so if needed because of developments during trial. Under revised Rule 37(c)(1) the court can permit use of unlisted documents the need for which could not reasonably have been anticipated in advance of trial.

Upon receipt of these final pretrial disclosures, other parties have 14 days (unless a different time is specified by the court) to disclose any objections they wish to preserve to the usability of the deposition testimony or to the admissibility of the documentary evidence (other than under Rules 402 and 403 of the Federal Rules of Evidence). Similar provisions have become commonplace either in pretrial orders or by local rules, and significantly expedite the presentation of evidence at trial, as well as eliminate the need to have available witnesses to provide "foundation" testimony for most items of documentary evidence. The listing of a potential objection does not constitute the making of that objection or require the court to rule on the objection; rather, it preserves the right of the party to make the objection when and as appropriate during trial. The court may, however, elect to treat the listing as a motion "in limine" and rule upon the objections in advance of trial to the extent appropriate.

The time specified in the rule for the final pretrial disclosures is relatively close to the trial date. The objective is to eliminate the time and expense in making these disclosures of evidence and objections in those cases that settle shortly before trial, while affording a reasonable time for final preparation for trial in those cases that do not settle. In many cases, it will be desirable for the court in a scheduling or pretrial order to set an earlier time for disclosures of evidence and provide more time for disclosing potential objections.

Paragraph (4). This paragraph prescribes the form of disclosures. A signed written statement is required, reminding the parties and counsel of the solemnity of the obligations imposed; and the signature on the initial or pretrial disclosure is a certification under subdivision (g)(1) that it is complete and correct as of the time when made. Consistent with Rule 5(d), these disclosures are to be filed with the court unless otherwise directed. It is anticipated that many courts will direct that expert reports required under paragraph (2)(B) not be filed until needed in connection with a motion or for trial.

Paragraph (5). This paragraph is revised to take note of the availability of revised Rule 45 for inspection from non-parties of documents and premises without the need for a deposition.

Subdivision (b). This subdivision is revised in several respects. First, former paragraph (1) is subdivided into two paragraphs for ease of reference and to avoid renumbering of paragraphs (3) and (4). Textual changes are then made in new paragraph (2) to enable the court to keep tighter rein on the extent of discovery. The information explosion of recent decades has greatly increased both the potential cost of wide-ranging discovery and the potential for discovery to be used as an instrument for delay or oppression. Amendments to Rules 30, 31, and 33 place presumptive limits on the number of depositions and interrogatories, subject to leave of court to pursue additional discovery. The revisions in Rule 26(b)(2) are intended to provide the court with broader discretion to impose additional restrictions on the scope and extent of discovery and to authorize courts that develop case tracking systems based on the complexity of cases to increase or decrease by local rule the presumptive number of depositions and interrogatories allowed in particular types or classifications of cases. The revision also dispels any doubt as to the power of the court to impose limitations on the length of depositions under Rule 30 or on the number of requests for admission under Rule 36.

Second, former paragraph (2), relating to insurance, has been relocated as part of the required initial disclosures under subdivision (a)(1)(D), and revised to provide for disclosure of the policy itself.

Third, paragraph (4)(A) is revised to provide that experts who are expected to be witnesses will be subject to deposition prior to trial, conforming the norm stated in the rule to the actual practice followed in most courts, in which depositions of experts have become standard. Concerns regarding the expense of such depositions should be mitigated by the fact that the expert's fees for the deposition will ordinarily be borne by the party taking the deposition. The requirement under subdivision (a)(2)(B) of a complete and detailed report of the expected testimony of certain forensic experts may, moreover, eliminate the need for some such depositions or at least reduce the length of the depositions. Accordingly, the deposition of an expert required by subdivision (a)(2)(B) to provide a written report may be taken only after the report has been served.

Paragraph (4)(C), bearing on compensation of experts, is revised to take account of the changes in paragraph (4)(A).

Paragraph (5) is a new provision. A party must notify other parties if it is withholding materials otherwise subject to disclosure under the rule or pursuant to a discovery request because it is asserting a claim of privilege or work product protection. To withhold materials without such notice is contrary to the rule, subjects the party to sanctions under Rule 37(b)(2), and may be viewed as a waiver of the privilege or protection.

The party must also provide sufficient information to enable other parties to evaluate the applicability of the claimed privilege or protection. Although the person from whom the discovery is sought decides whether to claim a privilege or protection, the court ultimately decides whether, if this claim is challenged, the privilege or protection applies. Providing information pertinent to the applicability of the privilege or protection should reduce the need for in camera examination of the documents.

The rule does not attempt to define for each case what information must be provided when a party asserts a claim of privilege or work product protection. Details concerning time, persons, general subject matter, etc., may be appropriate if only a few items are withheld, but may be unduly burdensome when voluminous documents are claimed to be privileged or protected, particularly if the items can be described by categories. A party can seek relief through a protective order under subdivision (c) if compliance with the requirement for providing this information would be an unreasonable burden. In rare circumstances some of the pertinent information affecting applicability of the claim, such as the identity of the client, may itself be privileged; the rule provides that such information need not be disclosed.

The obligation to provide pertinent information concerning withheld privileged materials applies only to items "otherwise discoverable." If a broad discovery request is made—for example, for all documents of a particular type during a twenty year period—and the responding party believes in good faith that production of documents for more than the past three years would be unduly burdensome, it should make its objection to the breadth of the request and, with respect to the documents generated in that three year period, produce the unprivileged documents and describe those withheld under the claim of privilege. If the court later rules that documents for a seven year period are properly discoverable, the documents for the additional four years should then be either produced (if not privileged) or described (if claimed to be privileged).

Subdivision (c). The revision requires that before filing a motion for a protective order the movant must confer—either in person or by telephone—with the other affected parties in a good faith effort to resolve the discovery dispute without the need for court intervention. If the movant is unable to get opposing parties even to discuss the matter, the efforts in attempting to arrange such a conference should be indicated in the certificate.

Subdivision (d). This subdivision is revised to provide that formal discovery—as distinguished from interviews of potential witnesses and other informal discovery—not commence until the parties have met and conferred as required by subdivision (f). Discovery can begin earlier if authorized under Rule 30(a)(2)(C) (deposition of person about to leave the country) or by local rule, order, or stipulation. This will be appropriate in some cases, such as those involving requests for a preliminary injunction or motions challenging personal jurisdiction. If a local rule exempts any types of cases in which discovery may be needed from the requirement of a meeting under Rule 26(f), it should specify when discovery may commence in those cases.

The meeting of counsel is to take place as soon as practicable and in any event at least 14 days before the date of the scheduling conference under Rule 16(b) or the date a scheduling order is due under Rule 16(b). The court can assure that discovery is not unduly delayed either by entering a special order or by setting the case for a scheduling conference.

Subdivision (e). This subdivision is revised to provide that the requirement for supplementation applies to all disclosures required by subdivisions (a)(1)–(3). Like the former rule, the duty, while imposed on a "party," applies whether the corrective information is learned by the client or by the attorney. Supplementations need not be made as each new item of information is learned but should be made at appropriate intervals during the discovery period, and with special promptness as the trial date approaches. It may be useful for the scheduling order to specify the time or times when supplementations should be made.

The revision also clarifies that the obligation to supplement responses to formal discovery requests applies to interrogatories, requests for production, and requests for admissions, but not ordinarily to deposition testimony. However, with respect to experts from whom a written report is required under subdivision (a)(2)(B), changes in the opinions expressed by the expert whether in the report or at a subsequent deposition are subject to a duty of supplemental disclosure under subdivision (e)(1).

The obligation to supplement disclosures and discovery responses applies whenever a party learns that its prior disclosures or responses are in some material respect incomplete or incorrect. There is, however, no obligation to provide supplemental or corrective information that has been otherwise made known to the parties in writing or during the discovery process, as when a witness not previously disclosed is identified during the taking of a deposition or when an expert during a deposition corrects information contained in an earlier report.

Subdivision (f). This subdivision was added in 1980 to provide a party threatened with abusive discovery with a special means for obtaining judicial intervention other than through discrete motions under Rules 26(c) and 37(a). The amendment envisioned a two-step process: first, the parties would attempt to frame a mutually agreeable plan; second, the court would hold a "discovery conference" and then enter an order establishing a schedule and limitations for the conduct of discovery. It was contemplated that the procedure, an elective one triggered on request of a party, would be used in special cases rather than as a routine matter. As expected, the device has been used only sparingly in most courts, and judicial controls over the discovery process have ordinarily been imposed through scheduling orders under Rule 16(b) or through rulings on discovery motions.

The provisions relating to a conference with the court are removed from subdivision (f). This change does not signal any lessening of the importance of judicial supervision. Indeed, there is a greater need for early judicial involvement to consider the scope and timing of the disclosure requirements of Rule 26(a) and the presumptive limits on discovery imposed under these rules or by local rules. Rather, the change is made because the provisions addressing the use of conferences with the court to control discovery are more properly included in Rule 16, which is being revised to highlight the court's powers regarding the discovery process.

The desirability of some judicial control of discovery can hardly be doubted. Rule 16, as revised, requires that the court set a time for completion of discovery and authorizes various other orders affecting the scope, timing, and extent of discovery and disclosures. Before entering such orders, the court should consider the views of the parties, preferably by means of a conference, but at the least through written submissions. Moreover, it is desirable that the parties' proposals regarding discovery be developed through a process where they meet in person, informally explore the nature and basis of the issues, and discuss how discovery can be conducted most efficiently and economically.

As noted above, former subdivision (f) envisioned the development of proposed discovery plans as an optional procedure to be used in relatively few cases. The revised rule directs that in all cases not exempted by local rule or special order the litigants must meet in person and plan for discovery. Following this meeting, the parties submit to the court their proposals for a discovery plan and can begin formal discovery. Their report will assist the court in seeing that the timing and scope of disclosures under revised Rule 26(a) and the limitations on the extent of discovery under these rules and local rules are tailored to the circumstances of the particular case.

To assure that the court has the litigants' proposals before deciding on a scheduling order and that the commencement of discovery is not delayed unduly, the rule provides that the meeting of the parties take place as soon as practicable and in any event at least 14 days before a scheduling conference is held or before a scheduling order is due under Rule 16(b). (Rule 16(b) requires that a scheduling order be entered within 90 days after the first appearance of a defendant or, if earlier, within 120 days after the complaint has been served on any defendant.) The obligation to participate in the planning process is imposed on all parties that have appeared in the case, including defendants who, because of a pending Rule 12 motion, may not have yet filed an answer in the case. Each such party should attend the meeting, either through one of its attorneys or in person if unrepresented. If more parties are joined or appear after the initial meeting, an additional meeting may be desirable.

Subdivision (f) describes certain matters that should be accomplished at the meeting and included in the proposed discovery plan. This listing does not exclude consideration of other subjects, such as the time when any dispositive motions should be filed and when the case should be ready for trial.

The parties are directed under subdivision (a)(1) to make the disclosures required by that subdivision at or within 10 days after this meeting. In many cases the parties should use the meeting to exchange, discuss, and clarify their respective disclosures. In other cases, it may be more useful if the disclosures are delayed until after the parties have discussed at the meeting the claims and defenses in order to define the issues with respect to which the initial disclosures should be made. As discussed in the Notes to subdivision (a)(1), the parties may also need to consider whether a stipulation extending this 10-day period would be appropriate, as when a defendant would otherwise have less than 60 days after being served in which to make its initial disclosure. The parties should also discuss at the meeting what additional information, although not subject to the disclosure requirements, can be made available informally without the necessity for formal discovery requests.

The report is to be submitted to the court within 10 days after the meeting and should not be difficult to prepare. In most cases counsel should be able to agree that one of them will be responsible for its preparation and submission to the court. Form 35 has been added in the Appendix to the Rules, both to illustrate the type of report that is contemplated and to serve as a checklist for the meeting.

The litigants are expected to attempt in good faith to agree on the contents of the proposed discovery plan. If they cannot agree on all aspects of the plan, their report to the court should indicate the competing proposals of the parties on those items, as well as the matters on which they agree. Unfortunately, there may be cases in which, because of disagreements about time or place or for other reasons, the meeting is not attended by all parties or, indeed, no meeting takes place. In such situations, the report—or reports—should describe the circumstances and the court may need to consider sanctions under Rule 37(g).

By local rule or special order, the court can exempt particular cases or types of cases from the meet-and-confer requirement of subdivision (f). In general this should include any types of cases which are exempted by local rule from the requirement for a scheduling order under Rule 16(b), such as cases in which there will be no discovery (*e.g.,* bankruptcy appeals and reviews of social security determinations). In addition, the court may want to exempt cases in which discovery is rarely needed (*e.g.,* government collection cases and proceedings to enforce administrative summonses) or in which a meeting of the parties might be impracticable (*e.g.,* actions by unrepresented prisoners). Note that if a court exempts from the requirements for a meeting any types of cases in which discovery may be needed, it should indicate when discovery may commence in those cases.

Subdivision (g). Paragraph (1) is added to require signatures on disclosures, a requirement that parallels the provisions of paragraph (2) with respect to discovery requests, responses, and objections. The provisions of paragraph (3) have been modified to be consistent with Rules 37(a)(4) and 37(c)(1); in combination, these rules establish sanctions for violation of the rules regarding disclosures and discovery matters. Amended Rule 11 no longer applies to such violations.

2000 Amendment

Purposes of amendments. The Rule 26(a)(1) initial disclosure provisions are amended to establish a nationally uniform practice. The scope of the disclosure obligation is narrowed to cover only information that the disclosing party may use to support its position. In addition, the rule exempts specified categories of proceedings from initial disclosure, and permits a party who contends that disclosure is not appropriate in the circumstances of the case to present its objections to the court, which must then determine whether disclosure should be made. Related changes are made in Rules 26(d) and (f).

The initial disclosure requirements added by the 1993 amendments permitted local rules directing that disclosure would not be required or altering its operation. The inclusion of the "opt out" provision reflected the strong opposition to initial disclosure felt in some districts, and permitted experimentation with differing disclosure rules in those districts that were favorable to disclosure. The local option also recognized that—partly in response to the first publication in 1991 of a proposed disclosure rule—many districts had adopted a variety of disclosure programs under the aegis of the Civil Justice Reform Act. It was hoped that developing experience under a variety of disclosure systems would support eventual refinement of a uniform national disclosure practice. In addition, there was hope that local experience could identify categories of actions in which disclosure is not useful.

A striking array of local regimes in fact emerged for disclosure and related features introduced in 1993. *See* D. Stienstra, *Implementation of Disclosure in United States District Courts, With Specific Attention to Courts' Responses to Selected Amendments to Federal Rule of Civil Procedure 26* (Federal Judicial Center, March 30, 1998) (describing and categorizing local regimes). In its final report to Congress on the CJRA experience, the Judicial Conference recommended reexamination of the need for national uniformity, particularly in regard to initial disclosure. Judicial Conference, *Alternative Proposals for Reduction of Cost and Delay: Assessment of Principles, Guidelines and Techniques,* 175 F.R.D. 62, 98 (1997).

At the Committee's request, the Federal Judicial Center undertook a survey in 1997 to develop information on current disclosure and discovery practices. *See* T. Willging, J. Shapard, D. Stienstra & D. Miletich, *Discovery and Disclosure Practice, Problems, and Proposals for Change* (Federal Judicial Center,

1997). In addition, the Committee convened two conferences on discovery involving lawyers from around the country and received reports and recommendations on possible discovery amendments from a number of bar groups. Papers and other proceedings from the second conference are published in 39 Boston Col. L. Rev. 517–840 (1998).

The Committee has discerned widespread support for national uniformity. Many lawyers have experienced difficulty in coping with divergent disclosure and other practices as they move from one district to another. Lawyers surveyed by the Federal Judicial Center ranked adoption of a uniform national disclosure rule second among proposed rule changes (behind increased availability of judges to resolve discovery disputes) as a means to reduce litigation expenses without interfering with fair outcomes. *Discovery and Disclosure Practice, supra*, at 44–45. National uniformity is also a central purpose of the Rules Enabling Act of 1934, as amended, 28 U.S.C. §§ 2072–2077.

These amendments restore national uniformity to disclosure practice. Uniformity is also restored to other aspects of discovery by deleting most of the provisions authorizing local rules that vary the number of permitted discovery events or the length of depositions. Local rule options are also deleted from Rules 26(d) and (f).

Subdivision (a)(1). The amendments remove the authority to alter or opt out of the national disclosure requirements by local rule, invalidating not only formal local rules but also informal "standing" orders of an individual judge or court that purport to create exemptions from—or limit or expand—the disclosure provided under the national rule. *See* Rule 83. Case-specific orders remain proper, however, and are expressly required if a party objects that initial disclosure is not appropriate in the circumstances of the action. Specified categories of proceedings are excluded from initial disclosure under subdivision (a)(1)(E). In addition, the parties can stipulate to forgo disclosure, as was true before. But even in a case excluded by subdivision (a)(1)(E) or in which the parties stipulate to bypass disclosure, the court can order exchange of similar information in managing the action under Rule 16.

The initial disclosure obligation of subdivisions (a)(1)(A) and (B) has been narrowed to identification of witnesses and documents that the disclosing party may use to support its claims or defenses. "Use" includes any use at a pretrial conference, to support a motion, or at trial. The disclosure obligation is also triggered by intended use in discovery, apart from use to respond to a discovery request; use of a document to question a witness during a deposition is a common example. The disclosure obligation attaches both to witnesses and documents a party intends to use and also to witnesses and to documents the party intends to use if— in the language of Rule 26(a)(3)—"the need arises."

A party is no longer obligated to disclose witnesses or documents, whether favorable or unfavorable, that it does not intend to use. The obligation to disclose information the party may use connects directly to the exclusion sanction of Rule 37(c)(1). Because the disclosure obligation is limited to material that the party may use, it is no longer tied to particularized allegations in the pleadings. Subdivision (e)(1), which is unchanged, requires supplementation if information later acquired would have been subject to the disclosure requirement. As case preparation continues, a party must supplement its disclosures when it determines that it may use a witness or document that it did not previously intend to use.

The disclosure obligation applies to "claims and defenses," and therefore requires a party to disclose information it may use to support its denial or rebuttal of the allegations, claim, or defense of another party. It thereby bolsters the requirements of Rule 11(b)(4), which authorizes denials "warranted on the evidence," and disclosure should include the identity of any witness or document that the disclosing party may use to support such denials.

Subdivision (a)(3) presently excuses pretrial disclosure of information solely for impeachment. Impeachment information is similarly excluded from the initial disclosure requirement.

Subdivisions (a)(1)(C) and (D) are not changed. Should a case be exempted from initial disclosure by Rule 26(a)(1)(E) or by agreement or order, the insurance information described by subparagraph (D) should be subject to discovery, as it would have been under the principles of former Rule 26(b)(2), which was added in 1970 and deleted in 1993 as redundant in light of the new initial disclosure obligation.

New subdivision (a)(1)(E) excludes eight specified categories of proceedings from initial disclosure. The objective of this listing is to identify cases in which there is likely to be little or no discovery, or in which initial disclosure appears unlikely to contribute to the effective development of the case. The list was developed after a review of the categories excluded by local rules in various districts from the operation of Rule 16(b) and the conference requirements of subdivision (f). Subdivision (a)(1)(E) refers to categories of "proceedings" rather than categories of "actions" because some might not properly be labeled "actions." Case designations made by the parties or the clerk's office at the time of filing do not control application of the exemptions. The descriptions in the rule are generic and are intended to be administered by the parties— and, when needed, the courts—with the flexibility needed to adapt to gradual evolution in the types of proceedings that fall within these general categories. The exclusion of an action for review on an administrative record, for example, is intended to reach a proceeding that is framed as an "appeal" based solely on an administrative record. The exclusion should not apply to a proceeding in a form that commonly permits admission of new evidence to supplement the record. Item (vii), excluding a proceeding ancillary to proceedings in other courts, does not refer to bankruptcy proceedings; application of the Civil Rules to bankruptcy proceedings is determined by the Bankruptcy Rules.

Subdivision (a)(1)(E) is likely to exempt a substantial proportion of the cases in most districts from the initial disclosure requirement. Based on 1996 and 1997 case filing statistics, Federal Judicial Center staff estimate that, nationwide, these categories total approximately one-third of all civil filings.

The categories of proceedings listed in subdivision (a)(1)(E) are also exempted from the subdivision (f) conference requirement and from the subdivision (d) moratorium on discovery. Although there is no restriction on commencement of discovery in these cases, it is not expected that this opportunity will often lead to abuse since there is likely to be little or no discovery in most such cases. Should a defendant need more time to respond to discovery requests filed at the beginning of an exempted action, it can seek relief by motion under Rule 26(c) if the plaintiff is unwilling to defer the due date by agreement.

Subdivision (a)(1)(E)'s enumeration of exempt categories is exclusive. Although a case-specific order can alter or excuse initial disclosure, local rules or "standing" orders that purport to create general exemptions are invalid. *See* Rule 83.

The time for initial disclosure is extended to 14 days after the subdivision (f) conference unless the court orders otherwise. This change is integrated with corresponding changes requiring that the subdivision (f) conference be held 21 days before the Rule 16(b) scheduling conference or scheduling order, and that the report on the subdivision (f) conference be submitted to the court 14 days after the meeting. These changes provide a more orderly opportunity for the parties to review the disclosures, and for the court to consider the report. In many instances, the subdivision (f) conference and the effective preparation of the case would benefit from disclosure before the conference, and earlier disclosure is encouraged.

The presumptive disclosure date does not apply if a party objects to initial disclosure during the subdivision (f) conference and states its objection in the subdivision (f) discovery plan. The right to object to initial disclosure is not intended to afford parties an opportunity to "opt out" of disclosure unilaterally. It does provide an opportunity for an objecting party to present to the court its position that disclosure would be "inappropriate in the circumstances of the action." Making the objection permits the objecting party to present the question to the judge before any party is required to make disclosure. The court must then rule on the objection and determine what disclosures—if any—should be made. Ordinarily, this determination would be included in the Rule 16(b) scheduling order, but the court could handle the matter in a different fashion. Even when circumstances warrant suspending some disclosure obligations, others—such as the damages and insurance information called for by subdivisions (a)(1)(C) and (D)—may continue to be appropriate.

The presumptive disclosure date is also inapplicable to a party who is "first served or otherwise joined" after the subdivision (f) conference. This phrase refers to the date of service of a claim on a party in a defensive posture (such as a defendant or third-party defendant), and the date of joinder of a party added as a claimant or an intervenor. Absent court order or stipulation, a new party has 30 days in which to make its initial disclosures. But it is expected that later-added parties will ordinarily be treated the same as the original parties when the original parties have stipulated to forgo initial disclosure, or the court has ordered disclosure in a modified form.

Subdivision (a)(3). The amendment to Rule 5(d) forbids filing disclosures under subdivisions (a)(1) and (a)(2) until they are used in the proceeding, and this change is reflected in an amendment to subdivision (a)(4). Disclosures under subdivision (a)(3), however, may be important to the court in connection with the final pretrial conference or otherwise in preparing for trial. The requirement that objections to certain matters be filed points up the court's need to be provided with these materials. Accordingly, the requirement that subdivision (a)(3) materials be filed has been moved from subdivision (a)(4) to subdivision (a)(3), and it has also been made clear that they—and any objections—should be filed "promptly."

Subdivision (a)(4). The filing requirement has been removed from this subdivision. Rule 5(d) has been amended to provide that disclosures under subdivisions (a)(1) and (a)(2) must not be filed until used in the proceeding. Subdivision (a)(3) has been amended to require that the disclosures it directs, and objections to them, be filed promptly. Subdivision (a)(4) continues to require that all disclosures under subdivisions (a)(1), (a)(2), and (a)(3) be in writing, signed, and served.

"Shall" is replaced by "must" under the program to conform amended rules to current style conventions when there is no ambiguity.

Gap Report

The Advisory Committee recommends that the amendments to Rules 26(a)(1)(A) and (B) be changed so that initial disclosure applies to information the disclosing party "may use to support" its claims or defenses. It also recommends changes in the Committee Note to explain that disclosure requirement. In addition, it recommends inclusion in the Note of further explanatory matter regarding the exclusion from initial disclosure provided in new Rule 26(a)(1)(E) for actions for review on an administrative record and the impact of these exclusions on bankruptcy proceedings. Minor wording improvements in the Note are also proposed.

Subdivision (b)(1). In 1978, the Committee published for comment a proposed amendment, suggested by the Section of Litigation of the American Bar Association, to refine the scope of discovery by deleting the "subject matter" language. This proposal was withdrawn, and the Committee has since then made other changes in the discovery rules to address concerns about overbroad discovery. Concerns about costs and delay of discovery have persisted nonetheless, and other bar groups have repeatedly renewed similar proposals for amendment to this subdivision to delete the "subject matter" language. Nearly one-third of the lawyers surveyed in 1997 by the Federal Judicial Center endorsed narrowing the scope of discovery as a means of reducing litigation expense without interfering with fair case resolutions. *Discovery and Disclosure Practice, supra,* at 44–45 (1997). The Committee has heard that in some instances, particularly cases involving large quantities of discovery, parties seek to justify discovery requests that sweep far beyond the claims and defenses of the parties on the ground that they nevertheless have a bearing on the "subject matter" involved in the action.

The amendments proposed for subdivision (b)(1) include one element of these earlier proposals but also differ from these proposals in significant ways. The similarity is that the amendments describe the scope of party-controlled discovery in terms of matter relevant to the claim or defense of any party. The court, however, retains authority to order discovery of any matter relevant to the subject matter involved in the action for good cause. The amendment is designed to involve the court more actively in regulating the breadth of sweeping or contentious discovery. The Committee has been informed repeatedly by lawyers that involvement of the court in managing discovery is an important method of controlling problems of inappropriately broad discovery. Increasing the availability of judicial officers to resolve discovery disputes and increasing court management of discovery were both strongly endorsed by the attorneys surveyed by the Federal Judicial Center. *See Discovery and Disclosure Practice, supra,* at 44. Under the amended provisions, if there is an objection that discovery goes beyond material relevant to the parties' claims or defenses, the court would become involved to determine whether the discovery is relevant to the claims or defenses and, if not, whether good cause exists for authorizing it so long as it is relevant to the subject matter of the action. The good-cause standard warranting broader discovery is meant to be flexible.

The Committee intends that the parties and the court focus on the actual claims and defenses involved in the action. The dividing line between information relevant to the claims and defenses and that relevant only to the subject matter of the action cannot be defined with precision. A variety of types of information not directly pertinent to the incident in suit could be relevant to the claims or defenses raised in a given action. For example, other incidents of the same type, or involving the same product, could be properly discoverable under the revised standard. Information about organizational arrangements or filing systems of a party could be discoverable if likely to yield or lead to the discovery of admissible information. Similarly, information that could be used to impeach a likely witness, although not otherwise relevant to the claims or defenses, might be properly discoverable. In each instance, the determination whether such information is discoverable because it is relevant to the claims or defenses depends on the circumstances of the pending action.

The rule change signals to the court that it has the authority to confine discovery to the claims and defenses asserted in the pleadings, and signals to the parties that they have no entitlement to discovery to develop new claims or defenses that are not already identified in the pleadings. In general, it is hoped that reasonable lawyers can cooperate to manage discovery without the need for judicial intervention. When judicial intervention is invoked, the actual scope of discovery should be determined according to the reasonable needs of the action. The court may permit broader discovery in a particular case depending on the circumstances of the case, the nature of the claims and defenses, and the scope of the discovery requested.

The amendments also modify the provision regarding discovery of information not admissible in evidence. As added in 1946, this sentence was designed to make clear that otherwise relevant material could not be withheld because it was hearsay or otherwise inadmissible. The Committee was concerned that the "reasonably calculated to lead to the discovery of admissible evidence" standard set forth in this sentence might swallow any other limitation on the scope of discovery. Accordingly, this sentence has been amended to clarify that information must be relevant to be discoverable, even though inadmissible, and that discovery of such material is permitted if reasonably calculated to lead to the discovery of admissible evidence. As used here, "relevant" means within the scope of discovery as defined in this subdivision, and it would include information relevant to the subject matter involved in the action if the court has ordered discovery to that limit based on a showing of good cause.

Finally, a sentence has been added calling attention to the limitations of subdivision (b)(2)(i), (ii), and (iii). These limitations apply to discovery that is otherwise within the scope of subdivision (b)(1). The Committee has been told repeatedly that courts have not implemented these limitations with the vigor that was contemplated. *See 8 Federal Practice & Procedure* § 2008.1 at 121. This otherwise redundant cross-reference has been added to emphasize the need for active judicial use of subdivision (b)(2) to control excessive discovery. *Cf. Crawford-El v. Britton*, 118 S. Ct. 1584, 1597 (1998) (quoting Rule 26(b)(2)(iii) and stating that "Rule 26 vests the trial judge with broad discretion to tailor discovery narrowly").

Gap Report

The Advisory Committee recommends changing the rule to authorize the court to expand discovery to any "matter"—not "information"—relevant to the subject matter involved in the action. In addition, it recommends additional clarifying material in the Committee Note about the impact of the change on some commonly disputed discovery topics, the relationship between cost-bearing under Rule 26(b)(2) and expansion of the scope of discovery on a showing of good cause, and the meaning of "relevant" in the revision to the last sentence of current subdivision (b)(1). In addition, some minor clarifications of language changes have been proposed for the Committee Note.

Subdivision (b)(2). Rules 30, 31, and 33 establish presumptive national limits on the numbers of depositions and interrogatories. New Rule 30(d)(2) establishes a presumptive limit on the length of depositions. Subdivision (b)(2) is amended to remove the previous permission for local rules that establish different presumptive limits on these discovery activities. There is no reason to believe that unique circumstances justify varying these nationally-applicable presumptive limits in certain districts. The limits can be modified by court order or agreement in an individual action, but "standing" orders imposing different presumptive limits are not authorized. Because there is no national rule limiting the number of Rule 36 requests for admissions, the rule continues to authorize local rules that impose numerical limits on them. This change is not intended to interfere with differentiated case management in districts that use this technique by case-specific order as part of their Rule 16 process.

Subdivision (d). The amendments remove the prior authority to exempt cases by local rule from the moratorium on discovery before the subdivision (f) conference, but the categories of proceedings exempted from initial disclosure under subdivision (a)(1)(E) are excluded from subdivision (d). The parties may agree to disregard the moratorium where it applies, and the court may so order in a case, but "standing" orders altering the moratorium are not authorized.

Subdivision (f). As in subdivision (d), the amendments remove the prior authority to exempt cases by local rule from the conference requirement. The Committee has been informed that the addition of the conference was one of the most successful changes made in the 1993 amendments, and it therefore has determined to apply the conference requirement nationwide. The categories of proceedings exempted from initial disclosure under subdivision (a)(1)(E) are exempted from the conference requirement for the reasons that warrant exclusion from initial disclosure. The court may order that the conference need not occur in a case where otherwise required, or that it occur in a case otherwise exempted by subdivision (a)(1)(E). "Standing" orders altering the conference requirement for categories of cases are not authorized.

The rule is amended to require only a "conference" of the parties, rather than a "meeting." There are important benefits to face-to-face discussion of the topics to be covered in the conference, and those benefits may be lost if other means of conferring were routinely used when face-to-face meetings would not impose burdens. Nevertheless, geographic conditions in some districts may exact costs far out of proportion to these benefits. The amendment allows the court by case-specific order to require a face-to-face meeting, but "standing" orders so requiring are not authorized.

As noted concerning the amendments to subdivision (a)(1), the time for the conference has been changed to at least 21 days before the Rule 16 scheduling conference, and the time for the report is changed to no more than 14 days after the Rule 26(f) conference. This should ensure that the court will have the report well in advance of the scheduling conference or the entry of the scheduling order.

Since Rule 16 was amended in 1983 to mandate some case management activities in all courts, it has included deadlines for Completing these tasks to ensure that all courts do so within a reasonable time. Rule 26(f) was fit into this scheme when it was adopted in 1993. It was never intended, however, that the national requirements that certain activities be completed by a certain time should delay case management in districts that move much faster than the national rules direct, and the rule is therefore amended to permit such a court to adopt a local rule that shortens the period specified for the completion of these tasks.

"Shall" is replaced by "must," "does," or an active verb under the program to conform amended rules to current style conventions when there is no ambiguity.

Gap Report

The Advisory Committee recommends adding a sentence to the published amendments to Rule 26(f) authorizing local rules shortening the time between the attorney conference and the court's action under Rule 16(b), and addition to the Committee Note of explanatory material about this change to the rule. This addition can be made without republication in response to public comments.

2006 Amendment

Subdivision (a). Rule 26(a)(1)(B) is amended to parallel Rule 34(a) by recognizing that a party must disclose electronically stored information as well as documents that it may use to support its claims or defenses. The term "electronically stored information" has the same broad meaning in Rule 26(a)(1) as in Rule 34(a). This amendment is consistent with the 1993 addition of Rule 26(a)(1)(B). The term "data compilations" is deleted as unnecessary because it is a subset of both documents and electronically stored information.

[Subdivision (a)(1)(E).] Civil forfeiture actions are added to the list of exemptions from Rule 26(a)(1) disclosure requirements. These actions are governed by new Supplemental Rule G. Disclosure is not likely to be useful.

Subdivision (b)(2). The amendment to Rule 26(b)(2) is designed to address issues raised by difficulties in locating, retrieving, and providing discovery of some electronically stored information. Electronic storage systems often make it easier to locate and retrieve information. These advantages are properly taken into account in determining the reasonable scope of discovery in a particular case. But some sources of electronically stored information can be accessed only with substantial burden and cost. In a particular case, these burdens and costs may make the information on such sources not reasonably accessible.

It is not possible to define in a rule the different types of technological features that may affect the burdens and costs of accessing electronically stored information. Information systems are designed to provide ready access to information used in regular ongoing activities. They also may be designed so as to provide ready access to information that is not regularly used. But a system may retain information on sources that are accessible only by incurring substantial burdens or costs. Subparagraph (B) is added to regulate discovery from such sources.

Under this rule, a responding party should produce electronically stored information that is relevant, not privileged, and reasonably accessible, subject to the (b)(2)(C) limitations that apply to all discovery. The responding party must also identify, by category or type, the sources containing potentially responsive information that it is neither searching nor producing. The identification should, to the extent possible, provide enough detail to enable the requesting party to evaluate the burdens and costs of providing the discovery and the likelihood of finding responsive information on the identified sources.

A party's identification of sources of electronically stored information as not reasonably accessible does not relieve the party of its common-law or statutory duties to preserve evidence. Whether a responding party is required to preserve unsearched sources of potentially responsive information that it believes are not reasonably accessible depends on the circumstances of each case. It is often useful for the parties to discuss this issue early in discovery.

The volume of—and the ability to search—much electronically stored information means that in many cases the responding party will be able to produce information from reasonably accessible sources that will fully satisfy the parties' discovery needs. In many circumstances the requesting party should obtain and evaluate the information from such sources before insisting that the responding party search and produce information contained on sources that are not reasonably accessible. If the requesting party continues to seek discovery of information from sources identified as not reasonably accessible, the parties should discuss the burdens and costs of accessing and retrieving the information, the needs that may establish good cause for requiring all or part of the requested discovery even if the information sought is not reasonably accessible, and conditions on obtaining and producing the information that may be appropriate.

If the parties cannot agree whether, or on what terms, sources identified as not reasonably accessible should be searched and discoverable information produced, the issue may be raised either by a motion to compel discovery or by a motion for a protective order. The parties must confer before bringing either motion. If the parties do not resolve the issue and the court must decide, the responding party must show that the identified sources of information are not reasonably accessible because of undue burden or cost. The requesting party may need discovery to test this assertion. Such discovery might take the form of requiring the responding party to conduct a sampling of information contained on the sources identified as not reasonably accessible; allowing some form of inspection of such sources; or taking depositions of witnesses knowledgeable about the responding party's information systems.

Once it is shown that a source of electronically stored information is not reasonably accessible, the requesting party may still obtain discovery by showing good cause, considering the limitations of Rule 26(b)(2)(C) that balance the costs and potential benefits of discovery. The decision whether to require a responding party to search for and produce information that is not reasonably accessible depends not only on the burdens and costs of doing so, but also on whether those burdens and costs can be justified in the circumstances of the case. Appropriate considerations may include: (1) the specificity of the discovery request; (2) the quantity of information available from other and more easily accessed sources; (3) the failure to produce relevant information that seems likely to have existed but is no longer available on more easily accessed sources; (4) the likelihood of finding relevant, responsive information that cannot be obtained from other, more easily accessed sources; (5) predictions as to the importance and usefulness of the further information; (6) the importance of the issues at stake in the litigation; and (7) the parties' resources.

The responding party has the burden as to one aspect of the inquiry—whether the identified sources are not reasonably accessible in light of the burdens and costs required to search for, retrieve, and produce whatever responsive information may be found. The requesting party has the burden of showing that its need for the discovery outweighs the burdens and costs of locating, retrieving, and producing the information. In some cases, the court will be able to determine whether the identified sources are not reasonably accessible and whether the requesting party has shown good cause for some or all of the discovery, consistent with the limitations of Rule 26(b)(2)(C), through a single proceeding or presentation. The good-cause determination, however, may be complicated because the court and parties may know little about what information the sources identified as not reasonably accessible might contain, whether it is relevant, or how valuable it may be to the litigation. In such cases, the parties may need some focused discovery, which may include sampling of the sources, to learn more about what burdens and costs are involved in accessing the information, what the information consists of, and how valuable it is for the litigation in light of information that can be obtained by exhausting other opportunities for discovery.

The good-cause inquiry and consideration of the Rule 26(b)(2)(C) limitations are coupled with the authority to set conditions for discovery. The conditions may take the form of limits on the amount, type, or sources of information required to be accessed and produced. The conditions may also include payment by the requesting party of part or all of the reasonable costs of obtaining information from sources that are not reasonably accessible. A requesting party's willingness to share or bear the access costs may be weighed by the court in determining whether there is good cause. But the producing party's burdens in reviewing the information for relevance and privilege may weigh against permitting the requested discovery.

The limitations of Rule 26(b)(2)(C) continue to apply to all discovery of electronically stored information, including that stored on reasonably accessible electronic sources.

Subdivision (b)(5). The Committee has repeatedly been advised that the risk of privilege waiver, and the work necessary to avoid it, add to the costs and delay of discovery. When the review is of electronically stored information, the risk of waiver, and the time and effort required to avoid it, can increase substantially because of the volume of electronically stored information and the difficulty in ensuring that all information to be produced has in fact been reviewed. Rule 26(b)(5)(A) provides a procedure for a party that has withheld information on the basis of privilege or protection as trial-preparation material to make the claim so that the requesting party can decide whether to contest the claim and the court can resolve the dispute. Rule 26(b)(5)(B) is added to provide a procedure for a party to assert a claim of privilege or trial-preparation material protection after information is produced in discovery in the action and, if the claim is contested, permit any party that received the information to present the matter to the court for resolution.

Rule 26(b)(5)(B) does not address whether the privilege or protection that is asserted after production was waived by the production. The courts have developed principles to determine whether, and under what circumstances, waiver results from inadvertent production of privileged or protected information. Rule 26(b)(5)(B) provides a procedure for presenting and addressing these issues. Rule 26(b)(5)(B) works in tandem with Rule 26(f), which is amended to direct the parties to discuss privilege issues in preparing their discovery plan, and which, with amended Rule 16(b), allows the parties to ask the court to include in an order any agreements the parties reach regarding issues of privilege or trial-preparation material protection. Agreements reached under Rule 26(f)(4) and orders including such agreements entered under Rule 16(b)(6) may be considered when a court determines whether a waiver has occurred. Such agreements and orders ordinarily control if they adopt procedures different from those in Rule 26(b)(5)(B).

A party asserting a claim of privilege or protection after production must give notice to the receiving party. That notice should be in writing unless the circumstances preclude it. Such circumstances could include the assertion of the claim during a deposition. The notice should be as specific as possible in identifying the information and stating the basis for the claim. Because the receiving party must decide whether to challenge the claim and may sequester the information and submit it to the court for a ruling on whether the claimed privilege or protection applies and whether it has been waived, the notice should be sufficiently detailed so as to enable the receiving party and the court to understand the basis for the claim and to determine whether waiver has occurred. Courts will continue to examine whether a claim of privilege or protection was made at a reasonable time when delay is part of the waiver determination under the governing law.

After receiving notice, each party that received the information must promptly return, sequester, or destroy the information and any copies it has. The option of sequestering or destroying the information is included in part because the receiving party may have incorporated the information in protected trial-preparation materials. No receiving party may use or disclose the information pending resolution of the privilege claim. The receiving party may present to the court the questions whether the information is privileged or protected as trial-preparation material, and whether the privilege or protection has been waived. If it does so, it must provide the court with the grounds for the privilege or protection specified in the producing party's notice, and serve all parties. In presenting the question, the party may use the content of the information only to the extent permitted by the applicable law of privilege, protection for trial-preparation material, and professional responsibility.

If a party disclosed the information to nonparties before receiving notice of a claim of privilege or protection as trial-preparation material, it must take reasonable steps to retrieve the information and to return it, sequester it until the claim is resolved, or destroy it.

Whether the information is returned or not, the producing party must preserve the information pending the court's ruling on whether the claim of privilege or of protection is properly asserted and whether it was waived. As with claims made under Rule 26(b)(5)(A), there may be no ruling if the other parties do not contest the claim.

Subdivision (f). Rule 26(f) is amended to direct the parties to discuss discovery of electronically stored information during their discovery-planning conference. The rule focuses on "issues relating to disclosure or discovery of electronically stored information"; the discussion is not required in cases not involving electronic discovery, and the amendment imposes no additional requirements in those cases. When the parties do anticipate disclosure or discovery of electronically stored information, discussion at the outset may avoid later difficulties or ease their resolution.

When a case involves discovery of electronically stored information, the issues to be addressed during the Rule 26(f) conference depend on the nature and extent of the contemplated discovery and of the parties' information systems. It may be important for the parties to discuss those systems, and accordingly important for counsel to become familiar with those systems before the conference. With that information, the parties can develop a discovery plan that takes into account the capabilities of their computer systems. In appropriate cases identification of, and early discovery from, individuals with special knowledge of a party's computer systems may be helpful.

The particular issues regarding electronically stored information that deserve attention during the discovery planning stage depend on the specifics of the given case. *See Manual for Complex Litigation* (4th) § 40.25(2) (listing topics for discussion in a proposed order regarding meet-and-confer sessions). For example, the parties may specify the topics for such discovery and the time period for which discovery will be sought. They may identify the various sources of such information within a party's control that should be searched for electronically stored information. They may discuss whether the information is reasonably accessible to the party that has it, including the burden or cost of retrieving and reviewing the information. *See* Rule 26(b)(2)(B). Rule 26(f)(3) explicitly directs the parties to discuss the form or forms in which electronically stored information might be produced. The parties may be able to reach agreement on the forms of production, making discovery more efficient. Rule 34(b) is amended to permit a requesting party to specify the form or forms in which it wants electronically stored information produced. If the requesting party does not specify a form, Rule 34(b) directs the responding party to state the forms it intends to use in the production. Early discussion of the forms of production may facilitate the application of Rule 34(b) by allowing the parties to determine what forms of production will meet both parties' needs. Early identification of disputes over the forms of production may help avoid the expense and delay of searches or productions using inappropriate forms.

Rule 26(f) is also amended to direct the parties to discuss any issues regarding preservation of discoverable information during their conference as they develop a discovery plan. This provision applies to all sorts of discoverable information, but can be particularly important with regard to electronically stored information. The volume and dynamic nature of electronically stored information may complicate preservation obligations. The ordinary operation of computers involves both the automatic creation and the automatic deletion or overwriting of certain information. Failure to address preservation issues early in the litigation increases uncertainty and raises a risk of disputes.

The parties' discussion should pay particular attention to the balance between the competing needs to preserve relevant evidence and to continue routine operations critical to ongoing activities. Complete or broad cessation of a party's routine computer operations could paralyze the party's activities. *Cf. Manual for Complex Litigation* (4th) § 11.422 ("A blanket preservation order may be prohibitively expensive and unduly burdensome for parties dependent on computer systems for their day-to-day operations.") The parties should take account of these considerations in their discussions, with the goal of agreeing on reasonable preservation steps.

The requirement that the parties discuss preservation does not imply that courts should routinely enter preservation orders. A preservation order entered over objections should be narrowly tailored. Ex parte preservation orders should issue only in exceptional circumstances.

Rule 26(f) is also amended to provide that the parties should discuss any issues relating to assertions of privilege or of protection as trial-preparation materials, including whether the parties can facilitate discovery by agreeing on procedures for asserting claims of privilege or protection after production and whether to ask the court to enter an order that includes any agreement the parties reach. The Committee has repeatedly been advised about the discovery difficulties that can result from efforts to guard against waiver of privilege and work-product protection. Frequently parties find it necessary to spend large amounts of time reviewing materials requested through discovery to avoid waiving privilege. These efforts are necessary because materials subject to a claim of privilege or protection are often difficult to identify. A failure to withhold even one such item may result in an argument that there has been a waiver of privilege as to all other privileged materials on that subject matter. Efforts to avoid the risk of waiver can impose substantial costs on the party producing the material and the time required for the privilege review can substantially delay access for the party seeking discovery.

These problems often become more acute when discovery of electronically stored information is sought. The volume of such data, and the informality that attends use of e-mail and some other types of electronically stored information, may make privilege determinations more difficult, and privilege review correspondingly more expensive and time consuming. Other aspects of electronically stored information pose particular difficulties for privilege review. For example, production may be sought of information automatically included in electronic files but not apparent to the creator or to readers. Computer programs may retain draft language, editorial comments, and other deleted matter (sometimes referred to as "embedded data" or "embedded edits") in an electronic file but not make them apparent to the reader. Information describing the history, tracking, or management of an electronic file (sometimes called "metadata") is usually not apparent to the reader viewing a hard copy or a screen image. Whether this information should be produced may be among the topics discussed in the Rule 26(f) conference. If it is, it may need to be reviewed to ensure that no privileged information is included, further complicating the task of privilege review.

Parties may attempt to minimize these costs and delays by agreeing to protocols that minimize the risk of waiver. They may agree that the responding party will provide certain requested materials for initial examination without waiving any privilege or protection—sometimes known as a "quick peek." The requesting party then designates the documents it wishes to have actually produced. This designation is the Rule 34 request. The responding party then responds in the usual course, screening only those documents actually requested for formal production and asserting privilege claims as provided in Rule 26(b)(5)(A). On other occasions, parties enter agreements—sometimes called "clawback agreements"—that production without intent to waive privilege or protection should not be a waiver so long as the responding party identifies the documents mistakenly produced, and that the documents should be returned under those circumstances. Other voluntary arrangements may be appropriate depending on the circumstances of each litigation. In most circumstances, a party who receives information under such an arrangement cannot assert that production of the information waived a claim of privilege or of protection as trial-preparation material.

Although these agreements may not be appropriate for all cases, in certain cases they can facilitate prompt and economical discovery by reducing delay before the discovering party obtains access to documents, and by reducing the cost and burden of review by the producing party. A case-management or other order including such agreements may further facilitate the discovery process. Form 35 is amended to include a report to the court about any agreement regarding protections against inadvertent forfeiture or waiver of privilege or protection that the parties have reached, and Rule 16(b) is amended to recognize that the court may include such an agreement in a case-management or other order. If the parties agree to entry of such an order, their proposal should be included in the report to the court.

Rule 26(b)(5)(B) is added to establish a parallel procedure to assert privilege or protection as trial-preparation material after production, leaving the question of waiver to later determination by the court.

2007 Amendment

The language of Rule 26 has been amended as part of the general restyling of the Civil Rules to make them more easily understood and to make style and terminology consistent throughout the rules. These changes are intended to be stylistic only.

Former Rule 26(a)(5) served as an index of the discovery methods provided by later rules. It was deleted as redundant. Deletion does not affect the right to pursue discovery in addition to disclosure.

Former Rule 26(b)(1) began with a general statement of the scope of discovery that appeared to function as a preface to each of the five numbered paragraphs that followed. This preface has been shifted to the text of paragraph (1) because it does not accurately reflect the limits embodied in paragraphs (2), (3), or (4), and because paragraph (5) does not address the scope of discovery.

The reference to discovery of "books" in former Rule 26(b)(1) was deleted to achieve consistent expression throughout the discovery rules. Books remain a proper subject of discovery.

Amended Rule 26(b)(3) states that a party may obtain a copy of the party's own previous statement "on request." Former Rule 26(b)(3) expressly made the request procedure available to a nonparty witness, but did not describe the procedure to be used by a party. This apparent gap is closed by adopting the request procedure, which ensures that a party need not invoke Rule 34 to obtain a copy of the party's own statement.

Rule 26(e) stated the duty to supplement or correct a disclosure or discovery response "to include information thereafter acquired." This apparent limit is not reflected in practice; parties recognize the duty to supplement or correct by providing information that was not originally provided although it was available at the time of the initial disclosure or response. These words are deleted to reflect the actual meaning of the present rule.

Former Rule 26(e) used different phrases to describe the time to supplement or correct a disclosure or discovery response. Disclosures were to be supplemented "at appropriate intervals." A prior discovery response must be "seasonably * * * amend[ed]." The fine distinction between these phrases has not been observed in practice. Amended Rule 26(e)(1)(A) uses the same phrase for disclosures and discovery responses. The party must supplement or correct "in a timely manner."

Former Rule 26(g)(1) did not call for striking an unsigned disclosure. The omission was an obvious drafting oversight. Amended Rule 26(g)(2) includes disclosures in the list of matters that the court must strike unless a signature is provided "promptly * * * after being called to the attorney's or party's attention."

Former Rule 26(b)(2)(A) referred to a "good faith" argument to extend existing law. Amended Rule 26(b)(1)(B)(i) changes this reference to a "nonfrivolous" argument to achieve consistency with Rule 11(b)(2).

As with the Rule 11 signature on a pleading, written motion, or other paper, disclosure and discovery signatures should include not only a postal address but also a telephone number and electronic-mail address. A signer who lacks one or more of those addresses need not supply a nonexistent item.

Rule 11(b)(2) recognizes that it is legitimate to argue for establishing new law. An argument to establish new law is equally legitimate in conducting discovery.

2010 Amendments

Rule 26. Rules 26(a)(2) and (b)(4) are amended to address concerns about expert discovery. The amendments to Rule 26(a)(2) require disclosure regarding expected expert testimony of those expert witnesses not required to provide expert reports and limit the expert report to facts or data (rather than "data or other information," as in the current rule) considered by the witness. Rule 26(b)(4) is amended to provide work-product protection against discovery regarding draft expert disclosures or reports and—with three specific exceptions—communications between expert witnesses and counsel.

In 1993, Rule 26(b)(4)(A) was revised to authorize expert depositions and Rule 26(a)(2) was added to provide disclosure, including—for many experts—an extensive report. Many courts read the disclosure provision to authorize discovery of all communications between counsel and expert witnesses and all draft reports. The Committee has been told repeatedly that routine discovery into attorney-expert communications and draft reports has had undesirable effects. Costs have risen. Attorneys may employ two sets of experts—one for purposes of consultation and another to testify at trial—because disclosure of their collaborative interactions with expert consultants would reveal their most sensitive and confidential case analyses. At the same time, attorneys often feel compelled to adopt a guarded attitude toward their interaction with testifying experts that impedes effective communication, and experts adopt strategies that protect against discovery but also interfere with their work.

Subdivision (a)(2)(B). Rule 26(a)(2)(B)(ii) is amended to provide that disclosure include all "facts or data considered by the witness in forming" the opinions to be offered, rather than the "data or other information" disclosure prescribed in 1993. This amendment is intended to alter the outcome in cases that have relied on the 1993 formulation in requiring disclosure of all attorney-expert communications and draft reports. The amendments to Rule 26(b)(4) make this change explicit by providing work-product protection against discovery regarding draft reports and disclosures or attorney-expert communications.

The refocus of disclosure on "facts or data" is meant to limit disclosure to material of a factual nature by excluding theories or mental impressions of counsel. At the same time, the intention is that "facts or data" be interpreted broadly to require disclosure of any material considered by the expert, from whatever source, that contains factual ingredients. The disclosure obligation extends to any facts or data "considered" by the expert in forming the opinions to be expressed, not only those relied upon by the expert.

Subdivision (a)(2)(C). Rule 26(a)(2)(C) is added to mandate summary disclosures of the opinions to be offered by expert witnesses who are not required to provide reports under Rule 26(a)(2)(B) and of the facts supporting those opinions. This disclosure is considerably less extensive than the report required by Rule 26(a)(2)(B). Courts must take care against requiring undue detail, keeping in mind that these witnesses have not been specially retained and may not be as responsive to counsel as those who have.

This amendment resolves a tension that has sometimes prompted courts to require reports under Rule 26(a)(2)(B) even from witnesses exempted from the report requirement. An (a)(2)(B) report is required only from an expert described in (a)(2)(B).

A witness who is not required to provide a report under Rule 26(a)(2)(B) may both testify as a fact witness and also provide expert testimony under Evidence Rule 702, 703, or 705. Frequent examples include physicians or other health care professionals and employees of a party who do not regularly provide expert testimony. Parties must identify such witnesses under Rule 26(a)(2)(A) and provide the disclosure required under Rule 26(a)(2)(C). The (a)(2)(C) disclosure obligation does not include facts unrelated to the expert opinions the witness will present.

Subdivision (a)(2)(D). This provision (formerly Rule 26(a)(2)(C)) is amended slightly to specify that the time limits for disclosure of contradictory or rebuttal evidence apply with regard to disclosures under new Rule 26(a)(2)(C), just as they do with regard to reports under Rule 26(a)(2)(B).

Subdivision (b)(4). Rule 26(b)(4)(B) is added to provide work-product protection under Rule 26(b)(3)(A) and (B) for drafts of expert reports or disclosures. This protection applies to all witnesses identified under Rule 26(a)(2)(A), whether they are required to provide reports under Rule 26(a)(2)(B) or are the subject of disclosure under Rule 26(a)(2)(C). It applies regardless of the form in which the draft is recorded, whether written, electronic, or otherwise. It also applies to drafts of any supplementation under Rule 26(e); *see* Rule 26(a)(2)(E).

Rule 26(b)(4)(C) is added to provide work-product protection for attorney-expert communications regardless of the form of the communications, whether oral, written, electronic, or otherwise. The addition of Rule 26(b)(4)(C) is designed to protect counsel's work product and ensure that lawyers may interact with retained experts without fear of exposing those communications to searching discovery. The protection is limited to communications between an expert witness required to provide a report under Rule 26(a)(2)(B) and the attorney for the party on whose behalf the witness will be testifying, including any "preliminary" expert opinions. Protected "communications" include those between the party's attorney and assistants of the expert witness. The rule does not itself protect communications between counsel and other expert witnesses, such as those for whom disclosure is required under Rule 26(a)(2)(C). The rule does not exclude protection under other doctrines, such as privilege or independent development of the work-product doctrine.

The most frequent method for discovering the work of expert witnesses is by deposition, but Rules 26(b)(4)(B) and (C) apply to all forms of discovery.

Rules 26(b)(4)(B) and (C) do not impede discovery about the opinions to be offered by the expert or the development, foundation, or basis of those opinions. For example, the expert's testing of material involved in litigation, and notes of any such testing, would not be exempted from discovery by this rule. Similarly, inquiry about communications the expert had with anyone other than the party's counsel about the opinions expressed is unaffected by the rule. Counsel are also free to question expert witnesses about alternative analyses, testing methods, or approaches to the issues on which they are testifying, whether or not the expert considered them in forming the opinions expressed. These discovery changes therefore do not affect the gatekeeping functions called for by *Daubert v. Merrell Dow Pharmaceuticals, Inc.,* 509 U.S. 579 (1993), and related cases.

The protection for communications between the retained expert and "the party's attorney" should be applied in a realistic manner, and often would not be limited to communications with a single lawyer or a single law firm. For example, a party may be involved in a number of suits about a given product or service, and may retain a particular expert witness to testify on that party's behalf in several of the cases. In such a situation, the protection applies to communications between the expert witness and the attorneys representing the party in any of those cases. Similarly, communications with in-house counsel for the party would often be regarded as protected even if the in-house attorney is not counsel of record in the action. Other situations may also justify a pragmatic application of the "party's attorney" concept.

Although attorney-expert communications are generally protected by Rule 26(b)(4)(C), the protection does not apply to the extent the lawyer and the expert communicate about matters that fall within three exceptions. But the discovery authorized by the exceptions does not extend beyond those specific topics. Lawyer-expert communications may cover many topics and, even when the excepted topics are included among those involved in a given communication, the protection applies to all other aspects of the communication beyond the excepted topics.

First, under Rule 26(b)(4)(C)(i) attorney-expert communications regarding compensation for the expert's study or testimony may be the subject of discovery. In some cases, this discovery may go beyond the disclosure requirement in Rule 26(a)(2)(B)(vi). It is not limited to compensation for work forming the opinions to be expressed, but extends to all compensation for the study and testimony provided in relation to the action. Any communications about additional benefits to the expert, such as further work in the event of a successful result in the present case, would be included. This exception includes compensation for work done by a person or organization associated with the expert. The objective is to permit full inquiry into such potential sources of bias.

Second, under Rule 26(b)(4)(C)(ii) discovery is permitted to identify facts or data the party's attorney provided to the expert and that the expert considered in forming the opinions to be expressed. The exception applies only to communications "identifying" the facts or data provided by counsel; further communications about the potential relevance of the facts or data are protected.

Third, under Rule 26(b)(4)(C)(iii) discovery regarding attorney-expert communications is permitted to identify any assumptions that counsel provided to the expert and that the expert relied upon in forming the opinions to be expressed. For example, the party's attorney may tell the expert to assume the truth of certain testimony or evidence, or the correctness of another expert's conclusions. This exception is limited to those assumptions that the expert actually did rely on in forming the opinions to be expressed. More general attorney-expert discussions about hypotheticals, or exploring possibilities based on hypothetical facts, are outside this exception.

Under the amended rule, discovery regarding attorney-expert communications on subjects outside the three exceptions in Rule 26(b)(4)(C), or regarding draft expert reports or disclosures, is permitted only in limited circumstances and by court order. A party seeking such discovery must make the showing specified in Rule 26(b)(3)(A)(ii)—that the party has a substantial need for the discovery and cannot obtain the substantial equivalent without undue hardship. It will be rare for a party to be able to make such a showing given the broad disclosure and discovery otherwise allowed regarding the expert's testimony. A party's failure to provide required disclosure or discovery does not show the need and hardship required by Rule 26(b)(3)(A); remedies are provided by Rule 37.

In the rare case in which a party does make this showing, the court must protect against disclosure of the attorney's mental impressions, conclusions, opinions, or legal theories under Rule 26(b)(3)(B). But this protection does not extend to the expert's own development of the opinions to be presented; those are subject to probing in deposition or at trial.

Former Rules 26(b)(4)(B) and (C) have been renumbered (D) and (E), and a slight revision has been made in (E) to take account of the renumbering of former (B).

2015 Amendment

Rule 26(b)(1) is changed in several ways.

Information is discoverable under revised Rule26(b)(1) if it is relevant to any party's claim or defense and is proportional to the needs of the case. The considerations that bear on proportionality are moved from present Rule 26(b)(2)(C)(iii), slightly rearranged and with one addition.

Most of what now appears in Rule 26(b)(2)(C)(iii) was first adopted in 1983. The 1983 provision was explicitly adopted as part of the scope of discovery defined by Rule 26(b)(1). Rule 26(b)(1) directed the court to limit the frequency or extent of use of discovery if it determined that "the discovery is unduly burdensome or expensive, taking into account the needs of the case, the amount in controversy, limitations on the parties' resources, and the importance of the issues at stake in the litigation." At the same time, Rule 26(g) was added. Rule 26(g) provided that signing a discovery request, response, or objection certified that the request, response, or objection was "not unreasonable or unduly burdensome or expensive, given the needs of the case, the discovery already had in the case, the amount in controversy, and the importance of the issues at stake in the litigation." The parties thus shared the responsibility to honor these limits on the scope of discovery.

The 1983 Committee Note stated that the new provisions were added "to deal with the problem of over-discovery. The objective is to guard against redundant or disproportionate discovery by giving the court authority to reduce the amount of discovery that may be directed to matters that are otherwise proper subjects of inquiry. The new sentence is intended to encourage judges to be more aggressive in identifying and discouraging discovery overuse. The grounds mentioned in the amended rule for limiting discovery reflect the existing practice of many courts in issuing protective orders under Rule 26(c). . . . On the whole, however, district judges have been reluctant to limit the use of the discovery devices."

The clear focus of the 1983 provisions may have been softened, although inadvertently, by the amendments made in 1993. The 1993 Committee Note explained: "[F]ormer paragraph (b)(1) [was] subdivided into two paragraphs for ease of reference and to avoid renumbering of paragraphs (3) and (4)." Subdividing the paragraphs, however, was done in a way that could be read to separate the proportionality provisions as "limitations," no longer an integral part of the (b)(1) scope provisions. That appearance was immediately offset by the next statement in the Note: "Textual changes are then made in new paragraph (2) to enable the court to keep tighter rein on the extent of discovery."

The 1993 amendments added two factors to the considerations that bear on limiting discovery: whether "the burden or expense of the proposed discovery outweighs its likely benefit," and "the importance of the proposed discovery in resolving the issues." Addressing these and other limitations added by the 1993 discovery amendments, the Committee Note stated that "[t]he revisions in Rule 26(b)(2) are intended to provide the court with broader discretion to impose additional restrictions on the scope and extent of discovery. . . ."

The relationship between Rule 26(b)(1) and (2) was further addressed by an amendment made in 2000 that added a new sentence at the end of (b)(1): "All discovery is subject to the limitations imposed by Rule 26(b)(2)(i), (ii), and (iii) [now Rule 26(b)(2)(C)]." The Committee Note recognized that "[t]hese limitations apply to discovery that is otherwise within the scope of subdivision (b)(1)." It explained that the Committee had been told repeatedly that courts were not using these limitations as originally intended. "This otherwise redundant cross-reference has been added to emphasize the need for active judicial use of subdivision (b)(2) to control excessive discovery."

The present amendment restores the proportionality factors to their original place in defining the scope of discovery. This change reinforces the Rule 26(g) obligation of the parties to consider these factors in making discovery requests, responses, or objections.

Restoring the proportionality calculation to Rule 26(b)(1) does not change the existing responsibilities of the court and the parties to consider proportionality, and the change does not place on the party seeking discovery the burden of addressing all proportionality considerations.

Nor is the change intended to permit the opposing party to refuse discovery simply by making a boilerplate objection that it is not proportional. The parties and the court have a collective responsibility to consider the proportionality of all discovery and consider it in resolving discovery disputes.

The parties may begin discovery without a full appreciation of the factors that bear on proportionality. A party requesting discovery, for example, may have little information about the burden or expense of responding. A party requested to provide discovery may have little information about the importance of the discovery in resolving the issues as understood by the requesting party. Many of these uncertainties should be addressed and reduced in the parties' Rule 26(f) conference and in scheduling and pretrial conferences with the court. But if the parties continue to disagree, the discovery dispute could be brought before the court and the parties' responsibilities would remain as they have been since 1983. A party claiming undue burden or expense ordinarily has far better information—perhaps the only information—with respect to that part of the determination. A party claiming that a request is important to resolve the issues should be able to explain the ways in which the underlying information bears on the issues as that party understands them. The court's responsibility, using all the information provided by the parties, is to consider these and all the other factors in reaching a case-specific determination of the appropriate scope of discovery.

The direction to consider the parties' relative access to relevant information adds new text to provide explicit focus on considerations already implicit in present Rule 26(b)(2)(C)(iii). Some cases involve what often is called "information asymmetry." One party—often an individual plaintiff—may have very little discoverable information. The other party may have vast amounts of information, including information that can be readily retrieved and information that is more difficult to retrieve. In practice these circumstances often mean that the burden of responding to discovery lies heavier on the party who has more information, and properly so.

Restoring proportionality as an express component of the scope of discovery warrants repetition of parts of the 1983 and 1993 Committee Notes that must not be lost from sight. The 1983 Committee Note explained that "[t]he rule contemplates greater judicial involvement in the discovery process and thus acknowledges the reality that it cannot always operate on a self-regulating basis." The 1993 Committee Note further observed that "[t]he information explosion of recent decades has greatly increased both the potential cost of wide-ranging discovery and the potential for discovery to be used as an instrument for delay or oppression." What seemed an explosion in 1993 has been exacerbated by the advent of e-discovery. The present amendment again reflects the need for continuing and close judicial involvement in the cases that do not yield readily to the ideal of effective party management. It is expected that discovery will be effectively managed by the parties in many cases. But there will be important occasions for judicial management, both when the parties are legitimately unable to resolve important differences and when the parties fall short of effective, cooperative management on their own.

It also is important to repeat the caution that the monetary stakes are only one factor, to be balanced against other factors. The 1983 Committee Note recognized "the significance of the substantive issues, as measured in philosophic, social, or institutional terms. Thus the rule recognizes that many cases in public policy spheres, such as employment practices, free speech, and other matters, may have importance far beyond the monetary amount involved." Many other substantive areas also may involve litigation that seeks relatively small amounts of money, or no money at all, but that seeks to vindicate vitally important personal or public values.

So too, consideration of the parties' resources does not foreclose discovery requests addressed to an impecunious party, nor justify unlimited discovery requests addressed to a wealthy party. The 1983 Committee Note cautioned that "[t]he court must apply the standards in an even-handed manner that will prevent use of discovery to wage a war of attrition or as a device to coerce a party, whether financially weak or affluent."

The burden or expense of proposed discovery should be determined in a realistic way. This includes the burden or expense of producing electronically stored information. Computer-based methods of searching such information continue to develop, particularly for cases involving large volumes of electronically stored information. Courts and parties should be willing to consider the opportunities for reducing the burden or expense of discovery as reliable means of searching electronically stored information become available.

A portion of present Rule 26(b)(1) is omitted from the proposed revision. After allowing discovery of any matter relevant to any party's claim or defense, the present rule adds: "including the existence, description, nature, custody, condition, and location of any documents or other tangible things and the identity and location of persons who know of any discoverable matter." Discovery of such matters is so deeply entrenched in practice that it is no longer necessary to clutter the long text of Rule 26 with these examples.

The discovery identified in these examples should still be permitted under the revised rule when relevant and proportional to the needs of the case. Framing intelligent requests for electronically stored information, for example, may require detailed information about another party's information systems and other information resources.

The amendment deletes the former provision authorizing the court, for good cause, to order discovery of any matter relevant to the subject matter involved in the action. The Committee has been informed that this language is rarely invoked. Proportional discovery relevant to any party's claim or defense suffices, given a proper understanding of what is relevant to a claim or defense. The distinction between matter relevant to a claim or defense and matter relevant to the subject matter was introduced in 2000. The 2000 Note offered three examples of information that, suitably focused, would be relevant to the parties' claims or defenses. The examples were "other incidents of the same type, or involving the same product"; "information about organizational arrangements or filing systems"; and "information that could be used to impeach a likely witness." Such discovery is not foreclosed by the amendments. Discovery that is relevant to the parties' claims or defenses may also support amendment of the pleadings to add a new claim or defense that affects the scope of discovery.

The former provision for discovery of relevant but inadmissible information that appears "reasonably calculated to lead to the discovery of admissible evidence" is also deleted. The phrase has been used by some, incorrectly, to define the scope of discovery. As the Committee Note to the 2000 amendments observed, use of the "reasonably calculated" phrase to define the scope of discovery "might swallow any other limitation on the scope of discovery." The 2000 amendments sought to prevent such misuse by adding the word "Relevant" at the beginning of the sentence, making clear that " 'relevant' means within the scope of discovery as defined in this subdivision. . . ." The "reasonably calculated" phrase has continued to create problems, however, and is removed by these amendments. It is replaced by the direct statement that "Information within this scope of discovery need not be admissible in evidence to be discoverable." Discovery of nonprivileged information not admissible in evidence remains available so long as it is otherwise within the scope of discovery.

Rule 26(b)(2)(C)(iii) is amended to reflect the transfer of the considerations that bear on proportionality to Rule 26(b)(1). The court still must limit the frequency or extent of proposed discovery, on motion or on its own, if it is outside the scope permitted by Rule 26(b)(1).

Rule 26(c)(1)(B) is amended to include an express recognition of protective orders that allocate expenses for disclosure or discovery. Authority to enter such orders is included in the present rule, and courts already exercise this authority. Explicit recognition will forestall the temptation some parties may feel to contest this authority. Recognizing the authority does not imply that cost-shifting should become a common practice. Courts and parties should continue to assume that a responding party ordinarily bears the costs of responding.

Rule 26(d)(2) is added to allow a party to deliver Rule 34 requests to another party more than 21 days after that party has been served even though the parties have not yet had a required Rule 26(f) conference. Delivery may be made by any party to the party that has been served, and by that party to any plaintiff and any other party that has been served. Delivery does not count as service; the requests are considered to be served at the first Rule 26(f) conference. Under Rule 34(b)(2)(A) the time to respond runs from service. This relaxation of the discovery moratorium is designed to facilitate focused discussion during the Rule 26(f) conference. Discussion at the conference may produce changes in the requests. The opportunity for advance scrutiny of requests delivered before the Rule 26(f) conference should not affect a decision whether to allow additional time to respond.

Rule 26(d)(3) is renumbered and amended to recognize that the parties may stipulate to case-specific sequences of discovery.

Rule 26(f)(3) is amended in parallel with Rule 16(b)(3) to add two items to the discovery plan—issues about preserving electronically stored information and court orders under Evidence Rule 502.

Gap Report

The published text of Rule 26(b)(1) is revised to place "the importance of the issues at stake" first in the list of factors to be considered in measuring proportionality, and to add a new factor, "the parties' relative access to relevant information." The proposal to amend Rule 26(b)(2)(A) to adjust for the proposal to add a presumptive numerical limit on Rule 36 requests to admit is omitted to reflect withdrawal of the Rule 36 proposal. The result restores the authority to limit the number of Rule 36 requests by local rule. The proposal to amend Rule 26(b)(2)(C) to adjust for elimination of the local-rule authority is withdrawn to reflect restoration of that authority. Style changes were made in Rule 26(d)(1), deleting the only proposed change, and in 26(d)(2). The Committee Note was expanded to emphasize the importance of observing proportionality by recounting the history of repeated efforts to encourage it. Other new material in the Note responds to concerns expressed in testimony and comments, particularly the concern that restoring proportionality to the scope of discovery might somehow change the "burdens" imposed on a party requesting discovery when faced with a proportionality objection.

Rule 27.　Depositions to Perpetuate Testimony

(a)　Before an Action Is Filed.

　(1)　*Petition.* A person who wants to perpetuate testimony about any matter cognizable in a United States court may file a verified petition in the district court for the district where any expected adverse party resides. The petition must ask for an order authorizing the petitioner to depose the named persons in order to perpetuate their testimony. The petition must be titled in the petitioner's name and must show:

　　(A)　that the petitioner expects to be a party to an action cognizable in a United States court but cannot presently bring it or cause it to be brought;

　　(B)　the subject matter of the expected action and the petitioner's interest;

　　(C)　the facts that the petitioner wants to establish by the proposed testimony and the reasons to perpetuate it;

　　(D)　the names or a description of the persons whom the petitioner expects to be adverse parties and their addresses, so far as known; and

　　(E)　the name, address, and expected substance of the testimony of each deponent.

　(2)　*Notice and Service.* At least 21 days before the hearing date, the petitioner must serve each expected adverse party with a copy of the petition and a notice stating the time and place of the hearing. The notice may be served either inside or outside the district or state in the manner provided in Rule 4. If that service cannot be made with reasonable diligence on an expected adverse party, the court may order service by publication or otherwise. The court must appoint an attorney to represent persons not served in the manner provided in Rule 4 and to cross-examine the deponent if an unserved person is not otherwise represented. If any expected adverse party is a minor or is incompetent, Rule 17(c) applies.

　(3)　*Order and Examination.* If satisfied that perpetuating the testimony may prevent a failure or delay of justice, the court must issue an order that designates or describes the persons whose depositions may be taken, specifies the subject matter of the examinations, and states whether the depositions will be taken orally or by written interrogatories. The depositions may then be taken under these rules, and the court may issue orders like those authorized by Rules 34 and 35. A reference in these rules to the court where an action is pending means, for purposes of this rule, the court where the petition for the deposition was filed.

　(4)　*Using the Deposition.* A deposition to perpetuate testimony may be used under Rule 32(a) in any later-filed district-court action involving the same subject matter if the deposition either was taken under these rules or, although not so taken, would be admissible in evidence in the courts of the state where it was taken.

(b)　Pending Appeal.

　(1)　*In General.* The court where a judgment has been rendered may, if an appeal has been taken or may still be taken, permit a party to depose witnesses to perpetuate their testimony for use in the event of further proceedings in that court.

(2) *Motion.* The party who wants to perpetuate testimony may move for leave to take the depositions, on the same notice and service as if the action were pending in the district court. The motion must show:

(A) the name, address, and expected substance of the testimony of each deponent; and

(B) the reasons for perpetuating the testimony.

(3) *Court Order.* If the court finds that perpetuating the testimony may prevent a failure or delay of justice, the court may permit the depositions to be taken and may issue orders like those authorized by Rules 34 and 35. The depositions may be taken and used as any other deposition taken in a pending district-court action.

(c) **Perpetuation by an Action.** This rule does not limit a court's power to entertain an action to perpetuate testimony.

(Amended December 27, 1946, effective March 19, 1948; December 29, 1948, effective October 20, 1949; March 1, 1971, effective July 1, 1971; March 2, 1987, effective August 1, 1987; April 25, 2005, effective December 1, 2005; April 30, 2007, effective December 1, 2007; March 26, 2009, effective December 1, 2009.)

ADVISORY COMMITTEE NOTES

1937 Adoption

Note to Subdivision (a). This rule offers a simple method of perpetuating testimony in cases where it is usually allowed under equity practice or under modern statutes. See *Arizona v. California,* 1934, 54 S.Ct. 735, 292 U.S. 341, 78 L.Ed. 1298; *Todd Engineering Dry Dock and Repair Co. v. United States,* C.C.A.5, 1929, 32 F.2d 734; *Hall v. Stout,* 4 Del.Ch. 269 (1871). For comparable state statutes see Ark.Civ.Code (Crawford, 1934) §§ 666 to 670; Calif.Code Civ.Proc. (Deering, 1937) 2083–2089; Smith-Hurd Ill.Stats. c. 51, §§ 39 to 46; Iowa Code (1935) §§ 11400 to 11407; 2 Mass.Gen.Laws (Ter.Ed., 1932) ch. 233, §§ 46 to 63; N.Y.C.P.A. (1937) § 295; Ohio Gen.Code Ann. (Throckmorton, 1936) §§ 12216 to 12222; Va.Code Ann. (Michie, 1936) § 6235; Wis.Stat. (1935) §§ 326.27 to 326.29. The appointment of an attorney to represent absent parties or parties not personally notified, or a guardian ad litem to represent minors and incompetents, is provided for in several of the above statutes.

Note to Subdivision (b). This follows the practice approved in *Richter v. Union Trust Co.,* 1885, 5 S.Ct. 1162, 115 U.S. 55, 29 L.Ed. 345, by extending the right to perpetuate testimony to cases pending an appeal.

Note to Subdivision (c). This preserves the right to employ a separate action to perpetuate testimony under U.S.C., Title 28, [former] § 644 (Depositions under *dedimus potestatem* and *in perpetuam*) as an alternate method.

1946 Amendment

Note. Since the second sentence in subdivision (a)(3) refers only to depositions, it is arguable that Rules 34 and 35 are inapplicable in proceedings to perpetuate testimony. The new matter [in subdivisions (a)(3) and (b)] clarifies. A conforming change is also made in subdivision (b).

1948 Amendment

The amendment effective October 1949, substituted the words "United States district court" in subdivision (a)(1) and (4) for "district court of the United States."

1971 Amendment

The reference intended in this subdivision is to the rule governing the use of depositions in court proceedings. Formerly Rule 26(d), that rule is now Rule 32(a). The subdivision is amended accordingly.

1987 Amendment

The amendments are technical. No substantive change is intended.

2005 Amendment

The outdated cross-reference to former Rule 4(d) is corrected to incorporate all Rule 4 methods of service. Former Rule 4(d) has been allocated to many different subdivisions of Rule 4. Former Rule 4(d) did not cover all categories of defendants or modes of service, and present Rule 4 reaches further than all of former Rule 4. But there is no reason to distinguish between the different categories of defendants and modes of service encompassed by Rule 4. Rule 4 service provides effective notice. Notice by such means should be provided to any expected adverse party that comes within Rule 4.

Other changes are made to conform Rule 27(a)(2) to current style conventions.

2007 Amendment

The language of Rule 27 has been amended as part of the general restyling of the Civil Rules to make them more easily understood and to make style and terminology consistent throughout the rules. These changes are intended to be stylistic only.

2009 Amendments

The time set in the former rule at 20 days has been revised to 21 days. See the Note to Rule 6.

Rule 28.   Persons Before Whom Depositions May Be Taken

(a) Within the United States.

   (1) *In General.* Within the United States or a territory or insular possession subject to United States jurisdiction, a deposition must be taken before:

   (A) an officer authorized to administer oaths either by federal law or by the law in the place of examination; or

   (B) a person appointed by the court where the action is pending to administer oaths and take testimony.

   (2) *Definition of "Officer".* The term "officer" in Rules 30, 31, and 32 includes a person appointed by the court under this rule or designated by the parties under Rule 29(a).

(b) In a Foreign Country.

   (1) *In General.* A deposition may be taken in a foreign country:

   (A) under an applicable treaty or convention;

   (B) under a letter of request, whether or not captioned a "letter rogatory";

   (C) on notice, before a person authorized to administer oaths either by federal law or by the law in the place of examination; or

   (D) before a person commissioned by the court to administer any necessary oath and take testimony.

   (2) *Issuing a Letter of Request or a Commission.* A letter of request, a commission, or both may be issued:

   (A) on appropriate terms after an application and notice of it; and

   (B) without a showing that taking the deposition in another manner is impracticable or inconvenient.

   (3) *Form of a Request, Notice, or Commission.* When a letter of request or any other device is used according to a treaty or convention, it must be captioned in the form prescribed by that treaty or convention. A letter of request may be addressed "To the Appropriate Authority in [name of country]." A deposition notice or a commission must designate by name or descriptive title the person before whom the deposition is to be taken.

(4) *Letter of Request—Admitting Evidence.* Evidence obtained in response to a letter of request need not be excluded merely because it is not a verbatim transcript, because the testimony was not taken under oath, or because of any similar departure from the requirements for depositions taken within the United States.

(c) Disqualification. A deposition must not be taken before a person who is any party's relative, employee, or attorney; who is related to or employed by any party's attorney; or who is financially interested in the action.

(Amended December 27, 1946, effective March 19, 1948; January 21, 1963, effective July 1, 1963; April 29, 1980, effective August 1, 1980; March 2, 1987, effective August 1, 1987; April 22, 1993, effective December 1, 1993; April 30, 2007, effective December 1, 2007.)

ADVISORY COMMITTEE NOTES

1937 Adoption

In effect this rule is substantially the same as U.S.C., Title 28, [former] § 639 (Depositions *de bene esse*; when and where taken; notice). U.S.C., Title 28, [former] § 642 (Depositions, acknowledgments, and affidavits taken by notaries public) does not conflict with subdivision (a).

1946 Amendments

Note. The added language [in subdivision (a)] provides for the situation, occasionally arising, when depositions must be taken in an isolated place where there is no one readily available who has the power to administer oaths and take testimony according to the terms of the rule as originally stated. In addition, the amendment affords a more convenient method of securing depositions in the case where state lines intervene between the location of various witnesses otherwise rather closely grouped. The amendment insures that the person appointed shall have adequate power to perform his duties. It has been held that a person authorized to act in the premises, as, for example, a master, may take testimony outside the district of his appointment. *Consolidated Fastener Co. v. Columbian Button & Fastener Co.,* C.C.N.D.N.Y.1898, 85 Fed. 54; *Mathieson Alkali Works v. Arnold, Hoffman & Co.,* C.C.A.1, 1929, 31 F.2d 1.

1963 Amendments

The amendment of clause (1) is designed to facilitate depositions in foreign countries by enlarging the class of persons before whom the depositions may be taken on notice. The class is no longer confined, as at present, to a secretary of embassy or legation, consul general, consul, vice consul, or consular agent of the United States. In a country that regards the taking of testimony by a foreign official in aid of litigation pending in a court of another country as an infringement upon its sovereignty, it will be expedient to notice depositions before officers of the country in which the examination is taken. See generally *Symposium, Letters Rogatory* (Grossman ed. 1956); Doyle, *Taking Evidence by Deposition and Letters Rogatory and Obtaining Documents in Foreign Territory,* Proc.A.B.A., Sec.Int'l & Comp.L. 37 (1959); Heilpern, *Procuring Evidence Abroad,* 14 Tul.L.Rev. 29 (1939); Jones, *International Judicial Assistance: Procedural Chaos and a Program for Reform,* 62 Yale L.J. 515, 526–29 (1953); Smit, *International Aspects of Federal Civil Procedure,* 61 Colum.L.Rev. 1031, 1056–58 (1961).

Clause (2) of amended subdivision (b), like the corresponding provision of subdivision (a) dealing with depositions taken in the United States, makes it clear that the appointment of a person by commission in itself confers power upon him to administer any necessary oath.

It has been held that a letter rogatory will not be issued unless the use of a notice or commission is shown to be impossible or impractical. See, e.g., *United States v. Matles,* 154 F.Supp. 574 (E.D.N.Y.1957); *The Edmund Fanning,* 89 F.Supp. 282 (E.D.N.Y.1950); *Branyan v. Koninklijke Luchtvaart Maatschappij,* 13 F.R.D. 425 (S.D.N.Y.1953). See also *Ali Akber Kiachif v. Philco International Corp.,* 10 F.R.D. 277 (S.D.N.Y.1950). The intent of the fourth sentence of the amended subdivision is to overcome this judicial antipathy and to permit a sound choice between depositions under a letter rogatory and on notice or by commission in the light of all the circumstances. In a case in which the foreign country will compel a witness to attend or testify in aid of a letter rogatory but not in aid of a commission, a letter rogatory may be preferred on the ground that it is less expensive to execute, even if there is plainly no need for compulsive process. A letter rogatory may also be preferred when it cannot be demonstrated that a witness will be recalcitrant or when the witness states that he is willing to testify voluntarily, but the contingency exists that he will change his mind at the last moment. In the latter case, it may be advisable to issue both a commission and a letter rogatory, the latter to be executed if the former fails. The choice between a letter rogatory and a commission may be conditioned by other factors, including the nature and extent of the assistance that the foreign country will give to the execution of either.

In executing a letter rogatory the courts of other countries may be expected to follow their customary procedure for taking testimony. See *United States v. Paraffin Wax,* 2255 Bags, 23 F.R.D. 289 (E.D.N.Y.1959). In many noncommon-law countries the judge questions the witness, sometimes without first administering an oath, the attorneys put any supplemental questions either to the witness or through the judge, and the judge dictates a summary of the testimony, which the witness acknowledges as correct. See *Jones, supra,* at 530–32; *Doyle, supra,* at 39–41. The last sentence of the amended subdivision provides, contrary to the implications of some authority, that evidence recorded in such a fashion need not be excluded on that account. See *The Mandu,* 11 F.Supp. 845 (E.D.N.Y.1935). But *cf. Nelson v. United States,* 17 Fed.Cas. 1340 (No. 10,116) (C.C.D.Pa.1816); *Winthrop v. Union Ins. Co.,* 30 Fed.Cas. 376 (No. 17901) (C.C.D.Pa.1807). The specific reference to the lack of an oath or a verbatim transcript is intended to be illustrative. Whether or to what degree the value or weight of the evidence may be affected by the method of taking or recording the testimony is left for determination according to the circumstances of the particular case, *cf. Uebersee Finanz-Korporation, A.G. v. Brownell,* 121 F.Supp. 420 (D.D.C.1954); *Danisch v. Guardian Life Ins. Co.,* 19 F.R.D. 235 (S.D.N.Y.1956); the testimony may indeed be so devoid of substance or probative value as to warrant its exclusion altogether.

Some foreign countries are hostile to allowing a deposition to be taken in their country, especially by notice or commission, or to lending assistance in the taking of a deposition. Thus compliance with the terms of amended subdivision (b) may not in all cases ensure completion of a deposition abroad. Examination of the law and policy of the particular foreign country in advance of attempting a deposition is therefore advisable. See 4 *Moore's Federal Practice* ¶¶ 28.05–28.08 (2d ed. 1950).

1980 Amendments

The amendments are clarifying.

1987 Amendments

The amendment is technical. No substantive change is intended.

1993 Amendments

This revision is intended to make effective use of the Hague Convention on the Taking of Evidence Abroad in Civil or Commercial Matters, and of any similar treaties that the United States may enter into in the future which provide procedures for taking depositions abroad. The party taking the deposition is ordinarily obliged to conform to an applicable treaty or convention if an effective deposition can be taken by such internationally approved means, even though a verbatim transcript is not available or testimony cannot be taken under oath. For a discussion of the impact of such treaties upon the discovery process, and of the application of principles of comity upon discovery in countries not signatories to a convention, see *Société Nationale Industrielle Aérospatiale v. United States District Court,* 482 U.S. 522 (1987).

The term "letter of request" has been substituted in the rule for the term "letter rogatory" because it is the primary method provided by the Hague Convention. A letter rogatory is essentially a form of letter of request. There are several other minor changes that are designed merely to carry out the intent of the other alterations.

2007 Amendment

The language of Rule 28 has been amended as part of the general restyling of the Civil Rules to make them more easily understood and to make style and terminology consistent throughout the rules. These changes are intended to be stylistic only.

HISTORICAL NOTES

Treaties and Conventions; Taking of Evidence Abroad in Civil or Commercial Matters; Observance On and After Oct. 7, 1972, by United States and Citizens and Persons Subject to Jurisdiction of United States

For text of Convention, see provisions set out as a note under section 1781 of Title 28.

Rule 29.   Stipulations About Discovery Procedure

Unless the court orders otherwise, the parties may stipulate that:

(a) a deposition may be taken before any person, at any time or place, on any notice, and in the manner specified—in which event it may be used in the same way as any other deposition; and

(b) other procedures governing or limiting discovery be modified—but a stipulation extending the time for any form of discovery must have court approval if it would interfere with the time set for completing discovery, for hearing a motion, or for trial.

(Amended March 30, 1970, effective July 1, 1970; April 22, 1993, effective December 1, 1993; April 30, 2007, effective December 1, 2007.)

ADVISORY COMMITTEE NOTES

1970 Amendment

There is no provision for stipulations varying the procedures by which methods of discovery other than depositions are governed. It is common practice for parties to agree on such variations, and the amendment recognizes such agreements and provides a formal mechanism in the rules for giving them effect. Any stipulation varying the procedures may be superseded by court order, and stipulations extending the time for response to discovery under Rules 33, 34, and 36 require court approval.

1993 Amendments

This rule is revised to give greater opportunity for litigants to agree upon modifications to the procedures governing discovery or to limitations upon discovery. Counsel are encouraged to agree on less expensive and time-consuming methods to obtain information, as through voluntary exchange of documents, use of interviews in lieu of depositions, etc. Likewise, when more depositions or interrogatories are needed than allowed under these rules or when more time is needed to complete a deposition than allowed under a local rule, they can, by agreeing to the additional discovery, eliminate the need for a special motion addressed to the court.

Under the revised rule, the litigants ordinarily are not required to obtain the court's approval of these stipulations. By order or local rule, the court can, however, direct that its approval be obtained for particular types of stipulations; and, in any event, approval must be obtained if a stipulation to extend the 30-day period for responding to interrogatories, requests for production, or requests for admissions would interfere with dates set by the court for completing discovery, for hearing of a motion, or for trial.

2007 Amendment

The language of Rule 29 has been amended as part of the general restyling of the Civil Rules to make them more easily understood and to make style and terminology consistent throughout the rules. These changes are intended to be stylistic only.

Rule 30.   Depositions by Oral Examination

(a) When a Deposition May Be Taken.

    (1) *Without Leave.* A party may, by oral questions, depose any person, including a party, without leave of court except as provided in Rule 30(a)(2). The deponent's attendance may be compelled by subpoena under Rule 45.

    (2) *With Leave.* A party must obtain leave of court, and the court must grant leave to the extent consistent with Rule 26(b)(1) and (2):

    (A) if the parties have not stipulated to the deposition and:

        (i) the deposition would result in more than 10 depositions being taken under this rule or Rule 31 by the plaintiffs, or by the defendants, or by the third-party defendants;

        (ii) the deponent has already been deposed in the case; or

        (iii) the party seeks to take the deposition before the time specified in Rule 26(d), unless the party certifies in the notice, with supporting facts, that the deponent is expected to leave the United States and be unavailable for examination in this country after that time; or

    (B) if the deponent is confined in prison.

(b) **Notice of the Deposition; Other Formal Requirements.**

    (1) *Notice in General.* A party who wants to depose a person by oral questions must give reasonable written notice to every other party. The notice must state the time and place of the deposition and, if known, the deponent's name and address. If the name is unknown, the notice must provide a general description sufficient to identify the person or the particular class or group to which the person belongs.

    (2) *Producing Documents.* If a subpoena duces tecum is to be served on the deponent, the materials designated for production, as set out in the subpoena, must be listed in the notice or in an attachment. The notice to a party deponent may be accompanied by a request under Rule 34 to produce documents and tangible things at the deposition.

    (3) *Method of Recording.*

        (A) *Method Stated in the Notice.* The party who notices the deposition must state in the notice the method for recording the testimony. Unless the court orders otherwise, testimony may be recorded by audio, audiovisual, or stenographic means. The noticing party bears the recording costs. Any party may arrange to transcribe a deposition.

        (B) *Additional Method.* With prior notice to the deponent and other parties, any party may designate another method for recording the testimony in addition to that specified in the original notice. That party bears the expense of the additional record or transcript unless the court orders otherwise.

    (4) *By Remote Means.* The parties may stipulate—or the court may on motion order—that a deposition be taken by telephone or other remote means. For the purpose of this rule and Rules 28(a), 37(a)(2), and 37(b)(1), the deposition takes place where the deponent answers the questions.

    (5) *Officer's Duties.*

        (A) *Before the Deposition.* Unless the parties stipulate otherwise, a deposition must be conducted before an officer appointed or designated under Rule 28. The officer must begin the deposition with an on-the-record statement that includes:

            (i) the officer's name and business address;

            (ii) the date, time, and place of the deposition;

            (iii) the deponent's name;

            (iv) the officer's administration of the oath or affirmation to the deponent; and

            (v) the identity of all persons present.

        (B) *Conducting the Deposition; Avoiding Distortion.* If the deposition is recorded non-stenographically, the officer must repeat the items in Rule 30(b)(5)(A)(i)–(iii) at the beginning of each unit of the recording medium. The deponent's and attorneys' appearance or demeanor must not be distorted through recording techniques.

(C) *After the Deposition.* At the end of a deposition, the officer must state on the record that the deposition is complete and must set out any stipulations made by the attorneys about custody of the transcript or recording and of the exhibits, or about any other pertinent matters.

(6) ***Notice or Subpoena Directed to an Organization.*** In its notice or subpoena, a party may name as the deponent a public or private corporation, a partnership, an association, a governmental agency, or other entity and must describe with reasonable particularity the matters for examination. The named organization must ~~then~~ designate one or more officers, directors, or managing agents, or designate other persons who consent to testify on its behalf; and it may set out the matters on which each person designated will testify. Before or promptly after the notice or subpoena is served, the serving party and the organization must confer in good faith about the matters for examination. A subpoena must advise a nonparty organization of its duty ~~to make this designation.~~ to confer with the serving party and to designate each person who will testify. The persons designated must testify about information known or reasonably available to the organization. This paragraph (6) does not preclude a deposition by any other procedure allowed by these rules.

(c) Examination and Cross-Examination; Record of the Examination; Objections; Written Questions.

(1) ***Examination and Cross-Examination.*** The examination and cross-examination of a deponent proceed as they would at trial under the Federal Rules of Evidence, except Rules 103 and 615. After putting the deponent under oath or affirmation, the officer must record the testimony by the method designated under Rule 30(b)(3)(A). The testimony must be recorded by the officer personally or by a person acting in the presence and under the direction of the officer.

(2) ***Objections.*** An objection at the time of the examination—whether to evidence, to a party's conduct, to the officer's qualifications, to the manner of taking the deposition, or to any other aspect of the deposition—must be noted on the record, but the examination still proceeds; the testimony is taken subject to any objection. An objection must be stated concisely in a nonargumentative and nonsuggestive manner. A person may instruct a deponent not to answer only when necessary to preserve a privilege, to enforce a limitation ordered by the court, or to present a motion under Rule 30(d)(3).

(3) ***Participating Through Written Questions.*** Instead of participating in the oral examination, a party may serve written questions in a sealed envelope on the party noticing the deposition, who must deliver them to the officer. The officer must ask the deponent those questions and record the answers verbatim.

(d) Duration; Sanction; Motion to Terminate or Limit.

(1) ***Duration.*** Unless otherwise stipulated or ordered by the court, a deposition is limited to 1 day of 7 hours. The court must allow additional time consistent with Rule 26(b)(1) and (2) if needed to fairly examine the deponent or if the deponent, another person, or any other circumstance impedes or delays the examination.

(2) ***Sanction.*** The court may impose an appropriate sanction—including the reasonable expenses and attorney's fees incurred by any party—on a person who impedes, delays, or frustrates the fair examination of the deponent.

(3) ***Motion to Terminate or Limit.***

(A) *Grounds.* At any time during a deposition, the deponent or a party may move to terminate or limit it on the ground that it is being conducted in bad faith or in a manner that unreasonably annoys, embarrasses, or oppresses the deponent or party. The motion may be filed in the court where the action is pending or the deposition is being taken. If the objecting deponent or party so demands, the deposition must be suspended for the time necessary to obtain an order.

(B) *Order.* The court may order that the deposition be terminated or may limit its scope and manner as provided in Rule 26(c). If terminated, the deposition may be resumed only by order of the court where the action is pending.

(C) *Award of Expenses.* Rule 37(a)(5) applies to the award of expenses.

(e) Review by the Witness; Changes.

(1) *Review; Statement of Changes.* On request by the deponent or a party before the deposition is completed, the deponent must be allowed 30 days after being notified by the officer that the transcript or recording is available in which:

(A) to review the transcript or recording; and

(B) if there are changes in form or substance, to sign a statement listing the changes and the reasons for making them.

(2) *Changes Indicated in the Officer's Certificate.* The officer must note in the certificate prescribed by Rule 30(f)(1) whether a review was requested and, if so, must attach any changes the deponent makes during the 30-day period.

(f) Certification and Delivery; Exhibits; Copies of the Transcript or Recording; Filing.

(1) *Certification and Delivery.* The officer must certify in writing that the witness was duly sworn and that the deposition accurately records the witness's testimony. The certificate must accompany the record of the deposition. Unless the court orders otherwise, the officer must seal the deposition in an envelope or package bearing the title of the action and marked "Deposition of [witness's name]" and must promptly send it to the attorney who arranged for the transcript or recording. The attorney must store it under conditions that will protect it against loss, destruction, tampering, or deterioration.

(2) *Documents and Tangible Things.*

(A) *Originals and Copies.* Documents and tangible things produced for inspection during a deposition must, on a party's request, be marked for identification and attached to the deposition. Any party may inspect and copy them. But if the person who produced them wants to keep the originals, the person may:

   (i) offer copies to be marked, attached to the deposition, and then used as originals—after giving all parties a fair opportunity to verify the copies by comparing them with the originals; or

   (ii) give all parties a fair opportunity to inspect and copy the originals after they are marked—in which event the originals may be used as if attached to the deposition.

(B) *Order Regarding the Originals.* Any party may move for an order that the originals be attached to the deposition pending final disposition of the case.

(3) *Copies of the Transcript or Recording.* Unless otherwise stipulated or ordered by the court, the officer must retain the stenographic notes of a deposition taken stenographically or a copy of the recording of a deposition taken by another method. When paid reasonable charges, the officer must furnish a copy of the transcript or recording to any party or the deponent.

(4) *Notice of Filing.* A party who files the deposition must promptly notify all other parties of the filing.

(g) Failure to Attend a Deposition or Serve a Subpoena; Expenses. A party who, expecting a deposition to be taken, attends in person or by an attorney may recover reasonable expenses for attending, including attorney's fees, if the noticing party failed to:

(1) attend and proceed with the deposition; or

(2) serve a subpoena on a nonparty deponent, who consequently did not attend.

(Amended January 21, 1963, effective July 1, 1963; March 30, 1970, effective July 1, 1970; March 1, 1971, effective July 1, 1971; November 20, 1972, effective July 1, 1975; April 29, 1980, effective August 1, 1980; March 2, 1987, effective August 1, 1987; April 22, 1993, effective December 1, 1993; April 17, 2000, effective December 1, 2000; April 30, 2007, effective December 1, 2007; April 29, 2015, effective December 1, 2015; April 27, 2020, effective December 1, 2020 absent congressional action.)

ADVISORY COMMITTEE NOTES

1937 Adoption

Note to Subdivision (a). This is in accordance with common practice. See U.S.C., Title 28, [former] § 639 (Depositions *de bene esse*; when and where taken; notice), the relevant provisions of which are incorporated in this rule; West's Ann.Code Civ.Proc. § 2031; and statutes cited in respect to notice in the Note to Rule 26(a). The provision for enlarging or shortening the time of notice has been added to give flexibility to the rule.

Note to Subdivisions (b) and (d). These are introduced as a safeguard for the protection of parties and deponents on account of the unlimited right of discovery given by Rule 26.

Note to Subdivisions (c) and (e). These follow the general plan of [former] Equity Rule 51 (Evidence Taken Before Examiners, Etc.) and U.S.C., Title 28, [former] §§ 640 (Depositions *de bene esse*; mode of taking), and [former] 641 (Same; transmission to court), but are more specific. They also permit the deponent to require the officer to make changes in the deposition if the deponent is not satisfied with it. See also [former] Equity Rule 50 (Stenographer—Appointment—Fees.)

Note to Subdivision (f). Compare [former] Equity Rule 55 (Depositions Deemed Published When Filed.)

Note to Subdivision (g). This is similar to 2 Minn.Stat. (Mason, 1927) § 9833, but is more extensive.

1963 Amendments

This amendment corresponds to the change in Rule 4(d)(4). See Advisory Committee's Note to that amendment.

1970 Amendments

Subdivision (a). This subdivision contains the provisions of existing Rule 26(a), transferred here as part of the rearrangement relating to Rule 26. Existing Rule 30(a) is transferred to 30(b). Changes in language have been made to conform to the new arrangement.

This subdivision is further revised in regard to the requirement of leave of court for taking a deposition. The present procedure, requiring a plaintiff to obtain leave of court if he serves notice of taking a deposition within 20 days after commencement of the action, is changed in several respects. First, leave is required by reference to the time the deposition is to be taken rather than the date of serving notice of taking. Second, the 20-day period is extended to 30 days and runs from the service of summons and complaint on any defendant, rather than the commencement of the action. *Cf.* Ill.S.Ct.R. 19–1 S-H Ill.Ann.Stat. § 101.19–1. Third, leave is not required beyond the time that defendant initiates discovery, thus showing that he has retained counsel. As under the present practice, a party not afforded a reasonable opportunity to appear at a deposition, because he has not yet been served with process, is protected against use of the deposition at trial against him. See Rule 32(a), transferred from 26(d). Moreover, he can later redepose the witness if he so desires.

The purpose of requiring the plaintiff to obtain leave of court is, as stated by the Advisory Committee that proposed the present language of Rule 26(a), to protect "a defendant who has not had an opportunity to retain counsel and inform himself as to the nature of the suit." Note to 1948 amendment of Rule 26(a), quoted in 3A Barron & Holtzoff, *Federal Practice and Procedure* 455–456 (Wright ed. 1958). In order to assure defendant of this opportunity, the period is lengthened to 30 days. This protection, however, is relevant to the time of taking the deposition, not to the time that notice is served. Similarly, the protective period should run from the service of process rather than the filing of the complaint with the court. As stated in the note to Rule 26(d), the courts have used the service of notice as a convenient reference point for assigning priority in taking depositions, but with the elimination of priority in new Rule 26(d) the reference point is no longer needed. The new procedure is consistent in principle with the provisions of Rules 33, 34, and 36 as revised.

Plaintiff is excused from obtaining leave even during the initial 30-day period if he gives the special notice provided in subdivision (b)(2). The required notice must state that the person to be examined is about to go out of the district where the action is pending and more than 100 miles from the place of trial, or out of the United States, or on a voyage to sea, and will be unavailable for examination unless deposed within the 30-day period. These events occur most often in maritime litigation, when seamen are transferred from one port to another or are about to go to sea. Yet, there are analogous situations in nonmaritime litigation, and although the maritime problems are more common, a rule limited to claims in the admiralty and maritime jurisdiction is not justified.

In the recent unification of the civil and admiralty rules, this problem was temporarily met through addition in Rule 26(a) of a provision that depositions *de bene esse* may continue to be taken as to admiralty and maritime claims within the meaning of Rule 9(h). It was recognized at the time that "a uniform rule applicable alike to what are now civil actions and suits in admiralty" was clearly preferable, but the de bene esse procedure was adopted "for the time being at least." See Advisory Committee's Note in Report of the Judicial Conference: Proposed Amendments to Rules of Civil Procedure 43–44 (1966).

The changes in Rule 30(a) and the new Rule 30(b)(2) provide a formula applicable to ordinary civil as well as maritime claims. They replace the provision for depositions *de bene esse*. They authorize an early deposition without leave of court where the witness is about to depart and, unless his deposition is promptly taken, (1) it will be impossible or very difficult to depose him before trial or (2) his deposition can later be taken but only with substantially increased effort and expense. *Cf. S.S. Hai Chang*, 1966 A.M.C. 2239 (S.D.N.Y.1966), in which the deposing party is required to prepay expenses and counsel fees of the other party's lawyer when the action is pending in New York and depositions are to be taken on the West Coast. Defendant is protected by a provision that the deposition cannot be used against him if he was unable through exercise of diligence to obtain counsel to represent him.

The distance of 100 miles from place of trial is derived from the *de bene esse* provision and also conforms to the reach of a subpoena of the trial court, as provided in Rule 45(e). See also S.D.N.Y. Civ.R. 5(a). Some parts of the *de bene esse* provision are omitted from Rule 30(b)(2). Modern deposition practice adequately covers the witness who lives more than 100 miles away from place of trial. If a witness is aged or infirm, leave of court can be obtained.

Subdivision (b). Existing Rule 30(b) on protective orders has been transferred to Rule 26(c), and existing Rule 30(a) relating to the notice of taking deposition has been transferred to this subdivision. Because new material has been added, subsection numbers have been inserted.

Subdivision (b)(1). If a subpoena duces tecum is to be served, a copy thereof or a designation of the materials to be produced must accompany the notice. Each party is thereby enabled to prepare for the deposition more effectively.

Subdivision (b)(2). This subdivision is discussed in the note to subdivision (a), to which it relates.

Subdivision (b)(3). This provision is derived from existing Rule 30(a), with a minor change of language.

Subdivision (b)(4). In order to facilitate less expensive procedures, provision is made for the recording of testimony by other than stenographic means—*e.g.*, by mechanical, electronic, or photographic means. Because these methods give rise to problems of accuracy and trustworthiness, the party taking the deposition is required to apply for a court order. The order is to specify how the testimony is to be recorded, preserved, and filed, and it may contain whatever additional safeguards the court deems necessary.

Subdivision (b)(5). A provision is added to enable a party, through service of notice, to require another party to produce documents or things at the taking of his deposition. This may now be done as to a nonparty deponent through use of a subpoena duces tecum as authorized by Rule 45, but some courts have held that documents may be secured from a party only under Rule 34. See 2A Barron & Holtzoff, *Federal Practice and Procedure* § 644.1 n. 83.2, § 792 n. 16 (Wright ed. 1961). With the elimination of "good cause" from Rule 34, the reason for this restrictive doctrine has disappeared. *Cf.* N.Y.C.P.L.R. § 3111.

Whether production of documents or things should be obtained directly under Rule 34 or at the deposition under this rule will depend on the nature and volume of the documents or things. Both methods are made available. When the documents are few and simple, and closely related to the oral examination, ability to proceed via this rule will facilitate discovery. If the discovering party insists on examining many and complex documents at the taking of the deposition, thereby causing undue burdens on others, the latter may, under Rules 26(c) or 30(d), apply for a court order that the examining party proceed via Rule 34 alone.

Subdivision (b)(6). A new provision is added, whereby a party may name a corporation, partnership, association, or governmental agency as the deponent and designate the matters on which he requests examination, and the organization shall then name one or more of its officers, directors, or managing agents, or other persons consenting to appear and testify on its behalf with respect to matters known or reasonably available to the organization. *Cf.* Alberta Sup.Ct.R. 255. The organization may designate persons other than officers, directors, and managing agents, but only with their consent. Thus, an employee or agent who has an independent or conflicting interest in the litigation—for example, in a personal injury case—can refuse to testify on behalf of the organization.

This procedure supplements the existing practice whereby the examining party designates the corporate official to be deposed. Thus, if the examining party believes that certain officials who have not testified pursuant to this subdivision have added information, he may depose them. On the other hand, a court's decision whether to issue a protective order may take account of the availability and use made of the procedures provided in this subdivision.

The new procedure should be viewed as an added facility for discovery, one which may be advantageous to both sides as well as an improvement in the deposition process. It will reduce the difficulties now encountered in determining, prior to the taking of a deposition, whether a particular employee or agent is a "managing agent." See Note, *Discovery Against Corporations Under the Federal Rules*, 47 Iowa L.Rev. 1006–1016 (1962). It will curb the "bandying" by which officers or managing agents of a corporation are deposed in turn but each disclaims knowledge of facts that are clearly known to persons in the organization and thereby to it. *Cf. Haney v. Woodward & Lothrop, Inc.*, 330 F.2d 940, 944 (4th Cir. 1964). The provision should also assist organizations which find that an unnecessarily large number of their officers and agents are being deposed by a party uncertain of who in the organization has knowledge. Some courts have held that under the existing rules a corporation should not be burdened with choosing which person is to appear for it. E.g., *United States v. Gahagan Dredging Corp.*, 24 F.R.D. 328, 329 (S.D.N.Y.1958). This burden is not essentially different from that of answering interrogatories under Rule 33, and is in any case lighter than that of an examining party ignorant of who in the corporation has knowledge.

Subdivision (c). A new sentence is inserted at the beginning, representing the transfer of existing Rule 26(c) to this subdivision. Another addition conforms to the new provision in subdivision (b)(4).

The present rule provides that transcription shall be carried out unless all parties waive it. In view of the many depositions taken from which nothing useful is discovered, the revised language provides that transcription is to be performed if any party requests it. The fact of the request is relevant to the exercise of the court's discretion in determining who shall pay for transcription.

Parties choosing to serve written questions rather than participate personally in an oral deposition are directed to serve their questions on the party taking the deposition, since the officer is often not identified in advance. Confidentiality is preserved, since the questions may be served in a sealed envelope.

Subdivision (d). The assessment of expenses incurred in relation to motions made under this subdivision (d) is made subject to the provisions of Rule 37(a). The standards for assessment of expenses are more fully set out in Rule 37(a), and these standards should apply to the essentially similar motions of this subdivision.

Subdivision (e). The provision relating to the refusal of a witness to sign his deposition is tightened through insertion of a 30-day time period.

Subdivision (f)(1). A provision is added which codifies in a flexible way the procedure for handling exhibits related to the deposition and at the same time assures each party that he may inspect and copy documents and things produced by a nonparty witness in response to a subpoena duces tecum. As a general rule and in the absence of agreement to the contrary or order of the court, exhibits produced without objection are to be annexed to and returned with the deposition, but a witness may substitute copies for purposes of marking and he may obtain return of the exhibits. The right of the parties to inspect exhibits for identification and to make copies is assured. *Cf.* N.Y.C.P.L.R. § 3116(c).

1971 Amendments

The subdivision permits a party to name a corporation or other form of organization as a deponent in the notice of examination and to describe in the notice the matters about which discovery is desired. The organization is then obliged to designate natural persons to testify on its behalf. The amendment clarifies the procedure to be followed if a party desires to examine a non-party organization through persons designated by the organization. Under the rules, a subpoena rather than a notice of examination is served on a non-party to compel attendance at the taking of a deposition. The amendment provides that a subpoena may name a non-party organization as the deponent and may indicate the matters about which discovery is desired. In that event, the non-party organization must respond by designating natural persons, who are then obliged to testify as to matters known or reasonably available to the organization. To insure that a non-party organization that is not represented by counsel has knowledge of its duty to designate, the amendment directs the party seeking discovery to advise of the duty in the body of the subpoena.

1972 Amendments

Subdivision (c). Existing Rule 43(b), which is to be abrogated, deals with the use of leading questions, the calling, interrogation, impeachment, and scope of cross-examination of adverse parties, officers, etc. These topics are dealt with in many places in the Rules of Evidence. Moreover, many pertinent topics included in the Rules of Evidence are not mentioned in Rule 43(b), e.g. privilege. A reference to the Rules of Evidence generally is therefore made in subdivision (c) of Rule 30.

1980 Amendments

Subdivision (b)(4). It has been proposed that electronic recording of depositions be authorized as a matter of course, subject to the right of a party to seek an order that a deposition be recorded by stenographic means. The Committee is not satisfied that a case has been made for a reversal of present practice. The amendment is made to encourage parties to agree to the use of electronic recording of depositions so that conflicting claims with respect to the potential of electronic recording for reducing costs of depositions can be appraised in the light of greater experience. The provision that the parties may stipulate that depositions may be recorded by other than stenographic means seems implicit in Rule 29. The amendment makes it explicit. The provision that the stipulation or order shall designate the person before whom the deposition is to be taken is added to encourage the naming of the recording technician as that person, eliminating the necessity of the presence of one whose only function is to administer the oath. See Rules 28(a) and 29.

Subdivision (b)(7). Depositions by telephone are now authorized by Rule 29 upon stipulation of the parties. The amendment authorizes that method by order of the court. The final sentence is added to make it clear that when a deposition is taken by telephone it is taken in the district and at the place where the witness is to answer the questions rather than that where the questions are propounded.

Subdivision (f)(1). For the reasons set out in the Note following the amendment of Rule 5(d), the court may wish to permit the parties to retain depositions unless they are to be used in the action. The amendment of the first paragraph permits the court to so order.

The amendment of the second paragraph is clarifying. The purpose of the paragraph is to permit a person who produces materials at a deposition to offer copies for marking and annexation to the deposition. Such copies are a "substitute" for the originals, which are not to be marked and which can thereafter be used or even disposed of by the person who produces them. In the light of that purpose, the former language of the paragraph had been justly termed "opaque." Wright & Miller, *Federal Practice and Procedure: Civil* § 2114.

1987 Amendments

The amendments are technical. No substantive change is intended.

1993 Amendments

Subdivision (a). Paragraph (1) retains the first and third sentences from the former subdivision (a) without significant modification. The second and fourth sentences are relocated.

Paragraph (2) collects all provisions bearing on requirements of leave of court to take a deposition.

Paragraph (2)(A) is new. It provides a limit on the number of depositions the parties may take, absent leave of court or stipulation with the other parties. One aim of this revision is to assure judicial review under the standards stated in Rule 26(b)(2) before any side will be allowed to take more than ten depositions in a case without agreement of the other parties. A second objective is to emphasize that counsel have a professional obligation to develop a mutual cost-effective plan for discovery in the case. Leave to take additional depositions should be granted when consistent with the principles of Rule 26(b)(2), and in some cases the ten-per-side limit should be reduced in accordance with those same principles. Consideration should ordinarily be given at the planning meeting of the parties under Rule 26(f) and at the time of a scheduling conference under Rule 16(b) as to enlargements or reductions in the number of depositions, eliminating the need for special motions.

A deposition under Rule 30(b)(6) should, for purposes of this limit, be treated as a single deposition even though more than one person may be designated to testify.

In multi-party cases, the parties on any side are expected to confer and agree as to which depositions are most needed, given the presumptive limit on the number of depositions they can take without leave of court. If these disputes cannot be amicably resolved, the court can be requested to resolve the dispute or permit additional depositions.

Paragraph (2)(B) is new. It requires leave of court if any witness is to be deposed in the action more than once. This requirement does not apply when a deposition is temporarily recessed for convenience of counsel or the deponent or to enable additional materials to be gathered before resuming the deposition. If significant travel costs would be incurred to resume the deposition, the parties should consider the feasibility of conducting the balance of the examination by telephonic means.

Paragraph (2)(C) revises the second sentence of the former subdivision (a) as to when depositions may be taken. Consistent with the changes made in Rule 26(d), providing that formal discovery ordinarily not commence until after the litigants have met and conferred as directed in revised Rule 26(f), the rule requires leave of court or agreement of the parties if a deposition is to be taken before that time (except when a witness is about to leave the country).

Subdivision (b). The primary change in subdivision (b) is that parties will be authorized to record deposition testimony by nonstenographic means without first having to obtain permission of the court or agreement from other counsel.

Former subdivision (b)(2) is partly relocated in subdivision (a)(2)(C) of this rule. The latter two sentences of the first paragraph are deleted, in part because they are redundant to Rule 26(g) and in part because Rule 11 no longer applies to discovery requests. The second paragraph of the former subdivision (b)(2), relating to use of depositions at trial where a party was unable to obtain counsel in time for an accelerated deposition, is relocated in Rule 32.

New paragraph (2) confers on the party taking the deposition the choice of the method of recording, without the need to obtain prior court approval for one taken other than stenographically. A party choosing to record a deposition only by videotape or audiotape should understand that a transcript will be required by Rule 26(a)(3)(B) and Rule 32(c) if the deposition is later to be offered as evidence at trial or on a dispositive motion under Rule 56. Objections to the nonstenographic recording of a deposition, when warranted by the circumstances, can be presented to the court under Rule 26(c).

Paragraph (3) provides that other parties may arrange, at their own expense, for the recording of a deposition by a means (stenographic, visual, or sound) in addition to the method designated by the person noticing the deposition. The former provisions of this paragraph, relating to the court's power to change the date of a deposition, have been eliminated as redundant in view of Rule 26(c)(2).

Revised paragraph (4) requires that all depositions be recorded by an officer designated or appointed under Rule 28 and contains special provisions designed to provide basic safeguards to assure the utility and integrity of recordings taken other than stenographically.

Paragraph (7) is revised to authorize the taking of a deposition not only by telephone but also by other remote electronic means, such as satellite television, when agreed to by the parties or authorized by the court.

Subdivision (c). Minor changes are made in this subdivision to reflect those made in subdivision (b) and to complement the new provisions of subdivision (d)(1), aimed at reducing the number of interruptions during depositions.

In addition, the revision addresses a recurring problem as to whether other potential deponents can attend a deposition. Courts have disagreed, some holding that witnesses should be excluded through invocation of Rule 615 of the evidence rules, and others holding that witnesses may attend unless excluded by an order under Rule 26(c)(5). The revision provides that other witnesses are not automatically excluded from a deposition simply by the request of a party. Exclusion, however, can be ordered under Rule 26(c)(5) when appropriate; and, if exclusion is ordered, consideration should be given as to whether the excluded witnesses likewise should be precluded from reading, or being otherwise informed about, the testimony given in the earlier depositions. The revision addresses only the matter of attendance by potential deponents, and does not attempt to resolve issues concerning attendance by others, such as members of the public or press.

Subdivision (d). The first sentence of new paragraph (1) provides that any objections during a deposition must be made concisely and in a non-argumentative and non-suggestive manner. Depositions frequently have been unduly prolonged, if not unfairly frustrated, by lengthy objections and colloquy, often suggesting how the deponent should respond. While objections may, under the revised rule, be made during a deposition, they ordinarily should be limited to those that under Rule 32(d)(3) might be waived if not made at that time, *i.e.,* objections on grounds that might be immediately obviated, removed, or cured, such as to the form of a question or the responsiveness of an answer. Under Rule 32(b), other objections can, even without the so-called "usual stipulation" preserving objections, be raised for the first time at trial and therefore should be kept to a minimum during a deposition.

Directions to a deponent not to answer a question can be even more disruptive than objections. The second sentence of new paragraph (1) prohibits such directions except in the three circumstances indicated: to claim a privilege or protection against disclosure (*e.g.,* as work product), to enforce a court directive limiting the scope or length of permissible discovery, or to suspend a deposition to enable presentation of a motion under paragraph (3).

Paragraph (2) is added to this subdivision to dispel any doubts regarding the power of the court by order or local rule to establish limits on the length of depositions. The rule also explicitly authorizes the court to impose the cost resulting from obstructive tactics that unreasonably prolong a deposition on the person engaged in such obstruction. This sanction may be imposed on a non-party witness as well as a party or attorney, but is otherwise congruent with Rule 26(g).

It is anticipated that limits on the length of depositions prescribed by local rules would be presumptive only, subject to modification by the court or by agreement of the parties. Such modifications typically should be discussed by the parties in their meeting under Rule 26(f) and included in the scheduling order required by Rule 16(b). Additional time, moreover, should be allowed under the revised rule when justified under the principles stated in Rule 26(b)(2). To reduce the number of special motions, local rules should ordinarily permit—and indeed encourage—the parties to agree to additional time, as when, during the taking of a deposition, it becomes clear that some additional examination is needed.

Paragraph (3) authorizes appropriate sanctions not only when a deposition is unreasonably prolonged, but also when an attorney engages in other practices that improperly frustrate the fair examination of the deponent, such as making improper objections or giving directions not to answer prohibited by paragraph (1). In general, counsel should not engage in any conduct during a deposition that would not be allowed in the presence of a judicial officer. The making of an excessive number of unnecessary objections may itself constitute sanctionable conduct, as may the refusal of an attorney to agree with other counsel on a fair apportionment of the time allowed for examination of a deponent or a refusal to agree to a reasonable request for some additional time to complete a deposition, when that is permitted by the local rule or order.

Subdivision (e). Various changes are made in this subdivision to reduce problems sometimes encountered when depositions are taken stenographically. Reporters frequently have difficulties obtaining signatures—and the return of depositions—from deponents. Under the revision pre-filing review by the deponent is required only if requested before the deposition is completed. If review is requested, the deponent will be allowed 30 days to review the transcript or recording and to indicate any changes in form or substance. Signature of the deponent will be required only if review is requested and changes are made.

Subdivision (f). Minor changes are made in this subdivision to reflect those made in subdivision (b). In courts which direct that depositions not be automatically filed, the reporter can transmit the transcript or recording to the attorney taking the deposition (or ordering the transcript or record), who then becomes custodian for the court of the original record of the deposition. Pursuant to subdivision (f)(2), as under the prior rule, any other party is entitled to secure a copy of the deposition from the officer designated to take the deposition; accordingly, unless ordered or agreed, the officer must retain a copy of the recording or the stenographic notes.

2000 Amendment

Subdivision (d). Paragraph (1) has been amended to clarify the terms regarding behavior during depositions. The references to objections " to evidence" and limitations "on evidence" have been removed to avoid disputes about what is "evidence" and whether an objection is to, or a limitation is on, discovery instead. It is intended that the rule apply to any objection to a question or other issue arising during a deposition, and to any limitation imposed by the court in connection with a deposition, which might relate to duration or other matters.

The current rule places limitations on instructions that a witness not answer only when the instruction is made by a "party." Similar limitations should apply with regard to anyone who might purport to instruct a witness not to answer a question. Accordingly, the rule is amended to apply the limitation to instructions by any person. The amendment is not intended to confer new authority on nonparties to instruct witnesses to refuse to answer deposition questions. The amendment makes it clear that, whatever the legitimacy of giving such instructions, the nonparty is subject to the same limitations as parties.

Paragraph (2) imposes a presumptive durational limitation of one day of seven hours for any deposition. The Committee has been informed that overlong depositions can result in undue costs and delays in some circumstances. This limitation contemplates that there will be reasonable breaks during the day for lunch and other reasons, and that the only time to be counted is the time occupied by the actual deposition. For purposes of this durational limit, the deposition of each person designated under Rule 30(b)(6) should be considered a separate deposition. The presumptive duration may be extended, or otherwise altered, by agreement. Absent agreement, a court order is needed. The party seeking a court order to extend the examination, or otherwise alter the limitations, is expected to show good cause to justify such an order.

Parties considering extending the time for a deposition—and courts asked to order an extension— might consider a variety of factors. For example, if the witness needs an interpreter, that may prolong the examination. If the examination will cover events occurring over a long period of time, that may justify allowing additional time. In cases in which the witness will be questioned about numerous or lengthy documents, it is often desirable for the interrogating party to send copies of the documents to the witness sufficiently in advance of the deposition so that the witness can become familiar with them. Should the witness nevertheless not read the documents in advance, thereby prolonging the deposition, a court could consider that a reason for extending the time limit. If the examination reveals that documents have been requested but not produced, that may justify further examination once production has occurred. In multi-party cases, the need for each party to examine the witness may warrant additional time, although duplicative questioning should be avoided and parties with similar interests should strive to designate one lawyer to question about areas of common interest. Similarly, should the lawyer for the witness want to examine the witness, that may require additional time. Finally, with regard to expert witnesses, there may more often be a need for additional time—even after the submission of the report required by Rule 26(a)(2)— for full exploration of the theories upon which the witness relies.

It is expected that in most instances the parties and the witness will make reasonable accommodations to avoid the need for resort to the court. The limitation is phrased in terms of a single day on the assumption that ordinarily a single day would be preferable to a deposition extending over multiple days; if alternative arrangements would better suit the parties, they may agree to them. It is also assumed that there will be reasonable breaks during the day. Preoccupation with timing is to be avoided.

The rule directs the court to allow additional time where consistent with Rule 26(b)(2) if needed for a fair examination of the deponent. In addition, if the deponent or another person impedes or delays the examination, the court must authorize extra time. The amendment makes clear that additional time should also be allowed where the examination is impeded by an "other circumstance," which might include a power outage, a health emergency, or other event.

In keeping with the amendment to Rule 26(b)(2), the provision added in 1993 granting authority to adopt a local rule limiting the time permitted for depositions has been removed. The court may enter a case-specific order directing shorter depositions for all depositions in a case or with regard to a specific witness. The court may also order that a deposition be taken for limited periods on several days.

Paragraph (3) includes sanctions provisions formerly included in paragraph (2). It authorizes the court to impose an appropriate sanction on any person responsible for an impediment that frustrated the fair examination of the deponent. This could include the deponent, any party, or any other person involved in the deposition. If the impediment or delay results from an "other circumstance" under paragraph (2), ordinarily no sanction would be appropriate.

Former paragraph (3) has been renumbered (4) but is otherwise unchanged.

Subdivision (f)(1): This subdivision is amended because Rule 5(d) has been amended to direct that discovery materials, including depositions, ordinarily should not be filed. The rule already has provisions directing that the lawyer who arranged for the transcript or recording preserve the deposition. Rule 5(d) provides that, once the deposition is used in the proceeding, the attorney must file it with the court.

"Shall" is replaced by "must" or "may" under the program to conform amended rules to current style conventions when there is no ambiguity.

Gap Report

The Advisory Committee recommends deleting the requirement in the published proposed amendments that the deponent consent to extending a deposition beyond one day, and adding an amendment to Rule 30(f)(1) to conform to the published amendment to Rule 5(d) regarding filing of depositions. It also recommends conforming the Committee Note with regard to the deponent veto, and adding material to the Note to provide direction on computation of the durational limitation on depositions, to provide examples of situations in which the parties might agree—or the court order—that a deposition be extended, and to make clear that no new authority to instruct a witness is conferred by the amendment. One minor wording improvement in the Note is also suggested.

2007 Amendment

The language of Rule 30 has been amended as part of the general restyling of the Civil Rules to make them more easily understood and to make style and terminology consistent throughout the rules. These changes are intended to be stylistic only.

The right to arrange a deposition transcription should be open to any party, regardless of the means of recording and regardless of who noticed the deposition.

"[O]ther entity" is added to the list of organizations that may be named as deponent. The purpose is to ensure that the deposition process can be used to reach information known or reasonably available to an organization no matter what abstract fictive concept is used to describe the organization. Nothing is gained by wrangling over the place to fit into current rule language such entities as limited liability companies, limited partnerships, business trusts, more exotic common-law creations, or forms developed in other countries.

2015 Amendment

Rule 30 is amended in parallel with Rules 31 and 33 to reflect the recognition of proportionality in Rule 26(b)(1).

Gap Report

The proposals to reduce the presumptive number of depositions from 10 to 5, and to shorten the presumptive length of an oral deposition from one day of 7 hours to one day of 6 hours, were withdrawn. The Committee Note was changed accordingly.

2020 Amendment

[Effective Dec. 1, 2020 absent contrary congressional action.]

Rule 30(b)(6) is amended to respond to problems that have emerged in some cases. Particular concerns raised have included overlong or ambiguously worded lists of matters for examination and inadequately prepared witnesses. This amendment directs the serving party and the named organization to confer before or promptly after the notice or subpoena is served about the matters for examination. The amendment also requires that a subpoena notify a nonparty organization of its duty to confer and to designate each person who will testify. It facilitates collaborative efforts to achieve the proportionality goals of the 2015 amendments to Rules 1 and 26(b)(1).

Candid exchanges about the purposes of the deposition and the organization's information structure may clarify and focus the matters for examination, and enable the organization to designate and to prepare an appropriate witness or witnesses, thereby avoiding later disagreements. It may be productive also to discuss "process" issues, such as the timing and location of the deposition, the number of witnesses and the matters on which each witness will testify, and any other issue that might facilitate the efficiency and productivity of the deposition.

The amended rule directs that the parties confer either before or promptly after the notice or subpoena is served. If they begin to confer before service, the discussion may be more productive if the serving party provides a draft of the proposed list of matters for examination, which may then be refined as the parties confer. The process of conferring may be iterative. Consistent with Rule 1, the obligation is to confer in good faith about the matters for examination, but the amendment does not require the parties to reach agreement. In some circumstances, it may be desirable to seek guidance from the court.

When the need for a Rule 30(b)(6) deposition is known early in the case, the Rule 26(f) conference may provide an occasion for beginning discussion of these topics. In appropriate cases, it may also be helpful to include reference to Rule 30(b)(6) depositions in the discovery plan submitted to the court under Rule 26(f)(3) and in the matters considered at a pretrial conference under Rule 16.

Because a Rule 31 deposition relies on written questions rather than a description with reasonable particularity of the matters for examination, the duty to confer about the matters for examination does not apply when an organization is deposed under Rule 31(a)(4).

Rule 31.   Depositions by Written Questions

(a) When a Deposition May Be Taken.

(1) *Without Leave.* A party may, by written questions, depose any person, including a party, without leave of court except as provided in Rule 31(a)(2). The deponent's attendance may be compelled by subpoena under Rule 45.

(2) *With Leave.* A party must obtain leave of court, and the court must grant leave to the extent consistent with Rule 26(b)(1) and (2):

(A) if the parties have not stipulated to the deposition and:

(i)   the deposition would result in more than 10 depositions being taken under this rule or Rule 30 by the plaintiffs, or by the defendants, or by the third-party defendants;

(ii) the deponent has already been deposed in the case; or

269

        (iii) the party seeks to take a deposition before the time specified in Rule 26(d); or

    (B) if the deponent is confined in prison.

  (3) *Service; Required Notice.* A party who wants to depose a person by written questions must serve them on every other party, with a notice stating, if known, the deponent's name and address. If the name is unknown, the notice must provide a general description sufficient to identify the person or the particular class or group to which the person belongs. The notice must also state the name or descriptive title and the address of the officer before whom the deposition will be taken.

  (4) *Questions Directed to an Organization.* A public or private corporation, a partnership, an association, or a governmental agency may be deposed by written questions in accordance with Rule 30(b)(6).

  (5) *Questions from Other Parties.* Any questions to the deponent from other parties must be served on all parties as follows: cross-questions, within 14 days after being served with the notice and direct questions; redirect questions, within 7 days after being served with cross-questions; and recross-questions, within 7 days after being served with redirect questions. The court may, for good cause, extend or shorten these times.

(b) Delivery to the Officer; Officer's Duties. The party who noticed the deposition must deliver to the officer a copy of all the questions served and of the notice. The officer must promptly proceed in the manner provided in Rule 30(c), (e), and (f) to:

  (1) take the deponent's testimony in response to the questions;

  (2) prepare and certify the deposition; and

  (3) send it to the party, attaching a copy of the questions and of the notice.

(c) Notice of Completion or Filing.

  (1) *Completion.* The party who noticed the deposition must notify all other parties when it is completed.

  (2) *Filing.* A party who files the deposition must promptly notify all other parties of the filing.

(Amended March 30, 1970, effective July 1, 1970; March 2, 1987, effective August 1, 1987; April 22, 1993, effective December 1, 1993; April 30, 2007, effective December 1, 2007; April 29, 2015, effective December 1, 2015.)

ADVISORY COMMITTEE NOTES

1937 Adoption

This rule is in accordance with common practice. In most of the states listed in the Note to Rule 26(a), provisions similar to this rule will be found in the statutes which in their respective statutory compilations follow those cited in the Note to Rule 26(a).

1970 Amendment

Confusion is created by the use of the same terminology to describe both the taking of a deposition upon "written interrogatories" pursuant to this rule and the serving of "written interrogatories" upon parties pursuant to Rule 33. The distinction between these two modes of discovery will be more readily and clearly grasped through substitution of the word "questions" for "interrogatories" throughout this rule.

Subdivision (a). A new paragraph is inserted at the beginning of this subdivision to conform to the rearrangement of provisions in Rules 26(a), 30(a), and 30(b).

The revised subdivision permits designation of the deponent by general description or by class or group. This conforms to the practice for depositions on oral examination.

The new procedure provided in Rule 30(b)(6) for taking the deposition of a corporation or other organization through persons designated by the organization is incorporated by reference.

The service of all questions, including cross, redirect, and recross, is to be made on all parties. This will inform the parties and enable them to participate fully in the procedure.

The time allowed for service of cross, redirect, and recross questions has been extended. Experience with the existing time limits shows them to be unrealistically short. No special restriction is placed on the time for serving the notice of taking the deposition and the first set of questions. Since no party is required to serve cross questions less than 30 days after the notice and questions are served, the defendant has sufficient time to obtain counsel. The court may for cause shown enlarge or shorten the time.

Subdivision (d). Since new Rule 26(c) provides for protective orders with respect to all discovery, and expressly provides that the court may order that one discovery device be used in place of another, subdivision (d) is eliminated as unnecessary.

1987 Amendment

The amendments are technical. No substantive change is intended.

1993 Amendments

Subdivision (a). The first paragraph of subdivision (a) is divided into two subparagraphs, with provisions comparable to those made in the revision of Rule 30. Changes are made in the former third paragraph, numbered in the revision as paragraph (4), to reduce the total time for developing cross-examination, redirect, and recross questions from 50 days to 28 days.

2007 Amendment

The language of Rule 31 has been amended as part of the general restyling of the Civil Rules to make them more easily understood and to make style and terminology consistent throughout the rules. These changes are intended to be stylistic only.

The party who noticed a deposition on written questions must notify all other parties when the deposition is completed, so that they may make use of the deposition. A deposition is completed when it is recorded and the deponent has either waived or exercised the right of review under Rule 30(e)(1).

2015 Amendment

Rule 31 is amended in parallel with Rules 30 and 33 to reflect the recognition of proportionality in Rule 26(b)(1).

Gap Report

The proposal to reduce the presumptive number of depositions from 10 to 5 was withdrawn. The Committee Note was changed accordingly.

Rule 32.   Using Depositions in Court Proceedings

(a) Using Depositions.

    (1) *In General.* At a hearing or trial, all or part of a deposition may be used against a party on these conditions:

        (A) the party was present or represented at the taking of the deposition or had reasonable notice of it;

        (B) it is used to the extent it would be admissible under the Federal Rules of Evidence if the deponent were present and testifying; and

        (C) the use is allowed by Rule 32(a)(2) through (8).

    (2) *Impeachment and Other Uses.* Any party may use a deposition to contradict or impeach the testimony given by the deponent as a witness, or for any other purpose allowed by the Federal Rules of Evidence.

    (3) *Deposition of Party, Agent, or Designee.* An adverse party may use for any purpose the deposition of a party or anyone who, when deposed, was the party's officer, director, managing agent, or designee under Rule 30(b)(6) or 31(a)(4).

(4) *Unavailable Witness.* A party may use for any purpose the deposition of a witness, whether or not a party, if the court finds:

(A) that the witness is dead;

(B) that the witness is more than 100 miles from the place of hearing or trial or is outside the United States, unless it appears that the witness's absence was procured by the party offering the deposition;

(C) that the witness cannot attend or testify because of age, illness, infirmity, or imprisonment;

(D) that the party offering the deposition could not procure the witness's attendance by subpoena; or

(E) on motion and notice, that exceptional circumstances make it desirable—in the interest of justice and with due regard to the importance of live testimony in open court—to permit the deposition to be used.

(5) *Limitations on Use.*

(A) *Deposition Taken on Short Notice.* A deposition must not be used against a party who, having received less than 14 days' notice of the deposition, promptly moved for a protective order under Rule 26(c)(1)(B) requesting that it not be taken or be taken at a different time or place—and this motion was still pending when the deposition was taken.

(B) *Unavailable Deponent; Party Could Not Obtain an Attorney.* A deposition taken without leave of court under the unavailability provision of Rule 30(a)(2)(A)(iii) must not be used against a party who shows that, when served with the notice, it could not, despite diligent efforts, obtain an attorney to represent it at the deposition.

(6) *Using Part of a Deposition.* If a party offers in evidence only part of a deposition, an adverse party may require the offeror to introduce other parts that in fairness should be considered with the part introduced, and any party may itself introduce any other parts.

(7) *Substituting a Party.* Substituting a party under Rule 25 does not affect the right to use a deposition previously taken.

(8) *Deposition Taken in an Earlier Action.* A deposition lawfully taken and, if required, filed in any federal- or state-court action may be used in a later action involving the same subject matter between the same parties, or their representatives or successors in interest, to the same extent as if taken in the later action. A deposition previously taken may also be used as allowed by the Federal Rules of Evidence.

(b) **Objections to Admissibility.** Subject to Rules 28(b) and 32(d)(3), an objection may be made at a hearing or trial to the admission of any deposition testimony that would be inadmissible if the witness were present and testifying.

(c) **Form of Presentation.** Unless the court orders otherwise, a party must provide a transcript of any deposition testimony the party offers, but may provide the court with the testimony in nontranscript form as well. On any party's request, deposition testimony offered in a jury trial for any purpose other than impeachment must be presented in nontranscript form, if available, unless the court for good cause orders otherwise.

(d) **Waiver of Objections.**

(1) *To the Notice.* An objection to an error or irregularity in a deposition notice is waived unless promptly served in writing on the party giving the notice.

(2) *To the Officer's Qualification.* An objection based on disqualification of the officer before whom a deposition is to be taken is waived if not made:

   (A)   before the deposition begins; or

   (B)   promptly after the basis for disqualification becomes known or, with reasonable diligence, could have been known.

(3)   *To the Taking of the Deposition.*

   (A)   *Objection to Competence, Relevance, or Materiality.* An objection to a deponent's competence—or to the competence, relevance, or materiality of testimony—is not waived by a failure to make the objection before or during the deposition, unless the ground for it might have been corrected at that time.

   (B)   *Objection to an Error or Irregularity.* An objection to an error or irregularity at an oral examination is waived if:

      (i)   it relates to the manner of taking the deposition, the form of a question or answer, the oath or affirmation, a party's conduct, or other matters that might have been corrected at that time; and

      (ii)   it is not timely made during the deposition.

   (C)   *Objection to a Written Question.* An objection to the form of a written question under Rule 31 is waived if not served in writing on the party submitting the question within the time for serving responsive questions or, if the question is a recross-question, within 7 days after being served with it.

(4)   *To Completing and Returning the Deposition.* An objection to how the officer transcribed the testimony—or prepared, signed, certified, sealed, endorsed, sent, or otherwise dealt with the deposition—is waived unless a motion to suppress is made promptly after the error or irregularity becomes known or, with reasonable diligence, could have been known.

(Amended March 30, 1970, effective July 1, 1970; November 20, 1972, effective July 1, 1975; April 29, 1980, effective August 1, 1980; March 2, 1987, effective August 1, 1987; April 22, 1993, effective December 1, 1993; April 30, 2007, effective December 1, 2007; March 26, 2009, effective December 1, 2009.)

ADVISORY COMMITTEE NOTES

1937 Adoption

This rule is in accordance with common practice. In most of the states listed in the note to rule 26, provisions similar to this rule will be found in the statutes which in their respective statutory compilations follow those cited in the Note to Rule 26.

1970 Amendment

As part of the rearrangement of the discovery rules, existing subdivisions (d), (e), and (f) of Rule 26 are transferred to Rule 32 as new subdivisions (a), (b), and (c). The provisions of Rule 32 are retained as subdivision (d) of Rule 32 with appropriate changes in the lettering and numbering of subheadings. The new rule is given a suitable new title. A beneficial byproduct of the rearrangement is that provisions which are naturally related to one another are placed in one rule.

A change is made in new Rule 32(a), whereby it is made clear that the rules of evidence are to be applied to depositions offered at trial as though the deponent were then present and testifying at trial. This eliminates the possibility of certain technical hearsay objections which are based, not on the contents of deponent's testimony, but on his absence from court. The language of present Rule 26(d) does not appear to authorize these technical objections, but it is not entirely clear. Note present Rule 26(e), transferred to Rule 32(b); see 2A Barron & Holtzoff, *Federal Practice and Procedure* 164–166 (Wright ed. 1961).

An addition in Rule 32(a)(2) provides for use of a deposition of a person designated by a corporation or other organization, which is a party, to testify on its behalf. This complements the new procedure for taking the deposition of a corporation or other organization provided in Rules 30(b)(6) and 31(a). The addition is appropriate, since the deposition is in substance and effect that of the corporation or other organization which is a party.

A change is made in the standard under which a party offering part of a deposition in evidence may be required to introduce additional parts of the deposition. The new standard is contained in a proposal made by the Advisory Committee on Rules of Evidence. See Rule 1–07 and accompanying Note, *Preliminary Draft of Proposed Rules of Evidence for the United States District Courts and Magistrates* 21–22 (March, 1969).

References to other rules are changed to conform to the rearrangement, and minor verbal changes have been made for clarification. The time for objecting to written questions served under Rule 31 is slightly extended.

1972 Amendment

Subdivision (c). The concept of "making a person one's own witness" appears to have had significance principally in two respects: impeachment and waiver of incompetency. Neither retains any vitality under the Rules of Evidence. The old prohibition against impeaching one's own witness is eliminated by Evidence Rule 607. The lack of recognition in the Rules of Evidence of state rules of incompetency in the Dead Man's area renders it unnecessary to consider aspects of waiver arising from calling the incompetent party-witness. Subdivision (c) is deleted because it appears to be no longer necessary in the light of the Rules of Evidence.

1980 Amendment

Subdivision (a)(1). Rule 801(d) of the Federal Rules of Evidence permits a prior inconsistent statement of a witness in a deposition to be used as substantive evidence. And Rule 801(d)(2) makes the statement of an agent or servant admissible against the principal under the circumstances described in the Rule. The language of the present subdivision is, therefore, too narrow.

Subdivision (a)(4). The requirement that a prior action must have been dismissed before depositions taken for use in it can be used in a subsequent action was doubtless an oversight, and the courts have ignored it. See Wright & Miller, *Federal Practice and Procedure: Civil* § 2150. The final sentence is added to reflect the fact that the Federal Rules of Evidence permit a broader use of depositions previously taken under certain circumstances. For example, Rule 804(b)(1) of the Federal Rules of Evidence provides that if a witness is unavailable, as that term is defined by the rule, his deposition in any earlier proceeding can be used against a party to the prior proceeding who had an opportunity and similar motive to develop the testimony of the witness.

1987 Amendment

The amendment is technical. No substantive change is intended.

1993 Amendments

Subdivision (a). The last sentence of revised subdivision (a) not only includes the substance of the provisions formerly contained in the second paragraph of Rule 30(b)(2), but adds a provision to deal with the situation when a party, receiving minimal notice of a proposed deposition, is unable to obtain a court ruling on its motion for a protective order seeking to delay or change the place of the deposition. Ordinarily a party does not obtain protection merely by the filing of a motion for a protective order under Rule 26(c); any protection is dependent upon the court's ruling. Under the revision, a party receiving less than 11 days['] notice of a deposition can, provided its motion for a protective order is filed promptly, be spared the risks resulting from nonattendance at the deposition held before its motion is ruled upon. Although the revision of Rule 32(a) covers only the risk that the deposition could be used against the non-appearing movant, it should also follow that, when the proposed deponent is the movant, the deponent would have "just cause" for failing to appear for purposes of Rule 37(d)(1). Inclusion of this provision is not intended to signify that 11 days' notice is the minimum advance notice for all depositions or that greater than 10 days should necessarily be deemed sufficient in all situations.

Subdivision (c). This new subdivision, inserted at the location of a subdivision previously abrogated, is included in view of the increased opportunities for video-recording and audio-recording of depositions under revised Rule 30(b). Under this rule a party may offer deposition testimony in any of the forms authorized under Rule 30(b) but, if offering it in a nonstenographic form, must provide the court with a transcript of the portions so offered. On request of any party in a jury trial, deposition testimony offered other than for impeachment purposes is to be presented in a nonstenographic form if available, unless the court directs otherwise. Note that under Rule 26(a)(3)(B) a party expecting to use nonstenographic deposition testimony as substantive evidence is required to provide other parties with a transcript in advance of trial.

2007 Amendment

The language of Rule 32 has been amended as part of the general restyling of the Civil Rules to make them more easily understood and to make style and terminology consistent throughout the rules. These changes are intended to be stylistic only.

Former Rule 32(a) applied "[a]t the trial or upon the hearing of a motion or an interlocutory proceeding." The amended rule describes the same events as "a hearing or trial."

The final paragraph of former Rule 32(a) allowed use in a later action of a deposition "lawfully taken and duly filed in the former action." Because of the 2000 amendment of Rule 5(d), many depositions are not filed. Amended Rule 32(a)(8) reflects this change by excluding use of an unfiled deposition only if filing was required in the former action.

2009 Amendments

The times set in the former rule at less than 11 days and within 5 days have been revised to 14 days and 7 days. See the Note to Rule 6.

HISTORICAL NOTES

References in Text

The Federal Rules of Evidence, referred to in subd. (a)(1), (2) and (8), are set out in this title.

Effective Date of Amendment Proposed November 20, 1972

Amendment of this rule embraced by the order entered by the Supreme Court of the United States on November 20, 1972, effective on the 180th day beginning after January 2, 1975, see section 3 of Pub.L. 93–595, Jan. 2, 1975, 88 Stat. 1959, set out as a note under section 2071 of Title 28.

Rule 33. Interrogatories to Parties

(a) In General.

    (1) *Number.* Unless otherwise stipulated or ordered by the court, a party may serve on any other party no more than 25 written interrogatories, including all discrete subparts. Leave to serve additional interrogatories may be granted to the extent consistent with Rule 26(b)(1) and (2).

    (2) *Scope.* An interrogatory may relate to any matter that may be inquired into under Rule 26(b). An interrogatory is not objectionable merely because it asks for an opinion or contention that relates to fact or the application of law to fact, but the court may order that the interrogatory need not be answered until designated discovery is complete, or until a pretrial conference or some other time.

(b) Answers and Objections.

    (1) *Responding Party.* The interrogatories must be answered:

        (A) by the party to whom they are directed; or

        (B) if that party is a public or private corporation, a partnership, an association, or a governmental agency, by any officer or agent, who must furnish the information available to the party.

    (2) *Time to Respond.* The responding party must serve its answers and any objections within 30 days after being served with the interrogatories. A shorter or longer time may be stipulated to under Rule 29 or be ordered by the court.

    (3) ***Answering Each Interrogatory.*** Each interrogatory must, to the extent it is not objected to, be answered separately and fully in writing under oath.

    (4) ***Objections.*** The grounds for objecting to an interrogatory must be stated with specificity. Any ground not stated in a timely objection is waived unless the court, for good cause, excuses the failure.

    (5) ***Signature.*** The person who makes the answers must sign them, and the attorney who objects must sign any objections.

(c) **Use.** An answer to an interrogatory may be used to the extent allowed by the Federal Rules of Evidence.

(d) **Option to Produce Business Records.** If the answer to an interrogatory may be determined by examining, auditing, compiling, abstracting, or summarizing a party's business records (including electronically stored information), and if the burden of deriving or ascertaining the answer will be substantially the same for either party, the responding party may answer by:

    (1) specifying the records that must be reviewed, in sufficient detail to enable the interrogating party to locate and identify them as readily as the responding party could; and

    (2) giving the interrogating party a reasonable opportunity to examine and audit the records and to make copies, compilations, abstracts, or summaries.

(Amended December 27, 1946, effective March 19, 1948; March 30, 1970, effective July 1, 1970; April 29, 1980, effective August 1, 1980; April 22, 1993, effective December 1, 1993; April 12, 2006, effective December 1, 2006; April 30, 2007, effective December 1, 2007; April 29, 2015, effective December 1, 2015.)

ADVISORY COMMITTEE NOTES

1937 Adoption

This rule restates the substance of [former] Equity Rule 58 (Discovery—Interrogatories—Inspection and Production of Documents—Admission of Execution or Genuineness), with modifications to conform to these rules.

1946 Amendment

Note. The added second sentence in the first paragraph of Rule 33 conforms with a similar change in Rule 26(a) and will avoid litigation as to when the interrogatories may be served. Original Rule 33 does not state the times at which parties may serve written interrogatories upon each other. It has been the accepted view, however, that the times were the same in Rule 33 as those stated in Rule 26(a). *United States v. American Solvents & Chemical Corp. of California,* D.Del.1939, 30 F.Supp. 107; *Sheldon v. Great Lakes Transit Corp.,* W.D.N.Y.1942, 2 F.R.D. 272, 5 Fed.Rules Serv. 33.11, Case 3; *Musher Foundation, Inc., v. Alba Trading Co.,* S.D.N.Y.1941, 42 F.Supp. 281; 2 *Moore's Federal Practice,* 1938, 2621. The time within which leave of court must be secured by a plaintiff has been fixed at 10 days, in view of the fact that a defendant has 10 days within which to make objections in any case, which should give him ample time to engage counsel and prepare.

Further in the first paragraph of Rule 33, the word "service" is substituted for "delivery" in conformance with the use of the word "serve" elsewhere in the rule and generally throughout the rules. See also Note to Rule 13(a) herein. The portion of the rule dealing with practice on objections has been revised so as to afford a clearer statement of the procedure. The addition of the words "to interrogatories to which objection is made" insures that only the answers to the objectionable interrogatories may be deferred, and that the answers to interrogatories not objectionable shall be forthcoming within the time prescribed in the rule. Under the original wording, answers to all interrogatories may be withheld until objections, sometimes to but a few interrogatories, are determined. The amendment expedites the procedure of the rule and serves to eliminate the strike value of objections to minor interrogatories. The elimination of the last sentence of the original rule is in line with the policy stated subsequently in this note.

The added second paragraph in Rule 33 contributes clarity and specificity as to the use and scope of interrogatories to the parties. The field of inquiry will be as broad as the scope of examination under Rule 26(b). There is no reason why interrogatories should be more limited than depositions, particularly when the former represent an inexpensive means of securing useful information. See *Hoffman v. Wilson Line, Inc.*, E.D.Pa.1946, 9 Fed.Rules Serv. 33.514, Case 2; *Brewster v. Technicolor, Inc.*, N.Y.1941, 2 F.R.D. 186, 5 Fed.Rules Serv. 33.319, Case 3; *Kingsway Press, Inc. v. Farrell Publishing Corp.*, S.D.N.Y.1939, 30 F.Supp. 775. Under present Rule 33 some courts have unnecessarily restricted the breadth of inquiry on various grounds. See *Auer v. Hershey Creamery Co.*, D.N.J.1939, 2 Fed.Rules Serv. 33.31, Case 2, 1 F.R.D. 14; *Tudor v. Leslie,* D.Mass.1940, 1 F.R.D. 448, 4 Fed.Rules Serv. 33.324, Case 1. Other courts have read into the rule the requirement that interrogation should be directed only towards "important facts", and have tended to fix a more or less arbitrary limit as to the number of interrogatories which could be asked in any case. See *Knox v. Alter,* W.D.Pa.1942, 2 F.R.D. 337, 6 Fed.Rules Serv. 33.352, Case 1; *Byers Theaters, Inc. v. Murphy*, W.D.Va.1940, 3 Fed.Rules Serv. 33.31, Case 3, 1 F.R.D. 286; *Coca-Cola Co. v. Dixi-Cola Laboratories, Inc.*, D.Md.1939, 30 F.Supp. 275. See also comment on these restrictions in Holtzoff, *Instruments of Discovery under Federal Rules of Civil Procedure,* 1942, 41 Mich.L.Rev. 205, 216–217. Under amended Rule 33, the party interrogated is given the right to invoke such protective orders under Rule 30(b) as are appropriate to the situation. At the same time, it is provided that the number of or number of sets of interrogatories to be served may not be limited arbitrarily or as a general policy to any particular number, but that a limit may be fixed only as justice requires to avoid annoyance, expense, embarrassment or oppression in individual cases. The party interrogated, therefore, must show the necessity for limitation on that basis. It will be noted that in accord with this change the last sentence of the present rule, restricting the sets of interrogatories to be served, has been stricken. In *J. Schoeneman, Inc. v. Brauer,* W.D.Mo.1940, 1 F.R.D. 292, 3 Fed.Rules Serv. 33.31, Case 2, the court said: "Rule 33 * * * has been interpreted * * * as being just as broad in its implications as in the case of depositions * * * It makes no difference therefore, how many interrogatories are propounded. If the inquiries are pertinent the opposing party cannot complain." To the same effect, see *Canuso v. City of Niagara Falls,* W.D.N.Y.1945, 8 Fed.Rules Serv. 33.352, Case 1; *Hoffman v. Wilson Line, Inc.,* supra.

By virtue of express language in the added second paragraph of Rule 33, as amended, any uncertainty as to the use of the answers to interrogatories is removed. The omission of a provision on this score in the original rule has caused some difficulty. See, e.g., *Bailey v. New England Mutual Life Ins. Co.,* S.D.Cal.1940, 1 F.R.D. 494, 4 Fed.Rules Serv. 33.46, Case 1.

The second sentence of the second paragraph in Rule 33, as amended, concerns the situation where a party wishes to serve interrogatories on a party after having taken his deposition, or vice versa. It has been held that an oral examination of a party, after the submission to him and answer of interrogatories, would be permitted. *Howard v. State Marine Corp.*, S.D.N.Y.1940, 4 Fed.Rules Serv. 33.62, Case 1, 1 F.R.D. 499; *Stevens v. Minder Construction Co.,* S.D.N.Y.1943, 3 F.R.D. 498, 7 Fed.Rules Serv. 30b.31, Case 2. But objections have been sustained to interrogatories served after the oral deposition of a party had been taken. *McNally v. Simons,* S.D.N.Y.1940, 3 Fed.Rules Serv. 33.61, Case 1, 1 F.R.D. 254; *Currier v. Currier*, S.D.N.Y.1942, 3 F.R.D. 21, 6 Fed.Rules Serv. 33.61, Case 1. Rule 33, as amended, permits either interrogatories after a deposition or a deposition after interrogatories. It may be quite desirable or necessary to elicit additional information by the inexpensive method of interrogatories where a deposition has already been taken. The party to be interrogated, however, may seek a protective order from the court under Rule 30(b) where the additional deposition or interrogation works a hardship or injustice on the party from whom it is sought.

1970 Amendment

Subdivision (a). The mechanics of the operation of Rule 33 are substantially revised by the proposed amendment, with a view to reducing court intervention. There is general agreement that interrogatories spawn a greater percentage of objections and motions than any other discovery device. The Columbia Survey shows that, although half of the litigants resorted to depositions and about one-third used interrogatories, about 65 percent of the objections were made with respect to interrogatories and 26 percent related to depositions. See also Speck, *The Use of Discovery in United States District Courts,* 60 Yale L.J. 1132, 1144, 1151 (1951); Note, 36 Minn.L.Rev. 364, 379 (1952).

The procedures now provided in Rule 33 seem calculated to encourage objections and court motions. The time periods now allowed for responding to interrogatories—15 days for answers and 10 days for objections—are too short. The Columbia Survey shows that tardy response to interrogatories is common, virtually expected. The same was reported in Speck, *supra,* 60 Yale L.J. 1132, 1144. The time pressures tend to encourage objections as a means of gaining time to answer.

The time for objections is even shorter than for answers, and the party runs the risk that if he fails to object in time he may have waived his objections. *E.g., Cleminshaw v. Beech Aircraft Corp.,* 21 F.R.D. 300 (D.Del.1957); See 4 *Moore's Federal Practice,* ¶ 33.27 (2d ed. 1966); 2A Barron & Holtzoff, *Federal Practice and Procedure* 372–373 (Wright ed. 1961). It often seems easier to object than to seek an extension of time. Unlike Rules 30(d) and 37(a), Rule 33 imposes no sanction of expenses on a party whose objections are clearly unjustified.

Rule 33 assures that the objections will lead directly to court, through its requirement that they be served with a notice of hearing. Although this procedure does not preclude an out-of-court resolution of the dispute, the procedure tends to discourage informal negotiations. If answers are served and they are thought inadequate, the interrogating party may move under Rule 37(a) for an order compelling adequate answers. There is no assurance that the hearing on objections and that on inadequate answers will be heard together.

The amendment improves the procedure of Rule 33 in the following respects:

(1) The time allowed for response is increased to 30 days and this time period applies to both answers and objections, but a defendant need not respond in less than 45 days after service of the summons and complaint upon him. As is true under existing law, the responding party who believes that some parts or all of the interrogatories are objectionable may choose to seek a protective order under new Rule 26(c) or may serve objections under this rule. Unless he applies for a protective order, he is required to serve answers or objections in response to the interrogatories, subject to the sanctions provided in Rule 37(d). Answers and objections are served together, so that a response to each interrogatory is encouraged, and any failure to respond is easily noted.

(2) In view of the enlarged time permitted for response, it is no longer necessary to require leave of court for service of interrogatories. The purpose of this requirement—that defendant have time to obtain counsel before a response must be made—is adequately fulfilled by the requirement that interrogatories be served upon a party with or after service of the summons and complaint upon him.

Some would urge that the plaintiff nevertheless not be permitted to serve interrogatories with the complaint. They fear that a routine practice might be invited, whereby form interrogatories would accompany most complaints. More fundamentally, they feel that, since very general complaints are permitted in present-day pleading, it is fair that the defendant have a right to take the lead in serving interrogatories. (These views apply also to Rule 36.) The amendment of Rule 33 rejects these views, in favor of allowing both parties to go forward with discovery, each free to obtain the information he needs respecting the case.

(3) If objections are made, the burden is on the interrogating party to move under Rule 37(a) for a court order compelling answers, in the course of which the court will pass on the objections. The change in the burden of going forward does not alter the existing obligation of an objecting party to justify his objections. *E.g., Pressley v. Bochlke,* 33 F.R.D. 316 (W.D.N.C. 1963). If the discovering party asserts that an answer is incomplete or evasive, again he may look to Rule 37(a) for relief, and he should add this assertion to his motion to overrule objections. There is no requirement that the parties consult informally concerning their differences, but the new procedure should encourage consultation, and the court may by local rule require it.

The proposed changes are similar in approach to those adopted by California in 1961. See Calif.Code Civ.Proc. § 2030(a). The experience of the Los Angeles Superior Court is informally reported as showing that the California amendment resulted in a significant reduction in court motions concerning interrogatories. Rhode Island takes a similar approach. See R. 33, *R.I.R. Civ.Proc. Official Draft,* p. 74 (Boston Law Book Co.).

A change is made in subdivision (a) which is not related to the sequence of procedures. The restriction to "adverse" parties is eliminated. The courts have generally construed this restriction as precluding interrogatories unless an issue between the parties is disclosed by the pleadings—even though the parties may have conflicting interests. E.g., *Mozeika v. Kaufman Construction Co.,* 25 F.R.D. 233 (E.D.Pa.1960) (plaintiff and third-party defendant); *Biddle v. Hutchinson,* 24 F.R.D. 256 (M.D.Pa.1959) (codefendants). The resulting distinctions have often been highly technical. In *Schlagenhauf v. Holder,* 379 U.S. 104 (1964), the Supreme Court rejected a contention that examination under Rule 35 could be had only against an "opposing" party, as not in keeping "with the aims of a liberal, nontechnical application of the Federal Rules."

379 U.S. at 116. Eliminating the requirement of "adverse" parties from Rule 33 brings it into line with all other discovery rules.

A second change in subdivision (a) is the addition of the term "governmental agency" to the listing of organizations whose answers are to be made by any officer or agent of the organization. This does not involve any change in existing law. Compare the similar listing in Rule 30(b)(6).

The duty of a party to supplement his answers to interrogatories is governed by a new provision in Rule 26(e).

Subdivision (b). There are numerous and conflicting decisions on the question whether and to what extent interrogatories are limited to matters "of fact," or may elicit opinions, contentions, and legal conclusions. Compare, e.g., *Payer, Hewitt & Co. v. Bellanca Corp.,* 26 F.R.D. 219 (D.Del.1960) (opinions bad); *Zinsky v. New York Central R.R.,* 36 F.R.D. 680 (N.D.Ohio 1964) (factual opinion or contention good, but legal theory bad); *United States v. Carter Products, Inc.,* 28 F.R.D. 373 (S.D.N.Y.1961) (factual contentions and legal theories bad) with *Taylor v. Sound Steamship Lines, Inc.,* 100 F.Supp. 388 (D.Conn.1951) (opinions good); *Bynum v. United States,* 36 F.R.D. 14 (E.D.La.1964) (contentions as to facts constituting negligence good). For lists of the many conflicting authorities, see 4 *Moore's Federal Practice* ¶ 33.17 (2d ed. 1966); 2A Barron & Holtzoff, *Federal Practice and Procedure* § 768 (Wright ed. 1961).

Rule 33 is amended to provide that an interrogatory is not objectionable merely because it calls for an opinion or contention that relates to fact or the application of law to fact. Efforts to draw sharp lines between facts and opinions have invariably been unsuccessful, and the clear trend of the cases is to permit "factual" opinions. As to requests for opinions or contentions that call for the application of law to fact, they can be most useful in narrowing and sharpening the issues, which is a major purpose of discovery. See *Diversified Products Corp. v. Sports Center Co.,* 42 F.R.D. 3 (D.Md.1967); Moore, *supra*; Field & McKusick, *Maine Civil Practice* § 26.18 (1959). On the other hand, under the new language interrogatories may not extend to issues of "pure law," *i.e.,* legal issues unrelated to the facts of the case. *Cf. United States v. Maryland & Va. Milk Producers Assn., Inc.,* 22 F.R.D. 300 (D.D.C.1958).

Since interrogatories involving mixed questions of law and fact may create disputes between the parties which are best resolved after much or all of the other discovery has been completed, the court is expressly authorized to defer an answer. Likewise, the court may delay determination until pretrial conference, if it believes that the dispute is best resolved in the presence of the judge.

The principal question raised with respect to the cases permitting such interrogatories is whether they reintroduce undesirable aspects of the prior pleading practice, whereby parties were chained to misconceived contentions or theories, and ultimate determination on the merits was frustrated. See James, *The Revival of Bills of Particulars under the Federal Rules,* 71 Harv.L.Rev. 1473 (1958). But there are few if any instances in the recorded cases demonstrating that such frustration has occurred. The general rule governing the use of answers to interrogatories is that under ordinary circumstances they do not limit proof. See, *e.g., McElroy v. United Air Lines, Inc.,* 21 F.R.D. 100 (W.D.Mo.1967); *Pressley v. Boehlke,* 33 F.R.D. 316, 317 (W.D.N.C.1963). Although in exceptional circumstances reliance on an answer may cause such prejudice that the court will hold the answering party bound to his answer, *e.g., Zielinski v. Philadelphia Piers, Inc.,* 139 F.Supp. 408 (E.D.Pa.1956), the interrogating party will ordinarily not be entitled to rely on the unchanging character of the answers he receives and cannot base prejudice on such reliance. The rule does not affect the power of a court to permit withdrawal or amendment of answers to interrogatories.

The use of answers to interrogatories at trial is made subject to the rules of evidence. The provisions governing use of depositions, to which Rule 33 presently refers, are not entirely apposite to answers to interrogatories, since deposition practice contemplates that all parties will ordinarily participate through cross-examination. See 4 *Moore's Federal Practice* ¶ 33.29[1] (2d ed. 1966).

Certain provisions are deleted from subdivision (b) because they are fully covered by new Rule 26(c) providing for protective orders and Rules 26(a) and 26(d). The language of the subdivision is thus simplified without any change of substance.

Subdivision (c). This is a new subdivision, adapted from Calif.Code Civ.Proc. § 2030(c), relating especially to interrogatories which require a party to engage in burdensome or expensive research into his own business records in order to give an answer. The subdivision gives the party an option to make the records available and place the burden of research of the party who seeks the information. "This provision, without undermining the liberal scope of interrogatory discovery, places the burden of discovery upon its potential benefittee," Louisell, *Modern California Discovery,* 124–125 (1963), and alleviates a problem which in the past has troubled Federal courts. See Speck, *The Use of Discovery in United States District Courts,* 60 Yale L.J. 1132, 1142–1144 (1951). The interrogating party is protected against abusive use of this provision through the requirement that the burden of ascertaining the answer be substantially the same for both sides. A respondent may not impose on an interrogating party a mass of records as to which research is feasible only for one familiar with the records. At the same time, the respondent unable to invoke this subdivision does not on that account lose the protection available to him under new Rule 26(c) against oppressive or unduly burdensome or expensive interrogatories. And even when the respondent successfully invokes the subdivision, the court is not deprived of its usual power, in appropriate cases, to require that the interrogating party reimburse the respondent for the expense of assembling his records and making them intelligible.

1980 Amendment

Subdivision (c). The Committee is advised that parties upon whom interrogatories are served have occasionally responded by directing the interrogating party to a mass of business records or by offering to make all of their records available, justifying the response by the option provided by this subdivision. Such practices are an abuse of the option. A party who is permitted by the terms of this subdivision to offer records for inspection in lieu of answering an interrogatory should offer them in a manner than permits the same direct and economical access that is available to the party. If the information sought exists in the form of compilations, abstracts or summaries then available to the responding party, those should be made available to the interrogating party. The final sentence is added to make it clear that a responding party has the duty to specify, by category and location, the records from which answers to interrogatories can be derived.

1993 Amendments

Purpose of Revision. The purpose of this revision is to reduce the frequency and increase the efficiency of interrogatory practice. The revision is based on experience with local rules. For ease of reference, subdivision (a) is divided into two subdivisions and the remaining subdivisions renumbered.

Subdivision (a). Revision of this subdivision limits interrogatory practice. Because Rule 26(a)(1)–(3) requires disclosure of much of the information previously obtained by this form of discovery, there should be less occasion to use it. Experience in over half of the district courts has confirmed that limitations on the number of interrogatories are useful and manageable. Moreover, because the device can be costly and may be used as a means of harassment, it is desirable to subject its use to the control of the court consistent with the principles stated in Rule 26(b)(2), particularly in multi-party cases where it has not been unusual for the same interrogatory to be propounded to a party by more than one of its adversaries.

Each party is allowed to serve 25 interrogatories upon any other party, but must secure leave of court (or a stipulation from the opposing party) to serve a larger number. Parties cannot evade this presumptive limitation through the device of joining as "subparts" questions that seek information about discrete separate subjects. However, a question asking about communications of a particular type should be treated as a single interrogatory even though it requests that the time, place, persons present, and contents be stated separately for each such communication.

As with the number of depositions authorized by Rule 30, leave to serve additional interrogatories is to be allowed when consistent with Rule 26(b)(2). The aim is not to prevent needed discovery, but to provide judicial scrutiny before parties make potentially excessive use of this discovery device. In many cases it will be appropriate for the court to permit a larger number of interrogatories in the scheduling order entered under Rule 16(b).

Unless leave of court is obtained, interrogatories may not be served prior to the meeting of the parties under Rule 26(f).

When a case with outstanding interrogatories exceeding the number permitted by this rule is removed to federal court, the interrogating party must seek leave allowing the additional interrogatories, specify which twenty-five are to be answered, or resubmit interrogatories that comply with the rule. Moreover, under Rule 26(d), the time for response would be measured from the date of the parties' meeting under Rule 26(f). See Rule 81(c), providing that these rules govern procedures after removal.

Subdivision (b). A separate subdivision is made of the former second paragraph of subdivision (a). Language is added to paragraph (1) of this subdivision to emphasize the duty of the responding party to provide full answers to the extent not objectionable. If, for example, an interrogatory seeking information about numerous facilities or products is deemed objectionable, but an interrogatory seeking information about a lesser number of facilities or products would not have been objectionable, the interrogatory should be answered with respect to the latter even though an objection is raised as to the balance of the facilities or products. Similarly, the fact that additional time may be needed to respond to some questions (or to some aspects of questions) should not justify a delay in responding to those questions (or other aspects of questions) that can be answered within the prescribed time.

Paragraph (4) is added to make clear that objections must be specifically justified, and that unstated or untimely grounds for objection ordinarily are waived. Note also the provisions of revised Rule 26(b)(5), which require a responding party to indicate when it is withholding information under a claim of privilege or as trial preparation materials.

These provisions should be read in light of Rule 26(g), authorizing the court to impose sanctions on a party and attorney making an unfounded objection to an interrogatory.

Subdivisions (c) and (d). The provisions of former subdivisions (b) and (c) are renumbered.

2006 Amendment

Rule 33(d) is amended to parallel Rule 34(a) by recognizing the importance of electronically stored information. The term "electronically stored information" has the same broad meaning in Rule 33(d) as in Rule 34(a). Much business information is stored only in electronic form; the Rule 33(d) option should be available with respect to such records as well.

Special difficulties may arise in using electronically stored information, either due to its form or because it is dependent on a particular computer system. Rule 33(d) allows a responding party to substitute access to documents or electronically stored information for an answer only if the burden of deriving the answer will be substantially the same for either party. Rule 33(d) states that a party electing to respond to an interrogatory by providing electronically stored information must ensure that the interrogating party can locate and identify it "as readily as can the party served," and that the responding party must give the interrogating party a "reasonable opportunity to examine, audit, or inspect" the information. Depending on the circumstances, satisfying these provisions with regard to electronically stored information may require the responding party to provide some combination of technical support, information on application software, or other assistance. The key question is whether such support enables the interrogating party to derive or ascertain the answer from the electronically stored information as readily as the responding party. A party that wishes to invoke Rule 33(d) by specifying electronically stored information may be required to provide direct access to its electronic information system, but only if that is necessary to afford the requesting party an adequate opportunity to derive or ascertain the answer to the interrogatory. In that situation, the responding party's need to protect sensitive interests of confidentiality or privacy may mean that it must derive or ascertain and provide the answer itself rather than invoke Rule 33(d).

2007 Amendment

The language of Rule 33 has been amended as part of the general restyling of the Civil Rules to make them more easily understood and to make style and terminology consistent throughout the rules. These changes are intended to be stylistic only.

The final sentence of former Rule 33(a) was a redundant cross-reference to the discovery moratorium provisions of Rule 26(d). Rule 26(d) is now familiar, obviating any need to carry forward the redundant cross-reference.

Former Rule 33(b)(5) was a redundant reminder of Rule 37(a) procedure and is omitted as no longer useful.

Former Rule 33(c) stated that an interrogatory "is not necessarily objectionable merely because an answer * * * involves an opinion or contention * * *." "[I]s not necessarily" seemed to imply that the interrogatory might be objectionable merely for this reason. This implication has been ignored in practice. Opinion and contention interrogatories are used routinely. Amended Rule 33(a)(2) embodies the current meaning of Rule 33 by omitting "necessarily."

Rule 33 is amended in parallel with Rules 30 and 31 to reflect the recognition of proportionality in Rule 26(b)(1).

Gap Report

The proposal to reduce the presumptive number of interrogatories from 25 to 15 was withdrawn. The Committee Note was changed accordingly.

Rule 34. Producing Documents, Electronically Stored Information, and Tangible Things, or Entering onto Land, for Inspection and Other Purposes

(a) **In General.** A party may serve on any other party a request within the scope of Rule 26(b):

(1) to produce and permit the requesting party or its representative to inspect, copy, test, or sample the following items in the responding party's possession, custody, or control:

(A) any designated documents or electronically stored information—including writings, drawings, graphs, charts, photographs, sound recordings, images, and other data or data compilations—stored in any medium from which information can be obtained either directly or, if necessary, after translation by the responding party into a reasonably usable form; or

(B) any designated tangible things; or

(2) to permit entry onto designated land or other property possessed or controlled by the responding party, so that the requesting party may inspect, measure, survey, photograph, test, or sample the property or any designated object or operation on it.

(b) **Procedure.**

(1) *Contents of the Request.* The request:

(A) must describe with reasonable particularity each item or category of items to be inspected;

(B) must specify a reasonable time, place, and manner for the inspection and for performing the related acts; and

(C) may specify the form or forms in which electronically stored information is to be produced.

(2) *Responses and Objections.*

(A) *Time to Respond.* The party to whom the request is directed must respond in writing within 30 days after being served or—if the request was delivered under Rule 26(d)(2)— within 30 days after the parties' first Rule 26(f) conference. A shorter or longer time may be stipulated to under Rule 29 or be ordered by the court.

(B) *Responding to Each Item.* For each item or category, the response must either state that inspection and related activities will be permitted as requested or state with specificity the grounds for objecting to the request, including the reasons. The responding party may state that it will produce copies of the documents or of electronically stored information instead of permitting inspection. The production must then be completed no later than the time for inspection specified in the request or another reasonable time specified in the response.

(C) *Objections.* An objection must state whether any responsive materials are being withheld on the basis of that objection. An objection to part of a request must specify the part and permit inspection of the rest.

(D) *Responding to a Request for Production of Electronically Stored Information.* The response may state an objection to a requested form for producing electronically stored information. If the responding party objects to a requested form—or if no form was specified in the request—the party must state the form or forms it intends to use.

(E) *Producing the Documents or Electronically Stored Information.* Unless otherwise stipulated or ordered by the court, these procedures apply to producing documents or electronically stored information:

(i) A party must produce documents as they are kept in the usual course of business or must organize and label them to correspond to the categories in the request;

(ii) If a request does not specify a form for producing electronically stored information, a party must produce it in a form or forms in which it is ordinarily maintained or in a reasonably usable form or forms; and

(iii) A party need not produce the same electronically stored information in more than one form.

(c) Nonparties. As provided in Rule 45, a nonparty may be compelled to produce documents and tangible things or to permit an inspection.

(Amended December 27, 1946, effective March 19, 1948; March 30, 1970, effective July 1, 1970; April 29, 1980, effective August 1, 1980; March 2, 1987, effective August 1, 1987; April 30, 1991, effective December 1, 1991; April 22, 1993, effective December 1, 1993; April 12, 2006, effective December 1, 2006; April 30, 2007, effective December 1, 2007; April 29, 2015, effective December 1, 2015.)

ADVISORY COMMITTEE NOTES

1937 Adoption

In England orders are made for the inspection of documents, *English Rules Under the Judicature Act (The Annual Practice,* 1937) O. 31, r.r. 14, et seq., or for the inspection of tangible property or for entry upon land, O. 50, r. 3. Michigan provides for inspection of damaged property when such damage is the ground of the action. Mich.Court Rules Ann. (Searl, 1933) Rule 41, § 2.

Practically all states have statutes authorizing the court to order parties in possession or control of documents to permit other parties to inspect and copy them before trial. See Ragland, *Discovery Before Trial* (1932) Appendix, p. 267, setting out the statutes.

Compare [former] Equity Rule 58 (Discovery—Interrogatories—Inspection and Production of Documents—Admission of Execution or Genuineness) (fifth paragraph).

1946 Amendment

Note. The changes in clauses (1) and (2) correlate the scope of inquiry permitted under Rule 34 with that provided in Rule 26(b), and thus remove any ambiguity created by the former differences in language. As stated in *Olson Transportation Co. v. Socony-Vacuum Oil Co.,* E.D.Wis.1944, 8 Fed.Rules Serv. 34.41, Case 2, "* * * Rule 34 is a direct and simple method of discovery." At the same time the addition of the words following the term "parties" makes certain that the person in whose custody, possession, or control the evidence reposes may have the benefit of the applicable protective orders stated in Rule 30(b). This change should be considered in the light of the proposed expansion of Rule 30(b).

An objection has been made that the word "designated" in Rule 34 has been construed with undue strictness in some district court cases so as to require great and impracticable specificity in the description of documents, papers, books, etc., sought to be inspected. The Committee, however, believes that no amendment is needed, and that the proper meaning of "designated" as requiring specificity has already been delineated by the Supreme Court. *See Brown v. United States,* 1928, 48 S.Ct. 288, 276 U.S. 134, 143, 72 L.Ed. 500 ("The subpoena * * * specifies * * * with reasonable particularity the subjects to which the documents called for related."); *Consolidated Rendering Co. v. Vermont,* 1908, 28 S.Ct. 178, 207 U.S. 541, 543–544, 52 L.Ed. 327 ("We see no reason why all such books, papers and correspondence which related to the subject of inquiry, and were described with reasonable detail, should not be called for and the company directed to produce them. Otherwise, the State would be compelled to designate each particular paper which it desired, which presupposes an accurate knowledge of such papers, which the tribunal desiring the papers would probably rarely, if ever, have.").

1970 Amendment

Rule 34 is revised to accomplish the following major changes in the existing rule: (1) to eliminate the requirement of good cause; (2) to have the rule operate extrajudicially; (3) to include testing and sampling as well as inspecting or photographing tangible things; and (4) to make clear that the rule does not preclude an independent action for analogous discovery against persons not parties.

Subdivision (a). Good cause is eliminated because it has furnished an uncertain and erratic protection to the parties from whom production is sought and is now rendered unnecessary by virtue of the more specific provisions added to Rule 26(b) relating to materials assembled in preparation for trial and to experts retained or consulted by parties.

The good cause requirement was originally inserted in Rule 34 as a general protective provision in the absence of experience with the specific problems that would arise thereunder. As the note to Rule 26(b)(3) on trial preparation materials makes clear, good cause has been applied differently to varying classes of documents, though not without confusion. It has often been said in court opinions that good cause requires a consideration of need for the materials and of alternative means of obtaining them, i.e., something more than relevance and lack of privilege. But the overwhelming proportion of the cases in which the formula of good cause has been applied to require a special showing are those involving trial preparation. In practice, the courts have not treated documents as having a special immunity to discovery simply because of their being documents. Protection may be afforded to claims of privacy or secrecy or of undue burden or expense under what is now Rule 26(c) (previously Rule 30(b)). To be sure, an appraisal of "undue" burden inevitably entails consideration of the needs of the party seeking discovery. With special provisions added to govern trial preparation materials and experts, there is no longer any occasion to retain the requirement of good cause.

The revision of Rule 34 to have it operate extrajudicially, rather than by court order, is to a large extent a reflection of existing law office practice. The Columbia Survey shows that of the litigants seeking inspection of documents or things, only about 25 percent filed motions for court orders. This minor fraction nevertheless accounted for a significant number of motions. About half of these motions were uncontested and in almost all instances the party seeking production ultimately prevailed. Although an extrajudicial procedure will not drastically alter existing practice under Rule 34—it will conform to it in most cases—it has the potential of saving court time in a substantial though proportionately small number of cases tried annually.

The inclusion of testing and sampling of tangible things and objects or operations on land reflects a need frequently encountered by parties in preparation for trial. If the operation of a particular machine is the basis of a claim for negligent injury, it will often be necessary to test its operating parts or to sample and test the products it is producing. *Cf.* Mich.Gen.Ct.R. 310.1(1) (1963) (testing authorized).

The inclusive description of "documents" is revised to accord with changing technology. It makes clear that Rule 34 applies to electronics data compilations from which information can be obtained only with the use of detection devices, and that when the data can as a practical matter be made usable by the discovering party only through respondent's devices, respondent may be required to use his devices to translate the data into usable form. In many instances, this means that respondent will have to supply a print-out of computer data. The burden thus placed on respondent will vary from case to case, and the courts have ample power under Rule 26(c) to protect respondent against undue burden or expense, either by restricting discovery or requiring that the discovering party pay costs. Similarly, if the discovering party needs to check the electronic source itself, the court may protect respondent with respect to preservation of his records, confidentiality of nondiscoverable matters, and costs.

Subdivision (b). The procedure provided in Rule 34 is essentially the same as that in Rule 33, as amended, and the discussion in the note appended to that rule is relevant to Rule 34 as well. Problems peculiar to Rule 34 relate to the specific arrangements that must be worked out for inspection and related acts of copying, photographing, testing, or sampling. The rule provides that a request for inspection shall set forth the items to be inspected either by item or category, describing each with reasonable particularity, and shall specify a reasonable time, place, and manner of making the inspection.

Subdivision (c). Rule 34 as revised continues to apply only to parties. Comments from the bar make clear that in the preparation of cases for trial it is occasionally necessary to enter land or inspect large tangible things in the possession of a person not a party, and that some courts have dismissed independent actions in the nature of bills in equity for such discovery on the ground that Rule 34 is preemptive. While an ideal solution to this problem is to provide for discovery against persons not parties in Rule 34, both the jurisdictional and procedural problems are very complex. For the present, this subdivision makes clear that Rule 34 does not preclude independent actions for discovery against persons not parties.

1980 Amendment

Subdivision (b). The Committee is advised that, "It is apparently not rare for parties deliberately to mix critical documents with others in the hope of obscuring significance." *Report of the Special Committee for the Study of Discovery Abuse, Section of Litigation of the American Bar Association* (1977) 22. The sentence added by this subdivision follows the recommendation of the *Report*.

1987 Amendment

The amendment is technical. No substantive change is intended.

1991 Amendment

This amendment reflects the change effected by revision of Rule 45 to provide for subpoenas to compel non-parties to produce documents and things and to submit to inspections of premises. The deletion of the text of the former paragraph is not intended to preclude an independent action for production of documents or things or for permission to enter upon land, but such actions may no longer be necessary in light of this revision.

1993 Amendments

The rule is revised to reflect the change made by Rule 26(d), preventing a party from seeking formal discovery prior to the meeting of the parties required by Rule 26(f). Also, like a change made in Rule 33, the rule is modified to make clear that, if a request for production is objectionable only in part, production should be afforded with respect to the unobjectionable portions.

When a case with outstanding requests for production is removed to federal court, the time for response would be measured from the date of the parties' meeting. See Rule 81(c), providing that these rules govern procedures after removal.

2006 Amendment

Subdivision (a). As originally adopted, Rule 34 focused on discovery of "documents" and "things." In 1970, Rule 34(a) was amended to include discovery of data compilations, anticipating that the use of computerized information would increase. Since then, the growth in electronically stored information and in the variety of systems for creating and storing such information has been dramatic. Lawyers and judges interpreted the term "documents" to include electronically stored information because it was obviously improper to allow a party to evade discovery obligations on the basis that the label had not kept pace with changes in information technology. But it has become increasingly difficult to say that all forms of electronically stored information, many dynamic in nature, fit within the traditional concept of a "document." Electronically stored information may exist in dynamic databases and other forms far different from fixed expression on paper. Rule 34(a) is amended to confirm that discovery of electronically stored information stands on equal footing with discovery of paper documents. The change clarifies that Rule 34 applies to information that is fixed in a tangible form and to information that is stored in a medium from which it can be retrieved and examined. At the same time, a Rule 34 request for production of "documents" should be understood to encompass, and the response should include, electronically stored information unless discovery in the action has clearly distinguished between electronically stored information and "documents."

Discoverable information often exists in both paper and electronic form, and the same or similar information might exist in both. The items listed in Rule 34(a) show different ways in which information may be recorded or stored. Images, for example, might be hard-copy documents or electronically stored information. The wide variety of computer systems currently in use, and the rapidity of technological change, counsel against a limiting or precise definition of electronically stored information. Rule 34(a)(1) is expansive and includes any type of information that is stored electronically. A common example often sought in discovery is electronic communications, such as e-mail. The rule covers—either as documents or as electronically stored information—information "stored in any medium," to encompass future developments in computer technology. Rule 34(a)(1) is intended to be broad enough to cover all current types of computer-based information, and flexible enough to encompass future changes and developments.

References elsewhere in the rules to "electronically stored information" should be understood to invoke this expansive approach. A companion change is made to Rule 33(d), making it explicit that parties choosing to respond to an interrogatory by permitting access to responsive records may do so by providing access to electronically stored information. More generally, the term used in Rule 34(a)(1) appears in a number of other amendments, such as those to Rules 26(a)(1), 26(b)(2), 26(b)(5)(B), 26(f), 34(b), 37(f), and 45. In each of these rules, electronically stored information has the same broad meaning it has under Rule 34(a)(1). References to "documents" appear in discovery rules that are not amended, including Rules 30(f), 36(a), and 37(c)(2). These references should be interpreted to include electronically stored information as circumstances warrant.

The term "electronically stored information" is broad, but whether material that falls within this term should be produced, and in what form, are separate questions that must be addressed under Rules 26(b), 26(c), and 34(b).

The Rule 34(a) requirement that, if necessary, a party producing electronically stored information translate it into reasonably usable form does not address the issue of translating from one human language to another. *See In re Puerto Rico Elect. Power Auth.*, 687 F.2d 501, 504–510 (1st Cir. 1989).

Rule 34(a)(1) is also amended to make clear that parties may request an opportunity to test or sample materials sought under the rule in addition to inspecting and copying them. That opportunity may be important for both electronically stored information and hard-copy materials. The current rule is not clear that such testing or sampling is authorized; the amendment expressly permits it. As with any other form of discovery, issues of burden and intrusiveness raised by requests to test or sample can be addressed under Rules 26(b)(2) and 26(c). Inspection or testing of certain types of electronically stored information or of a responding party's electronic information system may raise issues of confidentiality or privacy. The addition of testing and sampling to Rule 34(a) with regard to documents and electronically stored information is not meant to create a routine right of direct access to a party's electronic information system, although such access might be justified in some circumstances. Courts should guard against undue intrusiveness resulting from inspecting or testing such systems.

Rule 34(a)(1) is further amended to make clear that tangible things must—like documents and land sought to be examined—be designated in the request.

Subdivision (b). Rule 34(b) provides that a party must produce documents as they are kept in the usual course of business or must organize and label them to correspond with the categories in the discovery request. The production of electronically stored information should be subject to comparable requirements to protect against deliberate or inadvertent production in ways that raise unnecessary obstacles for the requesting party. Rule 34(b) is amended to ensure similar protection for electronically stored information.

The amendment to Rule 34(b) permits the requesting party to designate the form or forms in which it wants electronically stored information produced. The form of production is more important to the exchange of electronically stored information than of hard-copy materials, although a party might specify hard copy as the requested form. Specification of the desired form or forms may facilitate the orderly, efficient, and cost-effective discovery of electronically stored information. The rule recognizes that different forms of production may be appropriate for different types of electronically stored information. Using current technology, for example, a party might be called upon to produce word processing documents, e-mail messages, electronic spreadsheets, different image or sound files, and material from databases. Requiring that such diverse types of electronically stored information all be produced in the same form could prove impossible, and even if possible could increase the cost and burdens of producing and using the information. The rule therefore provides that the requesting party may ask for different forms of production for different types of electronically stored information.

The rule does not require that the requesting party choose a form or forms of production. The requesting party may not have a preference. In some cases, the requesting party may not know what form the producing party uses to maintain its electronically stored information, although Rule 26(f)(3) is amended to call for discussion of the form of production in the parties' prediscovery conference.

The responding party also is involved in determining the form of production. In the written response to the production request that Rule 34 requires, the responding party must state the form it intends to use for producing electronically stored information if the requesting party does not specify a form or if the responding party objects to a form that the requesting party specifies. Stating the intended form before the production occurs may permit the parties to identify and seek to resolve disputes before the expense and work of the production occurs. A party that responds to a discovery request by simply producing electronically stored information in a form of its choice, without identifying that form in advance of the production in the response required by Rule 34(b), runs a risk that the requesting party can show that the produced form is not reasonably usable and that it is entitled to production of some or all of the information in an additional form. Additional time might be required to permit a responding party to assess the appropriate form or forms of production.

If the requesting party is not satisfied with the form stated by the responding party, or if the responding party has objected to the form specified by the requesting party, the parties must meet and confer under Rule 37(a)(2)(B) in an effort to resolve the matter before the requesting party can file a motion to compel. If they cannot agree and the court resolves the dispute, the court is not limited to the forms initially chosen by the requesting party, stated by the responding party, or specified in this rule for situations in which there is no court order or party agreement.

If the form of production is not specified by party agreement or court order, the responding party must produce electronically stored information either in a form or forms in which it is ordinarily maintained or in a form or forms that are reasonably usable. Rule 34(a) requires that, if necessary, a responding party "translate" information it produces into a "reasonably usable" form. Under some circumstances, the responding party may need to provide some reasonable amount of technical support, information on application software, or other reasonable assistance to enable the requesting party to use the information. The rule does not require a party to produce electronically stored information in the form it which it is ordinarily maintained, as long as it is produced in a reasonably usable form. But the option to produce in a reasonably usable form does not mean that a responding party is free to convert electronically stored information from the form in which it is ordinarily maintained to a different form that makes it more difficult or burdensome for the requesting party to use the information efficiently in the litigation. If the responding party ordinarily maintains the information it is producing in a way that makes it searchable by electronic means, the information should not be produced in a form that removes or significantly degrades this feature.

Some electronically stored information may be ordinarily maintained in a form that is not reasonably usable by any party. One example is "legacy" data that can be used only by superseded systems. The questions whether a producing party should be required to convert such information to a more usable form, or should be required to produce it at all, should be addressed under Rule 26(b)(2)(B).

Whether or not the requesting party specified the form of production, Rule 34(b) provides that the same electronically stored information ordinarily need be produced in only one form.

2007 Amendment

The language of Rule 34 has been amended as part of the general restyling of the Civil Rules to make them more easily understood and to make style and terminology consistent throughout the rules. These changes are intended to be stylistic only.

The final sentence in the first paragraph of former Rule 34(b) was a redundant cross-reference to the discovery moratorium provisions of Rule 26(d). Rule 26(d) is now familiar, obviating any need to carry forward the redundant cross-reference.

The redundant reminder of Rule 37(a) procedure in the second paragraph of former Rule 34(b) is omitted as no longer useful.

2015 Amendment

Several amendments are made in Rule 34, aimed at reducing the potential to impose unreasonable burdens by objections to requests to produce.

Rule 34(b)(2)(A) is amended to fit with new Rule 26(d)(2). The time to respond to a Rule 34 request delivered before the parties' Rule 26(f) conference is 30 days after the first Rule 26(f) conference.

Rule 34(b)(2)(B) is amended to require that objections to Rule 34 requests be stated with specificity. This provision adopts the language of Rule 33(b)(4), eliminating any doubt that less specific objections might be suitable under Rule 34. The specificity of the objection ties to the new provision in Rule 34(b)(2)(C) directing that an objection must state whether any responsive materials are being withheld on the basis of that objection. An objection may state that a request is overbroad, but if the objection recognizes that some part of the request is appropriate the objection should state the scope that is not overbroad. Examples would be a statement that the responding party will limit the search to documents or electronically stored information created within a given period of time prior to the events in suit, or to specified sources. When there is such an objection, the statement of what has been withheld can properly identify as matters "withheld" anything beyond the scope of the search specified in the objection.

Rule 34(b)(2)(B) is further amended to reflect the common practice of producing copies of documents or electronically stored information rather than simply permitting inspection. The response to the request must state that copies will be produced. The production must be completed either by the time for inspection specified in the request or by another reasonable time specifically identified in the response. When it is necessary to make the production in stages the response should specify the beginning and end dates of the production.

Rule 34(b)(2)(C) is amended to provide that an objection to a Rule 34 request must state whether anything is being withheld on the basis of the objection. This amendment should end the confusion that frequently arises when a producing party states several objections and still produces information, leaving the requesting party uncertain whether any relevant and responsive information has been withheld on the basis of the objections. The producing party does not need to provide a detailed description or log of all documents withheld, but does need to alert other parties to the fact that documents have been withheld and thereby facilitate an informed discussion of the objection. An objection that states the limits that have controlled the search for responsive and relevant materials qualifies as a statement that the materials have been "withheld."

Gap Report

Style changes were made in the published text of Rule 34(b)(2)(B). The Committee Note was expanded to emphasize the interplay between a specific objection that defines the scope of the search made for responsive information and the requirement to state whether any responsive materials are being withheld.

Rule 35. Physical and Mental Examinations

(a) Order for an Examination.

(1) *In General.* The court where the action is pending may order a party whose mental or physical condition—including blood group—is in controversy to submit to a physical or mental examination by a suitably licensed or certified examiner. The court has the same authority to order a party to produce for examination a person who is in its custody or under its legal control.

(2) *Motion and Notice; Contents of the Order.* The order:

(A) may be made only on motion for good cause and on notice to all parties and the person to be examined; and

(B) must specify the time, place, manner, conditions, and scope of the examination, as well as the person or persons who will perform it.

(b) Examiner's Report.

(1) *Request by the Party or Person Examined.* The party who moved for the examination must, on request, deliver to the requester a copy of the examiner's report, together with like reports of all earlier examinations of the same condition. The request may be made by the party against whom the examination order was issued or by the person examined.

(2) *Contents.* The examiner's report must be in writing and must set out in detail the examiner's findings, including diagnoses, conclusions, and the results of any tests.

(3) *Request by the Moving Party.* After delivering the reports, the party who moved for the examination may request—and is entitled to receive—from the party against whom the examination order was issued like reports of all earlier or later examinations of the same condition. But those reports need not be delivered by the party with custody or control of the person examined if the party shows that it could not obtain them.

(4) *Waiver of Privilege.* By requesting and obtaining the examiner's report, or by deposing the examiner, the party examined waives any privilege it may have—in that action or any other action involving the same controversy—concerning testimony about all examinations of the same condition.

(5) *Failure to Deliver a Report.* The court on motion may order—on just terms—that a party deliver the report of an examination. If the report is not provided, the court may exclude the examiner's testimony at trial.

(6) *Scope.* This subdivision (b) applies also to an examination made by the parties' agreement, unless the agreement states otherwise. This subdivision does not preclude obtaining an examiner's report or deposing an examiner under other rules.

(Amended March 30, 1970, effective July 1, 1970; March 2, 1987, effective August 1, 1987; amended by Pub.L. 100–690, Title VII, § 7047(b), November 18, 1988, 102 Stat. 4401; amended April 30, 1991, effective December 1, 1991; April 30, 2007, effective December 1, 2007.)

ADVISORY COMMITTEE NOTES

1937 Adoption

Physical examination of parties before trial is authorized by statute or rule in a number of states. See Ariz.Rev. Code Ann. (Struckmeyer, 1928) § 4468; Mich. Court Rules Ann. (Searl, 1933) Rule 41, § 2; 2 N.J.Comp.Stat. (1910); N.Y.C.P.A. (1937) § 306; 1 S.D.Comp.Laws (1929) § 2716A; 3 Wash.Rev.Stat.Ann. (Remington, 1932) § 1230–1.

Mental examination of parties is authorized in Iowa. Iowa Code (1935) ch. 491–F1. See McCash, *The Evolution of the Doctrine of Discovery and Its Present Status in Iowa,* 20 Ia.L.Rev. 68 (1934).

The constitutionality of legislation providing for physical examination of parties was sustained in *Lyon v. Manhattan Railway Co.,* 1894, 37 N.E. 113, 142 N.Y. 298, and *McGovern v. Hope,* 1899, 42 A. 830, 63 N.J.L. 76. In *Union Pacific Ry. Co. v. Botsford,* 1891, 11 S.Ct. 1000, 141 U.S. 250, 35 L.Ed. 734, it was held that the court could not order the physical examination of a party in the absence of statutory authority. But in *Camden and Suburban Ry. Co. v. Stetson,* 1900, 20 S.Ct. 617, 177 U.S. 172, 44 L.Ed. 721 where there was statutory authority for such examination, derived from a state statute made operative by the conformity act, the practice was sustained. Such authority is now found in the present rule made operative by the Act of June 19, 1934, c. 651, U.S.C., Title 28, § 2072, formerly §§ 723b (Rules in actions at law; Supreme Court authorized to make) and 723c (Union of equity and action at law rules; power of Supreme Court).

1970 Amendment

Subdivision (a). Rule 35(a) has hitherto provided only for an order requiring a party to submit to an examination. It is desirable to extend the rule to provide for an order against the party for examination of a person in his custody or under his legal control. As appears from the provisions of amended Rule 37(b)(2) and the comment under that rule, an order to "produce" the third person imposes only an obligation to use good faith efforts to produce the person.

The amendment will settle beyond doubt that a parent or guardian suing to recover for injuries to a minor may be ordered to produce the minor for examination. Further, the amendment expressly includes blood examination within the kinds of examinations that can be ordered under the rule. See *Beach v. Beach,* 114 F.2d 479 (D.C. Cir. 1940). Provisions similar to the amendment have been adopted in at least 10 States: Calif. Code Civ.Proc. § 2032; Ida.R.Civ.P. 35; Ill. S–H Ann. c. 110A, § 215; Md.R.P. 420; Mich.Gen.Ct.R. 311; Minn.R.Civ.P. 35; Mo.Vern.Ann.R.Civ.P. 60.01; N.Dak.R.Civ.P. 35; N.Y.C.P.L. § 3121; Wyo.R.Civ.P. 35.

The amendment makes no change in the requirements of Rule 35 that, before a court order may issue, the relevant physical or mental condition must be shown to be "in controversy" and "good cause" must be shown for the examination. Thus, the amendment has no effect on the recent decision of the Supreme Court in *Schlagenhauf v. Holder,* 379 U.S. 104 (1964), stressing the importance of these requirements and applying them to the facts of the case. The amendment makes no reference to employees of a party. Provisions relating to employees in the State statutes and rules cited above appear to have been virtually unused.

Subdivision (b)(1). This subdivision is amended to correct an imbalance in Rule 35(b)(1) as heretofore written. Under that text, a party causing a Rule 35(a) examination to be made is required to furnish to the party examined, on request, a copy of the examining physician's report. If he delivers this copy, he is in turn entitled to receive from the party examined reports of all examinations of the same condition previously or later made. But the rule has not in terms entitled the examined party to receive from the party causing the Rule 35(a) examination any reports of earlier examinations of the same condition to which the latter may have access. The amendment cures this defect. See La.Stat.Ann., Civ.Proc. art 1495 (1960); Utah R.Civ.P. 35(c).

The amendment specifies that the written report of the examining physician includes results of all tests made, such as results of X-rays and cardiograms. It also embodies changes required by the broadening of Rule 35(a) to take in persons who are not parties.

Subdivision (b)(3). This new subdivision removes any possible doubt that reports of examination may be obtained although no order for examination has been made under Rule 35(a). Examinations are very frequently made by agreement, and sometimes before the party examined has an attorney. The courts have uniformly ordered that reports be supplied, see 4 *Moore's Federal Practice* ¶ 35.06, n. 1 (2d ed. 1966); 2A Barron & Holtzoff, *Federal Practice and Procedure* § 823, n. 22 (Wright ed. 1961), and it appears best to fill the technical gap in the present rule.

The subdivision also makes clear that reports of examining physicians are discoverable not only under Rule 35(b), but under other rules as well. To be sure, if the report is privileged, then discovery is not permissible under any rule other than Rule 35(b) and it is permissible under Rule 35(b) only if the party requests a copy of the report of examination made by the other party's doctor. *Sher v. De Haven,* 199 F.2d 777 (D.C. Cir. 1952), *cert. denied* 345 U.S. 936 (1953). But if the report is unprivileged and is subject to discovery under the provisions of rules other than Rule 35(b)—such as Rules 34 or 26(b)(3) or (4)—discovery should not depend upon whether the person examined demands a copy of the report. Although a few cases have suggested the contrary, *e.g., Galloway v. National Dairy Products Corp.,* 24 F.R.D. 362 (E.D.Pa.1959), the better considered district court decisions hold that Rule 35(b) is not preemptive. *E.g., Leszynski v. Russ,* 29 F.R.D. 10, 12 (D.Md.1961) and cases cited. The question was recently given full consideration in *Buffington v. Wood,* 351 F.2d 292 (3d Cir. 1965), holding that Rule 35(b) is not preemptive.

1987 Amendment

The amendments are technical. No substantive change is intended.

1991 Amendment

The revision authorizes the court to require physical or mental examinations conducted by any person who is suitably licensed or certified.

The rule was revised in 1988 by Congressional enactment to authorize mental examinations by licensed clinical psychologists. This revision extends that amendment to include other certified or licensed professionals, such as dentists or occupational therapists, who are not physicians or clinical psychologists, but who may be well-qualified to give valuable testimony about the physical or mental condition that is the subject of dispute.

The requirement that the examiner be *suitably* licensed or certified is a new requirement. The court is thus expressly authorized to assess the credentials of the examiner to assure that no person is subjected to a court-ordered examination by an examiner whose testimony would be of such limited value that it would be unjust to require the person to undergo the invasion of privacy associated with the examination. This authority is not wholly new, for under the former rule, the court retained discretion to refuse to order an examination, or to restrict an examination. 8 WRIGHT & MILLER, FEDERAL PRACTICE & PROCEDURE § 2234 (1986 Supp.). The revision is intended to encourage the exercise of this discretion, especially with respect to examinations by persons having narrow qualifications.

The court's responsibility to determine the suitability of the examiner's qualifications applies even to a proposed examination by a physician. If the proposed examination and testimony calls for an expertise that the proposed examiner does not have, it should not be ordered, even if the proposed examiner is a physician. The rule does not, however, require that the license or certificate be conferred by the jurisdiction in which the examination is conducted.

2007 Amendment

The language of Rule 35 has been amended as part of the general restyling of the Civil Rules to make them more easily understood and to make style and terminology consistent throughout the rules. These changes are intended to be stylistic only.

Rule 36.   Requests for Admission

(a) Scope and Procedure.

(1) *Scope.* A party may serve on any other party a written request to admit, for purposes of the pending action only, the truth of any matters within the scope of Rule 26(b)(1) relating to:

(A) facts, the application of law to fact, or opinions about either; and

(B) the genuineness of any described documents.

(2) *Form; Copy of a Document.* Each matter must be separately stated. A request to admit the genuineness of a document must be accompanied by a copy of the document unless it is, or has been, otherwise furnished or made available for inspection and copying.

(3) *Time to Respond; Effect of Not Responding.* A matter is admitted unless, within 30 days after being served, the party to whom the request is directed serves on the requesting party a written answer or objection addressed to the matter and signed by the party or its attorney. A shorter or longer time for responding may be stipulated to under Rule 29 or be ordered by the court.

(4) *Answer.* If a matter is not admitted, the answer must specifically deny it or state in detail why the answering party cannot truthfully admit or deny it. A denial must fairly respond to the substance of the matter; and when good faith requires that a party qualify an answer or deny only a part of a matter, the answer must specify the part admitted and qualify or deny the rest. The answering party may assert lack of knowledge or information as a reason for failing to admit or deny only if the party states that it has made reasonable inquiry and that the information it knows or can readily obtain is insufficient to enable it to admit or deny.

(5) *Objections.* The grounds for objecting to a request must be stated. A party must not object solely on the ground that the request presents a genuine issue for trial.

(6) *Motion Regarding the Sufficiency of an Answer or Objection.* The requesting party may move to determine the sufficiency of an answer or objection. Unless the court finds an objection justified, it must order that an answer be served. On finding that an answer does not comply with this rule, the court may order either that the matter is admitted or that an amended answer be served. The court may defer its final decision until a pretrial conference or a specified time before trial. Rule 37(a)(5) applies to an award of expenses.

(b) Effect of an Admission; Withdrawing or Amending It. A matter admitted under this rule is conclusively established unless the court, on motion, permits the admission to be withdrawn or amended. Subject to Rule 16(e), the court may permit withdrawal or amendment if it would promote the presentation of the merits of the action and if the court is not persuaded that it would prejudice the requesting party in maintaining or defending the action on the merits. An admission under this rule is not an admission for any other purpose and cannot be used against the party in any other proceeding.

(Amended December 27, 1946, effective March 19, 1948; March 30, 1970, effective July 1, 1970; March 2, 1987, effective August 1, 1987; April 22, 1993, effective December 1, 1993; April 30, 2007, effective December 1, 2007.)

ADVISORY COMMITTEE NOTES

1937 Adoption

Compare similar rules: [Former] Equity Rule 58 (last paragraph, which provides for the admission of the execution and genuineness of documents); *English Rules Under the Judicature Act* (The Annual Practice, 1937) O. 32; Ill.Rev.Stat. (1937) ch. 110, § 182 and Rule 18 (Ill.Rev.Stat. (1937) ch. 110, § 259.18); 2 Mass.Gen.Laws (Ter.Ed., 1932) ch. 231, § 69; Mich. Court Rules Ann. (Searl, 1933) Rule 42; N.J. Comp.Stat. (2 Cum.Supp. 1911–1924); N.Y.C.P.A. (1937) §§ 322, 323; Wis.Stat. (1935) § 327.22.

1946 Amendment

Note. The first change in the first sentence of Rule 36(a) and the addition of the new second sentence, specifying when requests for admissions may be served, bring Rule 36 in line with amended Rules 26(a) and 33. There is no reason why these rules should not be treated alike. Other provisions of Rule 36(a) give the party whose admissions are requested adequate protection.

The second change in the first sentence of the rule [subdivision (a)] removes any uncertainty as to whether a party can be called upon to admit matters of fact other than those set forth in relevant documents described in and exhibited with the request. In *Smyth v. Kaufman,* C.C.A.2, 1940, 114 F.2d 40, it was held that the word "therein", now stricken from the rule [said subdivision] referred to the request and that a matter of fact not related to any document could be presented to the other party for admission or denial. The rule of this case is now clearly stated.

The substitution of the word "served" for "delivered" in the third sentence of the amended rule [said subdivision] is in conformance with the use of the word "serve" elsewhere in the rule and generally throughout the rules. See also Notes to Rules 13(a) and 33 herein. The substitution [in said subdivision] of "shorter or longer" for "further" will enable a court to designate a lesser period than 10 days for answer. This conforms with a similar provision already contained in Rule 33.

The addition of clause (1) [in said subdivision] specifies the method by which a party may challenge the propriety of a request to admit. There has been considerable difference of judicial opinion as to the correct method, if any, available to secure relief from an allegedly improper request. See Commentary, *Methods of Objecting to Notice to Admit,* 1942, 5 Fed.Rules Serv. 835; *International Carbonic Engineering Co. v. Natural Carbonic Products, Inc.,* S.D.Cal.1944, 57 F.Supp. 248. The changes in clause (1) are merely of a clarifying and conforming nature.

The first of the added last two sentences [in said subdivision] prevents an objection to a part of a request from holding up the answer, if any, to the remainder. See similar proposed change in Rule 33. The last sentence strengthens the rule by making the denial accurately reflect the party's position. It is taken, with necessary changes, from Rule 8(b).

1970 Amendment

Rule 36 serves two vital purposes, both of which are designed to reduce trial time. Admissions are sought, first to facilitate proof with respect to issues that cannot be eliminated from the case, and secondly, to narrow the issues by eliminating those that can be. The changes made in the rule are designed to serve these purposes more effectively. Certain disagreements in the courts about the proper scope of the rule are resolved. In addition, the procedural operation of the rule is brought into line with other discovery procedures, and the binding effect of an admission is clarified. See generally Finman, *The Request for Admissions in Federal Civil Procedure,* 71 Yale L.J. 371 (1962).

Subdivision (a). As revised, the subdivision provides that a request may be made to admit any matters within the scope of Rule 26(b) that relate to statements or opinions of fact or of the application of law to fact. It thereby eliminates the requirement that the matters be "of fact." This change resolves conflicts in the court decisions as to whether a request to admit matters of "opinion" and matters involving "mixed law and fact" is proper under the rule. As to "opinion," compare, *e.g., Jackson Buff Corp. v. Marcelle,* 20 F.R.D. 139 (E.D.N.Y.1957); *California v. The S. S. Jules Fribourg,* 19 F.R.D. 432 (N.D.Calif.1955), with *e.g.,*

Photon, Inc. v. Harris Intertype, Inc., 28 F.R.D. 327 (D.Mass.1961); *Hise v. Lockwood Grader Corp.,* 153 F.Supp. 276 (D.Nebr.1957). As to "mixed law and fact" the majority of courts sustain objections, *e.g., Minnesota Mining and Mfg. Co. v. Norton Co.,* 36 F.R.D. 1 (N.D.Ohio 1964), but *McSparran v. Hanigan,* 225 F.Supp. 628 (E.D.Pa.1963) is to the contrary.

Not only is it difficult as a practical matter to separate "fact" from "opinion," see 4 *Moore's Federal Practice* ¶ 36.04 (2d ed. 1966); cf. 2A Barron & Holtzoff, *Federal Practice and Procedure* 317 (Wright ed. 1961), but an admission on a matter of opinion may facilitate proof or narrow the issues or both. An admission of a matter involving the application of law to fact may, in a given case, even more clearly narrow the issues. For example, an admission that an employee acted in the scope of his employment may remove a major issue from the trial. In *McSparran v. Hanigan, supra,* plaintiff admitted that "the premises on which said accident occurred, were occupied or under the control" of one of the defendants, 225 F.Supp. at 636. This admission, involving law as well as fact, removed one of the issues from the lawsuit and thereby reduced the proof required at trial. The amended provision does not authorize requests for admissions of law unrelated to the facts of the case.

Requests for admission involving the application of law to fact may create disputes between the parties which are best resolved in the presence of the judge after much or all of the other discovery has been completed. Power is therefore expressly conferred upon the court to defer decision until a pretrial conference is held or until a designated time prior to trial. On the other hand, the court should not automatically defer decision; in many instances, the importance of the admission lies in enabling the requesting party to avoid the burdensome accumulation of proof prior to the pretrial conference.

Courts have also divided on whether an answering party may properly object to request for admission as to matters which that party regards as "in dispute." Compare, *e.g., Syracuse Broadcasting Corp. v. Newhouse,* 271 F.2d 910, 917 (2d Cir. 1959); *Driver v. Gindy Mfg. Corp.,* 24 F.R.D. 473 (E.D.Pa.1959); with, *e.g., McGonigle v. Baxter,* 27 F.R.D. 504 (E.D.Pa.1961); *United States v. Ehbauer,* 13 F.R.D. 462 (W.D.Mo.1952). The proper response in such cases is an answer. The very purpose of the request is to ascertain whether the answering party is prepared to admit or regards the matter as presenting a genuine issue for trial. In his answer, the party may deny, or he may give as his reason for inability to admit or deny the existence of a genuine issue. The party runs no risk of sanctions if the matter is genuinely in issue, since Rule 37(c) provides a sanction of costs only when there are no good reasons for a failure to admit.

On the other hand, requests to admit may be so voluminous and so framed that the answering party finds the task of identifying what is in dispute and what is not unduly burdensome. If so, the responding party may obtain a protective order under Rule 26(c). Some of the decisions sustaining objections on "disputability" grounds could have been justified by the burdensome character of the requests. See, *e.g., Syracuse Broadcasting Corp. v. Newhouse, supra.*

Another sharp split of authority exists on the question whether a party may base his answer on lack of information or knowledge without seeking out additional information. One line of cases has held that a party may answer on the basis of such knowledge as he has at the time he answers. *E.g., Jackson Buff Corp. v. Marcelle,* 20 F.R.D. 139 (E.D.N.Y.1957); *Sladek v. General Motors Corp.,* 16 F.R.D. 104 (S.D.Iowa 1954). A larger group of cases, supported by commentators, has taken the view that if the responding party lacks knowledge, he must inform himself in reasonable fashion. *E.g., Hise v. Lockwood Grader Corp.,* 153 F.Supp. 276 (D.Nebr. 1957); *E. H. Tate Co. v. Jiffy Enterprises, Inc.,* 16 F.R.D. 571 (E.D.Pa.1954); Finman, *supra,* 71 Yale L.J. 371, 404–409; 4 *Moore's Federal Practice* ¶ 36.04 (2d ed. 1966); 2A Barron & Holtzoff, *Federal Practice and Procedure* 509 (Wright ed. 1961).

The rule as revised adopts the majority view, as in keeping with a basic principle of the discovery rules that a reasonable burden may be imposed on the parties when its discharge will facilitate preparation for trial and ease the trial process. It has been argued against this view that one side should not have the burden of "proving" the other side's case. The revised rule requires only that the answering party make reasonable inquiry and secure such knowledge and information as are readily obtainable by him. In most instances, the investigation will be necessary either to his own case or to preparation for rebuttal. Even when it is not, the information may be close enough at hand to be "readily obtainable." Rule 36 requires only that the party state that he has taken these steps. The sanction for failure of a party to inform himself before he answers lies in the award of costs after trial, as provided in Rule 37(c).

The requirement that the answer to a request for admission be sworn is deleted, in favor of a provision that the answer be signed by the party or by his attorney. The provisions of Rule 36 make it clear that admissions function very much as pleadings do. Thus, when a party admits in part and denies in part, his admission is for purposes of the pending action only and may not be used against him in any other proceeding. The broadening of the rule to encompass mixed questions of law and fact reinforces this feature. Rule 36 does not lack a sanction for false answers; Rule 37(c) furnishes an appropriate deterrent.

The existing language describing the available grounds for objection to a request for admission is eliminated as neither necessary nor helpful. The statement that objection may be made to any request which is "improper" adds nothing to the provisions that the party serve an answer or objection addressed to each matter and that he state his reasons for any objection. None of the other discovery rules sets forth grounds for objection, except so far as all are subject to the general provisions of Rule 26.

Changes are made in the sequence of procedures in Rule 36 so that they conform to the new procedures in Rules 33 and 34. The major changes are as follows:

(1)   The normal time for response to a request for admissions is lengthened from 10 to 30 days, conforming more closely to prevailing practice. A defendant need not respond, however, in less than 45 days after service of the summons and complaint upon him. The court may lengthen or shorten the time when special situations require it.

(2)   The present requirement that the plaintiff wait 10 days to serve requests without leave of court is eliminated. The revised provision accords with those in Rules 33 and 34.

(3)   The requirement that the objecting party move automatically for a hearing on his objection is eliminated, and the burden is on the requesting party to move for an order. The change in the burden of going forward does not modify present law on burden of persuasion. The award of expenses incurred in relation to the motion is made subject to the comprehensive provisions of Rule 37(a)(4).

(4)   A problem peculiar to Rule 36 arises if the responding party serves answers that are not in conformity with the requirements of the rule—for example, a denial is not "specific," or the explanation of inability to admit or deny is not "in detail." Rule 36 now makes no provision for court scrutiny of such answers before trial, and it seems to contemplate that defective answers bring about admissions just as effectively as if no answer had been served. Some cases have so held. *E.g., Southern Ry. Co. v. Crosby,* 201 F.2d 878 (4th Cir. 1953); *United States v. Laney,* 96 F.Supp. 482 (E.D.S.C.1951).

Giving a defective answer the automatic effect of an admission may cause unfair surprise. A responding party who purported to deny or to be unable to admit or deny will for the first time at trial confront the contention that he has made a binding admission. Since it is not always easy to know whether a denial is "specific" or an explanation is "in detail," neither party can know how the court will rule at trial and whether proof must be prepared. Some courts, therefore, have entertained motions to rule on defective answers. They have at times ordered that amended answers be served, when the defects were technical, and at other times have declared that the matter was admitted. *E.g., Woods v. Stewart,* 171 F.2d 544 (5th Cir. 1948); *SEC v. Kaye, Real & Co.,* 122 F.Supp. 639 (S.D.N.Y.1954); *Sieb's Hatcheries, Inc. v. Lindley,* 13 F.R.D. 113 (W.D.Ark.1952). The rule as revised conforms to the latter practice.

Subdivision (b). The rule does not how indicate the extent to which a party is bound by his admission. Some courts view admissions as the equivalent of sworn testimony. *E.g., Ark-Tenn Distributing Corp. v. Breidt,* 209 F.2d 359 (3d Cir. 1954); *United States v. Lemons,* 125 F.Supp. 686 (W.D.Ark.1954); 4 *Moore's Federal Practice* ¶ 36.08 (2d ed. 1966 Supp.). At least in some jurisdictions a party may rebut his own testimony, *e.g., Alamo v. Del Rosario,* 98 F.2d 328 (D.C.Cir.1938), and by analogy an admission made pursuant to Rule 36 may likewise be thought rebuttable. The courts in *Ark-Tenn* and *Lemons, supra,* reasoned in this way, although the results reached may be supported on different grounds. In *McSparran v. Hanigan,* 225 F.Supp. 628, 636–637 (E.D.Pa.1963), the court held that an admission is conclusively binding, though noting the confusion created by prior decisions.

The new provisions give an admission a conclusively binding effect, for purposes only of the pending action, unless the admission is withdrawn or amended. In form and substance a Rule 36 admission is comparable to an admission in pleadings or a stipulation drafted by counsel for use at trial, rather than to an evidentiary admission of a party. Louisell, *Modern California Discovery* § 8.07 (1963); 2A Barron & Holtzoff, *Federal Practice and Procedure* § 838 (Wright ed. 1961). Unless the party securing an admission can depend on its binding effect, he cannot safely avoid the expense of preparing to prove the very matters on which he has secured the admission, and the purpose of the rule is defeated. Field v. McKusick, *Maine Civil Practice* § 36.4 (1959); Finman, *supra*, 71 Yale L.J. 371, 418–426; Comment, 56 Nw.U.L.Rev. 679, 682–683 (1961).

Provision is made for withdrawal or amendment of an admission. This provision emphasizes the importance of having the action resolved on the merits, while at the same time assuring each party that justified reliance on an admission in preparation for trial will not operate to his prejudice. *Cf. Moosman v. Joseph P. Blitz, Inc.*, 358 F.2d 686 (2d Cir. 1966).

1987 Amendment

The amendments are technical. No substantive change is intended.

1993 Amendments

The rule is revised to reflect the change made by Rule 26(d), preventing a party from seeking formal discovery until after the meeting of the parties required by Rule 26(f).

2007 Amendment

The language of Rule 36 has been amended as part of the general restyling of the Civil Rules to make them more easily understood and to make style and terminology consistent throughout the rules. These changes are intended to be stylistic only.

The final sentence of the first paragraph of former Rule 36(a) was a redundant cross-reference to the discovery moratorium provisions of Rule 26(d). Rule 26(d) is now familiar, obviating any need to carry forward the redundant cross-reference. The redundant reminder of Rule 37(c) in the second paragraph was likewise omitted.

2015 Amendments

Gap Report

The published proposal to add a presumptive limit of 25 requests to admit, not counting requests to admit the genuineness of described documents, was withdrawn.

Rule 37.   Failure to Make Disclosures or to Cooperate in Discovery; Sanctions

(a) Motion for an Order Compelling Disclosure or Discovery.

    (1) *In General.* On notice to other parties and all affected persons, a party may move for an order compelling disclosure or discovery. The motion must include a certification that the movant has in good faith conferred or attempted to confer with the person or party failing to make disclosure or discovery in an effort to obtain it without court action.

    (2) *Appropriate Court.* A motion for an order to a party must be made in the court where the action is pending. A motion for an order to a nonparty must be made in the court where the discovery is or will be taken.

    (3) *Specific Motions.*

        (A) *To Compel Disclosure.* If a party fails to make a disclosure required by Rule 26(a), any other party may move to compel disclosure and for appropriate sanctions.

        (B) *To Compel a Discovery Response.* A party seeking discovery may move for an order compelling an answer, designation, production, or inspection. This motion may be made if:

            (i) a deponent fails to answer a question asked under Rule 30 or 31;

            (ii) a corporation or other entity fails to make a designation under Rule 30(b)(6) or 31(a)(4);

            (iii) a party fails to answer an interrogatory submitted under Rule 33; or

        (iv) a party fails to produce documents or fails to respond that inspection will be permitted—or fails to permit inspection—as requested under Rule 34.

    (C) *Related to a Deposition.* When taking an oral deposition, the party asking a question may complete or adjourn the examination before moving for an order.

  (4) *Evasive or Incomplete Disclosure, Answer, or Response.* For purposes of this subdivision (a), an evasive or incomplete disclosure, answer, or response must be treated as a failure to disclose, answer, or respond.

  (5) *Payment of Expenses; Protective Orders.*

    (A) *If the Motion Is Granted* (or Disclosure or Discovery Is Provided After Filing). If the motion is granted—or if the disclosure or requested discovery is provided after the motion was filed—the court must, after giving an opportunity to be heard, require the party or deponent whose conduct necessitated the motion, the party or attorney advising that conduct, or both to pay the movant's reasonable expenses incurred in making the motion, including attorney's fees. But the court must not order this payment if:

        (i) the movant filed the motion before attempting in good faith to obtain the disclosure or discovery without court action;

        (ii) the opposing party's nondisclosure, response, or objection was substantially justified; or

        (iii) other circumstances make an award of expenses unjust.

    (B) *If the Motion Is Denied.* If the motion is denied, the court may issue any protective order authorized under Rule 26(c) and must, after giving an opportunity to be heard, require the movant, the attorney filing the motion, or both to pay the party or deponent who opposed the motion its reasonable expenses incurred in opposing the motion, including attorney's fees. But the court must not order this payment if the motion was substantially justified or other circumstances make an award of expenses unjust.

    (C) *If the Motion Is Granted in Part and Denied in Part.* If the motion is granted in part and denied in part, the court may issue any protective order authorized under Rule 26(c) and may, after giving an opportunity to be heard, apportion the reasonable expenses for the motion.

(b) **Failure to Comply with a Court Order.**

  (1) *Sanctions Sought in the District Where the Deposition Is Taken.* If the court where the discovery is taken orders a deponent to be sworn or to answer a question and the deponent fails to obey, the failure may be treated as contempt of court. If a deposition-related motion is transferred to the court where the action is pending, and that court orders a deponent to be sworn or to answer a question and the deponent fails to obey, the failure may be treated as contempt of either the court where the discovery is taken or the court where the action is pending.

  (2) *Sanctions Sought in the District Where the Action Is Pending.*

    (A) *For Not Obeying a Discovery Order.* If a party or a party's officer, director, or managing agent—or a witness designated under Rule 30(b)(6) or 31(a)(4)—fails to obey an order to provide or permit discovery, including an order under Rule 26(f), 35, or 37(a), the court where the action is pending may issue further just orders. They may include the following:

        (i) directing that the matters embraced in the order or other designated facts be taken as established for purposes of the action, as the prevailing party claims;

(ii) prohibiting the disobedient party from supporting or opposing designated claims or defenses, or from introducing designated matters in evidence;

(iii) striking pleadings in whole or in part;

(iv) staying further proceedings until the order is obeyed;

(v) dismissing the action or proceeding in whole or in part;

(vi) rendering a default judgment against the disobedient party; or

(vii) treating as contempt of court the failure to obey any order except an order to submit to a physical or mental examination.

(B) *For Not Producing a Person for Examination.* If a party fails to comply with an order under Rule 35(a) requiring it to produce another person for examination, the court may issue any of the orders listed in Rule 37(b)(2)(A)(i)–(vi), unless the disobedient party shows that it cannot produce the other person.

Sibbach

(C) *Payment of Expenses.* Instead of or in addition to the orders above, the court must order the disobedient party, the attorney advising that party, or both to pay the reasonable expenses, including attorney's fees, caused by the failure, unless the failure was substantially justified or other circumstances make an award of expenses unjust.

(c) Failure to Disclose, to Supplement an Earlier Response, or to Admit.

(1) *Failure to Disclose or Supplement.* If a party fails to provide information or identify a witness as required by Rule 26(a) or (e), the party is not allowed to use that information or witness to supply evidence on a motion, at a hearing, or at a trial, unless the failure was substantially justified or is harmless. In addition to or instead of this sanction, the court, on motion and after giving an opportunity to be heard:

(A) may order payment of the reasonable expenses, including attorney's fees, caused by the failure;

(B) may inform the jury of the party's failure; and

(C) may impose other appropriate sanctions, including any of the orders listed in Rule 37(b)(2)(A)(i)–(vi).

(2) *Failure to Admit.* If a party fails to admit what is requested under Rule 36 and if the requesting party later proves a document to be genuine or the matter true, the requesting party may move that the party who failed to admit pay the reasonable expenses, including attorney's fees, incurred in making that proof. The court must so order unless:

(A) the request was held objectionable under Rule 36(a);

(B) the admission sought was of no substantial importance;

(C) the party failing to admit had a reasonable ground to believe that it might prevail on the matter; or

(D) there was other good reason for the failure to admit.

(d) Party's Failure to Attend Its Own Deposition, Serve Answers to Interrogatories, or Respond to a Request for Inspection.

(1) *In General.*

(A) *Motion; Grounds for Sanctions.* The court where the action is pending may, on motion, order sanctions if:

(i) a party or a party's officer, director, or managing agent—or a person designated under Rule 30(b)(6) or 31(a)(4)—fails, after being served with proper notice, to appear for that person's deposition; or

    (ii) a party, after being properly served with interrogatories under Rule 33 or a request for inspection under Rule 34, fails to serve its answers, objections, or written response.

  (B) *Certification.* A motion for sanctions for failing to answer or respond must include a certification that the movant has in good faith conferred or attempted to confer with the party failing to act in an effort to obtain the answer or response without court action.

(2) *Unacceptable Excuse for Failing to Act.* A failure described in Rule 37(d)(1)(A) is not excused on the ground that the discovery sought was objectionable, unless the party failing to act has a pending motion for a protective order under Rule 26(c).

(3) *Types of Sanctions.* Sanctions may include any of the orders listed in Rule 37(b)(2)(A)(i)–(vi). Instead of or in addition to these sanctions, the court must require the party failing to act, the attorney advising that party, or both to pay the reasonable expenses, including attorney's fees, caused by the failure, unless the failure was substantially justified or other circumstances make an award of expenses unjust.

(e) **Failure to Preserve Electronically Stored Information.** If electronically stored information that should have been preserved in the anticipation or conduct of litigation is lost because a party failed to take reasonable steps to preserve it, and it cannot be restored or replaced through additional discovery, the court:

(1) upon finding prejudice to another party from loss of the information, may order measures no greater than necessary to cure the prejudice; or

(2) only upon finding that the party acted with the intent to deprive another party of the information's use in the litigation may:

  (A) presume that the lost information was unfavorable to the party;

  (B) instruct the jury that it may or must presume the information was unfavorable to the party; or

  (C) dismiss the action or enter a default judgment.

(f) **Failure to Participate in Framing a Discovery Plan.** If a party or its attorney fails to participate in good faith in developing and submitting a proposed discovery plan as required by Rule 26(f), the court may, after giving an opportunity to be heard, require that party or attorney to pay to any other party the reasonable expenses, including attorney's fees, caused by the failure.

(Amended December 29, 1948, effective October 20, 1949; March 30, 1970, effective July 1, 1970; April 29, 1980, effective August 1, 1980; amended by Pub.L. 96–481, Title II, § 205(a), October 21, 1980, 94 Stat. 2330, effective October 1, 1981; amended March 2, 1987, effective August 1, 1987; April 22, 1993, effective December 1, 1993; April 17, 2000, effective December 1, 2000; April 12, 2006, effective December 1, 2006; April 30, 2007, effective December 1, 2007; April 16, 2013, effective December 1, 2013; April 29, 2015, effective December 1, 2015.)

ADVISORY COMMITTEE NOTES

1937 Adoption

The provisions of this rule authorizing orders establishing facts or excluding evidence or striking pleadings, or authorizing judgments of dismissal or default, for refusal to answer questions or permit inspection or otherwise make discovery, are in accord with *Hammond Packing Co. v. Arkansas,* 1909, 29 S.Ct. 370, 212 U.S. 322, 53 L.Ed. 530, 15 Ann.Cas. 645, which distinguishes between the justifiable use of such measures as a means of compelling the production of evidence, and their unjustifiable use, as in *Hovey v. Elliott,* 1897, 17 S.Ct. 841, 167 U.S. 409, 42 L.Ed. 215, for the mere purpose of punishing for contempt.

1948 Amendment

The amendment effective October 1949, substituted the reference to "Title 28, U.S.C., § 1783" in subdivision (e) for the reference to "the Act of July 3, 1926, c. 762, § 1 (44 Stat. 835), U.S.C., Title 28, § 711."

1970 Amendment

Rule 37 provides generally for sanctions against parties or persons unjustifiably resisting discovery. Experience has brought to light a number of defects in the language of the rule as well as instances in which it is not serving the purposes for which it was designed. See Rosenberg, *Sanctions to Effectuate Pretrial Discovery,* 58 Col.L.Rev. 480 (1958). In addition, changes being made in other discovery rules require conforming amendments to Rule 37.

Rule 37 sometimes refers to a "failure" to afford discovery and at other times to a "refusal" to do so. Taking note of this dual terminology, courts have imported into "refusal" a requirement of "wilfullness." See *Roth v. Paramount Pictures Corp.,* 8 F.R.D. 31 (W.D.Pa.1948); *Campbell v. Johnson,* 101 F.Supp. 705, 707 (S.D.N.Y.1951). In *Societe Internationale v. Rogers,* 357 U.S. 197 (1958), the Supreme Court concluded that the rather random use of these two terms in Rule 37 showed no design to use them with consistently distinctive meanings, that "refused" in Rule 37(b)(2) meant simply a failure to comply, and that wilfullness was relevant only to the selection of sanctions, if any, to be imposed. Nevertheless, after the decision in *Societe,* the court in *Hinson v. Michigan Mutual Liability Co.,* 275 F.2d 537 (5th Cir. 1960) once again ruled that "refusal" required wilfullness. Substitution of "failure" for "refusal" throughout Rule 37 should eliminate this confusion and bring the rule into harmony with the *Societe Internationale* decision. See Rosenberg, *supra,* 58 Col.L.Rev. 480, 489–490 (1958).

Subdivision (a). Rule 37(a) provides relief to a party seeking discovery against one who, with or without stated objections, fails to afford the discovery sought. It has always fully served this function in relation to depositions, but the amendments being made to Rules 33 and 34 give Rule 37(a) added scope and importance. Under existing Rule 33, a party objecting to interrogatories must make a motion for court hearing on his objections. The changes now made in Rules 33 and 37(a) make it clear that the interrogating party must move to compel answers, and the motion is provided for in Rule 37(a). Existing Rule 34, since it requires a court order prior to production of documents or things or permission to enter on land, has no relation to Rule 37(a). Amendments of Rules 34 and 37(a) create a procedure similar to that provided for Rule 33.

Subdivision (a)(1). This is a new provision making clear to which court a party may apply for an order compelling discovery. Existing Rule 37(a) refers only to the court in which the deposition is being taken; nevertheless, it has been held that the court where the action is pending has "inherent power" to compel a party deponent to answer. *Lincoln Laboratories, Inc. v. Savage Laboratories, Inc.,* 27 F.R.D. 476 (D.Del.1961). In relation to Rule 33 interrogatories and Rule 34 requests for inspection, the court where the action is pending is the appropriate enforcing tribunal. The new provision eliminates the need to resort to inherent power by spelling out the respective roles of the court where the action is pending and the court where the deposition is taken. In some instances, two courts are available to a party seeking to compel answers from a party deponent. The party seeking discovery may choose the court to which he will apply, but the court has power to remit the party to the other court as a more appropriate forum.

Subdivision (a)(2). This subdivision contains the substance of existing provisions of Rule 37(a) authorizing motions to compel answers to questions put at depositions and to interrogatories. New provisions authorize motions for orders compelling designation under Rules 30(b)(6) and 31(a) and compelling inspection in accordance with a request made under Rule 34. If the court denies a motion, in whole or part, it may accompany the denial with issuance of a protective order. Compare the converse provision in Rule 26(c).

Subdivision (a)(3). This new provision makes clear that an evasive or incomplete answer is to be considered, for purposes of subdivision (a), a failure to answer. The courts have consistently held that they have the power to compel adequate answers. *E.g., Cone Mills Corp. v. Joseph Bancroft & Sons Co.,* 33 F.R.D. 318 (D.Del.1963). This power is recognized and incorporated into the rule.

Subdivision (a)(4). This subdivision amends the provisions for award of expenses, including reasonable attorney's fees, to the prevailing party or person when a motion is made for an order compelling discovery. At present, an award of expenses is made only if the losing party or person is found to have acted without substantial justification. The change requires that expenses be awarded unless the conduct of the losing party or person is found to have been substantially justified. The test of "substantial justification" remains, but the change in language is intended to encourage judges to be more alert to abuses occurring in the discovery process.

On many occasions, to be sure, the dispute over discovery between the parties is genuine, though ultimately resolved one way or the other by the court. In such cases, the losing party is substantially justified in carrying the matter to court. But the rules should deter the abuse implicit in carrying or forcing a discovery dispute to court when no genuine dispute exists. And the potential or actual imposition of expenses is virtually the sole formal sanction in the rules to deter a party from pressing to a court hearing frivolous requests for or objections to discovery.

The present provision of Rule 37(a) that the court shall require payment if it finds that the defeated party acted without "substantial justification" may appear adequate, but in fact it has been little used. Only a handful of reported cases include an award of expenses, and the Columbia Survey found that in only one instance out of about 50 motions decided under Rule 37(a) did the court award expenses. It appears that the courts do not utilize the most important available sanction to deter abusive resort to the judiciary.

The proposed change provides in effect that expenses should ordinarily be awarded unless a court finds that the losing party acted justifiably in carrying his point to court. At the same time, a necessary flexibility is maintained, since the court retains the power to find that other circumstances make an award of expenses unjust—as where the prevailing party also acted unjustifiably. The amendment does not significantly narrow the discretion of the court, but rather presses the court to address itself to abusive practices. The present provision that expenses may be imposed upon either the party or his attorney or both is unchanged. But it is not contemplated that expenses will be imposed upon the attorney merely because the party is indigent.

Subdivision (b). This subdivision deals with sanctions for failure to comply with a court order. The present captions for subsections (1) and (2) entitled, "Contempt" and "Other Consequences," respectively, are confusing. One of the consequences listed in (2) is the arrest of the party, representing the exercise of the contempt power. The contents of the subsections show that the first authorizes the sanction of contempt (and no other) by the court in which the deposition is taken, whereas the second subsection authorizes a variety of sanctions, including contempt, which may be imposed by the court in which the action is pending. The captions of the subsections are changed to reflect their contents.

The scope of Rule 37(b)(2) is broadened by extending it to include any order "to provide or permit discovery," including orders issued under Rules 37(a) and 35. Various rules authorize orders for discovery— e.g., Rule 35(b)(1), Rule 26(c) as revised, Rule 37(d). See Rosenberg, *supra*, 58 Col.L.Rev. 480, 484–486. Rule 37(b)(2) should provide comprehensively for enforcement of all these orders. *Cf. Societe Internationale v. Rogers,* 357 U.S. 197, 207 (1958). On the other hand, the reference to Rule 34 is deleted to conform to the changed procedure in that rule.

A new subsection (E) provides that sanctions which have been available against a party for failure to comply with an order under Rule 35(a) to submit to examination will now be available against him for his failure to comply with a Rule 35(a) order to produce a third person for examination, unless he shows that he is unable to produce the person. In this context, "unable" means in effect "unable in good faith." See *Societe Internationale v. Rogers,* 357 U.S. 197 (1958).

Subdivision (b)(2) is amplified to provide for payment of reasonable expenses caused by the failure to obey the order. Although Rules 37(b)(2) and 37(d) have been silent as to award of expenses, courts have nevertheless ordered them on occasion. *E.g., United Sheeplined Clothing Co. v. Arctic Fur Cap Corp.,* 165 F.Supp. 193 (S.D.N.Y.1958); *Austin Theatre, Inc. v. Warner Bros. Pictures, Inc.,* 22 F.R.D. 302 (S.D.N.Y.1958). The provision places the burden on the disobedient party to avoid expenses by showing that his failure is justified or that special circumstances make an award of expenses unjust. Allocating the burden in this way conforms to the changed provisions as to expenses in Rule 37(a), and is particularly appropriate when a court order is disobeyed.

An added reference to directors of a party is similar to a change made in subdivision (d) and is explained in the note to that subdivision. The added reference to persons designated by a party under Rules 30(b)(6) or 31(a) to testify on behalf of the party carries out the new procedure in those rules for taking a deposition of a corporation or other organization.

Subdivision (c). Rule 37(c) provides a sanction for the enforcement of Rule 36 dealing with requests for admission. Rule 36 provides the mechanism whereby a party may obtain from another party in appropriate instances either (1) an admission, or (2) a sworn and specific denial or (3) a sworn statement "setting forth in detail the reasons why he cannot truthfully admit or deny." If the party obtains the second or third of these responses, in proper form, Rule 36 does not provide for a pretrial hearing on whether the response is warranted by the evidence thus far accumulated. Instead, Rule 37(c) is intended to provide posttrial relief in the form of a requirement that the party improperly refusing the admission pay the expenses of the other side in making the necessary proof at trial.

Rule 37(c), as now written, addresses itself in terms only to the sworn denial and is silent with respect to the statement of reasons for an inability to admit or deny. There is no apparent basis for this distinction, since the sanction provided in Rule 37(c) should deter all unjustified failures to admit. This omission in the rule has caused confused and diverse treatment in the courts. One court has held that if a party give inadequate reasons, he should be treated before trial as having denied the request, so that Rule 37(c) may apply. *Bertha Bldg. Corp. v. National Theatres Corp.,* 15 F.R.D. 339 (E.D.N.Y.1954). Another has held that the party should be treated as having admitted the request. *Heng Hsin Co. v. Stern, Morgenthau & Co.,* 20 Fed.Rules Serv. 36a.52, Case 1 (S.D.N.Y. Dec. 10, 1954). Still another has ordered a new response, without indicating what the outcome should be if the new response were inadequate. *United States Plywood Corp. v. Hudson Lumber Co.,* 127 F.Supp. 489, 497–498 (S.D.N.Y.1954). See generally Finman, *The Request for Admissions in Federal Civil Procedure,* 71 Yale L.J. 371, 426–430 (1962). The amendment eliminates this defect in Rule 37(c) by bringing within its scope all failures to admit.

Additional provisions in Rule 37(c) protect a party from having to pay expenses if the request for admission was held objectionable under Rule 36(a) or if the party failing to admit had reasonable ground to believe that he might prevail on the matter. The latter provision emphasizes that the true test under Rule 37(c) is not whether a party prevailed at trial but whether he acted reasonably in believing that he might prevail.

Subdivision (d). The scope of subdivision (d) is broadened to include responses to requests for inspection under Rule 34, thereby conforming to the new procedures of Rule 34.

Two related changes are made in subdivision (d): the permissible sanctions are broadened to include such orders "as are just"; and the requirement that the failure to appear or respond be "wilful" is eliminated. Although Rule 37(d) in terms provides for only three sanctions, all rather severe, the courts have interpreted it as permitting softer sanctions than those which it sets forth. E.g., *Gill v. Stolow,* 240 F.2d 669 (2d Cir.1957); *Saltzman v. Birrell,* 156 F.Supp. 538 (S.D.N.Y.1957); 2A Barron & Holtzoff, *Federal Practice and Procedure* 554–557 (Wright ed. 1961). The rule is changed to provide the greater flexibility as to sanctions which the cases show is needed.

The resulting flexibility as to sanctions eliminates any need to retain the requirement that the failure to appear or respond be "wilful." The concept of "wilful failure" is at best subtle and difficult, and the cases do not supply a bright line. Many courts have imposed sanctions without referring to wilfullness. E.g., *Milewski v. Schneider Transportation Co.,* 238 F.2d 397 (6th Cir.1956); *Dictograph Products, Inc. v. Kentworth Corp.,* 7 F.R.D. 543 (W.D.Ky.1947). In addition, in view of the possibility of light sanctions, even a negligent failure should come within Rule 37(d). If default is caused by counsel's ignorance of Federal practice, cf. *Dunn v. Pa. R.R.,* 96 F.Supp. 597 (N.D.Ohio 1951), or by his preoccupation with another aspect of the case, *cf. Maurer-Neuer, Inc. v. United Packinghouse Workers,* 26 F.R.D. 139 (D.Kans.1960), dismissal of the action and default judgment are not justified, but the imposition of expenses and fees may well be. "Wilfullness" continues to play a role, along with various other factors, in the choice of sanctions. Thus, the scheme conforms to Rule 37(b) as construed by the Supreme Court in *Societe Internationale v. Rogers,* 357 U.S. 197, 208 (1958).

A provision is added to make clear that a party may not properly remain completely silent even when he regards a notice to take his deposition or a set of interrogatories or requests to inspect as improper and objectionable. If he desires not to appear or not to respond, he must apply for a protective order. The cases are divided on whether a protective order must be sought. Compare *Collins v. Wayland,* 139 F.2d 677 (9th Cir. 1944), *cert. den.* 322 U.S. 744; *Bourgeois v. El Paso Natural Gas Co.,* 20 F.R.D. 358 (S.D.N.Y.1957); *Loosley v. Stone,* 15 F.R.D. 373 (S.D.Ill.1954), with *Scarlatos v. Kulukundis,* 21 F.R.D. 185 (S.D.N.Y.1957); *Ross v. True Temper Corp.,* 11 F.R.D. 307 (N.D.Ohio 1951). Compare also Rosenberg, *supra,* 58 Col.L.Rev. 480, 496 (1958) with 2A Barron & Holtzoff, *Federal Practice and Procedure* 530–531 (Wright ed. 1961). The party from whom discovery is sought is afforded, through Rule 26(c), a fair and effective procedure whereby he can challenge the request made. At the same time, the total noncompliance with which Rule 37(d) is concerned may impose severe inconvenience or hardship on the discovering party and substantially delay the discovery process. Cf. 2B Barron & Holtzoff, *Federal Practice and Procedure* 306–307 (Wright ed. 1961) (response to a subpoena).

The failure of an officer or managing agent of a party to make discovery as required by present Rule 37(d) is treated as the failure of the party. The rule as revised provides similar treatment for a director of a party. There is slight warrant for the present distinction between officers and managing agents on the one hand and directors on the other. Although the legal power over a director to compel his making discovery may not be as great as over officers or managing agents, *Campbell v. General Motors Corp.,* 13 F.R.D. 331 (S.D.N.Y.1952), the practical differences are negligible. That a director's interests are normally aligned with those of his corporation is shown by the provisions of old Rule 26(d)(2), transferred to 32(a)(2) (deposition of director of party may be used at trial by an adverse party for any purpose) and of Rule 43(b) (director of party may be treated at trial as a hostile witness on direct examination by any adverse party). Moreover, in those rare instances when a corporation is unable through good faith efforts to compel a director to make discovery, it is unlikely that the court will impose sanctions. Cf. *Societe Internationale v. Rogers,* 357 U.S. 197 (1958).

Subdivision (e). The change in the caption conforms to the language of 28 U.S.C. § 1783, as amended in 1964.

Subdivision (f). Until recently, costs of a civil action could be awarded against the United States only when expressly provided by Act of Congress, and such provision was rarely made. See H.R.Rep.No. 1535, 89th Cong., 2d Sess., 2–3 (1966). To avoid any conflict with this doctrine, Rule 37(f) has provided that expenses and attorney's fees may not be imposed upon the United States under Rule 37. See 2A Barron & Holtzoff, *Federal Practice and Procedure* 857 (Wright ed. 1961).

A major change in the law was made in 1966, 80 Stat. 308, 28 U.S.C. § 2412 (1966), whereby a judgment for costs may ordinarily be awarded to the prevailing party in any civil action brought by or against the United States. Costs are not to include the fees and expenses of attorneys. In light of this legislative development, Rule 37(f) is amended to permit the award of expenses and fees against the United States under Rule 37, but only to the extent permitted by statute. The amendment brings Rule 37(f) into line with present and future statutory provisions.

1980 Amendment

Subdivision (b)(2). New Rule 26(f) provides that if a discovery conference is held, at its close the court shall enter an order respecting the subsequent conduct of discovery. The amendment provides that the sanctions available for violation of other court orders respecting discovery are available for violation of the discovery conference order.

Subdivision (e). Subdivision (e) is stricken. Title 28, U.S.C. § 1783 no longer refers to sanctions. The subdivision otherwise duplicates Rule 45(e)(2).

Subdivision (g). New Rule 26(f) imposes a duty on parties to participate in good faith in the framing of a discovery plan by agreement upon the request of any party. This subdivision authorizes the court to award to parties who participate in good faith in an attempt to frame a discovery plan the expenses incurred in the attempt if any party or his attorney fails to participate in good faith and thereby causes additional expense.

Failure of United States to Participate in Good Faith in Discovery. Rule 37 authorizes the court to direct that parties or attorneys who fail to participate in good faith in the discovery process pay the expenses, including attorneys' fees, incurred by other parties as a result of that failure. Since attorneys' fees cannot ordinarily be awarded against the United States (28 U.S.C. § 2412), there is often no practical remedy for the misconduct of its officers and attorneys. However, in the case of a government attorney who fails to participate in good faith in discovery, nothing prevents a court in an appropriate case from giving written notification of that fact to the Attorney General of the United States and other appropriate heads of offices or agencies thereof.

1987 Amendment

The amendments are technical. No substantive change is intended.

1993 Amendments

Subdivision (a). This subdivision is revised to reflect the revision of Rule 26(a), requiring disclosure of matters without a discovery request.

Pursuant to new subdivision (a)(2)(A), a party dissatisfied with the disclosure made by an opposing party may under this rule move for an order to compel disclosure. In providing for such a motion, the revised rule parallels the provisions of the former rule dealing with failures to answer particular interrogatories. Such a motion may be needed when the information to be disclosed might be helpful to the party seeking the disclosure but not to the party required to make the disclosure. If the party required to make the disclosure would need the material to support its own contentions, the more effective enforcement of the disclosure requirement will be to exclude the evidence not disclosed, as provided in subdivision (c)(1) of this revised rule.

Language is included in the new paragraph and added to the subparagraph (B) that requires litigants to seek to resolve discovery disputes by informal means before filing a motion with the court. This requirement is based on successful experience with similar local rules of court promulgated pursuant to Rule 83.

The last sentence of paragraph (2) is moved into paragraph (4).

Under revised paragraph (3), evasive or incomplete disclosures and responses to interrogatories and production requests are treated as failures to disclose or respond. Interrogatories and requests for production should not be read or interpreted in an artificially restrictive or hypertechnical manner to avoid disclosure of information fairly covered by the discovery request, and to do so is subject to appropriate sanctions under subdivision (a).

Revised paragraph (4) is divided into three subparagraphs for ease of reference, and in each the phrase "after opportunity for hearing" is changed to "after affording an opportunity to be heard" to make clear that the court can consider such questions on written submissions as well as on oral hearings.

Subparagraph (A) is revised to cover the situation where information that should have been produced without a motion to compel is produced after the motion is filed but before it is brought on for hearing. The rule also is revised to provide that a party should not be awarded its expenses for filing a motion that could have been avoided by conferring with opposing counsel.

Subparagraph (C) is revised to include the provision that formerly was contained in subdivision (a)(2) and to include the same requirement of an opportunity to be heard that is specified in subparagraphs (A) and (B).

Subdivision (c). The revision provides a self-executing sanction for failure to make a disclosure required by Rule 26(a), without need for a motion under subdivision (a)(2)(A).

Paragraph (1) prevents a party from using as evidence any witnesses or information that, without substantial justification, has not been disclosed as required by Rules 26(a) and 26(e)(1). This automatic sanction provides a strong inducement for disclosure of material that the disclosing party would expect to use as evidence, whether at a trial, at a hearing, or on a motion, such as one under Rule 56. As disclosure of evidence offered solely for impeachment purposes is not required under those rules, this preclusion sanction likewise does not apply to that evidence.

Limiting the automatic sanction to violations "without substantial justification," coupled with the exception for violations that are "harmless," is needed to avoid unduly harsh penalties in a variety of situations: *e.g.,* the inadvertent omission from a Rule 26(a)(1)(A) disclosure of the name of a potential witness known to all parties; the failure to list as a trial witness a person so listed by another party; or the lack of knowledge of a pro se litigant of the requirement to make disclosures. In the latter situation, however, exclusion would be proper if the requirement for disclosure had been called to the litigant's attention by either the court or another party.

Preclusion of evidence is not an effective incentive to compel disclosure of information that, being supportive of the position of the opposing party, might advantageously be concealed by the disclosing party. However, the rule provides the court with a wide range of other sanctions—such as declaring specified facts to be established, preventing contradictory evidence, or, like spoliation of evidence, allowing the jury to be informed of the fact of nondisclosure—that, though not self-executing, can be imposed when found to be warranted after a hearing. The failure to identify a witness or document in a disclosure statement would be admissible under the Federal Rules of Evidence under the same principles that allow a party's interrogatory answers to be offered against it.

Subdivision (d). This subdivision is revised to require that, where a party fails to file any response to interrogatories or a Rule 34 request, the discovering party should informally seek to obtain such responses before filing a motion for sanctions.

The last sentence of this subdivision is revised to clarify that it is the pendency of a motion for protective order that may be urged as an excuse for a violation of subdivision (d). If a party's motion has been denied, the party cannot argue that its subsequent failure to comply would be justified. In this connection, it should be noted that the filing of a motion under Rule 26(c) is not self-executing—the relief authorized under that rule depends on obtaining the court's order to that effect.

Subdivision (g). This subdivision is modified to conform to the revision of Rule 26(f).

2000 Amendment

Subdivision (c)(1). When this subdivision was added in 1993 to direct exclusion of materials not disclosed as required, the duty to supplement discovery responses pursuant to Rule 26(e)(2) was omitted. In the face of this omission, courts may rely on inherent power to sanction for failure to supplement as required by Rule 26(e)(2), *see 8 Federal Practice & Procedure* § 2050 at 607–09, but that is an uncertain and unregulated ground for imposing sanctions. There is no obvious occasion for a Rule 37(a) motion in connection with failure to supplement, and ordinarily only Rule 37(c)(1) exists as rule-based authority for sanctions if this supplementation obligation is violated.

The amendment explicitly adds failure to comply with Rule 26(e)(2) as a ground for sanctions under Rule 37(c)(1), including exclusion of withheld materials. The rule provides that this sanction power only applies when the failure to supplement was "without substantial justification." Even if the failure was not substantially justified, a party should be allowed to use the material that was not disclosed if the lack of earlier notice was harmless.

"Shall" is replaced by "is" under the program to conform amended rules to current style conventions when there is no ambiguity.

GAP Report

The Advisory Committee recommends that the published amendment proposal be modified to state that the exclusion sanction can apply to failure "to amend a prior response to discovery as required by Rule 26(e)(2)." In addition, one minor phrasing change is recommended for the Committee Note.

2006 Amendment

Subdivision (f). Subdivision (f) is new. It focuses on a distinctive feature of computer operations, the routine alteration and deletion of information that attends ordinary use. Many steps essential to computer operation may alter or destroy information, for reasons that have nothing to do with how that information might relate to litigation. As a result, the ordinary operation of computer systems creates a risk that a party may lose potentially discoverable information without culpable conduct on its part. Under Rule 37(f), absent exceptional circumstances, sanctions cannot be imposed for loss of electronically stored information resulting from the routine, good-faith operation of an electronic information system.

Rule 37(f) applies only to information lost due to the "routine operation of an electronic information system"—the ways in which such systems are generally designed, programmed, and implemented to meet the party's technical and business needs. The "routine operation" of computer systems includes the alteration and overwriting of information, often without the operator's specific direction or awareness, a feature with no direct counterpart in hard-copy documents. Such features are essential to the operation of electronic information systems.

Rule 37(f) applies to information lost due to the routine operation of an information system only if the operation was in good faith. Good faith in the routine operation of an information system may involve a party's intervention to modify or suspend certain features of that routine operation to prevent the loss of information, if that information is subject to a preservation obligation. A preservation obligation may arise from many sources, including common law, statutes, regulations, or a court order in the case. The good faith requirement of Rule 37(f) means that a party is not permitted to exploit the routine operation of an information system to thwart discovery obligations by allowing that operation to continue in order to destroy specific stored information that it is required to preserve. When a party is under a duty to preserve information because of pending or reasonably anticipated litigation, intervention in the routine operation of an information system is one aspect of what is often called a "litigation hold." Among the factors that bear on a party's good faith in the routine operation of an information system are the steps the party took to comply with a court order in the case or party agreement requiring preservation of specific electronically stored information.

Whether good faith would call for steps to prevent the loss of information on sources that the party believes are not reasonably accessible under Rule 26(b)(2) depends on the circumstances of each case. One factor is whether the party reasonably believes that the information on such sources is likely to be discoverable and not available from reasonably accessible sources.

The protection provided by Rule 37(f) applies only to sanctions "under these rules." It does not affect other sources of authority to impose sanctions or rules of professional responsibility.

This rule restricts the imposition of "sanctions." It does not prevent a court from making the kinds of adjustments frequently used in managing discovery if a party is unable to provide relevant responsive information. For example, a court could order the responding party to produce an additional witness for deposition, respond to additional interrogatories, or make similar attempts to provide substitutes or alternatives for some or all of the lost information.

2007 Amendment

The language of Rule 37 has been amended as part of the general restyling of the Civil Rules to make them more easily understood and to make style and terminology consistent throughout the rules. These changes are intended to be stylistic only.

2013 Amendment

Rule 37(b) is amended to conform to amendments made to Rule 45, particularly the addition of Rule 45(f) providing for transfer of a subpoena-related motion to the court where the action is pending. A second sentence is added to Rule 37(b)(1) to deal with contempt of orders entered after such a transfer. The Rule 45(f) transfer provision is explained in the Committee Note to Rule 45.

Changes Made After Publication and Comment

As described in the Report, the published preliminary draft was modified in several ways after the public comment period. The words "before trial" were restored to the notice provision that was moved to new Rule 45(a)(4). The place of compliance in new Rule 45(c)(2)(A) was changed to a place "within 100 miles of where the person resides, is employed, or regularly conducts business." In new Rule 45(f), the party consent feature was removed, meaning consent of the person subject to the subpoena is sufficient to permit transfer to the issuing court. In addition, style changes were made after consultation with the Standing Committee's Style Consultant. In the Committee Note, clarifications were made in response to points raised during the public comment period.

2015 Amendment

Subdivision (a). Rule 37(a)(3)(B)(iv) is amended to reflect the common practice of producing copies of documents or electronically stored information rather than simply permitting inspection. This change brings item (iv) into line with paragraph (B), which provides a motion for an order compelling "production, or inspection."

Subdivision (e). Present Rule 37(e), adopted in 2006, provides: "Absent exceptional circumstances, a court may not impose sanctions under these rules on a party for failing to provide electronically stored information lost as a result of the routine, good-faith operation of an electronic information system." This limited rule has not adequately addressed the serious problems resulting from the continued exponential growth in the volume of such information. Federal circuits have established significantly different standards for imposing sanctions or curative measures on parties who fail to preserve electronically stored information.

These developments have caused litigants to expend excessive effort and money on preservation in order to avoid the risk of severe sanctions if a court finds they did not do enough.

New Rule 37(e) replaces the 2006 rule. It authorizes and specifies measures a court may employ if information that should have been preserved is lost, and specifies the findings necessary to justify these measures. It therefore forecloses reliance on inherent authority or state law to determine when certain measures should be used. The rule does not affect the validity of an independent tort claim for spoliation if state law applies in a case and authorizes the claim.

The new rule applies only to electronically stored information, also the focus of the 2006 rule. It applies only when such information is lost. Because electronically stored information often exists in multiple locations, loss from one source may often be harmless when substitute information can be found elsewhere.

The new rule applies only if the lost information should have been preserved in the anticipation or conduct of litigation and the party failed to take reasonable steps to preserve it. Many court decisions hold that potential litigants have a duty to preserve relevant information when litigation is reasonably foreseeable. Rule 37(e) is based on this common-law duty; it does not attempt to create a new duty to preserve. The rule does not apply when information is lost before a duty to preserve arises.

In applying the rule, a court may need to decide whether and when a duty to preserve arose. Courts should consider the extent to which a party was on notice that litigation was likely and that the information would be relevant. A variety of events may alert a party to the prospect of litigation. Often these events provide only limited information about that prospective litigation, however, so that the scope of information that should be preserved may remain uncertain. It is important not to be blinded to this reality by hindsight arising from familiarity with an action as it is actually filed.

Although the rule focuses on the common-law obligation to preserve in the anticipation or conduct of litigation, courts may sometimes consider whether there was an independent requirement that the lost information be preserved. Such requirements arise from many sources—statutes, administrative regulations, an order in another case, or a party's own information-retention protocols. The court should be sensitive, however, to the fact that such independent preservation requirements may be addressed to a wide variety of concerns unrelated to the current litigation. The fact that a party had an independent obligation to preserve information does not necessarily mean that it had such a duty with respect to the litigation, and the fact that the party failed to observe some other preservation obligation does not itself prove that its efforts to preserve were not reasonable with respect to a particular case.

The duty to preserve may in some instances be triggered or clarified by a court order in the case. Preservation orders may become more common, in part because Rules 16(b)(3)(B)(iii) and 26(f)(3)(C) are amended to encourage discovery plans and orders that address preservation. Once litigation has commenced, if the parties cannot reach agreement about preservation issues, promptly seeking judicial guidance about the extent of reasonable preservation may be important.

The rule applies only if the information was lost because the party failed to take reasonable steps to preserve the information. Due to the ever-increasing volume of electronically stored information and the multitude of devices that generate such information, perfection in preserving all relevant electronically stored information is often impossible. As under the current rule, the routine, good-faith operation of an electronic information system would be a relevant factor for the court to consider in evaluating whether a party failed to take reasonable steps to preserve lost information, although the prospect of litigation may call for reasonable steps to preserve information by intervening in that routine operation. This rule recognizes that "reasonable steps" to preserve suffice; it does not call for perfection. The court should be sensitive to the party's sophistication with regard to litigation in evaluating preservation efforts; some litigants, particularly individual litigants, may be less familiar with preservation obligations than others who have considerable experience in litigation.

Because the rule calls only for reasonable steps to preserve, it is inapplicable when the loss of information occurs despite the party's reasonable steps to preserve. For example, the information may not be in the party's control. Or information the party has preserved may be destroyed by events outside the party's control—the computer room may be flooded, a "cloud" service may fail, a malign software attack may disrupt a storage system, and so on. Courts may, however, need to assess the extent to which a party knew of and protected against such risks.

Another factor in evaluating the reasonableness of preservation efforts is proportionality. The court should be sensitive to party resources; aggressive preservation efforts can be extremely costly, and parties (including governmental parties) may have limited staff and resources to devote to those efforts. A party may act reasonably by choosing a less costly form of information preservation, if it is substantially as effective as more costly forms. It is important that counsel become familiar with their clients' information systems and digital data—including social media—to address these issues. A party urging that preservation requests are disproportionate may need to provide specifics about these matters in order to enable meaningful discussion of the appropriate preservation regime.

When a party fails to take reasonable steps to preserve electronically stored information that should have been preserved in the anticipation or conduct of litigation, and the information is lost as a result, Rule 37(e) directs that the initial focus should be on whether the lost information can be restored or replaced through additional discovery. Nothing in the rule limits the court's powers under Rules 16 and 26 to authorize additional discovery. Orders under Rule 26(b)(2)(B) regarding discovery from sources that would ordinarily be considered inaccessible or under Rule 26(c)(1)(B) on allocation of expenses may be pertinent to solving such problems. If the information is restored or replaced, no further measures should be taken. At the same time, it is important to emphasize that efforts to restore or replace lost information through discovery should be proportional to the apparent importance of the lost information to claims or defenses in the litigation. For example, substantial measures should not be employed to restore or replace information that is marginally relevant or duplicative.

Subdivision (e)(1). This subdivision applies only if information should have been preserved in the anticipation or conduct of litigation, a party failed to take reasonable steps to preserve the information, information was lost as a result, and the information could not be restored or replaced by additional discovery. In addition, a court may resort to (e)(1) measures only "upon finding prejudice to another party from loss of the information." An evaluation of prejudice from the loss of information necessarily includes an evaluation of the information's importance in the litigation.

The rule does not place a burden of proving or disproving prejudice on one party or the other. Determining the content of lost information may be a difficult task in some cases, and placing the burden of proving prejudice on the party that did not lose the information may be unfair. In other situations, however, the content of the lost information may be fairly evident, the information may appear to be unimportant, or the abundance of preserved information may appear sufficient to meet the needs of all parties. Requiring the party seeking curative measures to prove prejudice may be reasonable in such situations. The rule leaves judges with discretion to determine how best to assess prejudice in particular cases.

Once a finding of prejudice is made, the court is authorized to employ measures "no greater than necessary to cure the prejudice." The range of such measures is quite broad if they are necessary for this purpose. There is no all-purpose hierarchy of the severity of various measures; of their effect on the particular case. But authority to order measures no greater than necessary to cure prejudice does not require the court to adopt measures to cure every possible prejudicial effect. Much is entrusted to the court's discretion.

In an appropriate case, it may be that serious measures are necessary to cure prejudice found by the court, such as forbidding the party that failed to preserve information from putting on certain evidence, permitting the parties to present evidence and argument to the jury regarding the loss of information, or giving the jury instructions to assist in its evaluation of such evidence or argument, other than instructions to which subdivision (e)(2) applies. Care must be taken, however, to ensure that curative measures under subdivision (e)(1) do not have the effect of measures that are permitted under subdivision (e)(2) only on a finding of intent to deprive another party of the lost information's use in the litigation. An example of an inappropriate (e)(1) measure might be an order striking pleadings related to, or precluding a party from offering any evidence in support of, the central or only claim or defense in the case. On the other hand, it may be appropriate to exclude a specific item of evidence to offset prejudice caused by failure to preserve other evidence that might contradict the excluded item of evidence.

Subdivision (e)(2). This subdivision authorizes courts to use specified and very severe measures to address or deter failures to preserve electronically stored information, but only on finding that the party that lost the information acted with the intent to deprive another party of the information's use in the litigation. It is designed to provide a uniform standard in federal court for use of these serious measures when addressing failure to preserve electronically stored information. It rejects cases such as *Residential Funding Corp. v. DeGeorge Financial Corp.*, 306 F.3d 99 (2d Cir. 2002), that authorize the giving of adverse-inference instructions on a finding of negligence or gross negligence.

Adverse-inference instructions were developed on the premise that a party's intentional loss or destruction of evidence to prevent its use in litigation gives rise to a reasonable inference that the evidence was unfavorable to the party responsible for loss or destruction of the evidence. Negligent or even grossly negligent behavior does not logically support that inference. Information lost through negligence may have been favorable to either party, including the party that lost it, and inferring that it was unfavorable to that party may tip the balance at trial in ways the lost information never would have. The better rule for the negligent or grossly negligent loss of electronically stored information is to preserve a broad range of measures to cure prejudice caused by its loss, but to limit the most severe measures to instances of intentional loss or destruction.

Similar reasons apply to limiting the court's authority to presume or infer that the lost information was unfavorable to the party who lost it when ruling on a pretrial motion or presiding at a bench trial. Subdivision(e)(2) limits the ability of courts to draw adverse inferences based on the loss of information in these circumstances, permitting them only when a court finds that the information was lost with the intent to prevent its use in litigation.

Subdivision (e)(2) applies to jury instructions that permit or require the jury to presume or infer that lost information was unfavorable to the party that lost it. Thus, it covers any instruction that directs or permits the jury to infer from the loss of information that it was in fact unfavorable to the party that lost it. The subdivision does not apply to jury instructions that do not involve such an inference. For example, subdivision (e)(2) would not prohibit a court from allowing the parties to present evidence to the jury concerning the loss and likely relevance of information and instructing the jury that it may consider that evidence, along with all the other evidence in the case, in making its decision. These measures, which would not involve instructing a jury it may draw an adverse inference from loss of information, would be available under subdivision (e)(1) if no greater than necessary to cure prejudice. In addition, subdivision (e)(2) does not limit the discretion of courts to give traditional missing evidence instructions based on a party's failure to present evidence it has in its possession at the time of trial.

Subdivision (e)(2) requires a finding that the party acted with the intent to deprive another party of the information's use in the litigation. This finding may be made by the court when ruling on a pretrial motion, when presiding at a bench trial, or when deciding whether to give an adverse inference instruction at trial. If a court were to conclude that the intent finding should be made by a jury, the court's instruction should make clear that the jury may infer from the loss of the information that it was unfavorable to the party that lost it only if the jury first finds that the party acted with the intent to deprive another party of the information's use in the litigation. If the jury does not make this finding, it may not infer from the loss that the information was unfavorable to the party that lost it.

Subdivision (e)(2) does not include a requirement that the court find prejudice to the party deprived of the information. This is because the finding of intent required by the subdivision can support not only an inference that the lost information was unfavorable to the party that intentionally destroyed it, but also an inference that the opposing party was prejudiced by the loss of information that would have favored its position. Subdivision (e)(2) does not require any further finding of prejudice.

Courts should exercise caution, however, in using the measures specified in (e)(2). Finding an intent to deprive another party of the lost information's use in the litigation does not require a court to adopt any of the measures listed in subdivision (e)(2). The remedy should fit the wrong, and the severe measures authorized by this subdivision should not be used when the information lost was relatively unimportant or lesser measures such as those specified in subdivision (e)(1) would be sufficient to redress the loss.

Gap Report

The revised rule is a modification of the published draft in several ways: (1) It applies only to electronically stored information; (2) It removes the provision in the published draft that authorized "sanctions" against a party that lacked the culpable state of mind called for in the rule if the loss of information caused "irreparable prejudice" to another party's ability to litigate; (3) It does not speak in terms of "sanctions" and no longer invokes the list of sanctions contained in Rule 37(b)(2)(A); (4) It places primary emphasis on measures to restore or replace lost electronically stored information; (5) On finding prejudice to a party due to loss of the information, it authorizes the court to order measures "no greater than necessary" to cure the prejudice; (6) It does not use the culpability standard "willful or bad faith", substituting the standard that the party "acted with the intent to deprive another party of the information's use in the litigation"; (7) Only when that culpability standard is met, it authorizes the court to presume that the lost information was unfavorable to the party that lost it, to instruct the jury it may so infer from the loss of the information, or to dismiss the action or enter a default judgment; (8) It no longer includes in the rule a list of factors for the court's consideration in applying the rule. Recognizing that these changes are substantial, the Civil Rules Advisory Committee unanimously decided that republication would not be necessary to achieve adequate public comment and would not assist the work of the rules committees.

TITLE VI. TRIALS

Rule 38.   Right to a Jury Trial; Demand

(a) Right Preserved. The right of trial by jury as declared by the Seventh Amendment to the Constitution—or as provided by a federal statute—is preserved to the parties inviolate.

(b) Demand. On any issue triable of right by a jury, a party may demand a jury trial by:

    (1) serving the other parties with a written demand—which may be included in a pleading—no later than 14 days after the last pleading directed to the issue is served; and

    (2) filing the demand in accordance with Rule 5(d).

(c) Specifying Issues. In its demand, a party may specify the issues that it wishes to have tried by a jury; otherwise, it is considered to have demanded a jury trial on all the issues so triable. If the party has demanded a jury trial on only some issues, any other party may—within 14 days after being served with the demand or within a shorter time ordered by the court—serve a demand for a jury trial on any other or all factual issues triable by jury.

(d) Waiver; Withdrawal. A party waives a jury trial unless its demand is properly served and filed. A proper demand may be withdrawn only if the parties consent.

(e) Admiralty and Maritime Claims. These rules do not create a right to a jury trial on issues in a claim that is an admiralty or maritime claim under Rule 9(h).

(Amended February 28, 1966, effective July 1, 1966; March 2, 1987, effective August 1, 1987; April 22, 1993, effective December 1, 1993; April 30, 2007, effective December 1, 2007; March 26, 2009, effective December 1, 2009.)

ADVISORY COMMITTEE NOTES

1937 Adoption

This rule provides for the preservation of the constitutional right of trial by jury as directed in the enabling act (act of June 19, 1934, 48 Stat. 1064, U.S.C., Title 28, § 723c [sec. 2072]), and it and the next rule make definite provision for claim and waiver of jury trial, following the method used in many American states and in England and the British Dominions. Thus the claim must be made at once on initial pleading or appearance under Ill.Rev.Stat. (1937) ch. 110, § 188; 6 Tenn.Code Ann. (Williams, 1934) § 8734; compare Wyo.Rev.Stat.Ann. (1931) § 89–1320 (with answer or reply); within 10 days after the pleadings are completed or the case is at issue under 2 Conn.Gen.Stat. (1930) § 5624; Hawaii Rev.Laws (1935) § 4101; 2 Mass.Gen.Laws (Ter.Ed.1932) ch. 231, § 60; 3 Mich.Comp.Laws (1929) § 14263; Mich. Court Rules Ann. (Searl, 1933) Rule 33 (15 days); England (until 1933) O. 36, r.r. 2 and 6; and Ontario Jud. Act (1927) § 57(1) (4 days, or, where prior notice of trial, 2 days from such notice); or at a definite time varying under different codes, from 10 days before notice of trial to 10 days after notice, or, as in many, when the case is called for assignment, Ariz.Rev.Code Ann. (Struckmeyer, 1928) § 3802; Calif. Code Civ.Proc. (Deering, 1937) § 631, par. 4; Iowa Code (1935) § 10724; 4 Nev.Comp.Laws (Hillyer, 1929) § 8782; N.M. Stat.Ann. (Courtright, 1929) § 105–814; N.Y.C.P.A. (1937) § 426, subdivision 5 (applying to New York, Bronx, Richmond, Kings, and Queens Counties); R.I. Pub. Laws (1929), ch. 1327, amending R.I. Gen.Laws (1923) ch. 337, § 6; Utah Rev.Stat.Ann. (1933) § 104–23–6; 2 Wash.Rev.Stat.Ann. (Remington, 1932) § 316; England (4 days after notice of trial), Administration of Justice Act (1933) § 6 and amended rule under the Judicature Act (The Annual Practice, 1937), O. 36, r. 1; Australia High Court Procedure Act (1921) § 12, Rules, O. 33, r. 2; Alberta Rules of Ct. (1914) 172, 183, 184; British Columbia Sup.Ct.Rules (1925) O. 36, r.r. 2, 6, 11, and 16; New Brunswick Jud. Act (1927) O. 36, r.r. 2 and 5. See James, Trial by Jury and the New Federal Rules of Procedure (1936), 45 Yale L.J. 1022.

Rule 81(c) provides for claim for jury trial in removed actions.

The right to trial by jury as declared in U.S.C., Title 28, § 770 (Trial of issues of fact; by jury; exceptions), and similar statutes, is unaffected by this rule. This rule modifies U.S.C., Title 28, [former] § 773 (Trial of issues of fact; by court).

1966 Amendments

See Note to Rule 9(h), supra.

1987 Amendments

The amendments are technical. No substantive change is intended.

1993 Amendments

Language requiring the filing of a jury demand as provided in subdivision (d) is added to subdivision (b) to eliminate an apparent ambiguity between the two subdivisions. For proper scheduling of cases, it is important that jury demands not only be served on other parties, but also be filed with the court.

2007 Amendment

The language of Rule 38 has been amended as part of the general restyling of the Civil Rules to make them more easily understood and to make style and terminology consistent throughout the rules. These changes are intended to be stylistic only.

2009 Amendments

The times set in the former rule at 10 days have been revised to 14 days. See the Note to Rule 6.

Rule 39.   Trial by Jury or by the Court

(a) **When a Demand Is Made.** When a jury trial has been demanded under Rule 38, the action must be designated on the docket as a jury action. The trial on all issues so demanded must be by jury unless:

    (1)   the parties or their attorneys file a stipulation to a nonjury trial or so stipulate on the record; or

    (2)   the court, on motion or on its own, finds that on some or all of those issues there is no federal right to a jury trial.

(b) **When No Demand Is Made.** Issues on which a jury trial is not properly demanded are to be tried by the court. But the court may, on motion, order a jury trial on any issue for which a jury might have been demanded.

(c) **Advisory Jury; Jury Trial by Consent.** In an action not triable of right by a jury, the court, on motion or on its own:

    (1)   may try any issue with an advisory jury; or

    (2)   may, with the parties' consent, try any issue by a jury whose verdict has the same effect as if a jury trial had been a matter of right, unless the action is against the United States and a federal statute provides for a nonjury trial.

(Amended April 30, 2007, effective December 1, 2007.)

ADVISORY COMMITTEE NOTES

1937 Adoption

The provisions for express waiver of jury trial found in U.S.C., Title 28, [former] § 773 (Trial of issues of fact; by court) are incorporated in this rule. See Rule 38, however, which extends the provisions for waiver of jury. U.S.C., Title 28, [former] § 772 (Trial of issues of fact; in equity in patent causes) is unaffected by this rule. When certain of the issues are to be tried by jury and others by the court, the court may determine the sequence in which such issues shall be tried. *See Liberty Oil Co. v. Condon Nat. Bank,* 260 U.S. 235, 43 S.Ct. 118, 67 L.Ed. 232 (1922).

A discretionary power in the courts to send issues of fact to the jury is common in state procedure. Compare Calif. Code Civ.Proc. (Deering, 1937) § 592; 1 Colo.Stat.Ann. (1935) Code Civ.Proc., ch. 12, § 191; Conn.Gen.Stat. (1930) § 5625; 2 Minn.Stat. (Mason, 1927) § 9288; 4 Mont.Rev.Codes Ann. (1935) § 9327; N.Y.C.P.A. (1937) § 430; 2 Ohio Gen.Code Ann. (Page, 1926) § 11380; 1 Okla.Stat.Ann. (Harlow, 1931) § 351 [12 Okl.St.Ann. § 557]; Utah Rev.Stat.Ann. (1933) § 104–23–5; 2 Wash.Rev.Stat.Ann. (Remington, 1932) § 315; Wis.Stat. (1935) § 270.07. See [former] Equity Rule 23 (Matters Ordinarily Determinable at Law When Arising in Suit in Equity to be Disposed of Therein) and U.S.C., Title 28 [former] § 772 (Trial of issues of fact; in equity in patent causes); *Colleton Merc. Mfg. Co. v. Savannah River Lumber Co.,* C.C.A.4, 1922, 280 F. 358; *Fed. Res. Bk. of San Francisco v. Idaho Grimm Alfalfa Seed Growers' Ass'n,* C.C.A.9, 1925, 8 F.2d 922, certiorari denied 46 S.Ct. 347, 270 U.S. 646, 70 L.Ed. 778 (1926); *Watt v. Starke,* 1879, 101 U.S. 247, 25 L.Ed. 826.

2007 Amendment

The language of Rule 39 has been amended as part of the general restyling of the Civil Rules to make them more easily understood and to make style and terminology consistent throughout the rules. These changes are intended to be stylistic only.

Rule 40.   Scheduling Cases for Trial

Each court must provide by rule for scheduling trials. The court must give priority to actions entitled to priority by a federal statute.

(Amended April 30, 2007, effective December 1, 2007.)

ADVISORY COMMITTEE NOTES

1937 Adoption

U.S.C., Title 28, [former] § 769 (Notice of case for trial) is modified. See former Equity Rule 56 (On Expiration of Time for Depositions, Case Goes on Trial Calendar). See also [former] Equity Rule 57 (Continuances).

For examples of statutes giving precedence, see U.S.C., Title 28, § 47 (now §§ 1253, 2101, 2325) (Injunctions as to orders of Interstate Commerce Commission); § 380 (now §§ 1253, 2101, 2284) (Injunctions; alleged unconstitutionality of state statutes); § 380a (now §§ 1253, 2101, 2284) (Same; Constitutionality of federal statute); [former] § 768 (Priority of cases where a state is party); Title 15, § 28 (Antitrust laws; suits against monopolies expedited); Title 22, § 240 (Petition for restoration of property seized as munitions of war, etc.); and Title 49, [former] § 44 (Proceedings in equity under interstate commerce laws; expedition of suits).

2007 Amendment

The language of Rule 40 has been amended as part of the general restyling of the Civil Rules to make them more easily understood and to make style and terminology consistent throughout the rules. These changes are intended to be stylistic only.

The best methods for scheduling trials depend on local conditions. It is useful to ensure that each district adopts an explicit rule for scheduling trials. It is not useful to limit or dictate the provisions of local rules.

Rule 41.   Dismissal of Actions

(a) Voluntary Dismissal.

    (1) *By the Plaintiff.*

        (A) *Without a Court Order.* Subject to Rules 23(e), 23.1(c), 23.2, and 66 and any applicable federal statute, the plaintiff may dismiss an action without a court order by filing:

            (i) a notice of dismissal before the opposing party serves either an answer or a motion for summary judgment; or

            (ii) a stipulation of dismissal signed by all parties who have appeared.

        (B) *Effect.* Unless the notice or stipulation states otherwise, the dismissal is without prejudice. But if the plaintiff previously dismissed any federal- or state-court action based on or including the same claim, a notice of dismissal operates as an adjudication on the merits.

    (2) *By Court Order; Effect.* Except as provided in Rule 41(a)(1), an action may be dismissed at the plaintiff's request only by court order, on terms that the court considers proper. If a defendant has pleaded a counterclaim before being served with the plaintiff's motion to dismiss, the action may be dismissed over the defendant's objection only if the counterclaim can remain pending for independent adjudication. Unless the order states otherwise, a dismissal under this paragraph (2) is without prejudice.

(b) Involuntary Dismissal; Effect. If the plaintiff fails to prosecute or to comply with these rules or a court order, a defendant may move to dismiss the action or any claim against it. Unless the dismissal order states otherwise, a dismissal under this subdivision (b) and any dismissal not under this rule—except one for lack of jurisdiction, improper venue, or failure to join a party under Rule 19—operates as an adjudication on the merits.

(c) Dismissing a Counterclaim, Crossclaim, or Third-Party Claim. This rule applies to a dismissal of any counterclaim, crossclaim, or third-party claim. A claimant's voluntary dismissal under Rule 41(a)(1)(A)(i) must be made:

    (1) before a responsive pleading is served; or

    (2) if there is no responsive pleading, before evidence is introduced at a hearing or trial.

(d) Costs of a Previously Dismissed Action. If a plaintiff who previously dismissed an action in any court files an action based on or including the same claim against the same defendant, the court:

    (1) may order the plaintiff to pay all or part of the costs of that previous action; and

    (2) may stay the proceedings until the plaintiff has complied.

(Amended December 27, 1946, effective March 19, 1948; January 21, 1963, effective July 1, 1963; February 28, 1966, effective July 1, 1966; December 4, 1967, effective July 1, 1968; March 2, 1987, effective August 1, 1987; April 30, 1991, effective December 1, 1991; April 30, 2007, effective December 1, 2007.)

ADVISORY COMMITTEE NOTES

1937 Adoption

Note to Subdivision (a). Compare Ill.Rev.Stat. (1937) c. 110, § 176, and *English Rules Under the Judicature Act* (The Annual Practice, 1937) O. 26.

Provisions regarding dismissal in such statutes as U.S.C., Title 8, § 164 [see 1329] (Jurisdiction of district courts in immigration cases) and U.S.C., Title 31, § 232 [now 3730] (Liability of persons making false claims against United States; suits) are preserved by paragraph (1).

Note to Subdivision (b). This provides for the equivalent of a nonsuit on motion by the defendant after the completion of the presentation of evidence by the plaintiff. Also, for actions tried without a jury, it provides the equivalent of the directed verdict practice for jury actions which is regulated by Rule 50.

1946 Amendment

Note. Subdivision (a). The insertion of the reference to Rule 66 correlates Rule 41(a)(1) with the express provisions concerning dismissal set forth in amended Rule 66 on receivers.

The change in Rule 41(a)(1)(i) gives the service of a motion for summary judgment by the adverse party the same effect in preventing unlimited dismissal as was originally given only to the service of an answer. The omission of reference to a motion for summary judgment in the original rule was subject to criticism. 3 *Moore's Federal Practice,* 1938, 3037–3038, n. 12. A motion for summary judgment may be forthcoming prior to answer, and if well taken will eliminate the necessity for an answer. Since such a motion may require even more research and preparation than the answer itself, there is good reason why the service of the motion, like that of the answer, should prevent a voluntary dismissal by the adversary without court approval.

The word "generally" has been stricken from Rule 41(a)(1)(ii) in order to avoid confusion and to conform with the elimination of the necessity for special appearance by original Rule 12(b).

Subdivision (b). In some cases tried without a jury, where at the close of plaintiff's evidence the defendant moves for dismissal under Rule 41(b) on the ground that plaintiff's evidence is insufficient for recovery, the plaintiff's own evidence may be conflicting or present questions of credibility. In ruling on the defendant's motion, questions arise as to the function of the judge in evaluating the testimony and whether findings should be made if the motion is sustained. Three circuits hold that as the judge is the trier of the facts in such a situation his function is not the same as on a motion to direct a verdict, where the jury is the trier of the facts, and that the judge in deciding such a motion in a non-jury case may pass on conflicts of evidence and credibility, and if he performs that function of evaluating the testimony and grants the motion on the merits, findings are required. *Young v. United States,* C.C.A.9, 1940, 111 F.2d 823; *Gary Theatre Co. v. Columbia Pictures Corporation,* C.C.A.7, 1941, 120 F.2d 891; *Bach v. Friden Calculating Machine Co., Inc.,* C.C.A.6, 1945, 148 F.2d 407. Cf. *Mateas v. Fred Harvey, a Corporation,* C.C.A.9, 1945, 146 F.2d 989. The Third Circuit has held that on such a motion the function of the court is the same as on a motion to direct in a jury case, and that the court should only decide whether there is evidence which would support a judgment for the plaintiff, and therefore, findings are not required by Rule 52. *Federal Deposit Insurance Corp. v. Mason,* C.C.A.3, 1940, 115 F.2d 548; *Schad v. Twentieth Century-Fox Film Corp.,* C.C.A.3, 1943, 136 F.2d 991. The added sentence in Rule 41(b) incorporates the view of the Sixth, Seventh and Ninth Circuits. See also 3 *Moore's Federal Practice,* 1938, Cum.Supplement § 41.03, under "Page 3045"; Commentary, *The Motion to Dismiss in Non-Jury Cases,* 1946, 9 Fed.Rules Serv., Comm.Pg. 41b.14.

1963 Amendment

Under the present text of the second sentence of this subdivision, the motion for dismissal at the close of the plaintiff's evidence may be made in a case tried to a jury as well as in a case tried without a jury. But, when made in a jury-tried case, this motion overlaps the motion for a directed verdict under Rule 50(a), which is also available in the same situation. It has been held that the standard to be applied in deciding the Rule 41(b) motion at the close of the plaintiff's evidence in a jury-tried case is the same as that used upon a motion for a directed verdict made at the same stage; and, just as the court need not make findings pursuant to Rule 52(a) when it directs a verdict, so in a jury-tried case it may omit these findings in granting the Rule 41(b) motion. See generally *O'Brien v. Westinghouse Electric Corp.,* 293 F.2d 1, 5–10 (3d Cir. 1961).

As indicated by the discussion in the *O'Brien* case, the overlap has caused confusion. Accordingly, the second and third sentences of Rule 41(b) are amended to provide that the motion for dismissal at the close of the plaintiff's evidence shall apply only to nonjury cases (including cases tried with an advisory jury). Hereafter the correct motion in jury-tried cases will be the motion for a directed verdict. This involves no change of substance. It should be noted that the court upon a motion for a directed verdict may in appropriate circumstances deny that motion and grant instead a new trial, or a voluntary dismissal without prejudice under Rule 41(a)(2). See 6 *Moore's Federal Practice* ¶ 59.08[5] (2d ed. 1954); *cf. Cone v. West Virginia Pulp & Paper Co.,* 330 U.S. 212, 217, 67 S.Ct. 752, 91 L.Ed. 849 (1947).

The first sentence of Rule 41(b), providing for dismissal for failure to prosecute or to comply with the Rules or any order of court, and the general provisions of the last sentence remain applicable in jury as well as nonjury cases.

The amendment of the last sentence of Rule 41(b) indicates that a dismissal for lack of an indispensable party does not operate as an adjudication on the merits. Such a dismissal does not bar a new action, for it is based merely "on a plaintiff's failure to comply with a precondition requisite to the Court's going forward to determine the merits of his substantive claim." See *Costello v. United States,* 365 U.S. 265, 284–288, 81 S.Ct. 534, 5 L.Ed.2d 551 & n. 5 (1961); *Mallow v. Hinde,* 12 Wheat. (25 U.S.) 193, 6 L.Ed. 599 (1827); Clark, *Code Pleading* 602 (2d ed. 1947); *Restatement of Judgments* § 49, comm. a, b (1942). This amendment corrects an omission from the rule and is consistent with an earlier amendment, effective in 1948, adding "the defense of failure to join an indispensable party" to clause (1) of Rule 12(h).

1966 Amendment

The terminology is changed to accord with the amendment of Rule 19. See that amended rule and the Advisory Committee's Note thereto.

1968 Amendment

The amendment corrects an inadvertent error in the reference to amended Rule 23.

1987 Amendment

The amendment is technical. No substantive change is intended.

1991 Amendment

Language is deleted that authorized the use of this rule as a means of terminating a non-jury action on the merits when the plaintiff has failed to carry a burden of proof in presenting the plaintiff's case. The device is replaced by the new provisions of Rule 52(c), which authorize entry of judgment against the defendant as well as the plaintiff, and earlier than the close of the case of the party against whom judgment is rendered. A motion to dismiss under Rule 41 on the ground that a plaintiff's evidence is legally insufficient should now be treated as a motion for judgment on partial findings as provided in Rule 52(c).

2007 Amendment

The language of Rule 41 has been amended as part of the general restyling of the Civil Rules to make them more easily understood and to make style and terminology consistent throughout the rules. These changes are intended to be stylistic only.

When Rule 23 was amended in 1966, Rules 23.1 and 23.2 were separated from Rule 23. Rule 41(a)(1) was not then amended to reflect the Rule 23 changes. In 1968 Rule 41(a)(1) was amended to correct the cross-reference to what had become Rule 23(e), but Rules 23.1 and 23.2 were inadvertently overlooked. Rules 23.1 and 23.2 are now added to the list of exceptions in Rule 41(a)(1)(A). This change does not affect established meaning. Rule 23.2 explicitly incorporates Rule 23(e), and thus was already absorbed directly into the exceptions in Rule 41(a)(1). Rule 23.1 requires court approval of a compromise or dismissal in language parallel to Rule 23(e) and thus supersedes the apparent right to dismiss by notice of dismissal.

Rule 42. Consolidation; Separate Trials

(a) Consolidation. If actions before the court involve a common question of law or fact, the court may:

(1) join for hearing or trial any or all matters at issue in the actions;

(2) consolidate the actions; or

(3) issue any other orders to avoid unnecessary cost or delay.

(b) Separate Trials. For convenience, to avoid prejudice, or to expedite and economize, the court may order a separate trial of one or more separate issues, claims, crossclaims, counterclaims, or third-party claims. When ordering a separate trial, the court must preserve any federal right to a jury trial.

(Amended February 28, 1966, effective July 1, 1966; April 30, 2007, effective December 1, 2007.)

ADVISORY COMMITTEE NOTES

1937 Adoption

Subdivision (a) is based upon U.S.C., Title 28, [former] § 734 (Orders to save costs; consolidation of causes of like nature) but in so far as the statute differs from this rule, it is modified.

For comparable statutes dealing with consolidation see Ark.Dig.Stat. (Crawford & Moses, 1921) § 1081; Calif.Code Civ.Proc. (Deering, 1937) § 1048; N.M.Stat.Ann. (Courtright, 1929) § 105–828; N.Y.C.P.A. (1937) §§ 96, 96a, and 97; American Judicature Society, Bulletin XIV, (1919) Art. 26.

For severance or separate trials see Calif.Code Civ.Proc. (Deering, 1937) § 1048; N.Y.C.P.A. (1937) § 96; American Judicature Society, Bulletin XIV (1919) Art. 3, § 2 and Art. 10, § 10. See also the third sentence of Equity Rule 29 (Defenses—How Presented) providing for discretionary separate hearing and disposition before trial of pleas in bar or abatement, and see also Rule 12(d) of these rules for preliminary hearings of defenses and objections.

For the entry of separate judgments, see Rule 54(b) (Judgment at Various Stages).

1966 Amendment

In certain suits in admiralty separation for trial of the issues of liability and damages (or of the extent of liability other than damages, such as salvage and general average) has been conducive to expedition and economy, especially because of the statutory right to interlocutory appeal in admiralty cases (which is of course preserved by these Rules). While separation of issues for trial is not to be routinely ordered, it is important that it be encouraged where experience has demonstrated its worth. Cf. Weinstein, *Routine Bifurcation of Negligence Trials,* 14 Vand.L.Rev. 831 (1961).

In cases (including some cases within the admiralty and maritime jurisdiction) in which the parties have a constitutional or statutory right of trial by jury, separation of issues may give rise to problems. See *e.g., United Air Lines, Inc. v. Wiener,* 286 F.2d 302 (9th Cir.1961). Accordingly, the proposed change in Rule 42 reiterates the mandate of Rule 38 respecting preservation of the right to jury trial.

2007 Amendment

The language of Rule 42 has been amended as part of the general restyling of the Civil Rules to make them more easily understood and to make style and terminology consistent throughout the rules. These changes are intended to be stylistic only.

Rule 43. Taking Testimony

(a) **In Open Court.** At trial, the witnesses' testimony must be taken in open court unless a federal statute, the Federal Rules of Evidence, these rules, or other rules adopted by the Supreme Court provide otherwise. For good cause in compelling circumstances and with appropriate safeguards, the court may permit testimony in open court by contemporaneous transmission from a different location.

(b) **Affirmation Instead of an Oath.** When these rules require an oath, a solemn affirmation suffices.

(c) **Evidence on a Motion.** When a motion relies on facts outside the record, the court may hear the matter on affidavits or may hear it wholly or partly on oral testimony or on depositions.

(d) **Interpreter.** The court may appoint an interpreter of its choosing; fix reasonable compensation to be paid from funds provided by law or by one or more parties; and tax the compensation as costs.

(Amended February 28, 1966, effective July 1, 1966; November 20, 1972, and December 18, 1972, effective July 1, 1975; March 2, 1987, effective August 1, 1987; April 23, 1996, effective December 1, 1996; April 30, 2007, effective December 1, 2007.)

ADVISORY COMMITTEE NOTES

1937 Adoption

Note to Subdivision (a). The first sentence is a restatement of the substance of U.S.C., Title 28, § 635 (Proof in common-law actions), [former] § 637 (see §§ 2072, 2073) (Proof in equity and admiralty), and [former] Equity Rule 46 (Trial—Testimony Usually Taken in Open Court—Rulings on Objections to Evidence). This rule abolishes in patent and trademark actions, the practice under [former] Equity Rule 48 of setting forth in affidavits the testimony in chief of expert witnesses whose testimony is directed to matters of opinion. The second and third sentences on admissibility of evidence and Subdivision (b) on contradiction and cross-examination modify U.S.C., Title 28, § 725 (now 1652) (Laws of states as rules of decision) insofar as that statute has been construed to prescribe conformity to state rules of evidence. Compare Callahan and Ferguson, *Evidence and the New Federal Rules of Civil Procedure,* 45 Yale L.J. 622 (1936), and *Same: 2,* 47 Yale L.J. 195 (1937). The last sentence modifies to the extent indicated U.S.C., Title 28, [former] § 631 (Competency of witnesses governed by State laws).

Note to Subdivision (b). See 4 *Wigmore on Evidence* (2d ed., 1923) § 1885 et seq.

Note to Subdivision (c). See [former] Equity Rule 46 (Trial—Testimony Usually Taken in Open Court-Rulings on Objections to Evidence). With the last sentence compare *Dowagiac v. Lochren,* 143 Fed. 211 (C.C.A. 8th, 1906). See also *Blease v. Garlington,* 92 U.S. 1, 23 L.Ed. 521 (1876); *Nelson v. United States,* 201 U.S. 92, 114, 26 S.Ct. 358, 50 L.Ed. 673 (1906); *Unkle v. Wills,* 281 Fed. 29 (C.C.A. 8th, 1922).

See Rule 61 for harmless error in either the admission or exclusion of evidence.

Note to Subdivision (d). See [former] Equity Rule 78 (Affirmation in Lieu of Oath) and U.S.C., Title 1, § 1 (Words importing singular number, masculine gender, etc.; extended application), providing for affirmation in lieu of oath.

1946 Report of the Advisory Committee

Supplementary Note of Advisory Committee Regarding Rules 43 and 44

Note. These rules have been criticized and suggested improvements offered by commentators. 1 *Wigmore on Evidence,* 3d ed. 1940, 200–204; Green, *The Admissibility of Evidence Under the Federal Rules,* 1941, 55 Harv.L.Rev. 197. Cases indicate, however, that the rule is working better than these commentators had expected. *Boerner v. United States,* C.C.A.2d, 1941, 117 F.2d 387, cert. den., 1941, 313 U.S. 587, 61 S.Ct. 1120; *Mosson v. Liberty Fast Freight Co.,* C.C.A.2d, 1942, 124 F.2d, 448; *Hartford Accident & Indemnity Co. v. Olivier,* C.C.A. 5th, 1941, 123 F.2d 709; *Anzano v. Metropolitan Life Ins. Co. of New York,* C.C.A.3d, 1941, 118 F.2d 430; *Franzen v. E. I. DuPont De Nemours & Co.,* C.C.A.3d, 1944, 146 F.2d 837; *Fakouri v. Cadais,* C.C.A. 5th, 1945, 147 F.2d 667; *In re C. & P. Co.,* S.D.Cal.1945, 63 F.Supp. 400, 408. But cf. *United States v. Aluminum Co. of America,* S.D.N.Y.1938, 1 Fed.Rules Serv. 43a.3, Case 1; Note, 1946, 46 Col.L.Rev. 267. While consideration of a comprehensive and detailed set of rules of evidence seems very desirable, it has not been feasible for the Committee so far to undertake this important task. Such consideration should include the adaptability to federal practice of all or parts of the proposed Code of Evidence of the American Law Institute. See Armstrong, *Proposed Amendments to Federal Rules of Civil Procedure,* 4 F.R.D. 124, 137–138.

1966 Amendment

Note to Subdivision (f). This new subdivision [subdivision (f)] authorizes the court to appoint interpreters (including interpreters for the deaf), to provide for their compensation, and to tax the compensation as costs. Compare proposed subdivision (b) of Rule 28 of the Federal Rules of Criminal Procedure.

1972 Amendment

Rule 43, entitled Evidence, has heretofore served as the basic rule of evidence for civil cases in federal courts. Its very general provisions are superseded by the detailed provisions of the new Rules of Evidence. The original title and many of the provisions of the rule are, therefore, no longer appropriate.

Subdivision (a). The provision for taking testimony in open court is not duplicated in the Rules of Evidence and is retained. Those dealing with admissibility of evidence and competency of witnesses, however, are no longer needed or appropriate since those topics are covered at large in the Rules of Evidence.

They are accordingly deleted. The language is broadened, however, to take account of acts of Congress dealing with the taking of testimony, as well as of the Rules of Evidence and any other rules adopted by the Supreme Court.

Subdivision (b). The subdivision is no longer needed or appropriate since the matters with which it deals are treated in the Rules of Evidence. The use of leading questions, both generally and in the interrogation of an adverse party or witness identified with him, is the subject of Evidence Rule 611(c). Who may impeach is treated in Evidence Rule 601 [sic; probably means 607], and scope of cross-examination is covered in Evidence Rule 611(b). The subdivision is accordingly deleted.

Subdivision (c). Offers of proof and making a record of excluded evidence are treated in Evidence Rule 103. The subdivision is no longer needed or appropriate and is deleted.

1987 Amendment

The amendment is technical. No substantive change is intended.

1996 Amendment

Rule 43(a) is revised to conform to the style conventions adopted for simplifying the present Civil Rules. The only intended changes of meaning are described below.

The requirement that testimony be taken "orally" is deleted. The deletion makes it clear that testimony of a witness may be given in open court by other means if the witness is not able to communicate orally. Writing or sign language are common examples. The development of advanced technology may enable testimony to be given by other means. A witness unable to sign or write by hand may be able to communicate through a computer or similar device.

Contemporaneous transmission of testimony from a different location is permitted only on showing good cause in compelling circumstances. The importance of presenting live testimony in court cannot be forgotten. The very ceremony of trial and the presence of the factfinder may exert a powerful force for truthtelling. The opportunity to judge the demeanor of a witness face-to-face is accorded great value in our tradition. Transmission cannot be justified merely by showing that it is inconvenient for the witness to attend the trial.

The most persuasive showings of good cause and compelling circumstances are likely to arise when a witness is unable to attend trial for unexpected reasons, such as accident or illness, but remains able to testify from a different place. Contemporaneous transmission may be better than an attempt to reschedule the trial, particularly if there is a risk that other—and perhaps more important—witnesses might not be available at a later time.

Other possible justifications for remote transmission must be approached cautiously. Ordinarily depositions, including video depositions, provide a superior means of securing the testimony of a witness who is beyond the reach of a trial subpoena, or of resolving difficulties in scheduling a trial that can be attended by all witnesses. Deposition procedures ensure the opportunity of all parties to be represented while the witness is testifying. An unforeseen need for the testimony of a remote witness that arises during trial, however, may establish good cause and compelling circumstances. Justification is particularly likely if the need arises from the interjection of new issues during trial or from the unexpected inability to present testimony as planned from a different witness.

Good cause and compelling circumstances may be established with relative ease if all parties agree that testimony should be presented by transmission. The court is not bound by a stipulation, however, and can insist on live testimony. Rejection of the parties' agreement will be influenced, among other factors, by the apparent importance of the testimony in the full context of the trial.

A party who could reasonably foresee the circumstances offered to justify transmission of testimony will have special difficulty in showing good cause and the compelling nature of the circumstances. Notice of a desire to transmit testimony from a different location should be given as soon as the reasons are known, to enable other parties to arrange a deposition, or to secure an advance ruling on transmission so as to know whether to prepare to be present with the witness while testifying.

No attempt is made to specify the means of transmission that may be used. Audio transmission without video images may be sufficient in some circumstances, particularly as to less important testimony. Video transmission ordinarily should be preferred when the cost is reasonable in relation to the matters in dispute, the means of the parties, and the circumstances that justify transmission. Transmission that merely produces the equivalent of a written statement ordinarily should not be used.

Safeguards must be adopted that ensure accurate identification of the witness and that protect against influence by persons present with the witness. Accurate transmission likewise must be assured.

Other safeguards should be employed to ensure that advance notice is given to all parties of foreseeable circumstances that may lead the proponent to offer testimony by transmission. Advance notice is important to protect the opportunity to argue for attendance of the witness at trial. Advance notice also ensures an opportunity to depose the witness, perhaps by video record, as a means of supplementing transmitted testimony.

2007 Amendment

The language of Rule 43 has been amended as part of the general restyling of the Civil Rules to make them more easily understood and to make style and terminology consistent throughout the rules. These changes are intended to be stylistic only.

HISTORICAL NOTES

Effective Date of Amendments Proposed November 20, 1972, and December 18, 1972

Amendments of this rule embraced by orders entered by the Supreme Court of the United States on November 20, 1972, and December 18, 1972, effective on the 180th day beginning after January 2, 1975, see section 3 of Pub.L. 93–595, Jan. 2, 1975, 88 Stat. 1959, set out as a note under section 2071 of Title 28.

Rule 44.   Proving an Official Record

(a) Means of Proving.

  (1) *Domestic Record.* Each of the following evidences an official record—or an entry in it—that is otherwise admissible and is kept within the United States, any state, district, or commonwealth, or any territory subject to the administrative or judicial jurisdiction of the United States:

    (A) an official publication of the record; or

    (B) a copy attested by the officer with legal custody of the record—or by the officer's deputy—and accompanied by a certificate that the officer has custody. The certificate must be made under seal:

      (i) by a judge of a court of record in the district or political subdivision where the record is kept; or

      (ii) by any public officer with a seal of office and with official duties in the district or political subdivision where the record is kept.

  (2) *Foreign Record.*

    (A) *In General.* Each of the following evidences a foreign official record—or an entry in it—that is otherwise admissible:

      (i) an official publication of the record; or

      (ii) the record—or a copy—that is attested by an authorized person and is accompanied either by a final certification of genuineness or by a certification under a treaty or convention to which the United States and the country where the record is located are parties.

    (B) *Final Certification of Genuineness.* A final certification must certify the genuineness of the signature and official position of the attester or of any foreign official whose certificate of genuineness relates to the attestation or is in a chain of certificates of genuineness relating to the attestation. A final certification may be made by a secretary of a United States embassy or legation; by a consul general, vice consul, or consular agent of the United States; or by a diplomatic or consular official of the foreign country assigned or accredited to the United States.

(C) *Other Means of Proof.* If all parties have had a reasonable opportunity to investigate a foreign record's authenticity and accuracy, the court may, for good cause, either:

(i) admit an attested copy without final certification; or

(ii) permit the record to be evidenced by an attested summary with or without a final certification.

(b) Lack of a Record. A written statement that a diligent search of designated records revealed no record or entry of a specified tenor is admissible as evidence that the records contain no such record or entry. For domestic records, the statement must be authenticated under Rule 44(a)(1). For foreign records, the statement must comply with (a)(2)(C)(ii).

(c) Other Proof. A party may prove an official record—or an entry or lack of an entry in it—by any other method authorized by law.

(Amended February 28, 1966, effective July 1, 1966; March 2, 1987, effective August 1, 1987; April 30, 1991, effective December 1, 1991; April 30, 2007, effective December 1, 2007.)

ADVISORY COMMITTEE NOTES
1937 Adoption

This rule provides a simple and uniform method of proving public records, and entry or lack of entry therein, in all cases including those specifically provided for by statutes of the United States. Such statutes are not superseded, however, and proof may also be made according to their provisions whenever they differ from this rule. Some of those statutes are:

U.S.C., Title 28 [former sections]:

§ 661 [now 1733] (Copies of department or corporation records and papers; admissibility; seal)

§ 662 [now 1733] (Same; in office of General Counsel of the Treasury)

§ 663 [now 1733] (Instruments and papers of Comptroller of Currency; admissibility)

§ 664 [now 1733] (Organization certificates of national banks; admissibility)

§ 665 [now 1733] (Transcripts from books of Treasury in suits against delinquents; admissibility)

§ 666 [now 1733] (Same; certificate by Secretary or Assistant Secretary)

§ 670 [now 1743] (Admissibility of copies of statements of demands by Post Office Department)

§ 671 [now 1733] (Admissibility of copies of post office records and statement of accounts)

§ 672 [former] (Admissibility of copies of records in General Land Office)

§ 673 [now 1744] (Admissibility of copies of records, and so forth, of Patent Office)

§ 674 [now 1745] (Copies of foreign letters patent as prima facie evidence)

§ 675 [former] (Copies of specifications and drawings of patents admissible)

§ 676 [now 1736] (Extracts from Journals of Congress admissible when injunction of secrecy removed)

§ 677 [now 1740] (Copies of records in offices of United States consuls admissible)

§ 678 [former] (Books and papers in certain district courts)

§ 679 [former] (Records in clerks' offices, Western District of North Carolina)

§ 680 [former] (Records in clerks' offices of former district of California)

§ 681 [now 1734] (Original records lost or destroyed; certified copy admissible)

§ 682 [now 1734] (Same; when certified copy not obtainable)

§ 685 [now 1735] (Same; certified copy of official papers)

§ 687 [now 1738] (Authentication of legislative acts; proof of judicial proceedings of State)

§ 688 [now 1739] (Proofs of records in offices not pertaining to courts)

§ 689 [now 1742] (Copies of foreign records relating to land titles)

§ 695 [now 1732] (Writings and records made in regular course of business; admissibility)

§ 695e [now 1741] (Foreign documents on record in public offices; certification)

U.S.C., Title 1:

§ 30 [now 112] (Statutes at large; contents; admissibility in evidence)

§ 30a [now 113] ("Little and Brown's" edition of laws and treaties competent evidence of Acts of Congress)

§ 54 [now 204] (Codes and supplements as establishing prima facie the laws of United States and District of Columbia, etc.)

§ 55 [now 208] (Copies of supplements to Code of Laws of United States and of District of Columbia Code and supplements; conclusive evidence of original)

U.S.C., Title 5:

§ 490 [former] (Records of Department of Interior; authenticated copies as evidence)

U.S.C., Title 6:

§ 7 [now Title 31, § 9306] (Surety Companies as sureties; appointment of agents; service of process)

U.S.C., Title 8:

§ 9a [see 1435(c)] (Citizenship of children of persons naturalized under certain laws; repatriation of native-born women married to aliens prior to September 22, 1922; copies of proceedings)

§ 356 [see 1443] (Regulations for execution of naturalization laws; certified copies of papers as evidence)

§ 399b(d) [see 1443] (Certifications of naturalization records; authorization; admissibility as evidence)

U.S.C., Title 11:

§ 44(d), (e), (f), (g) [former] (Bankruptcy court proceedings and orders as evidence)

§ 204 [former] (Extensions extended, etc.; evidence of confirmation)

§ 207(j) [former] (Corporate reorganizations; certified copy of decree as evidence)

U.S.C., Title 15:

§ 127 (Trade-mark records in Patent Office; copies as evidence)

U.S.C., Title 20:

§ 52 (Smithsonian Institution; evidence of title to site and buildings)

U.S.C., Title 25:

§ 6 (Bureau of Indian Affairs; seal; authenticated and certified documents; evidence)

U.S.C., Title 31:

§ 46 [now 704] (Laws governing General Accounting Office; copies of books, records, etc., thereof as evidence)

U.S.C., Title 38:

§ 11g [see 202] (Seal of Veterans' Administration; authentication of copies of records)

U.S.C., Title 40:

§ 238 [former 44 U.S.C.A. § 300h] (National Archives; seal; reproduction of archives; fee; admissibility in evidence of reproductions)

§ 270c [see now 40 U.S.C.A. § 3133(a)] (Bonds of contractors for public works; right of person furnishing labor or material to copy of bond)

U.S.C., Title 43:

§§ 57–59 (Copies of land surveys, etc., in certain states and districts admissible as evidence)

§ 83 (General Land Office registers and receivers; transcripts of records as evidence)

U.S.C., Title 46:

§ 823 (Records of Maritime Commission; copies; publication of reports; evidence)

U.S.C., Title 47:

§ 154(m) (Federal Communications Commission; copies of reports and decisions as evidence)

§ 412 (Documents filed with Federal Communications Commission as public records; prima facie evidence; confidential records)

U.S.C., Title 49:

§ 14(3) [now 10310] (Interstate Commerce Commission reports and decisions; printing and distribution of copies)

§ 16(13) [now 10303(b)] (Copies of schedules, tariffs, etc. filed with Interstate Commerce Commission as evidence)

§ 19a(i) [now 10785(c)] (Valuation of property of carriers by Interstate Commerce Commission; final published valuations as evidence)

1946 Report of the Advisory Committee

Supplementary Note of Advisory Committee Regarding Rules 43 and 44.

For supplementary note of Advisory Committee on this rule, see note under Rule 43.

1966 Amendment

Note to Subdivision (a)(1). These provisions on proof of official records kept within the United States are similar in substance to those heretofore appearing in Rule 44. There is a more exact description of the geographical areas covered. An official record kept in one of the areas enumerated qualifies for proof under subdivision (a)(1) even though it is not a United States official record. For example, an official record kept in one of these areas by a government in exile falls within subdivision (a)(1). It also falls within subdivision (a)(2) which may be availed of alternatively. Cf. *Banco de Espana v. Federal Reserve Bank,* 114 F.2d 438 (2d Cir. 1940).

Note to Subdivision (a)(2). Foreign official records may be proved, as heretofore, by means of official publications thereof. See *United States v. Aluminum Co. of America,* 1 F.R.D. 71 (S.D.N.Y.1939). Under this rule, a document that, on its face, appears to be an official publication, is admissible, unless a party opposing its admission into evidence shows that it lacks that character.

The rest of subdivision (a)(2) aims to provide greater clarity, efficiency, and flexibility in the procedure for authenticating copies of foreign official records.

The reference to attestation by "the officer having the legal custody of the record," hitherto appearing in Rule 44, has been found inappropriate for official records kept in foreign countries where the assumed relation between custody and the authority to attest does not obtain. See 2B Barron & Holtzoff, Federal Practice & Procedure § 992 (Wright ed. 1961). Accordingly it is provided that an attested copy may be obtained from any person authorized by the law of the foreign country to make the attestation without regard to whether he is charged with responsibility for maintaining the record or keeping it in his custody.

Under Rule 44 a United States foreign service officer has been called on to certify to the authority of the foreign official attesting the copy as well as the genuineness of his signature and his official position. See Schlesinger, *Comparative Law 57* (2d ed. 1959); Smit, *International Aspects of Federal Civil Procedure,*

61 Colum.L.Rev. 1031, 1063 (1961); 22 C.F.R. § 92.41(a), (e) (1958). This has created practical difficulties. For example, the question of the authority of the foreign officer might raise issues of foreign law which were beyond the knowledge of the United States officer. The difficulties are met under the amended rule by eliminating the element of the authority of the attesting foreign official from the scope of the certifying process, and by specifically permitting use of the chain-certificate method. Under this method, it is sufficient if the original attestation purports to have been issued by an authorized person and is accompanied by a certificate of another foreign official whose certificate may in turn be followed by that of a foreign official of higher rank. The process continues until a foreign official is reached as to whom the United States foreign service official (or a diplomatic or consular officer of the foreign country assigned or accredited to the United States) has adequate information upon which to base a "final certification." See *New York Life Ins. Co. v. Aronson,* 38 F.Supp. 687 (W.D.Pa.1941); 22 C.F.R. § 92.37 (1958).

The final certification (a term used in contradistinction to the certificates prepared by the foreign officials in a chain) relates to the incumbency and genuineness of signature of the foreign official who attested the copy of the record or, where the chain-certificate method is used, of a foreign official whose certificate appears in the chain, whether that certificate is the last in the chain or not. A final certification may be prepared on the basis of material on file in the consulate or any other satisfactory information.

Although the amended rule will generally facilitate proof of foreign official records, it is recognized that in some situations it may be difficult or even impossible to satisfy the basic requirements of the rule. There may be no United States consul in a particular foreign country; the foreign officials may not cooperate, peculiarities may exist or arise hereafter in the law or practice of a foreign country. See *United States v. Grabina,* 119 F.2d 863 (2d Cir. 1941); and, generally, Jones, *International Judicial Assistance: Procedural Chaos and a Program for Reform,* 62 Yale L.J. 515, 548–49 (1953). Therefore the final sentence of subdivision (a)(2) provides the court with discretion to admit an attested copy of a record without a final certification, or an attested summary of a record with or without a final certification. See Rep. of Comm. on Comparative Civ.Proc. & Prac., Proc. A.B.A., Sec. Int'l & Comp.L. 123, 130–31 (1952); Model Code of Evidence §§ 517, 519 (1942). This relaxation should be permitted only when it is shown that the party has been unable to satisfy the basic requirements of the amended rule despite his reasonable efforts. Moreover it is specially provided that the parties must be given a reasonable opportunity in these cases to examine into the authenticity and accuracy of the copy or summary.

Note to Subdivision (b). This provision relating to proof of lack of record is accommodated to the changes made in subdivision (a).

Note to Subdivision (c). The amendment insures that international agreements of the United States are unaffected by the rule. Several consular conventions contain provisions for reception of copies or summaries of foreign official records. See, e.g., Consular Conv. with Italy, May 8, 1878, art. X, 20 Stat. 725, T.S. No. 178 (Dept. State 1878). See also 28 U.S.C. §§ 1740–42, 1745; *Fakouri v. Cadais,* 149 F.2d 321 (5th Cir.1945), cert. denied 326 U.S. 742 (1945); 5 *Moore's Federal Practice,* par. 44.05 (2d ed. 1951).

1987 Amendment

The amendments are technical. No substantive change is intended.

1991 Amendment

The amendment to paragraph (a)(1) strikes the references to specific territories, two of which are no longer subject to the jurisdiction of the United States, and adds a generic term to describe governments having a relationship with the United States such that their official records should be treated as domestic records.

The amendment to paragraph (a)(2) adds a sentence to dispense with the final certification by diplomatic officers when the United States and the foreign country where the record is located are parties to a treaty or convention that abolishes or displaces the requirement. In that event the treaty or convention is to be followed. This changes the former procedure for authenticating foreign official records only with respect to records from countries that are parties to the Hague Convention Abolishing the Requirement of Legalization for Foreign Public Documents. Moreover, it does not affect the former practice of attesting the records, but only changes the method of certifying the attestation.

The Hague Public Documents Convention provides that the requirement of a final certification is abolished and replaced with a model *apostille,* which is to be issued by officials of the country where the records are located. See Hague Public Documents Convention, Arts. 2–4. The *apostille* certifies the signature, official position, and seal of the attesting officer. The authority who issues the *apostille* must maintain a register or card index showing the serial number of the *apostille* and other relevant information recorded on it. A foreign court can then check the serial number and information on the *apostille* with the issuing authority in order to guard against the use of fraudulent *apostilles*. This system provides a reliable method for maintaining the integrity of the authentication process, and the *apostille* can be accorded greater weight than the normal authentication procedure because foreign officials are more likely to know the precise capacity under their law of the attesting officer than would an American official. See generally Comment, *The United States and the Hague Convention Abolishing the Requirement of Legalization for Foreign Public Documents,* 11 HARV. INT'L L.J. 476, 482, 488 (1970).

2007 Amendment

The language of Rule 44 has been amended as part of the general restyling of the Civil Rules to make them more easily understood and to make style and terminology consistent throughout the rules. These changes are intended to be stylistic only.

TREATIES AND CONVENTIONS

CONVENTION ABOLISHING THE REQUIREMENT OF LEGALISATION FOR FOREIGN PUBLIC DOCUMENTS

The States signatory to the present Convention,

Desiring to abolish the requirement of diplomatic or consular legalisation for foreign public documents,

Have resolved to conclude a Convention to this effect and have agreed upon the following provisions:

ARTICLE 1

The present Convention shall apply to public documents which have been executed in the territory of one contracting State and which have to be produced in the territory of another contracting State.

For the purposes of the present Convention, the following are deemed to be public documents:

   (a)   Documents emanating from an authority or an official connected with the courts or tribunals of the State, including those emanating from a public prosecutor, a clerk of a court or a process server ("huissier de justice");

   (b)   Administrative documents;

   (c)   Notarial acts;

   (d)   Official certificates which are placed on documents signed by persons in their private capacity, such as official certificates recording the registration of a document or the fact that it was in existence on a certain date and official and notarial authentications of signatures.

However, the present Convention shall not apply:

   (a)   To documents executed by diplomatic or consular agents;

   (b)   To administrative documents dealing directly with commercial or customs operations.

ARTICLE 2

Each contracting State shall exempt from legalisation documents to which the present Convention applies and which have to be produced in its territory. For the purposes of the present Convention, legalisation means only the formality by which the diplomatic or consular agents of the country in which the document has to be produced certify the authenticity of the signature, the capacity in which the person signing the document has acted and, where appropriate, the identity of the seal or stamp which it bears.

ARTICLE 3

The only formality that may be required in order to certify the authenticity of the signature, the capacity in which the person signing the document has acted and, where appropriate, the identity of the seal or stamp which it bears, is the addition of the certificate described in Article 4, issued by the competent authority of the State from which the document emanates.

However, the formality mentioned in the preceding paragraph cannot be required when either the laws, regulations, or practice in force in the State where the document is produced or an agreement between two or more contracting States have abolished or simplified it, or exempt the document itself from legalisation.

ARTICLE 4

The certificate referred to in the first paragraph of Article 3 shall be placed on the document itself or on an "allonge"; it shall be in the form of the model annexed to the present Convention.

It may, however, be drawn up in the official language of the authority which issues it. The standard terms appearing therein may be in a second language also. The title "Apostille (Convention de La Haye du 5 octobre 1961)" shall be in the French language.

ARTICLE 5

The certificate shall be issued at the request of the person who has signed the document or of any bearer.

When properly filled in, it will certify the authenticity of the signature, the capacity in which the person signing the document has acted and, where appropriate, the identity of the seal or stamp which the document bears.

The signature, seal and stamp on the certificate are exempt from all certification.

ARTICLE 6

Each contracting State shall designate by reference to their official function, the authorities who are competent to issue the certificate referred to in the first paragraph of Article 3.

It shall give notice of such designation to the Ministry of Foreign Affairs of the Netherlands at the time it deposits its instrument of ratification or of accession or its declaration of extension. It shall also give notice of any change in the designated authorities.

ARTICLE 7

Each of the authorities designated in accordance with Article 6 shall keep a register or card index in which it shall record the certificates issued, specifying:

    (a) The number and date of the certificate,

    (b) The name of the person signing the public document and the capacity in which he has acted, or in the case of unsigned documents, the name of the authority which has affixed the seal or stamp.

At the request of any interested person, the authority which has issued the certificate shall verify whether the particulars in the certificate correspond with those in the register or card index.

ARTICLE 8

When a treaty, convention or agreement between two or more contracting States contains provisions which subject the certification of a signature, seal or stamp to certain formalities, the present Convention will only override such provisions if those formalities are more rigorous than the formality referred to in Articles 3 and 4.

ARTICLE 9

Each contracting State shall take the necessary steps to prevent the performance of legalisations by its diplomatic or consular agents in cases where the present Convention provides for exemption.

ARTICLE 10

The present Convention shall be open for signature by the States represented at the Ninth session of the Hague Conference on Private International Law and Iceland, Ireland, Liechtenstein and Turkey.

It shall be ratified, and the instruments of ratification shall be deposited with the Ministry of Foreign Affairs of the Netherlands.

ARTICLE 11

The present Convention shall enter into force on the sixtieth day after the deposit of the third instrument of ratification referred to in the second paragraph of Article 10.

The Convention shall enter into force for each signatory State which ratifies subsequently on the sixtieth day after the deposit of its instrument of ratification.

ARTICLE 12

Any State not referred to in Article 10 may accede to the present Convention after it has entered into force in accordance with the first paragraph of Article 11. The instrument of accession shall be deposited with the Ministry of Foreign Affairs of the Netherlands.

Such accession shall have effect only as regards the relations between the acceding State and those contracting States which have not raised an objection to its accession in the six months after the receipt of the notification referred to in sub-paragraph (d) of Article 15. Any such objection shall be notified to the Ministry of Foreign Affairs of the Netherlands.

The Convention shall enter into force as between the acceding State and the States which have raised no objection to its accession on the sixtieth day after the expiry of the period of six months mentioned in the preceding paragraph.

ARTICLE 13

Any State may, at the time of signature, ratification or accession, declare that the present Convention shall extend to all the territories for the international relations of which it is responsible, or to one or more of them. Such a declaration shall take effect on the date of entry into force of the Convention for the State concerned.

At any time thereafter, such extension shall be notified to the Ministry of Foreign Affairs of the Netherlands.

When the declaration of extension is made by a State which has signed and ratified, the Convention shall enter into force for the territories concerned in accordance with Article 11. When the declaration of extension is made by a State which has acceded, the Convention shall enter into force for the territories concerned in accordance with Article 12.

ARTICLE 14

The present Convention shall remain in force for five years from the date of its entry into force in accordance with the first paragraph of Article 11, even for States which have ratified it or acceded to it subsequently.

If there has been no denunciation, the Convention shall be renewed tacitly every five years.

Any denunciation shall be notified to the Ministry of Foreign Affairs of the Netherlands at least six months before the end of the five year period.

It may be limited to certain of the territories to which the Convention applies.

The denunciation will only have effect as regards the State which has notified it. The Convention shall remain in force for the other contracting States.

ARTICLE 15

The Ministry of Foreign Affairs of the Netherlands shall give notice to the States referred to in Article 10, and to the States which have acceded in accordance with Article 12, of the following:

  (a)   The notifications referred to in the second paragraph of Article 6;

(b) The signatures and ratifications referred to in Article 10;

(c) The date on which the present Convention enters into force in accordance with the first paragraph of Article 11;

(d) The accessions and objections referred to in Article 12 and the date on which such accessions take effect;

(e) The extensions referred to in Article 13 and the date on which they take effect;

(f) The denunciations referred to in the third paragraph of Article 14.

In witness whereof the undersigned, being duly authorised thereto, have signed the present Convention.

Done at The Hague the 5th October 1961, in French and in English, the French text prevailing in case of divergence between the two texts, in a single copy which shall be deposited in the archives of the Government of the Netherlands, and of which a certified copy shall be sent, through the diplomatic channel, to each of the States represented at the Ninth session of the Hague Conference on Private International Law and also to Iceland, Ireland, Liechtenstein and Turkey.

[Signatures omitted.]

––––––––

ANNEX TO THE CONVENTION
Model of certificate

The certificate will be in the form of a square
with sides at least 9 centimetres long

APOSTILLE

(Convention de La Haye du 5 octobre 1961)

1.   Country: ....
   This public document
2.   has been signed by ....
3.   acting in the capacity of ....
4.   bears the seal/stamp of ....

                            Certified

5.   at ....   6.   The ....
7.   by ....
8.   N° ....
9.   Seal/stamp: 10.   Signature:

....

––––––––

Convention abolishing the requirement of legalization for foreign public documents, with annex. Done at The Hague October 5, 1961; entered into force for the United States October 15, 1981. (T.I.A.S. 10072; 527 U.N.T.S. 189).

Rule 44.1. Determining Foreign Law

A party who intends to raise an issue about a foreign country's law must give notice by a pleading or other writing. In determining foreign law, the court may consider any relevant material or source, including testimony, whether or not submitted by a party or admissible under the Federal Rules of Evidence. The court's determination must be treated as a ruling on a question of law.

(Adopted February 28, 1966, effective July 1, 1966; amended November 20, 1972, effective July 1, 1975; March 2, 1987, effective August 1, 1987; April 30, 2007, effective December 1, 2007.)

ADVISORY COMMITTEE NOTES
1966 Adoption

Rule 44.1 is added by amendment to furnish Federal courts with a uniform and effective procedure for raising and determining an issue concerning the law of a foreign country.

To avoid unfair surprise, the *first sentence* of the new rule requires that a party who intends to raise an issue of foreign law shall give notice thereof. The uncertainty under Rule 8(a) about whether foreign law must be pleaded—compare *Siegelman v. Cunard White Star, Ltd.,* 221 F.2d 189 (2d Cir.1955), and *Pedersen v. United States,* 191 F.Supp. 95 (D. Guam 1961), with *Harrison v. United Fruit Co.,* 143 F.Supp. 598 (S.D.N.Y.1956)—is eliminated by the provision that the notice shall be "written" and "reasonable." It may, but need not be, incorporated in the pleadings. In some situations the pertinence of foreign law is apparent from the outset; accordingly the necessary investigation of that law will have been accomplished by the party at the pleading stage, and the notice can be given conveniently in the pleadings. In other situations the pertinence of foreign law may remain doubtful until the case is further developed. A requirement that notice of foreign law be given only through the medium of the pleadings would tend in the latter instances to force the party to engage in a peculiarly burdensome type of investigation which might turn out to be unnecessary; and correspondingly the adversary would be forced into a possible wasteful investigation. The liberal provisions for amendment of the pleadings afford help if the pleadings are used as the medium of giving notice of the foreign law; but it seems best to permit a written notice to be given outside of and later than the pleadings, provided the notice is reasonable.

The new rule does not attempt to set any definite limit on the party's time for giving the notice of an issue of foreign law; in some cases the issue may not become apparent until the trial and notice then given may still be reasonable. The stage which the case had reached at the time of the notice, the reason proffered by the party for his failure to give earlier notice, and the importance to the case as a whole of the issue of foreign law sought to be raised, are among the factors which the court should consider in deciding a question of the reasonableness of a notice. If notice is given by one party it need not be repeated by any other and serves as a basis for presentation of material on the foreign law by all parties.

The *second sentence* of the new rule describes the materials to which the court may resort in determining an issue of foreign law. Heretofore the district courts, applying Rule 43(a), have looked in certain cases to State law to find the rules of evidence by which the content of foreign-country law is to be established. The State laws vary; some embody procedures which are inefficient, time consuming and expensive. See, generally, Nussbaum, *Proving the Law of Foreign Countries,* 3 Am. J. Comp. L. 60 (1954). In all events the ordinary rules of evidence are often inapposite to the problem of determining foreign law and have in the past prevented examination of material which could have provided a proper basis for the determination. The new rule permits consideration by the court of any relevant material, including testimony, without regard to its admissibility under Rule 43. Cf. N.Y. Civ. Prac. Law & Rules, R. 4511 (effective Sept. 1, 1963); 2 Va. Code Ann. tit. 8, § 8–273; 2 W. Va. Code Ann. § 5711.

In further recognition of the peculiar nature of the issue of foreign law, the new rule provides that in determining this law the court is not limited by material presented by the parties; it may engage in its own research and consider any relevant material thus found. The court may have at its disposal better foreign law materials than counsel have presented, or may wish to reexamine and amplify material that has been presented by counsel in partisan fashion or in insufficient detail. On the other hand, the court is free to insist on a complete presentation by counsel.

There is no requirement that the court give formal notice to the parties of its intention to engage in its own research on an issue of foreign law which has been raised by them, or of its intention to raise and determine independently an issue not raised by them. Ordinarily the court should inform the parties of material it has found diverging substantially from the material which they have presented; and in general the court should give the parties an opportunity to analyze and counter new points upon which it proposes to rely. See Schlesinger, *Comparative Law* 142 (2d ed. 1959); Wyzanski, *A Trial Judge's Freedom and Responsibility,* 65 Harv.L.Rev. 1281, 1296 (1952); cf. *Siegelman v. Cunard White Star, Ltd.,* supra, 221 F.2d at 197. To require, however, that the court give formal notice from time to time as it proceeds with its study of the foreign law would add an element of undesirable rigidity to the procedure for determining issues of foreign law.

The new rule refrains from imposing an obligation on the court to take "judicial notice" of foreign law because this would put an extreme burden on the court in many cases; and it avoids use of the concept of "judicial notice" in any form because of the uncertain meaning of that concept as applied to foreign law. See, e.g., Stern, *Foreign Law in the Courts: Judicial Notice and Proof,* 45 Calif.L.Rev. 23, 43 (1957). Rather the rule provides flexible procedures for presenting and utilizing material on issues of foreign law by which a sound result can be achieved with fairness to the parties.

Under the *third sentence,* the court's determination of an issue of foreign law is to be treated as a ruling on a question of "law," not "fact," so that appellate review will not be narrowly confined by the "clearly erroneous" standard of Rule 52(a). *Cf. Uniform Judicial Notice of Foreign Law Act* § 3; Note, 72 Harv.L.Rev. 318 (1958).

The new rule parallels Article IV of the Uniform Interstate and International Procedure Act, approved by the Commissioners on Uniform State Laws in 1962, except that § 4.03 of Article IV states that "[t]he court, not the jury" shall determine foreign law. The new rule does not address itself to this problem, since the Rules refrain from allocating functions as between the court and the jury. See Rule 38(a). It has long been thought, however, that the jury is not the appropriate body to determine issues of foreign law. See, e.g., Story, *Conflict of Laws,* § 638 (1st ed. 1834, 8th ed. 1883); 1 Greenleaf, *Evidence,* § 486 (1st ed. 1842, 16th ed. 1899); 4 Wigmore, *Evidence* § 2558 (1st ed. 1905); 9 id. § 2558 (3d ed. 1940). The majority of the States have committed such issues to determination by the court. See Article 5 of the Uniform Judicial Notice of Foreign Law Act, adopted by twenty-six states, 9A U.L.A. 318 (1957) (Suppl.1961, at 134); N.Y.Civ.Prac.Law & Rules, R. 4511 (effective Sept. 1, 1963); Wigmore, loc. cit. And Federal courts that have considered the problem in recent years have reached the same conclusion without reliance on statute. See *Jansson v. Swedish American Line,* 185 F.2d 212, 216 (1st Cir.1950); *Bank of Nova Scotia v. San Miguel,* 196 F.2d 950, 957, n. 6 (1st Cir.1952); *Liechti v. Roche,* 198 F.2d 174 (5th Cir.1952); *Daniel Lumber Co. v. Empresas Hondurenas, S.A.,* 215 F.2d 465 (5th Cir.1954).

1972 Amendment

Since the purpose of the provision is to free the judge, in determining foreign law, from any restrictions imposed by evidence rules, a general reference to the Rules of Evidence is appropriate and is made.

1987 Amendment

The amendment is technical. No substantive change is intended.

2007 Amendment

The language of Rule 44.1 has been amended as part of the general restyling of the Civil Rules to make them more easily understood and to make style and terminology consistent throughout the rules. These changes are intended to be stylistic only.

HISTORICAL NOTES

Effective Date of Amendment Proposed November 20, 1972

Amendment of this rule embraced by the order entered by the Supreme Court of the United States on November 20, 1972, effective on the 180th day beginning after January 2, 1975, see section 3 of Pub.L. 93–595, Jan. 2, 1975, 88 Stat. 1959, set out as a note under section 2071 of Title 28.

Rule 45.   Subpoena

(a) In General.

    (1) *Form and Contents.*

        (A) *Requirements—In General.* Every subpoena must:

            (i)   state the court from which it issued;

            (ii) state the title of the action and its civil-action number;

            (iii) command each person to whom it is directed to do the following at a specified time and place: attend and testify; produce designated documents, electronically stored information, or tangible things in that person's possession, custody, or control; or permit the inspection of premises; and

(iv) set out the text of Rule 45(d) and (e).

(B) *Command to Attend a Deposition—Notice of the Recording Method.* A subpoena commanding attendance at a deposition must state the method for recording the testimony.

(C) *Combining or Separating a Command to Produce or to Permit Inspection; Specifying the Form for Electronically Stored Information.* A command to produce documents, electronically stored information, or tangible things or to permit the inspection of premises may be included in a subpoena commanding attendance at a deposition, hearing, or trial, or may be set out in a separate subpoena. A subpoena may specify the form or forms in which electronically stored information is to be produced.

(D) *Command to Produce; Included Obligations.* A command in a subpoena to produce documents, electronically stored information, or tangible things requires the responding person to permit inspection, copying, testing, or sampling of the materials.

(2) *Issuing Court.* A subpoena must issue from the court where the action is pending.

(3) *Issued by Whom.* The clerk must issue a subpoena, signed but otherwise in blank, to a party who requests it. That party must complete it before service. An attorney also may issue and sign a subpoena if the attorney is authorized to practice in the issuing court.

(4) *Notice to Other Parties Before Service.* If the subpoena commands the production of documents, electronically stored information, or tangible things or the inspection of premises before trial, then before it is served on the person to whom it is directed, a notice and a copy of the subpoena must be served on each party.

(b) **Service.**

(1) *By Whom and How; Tendering Fees.* Any person who is at least 18 years old and not a party may serve a subpoena. Serving a subpoena requires delivering a copy to the named person and, if the subpoena requires that person's attendance, tendering the fees for 1 day's attendance and the mileage allowed by law. Fees and mileage need not be tendered when the subpoena issues on behalf of the United States or any of its officers or agencies.

(2) *Service in the United States.* A subpoena may be served at any place within the United States.

(3) *Service in a Foreign Country.* 28 U.S.C. § 1783 governs issuing and serving a subpoena directed to a United States national or resident who is in a foreign country.

(4) *Proof of Service.* Proving service, when necessary, requires filing with the issuing court a statement showing the date and manner of service and the names of the persons served. The statement must be certified by the server.

(c) **Place of Compliance.**

(1) *For a Trial, Hearing, or Deposition.* A subpoena may command a person to attend a trial, hearing, or deposition only as follows:

(A) within 100 miles of where the person resides, is employed, or regularly transacts business in person; or

(B) within the state where the person resides, is employed, or regularly transacts business in person, if the person

(i) is a party or a party's officer; or

(ii) is commanded to attend a trial and would not incur substantial expense.

(2) *For Other Discovery.* A subpoena may command:

(A) production of documents, electronically stored information, or tangible things at a place within 100 miles of where the person resides, is employed, or regularly transacts business in person; and

(B) inspection of premises at the premises to be inspected.

(d) **Protecting a Person Subject to a Subpoena; Enforcement.**

(1) *Avoiding Undue Burden or Expense; Sanctions.* A party or attorney responsible for issuing and serving a subpoena must take reasonable steps to avoid imposing undue burden or expense on a person subject to the subpoena. The court for the district where compliance is required must enforce this duty and impose an appropriate sanction—which may include lost earnings and reasonable attorney's fees—on a party or attorney who fails to comply.

(2) *Command to Produce Materials or Permit Inspection.*

(A) *Appearance Not Required.* A person commanded to produce documents, electronically stored information, or tangible things, or to permit the inspection of premises, need not appear in person at the place of production or inspection unless also commanded to appear for a deposition, hearing, or trial.

(B) *Objections.* A person commanded to produce documents or tangible things or to permit inspection may serve on the party or attorney designated in the subpoena a written objection to inspecting, copying, testing, or sampling any or all of the materials or to inspecting the premises—or to producing electronically stored information in the form or forms requested. The objection must be served before the earlier of the time specified for compliance or 14 days after the subpoena is served. If an objection is made, the following rules apply:

(i) At any time, on notice to the commanded person, the serving party may move the court for the district where compliance is required for an order compelling production or inspection.

(ii) These acts may be required only as directed in the order, and the order must protect a person who is neither a party nor a party's officer from significant expense resulting from compliance.

(3) *Quashing or Modifying a Subpoena.*

(A) *When Required.* On timely motion, the court for the district where compliance is required must quash or modify a subpoena that:

(i) fails to allow a reasonable time to comply;

(ii) requires a person to comply beyond the geographical limits specified in Rule 45(c);

(iii) requires disclosure of privileged or other protected matter, if no exception or waiver applies; or

(iv) subjects a person to undue burden.

(B) *When Permitted.* To protect a person subject to or affected by a subpoena, the court for the district where compliance is required may, on motion, quash or modify the subpoena if it requires:

(i) disclosing a trade secret or other confidential research, development, or commercial information; or

(ii) disclosing an unretained expert's opinion or information that does not describe specific occurrences in dispute and results from the expert's study that was not requested by a party.

(C) *Specifying Conditions as an Alternative.* In the circumstances described in Rule 45(d)(3)(B), the court may, instead of quashing or modifying a subpoena, order appearance or production under specified conditions if the serving party:

    (i) shows a substantial need for the testimony or material that cannot be otherwise met without undue hardship; and

    (ii) ensures that the subpoenaed person will be reasonably compensated.

(e) Duties in Responding to a Subpoena.

    (1) *Producing Documents or Electronically Stored Information.* These procedures apply to producing documents or electronically stored information:

        (A) *Documents.* A person responding to a subpoena to produce documents must produce them as they are kept in the ordinary course of business or must organize and label them to correspond to the categories in the demand.

        (B) *Form for Producing Electronically Stored Information Not Specified.* If a subpoena does not specify a form for producing electronically stored information, the person responding must produce it in a form or forms in which it is ordinarily maintained or in a reasonably usable form or forms.

        (C) *Electronically Stored Information Produced in Only One Form.* The person responding need not produce the same electronically stored information in more than one form.

        (D) *Inaccessible Electronically Stored Information.* The person responding need not provide discovery of electronically stored information from sources that the person identifies as not reasonably accessible because of undue burden or cost. On motion to compel discovery or for a protective order, the person responding must show that the information is not reasonably accessible because of undue burden or cost. If that showing is made, the court may nonetheless order discovery from such sources if the requesting party shows good cause, considering the limitations of Rule 26(b)(2)(C). The court may specify conditions for the discovery.

    (2) *Claiming Privilege or Protection.*

        (A) *Information Withheld.* A person withholding subpoenaed information under a claim that it is privileged or subject to protection as trial-preparation material must:

            (i) expressly make the claim; and

            (ii) describe the nature of the withheld documents, communications, or tangible things in a manner that, without revealing information itself privileged or protected, will enable the parties to assess the claim.

        (B) *Information Produced.* If information produced in response to a subpoena is subject to a claim of privilege or of protection as trial-preparation material, the person making the claim may notify any party that received the information of the claim and the basis for it. After being notified, a party must promptly return, sequester, or destroy the specified information and any copies it has; must not use or disclose the information until the claim is resolved; must take reasonable steps to retrieve the information if the party disclosed it before being notified; and may promptly present the information under seal to the court for the district where compliance is required for a determination of the claim. The person who produced the information must preserve the information until the claim is resolved.

(f) Transferring a Subpoena-Related Motion. When the court where compliance is required did not issue the subpoena, it may transfer a motion under this rule to the issuing court if the person subject to the subpoena consents or if the court finds exceptional circumstances. Then, if the attorney for a person subject to a subpoena is authorized to practice in the court where the motion was made, the attorney may file papers and appear on the motion as an officer of the issuing court. To enforce its order, the issuing court may transfer the order to the court where the motion was made.

(g) Contempt. The court for the district where compliance is required—and also, after a motion is transferred, the issuing court—may hold in contempt a person who, having been served, fails without adequate excuse to obey the subpoena or an order related to it.

(Amended December 27, 1946, effective March 19, 1948; December 29, 1948, effective October 20, 1949; March 30, 1970, effective July 1, 1970; April 29, 1980, effective August 1, 1980; April 29, 1985, effective August 1, 1985; March 2, 1987, effective August 1, 1987; April 30, 1991, effective December 1, 1991; April 25, 2005, effective December 1, 2005; April 12, 2006, effective December 1, 2006; April 30, 2007, effective December 1, 2007; April 16, 2013, effective December 1, 2013.)

ADVISORY COMMITTEE NOTES

1937 Adoption

This rule applies to subpoenas ad testificandum and duces tecum issued by the district courts for attendance at a hearing or a trial, or to take depositions. It does not apply to the enforcement of subpoenas issued by administrative officers and commissions pursuant to statutory authority. The enforcement of such subpoenas by the district courts is regulated by appropriate statutes. Many of these statutes do not place any territorial limits on the validity of subpoenas so issued, but provide that they may be served anywhere within the United States. Among such statutes are the following:

U.S.C., Title 7, §§ 222 and 511n (Secretary of Agriculture)

U.S.C., Title 15, § 49 (Federal Trade Commission)

U.S.C., Title 15, §§ 77v(b), 78u(c), 79r(d) (Securities and Exchange Commission)

U.S.C., Title 16, §§ 797(g) and 825f (Federal Power Commission)

U.S.C., Title 19, § 1333(b) (Tariff Commission)

U.S.C., Title 22, §§ 268, 270d and 270e (International Commissions, etc.)

U.S.C., Title 26, §§ 614, 619(b) [see 7456] (Board of Tax Appeals)

U.S.C., Title 26, § 1523(a) [see 7608] (Internal Revenue Officers)

U.S.C., Title 29, § 161 (Labor Relations Board)

U.S.C., Title 33, § 506 (Secretary of Army)

U.S.C., Title 35, §§ 54 to 56 [now 24] (Patent Office proceedings)

U.S.C., Title 38, [former] § 133 (Veterans' Administration)

U.S.C., Title 41, § 6507 (Secretary of Labor)

U.S.C., Title 45, § 157 Third. (h) (Board of Arbitration under Railway Labor Act)

U.S.C., Title 45, § 222(b) (Investigation Commission under Railroad Retirement Act of 1935)

U.S.C., Title 46, § 1124(b) (Maritime Commission)

U.S.C., Title 47, § 409(c) and (d) (Federal Communications Commission)

U.S.C., Title 49, § 12(2) and (3) [now 10321] (Interstate Commerce Commission)

U.S.C., Title 49, § 173a [see 1484] (Secretary of Commerce)

Note to Subdivisions (a) and (b). These simplify the form of subpoena as provided in U.S.C., Title 28, [former] § 655 (Witnesses; subpoena; form; attendance under); and broaden U.S.C, Title 28, [former] § 636 (Production for books and writings) to include all actions, and to extend to any person. With the provision for relief from an oppressive or unreasonable subpoena duces tecum, compare N.Y.C.P.A. (1937) § 411.

Note to Subdivision (c). This provides for the simple and convenient method of service permitted under many state codes; e.g., N.Y.C.P.A. (1937) §§ 220, 404, J.Ct.Act, § 191; 3 Wash.Rev.Stat.Ann. (Remington, 1932) § 1218. Compare former Equity Rule 15 (Process, by Whom Served).

For statutes governing fees and mileage of witnesses see:

U.S.C., Title 28 former sections:

> 600a [now 1871] (Per diem; mileage)
>
> 600c [now 1821, 1823] (Amount per diem and mileage for witnesses; subsistence)
>
> 600d [former] (Fees and mileage in certain states)
>
> 601 [former] (Witnesses' fees; enumeration)
>
> 602 [now 1824] (Fees and mileage of jurors and witnesses)
>
> 603 [see Title 5, §§ 5515, 5537] (No officer of court to have witness fees)

Note to Subdivision (d). The method provided in paragraph (1) for the authorization of the issuance of subpoenas has been employed in some districts. See *Henning v. Boyle,* S.D.N.Y.1901, 112 F. 397. The requirement of an order for the issuance of a subpoena duces tecum is in accordance with U.S.C., Title 28, [former] § 647 (Deposition under dedimus potestatem; subpoena duces tecum). The provisions of paragraph (2) are in accordance with common practice. See U.S.C., Title 28, former § 648 (Deposition under dedimus potestatem; witnesses, when required to attend); N.Y.C.P.A. (1937) § 300; 1 N.J.Rev.Stat. (1937) 2:27–174.

Note to Subdivision (e). The first paragraph continues the substance of U.S.C., Title 28, [former] § 654 (Witnesses; subpoenas; may run into another district). Compare U.S.C., Title 11, [former] § 69 (Referees in bankruptcy; contempts before) (production of books and writings) which is not affected by this rule. For examples of statutes which allow the court, upon proper application and cause shown, to authorize the clerk of the court to issue a subpoena for a witness who lives in another district and at a greater distance than 100 miles from the place of the hearing or trial, see:

U.S.C., Title 15:

> § 23 (Suits by United States; subpoenas for witnesses) (under antitrust laws).

U.S.C., Title 38:

> § 445 [now 784] (Actions on claims; jurisdiction; parties; procedure; limitation; witnesses; definitions) (Veterans' insurance contracts).

The second paragraph continues the present procedure applicable to certain witnesses who are in foreign countries. See U.S.C., Title 28, §§ 711 [now 1783] (Letters rogatory to take testimony of witness, addressed to court of foreign country; failure of witness to appear; subpoena) and 713 [now 1783] (Service of Subpoena on witness in foreign country).

Note to Subdivision (f). Compare [former] Equity Rule 52 (Attendance of Witnesses Before Commissioner, Master, or Examiner).

1946 Amendment

Note to Subdivision (b). The added words, "or tangible things" in subdivision (b) merely make the rule for the subpoena duces tecum at the trial conform to that of subdivision (d) for the subpoena at the taking of depositions. The insertion of the words "or modify" in clause (1) affords desirable flexibility.

Subdivision (d). The added last sentence of amended subdivision (d)(1) properly gives the subpoena for documents or tangible things the same scope as provided in Rule 26(b), thus promoting uniformity. The requirement in the last sentence of original Rule 45(d)(1)—to the effect that leave of court should be obtained for the issuance of such a subpoena—has been omitted. This requirement is unnecessary and oppressive on both counsel and court, and it had been criticized by district judges. There is no satisfactory reason for a differentiation between a subpoena for the production of documentary evidence by a witness at a trial (Rule 45(a)) and for the production of the same evidence at the taking of a deposition. Under this amendment, the person subpoenaed may obtain the protection afforded by any of the orders permitted under Rule 30(b) or Rule 45(b). See *Application of Zenith Radio Corp.,* E.D.Pa.1941, 4 F.Rules Serv. 30b.21. Case 1, 1 F.R.D.

627; *Fox v. House,* Okla.1939, 29 F.Supp. 673; *United States of America for the Use of Tilo Roofing Co., Inc. v. J. Slotnik Co.,* Conn.1944, 3 F.R.D. 408.

The changes in subdivisions (d)(2) give the court the same power in the case of residents of the district as is conferred in the case of non-residents, and permit the court to fix a place for attendance which may be more convenient and accessible for the parties than that specified in the rule.

1948 Amendment

The amendment effective October 1949, substituted the reference to "Title 28, U.S.C., § 1783" at the end of subdivision (e)(2) for the reference to "the Act of July 3, 1926, c. 762, §§ 1, 3 (44 Stat. 835), U.S.C., Title 28, § 713."

1970 Amendment

At present, when a subpoena duces tecum is issued to a deponent, he is required to produce the listed materials at the deposition, but is under no clear compulsion to permit their inspection and copying. This results in confusion and uncertainty before the time the deposition is taken, with no mechanism provided whereby the court can resolve the matter. Rule 45(d)(1), as revised, makes clear that the subpoena authorizes inspection and copying of the materials produced. The deponent is afforded full protection since he can object, thereby forcing the party serving the subpoena to obtain a court order if he wishes to inspect and copy. The procedure is thus analogous to that provided in Rule 34.

The changed references to other rules conform to changes made in those rules. The deletion of words in the clause describing the proper scope of the subpoena conforms to a change made in the language of Rule 34. The reference to Rule 26(b) is unchanged but encompasses new matter in that subdivision. The changes make it clear that the scope of discovery through a subpoena is the same as that applicable to Rule 34 and the other discovery rules.

1980 Amendment

Subdivision (d)(1). The amendment defines the term "proof of service" as used in the first sentence of the present subdivision. For want of a definition, the district court clerks have been obliged to fashion their own, with results that vary from district to district. All that seems required is a simple certification on a copy of the notice to take a deposition that the notice has been served on every other party to the action. That is the proof of service required by Rule 25(d) of both the Federal Rules of Appellate Procedure and the Supreme Court Rules.

Subdivision (e)(1). The amendment makes the reach of a subpoena of a district court at least as extensive as that of the state courts of general jurisdiction in the state in which the district court is held. Under the present rule the reach of a district court subpoena is often greater, since it extends throughout the district. No reason appears why it should be less, as it sometimes is because of the accident of district lines. Restrictions upon the reach of subpoenas are imposed to prevent undue inconvenience to witnesses. State statutes and rules of court are quite likely to reflect the varying degrees of difficulty and expense attendant upon local travel.

1985 Amendment

Present Rule 45(d)(2) has two sentences setting forth the territorial scope of deposition subpoenas. The first sentence is directed to depositions taken in the judicial district in which the deponent resides; the second sentence addresses situations in which the deponent is not a resident of the district in which the deposition is to take place. The Rule, as currently constituted, creates anomalous situations that often cause logistical problems in conducting litigation.

The first sentence of the present Rule states that a deponent may be required to attend only in the *county* wherein that person resides or is employed or transacts business in person, that is, where the person lives or works. Under this provision a deponent can be compelled, without court order, to travel from one end of that person's home county to the other, no matter how far that may be. The second sentence of the Rule is somewhat more flexible, stating that someone who does not reside in the district in which the deposition is to be taken can be required to attend in the county where the person is served with the subpoena, *or* within 40 miles from the place of service.

Under today's conditions there is no sound reason for distinguishing between residents of the district or county in which a deposition is to be taken and nonresidents, and the Rule is amended to provide that any person may be subpoenaed to attend a deposition within a specified radius from that person's residence, place of business, or where the person was served. The 40-mile radius has been increased to 100 miles.

1987 Amendment

The amendments are technical. No substantive change is intended.

1991 Amendment

Purposes of Revision. The purposes of this revision are (1) to clarify and enlarge the protections afforded persons who are required to assist the court by giving information or evidence; (2) to facilitate access outside the deposition procedure provided by Rule 30 to documents and other information in the possession of persons who are not parties; (3) to facilitate service of subpoenas for depositions or productions of evidence at places distant from the district in which an action is proceeding; (4) to enable the court to compel a witness found within the state in which the court sits to attend trial; (5) to clarify the organization of the text of the rule.

Subdivision (a). This subdivision is amended in seven significant respects.

First, Paragraph (a)(3) modifies the requirement that a subpoena be issued by the clerk of court. Provision is made for the issuance of subpoenas by attorneys as officers of the court. This revision perhaps culminates an evolution. Subpoenas were long issued by specific order of the court. As this became a burden to the court, general orders were made authorizing clerks to issue subpoenas on request. Since 1948, they have been issued in blank by the clerk of any federal court to any lawyer, the clerk serving as stationer to the bar. In allowing counsel to issue the subpoena, the rule is merely a recognition of present reality.

Although the subpoena is in a sense the command of the attorney who completes the form, defiance of a subpoena is nevertheless an act in defiance of a court order and exposes the defiant witness to contempt sanctions. In *ICC v. Brimson,* 154 U.S. 447 (1894), the Court upheld a statute directing federal courts to issue subpoenas to compel testimony before the ICC. In *CAB v. Hermann,* 353 U.S. 322 (1957), the Court approved as established practice the issuance of administrative subpoenas as a matter of absolute agency right. And in *NLRB v. Warren Co.,* 350 U.S. 107 (1955), the Court held that the lower court had no discretion to withhold sanctions against a contemnor who violated such subpoenas. The 1948 revision of Rule 45 put the attorney in a position similar to that of the administrative agency, as a public officer entitled to use the court's contempt power to investigate facts in dispute. Two courts of appeals have touched on the issue and have described lawyer-issued subpoenas as mandates of the court. *Waste Conversion, Inc. v. Rollins Environmental Services (NJ), Inc.,* 893 F.2d 605 (3d Cir., 1990); *Fisher v. Marubent Cotton Corp.,* 526 F.2d 1338, 1340 (8th Cir., 1975). Cf. *Young v. United States ex rel. Vuitton et Fils S.A.,* 481 U.S. 787, 821 (1987) (Scalia, J., concurring). This revision makes the rule explicit that the attorney acts as an officer of the court in issuing and signing subpoenas.

Necessarily accompanying the evolution of this power of the lawyer as officer of the court is the development of increased responsibility and liability for the misuse of this power. The latter development is reflected in the provisions of subdivision (c) of this rule, and also in the requirement imposed by paragraph (3) of this subdivision that the attorney issuing a subpoena must sign it.

Second, Paragraph (a)(3) authorizes attorneys in distant districts to serve as officers authorized to issue commands in the name of the court. Any attorney permitted to represent a client in a federal court, even one admitted pro haec vice, has the same authority as a clerk to issue a subpoena from any federal court for the district in which the subpoena is served and enforced. In authorizing attorneys to issue subpoenas from distant courts, the amended rule effectively authorizes service of a subpoena anywhere in the United States by an attorney representing any party. This change is intended to ease the administrative burdens of inter-district law practice. The former rule resulted in delay and expense caused by the need to secure forms from clerks' offices some distance from the place at which the action proceeds. This change does not enlarge the burden on the witness.

Pursuant to Paragraph (a)(2), a subpoena for a deposition must still issue from the court in which the deposition or production would be compelled. Accordingly, a motion to quash such a subpoena if it overbears the limits of the subpoena power must, as under the previous rule, be presented to the court for the district in which the deposition would occur. Likewise, the court in whose name the subpoena is issued is responsible for its enforcement.

Third, in order to relieve attorneys of the need to secure an appropriate seal to affix to a subpoena issued as an officer of a distant court, the requirement that a subpoena be under seal is abolished by the provisions of Paragraph (a)(1).

Fourth, Paragraph (a)(1) authorizes the issuance of a subpoena to compel a non-party to produce evidence independent of any deposition. This revision spares the necessity of a deposition of the custodian of evidentiary material required to be produced. A party seeking additional production from a person subject to such a subpoena may serve an additional subpoena requiring additional production at the same time and place.

Fifth, Paragraph (a)(2) makes clear that the person subject to the subpoena is required to produce materials in that person's control whether or not the materials are located within the district or within the territory within which the subpoena can be served. The non-party witness is subject to the same scope of discovery under this rule as that person would be as a party to whom a request is addressed pursuant to Rule 34.

Sixth, Paragraph (a)(1) requires that the subpoena include a statement of the rights and duties of witnesses by setting forth in full the text of the new subdivisions (c) and (d).

Seventh, the revised rule authorizes the issuance of a subpoena to compel the inspection of premises in the possession of a non-party. Rule 34 has authorized such inspections of premises in the possession of a party as discovery compelled under Rule 37, but prior practice required an independent proceeding to secure such relief ancillary to the federal proceeding when the premises were not in the possession of a party. Practice in some states has long authorized such use of a subpoena for this purpose without apparent adverse consequence.

Subdivision (b). Paragraph (b)(1) retains the text of the former subdivision (c) with minor changes.

The reference to the United States marshal and deputy marshal is deleted because of the infrequency of the use of these officers for this purpose. Inasmuch as these officers meet the age requirement, they may still be used if available.

A provision requiring service of prior notice pursuant to Rule 5 of compulsory pretrial production or inspection has been added to paragraph (b)(1). The purpose of such notice is to afford other parties an opportunity to object to the production or inspection, or to serve a demand for additional documents or things. Such additional notice is not needed with respect to a deposition because of the requirement of notice imposed by Rule 30 or 31. But when production or inspection is sought independently of a deposition, other parties may need notice in order to monitor the discovery and in order to pursue access to any information that may or should be produced.

Paragraph (b)(2) retains language formerly set forth in subdivision (e) and extends its application to subpoenas for depositions or production.

Paragraph (b)(3) retains language formerly set forth in paragraph (d)(1) and extends its applications to subpoenas for trial or hearing or production.

Subdivision (c). This provision is new and states the rights of witnesses. It is not intended to diminish rights conferred by Rules 26–37 or any other authority.

Paragraph (c)(1) gives specific application to the principle stated in Rule 26(g) and specifies liability for earnings lost by a non-party witness as a result of a misuse of the subpoena. No change in existing law is thereby effected. Abuse of a subpoena is an actionable tort, *Board of Ed. v. Farmingdale Classroom Teach. Ass'n,* 38 N.Y.2d 397, 380 N.Y.S.2d 635, 343 N.E.2d 278 (1975), and the duty of the attorney to the non-party is also embodied in Model Rule of Professional Conduct 4.4. The liability of the attorney is correlative to the expanded power of the attorney to issue subpoenas. The liability may include the cost of fees to collect attorneys' fees owed as a result of a breach of this duty.

Paragraph (c)(2) retains language from the former subdivision (b) and paragraph (d)(1). The 10-day period for response to a subpoena is extended to 14 days to avoid the complex calculations associated with short time periods under Rule 6 and to allow a bit more time for such objections to be made.

A non-party required to produce documents or materials is protected against significant expense resulting from involuntary assistance to the court. This provision applies, for example, to a non-party required to provide a list of class members. The court is not required to fix the costs in advance of production, although this will often be the most satisfactory accommodation to protect the party seeking discovery from excessive costs. In some instances, it may be preferable to leave uncertain costs to be determined after the materials have been produced, provided that the risk of uncertainty is fully disclosed to the discovering party. See, *e.g., United States v. Columbia Broadcasting Systems, Inc.,* 666 F.2d 364 (9th Cir.1982).

Paragraph (c)(3) explicitly authorizes the quashing of a subpoena as a means of protecting a witness from misuse of the subpoena power. It replaces and enlarges on the former subdivision (b) of this rule and tracks the provisions of Rule 26(c). While largely repetitious, this rule is addressed to the witness who may read it on the subpoena, where it is required to be printed by the revised paragraph (a)(1) of this rule.

Subparagraph (c)(3)(A) identifies those circumstances in which a subpoena must be quashed or modified. It restates the former provisions with respect to the limits of mandatory travel that are set forth in the former paragraphs (d)(2) and (e)(1), with one important change. Under the revised rule, a federal court can compel a witness to come from any place in the state to attend trial, whether or not the local state law so provides. This extension is subject to the qualification provided in the next paragraph, which authorizes the court to condition enforcement of a subpoena compelling a non-party witness to bear substantial expense to attend trial. The traveling non-party witness may be entitled to reasonable compensation for the time and effort entailed.

Clause (c)(3)(A)(iv) requires the court to protect all persons from undue burden imposed by the use of the subpoena power. Illustratively, it might be unduly burdensome to compel an adversary to attend trial as a witness if the adversary is known to have no personal knowledge of matters in dispute, especially so if the adversary would be required to incur substantial travel burdens.

Subparagraph (c)(3)(B) identifies circumstances in which a subpoena should be quashed unless the party serving the subpoena shows a substantial need and the court can devise an appropriate accommodation to protect the interests of the witness. An additional circumstance in which such action is required is a request for costly production of documents; that situation is expressly governed by subparagraph (b)(2)(B)*.

Clause (c)(3)(B)(i) authorizes the court to quash, modify, or condition a subpoena to protect the person subject to or affected by the subpoena from unnecessary or unduly harmful disclosures of confidential information. It corresponds to Rule 26(c)(7).

Clause (c)(3)(B)(ii) provides appropriate protection for the intellectual property of the non-party witness; it does not apply to the expert retained by a party, whose information is subject to the provisions of Rule 26(b)(4). A growing problem has been the use of subpoenas to compel the giving of evidence and information by unretained experts. Experts are not exempt from the duty to give evidence, even if they cannot be compelled to prepare themselves to give effective testimony, *e.g., Carter-Wallace, Inc. v. Otte,* 474 F.2d 529 (2d Cir.1972), but compulsion to give evidence may threaten the intellectual property of experts denied the opportunity to bargain for the value of their services. See generally Maurer, *Compelling the Expert Witness: Fairness and Utility Under the Federal Rules of Civil Procedure,* 19 GA.L.REV. 71 (1984); Note, *Discovery and Testimony of Unretained Experts,* 1987 DUKE L.J. 140. Arguably the compulsion to testify can be regarded as a "taking" of intellectual property. The rule establishes the right of such persons to withhold their expertise, at least unless the party seeking it makes the kind of showing required for a conditional denial of a motion to quash as provided in the final sentence of subparagraph (c)(3)(B); that requirement is the same as that necessary to secure work product under Rule 26(b)(3) and gives assurance of reasonable compensation. The Rule thus approves the accommodation of competing interests exemplified in *United States v. Columbia Broadcasting Systems Inc.,* 666 F.2d 364 (9th Cir.1982). See also *Wright v. Jeep Corporation,* 547 F.Supp. 871 (E.D.Mich.1982).

As stated in *Kaufman v. Edelstein,* 539 F.2d 811, 822 (2d Cir.1976), the district court's discretion in these matters should be informed by "the degree to which the expert is being called because of his knowledge of facts relevant to the case rather than in order to give opinion testimony; the difference between testifying to a previously formed or expressed opinion and forming a new one; the possibility that, for other reasons,

---

*   [So in original. Probably should be "subparagraph (c)(2)(B)". Ed.]

the witness is a unique expert; the extent to which the calling party is able to show the unlikelihood that any comparable witness will willingly testify; and the degree to which the witness is able to show that he has been oppressed by having continually to testify. . . ."

Clause (c)(3)(B)(iii) protects non-party witnesses who may be burdened to perform the duty to travel in order to provide testimony at trial. The provision requires the court to condition a subpoena requiring travel of more than 100 miles on reasonable compensation.

Subdivision (d). This provision is new. Paragraph (d)(1) extends to non-parties the duty imposed on parties by the last paragraph of Rule 34(b), which was added in 1980.

Paragraph (d)(2) is new and corresponds to the new Rule 26(b)(5) [paragraph (5) in Rule 26(b) was a proposed paragraph which was withdrawn by the Supreme Court]. Its purpose is to provide a party whose discovery is constrained by a claim of privilege or work product protection with information sufficient to evaluate such a claim and to resist if it seems unjustified. The person claiming a privilege or protection cannot decide the limits of that party's own entitlement.

A party receiving a discovery request who asserts a privilege or protection but fails to disclose that claim is at risk of waiving the privilege or protection. A person claiming a privilege or protection who fails to provide adequate information about the privilege or protection claim to the party seeking the information is subject to an order to show cause why the person should not be held in contempt under subdivision (e). Motions for such orders and responses to motions are subject to the sanctions provisions of Rules 7 and 11.

A person served a subpoena that is too broad may be faced with a burdensome task to provide full information regarding all that person's claims to privilege or work product protection. Such a person is entitled to protection that may be secured through an objection made pursuant to paragraph (c)(2).

Subdivision (e). This provision retains most of the language of the former subdivision (f).

"Adequate cause" for a failure to obey a subpoena remains undefined. In at least some circumstances, a non-party might be guilty of contempt for refusing to obey a subpoena even though the subpoena manifestly overreaches the appropriate limits of the subpoena power. *E.g., Walker v. City of Birmingham,* 388 U.S. 307 (1967). But, because the command of the subpoena is not in fact one uttered by a judicial officer, contempt should be very sparingly applied when the non-party witness has been overborne by a party or attorney. The language added to subdivision (f) is intended to assure that result where a non-party has been commanded, on the signature of an attorney, to travel greater distances than can be compelled pursuant to this rule.

2005 Amendments

This amendment closes a small gap in regard to notifying witnesses of the manner for recording a deposition. A deposition subpoena must state the method for recording the testimony.

Rule 30(b)(2) directs that the party noticing a deposition state in the notice the manner for recording the testimony, but the notice need not be served on the deponent. The deponent learns of the recording method only if the deponent is a party or is informed by a party. Rule 30(b)(3) permits another party to designate an additional method of recording with prior notice to the deponent and the other parties. The deponent thus has notice of the recording method when an additional method is designated. This amendment completes the notice provisions to ensure that a nonparty deponent has notice of the recording method when the recording method is described only in the deposition notice.

A subpoenaed witness does not have a right to refuse to proceed with a deposition due to objections to the manner of recording. But under rare circumstances, a nonparty witness might have a ground for seeking a protective order under Rule 26(c) with regard to the manner of recording or the use of the deposition if recorded in a certain manner. Should such a witness not learn of the manner of recording until the deposition begins, undesirable delay or complication might result. Advance notice of the recording method affords an opportunity to raise such protective issues.

Other changes are made to conform Rule 45(a)(2) to current style conventions.

2006 Amendments

Rule 45 is amended to conform the provisions for subpoenas to changes in other discovery rules, largely related to discovery of electronically stored information. Rule 34 is amended to provide in greater detail for the production of electronically stored information. Rule 45(a)(1)(C) is amended to recognize that electronically stored information, as defined in Rule 34(a), can also be sought by subpoena. Like Rule 34(b), Rule 45(a)(1) is amended to provide that the subpoena can designate a form or forms for production of electronic data. Rule 45(c)(2) is amended, like Rule 34(b), to authorize the person served with a subpoena to object to the requested form or forms. In addition, as under Rule 34(b), Rule 45(d)(1)(B) is amended to provide that if the subpoena does not specify the form or forms for electronically stored information, the person served with the subpoena must produce electronically stored information in a form or forms in which it is usually maintained or in a form or forms that are reasonably usable. Rule 45(d)(1)(C) is added to provide that the person producing electronically stored information should not have to produce the same information in more than one form unless so ordered by the court for good cause.

As with discovery of electronically stored information from parties, complying with a subpoena for such information may impose burdens on the responding person. Rule 45(c) provides protection against undue impositions on nonparties. For example, Rule 45(c)(1) directs that a party serving a subpoena "shall take reasonable steps to avoid imposing undue burden or expense on a person subject to the subpoena," and Rule 45(c)(2)(B) permits the person served with the subpoena to object to it and directs that an order requiring compliance "shall protect a person who is neither a party nor a party's officer from significant expense resulting from" compliance. Rule 45(d)(1)(D) is added to provide that the responding person need not provide discovery of electronically stored information from sources the party identifies as not reasonably accessible, unless the court orders such discovery for good cause, considering the limitations of Rule 26(b)(2)(C), on terms that protect a nonparty against significant expense. A parallel provision is added to Rule 26(b)(2).

Rule 45(a)(1)(B) is also amended, as is Rule 34(a), to provide that a subpoena is available to permit testing and sampling as well as inspection and copying. As in Rule 34, this change recognizes that on occasion the opportunity to perform testing or sampling may be important, both for documents and for electronically stored information. Because testing or sampling may present particular issues of burden or intrusion for the person served with the subpoena, however, the protective provisions of Rule 45(c) should be enforced with vigilance when such demands are made. Inspection or testing of certain types of electronically stored information or of a person's electronic information system may raise issues of confidentiality or privacy. The addition of sampling and testing to Rule 45(a) with regard to documents and electronically stored information is not meant to create a routine right of direct access to a person's electronic information system, although such access might be justified in some circumstances. Courts should guard against undue intrusiveness resulting from inspecting or testing such systems.

Rule 45(d)(2) is amended, as is Rule 26(b)(5), to add a procedure for assertion of privilege or of protection as trial-preparation materials after production. The receiving party may submit the information to the court for resolution of the privilege claim, as under Rule 26(b)(5)(B).

Other minor amendments are made to conform the rule to the changes described above.

2007 Amendment

The language of Rule 45 has been amended as part of the general restyling of the Civil Rules to make them more easily understood and to make style and terminology consistent throughout the rules. These changes are intended to be stylistic only.

The reference to discovery of "books" in former Rule 45(a)(1)(C) was deleted to achieve consistent expression throughout the discovery rules. Books remain a proper subject of discovery.

Former Rule 45(b)(1) required "prior notice" to each party of any commanded production of documents and things or inspection of premises. Courts have agreed that notice must be given "prior" to the return date, and have tended to converge on an interpretation that requires notice to the parties before the subpoena is served on the person commanded to produce or permit inspection. That interpretation is adopted in amended Rule 45(b)(1) to give clear notice of general present practice.

The language of former Rule 45(d)(2) addressing the manner of asserting privilege is replaced by adopting the wording of Rule 26(b)(5). The same meaning is better expressed in the same words.

2013 Amendment

Rule 45 was extensively amended in 1991. The goal of the present amendments is to clarify and simplify the rule. The amendments recognize the court where the action is pending as the issuing court, permit nationwide service of a subpoena, and collect in a new subdivision (c) the previously scattered provisions regarding place of compliance. These changes resolve a conflict that arose after the 1991 amendment about a court's authority to compel a party or party officer to travel long distances to testify at trial; such testimony may now be required only as specified in new Rule 45(c). In addition, the amendments introduce authority in new Rule 45(f) for the court where compliance is required to transfer a subpoena-related motion to the court where the action is pending on consent of the person subject to the subpoena or in exceptional circumstances.

Subdivision (a). This subdivision is amended to provide that a subpoena issues from the court where the action is pending. Subdivision (a)(3) specifies that an attorney authorized to practice in that court may issue a subpoena, which is consistent with current practice.

In Rule 45(a)(1)(D), "person" is substituted for "party" because the subpoena may be directed to a nonparty.

Rule 45(a)(4) is added to highlight and slightly modify a notice requirement first included in the rule in 1991. Under the 1991 amendments, Rule 45(b)(1) required prior notice of the service of a "documents only" subpoena to the other parties. Rule 45(b)(1) was clarified in 2007 to specify that this notice must be served before the subpoena is served on the witness.

The Committee has been informed that parties serving subpoenas frequently fail to give the required notice to the other parties. The amendment moves the notice requirement to a new provision in Rule 45(a) and requires that the notice include a copy of the subpoena. The amendments are intended to achieve the original purpose of enabling the other parties to object or to serve a subpoena for additional materials.

Parties desiring access to information produced in response to the subpoena will need to follow up with the party serving it or the person served to obtain such access. The rule does not limit the court's authority to order notice of receipt of produced materials or access to them. The party serving the subpoena should in any event make reasonable provision for prompt access.

Subdivision (b). The former notice requirement in Rule 45(b)(1) has been moved to new Rule 45(a)(4).

Rule 45(b)(2) is amended to provide that a subpoena may be served at any place within the United States, removing the complexities prescribed in prior versions.

Subdivision (c). Subdivision (c) is new. It collects the various provisions on where compliance can be required and simplifies them. Unlike the prior rule, place of service is not critical to place of compliance. Although Rule 45(a)(1)(A)(iii) permits the subpoena to direct a place of compliance, that place must be selected under Rule 45(c).

Rule 45(c)(1) addresses a subpoena to testify at a trial, hearing, or deposition. Rule 45(c)(1)(A) provides that compliance may be required within 100 miles of where the person subject to the subpoena resides, is employed, or regularly conducts business in person. For parties and party officers, Rule 45(c)(1)(B)(i) provides that compliance may be required anywhere in the state where the person resides, is employed, or regularly conducts business in person. When an order under Rule 43(a) authorizes testimony from a remote location, the witness can be commanded to testify from any place described in Rule 45(c)(1).

Under Rule 45(c)(1)(B)(ii), nonparty witnesses can be required to travel more than 100 miles within the state where they reside, are employed, or regularly transact business in person only if they would not, as a result, incur "substantial expense." When travel over 100 miles could impose substantial expense on the witness, the party that served the subpoena may pay that expense and the court can condition enforcement of the subpoena on such payment.

Because Rule 45(c) directs that compliance may be commanded only as it provides, these amendments resolve a split in interpreting Rule 45's provisions for subpoenaing parties and party officers. *Compare In re Vioxx Products Liability Litigation*, 438 F. Supp. 2d 664 (E.D. La. 2006) (finding authority to compel a party officer from New Jersey to testify at trial in New Orleans), *with Johnson v. Big Lots Stores, Inc.*, 251 F.R.D. 213 (E.D. La. 2008) (holding that Rule 45 did not require attendance of plaintiffs at trial in New

Orleans when they would have to travel more than 100 miles from outside the state). Rule 45(c)(1)(A) does not authorize a subpoena for trial to require a party or party officer to travel more than 100 miles unless the party or party officer resides, is employed, or regularly transacts business in person in the state.

Depositions of parties, and officers, directors, and managing agents of parties need not involve use of a subpoena. Under Rule 37(d)(1)(A)(i), failure of such a witness whose deposition was properly noticed to appear for the deposition can lead to Rule 37(b) sanctions (including dismissal or default but not contempt) without regard to service of a subpoena and without regard to the geographical limitations on compliance with a subpoena. These amendments do not change that existing law; the courts retain their authority to control the place of party depositions and impose sanctions for failure to appear under Rule 37(b).

For other discovery, Rule 45(c)(2) directs that inspection of premises occur at those premises, and that production of documents, tangible things, and electronically stored information may be commanded to occur at a place within 100 miles of where the person subject to the subpoena resides, is employed, or regularly conducts business in person. Under the current rule, parties often agree that production, particularly of electronically stored information, be transmitted by electronic means. Such arrangements facilitate discovery, and nothing in these amendments limits the ability of parties to make such arrangements.

Rule 45(d)(3)(A)(ii) directs the court to quash any subpoena that purports to compel compliance beyond the geographical limits specified in Rule 45(c).

Subdivision (d). Subdivision (d) contains the provisions formerly in subdivision (c). It is revised to recognize the court where the action is pending as the issuing court, and to take account of the addition of Rule 45(c) to specify where compliance with a subpoena is required.

Subdivision (f). Subdivision (f) is new. Under Rules 45(d)(2)(B), 45(d)(3), and 45(e)(2)(B), subpoena-related motions and applications are to be made to the court where compliance is required under Rule 45(c). Rule 45(f) provides authority for that court to transfer the motion to the court where the action is pending. It applies to all motions under this rule, including an application under Rule 45(e)(2)(B) for a privilege determination.

Subpoenas are essential to obtain discovery from nonparties. To protect local nonparties, local resolution of disputes about subpoenas is assured by the limitations of Rule 45(c) and the requirements in Rules 45(d) and (e) that motions be made in the court in which compliance is required under Rule 45(c). But transfer to the court where the action is pending is sometimes warranted. If the person subject to the subpoena consents to transfer, Rule 45(f) provides that the court where compliance is required may do so.

In the absence of consent, the court may transfer in exceptional circumstances, and the proponent of transfer bears the burden of showing that such circumstances are present. The prime concern should be avoiding burdens on local nonparties subject to subpoenas, and it should not be assumed that the issuing court is in a superior position to resolve subpoena-related motions. In some circumstances, however, transfer may be warranted in order to avoid disrupting the issuing court's management of the underlying litigation, as when that court has already ruled on issues presented by the motion or the same issues are likely to arise in discovery in many districts. Transfer is appropriate only if such interests outweigh the interests of the nonparty served with the subpoena in obtaining local resolution of the motion. Judges in compliance districts may find it helpful to consult with the judge in the issuing court presiding over the underlying case while addressing subpoena-related motions.

If the motion is transferred, judges are encouraged to permit telecommunications methods to minimize the burden a transfer imposes on nonparties, if it is necessary for attorneys admitted in the court where the motion is made to appear in the court in which the action is pending. The rule provides that if these attorneys are authorized to practice in the court where the motion is made, they may file papers and appear in the court in which the action is pending in relation to the motion as officers of that court.

After transfer, the court where the action is pending will decide the motion. If the court rules that discovery is not justified, that should end the matter. If the court orders further discovery, it is possible that retransfer may be important to enforce the order. One consequence of failure to obey such an order is contempt, addressed in Rule 45(g). Rule 45(g) and Rule 37(b)(1) are both amended to provide that disobedience of an order enforcing a subpoena after transfer is contempt of the issuing court and the court where compliance is required under Rule 45(c). In some instances, however, there may be a question about whether the issuing court can impose contempt sanctions on a distant nonparty. If such circumstances arise, or if it is better to supervise compliance in the court where compliance is required, the rule provides authority for retransfer for enforcement. Although changed circumstances may prompt a modification of such an order, it is not expected that the compliance court will reexamine the resolution of the underlying motion.

Subdivision (g). Subdivision (g) carries forward the authority of former subdivision (e) to punish disobedience of subpoenas as contempt. It is amended to make clear that, in the event of transfer of a subpoena-related motion, such disobedience constitutes contempt of both the court where compliance is required under Rule 45(c) and the court where the action is pending. If necessary for effective enforcement, Rule 45(f) authorizes the issuing court to transfer its order after the motion is resolved.

The rule is also amended to clarify that contempt sanctions may be applied to a person who disobeys a subpoena-related order, as well as one who fails entirely to obey a subpoena. In civil litigation, it would be rare for a court to use contempt sanctions without first ordering compliance with a subpoena, and the order might not require all the compliance sought by the subpoena. Often contempt proceedings will be initiated by an order to show cause, and an order to comply or be held in contempt may modify the subpoena's command. Disobedience of such an order may be treated as contempt.

The second sentence of former subdivision (e) is deleted as unnecessary.

TREATIES AND CONVENTIONS

Taking of Evidence Abroad in Civil or Commercial Matters; Observance On and After Oct. 7, 1972, by United States and Citizens and Persons Subject to Jurisdiction of United States

For text of Convention, see provisions set out as a note under section 1781 of Title 28.

Rule 46.   Objecting to a Ruling or Order

A formal exception to a ruling or order is unnecessary. When the ruling or order is requested or made, a party need only state the action that it wants the court to take or objects to, along with the grounds for the request or objection. Failing to object does not prejudice a party who had no opportunity to do so when the ruling or order was made.

(Amended March 2, 1987, effective August 1, 1987; April 30, 2007, effective December 1, 2007.)

ADVISORY COMMITTEE NOTES

1937 Adoption

Abolition of formal exceptions is often provided by statute. See Ill.Rev.Stat. (1937), ch. 110, § 204; Neb.Comp.Stat. (1929) § 20–1139; N.M.Stat.Ann. (Courtright, 1929) § 105–830; 2 N.D.Comp.Laws Ann. (1913) § 7653; Ohio Code Ann. (Throckmorton, 1936) § 11560; 1 S.D.Comp.Laws (1929) § 2542; Utah Rev.Stat.Ann. (1933) §§ 104–39–2, 104–24–18; Va.Rules of Court, Rule 22, 163 Va. v. xii (1935); Wis.Stat. (1935) § 270.39. Compare N.Y.C.P.A. (1937) §§ 583, 445, and 446, all as amended by L.1936, ch. 915. Rule 51 deals with objections to the court's instructions to the jury.

U.S.C., Title 28, [former] § 776 (Bill of exceptions; authentication; signing of by judge) and [former] § 875 (Review of findings in cases tried without a jury) are superseded insofar as they provide for formal exceptions, and a bill of exceptions.

1987 Amendment

The amendments are technical. No substantive change is intended.

2007 Amendments

The language of Rule 46 has been amended as part of the general restyling of the Civil Rules to make them more easily understood and to make style and terminology consistent throughout the rules. These changes are intended to be stylistic only.

Rule 47.   Selecting Jurors

(a) Examining Jurors. The court may permit the parties or their attorneys to examine prospective jurors or may itself do so. If the court examines the jurors, it must permit the parties or their attorneys to make any further inquiry it considers proper, or must itself ask any of their additional questions it considers proper.

(b) Peremptory Challenges. The court must allow the number of peremptory challenges provided by 28 U.S.C. § 1870.

(c) Excusing a Juror. During trial or deliberation, the court may excuse a juror for good cause.

(Amended February 28, 1966, effective July 1, 1966; April 30, 1991, effective December 1, 1991; April 30, 2007, effective December 1, 2007.)

ADVISORY COMMITTEE NOTES

1937 Adoption

Note to Subdivision (a). This permits a practice found very useful by Federal trial judges. For an example of a state practice in which the examination by the court is supplemented by further inquiry by counsel, see Rule 27 of the Code of Rules for the District Courts of Minnesota, 186 Minn. xxxiii (1932), 3 Minn.Stat. (Mason, Supp.1936) Appendix 4, p. 1062.

Note to Subdivision (b). The provision for an alternate juror is one often found in modern state codes. See N.C.Code (1935) § 2330(a); Ohio Gen.Code Ann. (Page, Supp.1926–1935) § 11419–47; Pa.Stat.Ann. (Purdon, Supp.1936) Title 17, § 1153; compare U.S.C., Title 28, [former] § 417a (Alternate jurors in criminal trials); 1 N.J.Rev.Stat. (1937) 2:91A–1, 2:91A–2, 2:91A–3.

Provisions for qualifying, drawing, and challenging of jurors are found in U.S.C., Title 28:

§ 411 [now 1861] (Qualifications and exemptions)

§ 412 [now 1864] (Manner of drawing)

§ 413 [now 1865] (Apportioned in district)

§ 415 [see 1862] (Not disqualified because of race or color)

§ 416 [now 1867] (Venire; service and return)

§ 417 [now 1866] (Talesmen for petit jurors)

§ 418 [now 1866] (Special juries)

§ 423 [now 1869] (Jurors not to serve more than once a year)

§ 424 [now 1870] (Challenges)

and D.C.Code (1930) Title 18, §§ 341 to 360 (Juries and Jury Commission) and Title 6, § 366 (Peremptory challenges).

1966 Amendment

The revision of this subdivision brings it into line with the amendment of Rule 24(c) of this Federal Rules of Criminal Procedure. That rule previously allowed four alternate jurors, as contrasted with the two allowed in civil cases, and the amendments increase the number to a maximum of six in all cases. The Advisory Committee's Note to amended Criminal Rule 24(c) points to experience demonstrating that four alternates may not be enough in some lengthy criminal trials; and the same may be said of civil trials. The Note adds:

"The words 'or are found to be' are added to the second sentence to make clear that an alternate juror may be called in the situation where it is first discovered during the trial that a juror was unable or disqualified to perform his duties at the time he was sworn."

1991 Amendment

Subdivision (b). The former provision for alternate jurors is stricken and the institution of the alternate juror abolished.

The former rule reflected the long-standing assumption that a jury would consist of exactly twelve members. It provided for additional jurors to be used as substitutes for jurors who are for any reason excused or disqualified from service after the commencement of the trial. Additional jurors were traditionally designated at the outset of the trial, and excused at the close of the evidence if they had not been promoted to full service on account of the elimination of one of the original jurors.

The use of alternate jurors has been a source of dissatisfaction with the jury system because of the burden it places on alternates who are required to listen to the evidence but denied the satisfaction of participating in its evaluation.

Subdivision (c). This provision makes it clear that the court may in appropriate circumstances excuse a juror during the jury deliberations without causing a mistrial. Sickness, family emergency or juror misconduct that might occasion a mistrial are examples of appropriate grounds for excusing a juror. It is not grounds for the dismissal of a juror that the juror refuses to join with fellow jurors in reaching a unanimous verdict.

2007 Amendments

The language of Rule 47 has been amended as part of the general restyling of the Civil Rules to make them more easily understood and to make style and terminology consistent throughout the rules. These changes are intended to be stylistic only.

Rule 48.   Number of Jurors; Verdict; Polling

(a) Number of Jurors. A jury must begin with at least 6 and no more than 12 members, and each juror must participate in the verdict unless excused under Rule 47(c).

(b) Verdict. Unless the parties stipulate otherwise, the verdict must be unanimous and must be returned by a jury of at least 6 members.

(c) Polling. After a verdict is returned but before the jury is discharged, the court must on a party's request, or may on its own, poll the jurors individually. If the poll reveals a lack of unanimity or lack of assent by the number of jurors that the parties stipulated to, the court may direct the jury to deliberate further or may order a new trial.

(Amended April 30, 1991, effective December 1, 1991; April 30, 2007, effective December 1, 2007; March 26, 2009, effective December 1, 2009.)

ADVISORY COMMITTEE NOTES

1937 Adoption

For provisions in state codes, compare Utah Rev.Stat.Ann. (1933) § 48–0–5 (In civil cases parties may agree in open court on lesser number of jurors); 2 Wash.Rev.Stat.Ann. (Remington, 1932) § 323 (Parties may consent to any number of jurors not less than three).

1991 Amendment

The former rule was rendered obsolete by the adoption in many districts of local rules establishing six as the standard size for a civil jury.

It appears that the minimum size of a jury consistent with the Seventh Amendment is six. *Cf. Ballew v. Georgia*, 435 U.S. 223 (1978) (holding that a conviction based on a jury of less than six is a denial of due process of law). If the parties agree to trial before a smaller jury, a verdict can be taken, but the parties should not other than in exceptional circumstances be encouraged to waive the right to a jury of six, not only because of the constitutional stature of the right, but also because smaller juries are more erratic and less effective in serving to distribute responsibility for the exercise of judicial power.

Because the institution of the alternate juror has been abolished by the proposed revision of Rule 47, it will ordinarily be prudent and necessary, in order to provide for sickness or disability among jurors, to seat more than six jurors. The use of jurors in excess of six increases the representativeness of the jury and harms no interest of a party. *Ray v. Parkside Surgery Center*, 13 F.R.Serv. 585 (6th Cir.1989).

If the court takes the precaution of seating a jury larger than six, an illness occurring during the deliberation period will not result in a mistrial, as it did formerly, because all seated jurors will participate in the verdict and a sufficient number will remain to render a unanimous verdict of six or more.

In exceptional circumstances, as where a jury suffers depletions during trial and deliberation that are greater than can reasonably be expected, the parties may agree to be bound by a verdict rendered by fewer than six jurors. The court should not, however, rely upon the availability of such an agreement, for the use of juries smaller than six is problematic for reasons fully explained in *Ballew v. Georgia*, supra.

2007 Amendments

The language of Rule 48 has been amended as part of the general restyling of the Civil Rules to make them more easily understood and to make style and terminology consistent throughout the rules. These changes are intended to be stylistic only.

2009 Amendments

Jury polling is added as new subdivision (c), which is drawn from Criminal Rule 31(d) with minor revisions to reflect Civil Rules Style and the parties' opportunity to stipulate to a nonunanimous verdict.

Rule 49.   Special Verdict; General Verdict and Questions

(a) Special Verdict.

(1) *In General.* The court may require a jury to return only a special verdict in the form of a special written finding on each issue of fact. The court may do so by:

(A) submitting written questions susceptible of a categorical or other brief answer;

(B) submitting written forms of the special findings that might properly be made under the pleadings and evidence; or

(C) using any other method that the court considers appropriate.

(2) *Instructions.* The court must give the instructions and explanations necessary to enable the jury to make its findings on each submitted issue.

(3) *Issues Not Submitted.* A party waives the right to a jury trial on any issue of fact raised by the pleadings or evidence but not submitted to the jury unless, before the jury retires, the party demands its submission to the jury. If the party does not demand submission, the court may make a finding on the issue. If the court makes no finding, it is considered to have made a finding consistent with its judgment on the special verdict.

(b) General Verdict with Answers to Written Questions.

(1) *In General.* The court may submit to the jury forms for a general verdict, together with written questions on one or more issues of fact that the jury must decide. The court must give the instructions and explanations necessary to enable the jury to render a general verdict and answer the questions in writing, and must direct the jury to do both.

(2) *Verdict and Answers Consistent.* When the general verdict and the answers are consistent, the court must approve, for entry under Rule 58, an appropriate judgment on the verdict and answers.

(3) *Answers Inconsistent with the Verdict.* When the answers are consistent with each other but one or more is inconsistent with the general verdict, the court may:

(A) approve, for entry under Rule 58, an appropriate judgment according to the answers, notwithstanding the general verdict;

(B) direct the jury to further consider its answers and verdict; or

(C) order a new trial.

(4) *Answers Inconsistent with Each Other and the Verdict.* When the answers are inconsistent with each other and one or more is also inconsistent with the general verdict, judgment must not be entered; instead, the court must direct the jury to further consider its answers and verdict, or must order a new trial.

(Amended January 21, 1963, effective July 1, 1963; March 2, 1987, effective August 1, 1987; April 30, 2007, effective December 1, 2007.)

ADVISORY COMMITTEE NOTES

1937 Adoption

The Federal courts are not bound to follow state statutes authorizing or requiring the court to ask a jury to find a special verdict or to answer interrogatories. *Victor American Fuel Co. v. Peccarich,* 209 Fed. 568 (C.C.A.8th, 1913), cert. den. 232 U.S. 727, 34 S.Ct. 603, 58 L.Ed. 817 (1914); *Spokane and I.E.R. Co. v. Campbell,* 217 Fed. 518 (C.C.A.9th, 1914), affd. 241 U.S. 497, 36 S.Ct. 683, 60 L.Ed. 1125 (1916); Simkins, *Federal Practice* (1934) § 186. The power of a territory to adopt by statute the practice under Subdivision (b) has been sustained. *Walker v. New Mexico and Southern Pacific R.R.,* 165 U.S. 593, 17 S.Ct. 421, 41 L.Ed. 837 (1897); *Southwestern Brewery and Ice Co. v. Schmidt,* 226 U.S. 162, 33 S.Ct. 68, 57 L.Ed. 170 (1912).

Compare Wis.Stat. (1935) §§ 270.27, 270.28 and 270.30; Green, *A New Development in Jury Trial* (1927), 13 A.B.A.J. 715; *Morgan, A Brief History of Special Verdicts and Special Interrogatories,* 1923, 32 Yale L.J. 575.

The provisions of U.S.C., Title 28, [former] § 400(3) (now §§ 2201, 2202) (Declaratory judgments authorized; procedure) permitting the submission of issues of fact to a jury are covered by this rule.

1963 Amendment

This amendment conforms to the amendment of Rule 58. See the Advisory Committee's Note to Rule 58, as amended.

1987 Amendment

The amendments are technical. No substantive change is intended.

2007 Amendments

The language of Rule 49 has been amended as part of the general restyling of the Civil Rules to make them more easily understood and to make style and terminology consistent throughout the rules. These changes are intended to be stylistic only.

Rule 50. Judgment as a Matter of Law in a Jury Trial; Related Motion for a New Trial; Conditional Ruling

(a) Judgment as a Matter of Law.

(1) *In General.* If a party has been fully heard on an issue during a jury trial and the court finds that a reasonable jury would not have a legally sufficient evidentiary basis to find for the party on that issue, the court may:

(A) resolve the issue against the party; and

(B) grant a motion for judgment as a matter of law against the party on a claim or defense that, under the controlling law, can be maintained or defeated only with a favorable finding on that issue.

(2) *Motion.* A motion for judgment as a matter of law may be made at any time before the case is submitted to the jury. The motion must specify the judgment sought and the law and facts that entitle the movant to the judgment.

(b) Renewing the Motion After Trial; Alternative Motion for a New Trial. If the court does not grant a motion for judgment as a matter of law made under Rule 50(a), the court is considered to have submitted the action to the jury subject to the court's later deciding the legal questions raised by the motion. No later than 28 days after the entry of judgment—or if the motion addresses a jury issue not decided by a verdict, no later than 28 days after the jury was discharged—the movant may file a renewed motion for judgment as a matter of law and may include an alternative or joint request for a new trial under Rule 59. In ruling on the renewed motion, the court may:

(1) allow judgment on the verdict, if the jury returned a verdict;

(2) order a new trial; or

(3) direct the entry of judgment as a matter of law.

(c) Granting the Renewed Motion; Conditional Ruling on a Motion for a New Trial.

(1) *In General.* If the court grants a renewed motion for judgment as a matter of law, it must also conditionally rule on any motion for a new trial by determining whether a new trial should be granted if the judgment is later vacated or reversed. The court must state the grounds for conditionally granting or denying the motion for a new trial.

(2) *Effect of a Conditional Ruling.* Conditionally granting the motion for a new trial does not affect the judgment's finality; if the judgment is reversed, the new trial must proceed unless the appellate court orders otherwise. If the motion for a new trial is conditionally denied, the appellee may assert error in that denial; if the judgment is reversed, the case must proceed as the appellate court orders.

(d) Time for a Losing Party's New-Trial Motion. Any motion for a new trial under Rule 59 by a party against whom judgment as a matter of law is rendered must be filed no later than 28 days after the entry of the judgment.

(e) Denying the Motion for Judgment as a Matter of Law; Reversal on Appeal. If the court denies the motion for judgment as a matter of law, the prevailing party may, as appellee, assert grounds entitling it to a new trial should the appellate court conclude that the trial court erred in denying the motion. If the appellate court reverses the judgment, it may order a new trial, direct the trial court to determine whether a new trial should be granted, or direct the entry of judgment.

(Amended January 21, 1963, effective July 1, 1963; March 2, 1987, effective August 1, 1987; April 30, 1991, effective December 1, 1991; April 22, 1993, effective December 1, 1993; April 27, 1995, effective December 1, 1995; April 12, 2006, effective December 1, 2006; April 30, 2007, effective December 1, 2007; March 26, 2009, effective December 1, 2009.)

ADVISORY COMMITTEE NOTES

1937 Adoption

Note to Subdivision (a). The present federal rule is changed to the extent that the formality of an express reservation of rights against waiver is no longer necessary. See *Sampliner v. Motion Picture Patents Co.,* 41 S.Ct. 79, 254 U.S. 233, 65 L.Ed. 240 (1920); *Union Indemnity Co. v. United States,* 74 F.2d 645 (C.C.A. 6th, 1935). The requirement that specific grounds for the motion for a directed verdict must be stated settles a conflict in the federal cases. See Simkins, *Federal Practice* (1934) § 189.

Note to Subdivision (b). For comparable state practice upheld under the conformity act, see *Baltimore and Carolina Line v. Redman,* 55 S.Ct. 890, 295 U.S. 654, 79 L.Ed. 1636 (1935); compare *Slocum v. New York Life Ins. Co.,* 33 S.Ct. 523, 228 U.S. 364, 57 L.Ed. 879, Ann.Cas.1914D, 1029 (1913).

See *Northern Ry. Co. v. Page,* 47 S.Ct. 491, 274 U.S. 65, 71 L.Ed. 929 (1927), following the Massachusetts practice of alternative verdicts, explained in Thorndike, *Trial by Jury in United States Courts,* 26 Harv.L.Rev. 732 (1913). See also Thayer, *Judicial Administration,* 63 U. of Pa.L.Rev. 585, 600–

601, and note 32 (1915); Scott, *Trial by Jury and the Reform of Civil Procedure,* 31 Harv.L.Rev. 669, 685 (1918); Comment, 34 Mich.L.Rev. 93, 98 (1935).

1963 Amendment

Subdivision (a). The practice, after the court has granted a motion for a directed verdict, of requiring the jury to express assent to a verdict they did not reach by their own deliberations serves no useful purpose and may give offense to the members of the jury. See 2B Barron & Holtzoff, *Federal Practice & Procedure* § 1072, at 367 (Wright ed. 1961); Blume, *Origin and Development of the Directed Verdict,* 48 Mich.L.Rev. 555, 582–85, 589–90 (1950). The final sentence of the subdivision, added by amendment, provides that the court's order granting a motion for a directed verdict is effective in itself, and that no action need be taken by the foreman or other members of the jury. See Ariz.R.Civ.P. 50(c); cf. Fed.R.Crim.P. 29(a). No change is intended in the standard to be applied in deciding the motion. To assure this interpretation, and in the interest of simplicity, the traditional term, "directed verdict," is retained.

Subdivision (b). A motion for judgment notwithstanding the verdict will not lie unless it was preceded by a motion for a directed verdict made at the close of all the evidence.

The amendment of the second sentence of this subdivision sets the time limit for making the motion for judgment n.o.v. at 10 days after the entry of judgment, rather than 10 days after the reception of the verdict. Thus the time provision is made consistent with that contained in Rule 59(b) (time for motion for new trial) and Rule 52(b) (time for motion to amend findings by the court).

Subdivision (c) deals with the situation where a party joins a motion for a new trial with his motion for judgment n.o.v., or prays for a new trial in the alternative, and the motion for judgment n.o.v. is granted. The procedure to be followed in making rulings on the motion for the new trial, and the consequences of the rulings thereon, were partly set out in *Montgomery Ward & Co. v. Duncan,* 311 U.S. 243, 253, 61 S.Ct. 189, 85 L.Ed. 147 (1940), and have been further elaborated in later cases. See *Cone v. West Virginia Pulp & Paper Co.,* 330 U.S. 212, 67 S.Ct. 752, 91 L.Ed. 849 (1947); *Globe Liquor Co., Inc. v. San Roman,* 332 U.S. 571, 68 S.Ct. 246, 92 L.Ed. 177 (1948); *Fountain v. Filson,* 336 U.S. 681, 69 S.Ct. 754, 93 L.Ed. 971 (1949); *Johnson v. New York, N.H. & H.R.R. Co.,* 344 U.S. 48, 73 S.Ct. 125, 97 L.Ed. 77 (1952). However, courts as well as counsel have often misunderstood the procedure, and it will be helpful to summarize the proper practice in the text of the rule. The amendments do not alter the effects of a jury verdict or the scope of appellate review.

In the situation mentioned, subdivision (c)(1) requires that the court make a "conditional" ruling on the new-trial motion, i.e., a ruling which goes on the assumption that the motion for judgment n.o.v. was erroneously granted and will be reversed or vacated; and the court is required to state its grounds for the conditional ruling. Subdivision (c)(1) then spells out the consequences of a reversal of the judgment in the light of the conditional ruling on the new-trial motion.

If the motion for new trial has been conditionally granted, and the judgment is reversed, "the new trial shall proceed unless the appellate court has otherwise ordered." The party against whom the judgment n.o.v. was entered below may, as appellant, besides seeking to overthrow that judgment, also attack the conditional grant of the new trial. And the appellate court, if it reverses the judgment n.o.v., may in an appropriate case also reverse the conditional grant of the new trial and direct that judgment be entered on the verdict. See *Bailey v. Slentz,* 189 F.2d 406 (10th Cir. 1951); *Moist Cold Refrigerator Co. v. Lou Johnson Co.,* 249 F.2d 246 (9th Cir. 1957), cert. denied, 356 U.S. 968, 78 S.Ct. 1008, 2 L.Ed.2d 1074 (1958); *Peters v. Smith,* 221 F.2d 721 (3d Cir. 1955); *Dailey v. Timmer,* 292 F.2d 824 (3d Cir. 1961), explaining *Lind v. Schenley Industries, Inc.,* 278 F.2d 79 (3d Cir.), cert. denied, 364 U.S. 835, 81 S.Ct. 58, 5 L.Ed.2d 60 (1960); *Cox v. Pennsylvania R.R.,* 120 A.2d 214 (D.C.Mun.Ct.App.1956); 3 Barron & Holtzoff, *Federal Practice & Procedure* § 1302.1 at 346–47 (Wright ed. 1958); 6 *Moore's Federal Practice* ¶ 59.16 at 3915 n. 8a (2d ed. 1954).

If the motion for a new trial has been conditionally denied, and the judgment is reversed, "subsequent proceedings shall be in accordance with the order of the appellate court." The party in whose favor judgment n.o.v. was entered below may, as appellee, besides seeking to uphold that judgment, also urge on the appellate court that the trial court committed error in conditionally denying the new trial. The appellee may assert this error in his brief, without taking a cross-appeal. *Cf. Patterson v. Pennsylvania R.R.,* 238 F.2d 645, 650 (6th Cir. 1956); *Hughes v. St. Louis Nat. L. Baseball Club, Inc.,* 359 Mo. 993, 997, 224 S.W.2d 989,

992 (1949). If the appellate court concludes that the judgment cannot stand, but accepts the appellee's contention that there was error in the conditional denial of the new trial, it may order a new trial in lieu of directing the entry of judgment upon the verdict.

Subdivision (c)(2), which also deals with the situation where the trial court has granted the motion for judgment n.o.v., states that the verdict-winner may apply to the trial court for a new trial pursuant to Rule 59 after the judgment n.o.v. has been entered against him. In arguing to the trial court in opposition to the motion for judgment n.o.v., the verdict-winner may, and often will, contend that he is entitled, at the least, to a new trial, and the court has a range of discretion to grant a new trial or (where plaintiff won the verdict) to order a dismissal of the action without prejudice instead of granting judgment n.o.v. See *Cone v. West Virginia Pulp & Paper Co.,* supra, 330 U.S. at 217, 218, 67 S.Ct. at 755, 756, 91 L.Ed. 849. Subdivision (c)(2) is a reminder that the verdict-winner is entitled, even after entry of judgment n.o.v. against him, to move for a new trial in the usual course. If in these circumstances the motion is granted, the judgment is superseded.

In some unusual circumstances, however, the grant of the new-trial motion may be only conditional, and the judgment will not be superseded. See the situation in *Tribble v. Bruin,* 279 F.2d 424 (4th Cir. 1960) (upon a verdict for plaintiff, defendant moves for and obtains judgment n.o.v.; plaintiff moves for a new trial on the ground of inadequate damages; trial court might properly have granted plaintiff's motion, conditional upon reversal of the judgment n.o.v.).

Even if the verdict-winner makes no motion for a new trial, he is entitled upon his appeal from the judgment n.o.v. not only to urge that that judgment should be reversed and judgment entered upon the verdict, but that errors were committed during the trial which at the least entitle him to a new trial.

Subdivision (d) deals with the situation where judgment has been entered on the jury verdict, the motion for judgment n.o.v. and any motion for a new trial having been denied by the trial court. The verdict-winner, as appellee, besides seeking to uphold the judgment may urge upon the appellate court that in case the trial court is found to have erred in entering judgment on the verdict, there are grounds for granting him a new trial instead of directing the entry of judgment for his opponent. In appropriate cases the appellate court is not precluded from itself directing that a new trial be had. See *Weade v. Dichmann, Wright & Pugh, Inc.,* 337 U.S. 801, 69 S.Ct. 1326, 93 L.Ed. 1704 (1949). Nor is it precluded in proper cases from remanding the case for a determination by the trial court as to whether a new trial should be granted. The latter course is advisable where the grounds urged are suitable for the exercise of trial court discretion.

Subdivision (d) does not attempt a regulation of all aspects of the procedure where the motion for judgment n.o.v. and any accompanying motion for a new trial are denied, since the problems have not been fully canvassed in the decisions and the procedure is in some respects still in a formative stage. It is, however, designed to give guidance on certain important features of the practice.

1987 Amendment

The amendments are technical. No substantive change is intended.

1991 Amendment

Subdivision (a). The revision of this subdivision aims to facilitate the exercise by the court of its responsibility to assure the fidelity of its judgment to the controlling law, a responsibility imposed by the Due Process Clause of the Fifth Amendment. *Cf. Galloway v. United States,* 319 U.S. 372 (1943).

The revision abandons the familiar terminology of *direction of verdict* for several reasons. The term is misleading as a description of the relationship between judge and jury. It is also freighted with anachronisms some of which are the subject of the text of former subdivision (a) of this rule that is deleted in this revision. Thus, it should not be necessary to state in the text of this rule that a motion made pursuant to it is not a waiver of the right to jury trial, and only the antiquities of directed verdict practice suggest that it might have been. The term "judgment as a matter of law" is an almost equally familiar term and appears in the text of Rule 56; its use in Rule 50 calls attention to the relationship between the two rules. Finally, the change enables the rule to refer to preverdict and post-verdict motions with a terminology that does not conceal the common identity of two motions made at different times in the proceeding.

If a motion is denominated a motion for directed verdict or for judgment notwithstanding the verdict, the party's error is merely formal. Such a motion should be treated as a motion for judgment as a matter of law in accordance with this rule.

Paragraph (a)(1) articulates the standard for the granting of a motion for judgment as a matter of law. It effects no change in the existing standard. That existing standard was not expressed in the former rule, but was articulated in long-standing case law. *See generally* Cooper, *Directions for Directed Verdicts: A Compass for Federal Courts,* 55 MINN.L.REV. 903 (1971). The expressed standard makes clear that action taken under the rule is a performance of the court's duty to assure enforcement of the controlling law and is not an intrusion on any responsibility for factual determinations conferred on the jury by the Seventh Amendment or any other provision of federal law. Because this standard is also used as a reference point for entry of summary judgment under 56(a), it serves to link the two related provisions.

The revision authorizes the court to perform its duty to enter judgment as a matter of law at any time during the trial, as soon as it is apparent that either party is unable to carry a burden of proof that is essential to that party's case. Thus, the second sentence of paragraph (a)(1) authorizes the court to consider a motion for judgment as a matter of law as soon as a party has completed a presentation on a fact essential to that party's case. Such early action is appropriate when economy and expedition will be served. In no event, however, should the court enter judgment against a party who has not been apprised of the materiality of the dispositive fact and been afforded an opportunity to present any available evidence bearing on that fact. In order further to facilitate the exercise of the authority provided by this rule, Rule 16 is also revised to encourage the court to schedule an order of trial that proceeds first with a presentation on an issue that is likely to be dispositive, if such an issue is identified in the course of pretrial. Such scheduling can be appropriate where the court is uncertain whether favorable action should be taken under Rule 56. Thus, the revision affords the court the alternative of denying a motion for summary judgment while scheduling a separate trial of the issue under Rule 42(b) or scheduling the trial to begin with a presentation on that essential fact which the opposing party seems unlikely to be able to maintain.

Paragraph (a)(2) retains the requirement that a motion for judgment be made prior to the close of the trial, subject to renewal after a jury verdict has been rendered. The purpose of this requirement is to assure the responding party an opportunity to cure any deficiency in that party's proof that may have been overlooked until called to the party's attention by a late motion for judgment. Cf. *Farley Transp. Co. v. Santa Fe Trail Transp. Co.,* 786 F.2d 1342 (9th Cir.1986) ("If the moving party is then permitted to make a later attack on the evidence through a motion for judgment notwithstanding the verdict or an appeal, the opposing party may be prejudiced by having lost the opportunity to present additional evidence before the case was submitted to the jury"); *Benson v. Allphin,* 786 F.2d 268 (7th Cir.1986) ("the motion for directed verdict at the close of all the evidence provides the nonmovant an opportunity to do what he can to remedy the deficiencies in his case . . .); *McLaughlin v. The Fellows Gear Shaper Co.,* 4 F.R.Serv.3d 607 (3d Cir.1986) (per Adams, J., dissenting: "This Rule serves important practical purposes in ensuring that neither party is precluded from presenting the most persuasive case possible and in preventing unfair surprise after a matter has been submitted to the jury"). At one time, this requirement was held to be of constitutional stature, being compelled by the Seventh Amendment. Cf. *Slocum v. New York Insurance Co.,* 228 U.S. 364 (1913). But cf. *Baltimore & Carolina Line v. Redman,* 295 U.S. 654 (1935).

The second sentence of paragraph (a)(2) does impose a requirement that the moving party articulate the basis on which a judgment as a matter of law might be rendered. The articulation is necessary to achieve the purpose of the requirement that the motion be made before the case is submitted to the jury, so that the responding party may seek to correct any overlooked deficiencies in the proof. The revision thus alters the result in cases in which courts have used various techniques to avoid the requirement that a motion for a directed verdict be made as a predicate to a motion for judgment notwithstanding the verdict. E.g., *Benson v. Allphin,* 788 F.2d 268 (7th Cir.1986) ("this circuit has allowed something less than a formal motion for directed verdict to preserve a party's right to move for judgment notwithstanding the verdict"). *See generally* 9 WRIGHT & MILLER, FEDERAL PRACTICE AND PROCEDURE § 2537 (1971 and Supp.). The information required with the motion may be supplied by explicit reference to materials and argument previously supplied to the court.

This subdivision deals only with the entry of judgment and not with the resolution of particular factual issues as a matter of law. The court may, as before, properly refuse to instruct a jury to decide an issue if a reasonable jury could on the evidence presented decide that issue in only one way.

Subdivision (b). This provision retains the concept of the former rule that the post-verdict motion is a renewal of an earlier motion made at the close of the evidence. One purpose of this concept was to avoid any question arising under the Seventh Amendment. *Montgomery Ward & Co. v. Duncan,* 311 U.S. 243 (1940). It remains useful as a means of defining the appropriate issue posed by the post-verdict motion. A post-trial motion for judgment can be granted only on grounds advanced in the pre-verdict motion. *E.g., Kutner Buick, Inc. v. American Motors Corp.,* 848 F.2d 614 (3d Cir.1989).

Often it appears to the court or to the moving party that a motion for judgment as a matter of law made at the close of the evidence should be reserved for a post-verdict decision. This is so because a jury verdict for the moving party moots the issue and because a preverdict ruling gambles that a reversal may result in a new trial that might have been avoided. For these reasons, the court may often wisely decline to rule on a motion for judgment as a matter of law made at the close of the evidence, and it is not inappropriate for the moving party to suggest such a postponement of the ruling until after the verdict has been rendered.

In ruling on such a motion, the court should disregard any jury determination for which there is no legally sufficient evidentiary basis enabling a reasonable jury to make it. The court may then decide such issues as a matter of law and enter judgment if all other material issues have been decided by the jury on the basis of legally sufficient evidence, or by the court as a matter of law.

The revised rule is intended for use in this manner with Rule 49. Thus, the court may combine facts established as a matter of law either before trial under Rule 56 or at trial on the basis of the evidence presented with other facts determined by the jury under instructions provided under Rule 49 to support a proper judgment under this rule.

This provision also retains the former requirement that a post-trial motion under the rule must be made within 10 days after entry of a contrary judgment. The renewed motion must be served and filed as provided by Rule 5. A purpose of this requirement is to meet the requirements of F.R.App.P. 4(a)(4).

Subdivision (c). Revision of this subdivision conforms the language to the change in diction set forth in subdivision (a) of this revised rule.

Subdivision (d). Revision of this subdivision conforms the language to that of the previous subdivisions.

1993 Amendments

This technical amendment corrects an ambiguity in the text of the 1991 revision of the rule, which, as indicated in the Notes, was not intended to change the existing standards under which "directed verdicts" could be granted. This amendment makes clear that judgments as a matter of law in jury trials may be entered against both plaintiffs and defendants and with respect to issues or defenses that may not be wholly dispositive of a claim or defense.

1995 Amendments

The only change, other than stylistic, intended by this revision is to prescribe a uniform explicit time for filing of post-judgment motions under this rule—no later than 10 days after entry of the judgment. Previously, there was an inconsistency in the wording of Rules 50, 52, and 59 with respect to whether certain post-judgment motions had to be filed, or merely served, during that period. This inconsistency caused special problems when motions for a new trial were joined with other post-judgment motions. These motions affect the finality of the judgment, a matter often of importance to third persons as well as the parties and the court. The Committee believes that each of these rules should be revised to require filing before end of the 10-day period. Filing is an event that can be determined with certainty from court records. The phrase "no later than" is used—rather than "within"—to include post-judgment motions that sometimes are filed before actual entry of the judgment by the clerk. It should be noted that under Rule 6(a) Saturdays, Sundays, and legal holidays are excluded in measuring the 10-day period, and that under Rule 5 the motions when filed are to contain a certificate of service on other parties.

2006 Amendment

The language of Rule 50(a) has been amended as part of the general restyling of the Civil Rules to make them more easily understood and to make style and terminology consistent throughout the rules. These changes are intended to be stylistic only.

Rule 50(b) is amended to permit renewal of any Rule 50(a) motion for judgment as a matter of law, deleting the requirement that a motion be made at the close of all the evidence. Because the Rule 50(b) motion is only a renewal of the preverdict motion, it can be granted only on grounds advanced in the preverdict motion. The earlier motion informs the opposing party of the challenge to the sufficiency of the evidence and affords a clear opportunity to provide additional evidence that may be available. The earlier motion also alerts the court to the opportunity to simplify the trial by resolving some issues, or even all issues, without submission to the jury. This fulfillment of the functional needs that underlie present Rule 50(b) also satisfies the Seventh Amendment. Automatic reservation of the legal questions raised by the motion conforms to the decision in *Baltimore & Carolina Line v. Redman*, 297 U.S. 654 (1935).

This change responds to many decisions that have begun to move away from requiring a motion for judgment as a matter of law at the literal close of all the evidence. Although the requirement has been clearly established for several decades, lawyers continue to overlook it. The courts are slowly working away from the formal requirement. The amendment establishes the functional approach that courts have been unable to reach under the present rule and makes practice more consistent and predictable.

Many judges expressly invite motions at the close of all the evidence. The amendment is not intended to discourage this useful practice.

Finally, an explicit time limit is added for making a posttrial motion when the trial ends without a verdict or with a verdict that does not dispose of all issues suitable for resolution by verdict. The motion must be made no later than 10 days after the jury was discharged.

2007 Amendments

The language of Rule 50 has been amended as part of the general restyling of the Civil Rules to make them more easily understood and to make style and terminology consistent throughout the rules. These changes are intended to be stylistic only.

Former Rule 50(b) stated that the court reserves ruling on a motion for judgment as a matter of law made at the close of all the evidence "[i]f, for any reason, the court does not grant" the motion. The words "for any reason" reflected the proposition that the reservation is automatic and inescapable. The ruling is reserved even if the court explicitly denies the motion. The same result follows under the amended rule. If the motion is not granted, the ruling is reserved.

Amended Rule 50(e) identifies the appellate court's authority to direct the entry of judgment. This authority was not described in former Rule 50(d), but was recognized in *Weisgram v. Marley Co.*, 528 U.S. 440 (2000), and in *Neely v. Martin K. Eby Construction Company*, 386 U.S. 317 (1967). When Rule 50(d) was drafted in 1963, the Committee Note stated that "[s]ubdivision (d) does not attempt a regulation of all aspects of the procedure where the motion for judgment n.o.v. and any accompanying motion for a new trial are denied * * * ." Express recognition of the authority to direct entry of judgment does not otherwise supersede this caution.

2009 Amendments

Former Rules 50, 52, and 59 adopted 10-day periods for their respective post-judgment motions. Rule 6(b) prohibits any expansion of those periods. Experience has proved that in many cases it is not possible to prepare a satisfactory post-judgment motion in 10 days, even under the former rule that excluded intermediate Saturdays, Sundays, and legal holidays. These time periods are particularly sensitive because Appellate Rule 4 integrates the time to appeal with a timely motion under these rules. Rather than introduce the prospect of uncertainty in appeal time by amending Rule 6(b) to permit additional time, the former 10-day periods are expanded to 28 days. Rule 6(b) continues to prohibit expansion of the 28-day period.

Rule 51.   Instructions to the Jury; Objections; Preserving a Claim of Error

(a) Requests.

    (1) *Before or at the Close of the Evidence.* At the close of the evidence or at any earlier reasonable time that the court orders, a party may file and furnish to every other party written requests for the jury instructions it wants the court to give.

    (2) *After the Close of the Evidence.* After the close of the evidence, a party may:

(A) file requests for instructions on issues that could not reasonably have been anticipated by an earlier time that the court set for requests; and

(B) with the court's permission, file untimely requests for instructions on any issue.

(b) Instructions. The court:

(1) must inform the parties of its proposed instructions and proposed action on the requests before instructing the jury and before final jury arguments;

(2) must give the parties an opportunity to object on the record and out of the jury's hearing before the instructions and arguments are delivered; and

(3) may instruct the jury at any time before the jury is discharged.

(c) Objections.

(1) *How to Make.* A party who objects to an instruction or the failure to give an instruction must do so on the record, stating distinctly the matter objected to and the grounds for the objection.

(2) *When to Make.* An objection is timely if:

(A) a party objects at the opportunity provided under Rule 51(b)(2); or

(B) a party was not informed of an instruction or action on a request before that opportunity to object, and the party objects promptly after learning that the instruction or request will be, or has been, given or refused.

(d) Assigning Error; Plain Error.

(1) *Assigning Error.* A party may assign as error:

(A) an error in an instruction actually given, if that party properly objected; or

(B) a failure to give an instruction, if that party properly requested it and—unless the court rejected the request in a definitive ruling on the record—also properly objected.

(2) *Plain Error.* A court may consider a plain error in the instructions that has not been preserved as required by Rule 51(d)(1) if the error affects substantial rights.

(Amended March 2, 1987, effective August 1, 1987; March 27, 2003, effective December 1, 2003; April 30, 2007, effective December 1, 2007.)

ADVISORY COMMITTEE NOTES

1937 Adoption

Supreme Court Rule 8 requires exceptions to the charge of the court to the jury which shall distinctly state the several matters of law in the charge to which exception is taken. Similar provisions appear in the rules of the various Circuit Courts of Appeals.

1987 Amendment

Although Rule 51 in its present form specifies that the court shall instruct the jury only after the arguments of the parties are completed, in some districts (typically those in states where the practice is otherwise) it is common for the parties to stipulate to instruction before the arguments. The purpose of the amendment is to give the court discretion to instruct the jury either before or after argument. Thus, the rule as revised will permit resort to the long-standing federal practice or to an alternative procedure, which has been praised because it gives counsel the opportunity to explain the instructions, argue their application to the facts and thereby give the jury the maximum assistance in determining the issues and arriving at a good verdict on the law and the evidence. As an ancillary benefit, this approach aids counsel by supplying a natural outline so that arguments may be directed to the essential fact issues which the jury must decide. See generally Raymond, *Merits and Demerits of the Missouri System of Instructing Juries,* 5 St. Louis U.L.J. 317 (1959). Moreover, if the court instructs before an argument, counsel then know the precise words the court has chosen and need not speculate as to the words the court will later use in its instructions. Finally, by instructing ahead of argument the court has the attention of the jurors when they are fresh and can give their full attention to the court's instructions. It is more difficult to hold the attention of jurors after lengthy arguments.

2003 Amendments

Rule 51 is revised to capture many of the interpretations that have emerged in practice. The revisions in text will make uniform the conclusions reached by a majority of decisions on each point. Additions also are made to cover some practices that cannot now be anchored in the text of Rule 51.

Scope. Rule 51 governs instructions to the trial jury on the law that governs the verdict. A variety of other instructions cannot practicably be brought within Rule 51. Among these instructions are preliminary instructions to a venire, and cautionary or limiting instructions delivered in immediate response to events at trial.

Requests. Subdivision (a) governs requests. Apart from the plain error doctrine recognized in subdivision (d)(2), a court is not obliged to instruct the jury on issues raised by the evidence unless a party requests an instruction. The revised rule recognizes the court's authority to direct that requests be submitted before trial.

The close-of-the-evidence deadline may come before trial is completed on all potential issues. Trial may be formally bifurcated or may be sequenced in some less formal manner. The close of the evidence is measured by the occurrence of two events: completion of all intended evidence on an identified phase of the trial and impending submission to the jury with instructions.

The risk in directing a pretrial request deadline is that trial evidence may raise new issues or reshape issues the parties thought they had understood. Courts need not insist on pretrial requests in all cases. Even if the request time is set before trial or early in the trial, subdivision (a)(2)(A) permits requests after the close of the evidence to address issues that could not reasonably have been anticipated at the earlier time for requests set by the court.

Subdivision (a)(2)(B) expressly recognizes the court's discretion to act on an untimely request. The most important consideration in exercising the discretion confirmed by subdivision (a)(2)(B) is the importance of the issue to the case—the closer the issue lies to the "plain error" that would be recognized under subdivision (d)(2), the better the reason to give an instruction. The cogency of the reason for failing to make a timely request also should be considered. To be considered under subdivision (a)(2)(B) a request should be made before final instructions and before final jury arguments. What is a "final" instruction and argument depends on the sequence of submitting the case to the jury. If separate portions of the case are submitted to the jury in sequence, the final arguments and final instructions are those made on submitting to the jury the portion of the case addressed by the arguments and instructions.

Instructions. Subdivision (b)(1) requires the court to inform the parties, before instructing the jury and before final jury arguments related to the instruction, of the proposed instructions as well as the proposed action on instruction requests. The time limit is addressed to final jury arguments to reflect the practice that allows interim arguments during trial in complex cases; it may not be feasible to develop final instructions before such interim arguments. It is enough that counsel know of the intended instructions before making final arguments addressed to the issue. If the trial is sequenced or bifurcated, the final arguments addressed to an issue may occur before the close of the entire trial.

Subdivision (b)(2) complements subdivision (b)(1) by carrying forward the opportunity to object established by present Rule 51. It makes explicit the opportunity to object on the record, ensuring a clear memorial of the objection.

Subdivision (b)(3) reflects common practice by authorizing instructions at any time after trial begins and before the jury is discharged.

Objections. Subdivision (c) states the right to object to an instruction or the failure to give an instruction. It carries forward the formula of present Rule 51 requiring that the objection state distinctly the matter objected to and the grounds of the objection, and makes explicit the requirement that the objection be made on the record. The provisions on the time to object make clear that it is timely to object promptly after learning of an instruction or action on a request when the court has not provided advance information as required by subdivision (b)(1). The need to repeat a request by way of objection is continued by new subdivision (d)(1)(B) except where the court made a definitive ruling on the record.

Preserving a claim of error and plain error. Many cases hold that a proper request for a jury instruction is not alone enough to preserve the right to appeal failure to give the instruction. The request must be renewed by objection. This doctrine is appropriate when the court may not have sufficiently focused on the request, or may believe that the request has been granted in substance although in different words. But this doctrine may also prove a trap for the unwary who fail to add an objection after the court has made it clear that the request has been considered and rejected on the merits. Subdivision (d)(1)(B) establishes authority to review the failure to grant a timely request, despite a failure to add an objection, when the court has made a definitive ruling on the record rejecting the request.

Many circuits have recognized that an error not preserved under Rule 51 may be reviewed in exceptional circumstances. The language adopted to capture these decisions in subdivision (d)(2) is borrowed from Criminal Rule 52. Although the language is the same, the context of civil litigation often differs from the context of criminal prosecution; actual application of the plain-error standard takes account of the differences. The Supreme Court has summarized application of Criminal Rule 52 as involving four elements: (1) there must be an error; (2) the error must be plain; (3) the error must affect substantial rights; and (4) the error must seriously affect the fairness, integrity, or public reputation of judicial proceedings. Johnson v. U.S., 520 U.S. 461, 466–467, 469–470 (1997). (The Johnson case quoted the fourth element from its decision in a civil action, U.S. v. Atkinson, 297 U.S. 157, 160 (1936): "In exceptional circumstances, especially in criminal cases, appellate courts, in the public interest, may, of their own motion, notice errors to which no exception has been taken, if the errors are obvious, or if they otherwise substantially affect the fairness, integrity, or public reputation of judicial proceedings.")

The court's duty to give correct jury instructions in a civil action is shaped by at least four factors.

The factor most directly implied by a "plain" error rule is the obviousness of the mistake. The importance of the error is a second major factor. The costs of correcting an error reflect a third factor that is affected by a variety of circumstances. In a case that seems close to the fundamental error line, account also may be taken of the impact a verdict may have on nonparties.

2007 Amendments

The language of Rule 51 has been amended as part of the general restyling of the Civil Rules to make them more easily understood and to make style and terminology consistent throughout the rules. These changes are intended to be stylistic only.

Rule 52. Findings and Conclusions by the Court; Judgment on Partial Findings

(a) Findings and Conclusions.

(1) *In General.* In an action tried on the facts without a jury or with an advisory jury, the court must find the facts specially and state its conclusions of law separately. The findings and conclusions may be stated on the record after the close of the evidence or may appear in an opinion or a memorandum of decision filed by the court. Judgment must be entered under Rule 58.

(2) *For an Interlocutory Injunction.* In granting or refusing an interlocutory injunction, the court must similarly state the findings and conclusions that support its action.

(3) *For a Motion.* The court is not required to state findings or conclusions when ruling on a motion under Rule 12 or 56 or, unless these rules provide otherwise, on any other motion.

(4) *Effect of a Master's Findings.* A master's findings, to the extent adopted by the court, must be considered the court's findings.

(5) *Questioning the Evidentiary Support.* A party may later question the sufficiency of the evidence supporting the findings, whether or not the party requested findings, objected to them, moved to amend them, or moved for partial findings.

(6) *Setting Aside the Findings.* Findings of fact, whether based on oral or other evidence, must not be set aside unless clearly erroneous, and the reviewing court must give due regard to the trial court's opportunity to judge the witnesses' credibility.

(b) Amended or Additional Findings. On a party's motion filed no later than 28 days after the entry of judgment, the court may amend its findings—or make additional findings—and may amend the judgment accordingly. The motion may accompany a motion for a new trial under Rule 59.

(c) Judgment on Partial Findings. If a party has been fully heard on an issue during a nonjury trial and the court finds against the party on that issue, the court may enter judgment against the party on a claim or defense that, under the controlling law, can be maintained or defeated only with a favorable finding on that issue. The court may, however, decline to render any judgment until the close of the evidence. A judgment on partial findings must be supported by findings of fact and conclusions of law as required by Rule 52(a).

(Amended December 27, 1946, effective March 19, 1948; January 21, 1963, effective July 1, 1963; April 28, 1983, effective August 1, 1983; April 29, 1985, effective August 1, 1985; April 30, 1991, effective December 1, 1991; April 22, 1993, effective December 1, 1993; April 27, 1995, effective December 1, 1995; April 30, 2007, effective December 1, 2007; March 26, 2009, effective December 1, 2009.)

ADVISORY COMMITTEE NOTES

1937 Adoption

See [former] Equity Rule 70½, as amended Nov. 25, 1935, (Findings of Fact and Conclusions of Law) and U.S.C., Title 28, [former] § 764 (Opinion, findings, and conclusions in action against United States) which are substantially continued in this rule. The provisions of U.S.C., Title 28, [former] §§ 773 (Trial of issues of fact; by court) and [former] 875 (Review in cases tried without a jury) are superseded in so far as they provide a different method of finding facts and a different method of appellate review. The rule stated in the third sentence of Subdivision (a) accords with the decisions on the scope of the review in modern federal equity practice. It is applicable to all classes of findings in cases tried without a jury whether the finding is of a fact concerning which there was conflict of testimony, or of a fact deduced or inferred from uncontradicted testimony. See *Silver King Coalition Mines Co. v. Silver King Consolidated Mining Co.,* C.C.A.8, 1913, 204 F. 166, certiorari denied 33 S.Ct. 1051, 229 U.S. 624, 57 L.Ed. 1356; *Warren v. Keep,* 1894, 15 S.Ct. 83, 155 U.S. 265, 39 L.Ed. 144; *Furrer v. Ferris,* 1892, 12 S.Ct. 821, 145 U.S. 132, 36 L.Ed. 649; *Tilghman v. Proctor,* 1888, 8 S.Ct. 894, 125 U.S. 136, 149, 31 L.Ed. 664; *Kimberly v. Arms,* 1889, 9 S.Ct. 355, 129 U.S. 512, 524, 32 L.Ed. 764. Compare *Kaeser & Blair Inc. v. Merchants' Ass'n,* C.C.A.6, 1933, 64 F.2d 575, 576; *Dunn v. Trefry,* C.C.A.1, 1919, 260 F. 147.

In the following states findings of fact are required in all cases tried without a jury (waiver by the parties being permitted as indicated at the end of the listing): Arkansas, Civ.Code (Crawford, 1934) § 364; California, Code Civ.Proc. (Deering, 1937) §§ 632, 634; Colorado, 1 Stat.Ann. (1935) Code Civ.Proc. §§ 232, 291 (in actions before referees or for possession of and damages to land); Connecticut, Gen.Stats. §§ 5660, 5664; Idaho, 1 Code Ann. (1932) §§ 7–302 through 7–305; Massachusetts (equity cases), 2 Gen.Laws (Ter.Ed., 1932) ch. 214, § 23; Minnesota, 2 Stat. (Mason, 1927) § 9311; Nevada, 4 Comp.Laws (Hillyer, 1929) §§ 8783–8784; New Jersey, Sup.Ct.Rule 113, 2 N.J.Misc. 1197, 1239 (1924); New Mexico, Stat.Ann. (Courtright, 1929) §§ 105–813; North Carolina, Code (1935) § 569; North Dakota, 2 Comp.Laws Ann. (1913) § 7641; Oregon, 2 Code Ann. (1930) §§ 2–502; South Carolina, Code (Michie, 1932) § 649; South Dakota, 1 Comp.Laws (1929) §§ 2525–2526; Utah, Rev.Stat.Ann. (1933) §§ 104–26–2, 104–26–3; Vermont (where jury trial waived), Pub.Laws (1933) § 2069; Washington, 2 Rev.Stat.Ann. (Remington, 1932) § 367; Wisconsin, Stat. (1935) § 270.33. The parties may waive this requirement for findings in California, Idaho, North Dakota, Nevada, New Mexico, Utah, and South Dakota.

In the following states the review of findings of fact in all non-jury cases, including jury waived cases, is assimilated to the equity review: Alabama, Code Ann. (Michie, 1928) §§ 9498, 8599; California, Code Civ.Proc. (Derring, 1937) § 956a; but see 20 Calif.Law Rev. 171 (1932); Colorado, *Johnson v. Kountze,* 1895, 43 P. 445, 21 Colo. 486, semble; Illinois, *Baker v. Hinricks,* 1934, 194 N.E. 284, 359 Ill. 138; *Weininger v. Metropolitan Fire Ins. Co.,* 1935, 195 N.E. 420, 359 Ill. 584, 98 A.L.R. 169; Minnesota, *State Bank of Gibbon v. Walter,* 1926, 208 N.W. 423, 167 Minn. 37; *Waldron v. Page,* 1934, 253 N.W. 894, 191 Minn. 302; New

Jersey N.J.S.A. 2:27–241, 2:27–363, as interpreted in *Bussy v. Hatch*, 1920, 111 A. 546, 95 N.J.L. 56; New York, *York Mortgage Corporation v. Clotar Const. Corp.*, 1930, 172 N.E. 265, 254 N.Y. 128; North Dakota, Comp.Laws Ann. (1913) § 7846, as amended by N.D.Laws 1933, c. 208; *Milnor Holding Co. v. Holt*, 1933, 248 N.W. 315, 63 N.D. 362, 370; Oklahoma, *Wichita Mining and Improvement Co. v. Hale*, 1908, 94 P. 530, 20 Okl. 159; South Dakota, *Randall v. Burk Township*, 4 S.D. 337, 57 N.W. 4 (1893); Texas, *Custard v. Flowers*, 1929, 14 S.W.2d 109; Utah, Rev.Stat.Ann. (1933) § 104–41–5; Vermont, *Roberge v. Troy*, 1933, 163 A. 770, 105 Vt. 134; Washington, 2 Rev.Stat.Ann. (Remington, 1932) §§ 309–316; *McCullough v. Puget Sound Realty Associates*, 1913, 136 Pac. 1146, 76 Wash. 700, but see *Cornwall v. Anderson*, 1915, 148 P. 1, 85 Wash. 369; West Virginia, *Kinsey v. Carr*, 1906, 55 S.E. 1004, 60 W.Va. 449, semble; Wisconsin, Stat. (1935) § 251.09; *Campbell v. Sutliff*, 1927, 214 N.W. 374, 193 Wis. 370; *Gessler v. Erwin Co.*, 1924, 193 N.W. 303, 182 Wis. 315.

For examples of an assimilation of the review of findings of fact in cases tried without a jury to the review at law as made in several states, see Clark and Stone, *Review of Findings of Fact*, 4 U. of Chi.L.Rev. 190, 215 (1937).

1946 Amendment

Note to Subdivision (a). The amended rule makes clear that the requirement for findings of fact and conclusions of law thereon applies in a case with an advisory jury. This removes an ambiguity in the rule as originally stated, but carries into effect what has been considered its intent. 3 *Moore's Federal Practice*, 1938, 3119. *Hurwitz v. Hurwitz*, 1943, 136 F.2d 796, 78 U.S.App.D.C. 66.

The two sentences added at the end of Rule 52(a) eliminate certain difficulties which have arisen concerning findings and conclusions. The first of the two sentences permits findings of fact and conclusions of law to appear in an opinion or memorandum of decision. See, e.g., *United States v. One 1941 Ford Sedan*, S.D.Tex.1946, 65 F.Supp. 84. Under original Rule 52(a) some courts have expressed the view that findings and conclusions could not be incorporated in an opinion. *Detective Comics, Inc. v. Bruns Publications*, S.D.N.Y.1939, 28 F.Supp. 399; *Pennsylvania Co. for Insurance on Lives & Granting Annuities v. Cincinnati & L.E.R. Co.*, S.D.Ohio 1941, 43 F.Supp. 5; *United States v. Aluminum Co. of America*, S.D.N.Y.1941, 2 F.R.D. 224, 5 Fed. Rules Serv. 52a.11, Case 3; see also s.c., 44 F.Supp. 97. But, to the contrary, see *Wellman v. United States*, D.Mass.1938, 25 F.Supp. 868; *Cook v. United States*, D.Mass.1939, 26 F.Supp. 253; *Proctor v. White*, D.Mass.1939, 28 F.Supp. 161; *Green Valley Creamery, Inc. v. United States*, C.C.A.1, 1939, 108 F.2d 342. See also *Matton Oil Transfer Corp. v. The Dynamic*, C.C.A.2, 1941, 123 F.2d 999; *Carter Coal Co. v. Litz*, C.C.A.4, 1944, 140 F.2d 934; *Woodruff v. Heiser*, C.C.A.10, 1945, 150 F.2d 869; *Coca Cola Co. v. Busch*, Pa.1943, 7 Fed. Rules Serv. 59b.2, Case 4; Oglebay, *Some Developments in Bankruptcy Law*, 1944, 18 J. of Nat'l Ass'n of Ref. 68, 69. Findings of fact aid in the process of judgment and in defining for future cases the precise limitations of the issues and the determination thereon. Thus they not only aid the appellate court on review, *Hurwitz v. Hurwitz*, App.D.C.1943, 136 F.2d 796, 78 U.S.App.D.C. 66, but they are an important factor in the proper application of the doctrines of res judicata and estoppel by judgment. Nordbye, *Improvements in Statement of Findings of Fact and Conclusions of Law*, 1 F.R.D. 25, 26–27; *United States v. Forness*, C.C.A.2, 1942, 125 F.2d 928, certiorari denied 1942, 62 S.Ct. 1293, 316 U.S. 694, 86 L.Ed. 1764. These findings should represent the judge's own determination and not the long, often argumentative statements of successful counsel. *United States v. Forness*, supra; *United States v. Crescent Amusement Co.*, 1944, 1945, 65 S.Ct. 254, 323 U.S. 173, 89 L.Ed. 160. Consequently, they should be a part of the judge's opinion and decision, either stated therein or stated separately. *Matton Oil Transfer Corp. v. The Dynamic*, supra. But the judge need only make brief, definite, pertinent findings and conclusions upon the contested matters; there is no necessity for over-elaboration of detail or particularization of facts. *United States v. Forness*, supra; *United States v. Crescent Amusement Co.*, supra. See also *Petterson Lighterage & Towing Corp. v. New York Central R. Co.*, C.C.A.2, 1942, 126 F.2d 992; *Brown Paper Mill Co., Inc. v. Irwin*, C.C.A.8, 1943, 134 F.2d 337; *Allen Bradley Co. v. Local Union No. 3, I.B.E.W.*, C.C.A.2, 1944, 145 F.2d 215, reversed on other grounds 65 S.Ct. 1533, 325 U.S. 797; *Young v. Murphy*, Ohio 1946, 9 Fed.Rules Serv. 52a.11, Case 2.

The last sentence of Rule 52(a) as amended will remove any doubt that findings and conclusions are unnecessary upon decision of a motion, particularly one under Rule 12 or Rule 56, except as provided in amended Rule 41(b). As so holding, see *Thomas v. Peyser*, App.D.C.1941, 118 F.2d 369; *Schad v. Twentieth Century-Fox Corp.*, C.C.A.3, 1943, 136 F.2d 991; *Prudential Ins. Co. of America v. Goldstein*, N.Y.1942, 43 F.Supp. 767; *Somers Coal Co. v. United States*, N.D.Ohio 1942, 2 F.R.D. 532, 6 Fed.Rules Serv. 52a.1, Case

1; *Pen-Ken Oil & Gas Corp. v. Warfield Natural Gas Co.,* E.D.Ky.1942, 2 F.R.D. 355, 5 Fed. Rules Serv. 52a.1, Case 3; also Commentary, *Necessity of Findings of Fact,* 1941, 4 Fed. Rules Serv. 936.

1963 Amendment

This amendment conforms to the amendment of Rule 58. See the Advisory Committee's Note to Rule 58, as amended.

1983 Amendment

Rule 52(a) has been amended to revise its penultimate sentence to provide explicitly that the district judge may make the findings of fact and conclusions of law required in nonjury cases orally. Nothing in the prior text of the rule forbids this practice, which is widely utilized by district judges. See Christensen, *A Modest Proposal for Immeasurable Improvement,* 64 A.B.A.J. 693 (1978). The objective is to lighten the burden on the trial court in preparing findings in nonjury cases. In addition, the amendment should reduce the number of published district court opinions that embrace written findings.

1985 Amendment

Rule 52(a) has been amended (1) to avoid continued confusion and conflicts among the circuits as to the standard of appellate review of findings of fact by the court, (2) to eliminate the disparity between the standard of review as literally stated in Rule 52(a) and the practice of some courts of appeals, and (3) to promote nationwide uniformity. See Note, *Rule 52(a): Appellate Review of Findings of Fact Based on Documentary or Undisputed Evidence,* 49 Va.L.Rev. 506, 536 (1963).

Some courts of appeal have stated that when a trial court's findings do not rest on demeanor evidence and evaluation of a witness' credibility, there is no reason to defer to the trial court's findings and the appellate court more readily can find them to be clearly erroneous. See, e.g., *Marcum v. United States,* 621 F.2d 142, 144–45 (5th Cir.1980). Others go further, holding that appellate review may be had without application of the "clearly erroneous" test since the appellate court is in as good a position as the trial court to review a purely documentary record. See, *e.g., Atari, Inc. v. North American Philips Consumer Electronics Corp.,* 672 F.2d 607, 614 (7th Cir.), cert. denied, 459 U.S. 880 (1982); *Lydle v. United States,* 635 F.2d 763, 765 n. 1 (6th Cir.1981); *Swanson v. Baker Indus., Inc.,* 615 F.2d 479, 483 (8th Cir.1980); *Taylor v. Lombard,* 606 F.2d 371, 372 (2d Cir.1979), cert. denied, 445 U.S. 946 (1980); *Jack Kahn Music Co. v. Baldwin Piano & Organ Co.,* 604 F.2d 755, 758 (2d Cir.1979); *John R. Thompson Co. v. United States,* 477 F.2d 164, 167 (7th Cir.1973).

A third group has adopted the view that the "clearly erroneous" rule applies in all nonjury cases even when findings are based solely on documentary evidence or on inferences from undisputed facts. See, *e.g., Maxwell v. Sumner,* 673 F.2d 1031, 1036 (9th Cir.), *cert. denied,* 459 U.S. 976 (1982); *United States v. Texas Education Agency,* 647 F.2d 504, 506–07 (5th Cir.1981), *cert. denied,* 454 U.S. 1143 (1982); *Constructora Maza, Inc. v. Banco de Ponce,* 616 F.2d 573, 576 (1st Cir.1980); *In re Sierra Trading Corp.,* 482 F.2d 333, 337 (10th Cir.1973); *Case v. Morrisette,* 475 F.2d 1300, 1306–07 (D.C.Cir.1973).

The commentators also disagree as to the proper interpretation of the Rule. *Compare* Wright, *The Doubtful Omniscience of Appellate Courts,* 41 Minn.L.Rev. 751, 769–70 (1957) (language and intent of Rule support view that "clearly erroneous" test should apply to all forms of evidence), *and* 9 C. Wright & A. Miller, *Federal Practice and Procedure: Civil § 2587,* at 740 (1971) (language of the Rule is clear), *with* 5A J. Moore, *Federal Practice* ¶ 52.04, 2687–88 (2d ed. 1982) (Rule as written supports broader review of findings based on non-demeanor testimony).

The Supreme Court has not clearly resolved the issue. See, *Bose Corp. v. Consumers Union of United States, Inc.,* 466 U.S. 485, 104 S.Ct. 1949, 1958 (1984); *Pullman Standard v. Swint,* 456 U.S. 273, 293 (1982); *United States v. General Motors Corp.,* 384 U.S. 127, 141 n. 16 (1966); *United States v. United States Gypsum Co.,* 333 U.S. 364, 394–96 (1948).

The principal argument advanced in favor of a more searching appellate review of findings by the district court based solely on documentary evidence is that the rationale of Rule 52(a) does not apply when the findings do not rest on the trial court's assessment of credibility of the witnesses but on an evaluation of documentary proof and the drawing of inferences from it, thus eliminating the need for any special deference to the trial court's findings. These considerations are outweighed by the public interest in the stability and judicial economy that would be promoted by recognizing that the trial court, not the appellate tribunal, should be the finder of the facts. To permit courts of appeals to share more actively in the fact-finding function would tend to undermine the legitimacy of the district courts in the eyes of litigants, multiply appeals by encouraging appellate retrial of some factual issues, and needlessly reallocate judicial authority.

1991 Amendment

Subdivision (c) is added. It parallels the revised Rule 50(a), but is applicable to non-jury trials. It authorizes the court to enter judgment at any time that it can appropriately make a dispositive finding of fact on the evidence.

The new subdivision replaces part of Rule 41(b), which formerly authorized a dismissal at the close of the plaintiff's case if the plaintiff had failed to carry an essential burden of proof. Accordingly, the reference to Rule 41 formerly made in subdivision (a) of this rule is deleted.

As under the former Rule 41(b), the court retains discretion to enter no judgment prior to the close of the evidence.

Judgment entered under this rule differs from a summary judgment under Rule 56 in the nature of the evaluation made by the court. A judgment on partial findings is made after the court has heard all the evidence bearing on the crucial issue of fact, and the finding is reversible only if the appellate court finds it to be "clearly erroneous." A summary judgment, in contrast, is made on the basis of facts established on account of the absence of contrary evidence or presumptions; such establishments of fact are rulings on questions of law as provided in Rule 56(a) and are not shielded by the "clear error" standard of review.

1993 Amendments

This technical amendment corrects an ambiguity in the text of the 1991 revision of the rule, similar to the revision being made to Rule 50. This amendment makes clear that judgments as a matter of law in nonjury trials may be entered against both plaintiffs and defendants and with respect to issues or defenses that may not be wholly dispositive of a claim or defense.

1995 Amendments

The only change, other than stylistic, intended by this revision is to require that any motion to amend or add findings after a nonjury trial must be filed no later than 10 days after entry of the judgment. Previously, there was an inconsistency in the wording of Rules 50, 52, and 59 with respect to whether certain post-judgment motions had to be filed, or merely served, during that period. This inconsistency caused special problems when motions for a new trial were joined with other post-judgment motions. These motions affect the finality of the judgment, a matter often of importance to third persons as well as the parties and the court. The Committee believes that each of these rules should be revised to require filing before end of the 10-day period. Filing is an event that can be determined with certainty from court records. The phrase "no later than" is used—rather than "within"—to include post-judgment motions that sometimes are filed before actual entry of the judgment by the clerk. It should be noted that under Rule 6(a) Saturdays, Sundays, and legal holidays are excluded in measuring the 10-day period, and that under Rule 5 the motions when filed are to contain a certificate of service on other parties.

2007 Amendments

The language of Rule 52 has been amended as part of the general restyling of the Civil Rules to make them more easily understood and to make style and terminology consistent throughout the rules. These changes are intended to be stylistic only.

Former Rule 52(a) said that findings are unnecessary on decisions of motions "except as provided in subdivision (c) of this rule." Amended Rule 52(a)(3) says that findings are unnecessary "unless these rules provide otherwise." This change reflects provisions in other rules that require Rule 52 findings on deciding motions. Rules 23(e), 23(h), and 54(d)(2)(C) are examples.

Amended Rule 52(a)(5) includes provisions that appeared in former Rule 52(a) and 52(b). Rule 52(a) provided that requests for findings are not necessary for purposes of review. It applied both in an action tried on the facts without a jury and also in granting or refusing an interlocutory injunction. Rule 52(b), applicable to findings "made in actions tried without a jury," provided that the sufficiency of the evidence might be "later questioned whether or not in the district court the party raising the question objected to the findings, moved to amend them, or moved for partial findings." Former Rule 52(b) did not explicitly apply to decisions granting or refusing an interlocutory injunction. Amended Rule 52(a)(5) makes explicit the application of this part of former Rule 52(b) to interlocutory injunction decisions.

Former Rule 52(c) provided for judgment on partial findings, and referred to it as "judgment as a matter of law." Amended Rule 52(c) refers only to "judgment," to avoid any confusion with a Rule 50 judgment as a matter of law in a jury case. The standards that govern judgment as a matter of law in a jury case have no bearing on a decision under Rule 52(c).

2009 Amendments

Former Rules 50, 52, and 59 adopted 10-day periods for their respective post-judgment motions. Rule 6(b) prohibits any expansion of those periods. Experience has proved that in many cases it is not possible to prepare a satisfactory post-judgment motion in 10 days, even under the former rule that excluded intermediate Saturdays, Sundays, and legal holidays. These time periods are particularly sensitive because Appellate Rule 4 integrates the time to appeal with a timely motion under these rules. Rather than introduce the prospect of uncertainty in appeal time by amending Rule 6(b) to permit additional time, the former 10-day periods are expanded to 28 days. Rule 6(b) continues to prohibit expansion of the 28-day period.

Rule 53.   Masters

(a) Appointment.

    (1) *Scope.* Unless a statute provides otherwise, a court may appoint a master only to:

        (A) perform duties consented to by the parties;

        (B) hold trial proceedings and make or recommend findings of fact on issues to be decided without a jury if appointment is warranted by:

            (i) some exceptional condition; or

            (ii) the need to perform an accounting or resolve a difficult computation of damages; or

        (C) address pretrial and posttrial matters that cannot be effectively and timely addressed by an available district judge or magistrate judge of the district.

    (2) *Disqualification.* A master must not have a relationship to the parties, attorneys, action, or court that would require disqualification of a judge under 28 U.S.C. § 455, unless the parties, with the court's approval, consent to the appointment after the master discloses any potential grounds for disqualification.

    (3) *Possible Expense or Delay.* In appointing a master, the court must consider the fairness of imposing the likely expenses on the parties and must protect against unreasonable expense or delay.

(b) Order Appointing a Master.

    (1) *Notice.* Before appointing a master, the court must give the parties notice and an opportunity to be heard. Any party may suggest candidates for appointment.

    (2) *Contents.* The appointing order must direct the master to proceed with all reasonable diligence and must state:

        (A) the master's duties, including any investigation or enforcement duties, and any limits on the master's authority under Rule 53(c);

        (B) the circumstances, if any, in which the master may communicate ex parte with the court or a party;

        (C) the nature of the materials to be preserved and filed as the record of the master's activities;

(D) the time limits, method of filing the record, other procedures, and standards for reviewing the master's orders, findings, and recommendations; and

(E) the basis, terms, and procedure for fixing the master's compensation under Rule 53(g).

(3) *Issuing.* The court may issue the order only after:

(A) the master files an affidavit disclosing whether there is any ground for disqualification under 28 U.S.C. § 455; and

(B) if a ground is disclosed, the parties, with the court's approval, waive the disqualification.

(4) *Amending.* The order may be amended at any time after notice to the parties and an opportunity to be heard.

(c) **Master's Authority.**

(1) *In General.* Unless the appointing order directs otherwise, a master may:

(A) regulate all proceedings;

(B) take all appropriate measures to perform the assigned duties fairly and efficiently; and

(C) if conducting an evidentiary hearing, exercise the appointing court's power to compel, take, and record evidence.

(2) *Sanctions.* The master may by order impose on a party any noncontempt sanction provided by Rule 37 or 45, and may recommend a contempt sanction against a party and sanctions against a nonparty.

(d) **Master's Orders.** A master who issues an order must file it and promptly serve a copy on each party. The clerk must enter the order on the docket.

(e) **Master's Reports.** A master must report to the court as required by the appointing order. The master must file the report and promptly serve a copy on each party, unless the court orders otherwise.

(f) **Action on the Master's Order, Report, or Recommendations.**

(1) *Opportunity for a Hearing; Action in General.* In acting on a master's order, report, or recommendations, the court must give the parties notice and an opportunity to be heard; may receive evidence; and may adopt or affirm, modify, wholly or partly reject or reverse, or resubmit to the master with instructions.

(2) *Time to Object or Move to Adopt or Modify.* A party may file objections to—or a motion to adopt or modify—the master's order, report, or recommendations no later than 21 days after a copy is served, unless the court sets a different time.

(3) *Reviewing Factual Findings.* The court must decide de novo all objections to findings of fact made or recommended by a master, unless the parties, with the court's approval, stipulate that:

(A) the findings will be reviewed for clear error; or

(B) the findings of a master appointed under Rule 53(a)(1)(A) or (C) will be final.

(4) *Reviewing Legal Conclusions.* The court must decide de novo all objections to conclusions of law made or recommended by a master.

(5) *Reviewing Procedural Matters.* Unless the appointing order establishes a different standard of review, the court may set aside a master's ruling on a procedural matter only for an abuse of discretion.

(g) Compensation.

    (1) *Fixing Compensation.* Before or after judgment, the court must fix the master's compensation on the basis and terms stated in the appointing order, but the court may set a new basis and terms after giving notice and an opportunity to be heard.

    (2) *Payment.* The compensation must be paid either:

        (A) by a party or parties; or

        (B) from a fund or subject matter of the action within the court's control.

    (3) *Allocating Payment.* The court must allocate payment among the parties after considering the nature and amount of the controversy, the parties' means, and the extent to which any party is more responsible than other parties for the reference to a master. An interim allocation may be amended to reflect a decision on the merits.

(h) Appointing a Magistrate Judge. A magistrate judge is subject to this rule only when the order referring a matter to the magistrate judge states that the reference is made under this rule.

(Amended February 28, 1966, effective July 1, 1966; April 28, 1983, effective August 1, 1983; March 2, 1987, effective August 1, 1987; April 30, 1991, effective December 1, 1991; April 22, 1993, effective December 1, 1993; March 27, 2003, effective December 1, 2003; April 30, 2007, effective December 1, 2007; March 26, 2009, effective December 1, 2009.)

ADVISORY COMMITTEE NOTES

1937 Adoption

    Note to Subdivision (a). This is a modification of former Equity Rule 68 (Appointment and Compensation of Masters).

    Note to Subdivision (b). This is substantially the first sentence of [former] Equity Rule 59 (Reference to Master—Exceptional, Not Usual) extended to actions formerly legal. See *Ex parte Peterson,* 1920, 40 S.Ct. 543, 253 U.S. 300, 64 L.Ed. 919.

    Note to Subdivision (c). This is [former] Equity Rules 62 (Powers of Master) and 65 (Claimants Before Master Examinable by Him) with slight modifications. Compare [former] Equity Rules 49 (Evidence Taken Before Examiners, Etc.) and 51 (Evidence Taken Before Examiners, Etc.).

    Note to Subdivision (d). (1) This is substantially a combination of the second sentence of [former] Equity Rule 59 (Reference to Master—Exceptional, Not Usual) and [former] Equity Rule 60 (Proceedings Before Master). Compare [former] Equity Rule 53 (Notice of Taking Testimony Before Examiner, Etc.).

    (2) This is substantially [former] Equity Rule 52 (Attendance of Witnesses Before Commissioner, Master, or Examiner).

    (3) This is substantially [former] Equity Rule 63 (Form of Accounts Before Master).

    Note to Subdivision (e). This contains the substance of [former] Equity Rules 61 (Master's Report—Documents Identified but not Set Forth), $61^{1}/_{2}$ (Master's Report—Presumption as to Correctness—Review), and 66 (Return of Master's Report—Exceptions—Hearing), with modifications as to the form and effect of the report and for inclusion of reports by auditors, referees, and examiners, and references in actions formerly legal. Compare [former] Equity Rules 49 (Evidence Taken Before Examiners, Etc.) and 67 (Costs on Exceptions to Master's Report). See *Camden v. Stuart,* 144 U.S. 104, 12 S.Ct. 585, 36 L.Ed. 363 (1892); *Ex parte Peterson,* 253 U.S. 300, 40 S.Ct. 543, 64 L.Ed. 919 (1920).

1966 Amendment

    These changes are designed to preserve the admiralty practice whereby difficult computations are referred to a commissioner or assessor, especially after an interlocutory judgment determining liability. As to separation of issues for trial see Rule 42(b).

1983 Amendment

Subdivision (a). The creation of full-time magistrates, who serve at government expense and have no nonjudicial duties competing for their time, eliminates the need to appoint standing masters. Thus the prior provision in Rule 53(a) authorizing the appointment of standing masters is deleted. Additionally, the definition of "master" in subdivision (a) now eliminates the superseded office of commissioner.

The term "special master" is retained in Rule 53 in order to maintain conformity with 28 U.S.C. § 636(b)(2), authorizing a judge to designate a magistrate "to serve as a special master pursuant to the applicable provisions of this title and the Federal Rules of Civil Procedure for the United States District Courts." Obviously, when a magistrate serves as a special master, the provisions for compensation of masters are inapplicable, and the amendment to subdivision (a) so provides.

Although the existence of magistrates may make the appointment of outside masters unnecessary in many instances, see, e.g., *Gautreaux v. Chicago Housing Authority,* 384 F.Supp. 37 (N.D.Ill.1974), mandamus denied *sub nom., Chicago Housing Authority v. Austin,* 511 F.2d 82 (7th Cir.1975); *Avco Corp. v. American Tel. & Tel. Co.,* 68 F.R.D. 532 (S.D.Ohio 1975), such masters may prove useful when some special expertise is desired or when a magistrate is unavailable for lengthy and detailed supervision of a case.

Subdivision (b). The provisions of 28 U.S.C. § 636(b)(2) not only permit magistrates to serve as masters under Rule 53(b) but also eliminate the exceptional condition requirement of Rule 53(b) when the reference is made with the consent of the parties. The amendment to subdivision (b) brings Rule 53 into harmony with the statute by exempting magistrates, appointed with the consent of the parties, from the general requirement that some exceptional condition requires the reference. It should be noted that subdivision (b) does not address the question, raised in recent decisional law and commentary, as to whether the exceptional condition requirement is applicable when *private masters* who are not magistrates are appointed with the consent of the parties. See Silberman, *Masters and Magistrates Part II: The American Analogue,* 50 N.Y.U.L.Rev. 1297, 1354 (1975).

Subdivision (c). The amendment recognizes the abrogation of Federal Rule 43(c) by the Federal Rules of Evidence.

Subdivision (f). The new subdivision responds to confusion flowing from the dual authority for references of pretrial matters to magistrates. Such references can be made, with or without the consent of the parties, pursuant to Rule 53 or under 28 U.S.C. § 636(b)(1)(A) and (b)(1)(B). There are a number of distinctions between references made under the statute and under the rule. For example, under the statute nondispositive pretrial matters may be referred to a magistrate, without consent, for final determination with reconsideration by the district judge if the magistrate's order is clearly erroneous or contrary to law. Under the rule, however, the appointment of a master, without consent of the parties, to supervise discovery would require some exceptional condition (Rule 53(b)) and would subject the proceedings to the report procedures of Rule 53(e). If an order of reference does not clearly articulate the source of the court's authority the resulting proceedings could be subject to attack on grounds of the magistrate's noncompliance with the provisions of Rule 53. This subdivision therefore establishes a presumption that the limitations of Rule 53 are not applicable unless the reference is specifically made subject to Rule 53.

A magistrate serving as a special master under 28 U.S.C. § 636(b)(2) is governed by the provisions of Rule 53, with the exceptional condition requirement lifted in the case of a consensual reference.

1987 Amendment

The amendments are technical. No substantive change is intended.

1991 Amendment

The purpose of the revision is to expedite proceedings before a master. The former rule required only a filing of the master's report, with the clerk then notifying the parties of the filing. To receive a copy, a party would then be required to secure it from the clerk. By transmitting directly to the parties, the master can save some efforts of counsel. Some local rules have previously required such action by the master.

1993 Amendments

This revision is made to conform the rule to changes made by the Judicial Improvements Act of 1990.

2003 Amendments

Rule 53 is revised extensively to reflect changing practices in using masters. From the beginning in 1938, Rule 53 focused primarily on special masters who perform trial functions. Since then, however, courts have gained experience with masters appointed to perform a variety of pretrial and post-trial functions. See Willging, Hooper, Leary, Miletich, Reagan, & Shapard, *Special Masters' Incidence and Activity* (Federal Judicial Center 2000). This revised Rule 53 recognizes that in appropriate circumstances masters may properly be appointed to perform these functions and regulates such appointments. Rule 53 continues to address trial masters as well, but permits appointment of a trial master in an action to be tried to a jury only if the parties consent. The new rule clarifies the provisions that govern the appointment and function of masters for all purposes. Rule 53(g) also changes the standard of review for findings of fact made or recommended by a master. The core of the original Rule 53 remains, including its prescription that appointment of a master must be the exception and not the rule.

Special masters are appointed in many circumstances outside the Civil Rules. Rule 53 applies only to proceedings that Rule 1 brings within its reach.

Subdivision (a)(1)

District judges bear primary responsibility for the work of their courts. A master should be appointed only in limited circumstances. Subdivision (a)(1) describes three different standards, relating to appointments by consent of the parties, appointments for trial duties, and appointments for pretrial or post-trial duties.

Consent Masters. Subparagraph (a)(1)(A) authorizes appointment of a master with the parties' consent. Party consent does not require that the court make the appointment; the court retains unfettered discretion to refuse appointment.

Trial Masters. Use of masters for the core functions of trial has been progressively limited. These limits are reflected in the provisions of subparagraph (a)(1)(B) that restrict appointments to exercise trial functions. The Supreme Court gave clear direction to this trend in *La Buy v. Howes Leather Co.*, 352 U.S. 249 (1957); earlier roots are sketched in *Los Angeles Brush Mfg. Corp. v. James*, 272 U.S. 701 (1927). As to nonjury trials, this trend has developed through elaboration of the "exceptional condition" requirement in present Rule 53(b). This phrase is retained, and will continue to have the same force as it has developed. Although the provision that a reference "shall be the exception and not the rule" is deleted, its meaning is embraced for this setting by the exceptional condition requirement.

Subparagraph (a)(1)(B)(ii) carries forward the approach of present Rule 53(b), which exempts from the "exceptional condition" requirement "matters of account and of difficult computation of damages." This approach is justified only as to essentially ministerial determinations that require mastery of much detailed information but that do not require extensive determinations of credibility. Evaluations of witness credibility should only be assigned to a trial master when justified by an exceptional condition.

The use of a trial master without party consent is abolished as to matters to be decided by a jury unless a statute provides for this practice.

Abolition of the direct power to appoint a trial master as to issues to be decided by a jury leaves the way free to appoint a trial master with the consent of all parties. A trial master should be appointed in a jury case, with consent of the parties and concurrence of the court, only if the parties waive jury trial with respect to the issues submitted to the master or if the master's findings are to be submitted to the jury as evidence in the manner provided by former Rule 53(e)(3). In no circumstance may a master be appointed to preside at a jury trial.

The central function of a trial master is to preside over an evidentiary hearing on the merits of the claims or defenses in the action. This function distinguishes the trial master from most functions of pretrial and post-trial masters. If any master is to be used for such matters as a preliminary injunction hearing or a determination of complex damages issues, for example, the master should be a trial master. The line, however, is not distinct. A pretrial master might well conduct an evidentiary hearing on a discovery dispute, and a post-trial master might conduct evidentiary hearings on questions of compliance.

Rule 53 has long provided authority to report the evidence without recommendations in nonjury trials. This authority is omitted from Rule 53(a)(1)(B). In some circumstances a master may be appointed under Rule 53(a)(1)(A) or (C) to take evidence and report without recommendations.

For nonjury cases, a master also may be appointed to assist the court in discharging trial duties other than conducting an evidentiary hearing.

Pretrial and Post-Trial Masters. Subparagraph (a)(1)(C) authorizes appointment of a master to address pretrial or post-trial matters. Appointment is limited to matters that cannot be addressed effectively and in a timely fashion by an available district judge or magistrate judge of the district. A master's pretrial or post-trial duties may include matters that could be addressed by a judge, such as reviewing discovery documents for privilege, or duties that might not be suitable for a judge. Some forms of settlement negotiations, investigations, or administration of an organization are familiar examples of duties that a judge might not feel free to undertake.

Magistrate Judges. Particular attention should be paid to the prospect that a magistrate judge may be available for special assignments. United States magistrate judges are authorized by statute to perform many pretrial functions in civil actions. 28 U.S.C. § 636(b)(1). Ordinarily a district judge who delegates these functions should refer them to a magistrate judge acting as magistrate judge.

There is statutory authority to appoint a magistrate judge as special master. 28 U.S.C. § 636(b)(2). In special circumstances, or when expressly authorized by a statute other than § 636(b)(2), it may be appropriate to appoint a magistrate judge as a master when needed to perform functions outside those listed in § 636(b)(1). There is no apparent reason to appoint a magistrate judge to perform as master duties that could be performed in the role of magistrate judge. Party consent is required for trial before a magistrate judge, moreover, and this requirement should not be undercut by resort to Rule 53 unless specifically authorized by statute; see 42 U.S.C. § 2000e–5(f)(5).

Pretrial Masters. The appointment of masters to participate in pretrial proceedings has developed extensively over the last two decades as some district courts have felt the need for additional help in managing complex litigation. This practice is not well regulated by present Rule 53, which focuses on masters as trial participants. Rule 53 is amended to confirm the authority to appoint—and to regulate the use of—pretrial masters.

A pretrial master should be appointed only when the need is clear. Direct judicial performance of judicial functions may be particularly important in cases that involve important public issues or many parties. At the extreme, a broad delegation of pretrial responsibility as well as a delegation of trial responsibilities can run afoul of Article III.

A master also may be appointed to address matters that blur the divide between pretrial and trial functions. The court's responsibility to interpret patent claims as a matter of law, for example, may be greatly assisted by appointing a master who has expert knowledge of the field in which the patent operates. Review of the master's findings will be de novo under Rule 53(g)(4), but the advantages of initial determination by a master may make the process more effective and timely than disposition by the judge acting alone. Determination of foreign law may present comparable difficulties. The decision whether to appoint a master to address such matters is governed by subdivision (a)(1)(C), not the trial-master provisions of subdivision (a)(1)(B).

Post-Trial Masters. Courts have come to rely on masters to assist in framing and enforcing complex decrees. Present Rule 53 does not directly address this practice. Amended Rule 53 authorizes appointment of post-trial masters for these and similar purposes. The constraint of subdivision (a)(1)(C) limits this practice to cases in which the master's duties cannot be performed effectively and in a timely fashion by an available district judge or magistrate judge of the district.

Reliance on a master is appropriate when a complex decree requires complex policing, particularly when a party has proved resistant or intransigent. This practice has been recognized by the Supreme Court, see *Local 28, Sheet Metal Workers' Internat. Assn. v. EEOC*, 478 U.S. 421, 481–482 (1986). The master's role in enforcement may extend to investigation in ways that are quite unlike the traditional role of judicial officers in an adversary system.

Expert Witness Overlap. This rule does not address the difficulties that arise when a single person is appointed to perform overlapping roles as master and as court-appointed expert witness under Evidence Rule 706. Whatever combination of functions is involved, the Rule 53(a)(1)(B) limit that confines trial masters to issues to be decided by the court does not apply to a person who also is appointed as an expert witness under Evidence Rule 706.

Subdivision (a)(2) and (3)

Masters are subject to the Code of Conduct for United States Judges, with exceptions spelled out in the Code. Special care must be taken to ensure that there is no actual or apparent conflict of interest involving a master. The standard of disqualification is established by 28 U.S.C. § 455. The affidavit required by Rule 53(b)(3) provides an important source of information about possible grounds for disqualification, but careful inquiry should be made at the time of making the initial appointment. The disqualification standards established by § 455 are strict. Because a master is not a public judicial officer, it may be appropriate to permit the parties to consent to appointment of a particular person as master in circumstances that would require disqualification of a judge. The judge must be careful to ensure that no party feels any pressure to consent, but with such assurances—and with the judge's own determination that there is no troubling conflict of interests or disquieting appearance of impropriety—consent may justify an otherwise barred appointment.

One potential disqualification issue is peculiar to the master's role. It may happen that a master who is an attorney represents a client whose litigation is assigned to the judge who appointed the attorney as master. Other parties to the litigation may fear that the attorney-master will gain special respect from the judge. A flat prohibition on appearance before the appointing judge during the time of service as master, however, might in some circumstances unduly limit the opportunity to make a desirable appointment. These matters may be regulated to some extent by state rules of professional responsibility. The question of present conflicts, and the possibility of future conflicts, can be considered at the time of appointment. Depending on the circumstances, the judge may consider it appropriate to impose a non-appearance condition on the lawyer-master, and perhaps on the master's firm as well.

Subdivision (b)

The order appointing a pretrial master is vitally important in informing the master and the parties about the nature and extent of the master's duties and authority. Care must be taken to make the order as precise as possible. The parties must be given notice and opportunity to be heard on the question whether a master should be appointed and on the terms of the appointment. To the extent possible, the notice should describe the master's proposed duties, time to complete the duties, standards of review, and compensation. Often it will be useful to engage the parties in the process of identifying the master, inviting nominations, and reviewing potential candidates. Party involvement may be particularly useful if a pretrial master is expected to promote settlement.

The hearing requirement of Rule 53(b)(1) can be satisfied by an opportunity to make written submissions unless the circumstances require live testimony.

Rule 53(b)(2) requires precise designation of the master's duties and authority. Clear identification of any investigating or enforcement duties is particularly important. Clear delineation of topics for any reports or recommendations is also an important part of this process. And it is important to protect against delay by establishing a time schedule for performing the assigned duties. Early designation of the procedure for fixing the master's compensation also may provide useful guidance to the parties.

Ex parte communications between a master and the court present troubling questions. Ordinarily the order should prohibit such communications, assuring that the parties know where authority is lodged at each step of the proceedings. Prohibiting ex parte communications between master and court also can enhance the role of a settlement master by assuring the parties that settlement can be fostered by confidential revelations that will not be shared with the court. Yet there may be circumstances in which the master's role is enhanced by the opportunity for ex parte communications with the court. A master assigned to help coordinate multiple proceedings, for example, may benefit from off-the-record exchanges with the court about logistical matters. The rule does not directly regulate these matters. It requires only that the court exercise its discretion and address the topic in the order of appointment.

Similarly difficult questions surround ex part e communications between a master and the parties. Ex parte communications may be essential in seeking to advance settlement. Ex parte communications also may prove useful in other settings, as with in camera review of documents to resolve privilege questions. In most settings, however, ex parte communications with the parties should be discouraged or prohibited. The rule requires that the court address the topic in the order of appointment.

Subdivision (b)(2)(C) provides that the appointment order must state the nature of the materials to be preserved and filed as the record of the master's activities, and (b)(2)(D) requires that the order state the method of filing the record. It is not feasible to prescribe the nature of the record without regard to the nature of the master's duties. The records appropriate to discovery duties may be different from those appropriate to encouraging settlement, investigating possible violations of a complex decree, or making recommendations for trial findings. A basic requirement, however, is that the master must make and file a complete record of the evidence considered in making or recommending findings of fact on the basis of evidence. The order of appointment should routinely include this requirement unless the nature of the appointment precludes any prospect that the master will make or recommend evidence-based findings of fact. In some circumstances it may be appropriate for a party to file materials directly with the court as provided by Rule 5(e), but in many circumstances filing with the court may be inappropriate. Confidentiality is important with respect to many materials that may properly be considered by a master. Materials in the record can be transmitted to the court, and filed, in connection with review of a master's order, report, or recommendations under subdivisions (f) and (g). Independently of review proceedings, the court may direct filing of any materials that it wishes to make part of the public record.

The provision in subdivision (b)(2)(D) that the order must state the standards for reviewing the master's orders, findings, or recommendations is a reminder of the provisions of subdivision (g)(3) that recognize stipulations for review less searching than the presumptive requirement of de novo decision by the court. Subdivision (b)(2)(D) does not authorize the court to supersede the limits of subdivision (g)(3).

In setting the procedure for fixing the master's compensation, it is useful at the outset to establish specific guidelines to control total expense. The court has power under subdivision (h) to change the basis and terms for determining compensation after notice to the parties.

Subdivision (b)(3) permits entry of the order appointing a master only after the master has filed an affidavit disclosing whether there is any ground for disqualification under 28 U.S.C. § 455. If the affidavit discloses a possible ground for disqualification, the order can enter only if the court determines that there is no ground for disqualification or if the parties, knowing of the ground for disqualification, consent with the court's approval to waive the disqualification.

The provision in Rule 53(b)(4) for amending the order of appointment is as import ant as the provisions for the initial order. Anything that could be done in the initial order can be done by amendment. The hearing requirement can be satisfied by an opportunity to make written submissions unless the circumstances require live testimony.

Subdivision (c)

Subdivision (c) is a simplification of the provisions scattered throughout present Rule 53. It is intended to provide the broad and flexible authority necessary to discharge the master's responsibilities. The most important delineation of a master's authority and duties is provided by the Rule 53(b) appointing order.

Subdivision (d)

The subdivision (d) provisions for evidentiary hearings are reduced from the extensive provisions in current Rule 53. This simplification of the rule is not intended to diminish the authority that may be delegated to a master. Reliance is placed on the broad and general terms of subdivision (c).

Subdivision (e)

Subdivision (e) provides that a master's order must be filed and entered on the docket. It must be promptly served on the parties, a task ordinarily accomplished by mailing or other means as permitted by Rule 5(b). In some circumstances it may be appropriate to have the clerk's office assist the master in mailing the order to the parties.

Subdivision (f)

Subdivision (f) restates some of the provisions of present Rule 53(e)(1). The report is the master's primary means of communication with the court. The materials to be provided to support review of the report will depend on the nature of the report. The master should provide all portions of the record preserved under Rule 53(b)(2)(C) that the master deems relevant to the report. The parties may designate additional materials from the record, and may seek permission to supplement the record with evidence. The court may direct that additional materials from the record be provided and filed. Given the wide array of tasks that may be assigned to a pretrial master, there may be circumstances that justify sealing a report or review record against public access—a report on continuing or failed settlement efforts is the most likely example. A post-trial master may be assigned duties in formulating a decree that deserve similar protection. Such circumstances may even justify denying access to the report or review materials by the parties, although this step should be taken only for the most compelling reasons. Sealing is much less likely to be appropriate with respect to a trial master's report.

Before formally making an order, report, or recommendations, a master may find it helpful to circulate a draft to the parties for review and comment. The usefulness of this practice depends on the nature of the master's proposed action.

Subdivision (g)

The provisions of subdivision (g)(1), describing the court's powers to afford a hearing, take evidence, and act on a master's order, report, or recommendations are drawn from present Rule 53(e)(2), but are not limited, as present Rule 53(e)(2) is limited, to the report of a trial master in a nonjury action. The requirement that the court must afford an opportunity to be heard can be satisfied by taking written submissions when the court acts on the report without taking live testimony.

The subdivision (g)(2) time limits for objecting to—or seeking adoption or modification of—a master's order, report, or recommendations, are important. They are not jurisdictional. Although a court may properly refuse to entertain untimely review proceedings, the court may excuse the failure to seek timely review. The basic time period is lengthened to 20 days because the present 10-day period may be too short to permit thorough study and response to a complex report dealing with complex litigation. If no party asks the court to act on a master's report, the court is free to adopt the master's action or to disregard it at any relevant point in the proceedings.

Subdivision (g)(3) establishes the standards of review for a master's findings of fact or recommended findings of fact. The court must decide de novo all objections to findings of fact made or recommended by the master unless the parties stipulate, with the court's consent, that the findings will be reviewed for clear error or—with respect to a master appointed on the parties' consent or appointed to address pretrial or post-trial matters—that the findings will be final. Clear-error review is more likely to be appropriate with respect to findings that do not go to the merits of the underlying claims or defenses, such as findings of fact bearing on a privilege objection to a discovery request. Even if no objection is made, the court is free to decide the facts de novo; to review for clear error if an earlier approved stipulation provided clear-error review; or to withdraw its consent to a stipulation for clear-error review or finality, and then to decide de novo. If the court withdraws its consent to a stipulation for finality or clear-error review, it may reopen the opportunity to object.

Under Rule 53(g)(4), the court must decide de novo all objections to conclusions of law made or recommended by a master. As with findings of fact, the court also may decide conclusions of law de novo when no objection is made.

Apart from factual and legal questions, masters often make determinations that, when made by a trial court, would be treated as matters of procedural discretion. The court may set a standard for review of such matters in the order of appointment, and may amend the order to establish the standard. If no standard is set by the original or amended order appointing the master, review of procedural matters is for abuse of discretion. The subordinate role of the master means that the trial court's review for abuse of discretion may be more searching than the review that an appellate court makes of a trial court.

If a master makes a recommendation on any matter that does not fall within Rule 53(g)(3), (4), or (5), the court may act on the recommendation under Rule 53(g)(1).

Subdivision (h)

The need to pay compensation is a substantial reason for care in appointing private persons as masters.

Payment of the master's fees must be allocated among the parties and any property or subject-matter within the court's control. The amount in controversy and the means of the parties may provide some guidance in making the allocation. The nature of the dispute also may be important—parties pursuing matters of public interest, for example, may deserve special protection. A party whose unreasonable behavior has occasioned the need to appoint a master, on the other hand, may properly be charged all or a major portion of the master's fees. It may be proper to revise an interim allocation after decision on the merits. The revision need not await a decision that is final for purposes of appeal, but may be made to reflect disposition of a substantial portion of the case.

The basis and terms for fixing compensation should be stated in the order of appointment. The court retains power to alter the initial basis and terms, after notice and an opportunity to be heard, but should protect the parties against unfair surprise.

The provision of former Rule 53(a) that the "provision for compensation shall not apply when a United States Magistrate Judge is designated to serve as a master" is deleted as unnecessary. Other provisions of law preclude compensation.

Subdivision (i)

Rule 53(i) carries forward unchanged former Rule 53(f).

2007 Amendments

The language of Rule 53 has been amended as part of the general restyling of the Civil Rules to make them more easily understood and to make style and terminology consistent throughout the rules. These changes are intended to be stylistic only.

2009 Amendments

The time set in the former rule at 20 days has been revised to 21 days. See the Note to Rule 6.

HISTORICAL NOTES

Change of Name

United States magistrate appointed under section 631 of Title 28, Judiciary and Judicial Procedure, to be known as United States magistrate judge after Dec. 1, 1990, with any reference to United States magistrate or magistrate in Title 28, in any other Federal statute, etc., deemed a reference to United States magistrate judge appointed under section 631 of Title 28, see section 321 of Pub.L. 101–650, set out as a note under section 631 of Title 28.

TITLE VII. JUDGMENT

Rule 54.   Judgment; Costs

(a) Definition; Form. "Judgment" as used in these rules includes a decree and any order from which an appeal lies. A judgment should not include recitals of pleadings, a master's report, or a record of prior proceedings.

(b) Judgment on Multiple Claims or Involving Multiple Parties. When an action presents more than one claim for relief—whether as a claim, counterclaim, crossclaim, or third-party claim—or when multiple parties are involved, the court may direct entry of a final judgment as to one or more, but fewer than all, claims or parties only if the court expressly determines that there is no just reason for delay. Otherwise, any order or other decision, however designated, that adjudicates fewer than all the claims or the rights and liabilities of fewer than all the parties does not end the action as to any of the claims or parties and may be revised at any time before the entry of a judgment adjudicating all the claims and all the parties' rights and liabilities.

(c) Demand for Judgment; Relief to Be Granted. A default judgment must not differ in kind from, or exceed in amount, what is demanded in the pleadings. Every other final judgment should grant the relief to which each party is entitled, even if the party has not demanded that relief in its pleadings.

(d) Costs; Attorney's Fees.

    (1) *Costs Other Than Attorney's Fees.* Unless a federal statute, these rules, or a court order provides otherwise, costs—other than attorney's fees—should be allowed to the prevailing party. But costs against the United States, its officers, and its agencies may be imposed only to the extent allowed by law. The clerk may tax costs on 14 days' notice. On motion served within the next 7 days, the court may review the clerk's action.

    (2) *Attorney's Fees.*

        (A) *Claim to Be by Motion.* A claim for attorney's fees and related nontaxable expenses must be made by motion unless the substantive law requires those fees to be proved at trial as an element of damages.

        (B) *Timing and Contents of the Motion.* Unless a statute or a court order provides otherwise, the motion must:

            (i) be filed no later than 14 days after the entry of judgment;

            (ii) specify the judgment and the statute, rule, or other grounds entitling the movant to the award;

            (iii) state the amount sought or provide a fair estimate of it; and

            (iv) disclose, if the court so orders, the terms of any agreement about fees for the services for which the claim is made.

        (C) *Proceedings.* Subject to Rule 23(h), the court must, on a party's request, give an opportunity for adversary submissions on the motion in accordance with Rule 43(c) or 78. The court may decide issues of liability for fees before receiving submissions on the value of services. The court must find the facts and state its conclusions of law as provided in Rule 52(a).

        (D) *Special Procedures by Local Rule; Reference to a Master or a Magistrate Judge.* By local rule, the court may establish special procedures to resolve fee-related issues without extensive evidentiary hearings. Also, the court may refer issues concerning the value of services to a special master under Rule 53 without regard to the limitations of Rule 53(a)(1), and may refer a motion for attorney's fees to a magistrate judge under Rule 72(b) as if it were a dispositive pretrial matter.

        (E) *Exceptions.* Subparagraphs (A)–(D) do not apply to claims for fees and expenses as sanctions for violating these rules or as sanctions under 28 U.S.C. § 1927.

(Amended December 27, 1946, effective March 19, 1948; April 17, 1961, effective July 19, 1961; March 2, 1987, effective August 1, 1987; April 22, 1993, effective December 1, 1993; April 29, 2002, effective December 1, 2002; March 27, 2003, effective December 1, 2003; April 30, 2007, effective December 1, 2007; March 26, 2009, effective December 1, 2009.)

ADVISORY COMMITTEE NOTES

1937 Adoption

    Note to Subdivision (a). The second sentence is derived substantially from [former] Equity Rule 71 (Form of Decree).

    Note to Subdivision (b). This provides for the separate judgment of equity and code practice. See Wis.Stat. (1935) § 270.54; Compare N.Y.C.P.A. (1937) § 476.

Note to Subdivision (c). For the limitation on default contained in the first sentence, see 2 N.D.Comp.Laws Ann. (1913) § 7680; N.Y.C.P.A. (1937) § 479. Compare *English Rules Under the Judicature Act* (The Annual Practice, 1937) O. 13, r.r. 3–12. The remainder is a usual code provision. It makes clear that a judgment should give the relief to which a party is entitled, regardless of whether it is legal or equitable or both. This necessarily includes the deficiency judgment in foreclosure cases formerly provided for by Equity Rule 10 (Decree for Deficiency in Foreclosures, Etc.).

Note to Subdivision (d). For the present rule in common law actions, see *Ex parte Peterson,* 253 U.S. 300, 40 S.Ct. 543, 64 L.Ed. 919 (1920); Payne, *Costs in Common Law Actions in the Federal Courts* (1935), 21 Va.L.Rev. 397.

The provisions as to costs in actions in forma pauperis contained in U.S.C., Title 28, former §§ 832–836 [now 1915] are unaffected by this rule. Other sections of U.S.C., Title 28, which are unaffected by this rule are: [former] §§ 815 (Costs; plaintiff not entitled to, when), 821 [now 1928] (Costs; infringement of patent; disclaimer), 825 (Costs; several actions), 829 [now 1927] (Costs; attorney liable for, when), and 830 [now 1920] (Costs; bill of; taxation).

The provisions of the following and similar statutes as to costs against the United States and its officers and agencies are specifically continued:

U.S.C., Title 15, §§ 77v(a), 78aa, 79y (Securities and Exchange Commission)

U.S.C., Title 16, § 825p (Federal Power Commission)

U.S.C., Title 26, [former] §§ 3679(d) and 3745(d) (Internal revenue actions)

U.S.C., Title 26, [former] § 3770(b)(2) (Reimbursement of costs of recovery against revenue officers)

U.S.C., Title 28, [former] § 817 (Internal revenue actions)

U.S.C., Title 28, § 836 [now 1915] (United States—actions in *forma pauperis*)

U.S.C., Title 28, § 842 [now 2006] (Actions against revenue officers)

U.S.C., Title 28, § 870 [now 2408] (United States—in certain cases)

U.S.C., Title 28, [former] § 906 (United States—foreclosure actions)

U.S.C., Title 47, § 401 (Communications Commission)

The provisions of the following and similar statutes as to costs are unaffected:

U.S.C., Title 7, § 210(f) (Actions for damages based on an order of the Secretary of Agriculture under Stockyards Act)

U.S.C., Title 7, § 499g(c) (Appeals from reparations orders of Secretary of Agriculture under Perishable Commodities Act)

U.S.C., Title 8, [former] § 45 (Action against district attorneys in certain cases)

U.S.C., Title 15, § 15 (Actions for injuries due to violation of antitrust laws)

U.S.C., Title 15, § 72 (Actions for violation of law forbidding importation or sale of articles at less than market value or wholesale prices)

U.S.C., Title 15, § 77k (Actions by persons acquiring securities registered with untrue statements under Securities Act of 1933)

U.S.C., Title 15, § 78i(e) (Certain actions under the Securities Exchange Act of 1934)

U.S.C., Title 15, § 78r (Similar to 78i(e))

U.S.C., Title 15, § 96 (Infringement of trade-mark—damages)

U.S.C., Title 15, § 99 (Infringement of trade-mark—injunctions)

U.S.C., Title 15, § 124 (Infringement of trade-mark—damages)

U.S.C., Title 19, § 274 (Certain actions under customs law)

U.S.C., Title 30, § 32 (Action to determine right to possession of mineral lands in certain cases)

U.S.C., Title 31, §§ 232 [now 3730] and 234 [former] (Action for making false claims upon United States)

U.S.C., Title 33, § 926 (Actions under Harbor Workers' Compensation Act)

U.S.C., Title 35, § 67 [now 281, 284] (Infringement of patent—damages)

U.S.C., Title 35, § 69 [now 282] (Infringement of patent—pleading and proof)

U.S.C., Title 35, § 71 [now 288] (Infringement of patent—when specification too broad)

U.S.C., Title 45, § 153p (Actions for non-compliance with an order of National R.R. Adjustment Board for payment of money)

U.S.C., Title 46, [former] § 38 (Action for penalty for failure to register vessel)

U.S.C., Title 46, § 829 (Action based on non-compliance with an order of Maritime Commission for payment of money)

U.S.C., Title 46, § 941 (Certain actions under Ship Mortgage Act)

U.S.C., Title 46, § 1227 (Actions for damages for violation of certain provisions of the Merchant Marine Act, 1936)

U.S.C., Title 47, § 206 (Actions for certain violations of Communications Act of 1934)

U.S.C., Title 49, § 16(2) [now 11705] (Action based on non-compliance with an order of I.C.C. for payment of money)

1946 Amendment

Note. The historic rule in the federal courts has always prohibited piecemeal disposal of litigation and permitted appeals only from final judgments except in those special instances covered by statute. *Hohorst v. Hamburg—American Packet Co.,* 1893, 13 S.Ct. 590, 148 U.S. 262, 37 L.Ed. 443; *Rexford v. Brunswick-Balke-Collender Co.,* 1913, 33 S.Ct. 515, 228 U.S. 339, 57 L.Ed. 864; *Collins v. Miller,* 1920, 40 S.Ct. 347, 252 U.S. 364, 64 L.Ed. 616. Rule 54(b) was originally adopted in view of the wide scope and possible content of the newly created "civil action" in order to avoid the possible injustice of a delay in judgment of a distinctly separate claim to await adjudication of the entire case. It was not designed to overturn the settled federal rule stated above, which, indeed, has more recently been reiterated in *Catlin v. United States,* 1945, 65 S.Ct. 631, 324 U.S. 229, 89 L.Ed. 911. See also *United States v. Florian,* 1941, 61 S.Ct. 713, 312 U.S. 656, 85 L.Ed. 1105; *Reeves v. Beardall,* 1942, 62 S.Ct. 1085, 316 U.S. 283, 86 L.Ed. 1478.

Unfortunately, this was not always understood, and some confusion ensued. Hence situations arose where district courts made a piecemeal disposition of an action and entered what the parties thought amounted to a judgment, although a trial remained to be had on other claims similar or identical with those disposed of. In the interim the parties did not know their ultimate rights, and accordingly took an appeal, thus putting the finality of the partial judgment in question. While most appellate courts have reached a result generally in accord with the intent of the rule, yet there have been divergent precedents and division of views which have served to render the issues more clouded to the parties appellant. It hardly seems a case where multiplicity of precedents will tend to remove the problem from debate. The problem is presented and discussed in the following cases: *Atwater v. North American Coal Corp.,* C.C.A.2, 1940, 111 F.2d 125; *Rosenblum v. Dingfelder,* C.C.A.2, 1940, 111 F.2d 406; *Audi-Vision, Inc. v. RCA Mfg. Co., Inc.,* C.C.A.2, 1943, 136 F.2d 621; *Zalkind v. Scheinman,* C.C.A.2, 1943, 139 F.2d 895; *Oppenheimer v. F. J. Young & Co., Inc.,* C.C.A.2, 1944, 144 F.2d 387; *Libbey-Owens-Ford Glass Co. v. Sylvania Industrial Corp.,* C.C.A.2, 1946, 154 F.2d 814, certiorari denied 1946, 66 S.Ct. 1353, 328 U.S. 859, 90 L.Ed. 1630; *Zarati Steamship Co. v. Park Bridge Corp.,* C.C.A.2, 1946, 154 F.2d 377; *Baltimore and Ohio R. Co. v. United Fuel Gas Co.,* C.C.A.4, 1946, 154 F.2d 545; *Jefferson Electric Co. v. Sola Electric Co.,* C.C.A.7, 1941, 122 F.2d 124; *Leonard v. Socony-Vacuum Oil Co.,* C.C.A.7, 1942, 130 F.2d 535; *Markham v. Kasper,* C.C.A.7, 1945, 152 F.2d 270; *Hanney v. Franklin Fire Ins. Co. of Philadelphia,* C.C.A.9, 1944, 142 F.2d 864; *Toomey v. Toomey,* App.D.C.1945, 149 F.2d 19, 80 U.S.App.D.C. 77.

In view of the difficulty thus disclosed, the Advisory Committee in its two preliminary drafts of proposed amendments attempted to redefine the original rule with particular stress upon the interlocutory nature of partial judgments which did not adjudicate all claims arising out of a single transaction or occurrence. This attempt appeared to meet with almost universal approval from those of the profession commenting upon it, although there were, of course, helpful suggestions for additional changes in language or clarification of detail. But cf. Circuit Judge Frank's dissenting opinion in *Libbey-Owens-Ford Glass Co. v. Sylvania Industrial Corp.,* supra, n. 21 of the dissenting opinion. The Committee, however, became convinced on careful study of its own proposals that the seeds of ambiguity still remained, and that it had not completely solved the problem of piecemeal appeals. After extended consideration, it concluded that a retention of the older federal rule was desirable, and that this rule needed only the exercise of a discretionary power to afford a remedy in the infrequent harsh case to provide a simple, definite, workable rule. This is afforded by amended Rule 54(b). It re-establishes an ancient policy with clarity and precision. For the possibility of staying execution where not all claims are disposed of under Rule 54(b), see amended Rule 62(h).

1961 Amendment

This rule permitting appeal, upon the trial court's determination of "no just reason for delay," from a judgment upon one or more but less than all the claims in an action, has generally been given a sympathetic construction by the courts and its validity is settled. *Reeves v. Beardall,* 316 U.S. 283 (1942); *Sears, Roebuck & Co. v. Mackey,* 351 U.S. 427 (1956); *Cold Metal Process Co. v. United Engineering & Foundry Co.,* 351 U.S. 445 (1956).

A serious difficulty has, however, arisen because the rule speaks of claims but nowhere mentions parties. A line of cases has developed in the circuits consistently holding the rule to be inapplicable to the dismissal, even with the requisite trial court determination, of one or more but less than all defendants jointly charged in an action, i.e. charged with various forms of concerted or related wrongdoing or related liability. See *Mull v. Ackerman,* 279 F.2d 25 (2d Cir. 1960); *Richards v. Smith,* 276 F.2d 652 (5th Cir. 1960); *Hardy v. Bankers Life & Cas. Co.,* 222 F.2d 827 (7th Cir. 1955); *Steiner v. 20th Century-Fox Film Corp.,* 220 F.2d 105 (9th Cir. 1955). For purposes of Rule 54(b) it was arguable that there were as many "claims" as there were parties defendant and that the rule in its present text applied where less than all of the parties were dismissed, cf. *United Artists Corp. v. Masterpiece Productions, Inc.,* 221 F.2d 213, 215 (2d Cir. 1955); *Bowling Machines, Inc. v. First Nat. Bank,* 283 F.2d 39 (1st Cir. 1960); but the Courts of Appeals are now committed to an opposite view.

The danger of hardship through delay of appeal until the whole action is concluded may be at least as serious in the multiple-parties situations as in multiple-claims cases, see *Pabellon v. Grace Line, Inc.,* 191 F.2d 169, 179 (2d Cir. 1951), cert. denied, 342 U.S. 893 (1951), and courts and commentators have urged that Rule 54(b) be changed to take in the former. See *Reagan v. Traders & General Ins. Co.,* 255 F.2d 845 (5th Cir. 1958); *Meadows v. Greyhound Corp.,* 235 F.2d 233 (5th Cir. 1956); *Steiner v. 20th Century-Fox Film Corp.,* supra; 6 Moore's Federal Practice ¶ 54.34[2] (2d ed. 1953); 3 Barron & Holtzoff, *Federal Practice & Procedure* § 1193.2 (Wright ed. 1958); *Developments in the Law—Multiparty Litigation,* 71 Harv.L.Rev. 874, 981 (1958); Note, 62 Yale L.J. 263, 271 (1953); Ill.Ann.Stat. ch. 110, § 50(2) (Smith-Hurd 1956). The amendment accomplishes this purpose by referring explicitly to parties.

There has been some recent indication that interlocutory appeal under the provisions of 28 U.S.C. § 1292(b), added in 1958, may now be available for the multiple-parties cases here considered. See *Jaftex Corp. v. Randolph Mills, Inc.,* 282 F.2d 508 (2d Cir. 1960). The Rule 54(b) procedure seems preferable for those cases, and § 1292(b) should be held inapplicable to them when the rule is enlarged as here proposed. See *Luckenbach Steamship Co., Inc., v. H. Muehlstein & Co., Inc.,* 280 F.2d 755, 757 (2d Cir. 1960); 1 Barron & Holtzoff, supra, § 58.1, p. 321 (Wright ed. 1960).

1987 Amendment

The amendment is technical. No substantive change is intended.

1993 Amendments

Subdivision (d). This revision adds paragraph (2) to this subdivision to provide for a frequently recurring form of litigation not initially contemplated by the rules—disputes over the amount of attorneys' fees to be awarded in the large number of actions in which prevailing parties may be entitled to such awards or in which the court must determine the fees to be paid from a common fund. This revision seeks to harmonize and clarify procedures that have been developed through case law and local rules.

Paragraph (1). Former subdivision (d), providing for taxation of costs by the clerk, is renumbered as paragraph (1) and revised to exclude applications for attorneys' fees.

Paragraph (2). This new paragraph establishes a procedure for presenting claims for attorneys' fees, whether or not denominated as "costs." It applies also to requests for reimbursement of expenses, not taxable as costs, when recoverable under governing law incident to the award of fees. *Cf. West Virginia Univ. Hosp. v. Casey,* 499 U.S. 83 (1991), holding, prior to the Civil Rights Act of 1991, that expert witness fees were not recoverable under 42 U.S.C. § 1988. As noted in subparagraph (A), it does not, however, apply to fees recoverable as an element of damages, as when sought under the terms of a contract; such damages typically are to be claimed in a pleading and may involve issues to be resolved by a jury. Nor, as provided in subparagraph (E), does it apply to awards of fees as sanctions authorized or mandated under these rules or under 28 U.S.C. § 1927.

Subparagraph (B) provides a deadline for motions for attorneys' fees—14 days after final judgment unless the court or a statute specifies some other time. One purpose of this provision is to assure that the opposing party is informed of the claim before the time for appeal has elapsed. Prior law did not prescribe any specific time limit on claims for attorneys' fees. *White v. New Hampshire Dep't of Employment Sec.,* 455 U.S. 445 (1982). In many nonjury cases the court will want to consider attorneys' fee issues immediately after rendering its judgment on the merits of the case. Note that the time for making claims is specifically stated in some legislation, such as the Equal Access to Justice Act, 28 U.S.C. § 2412(d)(1)(B) (30-day filing period).

Prompt filing affords an opportunity for the court to resolve fee disputes shortly after trial, while the services performed are freshly in mind. It also enables the court in appropriate circumstances to make its ruling on a fee request in time for any appellate review of a dispute over fees to proceed at the same time as review on the merits of the case.

Filing a motion for fees under this subdivision does not affect the finality or the appealability of a judgment, though revised Rule 58 provides a mechanism by which prior to appeal the court can suspend the finality to resolve a motion for fees. If an appeal on the merits of the case is taken, the court may rule on the claim for fees, may defer its ruling on the motion, or may deny the motion without prejudice, directing under subdivision (d)(2)(B) a new period for filing after the appeal has been resolved. A notice of appeal does not extend the time for filing a fee claim based on the initial judgment, but the court under subdivision (d)(2)(B) may effectively extend the period by permitting claims to be filed after resolution of the appeal. A new period for filing will automatically begin if a new judgment is entered following a reversal or remand by the appellate court or the granting of a motion under Rule 59.

The rule does not require that the motion be supported at the time of filing with the evidentiary material bearing on the fees. This material must of course be submitted in due course, according to such schedule as the court may direct in light of the circumstances of the case. What is required is the filing of a motion sufficient to alert the adversary and the court that there is a claim for fees, and the amount of such fees (or a fair estimate).

If directed by the court, the moving party is also required to disclose any fee agreement, including those between attorney and client, between attorneys sharing a fee to be awarded, and between adversaries made in partial settlement of a dispute where the settlement must be implemented by court action as may be required by Rules 23(e) and 23.1 or other like provisions. With respect to the fee arrangements requiring court approval, the court may also by local rule require disclosure immediately after such arrangements are agreed to. *E.g.,* Rule 5 of United States District Court for the Eastern District of New York; *cf. In re "Agent Orange" Product Liability Litigation (MDL 381),* 611 F.Supp. 1452, 1464 (E.D.N.Y.1985).

In the settlement of class actions resulting in a common fund from which fees will be sought, courts frequently have required that claims for fees be presented in advance of hearings to consider approval of the proposed settlement. The rule does not affect this practice, as it permits the court to require submissions of fee claims in advance of entry of judgment.

Subparagraph (C) assures the parties of an opportunity to make an appropriate presentation with respect to issues involving the evaluation of legal services. In some cases, an evidentiary hearing may be needed, but this is not required in every case. The amount of time to be allowed for the preparation of submissions both in support of and in opposition to awards should be tailored to the particular case.

The court is explicitly authorized to make a determination of the liability for fees before receiving submissions by the parties bearing on the amount of an award. This option may be appropriate in actions in which the liability issue is doubtful and the evaluation issues are numerous and complex.

The court may order disclosure of additional information, such as that bearing on prevailing local rates or on the appropriateness of particular services for which compensation is sought.

On rare occasion, the court may determine that discovery under Rules 26–37 would be useful to the parties. *Compare* Rules Governing Section 2254 Cases in the U.S. District Courts, Rule 6. *See* Note, *Determining the Reasonableness of Attorneys' Fees—the Discoverability of Billing Records,* 64 *B.U.L.Rev.* 241 (1984). In complex fee disputes, the court may use case management techniques to limit the scope of the dispute or to facilitate the settlement of fee award disputes.

Fee awards should be made in the form of a separate judgment under Rule 58 since such awards are subject to review in the court of appeals. To facilitate review, the paragraph provides that the court set forth its findings and conclusions as under Rule 52(a), though in most cases this explanation could be quite brief.

Subparagraph (D) explicitly authorizes the court to establish procedures facilitating the efficient and fair resolution of fee claims. A local rule, for example, might call for matters to be presented through affidavits, or might provide for issuance of proposed findings by the court, which would be treated as accepted by the parties unless objected to within a specified time. A court might also consider establishing a schedule reflecting customary fees or factors affecting fees within the community, as implicitly suggested by Justice O'Connor in *Pennsylvania v. Delaware Valley Citizens' Council,* 483 U.S. 711, 733 (1987) (O'Connor, J., concurring) (how particular markets compensate for contingency). *Cf. Thompson v. Kennickell,* 710 F.Supp. 1 (D.D.C.1989) (use of findings in other cases to promote consistency). The parties, of course, should be permitted to show that in the circumstances of the case such a schedule should not be applied or that different hourly rates would be appropriate.

The rule also explicitly permits, without need for a local rule, the court to refer issues regarding the amount of a fee award in a particular case to a master under Rule 53. The district judge may designate a magistrate judge to act as a master for this purpose or may refer a motion for attorneys' fees to a magistrate judge for proposed findings and recommendations under Rule 72(b). This authorization eliminates any controversy as to whether such references are permitted under Rule 53(b) as "matters of account and of difficult computation of damages" and whether motions for attorneys' fees can be treated as the equivalent of a dispositive pretrial matter that can be referred to a magistrate judge. For consistency and efficiency, all such matters might be referred to the same magistrate judge.

Subparagraph (E) excludes from this rule the award of fees as sanctions under these rules or under 28 U.S.C. § 1927.

2002 Amendments

Subdivision (d)(2)(C) is amended to delete the requirement that judgment on a motion for attorney fees be set forth in a separate document. This change complements the amendment of Rule 58(a)(1), which deletes the separate document requirement for an order disposing of a motion for attorney fees under Rule 54. These changes are made to support amendment of Rule 4 of the Federal Rules of Appellate Procedure. It continues to be important that a district court make clear its meaning when it intends an order to be the final disposition of a motion for attorney fees.

The requirement in subdivision (d)(2)(B) that a motion for attorney fees be not only filed but also served no later than 14 days after entry of judgment is changed to require filing only, to establish a parallel with Rules 50, 52, and 59. Service continues to be required under Rule 5(a).

2003 Amendments

Rule 54(d)(2)(D) is revised to reflect amendments to Rule 53.

2007 Amendments

The language of Rule 54 has been amended as part of the general restyling of the Civil Rules to make them more easily understood and to make style and terminology consistent throughout the rules. These changes are intended to be stylistic only.

The words "or class member" have been removed from Rule 54(d)(2)(C) because Rule 23(h)(2) now addresses objections by class members to attorney-fee motions. Rule 54(d)(2)(C) is amended to recognize that Rule 23(h) now controls those aspects of attorney-fee motions in class actions to which it is addressed.

2009 Amendments

Former Rule 54(d)(1) provided that the clerk may tax costs on 1 day's notice. That period was unrealistically short. The new 14-day period provides a better opportunity to prepare and present a response. The former 5-day period to serve a motion to review the clerk's action is extended to 7 days to reflect the change in the Rule 6(a) method for computing periods of less than 11 days.

HISTORICAL NOTES

Effective and Applicability Provisions

1961 Amendments. Amendment adopted on Apr. 17, 1961, effective July 19, 1961, see Rule 86(d).

Rule 55.   Default; Default Judgment

(a) Entering a Default. When a party against whom a judgment for affirmative relief is sought has failed to plead or otherwise defend, and that failure is shown by affidavit or otherwise, the clerk must enter the party's default.

(b) Entering a Default Judgment.

   (1) *By the Clerk.* If the plaintiff's claim is for a sum certain or a sum that can be made certain by computation, the clerk—on the plaintiff's request, with an affidavit showing the amount due—must enter judgment for that amount and costs against a defendant who has been defaulted for not appearing and who is neither a minor nor an incompetent person.

   (2) *By the Court.* In all other cases, the party must apply to the court for a default judgment. A default judgment may be entered against a minor or incompetent person only if represented by a general guardian, conservator, or other like fiduciary who has appeared. If the party against whom a default judgment is sought has appeared personally or by a representative, that party or its representative must be served with written notice of the application at least 7 days before the hearing. The court may conduct hearings or make referrals—preserving any federal statutory right to a jury trial—when, to enter or effectuate judgment, it needs to:

   (A) conduct an accounting;

   (B) determine the amount of damages;

   (C) establish the truth of any allegation by evidence; or

   (D) investigate any other matter.

(c) Setting Aside a Default or a Default Judgment. The court may set aside an entry of default for good cause, and it may set aside a final default judgment under Rule 60(b).

(d) Judgment Against the United States. A default judgment may be entered against the United States, its officers, or its agencies only if the claimant establishes a claim or right to relief by evidence that satisfies the court.

(Amended March 2, 1987, effective August 1, 1987; April 30, 2007, effective December 1, 2007; March 26, 2009, effective December 1, 2009; April 29, 2015, effective December 1, 2015.)

ADVISORY COMMITTEE NOTES

1937 Adoption

This represents the joining of the equity decree *pro confesso* (former Equity Rules 12 (Issue of Subpoena—Time for Answer), 16 (Defendant to Answer—Default—Decree *Pro Confesso*), 17 (Decree *Pro Confesso* to be Followed by Final Decree—Setting Aside Default), 29 (Defenses—How Presented), 31 (Reply—When Required—When Cause at Issue)) and the judgment by default now governed by U.S.C., Title 28, [former] § 724 (Conformity act). For dismissal of an action for failure to comply with these rules or any order of the court, see Rule 41(b).

Note to Subdivision (a). The provision for the entry of default comes from the Massachusetts practice, 2 Mass.Gen.Laws (Ter.Ed., 1932) ch. 231, § 57. For affidavit of default, see 2 Minn.Stat. (Mason, 1927) § 9256.

Note to Subdivision (b). The provision in paragraph (1) for the entry of judgment by the clerk when plaintiff claims a sum certain is found in the N.Y.C.P.A. (1937) § 485, in Calif.Code Civ.Proc. (Deering, 1937) § 585(1), and in Conn.Practice Book (1934) § 47. For provisions similar to paragraph (2), compare Calif.Code, *supra*, § 585(2); N.Y.C.P.A. (1937) § 490; 2 Minn.Stat. (Mason, 1927) § 9256(3); 2 Wash.Rev.Stat.Ann. (Remington, 1932) § 411(2). U.S.C., Title 28, § 1874, formerly § 785 (Action to recover forfeiture in bond) and similar statutes are preserved by the last clause of paragraph (2).

Note to Subdivision (e). This restates substantially the last clause of U.S.C., Title 28, [former] § 763 (Action against the United States under the Tucker Act). As this rule governs in all actions against the United States, U.S.C., Title 28, [former] § 45 (Practice and procedure in certain cases under the interstate commerce laws) and similar statutes are modified insofar as they contain anything inconsistent therewith.

Supplementary Note

Note. The operation of Rule 55(b) (Judgment) is directly affected by the Soldiers' and Sailors' Civil Relief Act of 1940, 50 U.S.C. Appendix, § 501 et seq. Section 200 of the Act [50 U.S.C. Appendix, § 520] imposes specific requirements which must be fulfilled before a default judgment can be entered, e.g., *Ledwith v. Storkan,* D.Neb.1942, 6 Fed.Rules Serv. 60b.24, Case 2, 2 F.R.D. 539, and also provides for the vacation of a judgment in certain circumstances. See discussion in Commentary, Effect of Conscription Legislation on the Federal Rules, 1940, 3 Fed.Rules Serv. 725; 3 *Moore's Federal Practice,* 1938, Cum.Supplement § 55.02.

1987 Amendment

The amendments are technical. No substantive change is intended.

2007 Amendments

The language of Rule 55 has been amended as part of the general restyling of the Civil Rules to make them more easily understood and to make style and terminology consistent throughout the rules. These changes are intended to be stylistic only.

Former Rule 55(a) directed the clerk to enter a default when a party failed to plead or otherwise defend "as provided by these rules." The implication from the reference to defending "as provided by these rules" seemed to be that the clerk should enter a default even if a party did something showing an intent to defend, but that act was not specifically described by the rules. Courts in fact have rejected that implication. Acts that show an intent to defend have frequently prevented a default even though not connected to any particular rule. "[A]s provided by these rules" is deleted to reflect Rule 55(a)'s actual meaning.

Amended Rule 55 omits former Rule 55(d), which included two provisions. The first recognized that Rule 55 applies to described claimants. The list was incomplete and unnecessary. Rule 55(a) applies Rule 55 to any party against whom a judgment for affirmative relief is requested. The second provision was a redundant reminder that Rule 54(c) limits the relief available by default judgment.

2009 Amendments

The time set in the former rule at 3 days has been revised to 7 days. See the Note to Rule 6.

2015 Amendment

Rule 55(c) is amended to make plain the interplay between Rules 54(b), 55(c), and 60(b). A default judgment that does not dispose of all of the claims among all parties is not a final judgment unless the court directs entry of final judgment under Rule 54(b). Until final judgment is entered, Rule 54(b) allows revision of the default judgment at any time. The demanding standards set by Rule 60(b) apply only in seeking relief from a final judgment.

Rule 56. Summary Judgment

(a) **Motion for Summary Judgment or Partial Summary Judgment.** A party may move for summary judgment, identifying each claim or defense—or the part of each claim or defense—on which summary judgment is sought. The court shall grant summary judgment if the movant shows that there is no genuine dispute as to any material fact and the movant is entitled to judgment as a matter of law. The court should state on the record the reasons for granting or denying the motion.

(b) **Time to File a Motion.** Unless a different time is set by local rule or the court orders otherwise, a party may file a motion for summary judgment at any time until 30 days after the close of all discovery.

(c) **Procedures.**

   (1) *Supporting Factual Positions.* A party asserting that a fact cannot be or is genuinely disputed must support the assertion by:

   (A) citing to particular parts of materials in the record, including depositions, documents, electronically stored information, affidavits or declarations, stipulations (including those made for purposes of the motion only), admissions, interrogatory answers, or other materials; or

   (B) showing that the materials cited do not establish the absence or presence of a genuine dispute, or that an adverse party cannot produce admissible evidence to support the fact.

   (2) *Objection That a Fact Is Not Supported by Admissible Evidence.* A party may object that the material cited to support or dispute a fact cannot be presented in a form that would be admissible in evidence.

   (3) *Materials Not Cited.* The court need consider only the cited materials, but it may consider other materials in the record.

   (4) *Affidavits or Declarations.* An affidavit or declaration used to support or oppose a motion must be made on personal knowledge, set out facts that would be admissible in evidence, and show that the affiant or declarant is competent to testify on the matters stated.

(d) **When Facts Are Unavailable to the Nonmovant.** If a nonmovant shows by affidavit or declaration that, for specified reasons, it cannot present facts essential to justify its opposition, the court may:

   (1) defer considering the motion or deny it;

   (2) allow time to obtain affidavits or declarations or to take discovery; or

   (3) issue any other appropriate order.

(e) **Failing to Properly Support or Address a Fact.** If a party fails to properly support an assertion of fact or fails to properly address another party's assertion of fact as required by Rule 56(c), the court may:

   (1) give an opportunity to properly support or address the fact;

   (2) consider the fact undisputed for purposes of the motion;

(3) grant summary judgment if the motion and supporting materials—including the facts considered undisputed—show that the movant is entitled to it; or

(4) issue any other appropriate order.

(f) Judgment Independent of the Motion. After giving notice and a reasonable time to respond, the court may:

(1) grant summary judgment for a nonmovant;

(2) grant the motion on grounds not raised by a party; or

(3) consider summary judgment on its own after identifying for the parties material facts that may not be genuinely in dispute.

(g) Failing to Grant All the Requested Relief. If the court does not grant all the relief requested by the motion, it may enter an order stating any material fact—including an item of damages or other relief—that is not genuinely in dispute and treating the fact as established in the case.

(h) Affidavit or Declaration Submitted in Bad Faith. If satisfied that an affidavit or declaration under this rule is submitted in bad faith or solely for delay, the court—after notice and a reasonable time to respond—may order the submitting party to pay the other party the reasonable expenses, including attorney's fees, it incurred as a result. An offending party or attorney may also be held in contempt or subjected to other appropriate sanctions.

(Amended December 27, 1946, effective March 19, 1948; January 21, 1963, effective July 1, 1963; March 2, 1987, effective August 1, 1987; April 30, 2007, effective December 1, 2007; March 26, 2009, effective December 1, 2009; April 28, 2010, effective December 1, 2010.)

ADVISORY COMMITTEE NOTES

1937 Adoption

This rule is applicable to all actions, including those against the United States or an officer or agency thereof.

Summary judgment procedure is a method for promptly disposing of actions in which there is no genuine issue as to any material fact. It has been extensively used in England for more than 50 years and has been adopted in a number of American states. New York, for example, has made great use of it. During the first nine years after its adoption there, the records of New York county alone show 5,600 applications for summary judgments. Report of the Commission on the Administration of Justice in New York State (1934), p. 383. See also *Third Annual Report of the Judicial Council of the State of New York* (1937), p. 30.

In England it was first employed only in cases of liquidated claims, but there has been a steady enlargement of the scope of the remedy until it is now used in actions to recover land or chattels and in all other actions at law, for liquidated or unliquidated claims, except for a few designated torts and breach of promise of marriage. *English Rules Under the Judicature Act* (The Annual Practice, 1937) O. 3, r. 6; Orders 14, 14A, and 15; see also O. 32, r. 6, authorizing an application for judgment at any time upon admissions. In Michigan (3 Comp.Laws (1929) § 14260) and Illinois (Smith-Hurd Ill.Stats. c. 110, §§ 181, 259.15, 259.16), it is not limited to liquidated demands. New York (N.Y.R.C.P. (1937) Rule 113; see also Rule 107) has brought so many classes of actions under the operation of the rule that the Commission on Administration of Justice in New York State (1934) recommend that all restrictions be removed and that the remedy be available "in any action" (p. 287). For the history and nature of the summary judgment procedure and citations of state statutes, see Clark and Samenow, *The Summary Judgment* (1929), 38 Yale L.J. 423.

Note to Subdivision (d). See Rule 16 (Pre-Trial Procedure; Formulating Issues) and the Note thereto.

Note to Subdivisions (e) and (f). These are similar to rules in Michigan. Mich.Court Rules Ann. (Searl, 1933) Rule 30.

1946 Amendment

Note to Subdivision (a). The amendment allows a claimant to move for a summary judgment at any time after the expiration of 20 days from the commencement of the action or after service of a motion for summary judgment by the adverse party. This will normally operate to permit an earlier motion by the claimant than under the original rule, where the phrase "at any time after the pleading in answer thereto has been served" operates to prevent a claimant from moving for summary judgment, even in a case clearly proper for its exercise, until a formal answer has been filed. Thus in *Peoples Bank v. Federal Reserve Bank of San Francisco,* N.D.Cal.1944, 58 F.Supp. 25, the plaintiff's countermotion for a summary judgment was stricken as premature, because the defendant had not filed an answer. Since Rule 12(a) allows at least 20 days for an answer, that time plus the 10 days required in Rule 56(c) means that under original Rule 56(a) a minimum period of 30 days necessarily has to elapse in every case before the claimant can be heard on his right to a summary judgment. An extension of time by the court or the service of preliminary motions of any kind will prolong that period even further. In many cases this merely represents unnecessary delay. See *United States v. Adler's Creamery, Inc.,* C.C.A.2, 1939, 107 F.2d 987. The changes are in the interest of more expeditious litigation. The 20-day period, as provided, gives the defendant an opportunity to secure counsel and determine a course of action. But in a case where the defendant himself makes a motion for summary judgment within that time, there is no reason to restrict the plaintiff and the amended rule so provides.

Subdivision (c). The amendment of Rule 56(c), by the addition of the final sentence, resolves a doubt expressed in *Sartor v. Arkansas Natural Gas Corp.,* 1944, 64 S.Ct. 724, 321 U.S. 620, 88 L.Ed. 967. See also Commentary, Summary Judgment as to Damages, 1944, 7 Fed.Rules Serv. 974; *Madeirense Do Brasil S/A v. Stulman-Emrick Lumber Co.,* C.C.A.2d, 1945, 147 F.2d 399, certiorari denied 1945, 65 S.Ct. 1201, 325 U.S. 861, 89 L.Ed. 1982. It makes clear that although the question of recovery depends on the amount of damages, the summary judgment rule is applicable and summary judgment may be granted in a proper case. If the case is not fully adjudicated it may be dealt with as provided in subdivision (d) of Rule 56, and the right to summary recovery determined by a preliminary order, interlocutory in character, and the precise amount of recovery left for trial.

Subdivision (d). Rule 54(a) defines "judgment" as including a decree and "any order from which an appeal lies." Subdivision (d) of Rule 56 indicates clearly, however, that a partial summary "judgment" is not a final judgment, and, therefore, that it is not appealable, unless in the particular case some statute allows an appeal from the interlocutory order involved. The partial summary judgment is merely a pretrial adjudication that certain issues shall be deemed established for the trial of the case. This adjudication is more nearly akin to the preliminary order under Rule 16, and likewise serves the purpose of speeding up litigation by eliminating before trial matters wherein there is no genuine issue of fact. See *Leonard v. Socony-Vacuum Oil Co.,* C.C.A.7, 1942, 130 F.2d 535; *Biggins v. Oltmer Iron Works,* C.C.A.7, 1946, 154 F.2d 214; 3 *Moore's Federal Practice,* 1938, 3190–3192. Since interlocutory appeals are not allowed, except where specifically provided by statute, see 3 Moore, op. cit. supra, 3155–3156, this interpretation is in line with that policy, *Leonard v. Socony-Vacuum Oil Co.,* supra. See also *Audi Vision Inc. v. RCA Mfg. Co.,* C.C.A.2, 1943, 136 F.2d 621; *Toomey v. Toomey,* 1945, 149 F.2d 19, 80 U.S.App.D.C. 77; *Biggins v. Oltmer Iron Works,* supra; *Catlin v. United States,* 1945, 65 S.Ct. 631, 324 U.S. 229, 89 L.Ed. 911.

1963 Amendment

Subdivision (c). By the amendment "answers to interrogatories" are included among the materials which may be considered on motion for summary judgment. The phrase was inadvertently omitted from the rule, see 3 Barron & Holtzoff, *Federal Practice & Procedure* 159–60 (Wright ed. 1958), and the courts have generally reached by interpretation the result which will hereafter be required by the text of the amended rule. See Annot., 74 A.L.R.2d 984 (1960).

Subdivision (e). The words "answers to interrogatories" are added in the third sentence of this subdivision to conform to the amendment of subdivision (c).

The last two sentences are added to overcome a line of cases, chiefly in the Third Circuit, which has impaired the utility of the summary judgment device. A typical case is as follows: A party supports his motion for summary judgment by affidavits or other evidentiary matter sufficient to show that there is no genuine issue as to a material fact. The adverse party, in opposing the motion, does not produce any evidentiary matter, or produces some but not enough to establish that there is a genuine issue for trial. Instead, the adverse party rests on averments of his pleadings which on their face present an issue. In this situation Third Circuit cases have taken the view that summary judgment must be denied, at least if the averments are "well-pleaded," and not suppositious, conclusory, or ultimate. See *Frederick Hart & Co., Inc. v. Recordgraph Corp.,* 169 F.2d 580 (3d Cir. 1948); *United States ex rel. Kolton v. Halpern,* 260 F.2d 590 (3d

Cir. 1958); *United States ex rel. Nobles v. Ivey Bros. Constr. Co., Inc.,* 191 F.Supp. 383 (D.Del.1961); *Jamison v. Pennsylvania Salt Mfg. Co.,* 22 F.R.D. 238 (W.D.Pa.1958); *Bunny Bear, Inc. v. Dennis Mitchell Industries,* 139 F.Supp. 542 (E.D.Pa.1956); *Levy v. Equitable Life Assur. Society,* 18 F.R.D. 164 (E.D.Pa.1955).

The very mission of the summary judgment procedure is to pierce the pleadings and to assess the proof in order to see whether there is a genuine need for trial. The Third Circuit doctrine, which permits the pleadings themselves to stand in the way of granting an otherwise justified summary judgment, is incompatible with the basic purpose of the rule. See 6 *Moore's Federal Practice* 2069 (2d ed. 1953); 3 Barron & Holtzoff, supra, § 1235.1.

It is hoped that the amendment will contribute to the more effective utilization of the salutary device of summary judgment.

The amendment is not intended to derogate from the solemnity of the pleadings. Rather it recognizes that, despite the best efforts of counsel to make his pleadings accurate, they may be overwhelmingly contradicted by the proof available to his adversary.

Nor is the amendment designed to affect the ordinary standards applicable to the summary judgment motion. So, for example: Where an issue as to a material fact cannot be resolved without observation of the demeanor of witnesses in order to evaluate their credibility, summary judgment is not appropriate. Where the evidentiary matter in support of the motion does not establish the absence of a genuine issue, summary judgment must be denied even if no opposing evidentiary matter is presented. And summary judgment may be inappropriate where the party opposing it shows under subdivision (f) that he cannot at the time present facts essential to justify his opposition.

1987 Amendment

The amendments are technical. No substantive change is intended.

2007 Amendments

The language of Rule 56 has been amended as part of the general restyling of the Civil Rules to make them more easily understood and to make style and terminology consistent throughout the rules. These changes are intended to be stylistic only.

Former Rule 56(a) and (b) referred to summary-judgment motions on or against a claim, counterclaim, or crossclaim, or to obtain a declaratory judgment. The list was incomplete. Rule 56 applies to third-party claimants, intervenors, claimants in interpleader, and others. Amended Rule 56(a) and (b) carry forward the present meaning by referring to a party claiming relief and a party against whom relief is sought.

Former Rule 56(c), (d), and (e) stated circumstances in which summary judgment "shall be rendered," the court "shall if practicable" ascertain facts existing without substantial controversy, and "if appropriate, shall" enter summary judgment. In each place "shall" is changed to "should." It is established that although there is no discretion to enter summary judgment when there is a genuine issue as to any material fact, there is discretion to deny summary judgment when it appears that there is no genuine issue as to any material fact. *Kennedy v. Silas Mason Co.,* 334 U.S. 249, 256–257 (1948). Many lower court decisions are gathered in 10A Wright, Miller & Kane, Federal Practice & Procedure: Civil 3d, § 2728. "Should" in amended Rule 56(c) recognizes that courts will seldom exercise the discretion to deny summary judgment when there is no genuine issue as to any material fact. Similarly sparing exercise of this discretion is appropriate under Rule 56(e)(2). Rule 56(d)(1), on the other hand, reflects the more open-ended discretion to decide whether it is practicable to determine what material facts are not genuinely at issue.

Former Rule 56(d) used a variety of different phrases to express the Rule 56(c) standard for summary judgment—that there is no genuine issue as to any material fact. Amended Rule 56(d) adopts terms directly parallel to Rule 56(c).

2009 Amendments

The timing provisions for summary judgment are outmoded. They are consolidated and substantially revised in new subdivision (c)(1). The new rule allows a party to move for summary judgment at any time, even as early as the commencement of the action. If the motion seems premature both subdivision (c)(1) and Rule 6(b) allow the court to extend the time to respond. The rule does set a presumptive deadline at 30 days after the close of all discovery.

The presumptive timing rules are default provisions that may be altered by an order in the case or by local rule. Scheduling orders are likely to supersede the rule provisions in most cases, deferring summary-judgment motions until a stated time or establishing different deadlines. Scheduling orders tailored to the needs of the specific case, perhaps adjusted as it progresses, are likely to work better than default rules. A scheduling order may be adjusted to adopt the parties' agreement on timing, or may require that discovery and motions occur in stages—including separation of expert-witness discovery from other discovery.

Local rules may prove useful when local docket conditions or practices are incompatible with the general Rule 56 timing provisions.

If a motion for summary judgment is filed before a responsive pleading is due from a party affected by the motion, the time for responding to the motion is 21 days after the responsive pleading is due.

2010 Amendments

Rule 56 is revised to improve the procedures for presenting and deciding summary-judgment motions and to make the procedures more consistent with those already used in many courts. The standard for granting summary judgment remains unchanged. The language of subdivision (a) continues to require that there be no genuine dispute as to any material fact and that the movant be entitled to judgment as a matter of law. The amendments will not affect continuing development of the decisional law construing and applying these phrases.

Subdivision (a). Subdivision (a) carries forward the summary-judgment standard expressed in former subdivision (c), changing only one word—genuine "issue" becomes genuine "dispute." "Dispute" better reflects the focus of a summary-judgment determination. As explained below, "shall" also is restored to the place it held from 1938 to 2007.

The first sentence is added to make clear at the beginning that summary judgment may be requested not only as to an entire case but also as to a claim, defense, or part of a claim or defense. The subdivision caption adopts the common phrase "partial summary judgment" to describe disposition of less than the whole action, whether or not the order grants all the relief requested by the motion.

"Shall" is restored to express the direction to grant summary judgment. The word "shall" in Rule 56 acquired significance over many decades of use. Rule 56 was amended in 2007 to replace "shall" with "should" as part of the Style Project, acting under a convention that prohibited any use of "shall." Comments on proposals to amend Rule 56, as published in 2008, have shown that neither of the choices available under the Style Project conventions—"must" or "should"—is suitable in light of the case law on whether a district court has discretion to deny summary judgment when there appears to be no genuine dispute as to any material fact. Compare *Anderson v. Liberty Lobby, Inc.*, 477 U.S. 242, 255 (1986) ("Neither do we suggest that the trial courts should act other than with caution in granting summary judgment or that the trial court may not deny summary judgment in a case in which there is reason to believe that the better course would be to proceed to a full trial. *Kennedy v. Silas Mason Co.*, 334 U.S. 249 * * * (1948)"), with *Celotex Corp. v. Catrett*, 477 U.S. 317, 322 (1986) ("In our view, the plain language of Rule 56(c) mandates the entry of summary judgment, after adequate time for discovery and upon motion, against a party who fails to make a showing sufficient to establish the existence of an element essential to that party's case, and on which that party will bear the burden of proof at trial."). Eliminating "shall" created an unacceptable risk of changing the summary-judgment standard. Restoring "shall" avoids the unintended consequences of any other word.

Subdivision (a) also adds a new direction that the court should state on the record the reasons for granting or denying the motion. Most courts recognize this practice. Among other advantages, a statement of reasons can facilitate an appeal or subsequent trial-court proceedings. It is particularly important to state the reasons for granting summary judgment. The form and detail of the statement of reasons are left to the court's discretion.

The statement on denying summary judgment need not address every available reason. But identification of central issues may help the parties to focus further proceedings.

Subdivision (b). The timing provisions in former subdivisions (a) and (c) are superseded. Although the rule allows a motion for summary judgment to be filed at the commencement of an action, in many cases the motion will be premature until the nonmovant has had time to file a responsive pleading or other pretrial proceedings have been had. Scheduling orders or other pretrial orders can regulate timing to fit the needs of the case.

Subdivision (c). Subdivision (c) is new. It establishes a common procedure for several aspects of summary-judgment motions synthesized from similar elements developed in the cases or found in many local rules.

Subdivision (c)(1) addresses the ways to support an assertion that a fact can or cannot be genuinely disputed. It does not address the form for providing the required support. Different courts and judges have adopted different forms including, for example, directions that the support be included in the motion, made part of a separate statement of facts, interpolated in the body of a brief or memorandum, or provided in a separate statement of facts included in a brief or memorandum.

Subdivision (c)(1)(A) describes the familiar record materials commonly relied upon and requires that the movant cite the particular parts of the materials that support its fact positions. Materials that are not yet in the record—including materials referred to in an affidavit or declaration—must be placed in the record. Once materials are in the record, the court may, by order in the case, direct that the materials be gathered in an appendix, a party may voluntarily submit an appendix, or the parties may submit a joint appendix. The appendix procedure also may be established by local rule. Pointing to a specific location in an appendix satisfies the citation requirement. So too it may be convenient to direct that a party assist the court in locating materials buried in a voluminous record.

Subdivision (c)(1)(B) recognizes that a party need not always point to specific record materials. One party, without citing any other materials, may respond or reply that materials cited to dispute or support a fact do not establish the absence or presence of a genuine dispute. And a party who does not have the trial burden of production may rely on a showing that a party who does have the trial burden cannot produce admissible evidence to carry its burden as to the fact.

Subdivision (c)(2) provides that a party may object that material cited to support or dispute a fact cannot be presented in a form that would be admissible in evidence. The objection functions much as an objection at trial, adjusted for the pretrial setting. The burden is on the proponent to show that the material is admissible as presented or to explain the admissible form that is anticipated. There is no need to make a separate motion to strike. If the case goes to trial, failure to challenge admissibility at the summary-judgment stage does not forfeit the right to challenge admissibility at trial.

Subdivision (c)(3) reflects judicial opinions and local rules provisions stating that the court may decide a motion for summary judgment without undertaking an independent search of the record. Nonetheless, the rule also recognizes that a court may consider record materials not called to its attention by the parties.

Subdivision (c)(4) carries forward some of the provisions of former subdivision (e)(1). Other provisions are relocated or omitted. The requirement that a sworn or certified copy of a paper referred to in an affidavit or declaration be attached to the affidavit or declaration is omitted as unnecessary given the requirement in subdivision (c)(1)(A) that a statement or dispute of fact be supported by materials in the record.

A formal affidavit is no longer required. 28 U.S.C. § 1746 allows a written unsworn declaration, certificate, verification, or statement subscribed in proper form as true under penalty of perjury to substitute for an affidavit.

Subdivision (d). Subdivision (d) carries forward without substantial change the provisions of former subdivision (f).

A party who seeks relief under subdivision (d) may seek an order deferring the time to respond to the summary-judgment motion.

Subdivision (e). Subdivision (e) addresses questions that arise when a party fails to support an assertion of fact or fails to properly address another party's assertion of fact as required by Rule 56(c). As explained below, summary judgment cannot be granted by default even if there is a complete failure to respond to the motion, much less when an attempted response fails to comply with Rule 56(c) requirements. Nor should it be denied by default even if the movant completely fails to reply to a nonmovant's response. Before deciding on other possible action, subdivision (e)(1) recognizes that the court may afford an opportunity to properly support or address the fact. In many circumstances this opportunity will be the court's preferred first step.

Subdivision (e)(2) authorizes the court to consider a fact as undisputed for purposes of the motion when response or reply requirements are not satisfied. This approach reflects the "deemed admitted" provisions in many local rules. The fact is considered undisputed only for purposes of the motion; if summary judgment is denied, a party who failed to make a proper Rule 56 response or reply remains free to contest the fact in further proceedings. And the court may choose not to consider the fact as undisputed, particularly if the court knows of record materials that show grounds for genuine dispute.

Subdivision (e)(3) recognizes that the court may grant summary judgment only if the motion and supporting materials—including the facts considered undisputed under subdivision (e)(2)—show that the movant is entitled to it. Considering some facts undisputed does not of itself allow summary judgment. If there is a proper response or reply as to some facts, the court cannot grant summary judgment without determining whether those facts can be genuinely disputed. Once the court has determined the set of facts—both those it has chosen to consider undisputed for want of a proper response or reply and any that cannot be genuinely disputed despite a procedurally proper response or reply—it must determine the legal consequences of these facts and permissible inferences from them.

Subdivision (e)(4) recognizes that still other orders may be appropriate. The choice among possible orders should be designed to encourage proper presentation of the record. Many courts take extra care with pro se litigants, advising them of the need to respond and the risk of losing by summary judgment if an adequate response is not filed. And the court may seek to reassure itself by some examination of the record before granting summary judgment against a pro se litigant.

Subdivision (f). Subdivision (f) brings into Rule 56 text a number of related procedures that have grown up in practice. After giving notice and a reasonable time to respond the court may grant summary judgment for the nonmoving party; grant a motion on legal or factual grounds not raised by the parties; or consider summary judgment on its own. In many cases it may prove useful first to invite a motion; the invited motion will automatically trigger the regular procedure of subdivision (c).

Subdivision (g). Subdivision (g) applies when the court does not grant all the relief requested by a motion for summary judgment. It becomes relevant only after the court has applied the summary-judgment standard carried forward in subdivision (a) to each claim, defense, or part of a claim or defense, identified by the motion. Once that duty is discharged, the court may decide whether to apply the summary-judgment standard to dispose of a material fact that is not genuinely in dispute. The court must take care that this determination does not interfere with a party's ability to accept a fact for purposes of the motion only. A nonmovant, for example, may feel confident that a genuine dispute as to one or a few facts will defeat the motion, and prefer to avoid the cost of detailed response to all facts stated by the movant. This position should be available without running the risk that the fact will be taken as established under subdivision (g) or otherwise found to have been accepted for other purposes.

If it is readily apparent that the court cannot grant all the relief requested by the motion, it may properly decide that the cost of determining whether some potential fact disputes may be eliminated by summary disposition is greater than the cost of resolving those disputes by other means, including trial. Even if the court believes that a fact is not genuinely in dispute it may refrain from ordering that the fact be treated as established. The court may conclude that it is better to leave open for trial facts and issues that may be better illuminated by the trial of related facts that must be tried in any event.

Subdivision (h). Subdivision (h) carries forward former subdivision (g) with three changes. Sanctions are made discretionary, not mandatory, reflecting the experience that courts seldom invoke the independent Rule 56 authority to impose sanctions. *See* Cecil & Cort, Federal Judicial Center Memorandum on Federal Rule of Civil Procedure 56(g) Motions for Sanctions (April 2, 2007). In addition, the rule text is expanded to recognize the need to provide notice and a reasonable time to respond. Finally, authority to impose other appropriate sanctions also is recognized.

Rule 57.   Declaratory Judgment

These rules govern the procedure for obtaining a declaratory judgment under 28 U.S.C. § 2201. Rules 38 and 39 govern a demand for a jury trial. The existence of another adequate remedy does not preclude a declaratory judgment that is otherwise appropriate. The court may order a speedy hearing of a declaratory-judgment action.

(Amended December 29, 1948, effective October 20, 1949; April 30, 2007, effective December 1, 2007.)

ADVISORY COMMITTEE NOTES

1937 Adoption

The fact that a declaratory judgment may be granted "whether or not further relief is or could be prayed" indicates that declaratory relief is alternative or cumulative and not exclusive or extraordinary. A declaratory judgment is appropriate when it will "terminate the controversy" giving rise on undisputed or relatively undisputed facts, it operates frequently as a summary proceeding, justifying docketing the case for early hearing as on a motion, as provided for in California (Code Civ.Proc. (Deering, 1937) § 1062a), Michigan (3 Comp.Laws (1929) § 13904), and Kentucky (Codes (Carroll, 1932) Civ.Pract. § 639a–3).

The "controversy" must necessarily be "of a justiciable nature, thus excluding an advisory decree upon a hypothetical state of facts." *Ashwander v. Tennessee Valley Authority,* 1936, 56 S.Ct. 466, 473, 297 U.S. 288, 80 L.Ed. 688. The existence or non-existence of any right, duty, power, liability, privilege, disability, or immunity or of any fact upon which such legal relations depend, or of a status, may be declared. The petitioner must have a practical interest in the declaration sought and all parties having an interest therein or adversely affected must be made parties or be cited. A declaration may not be rendered if a special statutory proceeding has been provided for the adjudication of some special type of case, but general ordinary or extraordinary legal remedies, whether regulated by statute or not, are not deemed special statutory proceedings.

When declaratory relief will not be effective in settling the controversy, the court may decline to grant it. But the fact that another remedy would be equally effective affords no ground for declining declaratory relief. The demand for relief shall state with precision the declaratory judgment relief, cumulatively or in the alternative; but when coercive relief only is sought but is deemed ungrantable, or inappropriate, the court may *sua sponte*, if it serves a useful purpose, grant instead a declaration of rights. *Hasselbring v. Koepke,* 1933, 248 N.W. 869, 263 Mich. 466, 93 A.L.R. 1170. Written instruments, including ordinances and statutes, may be construed before or after breach at the petition of a properly interested party, process being served on the private parties or public officials interested. In other respects the Uniform Declaratory Judgment Act affords a guide to the scope and function of the Federal act. Compare *Aetna Life Insurance Co. v. Haworth,* 1937, 57 S.Ct. 461, 300 U.S. 227, 81 L.Ed. 617, 108 A.L.R. 1000; *Nashville, Chattanooga & St. Louis Ry. v. Wallace,* 1933, 53 S.Ct. 345, 288 U.S. 249, 77 L.Ed. 730, 87 A.L.R. 1191; *Gully, Tax Collector v. Interstate Natural Gas Co.,* 82 F.2d 145 (C.C.A.5, 1936); *Ohio Casualty Ins. Co. v. Plummer,* Tex.1935, 13 F.Supp. 169; Borchard, Declaratory Judgments (1934), *passim.*

1948 Amendment

The amendment effective October 1949, substituted the reference to "Title 28, U.S.C., § 2201" in the first sentence for the reference to "Section 274(d) of the Judicial Code, as amended, U.S.C., Title 28, § 400".

2007 Amendments

The language of Rule 57 has been amended as part of the general restyling of the Civil Rules to make them more easily understood and to make style and terminology consistent throughout the rules. These changes are intended to be stylistic only.

Rule 58.   Entering Judgment

(a) **Separate Document.** Every judgment and amended judgment must be set out in a separate document, but a separate document is not required for an order disposing of a motion:

    (1)   for judgment under Rule 50(b);

    (2)   to amend or make additional findings under Rule 52(b);

    (3)   for attorney's fees under Rule 54;

    (4)   for a new trial, or to alter or amend the judgment, under Rule 59; or

    (5)   for relief under Rule 60.

(b) Entering Judgment.

    (1) *Without the Court's Direction.* Subject to Rule 54(b) and unless the court orders otherwise, the clerk must, without awaiting the court's direction, promptly prepare, sign, and enter the judgment when:

        (A) the jury returns a general verdict;

        (B) the court awards only costs or a sum certain; or

        (C) the court denies all relief.

    (2) *Court's Approval Required.* Subject to Rule 54(b), the court must promptly approve the form of the judgment, which the clerk must promptly enter, when:

        (A) the jury returns a special verdict or a general verdict with answers to written questions; or

        (B) the court grants other relief not described in this subdivision (b).

(c) Time of Entry. For purposes of these rules, judgment is entered at the following times:

    (1) if a separate document is not required, when the judgment is entered in the civil docket under Rule 79(a); or

    (2) if a separate document is required, when the judgment is entered in the civil docket under Rule 79(a) and the earlier of these events occurs:

        (A) it is set out in a separate document; or

        (B) 150 days have run from the entry in the civil docket.

(d) Request for Entry. A party may request that judgment be set out in a separate document as required by Rule 58(a).

(e) Cost or Fee Awards. Ordinarily, the entry of judgment may not be delayed, nor the time for appeal extended, in order to tax costs or award fees. But if a timely motion for attorney's fees is made under Rule 54(d)(2), the court may act before a notice of appeal has been filed and become effective to order that the motion have the same effect under Federal Rule of Appellate Procedure 4(a)(4) as a timely motion under Rule 59.

(Amended December 27, 1946, effective March 19, 1948; January 21, 1963, effective July 1, 1963; April 22, 1993, effective December 1, 1993; April 29, 2002, effective December 1, 2002; April 30, 2007, effective December 1, 2007.)

ADVISORY COMMITTEE NOTES

1937 Adoption

See Wis.Stat. (1935) § 270.31 (judgment entered forthwith on verdict of jury unless otherwise ordered), § 270.65 (where trial is by the court, entered by direction of the court), § 270.63 (entered by clerk on judgment on admitted claim for money). Compare 1 Idaho Code Ann. (1932) § 7–1101, and 4 Mont.Rev.Codes Ann. (1935) § 9403, which provide that judgment in jury cases be entered by clerk within 24 hours after verdict unless court otherwise directs. Conn.Practice Book (1934), § 200, provides that all judgments shall be entered within one week after rendition. In some States such as Washington, 2 Rev.Stat.Ann. (Remington, 1932), § 431, in jury cases the judgment is entered two days after the return of verdict to give time for making motion for new trial; § 435 (*ibid.*), provides that all judgments shall be entered by the clerk, subject to the court's direction.

1946 Amendment

Note. The reference to Rule 54(b) is made necessary by the amendment of that rule.

Two changes have been made in Rule 58 in order to clarify the practice. The substitution of the more inclusive phrase "all relief be denied" for the words "there be no recovery", makes it clear that the clerk shall enter the judgment forthwith in the situations specified without awaiting the filing of a formal judgment approved by the court. The phrase "all relief be denied" covers cases such as the denial of a bankrupt's discharge and similar situations where the relief sought is refused but there is literally no denial of a "recovery".

The addition of the last sentence in the rule emphasizes that judgments are to be entered promptly by the clerk without waiting for the taxing of costs. Certain district court rules, for example, Civil Rule 22 of the Southern District of New York—until its annulment Oct. 1, 1945, for conflict with this rule—and the like rule of the Eastern District of New York, are expressly in conflict with this provision, although the federal law is of long standing and well settled. *Fowler v. Hamill,* 1891, 11 S.Ct. 663, 139 U.S. 549, 35 L.Ed. 266; *Craig v. The Hartford,* C.C.Cal.1856, Fed.Cas. No. 3,333; *Tuttle v. Claflin,* C.C.A.2, 1895, 60 F. 7, certiorari denied 1897; 17 S.Ct. 992, 166 U.S. 721, 41 L.Ed. 1188; *Prescott & A.C. Ry. Co. v. Atchison, T. & S.F.R. Co.,* C.C.A.2, 1897, 84 F. 213; *Stallo v. Wagner,* C.C.A.2, 1917, 245 F. 636, 639–40; *Brown v. Parker,* C.C.A.8, 1899, 97 F. 446; *Allis-Chalmers v. United States,* C.C.A.7, 1908, 162 F. 679. And this applies even though state law is to the contrary. *United States v. Nordbye,* C.C.A.8, 1935, 75 F.2d 744, certiorari denied 56 S.Ct. 103, 296 U.S. 572, 80 L.Ed. 404. Inasmuch as it has been held that failure of the clerk thus to enter judgment is a "misprision" "not to be excused", *The Washington,* C.C.A.2, 1926, 16 F.2d 206, such a district court rule may have serious consequences for a district court clerk. Rules of this sort also provide for delay in entry of the judgment contrary to Rule 58. See *Commissioner of Internal Revenue v. Bedford's Estate,* 1945, 65 S.Ct. 1157, 325 U.S. 283, 91 L.Ed. 1611.

1963 Amendment

Under the present rule a distinction has sometimes been made between judgments on general jury verdicts, on the one hand, and, on the other, judgments upon decisions of the court that a party shall recover only money or costs or that all relief shall be denied. In the first situation, it is clear that the clerk should enter the judgment without awaiting a direction by the court unless the court otherwise orders. In the second situation it was intended that the clerk should similarly enter the judgment forthwith upon the court's decision; but because of the separate listing in the rule, and the use of the phrase "upon receipt . . . of the direction," the rule has sometimes been interpreted as requiring the clerk to await a separate direction of the court. All these judgments are usually uncomplicated, and should be handled in the same way. The amended rule accordingly deals with them as a single group in clause (1) (substituting the expression "only a sum certain" for the present expression "only money"), and requires the clerk to prepare, sign and enter them forthwith, without awaiting court direction, unless the court makes a contrary order. (The clerk's duty is ministerial and may be performed by a deputy clerk in the name of the clerk. See 28 U.S.C. § 956; cf. *Gilbertson v. United States,* 168 Fed. 672 (7th Cir. 1909).) The more complicated judgments described in clause (2) must be approved by the court before they are entered.

Rule 58 is designed to encourage all reasonable speed in formulating and entering the judgment when the case has been decided. Participation by the attorneys through the submission of forms of judgment involves needless expenditure of time and effort and promotes delay, except in special cases where counsel's assistance can be of real value. See *Matteson v. United States,* 240 F.2d 517, 518–19 (2d Cir. 1956). Accordingly, the amended rule provides that attorneys shall not submit forms of judgment unless directed to do so by the court. This applies to the judgments mentioned in clause (2) as well as clause (1).

Hitherto some difficulty has arisen, chiefly where the court has written an opinion or memorandum containing some apparently directive or dispositive words, e.g., "the plaintiff's motion [for summary judgment] is granted," see *United States v. F. & M. Schaefer Brewing Co.,* 356 U.S. 227, 229, 78 S.Ct. 674, 2 L.Ed.2d 721 (1958). Clerks on occasion have viewed these opinions or memoranda as being in themselves a sufficient basis for entering judgment in the civil docket as provided by Rule 79(a). However, where the opinion or memorandum has not contained all the elements of a judgment, or where the judge has later signed a formal judgment, it has become a matter of doubt whether the purported entry of judgment was effective, starting the time running for post-verdict motions and for the purpose of appeal. See id.; and compare *Blanchard v. Commonwealth Oil Co.,* 294 F.2d 834 (5th Cir. 1961); *United States v. Higginson,* 238 F.2d 439 (1st Cir. 1956); *Danzig v. Virgin Isle Hotel, Inc.,* 278 F.2d 580 (3d Cir. 1960); *Sears v. Austin,* 282 F.2d 340 (9th Cir. 1960), with *Matteson v. United States,* supra; *Erstling v. Southern Bell Tel. & Tel. Co.,* 255 F.2d 93 (5th Cir. 1958); *Barta v. Oglala Sioux Tribe,* 259 F.2d 553 (8th Cir. 1958) cert. denied, 358 U.S. 932, 79 S.Ct. 320, 3 L.Ed.2d 304 (1959); *Beacon Fed. S. & L. Assn. v. Federal Home L. Bank Bd.,* 266 F.2d 246 (7th Cir.), cert. denied, 361 U.S. 823, 80 S.Ct. 70, 4 L.Ed.2d 67 (1959); *Ram v. Paramount Film D. Corp.,* 278 F.2d 191 (4th Cir. 1960).

The amended rule eliminates these uncertainties by requiring that there be a judgment set out on a separate document—distinct from any opinion or memorandum—which provides the basis for the entry of judgment. That judgment shall be on separate documents is also indicated in Rule 79(b); and see General Rule 10 of the U.S. District Courts for the Eastern and Southern Districts of New York; *Ram v. Paramount Film D. Corp.*, supra, at 194.

See the amendment of Rule 79(a) and the new specimen forms of judgment, Forms 31 and 32.

See also Rule 55(b)(1) and (2) covering the subject of judgments by default.

1993 Amendments

Ordinarily the pendency or post-judgment filing of a claim for attorney's fees will not affect the time for appeal from the underlying judgment. See Budinich v. Becton Dickinson & Co., 486 U.S. 196 (1988). Particularly if the claim for fees involves substantial issues or is likely to be affected by the appellate decision, the district court may prefer to defer consideration of the claim for fees until after the appeal is resolved. However, in many cases it may be more efficient to decide fee questions before an appeal is taken so that appeals relating to the fee award can be heard at the same time as appeals relating to the merits of the case. This revision permits, but does not require, the court to delay the finality of the judgment for appellate purposes under revised Fed.R.App.P. 4(a) until the fee dispute is decided. To accomplish this result requires entry of an order by the district court before the time a notice of appeal becomes effective for appellate purposes. If the order is entered, the motion for attorney's fees is treated in the same manner as a timely motion under Rule 59.

2002 Amendments

Rule 58 has provided that a judgment is effective only when set forth on a separate document and entered as provided in Rule 79(a). This simple separate document requirement has been ignored in many cases. The result of failure to enter judgment on a separate document is that the time for making motions under Rules 50, 52, 54(d)(2)(B), 59, and some motions under Rule 60, never begins to run. The time to appeal under Appellate Rule 4(a) also does not begin to run. There have been few visible problems with respect to Rule 50, 52, 54(d)(2)(B), 59, or 60 motions, but there have been many and horridly confused problems under Appellate Rule 4(a). These amendments are designed to work in conjunction with Appellate Rule 4(a) to ensure that appeal time does not linger on indefinitely, and to maintain the integration of the time periods set for Rules 50, 52, 54(d)(2)(B), 59, and 60 with Appellate Rule 4(a).

Rule 58(a) preserves the core of the present separate document requirement, both for the initial judgment and for any amended judgment. No attempt is made to sort through the confusion that some courts have found in addressing the elements of a separate document. It is easy to prepare a separate document that recites the terms of the judgment without offering additional explanation or citation of authority. Forms 31 and 32 provide examples.

Rule 58 is amended, however, to address a problem that arises under Appellate Rule 4(a). Some courts treat such orders as those that deny a motion for new trial as a "judgment," so that appeal time does not start to run until the order is entered on a separate document. Without attempting to address the question whether such orders are appealable, and thus judgments as defined by Rule 54(a), the amendment provides that entry on a separate document is not required for an order disposing of the motions listed in Appellate Rule 4(a). The enumeration of motions drawn from the Appellate Rule 4(a) list is generalized by omitting details that are important for appeal time purposes but that would unnecessarily complicate the separate document requirement. As one example, it is not required that any of the enumerated motions be timely. Many of the enumerated motions are frequently made before judgment is entered. The exemption of the order disposing of the motion does not excuse the obligation to set forth the judgment itself on a separate document. And if disposition of the motion results in an amended judgment, the amended judgment must be set forth on a separate document.

Rule 58(b) discards the attempt to define the time when a judgment becomes "effective." Taken in conjunction with the Rule 54(a) definition of a judgment to include "any order from which an appeal lies," the former Rule 58 definition of effectiveness could cause strange difficulties in implementing pretrial orders that are appealable under interlocutory appeal provisions or under expansive theories of finality. Rule 58(b) replaces the definition of effectiveness with a new provision that defines the time when judgment is entered. If judgment is promptly set forth on a separate document, as should be done when required by Rule 58(a)(1), the new provision will not change the effect of Rule 58. But in the cases in which court and clerk fail to comply with this simple requirement, the motion time periods set by Rules 50, 52, 54, 59, and 60 begin to run after expiration of 150 days from entry of the judgment in the civil docket as required by Rule 79(a).

A companion amendment of Appellate Rule 4(a)(7) integrates these changes with the time to appeal.

The new all-purpose definition of the entry of judgment must be applied with common sense to other questions that may turn on the time when judgment is entered. If the 150-day provision in Rule 58(b)(2)(B)—designed to integrate the time for post-judgment motions with appeal time—serves no purpose, or would defeat the purpose of another rule, it should be disregarded. In theory, for example, the separate document requirement continues to apply to an interlocutory order that is appealable as a final decision under collateral-order doctrine. Appealability under collateral-order doctrine should not be complicated by failure to enter the order as a judgment on a separate document—there is little reason to force trial judges to speculate about the potential appealability of every order, and there is no means to ensure that the trial judge will always reach the same conclusion as the court of appeals. Appeal time should start to run when the collateral order is entered without regard to creation of a separate document and without awaiting expiration of the 150 days provided by Rule 58(b)(2). Drastic surgery on Rules 54(a) and 58 would be required to address this and related issues, however, and it is better to leave this conundrum to the pragmatic disregard that seems its present fate. The present amendments do not seem to make matters worse, apart from one false appearance. If a pretrial order is set forth on a separate document that meets the requirements of Rule 58(b), the time to move for reconsideration seems to begin to run, perhaps years before final judgment. And even if there is no separate document, the time to move for reconsideration seems to begin 150 days after entry in the civil docket. This apparent problem is resolved by Rule 54(b), which expressly permits revision of all orders not made final under Rule 54(b) "at any time before the entry of judgment adjudicating all the claims and the rights and liabilities of all the parties."

New Rule 58(d) replaces the provision that attorneys shall not submit forms of judgment except on direction of the court. This provision was added to Rule 58 to avoid the delays that were frequently encountered by the former practice of directing the attorneys for the prevailing party to prepare a form of judgment, and also to avoid the occasionally inept drafting that resulted from attorney-prepared judgments. See *11 Wright, Miller & Kane, Federal Practice & Procedure: Civil 2d, § 2786*. The express direction in Rule 58(a)(2) for prompt action by the clerk, and by the court if court action is required, addresses this concern. The new provision allowing any party to move for entry of judgment on a separate document will protect all needs for prompt commencement of the periods for motions, appeals, and execution or other enforcement.

Changes Made After Publication and Comment. Minor style changes were made. The definition of the time of entering judgment in Rule 58(b) was extended to reach all Civil Rules, not only the Rules described in the published version—Rules 50, 52, 54(d)(2)(B), 59, 60, and 62. And the time of entry was extended from 60 days to 150 days after entry in the civil docket without a required separate document.

2007 Amendments

The language of Rule 58 has been amended as part of the general restyling of the Civil Rules to make them more easily understood and to make style and terminology consistent throughout the rules. These changes are intended to be stylistic only.

Rule 59. New Trial; Altering or Amending a Judgment

(a) In General.

  (1) *Grounds for New Trial.* The court may, on motion, grant a new trial on all or some of the issues—and to any party—as follows:

  (A) after a jury trial, for any reason for which a new trial has heretofore been granted in an action at law in federal court; or

  (B) after a nonjury trial, for any reason for which a rehearing has heretofore been granted in a suit in equity in federal court.

  (2) *Further Action After a Nonjury Trial.* After a nonjury trial, the court may, on motion for a new trial, open the judgment if one has been entered, take additional testimony, amend findings of fact and conclusions of law or make new ones, and direct the entry of a new judgment.

(b) Time to File a Motion for a New Trial. A motion for a new trial must be filed no later than 28 days after the entry of judgment.

(c) Time to Serve Affidavits. When a motion for a new trial is based on affidavits, they must be filed with the motion. The opposing party has 14 days after being served to file opposing affidavits. The court may permit reply affidavits.

(d) New Trial on the Court's Initiative or for Reasons Not in the Motion. No later than 28 days after the entry of judgment, the court, on its own, may order a new trial for any reason that would justify granting one on a party's motion. After giving the parties notice and an opportunity to be heard, the court may grant a timely motion for a new trial for a reason not stated in the motion. In either event, the court must specify the reasons in its order.

(e) Motion to Alter or Amend a Judgment. A motion to alter or amend a judgment must be filed no later than 28 days after the entry of the judgment.

(Amended December 27, 1946, effective March 19, 1948; February 28, 1966, effective July 1, 1966; April 27, 1995, effective December 1, 1995; April 30, 2007, effective December 1, 2007; March 26, 2009, effective December 1, 2009.)

ADVISORY COMMITTEE NOTES

1937 Adoption

This rule represents an amalgamation of the petition for rehearing of [former] Equity Rule 69 (Petition for Rehearing) and the motion for new trial of 28 U.S.C., § 2111, formerly § 391 (New trials; harmless error), made in the light of the experience and provision of the code States. Compare Calif.Code Civ.Proc., Deering, 1937, §§ 656 to 663a, 28 U.S.C., § 2111, formerly § 391 (New trials; harmless error) is thus substantially continued in this rule. U.S.C., Title 28, [former] § 840 (Executions; stay on conditions) is modified insofar as it contains time provisions inconsistent with Subdivision (b). For the effect of the motion for new trial upon the time for taking an appeal see *Morse v. United States,* 1926, 46 S.Ct. 241, 270 U.S. 151, 70 L.Ed. 518; *Aspen Mining and Smelting Co. v. Billings,* 1893, 14 S.Ct. 4, 150 U.S. 31, 37 L.Ed. 986.

For partial new trials which are permissible under Subdivision (a), see *Gasoline Products Co., Inc. v. Champlin Refining Co.,* 1931, 51 S.Ct. 513, 283 U.S. 494, 75 L.Ed. 1188; *Schuerholz v. Roach,* C.C.A.4, 1932, 58 F.2d 32; *Simmons v. Fish,* 1912, 97 N.E. 102, 210 Mass. 563, Ann.Cas.1912D, 588 (sustaining and recommending the practice and citing federal cases and cases in accord from about sixteen States and contra from three States). The procedure in several States provides specifically for partial new trials. Ariz.Rev.Code Ann., Struckmeyer, 1928, § 3852; Calif.Code Civ.Proc., Deering, 1937, §§ 657, 662; Smith-Hurd Ill.Stats., 1937, c. 110, § 216 (Par. (f)); Md.Ann.Code, Bagby, 1924, Art. 5, §§ 25, 26; Mich.Court Rules Ann., Searl, 1933, Rule 47, § 2; Miss.Sup.Ct.Rule 12, 161 Miss. 903, 905, 1931; N.J.Sup.Ct.Rules 131, 132, 147, 2 N.J.Misc. 1197, 1246–1251, 1255, 1924; 2 N.D.Comp.Laws Ann., 1913, § 7844, as amended by N.D.Laws 1927, ch. 214.

1946 Amendment

Note. Subdivision (b). With the time for appeal to a circuit court of appeals reduced in general to 30 days by the proposed amendment of Rule 73(a), the utility of the original "except" clause, which permits a motion for a new trial on the ground of newly discovered evidence to be made before the expiration of the time for appeal, would have been seriously restricted. It was thought advisable, therefore, to take care of this matter in another way. By amendment of Rule 60(b), newly discovered evidence is made the basis for relief from a judgment, and the maximum time limit has been extended to one year. Accordingly the amendment of Rule 59(b) eliminates the "except" clause and its specific treatment of newly discovered evidence as a ground for a motion for new trial. This ground remains, however, as a basis for a motion for new trial served not later than 10 days after the entry of judgment. See also Rule 60(b).

As to the effect of a motion under subdivision (b) upon the running of appeal time, see amended Rule 73(a) and Note.

Note to Subdivision (e). This subdivision has been added to care for a situation such as that arising in *Boaz v. Mutual Life Ins. Co. of New York,* C.C.A.8, 1944, 146 F.2d 321, and makes clear that the district court possesses the power asserted in that case to alter or amend a judgment after its entry. The subdivision deals only with alteration or amendment of the original judgment in a case and does not relate to a judgment upon motion as provided in Rule 50(b). As to the effect of a motion under subdivision (e) upon the running of appeal time, see amended Rule 73(a) and Note.

The title of Rule 59 has been expanded to indicate the inclusion of this subdivision.

1966 Amendment

By narrow interpretation of Rule 59(b) and (d), it has been held that the trial court is without power to grant a motion for a new trial, timely served, by an order made more than 10 days after the entry of judgment, based upon a ground not stated in the motion but perceived and relied on by the trial court sua sponte. *Freid v. McGrath,* 133 F.2d 350 (D.C.Cir. 1942); *National Farmers Union Auto. & Cas. Co. v. Wood,* 207 F.2d 659 (10th Cir. 1953); *Bailey v. Slentz,* 189 F.2d 406 (10th Cir. 1951); *Marshall's U.S. Auto Supply, Inc. v. Cashman,* 111 F.2d 140 (10th Cir. 1940), cert. denied, 311 U.S. 667 (1940); but see *Steinberg v. Indemnity Ins. Co.,* 36 F.R.D. 253 (E.D.La.1964).

The result is undesirable. Just as the court has power under Rule 59(d) to grant a new trial of its own initiative within the 10 days, so it should have power, when an effective new trial motion has been made and is pending, to decide it on grounds thought meritorious by the court although not advanced in the motion. The second sentence added by amendment to Rule 59(d) confirms the court's power in the latter situation, with provision that the parties be afforded a hearing before the power is exercised. See 6 *Moore's Federal Practice,* par. 59.09[2] (2d ed. 1953).

In considering whether a given ground has or has not been advanced in the motion made by the party, it should be borne in mind that the particularity called for in stating the grounds for a new trial motion is the same as that required for all motions by Rule 7(b)(1). The latter rule does not require ritualistic detail but rather a fair indication to court and counsel of the substance of the grounds relied on. See *Lebeck v. William A. Jarvis Co.,* 250 F.2d 285 (3d Cir. 1957); *Tsai v. Rosenthal,* 297 F.2d 614 (8th Cir. 1961); *General Motors Corp. v. Perry,* 303 F.2d 544 (7th Cir. 1962); cf. *Grimm v. California Spray-Chemical Corp.,* 264 F.2d 145 (9th Cir. 1959); *Cooper v. Midwest Feed Products Co.,* 271 F.2d 177 (8th Cir. 1959).

1995 Amendments

The only change, other than stylistic, intended by this revision is to add explicit time limits for filing motions for a new trial, motions to alter or amend a judgment, and affidavits opposing a new trial motion. Previously, there was an inconsistency in the wording of Rules 50, 52, and 59 with respect to whether certain post-judgment motions had to be filed, or merely served, during the prescribed period. This inconsistency caused special problems when motions for a new trial were joined with other post-judgment motions. These motions affect the finality of the judgment, a matter often of importance to third persons as well as the parties and the court. The Committee believes that each of these rules should be revised to require filing before end of the 10-day period. Filing is an event that can be determined with certainty from court records. The phrase "no later than" is used—rather than "within"—to include post-judgment motions that sometimes are filed before actual entry of the judgment by the clerk. It should be noted that under Rule 5 the motions when filed are to contain a certificate of service on other parties. It also should be noted that under Rule 6(a) Saturdays, Sundays, and legal holidays are excluded in measuring the 10-day period, but that Bankruptcy Rule 9006(a) excludes intermediate Saturdays, Sundays, and legal holidays only in computing periods less than 8 days.

2007 Amendments

The language of Rule 59 has been amended as part of the general restyling of the Civil Rules to make them more easily understood and to make style and terminology consistent throughout the rules. These changes are intended to be stylistic only.

2009 Amendments

Former Rules 50, 52, and 59 adopted 10-day periods for their respective post-judgment motions. Rule 6(b) prohibits any expansion of those periods. Experience has proved that in many cases it is not possible to prepare a satisfactory post-judgment motion in 10 days, even under the former rule that excluded intermediate Saturdays, Sundays, and legal holidays. These time periods are particularly sensitive because Appellate Rule 4 integrates the time to appeal with a timely motion under these rules. Rather than introduce the prospect of uncertainty in appeal time by amending Rule 6(b) to permit additional time, the former 10-day periods are expanded to 28 days. Rule 6(b) continues to prohibit expansion of the 28-day period.

Former Rule 59(c) set a 10-day period after being served with a motion for new trial to file opposing affidavits. It also provided that the period could be extended for up to 20 days for good cause or by stipulation. The apparent 20-day limit on extending the time to file opposing affidavits seemed to conflict with the Rule 6(b) authority to extend time without any specific limit. This tension between the two rules may have been inadvertent. It is resolved by deleting the former Rule 59(c) limit. Rule 6(b) governs. The underlying 10-day period was extended to 14 days to reflect the change in the Rule 6(a) method for computing periods of less than 11 days.

Rule 60. Relief from a Judgment or Order

(a) Corrections Based on Clerical Mistakes; Oversights and Omissions. The court may correct a clerical mistake or a mistake arising from oversight or omission whenever one is found in a judgment, order, or other part of the record. The court may do so on motion or on its own, with or without notice. But after an appeal has been docketed in the appellate court and while it is pending, such a mistake may be corrected only with the appellate court's leave.

(b) Grounds for Relief from a Final Judgment, Order, or Proceeding. On motion and just terms, the court may relieve a party or its legal representative from a final judgment, order, or proceeding for the following reasons:

(1) mistake, inadvertence, surprise, or excusable neglect;

(2) newly discovered evidence that, with reasonable diligence, could not have been discovered in time to move for a new trial under Rule 59(b);

(3) fraud (whether previously called intrinsic or extrinsic), misrepresentation, or misconduct by an opposing party;

(4) the judgment is void;

(5) the judgment has been satisfied, released or discharged; it is based on an earlier judgment that has been reversed or vacated; or applying it prospectively is no longer equitable; or

(6) any other reason that justifies relief.

(c) Timing and Effect of the Motion.

(1) *Timing.* A motion under Rule 60(b) must be made within a reasonable time—and for reasons (1), (2), and (3) no more than a year after the entry of the judgment or order or the date of the proceeding.

(2) *Effect on Finality.* The motion does not affect the judgment's finality or suspend its operation.

(d) Other Powers to Grant Relief. This rule does not limit a court's power to:

(1) entertain an independent action to relieve a party from a judgment, order, or proceeding;

(2) grant relief under 28 U.S.C. § 1655 to a defendant who was not personally notified of the action; or

(3) set aside a judgment for fraud on the court.

(e) Bills and Writs Abolished. The following are abolished: bills of review, bills in the nature of bills of review, and writs of coram nobis, coram vobis, and audita querela.

(Amended December 27, 1946, effective March 19, 1948; December 29, 1948, effective October 20, 1949; March 2, 1987, effective August 1, 1987; April 30, 2007, effective December 1, 2007.)

ADVISORY COMMITTEE NOTES
1937 Adoption

Note to Subdivision (a). See [former] Equity Rule 72 (Correction of Clerical Mistakes in Orders and Decrees); Mich.Court Rules Ann. (Searl, 1933) Rule 48, § 3; 2 Wash.Rev.Stat.Ann. (Remington, 1932) § 464(3); Wyo.Rev.Stat.Ann. (Courtright, 1931) § 89–2301(3). For an example of a very liberal provision for the correction of clerical errors and for amendment after judgment, see Va.Code Ann. (Michie, 1936) §§ 6329, 6333.

Note to Subdivision (b). Application to the court under this subdivision does not extend the time for taking an appeal, as distinguished from the motion for new trial. This section is based upon Calif.Code Civ.Proc. (Deering, 1937) § 473. See also N.Y.C.P.A. (1937) § 108; 2 Minn.Stat. (Mason, 1927) § 9283.

For the independent action to relieve against mistake, etc., see Dobie, *Federal Procedure,* pages 760 to 765, compare 639; and Simkins, *Federal Practice,* ch. CXXI (pp. 820 to 830) and ch. CXXII (pp. 831 to 834), compare § 214.

1946 Amendment

Note. Subdivision (a). The amendment incorporates the view expressed in *Perlman v. 322 West Seventy-Second Street, Co., Inc.,* C.C.A.2d, 1942, 127 F.2d 716; 3 *Moore's Federal Practice,* 1938, 3276, and further permits correction after docketing, with leave of the appellate court. Some courts have thought that upon the taking of an appeal the district court lost its power to act. See *Schram v. Safety Investment Co.,* E.D.Mich.1942, 45 F.Supp. 636; also *Miller v. United States,* C.C.A.7th, 1940, 114 F.2d 267.

Subdivision (b). When promulgated, the rules contained a number of provisions, including those found in Rule 60(b), describing the practice by a motion to obtain relief from judgments, and these rules, coupled with the reservation in Rule 60(b) of the right to entertain a new action to relieve a party from a judgment, were generally supposed to cover the field. Since the rules have been in force, decisions have been rendered that the use of bills of review, coram nobis, or audita querela, to obtain relief from final judgments is still proper, and that various remedies of this kind still exist although they are not mentioned in the rules and the practice is not prescribed in the rules. It is obvious that the rules should be complete in this respect and define the practice with respect to any existing rights or remedies to obtain relief from final judgments. For extended discussion of the old common law writs and equitable remedies, the interpretation of Rule 60, and proposals for change, see Moore and Rogers, *Federal Relief from Civil Judgments,* 1946, 55 Yale L.J. 623. See also 3 *Moore's Federal Practice,* 1938, 3254 et seq.; Commentary, *Effect of Rule 60b on Other Methods of Relief From Judgment,* 1941, 4 Fed.Rules Serv. 942, 945; *Wallace v. United States,* C.C.A.2d, 1944, 142 F.2d 240, certiorari denied 65 S.Ct. 37, 323 U.S. 712, 89 L.Ed. 573.

The reconstruction of Rule 60(b) has for one of its purposes a clarification of this situation. Two types of procedure to obtain relief from judgments are specified in the rules as it is proposed to amend them. One procedure is by motion in the court and in the action in which the judgment was rendered. The other procedure is by a new or independent action to obtain relief from a judgment, which action may or may not be begun in the court which rendered the judgment. Various rules, such as the one dealing with a motion for new trial and for amendment of judgments, Rule 59, one for amended findings, Rule 52, and one for judgment notwithstanding the verdict, Rule 50(b), and including the provisions of Rule 60(b) as amended, prescribe the various types of cases in which the practice by motion is permitted. In each case there is a limit upon the time within which resort to a motion is permitted, and this time limit may not be enlarged under Rule 6(b). If the right to make a motion is lost by the expiration of the time limits fixed in these rules, the only other procedural remedy is by a new or independent action to set aside a judgment upon those principles which have heretofore been applied in such an action. Where the independent action is resorted to, the limitations of time are those of laches or statutes of limitations. The Committee has endeavored to ascertain all the remedies and types of relief heretofore available by coram nobis, coram vobis, audita querela, bill of review, or bill in the nature of a bill of review. See Moore and Rogers, *Federal Relief from Civil Judgments,* 1946, 55 Yale L.J. 623, 659 to 682. It endeavored then to amend the rules to permit, either by motion or by independent action, the granting of various kinds of relief from judgments which were permitted in the federal courts prior to the adoption of these rules, and the amendment concludes with a provision abolishing the use of bills of review and the other common law writs referred to, and requiring the practice to be by motion or by independent action.

To illustrate the operation of the amendment, it will be noted that under Rule 59(b) as it now stands, without amendment, a motion for new trial on the ground of newly discovered evidence is permitted within ten days after the entry of the judgment, or after that time upon leave of the court. It is proposed to amend Rule 59(b) by providing that under that rule a motion for new trial shall be served not later than ten days after the entry of the judgment, whatever the ground be for the motion, whether error by the court or newly discovered evidence. On the other hand, one of the purposes of the bill of review in equity was to afford relief on the ground of newly discovered evidence long after the entry of the judgment. Therefore, to permit relief by a motion similar to that heretofore obtained on bill of review, Rule 60(b) as amended permits an application for relief to be made by motion, on the ground of newly discovered evidence, within one year after judgment. Such a motion under Rule 60(b) does not affect the finality of the judgment, but a motion under Rule 59, made within 10 days, does affect finality and the running of the time for appeal.

If these various amendments, including principally those to Rule 60(b), accomplish the purpose for which they are intended, the federal rules will deal with the practice in every sort of case in which relief from final judgments is asked, and prescribe the practice. With reference to the question whether, as the rules now exist, relief by coram nobis, bills of review, and so forth, is permissible, the generally accepted view is that the remedies are still available, although the precise relief obtained in a particular case by use of these ancillary remedies is shrouded in ancient lore and mystery. See *Wallace v. United States,* C.C.A.2d, 1944, 142 F.2d 240, certiorari denied 65 S.Ct. 37, 323 U.S. 712, 89 L.Ed. 573; *Fraser v. Doing,* App.D.C.1942, 130 F.2d 617; *Jones v. Watts,* C.C.A.5th, 1944, 142 F.2d 575; *Preveden v. Hahn,* S.D.N.Y.1941, 36 F.Supp. 952; *Cavallo v. Agwilines, Inc.,* S.D.N.Y.1942, 6 Fed.Rules Serv. 60b.31, Case 2, 2 F.R.D. 526; *McGinn v. United States,* D.C.Mass.1942, 6 Fed.Rules Serv. 60b.51, Case 3, 2 F.R.D. 562; *City of Shattuck, Oklahoma ex rel. Versluis v. Oliver,* W.D.Okl.1945, 8 Fed.Rules Serv. 60b.31, Case 3; Moore and Rogers, *Federal Relief from Civil Judgments,* 1946, 55 Yale L.J. 623, 631 to 653; 3 *Moore's Federal Practice,* 1938, 3254 et seq.; Commentary, *Effect of Rule 60b on Other Methods of Relief From Judgment,* op. cit. supra. Cf. *Norris v. Camp,* C.C.A.10th, 1944, 144 F.2d 1; *Reed v. South Atlantic Steamship Co. of Delaware,* D.Del.1942, 2 F.R.D. 475, 6 Fed.Rules Serv. 60b.31, Case 1; *Laughlin v. Berens,* D.D.C.1945, 8 Fed.Rules Serv. 60b.51, Case 1, 73 W.L.R. 209.

The transposition of the words "the court" and the addition of the word "and" at the beginning of the first sentence are merely verbal changes. The addition of the qualifying word "final" emphasizes the character of the judgments, orders or proceedings from which Rule 60(b) affords relief; and hence interlocutory judgments are not brought within the restrictions of the rule, but rather they are left subject to the complete power of the court rendering them to afford such relief from them as justice requires.

The qualifying pronoun "his" has been eliminated on the basis that it is too restrictive, and that the subdivision should include the mistake or neglect of others which may be just as material and call just as much for supervisory jurisdiction as where the judgment is taken against the party through *his* mistake, inadvertence, etc.

Fraud, whether intrinsic or extrinsic, misrepresentation, or other misconduct of an adverse party are express grounds for relief by motion under amended subdivision (b). There is no sound reason for their exclusion. The incorporation of fraud and the like within the scope of the rule also removes confusion as to the proper procedure. It has been held that relief from a judgment obtained by extrinsic fraud could be secured by motion within a "reasonable time," which might be after the time stated in the rule had run. *Fiske v. Buder,* C.C.A.8th, 1942, 125 F.2d 841; see also inferentially *Bucy v. Nevada Construction Co.,* C.C.A.9th, 1942, 125 F.2d 213. On the other hand, it has been suggested that in view of the fact that fraud was omitted from original Rule 60(b) as a ground for relief, an independent action was the only proper remedy. Commentary, *Effect of Rule 60b on Other Methods of Relief From Judgment,* 1941, 4 Fed.Rules Serv. 942, 945. The amendment settles this problem by making fraud an express ground for relief by motion; and under the saving clause, fraud may be urged as a basis for relief by independent action insofar as established doctrine permits. See Moore and Rogers, *Federal Relief from Civil Judgments,* 1946, 55 Yale L.J. 623, 653 to 659; 3 Moore's Federal Practice, 1938, 3267 et seq. And the rule expressly does not limit the power of the court, when fraud has been perpetrated upon it, to give relief under the saving clause. As an illustration of this situation, see *Hazel-Atlas Glass Co. v. Hartford Empire Co.,* 1944, 64 S.Ct. 997, 322 U.S. 238, 88 L.Ed. 1250.

The time limit for relief by motion in the court and in the action in which the judgment was rendered has been enlarged from six months to one year.

It should be noted that Rule 60(b) does not assume to define the substantive law as to the grounds for vacating judgments, but merely prescribes the practice in proceedings to obtain relief. It should also be noted that under § 200(4) of the Soldiers' and Sailors' Civil Relief Act of 1940, § 501 et seq. [§ 520(4)] of the Appendix to Title 50, a judgment rendered in any action or proceeding governed by the section may be vacated under certain specified circumstances upon proper application to the court.

1948 Amendment

The amendment effective October, 1949 substituted the reference to "Title 28, U.S.C. § 1655," in the next to the last sentence of subdivision (b), for the reference to "Section 57 of the Judicial Code, U.S.C., Title 28, § 118".

1987 Amendment

The amendment is technical. No substantive change is intended.

2007 Amendments

The language of Rule 60 has been amended as part of the general restyling of the Civil Rules to make them more easily understood and to make style and terminology consistent throughout the rules. These changes are intended to be stylistic only.

The final sentence of former Rule 60(b) said that the procedure for obtaining any relief from a judgment was by motion as prescribed in the Civil Rules or by an independent action. That provision is deleted as unnecessary. Relief continues to be available only as provided in the Civil Rules or by independent action.

Rule 61.   Harmless Error

Unless justice requires otherwise, no error in admitting or excluding evidence—or any other error by the court or a party—is ground for granting a new trial, for setting aside a verdict, or for vacating, modifying, or otherwise disturbing a judgment or order. At every stage of the proceeding, the court must disregard all errors and defects that do not affect any party's substantial rights.

(Amended April 30, 2007, effective December 1, 2007.)

ADVISORY COMMITTEE NOTES

1937 Adoption

A combination of U.S.C., Title 28, § 2111, [former] § 391 (New trials; harmless error) and [former] § 777 (Defects of form; amendments) with modifications. See *McCandless v. United States,* 1936, 56 S.Ct. 764, 298 U.S. 342, 80 L.Ed. 1205. Compare [former] Equity Rule 72 (Correction of Clerical Mistakes in Orders and Decrees); and last sentence of [former] Equity Rule 46 (Trial—Testimony Usually Taken in Open Court—Rulings on Objections to Evidence). For the last sentence see the last sentence of [former] Equity Rule 19 (Amendments Generally).

2007 Amendments

The language of Rule 61 has been amended as part of the general restyling of the Civil Rules to make them more easily understood and to make style and terminology consistent throughout the rules. These changes are intended to be stylistic only.

Rule 62.   Stay of Proceedings to Enforce a Judgment

(a) **Automatic Stay.** Except as provided in Rule 62(c) and (d), execution on a judgment and proceedings to enforce it are stayed for 30 days after its entry, unless the court orders otherwise.

(b) **Stay by Bond or Other Security.** At any time after judgment is entered, a party may obtain a stay by providing a bond or other security. The stay takes effect when the court approves the bond or other security and remains in effect for the time specified in the bond or other security.

(c) **Stay of an Injunction, Receivership, or Patent Accounting Order.** Unless the court orders otherwise, the following are not stayed after being entered, even if an appeal is taken:

   (1) an interlocutory or final judgment in an action for an injunction or receivership; or

(2) a judgment or order that directs an accounting in an action for patent infringement.

(d) Injunction Pending an Appeal. While an appeal is pending from an interlocutory order or final judgment that grants, continues, modifies, refuses, dissolves, or refuses to dissolve or modify an injunction, the court may suspend, modify, restore, or grant an injunction on terms for bond or other terms that secure the opposing party's rights. If the judgment appealed from is rendered by a statutory three-judge district court, the order must be made either:

(1) by that court sitting in open session; or

(2) by the assent of all its judges, as evidenced by their signatures.

(e) Stay Without Bond on an Appeal by the United States, Its Officers, or Its Agencies. The court must not require a bond, obligation, or other security from the appellant when granting a stay on an appeal by the United States, its officers, or its agencies or on an appeal directed by a department of the federal government.

(f) Stay in Favor of a Judgment Debtor Under State Law. If a judgment is a lien on the judgment debtor's property under the law of the state where the court is located, the judgment debtor is entitled to the same stay of execution the state court would give.

(g) Appellate Court's Power Not Limited. This rule does not limit the power of the appellate court or one of its judges or justices:

(1) to stay proceedings—or suspend, modify, restore, or grant an injunction—while an appeal is pending; or

(2) to issue an order to preserve the status quo or the effectiveness of the judgment to be entered.

(h) Stay with Multiple Claims or Parties. A court may stay the enforcement of a final judgment entered under Rule 54(b) until it enters a later judgment or judgments, and may prescribe terms necessary to secure the benefit of the stayed judgment for the party in whose favor it was entered.

(Amended December 27, 1946, effective March 19, 1948; December 29, 1948, effective October 20, 1949; April 17, 1961, effective July 19, 1961; March 2, 1987, effective August 1, 1987; April 30, 2007, effective December 1, 2007; March 26, 2009, effective December 1, 2009; April 26, 2018, effective December 1, 2018.)

ADVISORY COMMITTEE NOTES

1937 Adoption

Note to Subdivision (a). The first sentence states the substance of the last sentence of U.S.C., Title 28, [former] § 874 (Supersedeas). The remainder of the subdivision states the substance of the last clause of U.S.C., Title 28, § 1292, [formerly] § 227 (Appeals in proceedings for injunctions; receivers; and admiralty), and of §§ 1292, 2107, [formerly] § 227a (Appeals in suits in equity for infringement of letters patent for inventions; stay of proceedings for accounting), but extended to include final as well as interlocutory judgments.

Note to Subdivision (b). This modifies U.S.C., Title 28, [former] § 840 (Executions; stay on conditions).

Note to Subdivision (c). Compare [former] Equity Rule 74 (Injunction Pending Appeal); and *Cumberland Telephone and Telegraph Co. v. Louisiana Public Service Commission,* 1922, 43 S.Ct. 75, 260 U.S. 212, 67 L.Ed. 217. See Simkins, Federal Practice (1934), § 916, in regard to the effect of appeal on injunctions and the giving of bonds. See U.S.C., [former] Title 6 (Official and Penal Bonds) for bonds by surety companies. For statutes providing for a specially constituted district court of three judges, see:

U.S.C., Title 7:

§ 217 (Proceedings for suspension of orders of Secretary of Agriculture under Stockyards Act)—by reference.

§ 499k (Injunctions; application of injunction laws governing orders of Interstate Commerce Commission to orders of Secretary of Agriculture under Perishable Commodities Act)—by reference.

U.S.C., Title 15:

§ 28 (Antitrust laws; suits against monopolies expedited)

U.S.C., Title 28, former:

§ 47 [now 2325 (repealed)] (Injunctions as to orders of Interstate Commerce Commission, etc.)

§ 380 [now 2284] (Injunctions; alleged unconstitutionality of State statutes)

§ 380a [now 2284] (Same; constitutionality of federal statute)

U.S.C., Title 49:

§ 44 [former] (Suits in equity under interstate commerce laws; expedition of suits)

Note to Subdivision (d). This modifies U.S.C., Title 28, [former] § 874 (Supersedeas). See Rule 36(2), Rules of the Supreme Court of the United States, which governs supersedeas bonds on direct appeals to the Supreme Court, and Rule 73(d), of these rules, which governs supersedeas bonds on appeals to a circuit court of appeals. The provisions governing supersedeas bonds in both kinds of appeals are substantially the same.

Note to Subdivision (e). This states the substance of U.S.C., Title 28, § 2408, formerly § 870 (Bond; not required of the United States).

Note to Subdivision (f). This states the substance of U.S.C., Title 28, [former] § 841 (Executions; stay of one term) with appropriate modification to conform to the provisions of Rule 6(c) as to terms of court.

1946 Amendment

Note. Subdivision (a). [This subdivision not amended]. Sections 203 and 204 of the Soldiers' and Sailors' Civil Relief Act of 1940, 50 U.S.C., Appendix, § 501 et seq. [§§ 523, 524], provide under certain circumstances for the issuance and continuance of a stay of execution of any judgment or order entered against a person in military service. See *Bowsman v. Peterson,* D.Neb.1942, 45 F.Supp. 741. Section 201 of the Act [50 U.S.C. App. § 521] permits under certain circumstances the issuance of a stay of any action or proceeding at any stage thereof, where either the plaintiff or defendant is a person in military service. See also note to Rule 64 herein.

Subdivision (b). This change was necessary because of the proposed addition to Rule 59 of subdivision (e).

Subdivision (h). In proposing to revise Rule 54(b), the Committee thought it advisable to include a separate provision in Rule 62 for stay of enforcement of a final judgment in cases involving multiple claims.

1948 Amendment

The amendment effective October 1949 deleted at the end of subdivision (g) the following language which originally appeared after the word "entered": "and these rules do not supersede the provisions of Section 210 of the Judicial Code, as amended, U.S.C., Title 28, [former] § 47a, or of other statutes of the United States to the effect that stays pending appeals to the Supreme Court may be granted only by that court or a justice thereof."

1961 Amendment

The amendment adopted Apr. 17, 1961, effective July 19, 1961, eliminated words "on some but not all of the claims presented in the action" which followed "final judgment".

1987 Amendment

The amendment is technical. No substantive change is intended.

2007 Amendments

The language of Rule 62 has been amended as part of the general restyling of the Civil Rules to make them more easily understood and to make style and terminology consistent throughout the rules. These changes are intended to be stylistic only.

The final sentence of former Rule 62(a) referred to Rule 62(c). It is deleted as an unnecessary. Rule 62(c) governs of its own force.

2009 Amendments

The time set in the former rule at 10 days has been revised to 14 days. See the Note to Rule 6.

2018 Amendments

Subdivisions (a), (b), (c), and (d) of former Rule 62 are reorganized and the provisions for staying a judgment are revised.

The provisions for staying an injunction, receivership, or order for a patent accounting are reorganized by consolidating them in new subdivisions (c) and (d). There is no change in meaning. The language is revised to include all of the words used in 28 U.S.C. § 1292(a)(1) to describe the right to appeal from interlocutory actions with respect to an injunction, but subdivisions (c) and (d) apply both to interlocutory injunction orders and to final judgments that grant, refuse, or otherwise deal with an injunction.

New Rule 62(a) extends the period of the automatic stay to 30 days. Former Rule 62(a) set the period at 14 days, while former Rule 62(b) provided for a court-ordered stay "pending disposition of" motions under Rules 50, 52, 59, and 60. The time for making motions under Rules 50, 52, and 59, however, was later extended to 28 days, leaving an apparent gap between expiration of the automatic stay and any of those motions (or a Rule 60 motion) made more than 14 days after entry of judgment. The revised rule eliminates any need to rely on inherent power to issue a stay during this period. Setting the period at 30 days coincides with the time for filing most appeals in civil actions, providing a would-be appellant the full period of appeal time to arrange a stay by other means. A 30-day automatic stay also suffices in cases governed by a 60-day appeal period.

Amended Rule 62(a) expressly recognizes the court's authority to dissolve the automatic stay or supersede it by a court-ordered stay. One reason for dissolving the automatic stay may be a risk that the judgment debtor's assets will be dissipated. Similarly, it may be important to allow immediate enforcement of a judgment that does not involve a payment of money. The court may address the risks of immediate execution by ordering dissolution of the stay only on condition that security be posted by the judgment creditor. Rather than dissolve the stay, the court may choose to supersede it by ordering a stay that lasts longer or requires security.

Subdivision 62(b) carries forward in modified form the supersedeas bond provisions of former Rule 62(d). A stay may be obtained under subdivision (b) at any time after judgment is entered. Thus a stay may be obtained before the automatic stay has expired, or after the automatic stay has been lifted by the court. The new rule's text makes explicit the opportunity to post security in a form other than a bond. The stay takes effect when the court approves the bond or other security and remains in effect for the time specified in the bond or security—a party may find it convenient to arrange a single bond or other security that persists through completion of post-judgment proceedings in the trial court and on through completion of all proceedings on appeal by issuance of the appellate mandate. This provision does not supersede the opportunity for a stay under 28 U.S.C. § 2101(f) pending review by the Supreme Court on certiorari. Finally, subdivision (b) changes the provision in former subdivision (d) that "an appellant" may obtain a stay. Under new subdivision (b), "a party" may obtain a stay. For example, a party may wish to secure a stay pending disposition of post-judgment proceedings after expiration of the automatic stay, not yet knowing whether it will want to appeal.

Rule 62.1. Indicative Ruling on a Motion for Relief That Is Barred by a Pending Appeal

(a) Relief Pending Appeal. If a timely motion is made for relief that the court lacks authority to grant because of an appeal that has been docketed and is pending, the court may:

(1) defer considering the motion;

(2) deny the motion; or

(3) state either that it would grant the motion if the court of appeals remands for that purpose or that the motion raises a substantial issue.

(b) Notice to the Court of Appeals. The movant must promptly notify the circuit clerk under Federal Rule of Appellate Procedure 12.1 if the district court states that it would grant the motion or that the motion raises a substantial issue.

(c) Remand. The district court may decide the motion if the court of appeals remands for that purpose.

(Added March 26, 2009, effective December 1, 2009.)

2009 Adoption

This new rule adopts for any motion that the district court cannot grant because of a pending appeal the practice that most courts follow when a party makes a Rule 60(b) motion to vacate a judgment that is pending on appeal. After an appeal has been docketed and while it remains pending, the district court cannot grant a Rule 60(b) motion without a remand. But it can entertain the motion and deny it, defer consideration, or state that it would grant the motion if the court of appeals remands for that purpose or state that the motion raises a substantial issue. Experienced lawyers often refer to the suggestion for remand as an "indicative ruling." (Appellate Rule 4(a)(4) lists six motions that, if filed within the relevant time limit, suspend the effect of a notice of appeal filed before or after the motion is filed until the last such motion is disposed of. The district court has authority to grant the motion without resorting to the indicative ruling procedure.)

This clear procedure is helpful whenever relief is sought from an order that the court cannot reconsider because the order is the subject of a pending appeal. Rule 62.1 does not attempt to define the circumstances in which an appeal limits or defeats the district court's authority to act in the face of a pending appeal. The rules that govern the relationship between trial courts and appellate courts may be complex, depending in part on the nature of the order and the source of appeal jurisdiction. Rule 62.1 applies only when those rules deprive the district court of authority to grant relief without appellate permission. If the district court concludes that it has authority to grant relief without appellate permission, it can act without falling back on the indicative ruling procedure.

To ensure proper coordination of proceedings in the district court and in the appellate court, the movant must notify the circuit clerk under Federal Rule of Appellate Procedure 12.1 if the district court states that it would grant the motion or that the motion raises a substantial issue. Remand is in the court of appeals' discretion under Appellate Rule 12.1.

Often it will be wise for the district court to determine whether it in fact would grant the motion if the court of appeals remands for that purpose. But a motion may present complex issues that require extensive litigation and that may either be mooted or be presented in a different context by decision of the issues raised on appeal. In such circumstances the district court may prefer to state that the motion raises a substantial issue, and to state the reasons why it prefers to decide only if the court of appeals agrees that it would be useful to decide the motion before decision of the pending appeal. The district court is not bound to grant the motion after stating that the motion raises a substantial issue; further proceedings on remand may show that the motion ought not be granted.

Rule 63. Judge's Inability to Proceed

If a judge conducting a hearing or trial is unable to proceed, any other judge may proceed upon certifying familiarity with the record and determining that the case may be completed without prejudice to the parties. In a hearing or a nonjury trial, the successor judge must, at a party's request, recall any witness whose testimony is material and disputed and who is available to testify again without undue burden. The successor judge may also recall any other witness.

(Amended March 2, 1987, effective August 1, 1987; April 30, 1991, effective December 1, 1991; April 30, 2007, effective December 1, 2007.)

ADVISORY COMMITTEE NOTES

1937 Adoption

This rule adapts and extends the provisions of U.S.C., Title 28, [former] § 776 (Bill of exceptions; authentication; signing of by judge) to include all duties to be performed by the judge after verdict or judgment. The statute is therefore superseded.

1987 Amendment

The amendments are technical. No substantive change is intended.

1991 Amendment

The revision substantially displaces the former rule. The former rule was limited to the disability of the judge, and made no provision for disqualification or possible other reasons for the withdrawal of the judge during proceedings. In making provision for other circumstances, the revision is not intended to encourage judges to discontinue participation in a trial for any but compelling reasons. Cf. *United States v. Lane,* 708 F.2d 1394, 1395–1397 (9th Cir.1983). Manifestly, a substitution should not be made for the personal convenience of the court, and the reasons for a substitution should be stated on the record.

The former rule made no provision for the withdrawal of the judge during the trial, but was limited to disqualification after trial. Several courts concluded that the text of the former rule prohibited substitution of a new judge prior to the points described in the rule, thus requiring a new trial, whether or not a fair disposition was within reach of a substitute judge. *E.g., Whalen v. Ford Motor Credit Co.*, 684 F.2d 272 (4th Cir.1982, en banc) *cert. denied*, 459 U.S. 910 (1982) (jury trial); *Arrow-Hart, Inc. v. Philip Carey Co.*, 552 F.2d 711 (6th Cir.1977) (non-jury trial). *See generally* Comment, *The Case of the Dead Judge: Fed.R.Civ.P. 63: Whalen v. Ford Motor Credit Co.*, 67 MINN.L.REV. 827 (1983).

The increasing length of federal trials has made it likely that the number of trials interrupted by the disability of the judge will increase. An efficient mechanism for completing these cases without unfairness is needed to prevent unnecessary expense and delay. To avoid the injustice that may result if the substitute judge proceeds despite unfamiliarity with the action, the new Rule provides, in language similar to Federal Rule of Criminal Procedure 25(a), that the successor judge must certify familiarity with the record and determine that the case may be completed before that judge without prejudice to the parties. This will necessarily require that there be available a transcript or a videotape of the proceedings prior to substitution. If there has been a long but incomplete jury trial, the prompt availability of the transcript or videotape is crucial to the effective use of this rule, for the jury cannot long be held while an extensive transcript is prepared without prejudice to one or all parties.

The revised text authorizes the substitute judge to make a finding of fact at a bench trial based on evidence heard by a different judge. This may be appropriate in limited circumstances. First, if a witness has become unavailable, the testimony recorded at trial can be considered by the successor judge pursuant to F.R.Ev. 804, being equivalent to a recorded deposition available for use at trial pursuant to Rule 32. For this purpose, a witness who is no longer subject to a subpoena to compel testimony at trial is unavailable. Secondly, the successor judge may determine that particular testimony is not material or is not disputed, and so need not be reheard. The propriety of proceeding in this manner may be marginally affected by the availability of a videotape record; a judge who has reviewed a trial on videotape may be entitled to greater confidence in his or her ability to proceed.

The court would, however, risk error to determine the credibility of a witness not seen or heard who is available to be recalled. Cf. *Anderson v. City of Bessemer City NC*, 470 U.S. 564, 575 (1985); *Marshall v. Jerrico Inc.,* 446 U.S. 238, 242 (1980). See also *United States v. Radatz*, 447 U.S. 667 (1980).

2007 Amendments

The language of Rule 63 has been amended as part of the general restyling of the Civil Rules to make them more easily understood and to make style and terminology consistent throughout the rules. These changes are intended to be stylistic only.

TITLE VIII. PROVISIONAL AND FINAL REMEDIES

Rule 64.   Seizing a Person or Property

(a) Remedies Under State Law—In General. At the commencement of and throughout an action, every remedy is available that, under the law of the state where the court is located, provides for seizing a person or property to secure satisfaction of the potential judgment. But a federal statute governs to the extent it applies.

(b) Specific Kinds of Remedies. The remedies available under this rule include the following—however designated and regardless of whether state procedure requires an independent action:

- arrest;
- attachment;
- garnishment;
- replevin;
- sequestration; and
- other corresponding or equivalent remedies.

(Amended April 30, 2007, effective December 1, 2007.)

ADVISORY COMMITTEE NOTES

1937 Adoption

This rule adopts the existing Federal law, except that it specifies the applicable State law to be that of the time when the remedy is sought. Under U.S.C., Title 28, [former] § 726 (Attachments as provided by State laws) the plaintiff was entitled to remedies by attachment or other process which were on June 1, 1872, provided by the applicable State law, and the district courts might, from time to time, by general rules, adopt such State laws as might be in force. This statute is superseded as are district court rules which are rendered unnecessary by the rule.

Lis pendens. No rule concerning lis pendens is stated, for this would appear to be a matter of substantive law affecting State laws of property. It has been held that in the absence of a State statute expressly providing for the recordation of notice of the pendency of Federal actions, the commencement of a Federal action is notice to all persons affected. *King v. Davis,* 137 F. 198 (W.D.Va., 1903). It has been held, however, that when a state statute does so provide expressly, its provisions are binding. *United States v. Calcasieu Timber Co.,* 236 F. 196 (C.C.A.5th, 1916).

For statutes of the United States on attachment, see, e.g.:

U.S.C., Title 28 former:

§ 737 [now 2710] (Attachment in postal suits)

§ 738 [now 2711] (Attachment; application for warrant)

§ 739 [now 2712] (Attachment; issue of warrant)

§ 740 [now 2713] (Attachment; trial of ownership of property)

§ 741 [now 2714] (Attachment; investment of proceeds of attached property)

§ 742 [now 2715] (Attachment; publication of attachment)

§ 743 [now 2716] (Attachment; personal notice of attachment)

§ 744 [now 2717] (Attachment; discharge; bond)

§ 745 [former] (Attachment; accrued rights not affected)

§ 746 (Attachments dissolved in conformity with State laws)

For statutes of the United States on garnishment, see, e.g.:

U.S.C., Title 28, former:

§ 748 [now 2405] (Garnishees in suits by United States against a corporation)

§ 749 [now 2405] (Same; issue tendered on denial of indebtedness)

§ 750 [now 2405] (Same; garnishee failing to appear)

For statutes of the United States on arrest, see, e.g.:

U.S.C., Title 28 former:

§ 376 [now 1651] (Writs of ne exeat)

§ 755 [former] (Special bail in suits for duties and penalties)

§ 756 [former] (Defendant giving bail in one district and committed in another)

§ 757 [former] (Defendant giving bail in one district and committed in another; defendant held until judgment in first suit)

§ 758 [former] (Bail and affidavits; taking by commissioners)

§ 759 [former] (Calling of bail in Kentucky)

§ 760 [former] (Clerks may take bail de bene esse)

§ 843 [now 2007] (Imprisonment for debt)

§ 844 [now 2007] (Imprisonment for debt; discharge according to State laws)

§ 845 [now 2007] (Imprisonment for debt; jail limits)

For statutes of the United States on replevin, see, e.g.:

U.S.C., Title 28:

§ 2463, formerly § 747 (Replevy of property taken under revenue laws).

Supplementary Note of Advisory Committee Regarding This Rule

Note. Sections 203 and 204 of the Soldiers' and Sailors' Civil Relief Act of 1940, 50 U.S.C.Appendix, § 501 et seq. [§§ 523 and 524], provide under certain circumstances for the issuance and continuance of a stay of the execution of any judgment entered against a person in military service, or the vacation or stay of any attachment or garnishment directed against such person's property, money, or debts in the hands of another. See also Note to Rule 62 herein.

2007 Amendments

The language of Rule 64 has been amended as part of the general restyling of the Civil Rules to make them more easily understood and to make style and terminology consistent throughout the rules. These changes are intended to be stylistic only.

Former Rule 64 stated that the Civil Rules govern an action in which any remedy available under Rule 64(a) is used. The Rules were said to govern from the time the action is commenced if filed in federal court, and from the time of removal if removed from state court. These provisions are deleted as redundant. Rule 1 establishes that the Civil Rules apply to all actions in a district court, and Rule 81(c)(1) adds reassurance that the Civil Rules apply to a removed action "after it is removed."

Rule 65. Injunctions and Restraining Orders

(a) **Preliminary Injunction.**

    (1) *Notice.* The court may issue a preliminary injunction only on notice to the adverse party.

    (2) *Consolidating the Hearing with the Trial on the Merits.* Before or after beginning the hearing on a motion for a preliminary injunction, the court may advance the trial on the merits and consolidate it with the hearing. Even when consolidation is not ordered, evidence that is received on the motion and that would be admissible at trial becomes part of the trial record and need not be repeated at trial. But the court must preserve any party's right to a jury trial.

(b) **Temporary Restraining Order.**

    (1) *Issuing Without Notice.* The court may issue a temporary restraining order without written or oral notice to the adverse party or its attorney only if:

        (A) specific facts in an affidavit or a verified complaint clearly show that immediate and irreparable injury, loss, or damage will result to the movant before the adverse party can be heard in opposition; and

        (B) the movant's attorney certifies in writing any efforts made to give notice and the reasons why it should not be required.

    (2) *Contents; Expiration.* Every temporary restraining order issued without notice must state the date and hour it was issued; describe the injury and state why it is irreparable; state why the order was issued without notice; and be promptly filed in the clerk's office and entered in the record. The order expires at the time after entry—not to exceed 14 days—that the court sets, unless before that time the court, for good cause, extends it for a like period or the adverse party consents to a longer extension. The reasons for an extension must be entered in the record.

    (3) *Expediting the Preliminary-Injunction Hearing.* If the order is issued without notice, the motion for a preliminary injunction must be set for hearing at the earliest possible time, taking precedence over all other matters except hearings on older matters of the same character. At the hearing, the party who obtained the order must proceed with the motion; if the party does not, the court must dissolve the order.

    (4) *Motion to Dissolve.* On 2 days' notice to the party who obtained the order without notice— or on shorter notice set by the court—the adverse party may appear and move to dissolve or modify the order. The court must then hear and decide the motion as promptly as justice requires.

(c) **Security.** The court may issue a preliminary injunction or a temporary restraining order only if the movant gives security in an amount that the court considers proper to pay the costs and damages sustained by any party found to have been wrongfully enjoined or restrained. The United States, its officers, and its agencies are not required to give security.

(d) **Contents and Scope of Every Injunction and Restraining Order.**

    (1) *Contents.* Every order granting an injunction and every restraining order must:

        (A) state the reasons why it issued;

        (B) state its terms specifically; and

        (C) describe in reasonable detail—and not by referring to the complaint or other document—the act or acts restrained or required.

    (2) *Persons Bound.* The order binds only the following who receive actual notice of it by personal service or otherwise:

    (A) the parties;

    (B) the parties' officers, agents, servants, employees, and attorneys; and

    (C) other persons who are in active concert or participation with anyone described in Rule 65(d)(2)(A) or (B).

(e) **Other Laws Not Modified.** These rules do not modify the following:

    (1) any federal statute relating to temporary restraining orders or preliminary injunctions in actions affecting employer and employee;

    (2) 28 U.S.C. § 2361, which relates to preliminary injunctions in actions of interpleader or in the nature of interpleader; or

    (3) 28 U.S.C. § 2284, which relates to actions that must be heard and decided by a three-judge district court.

(f) **Copyright Impoundment.** This rule applies to copyright-impoundment proceedings.

(Amended December 27, 1946, effective March 19, 1948; December 29, 1948, effective October 20, 1949; February 28, 1966, effective July 1, 1966; March 2, 1987, effective August 1, 1987; April 23, 2001, effective December 1, 2001; April 30, 2007, effective December 1, 2007; March 26, 2009, effective December 1, 2009.)

ADVISORY COMMITTEE NOTES

1937 Adoption

Note to Subdivisions (a) and (b). These are taken from U.S.C., Title 28, [former] § 381 (Injunctions; preliminary injunctions and temporary restraining orders).

Note to Subdivision (c). Except for the last sentence, this is substantially U.S.C., Title 28, [former] § 382 (Injunctions; security on issuance of). The last sentence continues the following and similar statutes which expressly except the United States or an officer or agency thereof from such security requirements: U.S.C. Title 15, §§ 77t(b), 78u(e), and 79r(f) (Securities and Exchange Commission). It also excepts the United States or an officer or agency thereof from such security requirements in any action in which a restraining order or interlocutory judgment of injunction issues in its favor whether there is an express statutory exception from such security requirements or not.

See U.S.C., [former] Title 6 (Official and Penal Bonds) for bonds by surety companies.

Note to Subdivision (d). This is substantially U.S.C., Title 28, [former] § 383 (Injunctions; requisites of order; binding effect).

Note to Subdivision (e). The words "relating to temporary restraining orders and preliminary injunctions in actions affecting employer and employee" are words of description and not of limitation.

Compare [former] Equity Rule 73 (Preliminary Injunctions and Temporary Restraining Orders) which is substantially equivalent to the statutes.

For other statutes dealing with injunctions which are continued, see e.g.:

U.S.C., Title 28 former:

    § 46 [now 2324] (Suits to enjoin orders of Interstate Commerce Commission to be against United States)

    § 47 [now 2325] (Injunctions as to orders of Interstate Commerce Commission; appeal to Supreme Court; time for taking)

    § 378 [former] (Injunctions; when granted)

    § 379 [now 2283] (Injunctions; stay in State courts)

    § 380 [now 1253, 2101, 2281, 2284] (Injunctions; alleged unconstitutionality of State statutes; appeal to Supreme Court)

§ 380a [now 1253, 2101, 2281, 2284] (Injunctions; constitutionality of Federal statute; application for hearing; appeal to Supreme Court)

U.S.C., Title 7:

§ 216 (Court proceedings to enforce orders; injunction)

§ 217 (Proceedings for suspension of orders)

U.S.C., Title 15:

§ 4 (Jurisdiction of courts; duty of district attorney; procedure)

§ 25 (Restraining violations; procedure)

§ 26 (Injunctive relief for private parties; exceptions)

§ 77t(b) (Injunctions and prosecution of offenses)

1946 Amendment

Note. It has been held that in actions on preliminary injunction bonds the district court has discretion to grant relief in the same proceeding or to require the institution of a new action on the bond. *Russell v. Farley,* 1881, 105 U.S. 433, 466. It is believed, however, that in all cases the litigant should have a right to proceed on the bond in the same proceeding, in the manner provided in Rule 73(f) for a similar situation. The paragraph added to Rule 65(c) insures this result and is in the interest of efficiency. There is no reason why Rules 65(c) and 73(f) should operate differently. Compare § 50, sub. n of the Bankruptcy Act, 11 U.S.C. § 78, sub. n, under which actions on all bonds furnished pursuant to the Act may be proceeded upon summarily in the bankruptcy court. See 2 *Collier on Bankruptcy,* 14th ed. by Moore and Oglebay, 1853–1854.

1948 Amendment

The amendment effective October 1949, changed subdivision (e) in the following respects: in the first clause the amendment substituted the words "any statute of the United States" for the words "the Act of October 15, 1914, c. 323, §§ 1 and 20 (38 Stat. 730), U.S.C., Title 29, §§ 52 and 53, or the Act of March 23, 1932, c. 90 (47 Stat. 70), U.S.C., Title 29, c. 6"; in the second clause of subdivision (e) the amendment substituted the reference to "Title 28, U.S.C., § 2361" for the reference to "Section 24(26) of the Judicial Code as amended, U.S.C., Title 28, § 41(26)"; and the third clause was amended to read "Title 28, U.S.C., § 2284," etc., as at present, instead of "the Act of August 24, 1937, c. 754, § 3, relating to actions to enjoin the enforcement of acts of Congress."

1966 Amendment

Subdivision (a)(2). This new subdivision provides express authority for consolidating the hearing of an application for a preliminary injunction with the trial on the merits. The authority can be exercised with particular profit when it appears that a substantial part of the evidence offered on the application will be relevant to the merits and will be presented in such form as to qualify for admission on the trial proper. Repetition of evidence is thereby avoided. The fact that the proceedings have been consolidated should cause no delay in the disposition of the application for the preliminary injunction, for the evidence will be directed in the first instance to that relief, and the preliminary injunction, if justified by the proof, may be issued in the course of the consolidated proceedings. Furthermore, to consolidate the proceedings will tend to expedite the final disposition of the action. It is believed that consolidation can be usefully availed of in many cases.

The subdivision further provides that even when consolidation is not ordered, evidence received in connection with an application for a preliminary injunction which would be admissible on the trial on the merits forms part of the trial record. This evidence need not be repeated on the trial. On the other hand, repetition is not altogether prohibited. That would be impractical and unwise. For example, a witness testifying comprehensively on the trial who has previously testified upon the application for a preliminary injunction might sometimes be hamstrung in telling his story if he could not go over some part of his prior testimony to connect it with his present testimony. So also, some repetition of testimony may be called for where the trial is conducted by a judge who did not hear the application for the preliminary injunction. In general, however, repetition can be avoided with an increase of efficiency in the conduct of the case and without any distortion of the presentation of evidence by the parties.

Since an application for a preliminary injunction may be made in an action in which, with respect to all or part of the merits, there is a right to trial by jury, it is appropriate to add the caution appearing in the last sentence of the subdivision. In such a case the jury will have to hear all the evidence bearing on its verdict, even if some part of the evidence has already been heard by the judge alone on the application for the preliminary injunction.

The subdivision is believed to reflect the substance of the best current practice and introduces no novel conception.

Subdivision (b). In view of the possibly drastic consequences of a temporary restraining order, the opposition should be heard, if feasible, before the order is granted. Many judges have properly insisted that, when time does not permit of formal notice of the application to the adverse party, some expedient, such as telephonic notice to the attorney for the adverse party, be resorted to if this can reasonably be done. On occasion, however, temporary restraining orders have been issued without any notice when it was feasible for some fair, although informal, notice to be given. See the emphatic criticisms in *Pennsylvania Rd. Co. v. Transport Workers Union*, 278 F.2d 693, 694 (3d Cir. 1960); *Arvida Corp. v. Sugarman*, 259 F.2d 428, 429 (2d Cir. 1958); *Lummus Co. v. Commonwealth Oil Ref. Co., Inc.*, 297 F.2d 80, 83 (2d Cir. 1961), cert. denied, 368 U.S. 986 (1962).

Heretofore the first sentence of subdivision (b), in referring to a notice "served" on the "adverse party" on which a "hearing" could be held, perhaps invited the interpretation that the order might be granted without notice if the circumstances did not permit of a formal hearing on the basis of a formal notice. The subdivision is amended to make it plain that informal notice, which may be communicated to the attorney rather than the adverse party, is to be preferred to no notice at all.

Before notice can be dispensed with, the applicant's counsel must give his certificate as to any efforts made to give notice and the reasons why notice should not be required. This certificate is in addition to the requirement of an affidavit or verified complaint setting forth the facts as to the irreparable injury which would result before the opposition could be heard.

The amended subdivision continues to recognize that a temporary restraining order may be issued without any notice when the circumstances warrant.

Subdivision (c). Original Rules 65 and 73 contained substantially identical provisions for summary proceedings against sureties on bonds required or permitted by the rules. There was fragmentary coverage of the same subject in the Admiralty Rules. Clearly, a single comprehensive rule is required, and is incorporated as Rule 65.1.

1987 Amendment

The amendments are technical. No substantive change is intended.

2001 Amendments

New subdivision (f) is added in conjunction with abrogation of the antiquated Copyright Rules of Practice adopted for proceedings under the 1909 Copyright Act. Courts have naturally turned to Rule 65 in response to the apparent inconsistency of the former Copyright Rules with the discretionary impoundment procedure adopted in 1976, 17 U.S.C. § 503(a). Rule 65 procedures also have assuaged well-founded doubts whether the Copyright Rules satisfy more contemporary requirements of due process. See, e.g., *Religious Technology Center v. Netcom On-Line Communications Servs., Inc.*, 923 F.Supp. 1231, 1260–1265 (N.D.Cal.1995); *Paramount Pictures Corp. v. Doe*, 821 F.Supp. 82 (E.D.N.Y.1993); *WPOW, Inc. v. MRLJ Enterprises*, 584 F.Supp. 132 (D.D.C.1984).

A common question has arisen from the experience that notice of a proposed impoundment may enable an infringer to defeat the court's capacity to grant effective relief. Impoundment may be ordered on an ex parte basis under subdivision (b) if the applicant makes a strong showing of the reasons why notice is likely to defeat effective relief. Such no-notice procedures are authorized in trademark infringement proceedings, see 15 U.S.C. § 1116(d), and courts have provided clear illustrations of the kinds of showings that support ex parte relief. See *Matter of Vuitton et Fils S.A.*, 606 F.2d 1 (2d Cir.1979); *Vuitton v. White*, 945 F.2d 569 (3d Cir.1991). In applying the tests for no-notice relief, the court should ask whether impoundment is necessary, or whether adequate protection can be had by a less intrusive form of no-notice relief shaped as a temporary restraining order.

This new subdivision (f) does not limit use of trademark procedures in cases that combine trademark and copyright claims. Some observers believe that trademark procedures should be adopted for all copyright cases, a proposal better considered by Congressional processes than by rulemaking processes.

2007 Amendments

The language of Rule 65 has been amended as part of the general restyling of the Civil Rules to make them more easily understood and to make style and terminology consistent throughout the rules. These changes are intended to be stylistic only.

The final sentence of former Rule 65(c) referred to Rule 65.1. It is deleted as unnecessary. Rule 65.1 governs of its own force.

Rule 65(d)(2) clarifies two ambiguities in former Rule 65(d). The former rule was adapted from former 28 U.S.C. § 363, but omitted a comma that made clear the common doctrine that a party must have actual notice of an injunction in order to be bound by it. Amended Rule 65(d) restores the meaning of the earlier statute, and also makes clear the proposition that an injunction can be enforced against a person who acts in concert with a party's officer, agent, servant, employee, or attorney.

2009 Amendments

The time set in the former rule at 10 days has been revised to 14 days. See the Note to Rule 6.

Rule 65.1. Proceedings Against a Security Provider

Whenever these rules (including the Supplemental Rules for Admiralty or Maritime Claims and Asset Forfeiture Actions) require or allow a party to give security, and security is given with one or more security providers, each provider submits to the court's jurisdiction and irrevocably appoints the court clerk as its agent for receiving service of any papers that affect its liability on the security. The security provider's liability may be enforced on motion without an independent action. The motion and any notice that the court orders may be served on the court clerk, who must promptly send a copy of each to every security provider whose address is known.

(Adopted February 28, 1966, effective July 1, 1966; amended March 2, 1987, effective August 1, 1987; April 12, 2006, effective December 1, 2006; April 30, 2007, effective December 1, 2007; April 24, 2018, effective December 1, 2018.)

ADVISORY COMMITTEE NOTES

1966 Addition

See Note to Rule 65.

1987 Amendment

The amendments are technical. No substantive change is intended.

2006 Amendment

Rule 65.1 is amended to conform to the changed title of the Supplemental Rules.

2007 Amendments

The language of Rule 65.1 has been amended as part of the general restyling of the Civil Rules to make them more easily understood and to make style and terminology consistent throughout the rules. These changes are intended to be stylistic only.

2018 Amendments

Rule 65.1 is amended to reflect the amendments of Rule 62. Rule 62 allows a party to obtain a stay of a judgment "by providing a bond or other security." Limiting Rule 65.1 enforcement procedures to sureties might exclude use of those procedures against a security provider that is not a surety. All security providers, including sureties, are brought into Rule 65.1 by these amendments. But the reference to "bond" is retained in Rule 62 because it has a long history.

The word "mail" is changed to "send" to avoid restricting the method of serving security providers.

Gap Report

The rule text was changed to eliminate references to "bond," "undertaking," and "surety." An explanation was added to the Committee Note.

Rule 66.   Receivers

These rules govern an action in which the appointment of a receiver is sought or a receiver sues or is sued. But the practice in administering an estate by a receiver or a similar court-appointed officer must accord with the historical practice in federal courts or with a local rule. An action in which a receiver has been appointed may be dismissed only by court order.

(Amended December 27, 1946, effective March 19, 1948; December 29, 1948, effective October 20, 1949; April 30, 2007, effective December 1, 2007.)

ADVISORY COMMITTEE NOTES

1946 Amendment

Note. The title of Rule 66 has been expanded to make clear the subject of the rule, i.e., federal equity receivers.

The first sentence added to Rule 66 prevents a dismissal by any party, after a federal equity receiver has been appointed, except upon leave of court. A party should not be permitted to oust the court and its officer without the consent of that court. See Civil Rule 31(e), Eastern District of Washington.

The second sentence added at the beginning of the rule deals with suits by or against a federal equity receiver. The first clause thereof eliminates the formal ceremony of an ancillary appointment before suit can be brought by a receiver, and is in accord with the more modern state practice, and with more expeditious and less expensive judicial administration. 2 *Moore's Federal Practice,* 1938, 2088–2091. For the rule necessitating ancillary appointment, see *Sterrett v. Second Nat. Bank,* 1918, 39 S.Ct. 27, 248 U.S. 73, 63 L.Ed. 135; *Kelley v. Queeney,* W.D.N.Y.1941, 41 F.Supp. 1015; see also *McCandless v. Furlaud,* 1934, 55 S.Ct. 42, 293 U.S. 67, 79 L.Ed. 202. This rule has been extensively criticized. First, *Extraterritorial Powers of Receivers,* 1932, 27 Ill.L.Rev. 271; Rose, *Extraterritorial Actions by Receivers,* 1933, 17 Minn.L.Rev. 704; Laughlin, *The Extraterritorial Powers of Receivers,* 1932, 45 Harv.L.Rev. 429; Clark and Moore, *A New Federal Civil Procedure—II, Pleadings and Parties,* 1935, 44 Yale L.J. 1291, 1312–1315; Note, 1932, 30 Mich.L.Rev. 1322. See also comment in *Bicknell v. Lloyd-Smith,* C.C.A.2d, 1940, 109 F.2d 527, certiorari denied 61 S.Ct. 15, 311 U.S. 650, 85 L.Ed. 416. The second clause of the sentence merely incorporates the well-known and general rule that, absent statutory authorization, a federal receiver cannot be sued without leave of the court which appointed him, applied in the federal courts since *Barton v. Barbour,* 1881, 104 U.S. 126. See also 1 *Clark on Receivers,* 2d ed., § 549. Under [§ 959 of this title, formerly] 28 U.S.C. § 125 leave of court is unnecessary when a receiver is sued "in respect of any act or transaction of his in carrying on the business" connected with the receivership property, but such suit is subject to the general equity jurisdiction of the court in which the receiver was appointed, so far as justice necessitates.

Capacity of a state court receiver to sue or be sued in Federal court is governed by Rule 17(b).

The last sentence added to Rule 66 assures the application of the rules in all matters except actual administration of the receivership estate itself. Since this implicitly carries with it the applicability of those rules relating to appellate procedure, the express reference thereto contained in Rule 66 has been stricken as superfluous. Under Rule 81(a)(1) the rules do not apply to bankruptcy proceedings except as they may be made applicable by order of the Supreme Court. Rule 66 is applicable to what is commonly known as a federal "chancery" or "equity" receiver, or similar type of court officer. It is not designed to regulate or affect receivers in bankruptcy, which are governed by the Bankruptcy Act and the General Orders. Since the Federal Rules are applicable in bankruptcy by virtue of General Orders in Bankruptcy 36 and 37 [see Appendix II following Rules of Bankruptcy Procedure, Title 11] only to the extent that they are not inconsistent with the Bankruptcy Act or the General Orders, Rule 66 is not applicable to bankruptcy receivers. See 1 *Collier on Bankruptcy,* 14th ed. by Moore and Oglebay, ¶¶ 2.23–2.36.

1948 Amendment

The amendment effective October 1949 deleted a sentence which formerly appeared immediately following the first sentence and which read as follows: "A receiver shall have the capacity to sue in any district court without ancillary appointment; but actions against a receiver may not be commenced without leave of the court appointing him except when authorized by a statute of the United States."

2007 Amendments

The language of Rule 66 has been amended as part of the general restyling of the Civil Rules to make them more easily understood and to make style and terminology consistent throughout the rules. These changes are intended to be stylistic only.

Rule 67.   Deposit into Court

(a) Depositing Property. If any part of the relief sought is a money judgment or the disposition of a sum of money or some other deliverable thing, a party—on notice to every other party and by leave of court—may deposit with the court all or part of the money or thing, whether or not that party claims any of it. The depositing party must deliver to the clerk a copy of the order permitting deposit.

(b) Investing and Withdrawing Funds. Money paid into court under this rule must be deposited and withdrawn in accordance with 28 U.S.C. §§ 2041 and 2042 and any like statute. The money must be deposited in an interest-bearing account or invested in a court-approved, interest-bearing instrument.

(Amended December 29, 1948, effective October 20, 1949; April 28, 1983, effective August 1, 1983; April 30, 2007, effective December 1, 2007.)

ADVISORY COMMITTEE NOTES

1937 Adoption

This rule provides for deposit in court generally, continuing similar special provisions contained in such statutes as U.S.C., Title 28, [§§ 1335, 1397, 2361, formerly] § 41(26) (Original jurisdiction of bills of interpleader, and of bills in the nature of interpleader). See generally *Howard v. United States,* 1902, 22 S.Ct. 543, 184 U.S. 676, 46 L.Ed. 754; United States Supreme Court Admiralty Rules (1920), Rules 37 (Bringing Funds into Court), 41 (Funds in Court Registry), and 42 (Claims Against Proceeds in Registry). With the first sentence, compare *English Rules Under the Judicature Act* (The Annual Practice, 1937) O. 22, r. 1(1).

1948 Amendment

The amendment effective October 1949 substituted the reference to "Title 28, U.S.C.A., §§ 2041, and 2042" for the reference to "Sections 995 and 996, Revised Statutes, as amended, U.S.C.A., Title 28, §§ 851, 852." The amendment also added the words "as amended" following the citation of the Act of June 26, 1934, c. 756, § 23, and, in the parenthetical citation immediately following, added the reference to "58 Stat. 845".

1983 Amendment

Rule 67 has been amended in three ways. The first change is the addition of the clause in the first sentence. Some courts have construed the present rule to permit deposit only when the party making it claims no interest in the fund or thing deposited. E.g., *Blasin-Stern v. Beech-Nut Life Savers Corp.,* 429 F.Supp. 533 (D. Puerto Rico 1975); *Dinkins v. General Aniline & Film Corp.,* 214 F.Supp. 281 (S.D.N.Y.1963). However, there are situations in which a litigant may wish to be relieved of responsibility for a sum or thing, but continue to claim an interest in all or part of it. In these cases the deposit-in-court procedure should be available; in addition to the advantages to the party making the deposit, the procedure gives other litigants assurance that any judgment will be collectable. The amendment is intended to accomplish that.

The second change is the addition of a requirement that the order of deposit be served on the clerk of the court in which the sum or thing is to be deposited. This is simply to assure that the clerk knows what is being deposited and what his responsibilities are with respect to the deposit. The latter point is particularly important since the rule as amended contemplates that deposits will be placed in interest-bearing accounts; the clerk must know what treatment has been ordered for the particular deposit.

The third change is to require that any money be deposited in an interest-bearing account or instrument approved by the court.

2007 Amendments

The language of Rule 67 has been amended as part of the general restyling of the Civil Rules to make them more easily understood and to make style and terminology consistent throughout the rules. These changes are intended to be stylistic only.

Rule 68.   Offer of Judgment

(a) Making an Offer; Judgment on an Accepted Offer. At least 14 days before the date set for trial, a party defending against a claim may serve on an opposing party an offer to allow judgment on specified terms, with the costs then accrued. If, within 14 days after being served, the opposing party serves written notice accepting the offer, either party may then file the offer and notice of acceptance, plus proof of service. The clerk must then enter judgment.

(b) Unaccepted Offer. An unaccepted offer is considered withdrawn, but it does not preclude a later offer. Evidence of an unaccepted offer is not admissible except in a proceeding to determine costs.

(c) Offer After Liability is Determined. When one party's liability to another has been determined but the extent of liability remains to be determined by further proceedings, the party held liable may make an offer of judgment. It must be served within a reasonable time—but at least 14 days—before the date set for a hearing to determine the extent of liability.

(d) Paying Costs After an Unaccepted Offer. If the judgment that the offeree finally obtains is not more favorable than the unaccepted offer, the offeree must pay the costs incurred after the offer was made.

(Amended December 27, 1946, effective March 19, 1948; February 28, 1966, effective July 1, 1966; March 2, 1987, effective August 1, 1987; April 30, 2007, effective December 1, 2007; March 26, 2009, effective December 1, 2009.)

ADVISORY COMMITTEE NOTES

1937 Adoption

See 2 Minn.Stat. (Mason, 1927) § 9323; 4 Mont.Rev.Codes Ann. (1935) § 9770; N.Y.C.P.A. (1937) § 177.

For the recovery of costs against the United States, see Rule 54(d).

1946 Amendment

Note. The third sentence of Rule 68 has been altered to make clear that evidence of an unaccepted offer is admissible in a proceeding to determine the costs of the action but is not otherwise admissible.

The two sentences substituted for the deleted last sentence of the rule assure a party the right to make a second offer where the situation permits—as, for example, where a prior offer was not accepted but the plaintiff's judgment is nullified and a new trial ordered, whereupon the defendant desires to make a second offer. It is implicit, however, that as long as the case continues—whether there be a first, second or third trial—and the defendant makes no further offer, his first and only offer will operate to save him the costs from the time of that offer if the plaintiff ultimately obtains a judgment less than the sum offered. In the case of successive offers not accepted, the offeror is saved the costs incurred after the making of the offer which was equal to or greater than the judgment ultimately obtained. These provisions should serve to encourage settlements and avoid protracted litigation.

The phrase "before the trial begins", in the first sentence of the rule, has been construed in *Cover v. Chicago Eye Shield Co.,* C.C.A.7th, 1943, 136 F.2d 374, certiorari denied 64 S.Ct. 53, 320 U.S. 749, 88 L.Ed. 445.

1966 Amendment

This logical extension of the concept of offer of judgment is suggested by the common admiralty practice of determining liability before the amount of liability is determined.

1987 Amendment

The amendments are technical. No substantive change is intended.

2007 Amendments

The language of Rule 68 has been amended as part of the general restyling of the Civil Rules to make them more easily understood and to make style and terminology consistent throughout the rules. These changes are intended to be stylistic only.

2009 Amendments

Former Rule 68 allowed service of an offer of judgment more than 10 days before the trial begins, or—if liability has been determined—at least 10 days before a hearing to determine the extent of liability. It may be difficult to know in advance when trial will begin or when a hearing will be held. The time is now measured from the date set for trial or hearing; resetting the date establishes a new time for serving the offer.

The former 10-day periods are extended to 14 days to reflect the change in the Rule 6(a) method for computing periods less than 11 days.

Rule 69. Execution

(a) In General.

    (1) *Money Judgment; Applicable Procedure.* A money judgment is enforced by a writ of execution, unless the court directs otherwise. The procedure on execution—and in proceedings supplementary to and in aid of judgment or execution—must accord with the procedure of the state where the court is located, but a federal statute governs to the extent it applies.

    (2) *Obtaining Discovery.* In aid of the judgment or execution, the judgment creditor or a successor in interest whose interest appears of record may obtain discovery from any person—including the judgment debtor—as provided in these rules or by the procedure of the state where the court is located.

(b) Against Certain Public Officers. When a judgment has been entered against a revenue officer in the circumstances stated in 28 U.S.C. § 2006, or against an officer of Congress in the circumstances stated in 2 U.S.C. § 118, the judgment must be satisfied as those statutes provide.

(Amended December 29, 1948, effective October 20, 1949; March 30, 1970, effective July 1, 1970; March 2, 1987 effective August 1, 1987; April 30, 2007, effective December 1, 2007.)

ADVISORY COMMITTEE NOTES

1937 Adoption

Note to Subdivision (a). This follows in substance U.S.C. Title 28, [former] §§ 727 (Executions as provided by State laws) and [former 729] [now Title 42, § 1988] (Proceedings in vindication of civil rights), except that, as in the similar case of attachments (see note to Rule 64), the rule specifies the applicable state law to be that of the time when the remedy is sought, and thus renders unnecessary, as well as supersedeas, local district court rules.

Statutes of the United States on execution, when applicable, govern under this rule. Among these are:

U.S.C., Title 12:

    § 91 (Transfers by bank and other acts in contemplation of insolvency)

    § 632 (Jurisdiction of United States district courts in cases arising out of foreign banking jurisdiction where Federal reserve bank a party)

U.S.C., Title 19:

§ 199 (Judgments for customs duties, how payable)

U.S.C., Title 26 [I.R.C.1939]:

§ 1610(a) [former] (Surrender of property subject to distraint)

U.S.C., Title 28 former:

§ 122 [now 1656] (Creation of new district or transfer of territory; lien)

§ 350 [now 2101] (Time for making application for appeal or certiorari; stay pending application for certiorari)

§ 489 [now 547] (District Attorneys; reports to Department of Justice)

§ 574 [now 1921] (Marshals, fees enumerated)

§ 786 [former] (Judgments for duties; collected in coin)

§ 811 [now 1961] (Interest on judgments)

§ 838 [former] (Executions; run in all districts of State)

§ 839 [now 2413] (Executions; run in every State and Territory)

§ 840 [former] (Executions; stay on conditions), as modified by Rule 62(b)

§ 841 [former] (Executions; stay of one term), as modified by Rule 62(f)

§ 842 [now 2006] (Executions; against officers of revenue in cases of probable cause), as incorporated in Subdivision (b) of this rule

§ 843 [now 2007] (Imprisonment for debt)

§ 844 [now 2007] (Imprisonment for debt; discharge according to State laws)

§ 845 [now 2007] (Imprisonment for debt; jail limits)

§ 846 [now 2005] (Fieri Facias; appraisal of goods; appraisers)

§ 847 [now 2001] (Sales; real property under order or decree)

§ 848 [now 2004] (Sales; personal property under order or decree)

§ 849 [now 2002] (Sales; necessity of notice)

§ 850 [now 2003] (Sales; death of marshal after levy or after sale)

§ 869 [former] (Bond in former error and on appeal), as incorporated in Rule 73(c)

§ 874 [former] (Supersedeas), as modified by Rules 62(d) and 73(d)

U.S.C., Title 31:

§ 195 [now 3715] (Purchase on execution)

U.S.C., Title 33:

§ 918 (Collection of defaulted payments)

U.S.C., Title 49:

§ 74(g) [former] (Causes of action arising out of Federal control of railroads; execution and other process)

Special statutes of the United States on exemption from execution are also continued. Among these are:

U.S.C., Title 2:

§ 118 (Actions against officers of Congress for official acts)

U.S.C., Title 5 former:

§ 729 [see 8346, 8470] (Federal employees retirement annuities not subject to assignment, execution, levy or other legal process)

U.S.C., Title 10 former:

§ 610 [now 3690, 8690] (Exemption of enlisted men from arrest on civil process)

U.S.C., Title 22 former:

§ 21(h) [see 4060] (Foreign service retirement and disability system; establishment; rules and regulations; annuities; nonassignable; exemption from legal process)

U.S.C., Title 33:

§ 916 (Assignment and exemption from claims of creditors) (Longshoremen's and Harborworkers' Compensation Act)

U.S.C., Title 38 former:

§ 54 [see 3101] (Attachment, levy or seizure of moneys due pensioners prohibited)

§ 393 [former] (Army and Navy Medal of Honor Roll; pensions additional to other pensions; liability to attachment, etc.) Compare [former] Title 34, § 365(c) (Medal of Honor Roll; special pension to persons enrolled)

§ 618 [see 3101] (Benefits exempt from seizure under process and taxation; no deductions for indebtedness to United States)

U.S.C., Title 43:

§ 175 (Exemption from execution of homestead land)

U.S.C., Title 48 former:

§ 1371o (Panama canal and railroad retirement annuities, exemption from execution and so forth.)

Supplementary Note

Note. With respect to the provisions of the Soldiers' and Sailors' Civil Relief Act of 1940, 50 U.S.C. Appendix, § 501 et seq., see notes to Rules 62 and 64 herein.

1948 Amendment

The amendment effective October 1949, substituted the citation of "Title 28, U.S.C., § 2006" in subdivision (b) in place of the citation to "Section 989, Revised Statutes, U.S.C., Title 28, § 842".

1970 Amendment

The amendment assures that, in aid of execution on a judgment, all discovery procedures provided in the rules are available and not just discovery via the taking of a deposition. Under the present language, one court had held that Rule 34 discovery is unavailable to the judgment creditor. *M. Lowenstein & Sons, Inc. v. American Underwear Mfg. Co.,* 11 F.R.D. 172 (E.D.Pa.1951). Notwithstanding the language, and relying heavily on legislative history referring to Rule 33, the Fifth Circuit has held that a judgment creditor may invoke Rule 33 interrogatories. *United States v. McWhirter,* 376 F.2d 102 (5th Cir. 1967). But the court's reasoning does not extend to discovery except as provided in Rules 26–33. One commentator suggests that the existing language might properly be stretched to all discovery, 7 *Moore's Federal Practice* ¶ 69.05[1] (2d ed. 1966), but another believes that a rules amendment is needed. 3 Barron & Holtzoff, *Federal Practice and Procedure* 1484 (Wright ed. 1958). Both commentators and the court in *McWhirter* are clear that, as a matter of policy, Rule 69 should authorize the use of all discovery devices provided in the rules.

1987 Amendment

The amendments are technical. No substantive change is intended.

2007 Amendments

The language of Rule 69 has been amended as part of the general restyling of the Civil Rules to make them more easily understood and to make style and terminology consistent throughout the rules. These changes are intended to be stylistic only.

Amended Rule 69(b) incorporates directly the provisions of 2 U.S.C. § 118 and 28 U.S.C. § 2006, deleting the incomplete statement in former Rule 69(b) of the circumstances in which execution does not issue against an officer.

Rule 70.   Enforcing a Judgment for a Specific Act

(a)   Party's Failure to Act; Ordering Another to Act. If a judgment requires a party to convey land, to deliver a deed or other document, or to perform any other specific act and the party fails to comply within the time specified, the court may order the act to be done—at the disobedient party's expense—by another person appointed by the court. When done, the act has the same effect as if done by the party.

(b)   Vesting Title. If the real or personal property is within the district, the court—instead of ordering a conveyance—may enter a judgment divesting any party's title and vesting it in others. That judgment has the effect of a legally executed conveyance.

(c)   Obtaining a Writ of Attachment or Sequestration. On application by a party entitled to performance of an act, the clerk must issue a writ of attachment or sequestration against the disobedient party's property to compel obedience.

(d)   Obtaining a Writ of Execution or Assistance. On application by a party who obtains a judgment or order for possession, the clerk must issue a writ of execution or assistance.

(e)   Holding in Contempt. The court may also hold the disobedient party in contempt.

(Amended April 30, 2007, effective December 1, 2007.)

ADVISORY COMMITTEE NOTES

1937 Adoption

Compare [former] Equity Rules 7 (Process, Mesne and Final), 8 (Enforcement of Final Decrees), and 9 (Writ of Assistance). To avoid possible confusion, both old and new denominations for attachment (sequestration) and execution (assistance) are used in this rule. Compare with the provision in this rule that the judgment may itself vest title, 6 Tenn.Ann.Code (Williams, 1934), § 10594; 2 Conn.Gen.Stat. (1930), § 5455; N.M.Stat.Ann. (Courtright, 1929), § 117–117; 2 Ohio Gen.Code Ann. (Page, 1926), § 11590; and England, Supreme Court of Judicature Act (1925), § 47.

2007 Amendments

The language of Rule 70 has been amended as part of the general restyling of the Civil Rules to make them more easily understood and to make style and terminology consistent throughout the rules. These changes are intended to be stylistic only.

Rule 71.   Enforcing Relief for or Against a Nonparty

When an order grants relief for a nonparty or may be enforced against a nonparty, the procedure for enforcing the order is the same as for a party.

(Amended March 2, 1987, effective August 1, 1987; April 30, 2007, effective December 1, 2007.)

ADVISORY COMMITTEE NOTES

1937 Adoption

Compare [former] Equity Rule 11 (Process in Behalf of and Against Persons Not Parties). Compare also *Terrell v. Allison,* 1875, 21 Wall. 289, 22 L.Ed. 634; *Farmers' Loan and Trust Co. v. Chicago and A. Ry. Co.,* C.C.Ind.1890, 44 F. 653; *Robert Findlay Mfg. Co. v. Hygrade Lighting Fixture Corp.,* E.D.N.Y.1923, 288 F. 80; *Thompson v. Smith,* C.C.Minn.1870, Fed.Cas. No. 13,977.

1987 Amendment

The amendments are technical. No substantive change is intended.

2007 Amendments

The language of Rule 71 has been amended as part of the general restyling of the Civil Rules to make them more easily understood and to make style and terminology consistent throughout the rules. These changes are intended to be stylistic only.

TITLE IX. SPECIAL PROCEEDINGS

Rule 71.1. Condemning Real or Personal Property

(a) Applicability of Other Rules. These rules govern proceedings to condemn real and personal property by eminent domain, except as this rule provides otherwise.

(b) Joinder of Properties. The plaintiff may join separate pieces of property in a single action, no matter whether they are owned by the same persons or sought for the same use.

(c) Complaint.

    (1) *Caption.* The complaint must contain a caption as provided in Rule 10(a). The plaintiff must, however, name as defendants both the property—designated generally by kind, quantity, and location—and at least one owner of some part of or interest in the property.

    (2) *Contents.* The complaint must contain a short and plain statement of the following:

        (A) the authority for the taking;

        (B) the uses for which the property is to be taken;

        (C) a description sufficient to identify the property;

        (D) the interests to be acquired; and

        (E) for each piece of property, a designation of each defendant who has been joined as an owner or owner of an interest in it.

    (3) *Parties.* When the action commences, the plaintiff need join as defendants only those persons who have or claim an interest in the property and whose names are then known. But before any hearing on compensation, the plaintiff must add as defendants all those persons who have or claim an interest and whose names have become known or can be found by a reasonably diligent search of the records, considering both the property's character and value and the interests to be acquired. All others may be made defendants under the designation "Unknown Owners."

    (4) *Procedure.* Notice must be served on all defendants as provided in Rule 71.1(d), whether they were named as defendants when the action commenced or were added later. A defendant may answer as provided in Rule 71.1(e). The court, meanwhile, may order any distribution of a deposit that the facts warrant.

    (5) *Filing; Additional Copies.* In addition to filing the complaint, the plaintiff must give the clerk at least one copy for the defendants' use and additional copies at the request of the clerk or a defendant.

(d) Process.

    (1) *Delivering Notice to the Clerk.* On filing a complaint, the plaintiff must promptly deliver to the clerk joint or several notices directed to the named defendants. When adding defendants, the plaintiff must deliver to the clerk additional notices directed to the new defendants.

(2) *Contents of the Notice.*

    (A) *Main Contents.* Each notice must name the court, the title of the action, and the defendant to whom it is directed. It must describe the property sufficiently to identify it, but need not describe any property other than that to be taken from the named defendant. The notice must also state:

        (i) that the action is to condemn property;

        (ii) the interest to be taken;

        (iii) the authority for the taking;

        (iv) the uses for which the property is to be taken;

        (v) that the defendant may serve an answer on the plaintiff's attorney within 21 days after being served with the notice;

        (vi) that the failure to so serve an answer constitutes consent to the taking and to the court's authority to proceed with the action and fix the compensation; and

        (vii) that a defendant who does not serve an answer may file a notice of appearance.

    (B) *Conclusion.* The notice must conclude with the name, telephone number, and e-mail address of the plaintiff's attorney and an address within the district in which the action is brought where the attorney may be served.

(3) *Serving the Notice.*

    (A) *Personal Service.* When a defendant whose address is known resides within the United States or a territory subject to the administrative or judicial jurisdiction of the United States, personal service of the notice (without a copy of the complaint) must be made in accordance with Rule 4.

    (B) *Service by Publication.*

        (i) A defendant may be served by publication only when the plaintiff's attorney files a certificate stating that the attorney believes the defendant cannot be personally served, because after diligent inquiry within the state where the complaint is filed, the defendant's place of residence is still unknown or, if known, that it is beyond the territorial limits of personal service. Service is then made by publishing the notice—once a week for at least 3 successive weeks—in a newspaper published in the county where the property is located or, if there is no such newspaper, in a newspaper with general circulation where the property is located. Before the last publication, a copy of the notice must also be mailed to every defendant who cannot be personally served but whose place of residence is then known. Unknown owners may be served by publication in the same manner by a notice addressed to "Unknown Owners."

        (ii) Service by publication is complete on the date of the last publication. The plaintiff's attorney must prove publication and mailing by a certificate, attach a printed copy of the published notice, and mark on the copy the newspaper's name and the dates of publication.

(4) *Effect of Delivery and Service.* Delivering the notice to the clerk and serving it have the same effect as serving a summons under Rule 4.

(5) *Amending the Notice; Proof of Service and Amending the Proof.* Rule 4(a)(2) governs amending the notice. Rule 4(*l*) governs proof of service and amending it.

(e) Appearance or Answer.

(1) ***Notice of Appearance.*** A defendant that has no objection or defense to the taking of its property may serve a notice of appearance designating the property in which it claims an interest. The defendant must then be given notice of all later proceedings affecting the defendant.

(2) ***Answer.*** A defendant that has an objection or defense to the taking must serve an answer within 21 days after being served with the notice. The answer must:

(A) identify the property in which the defendant claims an interest;

(B) state the nature and extent of the interest; and

(C) state all the defendant's objections and defenses to the taking.

(3) ***Waiver of Other Objections and Defenses; Evidence on Compensation.*** A defendant waives all objections and defenses not stated in its answer. No other pleading or motion asserting an additional objection or defense is allowed. But at the trial on compensation, a defendant—whether or not it has previously appeared or answered—may present evidence on the amount of compensation to be paid and may share in the award.

(f) Amending Pleadings. Without leave of court, the plaintiff may—as often as it wants—amend the complaint at any time before the trial on compensation. But no amendment may be made if it would result in a dismissal inconsistent with Rule 71.1(i)(1) or (2). The plaintiff need not serve a copy of an amendment, but must serve notice of the filing, as provided in Rule 5(b), on every affected party who has appeared and, as provided in Rule 71.1(d), on every affected party who has not appeared. In addition, the plaintiff must give the clerk at least one copy of each amendment for the defendants' use, and additional copies at the request of the clerk or a defendant. A defendant may appear or answer in the time and manner and with the same effect as provided in Rule 71.1(e).

(g) Substituting Parties. If a defendant dies, becomes incompetent, or transfers an interest after being joined, the court may, on motion and notice of hearing, order that the proper party be substituted. Service of the motion and notice on a nonparty must be made as provided in Rule 71.1(d)(3).

(h) Trial of the Issues.

(1) ***Issues Other Than Compensation; Compensation.*** In an action involving eminent domain under federal law, the court tries all issues, including compensation, except when compensation must be determined:

(A) by any tribunal specially constituted by a federal statute to determine compensation; or

(B) if there is no such tribunal, by a jury when a party demands one within the time to answer or within any additional time the court sets, unless the court appoints a commission.

(2) ***Appointing a Commission; Commission's Powers and Report.***

(A) *Reasons for Appointing.* If a party has demanded a jury, the court may instead appoint a three-person commission to determine compensation because of the character, location, or quantity of the property to be condemned or for other just reasons.

(B) *Alternate Commissioners.* The court may appoint up to two additional persons to serve as alternate commissioners to hear the case and replace commissioners who, before a decision is filed, the court finds unable or disqualified to perform their duties. Once the commission renders its final decision, the court must discharge any alternate who has not replaced a commissioner.

(C) *Examining the Prospective Commissioners.* Before making its appointments, the court must advise the parties of the identity and qualifications of each prospective commissioner and alternate, and may permit the parties to examine them. The parties may not suggest appointees, but for good cause may object to a prospective commissioner or alternate.

(D) *Commission's Powers and Report.* A commission has the powers of a master under Rule 53(c). Its action and report are determined by a majority. Rule 53(d), (e), and (f) apply to its action and report.

(i) Dismissal of the Action or a Defendant.

    (1) *Dismissing the Action.*

        (A) *By the Plaintiff.* If no compensation hearing on a piece of property has begun, and if the plaintiff has not acquired title or a lesser interest or taken possession, the plaintiff may, without a court order, dismiss the action as to that property by filing a notice of dismissal briefly describing the property.

        (B) *By Stipulation.* Before a judgment is entered vesting the plaintiff with title or a lesser interest in or possession of property, the plaintiff and affected defendants may, without a court order, dismiss the action in whole or in part by filing a stipulation of dismissal. And if the parties so stipulate, the court may vacate a judgment already entered.

        (C) *By Court Order.* At any time before compensation has been determined and paid, the court may, after a motion and hearing, dismiss the action as to a piece of property. But if the plaintiff has already taken title, a lesser interest, or possession as to any part of it, the court must award compensation for the title, lesser interest, or possession taken.

    (2) *Dismissing a Defendant.* The court may at any time dismiss a defendant who was unnecessarily or improperly joined.

    (3) *Effect.* A dismissal is without prejudice unless otherwise stated in the notice, stipulation, or court order.

(j) Deposit and Its Distribution.

    (1) *Deposit.* The plaintiff must deposit with the court any money required by law as a condition to the exercise of eminent domain and may make a deposit when allowed by statute.

    (2) *Distribution; Adjusting Distribution.* After a deposit, the court and attorneys must expedite the proceedings so as to distribute the deposit and to determine and pay compensation. If the compensation finally awarded to a defendant exceeds the amount distributed to that defendant, the court must enter judgment against the plaintiff for the deficiency. If the compensation awarded to a defendant is less than the amount distributed to that defendant, the court must enter judgment against that defendant for the overpayment.

(k) Condemnation Under a State's Power of Eminent Domain. This rule governs an action involving eminent domain under state law. But if state law provides for trying an issue by jury— or for trying the issue of compensation by jury or commission or both—that law governs.

(*l*) Costs. Costs are not subject to Rule 54(d).

(Adopted April 30, 1951, effective August 1, 1951; amended January 21, 1963, effective July 1, 1963; April 29, 1985, effective August 1, 1985; March 2, 1987, effective August 1, 1987; April 25, 1988, effective August 1, 1988; amended by Pub.L. 100–690, Title VII, § 7050, November 18, 1988, 102 Stat. 4401 (although amendment by Pub.L. 100–690 could not be executed due to prior amendment by Court order which made the same change effective August 1, 1988); amended April 22, 1993, effective December 1, 1993; March 27, 2003, effective December 1, 2003; April 30, 2007, effective December 1, 2007; March 26, 2009, effective December 1, 2009.)

ADVISORY COMMITTEE NOTES

1951 Addition

Supplementary Report of the Advisory Committee

MARCH 1951.

* * * [T]he Advisory Committee has given further consideration to the proposed rule, [ ] at a meeting of the Committee held at Washington April 6, 1950, and thereafter it adopted a number of amendments to the 1948 draft and now presents the revised draft to the Court with the recommendation that it be adopted. * * *

The Court will remember that at its conference on December 2, 1948, the discussion was confined to subdivision (h) of the rule (* * *), the particular question being whether the tribunal to award compensation should be a commission or a jury in cases where the Congress has not made specific provision on the subject. The Advisory Committee was agreed from the outset that a rule should not be promulgated which would overturn the decision of the Congress as to the kind of tribunal to fix compensation, provided that the system established by Congress was found to be working well. We found two instances where the Congress had specified the kind of tribunal to fix compensation. One case was the District of Columbia (U.S.C., Title 40, [former] §§ 361–386 [now D.C. Code, Title 16, § 1301 et seq.]) where a rather unique system exists under which the court is required in all cases to order the selection of a "jury" of five from among not less than twenty names drawn from "the special box provided by law." They must have the usual qualifications of jurors and in addition must be freeholders of the District and not in the service of the United States or the District. That system has been in effect for many years, and our inquiry revealed that it works well under the conditions prevailing in the District, and is satisfactory to the courts of the District, the legal profession and to property owners.

The other instance is that of the Tennessee Valley Authority, where the act of Congress (U.S.C., Title 16, § 831x) provides that compensation is fixed by three disinterested commissioners appointed by the court, whose award goes before the District Court for confirmation or modification. The Advisory Committee made a thorough inquiry into the practical operation of the TVA commission system. We obtained from counsel for the TVA the results of their experience, which afforded convincing proof that the commission system is preferable under the conditions affecting TVA and that the jury system would not work satisfactorily. We then, under date of February 6, 1947, wrote every Federal judge who had ever sat in a TVA condemnation case, asking his views as to whether the commission system is satisfactory and whether a jury system should be preferred. Of 21 responses from the judges 17 approved the commission system and opposed the substitution of a jury system for the TVA. Many of the judges went further and opposed the use of juries in any condemnation cases. Three of the judges preferred the jury system, and one dealt only with the TVA provision for a three judge district court. The Advisory Committee has not considered abolition of the three judge requirement of the TVA Act, because it seemed to raise a question of jurisdiction, which cannot be altered by rule. Nevertheless the Department of Justice continued its advocacy of the jury system for its asserted expedition and economy; and others favored a uniform procedure. In consequence of these divided counsels the Advisory Committee was itself divided, but in its May 1948 Report to the Court recommended the following rule as approved by a majority (* * *):

(h) Trial. If the action involves the exercise of the power of eminent domain under the law of the United States, any tribunal especially constituted by an Act of Congress governing the case for the trial of the issue of just compensation shall be the tribunal for the determination of that issue; but if there is no such specially constituted tribunal any party may have a trial by jury of the issue of just compensation by filing a demand therefor within the time allowed for answer or within such further time as the court may fix. Trial of all issues shall otherwise be by the court.

The effect of this was to preserve the existing systems in the District of Columbia and in TVA cases, but to provide for a jury to fix compensation in all other cases.

Before the Court's conference of December 2, 1948, the Chief Justice informed the Committee that the Court was particularly interested in the views expressed by Judge John Paul, Judge of the United States District Court for the Western District of Virginia, in a letter from him to the chairman of the Advisory Committee, dated February 13, 1947. Copies of all the letters from judges who had sat in TVA cases had been made available to the Court, and this letter from Judge Paul is one of them. Judge Paul strongly opposed jury trials and recommended the commission system in large projects like the TVA, and his views seemed to have impressed the Court and to have been the occasion for the conference.

The reasons which convinced the Advisory Committee that the use of commissioners instead of juries is desirable in TVA cases were these:

     1.   The TVA condemns large areas of land of similar kind, involving many owners. Uniformity in awards is essential. The commission system tends to prevent discrimination and provide for uniformity in compensation. The jury system tends to lack of uniformity. Once a reasonable and uniform standard of values for the area has been settled by a commission, litigation ends and settlements result.

     2.   Where large areas are involved many small landowners reside at great distances from the place where a court sits. It is a great hardship on humble people to have to travel long distances to attend a jury trial. A commission may travel around and receive the evidence of the owner near his home.

     3.   It is impracticable to take juries long distances to view the premises.

     4.   If the cases are tried by juries the burden on the time of the courts is excessive.

These considerations are the very ones Judge Paul stressed in his letter. He pointed out that they applied not only to the TVA but to other large governmental projects, such as flood control, hydroelectric power, reclamation, national forests, and others. So when the representatives of the Advisory Committee appeared at the Court's conference December 2, 1948, they found it difficult to justify the proposed provision in subdivision (h) of the rule that a jury should be used to fix compensation in all cases where Congress had not specified the tribunal. If our reasons for preserving the TVA system were sound, provision for a jury in similar projects of like magnitude seemed unsound.

Aware of the apparent inconsistency between the acceptance of the TVA system and the provision for a jury in all other cases, the members of the Committee attending the conference of December 2, 1948, then suggested that in the other cases the choice of jury or commission be left to the discretion of the District Court, going back to a suggestion previously made by Committee members and reported at page 15 of the Preliminary Draft of June 1947. They called the attention of the Court to the fact that the entire Advisory Committee had not been consulted about this suggestion and proposed that the draft be returned to the Committee for further consideration, and that was done.

The proposal we now make for subdivision (h) is as follows:

     (h)   **Trial.** If the action involves the exercise of the power of eminent domain under the law of the United States, any tribunal specially constituted by an Act of Congress governing the case for the trial of the issue of just compensation shall be the tribunal for the determination of that issue; but if there is no such specially constituted tribunal any party may have a trial by jury of the issue of just compensation by filing a demand therefor within the time allowed for answer or within such further time as the court may fix, unless the court in its discretion orders that, because of the character, location, or quantity of the property to be condemned, or for other reasons in the interest of justice, the issue of compensation shall be determined by a commission of three persons appointed by it. If a commission is appointed it shall have the powers of a master provided in subdivision (c) of Rule 53 and proceedings before it shall be governed by the provisions of paragraphs (1) and (2) of subdivision (d) of Rule 53. Its action and report shall be determined by a majority and its findings and report shall have the effect, and be dealt with by the court in accordance with the practice, prescribed in paragraph (2) of subdivision (e) of Rule 53. Trial of all issues shall otherwise be by the court.

In the 1948 draft the Committee had been almost evenly divided as between jury or commission and that made it easy for us to agree on the present draft. It would be difficult to state in a rule the various conditions to control the District Court in its choice and we have merely stated generally the matters which should be considered by the District Court.

The rule as now drafted seems to meet Judge Paul's objection. In large projects like the TVA the court may decide to use a commission. In a great number of cases involving only sites for buildings or other small areas, where use of a jury is appropriate, a jury may be chosen. The District Court's discretion may also be influenced by local preference or habit, and the preference of the Department of Justice and the reasons for its preference will doubtless be given weight. The Committee is convinced that there are some types of cases in which use of a commission is preferable and others in which a jury may be appropriately used, and that it would be a mistake to provide that the same kind of tribunal should be used in all cases. We think the available evidence clearly leads to that conclusion.

When this suggestion was made at the conference of December 2, 1948, representatives of the Department of Justice opposed it, expressing opposition to the use of a commission in any case. Their principal ground for opposition to commissions was then based on the assertion that the commission system is too expensive because courts allow commissioners too large compensation. The obvious answer to that is that the compensation of commissioners ought to be fixed or limited by law, as was done in the TVA Act, and the agency dealing with appropriations—either the Administrative Office or some other interested department of the government—should correct that evil, if evil there be, by obtaining such legislation. Authority to promulgate rules of procedure does not include power to fix compensation of government employees. The Advisory Committee is not convinced that even without such legislation the commission system is more expensive than the jury system. The expense of jury trials includes not only the per diem and mileage of the jurors impaneled for a case but like items for the entire venire. In computing cost of jury trials, the salaries of court officials, judges, clerks, marshals and deputies must be considered. No figures have been given to the Committee to establish that the cost of the commission system is the greater.

We earnestly recommend the rule as now drafted for promulgation by the Court, in the public interest.

The Advisory Committee have given more time to this rule, including time required for conferences with the Department of Justice to hear statements of its representatives, than has been required by any other rule. The rule may not be perfect but if faults develop in practice they may be promptly cured. Certainly the present conformity system is atrocious.

Under state practices, just compensation is normally determined by one of three methods: by commissioners; by commissioners with a right of appeal to and trial de novo before a jury; and by a jury, without a commission. A trial to the court or to the court including a master are, however, other methods that are occasionally used. Approximately 5 states use only commissioners; 23 states use commissioners with a trial de novo before a jury; and 18 states use only the jury. This classification is advisedly stated in approximate terms, since the same state may utilize diverse methods, depending upon different types of condemnations or upon the locality of the property, and since the methods used in a few states do not permit of a categorical classification. To reject the proposed rule and leave the situation as it is would not satisfy the views of the Department of Justice. The Department and the Advisory Committee agree that the use of a commission, with appeal to a jury, is a wasteful system.

The Department of Justice has a voluminous "Manual on Federal Eminent Domain," the 1940 edition of which has 948 pages with an appendix of 73 more pages. The title page informs us the preparation of the manual was begun during the incumbency of Attorney General Cummings, was continued under Attorney General Murphy, and completed during the incumbency of Attorney General Jackson. The preface contains the following statement:

It should also be mentioned that the research incorporated in the manual would be of invaluable assistance in the drafting of a new uniform code, or rules of court, for federal condemnation proceedings, which are now greatly confused, not only by the existence of over seventy federal statutes governing condemnations for different purposes—statutes which sometimes conflict with one another—but also by the countless problems occasioned by the requirements of conformity to state law. Progress of the work has already demonstrated that the need for such reform exists.

* * *

It is not surprising that more than once Attorneys General have asked the Advisory Committee to prepare a federal rule and rescue the government from this morass.

The Department of Justice has twice tried and failed to persuade the Congress to provide that juries shall be used in all condemnation cases. The debates in Congress show that part of the opposition to the Department of Justice's bills came from representatives opposed to jury trials in all cases, and in part from a preference for the conformity system. Our present proposal opens the door for district judges to yield to local preferences on the subject. It does much for the Department's points of view. It is a great improvement over the present so-called conformity system. It does away with the wasteful "double" system prevailing in 23 states where awards by commissions are followed by jury trials.

Aside from the question as to the choice of a tribunal to award compensation, the proposed rule would afford a simple and improved procedure.

We turn now to an itemized explanation of the other changes we have made in the 1948 draft. Some of these result from recent amendments to the Judicial Code. Others result from a reconsideration by the Advisory Committee of provisions which we thought could be improved.

     1.   In the amended Judicial Code, the district courts are designated as "United States District Courts" instead of "District Courts of the United States," and a corresponding change has been made in the rule.

     2.   After the 1948 draft was referred back to the committee, the provision in subdivision (c)(2), relating to naming defendants, * * * which provided that the plaintiff shall add as defendants all persons having or claiming an interest in that property whose names can be ascertained by a search of the records to the extent commonly made by competent searchers of title in the vicinity "in light of the type and value of the property involved," the phrase in quotation marks was changed to read "in the light of the character and value of the property involved and the interests to be acquired."

The Department of Justice made a counter proposal [that certain lines in the draft be deleted and] that there be substituted the words "reasonably diligent search of the records, considering the type." When the American Bar Association thereafter considered the draft, it approved the Advisory Committee's draft of this subdivision, but said that it had no objection to the Department's suggestion. Thereafter, in an effort to eliminate controversy, the Advisory Committee accepted the Department's suggestion as to (c)(2), using the word "character" instead of the word "type."

The Department of Justice also suggested that in subdivision (d)(3)(ii) relating to service by publication, the search for a defendant's residence as a preliminary to publication be limited to the state in which the complaint is filed. Here again the American Bar Association's report expressed the view that the Department's suggestion was unobjectionable and the Advisory Committee thereupon adopted it.

     3.   Subdivision (k) of the 1948 draft is as follows:

(k) Condemnation Under a State's Power of Eminent Domain. If the action involves the exercise of the power of eminent domain under the law of a state, the practice herein prescribed may be altered to the extent necessary to observe and enforce any condition affecting the substantial rights of a litigant attached by the state law to the exercise of the state's power of eminent domain.

Occasionally condemnation cases under a state's power of eminent domain reach a United States District Court because of diversity of citizenship. Such cases are rare, but provision should be made for them.

The 1948 draft of (k) required a district court to decide whether a provision of state law specifying the tribunal to award compensation is or is not a "condition" attached to the exercise of the state's power. On reconsideration we concluded that it would be wise to redraft (k) so as to avoid that troublesome question. As to conditions in state laws which affect the substantial rights of a litigant, the district courts would be bound to give them effect without any rule on the subject. Accordingly we present two alternative revisions. One suggestion supported by a majority of the Advisory Committee is as follows:

(k) Condemnation Under a State's Power of Eminent Domain. The practice herein prescribed governs in actions involving the exercise of the power of eminent domain under the law of a state, provided that if the state law makes provision for trial of any issue by jury, or for trial of the issue of compensation by jury or commission or both, that provision shall be followed.

The other is as follows:

(k) Condemnation Under a State's Power of Eminent Domain. The practice herein prescribed governs in actions involving the exercise of the power of eminent domain under the law of a state, provided that if the state law gives a right to a trial by jury such a trial shall in any case be allowed to the party demanding it within the time permitted by these rules, and in that event no hearing before a commission shall be had.

The first proposal accepts the state law as to the tribunals to fix compensation, and in that respect leaves the parties in precisely the same situation as if the case were pending in a state court, including the use of a commission with appeal to a jury, if the state law so provides. It has the effect of avoiding any question as to whether the decisions in *Erie R. Co. v. Tompkins* and later cases have application to a situation of this kind.

The second proposal gives the parties a right to a jury trial if that is provided for by state law, but prevents the use of both commission and jury. Those members of the Committee who favor the second proposal do so because of the obvious objections to the double trial, with a commission and appeal to a jury. As the decisions in *Erie R. Co. v. Tompkins* and later cases may have a bearing on this point, and the Committee is divided, we think both proposals should be placed before the Court.

4. The provision * * * of the 1948 draft * * * prescribing the effective date of the rule was drafted before the recent amendment of the Judicial Code on that subject. On May 10, 1950, the President approved an act which amended section 2072 of Title 28, United States Code, to read as follows:

Such rules shall not take effect until they have been reported to Congress by the Chief Justice at or after the beginning of a regular session thereof but not later than the first day of May, and until the expiration of ninety days after they have been thus reported.

To conform to the statute now in force, we suggest a provision as follows:

Effective Date. This Rule 71A and the amendment to Rule 81(a) will take effect on August 1, 1951. Rule 71A governs all proceedings in actions brought after it takes effect and also all further proceedings in actions then pending, except to the extent that in the opinion of the court its application in a particular action pending when the rule takes effect would not be feasible or would work injustice, in which event the former procedure applies.

If the rule is not reported to Congress by May 1, 1951, this provision must be altered.

[Par. 3 of Supreme Court Order adopted Apr. 30, 1951, setting out this rule and providing for the abrogation of par. (7) of Rule 81(a), and providing for the Effective Date, as stated herein, was transmitted to Congress on May 1, 1951 by the Chief Justice of the United States (House Document No. 121, May 1, 1951, 82nd Cong., 1st Sess.), in conformity with § 2072 of this title. As no action was taken by Congress within the 90-day period required by that section, this rule and the abrogation of par. (7) of Rule 81(a) took effect on Aug. 1, 1951, as provided in said order.]

5. We call attention to the fact that the proposed rule does not contain a provision for the procedure to be followed in order to exercise the right of the United States to take immediate possession or title, when the condemnation proceeding is begun. There are several statutes conferring such a right which are cited in the original notes to the May 1948 draft * * * . The existence of this right is taken into account in the rule. In subdivision (c)(2), * * * it is stated: "Upon the commencement of the action, the plaintiff need join as defendants only the persons having or claiming an interest in the property whose names are then known." That is to enable the United States to exercise the right to immediate title or possession without the delay involved in ascertaining the names of all interested parties. The right is also taken into account in the provision relating to dismissal (paragraph (i), subdivisions (1), (2), and (3), * * *); also in paragraph (j) relating to deposits and their distribution.

The Advisory Committee considered whether the procedure for exercising the right should be specified in the rule and decided against it, as the procedure now being followed seems to be giving no trouble, and to draft a rule to fit all the statutes on the subject might create confusion.

The American Bar Association has taken an active interest in a rule for condemnation cases. In 1944 its House of Delegates adopted a resolution which among other things resolved:

That before adoption by the Supreme Court of the United States of any redraft of the proposed rule, time and opportunity should be afforded to the bar to consider and make recommendations concerning any such redraft.

Accordingly, in 1950 the revised draft was submitted to the American Bar Association and its section of real property, probate and trust law appointed a committee to consider it. That committee was supplied with copies of the written statement from the Department of Justice giving the reasons relied on by the Department for preferring a rule to use juries in all cases. The Advisory Committee's report was approved at a meeting of the section of real property law, and by the House of Delegates at the annual meeting of September 1950. The American Bar Association report gave particular attention to the question whether juries or commissions should be used to fix compensation, approved the Advisory Committee's solution appearing in their latest draft designed to allow use of commissions in projects comparable to the TVA, and rejected the proposal for use of juries in all cases.

In November 1950 a committee of the Federal Bar Association, the chairman of which was a Special Assistant to the Attorney General, made a report which reflected the attitude of the Department of Justice on the condemnation rule.

Aside from subdivision (h) about the tribunal to award compensation the final draft of the condemnation rule here presented has the approval of the American Bar Association and, we understand, the Department of Justice, and we do not know of any opposition to it. Subdivision (h) has the unanimous approval of the Advisory Committee and has been approved by the American Bar Association. The use of commissions in TVA cases, and, by fair inference, in cases comparable to the TVA, is supported by 17 out of 20 judges who up to 1947 had sat in TVA cases. The legal staff of the TVA has vigorously objected to the substitution of juries for commissions in TVA cases. We regret to report that the Department of Justice still asks that subdivision (h) be altered to provide for jury trials in an cases where Congress has not specified the tribunal. We understand that the Department approves the proposal that the system prevailing in 23 states for the "double" trial, by commission with appeal to and trial de novo before a jury, should be abolished, and also asks that on demand a jury should be substituted for a commission, in those states where use of a commission alone is now required. The Advisory Committee has no evidence that commissions do not operate satisfactorily in the case of projects comparable to the TVA.

Original Report

General Statement. 1. Background. When the Advisory Committee was formulating its recommendations to the Court concerning rules of procedure, which subsequently became the Federal Rules of 1938, the Committee concluded at an early stage not to fix the procedure in condemnation cases. This is a matter principally involving the exercise of the federal power of eminent domain, as very few condemnation cases involving the state's power reach the United States District Courts. The Committee's reasons at that time were that inasmuch as condemnation proceedings by the United States are governed by statutes of the United States, prescribing different procedure for various agencies and departments of the government, or, in the absence of such statutes, by local state practice under the Conformity Act (former § 258 of Title 40), it would be extremely difficult to draft a uniform rule satisfactory to the various agencies and departments of the government and to private parties; and that there was no general demand for a uniform rule. The Committee continued in that belief until shortly before the preparation of the April 1937 Draft of the Rules, when the officials of the Department of Justice having to do with condemnation cases urgently requested the Committee to propose rules on this subject. The Committee undertook the task and drafted a Condemnation Rule which appeared for the first time as Rule 74 of the April 1937 Draft. After the publication and distribution of this initial draft many objections were urged against it by counsel for various governmental agencies, whose procedure in condemnation cases was prescribed by federal statutes. Some of these agencies wanted to be excepted in whole or in part from the operation of the uniform rule proposed in April 1937. And the Department of Justice changed its position and stated that it preferred to have government condemnations conducted by local attorneys familiar with the state practice, which was applied under the Conformity Act where the Acts of Congress do not prescribe the practice; that it preferred to work under the Conformity Act without a uniform rule of procedure. The profession generally showed little interest in the proposed uniform rule. For these reasons the Advisory Committee in its Final Report to the Court in November 1937 proposed that all of Rule 74 be stricken and that the Federal Rules be made applicable only to appeals in condemnation cases. See note to Rule 74 of the Final Report.

Some of six or seven years later when the Advisory Committee was considering the subject of amendments to the Federal Rules both government officials and the profession generally urged the adoption of some uniform procedure. This demand grew out of the volume of condemnation proceedings instituted during the war, and the general feeling of dissatisfaction with the diverse condemnation procedures that were applicable in the federal courts. A strongly held belief was that both the sovereign's power to condemn and the property owner's right to compensation could be promoted by a simplified rule. As a consequence the Committee proposed a Rule 71A on the subject of condemnation in its Preliminary Draft of May 1944. In the Second Preliminary Draft of May 1945 this earlier proposed Rule 71A was, however, omitted. The Committee did not then feel that it had sufficient time to prepare a revised draft satisfactorily to it which would meet legitimate objections made to the draft of May 1944. To avoid unduly delaying the proposed amendments to existing rules the Committee concluded to proceed in the regular way with the preparation of the amendments to these rules and deal with the question of a condemnation rule as an independent matter. As a consequence it made no recommendations to the Court on condemnation in its Final Report of Proposed Amendments of June 1946; and the amendments which the Court adopted in December 1946 did not deal with condemnation. After concluding its task relative to amendments, the Committee returned to a consideration of eminent domain, its proposed Rule 71A of May 1944, the suggestions and criticisms that had been presented in the interim, and in June 1947 prepared and distributed to the profession another draft of a proposed condemnation rule. This draft contained several alternative provisions, specifically called attention to and asked for opinion relative to these matters, and in particular as to the constitution of the tribunal to award compensation. The present draft was based on the June 1947 formulation, in light of the advice of the profession on both matters of substance and form.

2.   Statutory Provisions. The need for a uniform condemnation rule in the federal courts arises from the fact that by various statutes Congress has prescribed diverse procedures for certain condemnation proceedings, and, in the absence of such statutes, has prescribed conformity to local state practice under former § 258 of Title 40. This general conformity adds to the diversity of procedure since in the United States there are multifarious methods of procedure in existence. Thus in 1931 it was said that there were 269 different methods of judicial procedure in different classes of condemnation cases and 56 methods of nonjudicial or administrative procedure. First Report of Judicial Council of Michigan, 1931, § 46, pp. 55 to 56. These numbers have not decreased. Consequently, the general requirement of conformity to state practice and procedure, particularly where the condemnor is the United States, leads to expense, delay and uncertainty. In advocacy of a uniform federal rule, see Armstrong, *Proposed Amendments to Federal Rules for Civil Procedure,* 1944, 4 F.R.D. 124, 134; id., *Report of the Advisory Committee on Federal Rules of Civil Procedure Recommending Amendments,* 1946, 5 F.R.D. 339, 357.

There are a great variety of Acts of Congress authorizing the exercise of the power of eminent domain by the United States and its officers and agencies. These statutes for the most part do not specify the exact procedure to be followed, but where procedure is prescribed, it is by no means uniform.

The following are instances of Acts which merely authorize the exercise of the power without specific declaration as to the procedure:

U.S.C., Title 16:

§ 404c–11 (Mammoth Cave National Park; acquisition of lands, interests in lands or other property for park by the Secretary of the Interior).

§ 426d (Stones River National Park; acquisition of land for parks by the Secretary of the Army).

§ 450aa (George Washington Carver National Monument; acquisition of land by the Secretary of the Interior).

§ 517 (National forest reservation; title to lands to be acquired by the Secretary of Agriculture).

U.S.C., Title 42:

§§ 1805(b)(5), 1813(b) [now §§ 2061 and 2112, and §§ 2221 to 2224, respectively, of Title 42] (Atomic Energy Act).

The following are instances of Acts which authorized condemnation and declare that the procedure is to conform what that of similar actions in state courts:

U.S.C., Title 16:

§ 423k (Richmond National Battlefield Park; acquisition of lands by the Secretary of the Interior).

§ 814 (Exercise by water power licensee of power of eminent domain).

U.S.C., Title 24:

§ 78 [Repealed] (Condemnation of land for the former National Home for Disabled Volunteer Soldiers).

U.S.C., Title 33:

§ 591 (Condemnation of lands and materials for river and harbor improvement by the Secretary of the Army).

U.S.C., Title 40:

§ 257 [now § 3113] (Condemnation of realty for sites for public building and for other public uses by the Secretary of the Treasury authorized).

§ 258 [Omitted as superseded by this rule] (Same procedure).

U.S.C., Title 50:

§ 171 [Repealed and is now covered by § 2663 of Title 10] (Acquisition of land by the Secretary of the Army for national defense).

§ 172 [Repealed and is now covered by §§ 2664 and 2665 of Title 10] (Acquisition of property by the Secretary of the Army, etc., for production of lumber).

§ 632 App. [Omitted as terminated by § 645 of the Appendix to Title 50] (Second War Powers Act, 1942; acquisition of real property for war purposes by the Secretary of Army, the Secretary of the Navy and others).

The following are Acts in which a more or less complete code of procedure is set forth in connection with the taking:

U.S.C., Title 16:

§ 831x (Condemnation by Tennessee Valley Authority).

U.S.C., Title 40:

§ 361–386 [Repealed] [now D.C.Code, Title 16, § 1301 et seq.] (Acquisition of lands in District of Columbia for use of United States; condemnation).

3.   Adjustment of Rule to Statutory Provisions. While it was apparent that the principle of uniformity should be the basis for a rule to replace the multiple diverse procedures set out above, there remained a serious question as to whether an exception could properly be made relative to the method of determining compensation. Where Congress had provided for conformity to state law the following were the general methods in use: an initial determination by commissioners, with appeal to a judge; an initial award, likewise made by commissioners, but with the appeal to a jury; and determination by a jury without a previous award by commissioners. In two situations Congress had specified the tribunal to determine the issue of compensation: condemnation by the Tennessee Valley Authority; and condemnation in the District of Columbia. Under the TVA procedure the initial determination of value is by three disinterested commissioners, appointed by the court, from a locality other than the one in which the land lies. Either party may except to the award of the commission; in that case the exceptions are to be heard by three district judges (unless the parties stipulate for a lesser number), with a right of appeal to the circuit court of appeals. The TVA is a regional agency. It is faced with the necessity of acquiring a very substantial acreage within a relatively small area, and charged with the task of carrying on within the Tennessee Valley and in cooperation with the local people a permanent program involving navigation and flood control, electric power, soil conservation, and general regional development. The success of this program is partially dependent upon the good will and cooperation of the people of the Tennessee Valley, and this in turn partially depends upon the land acquisition program. Disproportionate awards among landowners would create dissatisfaction and ill will. To secure uniformity in treatment Congress provided the rather unique procedure of the three-judge court to review de novo the initial award of the commissioners. This procedure has worked to the satisfaction of the property owners and the TVA. A full statement of the TVA position and experience is set forth in Preliminary Draft of Proposed Rule to Govern Condemnation Cases (June, 1947) 15–19. A large majority of the district judges with experience under this procedure approve it, subject to some objection to the requirement for a three-judge district court to review commissioners' awards. A statutory three-judge requirement is, however, jurisdictional and must be strictly followed. *Stratton v. St. Louis, Southwestern Ry. Co.,* 1930, 51 S.Ct. 8, 282 U.S. 10, 75 L.Ed. 135; *Ayrshire Collieries Corp. v. United States,* 1947, 67 S.Ct. 1168, 331 U.S. 132, 91 L.Ed. 1391. Hence except insofar as the TVA statute itself authorizes the parties to stipulate for a court of less than three judges, the requirement must be followed, and would seem to be beyond alteration by court rule even if change were thought desirable. Accordingly the TVA procedure is retained for the determination of compensation in TVA condemnation cases. It was also thought desirable to retain the specific method Congress had prescribed for the District of Columbia, which is a so-called jury of five appointed by the court. This is a local matter and the specific treatment accorded by Congress has given local satisfaction.

Aside from the foregoing limited exceptions dealing with the TVA and the District of Columbia, the question was whether a uniform method for determining compensation should be a commission with appeal to a district judge, or a commission with appeal to a jury, or a jury without a commission. Experience with the commission on a nationwide basis, and in particular with the utilization of a commission followed by an appeal to a jury, has been that the commission is time consuming and expensive. Furthermore, it is largely a futile procedure where it is preparatory to jury trial. Since in the bulk of states a land owner is entitled eventually to a jury trial, since the jury is a traditional tribunal for the determination of questions of value, and since experience with juries has proved satisfactory to both government and land owner, the right to jury trial is adopted as the general rule. Condemnation involving the TVA and the District of Columbia are the two exceptions. See Note to Subdivision (h), infra.

Note to Subdivision (a). As originally promulgated the Federal Rules governed appeals in condemnation proceedings but were not otherwise applicable. Rule 81(a)(7). Pre-appeal procedure, in the main, conformed to state procedure. See statutes and discussion, supra. The purpose of Rule 71A is to provide a uniform procedure for condemnation in the federal district courts, including the District of Columbia. To achieve this purpose Rule 71A prescribes such specialized procedure as is required by condemnation proceedings, otherwise it utilizes the general framework of the Federal Rules where specific detail is unnecessary. The adoption of Rule 71A, of course, renders paragraph (7) of Rule 81(a) unnecessary.

The promulgation of a rule for condemnation procedure is within the rulemaking power. The Enabling Act [Act of June 19, 1934, c. 651, §§ 1, 2 (48 Stat. 1064), former §§ 723b, 723c, now § 2072, of this title] gives the Supreme Court "the power to prescribe, by general rules * * * the forms of process, writs, pleadings, and motions, and the practice and procedure in civil actions at law." Such rules, however, must not abridge, enlarge, or modify substantive rights. In *Kohl v. United States,* 1875, 91 U.S. 367, 23 L.Ed. 449, a proceeding instituted by the United States to appropriate land for a postoffice site under a statute enacted for such purpose, the Supreme Court held that "a proceeding to take land in virtue of the government's eminent domain, and determining the compensation to be made for it, is * * * a suit at common law, when initiated in a court." See, also, *Madisonville Traction Co. v. Saint Bernard Mining Co.,* 1905, 25 S.Ct. 251, 196 U.S. 239, 49 L.Ed. 462, infra, under subdivision (k). And the Conformity Act [former § 258 of Title 40], which is superseded by Rule 71A, deals only with "practice, pleadings, forms and proceedings and not with matters of substantive laws." *United States v. 243.22 Acres of Land in Village of Farmingdale, Town of Babylon, Suffolk County, N.Y.,* D.C.N.Y.1942, 43 F.Supp. 561, affirmed 129 F.2d 678, certiorari denied 63 S.Ct. 441, 317 U.S. 698, 87 L.Ed. 558.

Rule 71A affords a uniform procedure for all cases of condemnation invoking the national power of eminent domain, and, to the extent stated in subdivision (k), for cases invoking a state's power of eminent domain; and supplants all statutes prescribing a different procedure. While the almost exclusive utility of the rule is for the condemnation of real property, it also applies to the condemnation of personal property, either as an incident to real property or as the sole object of the proceeding, when permitted or required by statute. See former § 438j [now § 5001] of Title 38 (World War Veterans' Relief Act); former §§ 1805, 1811, and 1813 of Title 42 (Atomic Energy Act); former § 79 [now § 100] of Title 50 (Nitrates Act); former §§ 161 to 165 and § 166, of Title 50 (Helium Gas Act). Requisitioning of personal property with the right in the owner to sue the United States, where the compensation cannot be agreed upon (see former § 1813 [now §§ 2221 to 2224] of Title 42, for example) will continue to be the normal method of acquiring personal property and Rule 71A in no way interferes with or restricts any such right. Only where the law requires or permits the formal procedure of condemnation to be utilized will the rule have any applicability to the acquisition of personal property.

Rule 71A is not intended to and does not supersede the Act of February 26, 1931, c. 307, §§ 1 to 5 (46 Stat. 1421), §§ 258a to 258e of Title 40, which is a supplementary condemnation statute, permissive in its nature and designed to permit the prompt acquisition of title by the United States, pending the condemnation proceeding, upon a deposit in court. See *United States v. 76,800 Acres, More or Less, of Land, in Bryan and Liberty Counties, Ga.,* D.C.Ga.1942, 44 F.Supp. 653; *United States v. 17,280 Acres of Land, More or Less, Situated in Saunders County, Neb.,* D.C.Neb.1942, 47 F.Supp. 267. The same is true insofar as the following or any other statutes authorize the acquisition of title or the taking of immediate possession:

U.S.C., Title 33:

§ 594 (When immediate possession of land may be taken; for a work of river and harbor improvements.)

U.S.C., Title 42:

§ 1813(b) [now §§ 2221 to 2224 of Title 42] (When immediate possession may be taken under Atomic Energy Act).

U.S.C., Title 50:

§ 171 [Repealed and is now covered by § 2663 of Title 10] (Acquisition of land by the Secretary of the Army for national defense).

§ 632 App. [Omitted as terminated by § 645 of the Appendix to Title 50] (Second War Powers Act, 1942; acquisition of real property for war purposes by the Secretary of the Army, the Secretary of the Navy, and others).

Note to Subdivision (b). This subdivision provides for broad joinder in accordance with the tenor of other rules such as Rule 18. To require separate condemnation proceedings for each piece of property separately owned would be unduly burdensome and would serve no useful purpose. And a restriction that only properties may be joined which are to be acquired for the same public use would also cause difficulty. For example, a unified project to widen a street, construct a bridge across a navigable river, and for the construction of approaches to the level of the bridge on both sides of the river might involve acquiring property for different public uses. Yet it is eminently desirable that the plaintiff may in one proceeding condemn all the property interests and rights necessary to carry out this project. Rule 21 which allows the court to sever and proceed separately with any claim against a party, and Rule 42(b) giving the court broad discretion to order separate trials give adequate protection to all defendants in condemnation proceedings.

Note to Subdivision (c). Since a condemnation proceeding is in rem and since a great many property owners are often involved, paragraph (1) requires the property to be named and only one of the owners. In other respects and caption will contain the name of the court, the title of the action, file number, and a designation of the pleading as a complaint in accordance with Rule 10(a).

Since the general standards of pleading are stated in other rules, paragraph (2) prescribes only the necessary detail for condemnation proceedings. Certain statutes allow the United States to acquire title or possession immediately upon commencement of an action. See the Act of February 26, 1931, c. 307, §§ 1 to 5 (46 Stat. 1421), §§ 258a to 258e of Title 40; and § 594 of Title 33, former § 1813(b) of Title 42, former § 171 of Title 50, former § 632 of the Appendix to Title 50, supra. To carry out the purpose of such statutes and to aid the condemnor in instituting the action even where title is not acquired at the outset, the plaintiff is initially required to join as defendants only the persons having or claiming an interest in the property whose names are then known. This is no way prejudices the property owner, who must eventually be joined as a defendant, served with process, and allowed to answer before there can be any hearing involving the compensation to be paid for his piece of property. The rule requires the plaintiff to name all persons having or claiming an interest in the property of whom the plaintiff has learned and, more importantly, those appearing of record. By charging the plaintiff with the necessity to make "a search of the records of the extent commonly made by competent searches of title in the vicinity in light of the type and value of the property involved" both the plaintiff and property owner are protected. Where a short term interest in property of little value is involved, as a two or three year easement over a vacant land for purposes of ingress and egress to other property, a search of the records covering a long period of time is not required. Where on the other hand fee simple title in valuable property is being condemned the search must necessarily cover a much longer period of time and be commensurate with the interests involved. But even here the search is related to the type made by competent title searchers in the vicinity. A search that extends back to the original patent may be feasible in some midwestern and western states and be proper under certain circumstances. In the Atlantic seaboard states such a search is normally not feasible nor desirable. There is a common sense business accommodation of what title searchers can and should do. For state statutes requiring persons appearing as owners or otherwise interested in the property to be named as defendants, see 3 Colo.Stat.Ann., 1935, c. 61, § 2; Ill.Ann.Stat. (Smith-Hurd) c. 47, § 2; 1 Iowa Code, 1946, § 472.3; Kans.Stat.Ann., 1935, § 26–101; 2 Mass.Laws Ann., 1932, c. 80A, § 4; 7 Mich.Stat.Ann., 1936, § 8.2; 2 Minn.Stat., Mason 1927, § 6541; 20 N.J.Stat.Ann., 1939, § 1–2; 3 Wash.Revised Stat., Remington, 1932, Title 6, § 891. For state provisions allowing persons whose names are not known to be designated under the descriptive term of "unknown owner", see Hawaii Revised Laws, 1945, c. 8, § 310 ("such [unknown] defendant may be joined in the petition under a fictitious name."); Ill.Ann.Stat. (Smith-Hurd) c. 47, § 2 ("Persons interested, whose names are unknown, may be made parties defendant by the description of the unknown owners; * * * "); Maryland Code Ann., 1939, Art. 33A, § 1 ("In case any owner or owners is or are not known, he or they may be described in such petition as the unknown owner or owners, or the unknown heir or heirs of a deceased owner."); 2 Mass.Laws Ann., 1932, c. 80A, § 4 ("Persons not in being, unascertained or unknown who may have an interest in any of such land shall be made parties respondent by such description as seems appropriate, * * * "); New Mex.Stat.Ann., 1941, § 25–901 ("the owners * * * shall be parties defendant, by name, if the names are known, and by description of the unknown owners of the land therein described, if their names are unknown."); Utah Code Ann., 1943, § 104–61–7 ("The names of all owners and claimants of the property, if known, or a statement that they are unknown, who must be styled defendants").

The last sentence of paragraph (2) enables the court to expedite the distribution of a deposit, in whole or in part, as soon as pertinent facts of ownership, value and the like are established. See also subdivision (j).

The signing of the complaint is governed by Rule 11.

Note to Subdivision (d). In lieu of a summons, which is the initial process in other civil actions under Rule 4(a), subdivision (d) provides for a notice which is to contain sufficient information so that the defendant in effect obtains the plaintiff's statement of his claim against the defendant to whom the notice is directed. Since the plaintiff's attorney is an officer of the court and to prevent unduly burdening the clerk of the court, paragraph (1) of subdivision (d) provides that plaintiff's attorney shall prepare and deliver a notice or notices to the clerk. Flexibility is provided by the provision for joint or several notices, and for additional notices. Where there are only a few defendants it may be convenient to prepare but one notice directed to all the defendants. In other cases where there are many defendants it will be more convenient to prepare two or more notices; but in any event a notice must be directed to each named defendant. Paragraph (2) provides that the notice is to be signed by the plaintiff's attorney. Since the notice is to be delivered to the clerk, the issuance of the notice will appear of record in the court. The clerk should forthwith deliver the notice or notices for service to the marshal or to a person specially appointed to serve the notice. Rule 4(a). The form of the notice is such that, in addition to informing the defendant of the plaintiff's statement of claim, it tells the defendant precisely what his rights are. Failure on the part of the defendant to serve an answer constitutes a consent to the taking and to the authority of the court to proceed to fix compensation therefor, but it does not preclude the defendant from presenting evidence as to the amount of compensation due him or in sharing the award of distribution. See subdivision (e); Form 28.

While under Rule 4(f) the territorial limits of a summons are normally the territorial limits of the state in which the district court is held, the territorial limits for personal service of a notice under Rule 71A(d)(3) are those of the nation. This extension of process is here proper since the aim of the condemnation proceeding is not to enforce any personal liability and the property owner is helped, not imposed upon, by the best type of service possible. If personal service cannot be made either because the defendant's whereabouts cannot be ascertained, or, if ascertained, the defendant cannot be personally served, as where he resides in a foreign country such as Canada or Mexico, then service by publication is proper. The provisions for this type of service are set forth in the rule and are in no way governed by § 118 [now § 1655] of this title.

Note to Subdivision (e). Departing from the scheme of Rule 12, subdivision (e) requires all defenses and objections to be presented in an answer and does not authorize a preliminary motion. There is little need for the latter in condemnation proceedings. The general standard of pleading is governed by other rules, particularly Rule 8, and this subdivision (e) merely prescribes what matters the answer should set forth. Merely by appearing in the action a defendant can receive notice of all proceedings affecting him. And without the necessity of answering a defendant may present evidence as to the amount of compensation due him, and he may share in the distribution of the award. See also subdivision (d)(2); Form 28.

Note to Subdivision (f). Due to the number of persons who may be interested in the property to be condemned, there is a likelihood that the plaintiff will need to amend his complaint, perhaps many times, to add new parties or state new issues. This subdivision recognizes that fact and does not burden the court with applications by the plaintiff for leave to amend. At the same time all defendants are adequately protected; and their need to amend the answer is adequately protected by Rule 15, which is applicable by virtue of subdivision (a) of this Rule 71A.

Note to Subdivision (g). A condemnation action is a proceeding in rem. Commencement of the action as against a defendant by virtue of his joinder pursuant to subdivision (c)(2) is the point of cut-off and there is no mandatory requirement for substitution because of a subsequent change of interest, although the court is given ample power to require substitution. Rule 25 is inconsistent with subdivision (g) and hence inapplicable. Accordingly, the time periods of Rule 25 do not govern to require dismissal nor to prevent substitution.

Note to Subdivision (h). This subdivision prescribes the method for determining the issue of just compensation in cases involving the federal power of eminent domain. The method of jury trial provided by subdivision (h) will normally apply in cases involving the state power by virtue of subdivision (k).

Congress has specially constituted a tribunal for the trial of the issue of just compensation in two instances: condemnation under the Tennessee Valley Authority Act; and condemnation in the District of Columbia. These tribunals are retained for reasons set forth in the General Statement: 3. Adjustment of Rule to Statutory Provisions, supra. Subdivision (h) also has prospective application so that if Congress should create another special tribunal, that tribunal will determine the issue of just compensation. Subject to these exceptions the general method of trial of that issue is to be by jury if any party demands it, otherwise that issue, as well as all other issues, are to be tried by the court.

As to the TVA procedure that is continued, § 831x of Title 16 requires that three commissioners be appointed to fix the compensation; that exceptions to their award are to be heard by three district judges (unless the parties stipulate for a lesser number) and that the district judges try the question de novo; that an appeal to the circuit court of appeals may be taken within 30 days from the filing of the decision of the district judges; and that the circuit court of appeals shall on the record fix compensation "without regard to the awards of findings theretofore made by the commissioners or the district judges." The mode of fixing compensation in the District of Columbia, which is also continued, is prescribed in former §§ 361 to 386 of Title 40. Under former § 371 the court is required in all cases to order the selection of a jury of five from among not less than 20 names, drawn "from the special box provided by law." They must have the usual qualifications of jurors and in addition must be freeholders of the District, and not in the service of the United States or the District. A special oath is administered to the chosen jurors. The trial proceeds in the ordinary way, except that the jury is allowed to separate after they have begun to consider their verdict.

There is no constitutional right to jury trial in a condemnation proceeding. *Bauman v. Ross,* 1897, 17 S.Ct. 966, 167 U.S. 548, 42 L.Ed. 270. See, also, Hines, *Does the Seventh Amendment to the Constitution of the United States Require Jury Trials in all Condemnation Proceedings?,* 1925, 11 Va.L.Rev. 505; Blair, *Federal Condemnation Proceedings and the Seventh Amendment,* 1927, 41 Harv.L.Rev. 29; 3 *Moore's Federal Practice,* 1938, 3007. Prior to Rule 71A, jury trial in federal condemnation proceedings was, however, enjoyed under the general conformity statute, former § 258 of Title 40, in states which provided for jury trial. See generally, 2 Lewis, *Eminent Domain,* 3d ed. 1909, §§ 509, 510; 3 Moore, op. cit. supra. Since the general conformity statute is superseded by Rule 71A, see supra under subdivision (a), and since it was believed that the rule to be substituted should likewise give a right to jury trial, subdivision (h) establishes that method as the general one for determining the issue of just compensation.

Note to Subdivision (i). Both the right of the plaintiff to dismiss by filing a notice of dismissal and the right of the court to permit a dismissal are circumscribed to the extent that where the plaintiff has acquired the title or a lesser interest or possession, viz., any property interest for which just compensation should be paid, the action may not be dismissed, without the defendant's consent, and the property owner remitted to another court, such as the Court of Claims, to recover just compensation for the property right taken. Circuity of action is thus prevented without increasing the liability of the plaintiff to pay just compensation for any interest that is taken. Freedom of dismissal is accorded, where both the condemnor and condemnee agree, up to the time of the entry of judgment vesting plaintiff with title. And power is given to the court, where the parties agree, to vacate the judgment and thus revest title in the property owner. In line with Rule 21, the court may at any time drop a defendant who has been unnecessarily or improperly joined as where it develops that he has no interest.

Note to Subdivision (j). Whatever the substantive law is concerning the necessity of making a deposit will continue to govern. For statutory provisions concerning deposit in court in condemnation proceedings by the United States, see § 258a of [former] Title 40; § 594 of Title 33; acquisition of title and possession statutes referred to in note to subdivision (a), supra. If the plaintiff is invoking the state's power of eminent domain the necessity of deposit will be governed by the state law. For discussion of such law, see 1 Nichols, Eminent Domain, 2d ed. 1917, §§ 209 to 216. For discussion of the function of deposit and the power of the court to enter judgment in cases both of deficiency and overpayment, see *United States v. Miller,* 1943, 63 S.Ct. 276, 317 U.S. 369, 87 L.Ed. 336, 147 A.L.R. 55, rehearing denied 63 S.Ct. 557, 318 U.S. 798, 87 L.Ed. 1162 (judgment in favor of plaintiff for overpayment ordered).

The court is to make distribution of the deposit as promptly as the facts of the case warrant. See also subdivision (c)(2).

Note to Subdivision (k). While the overwhelming number of cases that will be brought in the federal courts under this rule will be actions involving the federal power of eminent domain, a small percentage of cases may be instituted in the federal court or removed thereto on the basis of diversity or alienage which will involve the power of eminent domain under the law of a state. See *Boom Co. v. Patterson,* 1878, 98 U.S. 403, 25 L.Ed. 206; *Searl v. School District No. 2,* 1888, 8 S.Ct. 460, 124 U.S. 197, 31 L.Ed. 415; *Madisonville Traction Co. v. Saint Bernard Mining Co.,* 1905, 25 S.Ct. 251, 196 U.S. 239, 49 L.Ed. 462. In the Madisonville case, and in cases cited therein, it has been held that condemnation actions brought by state corporations in the exercise of a power delegated by the state might be governed by procedure prescribed by the laws of the United States, whether the cases were begun in or removed to the federal court. See, also, *Franzen v. Chicago, M. & St. P. Ry. Co.,* C.C.A.7th, 1921, 278 F. 370, 372.

Any condition affecting the substantial right of a litigant attached by state law is to be observed and enforced, such as making a deposit in court where the power of eminent domain is conditioned upon so doing. (See also subdivision (j). Subject to this qualification, subdivision (k) provides that in cases involving the state power of eminent domain, the practice prescribed by other subdivisions of Rule 71A shall govern.

Note to Subdivision (l). Since the condemnor will normally be the prevailing party and since he should not recover his costs against the property owner, Rule 54(d), which provides generally that costs shall go to the prevailing party, is made inapplicable. Without attempting to state what the rule on costs is, the effect of subdivision (l) is that costs shall be awarded in accordance with the law that has developed in condemnation cases. This has been summarized as follows: "Costs of condemnation proceedings are not assessable against the condemnee, unless by stipulation he agrees to assume some or all of them. Such normal expenses of the proceeding as bills for publication of notice, commissioners' fees, the cost of transporting commissioners and jurors to take a view, fees for attorneys to represent defendants who have failed to answer, and witness' fees, are properly charged to the government, though not taxed as costs. Similarly, if it is necessary that a conveyance be executed by a commissioner, the United States pay his fees and those for recording the deed. However, the distribution of the award is a matter in which the United States has no legal interest. Expenses incurred in ascertaining the identity of distributees and deciding between conflicting claimants are properly chargeable against the award, not against the United States, although United States attorneys are expected to aid the court in such matters as amici curiae." Lands Division Manual 861. For other discussion and citation, see *Grand River Dam Authority v. Jarvis,* C.C.A.10th, 1942, 124 F.2d 914. Costs may not be taxed against the United States except to the extent permitted by law. *United States v. 125.71 Acres of Land in Loyalhanna Tp., Westmoreland County, Pa.,* D.C.Pa.1944, 54 F.Supp. 193; Lands Division Manual 859. Even if it were thought desirable to allow the property owner's costs to be taxed against the United States, this is a matter for legislation and not court rule.

1963 Amendment

This amendment conforms to the amendment of Rule 4(f).

1985 Amendment

Rule 71A(h) provides that except when Congress has provided otherwise, the issue of just compensation in a condemnation case may be tried by a jury if one of the parties so demands, unless the court in its discretion orders the issue determined by a commission of three persons. In 1980, the Comptroller General of the United States in a Report to Congress recommended that use of the commission procedure should be encouraged in order to improve and expedite the trial of condemnation cases. The Report noted that long delays were being caused in many districts by such factors as crowded dockets, the precedence given criminal cases, the low priority accorded condemnation matters, and the high turnover of Assistant United States Attorneys. The Report concluded that revising Rule 71A to make the use of the commission procedure more attractive might alleviate the situation.

Accordingly, Rule 71A(h) is being amended in a number of respects designed to assure the quality and utility of a Rule 71A commission. First, the amended Rule will give the court discretion to appoint, in addition to the three members of a commission, up to two additional persons as alternate commissioners who would hear the case and be available, at any time up to the filing of the decision by the three-member commission, to replace any commissioner who becomes unable or disqualified to continue. The discretion to appoint alternate commissioners can be particularly useful in protracted cases, avoiding expensive retrials that have been required in some cases because of the death or disability of a commissioner. Prior to replacing a commissioner an alternate would not be present at, or participate in, the commission's deliberations.

Second, the amended Rule requires the court, before appointment, to advise the parties of the identity and qualifications of each prospective commissioner and alternate. The court then may authorize the examination of prospective appointees by the parties and each party has the right to challenge for cause. The objective is to insure that unbiased and competent commissioners are appointed.

The amended Rule does not prescribe a qualification standard for appointment to a commission, although it is understood that only persons possessing background and ability to appraise real estate valuation testimony and to award fair and just compensation on the basis thereof would be appointed. In most situations the chairperson should be a lawyer and all members should have some background qualifying them to weigh proof of value in the real estate field and, when possible, in the particular real estate market embracing the land in question.

The amended Rule should give litigants greater confidence in the commission procedure by affording them certain rights to participate in the appointment of commission members that are roughly comparable to the practice with regard to jury selection. This is accomplished by giving the court permission to allow the parties to examine prospective commissioners and by recognizing the right of each party to object to the appointment of any person for cause.

1987 Amendment

The amendments are technical. No substantive change is intended.

1988 Amendment

The amendment is technical. No substantive change is intended.

1993 Amendments

The references to the subdivisions of Rule 4 are deleted in light of the revision of that rule.

2003 Amendments

The references to specific subdivisions of Rule 53 are deleted or revised to reflect amendments of Rule 53.

2007 Amendments

The language of Rule 71A has been amended as part of the general restyling of the Civil Rules to make them more easily understood and to make style and terminology consistent throughout the rules. These changes are intended to be stylistic only.

Former Rule 71A has been redesignated as Rule 71.1 to conform to the designations used for all other rules added with the original numbering system.

Rule 71.1(e) allows a defendant to appear without answering. Former form 28 (now form 60) includes information about this right in the Rule 71.1(d)(2) notice. It is useful to confirm this practice in the rule.

The information that identifies the attorney is changed to include telephone number and electronic-mail address, in line with similar amendments to Rules 11(a) and 26(g)(1).

2009 Amendments

The times set in the former rule at 20 days have been revised to 21 days. See the Note to Rule 6.

Rule 72.   Magistrate Judges: Pretrial Order

(a) Nondispositive Matters. When a pretrial matter not dispositive of a party's claim or defense is referred to a magistrate judge to hear and decide, the magistrate judge must promptly conduct the required proceedings and, when appropriate, issue a written order stating the decision. A party may serve and file objections to the order within 14 days after being served with a copy. A party may not assign as error a defect in the order not timely objected to. The district judge in the case must consider timely objections and modify or set aside any part of the order that is clearly erroneous or is contrary to law.

(b) Dispositive Motions and Prisoner Petitions.

   (1) *Findings and Recommendations.* A magistrate judge must promptly conduct the required proceedings when assigned, without the parties' consent, to hear a pretrial matter dispositive of a claim or defense or a prisoner petition challenging the conditions of confinement. A record must be made of all evidentiary proceedings and may, at the magistrate judge's discretion, be made of any other proceedings. The magistrate judge must enter a recommended disposition, including, if appropriate, proposed findings of fact. The clerk must promptly mail a copy to each party.

   (2) *Objections.* Within 14 days after being served with a copy of the recommended disposition, a party may serve and file specific written objections to the proposed findings and recommendations. A party may respond to another party's objections within 14 days after being served with a copy. Unless the district judge orders otherwise, the objecting party must promptly arrange for transcribing the record, or whatever portions of it the parties agree to or the magistrate judge considers sufficient.

   (3) *Resolving Objections.* The district judge must determine de novo any part of the magistrate judge's disposition that has been properly objected to. The district judge may accept, reject, or modify the recommended disposition; receive further evidence; or return the matter to the magistrate judge with instructions.

(Former Rule 72 abrogated December 4, 1967, effective July 1, 1968; new Rule 72 adopted April 28, 1983, effective August 1, 1983; amended April 30, 1991, effective December 1, 1991; April 22, 1993, effective December 1, 1993; April 30, 2007, effective December 1, 2007; March 26, 2009, effective December 1, 2009.)

ADVISORY COMMITTEE NOTES

1983 Addition

Subdivision (a). This subdivision addresses court-ordered referrals of nondispositive matters under 28 U.S.C. § 636(b)(1)(A). The rule calls for a written order of the magistrate's disposition to preserve the record and facilitate review. An oral order read into the record by the magistrate will satisfy this requirement.

No specific procedures or timetables for raising objections to the magistrate's rulings on nondispositive matters are set forth in the Magistrates Act. The rule fixes a 10-day period in order to avoid uncertainty and provide uniformity that will eliminate the confusion that might arise if different periods were prescribed by local rule in different districts. It also is contemplated that a party who is successful before the magistrate will be afforded an opportunity to respond to objections raised to the magistrate's ruling.

The last sentence of subdivision (a) specifies that reconsideration of a magistrate's order, as provided for in the Magistrates Act, shall be by the district judge to whom the case is assigned. This rule does not restrict experimentation by the district courts under 28 U.S.C. § 636(b)(3) involving references of matters other than pretrial matters, such as appointment of counsel, taking of default judgments, and acceptance of jury verdicts when the judge is unavailable.

Subdivision (b). This subdivision governs court-ordered referrals of dispositive pretrial matters and prisoner petitions challenging conditions of confinement, pursuant to statutory authorization in 28 U.S.C. § 636(b)(1)(B). This rule does not extend to habeas corpus petitions, which are covered by the specific rules relating to proceedings under Sections 2254 and 2255 of Title 28.

This rule implements the statutory procedures for making objections to the magistrate's proposed findings and recommendations. The 10-day period, as specified in the statute, is subject to Rule 6(e) which provides for an additional 3-day period when service is made by mail. Although no specific provision appears in the Magistrates Act, the rule specifies a 10-day period for a party to respond to objections to the magistrate's recommendation.

Implementing the statutory requirements, the rule requires the district judge to whom the case is assigned to make a de novo determination of those portions of the report, findings, or recommendations to which timely objection is made. The term "de novo" signifies that the magistrate's findings are not protected by the clearly erroneous doctrine, but does not indicate that a second evidentiary hearing is required. See *United States v. Raddatz,* 417 [447] U.S. 667 (1980). See also Silberman, *Masters and Magistrates Part II: The American Analogue,* 50 N.Y.U. L.Rev. 1297, 1367 (1975). When no timely objection is filed, the court need only satisfy itself that there is no clear error on the face of the record in order to accept the recommendation. See *Campbell v. United States Dist. Court,* 501 F.2d 196, 206 (9th Cir.1974), cert. denied, 419 U.S. 879, quoted in House Report No. 94–1609, 94th Cong.2d Sess. (1976) at 3. Compare *Park Motor Mart, Inc. v. Ford Motor Co.,* 616 F.2d 603 (1st Cir.1980). Failure to make timely objection to the magistrate's report prior to its adoption by the district judge may constitute a waiver of appellate review of the district judge's order. *See United States v. Walters,* 638 F.2d 947 (6th Cir.1981).

1991 Amendment

This amendment is intended to eliminate a discrepancy in measuring the 10 days for serving and filing objections to a magistrate's action under subdivisions (a) and (b) of this Rule. The rule as promulgated in 1983 required objections to the magistrate's handling of nondispositive matters to be served and filed within 10 days of entry of the order, but required objections to dispositive motions to be made within 10 days of being served with a copy of the recommended disposition. Subdivision (a) is here amended to conform to subdivision (b) to avoid any confusion or technical defaults, particularly in connection with magistrate orders that rule on both dispositive and nondispositive matters.

The amendment is also intended to assure that objections to magistrate's orders that are not timely made shall not be considered. *Compare* Rule 51.

1993 Amendments

This revision is made to conform the rule to changes made by the Judicial Improvements Act of 1990.

2007 Amendments

The language of Rule 72 has been amended as part of the general restyling of the Civil Rules to make them more easily understood and to make style and terminology consistent throughout the rules. These changes are intended to be stylistic only.

2009 Amendments

The times set in the former rule at 10 days have been revised to 14 days. See the Note to Rule 6.

HISTORICAL NOTES

Change of Name

Reference to United States magistrate or to magistrate deemed to refer to United States magistrate judge pursuant to section 321 of Pub.L. 101–650, set out as a note under section 631 of this title.

Rule 73.   Magistrate Judges: Trial by Consent; Appeal

(a) Trial by Consent. When authorized under 28 U.S.C. § 636(c), a magistrate judge may, if all parties consent, conduct a civil action or proceeding, including a jury or nonjury trial. A record must be made in accordance with 28 U.S.C. § 636(c)(5).

(b) Consent Procedure.

    (1) *In General.* When a magistrate judge has been designated to conduct civil actions or proceedings, the clerk must give the parties written notice of their opportunity to consent under 28 U.S.C. § 636(c). To signify their consent, the parties must jointly or separately file a statement consenting to the referral. A district judge or magistrate judge may be informed of a party's response to the clerk's notice only if all parties have consented to the referral.

    (2) *Reminding the Parties About Consenting.* A district judge, magistrate judge, or other court official may remind the parties of the magistrate judge's availability, but must also advise them that they are free to withhold consent without adverse substantive consequences.

    (3) *Vacating a Referral.* On its own for good cause—or when a party shows extraordinary circumstances—the district judge may vacate a referral to a magistrate judge under this rule.

(c) Appealing a Judgment. In accordance with 28 U.S.C. § 636(c)(3), an appeal from a judgment entered at a magistrate judge's direction may be taken to the court of appeals as would any other appeal from a district-court judgment.

(Former Rule 73 abrogated December 4, 1967, effective July 1, 1968; new Rule 73 adopted April 28, 1983, effective August 1, 1983; amended March 2, 1987, effective August 1, 1987; April 22, 1993, effective December 1, 1993; April 11, 1997, effective December 1, 1997; April 30, 2007, effective December 1, 2007.)

ADVISORY COMMITTEE NOTES

1983 Addition

Subdivision (a). This subdivision implements the broad authority of the 1979 amendments to the Magistrates Act, 28 U.S.C. § 636(c), which permit a magistrate to sit in lieu of a district judge and exercise civil jurisdiction over a case, when the parties consent. See McCabe, *The Federal Magistrate Act of 1979,* 16 Harv.J.Legis. 343, 364–79 (1979). In order to exercise this jurisdiction, a magistrate must be specially designated under 28 U.S.C. § 636(c)(1) by the district court or courts he serves. The only exception to a magistrate's exercise of civil jurisdiction, which includes the power to conduct jury and nonjury trials and decide dispositive motions, is the contempt power. A hearing on contempt is to be conducted by the district judge upon certification of the facts and an order to show cause by the magistrate. See 28 U.S.C. § 639(e). In view of 28 U.S.C. § 636(c)(1) and this rule, it is unnecessary to amend Rule 58 to provide that the decision of a magistrate is a "decision by the court" for the purposes of that rule and a "final decision of the district court" for purposes of 28 U.S.C. § 1291 governing appeals.

Subdivision (b). This subdivision implements the blind consent provision of 28 U.S.C. § 636(c)(2) and is designed to ensure that neither the judge nor the magistrate attempts to induce a party to consent to reference of a civil matter under this rule to a magistrate. See House Rep. No. 96–444, 96th Cong. 1st Sess. 8 (1979).

The rule opts for a uniform approach in implementing the consent provision by directing the clerk to notify the parties of their opportunity to elect to proceed before a magistrate and by requiring the execution and filing of a consent form or forms setting forth the election. However, flexibility at the local level is preserved in that local rules will determine how notice shall be communicated to the parties, and local rules will specify the time period within which an election must be made.

The last paragraph of subdivision (b) reiterates the provision in 28 U.S.C. § 636(c)(6) for vacating a reference to the magistrate.

Subdivision (c). Under 28 U.S.C. § 636(c)(3), the normal route of appeal from the judgment of a magistrate—the only route that will be available unless the parties otherwise agree in advance—is an appeal by the aggrieved party "directly to the appropriate United States court of appeals from the judgment of the magistrate in the same manner as an appeal from any other judgment of a district court." The quoted statutory language indicates Congress' intent that the same procedures and standards of appealability that govern appeals from district court judgments govern appeals from magistrates' judgments.

Subdivision (d). 28 U.S.C. § 636(c)(4) offers parties who consent to the exercise of civil jurisdiction by a magistrate an alternative appeal route to that provided in subdivision (c) of this rule. This optional appellate route was provided by Congress in recognition of the fact that not all civil cases warrant the same appellate treatment. In cases where the amount in controversy is not great and there are no difficult questions of law to be resolved, the parties may desire to avoid the expense and delay of appeal to the court of appeals by electing an appeal to the district judge. See McCabe, *The Federal Magistrate Act of 1979*, 16 Harv.J.Legis, 343, 388 (1979). This subdivision provides that the parties may elect the optional appeal route at the time of reference to a magistrate. To this end, the notice by the clerk under subdivision (b) of this rule shall explain the appeal option and the corollary restriction on review by the court of appeals. This approach will avoid later claims of lack of consent to the avenue of appeal. The choice of the alternative appeal route to the judge of the district court should be made by the parties in their forms of consent. Special appellate rules to govern appeals from a magistrate to a district judge appear in new Rules 74 through 76.

1987 Amendment

The amendment is technical. No substantive change is intended.

1993 Amendments

This revision is made to conform the rule to changes made by the Judicial Improvements Act of 1990. The Act requires that, when being reminded of the availability of a magistrate judge, the parties be advised that withholding of consent will have no "adverse substantive consequences." They may, however, be advised if the withholding of consent will have the adverse procedural consequence of a potential delay in trial.

1997 Amendments

The Federal Courts Improvement Act of 1996 repealed the former provisions of 28 U.S.C. § 636(c)(4) and (5) that enabled parties that had agreed to trial before a magistrate judge to agree also that appeal should be taken to the district court. Rule 73 is amended to conform to this change. Rules 74, 75, and 76 are abrogated for the same reason. The portions of Form 33 and Form 34 that referred to appeals to the district court also are deleted.

2007 Amendments

The language of Rule 73 has been amended as part of the general restyling of the Civil Rules to make them more easily understood and to make style and terminology consistent throughout the rules. These changes are intended to be stylistic only.

Rule 74.   Method of Appeal From Magistrate Judge to District Judge Under Title 28, U.S.C. § 636(c)(4) and Rule 73(d) [Abrogated]

(Former Rule 74 abrogated December 4, 1967, effective July 1, 1968; new Rule 74 adopted April 28, 1983, effective August 1, 1983; amended April 22, 1993, effective December 1, 1993; abrogated April 11, 1997, effective December 1, 1997; April 30, 2007, effective December 1, 2007.)

ADVISORY COMMITTEE NOTES

1997 Amendment

Rule 74 is abrogated for the reasons described in the Note to Rule 73.

2007 Amendment

Rule 74 was abrogated in 1997 to reflect repeal of the statute providing for appeal from a magistrate judge's judgment to the district court. The rule number is reserved for possible future use.

Rule 75.   Proceedings on Appeal From Magistrate Judge to District Judge under Rule 73(d) [Abrogated]

(Former Rule 75 abrogated December 4, 1967, effective July 1, 1968; new Rule 75 adopted April 28, 1983, effective August 1, 1983; amended March 2, 1987, effective August 1, 1987; April 22, 1993, effective December 1, 1993; abrogated April 11, 1997, effective December 1, 1997; April 30, 2007, effective December 1, 2007.)

ADVISORY COMMITTEE NOTES

1997 Amendment

Rule 75 is abrogated for the reasons described in the Note to Rule 73.

2007 Amendment

Rule 75 was abrogated in 1997 to reflect repeal of the statute providing for appeal from a magistrate judge's judgment to the district court. The rule number is reserved for possible future use.

Rule 76.   Judgment of the District Judge on The Appeal under Rule 73(d) and Costs [Abrogated]

(Former Rule 76 abrogated December 4, 1967, effective July 1, 1968; new Rule 76 adopted April 28, 1983, effective August 1, 1983; amended April 22, 1993, effective December 1, 1993; abrogated April 11, 1997, effective December 1, 1997; April 30, 2007, effective December 1, 2007.)

ADVISORY COMMITTEE NOTES

1997 Amendment

Rule 76 is abrogated for the reasons described in the Note to Rule 73.

2007 Amendment

Rule 76 was abrogated in 1997 to reflect repeal of the statute providing for appeal from a magistrate judge's judgment to the district court. The rule number is reserved for possible future use.

TITLE X. DISTRICT COURTS AND CLERKS: CONDUCTING BUSINESS; ISSUING ORDERS

Rule 77.   Conducting Business; Clerk's Authority; Notice of an Order or Judgment

(a) When Court Is Open. Every district court is considered always open for filing any paper, issuing and returning process, making a motion, or entering an order.

(b) Place for Trial and Other Proceedings. Every trial on the merits must be conducted in open court and, so far as convenient, in a regular courtroom. Any other act or proceeding may be done or conducted by a judge in chambers, without the attendance of the clerk or other court official, and anywhere inside or outside the district. But no hearing—other than one ex parte—may be conducted outside the district unless all the affected parties consent.

(c) Clerk's Office Hours; Clerk's Orders.

   (1) *Hours.* The clerk's office—with a clerk or deputy on duty—must be open during business hours every day except Saturdays, Sundays, and legal holidays. But a court may, by local rule or order, require that the office be open for specified hours on Saturday or a particular legal holiday other than one listed in Rule 6(a)(6)(A).

   (2) *Orders.* Subject to the court's power to suspend, alter, or rescind the clerk's action for good cause, the clerk may:

   (A) issue process;

   (B) enter a default;

    (C) enter a default judgment under Rule 55(b)(1); and

    (D) act on any other matter that does not require the court's action.

(d) Serving Notice of an Order or Judgment.

    (1) *Service.* Immediately after entering an order or judgment, the clerk must serve notice of the entry, as provided in Rule 5(b), on each party who is not in default for failing to appear. The clerk must record the service on the docket. A party also may serve notice of the entry as provided in Rule 5(b).

    (2) *Time to Appeal Not Affected by Lack of Notice.* Lack of notice of the entry does not affect the time for appeal or relieve—or authorize the court to relieve—a party for failing to appeal within the time allowed, except as allowed by Federal Rule of Appellate Procedure (4)(a).

(Amended December 27, 1946, effective March 19, 1948; January 21, 1963, effective July 1, 1963; December 4, 1967, effective July 1, 1968; March 1, 1971, effective July 1, 1971; March 2, 1987, effective August 1, 1987; April 30, 1991, effective December 1, 1991; April 23, 2001, effective December 1, 2001; April 30, 2007, effective December 1, 2007; April 25, 2014, December 1, 2014.)

ADVISORY COMMITTEE NOTES

1937 Adoption

This rule states the substance of U.S.C., Title 28, § 452, formerly § 13 (Courts open as courts of admiralty and equity). Compare [former] Equity Rules 1 (District Court Always Open For Certain Purposes—Orders at Chambers), 2 (Clerk's Office Always Open, Except, Etc.), 4 (Notice of Orders), and 5 (Motions Grantable of Course by Clerk).

1946 Amendment

Note. Rule 77(d) has been amended to avoid such situations as the one arising in *Hill v. Hawes,* 1944, 64 S.Ct. 334, 320 U.S. 520, 88 L.Ed. 283. In that case, an action instituted in the District Court for the District of Columbia, the clerk failed to give notice of the entry of a judgment for defendant as required by Rule 77(d). The time for taking an appeal then was 20 days under Rule 10 of the Court of Appeals (later enlarged by amendment to thirty days), and due to lack of notice of the entry of judgment the plaintiff failed to file his notice of appeal within the prescribed time. On this basis the trial court vacated the original judgment and then re-entered it, whereupon notice of appeal was filed. The Court of Appeals dismissed the appeal as taken too late. The Supreme Court, however, held that although rule 77(d) did not purport to attach any consequence to the clerk's failure to give notice as specified, the terms of the rule were such that the appellant was entitled to rely on it, and the trial court in such a case, in the exercise of a sound discretion, could vacate the former judgment and enter a new one, so that the appeal would be within the allowed time.

Because of Rule 6(c), which abolished the old rule that the expiration of the term ends a court's power over its judgment, the effect of the decision in *Hill v. Hawes* is to give the district court power, in its discretion and without time limit, and long after the term may have expired, to vacate a judgment and reenter it for the purpose of reviving the right of appeal. This seriously affects the finality of judgments. See also proposed Rule 6(c) and Note; proposed Rule 60(b) and Note; and proposed Rule 73(a) and Note.

Rule 77(d) as amended makes it clear that notification by the clerk of the entry of a judgment has nothing to do with the starting of the time for appeal; that time starts to run from the date of entry of judgment and not from the date of notice of the entry. Notification by the clerk is merely for the convenience of litigants. And lack of such notification in itself has no effect upon the time for appeal; but in considering an application for extension of time for appeal as provided in Rule 73(a), the court may take into account, as one of the factors affecting its decision, whether the clerk failed to give notice as provided in Rule 77(d) or the party failed to receive the clerk's notice. It need not, however, extend the time for appeal merely because the clerk's notice was not sent or received. It would, therefore, be entirely unsafe for a party to rely on absence of notice from the clerk of the entry of a judgment, or to rely on the adverse party's failure to serve notice of the entry of a judgment. Any party may, of course, serve timely notice of the entry of a judgment upon the adverse party and thus preclude a successful application, under Rule 73(a), for the extension of the time for appeal.

1963 Amendment

Subdivision (c). The amendment authorizes closing of the clerk's office on Saturday as far as civil business is concerned. However, a district court may require its clerk's office to remain open for specified hours on Saturdays or "legal holidays" other than those enumerated ("Legal holiday" is defined in Rule 6(a), as amended.) The clerk's offices of many district courts have customarily remained open on some of the days appointed as holidays by State law. This practice could be continued by local rule or order.

Subdivision (d). This amendment conforms to the amendment of Rule 5(a). See the Advisory Committee's Note to that amendment.

1968 Amendment

The provisions of Rule 73(a) are incorporated in Rule 4(a) of the Federal Rules of Appellate Procedure.

1971 Amendment

The amendment adds Columbus Day to the list of legal holidays. See the Note accompanying the amendment of Rule 6(a).

1987 Amendment

The amendments are technical. No substantive change is intended. The Birthday of Martin Luther King, Jr. is added to the list of national holidays in Rule 77.

1991 Amendment

This revision is a companion to the concurrent amendment to Rule 4 of the Federal Rules of Appellate Procedure. The purpose of the revisions is to permit district courts to ease strict sanctions now imposed on appellants whose notices of appeal are filed late because of their failure to receive notice of entry of a judgment. See, e.g. *Tucker v. Commonwealth Land Title Ins. Co.*, 800 F.2d 1054 (11th Cir.1986); *Ashby Enterprises, Ltd. v. Weitzman, Dym & Associates*, 780 F.2d 1043 (D.C.Cir.1986); *In re OPM Leasing Services, Inc.*, 769 F.2d 911 (2d Cir.1985); *Spika v. Village of Lombard, Ill.*, 763 F.2d 282 (7th Cir.1985); *Hall v. Community Mental Health Center of Beaver County*, 772 F.2d 42 (3d Cir.1985); *Wilson v. Atwood v. Stark*, 725 F.2d 255 (5th Cir. en banc), cert. dismissed, 105 S.Ct. 17 (1984); *Case v. BASF Wyandotte*, 727 F.2d 1034 (Fed.Cir.1984), cert. denied, 105 S.Ct. 386 (1984); *Hensley v. Chesapeake & Ohio R.R. Co.*, 651 F.2d 226 (4th Cir.1981); *Buckeye Cellulose Corp. v. Electric Construction Co.*, 569 F.2d 1036 (8th Cir.1978).

Failure to receive notice may have increased in frequency with the growth in the caseload in the clerks' offices. The present strict rule imposes a duty on counsel to maintain contact with the court while a case is under submission. Such contact is more difficult to maintain if counsel is outside the district, as is increasingly common, and can be a burden to the court as well as counsel.

The effect of the revisions is to place a burden on prevailing parties who desire certainty that the time for appeal is running. Such parties can take the initiative to assure that their adversaries receive effective notice. An appropriate procedure for such notice is provided in Rule 5.

The revised rule lightens the responsibility but not the workload of the clerk's offices, for the duty of that office to give notice of entry of judgment must be maintained.

2001 Amendments

Rule 77(d) is amended to reflect changes in Rule 5(b). A few courts have experimented with serving Rule 77(d) notices by electronic means on parties who consent to this procedure. The success of these experiments warrants express authorization. Because service is made in the manner provided in Rule 5(b), party consent is required for service by electronic or other means described in Rule 5(b)(2)(D). The same provision is made for a party who wishes to ensure actual communication of the Rule 77(d) notice by also serving notice.

Changes Made After Publication and Comments

Rule 77(d) was amended to correct an oversight in the published version. The clerk is to note "service," not "mailing," on the docket.

2007 Amendments

The language of Rule 77 has been amended as part of the general restyling of the Civil Rules to make them more easily understood and to make style and terminology consistent throughout the rules. These changes are intended to be stylistic only.

2014 Amendment

The amendment corrects an inadvertent failure to revise the cross-reference to Rule 6(a) when what was Rule 6(a)(4)(A) became Rule 6(a)(6)(A).

Rule 78.   Hearing Motions; Submission on Briefs

(a) **Providing a Regular Schedule for Oral Hearings.** A court may establish regular times and places for oral hearings on motions.

(b) **Providing for Submission on Briefs.** By rule or order, the court may provide for submitting and determining motions on briefs, without oral hearings.

(Amended March 2, 1987, effective August 1, 1987; April 30, 2007, effective December 1, 2007.)

ADVISORY COMMITTEE NOTES

1937 Adoption

Compare [former] Equity Rule 6 (Motion Day) with the first paragraph of this rule. The second paragraph authorizes a procedure found helpful for the expedition of business in some of the Federal and State courts. See Rule 43(e) of these rules dealing with evidence on motions. Compare *Civil Practice Rules of the Municipal Court of Chicago* (1935), Rules 269, 270, 271.

1987 Amendment

The amendment is technical. No substantive change is intended.

2007 Amendments

The language of Rule 78 has been amended as part of the general restyling of the Civil Rules to make them more easily understood and to make style and terminology consistent throughout the rules. These changes are intended to be stylistic only.

Rule 16 has superseded any need for the provision in former Rule 78 for orders for the advancement, conduct, and hearing of actions.

Rule 79.   Records Kept by the Clerk

(a) **Civil Docket.**

    (1) *In General.* The clerk must keep a record known as the "civil docket" in the form and manner prescribed by the Director of the Administrative Office of the United States Courts with the approval of the Judicial Conference of the United States. The clerk must enter each civil action in the docket. Actions must be assigned consecutive file numbers, which must be noted in the docket where the first entry of the action is made.

    (2) *Items to be Entered.* The following items must be marked with the file number and entered chronologically in the docket:

        (A) papers filed with the clerk;

        (B) process issued, and proofs of service or other returns showing execution; and

        (C) appearances, orders, verdicts, and judgments.

    (3) *Contents of Entries; Jury Trial Demanded.* Each entry must briefly show the nature of the paper filed or writ issued, the substance of each proof of service or other return, and the substance and date of entry of each order and judgment. When a jury trial has been properly demanded or ordered, the clerk must enter the word "jury" in the docket.

(b) Civil Judgments and Orders. The clerk must keep a copy of every final judgment and appealable order; of every order affecting title to or a lien on real or personal property; and of any other order that the court directs to be kept. The clerk must keep these in the form and manner prescribed by the Director of the Administrative Office of the United States Courts with the approval of the Judicial Conference of the United States.

(c) Indexes; Calendars. Under the court's direction, the clerk must:

   (1) keep indexes of the docket and of the judgments and orders described in Rule 79(b); and

   (2) prepare calendars of all actions ready for trial, distinguishing jury trials from nonjury trials.

(d) Other Records. The clerk must keep any other records required by the Director of the Administrative Office of the United States Courts with the approval of the Judicial Conference of the United States.

(Amended December 27, 1946, effective March 19, 1948; December 29, 1948, effective October 20, 1949; January 21, 1963, effective July 1, 1963; April 30, 2007, effective December 1, 2007.)

ADVISORY COMMITTEE NOTES
1937 Adoption

Compare [former] Equity Rule 3 (Books Kept by Clerk and Entries Therein). In connection with this rule, see also the following statutes of the United States:

U.S.C., Title 5 former:

   § 301 [See Title 28, § 526] (Officials for investigation of official acts, records and accounts of marshals, attorneys, clerks of courts, United States commissioners, referees and trustees)

   § 318 [former] (Accounts of district attorneys)

U.S.C., Title 28 former:

   § 556 [former] (Clerks of district courts; books open to inspection)

   § 567 [now 751] (Same; accounts)

   § 568 [now 751] (Same; reports and accounts of moneys received; dockets)

   § 813 [former] (Indices of judgment debtors to be kept by clerks)

And see "Instructions to United States Attorneys, Marshals, Clerks and Commissioners" issued by the Attorney General of the United States.

1946 Amendment

Note. Subdivision (a). The amendment substitutes the Director of the Administrative Office of the United States Courts, acting subject to the approval of the Judicial Conference of Senior Circuit Judges, in the place of the Attorney General as a consequence of and in accordance with the provisions of the act establishing the Administrative Office and transferring functions thereto. Act of August 7, 1939, c. 501, §§ 1 to 7, 53 Stat. 1223, 28 U.S.C.A. §§ 601 to 610, formerly §§ 444 to 450.

Subdivision (b). The change in this subdivision does not alter the nature of the judgments and orders to be recorded in permanent form but it does away with the express requirement that they be recorded in a book. This merely gives latitude for the preservation of court records in other than book form, if that shall seem advisable, and permits with the approval of the Judicial Conference the adoption of such modern, space-saving methods as microphotography. See *Proposed Improvements in the Administration of the Offices of Clerks of United States District Courts,* prepared by the Bureau of the Budget, 1941, 38–42. See also Rule 55, Federal Rules of Criminal Procedure.

Subdivision (c). The words "Separate and" have been deleted as unduly rigid. There is no sufficient reason for requiring that the indices in all cases be separate; on the contrary, the requirement frequently increases the labor of persons searching the records as well as the labor of the clerk's force preparing them. The matter should be left to administrative discretion.

The other changes in the subdivision merely conform with those made in subdivision (b) of the rule.

Subdivision (d). Subdivision (d) is a new provision enabling the Administrative Office, with the approval of the Judicial Conference, to carry out any improvements in clerical procedure with respect to books and records which may be deemed advisable. See report cited in Note to subdivision (b), supra.

1948 Amendment

The amendment effective October 1949, substituted the name, "Judicial Conference of the United States," for "Judicial Conference of Senior Circuit Judges," in the first sentence of subdivision (a), and in subdivisions (b) and (d).

1963 Amendment

The terminology is clarified without any change of the prescribed practice. See amended Rule 58, and the Advisory Committee's Note thereto.

2007 Amendments

The language of Rule 79 has been amended as part of the general restyling of the Civil Rules to make them more easily understood and to make style and terminology consistent throughout the rules. These changes are intended to be stylistic only.

Rule 80.   Stenographic Transcript as Evidence

If stenographically reported testimony at a hearing or trial is admissible in evidence at a later trial, the testimony may be proved by a transcript certified by the person who reported it.

(Amended December 27, 1946, effective March 19, 1948; April 30, 2007, effective December 1, 2007.)

ADVISORY COMMITTEE NOTES

1937 Adoption

Note to Subdivision (a). This follows substantially [former] Equity Rule 50 (Stenographer—Appointment—Fees). [This subdivision was abrogated in 1946. See amendment note of Advisory Committee below. Ed.]

Note to Subdivision (b). See *Reports of Conferences of Senior Circuit Judges with the Chief Justice of the United States* (1936), 22 A.B.A.J. 818, 819; (1937), 24 A.B.A.J. 75, 77. [This subdivision was abrogated in 1946. See amendment note of Advisory Committee below. Ed.]

Note to Subdivision (c). Compare Iowa Code (1935) § 11353.

1946 Amendment

Note. Subdivisions (a) and (b) of Rule 80 have been abrogated because of Public Law 222, 78th Cong., c. 3, 2d Sess., approved Jan. 20, 1944, 28 U.S.C. §§ 550, 604, 753, 1915, 1920, formerly § 9a, providing for the appointment of official stenographers for each district court, prescribing their duties, providing for the furnishing of transcripts, the taxation of the fees therefor as costs, and other related matters. This statute has now been implemented by Congressional appropriation available for the fiscal year beginning July 1, 1945.

Subdivision (c) of Rule 80 (Stenographic Report or Transcript as Evidence) has been retained unchanged.

2007 Amendments

The language of Rule 80 has been amended as part of the general restyling of the Civil Rules to make them more easily understood and to make style and terminology consistent throughout the rules. These changes are intended to be stylistic only.

TITLE XI. GENERAL PROVISIONS

Rule 81.   Applicability of the Rules in General; Removed Actions

(a) Applicability to Particular Proceedings.

    (1) *Prize Proceedings.* These rules do not apply to prize proceedings in admiralty governed by 10 U.S.C. §§ 7651–7681.

    (2) *Bankruptcy.* These rules apply to bankruptcy proceedings to the extent provided by the Federal Rules of Bankruptcy Procedure.

    (3) *Citizenship.* These rules apply to proceedings for admission to citizenship to the extent that the practice in those proceedings is not specified in federal statutes and has previously conformed to the practice in civil actions. The provisions of 8 U.S.C. § 1451 for service by publication and for answer apply in proceedings to cancel citizenship certificates.

    (4) *Special Writs.* These rules apply to proceedings for habeas corpus and for quo warranto to the extent that the practice in those proceedings:

        (A) is not specified in a federal statute, the Rules Governing Section 2254 Cases, or the Rules Governing Section 2255 Cases; and

        (B) has previously conformed to the practice in civil actions.

    (5) *Proceedings Involving a Subpoena.* These rules apply to proceedings to compel testimony or the production of documents through a subpoena issued by a United States officer or agency under a federal statute, except as otherwise provided by statute, by local rule, or by court order in the proceedings.

    (6) *Other Proceedings.* These rules, to the extent applicable, govern proceedings under the following laws, except as these laws provide other procedures:

        (A) 7 U.S.C. §§ 292, 499g(c), for reviewing an order of the Secretary of Agriculture;

        (B) 9 U.S.C., relating to arbitration;

        (C) 15 U.S.C. § 522, for reviewing an order of the Secretary of the Interior;

        (D) 15 U.S.C. § 715d(c), for reviewing an order denying a certificate of clearance;

        (E) 29 U.S.C. §§ 159, 160, for enforcing an order of the National Labor Relations Board;

        (F) 33 U.S.C. §§ 918, 921, for enforcing or reviewing a compensation order under the Longshore and Harbor Workers' Compensation Act; and

        (G) 45 U.S.C. § 159, for reviewing an arbitration award in a railway-labor dispute.

(b) Scire Facias and Mandamus. The writs of scire facias and mandamus are abolished. Relief previously available through them may be obtained by appropriate action or motion under these rules.

(c) Removed Actions.

    (1) *Applicability.* These rules apply to a civil action after it is removed from a state court.

    (2) *Further Pleading.* After removal, repleading is unnecessary unless the court orders it. A defendant who did not answer before removal must answer or present other defenses or objections under these rules within the longest of these periods:

        (A) 21 days after receiving—through service or otherwise—a copy of the initial pleading stating the claim for relief;

        (B) 21 days after being served with the summons for an initial pleading on file at the time of service; or

        (C) 7 days after the notice of removal is filed.

  (3) *Demand for a Jury Trial.*

        (A) *As Affected by State Law.* A party who, before removal, expressly demanded a jury trial in accordance with state law need not renew the demand after removal. If the state law did not require an express demand for a jury trial, a party need not make one after removal unless the court orders the parties to do so within a specified time. The court must so order at a party's request and may so order on its own. A party who fails to make a demand when so ordered waives a jury trial.

        (B) *Under Rule 38.* If all necessary pleadings have been served at the time of removal, a party entitled to a jury trial under Rule 38 must be given one if the party serves a demand within 14 days after:

            (i) it files a notice of removal; or

            (ii) it is served with a notice of removal filed by another party.

(d) **Law Applicable.**

  (1) *"State Law" Defined.* When these rules refer to state law, the term "law" includes the state's statutes and the state's judicial decisions.

  (2) *"State" Defined.* The term "state" includes, where appropriate, the District of Columbia and any United States commonwealth or territory.

  (3) *"Federal Statute" Defined in the District of Columbia.* In the United States District Court for the District of Columbia, the term "federal statute" includes any Act of Congress that applies locally to the District.

(Amended December 28, 1939, effective April 3, 1941; December 27, 1946, effective March 19, 1948; December 29, 1948, effective October 20, 1949; April 30, 1951, effective August 1, 1951; January 21, 1963, effective July 1, 1963; February 28, 1966, effective July 1, 1966; December 4, 1967, effective July 1, 1968; March 1, 1971, effective July 1, 1971; March 2, 1987, effective August 1, 1987; April 23, 2001, effective December 1, 2001; April 29, 2002, effective December 1, 2002; April 30, 2007, effective December 1, 2007; March 26, 2009, effective December 1, 2009.)

ADVISORY COMMITTEE NOTES

1937 Adoption

Note to Subdivision (a). Paragraph (1): Compare the enabling act, Act of June 19, 1934, U.S.C., Title 28, § 2072, formerly § 723b (Rules in actions at law; Supreme Court authorized to make) and § 2072, formerly § 723c (Union of equity and action at law rules; power of Supreme Court). For the application of these rules in bankruptcy and copyright proceedings, see Orders xxxvi and xxxvii in Bankruptcy and Rule 1 of Rules of Practice and Procedure under § 25 of the copyright act, Act of March 4, 1909, U.S.C., Title 17, former § 25 [see 412, 501 et seq.] (Infringement and rules of procedure).

For examples of statutes which are preserved by paragraph (2) see: U.S.C., Title 8, [former] ch. 9 (Naturalization); Title 28, former ch. 14 [now 153] (Habeas corpus); Title 28, former §§ 377a to 377c [now D.C.Code, Title 16 § 3501 et seq.] (Quo warranto); and such forfeiture statutes as U.S.C., Title 7, former § 116 (Misbranded seeds, confiscation), and Title 21, § 334(b), formerly § 14 (Pure Food and Drug Act—condemnation of adulterated or misbranded Food; procedure). See also *443 Cans of Frozen Eggs Product v. U.S.,* 1912, 33 S.Ct. 50, 226 U.S. 172, 57 L.Ed. 174.

For examples of statutes which under paragraph (7) will continue to govern procedure in condemnation cases, see U.S.C. [former] Title 40, [former] § 258 (Condemnation of realty for sites for public building, etc., procedure); U.S.C., Title 16, § 831x (Condemnation by Tennessee Valley Authority); U.S.C., [former] Title 40, § 120 (Acquisition of lands for public use in District of Columbia); [former] Title 40, ch. 7 [now D.C.Code, Title 16, § 1301 et seq.] (Acquisition of lands in District of Columbia for use of United States; condemnation).

Note to Subdivision (b). Some statutes which will be affected by this subdivision are;

U.S.C., Title 7:

§ 222 (Federal Trade Commission powers adopted for enforcement of Stockyards Act) (By reference to Title 15, § 49)

U.S.C., Title 15:

§ 49 (Enforcement of Federal Trade Commission orders and antitrust laws)

§ 77t(c) (Enforcement of Securities and Exchange Commission orders and Securities Act of 1933)

§ 78u(f) (Same; Securities Exchange Act of 1934)

§ 79r(g) (Same; Public Utility Holding Company Act of 1935)

U.S.C., Title 16:

§ 820 (Proceedings in equity for revocation or to prevent violations of license of Federal Power Commission licensee)

§ 825m(b) (Mandamus to compel compliance with Federal Water Power Act, etc.)

U.S.C., Title 19:

§ 1333(c) (Mandamus to compel compliance with orders of Tariff Commission, etc.)

U.S.C., Title 28, former:

§ 377 [now 1651] (Power to issue writs)

§ 572 [now 1923] (Fees, attorneys, solicitors and proctors)

§ 778 [former] (Death of parties; substitution of executor or administrator). Compare Rule 25(a) (Substitution of parties; death), and the note thereto.

U.S.C., Title 33:

§ 495 (Removal of bridges over navigable waters)

U.S.C., Title 45:

§ 88 (Mandamus against Union Pacific Railroad Company)

§ 153(p) (Mandamus to enforce orders of Adjustment Board under Railway Labor Act)

§ 185 (Same; National Air Transport Adjustment Board) (By reference to § 153)

U.S.C., Title 47:

§ 11 (Powers of Federal Communications Commission)

§ 401(a) (Enforcement of Federal Communications Act and orders of Commission)

§ 406 (Same; Compelling furnishing of facilities; mandamus)

U.S.C., Title 49:

§ 19a(*l*) [now 11703] (Mandamus to compel compliance with Interstate Commerce Act)

§ 20(9) [now 11703] (Jurisdiction to compel compliance with interstate commerce laws by mandamus)

For comparable provisions in state practice see Smith-Hurd Ill.Stats. c. 110, § 179 (1937); Calif.Code Civ.Proc. (Deering, 1937) § 802.

Note to Subdivision (c). Such statutes as the following dealing with the removal of actions are substantially continued and made subject to these rules:

U.S.C., Title 28 former:

§ 71 [now 1441, 1445, 1447] (Removal of suits from state courts)

§ 72 [now 1446, 1447] (Same; procedure)

§ 73 [former] (Same; suits under grants of land from different states)

§ 74 [now 1443, 1446, 1447] (Same; causes against persons denied civil rights)

§ 75 [now 1446] (Same; petitioner in actual custody of state court)

§ 76 [now 1442, 1446, 1447] (Same; suits and prosecutions against revenue officers)

§ 77 [now 1442] (Same; suits by aliens)

§ 78 [now 1449] (Same; copies of records refused by clerk of state court)

§ 79 [now 1450] (Same; previous attachment bonds or orders)

§ 80 [now 1359, 1447, 1919] (Same; dismissal or remand)

§ 81 [now 1447] (Same; proceedings in suits removed)

§ 82 [former] (Same; record; filing and return)

§ 83 [now 1447, 1448] (Service of process after removal)

U.S.C., Title 28, §§ 1446, 1447, formerly § 72, supra, however, is modified by shortening the time for pleading in removed actions.

Note to Subdivision (e). The last sentence of this subdivision modifies U.S.C., Title 28, § 1652, formerly § 725 (Laws of States as rules of decision) in so far as that statute has been construed to govern matters of procedure and to exclude state judicial decisions relative thereto.

1946 Amendment

Note to Subdivision (a). Despite certain dicta to the contrary, *Lynn v. United States,* C.C.A.5th, 1940, 110 F.2d 586; *Mount Tivy Winery, Inc. v. Lewis,* N.D.Cal.1942, 42 F.Supp. 636, it is manifest that the rules apply to actions against the United States under the Tucker Act [28 U.S.C., §§ 41(20), 250, 251, 254, 257, 258, 287, 289, 292, 761–765 [now 791, 1346, 1401, 1402, 1491, 1493, 1496, 1501, 1503, 2071, 2072, 2411, 2412, 2501, 2506, 2509, 2510]]. See United States to use of *Foster Wheeler Corp. v. American Surety Co. of New York,* E.D.N.Y.1939, 25 F.Supp. 700; *Boerner v. United States,* E.D.N.Y.1939, 26 F.Supp. 769; *United States v. Gallagher,* C.C.A.9th, 1945, 151 F.2d 556. Rules 1 and 81 provide that the rules shall apply to all suits of a civil nature, whether cognizable as cases at law or in equity except those specifically excepted; and the character of the various proceedings excepted by express statement in Rule 81, as well as the language of the rules generally, shows that the term "civil action" [Rule 2] includes actions against the United States. Moreover, the rules in many places expressly make provision for the situation wherein the United States is a party as either plaintiff or defendant. See Rules 4(d)(4), 12(a), 13(d), 25(d), 37(f), 39(c), 45(c), 54(d), 55(e), 62(e), and 65(c). In *United States v. Sherwood,* 1941, 61 S.Ct. 767, 312 U.S. 584, 85 L.Ed. 1058, the Solicitor General expressly conceded in his brief for the United States that the rules apply to Tucker Act cases. The Solicitor General stated: "The Government, of course, recognizes that the Federal Rules of Civil Procedure apply to cases brought under the Tucker Act." (Brief for the United States, p. 31). Regarding *Lynn v. United States,* supra, the Solicitor General said: "In *Lynn v. United States* . . . the Circuit Court of Appeals for the Fifth Circuit went beyond the Government's contention there, and held that an action under the Tucker Act is neither an action at law nor a suit in equity and, seemingly, that the Federal Rules of Civil Procedure are, therefore, inapplicable. We think the suggestion is erroneous. Rules 4(d), 12(a), 39(c), and 55(e) expressly contemplate suits against the United States, and nothing in the enabling Act (48 Stat. 1064, 28 U.S.C. §§ 723b, 723c [see 2072]) suggests that the Rules are inapplicable to Tucker Act proceedings, which in terms are to accord with court rules and their subsequent modifications (Sec. 4, Act of March 3, 1887, 24 Stat. 505, 28 U.S.C. § 761 [see 2071, 2072])." (Brief for the United States, p. 31, n. 17.)

United States v. Sherwood, supra, emphasizes, however, that the application of the rules in Tucker Act cases affects only matters of procedure and does not operate to extend jurisdiction. See also Rule 82. In the Sherwood case, the New York Supreme Court, acting under § 795 of the New York Civil Practice Act, made an order, authorizing Sherwood, as a judgment creditor, to maintain a suit under the Tucker Act to recover damages from the United States for breach of its contract with the judgment debtor, Kaiser, for construction of a post office building. Sherwood brought suit against the United States and Kaiser in the District Court for the Eastern District of New York. The question before the United States Supreme Court was whether a United States District Court had jurisdiction to entertain a suit against the United States wherein private parties were joined as parties defendant. It was contended that either the Federal Rules of Civil Procedure or the Tucker Act, or both, embodied the consent of the United States to be sued in litigations in which issues between the plaintiff and third persons were to be adjudicated. Regarding the effect of the Federal Rules, the Court declared that nothing in the rules, so far as they may be applicable in Tucker Act cases, authorized the maintenance of any suit against the United States to which it had not otherwise consented. The matter involved was not one of procedure but of jurisdiction, the limits of which were marked by the consent of the United States to be sued. The jurisdiction thus limited is unaffected by the Federal Rules of Civil Procedure.

Subdivision (a)(2). The added sentence makes it clear that the rules have not superseded the requirements of U.S.C., Title 28, § 2253, formerly § 466. *Schenk v. Plummer,* C.C.A.9, 1940, 113 F.2d 726.

For correct application of the rules in proceedings for forfeiture of property for violation of a statute of the United States, such as under U.S.C., Title 22, § 405 (seizure of war materials intended for unlawful export) or U.S.C., Title 21, § 334(b) (Federal Food, Drug, and Cosmetic Act; formerly Title 21, U.S.C. § 14, Pure Food and Drug Act), see *Reynal v. United States,* C.C.A.5, 1945, 153 F.2d 929; *United States v. 108 Boxes of Cheddar Cheese,* S.D.Iowa 1943, 3 F.R.D. 40.

Subdivision (a)(3). The added sentence makes it clear that the rules apply to appeals from proceedings to enforce administrative subpoenas. See *Perkins v. Endicott Johnson Corp.,* C.C.A.2d 1942, 128 F.2d 208, affirmed on other grounds 63 S.Ct. 339, 317 U.S. 501, 87 L.Ed. 424; *Walling v. News Printing Inc.,* C.C.A.3, 1945, 148 F.2d 57; *McCrone v. United States,* 1939, 59 S.Ct. 685, 307 U.S. 61, 83 L.Ed. 1108. And, although the provision allows full recognition of the fact that the rigid application of the rules in the proceedings themselves may conflict with the summary determination desired, *Goodyear Tire & Rubber Co. v. National Relations Board,* C.C.A.6, 1941, 122 F.2d 450; *Cudahy Packing Co. v. National Labor Relations Board,* C.C.A.10, 1941, 117 F.2d 692, it is drawn so as to permit application of any of the rules in the proceedings whenever the district court deems them helpful. See, e.g., *Peoples Natural Gas Co. v. Federal Power Commission,* App.D.C.1942, 127 F.2d 153, certiorari denied 62 S.Ct. 1298, 316 U.S. 700, 86 L.Ed. 1769; *Martin v. Chandis Securities Co.,* C.C.A.9th, 1942, 128 F.2d 731. Compare the application of the rules in summary proceedings in bankruptcy under General Order 37. See 1 *Collier on Bankruptcy,* 14th ed. by Moore and Oglebay, 326–327; 2 Collier, op.cit.supra, 1401–1402; 3 Collier, op.cit.supra, 228–231; 4 Collier, op.cit.supra, 1199–1202.

Subdivision (a)(6). Section 405 of U.S.C., Title 8 originally referred to in the last sentence of paragraph (6), has been repealed and § 738 [now 1451], U.S.C., Title 8, has been enacted in its stead. The last sentence of paragraph (6) has, therefore, been amended in accordance with this change. The sentence has also been amended so as to refer directly to the statute regarding the provision of time for answer, thus avoiding any confusion attendant upon a change in the statute.

That portion of subdivision (a)(6) making the rules applicable to proceedings for enforcement or review of compensation orders under the Longshoremen's and Harbor Workers' Compensation Act [33 U.S.C. § 901 et seq.] was added by an amendment made pursuant to order of the Court, December 28, 1939, effective three months subsequent to the adjournment of the 76th Congress, January 3, 1941.

Subdivision (c). The change in subdivision (c) effects more speedy trials in removed actions. In some states many of the courts have only two terms a year. A case, if filed 20 days before a term, is returnable to that term, but if filed less than 20 days before a term, is returnable to the following term, which convenes six months later. Hence, under the original wording of Rule 81(c), where a case is filed less than 20 days before the term and is removed within a few days but before answer, it is possible for the defendant to delay interposing his answer or presenting his defenses by motion for six months or more. The rule as amended prevents this result.

Subdivision (f). The use of the phrase "the United States or an officer or agency thereof" in the rules (as e.g., in Rule 12(a) and amended Rule 73(a)) could raise the question of whether "officer" includes a collector of internal revenue, a former collector, or the personal representative of a deceased collector, against whom suits for tax refunds are frequently instituted. Difficulty might ensue for the reason that a suit against a collector or his representative has been held to be a personal action. *Sage v. United States,* 1919, 39 S.Ct. 415, 250 U.S. 33, 63 L.Ed. 828; *Smietanka v. Indiana Steel Co.,* 1921, 42 S.Ct. 1, 257 U.S. 1, 66 L.Ed. 99; *United States v. Nunnally Investment Co.,* 1942, 62 S.Ct. 1064, 316 U.S. 258, 86 L.Ed. 1455. The addition of subdivision (f) to Rule 81 dispels any doubts on the matter and avoids further litigation.

1948 Amendment

The amendment effective October 1949, substituted the words "United States District Court" for the words "District Court of the United States" in the last sentence of subdivision (a)(1) and in the first and third sentences of subdivision (e). The amendment substituted the words "United States district courts" in lieu of "district courts of the United States" in subdivision (a)(4) and (5) and in the first sentence of subdivision (c).

The amendment effective October 20, 1949, also made the following changes:

In subdivision (a)(1), the reference to "Title 17, U.S.C." was substituted for the reference to "the Act of March 4, 1909, c. 320, § 25 (35 Stat. 1081), as amended, U.S.C., Title 17, § 25."

In subdivision (a)(2), the reference to "Title 28, U.S.C., § 2253" was substituted for "U.S.C., Title 28, § 466."

In subdivision (a)(3), the reference in the first sentence to "Title 9, U.S.C.," was substituted for "the Act of February 12, 1925, c. 213 (43 Stat. 883), U.S.C., Title 9".

In subdivision (a)(5), the words "as amended" were inserted after the parenthetical citation of "(49 Stat. 453)," and after the citations of "Title 29, §§ 159 and 160," former references to subdivisions "(e), (g), and (i)" were deleted.

In subdivision (a)(6), after the words "These rules" at the beginning of the first sentence, the following words were deleted: "do not apply to proceedings under the Act of September 13, 1888, c. 1015, § 13 (25 Stat. 479), as amended, U.S.C., Title 8, [former] § 282, relating to deportation of Chinese; they". Also in the first sentence, after the parenthetical citation of "(44 Stat. 1434, 1436)," the words "as amended" were added. In the last sentence, the words "October 14, 1940, c. 876, § 338 (54 Stat. 1158)" were inserted in lieu of the words "June 29, 1906, c. 3592, § 15 (34 Stat. 601), as amended."

In subdivision (c), the word "all" originally appearing in the first sentence between the words "govern" and "procedure" was deleted. In the third sentence, the portion beginning with the words "20 days after the receipt" and including all the remainder of that sentence was substituted for the following language: "the time allowed for answer by the law of the state or within 5 days after the filing of the transcript of the record in the district court of the United States, whichever period is longer, but in any event within 20 days after the filing of the transcript". In the fourth or last sentence, after the words at the beginning of the sentence, "If at the time of removal all necessary pleadings have been," the word "served" was inserted in lieu of the word "filed," and the concluding words of the sentence, "petition for removal is filed if he is the petitioner," together with the final clause immediately following, were substituted for the words "record of the action is filed in the district court of the United States."

1963 Amendment

Subdivision (a)(4). This change reflects the transfer of functions from the Secretary of Commerce to the Secretary of the Interior made by 1939 Reorganization Plan No. II, § 4(e), 53 Stat. 1433.

Subdivision (a)(6). The proper current reference is to the 1952 statute superseding the 1940 statute.

Subdivision (c). Most of the cases have held that a party who has made a proper express demand for jury trial in the State court is not required to renew the demand after removal of the action. *Zakoscielny v. Waterman Steamship Corp.,* 16 F.R.D. 314 (D.Md.1954); *Talley v. American Bakeries Co.,* 15 F.R.D. 391 (E.D.Tenn.1954); *Rehrer v. Service Trucking Co.,* 15 F.R.D. 113 (D.Del.1953); 5 *Moore's Federal Practice* ¶ 38.39[3] (2d ed. 1951); 1 Barron & Holtzoff, *Federal Practice & Procedure* § 132 (Wright ed. 1960). But there is some authority to the contrary. *Petsel v. Chicago, B. & Q.R. Co.,* 101 F.Supp. 1006 (S.D.Iowa 1951); *Nelson v. American Nat. Bank & Trust Co.,* 9 F.R.D. 680 (E.D.Tenn.1950). The amendment adopts the preponderant view.

In order still further to avoid unintended waivers of jury trial, the amendment provides that where by State law applicable in the court from which the case is removed a party is entitled to jury trial without making an express demand, he need not make a demand after removal. However, the district court for calendar or other purposes may on its own motion direct the parties to state whether they demand a jury, and the court must make such a direction upon the request of any party. Under the amendment a district

448

court may find it convenient to establish a routine practice of giving these directions to the parties in appropriate cases.

Subdivision (f). The amendment recognizes the change of nomenclature made by Treasury Dept. Order 150–26(2), 18 Fed.Reg. 3499 (1953).

As to a special problem arising under Rule 25 (Substitution of parties) in actions for refund of taxes, see the Advisory Committee's Note to the amendment of Rule 25(d), effective July 19, 1961; and 4 *Moore's Federal Practice* ¶ 25.09 at 531 (2d ed. 1950).

1966 Amendment

See Note to Rule 1, supra.

Statutory proceedings to forfeit property for violation of the laws of the United States, formerly governed by the admiralty rules, will be governed by the unified and supplemental rules. See Supplemental Rule A.

Upon the recommendation of the judges of the United States District Court for the District of Columbia, the Federal Rules of Civil Procedure are made applicable to probate proceedings in that court. The exception with regard to adoption proceedings is removed because the court no longer has jurisdiction of those matters; and the words "mental health" are substituted for "lunacy" to conform to the current characterization in the District.

The purpose of the amendment to paragraph (3) is to permit the deletion from Rule 73(a) of the clause "unless a shorter time is provided by law." The 10 day period fixed for an appeal under 45 U.S.C. § 159 is the only instance of a shorter time provided for appeals in civil cases. Apart from the unsettling effect of the clause, it is eliminated because its retention would preserve the 15 day period heretofore allowed by 28 U.S.C. § 2107 for appeals from interlocutory decrees in admiralty, it being one of the purposes of the amendment to make the time for appeals in civil and admiralty cases uniform under the unified rules. See Advisory Committee's Note to subdivision (a) of Rule 73.

1968 Amendment

The amendments eliminate inappropriate references to appellate procedure.

1971 Amendment

Title 28, U.S.C., § 2243 now requires that the custodian of a person detained must respond to an application for a writ of habeas corpus "within three days unless for good cause additional time, not exceeding twenty days, is allowed." The amendment increases to forty days the additional time that the district court may allow in habeas corpus proceedings involving persons in custody pursuant to a judgment of a state court. The substantial increase in the number of such proceedings in recent years has placed a considerable burden on state authorities. Twenty days has proved in practice too short a time in which to prepare and file the return in many such cases. Allowance of additional time should, of course, be granted only for good cause.

While the time allowed in such a case for the return of the writ may not exceed forty days, this does not mean that the state must necessarily be limited to that period of time to provide for the federal court the transcript of the proceedings of a state trial or plenary hearing if the transcript must be prepared after the habeas corpus proceeding has begun in the federal court.

1987 Amendment

The amendments are technical. No substantive change is intended.

2001 Amendments

Former Copyright Rule 1 made the Civil Rules applicable to copyright proceedings except to the extent the Civil Rules were inconsistent with Copyright Rules. Abrogation of the Copyright Rules leaves the Civil Rules fully applicable to copyright proceedings. Rule 81(a)(1) is amended to reflect this change.

The District of Columbia Court Reform and Criminal Procedure Act of 1970, Pub.L. 91–358, 84 Stat. 473, transferred mental health proceedings formerly held in the United States District Court for the District of Columbia to local District of Columbia courts. The provision that the Civil Rules do not apply to these proceedings is deleted as superfluous.

The reference to incorporation of the Civil Rules in the Federal Rules of Bankruptcy Procedure has been restyled.

Changes Made After Publication and Comments

The Committee Note was amended to correct the inadvertent omission of a negative. As revised, it correctly reflects the language that is stricken from the rule.

2002 Amendments

This amendment brings Rule 81(a)(2) into accord with the Rules Governing § 2254 and § 2255 proceedings. In its present form, Rule 81(a)(2) includes return-time provisions that are inconsistent with the provisions in the Rules Governing §§ 2254 and 2255. The inconsistency should be eliminated, and it is better that the time provisions continue to be set out in the other rules without duplication in Rule 81. Rule 81 also directs that the writ be directed to the person having custody of the person detained. Similar directions exist in the § 2254 and § 2255 rules, providing additional detail for applicants subject to future custody. There is no need for partial duplication in Rule 81.

The provision that the civil rules apply to the extent that practice is not set forth in the § 2254 and § 2255 rules dovetails with the provisions in Rule 11 of the § 2254 rules and Rule 12 of the § 2255 rules.

Changes Made After Publication and Comment. The only change since publication is deletion of an inadvertent reference to § 2241 proceedings.

2007 Amendments

The language of Rule 81 has been amended as part of the general restyling of the Civil Rules to make them more easily understood and to make style and terminology consistent throughout the rules. These changes are intended to be stylistic only.

Rule 81(c) has been revised to reflect the amendment of 28 U.S.C. § 1446(a) that changed the procedure for removal from a petition for removal to a notice of removal.

Former Rule 81(e), drafted before the decision in *Erie R.R. v. Tompkins*, 304 U.S. 64 (1938), defined state law to include "the statutes of that state and the state judicial decisions construing them." The *Erie* decision reinterpreted the Rules of Decision Act, now 28 U.S.C. § 1652, recognizing that the "laws" of the states include the common law established by judicial decisions. Long-established practice reflects this understanding, looking to state common law as well as statutes and court rules when a Civil Rule directs use of state law. Amended Rule 81(d)(1) adheres to this practice, including all state judicial decisions, not only those that construe state statutes.

Former Rule 81(f) is deleted. The office of district director of internal revenue was abolished by restructuring under the Internal Revenue Service Restructuring and Reform Act of 1998, Pub.L. 105–206, July 22, 1998, 26 U.S.C. § 1 Note.

2009 Amendments

The times set in the former rule at 5, 10, and 20 days have been revised to 7, 14, and 21 days, respectively. See the Note to Rule 6.

Several Rules incorporate local state practice. Rule 81(d) now provides that "the term 'state' includes, where appropriate, the District of Columbia." The definition is expanded to include any commonwealth or territory of the United States. As before, these entities are included only "where appropriate." They are included for the reasons that counsel incorporation of state practice. For example, state holidays are recognized in computing time under Rule 6(a). Other, quite different, examples are Rules 64(a), invoking state law for prejudgment remedies, and 69(a)(1), relying on state law for the procedure on execution. Including commonwealths and territories in these and other rules avoids the gaps that otherwise would result when the federal rule relies on local practice rather than provide a uniform federal approach. Including them also establishes uniformity between federal courts and local courts in areas that may involve strong local interests, little need for uniformity among federal courts, or difficulty in defining a uniform federal practice that integrates effectively with local practice.

Adherence to a local practice may be refused as not "appropriate" when the local practice would impair a significant federal interest.

HISTORICAL NOTES

Effective Date of Abrogation

Abrogation of par. (7) of subdivision (a) of this rule as effective Aug. 1, 1951, see Effective Date note incorporated within the Supplementary Report set out under the heading 1951 Addition in the Advisory Committee Notes appearing under Rule 71.1 of these rules.

Pending Actions

For applicability of Supreme Court amendments to pending cases, see Orders of the Supreme Court of the United States Adopting and Amending Rules set out preceding Rule 1 of these rules.

Rule 82. Jurisdiction and Venue Unaffected

These rules do not extend or limit the jurisdiction of the district courts or the venue of actions in those courts. An admiralty or maritime claim under Rule 9(h) is governed by 28 U.S.C. § 1390.

(Amended December 29, 1948, effective October 20, 1949; February 28, 1966, effective July 1, 1966; April 23, 2001, effective December 1, 2001; April 30, 2007, effective December 1, 2007; April 28, 2016, effective December 1, 2016.)

ADVISORY COMMITTEE NOTES

1937 Adoption

These rules grant extensive power of joining claims and counterclaims in one action, but, as this rule states, such grant does not extend federal jurisdiction. The rule is declaratory of existing practice under the [former] Federal Equity Rules with regard to such provisions as [former] Equity Rule 26 on Joinder of Causes of Action and [former] Equity Rule 30 on Counterclaims. Compare Shulman and Jaegerman, *Some Jurisdictional Limitations on Federal Procedure,* 45 Yale L.J. 393 (1936).

1948 Amendment

The amendment effective October 1949, substituted the words "United States district courts" for "district courts of the United States."

1966 Amendment

Title 28, U.S.C., § 1391(b) provides: "A civil action wherein jurisdiction is not founded solely on diversity of citizenship may be brought only in the judicial district where all defendants reside, except as otherwise provided by law." This provision cannot appropriately be applied to what were formerly suits in admiralty. The rationale of decisions holding it inapplicable rests largely on the use of the term "civil action": i.e., a suit in admiralty is not a "civil action" within the statute. By virtue of the amendment to Rule 1, the provisions of Rule 2 convert suits in admiralty into civil actions. The added sentence is necessary to avoid an undesirable change in existing law with respect to venue.

2001 Amendments

The final sentence of Rule 82 is amended to delete the reference to 28 U.S.C. § 1393, which has been repealed.

Style Comment

The recommendation that the change be made without publication carries with it a recommendation that style changes not be made. Styling would carry considerable risks. The first sentence of Rule 82, for example, states that the Civil Rules do not "extend or limit the jurisdiction of the United States district courts." That sentence is a flat lie if "jurisdiction" includes personal or quasi-in rem jurisdiction. The styling project on this rule requires publication and comment.

2007 Amendments

The language of Rule 82 has been amended as part of the general restyling of the Civil Rules to make them more easily understood and to make style and terminology consistent throughout the rules. These changes are intended to be stylistic only.

2016 Amendments

Rule 82 is amended to reflect the enactment of 28 U.S.C. § 1390 and the repeal of § 1392.

Rule 83.   Rules by District Courts; Judge's Directives

(a) **Local Rules.**

    (1) *In General.* After giving public notice and an opportunity for comment, a district court, acting by a majority of its district judges, may adopt and amend rules governing its practice. A local rule must be consistent with—but not duplicate—federal statutes and rules adopted under 28 U.S.C. §§ 2072 and 2075, and must conform to any uniform numbering system prescribed by the Judicial Conference of the United States. A local rule takes effect on the date specified by the district court and remains in effect unless amended by the court or abrogated by the judicial council of the circuit. Copies of rules and amendments must, on their adoption, be furnished to the judicial council and the Administrative Office of the United States Courts and be made available to the public.

    (2) *Requirement of Form.* A local rule imposing a requirement of form must not be enforced in a way that causes a party to lose any right because of a nonwillful failure to comply.

(b) **Procedure When There Is No Controlling Law.** A judge may regulate practice in any manner consistent with federal law, rules adopted under 28 U.S.C. §§ 2072 and 2075, and the district's local rules. No sanction or other disadvantage may be imposed for noncompliance with any requirement not in federal law, federal rules, or the local rules unless the alleged violator has been furnished in the particular case with actual notice of the requirement.

(Amended April 29, 1985, effective August 1, 1985; April 27, 1995, effective December 1, 1995; April 30, 2007, effective December 1, 2007.)

ADVISORY COMMITTEE NOTES

1937 Adoption

This rule substantially continues U.S.C., Title 28, § 2071, formerly § 731 (Rules of practice in district courts) with the additional requirement that copies of such rules and amendments be furnished to the Supreme Court of the United States. See [former] Equity Rule 79 (Additional Rules by District Court). With the last sentence compare United States Supreme Court Admiralty Rules, 1920, Rule 44 (Right of Trial Courts to Make Rules of Practice) (originally promulgated in 1842).

1985 Amendment

Rule 83, which has not been amended since the Federal Rules were promulgated in 1938, permits each district to adopt local rules not inconsistent with the Federal Rules by a majority of the judges. The only other requirement is that copies be furnished to the Supreme Court.

The widespread adoption of local rules and the modest procedural prerequisites for their promulgation have led many commentators to question the soundness of the process as well as the validity of some rules. See 12 C. Wright & A. Miller, *Federal Practice and Procedure: Civil* § 3152, at 217 (1973); Caballero, *Is There an Over-Exercise of Local Rule-Making Powers by the United States District Courts?,* 24 Fed.Bar News 325 (1977). Although the desirability of local rules for promoting uniform practice within a district is widely accepted, several commentators also have suggested reforms to increase the quality, simplicity, and uniformity of the local rules. See Note, *Rule 83 and the Local Federal Rules,* 67 Colum.L.Rev. 1251 (1967), and Comment, *The Local Rules of Civil Procedure in the Federal District Courts—A Survey,* 1966 Duke L.J. 1011.

The amended Rule attempts, without impairing the procedural validity of existing local rules, to enhance the local rulemaking process by requiring appropriate public notice of proposed rules and an opportunity to comment on them. Although some district courts apparently consult the local bar before promulgating rules, many do not, which has led to criticism of a process that has district judges consulting only with each other. See 12 C. Wright & A. Miller, *supra,* § 3152, at 217; Blair, *The New Local Rules for Federal Practice in Iowa,* 23 Drake L.Rev. 517 (1974). The new language subjects local rulemaking to scrutiny similar to that accompanying the Federal Rules, administrative rulemaking, and legislation. It attempts to assure that the expert advice of practitioners and scholars is made available to the district court before local rules are promulgated. See Weinstein, *Reform of Court Rule-Making Procedures* 84–87, 127–37, 151 (1977).

The amended Rule does not detail the procedure for giving notice and an opportunity to be heard since conditions vary from district to district. Thus, there is no explicit requirement for a public hearing, although a district may consider that procedure appropriate in all or some rulemaking situations. See generally, Weinstein, *supra,* at 117–37, 151. The new Rule does not foreclose any other form of consultation. For example, it can be accomplished through the mechanism of an "Advisory Committee" similar to that employed by the Supreme Court in connection with the Federal Rules themselves.

The amended Rule provides that a local rule will take effect upon the date specified by the district court and will remain in effect unless amended by the district court or abrogated by the judicial council. The effectiveness of a local rule should not be deferred until approved by the judicial council because that might unduly delay promulgation of a local rule that should become effective immediately, especially since some councils do not meet frequently. Similarly, it was thought that to delay a local rule's effectiveness for a fixed period of time would be arbitrary and that to require the judicial council to abrogate a local rule within a specified time would be inconsistent with its power under 28 U.S.C. § 332 (1976) to nullify a local rule at any time. The expectation is that the judicial council will examine all local rules, including those currently in effect, with an eye toward determining whether they are valid and consistent with the Federal Rules, promote inter-district uniformity and efficiency, and do not undermine the basic objectives of the Federal Rules.

The amended Rule requires copies of local rules to be sent upon their promulgation to the judicial council and the Administrative Office of the United States Courts rather than to the Supreme Court. The Supreme Court was the appropriate filing place in 1938, when Rule 83 originally was promulgated, but the establishment of the Administrative Office makes it a more logical place to develop a centralized file of local rules. This procedure is consistent with both the Criminal and the Appellate Rules. See Fed.R.Crim.P. 57(a); Fed.R.App.P. 47. The Administrative Office also will be able to provide improved utilization of the file because of its recent development of a Local Rules Index.

The practice pursued by some judges of issuing standing orders has been controversial, particularly among members of the practicing bar. The last sentence in Rule 83 has been amended to make certain that standing orders are not inconsistent with the Federal Rules or any local district court rules. Beyond that, it is hoped that each district will adopt procedures, perhaps by local rule, for promulgating and reviewing single-judge standing orders.

1995 Amendments

Subdivision (a). This rule is amended to reflect the requirement that local rules be consistent not only with the national rules but also with Acts of Congress. The amendment also states that local rules should not repeat Acts of Congress or national rules.

The amendment also requires that the numbering of local rules conform with any uniform numbering system that may be prescribed by the Judicial Conference. Lack of uniform numbering might create unnecessary traps for counsel and litigants. A uniform numbering system would make it easier for an increasingly national bar and for litigants to locate a local rule that applies to a particular procedural issue.

Paragraph (2) is new. Its aim is to protect against loss of rights in the enforcement of local rules relating to matters of form. For example, a party should not be deprived of a right to a jury trial because its attorney, unaware of—or forgetting—a local rule directing that jury demands be noted in the caption of the case, includes a jury demand only in the body of the pleading. The proscription of paragraph (2) is narrowly drawn—covering only violations attributable to nonwillful failure to comply and only those involving local rules directed to matters of form. It does not limit the court's power to impose substantive penalties upon a party if it or its attorney contumaciously or willfully violates a local rule, even one involving merely a matter of form. Nor does it affect the court's power to enforce local rules that involve more than mere matters of form—for example, a local rule requiring parties to identify evidentiary matters relied upon to support or oppose motions for summary judgment.

Subdivision (b). This rule provides flexibility to the court in regulating practice when there is no controlling law. Specifically, it permits the court to regulate practice in any manner consistent with Acts of Congress, with rules adopted under 28 U.S.C. §§ 2072 and 2075, and with the district local rules.

This rule recognizes that courts rely on multiple directives to control practice. Some courts regulate practice through the published Federal Rules and the local rules of the court. Some courts also have used internal operating procedures, standing orders, and other internal directives. Although such directives continue to be authorized, they can lead to problems. Counsel or litigants may be unaware of various directives. In addition, the sheer volume of directives may impose an unreasonable barrier. For example, it may be difficult to obtain copies of the directives. Finally, counsel or litigants may be unfairly sanctioned for failing to comply with a directive. For these reasons, the amendment to this rule disapproves imposing any sanction or other disadvantage on a person for noncompliance with such an internal directive, unless the alleged violator has been furnished actual notice of the requirement in a particular case.

There should be no adverse consequence to a party or attorney for violating special requirements relating to practice before a particular court unless the party or attorney has actual notice of those requirements. Furnishing litigants with a copy outlining the judge's practices—or attaching instructions to a notice setting a case for conference or trial—would suffice to give actual notice, as would an order in a case specifically adopting by reference a judge's standing order and indicating how copies can be obtained.

2007 Amendments

The language of Rule 83 has been amended as part of the general restyling of the Civil Rules to make them more easily understood and to make style and terminology consistent throughout the rules. These changes are intended to be stylistic only.

HISTORICAL NOTES

Change of Name

Reference to United States magistrate or to magistrate deemed to refer to United States magistrate judge pursuant to section 321 of Pub.L. 101–650, set out as a note under section 631 of this title.

Rule 84.   Forms [Abrogated (Apr. 29, 2015, eff. Dec. 1, 2015).]*

(Amended December 27, 1946, effective March 19, 1948; April 30, 2007, effective December 1, 2007; abrogated April 29, 2015, effective December 1, 2015.)

ADVISORY COMMITTEE NOTES

1937 Adoption

In accordance with the practice found useful in many codes, provision is here made for a limited number of official forms which may serve as guides in pleading. Compare 2 Mass. Gen. Laws (Ter.Ed., 1932) ch. 231, § 147, Forms 1–47; *English Annual Practice* (1937) Appendix A to M, inclusive; *Conn. Practice Book* (1934) Rules, 47–68, pp. 123 to 427.

1946 Amendment

Note. The amendment serves to emphasize that the forms contained in the Appendix of Forms are sufficient to withstand attack under the rules under which they are drawn, and that the practitioner using them may rely on them to that extent. The circuit courts of appeals generally have upheld the use of the forms as promoting desirable simplicity and brevity of statement. *Sierocinski v. E. I. DuPont DeNemours & Co.,* C.C.A.3, 1939, 103 F.2d 843; *Swift & Co. v. Young,* C.C.A.4, 1939, 107 F.2d 170; *Sparks v. England,*

---

*   [To learn more about the history and abrogation of Rule 84 and the Appendix of Forms, see A. Benjamin Spencer, *The Forms Had a Function: Rule 84 and the Appendix of Forms as Guardians of the Liberal Ethos in Civil Procedure*, 15 NEV. L.J. 1113 (2015). Ed.]

C.C.A.8, 1940, 113 F.2d 579; *Ramsouer v. Midland Valley R. Co.,* C.C.A.8, 1943, 135 F.2d 101. And the forms as a whole have met with widespread approval in the courts. See cases cited in 1 Moore's Federal Practice, 1938, Cum. Supplement § 8.07, under "Page 554"; see also Commentary, The Official Forms, 1941, 4 Fed.Rules Serv. 954. In Cook, "Facts" and "Statements of Fact", 1937, 4 U.Chi.L.Rev. 233, 245–246, it is said with reference to what is now Rule 84: ". . . pleaders in the federal courts are not to be left to guess as to the meaning of [the] language" in Rule 8(a) regarding the form of the complaint. "All of which is as it should be. In no other way can useless litigation be avoided." Ibid. The amended rule will operate to discourage isolated results such as those found in *Washburn v. Moorman Mfg. Co.,* S.D.Cal.1938, 25 F.Supp. 546; *Employers Mutual Liability Ins. Co. of Wisconsin v. Blue Line Transfer Co.,* W.D.Mo.1941, 2 F.R.D. 121, 5 Fed.Rules Serv. 12e.235, Case 2.

2007 Amendments

The language of Rule 84 has been amended as part of the general restyling of the Civil Rules to make them more easily understood and to make style and terminology consistent throughout the rules. These changes are intended to be stylistic only.

2015 Amendment

Rule 84 was adopted when the Civil Rules were established in 1938 "to indicate, subject to the provisions of these rules, the simplicity and brevity of statement which the rules contemplate." The purpose of providing illustrations for the rules, although useful when the rules were adopted, has been fulfilled. Accordingly, recognizing that there are many alternative sources for forms, including the website of the Administrative Office of the United States Courts, the websites of many district courts, and local law libraries that contain many commercially published forms, Rule 84 and the Appendix of Forms are no longer necessary and have been abrogated. The abrogation of Rule 84 does not alter existing pleading standards or otherwise change the requirements of Civil Rule 8.

Rule 85.   Title

These rules may be cited as the Federal Rules of Civil Procedure.

(Amended April 30, 2007, effective December 1, 2007.)

ADVISORY COMMITTEE NOTES*

2007 Amendments

The language of Rule 85 has been amended as part of the general restyling of the Civil Rules to make them more easily understood and to make style and terminology consistent throughout the rules. These changes are intended to be stylistic only.

Rule 86.   Effective Dates

(a) In General. These rules and any amendments take effect at the time specified by the Supreme Court, subject to 28 U.S.C. § 2074. They govern:

   (1)   proceedings in an action commenced after their effective date; and

   (2)   proceedings after that date in an action then pending unless:

      (A)   the Supreme Court specifies otherwise; or

      (B)   the court determines that applying them in a particular action would be infeasible or work an injustice.

(b) December 1, 2007 Amendments. If any provision in Rules 1–5.1, 6–73, or 77–86 conflicts with another law, priority in time for the purpose of 28 U.S.C. § 2072(b) is not affected by the amendments taking effect on December 1, 2007.

---

*   [When Rule 85 was adopted in 1937, no Advisory Committee Note accompanied the rule. Ed.]

(Amended December 27, 1946, effective March 19, 1948; December 29, 1948, effective October 20, 1949; April 17, 1961, effective July 19, 1961; January 21, 1963, and March 18, 1963, effective July 1, 1963; April 30, 2007, effective December 1, 2007.)

ADVISORY COMMITTEE NOTES

1937 Adoption

See former Equity Rule 81 (These Rules Effective February 1, 1913—Old Rules Abrogated).

2007 Amendments

The language of Rule 86 has been amended as part of the general restyling of the Civil Rules to make them more easily understood and to make style and terminology consistent throughout the rules. These changes are intended to be stylistic only.

The subdivisions that provided a list of the effective dates of the original Civil Rules and amendments made up to 1963 are deleted as no longer useful.

Rule 86(b) is added to clarify the relationship of amendments taking effect on December 1, 2007, to other laws for the purpose of applying the "supersession" clause in 28 U.S.C. § 2072(b). Section 2072(b) provides that a law in conflict with an Enabling Act Rule "shall be of no further force or effect after such rule[ ] ha[s] taken effect." The amendments that take effect on December 1, 2007, result from the general restyling of the Civil Rules and from a small number of technical revisions adopted on a parallel track. None of these amendments is intended to affect resolution of any conflict that might arise between a rule and another law. Rule 86(b) makes this intent explicit. Any conflict that arises should be resolved by looking to the date the specific conflicting rule provision first became effective.

HISTORICAL NOTES

Effective and Applicability Provisions

1948 Amendments. The first regular session of the 81st Congress adjourned sine die on Oct. 19, 1949, therefore the amendments to Rules 1, 17, 22, 24, 25, 27, 37, 45, 57, 60, 65, 66, 67, 69, 72–76, 79, 81, 82, and 86 and to forms 1, 19, 22, 23, and 27 became effective on Oct. 20, 1949, following the adjournment as provided for in subsection (c) of this rule.

1946 Amendments. The first regular session of the 80th Congress adjourned sine die on Friday, Dec. 19, 1947, therefore the amendments to Rules 6, 7, 12, 13, 14, 17, 24, 26, 27, 28, 33, 34, 36, 41, 45, 52, 54, 56, 58, 59, 60, 62, 65, 66, 68, 73, 75, 77, 79, 80, 81, 84, and 86, became effective Mar. 19, 1948 as provided for in subsection (b) of this rule.

Effective Date of 1970 Amendments; Transmission to Congress

Sections 2 and 3 of the Order of the Supreme Court, dated Mar. 30, 1970, provided:

"**2.** That the foregoing amendments to the Rules of Civil Procedure shall take effect on July 1, 1970, and shall govern all proceedings in actions brought thereafter and also in all further proceedings in actions then pending, except to the extent that in the opinion of the court their application in a particular action then pending would not be feasible or would work injustice, in which event the former procedure applies.

"**3.** That the Chief Justice be, and he hereby is, authorized to transmit to the Congress the foregoing amendments to the Rules of Civil Procedure in accordance with the provisions of Title 28, U.S.C. § 2072."

Effective Date of 1966 Amendment; Transmission to Congress; Rescission

Sections 2 to 4 of the Order of the Supreme Court, dated Feb. 28, 1966, 383 U.S. 1031, provided:

"**2.** That the foregoing amendments and additions to the Rules of Civil Procedure shall take effect on July 1, 1966, and shall govern all proceedings in actions brought thereafter and also in all further proceedings in actions then pending, except to the extent that in the opinion of the court their application in a particular action then pending would not be feasible or would work injustice, in which event the former procedure applies.

"**3.**   That the Chief Justice be, and he hereby is, authorized to transmit to the Congress the foregoing amendments and additions to the Rules of Civil Procedure in accordance with the provisions of Title 28, U.S.C., §§ 2072 and 2073.

"**4.**   That: (a) subdivision (c) of Rule 6 of the Rules of Civil Procedure for the United States District Courts promulgated by this court on December 20, 1937, effective September 16, 1938; (b) Rule 2 of the Rules for Practice and Procedure under section 25 of An Act To amend and consolidate the Acts respecting copyright, approved March 4, 1909, promulgated by this court on June 1, 1909, effective July 1, 1909; and (c) the Rules of Practice in Admiralty and Maritime Cases, promulgated by this court on December 6, 1920, effective March 7, 1921, as revised, amended and supplemented, be, and they hereby are, rescinded, effective July 1, 1966."

APPENDIX OF FORMS [Abrogated (Apr. 29, 2015, eff. Dec. 1, 2015).]*

---

*   [The Appendix of Forms were abrogated effective December 1, 2015. See the 2015 Committee Note accompanying Rule 84 for an explanation. A history of the official forms and their demise may be found at Spencer, *The Forms Had A Function*, 15 NEV. L.J. 1113 (2015). Ed.]

SUPPLEMENTAL RULES FOR ADMIRALTY OR MARITIME CLAIMS AND ASSET FORFEITURE ACTIONS

ADVISORY COMMITTEE NOTES*

1966 Adoption

The amendments to the Federal Rules of Civil Procedure to unify the civil and admiralty procedure, together with the Supplemental Rules for Certain Admiralty and Maritime Claims, completely superseded the Admiralty Rules, effective July 1, 1966. Accordingly, the latter were rescinded.

1985 Amendment

Since their promulgation in 1966, the Supplemental Rules for Certain Admiralty and Maritime Claims have preserved the special procedures of arrest and attachment unique to admiralty law. In recent years, however, these Rules have been challenged as violating the principles of procedural due process enunciated in the United States Supreme Court's decision in *Sniadach v. Family Finance Corp.*, 395 U.S. 337 (1969), and later developed in *Fuentes v. Shevin*, 407 U.S. 67 (1972); *Mitchell v. W.T. Grant Co.*, 416 U.S. 600 (1974); and *North Georgia Finishing, Inc. v. Di-Chem, Inc.*, 419 U.S. 601 (1975). These Supreme Court decisions provide five basic criteria for a constitutional seizure of property: (1) effective notice to persons having interests in the property seized, (2) judicial review prior to attachment, (3) avoidance of conclusory allegations in the complaint, (4) security posted by the plaintiff to protect the owner of the property under attachment, and (5) a meaningful and timely hearing after attachment.

Several commentators have found the Supplemental Rules lacking on some or all five grounds. *E.g.*, Batiza & Partridge, *The Constitutional Challenge to Maritime Seizures*, 26 Loy.L.Rev. 203 (1980); Morse, *The Conflict Between the Supreme Court Admiralty Rules and Sniadach-Fuentes: A Collision Course?*, 3 Fla.St.U.L.Rev. 1 (1975). The federal courts have varied in their disposition of challenges to the Supplemental Rules. The Fourth and Fifth Circuits have affirmed the constitutionality of Rule C. *Amstar Corp. v. S/S Alexandros T.*, 664 F.2d 904 (4th Cir.1981); *Merchants National Bank of Mobile v. The Dredge General G.L. Gillespie*, 663 F.2d 1338 (5th Cir.1981), *cert. dismissed*, 456 U.S. 966 (1982). However, a district court in the Ninth Circuit found Rule C unconstitutional. *Alyeska Pipeline Service Co. v. The Vessel Bay Ridge*, 509 F.Supp. 1115 (D. Alaska 1981), *appeal dismissed*, 703 F.2d 381 (9th Cir.1983). Rule B(1) has received similar inconsistent treatment. The Ninth and Eleventh Circuits have upheld its constitutionality. *Polar Shipping, Ltd. v. Oriental Shipping Corp.*, 680 F.2d 627 (9th Cir.1982); *Schiffahartsgesellschaft Leonhardt & Co. v. A. Bottacchi S.A. de Navegacion*, 732 F.2d 1543 (11th Cir.1984). On the other hand, a Washington district court has found it to be constitutionally deficient. *Grand Bahama Petroleum Co. v. Canadian Transportation Agencies, Ltd.*, 450 F.Supp. 447 (W.D. Wash. 1978). The constitutionality of both rules was questioned in *Techem Chem Co. v. M/T Choyo Maru*, 416 F.Supp. 960 (D. Md. 1976). Thus, there is uncertainty as to whether the current rules prescribe constitutionally sound procedures for guidance of courts and counsel. See generally Note, *Due Process in Admiralty Arrest and Attachment*, 56 Tex.L.Rev. 1091 (1978).

Due to the controversy and uncertainty that have surrounded the Supplemental Rules, local admiralty bars and the Maritime Law Association of the United States have sought to strengthen the constitutionality of maritime arrest and attachment by encouraging promulgation of local admiralty rules providing for prompt post-seizure hearings. Some districts also adopted rules calling for judicial scrutiny of applications for arrest or attachment. Nonetheless, the result has been a lack of uniformity and continued concern over the

---

*   [A table showing the distribution of the rescinded Rules of Practice in Admiralty and Maritime Cases across the Federal Rules of Civil Procedure and the Federal Rules of Appellate Procedure is omitted. Ed.]

constitutionality of the existing practice. The amendments that follow are intended to provide rules that meet the requirements prescribed by the Supreme Court and to develop uniformity in the admiralty practice.

Rule A.   Scope of Rules

(1) These Supplemental Rules apply to:

(A) the procedure in admiralty and maritime claims within the meaning of Rule 9(h) with respect to the following remedies:

(i) maritime attachment and garnishment,

(ii) actions in rem,

(iii) possessory, petitory, and partition actions, and

(iv) actions for exoneration from or limitation of liability;

(B) forfeiture actions in rem arising from a federal statute; and

(C) the procedure in statutory condemnation proceedings analogous to maritime actions in rem, whether within the admiralty and maritime jurisdiction or not. Except as otherwise provided, references in these Supplemental Rules to actions in rem include such analogous statutory condemnation proceedings.

(2) The Federal Rules of Civil Procedure also apply to the foregoing proceedings except to the extent that they are inconsistent with these Supplemental Rules.

(Added Feb. 28, 1966, eff. July 1, 1966; amended Apr. 12, 2006, eff. Dec. 1, 2006.)

ADVISORY COMMITTEE NOTES

1966 Adoption

Certain distinctively maritime remedies must be preserved in unified rules. The commencement of an action by attachment or garnishment has heretofore been practically unknown in federal jurisprudence except in admiralty, although the amendment of Rule 4(e) effective July 1, 1963, makes available that procedure in accordance with state law. The maritime proceeding in rem is unique, except as it has been emulated by statute, and is closely related to the substantive maritime law relating to liens. Arrest of the vessel or other maritime property is an historic remedy in controversies over title or right to possession, and in disputes among co-owners over the vessel's employment. The statutory right to limit liability is limited to owners of vessels, and has its own complexities. While the unified federal rules are generally applicable to these distinctive proceedings, certain special rules dealing with them are needed.

Arrest of the person and imprisonment for debt are not included because there remedies are not peculiarly maritime. The practice is not uniform but conforms to state law. See 2 Benedict § 286 [Note: reference is to the 6th Edition of Benedict on Admiralty * * *]; 28 U.S.C., § 2007; FRCP 64, 69. The relevant provisions of Admiralty Rules 2, 3, and 4 are unnecessary or obsolete.

No attempt is here made to compile a complete and self-contained code governing these distinctively maritime remedies. The more limited objective is to carry forward the relevant provisions of the former Rules of Practice for Admiralty and Maritime Cases, modernized and revised to some extent but still in the context of history and precedent. Accordingly, these Rules are not to be construed as limiting or impairing the traditional power of a district court, exercising the admiralty and maritime jurisdiction, to adapt its procedures and its remedies in the individual case, consistently with these rules, to secure the just, speedy, and inexpensive determination of every action. (See S*wift & Co., Packers v. Compania Columbiana Del Caribe, S/A,* 339 U.S. 684, (1950); Rule 1). In addition, of course, the district courts retain the power to make local rules not inconsistent with these rules. See Rule 83; cf. Admiralty Rule 44.

2006 Amendment

Rule A is amended to reflect the adoption of Rule G to govern procedure in civil forfeiture actions. Rule G(1) contemplates application of other Supplemental Rules to the extent that Rule G does not address an issue. One example is the Rule E(4)(c) provision for arresting intangible property.

Rule B.   In Personam Actions: Attachment and Garnishment

(1)   When Available; Complaint, Affidavit, Judicial Authorization, and Process. In an in personam action:

(a)   If a defendant is not found within the district when a verified complaint praying for attachment and the affidavit required by Rule B(1)(b) are filed, a verified complaint may contain a prayer for process to attach the defendant's tangible or intangible personal property—up to the amount sued for—in the hands of garnishees named in the process.

(b)   The plaintiff or the plaintiff's attorney must sign and file with the complaint an affidavit stating that, to the affiant's knowledge, or on information and belief, the defendant cannot be found within the district. The court must review the complaint and affidavit and, if the conditions of this Rule B appear to exist, enter an order so stating and authorizing process of attachment and garnishment. The clerk may issue supplemental process enforcing the court's order upon application without further court order.

(c)   If the plaintiff or the plaintiff's attorney certifies that exigent circumstances make court review impracticable, the clerk must issue the summons and process of attachment and garnishment. The plaintiff has the burden in any post-attachment hearing under Rule E(4)(f) to show that exigent circumstances existed.

(d)(i)   If the property is a vessel or tangible property on board a vessel, the summons, process, and any supplemental process must be delivered to the marshal for service.

(ii)   If the property is other tangible or intangible property, the summons, process, and any supplemental process must be delivered to a person or organization authorized to serve it, who may be (A) a marshal; (B) someone under contract with the United States; (C) someone specially appointed by the court for that purpose; or, (D) in an action brought by the United States, any officer or employee of the United States.

(e)   The plaintiff may invoke state-law remedies under Rule 64 for seizure of person or property for the purpose of securing satisfaction of the judgment.

(2)   Notice to Defendant. No default judgment may be entered except upon proof—which may be by affidavit—that:

(a)   the complaint, summons, and process of attachment or garnishment have been served on the defendant in a manner authorized by Rule 4;

(b)   the plaintiff or the garnishee has mailed to the defendant the complaint, summons, and process of attachment or garnishment, using any form of mail requiring a return receipt; or

(c)   the plaintiff or the garnishee has tried diligently to give notice of the action to the defendant but could not do so.

(3)   Answer.

(a)   By Garnishee. The garnishee shall serve an answer, together with answers to any interrogatories served with the complaint, within 21 days after service of process upon the garnishee. Interrogatories to the garnishee may be served with the complaint without leave of court. If the garnishee refuses or neglects to answer on oath as to the debts, credits, or effects of the defendant in the garnishee's hands, or any interrogatories concerning such debts, credits, and effects that may be propounded by the plaintiff, the court may award compulsory process against the garnishee. If the garnishee admits any debts, credits, or effects, they shall be held in the garnishee's hands or paid into the registry of the court, and shall be held in either case subject to the further order of the court.

(b)   By Defendant. The defendant shall serve an answer within 30 days after process has been executed, whether by attachment of property or service on the garnishee.

(Added Feb. 28, 1966, eff. July 1, 1966; amended Apr. 29, 1985, eff. Aug. 1, 1985; Mar. 2, 1987, eff. Aug. 1, 1987; Apr. 17, 2000, eff. Dec. 1, 2000; Apr. 25, 2005, eff. Dec. 1, 2005; Mar. 26, 2009, eff. Dec. 1, 2009.)

ADVISORY COMMITTEE NOTES

1966 Adoption

Subdivision (1)

This preserves the traditional maritime remedy of attachment and garnishment, and carries forward the relevant substance of Admiralty Rule 2. In addition, or in the alternative, provision is made for the use of similar state remedies made available by the amendment of Rule 4(e) effective July 1, 1963. On the effect of appearance to defend against attachment see Rule E(8).

The rule follows closely the language of Admiralty Rule 2. No change is made with respect to the property subject to attachment. No change is made in the condition that makes the remedy available. The rules have never defined the clause, "if the defendant shall not be found within the district," and no definition is attempted here. The subject seems one best left for the time being to development on a case-by-case basis. The proposal does shift from the marshal (on whom it now rests in theory) to the plaintiff the burden of establishing that the defendant cannot be found in the district.

A change in the context of the practice is brought about by Rule 4(f), which will enable summons to be served throughout the state instead of, as heretofore, only within the district. The Advisory Committee considered whether the rule on attachment and garnishment should be correspondingly changed to permit those remedies only when the defendant cannot be found within the state and concluded that the remedy should not be so limited.

The effect is to enlarge the class of cases in which the plaintiff may proceed by attachment or garnishment although jurisdiction of the person of the defendant may be independently obtained. This is possible at the present time where, for example, a corporate defendant has appointed an agent within the district to accept service of process but is not carrying on activities there sufficient to subject it to jurisdiction. (*Seawind Compania, S.A. v. Crescent Line, Inc.*, 320 F.2d 580 (2d Cir.1963)), or where, though the foreign corporation's activities in the district are sufficient to subject it personally to the jurisdiction, there is in the district no officer on whom process can be served (*United States v. Cia. Naviera Continental, S.A.*, 178 F.Supp. 561, (S.D.N.Y.1959)).

Process of attachment or garnishment will be limited to the district. See Rule E(3)(a).

Subdivision (2)

The former Admiralty Rules did not provide for notice to the defendant in attachment and garnishment proceedings. None is required by the principles of due process, since it is assumed that the garnishee or custodian of the property attached will either notify the defendant or be deprived of the right to plead the judgment as a defense in an action against him by the defendant. *Harris v. Balk,* 198 U.S. 215 (1905); *Pennoyer v. Neff,* 95 U.S. 714 (1878). Modern conceptions of fairness, however, dictate that actual notice be given to persons known to claim an interest in the property that is the subject of the action where that is reasonably practicable. In attachment and garnishment proceedings the persons whose interests will be affected by the judgment are identified by the complaint. No substantial burden is imposed on the plaintiff by a simple requirement that he notify the defendant of the action by mail.

In the usual case the defendant is notified of the pendency of the proceedings by the garnishee or otherwise, and appears to claim the property and to make his answer. Hence notice by mail is not routinely required in all cases, but only in those in which the defendant has not appeared prior to the time when a default judgment is demanded. The rule therefore provides only that no default judgment shall be entered except upon proof of notice, or of inability to give notice despite diligent efforts to do so. Thus the burden of giving notice is further minimized.

In some cases the plaintiff may prefer to give notice by serving process in the usual way instead of simply by mail. (Rule 4(d).) In particular, if the defendant is in a foreign country the plaintiff may wish to utilize the modes of notice recently provided to facilitate compliance with foreign laws and procedures (Rule 4(i)). The rule provides for these alternatives.

The rule does not provide for notice by publication because there is no problem concerning unknown claimants, and publication has little utility in proportion to its expense where the identity of the defendant is known.

Subdivision (3)

Subdivision (a) incorporates the substance of Admiralty Rule 36.

The Admiralty Rules were silent as to when the garnishee and the defendant were to answer. See also 2 Benedict ch. XXIV [Reference is to the 6th Edition of Benedict on Admiralty * * *].

The rule proceeds on the assumption that uniform and definite periods of time for responsive pleadings should be substituted for return days (see the discussion under Rule C(6), below). Twenty days seems sufficient time for the garnishee to answer (cf. FRCP 12(a)), and an additional 10 days should suffice for the defendant. When allowance is made for the time required for notice to reach the defendant this gives the defendant in attachment and garnishment approximately the same time that defendants have to answer when personally served.

1985 Amendment

Rule B(1) has been amended to provide for judicial scrutiny before the issuance of any attachment or garnishment process. Its purpose is to eliminate doubts as to whether the Rule is consistent with the principles of procedural due process enunciated by the Supreme Court in *Sniadach v. Family Finance Corp.*, 395 U.S. 337 (1969); and later developed in *Fuentes v. Shevin*, 407 U.S. 67 (1972); *Mitchell v. W.T. Grant Co.*, 416 U.S. 600 (1974); and *North Georgia Finishing, Inc. v. Di-Chem, Inc.*, 419 U.S. 601 (1975). Such doubts were raised in *Grand Bahama Petroleum Co. v. Canadian Transportation Agencies, Ltd.*, 450 F.Supp. 447 (W.D.Wash.1978); and *Schiffahartsgesellschaft Leonhardt & Co. v. A. Bottacchi S.A. de Navegacion*, 552 F.Supp. 771 (S.D.Ga.1982), which was reversed, 732 F.2d 1543 (11th Cir.1984). But compare *Polar Shipping Ltd. v. Oriental Shipping Corp.*, 680 F.2d 627 (9th Cir.1982), in which a majority of the panel upheld the constitutionality of Rule B because of the unique commercial context in which it is invoked. The practice described in Rule B(1) has been adopted in some districts by local rule. E.g., N.D. Calif. Local Rule 603.3; W.D.Wash. Local Admiralty Rule 15(d).

The rule envisions that the order will issue when the plaintiff makes a prima facie showing that he has a maritime claim against the defendant in the amount sued for and the defendant is not present in the district. A simple order with conclusory findings is contemplated. The reference to review by the "court" is broad enough to embrace review by a magistrate as well as by a district judge.

The new provision recognizes that in some situations, such as when the judge is unavailable and the ship is about to depart from the jurisdiction, it will be impracticable, if not impossible, to secure the judicial review contemplated by Rule B(1). When "exigent circumstances" exist, the rule enables the plaintiff to secure the issuance of the summons and process of attachment and garnishment, subject to a later showing that the necessary circumstances actually existed. This provision is intended to provide a safety valve without undermining the requirement of preattachment scrutiny. Thus, every effort to secure judicial review, including conducting a hearing by telephone, should be pursued before resorting to the exigent-circumstances procedure.

Rule B(1) also has been amended so that the garnishee shall be named in the "process" rather than in the "complaint." This should solve the problem presented in *Filia Compania Naviera, S.A. v. Petroship, S.A.*, 1983 A.M.C. 1 (S.D.N.Y.1982), and eliminate any need for an additional judicial review of the complaint and affidavit when a garnishee is added.

1987 Amendment

The amendments are technical. No substantive change is intended.

2000 Amendment

Rule B(1) is amended in two ways, and style changes have been made.

The service provisions of Rule C(3) are adopted in paragraph (d), providing alternatives to service by a marshal if the property to be seized is not a vessel or tangible property on board a vessel.

The provision that allows the plaintiff to invoke state attachment and garnishment remedies is amended to reflect the 1993 amendments of Civil Rule 4. Former Civil Rule 4(e), incorporated in Rule B(1), allowed general use of state quasi-in-rem jurisdiction if the defendant was not an inhabitant of, or found within, the state. Rule 4(e) was replaced in 1993 by Rule 4(n)(2), which permits use of state law to seize a defendant's assets only if personal jurisdiction over the defendant cannot be obtained in the district where the action is brought. Little purpose would be served by incorporating Rule 4(n)(2) in Rule B, since maritime attachment and garnishment are available whenever the defendant is not found within the district, a concept that allows attachment or garnishment even in some circumstances in which personal jurisdiction also can be asserted. In order to protect against any possibility that elimination of the reference to state quasi-in-rem jurisdiction remedies might seem to defeat continued use of state security devices, paragraph (e) expressly incorporates Civil Rule 64. Because Rule 64 looks only to security, not jurisdiction, the former reference to Rule E(8) is deleted as no longer relevant.

Rule B(2)(a) is amended to reflect the 1993 redistribution of the service provisions once found in Civil Rule 4(d) and (i). These provisions are now found in many different subdivisions of Rule 4. The new reference simply incorporates Rule 4, without designating the new subdivisions, because the function of Rule B(2) is simply to describe the methods of notice that suffice to support a default judgment. Style changes also have been made.

Gap Report*

Rule B(1)(a) was modified by moving "in an in personam action" out of paragraph (a) and into the first line of subdivision (1). This change makes it clear that all paragraphs of subdivision (1) apply when attachment is sought in an in personam action. Rule B(1)(d) was modified by changing the requirement that the clerk deliver the summons and process to the person or organization authorized to serve it. The new form requires only that the summons and process be delivered, not that the clerk effect the delivery. This change conforms to present practice in some districts and will facilitate rapid service. It matches the spirit of Civil Rule 4(b), which directs the clerk to issue the summons "to the plaintiff for service on the defendant." A parallel change is made in Rule C(3)(b).

2005 Amendments

Rule B(1) is amended to incorporate the decisions in *Heidmar, Inc. v. Anomina Ravennate Di Armamento Sp.A. of Ravenna*, 132 F.3d 264, 267–268 (5th Cir. 1998), and *Navieros InterAmericanos, S.A. v. M/V Vasilia Express*, 120 F.3d 304, 314–315 (1st Cir. 1997). The time for determining whether a defendant is "found" in the district is set at the time of filing the verified complaint that prays for attachment and the affidavit required by Rule B(1)(b). As provided by Rule B(1)(b), the affidavit must be filed with the complaint. A defendant cannot defeat the security purpose of attachment by appointing an agent for service of process after the complaint and affidavit are filed. The complaint praying for attachment need not be the initial complaint. So long as the defendant is not found in the district, the prayer for attachment may be made in an amended complaint; the affidavit that the defendant cannot be found must be filed with the amended complaint.

2009 Amendments

The time set in the former rule at 20 days has been revised to 21 days. See the Note to Rule 6.

---

*   [This Gap Report was mistakenly appended to the Committee Note pertaining to the 2000 amendments to Rule 14. This can be discerned from reading the Standing Committee Report for September 1999, which is available at www. uscourts.gov/sites/default/files/fr_import/ST9-1999.pdf. The Gap Report appears after all the civil amendments are reported, the last of which was the change to Rule 14. As a result, it appears that the Gap Report is for Rule 14 but in fact it only applies to post-comment changes to the proposed amendments to the Supplemental Rules. *See* Standing Committee Report, at Rules Appendix A-17 (Sept. 1999). Ed.]

Rule C.   In Rem Actions: Special Provisions

(1) When Available. An action in rem may be brought:

(a) To enforce any maritime lien;

(b) Whenever a statute of the United States provides for a maritime action in rem or a proceeding analogous thereto.

Except as otherwise provided by law a party who may proceed in rem may also, or in the alternative, proceed in personam against any person who may be liable.

Statutory provisions exempting vessels or other property owned or possessed by or operated by or for the United States from arrest or seizure are not affected by this rule. When a statute so provides, an action against the United States or an instrumentality thereof may proceed on in rem principles.

(2) Complaint. In an action in rem the complaint must:

(a) be verified;

(b) describe with reasonable particularity the property that is the subject of the action; and

(c) state that the property is within the district or will be within the district while the action is pending.

(3) Judicial Authorization and Process.

(a) Arrest Warrant.

(i) The court must review the complaint and any supporting papers. If the conditions for an in rem action appear to exist, the court must issue an order directing the clerk to issue a warrant for the arrest of the vessel or other property that is the subject of the action.

(ii) If the plaintiff or the plaintiff's attorney certifies that exigent circumstances make court review impracticable, the clerk must promptly issue a summons and a warrant for the arrest of the vessel or other property that is the subject of the action. The plaintiff has the burden in any post-arrest hearing under Rule E(4)(f) to show that exigent circumstances existed.

(b) Service.

(i) If the property that is the subject of the action is a vessel or tangible property on board a vessel, the warrant and any supplemental process must be delivered to the marshal for service.

(ii) If the property that is the subject of the action is other property, tangible or intangible, the warrant and any supplemental process must be delivered to a person or organization authorized to enforce it, who may be: (A) a marshal; (B) someone under contract with the United States; (C) someone specially appointed by the court for that purpose; or, (D) in an action brought by the United States, any officer or employee of the United States.

(c) Deposit in Court. If the property that is the subject of the action consists in whole or in part of freight, the proceeds of property sold, or other intangible property, the clerk must issue—in addition to the warrant—a summons directing any person controlling the property to show cause why it should not be deposited in court to abide the judgment.

(d) Supplemental Process. The clerk may upon application issue supplemental process to enforce the court's order without further court order.

(4) Notice. No notice other than execution of process is required when the property that is the subject of the action has been released under Rule E(5). If the property is not released within 14 days after execution, the plaintiff must promptly—or within the time that the court allows—give public notice of the action and arrest in a newspaper designated by court order and having general circulation in the district, but publication may be terminated if the property is released before publication is completed. The notice must specify the time under Rule C(6) to file a statement of interest in or right against the seized property and to answer. This rule does not affect the notice requirements in an action to foreclose a preferred ship mortgage under 46 U.S.C. §§ 31301 et seq., as amended.

(5) Ancillary Process. In any action in rem in which process has been served as provided by this rule, if any part of the property that is the subject of the action has not been brought within the control of the court because it has been removed or sold, or because it is intangible property in the hands of a person who has not been served with process, the court may, on motion, order any person having possession or control of such property or its proceeds to show cause why it should not be delivered into the custody of the marshal or other person or organization having a warrant for the arrest of the property, or paid into court to abide the judgment; and, after hearing, the court may enter such judgment as law and justice may require.

(6) Responsive Pleading; Interrogatories.

(a) Statement of Interest; Answer. In an action in rem:

(i) a person who asserts a right of possession or any ownership interest in the property that is the subject of the action must file a verified statement of right or interest:

(A) within 14 days after the execution of process, or

(B) within the time that the court allows;

(ii) the statement of right or interest must describe the interest in the property that supports the person's demand for its restitution or right to defend the action;

(iii) an agent, bailee, or attorney must state the authority to file a statement of right or interest on behalf of another; and

(iv) a person who asserts a right of possession or any ownership interest must serve an answer within 21 days after filing the statement of interest or right.

(b) Interrogatories. Interrogatories may be served with the complaint in an in rem action without leave of court. Answers to the interrogatories must be served with the answer to the complaint.

(Added Feb. 28, 1966, eff. July 1, 1966; amended Apr. 29, 1985, eff. Aug. 1, 1985; Mar. 2, 1987, eff. Aug. 1, 1987; Apr. 30, 1991, eff. Dec. 1, 1991; Apr. 17, 2000, eff. Dec. 1, 2000; Apr. 29, 2002, eff. Dec. 1, 2002; Apr. 25, 2005, eff. Dec. 1, 2005; Apr. 12, 2006, eff. Dec. 1, 2006; Apr. 23, 2008, eff. Dec. 1, 2008; Mar. 26, 2009, eff. Dec. 1, 2009.)

ADVISORY COMMITTEE NOTES

1966 Adoption

Subdivision (1).

This rule is designed not only to preserve the proceeding in rem as it now exists in admiralty cases, but to preserve the substance of Admiralty Rules 13–18. The general reference to enforcement of any maritime lien is believed to state the existing law, and is an improvement over the enumeration in the former Admiralty Rules, which is repetitious and incomplete (e.g., there was no reference to general average). The reference to any maritime lien is intended to include liens created by state law which are enforceable in admiralty.

The main concern of Admiralty Rules 13–18 was with the question whether certain actions might be brought in rem or also, or in the alternative, in personam. Essentially, therefore, these rules deal with questions of substantive law, for in general an action in rem may be brought to enforce any maritime lien, and no action in personam may be brought when the substantive law imposes no personal liability.

These rules may be summarized as follows:

1. Cases in which the plaintiff may proceed in rem and/or in personam:

    a. Suits for seamen's wages;

  b. Suits by materialmen for supplies, repairs, etc.;

  c. Suits for pilotage;

  d. Suits for collision damages;

  e. Suits founded on mere maritime hypothecation;

  f. Suits for salvage.

 2. Cases in which the plaintiff may proceed only in personam:

  a. Suits for assault and beating.

 3. Cases in which the plaintiff may proceed only in rem:

  a. Suits on bottomry bonds.

The coverage is incomplete, since the rules omit mention of many cases in which the plaintiff may proceed in rem or in personam. This revision proceeds on the principle that it is preferable to make a general statement as to the availability of the remedies, leaving out conclusions on matters of substantive law. Clearly it is not necessary to enumerate the cases listed under Item 1, above, nor to try to complete the list.

The rule eliminates the provision of Admiralty Rule 15 that actions for assault and beating may be brought only in personam. A preliminary study fails to disclose any reason for the rule. It is subject to so many exceptions that it is calculated to deceive rather than to inform. A seaman may sue in rem when he has been beaten by a fellow member of the crew so vicious as to render the vessel unseaworthy, *The Rolph,* 293 Fed. 269, aff'd 299 Fed. 52 (9th Cir. 1923), or where the theory of the action is that a beating by the master is a breach of the obligation under the shipping articles to treat the seaman with proper kindness, *The David Evans,* 187 Fed. 775 (D.Hawaii 1911); and a passenger may sue in rem on the theory that the assault is a breach of the contract of passage, *The Western States,* 159 Fed. 354 (2d Cir. 1908). To say that an action for money damages may be brought only in personam seems equivalent to saying that a maritime lien shall not exist; and that, in turn, seems equivalent to announcing a rule of substantive law rather than a rule of procedure. Dropping the rule will leave it to the courts to determine whether a lien exists as a matter of substantive law.

The specific reference to bottomry bonds is omitted because, as a matter of hornbook substantive law, there is no personal liability on such bonds.

Subdivision (2).

This incorporates the substance of Admiralty Rules 21 and 22.

Subdivision (3).

Derived from Admiralty Rules 10 and 37. The provision that the warrant is to be issued by the clerk is new, but is assumed to state existing law.

There is remarkably little authority bearing on Rule 37, although the subject would seem to be an important one. The rule appears on its face to have provided for a sort of ancillary process, and this may well be the case when tangible property, such as a vessel, is arrested, and intangible property such as freight is incidentally involved. It can easily happen, however, that the only property against which the action may be brought is intangible, as where the owner of a vessel under charter has a lien on subfreights. See 2 Benedict § 299 and cases cited. [Reference is to the 6th Edition of Benedict on Admiralty and not to the current 7th Edition]. In such cases it would seem that the order to the person holding the fund is equivalent to original process, taking the place of the warrant for arrest. That being so, it would also seem that (1) there should be some provision for notice, comparable to that given when tangible property is arrested, and (2) it should not be necessary, as Rule 37 provided, to petition the court for issuance of the process, but that it should issue as of course. Accordingly the substance of Rule 37 is included in the rule covering ordinary process, and notice will be required by Rule C(4). Presumably the rules omit any requirement of notice in these cases because the holder of the funds (e.g., the cargo owner) would be required on general principles (cf. *Harris v. Balk,* 198 U.S. 215 (1905)) to notify his obligee (e.g., the charterer); but in actions in rem such notice seems plainly inadequate because there may be adverse claims to the fund (e.g., there may be liens against the subfreights for seamen's wages, etc.). Compare Admiralty Rule 9.

Subdivision (4).

This carries forward the notice provision of Admiralty Rule 10, with one modification. Notice by publication is too expensive and ineffective a formality to be routinely required. When, as usually happens, the vessel or other property is released on bond or otherwise there is no point in publishing notice; the vessel is freed from the claim of the plaintiff and no other interest in the vessel can be affected by the proceedings. If, however, the vessel is not released, general notice is required in order that all persons, including unknown claimants, may appear and be heard, and in order that the judgment in rem shall be binding on all the world.

Subdivision (5).

This incorporates the substance of Admiralty Rule 9.

There are remarkably few cases dealing directly with the rule. In The *George Prescott,* 10 Fed.Cas. 222 (No. 5,339) (E.D.N.Y.1865), the master and crew of a vessel libeled her for wages, and other lienors also filed libels. One of the lienors suggested to the court that prior to the arrest of the vessel the master had removed the sails, and asked that he be ordered to produce them. He admitted removing the sails and selling them, justifying on the ground that he held a mortgage on the vessel. He was ordered to pay the proceeds into court. Cf. *United States v. The Zarko,* 187 F.Supp. 371 (S.D.Cal.1960), where an armature belonging to a vessel subject to a preferred ship mortgage was in possession of a repairman claiming a lien.

It is evident that, though the rule has had a limited career in the reported cases, it is a potentially important one. It is also evident that the rule is framed in terms narrower than the principle that supports it. There is no apparent reason for limiting it to ships and their appurtenances (2 Benedict § 299) [Reference is to the 6th Edition of Benedict on Admiralty and not to the current 7th Edition]. Also, the reference to "third parties" in the existing rule seems unfortunate. In *The George Prescott,* the person who removed and sold the sails was a plaintiff in the action, and relief against him was just as necessary as if he had been a stranger.

Another situation in which process of this kind would seem to be useful is that in which the principal property that is the subject of the action is a vessel, but her pending freight is incidentally involved. The warrant of arrest, and notice of its service, should be all that is required by way of original process and notice; ancillary process without notice should suffice as to the incidental intangibles.

The distinction between Admiralty Rules 9 and 37 is not at once apparent, but seems to be this: Where the action was against property that could not be seized by the marshal because it was intangible, the original process was required to be similar to that issued against a garnishee, and general notice was required (though not provided for by the present rule; cf. Advisory Committee's Note to Rule C(3)). Under Admiralty Rule 9 property had been arrested and general notice had been given, but some of the property had been removed or for some other reason could not be arrested. Here no further notice was necessary.

The rule also makes provision for this kind of situation: The proceeding is against a vessel's pending freight only; summons has been served on the person supposedly holding the funds, and general notice has been given; it develops that another person holds all or part of the funds. Ancillary process should be available here without further notice.

Subdivision (6).

Adherence to the practice of return days seems unsatisfactory. The practice varies significantly from district to district. A uniform rule should be provided so that any claimant or defendant can readily determine when he is required to file or serve a claim or answer.

A virtue of the return-day practice is that it requires claimants to come forward and identify themselves at an early stage of the proceedings—before they could fairly be required to answer. The draft is designed to preserve this feature of the present practice by requiring early filing of the claim. The time schedule contemplated in the draft is closely comparable to the present practice in the Southern District of New York, where the claimant has a minimum of 8 days to claim and three weeks thereafter to answer.

This rule also incorporates the substance of Admiralty Rule 25. The present rule's emphasis on "the true and bona fide owner" is omitted, since anyone having the right to possession can claim (2 Benedict § 324) [Reference is to the 6th Edition of Benedict on Admiralty and not to the current 7th Edition].

1985 Amendment

Rule C(3) has been amended to provide for judicial scrutiny before the issuance of any warrant of arrest. Its purpose is to eliminate any doubt as to the rule's constitutionality under the *Sniadach* line of cases. *Sniadach v. Family Finance Corp.,* 395 U.S. 337 (1969); *Fuentes v. Shevin,* 407 U.S. 67 (1972); *Mitchell v. W.T. Grant Co.,* 416 U.S. 600 (1974); and *North Georgia Finishing, Inc. v. Di-Chem, Inc.,* 419 U.S. 601 (1975). This was thought desirable even though both the Fourth and the Fifth Circuits have upheld the existing rule. *Amstar Corp. v. S/S Alexandros T.,* 664 F.2d 904 (4th Cir.1981); *Merchants National Bank of Mobile v. The Dredge General G.L. Gillespie,* 663 F.2d 1338 (5th Cir.1981), *cert. dismissed,* 456 U.S. 966 (1982). A contrary view was taken by Judge Tate in the *Merchants National Bank* case and by the district court in *Alyeska Pipeline Service Co. v. The Vessel Bay Ridge,* 509 F.Supp. 1115 (D.Alaska 1981), *appeal dismissed,* 703 F.2d 381 (9th Cir.1983).

The rule envisions that the order will issue upon a prima facie showing that the plaintiff has an action in rem against the defendant in the amount sued for and that the property is within the district. A simple order with conclusory findings is contemplated. The reference to review by the "court" is broad enough to embrace a magistrate as well as a district judge.

The new provision recognizes that in some situations, such as when a judge is unavailable and the vessel is about to depart from the jurisdiction, it will be impracticable, if not impossible, to secure the judicial review contemplated by Rule C(3). When "exigent circumstances" exist, the rule enables the plaintiff to secure the issuance of the summons and warrant of arrest, subject to a later showing that the necessary circumstances actually existed. This provision is intended to provide a safety valve without undermining the requirement of pre-arrest scrutiny. Thus, every effort to secure judicial review, including conducting a hearing by telephone, should be pursued before invoking the exigent-circumstances procedure.

The foregoing requirements for prior court review or proof of exigent circumstances do not apply to actions by the United States for forfeitures for federal statutory violations. In such actions a prompt hearing is not constitutionally required, *United States v. Eight Thousand Eight Hundred and Fifty Dollars,* 103 S.Ct. 2005 (1983); *Calero-Toledo v. Pearson Yacht Leasing Co.,* 416 U.S. 663 (1974), and could prejudice the government in its prosecution of the claimants as defendants in parallel criminal proceedings since the forfeiture hearing could be misused by the defendants to obtain by way of civil discovery information to which they would not otherwise be entitled and subject the government and the courts to the unnecessary burden and expense of two hearings rather than one.

1987 Amendment

The amendments are technical. No substantive change is intended.

1991 Amendment

These amendments are designed to conform the rule to Fed.R.Civ.P. 4, as amended. As with recent amendments to Rule 4, it is intended to relieve the Marshals Service of the burden of using its limited personnel and facilities for execution of process in routine circumstances. Doing so may involve a contractual arrangement with a person or organization retained by the government to perform these services, or the use of other government officers and employees, or the special appointment by the court of persons available to perform suitably.

The seizure of a vessel, with or without cargo, remains a task assigned to the Marshal. Successful arrest of a vessel frequently requires the enforcement presence of an armed government official and the cooperation of the United States Coast Guard and other governmental authorities. If the marshal is called upon to seize the vessel, it is expected that the same officer will also be responsible for the seizure of any property on board the vessel at the time of seizure that is to be the object of arrest or attachment.

2000 Amendment

Style changes have been made throughout the revised portions of Rule C. Several changes of meaning have been made as well.

Subdivision 2. In rem jurisdiction originally extended only to property within the judicial district. Since 1986, Congress has enacted a number of jurisdictional and venue statutes for forfeiture and criminal matters that in some circumstances permit a court to exercise authority over property outside the district.

28 U.S.C. § 1355(b)(1) allows a forfeiture action in the district where an act or omission giving rise to forfeiture occurred, or in any other district where venue is established by § 1395 or by any other statute. Section 1355(b)(2) allows an action to be brought as provided in (b)(1) or in the United States District Court for the District of Columbia when the forfeiture property is located in a foreign country or has been seized by authority of a foreign government. Section 1355(d) allows a court with jurisdiction under § 1355(b) to cause service in any other district of process required to bring the forfeiture property before the court. Section 1395 establishes venue of a civil proceeding for forfeiture in the district where the forfeiture accrues or the defendant is found; in any district where the property is found; in any district into which the property is brought, if the property initially is outside any judicial district; or in any district where the vessel is arrested if the proceeding is an admiralty proceeding to forfeit a vessel. Section 1395(e) deals with a vessel or cargo entering a port of entry closed by the President, and transportation to or from a state or section declared to be in insurrection. 18 U.S.C. § 981(h) creates expanded jurisdiction and venue over property located elsewhere that is related to a criminal prosecution pending in the district. These amendments, and related amendments of Rule E(3), bring these Rules into step with the new statutes. No change is made as to admiralty and maritime proceedings that do not involve a forfeiture governed by one of the new statutes.

Subdivision (2) has been separated into lettered paragraphs to facilitate understanding.

Subdivision (3). Subdivision (3) has been rearranged and divided into lettered paragraphs to facilitate understanding.

Paragraph (b)(i) is amended to make it clear that any supplemental process addressed to a vessel or tangible property on board a vessel, as well as the original warrant, is to be served by the marshal.

Subdivision (4). Subdivision (4) has required that public notice state the time for filing an answer, but has not required that the notice set out the earlier time for filing a statement of interest or claim. The amendment requires that both times be stated.

A new provision is added, allowing termination of publication if the property is released more than 10 days after execution but before publication is completed. Termination will save money, and also will reduce the risk of confusion as to the status of the property.

Subdivision (6). Subdivision (6) has applied a single set of undifferentiated provisions to civil forfeiture proceedings and to in rem admiralty proceedings. Because some differences in procedure are desirable, these proceedings are separated by adopting a new paragraph (a) for civil forfeiture proceedings and recasting the present rule as paragraph (b) for in rem admiralty proceedings. The provision for interrogatories and answers is carried forward as paragraph (c). Although this established procedure for serving interrogatories with the complaint departs from the general provisions of Civil Rule 26(d), the special needs of expedition that often arise in admiralty justify continuing the practice.

Both paragraphs (a) and (b) require a statement of interest or right rather than the "claim" formerly required. The new wording permits parallel drafting, and facilitates cross-references in other rules. The substantive nature of the statement remains the same as the former claim. The requirements of (a) and (b) are, however, different in some respects.

In a forfeiture proceeding governed by paragraph (a), a statement must be filed by a person who asserts an interest in or a right against the property involved. This category includes every right against the property, such as a lien, whether or not it establishes ownership or a right to possession. In determining who has an interest in or a right against property, courts may continue to rely on precedents that have developed the meaning of "claims" or "claimants" for the purpose of civil forfeiture proceedings.

In an admiralty and maritime proceeding governed by paragraph (b), a statement is filed only by a person claiming a right of possession or ownership. Other claims against the property are advanced by intervention under Civil Rule 24, as it may be supplemented by local admiralty rules. The reference to ownership includes every interest that qualifies as ownership under domestic or foreign law. If an ownership interest is asserted, it makes no difference whether its character is legal, equitable, or something else.

Paragraph (a) provides more time than paragraph (b) for filing a statement. Admiralty and maritime in rem proceedings often present special needs for prompt action that do not commonly arise in forfeiture proceedings.

Paragraphs (a) and (b) do not limit the right to make a restricted appearance under Rule E(8).

2002 Amendments

Rule C(3) is amended to reflect the provisions of 18 U.S.C. § 985, enacted by the Civil Asset Forfeiture Reform Act of 2000, 114 Stat. 202, 214–215. Section 985 provides, subject to enumerated exceptions, that real property that is the subject of a civil forfeiture action is not to be seized until an order of forfeiture is entered. A civil forfeiture action is initiated by filing a complaint, posting notice, and serving notice on the property owner. The summons and arrest procedure is no longer appropriate.

Rule C(6)(a)(i)(A) is amended to adopt the provision enacted by 18 U.S.C. § 983(a)(4)(A), shortly before Rule C(6)(a)(i)(A) took effect, that sets the time for filing a verified statement as 30 days rather than 20 days, and that sets the first alternative event for measuring the 30 days as the date of service of the Government's complaint.

Rule C(6)(a)(iii) is amended to give notice of the provision enacted by 18 U.S.C. § 983(a)(4)(B) that requires that the answer in a forfeiture proceeding be filed within 20 days. Without this notice, unwary litigants might rely on the provision of Rule 5(d) that allows a reasonable time for filing after service.

Rule C(6)(b)(iv) is amended to change the requirement that an answer be filed within 20 days to a requirement that it be served within 20 days. Service is the ordinary requirement, as in Rule 12(a). Rule 5(d) requires filing within a reasonable time after service.

Changes Made After Publication and Comment. No changes have been made since publication.

2005 Amendments

Rule C(6)(b)(i)(A) is amended to delete the reference to a time 10 days after completed publication under Rule C(4). This change corrects an oversight in the amendments made in 2000. Rule C(4) requires publication of notice only if the property that is the subject of the action is not released within 10 days after execution of process. Execution of process will always be earlier than publication.

2006 Amendment

Rule C is amended to reflect the adoption of Rule G to govern procedure in civil forfeiture actions.

2008 Amendments

Supplemental Rule C(6)(a)(i) is amended to correct an inadvertent omission in the 2006 amendment to Rule C. The amendment is technical and stylistic in nature. No substantive change is intended.

2009 Amendments

The times set in the former rule at 10 or 20 days have been revised to 14 or 21 days. See the Note to Rule 6.

Rule D.   Possessory, Petitory, and Partition Actions

In all actions for possession, partition, and to try title maintainable according to the course of the admiralty practice with respect to a vessel, in all actions so maintainable with respect to the possession of cargo or other maritime property, and in all actions by one or more part owners against the others to obtain security for the return of the vessel from any voyage undertaken without their consent, or by one or more part owners against the others to obtain possession of the vessel for any voyage on giving security for its safe return, the process shall be by a warrant of arrest of the vessel, cargo, or other property, and by notice in the manner provided by Rule B(2) to the adverse party or parties.

(Added Feb. 28, 1966, eff. July 1, 1966.)

ADVISORY COMMITTEE NOTES

1966 Adoption

This carries forward the substance of Admiralty Rule 19.

Rule 19 provided the remedy of arrest in controversies involving title and possession in general. See *The Tilton*, 23 Fed.Cas.1277 (No. 14,054) (C.C.D.Mass.1830). In addition it provided that remedy in controversies between co-owners respecting the employment of a vessel. It did not deal comprehensively with controversies between co-owners, omitting the remedy of partition. Presumably the omission is traceable to the fact that, when the rules were originally promulgated, concepts of substantive law (sometimes stated as concepts of jurisdiction) denied the remedy of partition except where the parties in disagreement were the owners of equal shares. See *The Steamboat Orleans,* 36 U.S. (11 Pet.) 175 (1837). The Supreme Court has now removed any doubt as to the jurisdiction of the district courts to partition a vessel, and has held in addition that no fixed principle of federal admiralty law limits the remedy to the case of equal shares. *Madruga v. Superior Court,* 346 U.S. 556 (1954). It is therefore appropriate to include a reference to partition in the rule.

Rule E.   Actions In Rem and Quasi In Rem: General Provisions

(1)   Applicability. Except as otherwise provided, this rule applies to actions in personam with process of maritime attachment and garnishment, actions in rem, and petitory, possessory, and partition actions, supplementing Rules B, C, and D.

(2)   Complaint; Security.

(a)   Complaint. In actions to which this rule is applicable the complaint shall state the circumstances from which the claim arises with such particularity that the defendant or claimant will be able, without moving for a more definite statement, to commence an investigation of the facts and to frame a responsive pleading.

(b)   Security for Costs. Subject to the provisions of Rule 54(d) and of relevant statutes, the court may, on the filing of the complaint or on the appearance of any defendant, claimant, or any other party, or at any later time, require the plaintiff, defendant, claimant, or other party to give security, or additional security, in such sum as the court shall direct to pay all costs and expenses that shall be awarded against the party by any interlocutory order or by the final judgment, or on appeal by any appellate court.

(3)   Process.

(a) In admiralty and maritime proceedings process in rem or of maritime attachment and garnishment may be served only within the district.

(b)   Issuance and Delivery. Issuance and delivery of process in rem, or of maritime attachment and garnishment, shall be held in abeyance if the plaintiff so requests.

(4)   Execution of Process; Marshal's Return; Custody of Property; Procedures for Release.

(a)   In General. Upon issuance and delivery of the process, or, in the case of summons with process of attachment and garnishment, when it appears that the defendant cannot be found within the district, the marshal or other person or organization having a warrant shall forthwith execute the process in accordance with this subdivision (4), making due and prompt return.

(b)   Tangible Property. If tangible property is to be attached or arrested, the marshal or other person or organization having the warrant shall take it into the marshal's possession for safe custody. If the character or situation of the property is such that the taking of actual possession is impracticable, the marshal or other person executing the process shall affix a copy thereof to the property in a conspicuous place and leave a copy of the complaint and process with the person having possession or the person's agent. In furtherance of the marshal's custody of any vessel the marshal is authorized to make a written request to the collector of customs not to grant clearance to such vessel until notified by the marshal or deputy marshal or by the clerk that the vessel has been released in accordance with these rules.

(c)   Intangible Property. If intangible property is to be attached or arrested the marshal or other person or organization having the warrant shall execute the process by leaving with the garnishee or other obligor a copy of the complaint and process requiring the garnishee or other obligor to answer as provided in Rules B(3)(a) and C(6); or the marshal may accept for payment into the registry of the court the amount owed to the extent of the amount claimed by the plaintiff with interest and costs, in which event the garnishee or other obligor shall not be required to answer unless alias process shall be served.

(d) Directions With Respect to Property in Custody. The marshal or other person or organization having the warrant may at any time apply to the court for directions with respect to property that has been attached or arrested, and shall give notice of such application to any or all of the parties as the court may direct.

(e) Expenses of Seizing and Keeping Property; Deposit. These rules do not alter the provisions of Title 28, U.S.C., § 1921, as amended, relative to the expenses of seizing and keeping property attached or arrested and to the requirement of deposits to cover such expenses.

(f) Procedure for Release From Arrest or Attachment. Whenever property is arrested or attached, any person claiming an interest in it shall be entitled to a prompt hearing at which the plaintiff shall be required to show why the arrest or attachment should not be vacated or other relief granted consistent with these rules. This subdivision shall have no application to suits for seamen's wages when process is issued upon a certification of sufficient cause filed pursuant to Title 46, U.S.C. §§ 603 and 604 or to actions by the United States for forfeitures for violation of any statute of the United States.

(5) Release of Property.

(a) Special Bond. Whenever process of maritime attachment and garnishment or process in rem is issued the execution of such process shall be stayed, or the property released, on the giving of security, to be approved by the court or clerk, or by stipulation of the parties, conditioned to answer the judgment of the court or of any appellate court. The parties may stipulate the amount and nature of such security. In the event of the inability or refusal of the parties so to stipulate the court shall fix the principal sum of the bond or stipulation at an amount sufficient to cover the amount of the plaintiff's claim fairly stated with accrued interest and costs; but the principal sum shall in no event exceed (i) twice the amount of the plaintiff's claim or (ii) the value of the property on due appraisement, whichever is smaller. The bond or stipulation shall be conditioned for the payment of the principal sum and interest thereon at 6 per cent per annum.

(b) General Bond. The owner of any vessel may file a general bond or stipulation, with sufficient surety, to be approved by the court, conditioned to answer the judgment of such court in all or any actions that may be brought thereafter in such court in which the vessel is attached or arrested. Thereupon the execution of all such process against such vessel shall be stayed so long as the amount secured by such bond or stipulation is at least double the aggregate amount claimed by plaintiffs in all actions begun and pending in which such vessel has been attached or arrested. Judgments and remedies may be had on such bond or stipulation as if a special bond or stipulation had been filed in each of such actions. The district court may make necessary orders to carry this rule into effect, particularly as to the giving of proper notice of any action against or attachment of a vessel for which a general bond has been filed. Such bond or stipulation shall be indorsed by the clerk with a minute of the actions wherein process is so stayed. Further security may be required by the court at any time.

If a special bond or stipulation is given in a particular case, the liability on the general bond or stipulation shall cease as to that case.

(c) Release by Consent or Stipulation; Order of Court or Clerk; Costs. Any vessel, cargo, or other property in the custody of the marshal or other person or organization having the warrant may be released forthwith upon the marshal's acceptance and approval of a stipulation, bond, or other security, signed by the party on whose behalf the property is detained or the party's attorney and expressly authorizing such release, if all costs and charges of the court and its officers shall have first been paid. Otherwise no property in the custody of the marshal, other person or organization having the warrant, or other officer of the court shall be released without an order of the court; but such order may be entered as of course by the clerk, upon the giving of approved security as provided by law and these rules, or upon the dismissal or discontinuance of the action; but the marshal or other person or organization having the warrant shall not deliver any property so released until the costs and charges of the officers of the court shall first have been paid.

(d) Possessory, Petitory, and Partition Actions. The foregoing provisions of this subdivision (5) do not apply to petitory, possessory, and partition actions. In such cases the property arrested shall be released only by order of the court, on such terms and conditions and on the giving of such security as the court may require.

(6) Reduction or Impairment of Security. Whenever security is taken the court may, on motion and hearing, for good cause shown, reduce the amount of security given; and if the surety shall be or become insufficient, new or additional sureties may be required on motion and hearing.

(7) Security on Counterclaim.

(a) When a person who has given security for damages in the original action asserts a counterclaim that arises from the transaction or occurrence that is the subject of the original action, a plaintiff for whose benefit the security has been given must give security for damages demanded in the counterclaim unless the court for cause shown, directs otherwise. Proceedings on the original claim must be stayed until this security is given unless the court directs otherwise.

(b) The plaintiff is required to give security under Rule E(7)(a) when the United States or its corporate instrumentality counterclaims and would have been required to give security to respond in damages if a private party but is relieved by law from giving security.

(8) Restricted Appearance. An appearance to defend against an admiralty and maritime claim with respect to which there has issued process in rem, or process of attachment and garnishment, may be expressly restricted to the defense of such claim, and in that event is not an appearance for the purposes of any other claim with respect to which such process is not available or has not been served.

(9) Disposition of Property; Sales.

(a) Interlocutory Sales; Delivery.

(i) On application of a party, the marshal, or other person having custody of the property, the court may order all or part of the property sold—with the sales proceeds, or as much of them as will satisfy the judgment, paid into court to await further orders of the court—if:

(A) the attached or arrested property is perishable, or liable to deterioration, decay, or injury by being detained in custody pending the action;

(B) the expense of keeping the property is excessive or disproportionate; or

(C) there is an unreasonable delay in securing release of the property.

(ii) In the circumstances described in Rule E(9)(a)(i), the court, on motion by a defendant or a person filing a statement of interest or right under Rule C(6), may order that the property, rather than being sold, be delivered to the movant upon giving security under these rules.

(b) Sales; Proceeds. All sales of property shall be made by the marshal or a deputy marshal, or by other person or organization having the warrant, or by any other person assigned by the court where the marshal or other person or organization having the warrant is a party in interest; and the proceeds of sale shall be forthwith paid into the registry of the court to be disposed of according to law.

(10) Preservation of Property. When the owner or another person remains in possession of property attached or arrested under the provisions of Rule E(4)(b) that permit execution of process without taking actual possession, the court, on a party's motion or on its own, may enter any order necessary to preserve the property and to prevent its removal.

(Added Feb. 28, 1966, eff. July 1, 1966; amended Apr. 29, 1985, eff. Aug. 1, 1985; Mar. 2, 1987, eff. Aug. 1, 1987; Apr. 30, 1991, eff. Dec. 1, 1991; Apr. 17, 2000, eff. Dec. 1, 2000; Apr. 12, 2006, eff. Dec. 1, 2006.)

ADVISORY COMMITTEE NOTES

1966 Adoption

Subdivisions (1), (2).

Adapted from Admiralty Rule 24. The rule is based on the assumption that there is no more need for security for costs in maritime personal actions than in civil cases generally, but that there is reason to retain the requirement for actions in which property is seized. As to proceedings for limitation of liability see Rule F(1).

Subdivision (3).

The Advisory Committee has concluded for practical reasons that process requiring seizure of property should continue to be served only within the geographical limits of the district. Compare Rule B(1), continuing the condition that process of attachment and garnishment may be served only if the defendant is not found within the district.

The provisions of Admiralty Rule 1 concerning the persons by whom process is to be served will be superseded by FRCP 4(c).

Subdivision (4).

This rule is intended to preserve the provisions of Admiralty Rules 10 and 36 relating to execution of process, custody of property seized by the marshal, and the marshal's return. It is also designed to make express provision for matters not heretofore covered.

The provision relating to clearance in subdivision (b) is suggested by Admiralty Rule 44 of the District of Maryland.

Subdivision (d) is suggested by English Rule 12, Order 75.

28 U.S.C., § 1921 as amended in 1962 contains detailed provisions relating to the expenses of seizing and preserving property attached or arrested.

Subdivision (5).

In addition to Admiralty Rule 11 (see Rule E(9)), the release of property seized on process of attachment or in rem was dealt with by Admiralty Rules 5, 6, 12, and 57, and 28 U.S.C., § 2464 (formerly Rev.Stat. § 941). The rule consolidates these provisions and makes them uniformly applicable to attachment and garnishment and actions in rem.

The rule restates the substance of Admiralty Rule 5. Admiralty Rule 12 dealt only with ships arrested on in rem process. Since the same ground appears to be covered more generally by 28 U.S.C., § 2464, the subject matter of Rule 12 is omitted. The substance of Admiralty Rule 57 is retained. 28 U.S.C., § 2464 is incorporated with changes of terminology, and with a substantial change as to the amount of the bond. See 2 Benedict 395 n. 1a [Reference is to the 6th Edition of Benedict on Admiralty and not to the current 7th Edition.] *The Lotosland,* 2 F.Supp. 42 (S.D.N.Y.1933). The provision for general bond is enlarged to include the contingency of attachment as well as arrest of the vessel.

Subdivision (6).

Adapted from Admiralty Rule 8.

Subdivision (7).

Derived from Admiralty Rule 50.

Title 46, U.S.C., § 783 extends the principle of Rule 50 to the Government when sued under the Public Vessels Act, presumably on the theory that the credit of the Government is the equivalent of the best security. The rule adopts this principle and extends it to all cases in which the Government is defendant although the Suits in Admiralty Act contains no parallel provisions.

Subdivision (8).

Under the liberal joinder provisions of unified rules the plaintiff will be enabled to join with maritime actions in rem, or maritime actions in personam with process of attachment and garnishment, claims with respect to which such process is not available, including nonmaritime claims. Unification should not, however, have the result that, in order to defend against an admiralty and maritime claim with respect to which process in rem or quasi in rem has been served, the claimant or defendant must subject himself personally to the jurisdiction of the court with reference to other claims with respect to which such process is not available or has not been served, especially when such other claims are nonmaritime. So far as attachment and garnishment are concerned this principle holds true whether process is issued according to admiralty tradition and the Supplemental Rules or according to Rule 4(e) as incorporated by Rule B(1).

A similar problem may arise with respect to civil actions other than admiralty and maritime claims within the meaning of Rule 9(h). That is to say, in an ordinary civil action, whether maritime or not, there may be joined in one action claims with respect to which process of attachment and garnishment is available under state law and Rule 4(e) and claims with respect to which such process is not available or has not been served. The general Rules of Civil Procedure do not specify whether an appearance in such cases to defend the claim with respect to which process of attachment and garnishment has issued is an appearance for the purposes of the other claims. In that context the question has been considered best left to case-by-case development. Where admiralty and maritime claims within the meaning of Rule 9(h) are concerned, however, it seems important to include a specific provision to avoid an unfortunate and unintended effect of unification. No inferences whatever as to the effect of such an appearance in an ordinary civil action should be drawn from the specific provision here and the absence of such a provision in the general Rules.

Subdivision (9).

Adapted from Admiralty Rules 11, 12, and 40. Subdivision (a) is necessary because of various provisions as to disposition of property in forfeiture proceedings. In addition to particular statutes, note the provisions of 28 U.S.C., §§ 2461–65.

The provision of Admiralty Rule 12 relating to unreasonable delay was limited to ships but should have broader application. See 2 Benedict 404 [Reference is to the 6th Edition of Benedict on Admiralty and not to the current 7th Edition]. Similarly, both Rules 11 and 12 were limited to actions in rem, but should equally apply to attached property.

1985 Amendment

Rule E(4)(f) makes available the type of prompt post-seizure hearing in proceedings under Supplemental Rules B and C that the Supreme Court has called for in a number of cases arising in other contexts. See *North Georgia Finishing, Inc. v. Di-Chem, Inc.,* 419 U.S. 601 (1975); *Mitchell v. W.T. Grant Co.,* 416 U.S. 600 (1974). Although post-attachment and post-arrest hearings always have been available on motion, an explicit statement emphasizing promptness and elaborating the procedure has been lacking in the Supplemental Rules. Rule E(4)(f) is designed to satisfy the constitutional requirement of due process by guaranteeing to the shipowner a prompt post-seizure hearing at which he can attack the complaint, the arrest, the security demanded, or any other alleged deficiency in the proceedings. The amendment also is intended to eliminate the previously disparate treatment under local rules of defendants whose property has been seized pursuant to Supplemental Rules B and C.

The new Rule E(4)(f) is based on a proposal by the Maritime Law Association of the United States and on local admiralty rules in the Eastern, Northern, and Southern Districts of New York. E.D.N.Y. Local Rule 13; N.D.N.Y. Local Rule 13; S.D.N.Y. Local Rule 12. Similar provisions have been adopted by other maritime districts. E.g., N.D.Calif. Local Rule 603.4; W.D.La. Local Admiralty Rule 21. Rule E(4)(f) will provide uniformity in practice and reduce constitutional uncertainties.

Rule E(4)(f) is triggered by the defendant or any other person with an interest in the property seized. Upon an oral or written application similar to that used in seeking a temporary restraining order, see Rule 65(b), the court is required to hold a hearing as promptly as possible to determine whether to allow the arrest or attachment to stand. The plaintiff has the burden of showing why the seizure should not be vacated. The hearing also may determine the amount of security to be granted or the propriety of imposing counter-security to protect the defendant from an improper seizure.

The foregoing requirements for prior court review or proof of exigent circumstances do not apply to actions by the United States for forfeitures for federal statutory violations. In such actions a prompt hearing is not constitutionally required, *United States v. Eight Thousand Eight Hundred and Fifty Dollars,* 103 S.Ct. 2005 (1983); *Calero-Toledo v. Pearson Yacht Leasing Co.,* 416 U.S. 663 (1974), and could prejudice the government in its prosecution of the claimants as defendants in parallel criminal proceedings since the forfeiture hearing could be misused by the defendants to obtain by way of civil discovery information to which they would not otherwise be entitled and subject the government and the courts to the unnecessary burden and expense of two hearings rather than one.

1987 Amendment

The amendments are technical. No substantive change is intended.

1991 Amendment

These amendments are designed to conform this rule to Fed.R.Civ.P. 4, as amended. They are intended to relieve the Marshals Service of the burden of using its limited personnel and facilities for execution of process in routine circumstances. Doing so may involve a contractual arrangement with a person or organization retained by the government to perform these services, or the use of other government officers and employees, or the special appointment by the court of persons available to perform suitably.

2000 Amendment

Style changes have been made throughout the revised portions of Rule E. Several changes of meaning have been made as well.

Subdivision (3). Subdivision (3) is amended to reflect the distinction drawn in Rule C(2)(c) and (d). Service in an admiralty or maritime proceeding still must be made within the district, as reflected in Rule C(2)(c), while service in forfeiture proceedings may be made outside the district when authorized by statute, as reflected in Rule C(2)(d).

Subdivision (7). Subdivision (7)(a) is amended to make it clear that a plaintiff need give security to meet a counterclaim only when the counterclaim is asserted by a person who has given security to respond in damages in the original action.

Subdivision (8). Subdivision (8) is amended to reflect the change in Rule B(1)(e) that deletes the former provision incorporating state quasi-in-rem jurisdiction. A restricted appearance is not appropriate when state law is invoked only for security under Civil Rule 64, not as a basis of quasi-in-rem jurisdiction. But if state law allows a special, limited, or restricted appearance as an incident of the remedy adopted from state law, the state practice applies through Rule 64 "in the manner provided by" state law.

Subdivision (9). Subdivision 9(b)(ii) is amended to reflect the change in Rule C(6) that substitutes a statement of interest or right for a claim.

Subdivision (10). Subdivision 10 is new. It makes clear the authority of the court to preserve and to prevent removal of attached or arrested property that remains in the possession of the owner or other person under Rule E(4)(b).

2006 Amendment

Rule E is amended to reflect the adoption of Rule G to govern procedure in civil forfeiture actions.

HISTORICAL NOTES

References in Text

Sections 603 and 604 of Title 46, referred to in subd. (4)(f), were repealed by Pub.L. 98–89, § 4(b), Aug. 26, 1983, 97 Stat. 600, section 1 of which enacted Title 46, Shipping.

Rule F.   Limitation of Liability

(1) Time for Filing Complaint; Security. Not later than six months after receipt of a claim in writing, any vessel owner may file a complaint in the appropriate district court, as provided in subdivision (9) of this rule, for limitation of liability pursuant to statute. The owner (a) shall deposit with the court, for the benefit of claimants, a sum equal to the amount or value of the owner's interest in the vessel and pending freight, or approved security therefor, and in addition such sums, or approved security therefor, as the court may from time to time fix as necessary to carry out the provisions of the statutes as amended; or (b) at the owner's option shall transfer to a trustee to be appointed by the court, for the benefit of claimants, the owner's interest in the vessel and pending freight, together with such sums, or approved security therefor, as the court may from time to time fix as necessary to carry out the provisions of the statutes as amended. The plaintiff shall also give security for costs and, if the plaintiff elects to give security, for interest at the rate of 6 percent per annum from the date of the security.

(2) Complaint. The complaint shall set forth the facts on the basis of which the right to limit liability is asserted and all facts necessary to enable the court to determine the amount to which the owner's liability shall be limited. The complaint may demand exoneration from as well as limitation of liability. It shall state the voyage if any, on which the demands sought to be limited arose, with the date and place of its termination; the amount of all demands including all unsatisfied liens or claims of lien, in contract or in tort or otherwise, arising on that voyage, so far as known to the plaintiff, and what actions and proceedings, if any, are pending thereon; whether the vessel was damaged, lost, or abandoned, and, if so, when and where; the value of the vessel at the close of the voyage or, in case of wreck, the value of her wreckage, strippings, or proceeds, if any, and where and in whose possession they are; and the amount of any pending freight recovered or recoverable. If the plaintiff elects to transfer the plaintiff's interest in the vessel to a trustee, the complaint must further show any prior paramount liens thereon, and what voyages or trips, if any, she has made since the voyage or trip on which the claims sought to be limited arose, and any existing liens arising upon any such subsequent voyage or trip, with the amounts and causes thereof, and the names and addresses of the lienors, so far as known; and whether the vessel sustained any injury upon or by reason of such subsequent voyage or trip.

(3) Claims Against Owner; Injunction. Upon compliance by the owner with the requirements of subdivision (1) of this rule all claims and proceedings against the owner or the owner's property with respect to the matter in question shall cease. On application of the plaintiff the court shall enjoin the further prosecution of any action or proceeding against the plaintiff or the plaintiff's property with respect to any claim subject to limitation in the action.

(4) Notice to Claimants. Upon the owner's compliance with subdivision (1) of this rule the court shall issue a notice to all persons asserting claims with respect to which the complaint seeks limitation, admonishing them to file their respective claims with the clerk of the court and to serve on the attorneys for the plaintiff a copy thereof on or before a date to be named in the notice. The date so fixed shall not be less than 30 days after issuance of the notice. For cause shown, the court may enlarge the time within which claims may be filed. The notice shall be published in such newspaper or newspapers as the court may direct once a week for four successive weeks prior to the date fixed for the filing of claims. The plaintiff not later than the day of second publication shall also mail a copy of the notice to every person known to have made any claim against the vessel or the plaintiff arising out of the voyage or trip on which the claims sought to be limited arose. In cases involving death a copy of such notice shall be mailed to the decedent at the decedent's last known address, and also to any person who shall be known to have made any claim on account of such death.

(5) Claims and Answer. Claims shall be filed and served on or before the date specified in the notice provided for in subdivision (4) of this rule. Each claim shall specify the facts upon which the claimant relies in support of the claim, the items thereof, and the dates on which the same accrued. If a claimant desires to contest either the right to exoneration from or the right to limitation of liability the claimant shall file and serve an answer to the complaint unless the claim has included an answer.

(6) Information to be Given Claimants. Within 30 days after the date specified in the notice for filing claims, or within such time as the court thereafter may allow, the plaintiff shall mail to the attorney for each claimant (or if the claimant has no attorney to the claimant) a list setting forth (a) the name of each claimant, (b) the name and address of the claimant's attorney (if the claimant is known to have one), (c) the nature of the claim, i.e., whether property loss, property damage, death, personal injury etc., and (d) the amount thereof.

(7) Insufficiency of Fund or Security. Any claimant may by motion demand that the funds deposited in court or the security given by the plaintiff be increased on the ground that they are less than the value of the plaintiff's interest in the vessel and pending freight. Thereupon the court shall cause due appraisement to be made of the value of the plaintiff's interest in the vessel and pending freight; and if the court finds that the deposit or security is either insufficient or excessive it shall order its increase or reduction. In like manner any claimant may demand that the deposit or security be increased on the ground that it is insufficient to carry out the provisions of the statutes relating to claims in respect of loss of life or bodily injury; and, after notice and hearing, the court may similarly order that the deposit or security be increased or reduced.

(8) Objections to Claims: Distribution of Fund. Any interested party may question or controvert any claim without filing an objection thereto. Upon determination of liability the fund deposited or secured, or the proceeds of the vessel and pending freight, shall be divided pro rata, subject to all relevant provisions of law, among the several claimants in proportion to the amounts of their respective claims, duly proved, saving, however, to all parties any priority to which they may be legally entitled.

(9) Venue; Transfer. The complaint shall be filed in any district in which the vessel has been attached or arrested to answer for any claim with respect to which the plaintiff seeks to limit liability; or, if the vessel has not been attached or arrested, then in any district in which the owner has been sued with respect to any such claim. When the vessel has not been attached or arrested to answer the matters aforesaid, and suit has not been commenced against the owner, the proceedings may be had in the district in which the vessel may be, but if the vessel is not within any district and no suit has been commenced in any district, then the complaint may be filed in any district. For the convenience of parties and witnesses, in the interest of justice, the court may transfer the action to any district; if venue is wrongly laid the court shall dismiss or, if it be in the interest of justice, transfer the action to any district in which it could have been brought. If the vessel shall have been sold, the proceeds shall represent the vessel for the purposes of these rules.

(Added Feb. 28, 1966, eff. July 1, 1966; amended Mar. 2, 1987, eff. Aug. 1, 1987.)

ADVISORY COMMITTEE NOTES

1966 Adoption

Subdivision (1).

The amendments of 1936 to the Limitation Act superseded to some extent the provisions of Admiralty Rule 51, especially with respect to the time of filing the complaint and with respect to security. The rule here incorporates in substance the 1936 amendment of the Act (46 U.S.C., § 185) with a slight modification to make it clear that the complaint may be filed at any time not later than six months after a claim has been lodged with the owner.

Subdivision (2).

Derived from Admiralty Rules 51 and 53.

Subdivision (3).

This is derived from the last sentence of 46 U.S.C. § 185 and the last paragraph of Admiralty Rule 51.

Subdivision (4).

Derived from Admiralty Rule 51.

Subdivision (5).

Derived from Admiralty Rules 52 and 53.

Subdivision (6).

Derived from Admiralty Rule 52.

Subdivision (7).

Derived from Admiralty Rule 52 and 46 U.S.C., § 185.

Subdivision (8).

Derived from Admiralty Rule 52.

Subdivision (9).

Derived from Admiralty Rule 54. The provision for transfer is revised to conform closely to the language of 28 U.S.C. §§ 1404(a) and 1406(a), though it retains the existing rule's provision for transfer to any district for convenience. The revision also makes clear what has been doubted: that the court may transfer if venue is wrongly laid.

1987 Amendment

The amendments are technical. No substantive change is intended.

Rule G.   Forfeiture Actions In Rem

(1) **Scope.** This rule governs a forfeiture action in rem arising from a federal statute. To the extent that this rule does not address an issue, Supplemental Rules C and E and the Federal Rules of Civil Procedure also apply.

(2) **Complaint.** The complaint must:

(a) be verified;

(b) state the grounds for subject-matter jurisdiction, in rem jurisdiction over the defendant property, and venue;

(c) describe the property with reasonable particularity;

(d) if the property is tangible, state its location when any seizure occurred and—if different—its location when the action is filed;

(e) identify the statute under which the forfeiture action is brought; and

(f) state sufficiently detailed facts to support a reasonable belief that the government will be able to meet its burden of proof at trial.

(3) **Judicial Authorization and Process.**

(a) **Real Property.** If the defendant is real property, the government must proceed under 18 U.S.C. § 985.

(b) **Other Property; Arrest Warrant.** If the defendant is not real property:

(i) the clerk must issue a warrant to arrest the property if it is in the government's possession, custody, or control;

(ii) the court—on finding probable cause—must issue a warrant to arrest the property if it is not in the government's possession, custody, or control and is not subject to a judicial restraining order; and

(iii) a warrant is not necessary if the property is subject to a judicial restraining order.

(c) Execution of Process.

(i) The warrant and any supplemental process must be delivered to a person or organization authorized to execute it, who may be: (A) a marshal or any other United States officer or employee; (B) someone under contract with the United States; or (C) someone specially appointed by the court for that purpose.

(ii) The authorized person or organization must execute the warrant and any supplemental process on property in the United States as soon as practicable unless:

(A) the property is in the government's possession, custody, or control; or

(B) the court orders a different time when the complaint is under seal, the action is stayed before the warrant and supplemental process are executed, or the court finds other good cause.

(iii) The warrant and any supplemental process may be executed within the district or, when authorized by statute, outside the district.

(iv) If executing a warrant on property outside the United States is required, the warrant may be transmitted to an appropriate authority for serving process where the property is located.

(4) Notice.

(a) Notice by Publication.

(i) When Publication Is Required. A judgment of forfeiture may be entered only if the government has published notice of the action within a reasonable time after filing the complaint or at a time the court orders. But notice need not be published if:

(A) the defendant property is worth less than $1,000 and direct notice is sent under Rule G(4)(b) to every person the government can reasonably identify as a potential claimant; or

(B) the court finds that the cost of publication exceeds the property's value and that other means of notice would satisfy due process.

(ii) Content of the Notice. Unless the court orders otherwise, the notice must:

(A) describe the property with reasonable particularity;

(B) state the times under Rule G(5) to file a claim and to answer; and

(C) name the government attorney to be served with the claim and answer.

(iii) Frequency of Publication. Published notice must appear:

(A) once a week for three consecutive weeks; or

(B) only once if, before the action was filed, notice of nonjudicial forfeiture of the same property was published on an official internet government forfeiture site for at least 30 consecutive days, or in a newspaper of general circulation for three consecutive weeks in a district where publication is authorized under Rule G(4)(a)(iv).

(iv) Means of Publication. The government should select from the following options a means of publication reasonably calculated to notify potential claimants of the action:

(A) if the property is in the United States, publication in a newspaper generally circulated in the district where the action is filed, where the property was seized, or where property that was not seized is located;

(B) if the property is outside the United States, publication in a newspaper generally circulated in a district where the action is filed, in a newspaper generally circulated in the country where the property is located, or in legal notices published and generally circulated in the country where the property is located; or

(C) instead of (A) or (B), posting a notice on an official internet government forfeiture site for at least 30 consecutive days.

(b) Notice to Known Potential Claimants.

(i) Direct Notice Required. The government must send notice of the action and a copy of the complaint to any person who reasonably appears to be a potential claimant on the facts known to the government before the end of the time for filing a claim under Rule G(5)(a)(ii)(B).

(ii) Content of the Notice. The notice must state:

(A) the date when the notice is sent;

(B) a deadline for filing a claim, at least 35 days after the notice is sent;

(C) that an answer or a motion under Rule 12 must be filed no later than 21 days after filing the claim; and

(D) the name of the government attorney to be served with the claim and answer.

(iii) Sending Notice.

(A) The notice must be sent by means reasonably calculated to reach the potential claimant.

(B) Notice may be sent to the potential claimant or to the attorney representing the potential claimant with respect to the seizure of the property or in a related investigation, administrative forfeiture proceeding, or criminal case.

(C) Notice sent to a potential claimant who is incarcerated must be sent to the place of incarceration.

(D) Notice to a person arrested in connection with an offense giving rise to the forfeiture who is not incarcerated when notice is sent may be sent to the address that person last gave to the agency that arrested or released the person.

(E) Notice to a person from whom the property was seized who is not incarcerated when notice is sent may be sent to the last address that person gave to the agency that seized the property.

(iv) When Notice Is Sent. Notice by the following means is sent on the date when it is placed in the mail, delivered to a commercial carrier, or sent by electronic mail.

(v) Actual Notice. A potential claimant who had actual notice of a forfeiture action may not oppose or seek relief from forfeiture because of the government's failure to send the required notice.

(5) Responsive Pleadings.

(a) Filing a Claim.

(i) A person who asserts an interest in the defendant property may contest the forfeiture by filing a claim in the court where the action is pending. The claim must:

(A) identify the specific property claimed;

(B) identify the claimant and state the claimant's interest in the property;

(C) be signed by the claimant under penalty of perjury; and

(D) be served on the government attorney designated under Rule G(4)(a)(ii)(C) or (b)(ii)(D).

(ii) Unless the court for good cause sets a different time, the claim must be filed:

(A) by the time stated in a direct notice sent under Rule G(4)(b);

(B) if notice was published but direct notice was not sent to the claimant or the claimant's attorney, no later than 30 days after final publication of newspaper notice or legal notice under Rule G(4)(a) or no later than 60 days after the first day of publication on an official internet government forfeiture site; or

(C) if notice was not published and direct notice was not sent to the claimant or the claimant's attorney:

(1) if the property was in the government's possession, custody, or control when the complaint was filed, no later than 60 days after the filing, not counting any time when the complaint was under seal or when the action was stayed before execution of a warrant issued under Rule G(3)(b); or

(2) if the property was not in the government's possession, custody, or control when the complaint was filed, no later than 60 days after the government complied with 18 U.S.C. § 985(c) as to real property, or 60 days after process was executed on the property under Rule G(3).

(iii) A claim filed by a person asserting an interest as a bailee must identify the bailor, and if filed on the bailor's behalf must state the authority to do so.

(b) **Answer.** A claimant must serve and file an answer to the complaint or a motion under Rule 12 within 21 days after filing the claim. A claimant waives an objection to in rem jurisdiction or to venue if the objection is not made by motion or stated in the answer.

(6) **Special Interrogatories.**

(a) **Time and Scope.** The government may serve special interrogatories limited to the claimant's identity and relationship to the defendant property without the court's leave at any time after the claim is filed and before discovery is closed. But if the claimant serves a motion to dismiss the action, the government must serve the interrogatories within 21 days after the motion is served.

(b) **Answers or Objections.** Answers or objections to these interrogatories must be served within 21 days after the interrogatories are served.

(c) **Government's Response Deferred.** The government need not respond to a claimant's motion to dismiss the action under Rule G(8)(b) until 21 days after the claimant has answered these interrogatories.

(7) **Preserving, Preventing Criminal Use, and Disposing of Property; Sales.**

(a) **Preserving and Preventing Criminal Use of Property.** When the government does not have actual possession of the defendant property the court, on motion or on its own, may enter any order necessary to preserve the property, to prevent its removal or encumbrance, or to prevent its use in a criminal offense.

(b) **Interlocutory Sale or Delivery.**

(i) **Order to Sell.** On motion by a party or a person having custody of the property, the court may order all or part of the property sold if:

(A) the property is perishable or at risk of deterioration, decay, or injury by being detained in custody pending the action;

(B) the expense of keeping the property is excessive or is disproportionate to its fair market value;

(C) the property is subject to a mortgage or to taxes on which the owner is in default; or

(D) the court finds other good cause.

(ii) Who Makes the Sale. A sale must be made by a United States agency that has authority to sell the property, by the agency's contractor, or by any person the court designates.

(iii) Sale Procedures. The sale is governed by 28 U.S.C. §§ 2001, 2002, and 2004, unless all parties, with the court's approval, agree to the sale, aspects of the sale, or different procedures.

(iv) Sale Proceeds. Sale proceeds are a substitute res subject to forfeiture in place of the property that was sold. The proceeds must be held in an interest-bearing account maintained by the United States pending the conclusion of the forfeiture action.

(v) Delivery on a Claimant's Motion. The court may order that the property be delivered to the claimant pending the conclusion of the action if the claimant shows circumstances that would permit sale under Rule G(7)(b)(i) and gives security under these rules.

(c) Disposing of Forfeited Property. Upon entry of a forfeiture judgment, the property or proceeds from selling the property must be disposed of as provided by law.

(8) Motions.

(a) Motion To Suppress Use of the Property as Evidence. If the defendant property was seized, a party with standing to contest the lawfulness of the seizure may move to suppress use of the property as evidence. Suppression does not affect forfeiture of the property based on independently derived evidence.

(b) Motion To Dismiss the Action.

(i) A claimant who establishes standing to contest forfeiture may move to dismiss the action under Rule 12(b).

(ii) In an action governed by 18 U.S.C. § 983(a)(3)(D) the complaint may not be dismissed on the ground that the government did not have adequate evidence at the time the complaint was filed to establish the forfeitability of the property. The sufficiency of the complaint is governed by Rule G(2).

(c) Motion To Strike a Claim or Answer.

(i) At any time before trial, the government may move to strike a claim or answer:

(A) for failing to comply with Rule G(5) or (6), or

(B) because the claimant lacks standing.

(ii) The motion:

(A) must be decided before any motion by the claimant to dismiss the action; and

(B) may be presented as a motion for judgment on the pleadings or as a motion to determine after a hearing or by summary judgment whether the claimant can carry the burden of establishing standing by a preponderance of the evidence.

(d) Petition To Release Property.

(i) If a United States agency or an agency's contractor holds property for judicial or nonjudicial forfeiture under a statute governed by 18 U.S.C. § 983(f), a person who has filed a claim to the property may petition for its release under § 983(f).

    (ii) If a petition for release is filed before a judicial forfeiture action is filed against the property, the petition may be filed either in the district where the property was seized or in the district where a warrant to seize the property issued. If a judicial forfeiture action against the property is later filed in another district—or if the government shows that the action will be filed in another district—the petition may be transferred to that district under 28 U.S.C. § 1404.

    (e) Excessive Fines. A claimant may seek to mitigate a forfeiture under the Excessive Fines Clause of the Eighth Amendment by motion for summary judgment or by motion made after entry of a forfeiture judgment if:

    (i) the claimant has pleaded the defense under Rule 8; and

    (ii) the parties have had the opportunity to conduct civil discovery on the defense.

    (9) Trial. Trial is to the court unless any party demands trial by jury under Rule 38.

(Added Apr. 12, 2006, eff. Dec. 1, 2006; amended Mar. 26, 2009, eff. Dec. 1, 2009.)

ADVISORY COMMITTEE NOTES

2006 Adoption

    Rule G is added to bring together the central procedures that govern civil forfeiture actions. Civil forfeiture actions are in rem proceedings, as are many admiralty proceedings. As the number of civil forfeiture actions has increased, however, reasons have appeared to create sharper distinctions within the framework of the Supplemental Rules. Civil forfeiture practice will benefit from distinctive provisions that express and focus developments in statutory, constitutional, and decisional law. Admiralty practice will be freed from the pressures that arise when the needs of civil forfeiture proceedings counsel interpretations of common rules that may not be suitable for admiralty proceedings.

    Rule G generally applies to actions governed by the Civil Asset Forfeiture Reform Act of 2000 (CAFRA) and also to actions excluded from it. The rule refers to some specific CAFRA provisions; if these statutes are amended, the rule should be adapted to the new provisions during the period required to amend the rule.

    Rule G is not completely self-contained. Subdivision (1) recognizes the need to rely at times on other Supplemental Rules and the place of the Supplemental Rules within the basic framework of the Civil Rules.

    Supplemental Rules A, C, and E are amended to reflect the adoption of Rule G.

Subdivision (1).

    Rule G is designed to include the distinctive procedures that govern a civil forfeiture action. Some details, however, are better supplied by relying on Rules C and E. Subdivision (1) incorporates those rules for issues not addressed by Rule G. This general incorporation is at times made explicit— subdivision (7)(b)(v), for example, invokes the security provisions of Rule E. But Rules C and E are not to be invoked to create conflicts with Rule G. They are to be used only when Rule G, fairly construed, does not address the issue.

    The Civil Rules continue to provide the procedural framework within which Rule G and the other Supplemental Rules operate. Both Rule G(1) and Rule A state this basic proposition. Rule G, for example, does not address pleadings amendments. Civil Rule 15 applies, in light of the circumstances of a forfeiture action.

Subdivision (2).

    Rule E(2)(a) requires that the complaint in an admiralty action "state the circumstances from which the claim arises with such particularity that the defendant or claimant will be able, without moving for a more definite statement, to commence an investigation of the facts and to frame a responsive pleading." Application of this standard to civil forfeiture actions has evolved to the standard stated in subdivision (2)(f). The complaint must state sufficiently detailed facts to support a reasonable belief that the government will be able to meet its burden of proof at trial. *See U. S. v. Mondragon*, 313 F.3d 862 (4th Cir. 2002). Subdivision (2)(f) carries this forfeiture case law forward without change.

Subdivision (3).

Subdivision (3) governs in rem process in a civil forfeiture action.

<u>Paragraph (a).</u> Paragraph (a) reflects the provisions of 18 U.S.C. § 985.

<u>Paragraph (b).</u> Paragraph (b) addresses arrest warrants when the defendant is not real property. Subparagraph (i) directs the clerk to issue a warrant if the property is in the government's possession, custody, or control. If the property is not in the government's possession, custody, or control and is not subject to a restraining order, subparagraph (ii) provides that a warrant issues only if the court finds probable cause to arrest the property. This provision departs from former Rule C(3)(a)(i), which authorized issuance of summons and warrant by the clerk without a probable-cause finding. The probable-cause finding better protects the interests of persons interested in the property. Subparagraph (iii) recognizes that a warrant is not necessary if the property is subject to a judicial restraining order. The government remains free, however, to seek a warrant if it anticipates that the restraining order may be modified or vacated.

<u>Paragraph (c).</u> Subparagraph (ii) requires that the warrant and any supplemental process be served as soon as practicable unless the property is already in the government's possession, custody, or control. But it authorizes the court to order a different time. The authority to order a different time recognizes that the government may have secured orders sealing the complaint in a civil forfeiture action or have won a stay after filing. The seal or stay may be ordered for reasons, such as protection of an ongoing criminal investigation, that would be defeated by prompt service of the warrant. Subparagraph (ii) does not reflect any independent ground for ordering a seal or stay, but merely reflects the consequences for execution when sealing or a stay is ordered. A court also may order a different time for service if good cause is shown for reasons unrelated to a seal or stay. Subparagraph (iv) reflects the uncertainty surrounding service of an arrest warrant on property not in the United States. It is not possible to identify in the rule the appropriate authority for serving process in all other countries. Transmission of the warrant to an appropriate authority, moreover, does not ensure that the warrant will be executed. The rule requires only that the warrant be transmitted to an appropriate authority.

Subdivision (4).

<u>Paragraph (a).</u> Paragraph (a) reflects the traditional practice of publishing notice of an in rem action.

Subparagraph (i) recognizes two exceptions to the general publication requirement. Publication is not required if the defendant property is worth less than $1,000 and direct notice is sent to all reasonably identifiable potential claimants as required by subdivision (4)(b). Publication also is not required if the cost would exceed the property's value and the court finds that other means of notice would satisfy due process. Publication on a government-established internet forfeiture site, as contemplated by subparagraph (iv), would be at a low marginal publication cost, which would likely be the cost to compare to the property value.

Subparagraph (iv) states the basic criterion for selecting the means and method of publication. The purpose is to adopt a means reasonably calculated to reach potential claimants. The government should choose from among these means a method that is reasonably likely to reach potential claimants at a cost reasonable in the circumstances.

If the property is in the United States and newspaper notice is chosen, publication may be where the action is filed, where the property was seized, or—if the property was not seized—where the property is located. Choice among these places is influenced by the probable location of potential claimants.

If the property is not in the United States, account must be taken of the sensitivities that surround publication of legal notices in other countries. A foreign country may forbid local publication. If potential claimants are likely to be in the United States, publication in the district where the action is filed may be the best choice. If potential claimants are likely to be located abroad, the better choice may be publication by means generally circulated in the country where the property is located.

Newspaper publication is not a particularly effective means of notice for most potential claimants. Its traditional use is best defended by want of affordable alternatives. Paragraph (iv)(C) contemplates a government-created internet forfeiture site that would provide a single easily identified means of notice. Such a site could allow much more direct access to notice as to any specific property than publication provides.

Paragraph (b). Paragraph (b) is entirely new. For the first time, Rule G expressly recognizes the due process obligation to send notice to any person who reasonably appears to be a potential claimant.

Subparagraph (i) states the obligation to send notice. Many potential claimants will be known to the government because they have filed claims during the administrative forfeiture stage. Notice must be sent, however, no matter what source of information makes it reasonably appear that a person is a potential claimant. The duty to send notice terminates when the time for filing a claim expires.

Notice of the action does not require formal service of summons in the manner required by Rule 4 to initiate a personal action. The process that begins an in rem forfeiture action is addressed by subdivision (3). This process commonly gives notice to potential claimants. Publication of notice is required in addition to this process. Due process requirements have moved beyond these traditional means of notice, but are satisfied by practical means that are reasonably calculated to accomplish actual notice.

Subparagraph (ii)(B) directs that the notice state a deadline for filing a claim that is at least 35 days after the notice is sent. This provision applies both in actions that fall within 18 U.S.C. § 983(a)(4)(A) and in other actions. Section 983(a)(4)(A) states that a claim should be filed no later than 30 days after service of the complaint. The variation introduced by subparagraph (ii)(B) reflects the procedure of § 983(a)(2)(B) for nonjudicial forfeiture proceedings. The nonjudicial procedure requires that a claim be filed "not later than the deadline set forth in a personal notice letter (which may be not earlier than 35 days after the date the letter is sent) * * * ." This procedure is as suitable in a civil forfeiture action as in a nonjudicial forfeiture proceeding. Thirty-five days after notice is sent ordinarily will extend the claim time by no more than a brief period; a claimant anxious to expedite proceedings can file the claim before the deadline; and the government has flexibility to set a still longer period when circumstances make that desirable.

Subparagraph (iii) begins by stating the basic requirement that notice must be sent by means reasonably calculated to reach the potential claimant. No attempt is made to list the various means that may be reasonable in different circumstances. It may be reasonable, for example, to rely on means that have already been established for communication with a particular potential claimant. The government's interest in choosing a means likely to accomplish actual notice is bolstered by its desire to avoid post-forfeiture challenges based on arguments that a different method would have been more likely to accomplish actual notice. Flexible rule language accommodates the rapid evolution of communications technology.

Notice may be directed to a potential claimant through counsel, but only to counsel already representing the claimant with respect to the seizure of the property, or in a related investigation, administrative forfeiture proceeding, or criminal case.

Subparagraph (iii)(C) reflects the basic proposition that notice to a potential claimant who is incarcerated must be sent to the place of incarceration. Notice directed to some other place, such as a pre-incarceration residence, is less likely to reach the potential claimant. This provision does not address due process questions that may arise if a particular prison has deficient procedures for delivering notice to prisoners. See Dusenbery v. U.S., 534 U.S. 161 (2002).

Items (D) and (E) of subparagraph (iii) authorize the government to rely on an address given by a person who is not incarcerated. The address may have been given to the agency that arrested or released the person, or to the agency that seized the property. The government is not obliged to undertake an independent investigation to verify the address.

Subparagraph (iv) identifies the date on which notice is considered to be sent for some common means, without addressing the circumstances for choosing among the identified means or other means. The date of sending should be determined by analogy for means not listed. Facsimile transmission, for example, is sent upon transmission. Notice by personal delivery is sent on delivery.

Subparagraph (v), finally, reflects the purpose to effect actual notice by providing that a potential claimant who had actual notice of a forfeiture proceeding cannot oppose or seek relief from forfeiture because the government failed to comply with subdivision (4)(b).

Subdivision (5).

Paragraph (a). Paragraph (a) establishes that the first step of contesting a civil forfeiture action is to file a claim. A claim is required by 18 U.S.C. § 983(a)(4)(A) for actions covered by § 983. Paragraph (a) applies this procedure as well to actions not covered by § 983. "Claim" is used to describe this first pleading because of the statutory references to claim and claimant. It functions in the same way as the statement of interest prescribed for an admiralty proceeding by Rule C(6), and is not related to the distinctive meaning of "claim" in admiralty practice.

If the claimant states its interest in the property to be as bailee, the bailor must be identified. A bailee who files a claim on behalf of a bailor must state the bailee's authority to do so.

The claim must be signed under penalty of perjury by the person making it. An artificial body that can act only through an agent may authorize an agent to sign for it. Excusable inability of counsel to obtain an appropriate signature may be grounds for an extension of time to file the claim.

Paragraph (a)(ii) sets the time for filing a claim. Item (C) applies in the relatively rare circumstance in which notice is not published and the government did not send direct notice to the claimant because it did not know of the claimant or did not have an address for the claimant.

Paragraph (b). Under 18 U.S.C. § 983(a)(4)(B), which governs many forfeiture proceedings, a person who asserts an interest by filing a claim "shall file an answer to the Government's complaint for forfeiture not later than 20 days after the date of the filing of the claim." Paragraph (b) recognizes that this statute works within the general procedures established by Civil Rule 12. Rule 12(a)(4) suspends the time to answer when a Rule 12 motion is served within the time allowed to answer. Continued application of this rule to proceedings governed by § 983(a)(4)(B) serves all of the purposes advanced by Rule 12(a)(4), *see U. S. v. $8,221,877.16*, 330 F.3d 141 (3d Cir. 2003); permits a uniform procedure for all civil forfeiture actions; and recognizes that a motion under Rule 12 can be made only after a claim is filed that provides background for the motion.

Failure to present an objection to in rem jurisdiction or to venue by timely motion or answer waives the objection. Waiver of such objections is familiar. An answer may be amended to assert an objection initially omitted. But Civil Rule 15 should be applied to an amendment that for the first time raises an objection to in rem jurisdiction by analogy to the personal jurisdiction objection provision in Civil Rule 12(h)(1)(B). The amendment should be permitted only if it is permitted as a matter of course under Rule 15(a).

A claimant's motion to dismiss the action is further governed by subdivisions (6)(c), (8)(b), and (8)(c).

Subdivision (6).

Subdivision (6) illustrates the adaptation of an admiralty procedure to the different needs of civil forfeiture. Rule C(6) permits interrogatories to be served with the complaint in an in rem action without limiting the subjects of inquiry. Civil forfeiture practice does not require such an extensive departure from ordinary civil practice. It remains useful, however, to permit the government to file limited interrogatories at any time after a claim is filed to gather information that bears on the claimant's standing. Subdivisions (8)(b) and (c) allow a claimant to move to dismiss only if the claimant has standing, and recognize the government's right to move to dismiss a claim for lack of standing. Subdivision (6) interrogatories are integrated with these provisions in that the interrogatories are limited to the claimant's identity and relationship to the defendant property. If the claimant asserts a relationship to the property as bailee, the interrogatories can inquire into the bailor's interest in the property and the bailee's relationship to the bailor. The claimant can accelerate the time to serve subdivision (6) interrogatories by serving a motion to dismiss—the interrogatories must be served within 20 days after the motion is served. Integration is further accomplished by deferring the government's obligation to respond to a motion to dismiss until 20 days after the claimant moving to dismiss has answered the interrogatories.

Special interrogatories served under Rule G(6) do not count against the presumptive 25-interrogatory limit established by Rule 33(a). Rule 33 procedure otherwise applies to these interrogatories.

Subdivision (6) supersedes the discovery "moratorium" of Rule 26(d) and the broader interrogatories permitted for admiralty proceedings by Rule C(6).

Subdivision (7).

Paragraph (a). Paragraph (a) is adapted from Rule E(9)(b). It provides for preservation orders when the government does not have actual possession of the defendant property. It also goes beyond Rule E(9) by recognizing the need to prevent use of the defendant property in ongoing criminal offenses.

Paragraph (b). Paragraph (b)(i)(C) recognizes the authority, already exercised in some cases, to order sale of property subject to a defaulted mortgage or to defaulted taxes. The authority is narrowly confined to mortgages and tax liens; other lien interests may be addressed, if at all, only through the general good-cause provision. The court must carefully weigh the competing interests in each case.

Paragraph (b)(i)(D) establishes authority to order sale for good cause. Good cause may be shown when the property is subject to diminution in value. Care should be taken before ordering sale to avoid diminished value.

Paragraph (b)(iii) recognizes that if the court approves, the interests of all parties may be served by their agreement to sale, aspects of the sale, or sale procedures that depart from governing statutory procedures.

Paragraph (c) draws from Rule E(9)(a), (b), and (c). Disposition of the proceeds as provided by law may require resolution of disputed issues. A mortgagee's claim to the property or sale proceeds, for example, may be disputed on the ground that the mortgage is not genuine. An undisputed lien claim, on the other hand, may be recognized by payment after an interlocutory sale.

Subdivision (8).

Subdivision (8) addresses a number of issues that are unique to civil forfeiture actions.

Paragraph (a). Standing to suppress use of seized property as evidence is governed by principles distinct from the principles that govern claim standing. A claimant with standing to contest forfeiture may not have standing to seek suppression. Rule G does not of itself create a basis of suppression standing that does not otherwise exist.

Paragraph (b). Paragraph (b)(i) is one element of the system that integrates the procedures for determining a claimant's standing to claim and for deciding a claimant's motion to dismiss the action. Under paragraph (c)(ii), a motion to dismiss the action cannot be addressed until the court has decided any government motion to strike the claim or answer. This procedure is reflected in the (b)(i) reminder that a motion to dismiss the forfeiture action may be made only by a claimant who establishes claim standing. The government, moreover, need not respond to a claimant's motion to dismiss until 20 days after the claimant has answered any subdivision (6) interrogatories.

Paragraph (b)(ii) mirrors 18 U.S.C. § 983(a)(3)(D). It applies only to an action independently governed by § 983(a)(3)(D), implying nothing as to actions outside § 983(a)(3)(D). The adequacy of the complaint is measured against the pleading requirements of subdivision (2), not against the quality of the evidence available to the government when the complaint was filed.

Paragraph (c). As noted with paragraph (b), paragraph (c) governs the procedure for determining whether a claimant has standing. It does not address the principles that govern claim standing.

Paragraph (c)(i)(A) provides that the government may move to strike a claim or answer for failure to comply with the pleading requirements of subdivision (5) or to answer subdivision (6) interrogatories. As with other pleadings, the court should strike a claim or answer only if satisfied that an opportunity should not be afforded to cure the defects under Rule 15. Not every failure to respond to subdivision (6) interrogatories warrants an order striking the claim. But the special role that subdivision (6) plays in the scheme for determining claim standing may justify a somewhat more demanding approach than the general approach to discovery sanctions under Rule 37.

Paragraph (c)(ii) directs that a motion to strike a claim or answer be decided before any motion by the claimant to dismiss the action. A claimant who lacks standing is not entitled to challenge the forfeiture on the merits.

Paragraph (c)(ii) further identifies three procedures for addressing claim standing. If a claim fails on its face to show facts that support claim standing, the claim can be dismissed by judgment on the pleadings. If the claim shows facts that would support claim standing, those facts can be tested by a motion for summary judgment. If material facts are disputed, precluding a grant of summary judgment, the court may hold an evidentiary hearing. The evidentiary hearing is held by the court without a jury. The claimant has the burden to establish claim standing at a hearing; procedure on a government summary judgment motion reflects this allocation of the burden.

Paragraph (d). The hardship release provisions of 18 U.S.C. § 983(f) do not apply to a civil forfeiture action exempted from § 983 by § 983(i).

Paragraph (d)(ii) reflects the venue provisions of 18 U.S.C. § 983(f)(3)(A) as a guide to practitioners. In addition, it makes clear the status of a civil forfeiture action as a "civil action" eligible for transfer under 28 U.S.C. § 1404. A transfer decision must be made on the circumstances of the particular proceeding. The district where the forfeiture action is filed has the advantage of bringing all related proceedings together, avoiding the waste that flows from consideration of different parts of the same forfeiture proceeding in the court where the warrant issued or the court where the property was seized. Transfer to that court would serve consolidation, the purpose that underlies nationwide enforcement of a seizure warrant. But there may be offsetting advantages in retaining the petition where it was filed. The claimant may not be able to litigate, effectively or at all, in a distant court. Issues relevant to the petition may be better litigated where the property was seized or where the warrant issued. One element, for example, is whether the claimant has sufficient ties to the community to provide assurance that the property will be available at the time of trial. Another is whether continued government possession would prevent the claimant from working. Determining whether seizure of the claimant's automobile prevents work may turn on assessing the realities of local public transit facilities.

Paragraph (e). The Excessive Fines Clause of the Eighth Amendment forbids an excessive forfeiture. *U.S. v. Bajakajian*, 524 U.S. 321 (1998). 18 U.S.C. § 983(g) provides a "petition" "to determine whether the forfeiture was constitutionally excessive" based on finding "that the forfeiture is grossly disproportional to the offense." Paragraph (e) describes the procedure for § 983(g) mitigation petitions and adopts the same procedure for forfeiture actions that fall outside § 983(g). The procedure is by motion, either for summary judgment or for mitigation after a forfeiture judgment is entered. The claimant must give notice of this defense by pleading, but failure to raise the defense in the initial answer may be cured by amendment under Rule 15. The issues that bear on mitigation often are separate from the issues that determine forfeiture. For that reason it may be convenient to resolve the issue by summary judgment before trial on the forfeiture issues. Often, however, it will be more convenient to determine first whether the property is to be forfeited. Whichever time is chosen to address mitigation, the parties must have had the opportunity to conduct civil discovery on the defense. The extent and timing of discovery are governed by the ordinary rules.

Subdivision (9).

Subdivision (9) serves as a reminder of the need to demand jury trial under Rule 38. It does not expand the right to jury trial. *See U.S. v. One Parcel of Property Located at 32 Medley Lane*, 2005 WL 465421 (D.Conn.2005), ruling that the court, not the jury, determines whether a forfeiture is constitutionally excessive.

2009 Amendments

The times set in the former rule at 20 days have been revised to 21 days. See the Note to Rule 6.

RULES OF PROCEDURE OF THE UNITED STATES JUDICIAL PANEL ON MULTIDISTRICT LITIGATION

(Current through June 15, 2020; most recently amended October 4, 2016)

I. RULES FOR MULTIDISTRICT LITIGATION UNDER 28 U.S.C. § 1407

II. RULES FOR MULTICIRCUIT PETITIONS FOR REVIEW UNDER 28 U.S.C. § 2112(a)(3)

III. CONVERSION TABLE

ELECTRONIC CASE FILING ADMINISTRATIVE POLICIES AND PROCEDURES

I. RULES FOR MULTIDISTRICT LITIGATION UNDER 28 U.S.C. § 1407

The United States Judicial Panel on Multidistrict Litigation promulgates these Rules pursuant to its authority under 28 U.S.C. § 1407(f).

Rule 1.1. Definitions

(a) "Panel" means the members of the United States Judicial Panel on Multidistrict Litigation appointed by the Chief Justice of the United States pursuant to 28 U.S.C. § 1407.

491

(b) "Chair" means the Chair of the Panel appointed by the Chief Justice of the United States pursuant to Section 1407, or the member of the Panel properly designated to act as Chair.

(c) "Clerk of the Panel" means the official that the Panel appoints to that position. The Clerk of the Panel shall perform such duties that the Panel or the Panel Executive delegates.

(d) "Electronic Case Filing (ECF)" refers to the Panel's automated system that receives and stores documents filed in electronic form. All attorneys filing pleadings with the Panel must do so using ECF. All pro se individuals are non-ECF users, unless the Panel orders otherwise.

(e) "MDL" means a multidistrict litigation docket which the Panel is either considering or has created by transferring cases to a transferee district for coordinated or consolidated pretrial proceedings pursuant to Section 1407.

(f) "Panel Executive" means the official appointed to act as the Panel's Chief Executive and Legal Officer. The Panel Executive may appoint, with the approval of the Panel, necessary deputies, clerical assistants and other employees to perform or assist in the performance of the duties of the Panel Executive. The Panel Executive, with the approval of the Panel, may make such delegations of authority as are necessary for the Panel's efficient operation.

(g) "Pleadings" means all papers, motions, responses, or replies of any kind filed with the Panel, including exhibits attached thereto, as well as all orders and notices that the Panel issues.

(h) "Tag-along action" refers to a civil action pending in a district court which involves common questions of fact with either (1) actions on a pending motion to transfer to create an MDL or (2) actions previously transferred to an existing MDL, and which the Panel would consider transferring under Section 1407.

(i) "Transferee district" is the federal district court to which the Panel transfers an action pursuant to Section 1407, for inclusion in an MDL.

(j) "Transferor district" is the federal district court where an action was pending prior to its transfer pursuant to Section 1407, for inclusion in an MDL, and where the Panel may remand that action at or before the conclusion of pretrial proceedings.

(Added May 3, 1993, eff. July 1, 1993; amended Sept. 1, 1998, eff. Nov. 2, 1998; Apr. 2, 2001, eff. Apr. 2, 2001; Sept. 8, 2010, eff. Oct. 4, 2010.)

Rule 2.1.   Rules and Practice

(a) Customary Practice. The Panel's customary practice shall govern, unless otherwise fixed by statute or these Rules.

(b) Failure to Comply with Rules. When a pleading does not comply with these Rules, the Clerk of the Panel may advise counsel of the deficiencies and set a date for full compliance. If counsel does not fully comply within the established time, the Clerk of the Panel shall file the non-complying pleading, but the Chair may thereafter order it stricken.

(c) Admission to Practice before the Panel. Every member in good standing of the Bar of any district court of the United States is entitled to practice before the Panel, provided, however, that he or she has established and maintains a CM/ECF account with any United States federal court. Any attorney of record in any action transferred under Section 1407 may continue to represent his or her client in any district court of the United States to which such action is transferred. Parties are not required to obtain local counsel.

(d) Pendency of Motion or Conditional Order. The pendency of a motion, order to show cause, conditional transfer order or conditional remand order before the Panel pursuant to 28 U.S.C. § 1407 does not affect or suspend orders and pretrial proceedings in any pending federal district court action and does not limit the pretrial jurisdiction of that court. An order to transfer or remand pursuant to 28 U.S.C. § 1407 shall be effective only upon its filing with the clerk of the transferee district court.

(e) Reassignment. If for any reason the transferee judge is unable to continue those responsibilities, the Panel shall make the reassignment of a new transferee judge.

(Former Rules 1.2, 1.3, 1.4, and 1.5 redesignated and amended Sept. 8, 2010, eff. Oct. 4, 2010.)

Rule 3.1. Electronic Records and Files; Copy Fees

(a) Electronic Record. Effective October 4, 2010, the official Panel record shall be the electronic file maintained on the Panel's servers. This record includes, but is not limited to, Panel pleadings, documents filed in paper and then scanned and made part of the electronic record, and Panel orders and notices filed. The official record also includes any documents or exhibits that may be impractical to scan. These documents and exhibits shall be kept in the Panel offices.

(b) Maintaining Records. Records and files generated prior to October 4, 2010, may be (i) maintained at the Panel offices, (ii) temporarily or permanently removed to such places at such times as the Clerk of the Panel or the Chair shall direct, or (iii) transferred whenever appropriate to the Federal Records Center.

(c) Fees. The Clerk of the Panel may charge fees for duplicating records and files, as prescribed by the Judicial Conference of the United States.

(Former Rule 5.1 redesignated and amended Sept. 8, 2010, eff. Oct. 4, 2010.)

Rule 3.2. ECF Users: Filing Requirements

(a) Form of Pleadings. This Rule applies to pleadings that ECF users file with the Panel.

(i) Each pleading shall bear the heading "Before the United States Judicial Panel on Multidistrict Litigation," the identification "MDL No. ___" and the descriptive title designated by the Panel. If the Panel has not yet designated a title, counsel shall use an appropriate description.

(ii) The final page of each pleading shall contain the name, address, telephone number, fax number and email address of the attorney or party designated to receive service of pleadings in the case, and the name of each party represented.

(iii) Each brief submitted with a motion and any response to it shall not exceed 20 pages, exclusive of exhibits. Each reply shall not exceed 10 pages and shall address arguments raised in the response(s). Absent exceptional circumstances and those set forth in Rule 6.1(d), the Panel will not grant motions to exceed page limits.

(iv) Each pleading shall be typed in size 12 point font (for both text and footnotes), double spaced (text only), in a letter size document (8½ × 11 inch) with sequentially numbered pages.

(v) Each exhibit shall be separately numbered and clearly identified.

(vi) Proposed Panel orders shall not be submitted.

(b) Place of Filing. Counsel shall sign and verify all pleadings electronically in accordance with these Rules and the Panel's Administrative Policies and Procedures for Electronic Case Filing found at www.jpml.uscourts.gov. A pleading filed electronically constitutes a written document for the purpose of these Rules and the Federal Rules of Civil Procedure and is deemed the electronically signed original thereof. All pleadings, except by pro se litigants, shall conform with this Rule beginning on October 4, 2010.

(i)* Pleadings shall not be transmitted directly to any Panel member.

---

*   [So in original. No (ii) promulgated. Ed.]

(c) Attorney Registration. Only attorneys identified, or to be identified, pursuant to Rule 4.1, shall file pleadings. Each of these attorneys must register as a Panel CM/ECF user through www.jpml. uscourts.gov. Registration/possession of a CM/ECF account with any United States federal court shall be deemed consent to receive electronic service of all Panel orders and notices as well as electronic service of pleadings from other parties before the Panel.

(d) Courtesy Copy of Specified Pleadings. Counsel shall serve the Clerk of the Panel, for delivery within 1 business day of filing, with a courtesy paper copy of the following pleadings: (i) a motion to transfer and its supporting brief; (ii) a response to a show cause order; (iii) a motion to vacate a conditional transfer order or a conditional remand order; and (iv) any response, reply, supplemental information or interested party response related to the pleadings listed in (i), (ii) and (iii). No courtesy copies of any other pleadings are required. Courtesy copies of pleadings totaling 10 pages or less (including any attachments) may be faxed to the Panel. The courtesy copy shall include all exhibits, shall be clearly marked "Courtesy Copy—Do Not File," shall contain the CM/ECF pleading number (if known), and shall be mailed or delivered to:

> Clerk of the Panel
> United States Judicial Panel on Multidistrict Litigation
> Thurgood Marshall Federal Judiciary Building
> One Columbus Circle, NE, Room G-255, North Lobby
> Washington, DC 20544–0005

(e) Privacy Protections. The privacy protections contained in Rule 5.2 of the Federal Rules of Civil Procedure shall apply to all Panel filings.

(Former Rules 5.1.1, 5.1.2, and 7.1 redesignated in part and amended Sept. 8, 2010, eff. Oct. 4, 2010; amended July 6, 2011, eff. July 6, 2011; technical revision eff. Oct. 4, 2016.)

Rule 3.3.   Non-ECF Users: Filing Requirements

(a) Definition of Non-ECF Users. Non-ECF users are all pro se individuals, unless the Panel orders otherwise. This Rule shall apply to all motions, responses and replies that non-ECF users file with the Panel.

(b) Form of Pleadings. Unless otherwise set forth in this Rule, the provisions of Rule 3.2 shall apply to non-ECF users.

(i) Each pleading shall be flat and unfolded; plainly written or typed in size 12 point font (for both text and footnotes), double spaced (text only), and printed single-sided on letter size (8 $^1/_2$ x 11 inch) white paper with sequentially numbered pages; and fastened at the top-left corner without side binding or front or back covers.

(ii) Each exhibit shall be separately numbered and clearly identified. Any exhibits exceeding a cumulative total of 50 pages shall be bound separately.

(c) Place of Filing. File an original and one copy of all pleadings with the Clerk of the Panel by mailing or delivering to:

Clerk of the Panel
United States Judicial Panel on Multidistrict Litigation
Thurgood Marshall Federal Judiciary Building
One Columbus Circle, NE, Room G-255, North Lobby
Washington, DC 20544–0005

(i) Pleadings not exceeding a total of 10 pages, including exhibits, may be faxed to the Panel office.

(ii) The Clerk of the Panel shall endorse the date for filing on all pleadings submitted for filing.

(Former Rules 5.1.1, 5.1.2, and 7.1 redesignated in part and amended Sept. 8, 2010, eff. Oct. 4, 2010.)

Rule 4.1.   Service of Pleadings

(a) Proof of Service. The Panel's notice of electronic filing shall constitute service of pleadings. Registration/possession by counsel of a CM/ECF account with any United States federal court shall be deemed consent to receive electronic service of all pleadings. All pleadings shall contain a proof of service on all other parties in all involved actions. The proof of service shall indicate the name and manner of service. If a party is not represented by counsel, the proof of service shall indicate the name of the party and the party's last known address. The proof of service shall indicate why any person named as a party in a constituent complaint was not served with the Section 1407 pleading.

(b) Service Upon Transferor Court. The proof of service pertaining to motions for a transfer or remand pursuant to 28 U.S.C. § 1407 shall certify that counsel has transmitted a copy of the motion for filing to the clerk of each district court where an affected action is pending.

(c) Notice of Appearance. Within 14 days after the issuance of a (i) notice of filing of a motion to initiate transfer under Rule 6.2, (ii) notice of filed opposition to a CTO under Rule 7.1, (iii) a show cause order under Rules* 8.1, (iv) notice of filed opposition to a CRO under Rule 10.2, or (v) notice of filing of a motion to remand under Rule 10.3, each party or designated attorney as required hereinafter shall file a Notice of Appearance notifying the Clerk of the Panel of the name, address and email address of the attorney designated to file and receive service of all pleadings. Each party shall designate only one attorney. Any party not represented by counsel shall be served by mailing such pleadings to the party's last known address. Except in extraordinary circumstances, the Panel will not grant requests for an extension of time to file the Notice of Appearance.

(d) Liaison Counsel. If the transferee district court appoints liaison counsel, this Rule shall be satisfied by serving each party in each affected action and all liaison counsel. Liaison counsel shall receive copies of all Panel orders concerning their particular litigation and shall be responsible for distribution to the parties for whom he or she serves as liaison counsel.

(Former Rule 5.2 redesignated and amended Sept. 8, 2010, eff. Oct. 4, 2010; technical revisions eff. July 6, 2011.)

Rule 5.1.   Corporate Disclosure Statement

(a) Requirements. A nongovernmental corporate party must file a disclosure statement that: (1) identifies any parent corporation and any publicly held corporation owning 10% or more of its stock; or (2) states that there is no such corporation.

(b) Deadline. A party shall file the corporate disclosure statement within 14 days after issuance of a notice of the filing of a motion to transfer or remand, an order to show cause, or a motion to vacate a conditional transfer order or a conditional remand order.

(c) Updating. Each party must update its corporate disclosure statement to reflect any change in the information therein (i) until the matter before the Panel is decided, and (ii) within 14 days after issuance of a notice of the filing of any subsequent motion to transfer or remand, order to show cause, or motion to vacate a conditional transfer order or a conditional remand order in that docket.

(Added May 3, 1993, eff. July 1, 1993; amended Sept. 1, 1998, eff. Nov. 2, 1998; Apr. 2, 2001, eff. Apr. 2, 2001; former Rule 5.3 redesignated and amended Sept. 8, 2010, eff. Oct. 4, 2010; amended July 6, 2011, eff. July 6, 2011.)

Rule 6.1.   Motion Practice

(a) Application. This Rule governs all motions requesting Panel action generally. More specific provisions may apply to motions to transfer (Rule 6.2), miscellaneous motions (Rule 6.3), conditional transfer orders (Rule 7.1), show cause orders (Rule 8.1), conditional remand orders (Rule 10.2) and motions to remand (Rule 10.3).

---

*   [So in original. Ed.]

(b)   Form of Motions. All motions shall briefly describe the action or relief sought and shall include:

(i)   a brief which concisely states the background of the litigation and movant's factual and legal contentions;

(ii)   a numbered schedule providing

(A)   the complete name of each action involved, listing the full name of each party included as such on the district court's docket sheet, not shortened by the use of references such as "et al." or "etc.";

(B)   the district court and division where each action is pending;

(C)   the civil action number of each action; and

(D)   the name of the judge assigned each action, if known;

(iii)   a proof of service providing

(A)   a service list listing the full name of each party included on the district court's docket sheet and the complaint, including opt-in plaintiffs not listed on the docket sheet; and

(B)   in actions where there are 25 or more plaintiffs listed on the docket sheet, list the first named plaintiff with the reference "et al." if all the plaintiffs are represented by the same attorney(s);

(iv)   a copy of all complaints and docket sheets for all actions listed on the Schedule; and

(v)   exhibits, if any, identified by number or letter and a descriptive title.

(c)   Responses and Joinders. Any other party may file a response within 21 days after filing of a motion. Failure to respond to a motion shall be treated as that party's acquiescence to it. A joinder in a motion shall not add any action to that motion.

(d)   Replies. The movant may file a reply within 7 days after the lapse of the time period for filing a response. Where a movant is replying to more than one response in opposition, the movant may file a consolidated reply with a limit of 20 pages.

(e)   Alteration of Time Periods. The Clerk of the Panel has the discretion to shorten or enlarge the time periods set forth in this Rule as necessary.

(f)   Notification of Developments. Counsel shall promptly notify the Clerk of the Panel of any development that would partially or completely moot any Panel matter.

(Former Rule 7.2 redesignated in part and amended Sept. 8, 2010, eff. Oct. 4, 2010.)

Rule 6.2.   Motions to Transfer for Coordinated or Consolidated Pretrial Proceedings

(a)   Initiation of Transfer. A party to an action may initiate proceedings to transfer under Section 1407 by filing a motion in accordance with these Rules. A copy of the motion shall be filed in each district court where the motion affects a pending action.

(b)   Notice of Filing of Motion to Transfer. Upon receipt of a motion, the Clerk of the Panel shall issue a "Notice of Filing of Motion to Transfer" to the service list recipients. The Notice shall contain the following: the filing date of the motion, caption, MDL docket number, briefing schedule and pertinent Panel policies. After a motion is filed, the Clerk of the Panel shall consider any other pleading to be a response unless the pleading adds an action. The Clerk of the Panel may designate such a pleading as a motion, and distribute a briefing schedule applicable to all or some of the parties, as appropriate.

(c)   Notice of Appearance. Within 14 days of issuance of a "Notice of the Filing of a Motion to Transfer," each party or designated attorney shall file a Notice of Appearance in accordance with Rule 4.1(c).

(d) Notice of Potential Tag-along Actions. Any party or counsel in a new group of actions under consideration for transfer under Section 1407 shall promptly notify the Clerk of the Panel of any potential tag-along actions in which that party is also named or in which that counsel appears.

(e) Interested Party Responses. Any party or counsel in one or more potential tag-along actions as well as amicus curiae may file a response to a pending motion to transfer. Such a pleading shall be deemed an Interested Party Response.

(f) Amendment to a Motion. Before amending a motion to transfer, a party shall first contact the Clerk of the Panel to ascertain whether such amendment is feasible and permissible considering the Panel's hearing schedule. Any such amendment shall be entitled "Amendment to Motion for Transfer," and shall clearly and specifically identify and describe the nature of the amendment.

(i) Where the amended motion includes new civil actions, the amending party shall file a "Schedule of Additional Actions" and a revised Proof of Service.

(ii) The Proof of Service shall state (A) that all new counsel have been served with a copy of the amendment and all previously-filed motion papers, and (B) that all counsel previously served with the original motion have been served with a copy of the amendment.

(iii) The Clerk of the Panel may designate the amendment with a different denomination (*e.g.*, a notice of potential tag-along action(s)) and treatment.

(h)* Oral Argument. The Panel shall schedule oral arguments as needed and as set forth in Rule 11.1.

(Added May 3, 1993, eff. July 1, 1993; amended Sept. 1, 1998, eff. Nov. 2, 1998; Apr. 2, 2001, eff. Apr. 2, 2001; former Rule 7.2 redesignated in part and amended Sept. 8, 2010, eff. Oct. 4, 2010; technical revisions eff. July 6, 2011.)

Rule 6.3. Motions for Miscellaneous Relief

(a) Definition. Motions for miscellaneous relief include, but are not limited to, requests for extensions of time, exemption from ECF requirements, page limit extensions, or expedited consideration of any motion.

(b) Panel Action. The Panel, through the Clerk, may act upon any motion for miscellaneous relief, at any time, without waiting for a response. A motion for extension of time to file a pleading or perform an act under these Rules must state specifically the revised date sought and must be filed before the deadline for filing the pleading or performing the act. Any party aggrieved by the Clerk of the Panel's action may file objections for consideration. Absent exceptional circumstances, the Panel will not grant any extensions of time to file a notice of opposition to either a conditional transfer order or a conditional remand order.

(Former Rule 6.2 redesignated and amended Sept. 8, 2010, eff. Oct. 4, 2010.)

Rule 7.1. Conditional Transfer Orders (CTO) for Tag-Along Actions

(a) Notice of Potential Tag-along Actions. Any party or counsel in actions previously transferred under Section 1407 shall promptly notify the Clerk of the Panel of any potential tag-along actions in which that party is also named or in which that counsel appears. The Panel has several options: (i) filing a CTO under Rule 7.1, (ii) filing a show cause order under Rule 8.1, or (iii) declining to act (Rule 7.1(b)(i)).

(b) Initiation of CTO. Upon learning of the pendency of a potential tag-along action, the Clerk of the Panel may enter a conditional order transferring that action to the previously designated transferee district court for the reasons expressed in the Panel's previous opinions and orders. The

---

*   [So in original. No (g) promulgated. Ed.]

Clerk of the Panel shall serve this order on each party to the litigation but shall not send the order to the clerk of the transferee district court until 7 days after its entry.

(i)* If the Clerk of the Panel determines that a potential tag-along action is not appropriate for inclusion in an MDL proceeding and does not enter a CTO, an involved party may move for its transfer pursuant to Rule 6.1.

(c) **Notice of Opposition to CTO.** Any party opposing the transfer shall file a notice of opposition with the Clerk of the Panel within the 7-day period. In such event, the Clerk of the Panel shall not transmit the transfer order to the clerk of the transferee district court, but shall notify the parties of the briefing schedule.

(d) **Failure to Respond.** Failure to respond to a CTO shall be treated as that party's acquiescence to it.

(e) **Notice of Appearance.** Within 14 days after the issuance of a "Notice of Filed Opposition" to a CTO, each opposing party or designated attorney shall file a Notice of Appearance in accordance with Rule 4.1(c).

(f) **Motion to Vacate CTO.** Within 14 days of the filing of its notice of opposition, the party opposing transfer shall file a motion to vacate the CTO and brief in support thereof. The Clerk of the Panel shall set the motion for the next appropriate hearing session. Failure to file and serve a motion and brief shall be treated as withdrawal of the opposition and the Clerk of the Panel shall forthwith transmit the order to the clerk of the transferee district court.

(g) **Notification of Developments.** Parties to an action subject to a CTO shall notify the Clerk of the Panel if that action is no longer pending in its transferor district court.

(h) **Effective Date of CTO.** CTOs are effective when filed with the clerk of the transferee district court.

(Added May 3, 1993, eff. July 1, 1993; amended Sept. 1, 1998, eff. Nov. 2, 1998; Apr. 2, 2001, eff. Apr. 2, 2001; former Rule 7.4 redesignated and amended Sept. 8, 2010, eff. Oct. 4, 2010; technical revisions eff. July 6, 2011.)

Rule 7.2. Miscellaneous Provisions Concerning Tag-Along Actions

(a) **Potential Tag-alongs in Transferee Court.** Potential tag-along actions filed in the transferee district do not require Panel action. A party should request assignment of such actions to the Section 1407 transferee judge in accordance with applicable local rules.

(b) **Failure to Serve.** Failure to serve one or more of the defendants in a potential tag-along action with the complaint and summons as required by Rule 4 of the Federal Rules of Civil Procedure does not preclude transfer of such action under Section 1407. Such failure, however, may constitute grounds for denying the proposed transfer where prejudice can be shown. The failure of the Clerk of the Panel to serve a CTO on all plaintiffs or defendants or their counsel may constitute grounds for the Clerk to reinstate the CTO or for the aggrieved party to seek § 1407(c) remand.

(Added May 3, 1993, eff. July 1, 1993; amended Sept. 1, 1998, eff. Nov. 2, 1998; Apr. 2, 2001, eff. Apr. 2, 2001; Nov. 23, 2009, eff. Dec. 1, 2009; former Rule 7.5 redesignated and amended Sept. 8, 2010, eff. Oct. 4, 2010; amended July 6, 2011, eff. July 6, 2011.)

Rule 8.1. Show Cause Orders

(a) **Entry of Show Cause Order.** When transfer of multidistrict litigation is being considered on the initiative of the Panel pursuant to 28 U.S.C. § 1407(c)(i), the Clerk of the Panel may enter an order directing the parties to show cause why a certain civil action or actions should not be transferred for coordinated or consolidated pretrial proceedings. Any party shall also promptly notify the Clerk of

---

* [So in original. No (ii) promulgated. Ed.]

the Panel whenever they learn of any other federal district court actions which are similar to those which the show cause order encompasses.

(b) Notice of Appearance. Within 14 days of the issuance of an order to show cause, each party or designated attorney shall file a Notice of Appearance in accordance with Rule 4.1(c).

(c) Responses. Unless otherwise provided by order, any party may file a response within 21 days of the filing of the show cause order. Failure to respond to a show cause order shall be treated as that party's acquiescence to the Panel action.

(d) Replies. Within 7 days after the lapse of the time period for filing a response, any party may file a reply.

(e) Notification of Developments. Counsel shall promptly notify the Clerk of the Panel of any development that would partially or completely moot any matter subject to a show cause order.

(Former Rule 7.3 redesignated and amended Sept. 8, 2010, eff. Oct. 4, 2010.)

Rule 9.1. Transfer of Files; Notification Requirements

(a) Notice to Transferee Court Clerk. The Clerk of the Panel, via a notice of electronic filing, will notify the clerk of the transferee district whenever a Panel transfer order should be filed in the transferee district court. Upon receipt of an electronically certified copy of a Panel transfer order from the clerk of the transferee district, the clerk of the transferor district shall transmit the record of each transferred action to the transferee district and then, unless Rule 9.1(b) applies, close the transferred action in the transferor district.

(b) Retention of Claims. If the transfer order provides for the separation and simultaneous remand of any claim, cross-claim, counterclaim, or third-party claim, the clerk of the transferor district shall retain jurisdiction over any such claim and shall not close the action.

(c) Notice to Clerk of Panel. The clerk of the transferee district shall promptly provide the Clerk of the Panel with the civil action numbers assigned to all transferred actions and the identity of liaison counsel, if or when designated. The clerk of the transferee district shall also promptly notify the Clerk of the Panel of any dispositive ruling that terminates a transferred action.

(Former Rule 1.6 redesignated in part and amended Sept. 8, 2010, eff. Oct. 4, 2010.)

Rule 10.1. Termination and Remand

(a) Termination. Where the transferee district court terminates an action by valid order, including but not limited to summary judgment, judgment of dismissal and judgment upon stipulation, the transferee district court clerk shall transmit a copy of that order to the Clerk of the Panel. The terminated action shall not be remanded to the transferor court and the transferee court shall retain the original files and records unless the transferee judge or the Panel directs otherwise.

(b) Initiation of Remand. Typically, the transferee judge recommends remand of an action, or a part of it, to the transferor court at any time by filing a suggestion of remand with the Panel. However, the Panel may remand an action or any separable claim, cross-claim, counterclaim or third-party claim within it, upon

    (i) the transferee court's suggestion of remand,

    (ii) the Panel's own initiative by entry of an order to show cause, a conditional remand order or other appropriate order, or

    (iii) motion of any party.

(Former Rule 7.6 redesignated in part and amended Sept. 8, 2010, eff. Oct. 4, 2010.)

Rule 10.2. Conditional Remand Orders (CRO)

(a) Entering a CRO. Upon the suggestion of the transferee judge or the Panel's own initiative, the Clerk of the Panel shall enter a conditional order remanding the action or actions to the transferor district court. The Clerk of the Panel shall serve this order on each party to the litigation but shall not send the order to the clerk of the transferee district court for 7 days from the entry thereof.

(i)* The Panel may, on its own initiative, also enter an order that the parties show cause why a matter should not be remanded. Rule 8.1 applies to responses and replies with respect to such a show cause order.

(b) Notice of Opposition. Any party opposing the CRO shall file a notice of opposition with the Clerk of the Panel within the 7-day period. In such event, the Clerk of the Panel shall not transmit the remand order to the clerk of the transferee district court and shall notify the parties of the briefing schedule.

(c) Failure to Respond. Failure to respond to a CRO shall be treated as that party's acquiescence to it.

(d) Notice of Appearance. Within 14 days after the issuance of a "Notice of Filed Opposition" to a CRO, each opposing party or designated attorney shall file a Notice of Appearance in accordance with Rule 4.1(c).

(e) Motion to Vacate CRO. Within 14 days of the filing of its notice of opposition, the party opposing remand shall file a motion to vacate the CRO and brief in support thereof. The Clerk of the Panel shall set the motion for the next appropriate Panel hearing session. Failure to file and serve a motion and brief shall be treated as a withdrawal of the opposition and the Clerk of the Panel shall forthwith transmit the order to the clerk of the transferee district court.

(f) Effective Date of CRO. CROs are not effective until filed with the clerk of the transferee district court.

(Former Rule 7.6 redesignated in part and amended Sept. 8, 2010, eff. Oct. 4, 2010; technical revisions eff. July 6, 2011.)

Rule 10.3. Motion to Remand

(a) Requirements of the Motion. If the Clerk of the Panel does not enter a CRO, a party may file a motion to remand to the transferor court pursuant to these Rules. Because the Panel is reluctant to order a remand absent the suggestion of the transferee judge, the motion must include:

(i) An affidavit reciting whether the movant has requested a suggestion of remand and the judge's response, whether the parties have completed common discovery and other pretrial proceedings, and whether the parties have complied with all transferee court orders.

(ii) A copy of the transferee district court's final pretrial order, if entered.

(b) Filing Copy of Motion. Counsel shall file a copy of the motion to remand in the affected transferee district court.

(c) Notice of Appearance. Within 14 days of the issuance of a "Notice of Filing" of a motion to remand, each party or designated attorney shall file a Notice of Appearance in accordance with Rule 4.1(c).

(Former Rule 7.6 redesignated in part and amended Sept. 8, 2010, eff. Oct. 4, 2010; technical revisions eff. July 6, 2011.)

---

* [So in original. No (ii) promulgated. Ed.]

Rule 10.4. Transfer of Files on Remand

(a) Designating the Record. Upon receipt of an order to remand from the Clerk of the Panel, the parties shall furnish forthwith to the transferee district clerk a stipulation or designation of the contents of the record or part thereof to be remanded.

(b) Transfer of Files. Upon receipt of an order to remand from the Clerk of the Panel, the transferee district shall transmit to the clerk of the transferor district the following concerning each remanded action:

(i) a copy of the individual docket sheet for each action remanded;

(ii) a copy of the master docket sheet, if applicable;

(iii) the entire file for each action remanded, as originally received from the transferor district and augmented as set out in this Rule;

(iv) a copy of the final pretrial order, if applicable; and

(v) a "record on remand" as designated by the parties in accordance with 10.4(a).

(Former Rule 1.6 redesignated in part and amended Sept. 8, 2010, eff. Oct. 4, 2010.)

Rule 11.1. Hearing Sessions and Oral Argument

(a) Schedule. The Panel shall schedule sessions for oral argument and consideration of other matters as desirable or necessary. The Chair shall determine the time, place and agenda for each hearing session. The Clerk of the Panel shall give appropriate notice to counsel for all parties. The Panel may continue its consideration of any scheduled matters.

(b) Oral Argument Statement. Any party affected by a motion may file a separate statement setting forth reasons why oral argument should, or need not, be heard. Such statements shall be captioned "Reasons Why Oral Argument Should [Need Not] Be Heard" and shall be limited to 2 pages.

(i)* The parties affected by a motion to transfer may agree to waive oral argument. The Panel will take this into consideration in determining the need for oral argument.

(c) Hearing Session. The Panel shall not consider transfer or remand of any action pending in a federal district court when any party timely opposes such transfer or remand without first holding a hearing session for the presentation of oral argument. The Panel may dispense with oral argument if it determines that:

(i) the dispositive issue(s) have been authoritatively decided; or

(ii) the facts and legal arguments are adequately presented and oral argument would not significantly aid the decisional process.

Unless otherwise ordered, the Panel shall consider all other matters, such as a motion for reconsideration, upon the basis of the pleadings.

(d) Notification of Oral Argument. The Panel shall promptly notify counsel of those matters in which oral argument is scheduled, as well as those matters that the Panel will consider on the pleadings. The Clerk of the Panel shall require counsel to file and serve notice of their intent to either make or waive oral argument. Failure to do so shall be deemed a waiver of oral argument. If counsel does not attend oral argument, the matter shall not be rescheduled and that party's position shall be treated as submitted for decision on the basis of the pleadings filed.

(i) Absent Panel approval and for good cause shown, only those parties to actions who have filed a motion or written response to a motion or order shall be permitted to present oral argument.

---

*   [So in original. No (ii) promulgated. Ed.]

(ii) The Panel will not receive oral testimony except upon notice, motion and an order expressly providing for it.

(e) Duty to Confer. Counsel in an action set for oral argument shall confer separately prior to that argument for the purpose of organizing their arguments and selecting representatives to present all views without duplication. Oral argument is a means for counsel to emphasize the key points of their arguments, and to update the Panel on any events since the conclusion of briefing.

(f) Time Limit for Oral Argument. Barring exceptional circumstances, the Panel shall allot a maximum of 20 minutes for oral argument in each matter. The time shall be divided among those with varying viewpoints. Counsel for the moving party or parties shall generally be heard first.

(Former Rule 16.1 redesignated and amended Sept. 8, 2010, eff. Oct. 4, 2010.)

Rules 12–15. [Reserved]

II. RULES FOR MULTICIRCUIT PETITIONS FOR REVIEW UNDER 28 U.S.C. § 2112(a)(3)

Rule 25.1. Definitions

The Panel promulgates these Rules pursuant to its authority under 28 U.S.C. § 2112(a)(3) to provide a means for the random selection of one circuit court of appeals to hear consolidated petitions for review of agency decisions.

An "Agency" means an agency, board, commission or officer of the United States government, that has received two or more petitions for review in a circuit court of appeals to enjoin, set aside, suspend, modify or otherwise review or enforce an action.

(Added May 3, 1993, eff. July 1, 1993; amended Sept. 1, 1998, eff. Nov. 2, 1998; Apr. 2, 2001, eff. Apr. 2, 2001; Sept. 8, 2010, eff. Oct. 4, 2010.)

Rule 25.2. Filing of Notices

(a) Submitting Notice. An affected agency shall submit a notice of multicircuit petitions for review pursuant to 28 U.S.C. § 2112(a)(3) to the Clerk of the Panel by electronic means in the manner these Rules require and in accordance with the Panel's Administrative Policies and Procedures for Electronic Case Filing, except that the portion of Rule 3.2(d) requiring a courtesy copy is suspended in its entirety.

(b) Accompaniments to Notices. All notices of multicircuit petitions for review shall include:

(i)   a copy of each involved petition for review as the petition for review is defined in 28 U.S.C. § 2112(a)(2);

(ii) a schedule giving

(A) the date of the relevant agency order;

(B) the case name of each petition for review involved;

(C) the circuit court of appeals in which each petition for review is pending;

(D) the appellate docket number of each petition for review;

(E) the date of filing by the court of appeals of each petition for review; and

(F) the date of receipt by the agency of each petition for review; and

(iii) proof of service (*see* Rule 25.3).

(c) Scope of Notice. All notices of multicircuit petitions for review shall embrace exclusively petitions for review filed in the courts of appeals within 10 days after issuance of an agency order and received by the affected agency from the petitioners within that 10-day period.

(d) Filing at the Panel. The Clerk of the Panel shall file the notice of multicircuit petitions for review and endorse thereon the date of filing.

(e) Filing With Each Circuit Clerk. The affected agency shall file copies of notices of multicircuit petitions for review with the clerk of each circuit court of appeals in which a petition for review is pending.

(Added May 3, 1993, eff. July 1, 1993; amended Sept. 1, 1998, eff. Nov. 2, 1998; Apr. 2, 2001, eff. Apr. 2, 2001; Sept. 8, 2010, eff. Oct. 4, 2010; technical revisions eff. July 6, 2011.)

Rule 25.3. Service of Notices

(a) Proof of Service. Notices of multicircuit petitions for review shall include proof of service on all other parties in the petitions for review included in the notice. Rule 25 of the Federal Rules of Appellate Procedure governs service and proof of service. The proof of service shall state the name, address and email address of each person served and shall indicate the party represented by each and the manner in which service was accomplished on each party. If a party is not represented by counsel, the proof of service shall indicate the name of the party and his or her last known address. The affected party shall submit proof of service for filing with the Clerk of the Panel and shall send copies thereof to each person included within the proof of service.

(b) Service on Clerk of Circuit. The proof of service pertaining to notices of multicircuit petitions for review shall certify the affected party has mailed or delivered copies of the notices to the clerk of each circuit court of appeals in which a petition for review is pending that is included in the notice. The Clerk shall file the notice with the circuit court.

(Added May 3, 1993, eff. July 1, 1993; amended Sept. 1, 1998, eff. Nov. 2, 1998; Apr. 2, 2001, eff. Apr. 2, 2001; Sept. 8, 2010, eff. Oct. 4, 2010.)

Rule 25.4. Form of Notices; Place of Filing

(a) Unless otherwise provided here, Rule 3.2 governs the form of a notice of multicircuit petitions for review. Each notice shall bear the heading Notice to the United States Judicial Panel on Multidistrict Litigation of Multicircuit Petitions for Review," followed by a brief caption identifying the involved agency, the relevant agency order, and the date of the order.

(b) Rule 3.2(b) and (c) govern the manner of filing a notice of multicircuit petitions for review.

(Added May 3, 1993, eff. July 1, 1993; amended Sept. 1, 1998, eff. Nov. 2, 1998; Apr. 2, 2001, eff. Apr. 2, 2001; Sept. 8, 2010, eff. Oct. 4, 2010.)

Rule 25.5. Random Selection

(a) Selection Process. Upon filing a notice of multicircuit petitions for review, the Clerk of the Panel shall randomly select a circuit court of appeals from a drum containing an entry for each circuit wherein a constituent petition for review is pending. Multiple petitions for review pending in a single circuit shall be allotted only a single entry in the drum. A designated deputy other than the random selector shall witness the random selection. Thereafter, an order on behalf of the Panel shall be issued, signed by the random selector and the witness,

> **(i)** consolidating the petitions for review in the court of appeals for the circuit that was randomly selected; and

> **(ii)** designating that circuit as the one in which the record is to be filed pursuant to Rules 16 and 17 of the Federal Rules of Appellate Procedure.

(b) Effective Date. A consolidation of petitions for review shall be effective when the Clerk of the Panel enters the consolidation order.

(Added May 3, 1993, eff. July 1, 1993; amended Sept. 1, 1998, eff. Nov. 2, 1998; Apr. 2, 2001, eff. Apr. 2, 2001; former Rule 17.1 redesignated and amended Sept. 8, 2010, eff. Oct. 4, 2010.)

Rule 25.6. Service of Panel Consolidation Order

(a) The Clerk of the Panel shall serve the Panel's consolidation order on the affected agency through the individual or individuals, as identified in Rule 25.2(a), who submitted the notice of multicircuit petitions for review on behalf of the agency.

(b) That individual or individuals, or anyone else designated by the agency, shall promptly serve the Panel's consolidation order on all other parties in all petitions for review included in the Panel's consolidation order, and shall promptly submit a proof of that service to the Clerk of the Panel. Rule 25.3 governs service.

(c) The Clerk of the Panel shall serve the Panel's consolidation order on the clerks of all circuit courts of appeals that were among the candidates for the Panel's random selection.

(Former Rule 25.5 redesignated and amended Sept. 8, 2010, eff. Oct. 4, 2010.)

III. CONVERSION TABLE—OCTOBER 2010

New to Old:

New Rule / Previous Rule		New Rule / Previous Rule	
1.1	1.1	9.1	1.6
2.1	1.2, 1.3, 1.4, 1.5	10.1	7.6
3.1	5.1	10.2	7.6
3.2	5.1.1, 5.1.2, 7.1	10.3	7.6
3.3	5.1.1, 5.1.2, 7.1	10.4	1.6
4.1	5.2	11.1	16.1
5.1	5.3	25.1	25.1
6.1	7.2	25.2	25.1, 25.2
6.2	7.2	25.3	25.3
6.3	6.2	25.4	25.1, 25.4
7.1	7.4	25.5	17.1
7.2	7.5	25.6	25.5
8.1	7.3		

Old to New:

Previous Rule / New Rule		Previous Rule / New Rule	
1.1	1.1	7.1	3.2, 3.3
1.2	2.1	7.2	6.1
1.3	2.1	7.3	8.1
1.4	2.1	7.4	7.1
1.5	2.1	7.5	7.2
1.6	10.4	7.6	10.1
5.1	3.1	16.1	11.1
5.1.1	3.2, 3.3	17.1	25.5
5.1.2	3.2, 3.3	25.1	25.1, 25.2, 25.4
5.1.3	-	25.2	25.2
5.2	4.1	25.3	25.3
5.3	5.1	25.4	25.4
6.2	6.3	25.5	25.6

ECF Policies

ELECTRONIC CASE FILING ADMINISTRATIVE POLICIES AND PROCEDURES*

1. DEFINITIONS.

1.1 "ELECTRONIC FILING SYSTEM" (ECF) refers to the United States Judicial Panel on Multidistrict Litigation's (the Panel's) automated system that receives and stores documents filed in electronic form. The program is part of the CM/ECF (Case Management/Electronic Case Files) software which was developed for the Federal Judiciary by the Administrative Office of the United States Courts.

1.2 "CLERK OF THE PANEL" means the official appointed by the Panel to act as Clerk of the Panel and shall include those deputized by the Clerk of the Panel to perform or assist in the performance of the duties of the Clerk of the Panel.

1.3 "FILING USER" is an individual who has a Panel-issued login and password to file documents electronically. In accordance with Rule 1.4 of the Rules of Procedure of the United States Judicial Panel on Multidistrict Litigation (the Panel Rules), every member in good standing of the Bar of any district court of the United States is entitled to practice before the Judicial Panel on Multidistrict Litigation.

1.4 "NOTICE OF ELECTRONIC FILING" (NEF) is a notice automatically generated by the Electronic Filing System at the time a document is filed with the system, setting forth the time of filing, the date the document is entered on the docket, the name of the party and attorney filing the document, the type of document, the text of the docket entry, the name of the party and/or attorney receiving the notice, and an electronic link (hyperlink) to the filed document, which allows recipients to retrieve the document automatically. A document shall not be considered filed for the purposes of the Panel's Rules until the filing party receives a system generated Notice of Electronic Filing with a hyperlink to the electronically filed document.

1.5 "PACER" (Public Access to Court Electronic Records) is an automated system that allows an individual to view, print and download Panel docket information over the Internet.

1.6 "PDF" (Portable Document Format). A document file created with a word processor, or a paper document which has been scanned, must be converted to portable document format to be filed electronically with the Panel. Converted files contain the extension ".pdf".

1.7 "TECHNICAL FAILURE" is defined as a failure of Panel owned/leased hardware, software, and/or telecommunications facility which results in the inability of a Filing User to submit a filing electronically. Technical failure does not include malfunctioning of a Filing User's equipment.

2. SCOPE OF ELECTRONIC FILING.

(a) All multidistrict litigation matters (MDLs) brought before the Panel under 28 U.S.C. § 1407 shall be assigned to the Electronic Filing System. Effective October 1, 2010, all MDLs, proceedings, motions, memoranda of law and other pleadings or documents filed with the Panel in new and existing dockets must be filed using CM/ECF unless otherwise specified herein.

(b) The filing of all MDL papers shall be accomplished electronically under procedures outlined in the Panel's CM/ECF User Manual.

(c) A party proceeding *pro se* shall not file electronically, unless otherwise permitted by the Panel. *Pro se* filers shall file paper originals of all documents. The clerk's office will scan these original documents into the JPML's electronic system, unless otherwise sealed.

---

*   [Available at https://www.jpml.uscourts.gov/sites/jpml/files/JPML_CMECF_Admin_Procedures-5-20-10.pdf. Ed.]

3. ELIGIBILITY, REGISTRATION, PASSWORDS.

(a)   Any attorney admitted to the Bar of any United States district court is eligible to practice before the Panel. Unless otherwise exempt as set forth herein, to become a Filing User, an attorney must register as a Filing User by completing the prescribed registration form and submitting it to the Clerk of the Panel.

(b)   Registration as a Filing User constitutes consent to electronic service of all documents filed with or issued by the Panel in accordance with the Panel Rules.

(c)   By submitting the online registration form, the Filing Users certify that they have read and are familiar with the Panel Rules and these administrative policies and procedures governing electronic filing and the method of training in the System used prior to becoming a Filing User. Filing users must also have a PACER account. An individual may register more than one Internet email address. The clerk's office will email the login and password to the attorney.

(d)   Once the registration is processed by the clerk, the Filing User shall protect the security of the User password and immediately notify the clerk if the Filing User learns that the password has been compromised. Filing Users may be subject to sanctions for failure to comply with this provision. After registering, attorneys may change their passwords. If an attorney comes to believe that the security of an existing password has been compromised and that a threat to the System exists, the attorney must change his or her password immediately.

(e)   Exemptions from mandatory electronic filing may be granted upon submission of a written request to the clerk. The written request shall include a supporting affidavit showing a substantial undue hardship. Final authority to grant such request is vested in the Clerk of the Panel or his/her designee.

(f)(1)   Each attorney is responsible for keeping his/her contact information up to date. If an attorney is leaving a law firm and is the attorney of record on an existing case and representation in the case will remain with the law firm, withdrawal and substitution of counsel must be made prior to the attorney's termination in the law firm, for the following reason:

The attorney leaving the firm has an email address with the law firm he or she is leaving on record with the Panel. This email address may be disabled by the law firm as soon as the attorney terminates his/her employment. The electronic notices in CM/ECF will continue to go to the terminated attorney's email address at the former firm. If the email address is disabled at the law firm, the attorney will not receive the electronic notice. If a withdrawal/substitution of counsel has not been filed prior to the attorney leaving the firm, the law firm should not disable the email account of the attorney leaving the firm until another attorney in the firm enters his/her appearance. The law firm should designate someone in the firm to check this email account for CM/ECF notices until substitution of counsel has been filed with the Panel.

(2)   If the attorney leaving the firm is taking active cases from the firm, the attorney needs to change his/her email address as soon as possible, otherwise the attorney will not receive electronic notices from CM/ECF. The email will continue to be sent to the former law firm's email address still on record. Procedures for changing an email address may be found in the Panel's CM/ECF User Manual.

4. ELECTRONIC FILING AND SERVICE OF DOCUMENTS.

(a)   Electronic transmission of a document to the Electronic Filing System in accordance with these procedures, together with the transmission of a (System) Notice of Electronic Filing from the Panel with a hyperlink to the electronically filed document, constitutes filing of the document for all purposes of the Panel Rules of Procedure.

(b)   Emailing a document to the clerk's office does not constitute filing the document. A document shall not be considered filed until the System generates a Notice of Electronic Filing (NEF) with a hyperlink to the electronically filed document.

(c)   Before filing a scanned document with the court, a Filing User must verify its legibility.

(d)   When a document has been filed electronically, the official record of that document is the electronic recording as stored by the Panel and the filing party is bound by the document as filed. A document filed electronically is deemed filed on the date and time stated on the Notice of Electronic Filing (NEF) from the Panel.

(e)   Filing a document electronically does not alter the filing deadline for that document. Filing must be completed before midnight, **EASTERN TIME**, in order to be considered timely filed that day. However, if time of day is of the essence, the Clerk of the Panel may order a document filed by a certain time.

(f)   Upon the filing of a document, a docket entry will be created using the information provided by the Filing User. The clerk will, where necessary and appropriate, modify the docket entry description to comply with quality control standards. In the event a Filing User electronically files a document in the wrong MDL or associated civil action, or the incorrect PDF document is attached, the Clerk of the Panel, or his/her designee, shall be authorized to strike the document from the record. A notice of the action striking a document from the record shall be served on all parties in the case.

(g)   By participating in the electronic filing process, the parties consent to the electronic service of all documents, and shall make available electronic mail addresses for service. Upon the filing of a document by a Filing User, a Notice of Electronic Filing (NEF), with a hyperlink to the electronic document and an email message will be automatically generated by the electronic filing system, and sent via electronic mail to the email addresses of all parties who have registered in the MDL. In addition to receiving email notifications of filing activity, the Filing User is strongly encouraged to sign on to the electronic filing system at regular intervals to check the docket in his/her MDL and/or civil action.

(h)   If the filing of an electronically submitted document requires leave of the Panel, such as a request to file out-of-time, the attorney shall attach the proposed document as an attachment to the motion requesting leave to file. If the Clerk of the Panel grants the motion, the document will be electronically filed without further action by the Filing User.

(i)   A certificate of service must be included with all documents filed electronically. Such certificate shall indicate that service was accomplished pursuant to the Panel's electronic filing procedures. Service by electronic mail shall constitute service pursuant to Panel Rule 5.2.

A party who is not a registered CM/ECF participant with any United States federal court is entitled to a paper copy of any electronically filed pleading, document, or order pursuant to Panel Rule 5.1.1(b). The filing party must therefore provide the non-registered attorney or party, including a terminated party or attorney, if appropriate, with the pleading, document, or order pursuant to Panel Rule 5.2. Under the Rule, they can be served with a paper copy of the electronically filed document, or they can consent in writing to service by any other method, including other forms of electronic service such as fax or direct email.

The following is a suggested certificate of service for electronic filing:

CERTIFICATE OF SERVICE

On [Date], I electronically filed this document through the CM/ECF system, which will send a notice of electronic filing to: [Attorney Name (attach list if necessary)]; and I [mailed] [hand delivered] [faxed] this document and the notice of electronic filing to: [Attorney/Party Name], [Address], [Parties Represented], [Civil Action(s)] (attach list if necessary).

                                  /s/ [typed name of attorney]
                                    Attorney's name
                                    Law Firm Name (if applicable)
                                    Address

Phone Number
Fax Number
Attorney's Email address
Attorney for:

5. ENTRY OF PANEL DOCUMENTS.

(a)   A document entered or issued by the Panel will be filed in accordance with these procedures and such filing shall constitute entry on the docket kept by the Clerk.

(b)   All signed orders will be electronically filed or entered. An order containing the electronic signature of a Panel Judge or the Clerk of the Panel shall have the same force and effect as if the Panel Judge or Clerk of the Panel had affixed a signature to a paper copy of the order and the order had been entered on the docket in a conventional manner.

(c)   Orders may also be issued as "text-only" entries on the docket, without an attached document. Such orders are official and binding.

6. NOTICE OF PANEL ORDERS AND NOTICES.

Immediately upon the entry of an order or notice by the Panel, the clerk will transmit to Filing Users in affected cases in the MDL, in electronic form, a Notice of Electronic Filing (NEF), with a hyperlink to the electronic document. Electronic transmission of the NEF, along with a hyperlink to the electronic document, constitutes the notice required by Panel Rule 5.2. The clerk must give notice in paper form to a pro se party or an attorney who is not a Filing User to the extent notice is required.

7. ATTACHMENTS AND EXHIBITS.

Documents referenced as exhibits or attachments shall be filed in accordance with these administrative policies and procedures and the Panel's CM/ECF User Manual, unless otherwise ordered by the Panel. A Filing User shall submit as exhibits or attachments only those excerpts of the referenced documents that are directly germane to the matter under consideration by the Panel. Excerpted material must be clearly and prominently identified as such. Filing Users who file excerpts of documents as exhibits or attachments under these procedures do so without prejudice to their right to file timely additional excerpts or the complete document. Responding parties may timely file additional excerpts or the complete document that they believe are directly germane. The Panel may require parties to file additional excerpts or the complete document.

8. SEALED DOCUMENTS.

To ensure proper storage of a document, a document subject to a sealing order must be filed with the Panel on paper in a sealed envelope marked "sealed", citing thereon the MDL docket number and title and the associated case caption and case number; or by attaching thereto a paper copy of the Panel's order sealing the document or a copy of the NEF citing the entry of the court's order sealing the document. The clerk may require the document to be accompanied by a disk or CD-ROM containing the document in .pdf format. Only a motion to file a document under seal may be filed electronically, unless prohibited by law. The order of the Panel authorizing the filing of documents under seal may be filed electronically, unless prohibited by law or otherwise directed by the Panel. If a document is filed under seal pursuant to the E-Government Act of 2002, the filing party is nevertheless required to file a redacted copy for the public record along with the unredacted sealed document.

9. SPECIAL FILING REQUIREMENTS AND EXCEPTIONS.

9.1   Special Filing Requirements

The documents listed below shall be presented for filing on paper. The clerk may require the document be accompanied by a disk or CD-ROM containing the document in .pdf format:

Sealed
MDL dockets involving Qui Tam Cases (under seal)

9.2   Exceptions

All documents shall be filed electronically unless otherwise ordered by the Panel or specifically exempt herein.

10. **RETENTION REQUIREMENTS.**

(a)   A document that is electronically filed and requires an original signature other than that of the Filing User must be maintained in paper form by counsel and/or the firm representing the party on whose behalf the document was filed until one year after all periods for appeals expire. On request of the Panel, said counsel must provide the original document for review.

(b)   The clerk's office may choose to discard certain documents brought to the clerk's office for filing in paper form after those documents are scanned and uploaded to the System (to include *pro se* filings). Therefore, counsel and *pro se* filers shall provide the Panel with a copy of the original documents with intrinsic value for scanning and maintain the original signature in accordance with 10(a).

11. **SIGNATURES.**

(a)   The user login and password required to submit documents to the Electronic Filing System serve as the Filing User signature on all electronic documents filed with the court. They serve as a signature for purposes of the Panel Rules and any other purpose for which a signature is required in connection with proceedings before the Panel.

(b)   Each document filed electronically must indicate in the caption that it has been electronically filed. An electronically filed document must include a signature block in compliance with Panel Rule 7.1(e), and must set forth the name, address, telephone number, fax number, and email address. In addition, the name of the Filing User under whose login and password the document is submitted must be preceded by an "/s/" and typed in the space where the signature would otherwise appear. No Filing User or other person may knowingly permit or cause to permit a Filing User password to be used by anyone other than an authorized agent of the Filing User.

(c)   A document requiring signatures of more than one party must be filed either by:

(1)   electronically filing a scanned document containing all necessary signatures; or

(2)   representing the consent of the other parties on the document; or

(3)   identifying on the document the party whose signature is required and by the submission of a notice of endorsement by the other parties no later than three (3) business days after filing; or

(4)   any other manner approved by the Panel.

(d)   A non-filing signatory or party who disputes the authenticity of an electronically filed document with a non-attorney signature, or the authenticity of the signature on that document; or the authenticity of an electronically filed document containing multiple signatures or the authenticity of the signature themselves, must file an objection to the document within fourteen (14) days of service of the document.

(e)   Any party challenging the authenticity of an electronically filed document or the attorney's signature on that document must file an objection to the document within fourteen (14) days of service of the document.

(f)   If a party wishes to challenge the authenticity of an electronically filed document or signature after the fourteen (14) day period, the party shall file a motion to seek a ruling from the Panel.

12. SERVICE OF DOCUMENTS BY ELECTRONIC MEANS.

12.1 Service

12.1.1 Filing User

Upon the electronic filing of a pleading or other document, the Panel's Electronic Case Filing System will automatically generate and send a Notice of Electronic Filing (NEF) to all Filing Users associated with that MDL and/or associated cases, along with a hyperlink to the electronic document. Transmission of the Notice of Electronic Filing with a hyperlink to the electronic document constitutes service of the filed document.

The NEF must include the time of filing, the date the document was entered on the docket, the name of the party and attorney filing the document, the type of document, the text of the docket entry, and an electronic link (hyperlink) to the filed document, allowing anyone receiving the notice by email to retrieve the document automatically. If the Filing User becomes aware that the NEF was not transmitted successfully to a party, or that the notice is deficient, *i.e.,* the electronic link to the document is defective, the filer shall serve the electronically filed document by email, hand, facsimile, or by first-class mail postage prepaid immediately upon notification of the NEF deficiency.

12.1.2 Individual who is not a Filing User

A non-registered participant is entitled to receive a paper copy of any electronically filed document from the party making such filing. Service of such paper copy must be made according to the Panel Rules.

13. TECHNICAL FAILURES.

(a)   If the site is unable to accept filings continuously or intermittently for more than one (1) hour occurring after 12:00 noon Eastern Time that day, the Clerk of the Panel shall deem the Panel's Electronic Case Filing web site to be subject to a technical failure.

(b)   If a Filing User experiences a technical failure as defined herein, the Filing User may submit the document to the Clerk of the Panel, provided that the document is accompanied by a certification, signed by the Filing User, that the Filing User has attempted to file the document electronically at least twice, with those unsuccessful attempts occurring at least one (1) hour apart after 12:00 noon Eastern Time that day. The Clerk may require the document to be accompanied by a disk or CD-ROM which contains the document in .pdf format.

(c)   The initial point of contact for a Filing User experiencing technical difficulty filing a document electronically will be the Panel's CM/ECF Help Desk at the numbers listed on the Panel's web site and in the CM/ECF User Manual.

(d)   A Filing User who suffers prejudice as a result of a technical failure as defined herein or a Filing User who cannot file a time-sensitive document electronically due to unforeseen technical difficulties, such as the malfunctioning of a Filing User's equipment, may seek relief from the Clerk of the Panel.

14. PUBLIC ACCESS.

14.1 (a)   A person may receive information from the Electronic Filing System at the Panel's Internet site by obtaining a PACER login and password. A person who has PACER access may retrieve docket sheets and documents (unless otherwise sealed or restricted) in MDL dockets and associated civil cases. Any case or document under seal shall not be available electronically or through any other means.

(b)   If a case or document has been restricted, a PACER user may retrieve the docket sheet over the Internet, but only a Filing User who is counsel of record may retrieve restricted documents electronically. However, a restricted case or document will be available for viewing by the public at the clerk's office.

(c)　Electronic access to electronic docket sheets and all documents filed in the System, unless sealed, is available to the public for viewing at no charge during regular business hours at the clerk's office. A copy fee for an electronic reproduction is required in accordance with 28 U.S.C. § 1932.

(d)　Conventional copies and certified copies of electronically filed documents may be purchased at the clerk's office. The fee for copying and certifying will be in accordance with 28 U.S.C. § 1932.

14.2 Sensitive Information

Since the public may access certain case information over the Internet through the Panel's Electronic Filing System, sensitive information should not be included in any document filed with the court unless such inclusion is necessary and relevant. In accordance with these Administrative Policies and Procedures, if sensitive information must be included, certain personal and identifying information such as Social Security numbers, financial account numbers, dates of birth and names of minor children shall be redacted from the pleading, whether it is filed electronically or on paper.

The Panel recognizes that parties may need to include in the record a document containing information such as driver's license number; medical records, treatment and diagnosis; employment history; individual financial information; and proprietary or trade secret information.

To avoid unnecessary disclosure of private, personal or financial information, a party may:

(a)　**RESTRICTED MDL DOCKETS OR DOCUMENTS.**

File a "Motion to Seal" or "Motion to Seal Document". The motion must state the reason and show good cause for restricting remote access to the case. If the motion is granted, remote access to documents will be limited to Filing Users who are counsel of record. However, the MDL docket sheet and/or documents will be available for viewing by the public at the clerk's office.

(b)　**EXHIBITS.**

File an exhibit containing private, personal or financial information as an attachment to a pleading entitled "Notice of Filing Restricted Exhibit". The notice and the attached exhibit shall be filed as a separate docket entry, rather than as an attachment to the pleading supported by the exhibit. Remote public access to the notice and exhibit will be limited to Filing Users who are counsel of record. The notice and exhibit will, however, be available for viewing by the public at the clerk's office.

(c)　**DOCUMENTS UNDER SEAL.**

(1)　File a redacted copy of a pleading or exhibit containing private, personal or financial information, whether electronically or on paper, while concurrently filing an unredacted copy under seal. This document shall be retained by the Panel as part of the record.

OR

(2)　File a reference list under seal. The reference list shall contain the complete personal data identifier(s) and the redacted identifier(s) used in its (their) place in the filing. All references in the case to the redacted identifier(s) included in the reference list will be construed to refer to the corresponding complete identifier. The reference list must be filed under seal, and may be amended as of right. It shall be retained by the Panel as part of the record.

(d)　**MOTION TO SEAL.**

File a motion to seal the document or MDL associated case. The motion must state the reason and show good cause for sealing the document or MDL associated case. If the motion to seal is granted, the document or case under seal will not be available electronically or through any other means.

It is the sole responsibility of counsel and the parties to ensure that all documents filed with the Panel comply with these Administrative Policies and Procedures, regarding public access to electronic case files. The Clerk will not review any document for redaction.

Counsel are strongly urged to share this information with all clients so that an informed decision about the inclusion, redaction, and/or exclusion of certain materials may be made.

[Effective May 2010.]

RULES GOVERNING SECTION 2254 CASES IN THE UNITED STATES DISTRICT COURTS

Effective February 1, 1977
Amendments received through May 1, 2020

Rule

APPENDIX OF FORMS

Petition for Relief From a Conviction or Sentence By a Person in State Custody. (Petition Under 28 U.S.C. § 2254 for a Writ of Habeas Corpus).

ORDERS OF THE SUPREME COURT OF THE UNITED STATES ADOPTING AND AMENDING RULES GOVERNING SECTION 2254 PROCEEDINGS IN THE UNITED STATES DISTRICT COURTS

ORDER OF APRIL 26, 1976 [425 U.S. 1169]

1.   That the rules and forms governing proceedings in the United States District Courts under Section 2254 and Section 2255 of Title 28, United States Code, as approved by the Judicial Conference of the United States be, and they hereby are, prescribed pursuant to Section 2072 of Title 28, United States Code and Sections 3771 and 3772 of Title 18, United States Code.

2.   That the aforementioned rules and forms shall take effect August 1, 1976, and shall be applicable to all proceedings then pending except to the extent that in the opinion of the court their application in a particular proceeding would not be feasible or would work injustice.

3.   That THE CHIEF JUSTICE be, and he hereby is, authorized to transmit the aforementioned rules and forms governing Section 2254 and Section 2255 proceedings to the Congress in accordance with the provisions of Section 2072 of Title 28 and Sections 3771 and 3772 of Title 18, United States Code.

CONGRESSIONAL ACTION ON PROPOSED RULES AND FORMS GOVERNING PROCEEDING UNDER 28 U.S.C. §§ 2254 AND 2255

Pub.L. 94–349, § 2, July 8, 1976, 90 Stat. 822, provided: "That, notwithstanding the provisions of section 2072 of title 28 of the United States Code, the rules and forms governing section 2254 cases in the United States district courts and the rules and forms governing section 2255 proceedings in the United States district courts which are embraced by the order entered by the United States Supreme Court on April 26, 1976, and which were transmitted to the Congress on or about April 26, 1976, shall not take effect until thirty days after the adjournment sine die of the 94th Congress, or until and to the extent approved by Act of Congress, whichever is earlier."

Pub.L. 94–426, § 1, Sept. 28, 1976, 90 Stat. 1334, provided: "That the rules governing section 2254 cases in the United States district courts and the rules governing section 2255 proceedings for the United States Supreme Court, which were delayed by the Act entitled 'An Act to delay the effective date of certain proposed amendments to the Federal Rules of Criminal Procedure and certain other rules promulgated by the United States Supreme Court' (Public Law 94–349), are approved with the amendments set forth in section 2 of this Act and shall take effect as so amended, with respect to petitions under section 2254 and motions under section 2255 of title 28 of the United States Code filed on or after February 1, 1977."

ORDER OF APRIL 30, 1979 [441 U.S. 1003]

1.   That Rule 10 of the Rules Governing Proceedings in the United States District Courts on application under Section 2254 of Title 28, United States Code, be, and hereby is, amended to read as follows:

[See amendment made thereby under Rule 10, post.]

2.   That Rules 10 and 11 of the Rules Governing Proceedings in the United States District Courts on a motion under Section 2255 of Title 28, United States Code, be, and they hereby are, amended to read as follows:

[See amendments made hereby under Rules 10 and 11 set out following section 2255.]

3.   That the foregoing amendments to the Rules Governing Proceedings in the United States District Courts under Section 2254 and Section 2255 of Title 28, United States Code, shall take effect on August 1, 1979, and shall be applicable to all proceedings then pending except to the extent that in the opinion of the court their application in a particular proceeding would not be feasible or would work injustice.

4.   That THE CHIEF JUSTICE be, and he hereby is, authorized to transmit the aforementioned amendments to the Rules Governing Section 2254 and Section 2255 Proceedings to the Congress in accordance with the provisions of Section 2072 of Title 28, United States Code, and Sections 3771 and 3772 of Title 18, United States Code.

ORDER OF APRIL 28, 1982 [456 U.S. 1033]

1.   That the rules and forms governing proceedings in the United States district courts under Section 2254 and Section 2255 of Title 28, United States Code, be, and they hereby are, amended by including therein an amendment to Rule 2(c) of the rules for Section 2254 cases, an amendment to Rule 2(b) of the rules for Section 2255 proceedings, and amendments to the model forms for use in applications under Section 2254 and motions under Section 2255, as hereinafter set forth:

*[See amendments made thereby under respective rules
and forms post and following section 2255.]*

2.   That the aforementioned amendments shall take effect August 1, 1982, and shall be applicable to all proceedings thereafter commenced and, insofar as just and practicable, all proceedings then pending.

3.   That THE CHIEF JUSTICE be, and he hereby is, authorized to transmit the aforementioned amendments to the Congress in accordance with Section 2072 of Title 28 and Sections 3771 and 3772 of Title 18, United States Code.

ORDER OF APRIL 26, 2004 [541 U.S. 1105]

1.   That the Federal Rules of Criminal Procedure be, and they hereby are, amended by including therein an amendment to Criminal Rule 35.

2.   That the rules and forms governing cases in the United States District Courts under Section 2254 and Section 2255 of Title 28, United States Code, be, and they hereby are, amended by including therein amendments to Rules 1 through 11 of the Rules Governing Section 2254 Cases in the United States District Courts, Rules 1 through 12 of the Rules Governing Section 2255 Cases in the United States District Courts, and forms for use in applications under Section 2254 and motions under Section 2255.

[See amendments made thereby under respective rules, post.]

3.   That the foregoing amendments to the Federal Rules of Criminal Procedure, the Rules Governing Section 2254 Cases in the United States District Courts, and the Rules Governing Section 2255 Cases in the United States District Courts shall take effect on December 1, 2004, and shall govern in all proceedings thereafter commenced and, insofar as just and practicable, all proceedings then pending.

4.   That THE CHIEF JUSTICE be, and hereby is, authorized to transmit to the Congress the foregoing amendments to the Federal Rules of Criminal Procedure, the Rules Governing Section 2254 Cases in the United States District Courts, and the Rules Governing Section 2255 Cases in the United States District Courts in accordance with the provisions of Section 2072 of Title 28, United States Code.

ORDER OF MARCH 26, 2009 [556 U.S. 1365]

1.   That the Federal Rules of Criminal Procedure be, and they hereby are, amended by including therein amendments to Criminal Rules 5.1, 7, 12.1, 12.3, 29, 32, 32.2, 33, 34, 35, 41, 45, 47, 58, and 59, and Rules 8 and 11, and new Rule 12 of the Rules Governing Section 2254 Cases in the United States District Courts, and Rules 8 and 11 of the Rules Governing Section 2255 Proceedings for the United States District Courts.

[See amendments made thereby under respective rules, post.]

2.   That the foregoing amendments to the Federal Rules of Criminal Procedure shall take effect on December 1, 2009, and shall govern in all proceedings thereafter commenced and, insofar as just and practicable, all proceedings then pending.

3.   That THE CHIEF JUSTICE be, and hereby is, authorized to transmit to the Congress the foregoing amendments to the Federal Rules of Criminal Procedure in accordance with the provisions of Section 2072 of Title 28, United States Code.

ORDER OF APRIL 25, 2019 [2018 J. Sup. Ct. U.S. 715]

1.   That the Federal Rules of Criminal Procedure are amended to include new Rule 16.1.

2.   The Rules Governing Section 2254 Cases in the United States District Courts are amended to include an amendment to Rule 5.

3.   The Rules Governing Section 2255 Proceedings for the United States District Courts are amended to include an amendment to Rule 5.

[See amendments made thereby under respective rules, post.]

4.   That the foregoing amendments to the Federal Rules of Criminal Procedure, the Rules Governing Section 2254 Cases in the United States District Courts, and the Rules Governing Section 2255 Proceedings for the United States District Courts shall take effect on December 1, 2019, and shall govern in all proceedings thereafter commenced and, insofar as just and practicable, all proceedings then pending.

5.   The Chief Justice is authorized to transmit to the Congress the foregoing amendments to the Federal Rules of Criminal Procedure, the Rules Governing Section 2254 Cases in the United States District Courts, and the Rules Governing Section 2255 Proceedings for the United States District Courts in accordance with the provisions of Section 2074 of Title 28, United States Code.

HISTORICAL NOTES

Effective Date of Rules; 1976 Act

Rules governing section 2254 cases, and the amendments thereto by Pub.L. 94–426, Sept. 28, 1976, 90 Stat. 1334, effective with respect to petitions under section 2254 of this title and motions under section 2255 of this title filed on or after Feb. 1, 1977, see section 1 of Pub.L. 94–426, set out as a note under section 2074 and 2254 of this title.

Rule 1.   Scope

(a) Cases Involving a Petition under 28 U.S.C. § 2254. These rules govern a petition for a writ of habeas corpus filed in a United States district court under 28 U.S.C. § 2254 by:

(1) a person in custody under a state-court judgment who seeks a determination that the custody violates the Constitution, laws, or treaties of the United States; and

(2) a person in custody under a state-court or federal-court judgment who seeks a determination that future custody under a state-court judgment would violate the Constitution, laws, or treaties of the United States.

(b) Other Cases. The district court may apply any or all of these rules to a habeas corpus petition not covered by Rule 1(a).

(As amended Apr. 26, 2004, eff. Dec. 1, 2004.)

ADVISORY COMMITTEE NOTES

1976 Adoption

Rule 1 provides that the habeas corpus rules are applicable to petitions by persons in custody pursuant to a judgment of a state court. See *Preiser v. Rodriguez,* 411 U.S. 475, 484 (1973). Whether the rules ought to apply to other situations (*e.g.,* person in active military service, *Glazier v. Hackel,* 440 F.2d 592 (9th Cir. 1971); or a reservist called to active duty but not reported, *Hammond v. Lenfest,* 398 F.2d 705 (2d Cir. 1968)) is left to the discretion of the court.

The basic scope of habeas corpus is prescribed by statute. 28 U.S.C. § 2241(c) provides that the "writ of habeas corpus shall not extend to a prisoner unless * * * (h)e is *in custody* in violation of the Constitution." 28 U.S.C. § 2254 deals specifically with state custody, providing that habeas corpus shall apply only "in behalf of a person in custody pursuant to a judgment of a state court * * * ."

In *Preiser v. Rodriguez, supra,* the court said: "It is clear . . . that the essence of habeas corpus is an attack by a person in custody upon the legality of that custody, and that the traditional function of the writ is to secure release from illegal custody." 411 U.S. at 484.

Initially the Supreme Court held that habeas corpus was appropriate only in those situations in which petitioner's claim would, if upheld, result in an immediate release from a present custody. *McNally v. Hill,* 293 U.S. 131 (1934). This was changed in *Peyton v. Rowe,* 391 U.S. 54 (1968), in which the court held that habeas corpus was a proper way to attack a consecutive sentence to be served in the future, expressing the view that consecutive sentences resulted in present custody under both judgments, not merely the one imposing the first sentence. This view was expanded in *Carafas v. LaVallee,* 391 U.S. 234 (1968), to recognize the propriety of habeas corpus in a case in which petitioner was in custody when the petition had been originally filed but had since been unconditionally released from custody.

See also *Preiser v. Rodriguez,* 411 U.S. at 486 et seq.

Since *Carafas,* custody has been construed more liberally by the courts so as to make a § 2255 motion or habeas corpus petition proper in more situations. "In custody" now includes a person who is: on parole, *Jones v. Cunningham,* 371 U.S. 236 (1963); at large on his own recognizance but subject to several conditions pending execution of his sentence, *Hensley v. Municipal Court,* 411 U.S. 345 (1973); or released on bail after conviction pending final disposition of his case, *Lefkowitz v. Newsome,* 95 S.Ct. 886 (1975). See also *United States v. Re,* 372 F.2d 641 (2d Cir.), cert. denied, 388 U.S. 912 (1967) (on probation); *Walker v. North Carolina,* 262 F.Supp. 102 (W.D.N.C.1966), aff'd per curiam, 372 F.2d 129 (4th Cir.), cert. denied, 388 U.S. 917 (1967) (recipient of a conditionally suspended sentence); *Burris v. Ryan,* 397 F.2d 553 (7th Cir. 1968); *Marden v. Purdy,* 409 F.2d 784 (5th Cir. 1969) (free on bail); *United States ex rel. Smith v. Dibella,* 314 F.Supp. 446 (D.Conn.1970) (release on own recognizance); *Choung v. California,* 320 F.Supp. 625 (E.D.Cal.1970) (federal stay of state court sentence); *United States ex rel. Meadows v. New York,* 426 F.2d 1176 (2d Cir. 1970), cert. denied, 401 U.S. 941 (1971) (subject to parole detainer warrant); *Capler v. City of Greenville,* 422 F.2d 299 (5th Cir. 1970) (released on appeal bond); *Glover v. North Carolina,* 301 F.Supp. 364 (E.D.N.C.1969) (sentence served, but as convicted felon disqualified from engaging in several activities).

The courts are not unanimous in dealing with the above situations, and the boundaries of custody remain somewhat unclear. In *Morgan v. Thomas,* 321 F.Supp. 565 (S.D.Miss.1970), the court noted:

It is axiomatic that actual physical custody or restraint is not required to confer habeas jurisdiction. Rather, the term is synonymous with restraint of liberty. The real question is how much restraint of one's liberty is necessary before the right to apply for the writ comes into play. * * *

It is clear however, that something more than moral restraint is necessary to make a case for habeas corpus.

321 F.Supp. at 573

Hammond v. Lenfest, 398 F.2d 705 (2d Cir. 1968), reviewed prior "custody" doctrine and reaffirmed a generalized flexible approach to the issue. In speaking about 28 U.S.C. § 2241, the first section in the habeas corpus statutes, the court said:

> While the language of the Act indicates that a writ of habeas corpus is appropriate only when a petitioner is "in custody" * * * the Act "does not attempt to mark the boundaries of 'custody' nor in any way other than by use of that word attempt to limit the situations in which the writ can be used." * * * And, recent Supreme Court decisions have made clear that "[i]t [habeas corpus] is not now and never has been a static, narrow, formalistic remedy; its scope has grown to achieve its grand purpose—the protection of individuals against erosion of their right to be free from wrongful restraints upon their liberty." * * * "[B]esides physical imprisonment, there are other restraints on a man's liberty, restraints not shared by the public generally, which have been thought sufficient in the English-speaking world to support the issuance of habeas corpus."

398 F.2d at 710–711

There is, as of now, no final list of the situations which are appropriate for habeas corpus relief. It is not the intent of these rules or notes to define or limit "custody."

It is, however, the view of the Advisory Committee that claims of improper conditions of custody or confinement (not related to the propriety of the custody itself), can better be handled by other means such as 42 U.S.C. § 1983 and other related statutes. In *Wilwording v. Swanson,* 404 U.S. 249 (1971), the court treated a habeas corpus petition by a state prisoner challenging the conditions of confinement as a claim for relief under 42 U.S.C. § 1983, the Civil Rights Act. Compare *Johnson v. Avery,* 393 U.S. 483 (1969).

The distinction between duration of confinement and conditions of confinement may be difficult to draw. Compare *Preiser v. Rodriguez,* 411 U.S. 475 (1973), with *Clutchette v. Procunier,* 497 F.2d 809 (9th Cir. 1974), modified, 510 F.2d 613 (1975).

2004 Amendments

The language of Rule 1 has been amended as part of general restyling of the rules to make them more easily understood and to make style and terminology consistent throughout the rules. These changes are intended to be stylistic and no substantive change is intended.

Changes Made After Publication and Comments. In response to at least one commentator on the published rules, the Committee modified Rule 1(b) to reflect the point that if the court was considering a habeas petition not covered by § 2254, the court could apply some or all of the rules.

Rule 2.   The Petition

(a) Current Custody; Naming the Respondent. If the petitioner is currently in custody under a state-court judgment, the petition must name as respondent the state officer who has custody.

(b) Future Custody; Naming the Respondents and Specifying the Judgment. If the petitioner is not yet in custody—but may be subject to future custody—under the state-court judgment being contested, the petition must name as respondents both the officer who has current custody and the attorney general of the state where the judgment was entered. The petition must ask for relief from the state-court judgment being contested.

(c) Form. The petition must:

   (1)   specify all the grounds for relief available to the petitioner;

   (2)   state the facts supporting each ground;

   (3)   state the relief requested;

   (4)   be printed, typewritten, or legibly handwritten; and

   (5)   be signed under penalty of perjury by the petitioner or by a person authorized to sign it for the petitioner under 28 U.S.C. § 2242.

(d) Standard Form. The petition must substantially follow either the form appended to these rules or a form prescribed by a local district-court rule. The clerk must make forms available to petitioners without charge.

(e) Separate Petitions for Judgments of Separate Courts. A petitioner who seeks relief from judgments of more than one state court must file a separate petition covering the judgment or judgments of each court.

(As amended Pub.L. 94–426, § 2(1), (2), Sept. 28, 1976, 90 Stat. 1334; Apr. 28, 1982, eff. Aug. 1, 1982; Apr. 26, 2004, eff. Dec. 1, 2004.)

ADVISORY COMMITTEE NOTES

1976 Adoption

Rule 2 describes the requirements of the actual petition, including matters relating to its form, contents, scope, and sufficiency. The rule provides more specific guidance for a petitioner and the court than 28 U.S.C. § 2242, after which it is patterned.

Subdivision (a) provides that an applicant challenging a state judgment, pursuant to which he is presently in custody, must make his application in the form of a petition for a writ of habeas corpus. It also requires that the state officer having custody of the applicant be named as respondent. This is consistent with 28 U.S.C. § 2242, which says in part, [Application for a writ of habeas corpus] shall allege * * * the name of the person who has custody over [the applicant] * * * ." The proper person to be served in the usual case is either the warden of the institution in which the petitioner is incarcerated (*Sanders v. Bennett,* 148 F.2d 19 (D.C.Cir. 1945)) or the chief officer in charge of state penal institutions.

Subdivision (b) prescribes the procedure to be used for a petition challenging a judgment under which the petitioner will be subject to custody in the future. In this event the relief sought will usually not be released from present custody, but rather for a declaration that the judgment being attacked is invalid. Subdivision (b) thus provides for a prayer for "appropriate relief." It is also provided that the attorney general of the state of the judgment as well as the state officer having actual custody of the petitioner shall be named as respondents. This is appropriate because no one will have custody of the petitioner in the state of the judgment being attacked, and the habeas corpus action will usually be defended by the attorney general. The attorney general is in the best position to inform the court as to who the proper party respondent is. If it is not the attorney general, he can move for a substitution of party.

Since the concept of "custody" requisite to the consideration of a petition for habeas corpus has been enlarged significantly in recent years, it may be worthwhile to spell out the various situations which might arise and who should be named as respondent(s) for each situation.

(1) The applicant is in jail, prison, or other actual physical restraint due to the state action he is attacking. The named respondent shall be the state officer who has official custody of the petitioner (for example, the warden of the prison).

(2) The applicant is on probation or parole due to the state judgment he is attacking. The named respondents shall be the particular probation or parole officer responsible for supervising the applicant, and the official in charge of the parole or probation agency, or the state correctional agency, as appropriate.

(3) The applicant is in custody in any other manner differing from (1) and (2) above due to the effects of the state action he seeks relief from. The named respondent should be the attorney general of the state wherein such action was taken.

(4) The applicant is in jail, prison, or other actual physical restraint but is attacking a state action which will cause him to be kept in custody in the future rather than the government action under which he is presently confined. The named respondents shall be the state or federal officer who has official custody of him at the time the petition is filed and the attorney general of the state whose action subjects the petitioner to future custody.

(5) The applicant is in custody, although not physically restrained, and is attacking a state action which will result in his future custody rather than the government action out of which his present custody arises. The named respondent(s) shall be the attorney general of the state whose action subjects the petitioner to future custody, as well as the government officer who has present official custody of the petitioner if there is such an officer and his identity is ascertainable.

In any of the above situations the judge may require or allow the petitioner to join an additional or different party as a respondent if to do so would serve the ends of justice.

As seen in rule 1 and paragraphs (4) and (5) above, these rules contemplate that a petitioner currently in federal custody will be permitted to apply for habeas relief from a state restraint which is to go into effect in the future. There has been disagreement in the courts as to whether they have jurisdiction of the habeas application under these circumstances (compare *Piper v. United States,* 306 F.Supp. 1259 (D.Conn.1969), with *United States ex rel. Meadows v. New York,* 426 F.2d 1176 (2d Cir. 1970), cert. denied, 401 U.S. 941 (1971)). This rule seeks to make clear that they do have such jurisdiction.

Subdivision (c) provides that unless a district court requires otherwise by local rule, the petition must be in the form annexed to these rules. Having a standard prescribed form has several advantages. In the past, petitions have frequently contained mere conclusions of law, unsupported by any facts. Since it is the relationship of the facts to the claim asserted that is important, these petitions were obviously deficient. In addition, lengthy and often illegible petitions, arranged in no logical order, were submitted to judges who have had to spend hours deciphering them. For example, in *Passic v. Michigan,* 98 F.Supp. 1015, 1016 (E.D.Mich.1951), the court dismissed a petition for habeas corpus, describing it as "two thousand pages of irrational, prolix and redundant pleadings * * * ."

Administrative convenience, of benefit to both the court and the petitioner, results from the use of a prescribed form. Judge Hubert L. Will briefly described the experience with the use of a standard form in the Northern District of Illinois:

Our own experience, though somewhat limited, has been quite satisfactory. * * *

In addition, [petitions] almost always contain the necessary basic information * * * . Very rarely do we get the kind of hybrid federal-state habeas corpus petition with civil rights allegations thrown in which were not uncommon in the past. * * * [W]hen a real constitutional issue is raised it is quickly apparent * * * .

33 F.R.D. 363, 384

Approximately 65 to 70% of all districts have adopted forms or local rules which require answers to essentially the same questions as contained in the standard form annexed to these rules. All courts using forms have indicated the petitions are time-saving and more legible. The form is particularly helpful in getting information about whether there has been an exhaustion of state remedies or, at least, where that information can be obtained.

The requirement of a standard form benefits the petitioner as well. His assertions are more readily apparent, and a meritorious claim is more likely to be properly raised and supported. The inclusion in the form of the ten most frequently raised grounds in habeas corpus petitions is intended to encourage the applicant to raise all his asserted grounds in one petition. It may better enable him to recognize if an issue he seeks to raise is cognizable under habeas corpus and hopefully inform him of those issues as to which he must first exhaust his state remedies.

Some commentators have suggested that the use of forms is of little help because the questions usually are too general, amounting to little more than a restatement of the statute. They contend the blanks permit a prisoner to fill in the same ambiguous answers he would have offered without the aid of a form. See Comment, Developments in the Law—Federal Habeas Corpus, 83 Harv.L.Rev. 1038, 1177–1178 (1970). Certainly, as long as the statute requires factual pleading, the adequacy of a petition will continue to be affected largely by the petitioner's intelligence and the legal advice available to him. On balance, however, the use of forms has contributed enough to warrant mandating their use.

Giving the petitioner a list of often—raised grounds may, it is said, encourage perjury. See Comment, Developments in the Law—Federal Habeas Corpus, 83 Harv.L.Rev. 1038, 1178 (1970). Most inmates are aware of, or have access to, some common constitutional grounds for relief. Thus, the risk of perjury is not likely to be substantially increased and the benefit of the list for some inmates seems sufficient to outweigh any slight risk that perjury will increase. There is a penalty for perjury, and this would seem the most appropriate way to try to discourage it.

Legal assistance is increasingly available to inmates either through paraprofessional programs involving law students or special programs staffed by members of the bar. See Jacob and Sharma, Justice After Trial: Prisoners' Need for Legal Services in the Criminal-Correctional Process, 18 Kan.L.Rev. 493 (1970). In these situations, the prescribed form can be filled out more competently, and it does serve to ensure a degree of uniformity in the manner in which habeas corpus claims are presented.

Subdivision (c) directs the clerk of the district court to make available to applicants upon request, without charge, blank petitions in the prescribed form.

Subdivision (c) also requires that all available grounds for relief be presented in the petition, including those grounds of which, by the exercise of reasonable diligence, the petitioner should be aware. This is reinforced by rule 9(b), which allows dismissal of a second petition which fails to allege new grounds or, if new grounds are alleged, the judge finds an inexcusable failure to assert the ground in the prior petition.

Both subdivision (c) and the annexed form require a legibly handwritten or typewritten petition. As required by 28 U.S.C. § 2242, the petition must be signed and sworn to by the petitioner (or someone acting in his behalf).

Subdivision (d) provides that a single petition may assert a claim only against the judgment or judgments of a single state court (*i.e.*, a court of the same county or judicial district or circuit). This permits, but does not require, an attack in a single petition on judgments based upon separate indictments or on separate counts even though sentences were imposed on separate days by the same court. A claim against a judgment of a court of a different political subdivision must be raised by means of a separate petition.

Subdivision (e) allows the clerk to return an insufficient petition to the petitioner, and it must be returned if the clerk is so directed by a judge of the court. Any failure to comply with the requirements of rule 2 or 3 is grounds for insufficiency. In situations where there may be arguable noncompliance with another rule, such as rule 9, the judge, not the clerk, must make the decision. If the petition is returned it must be accompanied by a statement of the reason for its return. No petitioner should be left to speculate as to why or in what manner his petition failed to conform to these rules.

Subdivision (e) also provides that the clerk shall retain one copy of the insufficient petition. If the prisoner files another petition, the clerk will be in a better position to determine the sufficiency of the new petition. If the new petition is insufficient, comparison with the prior petition may indicate whether the prisoner has failed to understand the clerk's prior explanation for its insufficiency, so that the clerk can make another, hopefully successful, attempt at transmitting this information to the petitioner. If the petitioner insists that the original petition was in compliance with the rules, a copy of the original petition is available for the consideration of the judge. It is probably better practice to make a photocopy of a petition which can be corrected by the petitioner, thus saving the petitioner the task of completing an additional copy.

1982 Amendment

Subdivision (c). The amendment takes into account 28 U.S.C. § 1746, enacted after adoption of the § 2254 rules. Section 1746 provides that in lieu of an affidavit an unsworn statement may be given under penalty of perjury in substantially the following form if executed within the United States, its territories, possessions or commonwealths: "I declare (or certify, verify, or state) under penalty of perjury that the foregoing is true and correct. Executed on (date). (Signature)." The statute is "intended to encompass prisoner litigation," and the statutory alternative is especially appropriate in such cases because a notary might not be readily available. *Carter v. Clark,* 616 F.2d 228 (5th Cir. 1980). The § 2254 forms have been revised accordingly.

2004 Amendments

The language of Rule 2 has been amended as part of general restyling of the rules to make them more easily understood and to make style and terminology consistent throughout the rules. These changes are intended to be stylistic and no substantive change is intended, except as described below.

Revised Rule 2(c)(5) has been amended by removing the requirement that the petition be signed personally by the petitioner. As reflected in 28 U.S.C. § 2242, an application for habeas corpus relief may be filed by the person who is seeking relief, or by someone acting on behalf of that person. *See, e.g., Whitmore v. Arkansas,* 495 U.S. 149 (1990) (discussion of requisites for "next friend" standing in petition for habeas corpus). Thus, under the, amended rule the petition may be signed by petitioner personally or by someone acting on behalf of the petitioner, assuming that the person is authorized to do so, for example, an attorney for the petitioner. The Committee envisions that the courts will apply third-party, or "next-friend," standing analysis in deciding whether the signer was actually authorized to sign the petition on behalf of the petitioner.

The language in new Rule 2(d) has been changed to reflect that a petitioner must substantially follow the standard form, which is appended to the rules, or a form provided by the court. The current rule, Rule 2(c), seems to indicate a preference for the standard "national" form. Under the amended rule, there is no stated preference. The Committee understood that current practice in some courts is that if the petitioner first files a petition using the national form, the courts may then ask the petitioner to supplement it with the local form.

Current Rule 2(e), which provided for returning an insufficient petition, has been deleted. The Committee believed that the approach in Federal Rule of Civil Procedure 5(e) was more appropriate for dealing with petitions that do not conform to the form requirements of the rule. That Rule provides that the clerk may not refuse to accept a filing solely for the reason that it fails to comply with these rules or local rules. Before the adoption of a one-year statute of limitations in the Antiterrorism and Effective Death Penalty Act of 1996, 110 Stat. 1214, the petitioner suffered no penalty, other than delay, if the petition was deemed insufficient. Now that a one-year statute of limitations applies to petitions filed under § 2254, *see* 28 U.S.C. § 2244(d)(1), the court's dismissal of a petition because it is not in proper form may pose a significant penalty for a petitioner, who may not be able to file another petition within the one-year limitations period. Now, under revised Rule 3(b), the clerk is required to file a petition, even though it may otherwise fail to comply with the provisions in revised Rule 2(c). The Committee believed that the better procedure was to accept the defective petition and require the petitioner to submit a corrected petition that conforms to Rule 2(c).

Changes Made After Publication and Comments. The Committee changed Rule 2(c)(2) to read "state the facts" rather then [sic] "briefly summarize the facts." As one commentator noted, the current language may actually mislead the petitioner and is also redundant. The Committee modified Rule 2(c)(5) to emphasize that any person, other than the petitioner, who signs the petition must be authorized to do so; the revised rule now specifically cites § 2242. The Note was changed to reflect that point.

Rule 2(c)(4) was modified to account for those cases where the petitioner prints the petition on a computer word-processing program.

Rule 3. Filing the Petition; Inmate Filing

(a) **Where to File; Copies; Filing Fee.** An original and two copies of the petition must be filed with the clerk and must be accompanied by:

(1) the applicable filing fee, or

(2) a motion for leave to proceed in forma pauperis, the affidavit required by 28 U.S.C. § 1915, and a certificate from the warden or other appropriate officer of the place of confinement showing the amount of money or securities that the petitioner has in any account in the institution.

(b) **Filing.** The clerk must file the petition and enter it on the docket.

(c) **Time to File.** The time for filing a petition is governed by 28 U.S.C. § 2244(d).

(d) **Inmate Filing.** A paper filed by an inmate confined in an institution is timely if deposited in the institution's internal mailing system on or before the last day for filing. If an institution has a system designed for legal mail, the inmate must use that system to receive the benefit of this rule. Timely filing may be shown by a declaration in compliance with 28 U.S.C. § 1746 or by a notarized statement, either of which must set forth the date of deposit and state that first-class postage has been prepaid.

(As amended Apr. 26, 2004, eff. Dec. 1, 2004.)

ADVISORY COMMITTEE NOTES

1976 Adoption

Rule 3 sets out the procedures to be followed by the petitioner and the court in filing the petition. Some of its provisions are currently dealt with by local rule or practice, while others are innovations. Subdivision (a) specifies the petitioner's responsibilities. It requires that the petition, which must be accompanied by two conformed copies thereof, be filed in the office of the clerk of the district court. The petition must be accompanied by the filing fee prescribed by law (presently $5; see 28 U.S.C. § 1914(a)), unless leave to prosecute the petition in forma pauperis is applied for and granted. In the event the petitioner desires to prosecute the petition in forma pauperis, he must file the affidavit required by 28 U.S.C. § 1915, together with a certificate showing the amount of funds in his institutional account.

Requiring that the petition be filed in the office of the clerk of the district court provides an efficient and uniform system of filing habeas corpus petitions.

Subdivision (b) requires the clerk to file the petition. If the filing fee accompanies the petition, it may be filed immediately, and, if not, it is contemplated that prompt attention will be given to the request to proceed in forma pauperis. The court may delegate the issuance of the order to the clerk in those cases in which it is clear from the petition that there is full compliance with the requirements to proceed in forma pauperis.

Requiring the copies of the petition to be filed with the clerk will have an impact not only upon administrative matters, but upon more basic problems as well. In districts with more than one judge, a petitioner under present circumstances may send a petition to more than one judge. If no central filing system exists for each district, two judges may independently take different action on the same petition. Even if the action taken is consistent, there may be needless duplication of effort.

The requirement of an additional two copies of the form of the petition is a current practice in many courts. An efficient filing system requires one copy for use by the court (central file), one for the respondent (under 3(b), the respondent receives a copy of the petition whether an answer is required or not), and one for petitioner's counsel, if appointed. Since rule 2 provides that blank copies of the petition in the prescribed form are to be furnished to the applicant free of charge, there should be no undue burden created by this requirement.

Attached to copies of the petition supplied in accordance with rule 2 is an affidavit form for the use of petitioners desiring to proceed in forma pauperis. The form requires information concerning the petitioner's financial resources.

In forma pauperis cases, the petition must also be accompanied by a certificate indicating the amount of funds in the petitioner's institution account. Usually the certificate will be from the warden. If the petitioner is on probation or parole, the court might want to require a certificate from the supervising officer. Petitions by persons on probation or parole are not numerous enough, however, to justify making special provision for this situation in the text of the rule.

The certificate will verify the amount of funds credited to the petitioner in an institution account. The district court may by local rule require that any amount credited to the petitioner, in excess of a stated maximum, must be used for the payment of the filing fee. Since prosecuting an action in forma pauperis is a privilege (see *Smart v. Heinze,* 347 F.2d 114, 116 (9th Cir. 1965), it is not to be granted when the petitioner has sufficient resources.

Subdivision (b) details the clerk's duties with regard to filing the petition. If the petition does not appear on its face to comply with the requirements of rules 2 and 3, it may be returned in accordance with rule 2(e). If it appears to comply, it must be filed and entered on the docket in the clerk's office. However, under this subdivision the respondent is not required to answer or otherwise move with respect to the petition unless so ordered by the court.

2004 Amendments

The language of Rule 3 has been amended as part of general restyling of the rules to make them more easily understood and to make style and terminology consistent throughout the rules. These changes are intended to be stylistic and no substantive change is intended except as described below.

The last sentence of current Rule 3(b), dealing with an answer being filed by the respondent, has been moved to revised Rule 5(a).

Revised Rule 3(b) is new and is intended to parallel Federal Rule of Civil Procedure 5(e), which provides that the clerk may not refuse to accept a filing solely for the reason that it fails to comply with these rules or local rules. Before the adoption of a one-year statute of limitations in the Antiterrorism and Effective Death Penalty Act of 1996, 110 Stat. 1214, the petitioner suffered no penalty, other than delay, if the petition was deemed insufficient. That Act, however, added a one-year statute of limitations to petitions filed under § 2254, see 28 U.S.C. § 2244(d)(1). Thus, a court's dismissal of a defective petition may pose a significant penalty for a petitioner who may not be able to file a corrected petition within the one-year limitations period. The Committee believed that the better procedure was to accept the defective petition and require the petitioner to submit a corrected petition that conforms to Rule 2. Thus, revised Rule 3(b) requires the clerk to file a petition, even though it may otherwise fail to comply with Rule 2. The rule, however, is not limited to those instances where the petition is defective only in form; the clerk would also be required, for example, to file the petition even though it lacked the requisite filing fee or an *in forma pauperis* form.

Revised Rule 3(c), which sets out a specific reference to 28 U.S.C. § 2244(d), is new and has been added to put petitioners on notice that a one-year statute of limitations applies to petitions filed under these Rules. Although the rule does not address the issue, every circuit that has addressed the issue has taken the position that equitable tolling of the statute of limitations is available in appropriate circumstances. *See, e.g., Smith v. McGinnis,* 208 F.3d 13, 17–18 (2d Cir. 2000); *Miller v. New Jersey State Department of Corrections,* 145 F.3d 616, 618–19 (3d Cir. 1998); *Harris v. Hutchinson,* 209 F.3d 325, 330 (4th Cir. 2000). The Supreme Court has not addressed the question directly. *See Duncan v. Walker,* 533 U.S. 167, 181 (2001) ("We . . . have no occasion to address the question that Justice Stevens raises concerning the availability of equitable tolling.").

Rule 3(d) is new and provides guidance on determining whether a petition from an inmate is considered to have been filed in a timely fashion. The new provision parallels Federal Rule of Appellate Procedure 25(a)(2)(C).

Changes Made After Publication and Comments. The Committee Note was changed to reflect that the clerk must file a petition, even in those instances where the necessary filing fee or in forma pauperis form is not attached. The Note also includes new language concerning the equitable tolling of the statute of limitations.

Rule 4.   Preliminary Review; Serving the Petition and Order

The clerk must promptly forward the petition to a judge under the court's assignment procedure, and the judge must promptly examine it. If it plainly appears from the petition and any attached exhibits that the petitioner is not entitled to relief in the district court, the judge must dismiss the petition and direct the clerk to notify the petitioner. If the petition is not dismissed, the judge must order the respondent to file an answer, motion, or other response within a fixed time, or to take other action the judge may order. In every case, the clerk must serve a copy of the petition and any order on the respondent and on the attorney general or other appropriate officer of the state involved.

(As amended Apr. 26, 2004, eff. Dec. 1, 2004.)

ADVISORY COMMITTEE NOTES

1976 Adoption

Rule 4 outlines the options available to the court after the petition is properly filed. The petition must be promptly presented to and examined by the judge to whom it is assigned. If it plainly appears from the face of the petition and any exhibits attached thereto that the petitioner is not entitled to relief in the district court, the judge must enter an order summarily dismissing the petition and cause the petitioner to be notified. If summary dismissal is not ordered, the judge must order the respondent to file an answer or to otherwise plead to the petition within a time period to be fixed in the order.

28 U.S.C. § 2243 requires that the writ shall be awarded, or an order to show cause issued, "unless it appears from the application that the applicant or person detained is not entitled thereto." Such consideration may properly encompass any exhibits attached to the petition, including, but not limited to,

transcripts, sentencing records, and copies of state court opinions. The judge may order any of these items for his consideration if they are not yet included with the petition. See 28 U.S.C. § 753(f) which authorizes payment for transcripts in habeas corpus cases.

It has been suggested that an answer should be required in every habeas proceeding, taking into account the usual petitioner's lack of legal expertise and the important functions served by the return. See Developments in the Law—Federal Habeas Corpus, 83 Harv.L.Rev. 1038, 1178 (1970). However, under § 2243 it is the duty of the court to screen out frivolous applications and eliminate the burden that would be placed on the respondent by ordering an unnecessary answer. *Allen v. Perini,* 424 F.2d 134, 141 (6th Cir. 1970). In addition, "notice" pleading is not sufficient, for the petition is expected to state facts that point to a "real possibility of constitutional error." See *Aubut v. State of Maine,* 431 F.2d 688, 689 (1st Cir. 1970).

In the event an answer is ordered under rule 4, the court is accorded greater flexibility than under § 2243 in determining within what time period an answer must be made. Under § 2243, the respondent must make a return within three days after being so ordered, with additional time of up to forty days allowed under the Federal Rules of Civil Procedure, Rule 81(a)(2), for good cause. In view of the widespread state of work overload in prosecutors' offices (see, *e.g., Allen,* 424 F.2d at 141), additional time is granted in some jurisdictions as a matter of course. Rule 4, which contains no fixed time requirement, gives the court the discretion to take into account various factors such as the respondent's workload and the availability of transcripts before determining a time within which an answer must be made.

Rule 4 authorizes the judge to "take such other action as the judge deems appropriate." This is designed to afford the judge flexibility in a case where either dismissal or an order to answer may be inappropriate. For example, the judge may want to authorize the respondent to make a motion to dismiss based upon information furnished by respondent, which may show that petitioner's claims have already been decided on the merits in a federal court; that petitioner has failed to exhaust state remedies; that the petitioner is not in custody within the meaning of 28 U.S.C. § 2254; or that a decision in the matter is pending in state court. In these situations, a dismissal may be called for on procedural grounds, which may avoid burdening the respondent with the necessity of filing an answer on the substantive merits of the petition. In other situations, the judge may want to consider a motion from respondent to make the petition more certain. Or the judge may want to dismiss some allegations in the petition, requiring the respondent to answer only those claims which appear to have some arguable merit.

Rule 4 requires that a copy of the petition and any order be served by certified mail on the respondent and the attorney general of the state involved. See 28 U.S.C. § 2252. Presently, the respondent often does not receive a copy of the petition unless the court directs an answer under 28 U.S.C. § 2243. Although the attorney general is served, he is not required to answer if it is more appropriate for some other agency to do so. Although the rule does not specifically so provide, it is assumed that copies of the court orders to respondent will be mailed to petitioner by the court.

2004 Amendments

The language of Rule 4 has been amended as part of general restyling of the rules to make them more easily understood and to make style and terminology consistent throughout the rules. These changes are intended to be stylistic and no substantive change is intended, except as described below.

The amended rule reflects that the response to a habeas petition may be a motion.

The requirement that in every case the clerk must serve a copy of the petition on the respondent by certified mail has been deleted. In addition, the current requirement that the petition be sent to the Attorney General of the state has been modified to reflect practice in some jurisdictions that the appropriate state official may be someone other than the Attorney General, for example, the officer in charge of a local confinement facility. This comports with a similar provision in 28 U.S.C. § 2252, which addresses notice of habeas corpus proceedings to the state's attorney general or other appropriate officer of the state.

Changes Made After Publication and Comments. The Rule was modified slightly to reflect the view of some commentators that it is common practice in some districts for the government to file a pre-answer motion to dismiss. The Committee agreed with that recommendation and changed the word "pleading" in the rule to "response." It also made several minor changes to the Committee Note.

Rule 5.   The Answer and the Reply

(a) When Required. The respondent is not required to answer the petition unless a judge so orders.

(b) Contents: Addressing the Allegations; Stating a Bar. The answer must address the allegations in the petition. In addition, it must state whether any claim in the petition is barred by a failure to exhaust state remedies, a procedural bar, non-retroactivity, or a statute of limitations.

(c) Contents: Transcripts. The answer must also indicate what transcripts (of pretrial, trial, sentencing, or post-conviction proceedings) are available, when they can be furnished, and what proceedings have been recorded but not transcribed. The respondent must attach to the answer parts of the transcript that the respondent considers relevant. The judge may order that the respondent furnish other parts of existing transcripts or that parts of untranscribed recordings be transcribed and furnished. If a transcript cannot be obtained, the respondent may submit a narrative summary of the evidence.

(d) Contents: Briefs on Appeal and Opinions. The respondent must also file with the answer a copy of:

(1) any brief that the petitioner submitted in an appellate court contesting the conviction or sentence, or contesting an adverse judgment or order in a post-conviction proceeding;

(2) any brief that the prosecution submitted in an appellate court relating to the conviction or sentence; and

(3) the opinions and dispositive orders of the appellate court relating to the conviction or the sentence.

(e) Reply. The petitioner may file a reply to the respondent's answer or other pleading. The judge must set the time to file unless the time is already set by local rule.

(As amended Apr. 26, 2004, eff. Dec. 1, 2004; Apr. 25, 2019, eff. Dec. 1, 2019.)

ADVISORY COMMITTEE NOTES

1976 Adoption

Rule 5 details the contents of the "answer". (This is a change in terminology from "return," which is still used below when referring to prior practice.) The answer plays an obviously important role in a habeas proceeding:

> The return serves several important functions: it permits the court and the parties to uncover quickly the disputed issues; it may reveal to the petitioner's attorney grounds for release that the petitioner did not know; and it may demonstrate that the petitioner's claim is wholly without merit.

Developments in the Law—Federal Habeas Corpus, 83 Harv.L.Rev. 1083, 1178 (1970).

The answer must respond to the allegations of the petition. While some districts require this by local rule (see, *e.g.,* E.D.N.C.R. 17(B)), under 28 U.S.C. § 2243 little specificity is demanded. As a result, courts occasionally receive answers which contain only a statement certifying the true cause of detention, or a series of delaying motions such as motions to dismiss. The requirement of the proposed rule that the "answer shall respond to the allegations of the petition" is intended to ensure that a responsive pleading will be filed and thus the functions of the answer fully served.

The answer must also state whether the petitioner has exhausted his state remedies. This is a prerequisite to eligibility for the writ under 28 U.S.C. § 2254(b) and applies to every ground the petitioner raises. Most form petitions now in use contain questions requiring information relevant to whether the petitioner has exhausted his remedies. However, the exhaustion requirement is often not understood by the unrepresented petitioner. The attorney general has both the legal expertise and access to the record and thus is in a much better position to inform the court on the matter of exhaustion of state remedies. An alleged failure to exhaust state remedies as to any ground in the petition may be raised by a motion by the attorney general, thus avoiding the necessity of a formal answer as to that ground.

The rule requires the answer to indicate what transcripts are available, when they can be furnished, and also what proceedings have been recorded and not transcribed. This will serve to inform the court and petitioner as to what factual allegations can be checked against the actual transcripts. The transcripts include pretrial transcripts relating, for example, to pretrial motions to suppress; transcripts of the trial or guilty plea proceeding; and transcripts of any post-conviction proceedings which may have taken place. The respondent is required to furnish those portions of the transcripts which he believes relevant. The court may order the furnishing of additional portions of the transcripts upon the request of petitioner or upon the court's own motion.

Where transcripts are unavailable, the rule provides that a narrative summary of the evidence may be submitted.

Rule 5 (and the general procedure set up by this entire set of rules) does not contemplate a traverse to the answer, except under special circumstances. See advisory committee note to rule 9. Therefore, the old common law assumption of verity of the allegations of a return until impeached, as codified in 28 U.S.C. § 2248, is no longer applicable. The meaning of the section, with its exception to the assumption "to the extent that the judge finds from the evidence that they (the allegations) are not true," has given attorneys and courts a great deal of difficulty. It seems that when the petition and return pose an issue of fact, no traverse is required; *Stewart v. Overholser*, 186 F.2d 339 (D.C.Cir. 1950).

We read § 2248 of the Judicial Code as not requiring a traverse when a factual issue has been clearly framed by the petition and the return or answer. This section provides that the allegations of a return or answer to an order to show cause shall be accepted as true if not traversed, except to the extent the judge finds from the evidence that they are not true. This contemplates that where the petition and return or answer do present an issue of fact material to the legality of detention, evidence is required to resolve that issue despite the absence of a traverse. This reference to evidence assumes a hearing on issues raised by the allegations of the petition and the return or answer to the order to show cause.

186 F.2d at 342, n. 5

In actual practice, the traverse tends to be a mere pro forma refutation of the return, serving little if any expository function. In the interests of a more streamlined and manageable habeas corpus procedure, it is not required except in those instances where it will serve a truly useful purpose. Also, under rule 11 the court is given the discretion to incorporate Federal Rules of Civil Procedure when appropriate, so civil rule 15(a) may be used to allow the petitioner to amend his petition when the court feels this is called for by the contents of the answer.

Rule 5 does not indicate who the answer is to be served upon, but it necessarily implies that it will be mailed to the petitioner (or to his attorney if he has one). The number of copies of the answer required is left to the court's discretion. Although the rule requires only a copy of petitioner's brief on appeal, respondent is free also to file a copy of respondent's brief. In practice, courts have found it helpful to have a copy of respondent's brief.

2004 Amendments

The language of Rule 5 has been amended as part of general restyling of the rules to make them more easily understood and to make style and terminology consistent throughout the rules. These changes are intended to be stylistic and no substantive change is intended, except as described below.

Revised Rule 5(a), which provides that the respondent is not required to file an answer to the petition, unless a judge so orders, is taken from current Rule 3(b). The revised rule does not address the practice in some districts, where the respondent files a pre-answer motion to dismiss the petition. But revised Rule 4 permits that practice and reflects the view that if the court does not dismiss the petition, it may require (or permit) the respondent to file a motion.

Rule 5(b) has been amended to require that the answer address not only failure to exhaust state remedies, but also procedural bars, non-retroactivity, and any statute of limitations. Although the latter three matters are not addressed in the current rule, the Committee intends no substantive change with the additional new language. *See, e.g.,* 28 U.S.C. § 2254(b)(3). Instead, the Committee believes that the explicit mention of those issues in the rule conforms to current case law and statutory provisions. *See, e.g.,* 28 U.S.C. § 2244(d)(1).

Revised Rule 5(d) includes new material. First, Rule 5(d)(2), requires a respondent—assuming an answer is filed—to provide the court with a copy of any brief submitted by the prosecution to the appellate court. And Rule 5(d)(3) now provides that the respondent also file copies of any opinions and dispositive orders of the appellate court concerning the conviction or sentence. These provisions are intended to ensure that the court is provided with additional information that may assist it in resolving the issues raised, or not raised, in the petition.

Finally, revised Rule 5(e) adopts the practice in some jurisdictions of giving the petitioner an opportunity to file a reply to the respondent's answer. Rather than using terms such as "traverse," *see* 28 U.S.C. § 2248, to identify the petitioner's response to the answer, the rule uses the more general term "reply." The Rule prescribes that the court set the time for such responses and in lieu of setting specific time limits in each case, the court may decide to include such time limits in its local rules.

Changes Made After Publication and Comments. Rule 5(a) was modified to read that the government is not required to "respond" to the petition unless the court so orders; the term "respond" was used because it leaves open the possibility that the government's first response (as it is in some districts) is in the form of a pre-answer motion to dismiss the petition. The Note has been changed to reflect the fact that although the rule itself does not reflect that particular motion, it is used in some districts and refers the reader to Rule 4.

The Committee also deleted the reference to "affirmative defenses," because the Committee believed that the term was a misnomer in the context of habeas petitions. The Note was also changed to reflect that there has been a potential substantive change from the current rule, to the extent that the published rule now requires that the answer address procedural bars and any statute of limitations. The Note states that the Committee believes the new language reflects current law.

The Note was modified to address the use of the term "traverse." One commentator noted that that is the term that is commonly used but that it does not appear in the rule itself.

2019 Amendments

The petitioner has a right to file a reply. Subsection (e), added in 2004, removed the discretion of the court to determine whether or not to allow the petitioner to file a reply in a case under § 2254. The current amendment was prompted by decisions holding that courts nevertheless retained the authority to bar a reply.

As amended, the first sentence of subsection (e) makes it even clearer that the petitioner has a right to file a reply to the respondent's answer or pleading. It retains the word "may," which is used throughout the federal rules to mean "is permitted to" or "has a right to." No change in meaning is intended by the substitution of "file" for "submit."

As amended, the second sentence of the rule retains the court's discretion to decide when the reply must be filed (but not whether it may be filed). To avoid uncertainty, the amended rule requires the court to set a time for filing if that time is not already set by local rule. Adding a reference to the time for the filing of any reply to the order requiring the government to file an answer or other pleading provides notice of that deadline to both parties.

Rule 6.   Discovery

(a) Leave of Court Required. A judge may, for good cause, authorize a party to conduct discovery under the Federal Rules of Civil Procedure and may limit the extent of discovery. If necessary for effective discovery, the judge must appoint an attorney for a petitioner who qualifies to have counsel appointed under 18 U.S.C. § 3006A.

(b) Requesting Discovery. A party requesting discovery must provide reasons for the request. The request must also include any proposed interrogatories and requests for admission, and must specify any requested documents.

(c) Deposition Expenses. If the respondent is granted leave to take a deposition, the judge may require the respondent to pay the travel expenses, subsistence expenses, and fees of the petitioner's attorney to attend the deposition.

(As amended Apr. 26, 2004, eff. Dec. 1, 2004.)

ADVISORY COMMITTEE NOTES

1976 Adoption

This rule prescribes the procedures governing discovery in habeas corpus cases. Subdivision (a) provides that any party may utilize the processes of discovery available under the Federal Rules of Civil Procedure (rules 26–37) if, and to the extent that, the judge allows. It also provides for the appointment of counsel for a petitioner who qualifies for this when counsel is necessary for effective utilization of discovery procedures permitted by the judge.

Subdivision (a) is consistent with *Harris v. Nelson,* 394 U.S. 286 (1969). In that case the court noted,

[I]t is clear that there was no intention to extend to habeas corpus, as a matter of right, the broad discovery provisions * * * of the new [Federal Rules of Civil Procedure].

394 U.S. at 295

However, citing the lack of methods for securing information in habeas proceedings, the court pointed to an alternative.

Clearly, in these circumstances * * * the courts may fashion appropriate modes of procedure, by analogy to existing rules or otherwise in conformity with judicial usage. * * * Their authority is expressly confirmed in the All Writs Act, 28 U.S.C. § 1651.

394 U.S. at 299

The court concluded that the issue of discovery in habeas corpus cases could best be dealt with as part of an effort to provide general rules of practice for habeas corpus cases:

In fact, it is our view that the rulemaking machinery should be invoked to formulate rules of practice with respect to federal habeas corpus and § 2255 proceedings, on a comprehensive basis and not merely one confined to discovery. The problems presented by these proceedings are materially different from those dealt with in the Federal Rules of Civil Procedure and the Federal Rules of Criminal Procedure, and reliance upon usage and the opaque language of Civil Rule 81(a)(2) is transparently inadequate. In our view the results of a meticulous formulation and adoption of special rules for federal habeas corpus and § 2255 proceedings would promise much benefit.

394 U.S. at 301 n. 7

Discovery may, in appropriate cases, aid in developing facts necessary to decide whether to order an evidentiary hearing or to grant the writ following an evidentiary hearing:

We are aware that confinement sometimes induces fantasy which has its basis in the paranoia of prison rather than in fact. But where specific allegations before the court show reason to believe that the petitioner may, if the facts are fully developed, be able to demonstrate that he is confined illegally and is therefore entitled to relief, it is the duty of the court to provide the necessary facilities and procedures for an adequate inquiry. Obviously, in exercising this power, the court may utilize familiar procedures, as appropriate, whether these are found in the civil or criminal rules or elsewhere in the "usages and principles."

Granting discovery is left to the discretion of the court, discretion to be exercised where there is a showing of good cause why discovery should be allowed. Several commentators have suggested that at least some discovery should be permitted without leave of court. It is argued that the courts will be burdened with weighing the propriety of requests to which the discovered party has no objection. Additionally, the availability of protective orders under Fed.R.Civ.P., Rules 30(b) and 31(d) will provide the necessary safeguards. See Developments in the Law—Federal Habeas Corpus, 83 Harv.L.Rev. 1038, 1186–87 (1970); Civil Discovery in Habeas Corpus, 67 Colum.L.Rev. 1296, 1310 (1967).

Nonetheless, it is felt the requirement of prior court approval of all discovery is necessary to prevent abuse, so this requirement is specifically mandated in the rule.

While requests for discovery in habeas proceedings normally follow the granting of an evidentiary hearing, there may be instances in which discovery would be appropriate beforehand. Such an approach was advocated in *Wagner v. United States*, 418 F.2d 618, 621 (9th Cir.1969), where the opinion stated the trial court could permit interrogatories, provide for deposing witnesses, "and take such other prehearing steps as may be appropriate." While this was an action under § 2255, the reasoning would apply equally well to petitions by state prisoners. Such pre-hearing discovery may show an evidentiary hearing to be unnecessary, as when there are "no disputed issues of law or fact." 83 Harv.L.Rev. 1038, 1181 (1970). The court in Harris alluded to such a possibility when it said "the court may * * * authorize such proceedings with respect to development, *before or in conjunction with the hearing* of the facts * * * ." [emphasis added] 394 U.S. at 300. Such pre-hearing discovery, like all discovery under rule 6, requires leave of court. In addition, the provisions in rule 7 for the use of an expanded record may eliminate much of the need for this type of discovery. While probably not as frequently sought or granted as discovery in conjunction with a hearing, it may nonetheless serve a valuable function.

In order to make pre-hearing discovery meaningful, subdivision (a) provides that the judge should appoint counsel for a petitioner who is without counsel and qualifies for appointment when this is necessary for the proper utilization of discovery procedures. Rule 8 provides for the appointment of counsel at the evidentiary hearing stage (see rule 8(b) and advisory committee note), but this would not assist the petitioner who seeks to utilize discovery to stave off dismissal of his petition (see rule 9 and advisory committee note) or to demonstrate that an evidentiary hearing is necessary. Thus, if the judge grants a petitioner's request for discovery prior to making a decision as to the necessity for an evidentiary hearing, he should determine whether counsel is necessary for the effective utilization of such discovery and, if so, appoint counsel for the petitioner if the petitioner qualifies for such appointment.

This rule contains very little specificity as to what types and methods of discovery should be made available to the parties in a habeas proceeding, or how, once made available, these discovery procedures should be administered. The purpose of this rule is to get some experience in how discovery would work in actual practice by letting district court judges fashion their own rules in the context of individual cases. When the results of such experience are available it would be desirable to consider whether further, more specific codification should take place.

Subdivision (b) provides for judicial consideration of all matters subject to discovery. A statement of the interrogatories, or requests for admission sought to be answered, and a list of any documents sought to be produced, must accompany a request for discovery. This is to advise the judge of the necessity for discovery and enable him to make certain that the inquiry is relevant and appropriately narrow.

Subdivision (c) refers to the situation where the respondent is granted leave to take the deposition of the petitioner or any other person. In such a case the judge may direct the respondent to pay the expenses and fees of counsel for the petitioner to attend the taking of the deposition, as a condition granting the respondent such leave. While the judge is not required to impose this condition subdivision (c) will give the court the means to do so. Such a provision affords some protection to the indigent petitioner who may be prejudiced by his inability to have counsel, often court-appointed, present at the taking of a deposition. It is recognized that under 18 U.S.C. § 3006A(g), court-appointed counsel in a § 2254 proceeding is entitled to receive up to $250 and reimbursement for expenses reasonably incurred. (Compare Fed.R.Crim.P. 15(c).) Typically, however, this does not adequately reimburse counsel if he must attend the taking of depositions or be involved in other pre-hearing proceedings. Subdivision (c) is intended to provide additional funds, if necessary, to be paid by the state government (respondent) to petitioner's counsel.

Although the rule does not specifically so provide, it is assumed that a petitioner who qualifies for the appointment of counsel under 18 U.S.C. § 3006A(g) and is granted leave to take a deposition will be allowed witness costs. This will include recording and transcription of the witness's statement. Such costs are payable pursuant to 28 U.S.C. § 1825. See Opinion of Comptroller General, February 28, 1974.

Subdivision (c) specifically recognizes the right of the respondent to take the deposition of the petitioner. Although the petitioner could not be called to testify against his will in a criminal trial, it is felt the nature of the habeas proceeding, along with the safeguards accorded by the Fifth Amendment and the presence of counsel, justify this provision. See 83 Harv.L.Rev. 1038, 1183–84 (1970).

2004 Amendments

The language of Rule 6 has been amended as part of general restyling of the rules to make them more easily understood and to make style and terminology consistent throughout the rules. These changes are intended to be stylistic and no substantive change is intended.

Although current Rule 6(b) contains no requirement that the parties provide reasons for the requested discovery, the revised rule does so and also includes a requirement that the request be accompanied by any proposed interrogatories and requests for admission, and must specify any requested documents. The Committee believes that the revised rule makes explicit what has been implicit in current practice.

Changes Made After Publication and Comments. Rule 6(b) was modified to require that discovery requests be supported by reasons, to assist the court in deciding what, if any, discovery should take place. The Committee believed that the change made explicit what has been implicit in current practice.

Rule 7.   Expanding the Record

(a) In General. If the petition is not dismissed, the judge may direct the parties to expand the record by submitting additional materials relating to the petition. The judge may require that these materials be authenticated.

(b) Types of Materials. The materials that may be required include letters predating the filing of the petition, documents, exhibits, and answers under oath to written interrogatories propounded by the judge. Affidavits may also be submitted and considered as part of the record.

(c) Review by the Opposing Party. The judge must give the party against whom the additional materials are offered an opportunity to admit or deny their correctness.

(As amended Apr. 26, 2004, eff. Dec. 1, 2004.)

ADVISORY COMMITTEE NOTES

1976 Adoption

This rule provides that the judge may direct that the record be expanded. The purpose is to enable the judge to dispose of some habeas petitions not dismissed on the pleadings, without the time and expense required for an evidentiary hearing. An expanded record may also be helpful when an evidentiary hearing is ordered.

The record may be expanded to include additional material relevant to the merits of the petition. While most petitions are dismissed either summarily or after a response has been made, of those that remain, by far the majority require an evidentiary hearing. In the fiscal year ending June 30, 1970, for example, of 8,423 § 2254 cases terminated, 8,231 required court action. Of these, 7,812 were dismissed before a prehearing conference and 469 merited further court action (*e.g.*, expansion of the record, prehearing conference, or an evidentiary hearing). Of the remaining 469 cases, 403 required an evidentiary hearing, often time-consuming, costly, and, at least occasionally, unnecessary. See Director of the Administrative Office of the United States Courts, Annual Report, 245a–245c (table C4) (1970). In some instances these hearings were necessitated by slight omissions in the state record which might have been cured by the use of an expanded record.

Authorizing expansion of the record will, hopefully, eliminate some unnecessary hearings. The value of this approach was articulated in *Raines v. United States*, 423 F.2d 526, 529–530 (4th Cir. 1970):

Unless it is clear from the pleadings and the files and records that the prisoner is entitled to no relief, the statute makes a hearing mandatory. We think there is a permissible intermediate step that may avoid the necessity for an expensive and time consuming evidentiary hearing in every Section 2255 case. It may instead be perfectly appropriate, depending upon the nature of the allegations, for the district court to proceed by requiring that the record be expanded to include letters, documentary evidence, and, in an appropriate case, even affidavits. *United States v. Carlino,* 400 F.2d 56 (2nd Cir. 1968); *Mirra v. United States,* 379 F.2d 782 (2nd Cir. 1967); *Accardi v. United States,* 379 F.2d 312 (2nd Cir. 1967). When the issue is one of credibility, resolution on the basis of affidavits can rarely be conclusive, but that is not to say they may not be helpful.

In *Harris v. Nelson,* 394 U.S. 286, 300 (1969), the court said:

> At any time in the proceedings * * * *either on [the court's] own motion* or upon cause shown by the petitioner, it may issue such writs and take or authorize such proceedings * * * *before* or in conjunction with the hearing of the facts * * * . [emphasis added]

Subdivision (b) specifies the materials which may be added to the record. These include, without limitation, letters predating the filing of the petition in the district court, documents, exhibits, and answers under oath directed to written interrogatories propounded by the judge. Under this subdivision affidavits may be submitted and considered part of the record. Subdivision (b) is consistent with 28 U.S.C. §§ 2246 and 2247 and the decision in *Raines* with regard to types of material that may be considered upon application for a writ of habeas corpus. See *United States v. Carlino,* 400 F.2d 56, 58 (2d Cir. 1968), and *Machibroda v. United States,* 368 U.S. 487 (1962).

Under subdivision (c) all materials proposed to be included in the record must be submitted to the party against whom they are to be offered.

Under subdivision (d) the judge can require authentication if he believes it desirable to do so.

2004 Amendments

The language of Rule 7 has been amended as part of general restyling of the rules to make them more easily understood and to make style and terminology consistent throughout the rules. These changes are intended to be stylistic and no substantive change is intended, except as noted below.

Revised Rule 7(a) is not intended to restrict the court's authority to expand the record through means other than requiring the parties themselves to provide the information. Further, the rule has been changed to remove the reference to the "merits" of the petition in the recognition that a court may wish to expand the record in order to assist it in deciding an issue other than the merits of the petition.

The language in current Rule 7(d), which deals with authentication of materials in the expanded record, has been moved to revised Rule 7(a).

Changes Made After Publication and Comments. The Committee modified Rule 7(a) by removing the reference to the "merits" of the petition. One commentator had commented that the court might wish to expand the record for purposes other than the merits of the case. The Committee agreed to the change and also changed the rule to reflect that someone other than a party may authenticate the materials.

Rule 8.   Evidentiary Hearing

   (a)   Determining Whether to Hold a Hearing. If the petition is not dismissed, the judge must review the answer, any transcripts and records of state-court proceedings, and any materials submitted under Rule 7 to determine whether an evidentiary hearing is warranted.

   (b)   Reference to a Magistrate Judge. A judge may, under 28 U.S.C. § 636(b), refer the petition to a magistrate judge to conduct hearings and to file proposed findings of fact and recommendations for disposition. When they are filed, the clerk must promptly serve copies of the proposed findings and recommendations on all parties. Within 14 days after being served, a party may file objections as provided by local court rule. The judge must determine de novo any proposed finding or recommendation to which objection is made. The judge may accept, reject, or modify any proposed finding or recommendation.

   (c)   Appointing Counsel; Time of Hearing. If an evidentiary hearing is warranted, the judge must appoint an attorney to represent a petitioner who qualifies to have counsel appointed under 18 U.S.C. § 3006A. The judge must conduct the hearing as soon as practicable after giving the attorneys adequate time to investigate and prepare. These rules do not limit the appointment of counsel under § 3006A at any stage of the proceeding.

(As amended Pub.L. 94–426, § 2(5), Sept. 28, 1976, 90 Stat. 1334; Pub.L. 94–577, § 2(a)(1), (b)(1), Oct. 21, 1976, 90 Stat. 2730, 2731; Apr. 26, 2004, eff. Dec. 1, 2004; Mar. 26, 2009, eff. Dec. 1, 2009.)

ADVISORY COMMITTEE NOTES

1976 Adoption

This rule outlines the procedure to be followed by the court immediately prior to and after the determination of whether to hold an evidentiary hearing.

The provisions are applicable if the petition has not been dismissed at a previous stage in the proceeding [including a summary dismissal under Rule 4; a dismissal pursuant to a motion by the respondent; a dismissal after the answer and petition are considered; or a dismissal after consideration of the pleadings and an expanded record].

If dismissal has not been ordered, the court must determine whether an evidentiary hearing is required. This determination is to be made upon a review of the answer, the transcript and record of state court proceedings, and if there is one, the expanded record. As the United States Supreme Court noted in *Townsend v. Sam,* 372 U.S. 293, 319 (1963):

> Ordinarily [the complete state-court] record—including the transcript of testimony (or if unavailable some adequate substitute, such as a narrative record), the pleadings, court opinions, and other pertinent documents—is indispensable to determining whether the habeas applicant received a full and fair state-court evidentiary hearing resulting in reliable findings.

Subdivision (a) contemplates that all of these materials, if available, will be taken into account. This is especially important in view of the standard set down in *Townsend* for determining *when* a hearing in the federal habeas proceeding is mandatory.

> The appropriate standard * * * is this: Where the facts are in dispute, the federal court in habeas corpus must hold an evidentiary hearing if the habeas applicant did not receive a full and fair evidentiary hearing in a state court, either at the time of the trial or in a collateral proceeding.

372 U.S. at 312

The circumstances under which a federal hearing is mandatory are now specified in 28 U.S.C. § 2254(d). The 1966 amendment clearly places the burden on the petitioner, when there has already been a state hearing, to show that it was not a fair or adequate hearing for one or more of the specifically enumerated reasons, in order to force a federal evidentiary hearing. Since the function of an evidentiary hearing is to try issues of fact (372 U.S. at 309), such a hearing is unnecessary when only issues of law are raised. See, *e.g.,* *Yeaman v. United States,* 326 F.2d 293 (9th Cir. 1963).

In situations in which an evidentiary hearing is not mandatory, the judge may nonetheless decide that an evidentiary hearing is desirable:

> The purpose of the test is to indicate the situations in which the holding of an evidentiary hearing is mandatory. In all other cases where the material facts are in dispute, the holding of such a hearing is in the discretion of the district judge.

372 U.S. at 318

If the judge decides that an evidentiary hearing is neither required nor desirable, he shall make such a disposition of the petition "as justice shall require." Most habeas petitions are dismissed before the prehearing conference stage (see Director of the Administrative Office of the United States Courts, Annual Report 245–245c (table C4) (1970)) and of those not dismissed, the majority raise factual issues that necessitate an evidentiary hearing. If no hearing is required, most petitions are dismissed, but in unusual cases the court may grant the relief sought without a hearing. This includes immediate release from custody or nullification of a judgment under which the sentence is to be served in the future.

Subdivision (b) provides that a magistrate, when so empowered by rule of the district court, may recommend to the district judge that an evidentiary hearing be held or that the petition be dismissed, provided he gives the district judge a sufficiently detailed description of the facts so that the judge may decide whether or not to hold an evidentiary hearing. This provision is not inconsistent with the holding in *Wingo v. Wedding,* 418 U.S. 461 (1974), that the Federal Magistrates Act did not change the requirement of the habeas corpus statute that federal judges personally conduct habeas evidentiary hearings, and that consequently a local district court rule was invalid insofar as it authorized a magistrate to hold such hearings. 28 U.S.C. § 636(b) provides that a district court may by rule authorize any magistrate to perform certain additional duties, including preliminary review of applications for posttrial relief made by individuals convicted of criminal offenses, and submission of a report and recommendations to facilitate the decision of the district judge having jurisdiction over the case as to whether there should be a hearing.

As noted in *Wingo*, review "by Magistrates of applications for post-trial relief is thus limited to review for the purpose of proposing, not holding, evidentiary hearings."

Utilization of the magistrate as specified in subdivision (b) will aid in the expeditious and fair handling of habeas petitions.

A qualified, experienced magistrate will, it is hoped, acquire an expertise in examining these [postconviction review] applications and summarizing their important contents for the district judge, thereby facilitating his decisions. Law clerks are presently charged with this responsibility by many judges, but judges have noted that the normal 1-year clerkship does not afford law clerks the time or experience necessary to attain real efficiency in handling such applications.

S.Rep. No. 371, 90th Cong., 1st Sess., 26 (1967).

Under subdivision (c) there are two provisions that differ from the procedure set forth in 28 U.S.C. § 2243. These are the appointment of counsel and standard for determining how soon the hearing will be held.

If an evidentiary hearing is required the judge must appoint counsel for a petitioner who qualified [sic] for appointment under the Criminal Justice Act. Currently, the appointment of counsel is not recognized as a right at any stage of a habeas proceeding. See, *e.g., United States ex rel. Marshall v. Wilkins,* 338 F.2d 404 (2d Cir. 1964). Some district courts have, however, by local rule, required that counsel must be provided for indigent petitioners in cases requiring a hearing. See, *e.g., D.N.M.R. 21(f), E.D.N.Y.R. 26(d).* Appointment of counsel at this stage is mandatory under subdivision (c). This requirement will not limit the authority of the court to provide counsel at an earlier stage if it is thought desirable to do so as is done in some courts under current practice. At the evidentiary hearing stage, however, an indigent petitioner's access to counsel should not depend on local practice and, for this reason, the furnishing of counsel is made mandatory.

Counsel can perform a valuable function benefiting both the court and the petitioner. The issues raised can be more clearly identified if both sides have the benefit of trained legal personnel. The presence of counsel at the prehearing conference may help to expedite the evidentiary hearing or make it unnecessary, and counsel will be able to make better use of available prehearing discovery procedures. Compare ABA Project on Standards for Criminal Justice, Standards Relating to Post-Conviction Remedies § 4.4, p. 66 (Approved Draft 1968). At a hearing, the petitioner's claims are more likely to be effectively and properly presented by counsel.

Under 18 U.S.C. § 3006A(g), payment is allowed counsel up to $250, plus reimbursement for expenses reasonably incurred. The standards of indigency under this section are less strict than those regarding eligibility to prosecute a petition in forma pauperis, and thus many who cannot qualify to proceed under 28 U.S.C. § 1915 will be entitled to the benefits of counsel under 18 U.S.C. § 3006A(g). Under Rule 6(c), the court may order the respondent to reimburse counsel from state funds for fees and expenses incurred as the result of the utilization of discovery procedures by the respondent.

Subdivision (c) provides that the hearing shall be conducted as promptly as possible, taking into account "the need of counsel for both parties for adequate time for investigation and preparation." This differs from the language of 28 U.S.C. § 2243, which requires that the day for the hearing be set "not more than five days after the return unless for good cause additional time is allowed." This time limit fails to take into account the function that may be served by a prehearing conference and the time required to prepare adequately for an evidentiary hearing. Although "additional time" is often allowed under § 2243, subdivision (c) provides more flexibility to take account of the complexity of the case, the availability of important materials, the workload of the attorney general, and the time required by appointed counsel to prepare.

While the rule does not make specific provision for a prehearing conference, the omission is not intended to cast doubt upon the value of such a conference:

The conference may limit the questions to be resolved, identify areas of agreement and dispute, and explore evidentiary problems that may be expected to arise. * * * [S]uch conferences may also disclose that a hearing is unnecessary * * * .

ABA Project on Standards for Criminal Justice, Standards Relating to Post-Conviction Remedies § 4.6, commentary pp. 74–75. (Approved Draft, 1968.)

See also Developments in the Law—Federal Habeas Corpus, 83 Harv.L.Rev. 1038, 1188 (1970).

The rule does not contain a specific provision on the subpoenaing of witnesses. It is left to local practice to determine the method for doing this. The implementation of 28 U.S.C. § 1825 on the payment of witness fees is dealt with in an opinion of the Comptroller General, February 28, 1974.

2004 Amendments

The language of Rule 8 has been amended as part of general restyling of the rules to make them more easily understood and to make style and terminology consistent throughout the rules. These changes are intended to be stylistic and no substantive change is intended.

Rule 8(a) is not intended to supersede the restrictions on evidentiary hearings contained in 28 U.S.C. § 2254(e)(2).

The requirement in current Rule 8(b)(2) that a copy of the magistrate judge's findings must be promptly mailed to all parties has been changed in revised Rule 8(b) to require that copies of those findings be served on all parties. As used in this rule, "service" means service consistent with Federal Rule of Civil Procedure 5(b), which allows mailing the copies.

Changes Made After Publication and Comments. The Committee changed the Committee Note to reflect the view that the amendments to Rule 8 were not intended to supercede the restrictions on evidentiary hearings contained in § 2254(e)(2).

2009 Amendments

The time set in the former rule at 10 days has been revised to 14 days. See the Committee Note to Federal Rules of Criminal Procedure 45(a).

HISTORICAL NOTES

Effective and Applicability Provisions

1976 Acts. Section 2(c) of Pub.L. 94–577 provided that: "The amendments made by this section [amending subdivs. (b) and (c) of this rule and Rule 8(b), (c) of the Rules Governing Proceedings Under Section 2255 of this title] shall take effect with respect to petitions under section 2254 and motions under section 2255 of title 28 of the United States Code filed on or after February 1, 1977."

Rule 9.   Second or Successive Petitions

Before presenting a second or successive petition, the petitioner must obtain an order from the appropriate court of appeals authorizing the district court to consider the petition as required by 28 U.S.C. § 2244(b)(3) and (4).

(As amended Pub.L. 94–426, § 2(7), (8), Sept. 28, 1976, 90 Stat. 1335; Apr. 26, 2004, eff. Dec. 1, 2004.)

ADVISORY COMMITTEE NOTES

1976 Adoption

This rule is intended to minimize abuse of the writ of habeas corpus by limiting the right to assert stale claims and to file multiple petitions. Subdivision (a) deals with the delayed petition. Subdivision (b) deals with the second or successive petition.

Subdivision (a) provides that a petition attacking the judgment of a state court may be dismissed on the grounds of delay if the petitioner knew or should have known of the existence of the grounds he is presently asserting in the petition and the delay has resulted in the state being prejudiced in its ability to respond to the petition. If the delay is more than five years after the judgment of conviction, prejudice is presumed, although this presumption is rebuttable by the petitioner. Otherwise, the state has the burden of showing such prejudice.

The assertion of stale claims is a problem which is not likely to decrease in frequency. Following the decisions in *Jones v. Cunningham,* 371 U.S. 236 (1963), and *Benson v. California,* 328 F.2d 159 (9th Cir. 1964), the concept of custody expanded greatly, lengthening the time period during which a habeas corpus petition may be filed. The petitioner who is not unconditionally discharged may be on parole or probation for many years. He may at some date, perhaps ten or fifteen years after conviction, decide to challenge the state court judgment. The grounds most often troublesome to the courts are ineffective counsel, denial of right of appeal, plea of guilty unlawfully induced, use of a coerced confession, and illegally constituted jury. The latter four grounds are often interlocked with the allegation of ineffective counsel. When they are asserted after the passage of many years, both the attorney for the defendant and the state have difficulty in ascertaining what the facts are. It often develops that the defense attorney has little or no recollection as to what took place and that many of the participants in the trial are dead or their whereabouts unknown. The court reporter's notes may have been lost or destroyed, thus eliminating any exact record of what transpired. If the case was decided on a guilty plea, even if the record is intact, it may not satisfactorily reveal the extent of the defense attorney's efforts in behalf of the petitioner. As a consequence, there is obvious difficulty in investigating petitioner's allegations.

The interest of both the petitioner and the government can best be served if claims are raised while the evidence is still fresh. The American Bar Association has recognized the interest of the state in protecting itself against stale claims by limiting the right to raise such claims after completion of service of a sentence imposed pursuant to a challenged judgment. See ABA Standards Relating to Post-Conviction Remedies § 2.4(c), p. 45 (Approved Draft, 1968). Subdivision (a) is not limited to those who have completed their sentence. Its reach is broader, extending to all instances where delay by the petitioner has prejudiced the state, subject to the qualifications and conditions contained in the subdivision.

In *McMann v. Richardson,* 397 U.S. 759 (1970), the court made reference to the issue of the stale claim:

> What is at stake in this phase of the case is not the integrity of the state convictions obtained on guilty pleas, *but whether, years later*, defendants must be permitted to withdraw their pleas, which were perfectly valid when made, and be given another choice between admitting their guilt and putting the State to its proof. [Emphasis added.]

397 U.S. at 773

The court refused to allow this, intimating its dislike of collateral attacks on sentences long since imposed which disrupt the state's interest in finality of convictions which were constitutionally valid when obtained.

Subdivision (a) is not a statute of limitations. Rather, the limitation is based on the equitable doctrine of laches. "Laches is such delay in enforcing one's rights as works disadvantage to another." 30A C.J.S. Equity § 112, p. 19. Also, the language of the subdivision, "a petition *may* be dismissed" [emphasis added], is permissive rather than mandatory. This clearly allows the court which is considering the petition to use discretion in assessing the equities of the particular situation.

The use of a flexible rule analogous to laches to bar the assertion of stale claims is suggested in ABA Standards Relating to Post-Conviction Remedies § 2.4, commentary at 48 (Approved Draft, 1968). Additionally, in *Fay v. Noia,* 372 U.S. 391 (1963), the Supreme Court noted:

> Furthermore, habeas corpus has traditionally been regarded as governed by equitable principles. *United States ex rel. Smith v. Baldi,* 344 U.S. 561, 573 (dissenting opinion). Among them is the principle that a suitor's conduct in relation to the matter at hand may disentitle him to the relief he seeks.

372 U.S. at 438

Finally, the doctrine of laches has been applied with reference to another postconviction remedy, the writ of coram nobis. See 24 C.J.S. Criminal Law § 1606(25), p. 779.

The standard used for determining if the petitioner shall be barred from asserting his claim is consistent with that used in laches provisions generally. The petitioner is held to a standard of reasonable diligence. Any inference or presumption arising by reason of the failure to attack collaterally a conviction may be disregarded where (1) there has been a change of law or fact (new evidence) or (2) where the court, in the interest of justice, feels that the collateral attack should be entertained and the prisoner makes a proper showing as to why he has not asserted a particular ground for relief.

Subdivision (a) establishes the presumption that the passage of more than five years from the time of the judgment of conviction to the time of filing a habeas petition is prejudicial to the state. "Presumption" has the meaning given it by Fed.R.Evid. 301. The prisoner has "the burden of going forward with evidence to rebut or meet the presumption" that the state has not been prejudiced by the passage of a substantial period of time. This does not impose too heavy a burden on the petitioner. He usually knows what persons are important to the issue of whether the state has been prejudiced. Rule 6 can be used by the court to allow petitioner liberal discovery to learn whether witnesses have died or whether other circumstances prejudicial to the state have occurred. Even if the petitioner should fail to overcome the presumption of prejudice to the state, he is not automatically barred from asserting his claim. As discussed previously, he may proceed if he neither knew nor, by the exercise of reasonable diligence, could have known of the grounds for relief.

The presumption of prejudice does not come into play if the time lag is not more than five years.

The time limitation should have a positive effect in encouraging petitioners who have knowledge of it to assert all their claims as soon after conviction as possible. The implementation of this rule can be substantially furthered by the development of greater legal resources for prisoners. See ABA Standards Relating to Post-Conviction Remedies § 3.1, pp. 49–50 (Approved Draft, 1968).

Subdivision (a) does not constitute an abridgement or modification of a substantive right under 28 U.S.C. § 2072. There are safeguards for the hardship case. The rule provides a flexible standard for determining when a petition will be barred.

Subdivision (b) deals with the problem of successive habeas petitions. It provides that the judge may dismiss a second or successive petition (1) if it fails to allege new or different grounds for relief or (2) if new or different grounds for relief are alleged and the judge finds the failure of the petitioner to assert those grounds in a prior petition is inexcusable.

In *Sanders v. United States,* 373 U.S. 1 (1963), the court, in dealing with the problem of successive applications, stated:

> Controlling weight *may* be given to denial of a prior application for federal habeas corpus or § 2255 relief only if (1) the same ground presented in the subsequent application was determined adversely to the applicant on the prior application, (2) the prior determination was on the merits, and (3) the ends of justice would not be served by reaching the merits of the subsequent application. [Emphasis added.]

373 U.S. at 15

The requirement is that the prior determination of the same ground has been on the merits. This requirement is in 28 U.S.C. § 2244(b) and has been reiterated in many cases since *Sanders.* See *Gains v. Allgood,* 391 F.2d 692 (5th Cir. 1968); *Hutchinson v. Craven,* 415 F.2d 278 (9th Cir. 1969); *Brown v. Peyton,* 435 F.2d 1352 (4th Cir. 1970).

With reference to a successive application asserting a new ground or one not previously decided on the merits, the court in *Sanders* noted:

> In either case, full consideration of the merits of the new application can be avoided only if there has been an abuse of the writ * * * and this the Government has the burden of pleading. * * *

Thus, for example, if a prisoner deliberately withholds one of two grounds for federal collateral relief at the time of filing his first application, * * * he may be deemed to have waived his right to a hearing on a second application presenting the withheld ground.

373 U.S. at 17–18

Subdivision (b) has incorporated this principle and requires that the judge find petitioner's failure to have asserted the new grounds in the prior petition to be inexcusable.

Sanders, 18 [sic] U.S.C. § 2244, and subdivision (b) make it clear that the court has discretion to entertain a successive application.

The burden is on the government to plead abuse of the writ. See *Sanders v. United States,* 373 U.S. 1, 10 (1963); *Dixon v. Jacobs,* 427 F.2d 589, 596 (D.C.Cir.1970); cf. *Johnson v. Copinger,* 420 F.2d 395 (4th Cir. 1969). Once the government has done this, the petitioner has the burden of proving that he has not abused the writ. In *Price v. Johnston,* 334 U.S. 266, 292 (1948), the court said:

> [I]f the Government chooses * * * to claim that the prisoner has abused the writ of *habeas corpus,* it rests with the Government to make that claim with clarity and particularity in its return to the order to show cause. That is not an intolerable burden. The Government is usually well acquainted with the facts that are necessary to make such a claim. Once a particular abuse has been alleged, the prisoner has the burden of answering that allegation and of proving that he has not abused the writ.

Subdivision (b) is consistent with the important and well established purpose of habeas corpus. It does not eliminate a remedy to which the petitioner is rightfully entitled. However, in *Sanders,* the court pointed out:

> Nothing in the traditions of habeas corpus requires the federal courts to tolerate needless piecemeal litigation, or to entertain collateral proceedings whose only purpose is to vex, harass, or delay.

373 U.S. at 18

There are instances in which petitioner's failure to assert a ground in a prior petition is excusable. A retroactive change in the law and newly discovered evidence are examples. In rare instances, the court may feel a need to entertain a petition alleging grounds that have already been decided on the merits. *Sanders,* 373 U.S. at 1, 16. However, abusive use of the writ should be discouraged, and instances of abuse are frequent enough to require a means of dealing with them. For example, a successive application, already decided on the merits, may be submitted in the hope of getting before a different judge in multijudge courts. A known ground may be deliberately withheld in the hope of getting two or more hearings or in the hope that delay will result in witnesses and records being lost. There are instances in which a petitioner will have three or four petitions pending at the same time in the same court. There are many hundreds of cases where the application is at least the second one by the petitioner. This subdivision is aimed at screening out the abusive petitions from this large volume, so that the more meritorious petitions can get quicker and fuller consideration.

The form petition, supplied in accordance with Rule 2(c), encourages the petitioner to raise all of his available grounds in one petition. It sets out the most common grounds asserted so that these may be brought to his attention.

Some commentators contend that the problem of abuse of the writ of habeas corpus is greatly overstated:

> Most prisoners, of course, are interested in being released as soon as possible; only rarely will one inexcusably neglect to raise all available issues in his first federal application. The purpose of the "abuse" bar is apparently to deter repetitious applications from those few bored or vindictive prisoners * * *.

83 Harv.L.Rev. at 1153–1154

See also ABA Standards Relating to Post-Conviction Remedies § 6.2, commentary at 92 (Approved Draft, 1968), which states: "The occasional, highly litigious prisoner stands out as the rarest exception." While no recent systematic study of repetitious applications exists, there is no reason to believe that the problem has decreased in significance in relation to the total number of § 2254 petitions filed. That number has increased from 584 in 1949 to 12,088 in 1971. See Director of the Administrative Office of the United States Courts, Annual Report, table 16 (1971). It is appropriate that action be taken by rule to allow the courts to deal with this problem, whatever its specific magnitude. The bar set up by subdivision (b) is not one of rigid application, but rather is within the discretion of the courts on a case-by-case basis.

If it appears to the court after examining the petition and answer (where appropriate) that there is a high probability that the petition will be barred under either subdivision of Rule 9, the court ought to afford petitioner an opportunity to explain his apparent abuse. One way of doing this is by the use of the form annexed hereto. The use of a form will ensure a full airing of the issue so that the court is in a better position to decide whether the petition should be barred. This conforms with *Johnson v. Copinger,* 420 F.2d 395 (4th Cir. 1969), where the court stated:

[T]he petitioner is obligated to present facts demonstrating that his earlier failure to raise his claims is excusable and does not amount to an abuse of the writ. However, it is inherent in this obligation placed upon the petitioner that he must be given an opportunity to make his explanation, if he has one. If he is not afforded such an opportunity, the requirement that he satisfy the court that he has not abused the writ is meaningless. Nor do we think that a procedure which allows the imposition of a forfeiture for abuse of the writ, without allowing the petitioner an opportunity to be heard on the issue, comports with the minimum requirements of fairness.

420 F.2d at 399

Use of the recommended form will contribute to an orderly handling of habeas petitions and will contribute to the ability of the court to distinguish the excusable from the inexcusable delay or failure to assert a ground for relief in a prior petition.

2004 Amendments

The language of Rule 9 has been amended as part of general restyling of the rules to make them more easily understood and to make style and terminology consistent throughout the rules. These changes are intended to be stylistic and no substantive change is intended, except as noted below.

First, current Rule 9(a) has been deleted as unnecessary in light of the applicable one-year statute of limitations for § 2254 petitions, added as part of the Antiterrorism and Effective Death Penalty Act of 1996, 28 U.S.C. § 2244(d).

Second, current Rule 9(b), now Rule 9, has been changed to also reflect provisions in the Antiterrorism and Effective Death Penalty Act of 1996, 28 U.S.C. § 2244(b)(3) and (4), which now require a petitioner to obtain approval from the appropriate court of appeals before filing a second or successive petition.

Finally, the title of Rule 9 has been changed to reflect the fact that the only topic now addressed in the rules is that of second or successive petitions.

Changes Made After Publication and Comments. The Committee made no changes to Rule 9.

Rule 10.   Powers of a Magistrate Judge

A magistrate judge may perform the duties of a district judge under these rules, as authorized under 28 U.S.C. § 636.

(As amended Pub.L. 94–426, § 2(11), Sept. 28, 1976, 90 Stat. 1335; Apr. 30, 1979, eff. Aug. 1, 1979; Apr. 26, 2004, eff. Dec. 1, 2004.)

ADVISORY COMMITTEE NOTES

1976 Adoption

Under this rule the duties imposed upon the judge of the district court by rules 2, 3, 4, 6, and 7 may be performed by a magistrate if and to the extent he is empowered to do so by a rule of the district court. However, when such duties involve the making of an order under rule 4 disposing of the petition, that order must be made by the court. The magistrate in such instances must submit to the court his report as to the facts and his recommendation with respect to the order.

The Federal Magistrates Act allows magistrates, when empowered by local rule, to perform certain functions in proceedings for post-trial relief. See 28 U.S.C. § 636(b)(3). The performance of such functions, when authorized, is intended to "afford some degree of relief to district judges and their law clerks, who are presently burdened with burgeoning numbers of habeas corpus petitions and applications under 28 U.S.C. § 2255." Committee on the Judiciary, The Federal Magistrates Act, S.Rep. No. 371, 90th Cong., 1st sess., 26 (1967).

Under 28 U.S.C. § 636(b), any district court,

by the concurrence of a majority of all the judges of such district court, may establish rules pursuant to which any full-time United States magistrate * * * may be assigned within the territorial jurisdiction of such court such additional duties as are not inconsistent with the Constitution and laws of the United States.

The proposed rule recognizes the limitations imposed by 28 U.S.C. § 636(b) upon the powers of magistrates to act in federal postconviction proceedings. These limitations are: (1) that the magistrate may act only pursuant to a rule passed by the majority of the judges in the district court in which the magistrate serves, and (2) that the duties performed by the magistrate pursuant to such rule be consistent with the Constitution and laws of the United States.

It has been suggested magistrates be empowered by law to hold hearings and make final decisions in habeas proceedings. See Proposed Reformation of Federal Habeas Corpus Procedure: Use of Federal Magistrates, 54 Iowa L.Rev. 1147, 1158 (1969). However, the Federal Magistrates Act does not authorize such use of magistrates. *Wingo v. Wedding,* 418 U.S. 461 (1974). See advisory committee note to Rule 8. While the use of magistrates can help alleviate the strain imposed on the district courts by the large number of unmeritorious habeas petitions, neither 28 U.S.C. § 636(b) nor this rule contemplate the abdication by the court of its decision-making responsibility. See also Developments in the Law—Federal Habeas Corpus, 83 Harv.L.Rev. 1038, 1188 (1970).

Where a full-time magistrate is not available, the duties contemplated by this rule may be assigned to a part-time magistrate.

2004 Amendments

The language of Rule 10 has been amended as part of general restyling of the rules to make them more easily understood and to make style and terminology consistent throughout the rules. These changes are intended to be stylistic and no substantive change is intended.

Changes Made After Publication and Comments. The Committee restyled the proposed rule.

HISTORICAL NOTES

Change of Name

United States magistrate appointed under section 631 of Title 28, Judiciary and Judicial Procedure, to be known as United States magistrate judge after Dec. 1, 1990, with any reference to United States magistrate or magistrate in Title 28, in any other Federal statute, etc., deemed a reference to United States magistrate judge appointed under section 631 of Title 28, see section 321 of Pub.L. 101–650, set out as a note under section 631 of Title 28.

Rule 11.   Certificate of Appealability; Time to Appeal

(a) Certificate of Appealability. The district court must issue or deny a certificate of appealability when it enters a final order adverse to the applicant. Before entering the final order, the court may direct the parties to submit arguments on whether a certificate should issue. If the court issues a certificate, the court must state the specific issue or issues that satisfy the showing required by 28 U.S.C. § 2253(c)(2). If the court denies a certificate, the parties may not appeal the denial but may seek a certificate from the court of appeals under Federal Rule of Appellate Procedure 22. A motion to reconsider a denial does not extend the time to appeal.

(b) Time to Appeal. Federal Rule of Appellate Procedure 4(a) governs the time to appeal an order entered under these rules. A timely notice of appeal must be filed even if the district court issues a certificate of appealability.

(Added Mar. 26, 2009, eff. Dec. 1, 2009.)

ADVISORY COMMITTEE NOTES

2009 Amendments

Subdivision (a). As provided in 28 U.S.C. § 2253(c), an applicant may not appeal to the court of appeals from a final order in a proceeding under § 2254 unless a judge issues a certificate of appealability (COA), identifying the specific issues for which the applicant has made a substantial showing of a denial of constitutional right. New Rule 11(a) makes the requirements concerning COAs more prominent by adding and consolidating them in the appropriate rule of the Rules Governing § 2254 Cases in the United States District Courts. Rule 11(a) also requires the district judge to grant or deny the certificate at the time a final order is issued. *See* 3d Cir. R. 22.2, 111.3. This will ensure prompt decision making when the issues are fresh, rather than postponing consideration of the certificate until after a notice of appeal is filed. These changes will expedite proceedings, avoid unnecessary remands, and help inform the applicant's decision whether to file a notice of appeal.

Subdivision (b). The new subdivision is designed to direct parties to the appropriate rule governing the timing of the notice of appeal and make it clear that the district court's grant of a COA does not eliminate the need to file a notice of appeal.

Changes Made to Proposed Amendment Released for Public Comment. In response to public comments, a sentence was added stating that prior to the entry of the final order the district court may direct the parties to submit arguments on whether or not a certificate should issue. This allows a court in complex cases (such as death penalty cases with numerous claims) to solicit briefing that might narrow the issues for appeal. For purposes of clarification, two sentences were added at the end of subdivision (a) stating that (1) although the district court's denial of a certificate is not appealable, a certificate may be sought in the court of appeals, and (2) a motion for reconsideration of a denial of a certificate does not extend the time to appeal.

Finally, a new subdivision (b) was added to mirror the information provided in subdivision (b) of Rule 11 of the Rules Governing § 2255 Proceedings, directing petitioners to Rule 4 of the appellate rules and indicating that notice of appeal must be filed even if a COA is issued.

Minor changes were also made to conform to style conventions.

HISTORICAL NOTES

Prior Provisions

Former Rule 11 concerning applicability of the Federal Rules of Civil Procedure redesignated as Rule 12.

Rule 12.   Applicability of the Federal Rules of Civil Procedure

The Federal Rules of Civil Procedure, to the extent that they are not inconsistent with any statutory provisions or these rules, may be applied to a proceeding under these rules.

(As amended Apr. 26, 2004, eff. Dec. 1, 2004; Rule 11 redesignated Rule 12 Mar. 26, 2009, eff. Dec. 1, 2009.)

ADVISORY COMMITTEE NOTES

1976 Adoption

Habeas corpus proceedings are characterized as civil in nature. See, *e.g., Fisher v. Baker,* 203 U.S. 174, 181 (1906). However, under Fed.R.Civ.P. 81(a)(2), the applicability of the civil rules to habeas corpus actions has been limited, although the various courts which have considered this problem have had difficulty in setting out the boundaries of this limitation. See *Harris v. Nelson,* 394 U.S. 286 (1969) at 289, footnote 1. Rule 11 [now redesignated as Rule 12] is intended to conform with the Supreme Court's approach in the *Harris* case. There the court was dealing with the petitioner's contention that Civil Rule 33 granting the right to discovery via written interrogatories is wholly applicable to habeas corpus proceedings. The court held:

> We agree with the Ninth Circuit that Rule 33 of the Federal Rules of Civil Procedure is not applicable to habeas corpus proceedings and that 28 U.S.C. § 2246 does not authorize interrogatories except in limited circumstances not applicable to this case; but we conclude that, in appropriate circumstances, a district court, confronted by a petition for habeas corpus which establishes a prima facie case for relief, may use or authorize the use of suitable discovery procedures, including interrogatories, reasonably fashioned to elicit facts necessary to help the court to "dispose of the matter as law and justice require" 28 U.S.C. § 2243.

394 U.S. at 290

The court then went on to consider the contention that the "conformity" provision of Rule 81(a)(2) should be rigidly applied so that the civil rules would be applicable only to the extent that habeas corpus practice had conformed to the practice in civil actions at the time of the adoption of the Federal Rules of Civil Procedure on September 16, 1938. The court said:

Although there is little direct evidence, relevant to the present problem, of the purpose of the "conformity" provision of Rule 81(a)(2), the concern of the draftsmen, as a general matter, seems to have been to provide for the continuing applicability of the "civil" rules in their new form to those areas of practice in habeas corpus and other enumerated proceedings in which the "specified" proceedings had theretofore utilized the modes of civil practice. Otherwise, those proceedings were to be considered outside of the scope of the rules without prejudice, of course, to the use of particular rules by analogy or otherwise, where appropriate.

394 U.S. at 294

The court then reiterated its commitment to judicial discretion in formulating rules and procedures for habeas corpus proceedings by stating:

[T]he habeas corpus jurisdiction and the duty to exercise it being present, the courts may fashion appropriate modes of procedure, by analogy to existing rules or otherwise in conformity with judicial usage. Where their duties require it, this is the inescapable obligation of the courts. Their authority is expressly confirmed in the All Writs Act, 28 U.S.C. § 1651.

394 U.S. at 299

Rule 6 of these proposed rules deals specifically with the issue of discovery in habeas actions in a manner consistent with *Harris*. Rule 11 [now Rule 12] extends this approach to allow the court considering the petition to use any of the rules of civil procedure (unless inconsistent with these rules of habeas corpus) when in its discretion the court decides they are appropriate under the circumstances of the particular case. The court does not have to rigidly apply rules which would be inconsistent or inequitable in the overall framework of habeas corpus. Rule 11 merely recognizes and affirms their discretionary power to use their judgment in promoting the ends of justice.

Rule 11 [now Rule 12] permits application of the civil rules only when it would be appropriate to do so. Illustrative of an inappropriate application is that rejected by the Supreme Court in *Pitchess v. Davis,* 95 S.Ct. 1748 (1975), holding that Fed.R.Civ.P. 60(b) should not be applied in a habeas case when it would have the effect of altering the statutory exhaustion requirement of 28 U.S.C. § 2254.

2004 Amendments

The language of Rule 11 [now Rule 12] has been amended as part of general restyling of the rules to make them more easily understood and to make style and terminology consistent throughout the rules. These changes are intended to be stylistic and no substantive change is intended.

Changes Made After Publication and Comments. The Committee made no changes to Rule 11 [now Rule 12].

2009 Amendments

The amendment renumbers current Rule 11 [to Rule 12] to accommodate the new rule on certificates of appealability.

APPENDIX OF FORMS

Petition for Relief From a Conviction or Sentence By a Person in State Custody*

(Petition Under 28 U.S.C. § 2254 for a Writ of Habeas Corpus)

Instructions

1. To use this form, you must be a person who is currently serving a sentence under a judgment against you in a state court. You are asking for relief from the conviction or the sentence. This form is your petition for relief.

2. You may also use this form to challenge a state judgment that imposed a sentence to be served in the future, but you must fill in the name of the state where the judgment was entered. If you want to challenge a federal judgment that imposed a sentence to be served in the future, you should file a motion under 28 U.S.C. § 2255 in the federal court that entered the judgment.

3. Make sure the form is typed or neatly written.

4. You must tell the truth and sign the form. If you make a false statement of a material fact, you may be prosecuted for perjury.

5. Answer all the questions. You do not need to cite law. You may submit additional pages if necessary. If you do not fill out the form properly, you will be asked to submit additional or correct information. If you want to submit a brief or arguments, you must submit them in a separate memorandum.

6. You must pay a fee of $5. If the fee is paid, your petition will be filed. If you cannot pay the fee, you may ask to proceed *in forma pauperis* (as a poor person). To do that, you must fill out the last page of this form. Also, you must submit a certificate signed by an officer at the institution where you are confined showing the amount of money that the institution is holding for you. If your account exceeds $___, you must pay the filing fee.

7. on, you may challenge the judgment entered by only one court. If you want to challenge a judgment entered by a different court (either in the same state or in different states), you must file a separate petition.

8. When you have completed the form, send the original and [two]† copies to the Clerk of the United States District Court at this address:

Clerk, United States District Court for
Address
City, State Zip Code

If you want a file-stamped copy of the petition, you must enclose an additional copy of the petition and ask the court to file-stamp it and return it to you.

9. **CAUTION: You must include in this petition all the grounds for relief from the conviction or sentence that you challenge. And you must state the facts that support each ground. If you fail to set forth all the grounds in this petition, you may be barred from presenting additional grounds at a later date.**

10. **CAPITAL CASES: If you are under a sentence of death, you are entitled to the assistance of counsel and should request the appointment of counsel.**

---

* [This form is AO 241, and is available for download at https://www.uscourts.gov/sites/default/files/AO_241_0.pdf. It was last revised on September 1, 2017. Ed.]

† [As this form appears on the website of the Administrative Office of the U.S. Courts, an underlined blank space appears instead of a number. The number included here is what the number was prior to the most recent revision. Ed.]

PETITION UNDER 28 U.S.C. § 2254 FOR WRIT OF
HABEAS CORPUS BY A PERSON IN STATE CUSTODY

United States District Court	District:
Name (under which you were convicted):	Docket or Case No.:
Place of Confinement:	Prisoner No.:
Petitioner (<u>include</u> the name under which you were convicted)	Respondent (authorized person having custody of petitioner)

v.

The Attorney General of the State of: _____

PETITION

1. (a) Name and location of court that entered the judgment of conviction you are challenging: _____
    _____
    _____

    (b) Criminal docket or case number (if you know): _____

2. (a) Date of the judgment of conviction (if you know): _____
    _____

    (b) Date of sentencing: _____

3. Length of sentence: _____

4. In this case, were you convicted on more than one count or of more than one crime? Yes ☐ No ☐

5. Identify all crimes of which you were convicted and sentenced in this case: _____
    _____
    _____
    _____
    _____
    _____

6. (a) What was your plea? (Check one)

    (1) Not guilty ☐   (3) Nolo contendere (no contest) ☐

    (2) Guilty ☐   (4) Insanity plea ☐

    (b) If you entered a guilty plea to one count or charge and a not guilty plea to another count or charge, what did you plead guilty to and what did you plead not guilty to? _____
    _____
    _____
    _____
    _____

    (c) If you went to trial, what kind of trial did you have? (Check one)

    Jury ☐   Judge only ☐

7. Did you testify at a pretrial hearing, trial, or a post-trial hearing?

    Yes ☐   No ☐

8.   Did you appeal from the judgment of conviction?

        Yes ☐   No ☐

9.   If you did appeal, answer the following:

    (a)   Name of court: _____

    (b)   Docket or case number (if you know): _____

    (c)   Result: _____

    (d)   Date of result (if you know): _____

    (e)   Citation to the case (if you know): _____

    (f)   Grounds raised: _____

                _____

                _____

                _____

    (g)   Did you seek further review by a higher state court? Yes ☐ No ☐
           If yes, answer the following:
           (1) Name of court: _____
           (2) Docket or case number (if you know): _____
           (3) Result: _____
           (4) Date of result (if you know): _____
           (5) Citation to the case (if you know): _____
           (6) Grounds raised: _____

                _____

                _____

                _____

                _____

    (h)   _____ Did you file a petition for certiorari in the United States Supreme Court?

        Yes ☐ No ☐

        If yes, answer the following:
        (1) Docket or case number (if you know): _____
        (2) Result: _____

                _____

        (3) Date of result (if you know): _____
        (4) Citation to the case (if you know): _____

10.   Other than the direct appeals listed above, have you previously filed any other petitions, applications, or motions concerning this judgment of conviction in any state court?

        Yes ☐ No ☐

11.   If your answer to Question 10 was "Yes," give the following information:

    (a)   (1) Name of court: _____
           (2) Docket or case number (if you know): _____
           (3) Date of filing (if you know): _____
           (4) Nature of the proceeding: _____
           (5) Grounds raised: _____

                _____

                _____

        (6) Did you receive a hearing where evidence was given on your petition, application, or motion?

           Yes ☐ No ☐

(7) Result: _____

(8) Date of result (if you know): _____

(b) If you filed any second petition, application, or motion, give the same information:

(1) Name of court:_____

(2) Docket or case number (if you know): _____

(3) Date of filing (if you know): _____

(4) Nature of the proceeding: _____

(5) Grounds raised: _____

_____

_____

_____

_____

_____

_____

_____

_____

(6) Did you receive a hearing where evidence was given on your petition, application, or motion?

Yes ☐   No ☐

(7) Result: _____

(8) Date of result (if you know): _____

(c) If you filed any third petition, application, or motion, give the same information:

(1) Name of court: _____

(2) Docket or case number (if you know): _____

(3) Date of filing (if you know): _____

(4) Nature of the proceeding: _____

(5) Grounds raised: _____

_____

_____

_____

_____

_____

(6) Did you receive a hearing where evidence was given on your petition, application, or motion?

Yes ☐   No ☐

(7) Result: _____

(8) Date of result (if you know):

(d) Did you appeal to the highest state court having jurisdiction over the action taken on your petition, application, or motion?

(1) First petition: Yes ☐   No ☐

(2) Second petition: Yes ☐   No ☐

(3) Third petition: Yes ☐   No ☐

(e) If you did not appeal to the highest state court having jurisdiction, explain why you did not: _____

_____

_____

12. For this petition, state every ground on which you claim that you are being held in violation of the Constitution, laws, or treaties of the United States. Attach additional pages if you have more than four grounds. State the facts supporting each ground. Any legal arguments must be submitted in a separate memorandum.

HABEAS CORPUS

CAUTION: To proceed in the federal court, you must ordinarily first exhaust (use up) your available state-court remedies on each ground on which you request action by the federal court. Also, if you fail to set forth all the grounds in this petition, you may be barred from presenting additional grounds at a later date.

GROUND ONE: _____

(a) Supporting facts (Do not argue or cite law. Just state the specific facts that support your claim.):

_____
_____
_____
_____
_____

(b) If you did not exhaust your state remedies on Ground One, explain why: _____

_____
_____
_____

(c) **Direct Appeal of Ground One:**
(1) If you appealed from the judgment of conviction, did you raise this issue?
Yes ☐   No ☐
(2) If you did <u>not</u> raise this issue in your direct appeal, explain why: _____

_____
_____

(d) **Post-Conviction Proceedings:**
(1) Did you raise this issue through a post-conviction motion or petition for habeas corpus in a state trial court?
Yes ☐   No ☐
(2) If your answer to Question (d)(1) is "Yes," state:
Type of motion or petition: _____
Name and location of the court where the motion or petition was filed: _____

_____
Docket or case number (if you know): _____
Date of the court's decision: _____
Result (attach a copy of the court's opinion or order, if available): _____

_____
_____

(3) Did you receive a hearing on your motion or petition?
Yes ☐   No ☐
(4) Did you appeal from the denial of your motion or petition?
Yes ☐   No ☐
(5) If your answer to Question (d)(4) is "Yes," did you raise this issue in the appeal?
Yes ☐   No ☐
(6) If your answer to Question (d)(4) is "Yes," state:
Name and location of the court where the appeal was filed: _____
Docket or case number (if you know): _____
Date of the court's decision: _____
Result (attach a copy of the court's opinion or order, if available): _____

_____
_____

(7) If your answer to Question (d)(4) or Question (d)(5) is "No," explain why you did not raise this issue: _____

_____
_____

(e) **Other Remedies:** Describe any other procedures (such as habeas corpus, administrative remedies, etc.) that you have used to exhaust your state remedies on Ground One: _____

_____

_____

GROUND TWO: _____

(a) Supporting facts (Do not argue or cite law. Just state the specific facts that support your claim.):

_____

_____

_____

_____

_____

_____

_____

(b) If you did not exhaust your state remedies on Ground Two, explain why: _____

_____

_____

_____

(c) **Direct Appeal of Ground Two:**
    (1) If you appealed from the judgment of conviction, did you raise this issue?
        Yes ☐   No ☐
    (2) If you did <u>not</u> raise this issue in your direct appeal, explain why: _____

    _____

    _____

(d) **Post-Conviction Proceedings:**
    (1) Did you raise this issue through a post-conviction motion or petition for habeas corpus in a state trial court?
        Yes ☐   No ☐
    (2) If your answer to Question (d)(1) is "Yes," state:
    Type of motion or petition: _____
    Name and location of the court where the motion or petition was filed: _____

    _____

    Docket or case number (if you know): _____
    Date of the court's decision: _____
    Result (attach a copy of the court's opinion or order, if available): _____

    _____

    _____

    (3) Did you receive a hearing on your motion or petition?
        Yes ☐   No ☐
    (4) Did you appeal from the denial of your motion or petition?
        Yes ☐   No ☐
    (5) If your answer to Question (d)(4) is "Yes," did you raise this issue in the appeal?
        Yes ☐   No ☐
    (6) If your answer to Question (d)(4) is "Yes," state:
    Name and location of the court where the appeal was filed: _____

    _____

    Docket or case number (if you know): _____
    Date of the court's decision: _____
    Result (attach a copy of the court's opinion or order, if available): _____

    _____

    _____

(7) If your answer to Question (d)(4) or Question (d)(5) is "No," explain why you did not raise this issue: _____
_____
_____
_____

(e) **Other Remedies:** Describe any other procedures (such as habeas corpus, administrative remedies, etc.) that you have used to exhaust your state remedies on Ground Two: _____
_____
_____
_____
_____

GROUND THREE: _____

(a) Supporting facts (Do not argue or cite law. Just state the specific facts that support your claim.):
_____
_____
_____
_____
_____
_____
_____

(b) If you did not exhaust your state remedies on Ground Three, explain why: _____
_____
_____

(c) **Direct Appeal of Ground Three:**
(1) If you appealed from the judgment of conviction, did you raise this issue?
Yes ☐   No ☐
(2) If you did not raise this issue in your direct appeal, explain why: _____
_____
_____

(d) **Post-Conviction Proceedings:**
(1) Did you raise this issue through a post-conviction motion or petition for habeas corpus in a state trial court?
Yes ☐   No ☐
(2) If your answer to Question (d)(1) is "Yes," state:
Type of motion or petition: _____
Name and location of the court where the motion or petition was filed: _____
Docket or case number (if you know): _____
Date of the court's decision: _____
Result (attach a copy of the court's opinion or order, if available): _____
_____
_____

(3) Did you receive a hearing on your motion or petition?
Yes ☐   No ☐
(4) Did you appeal from the denial of your motion or petition?
Yes ☐   No ☐
(5) If your answer to Question (d)(4) is "Yes," did you raise this issue in the appeal?
Yes ☐   No ☐
(6) If your answer to Question (d)(4) is "Yes," state:
Name and location of the court where the appeal was filed: _____
_____

Docket or case number (if you know): _____

Date of the court's decision: _____

Result (attach a copy of the court's opinion or order, if available): _____

_____

_____

(7) If your answer to Question (d)(4) or Question (d)(5) is "No," explain why you did not raise this issue: _____

_____

_____

_____

(e) **Other Remedies:** Describe any other procedures (such as habeas corpus, administrative remedies, etc.) that you have used to exhaust your state remedies on Ground Three: _____

_____

GROUND FOUR: _____

_____

(a) Supporting facts (Do not argue or cite law. Just state the specific facts that support your claim.): _

_____

_____

_____

_____

_____

_____

_____

(b) If you did not exhaust your state remedies on Ground Four, explain why: _____

_____

_____

_____

_____

(c) Direct Appeal of Ground Four:

(1) If you appealed from the judgment of conviction, did you raise this issue?
Yes ☐   No ☐

(2) If you did not raise this issue in your direct appeal, explain why:

(d) Post-Conviction Proceedings:

(1) Did you raise this issue through a post-conviction motion or petition for habeas corpus in a state trial court?
Yes ☐   No ☐

(2) If your answer to Question (d)(1) is "Yes," state:

Type of motion or petition: _____

Name and location of the court where the motion or petition was filed: _____

_____

Docket or case number (if you know): _____

Date of the court's decision: _____

Result (attach a copy of the court's opinion or order, if available): _____

_____

_____

(3) Did you receive a hearing on your motion or petition?
Yes ☐   No ☐

(4) Did you appeal from the denial of your motion or petition?
Yes ☐   No ☐

(5) If your answer to Question (d)(4) is "Yes," did you raise this issue in the appeal?
Yes ☐   No ☐

HABEAS CORPUS

(6) If your answer to Question (d)(4) is "Yes," state:

Name and location of the court where the appeal was filed: _____

_____

Docket or case number (if you know): _____

Date of the court's decision: _____

Result (attach a copy of the court's opinion or order, if available): _____

_____

_____

_____

(7) If your answer to Question (d)(4) or Question (d)(5) is "No," explain why you did not raise this issue: _____

_____

_____

_____

(e) **Other Remedies:** Describe any other procedures (such as habeas corpus, administrative remedies, etc.) that you have used to exhaust your state remedies on Ground Four:

_____

_____

13. Please answer these additional questions about the petition you are filing:

(a) Have all grounds for relief that you have raised in this petition been presented to the highest state court having jurisdiction? Yes ☐ No ☐

If your answer is "No," state which grounds have not been so presented and give your reason(s) for not presenting them:_____

_____

_____

_____

_____

(b) Is there any ground in this petition that has not been presented in some state or federal court? If so, which ground or grounds have not been presented, and state your reasons for not presenting them:_____

_____

_____

_____

_____

14. Have you previously filed any type of petition, application, or motion in a federal court regarding the conviction that you challenge in this petition? Yes ☐ No ☐

If "Yes," state the name and location of the court, the docket or case number, the type of proceeding, the issues raised, the date of the court's decision, and the result for each petition, application, or motion filed. Attach a copy of any court opinion or order, if available.

_____

_____

_____

_____

_____

_____

15. Do you have any petition or appeal <u>now pending</u> (filed and not decided yet) in any court, either state or federal, for the judgment you are challenging? Yes ☐ No ☐

If "Yes," state the name and location of the court, the docket or case number, the type of proceeding, and the issues raised. _____

_____

_____

_____

16. Give the name and address, if you know, of each attorney who represented you in the following stages of the judgment you are challenging:

    (a) At preliminary hearing: _____

    (b) At arraignment and plea: _____

    (c) At trial: _____

    (d) At sentencing: _____

    (e) On appeal: _____

    (f) In any post-conviction proceeding: _____

    (g) On appeal from any ruling against you in a post-conviction proceeding: _____

17. Do you have any future sentence to serve after you complete the sentence for the judgment that you are challenging? Yes ☐ No ☐

    (a) If so, give name and location of court that imposed the other sentence you will serve in the future: _____

    (b) Give the date the other sentence was imposed: _____

    (c) Give the length of the other sentence: _____

    (d) Have you filed, or do you plan to file, any petition that challenges the judgment or sentence to be served in the future? Yes ☐ No ☐

18. TIMELINESS OF PETITION: If your judgment of conviction became final over one year ago, you must explain why the one-year statute of limitations as contained in 28 U.S.C. § 2244(d) does not bar your petition.*

_____

_____

_____

_____

_____

_____

_____

_____

_____

_____

* The Antiterrorism and Effective Death Penalty Act of 1996 ("AEDPA") as contained in 28 U.S.C. § 2244(d) provides in part that:

(1) A one-year period of limitation shall apply to an application for a writ of habeas corpus by a person in custody pursuant to the judgment of a State court. The limitation period shall run from the latest of—

HABEAS CORPUS

(A) the date on which the judgment became final by the conclusion of direct review or the expiration of the time for seeking such review;

(B) the date on which the impediment to filing an application created by State action in violation of the Constitution or laws of the United States is removed, if the applicant was prevented from filing by such state action;

(C) the date on which the constitutional right asserted was initially recognized by the Supreme Court, if the right has been newly recognized by the Supreme Court and made retroactively applicable to cases on collateral review; or

(D) the date on which the factual predicate of the claim or claims presented could have been discovered through the exercise of due diligence.

(2) The time during which a properly filed application for State post-conviction or other collateral review with respect to the pertinent judgment or claim is pending shall not be counted toward any period of limitation under this subsection.

Therefore, petitioner asks that the Court grant the following relief: _____
_____
_____

or any other relief to which petitioner may be entitled.

_____
Signature of Attorney (if any)

I declare (or certify, verify, or state) under penalty of perjury that the foregoing is true and correct and that this Petition for Writ of Habeas Corpus was placed in the prison mailing system on _____(month, date, year).

_____
Executed (signed) on (date).

_____
Signature of Petitioner

If the person signing is not petitioner, state relationship to petitioner and explain why petitioner is not signing this petition. _____
_____
_____

RULES—SECTION 2254 CASES

IN FORMA PAUPERIS DECLARATION

[Insert appropriate court]

_____

(Petitioner)

v.

_____

(Respondent(s))

DECLARATION IN
SUPPORT
OF REQUEST
TO PROCEED
_IN FORMA
PAUPERIS_

I, _____, declare that I am the petitioner in the above entitled case; that in support of my motion to proceed without being required to prepay fees, costs or give security therefor, I state that because of my poverty I am unable to pay the costs of said proceeding or to give security therefor; that I believe I am entitled to relief.

1. Are you presently employed? Yes ☐ No ☐

   a. If the answer is "yes," state the amount of your salary or wages per month, and give the name and address of your employer.

   _____

   b. If the answer is "no," state the date of last employment and the amount of the salary and wages per month which you received.

   _____

2. Have you received within the past twelve months any money from any of the following sources?

   a. Business, profession or form of self-employment? Yes ☐ No ☐
   b. Rent payments, interest or dividends? Yes ☐ No ☐
   c. Pensions, annuities or life insurance payments? Yes ☐ No ☐
   d. Gifts or inheritances? Yes ☐ No ☐
   e. Any other sources? Yes ☐ No ☐
   If the answer to any of the above is "yes," describe each source of money and state the amount received from each during the past twelve months.

   _____
   _____
   _____
   _____

3. Do you own cash, or do you have money in a checking or savings account?

   Yes ☐ No ☐ (Include any funds in prison accounts.)
   If the answer is "yes," state the total value of the items owned.

   _____
   _____
   _____

4. Do you own any real estate, stocks, bonds, notes, automobiles, or other valuable property (excluding ordinary household furnishings and clothing)?

   Yes ☐ No ☐
   If the answer is "yes," describe the property and state its approximate value.

   _____
   _____
   _____

HABEAS CORPUS

5.   List the persons who are dependent upon you for support, state your relationship to those persons, and indicate how much you contribute toward their support.

_____

_____

_____

    I declare (or certify, verify, or state) under penalty of perjury that the foregoing is true and correct. Executed on _____.
             (date)

_____
Signature of Petitioner

CERTIFICATE

    I hereby certify that the petitioner herein has the sum of $_____ on account to his credit at the _____ institution where he is confined. I further certify that petitioner likewise has the following securities to his credit according to the records of said _____ institution:

_____

_____

_____

_____

_____
Authorized Officer of
Institution

(As amended Apr. 28, 1982, eff. Aug. 1, 1982; Apr. 26, 2004, eff. Dec. 1, 2004.)

RULES GOVERNING SECTION 2255 PROCEEDINGS FOR THE UNITED STATES DISTRICT COURTS

Effective February 1, 1977
Amendments received through May 1, 2020

APPENDIX OF FORMS

Motion to Vacate, Set Aside, or Correct a Sentence By a Person in Federal Custody (Motion Under 28 U.S.C. § 2255)

ORDERS OF THE SUPREME COURT OF THE UNITED STATES ADOPTING AND AMENDING RULES GOVERNING SECTION 2255 PROCEEDINGS

ORDER OF APRIL 26, 1976 [425 U.S. 1169]

1.   That the rules and forms governing proceedings in the United States District Courts under Section 2254 and Section 2255 of Title 28, United States Code, as approved by the Judicial Conference of the United States be, and they hereby are, prescribed pursuant to Section 2072 of Title 28, United States Code and Sections 3771 and 3772 of Title 18, United States Code.

2.   That the aforementioned rules and forms shall take effect August 1, 1976, and shall be applicable to all proceedings then pending except to the extent that in the opinion of the court their application in a particular proceeding would not be feasible or would work injustice.

3.   That THE CHIEF JUSTICE be, and he hereby is, authorized to transmit the aforementioned rules and forms governing Section 2254 and Section 2255 proceedings to the Congress in accordance with the provisions of Section 2072 of Title 28 and Sections 3771 and 3772 of Title 18, United States Code.

CONGRESSIONAL ACTION ON PROPOSED RULES AND FORMS GOVERNING PROCEEDING UNDER 28 U.S.C. §§ 2254 AND 2255

Pub.L. 94–349, § 2, July 8, 1976, 90 Stat. 822, provided: "That, notwithstanding the provisions of section 2072 of title 28 of the United States Code, the rules and forms governing section 2254 cases in the United States district courts and the rules and forms governing section 2255 proceedings in the United States district courts which are embraced by the order entered by the United States Supreme Court on April 26, 1976, and which were transmitted to the Congress on or about April 26, 1976, shall not take effect until thirty days after the adjournment sine die of the 94th Congress, or until and to the extent approved by Act of Congress, whichever is earlier."

Pub.L. 94–426, § 1, Sept. 28, 1976, 90 Stat. 1334, provided: "That the rules governing section 2254 cases in the United States district courts and the rules governing section 2255 proceedings for the United

States district courts, as proposed by the United States Supreme Court, which were delayed by the Act entitled 'An Act to delay the effective date of certain proposed amendments to the Federal Rules of Criminal Procedure and certain other rules promulgated by the United States Supreme Court' (Public Law 94–349), are approved with the amendments set forth in section 2 of this Act and shall take effect as so amended, with respect to petitions under section 2254 and motions under section 2255 of title 28 of the United States Code filed on or after February 1, 1977."

ORDER OF APRIL 30, 1979 [441 U.S. 1003]

1. That Rule 10 of the Rules Governing Proceedings in the United States District Courts on application under Section 2254 of Title 28, United States Code, be, and hereby is, amended to read as follows:

[See amendment made thereby under Rule 10 set out following section 2254.]

2. That Rules 10 and 11 of the Rules Governing Proceedings in the United States District Courts on a motion under Section 2255 of Title 28, United States Code, be, and they hereby are, amended to read as follows:

[See amendments made thereby under the respective rules, post.]

3. That the foregoing amendments to the Rules Governing Proceedings in the United States District Courts under Section 2254 and Section 2255 of Title 28, United States Code, shall take effect on August 1, 1979, and shall be applicable to all proceedings then pending except to the extent that in the opinion of the court their application in a particular proceeding would not be feasible or would work injustice.

4. That THE CHIEF JUSTICE be, and he hereby is, authorized to transmit the aforementioned amendments to the Rules Governing Section 2254 and Section 2255 Proceedings to the Congress in accordance with the provisions of Section 2072 of Title 28, United States Code, and Sections 3771 and 3772 of Title 18, United States Code.

ORDER OF APRIL 28, 1982 [456 U.S. 1033]

1. That the rules and forms governing proceedings in the United States district courts under Section 2254 and Section 2255 of Title 28, United States Code, be, and they hereby are, amended by including therein an amendment to Rule 2(c) of the rules for Section 2254 cases, an amendment to Rule 2(b) of the rules for Section 2255 proceedings, and amendments to the model forms for use in applications under Section 2254 and motions under Section 2255, as hereinafter set forth:

[See amendments made thereby under respective rules and
forms post and following section 2254.]

2. That the aforementioned amendments shall take effect August 1, 1982, and shall be applicable to all proceedings thereafter commenced and, insofar as just and practicable, all proceedings then pending.

3. That THE CHIEF JUSTICE be, and he hereby is, authorized to transmit the aforementioned amendments to the Congress in accordance with Section 2072 of Title 28 and Sections 3771 and 3772 of Title 18, United States Code.

ORDER OF APRIL 22, 1993 [507 U.S. 1163]

1. That the Federal Rules of Criminal Procedure for the United States District Courts be, and they hereby are, amended by including therein amendments to Criminal Rules 1, 3, 4, 5, 5.1, 6, 9, 12, 16, 17, 26.2, 32, 32.1, 40, 41, 44, 46, 49, 50, 54, 55, 57, and 58, and new Rule 26.3, and an amendment to Rule 8 of the Rules Governing Section 2255 Proceedings.

[See amendments made thereby under the respective rules set out in the
Federal Criminal Code and Rules and under Rule 8, post.]

2. That the foregoing amendments to the Federal Rules of Criminal Procedure shall take effect on December 1, 1993, and shall govern all proceedings in criminal cases thereafter commenced and, insofar as just and practicable, all proceedings in criminal cases then pending.

3. That THE CHIEF JUSTICE be, and he hereby is, authorized to transmit to the Congress the foregoing amendments to the Federal Rules of Criminal Procedure in accordance with the provisions of Section 2072 of Title 28, United States Code.

MOTION ATTACKING SENTENCE

ORDER OF APRIL 26, 2004 [541 U.S. 1105]

1. That the Federal Rules of Criminal Procedure be, and they hereby are, amended by including therein an amendment to Criminal Rule 35.

2. That the rules and forms governing cases in the United States District Courts under Section 2254 and Section 2255 of Title 28, United States Code, be, and they hereby are, amended by including therein amendments to Rules 1 through 11 of the Rules Governing Section 2254 Cases in the United States District Courts, Rules 1 through 12 of the Rules Governing Section 2255 Cases in the United States District Courts, and forms for use in applications under Section 2254 and motions under Section 2255.

[See amendments made thereby under respective rules, post.]

3. That the foregoing amendments to the Federal Rules of Criminal Procedure, the Rules Governing Section 2254 Cases in the United States District Courts, and the Rules Governing Section 2255 Cases in the United States District Courts shall take effect on December 1, 2004, and shall govern in all proceedings thereafter commenced and, insofar as just and practicable, all proceedings then pending.

4. That the CHIEF JUSTICE be, and hereby is, authorized to transmit to the Congress the foregoing amendments to the Federal Rules of Criminal Procedure, the Rules Governing Section 2254 Cases in the United States District Courts, and the Rules Governing Section 2255 Cases in the United States District Courts in accordance with the provisions of Section 2072 of Title 28, United States Code.

ORDER OF MARCH 26, 2009 [556 U.S. 985]

1. That the Federal Rules of Criminal Procedure be, and they hereby are, amended by including therein amendments to Criminal Rules 5.1, 7, 12.1, 12.3, 29, 32, 32.2, 33, 34, 35, 41, 45, 47, 58, and 59, and Rules 8 and 11, and new Rule 12 of the Rules Governing Section 2254 Cases in the United States District Courts, and Rules 8 and 11 of the Rules Governing Section 2255 Proceedings for the United States District Courts.

[See amendments made thereby under respective rules, post.]

2. That the foregoing amendments to the Federal Rules of Criminal Procedure shall take effect on December 1, 2009, and shall govern in all proceedings thereafter commenced and, insofar as just and practicable, all proceedings then pending.

3. That the CHIEF JUSTICE be, and hereby is, authorized to transmit to the Congress the foregoing amendments to the Federal Rules of Criminal Procedure in accordance with the provisions of Section 2072 of Title 28, United States Code.

ORDER OF APRIL 25, 2019 [2018 J. Sup. Ct. U.S. 715]

1. That the Federal Rules of Criminal Procedure are amended to include new Rule 16.1.

2. The Rules Governing Section 2254 Cases in the United States District Courts are amended to include an amendment to Rule 5.

3. The Rules Governing Section 2255 Proceedings for the United States District Courts are amended to include an amendment to Rule 5.

[See amendments made thereby under respective rules, post.]

4. That the foregoing amendments to the Federal Rules of Criminal Procedure, the Rules Governing Section 2254 Cases in the United States District Courts, and the Rules Governing Section 2255 Proceedings for the United States District Courts shall take effect on December 1, 2019, and shall govern in all proceedings thereafter commenced and, insofar as just and practicable, all proceedings then pending.

5. The Chief Justice is authorized to transmit to the Congress the foregoing amendments to the Federal Rules of Criminal Procedure, the Rules Governing Section 2254 Cases in the United States District Courts, and the Rules Governing Section 2255 Proceedings for the United States District Courts in accordance with the provisions of Section 2074 of Title 28, United States Code.

HISTORICAL NOTES

Effective Date of Rules; 1976 Act

Rules, and the amendments thereto by Pub.L. 94–426, Sept. 28, 1976, 90 Stat. 1334, effective with respect to petitions under section 2254 of this title and motions under section 2255 of this title filed on or after Feb. 1, 1977, see section 1 of Pub.L. 94–426, set out as a note under section 2074 and 2255 of this title.

Rule 1.   Scope

These rules govern a motion filed in a United States district court under 28 U.S.C. § 2255 by:

(a) a person in custody under a judgment of that court who seeks a determination that:

    (1) the judgment violates the Constitution or laws of the United States;

    (2) the court lacked jurisdiction to enter the judgment;

    (3) the sentence exceeded the maximum allowed by law; or

    (4) the judgment or sentence is otherwise subject to collateral review; and

(b) a person in custody under a judgment of a state court or another federal court, and subject to future custody under a judgment of the district court, who seeks a determination that:

    (1) future custody under a judgment of the district court would violate the Constitution or laws of the United States;

    (2) the district court lacked jurisdiction to enter the judgment;

    (3) the district court's sentence exceeded the maximum allowed by law; or

    (4) the district court's judgment or sentence is otherwise subject to collateral review.

(As amended Apr. 26, 2004, eff. Dec. 1, 2004.)

ADVISORY COMMITTEE NOTES

1976 Adoption

The basic scope of this postconviction remedy is prescribed by 28 U.S.C. § 2255. Under these rules the person seeking relief from federal custody files a motion to vacate, set aside, or correct sentence, rather than a petition for habeas corpus. This is consistent with the terminology used in section 2255 and indicates the difference between this remedy and federal habeas for a state prisoner. Also, habeas corpus is available to the person in federal custody if his "remedy by motion is inadequate or ineffective to test the legality of his detention."

Whereas sections 2241–2254 (dealing with federal habeas corpus for those in state custody) speak of the district court judge "issuing the writ" as the operative remedy, section 2255 provides that, if the judge finds the movant's assertions to be meritorious, he "shall discharge the prisoner or resentence him or grant a new trial or correct the sentence as may appear appropriate." This is possible because a motion under § 2255 is a further step in the movant's criminal case and not a separate civil action, as appears from the legislative history of section 2 of S. 20, 80th Congress, the provisions of which were incorporated by the same Congress in title 28 U.S.C. as § 2255. In reporting S. 20 favorably the Senate Judiciary Committee said (Sen.Rep. 1526, 80th Cong.2d Sess., p. 2):

The two main advantages of such motion remedy over the present habeas corpus are as follows:

First, habeas corpus is a separate civil action and not a further step in the criminal case in which petitioner is sentenced (Ex parte *Tom Tong,* 108 U.S. 556, 559 (1883)). It is not a determination of guilt or innocence of the charge upon which petitioner was sentenced. Where a prisoner sustains his right to discharge in habeas corpus, it is usually because some right—such as lack of counsel—has been denied which reflects no determination of his guilt or innocence but affects solely the fairness of his earlier criminal trial. Even under the broad power in the statute "to dispose of the party as law and justice require" (28 U.S.C.A., sec. 461), the court or judge is by no means in the same advantageous position in habeas corpus to do justice as would be so if the matter were determined in the criminal proceeding (see *Medley,* petitioner,

134 U.S. 160, 174 (1890)). For instance, the judge (by habeas corpus) cannot grant a new trial in the criminal case. Since the motion remedy is in the criminal proceeding, this section 2 affords the opportunity and expressly gives the broad powers to set aside the judgment and to "discharge the prisoner or resentence him or grant a new trial or correct the sentence as may appear appropriate."

The fact that a motion under § 2255 is a further step in the movant's criminal case rather than a separate civil action has significance at several points in these rules. See, *e.g.,* advisory committee note to Rule 3 (re no filing fee), advisory committee note to Rule 4 (re availability of files, etc., relating to the judgment), advisory committee note to Rule 6 (re availability of discovery under criminal procedure rules), advisory committee note to Rule 11 (re no extension of time for appeal), and advisory committee note to Rule 12 (re applicability of federal criminal rules). However, the fact that Congress has characterized the motion as a further step in the criminal proceedings does *not* mean that proceedings upon such a motion are of necessity governed by the legal principles which are applicable at a criminal trial regarding such matters as counsel, presence, confrontation, self-incrimination, and burden of proof.

The challenge of decisions such as the revocation of probation or parole are not appropriately dealt with under 28 U.S.C. § 2255, which is a continuation of the original criminal action. Other remedies, such as habeas corpus, are available in such situations.

Although Rule 1 indicates that these rules apply to a motion for a determination that the judgment was imposed "in violation of the . . . laws of the United States," the language of 28 U.S.C. § 2255, it is not the intent of these rules to define or limit what is encompassed within that phrase. See *Davis v. United States,* 417 U.S. 333 (1974), holding that it is not true "that every asserted error of law can be raised on a § 2255 motion," and that the appropriate inquiry is "whether the claimed error of law was 'a fundamental defect which inherently results in a complete miscarriage of justice,' and whether '[i]t . . . present[s] exceptional circumstances where the need for the remedy afforded by the writ of habeas corpus is apparent.' "

For a discussion of the "custody" requirement and the intended limited scope of this remedy, see advisory committee note to § 2254 Rule 1.

2004 Amendments

The language of Rule 1 has been amended as part of general restyling of the rules to make them more easily understood and to make style and terminology consistent throughout the rules. These changes are intended to be stylistic and no substantive change is intended.

Rule 2.   The Motion

(a) **Applying for Relief.** The application must be in the form of a motion to vacate, set aside, or correct the sentence.

(b) **Form.** The motion must:

(1)   specify all the grounds for relief available to the moving party;

(2)   state the facts supporting each ground;

(3)   state the relief requested;

(4)   be printed, typewritten, or legibly handwritten; and

(5)   be signed under penalty of perjury by the movant or by a person authorized to sign it for the movant.

(c) **Standard Form.** The motion must substantially follow either the form appended to these rules or a form prescribed by a local district-court rule. The clerk must make forms available to moving parties without charge.

(d) **Separate Motions for Separate Judgments.** A moving party who seeks relief from more than one judgment must file a separate motion covering each judgment.

(As amended Pub.L. 94–426, § 2(3), (4), Sept. 28, 1976, 90 Stat. 1334; Apr. 28, 1982, eff. Aug. 1, 1982; Apr. 26, 2004, eff. Dec. 1, 2004.)

ADVISORY COMMITTEE NOTES
1976 Adoption

Under these rules the application for relief is in the form of a motion rather than a petition (see Rule 1 and advisory committee note). Therefore, there is no requirement that the movant name a respondent. This is consistent with 28 U.S.C. § 2255. The United States Attorney for the district in which the judgment under attack was entered is the proper party to oppose the motion since the federal government is the movant's adversary of record.

If the movant is attacking a federal judgment which will subject him to future custody, he must be in present custody (see Rule 1 and advisory committee note) as the result of a state or federal governmental action. He need not alter the nature of the motion by trying to include the government officer who presently has official custody of him as a pseudo-respondent, or third-party plaintiff, or other fabrication. The court hearing his motion attacking the future custody can exercise jurisdiction over those having him in present custody without the use of artificial pleading devices.

There is presently a split among the courts as to whether a person currently in state custody may use a § 2255 motion to obtain relief from a federal judgment under which he will be subjected to custody in the future. Negative, see *Newton v. United States,* 329 F.Supp. 90 (S.D. Texas 1971); affirmative, see *Desmond v. The United States Board of Parole,* 397 F.2d 386 (1st Cir.1968), *cert. denied,* 393 U.S. 919 (1968); and *Paolino v. United States,* 314 F.Supp. 875 (C.D.Cal.1970). It is intended that these rules settle the matter in favor of the prisoner's being able to file a § 2255 motion for relief under those circumstances. The proper district in which to file such a motion is the one in which is situated the court which rendered the sentence under attack.

Under Rule 35, Federal Rules of Criminal Procedure, the court may correct an illegal sentence or a sentence imposed in an illegal manner, or may reduce the sentence. This remedy should be used, rather than a motion under these § 2255 rules, whenever applicable, but there is some overlap between the two proceedings which has caused the courts difficulty.

The movant should not be barred from an appropriate remedy because he has misstyled his motion. See *United States v. Morgan,* 346 U.S. 502, 505 (1954). The court should construe it as whichever one is proper under the circumstances and decide it on its merits. For a § 2255 motion construed as a Rule 35 motion, see *Heflin v. United States,* 358 U.S. 415 (1959); and *United States v. Coke,* 404 F.2d 836 (2d Cir.1968). For writ of error coram nobis treated as a Rule 35 motion, see *Hawkins v. United States,* 324 F.Supp. 223 (E.D. Texas, Tyler Division 1971). For a Rule 35 motion treated as a § 2255 motion, see *Moss v. United States,* 263 F.2d 615 (5th Cir.1959); *Jones v. United States,* 400 F.2d 892 (8th Cir.1968), cert. denied 394 U.S. 991 (1969); and *United States v. Brown,* 413 F.2d 878 (9th Cir.1969), cert. denied, 397 U.S. 947 (1970).

One area of difference between § 2255 and Rule 35 motions is that for the latter there is no requirement that the movant be "in custody." *Heflin v. United States,* 358 U.S. 415, 418, 422 (1959); *Duggins v. United States,* 240 F.2d 479, 483 (6th Cir.1957). Compare with Rule 1 and advisory committee note for § 2255 motions. The importance of this distinction has decreased since *Peyton v. Rowe,* 391 U.S. 54 (1968), but it might still make a difference in particular situations.

A Rule 35 motion is used to attack the sentence imposed, not the basis for the sentence. The court in *Gilinsky v. United States,* 335 F.2d 914, 916 (9th Cir.1964), stated, "a Rule 35 motion presupposes a valid conviction. * * * [C]ollateral attack on errors allegedly committed at trial is not permissible under Rule 35." By illustration the court noted at page 917: "a Rule 35 proceeding contemplates the correction of a sentence of a court having jurisdiction. * * * [J]urisdictional defects * * * involve a collateral attack, they must ordinarily be presented under 28 U.S.C. § 2255." In *United States v. Semet,* 295 F.Supp. 1084 (E.D.Okla.1968), the prisoner moved under Rule 35 and § 2255 to invalidate the sentence he was serving on the grounds of his failure to understand the charge to which he pleaded guilty. The court said:

> As regards Defendant's Motion under Rule 35, said Motion must be denied as its [sic] presupposes a valid conviction of the offense with which he was charged and may be used only to attack the sentence. It may not be used to examine errors occurring prior to the imposition of sentence.

295 F.Supp. at 1085.

See also: *Moss v. United States*, 263 F.2d at 616; *Duggins v. United States*, 240 F.2d at 484; *Migdal v. United States*, 298 F.2d 513, 514 (9th Cir.1961); *Jones v. United States*, 400 F.2d at 894; *United States v. Coke*, 404 F.2d at 847; and *United States v. Brown*, 413 F.2d at 879.

A major difficulty in deciding whether Rule 35 or § 2255 is the proper remedy is the uncertainty as to what is meant by an "illegal sentence." The Supreme Court dealt with this issue in *Hill v. United States*, 368 U.S. 424 (1962). The prisoner brought a § 2255 motion to vacate sentence on the ground that he had not been given a Fed.R.Crim.P. 32(a) opportunity to make a statement in his own behalf at the time of sentencing. The majority held this was not an error subject to collateral attack under § 2255. The five-member majority considered the motion as one brought pursuant to Rule 35, but denied relief, stating:

> [T]he narrow function of Rule 35 is to permit correction at any time of an illegal *sentence,* not to re-examine errors occurring at the trial or other proceedings prior to the imposition of sentence. The sentence in this case was not illegal. The punishment meted out was not in excess of that prescribed by the relevant statutes, multiple terms were not imposed for the same offense, nor were the terms of the sentence itself legally or constitutionally invalid in any other respect.

368 U.S. at 430.

The four dissenters felt the majority definition of "illegal" was too narrow.

> [Rule 35] provides for the correction of an "illegal sentence" without regard to the reasons why that sentence is illegal and contains not a single word to support the Court's conclusion that only a sentence illegal by reason of the punishment it imposes is "illegal" within the meaning of the Rule. I would have thought that a sentence imposed in an illegal manner—whether the amount or form of the punishment meted out constitutes an additional violation of law or not—would be recognized as an "illegal sentence" under any normal reading of the English language.

368 U.S. at 431–432.

The 1966 amendment of Rule 35 added language permitting correction of a sentence imposed in an "illegal manner." However, there is a 120-day time limit on a motion to do this, and the added language does not clarify the intent of the rule or its relation to § 2255.

The courts have been flexible in considering motions under circumstances in which relief might appear to be precluded by *Hill v. United States.* In *Peterson v. United States,* 432 F.2d 545 (8th Cir.1970), the court was confronted with a motion for reduction of sentence by a prisoner claiming to have received a harsher sentence than his codefendants because he stood trial rather than plead guilty. He alleged that this violated his constitutional right to a jury trial. The court ruled that, even though it was past the 120-day time period for a motion to reduce sentence, the claim was still cognizable under Rule 35 as a motion to correct an illegal sentence.

The courts have made even greater use of § 2255 in these types of situations. In *United States v. Lewis,* 392 F.2d 440 (4th Cir.1968), the prisoner moved under § 2255 and Rule 35 for relief from a sentence he claimed was the result of the judge's misunderstanding of the relevant sentencing law. The court held that he could not get relief under Rule 35 because it was past the 120 days for correction of a sentence imposed in an illegal manner and under *Hill v. United States* it was not an illegal sentence. However, § 2255 was applicable because of its "otherwise subject to collateral attack" language. The flaw was not a mere trial error relating to the finding of guilt, but a rare and unusual error which amounted to "exceptional circumstances" embraced in § 2255's words "collateral attack." See 368 U.S. at 444 for discussion of other cases allowing use of § 2255 to attack the sentence itself in similar circumstances, especially where the judge has sentenced out of a misapprehension of the law.

In *United States v. McCarthy,* 433 F.2d 591, 592 (1st Cir.1970), the court allowed a prisoner who was past the time limit for a proper Rule 35 motion to use § 2255 to attack the sentence which he received upon a plea of guilty on the ground that it was induced by an unfulfilled promise of the prosecutor to recommend leniency. The court specifically noted that under § 2255 this was a proper collateral attack on the sentence and there was no need to attack the conviction as well.

The court in *United States v. Malcolm,* 432 F.2d 809, 814, 818 (2d Cir.1970), allowed a prisoner to challenge his sentence under § 2255 without attacking the conviction. It held Rule 35 inapplicable because the sentence was not illegal on its face, but the manner in which the sentence was imposed raised a question of the denial of due process in the sentencing itself which was cognizable under § 2255.

The flexible approach taken by the courts in the above cases seems to be the reasonable way to handle these situations in which Rule 35 and § 2255 appear to overlap. For a further discussion of this problem, see C. Wright, Federal Practice and Procedure: Criminal §§ 581–587 (1969, Supp. 1975).

See the advisory committee note to Rule 2 of the § 2254 rules for further discussion of the purposes and intent of Rule 2 of these § 2255 rules.

1982 Amendment

Subdivision (b). The amendment takes into account 28 U.S.C. § 1746, enacted after adoption of the § 2255 rules. Section 1746 provides that in lieu of an affidavit an unsworn statement may be given under penalty of perjury in substantially the following form if executed within the United States, its territories, possessions or commonwealths: "I declare (or certify, verify, or state) under penalty of perjury that the foregoing is true and correct. Executed on (date). (Signature)." The statute is "intended to encompass prisoner litigation," and the statutory alternative is especially appropriate in such cases because a notary might not be readily available. *Carter v. Clark,* 616 F.2d 228 (5th Cir.1980). The § 2255 forms have been revised accordingly.

2004 Amendments

The language of Rule 2 has been amended as part of general restyling of the rules to make them more easily understood and to make style and terminology consistent throughout the rules. These changes are intended to be stylistic and no substantive change is intended, except as described below.

Revised Rule 2(b)(5) has been amended by removing the requirement that the motion be signed personally by the moving party. Thus, under the amended rule the motion may be signed by movant personally or by someone acting on behalf of the movant, assuming that the person is authorized to do so, for example, an attorney for the movant. The Committee envisions that the courts would apply third-party, or "next-friend," standing analysis in deciding whether the signer was actually authorized to sign the motion on behalf of the movant. *See generally Whitmore v. Arkansas,* 495 U.S. 149 (1990) (discussion of requisites for "next friend" standing in habeas petitions). *See also* 28 U.S.C. § 2242 (application for state habeas corpus relief may be filed by the person who is seeking relief, or by someone acting on behalf of that person).

The language in new Rule 2(c) has been changed to reflect that a moving party must substantially follow the standard form, which is appended to the rules, or a form provided by the court. The current rule, Rule 2(c), seems to indicate a preference for the standard "national" form. Under the amended rule, there is no stated preference. The Committee understood that the current practice in some courts is that if the moving party first files a motion using the national form, that courts may ask the moving party to supplement it with the local form.

Current Rule 2(d), which provided for returning an insufficient motion has been deleted. The Committee believed that the approach in Federal Rule of Civil Procedure 5(e) was more appropriate for dealing with motions that do not conform to the form requirements of the rule. That Rule provides that the clerk may not refuse to accept a filing solely for the reason that it fails to comply with these rules or local rules. Before the adoption of a one-year statute of limitations in the Antiterrorism and Effective Death Penalty Act of 1996, 110 Stat. 1214, the moving party suffered no penalty, other than delay, if the motion was deemed insufficient. Now that a one-year statute of limitations applies to motions filed under § 2255, *see* 28 U.S.C. § 2244(d)(1), the court's dismissal of a motion because it is not in proper form may pose a significant penalty for a moving party, who may not be able to file another motion within the one-year limitations period. Now, under revised Rule 3(b), the clerk is required to file a motion, even though it may otherwise fail to comply with the provisions in revised Rule 2(b). The Committee believed that the better procedure was to accept the defective motion and require the moving party to submit a corrected motion that conforms to Rule 2(b).

Changes Made After Publication and Comments. The Committee changed Rule 2(b)(2) to read "state the facts" rather then [sic] "briefly summarize the facts." One commentator had written that the current language may actually mislead the petitioner and is also redundant.

Rule 2(b)(4) was also modified to reflect that some motions may be printed using a word processing program.

Finally, Rule 2(b)(5) was changed to emphasize that any person, other than the petitioner, who signs the petition must be authorized to do so.

Rule 3.   Filing the Motion; Inmate Filing

(a) **Where to File; Copies.** An original and two copies of the motion must be filed with the clerk.

(b) **Filing and Service.** The clerk must file the motion and enter it on the criminal docket of the case in which the challenged judgment was entered. The clerk must then deliver or serve a copy of the motion on the United States attorney in that district, together with a notice of its filing.

(c) **Time to File.** The time for filing a motion is governed by 28 U.S.C. § 2255 para. 6.

(d) **Inmate Filing.** A paper filed by an inmate confined in an institution is timely if deposited in the institution's internal mailing system on or before the last day for filing. If an institution has a system designed for legal mail, the inmate must use that system to receive the benefit of this rule. Timely filing may be shown by a declaration in compliance with 28 U.S.C. § 1746 or by a notarized statement, either of which must set forth the date of deposit and state that first-class postage has been prepaid.

(As amended Apr. 26, 2004, eff. Dec. 1, 2004.)

ADVISORY COMMITTEE NOTES

1976 Adoption

There is no filing fee required of a movant under these rules. This is a change from the practice of charging $15 and is done to recognize specifically the nature of a § 2255 motion as being a continuation of the criminal case whose judgment is under attack.

The long-standing practice of requiring a $15 filing fee has followed from 28 U.S.C. § 1914(a) whereby "parties instituting any civil action * * * pay a filing fee of $15, except that on an application for a writ of habeas corpus the filing fee shall be $5." This has been held to apply to a proceeding under § 2255 despite the rationale that such a proceeding is a motion and thus a continuation of the criminal action. (See note to Rule 1.)

> A motion under Section 2255 is a civil action and the clerk has no choice but to charge a $15.00 filing fee unless by leave of court it is filed in forma pauperis.

McCune v. United States, 406 F.2d 417, 419 (6th Cir.1969).

Although the motion has been considered to be a new civil action in the nature of habeas corpus for filing purposes, the reduced fee for habeas has been held not applicable. The Tenth Circuit considered the specific issue in *Martin v. United States,* 273 F.2d 775 (10th Cir.1960), cert. denied, 365 U.S. 853 (1961), holding that the reduced fee was exclusive to habeas petitions.

> Counsel for Martin insists that, if a docket fee must be paid, the amount is $5 rather than $15 and bases his contention on the exception contained in 28 U.S.C. § 1914 that in habeas corpus the fee is $5. This reads into § 1914 language which is not there. While an application under § 2255 may afford the same relief as that previously obtainable by habeas corpus, it is not a petition for a writ of habeas corpus. A change in § 1914 must come from Congress.

273 F.2d at 778

Although for most situations § 2255 is intended to provide to the federal prisoner a remedy equivalent to habeas corpus as used by state prisoners, there is a major distinction between the two. Calling a § 2255 request for relief a motion rather than a petition militates toward charging no new filing fee, not an increased one. In the absence of convincing evidence to the contrary, there is no reason to suppose that Congress did not mean what it said in making a § 2255 action a motion. Therefore, as in other motions filed in a criminal action, there is no requirement of a filing fee. It is appropriate that the present situation of docketing a § 2255 motion as a new action and charging a $15 filing fee be remedied by the rule when the whole question of § 2255 motions is thoroughly thought through and organized.

Even though there is no need to have a forma pauperis affidavit to proceed with the action since there is no requirement of a fee for filing the motion the affidavit remains attached to the form to be supplied potential movants. Most such movants are indigent, and this is a convenient way of getting this into the official record so that the judge may appoint counsel, order the government to pay witness fees, allow docketing of an appeal, and grant any other rights to which an indigent is entitled in the course of a § 2255 motion, when appropriate to the particular situation, without the need for an indigency petition and adjudication at such later point in the proceeding. This should result in a streamlining of the process to allow quicker disposition of these motions.

For further discussion of this rule, see the advisory committee note to Rule 3 of the § 2254 rules.

2004 Amendments

The language of Rule 3 has been amended as part of general restyling of the rules to make them more easily understood and to make style and terminology consistent throughout the rules. These changes are intended to be stylistic and no substantive change is intended, except as indicated below.

Revised Rule 3(b) is new and is intended to parallel Federal Rule of Civil Procedure 5(e), which provides that the clerk may not refuse to accept a filing solely for the reason that it fails to comply with these rules or local rules. Before the adoption of a one-year statute of limitations in the Antiterrorism and Effective Death Penalty Act of 1996, 110 Stat. 1214, the moving party suffered no penalty, other than delay, if the petition was deemed insufficient. That Act, however, added a one-year statute of limitations to motions filed under § 2255, *see* 28 U.S.C. § 2244(d)(1). Thus, a court's dismissal of a defective motion may pose a significant penalty for a moving party who may not be able to file a corrected motion within the one-year limitation period. The Committee believed that the better procedure was to accept the defective motion and require the moving party to submit a corrected motion that conforms to Rule 2. Thus, revised Rule 3(b) requires the clerk to file a motion, even though it may otherwise fail to comply with Rule 2.

Revised Rule 3(c), which sets out a specific reference to 28 U.S.C. § 2255, paragraph 6, is new and has been added to put moving parties on notice that a one-year statute of limitations applies to motions filed under these Rules. Although the rule does not address the issue, every circuit that has addressed the issue has taken the position that equitable tolling of the statute of limitations is available in appropriate circumstances. *See, e.g., Dunlap v. United States,* 250 F.3d 1001, 1004–07 (6th Cir. 2001); *Moore v. United States,* 173 F.3d 1131, 1133–35 (8th Cir. 1999); *Sandvik v. United States,* 177 F.3d 1269, 1270–72 (11th Cir. 1999). The Supreme Court has not addressed the question directly. *See Duncan v. Walker,* 533 U.S. 167, 181 (2001) ("We . . . have no occasion to address the question that Justice Stevens raises concerning the availability of equitable tolling.").

Rule 3(d) is new and provides guidance on determining whether a motion from an inmate is considered to have been filed in a timely fashion. The new provision parallels Federal Rule of Appellate Procedure 25(a)(2)(C).

Changes Made After Publication and Comments. The Committee modified the Committee Note to reflect that the clerk must file a motion, even in those instances where the necessary filing fee or in forma pauperis form is not attached. The Note also includes new language concerning the equitable tolling of the statute of limitations.

Rule 4.   Preliminary Review

(a) **Referral to a Judge.** The clerk must promptly forward the motion to the judge who conducted the trial and imposed sentence or, if the judge who imposed sentence was not the trial judge, to the judge who conducted the proceedings being challenged. If the appropriate judge is not available, the clerk must forward the motion to a judge under the court's assignment procedure.

(b) **Initial Consideration by the Judge.** The judge who receives the motion must promptly examine it. If it plainly appears from the motion, any attached exhibits, and the record of prior proceedings that the moving party is not entitled to relief, the judge must dismiss the motion and direct the clerk to notify the moving party. If the motion is not dismissed, the judge must order the

United States attorney to file an answer, motion, or other response within a fixed time, or to take other action the judge may order.

(As amended Apr. 26, 2004, eff. Dec. 1, 2004.)

ADVISORY COMMITTEE NOTES

1976 Adoption

Rule 4 outlines the procedure for assigning the motion to a specific judge of the district court and the options available to the judge and the government after the motion is properly filed.

The long-standing majority practice in assigning motions made pursuant to § 2255 has been for the trial judge to determine the merits of the motion. In cases where the § 2255 motion is directed against the sentence, the merits have traditionally been decided by the judge who imposed sentence. The reasoning for this was first noted in *Carvell v. United States,* 173 F.2d 348–349 (4th Cir.1949):

> Complaint is made that the judge who tried the case passed upon the motion. Not only was there no impropriety in this, but it is highly desirable in such cases that the motions be passed on by the judge who is familiar with the facts and circumstances surrounding the trial, and is consequently not likely to be misled by false allegations as to what occurred.

This case, and its reasoning, has been almost unanimously endorsed by other courts dealing with the issue.

Commentators have been critical of having the motion decided by the trial judge. See Developments in the Law—Federal Habeas Corpus, 83 Harv.L.Rev. 1038, 1206–1208 (1970).

> [T]he trial judge may have become so involved with the decision that it will be difficult for him to review it objectively. Nothing in the legislative history suggests that "court" refers to a specific judge, and the procedural advantages of section 2255 are available whether or not the trial judge presides at the hearing.

> The theory that Congress intended the trial judge to preside at a section 2255 hearing apparently originated in *Carvell v. United States,* 173 F.2d 348 (4th Cir.1949) (per curiam), where the panel of judges included Chief Judge Parker of the Fourth Circuit, chairman of the Judicial Conference committee which drafted section 2255. But the legislative history does not indicate that Congress wanted the trial judge to preside. Indeed the advantages of section 2255 can all be achieved if the case is heard in the sentencing district, regardless of which judge hears it. According to the Senate committee report the purpose of the bill was to make the proceeding a part of the criminal action so the court could resentence the applicant, or grant him a new trial. (A judge presiding over a habeas corpus action does not have these powers.) In addition, Congress did not want the cases heard in the district of confinement because that tended to concentrate the burden on a few districts, and made it difficult for witnesses and records to be produced.

83 Harv.L.Rev. at 1207–1208

The Court of Appeals for the First Circuit has held that a judge other than the trial judge should rule on the 2255 motion. See *Halliday v. United States,* 380 F.2d 270 (1st Cir.1967).

There is a procedure by which the movant can have a judge other than the trial judge decide his motion in courts adhering to the majority rule. He can file an affidavit alleging bias in order to disqualify the trial judge. And there are circumstances in which the trial judge will, on his own, disqualify himself. See, *e.g., Webster v. United States,* 330 F.Supp. 1080 (1972). However, there has been some questioning of the effectiveness of this procedure. See Developments in the Law—Federal Habeas Corpus, 83 Harv.L.Rev. 1038, 1200–1207 (1970).

Subdivision (a) adopts the majority rule and provides that the trial judge, or sentencing judge if different and appropriate for the particular motion, will decide the motion made pursuant to these rules, recognizing that, under some circumstances, he may want to disqualify himself. A movant is not without remedy if he feels this is unfair to him. He can file an affidavit of bias. And there is the right to appellate review if the trial judge refuses to grant his motion. Because the trial judge is thoroughly familiar with the case, there is obvious administrative advantage in giving him the first opportunity to decide whether there are grounds for granting the motion.

Since the motion is part of the criminal action in which was entered the judgment to which it is directed, the files, records, transcripts, and correspondence relating to that judgment are automatically available to the judge in his consideration of the motion. He no longer need order them incorporated for that purpose.

Rule 4 has its basis in § 2255 (rather than 28 U.S.C. § 2243 in the corresponding habeas corpus rule) which does not have a specific time limitation as to when the answer must be made. Also, under § 2255, the United States Attorney for the district is the party served with the notice and a copy of the motion and required to answer (when appropriate). Subdivision (b) continues this practice since there is no respondent involved in the motion (unlike habeas) and the United States Attorney, as prosecutor in the case in question, is the most appropriate one to defend the judgment and oppose the motion.

The judge has discretion to require an answer or other appropriate response from the United States Attorney. See advisory committee note to Rule 4 of the § 2254 rules.

2004 Amendments

The language of Rule 4 has been amended as part of general restyling of the rules to make them more easily understood and to make style and terminology consistent throughout the rules. These changes are intended to be stylistic and no substantive change is intended.

The amended rule reflects that the response to a Section 2255 motion may be a motion to dismiss or some other response.

Changes Made After Publication and Comments. The Committee modified Rule 4 to reflect the view of some commentators that it is common practice in some districts for the government to file a pre-answer motion to dismiss the § 2255 motion. The Committee agreed with that recommendation and changed the word "pleading" in the rule to "response." It also made several minor changes to the Committee Note.

Rule 5.   The Answer and the Reply

(a) **When Required.** The respondent is not required to answer the motion unless a judge so orders.

(b) **Contents.** The answer must address the allegations in the motion. In addition, it must state whether the moving party has used any other federal remedies, including any prior post-conviction motions under these rules or any previous rules, and whether the moving party received an evidentiary hearing.

(c) **Records of Prior Proceedings.** If the answer refers to briefs or transcripts of the prior proceedings that are not available in the court's records, the judge must order the government to furnish them within a reasonable time that will not unduly delay the proceedings.

(d) **Reply.** The moving party may file a reply to the respondent's answer or other pleading. The judge must set the time to file unless the time is already set by local rule.

(As amended Apr. 26, 2004, eff. Dec. 1, 2004; Apr. 25, 2019, eff. Dec. 1, 2019.)

ADVISORY COMMITTEE NOTES

1976 Adoption

Unlike the habeas corpus statutes (see 28 U.S.C. §§ 2243, 2248) § 2255 does not specifically call for a return or answer by the United States Attorney or set any time limits as to when one must be submitted. The general practice, however, if the motion is not summarily dismissed, is for the government to file an answer to the motion as well as counter-affidavits, when appropriate. Rule 4 provides for an answer to the motion by the United States Attorney, and Rule 5 indicates what its contents should be.

There is no requirement that the movant exhaust his remedies prior to seeking relief under § 2255. However, the courts have held that such a motion is inappropriate if the movant is simultaneously appealing the decision.

We are of the view that there is no jurisdictional bar to the District Court's entertaining a Section 2255 motion during the pendency of a direct appeal but that the orderly administration of criminal law precludes considering such a motion absent extraordinary circumstances.

Womack v. United States, 395 F.2d 630, 631 (D.C.Cir.1968).

Also see *Masters v. Eide,* 353 F.2d 517 (8th Cir.1965). The answer may thus cut short consideration of the motion if it discloses the taking of an appeal which was omitted from the form motion filed by the movant.

There is nothing in § 2255 which corresponds to the § 2248 requirement of a traverse to the answer. Numerous cases have held that the government's answer and affidavits are not conclusive against the movant, and if they raise disputed issues of fact a hearing must be held. *Machibroda v. United States,* 368 U.S. 487, 494, 495 (1962); *United States v. Salerno,* 290 F.2d 105, 106 (2d Cir.1961); *Romero v. United States,* 327 F.2d 711, 712 (5th Cir.1964); *Scott v. United States,* 349 F.2d 641, 642, 643 (6th Cir.1965); *Schiebelhut v. United States,* 357 F.2d 743, 745 (6th Cir.1966); and *Del Piano v. United States,* 362 F.2d 931, 932, 933 (3d Cir.1966). None of these cases make any mention of a traverse by the movant to the government's answer. As under Rule 5 of the § 2254 rules, there is no intention here that such a traverse be required, except under special circumstances. See advisory committee note to Rule 9.

Subdivision (b) provides for the government to supplement its answers with appropriate copies of transcripts or briefs if for some reason the judge does not already have them under his control. This is because the government will in all probability have easier access to such papers than the movant, and it will conserve the court's time to have the government produce them rather than the movant, who would in most instances have to apply in forma pauperis for the government to supply them for him anyway.

For further discussion, see the advisory committee note to Rule 5 of the § 2254 rules.

2004 Amendments

The language of Rule 5 has been amended as part of general restyling of the rules to make them more easily understood and to make style and terminology consistent throughout the rules. These changes are intended to be stylistic and no substantive change is intended.

Revised Rule 5(a), which provides that the respondent is not required to file an answer to the motion, unless a judge so orders, is taken from current Rule 3(b). The revised rule does not address the practice in some districts, where the respondent files a pre-answer motion to dismiss the motion. But revised Rule 4(b) contemplates that practice and has been changed to reflect the view that if the court does not dismiss the motion, it may require (or permit) the respondent to file a motion.

Finally, revised Rule 5(d) adopts the practice in some jurisdictions giving the movant an opportunity to file a reply to the respondent's answer. Rather than using terms such as "traverse," *see* 28 U.S.C. § 2248, to identify the movant's response to the answer, the rule uses the more general term "reply." The Rule prescribes that the court set the time for such responses, and in lieu of setting specific time limits in each case, the court may decide to include such time limits in its local rules.

Changes Made After Publication and Comments. Rule 5(a) was modified to read that the government is not required to "respond" to the motion unless the court so orders; the term "respond" was used because it leaves open the possibility that the government's first response (as it is in some districts) is in the form of a pre-answer motion to dismiss the petition. The Note has been changed to reflect the fact that although the rule itself does not reflect that particular motion, it is used in some districts and refers the reader to Rule 4.

Finally, the Committee changed the Note to address the use of the term "traverse," a point raised by one of the commentators on the proposed rule.

2019 Amendments

The moving party has a right to file a reply. Subsection (d), added in 2004, removed the discretion of the court to determine whether or not to allow the moving party to file a reply in a case under § 2255. The current amendment was prompted by decisions holding that courts nevertheless retained the authority to bar a reply.

As amended, the first sentence of subsection (d) makes it even clearer that the moving party has a right to file a reply to the respondent's answer or pleading. It retains the word "may," which is used throughout the federal rules to mean "is permitted to" or "has a right to." No change in meaning is intended by the substitution of "file" for "submit."

As amended, the second sentence of the rule retains the court's discretion to decide when the reply must be filed (but not whether it may be filed). To avoid uncertainty, the amended rule requires the court to set a time for filing if that time is not already set by local rule. Adding a reference to the time for the filing of any reply to the order requiring the government to file an answer or other pleading provides notice of that deadline to both parties.

Rule 6.   Discovery

(a) Leave of Court Required. A judge may, for good cause, authorize a party to conduct discovery under the Federal Rules of Criminal Procedure or Civil Procedure, or in accordance with the practices and principles of law. If necessary for effective discovery, the judge must appoint an attorney for a moving party who qualifies to have counsel appointed under 18 U.S.C. § 3006A.

(b) Requesting Discovery. A party requesting discovery must provide reasons for the request. The request must also include any proposed interrogatories and requests for admission, and must specify any requested documents.

(c) Deposition Expenses. If the government is granted leave to take a deposition, the judge may require the government to pay the travel expenses, subsistence expenses, and fees of the moving party's attorney to attend the deposition.

(As amended Apr. 26, 2004, eff. Dec. 1, 2004.)

ADVISORY COMMITTEE NOTES

1976 Adoption

This rule differs from the corresponding discovery rule under the § 2254 rules in that it includes the processes of discovery available under the Federal Rules of Criminal Procedure as well as the civil. This is because of the nature of a § 2255 motion as a continuing part of the criminal proceeding (see advisory committee note to Rule 1) as well as a remedy analogous to habeas corpus by state prisoners.

See the advisory committee note to rule 6 of the § 2254 rules. The discussion there is fully applicable to discovery under these rules for § 2255 motions.

2004 Amendments

The language of Rule 6 has been amended as part of general restyling of the rules to make them more easily understood and to make style and terminology consistent throughout the rules. These changes are intended to be stylistic and no substantive change is intended, except as indicated below.

Although current Rule 6(b) contains no requirement that the parties provide reasons for the requested discovery, the revised rule does so and also includes a requirement that the request be accompanied by any proposed interrogatories and requests for admission, and must specify any requested documents. The Committee believes that the revised rule makes explicit what has been implicit in current practice.

Changes Made After Publication and Comments. The Committee modified Rule 6(b), to require that discovery requests be supported by reasons, to assist the court in deciding what, if any, discovery should take place. The Committee amended the Note to reflect the view that it believed that the change made explicit what has been implicit in current practice.

Rule 7.   Expanding the Record

(a) In General. If the motion is not dismissed, the judge may direct the parties to expand the record by submitting additional materials relating to the motion. The judge may require that these materials be authenticated.

(b) Types of Materials. The materials that may be required include letters predating the filing of the motion, documents, exhibits, and answers under oath to written interrogatories propounded by the judge. Affidavits also may be submitted and considered as part of the record.

(c) Review by the Opposing Party. The judge must give the party against whom the additional materials are offered an opportunity to admit or deny their correctness.

(As amended Apr. 26, 2004, eff. Dec. 1, 2004.)

ADVISORY COMMITTEE NOTES

1976 Adoption

It is less likely that the court will feel the need to expand the record in a § 2255 proceeding than in a habeas corpus proceeding, because the trial (or sentencing) judge is the one hearing the motion (see Rule 4) and should already have a complete file on the case in his possession. However, Rule 7 provides a convenient method for supplementing his file if the case warrants it.

See the advisory committee note to Rule 7 of the § 2254 rules for a full discussion of reasons and procedures for expanding the record.

2004 Amendments

The language of Rule 7 has been amended as part of general restyling of the rules to make them more easily understood and to make style and terminology consistent throughout the rules. These changes are intended to be stylistic and no substantive change is intended.

Revised Rule 7(a) is not intended to restrict the court's authority to expand the record through means other than requiring the parties themselves to provide the information.

The language in current Rule 7(d), which deals with authentication of materials in the expanded record, has been moved to revised Rule 7(a).

Changes Made After Publication and Comments. Rule 7(a) was changed by removing the reference to the "merits" of the motion. One commentator had stated that the court may wish to expand the record for purposes other than the merits of the case. The Committee agreed and also changed the rule to reflect that someone other than a party may authenticate the materials.

Rule 8.   Evidentiary Hearing

(a) Determining Whether to Hold a Hearing. If the motion is not dismissed, the judge must review the answer, any transcripts and records of prior proceedings, and any materials submitted under Rule 7 to determine whether an evidentiary hearing is warranted.

(b) Reference to a Magistrate Judge. A judge may, under 28 U.S.C. § 636(b), refer the motion to a magistrate judge to conduct hearings and to file proposed findings of fact and recommendations for disposition. When they are filed, the clerk must promptly serve copies of the proposed findings and recommendations on all parties. Within 14 days after being served, a party may file objections as provided by local court rule. The judge must determine de novo any proposed finding or recommendation to which objection is made. The judge may accept, reject, or modify any proposed finding or recommendation.

(c) Appointing Counsel; Time of Hearing. If an evidentiary hearing is warranted, the judge must appoint an attorney to represent a moving party who qualifies to have counsel appointed under 18 U.S.C. § 3006A. The judge must conduct the hearing as soon as practicable after giving the attorneys adequate time to investigate and prepare. These rules do not limit the appointment of counsel under § 3006A at any stage of the proceeding.

(d) Producing a Statement. Federal Rule of Criminal Procedure 26.2(a)–(d) and (f) applies at a hearing under this rule. If a party does not comply with a Rule 26.2(a) order to produce a witness's statement, the court must not consider that witness's testimony.

(As amended Pub.L. 94–426, § 2(6), Sept. 28, 1976, 90 Stat. 1335; Pub.L. 94–577, § 2(a)(2), (b)(2), Oct. 21, 1976, 90 Stat. 2730, 2731; Apr. 22, 1993, eff. Dec. 1, 1993; Apr. 26, 2004, eff. Dec. 1, 2004; Mar. 26, 2009, eff. Dec. 1, 2009.)

ADVISORY COMMITTEE NOTES

1976 Adoption

The standards for § 2255 hearings are essentially the same as for evidentiary hearings under a habeas petition, except that the previous federal fact-finding proceeding is in issue rather than the state's. Also § 2255 does not set specific time limits for holding the hearing, as does § 2243 for a habeas action. With these minor differences in mind, see the advisory committee note to Rule 8 of § 2254 rules, which is applicable to Rule 8 of these § 2255 rules.

1993 Amendment

The amendment to Rule 8 is one of a series of parallel amendments to Federal Rules of Criminal Procedure 32, 32.1, and 46 which extend the scope of Rule 26.2 (Production of Witness Statements) to proceedings other than the trial itself. The amendments are grounded on the compelling need for accurate and credible information in making decisions concerning the defendant's liberty. *See* the Advisory Committee Note to Rule 26.2(g). A few courts have recognized the authority of a judicial officer to order production of prior statements by a witness at a Section 2255 hearing, see, e.g., *United States v. White,* 342 F.2d 379, 382, n. 4 (4th Cir.1959). The amendment to Rule 8 grants explicit authority to do so. The amendment is not intended to require production of a witness's statement before the witness actually presents oral testimony.

2004 Amendments

The language of Rule 8 has been amended as part of general restyling of the rules to make them more easily understood and to make style and terminology consistent throughout the rules. These changes are intended to be stylistic and no substantive change is intended, except as described below.

The requirement in current Rule 8(b)(2) that a copy of the magistrate judge's findings must be promptly mailed to all parties has been changed in revised Rule 8(b) to require that copies of those findings be served on all parties. As used in this rule, "service" means service consistent with Federal Rule of Civil Procedure 5(b), which allows mailing the copies.

2009 Amendments

The time set in the former rule at 10 days has been revised to 14 days. See the Committee Note to Federal Rules of Criminal Procedure 45(a).

HISTORICAL NOTES

Effective and Applicability Provisions

1976 Acts. Amendments made by Pub.L. 94–577 effective with respect to motions under section 2255 of this title filed on or after Feb. 1, 1977, see section 2(c) of Pub.L. 94–577, set out as a note under Rule 8 of the Rules Governing Cases Under Section 2254 of this title.

Rule 9.   Second or Successive Motions

Before presenting a second or successive motion, the moving party must obtain an order from the appropriate court of appeals authorizing the district court to consider the motion, as required by 28 U.S.C. § 2255, para. 8.

(As amended Pub.L. 94–426, § 2(9), (10), Sept. 28, 1976, 90 Stat. 1335; Apr. 26, 2004, eff. Dec. 1, 2004.)

ADVISORY COMMITTEE NOTES

1976 Adoption

Unlike the statutory provisions on habeas corpus (28 U.S.C. §§ 2241–2254), § 2255 specifically provides that "a motion for such relief may be made *at any time*." [Emphasis added.] Subdivision (a) provides that delayed motions may be barred from consideration if the government has been prejudiced in its ability to respond to the motion by the delay and the movant's failure to seek relief earlier is not excusable within the terms of the rule. Case law, dealing with this issue, is in conflict.

Some courts have held that the literal language of § 2255 precludes any possible time bar to a motion brought under it. In *Heflin v. United States,* 358 U.S. 415 (1959), the concurring opinion noted:

> The statute [28 U.S.C. § 2255] further provides: "A motion * * * may be made at any time." This * * * simply means that, as in habeas corpus, there is no statute of limitations, no *res judicata,* and that the doctrine of laches is inapplicable.

358 U.S. at 420

McKinney v. United States, 208 F.2d 844 (D.C.Cir.1953) reversed the district court's dismissal of a § 2255 motion for being too late, the court stating:

> McKinney's present application for relief comes late in the day: he has served some fifteen years in prison. But tardiness is irrelevant where a constitutional issue is raised and where the prisoner is still confined.

208 F.2d at 846, 847

In accord, see; *Juelich v. United States,* 300 F.2d 381, 383 (5th Cir.1962); *Conners v. United States,* 431 F.2d 1207, 1208 (9th Cir.1970); *Sturrup v. United States,* 218 F.Supp. 279, 281 (E.D.N.Car.1963); and *Banks v. United States,* 319 F.Supp. 649, 652 (S.D.N.Y.1970).

It has also been held that delay in filing a § 2255 motion does not bar the movant because of lack of reasonable diligence in pressing the claim.

> The statute [28 U.S.C. § 2255], when it states that the motion may be made at any time, excludes the addition of a showing of diligence in delayed filings. A number of courts have considered contentions similar to those made here and have concluded that there are no time limitations. This result excludes the requirement of diligence which is in reality a time limitation.

Haier v. United States, 334 F.2d 441, 442 (10th Cir.1964)

Other courts have recognized that delay may have a negative effect on the movant. In *Raines v. United States,* 423 F.2d 526 (4th Cir.1970), the court stated:

> [B]oth petitioners' silence for extended periods, one for 28 months and the other for nine years, serves to render their allegations less believable. "Although a delay in filing a section 2255 motion is not a controlling element * * * it may merit some consideration * * *."

423 F.2d at 531

In *Aiken v. United States,* 191 F.Supp. 43, 50 (M.D.N.Car.1961), aff'd 296 F.2d 604 (4th Cir.1961), the court said: "While motions under 28 U.S.C. § 2255 may be made at any time, the lapse of time affects the good faith and credibility of the moving party." For similar conclusions, see: *Parker v. United States,* 358 F.2d 50, 54 n. 4 (7th Cir.1965), cert. denied, 386 U.S. 916 (1967); *Le Clair v. United States,* 241 F.Supp. 819, 824 (N.D.Ind.1965); *Malone v. United States,* 299 F.2d 254, 256 (6th Cir.1962), cert. denied, 371 U.S. 863 (1962); *Howell v. United States,* 442 F.2d 265, 274 (7th Cir.1971); and *United States v. Wiggins,* 184 F.Supp. 673, 676 (D.C.Cir.1960).

There have been holdings by some courts that a delay in filing a § 2255 motion operates to increase the burden of proof which the movant must meet to obtain relief. The reasons for this, as expressed in *United States v. Bostic,* 206 F.Supp. 855 (D.C.Cir.1962), are equitable in nature.

> Obviously, the burden of proof on a motion to vacate a sentence under 28 U.S.C. § 2255 is on the moving party. . . . The burden is particularly heavy if the issue is one of fact and a long time has elapsed since the trial of the case. While neither the statute of limitations nor laches can bar the assertion of a constitutional right, nevertheless, the passage of time may make it impracticable to retry a case if the motion is granted and a new trial is ordered. No doubt, at times such a motion is a product of an afterthought. Long delay may raise a question of good faith.

206 F.Supp. at 856–857

See also *United States v. Wiggins,* 184 F.Supp. at 676.

A requirement that the movant display reasonable diligence in filing a § 2255 motion has been adopted by some courts dealing with delayed motions. The court in *United States v. Moore,* 166 F.2d 102 (7th Cir.1948), cert. denied, 334 U.S. 849 (1948), did this, again for equitable reasons.

> [W]e agree with the District Court that the petitioner has too long slept upon his rights. * * * [A]pparently there is no limitation of time within which * * * a motion to vacate may be filed, except that an applicant must show reasonable diligence in presenting his claim. * * *

> The reasons which support the rule requiring diligence seem obvious. * * * Law enforcement officials change, witnesses die, memories grow dim. The prosecuting tribunal is put to a disadvantage if an unexpected retrial should be necessary after long passage of time.

166 F.2d at 105

In accord see *Desmond v. United States,* 333 F.2d 378, 381 (1st Cir.1964), on remand, 345 F.2d 225 (1st Cir.1965).

One of the major arguments advanced by the courts which would penalize a movant who waits an unduly long time before filing a § 2255 motion is that such delay is highly prejudicial to the prosecution. In *Desmond v. United States,* writing of a § 2255 motion alleging denial of effective appeal because of deception by movant's own counsel, the court said:

> [A]pplications for relief such as this must be made promptly. It will not do for a prisoner to wait until government witnesses have become unavailable as by death, serious illness or absence from the country, or until the memory of available government witnesses has faded. It will not even do for a prisoner to wait any longer than is reasonably necessary to prepare appropriate moving papers, however inartistic, after discovery of the deception practiced upon him by his attorney.

333 F.2d at 381

In a similar vein are *United States v. Moore* and *United States v. Bostic*, supra, and *United States v. Wiggins*, 184 F.Supp. at 676.

Subdivision (a) provides a flexible, equitable time limitation based on laches to prevent movants from withholding their claims so as to prejudice the government both in meeting the allegations of the motion and in any possible retrial. It includes a reasonable diligence requirement for ascertaining possible grounds for relief. If the delay is found to be excusable, or nonprejudicial to the government, the time bar is inoperative.

Subdivision (b) is consistent with the language of § 2255 and relevant case law.

The annexed form is intended to serve the same purpose as the comparable one included in the § 2254 rules.

For further discussion applicable to this rule, see the advisory committee note to Rule 9 of the § 2254 rules.

2004 Amendments

The language of Rule 9 has been amended as part of general restyling of the rules to make them more easily understood and to make style and terminology consistent throughout the rules. These changes are intended to be stylistic and no substantive change is intended, except as indicated below.

First, current Rule 9(a) has been deleted as unnecessary in light of the applicable one-year statute of limitations for § 2255 motions, added as part of the Antiterrorism and Effective Death Penalty Act of 1996, 28 U.S.C. § 2255, para. 6.

Second, the remainder of revised Rule 9 reflects provisions in the Antiterrorism and Effective Death Penalty Act of 1996, 28 U.S.C. § 2255, para. 8, which now require a moving party to obtain approval from the appropriate court of appeals before filing a second or successive motion.

Finally, the title of the rule has been changed to reflect the fact that the revised version addresses only the topic of second or successive motions.

Rule 10.   Powers of a Magistrate Judge

A magistrate judge may perform the duties of a district judge under these rules, as authorized by 28 U.S.C. § 636.

(As amended Pub.L. 94–426, § 2(12), Sept. 28, 1976, 90 Stat. 1335; Apr. 30, 1979, eff. Aug. 1, 1979; Apr. 26, 2004, eff. Dec. 1, 2004.)

ADVISORY COMMITTEE NOTES

1976 Adoption

See the advisory committee note to Rule 10 of the § 2254 rules for a discussion fully applicable here as well.

1979 Amendment

This amendment conforms the rule to 18 U.S.C. § 636. See Advisory Committee Note to Rule 10 of the Rules Governing Section 2254 Cases in the United States District Courts.

2004 Amendments

The language of Rule 10 has been amended as part of general restyling of the rules to make them more easily understood and to make style and terminology consistent throughout the rules. These changes are intended to be stylistic and no substantive change is intended.

Changes Made After Publication and Comments. The Committee restyled the proposed rule.

HISTORICAL NOTES

Change of Name

United States magistrate appointed under section 631 of Title 28, Judiciary and Judicial Procedure, to be known as United States magistrate judge after Dec. 1, 1990, with any reference to United States magistrate or magistrate in Title 28, in any other Federal statute, etc., deemed a reference to United States magistrate judge appointed under section 631 of Title 28, see section 321 of Pub.L. 101–650, set out as a note under section 631 of Title 28.

Rule 11.   Certificate of Appealability; Time to Appeal

(a) Certificate of Appealability. The district court must issue or deny a certificate of appealability when it enters a final order adverse to the applicant. Before entering the final order, the court may direct the parties to submit arguments on whether a certificate should issue. If the court issues a certificate, the court must state the specific issue or issues that satisfy the showing required by 28 U.S.C. § 2253(c)(2). If the court denies a certificate, a party may not appeal the denial but may seek a certificate from the court of appeals under Federal Rule of Appellate Procedure 22. A motion to reconsider a denial does not extend the time to appeal.

(b) Time to Appeal. Federal Rule of Appellate Procedure 4(a) governs the time to appeal an order entered under these rules. A timely notice of appeal must be filed even if the district court issues a certificate of appealability. These rules do not extend the time to appeal the original judgment of conviction.

(As amended Apr. 30, 1979, eff. Aug. 1, 1979; Apr. 26, 2004, eff. Dec. 1, 2004; Mar. 26, 2009, eff. Dec. 1, 2009.)

ADVISORY COMMITTEE NOTES

1976 Adoption

Rule 11 is intended to make clear that, although a § 2255 action is a continuation of the criminal case, the bringing of a § 2255 action does not extend the time.

1979 Amendment

Prior to the promulgation of the Rules Governing Section 2255 Proceedings, the courts consistently held that the time for appeal in a section 2255 case is as provided in Fed.R.App.P. 4(a), that is, 60 days when the government is a party, rather than as provided in appellate rule 4(b), which says that the time is 10 days in criminal cases. This result has often been explained on the ground that rule 4(a) has to do with civil cases and that "proceedings under section 2255 are civil in nature." E.g., *Rothman v. United States,* 508 F.2d 648 (3d Cir.1975). Because the new section 2255 rules are based upon the premise "that a motion under § 2255 is a further step in the movant's criminal case rather than a separate civil action," see Advisory Committee Note to Rule 1, the question has arisen whether the new rules have the effect of shortening the time for appeal to that provided in appellate rule 4(b). A sentence has been added to Rule 11 in order to make it clear that this is not the case.

Even though section 2255 proceedings are a further step in the criminal case, the added sentence correctly states current law. In *United States v. Hayman,* 342 U.S. 205 (1952), the Supreme Court noted that such appeals "are governed by the civil rules applicable to appeals from final judgments in habeas corpus actions." In support, the Court cited *Mercado v. United States,* 183 F.2d 486 (1st Cir.1950), a case rejecting the argument that because § 2255 proceedings are criminal in nature the time for appeal is only 10 days. The *Mercado* court concluded that the situation was governed by that part of 28 U.S.C. § 2255 which reads: "An appeal may be taken to the court of appeals from the order entered on the motion as from a final judgment on application for a writ of habeas corpus." Thus, because appellate rule 4(a) is applicable in habeas cases, it likewise governs in § 2255 cases even though they are criminal in nature.

2004 Amendments

The language of Rule 11 has been amended as part of general restyling of the rules to make them more easily understood and to make style and terminology consistent throughout the rules. These changes are intended to be stylistic and no substantive change is intended.

2009 Amendments

Subdivision (a). As provided in 28 U.S.C. § 2253(c), an applicant may not appeal to the court of appeals from a final order in a proceeding under § 2255 unless a judge issues a COA, identifying the specific issues for which the applicant has made a substantial showing of a denial of constitutional right. New Rule 11(a) makes the requirements concerning certificates of appealability more prominent by adding and consolidating them in the appropriate rule of the Rules Governing § 2255 Proceedings for the United States District Courts. Rule 11(a) also requires the district judge to grant or deny the certificate at the time a final order is issued. *See* 3d Cir. R. 22.2, 111.3. This will ensure prompt decision making when the issues are fresh, rather than postponing consideration of the certificate until after a notice of appeal is filed. These changes will expedite proceedings, avoid unnecessary remands, and help to inform the applicant's decision whether to file a notice of appeal.

Subdivision (b). The amendment is designed to make it clear that the district court's grant of a COA does not eliminate the need to file a notice of appeal.

Changes Made to Proposed Amendment Released for Public Comment. In response to public comments, a sentence was added stating that prior to the entry of the final order the district court may direct the parties to submit arguments on whether or not a certificate should issue. This allows a court in complex cases (such as death penalty cases with numerous claims) to solicit briefing that might narrow the issues for appeal. For purposes of clarification, two sentences were added at the end of subdivision (a) stating that (1) although the district court's denial of a certificate is not appealable, a certificate may be sought in the court of appeals, and (2) a motion for reconsideration of a denial of a certificate does not extend the time to appeal. Finally, a sentence indicating that notice of appeal must be filed even if a COA is issued was added to subdivision (b).

Minor changes were also made to conform to style conventions.

Rule 12. Applicability of the Federal Rules of Civil Procedure and the Federal Rules of Criminal Procedure

The Federal Rules of Civil Procedure and the Federal Rules of Criminal Procedure, to the extent that they are not inconsistent with any statutory provisions or these rules, may be applied to a proceeding under these rules.

(As amended Apr. 26, 2004, eff. Dec. 1, 2004.)

ADVISORY COMMITTEE NOTES

1976 Adoption

This rule differs from rule 11 [redesignated as Rule 12] of the § 2254 rules in that it includes the Federal Rules of Criminal Procedure as well as the civil. This is because of the nature of a § 2255 motion as a continuing part of the criminal proceeding (see advisory committee note to Rule 1) as well as a remedy analogous to habeas corpus by state prisoners.

Since § 2255 has been considered analogous to habeas as respects the restrictions in Fed.R.Civ.P. 81(a)(2) (see *Sullivan v. United States,* 198 F.Supp. 624 (S.D.N.Y.1961)), Rule 12 is needed. For discussion, see the advisory committee note to Rule 11 [now Rule 12] of the § 2254 rules.

2004 Amendments

The language of Rule 12 has been amended as part of general restyling of the rules to make them more easily understood and to make style and terminology consistent throughout the rules. These changes are intended to be stylistic and no substantive change is intended.

HISTORICAL NOTES

References in Text

The Federal Rules of Criminal Procedure, referred to in text, are set out in Title 18, Crimes and Criminal Procedure.

The Federal Rules of Civil Procedure, referred to in text, are set out in this title.

APPENDIX OF FORMS

Motion to Vacate, Set Aside, or Correct a Sentence By a Person in Federal Custody*
(Motion Under 28 U.S.C. § 2255)
Instructions

1. To use this form, you must be a person who is serving a sentence under a judgment against you in a federal court. You are asking for relief from the conviction or the sentence. This form is your motion for relief.

2. You must file the form in the United States district court that entered the judgment that you are challenging. If you want to challenge a federal judgment that imposed a sentence to be served in the future, you should file the motion in the federal court that entered that judgment.

3. Make sure the form is typed or neatly written.

4. You must tell the truth and sign the form. If you make a false statement of a material fact, you may be prosecuted for perjury.

5. Answer all the questions. You do not need to cite law. You may submit additional pages if necessary. If you do not fill out the form properly, you will be asked to submit additional or correct information. If you want to submit a brief or arguments, you must submit them in a separate memorandum. Be aware that any such memorandum may be subject to page limits set forth in the local rules of the court where you file this motion.

6. If you cannot pay for the costs of this motion (such as costs for an attorney or transcripts), you may ask to proceed *in forma pauperis* (as a poor person). To do that, you must fill out the last page of this form. Also, you must submit a certificate signed by an officer at the institution where you are confined showing the amount of money that the institution is holding for you.

7. In this motion, you may challenge the judgment entered by only one court. If you want to challenge a judgment entered by a different judge or division (either in the same district or in a different district), you must file a separate motion.

8. When you have completed the form, send the original and [two]† copies to the Clerk of the United States District Court at this address:

    ### Clerk, United States District Court for
    ### Address
    ### City, State Zip Code

    If you want a file-stamped copy of the petition, you must enclose an additional copy of the petition and ask the court to file-stamp it and return it to you.

9. **<u>CAUTION:</u> You must include in this motion all the grounds for relief from the conviction or sentence that you challenge. And you must state the facts that support each ground. If you fail to set forth all the grounds in this motion, you may be barred from presenting additional grounds at a later date.**

10. **<u>CAPITAL CASES:</u> If you are under a sentence of death, you are entitled to the assistance of counsel and should request the appointment of counsel.**

---

* [This form is AO 243, and is available for download at https://www.uscourts.gov/file/22686/download. It was last revised on September 1, 2017. Ed.]

† [As this form appears on the website of the Administrative Office of the U.S. Courts, an underlined blank space appears instead of a number. The number included here is what the number was prior to the most recent revision. Ed.]

MOTION UNDER 28 U.S.C. § 2255 TO VACATE, SET ASIDE, OR CORRECT SENTENCE BY A PERSON IN FEDERAL CUSTODY

United States District Court	District
Name (*under which you were convicted*):	Docket or Case No.:
Place of Confinement:	Prisoner No.:
UNITED STATES OF AMERICA	Movant (*include name under which convicted*)

v.

MOTION

1. (a) Name and location of court that entered the judgment of conviction you are challenging: _____

    (b) Criminal docket or case number (if you know): _____

2. (a) Date of the judgment of conviction (if you know): _____

    (b) Date of sentencing: _____

3. Length of sentence: _____

4. Nature of crime (all counts): _____

5. (a) What was your plea? (Check one)

    (1) Not guilty ☐   (2) Guilty ☐   (3) Nolo contendere (no contest) ☐

    (b) If you entered a guilty plea to one count or indictment, and a not guilty plea to another count or indictment, what did you plead guilty to and what did you plead not guilty to? _____

6. If you went to trial, what kind of trial did you have? (Check one)   Jury ☐   Judge only ☐

7. Did you testify at a pretrial hearing, trial, or post-trial hearing?   Yes ☐   No ☐

8. Did you appeal from the judgment of conviction?   Yes ☐   No ☐

9. If you did appeal, answer the following:

    (a) Name of court: _____

    (b) Docket or case number (if you know): _____

    (c) Result: _____

    (d) Date of result (if you know): _____

    (e) Citation to the case (if you know): _____

    (f) Grounds raised: _____

MOTION ATTACKING SENTENCE

(g) Did you file a petition for certiorari in the United States Supreme Court?   Yes ☐ No ☐

If "Yes," answer the following:

(1) Docket or case number (if you know): _____

(2) Result:_____

_____

(3) Date of result (if you know): _____

(4) Citation to the case (if you know): _____

(5) Grounds raised: _____

_____

_____

_____

_____

_____

_____

10.   Other than the direct appeals listed above, have you previously filed any other motions, petitions, or applications concerning this judgment of conviction in any court?

Yes ☐ No ☐

11.   If your answer to Question 10 was "Yes," give the following information:

(a)   (1) Name of court: _____

(2) Docket or case number (if you know): _____

(3) Date of filing (if you know): _____

(4) Nature of the proceeding: _____

(5) Grounds raised: _____

_____

_____

_____

_____

_____

_____

(6) Did you receive a hearing where evidence was given on your motion, petition, or application?

Yes ☐ No ☐

(7) Result: _____

(8) Date of result (if you know): _____

(b)   If you filed any second motion, petition, or application, give the same information:

(1) Name of court: _____

(2) Docket or case number (if you know): _____

(3) Date of filing (if you know): _____

(4) Nature of the proceeding: _____

(5) Grounds raised: _____

_____

_____

_____

_____

_____

_____

(6) Did you receive a hearing where evidence was given on your motion, petition, or application?

      Yes ☐ No ☐

(7) Result: _____

(8) Date of result (if you know): _____

(c)   Did you appeal to a federal appellate court having jurisdiction over the action taken on your motion, petition, or application?

    (1) First petition: Yes ☐ No ☐

    (2) Second petition: Yes ☐ No ☐

(d)   If you did not appeal from the action on any motion, petition, or application, explain briefly why you did not: _____

_____

_____

12.   For this motion, state every ground on which you claim that you are being held in violation of the Constitution, laws, or treaties of the United States. Attach additional pages if you have more than four grounds. State the facts supporting each ground. Any legal arguments must be submitted in a separate memorandum.

GROUND ONE: _____

(a)   Supporting facts (Do not argue or cite law. Just state the specific facts that support your claim.):

_____

_____

_____

_____

_____

_____

_____

_____

_____

_____

(b)   **Direct Appeal of Ground One:**

    (1) If you appealed from the judgment of conviction, did you raise this issue?

        Yes ☐ No ☐

    (2) If you did not raise this issue in your direct appeal, explain why: _____

_____

_____

MOTION ATTACKING SENTENCE

(c) **Post-Conviction Proceedings:**

   (1) Did you raise this issue in any post-conviction motion, petition, or application?

   Yes ☐ No ☐

   (2) If your answer to Question (c)(1) is "Yes," state:

   Type of motion or petition: _____

   Name and location of the court where the motion or petition was filed: _____
   _____

   Docket or case number (if you know): _____

   Result (attach a copy of the court's opinion or order, if available): _____
   _____
   _____

   (3) Did you receive a hearing on your motion, petition, or application?

   Yes ☐ No ☐

   (4) Did you appeal from the denial of your motion, petition, or application?

   Yes ☐ No ☐

   (5) If your answer to Question (c)(4) is "Yes," did you raise this issue in the appeal?

   Yes ☐ No ☐

   (6) If your answer to Question (c)(4) is "Yes," state:

   Name and location of the court where the appeal was filed:_____
   _____

   Docket or case number (if you know):_____

   Date of the court's decision: _____

   Result (attach a copy of the court's opinion or order, if available): _____

   (7) If your answer to Question (c)(4) or Question (c)(5) is "No," explain why you did not appeal or raise this issue: _____
   _____
   _____
   _____
   _____

GROUND TWO: _____

(a) Supporting facts (Do not argue or cite law. Just state the specific facts that support your claim.):
   _____
   _____
   _____
   _____
   _____
   _____
   _____
   _____

(b) **Direct Appeal of Ground Two:**
    (1) If you appealed from the judgment of conviction, did you raise this issue?
       Yes ☐ No ☐
    (2) If you did not raise this issue in your direct appeal, explain why:_____
_____
_____

(c) **Post-Conviction Proceedings**
    (1) Did you raise this issue in any post-conviction motion, petition, or application?
       Yes ☐ No ☐
    (2) If your answer to Question (c)(1) is "Yes," state:
Type of motion or petition: _____
Name and location of the court where the motion or petition was filed: _____
_____
Docket or case number (if you know): _____
Date of the court's decision: _____
Result (attach a copy of the court's opinion or order, if available): _____
_____

    (3) Did you receive a hearing on your motion, petition, or application?
       Yes ☐ No ☐
    (4) Did you appeal from the denial of your motion, petition, or application?
       Yes ☐ No ☐
    (5) If your answer to Question (c)(4) is "Yes," did you raise this issue in the appeal?
       Yes ☐ No ☐
    (6) If your answer to Question (c)(4) is "Yes," state:
Name and location of the court where the appeal was filed: _____
_____
Docket or case number (if you know):_____
Date of the court's decision: _____
Result (attach a copy of the court's opinion or order, if available): _____
_____

    (7) If your answer to Question (c)(4) or Question (c)(5) is "No," explain why you did not
appeal or raise this issue: _____
_____
_____
_____

GROUND THREE: _____
_____

(a) Supporting facts (Do not argue or cite law. Just state the specific facts that support your claim.):
_____
_____
_____
_____
_____
_____
_____

(b) **Direct Appeal of Ground Three:**
    (1) If you appealed from the judgment of conviction, did you raise this issue?
       Yes ☐ No ☐

(2) If you did not raise this issue in your direct appeal, explain why: _____

_____

(c) **Post-Conviction Proceedings:**
(1) Did you raise this issue in any post-conviction motion, petition, or application?
Yes ☐ No ☐
(2) If your answer to Question (c)(1) is "Yes," state:
Type of motion or petition: _____
Name and location of the court where the motion or petition was filed: _____

_____

Docket or case number (if you know): _____
Date of the court's decision:
Result (attach a copy of the court's opinion or order, if available): _____

_____

(3) Did you receive a hearing on your motion, petition, or application?
Yes ☐ No ☐
(4) Did you appeal from the denial of your motion, petition, or application?
Yes ☐ No ☐
(5) If your answer to Question (c)(4) is "Yes," did you raise this issue in the appeal?
Yes ☐ No ☐
(6) If your answer to Question (c)(4) is "Yes," state:
Name and location of the court where the appeal was filed: _____

_____

Docket or case number (if you know): _____
Date of the court's decision: _____
Result (attach a copy of the court's opinion or order, if available): _____

_____

(7) If your answer to Question (c)(4) or Question (c)(5) is "No," explain why you did not appeal or
raise this issue: _____

_____

_____

_____

_____

GROUND FOUR: _____

_____

(a) Supporting facts (Do not argue or cite law. Just state the specific facts that support your claim.):

_____

_____

_____

_____

_____

_____

_____

(b) **Direct Appeal of Ground Four:**
(1) If you appealed from the judgment of conviction, did you raise this issue?
Yes ☐ No ☐
(2) If you did not raise this issue in your direct appeal, explain why: _____

_____

_____

(c)   **Post-Conviction Proceedings:**
    (1) Did you raise this issue in any post-conviction motion, petition, or application?
        Yes ☐ No ☐
    (2) If your answer to Question (c)(1) is "Yes," state:
    Type of motion or petition: _____
    Name and location of the court where the motion or petition was filed: _____
    Docket or case number (if you know): _____
    Date of the court's decision: _____
    Result (attach a copy of the court's opinion or order, if available): _____
    _____

    (3) Did you receive a hearing on your motion, petition, or application?
        Yes ☐ No ☐
    (4) Did you appeal from the denial of your motion, petition, or application?
        Yes ☐ No ☐
    (5) If your answer to Question (c)(4) is "Yes," did you raise this issue in the appeal?
        Yes ☐ No ☐
    (6) If your answer to Question (c)(4) is "Yes," state:
    Name and location of the court where the appeal was filed: _____
    _____
    Docket or case number (if you know): _____
    Date of the court's decision: _____
    Result (attach a copy of the court's opinion or order, if available): _____
    _____

    (7) If your answer to Question (c)(4) or Question (c)(5) is "No," explain why you did not appeal or raise this issue: _____
    _____

13. Is there any ground in this motion that you have <u>not</u> previously presented in some federal court? If so, which ground or grounds have not been presented, and state your reasons for not presenting them: _____
    _____
    _____

14. Do you have any motion, petition, or appeal <u>now pending</u> (filed and not decided yet) in any court for the judgment you are challenging? Yes ☐ No ☐
    If "Yes," state the name and location of the court, the docket or case number, the type of proceeding, and the issues raised. _____
    _____
    _____

15. Give the name and address, if known, of each attorney who represented you in the following stages of the judgment you are challenging:
    (a) At preliminary hearing: _____
    _____
    (b) At arraignment and plea: _____
    _____
    (c) At trial: _____
    _____
    (d) At sentencing: _____
    _____
    (e) On appeal: _____
    _____
    (f) In any post-conviction proceeding: _____
    _____

MOTION ATTACKING SENTENCE

(g) On appeal from any ruling against you in a post-conviction proceeding: _____

16. Were you sentenced on more than one count of an indictment, or on more than one indictment, in the same court and at the same time? Yes ☐ No ☐

17. Do you have any future sentence to serve after you complete the sentence for the judgment that you are challenging? Yes ☐ No ☐

    (a) If so, give name and location of court that imposed the other sentence you will serve in the future: _____

    (b) Give the date the other sentence was imposed: _____
    (c) Give the length of the other sentence: _____
    (d) Have you filed, or do you plan to file, any motion, petition, or application that challenges the judgment or sentence to be served in the future? Yes ☐ No ☐

18. TIMELINESS OF MOTION: If your judgment of conviction became final over one year ago, you must explain why the one-year statute of limitations as contained in 28 U.S.C. § 2255 does not bar your motion.* _____

* The Antiterrorism and Effective Death Penalty Act of 1996 ("AEDPA") as contained in 28 U.S.C. § 2255, paragraph 6, provides in part that:

A one-year period of limitation shall apply to a motion under this section. The limitation period shall run from the latest of—

(1) the date on which the judgment of conviction became final;

(2) the date on which the impediment to making a motion created by governmental action in violation of the Constitution or laws of the United States is removed, if the movant was prevented from making such a motion by such governmental action;

(3) the date on which the right asserted was initially recognized by the Supreme Court, if that right has been newly recognized by the Supreme Court and made retroactively applicable to cases on collateral review; or

(4) the date on which the facts supporting the claim or claims presented could have been discovered through the exercise of due diligence.

Therefore, movant asks that the Court grant the following relief: _____

or any other relief to which movant may be entitled.

_____
Signature of Attorney (if any)

I declare (or certify, verify, or state) under penalty of perjury that the foregoing is true and correct and that this Motion Under 28 U.S.C. § 2255 was placed in the prison mailing system on _____ (month, date, year).

Executed (signed) on _____ (date).

_____
Signature of Movant

If the person signing is not movant, state relationship to movant and explain why movant is not signing this motion. _____

IN FORMA PAUPERIS DECLARATION

[INSERT APPROPRIATE COURT]

United States	DECLARATION IN SUPPORT
v.	OF REQUEST TO PROCEED
_____	*IN FORMA*
(Movant)	*PAUPERIS*

I, _____, declare that I am the movant in the above entitled case; that in support of my motion to proceed without being required to prepay fees, costs or give security therefor, I state that because of my poverty, I am unable to pay the costs of said proceeding or to give security therefor; that I believe I am entitled to relief.

1. Are you presently employed? Yes ☐ No ☐
   a. If the answer is "yes," state the amount of your salary or wages per month, and give the name and address of your employer.

   _____

   b. If the answer is "no," state the date of last employment and the amount of the salary and wages per month which you received.

   _____

2. Have you received within the past twelve months any money from any of the following sources?
   a. Business, profession or form of self-employment? Yes ☐ No ☐
   b. Rent payments, interest or dividends? Yes ☐ No ☐
   c. Pensions, annuities or life insurance payments? Yes ☐ No ☐
   d. Gifts or inheritances? Yes ☐ No ☐
   e. Any other sources? Yes ☐ No ☐
   If the answer to any of the above is "yes," describe each source of money and state the amount received from each during the past twelve months.

   _____

   _____

3. Do you own any cash, or do you have money in a checking or savings account?
   Yes ☐ No ☐ (Include any funds in prison accounts)
   If the answer is "yes," state the total value of the items owned.

   _____

   _____

4. Do you own real estate, stocks, bonds, notes, automobiles, or other valuable property (excluding ordinary household furnishings and clothing)?
   Yes ☐ No ☐

   If the answer is "yes," describe the property and state its approximate value.

   _____

   _____

5. List the persons who are dependent upon you for support, state your relationship to those persons, and indicate how much you contribute toward their support.

   _____

MOTION ATTACKING SENTENCE

I declare (or certify, verify, or state) under penalty of perjury that the foregoing is true and correct. Executed on _____.
(date)

_____
Signature of Movant

CERTIFICATE

I hereby certify that the movant herein has the sum of $_____ on account to his credit at the _____ institution where he is confined. I further certify that movant likewise has the following securities to his credit according to the records of said _____ institution:

_____

_____

_____

_____

_____
Authorized Officer of Institution

(As amended Apr. 28, 1982, eff. Aug. 1, 1982; Apr. 26, 2004, eff. Dec. 1, 2004.)

FEDERAL RULES OF
APPELLATE PROCEDURE

Amendments received through April 27, 2020*

TITLE I. APPLICABILITY OF RULES

---

* [The Federal Rules of Appellate Procedure as reproduced herein include amendments to Appellate Rules 35 and 40 that have been approved by the U.S. Supreme Court. New material is indicated by <u>underlined type</u> and matter to be omitted is ~~stricken through~~. These amendments will become effective on December 1, 2020 absent contrary congressional action. Ed.]

RULES OF APPELLATE PROCEDURE

TITLE VI. HABEAS CORPUS; PROCEEDINGS IN FORMA PAUPERIS

TITLE VII. GENERAL PROVISIONS

APPENDIX OF FORMS

RULES OF APPELLATE PROCEDURE

ORDERS OF THE SUPREME COURT OF THE UNITED STATES ADOPTING AND AMENDING RULES

ORDER OF DECEMBER 4, 1967 [389 U.S. 1065]

ORDERED:

1. That the following rules, to be known as the Federal Rules of Appellate Procedure, be, and they hereby are, prescribed, pursuant to sections 3771 and 3772 of Title 18, United States Code, and sections 2072 and 2075 of Title 28, United States Code, to govern the procedure in appeals to United States courts of appeals from the United States district courts, in the review by United States courts of appeals of decisions of the Tax Court of the United States, in proceedings in the United States courts of appeals for the review or enforcement of orders of administrative agencies, boards, commissions and officers, and in applications for writs or other relief which a United States court of appeals or judge thereof is competent to give:

[See text of Rules of Appellate Procedure, post]

2. That the foregoing rules shall take effect on July 1, 1968, and shall govern all proceedings in appeals and petitions for review or enforcement of orders thereafter brought and in all such proceedings then pending, except to the extent that in the opinion of the court of appeals their application in a particular proceeding then pending would not be feasible or would work injustice, in which case the former procedure may be followed.

3. That Rules 6, 9, 41, 77 and 81 of the Rules of Civil Procedure for the United States District Courts be, and they hereby are, amended, effective July 1, 1968, as hereinafter set forth:

[See amendments made thereby under the Rules of Civil Procedure, ante]

4. That the chapter heading "IX. APPEALS", all of Rules 72, 73, 74, 75 and 76 of the Rules of Civil Procedure for the United States District Courts, and Form 27 annexed to the said rules, be, and they hereby are, abrogated, effective July 1, 1968.

5. That Rules 45, 49, 56 and 57 of the Rules of Criminal Procedure for the United States District Courts be, and they hereby are, amended, effective July 1, 1968, as hereinafter set forth:

[For text of amendments, see pamphlet containing Federal Rules of Criminal Procedure]

6. That the chapter heading "VIII. APPEAL", all of Rules 37 and 39, and subdivisions (b) and (c) of Rule 38, of the Rules of Criminal Procedure for the United States District Courts, and Forms 26 and 27 annexed to the said rules, be, and they hereby are, abrogated, effective July 1, 1968.

7. That the Chief Justice be, and he hereby is, authorized to transmit to the Congress the foregoing new rules and amendments to and abrogation of existing rules, in accordance with the provisions of Title 18, U.S.C., § 3771, and Title 28, U.S.C., §§ 2072 and 2075.

ORDER OF MARCH 30, 1970 [398 U.S. 973]

1. That subdivisions (a) and (c) of Rule 30 and subdivision (a) of Rule 31 of the Federal Rules of Appellate Procedure be, and they hereby are, amended as follows:

[See the amendments made thereby under the respective rules, post]

2. That the foregoing amendments to the Federal Rules of Appellate Procedure shall take effect on July 1, 1970, and shall govern all proceedings in actions brought thereafter and also in all further proceedings in actions then pending, except to the extent that in the opinion of the court their application in a particular action then pending would not be feasible or would work injustice, in which event the former procedure applies.

3. That the Chief Justice be, and he hereby is, authorized to transmit to the Congress the foregoing amendments to existing rules, in accordance with the provisions of Title 18, U.S.C., § 3772, and Title 28, U.S.C., §§ 2072 and 2075.

RULES OF APPELLATE PROCEDURE

ORDER OF MARCH 1, 1971 [401 U.S. 1019]

1. That subdivision (a) of Rule 6, paragraph (4) of subdivision (a) of Rule 27, paragraph (6) of subdivision (b) of Rule 30, subdivision (c) of Rule 77, and paragraph (2) of subdivision (a) of Rule 81 of the Federal Rules of Civil Procedure be, and hereby are, amended, effective July 1, 1971, to read as follows:

[See amendments made thereby under the Rules of Civil Procedure, ante]

2. That subdivision (a) of Rule 45 and all of Rule 56 of the Federal Rules of Criminal Procedure be, and they hereby are, amended, effective July 1, 1971, to read as follows:

[For text of amendments, see pamphlet containing Federal Rules of Criminal Procedure]

3. That subdivision (a) of Rule 26 and subdivision (a) of Rule 45 of the Federal Rules of Appellate Procedure be, and they hereby are, amended, effective July 1, 1971, to read as follows:

[See amendments made thereby under the respective rules, post]

4. That THE CHIEF JUSTICE be, and he hereby is, authorized to transmit to the Congress the foregoing amendments to the Rules of Civil, Criminal and Appellate Procedure, in accordance with the provisions of Title 18, U.S.C., § 3771, and Title 28, U.S.C., §§ 2072 and 2075.

MR. JUSTICE BLACK and MR. JUSTICE DOUGLAS dissent from the order entered by the Court today amending the Federal Rules of Civil Procedure, the Federal Rules of Criminal Procedure, and the Federal Rules of Appellate Procedure.

ORDER OF APRIL 24, 1972 [406 U.S. 981]

1. That Rules 1, 3, 4(b) & (c), 5, 5.1, 6(b), 7(c), 9(b), (c) & (d), 17(a) & (g), 31(e), 32(b), 38(a), 40, 41, 44, 46, 50, 54 and 55 of the Federal Rules of Criminal Procedure be, and they hereby are, amended effective October 1, 1972, to read as follows:

[For text of amendments, see pamphlet containing Federal Rules of Criminal Procedure]

2. That Rule 9(c) of the Federal Rules of Appellate Procedure be, and hereby is amended, effective October 1, 1972, to read as follows:

[See amendments made thereby under the respective rules, post]

3. That THE CHIEF JUSTICE be, and he hereby is, authorized to transmit to the Congress the foregoing amendments to Rules of Criminal and Appellate Procedure, in accordance with the provisions of Title 18, U.S.Code, §§ 3771 and 3772.

[MR. JUSTICE DOUGLAS dissented to adoption of Rule 50(b) of the Federal Rules of Criminal Procedure.]

ORDER OF APRIL 30, 1979 [441 U.S. 971]

1. That the Federal Rules of Appellate Procedure be, and they hereby are, amended by including therein amendments to Rules 1(a), 3(c), (d) and (e), 4(a), 5(d), 6(d), 7, 10(b), 11(a), (b), (c) and (d), 12, 13(a), 24(b), 27(b), 28(g) and (j), 34(a) and (b), 35(b) and (c), 39(c) and (d), and 40 as hereinafter set forth:

[See amendments made thereby under the respective rules, post]

2. That the foregoing amendments to the Federal Rules of Appellate Procedure shall take effect on August 1, 1979, and shall govern all appellate proceedings thereafter commenced and, insofar as just and practicable, all proceedings then pending.

3. That THE CHIEF JUSTICE be, and he hereby is, authorized to transmit to the Congress the foregoing amendments to the Federal Rules of Appellate Procedure in accordance with the provisions of Section 3772 of Title 18, United States Code, and Sections 2072 and 2075 of Title 28, United States Code.

ORDER OF MARCH 10, 1986 [475 U.S. 1155]

1. That the Federal Rules of Appellate Procedure be, and they hereby are, amended by including therein new Appellate Rules 3.1, 5.1 and 15.1 and amendments to Appellate Rules 3(d), 8(b), 10(b) and (c), 11(b), 12(a), 19, 23(b) and (c), 24(a), 25(a) and (b), 26(a) and (c), 28(c) and (j), 30(a), (b) and (c), 31(a) and (c), 34(a) and (e), 39(c) and (d), 43(a) and (c), 45(a), (b), and (d), and 46(a) and (b), as hereinafter set forth:

RULES OF APPELLATE PROCEDURE

[See amendments made thereby under the respective rules, post]

2.   That the foregoing additions to and changes in the Federal Rules of Appellate Procedure, shall take effect on July 1, 1986 and shall govern all proceedings in appellate actions thereafter commenced and, insofar as just and practicable, all proceedings in appellate actions then pending.

3.   That THE CHIEF JUSTICE be, and he hereby is, authorized to transmit to the Congress the foregoing additions to and changes in the rules of appellate procedure in accordance with the provisions of Section 3772 of Title 18 and Section 2072 of Title 28, United States Code.

ORDER OF APRIL 25, 1989 [490 U.S. 1127]

1.   That the Federal Rules of Appellate Procedure be, and they hereby are, amended by including therein amendments to Appellate Rules 1(a), 3(a), 26(a), 27(a), 28(g) and new Rules 6 and 26.1, and a new Form 5 as hereinafter set forth:

[See amendments made thereby under the respective rules, post]

2.   That the foregoing additions to and changes in the Federal Rules of Appellate Procedure, shall take effect on December 1, 1989 and shall govern all proceedings in appellate actions thereafter commenced and, insofar as just and practicable, all proceedings in appellate actions then pending.

3.   That THE CHIEF JUSTICE be, and he hereby is, authorized to transmit to the Congress the foregoing additions to and changes in the rules of appellate procedure in accordance with the provisions of Section 2072 of Title 28, United States Code.

ORDER OF APRIL 30, 1991 [500 U.S. 1009]

1.   That the Federal Rules of Appellate Procedure be, and they hereby are, amended by including therein amendments to Appellate Rules 4(a), 6, 10(c), 25(a), 26(a), 26.1, 28(a), (b), and (h), 30(b), and 34(d).

[See amendments made thereby under the respective rules, post]

2.   That the foregoing amendments to the Federal Rules of Appellate Procedure shall take effect on December 1, 1991, and shall govern all proceedings in appellate cases thereafter commenced and, insofar as just and practicable, all proceedings in appellate cases then pending.

3.   That THE CHIEF JUSTICE be, and he hereby is, authorized to transmit to the Congress the foregoing amendments to the Federal Rules of Appellate Procedure in accordance with the provisions of Section 2072 of Title 28, United States Code.

ORDER OF APRIL 22, 1993 [507 U.S. 1061]

1.   That the Federal Rules of Appellate Procedure be, and they hereby are, amended by including therein amendments to Appellate Rules 3, 3.1, 4, 5.1, 6, 10, 12, 15, 25, 28, and 34, and to Forms 1, 2, and 3.

[See amendments made thereby under the respective rules and forms, post.]

2.   That the foregoing amendments to the Federal Rules of Appellate Procedure shall take effect on December 1, 1993, and shall govern all proceedings in appellate cases thereafter commenced and, insofar as just and practicable, all proceedings in appellate cases then pending.

3.   That THE CHIEF JUSTICE be, and he hereby is, authorized to transmit to the Congress the foregoing amendments to the Federal Rules of Appellate Procedure in accordance with the provisions of Section 2072 of Title 28, United States Code.

ORDER OF APRIL 29, 1994 [511 U.S. 1157]

1.   That the Federal Rules of Appellate Procedure be, and they hereby are, amended by including therein amendments to Appellate Rules 1, 3, 5, 5.1, 9, 13, 21, 25, 26.1, 27, 28, 30, 31, 33, 35, 38, 40, 41, and 48.

[See amendments made hereby under respective rules, post]

2.   That the foregoing amendments to the Federal Rules of Appellate Procedure shall take effect on December 1, 1994, and shall govern all proceedings in appellate cases thereafter commenced and, insofar as just and practicable, all proceedings in appellate cases then pending.

RULES OF APPELLATE PROCEDURE

3.   That THE CHIEF JUSTICE be, and he hereby is, authorized to transmit to the Congress the foregoing amendments to the Federal Rules of Appellate Procedure in accordance with the provisions of Section 2072 of Title 28, United States Code.

ORDER OF APRIL 27, 1995 [514 U.S. 1139]

1.   That the Federal Rules of Appellate Procedure be, and they hereby are, amended by including therein amendments to Appellate Rules 4, 8, 10, and 47.

[See amendments made thereby under the respective rules, post.]

2.   That the foregoing amendments to the Federal Rules of Appellate Procedure shall take effect on December 1, 1995, and shall govern all proceedings in appellate cases thereafter commenced and, insofar as just and practicable, all proceedings in appellate cases then pending.

3.   That THE CHIEF JUSTICE be, and he hereby is, authorized to transmit to the Congress the foregoing amendments to the Federal Rules of Appellate Procedure in accordance with the provisions of Section 2072 of Title 28, United States Code.

ORDER OF APRIL 23, 1996 [517 U.S. 1257]

1.   That the Federal Rules of Appellate Procedure be, and they hereby are, amended by including therein amendments to Appellate Rules 21, 25, and 26.

[See amendments made thereby under respective rules, post]

2.   That the foregoing amendments to the Federal Rules of Appellate Procedure shall take effect on December 1, 1996, and shall govern all proceedings in appellate cases thereafter commenced and, insofar as just and practicable, all proceedings in appellate cases then pending.

3.   That THE CHIEF JUSTICE be, and hereby is, authorized to transmit to the Congress the foregoing amendments to the Federal Rules of Appellate Procedure in accordance with the provisions of Section 2072 of Title 28, United States Code.

ORDER OF APRIL 24, 1998 [523 U.S. 1149]

1.   That the Federal Rules of Appellate Procedure be, and they hereby are, amended by including therein amendments to Appellate Rules 1–48 and to Form 4.

[See amendments made thereby under respective rules, post]

2.   That the foregoing amendments to the Federal Rules of Appellate Procedure shall take effect on December 1, 1998, and shall govern in all proceedings thereafter commenced and, insofar as just and practicable, all proceedings then pending.

3.   That THE CHIEF JUSTICE be, and hereby is, authorized to transmit to the Congress the foregoing amendments to the Federal Rules of Appellate Procedure in accordance with the provisions of Section 2072 of Title 28, United States Code.

ORDER OF APRIL 29, 2002 [535 U.S. 1125]

1.   That the Federal Rules of Appellate Procedure be, and they hereby are, amended by including therein amendments to Appellate Rules 1, 4, 5, 21, 24, 25, 26, 26.1, 27, 28, 31, 32, 36, 41, 44, and 45 and new Form 6.

[See amendments made thereby under respective rules and forms, post]

2.   That the foregoing amendments to the Federal Rules of Appellate Procedure shall take effect on December 1, 2002, and shall govern in all proceedings in appellate cases thereafter commenced and, insofar as just and practicable, all proceedings then pending.

3.   That THE CHIEF JUSTICE be, and hereby is, authorized to transmit to the Congress the foregoing amendments to the Federal Rules of Appellate Procedure in accordance with the provisions of Section 2072 of Title 28, United States Code.

RULES OF APPELLATE PROCEDURE

ORDER OF MARCH 27, 2003 [538 U.S. 1073]

1.   That Forms 1, 2, 3, and 5 in the Appendix to the Federal Rules of Appellate Procedure be, and they hereby are, amended by replacing all references to "19___" with references to "20___."

[See amendments made thereby under respective forms, post]

2.   That the foregoing amendments to the forms in the Appendix to the Federal Rules of Appellate Procedure shall take effect on December 1, 2003, and shall govern in all proceedings in appellate cases thereafter commenced and, insofar as just and practicable, all proceedings then pending.

3.   That THE CHIEF JUSTICE be, and hereby is, authorized to transmit to the Congress the foregoing amendments to the Federal Rules of Appellate Procedure in accordance with the provisions of Section 2072 of Title 28, United States Code.

ORDER OF APRIL 25, 2005 [544 U.S.1153]

1.   That the Federal Rules of Appellate Procedure be, and they hereby are, amended by including therein amendments to Appellate Rules 4, 26, 27, 28, 32, 34, 35, 45, and new Rule 28.1.

[See amendments made thereby under respective rules, post]

2.   That the foregoing amendments to the Federal Rules of Appellate Procedure shall take effect on December 1, 2005, and shall govern in all proceedings thereafter commenced and, insofar as just and practicable, all proceedings then pending.

3.   That THE CHIEF JUSTICE be, and hereby is, authorized to transmit to the Congress the foregoing amendments to the Federal Rules of Appellate Procedure in accordance with the provisions of Section 2072 of Title 28, United States Code.

ORDER OF APRIL 12, 2006 [547 U.S. 1223]

1.   That the Federal Rules of Appellate Procedure be, and they hereby are, amended by including therein an amendment to Appellate Rule 25 and a new Rule 32.1.

[See amendments made thereby under respective rules, post]

2.   That the foregoing amendment and new rule shall take effect on December 1, 2006, and shall govern in all proceedings thereafter commenced and, insofar as just and practicable, all proceedings then pending.

3.   That the CHIEF JUSTICE be, and hereby is, authorized to transmit to the Congress the foregoing amendments to the Federal Rules of Appellate Procedure in accordance with the provisions of Section 2072 of Title 28, United States Code.

ORDER OF APRIL 30, 2007 [550 U.S. 985]

1.   That the Federal Rules of Appellate Procedure be, and they hereby are, amended by including therein an amendment to Appellate Rule 25.

[See amendments made thereby under respective rules, post]

2.   That the foregoing amendment to the Federal Rules of Appellate Procedure shall take effect on December 1, 2007, and shall govern in all proceedings thereafter commenced and, insofar as just and practicable, all proceedings then pending.

3.   That the CHIEF JUSTICE be, and hereby is, authorized to transmit to the Congress the foregoing amendment to the Federal Rules of Appellate Procedure in accordance with the provisions of Section 2072 of Title 28, United States Code.

ORDER OF MARCH 26, 2009 [556 U.S. 1293]

1.   That the Federal Rules of Appellate Procedure be, and they hereby are, amended by including therein amendments to Appellate Rules 4, 5, 6, 10, 12, 15, 19, 22, 25, 26, 27, 28.1, 30, 31, 39, and 41, and new Rule 12.1.

[See amendments made thereby under respective rules, post]

RULES OF APPELLATE PROCEDURE

2.   That the foregoing amendments to the Federal Rules of Appellate Procedure shall take effect on December 1, 2009, and shall govern in all proceedings in appellate cases thereafter commenced and, insofar as just and practicable, all proceedings then pending.

3.   That THE CHIEF JUSTICE be, and hereby is, authorized to transmit to the Congress the foregoing amendment to the Federal Rules of Appellate Procedure in accordance with the provisions of Section 2072 of Title 28, United States Code.

ORDER OF APRIL 28, 2010 [2009 J. Sup. Ct. U.S. 804]

1.   That the Federal Rules of Appellate Procedure be, and they hereby are, amended by including therein amendments to Appellate Rules 1, 4, and 29, and Form 4.

[See amendments made thereby under respective rules and form, post.]

2.   That the foregoing amendments to the Federal Rules of Appellate Procedure shall take effect on December 1, 2010, and shall govern in all proceedings in appellate cases thereafter commenced and, insofar as just and practicable, all proceedings then pending.

3.   That THE CHIEF JUSTICE be, and hereby is, authorized to transmit to the Congress the foregoing amendments to the Federal Rules of Appellate Procedure in accordance with the provisions of Section 2072 of Title 28, United States Code.

ORDER OF APRIL 26, 2011 [2010–2011 J. Sup. Ct. U.S. 820]

1.   That the Federal Rules of Appellate Procedure be, and they hereby are, amended by including therein amendments to Appellate Rules 4 and 40.

[See amendments made thereby under respective rules, post]

2.   That the foregoing amendments to the Federal Rules of Appellate Procedure shall take effect on December 1, 2011, and shall govern in all proceedings in appellate cases thereafter commenced and, insofar as just and practicable, all proceedings then pending.

3.   That THE CHIEF JUSTICE be, and hereby is, authorized to transmit to the Congress the foregoing amendments to the Federal Rules of Appellate Procedure in accordance with the provisions of Section 2072 of Title 28, United States Code.

ORDER OF APRIL 16, 2013 [2012–2013 J. Sup. Ct. U.S. 779]

1.   That the Federal Rules of Appellate Procedure be, and they hereby are, amended by including therein amendments to Appellate Rules 13, 14, 24, 28, and 28.1, and to Form 4.

[See amendments made thereby under respective rules, post]

2.   That the foregoing amendments to the Federal Rules of Appellate Procedure shall take effect on December 1, 2013, and shall govern in all proceedings in appellate cases thereafter commenced and, insofar as just and practicable, all proceedings then pending.

3.   That THE CHIEF JUSTICE be, and hereby is, authorized to transmit to the Congress the foregoing amendments to the Federal Rules of Appellate Procedure in accordance with the provisions of Section 2072 of Title 28, United States Code.

ORDER OF APRIL 25, 2014 [2013 J. Sup. Ct. U.S. 771]

1.   That the Federal Rules of Appellate Procedure be, and they hereby are, amended by including therein amendments to Appellate Rule 6.

[See amendments made thereby under Rule 6, post]

2.   That the foregoing amendments to the Federal Rules of Appellate Procedure shall take effect on December 1, 2014, and shall govern in all proceedings in appellate cases thereafter commenced and, insofar as just and practicable, all proceedings then pending.

3.   That THE CHIEF JUSTICE be, and hereby is, authorized to transmit to the Congress the foregoing amendments to the Federal Rules of Appellate Procedure in accordance with the provisions of Section 2072 of Title 28, United States Code.

RULES OF APPELLATE PROCEDURE

ORDER OF APRIL 28, 2016 [2015 J. Sup. Ct. U.S. 763]

1.   That the Federal Rules of Appellate Procedure be, and they hereby are, amended by including therein amendments to Appellate Rules 4, 5, 21, 25, 26, 27, 28, 28.1, 29, 32, 35, and 40, and Forms 1, 5, and 6, new Form 7, and new Appendix.

[See amendments made thereby under Rules 4, 5, 21, 25, 26, 27, 28, 28.1, 29, 32, 35, and 40, and Forms 1, 5, and 6, new Form 7, and new Appendix, post]

2.   That the foregoing amendments to the Federal Rules of Appellate Procedure shall take effect on December 1, 2016, and shall govern in all proceedings in appellate cases thereafter commenced and, insofar as just and practicable, all proceedings then pending.

3.   That THE CHIEF JUSTICE be, and hereby is, authorized to transmit to the Congress the foregoing amendments to the Federal Rules of Appellate Procedure in accordance with the provisions of Section 2072 of Title 28, United States Code.

ORDER OF APRIL 27, 2017 [2016 J. Sup. Ct. U.S. 701]

1.   That the Federal Rules of Appellate Procedure be, and they hereby are, amended by including therein an amendment to Appellate Rule 4.

[See amendment made thereby under Rule 4, post]

2.   That the foregoing amendments to the Federal Rules of Appellate Procedure shall take effect on December 1, 2017, and shall govern in all proceedings in appellate cases thereafter commenced and, insofar as just and practicable, all proceedings then pending.

3.   That The Chief Justice be, and hereby is, authorized to transmit to the Congress the foregoing amendment to the Federal Rules of Appellate Procedure in accordance with the provisions of Section 2074 of Title 28, United States Code.

ORDER OF APRIL 26, 2018 [2017 J. Sup. Ct. U.S. 699]

1.   That the Federal Rules of Appellate Procedure be, and they hereby are, amended by including therein amendments to Appellate Rules 8, 11, 25, 26, 28.1, 29, 31, 39, and 41, and Forms 4 and 7.

[See amendment made thereby under Rules 8, 11, 25, 26, 28.1, 29, 31, 39, and 41, and Forms 4 and 7, post]

2.   That the foregoing amendments to the Federal Rules of Appellate Procedure shall take effect on December 1, 2018, and shall govern in all proceedings in appellate cases thereafter commenced and, insofar as just and practicable, all proceedings then pending.

3.   That The Chief Justice be, and hereby is, authorized to transmit to the Congress the foregoing amendment to the Federal Rules of Appellate Procedure in accordance with the provisions of Section 2074 of Title 28, United States Code.

ORDER OF APRIL 25, 2019 [2018 J. Sup. Ct. U.S. 715]

1.   The Federal Rules of Appellate Procedure are amended to include amendments to Rules 3, 5, 13, 21, 25, 26, 26.1, 28, 32, and 39.

[See amendment made thereby under Rules 3, 5, 13, 21, 25, 26, 26.1, 28, 32, and 39, post]

2.   The foregoing amendments to the Federal Rules of Appellate Procedure shall take effect on December 1, 2019, and shall govern in all proceedings in appellate cases thereafter commenced and, insofar as just and practicable, all proceedings then pending.

3.   The Chief Justice is authorized to transmit to the Congress the foregoing amendments to the Federal Rules of Appellate Procedure in accordance with the provisions of Section 2074 of Title 28, United States Code.

ORDER OF APRIL 27, 2020

1.   The Federal Rules of Appellate Procedure are amended to include amendments to Rules 35 and 40.

[See amendments made thereby under Rules 35 and 40, post]

2.   The foregoing amendments to the Federal Rules of Appellate Procedure shall take effect on December 1, 2020, and shall govern in all proceedings in appellate cases thereafter commenced and, insofar as just and practicable, all proceedings then pending.

3.   THE CHIEF JUSTICE is authorized to transmit to the Congress the foregoing amendments to the Federal Rules of Appellate Procedure in accordance with the provisions of Section 2074 of Title 28, United States Code.

HISTORICAL NOTES

Effective and Applicability Provisions; Application; Transmission to Congress

The Federal Rules of Appellate Procedure were adopted by order of the Supreme Court on Dec. 4, 1967, transmitted to Congress by the Chief Justice on Jan. 15, 1968, and became effective on July 1, 1968.

The Rules have been amended Mar. 30, 1970, eff. July 1, 1970; Mar. 1, 1971, eff. July 1, 1971; Apr. 24, 1972, eff. Oct. 1, 1972; Apr. 30, 1979, eff. Aug. 1, 1979; Oct. 12, 1984, Pub.L. 98–473, Title II, § 210, 98 Stat. 1987; Mar. 10, 1986, eff. July 1, 1986; Nov. 18, 1988, Pub.L. 100–690, Title VII, § 7111, 102 Stat. 4419; Apr. 25, 1989, eff. Dec. 1, 1989; Apr. 30, 1991, eff. Dec. 1, 1991; Apr. 22, 1993, eff. Dec. 1, 1993; Apr. 29, 1994, eff. Dec. 1, 1994; Apr. 27, 1995, eff. Dec. 1, 1995; Apr. 23, 1996, eff. Dec. 1, 1996; Apr. 24, 1998, eff. Dec. 1, 1998; Apr. 29, 2002, eff. Dec. 1, 2002; Mar. 27, 2003, eff. Dec. 1, 2003; Apr. 25, 2005, eff. Dec. 1, 2005; Apr. 12, 2006, eff. Dec. 1, 2006; Apr. 30, 2007, eff. Dec. 1, 2007; Mar. 26, 2009, eff. Dec. 1, 2009; Apr. 28, 2010, eff. Dec. 1, 2010; Apr. 26, 2011, eff. Dec. 1, 2011; Apr. 16, 2013, eff. Dec. 1, 2013; Apr. 25, 2014, eff. Dec. 1, 2014; Apr. 28, 2016, eff. Dec. 1, 2016; Apr. 27, 2017, eff. Dec. 1, 2017; Apr. 26, 2018, eff. Dec. 1, 2018; Apr. 25, 2019, eff. Dec. 1, 2019; Apr. 27, 2020, eff. Dec. 1, 2020 absent contrary congressional action.

TITLE I. APPLICABILITY OF RULES

Rule 1.   Scope of Rules; Definition; Title

(a) Scope of Rules.

(1) These rules govern procedure in the United States courts of appeals.

(2) When these rules provide for filing a motion or other document in the district court, the procedure must comply with the practice of the district court.

(b) Definition. In these rules, "state" includes the District of Columbia and any United States commonwealth or territory.

(c) Title. These rules are to be known as the Federal Rules of Appellate Procedure.

(As amended Apr. 30, 1979, eff. Aug. 1, 1979; Apr. 25, 1989, eff. Dec. 1, 1989; Apr. 29, 1994, eff. Dec. 1, 1994; Apr. 24, 1998, eff. Dec. 1, 1998; Apr. 29, 2002, eff. Dec. 1, 2002; Apr. 28, 2010, eff. Dec. 1, 2010.)

ADVISORY COMMITTEE NOTES

1967 Adoption

These rules are drawn under the authority of 28 U.S.C. § 2072 as amended by the Act of November 6, 1966, 80 Stat. 1323 (1 U.S.Code Cong. & Ad.News, p. 1546 (1966)) (Rules of Civil Procedure); 28 U.S.C. § 2075 (Bankruptcy Rules); and 18 U.S.C. §§ 3771 [§ 3771 of Title 18, Crimes and Criminal Procedure] (Procedure to and including verdict) and 3772 [§ 3772 of Title 18] (Procedure after verdict). Those statutes combine to give to the Supreme Court power to make rules of practice and procedure for all cases within the jurisdiction of the courts of appeals. By the terms of the statutes, after the rules have taken effect all laws in conflict with them are of no further force or effect. Practice and procedure in the eleven courts of appeals are now regulated by rules promulgated by each court under the authority of 28 U.S.C. § 2071. Rule 47 expressly authorizes the courts of appeals to make rules of practice not inconsistent with these rules.

As indicated by the titles under which they are found, the following rules are of special application: Rules 3 through 12 apply to appeals from judgments and orders of the district courts; Rules 13 and 14 apply to appeals from decisions of the Tax Court (Rule 13 establishes an appeal as the mode of review of decisions of the Tax Court in place of the present petition for review); Rules 15 through 20 apply to proceedings for review or enforcement of orders of administrative agencies, boards, commissions and officers. Rules 22 through 24 regulate habeas corpus proceedings and appeals in forma pauperis. All other rules apply to all proceedings in the courts of appeals.

1979 Amendment

The Federal Rules of Appellate Procedure were designed as an integrated set of rules to be followed in appeals to the courts of appeals, covering all steps in the appellate process, whether they take place in the district court or in the court of appeals, and with their adoption Rules 72 to 76 of the F.R.C.P. [rules 72 to 76, Federal Rules of Civil Procedure] were abrogated. In some instances, however, the F.R.A.P. provide that a motion or application for relief may, or must, be made in the district court. See Rules 4(a), 10(b) and 24. The proposed amendment would make it clear that when this is so the motion or application is to be made in the form and manner prescribed by the F.R.C.P. or F.R.Cr.P. [Federal Rules Criminal Procedure] and local rules relating to the form and presentation of motions and is not governed by Rule 27 of the F.R.A.P. See Rule 7(b) of the F.R.C.P. [rule 7(b), Federal Rules of Civil Procedure] and Rule 47 of the F.R.Cr.P. [rule 47, Federal Rules of Criminal Procedure].

1989 Amendment

The amendment is technical. No substantive change is intended.

1994 Amendment

Subdivision (c). A new subdivision is added to the rule. The text of new subdivision (c) has been moved from Rule 48 to Rule 1 to allow the addition of new rules at the end of the existing set of appellate rules without burying the title provision among other rules. In a similar fashion the Bankruptcy Rules combine the provisions governing the scope of the rules and the title in the first rule.

1998 Amendments

The language and organization of the rule are amended to make the rule more easily understood. In addition to changes made to improve the understanding, the Advisory Committee has changed language to make style and terminology consistent throughout the appellate rules. These changes are intended to be stylistic only. The Advisory Committee recommends deleting the language in subdivision (a) that describes the different types of proceedings that may be brought in a court of appeals. The Advisory Committee believes that the language is unnecessary and that its omission does not work any substantive change.

2002 Amendments

Subdivision (b). Two recent enactments make it likely that, in the future, one or more of the Federal Rules of Appellate Procedure ("FRAP") will extend or limit the jurisdiction of the courts of appeals. In 1990, Congress amended the Rules Enabling Act to give the Supreme Court authority to use the federal rules of practice and procedure to define when a ruling of a district court is final for purposes of 28 U.S.C. § 1291. *See* 28 U.S.C. § 2072(c). In 1992, Congress amended 28 U.S.C. § 1292 to give the Supreme Court authority to use the federal rules of practice and procedure to provide for appeals of interlocutory decisions that are not already authorized by 28 U.S.C. § 1292. *See* 28 U.S.C. § 1292(e). Both § 1291 and § 1292 are unquestionably jurisdictional statutes, and thus, as soon as FRAP is amended to define finality for purposes of the former or to authorize interlocutory appeals not provided for by the latter, FRAP will "extend or limit the jurisdiction of the courts of appeals," and subdivision (b) will become obsolete. For that reason, subdivision (b) has been abrogated.

Changes Made After Publication and Comments. No changes were made to the text of the proposed amendment or to the Committee Note.

2010 Amendments

Subdivision (b). New subdivision (b) defines the term "state" to include the District of Columbia and any commonwealth or territory of the United States. Thus, as used in these Rules, "state" includes the District of Columbia, Guam, American Samoa, the U.S. Virgin Islands, the Commonwealth of Puerto Rico, and the Commonwealth of the Northern Mariana Islands.

Rule 2.   Suspension of Rules

On its own or a party's motion, a court of appeals may—to expedite its decision or for other good cause—suspend any provision of these rules in a particular case and order proceedings as it directs, except as otherwise provided in Rule 26(b).

(As amended Apr. 24, 1998, eff. Dec. 1, 1998.)

ADVISORY COMMITTEE NOTES

1967 Adoption

The primary purpose of this rule is to make clear the power of the courts of appeals to expedite the determination of cases of pressing concern to the public or to the litigants by prescribing a time schedule other than that provided by the rules. The rule also contains a general authorization to the courts to relieve litigants of the consequences of default where manifest injustice would otherwise result. Rule 26(b) prohibits a court of appeals from extending the time for taking appeal or seeking review.

1998 Amendments

The language of the rule is amended to make the rule more easily understood. In addition to changes made to improve the understanding, the Advisory Committee has changed the language to make style and terminology consistent throughout the appellate rules. These changes are intended to by stylistic only.

TITLE II. APPEAL FROM A JUDGMENT OR ORDER OF A DISTRICT COURT

Rule 3.   Appeal as of Right—How Taken

(a) Filing the Notice of Appeal.

    (1) An appeal permitted by law as of right from a district court to a court of appeals may be taken only by filing a notice of appeal with the district clerk within the time allowed by Rule 4. At the time of filing, the appellant must furnish the clerk with enough copies of the notice to enable the clerk to comply with Rule 3(d).

    (2) An appellant's failure to take any step other than the timely filing of a notice of appeal does not affect the validity of the appeal, but is ground only for the court of appeals to act as it considers appropriate, including dismissing the appeal.

    (3) An appeal from a judgment by a magistrate judge in a civil case is taken in the same way as an appeal from any other district court judgment.

    (4) An appeal by permission under 28 U.S.C. § 1292(b) or an appeal in a bankruptcy case may be taken only in the manner prescribed by Rules 5 and 6, respectively.

(b) Joint or Consolidated Appeals.

    (1) When two or more parties are entitled to appeal from a district-court judgment or order, and their interests make joinder practicable, they may file a joint notice of appeal. They may then proceed on appeal as a single appellant.

    (2) When the parties have filed separate timely notices of appeal, the appeals may be joined or consolidated by the court of appeals.

(c) Contents of the Notice of Appeal.

    (1) The notice of appeal must:

        (A) specify the party or parties taking the appeal by naming each one in the caption or body of the notice, but an attorney representing more than one party may describe those parties with such terms as "all plaintiffs," "the defendants," "the plaintiffs A, B, et al.," or "all defendants except X";

        (B) designate the judgment, order, or part thereof being appealed; and

(C) name the court to which the appeal is taken.

(2) A pro se notice of appeal is considered filed on behalf of the signer and the signer's spouse and minor children (if they are parties), unless the notice clearly indicates otherwise.

(3) In a class action, whether or not the class has been certified, the notice of appeal is sufficient if it names one person qualified to bring the appeal as representative of the class.

(4) An appeal must not be dismissed for informality of form or title of the notice of appeal, or for failure to name a party whose intent to appeal is otherwise clear from the notice.

(5) Form 1 in the Appendix of Forms is a suggested form of a notice of appeal.

(d) Serving the Notice of Appeal.

(1) The district clerk must serve notice of the filing of a notice of appeal by sending a copy to each party's counsel of record—excluding the appellant's—or, if a party is proceeding pro se, to the party's last known address. When a defendant in a criminal case appeals, the clerk must also serve a copy of the notice of appeal on the defendant. The clerk must promptly send a copy of the notice of appeal and of the docket entries—and any later docket entries—to the clerk of the court of appeals named in the notice. The district clerk must note, on each copy, the date when the notice of appeal was filed.

(2) If an inmate confined in an institution files a notice of appeal in the manner provided by Rule 4(c), the district clerk must also note the date when the clerk docketed the notice.

(3) The district clerk's failure to serve notice does not affect the validity of the appeal. The clerk must note on the docket the names of the parties to whom the clerk sends copies, with the date of sending. Service is sufficient despite the death of a party or the party's counsel.

(e) Payment of Fees. Upon filing a notice of appeal, the appellant must pay the district clerk all required fees. The district clerk receives the appellate docket fee on behalf of the court of appeals.

(As amended Apr. 30, 1979, eff. Aug. 1, 1979; Mar. 10, 1986, eff. July 1, 1986; Apr. 25, 1989, eff. Dec. 1, 1989; Apr. 22, 1993, eff. Dec. 1, 1993; Apr. 29, 1994, eff. Dec. 1, 1994; Apr. 24, 1998, eff. Dec. 1, 1998; Apr. 25, 2019, eff. Dec. 1, 2019.)

ADVISORY COMMITTEE NOTES

1967 Adoption

General Note. Rule 3 and Rule 4 combine to require that a notice of appeal be filed with the clerk of the district court within the time prescribed for taking an appeal. Because the timely filing of a notice of appeal is "mandatory and jurisdictional," *United States v. Robinson*, 361 U.S. 220, 224, 80 S.Ct. 282, 4 L.Ed.2d 259 (1960), compliance with the provisions of those rules is of the utmost importance. But the proposed rules merely restate, in modified form, provisions now found in the civil and criminal rules (FRCP 5(e), 73 [Rules 5(e) and 73, Federal Rules of Civil Procedure]; FRCrP 37 [rule 37, Federal Rules of Criminal Procedure], and decisions under the present rules which dispense with literal compliance in cases in which it cannot fairly be exacted should control interpretation of these rules. Illustrative decisions are: *Fallen v. United States*, 378 U.S. 139, 84 S.Ct. 1689, 12 L.Ed.2d 760 (1964) (notice of appeal by a prisoner, in the form of a letter delivered, well within the time fixed for appeal, to prison authorities for mailing to the clerk of the district court held timely filed notwithstanding that it was received by the clerk after expiration of the time for appeal; the appellant "did all he could" to effect timely filing); *Richey v. Wilkins*, 335 F.2d 1 (2d Cir. 1964) (notice filed in the court of appeals by a prisoner without assistance of counsel held sufficient); *Halfen v. United States*, 324 F.2d 52 (10th Cir. 1963) (notice mailed to district judge in time to have been received by him in normal course held sufficient); *Riffle v. United States*, 299 F.2d 802 (5th Cir. 1962) (letter of prisoner to judge of court of appeals held sufficient). Earlier cases evidencing "a liberal view of papers filed by indigent and incarcerated defendants" are listed in *Coppedge v. United States*, 369 U.S. 438, 442, n. 5, 82 S.Ct. 917, 8 L.Ed.2d 21 (1962).

Subdivision (a). The substance of this subdivision is derived from FRCP 73(a) [rule 73(a), Federal Rules of Civil Procedure] and FRCrP 37(a)(1) [rule 37(a)(1), Federal Rules of Criminal Procedure]. The proposed rule follows those rules in requiring nothing other than the filing of a notice of appeal in the district court for the perfection of the appeal. The petition for allowance (except for appeals governed by Rules 5 and 6), citations, assignments of error, summons and severance—all specifically abolished by earlier modern rules—are assumed to be sufficiently obsolete as no longer to require pointed abolition.

Subdivision (b). The first sentence is derived from FRCP 74 [rule 74, Federal Rules of Civil Procedure]. The second sentence is added to encourage consolidation of appeals whenever feasible.

Subdivision (c). This subdivision is identical with corresponding provisions in FRCP 73(b) [rule 73(b), Federal Rules of Civil Procedure] and FRCrP 37(a)(1) [rule 37(a)(1), Federal Rules of Criminal Procedure].

Subdivision (d). This subdivision is derived from FRCP 73(b) [rule 73(b), Federal Rules of Civil Procedure] and FRCrP 37(a)(1) [rule 37(a)(1), Federal Rules of Criminal Procedure]. The duty of the clerk to forward a copy of the notice of appeal and of the docket entries to the court of appeals in a criminal case is extended to habeas corpus and 28 U.S.C. § 2255 proceedings.

1979 Amendments

Subdivision (c). The proposed amendment would add the last sentence. Because of the fact that the timely filing of the notice of appeal has been characterized as jurisdictional (see, e.g., Brainerd v. Real (C.A. 7th, 1974) 498 F.2d 901, in which the filing of a notice of appeal one day late was fatal), it is important that the right to appeal not be lost by mistakes of mere form. In a number of decided cases it has been held that so long as the function of notice is met by the filing of a paper indicating an intention to appeal, the substance of the rule has been complied with. See, e.g., Cobb v. Lewis (C.A. 5th, 1974), 488 F.2d 41; *Holley v. Capps* (C.A. 5th, 1972) 468 F.2d 1366. The proposed amendment would give recognition to this practice.

When a notice of appeal is filed, the clerk should ascertain whether any judgment designated therein has been entered in compliance with Rules 58 and 79(a) of the F.R.C.P. [rules 58 and 79(a), Federal Rules of Civil Procedure]. See Note to Rule 4(a)(6), *infra*.

Subdivision (d). The proposed amendment would extend to civil cases the present provision applicable to criminal cases, habeas corpus cases, and proceedings under 28 U.S.C. § 2255, requiring the clerk of the district court to transmit to the clerk of the court of appeals a copy of the notice of appeal and of the docket entries, which should include reference to compliance with the requirements for payment of fees. See Note to (e), *infra*.

This requirement is the initial step in proposed changes in the rules to place in the court of appeals an increased practical control over the early steps in the appeal.

Subdivision (e). Proposed new Rule 3(e) represents the second step in shifting to the court of appeals the control of the early stages of an appeal. See Note to Rule 3(d) above. Under the present rules the payment of the fee prescribed by 28 U.S.C. 1917 is not covered. Under the statute, however, this fee is paid to the clerk of the district court at the time the notice of appeal is filed. Under present Rule 12, the "docket fee" fixed by the Judicial Conference of the United States under 28 U.S.C. § 1913 must be paid to the clerk of the court of appeals within the time fixed for transmission of the record, " . . . and the clerk shall thereupon enter the appeal upon the docket."

Under the proposed new Rule 3(e) both fees would be paid to the clerk of the district court at the time the notice of appeal is filed, the clerk of the district court receiving the docket fee on behalf of the court of appeals.

In view of the provision in Rule 3(a) that "[f]ailure of an appellant to take any step other than the timely filing of a notice of appeal does not affect the validity of the appeal, but is ground only for such action as the court of appeals deems appropriate, which may include dismissal of the appeal," the case law indicates that the failure to prepay the statutory filing fee does not constitute a jurisdictional defect. See *Parissi v. Telechron*, 349 U.S. 46 (1955); *Gould v. Members of N.J. Division of Water Policy & Supply*, 555 F.2d 340 (3d Cir. 1977). Similarly, under present Rule 12, failure to pay the docket fee within the time prescribed may be excused by the court of appeals. See, e.g., *Walker v. Mathews*, 546 F.2d 814 (9th Cir. 1976). Proposed new Rule 3(e) adopts the view of these cases, requiring that both fees be paid at the time the notice of appeal is filed, but subject to the provisions of Rule 26(b) preserving the authority of the court of appeals to permit late payment.

1986 Amendments

The amendments to Rule 3(d) are technical. No substantive change is intended.

1989 Amendments

The amendment is technical. No substantive change is intended.

1993 Amendments

Note to subdivision (c). The amendment is intended to reduce the amount of satellite litigation spawned by the Supreme Court's decision in Torres v. Oakland Scavenger Co., 487 U.S. 312 (1988). In Torres the Supreme Court held that the language in Rule 3(c) requiring a notice of appeal to "specify the party or parties taking the appeal" is a jurisdictional requirement and that naming the first named party and adding "et al.," without any further specificity is insufficient to identify the appellants. Since the Torres decision, there has been a great deal of litigation regarding whether a notice of appeal that contains some indication of the appellants' identities but does not name the appellants is sufficiently specific.

The amendment states a general rule that specifying the parties should be done by naming them. Naming an appellant in an otherwise timely and proper notice of appeal ensures that the appellant has perfected an appeal. However, in order to prevent the loss of a right to appeal through inadvertent omission of a party's name or continued use of such terms as "et al.," which are sufficient in all district court filings after the complaint, the amendment allows an attorney representing more than one party the flexibility to indicate which parties are appealing without naming them individually. The test established by the rule for determining whether such designations are sufficient is whether it is objectively clear that a party intended to appeal. A notice of appeal filed by a party proceeding pro se is filed on behalf of the party signing the notice and the signer's spouse and minor children, if they are parties, unless the notice clearly indicates a contrary intent.

In class actions, naming each member of a class as an appellant may be extraordinarily burdensome or even impossible. In class actions if class certification has been denied, named plaintiffs may appeal the order denying the class certification on their own behalf and on behalf of putative class members, *United States Parole Comm'n v. Geraghty*, 445 U.S. 388 (1980); or if the named plaintiffs choose not to appeal the order denying the class certification, putative class members may appeal, *United Airlines, Inc. v. McDonald*, 432 U.S. 385 (1977). If no class has been certified, naming each of the putative class members as an appellant would often be impossible. Therefore the amendment provides that in class actions, whether or not the class has been certified, it is sufficient for the notice to name one person qualified to bring the appeal as a representative of the class.

Finally, the rule makes it clear that dismissal of an appeal should not occur when it is otherwise clear from the notice that the party intended to appeal. If a court determines it is objectively clear that a party intended to appeal, there are neither administrative concerns nor fairness concerns that should prevent the appeal from going forward.

Note to subdivision (d). The amendment requires the district court clerk to send to the clerk of the court of appeals a copy of every docket entry in a case after the filing of a notice of appeal. This amendment accompanies the amendment to Rule 4(a)(4), which provides that when one of the posttrial motions enumerated in Rule 4(a)(4) is filed, a notice of appeal filed before the disposition of the motion becomes effective upon disposition of the motion. The court of appeals needs to be advised that the filing of a posttrial motion has suspended a notice of appeal. The court of appeals also needs to know when the district court has ruled on the motion. Sending copies of all docket entries after the filing of a notice of appeal should provide the courts of appeals with the necessary information.

1994 Amendments

Subdivision (a). The amendment requires a party filing a notice of appeal to provide the court with sufficient copies of the notice for service on all other parties.

1998 Amendments

The language and organization of the rule are amended to make the rule more easily understood. In addition to changes made to improve the understanding, the Advisory Committee has changed language to make style and terminology consistent throughout the appellate rules. These changes are generally intended to by stylistic only; in this rule, however, substantive changes are made in subdivisions (a), (b), and (d).

Subdivision (a). The provision in paragraph (a)(3) is transferred from former Rule 3.1(b). The Federal Courts Improvement Act of 1996, Pub.L. No. 104–317, repealed paragraphs (4) and (5) of 28 U.S.C. § 636(c). That statutory change made the continued separate existence of Rule 3.1 unnecessary. New paragraph (a)(3) of this rule simply makes it clear that an appeal from a judgment by a magistrate judge is taken in identical fashion to any other appeal from a district-court judgment.

Subdivision (b). A joint appeal is authorized only when two or more persons may appeal from a single judgment or order. A joint appeal is treated as a single appeal and the joint appellants file a single brief. Under existing Rule 3(b) parties decide whether to join their appeals. They may do so by filing a joint notice of appeal or by joining their appeals after filing separate notices of appeal.

In consolidated appeals the separate appeals do not merge into one. The parties do not proceed as a single appellant. Under existing Rule 3(b) it is unclear whether appeals may be consolidated without court order if the parties stipulate to consolidation. The language resolves that ambiguity by requiring court action.

The language also requires court action to join appeals after separate notices of appeal have been filed.

Subdivision (d). Paragraph (d)(2) has been amended to require that when an inmate files a notice of appeal by depositing the notice in the institution's internal mail system, the clerk must note the docketing date—rather than the receipt date—on the notice of appeal before serving copies of it. This change conforms to a change in Rule 4(c). Rule 4(c) is amended to provide that when an inmate files the first notice of appeal in a civil case by depositing the notice in an institution's internal mail system, the time for filing a cross-appeal runs from the date the district court dockets the inmate's notice of appeal. Existing Rule 4(c) says that in such a case the time for filing a cross-appeal runs from the date the district court receives the inmate's notice of appeal. A court may "receive" a paper when its mail is delivered to it even if the mail is not processed for a day or two, making the date of receipt uncertain. "Docketing" is an easily identified event. The change is made to eliminate the uncertainty.

2019 Amendments

Amendments to Subdivision (d) change the words "mailing" and "mails" to "sending" and "sends," and delete language requiring certain forms of service, to allow for electronic service. Other rules determine when a party or the clerk may or must send a notice electronically or non-electronically.

[Rule 3.1. Appeal From a Judgment of a Magistrate Judge in a Civil Case (Abrogated Apr. 24, 1998, eff. Dec. 1, 1998)]

ADVISORY COMMITTEE NOTES

1998 Amendments

The Federal Courts Improvement Act of 1996, Pub.L. No. 104–317, repealed paragraphs (4) and (5) of 28 U.S.C. § 636(c). That statutory change means that when parties consent to trial before a magistrate judge, appeal lies directly, and as a matter of right, to the court of appeals under § 636(c)(3). The parties may not choose to appeal first to a district judge and thereafter seek discretionary review in the court of appeals.

As a result of the statutory amendments, subdivision (a) of Rule 3.1 is no longer necessary. Since Rule 3.1 existed primarily because of the provisions in subdivision (a), subdivision (b) has been moved to Rule 3(a)(3) and Rule 3.1 has been abrogated.

HISTORICAL NOTES

The abrogated rule provided that: "When the parties consent to a trial before a magistrate judge under 28 U.S.C. § 636(c)(1), any appeal from the judgment must be heard by the court of appeals in accordance with 28 U.S.C. § 636(c)(3), unless the parties consent to an appeal on the record to a district judge and thereafter, by petition only, to the court of appeals, in accordance with 28 U.S.C. § 636(c)(4). An appeal under 28 U.S.C. § 636(c)(3) must be taken in identical fashion as an appeal from any other judgment of the district court."

Rule 4.   Appeal as of Right—When Taken

(a) Appeal in a Civil Case.

(1) Time for Filing a Notice of Appeal.

(A) In a civil case, except as provided in Rules 4(a)(1)(B), 4(a)(4), and 4(c), the notice of appeal required by Rule 3 must be filed with the district clerk within 30 days after entry of the judgment or order appealed from.

(B) The notice of appeal may be filed by any party within 60 days after entry of the judgment or order appealed from if one of the parties is:

(i) the United States;

(ii) a United States agency;

(iii) a United States officer or employee sued in an official capacity; or

(iv) a current or former United States officer or employee sued in an individual capacity for an act or omission occurring in connection with duties performed on the United States' behalf—including all instances in which the United States represents that person when the judgment or order is entered or files the appeal for that person.

(C) An appeal from an order granting or denying an application for a writ of error coram nobis is an appeal in a civil case for purposes of Rule 4(a).

(2) Filing Before Entry of Judgment. A notice of appeal filed after the court announces a decision or order—but before the entry of the judgment or order—is treated as filed on the date of and after the entry.

(3) Multiple Appeals. If one party timely files a notice of appeal, any other party may file a notice of appeal within 14 days after the date when the first notice was filed, or within the time otherwise prescribed by this Rule 4(a), whichever period ends later.

(4) Effect of a Motion on a Notice of Appeal.

(A) If a party files in the district court any of the following motions under the Federal Rules of Civil Procedure—and does so within the time allowed by those rules—the time to file an appeal runs for all parties from the entry of the order disposing of the last such remaining motion:

(i) for judgment under Rule 50(b);

(ii) to amend or make additional factual findings under Rule 52(b), whether or not granting the motion would alter the judgment;

(iii) for attorney's fees under Rule 54 if the district court extends the time to appeal under Rule 58;

(iv) to alter or amend the judgment under Rule 59;

(v) for a new trial under Rule 59; or

(vi) for relief under Rule 60 if the motion is filed no later than 28 days after the judgment is entered.

(B)(i) If a party files a notice of appeal after the court announces or enters a judgment—but before it disposes of any motion listed in Rule 4(a)(4)(A)—the notice becomes effective to appeal a judgment or order, in whole or in part, when the order disposing of the last such remaining motion is entered.

(ii) A party intending to challenge an order disposing of any motion listed in Rule 4(a)(4)(A), or a judgment's alteration or amendment upon such a motion, must file a notice of appeal, or an amended notice of appeal—in compliance with Rule 3(c)—within the time prescribed by this Rule measured from the entry of the order disposing of the last such remaining motion.

(iii) No additional fee is required to file an amended notice.

(5) Motion for Extension of Time.

(A) The district court may extend the time to file a notice of appeal if:

(i) a party so moves no later than 30 days after the time prescribed by this Rule 4(a) expires; and

(ii) regardless of whether its motion is filed before or during the 30 days after the time prescribed by this Rule 4(a) expires, that party shows excusable neglect or good cause.

(B) A motion filed before the expiration of the time prescribed in Rule 4(a)(1) or (3) may be ex parte unless the court requires otherwise. If the motion is filed after the expiration of the prescribed time, notice must be given to the other parties in accordance with local rules.

(C) No extension under this Rule 4(a)(5) may exceed 30 days after the prescribed time or 14 days after the date when the order granting the motion is entered, whichever is later.

(6) Reopening the Time to File an Appeal. The district court may reopen the time to file an appeal for a period of 14 days after the date when its order to reopen is entered, but only if all the following conditions are satisfied:

(A) the court finds that the moving party did not receive notice under Federal Rule of Civil Procedure 77(d) of the entry of the judgment or order sought to be appealed within 21 days after entry;

(B) the motion is filed within 180 days after the judgment or order is entered or within 14 days after the moving party receives notice under Federal Rule of Civil Procedure 77(d) of the entry, whichever is earlier; and

(C) the court finds that no party would be prejudiced.

(7) Entry Defined.

(A) A judgment or order is entered for purposes of this Rule 4(a):

(i) if Federal Rule of Civil Procedure 58(a) does not require a separate document, when the judgment or order is entered in the civil docket under Federal Rule of Civil Procedure 79(a); or

(ii) if Federal Rule of Civil Procedure 58(a) requires a separate document, when the judgment or order is entered in the civil docket under Federal Rule of Civil Procedure 79(a) and when the earlier of these events occurs:

- the judgment or order is set forth on a separate document, or

- 150 days have run from entry of the judgment or order in the civil docket under Federal Rule of Civil Procedure 79(a).

(B) A failure to set forth a judgment or order on a separate document when required by Federal Rule of Civil Procedure 58(a) does not affect the validity of an appeal from that judgment or order.

(b) Appeal in a Criminal Case.

(1) Time for Filing a Notice of Appeal.

(A) In a criminal case, a defendant's notice of appeal must be filed in the district court within 14 days after the later of:

(i) the entry of either the judgment or the order being appealed; or

(ii) the filing of the government's notice of appeal.

(B) When the government is entitled to appeal, its notice of appeal must be filed in the district court within 30 days after the later of:

(i) the entry of the judgment or order being appealed; or

(ii) the filing of a notice of appeal by any defendant.

(2) Filing Before Entry of Judgment. A notice of appeal filed after the court announces a decision, sentence, or order—but before the entry of the judgment or order—is treated as filed on the date of and after the entry.

(3) Effect of a Motion on a Notice of Appeal.

(A) If a defendant timely makes any of the following motions under the Federal Rules of Criminal Procedure, the notice of appeal from a judgment of conviction must be filed within 14 days after the entry of the order disposing of the last such remaining motion, or within 14 days after the entry of the judgment of conviction, whichever period ends later. This provision applies to a timely motion:

(i) for judgment of acquittal under Rule 29;

(ii) for a new trial under Rule 33, but if based on newly discovered evidence, only if the motion is made no later than 14 days after the entry of the judgment; or

(iii) for arrest of judgment under Rule 34.

(B) A notice of appeal filed after the court announces a decision, sentence, or order—but before it disposes of any of the motions referred to in Rule 4(b)(3)(A)—becomes effective upon the later of the following:

(i) the entry of the order disposing of the last such remaining motion; or

(ii) the entry of the judgment of conviction.

(C) A valid notice of appeal is effective—without amendment—to appeal from an order disposing of any of the motions referred to in Rule 4(b)(3)(A).

(4) Motion for Extension of Time. Upon a finding of excusable neglect or good cause, the district court may—before or after the time has expired, with or without motion and notice—extend the time to file a notice of appeal for a period not to exceed 30 days from the expiration of the time otherwise prescribed by this Rule 4(b).

(5) Jurisdiction. The filing of a notice of appeal under this Rule 4(b) does not divest a district court of jurisdiction to correct a sentence under Federal Rule of Criminal Procedure 35(a), nor does the filing of a motion under 35(a) affect the validity of a notice of appeal filed before entry of the order disposing of the motion. The filing of a motion under Federal Rule of Criminal Procedure 35(a) does not suspend the time for filing a notice of appeal from a judgment of conviction.

(6) Entry Defined. A judgment or order is entered for purposes of this Rule 4(b) when it is entered on the criminal docket.

(c) Appeal by an Inmate Confined in an Institution.

(1) If an institution has a system designed for legal mail, an inmate confined there must use that system to receive the benefit of this Rule 4(c)(1). If an inmate files a notice of appeal in either a civil or a criminal case, the notice is timely if it is deposited in the institution's internal mail system on or before the last day for filing and:

(A) it is accompanied by:

    (i) a declaration in compliance with 28 U.S.C. § 1746—or a notarized statement—setting out the date of deposit and stating that first-class postage is being prepaid; or

    (ii) evidence (such as a postmark or date stamp) showing that the notice was so deposited and that postage was prepaid; or

    (B) the court of appeals exercises its discretion to permit the later filing of a declaration or notarized statement that satisfies Rule 4(c)(1)(A)(i).

    (2) If an inmate files the first notice of appeal in a civil case under this Rule 4(c), the 14-day period provided in Rule 4(a)(3) for another party to file a notice of appeal runs from the date when the district court dockets the first notice.

    (3) When a defendant in a criminal case files a notice of appeal under this Rule 4(c), the 30-day period for the government to file its notice of appeal runs from the entry of the judgment or order appealed from or from the district court's docketing of the defendant's notice of appeal, whichever is later.

(d) Mistaken Filing in the Court of Appeals. If a notice of appeal in either a civil or a criminal case is mistakenly filed in the court of appeals, the clerk of that court must note on the notice the date when it was received and send it to the district clerk. The notice is then considered filed in the district court on the date so noted.

(As amended Apr. 30, 1979, eff. Aug. 1, 1979; Nov. 18, 1988, Pub.L. 100–690, Title VII, § 7111, 102 Stat. 4419; Apr. 30, 1991, eff. Dec. 1, 1991; Apr. 22, 1993, eff. Dec. 1, 1993; Apr. 27, 1995, eff. Dec. 1, 1995; Apr. 24, 1998, eff. Dec. 1, 1998; Apr. 29, 2002, eff. Dec. 1, 2002; Apr. 25, 2005, eff. Dec. 1, 2005; Mar. 26, 2009, eff. Dec. 1, 2009; Apr. 28, 2010, eff. Dec. 1, 2010; Apr. 26, 2011, eff. Dec. 1, 2011; Apr. 28, 2016, eff. Dec. 1, 2016; Apr. 27, 2017, eff. Dec. 1, 2017.)

ADVISORY COMMITTEE NOTES

1967 Adoption

    Subdivision (a). This subdivision is derived from FRCP 73(a) [rule 73(a), Federal Rules of Civil Procedure, this title] without any change of substance. The requirement that a request for an extension of time for filing the notice of appeal made after expiration of the time be made by motion and on notice codifies the result reached under the present provisions of FRCP 73(a) and 6(b) [rules 73(a) and 6(b), Federal Rules of Civil Procedure]. *North Umberland Mining Co. v. Standard Accident Ins. Co.*, 193 F.2d 951 (9th Cir., 1952); *Cohen v. Plateau Natural Gas Co.*, 303 F.2d 273 (10th Cir., 1962); *Plant Economy, Inc. v. Mirror Insulation Co.*, 308 F.2d 275 (3d Cir., 1962).

    Since this subdivision governs appeals in all civil cases, it supersedes the provisions of § 25 of the Bankruptcy Act (11 U.S.C. § 48). Except in cases to which the United States or an officer or agency thereof is a party, the change is a minor one, since a successful litigant in a bankruptcy proceeding may, under § 25, oblige an aggrieved party to appeal within 30 days after entry of judgment—the time fixed by this subdivision in cases involving private parties only—by serving him with notice of entry on the day thereof, and by the terms of § 25 and aggrieved party must in any event appeal within 40 days after entry of judgment. No reason appears why the time for appeal in bankruptcy should not be the same as that in civil cases generally. Furthermore, § 25 is a potential trap for the uninitiated. The time for appeal which it provides is not applicable to all appeals which may fairly be termed appeals in bankruptcy. Section 25 governs only those cause referred to in § 24 as "proceedings in bankruptcy" and "controversies arising in proceedings in bankruptcy." *Lowenstein v. Reikes*, 54 F.2d 481 (2d Cir., 1931), cert. den., 285 U.S. 539, 52 S.Ct. 311, 76 L.Ed. 932 (1932). The distinction between such cases and other cases which arise out of bankruptcy is often difficult to determine. See 2 Moore's Collier on Bankruptcy ¶ 24.12 through ¶ 24.36 (1962). As a result it is not always clear whether an appeal is governed by § 25 or by FRCP 73(a) [rule 73(a), Federal Rules of Civil Procedure, this title], which is applicable to such appeals in bankruptcy as are not governed by § 25.

In view of the unification of the civil and admiralty procedure accomplished by the amendments of the Federal Rules of Civil Procedure effective July 1, 1966, this subdivision governs appeals in those civil actions which involve admiralty or maritime claims and which prior to that date were known as suits in admiralty.

The only other change possibly effected by this subdivision is in the time for appeal from a decision of a district court on a petition for impeachment of an award of a board of arbitration under the Act of May 20, 1926, c. 347, § 9 (44 Stat. 585), 45 U.S.C. § 159. The act provides that a notice of appeal from such a decision shall be filed within 10 days of the decision. This singular provision was apparently repealed by the enactment in 1948 of 28 U.S.C. § 2107, which fixed 30 days from the date of entry of judgment as the time for appeal in all actions a civil nature except actions in admiralty or bankruptcy matters or those in which the United States is a party. But it was not expressly repealed, and its status is in doubt. See 7 Moore's Federal Practice ¶ 73.09[2] (1966). The doubt should be resolved, and no reason appears why appeals in such cases should not be taken within the time provided for civil cases generally.

Subdivision (b). This subdivision is derived from FRCrP 37(a)(2) [rule 37(a)(2), Federal Rules of Criminal Procedure] without change of substance.

1979 Amendment

Subdivision (a)(1). The words "(including a civil action which involves an admiralty or maritime claim and a proceeding in bankruptcy or a controversy arising therein)," which appear in the present rule are struck out as unnecessary and perhaps misleading in suggesting that there may be other categories that are not either civil or criminal within the meaning of Rule 4(a) and (b).

The phrases "within 30 days of such entry" and "within 60 days of such entry" have been changed to read "after" instead of "or." The change is for clarity only, since the word "of" in the present rule appears to be used to mean "after." Since the proposed amended rule deals directly with the premature filing of a notice of appeal, it was thought useful to emphasize the fact that except as provided, the period during which a notice of appeal may be filed is the 30 days, or 60 days as the case may be, following the entry of the judgment or order appealed from. See Notes to Rule 4(a)(2) and (4), below.

Subdivision (a)(2). The proposed amendment to Rule 4(a)(2) would extend to civil cases the provisions of Rule 4(b), dealing with criminal cases, designed to avoid the loss of the right to appeal by filing the notice of appeal prematurely. Despite the absence of such a provision in Rule 4(a) the courts of appeals quite generally have held premature appeals effective. See, e.g., *Matter of Grand Jury Empanelled Jan. 21, 1975*, 541 F.2d 373 (3d Cir. 1976); *Hodge v. Hodge*, 507 F.2d 87 (3d Cir. 1976); *Song Jook Suh v. Rosenberg*, 437 F.2d 1098 (9th Cir. 1971); *Ruby v. Secretary of the Navy*, 365 F.2d 385 (9th Cir. 1966); *Firchau v. Diamond Nat'l Corp.*, 345 F.2d 269 (9th Cir. 1965).

The proposed amended rule would recognize this practice but make an exception in cases in which a post trial motion has destroyed the finality of the judgment. See Note to Rule 4(a)(4) below.

Subdivision (a)(4). The proposed amendment would make it clear that after the filing of the specified post trial motions, a notice of appeal should await disposition of the motion. Since the proposed amendments to Rules 3, 10, and 12 contemplate that immediately upon the filing of the notice of appeal the fees will be paid and the case docketed in the court of appeals, and the steps toward its disposition set in motion, it would be undesirable to proceed with the appeal while the district court has before it a motion the granting of which would vacate or alter the judgment appealed from. See, e.g., *Keith v. Newcourt*, 530 F.2d 826 (8th Cir. 1976). Under the present rule, since docketing may not take place until the record is transmitted, premature filing is much less likely to involve waste effort. See, e.g. *Stockes v. Peyton's Inc.*, 508 F.2d 1287 (5th Cir. 1975). Further, since a notice of appeal filed before the disposition of a post trial motion, even if it were treated as valid for purposes of jurisdiction, would not embrace objections to the denial of the motion, it is obviously preferable to postpone the notice of appeal until after the motion is disposed of.

The present rule, since it provides for the "termination" of the "running" of the appeal time, is ambiguous in its application to a notice of appeal filed prior to a post trial motion filed within the 10 day limit. The amendment would make it clear that in such circumstances the appellant should not proceed with the appeal during pendency of the motion but should file a new notice of appeal after the motion is disposed of.

Subdivision (a)(5). Under the present rule it is provided that upon a showing of excusable neglect the district court at any time may extend the time for the filing of a notice of appeal for a period not to exceed 30 days from the expiration of the time otherwise prescribed by the rule, but that if the application is made after the original time has run, the order may be made only on motion with such notice as the court deems appropriate.

A literal reading of this provision would require that the extension be ordered and the notice of appeal filed within the 30 day period, but despite the surface clarity of the rule, it has produced considerable confusion. See the discussion by Judge Friendly in In re Orbitek, 520 F.2d 358 (2d Cir. 1975). The proposed amendment would make it clear that a motion to extend the time must be filed no later than 30 days after the expiration of the original appeal time, and that if the motion is timely filed the district court may act upon the motion at a later date, and may extend the time not in excess of 10 days measured from the date on which the order granting the motion is entered.

Under the present rule there is a possible implication that prior to the time the initial appeal time has run, the district court may extend the time on the basis of an informal application. The amendment would require that the application must be made by motion, though the motion may be made *ex parte*. After the expiration of the initial time a motion for the extension of the time must be made in compliance with the F.R.C.P. [Federal Rules of Civil Procedure] and local rules of the district court. See Note to proposed amended Rule 1, *supra*. And see Rules 6(d), 7(b) of the F.R.C.P. [rules 6(d) and 7(b), Federal Rules of Civil Procedure].

The proposed amended rule expands to some extent the standard for the grant of an extension of time. The present rule requires a "showing of excusable neglect." While this was an appropriate standard in cases in which the motion is made after the time for filing the notice of appeal has run, and remains so, it has never fit exactly the situation in which the appellant seeks an extension before the expiration of the initial time. In such a case "good cause," which is the standard that is applied in the granting of other extensions of time under Rule 26(b) seems to be more appropriate.

Subdivision (a)(6). The proposed amendment would call attention to the requirement of Rule 58 of the F.R.C.P. [Federal Rules of Civil Procedure] that the judgment constitute a separate document. See *United States v. Indrelunas*, 411 U.S. 216 (1973). When a notice of appeal is filed, the clerk should ascertain whether any judgment designated therein has been entered in compliance with Rules 58 and 79(a) and if not, so advise all parties and the district judge. While the requirement of Rule 58 is not jurisdictional, (see *Bankers Trust Co. v. Mallis*, 431 U.S. 928 (1977)), compliance is important since the time for the filing of a notice of appeal by other parties is measured by the time at which the judgment is properly entered.

1991 Amendment

The amendment provides a limited opportunity for relief in circumstances where the notice of entry of a judgment or order, required to be mailed by the clerk of the district court pursuant to Rule 77(d) of the Federal Rules of Civil Procedure, is either not received by a party or is received so late as to impair the opportunity to file a timely notice of appeal. The amendment adds a new subdivision (6) allowing a district court to reopen for a brief period the time for appeal upon a finding that notice of entry of a judgment or order was not received from the clerk or a party within 21 days of its entry and that no party would be prejudiced. By "prejudice" the Committee means some adverse consequence other than the cost of having to oppose the appeal and encounter the risk of reversal, consequences that are present in every appeal. Prejudice might arise, for example, if the appellee had taken some action in reliance on the expiration of the normal time period for filing a notice of appeal.

Reopening may be ordered only upon a motion filed within 180 days of the entry of a judgment or order or within 7 days of receipt of notice of such entry, whichever is earlier. This provision establishes an outer time limit of 180 days for a party who fails to receive timely notice of entry of a judgment to seek additional time to appeal and enables any winning party to shorten the 180-day period by sending (and establishing proof of receipt of) its own notice of entry of a judgment, as authorized by Fed.R.Civ.P. 77(d). Winning parties are encouraged to send their own notice in order to lessen the chance that a judge will accept a claim of non-receipt in the face of evidence that notices were sent by both the clerk and the winning party. Receipt of a winning party's notice will shorten only the time for reopening the time for appeal under this subdivision, leaving the normal time periods for appeal unaffected.

If the motion is granted, the district court may reopen the time for filing a notice of appeal only for a period of 14 days from the date of entry of the order reopening the time for appeal.

Transmittal Note: Upon transmittal of this rule to Congress, the Advisory Committee recommends that the attention of Congress be called to the fact that language in the fourth paragraph of 28 U.S.C. § 2107 might appropriately be revised in light of this proposed rule.

1993 Amendment

Note to Paragraph (a)(1). The amendment is intended to alert readers to the fact that paragraph (a)(4) extends the time for filing an appeal when certain posttrial motions are filed. The Committee hopes that awareness of the provisions of paragraph (a)(4) will prevent the filing of a notice of appeal when a posttrial tolling motion is pending.

Note to Paragraph (a)(2). The amendment treats a notice of appeal filed after the announcement of a decision or order, but before its formal entry, as if the notice had been filed after entry. The amendment deletes the language that made paragraph (a)(2) inapplicable to a notice of appeal filed after announcement of the disposition of a posttrial motion enumerated in paragraph (a)(4) but before the entry of the order, see *Acosta v. Louisiana Dep't of Health & Human Resources*, 478 U.S. 251 (1986) (per curiam); *Alerte v. McGinnis*, 898 F.2d 69 (7th Cir.1990). Because the amendment of paragraph (a)(4) recognizes all notices of appeal filed after announcement or entry of judgment—even those that are filed while the posttrial motions enumerated in paragraph (a)(4) are pending—the amendment of this paragraph is consistent with the amendment of paragraph (a)(4).

Note to Paragraph (a)(3). The amendment is technical in nature; no substantive change is intended.

Note to Paragraph (a)(4). The 1979 amendment of this paragraph created a trap for an unsuspecting litigant who files a notice of appeal before a posttrial motion, or while a posttrial motion is pending. The 1979 amendment requires a party to file a new notice of appeal after the motion's disposition. Unless a new notice is filed, the court of appeals lacks jurisdiction to hear the appeal. *Griggs v. Provident Consumer Discount Co.*, 459 U.S. 56 (1982). Many litigants, especially pro se litigants, fail to file the second notice of appeal, and several courts have expressed dissatisfaction with the rule. See, e.g., *Averhart v. Arrendondo*, 773 F.2d 919 (7th Cir.1985); *Harcon Barge Co. v. D & G Boat Rentals, Inc.*, 746 F.2d 278 (5th Cir.1984), cert. denied, 479 U.S. 930 (1986).

The amendment provides that a notice of appeal filed before the disposition of a specified posttrial motion will become effective upon disposition of the motion. A notice filed before the filing of one of the specified motions or after the filing of a motion but before disposition of the motion is, in effect, suspended until the motion is disposed of, whereupon, the previously filed notice effectively places jurisdiction in the court of appeals.

Because a notice of appeal will ripen into an effective appeal upon disposition of a posttrial motion, in some instances there will be an appeal from a judgment that has been altered substantially because the motion was granted in whole or in part. Many such appeals will be dismissed for want of prosecution when the appellant fails to meet the briefing schedule. But, the appellee may also move to strike the appeal. When responding to such a motion, the appellant would have an opportunity to state that, even though some relief sought in a posttrial motion was granted, the appellant still plans to pursue the appeal. Because the appellant's response would provide the appellee with sufficient notice of the appellant's intentions, the Committee does not believe that an additional notice of appeal is needed.

The amendment provides that a notice of appeal filed before the disposition of a posttrial tolling motion is sufficient to bring the underlying case, as well as any orders specified in the original notice, to the court of appeals. If the judgment is altered upon disposition of a posttrial motion, however, and if a party wishes to appeal from the disposition of the motion, the party must amend the notice to so indicate. When a party files an amended notice, no additional fees are required because the notice is an amendment of the original and not a new notice of appeal.

Paragraph (a)(4) is also amended to include, among motions that extend the time for filing a notice of appeal, a Rule 60 motion that is served within 10 days after entry of judgment. This eliminates the difficulty of determining whether a posttrial motion made within 10 days after entry of a judgment is a Rule 59(e) motion, which tolls the time for filing an appeal, or a Rule 60 motion, which historically has not tolled the time. The amendment comports with the practice in several circuits of treating all motions to alter or amend judgments that are made within 10 days after entry of judgment as Rule 59(e) motions for purposes of Rule 4(a)(4). See, e.g., *Finch v. City of Vernon*, 845 F.2d 256 (11th Cir.1988); *Rados v. Celotex Corp.*, 809 F.2d 170 (2d Cir.1986); *Skagerberg v. Oklahoma*, 797 F.2d 881 (10th Cir.1986). To conform to a recent Supreme Court decision, however—*Budinich v. Becton Dickinson and Co.*, 486 U.S. 196 (1988)—the amendment excludes motions for attorney's fees from the class of motions that extend the filing time unless a district court, acting under Rule 58, enters an order extending the time for appeal. This amendment is to be read in conjunction with the amendment of Fed.R.Civ.P. 58.

Note to subdivision (b). The amendment grammatically restructures the portion of this subdivision that lists the types of motions that toll the time for filing an appeal. This restructuring is intended to make the rule easier to read. No substantive change is intended other than to add a motion for judgment of acquittal under Criminal Rule 29 to the list of tolling motions. Such a motion is the equivalent of a Fed.R.Civ.P. 50(b) motion for judgment notwithstanding the verdict, which tolls the running of time for an appeal in a civil case.

The proposed amendment also eliminates an ambiguity from the third sentence of this subdivision. Prior to this amendment, the third sentence provided that if one of the specified motions was filed, the time for filing an appeal would run from the entry of an order denying the motion. That sentence, like the parallel provision in Rule 4(a)(4), was intended to toll the running of time for appeal if one of the posttrial motions is timely filed. In a criminal case, however, the time for filing the motions runs not from entry of judgment (as it does in civil cases), but from the verdict or finding of guilt. Thus, in a criminal case, a posttrial motion may be disposed of more than 10 days before sentence is imposed, i.e. before the entry of judgment. *United States v. Hashagen*, 816 F.2d 899, 902 n. 5 (3d Cir.1987). To make it clear that a notice of appeal need not be filed before entry of judgment, the amendment states that an appeal may be taken within 10 days after the entry of an order disposing of the motion, or within 10 days after the entry of judgment, whichever is later. The amendment also changes the language in the third sentence providing that an appeal may be taken within 10 days after the entry of an order *denying* the motion; the amendment says instead that an appeal may be taken within 10 days after the entry of an order *disposing* of the last such motion outstanding. (Emphasis added) The change recognizes that there may be multiple posttrial motions filed and that, although one or more motions may be granted in whole or in part, a defendant may still wish to pursue an appeal.

The amendment also states that a notice of appeal filed before the disposition of any of the posttrial tolling motions becomes effective upon disposition of the motions. In most circuits this language simply restates the current practice. See *United States v. Cortes*, 895 F.2d 1245 (9th Cir.), cert. denied, 495 U.S. 939 (1990). Two circuits, however, have questioned that practice in light of the language of the rule, see *United States v. Gargano*, 826 F.2d 610 (7th Cir.1987), and *United States v. Jones*, 669 F.2d 559 (8th Cir.1982), and the Committee wishes to clarify the rule. The amendment is consistent with the proposed amendment of Rule 4(a)(4).

Subdivision (b) is further amended in light of new Fed.R.Crim.P. 35(c), which authorizes a sentencing court to correct any arithmetical, technical, or other clear errors in sentencing within 7 days after imposing the sentence. The Committee believes that a sentencing court should be able to act under Criminal Rule 35(c) even if a notice of appeal has already been filed; and that a notice of appeal should not be affected by the filing of a Rule 35(c) motion or by correction of a sentence under Rule 35(c).

Note to subdivision (c). In *Houston v. Lack*, 487 U.S. 266 (1988), the Supreme Court held that a *pro se* prisoner's notice of appeal is "filed" at the moment of delivery to prison authorities for forwarding to the district court. The amendment reflects that decision. The language of the amendment is similar to that in Supreme Court Rule 29.2.

Permitting an inmate to file a notice of appeal by depositing it in an institutional mail system requires adjustment of the rules governing the filing of cross-appeals. In a civil case, the time for filing a cross-appeal ordinarily runs from the date when the first notice of appeal is filed. If an inmate's notice of appeal is filed by depositing it in an institution's mail system, it is possible that the notice of appeal will not arrive in the district court until several days after the "filing" date and perhaps even after the time for filing a cross-appeal has expired. To avoid that problem, subdivision (c) provides that in a civil case when an institutionalized person files a notice of appeal by depositing it in the institution's mail system, the time for filing a cross-appeal runs from the district court's receipt of the notice. The amendment makes a parallel change regarding the time for the government to appeal in a criminal case.

1995 Amendment

Subdivision (a). Fed.R.Civ.P. 50, 52, and 59 were previously inconsistent with respect to whether certain postjudgment motions had to be filed or merely served no later than 10 days after entry of judgment. As a consequence Rule 4(a)(4) spoke of making or serving such motions rather than filing them. Civil Rules 50, 52, and 59, are being revised to require filing before the end of the 10-day period. As a consequence, this rule is being amended to provide that 'filing' must occur within the 10-day period in order to affect the finality of the judgment and extend the period for filing a notice of appeal.

The Civil Rules require the filing of postjudgment motions 'no later than 10 days after entry of judgment'—rather than 'within' 10 days—to include postjudgment motions that are filed before actual entry of the judgment by the clerk. This rule is amended, therefore, to use the same terminology.

The rule is further amended to clarify the fact that a party who wants to obtain review of an alteration or amendment of a judgment must file a notice of appeal or amend a previously filed notice to indicate intent to appeal from the altered judgment.

1998 Amendments

The language and organization of the rule are amended to make the rule more easily understood. In addition to changes made to improve the understanding the Advisory Committee has changed language to make style and terminology consistent throughout the appellate rules. These changes are intended to be stylistic only; in this rule, however, substantive changes are made in paragraphs (a)(6) and (b)(4), and in subdivision (c).

Subdivision (a), paragraph (1). Although the Advisory Committee does not intend to make any substantive changes in this paragraph, cross-references to Rules 4(a)(1)(B) and (4)(c) have been added to subparagraph (a)(1)(A).

Subdivision (a), paragraph (4). Item (iv) in subparagraph (A) of Rule 4(a)(4) provides that filing a motion for relief under Fed.R.Civ.P. 60 will extend the time for filing a notice of appeal if the Rule 60 motion is filed no later than 10 days after judgment is entered. Again, the Advisory Committee does not intend to make any substantive change in this paragraph. But because Fed.R.Civ.P. 6(a) and Fed.R.App.P. 26(a) have different methods for computing time, one might be uncertain whether the 10-day period referred to in Rule 4(a)(4) is computed using Civil Rule 6(a) or Appellate Rule 26(a). Because the Rule 60 motion is filed in the district court, and because Fed.R.App.P. 1(a)(2) says that when the appellate rules provide for filing a motion in the district court, "the procedure must comply with the practice of the district court," the rule provides that the 10-day period is computed using Fed.R.Civ.P. 6(a)

Subdivision (a), paragraph (6). Paragraph (6) permits a district court to reopen the time for appeal if a party has not received notice of the entry of judgment and no party would be prejudiced by the reopening. Before reopening the time for appeal, the existing rule requires the district court to find that the moving party was entitled to notice of the entry of judgment and did not receive it "from the clerk or any party within 21 days of its entry." The Advisory Committee makes a substantive change. The finding must be that the movant did not receive notice "from the district court or any party within 21 days after entry." This change broadens the type of notice that can preclude reopening the time for appeal. The existing rule provides that only notice from a party or from the clerk bars reopening. The new language precludes reopening if the movant has received notice from "the court."

Subdivision (b). Two substantive changes are made in what will be paragraph (b)(4). The current rule permits an extension of time to file a notice of appeal if there is a "showing of excusable neglect." First, the rule is amended to permit a court to extend the time for "good cause" as well as for excusable neglect. Rule 4(a) permits extensions for both reasons in civil cases and the Advisory Committee believes that "good cause" should be sufficient in criminal cases as well. The amendment does not limit extensions for good cause to instances in which the motion for extension of time is filed before the original time has expired. The rule gives the district court discretion to grant extensions for good cause whenever the court believes it appropriate to do so provided that the extended period does not exceed 30 days after the expiration of the time otherwise prescribed by Rule 4(b). Second, paragraph (b)(4) is amended to require only a "finding" of excusable neglect or good cause and not a "showing" of them. Because the rule authorizes the court to provide an extension without a motion, a "showing" is obviously not required; a "finding" is sufficient.

Subdivision (c). Substantive amendments are made in this subdivision. The current rule provides that if an inmate confined in an institution files a notice of appeal by depositing it in the institution's internal mail system, the notice is timely filed if deposited on or before the last day for filing. Some institutions have special internal mail systems for handling legal mail; such systems often record the date of deposit of mail by an inmate, the date of delivery of mail to an inmate, etc. The Advisory Committee amends the rule to require an inmate to use the system designed for legal mail, if there is one, in order to receive the benefit of this subdivision.

When an inmate uses the filing method authorized by subdivision (c), the current rule provides that the time for other parties to appeal begins to run from the date the district court "receives" the inmate's notice of appeal. The rule is amended so that the time for other parties begins to run when the district court "dockets" the inmates appeal. A court may "receive" a paper when its mail is delivered to it even if the mail is not processed for a day or two, making the date of receipt uncertain. "Docketing" is an easily identified event. The change eliminates uncertainty. Paragraph (c)(3) is further amended to make it clear that the time for the government to file its appeal runs from the later of the entry of the judgment or order appealed from or the district court's docketing of a defendant's notice filed under this paragraph (c).

2002 Amendments

Subdivision (a)(1)(C). The federal courts of appeals have reached conflicting conclusions about whether an appeal from an order granting or denying an application for a writ of error *coram nobis* is governed by the time limitations of Rule 4(a) (which apply in civil cases) or by the time limitations of Rule 4(b) (which apply in criminal cases). *Compare United States v. Craig*, 907 F.2d 653, 655–57, *amended* 919 F.2d 57 (7th Cir. 1990); *United States v. Cooper*, 876 F.2d 1192, 1193–94 (5th Cir. 1989); and *United States v. Keogh*, 391 F.2d 138, 140 (2d Cir. 1968) (applying the time limitations of Rule 4(a)); *with Yasui v. United States*, 772 F.2d 1496, 1498–99 (9th Cir. 1985); and *United States v. Mills*, 430 F.2d 526, 527–28 (8th Cir. 1970) (applying the time limitations of Rule 4(b)). A new part (C) has been added to Rule 4(a)(1) to resolve this conflict by providing that the time limitations of Rule 4(a) will apply.

Subsequent to the enactment of Fed. R. Civ. P. 60(b) and 28 U.S.C. § 2255, the Supreme Court has recognized the continued availability of a writ of error *coram nobis* in at least one narrow circumstance. In 1954, the Court permitted a litigant who had been convicted of a crime, served his full sentence, and been released from prison, but who was continuing to suffer a legal disability on account of the conviction, to seek a writ of error *coram nobis* to set aside the conviction. *United States v. Morgan*, 346 U.S. 502 (1954). As the Court recognized, in the *Morgan* situation an application for a writ of error *coram nobis* "is of the same general character as [a motion] under 28 U.S.C. § 2255." *Id.* at 506 n.4. Thus, it seems appropriate that the time limitations of Rule 4(a), which apply when a district court grants or denies relief under 28 U.S.C. § 2255, should also apply when a district court grants or denies a writ of error *coram nobis*. In addition, the strong public interest in the speedy resolution of criminal appeals that is reflected in the shortened deadlines of Rule 4(b) is not present in the *Morgan* situation, as the party seeking the writ of error *coram nobis* has already served his or her full sentence.

Notwithstanding *Morgan*, it is not clear whether the Supreme Court continues to believe that the writ of error *coram nobis* is available in federal court. In civil cases, the writ has been expressly abolished by Fed. R. Civ. P. 60(b). In criminal cases, the Supreme Court has recently stated that it has become " 'difficult to conceive of a situation' " in which the writ " 'would be necessary or appropriate.' " *Carlisle v. United States*, 517 U.S. 416, 429 (1996) (quoting *United States v. Smith*, 331 U.S. 469, 475 n.4 (1947)). The amendment to Rule 4(a)(1) is not intended to express any view on this issue; rather, it is merely meant to specify time limitations for appeals.

Rule 4(a)(1)(C) applies only to motions that are in substance, and not merely in form, applications for writs of error *coram nobis*. Litigants may bring and label as applications for a writ of error *coram nobis* what are in reality motions for a new trial under Fed. R. Crim. P. 33 or motions for correction or reduction of a sentence under Fed. R. Crim. P. 35. In such cases, the time limitations of Rule 4(b), and not those of Rule 4(a), should be enforced.

Changes Made After Publication and Comments. No changes were made to the text of the proposed amendment or to the Committee Note.

Subdivision (a)(4)(A)(vi). Rule 4(a)(4)(A)(vi) has been amended to remove a parenthetical that directed that the 10-day deadline be "computed using Federal Rule of Civil Procedure 6(a)." That parenthetical has become superfluous because Rule 26(a)(2) has been amended to require that all deadlines under 11 days be calculated as they are under Fed. R. Civ. P. 6(a).

Changes Made After Publication and Comments. No changes were made to the text of the proposed amendment or to the Committee Note.

Subdivision (a)(5)(A)(ii). Rule 4(a)(5)(A) permits the district court to extend the time to file a notice of appeal if two conditions are met. First, the party seeking the extension must file its motion no later than 30 days after the expiration of the time originally prescribed by Rule 4(a). Second, the party seeking the extension must show either excusable neglect or good cause. The text of Rule 4(a)(5)(A) does not distinguish between motions filed prior to the expiration of the original deadline and those filed after the expiration of the original deadline. Regardless of whether the motion is filed before or during the 30 days after the original deadline expires, the district court may grant an extension if a party shows either excusable neglect or good cause.

Despite the text of Rule 4(a)(5)(A), most of the courts of appeals have held that the good cause standard applies only to motions brought prior to the expiration of the original deadline and that the excusable neglect standard applies only to motions brought during the 30 days following the expiration of the original deadline. *See Pontarelli v. Stone*, 930 F.2d 104, 109–10 (1st Cir. 1991) (collecting cases from the Second, Fifth, Sixth, Seventh, Eighth, Ninth, and Eleventh Circuits). These courts have relied heavily upon the Advisory Committee Note to the 1979 amendment to Rule 4(a)(5). But the Advisory Committee Note refers to a draft of the 1979 amendment that was ultimately rejected. The rejected draft directed that the good cause standard apply only to motions filed prior to the expiration of the original deadline. Rule 4(a)(5), as actually amended, did not. *See* 16A CHARLES ALAN WRIGHT, ET AL., FEDERAL PRACTICE AND PROCEDURE § 3950.3, at 148–49 (2d ed. 1996).

The failure of the courts of appeals to apply Rule 4(a)(5)(A) as written has also created tension between that rule and Rule 4(b)(4). As amended in 1998, Rule 4(b)(4) permits the district court to extend the time for filing a notice of appeal in a *criminal* case for an additional 30 days upon a finding of excusable neglect or good cause. Both Rule 4(b)(4) and the Advisory Committee Note to the 1998 amendment make it clear that an extension can be granted for either excusable neglect or good cause, regardless of whether a motion for an extension is filed before or during the 30 days following the expiration of the original deadline.

Rule 4(a)(5)(A)(ii) has been amended to correct this misunderstanding and to bring the rule in harmony in this respect with Rule 4(b)(4). A motion for an extension filed prior to the expiration of the original deadline may be granted if the movant shows either excusable neglect or good cause. Likewise, a motion for an extension filed during the 30 days following the expiration of the original deadline may be granted if the movant shows either excusable neglect or good cause.

The good cause and excusable neglect standards have "different domains." *Lorenzen v. Employees Retirement Plan*, 896 F.2d 228, 232 (7th Cir. 1990). They are not interchangeable, and one is not inclusive of the other. The excusable neglect standard applies in situations in which there is fault; in such situations, the need for an extension is usually occasioned by something within the control of the movant. The good cause standard applies in situations in which there is no fault—excusable or otherwise. In such situations, the need for an extension is usually occasioned by something that is not within the control of the movant.

Thus, the good cause standard can apply to motions brought during the 30 days following the expiration of the original deadline. If, for example, the Postal Service fails to deliver a notice of appeal, a movant might have good cause to seek a post-expiration extension. It may be unfair to make such a movant prove that its "neglect" was excusable, given that the movant may not have been neglectful at all. Similarly, the excusable neglect standard can apply to motions brought prior to the expiration of the original deadline. For example, a movant may bring a pre-expiration motion for an extension of time when an error committed by the movant makes it unlikely that the movant will be able to meet the original deadline.

Changes Made After Publication and Comments. No changes were made to the text of the proposed amendment. The stylistic changes to the Committee Note suggested by Judge Newman were adopted. In addition, two paragraphs were added at the end of the Committee Note to clarify the difference between the good cause and excusable neglect standards.

Subdivision (a)(7). Several circuit splits have arisen out of uncertainties about how Rule 4(a)(7)'s definition of when a judgment or order is "entered" interacts with the requirement in Fed. R. Civ. P. 58 that, to be "effective," a judgment must be set forth on a separate document. Rule 4(a)(7) and Fed. R. Civ. P. 58 have been amended to resolve those splits.

1.   The first circuit split addressed by the amendments to Rule 4(a)(7) and Fed. R. Civ. P. 58 concerns the extent to which orders that dispose of post-judgment motions must be set forth on separate documents. Under Rule 4(a)(4)(A), the filing of certain post-judgment motions tolls the time to appeal the underlying judgment until the "entry" of the order disposing of the last such remaining motion. Courts have disagreed about whether such an order must be set forth on a separate document before it is treated as "entered." This disagreement reflects a broader dispute among courts about whether Rule 4(a)(7) independently imposes a separate document requirement (a requirement that is distinct from the separate document requirement that is imposed by the Federal Rules of Civil Procedure ("FRCP")) or whether Rule 4(a)(7) instead incorporates the separate document requirement as it exists in the FRCP. Further complicating the matter, courts in the former "camp" disagree among themselves about the scope of the separate document requirement that they interpret Rule 4(a)(7) as imposing, and courts in the latter "camp" disagree among themselves about the scope of the separate document requirement imposed by the FRCP.

Rule 4(a)(7) has been amended to make clear that it simply incorporates the separate document requirement as it exists in Fed. R. Civ. P. 58. If Fed. R. Civ. P. 58 does not require that a judgment or order be set forth on a separate document, then neither does Rule 4(a)(7); the judgment or order will be deemed entered for purposes of Rule 4(a) when it is entered in the civil docket. If Fed. R. Civ. P. 58 requires that a judgment or order be set forth on a separate document, then so does Rule 4(a)(7); the judgment or order will not be deemed entered for purposes of Rule 4(a) until it is so set forth and entered in the civil docket (with one important exception, described below).

In conjunction with the amendment to Rule 4(a)(7), Fed. R. Civ. P. 58 has been amended to provide that orders disposing of the postjudgment motions listed in new Fed. R. Civ. P. 58(a)(1) (which postjudgment motions include, but are not limited to, the post-judgment motions that can toll the time to appeal under Rule 4(a)(4)(A)) do not have to be set forth on separate documents. *See* Fed. R. Civ. P. 58(a)(1). Thus, such orders are entered for purposes of Rule 4(a) when they are entered in the civil docket pursuant to Fed. R. Civ. P. 79(a). *See* Rule 4(a)(7)(A)(1).

2.   The second circuit split addressed by the amendments to Rule 4(a)(7) and Fed. R. Civ. P. 58 concerns the following question: When a judgment or order is required to be set forth on a separate document under Fed. R. Civ. P. 58 but is not, does the time to appeal the judgment or order—or the time to bring post-judgment motions, such as a motion for a new trial under Fed. R. Civ. P. 59—ever begin to run? According to every circuit except the First Circuit, the answer is "no." The First Circuit alone holds that parties will be deemed to have waived their right to have a judgment or order entered on a separate document three months after the judgment or order is entered in the civil docket. *See Fiore v. Washington County Community Mental Health Ctr.*, 960 F.2d 229, 236 (1st Cir. 1992) (en banc). Other circuits have rejected this cap as contrary to the relevant rules. *See, e.g., United States v. Haynes*, 158 F.3d 1327, 1331 (D.C. Cir. 1998); *Hammack v. Baroid Corp.*, 142 F.3d 266, 269–70 (5th Cir. 1998); *Rubin v. Schottenstein, Zox & Dunn*, 110 F.3d 1247, 1253 n.4 (6th Cir. 1997), *vacated on other grounds*, 143 F.3d 263 (6th Cir. 1998) (en banc). However, no court has questioned the wisdom of imposing such a cap as a matter of policy.

Both Rule 4(a)(7)(A) and Fed. R. Civ. P. 58 have been amended to impose such a cap. Under the amendments, a judgment or order is generally treated as entered when it is entered in the civil docket pursuant to Fed. R. Civ. P. 79(a). There is one exception: When Fed. R. Civ. P. 58(a)(1) requires the judgment or order to be set forth on a separate document, that judgment or order is not treated as entered until it is set forth on a separate document (in addition to being entered in the civil docket) or until the expiration of 150 days after its entry in the civil docket, whichever occurs first. This cap will ensure that parties will not be given forever to appeal (or to bring a postjudgment motion) when a court fails to set forth a judgment or order on a separate document in violation of Fed. R. Civ. P. 58(a)(1).

3.   The third circuit split—this split addressed only by the amendment to Rule 4(a)(7)—concerns whether the appellant may waive the separate document requirement over the objection of the appellee. In

Bankers Trust Co. v. Mallis, 435 U.S. 381, 387 (1978) (per curiam), the Supreme Court held that the "parties to an appeal may waive the separate-judgment requirement of Rule 58." Specifically, the Supreme Court held that when a district court enters an order and "clearly evidence[s] its intent that the . . . order . . . represent[s] the final decision in the case," the order is a "final decision" for purposes of 28 U.S.C. § 1291, even if the order has not been set forth on a separate document for purposes of Fed. R. Civ. P. 58. *Id.* Thus, the parties can choose to appeal without waiting for the order to be set forth on a separate document.

Courts have disagreed about whether the consent of all parties is necessary to waive the separate document requirement. Some circuits permit appellees to object to attempted *Mallis* waivers and to force appellants to return to the trial court, request that judgment be set forth on a separate document, and appeal a second time. *See, e.g., Selletti v. Carey*, 173 F.3d 104, 109–10 (2d Cir. 1999); *Williams v. Borg*, 139 F.3d 737, 739–40 (9th Cir. 1998); *Silver Star Enters., Inc. v. M/V Saramacca*, 19 F.3d 1008, 1013 (5th Cir. 1994). Other courts disagree and permit *Mallis* waivers even if the appellee objects. *See, e.g., Haynes*, 158 F.3d at 1331; *Miller v. Artistic Cleaners*, 153 F.3d 781, 783–84 (7th Cir. 1998); *Alvord-Polk, Inc. v. F. Schumacher & Co.*, 37 F.3d 996, 1006 n.8 (3d Cir. 1994).

New Rule 4(a)(7)(B) is intended both to codify the Supreme Court's holding in *Mallis* and to make clear that the decision whether to waive the requirement that the judgment or order be set forth on a separate document is the appellant's alone. It is, after all, the appellant who needs a clear signal as to when the time to file a notice of appeal has begun to run. If the appellant chooses to bring an appeal without waiting for the judgment or order to be set forth on a separate document, then there is no reason why the appellee should be able to object. All that would result from honoring the appellee's objection would be delay.

4.   The final circuit split addressed by the amendment to Rule 4(a)(7) concerns the question whether an appellant who chooses to waive the separate document requirement must appeal within 30 days (60 days if the government is a party) from the entry in the civil docket of the judgment or order that should have been set forth on a separate document but was not. In *Townsend v. Lucas*, 745 F.2d 933 (5th Cir. 1984), the district court dismissed a 28 U.S.C. § 2254 action on May 6, 1983, but failed to set forth the judgment on a separate document. The plaintiff appealed on January 10, 1984. The Fifth Circuit dismissed the appeal, reasoning that, if the plaintiff waived the separate document requirement, then his appeal would be from the May 6 order, and if his appeal was from the May 6 order, then it was untimely under Rule 4(a)(1). The Fifth Circuit stressed that the plaintiff could return to the district court, move that the judgment be set forth on a separate document, and appeal from that judgment within 30 days. *Id.* at 934. Several other cases have embraced the *Townsend* approach. *See, e.g., Armstrong v. Ahitow*, 36 F.3d 574, 575 (7th Cir. 1994) (per curiam); *Hughes v. Halifax County Sch. Bd.*, 823 F.2d 832, 835–36 (4th Cir. 1987); *Harris v. McCarthy*, 790 F.2d 753, 756 n.1 (9th Cir. 1986).

Those cases are in the distinct minority. There are numerous cases in which courts have heard appeals that were not filed within 30 days (60 days if the government was a party) from the judgment or order that should have been set forth on a separate document but was not. *See, e.g., Haynes*, 158 F.3d at 1330–31; *Clough v. Rush*, 959 F.2d 182, 186 (10th Cir. 1992); *McCalden v. California Library Ass'n*, 955 F.2d 1214, 1218–19 (9th Cir. 1990). In the view of these courts, the remand in *Townsend* was "precisely the purposeless spinning of wheels abjured by the Court in the [*Mallis*] case." 15B CHARLES ALAN WRIGHT ET AL., FEDERAL PRACTICE AND PROCEDURE § 3915, at 259 n.8 (3d ed. 1992).

The Committee agrees with the majority of courts that have rejected the *Townsend* approach. In drafting new Rule 4(a)(7)(B), the Committee has been careful to avoid phrases such as "otherwise timely appeal" that might imply an endorsement of *Townsend*.

Changes Made After Publication and Comments. No changes were made to the text of proposed Rule 4(a)(7)(B) or to the third or fourth numbered sections of the Committee Note, except that, in several places, references to a judgment being "entered" on a separate document were changed to references to a judgment being "set forth" on a separate document. This was to maintain stylistic consistency. The appellate rules and the civil rules consistently refer to "entering" judgments on the civil docket and to "setting forth" judgments on separate documents.

Two major changes were made to the text of proposed Rule 4(a)(7)(A)—one substantive and one stylistic. The substantive change was to increase the "cap" from 60 days to 150 days. The Appellate Rules Committee and the Civil Rules Committee had to balance two concerns that are implicated whenever a court fails to enter its final decision on a separate document. On the one hand, potential appellants need a clear signal that the time to appeal has begun to run, so that they do not unknowingly forfeit their rights. On the other hand, the time to appeal cannot be allowed to run forever. A party who receives no notice whatsoever of a judgment has only 180 days to move to reopen the time to appeal from that judgment. *See* Rule 4(a)(6)(A). It hardly seems fair to give a party who *does* receive notice of a judgment an unlimited amount of time to appeal, merely because that judgment was not set forth on a separate piece of paper. Potential appellees and the judicial system need *some* limit on the time within which appeals can be brought.

The 150-day cap properly balances these two concerns. When an order is not set forth on a separate document, what signals litigants that the order is final and appealable is a lack of further activity from the court. A 60-day period of inactivity is not sufficiently rare to signal to litigants that the court has entered its last order. By contrast, 150 days of inactivity is much less common and thus more clearly signals to litigants that the court is done with their case.

The major stylistic change to Rule 4(a)(7) requires some explanation. In the published draft, proposed Rule 4(a)(7)(A) provided that "[a] judgment or order is entered for purposes of this Rule 4(a) when it is entered for purposes of Rule 58(b) of the Federal Rules of Civil Procedure." In other words, Rule 4(a)(7)(A) told readers to look to FRCP 58(b) to ascertain when a judgment is entered for purposes of starting the running of the time to appeal. Sending appellate lawyers to the civil rules to discover when time began to run for purposes of the appellate rules was itself somewhat awkward, but it was made more confusing by the fact that, when readers went to proposed FRCP 58(b), they found this introductory clause: "Judgment is entered for purposes of Rules 50, 52, 54(d)(2)(B), 59, 60, and 62 when. . . ."

This introductory clause was confusing for both appellate lawyers and trial lawyers. It was confusing for appellate lawyers because Rule 4(a)(7) informed them that FRCP 58(b) would tell them when the time begins to run for purposes of the *appellate* rules, but when they got to FRCP 58(b) they found a rule that, by its terms, dictated only when the time begins to run for purposes of certain *civil* rules. The introductory clause was confusing for trial lawyers because FRCP 58(b) described when judgment is entered for some purposes under the civil rules, but then was completely silent about when judgment is entered for other purposes.

To avoid this confusion, the Civil Rules Committee, on the recommendation of the Appellate Rules Committee, changed the introductory clause in FRCP 58(b) to read simply: "Judgment is entered for purposes of *these Rules* when. . . ." In addition, Rule 4(a)(7)(A) was redrafted[1] so that the triggering events for the running of the time to appeal (entry in the civil docket, and being set forth on a separate document or passage of 150 days) were incorporated directly into Rule 4(a)(7), rather than indirectly through a reference to FRCP 58(b). This eliminates the need for appellate lawyers to examine Rule 58(b) and any chance that Rule 58(b)'s introductory clause (even as modified) might confuse them.

We do not believe that republication of Rule 4(a)(7) or FRCP 58 is necessary. In *substance*, rewritten Rule 4(a)(7)(A) and FRCP 58(b) operate identically to the published versions, except that the 60-day cap has been replaced with a 150-day cap—a change that was suggested by some of the commentators and that makes the cap more forgiving.

Subdivision (b)(5). Federal Rule of Criminal Procedure 35(a) permits a district court, acting within 7 days after the imposition of sentence, to correct an erroneous sentence in a criminal case. Some courts have held that the filing of a motion for correction of a sentence suspends the time for filing a notice of appeal from the judgment of conviction. *See, e.g., United States v. Carmouche*, 138 F.3d 1014, 1016 (5th Cir. 1998) (per curiam); *United States v. Morillo*, 8 F.3d 864, 869 (1st Cir. 1993). Those courts establish conflicting timetables for appealing a judgment of conviction after the filing of a motion to correct a sentence. In the First Circuit, the time to appeal is suspended only for the period provided by Fed. R. Crim. P. 35(a) for the district court to correct a sentence; the time to appeal begins to run again once 7 days have passed after sentencing, even if the motion is still pending. By contrast, in the Fifth Circuit, the time to appeal does not begin to run again until the district court actually issues an order disposing of the motion.

Rule 4(b)(5) has been amended to eliminate the inconsistency concerning the effect of a motion to correct a sentence on the time for filing a notice of appeal. The amended rule makes clear that the time to appeal continues to run, even if a motion to correct a sentence is filed. The amendment is consistent with

---

[1]   A redraft of Rule 4(a)(7) was faxed to members of the Appellate Rules Committee two weeks after our meeting in New Orleans. The Committee consented to the redraft without objection.

Rule 4(b)(3)(A), which lists the motions that toll the time to appeal, and notably omits any mention of a Fed. R. Crim. P. 35(a) motion. The amendment also should promote certainty and minimize the likelihood of confusion concerning the time to appeal a judgment of conviction.

If a district court corrects a sentence pursuant to Fed. R. Crim. P. 35(a), the time for filing a notice of appeal of the corrected sentence under Rule 4(b)(1) would begin to run when the court enters a new judgment reflecting the corrected sentence.

Changes Made After Publication and Comments. The reference to Federal Rule of Criminal Procedure 35(c) was changed to Rule 35(a) to reflect the pending amendment of Rule 35. The proposed amendment to Criminal Rule 35, if approved, will take effect at the same time that the proposed amendment to Appellate Rule 4 will take effect, if approved.

2005 Amendments

Rule 4(a)(6) has permitted a district court to reopen the time to appeal a judgment or order upon finding that four conditions were satisfied. First, the district court had to find that the appellant did not receive notice of the entry of the judgment or order from the district court or any party within 21 days after the judgment or order was entered. Second, the district court had to find that the appellant moved to reopen the time to appeal within 7 days after the appellant received notice of the entry of the judgment or order. Third, the district court had to find that the appellant moved to reopen the time to appeal within 180 days after the judgment or order was entered. Finally, the district court had to find that no party would be prejudiced by the reopening of the time to appeal.

Rule 4(a)(6) has been amended to specify more clearly what type of "notice" of the entry of a judgment or order precludes a party from later moving to reopen the time to appeal. In addition, Rule 4(a)(6) has been amended to address confusion about what type of "notice" triggers the 7-day period to bring a motion to reopen. Finally, Rule 4(a)(6) has been reorganized to set forth more logically the conditions that must be met before a district court may reopen the time to appeal.

Subdivision (a)(6)(A). Former subdivision (a)(6)(B) has been redesignated as subdivision (a)(6)(A), and one substantive change has been made. As amended, the subdivision will preclude a party from moving to reopen the time to appeal a judgment or order only if the party receives (within 21 days) formal notice of the entry of that judgment or order under Civil Rule 77(d). No other type of notice will preclude a party.

The reasons for this change take some explanation. Prior to 1998, former subdivision (a)(6)(B) permitted a district court to reopen the time to appeal if it found "that a party entitled to notice of the entry of a judgment or order did not receive such notice from the clerk or any party within 21 days of its entry." The rule was clear that the "notice" to which it referred was the notice required under Civil Rule 77(d), which must be served by the clerk pursuant to Civil Rule 5(b) and may also be served by a party pursuant to that same rule. In other words, prior to 1998, former subdivision (a)(6)(B) was clear that, if a party did not receive formal notice of the entry of a judgment or order under Civil Rule 77(d), that party could later move to reopen the time to appeal (assuming that the other requirements of subdivision (a)(6) were met).

In 1998, former subdivision (a)(6)(B) was amended to change the description of the type of notice that would preclude a party from moving to reopen. As a result of the amendment, former subdivision (a)(6)(B) no longer referred to the failure of the moving party to receive "*such* notice"—that is, the notice required by Civil Rule 77(d)—but instead referred to the failure of the moving party to receive "*the* notice." And former subdivision (a)(6)(B) no longer referred to the failure of the moving party to receive notice from "the *clerk* or any party," both of whom are explicitly mentioned in Civil Rule 77(d). Rather, former subdivision (a)(6)(B) referred to the failure of the moving party to receive notice from "the *district court* or any party."

The 1998 amendment meant, then, that the type of notice that precluded a party from moving to reopen the time to appeal was no longer limited to Civil Rule 77(d) notice. Under the 1998 amendment, *some* type of notice, in addition to Civil Rule 77(d) notice, precluded a party. But the text of the amended rule did not make clear what type of notice qualified. This was an invitation for litigation, confusion, and possible circuit splits.

To avoid such problems, former subdivision (a)(6)(B)—new subdivision (a)(6)(A)—has been amended to restore its pre-1998 simplicity. Under new subdivision (a)(6)(A), if the court finds that the moving party was not notified under Civil Rule 77(d) of the entry of the judgment or order that the party seeks to appeal within 21 days after that judgment or order was entered, then the court is authorized to reopen the time to appeal (if all of the other requirements of subdivision (a)(6) are met). Because Civil Rule 77(d) requires that notice of the entry of a judgment or order be formally served under Civil Rule 5(b), any notice that is not so served will not operate to preclude the reopening of the time to appeal under new subdivision (a)(6)(A).

Subdivision (a)(6)(B). Former subdivision (a)(6)(A) required a party to move to reopen the time to appeal "within 7 days after the moving party receives notice of the entry [of the judgment or order sought to be appealed]." Former subdivision (a)(6)(A) has been redesignated as subdivision (a)(6)(B), and one important substantive change has been made: The subdivision now makes clear that only formal notice of the entry of a judgment or order under Civil Rule 77(d) will trigger the 7-day period to move to reopen the time to appeal.

The circuits have been split over what type of "notice" is sufficient to trigger the 7-day period. The majority of circuits that addressed the question held that only *written* notice was sufficient, although nothing in the text of the rule suggested such a limitation. *See, e.g., Bass v. United States Dep't of Agric.*, 211 F.3d 959, 963 (5th Cir. 2000). By contrast, the Ninth Circuit held that while former subdivision (a)(6)(A) did not require written notice, "the quality of the communication [had to] rise to the functional equivalent of written notice." *Nguyen v. Southwest Leasing & Rental, Inc.*, 282 F.3d 1061, 1066 (9th Cir. 2002). Other circuits suggested in dicta that former subdivision (a)(6)(A) required only "actual notice," which, presumably, could have included oral notice that was not "the functional equivalent of written notice." *See, e.g., Lowry v. McDonnell Douglas Corp.*, 211 F.3d 457, 464 (8th Cir. 2000). And still other circuits read into former subdivision (a)(6)(A) restrictions that appeared only in former subdivision (a)(6)(B) (such as the requirement that notice be received "from the district court or any party," *see Benavides v. Bureau of Prisons*, 79 F.3d 1211, 1214 (D.C. Cir. 1996)) or that appeared in neither former subdivision (a)(6)(A) nor former subdivision (a)(6)(B) (such as the requirement that notice be served in the manner prescribed by Civil Rule 5, *see Ryan v. First Unum Life Ins. Co.*, 174 F.3d 302, 304–05 (2d Cir. 1999)).

Former subdivision (a)(6)(A)—new subdivision (a)(6)(B)—has been amended to resolve this circuit split by providing that only formal notice of the entry of a judgment or order under Civil Rule 77(d) will trigger the 7-day period. Using Civil Rule 77(d) notice as the trigger has two advantages: First, because Civil Rule 77(d) is clear and familiar, circuit splits are unlikely to develop over its meaning. Second, because Civil Rule 77(d) notice must be served under Civil Rule 5(b), establishing whether and when such notice was provided should generally not be difficult.

Using Civil Rule 77(d) notice to trigger the 7-day period will not unduly delay appellate proceedings. Rule 4(a)(6) applies to only a small number of cases—cases in which a party was not notified of a judgment or order by either the clerk or another party within 21 days after entry. Even with respect to those cases, an appeal cannot be brought more than 180 days after entry, no matter what the circumstances. In addition, Civil Rule 77(d) permits parties to serve notice of the entry of a judgment or order. The winning party can prevent Rule 4(a)(6) from even coming into play simply by serving notice of entry within 21 days. Failing that, the winning party can always trigger the 7-day deadline to move to reopen by serving belated notice.

2009 Amendments

Subdivision (a)(4)(A)(vi). Subdivision (a)(4) provides that certain timely post-trial motions extend the time for filing an appeal. Lawyers sometimes move under Civil Rule 60 for relief that is still available under another rule such as Civil Rule 59. Subdivision (a)(4)(A)(vi) provides for such eventualities by extending the time for filing an appeal so long as the Rule 60 motion is filed within a limited time. Formerly, the time limit under subdivision (a)(4)(A)(vi) was 10 days, reflecting the 10-day limits for making motions under Civil Rules 50(b), 52(b), and 59. Subdivision (a)(4)(A)(vi) now contains a 28-day limit to match the revisions to the time limits in the Civil Rules.

Subdivision (a)(4)(B)(ii). Subdivision (a)(4)(B)(ii) is amended to address problems that stemmed from the adoption—during the 1998 restyling project—of language referring to "a judgment altered or amended upon" a post-trial motion.

Prior to the restyling, subdivision (a)(4) instructed that "[a]ppellate review of an order disposing of any of [the post-trial motions listed in subdivision (a)(4)] requires the party, in compliance with Appellate Rule 3(c), to amend a previously filed notice of appeal. A party intending to challenge an alteration or amendment of the judgment shall file a notice, or amended notice, of appeal within the time prescribed by this Rule 4 measured from the entry of the order disposing of the last such motion outstanding." After the restyling, subdivision (a)(4)(B)(ii) provided: "A party intending to challenge an order disposing of any motion listed in Rule 4(a)(4)(A), or a judgment altered or amended upon such a motion, must file a notice of appeal, or an amended notice of appeal—in compliance with Rule 3(c)—within the time prescribed by this Rule measured from the entry of the order disposing of the last such remaining motion."

One court has explained that the 1998 amendment introduced ambiguity into the Rule: "The new formulation could be read to expand the obligation to file an amended notice to circumstances where the ruling on the post-trial motion alters the prior judgment in an insignificant manner or in a manner favorable to the appellant, even though the appeal is not directed against the alteration of the judgment." *Sorensen v. City of New York*, 413 F.3d 292, 296 n.2 (2d Cir. 2005). The current amendment removes that ambiguous reference to "a judgment altered or amended upon" a post-trial motion, and refers instead to "a judgment's alteration or amendment" upon such a motion. Thus, subdivision (a)(4)(B)(ii) requires a new or amended notice of appeal when an appellant wishes to challenge an order disposing of a motion listed in Rule 4(a)(4)(A) or a judgment's alteration or amendment upon such a motion.

Subdivision (a)(5)(C). The time set in the former rule at 10 days has been revised to 14 days. See the Note to Rule 26.

Subdivision (a)(6)(B). The time set in the former rule at 7 days has been revised to 14 days. Under the time-computation approach set by former Rule 26(a), "7 days" always meant at least 9 days and could mean as many as 11 or even 13 days. Under current Rule 26(a), intermediate weekends and holidays are counted. Changing the period from 7 to 14 days offsets the change in computation approach. See the Note to Rule 26.

Subdivisions (b)(1)(A) and (b)(3)(A). The times set in the former rule at 10 days have been revised to 14 days. See the Note to Rule 26.

2010 Amendments

Subdivision (a)(7). Subdivision (a)(7) is amended to reflect the renumbering of Civil Rule 58 as part of the 2007 restyling of the Civil Rules. References to Civil Rule "58(a)(1)" are revised to refer to Civil Rule "58(a)." No substantive change is intended.

2011 Amendments

Subdivision (a)(1)(B). Rule 4(a)(1)(B) has been amended to make clear that the 60-day appeal period applies in cases in which an officer or employee of the United States is sued in an individual capacity for acts or omissions occurring in connection with duties performed on behalf of the United States. (A concurrent amendment to Rule 40(a)(1) makes clear that the 45-day period to file a petition for panel rehearing also applies in such cases.)

The amendment to Rule 4(a)(1)(B) is consistent with a 2000 amendment to Civil Rule 12(a)(3), which specified an extended 60-day period to respond to complaints when "[a] United States officer or employee [is] sued in an individual capacity for an act or omission occurring in connection with duties performed on the United States' behalf." The Committee Note to the 2000 amendment explained: "Time is needed for the United States to determine whether to provide representation to the defendant officer or employee. If the United States provides representation, the need for an extended answer period is the same as in actions against the United States, a United States agency, or a United States officer sued in an official capacity." The same reasons justify providing additional time to the Solicitor General to decide whether to file an appeal.

However, because of the greater need for clarity of application when appeal rights are at stake, the amendment to Rule 4(a)(1)(B), and the corresponding legislative amendment to 28 U.S.C. § 2107 that is simultaneously proposed, include safe harbor provisions that parties can readily apply and rely upon. Under new subdivision 4(a)(1)(B)(iv), a case automatically qualifies for the 60-day appeal period if (1) a legal officer of the United States has appeared in the case, in an official capacity, as counsel for the current or former officer or employee and has not withdrawn the appearance at the time of the entry of the judgment or order appealed from or (2) a legal officer of the United States appears on the notice of appeal as counsel, in an official capacity, for the current or former officer or employee. There will be cases that do not fall within either safe harbor but that qualify for the longer appeal period. An example would be a case in which a federal employee is sued in an individual capacity for an act occurring in connection with federal duties and the United States does not represent the employee either when the judgment is entered or when the appeal is filed but the United States pays for private counsel for the employee.

2016 Amendments

[Subdivision (a).] A clarifying amendment is made to subdivision (a)(4). Former Rule 4(a)(4) provided that "[i]f a party timely files in the district court" certain post-judgment motions, "the time to file an appeal runs for all parties from the entry of the order disposing of the last such remaining motion." Responding to a circuit split concerning the meaning of "timely" in this provision, the amendment adopts the majority approach and rejects the approach taken in *National Ecological Foundation v. Alexander*, 496 F.3d 466 (6th Cir. 2007). A motion made after the time allowed by the Civil Rules will not qualify as a motion that, under Rule 4(a)(4)(A), re-starts the appeal time—and that fact is not altered by, for example, a court order that sets a due date that is later than permitted by the Civil Rules, another party's consent or failure to object to the motion's lateness, or the court's disposition of the motion without explicit reliance on untimeliness.

[Subdivision (c).] Rule 4(c)(1) is revised to streamline and clarify the operation of the inmate-filing rule.

The Rule requires the inmate to show timely deposit and prepayment of postage. The Rule is amended to specify that a notice is timely if it is accompanied by a declaration or notarized statement stating the date the notice was deposited in the institution's mail system and attesting to the prepayment of first-class postage. The declaration must state that first-class postage "is being prepaid," not (as directed by the former Rule) that first-class postage "has been prepaid." This change reflects the fact that inmates may need to rely upon the institution to affix postage after the inmate has deposited the document in the institution's mail system. New Form 7 in the Appendix of Forms sets out a suggested form of the declaration.

The amended rule also provides that a notice is timely without a declaration or notarized statement if other evidence accompanying the notice shows that the notice was deposited on or before the due date and that postage was prepaid. If the notice is not accompanied by evidence that establishes timely deposit and prepayment of postage, then the court of appeals has discretion to accept a declaration or notarized statement at a later date. The Rule uses the phrase "exercises its discretion to permit"—rather than simply "permits"—to help ensure that pro se inmate litigants are aware that a court will not necessarily forgive a failure to provide the declaration initially.

Changes Made After Publication and Comment

Rules 4(c)(1) and 25(a)(2)(C), as published, would have deleted the requirement that an inmate use a system designed for legal mail (if one is available) in order to receive the benefit of the inmate-filing rules. The Committee proposed deleting that requirement because it perceived no purpose for it. However, a commentator pointed out that correctional institutions in the State of Florida log the date of deposit of inmates' legal mail but do not log the date of deposit of inmates' non-legal mail. The Committee's subsequent inquiries revealed that a number of other States similarly record the date of inmates' legal mail but not their non-legal mail. This new information, in the view of the Committee, provides reason to retain the legal-mail-system requirement. Requiring an inmate to use a legal mail system where available serves a useful purpose by ensuring that mail is logged or date-stamped and avoiding unnecessary litigation over the timing of deposits. Accordingly, the Committee restored that requirement to proposed Rules 4(c)(1) and 25(a)(2)(C) and made conforming changes to the Committee Notes.

2017 Amendment

Subdivision (a)(4)(B)(iii). This technical amendment restores the former subdivision (a)(4)(B)(iii) that was inadvertently deleted in 2009.

Rule 5.   Appeal by Permission

(a) Petition for Permission to Appeal.

(1) To request permission to appeal when an appeal is within the court of appeals' discretion, a party must file a petition with the circuit clerk and serve it on all other parties to the district-court action.

(2) The petition must be filed within the time specified by the statute or rule authorizing the appeal or, if no such time is specified, within the time provided by Rule 4(a) for filing a notice of appeal.

(3) If a party cannot petition for appeal unless the district court first enters an order granting permission to do so or stating that the necessary conditions are met, the district court may amend its order, either on its own or in response to a party's motion, to include the required permission or statement. In that event, the time to petition runs from entry of the amended order.

(b) Contents of the Petition; Answer or Cross-Petition; Oral Argument.

(1) The petition must include the following:

(A) the facts necessary to understand the question presented;

(B) the question itself;

(C) the relief sought;

(D) the reasons why the appeal should be allowed and is authorized by a statute or rule; and

(E) an attached copy of:

(i) the order, decree, or judgment complained of and any related opinion or memorandum, and

(ii) any order stating the district court's permission to appeal or finding that the necessary conditions are met.

(2) A party may file an answer in opposition or a cross-petition within 10 days after the petition is served.

(3) The petition and answer will be submitted without oral argument unless the court of appeals orders otherwise.

(c) Form of Papers; Number of Copies; Length Limits. All papers must conform to Rule 32(c)(2). An original and 3 copies must be filed unless the court requires a different number by local rule or by order in a particular case. Except by the court's permission, and excluding the accompanying documents required by Rule 5(b)(1)(E):

(1) a paper produced using a computer must not exceed 5,200 words; and

(2) a handwritten or typewritten paper must not exceed 20 pages.

(d) Grant of Permission; Fees; Cost Bond; Filing the Record.

(1) Within 14 days after the entry of the order granting permission to appeal, the appellant must:

(A) pay the district clerk all required fees; and

(B) file a cost bond if required under Rule 7.

(2) A notice of appeal need not be filed. The date when the order granting permission to appeal is entered serves as the date of the notice of appeal for calculating time under these rules.

(3) The district clerk must notify the circuit clerk once the petitioner has paid the fees. Upon receiving this notice, the circuit clerk must enter the appeal on the docket. The record must be forwarded and filed in accordance with Rules 11 and 12(c).

(As amended Apr. 30, 1979, eff. Aug. 1, 1979; Apr. 29, 1994, eff. Dec. 1, 1994; Apr. 24, 1998, eff. Dec. 1, 1998; Apr. 29, 2002, eff. Dec. 1, 2002; Mar. 26, 2009, eff. Dec. 1, 2009; Apr 28, 2016, eff. Dec. 1, 2016; Apr. 25, 2019, eff. Dec. 1, 2019.)

ADVISORY COMMITTEE NOTES

1967 Adoption

This rule is derived in the main from Third Circuit Rule 11(2), which is similar to the rule governing appeals under 28 U.S.C. § 1292(b) in a majority of the circuits. The second sentence of subdivision (a) resolves a conflict over the question of whether the district court can amend an order by supplying the statement required by § 1292(b) at any time after entry of the order, with the result that the time fixed by the statute commences to run on the date of entry of the order as amended. Compare *Milbert v. Bison Laboratories*, 260 F.2d 431 (3d Cir., 1958) with *Sperry Rand Corporation v. Bell Telephone Laboratories*, 272 F.2d 29 (2d Cir., 1959), *Hadjipateras v. Pacifica, S.A.*, 290 F.2d 697 (5th Cir., 1961) and *Houston Fearless Corporation v. Teter*, 313 F.2d 91 (10th Cir., 1962). The view taken by the Second, Fifth and Tenth Circuits seems theoretically and practically sound, and the rule adopts it. Although a majority of the circuits now require the filing of a notice of appeal following the grant of permission to appeal, filing of the notice serves no function other than to provide a time from which the time for transmitting the record and docketing the appeal begins to run.

1979 Amendment

The proposed amendment [to subdivision (d)] adapts to the practice in appeals from interlocutory orders under 28 U.S.C. § 1292(b) the provisions of proposed Rule 3(e) above, requiring payment of all fees in the district court upon the filing of the notice of appeal. See Note to proposed amended Rule 3(e), *supra*.

1994 Amendments

Subdivision (c). The amendment makes it clear that a court may require a different number of copies either by rule or by order in an individual case. The number of copies of any document that a court of appeals needs varies depending upon the way in which the court conducts business. The internal operation of the courts of appeals necessarily varies from circuit to circuit because of differences in the number of judges, the geographic area included within the circuit, and other such factors. Uniformity could be achieved only by setting the number of copies artificially high so that parties in all circuits file enough copies to satisfy the needs of the court requiring the greatest number. Rather than do that, the Committee decided to make it clear that local rules may require a greater or lesser number of copies and that, if the circumstances of a particular case indicate the need for a different number of copies in that case, the court may so order.

1998 Amendments

In 1992 Congress added subsection (e) to 28 U.S.C. § 1292. Subsection (e) says that the Supreme Court has power to prescribe rules that "provide for an appeal of an interlocutory decision to the courts of appeals that is not otherwise provided for" in section 1292. The amendment of Rule 5 was prompted by the possibility of new rules authorizing additional interlocutory appeals. Rather than add a separate rule governing each such appeal, the Committee believes it is preferable to amend Rule 5 so that it will govern all such appeals.

In addition the Federal Courts Improvement Act of 12996, Pub.L. 104–317, abolished appeals by permission under 28 U.S.C. § 636(c)(5), making Rule 5.1 obsolete.

This new Rule 5 is intended to govern all discretionary appeals from district-court orders, judgments, or decrees. At this time that includes interlocutory appeals under 28 U.S.C. § 1292(b), (c)(1), (d)(1) & (2). If additional interlocutory appeals are authorized under § 1292(e), the new Rule is intended to govern them if the appeals are discretionary.

Subdivision (a). Paragraph (a)(1) says that when granting an appeal is within a court of appeals' discretion, a party may file a petition for permission to appeal. The time for filing provision states only that the petition must be filed within the time provided in the statute or rule authorizing the appeal or, if no such time is specified, within the time provided by Rule 4(a) for filing a notice of appeal.

Section 1292(b), (c), and (d) provide that the petition must be filed within 10 days after entry of the order containing the statement prescribed in the statute. Existing Rule 5(a) provides that if a district court amends an order to contain the prescribed statement, the petition must be filed within 10 days after entry of the amended order. The new rule similarly says that if a party cannot petition without the district court's permission or statement that necessary circumstances are present, the district court may amend its order to include such a statement and the time to petition runs from entry of the amended order.

The provision that the Rule 4(a) time for filing a notice of appeal should apply if the statute or rule is silent about the filing time was drawn from existing Rule 5.1

Subdivision (b). The changes made in the provisions in paragraph (b)(1) are intended only to broaden them sufficiently to make them appropriate for all discretionary appeals.

In paragraph (b)(2) a uniform time—7 days—is established for filing an answer in opposition or cross-petition. Seven days is the time for responding under existing Rule 5 and is an appropriate length of time when dealing with an interlocutory appeal. Although existing Rule 5.1 provides 14 days for responding, the Committee does not believe that the longer response time is necessary.

Subdivision (c). Subdivision (c) is substantively unchanged.

Subdivision (d). Paragraph (d)(2) is amended to state that "the date when the order granting permission to appeal is entered serves as the date of the notice of appeal" for purposes of calculating time under the rules. That language simply clarifies existing practice.

2002 Amendments

Subdivision (c). A petition for permission to appeal, a cross-petition for permission to appeal, and an answer to a petition or cross-petition for permission to appeal are all "other papers" for purposes of Rule 32(c)(2), and all of the requirements of Rule 32(a) apply to those papers, except as provided in Rule 32(c)(2). During the 1998 restyling of the Federal Rules of Appellate Procedure, Rule 5(c) was inadvertently changed to suggest that only the requirements of Rule 32(a)(1) apply to such papers. Rule 5(c) has been amended to correct that error.

Rule 5(c) has been further amended to limit the length of papers filed under Rule 5.

Changes Made After Publication and Comments. No changes were made to the text of the proposed amendment or to the Committee Note.

2009 Amendments

Subdivision (b)(2). Subdivision (b)(2) is amended in the light of the change in Rule 26(a)'s time computation rules. Subdivision (b)(2) formerly required that an answer in opposition to a petition for permission to appeal, or a cross-petition for permission to appeal, be filed "within 7 days after the petition is served." Under former Rule 26(a), "7 days" always meant at least 9 days and could mean as many as 11 or even 13 days. Under current Rule 26(a), intermediate weekends and holidays are counted. Changing the period from 7 to 10 days offsets the change in computation approach. See the Note to Rule 26.

Subdivision (d)(1). The time set in the former rule at 10 days has been revised to 14 days. See the Note to Rule 26.

2016 Amendments

The page limits previously employed in Rules 5, 21, 27, 35, and 40 have been largely overtaken by changes in technology. For papers produced using a computer, those page limits are now replaced by word limits. The word limits were derived from the current page limits using the assumption that one page is equivalent to 260 words. Papers produced using a computer must include the certificate of compliance required by Rule 32(g); Form 6 in the Appendix of Forms suffices to meet that requirement. Page limits are retained for papers prepared without the aid of a computer (i.e., handwritten or typewritten papers). For both the word limit and the page limit, the calculation excludes the accompanying documents required by Rule 5(b)(1)(E) and any items listed in Rule 32(f).

Changes Made After Publication and Comment

The Committee deleted the proposed line limit and revised the proposed word limit from 5,000 words to 5,200 words. The Committee also made conforming changes to the Committee Note and style changes to the Rule text.

2019 Amendments

Subdivision (a)(1) is amended to delete the reference to "proof of service" to reflect amendments to Rule 25(d) that eliminate the requirement of a proof of service when service is completed using a court's electronic filing system.

[Rule 5.1. Appeal by Leave Under 28 U.S.C. § 636(c)(5) (Abrogated Apr. 24, 1998, eff. Dec. 1, 1998)]

ADVISORY COMMITTEE NOTES

1998 Amendments

The Federal Courts Improvement Act of 1996, Pub.L. No. 104–317, abolished appeals by permission under 28 U.S.C. § 636(c)(5), making Rule 5.1 obsolete. Rule 5.1 is, therefore, abrogated.

HISTORICAL NOTES

The abrogated rule provided that:

"**(a) Petition for Leave to Appeal; Answer or Cross Petition.** An appeal from a district court judgment, entered after an appeal under 28 U.S.C. § 636(c)(4) to a district judge from a judgment entered upon direction of a magistrate judge in a civil case, may be sought by filing a petition for leave to appeal. An appeal on petition for leave to appeal is not a matter of right, but its allowance is a matter of sound judicial discretion. The petition shall be filed with the clerk of the court of appeals within the time provided by Rule 4(a) for filing a notice of appeal, with proof of service on all parties to the action in the district court. A notice of appeal need not be filed. Within 14 days after service of the petition, a party may file an answer in opposition or a cross petition.

"**(b) Content of Petition; Answer.** The petition for leave to appeal shall contain a statement of the facts necessary to an understanding of the questions to be presented by the appeal; a statement of those questions and of the relief sought; a statement of the reasons why in the opinion of the petitioner the appeal should be allowed; and a copy of the order, decree or judgment complained of and any opinion or memorandum relating thereto. The petition and answer shall be submitted to a panel of judges of the court of appeals without oral argument unless otherwise ordered.

"**(c) Form of Papers; Number of Copies.** All papers may be typewritten. An original and three copies must be filed unless the court requires the filing of a different number by local rule or by order in a particular case.

"**(d) Allowance of the Appeal; Fees; Cost Bond; Filing of Record.** Within 10 days after the entry of an order granting the appeal, the appellant shall (1) pay to the clerk of the district court the fees established by statute and the docket fee prescribed by the Judicial Conference of the United States and (2) file a bond for costs if required pursuant to Rule 7. The clerk of the district court shall notify the clerk of the court of appeals of the payment of the fees. Upon receipt of such notice, the clerk of the court of appeals shall enter the appeal upon the docket. The record shall be transmitted and filed in accordance with Rules 11 and 12(b)."

Rule 6. Appeal in a Bankruptcy Case

(a) Appeal From a Judgment, Order, or Decree of a District Court Exercising Original Jurisdiction in a Bankruptcy Case. An appeal to a court of appeals from a final judgment, order, or decree of a district court exercising jurisdiction under 28 U.S.C. § 1334 is taken as any other civil appeal under these rules.

(b) Appeal From a Judgment, Order, or Decree of a District Court or Bankruptcy Appellate Panel Exercising Appellate Jurisdiction in a Bankruptcy Case.

(1) **Applicability of Other Rules.** These rules apply to an appeal to a court of appeals under 28 U.S.C. § 158(d)(1) from a final judgment, order, or decree of a district court or bankruptcy appellate panel exercising appellate jurisdiction under 28 U.S.C. § 158(a) or (b), but with these qualifications:

(A) Rules 4(a)(4), 4(b), 9, 10, 11, 12(c), 13–20, 22–23, and 24(b) do not apply;

(B) the reference in Rule 3(c) to "Form 1 in the Appendix of Forms" must be read as a reference to Form 5;

(C) when the appeal is from a bankruptcy appellate panel, "district court," as used in any applicable rule, means "appellate panel"; and

(D) in Rule 12.1, "district court" includes a bankruptcy court or bankruptcy appellate panel.

(2) **Additional Rules.** In addition to the rules made applicable by Rule 6(b)(1), the following rules apply:

(A) **Motion for Rehearing.**

(i) If a timely motion for rehearing under Bankruptcy Rule 8022 is filed, the time to appeal for all parties runs from the entry of the order disposing of the motion. A notice of appeal filed after the district court or bankruptcy appellate panel announces or enters a judgment, order, or decree—but before disposition of the motion for rehearing—becomes effective when the order disposing of the motion for rehearing is entered.

(ii) If a party intends to challenge the order disposing of the motion—or the alteration or amendment of a judgment, order, or decree upon the motion—then the party, in compliance with Rules 3(c) and 6(b)(1)(B), must file a notice of appeal or amended notice of appeal. The notice or amended notice must be filed within the time prescribed by Rule 4—excluding Rules 4(a)(4) and 4(b)—measured from the entry of the order disposing of the motion.

(iii) No additional fee is required to file an amended notice.

(B) **The Record on Appeal.**

(i) Within 14 days after filing the notice of appeal, the appellant must file with the clerk possessing the record assembled in accordance with Bankruptcy Rule 8009—and serve on the appellee—a statement of the issues to be presented on appeal and a designation of the record to be certified and made available to the circuit clerk.

(ii) An appellee who believes that other parts of the record are necessary must, within 14 days after being served with the appellant's designation, file with the clerk and serve on the appellant a designation of additional parts to be included.

(iii) The record on appeal consists of:

- the redesignated record as provided above;
- the proceedings in the district court or bankruptcy appellate panel; and
- a certified copy of the docket entries prepared by the clerk under Rule 3(d).

(C) **Making the Record Available.**

(i) When the record is complete, the district clerk or bankruptcy-appellate-panel clerk must number the documents constituting the record and promptly make it available to the circuit clerk. If the clerk makes the record available in paper form, the clerk will not send documents of unusual bulk or weight, physical exhibits other than documents, or other parts of the record designated for omission by local rule of the court of appeals, unless directed to do so by a party or the circuit clerk. If unusually bulky or heavy exhibits are to be made available in paper form, a party must arrange with the clerks in advance for their transportation and receipt.

(ii) All parties must do whatever else is necessary to enable the clerk to assemble the record and make it available. When the record is made available in paper form, the court of appeals may provide by rule or order that a certified copy of the docket entries be made available in place of the redesignated record. But any party may request at any time during the pendency of the appeal that the redesignated record be made available.

(D) **Filing the Record.** When the district clerk or bankruptcy-appellate-panel clerk has made the record available, the circuit clerk must note that fact on the docket. The date noted on the docket serves as the filing date of the record. The circuit clerk must immediately notify all parties of the filing date.

(c) **Direct Review by Permission Under 28 U.S.C. § 158(d)(2).**

(1) **Applicability of Other Rules.** These rules apply to a direct appeal by permission under 28 U.S.C. § 158(d)(2), but with these qualifications:

(A) Rules 3–4, 5(a)(3), 6(a), 6(b), 8(a), 8(c), 9–12, 13–20, 22–23, and 24(b) do not apply;

(B) as used in any applicable rule, "district court" or "district clerk" includes—to the extent appropriate—a bankruptcy court or bankruptcy appellate panel or its clerk; and

(C) the reference to "Rules 11 and 12(c)" in Rule 5(d)(3) must be read as a reference to Rules 6(c)(2)(B) and (C).

(2) **Additional Rules.** In addition, the following rules apply:

(A) **The Record on Appeal.** Bankruptcy Rule 8009 governs the record on appeal.

(B) **Making the Record Available.** Bankruptcy Rule 8010 governs completing the record and making it available.

(C) **Stays Pending Appeal.** Bankruptcy Rule 8007 applies to stays pending appeal.

(D) **Duties of the Circuit Clerk.** When the bankruptcy clerk has made the record available, the circuit clerk must note that fact on the docket. The date noted on the docket serves as the filing date of the record. The circuit clerk must immediately notify all parties of the filing date.

(E) **Filing a Representation Statement.** Unless the court of appeals designates another time, within 14 days after entry of the order granting permission to appeal, the attorney who sought permission must file a statement with the circuit clerk naming the parties that the attorney represents on appeal.

(Added Apr. 25, 1989, eff. Dec. 1, 1989; amended Apr. 30, 1991, eff. Dec. 1, 1991; Apr. 22, 1993, eff. Dec. 1, 1993; Apr. 24, 1998, eff. Dec. 1, 1998; Mar. 26, 2009, eff. Dec. 1, 2009; Apr. 25, 2014, eff. Dec. 1, 2014.)

ADVISORY COMMITTEE NOTES

1989 Addition

A new Rule 6 is proposed. The Bankruptcy Reform Act of 1978, Pub.L. No. 95–598, 92 Stat. 2549, the Supreme Court decision in *Northern Pipeline Construction Co. v. Marathon Pipe Line Co.,* 458 U.S. 50 (1982), and the Bankruptcy Amendments and Federal Judgeship Act of 1984, Pub.L. No. 98–353, 98 Stat. 333, have made the existing Rule 6 obsolete.

Subdivision (a). Subdivision (a) provides that when a district court exercises original jurisdiction in a bankruptcy matter, rather than referring it to a bankruptcy judge for a final determination, the appeal should be taken in identical fashion as appeals from district court decisions in other civil actions. A district court exercises original jurisdiction and this subdivision applies when the district court enters a final order or judgment upon consideration of a bankruptcy judge's proposed findings of fact and conclusions of law in a non-core proceeding pursuant to 28 U.S.C. § 157(c)(1) or when a district court withdraws a proceeding pursuant to 28 U.S.C. § 157(d). This subdivision is included to avoid uncertainty arising from the question of whether a bankruptcy case is a civil case. The rules refer at various points to the procedure "in a civil case", *see,* e.g. Rule 4(a)(1). Subdivision (a) makes it clear that such rules apply to an appeal from a district court bankruptcy decision.

Subdivision (b). Subdivision (b) governs appeals that follow intermediate review of a bankruptcy judge's decision by a district court or a bankruptcy appellate panel.

Subdivision (b)(1). Subdivision (b)(1) provides for the general applicability of the Federal Rules of Appellate Procedure, with specified exceptions, to appeals covered by subdivision (b) and makes necessary word adjustments.

Subdivision (b)(2). Paragraph (i) provides that the time for filing a notice of appeal shall begin to run anew from the entry of an order denying a rehearing or from the entry of a subsequent judgment. The Committee deliberately omitted from the rule any provision governing the validity of a notice of appeal filed prior to the entry of an order denying a rehearing; the Committee intended to leave undisturbed the current state of the law on that issue. Paragraph (ii) calls for a redesignation of the appellate record assembled in the bankruptcy court pursuant to Rule 8006 of the Rules of Bankruptcy Procedure. After an intermediate appeal, a party may well narrow the focus of its efforts on the second appeal and a redesignation of the record may eliminate unnecessary material. The proceedings during the first appeal are included to cover the possibility that independent error in the intermediate appeal, for example failure to follow appropriate procedures, may be assigned in the court of appeals. Paragraph (iii) provides for the transmission of the record and tracks the appropriate subsections of Rule 11. Paragraph (iv) provides for the filing of the record and notices to the parties. Paragraph (ii) and Paragraph (iv) both refer to "a certified copy of the docket entries". The "docket entries" referred to are the docket entries in the district court or the bankruptcy appellate panel, not the entire docket in the bankruptcy court.

1993 Amendments

Note to Subparagraph (b)(2)(i). The amendment accompanies concurrent changes to Rule 4(a)(4). Although Rule 6 never included language such as that being changed in Rule 4(a)(4), language that made a notice of appeal void if it was filed before, or during the pendency of, certain posttrial motions, courts have found that a notice of appeal is premature if it is filed before the court disposes of a motion for rehearing. See, e.g., *In re X-Cel, Inc.*, 823 F.2d 192 (7th Cir.1987); *In re Shah*, 859 F.2d 1463 (10th Cir.1988). The Committee wants to achieve the same result here as in Rule 4, the elimination of a procedural trap.

1998 Amendments

The language and organization of the rule are amended to make the rule more easily understood. In addition to changes made to improve the understanding, the Advisory Committee has changed language to make style and terminology consistent throughout the appellate rules. These changes are intended to be stylistic only.

Subdivision (b). Language is added to Rule 6(b)(2)(A)(ii) to conform with the corresponding provision in Rule 4(a)(4). The new language is clarifying rather than substantive. The existing rule states that a party intending to challenge an alteration or amendment of a judgment must file an amended notice of appeal. Of course, if a party has not previously filed a notice of appeal, the party would simply file a notice of appeal not an amended one. The new language states that the party must file "a notice of appeal or amended notice of appeal."

2009 Amendments

Subdivision (b)(2)(B). The times set in the former rule at 10 days have been revised to 14 days. See the Note to Rule 26.

2014 Amendments

Subdivision (b)(1). Subdivision (b)(1) is updated to reflect the renumbering of 28 U.S.C. § 158(d) as 28 U.S.C. § 158(d)(1). Subdivision (b)(1)(A) is updated to reflect the renumbering of Rule 12(b) as Rule 12(c). New subdivision (b)(1)(D) provides that references in Rule 12.1 to the "district court" include—as appropriate—a bankruptcy court or bankruptcy appellate panel.

Subdivision (b)(2). Subdivision (b)(2)(A)(i) is amended to refer to Bankruptcy Rule 8022 (in accordance with the renumbering of Part VIII of the Bankruptcy Rules).

Subdivision (b)(2)(A)(ii) is amended to address problems that stemmed from the adoption—during the 1998 restyling project—of language referring to challenges to "an altered or amended judgment, order, or decree." Current Rule 6(b)(2)(A)(ii) states that "[a] party intending to challenge an altered or amended judgment, order, or decree must file a notice of appeal or amended notice of appeal . . . " Before the 1998 restyling, the comparable subdivision of Rule 6 instead read "[a] party intending to challenge an alteration or amendment of the judgment, order, or decree shall file an amended notice of appeal . . . " The 1998 restyling made a similar change in Rule 4(a)(4). One court has explained that the 1998 amendment introduced ambiguity into that Rule: "The new formulation could be read to expand the obligation to file an amended notice to circumstances where the ruling on the post-trial motion alters the prior judgment in an insignificant manner or in a manner favorable to the appellant, even though the appeal is not directed against the alteration of the judgment." *Sorensen v. City of New York,* 413 F.3d 292, 296 n.2 (2d Cir. 2005). Though the *Sorensen* court was writing of Rule 4(a)(4), a similar concern arises with respect to Rule 6(b)(2)(A)(ii). Rule 4(a)(4) was amended in 2009 to remove the ambiguity identified by the *Sorensen* court. The current amendment follows suit by removing Rule 6(b)(2)(A)(ii)'s reference to challenging "an altered or amended judgment, order, or decree," and referring instead to challenging "the alteration or amendment of a judgment, order, or decree."

Subdivision (b)(2)(B)(i) is amended to refer to Rule 8009 (in accordance with the renumbering of Part VIII of the Bankruptcy Rules).

Due to the shift to electronic filing, in some appeals the record will no longer be transmitted in paper form. Subdivisions (b)(2)(B)(i), (b)(2)(C), and (b)(2)(D) are amended to reflect the fact that the record sometimes will be made available electronically.

Subdivision (b)(2)(D) sets the duties of the circuit clerk when the record has been made available. Because the record may be made available in electronic form, subdivision (b)(2)(D) does not direct the clerk to "file" the record. Rather, it directs the clerk to note on the docket the date when the record was made available and to notify the parties of that date, which shall serve as the date of filing the record for purposes of provisions in these Rules that calculate time from that filing date.

Subdivision (c). New subdivision (c) is added to govern permissive direct appeals from the bankruptcy court to the court of appeals under 28 U.S.C. § 158(d)(2). For further provisions governing such direct appeals, see Bankruptcy Rule 8006.

Subdivision (c)(1). Subdivision (c)(1) provides for the general applicability of the Federal Rules of Appellate Procedure, with specified exceptions, to appeals covered by subdivision (c) and makes necessary word adjustments.

Subdivision (c)(2). Subdivision (c)(2)(A) provides that the record on appeal is governed by Bankruptcy Rule 8009. Subdivision (c)(2)(B) provides that the record shall be made available as stated in Bankruptcy Rule 8010. Subdivision (c)(2)(C) provides that Bankruptcy Rule 8007 applies to stays pending appeal; in addition, Appellate Rule 8(b) applies to sureties on bonds provided in connection with stays pending appeal.

Subdivision (c)(2)(D), like subdivision (b)(2)(D), directs the clerk to note on the docket the date when the record was made available and to notify the parties of that date, which shall serve as the date of filing the record for purposes of provisions in these Rules that calculate time from that filing date.

Subdivision (c)(2)(E) is modeled on Rule 12(b), with appropriate adjustments.

Changes Made After Publication and Comment

No changes were made after publication and comment.

Rule 7.   Bond for Costs on Appeal in a Civil Case

In a civil case, the district court may require an appellant to file a bond or provide other security in any form and amount necessary to ensure payment of costs on appeal. Rule 8(b) applies to a surety on a bond given under this rule.

(As amended Apr. 30, 1979, eff. Aug. 1, 1979; Apr. 24, 1998, eff. Dec. 1, 1998.)

ADVISORY COMMITTEE NOTES

1967 Adoption

This rule is derived from FRCP 73(c) [rule 73(c), Federal Rules of Civil Procedure, this title] without change in substance.

1979 Amendment

The amendment would eliminate the provision of the present rule that requires the appellant to file a $250 bond for costs on appeal at the time of filing his notice of appeal. The $250 provision was carried forward in the F.R.App.P. [these rules] from former Rule 73(c) of the F.R.Civ.P. [rule 73(c), Federal Rules of Civil Procedure], and the $250 figure has remained unchanged since the adoption of that rule in 1937. Today it bears no relationship to actual costs. The amended rule would leave the question of the need for a bond for costs and its amount in the discretion of the court.

1998 Amendments

The language of the rule is amended to make the rule more easily understood. In addition to changes made to improve the understanding, the Advisory Committee has changed language to make style and terminology consistent throughout the appellate rules. These changes are intended to be stylistic only.

Rule 8.   Stay or Injunction Pending Appeal

(a) Motion for Stay.

(1) Initial Motion in the District Court. A party must ordinarily move first in the district court for the following relief:

(A) a stay of the judgment or order of a district court pending appeal;

(B) approval of a bond or other security provided to obtain a stay of judgment; or

(C) an order suspending, modifying, restoring, or granting an injunction while an appeal is pending.

(2) Motion in the Court of Appeals; Conditions on Relief. A motion for the relief mentioned in Rule 8(a)(1) may be made to the court of appeals or to one of its judges.

(A) The motion must:

(i) show that moving first in the district court would be impracticable; or

(ii) state that, a motion having been made, the district court denied the motion or failed to afford the relief requested and state any reasons given by the district court for its action.

(B) The motion must also include:

(i) the reasons for granting the relief requested and the facts relied on;

(ii) originals or copies of affidavits or other sworn statements supporting facts subject to dispute; and

(iii) relevant parts of the record.

(C) The moving party must give reasonable notice of the motion to all parties.

(D) A motion under this Rule 8(a)(2) must be filed with the circuit clerk and normally will be considered by a panel of the court. But in an exceptional case in which time requirements make that procedure impracticable, the motion may be made to and considered by a single judge.

(E) The court may condition relief on a party's filing a bond or other appropriate security in the district court.

(b) Proceeding Against a Security Provider. If a party gives security with one or more security providers, each provider submits to the jurisdiction of the district court and irrevocably appoints the district clerk as its agent on whom any papers affecting its liability on the security may be served. On motion, a security provider's liability may be enforced in the district court without the necessity of an independent action. The motion and any notice that the district court prescribes may be served on the district clerk, who must promptly send a copy to each security provider whose address is known.

(c) Stay in a Criminal Case. Rule 38 of the Federal Rules of Criminal Procedure governs a stay in a criminal case.

(As amended Mar. 10, 1986, eff. July 1, 1986; Apr. 27, 1995, eff. Dec. 1, 1995; Apr. 24, 1998, eff. Dec. 1, 1998; Apr. 26, 2018, eff. Dec. 1, 2018.)

ADVISORY COMMITTEE NOTES

1967 Adoption

Subdivision (a). While the power of a court of appeals to stay proceedings in the district court during the pendency of an appeal is not explicitly conferred by statute, it exists by virtue of the all writs statute, 28 U.S.C. § 1651. *Eastern Greyhound Lines v. Fusco*, 310 F.2d 632 (6th Cir., 1962); *United States v. Lynd*, 301 F.2d 818 (5th Cir., 1962); *Public Utilities Commission of Dist. of Col. v. Capital Transit Co.*, 94 U.S.App.D.C. 140, 214 F.2d 242 (1954). And the Supreme Court has termed the power "inherent" (*In re McKenzie*, 180 U.S. 536, 551, 21 S.Ct. 468, 45 L.Ed. 657 (1901)) and "part of its (the court of appeals') traditional equipment for the administration of justice." (*Scripps-Howard Radio v. F.C.C.*, 316 U.S. 4, 9–10, 62 S.Ct. 875, 86 L.Ed. 1229 (1942)). The power of a single judge of the court of appeals to grant a stay pending appeal was recognized in *In re McKenzie, supra. Alexander v. United States*, 173 F.2d 865 (9th Cir., 1949) held that a single judge could not stay the judgment of a district court, but it noted the absence of a rule of court authorizing the practice. FRCP 62(g) [rule 62(g), Federal Rules of Civil Procedure] adverts to the grant of a stay by a single judge of the appellate court. The requirement that application be first made to the district court is the case law rule. *Cumberland Tel. & Tel. Co. v. Louisiana Public Service Commission*, 260 U.S. 212, 219, 43 S.Ct. 75, 67 L.Ed. 217 (1922); *United States v. El-O-Pathic Pharmacy*, 192 F.2d 62 (9th Cir., 1951); *United States v. Hansell*, 109 F.2d 613 (2d Cir., 1940). The requirement is explicitly stated in FRCrP 38(c) [rule 38(c), Federal Rules of Criminal Procedure] and in the rules of the First, Third, Fourth and Tenth Circuits. See also Supreme Court Rules 18 and 27.

The statement of the requirement in the proposed rule would work a minor change in present practice. FRCP 73(e) [rule 73(e), Federal Rules of Civil Procedure] requires that if a bond for costs on appeal or a supersedeas bond is offered after the appeal is docketed, leave to file the bond must be obtained from the court of appeals. There appears to be no reason why matters relating to supersedeas and cost bonds should not be initially presented to the district court whenever they arise prior to the disposition of the appeal. The requirement of FRCP 73(e) appears to be a concession of the view that once an appeal is perfected, the district court loses all power over its judgment. See *In re Federal Facilities Realty Trust*, 227 F.2d 651 (7th Cir., 1955) and cases cited at 654–655. No reason appears why all questions related to supersedeas or the bond for costs on appeal should not be presented in the first instance to the district court in the ordinary case.

Subdivision (b). The provisions respecting a surety upon a bond or other undertaking are based upon FRCP 65.1 [rule 65.1, Federal Rules of Civil Procedure].

1986 Amendment

The amendments to Rule 8(b) are technical. No substantive change is intended.

1995 Amendment

Subdivision (c). The amendment conforms subdivision (c) to previous amendments to Fed.R.Crim.P. 38. This amendment strikes the reference to subdivision (a) of Fed.R.Crim.P. 38 so that Fed.R.App.P. 8(c) refers instead to all of Criminal Rule 38. When Rule 8(c) was adopted Fed.R.Crim.P. 38(a) included the procedures for obtaining a stay of execution when the sentence in question was death, imprisonment, a fine, or probation. Criminal Rule 38 was later amended and now addresses those topics in separate subdivisions. Subdivision 38(a) now addresses only stays of death sentences. The proper cross reference is to all of Criminal Rule 38.

1998 Amendments

The language and organization of the rule are amended to make the rule more easily understood. In addition to changes made to improve the understanding, the Advisory Committee has changed language to make style and terminology consistent throughout the appellate rules. These changes are intended to by stylistic only.

2018 Amendments

The amendments to subdivisions (a) and (b) conform this rule with the amendment of Federal Rule of Civil Procedure 62. Rule 62 formerly required a party to provide a "supersedeas bond" to obtain a stay of the judgment and proceedings to enforce the judgment. As amended, Rule 62(b) allows a party to obtain a stay by providing a "bond or other security." The word "mail" is changed to "send" to avoid restricting the method of serving security providers. Other rules specify the permissible manners of service.

Rule 9.   Release in a Criminal Case

(a)   Release Before Judgment of Conviction.

(1)   The district court must state in writing, or orally on the record, the reasons for an order regarding the release or detention of a defendant in a criminal case. A party appealing from the order must file with the court of appeals a copy of the district court's order and the court's statement of reasons as soon as practicable after filing the notice of appeal. An appellant who questions the factual basis for the district court's order must file a transcript of the release proceedings or an explanation of why a transcript was not obtained.

(2)   After reasonable notice to the appellee, the court of appeals must promptly determine the appeal on the basis of the papers, affidavits, and parts of the record that the parties present or the court requires. Unless the court so orders, briefs need not be filed.

(3)   The court of appeals or one of its judges may order the defendant's release pending the disposition of the appeal.

(b)   Release After Judgment of Conviction. A party entitled to do so may obtain review of a district-court order regarding release after a judgment of conviction by filing a notice of appeal from that order in the district court, or by filing a motion in the court of appeals if the party has already filed a notice of appeal from the judgment of conviction. Both the order and the review are subject to Rule 9(a). The papers filed by the party seeking review must include a copy of the judgment of conviction.

(c)   Criteria for Release. The court must make its decision regarding release in accordance with the applicable provisions of 18 U.S.C. §§ 3142, 3143, and 3145(c).

(As amended Apr. 24, 1972, eff. Oct. 1, 1972; Oct. 12, 1984, Pub.L. 98–473, Title II, § 210, 98 Stat. 1987; Apr. 29, 1994, eff. Dec. 1, 1994; Apr. 24, 1998, eff. Dec. 1, 1998.)

ADVISORY COMMITTEE NOTES

1967 Adoption

Subdivision (a). The appealability of release orders entered prior to a judgment of conviction is determined by the provisions of 18 U.S.C. § 3147, as qualified by 18 U.S.C. § 3148, and by the rule announced in *Stack v. Boyle*, 342 U.S. 1, 72 S.Ct. 1, 96 L.Ed. 3 (1951), holding certain orders respecting release appealable as final orders under 28 U.S.C. § 1291. The language of the rule, "(a)n appeal authorized by law from an order refusing or imposing conditions of release," is intentionally broader than that used in 18 U.S.C. § 3147 in describing orders made appealable by that section. The summary procedure ordained by the rule is intended to apply to all appeals from orders respecting release, and it would appear that at least some orders not made appealable by 18 U.S.C. § 3147 are nevertheless appealable under the *Stack v. Boyle* rationale. See, for example, *United States v. Foster*, 278 F.2d 567 (2d Cir., 1960), holding appealable an order refusing to extend bail limits. Note also the provisions of 18 U.S.C. § 3148, which after withdrawing from persons charged with an offense punishable by death and from those who have been convicted of an offense the right of appeal granted by 18 U.S.C. § 3147, expressly preserves "other rights to judicial review of conditions of release or orders of detention."

The purpose of the subdivision is to insure the expeditious determination of appeals respecting release orders, an expedition commanded by 18 U.S.C. § 3147 and by the Court in *Stack v. Boyle*, supra. It permits such appeals to be heard on an informal record without the necessity of briefs and on reasonable notice. Equally important to the just and speedy disposition of these appeals is the requirement that the district court state the reasons for its decision. See *Jones v. United States*, 358 F.2d 543 (D.C.Cir., 1966); *Rhodes v. United States*, 275 F.2d 78 (4th Cir., 1960); *United States v. Williams*, 253 F.2d 144 (7th Cir., 1958).

Subdivision (b). This subdivision regulates procedure for review of an order respecting release at a time when the jurisdiction of the court of appeals has already attached by virtue of an appeal from the judgment of conviction. Notwithstanding the fact that jurisdiction has passed to the court of appeals, both 18 U.S.C. § 3148 and FRCrP 38(c) [rule 38(c), Federal Rules of Criminal Procedure] contemplate that the initial determination of whether a convicted defendant is to be released pending the appeal is to be made by the district court. But at this point there is obviously no need for a separate appeal from the order of the district court respecting release. The court of appeals or a judge thereof has power to effect release on motion as an incident to the pending appeal. See FRCrP 38(c) and 46(a)(2) [rules 38(c) and 46(a)(2), Federal Rules of Criminal Procedure. But the motion is functionally identical with the appeal regulated by subdivision (a) and requires the same speedy determination if relief is to be effective. Hence the similarity of the procedure outlined in the two subdivisions.

1972 Amendment

Subdivision (c) is intended to bring the rule into conformity with 18 U.S.C. § 3148 and to allocate to the defendant the burden of establishing that he will not flee and that he poses no danger to pay other person or to the community. The burden is placed upon the defendant in the view that the fact of his conviction justifies retention in custody in situations where doubt exists as to whether he can be safely released pending disposition of his appeal. Release pending appeal may also be denied if "it appears that an appeal is frivolous or taken for delay." 18 U.S.C. § 3148. The burden of establishing the existence of these criteria remains with the government.

1994 Amendments

Rule 9 has been entirely rewritten. The basic structure of the rule has been retained. Subdivision (a) governs appeals from bail decisions made before the judgment of conviction is entered at the time of sentencing. Subdivision (b) governs review of bail decisions made after sentencing and pending appeal.

Subdivision (a). The subdivision applies to appeals from "an order regarding release or detention" of a criminal defendant before judgment of conviction, *i.e.,* before sentencing. See Fed. R. Crim. P. 32. The old rule applied only to a defendant's appeal from an order "refusing or imposing conditions of release." The new broader language is needed because the government is now permitted to appeal bail decisions in certain circumstances. 18 U.S.C. §§ 3145 and 3731. For the same reason, the rule now requires a district court to state reasons for its decision in all instances, not only when it refuses release or imposes conditions on release.

The rule requires a party appealing from a district court's decision to supply the court of appeals with a copy of the district court's order and its statement of reasons. In addition, an appellant who questions the factual basis for the district court's decision must file a transcript of the release proceedings, if possible. The rule also permits a court to require additional papers. A court must act promptly to decide these appeals; lack of pertinent information can cause delays. The old rule left the determination of what should be filed entirely within the party's, discretion; it stated that the court of appeals would hear the appeal "upon such papers, affidavits, and portions of the record as the parties shall present."

Subdivision (b). This subdivision applies to review of a district court's decision regarding release made after judgment of conviction. As in subdivision (a), the language has been changed to accommodate the government's ability to seek review.

The word "review" is used in this subdivision, rather than "appeal" because review may be obtained, in some instances, upon motion. Review may be obtained by motion if the party has already filed a notice of appeal from the judgment of conviction. If the party desiring review of the release decision has not filed such a notice of appeal, review may be obtained only by filing a notice of appeal from the order regarding release.

The requirements of subdivision (a) apply to both the order and the review. That is, the district court must state its reasons for the order. The party seeking review must supply the court of appeals with the same information required by subdivision (a). In addition, the party seeking review must also supply the court with information about the conviction and the sentence.

Subdivision (c). This subdivision has been amended to include references to the correct statutory provisions.

1998 Amendments

The language and organization of the rule are amended to make the rule more easily understood. In addition to changes made to improve the understanding, the Advisory Committee has changed language to make style and terminology consistent throughout the appellate rules. These changes are intended to by stylistic only.

Rule 10.   The Record on Appeal

(a)   **Composition of the Record on Appeal.** The following items constitute the record on appeal:

   (1)   the original papers and exhibits filed in the district court;

   (2)   the transcript of proceedings, if any; and

   (3)   a certified copy of the docket entries prepared by the district clerk.

(b)   **The Transcript of Proceedings.**

   (1)   **Appellant's Duty to Order.** Within 14 days after filing the notice of appeal or entry of an order disposing of the last timely remaining motion of a type specified in Rule 4(a)(4)(A), whichever is later, the appellant must do either of the following:

      (A)   order from the reporter a transcript of such parts of the proceedings not already on file as the appellant considers necessary, subject to a local rule of the court of appeals and with the following qualifications:

         (i)   the order must be in writing;

         (ii)   if the cost of the transcript is to be paid by the United States under the Criminal Justice Act, the order must so state; and

         (iii)   the appellant must, within the same period, file a copy of the order with the district clerk; or

      (B)   file a certificate stating that no transcript will be ordered.

   (2)   **Unsupported Finding or Conclusion.** If the appellant intends to urge on appeal that a finding or conclusion is unsupported by the evidence or is contrary to the evidence, the appellant must include in the record a transcript of all evidence relevant to that finding or conclusion.

(3) Partial Transcript. Unless the entire transcript is ordered:

(A) the appellant must—within the 14 days provided in Rule 10(b)(1)—file a statement of the issues that the appellant intends to present on the appeal and must serve on the appellee a copy of both the order or certificate and the statement;

(B) if the appellee considers it necessary to have a transcript of other parts of the proceedings, the appellee must, within 14 days after the service of the order or certificate and the statement of the issues, file and serve on the appellant a designation of additional parts to be ordered; and

(C) unless within 14 days after service of that designation the appellant has ordered all such parts, and has so notified the appellee, the appellee may within the following 14 days either order the parts or move in the district court for an order requiring the appellant to do so.

(4) Payment. At the time of ordering, a party must make satisfactory arrangements with the reporter for paying the cost of the transcript.

(c) Statement of the Evidence When the Proceedings Were Not Recorded or When a Transcript Is Unavailable. If the transcript of a hearing or trial is unavailable, the appellant may prepare a statement of the evidence or proceedings from the best available means, including the appellant's recollection. The statement must be served on the appellee, who may serve objections or proposed amendments within 14 days after being served. The statement and any objections or proposed amendments must then be submitted to the district court for settlement and approval. As settled and approved, the statement must be included by the district clerk in the record on appeal.

(d) Agreed Statement as the Record on Appeal. In place of the record on appeal as defined in Rule 10(a), the parties may prepare, sign, and submit to the district court a statement of the case showing how the issues presented by the appeal arose and were decided in the district court. The statement must set forth only those facts averred and proved or sought to be proved that are essential to the court's resolution of the issues. If the statement is truthful, it—together with any additions that the district court may consider necessary to a full presentation of the issues on appeal—must be approved by the district court and must then be certified to the court of appeals as the record on appeal. The district clerk must then send it to the circuit clerk within the time provided by Rule 11. A copy of the agreed statement may be filed in place of the appendix required by Rule 30.

(e) Correction or Modification of the Record.

(1) If any difference arises about whether the record truly discloses what occurred in the district court, the difference must be submitted to and settled by that court and the record conformed accordingly.

(2) If anything material to either party is omitted from or misstated in the record by error or accident, the omission or misstatement may be corrected and a supplemental record may be certified and forwarded:

(A) on stipulation of the parties;

(B) by the district court before or after the record has been forwarded; or

(C) by the court of appeals.

(3) All other questions as to the form and content of the record must be presented to the court of appeals.

(As amended Apr. 30, 1979, eff. Aug. 1, 1979; Mar. 10, 1986, eff. July 1, 1986; Apr. 30, 1991, eff. Dec. 1, 1991; Apr. 22, 1993, eff. Dec. 1, 1993; Apr. 27, 1995, eff. Dec. 1, 1995; Apr. 24, 1998, eff. Dec. 1, 1998; Mar. 26, 2009, eff. Dec. 1, 2009.)

ADVISORY COMMITTEE NOTES

1967 Adoption

This rule is derived from FRCP 75(a), (b), (c) and (d) and FRCP 76 [rule 75(a), (b), (c) and (d) and rule 76, Federal Rules of Civil Procedure], without change in substance.

1979 Amendment

The proposed amendments to Rule 10(b) would require the appellant to place with the reporter a written order for the transcript of proceedings and file a copy with the clerk, and to indicate on the order if the transcript is to be provided under the Criminal Justice Act. If the appellant does not plan to order a transcript of any of the proceedings, he must file a certificate to that effect. These requirements make the appellant's steps in readying the appeal a matter of record and give the district court notice of requests for transcripts at the expense of the United States under the Criminal Justice Act. They are also the third step in giving the court of appeals some control over the production and transmission of the record. See Note to Rules 3(d)(e) above and Rule 11 below.

In the event the appellant orders no transcript, or orders a transcript of less than all the proceedings, the procedure under the proposed amended rule remains substantially as before. The appellant must serve on the appellee a copy of his order or in the event no order is placed, of the certificate to that effect, and a statement of the issues he intends to present on appeal, and the appellee may thereupon designate additional parts of the transcript to be included, and upon appellant's refusal to order the additional parts, may either order them himself or seek an order requiring the appellant to order them. The only change proposed in this procedure is to place a 10 day time limit on motions to require the appellant to order the additional portions.

Rule 10(b) is made subject to local rules of the courts of appeals in recognition of the practice in some circuits in some classes of cases, e.g., appeals by indigents in criminal cases after a short trial, of ordering immediate preparation of a complete transcript, thus making compliance with the rule unnecessary.

1986 Amendment

The amendments to Rules 10(b) and (c) are technical. No substantive change is intended.

1993 Amendment

The amendment is technical and no substantive change is intended.

1995 Amendment

Subdivision (b)(1). The amendment conforms this rule to amendments made in Rule 4(a)(4) in 1993. The amendments to Rule 4(a)(4) provide that certain postjudgment motions have the effect of suspending a filed notice of appeal until the disposition of the last of such motions. The purpose of this amendment is to suspend the 10-day period for ordering a transcript if a timely postjudgment motion is made and a notice of appeal is suspended under Rule 4(a)(4). The 10-day period set forth in the first sentence of this rule begins to run when the order disposing of the last of such postjudgment motions outstanding is entered.

1998 Amendments

The language and organization of the rule are amended to make the rule more easily understood. In addition to changes made to improve the understanding, the Advisory Committee has changed language to make style and terminology consistent throughout the appellate rules. These changes are intended to by stylistic only.

2009 Amendments

Subdivisions (b)(1), (b)(3), and (c). The times set in the former rule at 10 days have been revised to 14 days. See the Note to Rule 26.

HISTORICAL NOTES

References in Text

The Criminal Justice Act, referred to in subd. (b)(1), probably means the Criminal Justice Act of 1964, Pub.L. 88–455, Aug. 20, 1964, 78 Stat. 552, which is classified to § 3006A of Title 18, Crimes and Criminal Procedure.

Rule 11.   Forwarding the Record

(a) Appellant's Duty. An appellant filing a notice of appeal must comply with Rule 10(b) and must do whatever else is necessary to enable the clerk to assemble and forward the record. If there are multiple appeals from a judgment or order, the clerk must forward a single record.

(b) Duties of Reporter and District Clerk.

(1) Reporter's Duty to Prepare and File a Transcript. The reporter must prepare and file a transcript as follows:

(A) Upon receiving an order for a transcript, the reporter must enter at the foot of the order the date of its receipt and the expected completion date and send a copy, so endorsed, to the circuit clerk.

(B) If the transcript cannot be completed within 30 days of the reporter's receipt of the order, the reporter may request the circuit clerk to grant additional time to complete it. The clerk must note on the docket the action taken and notify the parties.

(C) When a transcript is complete, the reporter must file it with the district clerk and notify the circuit clerk of the filing.

(D) If the reporter fails to file the transcript on time, the circuit clerk must notify the district judge and do whatever else the court of appeals directs.

(2) District Clerk's Duty to Forward. When the record is complete, the district clerk must number the documents constituting the record and send them promptly to the circuit clerk together with a list of the documents correspondingly numbered and reasonably identified. Unless directed to do so by a party or the circuit clerk, the district clerk will not send to the court of appeals documents of unusual bulk or weight, physical exhibits other than documents, or other parts of the record designated for omission by local rule of the court of appeals. If the exhibits are unusually bulky or heavy, a party must arrange with the clerks in advance for their transportation and receipt.

(c) Retaining the Record Temporarily in the District Court for Use in Preparing the Appeal. The parties may stipulate, or the district court on motion may order, that the district clerk retain the record temporarily for the parties to use in preparing the papers on appeal. In that event the district clerk must certify to the circuit clerk that the record on appeal is complete. Upon receipt of the appellee's brief, or earlier if the court orders or the parties agree, the appellant must request the district clerk to forward the record.

(d) [Abrogated.]

(e) Retaining the Record by Court Order.

(1) The court of appeals may, by order or local rule, provide that a certified copy of the docket entries be forwarded instead of the entire record. But a party may at any time during the appeal request that designated parts of the record be forwarded.

(2) The district court may order the record or some part of it retained if the court needs it while the appeal is pending, subject, however, to call by the court of appeals.

(3) If part or all of the record is ordered retained, the district clerk must send to the court of appeals a copy of the order and the docket entries together with the parts of the original record allowed by the district court and copies of any parts of the record designated by the parties.

(f) Retaining Parts of the Record in the District Court by Stipulation of the Parties. The parties may agree by written stipulation filed in the district court that designated parts of the record be retained in the district court subject to call by the court of appeals or request by a party. The parts of the record so designated remain a part of the record on appeal.

(g) Record for a Preliminary Motion in the Court of Appeals. If, before the record is forwarded, a party makes any of the following motions in the court of appeals:

- for dismissal;

- for release;

- for a stay pending appeal;

- for additional security on the bond on appeal or on a bond or other security provided to obtain a stay of judgment; or

- for any other intermediate order—

the district clerk must send the court of appeals any parts of the record designated by any party.

(As amended Apr. 30, 1979, eff. Aug. 1, 1979; Mar. 10, 1986, eff. July 1, 1986; Apr. 24, 1998, eff. Dec. 1, 1998; Apr. 26, 2018, eff. Dec. 1, 2018.)

ADVISORY COMMITTEE NOTES

1967 Adoption

Subdivisions (a) and (b). These subdivisions are derived from FRCP 73(g) and FRCP 75(e) [rules 73(g) and 75(e), Federal Rules of Civil Procedure]. FRCP 75(e) presently directs the clerk of the district court to transmit the record within the time allowed or fixed for its filing, which, under the provisions of FRCP 73(g) is within 40 days from the date of filing the notice of appeal, unless an extension is obtained from the district court. The precise time at which the record must be transmitted thus depends upon the time required for delivery of the record from the district court to the court of appeals, since, to permit its timely filing, it must reach the court of appeals before expiration of the 40-day period or an extension thereof. Subdivision (a) of this rule provides that the record is to be transmitted within the 40-day period, or any extension thereof; subdivision (b) provides that transmission is effected when the clerk of the district court mails or otherwise forwards the record to the clerk of the court of appeals; Rule 12(b) directs the clerk of the court of appeals to file the record upon its receipt following timely docketing and transmittal. It can thus be determined with certainty precisely when the clerk of the district court must forward the record to the clerk of the court of appeals in order to effect timely filing: the final day of the 40-day period or of any extension thereof.

Subdivision (c). This subdivision is derived from FRCP 75(e) [rule 75(e), Federal Rules of Civil Procedure] without change of substance.

Subdivision (d). This subdivision is derived from FRCP 73(g) [rule 73(g), Federal Rules of Civil Procedure] and FRCrP 39(c) [rule 39(c), Federal Rules of Criminal Procedure]. Under present rules the district court is empowered to extend the time for filing the record and docketing the appeal. Since under the proposed rule timely transmission now insures timely filing (see note to subdivisions (a) and (b) above) the power of the district court is expressed in terms of its power to extend the time for transmitting the record. Restriction of that power to a period of 90 days after the filing of the notice of appeal represents a change in the rule with respect to appeals in criminal cases. FRCrP 39(c) now permits the district court to extend the time for filing and docketing without restriction. No good reason appears for a difference between the civil and criminal rule in this regard, and subdivision (d) limits the power of the district court to extend the time for transmitting the record in all cases to 90 days from the date of filing the notice of appeal, just as its power is now limited with respect to docketing and filing in civil cases. Subdivision (d) makes explicit the power of the court of appeals to permit the record to be filed at any time. See *Pyramid Motor Freight Corporation v. Ispass*, 330 U.S. 695, 67 S.Ct. 954, 91 L.Ed. 1184 (1947).

Subdivisions (e), (f) and (g). These subdivisions are derived from FRCP 75(f) [rule 75(f), Federal Rules of Civil Procedure], (a) and (g), respectively, without change of substance.

1979 Amendment

Under present Rule 11(a) it is provided that the record shall be transmitted to the court of appeals within 40 days after the filing of the notice of appeal. Under present Rule 11(d) the district court, on request made during the initial time or any extension thereof, and cause shown, may extend the time for the transmission of the record to a point not more than 90 days after the filing of the first notice of appeal. If the district court is without authority to grant a request to extend the time, or denies a request for extension, the appellant may make a motion for extension of time in the court of appeals. Thus the duty to see that the record is transmitted is placed on the appellant. Aside from ordering the transcript within the time prescribed the appellant has no control over the time at which the record is transmitted, since all steps beyond this point are in the hands of the reporter and the clerk. The proposed amendments recognize this fact and place the duty directly on the reporter and the clerk. After receiving the written order for the transcript (See Note to Rule 10(b) above), the reporter must acknowledge its receipt, indicate when he expects to have it completed, and mail the order so endorsed to the clerk of the court of appeals. Requests for extensions of time must be made by the reporter to the clerk of the court of appeals and action on such requests is entered on the docket. Thus from the point at which the transcript is ordered the clerk of the court of appeals is made aware of any delays. If the transcript is not filed on time, the clerk of the court of appeals will notify the district judge.

Present Rule 11(b) provides that the record shall be transmitted when it is "complete for the purposes of the appeal." The proposed amended rule continues this requirement. The record is complete for the purposes of the appeal when it contains the original papers on file in the clerk's office, all necessary exhibits, and the transcript, if one is to be included. Cf. present Rule 11(c). The original papers will be in the custody of the clerk of the district court at the time the notice of appeal is filed. See Rule 5(e) of the F.R.C.P. [rule 5(e), Federal Rules of Civil Procedure]. The custody of exhibits is often the subject of local rules. Some of them require that documentary exhibits must be deposited with the clerk. See Local Rule 13 of the Eastern District of Virginia. Others leave exhibits with counsel, subject to order of the court. See Local Rule 33 of the Northern District of Illinois. If under local rules the custody of exhibits is left with counsel, the district court should make adequate provision for their preservation during the time during which an appeal may be taken, the prompt deposit with the clerk of such as under Rule 11(b) are to be transmitted to the court of appeals, and the availability of others in the event that the court of appeals should require their transmission. Cf. Local Rule 11 of the Second Circuit [rule 11, U.S.Ct. of App. 2d Cir.].

Usually the record will be complete with the filing of the transcript. While the proposed amendment requires transmission "forthwith" when the record is complete, it was not designed to preclude a local requirement by the court of appeals that the original papers and exhibits be transmitted when complete without awaiting the filing of the transcript.

The proposed amendments continue the provision in the present rule that documents of unusual bulk or weight and physical exhibits other than documents shall not be transmitted without direction by the parties or by the court of appeals, and the requirement that the parties make special arrangements for transmission and receipt of exhibits of unusual bulk or weight. In addition, they give recognition to local rules that make transmission of other record items subject to order of the court of appeals. See Local Rule 4 of the Seventh Circuit [rule 4, U.S.Ct. of App. 7th Cir., this title].

1986 Amendment

The amendments to Rule 11(b) are technical. No substantive change is intended.

1998 Amendments

The language and organization of the rule are amended to make the rule more easily understood. In addition to changes made to improve the understanding, the Advisory Committee has changed language to make style and terminology consistent throughout the appellate rules. These changes are intended to be stylistic only.

2018 Amendment

The amendment of subdivision (g) conforms this rule with the amendment of Federal Rule of Civil Procedure 62. Rule 62 formerly required a party to provide a "supersedeas bond" to obtain a stay of the judgment and proceedings to enforce the judgment. As amended, Rule 62(b) allows a party to obtain a stay by providing a "bond or other security."

Rule 12.   Docketing the Appeal; Filing a Representation Statement; Filing the Record

(a) Docketing the Appeal. Upon receiving the copy of the notice of appeal and the docket entries from the district clerk under Rule 3(d), the circuit clerk must docket the appeal under the title of the district-court action and must identify the appellant, adding the appellant's name if necessary.

(b) Filing a Representation Statement. Unless the court of appeals designates another time, the attorney who filed the notice of appeal must, within 14 days after filing the notice, file a statement with the circuit clerk naming the parties that the attorney represents on appeal.

(c) Filing the Record, Partial Record, or Certificate. Upon receiving the record, partial record, or district clerk's certificate as provided in Rule 11, the circuit clerk must file it and immediately notify all parties of the filing date.

(As amended Apr. 30, 1979, eff. Aug. 1, 1979; Mar. 10, 1986, eff. July 1, 1986; Apr. 22, 1993, eff. Dec. 1, 1993; Apr. 24, 1998, eff. Dec. 1, 1998; Mar. 26, 2009, eff. Dec. 1, 2009.)

ADVISORY COMMITTEE NOTES

1967 Adoption

Subdivision (a). All that is involved in the docketing of an appeal is the payment of the docket fee. In practice, after the clerk of the court of appeals receives the record from the clerk of the district court he notifies the appellant of its receipt and requests payment of the fee. Upon receipt of the fee, the clerk enters the appeal upon the docket and files the record. The appellant is allowed to pay the fee at any time within the time allowed or fixed for transmission of the record and thereby to discharge his responsibility for docketing. The final sentence is added in the interest of facilitating future reference and citation and location of cases in indexes. Compare 3d Cir.Rule 10(2) [rule 10(2), U.S.Ct. of App. 3d Cir.]; 4th Cir.Rule 9(8) [rule 9(8), U.S.Ct. of App. 4th Cir.]; 6th Cir.Rule 14(1) [rule 14(1), U.S.Ct. of App. 6th Cir.].

Subdivision (c). The rules of the circuits generally permit the appellee to move for dismissal in the event the appellant fails to effect timely filing of the record. See 1st Cir.Rule 21(3) [rule 21(3), U.S.Ct. of App. 1st Cir.]; 3d Cir.Rule 21(4) [rule 21(4), U.S.Ct. of App. 3d Cir.]; 5th Cir.Rule 16(1) [rule 16(1), U.S.Ct. of App. 5th Cir.]; 8th Cir.Rule 7(d) [rule 7(d), U.S.Ct. of App. 8th Cir.].

1979 Amendments

Subdivision (a). Under present Rule 12(a) the appellant must pay the docket fee within the time fixed for the transmission of the record, and upon timely payment of the fee, the appeal is docketed. The proposed amendment takes the docketing out of the hands of the appellant. The fee is paid at the time the notice of appeal is filed and the appeal is entered on the docket upon receipt of a copy of the notice of appeal and of the docket entries, which are sent to the court of appeals under the provisions of Rule 3(d). This is designed to give the court of appeals control of its docket at the earliest possible time so that within the limits of its facilities and personnel it can screen cases for appropriately different treatment, expedite the proceedings through prehearing conferences or otherwise, and in general plan more effectively for the prompt disposition of cases.

Subdivision (b). The proposed amendment conforms the provision to the changes in Rule 11.

1986 Amendments

The amendment to Rule 12(a) is technical. No substantive change is intended.

1993 Amendments

Note to new subdivision (b). This amendment is a companion to the amendment of Rule 3(c). The Rule 3(c) amendment allows an attorney who represents more than one party on appeal to "specify" the appellants by general description rather than by naming them individually. The requirement added here is that whenever an attorney files a notice of appeal, the attorney must soon thereafter file a statement indicating all parties represented on the appeal by that attorney. Although the notice of appeal is the jurisdictional document and it must clearly indicate who is bringing the appeal, the representation statement will be helpful especially to the court of appeals in identifying the individual appellants.

The rule allows a court of appeals to require the filing of the representation statement at some time other than specified in the rule so that if a court of appeals requires a docketing statement or appearance form the representation statement may be combined with it.

1998 Amendments

The language of the rule are amended to make the rule more easily understood. In addition to changes made to improve the understanding, the Advisory Committee has changed language to make style and terminology consistent throughout the appellate rules. These changes are intended to by stylistic only.

2009 Amendments

Subdivision (b). The time set in the former rule at 10 days has been revised to 14 days. See the Note to Rule 26.

Rule 12.1. Remand After an Indicative Ruling by the District Court on a Motion for Relief That Is Barred by a Pending Appeal

(a) Notice to the Court of Appeals. If a timely motion is made in the district court for relief that it lacks authority to grant because of an appeal that has been docketed and is pending, the movant must promptly notify the circuit clerk if the district court states either that it would grant the motion or that the motion raises a substantial issue.

(b) Remand After an Indicative Ruling. If the district court states that it would grant the motion or that the motion raises a substantial issue, the court of appeals may remand for further proceedings but retains jurisdiction unless it expressly dismisses the appeal. If the court of appeals remands but retains jurisdiction, the parties must promptly notify the circuit clerk when the district court has decided the motion on remand.

(Added Mar. 26, 2009, eff. Dec. 1, 2009.)

ADVISORY COMMITTEE NOTES

2009 Adoption

This new rule corresponds to Federal Rule of Civil Procedure 62.1, which adopts for any motion that the district court cannot grant because of a pending appeal the practice that most courts follow when a party moves under Civil Rule 60(b) to vacate a judgment that is pending on appeal. After an appeal has been docketed and while it remains pending, the district court cannot grant relief under a rule such as Civil Rule 60(b) without a remand. But it can entertain the motion and deny it, defer consideration, state that it would grant the motion if the court of appeals remands for that purpose, or state that the motion raises a substantial issue. Experienced lawyers often refer to the suggestion for remand as an "indicative ruling." (Appellate Rule 4(a)(4) lists six motions that, if filed within the relevant time limit, suspend the effect of a notice of appeal filed before or after the motion is filed until the last such motion is disposed of. The district court has authority to grant the motion without resorting to the indicative ruling procedure.)

The procedure formalized by Rule 12.1 is helpful when relief is sought from an order that the court cannot reconsider because the order is the subject of a pending appeal. In the criminal context, the Committee anticipates that Rule 12.1 will be used primarily if not exclusively for newly discovered evidence motions under Criminal Rule 33(b)(1) (*see United States v. Cronic*, 466 U.S. 648, 667 n.42 (1984)), reduced sentence motions under Criminal Rule 35(b), and motions under 18 U.S.C. § 3582(c).

Rule 12.1 does not attempt to define the circumstances in which an appeal limits or defeats the district court's authority to act in the face of a pending appeal. The rules that govern the relationship between trial courts and appellate courts may be complex, depending in part on the nature of the order and the source of appeal jurisdiction. Appellate Rule 12.1 applies only when those rules deprive the district court of authority to grant relief without appellate permission.

To ensure proper coordination of proceedings in the district court and in the court of appeals, the movant must notify the circuit clerk if the district court states that it would grant the motion or that the motion raises a substantial issue. The "substantial issue" standard may be illustrated by the following hypothetical: The district court grants summary judgment dismissing a case. While the plaintiff's appeal is pending, the plaintiff moves for relief from the judgment, claiming newly discovered evidence and also possible fraud by the defendant during the discovery process. If the district court reviews the motion and indicates that the motion "raises a substantial issue," the court of appeals may well wish to remand rather than proceed to determine the appeal.

If the district court states that it would grant the motion or that the motion raises a substantial issue, the movant may ask the court of appeals to remand so that the district court can make its final ruling on the motion. In accordance with Rule 47(a)(1), a local rule may prescribe the format for the litigants' notifications and the district court's statement.

Remand is in the court of appeals' discretion. The court of appeals may remand all proceedings, terminating the initial appeal. In the context of postjudgment motions, however, that procedure should be followed only when the appellant has stated clearly its intention to abandon the appeal. The danger is that if the initial appeal is terminated and the district court then denies the requested relief, the time for appealing the initial judgment will have run out and a court might rule that the appellant is limited to appealing the denial of the postjudgment motion. The latter appeal may well not provide the appellant with the opportunity to raise all the challenges that could have been raised on appeal from the underlying judgment. *See, e.g., Browder v. Dir., Dep't of Corrections of Ill.*, 434 U.S. 257, 263 n.7 (1978) ("[A]n appeal from denial of Rule 60(b) relief does not bring up the underlying judgment for review."). The Committee does not endorse the notion that a court of appeals should decide that the initial appeal was abandoned—despite the absence of any clear statement of intent to abandon the appeal—merely because an unlimited remand occurred, but the possibility that a court might take that troubling view underscores the need for caution in delimiting the scope of the remand.

The court of appeals may instead choose to remand for the sole purpose of ruling on the motion while retaining jurisdiction to proceed with the appeal after the district court rules on the motion (if the appeal is not moot at that point and if any party wishes to proceed). This will often be the preferred course in the light of the concerns expressed above. It is also possible that the court of appeals may wish to proceed to hear the appeal even after the district court has granted relief on remand; thus, even when the district court indicates that it would grant relief, the court of appeals may in appropriate circumstances choose a limited rather than unlimited remand.

If the court of appeals remands but retains jurisdiction, subdivision (b) requires the parties to notify the circuit clerk when the district court has decided the motion on remand. This is a joint obligation that is discharged when the required notice is given by any litigant involved in the motion in the district court.

When relief is sought in the district court during the pendency of an appeal, litigants should bear in mind the likelihood that a new or amended notice of appeal will be necessary in order to challenge the district court's disposition of the motion. *See, e.g., Jordan v. Bowen*, 808 F.2d 733, 736–37 (10th Cir. 1987) (viewing district court's response to appellant's motion for indicative ruling as a denial of appellant's request for relief under Rule 60(b), and refusing to review that denial because appellant had failed to take an appeal from the denial); *TAAG Linhas Aereas de Angola v. Transamerica Airlines, Inc.*, 915 F.2d 1351, 1354 (9th Cir. 1990) ("[W]here a 60(b) motion is filed subsequent to the notice of appeal and considered by the district court after a limited remand, an appeal specifically from the ruling on the motion must be taken if the issues raised in that motion are to be considered by the Court of Appeals.").

TITLE III. REVIEW OF A DECISION OF THE UNITED STATES TAX COURT

Rule 13.   Appeals From the Tax Court

(a) Appeal as of Right.

(1) How Obtained; Time for Filing a Notice of Appeal.

(A) An appeal as of right from the United States Tax Court is commenced by filing a notice of appeal with the Tax Court clerk within 90 days after the entry of the Tax Court's decision. At the time of filing, the appellant must furnish the clerk with enough copies of the notice to enable the clerk to comply with Rule 3(d). If one party files a timely notice of appeal, any other party may file a notice of appeal within 120 days after the Tax Court's decision is entered.

(B) If, under Tax Court rules, a party makes a timely motion to vacate or revise the Tax Court's decision, the time to file a notice of appeal runs from the entry of the order disposing of the motion or from the entry of a new decision, whichever is later.

(2) Notice of Appeal; How Filed. The notice of appeal may be filed either at the Tax Court clerk's office in the District of Columbia or by sending it to the clerk. If sent by mail the notice is considered filed on the postmark date, subject to § 7502 of the Internal Revenue Code, as amended, and the applicable regulations.

(3) Contents of the Notice of Appeal; Service; Effect of Filing and Service. Rule 3 prescribes the contents of a notice of appeal, the manner of service, and the effect of its filing and service. Form 2 in the Appendix of Forms is a suggested form of a notice of appeal.

(4) The Record on Appeal; Forwarding; Filing.

(A) Except as otherwise provided under Tax Court rules for the transcript of proceedings, the appeal is governed by the parts of Rules 10, 11, and 12 regarding the record on appeal from a district court, the time and manner of forwarding and filing, and the docketing in the court of appeals.

(B) If an appeal is taken to more than one court of appeals, the original record must be sent to the court named in the first notice of appeal filed. In an appeal to any other court of appeals, the appellant must apply to that other court to make provision for the record.

(b) Appeal by Permission. An appeal by permission is governed by Rule 5.

(As amended Apr. 30, 1979, eff. Aug. 1, 1979; Apr. 29, 1994, eff. Dec. 1, 1994; Apr. 24, 1998, eff. Dec. 1, 1998; Apr. 16, 2013, eff. Dec. 1, 2013; Apr. 25, 2019, eff. Dec. 1, 2019.)

ADVISORY COMMITTEE NOTES

1967 Adoption

Subdivision (a). This subdivision effects two changes in practice respecting review of Tax Court decisions: (1) § 7483 of the Internal Revenue Code, 68A Stat. 891, 26 U.S.C. § 7483, provides that review of a Tax Court decision may be obtained by filing a petition for review. The subdivision provides for review by the filing of the simple and familiar notice of appeal used to obtain review of district court judgments; (2) § 7483, supra, requires that a petition for review be filed within 3 months after a decision is rendered, and provides that if a petition is so filed by one party, any other party may file a petition for review within 4 months after the decision is rendered. In the interest of fixing the time for review with precision, the proposed rule substitutes "90 days" and "120 days" for the statutory "3 months" and "4 months", respectively. The power of the Court to regulate these details of practice is clear. Title 28 U.S.C. § 2072, as amended by the Act of November 6, 1966, 80 Stat. 1323 (1 U.S.Code Cong. & Ad. News, p. 1546 (1966)), authorizes the Court to regulate ". . . practice and procedure in proceedings for the review by the courts of appeals of decisions of the Tax Court of the United States. . . ."

The second paragraph states the settled teaching of the case law. See *Robert Louis Stevenson Apartments, Inc. v. C.I.R.*, 337 F.2d 681, 10 A.L.R.3d 112 (8th Cir., 1964); *Denholm & McKay Co. v. C.I.R.*,

132 F.2d 243 (1st Cir., 1942); *Helvering v. Continental Oil Co.*, 63 App.D.C. 5, 68 F.2d 750 (1934); *Burnet v. Lexington Ice & Coal Co.*, 62 F.2d 906 (4th Cir.1933); *Griffiths v. C.I.R.*, 50 F.2d 782 (7th Cir., 1931).

Subdivision (b). The subdivision incorporates the statutory provision (Title 26, U.S.C., § 7502) that timely mailing is to be treated as timely filing. The statute contains special provisions respecting other than ordinary mailing. If the notice of appeal is sent by registered mail, registration is deemed prima facie evidence that the notice was delivered to the clerk of the Tax Court, and the date of registration is deemed the postmark date. If the notice of appeal is sent by certified mail, the effect of certification with respect to prima facie evidence of delivery and the postmark date depends upon regulations of the Secretary of the Treasury. The effect of a postmark made other than by the United States Post Office likewise depends upon regulations of the Secretary. Current regulations are found in 26 CFR § 301.7502–1.

1979 Amendments

The proposed amendment reflects the change in the title of the Tax Court to "United States Tax Court." See 26 U.S.C. § 7441.

1994 Amendments

Subdivision (a). The amendment requires a party filing a notice of appeal to provide the court with sufficient copies of the notice for service on all other parties.

1998 Amendments

The language and organization of the rule are amended to make the rule more easily understood. In addition to changes made to improve the understanding, the Advisory Committee has changed language to make style and terminology consistent throughout the appellate rules. These changes are intended to by stylistic only.

2013 Amendments

Rules 13 and 14 are amended to address the treatment of permissive interlocutory appeals from the Tax Court under 26 U.S.C. § 7482(a)(2). Rules 13 and 14 do not currently address such appeals; instead, those Rules address only appeals as of right from the Tax Court. The existing Rule 13—governing appeals as of right—is revised and becomes Rule 13(a). New subdivision (b) provides that Rule 5 governs appeals by permission. The definition of district court and district clerk in current subdivision (d)(1) is deleted; definitions are now addressed in Rule 14. The caption of Title III is amended to reflect the broadened application of this Title.

Changes Made After Publication and Comment

No changes were made after publication and comment.

2019 Amendment

The amendment to subdivision (a)(2) will allow an appellant to send a notice of appeal to the Tax Court clerk by means other than mail. Other rules determine when a party must send a notice electronically or non-electronically.

Rule 14.   Applicability of Other Rules to Appeals From the Tax Court

All provisions of these rules, except Rules 4, 6–9, 15–20, and 22–23, apply to appeals from the Tax Court. References in any applicable rule (other than Rule 24(a)) to the district court and district clerk are to be read as referring to the Tax Court and its clerk.

(As amended Apr. 24, 1998, eff. Dec. 1, 1998; Apr. 16, 2013, eff. Dec. 1, 2013.)

ADVISORY COMMITTEE NOTES

1967 Adoption

The proposed rule continues the present uniform practice of the circuits of regulating review of decisions of the Tax Court by the general rules applicable to appeals from judgments of the district courts.

1998 Amendments

The language of the rule are amended to make the rule more easily understood. In addition to changes made to improve the understanding, the Advisory Committee has changed language to make style and terminology consistent throughout the appellate rules. These changes are intended to by stylistic only.

2013 Amendments

Rule 13 currently addresses appeals as of right from the Tax Court, and Rule 14 currently addresses the applicability of the Appellate Rules to such appeals. Rule 13 is amended to add a new subdivision (b) treating permissive interlocutory appeals from the Tax Court under 26 U.S.C. § 7482(a)(2). Rule 14 is amended to address the applicability of the Appellate Rules to both appeals as of right and appeals by permission. Because the latter are governed by Rule 5, that rule is deleted from Rule 14's list of inapplicable provisions. Rule 14 is amended to define the terms "district court" and "district clerk" in applicable rules (excluding Rule 24(a)) to include the Tax Court and its clerk. Rule 24(a) is excluded from this definition because motions to appeal from the Tax Court in forma pauperis are governed by Rule 24(b), not Rule 24(a).

TITLE IV. REVIEW OR ENFORCEMENT OF AN ORDER OF AN ADMINISTRATIVE AGENCY, BOARD, COMMISSION, OR OFFICER

Rule 15.   Review or Enforcement of an Agency Order—How Obtained; Intervention

(a) Petition for Review; Joint Petition.

(1) Review of an agency order is commenced by filing, within the time prescribed by law, a petition for review with the clerk of a court of appeals authorized to review the agency order. If their interests make joinder practicable, two or more persons may join in a petition to the same court to review the same order.

(2) The petition must:

(A) name each party seeking review either in the caption or the body of the petition—using such terms as "et al.," "petitioners," or "respondents" does not effectively name the parties;

(B) name the agency as a respondent (even though not named in the petition, the United States is a respondent if required by statute); and

(C) specify the order or part thereof to be reviewed.

(3) Form 3 in the Appendix of Forms is a suggested form of a petition for review.

(4) In this rule "agency" includes an agency, board, commission, or officer; "petition for review" includes a petition to enjoin, suspend, modify, or otherwise review, or a notice of appeal, whichever form is indicated by the applicable statute.

(b) Application or Cross-Application to Enforce an Order; Answer; Default.

(1) An application to enforce an agency order must be filed with the clerk of a court of appeals authorized to enforce the order. If a petition is filed to review an agency order that the court may enforce, a party opposing the petition may file a cross-application for enforcement.

(2) Within 21 days after the application for enforcement is filed, the respondent must serve on the applicant an answer to the application and file it with the clerk. If the respondent fails to answer in time, the court will enter judgment for the relief requested.

(3) The application must contain a concise statement of the proceedings in which the order was entered, the facts upon which venue is based, and the relief requested.

(c) Service of the Petition or Application.
The circuit clerk must serve a copy of the petition for review, or an application or cross-application to enforce an agency order, on each respondent as prescribed by Rule 3(d), unless a different manner of service is prescribed by statute. At the time of filing, the petitioner must:

(1) serve, or have served, a copy on each party admitted to participate in the agency proceedings, except for the respondents;

(2) file with the clerk a list of those so served; and

(3) give the clerk enough copies of the petition or application to serve each respondent.

(d) Intervention. Unless a statute provides another method, a person who wants to intervene in a proceeding under this rule must file a motion for leave to intervene with the circuit clerk and serve a copy on all parties. The motion—or other notice of intervention authorized by statute—must be filed within 30 days after the petition for review is filed and must contain a concise statement of the interest of the moving party and the grounds for intervention.

(e) Payment of Fees. When filing any separate or joint petition for review in a court of appeals, the petitioner must pay the circuit clerk all required fees.

(As amended Apr. 22, 1993, eff. Dec. 1, 1993; Apr. 24, 1998, eff. Dec. 1, 1998; Mar. 26, 2009, eff. Dec. 1, 2009.)

ADVISORY COMMITTEE NOTES

1967 Adoption

General Note. The power of the Supreme Court to prescribe rules of practice and procedure for the judicial review or enforcement of orders of administrative agencies, boards, commissions, and officers is conferred by 28 U.S.C. § 2072, as amended by the Act of November 6, 1966, § 1, 80 Stat. 1323 (1 U.S.Code Cong. & Ad. News, p. 1546 (1966). Section 11 of the Hobbs Administrative Orders Review Act of 1950, 64 Stat. 1132, reenacted as 28 U.S.C. § 2352 (28 U.S.C.A. § 2352 (Supp.1966)), repealed by the Act of November 6, 1966, § 4, supra, directed the courts of appeals to adopt and promulgate, subject to approval by the Judicial Conference rules governing practice and procedure in proceedings to review the orders of boards, commissions and officers whose orders were made reviewable in the courts of appeals by the Act. Thereafter, the Judicial Conference approved a uniform rule, and that rule, with minor variations, is now in effect in all circuits. Third Circuit Rule 18 [rule 18, U.S.Ct. of App. 3rd Cir.] is a typical circuit rule, and for convenience it is referred to as the uniform rule in the notes which accompany rules under this Title.

Subdivision (a). The uniform rule (see General Note above) requires that the petition for review contain "a concise statement, in barest outline, of the nature of the proceedings as to which relief is sought, the facts upon which venue is based, the grounds upon which relief is sought, and the relief prayed." That language is derived from § 4 of the Hobbs Administrative Orders Review Act of 1950, 64 Stat. 1130, reenacted as 28 U.S.C. § 2344 (28 U.S.C.A. § 2344 (Supp.1966)). A few other statutes also prescribe the content of the petition, but the great majority are silent on the point. The proposed rule supersedes 28 U.S.C. § 2344 and other statutory provisions prescribing the form of the petition for review and permits review to be initiated by the filing of a simple petition similar in form to the notice of appeal used in appeals from judgments of district courts. The more elaborate form of petition for review now required is rarely useful either to the litigants or to the courts. There is no effective, reasonable way of obliging petitioners to come to the real issues before those issues are formulated in the briefs. Other provisions of this subdivision are derived from §§ 1 and 2 of the uniform rule.

Subdivision (b). This subdivision is derived from §§ 3, 4 and 5 of the uniform rule.

Subdivision (c). This subdivision is derived from § 1 of the uniform rule.

Subdivision (d). This subdivision is based upon § 6 of the uniform rule. Statutes occasionally permit intervention by the filing of a notice of intention to intervene. The uniform rule does not fix a time limit for intervention, and the only time limits fixed by statute are the 30-day periods found in the Communications Act Amendments, 1952, § 402(e), 66 Stat. 719, 47 U.S.C. § 402(e), and the Sugar Act of 1948, § 205(d), 61 Stat. 927, 7 U.S.C. § 1115(d).

1993 Amendments

Subdivision (a). The amendment is a companion to the amendment of Rule 3(c). Both Rule 3(c) and Rule 15(a) state that a notice of appeal or petition for review must name the parties seeking appellate review. Rule 3(c), however, provides an attorney who represents more than one party on appeal the flexibility to describe the parties in general terms rather than naming them individually. Rule 15(a) does not allow that flexibility; each petitioner must be named. A petition for review of an agency decision is the first filing in any court and, therefore, is analogous to a complaint in which all parties must be named.

Subdivision (e). The amendment adds subdivision (e). Subdivision (e) parallels Rule 3(e) that requires the payment of fees when filing a notice of appeal. The omission of such a requirement from Rule 15 is an apparent oversight. Five circuits have local rules requiring the payment of such fees, see, e.g., Fifth Cir.Loc.R. 15.1, and Fed.Cir.Loc.R. 15(a)(2).

1998 Amendments

The language and organization of the rule are amended to make the rule more easily understood. In addition to changes made to improve the understanding, the Advisory Committee has changed language to make style and terminology consistent throughout the appellate rules. These changes are intended to by stylistic only.

2009 Amendments

Subdivision (b)(2). The time set in the former rule at 20 days has been revised to 21 days. See the Note to Rule 26.

Rule 15.1. Briefs and Oral Argument in a National Labor Relations Board Proceeding

In either an enforcement or a review proceeding, a party adverse to the National Labor Relations Board proceeds first on briefing and at oral argument, unless the court orders otherwise.

(Added Mar. 10, 1986, eff. July 1, 1986; amended Apr. 24, 1998, eff. Dec. 1, 1998.)

ADVISORY COMMITTEE NOTES

1986 Addition

This rule simply confirms the existing practice in most circuits.

1998 Amendments

The language of the rule are amended to make the rule more easily understood. In addition to changes made to improve the understanding, the Advisory Committee has changed language to make style and terminology consistent throughout the appellate rules. These changes are intended to by stylistic only.

Rule 16. The Record on Review or Enforcement

(a) Composition of the Record. The record on review or enforcement of an agency order consists of:

(1) the order involved;

(2) any findings or report on which it is based; and

(3) the pleadings, evidence, and other parts of the proceedings before the agency.

(b) Omissions From or Misstatements in the Record. The parties may at any time, by stipulation, supply any omission from the record or correct a misstatement, or the court may so direct. If necessary, the court may direct that a supplemental record be prepared and filed.

(As amended Apr. 24, 1998, eff. Dec. 1, 1998.)

ADVISORY COMMITTEE NOTES

1967 Adoption

Subdivision (a) is based upon 28 U.S.C § 2112(b). There is no distinction between the record compiled in the agency proceeding and the record on review; they are one and the same. The record in agency cases is thus the same as that in appeals from the district court—the original papers, transcripts and exhibits in the proceeding below. Subdivision (b) is based upon § 8 of the uniform rule (see General Note following Rule 15).

1998 Amendments

The language and organization of the rule are amended to make the rule more easily understood. In addition to changes made to improve the understanding, the Advisory Committee has changed language to make style and terminology consistent throughout the appellate rules. These changes are intended to by stylistic only.

Rule 17.   Filing the Record

(a) Agency to File; Time for Filing; Notice of Filing. The agency must file the record with the circuit clerk within 40 days after being served with a petition for review, unless the statute authorizing review provides otherwise, or within 40 days after it files an application for enforcement unless the respondent fails to answer or the court orders otherwise. The court may shorten or extend the time to file the record. The clerk must notify all parties of the date when the record is filed.

(b) Filing—What Constitutes.

 (1) The agency must file:

  (A) the original or a certified copy of the entire record or parts designated by the parties; or

  (B) a certified list adequately describing all documents, transcripts of testimony, exhibits, and other material constituting the record, or describing those parts designated by the parties.

 (2) The parties may stipulate in writing that no record or certified list be filed. The date when the stipulation is filed with the circuit clerk is treated as the date when the record is filed.

 (3) The agency must retain any portion of the record not filed with the clerk. All parts of the record retained by the agency are a part of the record on review for all purposes and, if the court or a party so requests, must be sent to the court regardless of any prior stipulation.

(As amended Apr. 24, 1998, eff. Dec. 1, 1998.)

ADVISORY COMMITTEE NOTES

1967 Adoption

Subdivision (a). This subdivision is based upon § 7 of the uniform rule (see General Note following Rule 15). That rule does not prescribe a time for filing the record in enforcement cases. Forty days are allowed in order to avoid useless preparation of the record or certified list in cases where the application for enforcement is not contested.

Subdivision (b). This subdivision is based upon 28 U.S.C. § 2112 and § 7 of the uniform rule. It permits the agency to file either the record itself or a certified list of its contents. It also permits the parties to stipulate against transmission of designated parts of the record without the fear that an inadvertent stipulation may "diminish" the record. Finally, the parties may, in cases where consultation of the record is unnecessary, stipulate that neither the record nor a certified list of its contents be filed.

1998 Amendments

The language and organization of the rule are amended to make the rule more easily understood. In addition to changes made to improve the understanding, the Advisory Committee has changed language to make style and terminology consistent throughout the appellate rules. These changes are intended to by stylistic only; a substantive change is made, however, in subdivision (b).

Subdivision (b). The current rule provides that when a court of appeals is asked to review or enforce an agency order, the agency must file either "the entire record or such parts thereof as the parties may designate by stipulation filed with the agency" or a certified list describing the documents, transcripts, exhibits, and other material constituting the record. If the agency is not filing a certified list, the current rule requires the agency to file the entire record unless the parties file a "stipulation" designating only parts of the record. Such a "stipulation" presumably requires agreement of the parties as to the parts to be filed. The amended language in subparagraph (b)(1)(A) permits the filing of less than the entire record even when the parties do not agree as to which parts should be filed. Each party can designate the parts that it wants filed; the agency can then forward the parts designated by each party. In contrast, paragraph (b)(2) continues to require stipulation, that is agreement of the parties, that the agency need not file either the record or a certified list.

Rule 18.   Stay Pending Review

(a) Motion for a Stay.

(1) Initial Motion Before the Agency. A petitioner must ordinarily move first before the agency for a stay pending review of its decision or order.

(2) Motion in the Court of Appeals. A motion for a stay may be made to the court of appeals or one of its judges.

(A) The motion must:

(i)   show that moving first before the agency would be impracticable; or

(ii)   state that, a motion having been made, the agency denied the motion or failed to afford the relief requested and state any reasons given by the agency for its action.

(B) The motion must also include:

(i)   the reasons for granting the relief requested and the facts relied on;

(ii)   originals or copies of affidavits or other sworn statements supporting facts subject to dispute; and

(iii) relevant parts of the record.

(C) The moving party must give reasonable notice of the motion to all parties.

(D) The motion must be filed with the circuit clerk and normally will be considered by a panel of the court. But in an exceptional case in which time requirements make that procedure impracticable, the motion may be made to and considered by a single judge.

(b) Bond. The court may condition relief on the filing of a bond or other appropriate security.

(As amended Apr. 24, 1998, eff. Dec. 1, 1998.)

ADVISORY COMMITTEE NOTES

1967 Adoption

While this rule has no counterpart in present rules regulating review of agency proceedings, it merely assimilates the procedure for obtaining stays in agency proceedings with that for obtaining stays in appeals from the district courts. The same considerations which justify the requirement of an initial application to the district court for a stay pending appeal support the requirement of an initial application to the agency pending review. See Note accompanying Rule 8. Title 5, U.S.C. § 705 (5 U.S.C.A. § 705 (1966 Pamphlet)), confers general authority on both agencies and reviewing courts to stay agency action pending review. Many of the statutes authorizing review of agency action by the courts of appeals deal with the question of stays, and at least one, the Act of June 15, 1936, 49 Stat. 1499 (7 U.S.C. § 10a), prohibits a stay pending review. The proposed rule in nowise affects such statutory provisions respecting stays. By its terms, it simply indicates the procedure to be followed when a stay is sought.

1998 Amendments

The language and organization of the rule are amended to make the rule more easily understood. In addition to changes made to improve the understanding, the Advisory Committee has changed language to make style and terminology consistent throughout the appellate rules. These changes are intended to by stylistic only.

Rule 19. Settlement of a Judgment Enforcing an Agency Order in Part

When the court files an opinion directing entry of judgment enforcing the agency's order in part, the agency must within 14 days file with the clerk and serve on each other party a proposed judgment conforming to the opinion. A party who disagrees with the agency's proposed judgment must within 10 days file with the clerk and serve the agency with a proposed judgment that the party believes conforms to the opinion. The court will settle the judgment and direct entry without further hearing or argument.

(As amended Mar. 10, 1986, eff. July 1, 1986; Apr. 24, 1998, eff. Dec. 1, 1998; Mar. 26, 2009, eff. Dec. 1, 2009.)

ADVISORY COMMITTEE NOTES

1967 Adoption

This is § 12 of the uniform rule (see General Note following Rule 15) with changes in phraseology.

1986 Amendment

The deletion of the words "in whole or" is designed to eliminate delay in the issuance of a judgment when the court of appeals has either enforced completely the order of an agency or denied completely such enforcement. In such a clear-cut situation, it serves no useful purpose to delay the issuance of the judgment until a proposed judgment is submitted by the agency and reviewed by the respondent. This change conforms the Rule to the existing practice in most circuits. Other amendments are technical and no substantive change is intended.

1998 Amendments

The language of the rule are amended to make the rule more easily understood. In addition to changes made to improve the understanding, the Advisory Committee has changed language to make style and terminology consistent throughout the appellate rules. These changes are intended to by stylistic only.

2009 Amendments

Rule 19 formerly required a party who disagreed with the agency's proposed judgment to file a proposed judgment "within 7 days." Under former Rule 26(a), "7 days" always meant at least 9 days and could mean as many as 11 or even 13 days. Under current Rule 26(a), intermediate weekends and holidays are counted. Changing the period from 7 to 10 days offsets the change in computation approach. See the Note to Rule 26.

Rule 20. Applicability of Rules to the Review or Enforcement of an Agency Order

All provisions of these rules, except Rules 3–14 and 22–23, apply to the review or enforcement of an agency order. In these rules, "appellant" includes a petitioner or applicant, and "appellee" includes a respondent.

(As amended Apr. 24, 1998, eff. Dec. 1, 1998.)

ADVISORY COMMITTEE NOTES

1967 Adoption

The proposed rule continues the present uniform practice of the circuits of regulating agency review or enforcement proceedings by the general rules applicable to appeals from judgments of the district courts.

1998 Amendments

The language of the rule are amended to make the rule more easily understood. In addition to changes made to improve the understanding, the Advisory Committee has changed language to make style and terminology consistent throughout the appellate rules. These changes are intended to by stylistic only.

TITLE V. EXTRAORDINARY WRITS

Rule 21.   Writs of Mandamus and Prohibition, and Other Extraordinary Writs

(a) Mandamus or Prohibition to a Court: Petition, Filing, Service, and Docketing.

(1) A party petitioning for a writ of mandamus or prohibition directed to a court must file the petition with the circuit clerk and serve it on all parties to the proceeding in the trial court. The party must also provide a copy to the trial-court judge. All parties to the proceeding in the trial court other than the petitioner are respondents for all purposes.

(2)(A) The petition must be titled "In re [name of petitioner]."

    (B) The petition must state:

        (i)   the relief sought;

        (ii)   the issues presented;

        (iii) the facts necessary to understand the issue presented by the petition; and

        (iv) the reasons why the writ should issue.

    (C)   The petition must include a copy of any order or opinion or parts of the record that may be essential to understand the matters set forth in the petition.

(3)   Upon receiving the prescribed docket fee, the clerk must docket the petition and submit it to the court.

(b) Denial; Order Directing Answer; Briefs; Precedence.

(1)   The court may deny the petition without an answer. Otherwise, it must order the respondent, if any, to answer within a fixed time.

(2)   The clerk must serve the order to respond on all persons directed to respond.

(3)   Two or more respondents may answer jointly.

(4)   The court of appeals may invite or order the trial-court judge to address the petition or may invite an amicus curiae to do so. The trial-court judge may request permission to address the petition but may not do so unless invited or ordered to do so by the court of appeals.

(5)   If briefing or oral argument is required, the clerk must advise the parties, and when appropriate, the trial-court judge or amicus curiae.

(6)   The proceeding must be given preference over ordinary civil cases.

(7)   The circuit clerk must send a copy of the final disposition to the trial-court judge.

(c) Other Extraordinary Writs. An application for an extraordinary writ other than one provided for in Rule 21(a) must be made by filing a petition with the circuit clerk and serving it on the respondents. Proceedings on the application must conform, so far as is practicable, to the procedures prescribed in Rule 21(a) and (b).

(d) Form of Papers; Number of Copies; Length Limits. All papers must conform to Rule 32(c)(2). An original and 3 copies must be filed unless the court requires the filing of a different number by local rule or by order in a particular case. Except by the court's permission, and excluding the accompanying documents required by Rule 21(a)(2)(C):

(1)   a paper produced using a computer must not exceed 7,800 words; and

(2)   a handwritten or typewritten paper must not exceed 30 pages.

(As amended Apr. 29, 1994, eff. Dec. 1, 1994; Apr. 23, 1996, eff. Dec. 1, 1996; Apr. 24, 1998, eff. Dec. 1, 1998; Apr. 29, 2002, eff. Dec. 1, 2002; Apr. 28, 2016; eff. Dec. 1, 2016; Apr. 25, 2019, eff. Dec. 1, 2019.)

ADVISORY COMMITTEE NOTES
1967 Adoption

The authority of courts of appeals to issue extraordinary writs is derived from 28 U.S.C. § 1651. Subdivisions (a) and (b) regulate in detail the procedure surrounding the writs most commonly sought—mandamus or prohibition directed to a judge or judges. Those subdivisions are based upon Supreme Court Rule 31, with certain changes which reflect the uniform practice among the circuits (Seventh Circuit Rule 19 is a typical circuit rule). Subdivision (c) sets out a very general procedure to be followed in applications for the variety of other writs which may be issued under the authority of 28 U.S.C. § 1651.

1994 Amendments

Subdivision (d). The amendment makes it clear that a court may require a different number of copies either by rule or by order in an individual case. The number of copies of any document that a court of appeals needs varies depending upon the way in which the court conducts business. The internal operation of the courts of appeals necessarily varies from circuit to circuit because of differences in the number of judges, the geographic area included within the circuit, and other such factors. Uniformity could be achieved only by setting the number of copies artificially high so that parties in all circuits file enough copies to satisfy the needs of the courts requiring the greatest number. Rather than do that, the Committee decided to make it clear that local rules may require a greater or lesser number of copies and that, if the circumstances of a particular case indicate the need for a different number of copies in that case, the court may so order.

1996 Amendments

In most instances, a writ of mandamus or prohibition is not actually directed to a judge in any more personal way than is an order reversing a court's judgment. Most often a petition for a writ of mandamus seeks review of the intrinsic merits of a judge's action and is in reality an adversary proceeding between the parties. See, *e.g., Walker v. Columbia Broadcasting System, Inc.,* 443 F.2d 33 (7th Cir.1971). In order to change the tone of the rule and of mandamus proceedings generally, the rule is amended so that the judge is not treated as a respondent. The caption and subdivision (a) are amended by deleting the reference to the writs as being "directed to a judge or judges."

Subdivision (a). Subdivision (a) applies to writs of mandamus or prohibition directed to a court, but it is amended so that a petition for a writ of mandamus or prohibition does not bear the name of the judge. The amendments to subdivision (a) speak, however, about mandamus or prohibition "directed to a court." This language is inserted to distinguish subdivision (a) from subdivision (c). Subdivision (c) governs all other extraordinary writs, including a writ of mandamus or prohibition directed to an administrative agency rather than to a court and a writ of habeas corpus.

The amendments require the petitioner to provide a copy of the petition to the trial court judge. This will alert the judge to the filing of the petition. This is necessary because the trial court judge is not treated as a respondent and, as a result, is not served. A companion amendment is made in subdivision (b). It requires the circuit clerk to send a copy of the disposition of the petition to the trial court judge.

Subdivision (b). The amendment provides that even if relief is requested of a particular judge, although the judge may request permission to respond, the judge may not do so unless the court invites or orders a response.

The court of appeals ordinarily will be adequately informed not only by the opinions or statements made by the trial court judge contemporaneously with the entry of the challenged order but also by the arguments made on behalf of the party opposing the relief. The latter does not create an attorney-client relationship between the party's attorney and the judge whose action is challenged, nor does it give rise to any right to compensation from the judge.

If the court of appeals desires to hear from the trial court judge, however, the court may invite or order the judge to respond. In some instances, especially those involving court administration or the failure of a judge to act, it may be that no one other than the judge can provide a thorough explanation of the matters at issue. Because it is ordinarily undesirable to place the trial court judge, even temporarily, in an adversarial posture with a litigant, the rule permits a court of appeals to invite an *amicus curiae* to provide a response to the petition. In those instances in which the respondent does not oppose issuance of the writ or does not have sufficient perspective on the issue to provide an adequate response, participation of an *amicus* may avoid the need for the trial judge to participate.

Subdivision (c). The changes are stylistic only. No substantive changes are intended.

1998 Amendments

The language and organization of the rule are amended to make the rule more easily understood. In addition to changes made to improve the understanding, the Advisory Committee has changed language to make style and terminology consistent throughout the appellate rules. These changes are intended to by stylistic only.

2002 Amendments

Subdivision (d). A petition for a writ of mandamus or prohibition, an application for another extraordinary writ, and an answer to such a petition or application are all "other papers" for purposes of Rule 32(c)(2), and all of the requirements of Rule 32(a) apply to those papers, except as provided in Rule 32(c)(2). During the 1998 restyling of the Federal Rules of Appellate Procedure, Rule 21(d) was inadvertently changed to suggest that only the requirements of Rule 32(a)(1) apply to such papers. Rule 21(d) has been amended to correct that error.

Rule 21(d) has been further amended to limit the length of papers filed under Rule 21.

Changes Made After Publication and Comments. No changes were made to the text of the proposed amendment or to the Committee Note, except that the page limit was increased from 20 pages to 30 pages. The Committee was persuaded by some commentators that petitions for extraordinary writs closely resemble principal briefs on the merits and should be allotted more than 20 pages.

2016 Amendments

The page limits previously employed in Rules 5, 21, 27, 35, and 40 have been largely overtaken by changes in technology. For papers produced using a computer, those page limits are now replaced by word limits. The word limits were derived from the current page limits using the assumption that one page is equivalent to 260 words. Papers produced using a computer must include the certificate of compliance required by Rule 32(g); Form 6 in the Appendix of Forms suffices to meet that requirement. Page limits are retained for papers prepared without the aid of a computer (i.e., handwritten or typewritten papers). For both the word limit and the page limit, the calculation excludes the accompanying documents required by Rule 21(a)(2)(C) and any items listed in Rule 32(f).

Changes Made After Publication and Comments

The Committee deleted the proposed line limit and revised the proposed word limit from 7,500 words to 7,800 words. The Committee also made conforming changes to the Committee Note and style changes to the Rule text.

2019 Amendments

The term "proof of service" in subdivisions (a)(1) and (c) is deleted to reflect amendments to Rule 25(d) that eliminate the requirement of a proof of service when service is completed using a court's electronic filing system.

TITLE VI. HABEAS CORPUS; PROCEEDINGS IN FORMA PAUPERIS

Rule 22.   Habeas Corpus and Section 2255 Proceedings

(a) Application for the Original Writ. An application for a writ of habeas corpus must be made to the appropriate district court. If made to a circuit judge, the application must be transferred to the appropriate district court. If a district court denies an application made or transferred to it, renewal of the application before a circuit judge is not permitted. The applicant may, under 28 U.S.C. § 2253, appeal to the court of appeals from the district court's order denying the application.

(b) Certificate of Appealability.

(1)   In a habeas corpus proceeding in which the detention complained of arises from process issued by a state court, or in a 28 U.S.C. § 2255 proceeding, the applicant cannot take an appeal unless a circuit justice or a circuit or district judge issues a certificate of appealability under 28 U.S.C. § 2253(c). If an applicant files a notice of appeal, the district clerk must send to the court of appeals the certificate (if any) and the statement described in Rule 11(a) of the Rules Governing Proceedings Under 28 U.S.C. § 2254 or § 2255 (if any), along with the notice of appeal and the file of the district-court proceedings. If the district judge has denied the certificate, the applicant may request a circuit judge to issue it.

(2)   A request addressed to the court of appeals may be considered by a circuit judge or judges, as the court prescribes. If no express request for a certificate is filed, the notice of appeal constitutes a request addressed to the judges of the court of appeals.

(3)   A certificate of appealability is not required when a state or its representative or the United States or its representative appeals.

(As amended Pub.L. 104–132, Title I, § 103, Apr. 24, 1996, 110 Stat. 1218; Apr. 24, 1998, eff. Dec. 1, 1998; Mar. 26, 2009, eff. Dec. 1, 2009.)

ADVISORY COMMITTEE NOTES

1967 Adoption

Subdivision (a). Title 28 U.S.C. § 2241(a) authorizes circuit judges to issue the writ of habeas corpus. Section 2241(b) [§ 2241(b) of this title], however, authorizes a circuit judge to decline to entertain an application and to transfer it to the appropriate district court, and this is the usual practice. The first two sentences merely make present practice explicit. Title 28 U.S.C. § 2253 seems clearly to contemplate that once an application is presented to a district judge and is denied by him, the remedy is an appeal from the order of denial. But the language of 28 U.S.C. § 2241 seems to authorize a second original application to a circuit judge following a denial by a district judge. *In re Gersing*, 79 U.S.App.D.[C.] 245, 145 F.2d 481 (D.C.Cir., 1944) and *Chapman v. Teets*, 241 F.2d 186 (9th Cir., 1957) acknowledge the availability of such a procedure. But the procedure is ordinarily a waste of time for all involved, and the final sentence attempts to discourage it.

A court of appeals has no jurisdiction as a court to grant an original writ of habeas corpus, and courts of appeals have dismissed applications addressed to them. *Loum v. Alvis*, 263 F.2d 836 (6th Cir., 1959); *In re Berry*, 221 F.2d 798 (9th Cir., 1955); *Posey v. Dowd*, 134 F.2d 613 (7th Cir., 1943). The fairer and more expeditious practice is for the court of appeals to regard an application addressed to it as being addressed to one of its members, and to transfer the application to the appropriate district court in accordance with the provisions of this rule. Perhaps such a disposition is required by the rationale of *In re Burwell*, 350 U.S. 521, 76 S.Ct. 539, 100 L.Ed. 666 (1956).

Subdivision (b). Title 28 U.S.C. § 2253 provides that an appeal may not be taken in a habeas corpus proceeding where confinement is under a judgment of a state court unless the judge who rendered the order in the habeas corpus proceeding, or a circuit justice or judge, issues a certificate of probable cause. In the interest of insuring that the matter of the certificate will not be overlooked and that, if the certificate is denied, the reasons for denial in the first instance will be available on any subsequent application, the proposed rule requires the district judge to issue the certificate or to state reasons for its denial.

While 28 U.S.C. § 2253 does not authorize the court of appeals as a court to grant a certificate of probable cause, *In re Burwell*, 350 U.S. 521, 76 S.Ct. 539, 100 L.Ed. 666 (1956) makes it clear that a court of appeals may not decline to consider a request for the certificate addressed to it as a court but must regard the request as made to the judges thereof. The fourth sentence incorporates the Burwell rule.

Although 28 U.S.C. § 2253 appears to require a certificate of probable cause even when an appeal is taken by a state or its representative, the legislative history strongly suggests that the intention of Congress was to require a certificate only in the case in which an appeal is taken by an applicant for the writ. See *United States ex rel. Tillery v. Cavell*, 294 F.2d 12 (3d Cir., 1960). Four of the five circuits which have ruled on the point have so interpreted § 2253. *United States ex rel. Tillery v. Cavell*, supra; *Buder v. Bell*, 306 F.2d

71 (6th Cir., 1962); *United States ex rel. Calhoun v. Pate*, 341 F.2d 885 (7th Cir., 1965); *State of Texas v. Graves*, 352 F.2d 514 (5th Cir., 1965). Cf. *United States ex rel. Carrol v. LaVallee*, 342 F.2d 641 (2d Cir., 1965). The final sentence makes it clear that a certificate of probable cause is not required of a state or its representative.

1998 Amendments

The language and organization of the rule are amended to make the rule more easily understood. In addition to changes made to improve the understanding, the Advisory Committee has changed language to make style and terminology consistent throughout the appellate rules. These changes are intended to by stylistic only; in this rule, however, substantive changes are made in paragraphs (b)(1) and (b)(3).

Subdivision (b), paragraph (1). Two substantive changes are made in this paragraph. First, the paragraph is made applicable to 28 U.S.C. § 2255 proceedings. This brings the rule into conformity with 28 U.S.C. § 2253 as amended by the Antiterrorism and Effective Death Penalty Act of 1996, Pub.L. No. 104–132. Second, the rule states that a certificate of appealability may be issued by a "circuit justice or a circuit or district judge." That language adds a reference to the circuit justice which also brings the rule into conformity with section 2253. The language continues to state that in addition to the circuit justice, both a circuit and a district judge may issue a certificate of appealability. The language of section 2253 is ambiguous; it states that a certificate of appealability may be issued by "a circuit justice or judge." Since the enactment of the Antiterrorism and Effective Death Penalty Act, three circuits have held that both district and circuit judges, as well as the circuit justice, may issue a certificate of appealability. *Else v. Johnson*, 104 F.3d 82 (5th Cir. 1997); *Lyons v. Ohio Adult Parole Authority*, 105 F.3d 1063 (6th Cir. 1997); and *Hunter v. United States*, 101 F.3d 1565 (11th Cir. 1996). The approach taken by the rule is consistent with those decisions.

Subdivision (b), paragraph (3). The Antiterrorism and Effective Death Penalty Act of 1996, Pub.L. No. 104–132, amended 28 U.S.C. § 2253 to make it applicable to § 2255 proceedings. Accordingly, paragraph (3) is amended to provide that when the United States or its representative appeals, a certificate of appealability is not required.

2009 Amendments

Subdivision (b)(1). The requirement that the district judge who rendered the judgment either issue a certificate of appealability or state why a certificate should not issue has been deleted from subdivision (b)(1). Rule 11(a) of the Rules Governing Proceedings under 28 U.S.C. § 2254 or § 2255 now delineates the relevant requirement. When an applicant has filed a notice of appeal, the district clerk must transmit the record to the court of appeals; if the district judge has issued a certificate of appealability, the district clerk must include in this transmission the certificate and the statement of reasons for grant of the certificate.

Rule 23.   Custody or Release of a Prisoner in a Habeas Corpus Proceeding

(a) Transfer of Custody Pending Review. Pending review of a decision in a habeas corpus proceeding commenced before a court, justice, or judge of the United States for the release of a prisoner, the person having custody of the prisoner must not transfer custody to another unless a transfer is directed in accordance with this rule. When, upon application, a custodian shows the need for a transfer, the court, justice, or judge rendering the decision under review may authorize the transfer and substitute the successor custodian as a party.

(b) Detention or Release Pending Review of Decision Not to Release. While a decision not to release a prisoner is under review, the court or judge rendering the decision, or the court of appeals, or the Supreme Court, or a judge or justice of either court, may order that the prisoner be:

    (1)   detained in the custody from which release is sought;

    (2)   detained in other appropriate custody; or

    (3)   released on personal recognizance, with or without surety.

(c) Release Pending Review of Decision Ordering Release. While a decision ordering the release of a prisoner is under review, the prisoner must—unless the court or judge rendering the decision, or the court of appeals, or the Supreme Court, or a judge or justice of either court orders otherwise—be released on personal recognizance, with or without surety.

(d) Modification of the Initial Order on Custody. An initial order governing the prisoner's custody or release, including any recognizance or surety, continues in effect pending review unless for special reasons shown to the court of appeals or the Supreme Court, or to a judge or justice of either court, the order is modified or an independent order regarding custody, release, or surety is issued.

(As amended Mar. 10, 1986, eff. July 1, 1986; Apr. 24, 1998, eff. Dec. 1, 1998.)

ADVISORY COMMITTEE NOTES

1967 Adoption

The rule is the same as Supreme Court Rule 49 as amended on June 12, 1967, effective October 2, 1967.

1986 Amendment

The amendments to Rules 23(b) and (c) are technical. No substantive change is intended.

1998 Amendments

The language and organization of the rule are amended to make the rule more easily understood. In addition to changes made to improve the understanding, the Advisory Committee has changed language to make style and terminology consistent throughout the appellate rules. These changes are intended to by stylistic only.

Subdivision (d). The current rule states that the initial order governing custody or release "shall govern review" in the court of appeals. The amended language says that the initial order generally "continues in effect" pending review.

When Rule 23 was adopted it used the same language as Supreme Court Rule 49, which then governed custody of prisoners in habeas corpus proceedings. The "shall govern review" language was drawn from the Supreme Court Rule. The Supreme Court has since amended its rule, now Rule 36, to say that the initial order "shall continue in effect" unless for reasons shown it is modified or a new order is entered. Rule 23 is amended to similarly state that the initial order "continues in effect." The new language is clearer. It removes the possible implication that the initial order created law of the case, a strange notion to attach to an order regarding custody or release.

Rule 24.   Proceeding In Forma Pauperis

(a) Leave to Proceed In Forma Pauperis.

(1) Motion in the District Court. Except as stated in Rule 24(a)(3), a party to a district-court action who desires to appeal in forma pauperis must file a motion in the district court. The party must attach an affidavit that:

(A) shows in the detail prescribed by Form 4 of the Appendix of Forms the party's inability to pay or to give security for fees and costs;

(B) claims an entitlement to redress; and

(C) states the issues that the party intends to present on appeal.

(2) Action on the Motion. If the district court grants the motion, the party may proceed on appeal without prepaying or giving security for fees and costs, unless a statute provides otherwise. If the district court denies the motion, it must state its reasons in writing.

(3) Prior Approval. A party who was permitted to proceed in forma pauperis in the district-court action, or who was determined to be financially unable to obtain an adequate defense in a criminal case, may proceed on appeal in forma pauperis without further authorization, unless:

(A) the district court—before or after the notice of appeal is filed—certifies that the appeal is not taken in good faith or finds that the party is not otherwise entitled to proceed in forma pauperis and states in writing its reasons for the certification or finding; or

(B) a statute provides otherwise.

(4) Notice of District Court's Denial. The district clerk must immediately notify the parties and the court of appeals when the district court does any of the following:

(A) denies a motion to proceed on appeal in forma pauperis;

(B) certifies that the appeal is not taken in good faith; or

(C) finds that the party is not otherwise entitled to proceed in forma pauperis.

(5) Motion in the Court of Appeals. A party may file a motion to proceed on appeal in forma pauperis in the court of appeals within 30 days after service of the notice prescribed in Rule 24(a)(4). The motion must include a copy of the affidavit filed in the district court and the district court's statement of reasons for its action. If no affidavit was filed in the district court, the party must include the affidavit prescribed by Rule 24(a)(1).

(b) Leave to Proceed In Forma Pauperis on Appeal from the United States Tax Court or on Appeal or Review of an Administrative-Agency Proceeding. A party may file in the court of appeals a motion for leave to proceed on appeal in forma pauperis with an affidavit prescribed by Rule 24(a)(1):

(1) in an appeal from the United States Tax Court; and

(2) when an appeal or review of a proceeding before an administrative agency, board, commission, or officer proceeds directly in the court of appeals.

(c) Leave to Use Original Record. A party allowed to proceed on appeal in forma pauperis may request that the appeal be heard on the original record without reproducing any part.

(As amended Apr. 30, 1979, eff. Aug. 1, 1979; Mar. 10, 1986, eff. July 1, 1986; Apr. 24, 1998, eff. Dec. 1, 1998; Apr. 29, 2002, eff. Dec. 1, 2002; Apr. 16, 2013, eff. Dec. 1, 2013.)

ADVISORY COMMITTEE NOTES

1967 Adoption

Subdivision (a). Authority to allow prosecution of an appeal in forma pauperis is vested in "[a]ny court of the United States" by 28 U.S.C. § 1915(a). The second paragraph of § 1915(a) seems to contemplate initial application to the district court for permission to proceed in forma pauperis, and although the circuit rules are generally silent on the question, the case law requires initial application to the district court. *Hayes v. United States*, 258 F.2d 400 (5th Cir., 1958), cert. den. 358 U.S. 856, 79 S.Ct. 87, 3 L.Ed.2d 89 (1958); *Elkins v. United States*, 250 F.2d 145 (9th Cir., 1957) see 364 U.S. 206, 80 S.Ct. 1437, 4 L.Ed.2d 1669 (1960); *United States v. Farley*, 238 F.2d 575 (2d Cir., 1956) see 354 U.S. 521, 77 S.Ct. 1371, 1 L.Ed.2d 1529 (1957). D.C.Cir. Rule 41(a) requires initial application to the district court. The content of the affidavit follows the language of the statute; the requirement of a statement of the issues comprehends the statutory requirement of a statement of "the nature of the . . . appeal. . . ." The second sentence is in accord with the decision in *McGann v. United States*, 362 U.S. 309, 80 S.Ct. 725, 4 L.Ed.2d 734 (1960). The requirement contained in the third sentence has no counterpart in present circuit rules, but it has been imposed by decision in at least two circuits. *Ragan v. Cox*, 305 F.2d 58 (10th Cir., 1962); *United States ex rel. Breedlove v. Dowd*, 269 F.2d 693 (7th Cir., 1959).

The second paragraph permits one whose indigency has been previously determined by the district court to proceed on appeal in forma pauperis without the necessity of a redetermination of indigency, while reserving to the district court its statutory authority to certify that the appeal is not taken in good faith, 28 U.S.C. § 1915(a), and permitting an inquiry into whether the circumstances of the party who was originally entitled to proceed in forma pauperis have changed during the course of the litigation. Cf. Sixth Circuit Rule 26 [rule 26, U.S.Ct. of App. 6th Cir.].

The final paragraph establishes a subsequent motion in the court of appeals, rather than an appeal from the order of denial or from the certification of lack of good faith, as the proper procedure for calling in question the correctness of the action of the district court. The simple and expeditious motion procedure seems clearly preferable to an appeal. This paragraph applies only to applications for leave to appeal in forma pauperis. The order of a district court refusing leave to initiate an action in the district court in forma pauperis is reviewable on appeal. See *Roberts v. United States District Court*, 339 U.S. 844, 70 S.Ct. 954, 94 L.Ed. 1326 (1950).

Subdivision (b). Authority to allow prosecution in forma pauperis is vested only in a "court of the United States" (see Note to subdivision (a), above). Thus in proceedings brought directly in a court of appeals to review decisions of agencies or of the Tax Court, authority to proceed in forma pauperis should be sought in the court of appeals. If initial review of agency action is had in a district court, an application to appeal to a court of appeals in forma pauperis from the judgment of the district court is governed by the provisions of subdivision (a).

1979 Amendment

The proposed amendment reflects the change in the title of the Tax Court to "United States Tax Court." See 26 U.S.C. § 7441.

1986 Amendment

The amendments to Rule 24(a) are technical. No substantive change is intended.

1998 Amendments

The language and organization of the rule are amended to make the rule more easily understood. In addition to changes made to improve the understanding, the Advisory Committee has changed language to make style and terminology consistent throughout the appellate rules. These changes are intended to by stylistic only. The Advisory Committee deletes the language in subdivision (c) authorizing a party proceeding in forma pauperis to file papers in typewritten form because the authorization is unnecessary. The rules permit all parties to file typewritten documents.

2002 Amendments

Subdivision (a)(2). Section 804 of the Prison Litigation Reform Act of 1995 ("PLRA") amended 28 U.S.C. § 1915 to require that prisoners who bring civil actions or appeals from civil actions must "pay the full amount of a filing fee." 28 U.S.C. § 1915(b)(1). Prisoners who are unable to pay the full amount of the filing fee at the time that their actions or appeals are filed are generally required to pay part of the fee and then to pay the remainder of the fee in installments. 28 U.S.C. § 1915(b). By contrast, Rule 24(a)(2) has provided that, after the district court grants a litigant's motion to proceed on appeal in forma pauperis, the litigant may proceed "without prepaying or giving security for fees and costs." Thus, the PLRA and Rule 24(a)(2) appear to be in conflict.

Rule 24(a)(2) has been amended to resolve this conflict. Recognizing that future legislation regarding prisoner litigation is likely, the Committee has not attempted to incorporate into Rule 24 all of the requirements of the current version of 28 U.S.C. § 1915. Rather, the Committee has amended Rule 24(a)(2) to clarify that the rule is not meant to conflict with anything required by the PLRA or any other statute.

Subdivision (a)(3). Rule 24(a)(3) has also been amended to eliminate an apparent conflict with the PLRA. Rule 24(a)(3) has provided that a party who was permitted to proceed in forma pauperis in the district court may continue to proceed in forma pauperis in the court of appeals without further authorization, subject to certain conditions. The PLRA, by contrast, provides that a prisoner who was permitted to proceed in forma pauperis in the district court and who wishes to continue to proceed in forma pauperis on appeal may not do so "automatically," but must seek permission. *See, e.g., Morgan v. Haro*, 112 F.3d 788, 789 (5th Cir. 1997) ("A prisoner who seeks to proceed IFP on appeal must obtain leave to so proceed despite proceeding IFP in the district court.").

Rule 24(a)(3) has been amended to resolve this conflict. Again, recognizing that future legislation regarding prisoner litigation is likely, the Committee has not attempted to incorporate into Rule 24 all of the requirements of the current version of 28 U.S.C. § 1915. Rather, the Committee has amended Rule

24(a)(3) to clarify that the rule is not meant to conflict with anything required by the PLRA or any other statute.

Changes Made After Publication and Comments. No changes were made to the text of the proposed amendment or to the Committee Note, except that "a statute provides otherwise" was substituted in place of "the law requires otherwise" in the text of the rule and conforming changes (as well as a couple of minor stylistic changes) were made to the Committee Note.

2013 Amendments

Rule 24(b) currently refers to review of proceedings "before an administrative agency, board, commission, or officer (including for the purpose of this rule the United States Tax Court)." Experience suggests that Rule 24(b) contributes to confusion by fostering the impression that the Tax Court is an executive branch agency rather than a court. (As a general example of that confusion, appellate courts have returned Tax Court records to the Internal Revenue Service, believing the Tax Court to be part of that agency.) To remove this possible source of confusion, the quoted parenthetical is deleted from subdivision (b) and appeals from the Tax Court are separately listed in subdivision (b)'s heading and in new subdivision (b)(1).

Changes Made After Publication and Comment

No changes were made after publication and comment.

TITLE VII. GENERAL PROVISIONS

Rule 25.   Filing and Service

(a) Filing.

(1) Filing with the Clerk. A paper required or permitted to be filed in a court of appeals must be filed with the clerk.

(2) Filing: Method and Timeliness.

(A) Nonelectronic Filing.

(i) In General. For a paper not filed electronically, filing may be accomplished by mail addressed to the clerk, but filing is not timely unless the clerk receives the papers within the time fixed for filing.

(ii) A Brief or Appendix. A brief or appendix not filed electronically is timely filed, however, if on or before the last day for filing, it is:

- mailed to the clerk by first-class mail, or other class of mail that is at least as expeditious, postage prepaid; or

- dispatched to a third-party commercial carrier for delivery to the clerk within 3 days.

(iii) Inmate Filing. If an institution has a system designed for legal mail, an inmate confined there must use that system to receive the benefit of this Rule 25(a)(2)(A)(iii). A paper not filed electronically by an inmate is timely if it is deposited in the institution's internal mail system on or before the last day for filing and:

- it is accompanied by: a declaration in compliance with 28 U.S.C. § 1746—or a notarized statement—setting out the date of deposit and stating that first-class postage is being prepaid; or evidence (such as a postmark or date stamp) showing that the paper was so deposited and that postage was prepaid; or

- the court of appeals exercises its discretion to permit the later filing of a declaration or notarized statement that satisfies Rule 25(a)(2)(A)(iii).

(B)   Electronic Filing and Signing.

(i)   By a Represented Person—Generally Required; Exceptions. A person represented by an attorney must file electronically, unless nonelectronic filing is allowed by the court for good cause or is allowed or required by local rule.

(ii)   By an Unrepresented Person—When Allowed or Required. A person not represented by an attorney:

- may file electronically only if allowed by court order or by local rule; and

- may be required to file electronically only by court order, or by a local rule that includes reasonable exceptions.

(iii) Signing. A filing made through a person's electronic-filing account and authorized by that person, together with that person's name on a signature block, constitutes the person's signature.

(iv) Same as a Written Paper. A paper filed electronically is a written paper for purposes of these rules.

(3)   Filing a Motion with a Judge. If a motion requests relief that may be granted by a single judge, the judge may permit the motion to be filed with the judge; the judge must note the filing date on the motion and give it to the clerk.

(4)   Clerk's Refusal of Documents. The clerk must not refuse to accept for filing any paper presented for that purpose solely because it is not presented in proper form as required by these rules or by any local rule or practice.

(5)   Privacy Protection. An appeal in a case whose privacy protection was governed by Federal Rule of Bankruptcy Procedure 9037, Federal Rule of Civil Procedure 5.2, or Federal Rule of Criminal Procedure 49.1 is governed by the same rule on appeal. In all other proceedings, privacy protection is governed by Federal Rule of Civil Procedure 5.2, except that Federal Rule of Criminal Procedure 49.1 governs when an extraordinary writ is sought in a criminal case.

(b)   Service of All Papers Required. Unless a rule requires service by the clerk, a party must, at or before the time of filing a paper, serve a copy on the other parties to the appeal or review. Service on a party represented by counsel must be made on the party's counsel.

(c)   Manner of Service.

(1)   Nonelectronic service may be any of the following:

(A)   personal, including delivery to a responsible person at the office of counsel;

(B)   by mail; or

(C)   by third-party commercial carrier for delivery within 3 days.

(2)   Electronic service of a paper may be made (A) by sending it to a registered user by filing it with the court's electronic-filing system or (B) by sending it by other electronic means that the person to be served consented to in writing.

(3)   When reasonable considering such factors as the immediacy of the relief sought, distance, and cost, service on a party must be by a manner at least as expeditious as the manner used to file the paper with the court.

(4)   Service by mail or by commercial carrier is complete on mailing or delivery to the carrier. Service by electronic means is complete on filing or sending, unless the party making service is notified that the paper was not received by the party served.

(d) Proof of Service.

(1) A paper presented for filing must contain either of the following if it was served other than through the court's electronic-filing system:

(A) an acknowledgment of service by the person served; or

(B) proof of service consisting of a statement by the person who made service certifying:

(i) the date and manner of service;

(ii) the names of the persons served; and

(iii) their mail or electronic addresses, facsimile numbers, or the addresses of the places of delivery, as appropriate for the manner of service.

(2) When a brief or appendix is filed by mailing or dispatch in accordance with Rule 25(a)(2)(A)(ii), the proof of service must also state the date and manner by which the document was mailed or dispatched to the clerk.

(3) Proof of service may appear on or be affixed to the papers filed.

(e) Number of Copies. When these rules require the filing or furnishing of a number of copies, a court may require a different number by local rule or by order in a particular case.

(As amended Mar. 10, 1986, eff. July 1, 1986; Apr. 30, 1991, eff. Dec. 1, 1991; Apr. 22, 1993, eff. Dec. 1, 1993; Apr. 29, 1994, eff. Dec. 1, 1994; Apr. 23, 1996, eff. Dec. 1, 1996; Apr. 24, 1998, eff. Dec. 1, 1998; Apr. 29, 2002, eff. Dec. 1, 2002; Apr. 12, 2006, eff. Dec. 1, 2006; Apr. 30, 2007, eff. Dec. 1, 2007; Mar. 26, 2009, eff. Dec. 1, 2009; Apr. 28, 2016, eff. Dec. 1, 2016; Apr. 26, 2018, eff. Dec. 1, 2018; Apr. 25, 2019, eff. Dec. 1, 2019.)

ADVISORY COMMITTEE NOTES

1967 Adoption

The rule that filing is not timely unless the papers filed are received within the time allowed is the familiar one. *Ward v. Atlantic Coast Line R.R. Co.*, 265 F.2d 75 (5th Cir., 1959), rev'd on other grounds 362 U.S. 396, 80 S.Ct. 789, 4 L.Ed.2d 820 (1960); *Kahler-Ellis Co. v. Ohio Turnpike Commission*, 225 F.2d 922 (6th Cir., 1955). An exception is made in the case of briefs and appendices in order to afford the parties the maximum time for their preparation. By the terms of the exception, air mail delivery must be used whenever it is the most expeditious manner of delivery.

A majority of the circuits now require service of all papers filed with the clerk. The usual provision in present rules is for service on "adverse" parties. In view of the extreme simplicity of service by mail, there seems to be no reason why a party who files a paper should not be required to serve all parties to the proceeding in the court of appeals, whether or not they may be deemed adverse. The common requirement of proof of service is retained, but the rule permits it to be made by simple certification, which may be endorsed on the copy which is filed.

1986 Amendment

The amendments to Rules 25(a) and (b) are technical. No substantive change is intended.

1991 Amendment

Subdivision (a). The amendment permits, but does not require, courts of appeals to adopt local rules that allow filing of papers by electronic means. However, courts of appeals cannot adopt such local rules until the Judicial Conference of the United States authorizes filing by facsimile or other electronic means.

1993 Amendment

The amendment accompanies new subdivision (c) of Rule 4 and extends the holding in *Houston v. Lack*, 487 U.S. 266 (1988), to all papers filed in the courts of appeals by persons confined in institutions.

1994 Amendment

Subdivision (a). Several circuits have local rules that authorize the office of the clerk to refuse to accept for filing papers that are not in the form required by these rules or by local rules. This is not a suitable role for the office of the clerk and the practice exposes litigants to the hazards of time bars; for these reasons, such rules are proscribed by this rule. This provision is similar to Fed.R.Civ.P. 5(e) and Fed.R.Bankr.P. 5005.

The Committee wishes to make it clear that the provision prohibiting a clerk from refusing a document does not mean that a clerk's office may no longer screen documents to determine whether they comply with the rules. A court may delegate to the clerk authority to inform a party about any noncompliance with the rules and, if the party is willing to correct the document, to determine a date by which the corrected document must be resubmitted. If a party refuses to take the steps recommended by the clerk or if in the clerk's judgment the party fails to correct the noncompliance, the clerk must refer the matter to the court for a ruling.

Subdivision (d). Two changes have been made in this subdivision. Subdivision (d) provides that a paper presented for filing must contain proof of service.

The last sentence of subdivision (d) has been deleted as unnecessary. That sentence stated that a clerk could permit papers to be filed without the acknowledgment or proof of service but must require that it be filed promptly thereafter. In light of the change made in subdivision (a) which states that a clerk may not refuse to accept for filing a document because it is not in the proper form, there is no further need for a provision stating that a clerk may accept a paper lacking a proof of service. The clerk must accept such a paper. That portion of the deleted sentence stating that the clerk must require that proof of service be filed promptly after the filing of the document if the proof is not filed concurrently with the document is also unnecessary.

The second amendment requires that the certificate of service must state the addresses to which the papers were mailed or at which they were delivered. The Federal Circuit has a similar local rule, Fed.Cir.R. 25.

Subdivision (e). Subdivision (e) is a new subdivision. It makes it clear that whenever these rules require a party to file or furnish a number of copies a court may require a different number of copies either by rule or by order in an individual case. The number of copies of any document that a court of appeals needs varies depending upon the way in which the court conducts business. The internal operation of the courts of appeals necessarily varies from circuit to circuit because of differences in the number of judges, the geographic area included within the circuit, and other such factors. Uniformity could be achieved only by setting the number of copies artificially high so that parties in all circuits file enough copies to satisfy the needs of the court requiring the greatest number. Rather than do that, the Committee decided to make it clear that local rules may require a greater or lesser number of copies and that, if the circumstances of a particular case indicate the need for a different number of copies in that case, the court may so order.

A party must consult local rules to determine whether the court requires a different number than that specified in these national rules. The Committee believes it would be helpful if each circuit either: 1) included a chart at the beginning of its local rules showing the number of copies of each document required to be filed with the court along with citation to the controlling rule; or 2) made available such a chart to each party upon commencement of an appeal; or both. If a party fails to file the required number of copies, the failure does not create a jurisdictional defect. Rule 3(a) states: "Failure of an appellant to take any step other than the timely filing of a notice of appeal does not affect the validity of the appeal, but is ground only for such action as the court of appeals deems appropriate. . . ."

1996 Amendments

Subdivision (a). The amendment deletes the language requiring a party to use "the most expeditious form of delivery by mail, except special delivery" in order to file a brief using the mailbox rule. That language was adopted before the Postal Service offered Express Mail and other expedited delivery services. The amendment makes it clear that it is sufficient to use First-Class Mail. Other equally or more expeditious classes of mail service, such as Express Mail, also may be used. In addition, the amendment permits the use of commercial carriers. The use of private, overnight courier services has become commonplace in law practice. Expedited services offered by commercial carriers often provide faster delivery than First-Class Mail; therefore, there should be no objection to the use of commercial carriers as long as they are reliable. In order to make use of the mailbox rule when using a commercial carrier, the amendment requires that the filer employ a carrier who undertakes to deliver the document in no more than three calendar days. The three-calendar-day period coordinates with the three-day extension provided by Rule 26(c).

Subdivision (c). The amendment permits service by commercial carrier if the carrier is to deliver the paper to the party being served within three days of the carrier's receipt of the paper. The amendment also expresses a desire that when reasonable, service on a party be accomplished by a manner as expeditious as the manner used to file the paper with the court. When a brief or motion is filed with the court by hand delivering the paper to the clerk's office, or by overnight courier, the copies should be served on the other parties by an equally expeditious manner—meaning either by personal service, if distance permits, or by overnight courier, if mail delivery to the party is not ordinarily accomplished overnight. The reasonableness standard is included so that if a paper is hand delivered to the clerk's office for filing but the other parties must be served in a different city, state, or region, personal service on them ordinarily will not be expected. If use of an equally expeditious manner of service is not reasonable, use of the next most expeditious manner may be. For example, if the paper is filed by hand delivery to the clerk's office but the other parties reside in distant cities, service on them need not be personal but in most instances should be by overnight courier. Even that may not be required, however, if the number of parties that must be served would make the use of overnight service too costly. A factor that bears upon the reasonableness of serving parties expeditiously is the immediacy of the relief requested.

Subdivision (d). The amendment adds a requirement that when a brief or appendix is filed by mail or commercial carrier, the certificate of service state the date and manner by which the document was mailed or dispatched to the clerk. Including that information in the certificate of service avoids the necessity for a separate certificate concerning the date and manner of filing.

1998 Amendments

The language and organization of the rule are amended to make the rule more easily understood. In addition to changes made to improve the understanding, the Advisory Committee has changed language to make style and terminology consistent throughout the appellate rules. These changes are intended to by stylistic only; a substantive amendment is made, however, in subdivision (a).

Subdivision (a). The substantive amendment in this subdivision is in subparagraph (a)(2)(C) and is a companion to an amendment in Rule 4(c). Currently Rule 25(a)(2(C) provides that if an inmate confined in an institution files a document by depositing it in the institution's internal mail system, the document is timely filed if deposited on or before the last day for filing. Some institutions have special internal mail systems for handling legal mail; such systems often record the date of deposit of mail by an inmate, the date of delivery of mail to an inmate, etc. The Advisory Committee amends the rule to require an inmate to use the system designed for legal mail, if there is one, in order to receive the benefit of this subparagraph

2002 Amendments

Rule 25(a)(2)(D) presently authorizes the courts of appeals to permit papers to be *filed* by electronic means. Rule 25 has been amended in several respects to permit papers also to be *served* electronically. In addition, Rule 25(c) has been reorganized and subdivided to make it easier to understand.

Subdivision (c)(1)(D). New subdivision (c)(1)(D) has been added to permit service to be made electronically, such as by e-mail or fax. No party may be served electronically, either by the clerk or by another party, unless the party has consented in writing to such service.

A court of appeals may not, by local rule, forbid the use of electronic service on a party that has consented to its use. At the same time, courts have considerable discretion to use local rules to regulate electronic service. Difficult and presently unforeseeable questions are likely to arise as electronic service becomes more common. Courts have the flexibility to use their local rules to address those questions. For example, courts may use local rules to set forth specific procedures that a party must follow before the party will be deemed to have given written consent to electronic service.

Parties also have the flexibility to define the terms of their consent; a party's consent to electronic service does not have to be "all-or-nothing." For example, a party may consent to service by facsimile transmission, but not by electronic mail; or a party may consent to electronic service only if "courtesy" copies of all transmissions are mailed within 24 hours; or a party may consent to electronic service of only documents that were created with Corel WordPerfect.

Subdivision (c)(2). The courts of appeals are authorized under Rule 25(a)(2)(D) to permit papers to be filed electronically. Technological advances may someday make it possible for a court to forward an electronically filed paper to all parties automatically or semi-automatically. When such court-facilitated service becomes possible, courts may decide to permit parties to use the courts' transmission facilities to serve electronically filed papers on other parties who have consented to such service. Court personnel would use the court's computer system to forward the papers, but the papers would be considered served by the filing parties, just as papers that are carried from one address to another by the United States Postal Service are considered served by the sending parties. New subdivision (c)(2) has been added so that the courts of appeals may use local rules to authorize such use of their transmission facilities, as well as to address the many questions that court-facilitated electronic service is likely to raise.

Subdivision (c)(4). The second sentence of new subdivision (c)(4) has been added to provide that electronic service is complete upon transmission. Transmission occurs when the sender performs the last act that he or she must perform to transmit a paper electronically; typically, it occurs when the sender hits the "send" or "transmit" button on an electronic mail program. There is one exception to the rule that electronic service is complete upon transmission: If the sender is notified—by the sender's e-mail program or otherwise—that the paper was not received, service is not complete, and the sender must take additional steps to effect service. A paper has been "received" by the party on which it has been served as long as the party has the ability to retrieve it. A party cannot defeat service by choosing not to access electronic mail on its server.

Changes Made After Publication and Comments. No changes were made to the text of the proposed amendment. A paragraph was added to the Committee Note to clarify that consent to electronic service is not an "all-or-nothing" matter.

Subdivision (d)(1)(B)(iii). Subdivision (d)(1)(B)(iii) has been amended to require that, when a paper is served electronically, the proof of service of that paper must include the electronic address or facsimile number to which the paper was transmitted.

Changes Made After Publication and Comments. The text of the proposed amendment was changed to refer to "electronic" addresses (instead of to "e-mail" addresses), to include "facsimile numbers," and to add the concluding phrase "as appropriate for the manner of service." Conforming changes were made to the Committee Note.

2006 Amendment

Subdivision (a)(2)(D). Amended Rule 25(a)(2)(D) acknowledges that many courts have required electronic filing by means of a standing order, procedures manual, or local rule. These local practices reflect the advantages that courts and most litigants realize from electronic filing. Courts that mandate electronic filing recognize the need to make exceptions when requiring electronic filing imposes a hardship on a party. Under Rule 25(a)(2)(D), a local rule that requires electronic filing must include reasonable exceptions, but Rule 25(a)(2)(D) does not define the scope of those exceptions. Experience with the local rules that have been adopted and that will emerge will aid in drafting new local rules and will facilitate gradual convergence on uniform exceptions, whether in local rules or in an amended Rule 25(a)(2)(D).

A local rule may require that both electronic and "hard" copies of a paper be filed. Nothing in the last sentence of Rule 25(a)(2)(D) is meant to imply otherwise.

2007 Amendments

Subdivision (a)(5). Section 205(c)(3)(A)(i) of the E-Government Act of 2002 (Public Law 107–347, as amended by Public Law 108–281) requires that the rules of practice and procedure be amended "to protect privacy and security concerns relating to electronic filing of documents and the public availability . . . of documents filed electronically." In response to that directive, the Federal Rules of Bankruptcy, Civil, and Criminal Procedure have been amended, not merely to address the privacy and security concerns raised by documents that are filed electronically, but also to address similar concerns raised by documents that are filed in paper form. *See* Fed. R. Bankr. P. 9037; Fed. R. Civ. P. 5.2; and Fed. R. Crim. P. 49.1.

Appellate Rule 25(a)(5) requires that, in cases that arise on appeal from a district court, bankruptcy appellate panel, or bankruptcy court, the privacy rule that applied to the case below will continue to apply to the case on appeal. With one exception, all other cases—such as cases involving the review or enforcement of an agency order, the review of a decision of the tax court, or the consideration of a petition for an extraordinary writ—will be governed by Civil Rule 5.2. The only exception is when an extraordinary writ is sought in a criminal case—that is, a case in which the related trial-court proceeding is governed by Criminal Rule 49.1. In such a case, Criminal Rule 49.1 will govern in the court of appeals as well.

2009 Amendments

Under former Rule 26(a), short periods that span weekends or holidays were computed without counting those weekends or holidays. To specify that a period should be calculated by counting all intermediate days, including weekends or holidays, the Rules used the term "calendar days." Rule 26(a) now takes a "days-are-days" approach under which all intermediate days are counted, no matter how short the period. Accordingly, "3 calendar days" in subdivisions (a)(2)(B)(ii) and (c)(1)(C) is amended to read simply "3 days."

2016 Amendments

Rule 25(a)(2)(C) is revised to streamline and clarify the operation of the inmate-filing rule.

The Rule requires the inmate to show timely deposit and prepayment of postage. The Rule is amended to specify that a paper is timely if it is accompanied by a declaration or notarized statement stating the date the paper was deposited in the institution's mail system and attesting to the prepayment of first-class postage. The declaration must state that first-class postage "is being prepaid," not (as directed by the former Rule) that first-class postage "has been prepaid." This change reflects the fact that inmates may need to rely upon the institution to affix postage after the inmate has deposited the document in the institution's mail system. New Form 7 in the Appendix of Forms sets out a suggested form of the declaration.

The amended rule also provides that a paper is timely without a declaration or notarized statement if other evidence accompanying the paper shows that the paper was deposited on or before the due date and that postage was prepaid. If the paper is not accompanied by evidence that establishes timely deposit and prepayment of postage, then the court of appeals has discretion to accept a declaration or notarized statement at a later date. The Rule uses the phrase "exercises its discretion to permit"—rather than simply "permits"—to help ensure that pro se inmate litigants are aware that a court will not necessarily forgive a failure to provide the declaration initially.

Changes Made After Publication and Comment

Rules 4(c)(1) and 25(a)(2)(C), as published, would have deleted the requirement that an inmate use a system designed for legal mail (if one is available) in order to receive the benefit of the inmate-filing rules. The Committee proposed deleting that requirement because it perceived no purpose for it. However, a commentator pointed out that correctional institutions in the State of Florida log the date of deposit of inmates' legal mail but do not log the date of deposit of inmates' non-legal mail. The Committee's subsequent inquiries revealed that a number of other States similarly record the date of inmates' legal mail but not their non-legal mail. This new information, in the view of the Committee, provides reason to retain the legal-mail-system requirement. Requiring an inmate to use a legal mail system where available serves a useful purpose by ensuring that mail is logged or date-stamped and avoiding unnecessary litigation over the timing of deposits. Accordingly, the Committee restored that requirement to proposed Rules 4(c)(1) and 25(a)(2)(C) and made conforming changes to the Committee Notes.

2018 Amendments

The amendments conform Rule 25 to the amendments to Federal Rule of Civil Procedure 5 on electronic filing, signature, service, and proof of service. They establish, in Rule 25(a)(2)(B), a new national rule that generally makes electronic filing mandatory. The rule recognizes exceptions for persons proceeding without an attorney, exceptions for good cause, and variations established by local rule. The amendments establish national rules regarding the methods of signing and serving electronic documents in Rule 25(a)(2)(B)(iii) and (c)(2).*

2019 Amendments

The amendment conforms Rule 25 to other federal rules regarding proof of service. As amended, subdivision (d) eliminates the requirement of proof of service or acknowledgment of service when service is made through a court's electronic-filing system. The notice of electronic filing generated by the court's system serves that purpose.

Rule 26. Computing and Extending Time

(a) **Computing Time.** The following rules apply in computing any time period specified in these rules, in any local rule or court order, or in any statute that does not specify a method of computing time.

(1) **Period Stated in Days or a Longer Unit.** When the period is stated in days or a longer unit of time:

(A) exclude the day of the event that triggers the period;

(B) count every day, including intermediate Saturdays, Sundays, and legal holidays; and

(C) include the last day of the period, but if the last day is a Saturday, Sunday, or legal holiday, the period continues to run until the end of the next day that is not a Saturday, Sunday, or legal holiday.

(2) **Period Stated in Hours.** When the period is stated in hours:

(A) begin counting immediately on the occurrence of the event that triggers the period;

(B) count every hour, including hours during intermediate Saturdays, Sundays, and legal holidays; and

(C) if the period would end on a Saturday, Sunday, or legal holiday, the period continues to run until the same time on the next day that is not a Saturday, Sunday, or legal holiday.

(3) **Inaccessibility of the Clerk's Office.** Unless the court orders otherwise, if the clerk's office is inaccessible:

(A) on the last day for filing under Rule 26(a)(1), then the time for filing is extended to the first accessible day that is not a Saturday, Sunday, or legal holiday; or

(B) during the last hour for filing under Rule 26(a)(2), then the time for filing is extended to the same time on the first accessible day that is not a Saturday, Sunday, or legal holiday.

(4) **"Last Day" Defined.** Unless a different time is set by a statute, local rule, or court order, the last day ends:

(A) for electronic filing in the district court, at midnight in the court's time zone;

(B) for electronic filing in the court of appeals, at midnight in the time zone of the circuit clerk's principal office;

---

*   [As originally published and proposed, the 2018 amendments to Rule 25 dispensed with the requirement of proof of service for electronic filings in Rule 25(d)(1). Although that amendment was approved by the Judicial Conference and submitted to the Supreme Court in 2017, it was withdrawn by the Standing Committee to allow for minor revisions. The revised proposal now appears among the 2019 amendments to the appellate rules and implements the amendment's original goal while also addressing the possibility that a document might be filed electronically and yet still need to be served on a party who does not participate in the court's electronic-filing system (most often a *pro se* litigant). Ed.]

(C) for filing under Rules 4(c)(1), 25(a)(2)(A)(ii), and 25(a)(2)(A)(iii)—and filing by mail under Rule 13(a)(2)—at the latest time for the method chosen for delivery to the post office, third-party commercial carrier, or prison mailing system; and

(D) for filing by other means, when the clerk's office is scheduled to close.

(5) **"Next Day" Defined.** The "next day" is determined by continuing to count forward when the period is measured after an event and backward when measured before an event.

(6) **"Legal Holiday" Defined.** "Legal holiday" means:

(A) the day set aside by statute for observing New Year's Day, Martin Luther King Jr.'s Birthday, Washington's Birthday, Memorial Day, Independence Day, Labor Day, Columbus Day, Veterans' Day, Thanksgiving Day, or Christmas Day;

(B) any day declared a holiday by the President or Congress; and

(C) for periods that are measured after an event, any other day declared a holiday by the state where either of the following is located: the district court that rendered the challenged judgment or order, or the circuit clerk's principal office.

(b) Extending Time. For good cause, the court may extend the time prescribed by these rules or by its order to perform any act, or may permit an act to be done after that time expires. But the court may not extend the time to file:

(1) a notice of appeal (except as authorized in Rule 4) or a petition for permission to appeal; or

(2) a notice of appeal from or a petition to enjoin, set aside, suspend, modify, enforce, or otherwise review an order of an administrative agency, board, commission, or officer of the United States, unless specifically authorized by law.

(c) Additional Time After Certain Kinds of Service. When a party may or must act within a specified time after being served, and the paper is not served electronically on the party or delivered to the party on the date stated in the proof of service, 3 days are added after the period would otherwise expire under Rule 26(a).

(As amended Mar. 1, 1971, eff. July 1, 1971; Mar. 10, 1986, eff. July 1, 1986; Apr. 25, 1989, eff. Dec. 1, 1989; Apr. 30, 1991, eff. Dec. 1, 1991; Apr. 23, 1996, eff. Dec. 1, 1996; Apr. 24, 1998, eff. Dec. 1, 1998; Apr. 29, 2002, eff. Dec. 1, 2002; Apr. 25, 2005, eff. Dec. 1, 2005; Mar. 26, 2009, eff. Dec. 1, 2009; Apr. 28, 2016; eff. Dec. 1, 2016; Apr. 26, 2018, eff. Dec. 1, 2018; Apr. 25, 2019, eff. Dec. 1, 2019.)

ADVISORY COMMITTEE NOTES

1967 Adoption

The provisions of this rule are based upon FRCP 6(a), (b) and (e) [rule 6(a), (b) and (e), Federal Rules of Civil Procedure]. See also Supreme Court Rule 34 and FRCrP 45 [rule 45, Federal Rules of Criminal Procedure]. Unlike FRCP 6(b), this rule, read with Rule 27, requires that every request for enlargement of time be made by motion, with proof of service on all parties. This is the simplest, most convenient way of keeping all parties advised of developments. By the terms of Rule 27(b) a motion for enlargement of time under Rule 26(b) may be entertained and acted upon immediately, subject to the right of any party to seek reconsideration. Thus the requirement of motion and notice will not delay the granting of relief of a kind which a court is inclined to grant as of course. Specifically, if a court is of the view that an extension of time sought before expiration of the period originally prescribed or as extended by a previous order ought to be granted in effect ex parte, as FRCP 6(b) permits, it may grant motions seeking such relief without delay.

1971 Amendments

The amendment adds Columbus Day to the list of legal holidays to conform the subdivision to the Act of June 28, 1968, 82 Stat. 250, which constituted Columbus Day a legal holiday effective after January 1, 1971.

The Act, which amended Title 5, U.S.C. § 6103(a), changes the day on which certain holidays are to be observed. Washington's Birthday, Memorial Day and Veterans Day are to be observed on the third Monday in February, the last Monday in May and the fourth Monday in October, respectively, rather than, as heretofore, on February 22, May 30, and November 11, respectively. Columbus Day is to be observed on the second Monday in October. New Year's Day, Independence Day, Thanksgiving Day and Christmas continue to be observed on the traditional days.

1986 Amendments

The Birthday of Martin Luther King, Jr. is added to the list of national holidays in Rule 26(a). The amendment to Rule 26(c) is technical. No substantive change is intended.

1989 Amendments

The proposed amendment brings Rule 26(a) into conformity with the provisions of Rule 6(a) of the Rules of Civil Procedure, Rule 45(a) of the Rules of Criminal Procedure, and Rule 9006(a) of the Rules of Bankruptcy Procedure which allow additional time for filing whenever a clerk's office is inaccessible on the last day for filing due to weather or other conditions.

1996 Amendments

The amendment is a companion to the proposed amendments to Rule 25 that permit service on a party by commercial carrier. The amendments to subdivision (c) of this rule make the three-day extension applicable not only when service is accomplished by mail, but whenever delivery to the party being served occurs later than the date of service stated in the proof of service. When service is by mail or commercial carrier, the proof of service recites the date of mailing or delivery to the commercial carrier. If the party being served receives the paper on a later date, the three-day extension applies. If the party being served receives the paper on the same date as the date of service recited in the proof of service, the three-day extension is not available.

The amendment also states that the three-day extension is three calendar days. Rule 26(a) states that when a period prescribed or allowed by the rules is less than seven days, intermediate Saturdays, Sundays, and legal holidays do not count. Whether the three-day extension in Rule 26(c) is such a period, meaning that three-days could actually be five or even six days, is unclear. The D.C. Circuit recently held that the parallel three-day extension provided in the Civil Rules is not such a period and that weekends and legal holidays do count. *CNPq v. Inter-Trade,* 50 F.3d 56 (D.C.Cir.1995). The Committee believes that is the right result and that the issue should be resolved. Providing that the extension is three calendar days means that if a period would otherwise end on Thursday but the three-day extension applies, the paper must be filed on Monday. Friday, Saturday, and Sunday are the extension days. Because the last day of the period as extended is Sunday, the paper must be filed the next day, Monday.

1998 Amendments

The language and organization of the rule are amended to make the rule more easily understood. In addition to changes made to improve the understanding, the Advisory Committee has changed language to make style and terminology consistent throughout the appellate rules. These changes are intended to by stylistic only; two substantive changes are made, however, in subdivision (a).

Subdivision (a). First, the amendments make the computation method prescribed in this rule applicable to any time period imposed by a local rule. This means that if a local rule establishing a time limit is permitted, the national rule will govern the computation of that period.

Second, paragraph (a)(2) includes language clarifying that whenever the rules establish a time period in "calendar days," weekends and legal holidays are counted.

2002 Amendments

Subdivision (a)(2). The Federal Rules of Civil Procedure and the Federal Rules of Criminal Procedure compute time differently than the Federal Rules of Appellate Procedure. Fed. R. Civ. P. 6(a) and Fed. R. Crim. P. 45(a) provide that, in computing any period of time, "[w]hen the period of time prescribed or allowed is less than 11 days, intermediate Saturdays, Sundays, and legal holidays shall be excluded in the computation." By contrast, Rule 26(a)(2) provides that, in computing any period of time, a litigant should "[e]xclude intermediate Saturdays, Sundays, and legal holidays when the period is less than 7 days, unless stated in calendar days." Thus, deadlines of 7, 8, 9, and 10 days are calculated differently under the rules of civil and criminal procedure than they are under the rules of appellate procedure. This creates a trap for unwary litigants. No good reason for this discrepancy is apparent, and thus Rule 26(a)(2) has been amended so that, under all three sets of rules, intermediate Saturdays, Sundays, and legal holidays will be excluded when computing deadlines under 11 days but will be counted when computing deadlines of 11 days and over.

Changes Made After Publication and Comments. No changes were made to the text of the proposed amendment or to the Committee Note.

Subdivision (c). Rule 26(c) has been amended to provide that when a paper is served on a party by electronic means, and that party is required or permitted to respond to that paper within a prescribed period, 3 calendar days are added to the prescribed period. Electronic service is usually instantaneous, but sometimes it is not, because of technical problems. Also, if a paper is electronically transmitted to a party on a Friday evening, the party may not realize that he or she has been served until two or three days later. Finally, extending the "3-day rule" to electronic service will encourage parties to consent to such service under Rule 25(c).

Changes Made After Publication and Comments. No changes were made to the text of the proposed amendment or to the Committee Note.

2005 Amendments

Subdivision (a)(4). Rule 26(a)(4) has been amended to refer to the third Monday in February as "Washington's Birthday." A federal statute officially designates the holiday as "Washington's Birthday," reflecting the desire of Congress specially to honor the first president of the United States. *See* 5 U.S.C. § 6103(a). During the 1998 restyling of the Federal Rules of Appellate Procedure, references to "Washington's Birthday" were mistakenly changed to "Presidents' Day." The amendment corrects that error.

2009 Amendments

Subdivision (a). Subdivision (a) has been amended to simplify and clarify the provisions that describe how deadlines are computed. Subdivision (a) governs the computation of any time period found in a statute that does not specify a method of computing time, a Federal Rule of Appellate Procedure, a local rule, or a court order. In accordance with Rule 47(a)(1), a local rule may not direct that a deadline be computed in a manner inconsistent with subdivision (a).

The time-computation provisions of subdivision (a) apply only when a time period must be computed. They do not apply when a fixed time to act is set. The amendments thus carry forward the approach taken in *Violette v. P.A. Days, Inc.*, 427 F.3d 1015, 1016 (6th Cir. 2005) (holding that Civil Rule 6(a) "does not apply to situations where the court has established a specific calendar day as a deadline"), and reject the contrary holding of *In re American Healthcare Management, Inc.*, 900 F.2d 827, 832 (5th Cir. 1990) (holding that Bankruptcy Rule 9006(a) governs treatment of date-certain deadline set by court order). If, for example, the date for filing is "no later than November 1, 2007," subdivision (a) does not govern. But if a filing is required to be made "within 10 days" or "within 72 hours," subdivision (a) describes how that deadline is computed.

Subdivision (a) does not apply when computing a time period set by a statute if the statute specifies a method of computing time. *See, e.g.,* 20 U.S.C. § 7711(b)(1) (requiring certain petitions for review by a local educational agency or a state to be filed "within 30 working days (as determined by the local educational agency or State) after receiving notice of" federal agency decision).

Subdivision (a)(1). New subdivision (a)(1) addresses the computation of time periods that are stated in days. It also applies to time periods that are stated in weeks, months, or years; though no such time period currently appears in the Federal Rules of Appellate Procedure, such periods may be set by other covered provisions such as a local rule. *See, e.g.,* Third Circuit Local Appellate Rule 46.3(c)(1). Subdivision (a)(1)(B)'s directive to "count every day" is relevant only if the period is stated in days (not weeks, months or years).

Under former Rule 26(a), a period of 11 days or more was computed differently than a period of less than 11 days. Intermediate Saturdays, Sundays, and legal holidays were included in computing the longer periods, but excluded in computing the shorter periods. Former Rule 26(a) thus made computing deadlines unnecessarily complicated and led to counterintuitive results. For example, a 10-day period and a 14-day period that started on the same day usually ended on the same day—and the 10-day period not infrequently ended later than the 14-day period. *See Miltimore Sales, Inc. v. Int'l Rectifier, Inc.*, 412 F.3d 685, 686 (6th Cir. 2005).

Under new subdivision (a)(1), all deadlines stated in days (no matter the length) are computed in the same way. The day of the event that triggers the deadline is not counted. All other days—including intermediate Saturdays, Sundays, and legal holidays—are counted, with only one exception: If the period ends on a Saturday, Sunday, or legal holiday, then the deadline falls on the next day that is not a Saturday, Sunday, or legal holiday. An illustration is provided below in the discussion of subdivision (a)(5). Subdivision (a)(3) addresses filing deadlines that expire on a day when the clerk's office is inaccessible.

Where subdivision (a) formerly referred to the "act, event, or default" that triggers the deadline, new subdivision (a) refers simply to the "event" that triggers the deadline; this change in terminology is adopted for brevity and simplicity, and is not intended to change meaning.

Periods previously expressed as less than 11 days will be shortened as a practical matter by the decision to count intermediate Saturdays, Sundays, and legal holidays in computing all periods. Many of those periods have been lengthened to compensate for the change. *See, e.g.*, Rules 5(b)(2), 5(d)(1), 28.1(f), & 31(a).

Most of the 10-day periods were adjusted to meet the change in computation method by setting 14 days as the new period. A 14-day period corresponds to the most frequent result of a 10-day period under the former computation method—two Saturdays and two Sundays were excluded, giving 14 days in all. A 14-day period has an additional advantage. The final day falls on the same day of the week as the event that triggered the period—the 14th day after a Monday, for example, is a Monday. This advantage of using week-long periods led to adopting 7-day periods to replace some of the periods set at less than 10 days, and 21-day periods to replace 20-day periods. Thirty-day and longer periods, however, were retained without change.

Subdivision (a)(2). New subdivision (a)(2) addresses the computation of time periods that are stated in hours. No such deadline currently appears in the Federal Rules of Appellate Procedure. But some statutes contain deadlines stated in hours, as do some court orders issued in expedited proceedings.

Under subdivision (a)(2), a deadline stated in hours starts to run immediately on the occurrence of the event that triggers the deadline. The deadline generally ends when the time expires. If, however, the time period expires at a specific time (say, 2:17 p.m.) on a Saturday, Sunday, or legal holiday, then the deadline is extended to the same time (2:17 p.m.) on the next day that is not a Saturday, Sunday, or legal holiday. Periods stated in hours are not to be "rounded up" to the next whole hour. Subdivision (a)(3) addresses situations when the clerk's office is inaccessible during the last hour before a filing deadline expires.

Subdivision (a)(2)(B) directs that every hour be counted. Thus, for example, a 72-hour period that commences at 10:00 a.m. on Friday, November 2, 2007, will run until 9:00 a.m. on Monday, November 5; the discrepancy in start and end times in this example results from the intervening shift from daylight saving time to standard time.

Subdivision (a)(3). When determining the last day of a filing period stated in days or a longer unit of time, a day on which the clerk's office is not accessible because of the weather or another reason is treated like a Saturday, Sunday, or legal holiday. When determining the end of a filing period stated in hours, if the clerk's office is inaccessible during the last hour of the filing period computed under subdivision (a)(2) then the period is extended to the same time on the next day that is not a weekend, holiday or day when the clerk's office is inaccessible.

Subdivision (a)(3)'s extensions apply "[u]nless the court orders otherwise." In some circumstances, the court might not wish a period of inaccessibility to trigger a full 24-hour extension; in those instances, the court can specify a briefer extension.

The text of the rule no longer refers to "weather or other conditions" as the reason for the inaccessibility of the clerk's office. The reference to "weather" was deleted from the text to underscore that inaccessibility can occur for reasons unrelated to weather, such as an outage of the electronic filing system. Weather can still be a reason for inaccessibility of the clerk's office. The rule does not attempt to define inaccessibility. Rather, the concept will continue to develop through caselaw, *see, e.g., Tchakmakjian v. Department of*

Defense, 57 Fed. Appx. 438, 441 (Fed. Cir. 2003) (unpublished per curiam opinion) (inaccessibility "due to anthrax concerns"); *cf.* William G. Phelps, *When Is Office of Clerk of Court Inaccessible Due to Weather or Other Conditions for Purpose of Computing Time Period for Filing Papers under Rule 6(a) of Federal Rules of Civil Procedure*, 135 A.L.R. Fed. 259 (1996) (collecting cases). In addition, local provisions may address inaccessibility for purposes of electronic filing.

Subdivision (a)(4). New subdivision (a)(4) defines the end of the last day of a period for purposes of subdivision (a)(1). Subdivision (a)(4) does not apply in computing periods stated in hours under subdivision (a)(2), and does not apply if a different time is set by a statute, local rule, or order in the case. A local rule may, for example, address the problems that might arise under subdivision (a)(4)(A) if a single district has clerk's offices in different time zones, or provide that papers filed in a drop box after the normal hours of the clerk's office are filed as of the day that is date-stamped on the papers by a device in the drop box.

28 U.S.C. § 452 provides that "[a]ll courts of the United States shall be deemed always open for the purpose of filing proper papers, issuing and returning process, and making motions and orders." A corresponding provision exists in Rule 45(a)(2). Some courts have held that these provisions permit an after-hours filing by handing the papers to an appropriate official. *See, e.g., Casalduc v. Diaz*, 117 F.2d 915, 917 (1st Cir. 1941). Subdivision (a)(4) does not address the effect of the statute on the question of after-hours filing; instead, the rule is designed to deal with filings in the ordinary course without regard to Section 452.

Subdivision (a)(4)(A) addresses electronic filings in the district court. For example, subdivision (a)(4)(A) would apply to an electronically-filed notice of appeal. Subdivision (a)(4)(B) addresses electronic filings in the court of appeals.

Subdivision (a)(4)(C) addresses filings by mail under Rules 25(a)(2)(B)(i) and 13(b), filings by third-party commercial carrier under Rule 25(a)(2)(B)(ii), and inmate filings under Rules 4(c)(1) and 25(a)(2)(C). For such filings, subdivision (a)(4)(C) provides that the "last day" ends at the latest time (prior to midnight in the filer's time zone) that the filer can properly submit the filing to the post office, third-party commercial carrier, or prison mail system (as applicable) using the filer's chosen method of submission. For example, if a correctional institution's legal mail system's rules of operation provide that items may only be placed in the mail system between 9:00 a.m. and 5:00 p.m., then the "last day" for filings under Rules 4(c)(1) and 25(a)(2)(C) by inmates in that institution ends at 5:00 p.m. As another example, if a filer uses a drop box maintained by a third-party commercial carrier, the "last day" ends at the time of that drop box's last scheduled pickup. Filings by mail under Rule 13(b) continue to be subject to § 7502 of the Internal Revenue Code, as amended, and the applicable regulations.

Subdivision (a)(4)(D) addresses all other non-electronic filings; for such filings, the last day ends under (a)(4)(D) when the clerk's office in which the filing is made is scheduled to close.

Subdivision (a)(5). New subdivision (a)(5) defines the "next" day for purposes of subdivisions (a)(1)(C) and (a)(2)(C). The Federal Rules of Appellate Procedure contain both forward-looking time periods and backward-looking time periods. A forward-looking time period requires something to be done within a period of time *after* an event. *See, e.g.,* Rule 4(a)(1)(A) (subject to certain exceptions, notice of appeal in a civil case must be filed "within 30 days after the judgment or order appealed from is entered"). A backward-looking time period requires something to be done within a period of time *before* an event. *See, e.g.,* Rule 31(a)(1) ("[A] reply brief must be filed at least 7 days before argument, unless the court, for good cause, allows a later filing."). In determining what is the "next" day for purposes of subdivisions (a)(1)(C) and (a)(2)(C), one should continue counting in the same direction—that is, forward when computing a forward-looking period and backward when computing a backward-looking period. If, for example, a filing is due within 10 days *after* an event, and the tenth day falls on Saturday, September 1, 2007, then the filing is due on Tuesday, September 4, 2007 (Monday, September 3, is Labor Day). But if a filing is due 10 days *before* an event, and the tenth day falls on Saturday, September 1, then the filing is due on Friday, August 31. If the clerk's office is inaccessible on August 31, then subdivision (a)(3) extends the filing deadline forward to the next accessible day that is not a Saturday, Sunday or legal holiday—no earlier than Tuesday, September 4.

Subdivision (a)(6). New subdivision (a)(6) defines "legal holiday" for purposes of the Federal Rules of Appellate Procedure, including the time-computation provisions of subdivision (a). Subdivision (a)(6) continues to include within the definition of "legal holiday" days that are declared a holiday by the President or Congress.

For forward-counted periods—i.e., periods that are measured after an event—subdivision (a)(6)(C) includes certain state holidays within the definition of legal holidays. However, state legal holidays are not recognized in computing backward-counted periods. For both forward- and backward-counted periods, the rule thus protects those who may be unsure of the effect of state holidays. For forward-counted deadlines, treating state holidays the same as federal holidays extends the deadline. Thus, someone who thought that the federal courts might be closed on a state holiday would be safeguarded against an inadvertent late filing. In contrast, for backward-counted deadlines, not giving state holidays the treatment of federal holidays allows filing on the state holiday itself rather than the day before. Take, for example, Monday, April 21, 2008 (Patriot's Day, a legal holiday in the relevant state). If a filing is due 14 days after an event, and the fourteenth day is April 21, then the filing is due on Tuesday, April 22 because Monday, April 21 counts as a legal holiday. But if a filing is due 14 days before an event, and the fourteenth day is April 21, the filing is due on Monday, April 21; the fact that April 21 is a state holiday does not make April 21 a legal holiday for purposes of computing this backward-counted deadline. But note that if the clerk's office is inaccessible on Monday, April 21, then subdivision (a)(3) extends the April 21 filing deadline forward to the next accessible day that is not a Saturday, Sunday or legal holiday—no earlier than Tuesday, April 22.

Subdivision (c). To specify that a period should be calculated by counting all intermediate days, including weekends or holidays, the Rules formerly used the term "calendar days." Because new subdivision (a) takes a "days-are-days" approach under which all intermediate days are counted, no matter how short the period, "3 calendar days" in subdivision (c) is amended to read simply "3 days."

Subdivision (c). Rule 26(c) has been amended to eliminate uncertainty about application of the 3-day rule. Civil Rule 6(e) was amended in 2004 to eliminate similar uncertainty in the Civil Rules.

Under the amendment, a party that is required or permitted to act within a prescribed period should first calculate that period, without reference to the 3-day rule provided by Rule 26(c), but with reference to the other time computation provisions of the Appellate Rules. After the party has identified the date on which the prescribed period would expire but for the operation of Rule 26(c), the party should add 3 calendar days. The party must act by the third day of the extension, unless that day is a Saturday, Sunday, or legal holiday, in which case the party must act by the next day that is not a Saturday, Sunday, or legal holiday.

To illustrate: A paper is served by mail on Thursday, November 1, 2007. The prescribed time to respond is 30 days. The prescribed period ends on Monday, December 3 (because the 30th day falls on a Saturday, the prescribed period extends to the following Monday). Under Rule 26(c), three calendar days are added— Tuesday, Wednesday, and Thursday—and thus the response is due on Thursday, December 6.

2016 Amendments

Subdivision (a)(4)(C). The reference to Rule 13(b) is revised to refer to Rule 13(a)(2) in light of a 2013 amendment to Rule 13. The amendment to subdivision (a)(4)(C) is technical and no substantive change is intended.

[Subdivision (c).] Rule 26(c) is amended to remove service by electronic means under Rule 25(c)(1)(D) from the modes of service that allow 3 added days to act after being served.

Rule 25(c) was amended in 2002 to provide for service by electronic means. Although electronic transmission seemed virtually instantaneous even then, electronic service was included in the modes of service that allow 3 added days to act after being served. There were concerns that the transmission might be delayed for some time, and particular concerns that incompatible systems might make it difficult or impossible to open attachments. Those concerns have been substantially alleviated by advances in technology and widespread skill in using electronic transmission.

A parallel reason for allowing the 3 added days was that electronic service was authorized only with the consent of the person to be served. Concerns about the reliability of electronic transmission might have led to refusals of consent; the 3 added days were calculated to alleviate these concerns.

Diminution of the concerns that prompted the decision to allow the 3 added days for electronic transmission is not the only reason for discarding this indulgence. Many rules have been changed to ease the task of computing time by adopting 7-, 14-, 21-, and 28-day periods that allow "day-of-the-week" counting. Adding 3 days at the end complicated the counting, and increased the occasions for further complication by invoking the provisions that apply when the last day is a Saturday, Sunday, or legal holiday.

The ease of making electronic service after business hours, or just before or during a weekend or holiday, may result in a practical reduction in the time available to respond. Extensions of time may be warranted to prevent prejudice.

Rule 26(c) has also been amended to refer to instances when a party "may or must act . . . after being served" rather than to instances when a party "may or must act . . . after service." If, in future, an Appellate Rule sets a deadline for a party to act after that party itself effects service on another person, this change in language will clarify that Rule 26(c)'s three added days are not accorded to the party who effected service.

Changes Made After Publication and Comment

The Committee added language to the Committee Note to recognize the need for extensions of time in appropriate cases.

2018 Amendments

The amendments adjust references to subdivisions of Rule 25 that have been renumbered.

2019 Amendments

The amendment in subdivision (c) simplifies the expression of the current rules for when three days are added. In addition, the amendment revises the subdivision to conform to the amendments to Rule 25(d).

Rule 26.1.　　Disclosure Statement

(a) Nongovernmental Corporations. Any nongovernmental corporation that is a party to a proceeding in a court of appeals must file a statement that identifies any parent corporation and any publicly held corporation that owns 10% or more of its stock or states that there is no such corporation. The same requirement applies to a nongovernmental corporation that seeks to intervene.

(b) Organizational Victims in Criminal Cases. In a criminal case, unless the government shows good cause, it must file a statement that identifies any organizational victim of the alleged criminal activity. If the organizational victim is a corporation, the statement must also disclose the information required by Rule 26.1(a) to the extent it can be obtained through due diligence.

(c) Bankruptcy Cases. In a bankruptcy case, the debtor, the trustee, or, if neither is a party, the appellant must file a statement that:

> **(1)** identifies each debtor not named in the caption; and

> **(2)** for each debtor that is a corporation, discloses the information required by Rule 26.1(a).

(d) Time for Filing; Supplemental Filing. The Rule 26.1 statement must:

> **(1)** be filed with the principal brief or upon filing a motion, response, petition, or answer in the court of appeals, whichever occurs first, unless a local rule requires earlier filing;

> **(2)** be included before the table of contents in the principal brief; and

> **(3)** be supplemented whenever the information required under Rule 26.1 changes.

(e) Number of Copies. If the Rule 26.1 statement is filed before the principal brief, or if a supplemental statement is filed, an original and 3 copies must be filed unless the court requires a different number by local rule or by order in a particular case.

(Added Apr. 25, 1989, eff. Dec. 1, 1989; amended Apr. 30, 1991, eff. Dec. 1, 1991; Apr. 29, 1994, eff. Dec. 1, 1994; Apr. 24, 1998, eff. Dec. 1, 1998; Apr. 29, 2002, eff. Dec. 1, 2002; Apr. 25, 2019, eff. Dec. 1, 2019.)

ADVISORY COMMITTEE NOTES

1989 Addition

The purpose of this rule is to assist judges in making a determination of whether they have any interests in any of a party's related corporate entities that would disqualify the judges from hearing the appeal. The committee believes that this rule represents minimum disclosure requirements. If a Court of Appeals wishes to require additional information, a court is free to do so by local rule. However, the committee requests the courts to consider the desirability of uniformity and the burden that varying circuit rules creates on attorneys who practice in many circuits.

1994 Amendment

The amendment requires a party to file three copies of the disclosure statement whenever the statement is filed before the party's principle brief. Because the statement is included in each copy of the party's brief, there is no need to require the filing of additional copies at that time. A court of appeals may require the filing of a different number of copies by local rule or by order in a particular case.

1998 Amendments

The language and organization of the rule are amended to make the rule more easily understood. In addition to changes made to improve the understanding, the Advisory Committee has changed language to make style and terminology consistent throughout the appellate rules. These changes are intended to by stylistic only; a substantive change is made, however, in subdivision (a).

Subdivision (a). The amendment deletes the requirement that a corporate party identify subsidiaries and affiliates that have issued shares to the public. Although several circuit rules require identification of such entities, the Committee believes that such disclosure is unnecessary.

A disclosure statement assists a judge in ascertaining whether or not the judge has an interest that should cause the judge to recuse himself or herself from the case. Given that purpose, disclosure of entities that would not be adversely affected by a decision in the case is unnecessary.

Disclosure of a party's parent corporation is necessary because a judgment against a subsidiary can negatively impact the parent. A judge who owns stock in the parent corporation, therefore, has an interest in litigation involving the subsidiary. The rule requires disclosure of all of a party's parent corporations meaning grandparent and great grandparent corporations as well. For example, if a party is a closely held corporation, the majority shareholder of which is a corporation formed by a publicly traded corporation for the purpose of acquiring and holding the shares of the party, the publicly traded grandparent corporation should be disclosed. Conversely, disclosure of a party's subsidiaries or affiliated corporations is ordinarily unnecessary. For example, if a party is a part owner of a corporation in which a judge owns stock, the possibility is quite remote that the judge might be biased by the fact that the judge and the litigant are co-owners of a corporation.

The amendment, however, adds a requirement that the party lists all its stockholders that are publicly held companies owning 10% or more of the stock of the party. A judgment against a corporate party can adversely affect the value of the company's stock and, therefore, persons owning stock in the party have an interest in the outcome of the litigation. A judge owning stock in a corporate party ordinarily recuses himself or herself. The new requirement takes the analysis one step further and assumes that if a judge owns stock in a publicly held corporation which in turn owns 10% or more of the stock in the party, the judge may have sufficient interest in the litigation to require recusal. The 10% threshold ensures that the corporation in which the judge may own stock is itself sufficiently invested in the party that a judgment adverse to the party could have an adverse impact upon the investing corporation in which the judge may own stock. This requirement is modeled on the Seventh Circuit's disclosure requirement.

Subdivision (b). The language requiring inclusion of the disclosure statement in a party's principal brief is moved to this subdivision because it deals with the time for filing the statement.

2002 Amendments

Subdivision (a). Rule 26.1(a) requires nongovernmental corporate parties to file a "corporate disclosure statement." In that statement, a nongovernmental corporate party is required to identify all of its parent corporations and all publicly held corporations that own 10% or more of its stock. The corporate disclosure statement is intended to assist judges in determining whether they must recuse themselves by reason of "a financial interest in the subject matter in controversy." Code of Judicial Conduct, Canon 3C(1)(c) (1972).

Rule 26.1(a) has been amended to require that nongovernmental corporate parties who have not been required to file a corporate disclosure statement—that is, nongovernmental corporate parties who do not have any parent corporations and at least 10% of whose stock is not owned by any publicly held corporation—inform the court of that fact. At present, when a corporate disclosure statement is not filed, courts do not know whether it has not been filed because there was nothing to report or because of ignorance of Rule 26.1.

Subdivision (b). Rule 26.1(b) has been amended to require parties to file supplemental disclosure statements whenever there is a change in the information that Rule 26.1(a) requires the parties to disclose. For example, if a publicly held corporation acquires 10% or more of a party's stock after the party has filed its disclosure statement, the party should file a supplemental statement identifying that publicly held corporation.

Subdivision (c). Rule 26.1(c) has been amended to provide that a party who is required to file a supplemental disclosure statement must file an original and 3 copies, unless a local rule or an order entered in a particular case provides otherwise.

Changes Made After Publication and Comments. The Committee is submitting two versions of proposed Rule 26.1 for the consideration of the Standing Committee.

The first version—"Alternative One"—is the same as the version that was published, except that the rule has been amended to refer to "any information that may be *publicly designated* by the Judicial Conference" instead of to "any information that may be *required* by the Judicial Conference." At its April meeting, the Committee gave unconditional approval to all of "Alternative One," except the Judicial Conference provisions. The Committee conditioned its approval of the Judicial Conference provisions on the Standing Committee's assuring itself that lawyers would have ready access to any standards promulgated by the Judicial Conference and that the Judicial Conference provisions were consistent with the Rules Enabling Act.

The second version—"Alternative Two"—is the same as the version that was published, except that the Judicial Conference provisions have been eliminated. The Civil Rules Committee met several days after the Appellate Rules Committee and joined the Bankruptcy Rules Committee in disapproving the Judicial Conference provisions. Given the decreasing likelihood that the Judicial Conference provisions will be approved by the Standing Committee, I asked Prof. Schiltz to draft, and the Appellate Rules Committee to approve, a version of Rule 26.1 that omitted those provisions. "Alternative Two" was circulated to and approved by the Committee in late April.

I should note that, at its April meeting, the Appellate Rules Committee discussed the financial disclosure provision that was approved by the Bankruptcy Rules Committee. That provision defines the scope of the financial disclosure obligation much differently than the provisions approved by the Appellate, Civil, and Criminal Rules Committees, which are based on existing Rule 26.1. For example, the bankruptcy provision requires disclosure when a party "directly or indirectly" owns 10 percent or more of "any class" of a publicly *or* privately held corporation's "equity interests." Members of the Appellate Rules Committee expressed several concerns about the provision approved by the Bankruptcy Rules Committee, objecting both to its substance and to its ambiguity.

2019 Amendments

These amendments are designed to help judges determine whether they must recuse themselves because of an "interest that could be affected substantially by the outcome of the proceeding." Code of Judicial Conduct, Canon 3(C)(1)(c) (2009).

Subdivision (a) is amended to encompass nongovernmental corporations that seek to intervene on appeal.

New subdivision (b) corresponds to the disclosure requirement in Criminal Rule 12.4(a)(2). Like Criminal Rule 12.4(a)(2), subdivision (b) requires the government to identify organizational victims to help judges comply with their obligations under the Code of Judicial Conduct. In some cases, there are many organizational victims, but the effect of the crime on each one is relatively small. In such cases, the amendment allows the government to show good cause to be relieved of making the disclosure statements because the organizations' interests could not be "affected substantially by the outcome of the proceedings."

New subdivision (c) requires disclosure of the names of all the debtors in bankruptcy cases, because the names of the debtors are not always included in the caption in appeals. Subdivision (c) also imposes disclosure requirements concerning the ownership of corporate debtors.

Subdivisions (d) and (e) (formerly subdivisions (b) and (c)) apply to all the disclosure requirements in Rule 26.1.

Rule 27. Motions

(a) In General.

(1) Application for Relief. An application for an order or other relief is made by motion unless these rules prescribe another form. A motion must be in writing unless the court permits otherwise.

(2) Contents of a Motion.

(A) Grounds and relief sought. A motion must state with particularity the grounds for the motion, the relief sought, and the legal argument necessary to support it.

(B) Accompanying documents.

(i) Any affidavit or other paper necessary to support a motion must be served and filed with the motion.

(ii) An affidavit must contain only factual information, not legal argument.

(iii) A motion seeking substantive relief must include a copy of the trial court's opinion or agency's decision as a separate exhibit.

(C) Documents barred or not required.

(i) A separate brief supporting or responding to a motion must not be filed.

(ii) A notice of motion is not required.

(iii) A proposed order is not required.

(3) Response.

(A) Time to file. Any party may file a response to a motion; Rule 27(a)(2) governs its contents. The response must be filed within 10 days after service of the motion unless the court shortens or extends the time. A motion authorized by Rules 8, 9, 18, or 41 may be granted before the 10-day period runs only if the court gives reasonable notice to the parties that it intends to act sooner.

(B) Request for affirmative relief. A response may include a motion for affirmative relief. The time to respond to the new motion, and to reply to that response, are governed by Rule 27(a)(3)(A) and (a)(4). The title of the response must alert the court to the request for relief.

(4) Reply to Response. Any reply to a response must be filed within 7 days after service of the response. A reply must not present matters that do not relate to the response.

(b) Disposition of a Motion for a Procedural Order. The court may act on a motion for a procedural order—including a motion under Rule 26(b)—at any time without awaiting a response, and may, by rule or by order in a particular case, authorize its clerk to act on specified types of procedural motions. A party adversely affected by the court's, or the clerk's, action may file a motion to reconsider, vacate, or modify that action. Timely opposition filed after the motion is granted in whole or in part does not constitute a request to reconsider, vacate, or modify the disposition; a motion requesting that relief must be filed.

(c) Power of a Single Judge to Entertain a Motion. A circuit judge may act alone on any motion, but may not dismiss or otherwise determine an appeal or other proceeding. A court of appeals may provide by rule or by order in a particular case that only the court may act on any motion or class of motions. The court may review the action of a single judge.

(d) Form of Papers; Length Limits; Number of Copies.

(1) Format.

(A) Reproduction. A motion, response, or reply may be reproduced by any process that yields a clear black image on light paper. The paper must be opaque and unglazed. Only one side of the paper may be used.

(B) Cover. A cover is not required, but there must be a caption that includes the case number, the name of the court, the title of the case, and a brief descriptive title indicating the purpose of the motion and identifying the party or parties for whom it is filed. If a cover is used, it must be white.

(C) Binding. The document must be bound in any manner that is secure, does not obscure the text, and permits the document to lie reasonably flat when open.

(D) Paper size, line spacing, and margins. The document must be on $8^1/_2$ by 11 inch paper. The text must be double-spaced, but quotations more than two lines long may be indented and single-spaced. Headings and footnotes may be single-spaced. Margins must be at least one inch on all four sides. Page numbers may be placed in the margins, but no text may appear there.

(E) Typeface and type styles. The document must comply with the typeface requirements of Rule 32(a)(5) and the type-style requirements of Rule 32(a)(6).

(2) Length Limits. Except by the court's permission, and excluding the accompanying documents authorized by Rule 27(a)(2)(B):

(A) a motion or response to a motion produced using a computer must not exceed 5,200 words;

(B) a handwritten or typewritten motion or response to a motion must not exceed 20 pages;

(C) a reply produced using a computer must not exceed 2,600 words; and

(D) a handwritten or typewritten reply to a response must not exceed 10 pages.

(3) Number of Copies. An original and 3 copies must be filed unless the court requires a different number by local rule or by order in a particular case.

(e) Oral Argument. A motion will be decided without oral argument unless the court orders otherwise.

(As amended Apr. 30, 1979, eff. Aug. 1, 1979; Apr. 25, 1989, eff. Dec. 1, 1989; Apr. 29, 1994, eff. Dec. 1, 1994; Apr. 24, 1998, eff. Dec. 1, 1998; Apr. 29, 2002, eff. Dec. 1, 2002; Apr. 25, 2005, eff. Dec. 1, 2005; Mar. 26, 2009, eff. Dec. 1, 2009; Apr. 28, 2016; eff. Dec. 1, 2016.)

ADVISORY COMMITTEE NOTES

1967 Adoption

Subdivisions (a) and (b). Many motions seek relief of a sort which is ordinarily unopposed or which is granted as of course. The provision of subdivision (a) which permits any party to file a response in opposition to a motion within 7 days after its service upon him assumes that the motion is one of substance which ought not be acted upon without affording affected parties an opportunity to reply. A motion to dismiss or otherwise determine an appeal is clearly such a motion. Motions authorized by Rules 8, 9, 18 and 41 are likewise motions of substance; but in the nature of the relief sought, to afford an adversary an automatic delay of at least 7 days is undesirable, thus such motions may be acted upon after notice which is reasonable under the circumstances.

The term "motions for procedural orders" is used in subdivision (b) to describe motions which do not substantially affect the rights of the parties or the ultimate disposition of the appeal. To prevent delay in the disposition of such motions, subdivision (b) provides that they may be acted upon immediately without awaiting a response, subject to the right of any party who is adversely affected by the action to seek reconsideration.

Subdivision (c). Within the general consideration of procedure on motions is the problem of the power of a single circuit judge. Certain powers are granted to a single judge of a court of appeals by statute. Thus, under 28 U.S.C. § 2101(f) a single judge may stay execution and enforcement of a judgment to enable a party aggrieved to obtain certiorari; under 28 U.S.C. § 2251 a judge before whom a habeas corpus proceeding involving a person detained by state authority is pending may stay any proceeding against the person; under 28 U.S.C. § 2253 a single judge may issue a certificate of probably cause. In addition, certain of these rules expressly grant power to a single judge. See Rules 8, 9 and 18.

This subdivision empowers a single circuit judge to act upon virtually all requests for intermediate relief which may be made during the course of an appeal or other proceeding. By its terms he may entertain and act upon any motion other than a motion to dismiss or otherwise determine an appeal or other proceeding. But the relief sought must be "relief which under these rules may properly be sought by motion."

Examples of the power conferred on a single judge by this subdivision are: to extend the time for transmitting the record or docketing the appeal (Rules 11 and 12); to permit intervention in agency cases (Rule 15), or substitution in any case (Rule 43); to permit an appeal in forma pauperis (Rule 24); to enlarge any time period fixed by the rules other than that for initiating a proceeding in the court of appeals (Rule 26(b)); to permit the filing of a brief by amicus curiae (Rule 29); to authorize the filing of a deferred appendix (Rule 30(c)), or dispense with the requirement of an appendix in a specific case (Rule 30(f)), or permit carbon copies of briefs or appendices to be used (Rule 32(a)); to permit the filing of additional briefs (Rule 28(c)), or the filing of briefs of extraordinary length (Rule 28(g)); to postpone oral argument (Rule 34(a)), or grant additional time therefor (Rule 34(b)).

Certain rules require that application for the relief or orders which they authorize be made by petition. Since relief under those rules may not properly be sought by motion, a single judge may not entertain requests for such relief. Thus a single judge may not act upon requests for permission to appeal (see Rules 5 and 6); or for mandamus or other extraordinary writs (see Rule 21), other than for stays or injunctions *pendente lite*, authority to grant which is "expressly conferred by these rules" on a single judge under certain circumstances (see Rules 8 and 18); or upon petitions for rehearing (see Rule 40).

A court of appeals may by order or rule abridge the power of a single judge if it is of the view that a motion or a class of motions should be disposed of by a panel. Exercise of any power granted a single judge is discretionary with the judge. The final sentence in this subdivision makes the disposition of any matter by a single judge subject to review by the court.

1979 Amendment

The proposed amendment would give sanction to local rules in a number of circuits permitting the clerk to dispose of specified types of procedural motions.

1989 Amendment

The amendment is technical. No substantive change is intended.

1994 Amendments

Subdivision (d). The amendment makes it clear that a court may require a different number of copies either by rule or by order in an individual case. The number of copies of any document that a court of appeals needs varies depending upon the way in which the court conducts business. The internal operation of the courts of appeals necessarily varies from circuit to circuit because of differences in the number of judges, the geographic area included within the circuit, and other such factors. Uniformity could be achieved only by setting the number of copies artificially high so that parties in all circuits file enough copies to satisfy the needs of the court requiring the greatest number. Rather than do that, the Committee decided to make it clear that local rules may require a greater or lesser number of copies and that, if the circumstances of a particular case indicate the need for a different number of copies in that case, the court may so order.

1998 Amendments

In addition to amending Rule 27 to conform to uniform drafting standards, several substantive amendments are made. The Advisory Committee had been working on substantive amendments to Rule 27 just prior to completion of this larger project.

Subdivision (a). Paragraph (1) retains the language of the existing rule indicating that an application for an order or other relief is made by filing a motion unless another form is required by some other provision in the rules.

Paragraph (1) also states that a motion must be in writing unless the court permits otherwise. The writing requirement has been implicit in the rule; the Advisory Committee decided to make it explicit. There are, however, instances in which a court may permit oral motions. Perhaps the most common such instance would be a motion made during oral argument in the presence of opposing counsel; for example, a request for permission to submit a supplemental brief on an issue raised by the court for the first time at oral argument. Rather than limit oral motions to those made during oral argument or, conversely, assume the propriety of making even extremely complex motions orally during argument, the Advisory Committee decided that it is better to leave the determination of the propriety of an oral motion to the court's discretion. The provision does not disturb the practice in those circuits that permit certain procedural motions, such as a motion for extension of time for filing a brief, to be made by telephone and ruled upon by the clerk.

Paragraph (2) outlines the contents of a motion. It begins with the general requirement from the current rule that a motion must state with particularity the grounds supporting it and the relief requested. It adds a requirement that all legal arguments should be presented in the body of the motion; a separate brief or memorandum supporting or responding to a motion must not be filed. The Supreme Court uses this single document approach. Sup. Ct. R. 21.1. In furtherance of the requirement that all legal argument must be contained in the body of the motion, paragraph (2) also states that an affidavit that is attached to a motion should contain only factual information and not legal argument.

Paragraph (2) further states that whenever a motion requests substantive relief, a copy of the trial court's opinion or agency's decision must be attached.

Although it is common to present a district court with a proposed order along with the motion requesting relief, that is not the practice in the courts of appeals. A proposed order is not required and is not expected or desired. Nor is a notice of motion required.

Paragraph (3) retains the provisions of the current rule concerning the filing of a response to a motion except that the time for responding has been expanded to 10 days rather than 7 days. Because the time periods in the rule apply to a substantive motion as well as a procedural motion, the longer time period may help reduce the number of motions for extension of time, or at least provide a more realistic time frame within which to make and dispose of such a motion.

A party filing a response in opposition to a motion may also request affirmative relief. It is the Advisory Committee's judgment that it is permissible to combine the response and the new motion in the same document. Indeed, because there may be substantial overlap of arguments in the response and in the request for affirmative relief, a combined document may be preferable. If a request for relief is combined with a response, the caption of the document must alert the court to the request for relief. The time for a response to such a new request and for reply to that response are governed by the general rules regulating responses and replies.

Paragraph (4) is new. Two circuits currently have rules authorizing a reply. As a general matter, a reply should not reargue propositions presented in the motion or present matters that do not relate to the response. Sometimes matters relevant to the motion arise after the motion is filed; treatment of such matters in the reply is appropriate even though strictly speaking it may not relate to the response.

Subdivision (b). The material in this subdivision remains substantively unchanged except to clarify that one may file a motion for reconsideration, etc. of a disposition by either the court or the clerk. A new sentence is added indicating that if a motion is granted in whole or in part before the filing of timely opposition to the motion, the filing of the opposition is not treated as a request for reconsideration, etc., A party wishing to have the court reconsider, vacate, or modify the disposition must file a new motion that addresses the order granting the motion.

Although the rule does not require a court to do so, it would be helpful if, whenever a motion is disposed of before receipt of any response from the opposing party, the ruling indicates that it was issued without awaiting a response. Such a statement will aid the opposing party in deciding whether to request reconsideration. The opposing party may have mailed a response about the time of the ruling and be uncertain whether the court has considered it.

Subdivision (c). The changes in this subdivision are stylistic only. No substantive changes are intended.

Subdivision (d). This subdivision has been substantially revised.

The format requirements have been moved from Rule 32(b) to paragraph (1) of this subdivision. No cover is required, but a caption is needed as well as a descriptive title indicating the purpose of the motion and identifying the party or parties for whom it is filed. Spiral binding or secure stapling at the upper left-hand corner satisfies the binding requirement. But they are not intended to be the exclusive methods of binding.

Paragraph (2) establishes page limits; twenty pages for a motion or a response, and ten pages for a reply. Three circuits have established page limits by local rule. This rule does not establish special page limits for those instances in which a party combines a response to a motion with a new request for affirmative relief. Because a combined document most often will be used when there is substantial overlap in the argument in opposition to the motion and in the argument for the affirmative relief, twenty pages may be sufficient in most instances. If it is not, the party may request additional pages. If ten pages is insufficient for the original movant to both reply to the response, and respond to the new request for affirmative relief, two separate documents may be used or a request for additional pages may be made.

The changes in paragraph (4) are stylistic only. No substantive changes are intended.

Subdivision (e). This new provision makes it clear that there is no right to oral argument on a motion. Seven circuits have local rules stating that oral argument of motions will not be held unless the court orders it.

2002 Amendments

Subdivision (a)(3)(A). Subdivision (a)(3)(A) presently requires that a response to a motion be filed within 10 days after service of the motion. Intermediate Saturdays, Sundays, and legal holidays are counted in computing that 10-day deadline, which means that, except when the 10-day deadline ends on a weekend or legal holiday, parties generally must respond to motions within 10 actual days.

Fed. R. App. P. 26(a)(2) has been amended to provide that, in computing any period of time, a litigant should "[e]xclude intermediate Saturdays, Sundays, and legal holidays when the period is less than 11 days, unless stated in calendar days." This change in the method of computing deadlines means that 10-day deadlines (such as that in subdivision (a)(3)(A)) have been lengthened as a practical matter. Under the new computation method, parties would never have less than 14 actual days to respond to motions, and legal holidays could extend that period to as much as 18 days.

Permitting parties to take two weeks or more to respond to motions would introduce significant and unwarranted delay into appellate proceedings. For that reason, the 10-day deadline in subdivision (a)(3)(A) has been reduced to 8 days. This change will, as a practical matter, ensure that every party will have at least 10 actual days—but, in the absence of a legal holiday, no more than 12 actual days—to respond to motions. The court continues to have discretion to shorten or extend that time in appropriate cases.

Changes Made After Publication and Comments. In response to the objections of commentators, the time to respond to a motion was increased from the proposed 7 days to 8 days. No other changes were made to the text of the proposed amendment or to the Committee Note.

Subdivision (a)(4). Subdivision (a)(4) presently requires that a reply to a response to a motion be filed within 7 days after service of the response. Intermediate Saturdays, Sundays, and legal holidays are counted in computing that 7-day deadline, which means that, except when the 7-day deadline ends on a weekend or legal holiday, parties generally must reply to responses to motions within one week.

Fed. R. App. P. 26(a)(2) has been amended to provide that, in computing any period of time, a litigant should "[e]xclude intermediate Saturdays, Sundays, and legal holidays when the period is less than 11 days, unless stated in calendar days." This change in the method of computing deadlines means that 7-day deadlines (such as that in subdivision (a)(4)) have been lengthened as a practical matter. Under the new computation method, parties would never have less than 9 actual days to reply to responses to motions, and legal holidays could extend that period to as much as 13 days.

Permitting parties to take 9 or more days to reply to a response to a motion would introduce significant and unwarranted delay into appellate proceedings. For that reason, the 7-day deadline in subdivision (a)(4) has been reduced to 5 days. This change will, as a practical matter, ensure that every party will have 7 actual days to file replies to responses to motions (in the absence of a legal holiday).

Changes Made After Publication and Comments. No changes were made to the text of the proposed amendment or to the Committee Note.

Subdivision (d)(1)(B). A cover is not required on motions, responses to motions, or replies to responses to motions. However, Rule 27(d)(1)(B) has been amended to provide that if a cover is nevertheless used on such a paper, the cover must be white. The amendment is intended to promote uniformity in federal appellate practice.

Changes Made After Publication and Comments. No changes were made to the text of the proposed amendment or to the Committee Note.

2005 Amendments

Subdivision (d)(1)(E). A new subdivision (E) has been added to Rule 27(d)(1) to provide that a motion, a response to a motion, and a reply to a response to a motion must comply with the typeface requirements of Rule 32(a)(5) and the type-style requirements of Rule 32(a)(6). The purpose of the amendment is to promote uniformity in federal appellate practice and to prevent the abuses that might occur if no restrictions were placed on the size of typeface used in motion papers.

2009 Amendments

Subdivision (a)(3)(A). Subdivision (a)(3)(A) formerly required that a response to a motion be filed "within 8 days after service of the motion unless the court shortens or extends the time." Prior to the 2002 amendments to Rule 27, subdivision (a)(3)(A) set this period at 10 days rather than 8 days. The period was changed in 2002 to reflect the change from a time-computation approach that counted intermediate weekends and holidays to an approach that did not. (Prior to the 2002 amendments, intermediate weekends and holidays were excluded only if the period was less than 7 days; after those amendments, such days were excluded if the period was less than 11 days.) Under current Rule 26(a), intermediate weekends and holidays are counted for all periods. Accordingly, revised subdivision (a)(3)(A) once again sets the period at 10 days.

Subdivision (a)(4). Subdivision (a)(4) formerly required that a reply to a response be filed "within 5 days after service of the response." Prior to the 2002 amendments, this period was set at 7 days; in 2002 it was shortened in the light of the 2002 change in time-computation approach (discussed above). Under current Rule 26(a), intermediate weekends and holidays are counted for all periods, and revised subdivision (a)(4) once again sets the period at 7 days.

2016 Amendments

The page limits previously employed in Rules 5, 21, 27, 35, and 40 have been largely overtaken by changes in technology. For papers produced using a computer, those page limits are now replaced by word limits. The word limits were derived from the current page limits using the assumption that one page is equivalent to 260 words. Papers produced using a computer must include the certificate of compliance required by Rule 32(g); Form 6 in the Appendix of Forms suffices to meet that requirement. Page limits are retained for papers prepared without the aid of a computer (i.e., handwritten or typewritten papers). For both the word limit and the page limit, the calculation excludes the accompanying documents required by Rule 27(a)(2)(B) and any items listed in Rule 32(f).

Changes Made After Publication and Comment

The Committee deleted the proposed line limits. The Committee revised the proposed word limit for motions and responses from 5,000 words to 5,200 words, and revised the proposed word limit for replies from 2,500 words to 2,600 words. The Committee also made conforming changes to the Committee Note and style changes to the Rule text.

Rule 28.   Briefs

(a)   Appellant's Brief. The appellant's brief must contain, under appropriate headings and in the order indicated:

(1)   a disclosure statement if required by Rule 26.1;

(2)   a table of contents, with page references;

(3)   a table of authorities—cases (alphabetically arranged), statutes, and other authorities—with references to the pages of the brief where they are cited;

(4)   a jurisdictional statement, including:

(A)   the basis for the district court's or agency's subject-matter jurisdiction, with citations to applicable statutory provisions and stating relevant facts establishing jurisdiction;

(B)   the basis for the court of appeals' jurisdiction, with citations to applicable statutory provisions and stating relevant facts establishing jurisdiction;

(C)   the filing dates establishing the timeliness of the appeal or petition for review; and

(D)   an assertion that the appeal is from a final order or judgment that disposes of all parties' claims, or information establishing the court of appeals' jurisdiction on some other basis;

(5)   a statement of the issues presented for review;

(6)   a concise statement of the case setting out the facts relevant to the issues submitted for review, describing the relevant procedural history, and identifying the rulings presented for review, with appropriate references to the record (see Rule 28(e));

(7)   a summary of the argument, which must contain a succinct, clear, and accurate statement of the arguments made in the body of the brief, and which must not merely repeat the argument headings;

(8)   the argument, which must contain:

(A)   appellant's contentions and the reasons for them, with citations to the authorities and parts of the record on which the appellant relies; and

(B)   for each issue, a concise statement of the applicable standard of review (which may appear in the discussion of the issue or under a separate heading placed before the discussion of the issues);

(9)   a short conclusion stating the precise relief sought; and

(10) the certificate of compliance, if required by Rule 32(g)(1).

(b)   Appellee's Brief. The appellee's brief must conform to the requirements of Rule 28(a)(1)–(8) and (10), except that none of the following need appear unless the appellee is dissatisfied with the appellant's statement:

(1)   the jurisdictional statement;

(2)   the statement of the issues;

(3)   the statement of the case; and

(4)   the statement of the standard of review.

(c)   Reply Brief. The appellant may file a brief in reply to the appellee's brief. Unless the court permits, no further briefs may be filed. A reply brief must contain a table of contents, with page references, and a table of authorities—cases (alphabetically arranged), statutes, and other authorities—with references to the pages of the reply brief where they are cited.

(d) References to Parties. In briefs and at oral argument, counsel should minimize use of the terms "appellant" and "appellee." To make briefs clear, counsel should use the parties' actual names or the designations used in the lower court or agency proceeding, or such descriptive terms as "the employee," "the injured person," "the taxpayer," "the ship," "the stevedore."

(e) References to the Record. References to the parts of the record contained in the appendix filed with the appellant's brief must be to the pages of the appendix. If the appendix is prepared after the briefs are filed, a party referring to the record must follow one of the methods detailed in Rule 30(c). If the original record is used under Rule 30(f) and is not consecutively paginated, or if the brief refers to an unreproduced part of the record, any reference must be to the page of the original document. For example:

- Answer p. 7;

- Motion for Judgment p. 2;

- Transcript p. 231.

Only clear abbreviations may be used. A party referring to evidence whose admissibility is in controversy must cite the pages of the appendix or of the transcript at which the evidence was identified, offered, and received or rejected.

(f) Reproduction of Statutes, Rules, Regulations, etc. If the court's determination of the issues presented requires the study of statutes, rules, regulations, etc., the relevant parts must be set out in the brief or in an addendum at the end, or may be supplied to the court in pamphlet form.

(g) [Reserved]

(h) [Deleted]

(i) Briefs in a Case Involving Multiple Appellants or Appellees. In a case involving more than one appellant or appellee, including consolidated cases, any number of appellants or appellees may join in a brief, and any party may adopt by reference a part of another's brief. Parties may also join in reply briefs.

(j) Citation of Supplemental Authorities. If pertinent and significant authorities come to a party's attention after the party's brief has been filed—or after oral argument but before decision—a party may promptly advise the circuit clerk by letter, with a copy to all other parties, setting forth the citations. The letter must state the reasons for the supplemental citations, referring either to the page of the brief or to a point argued orally. The body of the letter must not exceed 350 words. Any response must be made promptly and must be similarly limited.

(As amended Apr. 30, 1979, eff. Aug. 1, 1979; Mar. 10, 1986, eff. July 1, 1986; Apr. 25, 1989, eff. Dec. 1, 1989; Apr. 30, 1991, eff. Dec. 1, 1991; Apr. 22, 1993, eff. Dec. 1, 1993; Apr. 29, 1994, eff. Dec. 1, 1994; Apr. 24, 1998, eff. Dec. 1, 1998; Apr. 29, 2002, eff. Dec. 1, 2002; Apr. 25, 2005, eff. Dec. 1, 2005; Apr. 16, 2013, eff. Dec. 1, 2013; Apr. 28, 2016, eff. Dec. 1, 2016; Apr. 25, 2019, eff. Dec. 1, 2019.)

ADVISORY COMMITTEE NOTES

1967 Adoption

This rule is based upon Supreme Court Rule 40. For variations in present circuit rules on briefs see 2d Cir. Rule 17 [rule 17, U.S.Ct. of App. 2d Cir.], 3d Cir. Rule 24 [rule 24, U.S.Ct. of App. 3d Cir.], 5th Cir. Rule 24 [rule 24, U.S.Ct. of App. 5th Cir.], and 7th Cir. Rule 17 [rule 17, U.S.Ct. of App. 7th Cir.]. All circuits now limit the number of pages of briefs, a majority limiting the brief to 50 pages of standard typographic printing. Fifty pages of standard typographic printing is the approximate equivalent of 70 pages of typewritten text, given the page sizes required by Rule 32 and the requirement set out there that text produced by a method other than standard typographic must be double spaced.

1979 Amendments

Subdivision (g). The proposed amendment eliminates the distinction appearing in the present rule between the permissible length in pages of printed and typewritten briefs, investigation of the matter having disclosed that the number of words on the printed page is little if any larger than the number on a page typed in standard elite type.

The provision is made subject to local rule to permit the court of appeals to require that typewritten briefs be typed in larger type and permit a correspondingly larger number of pages.

Subdivision (j). Proposed new Rule 28(j) makes provision for calling the court's attention to authorities that come to the party's attention after the brief has been filed. It is patterned after the practice under local rule in some of the circuits.

1986 Amendments

While Rule 28(g) can be read as requiring that tables of authorities be included in a reply brief, such tables are often not included. Their absence impedes efficient use of the reply brief to ascertain the appellant's response to a particular argument of the appellee or to the appellee's use of a particular authority. The amendment to Rule 28(c) is intended to make it clear that such tables are required in reply briefs.

The amendment to Rule 28(j) is technical. No substantive change is intended.

1989 Amendments

The amendment provides that the corporate disclosure statement required by new Rule 26.1 shall be treated similarly to tables of contents and tables of citations and shall not be counted for purposes of the number of pages allowed in a brief.

1991 Amendments

Subdivision (a). The amendment adds a new subparagraph (2) that requires an appellant to include a specific jurisdictional statement in the appellant's brief to aid the court of appeals in determining whether it has both federal subject matter and appellate jurisdiction.

Subdivision (b). The amendment requires the appellee to include a jurisdictional statement in the appellee's brief except that the appellee need not include the statement if the appellee is satisfied with the appellant's jurisdictional statement.

Subdivision (h). The amendment provides that when more than one party appeals from a judgment or order, the party filing the first appeal is normally treated as the appellant for purposes of this rule and Rules 30 and 31. The party who first files an appeal usually is the principal appellant and should be treated as such. Parties who file a notice of appeal after the first notice often bring protective appeals and they should be treated as cross appellants. Local rules in the Fourth and Federal Circuits now take that approach. If notices of appeal are filed on the same day, the rule follows the old approach of treating the plaintiff below as the appellant. For purposes of this rule, in criminal cases "the plaintiff" means the United States. In those instances where the designations provided by the rule are inappropriate, they may be altered by agreement of the parties or by an order of the court.

1993 Amendments

Note to paragraph (a)(5). The amendment requires an appellant's brief to state the standard of review applicable to each issue on appeal. Five circuits currently require these statements. Experience in those circuits indicates that requiring a statement of the standard of review generally results in arguments that are properly shaped in light of the standard.

1994 Amendments

Subdivision (a). The amendment adds a requirement that an appellant's brief contain a summary of the argument. A number of circuits have local rules requiring a summary and the courts report that they find the summary useful. See, D.C. Cir.R. 11(a)(5); 5th Cir.R. 28.2.2; 8th Cir.R. 28A(i)(6); 11th Cir.R. 28–2(i); and Fed. Cir.R. 28.

Subdivision (b). The amendment adds a requirement that an appellee's brief contain a summary of the argument.

Subdivision (g). The amendment adds proof of service to the list of items in a brief that do not count for purposes of the page limitation. The concurrent amendment to Rule 25(d) requires a certificate of service to list the addresses to which a paper was mailed or at which it was delivered. When a number of parties must be served, the listing of addresses may run to several pages and those pages should not count for purposes of the page limitation.

1998 Amendments

The language and organization of the rule are amended to make the rule more easily understood. In addition to changes made to improve the understanding, the Advisory Committee has changed language to make style and terminology consistent throughout the appellate rules. These changes are intended to by stylistic only.

Several substantive changes are made in this rule, however. Most of them are necessary to confirm Rule 28 with changes recommended in Rule 32.

Subdivision (a). The current rule requires a brief to include a statement of the case which includes a description of the nature of the case, the course of proceedings, the disposition of the case—all of which might be described as the procedural history—as well as a statement of the facts. The amendments separate this into two statements; one procedural, called the statement of the case; and one factual, called the statement of the facts. The Advisory Committee believes that the separation will be helpful to the judges. The table of contents and table of authorities have also been separated into two distinct items.

An additional amendment of subdivision (a) is made to conform it with an amendment being made to Rule 32. Rule 32(a)(7) generally requires a brief to include a certificate of compliance with type-volume limitations contained in that rule. (No certificate is required if a brief does not exceed 30 pages, or 15 pages for a reply brief.) Rule 28(a) is amended to include that certificate in the list of items that must be included in a brief whenever it is required by Rule 32.

Subdivision (g). The amendments delete subdivision (g) that limited a principal brief to 50 pages and a reply brief to 25 pages. The length limitations have been moved to Rule 32. Rule 32 deals generally with the format for a brief or appendix.

Subdivision (h). The amendment requires an appellee's brief to comply with Rule 28(a)(1) through (11) with regard to a cross-appeal. The addition of separate paragraphs requiring a corporate disclosure statement, table of authorities, statement of facts, and certificate of compliance increased the relevant paragraphs of subdivision (a) from (7) to (11). The other changes are stylistic; no substantive changes are intended.

2002 Amendments

Subdivision (j). In the past, Rule 28(j) has required parties to describe supplemental authorities "without argument." Enforcement of this restriction has been lax, in part because of the difficulty of distinguishing "state[ment] . . . [of] the reasons for the supplemental citations," which is required, from "argument" about the supplemental citations, which is forbidden.

As amended, Rule 28(j) continues to require parties to state the reasons for supplemental citations, with reference to the part of a brief or oral argument to which the supplemental citations pertain. But Rule 28(j) no longer forbids "argument." Rather, Rule 28(j) permits parties to decide for themselves what they wish to say about supplemental authorities. The only restriction upon parties is that the body of a Rule 28(j) letter—that is, the part of the letter that begins with the first word after the salutation and ends with the last word before the complimentary close—cannot exceed 350 words. All words found in footnotes will count toward the 350-word limit.

Changes Made After Publication and Comments. No changes were made to the text of the proposed amendment or to the Committee Note, except that the word limit was increased from 250 to 350 in response to the complaint of some commentators that parties would have difficulty bringing multiple supplemental authorities to the attention of the court in one 250-word letter.

2005 Amendments

Subdivision (c). Subdivision (c) has been amended to delete a sentence that authorized an appellee who had cross-appealed to file a brief in reply to the appellant's response. All rules regarding briefing in cases involving cross-appeals have been consolidated into new Rule 28.1.

Subdivision (h). Subdivision (h)—regarding briefing in cases involving cross-appeals—has been deleted. All rules regarding such briefing have been consolidated into new Rule 28.1.

2013 Amendments

Subdivision (a). Rule 28(a) is amended to remove the requirement of separate statements of the case and of the facts. Currently Rule 28(a)(6) provides that the statement of the case must "indicat[e] the nature of the case, the course of proceedings, and the disposition below," and it precedes Rule 28(a)(7)'s requirement that the brief include "a statement of facts." Experience has shown that these requirements have generated confusion and redundancy. Rule 28(a) is amended to consolidate subdivisions (a)(6) and (a)(7) into a new subdivision (a)(6) that provides for one "statement," much like Supreme Court Rule 24.1(g) (which requires "[a] concise statement of the case, setting out the facts material to the consideration of the questions presented, with appropriate references to the joint appendix . . . "). This permits but does not require the lawyer to present the factual and procedural history chronologically. Conforming changes are made by renumbering Rules 28(a)(8) through (11) as Rules 28(a)(7) through (10).

The statement of the case should describe the nature of the case, which includes (1) the facts relevant to the issues submitted for review; (2) those aspects of the case's procedural history that are necessary to understand the posture of the appeal or are relevant to the issues submitted for review; and (3) the rulings presented for review. The statement should be concise, and can include subheadings, particularly for the purpose of highlighting the rulings presented for review.

Subdivision (b). Rule 28(b) is amended to accord with the amendment to Rule 28(a). Current Rules 28(b)(3) and (4) are consolidated into new Rule 28(b)(3), which refers to "the statement of the case." Rule 28(b)(5) becomes Rule 28(b)(4). And Rule 28(b)'s reference to certain subdivisions of Rule 28(a) is updated to reflect the renumbering of those subdivisions.

Changes Made After Publication and Comment

After publication and comment, the Committee made one change to the text of the proposal and two changes to the Committee Note.

During the comment period, concerns were raised that the deletion of current Rule 28(a)(6)'s reference to "the nature of the case, the course of proceedings, and the disposition below" might lead readers to conclude that those items may no longer be included in the statement of the case. The Committee rejected that concern with respect to the "nature of the case" and the "disposition below," because the Rule as published would naturally be read to permit continued inclusion of those items in the statement of the case. The Committee adhered to its view that the deletion of "course of proceedings" is useful because that phrase tends to elicit unnecessary detail; but to address the commenters' concerns, the Committee added, to the revised Rule text, the phrase "describing the relevant procedural history."

The Committee augmented the Note to Rule 28(a) in two respects. It added a reference to Supreme Court Rule 24.1(g), upon which the proposed revision to Rule 28(a)(6) is modeled. And it added—as a second paragraph in the Note—a discussion of the contents of the statement of the case.

2016 Amendments

Rule 28(a)(10) is revised to refer to Rule 32(g)(1) instead of Rule 32(a)(7), to reflect the relocation of the certificate-of-compliance requirement.

2019 Amendments

The phrase "corporate disclosure statement" is changed to "disclosure statement" to reflect the revision of Rule 26.1.

Rule 28.1.   Cross-Appeals

(a) Applicability. This rule applies to a case in which a cross-appeal is filed. Rules 28(a)–(c), 31(a)(1), 32(a)(2), and 32(a)(7)(A)–(B) do not apply to such a case, except as otherwise provided in this rule.

(b) Designation of Appellant. The party who files a notice of appeal first is the appellant for the purposes of this rule and Rules 30 and 34. If notices are filed on the same day, the plaintiff in the proceeding below is the appellant. These designations may be modified by the parties' agreement or by court order.

(c) **Briefs.** In a case involving a cross-appeal:

(1) **Appellant's Principal Brief.** The appellant must file a principal brief in the appeal. That brief must comply with Rule 28(a).

(2) **Appellee's Principal and Response Brief.** The appellee must file a principal brief in the cross-appeal and must, in the same brief, respond to the principal brief in the appeal. That appellee's brief must comply with Rule 28(a), except that the brief need not include a statement of the case unless the appellee is dissatisfied with the appellant's statement.

(3) **Appellant's Response and Reply Brief.** The appellant must file a brief that responds to the principal brief in the cross-appeal and may, in the same brief, reply to the response in the appeal. That brief must comply with Rule 28(a)(2)–(8) and (10), except that none of the following need appear unless the appellant is dissatisfied with the appellee's statement in the cross-appeal:

(A) the jurisdictional statement;

(B) the statement of the issues;

(C) the statement of the case; and

(D) the statement of the standard of review.

(4) **Appellee's Reply Brief.** The appellee may file a brief in reply to the response in the cross-appeal. That brief must comply with Rule 28(a)(2)–(3) and (10) and must be limited to the issues presented by the cross-appeal.

(5) **No Further Briefs.** Unless the court permits, no further briefs may be filed in a case involving a cross-appeal.

(d) **Cover.** Except for filings by unrepresented parties, the cover of the appellant's principal brief must be blue; the appellee's principal and response brief, red; the appellant's response and reply brief, yellow; the appellee's reply brief, gray; an intervenor's or amicus curiae's brief, green; and any supplemental brief, tan. The front cover of a brief must contain the information required by Rule 32(a)(2).

(e) **Length.**

(1) **Page Limitation.** Unless it complies with Rule 28.1(e)(2), the appellant's principal brief must not exceed 30 pages; the appellee's principal and response brief, 35 pages; the appellant's response and reply brief, 30 pages; and the appellee's reply brief, 15 pages.

(2) **Type-Volume Limitation.**

(A) The appellant's principal brief or the appellant's response and reply brief is acceptable if it:

(i) contains no more than 13,000 words; or

(ii) uses a monospaced face and contains no more than 1,300 lines of text.

(B) The appellee's principal and response brief is acceptable if it:

(i) contains no more than 15,300 words; or

(ii) uses a monospaced face and contains no more than 1,500 lines of text.

(C) The appellee's reply brief is acceptable if it contains no more than half of the type volume specified in Rule 28.1(e)(2)(A).

(f) **Time to Serve and File a Brief.** Briefs must be served and filed as follows:

(1) the appellant's principal brief, within 40 days after the record is filed;

(2) the appellee's principal and response brief, within 30 days after the appellant's principal brief is served;

(3) the appellant's response and reply brief, within 30 days after the appellee's principal and response brief is served; and

(4) the appellee's reply brief, within 21 days after the appellant's response and reply brief is served, but at least 7 days before argument unless the court, for good cause, allows a later filing.

(As added April 25, 2005, eff. Dec. 1, 2005; amended Mar. 26, 2009, eff. Dec. 1, 2009; Apr. 16, 2013, eff. Dec. 1, 2013; Apr. 28, 2016, eff. Dec. 1, 2016; Apr. 26, 2018, eff. Dec. 1, 2018.)

ADVISORY COMMITTEE NOTES

2005 Adoption

The Federal Rules of Appellate Procedure have said very little about briefing in cases involving cross-appeals. This vacuum has frustrated judges, attorneys, and parties who have sought guidance in the rules. More importantly, this vacuum has been filled by conflicting local rules regarding such matters as the number and length of briefs, the colors of the covers of briefs, and the deadlines for serving and filing briefs. These local rules have created a hardship for attorneys who practice in more than one circuit.

New Rule 28.1 provides a comprehensive set of rules governing briefing in cases involving cross-appeals. The few existing provisions regarding briefing in such cases have been moved into new Rule 28.1, and several new provisions have been added to fill the gaps in the existing rules. The new provisions reflect the practices of the large majority of circuits and, to a significant extent, the new provisions have been patterned after the requirements imposed by Rules 28, 31, and 32 on briefs filed in cases that do not involve cross-appeals.

Subdivision (a). Subdivision (a) makes clear that, in a case involving a cross-appeal, briefing is governed by new Rule 28.1, and not by Rules 28(a), 28(b), 28(c), 31(a)(1), 32(a)(2), 32(a)(7)(A), and 32(a)(7)(B), except to the extent that Rule 28.1 specifically incorporates those rules by reference.

Subdivision (b). Subdivision (b) defines who is the "appellant" and who is the "appellee" in a case involving a cross-appeal. Subdivision (b) is taken directly from former Rule 28(h), except that subdivision (b) refers to a party being designated as an appellant "for the purposes of this rule and Rules 30 and 34," whereas former Rule 28(h) also referred to Rule 31. Because the matter addressed by Rule 31(a)(1)—the time to serve and file briefs—is now addressed directly in new Rule 28.1(f), the cross-reference to Rule 31 is no longer necessary. In Rule 31 and in all rules other than Rules 28.1, 30, and 34, references to an "appellant" refer both to the appellant in an appeal and to the cross-appellant in a cross-appeal, and references to an "appellee" refer both to the appellee in an appeal and to the cross-appellee in a cross-appeal. Cf. Rule 31(c).

Subdivision (c). Subdivision (c) provides for the filing of four briefs in a case involving a cross-appeal. This reflects the practice of every circuit except the Seventh. *See* 7th Cir. R. 28(d)(1)(a).

The first brief is the "appellant's principal brief." That brief—like the appellant's principal brief in a case that does not involve a cross-appeal—must comply with Rule 28(a).

The second brief is the "appellee's principal and response brief." Because this brief serves as the appellee's principal brief on the merits of the cross-appeal, as well as the appellee's response brief on the merits of the appeal, it must also comply with Rule 28(a), with the limited exceptions noted in the text of the rule.

The third brief is the "appellant's response and reply brief." Like a response brief in a case that does not involve a cross-appeal—that is, a response brief that does not also serve as a principal brief on the merits of a cross-appeal—the appellant's response and reply brief must comply with Rule 28(a)(2)–(9) and (11), with the exceptions noted in the text of the rule. *See* Rule 28(b). The one difference between the appellant's response and reply brief, on the one hand, and a response brief filed in a case that does not involve a cross-appeal, on the other, is that the latter must include a corporate disclosure statement. *See* Rule 28(a)(1) and (b). An appellant filing a response and reply brief in a case involving a cross-appeal has already filed a corporate disclosure statement with its principal brief on the merits of the appeal.

The fourth brief is the "appellee's reply brief." Like a reply brief in a case that does not involve a cross-appeal, it must comply with Rule 28(c), which essentially restates the requirements of Rule 28(a)(2)–(3) and (11). (Rather than restating the requirements of Rule 28(a)(2)–(3) and (11), as Rule 28(c) does, Rule 28.1(c)(4) includes a direct cross-reference.) The appellee's reply brief must also be limited to the issues presented by the cross-appeal.

Subdivision (d). Subdivision (d) specifies the colors of the covers on briefs filed in a case involving a cross-appeal. It is patterned after Rule 32(a)(2), which does not specifically refer to cross-appeals.

Subdivision (e). Subdivision (e) sets forth limits on the length of the briefs filed in a case involving a cross-appeal. It is patterned after Rule 32(a)(7), which does not specifically refer to cross-appeals. Subdivision (e) permits the appellee's principal and response brief to be longer than a typical principal brief on the merits because this brief serves not only as the principal brief on the merits of the cross-appeal, but also as the response brief on the merits of the appeal. Likewise, subdivision (e) permits the appellant's response and reply brief to be longer than a typical reply brief because this brief serves not only as the reply brief in the appeal, but also as the response brief in the cross-appeal. For purposes of determining the maximum length of an amicus curiae's brief filed in a case involving a cross-appeal, Rule 29(d)'s reference to "the maximum length authorized by these rules for a party's principal brief" should be understood to refer to subdivision (e)'s limitations on the length of an appellant's principal brief.

Subdivision (f). Subdivision (f) provides deadlines for serving and filing briefs in a cross-appeal. It is patterned after Rule 31(a)(1), which does not specifically refer to cross-appeals.

2009 Amendments

Subdivision (f)(4). Subdivision (f)(4) formerly required that the appellee's reply brief be served "at least 3 days before argument unless the court, for good cause, allows a later filing." Under former Rule 26(a), "3 days" could mean as many as 5 or even 6 days. See the Note to Rule 26. Under revised Rule 26(a), intermediate weekends and holidays are counted. Changing "3 days" to "7 days" alters the period accordingly. Under revised Rule 26(a), when a period ends on a weekend or holiday, one must continue to count in the same direction until the next day that is not a weekend or holiday; the choice of the 7-day period for subdivision (f)(4) will minimize such occurrences.

2013 Amendments

Subdivision (c). Subdivision (c) is amended to accord with the amendments to Rule 28(a). Rule 28(a) is amended to consolidate subdivisions (a)(6) and (a)(7) into a new subdivision (a)(6) that provides for one "statement of the case setting out the facts relevant to the issues submitted for review, describing the relevant procedural history, and identifying the rulings presented for review . . . " Rule 28.1(c) is amended to refer to that consolidated "statement of the case," and references to subdivisions of Rule 28(a) are revised to reflect the re-numbering of those subdivisions.

Changes Made After Publication and Comment

No changes were made to the text of the proposed amendment to Rule 28.1 after publication and comment. The Committee revised a quotation in the Committee Note to Rule 28.1(c) to conform to the changes (described above) to the text of proposed Rule 28(a)(6).

2016 Amendments

When Rule 28.1 was adopted in 2005, it modeled its type-volume limits on those set forth in Rule 32(a)(7) for briefs in cases that did not involve a cross-appeal. At that time, Rule 32(a)(7)(B) set word limits based on an estimate of 280 words per page.

In the course of adopting word limits for the length limits in Rules 5, 21, 27, 35, and 40, and responding to concern about the length of briefs, the Committee has reevaluated the conversion ratio (from pages to words) and decided to apply a conversion ratio of 260 words per page. Rules 28.1 and 32(a)(7)(B) are amended to reduce the word limits accordingly.

In a complex case, a party may need to file a brief that exceeds the type-volume limitations specified in these rules, such as to include unusually voluminous information explaining relevant background or legal provisions or to respond to multiple briefs by opposing parties or amici. The Committee expects that courts will accommodate those situations by granting leave to exceed the type-volume limitations as appropriate.

Changes Made After Publication and Comment

The Committee revised the proposed word limit for the appellant's principal brief and the appellant's response and reply brief from 12,500 words to 13,000 words, and revised the proposed word limit for the appellee's principal and response brief from 14,700 words to 15,300 words. The Committee made conforming changes to the Committee Note and style changes to the Rule text. The Committee also added language to the Committee Note to recognize the need for extra length in appropriate cases.

2018 Amendment

Subdivision (f)(4) is amended to extend the period for filing a reply brief from 14 days to 21 days. Before the elimination of the "three-day rule" in Rule 26(c), attorneys were accustomed to a period of 17 days within which to file a reply brief, and the committee concluded that shortening the period from 17 days to 14 days could adversely affect the preparation of useful reply briefs. Because time periods are best measured in increments of 7 days, the period is extended to 21 days.

Rule 29.   Brief of an Amicus Curiae

(a) During Initial Consideration of a Case on the Merits.

(1) Applicability. This Rule 29(a) governs amicus filings during a court's initial consideration of a case on the merits.

(2) When Permitted. The United States or its officer or agency or a state may file an amicus brief without the consent of the parties or leave of court. Any other amicus curiae may file a brief only by leave of court or if the brief states that all parties have consented to its filing, but a court of appeals may prohibit the filing of or may strike an amicus brief that would result in a judge's disqualification.

(3) Motion for Leave to File. The motion must be accompanied by the proposed brief and state:

(A) the movant's interest; and

(B) the reason why an amicus brief is desirable and why the matters asserted are relevant to the disposition of the case.

(4) Contents and Form. An amicus brief must comply with Rule 32. In addition to the requirements of Rule 32, the cover must identify the party or parties supported and indicate whether the brief supports affirmance or reversal. An amicus brief need not comply with Rule 28, but must include the following:

(A) if the amicus curiae is a corporation, a disclosure statement like that required of parties by Rule 26.1;

(B) a table of contents, with page references;

(C) a table of authorities—cases (alphabetically arranged), statutes, and other authorities—with references to the pages of the brief where they are cited;

(D) a concise statement of the identity of the amicus curiae, its interest in the case, and the source of its authority to file;

(E) unless the amicus curiae is one listed in the first sentence of Rule 29(a)(2), a statement that indicates whether:

(i) a party's counsel authored the brief in whole or in part;

(ii) a party or a party's counsel contributed money that was intended to fund preparing or submitting the brief; and

(iii) a person—other than the amicus curiae, its members, or its counsel—contributed money that was intended to fund preparing or submitting the brief and, if so, identifies each such person;

(F) an argument, which may be preceded by a summary and which need not include a statement of the applicable standard of review; and

(G) a certificate of compliance under Rule 32(g)(1), if length is computed using a word or line limit.

(5) Length. Except by the court's permission, an amicus brief may be no more than one-half the maximum length authorized by these rules for a party's principal brief. If the court grants a party permission to file a longer brief, that extension does not affect the length of an amicus brief.

(6) Time for Filing. An amicus curiae must file its brief, accompanied by a motion for filing when necessary, no later than 7 days after the principal brief of the party being supported is filed. An amicus curiae that does not support either party must file its brief no later than 7 days after the appellant's or petitioner's principal brief is filed. A court may grant leave for later filing, specifying the time within which an opposing party may answer.

(7) Reply Brief. Except by the court's permission, an amicus curiae may not file a reply brief.

(8) Oral Argument. An amicus curiae may participate in oral argument only with the court's permission.

(b) During Consideration of Whether to Grant Rehearing.

(1) Applicability. This Rule 29(b) governs amicus filings during a court's consideration of whether to grant panel rehearing or rehearing en banc, unless a local rule or order in a case provides otherwise.

(2) When Permitted. The United States or its officer or agency or a state may file an amicus brief without the consent of the parties or leave of court. Any other amicus curiae may file a brief only by leave of court.

(3) Motion for Leave to File. Rule 29(a)(3) applies to a motion for leave.

(4) Contents, Form, and Length. Rule 29(a)(4) applies to the amicus brief. The brief must include a certificate under Rule 32(g) and not exceed 2,600 words.

(5) Time for Filing. An amicus curiae supporting the petition for rehearing or supporting neither party must file its brief, accompanied by a motion for filing when necessary, no later than 7 days after the petition is filed. An amicus curiae opposing the petition must file its brief, accompanied by a motion for filing when necessary, no later than the date set by the court for the response.

(As amended Apr. 24, 1998, eff. Dec. 1, 1998; Apr. 28, 2010, eff. Dec. 1, 2010; Apr. 28, 2016; eff. Dec. 1, 2016; Apr. 26, 2018; eff. Dec. 1, 2018.)

ADVISORY COMMITTEE NOTES

1967 Adoption

Only five circuits presently regulate the filing of the brief of an amicus curiae. See D.C.Cir. Rule 18(j) [rule 18(j), U.S.Ct. of App.Dist. of Col.Cir., this title]; 1st Cir. Rule 23(10) [rule 23(10), U.S.Ct. of App. 1st Cir.]; 6th Cir. Rule 17(4) [rule 17(4), U.S.Ct. of App. 6th Cir.]; 9th Cir. Rule 18(9) [rule 18(9), U.S.Ct. of App. 9th Cir.]; 10th Cir. Rule 20 [rule 20, U.S.Ct. of App. 10th Cir.]. This rule follows the practice of a majority of circuits in requiring leave of court to file an amicus brief except under the circumstances stated therein. Compare Supreme Court Rule 42.

1998 Amendments

The language and organization of the rule are amended to make the rule more easily understood. In addition to changes made to improve the understanding, the Advisory Committee has changed language to make style and terminology consistent through the appellate rules. These changes are intended to be stylistic only.

Several substantive changes are made in this rule, however.

Subdivision (a). The major change in this subpart is that when a brief is filed with the consent of all parties, it is no longer necessary to obtain the parties' written consent and to file the consents with the brief. It is sufficient to obtain the parties' oral consent and to state in the brief that all parties have consented. It is sometimes difficult to obtain all the written consents by the filing deadline and it is not unusual for counsel to represent that parties have consented; for example, in a motion for extension of time to file a brief it is not unusual for the movant to state that the other parties have been consulted and they do not object to the extension. If a party's consent has been misrepresented, the party will be able to take action before the court considers the amicus brief.

The District of Columbia is added to the list of entities allowed to file an amicus brief without consent of all parties. The other changes in this material are stylistic.

Subdivision (b). The provision in the former rule, granting permission to conditionally file the brief with the motion, is changed to one requiring that the brief accompany the motion. Sup. Ct. R. 37.4 requires that the proposed brief be presented with the motion.

The former rule only required the motion to identify the applicant's interest and to generally state the reasons why an amicus brief is desirable. The amended rule additionally requires that the motion state the relevance of the matters asserted to the disposition of the case. As Sup. Ct. R. 37.1 states:

An *amicus curiae* brief which brings relevant matter to the attention of the Court that has not already been brought to its attention by the parties is of considerable help to the Court. An *amicus curiae* brief which does not serve this purpose simply burdens the staff and facilities of the Court and its filing is not favored.

Because the relevance of the matters asserted by an amicus is ordinarily the most compelling reason for granting leave to file, the Committee believes that it is helpful to explicitly require such a showing.

Subdivision (c). The provisions in this subdivision are entirely new. Previously there was confusion as to whether an amicus brief must include all of the items listed in Rule 28. Out of caution practitioners in some circuits included all those items. Ordinarily that is unnecessary.

The requirement that the cover identify the party supported and indicate whether the amicus supports affirmance or reversal is an administrative aid.

Paragraph (c)(3) requires an amicus to state the source of its authority to file. The amicus simply must identify which of the provisions in Rule 29(a) provides the basis for the amicus to file its brief.

Subdivision (d). This new provision imposes a shorter page limit for an amicus brief than for a party's brief. This is appropriate for two reasons. First, an amicus may omit certain items that must be included in a party's brief. Second, an amicus brief is supplemental. It need not address all issues or all facets of a case. It should treat only matter not adequately addressed by a party.

Subdivision (e). The time limit for filing is changed. An amicus brief must be filed no later than 7 days after the principal brief of the party being supported is filed. Occasionally, an amicus supports neither party; in such instances, the amendment provides that the amicus brief must be filed no later than 7 days after the appellant's or petitioner's principal brief is filed. Note that in both instances the 7-day period runs from when a brief is filed. The passive voice—"is filed"—is used deliberately. A party or amicus can send its brief to a court for filing and, under Rule 25, the brief is timely if mailed within the filing period. Although the brief is timely if mailed within the filing period, it is not "filed" until the court receives it and file stamps it. "Filing" is done by the court, not by the party. It may be necessary for an amicus to contact the court to ascertain the filing date.

The 7-day stagger was adopted because it is long enough to permit an amicus to review the completed brief of the party being supported and avoid repetitious argument. A 7-day period also is short enough that no adjustment need be made in the opposing party's briefing schedule. The opposing party will have sufficient time to review arguments made by the amicus and address them in the party's responsive pleading. The timetable for filing the parties' briefs is unaffected by this change.

A court may grant permission to file an amicus brief in a context in which the party does not file a "principal brief"; for example, an amicus may be permitted to file in support of a party's petition for rehearing. In such instances the court will establish the filing time for the amicus.

The former rule's statement that a court may, for cause shown, grant leave for later filing is unnecessary. Rule 26(b) grants general authority to enlarge the time prescribed in these rules for good cause shown. This new rule, however, states that when a court grants permission for later filing, the court must specify the period within which an opposing party may answer the arguments of the amicus.

Subdivision (f). This subdivision generally prohibits the filing of a reply brief by an amicus curiae. Sup. Ct. R. 37 and local rules of the D.C., Ninth, and Federal Circuits state that an amicus may not file a reply brief. The role of an amicus should not require the use of a reply brief.

Subdivision (g). The language of this subdivision stating that an amicus will be granted permission to participate in oral argument "only for extraordinary reasons" has been deleted. The change is made to reflect more accurately the current practice in which it is not unusual for a court to permit an amicus to argue when a party is willing to share its argument time with the amicus. The Committee does not intend, however, to suggest that in other instances an amicus will be permitted to argue absent extraordinary circumstances.

2010 Amendments

Subdivision (a). New Rule 1(b) defines the term "state" to include "the District of Columbia and any United States commonwealth or territory." That definition renders subdivision (a)'s reference to a "Territory, Commonwealth, or the District of Columbia" redundant. Accordingly, subdivision (a) is amended to refer simply to "[t]he United States or its officer or agency or a state."

Subdivision (c). The subparts of subdivision (c) are renumbered due to the relocation of an existing provision in new subdivision (c)(1) and the addition of a new provision in new subdivision (c)(5). Existing subdivisions (c)(1) through (c)(5) are renumbered, respectively, (c)(2), (c)(3), (c)(4), (c)(6) and (c)(7). The new ordering of the subdivisions tracks the order in which the items should appear in the brief.

Subdivision (c)(1). The requirement that corporate amici include a disclosure statement like that required of parties by Rule 26.1 was previously stated in the third sentence of subdivision (c). The requirement has been moved to new subdivision (c)(1) for ease of reference.

Subdivision (c)(5). New subdivision (c)(5) sets certain disclosure requirements concerning authorship and funding. Subdivision (c)(5) exempts from the authorship and funding disclosure requirements entities entitled under subdivision (a) to file an amicus brief without the consent of the parties or leave of court. Subdivision (c)(5) requires amicus briefs to disclose whether counsel for a party authored the brief in whole or in part and whether a party or a party's counsel contributed money with the intention of funding the preparation or submission of the brief. A party's or counsel's payment of general membership dues to an amicus need not be disclosed. Subdivision (c)(5) also requires amicus briefs to state whether any other "person" (other than the amicus, its members, or its counsel) contributed money with the intention of funding the brief's preparation or submission, and, if so, to identify all such persons. "Person," as used in subdivision (c)(5), includes artificial persons as well as natural persons.

The disclosure requirement, which is modeled on Supreme Court Rule 37.6, serves to deter counsel from using an amicus brief to circumvent page limits on the parties' briefs. *See Glassroth v. Moore*, 347 F.3d 916, 919 (11th Cir. 2003) (noting the majority's suspicion "that amicus briefs are often used as a means of evading the page limitations on a party's briefs"). It also may help judges to assess whether the amicus itself considers the issue important enough to sustain the cost and effort of filing an amicus brief.

It should be noted that coordination between the amicus and the party whose position the amicus supports is desirable, to the extent that it helps to avoid duplicative arguments. This was particularly true prior to the 1998 amendments, when deadlines for amici were the same as those for the party whose position they supported. Now that the filing deadlines are staggered, coordination may not always be essential in order to avoid duplication. In any event, mere coordination—in the sense of sharing drafts of briefs—need not be disclosed under subdivision (c)(5). *Cf.* Eugene Gressman et al., Supreme Court Practice 739 (9th ed. 2007) (Supreme Court Rule 37.6 does not "require disclosure of any coordination and discussion between party counsel and amici counsel regarding their respective arguments . . . ").

2016 Amendments

Rule 29 is amended to address amicus filings in connection with requests for panel rehearing and rehearing en banc.

Existing Rule 29 is renumbered Rule 29(a), and language is added to that subdivision (a) to state that its provisions apply to amicus filings during the court's initial consideration of a case on the merits. Rule 29(c)(7) becomes Rule 29(a)(4)(G) and is revised to accord with the relocation and revision of the certificate-of-compliance requirement. New Rule 32(g)(1) states that "[a] brief submitted under Rules 28.1(e)(2), 29(b)(4), or 32(a)(7)(B) . . . must include" a certificate of compliance. An amicus brief submitted during initial consideration of a case on the merits counts as a "brief submitted under Rule[ ] . . . 32(a)(7)(B)" if the amicus computes Rule 29(a)(5)'s length limit by taking half of the type-volume limit in Rule 32(a)(7)(B). Rule 29(a)(4)(G) restates Rule 32(g)(1)'s requirement functionally, by providing that a certificate of compliance is required if an amicus brief's length is computed using a word or line limit.

New subdivision (b) is added to address amicus filings in connection with a petition for panel rehearing or rehearing en banc. Subdivision (b) sets default rules that apply when a court does not provide otherwise by local rule or by order in a case. A court remains free to adopt different rules governing whether amicus filings are permitted in connection with petitions for rehearing, and governing the procedures when such filings are permitted.

Changes Made After Publication and Comment

The Committee changed the presumptive length limit under Rule 29(b)(4) from 2,000 words to 2,600 words and deleted the alternative line limit. The Committee changed Rule 29(b)(5)'s presumptive deadline for amicus filings in support of a rehearing petition (or in support of neither party) from three days after the petition's filing to seven days after the petition's filing.

2018 Amendments

The amendment to subdivision (a)(2) authorizes orders or local rules that prohibit the filing of or permit the striking of an amicus brief if the brief would result in a judge's disqualification. The amendment does not alter or address the standards for when an amicus brief requires a judge's disqualification. A comparable amendment to subdivision (b) is not necessary. Subdivision (b)(1) currently authorizes local rules and orders governing filings during a court's consideration of whether to grant panel rehearing or rehearing en banc. These local rules or orders may prohibit the filing of or permit the striking of an amicus brief that would result in a judge's disqualification. In addition, under subdivision (b)(2), a court may deny leave to file an amicus brief that would result in a judge's disqualification.

Rule 30. Appendix to the Briefs

(a) Appellant's Responsibility.

(1) **Contents of the Appendix.** The appellant must prepare and file an appendix to the briefs containing:

(A) the relevant docket entries in the proceeding below;

(B) the relevant portions of the pleadings, charge, findings, or opinion;

(C) the judgment, order, or decision in question; and

(D) other parts of the record to which the parties wish to direct the court's attention.

(2) **Excluded Material.** Memoranda of law in the district court should not be included in the appendix unless they have independent relevance. Parts of the record may be relied on by the court or the parties even though not included in the appendix.

(3) **Time to File; Number of Copies.** Unless filing is deferred under Rule 30(c), the appellant must file 10 copies of the appendix with the brief and must serve one copy on counsel for each party separately represented. An unrepresented party proceeding in forma pauperis must file 4 legible copies with the clerk, and one copy must be served on counsel for each separately represented party. The court may by local rule or by order in a particular case require the filing or service of a different number.

(b) All Parties' Responsibilities.

(1) **Determining the Contents of the Appendix.** The parties are encouraged to agree on the contents of the appendix. In the absence of an agreement, the appellant must, within 14 days after the record is filed, serve on the appellee a designation of the parts of the record the appellant intends to include in the appendix and a statement of the issues the appellant intends to present for review. The appellee may, within 14 days after receiving the designation, serve on the appellant a designation of additional parts to which it wishes to direct the court's attention. The appellant must include the designated parts in the appendix. The parties must not engage in unnecessary designation of parts of the record, because the entire record is available to the court. This paragraph applies also to a cross-appellant and a cross-appellee.

(2) **Costs of Appendix.** Unless the parties agree otherwise, the appellant must pay the cost of the appendix. If the appellant considers parts of the record designated by the appellee to be unnecessary, the appellant may advise the appellee, who must then advance the cost of including those parts. The cost of the appendix is a taxable cost. But if any party causes unnecessary parts of the record to be included in the appendix, the court may impose the cost of those parts on that party. Each circuit must, by local rule, provide for sanctions against attorneys who unreasonably and vexatiously increase litigation costs by including unnecessary material in the appendix.

(c) Deferred Appendix.

(1) **Deferral Until After Briefs Are Filed.** The court may provide by rule for classes of cases or by order in a particular case that preparation of the appendix may be deferred until after the briefs have been filed and that the appendix may be filed 21 days after the appellee's brief is served. Even though the filing of the appendix may be deferred, Rule 30(b) applies; except that a party must designate the parts of the record it wants included in the appendix when it serves its brief, and need not include a statement of the issues presented.

(2) **References to the Record.**

(A) If the deferred appendix is used, the parties may cite in their briefs the pertinent pages of the record. When the appendix is prepared, the record pages cited in the briefs must be indicated by inserting record page numbers, in brackets, at places in the appendix where those pages of the record appear.

(B) A party who wants to refer directly to pages of the appendix may serve and file copies of the brief within the time required by Rule 31(a), containing appropriate references to pertinent pages of the record. In that event, within 14 days after the appendix is filed, the party must serve and file copies of the brief, containing references to the pages of the appendix in place of or in addition to the references to the pertinent pages of the record. Except for the correction of typographical errors, no other changes may be made to the brief.

(d) Format of the Appendix. The appendix must begin with a table of contents identifying the page at which each part begins. The relevant docket entries must follow the table of contents. Other parts of the record must follow chronologically. When pages from the transcript of proceedings are placed in the appendix, the transcript page numbers must be shown in brackets immediately before the included pages. Omissions in the text of papers or of the transcript must be indicated by asterisks. Immaterial formal matters (captions, subscriptions, acknowledgments, etc.) should be omitted.

(e) Reproduction of Exhibits. Exhibits designated for inclusion in the appendix may be reproduced in a separate volume, or volumes, suitably indexed. Four copies must be filed with the appendix, and one copy must be served on counsel for each separately represented party. If a transcript of a proceeding before an administrative agency, board, commission, or officer was used in a district-court action and has been designated for inclusion in the appendix, the transcript must be placed in the appendix as an exhibit.

(f) Appeal on the Original Record Without an Appendix. The court may, either by rule for all cases or classes of cases or by order in a particular case, dispense with the appendix and permit an appeal to proceed on the original record with any copies of the record, or relevant parts, that the court may order the parties to file.

(As amended Mar. 30, 1970, eff. July 1, 1970; Mar. 10, 1986, eff. July 1, 1986; Apr. 30, 1991, eff. Dec. 1, 1991; Apr. 29, 1994, eff. Dec. 1, 1994; Apr. 24, 1998, eff. Dec. 1, 1998; Mar. 26, 2009, eff. Dec. 1, 2009.)

ADVISORY COMMITTEE NOTES

1967 Adoption

Subdivision (a). Only two circuits presently require a printed record (5th Cir. Rule 23(a) [rule 23(a), U.S.Ct. of App. 5th Cir.]; 8th Cir. Rule 10 [rule 10, U.S.Ct. of App. 8th Cir.] (in civil appeals only)), and the rules and practice in those circuits combine to make the difference between a printed record and the appendix, which is now used in eight circuits and in the Supreme Court in lieu of the printed record, largely nominal. The essential characteristics of the appendix method are: (1) the entire record may not be reproduced; (2) instead, the parties are to set out in an appendix to the briefs those parts of the record which in their judgment the judges must consult in order to determine the issues presented by the appeal; (3) the appendix is not the record but merely a selection therefrom for the convenience of the judges of the court of appeals; the record is the actual trial court record, and the record itself is always available to supply inadvertent omissions from the appendix. These essentials are incorporated, either by rule or by practice, in the circuits that continue to require the printed record rather than the appendix. See 5th Cir. Rule 23(a)(9) [23(a)(9), U.S.Ct. of App. 5th Cir.] and 8th Cir. Rule 10(a)–(d) [rule 10(a)–(d), U.S.Ct. of App. 8th Cir.].

Subdivision (b). Under the practice in six of the eight circuits which now use the appendix method, unless the parties agree to use a single appendix, the appellant files with his brief an appendix containing the parts of the record which he deems it essential that the court read in order to determine the questions presented. If the appellee deems additional parts of the record necessary he must include such parts as an appendix to his brief. The proposed rule differs from that practice. By the new rule a single appendix is to be filed. It is to be prepared by the appellant, who must include therein those parts which he deems essential and those which the appellee designates as essential.

Under the practice by which each party files his own appendix the resulting reproduction of essential parts of the record is often fragmentary; it is not infrequently necessary to piece several appendices together to arrive at a usable reproduction. Too, there seems to be a tendency on the part of some appellants to reproduce less than what is necessary for a determination of the issues presented (see *Moran Towing Corp. v. M. A. Gammino Construction Co.*, 363 F.2d 108 (1st Cir. 1966); *Walters v. Shari Music Publishing Corp.*, 298 F.2d 206 (2d Cir. 1962) and cases cited therein; *Morrison v. Texas Co.*, 289 F.2d 382 (7th Cir. 1961) and cases cited therein), a tendency which is doubtless encouraged by the requirement in present rules that the appellee reproduce in his separately prepared appendix such necessary parts of the record as are not included by the appellant.

Under the proposed rule responsibility for the preparation of the appendix is placed on the appellant. If the appellee feels that the appellant has omitted essential portions of the record, he may require the appellant to include such portions in the appendix. The appellant is protected against a demand that he reproduce parts which he considers unnecessary by the provisions entitling him to require the appellee to advance the costs of reproducing such parts and authorizing denial of costs for matter unnecessarily reproduced.

Subdivision (c). This subdivision permits the appellant to elect to defer the production of the appendix to the briefs until the briefs of both sides are written, and authorizes a court of appeals to require such deferred filing by rule or order. The advantage of this method of preparing the appendix is that it permits the parties to determine what parts of the record need to be reproduced in the light of the issues actually presented by the briefs. Often neither side is in a position to say precisely what is needed until the briefs are completed. Once the argument on both sides is known, it should be possible to confine the matter reproduced in the appendix to that which is essential to a determination of the appeal or review. This method of preparing the appendix is presently in use in the Tenth Circuit (Rule 17) [rule 17, U.S.Ct. of App. 10th Cir.] and in other circuits in review of agency proceedings, and it has proven its value in reducing the volume required to be reproduced. When the record is long, use of this method is likely to result in substantial economy to the parties.

Subdivision (e). The purpose of this subdivision is to reduce the cost of reproducing exhibits. While subdivision (a) requires that 10 copies of the appendix be filed, unless the court requires a lesser number, subdivision (e) permits exhibits necessary for the determination of an appeal to be bound separately, and requires only 4 copies of such a separate volume or volumes to be filed and a single copy to be served on counsel.

Subdivision (f). The subdivision authorizes a court of appeals to dispense with the appendix method of reproducing parts of the record and to hear appeals on the original record and such copies of it as the court may require.

Since 1962 the Ninth Circuit has permitted all appeals to be heard on the original record and a very limited number of copies. Under the practice as adopted in 1962, any party to an appeal could elect to have the appeal heard on the original record and two copies thereof rather than on the printed record theretofore required. The resulting substantial saving of printing costs led to the election of the new practice in virtually all cases, and by 1967 the use of printed records had ceased. By a recent amendment, the Ninth Circuit has abolished the printed record altogether. Its rules now provide that all appeals are to be heard on the original record, and it has reduced the number of copies required to two sets of copies of the transmitted original papers (excluding copies of exhibits, which need not be filed unless specifically ordered). See 9 Cir. Rule 10 [rule 10 U.S.Ct. of App. 9th Cir.], as amended June 2, 1967, effective September 1, 1967. The Eighth Circuit permits appeals in criminal cases and in habeas corpus and 28 U.S.C. § 2255 proceedings to be heard on the original record and two copies thereof. See 8 Cir. Rule 8(i)–(j) [rule 8(i)–(j), U.S.Ct. of App. 8th Cir.]. The Tenth Circuit permits appeals in all cases to be heard on the original record and four copies thereof whenever the record consists of two hundred pages or less. See 10 Cir. Rule 17(a) [rule 17(a), U.S.Ct. of App. 10th Cir.]. This subdivision expressly authorizes the continuation of the practices in the Eighth, Ninth and Tenth Circuits.

The judges of the Court of Appeals for the Ninth Circuit have expressed complete satisfaction with the practice there in use and have suggested that attention be called to the advantages which it offers in terms of reducing cost.

1970 Amendments

Subdivision (a). The amendment of subdivision (a) is related to the amendment of Rule 31(a), which authorizes a court of appeals to shorten the time for filing briefs. By virtue of this amendment, if the time for filing the brief of the appellant is shortened the time for filing the appendix is likewise shortened.

Subdivision (c). As originally written, subdivision (c) permitted the appellant to elect to defer filing of the appendix until 21 days after service of the brief of the appellee. As amended, subdivision (c) requires that an order of court be obtained before filing of the appendix can be deferred, unless a court permits deferred filing by local rule. The amendment should not cause use of the deferred appendix to be viewed with disfavor. In cases involving lengthy records, permission to defer filing of the appendix should be freely granted as an inducement to the parties to include in the appendix only matter that the briefs show to be necessary for consideration by the judges. But the Committee is advised that appellants have elected to defer filing of the appendix in cases involving brief records merely to obtain the 21 day delay. The subdivision is amended to prevent that practice.

1986 Amendments

Subdivision (a). During its study of the separate appendix [see Report of the Advisory Committee on the Federal Appellate Rules on the Operation of Rule 30, FRD (1985)], the Advisory Committee found that this document was frequently encumbered with memoranda submitted to the trial court. *United States v.*

Noall, 587 F.2d 123, 125 n. 1 (2nd Cir.1978). See generally *Drewett v. Aetna Cas. & Sur. Co.,* 539 F.2d 496, 500 (5th Cir.1976); *Volkswagenwerk Aktiengesellschaft v. Church,* 413 F.2d 1126, 1128 (9th Cir.1969). Inclusion of such material makes the appendix more bulky and therefore less useful to the appellate panel. It also can increase significantly the costs of litigation.

There are occasions when such trial court memoranda have independent relevance in the appellate litigation. For instance, there may be a dispute as to whether a particular point was raised or whether a concession was made in the district court. In such circumstances, it is appropriate to include pertinent sections of such memoranda in the appendix.

Subdivision (b). The amendment to subdivision (b) is designed to require the circuits, by local rule, to establish a procedural mechanism for the imposition of sanctions against those attorneys who conduct appellate litigation in bad faith. Both 28 U.S.C. § 1927 and the inherent power of the court authorize such sanctions. See *Brennan v. Local 357, International Brotherhood of Teamsters,* 709 F.2d 611 (9th Cir.1983). See generally *Roadway Express, Inc. v. Piper,* 447 U.S. 752 (1980). While considerations of uniformity are important and doubtless will be taken into account by the judges of the respective circuits, the Advisory Committee believes that, at this time, the circuits need the flexibility to tailor their approach to the conditions of local practice. The local rule shall provide for notice and opportunity to respond before the imposition of any sanction.

Technical amendments also are made to subdivisions (a), (b) and (c) which are not intended to be substantive changes.

1991 Amendments

Subdivision (b). The amendment requires a cross appellant to serve the appellant with a statement of the issues that the cross appellant intends to pursue on appeal. No later than ten days after the record is filed, the appellant and cross appellant must serve each other with a statement of the issues each intends to present for review and with a designation of the parts of the record that each wants included in the appendix. Within the next ten days, both the appellee and the cross appellee may designate additional materials for inclusion in the appendix. The appellant must then include in the appendix the parts thus designated for both the appeal and any cross appeals. The Committee expects that simultaneous compliance with this subdivision by an appellant and a cross appellant will be feasible in most cases. If a cross appellant cannot fairly be expected to comply until receipt of the appellant's statement of issues, relief may be sought by motion in the court of appeals.

1994 Amendments

Subdivision (a). The only substantive change is to allow a court to require the filing of a greater number of copies of an appendix as well as a lesser number.

1998 Amendments

The language and organization of the new rule are amended to make the rule more easily understood. In addition to changes made to improve the understanding, the Advisory Committee has changed language to make style and terminology consistent throughout the appellate Rules. These changes are intended to be stylistic only.

Subdivision (a). Paragraph (a)(3) is amended so that it is consistent with Rule 31(b). An unrepresented party proceeding in forma pauperis is only required to file 4 copies of the appendix rather than 10.

Subdivision (c). When a deferred appendix is used, a brief must make reference to the original record rather than to the appendix because it does not exist when the briefs are prepared. Unless a party later files an amended brief with direct references to the pages of the appendix (as provided in subparagraph (c)(2)(B)), the material in the appendix must indicate the pages of the original record from which it was drawn so that a reader of the brief can make meaningful use of the appendix. The instructions in the current rule for cross-referencing the appendix materials to the original record are unclear. The language in paragraph (c)(2) has been amended to try to clarify the procedure.

Subdivision (d). In recognition of the fact that use of a typeset appendix is exceedingly rare in the courts of appeals, the last sentence—permitting a question and answer (as from a transcript) to be in a single paragraph—has been omitted.

2009 Amendments

Subdivision (b)(1). The times set in the former rule at 10 days have been revised to 14 days. See the Note to Rule 26.

HISTORICAL NOTES

Taxation of Fees in Appeals in Which Requirement of Appendix is Dispensed With

See item (6) in the Judicial Conference Schedule of Fees note under 28 U.S.C.A. § 1913.

Rule 31.   Serving and Filing Briefs

(a)   Time to Serve and File a Brief.

(1)   The appellant must serve and file a brief within 40 days after the record is filed. The appellee must serve and file a brief within 30 days after the appellant's brief is served. The appellant may serve and file a reply brief within 21 days after service of the appellee's brief but a reply brief must be filed at least 7 days before argument, unless the court, for good cause, allows a later filing.

(2)   A court of appeals that routinely considers cases on the merits promptly after the briefs are filed may shorten the time to serve and file briefs, either by local rule or by order in a particular case.

(b)   Number of Copies. Twenty-five copies of each brief must be filed with the clerk and 2 copies must be served on each unrepresented party and on counsel for each separately represented party. An unrepresented party proceeding in forma pauperis must file 4 legible copies with the clerk, and one copy must be served on each unrepresented party and on counsel for each separately represented party. The court may by local rule or by order in a particular case require the filing or service of a different number.

(c)   Consequence of Failure to File. If an appellant fails to file a brief within the time provided by this rule, or within an extended time, an appellee may move to dismiss the appeal. An appellee who fails to file a brief will not be heard at oral argument unless the court grants permission.

(As amended Mar. 30, 1970, eff. July 1, 1970; Mar. 10, 1986, eff. July 1, 1986; Apr. 29, 1994, eff. Dec. 1, 1994; Apr. 24, 1998, eff. Dec. 1, 1998; Apr. 29, 2002, eff. Dec. 1, 2002; Mar. 26, 2009, eff. Dec. 1, 2009; Apr. 26, 2018, eff. Dec. 1, 2018.)

ADVISORY COMMITTEE NOTES

1967 Adoption

A majority of the circuits now require the brief of the appellant to be filed within 30 days from the date on which the record is filed. But in those circuits an exchange of designations is unnecessary in the preparation of the appendix. The appellant files with his brief an appendix containing the parts of the record which he deems essential. If the appellee considers other parts essential, he includes those parts in his own appendix. Since the proposed rule requires the appellant to file with his brief an appendix containing necessary parts of the record as designated by both parties, the rule allows the appellant 40 days in order to provide time for the exchange of designations respecting the content of the appendix (see Rule 30(b)).

1970 Amendment

The time prescribed by Rule 31(a) for preparing briefs—40 days to the appellant, 30 days to the appellee—is well within the time that must ordinarily elapse in most circuits before an appeal can be reached for consideration. In those circuits, the time prescribed by the Rule should not be disturbed. But if a court of appeals maintains a current calendar, that is, if an appeal can be heard as soon as the briefs have been filed, or if the practice of the court permits the submission of appeals for preliminary consideration as soon as the briefs have been filed, the court should be free to prescribe shorter periods in the interest of expediting decision.

1986 Amendment

The amendments to Rules 31(a) and (c) are technical. No substantive change is intended.

1994 Amendments

Subdivision (b). The amendment allows a court of appeals to require the filing of a greater, as well as a lesser, number of copies of briefs. The amendment also allows the required number to be prescribed by local rule as well as by order in a particular case.

1998 Amendments

The language and organization of the rule are amended to make the rule more easily understood. In addition to changes made to improve the understanding, the advisory committee has changed language to make style and terminology consistent throughout the appellate rules. These changes are intended to by stylistic only; a substantive change is made, however, in subdivision (b).

Subdivision (a). Paragraph (a)(2) explicitly authorizes a court of appeals to shorten a briefing schedule if the court routinely considers cases on the merits promptly after the briefs are filed. Extensions of the briefing schedule, by order, are permitted under the general provisions of Rule 26(b).

Subdivision (b). The current rules says that a party who is permitted to file "typewritten ribbon and carbon copies of the brief" need only file and original and three copies of the brief. The quoted language, in conjunction with current rule 24(c), means that a party allowed to proceed in forma pauperis need not file 25 copies of the brief. Two changes are made in this subdivision. First, it is anachronistic to refer to a party who is allowed to file a typewritten brief as if that would distinguish the party from all other parties; any party is permitted to file a typewritten brief. The amended rule states directly that it applies to a party to proceed in forma pauperis. Second, the amended rule does not generally permit parties who are represented by counsel to file the lesser number of brief. Inexpensive methods of copying are generally available. Unless it would impose hardship, in which case a motion to file a lesser number should be filed, a represented party must file the usual number of briefs.

2002 Amendments

Subdivision (b). In requiring that two copies of each brief "must be served on counsel for each separately represented party," Rule 31(b) may be read to imply that copies of briefs need not be served on unrepresented parties. The Rule has been amended to clarify that briefs must be served on all parties, including those who are not represented by counsel.

Changes Made After Publication and Comments. No changes were made to the text of the proposed amendment or to the Committee Note.

2009 Amendments

Subdivision (a)(1). Subdivision (a)(1) formerly required that the appellant's reply brief be served "at least 3 days before argument, unless the court, for good cause, allows a later filing." Under former Rule 26(a), "3 days" could mean as many as 5 or even 6 days. See the Note to Rule 26. Under revised Rule 26(a), intermediate weekends and holidays are counted. Changing "3 days" to "7 days" alters the period accordingly. Under revised Rule 26(a), when a period ends on a weekend or holiday, one must continue to count in the same direction until the next day that is not a weekend or holiday; the choice of the 7-day period for subdivision (a)(1) will minimize such occurrences.

2018 Amendments

Subdivision (a)(1) is revised to extend the period for filing a reply brief from 14 days to 21 days. Before the elimination of the "three-day rule" in Rule 26(c), attorneys were accustomed to a period of 17 days within which to file a reply brief, and the committee concluded that shortening the period from 17 days to 14 days could adversely affect the preparation of useful reply briefs. Because time periods are best measured in increments of 7 days, the period is extended to 21 days.

Rule 32.   Form of Briefs, Appendices, and Other Papers

(a)   Form of a Brief.

(1)   Reproduction.

(A) A brief may be reproduced by any process that yields a clear black image on light paper. The paper must be opaque and unglazed. Only one side of the paper may be used.

(B) Text must be reproduced with a clarity that equals or exceeds the output of a laser printer.

(C) Photographs, illustrations, and tables may be reproduced by any method that results in a good copy of the original; a glossy finish is acceptable if the original is glossy.

(2)   Cover. Except for filings by unrepresented parties, the cover of the appellant's brief must be blue; the appellee's, red; an intervenor's or amicus curiae's, green; any reply brief, gray; and any supplemental brief, tan. The front cover of a brief must contain:

(A) the number of the case centered at the top;

(B) the name of the court;

(C) the title of the case (see Rule 12(a));

(D) the nature of the proceeding (e.g., Appeal, Petition for Review) and the name of the court, agency, or board below;

(E) the title of the brief, identifying the party or parties for whom the brief is filed; and

(F) the name, office address, and telephone number of counsel representing the party for whom the brief is filed.

(3)   Binding. The brief must be bound in any manner that is secure, does not obscure the text, and permits the brief to lie reasonably flat when open.

(4)   Paper Size, Line Spacing, and Margins. The brief must be on $8\frac{1}{2}$ by 11 inch paper. The text must be double-spaced, but quotations more than two lines long may be indented and single-spaced. Headings and footnotes may be single-spaced. Margins must be at least one inch on all four sides. Page numbers may be placed in the margins, but no text may appear there.

(5)   Typeface. Either a proportionally spaced or a monospaced face may be used.

(A) A proportionally spaced face must include serifs, but sans-serif type may be used in headings and captions. A proportionally spaced face must be 14-point or larger.

(B) A monospaced face may not contain more than $10\frac{1}{2}$ characters per inch.

(6)   Type Styles. A brief must be set in a plain, roman style, although italics or boldface may be used for emphasis. Case names must be italicized or underlined.

(7)   Length.

(A)   Page limitation. A principal brief may not exceed 30 pages, or a reply brief 15 pages, unless it complies with Rule 32(a)(7)(B).

(B)   Type-volume limitation.

(i) A principal brief is acceptable if it:

- contains no more than 13,000 words; or

- uses a monospaced face and contains no more than 1,300 lines of text.

(ii) A reply brief is acceptable if it contains no more than half of the type volume specified in Rule 32(a)(7)(B)(i).

(b)   Form of an Appendix. An appendix must comply with Rule 32(a)(1), (2), (3), and (4), with the following exceptions:

   (1)   The cover of a separately bound appendix must be white.

   (2)   An appendix may include a legible photocopy of any document found in the record or of a printed judicial or agency decision.

   (3)   When necessary to facilitate inclusion of odd-sized documents such as technical drawings, an appendix may be a size other than 8½ by 11 inches, and need not lie reasonably flat when opened.

(c)   Form of Other Papers.

   (1)   Motion. The form of a motion is governed by Rule 27(d).

   (2)   Other Papers. Any other paper, including a petition for panel rehearing and a petition for hearing or rehearing en banc, and any response to such a petition, must be reproduced in the manner prescribed by Rule 32(a), with the following exceptions:

      (A)   A cover is not necessary if the caption and signature page of the paper together contain the information required by Rule 32(a)(2). If a cover is used, it must be white.

      (B)   Rule 32(a)(7) does not apply.

(d)   Signature. Every brief, motion, or other paper filed with the court must be signed by the party filing the paper or, if the party is represented, by one of the party's attorneys.

(e)   Local Variation. Every court of appeals must accept documents that comply with the form requirements of this rule and the length limits set by these rules. By local rule or order in a particular case, a court of appeals may accept documents that do not meet all the form requirements of this rule or the length limits set by these rules.

(f)   Items Excluded from Length. In computing any length limit, headings, footnotes, and quotations count toward the limit but the following items do not:

- cover page;
- disclosure statement;
- table of contents;
- table of citations;
- statement regarding oral argument;
- addendum containing statutes, rules, or regulations;
- certificates of counsel;
- signature block;
- proof of service; and
- any item specifically excluded by these rules or by local rule.

(g)   Certificate of Compliance.

   (1)   Briefs and Papers That Require a Certificate. A brief submitted under Rules 28.1(e)(2), 29(b)(4), or 32(a)(7)(B)—and a paper submitted under Rules 5(c)(1), 21(d)(1), 27(d)(2)(A), 27(d)(2)(C), 35(b)(2)(A), or 40(b)(1)—must include a certificate by the attorney, or an unrepresented party, that the document complies with the type-volume limitation. The person preparing the certificate may rely on the word or line count of the word-processing system used to prepare the document. The certificate must state the number of words—or the number of lines of monospaced type—in the document.

(2) Acceptable Form. Form 6 in the Appendix of Forms meets the requirements for a certificate of compliance.

(As amended Apr. 24, 1998, eff. Dec. 1, 1998; Apr. 29, 2002, eff. Dec. 1, 2002; Apr. 25, 2005, eff. Dec. 1, 2005; Apr. 28, 2016; eff. Dec. 1, 2016; Apr. 25, 2019, eff. Dec. 1, 2019.)

ADVISORY COMMITTEE NOTES

1967 Adoption

Only two methods of printing are now generally recognized by the circuits—standard typographic printing and the offset duplicating process (multilith). A third, mimeographing, is permitted in the Fifth Circuit. The District of Columbia, Ninth, and Tenth Circuits permit records to be reproduced by copying processes. The Committee feels that recent and impending advances in the arts of duplicating and copying warrant experimentation with less costly forms of reproduction than those now generally authorized. The proposed rule permits, in effect, the use of any process other than the carbon copy process which produces a clean, readable page. What constitutes such is left in first instance to the parties and ultimately to the court to determine. The final sentence of the first paragraph of subdivision (a) is added to allow the use of multilith, mimeograph, or other forms of copies of the reporter's original transcript whenever such are available.

1998 Amendments

In addition to amending Rule 32 to conform to uniform drafting standards, several substantive amendments are made. The Advisory Committee had been working on substantive amendments to Rule 32 for some time prior to completion of this larger project.

Subdivision (a). Form of a Brief.

Paragraph (a)(1). Reproduction.

The rule permits the use of "light" paper, not just "white" paper. Cream and buff colored paper, including recycled paper, are acceptable. The rule permits printing on only one side of the paper. Although some argue that paper could be saved by allowing double-sided printing, others argue that in order to preserve legibility a heavier weight paper would be needed, resulting in little, if any, paper saving. In addition, the blank sides of a brief are commonly used by judges and their clerks for making notes about the case.

Because photocopying is inexpensive and widely available and because use of carbon paper is now very rare, all references to the use of carbon copies have been deleted.

The rule requires that the text be reproduced with a clarity that equals or exceeds the output of a laser printer. That means that the method used must have a print resolution of 300 dots per inch (dpi) or more. This will ensure the legibility of the brief. A brief produced by a typewriter or a daisy wheel printer, as well as one produced by a laser printer, has a print resolution of 300 dpi or more. But a brief produced by a dot-matrix printer, fax machine, or portable printer that uses head or dye to transfer methods does not. Some ink jet printers are 300 dpi or more, but some are 216 dpi and would not be sufficient.

Photographs, illustrations, and tables may be reproduced by any method that results in a good copy.

Paragraph (a)(2). Cover.

The rule requires that the number of the case be centered at the top of the front cover of a brief. This will aid in identification of the brief. The idea was drawn from a local rule. The rule also requires that the title of the brief identify the party or parties on whose behalf the brief is filed. When there are multiple appellants or appellees, the information is necessary to the court. If, however, the brief is filed on behalf of all appellants or appellees, it may so indicate. Further, it may be possible to identify the class of parties on whose behalf the brief is filed. Otherwise, it may be necessary to name each party. The rule also requires that attorneys' telephone numbers appear on the front cover of a brief or appendix.

Paragraph (a)(3). Binding.

The rule requires a brief to be bound in any manner that is secure, does not obscure the text, and that permits the brief to lie reasonable flat when open. Many judges and most court employees do much of their work at computer keyboards and a brief that lies flat when open is significantly more convenient. One circuit already has such a requirement and another states a preference for it. While a spiral binding would comply with this requirement, it is not intended to be the exclusive method of binding. Stapling a brief at the upper left-hand corner also satisfies this requirement as long as it is sufficiently secure.

Paragraph (a)(4). Paper Size, Line Spacing, and Margins.

The provisions for pamphlet-size briefs are deleted because their use is so rare. If a circuit wishes to authorize their use, it has authority to do so under subdivision (d) of this rule.

Paragraph (a)(5). Typeface.

This paragraph and the next one, governing type style, are new. The existing rule simply states that a brief produced by the standard typographic process must be printed in at least 11 point type, or if produced in any other manner, the lines of text must be double spaced. Today few briefs are produced by commercial printers or by typewriters; most are produced on and printed by computer. The availability of computer fonts in a variety of sizes and styles has given rise to local rules limiting type styles. The Advisory Committee believes that some standards are needed both to ensure that all litigants have an equal opportunity to present their material and to ensure that the briefs are easily legible.

With regard to typeface there are two options; proportionally-spaced typeface or monospaced typeface.

A proportionally-spaced typeface gives a different amount of horizontal space to characters depending upon the width of the character. A capital "M" is given more horizontal space than a lower case "i". The rule requires that a proportionally-spaced typeface have serifs. Serifs are small horizontal or vertical strokes at the ends of the lines that make up the letters and numbers. Studies have shown that long passages of serif type are easier to read and comprehend than long passages of sans-serif type. The rule accordingly limits the principal sections of submissions to serif type although sans-serif type may be used in headings and captions. This is the same approach magazines, newspapers, and commercial printers take. Look at a professionally printed brief; you will find sans-serif type confined to captions, if it is used at all. The next line shows two characters enlarged for detail. The first has serifs, the second does not. [characters omitted] [For original representation of characters, see House Document 105–269 of the 105th Congress, 2d Session dated May 11, 1998 entitled "Amendments to the Federal Rules of Appellate Procedure . . . (Executive Communication No. 9072)."]

So that the type is easily legible, the rule requires a minimum type size of 14 points for proportionally-spaced typeface.

A monospaced typeface is one in which all characters have the same advance width. That means that each character is given the same horizontal space on the line. A wide letter such as a capital "M" and a narrow letter such as a lower case "i" are given the same space. Most typewriters produce mono-spaced type, and most computers also can do so using fonts with names such as "Courier." [sample sentences omitted] [For original representation of characters, see House Document 105–269 of the 105th Congress, 2d Session dated May 11, 1998 entitled "Amendments to the Federal Rules of Appellate Procedure . . . (Executive Communication No. 9072)."]

The rule requires use of a monospaced typeface that produces no more than 10½ characters per inch. A standard typewriter with pica type produces a monospaced typeface with 10 characters per inch (cpi). That is the ideal monospaced typeface. The rule permits up to 10½ cpi because some computer software programs contain monospaced fonts that purport to produce 10 cpi but that in fact produce slightly more than 10 cpi. In order to avoid the need to reprint a brief produced in good faith reliance upon such a program, the rule permits a bit of leeway. A monospaced typeface with no more than 10 cpi is preferred.

Paragraph (a)(6). Type Styles.

The rule requires use of plain roman, that is not italic or script, type. Italics and boldface may be used for emphasis. Italicizing case names is preferred but underlining may be used.

Paragraph (a)(7). Type-Volume Limitation.

Subparagraph (a)(7)(A) contains a safe-harbor provision. A principal brief that does not exceed 30 pages complies with the type-volume limitation without further question or certification. A reply brief that does not exceed 15 pages is similarly treated. The current limit is 50 pages but that limit was established when most briefs were produced on typewriters. The widespread use of personal computers has made a multitude of printing options available to practitioners. Use of a proportional typeface alone can greatly increase the amount of material per page as compared with use of a monospaced typeface. Even though the rule requires use of 14-point proportional type, there is great variation in the x-height of different 14-point typefaces. Selection of a typeface with a small x-height increases the amount of text per page. Computers also make possible fine gradations in spacing between lines and tight tracking between letters and words. All of this, and more, have made the 50-page limit virtually meaningless. Establishing a safe-harbor of 50 pages would permit a person who makes use of the multitude of printing "tricks" available with most personal computers to file a brief far longer than the "old" 50-page brief. Therefore, as to those briefs not subject to any other volume control than a page limit, a 30-page limit is imposed.

The limits in subparagraph (B) approximate the current 50-page limit and compliance with them is easy even for a person without a personal computer. The aim of these provisions is to create a level playing field. The rule gives every party an equal opportunity to make arguments, without permitting those with the best in-house typesetting an opportunity to expand their submissions.

The length can be determined either by counting words or lines. That is, the length of a brief is determined not by the number of pages but by the number or words or lines in the brief. This gives every party the same opportunity to present an argument without regard to the typeface used and eliminates any incentive to use footnotes or typographical "tricks" to squeeze more material onto a page.

The word counting method can be used with any typeface.

A monospaced brief can meet the volume limitation by using the word or a line count. If the line counting method is used, the number of lines may not exceed 1,300—26 lines per page in a 50-page brief. The number of lines is easily counted manually. Line counting is not sufficient if a proportionally spaced typeface is used, because the amount of material per line can vary widely.

A brief using the type-volume limitations in subparagraph (B) must include a certificate by the attorney, or party proceeding pro se, that the brief complies with the limitation. The rule permits the person preparing the certification to rely upon the word or line count of the word-processing system used to prepare the brief.

Currently, Rule 28(g) governs the length of a brief. Rule 28(g) begins with the words "[e]xcept by permission of the court," signaling that a party may file a motion to exceed the limits established in the rule. The absence of similar language in Rule 32 does not mean that the Advisory Committee intends to prohibit motions to deviate from the requirements of the rule. The Advisory Committee does not believe that any such language is needed to authorize such a motion.

Subdivision (b). Form of an Appendix.

The provisions governing the form of a brief generally apply to an appendix. The rule recognizes, however, that an appendix is usually produced by photocopying existing documents. The rule requires that the photocopies be legible.

The rule permits inclusion not only of documents from the record but also copies of a printed judicial or agency decision. If a decision that is part of the record in the case has been published, it is helpful to provide a copy of the published decision in place of a copy of the decision from the record.

Subdivision (c). Form of Other Papers.

The old rule required a petition for rehearing to be produced in the same manner as a brief or appendix. The new rule also requires that a petition for rehearing en banc and a response to either a petition for panel rehearing or a petition for rehearing en banc be prepared in the same manner. But the length limitations of paragraph (a)(7) do not apply to those documents and a cover is not required if all the formation needed by the court to properly identify the document and the parties is included in the caption or signature page.

Existing subdivision (b) states that other papers may be produced in like manner, or "they may be typewritten upon opaque, unglazed paper 8½ by 11 inches in size." The quoted language is deleted but that method of preparing documents is not eliminated because (a)(5)(b) permits use of standard pica type. The only change is that the new rule now specifies margins for typewritten documents.

Subdivision (d). Local Variation.

A brief that complies with the national rule should be acceptable in every court. Local rules may move in one direction only; they may authorize noncompliance with certain of the national norms. For example, a court that wishes to do so may authorize printing of briefs on both sides of the paper, or the use of smaller type size or sans-serif proportional type. A local rules may not, however, impose requirements that are not in the national rule.

2002 Amendments

Subdivision (a)(2). On occasion, a court may permit or order the parties to file supplemental briefs addressing an issue that was not addressed—or adequately addressed—in the principal briefs. Rule 32(a)(2) has been amended to require that tan covers be used on such supplemental briefs. The amendment is intended to promote uniformity in federal appellate practice. At present, the local rules of the circuit courts conflict. *See, e.g.,* D.C. Cir. R. 28(g) (requiring yellow covers on supplemental briefs); 11th Cir. R. 32, I.O.P. 1 (requiring white covers on supplemental briefs).

Changes Made After Publication and Comments. No changes were made to the text of the proposed amendment or to the Committee Note.

Subdivision (a)(7)(C). If the principal brief of a party exceeds 30 pages, or if the reply brief of a party exceeds 15 pages, Rule 32(a)(7)(C) provides that the party or the party's attorney must certify that the brief complies with the type-volume limitation of Rule 32(a)(7)(B). Rule 32(a)(7)(C) has been amended to refer to Form 6 (which has been added to the Appendix of Forms) and to provide that a party or attorney who uses Form 6 has complied with Rule 32(a)(7)(C). No court may provide to the contrary, in its local rules or otherwise.

Form 6 requests not only the information mandated by Rule 32(a)(7)(C), but also information that will assist courts in enforcing the typeface requirements of Rule 32(a)(5) and the type style requirements of Rule 32(a)(6). Parties and attorneys are not required to use Form 6, but they are encouraged to do so.

Subdivision (c)(2)(A). Under Rule 32(c)(2)(A), a cover is not required on a petition for panel rehearing, petition for hearing or rehearing en banc, answer to a petition for panel rehearing, response to a petition for hearing or rehearing en banc, or any other paper. Rule 32(d) makes it clear that no court can require that a cover be used on any of these papers. However, nothing prohibits a court from providing in its local rules that if a cover on one of these papers is "voluntarily" used, it must be a particular color. Several circuits have adopted such local rules. *See, e.g.,* Fed. Cir. R. 35(c) (requiring yellow covers on petitions for hearing or rehearing en banc and brown covers on responses to such petitions); Fed. Cir. R. 40(a) (requiring yellow covers on petitions for panel rehearing and brown covers on answers to such petitions); 7th Cir. R. 28 (requiring blue covers on petitions for rehearing filed by appellants or answers to such petitions, and requiring red covers on petitions for rehearing filed by appellees or answers to such petitions); 9th Cir. R. 40–1 (requiring blue covers on petitions for panel rehearing filed by appellants and red covers on answers to such petitions, and requiring red covers on petitions for panel rehearing filed by appellees and blue covers on answers to such petitions); 11th Cir. R. 35–6 (requiring white covers on petitions for hearing or rehearing en banc).

These conflicting local rules create a hardship for counsel who practice in more than one circuit. For that reason, Rule 32(c)(2)(A) has been amended to provide that if a party chooses to use a cover on a paper that is not required to have one, that cover must be white. The amendment is intended to preempt all local rulemaking on the subject of cover colors and thereby promote uniformity in federal appellate practice.

Changes Made After Publication and Comments. No changes were made to the text of the proposed amendment or to the Committee Note.

Subdivisions (d) and (e). Former subdivision (d) has been redesignated as subdivision (e), and a new subdivision (d) has been added. The new subdivision (d) requires that every brief, motion, or other paper filed with the court be signed by the attorney or unrepresented party who files it, much as Fed. R. Civ. P. 11(a) imposes a signature requirement on papers filed in district court. Only the original copy of every paper must be signed. An appendix filed with the court does not have to be signed at all.

By requiring a signature, subdivision (d) ensures that a readily identifiable attorney or party takes responsibility for every paper. The courts of appeals already have authority to sanction attorneys and parties who file papers that contain misleading or frivolous assertions, *see, e.g.,* 28 U.S.C. § 1912, Fed. R. App. P. 38 & 46(b)(1)(B), and thus subdivision (d) has not been amended to incorporate provisions similar to those found in Fed. R. Civ. P. 11(b) and 11(c).

Changes Made After Publication and Comments. No changes were made to the text of the proposed amendment. A line was added to the Committee Note to clarify that only the original copy of a paper needs to be signed.

2005 Amendments

Subdivision (a)(7)(C). Rule 32(a)(7)(C) has been amended to add cross-references to new Rule 28.1, which governs briefs filed in cases involving cross-appeals. Rule 28.1(e)(2) prescribes type-volume limitations that apply to such briefs, and Rule 28.1(e)(3) requires parties to certify compliance with those type-volume limitations under Rule 32(a)(7)(C).

2016 Amendments

When Rule 32(a)(7)(B)'s type-volume limits for briefs were adopted in 1998, the word limits were based on an estimate of 280 words per page. In the course of adopting word limits for the length limits in Rules 5, 21, 27, 35, and 40, and responding to concern about the length of briefs, the Committee has re-evaluated the conversion ratio (from pages to words) and decided to apply a conversion ratio of 260 words per page. Rules 28.1 and 32(a)(7)(B) are amended to reduce the word limits accordingly.

In a complex case, a party may need to file a brief that exceeds the type-volume limitations specified in these rules, such as to include unusually voluminous information explaining relevant background or legal provisions or to respond to multiple briefs by opposing parties or amici. The Committee expects that courts will accommodate those situations by granting leave to exceed the type-volume limitations as appropriate.

Subdivision (e) is amended to make clear a court's ability (by local rule or order in a case) to increase the length limits for briefs and other documents. Subdivision (e) already established this authority as to the length limits in Rule 32(a)(7); the amendment makes clear that this authority extends to all length limits in the Appellate Rules.

A new subdivision (f) is added to set out a global list of items excluded from length computations, and the list of exclusions in former subdivision (a)(7)(B)(iii) is deleted. The certificate-of-compliance provision formerly in Rule 32(a)(7)(C) is relocated to a new Rule 32(g) and now applies to filings under all type-volume limits (other than Rule 28(j)'s word limit)—including the new word limits in Rules 5, 21, 27, 29, 35, and 40. Conforming amendments are made to Form 6.

Changes Made After Publication and Comment

The Committee revised the proposed word limit for principal briefs from 12,500 words to 13,000 words. The Committee added an amendment to Rule 32(e) to highlight a circuit court's ability to increase any or all of the Appellate Rules' length limits by local rule. A cross-reference in Rule 32(a)(7)(A) was updated. A reference to Rule 29(b)(4) was added to Rule 32(g)(1), to reflect the Committee's approval of a proposed amendment to Rule 29. The Committee made conforming changes to the Committee Note and style changes to the Rule text. The Committee also added language to the Committee Note to recognize the need for extra length in appropriate cases.

2019 Amendments

The phrase "corporate disclosure statement" is changed to "disclosure statement" to reflect the revision of Rule 26.1. The other amendment to subdivision (f) does not change the substance of the current rule, but removes the articles before each item because a document will not always include these items.

Rule 32.1.   Citing Judicial Dispositions

(a) Citation Permitted. A court may not prohibit or restrict the citation of federal judicial opinions, orders, judgments, or other written dispositions that have been:

    (i) designated as "unpublished," "not for publication," "non-precedential," "not precedent," or the like; and

    (ii) issued on or after January 1, 2007.

  (b) Copies Required. If a party cites a federal judicial opinion, order, judgment, or other written disposition that is not available in a publicly accessible electronic database, the party must file and serve a copy of that opinion, order, judgment, or disposition with the brief or other paper in which it is cited.

(Added Apr. 12, 2006, eff. Dec. 1, 2006.)

ADVISORY COMMITTEE NOTES

2006 Adoption

    Rule 32.1 is a new rule addressing the citation of judicial opinions, orders, judgments, or other written dispositions that have been designated by a federal court as "unpublished," "not for publication," "non-precedential," "not precedent," or the like. This Committee Note will refer to these dispositions collectively as "unpublished" opinions.

    Rule 32.1 is extremely limited. It does not require any court to issue an unpublished opinion or forbid any court from doing so. It does not dictate the circumstances under which a court may choose to designate an opinion as "unpublished" or specify the procedure that a court must follow in making that determination. It says nothing about what effect a court must give to one of its unpublished opinions or to the unpublished opinions of another court. Rule 32.1 addresses only the *citation* of federal judicial dispositions that have been *designated* as "unpublished" or "non-precedential"—whether or not those dispositions have been published in some way or are precedential in some sense.

    Subdivision (a). Every court of appeals has allowed unpublished opinions to be cited in some circumstances, such as to support a contention of issue preclusion or claim preclusion. But the circuits have differed dramatically with respect to the restrictions that they have placed on the citation of unpublished opinions for their persuasive value. Some circuits have freely permitted such citation, others have discouraged it but permitted it in limited circumstances, and still others have forbidden it altogether.

    Rule 32.1(a) is intended to replace these inconsistent standards with one uniform rule. Under Rule 32.1(a), a court of appeals may not prohibit a party from citing an unpublished opinion of a federal court for its persuasive value or for any other reason. In addition, under Rule 32.1(a), a court may not place any restriction on the citation of such opinions. For example, a court may not instruct parties that the citation of unpublished opinions is discouraged, nor may a court forbid parties to cite unpublished opinions when a published opinion addresses the same issue.

    Rule 32.1(a) applies only to unpublished opinions issued on or after January 1, 2007. The citation of unpublished opinions issued before January 1, 2007, will continue to be governed by the local rules of the circuits.

    Subdivision (b). Under Rule 32.1(b), a party who cites an opinion of a federal court must provide a copy of that opinion to the court of appeals and to the other parties, unless that opinion is available in a publicly accessible electronic database—such as a commercial database maintained by a legal research service or a database maintained by a court. A party who is required under Rule 32.1(b) to provide a copy of an opinion must file and serve the copy with the brief or other paper in which the opinion is cited. Rule 32.1(b) applies to all unpublished opinions, regardless of when they were issued.

Rule 33.   Appeal Conferences

    The court may direct the attorneys—and, when appropriate, the parties—to participate in one or more conferences to address any matter that may aid in disposing of the proceedings, including simplifying the issues and discussing settlement. A judge or other person designated by the court may preside over the conference, which may be conducted in person or by telephone. Before a settlement conference, the attorneys must consult with their clients and obtain as much authority as feasible to settle the case. The court may, as a result of the conference, enter an order controlling the course of the proceedings or implementing any settlement agreement.

(As amended Apr. 29, 1994, eff. Dec. 1, 1994; Apr. 24, 1998, eff. Dec. 1, 1998.)

ADVISORY COMMITTEE NOTES

1967 Adoption

The uniform rule for review or enforcement of orders of administrative agencies, boards, commissions or officers (see the general note following Rule 15) authorizes a prehearing conference in agency review proceedings. The same considerations which make a prehearing conference desirable in such proceedings may be present in certain cases on appeal from the district courts. The proposed rule is based upon subdivision 11 of the present uniform rule for review of agency orders.

1994 Amendment

Rule 33 has been entirely rewritten. The new rule makes several changes.

The caption of the rule has been changed from "Prehearing Conference" to "Appeal Conferences" to reflect the fact that occasionally a conference is held after oral argument.

The rule permits the court to require the parties to attend the conference in appropriate cases. The Committee does not contemplate that attendance of the parties will become routine, but in certain instances the parties' presence can be useful. The language of the rule is broad enough to allow a court to determine that an executive or an employee (other than the general counsel) of a corporation or government agency with authority regarding the matter at issue, constitutes "the party."

The rule includes the possibility of settlement among the possible conference topics.

The rule recognizes that conferences are often held by telephone.

The rule allows a judge or other person designated by the court to preside over a conference. A number of local rules permit persons other than judges to preside over conferences. 1st Cir. R. 47.5; 6th Cir. R. 18; 8th Cir. R. 33A; 9th Cir. R. 33–1; and 10th Cir. R. 33.

The rule requires an attorney to consult with his or her client before a settlement conference and obtain as much authority as feasible to settle the case. An attorney can never settle a case without his or her client's consent. Certain entities, especially government entities, have particular difficulty obtaining authority to settle a case. The rule requires counsel to obtain only as much authority "as feasible."

1998 Amendments

The language of the rule is amended to make the rule more easily understood. In addition to changes made to improve the understanding, the Advisory Committee has changed language to make style and terminology consistent throughout the appellate rules. These changes are intended to be stylistic only.

Rule 34.   Oral Argument

(a) In General.

(1) Party's Statement. Any party may file, or a court may require by local rule, a statement explaining why oral argument should, or need not, be permitted.

(2) Standards. Oral argument must be allowed in every case unless a panel of three judges who have examined the briefs and record unanimously agrees that oral argument is unnecessary for any of the following reasons:

(A) the appeal is frivolous;

(B) the dispositive issue or issues have been authoritatively decided; or

(C) the facts and legal arguments are adequately presented in the briefs and record, and the decisional process would not be significantly aided by oral argument.

(b) Notice of Argument; Postponement. The clerk must advise all parties whether oral argument will be scheduled, and, if so, the date, time, and place for it, and the time allowed for each side. A motion to postpone the argument or to allow longer argument must be filed reasonably in advance of the hearing date.

(c) Order and Contents of Argument. The appellant opens and concludes the argument. Counsel must not read at length from briefs, records, or authorities.

(d) Cross-Appeals and Separate Appeals. If there is a cross-appeal, Rule 28.1(b) determines which party is the appellant and which is the appellee for purposes of oral argument. Unless the court directs otherwise, a cross-appeal or separate appeal must be argued when the initial appeal is argued. Separate parties should avoid duplicative argument.

(e) Nonappearance of a Party. If the appellee fails to appear for argument, the court must hear appellant's argument. If the appellant fails to appear for argument, the court may hear the appellee's argument. If neither party appears, the case will be decided on the briefs, unless the court orders otherwise.

(f) Submission on Briefs. The parties may agree to submit a case for decision on the briefs, but the court may direct that the case be argued.

(g) Use of Physical Exhibits at Argument; Removal. Counsel intending to use physical exhibits other than documents at the argument must arrange to place them in the courtroom on the day of the argument before the court convenes. After the argument, counsel must remove the exhibits from the courtroom, unless the court directs otherwise. The clerk may destroy or dispose of the exhibits if counsel does not reclaim them within a reasonable time after the clerk gives notice to remove them.

(As amended Apr. 30, 1979, eff. Aug. 1, 1979; Mar. 10, 1986, eff. July 1, 1986; Apr. 30, 1991, eff. Dec. 1, 1991; Apr. 22, 1993, eff. Dec. 1, 1993; Apr. 24, 1998, eff. Dec. 1, 1998; Apr. 25, 2005, eff. Dec. 1, 2005.)

ADVISORY COMMITTEE NOTES

1967 Adoption

A majority of circuits now limit oral argument to thirty minutes for each side, with the provision that additional time may be made available upon request. The Committee is of the view that thirty minutes to each side is sufficient in most cases, but that where additional time is necessary it should be freely granted on a proper showing of cause therefor. It further feels that the matter of time should be left ultimately to each court of appeals, subject to the spirit of the rule that a reasonable time should be allowed for argument. The term "side" is used to indicate that the time allowed by the rule is afforded to opposing interests rather than to individual parties. Thus if multiple appellants or appellees have a common interest, they constitute only a single side. If counsel for multiple parties who constitute a single side feel that additional time is necessary, they may request it. In other particulars this rule follows the usual practice among the circuits. See 3d Cir. Rule 31 [rule 31, U.S.Ct. of App.3rd Cir.]; 6th Cir. Rule 20 [rule 20, U.S.Ct. of App.6th Cir.]; 10th Cir. Rule 23 [rule 23, U.S.Ct. of App.10th Cir.].

1979 Amendment

The proposed amendment, patterned after the recommendations in the Report of the Commission on Revision of the Federal Court Appellate System, *Structure and Internal Procedures: Recommendations for Change,* 1975, created by Public Law 489 of the 92nd Cong.2nd Sess., 86 Stat. 807, sets forth general principles and minimum standards to be observed in formulating any local rule.

1986 Amendment

The amendments to Rules 34(a) and (e) are technical. No substantive change is intended.

1991 Amendment

Subdivision (d). The amendment of subdivision (d) conforms this rule with the amendment of Rule 28(h).

1993 Amendment

Subdivision (c). The amendment deletes the requirement that the opening argument must include a fair statement of the case. The Committee proposed the change because in some circuits the court does not want appellants to give such statements. In those circuits, the rule is not followed and is misleading. Nevertheless, the Committee does not want the deletion of the requirement to indicate disapproval of the practice. Those circuits that desire a statement of the case may continue the practice.

1998 Amendments

The language of the rule is amended to make the rule more easily understood. In addition to changes made to improve the understanding, the Advisory Committee has changed language to make style and terminology consistent throughout the appellate rules. These changes are intended to be stylistic only. Substantive changes are made in subdivision (a).

Subdivision (a). Currently subdivision (a) says that oral argument must be permitted unless, applying a local rule, a panel of three judges unanimously agrees that oral argument is not necessary. Rule 34 then outlines the criteria to be used to determine whether oral argument is needed and requires any local rule to "conform substantially" to the "minimum standard[s]" established in the national rule. The amendments omit the local rule requirement and make the criteria applicable by force of the national rule. The local rule is an unnecessary instrument.

Paragraph (a)(2) states that one reason for deciding that oral argument is unnecessary is that the dispositive issue has been authoritatively decided. the amended language no longer states that the issue must have been "recently" decided. The Advisory Committee does not intend any substantive change, but thinks that the use of "recently" may be misleading.

Subdivision (d). A cross-reference to Rule 28(h) has been substituted for a reiteration of the provisions of Rule 28(h).

2005 Amendments

Subdivision (d). A cross-reference in subdivision (d) has been changed to reflect the fact that, as part of an effort to collect within one rule all provisions regarding briefing in cases involving cross-appeals, former Rule 28(h) has been abrogated and its contents moved to new Rule 28.1(b).

Rule 35.   En Banc Determination

(a)   When Hearing or Rehearing En Banc May Be Ordered. A majority of the circuit judges who are in regular active service and who are not disqualified may order that an appeal or other proceeding be heard or reheard by the court of appeals en banc. An en banc hearing or rehearing is not favored and ordinarily will not be ordered unless:

(1) en banc consideration is necessary to secure or maintain uniformity of the court's decisions; or

(2) the proceeding involves a question of exceptional importance.

(b)   Petition for Hearing or Rehearing En Banc. A party may petition for a hearing or rehearing en banc.

(1) The petition must begin with a statement that either:

(A) the panel decision conflicts with a decision of the United States Supreme Court or of the court to which the petition is addressed (with citation to the conflicting case or cases) and consideration by the full court is therefore necessary to secure and maintain uniformity of the court's decisions; or

(B) the proceeding involves one or more questions of exceptional importance, each of which must be concisely stated; for example, a petition may assert that a proceeding presents a question of exceptional importance if it involves an issue on which the panel decision conflicts with the authoritative decisions of other United States Courts of Appeals that have addressed the issue.

(2) Except by the court's permission:

(A) a petition for an en banc hearing or rehearing produced using a computer must not exceed 3,900 words; and

(B) a handwritten or typewritten petition for an en banc hearing or rehearing must not exceed 15 pages.

(3) For purposes of the limits in Rule 35(b)(2), if a party files both a petition for panel rehearing and a petition for rehearing en banc, they are considered a single document even if they are filed separately, unless separate filing is required by local rule.

(c) Time for Petition for Hearing or Rehearing En Banc. A petition that an appeal be heard initially en banc must be filed by the date when the appellee's brief is due. A petition for a rehearing en banc must be filed within the time prescribed by Rule 40 for filing a petition for rehearing.

(d) Number of Copies. The number of copies to be filed must be prescribed by local rule and may be altered by order in a particular case.

(e) Response. No response may be filed to a petition for an en banc consideration unless the court orders a response. The length limits in Rule 35(b)(2) apply to a response.

(f) Call for a Vote. A vote need not be taken to determine whether the case will be heard or reheard en banc unless a judge calls for a vote.

(As amended Apr. 30, 1979, eff. Aug. 1, 1979; Apr. 29, 1994, eff. Dec. 1, 1994; Apr. 24, 1998, eff. Dec. 1, 1998; Apr. 25, 2005, eff. Dec. 1, 2005; Apr. 28, 2016; eff. Dec. 1, 2016; Apr. 27, 2020; eff. Dec. 1, 2020 absent contrary congressional action.)

ADVISORY COMMITTEE NOTES

1967 Adoption

Statutory authority for in banc hearings is found in 28 U.S.C. § 46(c). The proposed rule is responsive to the Supreme Court's view in *Western Pacific Ry. Corp. v. Western Pacific Ry. Co.*, 345 U.S. 247, 73 S.Ct. 656, 97 L.Ed. 986 (1953), that litigants should be free to suggest that a particular case is appropriate for consideration by all the judges of a court of appeals. The rule is addressed to the procedure whereby a party may suggest the appropriateness of convening the court in banc. It does not affect the power of a court of appeals to initiate in banc hearings *sua sponte*.

The provision that a vote will not be taken as a result of the suggestion of the party unless requested by a judge of the court in regular active service or by a judge who was a member of the panel that rendered a decision sought to be reheard is intended to make it clear that a suggestion of a party as such does not require any action by the court. See *Western Pacific Ry. Corp. v. Western Pacific Ry. Co.*, supra, 345 U.S. at 262, 73 S.Ct. 656. The rule merely authorizes a suggestion, imposes a time limit on suggestions for rehearings in banc, and provides that suggestions will be directed to the judges of the court in regular active service.

In practice, the suggestion of a party that a case be reheard in banc is frequently contained in a petition for rehearing, commonly styled "petition for rehearing in banc." Such a petition is in fact merely a petition for a rehearing, with a suggestion that the case be reheard in banc. Since no response to the suggestion, as distinguished from the petition for rehearing, is required, the panel which heard the case may quite properly dispose of the petition without reference to the suggestion. In such a case the fact that no response has been made to the suggestion does not affect the finality of the judgment or the issuance of the mandate, and the final sentence of the rule expressly so provides.

1979 Amendment

Under the present rule there is no specific provision for a response to a suggestion that an appeal be heard in banc. This has led to some uncertainty as to whether such a response may be filed. The proposed amendment would resolve this uncertainty.

While the present rule provides a time limit for suggestions for rehearing in banc, it does not deal with the timing of a request that the appeal be heard in banc initially. The proposed amendment fills this gap as well, providing that the suggestion must be made by the date of which the appellee's brief is filed.

Provision is made for circulating the suggestions to members of the panel despite the fact that senior judges on the panel would not be entitled to vote on whether a suggestion will be granted.

1994 Amendment

Subdivision (d). Subdivision (d) is added; it authorizes the courts of appeals to prescribe the number of copies of suggestions for hearing or rehearing in banc that must be filed. Because the number of copies needed depends directly upon the number of judges in the circuit, local rules are the best vehicle for setting the required number of copies.

1998 Amendments

The language and organization of the rule are amended to make the rule more easily understood. In addition to changes made to improve the understanding, the Advisory Committee has changed language to make style and terminology consistent throughout the appellate rules. These changes are intended to be stylistic only.

Several substantive changes are made to this rule, however.

One of the purposes of the substantive amendments is to treat a request for a rehearing en banc like a petition for panel rehearing so that a request for a rehearing en banc will suspend the finality of the court of appeals' judgment and delay the running of the period for filing a petition for writ of certiorari. Companion amendments are made to Rule 41.

Subdivision (a). The title of this subdivision is changed from "When hearing or rehearing in banc *will* be ordered" to "When Hearing or Rehearing En Banc *May* Be Ordered." The change emphasizes the discretion a court has with regard to granting en banc review.

Subdivision (b). The term "petition" for rehearing en banc is substituted for the term "suggestion" for rehearing en banc. The terminology change reflects the Committee's intent to treat similarly a petition for panel rehearing and a request for a rehearing en banc. The terminology change also delays the running of the time for filing a petition for a writ of certiorari because Sur. Ct. R. 13.3 says:

> if a petition for rehearing is timely filed in the lower court by any party, the time to file the petition for a writ of certiorari for all parties . . . runs from the date of the denial of the petition for rehearing or, if the petition for rehearing is granted, the subsequent entry of judgment.

The amendments also require each petition for en banc consideration to begin with a statement concisely demonstrating that the case meets the usual criteria for en banc consideration. It is the Committee's hope that requiring such a statement will cause the drafter of a petition to focus on the narrow grounds that support en banc consideration and to realize that a petition should not be filed unless the case meets those rigid standards.

Intercircuit conflict is cited as one reason for asserting that a proceeding involves a question of "exceptional importance." Intercircuit conflicts create problems. When the circuits construe the same federal law differently, parties' rights and duties depend upon where a case is litigated. Given the increase in the number of cases decided by the federal courts and the limitation on the number of cases the Supreme Court can hear, conflicts between the circuits may remain unresolved by the Supreme Court for an extended period of time. The existence of an intercircuit conflict often generates additional litigation in the other circuits as well as in the circuits that are already in conflict. Although an en banc proceeding will not necessarily prevent intercircuit conflicts, an en banc proceeding provides a safeguard against unnecessary intercircuit conflicts.

Some circuits have had rules or internal operating procedures that recognize a conflict with another circuit as a legitimate basis for granting a rehearing en banc. An intercircuit conflict may present a question of "exceptional importance" because of the costs that intercircuit conflicts impose on the system as a whole, in addition to the significance of the issues involved. It is not, however, the Committee's intent to make the granting of a hearing or rehearing en banc mandatory whenever there is an intercircuit conflict.

The amendment states that "a petition may assert that a proceeding presents a question of exceptional importance if it involves an issue on which the panel decision conflicts with the authoritative decisions of every other United States Court of Appeals that has addressed the issue." That language contemplates two situations in which a rehearing en banc may be appropriate. The first is when a panel decision creates a conflict. A panel decision creates a conflict when it conflicts with the decisions of all other circuits that have considered the issue. If a panel decision simply joins one side of an already existing conflict, a rehearing en banc may not be as important because it cannot avoid the conflict. The Second situation that may be a strong candidate for a rehearing en banc is one in which the circuit persists in a conflict created by a pre-existing decision of the same circuit and no other circuits have joined on that side of the conflict. The amendment states that the conflict must be with an "authoritative" decision of another circuit. "Authoritative" is used rather than "published" because in some circuits unpublished opinions may be treated as authoritative.

Counsel are reminded that their duty is fully discharged without filing a petition for rehearing en banc unless the case meets the rigid standards of subdivision (a) of this rule and even then the granting of a petition is entirely within the court's discretion.

Paragraph (2) of this subdivision establishes a maximum length for a petition. Fifteen pages is the length currently used in several circuits. Each request for en banc consideration must be studied by every active judge of the court and is a serious call on limited judicial resources. The extraordinary nature of the issue or the threat to uniformity of the court's decision can be established in most cases in less than fifteen pages. A court may shorten the maximum length on a case by case basis but the rule does not permit a circuit to shorten the length by local rule. The Committee has retained page limits rather than using word or line counts similar to those in amended Rule 32 because there has not been a serious enough problem to justify importing the word and line-count and typeface requirement that are applicable to briefs into other contexts.

Paragraph (3), although similar to (2), is separate because it deals with those instances in which a party files both a petition for rehearing en banc under this rule and a petition for panel rehearing under Rule 40.

To improve the clarity of the rule, the material dealing with filing a response to a petition and with voting on a petition have been moved to new subdivisions (e) and (f).

Subdivision (c). Two changes are made in this subdivision. First, the sentence stating that a request for a rehearing en banc does not affect the finality of the judgment or stay the issuance of the mandate is deleted. Second, the language permitting a party to include a request for rehearing en banc in a petition for panel rehearing is deleted. The Committee believes that those circuits that want to require two separate documents should have the option to do so.

Subdivision (e). This is a new subdivision. The substance of the subdivision, however, was drawn from former subdivision (b). The only changes are stylistic; no substantive changes are intended.

Subdivision (f). This is a new subdivision. The substance of the subdivision, however, was drawn from former subdivision (b).

Because of the discretionary nature of the en banc procedure, the filing of a suggestion for rehearing en banc has not required a vote; a vote is taken only when requested by a judge. It is not the Committee's intent to change the discretionary nature of the procedure or to require a vote on a petition for rehearing en banc. The rule continues, therefore, to provide that a court is not obligated to vote on such petitions. It is necessary, however, that each court develop a procedure for disposing of such petitions because they will suspend the finality of the court's judgment and toll the time for filing a petition for certiorari.

Former subdivision (b) contained language directing the clerk to distribute a "suggestion" to certain judges and indicating which judges may call for a vote. New subdivision (f) does not address those issues because they deal with internal court procedures.

2005 Amendments

Subdivision (a). Two national standards—28 U.S.C. § 46(c) and Rule 35(a)—provide that a hearing or rehearing en banc may be ordered by "a majority of the circuit judges who are in regular active service." Although these standards apply to all of the courts of appeals, the circuits are deeply divided over the interpretation of this language when one or more active judges are disqualified.

The Supreme Court has never addressed this issue. In *Shenker v. Baltimore & Ohio R.R. Co.*, 374 U.S. 1 (1963), the Court rejected a petitioner's claim that his rights under § 46(c) had been violated when the Third Circuit refused to rehear his case en banc. The Third Circuit had 8 active judges at the time; 4 voted in favor of rehearing the case, 2 against, and 2 abstained. No judge was disqualified. The Supreme Court ruled against the petitioner, holding, in essence, that § 46(c) did not provide a cause of action, but instead simply gave litigants "the right to know the administrative machinery that will be followed and the right to suggest that the *en banc* procedure be set in motion in his case." *Id.* at 5. *Shenker* did stress that a court of appeals has broad discretion in establishing internal procedures to handle requests for rehearings—or, as *Shenker* put it, " 'to devise its own administrative machinery to provide the *means* whereby a majority may order such a hearing.' " *Id.* (quoting *Western Pac. R.R. Corp. v. Western Pac. R.R. Co.*, 345 U.S. 247, 250 (1953) (emphasis added)). But *Shenker* did not address what is meant by "a majority" in § 46(c) (or Rule 35(a), which did not yet exist)—and *Shenker* certainly did not suggest that the phrase should have different meanings in different circuits.

In interpreting that phrase, 7 of the courts of appeals follow the "absolute majority" approach. *See* Marie Leary, Defining the "Majority" Vote Requirement in Federal Rule of Appellate Procedure 35(a) for Rehearings En Banc in the United States Courts of Appeals 8 tbl.1 (Federal Judicial Center 2002). Under this approach, disqualified judges are counted in the base in calculating whether a majority of judges have voted to hear a case en banc. Thus, in a circuit with 12 active judges, 7 must vote to hear a case en banc. If 5 of the 12 active judges are disqualified, all 7 non-disqualified judges must vote to hear the case en banc. The votes of 6 of the 7 non-disqualified judges are not enough, as 6 is not a majority of 12.

Six of the courts of appeals follow the "case majority" approach. *Id.* Under this approach, disqualified judges are not counted in the base in calculating whether a majority of judges have voted to hear a case en banc. Thus, in a case in which 5 of a circuit's 12 active judges are disqualified, only 4 judges (a majority of the 7 non-disqualified judges) must vote to hear a case en banc. (The First and Third Circuits explicitly qualify the case majority approach by providing that a case cannot be heard en banc unless a majority of all active judges—disqualified and non-disqualified—are eligible to participate.)

Rule 35(a) has been amended to adopt the case majority approach as a uniform national interpretation of § 46(c). The federal rules of practice and procedure exist to "maintain consistency," which Congress has equated with "promot[ing] the interest of justice." 28 U.S.C. § 2073(b). The courts of appeals should not follow two inconsistent approaches in deciding whether sufficient votes exist to hear a case en banc, especially when there is a governing statute and governing rule that apply to all circuits and that use identical terms, and especially when there is nothing about the local conditions of each circuit that justifies conflicting approaches.

The case majority approach represents the better interpretation of the phrase "the circuit judges . . . in regular active service" in the first sentence of § 46(c). The second sentence of § 46(c)—which defines which judges are eligible to participate in a case being heard or reheard en banc—uses the similar expression "all circuit judges in regular active service." It is clear that "all circuit judges in regular active service" in the second sentence does not include disqualified judges, as disqualified judges clearly cannot participate in a case being heard or reheard en banc. Therefore, assuming that two nearly identical phrases appearing in adjacent sentences in a statute should be interpreted in the same way, the best reading of "the circuit judges . . . in regular active service" in the first sentence of § 46(c) is that it, too, does not include disqualified judges.

This interpretation of § 46(c) is bolstered by the fact that the case majority approach has at least two major advantages over the absolute majority approach:

First, under the absolute majority approach, a disqualified judge is, as a practical matter, counted as voting against hearing a case en banc. This defeats the purpose of recusal. To the extent possible, the disqualification of a judge should not result in the equivalent of a vote for or against hearing a case en banc.

Second, the absolute majority approach can leave the en banc court helpless to overturn a panel decision with which almost all of the circuit's active judges disagree. For example, in a case in which 5 of a circuit's 12 active judges are disqualified, the case cannot be heard en banc even if 6 of the 7 non-disqualified judges strongly disagree with the panel opinion. This permits one active judge—perhaps sitting on a panel with a visiting judge—effectively to control circuit precedent, even over the objection of all of his or her colleagues. *See Gulf Power Co. v. FCC*, 226 F.3d 1220, 1222–23 (11th Cir. 2000) (Carnes, J., concerning the denial of reh'g en banc), *rev'd sub nom. National Cable & Telecomm. Ass'n, Inc. v. Gulf Power Co.*, 534 U.S. 327 (2002). Even though the en banc court may, in a future case, be able to correct an erroneous legal interpretation, the en banc court will never be able to correct the injustice inflicted by the panel on the parties to the case. Moreover, it may take many years before sufficient non-disqualified judges can be mustered to overturn the panel's erroneous legal interpretation. In the meantime, the lower courts of the circuit must apply—and the citizens of the circuit must conform their behavior to—an interpretation of the law that almost all of the circuit's active judges believe is incorrect.

The amendment to Rule 35(a) is not meant to alter or affect the quorum requirement of 28 U.S.C. § 46(d). In particular, the amendment is not intended to foreclose the possibility that § 46(d) might be read to require that more than half of all circuit judges in regular active service be eligible to participate in order for the court to hear or rehear a case en banc.

2016 Amendment

The page limits previously employed in Rules 5, 21, 27, 35, and 40 have been largely overtaken by changes in technology. For papers produced using a computer, those page limits are now replaced by word limits. The word limits were derived from the current page limits using the assumption that one page is equivalent to 260 words. Papers produced using a computer must include the certificate of compliance required by Rule 32(g); Form 6 in the Appendix of Forms suffices to meet that requirement. Page limits are retained for papers prepared without the aid of a computer (i.e., handwritten or typewritten papers). For both the word limit and the page limit, the calculation excludes any items listed in Rule 32(f).

Changes Made After Publication and Comment

The Committee deleted the proposed line limit and revised the proposed word limit from 3,750 words to 3,900 words. The Committee also made conforming changes to the Committee Note and style changes to the Rule text.

2020 Amendments

[Effective Dec. 1, 2020 absent contrary congressional action]

The amendment to Rule 35(e) clarifies that the length limits applicable to a petition for hearing or rehearing en banc also apply to a response to such a petition, if the court orders one.

Rule 36.   Entry of Judgment; Notice

(a)   Entry. A judgment is entered when it is noted on the docket. The clerk must prepare, sign, and enter the judgment:

(1)   after receiving the court's opinion—but if settlement of the judgment's form is required, after final settlement; or

(2)   if a judgment is rendered without an opinion, as the court instructs.

(b)   Notice. On the date when judgment is entered, the clerk must serve on all parties a copy of the opinion—or the judgment, if no opinion was written—and a notice of the date when the judgment was entered.

(As amended Apr. 24, 1998, eff. Dec. 1, 1998; Apr. 29, 2002, eff. Dec. 1, 2002.)

ADVISORY COMMITTEE NOTES

1967 Adoption

This is the typical rule. See 1st Cir. Rule 29 [rule 29, U.S.Ct. of App. 1st Cir.]; 3d Cir. Rule 32 [rule 32, U.S.Ct. of App. 3rd Cir.]; 6th Cir. Rule 21 [rule 21, U.S.Ct. of App. 6th Cir.]. At present, uncertainty exists as to the date of entry of judgment when the opinion directs subsequent settlement of the precise terms of the judgment, a common practice in cases involving enforcement of agency orders. See Stern and Gressman, Supreme Court Practice, p. 203 (3d Ed., 1962). The principle of finality suggests that in such cases entry of judgment should be delayed until approval of the judgment in final form.

1998 Amendments

The language and organization of the rule are amended to make the rule more easily understood. In addition to changes made to improve the understanding, the Advisory Committee has changed language to make style and terminology consistent throughout the appellate rules. These changes are intended to be stylistic only.

2002 Amendments

Subdivision (b). Subdivision (b) has been amended so that the clerk may use electronic means to serve a copy of the opinion or judgment or to serve notice of the date when judgment was entered upon parties who have consented to such service.

Changes Made After Publication and Comments. No changes were made to the text of the proposed amendment or to the Committee Note.

Rule 37.　Interest on Judgment

(a)　When the Court Affirms. Unless the law provides otherwise, if a money judgment in a civil case is affirmed, whatever interest is allowed by law is payable from the date when the district court's judgment was entered.

(b)　When the Court Reverses. If the court modifies or reverses a judgment with a direction that a money judgment be entered in the district court, the mandate must contain instructions about the allowance of interest.

(As amended Apr. 24, 1998, eff. Dec. 1, 1998.)

ADVISORY COMMITTEE NOTES

1967 Adoption

The first sentence makes it clear that if a money judgment is affirmed in the court of appeals, the interest which attaches to money judgments by force of law (see 28 U.S.C. § 1961 and § 2411) upon their initial entry is payable as if no appeal had been taken, whether or not the mandate makes mention of interest. There has been some confusion on this point. *See Blair v. Durham*, 139 F.2d 260 (6th Cir., 1943) and cases cited therein.

In reversing or modifying the judgment of the district court, the court of appeals may direct the entry of a money judgment, as, for example, when the court of appeals reverses a judgment notwithstanding the verdict and directs entry of judgment on the verdict. In such a case the question may arise as to whether interest is to run from the date of entry of the judgment directed by the court of appeals or from the date on which the judgment would have been entered in the district court except for the erroneous ruling corrected on appeal. In *Briggs v. Pennsylvania R. Co.*, 334 U.S. 304, 68 S.Ct. 1039, 92 L.Ed. 1403 (1948), the Court held that where the mandate of the court of appeals directed entry of judgment upon a verdict but made no mention of interest from the date of the verdict to the date of the entry of the judgment directed by the mandate, the district court was powerless to add such interest. The second sentence of the proposed rule is a reminder to the court, the clerk and counsel of the *Briggs* rule. Since the rule directs that the matter of interest be disposed of by the mandate, in cases where interest is simply overlooked, a party who conceives himself entitled to interest from a date other than the date of entry of judgment in accordance with the mandate should be entitled to seek recall of the mandate for determination of the question.

1998 Amendments

The language and organization of the rule are amended to make the rule more easily understood. In addition to changes made to improve the understanding, the Advisory Committee has changed language to make style and terminology consistent throughout the appellate rules. These changes are intended to be stylistic only.

Rule 38.　Frivolous Appeal—Damages and Costs

If a court of appeals determines that an appeal is frivolous, it may, after a separately filed motion or notice from the court and reasonable opportunity to respond, award just damages and single or double costs to the appellee.

(As amended Apr. 29, 1994, eff. Dec. 1, 1994; Apr. 24, 1998, eff. Dec. 1, 1998.)

ADVISORY COMMITTEE NOTES

1967 Adoption

Compare 28 U.S.C. § 1912. While both the statute and the usual rule on the subject by courts of appeals (Fourth Circuit Rule 20 [rule 20, U.S.Ct. of App. 4th Cir.] is a typical rule) speak of "damages for delay," the courts of appeals quite properly allow damages, attorney's fees and other expenses incurred by an appellee if the appeal is frivolous without requiring a showing that the appeal resulted in delay. See *Dunscombe v. Sayle*, 340 F.2d 311 (5th Cir., 1965), cert. den., 382 U.S. 814, 86 S.Ct. 32, 15 L.Ed.2d 62 (1965); *Lowe v. Willacy*, 239 F.2d 179 (9th Cir., 1956); *Griffin Wellpoint Corp. v. Munro-Langstroth, Inc.*, 269 F.2d 64 (1st Cir., 1959); *Ginsburg v. Stern*, 295 F.2d 698 (3d Cir., 1961). The subjects of interest and damages are separately regulated, contrary to the present practice of combining the two (see Fourth Circuit Rule 20) to make it clear that the awards are distinct and independent. Interest is provided for by law; damages are awarded by the court in its discretion in the case of a frivolous appeal as a matter of justice to the appellee and as a penalty against the appellant.

1994 Amendments

The amendment requires that before a court of appeals may impose sanctions, the person to be sanctioned must have notice and an opportunity to respond. The amendment reflects the basic principle enunciated in the Supreme Court's opinion in *Roadway Express, Inc. v. Piper*, 447 U.S. 752, 767 (1980), that notice and opportunity to respond must precede the imposition of sanctions. A separately filed motion requesting sanctions constitutes notice. A statement inserted in a party's brief that the party moves for sanctions is not sufficient notice. Requests in briefs for sanctions have become so commonplace that it is unrealistic to expect careful responses to such requests without any indication that the court is actually contemplating such measures. Only a motion, the purpose of which is to request sanctions, is sufficient. If there is no such motion filed, notice must come from the court. The form of notice from the court and of the opportunity for comment purposely are left to the court's discretion.

1998 Amendments

Only the caption of this rule has been amended. The changes are intended to be stylistic only.

Rule 39.   Costs

(a) **Against Whom Assessed.** The following rules apply unless the law provides or the court orders otherwise:

   (1) if an appeal is dismissed, costs are taxed against the appellant, unless the parties agree otherwise;

   (2) if a judgment is affirmed, costs are taxed against the appellant;

   (3) if a judgment is reversed, costs are taxed against the appellee;

   (4) if a judgment is affirmed in part, reversed in part, modified, or vacated, costs are taxed only as the court orders.

(b) **Costs For and Against the United States.** Costs for or against the United States, its agency, or officer will be assessed under Rule 39(a) only if authorized by law.

(c) **Costs of Copies.** Each court of appeals must, by local rule, fix the maximum rate for taxing the cost of producing necessary copies of a brief or appendix, or copies of records authorized by Rule 30(f). The rate must not exceed that generally charged for such work in the area where the clerk's office is located and should encourage economical methods of copying.

(d) **Bill of Costs: Objections; Insertion in Mandate.**

   (1) A party who wants costs taxed must—within 14 days after entry of judgment—file with the circuit clerk and serve an itemized and verified bill of costs.

   (2) Objections must be filed within 14 days after service of the bill of costs, unless the court extends the time.

(3) The clerk must prepare and certify an itemized statement of costs for insertion in the mandate, but issuance of the mandate must not be delayed for taxing costs. If the mandate issues before costs are finally determined, the district clerk must—upon the circuit clerk's request—add the statement of costs, or any amendment of it, to the mandate.

(e) **Costs on Appeal Taxable in the District Court.** The following costs on appeal are taxable in the district court for the benefit of the party entitled to costs under this rule:

(1) the preparation and transmission of the record;

(2) the reporter's transcript, if needed to determine the appeal;

(3) premiums paid for a bond or other security to preserve rights pending appeal; and

(4) the fee for filing the notice of appeal.

(As amended Apr. 30, 1979, eff. Aug. 1, 1979; Mar. 10, 1986, eff. July 1, 1986; Apr. 24, 1998, eff. Dec. 1, 1998; Mar. 26, 2009, eff. Dec. 1, 2009; Apr. 26, 2018, eff. Dec. 1, 2018; Apr. 25, 2019, eff. Dec. 1, 2019.)

ADVISORY COMMITTEE NOTES

1967 Adoption

Subdivision (a). Statutory authorization for taxation of costs is found in 28 U.S.C. § 1920. The provisions of this subdivision follow the usual practice in the circuits. A few statutes contain specific provisions in derogation of these general provisions. (See 28 U.S.C. § 1928, which forbids the award of costs to a successful plaintiff in a patent infringement action under the circumstances described by the statute). These statutes are controlling in cases to which they apply.

Subdivision (b). The rules of the courts of appeals at present commonly deny costs to the United States except as allowance may be directed by statute. Those rules were promulgated at a time when the United States was generally invulnerable to an award of costs against it, and they appear to be based on the view that if the United States is not subject to costs if it loses, it ought not be entitled to recover costs if it wins.

The number of cases affected by such rules has been greatly reduced by the Act of July 18, 1966, 80 Stat. 308 (1 U.S.Code Cong. & Ad.News, p. 349 (1966), 89th Cong., 2d Sess., which amended 28 U.S.C. § 2412, the former general bar to the award of costs against the United States. Section 2412 as amended generally places the United States on the same footing as private parties with respect to the award of costs in civil cases. But the United States continues to enjoy immunity from costs in certain cases. By its terms amended § 2412 authorizes an award of costs against the United States only in civil actions, and it excepts from its general authorization of an award of costs against the United States cases which are "otherwise specifically provided (for) by statute." Furthermore, the Act of July 18, 1966, *supra*, provides that the amendments of § 2412 which it effects shall apply only to actions filed subsequent to the date of its enactment. The second clause continues in effect, for these and all other cases in which the United States enjoys immunity from costs, the presently prevailing rule that the United States may recover costs as the prevailing party only if it would have suffered them as the losing party.

Subdivision (c). While only five circuits (D.C.Cir. Rule 20(d) [rule 20(d), U.S.Ct. of App. Dist. of Col.]; 1st Cir. Rule 31(4) [rule 31(4), U.S.Ct. of App. 1st Cir.]; 3d Cir. Rule 35(4) [rule 35(4), U.S.Ct. of App. 3rd Cir.]; 4th Cir. Rule 21(4) [rule 21(4) U.S.Ct. of App. 4th Cir.]; 9th Cir. Rule 25 [rule 25, U.S.Ct. of App.9th Cir.], as amended June 2, 1967) presently tax the cost of printing briefs, the proposed rule makes the cost taxable in keeping with the principle of this rule that all cost items expended in the prosecution of a proceeding should be borne by the unsuccessful party.

Subdivision (e). The costs described in this subdivision are costs of the appeal and, as such, are within the undertaking of the appeal bond. They are made taxable in the district court for general convenience. Taxation of the cost of the reporter's transcript is specifically authorized by 28 U.S.C. § 1920, but in the absence of a rule some district courts have held themselves without authority to tax the cost (*Perlman v. Feldmann*, 116 F.Supp. 102 (D. Conn., 1953); *Firtag v. Gendleman*, 152 F.Supp. 226 (D.D.C., 1957); *Todd Atlantic Shipyards Corp. v. The Southport*, 100 F.Supp. 763 (E.D.S.C., 1951). Provision for taxation of the cost of premiums paid for supersedeas bonds is common in the local rules of district courts and the practice is established in the Second, Seventh, and Ninth Circuits. *Berner v. British Commonwealth Pacific Air Lines, Ltd.*, 362 F.2d 799 (2d Cir. 1966); *Land Oberoesterreich v. Gude*, 93 F.2d 292 (2d Cir., 1937); *In re Northern Ind. Oil Co.*, 192 F.2d 139 (7th Cir., 1951); *Lunn v. F. W. Woolworth*, 210 F.2d 159 (9th Cir., 1954).

1979 Amendment

Subdivision (c). The proposed amendment would permit variations among the circuits in regulating the maximum rates taxable as costs for printing or otherwise reproducing briefs, appendices, and copies of records authorized by Rule 30(f). The present rule has had a different effect in different circuits depending upon the size of the circuit, the location of the clerk's office, and the location of other cities. As a consequence there was a growing sense that strict adherence to the rule produces some unfairness in some of the circuits and the matter should be made subject to local rule.

Subdivision (d). The present rule makes no provision for objections to a bill of costs. The proposed amendment would allow 10 days for such objections. Cf. Rule 54(d) of the F.R.C.P. [rule 54(d), Federal Rules of Civil Procedure]. It provides further that the mandate shall not be delayed for taxation of costs.

1986 Amendment

The amendment to subdivision (c) is intended to increase the degree of control exercised by the courts of appeals over rates for printing and copying recoverable as costs. It further requires the courts of appeals to encourage cost-consciousness by requiring that, in fixing the rate, the court consider the most economical methods of printing and copying.

The amendment to subdivision (d) is technical. No substantive change is intended.

1998 Amendments

The language and organization of the rule are amended to make the rule more easily understood. In addition to changes made to improve the understanding, the Advisory Committee has changed language to make style and terminology consistent throughout the appellate rules. These changes are intended to be stylistic only. All references to the cost of "printing" have been deleted from subdivision (c) because commercial printing is so rarely used for preparation of documents filed with a court of appeals.

2009 Amendments

Subdivision (d)(2). The time set in the former rule at 10 days has been revised to 14 days. See the Note to Rule 26.

2018 Amendments

The amendment of subdivision (e)(3) conforms this rule with the amendment of Federal Rule of Civil Procedure 62. Rule 62 formerly required a party to provide a "supersedeas bond" to obtain a stay of the judgment and proceedings to enforce the judgment. As amended, Rule 62(b) allows a party to obtain a stay by providing a "bond or other security."

2019 Amendments

In subdivision (d)(1) the words "with proof of service" are deleted and replaced with "and serve" to conform with amendments to Rule 25(d) regarding when proof of service or acknowledgement of service is required for filed papers.

Rule 40.   Petition for Panel Rehearing

(a) Time to File; Contents; ~~Answer~~Response; Action by the Court if Granted.

(1) Time. Unless the time is shortened or extended by order or local rule, a petition for panel rehearing may be filed within 14 days after entry of judgment. But in a civil case, unless an order shortens or extends the time, the petition may be filed by any party within 45 days after entry of judgment if one of the parties is:

(A) the United States;

(B) a United States agency;

(C) a United States officer or employee sued in an official capacity; or

(D) a current or former United States officer or employee sued in an individual capacity for an act or omission occurring in connection with duties performed on the United States' behalf—including all instances in which the United States represents that person when the court of appeals' judgment is entered or files the petition for that person.

(2)   Contents. The petition must state with particularity each point of law or fact that the petitioner believes the court has overlooked or misapprehended and must argue in support of the petition. Oral argument is not permitted.

(3)   ~~Answer~~Response. Unless the court requests, no ~~answer~~response to a petition for panel rehearing is permitted. ~~But o~~Ordinarily, rehearing will not be granted in the absence of such a request. If a response is requested, the requirements of Rule 40(b) apply to the response.

(4)   Action by the Court. If a petition for panel rehearing is granted, the court may do any of the following:

(A)   make a final disposition of the case without reargument;

(B)   restore the case to the calendar for reargument or resubmission; or

(C)   issue any other appropriate order.

(b)   Form of Petition; Length. The petition must comply in form with Rule 32. Copies must be served and filed as Rule 31 prescribes. Except by the court's permission:

(1)   a petition for panel rehearing produced using a computer must not exceed 3,900 words; and

(2)   a handwritten or typewritten petition for panel rehearing must not exceed 15 pages.

(As amended Apr. 30, 1979, eff. Aug. 1, 1979; Apr. 29, 1994, eff. Dec. 1, 1994; Apr. 24, 1998, eff. Dec. 1, 1998; Apr. 26, 2011, eff. Dec. 1, 2011; Apr. 28, 2016, eff. Dec. 1, 2016; Apr. 27, 2020, eff. Dec. 1, 2020 absent contrary congressional action.)

ADVISORY COMMITTEE NOTES

1967 Adoption

This is the usual rule among the circuits, except that the express prohibition against filing a reply to the petition is found only in the rules of the Fourth, Sixth and Eighth Circuits (it is also contained in Supreme Court Rule 58(3) [rule 58(3), U.S.Sup.Ct.Rules). It is included to save time and expense to the party victorious on appeal. In the very rare instances in which a reply is useful, the court will ask for it.

1979 Amendment

Subdivision (a). The Standing Committee added to the first sentence of Rule 40(a) the words "or by local rule," to conform to current practice in the circuits. The Standing Committee believes the change noncontroversial.

Subdivision (b). The proposed amendment would eliminate the distinction drawn in the present rule between printed briefs and those duplicated from typewritten pages in fixing their maximum length. See Note to Rule 28. Since petitions for rehearing must be prepared in a short time, making typographic printing less likely, the maximum number of pages is fixed at 15, the figure used in the present rule for petitions duplicated by means other than typographic printing.

1994 Amendment

Subdivision (a). The amendment lengthens the time for filing a petition for rehearing from 14 to 45 days in civil cases involving the United States or its agencies or officers. It has no effect upon the time for filing in criminal cases. The amendment makes nation-wide the current practice in the District of Columbia and the Tenth Circuits, *see* D.C. Cir. R. 15 (a), 10th Cir. R. 40.3. This amendment, analogous to the provision in Rule 4(a) extending the time for filing a notice of appeal in cases involving the United States, recognizes that the Solicitor General needs time to conduct a thorough review of the merits of a case before requesting a rehearing. In a case in which a court of appeals believes it necessary to restrict the time for filing a rehearing petition, the amendment provides that the court may do so by order. Although the first sentence of Rule 40 permits a court of appeals to shorten or lengthen the usual 14 day filing period by order or by local rule, the sentence governing appeals in civil cases involving the United States purposely limits a court's power to alter the 45 day period to orders in specific cases. If a court of appeals could adopt a local rule shortening the time for filing a petition for rehearing in all cases involving the United States, the purpose of the amendment would be defeated.

1998 Amendments

The language and organization of the rule are amended to make the rule more easily understood. In addition to changes made to improve the understanding, the Advisory Committee has changed language to make style and terminology consistent throughout the appellate rules. These changes are intended to be stylistic only.

2011 Amendments

Subdivision (a)(1). Rule 40(a)(1) has been amended to make clear that the 45-day period to file a petition for panel rehearing applies in cases in which an officer or employee of the United States is sued in an individual capacity for acts or omissions occurring in connection with duties performed on behalf of the United States. (A concurrent amendment to Rule 4(a)(1)(B) makes clear that the 60-day period to file an appeal also applies in such cases.) In such cases, the Solicitor General needs adequate time to review the merits of the panel decision and decide whether to seek rehearing, just as the Solicitor General does when an appeal involves the United States, a United States agency, or a United States officer or employee sued in an official capacity.

To promote clarity of application, the amendment to Rule 40(a)(1) includes safe harbor provisions that parties can readily apply and rely upon. Under new subdivision 40(a)(1)(D), a case automatically qualifies for the 45-day period if (1) a legal officer of the United States has appeared in the case, in an official capacity, as counsel for the current or former officer or employee and has not withdrawn the appearance at the time of the entry of the court of appeals' judgment that is the subject of the petition or (2) a legal officer of the United States appears on the petition as counsel, in an official capacity, for the current or former officer or employee. There will be cases that do not fall within either safe harbor but that qualify for the longer petition period. An example would be a case in which a federal employee is sued in an individual capacity for an act occurring in connection with federal duties and the United States does not represent the employee either when the court of appeals' judgment is entered or when the petition is filed but the United States pays for private counsel for the employee.

2016 Amendments

The page limits previously employed in Rules 5, 21, 27, 35, and 40 have been largely overtaken by changes in technology. For papers produced using a computer, those page limits are now replaced by word limits. The word limits were derived from the current page limits using the assumption that one page is equivalent to 260 words. Papers produced using a computer must include the certificate of compliance required by Rule 32(g); Form 6 in the Appendix of Forms suffices to meet that requirement. Page limits are retained for papers prepared without the aid of a computer (i.e., handwritten or typewritten papers). For both the word limit and the page limit, the calculation excludes any items listed in Rule 32(f).

Changes Made After Publication and Comment

The Committee deleted the proposed line limit and revised the proposed word limit from 3,750 words to 3,900 words. The Committee also made conforming changes to the Committee Note and style changes to the Rule text.

2020 Amendments

[Effective Dec. 1, 2020 absent contrary congressional action]

The amendment to Rule 40(a)(3) clarifies that the provisions of Rule 40(b) regarding a petition for panel rehearing also apply to a response to such a petition, if the court orders a response. The amendment also changes the language to refer to a "response," rather than an "answer," to make the terminology consistent with Rule 35; this change is intended to be stylistic only.

Rule 41.   Mandate: Contents; Issuance and Effective Date; Stay

(a) Contents. Unless the court directs that a formal mandate issue, the mandate consists of a certified copy of the judgment, a copy of the court's opinion, if any, and any direction about costs.

(b) When Issued. The court's mandate must issue 7 days after the time to file a petition for rehearing expires, or 7 days after entry of an order denying a timely petition for panel rehearing, petition for rehearing en banc, or motion for stay of mandate, whichever is later. The court may shorten or extend the time by order.

(c) Effective Date. The mandate is effective when issued.

(d) Staying the Mandate Pending a Petition for Certiorari.

(1) Motion to Stay. A party may move to stay the mandate pending the filing of a petition for a writ of certiorari in the Supreme Court. The motion must be served on all parties and must show that the certiorari petition would present a substantial question and that there is good cause for a stay.

(2) Duration of Stay; Extensions. The stay must not exceed 90 days, unless:

(A) the period is extended for good cause; or

(B) the party who obtained the stay notifies the circuit clerk in writing within the period of the stay:

(i) that the time for filing a petition has been extended, in which case the stay continues for the extended period; or

(ii) that the petition has been filed, in which case the stay continues until the Supreme Court's final disposition.

(3) Security. The court may require a bond or other security as a condition to granting or continuing a stay of the mandate.

(4) Issuance of Mandate. The court of appeals must issue the mandate immediately on receiving a copy of a Supreme Court order denying the petition, unless extraordinary circumstances exist.

(As amended Apr. 29, 1994, eff. Dec. 1, 1994; Apr. 24, 1998, eff. Dec. 1, 1998; Apr. 29, 2002, eff. Dec. 1, 2002; Mar. 26, 2009, eff. Dec. 1, 2009; Apr. 26, 2018, eff. Dec. 1, 2018.)

ADVISORY COMMITTEE NOTES

1967 Adoption

The proposed rule follows the rule or practice in a majority of circuits by which copies of the opinion and the judgment serve in lieu of a formal mandate in the ordinary case. Compare Supreme Court Rule 59. Although 28 U.S.C. § 2101(c) permits a writ of certiorari to be filed within 90 days after entry of judgment, seven of the eight circuits which now regulate the matter of stays pending application for certiorari limit the initial stay of the mandate to the 30-day period provided in the proposed rule. Compare D.C.Cir. Rule 27(e) [rule 27(e), U.S.Ct. of App. Dist. of Col.].

1994 Amendment

Subdivision (a). The amendment conforms Rule 41(a) to the amendment made to Rule 40(a). The amendment keys the time for issuance of the mandate to the expiration of the time for filing a petition for rehearing, unless such a petition is filed in which case the mandate issues 7 days after the entry of the order denying the petition. Because the amendment to Rule 40(a) lengthens the time for filing a petition for rehearing in civil cases involving the United States from 14 to 45 days, the rule requiring the mandate to issue 21 days after the entry of judgment would cause the mandate to issue while the government is still considering requesting a rehearing. Therefore, the amendment generally requires the mandate to issue 7 days after the expiration of the time for filing a petition for rehearing.

Subdivision (b). The amendment requires a party who files a motion requesting a stay of mandate to file, at the same time, proof of service on all other parties. The old rule required the party to give notice to the other parties; the amendment merely requires the party to provide the court with evidence of having done so.

The amendment also states that the motion must show that a petition for certiorari would present a substantial question and that there is good cause for a stay. The amendment is intended to alert the parties to the fact that a stay of mandate is not granted automatically and to the type of showing that needs to be made. The Supreme Court has established conditions that must be met before it will stay a mandate. *See* Robert L. Stern et al., Supreme Court Practice § 17.19 (6th ed. 1986).

1998 Amendments

The language and organization of the rule are amended to make the rule more easily understood. In addition to changes made to improve the understanding, the Advisory Committee has changed language to make style and terminology consistent throughout the appellate rules. These changes are intended to be stylistic only.

Several substantive changes are made in this rule, however.

Subdivision (b). The existing rule provides that the mandate issues 7 days after the time to file a petition for panel rehearing expires unless such a petition for rehearing en banc or motion for stay of mandate is filed, the mandate does not issue until 7 days after entry of an order denying the last of all such requests. If a petition for rehearing or a petition for rehearing en banc is granted, the court enters a new judgment after the rehearing and the mandate issues within the normal time after entry of that judgment.

Subdivision (c). Subdivision (c) is new. It provides that the mandate is effective when the court issues it. A court of appeals' judgment or order is not final until issuance of the mandate; at that time the parties' obligations become fixed. This amendment is intended to make it clear that the mandate is effective upon issuance and that its effectiveness is not delayed until receipt of the mandate by the trial court or agency, or until the trial court or agency acts upon it. This amendment is consistent with the current understanding. Unless the court orders that the mandate issue earlier than provided in the rule, the parties can easily calculate the anticipated date of issuance and verify issuance of the mandate, the entry of the order on the docket alerts the parties to that fact.

Subdivision (d). Amended paragraph (1) provides that the filing of a petition for panel rehearing, a petition for rehearing en banc or a motion for a stay of mandate pending petition to the Supreme Court for a writ of certiorari stays the issuance of the mandate until the court disposes of the petition or motion. The provision that a petition for rehearing en banc stays the mandate is a companion to the amendment of Rule 35 that deletes the language stating that a request for a rehearing en banc does not affect the finality of the judgment or stay the issuance of the mandate. The Committee's objective is to treat a request for a rehearing en banc like a petition for panel rehearing so that a request for a rehearing en banc will suspend the finality of the court of appeals' judgment and delay the running of the period for filing a petition for writ of certiorari. Because the filing of a petition for rehearing en banc will stay the mandate, a court of appeals will need to take final action on the petition but the procedure for doing so is left to local practice.

Paragraph (1) also provides that the filing of a motion for a stay of mandate pending petition to the Supreme Court for a writ of certiorari stays the mandate until the court disposes of the motion. If the court denies the motion, the court must issue the mandate 7 days after entering the order denying the motion. If the court grants the motion, the mandate is stayed according to the terms of the order granting the stay. Delaying issuance of the mandate eliminates the need to recall the mandate if the motion for a stay is granted. If, however, the court believes that it would be inappropriate to delay issuance of the mandate until disposition of the motion for a stay, the court may order that the mandate issue immediately.

Paragraph (2). The amendment changes the maximum period for a stay of mandate, absent the court of appeals granting an extension for cause, to 90 days. The presumptive 30-day period was adopted when a party had to file a petition for a writ of certiorari in criminal cases within 30 days after entry of judgment. Supreme Court Rule 13.1 now provides that a party has 90 days after entry of judgment by a court of appeals to file a petition for a writ of certiorari whether the case is civil or criminal.

The amendment does not require a court of appeals to grant a stay of mandate that is coextensive with the period granted for filing a petition for a writ of certiorari. The granting of a stay and the length of the stay remain within the discretion of the court of appeals. The amendment means only that a 90-day stay may be granted without a need to show cause for a stay longer than 30 days.

Subparagraph (C) is not new; it has been moved from the end of the rule to this position.

2002 Amendments

Subdivision (b). Subdivision (b) directs that the mandate of a court must issue 7 days after the time to file a petition for rehearing expires or 7 days after the court denies a timely petition for panel rehearing, petition for rehearing en banc, or motion for stay of mandate, whichever is later. Intermediate Saturdays, Sundays, and legal holidays are counted in computing that 7-day deadline, which means that, except when the 7-day deadline ends on a weekend or legal holiday, the mandate issues exactly one week after the triggering event.

Fed. R. App. P. 26(a)(2) has been amended to provide that, in computing any period of time, one should "[e]xclude intermediate Saturdays, Sundays, and legal holidays when the period is less than 11 days, unless stated in calendar days." This change in the method of computing deadlines means that 7-day deadlines (such as that in subdivision (b)) have been lengthened as a practical matter. Under the new computation method, a mandate would never issue sooner than 9 actual days after a triggering event, and legal holidays could extend that period to as much as 13 days.

Delaying mandates for 9 or more days would introduce significant and unwarranted delay into appellate proceedings. For that reason, subdivision (b) has been amended to require that mandates issue 7 *calendar* days after a triggering event.

Changes Made After Publication and Comments. No changes were made to the text of the proposed amendment or to the Committee Note.

2009 Amendments

Under former Rule 26(a), short periods that span weekends or holidays were computed without counting those weekends or holidays. To specify that a period should be calculated by counting all intermediate days, including weekends or holidays, the Rules used the term "calendar days." Rule 26(a) now takes a "days-are-days" approach under which all intermediate days are counted, no matter how short the period. Accordingly, "7 calendar days" in subdivision (b) is amended to read simply "7 days."

2018 Amendments

Subdivision (b). Subdivision (b) is revised to clarify that an order is required for a stay of the mandate.

Before 1998, the rule referred to a court's ability to shorten or enlarge the time for the mandate's issuance "by order." The phrase "by order" was deleted as part of the 1998 restyling of the rule. Though the change appears to have been intended as merely stylistic, it has caused uncertainty concerning whether a court of appeals can stay its mandate through mere inaction or whether such a stay requires an order. There are good reasons to require an affirmative act by the court. Litigants—particularly those not well versed in appellate procedure—may overlook the need to check that the court of appeals has issued its mandate in due course after handing down a decision. And, in *Bell v. Thompson*, 545 U.S. 794, 804 (2005), the lack of notice of a stay was one of the factors that contributed to the Court's holding that staying the mandate was an abuse of discretion. Requiring stays of the mandate to be accomplished by court order will provide notice to litigants and can also facilitate review of the stay.

Subdivision (d). Three changes are made in subdivision (d).

Subdivision (d)(1)—which formerly addressed stays of the mandate upon the timely filing of a motion to stay the mandate or a petition for panel or en banc rehearing—has been deleted and the rest of subdivision (d) has been renumbered and renamed accordingly. In instances where such a petition or motion is timely filed, subdivision (b) sets the presumptive date for issuance of the mandate at 7 days after entry of an order denying the petition or motion. Thus, it seems redundant to state (as subdivision (d)(1) did) that timely filing of such a petition or motion stays the mandate until disposition of the petition or motion. The deletion of subdivision (d)(1) is intended to streamline the rule; no substantive change is intended.

Under the new subdivision (d)(2)(B), if the court of appeals issues a stay of the mandate for a party to file a petition for certiorari, and a Justice of the Supreme Court subsequently extends the time for filing the petition, the stay automatically continues for the extended period.

Subdivision (d)(4)—i.e., former subdivision (d)(2)(D)—is amended to specify that a mandate stayed pending a petition for certiorari must issue immediately once the court of appeals receives a copy of the Supreme Court's order denying certiorari, unless the court of appeals finds that extraordinary circumstances justify a further stay. Without deciding whether the prior version of Rule 41 provided authority for a further stay of the mandate after denial of certiorari, the Supreme Court ruled that any such authority could be exercised only in "extraordinary circumstances." *Ryan v. Schad*, 133 S. Ct. 2548, 2551 (2013) (per curiam). The amendment to subdivision (d)(4) makes explicit that the court may stay the mandate after the denial of certiorari, and also makes explicit that such a stay is permissible only in extraordinary circumstances. Such a stay cannot occur through mere inaction but rather requires an order.

The reference in prior subdivision (d)(2)(D) to the *filing* of a copy of the Supreme Court's order is replaced by a reference to the court of appeals' *receipt* of a copy of the Supreme Court's order. The filing of the copy and its receipt by the court of appeals amount to the same thing (*cf.* Rule 25(a)(2)(A)(i), setting a general rule that "filing is not timely unless the clerk receives the papers within the time fixed for filing"), but "on receiving a copy" is more specific and, hence, clearer.

Rule 42.   Voluntary Dismissal

(a) Dismissal in the District Court. Before an appeal has been docketed by the circuit clerk, the district court may dismiss the appeal on the filing of a stipulation signed by all parties or on the appellant's motion with notice to all parties.

(b) Dismissal in the Court of Appeals. The circuit clerk may dismiss a docketed appeal if the parties file a signed dismissal agreement specifying how costs are to be paid and pay any fees that are due. But no mandate or other process may issue without a court order. An appeal may be dismissed on the appellant's motion on terms agreed to by the parties or fixed by the court.

(As amended Apr. 24, 1998, eff. Dec. 1, 1998.)

ADVISORY COMMITTEE NOTES
1967 Adoption

Subdivision (a). This subdivision is derived from FRCP 73(a) [rule 73(a), Federal Rules of Civil Procedure] without change of substance.

Subdivision (b). The first sentence is a common provision in present circuit rules. The second sentence is added. Compare Supreme Court Rule 60.

1998 Amendments

The language of the rule is amended to make the rule more easily understood. In addition to changes made to improve the understanding, the Advisory Committee has changed language to make style and terminology consistent throughout the appellate rules. These changes are intended to be stylistic only.

Rule 43.   Substitution of Parties

(a) Death of a Party.

(1) After Notice of Appeal Is Filed. If a party dies after a notice of appeal has been filed or while a proceeding is pending in the court of appeals, the decedent's personal representative may be substituted as a party on motion filed with the circuit clerk by the representative or by any party. A party's motion must be served on the representative in accordance with Rule 25. If the decedent has no representative, any party may suggest the death on the record, and the court of appeals may then direct appropriate proceedings.

(2) Before Notice of Appeal Is Filed—Potential Appellant. If a party entitled to appeal dies before filing a notice of appeal, the decedent's personal representative—or, if there is no personal representative, the decedent's attorney of record—may file a notice of appeal within the time prescribed by these rules. After the notice of appeal is filed, substitution must be in accordance with Rule 43(a)(1).

(3) Before Notice of Appeal Is Filed—Potential Appellee. If a party against whom an appeal may be taken dies after entry of a judgment or order in the district court, but before a notice of appeal is filed, an appellant may proceed as if the death had not occurred. After the notice of appeal is filed, substitution must be in accordance with Rule 43(a)(1).

(b) Substitution for a Reason Other Than Death. If a party needs to be substituted for any reason other than death, the procedure prescribed in Rule 43(a) applies.

(c) Public Officer: Identification; Substitution.

(1) Identification of Party. A public officer who is a party to an appeal or other proceeding in an official capacity may be described as a party by the public officer's official title rather than by name. But the court may require the public officer's name to be added.

(2) Automatic Substitution of Officeholder. When a public officer who is a party to an appeal or other proceeding in an official capacity dies, resigns, or otherwise ceases to hold office, the action does not abate. The public officer's successor is automatically substituted as a party. Proceedings following the substitution are to be in the name of the substituted party, but any misnomer that does not affect the substantial rights of the parties may be disregarded. An order of substitution may be entered at any time, but failure to enter an order does not affect the substitution.

(As amended Mar. 10, 1986, eff. July 1, 1986; Apr. 24, 1998, eff. Dec. 1, 1998.)

ADVISORY COMMITTEE NOTES

1967 Adoption

Subdivision (a). The first three sentences describe a procedure similar to the rule on substitution in civil actions in the district court. See FRCP 25(a) [rule 25(a), Federal Rules of Civil Procedure]. The fourth sentence expressly authorizes an appeal to be taken against one who has died after the entry of judgment. Compare FRCP 73(b) [rule 73(b), Federal Rules of Civil Procedure], which impliedly authorizes such an appeal.

The sixth sentence authorizes an attorney of record for the deceased to take an appeal on behalf of successors in interest if the deceased has no representative. At present, if a party entitled to appeal dies before the notice of appeal is filed, the appeal can presumably be taken only by his legal representative and must be taken within the time ordinarily prescribed. 13 Cyclopedia of Federal Procedure (3d Ed.) § 63.21. The states commonly make special provision for the even[t] of the death of a party entitled to appeal, usually by extending the time otherwise prescribed. Rules of Civil Procedure for Superior Courts of Arizona, Rule 73(t), 16 A.R.S.; New Jersey Rev.Rules 1:3–3; New York Civil Practice Law and Rules, § 1022; Wisconsin Statutes Ann. 274.01(2). The Provision in the proposed rule is derived from California Code of Civil Procedure, § 941.

Subdivision (c). This subdivision is derived from FRCP 25(d) [rule 25(d), Federal Rules of Civil Procedure] and Supreme Court Rule 48, with appropriate changes.

1986 Amendment

The amendments to Rules 43(a) and (c) are technical. No substantive change is intended.

1998 Amendments

The language and organization of the rule are amended to make the rule more easily understood. In addition to changes made to improve the understanding, the Advisory Committee has changed language to make style and terminology consistent throughout the appellate rules. These changes are intended to be stylistic only.

Rule 44. Case Involving a Constitutional Question When the United States or the Relevant State Is Not a Party

(a) Constitutional Challenge to Federal Statute. If a party questions the constitutionality of an Act of Congress in a proceeding in which the United States or its agency, officer, or employee is not a party in an official capacity, the questioning party must give written notice to the circuit clerk immediately upon the filing of the record or as soon as the question is raised in the court of appeals. The clerk must then certify that fact to the Attorney General.

(b) Constitutional Challenge to State Statute. If a party questions the constitutionality of a statute of a State in a proceeding in which that State or its agency, officer, or employee is not a party in an official capacity, the questioning party must give written notice to the circuit clerk immediately upon the filing of the record or as soon as the question is raised in the court of appeals. The clerk must then certify that fact to the attorney general of the State.

(As amended Apr. 24, 1998, eff. Dec. 1, 1998; Apr. 29, 2002, eff. Dec. 1, 2002.)

ADVISORY COMMITTEE NOTES

1967 Adoption

This rule is now found in the rules of a majority of the circuits. It is in response to the Act of August 24, 1937 (28 U.S.C. § 2403), which requires all courts of the United States to advise the Attorney General of the existence of an action or proceeding of the kind described in the rule.

1998 Amendments

The language of the rule is amended to make the rule more easily understood. In addition to changes made to improve the understanding, the Advisory Committee has changed language to make style and terminology consistent throughout the appellate rules. These changes are intended to be stylistic only.

2002 Amendments

Rule 44 requires that a party who "questions the constitutionality of an Act of Congress" in a proceeding in which the United States is not a party must provide written notice of that challenge to the clerk. Rule 44 is designed to implement 28 U.S.C. § 2403(a), which states that:

In any action, suit or proceeding in a court of the United States to which the United States or any agency, officer or employee thereof is not a party, wherein the constitutionality of any Act of Congress affecting the public interest is drawn in question, the court shall certify such fact to the Attorney General, and shall permit the United States to intervene . . . for argument on the question of constitutionality.

The subsequent section of the statute—§ 2403(*b*)—contains virtually identical language imposing upon the courts the duty to notify the attorney general of a *state* of a constitutional challenge to any statute of that state. But § 2403(b), unlike § 2403(a), was not implemented in Rule 44.

Rule 44 has been amended to correct this omission. The text of former Rule 44 regarding constitutional challenges to federal statutes now appears as Rule 44(a), while new language regarding constitutional challenges to state statutes now appears as Rule 44(b).

Changes Made After Publication and Comments. No changes were made to the text of the proposed amendment or to the Committee Note.

Rule 45. Clerk's Duties

(a) General Provisions.

(1) Qualifications. The circuit clerk must take the oath and post any bond required by law. Neither the clerk nor any deputy clerk may practice as an attorney or counselor in any court while in office.

(2) When Court Is Open. The court of appeals is always open for filing any paper, issuing and returning process, making a motion, and entering an order. The clerk's office with the clerk or a deputy in attendance must be open during business hours on all days except Saturdays,

Sundays, and legal holidays. A court may provide by local rule or by order that the clerk's office be open for specified hours on Saturdays or on legal holidays other than New Year's Day, Martin Luther King, Jr.'s Birthday, Washington's Birthday, Memorial Day, Independence Day, Labor Day, Columbus Day, Veterans' Day, Thanksgiving Day, and Christmas Day.

(b) Records.

(1) The Docket. The circuit clerk must maintain a docket and an index of all docketed cases in the manner prescribed by the Director of the Administrative Office of the United States Courts. The clerk must record all papers filed with the clerk and all process, orders, and judgments.

(2) Calendar. Under the court's direction, the clerk must prepare a calendar of cases awaiting argument. In placing cases on the calendar for argument, the clerk must give preference to appeals in criminal cases and to other proceedings and appeals entitled to preference by law.

(3) Other Records. The clerk must keep other books and records required by the Director of the Administrative Office of the United States Courts, with the approval of the Judicial Conference of the United States, or by the court.

(c) Notice of an Order or Judgment. Upon the entry of an order or judgment, the circuit clerk must immediately serve a notice of entry on each party, with a copy of any opinion, and must note the date of service on the docket. Service on a party represented by counsel must be made on counsel.

(d) Custody of Records and Papers. The circuit clerk has custody of the court's records and papers. Unless the court orders or instructs otherwise, the clerk must not permit an original record or paper to be taken from the clerk's office. Upon disposition of the case, original papers constituting the record on appeal or review must be returned to the court or agency from which they were received. The clerk must preserve a copy of any brief, appendix, or other paper that has been filed.

(As amended Mar. 1, 1971, eff. July 1, 1971; Mar. 10, 1986, eff. July 1, 1986; Apr. 24, 1998, eff. Dec. 1, 1998; Apr. 29, 2002, eff. Dec. 1, 2002; Apr. 25, 2005, eff. Dec. 1, 2005.)

ADVISORY COMMITTEE NOTES

1967 Adoption

The duties imposed upon clerks of the courts of appeals by this rule are those imposed by rule or practice in a majority of the circuits. The second sentence of subdivision (a) authorizing the closing of the clerk's office on Saturday and non-national legal holidays follows a similar provision respecting the district court clerk's office found in FRCP 77(c) [rule 77(c), Federal Rules of Civil Procedure] and in FRCrP 56 [rule 56, Federal Rules of Criminal Procedure].

1971 Amendment

The amendment adds Columbus Day to the list of legal holidays. See the Note accompanying the amendment of Rule 26(a).

1986 Amendment

The amendment to Rule 45(b) permits the courts of appeals to maintain computerized dockets. The Committee believes that the Administrative Office of the United States Courts ought to have maximum flexibility in prescribing the format of this docket in order to ensure a smooth transition from manual to automated systems and subsequent adaptation to technological improvements.

The amendments to Rules 45(a) and (d) are technical. No substantive change is intended. The Birthday of Martin Luther King, Jr. has been added to the list of national holidays.

1998 Amendments

The language and organization of the rule are amended to make the rule more easily understood. In addition to changes made to improve the understanding, the Advisory Committee has changed language to make style and terminology consistent throughout the appellate rules. These changes are intended to be stylistic only.

2002 Amendments

Subdivision (c). Subdivision (c) has been amended so that the clerk may use electronic means to serve notice of entry of an order or judgment upon parties who have consented to such service.

Changes Made After Publication and Comments. No changes were made to the text of the proposed amendment or to the Committee Note.

2005 Amendments

Subdivision (a)(2). Rule 45(a)(2) has been amended to refer to the third Monday in February as "Washington's Birthday." A federal statute officially designates the holiday as "Washington's Birthday," reflecting the desire of Congress specially to honor the first president of the United States. *See* 5 U.S.C. § 6103(a). During the 1998 restyling of the Federal Rules of Appellate Procedure, references to "Washington's Birthday" were mistakenly changed to "Presidents' Day." The amendment corrects that error.

Rule 46. Attorneys

(a) Admission to the Bar.

(1) Eligibility. An attorney is eligible for admission to the bar of a court of appeals if that attorney is of good moral and professional character and is admitted to practice before the Supreme Court of the United States, the highest court of a state, another United States court of appeals, or a United States district court (including the district courts for Guam, the Northern Mariana Islands, and the Virgin Islands).

(2) Application. An applicant must file an application for admission, on a form approved by the court that contains the applicant's personal statement showing eligibility for membership. The applicant must subscribe to the following oath or affirmation:

"I, _____, do solemnly swear [or affirm] that I will conduct myself as an attorney and counselor of this court, uprightly and according to law; and that I will support the Constitution of the United States."

(3) Admission Procedures. On written or oral motion of a member of the court's bar, the court will act on the application. An applicant may be admitted by oral motion in open court. But, unless the court orders otherwise, an applicant need not appear before the court to be admitted. Upon admission, an applicant must pay the clerk the fee prescribed by local rule or court order.

(b) Suspension or Disbarment.

(1) Standard. A member of the court's bar is subject to suspension or disbarment by the court if the member:

(A) has been suspended or disbarred from practice in any other court; or

(B) is guilty of conduct unbecoming a member of the court's bar.

(2) Procedure. The member must be given an opportunity to show good cause, within the time prescribed by the court, why the member should not be suspended or disbarred.

(3) Order. The court must enter an appropriate order after the member responds and a hearing is held, if requested, or after the time prescribed for a response expires, if no response is made.

(c) Discipline.
A court of appeals may discipline an attorney who practices before it for conduct unbecoming a member of the bar or for failure to comply with any court rule. First, however, the court must afford the attorney reasonable notice, an opportunity to show cause to the contrary, and, if requested, a hearing.

(As amended Mar. 10, 1986, eff. July 1, 1986; Apr. 24, 1998, eff. Dec. 1, 1998.)

ADVISORY COMMITTEE NOTES

1967 Adoption

Subdivision (a). The basic requirement of membership in the bar of the Supreme Court, or of the highest court of a state, or in another court of appeals or a district court is found, with minor variations, in the rules of ten circuits. The only other requirement in those circuits is that the applicant be of good moral and professional character. In the District of Columbia Circuit applicants other than members of the District of Columbia District bar or the Supreme Court bar must claim membership in the bar of the highest court of a state, territory or possession for three years prior to application for admission (D.C.Cir. Rule 7 [rule 7, U.S.Ct. of App.Dist. of Col.]). Members of the District of Columbia District bar and the Supreme Court bar again excepted, applicants for admission to the District of Columbia Circuit bar must meet precisely defined prelaw and law school study requirements (D.C.Cir. Rule 7½ [rule 7½, U.S.Ct. of App.Dist. of Col.]).

A few circuits now require that application for admission be made by oral motion by a sponsor member in open court. The proposed rule permits both the application and the motion by the sponsor member to be in writing, and permits action on the motion without the appearance of the applicant or the sponsor, unless the court otherwise orders.

Subdivision (b). The provision respecting suspension or disbarment is uniform. Third Circuit Rule 8(3) [rule 8(3), U.S.Ct. of App. 3rd Cir.] is typical.

Subdivision (c). At present only Fourth Circuit Rule 36 [rule 36, U.S.Ct. of App. 4th Cir.] contains an equivalent provision. The purpose of this provision is to make explicit the power of a court of appeals to impose sanctions less serious than suspension or disbarment for the breach of rules. It also affords some measure of control over attorneys who are not members of the bar of the court. Several circuits permit a non-member attorney to file briefs and motions, membership being required only at the time of oral argument. And several circuits permit argument pro hac vice by non-member attorneys.

1986 Amendments

The amendments to Rules 46(a) and (b) are technical. No substantive change is intended.

1998 Amendments

The language and organization of the rule are amended to make the rule more easily understood. In addition to changes made to improve the understanding, the Advisory Committee has changed language to make style and terminology consistent throughout the appellate rules. These changes are intended to be stylistic only.

Rule 47.   Local Rules by Courts of Appeals

(a) Local Rules.

    (1) Each court of appeals acting by a majority of its judges in regular active service may, after giving appropriate public notice and opportunity for comment, make and amend rules governing its practice. A generally applicable direction to parties or lawyers regarding practice before a court must be in a local rule rather than an internal operating procedure or standing order. A local rule must be consistent with—but not duplicative of—Acts of Congress and rules adopted under 28 U.S.C. § 2072 and must conform to any uniform numbering system prescribed by the Judicial Conference of the United States. Each circuit clerk must send the Administrative Office of the United States Courts a copy of each local rule and internal operating procedure when it is promulgated or amended.

    (2) A local rule imposing a requirement of form must not be enforced in a manner that causes a party to lose rights because of a nonwillful failure to comply with the requirement.

(b) Procedure When There Is No Controlling Law. A court of appeals may regulate practice in a particular case in any manner consistent with federal law, these rules, and local rules of the circuit. No sanction or other disadvantage may be imposed for noncompliance with any requirement not in federal law, federal rules, or the local circuit rules unless the alleged violator has been furnished in the particular case with actual notice of the requirement.

(As amended Apr. 27, 1995, eff. Dec. 1, 1995; Apr. 24, 1998, eff. Dec. 1, 1998.)

ADVISORY COMMITTEE NOTES

1967 Adoption

This rule continues the authority now vested in individual courts of appeals by 28 U.S.C. § 2071 to make rules consistent with rules of practice and procedure promulgated by the Supreme Court.

1995 Amendments

Subdivision (a). This rule is amended to require that a generally applicable direction regarding practice before a court of appeals must be in a local rule rather than an internal operating procedure or some other general directive. It is the intent of this rule that a local rule may not bar any practice that these rules explicitly or implicitly permit. Subdivision (b) allows a court of appeals to regulate practice in an individual case by entry of an order in the case. The amendment also reflects the requirement that local rules be consistent not only with the national rules but also with Acts of Congress. The amendment also states that local rules should not repeat national rules and Acts of Congress.

The amendment also requires that the numbering of local rules conform with any uniform numbering system that may be prescribed by the Judicial Conference. Lack of uniform numbering might create unnecessary traps for counsel and litigants. A uniform numbering system would make it easier for an increasingly national bar and for litigants to locate a local rule that applies to a particular procedural issue.

Paragraph (2) is new. Its aim is to protect against loss of rights in the enforcement of local rules relating to matters of form. The proscription of paragraph (2) is narrowly drawn—covering only violations that are not willful and only those involving local rules directed to matters of form. It does not limit the court's power to impose substantive penalties upon a party if it or its attorney stubbornly or repeatedly violates a local rule, even one involving merely a matter of form. Nor does it affect the court's power to enforce local rules that involve more than mere matters of form.

Subdivision (b). This rule provides flexibility to the court in regulating practice in a particular case when there is no controlling law. Specifically, it permits the court to regulate practice in any manner consistent with Acts of Congress, with rules adopted under 28 U.S.C. § 2072, and with the circuit's local rules.

The amendment to this rule disapproves imposing any sanction or other disadvantage on a person for noncompliance with such a directive, unless the alleged violator has been furnished in a particular case with actual notice of the requirement. There should be no adverse consequence to a party or attorney for violating special requirements relating to practice before a particular court unless the party or attorney has actual notice of those requirements.

1998 Amendments

The language of the rule is amended to make the rule more easily understood. In addition to changes made to improve the understanding, the Advisory Committee has changed language to make style and terminology consistent throughout the appellate rules. These changes are intended to be stylistic only.

Rule 48.   Masters

(a) Appointment; Powers. A court of appeals may appoint a special master to hold hearings, if necessary, and to recommend factual findings and disposition in matters ancillary to proceedings in the court. Unless the order referring a matter to a master specifies or limits the master's powers, those powers include, but are not limited to, the following:

    (1)   regulating all aspects of a hearing;

    (2)   taking all appropriate action for the efficient performance of the master's duties under the order;

    (3)   requiring the production of evidence on all matters embraced in the reference; and

(4) administering oaths and examining witnesses and parties.

(b) Compensation. If the master is not a judge or court employee, the court must determine the master's compensation and whether the cost is to be charged to any party.

(As amended Apr. 29, 1994, eff. Dec. 1, 1994; Apr. 24, 1998, eff. Dec. 1, 1998.)

ADVISORY COMMITTEE NOTES

1994 Amendments

The text of the existing Rule 48 concerning the title was moved to Rule 1.

This new Rule 48 authorizes a court of appeals to appoint a special master to make recommendations concerning ancillary matters. The courts of appeals have long used masters in contempt proceedings where the issue is compliance with an enforcement order. See *Polish National Alliance v. NLRB*, 159 F.2d 38 (7th Cir. 1946); *NLRB v. Arcade-Sunshine Co.*, 132 F.2d 8 (D.C. Cir. 1942); *NLRB v. Remington Rand, Inc.*, 130 F.2d 919 (2d Cir. 1942). There are other instances when the question before a court of appeals requires a factual determination. An application for fees or eligibility for Criminal Justice Act status on appeal are examples.

Ordinarily when a factual issue is unresolved, a court of appeals remands the case to the district court or agency that originally heard the case. It is not the Committee's intent to alter that practice. However, when factual issues arise in the first instance in the court of appeals, such as fees for representation on appeal, it would be useful to have authority to refer such determinations to a master for a recommendation.

1998 Amendments

The language and organization of the rule are amended to make the rule more easily understood. In addition to changes made to improve the understanding, the Advisory Committee has changed language to make style and terminology consistent throughout the appellate rules. These changes are intended to be stylistic only.

APPENDIX OF FORMS

Form 1.   **Notice of Appeal to a Court of Appeals From a Judgment or Order of a District Court**

United States District Court for the _____

District of _____

File Number _____

A.B., Plaintiff	)	
	)	
v.	)	Notice of Appeal
	)	
C.D., Defendant	)	

Notice is hereby given that _____(here name all parties taking the appeal)_____, (plaintiffs) (defendants) in the above named case,* hereby appeal to the United States Court of Appeals for the _____ Circuit (from the final judgment) (from an order (describing it)) entered in this action on the _____ day of _____, 20___.

(s)   _____

Attorney for _____

Address:_____

[***Note to inmate filers***: *If you are an inmate confined in an institution and you seek the timing benefit of Fed. R. App. P. 4(c)(1), complete Form 7 (Declaration of Inmate Filing) and file that declaration along with the Notice of Appeal.*]

(As amended Apr. 22, 1993, eff. Dec. 1, 1993; Mar. 27, 2003, eff. Dec. 1, 2003; Apr. 28, 2016, eff. Dec. 1, 2016.)

---

*   See Rule 3(c) for permissible ways of identifying appellants.

Form 2.   Notice of Appeal to a Court of Appeals From a Decision of the United States Tax Court

UNITED STATES TAX COURT

Washington, D.C.

A.B., Petitioner   )
)
     v.   ) Docket No. _____
)
Commissioner of Internal Revenue,)
    Respondent   )

Notice of Appeal

Notice is hereby given that _____(here name all parties taking the appeal)*_____ hereby appeal to the United States Court of Appeals for the _____ Circuit from (that part of) the decision of this court entered in the above captioned proceeding on the _____ day of _____, 20___ (relating to _____).

              (s)_____

                Counsel for _____

                *Address:*_____

* See Rule 3(c) for permissible ways of identifying appellants.

(As amended Apr. 22, 1993, eff. Dec. 1, 1993; Mar. 27, 2003, eff. Dec. 1, 2003.)

Form 3.   Petition for Review of Order of an Agency, Board, Commission or Officer

United States Court of Appeals
for the _____ Circuit

A.B., Petitioner   )
)
     v.   ) Petition for Review
XYZ Commission, Respondent   )

_____(here name all parties bringing the petition)*_____ hereby petition the court for review of the Order of the XYZ Commission (describe the order) entered on _____, 20___.

              (s)_____

               Attorney for Petitioners

                *Address:*_____

* See Rule 15.

(As amended Apr. 22, 1993, eff. Dec. 1, 1993; Mar. 27, 2003, eff. Dec. 1, 2003.)

Form 4.   **Affidavit Accompanying Motion for Permission to Appeal In Forma Pauperis**

UNITED STATES DISTRICT COURT
for the
<_____> DISTRICT OF <_____>

<Name(s) of plaintiff(s)>,	)	
	)	
Plaintiff(s)	)	
	)	
v.	)	
	)	Case No. <Number>
<Name(s) of defendant(s)>,	)	
	)	
Defendant(s)	)	
	)	

AFFIDAVIT ACCOMPANYING MOTION FOR
PERMISSION TO APPEAL IN FORMA PAUPERIS

Affidavit in Support of Motion	**Instructions**
I swear or affirm under penalty of perjury that, because of my poverty, I cannot prepay the docket fees of my appeal or post a bond for them. I believe I am entitled to redress. I swear or affirm under penalty of perjury under United States laws that my answers on this form are true and correct. (28 U.S.C. § 1746; 18 U.S.C. § 1621.)	Complete all questions in this application and then sign it. Do not leave any blanks: if the answer to a question is "0," "none," or "not applicable (N/A)," write in that response. If you need more space to answer a question or to explain your answer, attach a separate sheet of paper identified with your name, your case's docket number, and the question number.
Signed: _____	Date: _____

My issues on appeal are:

1.   *For both you and your spouse estimate the average amount of money received from each of the following sources during the past 12 months. Adjust any amount that was received weekly, biweekly, quarterly, semiannually, or annually to show the monthly rate. Use gross amounts, that is, amounts before any deductions for taxes or otherwise.*

Income source	Average monthly amount during the past 12 months		Amount expected next month	
	You	**Spouse**	**You**	**Spouse**
Employment	$_____	$_____	$_____	$_____
Self-employment	$_____	$_____	$_____	$_____
Income from real property (such as rental income)	$_____	$_____	$_____	$_____
Interest and dividends	$_____	$_____	$_____	$_____
Gifts	$_____	$_____	$_____	$_____

Alimony	$_____	$_____	$_____	$_____
Child support	$_____	$_____	$_____	$_____
Retirement (such as social security, pensions, annuities, insurance)	$_____	$_____	$_____	$_____
Disability (such as social security, insurance payments)	$_____	$_____	$_____	$_____
Unemployment payments	$_____	$_____	$_____	$_____
Public-assistance (such as welfare)	$_____	$_____	$_____	$_____
Other (specify): _____	$_____	$_____	$_____	$_____
Total monthly income:	$_____	$_____	$_____	$_____

2.   *List your employment history for the past two years, most recent employer first. (Gross monthly pay is before taxes or other deductions.)*

Employer	Address	Dates of employment	Gross monthly pay
			$
			$
			$

3.   *List your spouse's employment history for the past two years, most recent employer first. (Gross monthly pay is before taxes or other deductions.)*

Employer	Address	Dates of employment	Gross monthly pay
			$
			$
			$

4.   *How much cash do you and your spouse have? $_____*

Below, state any money you or your spouse have in bank accounts or in any other financial institution.

Financial institution	Type of account	Amount you have	Amount your spouse has
		$	$
		$	$
		$	$

If you are a prisoner seeking to appeal a judgment in a civil action or proceeding, you must attach a statement certified by the appropriate institutional officer showing all receipts, expenditures, and balances during the last six months in your institutional accounts. If you have multiple accounts, perhaps because you have been in multiple institutions, attach one certified statement of each account.

5. *List the assets, and their values, which you own or your spouse owns. Do not list clothing and ordinary household furnishings.*

Home	Other real estate	Motor vehicle #1
(Value) $	(Value) $	(Value) $
		Make & year:
		Model:
		Registration #:
Motor vehicle #2	**Other assets**	**Other assets**
(Value) $	(Value) $	(Value) $
Make & year:		
Model:		
Registration #:		

6. *State every person, business, or organization owing you or your spouse money, and the amount owed.*

Person owing you or your spouse money	Amount owed to you	Amount owed to your spouse
	$	$
	$	$
	$	$

7. *State the persons who rely on you or your spouse for support.*

Name [or, if under 18, initials only]	Relationship	Age

8. *Estimate the average monthly expenses of you and your family. Show separately the amounts paid by your spouse. Adjust any payments that are made weekly, biweekly, quarterly, semiannually, or annually to show the monthly rate.*

	You	Your Spouse
Rent or home-mortgage payment (include lot rented for mobile home) Are real-estate taxes included? ☐ Yes ☐ No Is property insurance included? ☐ Yes ☐ No	$	$
Utilities (electricity, heating fuel, water, sewer, and Telephone)	$	$
Home maintenance (repairs and upkeep)	$	$
Food	$	$
Clothing	$	$
Laundry and dry-cleaning	$	$
Medical and dental expenses	$	$
Transportation (not including motor vehicle payments)	$	$
Recreation, entertainment, newspapers, magazines, etc.	$	$

Insurance (not deducted from wages or included in mortgage payments)		
Homeowner's or renter's:	$	$
Life:	$	$
Health:	$	$
Motor Vehicle:	$	$
Other: _____	$	$
Taxes (not deducted from wages or included in mortgage payments) (specify):	$	$
Installment payments		
Motor Vehicle:	$	$
Credit card (name):	$	$
Department store (name):	$	$
Other:	$	$
Alimony, maintenance, and support paid to others	$	$
Regular expenses for operation of business, profession, or farm (attach detailed statement)	$	$
Other (specify):	$	$
Total monthly expenses:	$	$

9. *Do you expect any major changes to your monthly income or expenses or in your assets or liabilities during the next 12 months?*

☐ Yes ☐ No   If yes, describe on an attached sheet.

10. *Have you spent—or will you be spending—any money for expenses or attorney fees in connection with this lawsuit?* ☐ Yes ☐ No

If yes, how much? $_____

11. *Provide any other information that will help explain why you cannot pay the docket fees for your appeal.*

12. *State the city and state of your legal residence.*

Your daytime phone number: (___) _____

Your age: _____ *Your years of schooling:* _____

(As amended Apr. 24, 1998, eff. Dec. 1, 1998; Apr. 28, 2010, eff. Dec. 1, 2010; Apr. 16, 2013, eff. Dec. 1, 2013; Apr. 26, 2018, eff. Dec. 1, 2018.)

Form 5.   **Notice of Appeal to a Court of Appeals from a Judgment or Order of a District Court or a Bankruptcy Appellate Panel**

United States District Court for the _____

District of _____

In re	)
	)
	)
_____,	)
Debtor	)
	) File No. _____
_____,	)
Plaintiff	)
	)
v.	)
	)
	)
_____,	)
Defendant	)

Notice of Appeal to United States Court of Appeals for the
_____ Circuit

_____, the plaintiff [or defendant or other party] appeals to the United States Court of Appeals for the _____ Circuit from the final judgment [or order or decree] of the district court for the district of _____ [or bankruptcy appellate panel of the _____ circuit], entered in this case on _____, 20___ [here describe the judgment, order, or decree] _____.

The parties to the judgment [or order or decree] appealed from and the names and addresses of their respective attorneys are as follows:

Dated _____

Signed _____
Attorney for Appellant

Address: _____

_____

[***Note to inmate filers:*** *If you are an inmate confined in an institution and you seek the timing benefit of Fed. R. App. P. 4(c)(1), complete Form 7 (Declaration of Inmate Filing) and file that declaration along with the Notice of Appeal.*]

(As added Apr. 25, 1989, eff. Dec. 1, 1989; amended Mar. 27, 2003, eff. Dec. 1, 2003; Apr. 28, 2016, eff. Dec. 1, 2016.)

Form 6.　　**Certificate of Compliance with Type-Volume Limit**

Certificate of Compliance With Type-Volume Limit
Typeface Requirements, and Type-Style Requirements

1.　　This document complies with the [type-volume limit of Fed. R. App. P. [*insert Rule citation; e.g., 32(a)(7)(B)*]] [the word limit of Fed. R. App. P. [*insert Rule citation; e.g., 5(c)(1)*]] because, excluding the parts of the document exempted by Fed. R. App. P. 32(f) [and [*insert applicable Rule citation, if any*]]:

☐　　this document contains [*state the number of*] words, **or**

☐　　this brief uses a monospaced typeface and contains [*state the number of*] lines of text.

2.　　This document complies with the typeface requirements of Fed. R. App. P. 32(a)(5) and the type-style requirements of Fed. R. App. P. 32(a)(6) because:

☐　　this document has been prepared in a proportionally spaced typeface using [*state name and version of word-processing program*] in [*state font size and name of type style*], **or**

☐　　this document has been prepared in a monospaced typeface using [*state name and version of word-processing program*] with [*state number of characters per inch and name of type style*].

(s)_____

Attorney for _____

Dated: _____

(As added Apr. 29, 2002, eff. Dec. 1, 2002; amended Apr. 28, 2016, Dec. 1, 2016.)

ADVISORY COMMITTEE NOTES

2016 Amendment

Changes Made After Publication and Comment

The Committee revised the proposed amendments to Form 6 to reflect the deletion of the proposed line limits for documents other than briefs. The Committee also made style changes to the Form.

Form 7.   Declaration of Inmate Filing

_____

[insert name of court; for example,
United States District Court for the District of Minnesota]

A.B., Plaintiff	)	
	)	
v.	)	
	)	Case No. _____
	)	
C.D., Defendant	)	
	)	

I am an inmate confined in an institution. Today, _____ *[insert date]*, I am depositing the _____ *[insert title of document; for example, "notice of appeal"]* in this case in the institution's internal mail system. First-class postage is being prepaid either by me or by the institution on my behalf.

I declare under penalty of perjury that the foregoing is true and correct (see 28 U.S.C. § 1746; 18 U.S.C. § 1621).

Sign your name here_____

Signed on _____ *[insert date]*

*[**Note to inmate filers:** If your institution has a system designed for legal mail, you must use that system in order to receive the timing benefit of Fed. R. App. P. 4(c)(1) or Fed. R. App. P. 25(a)(2)(A)(iii).]*

(As added Apr. 28, 2016, eff. Dec. 1, 2016; amended Apr. 26, 2018, eff. Dec. 1, 2018.)

ADVISORY COMMITTEE NOTES

2016 Adoption

Changes Made After Publication and Comment

The Committee revised Form 7 to use the present tense ("Today . . . I am depositing") rather than the past tense ("I deposited . . . "), to reflect the fact that the inmate will fill out the declaration before depositing both the declaration and the underlying filing in the institution's mail system. The Committee added a "Note to inmate filers" pointing out the legal-mail-system requirement in Rules 4(c)(1) and 25(a)(2)(C). The Committee also made style changes.

APPENDIX:

Length Limits Stated in the
Federal Rules of Appellate Procedure

This chart summarizes the length limits stated in the Federal Rules of Appellate Procedure. Please refer to the rules for precise requirements, and bear in mind the following:

- In computing these limits, you can exclude the items listed in Rule 32(f).

- If you use a word limit or a line limit (other than the word limit in Rule 28(j)), you must file the certificate required by Rule 32(g).

- For the limits in Rules 5, 21, 27, 35, and 40:

  - You must use the word limit if you produce your document on a computer; and

  - You must use the page limit if you handwrite your document or type it on a typewriter.

- For the limits in Rules 28.1, 29(a)(5), and 32:

  - You must use the word limit or page limit, regardless of how you produce the document; or

  - You may use the line limit if you type or print your document with a monospaced typeface. A typeface is monospaced when each character occupies the same amount of horizontal space.

	Rule	Document type	Word limit	Page limit	Line limit
Permission to appeal	5(c)	• Petition for permission to appeal • Answer in opposition • Cross-petition	5,200	20	Not applicable
Extraordinary Writs	21(d)	• Petition for writ of mandamus or prohibition or other extraordinary writ • Answer	7,800	30	Not applicable
Motions	27(d)(2)	• Motion • Response to a motion	5,200	20	Not applicable
	27(d)(2)	• Reply to a response to a motion	2,600	10	Not applicable
Parties' briefs (where no cross-appeal)	32(a)(7)	• Principal brief	13,000	30	1,300
	32(a)(7)	• Reply brief	6,500	15	650
Parties' briefs (where cross-appeal)	28.1(e)	• Appellant's principal brief • Appellant's response and reply brief	13,000	30	1,300
	28.1(e)	• Appellee's principal and response brief	15,300	35	1,500
	28.1(e)	• Appellee's reply brief	6,500	15	650

Party's supplemental letter	28(j)	• Letter citing supplemental authorities	350	Not applicable	Not applicable
Amicus briefs	29(a)(5)	• Amicus brief during initial consideration of case on merits	One-half the length set by the Appellate Rules for a party's principal brief	One-half the length set by the Appellate Rules for a party's principal brief	One-half the length set by the Appellate Rules for a party's principal brief
	29(b)(4)	• Amicus brief during consideration of whether to grant rehearing	2,600	Not applicable	Not applicable
Rehearing and en banc filings*	35(b)(2) & 40(b)	• Petition for hearing en banc • Petition for panel rehearing; petition for rehearing en banc	3,900	15	Not applicable

(As added Apr. 28, 2016, eff. Dec. 1, 2016.)

ADVISORY COMMITTEE NOTES
2016 Adoption
Changes Made After Publication and Comment

The Committee added the Appendix after the public comment period, as an aid to understanding the various length limits that will now be stated in the Appellate Rules.

---

* [Amendments to Rules 35 and 40 that are set to take effect December 1, 2020 (absent contrary congressional action) subject a response to a petition for hearing en banc and a response to a petition for panel rehearing to the same page limit that applies to the petitions themselves. The Advisory Committee has not yet updated this Appendix to reflect those changes. Ed.]

RULES OF THE SUPREME COURT OF THE UNITED STATES

Adopted April 18, 2019
Effective July 1, 2019

PART I. THE COURT

PART II. ATTORNEYS AND COUNSELORS

PART III. JURISDICTION ON WRIT OF CERTIORARI

PART IV. OTHER JURISDICTION

PART V. MOTIONS AND APPLICATIONS

PART VI. BRIEFS ON THE MERITS AND ORAL ARGUMENT

SUPREME COURT RULES

Part VII. Practice and Procedure

Part VIII. Disposition of Cases

Part IX. Definitions and Effective Date

ELECTRONIC FILING

TABLE OF CORRESPONDING SUPREME COURT RULES

This table shows corresponding relationship between the rules effective July 1, 1925, the rules effective July 1, 1928, the rules effective Feb. 27, 1939, the rules effective July 1, 1954, the rules effective Oct. 2, 1967, the rules effective July 1, 1970, and the rules effective June 30, 1980. Additional revisions were effective in 1990, 1995, 1997, 1999, 2003, 2005, 2007, 2010, 2013, and 2017.

1925	1928	1939	1954	1967	1970	1980
1	1	1	1	1	1	1
2	2	2	5, 6, 8	5, 6, 8	5, 6, 8	5, 6, 8
	3	3	7	7	7	7
3	4	4	2	2	2	2
		5	9	9	9	9
4	5					
5	6	6	9, 59	9, 59	9, 59	9, 52
6	7	7	16, 20, 24, 35, 44	16, 20, 24, 35, 44	16, 20, 24, 35, 44	16, 18, 22, 23, 28
7	8	8				
8	9	9				
9	10	10	12	12	12	13
10	11	11	13, 14	13, 14	13, 14	12, 14
	12	12	15, 16	15, 16	15, 16	15, 16
11	13	13	17, 26, 36	17, 26, 36	17, 26, 36	30
12	14	14	37	37	37	31
13	15	15				

SUPREME COURT RULES

1925	1928	1939	1954	1967	1970	1980
14	16	16				
15	17	17	32	32	32	
16	18	18	38	38	38	32
17	19	19	48	48	48	40
18	20	20	35, 43	35, 43	35, 43	37, 42
19	21	21				
20	22	22				
21	23	23				
22	24	24				
23	25	25	45	45	45	38
24	26	26	39	39	39	33
25	27	27	40 to 42	40 to 42	40 to 42	34 to 36
26	28	28	44	44	44	38
27	29	29	55	55	55	48
28	30	30	56	56	56	49
	31	31				
29	32	32	52, 57	52, 57	52, 57	45, 50
30	33	33	58	58	58	51
31	34	34	25, 59	25, 59	25, 59	23, 52
32	35	35	60	60	60	53
33	36	36	18	18	18	44
34	37	37	28	28	28	24
35	38	38	19, 21 to 24, 27, 36	19, 21 to 24, 27, 36	19, 21 to 24, 27, 36	17, 19 to 22, 30, 44
		38½	11, 22	11, 22	11, 22	11, 20
36	39	39	20	20	20	18
37	40	40	28	28	28	24
38	41	41	19	19	19	17
39	42	42	19	19	19	17
40	43	43	25	25	25	23
41	44	44				
42	45	45	49	49	49	41
	46	46				
	46½	47				
		48	46	46	46	10, 19
43	47	49	4	4	4	4
44	48	50	3	3	3	3
45	49	51	61	62	62	55
			62	61	61	54

PART I. THE COURT

Rule 1. Clerk

1. The Clerk receives documents for filing with the Court and has authority to reject any submitted filing that does not comply with these Rules.

2. The Clerk maintains the Court's records and will not permit any of them to be removed from the Court building except as authorized by the Court. Any document filed with the Clerk and made a part of the Court's records may not thereafter be withdrawn from the official Court files. After the conclusion of proceedings in this Court, original records and documents transmitted to this Court by any other court will be returned to the court from which they were received.

3. Unless the Court or the Chief Justice orders otherwise, the Clerk's office is open from 9 a.m. to 5 p.m., Monday through Friday, except on federal legal holidays listed in 5 U.S.C. § 6103.

Rule 2. Library

1. The Court's library is available for use by appropriate personnel of this Court, members of the Bar of this Court, Members of Congress and their legal staffs, and attorneys for the United States and for federal departments and agencies.

2. The library's hours are governed by regulations made by the Librarian with the approval of the Chief Justice or the Court.

3. Library books may not be removed from the Court building, except by a Justice or a member of a Justice's staff.

Rule 3. Term

The Court holds a continuous annual Term commencing on the first Monday in October and ending on the day before the first Monday in October of the following year. See 28 U.S.C. § 2. At the end of each Term, all cases pending on the docket are continued to the next Term.

Rule 4. Sessions and Quorum

1. Open sessions of the Court are held beginning at 10 a.m. on the first Monday in October of each year, and thereafter as announced by the Court. Unless it orders otherwise, the Court sits to hear arguments from 10 a.m. until noon and from 1 p.m. until 3 p.m.

2. Six Members of the Court constitute a quorum. See 28 U.S.C. § 1. In the absence of a quorum on any day appointed for holding a session of the Court, the Justices attending—or if no Justice is present, the Clerk or a Deputy Clerk—may announce that the Court will not meet until there is a quorum.

3. When appropriate, the Court will direct the Clerk or the Marshal to announce recesses.

PART II. ATTORNEYS AND COUNSELORS

Rule 5. Admission to the Bar

1. To qualify for admission to the Bar of this Court, an applicant must have been admitted to practice in the highest court of a State, Commonwealth, Territory or Possession, or the District of Columbia for a period of at least three years immediately before the date of application; must not have been the subject of any adverse disciplinary action pronounced or in effect during that 3-year period; and must appear to the Court to be of good moral and professional character.

2. Each applicant shall file with the Clerk (1) a certificate from the presiding judge, clerk, or other authorized official of that court evidencing the applicant's admission to practice there and the applicant's current good standing, and (2) a completely executed copy of the form approved by this

Court and furnished by the Clerk containing (a) the applicant's personal statement, and (b) the statement of two sponsors endorsing the correctness of the applicant's statement, stating that the applicant possesses all the qualifications required for admission, and affirming that the applicant is of good moral and professional character. Both sponsors must be members of the Bar of this Court who personally know, but are not related to, the applicant.

3.   If the documents submitted demonstrate that the applicant possesses the necessary qualifications, and if the applicant has signed the oath or affirmation and paid the required fee, the Clerk will notify the applicant of acceptance by the Court as a member of the Bar and issue a certificate of admission. An applicant who so wishes may be admitted in open court on oral motion by a member of the Bar of this Court, provided that all other requirements for admission have been satisfied.

4.   Each applicant shall sign the following oath or affirmation: I, ..., do solemnly swear (or affirm) that as an attorney and as a counselor of this Court, I will conduct myself uprightly and according to law, and that I will support the Constitution of the United States.

5.   The fee for admission to the Bar and a certificate bearing the seal of the Court is $200, payable to the United States Supreme Court. The Marshal will deposit such fees in a separate fund to be disbursed by the Marshal at the direction of the Chief Justice for the costs of admissions, for the benefit of the Court and its Bar, and for related purposes.

6.   The fee for a duplicate certificate of admission to the Bar bearing the seal of the Court is $15, and the fee for a certificate of good standing is $10, payable to the United States Supreme Court. The proceeds will be maintained by the Marshal as provided in paragraph 5 of this Rule.

(As amended Jan. 11, 1999, eff. May 3, 1999; July 17, 2007, eff. Oct. 1, 2007.)

Rule 6.   Argument *Pro Hac Vice*

1.   An attorney not admitted to practice in the highest court of a State, Commonwealth, Territory or Possession, or the District of Columbia for the requisite three years, but otherwise eligible for admission to practice in this Court under Rule 5.1, may be permitted to argue *pro hac vice.*

2.   An attorney qualified to practice in the courts of a foreign state may be permitted to argue *pro hac vice.*

3.   Oral argument *pro hac vice* is allowed only on motion of the counsel of record for the party on whose behalf leave is requested. The motion shall state concisely the qualifications of the attorney who is to argue *pro hac vice.* It shall be filed with the Clerk, in the form required by Rule 21, no later than the date on which the respondent's or appellee's brief on the merits is due to be filed, and it shall be accompanied by proof of service as required by Rule 29.

Rule 7.   Prohibition Against Practice

No employee of this Court shall practice as an attorney or counselor in any court or before any agency of government while employed by the Court; nor shall any person after leaving such employment participate in any professional capacity in any case pending before this Court or in any case being considered for filing in this Court, until two years have elapsed after separation; nor shall a former employee ever participate in any professional capacity in any case that was pending in this Court during the employee's tenure.

Rule 8.   Disbarment and Disciplinary Action

1.   Whenever a member of the Bar of this Court has been disbarred or suspended from practice in any court of record, or has engaged in conduct unbecoming a member of the Bar of this Court, the Court will enter an order suspending that member from practice before this Court and affording the member an opportunity to show cause, within 40 days, why a disbarment order should not be entered. Upon response, or if no response is timely filed, the Court will enter an appropriate order.

2.   After reasonable notice and an opportunity to show cause why disciplinary action should not be taken, and after a hearing if material facts are in dispute, the Court may take any appropriate disciplinary action against any attorney who is admitted to practice before it for conduct unbecoming a member of the Bar or for failure to comply with these Rules or any Rule or order of the Court.

Rule 9.   Appearance of Counsel

1.   An attorney seeking to file a document in this Court in a representative capacity must first be admitted to practice before this Court as provided in Rule 5, except that admission to the Bar of this Court is not required for an attorney appointed under the Criminal Justice Act of 1964, see 18 U.S.C. § 3006A(d)(7), or under any other applicable federal statute. The attorney whose name, address, and telephone number appear on the cover of a document presented for filing is considered counsel of record. If the name of more than one attorney is shown on the cover of the document, the attorney who is counsel of record shall be clearly identified. See Rule 34.1(f).

2.   An attorney representing a party who will not be filing a document shall enter a separate notice of appearance as counsel of record indicating the name of the party represented. A separate notice of appearance shall also be entered whenever an attorney is substituted as counsel of record in a particular case.

(As amended July 17, 2007, eff. Oct. 1, 2007; Sept. 27, 2017, eff. Nov. 13, 2017.)

PART III. JURISDICTION ON WRIT OF CERTIORARI

Rule 10.   Considerations Governing Review on Certiorari

Review on a writ of certiorari is not a matter of right, but of judicial discretion. A petition for a writ of certiorari will be granted only for compelling reasons. The following, although neither controlling nor fully measuring the Court's discretion, indicate the character of the reasons the Court considers:

(a)   a United States court of appeals has entered a decision in conflict with the decision of another United States court of appeals on the same important matter; has decided an important federal question in a way that conflicts with a decision by a state court of last resort; or has so far departed from the accepted and usual course of judicial proceedings, or sanctioned such a departure by a lower court, as to call for an exercise of this Court's supervisory power;

(b)   a state court of last resort has decided an important federal question in a way that conflicts with the decision of another state court of last resort or of a United States court of appeals;

(c)   a state court or a United States court of appeals has decided an important question of federal law that has not been, but should be, settled by this Court, or has decided an important federal question in a way that conflicts with relevant decisions of this Court.

A petition for a writ of certiorari is rarely granted when the asserted error consists of erroneous factual findings or the misapplication of a properly stated rule of law.

Rule 11.   Certiorari to a United States Court of Appeals Before Judgment

A petition for a writ of certiorari to review a case pending in a United States court of appeals, before judgment is entered in that court, will be granted only upon a showing that the case is of such imperative public importance as to justify deviation from normal appellate practice and to require immediate determination in this Court. See 28 U.S.C. § 2101(e).

Rule 12.   Review on Certiorari: How Sought; Parties

1.   Except as provided in paragraph 2 of this Rule, the petitioner shall file 40 copies of a petition for a writ of certiorari, prepared as required by Rule 33.1, and shall pay the Rule 38(a) docket fee.

2. A petitioner proceeding *in forma pauperis* under Rule 39 shall file an original and 10 copies of a petition for a writ of certiorari prepared as required by Rule 33.2, together with an original and 10 copies of the motion for leave to proceed *in forma pauperis*. A copy of the motion shall precede and be attached to each copy of the petition. An inmate confined in an institution, if proceeding *in forma pauperis* and not represented by counsel, need file only an original petition and motion.

3. Whether prepared under Rule 33.1 or Rule 33.2, the petition shall comply in all respects with Rule 14 and shall be submitted with proof of service as required by Rule 29. The case then will be placed on the docket. It is the petitioner's duty to notify all respondents promptly, on a form supplied by the Clerk, of the date of filing, the date the case was placed on the docket, and the docket number of the case. The notice shall be served as required by Rule 29.

4. Parties interested jointly, severally, or otherwise in a judgment may petition separately for a writ of certiorari; or any two or more may join in a petition. A party not shown on the petition as joined therein at the time the petition is filed may not later join in that petition. When two or more judgments are sought to be reviewed on a writ of certiorari to the same court and involve identical or closely related questions, a single petition for a writ of certiorari covering all the judgments suffices. A petition for a writ of certiorari may not be joined with any other pleading, except that any motion for leave to proceed *in forma pauperis* shall be attached.

5. No more than 30 days after a case has been placed on the docket, a respondent seeking to file a conditional cross-petition (*i.e.*, a cross-petition that otherwise would be untimely) shall file, with proof of service as required by Rule 29, 40 copies of the cross-petition prepared as required by Rule 33.1, except that a cross-petitioner proceeding *in forma pauperis* under Rule 39 shall comply with Rule 12.2. The cross-petition shall comply in all respects with this Rule and Rule 14, except that material already reproduced in the appendix to the opening petition need not be reproduced again. A cross-petitioning respondent shall pay the Rule 38(a) docket fee or submit a motion for leave to proceed *in forma pauperis*. The cover of the cross-petition shall indicate clearly that it is a conditional cross-petition. The cross-petition then will be placed on the docket, subject to the provisions of Rule 13.4. It is the cross-petitioner's duty to notify all cross-respondents promptly, on a form supplied by the Clerk, of the date of filing, the date the cross-petition was placed on the docket, and the docket number of the cross-petition. The notice shall be served as required by Rule 29. A cross-petition for a writ of certiorari may not be joined with any other pleading, except that any motion for leave to proceed *in forma pauperis* shall be attached. The time to file a conditional cross-petition will not be extended.

6. All parties to the proceeding in the court whose judgment is sought to be reviewed are deemed parties entitled to file documents in this Court, unless the petitioner notifies the Clerk of this Court in writing of the petitioner's belief that one or more of the parties below have no interest in the outcome of the petition. A copy of such notice shall be served as required by Rule 29 on all parties to the proceeding below. A party noted as no longer interested may remain a party by notifying the Clerk promptly, with service on the other parties, of an intention to remain a party. All parties other than the petitioner are considered respondents, but any respondent who supports the position of a petitioner shall meet the petitioner's time schedule for filing documents, with the following exception: A response of a party aligned with petitioner below who supports granting the petition shall be filed within 30 days after the case is placed on the docket, and that time will not be extended. Counsel for such respondent shall ensure that counsel of record for all parties receive notice of its intention to file a brief in support within 20 days after the case is placed on the docket. A respondent not aligned with petitioner below who supports granting the petition, or a respondent aligned with petitioner below who takes the position that the petition should be denied, is not subject to the notice requirement and may file a response within the time otherwise provided by Rule 15.3. Parties who file no document will not qualify for any relief from this Court.

7. The clerk of the court having possession of the record shall keep it until notified by the Clerk of this Court to certify and transmit it. In any document filed with this Court, a party may cite or quote from the record, even if it has not been transmitted to this Court. When requested by the Clerk of this Court to certify and transmit the record, or any part of it, the clerk of the court having possession of the record shall number the documents to be certified and shall transmit therewith a numbered list specifically identifying each document transmitted. If the record, or stipulated portions, have been printed for the use of the court below, that printed record, plus the proceedings in the court below, may be certified as the record unless one of the parties or the Clerk of this Court requests otherwise. The record may consist of certified copies, but if the lower court is of the view that original documents of any kind should be seen by this Court, that court may provide by order for the transport, safekeeping, and return of such originals.

(As amended Apr. 19, 2013, eff. July 1, 2013.)

Rule 13. Review on Certiorari: Time for Petitioning

1. Unless otherwise provided by law, a petition for a writ of certiorari to review a judgment in any case, civil or criminal, entered by a state court of last resort or a United States court of appeals (including the United States Court of Appeals for the Armed Forces) is timely when it is filed with the Clerk of this Court within 90 days after entry of the judgment. A petition for a writ of certiorari seeking review of a judgment of a lower state court that is subject to discretionary review by the state court of last resort is timely when it is filed with the Clerk within 90 days after entry of the order denying discretionary review.

2. The Clerk will not file any petition for a writ of certiorari that is jurisdictionally out of time. *See, e.g.,* 28 U.S.C. § 2101(c).

3. The time to file a petition for a writ of certiorari runs from the date of entry of the judgment or order sought to be reviewed, and not from the issuance date of the mandate (or its equivalent under local practice). But if a petition for rehearing is timely filed in the lower court by any party, or if the lower court appropriately entertains an untimely petition for rehearing or sua sponte considers rehearing, the time to file the petition for a writ of certiorari for all parties (whether or not they requested rehearing or joined in the petition for rehearing) runs from the date of the denial of rehearing or, if rehearing is granted, the subsequent entry of judgment.

4. A cross-petition for a writ of certiorari is timely when it is filed with the Clerk as provided in paragraphs 1, 3, and 5 of this Rule, or in Rule 12.5. However, a conditional cross-petition (which except for Rule 12.5 would be untimely) will not be granted unless another party's timely petition for a writ of certiorari is granted.

5. For good cause, a Justice may extend the time to file a petition for a writ of certiorari for a period not exceeding 60 days. An application to extend the time to file shall set out the basis for jurisdiction in this Court, identify the judgment sought to be reviewed, include a copy of the opinion and any order respecting rehearing, and set out specific reasons why an extension of time is justified. The application must be filed with the Clerk at least 10 days before the date the petition is due, except in extraordinary circumstances. The application must clearly identify each party for whom an extension is being sought, as any extension that might be granted would apply solely to the party or parties named in the application. For the time and manner of presenting the application, see Rules 21, 22, 30, and 33.2. An application to extend the time to file a petition for a writ of certiorari is not favored.

(As amended Jan. 11, 1999, eff. May 3, 1999; Jan. 27, 2003, eff. May 1, 2003; Mar. 14, 2005, eff. May 2, 2005; Apr. 19, 2013, eff. July 1, 2013.)

Rule 14. Content of a Petition for a Writ of Certiorari

1. A petition for a writ of certiorari shall contain, in the order indicated:

(a) The questions presented for review, expressed concisely in relation to the circumstances of the case, without unnecessary detail. The questions should be short and should not be argumentative or repetitive. If the petitioner or respondent is under a death sentence that may be affected by the disposition of the petition, the notation "capital case" shall precede the questions presented. The questions shall be set out on the first page following the cover, and no other information may appear on that page. The statement of any question presented is deemed to comprise every subsidiary question fairly included therein. Only the questions set out in the petition, or fairly included therein, will be considered by the Court.

(b) **(i)** A list of all parties to the proceeding in the court whose judgment is sought to be reviewed (unless the caption of the case contains the names of all the parties);

(ii) a corporate disclosure statement as required by Rule 29.6; and

(iii) a list of all proceedings in state and federal trial and appellate courts, including proceedings in this Court, that are directly related to the case in this Court. For each such proceeding, the list should include the court in question, the docket number and case caption for the proceeding, and the date of entry of the judgment. For the purposes of this rule, a case is "directly related" if it arises from the same trial court case as the case in this Court (including the proceedings directly on review in this case), or if it challenges the same criminal conviction or sentence as is challenged in this Court, whether on direct appeal or through state or federal collateral proceedings.

(c) If the petition prepared under Rule 33.1 exceeds 1,500 words or exceeds five pages if prepared under Rule 33.2, a table of contents and a table of cited authorities. The table of contents shall include the items contained in the appendix.

(d) Citations of the official and unofficial reports of the opinions and orders entered in the case by courts or administrative agencies.

(e) A concise statement of the basis for jurisdiction in this Court, showing:

(i) the date the judgment or order sought to be reviewed was entered (and, if applicable, a statement that the petition is filed under this Court's Rule 11);

(ii) the date of any order respecting rehearing, and the date and terms of any order granting an extension of time to file the petition for a writ of certiorari;

(iii) express reliance on Rule 12.5, when a cross-petition for a writ of certiorari is filed under that Rule, and the date of docketing of the petition for a writ of certiorari in connection with which the cross-petition is filed;

(iv) the statutory provision believed to confer on this Court jurisdiction to review on a writ of certiorari the judgment or order in question; and

(v) if applicable, a statement that the notifications required by Rule 29.4(b) or (c) have been made.

(f) The constitutional provisions, treaties, statutes, ordinances, and regulations involved in the case, set out verbatim with appropriate citation. If the provisions involved are lengthy, their citation alone suffices at this point, and their pertinent text shall be set out in the appendix referred to in subparagraph 1(i).

(g) A concise statement of the case setting out the facts material to consideration of the questions presented, and also containing the following:

(i) If review of a state-court judgment is sought, specification of the stage in the proceedings, both in the court of first instance and in the appellate courts, when the federal questions sought to be reviewed were raised; the method or manner of raising them and the way in which they were passed on by those courts; and pertinent quotations of specific portions of the record or summary thereof, with specific reference to the places in the record where the matter appears (*e.g.*, court opinion, ruling on exception, portion of court's charge and exception thereto, assignment of error), so as to show that the federal question was timely and properly raised and that this Court has jurisdiction to review the judgment on a writ of certiorari. When the portions of the record relied on under this subparagraph are voluminous, they shall be included in the appendix referred to in subparagraph 1(i).

(ii) If review of a judgment of a United States court of appeals is sought, the basis for federal jurisdiction in the court of first instance.

(h) A direct and concise argument amplifying the reasons relied on for allowance of the writ. See Rule 10.

(i) An appendix containing, in the order indicated:

(i) the opinions, orders, findings of fact, and conclusions of law, whether written or orally given and transcribed, entered in conjunction with the judgment sought to be reviewed;

(ii) any other relevant opinions, orders, findings of fact, and conclusions of law entered in the case by courts or administrative agencies, and, if reference thereto is necessary to ascertain the grounds of the judgment, of those in companion cases (each document shall include the caption showing the name of the issuing court or agency, the title and number of the case, and the date of entry);

(iii) any order on rehearing, including the caption showing the name of the issuing court, the title and number of the case, and the date of entry;

(iv) the judgment sought to be reviewed if the date of its entry is different from the date of the opinion or order required in sub-subparagraph (i) of this subparagraph;

(v) material required by subparagraphs 1(f) or 1(g)(i); and

(vi) any other material the petitioner believes essential to understand the petition.

If the material required by this subparagraph is voluminous, it may be presented in a separate volume or volumes with appropriate covers.

2. All contentions in support of a petition for a writ of certiorari shall be set out in the body of the petition, as provided in subparagraph 1(h) of this Rule. No separate brief in support of a petition for a writ of certiorari may be filed, and the Clerk will not file any petition for a writ of certiorari to which any supporting brief is annexed or appended.

3. A petition for a writ of certiorari should be stated briefly and in plain terms and may not exceed the word or page limitations specified in Rule 33.

4. The failure of a petitioner to present with accuracy, brevity, and clarity whatever is essential to ready and adequate understanding of the points requiring consideration is sufficient reason for the Court to deny a petition.

5. If the Clerk determines that a petition submitted timely and in good faith is in a form that does not comply with this Rule or with Rule 33 or Rule 34, the Clerk will return it with a letter indicating the deficiency. A corrected petition submitted in accordance with Rule 29.2 no more than 60 days after the date of the Clerk's letter will be deemed timely.

(As amended July 17, 2007, eff. Oct. 1, 2007; Apr. 19, 2013, eff. July 1, 2013; Apr. 18, 2019, eff. July 1, 2019.)

Rule 15. Briefs in Opposition; Reply Briefs; Supplemental Briefs

1. A brief in opposition to a petition for a writ of certiorari may be filed by the respondent in any case, but is not mandatory except in a capital case, see Rule 14.1(a), or when ordered by the Court.

2. A brief in opposition should be stated briefly and in plain terms and may not exceed the word or page limitations specified in Rule 33. In addition to presenting other arguments for denying the petition, the brief in opposition should address any perceived misstatement of fact or law in the petition that bears on what issues properly would be before the Court if certiorari were granted. Counsel are admonished that they have an obligation to the Court to point out in the brief in opposition, and not later, any perceived misstatement made in the petition. Any objection to consideration of a question presented based on what occurred in the proceedings below, if the objection does not go to jurisdiction, may be deemed waived unless called to the Court's attention in the brief in opposition. A brief in opposition should identify any directly related cases that were not identified in the petition under Rule 14.1(b)(iii), including for each such case the information called for by Rule 14.1(b)(iii).

3. Any brief in opposition shall be filed within 30 days after the case is placed on the docket, unless the time is extended by the Court or a Justice, or by the Clerk under Rule 30.4. Forty copies shall be filed, except that a respondent proceeding *in forma pauperis* under Rule 39, including an inmate of an institution, shall file the number of copies required for a petition by such a person under Rule 12.2, together with a motion for leave to proceed *in forma pauperis*, a copy of which shall precede and be attached to each copy of the brief in opposition. If the petitioner is proceeding *in forma pauperis*, the respondent shall prepare its brief in opposition, if any, as required by Rule 33.2, and shall file an original and 10 copies of that brief. Whether prepared under Rule 33.1 or Rule 33.2, the brief in opposition shall comply with the requirements of Rule 24 governing a respondent's brief, except that no summary of the argument is required. A brief in opposition may not be joined with any other pleading, except that any motion for leave to proceed *in forma pauperis* shall be attached. The brief in opposition shall be served as required by Rule 29.

4. No motion by a respondent to dismiss a petition for a writ of certiorari may be filed. Any objections to the jurisdiction of the Court to grant a petition for a writ of certiorari shall be included in the brief in opposition.

5. The Clerk will distribute the petition to the Court for its consideration upon receiving an express waiver of the right to file a brief in opposition, or, if no waiver or brief in opposition is filed, upon the expiration of the time allowed for filing. If a brief in opposition is timely filed, the Clerk will distribute the petition, brief in opposition, and any reply brief to the Court for its consideration no less than 14 days after the brief in opposition is filed, unless the petitioner expressly waives the 14-day waiting period.

6. Any petitioner may file a reply brief addressed to new points raised in the brief in opposition, but distribution and consideration by the Court under paragraph 5 of this Rule will not be deferred pending its receipt. Forty copies shall be filed, except that a petitioner proceeding *in forma pauperis* under Rule 39, including an inmate of an institution, shall file the number of copies required for a petition by such a person under Rule 12.2. The reply brief shall be served as required by Rule 29.

7. If a cross-petition for a writ of certiorari has been docketed, distribution of both petitions will be deferred until the cross-petition is due for distribution under this Rule.

8. Any party may file a supplemental brief at any time while a petition for a writ of certiorari is pending, calling attention to new cases, new legislation, or other intervening matter not available at the time of the party's last filing. A supplemental brief shall be restricted to new matter and shall follow, insofar as applicable, the form for a brief in opposition prescribed by this Rule. Forty copies shall be filed, except that a party proceeding *in forma pauperis* under Rule 39, including an inmate of an institution, shall file the number of copies required for a petition by such a person under Rule 12.2. The supplemental brief shall be served as required by Rule 29.

(As amended July 17, 2007, eff. Oct. 1, 2007; Apr. 19, 2013, eff. July 1, 2013; Apr. 18, 2019, eff. July 1, 2019.)

Rule 16. Disposition of a Petition for a Writ of Certiorari

1. After considering the documents distributed under Rule 15, the Court will enter an appropriate order. The order may be a summary disposition on the merits.

2. Whenever the Court grants a petition for a writ of certiorari, the Clerk will prepare, sign, and enter an order to that effect and will notify forthwith counsel of record and the court whose judgment is to be reviewed. The case then will be scheduled for briefing and oral argument. If the

record has not previously been filed in this Court, the Clerk will request the clerk of the court having possession of the record to certify and transmit it. A formal writ will not issue unless specially directed.

3.   Whenever the Court denies a petition for a writ of certiorari, the Clerk will prepare, sign, and enter an order to that effect and will notify forthwith counsel of record and the court whose judgment was sought to be reviewed. The order of denial will not be suspended pending disposition of a petition for rehearing except by order of the Court or a Justice.

PART IV. OTHER JURISDICTION

Rule 17.   Procedure in an Original Action

1.   This Rule applies only to an action invoking the Court's original jurisdiction under Article III of the Constitution of the United States. See also 28 U.S.C. § 1251 and U.S. Const., Amdt. 11. A petition for an extraordinary writ in aid of the Court's appellate jurisdiction shall be filed as provided in Rule 20.

2.   The form of pleadings and motions prescribed by the Federal Rules of Civil Procedure is followed. In other respects, those Rules and the Federal Rules of Evidence may be taken as guides.

3.   The initial pleading shall be preceded by a motion for leave to file, and may be accompanied by a brief in support of the motion. Forty copies of each document shall be filed, with proof of service. Service shall be as required by Rule 29, except that when an adverse party is a State, service shall be made on both the Governor and the Attorney General of that State.

4.   The case will be placed on the docket when the motion for leave to file and the initial pleading are filed with the Clerk. The Rule 38(a) docket fee shall be paid at that time.

5.   No more than 60 days after receiving the motion for leave to file and the initial pleading, an adverse party shall file 40 copies of any brief in opposition to the motion, with proof of service as required by Rule 29. The Clerk will distribute the filed documents to the Court for its consideration upon receiving an express waiver of the right to file a brief in opposition, or, if no waiver or brief is filed, upon the expiration of the time allowed for filing. If a brief in opposition is timely filed, the Clerk will distribute the filed documents to the Court for its consideration no less than 10 days after the brief in opposition is filed. A reply brief may be filed, but consideration of the case will not be deferred pending its receipt. The Court thereafter may grant or deny the motion, set it for oral argument, direct that additional documents be filed, or require that other proceedings be conducted.

6.   A summons issued out of this Court shall be served on the defendant 60 days before the return day specified therein. If the defendant does not respond by the return day, the plaintiff may proceed *ex parte*.

7.   Process against a State issued out of this Court shall be served on both the Governor and the Attorney General of that State.

Rule 18.   Appeal from a United States District Court

1.   When a direct appeal from a decision of a United States district court is authorized by law, the appeal is commenced by filing a notice of appeal with the clerk of the district court within the time provided by law after entry of the judgment sought to be reviewed. The time to file may not be extended. The notice of appeal shall specify the parties taking the appeal, designate the judgment, or part thereof, appealed from and the date of its entry, and specify the statute or statutes under which the appeal is taken. A copy of the notice of appeal shall be served on all parties to the proceeding as required by Rule 29, and proof of service shall be filed in the district court together with the notice of appeal.

2.   All parties to the proceeding in the district court are deemed parties entitled to file documents in this Court, but a party having no interest in the outcome of the appeal may so notify the Clerk of this Court and shall serve a copy of the notice on all other parties. Parties interested jointly,

severally, or otherwise in the judgment may appeal separately, or any two or more may join in an appeal. When two or more judgments involving identical or closely related questions are sought to be reviewed on appeal from the same court, a notice of appeal for each judgment shall be filed with the clerk of the district court, but a single jurisdictional statement covering all the judgments suffices. Parties who file no document will not qualify for any relief from this Court.

   3.   No more than 60 days after filing the notice of appeal in the district court, the appellant shall file 40 copies of a jurisdictional statement and shall pay the Rule 38 docket fee, except that an appellant proceeding *in forma pauperis* under Rule 39, including an inmate of an institution, shall file the number of copies required for a petition by such a person under Rule 12.2, together with a motion for leave to proceed *in forma pauperis*, a copy of which shall precede and be attached to each copy of the jurisdictional statement. The jurisdictional statement shall follow, insofar as applicable, the form for a petition for a writ of certiorari prescribed by Rule 14, and shall be served as required by Rule 29. The case will then be placed on the docket. It is the appellant's duty to notify all appellees promptly, on a form supplied by the Clerk, of the date of filing, the date the case was placed on the docket, and the docket number of the case. The notice shall be served as required by Rule 29. The appendix shall include a copy of the notice of appeal showing the date it was filed in the district court. For good cause, a Justice may extend the time to file a jurisdictional statement for a period not exceeding 60 days. An application to extend the time to file a jurisdictional statement shall set out the basis for jurisdiction in this Court; identify the judgment sought to be reviewed; include a copy of the opinion, any order respecting rehearing, and the notice of appeal; and set out specific reasons why an extension of time is justified. For the time and manner of presenting the application, see Rules 21, 22, and 30. An application to extend the time to file a jurisdictional statement is not favored.

   4.   No more than 30 days after a case has been placed on the docket, an appellee seeking to file a conditional cross-appeal (*i.e.*, a cross-appeal that otherwise would be untimely) shall file, with proof of service as required by Rule 29, a jurisdictional statement that complies in all respects (including number of copies filed) with paragraph 3 of this Rule, except that material already reproduced in the appendix to the opening jurisdictional statement need not be reproduced again. A cross-appealing appellee shall pay the Rule 38 docket fee or submit a motion for leave to proceed *in forma pauperis*. The cover of the cross-appeal shall indicate clearly that it is a conditional cross-appeal. The cross-appeal then will be placed on the docket. It is the cross-appellant's duty to notify all cross-appellees promptly, on a form supplied by the Clerk, of the date of filing, the date the cross-appeal was placed on the docket, and the docket number of the cross-appeal. The notice shall be served as required by Rule 29. A cross-appeal may not be joined with any other pleading, except that any motion for leave to proceed *in forma pauperis* shall be attached. The time to file a cross-appeal will not be extended.

   5.   After a notice of appeal has been filed in the district court, but before the case is placed on this Court's docket, the parties may dismiss the appeal by stipulation filed in the district court, or the district court may dismiss the appeal on the appellant's motion, with notice to all parties. If a notice of appeal has been filed, but the case has not been placed on this Court's docket within the time prescribed for docketing, the district court may dismiss the appeal on the appellee's motion, with notice to all parties, and may make any just order with respect to costs. If the district court has denied the appellee's motion to dismiss the appeal, the appellee may move this Court to docket and dismiss the appeal by filing an original and 10 copies of a motion presented in conformity with Rules 21 and 33.2. The motion shall be accompanied by proof of service as required by Rule 29, and by a certificate from the clerk of the district court, certifying that a notice of appeal was filed and that the appellee's motion to dismiss was denied. The appellant may not thereafter file a jurisdictional statement without special leave of the Court, and the Court may allow costs against the appellant.

   6.   Within 30 days after the case is placed on this Court's docket, the appellee may file a motion to dismiss, to affirm, or in the alternative to affirm or dismiss. Forty copies of the motion shall be filed, except that an appellee proceeding *in forma pauperis* under Rule 39, including an inmate of an institution, shall file the number of copies required for a petition by such a person under Rule 12.2, together with a motion for leave to proceed *in forma pauperis*, a copy of which shall precede and be attached to each copy of the motion to dismiss, to affirm, or in the alternative to affirm or dismiss. The

motion shall follow, insofar as applicable, the form for a brief in opposition prescribed by Rule 15, and shall comply in all respects with Rule 21.

7. The Clerk will distribute the jurisdictional statement to the Court for its consideration upon receiving an express waiver of the right to file a motion to dismiss or to affirm or, if no waiver or motion is filed, upon the expiration of the time allowed for filing. If a motion to dismiss or to affirm is timely filed, the Clerk will distribute the jurisdictional statement, motion, and any brief opposing the motion to the Court for its consideration no less than 14 days after the motion is filed, unless the appellant expressly waives the 14-day waiting period.

8. Any appellant may file a brief opposing a motion to dismiss or to affirm, but distribution and consideration by the Court under paragraph 7 of this Rule will not be deferred pending its receipt. Forty copies shall be filed, except that an appellant proceeding *in forma pauperis* under Rule 39, including an inmate of an institution, shall file the number of copies required for a petition by such a person under Rule 12.2. The brief shall be served as required by Rule 29.

9. If a cross-appeal has been docketed, distribution of both jurisdictional statements will be deferred until the cross-appeal is due for distribution under this Rule.

10. Any party may file a supplemental brief at any time while a jurisdictional statement is pending, calling attention to new cases, new legislation, or other intervening matter not available at the time of the party's last filing. A supplemental brief shall be restricted to new matter and shall follow, insofar as applicable, the form for a brief in opposition prescribed by Rule 15. Forty copies shall be filed, except that a party proceeding *in forma pauperis* under Rule 39, including an inmate of an institution, shall file the number of copies required for a petition by such a person under Rule 12.2. The supplemental brief shall be served as required by Rule 29.

11. The clerk of the district court shall retain possession of the record until notified by the Clerk of this Court to certify and transmit it. See Rule 12.7.

12. After considering the documents distributed under this Rule, the Court may dispose summarily of the appeal on the merits, note probable jurisdiction, or postpone consideration of jurisdiction until a hearing of the case on the merits. If not disposed of summarily, the case stands for briefing and oral argument on the merits. If consideration of jurisdiction is postponed, counsel, at the outset of their briefs and at oral argument, shall address the question of jurisdiction. If the record has not previously been filed in this Court, the Clerk of this Court will request the clerk of the court in possession of the record to certify and transmit it.

13. If the Clerk determines that a jurisdictional statement submitted timely and in good faith is in a form that does not comply with this Rule or with Rule 33 or Rule 34, the Clerk will return it with a letter indicating the deficiency. If a corrected jurisdictional statement is submitted in accordance with Rule 29.2 no more than 60 days after the date of the Clerk's letter it will be deemed timely.

(As amended July 17, 2007, eff. Oct. 1, 2007; Apr. 19, 2013, eff. July 1, 2013.)

Rule 19.   Procedure on a Certified Question

1. A United States court of appeals may certify to this Court a question or proposition of law on which it seeks instruction for the proper decision of a case. The certificate shall contain a statement of the nature of the case and the facts on which the question or proposition of law arises. Only questions or propositions of law may be certified, and they shall be stated separately and with precision. The certificate shall be prepared as required by Rule 33.2 and shall be signed by the clerk of the court of appeals.

2. When a question is certified by a United States court of appeals, this Court, on its own motion or that of a party, may consider and decide the entire matter in controversy. See 28 U.S.C. § 1254(2).

3. When a question is certified, the Clerk will notify the parties and docket the case. Counsel shall then enter their appearances. After docketing, the Clerk will submit the certificate to the Court for a preliminary examination to determine whether the case should be briefed, set for argument, or dismissed. No brief may be filed until the preliminary examination of the certificate is completed.

4. If the Court orders the case briefed or set for argument, the parties will be notified and permitted to file briefs. The Clerk of this Court then will request the clerk of the court in possession of the record to certify and transmit it. Any portion of the record to which the parties wish to direct the Court's particular attention should be printed in a joint appendix, prepared in conformity with Rule 26 by the appellant or petitioner in the court of appeals, but the fact that any part of the record has not been printed does not prevent the parties or the Court from relying on it.

5. A brief on the merits in a case involving a certified question shall comply with Rules 24, 25, and 33.1, except that the brief for the party who is the appellant or petitioner below shall be filed within 45 days of the order requiring briefs or setting the case for argument.

Rule 20. Procedure on a Petition for an Extraordinary Writ

1. Issuance by the Court of an extraordinary writ authorized by 28 U.S.C. § 1651(a) is not a matter of right, but of discretion sparingly exercised. To justify the granting of any such writ, the petition must show that the writ will be in aid of the Court's appellate jurisdiction, that exceptional circumstances warrant the exercise of the Court's discretionary powers, and that adequate relief cannot be obtained in any other form or from any other court.

2. A petition seeking a writ authorized by 28 U.S.C. § 1651(a), § 2241, or § 2254(a) shall be prepared in all respects as required by Rules 33 and 34. The petition shall be captioned "*In re* [name of petitioner]" and shall follow, insofar as applicable, the form of a petition for a writ of certiorari prescribed by Rule 14. All contentions in support of the petition shall be included in the petition. The case will be placed on the docket when 40 copies of the petition are filed with the Clerk and the docket fee is paid, except that a petitioner proceeding *in forma pauperis* under Rule 39, including an inmate of an institution, shall file the number of copies required for a petition by such a person under Rule 12.2, together with a motion for leave to proceed *in forma pauperis,* a copy of which shall precede and be attached to each copy of the petition. The petition shall be served as required by Rule 29 (subject to subparagraph 4(b) of this Rule).

3. **(a)** A petition seeking a writ of prohibition, a writ of mandamus, or both in the alternative shall state the name and office or function of every person against whom relief is sought and shall set out with particularity why the relief sought is not available in any other court. A copy of the judgment with respect to which the writ is sought, including any related opinion, shall be appended to the petition together with any other document essential to understanding the petition.

(b) The petition shall be served on every party to the proceeding with respect to which relief is sought. Within 30 days after the petition is placed on the docket, a party shall file 40 copies of any brief or briefs in opposition thereto, which shall comply fully with Rule 15. If a party named as a respondent does not wish to respond to the petition, that party may so advise the Clerk and all other parties by letter. All persons served are deemed respondents for all purposes in the proceedings in this Court.

4. **(a)** A petition seeking a writ of habeas corpus shall comply with the requirements of 28 U.S.C. §§ 2241 and 2242, and in particular with the provision in the last paragraph of § 2242, which requires a statement of the "reasons for not making application to the district court of the district in which the applicant is held." If the relief sought is from the judgment of a state court, the petition shall set out specifically how and where the petitioner has exhausted available remedies in the state courts or otherwise comes within the provisions of 28 U.S.C. § 2254(b). To justify the granting of a writ of habeas corpus, the petitioner must show that exceptional circumstances warrant the exercise of the Court's discretionary powers, and that adequate relief cannot be obtained in any other form or from any other court. This writ is rarely granted.

(b) Habeas corpus proceedings, except in capital cases, are *ex parte,* unless the Court requires the respondent to show cause why the petition for a writ of habeas corpus should not be granted. A response, if ordered, or in a capital case, shall comply fully with Rule 15. Neither the denial of the petition, without more, nor an order of transfer to a district court under the authority of 28 U.S.C. § 2241(b), is an adjudication on the merits, and therefore does not preclude further application to another court for the relief sought.

5.   The Clerk will distribute the documents to the Court for its consideration when a brief in opposition under subparagraph 3(b) of this Rule has been filed, when a response under subparagraph 4(b) has been ordered and filed, when the time to file has expired, or when the right to file has been expressly waived.

6.   If the Court orders the case set for argument, the Clerk will notify the parties whether additional briefs are required, when they shall be filed, and, if the case involves a petition for a common-law writ of certiorari, that the parties shall prepare a joint appendix in accordance with Rule 26.

PART V. MOTIONS AND APPLICATIONS

Rule 21.   Motions to the Court

1.   Every motion to the Court shall clearly state its purpose and the facts on which it is based and may present legal argument in support thereof. No separate brief may be filed. A motion should be concise and shall comply with any applicable page limits. Non-dispositive motions and applications in cases in which certiorari has been granted, probable jurisdiction noted, or consideration of jurisdiction postponed shall state the position on the disposition of the motion or application of the other party or parties to the case. Rule 22 governs an application addressed to a single Justice.

2.   **(a)** A motion in any action within the Court's original jurisdiction shall comply with Rule 17.3.

(b) A motion to dismiss as moot (or a suggestion of mootness), a motion for leave to file a brief as *amicus curiae*, and any motion the granting of which would dispose of the entire case or would affect the final judgment to be entered (other than a motion to docket and dismiss under Rule 18.5 or a motion for voluntary dismissal under Rule 46) shall be prepared as required by Rule 33.1, and 40 copies shall be filed, except that a movant proceeding *in forma pauperis* under Rule 39, including an inmate of an institution, shall file a motion prepared as required by Rule 33.2, and shall file the number of copies required for a petition by such a person under Rule 12.2. The motion shall be served as required by Rule 29.

(c) Any other motion to the Court shall be prepared as required by Rule 33.2; the moving party shall file an original and 10 copies. The Court subsequently may order the moving party to prepare the motion as required by Rule 33.1; in that event, the party shall file 40 copies.

3.   A motion to the Court shall be filed with the Clerk and shall be accompanied by proof of service as required by Rule 29. No motion may be presented in open Court, other than a motion for admission to the Bar, except when the proceeding to which it refers is being argued. Oral argument on a motion will not be permitted unless the Court so directs.

4.   Any response to a motion shall be filed as promptly as possible considering the nature of the relief sought and any asserted need for emergency action, and, in any event, within 10 days of receipt, unless the Court or a Justice, or the Clerk under Rule 30.4, orders otherwise. A response to a motion prepared as required by Rule 33.1, except a response to a motion for leave to file an *amicus curiae* brief (see Rule 37.5), shall be prepared in the same manner if time permits. In an appropriate case, the Court may act on a motion without waiting for a response.

(As amended Apr. 19, 2013, eff. July 1, 2013.)

Rule 22.   Applications to Individual Justices

1.   An application addressed to an individual Justice shall be filed with the Clerk, who will transmit it promptly to the Justice concerned if an individual Justice has authority to grant the sought relief.

2.   The original and two copies of any application addressed to an individual Justice shall be prepared as required by Rule 33.2, and shall be accompanied by proof of service as required by Rule 29.

3.   An application shall be addressed to the Justice allotted to the Circuit from which the case arises. An application arising from the United States Court of Appeals for the Armed Forces shall be addressed to the Chief Justice. When the Circuit Justice is unavailable for any reason, the application addressed to that Justice will be distributed to the Justice then available who is next junior to the Circuit Justice; the turn of the Chief Justice follows that of the most junior Justice.

4.   A Justice denying an application will note the denial thereon. Thereafter, unless action thereon is restricted by law to the Circuit Justice or is untimely under Rule 30.2, the party making an application, except in the case of an application for an extension of time, may renew it to any other Justice, subject to the provisions of this Rule. Except when the denial is without prejudice, a renewed application is not favored. Renewed application is made by a letter to the Clerk, designating the Justice to whom the application is to be directed, and accompanied by 10 copies of the original application and proof of service as required by Rule 29.

5.   A Justice to whom an application for a stay or for bail is submitted may refer it to the Court for determination.

6.   The Clerk will advise all parties concerned, by appropriately speedy means, of the disposition made of an application.

(As amended July 17, 2007, effective Oct. 1, 2007.)

Rule 23.   Stays

1.   A stay may be granted by a Justice as permitted by law.

2.   A party to a judgment sought to be reviewed may present to a Justice an application to stay the enforcement of that judgment. See 28 U.S.C. § 2101(f).

3.   An application for a stay shall set out with particularity why the relief sought is not available from any other court or judge. Except in the most extraordinary circumstances, an application for a stay will not be entertained unless the relief requested was first sought in the appropriate court or courts below or from a judge or judges thereof. An application for a stay shall identify the judgment sought to be reviewed and have appended thereto a copy of the order and opinion, if any, and a copy of the order, if any, of the court or judge below denying the relief sought, and shall set out specific reasons why a stay is justified. The form and content of an application for a stay are governed by Rules 22 and 33.2.

4.   A judge, court, or Justice granting an application for a stay pending review by this Court may condition the stay on the filing of a supersedeas bond having an approved surety or sureties. The bond will be conditioned on the satisfaction of the judgment in full, together with any costs, interest, and damages for delay that may be awarded. If a part of the judgment sought to be reviewed has already been satisfied, or is otherwise secured, the bond may be conditioned on the satisfaction of the part of the judgment not otherwise secured or satisfied, together with costs, interest, and damages.

PART VI. BRIEFS ON THE MERITS AND ORAL ARGUMENT

Rule 24.   Briefs on the Merits: In General

1.   A brief on the merits for a petitioner or an appellant shall comply in all respects with Rules 33.1 and 34 and shall contain in the order here indicated:

(a) The questions presented for review under Rule 14.1(a). The questions shall be set out on the first page following the cover, and no other information may appear on that page. The phrasing of the questions presented need not be identical with that in the petition for a writ of certiorari or the jurisdictional statement, but the brief may not raise additional questions or change the substance of the questions already presented in those documents. At its option, however, the Court may consider a plain error not among the questions presented but evident from the record and otherwise within its jurisdiction to decide.

(b) A list of all parties to the proceeding in the court whose judgment is under review (unless the caption of the case in this Court contains the names of all parties). Any amended corporate disclosure statement as required by Rule 29.6 shall be placed here.

(c) If the brief exceeds 1,500 words, a table of contents and a table of cited authorities.

(d) Citations of the official and unofficial reports of the opinions and orders entered in the case by courts and administrative agencies.

(e) A concise statement of the basis for jurisdiction in this Court, including the statutory provisions and time factors on which jurisdiction rests.

(f) The constitutional provisions, treaties, statutes, ordinances, and regulations involved in the case, set out verbatim with appropriate citation. If the provisions involved are lengthy, their citation alone suffices at this point, and their pertinent text, if not already set out in the petition for a writ of certiorari, jurisdictional statement, or an appendix to either document, shall be set out in an appendix to the brief.

(g) A concise statement of the case, setting out the facts material to the consideration of the questions presented, with appropriate references to the joint appendix, *e.g.*, App. 12, or to the record, *e.g.*, Record 12.

(h) A summary of the argument, suitably paragraphed. The summary should be a clear and concise condensation of the argument made in the body of the brief; mere repetition of the headings under which the argument is arranged is not sufficient.

(i) The argument, exhibiting clearly the points of fact and of law presented and citing the authorities and statutes relied on.

(j) A conclusion specifying with particularity the relief the party seeks.

2. A brief on the merits for a respondent or an appellee shall conform to the foregoing requirements, except that items required by subparagraphs 1(a), (b), (d), (e), (f), and (g) of this Rule need not be included unless the respondent or appellee is dissatisfied with their presentation by the opposing party.

3. A brief on the merits may not exceed the word limitations specified in Rule 33.1(g). An appendix to a brief may include only relevant material, and counsel are cautioned not to include in an appendix arguments or citations that properly belong in the body of the brief.

4. A reply brief shall conform to those portions of this Rule applicable to the brief for a respondent or an appellee, but, if appropriately divided by topical headings, need not contain a summary of the argument.

5. A reference to the joint appendix or to the record set out in any brief shall indicate the appropriate page number. If the reference is to an exhibit, the page numbers at which the exhibit appears, at which it was offered in evidence, and at which it was ruled on by the judge shall be indicated, *e.g.*, Pl. Exh. 14, Record 199, 2134.

6. A brief shall be concise, logically arranged with proper headings, and free of irrelevant, immaterial, or scandalous matter. The Court may disregard or strike a brief that does not comply with this paragraph.

(As amended July 17, 2007, eff. Oct. 1, 2007; Apr. 19, 2013, eff. July 1, 2013.)

Rule 25.   Briefs on the Merits: Number of Copies and Time to File

1.   The petitioner or appellant shall file 40 copies of the brief on the merits within 45 days of the order granting the writ of certiorari, noting probable jurisdiction, or postponing consideration of jurisdiction. Any respondent or appellee who supports the petitioner or appellant shall meet the petitioner's or appellant's time schedule for filing documents.

2.   The respondent or appellee shall file 40 copies of the brief on the merits within 30 days after the brief for the petitioner or appellant is filed.

3.   The petitioner or appellant shall file 40 copies of the reply brief, if any, within 30 days after the brief for the respondent or appellee is filed, but any reply brief must actually be received by the Clerk not later than 2 p.m. 10 days before the date of oral argument. Any respondent or appellee supporting the petitioner or appellant may file a reply brief.

4.   If cross-petitions or cross-appeals have been consolidated for argument, the Clerk, upon request of the parties, may designate one of the parties to file an initial brief and reply brief as provided in paragraphs 1 and 3 of this Rule (as if the party were petitioner or appellant), and may designate the other party to file an initial brief as provided in paragraph 2 of this Rule and, to the extent appropriate, a supplemental brief following the submission of the reply brief. In such a case, the Clerk may establish the time for the submission of the briefs and alter the otherwise applicable word limits. Except as approved by the Court or a Justice, the total number of words permitted for the briefs of the parties cumulatively shall not exceed the maximum that would have been allowed in the absence of an order under this paragraph.

5.   The time periods stated in paragraphs 1, 2, and 3 of this Rule may be extended as provided in Rule 30. An application to extend the time to file a brief on the merits is not favored. If a case is advanced for hearing, the time to file briefs on the merits may be abridged as circumstances require pursuant to an order of the Court on its own motion or that of a party.

6.   A party wishing to present late authorities, newly enacted legislation, or other intervening matter that was not available in time to be included in a brief may file 40 copies of a supplemental brief, restricted to such new matter and otherwise presented in conformity with these Rules, up to the time the case is called for oral argument or by leave of the Court thereafter.

7.   After a case has been argued or submitted, the Clerk will not file any brief, except that of a party filed by leave of the Court.

8.   The Clerk will not file any brief that is not accompanied by proof of service as required by Rule 29.

(As amended Jan. 11, 1999, eff. May 3, 1999; Jan. 27, 2003, eff. May 1, 2003; July 17, 2007, eff. Oct. 1, 2007; Jan. 12, 2010, eff. Feb. 16, 2010; Sept. 27, 2017, eff. Nov. 13, 2017; Apr. 18, 2019, eff. July 1, 2019.)

Rule 26.   Joint Appendix

1.   Unless the Clerk has allowed the parties to use the deferred method described in paragraph 4 of this Rule, the petitioner or appellant, within 45 days after entry of the order granting the writ of certiorari, noting probable jurisdiction, or postponing consideration of jurisdiction, shall file 40 copies of a joint appendix, prepared as required by Rule 33.1. The joint appendix shall contain: (1) the relevant docket entries in all the courts below; (2) any relevant pleadings, jury instructions, findings, conclusions, or opinions; (3) the judgment, order, or decision under review; and (4) any other parts of the record that the parties particularly wish to bring to the Court's attention. Any of the foregoing items already reproduced in a petition for a writ of certiorari, jurisdictional statement, brief in opposition to a petition for a writ of certiorari, motion to dismiss or affirm, or any appendix to the foregoing, that was prepared as required by Rule 33.1, need not be reproduced again in the joint appendix. The petitioner or appellant shall serve three copies of the joint appendix on each of the other parties to the proceeding as required by Rule 29.

2. The parties are encouraged to agree on the contents of the joint appendix. In the absence of agreement, the petitioner or appellant, within 10 days after entry of the order granting the writ of certiorari, noting probable jurisdiction, or postponing consideration of jurisdiction, shall serve on the respondent or appellee a designation of parts of the record to be included in the joint appendix. Within 10 days after receiving the designation, a respondent or appellee who considers the parts of the record so designated insufficient shall serve on the petitioner or appellant a designation of additional parts to be included in the joint appendix, and the petitioner or appellant shall include the parts so designated. If the Court has permitted the respondent or appellee to proceed *in forma pauperis*, the petitioner or appellant may seek by motion to be excused from printing portions of the record the petitioner or appellant considers unnecessary. In making these designations, counsel should include only those materials the Court should examine; unnecessary designations should be avoided. The record is on file with the Clerk and available to the Justices, and counsel may refer in briefs and in oral argument to relevant portions of the record not included in the joint appendix.

3. When the joint appendix is filed, the petitioner or appellant immediately shall file with the Clerk a statement of the cost of printing 50 copies and shall serve a copy of the statement on each of the other parties as required by Rule 29. Unless the parties agree otherwise, the cost of producing the joint appendix shall be paid initially by the petitioner or appellant; but a petitioner or appellant who considers that parts of the record designated by the respondent or appellee are unnecessary for the determination of the issues presented may so advise the respondent or appellee, who then shall advance the cost of printing the additional parts, unless the Court or a Justice otherwise fixes the initial allocation of the costs. The cost of printing the joint appendix is taxed as a cost in the case, but if a party unnecessarily causes matter to be included in the joint appendix or prints excessive copies, the Court may impose these costs on that party.

4. (a) On the parties' request, the Clerk may allow preparation of the joint appendix to be deferred until after the briefs have been filed. In that event, the petitioner or appellant shall file the joint appendix no more than 14 days after receiving the brief for the respondent or appellee. The provisions of paragraphs 1, 2, and 3 of this Rule shall be followed, except that the designations referred to therein shall be made by each party when that party's brief is served. Deferral of the joint appendix is not favored.

(b) If the deferred method is used, the briefs on the merits may refer to the pages of the record. In that event, the joint appendix shall include in brackets on each page thereof the page number of the record where that material may be found. A party wishing to refer directly to the pages of the joint appendix may serve and file copies of its brief prepared as required by Rule 33.2 within the time provided by Rule 25, with appropriate references to the pages of the record. In that event, within 10 days after the joint appendix is filed, copies of the brief prepared as required by Rule 33.1 containing references to the pages of the joint appendix in place of, or in addition to, the initial references to the pages of the record, shall be served and filed. No other change may be made in the brief as initially served and filed, except that typographical errors may be corrected.

5. The joint appendix shall be prefaced by a table of contents showing the parts of the record that it contains, in the order in which the parts are set out, with references to the pages of the joint appendix at which each part begins. The relevant docket entries shall be set out after the table of contents, followed by the other parts of the record in chronological order. When testimony contained in the reporter's transcript of proceedings is set out in the joint appendix, the page of the transcript at which the testimony appears shall be indicated in brackets immediately before the statement that is set out. Omissions in the transcript or in any other document printed in the joint appendix shall be indicated by asterisks. Immaterial formal matters (*e.g.*, captions, subscriptions, acknowledgments) shall be omitted. A question and its answer may be contained in a single paragraph.

6. Two lines must appear at the bottom of the cover of the joint appendix: (1) The first line must indicate the date the petition for the writ of certiorari was filed or the date the appeal was docketed; (2) the second line must indicate the date certiorari was granted or the date jurisdiction of the appeal was noted or postponed.

7.   Exhibits designated for inclusion in the joint appendix may be contained in a separate volume or volumes suitably indexed. The transcript of a proceeding before an administrative agency, board, commission, or officer used in an action in a district court or court of appeals is regarded as an exhibit for the purposes of this paragraph.

8.   The Court, on its own motion or that of a party, may dispense with the requirement of a joint appendix and may permit a case to be heard on the original record (with such copies of the record, or relevant parts thereof, as the Court may require) or on the appendix used in the court below, if it conforms to the requirements of this Rule.

9.   For good cause, the time limits specified in this Rule may be shortened or extended by the Court or a Justice, or by the Clerk under Rule 30.4.

(As amended Jan. 12, 2010, eff. Feb. 16, 2010.)

Rule 27.   Calendar

1.   From time to time, the Clerk will prepare a calendar of cases ready for argument. A case ordinarily will not be called for argument less than two weeks after the brief on the merits for the respondent or appellee is due.

2.   The Clerk will advise counsel when they are required to appear for oral argument and will publish a hearing list in advance of each argument session for the convenience of counsel and the information of the public.

3.   The Court, on its own motion or that of a party, may order that two or more cases involving the same or related questions be argued together as one case or on such other terms as the Court may prescribe.

Rule 28.   Oral Argument

1.   Oral argument should emphasize and clarify the written arguments in the briefs on the merits. Counsel should assume that all Justices have read the briefs before oral argument. Oral argument read from a prepared text is not favored.

2.   The petitioner or appellant shall open and may conclude the argument. A cross-writ of certiorari or cross-appeal will be argued with the initial writ of certiorari or appeal as one case in the time allowed for that one case, and the Court will advise the parties who shall open and close.

3.   Unless the Court directs otherwise, each side is allowed one-half hour for argument. Counsel is not required to use all the allotted time. Any request for additional time to argue shall be presented by motion under Rule 21 in time to be considered at a scheduled Conference prior to the date of oral argument and no later than 7 days after the respondent's or appellee's brief on the merits is filed, and shall set out specifically and concisely why the case cannot be presented within the half-hour limitation. Additional time is rarely accorded.

4.   Only one attorney will be heard for each side, except by leave of the Court on motion filed in time to be considered at a scheduled Conference prior to the date of oral argument and no later than 7 days after the respondent's or appellee's brief on the merits is filed. Any request for divided argument shall be presented by motion under Rule 21 and shall set out specifically and concisely why more than one attorney should be allowed to argue. Divided argument is not favored.

5.   Regardless of the number of counsel participating in oral argument, counsel making the opening argument shall present the case fairly and completely and not reserve points of substance for rebuttal.

6.   Oral argument will not be allowed on behalf of any party for whom a brief has not been filed.

7.   By leave of the Court, and subject to paragraph 4 of this Rule, counsel for an *amicus curiae* whose brief has been filed as provided in Rule 37 may argue orally on the side of a party, with the consent of that party. In the absence of consent, counsel for an *amicus curiae* may seek leave of the Court to argue orally by a motion setting out specifically and concisely why oral argument would provide assistance to the Court not otherwise available. Such a motion will be granted only in the most extraordinary circumstances.

8.   Oral arguments may be presented only by members of the Bar of this Court. Attorneys who are not members of the Bar of this Court may make a motion to argue pro hac vice under the provisions of Rule 6.

(As amended July 17, 2007, eff. Oct. 1, 2007; Apr. 19, 2013, eff. July 1, 2013.)

PART VII. PRACTICE AND PROCEDURE

Rule 29.   Filing and Service of Documents; Special Notifications; Corporate Listing

1.   Any document required or permitted to be presented to the Court or to a Justice shall be filed with the Clerk in paper form.

2.   A document is timely filed if it is received by the Clerk in paper form within the time specified for filing; or if it is sent to the Clerk through the United States Postal Service by first-class mail (including express or priority mail), postage prepaid, and bears a postmark, other than a commercial postage meter label, showing that the document was mailed on or before the last day for filing; or if it is delivered on or before the last day for filing to a third-party commercial carrier for delivery to the Clerk within 3 calendar days. If submitted by an inmate confined in an institution, a document is timely filed if it is deposited in the institution's internal mail system on or before the last day for filing and is accompanied by a notarized statement or declaration in compliance with 28 U.S.C. § 1746 setting out the date of deposit and stating that first-class postage has been prepaid. If the postmark is missing or not legible, or if the third-party commercial carrier does not provide the date the document was received by the carrier, the Clerk will require the person who sent the document to submit a notarized statement or declaration in compliance with 28 U.S.C. § 1746 setting out the details of the filing and stating that the filing took place on a particular date within the permitted time.

3.   Any document required by these Rules to be served may be served personally, by mail, or by third-party commercial carrier for delivery within 3 calendar days on each party to the proceeding at or before the time of filing. If the document has been prepared as required by Rule 33.1, three copies shall be served on each other party separately represented in the proceeding. If the document has been prepared as required by Rule 33.2, service of a single copy on each other separately represented party suffices. If personal service is made, it shall consist of delivery at the office of the counsel of record, either to counsel or to an employee therein. If service is by mail or third-party commercial carrier, it shall consist of depositing the document with the United States Postal Service, with no less than first-class postage prepaid, or delivery to the carrier for delivery within 3 calendar days, addressed to counsel of record at the proper address. When a party is not represented by counsel, service shall be made on the party, personally, by mail, or by commercial carrier. Ordinarily, service on a party must be by a manner at least as expeditious as the manner used to file the document with the Court. An electronic version of the document shall also be transmitted to all other parties at the time of filing or reasonably contemporaneous therewith, unless the party filing the document is proceeding *pro se* and *in forma pauperis* or the electronic service address of the party being served is unknown and not identifiable through reasonable efforts.

4.   (a)   If the United States or any federal department, office, agency, officer, or employee is a party to be served, service shall be made on the Solicitor General of the United States, Room 5616, Department of Justice, 950 Pennsylvania Ave., N.W., Washington, DC 20530–0001. When an agency of the United States that is a party is authorized by law to appear before this Court on its own behalf,

or when an officer or employee of the United States is a party, the agency, officer, or employee shall be served in addition to the Solicitor General.

(b) In any proceeding in this Court in which the constitutionality of an Act of Congress is drawn into question, and neither the United States nor any federal department, office, agency, officer, or employee is a party, the initial document filed in this Court shall recite that 28 U.S.C. § 2403(a) may apply and shall be served on the Solicitor General of the United States, Room 5616, Department of Justice, 950 Pennsylvania Ave., N.W., Washington, DC 20530–0001. In such a proceeding from any court of the United States, as defined by 28 U.S.C. § 451, the initial document also shall state whether that court, pursuant to 28 U.S.C. § 2403(a), certified to the Attorney General the fact that the constitutionality of an Act of Congress was drawn into question. See Rule 14.1(e)(v).

(c) In any proceeding in this Court in which the constitutionality of any statute of a State is drawn into question, and neither the State nor any agency, officer, or employee thereof is a party, the initial document filed in this Court shall recite that 28 U.S.C. § 2403(b) may apply and shall be served on the Attorney General of that State. In such a proceeding from any court of the United States, as defined by 28 U.S.C. § 451, the initial document also shall state whether that court, pursuant to 28 U.S.C. § 2403(b), certified to the State Attorney General the fact that the constitutionality of a statute of that State was drawn into question. See Rule 14.1(e)(v).

5. Proof of service, when required by these Rules, shall accompany the document when it is presented to the Clerk for filing and shall be separate from it. Proof of service shall contain, or be accompanied by, a statement that all parties required to be served have been served, together with a list of the names, addresses, and telephone numbers of counsel indicating the name of the party or parties each counsel represents. It is not necessary that service on each party required to be served be made in the same manner or evidenced by the same proof. Proof of service may consist of any one of the following:

(a) an acknowledgment of service, signed by counsel of record for the party served, and bearing the address and telephone number of such counsel;

(b) a certificate of service, reciting the facts and circumstances of service in compliance with the appropriate paragraph or paragraphs of this Rule, and signed by a member of the Bar of this Court representing the party on whose behalf service is made or by an attorney appointed to represent that party under the Criminal Justice Act of 1964, see 18 U.S.C. § 3006A(d)(7), or under any other applicable federal statute; or

(c) a notarized affidavit or declaration in compliance with 28 U.S.C. § 1746, reciting the facts and circumstances of service in accordance with the appropriate paragraph or paragraphs of this Rule, whenever service is made by any person not a member of the Bar of this Court and not an attorney appointed to represent a party under the Criminal Justice Act of 1964, see 18 U.S.C. § 3006A(d)(7), or under any other applicable federal statute.

6. Every document, except a joint appendix or *amicus curiae* brief, filed by or on behalf of a nongovernmental corporation shall contain a corporate disclosure statement identifying the parent corporations and listing any publicly held company that owns 10% or more of the corporation's stock. If there is no parent or publicly held company owning 10% or more of the corporation's stock, a notation to this effect shall be included in the document. If a statement has been included in a document filed earlier in the case, reference may be made to the earlier document (except when the earlier statement appeared in a document prepared under Rule 33.2), and only amendments to the statement to make it current need be included in the document being filed. In addition, whenever there is a material change in the identity of the parent corporation or publicly held companies that own 10% or more of the corporation's stock, counsel shall promptly inform the Clerk by letter and include, within that letter, any amendment needed to make the statement current.

7. In addition to the filing requirements set forth in this Rule, all filers who are represented by counsel must submit documents to the Court's electronic filing system in conformity with the "Guidelines for the Submission of Documents to the Supreme Court's Electronic Filing System" issued by the Clerk.

(As amended Jan. 11, 1999, eff. May 3, 1999; Jan. 27, 2003, eff. May 1, 2003; Apr. 19, 2013, eff. July 1, 2013; Sept. 27, 2017, eff. Nov. 13, 2017; Apr. 18, 2019, eff. July 1, 2019.)

Rule 30. Computation and Extension of Time

1. In the computation of any period of time prescribed or allowed by these Rules, by order of the Court, or by an applicable statute, the day of the act, event, or default from which the designated period begins to run is not included. The last day of the period shall be included, unless it is a Saturday, Sunday, federal legal holiday listed in 5 U.S.C. § 6103, or day on which the Court building is closed by order of the Court or the Chief Justice, in which event the period shall extend until the end of the next day that is not a Saturday, Sunday, federal legal holiday, or day on which the Court building is closed.

2. Whenever a Justice or the Clerk is empowered by law or these Rules to extend the time to file any document, an application or motion seeking an extension shall be filed within the period sought to be extended. An application to extend the time to file a petition for a writ of certiorari or to file a jurisdictional statement must be filed at least 10 days before the specified final filing date as computed under these Rules; if filed less than 10 days before the final filing date, such application will not be granted except in the most extraordinary circumstances.

3. An application to extend the time to file a petition for a writ of certiorari, to file a jurisdictional statement, to file a reply brief on the merits, or to file a petition for rehearing of any judgment or decision of the Court on the merits shall be made to an individual Justice and presented and served on all other parties as provided by Rule 22. Once denied, such an application may not be renewed.

4. A motion to extend the time to file any document or paper other than those specified in paragraph 3 of this Rule may be presented in the form of a letter to the Clerk setting out specific reasons why an extension of time is justified. The letter shall be served on all other parties as required by Rule 29. The motion may be acted on by the Clerk in the first instance, and any party aggrieved by the Clerk's action may request that the motion be submitted to a Justice or to the Court. The Clerk will report action under this paragraph to the Court as instructed.

(As amended Jan. 27, 2003, eff. May 1, 2003; Apr. 19, 2013, eff. July 1, 2013; Sept. 27, 2017, eff. Nov. 13, 2017.)

Rule 31. Translations

Whenever any record to be transmitted to this Court contains material written in a foreign language without a translation made under the authority of the lower court, or admitted to be correct, the clerk of the court transmitting the record shall advise the Clerk of this Court immediately so that this Court may order that a translation be supplied and, if necessary, printed as part of the joint appendix.

Rule 32. Models, Diagrams, Exhibits, and Lodgings

1. Models, diagrams, and exhibits of material forming part of the evidence taken in a case and brought to this Court for its inspection shall be placed in the custody of the Clerk at least two weeks before the case is to be heard or submitted.

2. All models, diagrams, exhibits, and other items placed in the custody of the Clerk shall be removed by the parties no more than 40 days after the case is decided. If this is not done, the Clerk will notify counsel to remove the articles forthwith. If they are not removed within a reasonable time thereafter, the Clerk will destroy them or dispose of them in any other appropriate way.

3. Any party or *amicus curiae* desiring to lodge non-record material with the Clerk must set out in a letter, served on all parties, a description of the material proposed for lodging and the reasons why the non-record material may properly be considered by the Court. The material proposed for lodging may not be submitted until and unless requested by the Clerk.

(As amended Jan. 11, 1999, eff. May 3, 1999; Jan. 27, 2003, eff. May 1, 2003.)

Rule 33. Document Preparation: Booklet Format; 8½- by 11-inch Paper Format

1. **Booklet Format: (a)** Except for a document expressly permitted by these Rules to be submitted on 8½- by 11-inch paper, see, *e.g.*, Rules 21, 22, and 39, every document filed with the Court shall be prepared in a 6⅛ by 9¼-inch booklet format using a standard typesetting process (*e.g.*, hot metal, photocomposition, or computer typesetting) to produce text printed in typographic (as opposed to typewriter) characters. The process used must produce a clear, black image on white paper. The text must be reproduced with a clarity that equals or exceeds the output of a laser printer.

(b) The text of every booklet-format document, including any appendix thereto, shall be typeset in a Century family (*e.g.*, Century Expanded, New Century Schoolbook, or Century Schoolbook) 12-point type with 2-point or more leading between lines. Quotations in excess of 50 words shall be indented. The typeface of footnotes shall be 10-point type with 2-point or more leading between lines. The text of the document must appear on both sides of the page.

(c) Every booklet-format document shall be produced on paper that is opaque, unglazed, and not less than 60 pounds in weight, and shall have margins of at least three-fourths of an inch on all sides. The text field, including footnotes, may not exceed 4⅛ by 7⅛ inches. The document shall be bound firmly in at least two places along the left margin (saddle stitch or perfect binding preferred) so as to permit easy opening, and no part of the text should be obscured by the binding. Spiral, plastic, metal, or string bindings may not be used. Copies of patent documents, except opinions, may be duplicated in such size as is necessary in a separate appendix.

(d) Every booklet-format document shall comply with the word limits shown on the chart in subparagraph 1(g) of this Rule. The word limits do not include the questions presented, the list of parties and the corporate disclosure statement, the table of contents, the table of cited authorities, the listing of counsel at the end of the document, or any appendix. The word limits include footnotes. Verbatim quotations required under Rule 14.1(f) and Rule 24.1(f), if set out in the text of a brief rather than in the appendix, are also excluded. For good cause, the Court or a Justice may grant leave to file a document in excess of the word limits, but application for such leave is not favored. An application to exceed word limits shall comply with Rule 22 and must be received by the Clerk at least 15 days before the filing date of the document in question, except in the most extraordinary circumstances.

(e) Every booklet-format document shall have a suitable cover consisting of 65-pound weight paper in the color indicated on the chart in subparagraph 1(g) of this Rule. If a separate appendix to any document is filed, the color of its cover shall be the same as that of the cover of the document it supports. The Clerk will furnish a color chart upon request. Counsel shall ensure that there is adequate contrast between the printing and the color of the cover. A document filed by the United States, or by any other federal party represented by the Solicitor General, shall have a gray cover. A joint appendix, answer to a bill of complaint, motion for leave to intervene, and any other document not listed in subparagraph 1(g) of this Rule shall have a tan cover.

(f) Forty copies of a booklet-format document shall be filed, and one unbound copy of the document on 8½- by 11-inch paper shall also be submitted.

(g) Word limits and cover colors for booklet-format documents are as follows:

	Type of Document	Word Limits	Color of Cover
(i)	Petition for a Writ of Certiorari (Rule 14); Motion for Leave to File a Bill of Complaint and Brief in Support (Rule 17.3); Jurisdictional Statement (Rule 18.3); Petition for an Extraordinary Writ (Rule 20.2)	9,000	white
(ii)	Brief in Opposition (Rule 15.3); Brief in Opposition to Motion for Leave to File an Original Action (Rule 17.5); Motion to Dismiss or Affirm (Rule 18.6); Brief in Opposition to Mandamus or Prohibition (Rule 20.3(b)); Response to a Petition for Habeas Corpus (Rule 20.4); Respondent's Brief in Support of Certiorari (Rule 12.6)	9,000	orange
(iii)	Reply to Brief in Opposition (Rules 15.6 and 17.5); Brief Opposing a Motion to Dismiss or Affirm (Rule 18.8)	3,000	tan
(iv)	Supplemental Brief (Rules 15.8, 17, 18.10, and 25.6)	3,000	tan
(v)	Brief on the Merits for Petitioner or Appellant (Rule 24); Exceptions by Plaintiff to Report of Special Master (Rule 17)	13,000	light blue
(vi)	Brief on the Merits for Respondent or Appellee (Rule 24.2); Brief on the Merits for Respondent or Appellee Supporting Petitioner or Appellant (Rule 12.6); Exceptions by Party Other Than Plaintiff to Report of Special Master (Rule 17)	13,000	light red
(vii)	Reply Brief on the Merits (Rule 24.4)	6,000	yellow
(viii)	Reply to Plaintiff's Exceptions to Report of Special Master (Rule 17)	13,000	orange
(ix)	Reply to Exceptions by Party Other Than Plaintiff to Report of Special Master (Rule 17)	13,000	yellow
(x)	Brief for an *Amicus Curiae* at the Petition Stage or pertaining to a Motion for Leave to file a Bill of Complaint (Rule 37.2)	6,000	cream
(xi)	Brief for an *Amicus Curiae* Identified in Rule 37.4 in Support of the Plaintiff, Petitioner, or Appellant, or in Support of Neither Party, on the Merits or in an Original Action at the Exceptions Stage (Rule 37.3)	9,000	light green
(xii)	Brief for any Other *Amicus Curiae* in Support of the Plaintiff, Petitioner, or Appellant, or in Support of Neither Party, on the Merits or in an Original Action at the Exceptions Stage (Rule 37.3)	8,000	light green
(xiii)	Brief for an *Amicus Curiae* Identified in Rule 37.4 in Support of the Defendant, Respondent, or Appellee, on the Merits or in an Original Action at the Exceptions Stage (Rule 37.3)	9,000	dark green
(xiv)	Brief for any Other *Amicus Curiae* in Support of the Defendant, Respondent, or Appellee, on the Merits or in an Original Action at the Exceptions Stage (Rule 37.3)	8,000	dark green
(xv)	Petition for Rehearing (Rule 44)	3,000	tan

(h) A document prepared under Rule 33.1 must be accompanied by a certificate signed by the attorney, the unrepresented party, or the preparer of the document stating that the brief complies with the word limitations. The person preparing the certificate may rely on the word count of the word-processing system used to prepare the document. The word-processing system must be set to include footnotes in the word count. The certificate must state the number of words in the document. The certificate shall accompany the document when it is presented to the Clerk for filing and shall be separate from it. If the certificate is signed by a person other than a member of the Bar of this Court, the counsel of record, or the unrepresented party, it must contain a notarized affidavit or declaration in compliance with 28 U.S.C. § 1746.

2.   8$^1/_2$- by 11-Inch Paper Format: (a) The text of every document, including any appendix thereto, expressly permitted by these Rules to be presented to the Court on 8$^1/_2$- by 11-inch paper shall appear double spaced, except for indented quotations, which shall be single spaced, on opaque, unglazed, white paper. The document shall be stapled or bound at the upper left-hand corner. Copies, if required, shall be produced on the same type of paper and shall be legible. The original of any such document (except a motion to dismiss or affirm under Rule 18.6) shall be signed by the party proceeding pro se or by counsel of record who must be a member of the Bar of this Court or an attorney appointed under the Criminal Justice Act of 1964, see 18 U.S.C. § 3006A(d)(7), or under any other applicable federal statute. Subparagraph 1(g) of this Rule does not apply to documents prepared under this paragraph.

(b) Page limits for documents presented on 8$^1/_2$- by 11-inch paper are: 40 pages for a petition for a writ of certiorari, jurisdictional statement, petition for an extraordinary writ, brief in opposition, or motion to dismiss or affirm; and 15 pages for a reply to a brief in opposition, brief opposing a motion to dismiss or affirm, supplemental brief, or petition for rehearing. The exclusions specified in subparagraph 1(d) of this Rule apply.

(As amended Jan. 11, 1999, eff. May 3, 1999; July 17, 2007, eff. Oct. 1, 2007; Jan. 12, 2010, eff. Feb. 16, 2010; Apr. 19, 2013, eff. July 1, 2013; Sept. 27, 2017, eff. Nov. 13, 2017; Apr. 18, 2019, eff. July 1, 2019.)

Rule 34.   Document Preparation: General Requirements

Every document, whether prepared under Rule 33.1 or Rule 33.2, shall comply with the following provisions:

1.   Each document shall bear on its cover, in the order indicated, from the top of the page:

(a)   the docket number of the case or, if there is none, a space for one;

(b)   the name of this Court;

(c)   the caption of the case as appropriate in this Court;

(d)   the nature of the proceeding and the name of the court from which the action is brought (*e.g.*, "On Petition for Writ of Certiorari to the United States Court of Appeals for the Fifth Circuit"; or, for a merits brief, "On Writ of Certiorari to the United States Court of Appeals for the Fifth Circuit");

(e)   the title of the document (*e.g.*, "Petition for Writ of Certiorari," "Brief for Respondent," "Joint Appendix");

(f)   the name of the attorney who is counsel of record for the party concerned (who must be a member of the Bar of this Court except as provided in Rule 9.1) and on whom service is to be made, with a notation directly thereunder identifying the attorney as counsel of record and setting out counsel's office address, e-mail address, and telephone number. Only one counsel of record may be noted on a single document, except that counsel of record for each party must be listed on the cover of a joint appendix. The names of other members of the Bar of this Court or of the bar of the highest court of State acting as counsel, and, if desired, their addresses, may be added, but counsel of record shall be clearly identified. Names of persons other than attorneys admitted to a state bar may not be listed, unless the party is appearing pro se, in which case the party's name, address, and telephone number shall appear.

(g) The foregoing shall be displayed in an appropriate typographical manner and, except for identification of counsel, may not be set in type smaller than standard 11-point, if the document is prepared as required by Rule 33.1.

2. Every document (other than a joint appendix), that exceeds 1,500 words when prepared under Rule 33.1, or that exceeds five pages when prepared under Rule 33.2, shall contain a table of contents and a table of cited authorities (*i.e.*, cases alphabetically arranged, constitutional provisions, statutes, treatises, and other materials) with references to the pages in the document where such authorities are cited.

3. The body of every document shall bear at its close the name of counsel of record and such other counsel, identified on the cover of the document in conformity with subparagraph 1(f) of this Rule, as may be desired.

4. Every appendix to a document must be preceded by a table of contents that provides a description of each document in the appendix.

5. All references to a provision of federal statutory law should ordinarily be cited to the United States Code, if the provision has been codified therein. In the event the provision has not been classified to the United States Code, citation should be to the Statutes at Large. Additional or alternative citations should be provided only if there is a particular reason why those citations are relevant or necessary to the argument.

6. A case in which privacy protection was governed by Federal Rule of Appellate Procedure 25(a)(5), Federal Rule of Bankruptcy Procedure 9037, Federal Rule of Civil Procedure 5.2, or Federal Rule of Criminal Procedure 49.1 is governed by the same Rule in this Court. In any other case, privacy protection is governed by Federal Rule of Civil Procedure 5.2, except that Federal Rule of Criminal Procedure 49.1 governs when an extraordinary writ is sought in a criminal case. If the Court schedules briefing and oral argument in a case that was governed by Federal Rule of Civil Procedure 5.2(c) or Federal Rule of Criminal Procedure 49.1(c), the parties shall submit electronic versions of all prior and subsequent filings with this Court in the case, subject to the redaction Rules set forth above.

(As amended Jan. 11, 1999, eff. May 3, 1999; July 17, 2007, eff. Oct. 1, 2007; Jan. 12, 2010, eff. Feb. 16, 2010; Apr. 19, 2013, eff. July 1, 2013; Sept. 27, 2017, eff. Nov. 13, 2017.)

Rule 35.   Death, Substitution, and Revivor; Public Officers

1. If a party dies after the filing of a petition for a writ of certiorari to this Court, or after the filing of a notice of appeal, the authorized representative of the deceased party may appear and, on motion, be substituted as a party. If the representative does not voluntarily become a party, any other party may suggest the death on the record and, on motion, seek an order requiring the representative to become a party within a designated time. If the representative then fails to become a party, the party so moving, if a respondent or appellee, is entitled to have the petition for a writ of certiorari or the appeal dismissed, and if a petitioner or appellant, is entitled to proceed as in any other case of nonappearance by a respondent or appellee. If the substitution of a representative of the deceased is not made within six months after the death of the party, the case shall abate.

2. Whenever a case cannot be revived in the court whose judgment is sought to be reviewed, because the deceased party's authorized representative is not subject to that court's jurisdiction, proceedings will be conducted as this Court may direct.

3. When a public officer who is a party to a proceeding in this Court in an official capacity dies, resigns, or otherwise ceases to hold office, the action does not abate and any successor in office is automatically substituted as a party. The parties shall notify the Clerk in writing of any such successions. Proceedings following the substitution shall be in the name of the substituted party, but any misnomer not affecting substantial rights of the parties will be disregarded.

4. A public officer who is a party to a proceeding in this Court in an official capacity may be described as a party by the officer's official title rather than by name, but the Court may require the name to be added.

(As amended Jan. 11, 1999, eff. May 3, 1999.)

Rule 36.   Custody of Prisoners in Habeas Corpus Proceedings

1. Pending review in this Court of a decision in a habeas corpus proceeding commenced before a court, Justice, or judge of the United States, the person having custody of the prisoner may not transfer custody to another person unless the transfer is authorized under this Rule.

2. Upon application by a custodian, the court, Justice, or judge who entered the decision under review may authorize transfer and the substitution of a successor custodian as a party.

3. **(a)** Pending review of a decision failing or refusing to release a prisoner, the prisoner may be detained in the custody from which release is sought or in other appropriate custody or may be enlarged on personal recognizance or bail, as may appear appropriate to the court, Justice, or judge who entered the decision, or to the court of appeals, this Court, or a judge or Justice of either court.

(b) Pending review of a decision ordering release, the prisoner shall be enlarged on personal recognizance or bail, unless the court, Justice, or judge who entered the decision, or the court of appeals, this Court, or a judge or Justice of either court, orders otherwise.

4. An initial order respecting the custody or enlargement of the prisoner, and any recognizance or surety taken, shall continue in effect pending review in the court of appeals and in this Court unless for reasons shown to the court of appeals, this Court, or a judge or Justice of either court, the order is modified or an independent order respecting custody, enlargement, or surety is entered.

Rule 37.   Brief for an *Amicus Curiae*

1. An *amicus curiae* brief that brings to the attention of the Court relevant matter not already brought to its attention by the parties may be of considerable help to the Court. An *amicus curiae* brief that does not serve this purpose burdens the Court, and its filing is not favored. An *amicus curiae* brief may be filed only by an attorney admitted to practice before this Court as provided in Rule 5.

2. **(a)** An *amicus curiae* brief submitted before the Court's consideration of a petition for a writ of certiorari, motion for leave to file a bill of complaint, jurisdictional statement, or petition for an extraordinary writ may be filed if it reflects that written consent of all parties has been provided, or if the Court grants leave to file under subparagraph 2(b) of this Rule. An *amicus curiae* brief in support of a petitioner or appellant shall be filed within 30 days after the case is placed on the docket or a response is called for by the Court, whichever is later, and that time will not be extended. An *amicus curiae* brief in support of a motion of a plaintiff for leave to file a bill of complaint in an original action shall be filed within 60 days after the case is placed on the docket, and that time will not be extended. An *amicus curiae* brief in support of a respondent, an appellee, or a defendant shall be submitted within the time allowed for filing a brief in opposition or a motion to dismiss or affirm. An *amicus curiae* filing a brief under this subparagraph shall ensure that the counsel of record for all parties receive notice of its intention to file an *amicus curiae* brief at least 10 days prior to the due date for the *amicus curiae* brief, unless the *amicus curiae* brief is filed earlier than 10 days before the due date. Only one signatory to any *amicus curiae* brief filed jointly by more than one *amicus curiae* must timely notify the parties of its intent to file that brief. The *amicus curiae* brief shall indicate that counsel of record received timely notice of the intent to file the brief under this Rule and shall specify whether consent was granted, and its cover shall identify the party supported. Only one signatory to an *amicus curiae* brief filed jointly by more than one *amicus curiae* must obtain consent of the parties to file that brief. A petitioner or respondent may submit to the Clerk a letter granting blanket consent to *amicus curiae* briefs, stating that the party consents to the filing of *amicus curiae* briefs in support of either or of neither party. The Clerk will note all notices of blanket consent on the docket.

(b) When a party to the case has withheld consent, a motion for leave to file an *amicus curiae* brief before the Court's consideration of a petition for a writ of certiorari, motion for leave to file a bill of complaint, jurisdictional statement, or petition for an extraordinary writ may be presented to the Court. The motion, prepared as required by Rule 33.1 and as one document with the brief sought to be filed, shall be submitted within the time allowed for filing an *amicus curiae* brief, and shall indicate the party or parties who have withheld consent and state the nature of the movant's interest. Such a motion is not favored.

3.   (a) An *amicus curiae* brief in a case before the Court for oral argument may be filed if it reflects that written consent of all parties has been provided, or if the Court grants leave to file under subparagraph 3(b) of this Rule. The brief shall be submitted within 7 days after the brief for the party supported is filed, or if in support of neither party, within 7 days after the time allowed for filing the petitioner's or appellant's brief. Motions to extend the time for filing an *amicus curiae* brief will not be entertained. The 10-day notice requirement of subparagraph 2(a) of this Rule does not apply to an *amicus curiae* brief in a case before the Court for oral argument. The *amicus curiae* brief shall specify whether consent was granted, and its cover shall identify the party supported or indicate whether it suggests affirmance or reversal. The Clerk will not file a reply brief for an *amicus curiae*, or a brief for an *amicus curiae* in support of, or in opposition to, a petition for rehearing. Only one signatory to an *amicus curiae* brief filed jointly by more than one *amicus curiae* must obtain consent of the parties to file that brief. A petitioner or respondent may submit to the Clerk a letter granting blanket consent to *amicus curiae* briefs, stating that the party consents to the filing of *amicus curiae* briefs in support of either or of neither party. The Clerk will note all notices of blanket consent on the docket.

(b) When a party to a case before the Court for oral argument has withheld consent, a motion for leave to file an *amicus curiae* brief may be presented to the Court. The motion, prepared as required by Rule 33.1 and as one document with the brief sought to be filed, shall be submitted within the time allowed for filing an *amicus curiae* brief, and shall indicate the party or parties who have withheld consent and state the nature of the movant's interest.

4. No motion for leave to file an *amicus curiae* brief is necessary if the brief is presented on behalf of the United States by the Solicitor General; on behalf of any agency of the United States allowed by law to appear before this Court when submitted by the agency's authorized legal representative; on behalf of a State, Commonwealth, Territory, or Possession when submitted by its Attorney General; or on behalf of a city, county, town, or similar entity when submitted by its authorized law officer.

5. A brief or motion filed under this Rule shall be accompanied by proof of service as required by Rule 29, and shall comply with the applicable provisions of Rules 21, 24, and 33.1 (except that it suffices to set out in the brief the interest of the *amicus curiae*, the summary of the argument, the argument, and the conclusion). A motion for leave to file may not exceed 1,500 words. A party served with the motion may file an objection thereto, stating concisely the reasons for withholding consent; the objection shall be prepared as required by Rule 33.2.

6. Except for briefs presented on behalf of *amicus curiae* listed in Rule 37.4, a brief filed under this Rule shall indicate whether counsel for a party authored the brief in whole or in part and whether such counsel or a party made a monetary contribution intended to fund the preparation or submission of the brief, and shall identify every person other than the *amicus curiae*, its members, or its counsel, who made such a monetary contribution. The disclosure shall be made in the first footnote on the first page of text.

(As amended July 17, 2007, eff. Oct. 1, 2007; Jan. 12, 2010, eff. Feb. 16, 2010; Apr. 19, 2013, eff. July 1, 2013; Sept. 27, 2017, eff. Nov. 13, 2017.)

Rule 38. Fees

Under 28 U.S.C. § 1911, the fees charged by the Clerk are:

(a) for docketing a case on a petition for a writ of certiorari or on appeal or for docketing any other proceeding, except a certified question or a motion to docket and dismiss an appeal under Rule 18.5, $300;

(b) for filing a petition for rehearing or a motion for leave to file a petition for rehearing, $200;

(c) for reproducing and certifying any record or paper, $1 per page; and for comparing with the original thereof any photographic reproduction of any record or paper, when furnished by the person requesting its certification, $.50 per page;

(d) for a certificate bearing the seal of the Court, $10; and

(e) for a check paid to the Court, Clerk, or Marshal that is returned for lack of funds, $35.

Rule 39. Proceedings *In Forma Pauperis*

1. A party seeking to proceed *in forma pauperis* shall file a motion for leave to do so, together with the party's notarized affidavit or declaration (in compliance with 28 U.S.C. § 1746) in the form prescribed by the Federal Rules of Appellate Procedure, Form 4. The motion shall state whether leave to proceed *in forma pauperis* was sought in any other court and, if so, whether leave was granted. If the court below appointed counsel for an indigent party, no affidavit or declaration is required, but the motion shall cite the provision of law under which counsel was appointed, or a copy of the order of appointment shall be appended to the motion.

2. If leave to proceed *in forma pauperis* is sought for the purpose of filing a document, the motion, and an affidavit or declaration if required, shall be filed together with that document and shall comply in every respect with Rule 21. As provided in that Rule, it suffices to file an original and 10 copies, unless the party is an inmate confined in an institution and is not represented by counsel, in which case the original, alone, suffices. A copy of the motion, and affidavit or declaration if required, shall precede and be attached to each copy of the accompanying document.

3. Except when these Rules expressly provide that a document shall be prepared as required by Rule 33.1, every document presented by a party proceeding under this Rule shall be prepared as required by Rule 33.2 (unless such preparation is impossible). Every document shall be legible. While making due allowance for any case presented under this Rule by a person appearing *pro se*, the Clerk will not file any document if it does not comply with the substance of these Rules or is jurisdictionally out of time.

4. When the documents required by paragraphs 1 and 2 of this Rule are presented to the Clerk, accompanied by proof of service as required by Rule 29, they will be placed on the docket without the payment of a docket fee or any other fee.

5. The respondent or appellee in a case filed *in forma pauperis* shall respond in the same manner and within the same time as in any other case of the same nature, except that the filing of an original and 10 copies of a response prepared as required by Rule 33.2, with proof of service as required by Rule 29, suffices. The respondent or appellee may challenge the grounds for the motion for leave to proceed *in forma pauperis* in a separate document or in the response itself.

6. Whenever the Court appoints counsel for an indigent party in a case set for oral argument, the briefs on the merits submitted by that counsel, unless otherwise requested, shall be prepared under the Clerk's supervision. The Clerk also will reimburse appointed counsel for any necessary travel expenses to Washington, D.C., and return in connection with the argument.

7. In a case in which certiorari has been granted, probable jurisdiction noted, or consideration of jurisdiction postponed, this Court may appoint counsel to represent a party financially unable to afford an attorney to the extent authorized by the Criminal Justice Act of 1964, 18 U.S.C. § 3006A, or by any other applicable federal statute.

    8.   If satisfied that a petition for a writ of certiorari, jurisdictional statement, or petition for an extraordinary writ is frivolous or malicious, the Court may deny leave to proceed *in forma pauperis.*

(As amended Jan. 27, 2003, eff. May 1, 2003; Apr. 19, 2013, eff. July 1, 2013.)

Rule 40.   Veterans, Seamen, and Military Cases

    1.   A veteran suing under any provision of law exempting veterans from the payment of fees or court costs, may proceed without prepayment of fees or costs or furnishing security therefor and may file a motion for leave to proceed on papers prepared as required by Rule 33.2. The motion shall ask leave to proceed as a veteran and be accompanied by an affidavit or declaration setting out the moving party's veteran status. A copy of the motion shall precede and be attached to each copy of the petition for a writ of certiorari or other substantive document filed by the veteran.

    2.   A seaman suing under 28 U.S.C. § 1916 may proceed without prepayment of fees or costs or furnishing security therefor and may file a motion for leave to proceed on papers prepared as required by Rule 33.2. The motion shall ask leave to proceed as a seaman and be accompanied by an affidavit or declaration setting out the moving party's seaman status. A copy of the motion shall precede and be attached to each copy of the petition for a writ of certiorari or other substantive document filed by the seaman.

    3.   An accused person petitioning for a writ of certiorari to review a decision of the United States Court of Appeals for the Armed Forces under 28 U.S.C. § 1259 may proceed without prepayment of fees or costs or furnishing security therefor and without filing an affidavit of indigency, but is not entitled to proceed on papers prepared as required by Rule 33.2, except as authorized by the Court on separate motion under Rule 39.

(As amended July 17, 2007, eff. Oct. 1, 2007.)

PART VIII. DISPOSITION OF CASES

Rule 41.   Opinions of the Court

    Opinions of the Court will be released by the Clerk immediately upon their announcement from the bench, or as the Court otherwise directs. Thereafter, the Clerk will cause the opinions to be issued in slip form, and the Reporter of Decisions will prepare them for publication in the preliminary prints and bound volumes of the United States Reports.

Rule 42.   Interest and Damages

    1.   If a judgment for money in a civil case is affirmed, any interest allowed by law is payable from the date the judgment under review was entered. If a judgment is modified or reversed with a direction that a judgment for money be entered below, the courts below may award interest to the extent permitted by law. Interest in cases arising in a state court is allowed at the same rate that similar judgments bear interest in the courts of the State in which judgment is directed to be entered. Interest in cases arising in a court of the United States is allowed at the interest rate authorized by law.

    2.   When a petition for a writ of certiorari, an appeal, or an application for other relief is frivolous, the Court may award the respondent or appellee just damages, and single or double costs under Rule 43. Damages or costs may be awarded against the petitioner, appellant, or applicant, against the party's counsel, or against both party and counsel.

(As amended Jan. 12, 2010, eff. Feb. 16, 2010.)

Rule 43.   Costs

1.   If the Court affirms a judgment, the petitioner or appellant shall pay costs unless the Court otherwise orders.

2.   If the Court reverses or vacates a judgment, the respondent or appellee shall pay costs unless the Court otherwise orders.

3.   The Clerk's fees and the cost of printing the joint appendix are the only taxable items in this Court. The cost of the transcript of the record from the court below is also a taxable item, but shall be taxable in that court as costs in the case. The expenses of printing briefs, motions, petitions, or jurisdictional statements are not taxable.

4.   In a case involving a certified question, costs are equally divided unless the Court otherwise orders, except that if the Court decides the whole matter in controversy, as permitted by Rule 19.2, costs are allowed as provided in paragraphs 1 and 2 of this Rule.

5.   To the extent permitted by 28 U.S.C. § 2412, costs under this Rule are allowed for or against the United States or an officer or agent thereof, unless expressly waived or unless the Court otherwise orders.

6.   When costs are allowed in this Court, the Clerk will insert an itemization of the costs in the body of the mandate or judgment sent to the court below. The prevailing side may not submit a bill of costs.

7.   In extraordinary circumstances the Court may adjudge double costs.

Rule 44.   Rehearing

1.   Any petition for the rehearing of any judgment or decision of the Court on the merits shall be filed within 25 days after entry of the judgment or decision, unless the Court or a Justice shortens or extends the time. The petitioner shall file 40 copies of the rehearing petition and shall pay the filing fee prescribed by Rule 38(b), except that a petitioner proceeding in forma pauperis under Rule 39, including an inmate of an institution, shall file the number of copies required for a petition by such a person under Rule 12.2. The petition shall state its grounds briefly and distinctly and shall be served as required by Rule 29. The petition shall be presented together with certification of counsel (or of a party unrepresented by counsel) that it is presented in good faith and not for delay; one copy of the certificate shall bear the signature of counsel (or of a party unrepresented by counsel). A copy of the certificate shall follow and be attached to each copy of the petition. A petition for rehearing is not subject to oral argument and will not be granted except by a majority of the Court, at the instance of a Justice who concurred in the judgment or decision.

2.   Any petition for the rehearing of an order denying a petition for a writ of certiorari or extraordinary writ shall be filed within 25 days after the date of the order of denial and shall comply with all the form and filing requirements of paragraph 1 of this Rule, including the payment of the filing fee if required, but its grounds shall be limited to intervening circumstances of a substantial or controlling effect or to other substantial grounds not previously presented. The time for filing a petition for the rehearing of an order denying a petition for a writ of certiorari or extraordinary writ will not be extended. The petition shall be presented together with certification of counsel (or of a party unrepresented by counsel) that it is restricted to the grounds specified in this paragraph and that it is presented in good faith and not for delay; one copy of the certificate shall bear the signature of counsel (or of a party unrepresented by counsel). The certificate shall be bound with each copy of the petition. The Clerk will not file a petition without a certificate. The petition is not subject to oral argument.

3.   The Clerk will not file any response to a petition for rehearing unless the Court requests a response. In the absence of extraordinary circumstances, the Court will not grant a petition for rehearing without first requesting a response.

4.   The Clerk will not file consecutive petitions and petitions that are out of time under this Rule.

5. The Clerk will not file any brief for an *amicus curiae* in support of, or in opposition to, a petition for rehearing.

6. If the Clerk determines that a petition for rehearing submitted timely and in good faith is in a form that does not comply with this Rule or with Rule 33 or Rule 34, the Clerk will return it with a letter indicating the deficiency. A corrected petition for rehearing submitted in accordance with Rule 29.2 no more than 15 days after the date of the Clerk's letter will be deemed timely.

(As amended Jan. 11, 1999, eff. May 3, 1999; Jan. 27, 2003, eff. May 1, 2003; July 17, 2007, eff. Oct. 1, 2007; Apr. 19, 2013, eff. July 1, 2013.)

Rule 45.   Process; Mandates

1. All process of this Court issues in the name of the President of the United States.

2. In a case on review from a state court, the mandate issues 25 days after entry of the judgment, unless the Court or a Justice shortens or extends the time, or unless the parties stipulate that it issue sooner. The filing of a petition for rehearing stays the mandate until disposition of the petition, unless the Court orders otherwise. If the petition is denied, the mandate issues forthwith.

3. In a case on review from any court of the United States, as defined by 28 U.S.C. § 451, a formal mandate does not issue unless specially directed; instead, the Clerk of this Court will send the clerk of the lower court a copy of the opinion or order of this Court and a certified copy of the judgment. The certified copy of the judgment, prepared and signed by this Court's Clerk, will provide for costs if any are awarded. In all other respects, the provisions of paragraph 2 of this Rule apply.

Rule 46.   Dismissing Cases

1. At any stage of the proceedings, whenever all parties file with the Clerk an agreement in writing that a case be dismissed, specifying the terms for payment of costs, and pay to the Clerk any fees then due, the Clerk, without further reference to the Court, will enter an order of dismissal.

2. (a) A petitioner or appellant may file a motion to dismiss the case, with proof of service as required by Rule 29, tendering to the Clerk any fees due and costs payable. No more than 15 days after service thereof, an adverse party may file an objection, limited to the amount of damages and costs in this Court alleged to be payable or to showing that the moving party does not represent all petitioners or appellants. The Clerk will not file any objection not so limited.

(b) When the objection asserts that the moving party does not represent all the petitioners or appellants, the party moving for dismissal may file a reply within 10 days, after which time the matter will be submitted to the Court for its determination.

(c) If no objection is filed—or if upon objection going only to the amount of damages and costs in this Court, the party moving for dismissal tenders the additional damages and costs in full within 10 days of the demand therefor—the Clerk, without further reference to the Court, will enter an order of dismissal. If, after objection as to the amount of damages and costs in this Court, the moving party does not respond by a tender within 10 days, the Clerk will report the matter to the Court for its determination.

3. No mandate or other process will issue on a dismissal under this Rule without an order of the Court.

PART IX. DEFINITIONS AND EFFECTIVE DATE

Rule 47.   Reference to "State Court" and "State Law"

The term "state court," when used in these Rules, includes the District of Columbia Court of Appeals, the Supreme Court of the Commonwealth of Puerto Rico, the courts of the Northern Mariana Islands, the local courts of Guam, and the Supreme Court of the Virgin Islands. References in these Rules to the statutes of a State include the statutes of the District of Columbia, the Commonwealth of

Puerto Rico, the Commonwealth of the Northern Mariana Islands, the Territory of Guam, and the Territory of the Virgin Islands.

(As amended Mar. 14, 2005, eff. May 2, 2005; Apr. 19, 2013, eff. July 1, 2013.)

Rule 48.   Effective Date of Rules

1.   These Rules, adopted April 18, 2019, will be effective July 1, 2019.

2.   The Rules govern all proceedings after their effective date except that the amendments to Rules 25.3 and 33.1(g) will apply only to cases in which certiorari was granted, or a direct appeal or original action was set for argument, after the effective date.

(As amended July 17, 2007, eff. Oct. 1, 2007; Jan. 12, 2010, eff. Feb. 16, 2010; Apr. 19, 2013, eff. July 1, 2013; Sept. 27, 2017, eff. Nov. 13, 2017; Apr. 18, 2019, eff. July 1, 2019.)

ELECTRONIC FILING

Guidelines for the Submission of Documents to the Supreme Court's Electronic Filing System

These guidelines govern the submission of documents to the electronic filing system at the Supreme Court of the United States. They are issued pursuant to Supreme Court Rule 29.7, and are effective beginning November 13, 2017.

1.   Electronic Submission Requirement. Filings submitted by parties represented by counsel (with the exception of material addressed in paragraphs 7, 9 and 14 below) must be submitted through the Court's electronic filing system. This requirement is in addition to the existing requirements concerning the paper filing of documents with the Court. This requirement applies to all documents required or permitted to be presented to the Court or a Justice, unless otherwise directed by Court Rule, these Guidelines, or other communication from the Clerk's Office. Documents should be submitted through the electronic filing system contemporaneously with their filing pursuant to Rule 29.2, *i.e.*, at or near the time they are delivered to the Court, placed in the mail, delivered to a third-party carrier, etc.

Only the following types of letters to the Court should be submitted through the electronic filing system: (1) motions for an extension of time under Rule 30.4, and responses thereto; (2) notices under Rule 12.6 of a petitioner's view that a party below no longer has an interest in the outcome of a petition, and responses thereto; (3) amendments to corporate disclosure statements or party name changes; (4) substitutions of public officers under Rule 35.3; (5) renewed applications under Rule 22.4; (6) waivers of the 14-day waiting period under Rule 15.5; (7) blanket consents to the filing of *amicus* briefs; and (8) letters that are submitted in response to a specific request from the Court. Any other letters or correspondence to the Court should be submitted in paper form only.

2.   Registration. Before submitting documents through the electronic filing system, attorneys must register at https://file.supremecourt.gov. Only members of the Supreme Court Bar and attorneys appointed for a particular case under the federal Criminal Justice Act are eligible to register. As part of the registration process, an attorney will establish a username and password that will enable the attorney to submit documents through the system. Users must protect the security of their username and password, and must notify the Clerk's Office immediately upon learning that either has been compromised. Users also have a responsibility to keep contact information up-to-date; changes to contact information can be made through the "My Account" link on the electronic filing system home page.

3.   Notice of Appearance. Attorneys are required to enter a notice of appearance in a case before submitting filings on behalf of a party or *amicus curiae* in that case. The submission of a case-initiating document (e.g., a petition for a writ of certiorari, a jurisdictional statement, a petition for an extraordinary writ, or an application not connected to an existing case) will serve as a notice of appearance for the filer. But a filer seeking to submit any other filings in a case will be required to enter a notice of appearance in that case. The notice of appearance is created and submitted entirely though the system itself; no separate paper document need be submitted, and no PDF need be uploaded. While it is permissible for multiple attorneys to submit notices of appearance on behalf of the same party, the requirement that a party have a single counsel of record remains in effect. If an attorney no longer represents a party in this Court, the attorney should submit a withdrawal of appearance through the system. This withdrawal will also be entirely electronic; no paper document need be submitted, and no PDF need be uploaded.

4.   Format of Documents. Documents submitted through the electronic filing system should be in the PDF/A format. Where possible, the electronic file should be created from a word processing document and should be text searchable. Items included in an appendix to a filing may be scanned if a word-processing document is not available. A document submitted through the electronic filing system may contain hyperlinks to another part of the same document, or to an external source cited in the document.

5.   Maximum Size of Documents. The maximum size of any single computer file that can be uploaded to the electronic filing system is 100MB. Documents larger than 100MB should be separated into multiple parts to allow each part to be under this limit.

6.   Viruses and Malware. Before submitting any document through the electronic filing system, the filer should ensure that the document has been scanned for viruses and malware. The electronic filing system will also perform a scan for viruses and malware, and it will not accept a filing until the scan has determined that the entire document does not pose a risk of infection for the system. In most instances, the scan should be completed within 3–5 minutes of the time that a document has been uploaded. (Note that the "Summary" page for a filing will update automatically to reflect when the scan has been completed.)

7.   Documents Containing Sealed Material. Documents containing material that is under seal, including documents filed under seal in lower courts and motions to file documents under seal in this Court, should not be submitted through the electronic filing system. Those documents (including redacted versions for the public record) should be submitted only in paper form. Such documents also should not be served upon other parties electronically. Filers are admonished to pay strict attention to the prohibition, since documents submitted through the electronic filing system may be posted publicly before personal review by Clerk's Office staff.

8.   Redaction of Personal Identifying Information. Personal identifying information contained in filings must be redacted in keeping with the standards set forth in Rule 34.6. No motion is required to make redactions to conform with this rule. Nothing in the rule precludes a party from filing a motion to redact additional information in appropriate circumstances. The responsibility to redact this information rests with counsel and the parties.

9.   Cases Governed by Fed. R. Civ. P. 5.2(c). In cases governed below by Federal Rule of Civil Procedure 5.2(c), including immigration cases addressed in Federal Rule of Criminal Procedure 49.1(c), filings by the parties should not be submitted through the electronic filing system. *A cover letter provided along with the petition for a writ of certiorari, application for an extension of time to file a petition for a writ of certiorari, or other case-initiating document should clearly state that the case was governed by Rule 5.2(c).*

10.   Posting of Documents. Electronic versions of all documents filed with the Court (except those containing sealed material or otherwise exempt from electronic posting) will be made available to the public without charge on the Supreme Court's website at http://www.supremecourt.gov.

(a)   Filings that initiate a new case at the Supreme Court will be posted on the Court's website only after the Clerk's Office has received and reviewed the paper version of the filing, determined that it should be accepted for filing, and assigned a case number.

(b)   Subsequent filings from represented parties that are submitted through the electronic filing system will be posted upon electronic submission to the system. Such filings will initially be noted on the docket as "Submitted." Once the Clerk's Office has received and reviewed the paper version of the document and determined that it should be accepted for filing, the docket will reflect that the document has been "Filed." If a document is not accepted for filing, the docket entry will reflect that it is "Not Accepted for Filing," and an electronic version of the document will no longer be accessible.

(c) Paper filings from parties not represented by counsel will be scanned by the Clerk's Office and posted on the Court's website once the Clerk's Office has reviewed the filing and determined that it should be accepted for filing

11. Service and Notification of Case Activity. Registered users who have entered an appearance in a given case will receive automated email notification of all action in that case, including filings by other parties. This notification does not constitute official service, and parties remain obligated to effect formal service as outlined in the Rules of the Court. The system will also have the ability to provide notification of case activity to email addresses of attorneys and other legal professionals actually working on the case.

12. Changes to Filings. Once a document is submitted through the electronic filing system, the filer will no longer have the ability to withdraw the electronic filing or make changes to it through the system. In the event that a filer needs to make a change to the document that was submitted, the filer should contact the Clerk's Office.

13. Filing Fees. Filers submitting through the electronic filing system will continue to pay filing fees, where applicable, by check. If a fee is required, the filing will not be docketed until the fee is received.

14. Supreme Court Bar Matters. Documents relating to membership in the Supreme Court Bar, including responses to rules to show cause why a member of the Court's Bar should not be disbarred, should not be submitted through the electronic filing system. Such documents should be submitted only on paper.

15. Technical Problems. A filer who is unable to submit documents through the system due to technical problems can contact the Clerk's Office for assistance at efilingsupport@supremecourt.gov or 202-479-5660. Clerk's Office personnel will be available to respond to telephone inquiries between 9:00 am and 5:00 pm on days that the Clerk's Office is open under Rule 1.3. In the event that a technical problem is discovered after working hours and the deadline to file is before the Clerk's Office reopens, the filing should be emailed to other parties and to efilingsupport@supremecourt.gov. The inability to submit a document through the electronic filing system due to technical problems does not affect the timeliness of the filing, but the Clerk's Office generally will not docket filings from attorneys until they are submitted through the electronic filing system.

Updated: November 20, 2017

TITLE 28, U.S. CODE,
JUDICIARY AND JUDICIAL PROCEDURE
(SELECTED PROVISIONS)

Current through Pub.L. No. 116–139, enacted April 24, 2020

CONSTITUTIONAL PROVISIONS

The Constitution of the United States, Article 3, § 1, provides that: "The judicial Power of the United States, shall be vested in one supreme Court, and in such inferior Courts as the Congress may from time to time ordain and establish. The Judges, both of the supreme and inferior Courts, shall hold their Offices during good Behaviour, and shall, at stated Times, receive for their Services, a Compensation, which shall not be diminished during their Continuance in Office."

Article 2, § 2, authorizes the President of the United States to nominate and, by and with the advice and consent of the senate, to appoint judges of the supreme court, and all other officers of the United States, whose appointments are not "herein" otherwise provided for, and which shall be established by law.

Section 2 of Article 3 provides as follows: "The judicial Power shall extend to all Cases, in Law and Equity, arising under this Constitution, the Laws of the United States, and Treaties made, or which shall be made, under their Authority;—to all Cases affecting Ambassadors, other public Ministers and Consuls;—to all Cases of admiralty and maritime Jurisdiction;—to Controversies to which the United States shall be a Party;—to Controversies between two or more States;—between a State and Citizens of another State;—between Citizens of different States,—between Citizens of the same State claiming Lands under Grants of different States, and between a State, or the Citizens thereof, and foreign States, Citizens or Subjects.

"In all Cases affecting Ambassadors, other public Ministers and Consuls, and those in which a State shall be Party, the supreme Court shall have original Jurisdiction. In all the other Cases before mentioned, the supreme Court shall have appellate Jurisdiction, both as to Law and Fact, with such Exceptions, and under such Regulations as the Congress shall make."

Section 8 of Article 1 authorizes the Congress "To constitute Tribunals inferior to the Supreme Court".

Amendment 7 provides that: "In Suits at common law, where the value in controversy shall exceed twenty dollars, the right of trial by jury shall be preserved, and no fact tried by a jury, shall be otherwise reexamined in any Court of the United States, than according to the rules of the common law."

Under Amendment 11, the "Judicial power of the United States shall not be construed to extend to any suit in law or equity, commenced or prosecuted against one of the United States by Citizens of another State, or by Citizens or Subjects of any Foreign State."

HISTORICAL AND STATUTORY NOTES

Effective and Applicability Provisions

Section 38 of Act June 25, 1948, c. 646, 62 Stat. 992, provided that: "The provisions of this Act shall take effect on Sept. 1, 1948."

Separability of Provisions

Section 34 of Act June 25, 1948, c. 646, 62 Stat. 991, provided that: "If any part of Title 28, Judiciary and Judicial Procedure, as set out in section 1 of this Act, shall be held invalid, the remainder shall not be affected thereby."

Enactment into Law; Citation

Section 1 of Act June 25, 1948, c. 646, 62 Stat. 869, provided in part: "That title 28 of the United States Code, entitled 'Judicial Code and Judiciary' is hereby revised, codified, and enacted into law, and may be cited as 'Title 28, United States Code, section ___.'"

ORGANIZATION OF COURTS

Miscellaneous Provisions

Sections 2 to 32 of Act June 25, 1948, c. 646, 62 Stat. 985 to 991 contained certain executing provisions and conforming amendments to sections in other titles of the United States Code. For text of sections 2 to 32, see "Act June 25, 1948, c. 646, §§ 2 to 39, 62 Stat. 985 to 991," set out following the last section of Title 28.

Section 35 of Act June 25, 1948, c. 646, 62 Stat. 991, was not classified to the United States Code. For text of section 35, see "Act June 25, 1948, c. 646, §§ 2 to 39, 62 Stat. 985 to 991" set out following the last section of Title 28.

Sections 36 and 37 of Act June 25, 1948, c. 646, 62 Stat. 991, 992, contained certain executing provisions and conforming amendments to sections in other titles of the United States Code. For text of sections 36 and 37, see "Act June 25, 1948, c. 646, §§ 2 to 39, 62 Stat. 985 to 991", set out following the last section of Title 28.

Legislative Construction

Section 33 of Act June 25, 1948, c. 646, 62 Stat. 991, provided that: "No inference of a legislative construction is to be drawn by reason of the chapter in Title 28, Judiciary and Judicial Procedure, as set out in section 1 of this Act, in which any section is placed, nor by reason of the catchlines used in such title."

Repeals; Rights and Liabilities Saved

Section 39 of Act June 25, 1948, c. 646, 62 Stat. 992, repealed the sections or parts thereof of the Revised Statutes of the United States, Statutes at Large, or the Revised Statutes of the District of Columbia covering provisions codified in this title, but saved any rights or liabilities then existing under said sections or parts thereof.

Writs of Error

Act Jan. 31, 1928, c. 14, § 1, 45 Stat. 54 [section 861a of former Title 28, Judicial Code and Judiciary], provided that: "The writ of error in cases, civil and criminal, is abolished. All relief which heretofore [Jan. 31, 1928] could be obtained by writ of error shall hereafter be obtainable by appeal." This provision was omitted from the 1948 Revised Judicial Code as obsolete, and repealed by Act June 25, 1948, c. 646, § 39, 62 Stat. 992.

R.S. § 1012 as affected by Act Mar. 3, 1911, c. 231, § 291, 36 Stat. 1167 [Section 880 of former Title 28, Judicial Code and Judiciary], provided that appeals from district courts shall be subject to the same rules, regulations, and restrictions as are or may be prescribed in law in cases of writs of error. This provision was repealed by Act June 25, 1948, c. 646, § 39, 62 Stat. 992. Section 2 of Act Jan. 31, 1928, c. 14, 45 Stat. 54, as amended Apr. 26, 1928, c. 440, 45 Stat. 466; June 25, 1948, c. 646, § 23, 62 Stat. 990 [section 861b of former Title 28, Judicial Code and Judiciary], provided that: "All Acts of Congress referring to writs of error shall be construed as amended to the extent necessary to substitute appeal for writ of error."

Title 28 as Continuation of Existing Law; Change of Name of Circuit Courts of Appeals

Section 2(b) of Act June 25, 1948, c. 646, 62 Stat. 985, provided that: "The provisions of Title 28, Judiciary and Judicial Procedure, of the United States Code, set out in section 1 of this Act, with respect to the organization of each of the several courts therein provided for and of the Administrative Office of the United States Courts, shall be construed as continuations of existing law, and the tenure of the judges, officers, and employees thereof and of the United States attorneys and marshals and their deputies and assistants, in office on the effective date of this Act [Sept. 1, 1948], shall not be affected by its enactment, but each of them shall continue to serve in the same capacity under the appropriate provisions of title 28, as set out in section 1 of this Act, pursuant to his prior appointment: *Provided, however,* That each circuit court of appeals shall, as in said title 28 set out, hereafter be known as a United States court of appeals. No loss of rights, interruption of jurisdiction, or prejudice to matters pending in any of such courts on the effective date of this Act shall result from its enactment."

PART I—ORGANIZATION OF COURTS

HISTORICAL AND STATUTORY NOTES

Codifications

Analysis of chapters comprising Part I was amended by Pub.L. 95–598, Title II, § 201(b), Nov. 6, 1978, 92 Stat. 2660, effective June 28, 1984, pursuant to Pub.L. 95–598, Title IV, § 402(b), Nov. 6, 1978, 92 Stat. 2682, as amended by Pub.L. 98–249, § 1(a), Mar. 31, 1984, 98 Stat. 116; Pub.L. 98–271, § 1(a), Apr. 30, 1984, 98 Stat. 163; Pub.L. 98–299, § 1(a), May 25, 1984, 98 Stat. 214; Pub.L. 98–325, § 1(a), June 20, 1984, 98 Stat. 268, by adding:

"6. Bankruptcy courts ....151".

Section 402(b) of Pub.L. 95–598 was amended by section 113 of Pub.L. 98–353, Title I, July 10, 1984, 98 Stat. 343, by substituting "shall not be effective" for "shall take effect on June 28, 1984", thereby eliminating the amendment by section 201(b) of Pub.L. 95–598, effective June 27, 1984, pursuant to section 122(c) of Pub.L. 98–353, set out as an Effective Date note under section 151 of the title.

Section 121(a) of Pub.L. 98–353 directed that section 402(b) of Pub.L. 95–598 be amended by substituting "the date of enactment of the Bankruptcy Amendments and Federal Judgeship Act of 1984 [i.e. July 10, 1984]" for "June 28, 1984". This amendment was not executed in view of the prior amendment to section 402(b) of Pub.L. 95–598 by section 113 of Pub.L. 98–353.

Change of Name

References to United States Claims Court deemed to refer to United States Court of Federal Claims and references to Claims Court deemed to refer to Court of Federal Claims, see section 902(b) of Pub.L. 102–572, set out as a note under section 171 of Title

28, Judiciary and Judicial Procedure.

CHAPTER 1—SUPREME COURT

§ 1.   Number of justices; quorum

The Supreme Court of the United States shall consist of a Chief Justice of the United States and eight associate justices, any six of whom shall constitute a quorum.

(June 25, 1948, c. 646, 62 Stat. 869.)

§ 2.   Terms of court

The Supreme Court shall hold at the seat of government a term of court commencing on the first Monday in October of each year and may hold such adjourned or special terms as may be necessary.

(June 25, 1948, c. 646, 62 Stat. 869.)

§ 3.   Vacancy in office of Chief Justice; disability

Whenever the Chief Justice is unable to perform the duties of his office or the office is vacant, his powers and duties shall devolve upon the associate justice next in precedence who is able to act, until such disability is removed or another Chief Justice is appointed and duly qualified.

(June 25, 1948, c. 646, 62 Stat. 869.)

§ 4.   Precedence of associate justices

Associate justices shall have precedence according to the seniority of their commissions. Justices whose commissions bear the same date shall have precedence according to seniority in age.

(June 25, 1948, c. 646, 62 Stat. 869.)

§ 5.   Salaries of justices

The Chief Justice and each associate justice shall each receive a salary at annual rates determined under section 225 of the Federal Salary Act of 1967 (2 U.S.C. 351–361), as adjusted by section 461 of this title.

(June 25, 1948, c. 646, 62 Stat. 870; Mar. 2, 1955, c. 9, § 1(a), 69 Stat. 9; Aug. 14, 1964, Pub.L. 88–426, Title IV, § 403(a), 78 Stat. 434; Aug. 9, 1975, Pub.L. 94–82, Title II, § 205(b)(1), 89 Stat. 422.)

§ 6.   Records of former court of appeals

The records and proceedings of the court of appeals, appointed previous to the adoption of the Constitution, shall be kept until deposited with the National Archives of the United States in the office of the clerk of the Supreme Court, who shall furnish copies thereof to any person requiring and paying for them, in the manner provided by law for giving copies of the records and proceedings of the Supreme Court. Such copies shall have the same faith and credit as proceedings of the Supreme Court.

(June 25, 1948, c. 646, 62 Stat. 870; Oct. 25, 1951, c. 562, § 4(7), 65 Stat. 640.)

CHAPTER 3—COURTS OF APPEALS

§ 41.   Number and composition of circuits

The thirteen judicial circuits of the United States are constituted as follows:

Circuits	Composition
District of Columbia	District of Columbia.
First	Maine, Massachusetts, New Hampshire, Puerto Rico, Rhode Island.
Second	Connecticut, New York, Vermont.
Third	Delaware, New Jersey, Pennsylvania, Virgin Islands.
Fourth	Maryland, North Carolina, South Carolina, Virginia, West Virginia.

Circuit	States
Fifth	District of the Canal Zone, Louisiana, Mississippi, Texas.
Sixth	Kentucky, Michigan, Ohio, Tennessee.
Seventh	Illinois, Indiana, Wisconsin.
Eighth	Arkansas, Iowa, Minnesota, Missouri, Nebraska, North Dakota, South Dakota.
Ninth	Alaska, Arizona, California, Idaho, Montana, Nevada, Oregon, Washington, Guam, Hawaii.
Tenth	Colorado, Kansas, New Mexico, Oklahoma, Utah, Wyoming.
Eleventh	Alabama, Florida, Georgia.
Federal	All Federal judicial districts.

(June 25, 1948, c. 646, 62 Stat. 870; Oct. 31, 1951, c. 655, § 34, 65 Stat. 723; Oct. 14, 1980, Pub.L. 96–452, § 2, 94 Stat. 1994; Apr. 2, 1982, Pub.L. 97–164, Title I, § 101, 96 Stat. 25.)

§ 42.   Allotment of Supreme Court justices to circuits

The Chief Justice of the United States and the associate justices of the Supreme Court shall from time to time be allotted as circuit justices among the circuits by order of the Supreme Court. The Chief Justice may make such allotments in vacation.

A justice may be assigned to more than one circuit, and two or more justices may be assigned to the same circuit.

(June 25, 1948, c. 646, 62 Stat. 870.)

§ 43.   Creation and composition of courts

(a) There shall be in each circuit a court of appeals, which shall be a court of record, known as the United States Court of Appeals for the circuit.

(b) Each court of appeals shall consist of the circuit judges of the circuit in regular active service. The circuit justice and justices or judges designated or assigned shall be competent to sit as judges of the court.

(June 25, 1948, c. 646, 62 Stat. 870; Nov. 13, 1963, Pub.L. 88–176, § 1(a), 77 Stat. 331.)

§ 44.   Appointment, tenure, residence and salary of circuit judges

(a) The President shall appoint, by and with the advice and consent of the Senate, circuit judges for the several circuits as follows:

Circuits	Number of Judges
District of Columbia	11
First	6
Second	13
Third	14
Fourth	15
Fifth	17
Sixth	16
Seventh	11
Eighth	11
Ninth	29
Tenth	12

(b) Circuit judges shall hold office during good behavior.

(c) Except in the District of Columbia, each circuit judge shall be a resident of the circuit for which appointed at the time of his appointment and thereafter while in active service. While in active service, each circuit judge of the Federal judicial circuit appointed after the effective date of the Federal Courts Improvement Act of 1982, and the chief judge of the Federal judicial circuit, whenever appointed, shall reside within fifty miles of the District of Columbia. In each circuit (other than the Federal judicial circuit) there shall be at least one circuit judge in regular active service appointed from the residents of each state[1] in that circuit.

(d) Each circuit judge shall receive a salary at an annual rate determined under section 225 of the Federal Salary Act of 1967 (2 U.S.C. 351–361), as adjusted by section 461 of this title.

(June 25, 1948, c. 646, 62 Stat. 871; Aug. 3, 1949, c. 387, § 1, 63 Stat. 493; Feb. 10, 1954, c. 6, § 1, 68 Stat. 8; Mar. 2, 1955, c. 9, § 1(b), 69 Stat. 10; May 19, 1961, Pub.L. 87–36, § 1(b), 75 Stat. 80; Aug. 14, 1964, Pub.L. 88–426, Title IV, § 403(b), 78 Stat. 434; Mar. 18, 1966, Pub.L. 89–372, § 1(b), 80 Stat. 75; June 18, 1968, Pub.L. 90–347, § 3, 82 Stat. 184; Aug. 9, 1975, Pub.L. 94–82, Title II, § 205(b)(2), 89 Stat. 422; Oct. 20, 1978, Pub.L. 95–486, § 3(b), 92 Stat. 1632; Oct. 14, 1980, Pub.L. 96–452, § 3, 94 Stat. 1994; Apr. 2, 1982, Pub.L. 97–164, Title I, § 102, 96 Stat. 25; July 10, 1984, Pub.L. 98–353, Title II, § 201(b), 98 Stat. 346; Dec. 1, 1990, Pub.L. 101–650, Title II, § 202(b), 104 Stat. 5099; Dec. 9, 1991, Pub.L. 102–198, § 10(c), 105 Stat. 1626; Nov. 26, 1997, Pub.L. 105–119, Title III, § 307, 111 Stat. 2493; Jan. 7, 2008, Pub.L. 110–177, Title V, § 509(a), 121 Stat. 2543.)

§ 45.　　Chief judges; precedence of judges

(a)(1) The chief judge of the circuit shall be the circuit judge in regular active service who is senior in commission of those judges who—

　　(A) are sixty-four years of age or under;

　　(B) have served for one year or more as a circuit judge; and

　　(C) have not served previously as chief judge.

(2)(A) In any case in which no circuit judge meets the qualifications of paragraph (1), the youngest circuit judge in regular active service who is sixty-five years of age or over and who has served as circuit judge for one year or more shall act as the chief judge.

　　(B) In any case under subparagraph (A) in which there is no circuit judge in regular active service who has served as a circuit judge for one year or more, the circuit judge in regular active service who is senior in commission and who has not served previously as chief judge shall act as the chief judge.

(3)(A) Except as provided in subparagraph (C), the chief judge of the circuit appointed under paragraph (1) shall serve for a term of seven years and shall serve after expiration of such term until another judge is eligible under paragraph (1) to serve as chief judge of the circuit.

　　(B) Except as provided in subparagraph (C), a circuit judge acting as chief judge under subparagraph (A) or (B) of paragraph (2) shall serve until a judge has been appointed who meets the qualifications under paragraph (1).

　　(C) No circuit judge may serve or act as chief judge of the circuit after attaining the age of seventy years unless no other circuit judge is qualified to serve as chief judge of the circuit under paragraph (1) or is qualified to act as chief judge under paragraph (2).

(b) The chief judge shall have precedence and preside at any session of the court which he attends. Other circuit judges of the court in regular active service shall have precedence and preside

---

　　[1]　So in original. Probably should be capitalized.

according to the seniority of their commissions. Judges whose commissions bear the same date shall have precedence according to seniority in age. The circuit justice, however, shall have precedence over all the circuit judges and shall preside at any session which he attends.

(c) If the chief judge desires to be relieved of his duties as chief judge while retaining his active status as circuit judge, he may so certify to the Chief Justice of the United States, and thereafter the chief judge of the circuit shall be such other circuit judge who is qualified to serve or act as chief judge under subsection (a).

(d) If a chief judge is temporarily unable to perform his duties as such, they shall be performed by the circuit judge in active service, present in the circuit and able and qualified to act, who is next in precedence.

(June 25, 1948, c. 646, 62 Stat. 871; Oct. 31, 1951, c. 655, § 35, 65 Stat. 723; Aug. 6, 1958, Pub.L. 85–593, § 1, 72 Stat. 497; Apr. 2, 1982, Pub.L. 97–164, Title II, §§ 201, 204, 96 Stat. 51, 53.)

§ 46. Assignment of judges; panels; hearings; quorum

(a) Circuit judges shall sit on the court and its panels in such order and at such times as the court directs.

(b) In each circuit the court may authorize the hearing and determination of cases and controversies by separate panels, each consisting of three judges, at least a majority of whom shall be judges of that court, unless such judges cannot sit because recused or disqualified, or unless the chief judge of that court certifies that there is an emergency including, but not limited to, the unavailability of a judge of the court because of illness. Such panels shall sit at the times and places and hear the cases and controversies assigned as the court directs. The United States Court of Appeals for the Federal Circuit shall determine by rule a procedure for the rotation of judges from panel to panel to ensure that all of the judges sit on a representative cross section of the cases heard and, notwithstanding the first sentence of this subsection, may determine by rule the number of judges, not less than three, who constitute a panel.

(c) Cases and controversies shall be heard and determined by a court or panel of not more than three judges (except that the United States Court of Appeals for the Federal Circuit may sit in panels of more than three judges if its rules so provide), unless a hearing or rehearing before the court in banc is ordered by a majority of the circuit judges of the circuit who are in regular active service. A court in banc shall consist of all circuit judges in regular active service, or such number of judges as may be prescribed in accordance with section 6 of Public Law 95–486 (92 Stat. 1633), except that any senior circuit judge of the circuit shall be eligible (1) to participate, at his election and upon designation and assignment pursuant to section 294(c) of this title and the rules of the circuit, as a member of an in banc court reviewing a decision of a panel of which such judge was a member, or (2) to continue to participate in the decision of a case or controversy that was heard or reheard by the court in banc at a time when such judge was in regular active service.

(d) A majority of the number of judges authorized to constitute a court or panel thereof, as provided in paragraph (c), shall constitute a quorum.

(June 25, 1948, c. 646, 62 Stat. 871; Nov. 13, 1963, Pub.L. 88–176, § 1(b), 77 Stat. 331; Oct. 20, 1978, Pub.L. 95–486, § 5(a), (b), 92 Stat. 1633; Apr. 2, 1982, Pub.L. 97–164, Title I, § 103, Title II, § 205, 96 Stat. 25, 53; Aug. 6, 1996, Pub.L. 104–175, § 1, 110 Stat. 1556.)

CHIEF CIRCUIT JUDGE (FIFTH CIRCUIT): ORDER
DECLARING AN EMERGENCY UNDER
28 U.S.C. § 46(b)

This court is authorized 17 judges in active service. Today the number of active judges is 14. One of the vacancies has been in existence for two and one-half years. Two nominations have been sent to the Senate for its advice and consent and are pending. In addition, one active judge was recently injured seriously in an automobile accident and will be unavailable to perform his judicial duties for an indefinite period of time needed for his recuperation and rehabilitation. Effectively this places the court's strength at 13 active judges.

As of June 30, 1999, the court's workload is nearly at its historical record, with some 8,325 new filings and 5,430 pending actions.

During the last nine years, the court's filings have increased 65%, but the court has resisted an increase in the number of authorized judgeships, believing that efficiency and economy would thereby be promoted. The result has been an extremely heavy per judge workload even when operating with a full complement of judges. We have now reached the point where we are so far below our authorized strength that the timeliness and quality of our work will be jeopardized if we are unable to enlist the aid of visiting judges in greater numbers.

In sum, the three judicial vacancies, the injury to an active judge and the sustained high level of case filings have created a judicial emergency in the court. Until such time as the injured judge can return to his judicial duties and until the President has nominated and the Congress has advised and consented to the appointment of the number of judges in regular active service provided by law, a judicial emergency exists. This emergency prevents the routine empaneling of three-judge panels consisting of judges at least a majority of whom are judges of this court.

During the continuation of this declared emergency, the hearing and determination of cases and controversies may be conducted by panels of three judges selected without regard to the qualification in 28 U.S.C. § 46(b) that a majority of each panel be composed of judges of this court.

Signed this 28th day of September, 1999.

CAROLYN DINEEN KING
CHIEF JUDGE

Filed: Sept. 28, 1999

CHIEF CIRCUIT JUDGE (FOURTH CIRCUIT): ORDER REGARDING PERFORMANCE OF JUDICIAL DUTIES

Pursuant to the authority set forth in 28 U.S.C. § 46(c) and 28 U.S.C. § 294(c), all senior circuit judges in this circuit are hereby assigned to perform all judicial duties in any case, or in the decision of any matter, such as a motion or any other procedural or administrative matter, which has been properly assigned to them, whether in the ordinary course of business or otherwise. Any senior circuit judge who undertakes the performance of any official duties pursuant to this designation consents to participate (except upon absence from duty station or the like) in the consideration of the same until terminated, including, but not exclusively, participation in in banc consideration of the matter.

ENTERED this 31st day of March, 1993.

SAM J. ERVIN, III
CHIEF CIRCUIT JUDGE

§ 47.   Disqualification of trial judge to hear appeal

No judge shall hear or determine an appeal from the decision of a case or issue tried by him.

(June 25, 1948, c. 646, 62 Stat. 872.)

§ 48.   Terms of court

(a) The courts of appeals shall hold regular sessions at the places listed below, and at such other places within the respective circuit as each court may designate by rule.

Circuits	Places
District of Columbia	Washington.
First	Boston.
Second	New York.
Third	Philadelphia.

Fourth	Richmond, Asheville.
Fifth	New Orleans, Fort Worth, Jackson.
Sixth	Cincinnati.
Seventh	Chicago.
Eighth	St. Louis, Kansas City, Omaha, St. Paul.
Ninth	San Francisco, Los Angeles, Portland, Seattle.
Tenth	Denver, Wichita, Oklahoma City.
Eleventh	Atlanta, Jacksonville, Montgomery.
Federal	District of Columbia, and in any other place listed above as the court by rule directs.

(b) Each court of appeals may hold special sessions at any place within its circuit as the nature of the business may require, and upon such notice as the court orders. The court may transact any business at a special session which it might transact at a regular session.

(c) Any court of appeals may pretermit any regular session of court at any place for insufficient business or other good cause.

(d) The times and places of the sessions of the Court of Appeals for the Federal Circuit shall be prescribed with a view to securing reasonable opportunity to citizens to appear before the court with as little inconvenience and expense to citizens as is practicable.

(e) Each court of appeals may hold special sessions at any place within the United States outside the circuit as the nature of the business may require and upon such notice as the court orders, upon a finding by either the chief judge of the court of appeals (or, if the chief judge is unavailable, the most senior available active judge of the court of appeals) or the judicial council of the circuit that, because of emergency conditions, no location within the circuit is reasonably available where such special sessions could be held. The court may transact any business at a special session outside the circuit which it might transact at a regular session.

(f) If a court of appeals issues an order exercising its authority under subsection (e), the court—

    (1) through the Administrative Office of the United States Courts, shall—

        (A) send notice of such order, including the reasons for the issuance of such order, to the Committee on the Judiciary of the Senate and the Committee on the Judiciary of the House of Representatives; and

        (B) not later than 180 days after the expiration of such court order submit a brief report to the Committee on the Judiciary of the Senate and the Committee on the Judiciary of the House of Representatives describing the impact of such order, including—

            (i) the reasons for the issuance of such order;

            (ii) the duration of such order;

            (iii) the impact of such order on litigants; and

            (iv) the costs to the judiciary resulting from such order; and

    (2) shall provide reasonable notice to the United States Marshals Service before the commencement of any special session held pursuant to such order.

(June 25, 1948, c. 646, 62 Stat. 872; Oct. 31, 1951, c. 655, § 36, 65 Stat. 723; Oct. 14, 1980, Pub.L. 96–452, § 4, 94 Stat. 1994; Apr. 2, 1982, Pub.L. 97–164, Title I, § 104, 96 Stat. 26; Oct. 29, 1992, Pub.L. 102–572, Title V, § 501, 106 Stat. 4512; Sept. 9, 2005, Pub.L. 109–63, § 2(a), 119 Stat. 1993.)

§ 49.   Assignment of judges to division to appoint independent counsels

(a)   Beginning with the two-year period commencing on the date of the enactment of this section, three judges or justices shall be assigned for each successive two-year period to a division of the United States Court of Appeals for the District of Columbia to be the division of the court for the purpose of appointing independent counsels. The Clerk of the United States Court of Appeals for the District of Columbia Circuit shall serve as the clerk of such division of the court and shall provide such services as are needed by such division of the court.

(b)   Except as provided under subsection (f) of this section, assignment to such division of the court shall not be a bar to other judicial assignments during the term of such division.

(c)   In assigning judges or justices to sit on such division of the court, priority shall be given to senior circuit judges and retired justices.

(d)   The Chief Justice of the United States shall designate and assign three circuit court judges or justices, one of whom shall be a judge of the United States Court of Appeals for the District of Columbia, to such division of the court. Not more than one judge or justice or senior or retired judge or justice may be named to such division from a particular court.

(e)   Any vacancy in such division of the court shall be filled only for the remainder of the two-year period in which such vacancy occurs and in the same manner as initial assignments to such division were made.

(f)   Except as otherwise provided in chapter 40 of this title, no member of such division of the court who participated in a function conferred on the division under chapter 40 of this title involving an independent counsel shall be eligible to participate in any judicial proceeding concerning a matter which involves such independent counsel while such independent counsel is serving in that office or which involves the exercise of such independent counsel's official duties, regardless of whether such independent counsel is still serving in that office.

(Added Pub.L. 95–521, Title VI, § 602(a), Oct. 26, 1978, 92 Stat. 1873; amended Pub.L. 97–409, § 2(b)(1), Jan. 3, 1983, 96 Stat. 2039; Pub.L. 99–554, Title I, § 144(g)(3), Oct. 27, 1986, 100 Stat. 3097; Pub.L. 100–191, §§ 4, 5(a), Dec. 15, 1987, 101 Stat. 1307.)

CHAPTER 5—DISTRICT COURTS

§ 81.   Alabama

Alabama is divided into three judicial districts to be known as the Northern, Middle, and Southern Districts of Alabama.

Northern District

(a)　The Northern District comprises seven divisions.

(1)　The Northwestern Division comprises the counties of Colbert, Franklin, and Lauderdale.

Court for the Northwestern Division shall be held at Florence.

(2)　The Northeastern Division comprises the counties of Cullman, Jackson, Lawrence, Limestone, Madison, and Morgan.

Court for the Northeastern Division shall be held at Huntsville and Decatur.

(3)　The Southern Division comprises the counties of Blount, Jefferson, and Shelby.

Court for the Southern Division shall be held at Birmingham.

(4)　The Eastern Division comprises the counties of Calhoun, Clay, Cleburne, and Talladega.

Court for the Eastern Division shall be held at Anniston.

(5)　The Western Division comprises the counties of Bibb, Greene, Pickens, Sumter, and Tuscaloosa.

Court for the Western Division shall be held at Tuscaloosa.

(6)　The Middle Division comprises the counties of Cherokee, De Kalb, Etowah, Marshall, and Saint Clair.

Court for the Middle Division shall be held at Gadsden.

(7)　The Jasper Division comprises the counties of Fayette, Lamar, Marion, Walker, and Winston.

Court for the Jasper Division shall be held at Jasper.

Middle District

(b)　The Middle District comprises three divisions.

(1)　The Northern Division comprises the counties of Autauga, Barbour, Bullock, Butler, Chilton, Coosa, Covington, Crenshaw, Elmore, Lowndes, Montgomery, and Pike.

Court for the Northern Division shall be held at Montgomery.

(2)　The Southern Division comprises the counties of Coffee, Dale, Geneva, Henry, and Houston.

Court for the Southern Division shall be held at Dothan.

(3)　The Eastern Division comprises the counties of Chambers, Lee, Macon, Randolph, Russell, and Tallapoosa.

Court for the Eastern Division shall be held at Opelika.

Southern District

(c)　The Southern District comprises two divisions.

(1)　The Northern Division comprises the counties of Dallas, Hale, Marengo, Perry, and Wilcox.

Court for the Northern Division shall be held at Selma.

(2)　The Southern Division comprises the counties of Baldwin, Choctaw, Clarke, Conecuh, Escambia, Mobile, Monroe, and Washington.

Court for the Southern Division shall be held at Mobile.

(June 25, 1948, c. 646, 62 Stat. 873; May 19, 1961, Pub.L. 87–36, § 3(a), 75 Stat. 83.)

§ 81A. Alaska

Alaska constitutes one judicial district.

Court shall be held at Anchorage, Fairbanks, Juneau, Ketchikan, and Nome.

(Added Pub.L. 85–508, § 12(b), July 7, 1958, 72 Stat. 348; amended Pub.L. 86–70, § 23(b), June 25, 1959, 73 Stat. 147.)

§ 82. Arizona

Arizona constitutes one judicial district.

Court shall be held at Flagstaff, Globe, Phoenix, Prescott, Tucson, and Yuma.

(June 25, 1948, c. 646, 62 Stat. 874; Pub.L. 116–40, § 1, Aug. 9, 2019, 133 Stat. 1063.)

§ 83. Arkansas

Arkansas is divided into two judicial districts to be known as the Eastern and Western Districts of Arkansas.

Eastern District

(a) The Eastern District comprises three divisions.

(1) The Central Division comprises the counties of Cleburne, Cleveland, Conway, Dallas, Drew, Faulkner, Grant, Jefferson, Lincoln, Lonoke, Perry, Pope, Prairie, Pulaski, Saline, Stone, Van Buren, White, and Yell.

Court for the Central Division shall be held at Little Rock.

(2) The Delta Division comprises the counties of Arkansas, Chicot, Crittenden, Desha, Lee, Monroe, Phillips, and St. Francis.

Court for the Delta Division shall be held at Helena.

(3) The Northern Division comprises the counties of Clay, Craighead, Cross, Fulton, Greene, Independence, Izard, Jackson, Lawrence, Mississippi, Poinsett, Randolph, Sharp, and Woodruff.

Court for the Northern Division shall be held at Jonesboro.

Western District

(b) The Western District comprises six divisions.

(1) The Texarkana Division comprises the counties of Hempstead, Howard, Lafayette, Little River, Miller, Nevada, and Sevier.

Court for the Texarkana Division shall be held at Texarkana, and may be held anywhere within the Federal courthouse in Texarkana that is located astride the State line between Texas and Arkansas.

(2) The El Dorado Division comprises the counties of Ashley, Bradley, Calhoun, Columbia, Ouachita, and Union.

Court for the El Dorado Division shall be held at El Dorado.

(3) The Fort Smith Division comprises the counties of Crawford, Franklin, Johnson, Logan, Polk, Scott, and Sebastian.

Court for the Fort Smith Division shall be held at Fort Smith.

(4) The Harrison Division comprises the counties of Baxter, Boone, Carroll, Marion, Newton, and Searcy.

Court for the Harrison Division shall be held at Harrison.

(5) The Fayetteville Division comprises the counties of Benton, Madison, and Washington.

Court for the Fayetteville Division shall be held at Fayetteville.

(6) The Hot Springs Division comprises the counties of Clark, Garland, Hot Springs, Montgomery, and Pike.

Court for the Hot Springs Division shall be held at Hot Springs.

(June 25, 1948, c. 646, 62 Stat. 874; May 19, 1961, Pub.L. 87–36, § 5, 75 Stat. 84; Dec. 10, 2004, Pub.L. 108–455, § 3, 118 Stat. 3628; Pub.L. 116–73, § 2, Nov. 26, 2019, 133 Stat. 1154.)

§ 84.   California

California is divided into four judicial districts to be known as the Northern, Eastern, Central, and Southern Districts of California.

Northern District

(a) The Northern District comprises the counties of Alameda, Contra Costa, Del Norte, Humboldt, Lake, Marin, Mendocino, Monterey, Napa, San Benito, Santa Clara, Santa Cruz, San Francisco, San Mateo, and Sonoma.

> Court for the Northern District shall be held at Eureka, Oakland, San Francisco, and San Jose.

Eastern District

(b) The Eastern District comprises the counties of Alpine, Amador, Butte, Calaveras, Colusa, El Dorado, Fresno, Glenn, Inyo, Kern, Kings, Lassen, Madera, Mariposa, Merced, Modoc, Mono, Nevada, Placer, Plumas, Sacramento, San Joaquin, Shasta, Sierra, Siskiyou, Solano, Stanislaus, Sutter, Tehama, Trinity, Tulare, Tuolumne, Yolo, and Yuba.

> Court for the Eastern District shall be held at Bakersfield, Fresno, Redding, and Sacramento.

Central District

(c) The Central District comprises 3 divisions.

(1) The Eastern Division comprises the counties of Riverside and San Bernardino.

Court for the Eastern Division shall be held at a suitable site in the city of Riverside, the city of San Bernardino, or not more than 5 miles from the boundary of either such city.

(2) The Western Division comprises the counties of Los Angeles, San Luis Obispo, Santa Barbara, and Ventura.

Court for the Western Division shall be held at Los Angeles.

(3) The Southern Division comprises Orange County.

Court for the Southern Division shall be held at Santa Ana.

Southern District

(d) The Southern District comprises the counties of Imperial and San Diego.

Court for the Southern District shall be held at San Diego.

(June 25, 1948, c. 646, 62 Stat. 875; Mar. 18, 1966, Pub.L. 89–372, § 3(a), 80 Stat. 75; Oct. 15, 1980, Pub.L. 96–462, § 2, 94 Stat. 2053; Aug. 26, 1992, Pub.L. 102–357, § 2, 106 Stat. 958; Dec. 16, 2014, Pub. L. 113–235, § 307, 128 Stat. 2130.)

§ 85. Colorado

Colorado constitutes one judicial district.

> Court shall be held at Boulder, Colorado Springs, Denver, Durango, Grand Junction, Montrose, Pueblo, and Sterling.

(June 25, 1948, c. 646, 62 Stat. 875; Nov. 8, 1984, Pub.L. 98–620, Title IV, § 409, 98 Stat. 3362; Dec. 10, 2004, Pub.L. 108–455, § 5, 118 Stat. 3629; Dec. 23, 2004, Pub.L. 108–482, Title III, § 301, 118 Stat. 3918.)

§ 86. Connecticut

Connecticut constitutes one judicial district.

> Court shall be held at Bridgeport, Hartford, New Haven, New London, and Waterbury.

(June 25, 1948, c. 646, 62 Stat. 875; May 19, 1961, Pub.L. 87–36, § 3(b), 75 Stat. 83; Sept. 7, 1966, Pub.L. 89–558, 80 Stat. 705.)

§ 87. Delaware

Delaware constitutes one judicial district.

> Court shall be held at Wilmington.

(June 25, 1948, c. 646, 62 Stat. 875.)

§ 88. District of Columbia

The District of Columbia constitutes one judicial district.

> Court shall be held at Washington.

(June 25, 1948, c. 646, 62 Stat. 875.)

§ 89. Florida

Florida is divided into three judicial districts to be known as the Northern, Middle, and Southern Districts of Florida.

Northern District

(a) The Northern District comprises the counties of Alachua, Bay, Calhoun, Dixie, Escambia, Franklin, Gadsden, Gilchrist, Gulf, Holmes, Jackson, Jefferson, Lafayette, Leon, Levy, Liberty, Madison, Okaloosa, Santa Rosa, Taylor, Wakulla, Walton, and Washington.

> Court for the Northern District shall be held at Gainesville, Marianna, Panama City, Pensacola, and Tallahassee.

Middle District

(b) The Middle District comprises the counties of Baker, Bradford, Brevard, Charlotte, Citrus, Clay, Collier, Columbia, De Soto, Duval, Flagler, Glades, Hamilton, Hardee, Hendry, Hernando, Hillsborough, Lake, Lee, Manatee, Marion, Nassau, Orange, Osceola, Pasco, Pinellas, Polk, Putnam, St. Johns, Sarasota, Seminole, Sumter, Suwannee, Union, and Volusia.

> Court for the Middle District shall be held at Fernandina, Fort Myers, Jacksonville, Live Oak, Ocala, Orlando, Saint Petersburg, and Tampa.

Southern District

(c) The Southern District comprises the counties of Broward, Dade, Highlands, Indian River, Martin, Monroe, Okeechobee, Palm Beach, and Saint Lucie.

Court for the Southern District shall be held at Fort Lauderdale, Fort Pierce, Key West, Miami, and West Palm Beach.

(June 25, 1948, c. 646, 62 Stat. 876; July 17, 1952, c. 929, 66 Stat. 757; May 19, 1961, Pub.L. 87–36, § 3(f), 75 Stat. 83; July 30, 1962, Pub.L. 87–562, § 1, 76 Stat. 247; June 2, 1970, Pub.L. 91–272, § 10, 84 Stat. 298; Oct. 2, 1978, Pub.L. 95–408, § 4(a), 92 Stat. 884; Nov. 19, 1988, Pub.L. 100–702, Title X, § 1021(a), 102 Stat. 4672.)

§ 90. Georgia

Georgia is divided into three judicial districts to be known as the Northern, Middle, and Southern Districts of Georgia.

Northern District

(a) The Northern District comprises four divisions.

  (1) The Gainesville Division comprises the counties of Banks, Barrow, Dawson, Fannin, Forsyth, Gilmer, Habersham, Hall, Jackson, Lumpkin, Pickens, Rabun, Stephens, Towns, Union, and White.

Court for the Gainesville Division shall be held at Gainesville.

  (2) The Atlanta Division comprises the counties of Cherokee, Clayton, Cobb, De Kalb, Douglas, Fulton, Gwinnett, Henry, Newton, and Rockdale.

Court for the Atlanta Division shall be held at Atlanta.

  (3) The Rome Division comprises the counties of Bartow, Catoosa, Chattooga, Dade, Floyd, Gordon, Murray, Paulding, Polk, Walker, and Whitfield.

Court for the Rome Division shall be held at Rome.

  (4) The Newnan Division comprises the counties of Carroll, Coweta, Fayette, Haralson, Heard, Meriwether, Pike, Spalding, and Troup.

Court for the Newnan Division shall be held at Newnan.

Middle District

(b) The Middle District comprises seven divisions.

  (1) The Athens Division comprises the counties of Clarke, Elbert, Franklin, Greene, Hart, Madison, Morgan, Oconee, Oglethorpe, and Walton.

Court for the Athens Division shall be held at Athens.

  (2) The Macon Division comprises the counties of Baldwin, Bibb, Bleckley, Butts, Crawford, Hancock, Houston, Jasper, Jones, Lamar, Monroe, Peach, Pulaski, Putnam, Twiggs, Upson, Washington, and Wilkinson.

Court for the Macon Division shall be held at Macon.

  (3) The Columbus Division comprises the counties of Chattahoochee, Clay, Harris, Marion, Muscogee, Quitman, Randolph, Stewart, Talbot, and Taylor.

Court for the Columbus Division shall be held at Columbus.

  (4) The Americus Division comprises the counties of Ben Hill, Crisp, Dooly, Lee, Macon, Schley, Sumter, Terrell, Webster, and Wilcox.

Court for the Americus Division shall be held at Americus.

(5) The Albany Division comprises the counties of Baker, Calhoun, Dougherty, Early, Miller, Mitchell, Turner, and Worth.

Court for the Albany Division shall be held at Albany.

(6) The Valdosta Division comprises the counties of Berrien, Clinch, Cook, Echols, Irwin, Lanier, Lowndes, and Tift.

Court for the Valdosta Division shall be held at Valdosta.

(7) The Thomasville Division comprises the counties of Brooks, Colquitt, Decatur, Grady, Seminole, and Thomas.

Court for the Thomasville Division shall be held at Thomasville.

Southern District

(c) The Southern District comprises six divisions.

(1) The Augusta Division comprises the counties of Burke, Columbia, Glascock, Jefferson, Lincoln, McDuffie, Richmond, Taliaferro, Warren, and Wilkes.

Court for the Augusta Division shall be held at Augusta.

(2) The Dublin Division comprises the counties of Dodge, Johnson, Laurens, Montgomery, Telfair, Treutlen, and Wheeler.

Court for the Dublin Division shall be held at Dublin.

(3) The Savannah Division comprises the counties of Bryan, Chatham, Effingham, and Liberty.

Court for the Savannah Division shall be held at Savannah.

(4) The Waycross Division comprises the counties of Atkinson, Bacon, Brantley, Charlton, Coffee, Pierce, and Ware.

Court for the Waycross Division shall be held at Waycross.

(5) The Brunswick Division comprises the counties of Appling, Camden, Glynn, Jeff Davis, Long, McIntosh, and Wayne.

Court for the Brunswick Division shall be held at Brunswick.

(6) The Statesboro Division comprises the counties of Bulloch, Candler, Emanuel, Evans, Jenkins, Screven, Tattnall, and Toombs.

Court for the Statesboro Division shall be held at Statesboro.

(June 25, 1948, c. 646, 62 Stat. 876; Aug. 16, 1949, c. 444, 63 Stat. 610; Oct. 31, 1951, c. 655, § 36a, 65 Stat. 723; Nov. 8, 1984, Pub.L. 98–620, Title IV, § 408(a)–(c), 98 Stat. 3362; Nov. 14, 1986, Pub.L. 99–657, § 3, 100 Stat. 3670.)

§ 91.   Hawaii

Hawaii constitutes one judicial district which includes the Midway Islands, Wake Island, Johnston Island, Sand Island, Kingman Reef, Palmyra Island, Baker Island, Howland Island, Jarvis Island,* Canton Island, and Enderbury Island: *Provided,* That the inclusion of Canton and Enderbury Islands in such judicial district shall in no way be construed to be prejudicial to the claims of the United Kingdom to said Islands in accordance with the agreement of April 6, 1939, between the

---

   * [With the exception of Sand Island, which is within Honolulu in the State of Hawaii, the aforementioned islands comprise the U.S. Minor Outlying Islands and are territories of the United States. Palmyra Island was part of the Territory of Hawaii until Hawaii became a U.S. state. Ed.]

Governments of the United States and of the United Kingdom to set up a regime for their use in common.*

Court shall be held at Honolulu.

(June 25, 1948, c. 646, 62 Stat. 877; May 24, 1949, c. 139, § 64a, 63 Stat. 99; Mar. 18, 1959, Pub.L. 86–3, § 14(i), 73 Stat. 11; July 12, 1960, Pub.L. 86–624, § 19, 74 Stat. 416.)

§ 92.   Idaho

Idaho, exclusive of Yellowstone National Park,** constitutes one judicial district.

Court shall be held at Boise, Coeur d'Alene, Moscow, and Pocatello.

(June 25, 1948, c. 646, 62 Stat. 877; June 2, 1970, Pub.L. 91–272, § 5, 84 Stat. 297.)

§ 93.   Illinois

Illinois is divided into three judicial districts to be known as the Northern, Central, and Southern Districts of Illinois.

Northern District

(a) The Northern District comprises two divisions.

  (1) The Eastern Division comprises the counties of Cook, Du Page, Grundy, Kane, Kendall, Lake, La Salle, and Will.

Court for the Eastern Division shall be held at Chicago and Wheaton.

  (2) The Western Division comprises the counties of Boone, Carroll, De Kalb, Jo Daviess, Lee, McHenry, Ogle, Stephenson, Whiteside, and Winnebago.

Court for the Western Division shall be held at Freeport and Rockford.

Central District

(b) The Central District comprises the counties of Adams, Brown, Bureau, Cass, Champaign, Christian, Coles, De Witt, Douglas, Edgar, Ford, Fulton, Greene, Hancock, Henderson, Henry, Iroquois, Kankakee, Knox, Livingston, Logan, McDonough, McLean, Macoupin, Macon, Marshall, Mason, Menard, Mercer, Montgomery, Morgan, Moultrie, Peoria, Piatt, Pike, Putnam, Rock Island, Sangamon, Schuyler, Scott, Shelby, Stark, Tazewell, Vermilion, Warren, and Woodford.

Court for the Central District shall be held at Champaign/Urbana, Danville, Peoria, Quincy, Rock Island, and Springfield.

Southern District

(c) The Southern District comprises the counties of Alexander, Bond, Calhoun, Clark, Clay, Clinton, Crawford, Cumberland, Edwards, Effingham, Fayette, Franklin, Gallatin, Hamilton, Hardin, Jackson, Jasper, Jefferson, Jersey, Johnson, Lawrence, Madison, Marion, Massac, Monroe, Perry, Pope, Pulaski, Randolph, Richland, St. Clair, Saline, Union, Wabash, Washington, Wayne, White, and Williamson.

Court for the Southern District shall be held at Alton, Benton, Cairo, and East Saint Louis.

(June 25, 1948, c. 646, 62 Stat. 878; Aug. 10, 1950, c. 675, § 1, 64 Stat. 438; May 19, 1961, Pub.L. 87–36, § 3(c), 75 Stat. 83; June 2, 1970, Pub.L. 91–272, § 8, 84 Stat. 297; Oct. 2, 1978, Pub.L. 95–408, § 4(b)(1), 92

---

* [The Canton and Enderbury Islands are not part of the State of Hawaii but rather are two coral atolls approximately 1,850 miles south of Hawaii in the Pacific Ocean and are a jointly administered U.S.–U.K. "condominium" under international law. Ed.]

** [Yellowstone National Park is assigned in its entirety to the District of Wyoming. *See* 28 U.S.C. § 131. Ed.]

Stat. 884; Nov. 2, 1978, Pub.L. 95–573, § 1, 92 Stat. 2458; Nov. 8, 1984, Pub.L. 98–620, Title IV, § 406(a), (c), 98 Stat. 3361; Dec. 6, 1999, Pub.L. 106–130, § 2, 113 Stat. 1677.)

§ 94. Indiana

Indiana is divided into two judicial districts to be known as the Northern and Southern Districts of Indiana.

Northern District

(a) The Northern District comprises three divisions.

(1) The Fort Wayne Division comprises the counties of Adams, Allen, Blackford, De Kalb, Grant, Huntington, Jay, Lagrange, Noble, Steuben, Wells, and Whitley.

Court for the Fort Wayne Division shall be held at Fort Wayne.

(2) The South Bend Division comprises the counties of Cass, Elkhart, Fulton, Kosciusko, La Porte, Marshall, Miami, Pulaski, St. Joseph, Starke, and Wabash.

Court for the South Bend Division shall be held at South Bend.

(3) The Hammond Division comprises the counties of Benton, Carroll, Jasper, Lake, Newton, Porter, Tippecanoe, Warren, and White.

Court for the Hammond Division shall be held at Hammond and Lafayette.

Southern District

(b) The Southern District comprises four divisions.

(1) The Indianapolis Division comprises the counties of Bartholomew, Boone, Brown, Clinton, Decatur, Delaware, Fayette, Fountain, Franklin, Hamilton, Hancock, Hendricks, Henry, Howard, Johnson, Madison, Marion, Monroe, Montgomery, Morgan, Randolph, Rush, Shelby, Tipton, Union, and Wayne.

Court for the Indianapolis Division shall be held at Indianapolis and Richmond.

(2) The Terre Haute Division comprises the counties of Clay, Greene, Knox, Owen, Parke, Putnam, Sullivan, Vermilion, and Vigo.

Court for the Terre Haute Division shall be held at Terre Haute.

(3) The Evansville Division comprises the counties of Davies, Dubois, Gibson, Martin, Perry, Pike, Posey, Spencer, Vanderburgh, and Warrick.

Court for the Evansville Division shall be held at Evansville.

(4) The New Albany Division comprises the counties of Clark, Crawford, Dearborn, Floyd, Harrison, Jackson, Jefferson, Jennings, Lawrence, Ohio, Orange, Ripley, Scott, Switzerland, and Washington.

Court for the New Albany Division shall be held at New Albany.

(June 25, 1948, c. 646, 62 Stat. 878; Feb. 10, 1954, c. 6, § 2(b)(7), 68 Stat. 11; June 2, 1970, Pub.L. 91–272, § 9, 84 Stat. 298.)

§ 95. Iowa

Iowa is divided into two judicial districts to be known as the Northern and Southern Districts of Iowa.

Northern District

(a) The Northern District comprises four divisions.

    (1) The Cedar Rapids Division comprises the counties of Benton, Cedar, Grundy, Hardin, Iowa, Jones, Linn, and Tama.

Court for the Cedar Rapids Division shall be held at Cedar Rapids.

    (2) The Eastern Division comprises the counties of Allamakee, Black Hawk, Bremer, Buchanan, Chickasaw, Clayton, Delaware, Dubuque, Fayette, Floyd, Howard, Jackson, Mitchell, and Winneshiek.

Court for the Eastern Division shall be held at Dubuque and Waterloo.

    (3) The Western Division comprises the counties of Buena Vista, Cherokee, Clay, Crawford, Dickinson, Ida, Lyon, Monona, O'Brien, Osceola, Plymouth, Sac, Sioux, and Woodbury.

Court for the Western Division shall be held at Sioux City.

    (4) The Central Division comprises the counties of Butler, Calhoun, Carroll, Cerro Gordo, Emmet, Franklin, Hamilton, Hancock, Humboldt, Kossuth, Palo Alto, Pocahontas, Webster, Winnebago, Worth, and Wright.

Court for the Central Division shall be held at Fort Dodge and Mason City.

Southern District

(b) The Southern District comprises six divisions.

    (1) The Central Division comprises the counties of Boone, Dallas, Greene, Guthrie, Jasper, Madison, Marion, Marshall, Polk, Poweshiek, Story, and Warren.

Court for the Central Division shall be held at Des Moines.

    (2) The Eastern Division comprises the counties of Des Moines, Henry, Lee, Louisa, and Van Buren.

Court for the Eastern Division shall be held at Keokuk.

    (3) The Western Division comprises the counties of Audubon, Cass, Fremont, Harrison, Mills, Montgomery, Page, Pottawattamie, and Shelby.

Court for the Western Division shall be held at Council Bluffs.

    (4) The Southern Division comprises the counties of Adair, Adams, Clarke, Decatur, Lucas, Ringgold, Taylor, Union, and Wayne.

Court for the Southern Division shall be held at Creston.

    (5) The Davenport Division comprises the counties of Clinton, Johnson, Muscatine, Scott, and Washington.

Court for the Davenport Division shall be held at Davenport.

    (6) The Ottumwa Division comprises the counties of Appanoose, Davis, Jefferson, Keokuk, Mahaska, Monroe, and Wapello.

Court for the Ottumwa Division shall be held at Ottumwa.

(June 25, 1948, c. 646, 62 Stat. 879; Oct. 15, 1980, Pub.L. 96–462, § 3(a), 94 Stat. 2053.)

§ 96.　Kansas

Kansas constitutes one judicial district.

　　Court shall be held at Kansas City, Lawrence, Leavenworth, Salina, Topeka, Hutchinson, Wichita, Dodge City, and Fort Scott.

(June 25, 1948, c. 646, 62 Stat. 880; Aug. 27, 1949, c. 516, 63 Stat. 666; Oct. 27, 1986, Pub.L. 99–554, Title I, § 141, 100 Stat. 3096.)

HISTORICAL AND STATUTORY NOTES

Effective and Applicability Provisions

　　1986 Acts. Amendment by Pub.L. 99–554 effective 30 days after Oct. 27, 1986, see section 302(a) of Pub.L. 99–554, set out as a note under section 581 of this title.

§ 97.　Kentucky

Kentucky is divided into two judicial districts to be known as the Eastern and Western Districts of Kentucky.

Eastern District

　　(a)　The Eastern District comprises the counties of Anderson, Bath, Bell, Boone, Bourbon, Boyd, Boyle, Bracken, Breathitt, Campbell, Carroll, Carter, Clark, Clay, Elliott, Estill, Fayette, Fleming, Floyd, Franklin, Gallatin, Garrard, Grant, Greenup, Harlan, Harrison, Henry, Jackson, Jessamine, Johnson, Kenton, Knott, Knox, Laurel, Lawrence, Lee, Leslie, Letcher, Lewis, Lincoln, McCreary, Madison, Magoffin, Martin, Mason, Menifee, Mercer, Montgomery, Morgan, Nicholas, Owen, Owsley, Pendleton, Perry, Pike, Powell, Pulaski, Robertson, Rockcastle, Rowan, Scott, Shelby, Trimble, Wayne, Whitley, Wolfe, and Woodford.

　　Court for the Eastern District shall be held at Ashland, Catlettsburg, Covington, Frankfort, Jackson, Lexington, London, Pikeville, and Richmond.

Western District

　　(b)　The Western District comprises the counties of Adair, Allen, Ballard, Barren, Breckenridge, Bullitt, Butler, Caldwell, Calloway, Carlisle, Casey, Christian, Clinton, Crittenden, Cumberland, Daviess, Edmonson, Fulton, Graves, Grayson, Green, Hancock, Hardin, Hart, Henderson, Hickman, Hopkins, Jefferson, Larue, Livingston, Logan, Lyon, McCracken, McLean, Marion, Marshall, Meade, Metcalfe, Monroe, Muhlenberg, Nelson, Ohio, Oldham, Russell, Simpson, Spencer, Taylor, Todd, Trigg, Union, Warren, Washington, and Webster.

　　Court for the Western District shall be held at Bowling Green, Louisville, Owensboro, and Paducah.

(June 25, 1948, c. 646, 62 Stat. 880; Oct. 2, 1978, Pub.L. 95–408, § 2(a), 92 Stat. 883.)

§ 98.　Louisiana

Louisiana is divided into three judicial districts to be known as the Eastern, Middle, and Western Districts of Louisiana.

Eastern District

　　(a)　The Eastern District comprises the parishes of Assumption, Jefferson, Lafourche, Orleans, Plaquemines, Saint Bernard, Saint Charles, Saint James, Saint John the Baptist, Saint Tammany, Tangipahoa, Terrebonne, and Washington.

　　Court for the Eastern District shall be held at New Orleans, and Houma.

Middle District

(b) The Middle District comprises the parishes of Ascension, East Baton Rouge, East Feliciana, Iberville, Livingston, Pointe Coupee, Saint Helena, West Baton Rouge, and West Feliciana.

Court for the Middle District shall be held at Baton Rouge.

Western District

(c) The Western District comprises the parishes of Acadia, Allen, Avoyelles, Beauregard, Bienville, Bossier, Caddo, Calcasieu, Caldwell, Cameron, Catahoula, Claiborne, Concordia, Jefferson Davis, De Soto, East Carroll, Evangeline, Franklin, Grant, Iberia, Jackson, Lafayette, La Salle, Lincoln, Madison, Morehouse, Natchitoches, Ouachita, Rapides, Red River, Richland, Sabine, Saint Landry, Saint Martin, Saint Mary, Tensas, Union, Vermilion, Vernon, Webster, West Carroll, and Winn.

Court for the Western District shall be held at Alexandria, Lafayette, Lake Charles, Monroe, Opelousas, and Shreveport.

(June 25, 1948, c. 646, 62 Stat. 881; May 19, 1961, Pub.L. 87–36, § 4, 75 Stat. 83; Dec. 18, 1971, Pub.L. 92–208, § 3(a), 85 Stat. 741; Oct. 2, 1978, Pub.L. 95–408, § 3(a), 92 Stat. 883; July 10, 1984, Pub.L. 98–353, Title II, § 203(b), 98 Stat. 350.)

§ 99. Maine

Maine constitutes one judicial district.

Court shall be held at Bangor and Portland.

(June 25, 1948, c. 646, 62 Stat. 881; Nov. 2, 1978, Pub.L. 95–573, § 2, 92 Stat. 2458.)

§ 100. Maryland

Maryland constitutes one judicial district comprising two divisions.

(1) The Northern Division comprises the counties of Allegany, Anne Arundel, Baltimore, Caroline, Carroll, Cecil, Dorchester, Frederick, Garrett, Harford, Howard, Kent, Queen Anne's, Somerset, Talbot, Washington, Wicomico, and Worcester, and the City of Baltimore.

Court for the Northern Division shall be held at Baltimore, Cumberland, and Denton.

(2) The Southern Division comprises the counties of Calvert, Charles, Montgomery, Prince George's, and St. Mary's.

Court for the Southern Division shall be held at a suitable site in Montgomery or Prince George's County not more than five miles from the boundary of Montgomery and Prince George's Counties.

(June 25, 1948, c. 646, 62 Stat. 882; Dec. 14, 1970, Pub.L. 91–546, § 4, 84 Stat. 1412; Oct. 14, 1988, Pub.L. 100–487, § 1, 102 Stat. 2431.)

§ 101. Massachusetts

Massachusetts constitutes one judicial district.

Court shall be held at Boston, New Bedford, Springfield, and Worcester.

(June 25, 1948, c. 646, 62 Stat. 882.)

§ 102. Michigan

Michigan is divided into two judicial districts to be known as the Eastern and Western Districts of Michigan.

Eastern District

(a) The Eastern District comprises two divisions.

    (1) The Southern Division comprises the counties of Genesee, Jackson, Lapeer, Lenawee, Livingston, Macomb, Monroe, Oakland, Saint Clair, Sanilac, Shiawassee, Washtenaw, and Wayne.

Court for the Southern Division shall be held at Ann Arbor, Detroit, Flint, and Port Huron.

    (2) The Northern Division comprises the counties of Alcona, Alpena, Arenac, Bay, Cheboygan, Clare, Crawford, Gladwin, Gratiot, Huron, Iosco, Isabella, Midland, Montmorency, Ogemaw, Oscoda, Otsego, Presque Isle, Roscommon, Saginaw, and Tuscola.

Court for the Northern Division shall be held at Bay City.

Western District

(b) The Western District comprises two divisions.

    (1) The Southern Division comprises the counties of Allegan, Antrim, Barry, Benzie, Berrien, Branch, Calhoun, Cass, Charlevoix, Clinton, Eaton, Emmet, Grand Traverse, Hillsdale, Ingham, Ionia, Kalamazoo, Kalkaska, Kent, Lake, Leelanau, Manistee, Mason, Mecosta, Missaukee, Montcalm, Muskegon, Newaygo, Oceana, Osceola, Ottawa, Saint Joseph, Van Buren, and Wexford.

Court for the Southern Division shall be held at Grand Rapids, Kalamazoo, Lansing, and Traverse City.

    (2) The Northern Division comprises the counties of Alger, Baraga, Chippewa, Delta, Dickinson, Gogebic, Houghton, Iron, Keweenaw, Luce, Mackinac, Marquette, Menominee, Ontonagon, and Schoolcraft.

Court for the Northern Division shall be held at Marquette and Sault Sainte Marie.

(June 25, 1948, c. 646, 62 Stat. 882; Feb. 10, 1954, c. 6, § 2(b)(8), 68 Stat. 11; May 19, 1961, Pub.L. 87–36, § 3(d), 75 Stat. 83; Oct. 6, 1964, Pub.L. 88–627, 78 Stat. 1003; June 2, 1970, Pub.L. 91–272, § 11, 84 Stat. 298.)

§ 103.   Minnesota

Minnesota constitutes one judicial district comprising six divisions.

    (1) The First Division comprises the counties of Dodge, Fillmore, Houston, Mower, Olmsted, Steele, Wabasha, and Winona.

Court for the First Division shall be held at Winona.

    (2) The Second Division comprises the counties of Blue Earth, Brown, Cottonwood, Faribault, Freeborn, Jackson, Lac qui Parle, Le Sueur, Lincoln, Lyon, Martin, Murray, Nicollet, Nobles, Pipestone, Redwood, Rock, Sibley, Waseca, Watonwan, and Yellow Medicine.

Court for the Second Division shall be held at Mankato.

    (3) The Third Division comprises the counties of Chisago, Dakota, Goodhue, Ramsey, Rice, Scott, and Washington.

Court for the Third Division shall be held at Saint Paul.

    (4) The Fourth Division comprises the counties of Anoka, Carver, Chippewa, Hennepin, Isanti, Kandiyohi, McLeod, Meeker, Renville, Sherburne, Swift, and Wright.

Court for the Fourth Division shall be held at Minneapolis.

(5) The Fifth Division comprises the counties of Aitkin, Benton, Carlton, Cass, Cook, Crow Wing, Itasca, Kanabec, Koochiching, Lake, Mille Lacs, Morrison, Pine, and Saint Louis.

Court for the Fifth Division shall be held at Duluth.

(6) The Sixth Division comprises the counties of Becker, Beltrami, Big Stone, Clay, Clearwater, Douglas, Grant, Hubbard, Kittson, Lake of the Woods, Mahnomen, Marshall, Norman, Otter Tail, Pennington, Polk, Pope, Red Lake, Roseau, Stearns, Stevens, Todd, Traverse, Wadena, and Wilkin.

Court for the Sixth Division shall be held at Fergus Falls and Bemidji.

(June 25, 1948, c. 646, 62 Stat. 882; Oct. 13, 2008, Pub.L. 110–406, § 18, 122 Stat. 4295.)

§ 104. Mississippi

Mississippi is divided into two judicial districts to be known as the northern and southern districts of Mississippi.

Northern District

(a) The northern district comprises three divisions.

(1) The Aberdeen Division comprises the counties of Alcorn, Chickasaw, Choctaw, Clay, Itawamba, Lee, Lowndes, Monroe, Oktibbeha, Prentiss, Tishomingo, Webster, and Winston.

Court for the Aberdeen Division shall be held at Aberdeen, Ackerman, and Corinth.

(2) The Oxford Division comprises the counties of Benton, Calhoun, DeSoto, Lafayette, Marshall, Panola, Pontotoc, Quitman, Tallahatchie, Tate, Tippah, Tunica, Union, and Yalobusha.

Court for the Oxford Division shall be held at Oxford.

(3) The Greenville Division comprises the counties of Attala, Bolivar, Carroll, Coahoma, Grenada, Humphreys, Leflore, Montgomery, Sunflower, and Washington.

Court for the Greenville Division shall be held at Clarksdale, Cleveland, and Greenville.

Southern District

(b) The southern district comprises four divisions.

(1) The Northern Division comprises the counties of Copiah, Hinds, Holmes, Issaquena, Kemper, Lauderdale, Leake, Madison, Neshoba, Newton, Noxubee, Rankin, Scott, Simpson, Sharkey, Smith, Warren, and Yazoo.

Court for the Northern Division shall be held at Jackson.

(2) The Southern Division comprises the counties of George, Greene, Hancock, Harrison, Jackson, Pearl River, and Stone.

Court for the Southern Division shall be held at Gulfport.

(3) The Eastern Division comprises the counties of Clarke, Covington, Forrest, Jasper, Jefferson Davis, Jones, Lamar, Lawrence, Marion, Perry, Wayne, and Walthall.

Court for the Eastern Division shall be held at Hattiesburg.

(4) The Western Division comprises the counties of Adams, Amite, Claiborne, Franklin, Jefferson, Lincoln, Pike, and Wilkinson.

Court for the Western Division shall be held at Natchez.

(June 25, 1948, c. 646, 62 Stat. 883; Aug. 7, 1950, c. 601, 64 Stat. 415; Sept. 27, 1967, Pub.L. 90–92, 81 Stat. 229; Dec. 14, 1970, Pub.L. 91–546, §§ 2, 3, 84 Stat. 1412; Oct. 2, 1978, Pub.L. 95–408, § 2(b), 92 Stat. 883;

Dec. 6, 1999, Pub.L. 106–130, § 1, 113 Stat. 1677; Dec. 10, 2004, Pub.L. 108–455, § 2, 118 Stat. 3628; Pub.L. 112–188, § 3, Oct. 5, 2012, 126 Stat. 1433; Pub.L. 113–61, § 1, Dec. 20, 2013, 127 Stat. 665.)

§ 105. Missouri

Missouri is divided into two judicial districts to be known as the Eastern and Western Districts of Missouri.

Eastern District

(a) The Eastern District comprises three divisions.

(1) The Eastern Division comprises the counties of Crawford, Dent, Franklin, Gasconade, Jefferson, Lincoln, Maries, Phelps, Saint Charles, Saint Francois, Saint Louis, Warren, and Washington, and the city of Saint Louis.

Court for the Eastern Division shall be held at Saint Louis.

(2) The Northern Division comprises the counties of Adair, Audrain, Chariton, Clark, Knox, Lewis, Linn, Macon, Marion, Monroe, Montgomery, Pike, Ralls, Randolph, Schuyler, Scotland, and Shelby.

Court for the Northern Division shall be held at Hannibal.

(3) The Southeastern Division comprises the counties of Bollinger, Butler, Cape Girardeau, Carter, Dunklin, Iron, Madison, Mississippi, New Madrid, Pemiscot, Perry, Reynolds, Ripley, Saint Genevieve, Scott, Shannon, Stoddard, and Wayne.

Court for the Southeastern Division shall be held at Cape Girardeau.

Western District

(b) The Western District comprises five divisions.

(1) The Western Division comprises the counties of Bates, Carroll, Cass, Clay, Henry, Jackson, Johnson, Lafayette, Ray, Saint Clair, and Saline.

Court for the Western Division shall be held at Kansas City.

(2) The Southwestern Division comprises the counties of Barton, Barry, Jasper, Lawrence, McDonald, Newton, Stone, and Vernon.

Court for the Southwestern Division shall be held at Joplin.

(3) The Saint Joseph Division comprises the counties of Andrew, Atchison, Buchanan, Caldwell, Clinton, Daviess, De Kalb, Gentry, Grundy, Harrison, Holt, Livingston, Mercer, Nodaway, Platte, Putnam, Sullivan, and Worth.

Court for the Saint Joseph Division shall be held at Saint Joseph.

(4) The Central Division comprises the counties of Benton, Boone, Callaway, Camden, Cole, Cooper, Hickory, Howard, Miller, Moniteau, Morgan, Osage, and Pettis.

Court for the Central Division shall be held at Jefferson City.

(5) The Southern Division comprises the counties of Cedar, Christian, Dade, Dallas, Douglas, Greene, Howell, Laclede, Oregon, Ozark, Polk, Pulaski, Taney, Texas, Webster, and Wright.

Court for the Southern Division shall be held at Springfield.

(June 25, 1948, c. 646, 62 Stat. 884; May 31, 1962, Pub.L. 87–461, 76 Stat. 85; Oct. 15, 1980, Pub.L. 96–462, § 4(a), 94 Stat. 2053; Pub.L. 112–188, § 2, Oct. 5, 2012, 126 Stat. 1433.)

§ 106. Montana

Montana, exclusive of Yellowstone National Park,* constitutes one judicial district.

Court shall be held at Billings, Butte, Glasgow, Great Falls, Havre, Helena, Kalispell, Lewistown, Livingston, Miles City, and Missoula.

(June 25, 1948, c. 646, 62 Stat. 884.)

§ 107. Nebraska

Nebraska constitutes one judicial district.

Court shall be held at Lincoln, North Platte, and Omaha.

(June 25, 1948, c. 646, 62 Stat. 884; Aug. 9, 1955, c. 627, § 1, 69 Stat. 546.)

§ 108. Nevada

Nevada constitutes one judicial district.

Court shall be held at Carson City, Elko, Las Vegas, Reno, Ely, and Lovelock.

(June 25, 1948, c. 646, 62 Stat. 885; Dec. 1, 1990, Pub.L. 101–650, Title III, § 324(a)(1), 104 Stat. 5120.)

§ 109. New Hampshire

New Hampshire constitutes one judicial district.

Court shall be held at Concord and Littleton.

(June 25, 1948, c. 646, 62 Stat. 885.)

§ 110. New Jersey

New Jersey constitutes one judicial district.

Court shall be held at Camden, Newark and Trenton.

(June 25, 1948, c. 646, 62 Stat. 885.)

§ 111. New Mexico

New Mexico constitutes one judicial district.

Court shall be held at Albuquerque, Las Cruces, Las Vegas, Roswell, Santa Fe, and Silver City.

(June 25, 1948, c. 646, 62 Stat. 885.)

§ 112. New York

New York is divided into four judicial districts to be known as the Northern, Southern, Eastern, and Western Districts of New York.

Northern District

(a) The Northern District comprises the counties of Albany, Broome, Cayuga, Chenango, Clinton, Columbia, Cortland, Delaware, Essex, Franklin, Fulton, Greene, Hamilton, Herkimer, Jefferson, Lewis, Madison, Montgomery, Oneida, Onondaga, Oswego, Otsego, Rensselaer, Saint Lawrence, Saratoga, Schenectady, Schoharie, Tioga, Tompkins, Ulster, Warren, and Washington.

---

* [Yellowstone National Park is assigned in its entirety to the District of Wyoming. *See* 28 U.S.C. § 131. Ed.]

Court for the Northern District shall be held at Albany, Auburn, Binghamton, Malone, Plattsburgh,[1] Syracuse, Utica, Watertown, and Plattsburgh.[1]

Southern District

(b) The Southern District comprises the counties of Bronx, Dutchess, New York, Orange, Putnam, Rockland, Sullivan, and Westchester and concurrently with the Eastern District, the waters within the Eastern District.

> Court for the Southern District shall be held at New York, White Plains, and in the Middletown-Wallkill area of Orange County or such nearby location as may be deemed appropriate.

Eastern District

(c) The Eastern District comprises the counties of Kings, Nassau, Queens, Richmond, and Suffolk and concurrently with the Southern District, the waters within the counties of Bronx and New York.

> Court for the Eastern District shall be held at Brooklyn, Hauppauge, Hempstead (including the village of Uniondale), and Central Islip.

Western District

(d) The Western District comprises the counties of Allegany, Cattaraugus, Chautauqua, Chemung, Erie, Genesee, Livingston, Monroe, Niagara, Ontario, Orleans, Schuyler, Seneca, Steuben, Wayne, Wyoming, and Yates.

> Court for the Western District shall be held at Buffalo, Canandaigua, Elmira, Jamestown, and Rochester.

(June 25, 1948, c. 646, 62 Stat. 885; Dec. 18, 1967, Pub.L. 90–217, 81 Stat. 662; Dec. 14, 1970, Pub.L. 91–546, § 1, 84 Stat. 1412; Apr. 28, 1978, Pub.L. 95–271, § 1, 92 Stat. 221; Oct. 2, 1978, Pub.L. 95–408, § 4(c), 92 Stat. 885; Nov. 2, 1978, Pub.L. 95–573, § 3, 92 Stat. 2458; Nov. 8, 1984, Pub.L. 98–620, Title IV, § 405, 98 Stat. 3361; Dec. 1, 1990, Pub.L. 101–650, Title III, § 324(a)(2), 104 Stat. 5120; Oct. 19, 1996, Pub.L. 104–317, Title VI, § 609, 110 Stat. 3860; Nov. 29, 1999, Pub.L. 106–113, Div. B, § 1000(a)(1) [Title III, § 306], 113 Stat. 1535, 1501A–37; Dec. 10, 2004, Pub.L. 108–455, § 4, 118 Stat. 3628; Dec. 23, 2004, Pub.L. 108–482, Title III, § 302, 118 Stat. 3918.)

§ 113.   North Carolina

North Carolina is divided into three judicial districts to be known as the Eastern, Middle, and Western Districts of North Carolina.

Eastern District

(a) The Eastern District comprises the counties of Beaufort, Bertie, Bladen, Brunswick, Camden, Carteret, Chowan, Columbus, Craven, Cumberland, Currituck, Dare, Duplin, Edgecombe, Franklin, Gates, Granville, Greene, Halifax, Harnett, Hertford, Hyde, Johnston, Jones, Lenoir, Martin, Nash, New Hanover, Northampton, Onslow, Pamlico, Pasquotank, Pender, Perquimans, Pitt, Robeson, Sampson, Tyrrell, Vance, Wake, Warren, Washington, Wayne, and Wilson and that portion of Durham County encompassing the Federal Correctional Institution, Butner, North Carolina.

> Court for the Eastern District shall be held at Elizabeth City, Fayetteville, Greenville, New Bern, Raleigh, Wilmington, and Wilson.

Middle District

(b) The Middle District comprises the counties of Alamance, Cabarrus, Caswell, Chatham, Davidson, Davie, Durham (excluding that portion of Durham County encompassing the Federal Correctional Institution, Butner, North Carolina), Forsythe, Guilford, Hoke, Lee, Montgomery, Moore,

---

[1]   So in original. "Plattsburgh" appears twice.

Orange, Person, Randolph, Richmond, Rockingham, Rowan, Scotland, Stanly, Stokes, Surry, and Yadkin.

Court for the Middle District shall be held at Durham, Greensboro, and Winston-Salem.

Western District

(c)　The Western District comprises the counties of Alexander, Alleghany, Anson, Ashe, Avery, Buncombe, Burke, Caldwell, Catawba, Cherokee, Clay, Cleveland, Gaston, Graham, Haywood, Henderson, Iredell, Jackson, Lincoln, McDowell, Macon, Madison, Mecklenburg, Mitchell, Polk, Rutherford, Swain, Transylvania, Union, Watauga, Wilkes, and Yancey.

Court for the Western District shall be held at Asheville, Bryson City, Charlotte, Shelby, and Statesville.

(June 25, 1948, c. 646, 62 Stat. 886; Nov. 2, 1965, Pub.L. 89–319, 79 Stat. 1186; Oct. 15, 1980, Pub.L. 96–462, § 5(a)–(c), 94 Stat. 2053, 2054; Apr. 21, 1992, Pub.L. 102–272, 106 Stat. 112.)*

§ 114.　North Dakota

North Dakota constitutes one judicial district.

Court shall be held at Bismarck, Fargo, Grand Forks, and Minot.

(Added Pub.L. 111–174, § 3, May 27, 2010, 124 Stat. 1216.)

HISTORICAL AND STATUTORY NOTES

Prior Provisions

A prior section 114, June 25, 1948, c. 646, 62 Stat. 886; Oct. 2, 1978, Pub.L. 95–408, § 3(b), 92 Stat. 883, which identified the judicial district of North Dakota as one judicial district comprising four divisions, was repealed by Pub.L. 111–174, § 3, May 27, 2010, 124 Stat. 1216.

§ 115.　Ohio

Ohio is divided into two judicial districts to be known as the Northern and Southern Districts of Ohio.

Northern District

(a)　The Northern District comprises two divisions.

(1)　The Eastern Division comprises the counties of Ashland, Ashtabula, Carroll, Columbiana, Crawford, Cuyahoga, Geauga, Holmes, Lake, Lorain, Mahoning, Medina, Portage, Richland, Stark, Summit, Trumbull, Tuscarawas, and Wayne.

Court for the Eastern Division shall be held at Cleveland, Youngstown, and Akron.

(2)　The Western Division comprises the counties of Allen, Auglaize, Defiance, Erie, Fulton, Hancock, Hardin, Henry, Huron, Lucas, Marion, Mercer, Ottawa, Paulding, Putnam, Sandusky, Seneca, Van Wert, Williams, Woods, and Wyandot.

Court for the Western Division shall be held at Lima and Toledo.

Southern District

(b)　The Southern District comprises two divisions.

(1)　The Western Division comprises the counties of Adams, Brown, Butler, Champaign, Clark, Clermont, Clinton, Darke, Greene, Hamilton, Highland, Lawrence, Miami, Montgomery, Preble, Scioto, Shelby, and Warren.

---

*　[Proposed legislation that has passed the U.S. Senate, S. 929, would move portions of four counties encompassing the Fort Bragg Military Reservation and Camp Mackall from the Middle District to the Eastern District of North Carolina. Ed.]

Court for the Western Division shall be held at Cincinnati and Dayton.

(2) The Eastern Division comprises the counties of Athens, Belmont, Coshocton, Delaware, Fairfield, Fayette, Franklin, Gallia, Guernsey, Harrison, Hocking, Jackson, Jefferson, Knox, Licking, Logan, Madison, Meigs, Monroe, Morgan, Morrow, Muskingum, Noble, Perry, Pickaway, Pike, Ross, Union, Vinton, and Washington.

Court for the Eastern Division shall be held at Columbus[1] St. Clairsville, and Steubenville.

(June 25, 1948, c. 646, 62 Stat. 887; Feb. 10, 1954, c. 6, § 2(b)(9), 68 Stat. 11; Nov. 2, 2002, Pub.L. 107–273, Div. C, Title I, § 11021, 116 Stat. 1829.)

§ 116. Oklahoma

Oklahoma is divided into three judicial districts to be known as the Northern, Eastern, and Western Districts of Oklahoma.

Northern District

(a) The Northern District comprises the counties of Craig, Creek, Delaware, Mayes, Nowata, Osage, Ottawa, Pawnee, Rogers, Tulsa, and Washington.

> Court for the Northern District shall be held at Bartlesville, Miami, Pawhuska, Tulsa, and Vinita.

Eastern District

(b) The Eastern District comprises the counties of Adair, Atoka, Bryan, Carter, Cherokee, Choctaw, Coal, Haskell, Hughes, Johnston, Latimer, Le Flore, Love, McCurtain, McIntosh, Marshall, Murray, Muskogee, Okfuskee, Okmulgee, Pittsburg, Pontotoc, Pushmataha, Seminole, Sequoyah, and Wagoner.

> Court for the Eastern District shall be held at Ada, Ardmore, Durant, Hugo, Muskogee, Okmulgee, Poteau, and S. McAlester.

Western District

(c) The Western District comprises the counties of Alfalfa, Beaver, Beckham, Blaine, Caddo, Canadian, Cimarron, Cleveland, Comanche, Cotton, Custer, Dewey, Ellis, Garfield, Garvin, Grady, Grant, Greer, Harmon, Harper, Jackson, Jefferson, Kay, Kingfisher, Kiowa, Lincoln, Logan, McClain, Major, Noble, Oklahoma, Payne, Pottawatomie, Roger Mills, Stephens, Texas, Tillman, Washita, Woods, and Woodward.

> Court for the Western District shall be held at Chickasha, Enid, Guthrie, Lawton, Mangum, Oklahoma City, Pauls Valley, Ponca City, Shawnee, and Woodward.

(June 25, 1948, c. 646, 62 Stat. 887; Aug. 4, 1966, Pub.L. 89–526, § 1, 80 Stat. 335.)

§ 117. Oregon

Oregon constitutes one judicial district.

> Court shall be held at Coquille, Eugene or Springfield, Klamath Falls, Medford, Pendleton, and Portland.

(June 25, 1948, c. 646, 62 Stat. 888; Aug. 3, 1950, c. 514, 64 Stat. 393; June 2, 1970, Pub.L. 91–272, § 7, 84 Stat. 297; Nov. 13, 2000, Pub.L. 106–518, Title V, § 502, 114 Stat. 2422.)

---

[1]   [Footnote to 28 U.S.C. § 115:] So in original. Probably should be followed by a comma.

§ 118. Pennsylvania

Pennsylvania is divided into three judicial districts to be known as the Eastern, Middle, and Western Districts of Pennsylvania.

Eastern District

(a)   The Eastern District comprises the counties of Berks, Bucks, Chester, Delaware, Lancaster, Lehigh, Montgomery, Northampton, and Philadelphia.

> Court for the Eastern District shall be held at Allentown, Easton, Lancaster, Reading, and Philadelphia.

Middle District

(b)   The Middle District comprises the counties of Adams, Bradford, Cameron, Carbon, Centre, Clinton, Columbia, Cumberland, Dauphin, Franklin, Fulton, Huntingdon, Juniata, Lackawanna, Lebanon, Luzerne, Lycoming, Mifflin, Monroe, Montour, Northumberland, Perry, Pike, Potter, Schuylkill, Snyder, Sullivan, Susquehanna, Tioga, Union, Wayne, Wyoming, and York.

> Court for the Middle District shall be held at Harrisburg, Lewisburg, Scranton, Wilkes-Barre, and Williamsport.

Western District

(c)   The Western District comprises the counties of Allegheny, Armstrong, Beaver, Bedford, Blair, Butler, Cambria, Clarion, Clearfield, Crawford, Elk, Erie, Fayette, Forest, Greene, Indiana, Jefferson, Lawrence, McKean, Mercer, Somerset, Venango, Warren, Washington, and Westmoreland.

> Court for the Western District shall be held at Erie, Johnstown, and Pittsburgh.

(June 25, 1948, c. 646, 62 Stat. 888; June 2, 1970, Pub.L. 91–272, § 6, 84 Stat. 297; Nov. 2, 1978, Pub.L. 95–573, § 4, 92 Stat. 2458; Oct. 6, 1992, Pub.L. 102–396, Title IX, § 9161, 106 Stat. 1947; Oct. 21, 1998, Pub.L. 105–277, Div. A, § 101(b) [Title VI, § 624(a)], 112 Stat. 2681–116.)

§ 119. Puerto Rico

Puerto Rico constitutes one judicial district.

> Court shall be held at Mayaguez, Ponce, and San Juan.

(June 25, 1948, c. 646, 62 Stat. 889.)

§ 120. Rhode Island

Rhode Island constitutes one judicial district.

> Court shall be held at Providence.

(June 25, 1948, c. 646, 62 Stat. 889.)

§ 121. South Carolina

South Carolina constitutes one judicial district comprising eleven divisions.

(1)   The Charleston Division comprises the counties of Berkeley, Charleston, Clarendon, Colleton, Dorchester, and Georgetown.

Court for the Charleston Division shall be held at Charleston.

(2)   The Columbia Division comprises the counties of Kershaw, Lee, Lexington, Richland, and Sumter.

Court for the Columbia Division shall be held at Columbia.

(3)   The Florence Division comprises the counties of Chesterfield, Darlington, Dillon, Florence, Horry, Marion, Marlboro, and Williamsburg

Court for the Florence Division shall be held at Florence.

(4) The Aiken Division comprises the counties of Aiken, Allendale, and Barnwell.

Court for the Aiken Division shall be held at Aiken.

(5) The Orangeburg Division comprises the counties of Bamberg, Calhoun, and Orangeburg.

Court for the Orangeburg Division shall be held at Orangeburg.

(6) The Greenville Division comprises the counties of Greenville and Laurens.

Court for the Greenville Division shall be held at Greenville.

(7) The Rock Hill Division comprises the counties of Chester, Fairfield, Lancaster, and York.

Court for the Rock Hill Division shall be held at Rock Hill.

(8) The Greenwood Division comprises the counties of Abbeville, Edgefield, Greenwood, McCormick, Newberry, and Saluda.

Court for the Greenwood Division shall be held at Greenwood.

(9) The Anderson Division comprises the counties of Anderson, Oconee, and Pickens.

Court for the Anderson Division shall be held at Anderson.

(10) The Spartanburg Division comprises the counties of Cherokee, Spartanburg, and Union.

Court for the Spartanburg Division shall be held at Spartanburg.

(11) The Beaufort Division comprises the counties of Beaufort, Hampton, and Jasper.

Court for the Beaufort Division shall be held at Beaufort.

(June 25, 1948, c. 646, 62 Stat. 889; Oct. 7, 1965, Pub.L. 89–242, § 1(a), 79 Stat. 951; Nov. 14, 1986, Pub.L. 99–657, § 2, 100 Stat. 3670; Oct. 28, 1991, Pub.L. 102–140, Title III, § 304, 105 Stat. 810.)

§ 122. South Dakota

South Dakota constitutes one judicial district comprising four divisions.

(1) The Northern Division comprises the counties of Brown, Campbell, Clark, Codington, Corson, Day, Deuel, Edmonds, Grant, Hamlin, McPherson, Marshall, Roberts, Spink, and Walworth.

Court for the Northern Division shall be held at Aberdeen.

(2) The Southern Division comprises the counties of Aurora, Beadle, Bon Homme, Brookings, Brule, Charles Mix, Clay, Davison, Douglas, Hanson, Hutchinson, Kingsbury, Lake, Lincoln, McCook, Miner, Minnehaha, Moody, Sanborn, Turner, Union, and Yankton.

Court for the Southern Division shall be held at Sioux Falls.

(3) The central division comprises the counties of Buffalo, Dewey, Faulk, Gregory, Haakon, Hand, Hughes, Hyde, Jerauld, Jones, Lyman, Mellette, Potter, Stanley, Sully, Todd, Tripp, and Ziebach.

Court for the Central Division shall be held at Pierre.

(4) The Western Division comprises the counties of Bennett, Butte, Custer, Fall River, Harding, Jackson, Lawrence, Meade, Pennington, Perkins, and Shannon.

Court for the Western Division shall be held at Deadwood and Rapid City.

(June 25, 1948, c. 646, 62 Stat. 889; Oct. 10, 1966, Pub.L. 89–638, 80 Stat. 883; Aug. 10, 1972, Pub.L. 92–376, 86 Stat. 529; Dec. 1, 1990, Pub.L. 101–650, Title III, § 324(b), 104 Stat. 5120.)

§ 123.　Tennessee

Tennessee is divided into three judicial districts to be known as the Eastern, Middle, and Western Districts of Tennessee.

Eastern District

(a)　The Eastern District comprises four divisions.

　(1)　The Northern Division comprises the counties of Anderson, Blount, Campbell, Claiborne, Grainger, Jefferson, Knox, Loudon, Monroe, Morgan, Roane, Scott, Sevier, and Union.

Court for the Northern Division shall be held at Knoxville.

　(2)　The Northeastern Division comprises the counties of Carter, Cocke, Greene, Hamblen, Hancock, Hawkins, Johnson, Sullivan, Unicoi, and Washington.

Court for the Northeastern Division shall be held at Greenville.

　(3)　The Southern Division comprises the counties of Bledsoe, Bradley, Hamilton, McMinn, Marion, Meigs, Polk, Rhea, and Sequatchie.

Court for the Southern Division shall be held at Chattanooga.

　(4)　The Winchester Division comprises the counties of Bedford, Coffee, Franklin, Grundy, Lincoln, Moore, Van Buren, and Warren.

Court for the Winchester Division shall be held at Winchester.

Middle District

(b)　The Middle District comprises three divisions.

　(1)　The Nashville Division comprises the counties of Cannon, Cheatham, Davidson, Dickson, Houston, Humphreys, Montgomery, Robertson, Rutherford, Stewart, Sumner, Trousdale, Williamson, and Wilson.

Court for the Nashville Division shall be held at Nashville.

　(2)　The Northeastern Division comprises the counties of Clay, Cumberland, De Kalb, Fentress, Jackson, Macon, Overton, Pickett, Putnam, Smith, and White.

Court for the Northeastern Division shall be held at Cookeville.

　(3)　The Columbia Division comprises the counties of Giles, Hickman, Lawrence, Lewis, Marshall, Maury, and Wayne.

Court for the Columbia Division shall be held at Columbia.

Western District

(c)　The Western District comprises two divisions.

　(1)　The Eastern Division comprises the counties of Benton, Carroll, Chester, Crockett, Decatur, Dyer, Gibson, Hardeman, Hardin, Haywood, Henderson, Henry, Lake, McNairy, Madison, Obion, Perry, and Weakley.

The Eastern Division also includes the waters of Tennessee River to low-water mark on the eastern shore wherever such river forms the boundary between the western and middle districts from the north line of Alabama north to the point in Henry County, Tennessee, where the south boundary of Kentucky strikes the east bank of the river.

Court for the Eastern Division shall be held at Jackson and Dyersburg.

(2)   The Western Division comprises the counties of Fayette, Lauderdale, Shelby, and Tipton.

Court for the Western Division shall be held at Memphis.

The district judge for the Eastern District in office on November 27, 1940, shall hold court in the Northern and Northeastern Divisions. The other judge of that district shall hold the terms of court in the Southern and Winchester Divisions. Each may appoint and remove all officers and employees of the court whose official headquarters are located in the divisions within which he holds court and whose appointments are vested by law in a district judge or chief judge of a district.

(June 25, 1948, c. 646, 62 Stat. 890; May 19, 1961, Pub.L. 87–36, § 3(e), 75 Stat. 83; July 11, 1961, Pub.L. 87–86, 75 Stat. 203; June 2, 1970, Pub.L. 91–272, § 12, 84 Stat. 298; Oct. 13, 2008, Pub.L. 110–406, § 2(a), 122 Stat. 4291.)

§ 124.   Texas

Texas is divided into four judicial districts to be known as the Northern, Southern, Eastern, and Western Districts of Texas.

Northern District

(a)   The Northern District comprises seven divisions.

(1)   The Dallas Division comprises the counties of Dallas, Ellis, Hunt, Johnson, Kaufman, Navarro, and Rockwall.

Court for the Dallas Division shall be held at Dallas.

(2)   The Fort Worth Division comprises the counties of Comanche, Erath, Hood, Jack, Palo Pinto, Parker, Tarrant, and Wise.

Court for the Fort Worth Division shall be held at Fort Worth.

(3)   The Abilene Division comprises the counties of Callahan, Eastland, Fisher, Haskell, Howard, Jones, Mitchell, Nolan, Shackleford, Stephens, Stonewall, Taylor, and Throckmorton.

Court for the Abilene Division shall be held at Abilene.

(4)   The San Angelo Division comprises the counties of Brown, Coke, Coleman, Concho, Crockett, Glasscock, Irion, Menard, Mills, Reagan, Runnels, Schleicher, Sterling, Sutton, and Tom Green.

Court for the San Angelo Division shall be held at San Angelo.

(5)   The Amarillo Division comprises the counties of Armstrong, Brisco, Carson, Castro, Childress, Collingsworth, Dallam, Deaf Smith, Donley, Gray, Hall, Hansford, Hartley, Hemphill, Hutchinson, Lipscomb, Moore, Ochiltree, Oldham, Parmer, Potter, Randall, Roberts, Sherman, Swisher, and Wheeler.

Court for the Amarillo Division shall be held at Amarillo.

(6)   The Wichita Falls Division comprises the counties of Archer, Baylor, Clay, Cottle, Foard, Hardeman, King, Knox, Montague, Wichita, Wilbarger, and Young.

Court for the Wichita Falls Division shall be held at Wichita Falls.

(7)   The Lubbock Division comprises the counties of Bailey, Borden, Cochran, Crosby, Dawson, Dickens, Floyd, Gaines, Garza, Hale, Hockley, Kent, Lamb, Lubbock, Lynn, Motley, Scurry, Terry, and Yoakum.

Court for the Lubbock Division shall be held at Lubbock.

Southern District

(b) The Southern District comprises seven divisions.

(1) The Galveston Division comprises the counties of Brazoria, Chambers, Galveston, and Matagorda.

Court for the Galveston Division shall be held at Galveston.

(2) The Houston Division comprises the counties of Austin, Brazos, Colorado, Fayette, Fort Bend, Grimes, Harris, Madison, Montgomery, San Jacinto, Walker, Waller, and Wharton.

Court for the Houston Division shall be held at Houston.

(3) The Laredo Division comprises the counties of Jim Hogg, La Salle, McMullen, Webb, and Zapata.

Court for the Laredo Division shall be held at Laredo.

(4) The Brownsville Division comprises the counties of Cameron and Willacy.

Court for the Brownsville Division shall be held at Brownsville.

(5) The Victoria Division comprises the counties of Calhoun, DeWitt, Goliad, Jackson, Lavaca, Refugio, and Victoria.

Court for the Victoria Division shall be held at Victoria.

(6) The Corpus Christi Division comprises the counties of Aransas, Bee, Brooks, Duval, Jim Wells, Kenedy, Kleberg, Live Oak, Nueces, and San Patricio.

Court for the Corpus Christi Division shall be held at Corpus Christi.

(7) The McAllen Division comprises the counties of Hidalgo and Starr.

Court for the McAllen Division shall be held at McAllen.

Eastern District

(c) The Eastern District comprises seven divisions.

(1) The Tyler Division comprises the counties of Anderson, Cherokee, Gregg, Henderson, Panola, Rains, Rusk, Smith, Van Zandt, and Wood.

Court for Tyler Division will be held at Tyler.

(2) The Beaumont Division comprises the counties of Hardin, Jasper, Jefferson, Liberty, Newton, and Orange.

Court for the Beaumont Division is to be held at Beaumont.

(3) The Sherman Division comprises the counties of Collin, Cook, Delta, Denton, Fannin, Grayson, Hopkins, and Lamar.

Court for the Sherman Division shall be held at Sherman and Plano.

(4) The Marshall Division comprises the counties of Camp, Cass, Harrison, Marion, Morris, and Upshur.

Court for the Marshall Division shall be held at Marshall.

(5) The Texarkana Division comprises the counties of Bowie, Franklin, Red River, and Titus.

Court for the Texarkana Division shall be held at Texarkana, and may be held anywhere within the Federal courthouse in Texarkana that is located astride the State line between Texas and Arkansas.

(6)   The Lufkin Division comprises the counties of Angelina, Houston, Nacogdoches, Polk, Sabine, San Augustine, Shelby, Trinity, and Tyler.

Court for the Lufkin Division shall be held at Lufkin.

Western District

(d)   The Western District comprises seven divisions.

(1)   The Austin Division comprises the counties of Bastrop, Blanco, Burleson, Burnet, Caldwell, Gillespie, Hays, Kimble, Lampasas, Lee, Llano, Mason, McCulloch, San Saba, Travis, Washington, and Williamson.

Court for the Austin Division shall be held at Austin.

(2)   The Waco Division comprises the counties of Bell, Bosque, Coryell, Falls, Freestone, Hamilton, Hill, Leon, Limestone, McLennan, Milam, Robertson, and Somervell.

Court for the Waco Division shall be held at Waco.

(3)   The El Paso Division comprises the county of El Paso.

Court for the El Paso Division shall be held at El Paso.

(4)   The San Antonio Division comprises the counties of Atascosa, Bandera, Bexar, Comal, Dimmit, Frio, Gonzales, Guadalupe, Karnes, Kendall, Kerr, Medina, Real, and Wilson.

Court for the San Antonio Division shall be held at San Antonio.

(5)   The Del Rio Division comprises the counties of Edwards, Kinney, Maverick, Terrell, Uvalde, Val Verde, and Zavalla.

Court for the Del Rio Division shall be held at Del Rio.

(6)   The Pecos Division comprises the counties of Brewster, Culberson, Jeff Davis, Hudspeth, Loving, Pecos, Presidio, Reeves, Ward, and Winkler.

Court for the Pecos Division shall be held at Pecos.

(7)   The Midland-Odessa Division comprises the counties of Andrews, Crane, Ector, Martin, Midland, and Upton.

Court for the Midland-Odessa Division shall be held at Midland. Court may be held, in the discretion of the court, in Odessa, when courtroom facilities are made available at no expense to the Government.

(June 25, 1948, c. 646, 62 Stat. 891; Feb. 10, 1954, c. 6, § 2(b)(9)(a), (b), 68 Stat. 11; Sept. 4, 1957, Pub.L. 85–298, §§ 1, 2, 71 Stat. 618; Oct. 4, 1961, Pub.L. 87–352, 75 Stat. 772; Mar. 11, 1964, Pub.L. 88–282, 78 Stat. 163; Aug. 30, 1964, Pub.L. 88–512, 78 Stat. 695; Dec. 18, 1967, Pub.L. 90–216, 81 Stat. 661; Oct. 15, 1980, Pub.L. 96–462, § 6, 94 Stat. 2054; Nov. 8, 1984, Pub.L. 98–620, Title IV, § 407(a), 98 Stat. 3362; Dec. 3, 2003, Pub.L. 108–157, § 1(a), 117 Stat. 1947; Dec. 10, 2004, Pub.L. 108–455, § 3, 118 Stat. 3628.)

§ 125.   Utah

Utah constitutes one judicial district comprising two divisions.

(1)   The Northern Division comprises the counties of Box Elder, Cache, Davis, Morgan, Rich, and Weber.

Court for the Northern Division shall be held at Salt Lake City and Ogden.

(2)   The Central Division comprises the counties of Beaver, Carbon, Daggett, Duchesne, Emery, Garfield, Grand, Iron, Juab, Kane, Millard, Piute, Salt Lake, San Juan, Sanpete, Sevier, Summit, Tooele, Uintah, Utah, Wasatch, Washington, and Wayne.

Court for the Central Division shall be held at Salt Lake City, Provo, and St. George.

(June 25, 1948, c. 646, 62 Stat. 893; Oct. 19, 1996, Pub.L. 104–317, Title VI, § 606, 110 Stat. 3859.)

§ 126. Vermont

Vermont constitutes one judicial district.

> Court shall be held at Bennington, Brattleboro, Burlington, Montpelier, Rutland, Saint Johnsbury, and Windsor.

(June 25, 1948, c. 646, 62 Stat. 893; May 28, 1964, Pub.L. 88–312, 78 Stat. 201; Nov. 8, 1984, Pub.L. 98–620, Title IV, § 410, 98 Stat. 3362.)

§ 127. Virginia

Virginia is divided into two judicial districts, to be known as the Eastern and Western Districts of Virginia.

Eastern District

(a) The Eastern District comprises the counties of Accomac, Amelia, Arlington, Brunswick, Caroline, Charles City, Chesterfield, Dinwiddie, Elizabeth City, Essex, Fairfax, Fauquier, Gloucester, Goochland, Greensville, Hanover, Henrico, Isle of Wight, James City, King and Queen, King George, King William, Lancaster, Loudoun, Lunenburg, Mathews, Mecklenburg, Middlesex, Nansemond, New Kent, Norfolk, Northampton, Northumberland, Nottoway, Powhatan, Prince Edward, Prince George, Prince William, Princess Anne, Richmond, Southampton, Spotsylvania, Stafford, Surry, Sussex, Warwick, Westmoreland, and York.

> Court for the Eastern District shall be held at Alexandria, Newport News, Norfolk, and Richmond.

Western District

(b) The Western District comprises the counties of Albemarle, Alleghany, Amherst, Appomattox, Augusta, Bath, Bedford, Bland, Botetourt, Buchanan, Buckingham, Campbell, Carroll, Charlotte, Clarke, Craig, Culpeper, Cumberland, Dickenson, Floyd, Fluvanna, Franklin, Frederick, Giles, Grayson, Greene, Halifax, Henry, Highland, Lee, Louisa, Madison, Montgomery, Nelson, Orange, Page, Patrick, Pittsylvania, Pulaski, Rappahannock, Roanoke, Rockbridge, Rockingham, Russell, Scott, Shenandoah, Smyth, Tazewell, Warren, Washington, Wise, and Wythe.

> Court for the Western District shall be held at Abingdon, Big Stone Gap, Charlottesville, Danville, Harrisonburg, Lynchburg, and Roanoke.

(c) Cities and incorporated towns are included in that district in which are included the counties within the exterior boundaries of which such cities and incorporated towns are geographically located or out of the territory of which they have been incorporated.

(June 25, 1948, c. 646, 62 Stat. 893; July 5, 1968, Pub.L. 90–383, 82 Stat. 292; Dec. 10, 1991, Pub.L. 102–200, § 1, 105 Stat. 1630.)

§ 128. Washington

Washington is divided into two judicial districts to be known as the Eastern and Western Districts of Washington.

Eastern District

(a) The Eastern District comprises the counties of Adams, Asotin, Benton, Chelan, Columbia, Douglas, Ferry, Franklin, Garfield, Grant, Kittitas, Klickitat, Lincoln, Okanogan, Pend Oreille, Spokane, Stevens, Walla Walla, Whitman, and Yakima.

> Court for the Eastern District shall be held at Spokane, Yakima, Walla Walla, and Richland.

Western District

(b) The Western District comprises the counties of Clallam, Clark, Cowlitz, Grays Harbor, Island, Jefferson, King, Kitsap, Lewis, Mason, Pacific, Pierce, San Juan, Skagit, Skamania, Snohomish, Thurston, Wahkiakum, and Whatcom.

Court for the Western District shall be held at Bellingham, Seattle, Tacoma, and Vancouver.

(June 25, 1948, c. 646, 62 Stat. 894; Sept. 25, 1962, Pub.L. 87–699, 76 Stat. 598; June 2, 1970, Pub.L. 91–272, § 4, 84 Stat. 297; Dec. 26, 2007, Pub.L. 110–161, Div. D, Title III, § 308, 121 Stat. 1990.)

§ 129. West Virginia

West Virginia is divided into two judicial districts to be known as the Northern and Southern Districts of West Virginia.

Northern District

(a) The Northern District comprises the counties of Barbour, Berkeley, Braxton, Brooke, Calhoun, Doddridge, Gilmer, Grant, Hampshire, Hancock, Hardy, Harrison, Jefferson, Lewis, Marion, Marshall, Mineral, Monongalia, Morgan, Ohio, Pendleton, Pleasants, Pocahontas, Preston, Randolph, Ritchie, Taylor, Tucker, Tyler, Upshur, Webster, and Wetzel.

Court for the Northern District shall be held at Clarksburg, Elkins, Fairmont, Martinsburg, and Wheeling.

Southern District

(b) The Southern District comprises the counties of Boone, Cabell, Clay, Fayette, Greenbrier, Jackson, Kanawha, Lincoln, Logan, McDowell, Mason, Mercer, Mingo, Monroe, Nicholas, Putnam, Raleigh, Roane, Summers, Wayne, Wirt, Wood, and Wyoming.

Court for the Southern District shall be held at Beckley, Bluefield, Charleston, Huntington, Lewisburg, and Parkersburg.

(June 25, 1948, c. 646, 62 Stat. 894; Jan. 14, 1983, Pub.L. 97–471, § 1, 96 Stat. 2601.)

§ 130. Wisconsin

Wisconsin is divided into two judicial districts to be known as the Eastern and Western districts of Wisconsin.

Eastern District

(a) The Eastern District comprises the counties of Brown, Calumet, Dodge, Door, Florence, Fond du Lac, Forest, Green Lake, Kenosha, Kewaunee, Langlade, Manitowoc, Marinette, Marquette, Menominee, Milwaukee, Oconto, Outagamie, Ozaukee, Racine, Shawano, Sheboygan, Walworth, Washington, Waukesha, Waupaca, Waushara, and Winnebago.

Court for the Eastern District shall be held at Green Bay, Milwaukee, and Oshkosh.

Western District

(b) The Western District comprises the counties of Adams, Ashland, Barron, Bayfield, Buffalo, Burnett, Chippewa, Clark, Columbia, Crawford, Dane, Douglas, Dunn, Eau Claire, Grant, Green, Iowa, Iron, Jackson, Jefferson, Juneau, La Crosse, Lafayette, Lincoln, Marathon, Monroe, Oneida, Pepin, Pierce, Polk, Portage, Price, Richland, Rock, Rusk, Saint Croix, Sauk, Sawyer, Taylor, Trempealeau, Vernon, Vilas, Washburn, and Wood.

Court for the Western District shall be held at Eau Claire, La Crosse, Madison, Superior, and Wausau.

(June 25, 1948, c. 646, 62 Stat. 894; Aug. 6, 1962, Pub.L. 87–573, 76 Stat. 307.)

§ 131. Wyoming

Wyoming and those portions of Yellowstone National Park situated in Montana and Idaho constitute one judicial district.

Court shall be held at Casper, Cheyenne, Evanston, Lander, Jackson, and Sheridan.

(June 25, 1948, c. 646, 62 Stat. 895; July 10, 1984, Pub.L. 98–353, Title II, § 203(a), 98 Stat. 350.)

§ 132. Creation and composition of district courts

(a)   There shall be in each judicial district a district court which shall be a court of record known as the United States District Court for the district.

(b)   Each district court shall consist of the district judge or judges for the district in regular active service. Justices or judges designated or assigned shall be competent to sit as judges of the court.

(c)   Except as otherwise provided by law, or rule or order of court, the judicial power of a district court with respect to any action, suit or proceeding may be exercised by a single judge, who may preside alone and hold a regular or special session of court at the same time other sessions are held by other judges.

(June 25, 1948, c. 646, 62 Stat. 895; Nov. 13, 1963, Pub.L. 88–176, § 2, 77 Stat. 331.)

§ 133. Appointment and number of district judges

(a)   The President shall appoint, by and with the advice and consent of the Senate, district judges for the several judicial districts, as follows:

DISTRICTS	JUDGES
Alabama:	
Northern	7
Middle	3
Southern	3
Alaska	3
Arizona	12
Arkansas:	
Eastern	5
Western	3
California:	
Northern	14
Eastern	6
Central	27
Southern	13
Colorado	7
Connecticut	8
Delaware	4
District of Columbia	15
Florida:	
Northern	4
Middle	15
Southern	17
Georgia:	
Northern	11
Middle	4
Southern	3
Hawaii	3
Idaho	2

Illinois:
    Northern 22
    Central 4
    Southern 4
Indiana:
    Northern 5
    Southern 5
Iowa:
    Northern 2
    Southern 3
Kansas 5
Kentucky:
    Eastern 5
    Western 4
    Eastern and Western 1
Louisiana:
    Eastern 12
    Middle 3
    Western 7
Maine 3
Maryland 10
Massachusetts 13
Michigan:
    Eastern 15
    Western 4
Minnesota 7
Mississippi:
    Northern 3
    Southern 6
Missouri:
    Eastern 6
    Western 5
    Eastern and Western 2
Montana 3
Nebraska 3
Nevada 7
New Hampshire 3
New Jersey 17
New Mexico 6
New York:
    Northern 5
    Southern 28
    Eastern 15
    Western 4
North Carolina:
    Eastern 4
    Middle 4
    Western 4
North Dakota 2
Ohio:
    Northern 11
    Southern 8

Oklahoma:
    Northern 3
    Eastern.. 1
    Western.. 6
    Northern, Eastern, and Western... 1
Oregon.. 6
Pennsylvania:
    Eastern... 22
    Middle 6
    Western.. 10
Puerto Rico.. 7
Rhode Island 3
South Carolina... 10
South Dakota 3
Tennessee:
    Eastern.. 5
    Middle 4
    Western.. 5
Texas:
    Northern 12
    Southern 19
    Eastern.. 7
    Western.. 13
Utah 5
Vermont 2
Virginia:
    Eastern.. 11
    Western.. 4
Washington:
    Eastern.. 4
    Western.. 7
West Virginia:
    Northern 3
    Southern 5
Wisconsin:
    Eastern.. 5
    Western.. 2
Wyoming .... 3.

    (b)(1) In any case in which a judge of the United States (other than a senior judge) assumes the duties of a full-time office of Federal judicial administration, the President shall appoint, by and with the advice and consent of the Senate, an additional judge for the court on which such judge serves. If the judge who assumes the duties of such full-time office leaves that office and resumes the duties as an active judge of the court, then the President shall not appoint a judge to fill the first vacancy which occurs thereafter in that court.

    (2) For purposes of paragraph (1), the term "office of Federal judicial administration" means a position as Director of the Federal Judicial Center, Director of the Administrative Office of the United States Courts, or Counselor to the Chief Justice.

(June 25, 1948, c. 646, 62 Stat. 895; Aug. 3, 1949, c. 387, § 2(a), 63 Stat. 493; Aug. 14, 1950, c. 708, 64 Stat. 443; Aug. 29, 1950, c. 819, § 1, 64 Stat. 562; Sept. 5, 1950, c. 848, § 1, 64 Stat. 578; Feb. 10, 1954, c. 6, § 2(a)(3), 68 Stat. 9; Sept. 7, 1957, Pub.L. 85–310, 71 Stat. 631; July 7, 1958, Pub.L. 85–508, § 12(c), 72 Stat. 348; Mar. 18, 1959, Pub.L. 86–3, § 9(b), 73 Stat. 8; May 19, 1961, Pub.L. 87–36, § 2(d), 75 Stat. 81; July 30, 1962, Pub.L. 87–562, § 3, 76 Stat. 248; Oct. 7, 1965, Pub.L. 89–242, § 1(c), 79 Stat. 951; Mar. 18, 1966, Pub.L.

89–372, § 4, 80 Stat. 77; June 2, 1970, Pub.L. 91–272, § 1(d), 84 Stat. 295; Dec. 18, 1971, Pub.L. 92–208, § 3(d), 85 Stat. 742; Oct. 2, 1978, Pub.L. 95–408, § 4(b)(2), 92 Stat. 883; Oct. 20, 1978, Pub.L. 95–486, § 1(c), 92 Stat. 1630; Jan. 14, 1983, Pub.L. 97–471, § 3, 96 Stat. 2601; July 10, 1984, Pub.L. 98–353, Title II, § 202(e), 98 Stat. 348; Dec. 1, 1990, Pub.L. 101–650, Title II, § 203(d), Title III, § 303, 104 Stat. 5101, 5105; Oct. 6, 1997, Pub.L. 105–53, § 4, 111 Stat. 1174; Nov. 29, 1999, Pub.L. 106–113, Div. B, § 1000(a)(1) [Title III, § 309(b)], 113 Stat. 1535, 1501A–37; Dec. 21, 2000, Pub.L. 106–553, § 1(a)(2) [Title III, § 305(b)], 114 Stat. 2762, 2762A–85; Nov. 2, 2002, Pub.L. 107–273, Div. A, Title III, § 312(a)(2), (b)(2), 116 Stat. 1787, 1788; Oct. 13, 2008, Pub.L. 110–402, § 1(b)(1), 122 Stat. 4254.)

§ 134.   Tenure and residence of district judges

    (a)   The district judges shall hold office during good behavior.

    (b)   Each district judge, except in the District of Columbia, the Southern District of New York, and the Eastern District of New York, shall reside in the district or one of the districts for which he is appointed. Each district judge of the Southern District of New York and the Eastern District of New York may reside within 20 miles of the district to which he or she is appointed.

    (c)   If the public interest and the nature of the business of a district court require that a district judge should maintain his abode at or near a particular place for holding court in the district or within a particular part of the district the judicial council of the circuit may so declare and may make an appropriate order. If the district judges of such a district are unable to agree as to which of them shall maintain his abode at or near the place or within the area specified in such an order the judicial council of the circuit may decide which of them shall do so.

(June 25, 1948, c. 646, 62 Stat. 896; Aug. 3, 1949, c. 387, § 2(b)(1), 63 Stat. 495; Feb. 10, 1954, c. 6, § 2(b)(13)(a), 68 Stat. 12; Mar. 18, 1959, Pub.L. 86–3, § 9(c), 73 Stat. 8; May 19, 1961, Pub.L. 87–36, § 2(e)(3), 75 Stat. 83; Sept. 12, 1966, Pub.L. 89–571, § 1, 80 Stat. 764; Dec. 18, 1971, Pub.L. 92–208, § 3(e), 85 Stat. 742; Oct. 19, 1996, Pub.L. 104–317, Title VI, § 607, 110 Stat. 3860.)

§ 135.   Salaries of district judges

    Each judge of a district court of the United States shall receive a salary at an annual rate determined under section 225 of the Federal Salary Act of 1967 (2 U.S.C. 351–361), as adjusted by section 461 of this title.

(June 25, 1948, c. 646, 62 Stat. 897; Mar. 2, 1955, c. 9, § 1(c), 69 Stat. 10; Aug. 14, 1964, Pub.L. 88–426, Title IV, § 403(c), 78 Stat. 434; Aug. 9, 1975, Pub.L. 94–82, Title II, § 205(b)(3), 89 Stat. 422.)

§ 136.   Chief judges; precedence of district judges

    (a)(1)   In any district having more than one district judge, the chief judge of the district shall be the district judge in regular active service who is senior in commission of those judges who—

        (A)   are sixty-four years of age or under;

        (B)   have served for one year or more as a district judge; and

        (C)   have not served previously as chief judge.

    (2)(A)   In any case in which no district judge meets the qualifications of paragraph (1), the youngest district judge in regular active service who is sixty-five years of age or over and who has served as district judge for one year or more shall act as the chief judge.

        (B)   In any case under subparagraph (A) in which there is no district judge in regular active service who has served as a district judge for one year or more, the district judge in regular active service who is senior in commission and who has not served previously as chief judge shall act as the chief judge.

(3)(A)   Except as provided in subparagraph (C), the chief judge of the district appointed under paragraph (1) shall serve for a term of seven years and shall serve after expiration of such term until another judge is eligible under paragraph (1) to serve as chief judge of the district.

(B)   Except as provided in subparagraph (C), a district judge acting as chief judge under subparagraph (A) or (B) of paragraph (2) shall serve until a judge has been appointed who meets the qualifications under paragraph (1).

(C)   No district judge may serve or act as chief judge of the district after attaining the age of seventy years unless no other district judge is qualified to serve as chief judge of the district under paragraph (1) or is qualified to act as chief judge under paragraph (2).

(b)   The chief judge shall have precedence and preside at any session which he attends.

Other district judges shall have precedence and preside according to the seniority of their commissions. Judges whose commissions bear the same date shall have precedence according to seniority in age.

(c)   A judge whose commission extends over more than one district shall be junior to all district judges except in the district in which he resided at the time he entered upon the duties of his office.

(d)   If the chief judge desires to be relieved of his duties as chief judge while retaining his active status as district judge, he may so certify to the Chief Justice of the United States, and thereafter, the chief judge of the district shall be such other district judge who is qualified to serve or act as chief judge under subsection (a).

(e)   If a chief judge is temporarily unable to perform his duties as such, they shall be performed by the district judge in active service, present in the district and able and qualified to act, who is next in precedence.

(June 25, 1948, c. 646, 62 Stat. 897; Oct. 31, 1951, c. 655, § 37, 65 Stat. 723; Aug. 6, 1958, Pub.L. 85–593, § 2, 72 Stat. 497; Apr. 2, 1982, Pub.L. 97–164, Title II, § 202, 96 Stat. 52.)

§ 137.   Division of business among district judges

(a)   In general.—The business of a court having more than one judge shall be divided among the judges as provided by the rules and orders of the court.

The chief judge of the district court shall be responsible for the observance of such rules and orders, and shall divide the business and assign the cases so far as such rules and orders do not otherwise prescribe.

If the district judges in any district are unable to agree upon the adoption of rules or orders for that purpose the judicial council of the circuit shall make the necessary orders.

(b)   Random assignment of rate court proceedings.—

(1)   In general.—

(A)   Definition.—In this paragraph, the term "performing rights society" has the meaning given the term in section 101 of title 17.

(B)   Determination of license fee.—Except as provided in subparagraph (C), in the case of any performing rights society subject to a consent decree, any application for the determination of a license fee for the public performance of music in accordance with the applicable consent decree shall be made in the district court with jurisdiction over that consent decree and randomly assigned to a judge of that district court according to the rules of that court for the division of business among district judges, provided that any such application shall not be assigned to—

    (i) a judge to whom continuing jurisdiction over any performing rights society for any performing rights society consent decree is assigned or has previously been assigned; or

    (ii) a judge to whom another proceeding concerning an application for the determination of a reasonable license fee is assigned at the time of the filing of the application.

    (C) Exception.—Subparagraph (B) does not apply to an application to determine reasonable license fees made by individual proprietors under section 513 of title 17.

    (2) Rule of construction.—Nothing in paragraph (1) shall modify the rights of any party to a consent decree or to a proceeding to determine reasonable license fees, to make an application for the construction of any provision of the applicable consent decree. Such application shall be referred to the judge to whom continuing jurisdiction over the applicable consent decree is currently assigned. If any such application is made in connection with a rate proceeding, such rate proceeding shall be stayed until the final determination of the construction application. Disputes in connection with a rate proceeding about whether a licensee is similarly situated to another licensee shall not be subject to referral to the judge with continuing jurisdiction over the applicable consent decree.

(June 25, 1948, c. 646, 62 Stat. 897; Pub.L. 115–264, Title I, § 104, Oct. 11, 2018, 132 Stat. 3726.)

§ 138. Terms abolished

The district court shall not hold formal terms.

(June 25, 1948, c. 646, 62 Stat. 897; Oct. 16, 1963, Pub.L. 88–139, § 1, 77 Stat. 248.)

§ 139. Times for holding regular sessions

The times for commencing regular sessions of the district court for transacting judicial business at the places fixed by this chapter shall be determined by the rules or orders of the court. Such rules or orders may provide that at one or more of such places the court shall be in continuous session for such purposes on all business days throughout the year. At other places a session of the court shall continue for such purposes until terminated by order of final adjournment or by commencement of the next regular session at the same place.

(June 25, 1948, c. 646, 62 Stat. 897; Oct. 16, 1963, Pub.L. 88–139, § 1, 77 Stat. 248.)

§ 140. Adjournment

    (a) Any district court may, by order made anywhere within its district, adjourn or, with the consent of the judicial council of the circuit, pretermit any regular session of court for insufficient business or other good cause.

    (b) If the judge of a district court is unable to attend and unable to make an order of adjournment, the clerk may adjourn the court to the next regular session or to any earlier day which he may determine.

(June 25, 1948, c. 646, 62 Stat. 897; Oct. 16, 1963, Pub.L. 88–139, § 1, 77 Stat. 248.)

§ 141. Special sessions; places; notice

    (a)(1) Special sessions of the district court may be held at such places in the district as the nature of the business may require, and upon such notice as the court orders.

    (2) Any business may be transacted at a special session which might be transacted at a regular session.

    (b)(1) Special sessions of the district court may be held at such places within the United States outside the district as the nature of the business may require and upon such notice as the court orders, upon a finding by either the chief judge of the district court (or, if the chief judge is unavailable, the most senior available active judge of the district court) or the judicial council of the circuit that, because of emergency conditions, no location within the district is reasonably available where such special sessions could be held.

(2) Pursuant to this subsection, any business which may be transacted at a regular session of a district court may be transacted at a special session conducted outside the district, except that a criminal trial may not be conducted at a special session outside the State in which the crime has been committed unless the defendant consents to such a criminal trial.

(3) Notwithstanding any other provision of law, in any case in which special sessions are conducted pursuant to this section, the district court may summon jurors—

(A) in civil proceedings, from any part of the district in which the court ordinarily conducts business or the district in which it is holding a special session; and

(B) in criminal trials, from any part of the district in which the crime has been committed and, if the defendant so consents, from any district in which the court is conducting business pursuant to this section.

(4) If a district court issues an order exercising its authority under paragraph (1), the court—

(A) through the Administrative Office of the United States Courts, shall—

(i) send notice of such order, including the reasons for the issuance of such order, to the Committee on the Judiciary of the Senate and the Committee on the Judiciary of the House of Representatives; and

(ii) not later than 180 days after the expiration of such court order submit a brief report to the Committee on the Judiciary of the Senate and the Committee on the Judiciary of the House of Representatives describing the impact of such order, including—

(I) the reasons for the issuance of such order;

(II) the duration of such order;

(III) the impact of such order on litigants; and

(IV) the costs to the judiciary resulting from such order; and

(B) shall provide reasonable notice to the United States Marshals Service before the commencement of any special session held pursuant to such order.

(5) If a district court issues an order exercising its authority under paragraph (1), the court shall direct the United States marshal of the district where the court is meeting to furnish transportation and subsistence to the same extent as that provided in sections 4282 and 4285 of title 18.

(June 25, 1948, c. 646, 62 Stat. 897; Oct. 16, 1963, Pub.L. 88–139, § 1, 77 Stat. 248; Sept. 9, 2005, Pub.L. 109–63, § 2(b), 119 Stat. 1994; Jan. 5, 2006, Pub.L. 109–162, Title XI, § 1198(a), 119 Stat. 3132.)

[§ 142. Repealed. Pub.L. 97–164, Title I, § 115(c)(3), Apr. 2, 1982, 96 Stat. 32]

HISTORICAL AND STATUTORY NOTES

Section, Acts June 25, 1948, c. 646, 62 Stat. 898; Oct. 9, 1962, Pub.L. 87–764, 76 Stat. 762; Nov. 19, 1977, Pub.L. 95–196, 91 Stat. 1420, related to the providing of accommodations at places for holding court. See section 462 of this title.

§ 143. Vacant judgeship as affecting proceedings

When the office of a district judge becomes vacant, all pending process, pleadings and proceedings shall, when necessary, be continued by the clerk until a judge is appointed or designated to hold such court.

(June 25, 1948, c. 646, 62 Stat. 898.)

§ 144. Bias or prejudice of judge

Whenever a party to any proceeding in a district court makes and files a timely and sufficient affidavit that the judge before whom the matter is pending has a personal bias or prejudice either against him or in favor of any adverse party, such judge shall proceed no further therein, but another judge shall be assigned to hear such proceeding.

The affidavit shall state the facts and the reasons for the belief that bias or prejudice exists, and shall be filed not less than ten days before the beginning of the term at which the proceeding is to be heard, or good cause shall be shown for failure to file it within such time. A party may file only one such affidavit in any case. It shall be accompanied by a certificate of counsel of record stating that it is made in good faith.

(June 25, 1948, c. 646, 62 Stat. 898; May 24, 1949, c. 139, § 65, 63 Stat. 99.)

CHAPTER 6—BANKRUPTCY JUDGES

§ 151. Designation of bankruptcy courts

In each judicial district, the bankruptcy judges in regular active service shall constitute a unit of the district court to be known as the bankruptcy court for that district. Each bankruptcy judge, as a judicial officer of the district court, may exercise the authority conferred under this chapter with respect to any action, suit, or proceeding and may preside alone and hold a regular or special session of the court, except as otherwise provided by law or by rule or order of the district court.

(Added Pub.L. 98–353, Title I, § 104(a), July 10, 1984, 98 Stat. 336.)

§ 152. Appointment of bankruptcy judges

(a)(1) Each bankruptcy judge to be appointed for a judicial district, as provided in paragraph (2), shall be appointed by the court of appeals of the United States for the circuit in which such district is located. Such appointments shall be made after considering the recommendations of the Judicial Conference submitted pursuant to subsection (b). Each bankruptcy judge shall be appointed for a term of fourteen years, subject to the provisions of subsection (e). However, upon the expiration of the term, a bankruptcy judge may, with the approval of the judicial council of the circuit, continue to perform the duties of the office until the earlier of the date which is 180 days after the expiration of the term

---

[1]   [Footnote to Chapter 6 table entry:] So in original. Does not conform to section catchline.

or the date of the appointment of a successor. Bankruptcy judges shall serve as judicial officers of the United States district court established under Article III of the Constitution.

(2) The bankruptcy judges appointed pursuant to this section shall be appointed for the several judicial districts as follows:

Districts	Judges
Alabama:	
Northern	5
Middle	2
Southern	2
Alaska	2
Arizona	7
Arkansas:	
Eastern and Western	3
California:	
Northern	9
Eastern	6
Central	21
Southern	4
Colorado	5
Connecticut	3
Delaware	1
District of Columbia	1
Florida:	
Northern	1
Middle	8
Southern	5
Georgia:	
Northern	8
Middle	3
Southern	2
Hawaii	1
Idaho	2
Illinois:	
Northern	10
Central	3
Southern	1
Indiana:	
Northern	3
Southern	4
Iowa:	
Northern	2
Southern	2
Kansas	4
Kentucky:	
Eastern	2
Western	3
Louisiana:	
Eastern	2

Middle	3
Western	4
Texas:	
Northern	6
Eastern	2
Southern	6
Western	4
Utah	3
Vermont	1
Virginia:	
Eastern	5
Western	3
Washington:	
Eastern	2
Western	5
West Virginia:	
Northern	1
Southern	1
Wisconsin:	
Eastern	4
Western	2
Wyoming	1.

(3) Whenever a majority of the judges of any court of appeals cannot agree upon the appointment of a bankruptcy judge, the chief judge of such court shall make such appointment.

(4) The judges of the district courts for the territories shall serve as the bankruptcy judges for such courts. The United States court of appeals for the circuit within which such a territorial district court is located may appoint bankruptcy judges under this chapter for such district if authorized to do so by the Congress of the United States under this section.

(b)(1) The Judicial Conference of the United States shall, from time to time, and after considering the recommendations submitted by the Director of the Administrative Office of the United States Courts after such Director has consulted with the judicial council of the circuit involved, determine the official duty stations of bankruptcy judges and places of holding court.

(2) The Judicial Conference shall, from time to time, submit recommendations to the Congress regarding the number of bankruptcy judges needed and the districts in which such judges are needed.

(3) Not later than December 31, 1994, and not later than the end of each 2-year period thereafter, the Judicial Conference of the United States shall conduct a comprehensive review of all judicial districts to assess the continuing need for the bankruptcy judges authorized by this section, and shall report to the Congress its findings and any recommendations for the elimination of any authorized position which can be eliminated when a vacancy exists by reason of resignation, retirement, removal, or death.

(c)(1) Each bankruptcy judge may hold court at such places within the judicial district, in addition to the official duty station of such judge, as the business of the court may require.

(2)(A) Bankruptcy judges may hold court at such places within the United States outside the judicial district as the nature of the business of the court may require, and upon such notice as the court orders, upon a finding by either the chief judge of the bankruptcy court (or, if the chief judge is unavailable, the most senior available bankruptcy judge) or by the judicial council of the circuit that, because of emergency conditions, no location within the district is reasonably available where the bankruptcy judges could hold court.

(B) Bankruptcy judges may transact any business at special sessions of court held outside the district pursuant to this paragraph that might be transacted at a regular session.

(C) If a bankruptcy court issues an order exercising its authority under subparagraph (A), the court—

    (i) through the Administrative Office of the United States Courts, shall—

        (I) send notice of such order, including the reasons for the issuance of such order, to the Committee on the Judiciary of the Senate and the Committee on the Judiciary of the House of Representatives; and

        (II) not later than 180 days after the expiration of such court order submit a brief report to the Committee on the Judiciary of the Senate and the Committee on the Judiciary of the House of Representatives describing the impact of such order, including—

            (aa) the reasons for the issuance of such order;

            (bb) the duration of such order;

            (cc) the impact of such order on litigants; and

            (dd) the costs to the judiciary resulting from such order; and

    (ii) shall provide reasonable notice to the United States Marshals Service before the commencement of any special session held pursuant to such order.

(d) With the approval of the Judicial Conference and of each of the judicial councils involved, a bankruptcy judge may be designated to serve in any district adjacent to or near the district for which such bankruptcy judge was appointed.

(e) A bankruptcy judge may be removed during the term for which such bankruptcy judge is appointed, only for incompetence, misconduct, neglect of duty, or physical or mental disability and only by the judicial council of the circuit in which the judge's official duty station is located. Removal may not occur unless a majority of all of the judges of such council concur in the order of removal. Before any order of removal may be entered, a full specification of charges shall be furnished to such bankruptcy judge who shall be accorded an opportunity to be heard on such charges.

(Added Pub.L. 98–353, Title I, § 104(a), July 10, 1984, 98 Stat. 336; amended Pub.L. 99–554, Title I, § 101, Oct. 27, 1986, 100 Stat. 3088; Pub.L. 100–587, Nov. 3, 1988, 102 Stat. 2982; Pub.L. 101–650, Title III, § 304, Dec. 1, 1990, 104 Stat. 5105; Pub.L. 102–361, §§ 2, 4, Aug. 26, 1992, 106 Stat. 965, 966; Pub.L. 109–8, Title XII, § 1223(d), Apr. 20, 2005, 119 Stat. 198; Pub.L. 109–63, § 2(c), Sept. 9, 2005, 119 Stat. 1994.)

§ 153. Salaries; character of service

(a) Each bankruptcy judge shall serve on a full-time basis and shall receive as full compensation for his services, a salary at an annual rate that is equal to 92 percent of the salary of a judge of the district court of the United States as determined pursuant to section 135, to be paid at such times as the Judicial Conference of the United States determines.

(b) A bankruptcy judge may not engage in the practice of law and may not engage in any other practice, business, occupation, or employment inconsistent with the expeditious, proper, and impartial performance of such bankruptcy judge's duties as a judicial officer. The Conference may promulgate appropriate rules and regulations to implement this subsection.

(c) Each individual appointed under this chapter shall take the oath or affirmation prescribed by section 453 of this title before performing the duties of the office of bankruptcy judge.

(d) A bankruptcy judge appointed under this chapter shall be exempt from the provisions of subchapter I of chapter 63 of title 5.

(Added Pub.L. 98–353, Title I, § 104(a), July 10, 1984, 98 Stat. 338; amended Pub.L. 100–202, § 101(a) [Title IV, § 408(a)], Dec. 22, 1987, 101 Stat. 1329–26; Pub.L. 100–702, Title X, § 1003(a)(1), Nov. 19, 1988, 102 Stat. 4665.)

§ 154. Division of businesses;* chief judge

(a) Each bankruptcy court for a district having more than one bankruptcy judge shall by majority vote promulgate rules for the division of business among the bankruptcy judges to the extent that the division of business is not otherwise provided for by the rules of the district court.

(b) In each district court having more than one bankruptcy judge the district court shall designate one judge to serve as chief judge of such bankruptcy court. Whenever a majority of the judges of such district court cannot agree upon the designation as chief judge, the chief judge of such district court shall make such designation. The chief judge of the bankruptcy court shall ensure that the rules of the bankruptcy court and of the district court are observed and that the business of the bankruptcy court is handled effectively and expeditiously.

(Added Pub.L. 98–353, Title I, § 104(a), July 10, 1984, 98 Stat. 339.)

§ 155. Temporary transfer of bankruptcy judges

(a) A bankruptcy judge may be transferred to serve temporarily as a bankruptcy judge in any judicial district other than the judicial district for which such bankruptcy judge was appointed upon the approval of the judicial council of each of the circuits involved.

(b) A bankruptcy judge who has retired may, upon consent, be recalled to serve as a bankruptcy judge in any judicial district by the judicial council of the circuit within which such district is located. Upon recall, a bankruptcy judge may receive a salary for such service in accordance with regulations promulgated by the Judicial Conference of the United States, subject to the restrictions on the payment of an annuity in section 377 of this title or in subchapter III of chapter 83, and chapter 84, of title 5 which are applicable to such judge.

(Added Pub.L. 98–353, Title I, § 104(a), July 10, 1984, 98 Stat. 339; amended Pub.L. 99–651, Title II, § 202(a), Nov. 14, 1986, 100 Stat. 3648; Pub.L. 100–659, § 4(a), Nov. 15, 1988, 102 Stat. 3918.)

§ 156. Staff; expenses

(a) Each bankruptcy judge may appoint a secretary, a law clerk, and such additional assistants as the Director of the Administrative Office of the United States Courts determines to be necessary. A law clerk appointed under this section shall be exempt from the provisions of subchapter I of chapter 63 of title 5, unless specifically included by the appointing judge or by local rule of court.

(b) Upon certification to the judicial council of the circuit involved and to the Director of the Administrative Office of the United States Courts that the number of cases and proceedings pending within the jurisdiction under section 1334 of this title within a judicial district so warrants, the bankruptcy judges for such district may appoint an individual to serve as clerk of such bankruptcy court. The clerk may appoint, with the approval of such bankruptcy judges, and in such number as may be approved by the Director, necessary deputies, and may remove such deputies with the approval of such bankruptcy judges.

(c) Any court may utilize facilities or services, either on or off the court's premises, which pertain to the provision of notices, dockets, calendars, and other administrative information to parties in cases filed under the provisions of title 11, United States Code, where the costs of such facilities or services are paid for out of the assets of the estate and are not charged to the United States. The

---

*   [Footnote to 28 U.S.C. § 154: So in original. Probably should be "business." Ed.]

utilization of such facilities or services shall be subject to such conditions and limitations as the pertinent circuit council may prescribe.

(d) No office of the bankruptcy clerk of court may be consolidated with the district clerk of court office without the prior approval of the Judicial Conference and the Congress.

(e) In a judicial district where a bankruptcy clerk has been appointed pursuant to subsection (b), the bankruptcy clerk shall be the official custodian of the records and dockets of the bankruptcy court.

(f) For purposes of financial accountability in a district where a bankruptcy clerk has been certified, such clerk shall be accountable for and pay into the Treasury all fees, costs, and other monies collected by such clerk except uncollected fees not required by an Act of Congress to be prepaid. Such clerk shall make returns thereof to the Director of the Administrative Office of the United States Courts and the Director of the Executive Office For United States Trustees, under regulations prescribed by such Directors.

(Added Pub.L. 98–353, Title I, § 104(a), July 10, 1984, 98 Stat. 339; amended Pub.L. 99–554, Title I, §§ 103, 142, 144(a), Oct. 27, 1986, 100 Stat. 3090, 3096; Pub.L. 100–702, Title X, § 1003(a)(3), Nov. 19, 1988, 102 Stat. 4665.)

§ 157.   Procedures

(a) Each district court may provide that any or all cases under title 11 and any or all proceedings arising under title 11 or arising in or related to a case under title 11 shall be referred to the bankruptcy judges for the district.

(b)(1) Bankruptcy judges may hear and determine all cases under title 11 and all core proceedings arising under title 11, or arising in a case under title 11, referred under subsection (a) of this section, and may enter appropriate orders and judgments, subject to review under section 158 of this title.

(2) Core proceedings include, but are not limited to—

(A) matters concerning the administration of the estate;

(B) allowance or disallowance of claims against the estate or exemptions from property of the estate, and estimation of claims or interests for the purposes of confirming a plan under chapter 11, 12, or 13 of title 11 but not the liquidation or estimation of contingent or unliquidated personal injury tort or wrongful death claims against the estate for purposes of distribution in a case under title 11;

(C) counterclaims by the estate against persons filing claims against the estate;

(D) orders in respect to obtaining credit;

(E) orders to turn over property of the estate;

(F) proceedings to determine, avoid, or recover preferences;

(G) motions to terminate, annul, or modify the automatic stay;

(H) proceedings to determine, avoid, or recover fraudulent conveyances;

(I) determinations as to the dischargeability of particular debts;

(J) objections to discharges;

(K) determinations of the validity, extent, or priority of liens;

(L) confirmations of plans;

(M) orders approving the use or lease of property, including the use of cash collateral;

(N) orders approving the sale of property other than property resulting from claims brought by the estate against persons who have not filed claims against the estate;

(O) other proceedings affecting the liquidation of the assets of the estate or the adjustment of the debtor-creditor or the equity security holder relationship, except personal injury tort or wrongful death claims; and

(P) recognition of foreign proceedings and other matters under chapter 15 of title 11.

(3) The bankruptcy judge shall determine, on the judge's own motion or on timely motion of a party, whether a proceeding is a core proceeding under this subsection or is a proceeding that is otherwise related to a case under title 11. A determination that a proceeding is not a core proceeding shall not be made solely on the basis that its resolution may be affected by State law.

(4) Non-core proceedings under section 157(b)(2)(B) of title 28, United States Code, shall not be subject to the mandatory abstention provisions of section 1334(c)(2).

(5) The district court shall order that personal injury tort and wrongful death claims shall be tried in the district court in which the bankruptcy case is pending, or in the district court in the district in which the claim arose, as determined by the district court in which the bankruptcy case is pending.

(c)(1) A bankruptcy judge may hear a proceeding that is not a core proceeding but that is otherwise related to a case under title 11. In such proceeding, the bankruptcy judge shall submit proposed findings of fact and conclusions of law to the district court, and any final order or judgment shall be entered by the district judge after considering the bankruptcy judge's proposed findings and conclusions and after reviewing de novo those matters to which any party has timely and specifically objected.

(2) Notwithstanding the provisions of paragraph (1) of this subsection, the district court, with the consent of all the parties to the proceeding, may refer a proceeding related to a case under title 11 to a bankruptcy judge to hear and determine and to enter appropriate orders and judgments, subject to review under section 158 of this title.

(d) The district court may withdraw, in whole or in part, any case or proceeding referred under this section, on its own motion or on timely motion of any party, for cause shown. The district court shall, on timely motion of a party, so withdraw a proceeding if the court determines that resolution of the proceeding requires consideration of both title 11 and other laws of the United States regulating organizations or activities affecting interstate commerce.

(e) If the right to a jury trial applies in a proceeding that may be heard under this section by a bankruptcy judge, the bankruptcy judge may conduct the jury trial if specially designated to exercise such jurisdiction by the district court and with the express consent of all the parties.

(Added Pub.L. 98–353, Title I, § 104(a), July 10, 1984, 98 Stat. 340; amended Pub.L. 99–554, Title I, §§ 143, 144(b), Oct. 27, 1986, 100 Stat. 3096; Pub.L. 103–394, Title I, § 112, Oct. 22, 1994, 108 Stat. 4117; Pub.L. 109–8, Title VIII, § 802(c)(1), Apr. 20, 2005, 119 Stat. 145.)

§ 158. Appeals

(a) The district courts of the United States shall have jurisdiction to hear appeals

(1) from final judgments, orders, and decrees;

(2) from interlocutory orders and decrees issued under section 1121(d) of title 11 increasing or reducing the time periods referred to in section 1121 of such title; and

(3) with leave of the court, from other interlocutory orders and decrees;

and, with leave of the court, from interlocutory orders and decrees, of bankruptcy judges entered in cases and proceedings referred to the bankruptcy judges under section 157 of this title. An appeal under this subsection shall be taken only to the district court for the judicial district in which the bankruptcy judge is serving.

(b)(1) The judicial council of a circuit shall establish a bankruptcy appellate panel service composed of bankruptcy judges of the districts in the circuit who are appointed by the judicial council in accordance with paragraph (3), to hear and determine, with the consent of all the parties, appeals under subsection (a) unless the judicial council finds that—

> **(A)** there are insufficient judicial resources available in the circuit; or

> **(B)** establishment of such service would result in undue delay or increased cost to parties in cases under title 11.

Not later than 90 days after making the finding, the judicial council shall submit to the Judicial Conference of the United States a report containing the factual basis of such finding.

> **(2)(A)** A judicial council may reconsider, at any time, the finding described in paragraph (1).

> **(B)** On the request of a majority of the district judges in a circuit for which a bankruptcy appellate panel service is established under paragraph (1), made after the expiration of the 1-year period beginning on the date such service is established, the judicial council of the circuit shall determine whether a circumstance specified in subparagraph (A) or (B) of such paragraph exists.

> **(C)** On its own motion, after the expiration of the 3-year period beginning on the date a bankruptcy appellate panel service is established under paragraph (1), the judicial council of the circuit may determine whether a circumstance specified in subparagraph (A) or (B) of such paragraph exists.

> **(D)** If the judicial council finds that either of such circumstances exists, the judicial council may provide for the completion of the appeals then pending before such service and the orderly termination of such service.

> **(3)** Bankruptcy judges appointed under paragraph (1) shall be appointed and may be reappointed under such paragraph.

> **(4)** If authorized by the Judicial Conference of the United States, the judicial councils of 2 or more circuits may establish a joint bankruptcy appellate panel comprised of bankruptcy judges from the districts within the circuits for which such panel is established, to hear and determine, upon the consent of all the parties, appeals under subsection (a) of this section.

> **(5)** An appeal to be heard under this subsection shall be heard by a panel of 3 members of the bankruptcy appellate panel service, except that a member of such service may not hear an appeal originating in the district for which such member is appointed or designated under section 152 of this title.

> **(6)** Appeals may not be heard under this subsection by a panel of the bankruptcy appellate panel service unless the district judges for the district in which the appeals occur, by majority vote, have authorized such service to hear and determine appeals originating in such district.

(c)(1) Subject to subsections (b) and (d)(2), each appeal under subsection (a) shall be heard by a 3-judge panel of the bankruptcy appellate panel service established under subsection (b)(1) unless—

> **(A)** the appellant elects at the time of filing the appeal; or

> **(B)** any other party elects, not later than 30 days after service of notice of the appeal;

to have such appeal heard by the district court.

> **(2)** An appeal under subsections (a) and (b) of this section shall be taken in the same manner as appeals in civil proceedings generally are taken to the courts of appeals from the district courts and in the time provided by Rule 8002 of the Bankruptcy Rules.

(d)(1)   The courts of appeals shall have jurisdiction of appeals from all final decisions, judgments, orders, and decrees entered under subsections (a) and (b) of this section.

(2)(A)   The appropriate court of appeals shall have jurisdiction of appeals described in the first sentence of subsection (a) if the bankruptcy court, the district court, or the bankruptcy appellate panel involved, acting on its own motion or on the request of a party to the judgment, order, or decree described in such first sentence, or all the appellants and appellees (if any) acting jointly, certify that—

(i)   the judgment, order, or decree involves a question of law as to which there is no controlling decision of the court of appeals for the circuit or of the Supreme Court of the United States, or involves a matter of public importance;

(ii)   the judgment, order, or decree involves a question of law requiring resolution of conflicting decisions; or

(iii)   an immediate appeal from the judgment, order, or decree may materially advance the progress of the case or proceeding in which the appeal is taken;

and if the court of appeals authorizes the direct appeal of the judgment, order, or decree.

(B)   If the bankruptcy court, the district court, or the bankruptcy appellate panel—

(i)   on its own motion or on the request of a party, determines that a circumstance specified in clause (i), (ii), or (iii) of subparagraph (A) exists; or

(ii)   receives a request made by a majority of the appellants and a majority of appellees (if any) to make the certification described in subparagraph (A);

then the bankruptcy court, the district court, or the bankruptcy appellate panel shall make the certification described in subparagraph (A).

(C)   The parties may supplement the certification with a short statement of the basis for the certification.

(D)   An appeal under this paragraph does not stay any proceeding of the bankruptcy court, the district court, or the bankruptcy appellate panel from which the appeal is taken, unless the respective bankruptcy court, district court, or bankruptcy appellate panel, or the court of appeals in which the appeal is pending, issues a stay of such proceeding pending the appeal.

(E)   Any request under subparagraph (B) for certification shall be made not later than 60 days after the entry of the judgment, order, or decree.

(Added Pub.L. 98–353, Title I, § 104(a), July 10, 1984, 98 Stat. 341; amended Pub.L. 101–650, Title III, § 305, Dec. 1, 1990, 104 Stat. 5105; Pub.L. 103–394, Title I, §§ 102, 104(c), (d), Oct. 22, 1994, 108 Stat. 4108–4110; Pub.L. 109–8, Title XII, § 1233(a), Apr. 20, 2005, 119 Stat. 202; Pub.L. 111–327, § 2(c)(1), Dec. 22, 2010, 124 Stat. 3563.)

§ 159.   Bankruptcy statistics

(a)   The clerk of the district court, or the clerk of the bankruptcy court if one is certified pursuant to section 156(b) of this title, shall collect statistics regarding debtors who are individuals with primarily consumer debts seeking relief under chapters 7, 11, and 13 of title 11. Those statistics shall be in a standardized format prescribed by the Director of the Administrative Office of the United States Courts (referred to in this section as the "Director").

(b)   The Director shall—

(1)   compile the statistics referred to in subsection (a);

(2)   make the statistics available to the public; and

(3) not later than July 1, 2008, and annually thereafter, prepare, and submit to Congress a report concerning the information collected under subsection (a) that contains an analysis of the information.

(c) The compilation required under subsection (b) shall—

(1) be itemized, by chapter, with respect to title 11;

(2) be presented in the aggregate and for each district; and

(3) include information concerning—

(A) the total assets and total liabilities of the debtors described in subsection (a), and in each category of assets and liabilities, as reported in the schedules prescribed pursuant to section 2075 of this title and filed by debtors;

(B) the current monthly income, average income, and average expenses of debtors as reported on the schedules and statements that each such debtor files under sections 521 and 1322 of title 11;

(C) the aggregate amount of debt discharged in cases filed during the reporting period, determined as the difference between the total amount of debt and obligations of a debtor reported on the schedules and the amount of such debt reported in categories which are predominantly nondischargeable;

(D) the average period of time between the date of the filing of the petition and the closing of the case for cases closed during the reporting period;

(E) for cases closed during the reporting period—

(i) the number of cases in which a reaffirmation agreement was filed; and

(ii)(I) the total number of reaffirmation agreements filed;

(II) of those cases in which a reaffirmation agreement was filed, the number of cases in which the debtor was not represented by an attorney; and

(III) of those cases in which a reaffirmation agreement was filed, the number of cases in which the reaffirmation agreement was approved by the court;

(F) with respect to cases filed under chapter 13 of title 11, for the reporting period—

(i)(I) the number of cases in which a final order was entered determining the value of property securing a claim in an amount less than the amount of the claim; and

(II) the number of final orders entered determining the value of property securing a claim;

(ii) the number of cases dismissed, the number of cases dismissed for failure to make payments under the plan, the number of cases refiled after dismissal, and the number of cases in which the plan was completed, separately itemized with respect to the number of modifications made before completion of the plan, if any; and

(iii) the number of cases in which the debtor filed another case during the 6-year period preceding the filing;

(G) the number of cases in which creditors were fined for misconduct and any amount of punitive damages awarded by the court for creditor misconduct; and

(H) the number of cases in which sanctions under rule 9011 of the Federal Rules of Bankruptcy Procedure were imposed against the debtor's attorney or damages awarded under such Rule.

(Added Pub.L. 109–8, Title VI, § 601(a), Apr. 20, 2005, 119 Stat. 119; amended Pub.L. 111–327, § 2(c)(2), Dec. 22, 2010, 124 Stat. 3563.)

[CHAPTER 9—REPEALED]

[§§ 211 to 216.   Repealed. Pub.L. 97–164, Title I, § 106, Apr. 2, 1982, 96 Stat. 28]

HISTORICAL AND STATUTORY NOTES

Section 211, Acts June 25, 1948, c. 646, 62 Stat. 899; Aug. 25, 1958, Pub.L. 85–755, § 1, 72 Stat. 848, provided for the creation of the United States Court of Customs and Patent Appeals under article III of the United States Constitution and for the appointment of a chief judge and four associate judges for that court.

Section 212, Act June 25, 1948, c. 646, 62 Stat. 899, provided for the order of precedence of the chief judge and associate judges of the Court of Customs and Patent Appeals.

Section 213, Acts June 25, 1948, c. 646, 62 Stat. 899; Mar. 2, 1955, c. 9, § 1(e), 69 Stat. 10; Aug. 14, 1964, Pub.L. 88–426, Title IV, § 403(e), 78 Stat. 434; Aug. 9, 1975, Pub.L. 94–82, Title II, § 205(b)(5), 89 Stat. 422, provided for the tenure and salaries of the judges of the Court of Customs and Patent Appeals.

Section 214, Act June 25, 1948, c. 646, 62 Stat. 899, authorized the Court of Customs and Patent Appeals to hold court at such times and places as it might fix by rule.

Section 215, Act June 25, 1948, c. 646, 62 Stat. 899, provided that three judges of the Court of Customs and Patent Appeals constituted a quorum and that the concurrence of three judges was necessary to any decision.

Section 216, Act June 25, 1948, c. 646, 62 Stat. 899, provided for the filing of written opinions by the Court of Customs and Patent Appeals on appeals from decisions of the Patent Office and the recording of those opinions in the Patent Office.

Effective Date of Repeal

Repeal effective Oct. 1, 1982, see section 402 of Pub.L. 97–164, set out as a note under section 171 of this title.

Transfer of Matters and Petitions Pending in United States Court of Customs and Patent Appeals on October 1, 1982

For provisions that any matter pending before the United States Court of Customs and Patent Appeals on Oct. 1, 1982, and any petition for rehearing, reconsideration, alteration, modification, or other change in any decision of the United States Court of Customs and Patent Appeals rendered prior to Oct. 1, 1982, that has not been determined on that date or that is filed after that date, be determined by the United States Court of Appeals for the Federal Circuit, see section 403(b), (c) of Pub.L. 97–164, set out as a note under section 171 of this title.

CHAPTER 13—ASSIGNMENT OF JUDGES TO OTHER COURTS

§ 291.   Circuit judges

(a) The Chief Justice of the United States may, in the public interest, designate and assign temporarily any circuit judge to act as circuit judge in another circuit upon request by the chief judge or circuit justice of such circuit.

(b) The chief judge of a circuit or the circuit justice may, in the public interest, designate and assign temporarily any circuit judge within the circuit, including a judge designated and assigned to temporary duty therein, to hold a district court in any district within the circuit.

(June 25, 1948, c. 646, 62 Stat. 900; July 28, 1953, c. 253, § 2, 67 Stat. 226; Sept. 3, 1954, c. 1263, § 39(b), 68 Stat. 1240; July 9, 1956, c. 517, § 1(a), 70 Stat. 497; Aug. 25, 1958, Pub.L. 85–755, § 2, 72 Stat. 848; Nov. 6, 1978, Pub.L. 95–598, Title II, § 202, 92 Stat. 2660; Apr. 2, 1982, Pub.L. 97–164, Title I, § 108, 96 Stat. 28; Oct. 29, 1992, Pub.L. 102–572, Title I, § 104, 106 Stat. 4507.)

§ 292. District judges

(a) The chief judge of a circuit may designate and assign one or more district judges within the circuit to sit upon the court of appeals or a division thereof whenever the business of that court so requires. Such designations or assignments shall be in conformity with the rules or orders of the court of appeals of the circuit.

(b) The chief judge of a circuit may, in the public interest, designate and assign temporarily any district judge of the circuit to hold a district court in any district within the circuit.

(c) The chief judge of the United States Court of Appeals for the District of Columbia Circuit may, upon presentation of a certificate of necessity by the chief judge of the Superior Court of the District of Columbia pursuant to section 11–908(c) of the District of Columbia Code, designate and assign temporarily any district judge of the circuit to serve as a judge of such Superior Court, if such assignment (1) is approved by the Attorney General of the United States following a determination by him to the effect that such assignment is necessary to meet the ends of justice, and (2) is approved by the chief judge of the United States District Court for the District of Columbia.

(d) The Chief Justice of the United States may designate and assign temporarily a district judge of one circuit for service in another circuit, either in a district court or court of appeals, upon presentation of a certificate of necessity by the chief judge or circuit justice of the circuit wherein the need arises.

(e) The Chief Justice of the United States may designate and assign temporarily any district judge to serve as a judge of the Court of International Trade upon presentation to him of a certificate of necessity by the chief judge of the court.

(June 25, 1948, c. 646, 62 Stat. 901; July 28, 1953, c. 253, § 3, 67 Stat. 226; Sept. 3, 1954, c. 1263, § 39(c), 68 Stat. 1240; July 9, 1956, c. 517, § 1(b), 70 Stat. 497; July 14, 1956, c. 589, § 2, 70 Stat. 532; Aug. 25, 1958, Pub.L. 85–755, § 3, 72 Stat. 848; July 29, 1970, Pub.L. 91–358, Title I, § 172(e), 84 Stat. 591; Nov. 6, 1978, Pub.L. 95–598, Title II, §§ 203, 204, 92 Stat. 2660; Oct. 10, 1980, Pub.L. 96–417, Title V, § 501(7), 94 Stat. 1742; Apr. 2, 1982, Pub.L. 97–164, Title I, § 109, 96 Stat. 28.)

§ 293. Judges of the Court of International Trade

(a)[1] The Chief Justice of the United States may designate and assign temporarily any judge of the Court of International Trade to perform judicial duties in any circuit, either in a court of appeals or district court, upon presentation of a certificate of necessity by the chief judge or circuit justice of the circuit in which the need arises.

(June 25, 1948, c. 646, 62 Stat. 901; July 14, 1956, c. 589, § 3(a), 70 Stat. 532; Aug. 25, 1958, Pub.L. 85–755, § 4, 72 Stat. 848; Nov. 6, 1978, Pub.L. 95–598, Title II, § 205, 92 Stat. 2660; Oct. 10, 1980, Pub.L. 96–417, Title I, § 102, Title V, § 501(8), 94 Stat. 1727, 1742; Apr. 2, 1982, Pub.L. 97–164, Title I, § 110(a), (b), 96 Stat. 29.)

---

[1]   [Footnote to 28 U.S.C. § 293:] So in original. No subsec. (b) has been enacted.

§ 294. Assignment of retired Justices or judges to active duty

(a) Any retired Chief Justice of the United States or Associate Justice of the Supreme Court may be designated and assigned by the Chief Justice of the United States to perform such judicial duties in any circuit, including those of a circuit justice, as he is willing to undertake.

(b) Any judge of the United States who has retired from regular active service under section 371(b) or 372(a) of this title shall be known and designated as a senior judge and may continue to perform such judicial duties as he is willing and able to undertake, when designated and assigned as provided in subsections (c) and (d).

(c) Any retired circuit or district judge may be designated and assigned by the chief judge or judicial council of his circuit to perform such judicial duties within the circuit as he is willing and able to undertake. Any other retired judge of the United States may be designated and assigned by the chief judge of his court to perform such judicial duties in such court as he is willing and able to undertake.

(d) The Chief Justice of the United States shall maintain a roster of retired judges of the United States who are willing and able to undertake special judicial duties from time to time outside their own circuit, in the case of a retired circuit or district judge, or in a court other than their own, in the case of other retired judges, which roster shall be known as the roster of senior judges. Any such retired judge of the United States may be designated and assigned by the Chief Justice to perform such judicial duties as he is willing and able to undertake in a court outside his own circuit, in the case of a retired circuit or district judge, or in a court other than his own, in the case of any other retired judge of the United States. Such designation and assignment to a court of appeals or district court shall be made upon the presentation of a certificate of necessity by the chief judge or circuit justice of the circuit wherein the need arises and to any other court of the United States upon the presentation of a certificate of necessity by the chief judge of such court. No such designation or assignment shall be made to the Supreme Court.

(e) No retired Justice or judge shall perform judicial duties except when designated and assigned.

(June 25, 1948, c. 646, 62 Stat. 901; July 9, 1956, c. 517, § 1(c), 70 Stat. 497; Aug. 29, 1957, Pub.L. 85–219, 71 Stat. 495; Aug. 25, 1958, Pub.L. 85–755, § 5, 72 Stat. 849; Nov. 6, 1978, Pub.L. 95–598, Title II, § 206, 92 Stat. 2660.)

§ 295. Conditions upon designation and assignment

No designation and assignment of a circuit or district judge in active service shall be made without the consent of the chief judge or judicial council of the circuit from which the judge is to be designated and assigned. No designation and assignment of a judge of any other court of the United States in active service shall be made without the consent of the chief judge of such court.

All designations and assignments of justices and judges shall be filed with the clerks and entered on the minutes of the courts from and to which made.

The Chief Justice of the United States, a circuit justice or a chief judge of a circuit may make new designation and assignments in accordance with the provisions of this chapter and may revoke those previously made by him.

(June 25, 1948, c. 646, 62 Stat. 901; Sept. 3, 1954, c. 1263, § 39(d), 68 Stat. 1240; July 14, 1956, c. 589, § 3(b), 70 Stat. 532; Aug. 25, 1958, Pub.L. 85–755, § 6, 72 Stat. 850; Nov. 6, 1978, Pub.L. 95–598, Title II, § 207, 92 Stat. 2660.)

§ 296. Powers upon designation and assignment

A justice or judge shall discharge, during the period of his designation and assignment, all judicial duties for which he is designated and assigned. He may be required to perform any duty which might be required of a judge of the court or district or circuit to which he is designated and assigned.

Such justice or judge shall have all the powers of a judge of the court, circuit or district to which he is designated and assigned, except the power to appoint any person to a statutory position or to designate permanently a depository of funds or a newspaper for publication of legal notices. However, a district judge who has retired from regular active service under section 371(b) of this title, when designated and assigned to the court to which such judge was appointed, having performed in the preceding calendar year an amount of work equal to or greater than the amount of work an average judge in active service on that court would perform in 6 months, and having elected to exercise such powers, shall have the powers of a judge of that court to participate in appointment of court officers and magistrate judges, rulemaking, governance, and administrative matters.

A justice or judge who has sat by designation and assignment in another district or circuit may, notwithstanding his absence from such district or circuit or the expiration of the period of his designation and assignment, decide or join in the decision and final disposition of all matters submitted to him during such period and in the consideration and disposition of applications for rehearing or further proceedings in such matters.

(June 25, 1948, c. 646, 62 Stat. 901; Jan. 7, 2008, Pub.L. 110–177, Title V, § 503, 121 Stat. 2542.)

§ 297. Assignment of judges to courts of the freely associated compact states*

(a) The Chief Justice or the chief judge of the United States Court of Appeals for the Ninth Circuit may assign any circuit, district, magistrate, or territorial judge of a court of the Ninth Circuit, with the consent of the judge so assigned, to serve temporarily as a judge of any duly constituted court of the freely associated compact states whenever an official duly authorized by the laws of the respective compact state requests such assignment and such assignment is necessary for the proper dispatch of the business of the respective court.

(b) The Congress consents to the acceptance and retention by any judge so authorized of reimbursement from the countries referred to in subsection (a) of all necessary travel expenses, including transportation, and of subsistence, or of a reasonable per diem allowance in lieu of subsistence. The judge shall report to the Administrative Office of the United States Courts any amount received pursuant to this subsection.

(Added Pub.L. 100–702, Title X, § 1022(1), Nov. 19, 1988, 102 Stat. 4672; amended Pub.L. 112–149, § 3, July 26, 2012, 126 Stat. 1145.)

CHAPTER 15—CONFERENCES AND COUNCILS OF JUDGES

§ 331. Judicial Conference of the United States

The Chief Justice of the United States shall summon annually the chief judge of each judicial circuit, the chief judge of the Court of International Trade, and a district judge from each judicial circuit to a conference at such time and place in the United States as he may designate. He shall preside at such conference which shall be known as the Judicial Conference of the United States.

---

* [Footnote to 28 U.S.C. § 297: The freely associated compact states are the Federated States of Micronesia, the Republic of the Marshall Islands, and the Republic of Palau, which are each located in the Pacific Ocean. These are independent nations in "free association" with the United States. The United States provides funding and military protection for these nations and permits their citizens to enter the United States as legal non-immigrants—visa-free—to live, work, or study for an unlimited period of time. Ed.]

Special sessions of the Conference may be called by the Chief Justice at such times and places as he may designate.

The district judge to be summoned from each judicial circuit shall be chosen by the circuit and district judges of the circuit and shall serve as a member of the Judicial Conference of the United States for a term of not less than 3 successive years nor more than 5 successive years, as established by majority vote of all circuit and district judges of the circuit. A district judge serving as a member of the Judicial Conference may be either a judge in regular active service or a judge retired from regular active service under section 371(b) of this title.

If the chief judge of any circuit, the chief judge of the Court of International Trade, or the district judge chosen by the judges of the circuit is unable to attend, the Chief Justice may summon any other circuit or district judge from such circuit or any other judge of the Court of International Trade, as the case may be. Every judge summoned shall attend and, unless excused by the Chief Justice, shall remain throughout the sessions of the conference and advise as to the needs of his circuit or court and as to any matters in respect of which the administration of justice in the courts of the United States may be improved.

The Conference shall make a comprehensive survey of the condition of business in the courts of the United States and prepare plans for assignment of judges to or from circuits or districts where necessary. It shall also submit suggestions and recommendations to the various courts to promote uniformity of management procedures and the expeditious conduct of court business. The Conference is authorized to exercise the authority provided in chapter 16 of this title as the Conference, or through a standing committee. If the Conference elects to establish a standing committee, it shall be appointed by the Chief Justice and all petitions for review shall be reviewed by that committee. The Conference or the standing committee may hold hearings, take sworn testimony, issue subpoenas and subpoenas duces tecum, and make necessary and appropriate orders in the exercise of its authority. Subpoenas and subpoenas duces tecum shall be issued by the clerk of the Supreme Court or by the clerk of any court of appeals, at the direction of the Chief Justice or his designee and under the seal of the court, and shall be served in the manner provided in rule 45(c) of the Federal Rules of Civil Procedure for subpoenas and subpoenas duces tecum issued on behalf of the United States or an officer or any agency thereof. The Conference may also prescribe and modify rules for the exercise of the authority provided in chapter 16 of this title. All judicial officers and employees of the United States shall promptly carry into effect all orders of the Judicial Conference or the standing committee established pursuant to this section.

The Conference shall also carry on a continuous study of the operation and effect of the general rules of practice and procedure now or hereafter in use as prescribed by the Supreme Court for the other courts of the United States pursuant to law. Such changes in and additions to those rules as the Conference may deem desirable to promote simplicity in procedure, fairness in administration, the just determination of litigation, and the elimination of unjustifiable expense and delay shall be recommended by the Conference from time to time to the Supreme Court for its consideration and adoption, modification or rejection, in accordance with law.

The Judicial Conference shall review rules prescribed under section 2071 of this title by the courts, other than the Supreme Court and the district courts, for consistency with Federal law. The Judicial Conference may modify or abrogate any such rule so reviewed found inconsistent in the course of such a review.

The Attorney General shall, upon request of the Chief Justice, report to such Conference on matters relating to the business of the several courts of the United States, with particular reference to cases to which the United States is a party.

The Chief Justice shall submit to Congress an annual report of the proceedings of the Judicial Conference and its recommendations for legislation.

The Judicial Conference shall consult with the Director of United States Marshals Service on a continuing basis regarding the security requirements for the judicial branch of the United States

Government, to ensure that the views of the Judicial Conference regarding the security requirements for the judicial branch of the Federal Government are taken into account when determining staffing levels, setting priorities for programs regarding judicial security, and allocating judicial security resources. In this paragraph, the term "judicial security" includes the security of buildings housing the judiciary, the personal security of judicial officers, the assessment of threats made to judicial officers, and the protection of all other judicial personnel. The United States Marshals Service retains final authority regarding security requirements for the judicial branch of the Federal Government.

(June 25, 1948, c. 646, 62 Stat. 902; July 9, 1956, c. 517, § 1(d), 70 Stat. 497; Aug. 28, 1957, Pub.L. 85–202, 71 Stat. 476; July 11, 1958, Pub.L. 85–513, 72 Stat. 356; Sept. 19, 1961, Pub.L. 87–253, §§ 1, 2, 75 Stat. 521; Nov. 6, 1978, Pub.L. 95–598, Title II, § 208, 92 Stat. 2660; Oct. 15, 1980, Pub.L. 96–458, § 4, 94 Stat. 2040; Apr. 2, 1982, Pub.L. 97–164, Title I, § 111, 96 Stat. 29; Oct. 14, 1986, Pub.L. 99–466, § 1, 100 Stat. 1190; Nov. 19, 1988, Pub.L. 100–702, Title IV, § 402(b), 102 Stat. 4650; Oct. 19, 1996, Pub.L. 104–317, Title VI, § 601(a), 110 Stat. 3857; Nov. 2, 2002, Pub.L. 107–273, Div. C, Title I, § 110403(b), 116 Stat. 1855; Jan. 7, 2008, Pub.L. 110–177, Title I, § 101(b), 121 Stat. 2534.)

§ 332.   Judicial councils of circuits

(a)(1)   The chief judge of each judicial circuit shall call, at least twice in each year and at such places as he or she may designate, a meeting of the judicial council of the circuit, consisting of the chief judge of the circuit, who shall preside, and an equal number of circuit judges and district judges of the circuit, as such number is determined by majority vote of all such judges of the circuit in regular active service.

(2)   Members of the council shall serve for terms established by a majority vote of all judges of the circuit in regular active service.

(3)   Except for the chief judge of the circuit, either judges in regular active service or judges retired from regular active service under section 371(b) of this title may serve as members of the council. Service as a member of a judicial council by a judge retired from regular active service under section 371(b) may not be considered for meeting the requirements of section 371(f)(1)(A), (B), or (C).

(4)   No more than one district judge from any one district shall serve simultaneously on the council, unless at least one district judge from each district within the circuit is already serving as a member of the council.

(5)   In the event of the death, resignation, retirement under section 371(a) or 372(a) of this title, or disability of a member of the council, a replacement member shall be designated to serve the remainder of the unexpired term by the chief judge of the circuit.

(6)   Each member of the council shall attend each council meeting unless excused by the chief judge of the circuit.

(b)   The council shall be known as the Judicial Council of the circuit.

(c)   The chief judge shall submit to the council the semiannual reports of the Director of the Administrative Office of the United States Courts. The council shall take such action thereon as may be necessary.

(d)(1)   Each judicial council shall make all necessary and appropriate orders for the effective and expeditious administration of justice within its circuit. Any general order relating to practice and procedure shall be made or amended only after giving appropriate public notice and an opportunity for comment. Any such order so relating shall take effect upon the date specified by such judicial council. Copies of such orders so relating shall be furnished to the Judicial Conference and the Administrative Office of the United States Courts and be made available to the public. Each council is authorized to hold hearings, to take sworn testimony, and to issue subpoenas and subpoenas duces tecum. Subpoenas and subpoenas duces tecum shall be issued by the clerk of the court of appeals, at the direction of the chief judge of the circuit or his designee and under the seal of the court, and shall be served in the manner provided in rule 45(c) of the Federal Rules of Civil Procedure for subpoenas and subpoenas duces tecum issued on behalf of the United States or an officer or agency thereof.

(2)   All judicial officers and employees of the circuit shall promptly carry into effect all orders of the judicial council. In the case of failure to comply with an order made under this subsection or a subpoena issued under chapter 16 of this title, a judicial council or a special committee appointed under section 353 of this title may institute a contempt proceeding in any district court in which the judicial officer or employee of the circuit who fails to comply with the order made under this subsection shall be ordered to show cause before the court why he or she should not be held in contempt of court.

(3)   Unless an impediment to the administration of justice is involved, regular business of the courts need not be referred to the council.

(4)   Each judicial council shall periodically review the rules which are prescribed under section 2071 of this title by district courts within its circuit for consistency with rules prescribed under section 2072 of this title. Each council may modify or abrogate any such rule found inconsistent in the course of such a review.

(e)   The judicial council of each circuit may appoint a circuit executive. In appointing a circuit executive, the judicial council shall take into account experience in administrative and executive positions, familiarity with court procedures, and special training. The circuit executive shall exercise such administrative powers and perform such duties as may be delegated to him by the circuit council. The duties delegated to the circuit executive of each circuit may include but need not be limited to:

(1)   Exercising administrative control of all nonjudicial activities of the court of appeals of the circuit in which he is appointed.

(2)   Administering the personnel system of the court of appeals of the circuit.

(3)   Administering the budget of the court of appeals of the circuit.

(4)   Maintaining a modern accounting system.

(5)   Establishing and maintaining property control records and undertaking a space management program.

(6)   Conducting studies relating to the business and administration of the courts within the circuit and preparing appropriate recommendations and reports to the chief judge, the circuit council, and the Judicial Conference.

(7)   Collecting, compiling, and analyzing statistical data with a view to the preparation and presentation of reports based on such data as may be directed by the chief judge, the circuit council, and the Administrative Office of the United States Courts.

(8)   Representing the circuit as its liaison to the courts of the various States in which the circuit is located, the marshal's office, State and local bar associations, civic groups, news media, and other private and public groups having a reasonable interest in the administration of the circuit.

(9)   Arranging and attending meetings of the judges of the circuit and of the circuit council, including preparing the agenda and serving as secretary in all such meetings.

(10) Preparing an annual report to the circuit and to the Administrative Office of the United States Courts for the preceding calendar year, including recommendations for more expeditious disposition of the business of the circuit.

All duties delegated to the circuit executive shall be subject to the general supervision of the chief judge of the circuit.

(f)(1)   Each circuit executive shall be paid at a salary to be established by the Judicial Conference of the United States not to exceed the annual rate of level IV of the Executive Schedule pay rates under section 5315 of title 5.

(2)   The circuit executive shall serve at the pleasure of the judicial council of the circuit.

(3)   The circuit executive may appoint, with the approval of the council, necessary employees in such number as may be approved by the Director of the Administrative Office of the United States Courts.

(4)   The circuit executive and his staff shall be deemed to be officers and employees of the judicial branch of the United States Government within the meaning of subchapter III of chapter 83 (relating to civil service retirement), chapter 87 (relating to Federal employees' life insurance program), and chapter 89 (relating to Federal employees' health benefits program) of title 5, United States Code.

(g)   No later than January 31 of each year, each judicial council shall submit a report to the Administrative Office of the United States Courts on the number and nature of orders entered under this section during the preceding calendar year that relate to judicial misconduct or disability.

(h)(1)   The United States Court of Appeals for the Federal Circuit may appoint a circuit executive, who shall serve at the pleasure of the court. In appointing a circuit executive, the court shall take into account experience in administrative and executive positions, familiarity with court procedures, and special training. The circuit executive shall exercise such administrative powers and perform such duties as may be delegated by the court. The duties delegated to the circuit executive may include the duties specified in subsection (e) of this section, insofar as such duties are applicable to the Court of Appeals for the Federal Circuit.

(2)   The circuit executive shall be paid the salary for circuit executives established under subsection (f) of this section.

(3)   The circuit executive may appoint, with the approval of the court, necessary employees in such number as may be approved by the Director of the Administrative Office of the United States Courts.

(4)   The circuit executive and staff shall be deemed to be officers and employees of the United States within the meaning of the statutes specified in subsection (f)(4).

(5)   The court may appoint either a circuit executive under this subsection or a clerk under section 711 of this title, but not both, or may appoint a combined circuit executive/clerk who shall be paid the salary of a circuit executive.

(June 25, 1948, c. 646, 62 Stat. 902; Nov. 13, 1963, Pub.L. 88–176, § 3, 77 Stat. 331; Jan. 5, 1971, Pub.L. 91–647, 84 Stat. 1907; Nov. 6, 1978, Pub.L. 95–598, Title II, § 209, 92 Stat. 2661; Oct. 15, 1980, Pub.L. 96–458, § 2(a) to (d)(1), 94 Stat. 2035, 2036; Oct. 1, 1988, Pub.L. 100–459, Title IV, § 407, 102 Stat. 2213; Nov. 19, 1988, Pub.L. 100–702, Title IV, § 403(a)(2), (b), Title X, §§ 1018, 1020(a)(1), 102 Stat. 4651, 4670, 4671; Dec. 1, 1990, Pub.L. 101–650, Title III, §§ 323, 325(b)(1), Title IV, § 403, 104 Stat. 5120, 5121, 5124; Dec. 9, 1991, Pub.L. 102–198, § 1, 105 Stat. 1623; Oct. 19, 1996, Pub.L. 104–317, Title II, § 208, 110 Stat. 3851; Nov. 13, 2000, Pub.L. 106–518, Title II, § 205, Title III, § 306, 114 Stat. 2414, 2418; Dec. 21, 2000, Pub.L. 106–553, § 1(a)(2) [Title III, § 306], 114 Stat. 2762, 2762A–85; Nov. 2, 2002, Pub.L. 107–273, Div. C, Title I, § 11043(c), 116 Stat. 1855.)

§ 333.   Judicial conferences of circuits

The chief judge of each circuit may summon biennially, and may summon annually, the circuit, district, magistrate, and bankruptcy judges of the circuit, in active service, to a conference at a time and place that he designates, for the purpose of considering the business of the courts and advising means of improving the administration of justice within such circuit. He may preside at such conference, which shall be known as the Judicial Conference of the circuit. The judges of the District Court of Guam, the District Court of the Virgin Islands, and the District Court of the Northern

Mariana Islands may also be summoned biennially, and may be summoned annually, to the conferences of their respective circuits.

Every judge summoned may attend.

The court of appeals for each circuit shall provide by its rules for representation and active participation at such conference by members of the bar of such circuit.

(June 25, 1948, c. 646, 62 Stat. 903; Dec. 29, 1950, c. 1185, 64 Stat. 1128; Oct. 31, 1951, c. 655, § 38, 65 Stat. 723; July 7, 1958, Pub.L. 85–508, § 12(e), 72 Stat. 348; Nov. 6, 1978, Pub.L. 95–598, Title II, § 210, 92 Stat. 2661; Dec. 1, 1990, Pub.L. 101–650, Title III, § 320, 104 Stat. 5117; Apr. 26, 1996, Pub.L. 104–134, Title I, § 101[(a)][Title III, § 305], 110 Stat. 1321–36; renumbered Title I May 2, 1996, Pub.L. 104–140, § 1(a), 110 Stat. 1327; Oct. 13, 2008, Pub.L. 110–406, § 9, 122 Stat. 4293.)

§ 334. Institutes and joint councils on sentencing

(a) In the interest of uniformity in sentencing procedures, there is hereby authorized to be established under the auspices of the Judicial Conference of the United States, institutes and joint councils on sentencing. The Attorney General and/or the chief judge of each circuit may at any time request, through the Director of the Administrative Office of the United States Courts, the Judicial Conference to convene such institutes and joint councils for the purpose of studying, discussing, and formulating the objectives, policies, standards, and criteria for sentencing those convicted of crimes and offenses in the courts of the United States. The agenda of the institutes and joint councils may include but shall not be limited to: (1) The development of standards for the content and utilization of presentence reports; (2) the establishment of factors to be used in selecting cases for special study and observation in prescribed diagnostic clinics; (3) the determination of the importance of psychiatric, emotional, sociological and physiological factors involved in crime and their bearing upon sentences; (4) the discussion of special sentencing problems in unusual cases such as treason, violation of public trust, subversion, or involving abnormal sex behavior, addiction to drugs or alcohol, and mental or physical handicaps; (5) the formulation of sentencing principles and criteria which will assist in promoting the equitable administration of the criminal laws of the United States.

(b) After the Judicial Conference has approved the time, place, participants, agenda, and other arrangements for such institutes and joint councils, the chief judge of each circuit is authorized to invite the attendance of district judges under conditions which he thinks proper and which will not unduly delay the work of the courts.

(c) The Attorney General is authorized to select and direct the attendance at such institutes and meetings of United States attorneys and other officials of the Department of Justice and may invite the participation of other interested Federal officers. He may also invite specialists in sentencing methods, criminologists, psychiatrists, penologists, and others to participate in the proceedings.

(d) The expenses of attendance of judges shall be paid from applicable appropriations for the judiciary of the United States. The expenses connected with the preparation of the plans and agenda for the conference and for the travel and other expenses incident to the attendance of officials and other participants invited by the Attorney General shall be paid from applicable appropriations of the Department of Justice.

(Added Pub.L. 85–752, § 1, Aug. 25, 1958, 72 Stat. 845.)

§ 335. Judicial Conference of the Court of International Trade

(a) The chief judge of the Court of International Trade is authorized to summon annually the judges of such court to a judicial conference, at a time and place that such chief judge designates, for the purpose of considering the business of such court and improvements in the administration of justice in such court.

(b) The Court of International Trade shall provide by its rules for representation and active participation at such conference by members of the bar.

(Added Pub.L. 99–466, § 2(a), Oct. 14, 1986, 100 Stat. 1190.)

CHAPTER 17—RESIGNATION AND RETIREMENT
OF JUSTICES AND JUDGES

§ 371.   Retirement on salary; retirement in senior status

(a)   Any justice or judge of the United States appointed to hold office during good behavior may retire from the office after attaining the age and meeting the service requirements, whether continuous or otherwise, of subsection (c) and shall, during the remainder of his lifetime, receive an annuity equal to the salary he was receiving at the time he retired.

(b)(1)   Any justice or judge of the United States appointed to hold office during good behavior may retain the office but retire from regular active service after attaining the age and meeting the service requirements, whether continuous or otherwise, of subsection (c) of this section and shall, during the remainder of his or her lifetime, continue to receive the salary of the office if he or she meets the requirements of subsection (e).

(2)   In a case in which a justice or judge who retires under paragraph (1) does not meet the requirements of subsection (e), the justice or judge shall continue to receive the salary that he or she was receiving when he or she was last in active service or, if a certification under subsection (e) was made for such justice or judge, when such a certification was last in effect. The salary of such justice or judge shall be adjusted under section 461 of this title.

(c)   The age and service requirements for retirement under this section are as follows:

Attained Age:	Years of Service:
65	15
66	14
67	13
68	12
69	11
70	10

(d)   The President shall appoint, by and with the advice and consent of the Senate, a successor to a justice or judge who retires under this section.

(e)(1)   In order to continue receiving the salary of the office under subsection (b), a justice must be certified in each calendar year by the Chief Justice, and a judge must be certified by the chief judge of the circuit in which the judge sits, as having met the requirements set forth in at least one of the following subparagraphs:

(A)   The justice or judge must have carried in the preceding calendar year a caseload involving courtroom participation which is equal to or greater than the amount of work involving courtroom participation which an average judge in active service would perform in three months. In the instance of a justice or judge who has sat on both district courts and courts of appeals, the caseload of appellate work and trial work shall be determined separately and the results of those determinations added together for purposes of this paragraph.

(B) The justice or judge performed in the preceding calendar year substantial judicial duties not involving courtroom participation under subparagraph (A), including settlement efforts, motion decisions, writing opinions in cases that have not been orally argued, and administrative duties for the court to which the justice or judge is assigned. Any certification under this subparagraph shall include a statement describing in detail the nature and amount of work and certifying that the work done is equal to or greater than the work described in this subparagraph which an average judge in active service would perform in three months.

(C) The justice or judge has, in the preceding calendar year, performed work described in subparagraphs (A) and (B) in an amount which, when calculated in accordance with such subparagraphs, in the aggregate equals at least 3 months [*sic*] work.

(D) The justice or judge has, in the preceding calendar year, performed substantial administrative duties directly related to the operation of the courts, or has performed substantial duties for a Federal or State governmental entity. A certification under this subparagraph shall specify that the work done is equal to the full-time work of an employee of the judicial branch. In any year in which a justice or judge performs work described under this subparagraph for less than the full year, one-half of such work may be aggregated with work described under subparagraph (A), (B), or (C) of this paragraph for the purpose of the justice or judge satisfying the requirements of such subparagraph.

(E) The justice or judge was unable in the preceding calendar year to perform judicial or administrative work to the extent required by any of subparagraphs (A) through (D) because of a temporary or permanent disability. A certification under this subparagraph shall be made to a justice who certifies in writing his or her disability to the Chief Justice, and to a judge who certifies in writing his or her disability to the chief judge of the circuit in which the judge sits. A justice or judge who is certified under this subparagraph as having a permanent disability shall be deemed to have met the requirements of this subsection for each calendar year thereafter.

(2) Determinations of work performed under subparagraphs (A), (B), (C), and (D) of paragraph (1) shall be made pursuant to rules promulgated by the Judicial Conference of the United States. In promulgating such criteria, the Judicial Conference shall take into account existing standards promulgated by the Conference for allocation of space and staff for senior judges.

(3) If in any year a justice or judge who retires under subsection (b) does not receive a certification under this subsection (except as provided in paragraph (1)(E)), he or she may thereafter receive a certification for that year by satisfying the requirements of subparagraph (A), (B), (C), or (D) of paragraph (1) of this subsection in a subsequent year and attributing a sufficient part of the work performed in such subsequent year to the earlier year so that the work so attributed, when added to the work performed during such earlier year, satisfies the requirements for certification for that year. However, a justice or judge may not receive credit for the same work for purposes of certification for more than 1 year.

(4) In the case of any justice or judge who retires under subsection (b) during a calendar year, there shall be included in the determination under this subsection of work performed during that calendar year all work performed by that justice or judge (as described in subparagraphs (A), (B), (C), and (D) of paragraph (1)) during that calendar year before such retirement.

(June 25, 1948, c. 646, 62 Stat. 903; Oct. 31, 1951, c. 655, § 39, 65 Stat. 724; Feb. 10, 1954, c. 6, § 4(a), 68 Stat. 12; July 10, 1984, Pub.L. 98–353, Title II, § 204(a), 98 Stat. 350; Nov. 19, 1988, Pub.L. 100–702, Title X, § 1005(a), 102 Stat. 4666; Nov. 30, 1989, Pub.L. 101–194, Title VII, § 705(a), 103 Stat. 1770; Oct. 19, 1996,

Pub.L. 104–317, Title III, § 301, 110 Stat. 3851; Oct. 30, 2000, Pub.L. 106–398, § 1 [Div. A, Title VI, § 654(a)], 114 Stat. 1654, 1654A–165; Nov. 13, 2000, Pub.L. 106–518, Title III, § 303, 114 Stat. 2417.)

§ 372. Retirement for disability; substitute judge on failure to retire

(a) Any justice or judge of the United States appointed to hold office during good behavior who becomes permanently disabled from performing his duties may retire from regular active service, and the President shall, by and with the advice and consent of the Senate, appoint a successor.

Any justice or judge of the United States desiring to retire under this section shall certify to the President his disability in writing.

Whenever an associate justice of the Supreme Court, a chief judge of a circuit or the chief judge of the Court of International Trade, desires to retire under this section, he shall furnish to the President a certificate of disability signed by the Chief Justice of the United States.

A circuit or district judge, desiring to retire under this section, shall furnish to the President a certificate of disability signed by the chief judge of his circuit.

A judge of the Court of International Trade desiring to retire under this section, shall furnish to the President a certificate of disability signed by the chief judge of his court.

Each justice or judge retiring under this section after serving ten years continuously or otherwise shall, during the remainder of his lifetime, receive the salary of the office. A justice or judge retiring under this section who has served less than ten years in all shall, during the remainder of his lifetime, receive one-half the salary of the office.

(b) Whenever any judge of the United States appointed to hold office during good behavior who is eligible to retire under this section does not do so and a certificate of his disability signed by a majority of the members of the Judicial Council of his circuit in the case of a circuit or district judge, or by the Chief Justice of the United States in the case of the Chief Judge of the Court of International Trade, or by the chief judge of his court in the case of a judge of the Court of International Trade, is presented to the President and the President finds that such judge is unable to discharge efficiently all the duties of his office by reason of permanent mental or physical disability and that the appointment of an additional judge is necessary for the efficient dispatch of business, the President may make such appointment by and with the advice and consent of the Senate. Whenever any such additional judge is appointed, the vacancy subsequently caused by the death, resignation, or retirement of the disabled judge shall not be filled. Any judge whose disability causes the appointment of an additional judge shall, for purpose of precedence, service as chief judge, or temporary performance of the duties of that office, be treated as junior in commission to the other judges of the circuit, district, or court.

[**(c)** Repealed. Pub.L. 107–273, Div. C, Title I, § 11043(a)(1)(B), Nov. 2, 2002, 116 Stat. 1855]

(June 25, 1948, c. 646, 62 Stat. 903; May 24, 1949, c. 139, § 67, 63 Stat. 99; Feb. 10, 1954, c. 6, § 4(a), 68 Stat. 12; Sept. 2, 1957, Pub.L. 85–261, 71 Stat. 586; Oct. 10, 1980, Pub.L. 96–417, Title V, § 501(9), 94 Stat. 1742; Oct. 15, 1980, Pub.L. 96–458, § 3(a), (b), 94 Stat. 2036, 2040; Apr. 2, 1982, Pub.L. 97–164, Title I, § 112, 96 Stat. 29; July 10, 1984, Pub.L. 98–353, Title I, § 107, 98 Stat. 342; Nov. 19, 1988, Pub.L. 100–702, Title IV, § 403(c), 102 Stat. 4651; Dec. 1, 1990, Pub.L. 101–650, Title III, § 321, Title IV, § 402, 104 Stat. 5117, 5122; Oct. 29, 1992, Pub.L. 102–572, Title IX, § 902(b)(1), 106 Stat. 4516; Nov. 2, 2002, Pub.L. 107–273, Div. C, Title I, § 11043(a)(1), 116 Stat. 1855.)

§ 373. Judges in Territories and Possessions

(a) Any judge of the District Court of Guam, the District Court of the Northern Mariana Islands, or the District Court of the Virgin Islands who retires from office after attaining the age and meeting the service requirements whether continuous or otherwise, of subsection (b) shall, during the remainder of his lifetime, receive an annuity equal to the salary he is receiving at the time he retires.

(b) The age and service requirements for retirement under subsection (a) of this section are as follows:

Attained Age:	Years of Service:
65	15
66	14
67	13
68	12
69	11
70	10

(c)(1) Any judge or former judge who is receiving an annuity pursuant to this section may elect to become a senior judge of the court upon which he served before retiring.

(2) The chief judge of a judicial circuit may recall any such senior judge, with the judge's consent, to perform, for the court from which he retired, such judicial duties for such periods of time as the chief judge may specify.

(3) Any act or failure to act by a senior judge performing judicial duties pursuant to recall under paragraph (2) of this subsection shall have the same force and effect as if it were an act or failure to act of a judge on active duty; but such senior judge shall not be counted as a judge of the court on which he is serving as a recalled annuitant for purposes of the number of judgeships authorized for that court.

(4) Any senior judge performing judicial duties pursuant to recall under paragraph (2) of this subsection shall be paid, while performing such duties, the same compensation (in lieu of the annuity payable under subsection (a) of this section) and the same allowances for travel and other expenses as a judge on active duty with the court being served.

(5) Any senior judge performing judicial duties pursuant to recall under paragraph (2) of this subsection shall at all times be governed by the code of judicial conduct for United States judges approved by the Judicial Conference of the United States.

(d) Any judge who elects to become a senior judge under subsection (c) of this section and who thereafter—

(1) accepts civil office or employment under the Government of the United States (other than the performance of judicial duties pursuant to recall under subsection (c) of this section);

(2) engages in the practice of law; or

(3) materially violates the code of judicial conduct for United States judges,

shall cease to be a senior judge and to be eligible for recall pursuant to subsection (c) of this section.

(e) Any judge of the District Court of Guam, the District Court of the Northern Mariana Islands, or the District Court of the Virgin Islands who is removed by the President of the United States upon the sole ground of mental or physical disability, or who is not reappointed (as judge of such court), shall be entitled, upon attaining the age of sixty-five years or upon relinquishing office if he is then beyond the age of sixty-five years, (1) if his judicial service, continuous or otherwise, aggregates fifteen years or more, to receive during the remainder of his life an annuity equal to the salary he received when he left office, or (2) if his judicial service, continuous or otherwise, aggregated less than fifteen years but not less than ten years, to receive during the remainder of his life an annuity equal to that proportion of such salary which the aggregate number of his years of his judicial service bears to fifteen.

(f) Service at any time as a judge of the courts referred to in subsection (a) or of any other court of the United States, as defined by section 451 of this title, shall be included in the computation of aggregate years of judicial service for purposes of this section.

(g) Any retired judge who is entitled to receive an annuity under subsection (a) shall be entitled to a cost of living adjustment in the amount payable to him computed as specified in section 8340(b) of title 5, except that in no case may the annuity payable to such retired judge, as increased under this subsection, exceed 95 per centum of the salary of a United States district judge in regular active service.

(June 25, 1948, c. 646, 62 Stat. 904; Oct. 31, 1951, c. 655, § 40, 65 Stat. 724; Feb. 10, 1954, c. 6, § 5, 68 Stat. 13; July 7, 1958, Pub.L. 85–508, § 12(d), 72 Stat. 348; Mar. 18, 1959, Pub.L. 86–3, § 14(d), 73 Stat. 10; Sept. 12, 1966, Pub.L. 89–571, § 2, 80 Stat. 764; Oct. 11, 1976, Pub.L. 94–470, 90 Stat. 2052; Aug. 27, 1986, Pub.L. 99–396, § 21(a), 100 Stat. 844.)

§ 374. Residence of retired judges; official station

Retired judges of the United States are not subject to restrictions as to residence. The place where a retired judge maintains the actual abode in which he customarily lives shall be deemed to be his official station for the purposes of section 456 of this title. The place where a judge or magistrate judge recalled under section 155, 375, 636, or 797 of this title maintains the actual abode in which the judge or magistrate judge customarily lives shall be deemed to be the official station of such judge or magistrate judge for purposes of section 604(a)(7) of this title.

(June 25, 1948, c. 646, 62 Stat. 904; Sept. 21, 1959, Pub.L. 86–312, § 1, 73 Stat. 587; Nov. 14, 1986, Pub.L. 99–651, Title II, § 202(b), 100 Stat. 3648; Dec. 1, 1990, Pub.L. 101–650, Title III, § 321, 104 Stat. 5117.)

HISTORICAL AND STATUTORY NOTES

Change of Name

"United States magistrate judge" substituted for "United States magistrate" in text pursuant to section 321 of Pub.L. 101–650, set out as a note under 28 U.S.C.A. § 631.

§ 375. Recall of certain judges and magistrate judges

(a)(1) A bankruptcy judge or a United States magistrate judge appointed under chapter 43 of this title, who has retired under the provisions of section 377 of this title or under the applicable provisions of title 5 upon attaining the age and years of service requirements established in section 371(c) of this title, may agree to be recalled to serve under this section for a period of five years as a bankruptcy judge or magistrate judge, as the case may be, upon certification that substantial service is expected to be performed by such retired judge or magistrate judge during such 5-year period. With the agreement of the judge or magistrate judge involved, a certification under this subsection may be renewed for successive 5-year periods.

(2) For purposes of paragraph (1) of this subsection, a certification may be made, in the case of a bankruptcy judge or a United States magistrate,[1] by the judicial council of the circuit in which the official duty station of the judge or magistrate at the time of retirement was located.

(3) For purposes of this section, the term "bankruptcy judge" means a bankruptcy judge appointed under chapter 6 of this title or serving as a bankruptcy judge on March 31, 1984.

(b) A judge or magistrate judge recalled under this section may exercise all of the powers and duties of the office of judge or magistrate judge held at the time of retirement, including the ability to serve in any other judicial district to the extent applicable, but may not engage in the practice of law or engage in any other business, occupation, or employment inconsistent with the expeditious, proper, and impartial performance of duties as a judicial officer.

(c) During the 5-year period in which a certification under subsection (a) is in effect, the judge or magistrate judge involved shall receive, in addition to the annuity provided under the provisions of section 377 of this title or under the applicable provisions of title 5, an amount equal to the difference between that annuity and the current salary of the office to which the judge or magistrate judge is

---

[1] [Footnote to 28 U.S.C. § 375(a)(2):] So in original. Probably should be "United States magistrate judge."

recalled. The annuity of a bankruptcy judge or magistrate judge who completes that 5-year period of service, whose certification is not renewed, and who retired under section 377 of this title shall be equal to the salary in effect, at the end of that 5-year period, for the office from which he or she retired.

(d) A certification under subsection (a) may be terminated in accordance with chapter 16 of this title, and such a certification shall be terminated upon the death of the recalled judge or magistrate judge involved.

(e) Except as provided in subsection (b), nothing in this section shall affect the right of judges or magistrate judges who retire under the provisions of chapter 83 or chapter 84 of title 5 to serve as reemployed annuitants in accordance with the provisions of title 5. A judge or magistrate judge to whom this section applies may be recalled under section 155, 636(h), or 797 of this title, as the case may be, other than during a 5-year period in which a certification under subsection (a) is in effect with respect to that judge or magistrate judge.

(f) For purposes of determining the years of service requirements in order to be eligible for recall under this section, any service as a bankruptcy judge or a United States magistrate judge, and any prior service as a referee in bankruptcy or a United States commissioner, may be credited.

(g) Except as provided in subsection (c), a judge or magistrate judge recalled under this section who retired under the applicable provisions of title 5 shall be considered to be a reemployed annuitant under chapter 83 or chapter 84, as the case may be, of title 5.

(h) The Judicial Conference of the United States may promulgate regulations to implement this section.

(Added Pub.L. 99–651, Title II, § 201(b)(1), Nov. 14, 1986, 100 Stat. 3647; amended Pub.L. 100–659, § 4(b), Nov. 15, 1988, 102 Stat. 3918; Pub.L. 101–650, Title III, §§ 321, 325(b)(2), Dec. 1, 1990, 104 Stat. 5117, 5121; Pub.L. 102–572, Title IX, § 904(a), Oct. 29, 1992, 106 Stat. 4517; Pub.L. 107–273, Div. C, Title I, § 11043(d), Nov. 2, 2002, 116 Stat. 1855.)

§ 376. Annuities for survivors of certain judicial officials of the United States

(a) For the purposes of this section—

(1) "judicial official" means:

(A) a Justice or judge of the United States, as defined by section 451 of this title;

(B) a judge of the District Court of Guam, the District Court of the Northern Mariana Islands, or the District Court of the Virgin Islands;

(C) a Director of the Administrative Office of the United States Courts, after he or she has filed a waiver under subsection (a) of section 611 of this title;

(D) a Director of the Federal Judicial Center, after he or she has filed a waiver under subsection (a) of section 627 of this title;

(E) a Counselor to the Chief Justice of the United States, after he or she has filed a waiver in accordance with both subsection (a) of section 677 and subsection (a) of section 611 of this title;

(F) a full-time bankruptcy judge or a full-time United States magistrate judge; or

(G) a judge of the United States Court of Federal Claims;

who notifies the Director of the Administrative Office of the United States Courts in writing of his or her intention to come within the purview of this section within six months after (i) the date upon which he or she takes office, (ii) the date upon which he or she marries, (iii) January 1, 1977, (iv) October 1, 1986, (v) the date of the enactment of the Retirement and Survivors' Annuities for Bankruptcy Judges and Magistrates Act of 1988, in the case of a full-time bankruptcy judge or United States magistrate judge in active service on that date, (vi) the date of the enactment of the Federal Courts Study Committee Implementation Act of 1990, in the case of a full-time judge of the Court of Federal Claims in active service on that date, or (vii) the date of the enactment of the Federal Courts Administration Act of 1992;

(2) "retirement salary" means:

(A) in the case of a Justice or judge of the United States, as defined by section 451 of this title, salary paid (i) after retirement from regular active service under subsection (b) of section 371 or subsection (a) of section 372 of this title, or (ii) after retirement from office by resignation on salary under subsection (a) of section 371 of this title;

(B) in the case of a judge of the District Court of Guam, the District Court of the Northern Mariana Islands, or the District Court of the Virgin Islands, (i) an annuity paid under subsection (a) of section 373 of this title or (ii) compensation paid under paragraph (4) of subsection (c) of section 373 of this title;

(C) in the case of a Director of the Administrative Office of the United States Courts, an annuity paid under subsection (b) or (c) of section 611 of this title;

(D) in the case of a Director of the Federal Judicial Center, an annuity paid under subsection (b) or (c) of section 627 of this title;

(E) in the case of a Counselor to the Chief Justice of the United States, an annuity paid in accordance with both subsection (a) of section 677 and subsection (a) of section 611 of this title;

(F) in the case of a bankruptcy judge or United States magistrate judge, an annuity paid under section 377 of this title; and

(G) in the case of a judge of the United States Court of Federal Claims, an annuity paid under section 178 of this title;

(3) "widow" means the surviving wife of a "judicial official", who:

(A) has been married to him for at least one year on the day of his death; or

(B) is the mother of issue by that marriage;

(4) "widower" means the surviving husband of a "judicial official", who:

(A) has been married to her for at least one year on the day of her death; or

(B) is the father of issue by that marriage;

(5) "child" means:

(A) an unmarried child under eighteen years of age, including (i) an adopted child and (ii) a stepchild or recognized natural child who lived with the judicial official in a regular parent-child relationship;

(B) such unmarried child between eighteen and twenty-two years of age who is a student regularly pursuing a full-time course of study or training in residence in a high school, trade school, technical or vocational institute, junior college, college, university, or comparable educational institution. A child whose twenty-second birthday occurs before July 1, or after August 31, of a calendar year, and while he or she is regularly pursuing such a course of study or training, is deemed to have become twenty-two years of age on the first day of July immediately following that birthday. A child who is a student is deemed not to have ceased being a student during an interim period between school years, if that interim period lasts no longer than five consecutive months and if that child shows, to the satisfaction of the Director of the Administrative Office of the United States Courts, that he or she has a bona fide intention of continuing to pursue a course of study or training in the same or a different school during the school semester, or other period into which the school year is divided, immediately following that interim period; or

(C) such unmarried child, regardless of age, who is incapable of self-support because of a mental or physical disability incurred either (i) before age eighteen, or (ii) in the case of a child who is receiving an annuity as a full-time student under paragraph (5)(B) of this subsection, before the termination of that annuity;

(6) "former spouse" means a former spouse of a judicial official if the former spouse was married to such judicial official for at least 9 months; and

(7) "assassinated" and "assassination" mean the killing of a judicial official described in paragraph (1)(A), (B), (F), or (G) of this subsection that is motivated by the performance by that judicial official of his or her official duties.

(b)(1) Every judicial official who files a written notification of his or her intention to come within the purview of this section, in accordance with paragraph (1) of subsection (a) of this section, shall be deemed thereby to consent and agree to having deducted and withheld from his or her salary a sum equal to 2.2 percent of that salary, and a sum equal to 3.5 percent of his or her retirement salary. The deduction from any retirement salary—

(A) of a justice or judge of the United States retired from regular active service under section 371(b) or section 372(a) of this title,

(B) of a judge of the United States Court of Federal Claims retired under section 178 of this title, or

(C) of a judicial official on recall under section 155(b), 373(c)(4), 375, or 636(h) of this title,

shall be an amount equal to 2.2 percent of retirement salary.

(2) A judicial official who is not entitled to receive an immediate retirement salary upon leaving office but who is eligible to receive a deferred retirement salary on a later date shall file, within 90 days before leaving office, a written notification of his or her intention to remain within the purview of this section under such conditions and procedures as may be determined by the Director of the Administrative Office of the United States Courts. Every judicial official who files a written notification in accordance with this paragraph shall be deemed to consent to contribute, during the period before such a judicial official begins to receive his or her retirement salary, a sum equal to 3.5 percent of the deferred retirement salary which that judicial official is entitled to receive. Any judicial official who fails to file a written notification under this paragraph shall be deemed to have revoked his or her election under subsection (a) of this section.

(3) The amounts deducted and withheld from the salary of each judicial official under paragraphs (1) and (2) of this subsection shall, in accordance with such procedures as may be prescribed by the Comptroller General of the United States, be covered into the Treasury of the United States and credited to the "Judicial Survivors' Annuities Fund" established by section 3 of the Judicial Survivors' Annuities Reform Act. Such fund shall be used for the payment of annuities, refunds, and allowances as provided by this section. Payment of such salary less such deductions (and any deductions made under section 178 or 377 of this title or under subchapter III of chapter 83, or chapter 84, of title 5) shall be a full and complete discharge and acquittance of all claims and demands whatsoever for all services rendered by such judicial official during the period covered by such payment, except the rights to those benefits to which such judicial official, or his or her survivors, shall be entitled under the provisions of this section (and under section 178 or 377 of this title or under subchapter III of chapter 83, or chapter 84, of title 5).

(c)(1) There shall also be deposited to the credit of the Judicial Survivors' Annuities Fund, in accordance with such procedures as the Comptroller General of the United States may prescribe, amounts required to reduce to zero the unfunded liability of the Judicial Survivors' Annuities Fund: *Provided,* That such amounts shall not exceed the equivalent of 9 percent of salary or retirement salary. Such deposits shall, subject to appropriations Acts, be taken from the fund used to pay the compensation of the judicial official, and shall immediately become an integrated part of the Judicial Survivors' Annuities Fund for any use required under this section.

(2) For purposes of paragraph (1), the term "unfunded liability" means the estimated excess, determined on an annual basis in accordance with the provisions of section 9503 of title 31, United States Code, of the present value of all benefits payable from the Judicial Survivors' Annuities Fund, over the sum of—

(A) the present value of deductions to be withheld from the future basic pay of judicial officials; plus

(B) the balance in the Fund as of the date the unfunded liability is determined.

In making any determination under this paragraph, the Comptroller General shall use the applicable information contained in the reports filed pursuant to section 9503 of title 31, United States Code, with respect to the judicial survivors' annuities plan established by this section.

(3) There are authorized to be appropriated such sums as may be necessary to carry out this subsection.

(d) Each judicial official shall deposit, with interest at 4 percent per annum to December 31, 1947, and at 3 percent per annum thereafter, compounded on December 31 of each year, to the credit of the "Judicial Survivors' Annuities Fund":

(1) a sum equal to 3.5 percent of that salary, including "retirement salary", which he or she has received for serving in any of the offices designated in paragraph (1) of subsection (a) of this section prior to the date upon which he or she filed notice of an intention to come within the purview of this section with the Director of the Administrative Office of the United States Courts; and

(2) a sum equal to 3.5 percent of the basic salary, pay, or compensation which he or she has received for serving as a Senator, Representative, Delegate, or Resident Commissioner in Congress, or for serving as an "employee", as that term is defined in subsection (1) of section 8331 of title 5, prior to assuming the responsibilities of any of the offices designated in paragraph (1) of subsection (a) of this section.

The interest otherwise required by this subsection shall not be required for any period during which a judicial official was separated from all such service and was not receiving any retirement salary.

Each such judicial official may elect to make such deposits in installments, during the continuance of his or her service in those offices designated in paragraph (1) of subsection (a) of this section, in such amounts and under such conditions as may be determined in each instance by the Director of the Administrative Office of the United States Courts: *Provided*, That, in each instance in which a judicial official does elect to make such deposits in installments, the Director shall require (i) that the first installment payment made shall be in an amount no smaller than that amount necessary to cover at least the last eighteen months of prior creditable civilian service, and (ii) that at least one additional installment payment shall be made every eighteen months thereafter until the total of all such deposits have been made.

Notwithstanding the failure of any such judicial official to make all such deposits or installment payments, credit shall be allowed for the service rendered, but the annuity of that judicial official's widow or widower shall be reduced by an amount equal to 10 percent of the amount of such deposits, computed as of the date of the death of such judicial official, unless such widow or widower shall elect to eliminate such service entirely from credit under subsection (k) of this section: *Provided*, That no deposit shall be required from any such judicial official for any honorable active duty service in the Army, Navy, Air Force, Marine Corps, or Coast Guard of the United States, or for any other creditable service rendered prior to August 1, 1920.

(e) The amounts deducted and withheld in accordance with subsection (b) of this section, and the amounts deposited in accordance with subsection (d) of this section, shall be credited to individual accounts in the name of each judicial official from whom such amounts are received, for credit to the "Judicial Survivors' Annuities Fund".

(f) The Secretary of the Treasury shall invest, from time to time, in interest bearing securities of the United States or Federal farm loan bonds, those portions of the "Judicial Survivors' Annuities Fund" which in his judgment may not be immediately required for the payment of annuities, refunds, and allowances as provided in this section. The income derived from such investments shall constitute a part of such fund for the purposes of paying annuities and carrying out the provisions of subsections (g), (h), (m), (o), (p), and (q) of this section.

(g) If any judicial official leaves office and is ineligible to receive a retirement salary or leaves office and is entitled to a deferred retirement salary but fails to make an election under subsection (b)(2) of this section, all amounts credited to his or her account established under subsection (e), together with interest at 4 percent per annum to December 31, 1947, and at 3 percent per annum thereafter, compounded on December 31 of each year, to the date of his or her relinquishment of office, minus a sum equal to 2.2 percent of salary for service while deductions were withheld under subsection (b) or for which a deposit was made by the judicial official under subsection (d), shall be returned to that judicial official in a lump-sum payment within a reasonable period of time following the date of his or her relinquishment of office. For the purposes of this section, a "reasonable period of time" shall be presumed to be no longer than 1 year following the date upon which such judicial official relinquishes his or her office.

(h) Annuities payable under this section shall be paid only in accordance with the following provisions:

(1) In any case in which a judicial official dies while in office, while receiving retirement salary, or after filing an election and otherwise complying with the conditions under subsection (b)(2) of this section (A) after having completed at least eighteen months of creditable civilian service, as computed in accordance with subsection (k) of this section, for the last eighteen months of which the salary deductions provided by subsection (b) of this section or, in lieu thereof, the deposits required by subsection (d) of this section have actually been made, or (B) if the death of such judicial official was by assassination, before having satisfied the requirements of clause (A) if, for the period of such service, the deductions provided by subsection (b) or, in lieu thereof, the deposits required by subsection (d) have actually been made—

(i) if such judicial official is survived by a widow or widower, but not by a child, there shall be paid to such widow or widower an annuity, beginning on the day on which such judicial official died, in an amount computed as provided in subsection (*l*) of this section; or

(ii) if such judicial official is survived by a widow or widower and a child or children, there shall be paid to such widow or widower an annuity, beginning on the day on which such judicial official died, in an amount computed as provided in subsection (*l*) of this section, and there shall also be paid to or on behalf of each such child an immediate annuity equal to:

(I) 10 percent of the average annual salary determined under subsection (*l*)(1) of this section; or

(II) 20 percent of such average annual salary, divided by the number of children;

whichever is smallest; or

(iii) if such judicial official leaves no surviving widow or widower, but does leave a surviving child or children, there shall be paid to or on behalf of each such child an immediate annuity equal to:

(I) the amount of the annuity to which the judicial official's widow or widower would have been entitled under clause (i) of this paragraph, had such widow or widower survived the judicial official, divided by the number of children; or

(II) 20 percent of the average annual salary determined under subsection (*l*)(1) of this section; or

(III) 40 percent of such average annual salary amount, divided by the number of children;

whichever is smallest.

(2) An annuity payable to a widow or widower under clause (i) or (ii) of paragraph (1) of this subsection shall be terminated upon his or her death or remarriage before attaining age 55, subject to subsection (w).

(3) An annuity payable to a child under this subsection shall terminate:

(A) if such child is receiving an annuity based upon his or her status under paragraph (5)(A) of subsection (a) of this section, on the last day of the month during which he or she becomes eighteen years of age;

(B) if such child is receiving an annuity based upon his or her status under paragraph (5)(B) of subsection (a) of this section, either (i) on the first day of July immediately following his or her twenty-second birthday or (ii) on the last day of the month during which he or she ceases to be a full-time student in accordance with paragraph (5)(B) of subsection (a) of this section, whichever occurs first: *Provided*, That if such child is rendered incapable of self-support because of a mental or physical disability incurred while receiving that annuity, that annuity shall not terminate, but shall continue without interruption and shall be deemed to have become, as of the date of disability, an annuity based upon his or her status under clause (ii) of paragraph (5)(C) of subsection (a) of this section;

(C) if such child is receiving an annuity based upon his or her status under paragraph (5)(C) of subsection (a) of this section, on the last day of the month during which he or she ceases to be incapable of self-support because of mental or physical disability; or

(D) on the last day of the month during which such child dies or marries.

(4) An annuity payable to a child or children under paragraph (1)(ii) of this subsection shall be recomputed and paid as provided in paragraph (1)(iii) of this subsection upon the death, but not upon the remarriage, of the widow or widower who is receiving an annuity under paragraph (1)(ii) of this subsection.

(5) In any case in which the annuity of a child is terminated, the annuity of each remaining child which is based upon the service of the same judicial official shall be recomputed and paid as though the child whose annuity has been terminated had not survived that judicial official.

(6) In the case of the survivor or survivors of a judicial official to whom paragraph (1)(B) applies, there shall be deducted from the annuities otherwise payable under this section an amount equal to the amount of salary deductions that would have been made if such deductions had been made for 18 months prior to the judicial official's death.

(i)(1) All questions of dependency and disability arising under this section shall be determined by the Director of the Administrative Office of the United States Courts, subject to review only by the Judicial Conference of the United States, and the decision of the Judicial Conference of the United States shall be final and conclusive. The Director may order or direct at any time such medical or other examinations as he deems necessary to determine the facts relative to the nature and degree of disability of any child who is an annuitant, or an applicant for an annuity, under this section, and may suspend or deny any such annuity for failure to submit to any such examination.

(2) The Director of the Administrative Office of the United States Courts shall determine whether the killing of a judicial official was an assassination, subject to review only by the Judicial Conference of the United States. The head of any Federal agency that investigates the killing of a judicial official shall provide information to the Director that would assist the Director in making such determination.

(j) In any case in which a payment under this section is to be made to a minor, or to a person mentally incompetent or under other legal disability, as determined by a court of competent jurisdiction, such payment may be made to the person who is constituted guardian or other fiduciary of such claimant by the laws of the State of residence of such claimant, or to any other person who is otherwise legally vested with the care of the claimant or of the claimant's estate, and need not be made directly to such claimant. The Director of the Administrative Office of the United States Courts may, at his or her discretion, determine whether such payment is made directly to such claimant or to such guardian, fiduciary, or other person legally vested with the care of such claimant or the claimant's estate. Where no guardian or other fiduciary of such minor or such person under legal disability has been appointed under the laws of the State of residence of such claimant, the Director of the Administrative Office of the United States Courts shall determine the person who is otherwise legally vested with the care of the claimant or of the claimant's estate.

(k) The years of service rendered by a judicial official which may be creditable in calculating the amount of an annuity for such judicial official's widow or widower under subsection (*l*) of this section shall include—

(1) those years during which such judicial official served in any of the offices designated in paragraph (1) of subsection (a) of this section, including in the case of a Justice or judge of the United States those years during which he or she continued to hold office following retirement from regular active service under section 371 or subsection (a) of section 372 of this title;

(2) those years during which such judicial official served as a Senator, Representative, Delegate, or Resident Commissioner in Congress, prior to assuming the responsibilities of any of the offices designated in paragraph (1) of subsection (a) of this section;

(3) those years during which such judicial official honorably served on active duty in the Army, Navy, Air Force, Marine Corps, or Coast Guard of the United States, prior to assuming the responsibilities of any of the offices designated in paragraph (1) of subsection (a) of this section: *Provided*, That those years of such military service for which credit has been allowed for the purposes of retirement or retired pay under any other provision of law shall not be included as allowable years of such service under this section;

(4) those years during which such judicial official served as an "employee", as that term is defined in subsection (1) of section 8331 of title 5, prior to assuming the responsibilities of any of the offices designated in paragraph (1) of subsection (a) of this section,[1] and

(5) those years during which such judicial official had deductions withheld from his or her retirement salary in accordance with subsection (b)(1) or (2) of this section.

For the purposes of this subsection the term "years" shall mean full years and twelfth parts thereof, excluding from the aggregate any fractional part of a month which numbers less than fifteen full days and including, as one full month, any fractional part of a month which numbers fifteen full days or more. Nothing in this subsection shall be interpreted as waiving or canceling that reduction in the annuity of a widow or widower which is required by subsection (d) of this section due to the failure of a judicial official to make those deposits required by subsection (d) of this section.

(*l*) The annuity of a widow or widower of a judicial official shall be an amount equal to the sum of—

(1) 1.5 percent of the average annual salary, including retirement salary, which such judicial official received for serving in any of the offices designated in paragraph (1) of subsection (a) of this section (i) during those three years of such service, or during those three years while receiving a retirement salary, in which his or her annual salary or retirement salary was greatest, or (ii) if such judicial official has so served less than three years, then during the total period of such service prior to his or her death, multiplied by the total of:

---

[1]   [Footnote to 28 U.S.C. § 376(k)(4):] So in original. Comma probably should be a semicolon.

(A) the number of years of creditable service tabulated in accordance with paragraph (1) of subsection (k) of this section; plus

(B) the number of years of creditable service tabulated in accordance with paragraph (2) of subsection (k) of this section; plus

(C) the number of years of creditable service tabulated in accordance with paragraph (3) of subsection (k) of this section; plus

(D) the number of years during which the judicial official had deductions withheld from his or her retirement salary under subsection (b)(1) or (2) of this section; plus

(E) the number of years up to, but not exceeding, fifteen of creditable service tabulated in accordance with paragraph (4) of subsection (k) of this section,

plus:

(2) three-fourths of 1 percent of such average annual salary, multiplied by the number of years of any prior creditable service, as tabulated in accordance with subsection (k) of this section, not applied under paragraph (1) of this subsection;

except that such annuity shall not exceed an amount equal to 50 percent of such average annual salary, nor be less than an amount equal to 25 percent of such average annual salary. Any annuity determined in accordance with the provisions of this subsection shall be reduced to the extent required by subsection (d) of this section, and by the amount of any annuity payable to a former spouse under subsection (t).

(m) Each time that an increase is made under section 8340(b) of title 5 in annuities paid under subchapter III of chapter 83 of such title, each annuity payable from the Judicial Survivors' Annuities Fund shall be increased at the same time by the same percentage by which annuities are increased under that section.

(n) Each annuity authorized under this section shall accrue monthly and shall be due and payable in monthly installments on the first business day of the month following the month or other period for which the annuity shall have accrued. No annuity authorized under this section shall be assignable, either in law or in equity, except as provided in subsections (s) and (t), or subject to execution, levy, attachment, garnishment, or other legal process.

(o)(1) In any case in which a judicial official dies while in office, while receiving retirement salary, or after filing an election and otherwise complying with the conditions under subsection (b)(2) of this section, and;

(A) subject to paragraph (2) of this subsection, before having completed eighteen months of civilian service, computed in accordance with subsection (k) of this section, during which the salary deductions provided by subsection (b) of this section or the deposit required by subsection (d) of this section have actually been made; or

(B) after having completed eighteen months of civilian service, computed in accordance with subsection (k) of this section, during which all such deductions or deposits have been made, but without a survivor or survivors who are entitled to receive the annuity benefits provided by subsection (h) or (t) of this section; or

(C) the rights of all persons entitled to receive the annuity benefits provided by subsection (h) or (t) of this section terminate before a valid claim therefor has been established;

the total amount credited to the individual account of that judicial official, established under subsection (e) of this section, with interest at 4 percent per annum to December 31, 1947, and at 3 percent per annum thereafter, compounded on December 31, of each year, to the date of that judicial official's death, shall be paid, upon the establishment of a valid claim therefor, to the person or persons surviving at the date title to the payment arises, in the following order of precedence:

First, to the beneficiary or beneficiaries whom that judicial official may have designated in a writing received by the Administrative Office of the United States Courts prior to his or her death;

Second, if there be no such beneficiary, to the widow or widower of such judicial official;

Third, if none of the above, to the child or children of such judicial official and the descendants of any deceased children by representation;

Fourth, if none of the above, to the parents of such judicial official or the survivor of them;

Fifth, if none of the above, to the duly appointed executor, executrix, administrator, or administratrix of the estate of such judicial official;

Sixth, if none of the above, to such other next of kin of such judicial official, as may be determined by the Director of the Administrative Office of the United States Courts to be entitled to such payment, under the laws of the domicile of such judicial official, at the time of his or her death.

Such payment shall be a bar to recovery by any other person. For the purposes of this subsection only, a determination that an individual is a widow, widower, or child of a judicial official may be made by the Director of the Administrative Office of the United States Courts without regard to the definitions of those terms contained in paragraphs (3), (4), and (5) of subsection (a) of this section.

(2) In cases in which a judicial official dies as a result of assassination and leaves a survivor or survivors who are entitled to receive the annuity benefits provided by subsection (h) or (t) of this section, paragraph (1)(A) of this subsection shall not apply.

(p) In any case in which all the annuities which are authorized by this section and based upon the service of a given official terminate before the aggregate amount of annuity payments received by the annuitant or annuitants equals the total amount credited to the individual account of such judicial official, established under subsection (e) of this section with interest at 4 percent per annum to December 31, 1947, and at 3 percent per annum thereafter, compounded on December 31, of each year, to the date of that judicial official's death, the difference between such total amount, with such interest, and such aggregate amount shall be paid, upon establishment of a valid claim therefor, in the order of precedence prescribed in subsection (o) of this section.

(q) Any accrued annuity benefits remaining unpaid upon the termination of an annuity, other than by the death of an annuitant, shall be paid to that annuitant. Any accrued annuity benefits remaining unpaid upon the death of an annuitant shall be paid, upon the establishment of a valid claim therefor, in the following order of precedence:

First, to the duly appointed executor, executrix, administrator, or administratrix of the estate of such annuitant;

Second, if there is no such executor, executrix, administrator, or administratrix, payments shall be made, after the expiration of sixty days from the date of death of such annuitant, to such individual or individuals as may appear, in the judgment of the Director of the Administrative Office of the United States Courts, to be legally entitled thereto, and such payment shall be a bar to recovery by any other individual.

(r) Nothing contained in this section shall be interpreted to prevent a widow or widower eligible for an annuity under this section from simultaneously receiving such an annuity while also receiving any other annuity to which such widow or widower may also be entitled under any other law without regard to this section: *Provided*, That service used in the computation of the annuity conferred by this section shall not also be credited in computing any such other annuity.

(s) A judicial official who has a former spouse may elect, under procedures prescribed by the Director of the Administrative Office of the United States Courts, to provide a survivor annuity for such former spouse under subsection (t). An election under this subsection shall be made at the time of retirement, or, if later, within 2 years after the date on which the marriage of the former spouse to the judicial official is dissolved. An election under this subsection—

(1) shall not be effective to the extent that it—

(A) conflicts with—

(i) any court order or decree referred to in subsection (t)(1), which was issued before the date of such election, or

(ii) any agreement referred to in such subsection which was entered into before such date; or

(B) would cause the total of survivor annuities payable under subsections (h) and (t) based on the service of the judicial official to exceed 55 percent of the average annual salary (as such term is used in subsection (*l*)) of such official; and

(2) shall not be effective, in the case of a judicial official who is then married, unless it is made with the spouse's written consent.

The Director of the Administrative Office of the United States Courts shall provide by regulation that paragraph (2) of this subsection may be waived if the judicial official establishes to the satisfaction of the Director that the spouse's whereabouts cannot be determined, or that, due to exceptional circumstances, requiring the judicial official to seek the spouse's consent would otherwise be inappropriate.

(t)(1) Subject to paragraphs (2) through (4) of this subsection, a former spouse of a deceased judicial official is entitled to a survivor annuity under this section if and to the extent expressly provided for in an election under subsection (s), or in the terms of any decree of divorce or annulment or any court order or court-approved property settlement agreement incident to such decree.

(2) The annuity payable to a former spouse under this subsection may not exceed the difference between—

(A) the maximum amount that would be payable as an annuity to a widow or widower under subsection (*l*), determined without taking into account any reduction of such annuity caused by payment of an annuity to a former spouse; and

(B) the amount of any annuity payable under this subsection to any other former spouse of the judicial official, based on an election previously made under subsection (s), or a court order previously issued.

(3) The commencement and termination of an annuity payable under this subsection shall be governed by the terms of the applicable order, decree, agreement, or election, as the case may be, except that any such annuity—

(A) shall not commence before—

(i) the day after the judicial official dies, or

(ii) the first day of the second month beginning after the date on which the Director of the Administrative Office of the United States Courts receives written notice of the order, decree, agreement, or election, as the case may be, together with such additional information or documentation as the Director may prescribe,

whichever is later, and

(B) shall terminate no later than the last day of the month before the former spouse remarries before becoming 55 years of age or dies.

(4) For purposes of this section, a modification in a decree, order, agreement, or election referred to in paragraph (1) of this subsection shall not be effective—

(A) if such modification is made after the retirement of the judicial official concerned, and

(B) to the extent that such modification involves an annuity under this subsection.

(u) In the case of a judicial official who is assassinated, an annuity shall be paid under this section notwithstanding a survivor's eligibility for or receipt of benefits under chapter 81 of title 5, except that the annuity for which a surviving spouse is eligible under this section shall be reduced to the extent that the total benefits paid under this section and chapter 81 of title 5 for any year would exceed the current salary for that year of the office of the judicial official.

(v) Subject to the terms of a decree, court order, or agreement described in subsection (t)(1), if any judicial official ceases to be married after making the election under subsection (a), he or she may revoke such election in writing by notifying the Director of the Administrative Office of the United States Courts. The judicial official shall also notify any spouse or former spouse of the application for revocation in accordance with such requirements as the Director of the Administrative Office of the United States Courts shall by regulation prescribe. The Director may provide under such regulations that the notification requirement may be waived with respect to a spouse or former spouse if the judicial official establishes to the satisfaction of the Director that the whereabouts of such spouse or former spouse cannot be determined.

(w) In the case of a widow or widower whose annuity under clause (i) or (ii) of subsection (h)(1) is terminated because of remarriage before attaining 55 years of age, the annuity shall be restored at the same rate commencing on the day the remarriage is dissolved by death, divorce, or annulment, if—

(1) the widow or widower elects to receive this annuity instead of any other survivor annuity to which such widow or widower may be entitled, under this chapter or under another retirement system for Government employees, by reason of the remarriage; and

(2) any payment made to such widow or widower under subsection (*o*) or (p) on termination of the annuity is returned to the Judicial Survivors' Annuities Fund.

(x) For each year of Federal judicial service completed, judicial officials who are enrolled in the Judicial Survivors' Annuities System on the date of enactment of the Judicial Survivors Protection Act of 2009 may purchase, in 3-month increments, up to an additional year of service credit, under the terms set forth in this section. In the case of judicial officials who elect to enroll in the Judicial Survivors' Annuities System during the statutory open enrollment period authorized under the Judicial Survivors Protection Act of 2009, for each year of Federal judicial service completed, such an official may purchase, in 3-month increments, up to an additional year of service credit for each year of Federal judicial service completed, under the terms set forth in section 4(a) of that Act.

(Added Aug. 3, 1956, c. 944, § 2, 70 Stat. 1021; amended July 7, 1958, Pub.L. 85–508, § 12(n), 72 Stat. 348; Dec. 20, 1967, Pub.L. 90–219, Title II, § 202, 81 Stat. 668; Aug. 8, 1968, Pub.L. 90–466, § 1(a), 82 Stat. 662; Aug. 22, 1972, Pub.L. 92–397, §§ 2, 3(c), 86 Stat. 579, 580; Oct. 19, 1976, Pub.L. 94–554, § 2, 90 Stat. 2603; Nov. 6, 1978, Pub.L. 95–598, Title II, § 211, 92 Stat. 2661; June 19, 1986, Pub.L. 99–336, § 2(a), (d)(1) to (3), (e), 100 Stat. 633, 635 to 637; Aug. 27, 1986, Pub.L. 99–396, § 21(b), 100 Stat. 846; Nov. 15, 1988, Pub.L. 100–659, § 3(a), 102 Stat. 3917; Nov. 19, 1988, Pub.L. 100–702, Title X, § 1017(a), 102 Stat. 4670; Dec. 1, 1990, Pub.L. 101–650, Title III, §§ 306(b), 321, 322(a) to (f), (g) [(h)], 104 Stat. 5109, 5117 to 5120; Oct. 29, 1992, Pub.L. 102–572, Title II, § 201(a) to (i), Title IX, § 902(b), 106 Stat. 4508 to 4510, 4516; Oct. 19, 1996, Pub.L. 104–317, Title III, §§ 302, 308, 110 Stat. 3851, 3853; Nov. 13, 2000, Pub.L. 106–518, Title III, § 312(b), 114 Stat. 2421; Oct. 13, 2008, Pub.L. 110–402, § 1(b)(2), 122 Stat. 4254; Oct. 15, 2008, Pub.L. 110–428, § 3(a), (b), 122 Stat. 4840; Aug. 12, 2009, Pub.L. 111–49, § 6, 123 Stat. 1977; Pub.L. 112–234, § 2(b), Dec. 28, 2012, 126 Stat. 1624.)

§ 377. Retirement of bankruptcy judges and magistrate judges

(a) Retirement based on years of service.—A bankruptcy judge or magistrate judge to whom this section applies and who retires from office after attaining the age of 65 years and serving at least 14 years, whether continuously or otherwise, as such bankruptcy judge or magistrate judge shall, subject to subsection (f), be entitled to receive, during the remainder of the judge's or magistrate judge's lifetime, an annuity equal to the salary being received at the time the judge or magistrate judge leaves office.

(b) **Retirement upon failure of reappointment.**—A bankruptcy judge or magistrate judge to whom this section applies, who is not reappointed following the expiration of the term of office of such judge or magistrate judge, and who retires upon the completion of the term shall, subject to subsection (f), be entitled to receive, upon attaining the age of 65 years and during the remainder of such bankruptcy judge's or magistrate judge's lifetime, an annuity equal to that portion of the salary being received at the time the judge or magistrate judge leaves office which the aggregate number of years of service, not to exceed 14, bears to 14, if—

(1) such judge or magistrate judge has served at least 1 full term as a bankruptcy judge or magistrate judge, and

(2) not earlier than 9 months before the date on which the term of office of such judge or magistrate judge expires, and not later than 6 months before such date, such judge or magistrate judge notified the appointing authority in writing that such judge or magistrate judge was willing to accept reappointment to the position in which such judge or magistrate judge was serving.

For purposes of this subsection, in the case of a bankruptcy judge, the written notice required by paragraph (2) shall be given to the chief judge of the circuit in which such bankruptcy judge is serving and, in the case of a magistrate judge, such notice shall be given to the chief judge of the district court in which the magistrate judge is serving.

(c) **Service of at least 8 years.**—A bankruptcy judge or magistrate judge to whom this section applies and who retires after serving at least 8 years, whether continuously or otherwise, as such a bankruptcy judge or magistrate judge shall, subject to subsection (f), be entitled to receive, upon attaining the age of 65 years and during the remainder of the judge's or magistrate judge's lifetime, an annuity equal to that portion of the salary being received at the time the judge or magistrate judge leaves office which the aggregate number of years of service, not to exceed 14, bears to 14. Such annuity shall be reduced by $1/6$ of 1 percent for each full month such bankruptcy judge or magistrate judge was under the age of 65 at the time the judge or magistrate judge left office, except that such reduction shall not exceed 20 percent.

(d) **Retirement for disability.**—A bankruptcy judge or magistrate judge to whom this section applies, who has served at least 5 years, whether continuously or otherwise, as such a bankruptcy judge or magistrate judge, and who retires or is removed from office upon the sole ground of mental or physical disability shall, subject to subsection (f), be entitled to receive, during the remainder of the judge's or magistrate judge's lifetime, an annuity equal to 40 percent of the salary being received at the time of retirement or removal or, in the case of a judge or magistrate judge who has served for at least 10 years, an amount equal to that proportion of the salary being received at the time of retirement or removal which the aggregate number of years of service, not to exceed 14, bears to 14.

(e) **Cost-of-living adjustments.**—A bankruptcy judge or magistrate judge who is entitled to an annuity under this section is also entitled to a cost-of-living adjustment in such annuity, calculated and payable in the same manner as adjustments under section 8340(b) of title 5, except that any such annuity, as increased under this subsection, may not exceed the salary then payable for the position from which the judge or magistrate judge retired or was removed.

(f) **Election; annuity in lieu of other annuities.**—A bankruptcy judge or magistrate judge shall be entitled to an annuity under this section if the judge or magistrate judge elects an annuity under this section by notifying the Director of the Administrative Office of the United States Courts. A bankruptcy judge or magistrate judge who elects to receive an annuity under this section shall not be entitled to receive[1]

---

[1] [Footnote to 28 U.S.C. § 377(f):] So in original. Probably should be "receive—".

(1) any annuity to which such judge or magistrate judge would otherwise have been entitled under subchapter III of chapter 83, or under chapter 84 (except for subchapters III and VII), of title 5, for service performed as such a judge or magistrate judge or otherwise;

(2) an annuity or salary in senior status or retirement under section 371 or 372 of this title;

(3) retired pay under section 7447 of the Internal Revenue Code of 1986; or

(4) retired pay under section 7296 of title 38.

(g) **Calculation of service.**—(1) For purposes of calculating an annuity under this section—

(A) full-time service as a bankruptcy judge or magistrate judge to whom this section applies may be credited; and

(B) each month of service shall be credited as one-twelfth of a year, and the fractional part of any month shall not be credited.

(2)(A) In the case of an individual who is a bankruptcy judge to whom this section applies and who retires under this section or who is removed from office under subsection (d) upon the sole ground of mental or physical disability, any service of that individual as a United States magistrate judge to whom this section applies, and any service of that individual as a full-time judicial officer who performed the duties of a magistrate judge and a bankruptcy judge at the same time, shall be included for purposes of calculating years of service under subsection (a), (b), (c), or (d), as the case may be.

(B) In the case of an individual who is a magistrate judge to whom this section applies and who retires under this section or who is removed from office under subsection (d) upon the sole ground of mental or physical disability, any service of that individual as a bankruptcy judge to whom this section applies, and any service of that individual as a full-time judicial officer who performed the duties of magistrate judge and a bankruptcy judge at the same time, shall be included for purposes of calculating years of service under subsection (a), (b), (c), or (d), as the case may be.

(h) **Covered positions and service.**—This section applies to—

(1) any bankruptcy judge appointed under—

(A) section 152 of this title;

(B) section 34 of the Bankruptcy Act before the repeal of that Act by section 401 of the Act of November 6, 1978 (Public Law 95–598; 92 Stat. 2682); or

(C) section 404 of the Act of November 6, 1978 (Public Law 95–598; 92 Stat. 2549); and

(2) any United States magistrate judge appointed under section 631 of this title,

only with respect to service on or after October 1, 1979, as such a bankruptcy judge or magistrate judge.

(i) **Payments pursuant to court order.**—(1) Payments under this section which would otherwise be made to a bankruptcy judge or magistrate judge based upon his or her service shall be paid (in whole or in part) by the Director of the Administrative Office of the United States Courts to another person if and to the extent expressly provided for in the terms of any court decree of divorce, annulment, or legal separation, or the terms of any court order or court-approved property settlement agreement incident to any court decree of divorce, annulment, or legal separation. Any payment under this paragraph to a person bars recovery by any other person.

(2) Paragraph (1) shall apply only to payments made by the Director of the Administrative Office of the United States Courts after the date of receipt by the Director of written notice of such decree, order, or agreement, and such additional information as the Director may prescribe.

(3) As used in this subsection, the term "court" means any court of any State, the District of Columbia, the Commonwealth of Puerto Rico, Guam, the Northern Mariana Islands, or the Virgin Islands, and any Indian tribal court or courts of Indian offense.

(j) Deductions, contributions, and deposits.—

(1) Deductions.—Beginning with the next pay period after the Director of the Administrative Office of the United States Courts receives a notice under subsection (f) that a bankruptcy judge or magistrate judge has elected an annuity under this section, the Director shall deduct and withhold 1 percent of the salary of such bankruptcy judge or magistrate judge. Amounts shall be so deducted and withheld in a manner determined by the Director. Amounts deducted and withheld under this subsection shall be deposited in the Treasury of the United States to the credit of the Judicial Officers' Retirement Fund. Deductions under this subsection from the salary of a bankruptcy judge or magistrate judge shall terminate upon the retirement of the bankruptcy judge or magistrate judge or upon completing 14 years of service for which contributions under this section have been made, whether continuously or otherwise, as calculated under subsection (g), whichever occurs first.

(2) Consent to deductions; discharge of claims.—Each bankruptcy judge or magistrate judge who makes an election under subsection (f) shall be deemed to consent and agree to the deductions from salary which are made under paragraph (1). Payment of such salary less such deductions (and any deductions made under section 376 of this title) is a full and complete discharge and acquittance of all claims and demands for all services rendered by such bankruptcy judge or magistrate judge during the period covered by such payment, except the right to those benefits to which the bankruptcy judge or magistrate judge is entitled under this section (and section 376).

(k) Deposits for prior service.—Each bankruptcy judge or magistrate judge who makes an election under subsection (f) may deposit, for service performed before such election for which contributions may be made under this section, an amount equal to 1 percent of the salary received for that service. Credit for any period covered by that service may not be allowed for purposes of an annuity under this section until a deposit under this subsection has been made for that period.

(*l*) Individual retirement records.—The amounts deducted and withheld under subsection (j), and the amounts deposited under subsection (k), shall be credited to individual accounts in the name of each bankruptcy judge or magistrate judge from whom such amounts are received, for credit to the Judicial Officers' Retirement Fund.

(m) Annuities affected in certain cases.—

(1) Practicing law after retirement.—

(A) Forfeiture of annuity.—Subject to subparagraph (B), any bankruptcy judge or magistrate judge who retires under this section and who thereafter practices law shall forfeit all rights to an annuity under this section for all periods beginning on or after the first day on which he or she so practices law.

(B) Forfeiture not to apply where individual elects to freeze amount of annuity.—(i) If a bankruptcy judge or magistrate judge makes an election to practice law after retirement under this section—

(I) subparagraph (A) shall not apply to such bankruptcy judge or magistrate judge beginning on the date such election takes effect, and

(II) the annuity payable under this section to such bankruptcy judge or magistrate judge, for periods beginning on or after the date such election takes effect, shall be equal to the annuity to which such bankruptcy judge or magistrate judge is entitled on the day before such effective date.

(ii) An election under clause (i)—

(I) may be made by a bankruptcy judge or magistrate judge eligible for retirement under this section, and

(II) shall be filed with the Director of the Administrative Office of the United States Courts.

Such an election, once it takes effect, shall be irrevocable.

(iii) Any election under this subparagraph shall take effect on the first day of the first month following the month in which the election is made.

(2) Recall not permitted.—Any bankruptcy judge or magistrate judge who retires under this section and who thereafter practices law shall not be eligible for recall under section 155(b), 375, or 636(h) of this title.

(3) Accepting other employment.—Any bankruptcy judge or magistrate judge who retires under this section and thereafter accepts compensation for civil office or employment under the United States Government (other than for the performance of functions as a bankruptcy judge or magistrate judge under section 155(b), 375, or 636(h) of this title) shall forfeit all rights to an annuity under this section for the period for which such compensation is received. For purposes of this paragraph, the term "compensation" includes retired pay or salary received in retired status.

(n) Lump-sum payments.—

(1) Eligibility.—**(A)** Subject to paragraph (2), an individual who serves as a bankruptcy judge or magistrate judge and—

(i) who leaves office and is not reappointed as a bankruptcy judge or magistrate judge for at least 31 consecutive days;

(ii) who files an application with the Administrative Office of the United States Courts for payment of the lump-sum credit;

(iii) is not serving as a bankruptcy judge or magistrate judge at the time of filing of the application; and

(iv) will not become eligible to receive an annuity under this section within 31 days after filing the application;

is entitled to be paid the lump-sum credit. Payment of the lump-sum credit voids all rights to an annuity under this section based on the service on which the lump-sum credit is based, until that individual resumes office as a bankruptcy judge or magistrate judge.

(B) Lump-sum benefits authorized by subparagraphs (C), (D), and (E) of this paragraph shall be paid to the person or persons surviving the bankruptcy judge or magistrate judge and alive on the date title to the payment arises, in the order of precedence set forth in subsection (*o*) of section 376 of this title, and in accordance with the last two sentences of that subsection. For purposes of the preceding sentence, the term "judicial official" as used in subsection (*o*) of section 376 shall be deemed to mean "bankruptcy judge or magistrate judge".

(C) If a bankruptcy judge or magistrate judge dies before receiving an annuity under this section, the lump-sum credit shall be paid.

(D) If all annuity rights under this section based on the service of a deceased bankruptcy judge or magistrate judge terminate before the total annuity paid equals the lump-sum credit, the difference shall be paid.

(E) If a bankruptcy judge or magistrate judge who is receiving an annuity under this section dies, annuity accrued and unpaid shall be paid.

(F) Annuity accrued and unpaid on the termination, except by death, of the annuity of a bankruptcy judge or magistrate judge shall be paid to that individual.

(G) Subject to paragraph (2), a bankruptcy judge or magistrate judge who forfeits rights to an annuity under subsection (m)(3) before the total annuity paid equals the lump-sum credit, shall be entitled to be paid the difference if the bankruptcy judge or magistrate judge files an application with the Administrative Office of the United States Courts for payment of that difference. A payment under this subparagraph voids all rights to an annuity on which the payment is based.

(2) Spouses and former spouses.—(A) Payment of the lump-sum credit under paragraph (1)(A) or a payment under paragraph (1)(G)—

(i) may be made only if any current spouse and any former spouse of the bankruptcy judge or magistrate judge are notified of the bankruptcy judge's or magistrate judge's application; and

(ii) shall be subject to the terms of a court decree of divorce, annulment, or legal separation or any court or court approved property settlement agreement incident to such decree, if—

(I) the decree, order, or agreement expressly relates to any portion of the lump-sum credit or other payment involved; and

(II) payment of the lump-sum credit or other payment would extinguish entitlement of the bankruptcy judge's or magistrate judge's spouse or former spouse to any portion of an annuity under subsection (i).

(B) Notification of a spouse or former spouse under this paragraph shall be made in accordance with such requirements as the Director of the Administrative Office of the United States Courts shall by regulation prescribe. The Director may provide under such regulations that subparagraph (A)(i) may be waived with respect to a spouse or former spouse if the bankruptcy judge or magistrate judge establishes to the satisfaction of the Director that the whereabouts of such spouse or former spouse cannot be determined.

(C) The Director shall prescribe regulations under which this paragraph shall be applied in any case in which the Director receives two or more orders or decrees described in subparagraph (A).

(3) Definition.—For purposes of this subsection, the term "lump-sum credit" means the unrefunded amount consisting of—

(A) retirement deductions made under this section from the salary of a bankruptcy judge or magistrate judge;

(B) amounts deposited under subsection (k) by a bankruptcy judge or magistrate judge covering earlier service; and

(C) interest on the deductions and deposits which, for any calendar year, shall be equal to the overall average yield to the Judicial Officers' Retirement Fund during the preceding fiscal year from all obligations purchased by the Secretary of the Treasury during such fiscal year under subsection (*o*);

but does not include interest—

(i) if the service covered thereby aggregates 1 year or less; or

(ii) for the fractional part of a month in the total service.

(*o*) **Judicial Officers' Retirement Fund.—**

(1) **Establishment.—**There is established in the Treasury a fund which shall be known as the "Judicial Officers' Retirement Fund". The Fund is appropriated for the payment of annuities, refunds, and other payments under this section.

(2) **Investment of Fund.—**The Secretary of the Treasury shall invest, in interest bearing securities of the United States, such currently available portions of the Judicial Officers' Retirement Fund as are not immediately required for payments from the Fund. The income derived from these investments constitutes a part of the Fund.

(3) **Unfunded liability.—(A)** There are authorized to be appropriated to the Judicial Officers' Retirement Fund amounts required to reduce to zero the unfunded liability of the Fund.

(B) For purposes of subparagraph (A), the term "unfunded liability" means the estimated excess, determined on an annual basis in accordance with the provisions of section 9503 of title 31, of the present value of all benefits payable from the Judicial Officers' Retirement Fund over the sum of—

(i) the present value of deductions to be withheld under this section from the future basic pay of bankruptcy judges and magistrate judges; plus

(ii) the balance in the Fund as of the date the unfunded liability is determined.

In making any determination under this subparagraph, the Comptroller General shall use the applicable information contained in the reports filed pursuant to section 9503 of title 31, with respect to the retirement annuities provided for in this section.

(C) There are authorized to be appropriated such sums as may be necessary to carry out this paragraph.

(Added Pub.L. 100–659, § 2(a), Nov. 15, 1988, 102 Stat. 3910; amended Pub.L. 101–650, Title III, §§ 321, 325(b)(3), Dec. 1, 1990, 104 Stat. 5117, 5121; Pub.L. 102–40, Title IV, § 402(d)(2), May 7, 1991, 105 Stat. 239.)

CHAPTER 19—DISTRIBUTION OF REPORTS AND DIGESTS

§ 411. Supreme Court reports; printing, binding, and distribution

(a) The decisions of the Supreme Court of the United States shall be printed, bound, and distributed in the preliminary prints and bound volumes of the United States Reports as soon as practicable after rendition, to be charged to the proper appropriation for the judiciary. The number and distribution of the copies shall be under the control of the Joint Committee on Printing.

(b) Reports printed prior to June 12, 1926, shall not be furnished the Secretary of the Army, the Secretary of the Navy, or the Secretary of the Air Force.

(c) The Director of the Government Publishing Office, or other printer designated by the Supreme Court of the United States, upon request, shall furnish to the Superintendent of Documents the reports required to be distributed under the provisions of this section.

(June 25, 1948, c. 646, 62 Stat. 904; May 24, 1949, c. 139, § 68, 63 Stat. 99; Oct. 31, 1951, c. 655, § 41, 65 Stat. 725; July 10, 1952, c. 632, § 4, 66 Stat. 540; Dec. 16, 2014, Pub. L. 113–235, 128 Stat. 2130.)

§ 412. Sale of Supreme Court reports

The Director of the Government Publishing Office, or other printer designated by the Supreme Court of the United States shall print such additional bound volumes and preliminary prints of such reports as may be required for sale to the public. Such additional copies shall be sold by the Superintendent of Documents, as provided by law.

(June 25, 1948, c. 646, 62 Stat. 906; July 10, 1952, c. 632, § 5, 66 Stat. 541; Dec. 16, 2014, Pub. L. 113–235, 128 Stat. 2130.)

§ 413. Publications; distribution to courts

Distribution of publications to Federal courts in accordance with the provisions of this chapter shall not be made to any place where such court is held in a building not owned or controlled by the United States unless such publications are committed to the custody of an officer of the United States at such building.

The Attorney General and the Director in the procurement of law books, books of reference or periodicals may exchange or sell similar items and apply the allowance or proceeds to payment in whole or in part of the cost of the items procured.

(June 25, 1948, c. 646, 62 Stat. 906; May 24, 1949, c. 139, § 69, 63 Stat. 100; July 10, 1952, c. 632, § 6, 66 Stat. 541.)

§ 414. Transmittal of books to successors

All government publications and law books furnished to justices, judges, clerks of courts, and United States attorneys of the United States and its territories and possessions, and other officers of the United States or an agency thereof shall be transmitted to their successors in office. All permanent or bound books and publications furnished under this chapter except those books furnished to the Library of Congress for international exchange shall remain the property of the United States and shall be marked plainly, "The Property of the United States".

(June 25, 1948, c. 646, 62 Stat. 906; Oct. 18, 1962, Pub.L. 87–845, § 7, 76A Stat. 699.)

[§ 415. Repealed. Pub.L. 97–164, Title I, § 113, Apr. 2, 1982, 96 Stat. 29]

HISTORICAL AND STATUTORY NOTES

Section, Acts June 25, 1948, c. 646, 62 Stat. 906; May 24, 1949, c. 139, § 70, 63 Stat. 100, provided for the distribution of copies of the decisions of the Court of Claims. See section 174(b) of this title.

CHAPTER 21—GENERAL PROVISIONS APPLICABLE TO COURTS AND JUDGES

HISTORICAL AND STATUTORY NOTES

Change of Name

"United States magistrate judge" substituted for "United States magistrate" in item 455 pursuant to section 321 of Pub.L. 101–650, set out as a note under 28 U.S.C.A. § 631.

§ 451. Definitions

As used in this title:

The term "court of the United States" includes the Supreme Court of the United States, courts of appeals, district courts constituted by chapter 5 of this title, including the Court of International Trade and any court created by Act of Congress the judges of which are entitled to hold office during good behavior.

The terms "district court" and "district court of the United States" mean the courts constituted by chapter 5 of this title.

The term "judge of the United States" includes judges of the courts of appeals, district courts, Court of International Trade and any court created by Act of Congress, the judges of which are entitled to hold office during good behavior.

The term "justice of the United States" includes the Chief Justice of the United States and the associate justices of the Supreme Court.

The term "district" and "judicial district" mean the districts enumerated in Chapter 5 of this title.

The term "department" means one of the executive departments enumerated in section 1 of Title 5, unless the context shows that such term was intended to describe the executive, legislative, or judicial branches of the government.

The term "agency" includes any department, independent establishment, commission, administration, authority, board or bureau of the United States or any corporation in which the United States has a proprietary interest, unless the context shows that such term was intended to be used in a more limited sense.

(June 25, 1948, c. 646, 62 Stat. 907; Mar. 18, 1959, Pub.L. 86–3, § 10, 73 Stat. 9; Sept. 12, 1966, Pub.L. 89–571, § 3, 80 Stat. 764; Nov. 6, 1978, Pub.L. 95–598, Title II, § 213, 92 Stat. 2661; Oct. 10, 1980, Pub.L. 96–417, Title V, § 501(10), 94 Stat. 1742; Apr. 2, 1982, Pub.L. 97–164, Title I, § 114, 96 Stat. 29.)

§ 452. Courts always open; powers unrestricted by expiration of sessions

All courts of the United States shall be deemed always open for the purpose of filing proper papers, issuing and returning process, and making motions and orders.

The continued existence or expiration of a session of a court in no way affects the power of the court to do any act or take any proceeding.

(June 25, 1948, c. 646, 62 Stat. 907; Oct. 16, 1963, Pub.L. 88–139, § 2, 77 Stat. 248.)

§ 453. Oaths of justices and judges

Each justice or judge of the United States shall take the following oath or affirmation before performing the duties of his office: "I, _____ _____, do solemnly swear (or affirm) that I will administer justice without respect to persons, and do equal right to the poor and to the rich, and that I will faithfully and impartially discharge and perform all the duties incumbent upon me as _____ under the Constitution and laws of the United States. So help me God."

(June 25, 1948, c. 646, 62 Stat. 907; Dec. 1, 1990, Pub.L. 101–650, Title IV, § 404, 104 Stat. 5124.)

§ 454. Practice of law by justices and judges

Any justice or judge appointed under the authority of the United States who engages in the practice of law is guilty of a high misdemeanor.

(June 25, 1948, c. 646, 62 Stat. 908.)

§ 455. Disqualification of justice, judge, or magistrate judge

(a) Any justice, judge, or magistrate judge of the United States shall disqualify himself in any proceeding in which his impartiality might reasonably be questioned.

(b) He shall also disqualify himself in the following circumstances:

(1) Where he has a personal bias or prejudice concerning a party, or personal knowledge of disputed evidentiary facts concerning the proceeding;

(2) Where in private practice he served as lawyer in the matter in controversy, or a lawyer with whom he previously practiced law served during such association as a lawyer concerning the matter, or the judge or such lawyer has been a material witness concerning it;

(3) Where he has served in governmental employment and in such capacity participated as counsel, adviser or material witness concerning the proceeding or expressed an opinion concerning the merits of the particular case in controversy;

(4) He knows that he, individually or as a fiduciary, or his spouse or minor child residing in his household, has a financial interest in the subject matter in controversy or in a party to the proceeding, or any other interest that could be substantially affected by the outcome of the proceeding;

(5) He or his spouse, or a person within the third degree of relationship to either of them, or the spouse of such a person:

(i) Is a party to the proceeding, or an officer, director, or trustee of a party;

(ii) Is acting as a lawyer in the proceeding;

(iii) Is known by the judge to have an interest that could be substantially affected by the outcome of the proceeding;

(iv) Is to the judge's knowledge likely to be a material witness in the proceeding.

(c) A judge should inform himself about his personal and fiduciary financial interests, and make a reasonable effort to inform himself about the personal financial interests of his spouse and minor children residing in his household.

(d) For the purposes of this section the following words or phrases shall have the meaning indicated:

(1) "proceeding" includes pretrial, trial, appellate review, or other stages of litigation;

(2) the degree of relationship is calculated according to the civil law system;

(3) "fiduciary" includes such relationships as executor, administrator, trustee, and guardian;

(4) "financial interest" means ownership of a legal or equitable interest, however small, or a relationship as director, adviser, or other active participant in the affairs of a party, except that:

(i) Ownership in a mutual or common investment fund that holds securities is not a "financial interest" in such securities unless the judge participates in the management of the fund;

(ii) An office in an educational, religious, charitable, fraternal, or civic organization is not a "financial interest" in securities held by the organization;

(iii) The proprietary interest of a policyholder in a mutual insurance company, of a depositor in a mutual savings association, or a similar proprietary interest, is a "financial interest" in the organization only if the outcome of the proceeding could substantially affect the value of the interest;

(iv) Ownership of government securities is a "financial interest" in the issuer only if the outcome of the proceeding could substantially affect the value of the securities.

(e) No justice, judge, or magistrate judge shall accept from the parties to the proceeding a waiver of any ground for disqualification enumerated in subsection (b). Where the ground for disqualification arises only under subsection (a), waiver may be accepted provided it is preceded by a full disclosure on the record of the basis for disqualification.

(f) Notwithstanding the preceding provisions of this section, if any justice, judge, magistrate judge, or bankruptcy judge to whom a matter has been assigned would be disqualified, after substantial judicial time has been devoted to the matter, because of the appearance or discovery, after the matter was assigned to him or her, that he or she individually or as a fiduciary, or his or her spouse or minor child residing in his or her household, has a financial interest in a party (other than an interest that could be substantially affected by the outcome), disqualification is not required if the justice, judge, magistrate judge, bankruptcy judge, spouse or minor child, as the case may be, divests himself or herself of the interest that provides the grounds for the disqualification.

(June 25, 1948, c. 646, 62 Stat. 908; Dec. 5, 1974, Pub.L. 93–512, § 1, 88 Stat. 1609; Nov. 6, 1978, Pub.L. 95–598, Title II, § 214(a), (b), 92 Stat. 2661; Nov. 19, 1988, Pub.L. 100–702, Title X, § 1007, 102 Stat. 4667; Dec. 1, 1990, Pub.L. 101–650, Title III, § 321, 104 Stat. 5117.)

§ 456. Traveling expenses of justices and judges; official duty stations

(a) The Director of the Administrative Office of the United States Courts shall pay each justice or judge of the United States, and each retired justice or judge recalled or designated and assigned to active duty, while attending court or transacting official business at a place other than his official duty station for any continuous period of less than thirty calendar days (1) all necessary transportation expenses certified by the justice or judge; and (2) payments for subsistence expenses at rates or in amounts which the Director establishes, in accordance with regulations which the Director shall prescribe with the approval of the Judicial Conference of the United States and after considering the rates or amounts set by the Administrator of General Services and the President pursuant to section 5702 of title 5. The Director of the Administrative Office of the United States Courts shall also pay each justice or judge of the United States, and each retired justice or judge recalled or designated and assigned to active duty, while attending court or transacting official business under an assignment authorized under chapter 13 of this title which exceeds in duration a continuous period of thirty calendar days, all necessary transportation expenses and actual and necessary expenses of subsistence actually incurred, notwithstanding the provisions of section 5702 of title 5, in accordance with regulations which the Director shall prescribe with the approval of the Judicial Conference of the United States.

(b) The official duty station of the Chief Justice of the United States, the Justices of the Supreme Court of the United States, and the judges of the United States Court of Appeals for the District of Columbia Circuit, the United States Court of Appeals for the Federal Circuit, and the United States District Court for the District of Columbia shall be the District of Columbia.

(c) The official duty station of the judges of the United States Court of International Trade shall be New York City.

(d) The official duty station of each district judge shall be that place where a district court holds regular sessions at or near which the judge performs a substantial portion of his judicial work, which is nearest the place where he maintains his actual abode in which he customarily lives.

(e) The official duty station of a circuit judge shall be that place where a circuit or district court holds regular sessions at or near which the judge performs a substantial portion of his judicial work, or that place where the Director provides chambers to the judge where he performs a substantial portion of his judicial work, which is nearest the place where he maintains his actual abode in which he customarily lives.

(f) The official duty station of a retired judge shall be established in accordance with section 374 of this title.

(g) Each circuit or district judge whose official duty station is not fixed expressly by this section shall notify the Director of the Administrative Office of the United States Courts in writing of his actual abode and official duty station upon his appointment and from time to time thereafter as his official duty station may change.

(June 25, 1948, c. 646, 62 Stat. 908; Aug. 8, 1953, c. 376, 67 Stat. 488; Aug. 7, 1959, Pub.L. 86–138, 73 Stat. 285; Nov. 6, 1978, Pub.L. 95–598, Title II, § 215, 92 Stat. 2661; Oct. 10, 1980, Pub.L. 96–417, Title V, § 501(11), 94 Stat. 1742; Apr. 2, 1982, Pub.L. 97–164, Title I, § 115(a)(1), 96 Stat. 30; Jan. 2, 1986, Pub.L. 99–234, Title I, § 107(d), 99 Stat. 1759.)

§ 457. Records; obsolete papers

The records of district courts and of courts of appeals shall be kept at one or more of the places where court is held. Such places shall be designated by the respective courts except when otherwise directed by the judicial council of the circuit.

Papers of any court established by Act of Congress which have become obsolete and are no longer necessary or useful, may be disposed of with the approval of the court concerned in the manner provided by sections 366–380 of Title 44 and in accordance with the rules of the Judicial Conference of the United States.

(June 25, 1948, c. 646, 62 Stat. 908; Nov. 6, 1978, Pub.L. 95–598, Title II, § 216, 92 Stat. 2661.)

§ 458. Relative of justice or judge ineligible to appointment

(a)(1) No person shall be appointed to or employed in any office or duty in any court who is related by affinity or consanguinity within the degree of first cousin to any justice or judge of such court.

(2) With respect to the appointment of a judge of a court exercising judicial power under article III of the United States Constitution [U.S.C.A. Const. Art. III] (other than the Supreme Court), subsection (b) shall apply in lieu of this subsection.

(b)(1) In this subsection, the term—

    (A) "same court" means—

        (i) in the case of a district court, the court of a single judicial district; and

        (ii) in the case of a court of appeals, the court of appeals of a single circuit; and

    (B) "member"—

        (i) means an active judge or a judge retired in senior status under section 371(b); and

        (ii) shall not include a retired judge, except as described under clause (i).

(2) No person may be appointed to the position of judge of a court exercising judicial power under article III of the United States Constitution [U.S.C.A. Const. Art. III] (other than the Supreme Court) who is related by affinity or consanguinity within the degree of first cousin to any judge who is a member of the same court.

(June 25, 1948, c. 646, 62 Stat. 908; Oct. 27, 1998, Pub.L. 105–300, § 1(a), 112 Stat. 2836.)

§ 459. Administration of oaths and acknowledgments

Each justice or judge of the United States may administer oaths and affirmations and take acknowledgments.

(June 25, 1948, c. 646, 62 Stat. 908.)

§ 460. Application to other courts

(a) Sections 452 through 459 and section 462 of this chapter shall also apply to the United States Court of Federal Claims, to each court created by Act of Congress in a territory which is invested with any jurisdiction of a district court of the United States, and to the judges thereof.

(b) The official duty station of each judge referred to in subsection (a) which is not otherwise established by law shall be that place where the court holds regular sessions at or near which the judge performs a substantial portion of his judicial work, which is nearest the place where he maintains his actual abode in which he customarily lives.

(June 25, 1948, c. 646, 62 Stat. 908; Oct. 31, 1951, c. 655, § 43(a), 65 Stat. 725; July 7, 1958, Pub.L. 85–508, § 12(e), 72 Stat. 348; Nov. 6, 1978, Pub.L. 95–598, Title II, § 217(a), 92 Stat. 2661; Apr. 2, 1982, Pub.L. 97–164, Title I, § 115(b)(1), 96 Stat. 31; Oct. 29, 1992, Pub.L. 102–572, Title IX, § 902(b)(1), 106 Stat. 4516.)

§ 461. Adjustments in certain salaries

(a)(1) Subject to paragraph (2), effective at the beginning of the first applicable pay period commencing on or after the first day of the month in which an adjustment takes effect under section 5303 of title 5 in the rates of pay under the General Schedule (except as provided in subsection (b)), each salary rate which is subject to adjustment under this section shall be adjusted by an amount, rounded to the nearest multiple of $100 (or if midway between multiples of $100, to the next higher multiple of $100) equal to the percentage of such salary rate which corresponds to the most recent percentage change in the ECI (relative to the date described in the next sentence), as determined under section 704(a)(1) of the Ethics Reform Act of 1989. The appropriate date under this sentence is the first day of the fiscal year in which such adjustment in the rates of pay under the General Schedule takes effect.

(2) In no event shall the percentage adjustment taking effect under paragraph (1) in any calendar year (before rounding), in any salary rate, exceed the percentage adjustment taking effect in such calendar year under section 5303 of title 5 in the rates of pay under the General Schedule.

(b) Subsection (a) shall not apply to the extent it would reduce the salary of any individual whose compensation may not, under section 1 of article III of the Constitution of the United States, be diminished during such individual's continuance in office.

(Added Pub.L. 94–82, Title II, § 205(a)(1), Aug. 9, 1975, 89 Stat. 422; amended Pub.L. 101–194, Title VII, § 704(a)(2)(A), Nov. 30, 1989, 103 Stat. 1769; Pub.L. 101–509, Title V, § 529 [Title I, § 101(b)(4)(J)], Nov. 5, 1990, 104 Stat. 1427, 1440; Pub.L. 103–356, Title I, § 101(4), Oct. 13, 1994, 108 Stat. 3411.)

§ 462. Court accommodations

(a) Sessions of courts of the United States (except the Supreme Court) shall be held only at places where the Director of the Administrative Office of the United States Courts provides accommodations, or where suitable accommodations are furnished without cost to the judicial branch.

(b) The Director of the Administrative Office of the United States Courts shall provide accommodations, including chambers and courtrooms, only at places where regular sessions of court are authorized by law to be held, but only if the judicial council of the appropriate circuit has approved the accommodations as necessary.

(c) The limitations and restrictions contained in subsection (b) of this section shall not prevent the Director from furnishing chambers to circuit judges at places within the circuit other than where regular sessions of court are authorized by law to be held, when the judicial council of the circuit approves.

(d) The Director of the Administrative Office of the United States Courts shall provide permanent accommodations for the United States Court of Appeals for the Federal Circuit and for the United States Court of Federal Claims only at the District of Columbia. However, each such court may hold regular and special sessions at other places utilizing the accommodations which the Director provides to other courts.

(e) The Director of the Administrative Office of the United States Courts shall provide accommodations for probation officers, pretrial service officers, and Federal Public Defender Organizations at such places as may be approved by the judicial council of the appropriate circuit.

(f) Upon the request of the Director, the Administrator of General Services is authorized and directed to provide the accommodations the Director requests, and to close accommodations which the Director recommends for closure with the approval of the Judicial Conference of the United States.

(Added Pub.L. 97–164, Title I, § 115(c)(1), Apr. 2, 1982, 96 Stat. 31; amended Pub.L. 100–702, Title X, § 1015, Nov. 19, 1988, 102 Stat. 4669; Pub.L. 102–572, Title IX, § 902(b)(1), Oct. 29, 1992, 106 Stat. 4516.)

§ 463. Expenses of litigation

Whenever a Chief Justice, justice, judge, officer, or employee of any United States court is sued in his official capacity, or is otherwise required to defend acts taken or omissions made in his official capacity, and the services of an attorney for the Government are not reasonably available pursuant to chapter 31 of this title, the Director of the Administrative Office of the United States Courts may pay the costs of his defense. The Director shall prescribe regulations for such payments subject to the approval of the Judicial Conference of the United States.

(Added Pub.L. 97–164, Title I, § 116(a), Apr. 2, 1982, 96 Stat. 32.)

PART III—COURT OFFICERS AND EMPLOYEES*

CHAPTER 43—UNITED STATES MAGISTRATE JUDGES

HISTORICAL AND STATUTORY NOTES

Change of Name

"United States magistrate judge" substituted for "United States magistrate" in the chapter heading pursuant to section 321 of Pub.L. 101–650, set out as a note under 28 U.S.C.A. § 631.

§ 631. Appointment and tenure

(a) The judges of each United States district court and the district courts of the Virgin Islands, Guam, and the Northern Mariana Islands shall appoint United States magistrate judges in such numbers and to serve at such locations within the judicial districts as the Judicial Conference may determine under this chapter. In the case of a magistrate judge appointed by the district court of the Virgin Islands, Guam, or the Northern Mariana Islands, this chapter shall apply as though the court appointing such a magistrate judge were a United States district court. Where there is more than one judge of a district court, the appointment, whether an original appointment or a reappointment, shall be by the concurrence of a majority of all the judges of such district court, and when there is no such concurrence, then by the chief judge. Where the conference deems it desirable, a magistrate judge may be designated to serve in one or more districts adjoining the district for which he is appointed. Such a designation shall be made by the concurrence of a majority of the judges of each of the district courts involved and shall specify the duties to be performed by the magistrate judge in the adjoining district or districts.

(b) No individual may be appointed or reappointed to serve as a magistrate judge under this chapter unless:

(1) He has been for at least five years a member in good standing of the bar of the highest court of a State, the District of Columbia, the Commonwealth of Puerto Rico, the Territory of Guam, the Commonwealth of the Northern Mariana Islands, or the Virgin Islands of the United States, except that an individual who does not meet the bar membership requirements of this paragraph may be appointed and serve as a part-time magistrate judge if the appointing court or courts and the conference find that no qualified individual who is a member of the bar is available to serve at a specific location;

(2) He is determined by the appointing district court or courts to be competent to perform the duties of the office;

(3) In the case of an individual appointed to serve in a national park, he resides within the exterior boundaries of that park, or at some place reasonably adjacent thereto;

---

*   [Part II of Title 28, which pertains to the Department of Justice, is omitted. Ed.]

(4) He is not related by blood or marriage to a judge of the appointing court or courts at the time of his initial appointment; and

(5) He is selected pursuant to standards and procedures promulgated by the Judicial Conference of the United States. Such standards and procedures shall contain provision for public notice of all vacancies in magistrate judge positions and for the establishment by the district courts of merit selection panels, composed of residents of the individual judicial districts, to assist the courts in identifying and recommending persons who are best qualified to fill such positions.

(c) A magistrate judge may hold no other civil or military office or employment under the United States: *Provided, however*, That, with the approval of the conference, a part-time referee in bankruptcy or a clerk or deputy clerk of a court of the United States may be appointed and serve as a part-time United States magistrate judge, but the conference shall fix the aggregate amount of compensation to be received for performing the duties of part-time magistrate judge and part-time referee in bankruptcy, clerk or deputy clerk: *And provided further*, That retired officers and retired enlisted personnel of the Regular and Reserve components of the Army, Navy, Air Force, Marine Corps, and Coast Guard, members of the Reserve components of the Army, Navy, Air Force, Marine Corps, and Coast Guard, and members of the Army National Guard of the United States, the Air National Guard of the United States, and the Naval Militia and of the National Guard of a State, territory, or the District of Columbia, except the National Guard disbursing officers who are on a full-time salary basis, may be appointed and serve as United States magistrate judges.

(d) Except as otherwise provided in sections 375 and 636(h) of this title, no individual may serve under this chapter after having attained the age of seventy years: *Provided, however*, That upon a majority vote of all the judges of the appointing court or courts, which is taken upon the magistrate judge's attaining age seventy and upon each subsequent anniversary thereof, a magistrate judge who has attained the age of seventy years may continue to serve and may be reappointed under this chapter.

(e) The appointment of any individual as a full-time magistrate judge shall be for a term of eight years, and the appointment of any individuals as a part-time magistrate judge shall be for a term of four years, except that the term of a full-time or part-time magistrate judge appointed under subsection (k) shall expire upon—

(1) the expiration of the absent magistrate judge's term,

(2) the reinstatement of the absent magistrate judge in regular service in office as a magistrate judge,

(3) the failure of the absent magistrate judge to make timely application under subsection (j) of this section for reinstatement in regular service in office as a magistrate judge after discharge or release from military service,

(4) the death or resignation of the absent magistrate judge, or

(5) the removal from office of the absent magistrate judge pursuant to subsection (i) of this section,

whichever may first occur.

(f) Upon the expiration of his term, a magistrate judge may, by a majority vote of the judges of the appointing district court or courts and with the approval of the judicial council of the circuit, continue to perform the duties of his office until his successor is appointed, or for 180 days after the date of the expiration of the magistrate judge's term, whichever is earlier.

(g) Each individual appointed as a magistrate judge under this section shall take the oath or affirmation prescribed by section 453 of this title before performing the duties of his office.

(h) Each appointment made by a judge or judges of a district court shall be entered of record in such court, and notice of such appointment shall be given at once by the clerk of that court to the Director.

(i) Removal of a magistrate judge during the term for which he is appointed shall be only for incompetency, misconduct, neglect of duty, or physical or mental disability, but a magistrate judge's office shall be terminated if the conference determines that the services performed by his office are no longer needed. Removal shall be by the judges of the district court for the judicial district in which the magistrate judge serves; where there is more than one judge of a district court, removal shall not occur unless a majority of all the judges of such court concur in the order of removal; and when there is a tie vote of the judges of the district court on the question of the removal or retention in office of a magistrate judge, then removal shall be only by a concurrence of a majority of all the judges of the council. In the case of a magistrate judge appointed under the third sentence of subsection (a) of this section, removal shall not occur unless a majority of all the judges of the appointing district courts concur in the order of removal; and where there is a tie vote on the question of the removal or retention in office of a magistrate judge, then removal shall be only by a concurrence of a majority of all the judges of the council or councils. Before any order or removal shall be entered, a full specification of the charges shall be furnished to the magistrate judge, and he shall be accorded by the judge or judges of the removing court, courts, council, or councils an opportunity to be heard on the charges.

(j) Upon the grant by the appropriate district court or courts of a leave of absence to a magistrate judge entitled to such relief under chapter 43 of title 38, such court or courts may proceed to appoint, in the manner specified in subsection (a) of this section, another magistrate judge, qualified for appointment and service under subsections (b), (c), and (d) of this section, who shall serve for the period specified in subsection (e) of this section.

(k) A United States magistrate judge appointed under this chapter shall be exempt from the provisions of subchapter I of chapter 63 of title 5.

(June 25, 1948, c. 646, 62 Stat. 915; May 24, 1949, c. 139, § 73, 63 Stat. 100; July 9, 1952, c. 609, § 1, 66 Stat. 509; July 25, 1956, c. 722, 70 Stat. 642; Oct. 17, 1968, Pub.L. 90–578, Title I, § 101, 82 Stat. 1108; Oct. 17, 1976, Pub.L. 94–520, § 2, 90 Stat. 2458; Nov. 6, 1978, Pub.L. 95–598, Title II, § 231, 92 Stat. 2665; Oct. 10, 1979, Pub.L. 96–82, § 3(a)–(d), 93 Stat. 644, 645; Aug. 6, 1982, Pub.L. 97–230, 96 Stat. 255; Nov. 14, 1986, Pub.L. 99–651, Title II, § 201(a)(1), 100 Stat. 3646; Nov. 15, 1988, Pub.L. 100–659, § 5, 102 Stat. 3918; Nov. 19, 1988, Pub.L. 100–702, Title X, § 1003(a)(2), 102 Stat. 4665; June 30, 1989, Pub.L. 101–45, Title II, § 104, 103 Stat. 122; Dec. 1, 1990, Pub.L. 101–650, Title III, §§ 308(b), 321, 104 Stat. 5112, 5117; Oct. 13, 1994, Pub.L. 103–353, § 2(c), 108 Stat. 3169; Nov. 13, 2000, Pub.L. 106–518, Title II, § 201, 114 Stat. 2412; Jan. 7, 2008, Pub.L. 110–177, Title V, § 504, 121 Stat. 2542; Pub.L. 111–174, § 2, May 27, 2010, 124 Stat. 1216.)

§ 632. Character of service

(a) Full-time United States magistrate judges may not engage in the practice of law, and may not engage in any other business, occupation, or employment inconsistent with the expeditious, proper, and impartial performance of their duties as judicial officers.

(b) Part-time United States magistrate judges shall render such service as judicial officers as is required by law. While so serving they may engage in the practice of law, but may not serve as counsel in any criminal action in any court of the United States, nor act in any capacity that is, under such regulations as the conference may establish, inconsistent with the proper discharge of their office. Within such restrictions, they may engage in any other business, occupation, or employment which is not inconsistent with the expeditious, proper, and impartial performance of their duties as judicial officers.

(June 25, 1948, c. 646, 62 Stat. 916; Oct. 17, 1968, Pub.L. 90–578, Title I, § 101, 82 Stat. 1110; Pub.L. 101–650, Title III, § 321, Dec. 1 1990, 104 Stat. 5117.)

§ 633. Determination of number, locations, and salaries of magistrates

(a) **Surveys by the Director.**[*]—

(1) The Director shall, within one year immediately following the date of the enactment of the Federal Magistrates Act, make a careful survey of conditions in judicial districts to determine (A) the number of appointments of full-time magistrates and part-time magistrates required to be made under this chapter to provide for the expeditious and effective administration of justice, (B) the locations at which such officers shall serve, and (C) their respective salaries under section 634 of this title. Thereafter, the Director shall, from time to time, make such surveys, general or local, as the conference shall deem expedient.

(2) In the course of any survey, the Director shall take into account local conditions in each judicial district, including the areas and the populations to be served, the transportation and communications facilities available, the amount and distribution of business of the type expected to arise before officers appointed under this chapter (including such matters as may be assigned under section 636(b) of this chapter), and any other material factors. The Director shall give consideration to suggestions from any interested parties, including district judges, United States magistrate judges or officers appointed under this chapter, United States attorneys, bar associations, and other parties having relevant experience or information.

(3) The surveys shall be made with a view toward creating and maintaining a system of full-time United States magistrate judges. However, should the Director find, as a result of any such surveys, areas in which the employment of a full-time magistrate judge would not be feasible or desirable, he shall recommend the appointment of part-time United States magistrate judges in such numbers and at such locations as may be required to permit prompt and efficient issuance of process and to permit individuals charged with criminal offenses against the United States to be brought before a judicial officer of the United States promptly after arrest.

(b) **Determination by the conference.**—Upon the completion of the initial surveys required by subsection (a) of this section, the Director shall report to the district courts, the councils, and the conference his recommendations concerning the number of full-time magistrates and part-time magistrates, their respective locations, and the amount of their respective salaries under section 634 of this title. The district courts shall advise their respective councils, stating their recommendations and the reasons therefor; the councils shall advise the conference, stating their recommendations and the reasons therefor, and shall also report to the conference the recommendations of the district courts. The conference shall determine, in the light of the recommendations of the Director, the district courts, and the councils, the number of full-time United States magistrates and part-time United States magistrates, the locations at which they shall serve, and their respective salaries. Such determinations shall take effect in each judicial district at such time as the district court for such judicial district shall determine, but in no event later than one year after they are promulgated.

(c) **Changes in number, locations, and salaries.**—Except as otherwise provided in this chapter, the conference may, from time to time, in the light of the recommendations of the Director, the district courts, and the councils, change the number, locations, and salaries of full-time and part-time magistrate judges, as the expeditious administration of justice may require.

(June 25, 1948, c. 646, 62 Stat. 916; Aug. 13, 1954, c. 728, § 1(a), (b), 68 Stat. 703, 704; Sept. 2, 1957, Pub.L. 85–276, §§ 1, 2, 71 Stat. 600; Oct. 17, 1968, Pub.L. 90–578, Title I, § 101, 82 Stat. 1111; Oct. 10, 1979, Pub.L. 96–82, § 4, 93 Stat. 645; Nov. 14, 1986, Pub.L. 99–651, Title II, § 202(d), 100 Stat. 3648; Dec. 1, 1990, Pub.L. 101–650, Title III, § 321, 104 Stat. 5117.)

---

[*]   [The Director referred to here and throughout is the Director of the Administrative Office of the United States Courts. *See* 28 U.S.C. § 604. Ed.]

§ 634. Compensation

(a) Officers appointed under this chapter shall receive, as full compensation for their services, salaries to be fixed by the conference pursuant to section 633, at rates for full-time United States magistrate judges up to an annual rate equal to 92 percent of the salary of a judge of the district court of the United States, as determined pursuant to section 135, and at rates for part-time magistrate judges of not less than an annual salary of $100, nor more than one-half the maximum salary payable to a full-time magistrate judge. In fixing the amount of salary to be paid to any officer appointed under this chapter, consideration shall be given to the average number and the nature of matters that have arisen during the immediately preceding period of five years, and that may be expected thereafter to arise, over which such officer would have jurisdiction and to such other factors as may be material. Disbursement of salaries shall be made by or pursuant to the order of the Director.

(b) Except as provided by section 8344, title 5, relating to reductions of the salaries of reemployed annuitants under subchapter III of chapter 83 of such title and unless the office has been terminated as provided in this chapter, the salary of a full-time United States magistrate judge shall not be reduced, during the term in which he is serving, below the salary fixed for him at the beginning of that term.

(c) All United States magistrate judges, effective upon their taking the oath or affirmation of office, and all necessary legal, clerical, and secretarial assistants employed in the offices of full-time United States magistrate judges shall be deemed to be officers and employees in the judicial branch of the United States Government within the meaning of subchapter III (relating to civil service retirement) of chapter 83, chapter 87 (relating to Federal employees' group life insurance), and chapter 89 (relating to Federal employees' health benefits program) of title 5. Part-time magistrate judges shall not be excluded from coverage under these chapters solely for lack of a prearranged regular tour of duty. A legal assistant appointed under this section shall be exempt from the provisions of subchapter I of chapter 63 of title 5, unless specifically included by the appointing judge or by local rule of court.

(June 25, 1948, c. 646, 62 Stat. 917; Oct. 17, 1968, Pub.L. 90–578, Title I, § 101, 82 Stat. 1112; Sept. 21, 1972, Pub.L. 92–428, 86 Stat. 721; Oct. 17, 1976, Pub.L. 94–520, § 1, 90 Stat. 2458; Nov. 6, 1978, Pub.L. 95–598, Title II, § 232, 92 Stat. 2665; Oct. 10, 1979, Pub.L. 96–82, § 8(b), 93 Stat. 647; July 10, 1984, Pub.L. 98–353, Title I, § 108(a), Title II, § 210, 98 Stat. 342, 351; Dec. 22, 1987, Pub.L. 100–202, § 101(a) [Title IV, § 408 (b)], 101 Stat. 1329, 1329–27; Nov. 19, 1988, Pub.L. 100–702, Title X, § 1003(a)(4), 102 Stat. 4665; Dec. 1, 1990, Pub.L. 101–650, Title III, § 321, 104 Stat. 5117.)

§ 635. Expenses

(a) Full-time United States magistrate judges serving under this chapter shall be allowed their actual and necessary expenses incurred in the performance of their duties, including the compensation of such legal assistants as the Judicial Conference, on the basis of the recommendations of the judicial councils of the circuits, considers necessary, and the compensation of necessary clerical and secretarial assistance. Such expenses and compensation shall be determined and paid by the Director under such regulations as the Director shall prescribe with the approval of the conference. The Administrator of General Services shall provide such magistrate judges with necessary courtrooms, office space, furniture and facilities within United States courthouses or office buildings owned or occupied by departments or agencies of the United States, or should suitable courtroom and office space not be available within any such courthouse or office building, the Administrator of General Services, at the request of the Director, shall procure and pay for suitable courtroom and office space, furniture and facilities for such magistrate judge in another building, but only if such request has been approved as necessary by the judicial council of the appropriate circuit.

(b) Under such regulations as the Director shall prescribe with the approval of the conference, the Director shall reimburse part-time magistrate judges for actual expenses necessarily incurred by them in the performance of their duties under this chapter. Such reimbursement may be made, at rates not exceeding those prescribed by such regulations, for expenses incurred by such part-time magistrate judges for clerical and secretarial assistance, stationery, telephone and other communications services, travel, and such other expenses as may be determined to be necessary for the proper performance of the duties of such officers: *Provided, however,* That no reimbursement shall be made for all or any portion of the expense incurred by such part-time magistrate judges for the procurement of office space.

(June 25, 1948, c. 646, 62 Stat. 917; Oct. 17, 1968, Pub.L. 90–578, Title I, § 101, 82 Stat. 1112; Oct. 10, 1979, Pub.L. 96–82, § 8(a), 93 Stat. 646; Dec. 1, 1990, Pub.L. 101–650, title III, § 321, 104 Stat. 5117.)

§ 636. Jurisdiction, powers, and temporary assignment

(a) Each United States magistrate judge serving under this chapter shall have within the district in which sessions are held by the court that appointed the magistrate judge, at other places where that court may function, and elsewhere as authorized by law—

(1) all powers and duties conferred or imposed upon United States commissioners by law or by the Rules of Criminal Procedure for the United States District Courts;

(2) the power to administer oaths and affirmations, issue orders pursuant to section 3142 of title 18 concerning release or detention of persons pending trial, and take acknowledgements, affidavits, and depositions;

(3) the power to conduct trials under section 3401, title 18, United States Code, in conformity with and subject to the limitations of that section;

(4) the power to enter a sentence for a petty offense; and

(5) the power to enter a sentence for a class A misdemeanor in a case in which the parties have consented.

(b)(1) Notwithstanding any provision of law to the contrary—

(A) a judge may designate a magistrate judge to hear and determine any pretrial matter pending before the court, except a motion for injunctive relief, for judgment on the pleadings, for summary judgment, to dismiss or quash an indictment or information made by the defendant, to suppress evidence in a criminal case, to dismiss or to permit maintenance of a class action, to dismiss for failure to state a claim upon which relief can be granted, and to involuntarily dismiss an action. A judge of the court may reconsider any pretrial matter under this subparagraph (A) where it has been shown that the magistrate judge's order is clearly erroneous or contrary to law.

(B) a judge may also designate a magistrate judge to conduct hearings, including evidentiary hearings, and to submit to a judge of the court proposed findings of fact and recommendations for the disposition, by a judge of the court, of any motion excepted in subparagraph (A), of applications for posttrial[1] relief made by individuals convicted of criminal offenses and of prisoner petitions challenging conditions of confinement.

(C) the magistrate judge shall file his proposed findings and recommendations under subparagraph (B) with the court and a copy shall forthwith be mailed to all parties.

Within fourteen days after being served with a copy, any party may serve and file written objections to such proposed findings and recommendations as provided by rules of court. A judge of the court shall make a de novo determination of those portions of the report or specified proposed findings or recommendations to which objection is made. A judge of the court may accept, reject, or modify, in whole or in part, the findings or recommendations made by the magistrate judge. The judge may also receive further evidence or recommit the matter to the magistrate judge with instructions.

(2) A judge may designate a magistrate judge to serve as a special master pursuant to the applicable provisions of this title and the Federal Rules of Civil Procedure for the United States

---

[1]   [Footnote to 28 U.S.C. § 636(b)(1)(B):] So in original. Probably should be "post-trial".

district courts. A judge may designate a magistrate judge to serve as a special master in any civil case, upon consent of the parties, without regard to the provisions of rule 53(b) of the Federal Rules of Civil Procedure for the United States district courts.

(3) A magistrate judge may be assigned such additional duties as are not inconsistent with the Constitution and laws of the United States.

(4) Each district court shall establish rules pursuant to which the magistrate judges shall discharge their duties.

(c) Notwithstanding any provision of law to the contrary—

(1) Upon the consent of the parties, a full-time United States magistrate judge or a part-time United States magistrate judge who serves as a full-time judicial officer may conduct any or all proceedings in a jury or nonjury civil matter and order the entry of judgment in the case, when specially designated to exercise such jurisdiction by the district court or courts he serves. Upon the consent of the parties, pursuant to their specific written request, any other part-time magistrate judge may exercise such jurisdiction, if such magistrate judge meets the bar membership requirements set forth in section 631(b)(1) and the chief judge of the district court certifies that a full-time magistrate judge is not reasonably available in accordance with guidelines established by the judicial council of the circuit. When there is more than one judge of a district court, designation under this paragraph shall be by the concurrence of a majority of all the judges of such district court, and when there is no such concurrence, then by the chief judge.

(2) If a magistrate judge is designated to exercise civil jurisdiction under paragraph (1) of this subsection, the clerk of court shall, at the time the action is filed, notify the parties of the availability of a magistrate judge to exercise such jurisdiction. The decision of the parties shall be communicated to the clerk of court. Thereafter, either the district court judge or the magistrate judge may again advise the parties of the availability of the magistrate judge, but in so doing, shall also advise the parties that they are free to withhold consent without adverse substantive consequences. Rules of court for the reference of civil matters to magistrate judges shall include procedures to protect the voluntariness of the parties' consent.

(3) Upon entry of judgment in any case referred under paragraph (1) of this subsection, an aggrieved party may appeal directly to the appropriate United States court of appeals from the judgment of the magistrate judge in the same manner as an appeal from any other judgment of a district court. The consent of the parties allows a magistrate judge designated to exercise civil jurisdiction under paragraph (1) of this subsection to direct the entry of a judgment of the district court in accordance with the Federal Rules of Civil Procedure. Nothing in this paragraph shall be construed as a limitation of any party's right to seek review by the Supreme Court of the United States.

(4) The court may, for good cause shown on its own motion, or under extraordinary circumstances shown by any party, vacate a reference of a civil matter to a magistrate judge under this subsection.

(5) The magistrate judge shall, subject to guidelines of the Judicial Conference, determine whether the record taken pursuant to this section shall be taken by electronic sound recording, by a court reporter, or by other means.

(d) The practice and procedure for the trial of cases before officers serving under this chapter shall conform to rules promulgated by the Supreme Court pursuant to section 2072 of this title.

(e) Contempt authority.—

(1) In general.—A United States magistrate judge serving under this chapter shall have within the territorial jurisdiction prescribed by the appointment of such magistrate judge the power to exercise contempt authority as set forth in this subsection.

(2) Summary criminal contempt authority.—A magistrate judge shall have the power to punish summarily by fine or imprisonment, or both, such contempt of the authority of such magistrate judge constituting misbehavior of any person in the magistrate judge's presence so as to obstruct the administration of justice. The order of contempt shall be issued under the Federal Rules of Criminal Procedure.

(3) Additional criminal contempt authority in civil consent and misdemeanor cases.—In any case in which a United States magistrate judge presides with the consent of the parties under subsection (c) of this section, and in any misdemeanor case proceeding before a magistrate judge under section 3401 of title 18, the magistrate judge shall have the power to punish, by fine or imprisonment, or both, criminal contempt constituting disobedience or resistance to the magistrate judge's lawful writ, process, order, rule, decree, or command. Disposition of such contempt shall be conducted upon notice and hearing under the Federal Rules of Criminal Procedure.

(4) Civil contempt authority in civil consent and misdemeanor cases.—In any case in which a United States magistrate judge presides with the consent of the parties under subsection (c) of this section, and in any misdemeanor case proceeding before a magistrate judge under section 3401 of title 18, the magistrate judge may exercise the civil contempt authority of the district court. This paragraph shall not be construed to limit the authority of a magistrate judge to order sanctions under any other statute, the Federal Rules of Civil Procedure, or the Federal Rules of Criminal Procedure.

(5) Criminal contempt penalties.—The sentence imposed by a magistrate judge for any criminal contempt provided for in paragraphs (2) and (3) shall not exceed the penalties for a Class C misdemeanor as set forth in sections 3581(b)(8) and 3571(b)(6) of title 18.

(6) Certification of other contempts to the district court.—Upon the commission of any such act—

(A) in any case in which a United States magistrate judge presides with the consent of the parties under subsection (c) of this section, or in any misdemeanor case proceeding before a magistrate judge under section 3401 of title 18, that may, in the opinion of the magistrate judge, constitute a serious criminal contempt punishable by penalties exceeding those set forth in paragraph (5) of this subsection, or

(B) in any other case or proceeding under subsection (a) or (b) of this section, or any other statute, where—

(i) the act committed in the magistrate judge's presence may, in the opinion of the magistrate judge, constitute a serious criminal contempt punishable by penalties exceeding those set forth in paragraph (5) of this subsection,

(ii) the act that constitutes a criminal contempt occurs outside the presence of the magistrate judge, or

(iii) the act constitutes a civil contempt,

the magistrate judge shall forthwith certify the facts to a district judge and may serve or cause to be served, upon any person whose behavior is brought into question under this paragraph, an order requiring such person to appear before a district judge upon a day certain to show cause why that person should not be adjudged in contempt by reason of the facts so certified. The district judge shall thereupon hear the evidence as to the act or conduct complained of and, if it is such as to warrant punishment, punish such person in the same manner and to the same extent as for a contempt committed before a district judge.

(7) Appeals of magistrate judge contempt orders.—The appeal of an order of contempt under this subsection shall be made to the court of appeals in cases proceeding under subsection (c) of this section. The appeal of any other order of contempt issued under this section shall be made to the district court.

(f) In an emergency and upon the concurrence of the chief judges of the districts involved, a United States magistrate judge may be temporarily assigned to perform any of the duties specified in subsection (a), (b), or (c) of this section in a judicial district other than the judicial district for which he has been appointed. No magistrate judge shall perform any of such duties in a district to which he has been temporarily assigned until an order has been issued by the chief judge of such district specifying (1) the emergency by reason of which he has been transferred, (2) the duration of his assignment, and (3) the duties which he is authorized to perform. A magistrate judge so assigned shall not be entitled to additional compensation but shall be reimbursed for actual and necessary expenses incurred in the performance of his duties in accordance with section 635.

(g) A United States magistrate judge may perform the verification function required by section 4107 of title 18, United States Code. A magistrate judge may be assigned by a judge of any United States district court to perform the verification required by section 4108 and the appointment of counsel authorized by section 4109 of title 18, United States Code, and may perform such functions beyond the territorial limits of the United States. A magistrate judge assigned such functions shall have no authority to perform any other function within the territory of a foreign country.

(h) A United States magistrate judge who has retired may, upon the consent of the chief judge of the district involved, be recalled to serve as a magistrate judge in any judicial district by the judicial council of the circuit within which such district is located. Upon recall, a magistrate judge may receive a salary for such service in accordance with regulations promulgated by the Judicial Conference, subject to the restrictions on the payment of an annuity set forth in section 377 of this title or in subchapter III of chapter 83, and chapter 84, of title 5 which are applicable to such magistrate judge. The requirements set forth in subsections (a), (b)(3), and (d) of section 631, and paragraph (1) of subsection (b) of such section to the extent such paragraph requires membership of the bar of the location in which an individual is to serve as a magistrate judge, shall not apply to the recall of a retired magistrate judge under this subsection or section 375 of this title. Any other requirement set forth in section 631(b) shall apply to the recall of a retired magistrate judge under this subsection or section 375 of this title unless such retired magistrate judge met such requirement upon appointment or reappointment as a magistrate judge under section 361.

(June 25, 1948, c. 646, 62 Stat. 917; Oct. 17, 1968, Pub.L. 90–578, Title I, § 101, 82 Stat. 1113; Mar. 1, 1972, Pub.L. 92–239, §§ 1, 2, 86 Stat. 47; Oct. 21, 1976, Pub.L. 94–577, § 1, 90 Stat. 2729; Oct. 28, 1977, Pub.L. 95–144, § 2, 91 Stat. 1220; Oct. 10, 1979, Pub.L. 96–82, § 2, 93 Stat. 643; Oct. 12, 1984, Pub.L. 98–473, Title II, § 208, 98 Stat. 1986; Nov. 8, 1984, Pub.L. 98–620, Title IV, § 402(29)(B), 98 Stat. 3359; Nov. 14, 1986, Pub.L. 99–651, Title II, § 201(a)(2), 100 Stat. 3647; Nov. 15, 1988, Pub.L. 100–659, § 4(c), 102 Stat. 3918; Nov. 18, 1988, Pub.L. 100–690, Title VII, § 7322, 102 Stat. 4467; Nov. 19, 1988, Pub.L. 100–702, Title IV, § 404(b)(1), Title X, § 1014, 102 Stat. 4651, 4669; Dec. 1, 1990, Pub.L. 101–650, Title III, §§ 308(a), 321, 104 Stat. 5112, 5117; Oct. 19, 1996, Pub.L. 104–317, Title II, §§ 201, 202(b), 207, 110 Stat. 3848, 3849, 3851; Nov. 13, 2000, Pub.L. 106–518, Title II, §§ 202, 203(b), 114 Stat. 2412, 2414; Nov. 2, 2002, Pub.L. 107–273, Div. B, Title III, § 3002(b), 116 Stat. 1805; Sept. 9, 2005, Pub.L. 109–63, § 2(d), 119 Stat. 1995; May 7, 2009, Pub.L. 111–16, § 6(1), 123 Stat. 1608.)

§ 637. Training

The Federal Judicial Center shall conduct periodic training programs and seminars for both full-time and part-time United States magistrate judges, including an introductory training program for new magistrate judges, to be held within one year after initial appointment.

(June 25, 1948, c. 646, 62 Stat. 917; Oct. 17, 1968, Pub.L. 90–578, Title I, § 101, 82 Stat. 1114; Dec. 1, 1990, Pub.L. 101–650, Title III, § 321, 104 Stat. 5117.)

§ 638.   Dockets and forms; United States Code; seals

(a) The Director shall furnish to United States magistrate judges adequate docket books and forms prescribed by the Director. The Director shall also furnish to each such officer a copy of the current edition of the United States Code.

(b) All property furnished to any such officer shall remain the property of the United States and, upon the termination of his term of office, shall be transmitted to his successor in office or otherwise disposed of as the Director orders.

(c) The Director shall furnish to each United States magistrate judge appointed under this chapter an official impression seal in a form prescribed by the conference. Each such officer shall affix his seal to every jurat or certificate of his official acts without fee.

(June 25, 1948, c. 646, 62 Stat. 917; Oct. 17, 1968, Pub.L. 90–578, Title I, § 101, 82 Stat. 1114; Dec. 1, 1990, Pub.L. 101–650, Title III, § 321, 104 Stat. 5117.)

§ 639.   Definitions

As used in this chapter—

(1) "Conference" shall mean the Judicial Conference of the United States;

(2) "Council" shall mean the Judicial Council of the Circuit;

(3) "Director" shall mean the Director of the Administrative Office of the United States Courts;

(4) "Full-time magistrate judge" shall mean a full-time United States magistrate judge;

(5) "Part-time magistrate judge" shall mean a part-time United States magistrate judge; and

(6) "United States magistrate judge" and "magistrate judge" shall mean both full-time and part-time United States magistrate judges.

(June 25, 1948, c. 646, 62 Stat. 917; Oct. 17, 1968, Pub.L. 90–578, Title I, § 101, 82 Stat. 1114; Dec. 1, 1990, Pub.L. 101–650, Title III, § 321, 104 Stat. 5117.)

CHAPTER 44—ALTERNATIVE DISPUTE RESOLUTION

Sec.
651.	Authorization of alternative dispute resolution.
652.	Jurisdiction.
653.	Neutrals.
654.	Arbitration.
655.	Arbitrators.
656.	Subpoenas.
657.	Arbitration award and judgment.
658.	Compensation of arbitrators and neutrals.

§ 651.   Authorization of alternative dispute resolution

(a) **Definition.**—For purposes of this chapter, an alternative dispute resolution process includes any process or procedure, other than an adjudication by a presiding judge, in which a neutral third party participates to assist in the resolution of issues in controversy, through processes such as early neutral evaluation, mediation, minitrial, and arbitration as provided in sections 654 through 658.

(b) **Authority.**—Each United States district court shall authorize, by local rule adopted under section 2071(a), the use of alternative dispute resolution processes in all civil actions, including adversary proceedings in bankruptcy, in accordance with this chapter, except that the use of arbitration may be authorized only as provided in section 654. Each United States district court shall devise and implement its own alternative dispute resolution program, by local rule adopted under section 2071(a), to encourage and promote the use of alternative dispute resolution in its district.

(c) Existing alternative dispute resolution programs.—In those courts where an alternative dispute resolution program is in place on the date of the enactment of the Alternative Dispute Resolution Act of 1998, the court shall examine the effectiveness of that program and adopt such improvements to the program as are consistent with the provisions and purposes of this chapter [28 U.S.C.A. § 651 et seq.].

(d) Administration of alternative dispute resolution programs.—Each United States district court shall designate an employee, or a judicial officer, who is knowledgeable in alternative dispute resolution practices and processes to implement, administer, oversee, and evaluate the court's alternative dispute resolution program. Such person may also be responsible for recruiting, screening, and training attorneys to serve as neutrals and arbitrators in the court's alternative dispute resolution program.

(e) Title 9 not affected.—This chapter shall not affect title 9, United States Code.

(f) Program support.—The Federal Judicial Center and the Administrative Office of the United States Courts are authorized to assist the district courts in the establishment and improvement of alternative dispute resolution programs by identifying particular practices employed in successful programs and providing additional assistance as needed and appropriate.

(Added Pub.L. 100–702, Title IX, § 901(a), Nov. 19, 1988, 102 Stat. 4659; amended Pub.L. 105–315, § 3, Oct. 30, 1998, 112 Stat. 2993.)

§ 652. Jurisdiction

(a) Consideration of alternative dispute resolution in appropriate cases.— Notwithstanding any provision of law to the contrary and except as provided in subsections (b) and (c), each district court shall, by local rule adopted under section 2071(a), require that litigants in all civil cases consider the use of an alternative dispute resolution process at an appropriate stage in the litigation. Each district court shall provide litigants in all civil cases with at least one alternative dispute resolution process, including, but not limited to, mediation, early neutral evaluation, minitrial, and arbitration as authorized in sections 654 through 658. Any district court that elects to require the use of alternative dispute resolution in certain cases may do so only with respect to mediation, early neutral evaluation, and, if the parties consent, arbitration.

(b) Actions exempted from consideration of alternative dispute resolution.—Each district court may exempt from the requirements of this section specific cases or categories of cases in which use of alternative dispute resolution would not be appropriate. In defining these exemptions, each district court shall consult with members of the bar, including the United States Attorney for that district.

(c) Authority of the Attorney General.—Nothing in this section shall alter or conflict with the authority of the Attorney General to conduct litigation on behalf of the United States, with the authority of any Federal agency authorized to conduct litigation in the United States courts, or with any delegation of litigation authority by the Attorney General.

(d) Confidentiality provisions.—Until such time as rules are adopted under chapter 131 of this title [28 U.S.C.A. § 2071 et seq.] providing for the confidentiality of alternative dispute resolution processes under this chapter [28 U.S.C.A. § 651 et seq.], each district court shall, by local rule adopted under section 2071(a), provide for the confidentiality of the alternative dispute resolution processes and to prohibit disclosure of confidential dispute resolution communications.

(Added Pub.L. 100–702, Title IX, § 901(a), Nov. 19, 1988, 102 Stat. 4659; amended Pub.L. 105–315, § 4, Oct. 30, 1998, 112 Stat. 2994.)

§ 653. Neutrals

(a) Panel of neutrals.—Each district court that authorizes the use of alternative dispute resolution processes shall adopt appropriate processes for making neutrals available for use by the parties for each category of process offered. Each district court shall promulgate its own procedures and criteria for the selection of neutrals on its panels.

(b) Qualifications and training.—Each person serving as a neutral in an alternative dispute resolution process should be qualified and trained to serve as a neutral in the appropriate alternative dispute resolution process. For this purpose, the district court may use, among others, magistrate judges who have been trained to serve as neutrals in alternative dispute resolution processes, professional neutrals from the private sector, and persons who have been trained to serve as neutrals in alternative dispute resolution processes. Until such time as rules are adopted under chapter 131 of this title [28 U.S.C.A. § 2071 et seq.] relating to the disqualification of neutrals, each district court shall issue rules under section 2071(a) relating to the disqualification of neutrals (including, where appropriate, disqualification under section 455 of this title, other applicable law, and professional responsibility standards).

(Added Pub.L. 100–702, Title IX, § 901(a), Nov. 19, 1988, 102 Stat. 4660; amended Pub.L. 105–315, § 5, Oct. 30, 1998, 112 Stat. 2995.)

§ 654. Arbitration

(a) Referral of actions to arbitration.—Notwithstanding any provision of law to the contrary and except as provided in subsections (a), (b), and (c) of section 652 and subsection (d) of this section, a district court may allow the referral to arbitration of any civil action (including any adversary proceeding in bankruptcy) pending before it when the parties consent, except that referral to arbitration may not be made where—

    (1) the action is based on an alleged violation of a right secured by the Constitution of the United States;

    (2) jurisdiction is based in whole or in part on section 1343 of this title; or

    (3) the relief sought consists of money damages in an amount greater than $150,000.

(b) Safeguards in consent cases.—Until such time as rules are adopted under chapter 131 of this title relating to procedures described in this subsection, the district court shall, by local rule adopted under section 2071(a), establish procedures to ensure that any civil action in which arbitration by consent is allowed under subsection (a)—

    (1) consent to arbitration is freely and knowingly obtained; and

    (2) no party or attorney is prejudiced for refusing to participate in arbitration.

(c) Presumptions.—For purposes of subsection (a)(3), a district court may presume damages are not in excess of $150,000 unless counsel certifies that damages exceed such amount.

(d) Existing programs.—Nothing in this chapter is deemed to affect any program in which arbitration is conducted pursuant to section[1] title IX of the Judicial Improvements and Access to Justice Act (Public Law 100–702), as amended by section 1 of Public Law 105–53.

(Added Pub.L. 100–702, Title IX, § 901(a), Nov. 19, 1988, 102 Stat. 4660; amended Pub.L. 105–315, § 6, Oct. 30, 1998, 112 Stat. 2995.)

---

[1] So in original. The word "section" probably should not appear.

§ 655. Arbitrators

(a) Powers of arbitrators.—An arbitrator to whom an action is referred under section 654 shall have the power, within the judicial district of the district court which referred the action to arbitration—

    (1) to conduct arbitration hearings;

    (2) to administer oaths and affirmations; and

    (3) to make awards.

(b) Standards for certification.—Each district court that authorizes arbitration shall establish standards for the certification of arbitrators and shall certify arbitrators to perform services in accordance with such standards and this chapter. The standards shall include provisions requiring that any arbitrator—

    (1) shall take the oath or affirmation described in section 453; and

    (2) shall be subject to the disqualification rules under section 455.

(c) Immunity.—All individuals serving as arbitrators in an alternative dispute resolution program under this chapter are performing quasi-judicial functions and are entitled to the immunities and protections that the law accords to persons serving in such capacity.

(Added Pub.L. 100–702, Title IX, § 901(a), Nov. 19, 1988, 102 Stat. 4661; amended Pub.L. 105–315, § 7, Oct. 30, 1998, 112 Stat. 2996.)

§ 656. Subpoenas

Rule 45 of the Federal Rules of Civil Procedure (relating to subpoenas) applies to subpoenas for the attendance of witnesses and the production of documentary evidence at an arbitration hearing under this chapter.

(Added Pub.L. 100–702, Title IX, § 901(a), Nov. 19, 1988, 102 Stat. 4662; amended Pub.L. 105–315, § 8, Oct. 30, 1998, 112 Stat. 2996.)

§ 657. Arbitration award and judgment

(a) Filing and effect of arbitration award.—An arbitration award made by an arbitrator under this chapter, along with proof of service of such award on the other party by the prevailing party or by the plaintiff, shall be filed promptly after the arbitration hearing is concluded with the clerk of the district court that referred the case to arbitration. Such award shall be entered as the judgment of the court after the time has expired for requesting a trial de novo. The judgment so entered shall be subject to the same provisions of law and shall have the same force and effect as a judgment of the court in a civil action, except that the judgment shall not be subject to review in any other court by appeal or otherwise.

(b) Sealing of arbitration award.—The district court shall provide, by local rule adopted under section 2071(a), that the contents of any arbitration award made under this chapter shall not be made known to any judge who might be assigned to the case until the district court has entered final judgment in the action or the action has otherwise terminated.

(c) Trial de novo of arbitration awards.—

    (1) Time for filing demand.—Within 30 days after the filing of an arbitration award with a district court under subsection (a), any party may file a written demand for a trial de novo in the district court.

    (2) Action restored to court docket.—Upon a demand for a trial de novo, the action shall be restored to the docket of the court and treated for all purposes as if it had not been referred to arbitration.

(3) **Exclusion of evidence of arbitration.**—The court shall not admit at the trial de novo any evidence that there has been an arbitration proceeding, the nature or amount of any award, or any other matter concerning the conduct of the arbitration proceeding, unless—

(A) the evidence would otherwise be admissible in the court under the Federal Rules of Evidence; or

(B) the parties have otherwise stipulated.

(Added Pub.L. 100–702, Title IX, § 901(a), Nov. 19, 1988, 102 Stat. 4662; amended Pub.L. 105–315, § 9, Oct. 30, 1998, 112 Stat. 2997.)

§ 658. Compensation of arbitrators and neutrals

(a) **Compensation.**—The district court shall, subject to regulations approved by the Judicial Conference of the United States, establish the amount of compensation, if any, that each arbitrator or neutral shall receive for services rendered in each case under this chapter.

(b) **Transportation allowances.**—Under regulations prescribed by the Director of the Administrative Office of the United States Courts, a district court may reimburse arbitrators and other neutrals for actual transportation expenses necessarily incurred in the performance of duties under this chapter.

(Added Pub.L. 100–702, Title IX, § 901(a), Nov. 19, 1988, 102 Stat. 4662; amended Pub.L. 105–315, § 10, Oct. 30, 1998, 112 Stat. 2997.)

PART IV—JURISDICTION AND VENUE

HISTORICAL AND STATUTORY NOTES

Codifications

The analysis of chapters comprising Part IV was amended by Pub.L. 95–598, Title II, § 241(b), Nov. 6, 1978, 92 Stat. 2671, effective June 28, 1984, pursuant to Pub.L. 95–598, Title IV, § 402(b), Nov. 6, 1978, 92 Stat. 2682, as amended by Pub.L. 98–249, § 1(a), Mar. 31, 1984, 98 Stat. 116; Pub.L. 98–271, § 1(a), Apr. 30, 1984, 98 Stat. 163; Pub.L. 98–299, § 1(a), May 25, 1984, 98 Stat. 214; Pub.L. 98–325, § 1(a), June 20, 1984, 98 Stat. 268, set out as an Effective Date note preceding section 101 of Title 11, Bankruptcy, by adding:

Section 402(b) of Pub.L. 95–598 was amended by section 113 of Pub.L. 98–353, Title I, July 10, 1984, 98 Stat. 343, by substituting "shall not be effective" for "shall take effect on June 28, 1984", thereby eliminating the amendment by section 241(b) of Pub.L. 95–598, effective June 27, 1984, pursuant to section 122(c) of Pub.L. 98–353, set out as an Effective and Applicability Provisions note under section 151 of this title.

Section 121(a) of Pub.L. 98–353 directed that section 402(b) of Pub.L. 95–598 be amended by substituting "the date of enactment of the Bankruptcy Amendments and Federal Judgeship Act of 1984 [i.e. July 10, 1984]" for "June 28, 1984". This amendment was not executed in view of the prior amendment to section 402(b) of Pub.L. 95–598 by section 113 of Pub.L. 98–353.

Change of Name

References to United States Claims Court deemed to refer to United States Court of Federal Claims and references to Claims Court deemed to refer to Court of Federal Claims, see section 902(b) of Pub.L. 102–572, set out as a note under section 171 of Title 28, Judiciary and Judicial Procedure.

CHAPTER 81—SUPREME COURT

HISTORICAL AND STATUTORY NOTES

Definitions of Courts and Judges

Section 32 of Act June 25, 1948, as amended by Act May 24, 1949, c. 139, § 127, 63 Stat. 107, provided:

"**(a)** All laws of the United States in force on September 1, 1948, in which reference is made to a 'circuit court of appeals'; 'senior circuit judge'; 'senior district judge'; 'presiding judge'; 'chief justice', except when reference to the Chief Justice of the United States is intended; or 'justice', except when used with respect to a justice of the Supreme Court of the United States in his capacity as such or as a circuit justice, are hereby amended by substituting 'court of appeals' for 'circuit court of appeals'; 'chief judge of the circuit' for 'senior circuit judge'; 'chief judge of the district court' for 'senior district judge'; 'chief judge' for 'presiding judge'; 'chief judge' for 'chief justice', except when reference to the Chief Justice of the United States is intended; and 'judge' for 'justice', except when the latter term is used with respect to a justice of the Supreme Court of the United States in his capacity as such or as a circuit justice.

"**(b)** All laws of the United States in force on September 1, 1948, in which reference is made to the Supreme Court of the District of Columbia or to the District Court of the United States for the District of

Columbia are amended by substituting 'United States District Court for the District of Columbia' for such designations.

"**(c)** All laws of the United States in force on September 1, 1948, in which reference is made to the 'Conference of Senior Circuit Judges', or to the 'Judicial Conference of Senior Circuit Judges' are amended by substituting 'Judicial Conference of the United States' for such designations.

"**(d)** This section shall not be construed to amend historical references to courts or judicial offices which have no present or future application to such courts or offices."

§ 1251.   Original jurisdiction

(a) The Supreme Court shall have original and exclusive jurisdiction of all controversies between two or more States.

(b) The Supreme Court shall have original but not exclusive jurisdiction of:

    (1) All actions or proceedings to which ambassadors, other public ministers, consuls, or vice consuls of foreign states are parties;

    (2) All controversies between the United States and a State;

    (3) All actions or proceedings by a State against the citizens of another State or against aliens.

(June 25, 1948, c. 646, 62 Stat. 927; Sept. 30, 1978, Pub.L. 95–393, § 8(b), 92 Stat. 810.)

HISTORICAL AND STATUTORY NOTES

Effective and Applicability Provisions

1978 Acts. Amendment by Pub.L. 95–393 effective at the end of the 90-day period beginning on Sept. 30, 1978, see section 9 of Pub.L. 95–393, set out as a note under section 254a of Title 22, Foreign Relations and Intercourse.

Statutes Governing Writs of Error to Apply to Appeals

Act Jan. 31, 1928, c. 14, § 2, 45 Stat. 54, amended Apr. 26, 1928, c. 440, 45 Stat. 466; June 25, 1948, c. 646, § 23, 62 Stat. 990, provided that: "All Acts of Congress referring to writs of error shall be construed as amended to the extent necessary to substitute appeal for writ of error." See, also, notes preceding section 1 of this title.

[§ 1252.   Repealed. Pub.L. 100–352, § 1, June 27, 1988, 102 Stat. 662]

HISTORICAL AND STATUTORY NOTES

Section, Acts June 25, 1948, c. 646, 62 Stat. 928; Oct. 31, 1951, c. 655, § 47, 65 Stat. 726; July 7, 1958, Pub.L. 85–508, § 12(e), (f), 72 Stat. 348; Mar. 18, 1959, Pub.L. 86–3, § 14(a), 73 Stat. 10, provided for direct appeals to Supreme Court from decisions invalidating Acts of Congress.

Effective Date of Repeal

Repeal of section effective ninety days after June 27, 1988, except that such repeal shall not apply to cases pending in the Supreme Court on such effective date or affect the right to review or the manner of reviewing the judgment or decree of a court which was entered before such effective date, see section 7 of Pub.L. 100–352, set out as a note under section 1254 of this title.

§ 1253.   Direct appeals from decisions of three-judge courts

Except as otherwise provided by law, any party may appeal to the Supreme Court from an order granting or denying, after notice and hearing, an interlocutory or permanent injunction in any civil action, suit or proceeding required by any Act of Congress to be heard and determined by a district court of three judges.

(June 25, 1948, c. 646, 62 Stat. 928.)

§ 1254.   Courts of appeals; certiorari; certified questions

Cases in the courts of appeals may be reviewed by the Supreme Court by the following methods:

     (1)   By writ of certiorari granted upon the petition of any party to any civil or criminal case, before or after rendition of judgment or decree;

     (2)   By certification at any time by a court of appeals of any question of law in any civil or criminal case as to which instructions are desired, and upon such certification the Supreme Court may give binding instructions or require the entire record to be sent up for decision of the entire matter in controversy.

(June 25, 1948, c. 646, 62 Stat. 928; June 27, 1988, Pub.L. 100–352, § 2(a), (b), 102 Stat. 662.)

[§§ 1255, 1256.   Repealed. Pub.L. 97–164, Title I, § 123, Apr. 2, 1982, 96 Stat. 36]

HISTORICAL AND STATUTORY NOTES

Section 1255, Act June 25, 1948, c. 646, 62 Stat. 928, authorized the Supreme Court to review cases in the Court of Claims by writ of certiorari and by certification of questions of law.

Section 1256, Act June 25, 1948, c. 646, 62 Stat. 928, authorized the Supreme Court to review cases in the Court of Customs and Patent Appeals by writ of certiorari.

Effective Date of Repeal

Repeal effective Oct. 1, 1982, see section 402 of Pub.L. 97–164, set out as Effective and Applicability Provisions of 1982 Amendments note under section 171 of this title.

§ 1257.   State courts; certiorari

     (a)   Final judgments or decrees rendered by the highest court of a State in which a decision could be had, may be reviewed by the Supreme Court by writ of certiorari where the validity of a treaty or statute of the United States is drawn in question or where the validity of a statute of any State is drawn in question on the ground of its being repugnant to the Constitution, treaties, or laws of the United States, or where any title, right, privilege, or immunity is specially set up or claimed under the Constitution or the treaties or statutes of, or any commission held or authority exercised under, the United States.

     (b)   For the purposes of this section, the term "highest court of a State" includes the District of Columbia Court of Appeals.

(June 25, 1948, c. 646, 62 Stat. 929; July 29, 1970, Pub.L. 91–358, Title I, § 172(a)(1), 84 Stat. 590; June 27, 1988, Pub.L. 100–352, § 3, 102 Stat. 662.)

§ 1258.   Supreme Court of Puerto Rico; certiorari

Final judgments or decrees rendered by the Supreme Court of the Commonwealth of Puerto Rico may be reviewed by the Supreme Court by writ of certiorari where the validity of a treaty or statute of the United States is drawn in question or where the validity of a statute of the Commonwealth of Puerto Rico is drawn in question on the ground of its being repugnant to the Constitution, treaties, or laws of the United States, or where any title, right, privilege, or immunity is specially set up or claimed under the Constitution or the treaties or statutes of, or any commission held or authority exercised under, the United States.

(Added Pub.L. 87–189, § 1, Aug. 30, 1961, 75 Stat. 417; amended, Pub.L. 100–352, § 4, June 27, 1988, 102 Stat. 662.)

§ 1259.   Court of Appeals for the Armed Forces; certiorari

Decisions of the United States Court of Appeals for the Armed Forces may be reviewed by the Supreme Court by writ of certiorari in the following cases:

(1) Cases reviewed by the Court of Appeals for the Armed Forces under section 867(a)(1) of title 10.

(2) Cases certified to the Court of Appeals for the Armed Forces by the Judge Advocate General under section 867(a)(2) of title 10.

(3) Cases in which the Court of Appeals for the Armed Forces granted a petition for review under section 867(a)(3) of title 10.

(4) Cases, other than those described in paragraphs (1), (2), and (3) of this subsection, in which the Court of Appeals for the Armed Forces granted relief.

(Added Pub.L. 98–209, § 10(a)(1), Dec. 6, 1983, 97 Stat. 1405; amended Pub.L. 101–189, Div. A, Title XIII, § 1304(b)(3), Nov. 29, 1989, 103 Stat. 1577; Pub.L. 103–337, Div. A, Title IX, § 924(d)(1)(C), (2)(A), Oct. 5, 1994, 108 Stat. 2832.)

HISTORICAL AND STATUTORY NOTES

Effective and Applicability Provisions

1983 Acts. Section effective on the first day of the eighth calendar month beginning after Dec. 6, 1983, see section 12(a)(1) of Pub.L 98–209, set out as a note under section 801 of Title 10, Armed Forces.

§ 1260.   Supreme Court of the Virgin Islands; certiorari

Final judgments or decrees rendered by the Supreme Court of the Virgin Islands may be reviewed by the Supreme Court by writ of certiorari where the validity of a treaty or statute of the United States is drawn in question or where the validity of a statute of the Virgin Islands is drawn in question on the ground of its being repugnant to the Constitution, treaties, or laws of the United States, or where any title, right, privilege, or immunity is specially set up or claimed under the Constitution or the treaties or statutes of, or any commission held or authority exercised under, the United States.

(Added Pub.L. 112–226, § 2(a), Dec. 28, 2012, 126 Stat. 1606.)

CHAPTER 83—COURTS OF APPEALS

§ 1291.   Final decisions of district courts

The courts of appeals (other than the United States Court of Appeals for the Federal Circuit) shall have jurisdiction of appeals from all final decisions of the district courts of the United States, the United States District Court for the District of the Canal Zone, the District Court of Guam, and the District Court of the Virgin Islands, except where a direct review may be had in the Supreme Court. The jurisdiction of the United States Court of Appeals for the Federal Circuit shall be limited to the jurisdiction described in sections 1292(c) and (d) and 1295 of this title.

(June 25, 1948, c. 646, 62 Stat. 929; Oct. 31, 1951, c. 655, § 48, 65 Stat. 726; July 7, 1958, Pub.L. 85–508, § 12(e), 72 Stat. 348; Apr. 2, 1982, Pub.L. 97–164, Title I, § 124, 96 Stat. 36.)

§ 1292.   Interlocutory decisions

(a) Except as provided in subsections (c) and (d) of this section, the courts of appeals shall have jurisdiction of appeals from:

(1)   Interlocutory orders of the district courts of the United States, the United States District Court for the District of the Canal Zone, the District Court of Guam, and the District Court of the Virgin Islands, or of the judges thereof, granting, continuing, modifying, refusing or dissolving injunctions, or refusing to dissolve or modify injunctions, except where a direct review may be had in the Supreme Court;

(2)   Interlocutory orders appointing receivers, or refusing orders to wind up receiverships or to take steps to accomplish the purposes thereof, such as directing sales or other disposals of property;

(3)   Interlocutory decrees of such district courts or the judges thereof determining the rights and liabilities of the parties to admiralty cases in which appeals from final decrees are allowed.

(b)   When a district judge, in making in a civil action an order not otherwise appealable under this section, shall be of the opinion that such order involves a controlling question of law as to which there is substantial ground for difference of opinion and that an immediate appeal from the order may materially advance the ultimate termination of the litigation, he shall so state in writing in such order. The Court of Appeals which would have jurisdiction of an appeal of such action may thereupon, in its discretion, permit an appeal to be taken from such order, if application is made to it within ten days after the entry of the order: *Provided, however,* That application for an appeal hereunder shall not stay proceedings in the district court unless the district judge or the Court of Appeals or a judge thereof shall so order.

(c)   The United States Court of Appeals for the Federal Circuit shall have exclusive jurisdiction—

(1)   of an appeal from an interlocutory order or decree described in subsection (a) or (b) of this section in any case over which the court would have jurisdiction of an appeal under section 1295 of this title; and

(2)   of an appeal from a judgment in a civil action for patent infringement which would otherwise be appealable to the United States Court of Appeals for the Federal Circuit and is final except for an accounting.

(d)(1)   When the chief judge of the Court of International Trade issues an order under the provisions of section 256(b) of this title, or when any judge of the Court of International Trade, in issuing any other interlocutory order, includes in the order a statement that a controlling question of law is involved with respect to which there is a substantial ground for difference of opinion and that an immediate appeal from that order may materially advance the ultimate termination of the litigation, the United States Court of Appeals for the Federal Circuit may, in its discretion, permit an appeal to be taken from such order, if application is made to that Court within ten days after the entry of such order.

(2)   When the chief judge of the United States Court of Federal Claims issues an order under section 798(b) of this title, or when any judge of the United States Court of Federal Claims, in issuing an interlocutory order, includes in the order a statement that a controlling question of law is involved with respect to which there is a substantial ground for difference of opinion and that an immediate appeal from that order may materially advance the ultimate termination of the litigation, the United States Court of Appeals for the Federal Circuit may, in its discretion, permit an appeal to be taken from such order, if application is made to that Court within ten days after the entry of such order.

(3)   Neither the application for nor the granting of an appeal under this subsection shall stay proceedings in the Court of International Trade or in the Court of Federal Claims, as the case may be, unless a stay is ordered by a judge of the Court of International Trade or of the Court of Federal Claims or by the United States Court of Appeals for the Federal Circuit or a judge of that court.

(4)(A) The United States Court of Appeals for the Federal Circuit shall have exclusive jurisdiction of an appeal from an interlocutory order of a district court of the United States, the District Court of Guam, the District Court of the Virgin Islands, or the District Court for the Northern Mariana Islands, granting or denying, in whole or in part, a motion to transfer an action to the United States Court of Federal Claims under section 1631 of this title.

(B) When a motion to transfer an action to the Court of Federal Claims is filed in a district court, no further proceedings shall be taken in the district court until 60 days after the court has ruled upon the motion. If an appeal is taken from the district court's grant or denial of the motion, proceedings shall be further stayed until the appeal has been decided by the Court of Appeals for the Federal Circuit. The stay of proceedings in the district court shall not bar the granting of preliminary or injunctive relief, where appropriate and where expedition is reasonably necessary. However, during the period in which proceedings are stayed as provided in this subparagraph, no transfer to the Court of Federal Claims pursuant to the motion shall be carried out.

(e) The Supreme Court may prescribe rules, in accordance with section 2072 of this title, to provide for an appeal of an interlocutory decision to the courts of appeals that is not otherwise provided for under subsection (a), (b), (c), or (d).

(June 25, 1948, c. 646, 62 Stat. 929; Oct. 31, 1951, c. 655, § 49, 65 Stat. 726; July 7, 1958, Pub.L. 85–508, § 12(e), 72 Stat. 348; Sept. 2, 1958, Pub.L. 85–919, 72 Stat. 1770; Apr. 2, 1982, Pub.L. 97–164, Title I, § 125, 96 Stat. 36; Nov. 8, 1984, Pub.L. 98–620, Title IV, § 412, 98 Stat. 3362; Nov. 19, 1988, Pub.L. 100–702, Title V, § 501, 102 Stat. 4652; Oct. 29, 1992, Pub.L. 102–572, Title I, § 101, Title IX, §§ 902(b), 906(c), 106 Stat. 4506, 4516, 4518.)

[§ 1293.   Repealed. Pub.L. 87–189, § 3, Aug. 30, 1961, 75 Stat. 417]

HISTORICAL AND STATUTORY NOTES

Section, Acts June 25, 1948, c. 646, 62 Stat. 929; Mar. 18, 1959, Pub.L. 86–3, § 14(b), 73 Stat. 10, provided for appeal from supreme court of Puerto Rico to court of appeals for first circuit. See section 1258 of this title.

§ 1294.   Circuits in which decisions reviewable

Except as provided in sections 1292(c), 1292(d), and 1295 of this title, appeals from reviewable decisions of the district and territorial courts shall be taken to the courts of appeals as follows:

(1) From a district court of the United States to the court of appeals for the circuit embracing the district;

(2) From the United States District Court for the District of the Canal Zone, to the Court of Appeals for the Fifth Circuit;

(3) From the District Court of the Virgin Islands, to the Court of Appeals for the Third Circuit;

(4) From the District Court of Guam, to the Court of Appeals for the Ninth Circuit.

(June 25, 1948, c. 646, 62 Stat. 930; Oct. 31, 1951, c. 655, § 50(a), 65 Stat. 727; July 7, 1958, Pub.L. 85–508, § 12(g), 72 Stat. 348; Mar. 18, 1959, Pub.L. 86–3, § 14(c), 73 Stat. 10; Aug. 30, 1961, Pub.L. 87–189, § 5, 75 Stat. 417; Nov. 6, 1978, Pub.L. 95–598, Title II, § 237, 92 Stat. 2667; Apr. 2, 1982, Pub.L. 97–164, Title I, § 126, 96 Stat. 37.)

§ 1295.   Jurisdiction of the United States Court of Appeals for the Federal Circuit

(a) The United States Court of Appeals for the Federal Circuit shall have exclusive jurisdiction—

(1) of an appeal from a final decision of a district court of the United States, the District Court of Guam, the District Court of the Virgin Islands, or the District Court of the Northern

Mariana Islands, in any civil action arising under, or in any civil action in which a party has asserted a compulsory counterclaim arising under, any Act of Congress relating to patents or plant variety protection;

(2) of an appeal from a final decision of a district court of the United States, the United States District Court for the District of the Canal Zone, the District Court of Guam, the District Court of the Virgin Islands, or the District Court for the Northern Mariana Islands, if the jurisdiction of that court was based, in whole or in part, on section 1346 of this title, except that jurisdiction of an appeal in a case brought in a district court under section 1346(a)(1), 1346(b), 1346(e), or 1346(f) of this title or under section 1346(a)(2) when the claim is founded upon an Act of Congress or a regulation of an executive department providing for internal revenue shall be governed by sections 1291, 1292, and 1294 of this title;

(3) of an appeal from a final decision of the United States Court of Federal Claims;

(4) of an appeal from a decision of—

(A) the Patent Trial and Appeal Board of the United States Patent and Trademark Office with respect to a patent application, derivation proceeding, reexamination, post-grant review, or inter partes review under title 35, at the instance of a party who exercised that party's right to participate in the applicable proceeding before or appeal to the Board, except that an applicant or a party to a derivation proceeding may also have remedy by civil action pursuant to section 145 or 146 of title 35; an appeal under this subparagraph of a decision of the Board with respect to an application or derivation proceeding shall waive the right of such applicant or party to proceed under section 145 or 146 of title 35;

(B) the Under Secretary of Commerce for Intellectual Property and Director of the United States Patent and Trademark Office or the Trademark Trial and Appeal Board with respect to applications for registration of marks and other proceedings as provided in section 21 of the Trademark Act of 1946 (15 U.S.C. 1071); or

(C) a district court to which a case was directed pursuant to section 145, 146, or 154(b) of title 35;

(5) of an appeal from a final decision of the United States Court of International Trade;

(6) to review the final determinations of the United States International Trade Commission relating to unfair practices in import trade, made under section 337 of the Tariff Act of 1930 (19 U.S.C. 1337);

(7) to review, by appeal on questions of law only, findings of the Secretary of Commerce under U.S. note 6 to subchapter X of chapter 98 of the Harmonized Tariff Schedule of the United States (relating to importation of instruments or apparatus);

(8) of an appeal under section 71 of the Plant Variety Protection Act (7 U.S.C. 2461);

(9) of an appeal from a final order or final decision of the Merit Systems Protection Board, pursuant to sections 7703(b)(1) and 7703(d) of title 5;

(10) of an appeal from a final decision of an agency board of contract appeals pursuant to section 7107(a)(1) of title 41;

(11) of an appeal under section 211 of the Economic Stabilization Act of 1970;

(12) of an appeal under section 5 of the Emergency Petroleum Allocation Act of 1973;

(13) of an appeal under section 506(c) of the Natural Gas Policy Act of 1978; and

(14) of an appeal under section 523 of the Energy Policy and Conservation Act.

(b) The head of any executive department or agency may, with the approval of the Attorney General, refer to the Court of Appeals for the Federal Circuit for judicial review any final decision rendered by a board of contract appeals pursuant to the terms of any contract with the United States awarded by that department or agency which the head of such department or agency has concluded is not entitled to finality pursuant to the review standards specified in section 7107(b) of title 41. The head of each executive department or agency shall make any referral under this section within one hundred and twenty days after the receipt of a copy of the final appeal decision.

(c)   The Court of Appeals for the Federal Circuit shall review the matter referred in accordance with the standards specified in section 7107(b) of title 41. The court shall proceed with judicial review on the administrative record made before the board of contract appeals on matters so referred as in other cases pending in such court, shall determine the issue of finality of the appeal decision, and shall, if appropriate, render judgment thereon, or remand the matter to any administrative or executive body or official with such direction as it may deem proper and just.

(Added Pub.L. 97–164, Title I, § 127(a), Apr. 2, 1982, 96 Stat. 37; amended Pub.L. 98–622, Title II, § 205(a), Nov. 8, 1984, 98 Stat. 3388; Pub.L. 100–418, Title I, § 1214(a)(3), Aug. 23, 1988, 102 Stat. 1156; Pub.L. 100–702, Title X, § 1020(a)(3), Nov. 19, 1988, 102 Stat. 4671; Pub.L. 102–572, Title I, § 102(c), Title IX, § 902(b)(1), Oct. 29, 1992, 106 Stat. 4507, 4516; Pub.L. 106–113, Div. B, § 1000(a)(9) [Title IV, §§ 4402(b)(2), 4732(b)(14)], Nov. 29, 1999, 113 Stat. 1536, 1501A–560, 1501A–584; Pub.L. 111–350, § 5(g)(5), Jan. 4, 2011, 124 Stat. 3848; Pub.L. 112–29, §§ 7(c)(2), 19(b), Sept. 16, 2011, 125 Stat. 314, 332.)

§ 1296.   Review of certain agency actions

(a)   **Jurisdiction.**—Subject to the provisions of chapter 179, the United States Court of Appeals for the Federal Circuit shall have jurisdiction over a petition for review of a final decision under chapter 5 of title 3 of—

(1)   an appropriate agency (as determined under section 454 of title 3);

(2)   the Federal Labor Relations Authority made under part D of subchapter II of chapter 5 of title 3, notwithstanding section 7123 of title 5; or

(3)   the Secretary of Labor or the Occupational Safety and Health Review Commission, made under part C of subchapter II of chapter 5 of title 3.

(b)   **Filing of petition.**—Any petition for review under this section must be filed within 30 days after the date the petitioner receives notice of the final decision.

(Added Pub.L. 104–331, § 3(a)(1), Oct. 26, 1996, 110 Stat. 4069.)

CHAPTER 85—DISTRICT COURTS; JURISDICTION

§ 1330.   Actions against foreign states

(a) The district courts shall have original jurisdiction without regard to amount in controversy of any nonjury civil action against a foreign state as defined in section 1603(a) of this title as to any claim for relief in personam with respect to which the foreign state is not entitled to immunity either under sections 1605–1607 of this title or under any applicable international agreement.

(b) Personal jurisdiction over a foreign state shall exist as to every claim for relief over which the district courts have jurisdiction under subsection (a) where service has been made under section 1608 of this title.

(c) For purposes of subsection (b), an appearance by a foreign state does not confer personal jurisdiction with respect to any claim for relief not arising out of any transaction or occurrence enumerated in sections 1605–1607 of this title.

(Added Pub.L. 94–583, § 2(a), Oct. 21, 1976, 90 Stat. 2891.)

§ 1331.   Federal question

The district courts shall have original jurisdiction of all civil actions arising under the Constitution, laws, or treaties of the United States.

(June 25, 1948, c. 646, 62 Stat. 930; July 25, 1958, Pub.L. 85–554, § 1, 72 Stat. 415; Oct. 21, 1976, Pub.L. 94–574, § 2, 90 Stat. 2721; Dec. 1, 1980, Pub.L. 96–486, § 2(a), 94 Stat. 2369.)

§ 1332.   Diversity of citizenship; amount in controversy; costs*

(a)   The district courts shall have original jurisdiction of all civil actions where the matter in controversy exceeds the sum or value of $75,000, exclusive of interest and costs, and is between—

(1)   citizens of different States;

(2)   citizens of a State and citizens or subjects of a foreign state, except that the district courts shall not have original jurisdiction under this subsection of an action between citizens of a State and citizens or subjects of a foreign state who are lawfully admitted for permanent residence in the United States and are domiciled in the same State;

(3)   citizens of different States and in which citizens or subjects of a foreign state are additional parties; and

(4)   a foreign state, defined in section 1603(a) of this title, as plaintiff and citizens of a State or of different States.

(b)   Except when express provision therefor is otherwise made in a statute of the United States, where the plaintiff who files the case originally in the Federal courts is finally adjudged to be entitled to recover less than the sum or value of $75,000, computed without regard to any setoff or counterclaim to which the defendant may be adjudged to be entitled, and exclusive of interest and costs, the district court may deny costs to the plaintiff and, in addition, may impose costs on the plaintiff.

(c)   For the purposes of this section and section 1441 of this title—

(1)   a corporation shall be deemed to be a citizen of every State and foreign state by which it has been incorporated and of the State or foreign state where it has its principal place of business, except that in any direct action against the insurer of a policy or contract of liability insurance, whether incorporated or unincorporated, to which action the insured is not joined as a party-defendant, such insurer shall be deemed a citizen of—

(A)   every State and foreign state of which the insured is a citizen;

(B)   every State and foreign state by which the insurer has been incorporated; and

(C)   the State or foreign state where the insurer has its principal place of business; and

(2)   the legal representative of the estate of a decedent shall be deemed to be a citizen only of the same State as the decedent, and the legal representative of an infant or incompetent shall be deemed to be a citizen only of the same State as the infant or incompetent.

(d)(1)   In this subsection—

(A)   the term "class" means all of the class members in a class action;

(B)   the term "class action" means any civil action filed under rule 23 of the Federal Rules of Civil Procedure or similar State statute or rule of judicial procedure authorizing an action to be brought by 1 or more representative persons as a class action;

(C)   the term "class certification order" means an order issued by a court approving the treatment of some or all aspects of a civil action as a class action; and

(D)   the term "class members" means the persons (named or unnamed) who fall within the definition of the proposed or certified class in a class action.

(2)   The district courts shall have original jurisdiction of any civil action in which the matter in controversy exceeds the sum or value of $5,000,000, exclusive of interest and costs, and is a class action in which—

---

*   [Proposed legislation introduced in the 116th Congress, 1st Session (S. 297—Federal Courts Access Act of 2019), would modify 28 U.S.C. § 1332 to increase the amount in controversy to $125,000 and to eliminate the complete diversity requirement. No assessment is offered here regarding the prospect that this proposal will be enacted into law. Ed.]

(A) any member of a class of plaintiffs is a citizen of a State different from any defendant;

(B) any member of a class of plaintiffs is a foreign state or a citizen or subject of a foreign state and any defendant is a citizen of a State; or

(C) any member of a class of plaintiffs is a citizen of a State and any defendant is a foreign state or a citizen or subject of a foreign state.

(3) A district court may, in the interests of justice and looking at the totality of the circumstances, decline to exercise jurisdiction under paragraph (2) over a class action in which greater than one-third but less than two-thirds of the members of all proposed plaintiff classes in the aggregate and the primary defendants are citizens of the State in which the action was originally filed based on consideration of—

(A) whether the claims asserted involve matters of national or interstate interest;

(B) whether the claims asserted will be governed by laws of the State in which the action was originally filed or by the laws of other States;

(C) whether the class action has been pleaded in a manner that seeks to avoid Federal jurisdiction;

(D) whether the action was brought in a forum with a distinct nexus with the class members, the alleged harm, or the defendants;

(E) whether the number of citizens of the State in which the action was originally filed in all proposed plaintiff classes in the aggregate is substantially larger than the number of citizens from any other State, and the citizenship of the other members of the proposed class is dispersed among a substantial number of States; and

(F) whether, during the 3-year period preceding the filing of that class action, 1 or more other class actions asserting the same or similar claims on behalf of the same or other persons have been filed.

(4) A district court shall decline to exercise jurisdiction under paragraph (2)—

(A)(i) over a class action in which—

(I) greater than two-thirds of the members of all proposed plaintiff classes in the aggregate are citizens of the State in which the action was originally filed;

(II) at least 1 defendant is a defendant—

(aa) from whom significant relief is sought by members of the plaintiff class;

(bb) whose alleged conduct forms a significant basis for the claims asserted by the proposed plaintiff class; and

(cc) who is a citizen of the State in which the action was originally filed; and

(III) principal injuries resulting from the alleged conduct or any related conduct of each defendant were incurred in the State in which the action was originally filed; and

(ii) during the 3-year period preceding the filing of that class action, no other class action has been filed asserting the same or similar factual allegations against any of the defendants on behalf of the same or other persons; or

(B) [over a class action in which]* two-thirds or more of the members of all proposed plaintiff classes in the aggregate, and the primary defendants, are citizens of the State in which the action was originally filed.

(5) Paragraphs (2) through (4) shall not apply to any class action in which—

(A) the primary defendants are States, State officials, or other governmental entities against whom the district court may be foreclosed from ordering relief; or

(B) the number of members of all proposed plaintiff classes in the aggregate is less than 100.

(6) In any class action, the claims of the individual class members shall be aggregated to determine whether the matter in controversy exceeds the sum or value of $5,000,000, exclusive of interest and costs.

(7) Citizenship of the members of the proposed plaintiff classes shall be determined for purposes of paragraphs (2) through (6) as of the date of filing of the complaint or amended complaint, or, if the case stated by the initial pleading is not subject to Federal jurisdiction, as of the date of service by plaintiffs of an amended pleading, motion, or other paper, indicating the existence of Federal jurisdiction.

(8) This subsection shall apply to any class action before or after the entry of a class certification order by the court with respect to that action.

(9) Paragraph (2) shall not apply to any class action that solely involves a claim—

(A) concerning a covered security as defined under 16(f)(3)[1] of the Securities Act of 1933 (15 U.S.C. 78p(f)(3)[2]) and section 28(f)(5)(E) of the Securities Exchange Act of 1934 (15 U.S.C. 78bb(f)(5)(E));

(B) that relates to the internal affairs or governance of a corporation or other form of business enterprise and that arises under or by virtue of the laws of the State in which such corporation or business enterprise is incorporated or organized; or

(C) that relates to the rights, duties (including fiduciary duties), and obligations relating to or created by or pursuant to any security (as defined under section 2(a)(1) of the Securities Act of 1933 (15 U.S.C. 77b(a)(1)) and the regulations issued thereunder).

(10) For purposes of this subsection and section 1453, an unincorporated association shall be deemed to be a citizen of the State where it has its principal place of business and the State under whose laws it is organized.

(11)(A) For purposes of this subsection and section 1453, a mass action shall be deemed to be a class action removable under paragraphs (2) through (10) if it otherwise meets the provisions of those paragraphs.

(B)(i) As used in subparagraph (A), the term "mass action" means any civil action (except a civil action within the scope of section 1711(2)) in which monetary relief claims of 100 or more persons are proposed to be tried jointly on the ground that the plaintiffs' claims involve common questions of law or fact, except that jurisdiction shall exist only over those plaintiffs whose claims in a mass action satisfy the jurisdictional amount requirements under subsection (a).

---

* [Footnote to 28 U.S.C. § 1332(d)(4)(B): Due to what may have been a drafting error, the bracketed language inserted here appears to be missing from the enacted version of this provision. These words are added to clarify what appears to be the intended meaning; however, readers should not treat this bracketed language as part of the statute. Ed.]

[1] [Footnote to 28 U.S.C. § 1332(d)(9)(A):] So in original. Reference to "16(f)(3)" probably should be preceded by "section".

[2] [Footnote to 28 U.S.C. § 1332(d)(9)(A):] So in original. Probably should be "77p(f)(3)".

(ii) As used in subparagraph (A), the term "mass action" shall not include any civil action in which—

    (I) all of the claims in the action arise from an event or occurrence in the State in which the action was filed, and that allegedly resulted in injuries in that State or in States contiguous to that State;

    (II) the claims are joined upon motion of a defendant;

    (III) all of the claims in the action are asserted on behalf of the general public (and not on behalf of individual claimants or members of a purported class) pursuant to a State statute specifically authorizing such action; or

    (IV) the claims have been consolidated or coordinated solely for pretrial proceedings.

(C)(i) Any action(s) removed to Federal court pursuant to this subsection shall not thereafter be transferred to any other court pursuant to section 1407, or the rules promulgated thereunder, unless a majority of the plaintiffs in the action request transfer pursuant to section 1407.

    (ii) This subparagraph will not apply—

        (I) to cases certified pursuant to rule 23 of the Federal Rules of Civil Procedure; or

        (II) if plaintiffs propose that the action proceed as a class action pursuant to rule 23 of the Federal Rules of Civil Procedure.

(D) The limitations periods on any claims asserted in a mass action that is removed to Federal court pursuant to this subsection shall be deemed tolled during the period that the action is pending in Federal court.

(e) The word "States", as used in this section, includes the Territories, the District of Columbia, and the Commonwealth of Puerto Rico.

(June 25, 1948, c. 646, 62 Stat. 930; July 26, 1956, c. 740, 70 Stat. 658; July 25, 1958, Pub.L. 85–554, § 2, 72 Stat. 415; Aug. 14, 1964, Pub.L. 88–439, § 1, 78 Stat. 445; Oct. 21, 1976, Pub.L. 94–583, § 3, 90 Stat. 2891; Nov. 19, 1988, Pub.L. 100–702, Title II, §§ 201(a), 202(a), 203(a), 102 Stat. 4646; Oct. 19, 1996, Pub.L. 104–317, Title II, § 205(a), 110 Stat. 3850; Feb. 18, 2005, Pub.L. 109–2, § 4(a), 119 Stat. 9; Pub.L. 112–63, Title I, §§ 101, 102, Dec. 7, 2011, 125 Stat. 758.)

§ 1333.   Admiralty, maritime and prize cases

The district courts shall have original jurisdiction, exclusive of the courts of the States, of:

    (1) Any civil case of admiralty or maritime jurisdiction, saving to suitors in all cases all other remedies to which they are otherwise entitled.

    (2) Any prize brought into the United States and all proceedings for the condemnation of property taken as prize.

(June 25, 1948, c. 646, 62 Stat. 931; May 24, 1949, c. 139, § 79, 63 Stat. 101.)

§ 1334.   Bankruptcy cases and proceedings

(a) Except as provided in subsection (b) of this section, the district courts shall have original and exclusive jurisdiction of all cases under title 11.

(b) Except as provided in subsection (e)(2), and notwithstanding any Act of Congress that confers exclusive jurisdiction on a court or courts other than the district courts, the district courts shall have original but not exclusive jurisdiction of all civil proceedings arising under title 11, or arising in or related to cases under title 11.

(c)(1)　Except with respect to a case under chapter 15 of title 11, nothing in this section prevents a district court in the interest of justice, or in the interest of comity with State courts or respect for State law, from abstaining from hearing a particular proceeding arising under title 11 or arising in or related to a case under title 11.

(2)　Upon timely motion of a party in a proceeding based upon a State law claim or State law cause of action, related to a case under title 11 but not arising under title 11 or arising in a case under title 11, with respect to which an action could not have been commenced in a court of the United States absent jurisdiction under this section, the district court shall abstain from hearing such proceeding if an action is commenced, and can be timely adjudicated, in a State forum of appropriate jurisdiction.

(d)　Any decision to abstain or not to abstain made under subsection (c) (other than a decision not to abstain in a proceeding described in subsection (c)(2)) is not reviewable by appeal or otherwise by the court of appeals under section 158(d), 1291, or 1292 of this title or by the Supreme Court of the United States under section 1254 of this title. Subsection (c) and this subsection shall not be construed to limit the applicability of the stay provided for by section 362 of title 11, United States Code, as such section applies to an action affecting the property of the estate in bankruptcy.

(e)　The district court in which a case under title 11 is commenced or is pending shall have exclusive jurisdiction—

(1)　of all the property, wherever located, of the debtor as of the commencement of such case, and of property of the estate; and

(2)　over all claims or causes of action that involve construction of section 327 of title 11, United States Code, or rules relating to disclosure requirements under section 327.

(June 25, 1948, c. 646, 62 Stat. 931; Nov. 6, 1978, Pub.L. 95–598, Title II, § 238(a), 92 Stat. 2667; July 10, 1984, Pub.L. 98–353, Title I, § 101(a), 98 Stat. 333; Oct. 27, 1986, Pub.L. 99–554, Title I, § 144(e), 100 Stat. 3096; Dec. 1, 1990, Pub.L. 101–650, Title III, § 309(b), 104 Stat. 5113; Oct. 22, 1994, Pub.L. 103–394, Title I, § 104(b), 108 Stat. 4109; Apr. 20, 2005, Pub.L. 109–8, Title III, § 324(a), Title VIII, § 802(c)(2), Title XII, § 1219, 119 Stat. 98, 145, 195.)

§ 1335.　　Interpleader

(a)　The district courts shall have original jurisdiction of any civil action of interpleader or in the nature of interpleader filed by any person, firm, or corporation, association, or society having in his or its custody or possession money or property of the value of $500 or more, or having issued a note, bond, certificate, policy of insurance, or other instrument of value or amount of $500 or more, or providing for the delivery or payment or the loan of money or property of such amount or value, or being under any obligation written or unwritten to the amount of $500 or more, if

(1)　Two or more adverse claimants, of diverse citizenship as defined in subsection (a) or (d) of section 1332 of this title, are claiming or may claim to be entitled to such money or property, or to any one or more of the benefits arising by virtue of any note, bond, certificate, policy or other instrument, or arising by virtue of any such obligation; and if

(2)　the plaintiff has deposited such money or property or has paid the amount of or the loan or other value of such instrument or the amount due under such obligation into the registry of the court, there to abide the judgment of the court, or has given bond payable to the clerk of the court in such amount and with such surety as the court or judge may deem proper, conditioned upon the compliance by the plaintiff with the future order or judgment of the court with respect to the subject matter of the controversy.

(b)　Such an action may be entertained although the titles or claims of the conflicting claimants do not have a common origin, or are not identical, but are adverse to and independent of one another.

(June 25, 1948, c. 646, 62 Stat. 931; Feb. 18, 2005, Pub.L. 109–2, § 4(b)(1), 119 Stat. 12.)

§ 1336.   Surface Transportation Board's orders

(a) Except as otherwise provided by Act of Congress, the district courts shall have jurisdiction of any civil action to enforce, in whole or in part, any order of the Surface Transportation Board, and to enjoin or suspend, in whole or in part, any order of the Surface Transportation Board for the payment of money or the collection of fines, penalties, and forfeitures.

(b) When a district court or the United States Court of Federal Claims refers a question or issue to the Surface Transportation Board for determination, the court which referred the question or issue shall have exclusive jurisdiction of a civil action to enforce, enjoin, set aside, annul, or suspend, in whole or in part, any order of the Surface Transportation Board arising out of such referral.

(c) Any action brought under subsection (b) of this section shall be filed within 90 days from the date that the order of the Surface Transportation Board becomes final.

(June 25, 1948, c. 646, 62 Stat. 931; Aug. 30, 1964, Pub.L. 88–513, § 1, 78 Stat. 695; Jan. 2, 1975, Pub.L. 93–584, § 1, 88 Stat. 1917; Apr. 2, 1982, Pub.L. 97–164, Title I, § 128, 96 Stat. 39; Oct. 29, 1992, Pub.L. 102–572, Title IX, § 902(b)(1), 106 Stat. 4516; Dec. 29, 1995, Pub.L. 104–88, Title III, § 305(a)(1), (2), 109 Stat. 944.)

§ 1337.   Commerce and antitrust regulations; amount in controversy, costs

(a) The district courts shall have original jurisdiction of any civil action or proceeding arising under any Act of Congress regulating commerce or protecting trade and commerce against restraints and monopolies: *Provided, however,* That the district courts shall have original jurisdiction of an action brought under section 11706 or 14706 of title 49, only if the matter in controversy for each receipt or bill of lading exceeds $10,000, exclusive of interest and costs.

(b) Except when express provision therefor is otherwise made in a statute of the United States, where a plaintiff who files the case under section 11706 or 14706 of title 49, originally in the Federal courts is finally adjudged to be entitled to recover less than the sum or value of $10,000, computed without regard to any setoff or counterclaim to which the defendant may be adjudged to be entitled, and exclusive of any interest and costs, the district court may deny costs to the plaintiff and, in addition, may impose costs on the plaintiff.

(c) The district courts shall not have jurisdiction under this section of any matter within the exclusive jurisdiction of the Court of International Trade under chapter 95 of this title.

(June 25, 1948, c. 646, 62 Stat. 931; Oct. 20, 1978, Pub.L. 95–486, § 9(a), 92 Stat. 1633; Oct. 10, 1980, Pub.L. 96–417, Title V, § 505, 94 Stat. 1743; Jan. 12, 1983, Pub.L. 97–449, § 5(f), 96 Stat. 2442; Dec. 29, 1995, Pub.L. 104–88, Title III, § 305(a)(3), 109 Stat. 944.)

§ 1338.   Patents, plant variety protection, copyrights, mask works, designs, trademarks, and unfair competition

(a) The district courts shall have original jurisdiction of any civil action arising under any Act of Congress relating to patents, plant variety protection, copyrights and trademarks. No State court shall have jurisdiction over any claim for relief arising under any Act of Congress relating to patents, plant variety protection, or copyrights. For purposes of this subsection, the term "State" includes any State of the United States, the District of Columbia, the Commonwealth of Puerto Rico, the United States Virgin Islands, American Samoa, Guam, and the Northern Mariana Islands.

(b) The district courts shall have original jurisdiction of any civil action asserting a claim of unfair competition when joined with a substantial and related claim under the copyright, patent, plant variety protection or trademark laws.

(c) Subsections (a) and (b) apply to exclusive rights in mask works under chapter 9 of title 17, and to exclusive rights in designs under chapter 13 of title 17, to the same extent as such subsections apply to copyrights.

(June 25, 1948, c. 646, 62 Stat. 931; Dec. 24, 1970, Pub.L. 91–577, Title III, § 143(b), 84 Stat. 1559; Nov. 19, 1988, Pub.L. 100–702, Title X, § 1020(a)(4), 102 Stat. 4671; Oct. 28, 1998, Pub.L. 105–304, Title V, § 503(b)(1), (2)(A), 112 Stat. 2917; Nov. 29, 1999, Pub.L. 106–113, Div. B, § 1000(a)(9) [Title III, § 3009(1)], 113 Stat. 1536, 1501A–551; Pub.L. 112–29, § 19(a), Sept. 16, 2011, 125 Stat. 331.)

§ 1339.   Postal matters

The district courts shall have original jurisdiction of any civil action arising under any Act of Congress relating to the postal service.

(June 25, 1948, c. 646, 62 Stat. 932.)

§ 1340.   Internal revenue; customs duties

The district courts shall have original jurisdiction of any civil action arising under any Act of Congress providing for internal revenue, or revenue from imports or tonnage except matters within the jurisdiction of the Court of International Trade.

(June 25, 1948, c. 646, 62 Stat. 932; Oct. 10, 1980, Pub.L. 96–417, Title V, § 501(21), 94 Stat. 1742.)

§ 1341.   Taxes by States

The district courts shall not enjoin, suspend or restrain the assessment, levy or collection of any tax under State law where a plain, speedy and efficient remedy may be had in the courts of such State.

(June 25, 1948, c. 646, 62 Stat. 932.)

HISTORICAL AND STATUTORY NOTES

Short Title

1948 Acts. This section is commonly known as the Tax Injunction Act.

§ 1342.   Rate orders of State agencies

The district courts shall not enjoin, suspend or restrain the operation of, or compliance with, any order affecting rates chargeable by a public utility and made by a State administrative agency or a rate-making body of a State political subdivision, where:

(1)   Jurisdiction is based solely on diversity of citizenship or repugnance of the order to the Federal Constitution; and,

(2)   The order does not interfere with interstate commerce; and,

(3)   The order has been made after reasonable notice and hearing; and,

(4)   A plain, speedy and efficient remedy may be had in the courts of such State.

(June 25, 1948, c. 646, 62 Stat. 932.)

§ 1343.   Civil rights and elective franchise

(a)   The district courts shall have original jurisdiction of any civil action authorized by law to be commenced by any person:

(1)   To recover damages for injury to his person or property, or because of the deprivation of any right or privilege of a citizen of the United States, by any act done in furtherance of any conspiracy mentioned in section 1985 of Title 42;

(2)   To recover damages from any person who fails to prevent or to aid in preventing any wrongs mentioned in section 1985 of Title 42 which he had knowledge were about to occur and power to prevent;

(3)   To redress the deprivation, under color of any State law, statute, ordinance, regulation, custom or usage, of any right, privilege or immunity secured by the Constitution of the United

States or by any Act of Congress providing for equal rights of citizens or of all persons within the jurisdiction of the United States;

    (4)   To recover damages or to secure equitable or other relief under any Act of Congress providing for the protection of civil rights, including the right to vote.

  (b)   For purposes of this section—

    (1)   the District of Columbia shall be considered to be a State; and

    (2)   any Act of Congress applicable exclusively to the District of Columbia shall be considered to be a statute of the District of Columbia.

(June 25, 1948, c. 646, 62 Stat. 932; Sept. 3, 1954, c. 1263, § 42, 68 Stat. 1241; Sept. 9, 1957, Pub.L. 85–315, Part III, § 121, 71 Stat. 637; Dec. 29, 1979, Pub.L. 96–170, § 2, 93 Stat. 1284.)

§ 1344.   Election disputes

The district courts shall have original jurisdiction of any civil action to recover possession of any office, except that of elector of President or Vice President, United States Senator, Representative in or delegate to Congress, or member of a state legislature, authorized by law to be commenced, wherein it appears that the sole question touching the title to office arises out of denial of the right to vote, to any citizen offering to vote, on account of race, color or previous condition of servitude.

The jurisdiction under this section shall extend only so far as to determine the rights of the parties to office by reason of the denial of the right, guaranteed by the Constitution of the United States and secured by any law, to enforce the right of citizens of the United States to vote in all the States.

(June 25, 1948, c. 646, 62 Stat. 932.)

§ 1345.   United States as plaintiff

Except as otherwise provided by Act of Congress, the district courts shall have original jurisdiction of all civil actions, suits or proceedings commenced by the United States, or by any agency or officer thereof expressly authorized to sue by Act of Congress.

(June 25, 1948, c. 646, 62 Stat. 933.)

§ 1346.   United States as defendant

  (a)   The district courts shall have original jurisdiction, concurrent with the United States Court of Federal Claims, of:

    (1)   Any civil action against the United States for the recovery of any internal-revenue tax alleged to have been erroneously or illegally assessed or collected, or any penalty claimed to have been collected without authority or any sum alleged to have been excessive or in any manner wrongfully collected under the internal-revenue laws;

    (2)   Any other civil action or claim against the United States, not exceeding $10,000 in amount, founded either upon the Constitution, or any Act of Congress, or any regulation of an executive department, or upon any express or implied contract with the United States, or for liquidated or unliquidated damages in cases not sounding in tort, except that the district courts shall not have jurisdiction of any civil action or claim against the United States founded upon any express or implied contract with the United States or for liquidated or unliquidated damages in cases not sounding in tort which are subject to sections 7104(b)(1) and 7107(a)(1) of title 41. For the purpose of this paragraph, an express or implied contract with the Army and Air Force Exchange Service, Navy Exchanges, Marine Corps Exchanges, Coast Guard Exchanges, or Exchange Councils of the National Aeronautics and Space Administration shall be considered an express or implied contract with the United States.

(b)(1)　Subject to the provisions of chapter 171 of this title, the district courts, together with the United States District Court for the District of the Canal Zone and the District Court of the Virgin Islands, shall have exclusive jurisdiction of civil actions on claims against the United States, for money damages, accruing on and after January 1, 1945, for injury or loss of property, or personal injury or death caused by the negligent or wrongful act or omission of any employee of the Government while acting within the scope of his office or employment, under circumstances where the United States, if a private person, would be liable to the claimant in accordance with the law of the place where the act or omission occurred.

(2)　No person convicted of a felony who is incarcerated while awaiting sentencing or while serving a sentence may bring a civil action against the United States or an agency, officer, or employee of the Government, for mental or emotional injury suffered while in custody without a prior showing of physical injury or the commission of a sexual act (as defined in section 2246 of Title 18).

(c)　The jurisdiction conferred by this section includes jurisdiction of any set-off, counterclaim, or other claim or demand whatever on the part of the United States against any plaintiff commencing an action under this section.

(d)　The district courts shall not have jurisdiction under this section of any civil action or claim for a pension.

(e)　The district courts shall have original jurisdiction of any civil action against the United States provided in section 6226, 6228(a), 7426, or 7428 (in the case of the United States district court for the District of Columbia) or section 7429 of the Internal Revenue Code of 1986.

(f)　The district courts shall have exclusive original jurisdiction of civil actions under section 2409a to quiet title to an estate or interest in real property in which an interest is claimed by the United States.

(g)　Subject to the provisions of chapter 179, the district courts of the United States shall have exclusive jurisdiction over any civil action commenced under section 453(2) of title 3, by a covered employee under chapter 5 of such title.

(June 25, 1948, c. 646, 62 Stat. 933; Apr. 25, 1949, c. 92, § 2(a), 63 Stat. 62; May 24, 1949, c. 139, § 80(a), (b), 63 Stat. 101; Oct. 31, 1951, c. 655, § 50(b), 65 Stat. 727; July 30, 1954, c. 648, § 1, 68 Stat. 589; July 7, 1958, Pub.L. 85–508, § 12(e), 72 Stat. 348; Aug. 30, 1964, Pub.L. 88–519, 78 Stat. 699; Nov. 2, 1966, Pub.L. 89–719, Title II, § 202(a), 80 Stat. 1148; July 23, 1970, Pub.L. 91–350, § 1(a), 84 Stat. 449; Oct. 25, 1972, Pub.L. 92–562, § 1, 86 Stat. 1176; Oct. 4, 1976, Pub.L. 94–455, Title XII, § 1204(c)(1), Title XIII, § 1306(b)(7), 90 Stat. 1697, 1719; Nov. 1, 1978, Pub.L. 95–563, § 14(a), 92 Stat. 2389; Apr. 2, 1982, Pub.L. 97–164, Title I, § 129, 96 Stat. 39; Sept. 3, 1982, Pub.L. 97–248, Title IV, § 402(c) (17), 96 Stat. 669; Oct. 22, 1986, Pub.L. 99–514, § 2, 100 Stat. 2095; Oct. 29, 1992, Pub.L. 102–572, Title IX, § 902(b)(1), 106 Stat. 4516; Apr. 26, 1996, Pub.L. 104–134, Title I, § 101[(a)][Title VIII, § 806], 110 Stat. 1321–75; renumbered Title I May 2, 1996, Pub.L. 104–140, § 1(a), 110 Stat. 1327; amended Oct. 26, 1996, Pub.L. 104–331, § 3(b)(1), 110 Stat. 4069; Jan. 4, 2011, Pub.L. 111–350, § 5(g)(6), 124 Stat. 3848; Pub.L. 113–4, Title XI, § 1101(b), Mar. 7, 2013, 127 Stat. 134.)

§ 1347.　　Partition action where United States is joint tenant

The district courts shall have original jurisdiction of any civil action commenced by any tenant in common or joint tenant for the partition of lands where the United States is one of the tenants in common or joint tenants.

(June 25, 1948, c. 646, 62 Stat. 933.)

§ 1348.　　Banking association as party

The district courts shall have original jurisdiction of any civil action commenced by the United States, or by direction of any officer thereof, against any national banking association, any civil action to wind up the affairs of any such association, and any action by a banking association established in the district for which the court is held, under chapter 2 of Title 12, to enjoin the Comptroller of the Currency, or any receiver acting under his direction, as provided by such chapter.

All national banking associations shall, for the purposes of all other actions by or against them, be deemed citizens of the States in which they are respectively located.

(June 25, 1948, c. 646, 62 Stat. 933.)

§ 1349.   Corporation organized under federal law as party

The district courts shall not have jurisdiction of any civil action by or against any corporation upon the ground that it was incorporated by or under an Act of Congress, unless the United States is the owner of more than one-half of its capital stock.

(June 25, 1948, c. 646, 62 Stat. 934.)

§ 1350.   Alien's action for tort

The district courts shall have original jurisdiction of any civil action by an alien for a tort only, committed in violation of the law of nations or a treaty of the United States.

(June 25, 1948, c. 646, 62 Stat. 934.)

§ 1351.   Consuls, vice consuls, and members of a diplomatic mission as defendant

The district courts shall have original jurisdiction, exclusive of the courts of the States, of all civil actions and proceedings against—

     (1) consuls or vice consuls of foreign states; or

     (2) members of a mission or members of their families (as such terms are defined in section 2 of the Diplomatic Relations Act).

(June 25, 1948, c. 646, 62 Stat. 934; May 24, 1949, c. 139, § 80(c), 63 Stat. 101; Sept. 30, 1978, Pub.L. 95–393, § 8(a)(1), 92 Stat. 810.)

§ 1352.   Bonds executed under federal law

The district courts shall have original jurisdiction, concurrent with State courts, of any action on a bond executed under any law of the United States, except matters within the jurisdiction of the Court of International Trade under section 1582 of this title.

(June 25, 1948, c. 646, 62 Stat. 934; Oct. 10, 1980, Pub.L. 96–417, Title V, § 506, 94 Stat. 1743.)

§ 1353.   Indian allotments*

The district courts shall have original jurisdiction of any civil action involving the right of any person, in whole or in part of Indian blood or descent, to any allotment of land under any Act of Congress or treaty.

The judgment in favor of any claimant to an allotment of land shall have the same effect, when properly certified to the Secretary of the Interior, as if such allotment had been allowed and approved by him; but this provision shall not apply to any lands held on or before December 21, 1911, by either of the Five Civilized Tribes,* the Osage Nation of Indians, nor to any of the lands within the Quapaw Indian Agency.

---

   * [Footnote to 28 U.S.C. § 1353: To learn more about the complicated and problematic history of the Indian land allotment policy of the United States, which facilitated the widespread transfer of land out of Indian hands, visit the website of the Indian Land Tenure Foundation, at https://iltf.org/land-issues/history/. Ed.]

   * [Footnote to 28 U.S.C. § 1353: The so-called "Five Civilized Tribes" is a term that is meant to refer to the Cherokee, Chickasaw, Choctaw, Creek/Muscogee, and Seminole American Indian nations, each of whom were located principally in

(June 25, 1948, c. 646, 62 Stat. 934.)

§ 1354.   Land grants from different states

The district courts shall have original jurisdiction of actions between citizens of the same state claiming lands under grants from different states.

(June 25, 1948, c. 646, 62 Stat. 934.)

§ 1355.   Fine, penalty or forfeiture

(a) The district courts shall have original jurisdiction, exclusive of the courts of the States, of any action or proceeding for the recovery or enforcement of any fine, penalty, or forfeiture, pecuniary or otherwise, incurred under any Act of Congress, except matters within the jurisdiction of the Court of International Trade under section 1582 of this title.

(b)(1) A forfeiture action or proceeding may be brought in—

     (A) the district court for the district in which any of the acts or omissions giving rise to the forfeiture occurred, or

     (B) any other district where venue for the forfeiture action or proceeding is specifically provided for in section 1395 of this title or any other statute.

     (2) Whenever property subject to forfeiture under the laws of the United States is located in a foreign country, or has been detained or seized pursuant to legal process or competent authority of a foreign government, an action or proceeding for forfeiture may be brought as provided in paragraph (1), or in the United States District court[1] for the District of Columbia.

(c) In any case in which a final order disposing of property in a civil forfeiture action or proceeding is appealed, removal of the property by the prevailing party shall not deprive the court of jurisdiction. Upon motion of the appealing party, the district court or the court of appeals shall issue any order necessary to preserve the right of the appealing party to the full value of the property at issue, including a stay of the judgment of the district court pending appeal or requiring the prevailing party to post an appeal bond.

(d) Any court with jurisdiction over a forfeiture action pursuant to subsection (b) may issue and cause to be served in any other district such process as may be required to bring before the court the property that is the subject of the forfeiture action.

(June 25, 1948, c. 646, 62 Stat. 934; Oct. 10, 1980, Pub.L. 96–417, Title V, § 507, 94 Stat. 1743; Oct. 28, 1992, Pub.L. 102–550, Title XV, § 1521, 106 Stat. 4062.)

§ 1356.   Seizures not within admiralty and maritime jurisdiction

The district courts shall have original jurisdiction, exclusive of the courts of the States, of any seizure under any law of the United States on land or upon waters not within admiralty and maritime jurisdiction, except matters within the jurisdiction of the Court of International Trade under section 1582 of this title.

(June 25, 1948, c. 646, 62 Stat. 934; Oct. 10, 1980, Pub.L. 96–417, Title V, § 508, 94 Stat. 1743.)

§ 1357.   Injuries under Federal laws

The district courts shall have original jurisdiction of any civil action commenced by any person to recover damages for any injury to his person or property on account of any act done by him, under any

---

the Southeastern United States prior to their forced relocation to Indian Territory through what became known as the Trail of Tears. Ed.]

    [1]   [Footnote to 28 U.S.C. § 1355(b)(2):] So in original. Probably should be capitalized.

Act of Congress, for the protection or collection of any of the revenues, or to enforce the right of citizens of the United States to vote in any State.

(June 25, 1948, c. 646, 62 Stat. 934.)

§ 1358.　　Eminent domain

The district courts shall have original jurisdiction of all proceedings to condemn real estate for the use of the United States or its departments or agencies.

(June 25, 1948, c. 646, 62 Stat. 935.)

§ 1359.　　Parties collusively joined or made

A district court shall not have jurisdiction of a civil action in which any party, by assignment or otherwise, has been improperly or collusively made or joined to invoke the jurisdiction of such court.

(June 25, 1948, c. 646, 62 Stat. 935.)

§ 1360.　　State civil jurisdiction in actions to which Indians are parties

(a) Each of the States listed in the following table shall have jurisdiction over civil causes of action between Indians or to which Indians are parties which arise in the areas of Indian country* listed opposite the name of the State to the same extent that such State has jurisdiction over other civil causes of action, and those civil laws of such State that are of general application to private persons or private property shall have the same force and effect within such Indian country as they have elsewhere within the State:

State of	Indian country affected
Alaska	All Indian country within the State
California	All Indian country within the State
Minnesota	All Indian country within the State, except the Red Lake Reservation
Nebraska	All Indian country within the State
Oregon	All Indian country within the State, except the Warm Springs Reservation
Wisconsin	All Indian country within the State

(b) Nothing in this section shall authorize the alienation, encumbrance, or taxation of any real or personal property, including water rights, belonging to any Indian or any Indian tribe, band, or community that is held in trust by the United States or is subject to a restriction against alienation imposed by the United States; or shall authorize regulation of the use of such property in a manner inconsistent with any Federal treaty, agreement, or statute or with any regulation made pursuant thereto; or shall confer jurisdiction upon the State to adjudicate, in probate proceedings or otherwise, the ownership or right to possession of such property or any interest therein.

(c) Any tribal ordinance or custom heretofore or hereafter adopted by an Indian tribe, band, or community in the exercise of any authority which it may possess shall, if not inconsistent with any applicable civil law of the State, be given full force and effect in the determination of civil causes of action pursuant to this section.

(Added Aug. 15, 1953, c. 505, § 4, 67 Stat. 589; amended Aug. 24, 1954, c. 910, § 2, 68 Stat. 795; Aug. 8, 1958, Pub.L. 85–615, § 2, 72 Stat. 545; Nov. 6, 1978, Pub.L. 95–598, Title II, § 239, 92 Stat. 2668; July 10, 1984, Pub.L. 98–353, Title I, § 110, 98 Stat. 342.)

---

* [Footnote to 28 U.S.C. § 1360(a): The term "Indian country" refers to land within any Indian reservation, dependent Indian communities within the United States, and all Indian allotments for which the Indian titles have not been extinguished. See 18 U.S.C. § 1151. Ed.]

§ 1361.   Action to compel an officer of the United States to perform his duty

The district courts shall have original jurisdiction of any action in the nature of mandamus to compel an officer or employee of the United States or any agency thereof to perform a duty owed to the plaintiff.

(Added Pub.L. 87–748, § 1(a), Oct. 5, 1962, 76 Stat. 744.)

§ 1362.   Indian tribes

The district courts shall have original jurisdiction of all civil actions, brought by any Indian tribe or band with a governing body duly recognized by the Secretary of the Interior, wherein the matter in controversy arises under the Constitution, laws, or treaties of the United States.

(Added Pub.L. 89–635, § 1, Oct. 10, 1966, 80 Stat. 880.)

§ 1363.   Jurors' employment rights

The district courts shall have original jurisdiction of any civil action brought for the protection of jurors' employment under section 1875 of this title.

(Added Pub.L. 95–572, § 6(b)(1), Nov. 2, 1978, 92 Stat. 2457.)

§ 1364.   Direct actions against insurers of members of diplomatic missions and their families

(a) The district courts shall have original and exclusive jurisdiction, without regard to the amount in controversy, of any civil action commenced by any person against an insurer who by contract has insured an individual, who is, or was at the time of the tortious act or omission, a member of a mission (within the meaning of section 2(3) of the Diplomatic Relations Act (22 U.S.C. 254a(3))) or a member of the family of such a member of a mission, or an individual described in section 19 of the Convention on Privileges and Immunities of the United Nations of February 13, 1946, against liability for personal injury, death, or damage to property.

(b) Any direct action brought against an insurer under subsection (a) shall be tried without a jury, but shall not be subject to the defense that the insured is immune from suit, that the insured is an indispensable party, or in the absence of fraud or collusion, that the insured has violated a term of the contract, unless the contract was cancelled before the claim arose.

(Added Pub.L. 95–393, § 7(a), Sept. 30, 1978, 92 Stat. 809; amended Pub.L. 97–241, Title II, § 203(b)(4), Aug. 24, 1982, 96 Stat. 291; Pub.L. 100–204, Title I, § 138(a), Dec. 22, 1987, 101 Stat. 1347.)

§ 1365.   Senate actions

(a) The United States District Court for the District of Columbia shall have original jurisdiction, without regard to the amount in controversy, over any civil action brought by the Senate or any authorized committee or subcommittee of the Senate to enforce, to secure a declaratory judgment concerning the validity of, or to prevent a threatened refusal or failure to comply with, any subpena or order issued by the Senate or committee or subcommittee of the Senate to any entity acting or purporting to act under color or authority of State law or to any natural person to secure the production of documents or other materials of any kind or the answering of any deposition or interrogatory or to secure testimony or any combination thereof. This section shall not apply to an action to enforce, to secure a declaratory judgment concerning the validity of, or to prevent a threatened refusal to comply with, any subpena or order issued to an officer or employee of the executive branch of the Federal Government acting within his or her official capacity, except that this section shall apply if the refusal to comply is based on the assertion of a personal privilege or objection and is not based on a governmental privilege or objection the assertion of which has been authorized by the executive branch of the Federal Government.

(b) Upon application by the Senate or any authorized committee or subcommittee of the Senate, the district court shall issue an order to an entity or person refusing, or failing to comply with, or threatening to refuse or not to comply with, a subpena or order of the Senate or committee or subcommittee of the Senate requiring such entity or person to comply forthwith. Any refusal or failure to obey a lawful order of the district court issued pursuant to this section may be held by such court to be a contempt thereof. A contempt proceeding shall be commenced by an order to show cause before the court why the entity or person refusing or failing to obey the court order should not be held in contempt of court. Such contempt proceeding shall be tried by the court and shall be summary in manner. The purpose of sanctions imposed as a result of such contempt proceeding shall be to compel obedience to the order of the court. Process in any such action or contempt proceeding may be served in any judicial district wherein the entity or party refusing, or failing to comply, or threatening to refuse or not to comply, resides, transacts business, or may be found, and subpenas for witnesses who are required to attend such proceeding may run into any other district. Nothing in this section shall confer upon such court jurisdiction to affect by injunction or otherwise the issuance or effect of any subpena or order of the Senate or any committee or subcommittee of the Senate or to review, modify, suspend, terminate, or set aside any such subpena or order. An action, contempt proceeding, or sanction brought or imposed pursuant to this section shall not abate upon adjournment sine die by the Senate at the end of a Congress if the Senate or the committee or subcommittee of the Senate which issued the subpena or order certifies to the court that it maintains its interest in securing the documents, answers, or testimony during such adjournment.

[**(c)** Repealed. Pub.L. 98–620, Title IV, § 402(29)(D), Nov. 8, 1984, 98 Stat. 3359]

(d) The Senate or any committee or subcommittee of the Senate commencing and prosecuting a civil action or contempt proceeding under this section may be represented in such action by such attorneys as the Senate may designate.

(e) A civil action commenced or prosecuted under this section, may not be authorized pursuant to the Standing Order of the Senate "authorizing suits by Senate Committees" (S. Jour. 572, May 28, 1928).

(f) For the purposes of this section the term "committee" includes standing, select, or special committees of the Senate established by law or resolution.

(Added Pub.L. 95–521, Title VII, § 705(f)(1), Oct. 26, 1978, 92 Stat. 1879, § 1364; amended Pub.L. 98–620, Title IV, § 402(29)(D), Nov. 8, 1984, 98 Stat. 3359; renumbered § 1365, Pub.L. 99–336, § 6(a)(1)(B), June 19, 1986, 100 Stat. 638; Pub.L. 104–292, § 4, Oct. 11, 1996, 110 Stat. 3460.)

§ 1366.   Construction of references to laws of the United States or Acts of Congress

For the purposes of this chapter, references to laws of the United States or Acts of Congress do not include laws applicable exclusively to the District of Columbia.

(Added Pub.L. 91–358, Title I, § 172(c)(1), July 29, 1970, 84 Stat. 590, § 1363; renumbered § 1364, Pub.L. 95–572, § 6(b)(1), Nov. 2, 1978, 92 Stat. 2456; renumbered § 1366, Pub.L. 99–336, § 6(a)(1)(C), June 19, 1986, 100 Stat. 639.)

§ 1367.   Supplemental jurisdiction

(a) Except as provided in subsections (b) and (c) or as expressly provided otherwise by Federal statute, in any civil action of which the district courts have original jurisdiction, the district courts shall have supplemental jurisdiction over all other claims that are so related to claims in the action within such original jurisdiction that they form part of the same case or controversy under Article III of the United States Constitution. Such supplemental jurisdiction shall include claims that involve the joinder or intervention of additional parties.

(b) In any civil action of which the district courts have original jurisdiction founded solely on section 1332 of this title, the district courts shall not have supplemental jurisdiction under subsection (a) over claims by plaintiffs against persons made parties under Rule 14, 19, 20, or 24 of the Federal

Rules of Civil Procedure, or over claims by persons proposed to be joined as plaintiffs under Rule 19 of such rules, or seeking to intervene as plaintiffs under Rule 24 of such rules, when exercising supplemental jurisdiction over such claims would be inconsistent with the jurisdictional requirements of section 1332.

(c) The district courts may decline to exercise supplemental jurisdiction over a claim under subsection (a) if—

(1) the claim raises a novel or complex issue of State law,

(2) the claim substantially predominates over the claim or claims over which the district court has original jurisdiction,

(3) the district court has dismissed all claims over which it has original jurisdiction, or

(4) in exceptional circumstances, there are other compelling reasons for declining jurisdiction.

(d) The period of limitations for any claim asserted under subsection (a), and for any other claim in the same action that is voluntarily dismissed at the same time as or after the dismissal of the claim under subsection (a), shall be tolled while the claim is pending and for a period of 30 days after it is dismissed unless State law provides for a longer tolling period.

(e) As used in this section, the term "State" includes the District of Columbia, the Commonwealth of Puerto Rico, and any territory or possession of the United States.

(Added Pub.L. 101–650, Title III, § 310(a), Dec. 1, 1990, 104 Stat. 5113.)

§ 1368.   Counterclaims in unfair practices in international trade

The district courts shall have original jurisdiction of any civil action based on a counterclaim raised pursuant to section 337(c) of the Tariff Act of 1930, to the extent that it arises out of the transaction or occurrence that is the subject matter of the opposing party's claim in the proceeding under section 337(a) of that Act.

(Added Pub.L. 103–465, Title III, § 321(b)(3)(A), Dec. 8, 1994, 108 Stat. 4946.)

HISTORICAL AND STATUTORY NOTES

References in Text

Section 337 of the Tariff Act of 1930, referred to in text, is section 337 of Act June 17, 1930, c. 497, Title III, 46 Stat. 703, which is classified to section 1337 of Title 19, Customs Duties.

Effective and Applicability Provisions

1994 Acts. Section applicable with respect to complaints filed under section 1337 of Title 19, Customs Duties, on or after the date on which the WTO Agreement enters into force with respect to the United States, Jan. 1, 1995, or in cases under section 1337 of Title 19 in which no complaint is filed, with respect to investigations initiated under such section on or after such date, see section 322 of Pub.L. 103–465, set out as a note under section 1337 of Title 19.

§ 1369.   Multiparty, multiforum jurisdiction

(a) **In general.**—The district courts shall have original jurisdiction of any civil action involving minimal diversity between adverse parties that arises from a single accident, where at least 75 natural persons have died in the accident at a discrete location, if—

(1) a defendant resides in a State and a substantial part of the accident took place in another State or other location, regardless of whether that defendant is also a resident of the State where a substantial part of the accident took place;

(2) any two defendants reside in different States, regardless of whether such defendants are also residents of the same State or States; or

(3)   substantial parts of the accident took place in different States.

(b) Limitation of jurisdiction of district courts.—The district court shall abstain from hearing any civil action described in subsection (a) in which—

(1)   the substantial majority of all plaintiffs are citizens of a single State of which the primary defendants are also citizens; and

(2)   the claims asserted will be governed primarily by the laws of that State.

(c) Special rules and definitions.—For purposes of this section—

(1)   minimal diversity exists between adverse parties if any party is a citizen of a State and any adverse party is a citizen of another State, a citizen or subject of a foreign state, or a foreign state as defined in section 1603(a) of this title;

(2)   a corporation is deemed to be a citizen of any State, and a citizen or subject of any foreign state, in which it is incorporated or has its principal place of business, and is deemed to be a resident of any State in which it is incorporated or licensed to do business or is doing business;

(3)   the term "injury" means—

(A)   physical harm to a natural person; and

(B)   physical damage to or destruction of tangible property, but only if physical harm described in subparagraph (A) exists;

(4)   the term "accident" means a sudden accident, or a natural event culminating in an accident, that results in death incurred at a discrete location by at least 75 natural persons; and

(5)   the term "State" includes the District of Columbia, the Commonwealth of Puerto Rico, and any territory or possession of the United States.

(d) Intervening parties.—In any action in a district court which is or could have been brought, in whole or in part, under this section, any person with a claim arising from the accident described in subsection (a) shall be permitted to intervene as a party plaintiff in the action, even if that person could not have brought an action in a district court as an original matter.

(e) Notification of judicial panel on multidistrict litigation.—A district court in which an action under this section is pending shall promptly notify the judicial panel on multidistrict litigation of the pendency of the action.

(Added Pub.L. 107–273, Div. C, Title I, § 11020(b)(1)(A), Nov. 2, 2002, 116 Stat. 1826.)

CHAPTER 87—DISTRICT COURTS; VENUE

§ 1390.   Scope

(a) **Venue Defined.**—As used in this chapter, the term "venue" refers to the geographic specification of the proper court or courts for the litigation of a civil action that is within the subject-matter jurisdiction of the district courts in general, and does not refer to any grant or restriction of subject-matter jurisdiction providing for a civil action to be adjudicated only by the district court for a particular district or districts.

(b) **Exclusion of Certain Cases.**—Except as otherwise provided by law, this chapter shall not govern the venue of a civil action in which the district court exercises the jurisdiction conferred by section 1333, except that such civil actions may be transferred between district courts as provided in this chapter.

(c) **Clarification Regarding Cases Removed from State Courts.**—This chapter shall not determine the district court to which a civil action pending in a State court may be removed, but shall govern the transfer of an action so removed as between districts and divisions of the United States district courts.

(Added Pub.L. 112–63, Title II, § 201(a), Dec. 7, 2011, 125 Stat. 762.)

HISTORICAL AND STATUTORY NOTES

Effective and Applicability Provisions

2011 Acts. Pub.L. 112–63, Title II, § 205, Dec. 7, 2011, 125 Stat. 764, provided that:

"The amendments made by this title [Title II of Pub.L. 112–63, enacting this section, amending 28 U.S.C.A. §§ 1391 and 1404, and repealing 28 U.S.C.A. § 1392]—

"**(1)** shall take effect upon the expiration of the 30-day period beginning on the date of the enactment of this Act [Dec. 7, 2011]; and

"**(2)** Shall apply to—

"**(A)** any action that is commenced in a United States district court on or after such effective date; and

"**(B)** any action that is removed from a State court to a United States district court and that had been commenced, within the meaning of State law, on or after such effective date."

§ 1391.   Venue generally

(a) **Applicability of Section.**—Except as otherwise provided by law—

(1) this section shall govern the venue of all civil actions brought in district courts of the United States; and

(2) the proper venue for a civil action shall be determined without regard to whether the action is local or transitory in nature.

(b) Venue in General.—A civil action may be brought in—

    (1) a judicial district in which any defendant resides, if all defendants are residents of the State in which the district is located;

    (2) a judicial district in which a substantial part of the events or omissions giving rise to the claim occurred, or a substantial part of property that is the subject of the action is situated; or

    (3) if there is no district in which an action may otherwise be brought as provided in this section, any judicial district in which any defendant is subject to the court's personal jurisdiction with respect to such action.

(c) Residency.—For all venue purposes—

    (1) a natural person, including an alien lawfully admitted for permanent residence in the United States, shall be deemed to reside in the judicial district in which that person is domiciled;

    (2) an entity with the capacity to sue and be sued in its common name under applicable law, whether or not incorporated, shall be deemed to reside, if a defendant, in any judicial district in which such defendant is subject to the court's personal jurisdiction with respect to the civil action in question and, if a plaintiff, only in the judicial district in which it maintains its principal place of business; and

    (3) a defendant not resident in the United States may be sued in any judicial district, and the joinder of such a defendant shall be disregarded in determining where the action may be brought with respect to other defendants.

(d) Residency of Corporations in States With Multiple Districts.—For purposes of venue under this chapter, in a State which has more than one judicial district and in which a defendant that is a corporation is subject to personal jurisdiction at the time an action is commenced, such corporation shall be deemed to reside in any district in that State within which its contacts would be sufficient to subject it to personal jurisdiction if that district were a separate State, and, if there is no such district, the corporation shall be deemed to reside in the district within which it has the most significant contacts.

(e) Actions Where Defendant Is Officer or Employee of the United States.—

    (1) In general.—A civil action in which a defendant is an officer or employee of the United States or any agency thereof acting in his official capacity or under color of legal authority, or an agency of the United States, or the United States, may, except as otherwise provided by law, be brought in any judicial district in which (A) a defendant in the action resides, (B) a substantial part of the events or omissions giving rise to the claim occurred, or a substantial part of property that is the subject of the action is situated, or (C) the plaintiff resides if no real property is involved in the action. Additional persons may be joined as parties to any such action in accordance with the Federal Rules of Civil Procedure and with such other venue requirements as would be applicable if the United States or one of its officers, employees, or agencies were not a party.

    (2) Service.—The summons and complaint in such an action shall be served as provided by the Federal Rules of Civil Procedure except that the delivery of the summons and complaint to the officer or agency as required by the rules may be made by certified mail beyond the territorial limits of the district in which the action is brought.

(f) Civil Actions Against a Foreign State.—A civil action against a foreign state as defined in section 1603(a) of this title may be brought—

    (1) in any judicial district in which a substantial part of the events or omissions giving rise to the claim occurred, or a substantial part of property that is the subject of the action is situated;

    (2) in any judicial district in which the vessel or cargo of a foreign state is situated, if the claim is asserted under section 1605(b) of this title;

(3)   in any judicial district in which the agency or instrumentality is licensed to do business or is doing business, if the action is brought against an agency or instrumentality of a foreign state as defined in section 1603(b) of this title; or

(4)   in the United States District Court for the District of Columbia if the action is brought against a foreign state or political subdivision thereof.

(g)   **Multiparty, Multiforum Litigation.**—A civil action in which jurisdiction of the district court is based upon section 1369 of this title may be brought in any district in which any defendant resides or in which a substantial part of the accident giving rise to the action took place.

(June 25, 1948, c. 646, 62 Stat. 935; Oct. 5, 1962, Pub.L. 87–748, § 2, 76 Stat. 744; Dec. 23, 1963, Pub.L. 88–234, 77 Stat. 473; Nov. 2, 1966, Pub.L. 89–714, §§ 1, 2, 80 Stat. 1111; Oct. 21, 1976, Pub.L. 94–574, § 3, 90 Stat. 2721; Oct. 21, 1976, Pub.L. 94–583, § 5, 90 Stat. 2897; Nov. 19, 1988, Pub.L. 100–702, Title X, § 1013(a), 102 Stat. 4669; Dec. 1, 1990, Pub.L. 101–650, Title III, § 311, 104 Stat. 5114; Dec. 9, 1991, Pub.L. 102–198, § 3, 105 Stat. 1623; Oct. 29, 1992, Pub.L. 102–572, Title V, § 504, 106 Stat. 4513; Oct. 3, 1995, Pub.L. 104–34, § 1, 109 Stat. 293; Nov. 2, 2002, Pub.L. 107–273, Div. C, Title I, § 11020(b)(2), 116 Stat. 1827; Pub.L. 112–63, Title II, § 202, Dec. 7, 2011, 125 Stat. 763.)

[§ 1392.   Repealed. Pub.L. 112–63, Title II, § 203, Dec. 7, 2011, 125 Stat. 764]

HISTORICAL AND STATUTORY NOTES

Section, June 25, 1948, c. 646, 62 Stat. 935; Oct. 1, 1996, Pub.L. 104–220, § 1, 110 Stat. 3023, related to venue for civil actions involving defendants or property located in different districts in the same State.

Effective and Applicability Provisions

2011 Acts. Repeal of section by Title II of Pub.L. 112–63 takes effect upon the expiration of the 30 day period beginning on Dec. 7, 2011, and shall apply to actions commenced in U.S. District courts on or after such effective date and actions removed from State courts to U.S. District courts that had been commenced on or after such effective date, see Pub.L. 112–63, § 205, set out as a note under 28 U.S.C.A. § 1390.

[§ 1393.   Repealed. Pub.L. 100–702, Title X, § 1001(a), Nov. 19, 1988, 102 Stat. 4664]

HISTORICAL AND STATUTORY NOTES

Section, Act June 25, 1948, c. 646, 62 Stat. 935, related to divisional venue in civil cases of a single defendant or defendants in different divisions.

§ 1394.   Banking association's action against Comptroller of Currency

Any civil action by a national banking association to enjoin the Comptroller of the Currency, under the provisions of any Act of Congress relating to such associations, may be prosecuted in the judicial district where such association is located.

(June 25, 1948, c. 646, 62 Stat. 935.)

§ 1395.   Fine, penalty or forfeiture

(a)   A civil proceeding for the recovery of a pecuniary fine, penalty or forfeiture may be prosecuted in the district where it accrues or the defendant is found.

(b)   A civil proceeding for the forfeiture of property may be prosecuted in any district where such property is found.

(c)   A civil proceeding for the forfeiture of property seized outside any judicial district may be prosecuted in any district into which the property is brought.

(d)   A proceeding in admiralty for the enforcement of fines, penalties and forfeitures against a vessel may be brought in any district in which the vessel is arrested.

(e) Any proceeding for the forfeiture of a vessel or cargo entering a port of entry closed by the President in pursuance of law, or of goods and chattels coming from a State or section declared by proclamation of the President to be in insurrection, or of any vessel or vehicle conveying persons or property to or from such State or section or belonging in whole or in part to a resident thereof, may be prosecuted in any district into which the property is taken and in which the proceeding is instituted.

(June 25, 1948, c. 646, 62 Stat. 936.)

HISTORICAL AND STATUTORY NOTES

Senate Revision Amendment

While section 3745(c) of Title 26, U.S.C., Internal Revenue Code, is one of the sources of this section, it was eliminated from the schedule of repeals by Senate amendment. Therefore, such section 3745(c) remains in Title 26. See 80th Congress Senate Report No. 1559.

Said section 3745(c) was subsequently repealed by Act May 24, 1949, c. 139, § 142, 63 Stat. 110.

§ 1396.   Internal revenue taxes

Any civil action for the collection of internal revenue taxes may be brought in the district where the liability for such tax accrues, in the district of the taxpayer's residence, or in the district where the return was filed.

(June 25, 1948, c. 646, 62 Stat. 936.)

HISTORICAL AND STATUTORY NOTES

Senate Revision Amendment

While section 3744 of Title 26, U.S.C., Internal Revenue Code [1939], is one of the sources of this section, it was eliminated from the schedule of repeals by Senate amendment. Therefore, it remains in Title 26 [I.R.C.1939]. See 80th Congress Senate Report No. 1559.

Said section 3744 was subsequently repealed by Act May 24, 1949, c. 139, § 142, 63 Stat. 110.

§ 1397.   Interpleader

Any civil action of interpleader or in the nature of interpleader under section 1335 of this title may be brought in the judicial district in which one or more of the claimants reside.

(June 25, 1948, c. 646, 62 Stat. 936.)

§ 1398.   Interstate Commerce Commission's orders

(a) Except as otherwise provided by law, a civil action brought under section 1336(a) of this title shall be brought only in a judicial district in which any of the parties bringing the action resides or has its principal office.

(b) A civil action to enforce, enjoin, set aside, annul, or suspend, in whole or in part, an order of the Interstate Commerce Commission made pursuant to the referral of a question or issue by a district court or by the United States Court of Federal Claims, shall be brought only in the court which referred the question or issue.

(June 25, 1948, c. 646, 62 Stat. 936; Aug. 30, 1964, Pub.L. 88–513, § 2, 78 Stat. 695; Jan. 2, 1975, Pub.L. 93–584, § 2, 88 Stat. 1917; Apr. 2, 1982, Pub.L. 97–164, Title I, § 130, 96 Stat. 39; Oct. 29, 1992, Pub.L. 102–572, Title IX, § 902(b)(1), 106 Stat. 4516.)

HISTORICAL AND STATUTORY NOTES

Abolition of Interstate Commerce Commission and Transfer of Functions

Interstate Commerce Commission abolished and functions of Commission transferred, except as otherwise provided in Pub.L. 104–88, to Surface Transportation Board effective Jan. 1, 1996, by sections 702 of Title 49, Transportation, and section 101 of Pub.L. 104–88, set out as a note under section 701 of title

49. References to Interstate Commerce Commission deemed to refer to Surface Transportation Board, a member or employee of the Board, or Secretary of Transportation, as appropriate, see section 205 of Pub.L. 104–88, set out as a note under section 701 of Title 49.

§ 1399. Partition action involving United States

Any civil action by any tenant in common or joint tenant for the partition of lands, where the United States is one of the tenants in common or joint tenants, may be brought only in the judicial district where such lands are located or, if located in different districts in the same State, in any of such districts.

(June 25, 1948, c. 646, 62 Stat. 936.)

§ 1400. Patents and copyrights, mask works, and designs

(a) Civil actions, suits, or proceedings arising under any Act of Congress relating to copyrights or exclusive rights in mask works or designs may be instituted in the district in which the defendant or his agent resides or may be found.

(b) Any civil action for patent infringement may be brought in the judicial district where the defendant resides, or where the defendant has committed acts of infringement and has a regular and established place of business.

(June 25, 1948, c. 646, 62 Stat. 936; Nov. 19, 1988, Pub.L. 100–702, Title X, § 1020(a)(5), 102 Stat. 4671; Oct. 28, 1998, Pub.L. 105–304, Title V, § 503(c)(1), (2), 112 Stat. 2917; Aug. 5, 1999, Pub.L. 106–44, § 2(a), 113 Stat. 223.)

§ 1401. Stockholder's derivative action

Any civil action by a stockholder on behalf of his corporation may be prosecuted in any judicial district where the corporation might have sued the same defendants.

(June 25, 1948, c. 646, 62 Stat. 936.)

§ 1402. United States as defendant

(a) Any civil action in a district court against the United States under subsection (a) of section 1346 of this title may be prosecuted only:

(1) Except as provided in paragraph (2), in the judicial district where the plaintiff resides;

(2) In the case of a civil action by a corporation under paragraph (1) of subsection (a) of section 1346, in the judicial district in which is located the principal place of business or principal office or agency of the corporation; or if it has no principal place of business or principal office or agency in any judicial district (A) in the judicial district in which is located the office to which was made the return of the tax in respect of which the claim is made, or (B) if no return was made, in the judicial district in which lies the District of Columbia. Notwithstanding the foregoing provisions of this paragraph a district court, for the convenience of the parties and witnesses, in the interest of justice, may transfer any such action to any other district or division.

(b) Any civil action on a tort claim against the United States under subsection (b) of section 1346 of this title may be prosecuted only in the judicial district where the plaintiff resides or wherein the act or omission complained of occurred.

(c) Any civil action against the United States under subsection (e) of section 1346 of this title may be prosecuted only in the judicial district where the property is situated at the time of levy, or if no levy is made, in the judicial district in which the event occurred which gave rise to the cause of action.

(d) Any civil action under section 2409a to quiet title to an estate or interest in real property in which an interest is claimed by the United States shall be brought in the district court of the district where the property is located or, if located in different districts, in any of such districts.

(June 25, 1948, c. 646, 62 Stat. 937; Sept. 2, 1958, Pub.L. 85–920, 72 Stat. 1770; Nov. 2, 1966, Pub.L. 89–719, Title II, § 202(b), 80 Stat. 1149; Oct. 25, 1972, Pub.L. 92–562, § 2, 86 Stat. 1176; Apr. 2, 1982, Pub.L. 97–164, Title I, § 131, 96 Stat. 39.)

§ 1403.   Eminent domain

Proceedings to condemn real estate for the use of the United States or its departments or agencies shall be brought in the district court of the district where the land is located or, if located in different districts in the same State, in any of such districts.

(June 25, 1948, c. 646, 62 Stat. 937.)

§ 1404.   Change of venue

(a) For the convenience of parties and witnesses, in the interest of justice, a district court may transfer any civil action to any other district or division where it might have been brought or to any district or division to which all parties have consented.

(b) Upon motion, consent or stipulation of all parties, any action, suit or proceeding of a civil nature or any motion or hearing thereof, may be transferred, in the discretion of the court, from the division in which pending to any other division in the same district. Transfer of proceedings in rem brought by or on behalf of the United States may be transferred under this section without the consent of the United States where all other parties request transfer.

(c) A district court may order any civil action to be tried at any place within the division in which it is pending.

(d) Transfers from a district court of the United States to the District Court of Guam, the District Court for the Northern Mariana Islands, or the District Court of the Virgin Islands shall not be permitted under this section. As otherwise used in this section, the term "district court" includes the District Court of Guam, the District Court for the Northern Mariana Islands, and the District Court of the Virgin Islands, and the term "district" includes the territorial jurisdiction of each such court.

(June 25, 1948, c. 646, 62 Stat. 937; Oct. 18, 1962, Pub.L. 87–845, § 9, 76A Stat. 699; Oct. 19, 1996, Pub.L. 104–317, Title VI, § 610(a), 110 Stat. 3860; Pub.L. 112–63, Title II, § 204, Dec. 7, 2011, 125 Stat. 764.)

HISTORICAL AND STATUTORY NOTES

Termination of United States District Court for the District of the Canal Zone

For termination of the United States District Court for the District of the Canal Zone at end of the "transition period", being the 30-month period beginning Oct. 1, 1979, and ending midnight Mar. 31, 1982, see Paragraph 5 of Article XI of the Panama Canal Treaty of 1977 and sections 3831 and 3841 to 3843 of Title 22, Foreign Relations and Intercourse.

§ 1405.   Creation or alteration of district or division

Actions or proceedings pending at the time of the creation of a new district or division or transfer of a county or territory from one division or district to another may be tried in the district or division as it existed at the institution of the action or proceeding, or in the district or division so created or to which the county or territory is so transferred as the parties shall agree or the court direct.

(June 25, 1948, c. 646, 62 Stat. 937.)

§ 1406.　　Cure or waiver of defects

(a)　The district court of a district in which is filed a case laying venue in the wrong division or district shall dismiss, or if it be in the interest of justice, transfer such case to any district or division in which it could have been brought.

(b)　Nothing in this chapter shall impair the jurisdiction of a district court of any matter involving a party who does not interpose timely and sufficient objection to the venue.

(c)　As used in this section, the term "district court" includes the District Court of Guam, the District Court for the Northern Mariana Islands, and the District Court of the Virgin Islands, and the term "district" includes the territorial jurisdiction of each such court.

(June 25, 1948, c. 646, 62 Stat. 937; May 24, 1949, c. 139, § 81, 63 Stat. 101; Sept. 13, 1960, Pub.L. 86–770, § 1, 74 Stat. 912; Oct. 18, 1962, Pub.L. 87–845, § 10, 76A Stat. 699; Apr. 2, 1982, Pub.L. 97–164, Title I, § 132, 96 Stat. 39; Oct. 19, 1996, Pub.L. 104–317, Title VI, § 610(b), 110 Stat. 3860.)

§ 1407.　　Multidistrict litigation

(a)　When civil actions involving one or more common questions of fact are pending in different districts, such actions may be transferred to any district for coordinated or consolidated pretrial proceedings. Such transfers shall be made by the judicial panel on multidistrict litigation authorized by this section upon its determination that transfers for such proceedings will be for the convenience of parties and witnesses and will promote the just and efficient conduct of such actions. Each action so transferred shall be remanded by the panel at or before the conclusion of such pretrial proceedings to the district from which it was transferred unless it shall have been previously terminated: *Provided, however,* That the panel may separate any claim, cross-claim, counter-claim, or third-party claim and remand any of such claims before the remainder of the action is remanded.

(b)　Such coordinated or consolidated pretrial proceedings shall be conducted by a judge or judges to whom such actions are assigned by the judicial panel on multidistrict litigation. For this purpose, upon request of the panel, a circuit judge or a district judge may be designated and assigned temporarily for service in the transferee district by the Chief Justice of the United States or the chief judge of the circuit, as may be required, in accordance with the provisions of chapter 13 of this title. With the consent of the transferee district court, such actions may be assigned by the panel to a judge or judges of such district. The judge or judges to whom such actions are assigned, the members of the judicial panel on multidistrict litigation, and other circuit and district judges designated when needed by the panel may exercise the powers of a district judge in any district for the purpose of conducting pretrial depositions in such coordinated or consolidated pretrial proceedings.

(c)　Proceedings for the transfer of an action under this section may be initiated by—

(i)　the judicial panel on multidistrict litigation upon its own initiative, or

(ii)　motion filed with the panel by a party in any action in which transfer for coordinated or consolidated pretrial proceedings under this section may be appropriate. A copy of such motion shall be filed in the district court in which the moving party's action is pending.

The panel shall give notice to the parties in all actions in which transfers for coordinated or consolidated pretrial proceedings are contemplated, and such notice shall specify the time and place of any hearing to determine whether such transfer shall be made. Orders of the panel to set a hearing and other orders of the panel issued prior to the order either directing or denying transfer shall be filed in the office of the clerk of the district court in which a transfer hearing is to be or has been held. The panel's order of transfer shall be based upon a record of such hearing at which material evidence may be offered by any party to an action pending in any district that would be affected by the proceedings under this section, and shall be supported by findings of fact and conclusions of law based upon such record. Orders of transfer and such other orders as the panel may make thereafter shall be filed in the office of the clerk of the district court of the transferee district and shall be effective when thus filed. The clerk of the transferee district court shall forthwith transmit a certified copy of the panel's order to transfer to the clerk of the district court from which the action is being transferred. An order denying transfer shall be filed in each district wherein there is a case pending in which the motion for transfer has been made.

(d) The judicial panel on multidistrict litigation shall consist of seven circuit and district judges designated from time to time by the Chief Justice of the United States, no two of whom shall be from the same circuit. The concurrence of four members shall be necessary to any action by the panel.

(e) No proceedings for review of any order of the panel may be permitted except by extraordinary writ pursuant to the provisions of title 28, section 1651, United States Code. Petitions for an extraordinary writ to review an order of the panel to set a transfer hearing and other orders of the panel issued prior to the order either directing or denying transfer shall be filed only in the court of appeals having jurisdiction over the district in which a hearing is to be or has been held. Petitions for an extraordinary writ to review an order to transfer or orders subsequent to transfer shall be filed only in the court of appeals having jurisdiction over the transferee district. There shall be no appeal or review of an order of the panel denying a motion to transfer for consolidated or coordinated proceedings.

(f) The panel may prescribe rules for the conduct of its business not inconsistent with Acts of Congress and the Federal Rules of Civil Procedure.

(g) Nothing in this section shall apply to any action in which the United States is a complainant arising under the antitrust laws. "Antitrust laws" as used herein include those acts referred to in the Act of October 15, 1914, as amended (38 Stat. 730; 15 U.S.C. 12), and also include the Act of June 19, 1936 (49 Stat. 1526; 15 U.S.C. 13, 13a, and 13b) and the Act of September 26, 1914, as added March 21, 1938 (52 Stat. 116, 117; 15 U.S.C. 56); but shall not include section 4A of the Act of October 15, 1914, as added July 7, 1955 (69 Stat. 282; 15 U.S.C. 15a).

(h) Notwithstanding the provisions of section 1404 or subsection (f) of this section, the judicial panel on multidistrict litigation may consolidate and transfer with or without the consent of the parties, for both pretrial purposes and for trial, any action brought under section 4C of the Clayton Act.

(Added Pub.L. 90–296, § 1, Apr. 29, 1968, 82 Stat. 109; amended Pub.L. 94–435, Title III, § 303, Sept. 30, 1976, 90 Stat. 1396.)

§ 1408.　　　Venue of cases under title 11

Except as provided in section 1410 of this title, a case under title 11 may be commenced in the district court for the district—

(1) in which the domicile, residence, principal place of business in the United States, or principal assets in the United States, of the person or entity that is the subject of such case have been located for the one hundred and eighty days immediately preceding such commencement, or for a longer portion of such one-hundred-and-eighty-day period than the domicile, residence, or principal place of business, in the United States, or principal assets in the United States, of such person were located in any other district; or

(2) in which there is pending a case under title 11 concerning such person's affiliate, general partner, or partnership.

(Added Pub.L. 98–353, Title I, § 102(a), July 10, 1984, 98 Stat. 334.)

§ 1409.　　　Venue of proceedings arising under title 11 or arising in or related to cases under title 11

(a) Except as otherwise provided in subsections (b) and (d), a proceeding arising under title 11 or arising in or related to a case under title 11 may be commenced in the district court in which such case is pending.

(b) Except as provided in subsection (d) of this section, a trustee in a case under title 11 may commence a proceeding arising in or related to such case to recover a money judgment of or property worth less than $1,000[1] or a consumer debt of less than $15,000[1], or a debt (excluding a consumer debt) against a noninsider of less than $25,000[1], only in the district court for the district in which the defendant resides.

(c) Except as provided in subsection (b) of this section, a trustee in a case under title 11 may commence a proceeding arising in or related to such case as statutory successor to the debtor or creditors under section 541 or 544(b) of title 11 in the district court for the district where the State or Federal court sits in which, under applicable nonbankruptcy venue provisions, the debtor or creditors, as the case may be, may have commenced an action on which such proceeding is based if the case under title 11 had not been commenced.

(d) A trustee may commence a proceeding arising under title 11 or arising in or related to a case under title 11 based on a claim arising after the commencement of such case from the operation of the business of the debtor only in the district court for the district where a State or Federal court sits in which, under applicable nonbankruptcy venue provisions, an action on such claim may have been brought.

(e) A proceeding arising under title 11 or arising in or related to a case under title 11, based on a claim arising after the commencement of such case from the operation of the business of the debtor, may be commenced against the representative of the estate in such case in the district court for the district where the State or Federal court sits in which the party commencing such proceeding may, under applicable nonbankruptcy venue provisions, have brought an action on such claim, or in the district court in which such case is pending.

(Added Pub.L. 98–353, Title I, § 102(a), July 10, 1984, 98 Stat. 334; amended Pub.L. 109–8, Title IV, § 410, Apr. 20, 2005, 119 Stat. 106; Pub.L. 116–54, § 3(b), Aug. 23, 2019, 133 Stat. 1085.)

HISTORICAL AND STATUTORY NOTES

Adjustment of Dollar Amounts

The dollar amounts specified in this section were adjusted by notices of the Judicial Conference of the United States pursuant to section 104 of Title 11, Bankruptcy, as follows:

By notice published Feb. 12, 2019, 84 F.R. 3488, the Judicial Conference of the United States adjusted the dollar amounts in provisions specified in subsec. (b) of this section, effective Apr. 1, 2019, as follows: Adjusted $1,300 to $1,375. Adjusted $19,250 to $20,450. Adjusted $12,850 to $13,650 [which Congress subsequently adjusted to $25,000 effective August 23, 2019. Ed.].

By notice dated Feb. 16, 2016, 81 F.R. 8748, effective Apr. 1, 2016, in subsec. (b), dollar amounts "1,250", "18,675", and "12,475" were adjusted to "1,300", "19,250", and "12,850", respectively. See notice of the Judicial Conference of the United States set out as a note under section 104 of Title 11.

By notice dated Feb. 12, 2013, 78 F.R. 12089, effective Apr. 1, 2013, in subsec. (b), dollar amounts "1,175", "17,575", and "11,725" were adjusted to "1,250", "18,675", and "12,475", respectively.

By notice dated Feb. 19, 2010, 75 F.R. 8747, effective Apr. 1, 2010, in subsec. (b), dollar amounts "1,100", "16,425", and "10,950" were adjusted to "1,175", "17,575", and "11,725", respectively.

By notice dated Feb. 7, 2007, 72 F.R. 7082, effective Apr. 1, 2007, in subsec. (b), dollar amounts "1,000", "15,000", and "10,000" were adjusted to "1,100", "16,425", and "10,950", respectively.

§ 1410.   Venue of cases ancillary to foreign proceedings

A case under chapter 15 of title 11 may be commenced in the district court of the United States for the district—

---

[1]   [Footnote to 28 U.S.C. § 1409(b): Dollar amount as adjusted by the Judicial Conference of the United States. See adjustment of Dollar Amounts notes set out under this section and 11 U.S.C.A. § 104. [These adjustments are made every three years. Ed.]

   (1) in which the debtor has its principal place of business or principal assets in the United States;

   (2) if the debtor does not have a place of business or assets in the United States, in which there is pending against the debtor an action or proceeding in a Federal or State court; or

   (3) in a case other than those specified in paragraph (1) or (2), in which venue will be consistent with the interests of justice and the convenience of the parties, having regard to the relief sought by the foreign representative.

(Added Pub.L. 98–353, Title I, § 102(a), July 10, 1984, 98 Stat. 335; amended Pub.L. 109–8, Title VIII, § 802(c)(4), Apr. 20, 2005, 119 Stat. 146.)

§ 1411.   Jury trials

   (a) Except as provided in subsection (b) of this section, this chapter and title 11 do not affect any right to trial by jury that an individual has under applicable nonbankruptcy law with regard to a personal injury or wrongful death tort claim.

   (b) The district court may order the issues arising under section 303 of title 11 to be tried without a jury.

(Added Pub.L. 98–353, Title I, § 102(a), July 10, 1984, 98 Stat. 335.)

§ 1412.   Change of venue

   A district court may transfer a case or proceeding under title 11 to a district court for another district, in the interest of justice or for the convenience of the parties.

(Added Pub.L. 98–353, Title I, § 102(a), July 10, 1984, 98 Stat. 335.)

§ 1413.   Venue of cases under chapter 5 of title 3

   Notwithstanding the preceding provisions of this chapter, a civil action under section 1346(g) may be brought in the United States district court for the district in which the employee is employed or in the United States District Court for the District of Columbia.

(Added Pub.L. 104–331, § 3(b)(2)(A), Oct. 26, 1996, 110 Stat. 4069.)

CHAPTER 89—DISTRICT COURTS; REMOVAL OF CASES FROM STATE COURTS

---

   [1]   [Footnote to Chapter 89 table:] So in original. Does not conform to section catchline.

§ 1441.   Removal of civil actions

(a) **Generally.**—Except as otherwise expressly provided by Act of Congress, any civil action brought in a State court of which the district courts of the United States have original jurisdiction, may be removed by the defendant or the defendants, to the district court of the United States for the district and division embracing the place where such action is pending.

(b) **Removal based on diversity of citizenship.**—(1) In determining whether a civil action is removable on the basis of the jurisdiction under section 1332(a) of this title, the citizenship of defendants sued under fictitious names shall be disregarded.

(2) A civil action otherwise removable solely on the basis of the jurisdiction under section 1332(a) of this title may not be removed if any of the parties in interest properly joined and served as defendants is a citizen of the State in which such action is brought.

(c) **Joinder of Federal law claims and State law claims.**—(1) If a civil action includes—

(A) a claim arising under the Constitution, laws, or treaties of the United States (within the meaning of section 1331 of this title), and

(B) a claim not within the original or supplemental jurisdiction of the district court or a claim that has been made nonremovable by statute, the entire action may be removed if the action would be removable without the inclusion of the claim described in subparagraph (B).

(2) Upon removal of an action described in paragraph (1), the district court shall sever from the action all claims described in paragraph (1)(B) and shall remand the severed claims to the State court from which the action was removed. Only defendants against whom a claim described in paragraph (1)(A) has been asserted are required to join in or consent to the removal under paragraph (1).

(d) **Actions against foreign States.**—Any civil action brought in a State court against a foreign state as defined in section 1603(a) of this title may be removed by the foreign state to the district court of the United States for the district and division embracing the place where such action is pending. Upon removal the action shall be tried by the court without jury. Where removal is based upon this subsection, the time limitations of section 1446(b) of this chapter may be enlarged at any time for cause shown.

(e) **Multiparty, multiforum jurisdiction.**—(1) Notwithstanding the provisions of subsection (b) of this section, a defendant in a civil action in a State court may remove the action to the district court of the United States for the district and division embracing the place where the action is pending if—

(A) the action could have been brought in a United States district court under section 1369 of this title; or

(B) the defendant is a party to an action which is or could have been brought, in whole or in part, under section 1369 in a United States district court and arises from the same accident as the action in State court, even if the action to be removed could not have been brought in a district court as an original matter.

The removal of an action under this subsection shall be made in accordance with section 1446 of this title, except that a notice of removal may also be filed before trial of the action in State court within 30 days after the date on which the defendant first becomes a party to an action under section 1369 in a United States district court that arises from the same accident as the action in State court, or at a later time with leave of the district court.

(2) Whenever an action is removed under this subsection and the district court to which it is removed or transferred under section 1407(j)[1] has made a liability determination requiring further proceedings as to damages, the district court shall remand the action to the State court from which it had been removed for the determination of damages, unless the court finds that, for the convenience of parties and witnesses and in the interest of justice, the action should be retained for the determination of damages.

(3) Any remand under paragraph (2) shall not be effective until 60 days after the district court has issued an order determining liability and has certified its intention to remand the removed action for the determination of damages. An appeal with respect to the liability determination of the district court may be taken during that 60-day period to the court of appeals with appellate jurisdiction over the district court. In the event a party files such an appeal, the remand shall not be effective until the appeal has been finally disposed of. Once the remand has become effective, the liability determination shall not be subject to further review by appeal or otherwise.

(4) Any decision under this subsection concerning remand for the determination of damages shall not be reviewable by appeal or otherwise.

(5) An action removed under this subsection shall be deemed to be an action under section 1369 and an action in which jurisdiction is based on section 1369 of this title for purposes of this section and sections 1407, 1697, and 1785 of this title.

(6) Nothing in this subsection shall restrict the authority of the district court to transfer or dismiss an action on the ground of inconvenient forum.

(f) **Derivative removal jurisdiction.**—The court to which a civil action is removed under this section is not precluded from hearing and determining any claim in such civil action because the State court from which such civil action is removed did not have jurisdiction over that claim.

(June 25, 1948, c. 646, 62 Stat. 937; Oct. 21, 1976, Pub.L. 94–583, § 6, 90 Stat. 2898; June 19, 1986, Pub.L. 99–336, § 3(a), 100 Stat. 637; Nov. 19, 1988, Pub.L. 100–702, Title X, § 1016(a), 102 Stat. 4669; Dec. 1, 1990, Pub.L. 101–650, Title III, § 312, 104 Stat. 5114; Dec. 9, 1991, Pub.L. 102–198, § 4, 105 Stat. 1623; Nov. 2, 2002, Pub.L. 107–273, Div. C, Title I, § 11020(b)(3), 116 Stat. 1827; Pub.L. 112–63, Title I, § 103(a), Dec. 7, 2011, 125 Stat. 759.)

HISTORICAL AND STATUTORY NOTES

References in Text

Section 1407(j) of Title 28, referred to in subsec. (e)(2), does not exist.

§ 1442.   Federal officers or agencies sued or prosecuted

(a) A civil action or criminal prosecution that is commenced in a State court and that is against or directed to any of the following may be removed by them to the district court of the United States for the district and division embracing the place wherein it is pending:

(1) The United States or any agency thereof or any officer (or any person acting under that officer) of the United States or of any agency thereof, in an official or individual capacity, for or relating to any act under color of such office or on account of any right, title or authority claimed under any Act of Congress for the apprehension or punishment of criminals or the collection of the revenue.

(2) A property holder whose title is derived from any such officer, where such action or prosecution affects the validity of any law of the United States.

---

[1]   [Footnote to 28 U.S.C. § 1441(e)(2):] So in original. Section 1407 of this title does not contain a subsec. (j). [It is likely that subsection (a) is intended. Ed.]

(3) Any officer of the courts of the United States, for or relating to any act under color of office or in the performance of his duties;

(4) Any officer of either House of Congress, for or relating to any act in the discharge of his official duty under an order of such House.

(b) A personal action commenced in any State court by an alien against any citizen of a State who is, or at the time the alleged action accrued was, a civil officer of the United States and is a nonresident of such State, wherein jurisdiction is obtained by the State court by personal service of process, may be removed by the defendant to the district court of the United States for the district and division in which the defendant was served with process.

(c) Solely for purposes of determining the propriety of removal under subsection (a), a law enforcement officer, who is the defendant in a criminal prosecution, shall be deemed to have been acting under the color of his office if the officer—

(1) protected an individual in the presence of the officer from a crime of violence;

(2) provided immediate assistance to an individual who suffered, or who was threatened with, bodily harm; or

(3) prevented the escape of any individual who the officer reasonably believed to have committed, or was about to commit, in the presence of the officer, a crime of violence that resulted in, or was likely to result in, death or serious bodily injury.

(d) In this section, the following definitions apply:

(1) The terms "civil action" and "criminal prosecution" include any proceeding (whether or not ancillary to another proceeding) to the extent that in such proceeding a judicial order, including a subpoena for testimony or documents, is sought or issued. If removal is sought for a proceeding described in the previous sentence, and there is no other basis for removal, only that proceeding may be removed to the district court.

(2) The term "crime of violence" has the meaning given that term in section 16 of title 18.

(3) The term "law enforcement officer" means any employee described in subparagraph (A), (B), or (C) of section 8401(17) of title 5 and any special agent in the Diplomatic Security Service of the Department of State.

(4) The term "serious bodily injury" has the meaning given that term in section 1365 of title 18.

(5) The term "State" includes the District of Columbia, United States territories and insular possessions, and Indian country (as defined in section 1151 of title 18).

(6) The term "State court" includes the Superior Court of the District of Columbia, a court of a United States territory or insular possession, and a tribal court.

(June 25, 1948, c. 646, 62 Stat. 938; Pub.L. 104–317, Title II, § 206(a), Oct. 19, 1996, 110 Stat. 3850; Pub.L. 112–51, § 2(a), (b), Nov. 9, 2011, 125 Stat. 545; Pub.L. 112–239, Div. A, Title X, § 1087, Jan. 2, 2013, 126 Stat. 1969.)

§ 1442a.   Members of armed forces sued or prosecuted

A civil or criminal prosecution in a court of a State of the United States against a member of the armed forces of the United States on account of an act done under color of his office or status, or in respect to which he claims any right, title, or authority under a law of the United States respecting the armed forces thereof, or under the law of war, may at any time before the trial or final hearing thereof be removed for trial into the district court of the United States for the district where it is pending in the manner prescribed by law, and it shall thereupon be entered on the docket of the district court, which shall proceed as if the cause had been originally commenced therein and shall have full power to hear and determine the cause.

(Added Aug. 10, 1956, c. 1041, § 19(a), 70A Stat. 626.)

HISTORICAL AND STATUTORY NOTES

Codifications

Section was from the Uniform Code of Military Justice, Act May 5, 1950, c. 169, § 9, 64 Stat. 146, which was based on Article 117, Articles of War, Act June 4, 1920, c. 227, subch. II, § 1, 41 Stat. 811, as amended June 24, 1948, c. 625, Title II, § 242, 62 Stat. 642.

§ 1443.   Civil rights cases

Any of the following civil actions or criminal prosecutions, commenced in a State court may be removed by the defendant to the district court of the United States for the district and division embracing the place wherein it is pending:

(1) Against any person who is denied or cannot enforce in the courts of such State a right under any law providing for the equal civil rights of citizens of the United States, or of all persons within the jurisdiction thereof;

(2) For any act under color of authority derived from any law providing for equal rights, or for refusing to do any act on the ground that it would be inconsistent with such law.

(June 25, 1948, c. 646, 62 Stat. 938.)

§ 1444.   Foreclosure action against United States

Any action brought under section 2410 of this title against the United States in any State court may be removed by the United States to the district court of the United States for the district and division in which the action is pending.

(June 25, 1948, c. 646, 62 Stat. 938; May 24, 1949, c. 139, § 82, 63 Stat. 101.)

§ 1445.   Nonremovable actions

(a) A civil action in any State court against a railroad or its receivers or trustees, arising under sections 1–4 and 5–10 of the Act of April 22, 1908 (45 U.S.C. 51–54, 55–60), may not be removed to any district court of the United States.

(b) A civil action in any State court against a carrier or its receivers or trustees to recover damages for delay, loss, or injury of shipments, arising under section 11706 or 14706 of title 49, may not be removed to any district court of the United States unless the matter in controversy exceeds $10,000, exclusive of interest and costs.

(c) A civil action in any State court arising under the workmen's compensation laws of such State may not be removed to any district court of the United States.

(d) A civil action in any State court arising under section 40302 of the Violence Against Women Act of 1994 may not be removed to any district court of the United States.

(June 25, 1948, c. 646, 62 Stat. 939; July 25, 1958, Pub.L. 85–554, § 5, 72 Stat. 415; Oct. 17, 1978, Pub.L. 95–473, § 2(a)(3)(A), 92 Stat. 1465; Oct. 20, 1978, Pub.L. 95–486, § 9(b), 92 Stat. 1634; Sept. 13, 1994, Pub.L. 103–322, Title IV, § 40302(e)(5), 108 Stat. 1942; Dec. 29, 1995, Pub.L. 104–88, Title III, § 305(b), 109 Stat. 944; Oct. 11, 1996, Pub.L. 104–287, § 3, 110 Stat. 3388.)

HISTORICAL AND STATUTORY NOTES

References in Text

The Act of April 22, 1908, referred to in subsec. (a), popularly referred to as the [second] Employers' Liability Act, is Act Apr. 22, 1908, c. 149, 35 Stat. 65, as amended, which is classified generally to chapter 2 (section 51 et seq.) of Title 45, Railroads. For complete classification of this Act to the Code, see Short Title note set out under section 51 of Title 45 and Tables.

Section 40302 of the Violence Against Women Act of 1994, referred to in subsec. (d), means section 40302 of Pub.L. 103–322, the Violent Crime Control and Law Enforcement Act of 1994 (Title IV of such Act is the Violence Against Women Act of 1994), which is classified to section 13981 of Title 42, The Public Health and Welfare.

§ 1446.   Procedure for removal of civil actions

(a) Generally.—A defendant or defendants desiring to remove any civil action from a State court shall file in the district court of the United States for the district and division within which such action is pending a notice of removal signed pursuant to Rule 11 of the Federal Rules of Civil Procedure and containing a short and plain statement of the grounds for removal, together with a copy of all process, pleadings, and orders served upon such defendant or defendants in such action.

(b) Requirements; generally.—**(1)** The notice of removal of a civil action or proceeding shall be filed within 30 days after the receipt by the defendant, through service or otherwise, of a copy of the initial pleading setting forth the claim for relief upon which such action or proceeding is based, or within 30 days after the service of summons upon the defendant if such initial pleading has then been filed in court and is not required to be served on the defendant, whichever period is shorter.

(2)(A)   When a civil action is removed solely under section 1441(a), all defendants who have been properly joined and served must join in or consent to the removal of the action.

(B) Each defendant shall have 30 days after receipt by or service on that defendant of the initial pleading or summons described in paragraph (1) to file the notice of removal.

(C) If defendants are served at different times, and a later-served defendant files a notice of removal, any earlier-served defendant may consent to the removal even though that earlier-served defendant did not previously initiate or consent to removal.

(3) Except as provided in subsection (c), if the case stated by the initial pleading is not removable, a notice of removal may be filed within 30 days after receipt by the defendant, through service or otherwise, of a copy of an amended pleading, motion, order or other paper from which it may first be ascertained that the case is one which is or has become removable.

(c) Requirements; removal based on diversity of citizenship.—**(1)** A case may not be removed under subsection (b)(3) on the basis of jurisdiction conferred by section 1332 more than 1 year after commencement of the action, unless the district court finds that the plaintiff has acted in bad faith in order to prevent a defendant from removing the action.

(2) If removal of a civil action is sought on the basis of the jurisdiction conferred by section 1332(a), the sum demanded in good faith in the initial pleading shall be deemed to be the amount in controversy, except that—

(A) the notice of removal may assert the amount in controversy if the initial pleading seeks—

(i) nonmonetary relief; or

(ii) a money judgment, but the State practice either does not permit demand for a specific sum or permits recovery of damages in excess of the amount demanded; and

(B) removal of the action is proper on the basis of an amount in controversy asserted under subparagraph (A) if the district court finds, by the preponderance of the evidence, that the amount in controversy exceeds the amount specified in section 1332(a).

(3)(A)   If the case stated by the initial pleading is not removable solely because the amount in controversy does not exceed the amount specified in section 1332(a), information relating to the amount in controversy in the record of the State proceeding, or in responses to discovery, shall be treated as an 'other paper' under subsection (b)(3).

(B) If the notice of removal is filed more than 1 year after commencement of the action and the district court finds that the plaintiff deliberately failed to disclose the actual amount in controversy to prevent removal, that finding shall be deemed bad faith under paragraph (1).

(d) Notice to adverse parties and State court.—Promptly after the filing of such notice of removal of a civil action the defendant or defendants shall give written notice thereof to all adverse parties and shall file a copy of the notice with the clerk of such State court, which shall effect the removal and the State court shall proceed no further unless and until the case is remanded.

(e) Counterclaim in 337 proceeding.—With respect to any counterclaim removed to a district court pursuant to section 337(c) of the Tariff Act of 1930, the district court shall resolve such counterclaim in the same manner as an original complaint under the Federal Rules of Civil Procedure, except that the payment of a filing fee shall not be required in such cases and the counterclaim shall relate back to the date of the original complaint in the proceeding before the International Trade Commission under section 337 of that Act.

[(f) Redesignated (e)]

(g) Where the civil action or criminal prosecution that is removable under section 1442(a) is a proceeding in which a judicial order for testimony or documents is sought or issued or sought to be enforced, the 30-day requirement of subsection (b) of this section and paragraph (1) of section 1455(b) is satisfied if the person or entity desiring to remove the proceeding files the notice of removal not later than 30 days after receiving, through service, notice of any such proceeding.

(June 25, 1948, c. 646, 62 Stat. 939; May 24, 1949, c. 139, § 83, 63 Stat. 101; Sept. 29, 1965, Pub.L. 89–215, 79 Stat. 887; July 30, 1977, Pub.L. 95–78, § 3, 91 Stat. 321; Nov. 19, 1988, Pub.L. 100–702, Title X, § 1016(b), 102 Stat. 4669; Dec. 9, 1991, Pub.L. 102–198, § 10(a), 105 Stat. 1626; Dec. 8, 1994, Pub.L. 103–465, Title III, § 321(b)(2), 108 Stat. 4946; Oct. 19, 1996, Pub.L. 104–317, Title VI, § 603, 110 Stat. 3857; Pub.L. 112–51, § 2(c), Nov. 9, 2011, 125 Stat. 545; Pub.L. 112–63, Title I, §§ 103(b), 104, Dec. 7, 2011, 125 Stat. 760, 762.)

§ 1447.   Procedure after removal generally

(a) In any case removed from a State court, the district court may issue all necessary orders and process to bring before it all proper parties whether served by process issued by the State court or otherwise.

(b) It may require the removing party to file with its clerk copies of all records and proceedings in such State court or may cause the same to be brought before it by writ of certiorari issued to such State court.

(c) A motion to remand the case on the basis of any defect other than lack of subject matter jurisdiction must be made within 30 days after the filing of the notice of removal under section 1446(a). If at any time before final judgment it appears that the district court lacks subject matter jurisdiction, the case shall be remanded. An order remanding the case may require payment of just costs and any actual expenses, including attorney fees, incurred as a result of the removal. A certified copy of the order of remand shall be mailed by the clerk to the clerk of the State court. The State court may thereupon proceed with such case.

(d) An order remanding a case to the State court from which it was removed is not reviewable on appeal or otherwise, except that an order remanding a case to the State court from which it was removed pursuant to section 1442 or 1443 of this title shall be reviewable by appeal or otherwise.

(e) If after removal the plaintiff seeks to join additional defendants whose joinder would destroy subject matter jurisdiction, the court may deny joinder, or permit joinder and remand the action to the State court.

(June 25, 1948, c. 646, 62 Stat. 939; May 24, 1949, c. 139, § 84, 63 Stat. 102; July 2, 1964, Pub.L. 88–352, Title IX, § 901, 78 Stat. 266; Nov. 19, 1988, Pub.L. 100–702, Title X, § 1016(c), 102 Stat. 4670; Dec. 9, 1991,

Pub.L. 102–198, § 10(b), 105 Stat. 1626; Oct. 1, 1996, Pub.L. 104–219, § 1, 110 Stat. 3022; Pub.L. 112–51, § 2(d), Nov. 9, 2011, 125 Stat. 546.)

HISTORICAL AND STATUTORY NOTES

Exception to Subsection (d)

Section 3(c) of Act Aug. 4, 1947, c. 458, 61 Stat. 732, provided in part that the United States shall have the right to appeal from any order of remand entered in any case removed to a United States district court pursuant to the provisions of Act Apr. 12, 1926, c. 115, 44 Stat. 239. These Acts referred to herein relate to restrictions on land of the Five Civilized Tribes of Oklahoma and are set out as notes under section 355 of Title 25, Indians.

§ 1448.   Process after removal

In all cases removed from any State court to any district court of the United States in which any one or more of the defendants has not been served with process or in which the service has not been perfected prior to removal, or in which process served proves to be defective, such process or service may be completed or new process issued in the same manner as in cases originally filed in such district court.

This section shall not deprive any defendant upon whom process is served after removal of his right to move to remand the case.

(June 25, 1948, c. 646, 62 Stat. 940.)

§ 1449.   State court record supplied

Where a party is entitled to copies of the records and proceedings in any suit or prosecution in a State court, to be used in any district court of the United States, and the clerk of such State court, upon demand, and the payment or tender of the legal fees, fails to deliver certified copies, the district court may, on affidavit reciting such facts, direct such record to be supplied by affidavit or otherwise. Thereupon such proceedings, trial, and judgment may be had in such district court, and all such process awarded, as if certified copies had been filed in the district court.

(June 25, 1948, c. 646, 62 Stat. 940; May 24, 1949, c. 139, § 85, 63 Stat. 102.)

§ 1450.   Attachment or sequestration; securities

Whenever any action is removed from a State court to a district court of the United States, any attachment or sequestration of the goods or estate of the defendant in such action in the State court shall hold the goods or estate to answer the final judgment or decree in the same manner as they would have been held to answer final judgment or decree had it been rendered by the State court.

All bonds, undertakings, or security given by either party in such action prior to its removal shall remain valid and effectual notwithstanding such removal.

All injunctions, orders, and other proceedings had in such action prior to its removal shall remain in full force and effect until dissolved or modified by the district court.

(June 25, 1948, c. 646, 62 Stat. 940.)

§ 1451.   Definitions

For purposes of this chapter—

(1)   The term "State court" includes the Superior Court of the District of Columbia.

(2)   The term "State" includes the District of Columbia.

(Added Pub.L. 91–358, Title I, § 172(d)(1), July 29, 1970, 84 Stat. 591.)

§ 1452.   Removal of claims related to bankruptcy cases

(a)   A party may remove any claim or cause of action in a civil action other than a proceeding before the United States Tax Court or a civil action by a governmental unit to enforce such governmental unit's police or regulatory power, to the district court for the district where such civil action is pending, if such district court has jurisdiction of such claim or cause of action under section 1334 of this title.

(b)   The court to which such claim or cause of action is removed may remand such claim or cause of action on any equitable ground. An order entered under this subsection remanding a claim or cause of action, or a decision to not remand, is not reviewable by appeal or otherwise by the court of appeals under section 158(d), 1291, or 1292 of this title or by the Supreme Court of the United States under section 1254 of this title.

(Added Pub.L. 98–353, Title I, § 103(a), July 10, 1984, 98 Stat. 335; amended Pub.L. 101–650, Title III, § 309(c), Dec. 1, 1990, 104 Stat. 5113.)

§ 1453.   Removal of class actions

(a) Definitions.—In this section, the terms "class", "class action", "class certification order", and "class member" shall have the meanings given such terms under section 1332(d)(1).

(b) In general.—A class action may be removed to a district court of the United States in accordance with section 1446 (except that the 1-year limitation under section 1446(c)(1) shall not apply), without regard to whether any defendant is a citizen of the State in which the action is brought, except that such action may be removed by any defendant without the consent of all defendants.

(c) Review of remand orders.—

    (1) In general.—Section 1447 shall apply to any removal of a case under this section, except that notwithstanding section 1447(d), a court of appeals may accept an appeal from an order of a district court granting or denying a motion to remand a class action to the State court from which it was removed if application is made to the court of appeals not more than 10 days after entry of the order.

    (2) Time period for judgment.—If the court of appeals accepts an appeal under paragraph (1), the court shall complete all action on such appeal, including rendering judgment, not later than 60 days after the date on which such appeal was filed, unless an extension is granted under paragraph (3).

    (3) Extension of time period.—The court of appeals may grant an extension of the 60-day period described in paragraph (2) if—

       (A) all parties to the proceeding agree to such extension, for any period of time; or

       (B) such extension is for good cause shown and in the interests of justice, for a period not to exceed 10 days.

    (4) Denial of appeal.—If a final judgment on the appeal under paragraph (1) is not issued before the end of the period described in paragraph (2), including any extension under paragraph (3), the appeal shall be denied.

(d) Exception.—This section shall not apply to any class action that solely involves—

    (1) a claim concerning a covered security as defined under section 16(f)(3) of the Securities Act of 1933 (15 U.S.C. 78p(f)(3)[1]) and section 28(f)(5)(E) of the Securities Exchange Act of 1934 (15 U.S.C. 78bb(f)(5)(E));

---

[1]   [Footnote to 28 U.S.C. § 1453(d):] So in original. Probably should be "77p(f)(3)".

(2) a claim that relates to the internal affairs or governance of a corporation or other form of business enterprise and arises under or by virtue of the laws of the State in which such corporation or business enterprise is incorporated or organized; or

(3) a claim that relates to the rights, duties (including fiduciary duties), and obligations relating to or created by or pursuant to any security (as defined under section 2(a)(1) of the Securities Act of 1933 (15 U.S.C. 77b(a)(1)) and the regulations issued thereunder).

(Added Pub.L. 109–2, § 5(a), Feb. 18, 2005, 119 Stat. 12; amended Pub.L. 111–16, § 6(2), May 7, 2009, 123 Stat. 1608; Pub.L. 112–63, Title I, § 103(d)(2), Dec. 7, 2011, 125 Stat. 762.)

HISTORICAL AND STATUTORY NOTES

References in Text

Section 16(f)(3) of the Securities Act of 1933, referred to in subsec. (d)(1), is May 27, 1933, c. 38, Title I, § 16(f)(3), 48 Stat. 84, as amended, which is classified to 15 U.S.C.A. § 78p(f)(3).

Section 28(f)(5)(E) of the Securities Exchange Act of 1934, referred to in subsec. (d)(1), is May 27, 1933, c. 38, Title I, § 2(f)(5)(E), 48 Stat. 74, as amended, which is classified to 15 U.S.C.A. § 78bb(f)(5)(E).

Section 2(a)(1) of the Securities Act of 1933, referred to in subsec. (d)(3), is May 27, 1933, c. 38, Title I, § 2(a)(1), 48 Stat. 74, as amended, which is classified to 15 U.S.C.A. § 77b(a)(1).

Effective and Applicability Provisions

2011 Acts. Subject to certain conditions, amendments made by Title I of Pub.L. 112–63, shall take effect upon the expiration of the 30-day period beginning on Dec. 7, 2011, and shall apply to any action or prosecution commenced on or after such effective date, see Pub.L. 112–63, § 105(d), set out as a note under 28 U.S.C.A. § 1332.

2009 Acts. Amendments by Pub.L. 111–16 effective Dec. 1, 2009, see Pub.L. 111–16, § 7, set out as a note under 11 U.S.C.A. § 109.

2005 Acts. Amendments by Class Action Fairness Act of 2005, Pub.L. 109–2, Feb. 18, 2005, 119 Stat. 4, applicable to any civil action commenced on or after Feb. 18, 2005, see Pub.L. 109–2, § 9, set out as a note under 28 U.S.C.A. § 1332.

§ 1454.　　Patent, plant variety protection, and copyright cases

(a)　In general.—A civil action in which any party asserts a claim for relief arising under any Act of Congress relating to patents, plant variety protection, or copyrights may be removed to the district court of the United States for the district and division embracing the place where the action is pending.

(b)　Special rules.—The removal of an action under this section shall be made in accordance with section 1446, except that if the removal is based solely on this section—

(1) the action may be removed by any party; and

(2) the time limitations contained in section 1446(b) may be extended at any time for cause shown.

(c)　Clarification of jurisdiction in certain cases.—The court to which a civil action is removed under this section is not precluded from hearing and determining any claim in the civil action because the State court from which the civil action is removed did not have jurisdiction over that claim.

(d)　Remand.—If a civil action is removed solely under this section, the district court—

(1) shall remand all claims that are neither a basis for removal under subsection (a) nor within the original or supplemental jurisdiction of the district court under any Act of Congress; and

(2) may, under the circumstances specified in section 1367(c), remand any claims within the supplemental jurisdiction of the district court under section 1367.

(Added Pub.L. 112–29, § 19(c)(1), Sept. 16, 2011, 125 Stat. 332.)

HISTORICAL AND STATUTORY NOTES

Effective and Applicability Provisions

2011 Acts. Amendment by Pub.L. 112–29, § 19, shall apply to any civil action commenced on or after Sept. 16, 2011, see Pub.L. 112–29, § 19(e), set out as a note under 28 U.S.C.A. § 1295.

§ 1455.   Procedure for removal of criminal prosecutions

(a) **Notice of removal.**—A defendant or defendants desiring to remove any criminal prosecution from a State court shall file in the district court of the United States for the district and division within which such prosecution is pending a notice of removal signed pursuant to Rule 11 of the Federal Rules of Civil Procedure and containing a short and plain statement of the grounds for removal, together with a copy of all process, pleadings, and orders served upon such defendant or defendants in such action.

(b) **Requirements.**—(1) A notice of removal of a criminal prosecution shall be filed not later than 30 days after the arraignment in the State court, or at any time before trial, whichever is earlier, except that for good cause shown the United States district court may enter an order granting the defendant or defendants leave to file the notice at a later time.

(2) A notice of removal of a criminal prosecution shall include all grounds for such removal. A failure to state grounds that exist at the time of the filing of the notice shall constitute a waiver of such grounds, and a second notice may be filed only on grounds not existing at the time of the original notice. For good cause shown, the United States district court may grant relief from the limitations of this paragraph.

(3) The filing of a notice of removal of a criminal prosecution shall not prevent the State court in which such prosecution is pending from proceeding further, except that a judgment of conviction shall not be entered unless the prosecution is first remanded.

(4) The United States district court in which such notice is filed shall examine the notice promptly. If it clearly appears on the face of the notice and any exhibits annexed thereto that removal should not be permitted, the court shall make an order for summary remand.

(5) If the United States district court does not order the summary remand of such prosecution, it shall order an evidentiary hearing to be held promptly and, after such hearing, shall make such disposition of the prosecution as justice shall require. If the United States district court determines that removal shall be permitted, it shall so notify the State court in which prosecution is pending, which shall proceed no further.

(c) **Writ of habeas corpus.**—If the defendant or defendants are in actual custody on process issued by the State court, the district court shall issue its writ of habeas corpus, and the marshal shall thereupon take such defendant or defendants into the marshal's custody and deliver a copy of the writ to the clerk of such State court.

(Added Pub.L. 112–63, Title I, § 103(c), Dec. 7, 2011, 125 Stat. 761.)

[CHAPTER 90—DISTRICT COURTS AND BANKRUPTCY COURTS] [OMITTED]

HISTORICAL AND STATUTORY NOTES

Codifications

Chapter 90, consisting of sections 1471 to 1482, which was added by Pub.L.95–598, Title II, § 241(a), Nov. 6, 1978, 92 Stat. 2668, and which related to district courts and bankruptcy courts, did not become effective pursuant to section 402(b) of Pub.L. 95–598, as amended, set out as an Effective and Applicability Provisions note preceding section 101 of Title 11, Bankruptcy.

Transition to New Court System

Pub.L. 95–598, Title IV, § 409, Nov. 6, 1978, 92 Stat. 2687, as amended by Pub.L. 98–249, § 1(d), Mar. 31, 1984, 98 Stat. 116; Pub.L. 98–271, § 1(d), Apr. 30, 1984, 98 Stat. 163; Pub.L. 98–299, § 1(d), May 25, 1984, 98 Stat. 214; Pub.L. 98–325, § 1(d), June 20, 1984, 98 Stat. 268; Pub.L. 98–353, Title I, § 121(d), July 10, 1984, 98 Stat. 346, was repealed by Pub.L. 98–353, Title I, §§ 114, 122(a), July 10, 1984, 98 Stat. 343, 346, eff. July 10, 1984. The repealed section had provided for transfer to the new court system of 1) cases, and matters and proceedings in cases, under the Bankruptcy Act [former Title 11] pending at the end of Sept. 30, 1983, in the courts of bankruptcy continued under section 404(a) of Pub.L. 95–598, with certain exceptions, and 2) cases and proceedings arising under or related to cases under Title 11 pending at the end of July 9, 1984, in the courts of bankruptcy continued under section 404(a) of Pub.L. 95–598, and directed that civil actions pending on July 9, 1984, over which a bankruptcy court had jurisdiction on July 9, 1984, not abate, that actions not finally determined before Apr. 1, 1985, be removed to a bankruptcy court under this chapter, and that all law books, publications, etc., furnished bankruptcy judges as of July 9, 1984, be transferred to the United States bankruptcy courts under the supervision of the Director of the Administrative Office of the United States Courts.

CHAPTER 91—UNITED STATES COURT OF FEDERAL CLAIMS

§ 1491.   Claims against United States generally; actions involving Tennessee Valley Authority

(a)(1)   The United States Court of Federal Claims shall have jurisdiction to render judgment upon any claim against the United States founded either upon the Constitution, or any Act of Congress or any regulation of an executive department, or upon any express or implied contract with the United States, or for liquidated or unliquidated damages in cases not sounding in tort. For the purpose of this paragraph, an express or implied contract with the Army and Air Force Exchange Service, Navy Exchanges, Marine Corps Exchanges, Coast Guard Exchanges, or Exchange Councils of the National Aeronautics and Space Administration shall be considered an express or implied contract with the United States.

(2)   To provide an entire remedy and to complete the relief afforded by the judgment, the court may, as an incident of and collateral to any such judgment, issue orders directing restoration to office or position, placement in appropriate duty or retirement status, and correction of applicable records, and such orders may be issued to any appropriate official of the United States. In any case within its jurisdiction, the court shall have the power to remand appropriate matters to any administrative or executive body or official with such direction as it may deem proper and just. The Court of Federal Claims shall have jurisdiction to render judgment upon any claim by or against, or dispute with, a contractor arising under section 7104(b)(1) of title 41, including a dispute concerning termination of a contract, rights in tangible or intangible property, compliance with cost accounting standards, and other nonmonetary disputes on which a decision of the contracting officer has been issued under section 6[1] of that Act.

(b)(1) Both the Unites[2] States Court of Federal Claims and the district courts of the United States shall have jurisdiction to render judgment on an action by an interested party objecting to a solicitation by a Federal agency for bids or proposals for a proposed contract or to a proposed award or the award of a contract or any alleged violation of statute or regulation in connection with a procurement or a proposed procurement. Both the United States Court of Federal Claims and the district courts of the United States shall have jurisdiction to entertain such an action without regard to whether suit is instituted before or after the contract is awarded.

    (2) To afford relief in such an action, the courts may award any relief that the court considers proper, including declaratory and injunctive relief except that any monetary relief shall be limited to bid preparation and proposal costs.

    (3) In exercising jurisdiction under this subsection, the courts shall give due regard to the interests of national defense and national security and the need for expeditious resolution of the action.

    (4) In any action under this subsection, the courts shall review the agency's decision pursuant to the standards set forth in section 706 of title 5.

    (5) If an interested party who is a member of the private sector commences an action described in paragraph (1) with respect to a public-private competition conducted under Office of Management and Budget Circular A-76 regarding the performance of an activity or function of a Federal agency, or a decision to convert a function performed by Federal employees to private sector performance without a competition under Office of Management and Budget Circular A-76, then an interested party described in section 3551(2)(B) of title 31 shall be entitled to intervene in that action.

    (6) Jurisdiction over any action described in paragraph (1) arising out of a maritime contract, or a solicitation for a proposed maritime contract, shall be governed by this section and shall not be subject to the jurisdiction of the district courts of the United States under the Suits in Admiralty Act (chapter 309 of title 46) or the Public Vessels Act (chapter 311 of title 46).

(c) Nothing herein shall be construed to give the United States Court of Federal Claims jurisdiction of any civil action within the exclusive jurisdiction of the Court of International Trade, or of any action against, or founded on conduct of, the Tennessee Valley Authority, or to amend or modify the provisions of the Tennessee Valley Authority Act of 1933 with respect to actions by or against the Authority.

(June 25, 1948, c. 646, 62 Stat. 940; July 28, 1953, c. 253, § 7, 67 Stat. 226; Sept. 3, 1954, c. 1263, § 44(a), (b), 68 Stat. 1241; July 23, 1970, Pub.L. 91–350, § 1(b), 84 Stat. 449; Aug. 29, 1972, Pub.L. 92–415, § 1, 86 Stat. 652; Nov. 1, 1978, Pub.L. 95–563, § 14(i), 92 Stat. 2391; Oct. 10, 1980, Pub.L. 96–417, Title V, § 509, 94 Stat. 1743; Apr. 2, 1982, Pub.L. 97–164, Title I, § 133(a), 96 Stat. 39; Oct. 29, 1992, Pub.L. 102–572, Title IX, §§ 902(a), 907(b)(1), 106 Stat. 4516, 4519; Oct. 19, 1996, Pub.L. 104–320, § 12(a), 110 Stat. 3874; Dec. 26, 2007, Pub.L. 110–161, Div. D, Title VII, § 739(c)(2), 121 Stat. 2031; Jan. 28, 2008, Pub.L. 110–181, Div. A, Title III, § 326(c), 122 Stat. 63; Oct. 14, 2008, Pub.L. 110–417, Div. A, Title X, § 1061(d), 122 Stat. 4613;

---

[1]   See References in Text note below.

[2]   So in original. Probably should be "United".

Jan. 4, 2011, Pub.L. 111–350, § 5(g)(7), 124 Stat. 3848; Pub.L. 112–81, Div. A, Title VIII, § 861(a), Dec. 31, 2011, 125 Stat. 1521.)

HISTORICAL AND STATUTORY NOTES

References in Text

Section 6 of the Contract Disputes Act of 1978, referred to in subsec. (a)(2), was classified to section 605 of former Title 41, Public Contracts, and was repealed and restated as subsecs. (a) to (c)(1) and (d) to (h) of section 7103 of Title 41, Public Contracts, by Pub. L. 111–350, §§ 3, 7(b), Jan. 4, 2011, 124 Stat. 3677, 3855.

The Tennessee Valley Authority Act of 1933, referred to in subsec. (c), is act May 18, 1933, ch. 32, 48 Stat. 58, which is classified generally to chapter 12A (§ 831 et seq.) of Title 16, Conservation. For complete classification of this Act to the Code, see section 831 of Title 16 and Tables.

§ 1492. Congressional reference cases

Any bill, except a bill for a pension, may be referred by either House of Congress to the chief judge of the United States Court of Federal Claims for a report in conformity with section 2509 of this title.

(June 25, 1948, c. 646, 62 Stat. 941; Oct. 15, 1966, Pub.L. 89–681, § 1, 80 Stat. 958; Apr. 2, 1982, Pub.L. 97–164, Title I, § 133(b), 96 Stat. 40; Oct. 29, 1992, Pub.L. 102–572, Title IX, § 902(a)(1), 106 Stat. 4516.)

[§ 1493. Repealed. July 28, 1953, c. 253, § 8, 67 Stat. 226]

HISTORICAL AND STATUTORY NOTES

Section, Act June 25, 1948, c. 646, 62 Stat. 941, authorized the Court of Claims to give legal advice to the heads of executive departments in matters referred to it by such heads, if the Court had jurisdiction over such matters.

§ 1494. Accounts of officers, agents or contractors

The United States Court of Federal Claims shall have jurisdiction to determine the amount, if any, due to or from the United States by reason of any unsettled account of any officer or agent of, or contractor with, the United States, or a guarantor, surety or personal representative of any such officer, agent or contractor, and to render judgment thereof,[1] where—

 (1) claimant or the person he represents has applied to the proper department of the Government for settlement of the account;

 (2) three years have elapsed from the date of such application without settlement; and

 (3) no suit upon the same has been brought by the United States.

(June 25, 1948, c. 646, 62 Stat. 941; July 28, 1953, c. 253, § 9, 67 Stat. 226; Sept. 3, 1954, c. 1263, § 44(c), 68 Stat. 1242; Apr. 2, 1982, Pub.L. 97–164, Title I, § 133(c)(1), 96 Stat. 40; Oct. 29, 1992, Pub.L. 102–572, Title IX, § 902(a)(1), 106 Stat. 4516.)

§ 1495. Damages for unjust conviction and imprisonment; claim against United States

The United States Court of Federal Claims shall have jurisdiction to render judgment upon any claim for damages by any person unjustly convicted of an offense against the United States and imprisoned.

(June 25, 1948, c. 646, 62 Stat. 941; Apr. 2, 1982, Pub.L. 97–164, Title I, § 133(c)(1), 96 Stat. 40; Oct. 29, 1992, Pub.L. 102–572, Title IX, § 902(a)(1), 106 Stat. 4516.)

---

[1] [Footnote to 28 U.S.C. § 1494:] So in original. Probably should be "thereon".

§ 1496.   Disbursing officers' claims

The United States Court of Federal Claims shall have jurisdiction to render judgment upon any claim by a disbursing officer of the United States or by his administrator or executor for relief from responsibility for loss, in line of duty, of Government funds, vouchers, records or other papers in his charge.

(June 25, 1948, c. 646, 62 Stat. 941; Apr. 2, 1982, Pub.L. 97–164, Title I, § 133(c)(1), 96 Stat. 40; Oct. 29, 1992, Pub.L. 102–572, Title IX, § 902(a)(1), 106 Stat. 4516.)

§ 1497.   Oyster growers' damages from dredging operations

The United States Court of Federal Claims shall have jurisdiction to render judgment upon any claim for damages to oyster growers on private or leased lands or bottoms arising from dredging operations or use of other machinery and equipment in making river and harbor improvements authorized by Act of Congress.

(June 25, 1948, c. 646, 62 Stat. 941; Apr. 2, 1982, Pub.L. 97–164, Title I, § 133(c), 96 Stat. 40; Oct. 29, 1992, Pub.L. 102–572, Title IX, § 902(a)(1), 106 Stat. 4516.)

§ 1498.   Patent and copyright cases

(a) Whenever an invention described in and covered by a patent of the United States is used or manufactured by or for the United States without license of the owner thereof or lawful right to use or manufacture the same, the owner's remedy shall be by action against the United States in the United States Court of Federal Claims for the recovery of his reasonable and entire compensation for such use and manufacture. Reasonable and entire compensation shall include the owner's reasonable costs, including reasonable fees for expert witnesses and attorneys, in pursuing the action if the owner is an independent inventor, a nonprofit organization, or an entity that had no more than 500 employees at any time during the 5-year period preceding the use or manufacture of the patented invention by or for the United States. Nothwithstanding[1] the preceding sentences, unless the action has been pending for more than 10 years from the time of filing to the time that the owner applies for such costs and fees, reasonable and entire compensation shall not include such costs and fees if the court finds that the position of the United States was substantially justified or that special circumstances make an award unjust.

For the purposes of this section, the use or manufacture of an invention described in and covered by a patent of the United States by a contractor, a subcontractor, or any person, firm, or corporation for the Government and with the authorization or consent of the Government, shall be construed as use or manufacture for the United States.

The court shall not award compensation under this section if the claim is based on the use or manufacture by or for the United States of any article owned, leased, used by, or in the possession of the United States prior to July 1, 1918.

A Government employee shall have the right to bring suit against the Government under this section except where he was in a position to order, influence, or induce use of the invention by the Government. This section shall not confer a right of action on any patentee or any assignee of such patentee with respect to any invention discovered or invented by a person while in the employment or service of the United States, where the invention was related to the official functions of the employee, in cases in which such functions included research and development, or in the making of which Government time, materials or facilities were used.

(b) Hereafter, whenever the copyright in any work protected under the copyright laws of the United States shall be infringed by the United States, by a corporation owned or controlled by the United States, or by a contractor, subcontractor, or any person, firm, or corporation acting for the Government and with the authorization or consent of the Government, the exclusive action which may

---

[1]   [Footnote to 28 U.S.C. § 1498(a):] So in original. Probably should be "Notwithstanding".

be brought for such infringement shall be an action by the copyright owner against the United States in the Court of Federal Claims for the recovery of his reasonable and entire compensation as damages for such infringement, including the minimum statutory damages as set forth in section 504(c) of title 17, United States Code: *Provided,* That a Government employee shall have a right of action against the Government under this subsection except where he was in a position to order, influence, or induce use of the copyrighted work by the Government: *Provided, however,* That this subsection shall not confer a right of action on any copyright owner or any assignee of such owner with respect to any copyrighted work prepared by a person while in the employment or service of the United States, where the copyrighted work was prepared as a part of the official functions of the employee, or in the preparation of which Government time, material, or facilities were used: *And provided further,* That before such action against the United States has been instituted the appropriate corporation owned or controlled by the United States or the head of the appropriate department or agency of the Government, as the case may be, is authorized to enter into an agreement with the copyright owner in full settlement and compromise for the damages accruing to him by reason of such infringement and to settle the claim administratively out of available appropriations.

Except as otherwise provided by law, no recovery shall be had for any infringement of a copyright covered by this subsection committed more than three years prior to the filing of the complaint or counterclaim for infringement in the action, except that the period between the date of receipt of a written claim for compensation by the Department or agency of the Government or corporation owned or controlled by the United States, as the case may be, having authority to settle such claim and the date of mailing by the Government of a notice to the claimant that his claim has been denied shall not be counted as a part of the three years, unless suit is brought before the last-mentioned date.

(c)   The provisions of this section shall not apply to any claim arising in a foreign country.

(d)   Hereafter, whenever a plant variety protected by a certificate of plant variety protection under the laws of the United States shall be infringed by the United States, by a corporation owned or controlled by the United States, or by a contractor, subcontractor, or any person, firm, or corporation acting for the Government, and with the authorization and consent of the Government, the exclusive remedy of the owner of such certificate shall be by action against the United States in the Court of Federal Claims for the recovery of his reasonable and entire compensation as damages for such infringement: *Provided,* That a Government employee shall have a right of action against the Government under this subsection except where he was in a position to order, influence, or induce use of the protected plant variety by the Government: *Provided, however,* That this subsection shall not confer a right of action on any certificate owner or any assignee of such owner with respect to any protected plant variety made by a person while in the employment or service of the United States, where such variety was prepared as a part of the official functions of the employee, or in the preparation of which Government time, material, or facilities were used: *And provided further,* That before such action against the United States has been instituted, the appropriate corporation owned or controlled by the United States or the head of the appropriate agency of the Government, as the case may be, is authorized to enter into an agreement with the certificate owner in full settlement and compromise, for the damages accrued to him by reason of such infringement and to settle the claim administratively out of available appropriations.

(e)   Subsections (b) and (c) of this section apply to exclusive rights in mask works under chapter 9 of title 17, and to exclusive rights in designs under chapter 13 of title 17 [17 U.S.C.A. § 1301 et seq.], to the same extent as such subsections apply to copyrights.

(June 25, 1948, c. 646, 62 Stat. 941; May 24, 1949, c. 139, § 87, 63 Stat. 102; Oct. 31, 1951, c. 655, § 50(c), 65 Stat. 727; July 17, 1952, c. 930, 66 Stat. 757; Sept. 8, 1960, Pub.L. 86–726, §§ 1, 4, 74 Stat. 855, 856; Dec. 24, 1970, Pub.L. 91–577, Title III, § 143(d), 84 Stat. 1559; Oct. 19, 1976, Pub.L. 94–553, Title I, § 105(c), 90 Stat. 2599; Apr. 2, 1982, Pub.L. 97–164, Title I, § 133(d), 96 Stat. 40; Nov. 19, 1988, Pub.L. 100–702, Title X, § 1020(a)(6), 102 Stat. 4671; Oct. 29, 1992, Pub.L. 102–572, Title IX, § 902(a), 106 Stat. 4516; Oct. 19, 1996, Pub.L. 104–308, § 1(a), 110 Stat. 3814; Dec. 16, 1997, Pub.L. 105–147, § 3, 111 Stat. 2680; Oct. 28, 1998, Pub.L. 105–304, Title V, § 503(d), 112 Stat. 2917.)

HISTORICAL AND STATUTORY NOTES

References in Text

Hereafter, referred to in subsec. (b), probably means the date of enactment of Pub. L. 86–726 [which, among other changes, added subsec. (b)], which was approved on Sept. 8, 1960.

The copyright laws of the United States, referred to in subsec. (b), are classified generally to Title 17, Copyrights.

The "hereafter" set out at the beginning of subsec. (d) probably means after Dec. 24, 1970, the date of enactment of Pub.L. 91–577 which added subsec. (d).

Waiver of Immunity for Members of Congress

Section 2 of Pub.L. 86–726 provided that: "Nothing in this Act [amending this section and section 2386 of Title 10, Armed Forces] shall be construed to in any way waive any immunity provided for Members of Congress under article I of section 6 of the Constitution of the United States."

§ 1499.   Liquidated damages withheld from contractors under chapter 37 of title 40

The United States Court of Federal Claims shall have jurisdiction to render judgment upon any claim for liquidated damages withheld from a contractor or subcontractor under section 3703 of title 40.

(June 25, 1948, c. 646, 62 Stat. 942; Aug. 13, 1962, Pub.L. 87–581, Title II, § 202(a), 76 Stat. 360; Apr. 2, 1982, Pub.L. 97–164, Title I, § 133(e)(1), (2)(A), 96 Stat. 40, 41; Dec. 1, 1990, Pub.L. 101–650, Title III, § 325(b)(7), 104 Stat. 5121; Oct. 29, 1992, Pub.L. 102–572, Title IX, § 902(a)(1), 106 Stat. 4516; Aug. 21, 2002, Pub.L. 107–217, § 3(g)(3), 116 Stat. 1299; Sept. 27, 2006, Pub.L. 109–284, § 4(2), 120 Stat. 1211.)

§ 1500.   Pendency of claims in other courts

The United States Court of Federal Claims shall not have jurisdiction of any claim for or in respect to which the plaintiff or his assignee has pending in any other court any suit or process against the United States or any person who, at the time when the cause of action alleged in such suit or process arose, was, in respect thereto, acting or professing to act, directly or indirectly under the authority of the United States.

(June 25, 1948, c. 646, 62 Stat. 942; Apr. 2, 1982, Pub.L. 97–164, Title I, § 133(e)(1), 96 Stat. 40; Oct. 29, 1992, Pub.L. 102–572, Title IX, § 902(a)(1), 106 Stat. 4516.)

§ 1501.   Pensions

The United States Court of Federal Claims shall not have jurisdiction of any claim for a pension.

(June 25, 1948, c. 646, 62 Stat. 942; Apr. 2, 1982, Pub.L. 97–164, Title I, § 133(e)(1), 96 Stat. 40; Oct. 29, 1992, Pub.L. 102–572, Title IX, § 902(a)(1), 106 Stat. 4516.)

§ 1502.   Treaty cases

Except as otherwise provided by Act of Congress, the United States Court of Federal Claims shall not have jurisdiction of any claim against the United States growing out of or dependent upon any treaty entered into with foreign nations.

(June 25, 1948, c. 646, 62 Stat. 942; May 24, 1949, c. 139, § 88, 63 Stat. 102; Apr. 2, 1982, Pub.L. 97–164, Title I, § 133(e)(1), 96 Stat. 40; Oct. 29, 1992, Pub.L. 102–572, Title IX, § 902(a)(1), 106 Stat. 4516.)

§ 1503.   Set-offs

The United States Court of Federal Claims shall have jurisdiction to render judgment upon any set-off or demand by the United States against any plaintiff in such court.

(June 25, 1948, c. 646, 62 Stat. 942; Apr. 2, 1982, Pub.L. 97–164, Title I, § 133(e)(1), 96 Stat. 40; Oct. 29, 1992, Pub.L. 102–572, Title IX, § 902(a)(1), 106 Stat. 4516.)

[§ 1504.　　　Repealed. Pub.L. 97–164, Title I, § 133(f), Apr. 2, 1982, 96 Stat. 41]

HISTORICAL AND STATUTORY NOTES

Section, Act June 25, 1948, c. 646, 62 Stat. 942, directed that the Court of Claims [now Court of Federal Claims] have jurisdiction to review by appeal final judgments in the district courts in civil actions based on tort claims brought under section 1346(b) of this title if the notice of appeal filed in the district court had affixed to it a written consent on behalf of the appellees that the appeal be taken to the Court of Claims.

§ 1505.　　　Indian claims

The United States Court of Federal Claims shall have jurisdiction of any claim against the United States accruing after August 13, 1946, in favor of any tribe, band, or other identifiable group of American Indians residing within the territorial limits of the United States or Alaska whenever such claim is one arising under the Constitution, laws or treaties of the United States, or Executive orders of the President, or is one which otherwise would be cognizable in the Court of Federal Claims if the claimant were not an Indian tribe, band or group.

(Added May 24, 1949, c. 139, § 89(a), 63 Stat. 102; amended Apr. 2, 1982, Pub.L. 97–164, Title I, § 133(g), 96 Stat. 41; Oct. 29, 1992, Pub.L. 102–572, Title IX, § 902(a), 106 Stat. 4516.)

[§ 1506.　　　Repealed. Pub.L. 97–164, title I, § 133(h), Apr. 2, 1982, 96 Stat. 41]

HISTORICAL AND STATUTORY NOTES

Section, added Pub.L. 86–770, § 2(a), Sept. 13, 1960, 74 Stat. 912, provided that if a case within the exclusive jurisdiction of the district courts was filed in the Court of Claims [now Court of Federal Claims], the Court of Claims, if it were in the interest of justice, had to transfer such case to any district court in which it could have been brought at the time such case was filed, where the case would proceed as if it had been filed in the district court on the date it was filed in the Court of Claims.

§ 1507.　　　Jurisdiction for certain declaratory judgments

The United States Court of Federal Claims shall have jurisdiction to hear any suit for and issue a declaratory judgment under section 7428 of the Internal Revenue Code of 1986.

(Added Pub.L. 94–455, Title XIII, § 1306(b)(9)(A), Oct. 4, 1976, 90 Stat. 1720; amended Pub.L. 97–164, Title I, § 133(i), Apr. 2, 1982, 96 Stat. 41; Pub.L. 99–514, § 2, Oct. 22, 1986, 100 Stat. 2095; Pub.L. 102–572, Title IX, § 902(a)(1), Oct. 29, 1992, 106 Stat. 4516.)

§ 1508.　　　Jurisdiction for certain partnership proceedings

The Court of Federal Claims shall have jurisdiction to hear and to render judgment upon any petition under section 6226 or 6228(a) of the Internal Revenue Code of 1986.

(Added Pub.L. 97–248, Title IV, § 402(c)(18)(A), Sept. 3, 1982, 96 Stat. 669; amended Pub.L. 99–514, § 2, Oct. 22, 1986, 100 Stat. 2095; Pub.L. 102–572, Title IX, § 902(a)(2), Oct. 29, 1992, 106 Stat. 4516.)

HISTORICAL AND STATUTORY NOTES

References in Text

Sections 6226 and 6228(a) of the Internal Revenue Code of 1986, referred to in text, are classified to sections 6226 and 6228(a) of Title 26, Internal Revenue Code.

§ 1509.　　　No jurisdiction in cases involving refunds of tax shelter promoter and understatement penalties

The United States Court of Federal Claims shall not have jurisdiction to hear any action or proceeding for any refund or credit of any penalty imposed under section 6700 of the Internal Revenue Code of 1986 (relating to penalty for promoting abusive tax shelters, etc.) or section 6701 of such Code (relating to penalties for aiding and abetting understatement of tax liability).

(Added Pub.L. 98–369, Div. A, Title VII, § 714(g)(2), July 18, 1984, 98 Stat. 962; amended Pub.L. 99–514, § 2, Oct. 22, 1986, 100 Stat. 2095; Pub.L. 102–572, Title IX, § 902(a)(1), Oct. 29, 1992, 106 Stat. 4516.)

HISTORICAL AND STATUTORY NOTES

References in Text

Sections 6700 and 6701 of the Internal Revenue Code of 1986, referred to in text, are classified to sections 6700 and 6701, respectively, of Title 26, Internal Revenue Code.

[CHAPTER 93—REPEALED]

[§§ 1541 to 1546.　　Repealed. Pub.L. 97–164, Title I, § 134, Apr. 2, 1982, 96 Stat. 41]

HISTORICAL AND STATUTORY NOTES

Section 1541, Acts June 25, 1948, c. 646, 62 Stat. 942; June 2, 1970, Pub.L. 91–271, Title I, § 102, 84 Stat. 274; July 26, 1979, Pub.L. 96–39, Title X, § 1001(b)(4)(A), 93 Stat. 305; Oct. 10, 1980, Pub.L. 96–417, Title IV, § 401(a), Title V, § 501(23), (24), 94 Stat. 1740, 1742, gave the Court of Customs and Patent Appeals exclusive jurisdiction of appeals from all final decisions of the Court of International Trade and from interlocutory orders of the Court of International Trade granting, continuing, modifying, refusing, or dissolving injunctions, or refusing to dissolve or modify injunctions, and with discretion to entertain appeals from certain orders of the Court of International Trade. See section 1295(a)(5) of this title.

Section 1542, Acts June 25, 1948, c. 646, 62 Stat. 942; May 24, 1949, c. 139, § 89(b), 63 Stat. 102, gave the Court of Customs and Patent Appeals jurisdiction of appeals from decisions of the Board of Appeals and the Board of Interference Examiners of the Patent Office as to patent applications and interferences, at the instance of an applicant for a patent or any party to a patent interference, with such appeal by an applicant to waive his right to proceed under section 63 of Title 35, and the Commissioner of Patents as to trade-mark applications and proceedings as provided in section 1071 of Title 15. See section 1295(a)(4) of this title.

Section 1543, Acts June 25, 1948, c. 646, 62 Stat. 943; Oct. 10, 1980, Pub.L. 96–417, Title IV, § 401(b)(1), 94 Stat. 1740, gave the Court of Customs and Patent Appeals jurisdiction to review final determinations of the United States International Trade Commission made under section 337 of the Tariff Act of 1930 relating to unfair trade practices in import trade. See section 1295(a)(6) of this title.

Section 1544, added Pub.L. 89–651, § 8(c)(1), Oct. 14, 1966, 80 Stat. 901, gave the Court of Customs and Patent Appeals jurisdiction to review, by appeal on questions of law only, findings of the Secretary of Commerce under headnote 6 to schedule 8, part 4, of the Tariff Schedules of the United States (relating to importation of instruments or apparatus). See section 1295(a)(7) of this title.

Section 1545, added Pub.L. 91–577, Title III, § 143(a), Dec. 24, 1970, 84 Stat. 1558, gave the Court of Customs and Patent Appeals nonexclusive jurisdiction of appeals under section 71 of the Plant Variety Protection Act, classified to section 2461 of Title 7, Agriculture. See section 1295(a)(8) of this title.

Section 1546, added Pub.L. 96–417, Title IV, § 402(a), Oct. 10, 1980, 94 Stat. 1740, gave the Court of Customs and Patent Appeals all of the powers in law and in equity of, or conferred by statute upon, a court of appeals of the United States.

Effective Date of Repeal

Repeal effective Oct. 1, 1982, see section 402 of Pub.L. 97–164, set out as a note under section 171 of this title.

CHAPTER 95—COURT OF INTERNATIONAL TRADE

Sec.
1581.　Civil actions against the United States and agencies and officers thereof.
1582.　Civil actions commenced by the United States.
1583.　Counterclaims, cross-claims, and third-party actions.
1584.　Civil actions under the North American Free Trade Agreement or the United States–Canada Free-Trade Agreement.

1585.   Powers in law and equity.

HISTORICAL AND STATUTORY NOTES

Prior Provisions

A prior Chapter 95—Customs Court, comprising sections 1581 and 1582, was omitted from the Code upon the general revision of this chapter by Pub.L. 96–417, Title II, § 201, Oct. 10, 1980, 94 Stat. 1728.

§ 1581.   Civil actions against the United States and agencies and officers thereof

(a) The Court of International Trade shall have exclusive jurisdiction of any civil action commenced to contest the denial of a protest, in whole or in part, under section 515 of the Tariff Act of 1930.

(b) The Court of International Trade shall have exclusive jurisdiction of any civil action commenced under section 516 of the Tariff Act of 1930.

(c) The Court of International Trade shall have exclusive jurisdiction of any civil action commenced under section 516A or 517 of the Tariff Act of 1930.

(d) The Court of International Trade shall have exclusive jurisdiction of any civil action commenced to review—

     (1) any final determination of the Secretary of Labor under section 223 of the Trade Act of 1974 with respect to the eligibility of workers for adjustment assistance under such Act;

     (2) any final determination of the Secretary of Commerce under section 251 of the Trade Act of 1974 with respect to the eligibility of a firm for adjustment assistance under such Act;

     (3) any final determination of the Secretary of Commerce under section 273 of the Trade Act of 1974 with respect to the eligibility of a community for adjustment assistance under such Act; and

     (4) any final determination of the Secretary of Agriculture under section 293 or 296 of the Trade Act of 1974 (19 U.S.C. 2401b) with respect to the eligibility of a group of agricultural commodity producers for adjustment assistance under such Act.

(e) The Court of International Trade shall have exclusive jurisdiction of any civil action commenced to review any final determination of the Secretary of the Treasury under section 305(b)(1) of the Trade Agreements Act of 1979.

(f) The Court of International Trade shall have exclusive jurisdiction of any civil action involving an application for an order directing the administering authority or the International Trade Commission to make confidential information available under section 777(c)(2) of the Tariff Act of 1930.

(g) The Court of International Trade shall have exclusive jurisdiction of any civil action commenced to review—

     (1) any decision of the Secretary of the Treasury to deny a customs broker's license under section 641(b)(2) or (3) of the Tariff Act of 1930, or to deny a customs broker's permit under section 641(c)(1) of such Act, or to revoke a license or permit under section 641(b)(5) or (c)(2) of such Act;

     (2) any decision of the Secretary of the Treasury to revoke or suspend a customs broker's license or permit, or impose a monetary penalty in lieu thereof, under section 641(d)(2)(B) of the Tariff Act of 1930; and

     (3) any decision or order of the Customs Service to deny, suspend, or revoke accreditation of a private laboratory under section 499(b) of the Tariff Act of 1930.

(h) The Court of International Trade shall have exclusive jurisdiction of any civil action commenced to review, prior to the importation of the goods involved, a ruling issued by the Secretary of the Treasury, or a refusal to issue or change such a ruling, relating to classification, valuation, rate of duty, marking, restricted merchandise, entry requirements, drawbacks, vessel repairs, or similar matters, but only if the party commencing the civil action demonstrates to the court that he would be irreparably harmed unless given an opportunity to obtain judicial review prior to such importation.

(i) In addition to the jurisdiction conferred upon the Court of International Trade by subsections (a)–(h) of this section and subject to the exception set forth in subsection (j) of this section, the Court of International Trade shall have exclusive jurisdiction of any civil action commenced against the United States, its agencies, or its officers, that arises out of any law of the United States providing for—

    (1)(A) revenue from imports or tonnage;

    (B) tariffs, duties, fees, or other taxes on the importation of merchandise for reasons other than the raising of revenue;

    (C) embargoes or other quantitative restrictions on the importation of merchandise for reasons other than the protection of the public health or safety; or

    (D) administration and enforcement with respect to the matters referred to in subparagraphs (A) through (C) of this paragraph and subsections (a)–(h) of this section.

    (2) This subsection shall not confer jurisdiction over an antidumping or countervailing duty determination which is reviewable by—

    (A) the Court of International Trade under section 516A(a) of the Tariff Act of 1930 (19 U.S.C. 1516a(a)); or

    (B) a binational panel under section 516A(g) of the Tariff Act of 1930 (19 U.S.C. 1516a(g)).

(j) The Court of International Trade shall not have jurisdiction of any civil action arising under section 305 of the Tariff Act of 1930.

(Added Pub.L. 96–417, Title II, § 201, Oct. 10, 1980, 94 Stat. 1728; amended Pub.L. 98–573, Title II, § 212(b)(1), Oct. 30, 1984, 98 Stat. 2983; Pub.L. 99–514, Title XVIII, § 1891(1), Oct. 22, 1986, 100 Stat. 2926; Pub.L. 100–449, Title IV, § 402(a), Sept. 28, 1988, 102 Stat. 1883; Pub.L. 103–182, Title IV, § 414(a)(1), Title VI, § 684(a)(1), Dec. 8, 1993, 107 Stat. 2147, 2219; Pub.L. 111–5, Div. B, Title I, § 1873(b)(2), Feb. 17, 2009, 123 Stat. 414; Pub.L. 114–125, Title IV, § 421(b), Feb. 24, 2016, 130 Stat. 122; Pub.L. 116–113, Jan. 29, 2020, 134 Stat. 11.)

Termination of Amendment

For termination of amendment by section 501(c) of Pub.L. 100–449, see Sunset Provisions note set out under this section.

HISTORICAL AND STATUTORY NOTES

References in Text

Sections 515 and 516 of the Tariff Act of 1930, referred to in subsecs. (a) and (b), respectively, are classified, respectively, to sections 1515 and 1516 of Title 19, Customs Duties.

The Trade Act of 1974, referred to in subsec. (d), is Pub.L. 93–618, Jan. 3, 1975, 88 Stat.1978, as amended, which is classified principally to chapter 12 of Title 19, 19 U.S.C.A. § 2101 et seq. Sections 223, 251, 273, 293, and 296 of the Trade Act of 1974 are classified to 19 U.S.C.A. §§ 2273, 2341, 2371b, 2401b and 2401e, respectively. For complete classification, see References in Text note set out under 19 U.S.C.A. § 2101 and Tables.

Section 305(b)(1) of the Trade Agreements Act of 1979, referred to in subsec. (e), is classified to section 2515(b)(1) of Title 19, Customs Duties.

Sections 777(c)(2), 641(b), (c), (d), and 305 of the Tariff Act of 1930, referred to in subsecs. (f), (g), and (j), are classified to sections 1677f(c)(2), 1641, (b), (c), (d), and 1305, respectively, of Title 19, Customs Duties.

Section 499(b) of the Tariff Act of 1930, referred to in subsec. (g)(3), is classified to section 1499(b) of Title 19, Customs Duties.

Section 516A of the Tariff Act of 1930, referred to in subsec. (i), is classified to section 1516a of Title 19.

The United States-Canada Free-Trade Agreement, referred to in subsec. (i), was entered into on Jan. 2, 1988. The Agreement is not set out in the Code.

Sunset Provisions

For provisions relating to the effect of termination of NAFTA country status on the provisions of Pub.L. 103–182, §§ 401 to 416, see 19 U.S.C.A. § 3451.

For provisions directing that the amendments made by Pub.L. 100–449, which amended this section, shall cease to have effect on the date on which the United States-Canada Free-Trade Agreement ceases to be in force, see Pub.L. 100–449, § 501(c), set out in the note under 19 U.S.C.A. § 2112.

Transfer of Functions

For transfer of the functions, personnel, assets, and liabilities of the United States Customs Service of the Department of the Treasury, including the functions of the Secretary of the Treasury relating thereto, to the Secretary of Homeland Security, and for treatment of related references, see 6 U.S.C.A. §§ 203(1), 551(d), 552(d) and 557, and the Department of Homeland Security Reorganization Plan of November 25, 2002, as modified, set out as a note under 6 U.S.C.A. § 542.

Prior Provisions

A prior section 1581, Act June 25, 1948, c. 646, 62 Stat. 943, related to powers of the Customs Court generally and was omitted in the general revision of this chapter by Pub.L. 96–417. See section 1585 of this title.

Application of Amendments Relating to Accreditation of Private Laboratories

Section 684(b) of Pub.L. 103–182 provided that: "For purposes of applying the amendments made by subsection (a) [amending subsec. (g) of this section, and sections 2631, 2636, 2640 and 2642 of this title], any decision or order of the Customs Service denying, suspending, or revoking the accreditation of a private laboratory on or after the date of the enactment of this Act [Dec. 8, 1993] and before regulations to implement section 499(b) of the Tariff Act of 1930 [section 1499(b) of Title 19, Customs Duties] are issued shall be treated as having been denied, suspended, or revoked under such section 499(b)."

Prior History of Court

The United States Customs Court, the predecessor of the Court of International Trade, was omitted in the general revision of this chapter by Pub.L. 96–417.

The predecessor of the United States Customs Court was the Board of General Appraisers which was created by the Customs Administrative Act of June 10, 1890. The Board was under the administrative supervision of the Secretary of the Treasury.

From 1890 to 1926, the Board of General Appraisers had jurisdiction over all protests from decisions of the collectors of customs and appeals for reappraisement under sections 13 and 14 of the Customs Administrative Act of June 10, 1890, c. 407, 26 Stat. 136.

The Customs Court was established by Act May 28, 1926, c. 411, §§ 1, 2, 44 Stat. 669, sections 405a and 405b of Title 19, Customs Duties, and said act transferred to it all the jurisdiction and powers of the former Board of General Appraisers. The Tariff Act of June 1930, c. 497, Title IV, § 518, 46 Stat. 737, section 1518 of Title 19, continued the Customs Court as constituted on June 17, 1930 with, however, several important changes.

§ 1582. Civil actions commenced by the United States

The Court of International Trade shall have exclusive jurisdiction of any civil action which arises out of an import transaction and which is commenced by the United States—

   (1)   to recover a civil penalty under section 592, 593A, 641(b)(6), 641(d)(2)(A), 704(i)(2), or 734(i)(2) of the Tariff Act of 1930;

   (2)   to recover upon a bond relating to the importation of merchandise required by the laws of the United States or by the Secretary of the Treasury; or

   (3)   to recover customs duties.

(Added Pub.L. 96–417, Title II, § 201, Oct. 10, 1980, 94 Stat. 1729; amended Pub.L. 98–573, Title II, § 212(b)(2), Oct. 30, 1984, 98 Stat. 2983; Pub.L. 99–514, Title XVIII, § 1891(2), Oct. 22, 1986, 100 Stat. 2926; Pub.L. 103–182, Title VI, § 684(c), Dec. 8, 1993, 107 Stat. 2219.)

HISTORICAL AND STATUTORY NOTES

References in Text

   Sections 592, 593A, 641(b)(2), 641(d)(2)(A), 704(i)(2), and 734(i)(2) of the Tariff Act of 1930, referred to in par. (1), are classified to sections 1592, 1593a, 1641(b)(6), 1641(d)(2)(A), 1671c(i)(2), and 1673c(i)(2) of Title 19, Customs Duties.

§ 1583.   Counterclaims, cross-claims, and third-party actions

   In any civil action in the Court of International Trade, the court shall have exclusive jurisdiction to render judgment upon any counterclaim, cross-claim, or third-party action of any party, if (1) such claim or action involves the imported merchandise that is the subject matter of such civil action, or (2) such claim or action is to recover upon a bond or customs duties relating to such merchandise.

(Added Pub.L. 96–417, Title II, § 201, Oct. 10, 1980, 94 Stat. 1729.)

§ 1584.   Civil actions under the North American Free Trade Agreement or the United States–Canada Free-Trade Agreement

   The United States Court of International Trade shall have exclusive jurisdiction of any civil action which arises under section 777(f) of the Tariff Act of 1930 and is commenced by the United States to enforce administrative sanctions levied for violation of a protective order or an undertaking.

(Added Pub.L. 100–449, Title IV, § 402(d)(1), Sept. 28, 1988, 102 Stat. 1884; amended Pub.L. 103–182, Title IV, § 414(a)(2), Dec. 8, 1993, 107 Stat. 2147; Pub.L. 116–113, Jan. 29, 2020, 134 Stat. 11.)

Termination of Section

   For termination of section by section 501(c) of Pub.L. 100–449, see Sunset Provisions note set out under this section.

HISTORICAL AND STATUTORY NOTES

References in Text

   Section 777(f) of the Tariff Act of 1930, referred to in text, is classified to section 1677f(f) of Title 19, Customs Duties.

Sunset Provisions

   For provisions directing that the amendments made by Pub.L. 100–449, which amended this section, shall cease to have effect on the date on which the United States-Canada Free-Trade Agreement ceases to be in force, see section 501(c) of Pub.L. 100–449, set out in the note under 19 U.S.C.A. § 2112.

   For provisions relating to the effect of termination of NAFTA country status on the provisions of Pub.L. 103–182, §§ 401 to 416, see 19 U.S.C.A. § 3451.

   For provisions directing that the amendments made by Pub.L. 100–449, which amended this section, shall cease to have effect on the date on which the United States-Canada Free-Trade Agreement ceases to be in force, see Pub.L. 100–449, § 501(c), set out in the note under 19 U.S.C.A. § 2112.

Prior Provisions

A prior section 1584, added Pub.L. 96–417, Title II, § 201, Oct. 10, 1980, 94 Stat. 1729, which provided that if a civil action within the exclusive jurisdiction of the Court of International Trade were commenced in a district court of the United States, the district court, in the interest of justice, would transfer such civil action to the Court of International Trade, where such action proceeded as if it had been commenced in the Court of International Trade in the first instance, and that if a civil action within the exclusive jurisdiction of a district court, a court of appeals, or the Court of Customs and Patent Appeals were commenced in the Court of International Trade, the Court of International Trade, in the interest of justice, would transfer such civil action to the appropriate district court or court of appeals or to the Court of Customs and Patent Appeals where such action proceeded as if it had been commenced in such court in the first instance, was repealed by Pub.L. 97–164, Title I, § 135, Apr. 2, 1982, 96 Stat. 41, eff. Oct. 1, 1982.

Amendment of Section

Pub.L. 116–113, Title IV, §§ 423(a)(2), 432, Jan. 29, 2020, 134 Stat. 65, 66, provided that effective on the date on which the USMCA enters into force, but not applicable to any final determination described in pars. (a)(1)(B) or (a)(2)(B)(i) to (iii) of 19 U.S.C.A. § 1516a, or to a determination described in par. (a)(2)(B)(vi) of such section, or to any binational panel review under NAFTA, or any extraordinary challenge arising out of any such review, section heading is amended to read as follows: "Civil actions under the United States–Canada Free-Trade Agreement or the USMCA"

§ 1585.   Powers in law and equity

The Court of International Trade shall possess all the powers in law and equity of, or as conferred by statute upon, a district court of the United States.

(Added Pub.L. 96–417, Title II, § 201, Oct. 10, 1980, 94 Stat. 1730.)

CHAPTER 97—JURISDICTIONAL IMMUNITIES OF FOREIGN STATES

§ 1602.   Findings and declaration of purpose

The Congress finds that the determination by United States courts of the claims of foreign states to immunity from the jurisdiction of such courts would serve the interests of justice and would protect the rights of both foreign states and litigants in United States courts. Under international law, states are not immune from the jurisdiction of foreign courts insofar as their commercial activities are concerned, and their commercial property may be levied upon for the satisfaction of judgments rendered against them in connection with their commercial activities. Claims of foreign states to immunity should henceforth be decided by courts of the United States and of the States in conformity with the principles set forth in this chapter.

(Added Pub.L. 94–583, § 4(a), Oct. 21, 1976, 90 Stat. 2892.)

HISTORICAL AND STATUTORY NOTES

Separability of Provisions

Section 7 of Pub.L. 94–583 provided that: "If any provision of this Act [enacting this chapter and section 1330 of this title, amending sections 1332, 1391, and 1441 of this title, and enacting provisions set out as notes under this section and section 1 of this title] or the application thereof to any foreign state is held invalid, the invalidity does not affect other provisions or applications of the Act which can be given effect without the invalid provision or application, and to this end the provisions of this Act are severable."

Short Title

1976 Acts. Authorization to cite Pub.L. 94–583, which enacted this chapter, as the "Foreign Sovereign Immunities Act of 1976", see section 1 of Pub.L. 94–583, set out as a note under section 1 of this title.

§ 1603.   Definitions

For purposes of this chapter—

(a) A "foreign state", except as used in section 1608 of this title, includes a political subdivision of a foreign state or an agency or instrumentality of a foreign state as defined in subsection (b).

(b) An "agency or instrumentality of a foreign state" means any entity—

(1) which is a separate legal person, corporate or otherwise, and

(2) which is an organ of a foreign state or political subdivision thereof, or a majority of whose shares or other ownership interest is owned by a foreign state or political subdivision thereof, and

(3) which is neither a citizen of a State of the United States as defined in section 1332(c) and (e) of this title, nor created under the laws of any third country.

(c) The "United States" includes all territory and waters, continental or insular, subject to the jurisdiction of the United States.

(d) A "commercial activity" means either a regular course of commercial conduct or a particular commercial transaction or act. The commercial character of an activity shall be determined by reference to the nature of the course of conduct or particular transaction or act, rather than by reference to its purpose.

(e) A "commercial activity carried on in the United States by a foreign state" means commercial activity carried on by such state and having substantial contact with the United States.

(Added Pub.L. 94–583, § 4(a), Oct. 21, 1976, 90 Stat. 2892; amended Pub.L. 109–2, § 4(b)(2), Feb. 18, 2005, 119 Stat. 12.)

§ 1604.   Immunity of a foreign state from jurisdiction

Subject to existing international agreements to which the United States is a party at the time of enactment of this Act a foreign state shall be immune from the jurisdiction of the courts of the United States and of the States except as provided in sections 1605 to 1607 of this chapter.

(Added Pub.L. 94–583, § 4(a), Oct. 21, 1976, 90 Stat. 2892.)

HISTORICAL AND STATUTORY NOTES

References in Text

The time of enactment of this Act, referred to in text, probably means the time of enactment of Pub.L. 94–583, which was approved on Oct. 21, 1976.

§ 1605.   General exceptions to the jurisdictional immunity of a foreign state

(a)   A foreign state shall not be immune from the jurisdiction of courts of the United States or of the States in any case—

(1)   in which the foreign state has waived its immunity either explicitly or by implication, notwithstanding any withdrawal of the waiver which the foreign state may purport to effect except in accordance with the terms of the waiver;

(2)   in which the action is based upon a commercial activity carried on in the United States by the foreign state; or upon an act performed in the United States in connection with a commercial activity of the foreign state elsewhere; or upon an act outside the territory of the United States in connection with a commercial activity of the foreign state elsewhere and that act causes a direct effect in the United States;

(3)   in which rights in property taken in violation of international law are in issue and that property or any property exchanged for such property is present in the United States in connection with a commercial activity carried on in the United States by the foreign state; or that property or any property exchanged for such property is owned or operated by an agency or instrumentality of the foreign state and that agency or instrumentality is engaged in a commercial activity in the United States;

(4)   in which rights in property in the United States acquired by succession or gift or rights in immovable property situated in the United States are in issue;

(5)   not otherwise encompassed in paragraph (2) above, in which money damages are sought against a foreign state for personal injury or death, or damage to or loss of property, occurring in the United States and caused by the tortious act or omission of that foreign state or of any official or employee of that foreign state while acting within the scope of his office or employment; except this paragraph shall not apply to—

(A)   any claim based upon the exercise or performance or the failure to exercise or perform a discretionary function regardless of whether the discretion be abused, or

(B)   any claim arising out of malicious prosecution, abuse of process, libel, slander, misrepresentation, deceit, or interference with contract rights; or

(6)   in which the action is brought, either to enforce an agreement made by the foreign state with or for the benefit of a private party to submit to arbitration all or any differences which have arisen or which may arise between the parties with respect to a defined legal relationship, whether contractual or not, concerning a subject matter capable of settlement by arbitration under the laws of the United States, or to confirm an award made pursuant to such an agreement to arbitrate, if (A) the arbitration takes place or is intended to take place in the United States, (B) the agreement or award is or may be governed by a treaty or other international agreement in force for the United States calling for the recognition and enforcement of arbitral awards, (C) the underlying claim, save for the agreement to arbitrate, could have been brought in a United States court under this section or section 1607, or (D) paragraph (1) of this subsection is otherwise applicable.

(b)   A foreign state shall not be immune from the jurisdiction of the courts of the United States in any case in which a suit in admiralty is brought to enforce a maritime lien against a vessel or cargo of the foreign state, which maritime lien is based upon a commercial activity of the foreign state: *Provided*, That—

(1)   notice of the suit is given by delivery of a copy of the summons and of the complaint to the person, or his agent, having possession of the vessel or cargo against which the maritime lien is asserted; and if the vessel or cargo is arrested pursuant to process obtained on behalf of the party bringing the suit, the service of process of arrest shall be deemed to constitute valid delivery of such notice, but the party bringing the suit shall be liable for any damages sustained by the foreign state as a result of the arrest if the party bringing the suit had actual or constructive knowledge that the vessel or cargo of a foreign state was involved; and

(2) notice to the foreign state of the commencement of suit as provided in section 1608 of this title is initiated within ten days either of the delivery of notice as provided in paragraph (1) of this subsection or, in the case of a party who was unaware that the vessel or cargo of a foreign state was involved, of the date such party determined the existence of the foreign state's interest.

(c) Whenever notice is delivered under subsection (b)(1), the suit to enforce a maritime lien shall thereafter proceed and shall be heard and determined according to the principles of law and rules of practice of suits in rem whenever it appears that, had the vessel been privately owned and possessed, a suit in rem might have been maintained. A decree against the foreign state may include costs of the suit and, if the decree is for a money judgment, interest as ordered by the court, except that the court may not award judgment against the foreign state in an amount greater than the value of the vessel or cargo upon which the maritime lien arose. Such value shall be determined as of the time notice is served under subsection (b)(1). Decrees shall be subject to appeal and revision as provided in other cases of admiralty and maritime jurisdiction. Nothing shall preclude the plaintiff in any proper case from seeking relief in personam in the same action brought to enforce a maritime lien as provided in this section.

(d) A foreign state shall not be immune from the jurisdiction of the courts of the United States in any action brought to foreclose a preferred mortgage, as defined in section 31301 of title 46. Such action shall be brought, heard, and determined in accordance with the provisions of chapter 313 of title 46 and in accordance with the principles of law and rules of practice of suits in rem, whenever it appears that had the vessel been privately owned and possessed a suit in rem might have been maintained.

[(e), (f) Repealed. Pub.L. 110–181, Div. A, Title X, § 1083(b)(1)(B), Jan. 28, 2008, 122 Stat. 341.]

(g) **Limitation on discovery.—**

(1) **In general.—(A)** Subject to paragraph (2), if an action is filed that would otherwise be barred by section 1604, but for section 1605A, the court, upon request of the Attorney General, shall stay any request, demand, or order for discovery on the United States that the Attorney General certifies would significantly interfere with a criminal investigation or prosecution, or a national security operation, related to the incident that gave rise to the cause of action, until such time as the Attorney General advises the court that such request, demand, or order will no longer so interfere.

(B) A stay under this paragraph shall be in effect during the 12-month period beginning on the date on which the court issues the order to stay discovery. The court shall renew the order to stay discovery for additional 12-month periods upon motion by the United States if the Attorney General certifies that discovery would significantly interfere with a criminal investigation or prosecution, or a national security operation, related to the incident that gave rise to the cause of action.

(2) **Sunset.—(A)** Subject to subparagraph (B), no stay shall be granted or continued in effect under paragraph (1) after the date that is 10 years after the date on which the incident that gave rise to the cause of action occurred.

(B) After the period referred to in subparagraph (A), the court, upon request of the Attorney General, may stay any request, demand, or order for discovery on the United States that the court finds a substantial likelihood would—

(i) create a serious threat of death or serious bodily injury to any person;

(ii) adversely affect the ability of the United States to work in cooperation with foreign and international law enforcement agencies in investigating violations of United States law; or

    (iii) obstruct the criminal case related to the incident that gave rise to the cause of action or undermine the potential for a conviction in such case.

(3) Evaluation of evidence.—The court's evaluation of any request for a stay under this subsection filed by the Attorney General shall be conducted ex parte and in camera.

(4) Bar on motions to dismiss.—A stay of discovery under this subsection shall constitute a bar to the granting of a motion to dismiss under rules 12(b)(6) and 56 of the Federal Rules of Civil Procedure.

(5) Construction.—Nothing in this subsection shall prevent the United States from seeking protective orders or asserting privileges ordinarily available to the United States.

(h) Jurisdictional immunity for certain art exhibition activities.—

(1) In general.—If—

    (A) a work is imported into the United States from any foreign state pursuant to an agreement that provides for the temporary exhibition or display of such work entered into between a foreign state that is the owner or custodian of such work and the United States or one or more cultural or educational institutions within the United States;

    (B) the President, or the President's designee, has determined, in accordance with subsection (a) of Public Law 89–259 (22 U.S.C. 2459(a)), that such work is of cultural significance and the temporary exhibition or display of such work is in the national interest; and

    (C) the notice thereof has been published in accordance with subsection (a) of Public Law 89–259 (22 U.S.C. 2459(a)), any activity in the United States of such foreign state, or of any carrier, that is associated with the temporary exhibition or display of such work shall not be considered to be commercial activity by such foreign state for purposes of subsection (a)(3).

(2) Exceptions.—

    (A) Nazi-era claims.—Paragraph (1) shall not apply in any case asserting jurisdiction under subsection (a)(3) in which rights in property taken in violation of international law are in issue within the meaning of that subsection and—

        (i) the property at issue is the work described in paragraph (1);

        (ii) the action is based upon a claim that such work was taken in connection with the acts of a covered government during the covered period;

        (iii) the court determines that the activity associated with the exhibition or display is commercial activity, as that term is defined in section 1603(d); and

        (iv) a determination under clause (iii) is necessary for the court to exercise jurisdiction over the foreign state under subsection (a)(3).

    (B) Other culturally significant works.—In addition to cases exempted under subparagraph (A), paragraph (1) shall not apply in any case asserting jurisdiction under subsection (a)(3) in which rights in property taken in violation of international law are in issue within the meaning of that subsection and—

        (i) the property at issue is the work described in paragraph (1);

        (ii) the action is based upon a claim that such work was taken in connection with the acts of a foreign government as part of a systematic campaign of coercive confiscation or misappropriation of works from members of a targeted and vulnerable group;

        (iii) the taking occurred after 1900;

        (iv) the court determines that the activity associated with the exhibition or display is commercial activity, as that term is defined in section 1603(d); and

        (v) a determination under clause (iv) is necessary for the court to exercise jurisdiction over the foreign state under subsection (a)(3).

    (3) Definitions.—For purposes of this subsection—

        (A) the term "work" means a work of art or other object of cultural significance;

        (B) the term "covered government" means—

        (i) the Government of Germany during the covered period;

        (ii) any government in any area in Europe that was occupied by the military forces of the Government of Germany during the covered period;

        (iii) any government in Europe that was established with the assistance or cooperation of the Government of Germany during the covered period; and

        (iv) any government in Europe that was an ally of the Government of Germany during the covered period; and

        (C) the term "covered period" means the period beginning on January 30, 1933, and ending on May 8, 1945.

(Added Pub.L. 94–583, § 4(a), Oct. 21, 1976, 90 Stat. 2892; amended Pub.L. 100–640, § 1, Nov. 9, 1988, 102 Stat. 3333; Pub.L. 100–669, § 2, Nov. 16, 1988, 102 Stat. 3969; Pub.L. 101–650, Title III, § 325(b)(8), Dec. 1, 1990, 104 Stat. 5121; Pub.L. 104–132, Title II, § 221(a), Apr. 24, 1996, 110 Stat. 1241; Pub.L. 105–11, Apr. 25, 1997, 111 Stat. 22; Pub.L. 107–77, Title VI, § 626(c), Nov. 28, 2001, 115 Stat. 803; Pub.L. 107–117, Div. B, Ch. 2, § 208, Jan. 10, 2002, 115 Stat. 2299; Pub.L. 109–304, § 17(f)(2), Oct. 6, 2006, 120 Stat. 1708; Pub.L. 110–181, Title X, § 1083(b)(1), Jan. 28, 2008, 122 Stat. 341; Pub.L. 114–222, § 3(b)(2), Sept. 28, 2016, 130 Stat. 853; Pub.L. 114–319, § 2(a), Dec. 16, 2016, 130 Stat. 1618.)

HISTORICAL AND STATUTORY NOTES

References in Text

    Section 101(a)(22) of the Immigration and Nationality Act, referred to in subsec. (a)(7)(B)(ii), is classified to section 1101(a)(22) of Title 8, Aliens and Nationality.

    Chapter 313 of Title 46, referred to in subsec. (d), is Commercial Instruments and Maritime Liens, 46 U.S.C.A. § 31301 et seq.

    Section 3 of the Torture Victim Protection Act of 1991, referred to in subsec. (e)(1), is section 3 of Pub.L. 102–256, Mar. 12, 1992, 106 Stat. 73, set out in a note under section 1350 of this title.

Application of Pub.L. 110–181, Div. A, § 1083 to Pending Cases

    For application of amendments made by Pub.L. 110–181, Div. A, § 1083 to pending cases and treatment of prior actions, see Pub.L. 110–181, Div. A, § 1083(c), set out as a note under 28 U.S.C.A. § 1605A.

Application of Pub.L. 110–181, Div. A, § 1083 to Iraq

    For application of amendments made by Pub.L. 110–181, Div. A, § 1083 to Iraq, see Pub.L. 110–181, Div. A, § 1083(d), set out as a note under 28 U.S.C.A. § 1605A.

Severability

    If any provision of Pub.L. 110–181, Div. A, § 1083, or the amendments made by that section, or the application of such provision to any person or circumstance, is held invalid, the remainder of that section and such amendments, and the application of such provision to other persons not similarly situated or to other circumstances, shall not be affected by such invalidation, see Pub.L. 110–181, Div. A, § 1083(e), set out as a note under 28 U.S.C.A. § 1605A.

Civil Liability for Acts of State Sponsored Terrorism

Pub.L. 104–208, Div. A, Title I, § 101(c) [Title V, § 589], Sept. 30, 1996, 110 Stat. 3009–172, provided that:

"**(a)** An official, employee, or agent of a foreign state designated as a state sponsor of terrorism designated under section 6(j) of the Export Administration Act of 1979 [section 2405(j) of the Appendix to Title 50, War and National Defense] while acting within the scope of his or her office, employment, or agency shall be liable to a United States national or the national's legal representative for personal injury or death caused by acts of that official, employee, or agent for which the courts of the United States may maintain jurisdiction under section 1605(a)(7) of title 28, United States Code [subsec. (a)(7) of this section] for money damages which may include economic damages, solatium, pain, and suffering, and punitive damages if the acts were among those described in section 1605(a)(7) [subsec. (a)(7) of this section].

"**(b)** Provisions related to statute of limitations and limitations on discovery that would apply to an action brought under 28 U.S.C. 1605(f) and (g) [subsecs. (f) and (g) of this section] shall also apply to actions brought under this section.

No action shall be maintained under this action [SIC] if an official, employee, or agent of the United States, while acting within the scope of his or her office, employment, or agency would not be liable for such acts if carried out within the United States."

§ 1605A.   Terrorism exception to the jurisdictional immunity of a foreign state

(a) In general.—

(1) No immunity.—A foreign state shall not be immune from the jurisdiction of courts of the United States or of the States in any case not otherwise covered by this chapter in which money damages are sought against a foreign state for personal injury or death that was caused by an act of torture, extrajudicial killing, aircraft sabotage, hostage taking, or the provision of material support or resources for such an act if such act or provision of material support or resources is engaged in by an official, employee, or agent of such foreign state while acting within the scope of his or her office, employment, or agency.

(2) Claim heard.—The court shall hear a claim under this section if—

(A)(i)(I) the foreign state was designated as a state sponsor of terrorism at the time the act described in paragraph (1) occurred, or was so designated as a result of such act, and, subject to subclause (II), either remains so designated when the claim is filed under this section or was so designated within the 6-month period before the claim is filed under this section; or

(II) in the case of an action that is refiled under this section by reason of section 1083(c)(2)(A) of the National Defense Authorization Act for Fiscal Year 2008 or is filed under this section by reason of section 1083(c)(3) of that Act, the foreign state was designated as a state sponsor of terrorism when the original action or the related action under section 1605(a)(7) (as in effect before the enactment of this section) or section 589 of the Foreign Operations, Export Financing, and Related Programs Appropriations Act, 1997 (as contained in section 101(c) of division A of Public Law 104–208) was filed;

(ii) the claimant or the victim was, at the time the act described in paragraph (1) occurred—

(I) a national of the United States;

(II) a member of the armed forces; or

(III) otherwise an employee of the Government of the United States, or of an individual performing a contract awarded by the United States Government, acting within the scope of the employee's employment; and

(iii) in a case in which the act occurred in the foreign state against which the claim has been brought, the claimant has afforded the foreign state a reasonable opportunity to arbitrate the claim in accordance with the accepted international rules of arbitration; or

(B) the act described in paragraph (1) is related to Case Number 1:00CV03110 (EGS) in the United States District Court for the District of Columbia.

(b) Limitations.—An action may be brought or maintained under this section if the action is commenced, or a related action was commenced under section 1605(a)(7) (before the date of the enactment of this section) or section 589 of the Foreign Operations, Export Financing, and Related Programs Appropriations Act, 1997 (as contained in section 101(c) of division A of Public Law 104–208) not later than the latter of—

(1) 10 years after April 24, 1996; or

(2) 10 years after the date on which the cause of action arose.

(c) Private right of action.—A foreign state that is or was a state sponsor of terrorism as described in subsection (a)(2)(A)(i), and any official, employee, or agent of that foreign state while acting within the scope of his or her office, employment, or agency, shall be liable to—

(1) a national of the United States,

(2) a member of the armed forces,

(3) an employee of the Government of the United States, or of an individual performing a contract awarded by the United States Government, acting within the scope of the employee's employment, or

(4) the legal representative of a person described in paragraph (1), (2), or (3),

for personal injury or death caused by acts described in subsection (a)(1) of that foreign state, or of an official, employee, or agent of that foreign state, for which the courts of the United States may maintain jurisdiction under this section for money damages. In any such action, damages may include economic damages, solatium, pain and suffering, and punitive damages. In any such action, a foreign state shall be vicariously liable for the acts of its officials, employees, or agents.

(d) Additional damages.—After an action has been brought under subsection (c), actions may also be brought for reasonably foreseeable property loss, whether insured or uninsured, third party liability, and loss claims under life and property insurance policies, by reason of the same acts on which the action under subsection (c) is based.

(e) Special masters.—

(1) In general.—The courts of the United States may appoint special masters to hear damage claims brought under this section.

(2) Transfer of funds.—The Attorney General shall transfer, from funds available for the program under section 1404C of the Victims of Crime Act of 1984 (42 U.S.C. 10603c), to the Administrator of the United States district court in which any case is pending which has been brought or maintained under this section such funds as may be required to cover the costs of special masters appointed under paragraph (1). Any amount paid in compensation to any such special master shall constitute an item of court costs.

(f) Appeal.—In an action brought under this section, appeals from orders not conclusively ending the litigation may only be taken pursuant to section 1292(b) of this title.

(g) Property disposition.—

(1) In general.—In every action filed in a United States district court in which jurisdiction is alleged under this section, the filing of a notice of pending action pursuant to this section, to which is attached a copy of the complaint filed in the action, shall have the effect of establishing a lien of lis pendens upon any real property or tangible personal property that is—

  (A) subject to attachment in aid of execution, or execution, under section 1610;

  (B) located within that judicial district; and

  (C) titled in the name of any defendant, or titled in the name of any entity controlled by any defendant if such notice contains a statement listing such controlled entity.

 (2) Notice.—A notice of pending action pursuant to this section shall be filed by the clerk of the district court in the same manner as any pending action and shall be indexed by listing as defendants all named defendants and all entities listed as controlled by any defendant.

 (3) Enforceability.—Liens established by reason of this subsection shall be enforceable as provided in chapter 111 of this title.

(h) Definitions.—For purposes of this section—

 (1) the term "aircraft sabotage" has the meaning given that term in Article 1 of the Convention for the Suppression of Unlawful Acts Against the Safety of Civil Aviation;

 (2) the term "hostage taking" has the meaning given that term in Article 1 of the International Convention Against the Taking of Hostages;

 (3) the term "material support or resources" has the meaning given that term in section 2339A of title 18;

 (4) the term "armed forces" has the meaning given that term in section 101 of title 10;

 (5) the term "national of the United States" has the meaning given that term in section 101(a)(22) of the Immigration and Nationality Act (8 U.S.C. 1101(a)(22));

 (6) the term "state sponsor of terrorism" means a country the government of which the Secretary of State has determined, for purposes of section 6(j) of the Export Administration Act of 1979 (50 U.S.C. App. 2405(j)), section 620A of the Foreign Assistance Act of 1961 (22 U.S.C. 2371), section 40 of the Arms Export Control Act (22 U.S.C. 2780), or any other provision of law, is a government that has repeatedly provided support for acts of international terrorism; and

 (7) the terms "torture" and "extrajudicial killing" have the meaning given those terms in section 3 of the Torture Victim Protection Act of 1991 (28 U.S.C. 1350 note).

(Added Pub.L. 110–181, Div. A, Title X, § 1083(a)(1), Jan. 28, 2008, 122 Stat. 338.)

HISTORICAL AND STATUTORY NOTES

References in Text

 Section 1083(c) of the National Defense Authorization Act for Fiscal Year 2008, referred to in subsec. (a)(2)(A)(II), is Pub.L. 110–181, Div. A, Title X, § 1083(c), Jan. 28, 2008, 122 Stat. 342, which is set out as a note under this section.

 The enactment of this section, and the date of the enactment of this section, referred to in subsecs. (a)(2)(A)(II), (b), is Jan. 28, 2008, the approval date of Pub.L. 110–181, 122 Stat. 3, which enacted this section.

 The Foreign Operations, Export Financing, and Related Programs Appropriations Act, 1997, referred to in subsecs. (a)(2)(A)(II), (b), is Pub.L. 104–208, Div. A, Title I, § 101(c), [Title I to V], Sept. 30, 1996, 110 Stat. 3009. Section 589 of the Act is not classified to the Code; see Tables for complete classification.

 The Victims of Crime Act of 1984, referred to in subsec. (e)(2), is Pub.L. 98–473, Title II, ch. XIV, Oct. 12, 1984, 98 Stat. 2170, which is principally classified to Chapter 112 of Title 42, 42 U.S.C.A. § 10601 et seq. Section 1404C of the Act is classified to 42 U.S.C.A. § 10603c. For complete classification, see Short Title note set out under 42 U.S.C.A. § 10601 and Tables.

 Chapter 111 of this title, referred to in subsec. (g)(3), is 28 U.S.C.A. § 1651 et seq.

The Immigration and Nationality Act, referred to in subsec. (h)(5), is Act June 27, 1952, c. 477, 66 Stat. 163, as amended, also known as the INA, the McCarran Act, and the McCarran-Walter Act, which is classified principally to chapter 12 of Title 8, 8 U.S.C.A. § 1101 et seq. Section 101 of the Act is classified to 8 U.S.C.A. § 1101. For complete classification, see Short Title note set out under 8 U.S.C.A. § 1101 and Tables.

The Export Administration Act of 1979, referred to in subsec. (h)(6), is Pub.L. 96–72, Sept. 29, 1979, 93 Stat. 503, which is classified principally to 50 App. U.S.C.A. §§ 2401 to 2420. Section 6 of the Act is classified to 50 App. U.S.C.A. § 2405. See Tables for complete classification.

The Foreign Assistance Act of 1961, referred to in subsec. (h)(6), is Pub.L. 87–195, Sept. 4, 1961, 75 Stat. 424, as amended, also known as the Act for International Development of 1961 and the FAA, which is classified principally to chapter 32 of Title 22, 22 U.S.C.A. § 2151 et seq. Section 620A of the Act is classified to 22 U.S.C.A. § 2371. For complete classification, see Short Title note set out under 22 U.S.C.A. § 2151 and Tables.

The Arms Export Control Act, referred to in subsec. (h)(6), is Pub.L. 90–629, Oct. 22, 1968, 82 Stat. 1320, as amended, also known as the AECA and the Foreign Military Sales Act, which is classified principally to chapter 39 of Title 22, 22 U.S.C.A. § 2751 et seq. Section 40 of the Act is classified to 22 U.S.C.A. § 2780. For complete classification, see Short Title note set out under 22 U.S.C.A. § 2751 and Tables.

Section 3 of the Torture Victim Protection Act of 1991, referred to in subsec. (h)(7), is section 3 of Pub.L. 102–256, Mar. 12, 1992, 106 Stat. 73, set out in a note under section 28 U.S.C.A. § 1350.

Libyan Claims Resolution Act

Pub.L. 110–301, Aug. 4, 2008, 122 Stat. 2999, provided that:

"Section 1. Short title.

"This Act [enacting this note] may be cited as the 'Libyan Claims Resolution Act'.

"Sec. 2. Definitions.

"In this Act—

"**(1)** the term 'appropriate congressional committees' means the Committee on Foreign Relations and the Committee on the Judiciary of the Senate and the Committee on Foreign Affairs and the Committee on the Judiciary of the House of Representatives;

"**(2)** the term 'claims agreement' means an international agreement between the United States and Libya, binding under international law, that provides for the settlement of terrorism-related claims of nationals of the United States against Libya through fair compensation;

"**(3)** the term 'national of the United States' has the meaning given that term in section 101(a)(22) of the Immigration and Nationality Act (8 U.S.C. 1101(a)(22));

"**(4)** the term 'Secretary' means the Secretary of State; and

"**(5)** the term 'state sponsor of terrorism' means a country the government of which the Secretary has determined, for purposes of section 6(j) of the Export Administration Act of 1979 (50 U.S.C. App. 2405(j)), section 620A of the Foreign Assistance Act of 1961 (22 U.S.C. 2371), section 40 of the Arms Export Control Act (22 U.S.C. 2780), or any other provision of law, is a government that has repeatedly provided support for acts of international terrorism.

"Sec. 3. Sense of Congress.

"Congress supports the President in his efforts to provide fair compensation to all nationals of the United States who have terrorism-related claims against Libya through a comprehensive settlement of claims by such nationals against Libya pursuant to an international agreement between the United States and Libya as a part of the process of restoring normal relations between Libya and the United States.

"Sec. 4. Entity to assist in implementation of claims agreement.

"**(a) Designation of entity.—**

"**(1) Designation.**—The Secretary, by publication in the Federal Register, may, after consultation with the appropriate congressional committees, designate 1 or more entities to assist in providing compensation to nationals of the United States, pursuant to a claims agreement.

"**(2) Authority of the Secretary.**—The designation of an entity under paragraph (1) is within the sole discretion of the Secretary, and may not be delegated. The designation shall not be subject to judicial review.

"**(b) Immunity.**—

"**(1) Property.**—

"**(A) In general.**—Notwithstanding any other provision of law, if the Secretary designates any entity under subsection (a)(1), any property described in subparagraph (B) of this paragraph shall be immune from attachment or any other judicial process. Such immunity shall be in addition to any other applicable immunity.

"**(B) Property described.**—The property described in this subparagraph is any property that—

"**(i)** relates to the claims agreement; and

"**(ii)** For the purpose of implementing the claims agreement, is—

"**(I)** held by an entity designated by the Secretary under subsection (a)(1);

"**(II)** transferred to the entity; or

"**(III)** transferred from the entity.

"**(2) Other acts.**—An entity designated by the Secretary under subsection (a)(1), and any person acting through or on behalf of such entity, shall not be liable in any Federal or State court for any action taken to implement a claims agreement.

"**(c) Nonapplicability of the Government Corporation Control Act.**—An entity designated by the Secretary under subsection (a)(1) shall not be subject to chapter 91 of title 31, United States Code [31 U.S.C.A. § 9101 et seq.] (commonly known as the 'Government Corporation Control Act').

"**Sec. 5. Receipt of adequate funds; immunities of Libya.**

"**(a) Immunity.**—

"**(1) In general.**—Notwithstanding any other provision of law, upon submission of a certification described in paragraph (2)—

"**(A)** Libya, an agency or instrumentality of Libya, and the property of Libya or an agency or instrumentality of Libya, shall not be subject to the exceptions to immunity from jurisdiction, liens, attachment, and execution contained in section 1605A, 1605(a)(7), or 1610 (insofar as section 1610 relates to a judgment under such section 1605A or 1605(a)(7)) of title 28, United States Code;

"**(B)** section 1605A(c) of title 28, United States Code, section 1083(c) of the National Defense Authorization Act for Fiscal Year 2008 (Public Law 110–181; 122 Stat. 342; 28 U.S.C. 1605A note), section 589 of the Foreign Operations, Export Financing, and Related Programs Appropriations Act, 1997 (28 U.S.C. 1605 note), and any other private right of action relating to acts by a state sponsor of terrorism arising under Federal, State, or foreign law shall not apply with respect to claims against Libya, or any of its agencies, instrumentalities, officials, employees, or agents in any action in a Federal or State court; and

"**(C)** any attachment, decree, lien, execution, garnishment, or other judicial process brought against property of Libya, or property of any agency, instrumentality, official, employee, or agent of Libya, in connection with an action that would be precluded by subparagraph (A) or (B) shall be void.

"**(2) Certification.**—A certification described in this paragraph is a certification—

"**(A)** by the Secretary to the appropriate congressional committees; and

"**(B)** Stating that the United States Government has received funds pursuant to the claims agreement that are sufficient to ensure—

"**(i)** payment of the settlements referred to in section 654(b) of division J of the Consolidated Appropriations Act, 2008 (Public Law 110–161; 121 Stat. 2342); and

"**(ii)** fair compensation of claims of nationals of the United States for wrongful death or physical injury in cases pending on the date of enactment of this Act against Libya arising under section 1605A of title 28, United States Code (including any action brought under section 1605(a)(7) of title 28, United States Code, or section 589 of the Foreign Operations, Export Financing, and Related Programs Appropriations Act, 1997 (28 U.S.C. 1605 note), that has been given effect as if the action had originally been filed under 1605A(c) of title 28, United States Code, pursuant to section 1083(c) of the National Defense Authorization Act for Fiscal Year 2008 (Public Law 110–181; 122 Stat. 342; 28 U.S.C. 1605A note)).

"**(b) Temporal scope.**—Subsection (a) shall apply only with respect to any conduct or event occurring before June 30, 2006, regardless of whether, or the extent to which, application of that subsection affects any action filed before, on, or after that date.

"**(c) Authority of the Secretary.**—The certification by the Secretary referred to in subsection (a)(2) may not be delegated, and shall not be subject to judicial review."

Application of Pub.L. 110–181, Div. A, § 1083 to Pending Cases

Pub.L. 110–181, Div. A, Title X, § 1083(c), Jan. 28, 2008, 122 Stat. 342, provided that:

"**(1) In general.**—The amendments made by this section [enacting this section and amending 28 U.S.C.A. §§ 1605, 1607, 1610, and 42 U.S.C.A. § 10603c] shall apply to any claim arising under section 1605A of title 28, United States Code [this section].

"**(2) Prior actions.**—

"**(A) In general.**—With respect to any action that—

"**(i)** was brought under section 1605(a)(7) of title 28, United States Code, or section 589 of the Foreign Operations, Export Financing, and Related Programs Appropriations Act, 1997 (as contained in section 101(c) of division A of Public Law 104–208) [not classified to the Code], before the date of the enactment of this Act [Jan. 28, 2008],

"**(ii)** relied upon either such provision as creating a cause of action,

"**(iii)** has been adversely affected on the grounds that either or both of these provisions fail to create a cause of action against the state, and

"**(iv)** as of such date of enactment [Jan. 28, 2008], is before the courts in any form, including on appeal or motion under rule 60(b) of the Federal Rules of Civil Procedure,

that action, and any judgment in the action shall, on motion made by plaintiffs to the United States district court where the action was initially brought, or judgment in the action was initially entered, be given effect as if the action had originally been filed under section 1605A(c) of title 28, United States Code [subsec. (c) of this section].

"**(B) Defenses waived.**—The defenses of res judicata, collateral estoppel, and limitation period are waived—

"**(i)** in any action with respect to which a motion is made under subparagraph (A), or

"**(ii)** in any action that was originally brought, before the date of the enactment of this Act [Jan. 28, 2008], under section 1605(a)(7) of title 28, United States Code, or section 589 of the Foreign Operations, Export Financing, and Related Programs Appropriations Act, 1997 (as contained in section 101(c) of division A of Public Law 104–208) [not classified to the Code], and is refiled under section 1605A(c) of title 28, United States Code [subsec. (c) of this section],

to the extent such defenses are based on the claim in the action.

"**(C) Time limitations.**—A motion may be made or an action may be refiled under subparagraph (A) only—

"**(i)** If the original action was commenced not later than the latter of—

"**(I)** 10 years after April 24, 1996; or

"**(II)** 10 years after the cause of action arose; and

"**(ii)** within the 60-day period beginning on the date of the enactment of this Act [Jan. 28, 2008].

"**(3) Related actions.**—If an action arising out of an act or incident has been timely commenced under section 1605(a)(7) of title 28, United States Code, or section 589 of the Foreign Operations, Export Financing, and Related Programs Appropriations Act, 1997 (as contained in section 101(c) of division A of Public Law 104–208), any other action arising out of the same act or incident may be brought under section 1605A of title 28, United States Code [this section], if the action is commenced not later than the latter of 60 days after—

"**(A)** the date of the entry of judgment in the original action; or

"**(B)** the date of the enactment of this Act [Jan. 28, 2008].

"**(4) Preserving the jurisdiction of the courts.**—Nothing in section 1503 of the Emergency Wartime Supplemental Appropriations Act, 2003 (Public Law 108–11, 117 Stat. 579 [not classified to the Code]) has ever authorized, directly or indirectly, the making inapplicable of any provision of chapter 97 of title 28, United States Code [28 U.S.C.A. § 1602 et seq.], or the removal of the jurisdiction of any court of the United States."

[If any provision of Pub.L. 110–181, Div. A, § 1083, or the amendments made by that section, or the application of such provision to any person or circumstance, is held invalid, the remainder of that section and such amendments, and the application of such provision to other persons not similarly situated or to other circumstances, shall not be affected by such invalidation, see Pub.L. 110–181, Div. A, § 1083(e), set out as a note under this section.]

Application of Pub.L. 110–181, Div. A, § 1083 to Iraq

Pub.L. 110–181, Div. A, Title X, § 1083(d), Jan. 28, 2008, 122 Stat. 343, provided that:

"**(1) Applicability.**—The President may waive any provision of this section [enacting this section, amending 28 U.S.C.A. §§ 1605, 1607, 1610, and 42 U.S.C.A. § 10603c, and enacting provisions set out as notes under this section] with respect to Iraq, insofar as that provision may, in the President's determination, affect Iraq or any agency or instrumentality thereof, if the President determines that—

"**(A)** the waiver is in the national security interest of the United States;

"**(B)** the waiver will promote the reconstruction of, the consolidation of democracy in, and the relations of the United States with, Iraq; and

"**(C)** Iraq continues to be a reliable ally of the United States and partner in combating acts of international terrorism.

"**(2) Temporal scope.**—The authority under paragraph (1) shall apply—

"**(A)** with respect to any conduct or event occurring before or on the date of the enactment of this Act [Jan. 28, 2008];

"**(B)** with respect to any conduct or event occurring before or on the date of the exercise of that authority; and

"**(C)** regardless of whether, or the extent to which, the exercise of that authority affects any action filed before, on, or after the date of the exercise of that authority or of the enactment of this Act [Jan. 28, 2008].

"**(3) Notification to Congress.**—A waiver by the President under paragraph (1) shall cease to be effective 30 days after it is made unless the President has notified Congress in writing of the basis for the waiver as determined by the President under paragraph (1).

"**(4) Sense of Congress.**—It is the sense of the Congress that the President, acting through the Secretary of State, should work with the Government of Iraq on a state-to-state basis to ensure compensation for any meritorious claims based on terrorist acts committed by the Saddam Hussein regime against individuals who were United States nationals or members of the United States Armed Forces at the time of those terrorist acts and whose claims cannot be addressed in courts in the United States due to the exercise of the waiver authority under paragraph (1)."

[If any provision of Pub.L. 110–181, Div. A, § 1083, or the amendments made by that section, or the application of such provision to any person or circumstance, is held invalid, the remainder of that section and such amendments, and the application of such provision to other persons not similarly situated or to other circumstances, shall not be affected by such invalidation, see Pub.L. 110–181, Div. A, § 1083(e), set out as a note under this section.]

Severability

Pub.L. 110–181, Div. A, Title X, § 1083(e), Jan. 28, 2008, 122 Stat. 344, provided that: "If any provision of this section or the amendments made by this section [enacting this section, amending 28 U.S.C.A. §§ 1605, 1607, 1610, and 42 U.S.C.A. § 10603c, and enacting provisions set out as notes under this section], or the application of such provision to any person or circumstance, is held invalid, the remainder of this section and such amendments, and the application of such provision to other persons not similarly situated or to other circumstances, shall not be affected by such invalidation."

§ 1605B.   Responsibility of foreign states for international terrorism against the United States

    (a)   **Definition.**—In this section, the term "international terrorism"—

        (1)   has the meaning given the term in section 2331 of title 18, United States Code; and

        (2)   does not include any act of war (as defined in that section).

    (b)   **Responsibility of foreign states.**—A foreign state shall not be immune from the jurisdiction of the courts of the United States in any case in which money damages are sought against a foreign state for physical injury to person or property or death occurring in the United States and caused by—

        (1)   an act of international terrorism in the United States; and

        (2)   a tortious act or acts of the foreign state, or of any official, employee, or agent of that foreign state while acting within the scope of his or her office, employment, or agency, regardless where the tortious act or acts of the foreign state occurred.

    (c)   **Claims by nationals of the United States.**—Notwithstanding section 2337(2) of title 18, a national of the United States may bring a claim against a foreign state in accordance with section 2333 of that title if the foreign state would not be immune under subsection (b).

    (d)   **Rule of construction.**—A foreign state shall not be subject to the jurisdiction of the courts of the United States under subsection (b) on the basis of an omission or a tortious act or acts that constitute mere negligence.

(Added Pub.L. 114–222, § 3(a), Sept. 28, 2016, 130 Stat. 853.)

§ 1606.   Extent of liability

As to any claim for relief with respect to which a foreign state is not entitled to immunity under section 1605 or 1607 of this chapter, the foreign state shall be liable in the same manner and to the same extent as a private individual under like circumstances; but a foreign state except for an agency or instrumentality thereof shall not be liable for punitive damages; if, however, in any case wherein death was caused, the law of the place where the action or omission occurred provides, or has been construed to provide, for damages only punitive in nature, the foreign state shall be liable for actual or compensatory damages measured by the pecuniary injuries resulting from such death which were incurred by the persons for whose benefit the action was brought.

(Added Pub.L. 94–583, § 4(a), Oct. 21, 1976, 90 Stat. 2894; amended Pub.L. 105–277, Div. A, § 101(h) [Title I, § 117(b)], Oct. 21, 1998, 112 Stat. 2681–491; Pub.L. 106–386, Div. C, § 2002(f)(2), Oct. 28, 2000, 114 Stat. 1543; Pub.L. 107–297, Title II, § 201(c)(3), Nov. 26, 2002, 116 Stat. 2337.)

HISTORICAL AND STATUTORY NOTES

Waiver of Exception to Immunity from Attachment or Execution

Provisions formerly authorizing the President to waive the requirements of section 117(b) of Pub.L. 105–277 [Div. A, § 101(h), Title I], (which amended this section) in the interest of national security, set out in Pub.L. 105–277, Div. A, § 101(h) [Title I, § 117(d)], Oct. 21, 1998, 112 Stat. 2681–491, which formerly appeared as a note under section 1610 of this title, were repealed by Pub.L. 106–386, Div. C, § 2002(f)(2), Oct. 28, 2000, 114 Stat. 1543.

§ 1607.   Counterclaims

In any action brought by a foreign state, or in which a foreign state intervenes, in a court of the United States or of a State, the foreign state shall not be accorded immunity with respect to any counterclaim—

(a) for which a foreign state would not be entitled to immunity under section 1605 or 1605A of this chapter had such claim been brought in a separate action against the foreign state; or

(b) arising out of the transaction or occurrence that is the subject matter of the claim of the foreign state; or

(c) to the extent that the counterclaim does not seek relief exceeding in amount or differing in kind from that sought by the foreign state.

(Added Pub.L. 94–583, § 4(a), Oct. 21, 1976, 90 Stat. 2894; amended Pub.L. 110–181, Div. A, Title X, § 1083(b)(2), Jan. 28, 2008, 122 Stat. 341.)

HISTORICAL AND STATUTORY NOTES

Severability

If any provision of Pub.L. 110–181, Div. A, § 1083, or the amendments made by that section, or the application of such provision to any person or circumstance, is held invalid, the remainder of that section and such amendments, and the application of such provision to other persons not similarly situated or to other circumstances, shall not be affected by such invalidation, see Pub.L. 110–181, Div. A, § 1083(e), set out as a note under 28 U.S.C.A. § 1605A.

§ 1608.   Service; time to answer; default

(a) Service in the courts of the United States and of the States shall be made upon a foreign state or political subdivision of a foreign state:

(1) by delivery of a copy of the summons and complaint in accordance with any special arrangement for service between the plaintiff and the foreign state or political subdivision; or

(2) if no special arrangement exists, by delivery of a copy of the summons and complaint in accordance with an applicable international convention on service of judicial documents; or

(3) if service cannot be made under paragraphs (1) or (2), by sending a copy of the summons and complaint and a notice of suit, together with a translation of each into the official language of the foreign state, by any form of mail requiring a signed receipt, to be addressed and dispatched by the clerk of the court to the head of the ministry of foreign affairs of the foreign state concerned, or

(4) if service cannot be made within 30 days under paragraph (3), by sending two copies of the summons and complaint and a notice of suit, together with a translation of each into the official language of the foreign state, by any form of mail requiring a signed receipt, to be addressed and dispatched by the clerk of the court to the Secretary of State in Washington,

District of Columbia, to the attention of the Director of Special Consular Services—and the Secretary shall transmit one copy of the papers through diplomatic channels to the foreign state and shall send to the clerk of the court a certified copy of the diplomatic note indicating when the papers were transmitted.

As used in this subsection, a "notice of suit" shall mean a notice addressed to a foreign state and in a form prescribed by the Secretary of State by regulation.

(b) Service in the courts of the United States and of the States shall be made upon an agency or instrumentality of a foreign state:

(1) by delivery of a copy of the summons and complaint in accordance with any special arrangement for service between the plaintiff and the agency or instrumentality; or

(2) if no special arrangement exists, by delivery of a copy of the summons and complaint either to an officer, a managing or general agent, or to any other agent authorized by appointment or by law to receive service of process in the United States; or in accordance with an applicable international convention on service of judicial documents; or

(3) if service cannot be made under paragraphs (1) or (2), and if reasonably calculated to give actual notice, by delivery of a copy of the summons and complaint, together with a translation of each into the official language of the foreign state—

(A) as directed by an authority of the foreign state or political subdivision in response to a letter rogatory or request or

(B) by any form of mail requiring a signed receipt, to be addressed and dispatched by the clerk of the court to the agency or instrumentality to be served, or

(C) as directed by order of the court consistent with the law of the place where service is to be made.

(c) Service shall be deemed to have been made—

(1) in the case of service under subsection (a)(4), as of the date of transmittal indicated in the certified copy of the diplomatic note; and

(2) in any other case under this section, as of the date of receipt indicated in the certification, signed and returned postal receipt, or other proof of service applicable to the method of service employed.

(d) In any action brought in a court of the United States or of a State, a foreign state, a political subdivision thereof, or an agency or instrumentality of a foreign state shall serve an answer or other responsive pleading to the complaint within sixty days after service has been made under this section.

(e) No judgment by default shall be entered by a court of the United States or of a State against a foreign state, a political subdivision thereof, or an agency or instrumentality of a foreign state, unless the claimant establishes his claim or right to relief by evidence satisfactory to the court. A copy of any such default judgment shall be sent to the foreign state or political subdivision in the manner prescribed for service in this section.

(Added Pub.L. 94–583, § 4(a), Oct. 21, 1976, 90 Stat. 2894.)

§ 1609.   Immunity from attachment and execution of property of a foreign state

Subject to existing international agreements to which the United States is a party at the time of enactment of this Act the property in the United States of a foreign state shall be immune from attachment arrest and execution except as provided in sections 1610 and 1611 of this chapter.

(Added Pub.L. 94–583, § 4(a), Oct. 21, 1976, 90 Stat. 2895.)

HISTORICAL AND STATUTORY NOTES

References in Text

The time of enactment of this Act, referred to in text, probably means the time of enactment of Pub.L. 94–583, which was approved on Oct. 21, 1976.

§ 1610.   Exceptions to the immunity from attachment or execution

(a) The property in the United States of a foreign state, as defined in section 1603(a) of this chapter, used for a commercial activity in the United States, shall not be immune from attachment in aid of execution, or from execution, upon a judgment entered by a court of the United States or of a State after the effective date of this Act, if—

(1) the foreign state has waived its immunity from attachment in aid of execution or from execution either explicitly or by implication, notwithstanding any withdrawal of the waiver the foreign state may purport to effect except in accordance with the terms of the waiver, or

(2) the property is or was used for the commercial activity upon which the claim is based, or

(3) the execution relates to a judgment establishing rights in property which has been taken in violation of international law or which has been exchanged for property taken in violation of international law, or

(4) the execution relates to a judgment establishing rights in property—

(A) which is acquired by succession or gift, or

(B) which is immovable and situated in the United States: *Provided*, That such property is not used for purposes of maintaining a diplomatic or consular mission or the residence of the Chief of such mission, or

(5) the property consists of any contractual obligation or any proceeds from such a contractual obligation to indemnify or hold harmless the foreign state or its employees under a policy of automobile or other liability or casualty insurance covering the claim which merged into the judgment, or

(6) the judgment is based on an order confirming an arbitral award rendered against the foreign state, provided that attachment in aid of execution, or execution, would not be inconsistent with any provision in the arbitral agreement, or

(7) the judgment relates to a claim for which the foreign state is not immune under section 1605A or section 1605(a)(7) (as such section was in effect on January 27, 2008), regardless of whether the property is or was involved with the act upon which the claim is based.

(b) In addition to subsection (a), any property in the United States of an agency or instrumentality of a foreign state engaged in commercial activity in the United States shall not be immune from attachment in aid of execution, or from execution, upon a judgment entered by a court of the United States or of a State after the effective date of this Act, if—

(1) the agency or instrumentality has waived its immunity from attachment in aid of execution or from execution either explicitly or implicitly, notwithstanding any withdrawal of the waiver the agency or instrumentality may purport to effect except in accordance with the terms of the waiver, or

(2) the judgment relates to a claim for which the agency or instrumentality is not immune by virtue of section 1605(a)(2), (3), or (5) or 1605(b) of this chapter, regardless of whether the property is or was involved in the act upon which the claim is based, or

(3) the judgment relates to a claim for which the agency or instrumentality is not immune by virtue of section 1605A of this chapter or section 1605(a)(7) of this chapter (as such section was in effect on January 27, 2008), regardless of whether the property is or was involved in the act upon which the claim is based.

(c) No attachment or execution referred to in subsections (a) and (b) of this section shall be permitted until the court has ordered such attachment and execution after having determined that a reasonable period of time has elapsed following the entry of judgment and the giving of any notice required under section 1608(e) of this chapter.

(d) The property of a foreign state, as defined in section 1603(a) of this chapter, used for a commercial activity in the United States, shall not be immune from attachment prior to the entry of judgment in any action brought in a court of the United States or of a State, or prior to the elapse of the period of time provided in subsection (c) of this section, if—

(1) the foreign state has explicitly waived its immunity from attachment prior to judgment, notwithstanding any withdrawal of the waiver the foreign state may purport to effect except in accordance with the terms of the waiver, and

(2) the purpose of the attachment is to secure satisfaction of a judgment that has been or may ultimately be entered against the foreign state, and not to obtain jurisdiction.

(e) The vessels of a foreign state shall not be immune from arrest in rem, interlocutory sale, and execution in actions brought to foreclose a preferred mortgage as provided in section 1605(d).

(f)(1)(A) Notwithstanding any other provision of law, including but not limited to section 208(f) of the Foreign Missions Act (22 U.S.C. 4308(f)), and except as provided in subparagraph (B), any property with respect to which financial transactions are prohibited or regulated pursuant to section 5(b) of the Trading with the Enemy Act (50 U.S.C. App. 5(b)), section 620(a) of the Foreign Assistance Act of 1961 (22 U.S.C. 2370(a)), sections 202 and 203 of the International Emergency Economic Powers Act (50 U.S.C. 1701–1702), or any other proclamation, order, regulation, or license issued pursuant thereto, shall be subject to execution or attachment in aid of execution of any judgment relating to a claim for which a foreign state (including any agency or instrumentality or such state) claiming such property is not immune under section 1605(a)(7) (as in effect before the enactment of section 1605A) or section 1605A.

(B) Subparagraph (A) shall not apply if, at the time the property is expropriated or seized by the foreign state, the property has been held in title by a natural person or, if held in trust, has been held for the benefit of a natural person or persons.

(2)(A) At the request of any party in whose favor a judgment has been issued with respect to a claim for which the foreign state is not immune under section 1605(a)(7) (as in effect before the enactment of section 1605A) or section 1605A, the Secretary of the Treasury and the Secretary of State should make every effort to fully, promptly, and effectively assist any judgment creditor or any court that has issued any such judgment in identifying, locating, and executing against the property of that foreign state or any agency or instrumentality of such state.

(B) In providing such assistance, the Secretaries—

(i) may provide such information to the court under seal; and

(ii) should make every effort to provide the information in a manner sufficient to allow the court to direct the United States Marshal's office to promptly and effectively execute against that property.

(3) **Waiver.**—The President may waive any provision of paragraph (1) in the interest of national security.

(g) **Property in certain actions.**—

(1) **In general.**—Subject to paragraph (3), the property of a foreign state against which a judgment is entered under section 1605A, and the property of an agency or instrumentality of such a state, including property that is a separate juridical entity or is an interest held directly or indirectly in a separate juridical entity, is subject to attachment in aid of execution, and execution, upon that judgment as provided in this section, regardless of—

(A) the level of economic control over the property by the government of the foreign state;

(B) whether the profits of the property go to that government;

(C) the degree to which officials of that government manage the property or otherwise control its daily affairs;

(D) whether that government is the sole beneficiary in interest of the property; or

(E) whether establishing the property as a separate entity would entitle the foreign state to benefits in United States courts while avoiding its obligations.

(2) United States sovereign immunity inapplicable.—Any property of a foreign state, or agency or instrumentality of a foreign state, to which paragraph (1) applies shall not be immune from attachment in aid of execution, or execution, upon a judgment entered under section 1605A because the property is regulated by the United States Government by reason of action taken against that foreign state under the Trading With the Enemy Act or the International Emergency Economic Powers Act.

(3) Third-party joint property holders.—Nothing in this subsection shall be construed to supersede the authority of a court to prevent appropriately the impairment of an interest held by a person who is not liable in the action giving rise to a judgment in property subject to attachment in aid of execution, or execution, upon such judgment.

(Added Pub.L. 94–583, § 4(a), Oct. 21, 1976, 90 Stat. 2896; amended Pub.L. 100–640, § 2, Nov. 9, 1988, 102 Stat. 3333; Pub.L. 100–669, § 3, Nov. 16, 1988, 102 Stat. 3969; Pub.L. 101–650, Title III, § 325(b)(9), Dec. 1, 1990, 104 Stat. 5121; Pub.L. 104–132, Title II, § 221(b), Apr. 24, 1996, 110 Stat. 1243; Pub.L. 105–277, Div. A, § 101(h) [Title I, § 117(a)], Oct. 21, 1998, 112 Stat. 2681–491; Pub.L. 106–386, Div. C, § 2002(g)(1), Oct. 28, 2000, 114 Stat. 1543; Pub.L. 107–297, Title II, § 201(c)(3), Nov. 26, 2002, 116 Stat. 2337; Pub.L. 110–181, Div. A, Title X, § 1083(b)(3), Jan. 28, 2008, 122 Stat. 341; Pub.L. 112–158, Title V, § 502(e)(1), Aug. 10, 2012, 126 Stat. 1260.)

HISTORICAL AND STATUTORY NOTES

References in Text

The effective date of this Act, referred to in subsecs. (a) and (b), is 90 days after Oct. 21, 1976, see section 8 of Pub.L. 94–583, set out as an Effective and Applicability Provisions note under section 1602 of this title.

The enactment of section 1605A, referred to in subsec. (f), is Jan. 28, 2008, the approval date of National Defense Authorization Act for Fiscal Year 2008, Pub.L. 110–181, 122 Stat. 3, which enacted 28 U.S.C.A. § 1605A.

Severability

If any provision of Pub.L. 110–181, Div. A, § 1083, or the amendments made by that section, or the application of such provision to any person or circumstance, is held invalid, the remainder of that section and such amendments, and the application of such provision to other persons not similarly situated or to other circumstances, shall not be affected by such invalidation, see Pub.L. 110–181, Div. A, § 1083(e), set out as a note under 28 U.S.C.A. § 1605A.

Treatment of Terrorist Assets

Pub.L. 107–297, Title II, § 201(a), (b), (d), Nov. 26, 2002, 116 Stat. 2337, as amended Pub.L. 112–158, Title V, § 502(e)(2), Aug. 10, 2012, 126 Stat. 1260, provided that:

"**(a) In general.**—Notwithstanding any other provision of law, and except as provided in subsection (b) [of this note], in every case in which a person has obtained a judgment against a terrorist party on a claim based upon an act of terrorism, or for which a terrorist party is not immune under section 1605A or

1605(a)(7) (as such section was in effect on January 27, 2008) of title 28, United States Code, the blocked assets of that terrorist party (including the blocked assets of any agency or instrumentality of that terrorist party) shall be subject to execution or attachment in aid of execution in order to satisfy such judgment to the extent of any compensatory damages for which such terrorist party has been adjudged liable.

"**(b) Presidential waiver.**—

"**(1) In general.**—Subject to paragraph (2), upon determining on an asset-by-asset basis that a waiver is necessary in the national security interest, the President may waive the requirements of subsection (a) [of this note] in connection with (and prior to the enforcement of) any judicial order directing attachment in aid of execution or execution against any property subject to the Vienna Convention on Diplomatic Relations or the Vienna Convention on Consular Relations.

"**(2) Exception.**—A waiver under this subsection shall not apply to—

"**(A)** property subject to the Vienna Convention on Diplomatic Relations or the Vienna Convention on Consular Relations that has been used by the United States for any nondiplomatic purpose (including use as rental property), or the proceeds of such use; or

"**(B)** the proceeds of any sale or transfer for value to a third party of any asset subject to the Vienna Convention on Diplomatic Relations or the Vienna Convention on Consular Relations."

"**(d) Definitions.**—In this section [this note] the following definitions shall apply:

"**(1) Act of terrorism.**—The term 'act of terrorism' means—

"**(A)** any act or event certified under section 102(1) [Pub.L. 107–297, Title I, § 102(1), Nov. 26, 2002, 116 Stat. 2323, which is set out in a note under 15 U.S.C.A. § 6701]; or

"**(B)** to the extent not covered by subparagraph (A), any terrorist activity (as defined in section 212(a)(3)(B)(iii) of the Immigration and Nationality Act (8 U.S.C. 1182(a)(3)(B)(iii))).

"**(2) Blocked asset.**—The term 'blocked asset' means—

"**(A)** any asset seized or frozen by the United States under section 5(b) of the Trading With the Enemy Act (50 U.S.C. App. 5(b)) or under sections 202 and 203 of the International Emergency Economic Powers Act (50 U.S.C. 1701; 1702); and

"**(B)** does not include property that—

"**(i)** is subject to a license issued by the United States Government for final payment, transfer, or disposition by or to a person subject to the jurisdiction of the United States in connection with a transaction for which the issuance of such license has been specifically required by statute other than the International Emergency Economic Powers Act (50 U.S.C. 1701 et seq.) or the United Nations Participation Act of 1945 (22 U.S.C. 287 et seq.); or

"**(ii)** in the case of property subject to the Vienna Convention on Diplomatic Relations or the Vienna Convention on Consular Relations, or that enjoys equivalent privileges and immunities under the law of the United States, is being used exclusively for diplomatic or consular purposes.

"**(3) Certain property.**—The term 'property subject to the Vienna Convention on Diplomatic Relations or the Vienna Convention on Consular Relations' and the term 'asset subject to the Vienna Convention on Diplomatic Relations or the Vienna Convention on Consular Relations' mean any property or asset, respectively, the attachment in aid of execution or execution of which would result in a violation of an obligation of the United States under the Vienna Convention on Diplomatic Relations or the Vienna Convention on Consular Relations, as the case may be.

"**(4) Terrorist party.**—The term 'terrorist party' means a terrorist, a terrorist organization (as defined in section 212(a)(3)(B)(vi) of the Immigration and Nationality Act (8 U.S.C. 1182(a)(3)(B)(vi))), or a foreign state designated as a state sponsor of terrorism under section 6(j) of the Export Administration Act of 1979 (50 U.S.C. App. 2405(j)) or section 620A of the Foreign Assistance Act of 1961 (22 U.S.C. 2371)."

Waiver of Exception to Immunity from Attachment or Execution

Pub.L. 105–277, Div. A, § 101(h) [Title I, § 117(d)], Oct. 21, 1998, 112 Stat. 2681–491, which had provided authority for the President to waive the requirements of section 117 of Pub.L. 105–277 [amending this section and section 1606 of this title and enacting provisions set out as notes under this section] in the interest of national security, was repealed by Pub.L. 106–386, Div. C, § 2002(g)(2), Oct. 28, 2000, 114 Stat. 1543; Pub.L. 107–297, Title II, § 201(c)(3), Nov. 26, 2002, 116 Stat. 2337.

§ 1611.　　Certain types of property immune from execution

(a)　Notwithstanding the provisions of section 1610 of this chapter, the property of those organizations designated by the President as being entitled to enjoy the privileges, exemptions, and immunities provided by the International Organizations Immunities Act shall not be subject to attachment or any other judicial process impeding the disbursement of funds to, or on the order of, a foreign state as the result of an action brought in the courts of the United States or of the States.

(b)　Notwithstanding the provisions of section 1610 of this chapter, the property of a foreign state shall be immune from attachment and from execution, if—

　(1)　the property is that of a foreign central bank or monetary authority held for its own account, unless such bank or authority, or its parent foreign government, has explicitly waived its immunity from attachment in aid of execution, or from execution, notwithstanding any withdrawal of the waiver which the bank, authority or government may purport to effect except in accordance with the terms of the waiver; or

　(2)　the property is, or is intended to be, used in connection with a military activity and

　　(A)　is of a military character, or

　　(B)　is under the control of a military authority or defense agency.

(c)　Notwithstanding the provisions of section 1610 of this chapter, the property of a foreign state shall be immune from attachment and from execution in an action brought under section 302 of the Cuban Liberty and Democratic Solidarity (LIBERTAD) Act of 1996 to the extent that the property is a facility or installation used by an accredited diplomatic mission for official purposes.

(Added Pub.L. 94–583, § 4(a), Oct. 21, 1976, 90 Stat. 2897; amended Pub.L. 104–114, Title III, § 302(e), Mar. 12, 1996, 110 Stat. 818.)

HISTORICAL AND STATUTORY NOTES

References in Text

The International Organizations Immunities Act, referred to in subsec. (a), is Act Dec. 29, 1945, c. 652, Title I, 59 Stat. 669, as amended, which is classified principally to section 288 et seq. of Title 22, Foreign Relations and Intercourse. For complete classification of this Act to the Code, see Short Title note set out under section 288 of Title 22 and Tables.

Section 302 of the Cuban Liberty and Democratic Solidarity (LIBERTAD) Act of 1996, referred to in subsec. (c), is Pub.L. 104–114, Title III, § 302, Mar. 12, 1996, 110 Stat. 815, which is classified to section 6082 of Title 22, Foreign Relations and Intercourse.

CHAPTER 99—GENERAL PROVISIONS

Sec.
1631.　　　Transfer to cure want of jurisdiction.

§ 1631.　　Transfer to cure want of jurisdiction

Whenever a civil action is filed in a court as defined in section 610 of this title or an appeal, including a petition for review of administrative action, is noticed for or filed with such a court and that court finds that there is a want of jurisdiction, the court shall, if it is in the interest of justice, transfer such action or appeal to any other such court (or, for cases within the jurisdiction of the United States Tax Court, to that court) in which the action or appeal could have been brought at the time it was filed or noticed, and the action or appeal shall proceed as if it had been filed in or noticed for the court to which it is transferred on the date upon which it was actually filed in or noticed for the court from which it is transferred.

(Added Pub.L. 97–164, Title III, § 301(a), Apr. 2, 1982, 96 Stat. 55; amended Pub.L. 115–332, § 2, Dec. 19, 2018, 132 Stat. 4487.)

PART V—PROCEDURE

CHAPTER 111—GENERAL PROVISIONS

§ 1651. Writs

(a) The Supreme Court and all courts established by Act of Congress may issue all writs necessary or appropriate in aid of their respective jurisdictions and agreeable to the usages and principles of law.

(b) An alternative writ or rule nisi may be issued by a justice or judge of a court which has jurisdiction.

(June 25, 1948, c. 646, 62 Stat. 944; May 24, 1949, c. 139, § 90, 63 Stat. 102.)

HISTORICAL AND STATUTORY NOTES

Writ of Error

Act Jan. 31, 1928, c. 14, § 2, 45 Stat. 54, as amended Apr. 26, 1928, c. 440, 45 Stat. 466; June 25, 1948, c. 646, § 23, 62 Stat. 990, provided that: "All Acts of Congress referring to writs of error shall be construed as amended to the extent necessary to substitute appeal for writ of error."

§ 1652. State laws as rules of decision

The laws of the several states, except where the Constitution or treaties of the United States or Acts of Congress otherwise require or provide, shall be regarded as rules of decision in civil actions in the courts of the United States, in cases where they apply.

(June 25, 1948, c. 646, 62 Stat. 944.)

§ 1653. Amendment of pleadings to show jurisdiction

Defective allegations of jurisdiction may be amended, upon terms, in the trial or appellate courts.

(June 25, 1948, c. 646, 62 Stat. 944.)

§ 1654. Appearance personally or by counsel

In all courts of the United States the parties may plead and conduct their own cases personally or by counsel as, by the rules of such courts, respectively, are permitted to manage and conduct causes therein.

(June 25, 1948, c. 646, 62 Stat. 944; May 24, 1949, c. 139, § 91, 63 Stat. 103.)

§ 1655. Lien enforcement; absent defendants

In an action in a district court to enforce any lien upon or claim to, or to remove any incumbrance or lien or cloud upon the title to, real or personal property within the district, where any defendant cannot be served within the State, or does not voluntarily appear, the court may order the absent defendant to appear or plead by a day certain.

Such order shall be served on the absent defendant personally if practicable, wherever found, and also upon the person or persons in possession or charge of such property, if any. Where personal service is not practicable, the order shall be published as the court may direct, not less than once a week for six consecutive weeks.

If an absent defendant does not appear or plead within the time allowed, the court may proceed as if the absent defendant had been served with process within the State, but any adjudication shall, as regards the absent defendant without appearance, affect only the property which is the subject of the action. When a part of the property is within another district, but within the same state, such action may be brought in either district.

Any defendant not so personally notified may, at any time within one year after final judgment, enter his appearance, and thereupon the court shall set aside the judgment and permit such defendant to plead on payment of such costs as the court deems just.

(June 25, 1948, c. 646, 62 Stat. 944.)

§ 1656. Creation of new district or division or transfer of territory; lien enforcement

The creation of a new district or division or the transfer of any territory to another district or division shall not affect or divest any lien theretofore acquired in a district court upon property within such district, division or territory.

To enforce such lien, the clerk of the court in which the same is acquired, upon the request and at the cost of the party desiring the same, shall make a certified copy of the record thereof, which, when filed in the proper court of the district or division in which such property is situated after such creation or transfer shall be evidence in all courts and places equally with the original thereof; and, thereafter like proceedings shall be had thereon, and with the same effect, as though the case or proceeding had been originally instituted in such court.

(June 25, 1948, c. 646, 62 Stat. 944; Nov. 6, 1978, Pub.L. 95–598, Title II, § 242, 92 Stat. 2671.)

§ 1657. Priority of civil actions

(a) Notwithstanding any other provision of law, each court of the United States shall determine the order in which civil actions are heard and determined, except that the court shall expedite the consideration of any action brought under chapter 153 or section 1826 of this title, any action for temporary or preliminary injunctive relief, or any other action if good cause therefor is shown. For purposes of this subsection, "good cause" is shown if a right under the Constitution of the United States or a Federal Statute (including rights under section 552 of title 5) would be maintained in a factual context that indicates that a request for expedited consideration has merit.

(b) The Judicial Conference of the United States may modify the rules adopted by the courts to determine the order in which civil actions are heard and determined, in order to establish consistency among the judicial circuits.

(Added Pub.L. 98–620, Title IV, § 401(a), Nov. 8, 1984, 98 Stat. 3356.)

§ 1658. Time limitations on the commencement of civil actions arising under Acts of Congress

(a) Except as otherwise provided by law, a civil action arising under an Act of Congress enacted after the date of the enactment of this section may not be commenced later than 4 years after the cause of action accrues.

(b) Notwithstanding subsection (a), a private right of action that involves a claim of fraud, deceit, manipulation, or contrivance in contravention of a regulatory requirement concerning the securities laws, as defined in section 3(a)(47) of the Securities Exchange Act of 1934 (15 U.S.C. 78c(a)(47)), may be brought not later than the earlier of—

    (1)   2 years after the discovery of the facts constituting the violation; or

    (2)   5 years after such violation.

(Added Pub.L. 101–650, Title III, § 313(a), Dec. 1, 1990, 104 Stat. 5114; amended Pub.L. 107–204, Title VIII, § 804(a), July 30, 2002, 116 Stat. 801.)

HISTORICAL AND STATUTORY NOTES

References in Text

The date of the enactment of this section, referred to in text, is the date of enactment of this section by section 313(a) of Pub.L. 101–650, which was approved Dec. 1, 1990.

No Creation of Actions

Pub.L. 107–204, Title VIII, § 804(c), July 30, 2002, 116 Stat. 801, provided that: "Nothing in this section [Pub.L. 107–204, Title VIII, § 804, July 30, 2002, 116 Stat. 801, which amended this section and enacted provisions set out as a note under this section] shall create a new, private right of action."

§ 1659.   Stay of certain actions pending disposition of related proceedings before the United States International Trade Commission

(a)   Stay.—In a civil action involving parties that are also parties to a proceeding before the United States International Trade Commission under section 337 of the Tariff Act of 1930, at the request of a party to the civil action that is also a respondent in the proceeding before the Commission, the district court shall stay, until the determination of the Commission becomes final, proceedings in the civil action with respect to any claim that involves the same issues involved in the proceeding before the Commission, but only if such request is made within—

    (1)   30 days after the party is named as a respondent in the proceeding before the Commission, or

    (2)   30 days after the district court action is filed,

whichever is later.

(b)   Use of Commission record.—Notwithstanding section 337(n)(1) of the Tariff Act of 1930, after dissolution of a stay under subsection (a), the record of the proceeding before the United States International Trade Commission shall be transmitted to the district court and shall be admissible in the civil action, subject to such protective order as the district court determines necessary, to the extent permitted under the Federal Rules of Evidence and the Federal Rules of Civil Procedure.

(Added Pub.L. 103–465, Title III, § 321(b)(1)(A), Dec. 8, 1994, 108 Stat. 4945.)

HISTORICAL AND STATUTORY NOTES

References in Text

Section 337 of the Tariff Act of 1930, referred to in text, is section 337 of Act June 17, 1930, c. 497, Title III, 46 Stat. 703, which is classified to section 1337 of Title 19, Customs Duties.

CHAPTER 113—PROCESS

§ 1691.   Seal and teste of process

All writs and process issuing from a court of the United States shall be under the seal of the court and signed by the clerk thereof.

(June 25, 1948, c. 646, 62 Stat. 945.)

HISTORICAL AND STATUTORY NOTES

Immunity from Seizure under Judicial Process of Cultural Objects Imported for Temporary Exhibition or Display

Presidential determination of cultural significance of objects and exhibition or display thereof in the national interest, see section 2459 of Title 22, Foreign Relations and Intercourse.

§ 1692.   Process and orders affecting property in different districts

In proceedings in a district court where a receiver is appointed for property, real, personal, or mixed, situated in different districts, process may issue and be executed in any such district as if the property lay wholly within one district, but orders affecting the property shall be entered of record in each of such districts.

(June 25, 1948, c. 646, 62 Stat. 945.)

§ 1693.   Place of arrest in civil action

Except as otherwise provided by Act of Congress, no person shall be arrested in one district for trial in another in any civil action in a district court.

(June 25, 1948, c. 646, 62 Stat. 945.)

§ 1694.   Patent infringement action

In a patent infringement action commenced in a district where the defendant is not a resident but has a regular and established place of business, service of process, summons or subpoena upon such defendant may be made upon his agent or agents conducting such business.

(June 25, 1948, c. 646, 62 Stat. 945.)

§ 1695.   Stockholder's derivative action

Process in a stockholder's action in behalf of his corporation may be served upon such corporation in any district where it is organized or licensed to do business or is doing business.

(June 25, 1948, c. 646, 62 Stat. 945.)

§ 1696.   Service in foreign and international litigation

(a) The district court of the district in which a person resides or is found may order service upon him of any document issued in connection with a proceeding in a foreign or international tribunal. The order may be made pursuant to a letter rogatory issued, or request made, by a foreign or international tribunal or upon application of any interested person and shall direct the manner of service. Service pursuant to this subsection does not, of itself, require the recognition or enforcement in the United States of a judgment, decree, or order rendered by a foreign or international tribunal.

(b) This section does not preclude service of such a document without an order of court.

(Added Pub.L. 88–619, § 4(a), Oct. 3, 1964, 78 Stat. 995.)

HISTORICAL AND STATUTORY NOTES

Treaties and Conventions; Service Abroad of Judicial and Extrajudicial Documents in Civil or Commercial Matters; Observance On and After Feb. 10, 1969, by United States and Citizens and Persons Subject to Jurisdiction of United States

For text of Convention, see provisions set out as a note under Rule 4, Federal Rules of Civil Procedure, 28 U.S.C.A.

§ 1697.　　Service in multiparty, multiforum actions

When the jurisdiction of the district court is based in whole or in part upon section 1369 of this title, process, other than subpoenas, may be served at any place within the United States, or anywhere outside the United States if otherwise permitted by law.

(Added Pub.L. 107–273, Div. C, Title I, § 11020(b)(4)(A)(i), Nov. 2, 2002, 116 Stat. 1828.)

CHAPTER 114—CLASS ACTIONS

§ 1711.　　Definitions

In this chapter:

(1) **Class.**—The term "class" means all of the class members in a class action.

(2) **Class action.**—The term "class action" means any civil action filed in a district court of the United States under rule 23 of the Federal Rules of Civil Procedure or any civil action that is removed to a district court of the United States that was originally filed under a State statute or rule of judicial procedure authorizing an action to be brought by 1 or more representatives as a class action.

(3) **Class counsel.**—The term "class counsel" means the persons who serve as the attorneys for the class members in a proposed or certified class action.

(4) **Class members.**—The term "class members" means the persons (named or unnamed) who fall within the definition of the proposed or certified class in a class action.

(5) **Plaintiff class action.**—The term "plaintiff class action" means a class action in which class members are plaintiffs.

(6) **Proposed settlement.**—The term "proposed settlement" means an agreement regarding a class action that is subject to court approval and that, if approved, would be binding on some or all class members.

(Added Pub.L. 109–2, § 3(a), Feb. 18, 2005, 119 Stat. 5.)

HISTORICAL AND STATUTORY NOTES

References in Text

Rule 23 of the Federal Rules of Civil Procedure, referred to in par. (2), is set out following the code sections of this title.

Effective and Applicability Provisions

2005 Acts. Enactment of this section by Class Action Fairness Act of 2005, Pub.L. 109–2, Feb. 18, 2005, 119 Stat. 4, applicable to any civil action commenced on or after Feb. 18, 2005, see Pub.L. 109–2, § 9, set out as a note under 28 U.S.C.A. § 1332.

Findings and Purposes

Pub.L. 109–2, § 2, Feb. 18, 2005, 119 Stat. 4, provided that:

"**(a) Findings.**—Congress finds the following:

"**(1)** Class action lawsuits are an important and valuable part of the legal system when they permit the fair and efficient resolution of legitimate claims of numerous parties by allowing the claims to be aggregated into a single action against a defendant that has allegedly caused harm.

"**(2)** Over the past decade, there have been abuses of the class action device that have—

"**(A)** harmed class members with legitimate claims and defendants that have acted responsibly;

"**(B)** adversely affected interstate commerce; and

"**(C)** undermined public respect for our judicial system.

"**(3)** Class members often receive little or no benefit from class actions, and are sometimes harmed, such as where—

"**(A)** counsel are awarded large fees, while leaving class members with coupons or other awards of little or no value;

"**(B)** unjustified awards are made to certain plaintiffs at the expense of other class members; and

"**(C)** confusing notices are published that prevent class members from being able to fully understand and effectively exercise their rights.

"**(4)** Abuses in class actions undermine the National judicial system, the free flow of interstate commerce, and the concept of diversity jurisdiction as intended by the framers of the United States constitution, in that State and local courts are—

"**(A)** keeping cases of national importance out of Federal court;

"**(B)** sometimes acting in ways that demonstrate bias against out-of-State defendants; and

"**(C)** making judgments that impose their view of the law on other States and bind the rights of the residents of those States.

"**(b) Purposes.**—The purposes of this Act [the Class Action Fairness Act of 2005, which enacted this note, this chapter, and 28 U.S.C.A. § 1453, amended 28 U.S.C.A. §§ 1332, 1335, and 1603, and enacted provisions set out as notes under 28 U.S.C.A. §§ 1332, 2071, and 2074] are to—

"**(1)** assure fair and prompt recoveries for class members with legitimate claims;

"**(2)** restore the intent of the framers of the United States Constitution by providing for Federal court consideration of interstate cases of national importance under diversity jurisdiction; and

"**(3)** benefit society by encouraging innovation and lowering consumer prices."

[Enactment of this note by Class Action Fairness Act of 2005, Pub.L. 109–2, Feb. 18, 2005, 119 Stat. 4, applicable to any civil action commenced on or after Feb. 18, 2005, see Pub.L. 109–2, § 9, set out as a note under 28 U.S.C.A. § 1332.]

§ 1712.   Coupon settlements

(a) Contingent fees in coupon settlements.—If a proposed settlement in a class action provides for a recovery of coupons to a class member, the portion of any attorney's fee award to class counsel that is attributable to the award of the coupons shall be based on the value to class members of the coupons that are redeemed.

(b) Other attorney's fee awards in coupon settlements.—

    (1) In general.—If a proposed settlement in a class action provides for a recovery of coupons to class members, and a portion of the recovery of the coupons is not used to determine the attorney's fee to be paid to class counsel, any attorney's fee award shall be based upon the amount of time class counsel reasonably expended working on the action.

    (2) Court approval.—Any attorney's fee under this subsection shall be subject to approval by the court and shall include an appropriate attorney's fee, if any, for obtaining equitable relief, including an injunction, if applicable. Nothing in this subsection shall be construed to prohibit application of a lodestar with a multiplier method of determining attorney's fees.

(c) Attorney's fee awards calculated on a mixed basis in coupon settlements.—If a proposed settlement in a class action provides for an award of coupons to class members and also provides for equitable relief, including injunctive relief—

    (1) that portion of the attorney's fee to be paid to class counsel that is based upon a portion of the recovery of the coupons shall be calculated in accordance with subsection (a); and

    (2) that portion of the attorney's fee to be paid to class counsel that is not based upon a portion of the recovery of the coupons shall be calculated in accordance with subsection (b).

(d) Settlement valuation expertise.—In a class action involving the awarding of coupons, the court may, in its discretion upon the motion of a party, receive expert testimony from a witness qualified to provide information on the actual value to the class members of the coupons that are redeemed.

(e) Judicial scrutiny of coupon settlements.—In a proposed settlement under which class members would be awarded coupons, the court may approve the proposed settlement only after a hearing to determine whether, and making a written finding that, the settlement is fair, reasonable, and adequate for class members. The court, in its discretion, may also require that a proposed settlement agreement provide for the distribution of a portion of the value of unclaimed coupons to 1 or more charitable or governmental organizations, as agreed to by the parties. The distribution and redemption of any proceeds under this subsection shall not be used to calculate attorneys' fees under this section.

(Added Pub.L. 109–2, § 3(a), Feb. 18, 2005, 119 Stat. 6.)

HISTORICAL AND STATUTORY NOTES

Effective and Applicability Provisions

    2005 Acts. Enactment of this section by Class Action Fairness Act of 2005, Pub.L. 109–2, Feb. 18, 2005, 119 Stat. 4, applicable to any civil action commenced on or after Feb. 18, 2005, see Pub.L. 109–2, § 9, set out as a note under 28 U.S.C.A. § 1332.

§ 1713.   Protection against loss by class members

    The court may approve a proposed settlement under which any class member is obligated to pay sums to class counsel that would result in a net loss to the class member only if the court makes a written finding that nonmonetary benefits to the class member substantially outweigh the monetary loss.

(Added Pub.L. 109–2, § 3(a), Feb. 18, 2005, 119 Stat. 7.)

HISTORICAL AND STATUTORY NOTES

Effective and Applicability Provisions

2005 Acts. Enactment of this section by Class Action Fairness Act of 2005, Pub.L. 109–2, Feb. 18, 2005, 119 Stat. 4, applicable to any civil action commenced on or after Feb. 18, 2005, see Pub.L. 109–2, § 9, set out as a note under 28 U.S.C.A. § 1332.

§ 1714.   Protection against discrimination based on geographic location

The court may not approve a proposed settlement that provides for the payment of greater sums to some class members than to others solely on the basis that the class members to whom the greater sums are to be paid are located in closer geographic proximity to the court.

(Added Pub.L. 109–2, § 3(a), Feb. 18, 2005, 119 Stat. 7.)

HISTORICAL AND STATUTORY NOTES

Effective and Applicability Provisions

2005 Acts. Enactment of this section by Class Action Fairness Act of 2005, Pub.L. 109–2, Feb. 18, 2005, 119 Stat. 4, applicable to any civil action commenced on or after Feb. 18, 2005, see Pub.L. 109–2, § 9, set out as a note under 28 U.S.C.A. § 1332.

§ 1715.   Notifications to appropriate Federal and State officials

(a) Definitions.—

(1) Appropriate Federal official.—In this section, the term "appropriate Federal official" means—

(A) the Attorney General of the United States; or

(B) in any case in which the defendant is a Federal depository institution, a State depository institution, a depository institution holding company, a foreign bank, or a nondepository institution subsidiary of the foregoing (as such terms are defined in section 3 of the Federal Deposit Insurance Act (12 U.S.C. 1813)), the person who has the primary Federal regulatory or supervisory responsibility with respect to the defendant, if some or all of the matters alleged in the class action are subject to regulation or supervision by that person.

(2) Appropriate State official.—In this section, the term "appropriate State official" means the person in the State who has the primary regulatory or supervisory responsibility with respect to the defendant, or who licenses or otherwise authorizes the defendant to conduct business in the State, if some or all of the matters alleged in the class action are subject to regulation by that person. If there is no primary regulator, supervisor, or licensing authority, or the matters alleged in the class action are not subject to regulation or supervision by that person, then the appropriate State official shall be the State attorney general.

(b) In general.—Not later than 10 days after a proposed settlement of a class action is filed in court, each defendant that is participating in the proposed settlement shall serve upon the appropriate State official of each State in which a class member resides and the appropriate Federal official, a notice of the proposed settlement consisting of—

(1) a copy of the complaint and any materials filed with the complaint and any amended complaints (except such materials shall not be required to be served if such materials are made electronically available through the Internet and such service includes notice of how to electronically access such material);

(2) notice of any scheduled judicial hearing in the class action;

(3) any proposed or final notification to class members of—

(A)(i)   the members' rights to request exclusion from the class action; or

(ii)   if no right to request exclusion exists, a statement that no such right exists; and

(B)   a proposed settlement of a class action;

(4)   any proposed or final class action settlement;

(5)   any settlement or other agreement contemporaneously made between class counsel and counsel for the defendants;

(6)   any final judgment or notice of dismissal;

(7)(A)   if feasible, the names of class members who reside in each State and the estimated proportionate share of the claims of such members to the entire settlement to that State's appropriate State official; or

(B)   if the provision of information under subparagraph (A) is not feasible, a reasonable estimate of the number of class members residing in each State and the estimated proportionate share of the claims of such members to the entire settlement; and

(8)   any written judicial opinion relating to the materials described under subparagraphs (3) through (6).

(c)   **Depository institutions notification.—**

(1)   **Federal and other depository institutions.—**In any case in which the defendant is a Federal depository institution, a depository institution holding company, a foreign bank, or a non-depository institution subsidiary of the foregoing, the notice requirements of this section are satisfied by serving the notice required under subsection (b) upon the person who has the primary Federal regulatory or supervisory responsibility with respect to the defendant, if some or all of the matters alleged in the class action are subject to regulation or supervision by that person.

(2)   **State depository institutions.—**In any case in which the defendant is a State depository institution (as that term is defined in section 3 of the Federal Deposit Insurance Act (12 U.S.C. 1813)), the notice requirements of this section are satisfied by serving the notice required under subsection (b) upon the State bank supervisor (as that term is defined in section 3 of the Federal Deposit Insurance Act (12 U.S.C. 1813)) of the State in which the defendant is incorporated or chartered, if some or all of the matters alleged in the class action are subject to regulation or supervision by that person, and upon the appropriate Federal official.

(d)   **Final approval.—**An order giving final approval of a proposed settlement may not be issued earlier than 90 days after the later of the dates on which the appropriate Federal official and the appropriate State official are served with the notice required under subsection (b).

(e)   **Noncompliance if notice not provided.—**

(1)   **In general.—**A class member may refuse to comply with and may choose not to be bound by a settlement agreement or consent decree in a class action if the class member demonstrates that the notice required under subsection (b) has not been provided.

(2)   **Limitation.—**A class member may not refuse to comply with or to be bound by a settlement agreement or consent decree under paragraph (1) if the notice required under subsection (b) was directed to the appropriate Federal official and to either the State attorney general or the person that has primary regulatory, supervisory, or licensing authority over the defendant.

(3)   **Application of rights.—**The rights created by this subsection shall apply only to class members or any person acting on a class member's behalf, and shall not be construed to limit any other rights affecting a class member's participation in the settlement.

(f) Rule of construction.—Nothing in this section shall be construed to expand the authority of, or impose any obligations, duties, or responsibilities upon, Federal or State officials.

(Added Pub.L. 109–2, § 3(a), Feb. 18, 2005, 119 Stat. 7.)

HISTORICAL AND STATUTORY NOTES

References in Text

Section 3 of the Federal Deposit Insurance Act, referred to in subsecs. (a)(1)(B) and (c)(2), is Act Sept. 21, 1950, c. 967, § 2[3], 64 Stat. 873, as amended, which is classified to 12 U.S.C.A. § 1813. A Federal depository institution is defined in 12 U.S.C.A. § 1813(c)(4); a State depository institution, in 12 U.S.C.A. § 1813(c)(5); a depository institution holding company, in 12 U.S.C.A. § 1813(w)(1); a foreign bank, in 12 U.S.C.A. § 1813(s)(1); and State bank supervisor, in 12 U.S.C.A. § 1813(r)(1).

Effective and Applicability Provisions

2005 Acts. Enactment of this section by Class Action Fairness Act of 2005, Pub.L. 109–2, Feb. 18, 2005, 119 Stat. 4, applicable to any civil action commenced on or after Feb. 18, 2005, see Pub.L. 109–2, § 9, set out as a note under 28 U.S.C.A. § 1332.

CHAPTER 115—EVIDENCE; DOCUMENTARY

§ 1731.   Handwriting

The admitted or proved handwriting of any person shall be admissible, for purposes of comparison, to determine genuineness of other handwriting attributed to such person.

(June 25, 1948, c. 646, 62 Stat. 945.)

§ 1732.   Record made in regular course of business; photographic copies

If any business, institution, member of a profession or calling, or any department or agency of government, in the regular course of business or activity has kept or recorded any memorandum, writing, entry, print, representation or combination thereof, of any act, transaction, occurrence, or event, and in the regular course of business has caused any or all of the same to be recorded, copied,

---

[1] [Footnote to Chapter 115 table:] So in original. Does not conform to section catchline.

or reproduced by any photographic, photostatic, microfilm, micro-card, miniature photographic, or other process which accurately reproduces or forms a durable medium for so reproducing the original, the original may be destroyed in the regular course of business unless its preservation is required by law. Such reproduction, when satisfactorily identified, is as admissible in evidence as the original itself in any judicial or administrative proceeding whether the original is in existence or not and an enlargement or facsimile of such reproduction is likewise admissible in evidence if the original reproduction is in existence and available for inspection under direction of court. The introduction of a reproduced record, enlargement, or facsimile does not preclude admission of the original. This subsection[1] shall not be construed to exclude from evidence any document or copy thereof which is otherwise admissible under the rules of evidence.

(June 25, 1948, c. 646, 62 Stat. 945; Aug. 28, 1951, c. 351, §§ 1, 3, 65 Stat. 205, 206; Aug. 30, 1961, Pub.L. 87–183, 75 Stat. 413; Jan. 2, 1975, Pub.L. 93–595, § 2(b), 88 Stat. 1949.)

§ 1733.   Government records and papers; copies

(a) Books or records of account or minutes of proceedings of any department or agency of the United States shall be admissible to prove the act, transaction or occurrence as a memorandum of which the same were made or kept.

(b) Properly authenticated copies or transcripts of any books, records, papers or documents of any department or agency of the United States shall be admitted in evidence equally with the originals thereof.

(c) This section does not apply to cases, actions, and proceedings to which the Federal Rules of Evidence apply.

(June 25, 1948, c. 646, 62 Stat. 946; Jan. 2, 1975, Pub.L. 93–595, § 2(c), 88 Stat. 1949.)

HISTORICAL AND STATUTORY NOTES

References in Text

The Federal Rules of Evidence, referred to in subsec. (c), are set out in this title.

§ 1734.   Court record lost or destroyed, generally

(a) A lost or destroyed record of any proceeding in any court of the United States may be supplied on application of any interested party not at fault, by substituting a copy certified by the clerk of any court in which an authentic copy is lodged.

(b) Where a certified copy is not available, any interested person not at fault may file in such court a verified application for an order establishing the lost or destroyed record.

Every other interested person shall be served personally with a copy of the application and with notice of hearing on a day stated, not less than sixty days after service. Service may be made on any nonresident of the district anywhere within the jurisdiction of the United States or in any foreign country.

Proof of service in a foreign country shall be certified by a minister or consul of the United States in such country, under his official seal.

If, after the hearing, the court is satisfied that the statements contained in the application are true, it shall enter an order reciting the substance and effect of the lost or destroyed record. Such order, subject to intervening rights of third persons, shall have the same effect as the original record.

(June 25, 1948, c. 646, 62 Stat. 946.)

---

[1] [Footnote to 28 U.S.C. § 1732:] So in original. Probably should be read as "section". [Section formerly was subsection (b) of this section. Ed.]

§ 1735.   Court record lost or destroyed where United States interested

(a) When the record of any case or matter in any court of the United States to which the United States is a party, is lost or destroyed, a certified copy of any official paper of a United States attorney, United States marshal or clerk or other certifying or recording officer of any such court, made pursuant to law, on file in any department or agency of the United States and relating to such case or matter, shall, on being filed in the court to which it relates, have the same effect as an original paper filed in such court. If the copy so filed discloses the date and amount of a judgment or decree and the names of the parties thereto, the court may enforce the judgment or decree as though the original record had not been lost or destroyed.

(b) Whenever the United States is interested in any lost or destroyed records or files of a court of the United States, the clerk of such court and the United States attorney for the district shall take the steps necessary to restore such records or files, under the direction of the judges of such court.

(June 25, 1948, c. 646, 62 Stat. 946.)

§ 1736.   Congressional Journals

Extracts from the Journals of the Senate and the House of Representatives, and from the Executive Journal of the Senate when the injunction of secrecy is removed, certified by the Secretary of the Senate or the Clerk of the House of Representatives shall be received in evidence with the same effect as the originals would have.

(June 25, 1948, c. 646, 62 Stat. 947.)

HISTORICAL AND STATUTORY NOTES

Transfer of Functions

Any reference in any provision of law enacted before Jan. 4, 1995, to a function, duty, or authority of the Clerk of the House of Representatives treated as referring, with respect to that function, duty, or authority, to the officer of the House of Representatives exercising that function, duty, or authority, as determined by the Committee on House Oversight of the House of Representatives, see section 2(1) of Pub.L. 104–14, set out as a note preceding section 21 of Title 2, The Congress.

§ 1737.   Copy of officer's bond

Any person to whose custody the bond of any officer of the United States has been committed shall, on proper request and payment of the fee allowed by any Act of Congress, furnish certified copies thereof, which shall be prima facie evidence in any court of the execution, filing and contents of the bond.

(June 25, 1948, c. 646, 62 Stat. 947.)

§ 1738.   State and Territorial statutes and judicial proceedings; full faith and credit

The Acts of the legislature of any State, Territory, or Possession of the United States, or copies thereof, shall be authenticated by affixing the seal of such State, Territory or Possession thereto.

The records and judicial proceedings of any court of any such State, Territory or Possession, or copies thereof, shall be proved or admitted in other courts within the United States and its Territories and Possessions by the attestation of the clerk and seal of the court annexed, if a seal exists, together with a certificate of a judge of the court that the said attestation is in proper form.

Such Acts, records and judicial proceedings or copies thereof, so authenticated, shall have the same full faith and credit in every court within the United States and its Territories and Possessions as they have by law or usage in the courts of such State, Territory or Possession from which they are taken.

(June 25, 1948, c. 646, 62 Stat. 947.)

§ 1738A. Full faith and credit given to child custody determinations

(a) The appropriate authorities of every State shall enforce according to its terms, and shall not modify except as provided in subsections (f), (g), and (h) of this section, any custody determination or visitation determination made consistently with the provisions of this section by a court of another State.

(b) As used in this section, the term—

(1) "child" means a person under the age of eighteen;

(2) "contestant" means a person, including a parent or grandparent, who claims a right to custody or visitation of a child;

(3) "custody determination" means a judgment, decree, or other order of a court providing for the custody of a child, and includes permanent and temporary orders, and initial orders and modifications;

(4) "home State" means the State in which, immediately preceding the time involved, the child lived with his parents, a parent, or a person acting as parent, for at least six consecutive months, and in the case of a child less than six months old, the State in which the child lived from birth with any of such persons. Periods of temporary absence of any of such persons are counted as part of the six-month or other period;

(5) "modification" and "modify" refer to a custody or visitation determination which modifies, replaces, supersedes, or otherwise is made subsequent to, a prior custody or visitation determination concerning the same child, whether made by the same court or not;

(6) "person acting as a parent" means a person, other than a parent, who has physical custody of a child and who has either been awarded custody by a court or claims a right to custody;

(7) "physical custody" means actual possession and control of a child;

(8) "State" means a State of the United States, the District of Columbia, the Commonwealth of Puerto Rico, or a territory or possession of the United States; and

(9) "visitation determination" means a judgment, decree, or other order of a court providing for the visitation of a child and includes permanent and temporary orders and initial orders and modifications.

(c) A child custody or visitation determination made by a court of a State is consistent with the provisions of this section only if—

(1) such court has jurisdiction under the law of such State; and

(2) one of the following conditions is met:

(A) such State (i) is the home State of the child on the date of the commencement of the proceeding, or (ii) had been the child's home State within six months before the date of the commencement of the proceeding and the child is absent from such State because of his removal or retention by a contestant or for other reasons, and a contestant continues to live in such State;

(B) (i) it appears that no other State would have jurisdiction under subparagraph (A), and (ii) it is in the best interest of the child that a court of such State assume jurisdiction because (I) the child and his parents, or the child and at least one contestant, have a significant connection with such State other than mere physical presence in such State, and (II) there is available in such State substantial evidence concerning the child's present or future care, protection, training, and personal relationships;

(C) the child is physically present in such State and (i) the child has been abandoned, or (ii) it is necessary in an emergency to protect the child because the child, a sibling, or parent of the child has been subjected to or threatened with mistreatment or abuse;

(D) (i) it appears that no other State would have jurisdiction under subparagraph (A), (B), (C), or (E), or another State has declined to exercise jurisdiction on the ground that the State whose jurisdiction is in issue is the more appropriate forum to determine the custody or visitation of the child, and (ii) it is in the best interest of the child that such court assume jurisdiction; or

(E) the court has continuing jurisdiction pursuant to subsection (d) of this section.

(d) The jurisdiction of a court of a State which has made a child custody or visitation determination consistently with the provisions of this section continues as long as the requirement of subsection (c)(1) of this section continues to be met and such State remains the residence of the child or of any contestant.

(e) Before a child custody or visitation determination is made, reasonable notice and opportunity to be heard shall be given to the contestants, any parent whose parental rights have not been previously terminated and any person who has physical custody of a child.

(f) A court of a State may modify a determination of the custody of the same child made by a court of another State, if—

(1) it has jurisdiction to make such a child custody determination; and

(2) the court of the other State no longer has jurisdiction, or it has declined to exercise such jurisdiction to modify such determination.

(g) A court of a State shall not exercise jurisdiction in any proceeding for a custody or visitation determination commenced during the pendency of a proceeding in a court of another State where such court of that other State is exercising jurisdiction consistently with the provisions of this section to make a custody or visitation determination.

(h) A court of a State may not modify a visitation determination made by a court of another State unless the court of the other State no longer has jurisdiction to modify such determination or has declined to exercise jurisdiction to modify such determination.

(Added Pub.L. 96–611, § 8(a), Dec. 28, 1980, 94 Stat. 3569; amended Pub.L. 105–374, § 1, Nov. 12, 1998, 112 Stat. 3383; Pub.L. 106–386, Div. B, Title III, § 1303(d), Oct. 28, 2000, 114 Stat. 1512.)

HISTORICAL AND STATUTORY NOTES

Report on Effects of Parental Kidnapping Laws in Domestic Violence Cases

Pub.L. 106–386, Div. B, Title III, § 1303(a) to (c), Oct. 28, 2000, 114 Stat. 1512, provided that:

"**(a) In general.**—The Attorney General shall—

"**(1)** conduct a study of Federal and State laws relating to child custody, including custody provisions in protection orders, the Uniform Child Custody Jurisdiction and Enforcement Act adopted by the National Conference of Commissioners on Uniform State Laws in July 1997, the Parental Kidnaping Prevention Act of 1980 [Pub.L. 96–611, Dec. 28, 1980, 94 Stat. 3568] and the amendments made by that Act, and the effect of those laws on child custody cases in which domestic violence is a factor; and

"**(2)** submit to Congress a report describing the results of that study, including the effects of implementing or applying model State laws, and the recommendations of the Attorney General to reduce the incidence or pattern of violence against women or of sexual assault of the child.

"**(b) Sufficiency of defenses.**—In carrying out subsection (a) with respect to the Parental Kidnaping Prevention Act of 1980 [Pub.L. 96–611, Dec. 28, 1980, 94 Stat. 3568] and the amendments made by that Act [see Tables for classification], the Attorney General shall examine the sufficiency of defenses to parental abduction charges available in cases involving domestic violence, and the burdens and risks encountered by victims of domestic violence arising from jurisdictional requirements of that Act and the amendments made by that Act.

"**(c) Authorization of appropriations.**—There is authorized to be appropriated to carry out this section $200,000 for fiscal year 2001."

Congressional Findings and Declaration of Purpose

Section 7 of Pub.L. 96–611 provided that:

"**(a)** The Congress finds that—

"**(1)** there is a large and growing number of cases annually involving disputes between persons claiming rights of custody and visitation of children under the laws, and in the courts, of different States, the District of Columbia, the Commonwealth of Puerto Rico, and the territories and possessions of the United States;

"**(2)** the laws and practices by which the courts of those jurisdictions determine their jurisdiction to decide such disputes, and the effect to be given the decisions of such disputes by the courts of other jurisdictions, are often inconsistent and conflicting;

"**(3)** those characteristics of the law and practice in such cases, along with the limits imposed by a Federal system on the authority of each such jurisdiction to conduct investigations and take other actions outside its own boundaries, contribute to a tendency of parties involved in such disputes to frequently resort to the seizure, restraint, concealment, and interstate transportation of children, the disregard of court orders, excessive relitigation of cases, obtaining of conflicting orders by the courts of various jurisdictions, and interstate travel and communication that is so expensive and time consuming as to disrupt their occupations and commercial activities; and

"**(4)** among the results of those conditions and activities are the failure of the courts of such jurisdictions to give full faith and credit to the judicial proceedings of the other jurisdictions, the deprivation of rights of liberty and property without due process of law, burdens on commerce among such jurisdictions and with foreign nations, and harm to the welfare of children and their parents and other custodians.

"**(b)** For those reasons it is necessary to establish a national system for locating parents and children who travel from one such jurisdiction to another and are concealed in connection with such disputes, and to establish national standards under which the courts of such jurisdictions will determine their jurisdiction to decide such disputes and the effect to be given by each such jurisdiction to such decisions by the courts of other such jurisdictions.

"**(c)** The general purposes of sections 6 to 10 of this Act [enacting this section and sections 654(17) and 663 of Title 42, The Public Health and Welfare, amending section 655(a) of Title 42, and enacting provisions set out as notes under this section and sections 663 and 1305 of Title 42 and 1073 of Title 18, Crimes and Criminal Procedure] are to—

"**(1)** promote cooperation between State courts to the end that a determination of custody and visitation is rendered in the State which can best decide the case in the interest of the child;

"**(2)** promote and expand the exchange of information and other forms of mutual assistance between States which are concerned with the same child;

"**(3)** facilitate the enforcement of custody and visitation decrees of sister States;

"**(4)** discourage continuing interstate controversies over child custody in the interest of greater stability of home environment and of secure family relationships for the child;

"**(5)** avoid jurisdictional competition and conflict between State courts in matters of child custody and visitation which have in the past resulted in the shifting of children from State to State with harmful effects on their well-being; and

"**(6)** deter interstate abductions and other unilateral removals of children undertaken to obtain custody and visitation awards."

State Court Proceedings for Custody Determinations; Priority Treatment; Fees, Costs, and Other Expenses

Section 8(c) of Pub.L. 96–611 provided that: "In furtherance of the purposes of section 1738A of title 28, United States Code [this section], as added by subsection (a) of this section, State courts are encouraged to—

"**(1)** afford priority to proceedings for custody determinations; and

"**(2)** award to the person entitled to custody or visitation pursuant to a custody determination which is consistent with the provisions of such section 1738A [this section], necessary travel expenses, attorneys' fees, costs of private investigations, witness fees or expenses, and other expenses incurred in connection with such custody determination in any case in which—

"**(A)** a contestant has, without the consent of the person entitled to custody or visitation pursuant to a custody determination which is consistent with the provisions of such section 1738A [this section], (i) wrongfully removed the child from the physical custody of such person, or (ii) wrongfully retained the child after a visit or other temporary relinquishment of physical custody; or

"**(B)** the court determines it is appropriate."

§ 1738B. Full faith and credit for child support orders

(a) General rule.—The appropriate authorities of each State—

(1) shall enforce according to its terms a child support order made consistently with this section by a court of another State; and

(2) shall not seek or make a modification of such an order except in accordance with subsections (e), (f), and (i).

(b) Definitions.—In this section:

(1) The term "child" means—

(A) a person under 18 years of age; and

(B) a person 18 or more years of age with respect to whom a child support order has been issued pursuant to the laws of a State.

(2) The term "child's State" means the State in which a child resides.

(3) The term "child's home State" means the State in which a child lived with a parent or a person acting as parent for at least 6 consecutive months immediately preceding the time of filing of a petition or comparable pleading for support and, if a child is less than 6 months old, the State in which the child lived from birth with any of them. A period of temporary absence of any of them is counted as part of the 6-month period.

(4) The term "child support" means a payment of money, continuing support, or arrearages or the provision of a benefit (including payment of health insurance, child care, and educational expenses) for the support of a child.

(5) The term "child support order"—

(A) means a judgment, decree, or order of a court requiring the payment of child support in periodic amounts or in a lump sum; and

(B) includes—

(i) a permanent or temporary order; and

(ii) an initial order or a modification of an order.

(6) The term "contestant" means—

(A) a person (including a parent) who—

(i) claims a right to receive child support;

(ii) is a party to a proceeding that may result in the issuance of a child support order; or

(iii) is under a child support order; and

(B) a State or political subdivision of a State to which the right to obtain child support has been assigned.

(7) The term "court" means a court or administrative agency of a State that is authorized by State law to establish the amount of child support payable by a contestant or make a modification of a child support order.

(8) The term "modification" means a change in a child support order that affects the amount, scope, or duration of the order and modifies, replaces, supersedes, or otherwise is made subsequent to the child support order.

(9) The term "State" means a State of the United States, the District of Columbia, the Commonwealth of Puerto Rico, the territories and possessions of the United States, and Indian country (as defined in section 1151 of title 18).

(c) **Requirements of child support orders.**—A child support order made by a court of a State is made consistently with this section if—

(1) a court that makes the order, pursuant to the laws of the State in which the court is located and subsections (e), (f), and (g)—

(A) has subject matter jurisdiction to hear the matter and enter such an order; and

(B) has personal jurisdiction over the contestants; and

(2) reasonable notice and opportunity to be heard is given to the contestants.

(d) **Continuing jurisdiction.**—A court of a State that has made a child support order consistently with this section has continuing, exclusive jurisdiction over the order if the State is the child's State or the residence of any individual contestant unless the court of another State, acting in accordance with subsections (e) and (f), has made a modification of the order.

(e) **Authority to modify orders.**—A court of a State may modify a child support order issued by a court of another State if—

(1) the court has jurisdiction to make such a child support order pursuant to subsection (i); and

(2)(A) the court of the other State no longer has continuing, exclusive jurisdiction of the child support order because that State no longer is the child's State or the residence of any individual contestant; or

(B) each individual contestant has filed written consent with the State of continuing, exclusive jurisdiction for a court of another State to modify the order and assume continuing, exclusive jurisdiction over the order.

(f) **Recognition of child support orders.**—If 1 or more child support orders have been issued with regard to an obligor and a child, a court shall apply the following rules in determining which order to recognize for purposes of continuing, exclusive jurisdiction and enforcement:

(1) If only 1 court has issued a child support order, the order of that court must be recognized.

(2) If 2 or more courts have issued child support orders for the same obligor and child, and only 1 of the courts would have continuing, exclusive jurisdiction under this section, the order of that court must be recognized.

(3) If 2 or more courts have issued child support orders for the same obligor and child, and more than 1 of the courts would have continuing, exclusive jurisdiction under this section, an order issued by a court in the current home State of the child must be recognized, but if an order has not been issued in the current home State of the child, the order most recently issued must be recognized.

(4) If 2 or more courts have issued child support orders for the same obligor and child, and none of the courts would have continuing, exclusive jurisdiction under this section, a court having jurisdiction over the parties shall issue a child support order, which must be recognized.

(5) The court that has issued an order recognized under this subsection is the court having continuing, exclusive jurisdiction under subsection (d).

(g) Enforcement of modified orders.—A court of a State that no longer has continuing, exclusive jurisdiction of a child support order may enforce the order with respect to nonmodifiable obligations and unsatisfied obligations that accrued before the date on which a modification of the order is made under subsections (e) and (f).

(h) Choice of law.—

(1) In general.—In a proceeding to establish, modify, or enforce a child support order, the forum State's law shall apply except as provided in paragraphs (2) and (3).

(2) Law of State of issuance of order.—In interpreting a child support order including the duration of current payments and other obligations of support, a court shall apply the law of the State of the court that issued the order.

(3) Period of limitation.—In an action to enforce arrears under a child support order, a court shall apply the statute of limitation of the forum State or the State of the court that issued the order, whichever statute provides the longer period of limitation.

(i) Registration for modification.—If there is no individual contestant or child residing in the issuing State, the party or support enforcement agency seeking to modify, or to modify and enforce, a child support order issued in another State shall register that order in a State with jurisdiction over the nonmovant for the purpose of modification.

(Added Pub.L. 103–383, § 3(a), Oct. 22, 1994, 108 Stat. 4064; amended Pub.L. 104–193, Title III, § 322, Aug. 22, 1996, 110 Stat. 2221; Pub.L. 105–33, Title V, § 5554, Aug. 5, 1997, 111 Stat. 636; Pub.L. 113–183, Title III, § 301(f)(2)(C), Sept. 29, 2014, 128 Stat. 1945.)

AMENDMENT OF SUBSEC. (d)

Pub.L. 113–183, Title III, § 301(f)(2)(A), (3)(B), Sept. 29, 2014, 128 Stat. 1944, 1945, provided that effective on the date on which the Hague Convention of 23 November 2007 on the International Recovery of Child Support and Other Forms of Family Maintenance enters into force for the United States, subsec. (d) is amended by striking "individual contestant" and inserting "individual contestant or the parties have consented in a record or open court that the tribunal of the State may continue to exercise jurisdiction to modify its order,".

AMENDMENT OF SUBSEC. (e)(2)(A)

Pub.L. 113–183, Title III, § 301(f)(2)(B), (3)(B), Sept. 29, 2014, 128 Stat. 1944, 1945, provided that effective on the date on which the Hague Convention of 23 November 2007 on the International Recovery of Child Support and Other Forms of Family Maintenance enters into force for the United States, subsec. (e)(2)(A) is amended by striking "individual contestant" and inserting "individual contestant and the parties have not consented in a record or open court that the tribunal of the other State may continue to exercise jurisdiction to modify its order".

HISTORICAL AND STATUTORY NOTES

Effective and Applicability Provisions

1997 Acts. Amendments by Pub.L. 105–33 made by sections 5531 to 5556 to take effect as if included in the enactment of Title III of the Personal Responsibility and Work Opportunity Reconciliation Act of 1996 (Pub.L. 104–193, Aug. 22, 1996, 110 Stat. 2105), except for amendments made by section 5532(b)(2) (amending section 608(a)(3)(A) of Title 42, The Public Health and Welfare), see section 5557 of Pub.L. 105–33, set out as a note under section 608 of Title 42, The Public Health and Welfare.

1996 Acts. For effective date of Title III of Pub.L. 104–193, see section 395(a) to (c) of Pub.L. 104–193, set out as a note under section 654 of Title 42, The Public Health and Welfare.

Congressional Findings and Declaration of Purpose

Section 2 of Pub.L. 103–383 provided that:

"**(a) Findings.**—The Congress finds that—

"**(1)** there is a large and growing number of child support cases annually involving disputes between parents who reside in different States;

"**(2)** the laws by which the courts of different jurisdictions determine their authority to establish child support orders are not uniform;

"**(3)** those laws, along with the limits imposed by the Federal system on the authority of each State to take certain actions outside its own boundaries—

"**(A)** encourage noncustodial parents to relocate outside the States where their children and the custodial parents reside to avoid the jurisdiction of the courts of such States, resulting in an increase in the amount of interstate travel and communication required to establish and collect on child support orders and a burden on custodial parents that is expensive, time consuming, and disruptive of occupations and commercial activity;

"**(B)** contribute to the pressing problem of relatively low levels of child support payments in interstate cases and to inequities in child support payments levels that are based solely on the noncustodial parent's choice of residence;

"**(C)** encourage a disregard of court orders resulting in massive arrearages nationwide;

"**(D)** allow noncustodial parents to avoid the payment of regularly scheduled child support payments for extensive periods of time, resulting in substantial hardship for the children for whom support is due and for their custodians; and

"**(E)** lead to the excessive relitigation of cases and to the establishment of conflicting orders by the courts of various jurisdictions, resulting in confusion, waste of judicial resources, disrespect for the courts, and a diminution of public confidence in the rule of law; and

"**(4)** among the results of the conditions described in this subsection are—

"**(A)** the failure of the courts of the States to give full faith and credit to the judicial proceedings of the other States;

"**(B)** the deprivation of rights of liberty and property without due process of law;

"**(C)** burdens on commerce among the States; and

"**(D)** harm to the welfare of children and their parents and other custodians.

"**(b) Statement of policy.**—In view of the findings made in subsection (a), it is necessary to establish national standards under which the courts of the various States shall determine their jurisdiction to issue a child support order and the effect to be given by each State to child support orders issued by the courts of other States.

"**(c) Purposes.**—The purposes of this Act [enacting this section and a provision set out as a note under section 1 of this title] are—

"**(1)** to facilitate the enforcement of child support orders among the States;

"**(2)** to discourage continuing interstate controversies over child support in the interest of greater financial stability and secure family relationships for the child; and

"**(3)** to avoid jurisdictional competition and conflict among State courts in the establishment of child support orders."

§ 1738C.   Certain acts, records, and proceedings and the effect thereof

No State, territory, or possession of the United States, or Indian tribe, shall be required to give effect to any public act, record, or judicial proceeding of any other State, territory, possession, or tribe respecting a relationship between persons of the same sex that is treated as a marriage under the laws of such other State, territory, possession, or tribe, or a right or claim arising from such relationship.

(Added Pub.L. 104–199, § 2(a), Sept. 21, 1996, 110 Stat. 2419.)

HISTORICAL AND STATUTORY NOTES

Validity

For constitutionality of provisions of Pub.L. 104–199 [*i.e.*, 28 U.S.C. § 1738C], see United States v. Windsor, U.S.2013, 133 S.Ct. 2675, 186 L.Ed.2d 808 and Obergefell v. Hodges, U.S.2015, 135 S.Ct. 2584, 192 L.Ed.2d 609.

§ 1739.   State and Territorial nonjudicial records; full faith and credit

All nonjudicial records or books kept in any public office of any State, Territory, or Possession of the United States, or copies thereof, shall be proved or admitted in any court or office in any other State, Territory, or Possession by the attestation of the custodian of such records or books, and the seal of his office annexed, if there be a seal, together with a certificate of a judge of a court of record of the county, parish, or district in which such office may be kept, or of the Governor, or secretary of state, the chancellor or keeper of the great seal, of the State, Territory, or Possession that the said attestation is in due form and by the proper officers.

If the certificate is given by a judge, it shall be further authenticated by the clerk or prothonotary of the court, who shall certify, under his hand and the seal of his office, that such judge is duly commissioned and qualified; or, if given by such Governor, secretary, chancellor, or keeper of the great seal, it shall be under the great seal of the State, Territory, or Possession in which it is made.

Such records or books, or copies thereof, so authenticated, shall have the same full faith and credit in every court and office within the United States and its Territories and Possessions as they have by law or usage in the courts or offices of the State, Territory, or Possession from which they are taken.

(June 25, 1948, c. 646, 62 Stat. 947.)

§ 1740.   Copies of consular papers

Copies of all official documents and papers in the office of any consul or vice consul of the United States, and of all official entries in the books or records of any such office, authenticated by the consul or vice consul, shall be admissible equally with the originals.

(June 25, 1948, c. 646, 62 Stat. 947.)

§ 1741.   Foreign official documents

An official record or document of a foreign country may be evidenced by a copy, summary, or excerpt authenticated as provided in the Federal Rules of Civil Procedure.

(June 25, 1948, c. 646, 62 Stat. 948; May 24, 1949, c. 139, § 92(b), 63 Stat. 103; Oct. 3, 1964, Pub.L. 88–619, § 5(a), 78 Stat. 996.)

HISTORICAL AND STATUTORY NOTES

Treaties and Conventions; Taking of Evidence Abroad in Civil or Commercial Matters; Observance On and After Oct. 7, 1972, by United States and Citizens and Persons Subject to Jurisdiction of United States

For text of Convention, see provisions set out as a note under section 1781 of this title.

[§ 1742.   Repealed. Pub.L. 88–619, § 6(a), Oct. 3, 1964, 78 Stat. 996]

HISTORICAL AND STATUTORY NOTES

Section, Act June 25, 1948, c. 646, 62 Stat. 948, related to authentication and certification of copies of documents relating to land titles, by persons having custody of such of any foreign government or its agents, certification by an American minister or consul that they be true copies of the originals, the recording of such copies in the office of the General Counsel for the Department of the Treasury, and to the evidentiary value of such copies.

§ 1743.   Demand on postmaster

The certificate of the Postmaster General or the Government Accountability Office of the mailing to a postmaster of a statement of his account and that payment of the balance stated has not been received shall be sufficient evidence of a demand notwithstanding any allowances or credits subsequently made. A copy of such statement shall be attached to the certificate.

(June 25, 1948, c. 646, 62 Stat. 948; July 7, 2004, Pub.L. 108–271, § 8(b), 118 Stat. 814.)

HISTORICAL AND STATUTORY NOTES

Transfer of Functions

The office of Postmaster General of the Post Office Department was abolished and all functions, powers, and duties of the Postmaster General were transferred to the United States Postal Service by Pub.L. 91–375, § 4(a), Aug. 12, 1970, 84 Stat. 773, set out as a note under section 201 of Title 39, Postal Service.

§ 1744.   Copies of United States Patent and Trademark Office documents, generally

Copies of letters patent or of any records, books, papers, or drawings belonging to the United States Patent and Trademark Office and relating to patents, authenticated under the seal of the United States Patent and Trademark Office and certified by the Under Secretary of Commerce for Intellectual Property and Director of the United States Patent and Trademark Office, or by another officer of the United States Patent and Trademark Office authorized to do so by the Director, shall be admissible in evidence with the same effect as the originals.

Any person making application and paying the required fee may obtain such certified copies.

(June 25, 1948, c. 646, 62 Stat. 948; May 24, 1949, c. 139, § 92(c), 63 Stat. 103; Nov. 29, 1999, Pub.L. 106–113, Div. B, § 1000(a)(9) [Title IV, § 4732(b)(15)(B), (C)], 113 Stat. 1536, 1501A–584.)

HISTORICAL AND STATUTORY NOTES

Change of Name

Patent Office and Commissioner of Patents redesignated Patent and Trademark Office and Commissioner of Patents and Trademarks, respectively, by section 3 of Pub.L. 93–596, Jan. 2, 1975, 88 Stat. 1949, set out as a note under section 1 of Title 35, Patents.

Transfer of Functions

The functions of all officers of the Department of Commerce and all functions of all agencies and employees of such Department, were, with a few exceptions, transferred to the Secretary of Commerce, with power vested in him to authorize their performance or the performance of any of his functions by any of such officers, agencies, and employees, by 1950 Reorg. Plan No. 5, §§ 1, 2, eff. May 24, 1950, 15 F.R. 3174, 64 Stat. 1263, set out in Appendix 1 to Title 5, Government Organization and Employees. The Patent Office [now Patent and Trademark Office], referred to in this section, is an agency of the Department of Commerce, and the Commissioner of Patents [now Commissioner of Patents and Trademarks], referred to in this section, is an officer of such Department.

§ 1745.   Copies of foreign patent documents

Copies of the specifications and drawings of foreign letters patent, or applications for foreign letters patent, and copies of excerpts of the official journals and other official publications of foreign patent offices belonging to the United States Patent and Trademark Office, certified in the manner provided by section 1744 of this title are prima facie evidence of their contents and of the dates indicated on their face.

(June 25, 1948, c. 646, 62 Stat. 948, § 1746; renumbered § 1745 and amended May 24, 1949, c. 139, § 92(d), (e), 63 Stat. 103; Oct. 3, 1964, Pub.L. 88–619, § 7(a), 78 Stat. 996; Nov. 29, 1999, Pub.L. 106–113, Div. B, § 1000(a)(9) [Title IV, § 4732(b)(16)], 113 Stat. 1536, 1501A–585.)

HISTORICAL AND STATUTORY NOTES

Change of Name

Patent Office redesignated Patent and Trademark Office by section 3 of Pub.L. 93–596, Jan. 2, 1975, 88 Stat. 1949, set out as a note under section 1 of Title 35, Patents.

Prior Provisions

A prior section 1745, Act June 25, 1948, c. 646, 62 Stat. 948, related to printed copies of patent specifications and drawings, prior to repeal by Act May 24, 1949, c. 139, § 92(d), 63 Stat. 103.

§ 1746.   Unsworn declarations under penalty of perjury

Wherever, under any law of the United States or under any rule, regulation, order, or requirement made pursuant to law, any matter is required or permitted to be supported, evidenced, established, or proved by the sworn declaration, verification, certificate, statement, oath, or affidavit, in writing of the person making the same (other than a deposition, or an oath of office, or an oath required to be taken before a specified official other than a notary public), such matter may, with like force and effect, be supported, evidenced, established, or proved by the unsworn declaration, certificate, verification, or statement, in writing of such person which is subscribed by him, as true under penalty of perjury, and dated, in substantially the following form:

(1)   If executed without the United States: "I declare (or certify, verify, or state) under penalty of perjury under the laws of the United States of America that the foregoing is true and correct. Executed on (date).

(Signature)".

(2)   If executed within the United States, its territories, possessions, or commonwealths: "I declare (or certify, verify, or state) under penalty of perjury that the foregoing is true and correct. Executed on (date).

(Signature)".

(Added Pub.L. 94–550, § 1(a), Oct. 18, 1976, 90 Stat. 2534.)

HISTORICAL AND STATUTORY NOTES

Prior Provisions

A prior section 1746 was renumbered section 1745 of this title by Act May 24, 1949.

CHAPTER 117—EVIDENCE; DEPOSITIONS

HISTORICAL AND STATUTORY NOTES

Deposition in Admiralty Cases

Prior to the general unification of civil and admiralty procedure and the rescission of the Admiralty Rules on July 1, 1966, Revised Statutes, §§ 863 to 865, as amended, which related to depositions de bene esse, when and how taken, notice, mode of taking, and transmission to court, provided as follows:

"**Sec. 863.** The testimony of any witness may be taken in any civil cause depending in a district court by deposition de bene esse, when the witness lives at a greater distance from the place of trial than one hundred miles, or is bound on a voyage to sea, or is about to go out of the United States, or out of the district in which the case is to be tried, and to a greater distance than one hundred miles from the place of trial, before the time of trial, or when he is ancient and infirm. The deposition may be taken before any judge of any court of the United States, or any clerk of a district court, or any chancellor, justice, or judge of a supreme or superior court, mayor or chief magistrate of a city, judge of a county court or court of common pleas of any of the United States, or any notary public, not being of counsel or attorney to either of the parties, nor interested in the event of the cause. Reasonable notice must first be given in writing by the party or his attorney proposing to take such deposition, to the opposite party or his attorney of record, as either may be nearest, which notice shall state the name of the witness and the time and place of the taking of his deposition; and in all cases in rem, the person having the agency or possession of the property at the time of seizure shall be deemed the adverse party, until a claim shall have been put in; and whenever, by reason of the absence from the district and want of an attorney of record or other reason, the giving of the notice herein required shall be impracticable, it shall be lawful to take such depositions as there shall be urgent necessity for taking, upon such notice as any judge authorized to hold courts in such district shall think reasonable and direct. Any person may be compelled to appear and depose as provided by this section, in the same manner as witnesses may be compelled to appear and testify in court.

"**Sec. 864.** Every person deposing as provided in the preceding section [R.S. § 863] shall be cautioned and sworn to testify the whole truth, and carefully examined.

"His testimony shall be reduced to writing or typewriting by the officer taking the deposition, or by some person under his personal supervision, or by the deponent himself in the officer's presence, and by no other person, and shall, after it has been reduced to writing or typewriting, be subscribed by the deponent. [As amended May 23, 1900, c. 541, 31 Stat. 182.]

"**Sec. 865.** Every deposition taken under the two preceding sections [R.S. §§ 863, 864] shall be retained by the magistrate taking it, until he delivers it with his own hand into the court for which it is taken; or it shall, together with a certificate of the reasons as aforesaid of taking it and of the notice, if any, given to the adverse party, be by him sealed up and directed to such court, and remain under his seal until opened in court. But unless it appears to the satisfaction of the court that the witness is then dead, or gone out of the United States, or to a greater distance than one hundred miles from the place where the court is sitting, or that, by reason of age, sickness, bodily infirmity, or imprisonment, he is unable to travel and appear at court, such deposition shall not be used in the cause."

R.S. §§ 863 to 865, as amended, quoted above, were applicable to admiralty proceedings only. Proceedings in bankruptcy and copyright are governed by Rule 26 et seq. of Federal Rules of Civil Procedure. See also Rules of Bankruptcy Procedure set out in Title 11, Bankruptcy.

§ 1781.　　Transmittal of letter rogatory or request

(a) The Department of State has power, directly, or through suitable channels—

(1) to receive a letter rogatory issued, or request made, by a foreign or international tribunal, to transmit it to the tribunal, officer, or agency in the United States to whom it is addressed, and to receive and return it after execution; and

(2) to receive a letter rogatory issued, or request made, by a tribunal in the United States, to transmit it to the foreign or international tribunal, officer, or agency to whom it is addressed, and to receive and return it after execution.

(b) This section does not preclude—

(1) the transmittal of a letter rogatory or request directly from a foreign or international tribunal to the tribunal, officer, or agency in the United States to whom it is addressed and its return in the same manner; or

(2) the transmittal of a letter rogatory or request directly from a tribunal in the United States to the foreign or international tribunal, officer, or agency to whom it is addressed and its return in the same manner.

(June 25, 1948, c. 646, 62 Stat. 949; Oct. 3, 1964, Pub.L. 88–619, § 8(a), 78 Stat. 996.)

TREATIES AND CONVENTIONS

CONVENTION ON THE TAKING OF EVIDENCE ABROAD IN CIVIL OR COMMERCIAL MATTERS

The States signatory to the present Convention,

Desiring to facilitate the transmission and execution of Letters of Request and to further the accommodation of the different methods which they use for this purpose.

Desiring to improve mutual judicial co-operation in civil or commercial matters.

Have resolved to conclude a Convention to this effect and have agreed upon the following provisions—

*　　　*　　　*　　　*　　　*　　　*

CHAPTER I—LETTERS OF REQUEST

Article 1

In civil or commercial matters a judicial authority of a Contracting State may, in accordance with the provisions of the law of that State, request the competent authority of another Contracting State, by means of a Letter of Request, to obtain evidence, or to perform some other judicial act.

A Letter shall not be used to obtain evidence which is not intended for use in judicial proceedings, commenced or contemplated.

The expression "other judicial act" does not cover the service of judicial documents or the issuance of any process by which judgments or orders are executed or enforced, or orders for provisional or protective measures.

Article 2

A Contracting State shall designate a Central Authority which will undertake to receive Letters of Request coming from a judicial authority of another Contracting State and to transmit them to the authority competent to execute them. Each State shall organize the Central Authority in accordance with its own law.

Letters shall be sent to the Central Authority of the State of execution without being transmitted through any other authority of that State.

Article 3

A Letter of Request shall specify—

(a) the authority requesting its execution and the authority requested to execute it, if known to the requesting authority;

(b) the names and addresses of the parties to the proceedings and their representatives, if any;

(c) the nature of the proceedings for which the evidence is required, giving all necessary information in regard thereto;

(d) the evidence to be obtained or other judicial act to be performed.

Where appropriate, the Letter shall specify, inter alia—

(e) the names and addresses of the persons to be examined;

(f) the questions to be put to the persons to be examined or a statement of the subject-matter about which they are to be examined;

(g) the documents or other property, real or personal, to be inspected;

(h) any requirement that the evidence is to be given on oath or affirmation, and any special form to be used;

(i) any special method or procedure to be followed under Article 9.

A Letter may also mention any information necessary for the application of Article 11.

No legalization or other like formality may be required.

Article 4

A Letter of Request shall be in the language of the authority requested to execute it or be accompanied by a translation into that language.

Nevertheless, a Contracting State shall accept a Letter in either English or French, or a translation into one of these languages, unless it has made the reservation authorized by Article 33.

A Contracting State which has more than one official language and cannot, for reasons of internal law, accept Letters in one of these languages for the whole of its territory, shall, by declaration, specify the language in which the Letter or translation thereof shall be expressed for execution in the specified parts of its territory. In case of failure to comply with this declaration, without justifiable excuse, the costs of translation into the required language shall be borne by the State of origin.

A Contracting State may, by declaration, specify the language or languages other than those referred to in the preceding paragraphs, in which a Letter may be sent to its Central Authority.

Any translation accompanying a Letter shall be certified as correct, either by a diplomatic officer or consular agent or by a sworn translator or by any other person so authorized in either State.

Article 5

If the Central Authority considers that the request does not comply with the provisions of the present Convention, it shall promptly inform the authority of the State of origin which transmitted the Letter of Request, specifying the objections to the Letter.

Article 6

If the authority to whom a Letter of Request has been transmitted is not competent to execute it, the Letter shall be sent forthwith to the authority in the same State which is competent to execute it in accordance with the provisions of its own law.

Article 7

The requesting authority shall, if it so desires, be informed of the time when, and the place where, the proceedings will take place, in order that the parties concerned, and their representatives, if any, may be present. This information shall be sent directly to the parties or their representatives when the authority of the State of origin so requests.

Article 8

A Contracting State may declare that members of the judicial personnel of the requesting authority of another Contracting State may be present at the execution of a Letter of Request. Prior authorization by the competent authority designated by the declaring State may be required.

Article 9

The judicial authority which executes a Letter of Request shall apply its own law as to the methods and procedures to be followed.

However, it will follow a request of the requesting authority that a special method or procedure be followed, unless this is incompatible with the internal law of the State of execution or is impossible of performance by reason of its internal practice and procedure or by reason of practical difficulties.

A Letter of Request shall be executed expeditiously.

Article 10

In executing a Letter of Request the requested authority shall apply the appropriate measures of compulsion in the instances and to the same extent as are provided by its internal law for the execution of orders issued by the authorities of its own country or of requests made by parties in internal proceedings.

Article 11

In the execution of a Letter of Request the person concerned may refuse to give evidence in so far as he has a privilege or duty to refuse to give the evidence—

(a) under the law of the State of execution; or

(b) under the law of the State of origin, and the privilege or duty has been specified in the Letter, or, at the instance of the requested authority, has been otherwise confirmed to that authority by the requesting authority.

A Contracting State may declare that, in addition, it will respect privileges and duties existing under the law of States other than the State of origin and the State of execution, to the extent specified in that declaration.

Article 12

The execution of a Letter of Request may be refused only to the extent that—

(a) in the State of execution the execution of the Letter does not fall within the functions of the judiciary; or

(b) the State addressed considers that its sovereignty or security would be prejudiced thereby.

Execution may not be refused solely on the ground that under its internal law the State of execution claims exclusive jurisdiction over the subject-matter of the action or that its internal law would not admit a right of action on it.

Article 13

The documents establishing the execution of the Letter of Request shall be sent by the requested authority to the requesting authority by the same channel which was used by the latter.

In every instance where the Letter is not executed in whole or in part, the requesting authority shall be informed immediately through the same channel and advised of the reasons.

Article 14

The execution of the Letter of Request shall not give rise to any reimbursement of taxes or costs of any nature.

Nevertheless, the State of execution has the right to require the State of origin to reimburse the fees paid to experts and interpreters and the costs occasioned by the use of a special procedure requested by the State of origin under Article 9, paragraph 2.

The requested authority whose law obliges the parties themselves to secure evidence, and which is not able itself to execute the Letter, may, after having obtained the consent of the requesting authority, appoint a suitable person to do so. When seeking this consent the requested authority shall indicate the approximate costs which would result from this procedure. If the requesting authority gives its consent it shall reimburse any costs incurred; without such consent the requesting authority shall not be liable for the costs.

CHAPTER II—TAKING OF EVIDENCE BY DIPLOMATIC OFFICERS, CONSULAR AGENTS AND COMMISSIONERS

Article 15

In a civil or commercial matter, a diplomatic officer or consular agent of a Contracting State may, in the territory of another Contracting State and within the area where he exercises his functions, take the evidence without compulsion of nationals of a State which he represents in aid of proceedings commenced in the courts of a State which he represents.

A Contracting State may declare that evidence may be taken by a diplomatic officer or consular agent only if permission to that effect is given upon application made by him or on his behalf to the appropriate authority designated by the declaring State.

Article 16

A diplomatic officer or consular agent of a Contracting State may, in the territory of another Contracting State and within the area where he exercises his functions, also take the evidence, without compulsion, of nationals of the State in which he exercises his functions or of a third State, in aid of proceedings commenced in the courts of a State which he represents, if—

(a) a competent authority designated by the State in which he exercises his functions has given its permission either generally or in the particular case, and

(b) he complies with the conditions which the competent authority has specified in the permission.

A Contracting State may declare that evidence may be taken under this Article without its prior permission.

Article 17

In a civil or commercial matter, a person duly appointed as a commissioner for the purpose may, without compulsion, take evidence in the territory of a Contracting State in aid of proceedings commenced in the courts of another Contracting State if—

(a) a competent authority designated by the State where the evidence is to be taken has given its permission either generally or in the particular case; and

(b) he complies with the conditions which the competent authority has specified in the permission.

A Contracting State may declare that evidence may be taken under this Article without its prior permission.

Article 18

A Contracting State may declare that a diplomatic officer, consular agent or commissioner authorized to take evidence under Articles 15, 16 or 17, may apply to the competent authority designated by the declaring State for appropriate assistance to obtain the evidence by compulsion. The declaration may contain such conditions as the declaring State may see fit to impose.

If the authority grants the application it shall apply any measures of compulsion which are appropriate and are prescribed by its law for use in internal proceedings.

Article 19

The competent authority, in giving the permission referred to in Articles 15, 16 or 17, or in granting the application referred to in Article 18, may lay down such conditions as it deems fit, *inter alia*, as to the time and place of the taking of the evidence. Similarly it may require that it be given reasonable advance notice of the time, date and place of the taking of the evidence; in such a case a representative of the authority shall be entitled to be present at the taking of the evidence.

Article 20

In the taking of evidence under any Article of this Chapter persons concerned may be legally represented.

Article 21

Where a diplomatic officer, consular agent or commissioner is authorized under Articles 15, 16 or 17 to take evidence—

(a)   he may take all kinds of evidence which are not incompatible with the law of the State where the evidence is taken or contrary to any permission granted pursuant to the above Articles, and shall have power within such limits to administer an oath or take an affirmation;

(b)   a request to a person to appear or to give evidence shall, unless the recipient is a national of the State where the action is pending, be drawn up in the language of the place where the evidence is taken or be accompanied by a translation into such language;

(c)   the request shall inform the person that he may be legally represented and, in any State that has not filed a declaration under Article 18, shall also inform him that he is not compelled to appear or to give evidence;

(d)   the evidence may be taken in the manner provided by the law applicable to the court in which the action is pending provided that such manner is not forbidden by the law of the State where the evidence is taken;

(e)   a person requested to give evidence may invoke the privileges and duties to refuse to give the evidence contained in Article 11.

Article 22

The fact that an attempt to take evidence under the procedure laid down in this Chapter has failed, owing to the refusal of a person to give evidence, shall not prevent an application being subsequently made to take the evidence in accordance with Chapter I.

CHAPTER III—GENERAL CLAUSES

Article 23

A Contracting State may at the time of signature, ratification or accession, declare that it will not execute Letters of Request issued for the purpose of obtaining pretrial discovery of documents as known in Common Law countries.

Article 24

A Contracting State may designate other authorities in addition to the Central Authority and shall determine the extent of their competence. However, Letters of Request may in all cases be sent to the Central Authority.

Federal States shall be free to designate more than one Central Authority.

Article 25

A Contracting State which has more than one legal system may designate the authorities of one of such systems, which shall have exclusive competence to execute Letters of Request pursuant to this Convention.

Article 26

A Contracting State, if required to do so because of constitutional limitations, may request the reimbursement by the State of origin of fees and costs, in connection with the execution of Letters of Request, for the service of process necessary to compel the appearance of a person to give evidence, the costs of attendance of such persons, and the cost of any transcript of the evidence.

Where a State has made a request pursuant to the above paragraph, any other Contracting State may request from that State the reimbursement of similar fees and costs.

Article 27

The provisions of the present Convention shall not prevent a Contracting State from—

(a) declaring that Letters of Request may be transmitted to its judicial authorities through channels other than those provided for in Article 2;

(b) permitting, by internal law or practice, any act provided for in this Convention to be performed upon less restrictive conditions;

(c) permitting, by internal law or practice, methods of taking evidence other than those provided for in this Convention.

Article 28

The present Convention shall not prevent an agreement between any two or more Contracting States to derogate from—

(a) the provisions of Article 2 with respect to methods of transmitting Letters of Request;

(b) the provisions of Article 4 with respect to the languages which may be used;

(c) the provisions of Article 8 with respect to the presence of judicial personnel at the execution of Letters;

(d) the provisions of Article 11 with respect to the privileges and duties of witnesses to refuse to give evidence;

(e) the provisions of Article 13 with respect to the methods of returning executed Letters to the requesting authority;

(f) the provisions of Article 14 with respect to fees and costs;

(g) the provisions of Chapter II.

Article 29

Between Parties to the present Convention who are also Parties to one or both of the Conventions on Civil Procedure signed at the Hague on the 17th of July 1905 [99 British Foreign and State Papers 990] and the 1st of March 1954 [286 UNTS 265], this Convention shall replace Articles 8–16 of the earlier Conventions.

Article 30

The present Convention shall not affect the application of Article 23 of the Convention of 1905, or of Article 24 of the Convention of 1954.

Article 31

Supplementary Agreements between Parties to the Conventions of 1905 and 1954 shall be considered as equally applicable to the present Convention unless the Parties have otherwise agreed.

Article 32

Without prejudice to the provisions of Articles 29 and 31, the present Convention shall not derogate from conventions containing provisions on the matters covered by this Convention to which the Contracting States are, or shall become Parties.

Article 33

A State may, at the time of signature, ratification or accession exclude, in whole or in part, the application of the provisions of paragraph 2 of Article 4 and of Chapter II. No other reservation shall be permitted.

Each Contracting State may at any time withdraw a reservation it has made; the reservation shall cease to have effect on the sixtieth day after notification of the withdrawal.

When a State has made a reservation, any other State affected thereby may apply the same rule against the reserving State.

Article 34

A State may at any time withdraw or modify a declaration.

Article 35

A Contracting State shall, at the time of the deposit of its instrument of ratification or accession, or at a later date, inform the Ministry of Foreign Affairs of the Netherlands of the designation of authorities, pursuant to Articles 2, 8, 24 and 25.

A Contracting State shall likewise inform the Ministry, where appropriate, of the following—

(a) the designation of the authorities to whom notice must be given, whose permission may be required, and whose assistance may be invoked in the taking of evidence by diplomatic officers and consular agents, pursuant to Articles 15, 16 and 18 respectively;

(b) the designation of the authorities whose permission may be required in the taking of evidence by commissioners pursuant to Article 17 and of those who may grant the assistance provided for in Article 18;

(c) declarations pursuant to Articles 4, 8, 11, 15, 16, 17, 18, 23 and 27;

(d) any withdrawal or modification of the above designations and declarations;

(e) the withdrawal of any reservation.

Article 36

Any difficulties which may arise between Contracting States in connection with the operation of this Convention shall be settled through diplomatic channels.

Article 37

The present Convention shall be open for signature by the States represented at the Eleventh Session of the Hague Conference on Private International Law.

It shall be ratified, and the instruments of ratification shall be deposited with the Ministry of Foreign Affairs of the Netherlands.

Article 38

The present Convention shall enter into force on the sixtieth day after the deposit of the third instrument of ratification referred to in the second paragraph of Article 37.

The Convention shall enter into force for each signatory State which ratifies subsequently on the sixtieth day after the deposit of its instrument of ratification.

Article 39

Any State not represented at the Eleventh Session of the Hague Conference on Private International Law which is a Member of this Conference or of the United Nations or of a specialized agency of that Organization, or a Party to the Statute of the International Court of Justice may accede to the present Convention after it has entered into force in accordance with the first paragraph of Article 38.

The instrument of accession shall be deposited with the Ministry of Foreign Affairs of the Netherlands.

The Convention shall enter into force for a State acceding to it on the sixtieth day after the deposit of its instrument of accession.

The accession will have effect only as regards the relations between the acceding State and such Contracting States as will have declared their acceptance of the accession. Such declaration shall be deposited at the Ministry of Foreign Affairs of the Netherlands; this Ministry shall forward, through diplomatic channels, a certified copy to each of the Contracting States.

The Convention will enter into force as between the acceding State and the State that has declared its acceptance of the accession on the sixtieth day after the deposit of the declaration of acceptance.

Article 40

Any State may, at the time of signature, ratification or accession, declare that the present Convention shall extend to all the territories for the international relations of which it is responsible, or to one or more of them. Such a declaration shall take effect on the date of entry into force of the Convention for the State concerned.

At any time thereafter, such extensions shall be notified to the Ministry of Foreign Affairs of the Netherlands.

The Convention shall enter into force for the territories mentioned in such an extension on the sixtieth day after the notification indicated in the preceding paragraph.

Article 41

The present Convention shall remain in force for five years from the date of its entry into force in accordance with the first paragraph of Article 38, even for States which have ratified it or acceded to it subsequently.

If there has been no denunciation, it shall be renewed tacitly every five years.

Any denunciation shall be notified to the Ministry of Foreign Affairs of the Netherlands at least six months before the end of the five year period.

It may be limited to certain of the territories to which the Convention applies.

The denunciation shall have effect only as regards the State which has notified it. The Convention shall remain in force for the other Contracting States.

Article 42

The Ministry of Foreign Affairs of the Netherlands shall give notice to the States referred to in Article 37, and to the States which have acceded in accordance with Article 39, of the following—

(a) the signatures and ratifications referred to in Article 37;

(b) the date on which the present Convention enters into force in accordance with the first paragraph of Article 38;

(c) the accessions referred to in Article 39 and the dates on which they take effect;

(d) the extensions referred to in Article 40 and the dates on which they take effect;

(e) the designations, reservations and declarations referred to in Articles 33 and 35;

(f) the denunciations referred to in the third paragraph of Article 41.

IN WITNESS WHEREOF the undersigned, being duly authorized thereto, have signed the present Convention.

DONE at The Hague, on the 18th day of March 1970, in the English and French languages, both texts being equally authentic, in a single copy which shall be deposited in the archives of the Government of the Netherlands, and of which a certified copy shall be sent, through the diplomatic channel, to each of the States represented at the Eleventh Session of the Hague Conference on Private International Law. [Signatures omitted.]

Convention on the taking of evidence abroad in civil or commercial matters. Done at The Hague March 18, 1970; entered into force for the United States October 7, 1972. T.I.A.S. 7444; 23 U.S.T. 2555

Annotations to the Convention

"Report of the U.S. Delegation on the Evidence Convention", 8 Int'l Legal Materials 804 (1969).

Amram, "Explanatory Report on the Convention on the Taking of Evidence Abroad in Civil and Commercial Matters—Message from the President of the United States", Sen.Exec. A, 92nd Cong., 2d Sess. (Feb. 1, 1972).

Edwards, "Taking of Evidence Abroad in Civil or Commercial Matters", 18 Int'l and Comp.L.Q. 646 (1969).

Amram, "U.S. Ratification of the Hague Convention on the Taking of Evidence Abroad" 67 Am.J. Int'l L. 104 (1973).

————————

Model for Letters of Request Recommended for Use in Applying the Hague Convention of 18 March 1970 on the Taking of Evidence Abroad in Civil or Commercial Matters

Request for International Judicial Assistance Pursuant to the Hague Convention of 18 March 1970 on the Taking of Evidence in Civil or Commercial Matters

N.B.   *Under the first paragraph of article 4, the Letter of Request shall be in the language of the authority requested to execute it or be accompanied by a translation into that language. However, the provisions of the second and third paragraphs may permit use of other languages.*

In order to avoid confusion, please spell out the name of the month in each date.

I.   *(Items to be included in all Letters of Request.)*

1.   Sender   _____*(identity and address)*_____

2.   Central Authority of the
      Requested State   _____*(identity and address)*_____

3.   Person to whom the executed   _____*(identity and address)*_____
      request is to be returned

II.   *(Items to be included in all Letters of Request.)*

4.   In conformity with article 3 of the Convention, the undersigned applicant has the honour to submit the following request:

5.   *a*   Requesting judicial authority
      (article 3, *a*)   _____*(identity and address)*_____

      b   To the competent authority of
      (article 3, *a*)   _____*(the requested State)*_____

6.   Names and addresses of the
      parties and their representatives
      (article 3, *b*)

    a   Plaintiff   _____

                                _____

                                _____

    b   Defendant   _____

                                _____

                                _____

    c   Other parties   _____

                                _____

                                _____

7.   Nature and purpose of the   _____
      proceedings and summary of the   _____
      facts (article 3, *c*)   _____

8.   Evidence to be obtained or other   _____
      judicial act to be performed   _____
      (article 3, *d*)   _____

III.   *(Items to be completed where applicable.)*

9.   Identity and address of any person   _____
      to be examined (article 3, *e*)   _____

                                  _____

10.   Questions to be put to the persons
      to be examined or statement   _____
      of the subject-matter   _____*(or see attached list)*_____
      about which they are to be   _____
      examined (article 3, *f*)   _____

11.   Documents or other property   _____*(specify whether it is to be*
      to be inspected (article 3, *g*)   *produced, copied, valued, etc.)*_____

                                  _____

12.   Any requirement that the   _____
      evidence be given on oath or   _____*(In the event that the evidence*
      affirmation and any special   *cannot be taken in the manner requested,*
      form to be used (article 3, *h*)   *specify whether it is to be taken in such*
                                  manner as provided by local law for the
                                  formal taking of evidence.) _____

                                  _____

13.   Special methods or procedure   _____
      to be followed   _____
      (articles 3, *i* and 9)   _____

14. Request for notification of the time and place for the execution of the Request and identity and address of any person to be notified (article 7)

——————————————————
——————————————————
——————————————————
——————————————————

15. Request for attendance or participation of judicial personnel of the requesting authority at the execution of the Letter of Request

——————————————————
——————————————————
——————————————————

16. Specification of privilege or duty to refuse to give evidence under the law of the State of origin (article 11, *b*)

——————————————————
——————————————————
——————————————————
——————————————————

17. The fees and costs incurred which are reimbursable under the second paragraph of article 14 or under article 26 of the Convention will be borne by

————*(identity and address)*————
——————————————————
——————————————————
——————————————————
——————————————————

IV. *(Items to be included in all Letters of Request.)*

18. Date of request

——————————————————

19. Signature and seal of the requesting authority

——————————————————
——————————————————

TREATIES AND CONVENTIONS

INTER-AMERICAN CONVENTION ON LETTERS ROGATORY

The Governments of the Member States of the Organization of American States, desirous of concluding a convention on letters rogatory, have agreed as follows:

I. USE OF TERMS

Article 1

For the purposes of this Convention the terms "exhortos" and "cartas rogatorias" are synonymous in the Spanish text. The terms "letters rogatory", "commissions rogatoires", and "cartas rogatórias" used in the English, French and Portuguese texts, respectively, cover both "exhortos" and "cartas rogatorias".

II. SCOPE OF THE CONVENTION

Article 2

This Convention shall apply to letters rogatory, issued in conjunction with proceedings in civil and commercial matters held before the appropriate judicial or other adjudicatory authority of one of the States Parties to this Convention, that have as their purpose:

a.   The performance of procedural acts of a merely formal nature, such as service of process, summonses or subpoenas abroad;

b.   The taking of evidence and the obtaining of information abroad, unless a reservation is made in this respect.

Article 3

This Convention shall not apply to letters rogatory relating to procedural acts other than those specified in the preceding article; and in particular it shall not apply to acts involving measures of compulsion.

III. TRANSMISSION OF LETTERS ROGATORY

Article 4

Letters rogatory may be transmitted to the authority to which they are addressed by the interested parties, through judicial channels, diplomatic or consular agents, or the Central Authority of the State of origin or of the State of destination, as the case may be.

Each State Party shall inform the General Secretariat of the Organization of American States of the Central Authority competent to receive and distribute letters rogatory.

IV. REQUIREMENTS FOR EXECUTION

Article 5

Letters rogatory shall be executed in the States Parties provided they meet the following requirements:

a.   The letter rogatory is legalized, except as provided for in Articles 6 and 7 of this Convention. The letter rogatory shall be presumed to be duly legalized in the State of origin when legalized by the competent consular or diplomatic agent;

b.   The letter rogatory and the appended documentation are duly translated into the official language of the State of destination.

Article 6

Whenever letters rogatory are transmitted through consular or diplomatic channels or through the Central Authority, legalization shall not be required.

Article 7

Courts in border areas of the States Parties may directly execute the letters rogatory contemplated in this Convention and such letters shall not require legalization.

Article 8

Letters rogatory shall be accompanied by the following documents to be delivered to the person on whom process, summons or subpoena is being served:

a.   An authenticated copy of the complaint with its supporting documents, and of other exhibits or rulings that serve as the basis for the measure requested;

b.   Written information identifying the judicial or other adjudicatory authority issuing the letter, indicating the time-limits allowed the person affected to act upon the request, and warning of the consequences of failure to do so;

c.   Where appropriate, information on the existence and address of the court-appointed defense counsel or of competent legal-aid societies in the State of origin.

Article 9

Execution of letters rogatory shall not imply ultimate recognition of the jurisdiction of the judicial or other adjudicatory authority issuing the letter rogatory or a commitment to recognize the validity of the judgment it may render or to execute it.

V. EXECUTION

Article 10

Letters rogatory shall be executed in accordance with the laws and procedural rules of the State of destination.

At the request of the judicial or other adjudicatory authority issuing the letter rogatory, the authority of the State of destination may execute the letter through a special procedure, or accept the observance of additional formalities in performing the act requested, provided this procedure or the observance of those formalities is not contrary to the law of the State of destination.

Article 11

The authority of the State of destination shall have jurisdiction to determine any issue arising as a result of the execution of the measure requested in the letter rogatory.

Should such authority find that it lacks jurisdiction to execute the letter rogatory, it shall ex officio forward the documents and antecedents of the case to the authority of the State which has jurisdiction.

Article 12

The costs and other expenses involved in the processing and execution of letters rogatory shall be borne by the interested parties.

The State of destination may, in its discretion, execute a letter rogatory that does not indicate the person to be held responsible for costs and other expenses when incurred. The identity of the person empowered to represent the applicant for legal purposes may be indicated in the letter rogatory or in the documents relating to its execution.

The effects of a declaration in forma pauperis shall be regulated by the law of the State of destination.

Article 13

Consular or diplomatic agents of the States Parties to this Convention may perform the acts referred to in Article 2 in the State in which they are accredited, provided the performance of such acts is not contrary to the laws of that State. In so doing, they shall not perform any acts involving measures of compulsion.

VI. GENERAL PROVISIONS

Article 14

States Parties belonging to economic integration systems may agree directly between themselves upon special methods and procedures more expeditious than those provided for in this Convention. These agreements may be extended to include other States in the manner in which the parties may agree.

Article 15

This Convention shall not limit any provisions regarding letters rogatory in bilateral or multilateral agreements that may have been signed or may be signed in the future by the States Parties or preclude the continuation of more favorable practices in this regard that may be followed by these States.

Article 16

The States Parties to this Convention may declare that its provisions cover the execution of letters rogatory in criminal, labor, and "contentious-administrative" cases, as well as in arbitrations and other matters within the jurisdiction of special courts. Such declarations shall be transmitted to the General Secretariat of the Organization of American States.

Article 17

The State of destination may refuse to execute a letter rogatory that is manifestly contrary to its public policy ("ordre public").

Article 18

The States Parties shall inform the General Secretariat of the Organization of American States of the requirements stipulated in their laws for the legalization and the translation of letters rogatory.

VII. FINAL PROVISIONS

Article 19

This Convention shall be open for signature by the Member States of the Organization of American States.

Article 20

This Convention is subject to ratification. The instruments of ratification shall be deposited with the General Secretariat of the Organization of American States.

Article 21

This Convention shall remain open for accession by any other State. The instrument of accession shall be deposited with the General Secretariat of the Organization of American States.

Article 22

This Convention shall enter into force on the thirtieth day following the date of deposit of the second instrument of ratification.

For each State ratifying or acceding to the Convention after the deposit of the second instrument of ratification, the Convention shall enter into force on the thirtieth day after deposit by such State of its instrument of ratification or accession.

Article 23

If a State Party has two or more territorial units in which different systems of law apply in relation to the matters dealt with in this Convention, it may, at the time of signature, ratification or accession, declare that this Convention shall extend to all its territorial units or only to one or more of them.

Such declaration may be modified by subsequent declarations, which shall expressly indicate the territorial unit or units to which the Convention applies. Such subsequent declarations shall be transmitted to the General Secretariat of the Organization of American States, and shall become effective thirty days after the date of their receipt.

Article 24

This Convention shall remain in force indefinitely, but any of the States Parties may denounce it. The instrument of denunciation shall be deposited with the General Secretariat of the Organization of American States. After one year from the date of deposit of the instrument of denunciation, the Convention shall no longer be in effect for the denouncing State, but shall remain in effect for the other States Parties.

Article 25

The original instrument of this Convention, the English, French, Portuguese and Spanish texts of which are equally authentic, shall be deposited with the General Secretariat of the Organization of American States. The Secretariat shall notify the Member States of the Organization of American States and the States that have acceded to the Convention of the signatures, deposits of instruments of ratification, accession, and denunciation as well as of reservations, if any. It shall also transmit the information mentioned in the second paragraph of Article 4 and in Article 18 and the declarations referred to in Articles 16 and 23 of this Convention.

IN WITNESS WHEREOF the undersigned Plenipotentiaries, being duly authorized thereto by their respective Governments, have signed this Convention.

DONE AT PANAMA CITY, Republic of Panama, this thirtieth day of January one thousand nine hundred and seventy-five.

[Signatures omitted]

Inter-American Convention on Letters Rogatory.

Done at Panama January 30, 1975; entered into force for the United States August 27, 1988.

ADDITIONAL PROTOCOL TO THE INTER-AMERICAN CONVENTION ON LETTERS ROGATORY

The Governments of the Member States of the Organization of American States, desirous of strengthening and facilitating international cooperation in judicial procedures as provided for in the Inter-American Convention on Letters Rogatory done in Panama on January 30, 1975, have agreed as follows:

I. SCOPE OF PROTOCOL

Article 1

This Protocol shall apply only to those procedural acts set forth in Article 2(a) of the Inter-American Convention on Letters Rogatory, hereinafter referred to as "the Convention". For the purposes of this Protocol, such acts shall be understood to mean procedural acts (pleadings, motions, orders, and subpoenas) that are served and requests for information that are made by a judicial or other adjudicatory authority of a State Party to a judicial or administrative authority of another State Party and are transmitted by a letter rogatory from the Central Authority of the State of origin to the Central Authority of the State of destination.

II. CENTRAL AUTHORITY

Article 2

Each State Party shall designate a central authority that shall perform the functions assigned to it in the Convention and in this Protocol. At the time of deposit of their instruments of ratification or accession to this Protocol, the States Parties shall communicate the designations to the General Secretariat of the Organization of American States, which shall distribute to the States Parties to the Convention a list containing the designations received. The Central Authority designated by a State Party in accordance with Article 4 of the Convention may be changed at any time. The State Party shall inform the above-mentioned Secretariat of such change as promptly as possible.

III. PREPARATION OF LETTERS ROGATORY

Article 3

Letters rogatory shall be prepared on forms that are printed in the four official languages of the Organization of American States or in the languages of the State of origin and of the State of destination and conform to Form A contained in the Annex to this Protocol.

Letters rogatory shall be accompanied by the following:

a.   Copy of the complaint or pleading that initiated the action in which the letter rogatory was issued, as well as a translation thereof into the language of the State of destination;

b.   Untranslated copy of the documents attached to the complaint or pleading;

c.   Untranslated copy of any rulings ordering issuance of the letter rogatory;

d.   Form conforming to Form B annexed to this Protocol and containing essential information for the person to be served or the authority to receive the documents; and

e.   Certificate conforming to Form C annexed to this Protocol on which the Central Authority of the State of destination shall attest to execution or non-execution of the letter rogatory.

The copies shall be regarded as authenticated for the purposes of Article 8(a) of the Convention if they bear the seal of the judicial or other adjudicatory authority that issued the letter rogatory.

A copy of the letter rogatory together with Form B and the copies referred to in items a, b, and c of this Article shall be delivered to the person notified or to the authority to which the request is addressed. One of the copies of the letter rogatory and the documents attached to it shall remain in the possession of the State of destination; the untranslated original, the certificate of execution and the documents attached to them shall be returned to the Central Authority of the State of origin through appropriate channels.

If a State Party has more than one official language, it shall, at the time of signature, ratification or accession to this Protocol, declare which language or languages shall be considered official for the purposes of the Convention and of this Protocol. If a State Party comprises territorial units that have different official languages, it shall, at the time of signature, ratification or accession to this Protocol, declare which language or languages in each territorial unit shall be considered official for the purposes of the Convention and of this Protocol. The General Secretariat of the Organization of American States shall distribute to the States Parties to this Protocol the information contained in such declarations.

IV. TRANSMISSION AND PROCESSING OF LETTERS ROGATORY

Article 4

Upon receipt of a letter rogatory from the Central Authority in another State Party, the Central Authority in the State of destination shall transmit the letter rogatory to the appropriate judicial or administrative authority for processing in accordance with the applicable local law.

Upon execution of the letter rogatory, the judicial or administrative authority or authorities that processed it shall attest to the execution thereof in the manner prescribed in their local law, and shall transmit it with the relevant documents to the Central Authority. The Central Authority of the State Party of destination shall certify execution of the letter rogatory to the Central Authority of the State Party of origin on a form conforming to Form C of the Annex, which shall not require legalization. In addition, the Central Authority of the State of destination shall return the letter rogatory and attached documents to the Central Authority of the State of origin for delivery to the judicial or other adjudicatory authority that issued it.

V. COSTS AND EXPENSES

Article 5

The processing of letters rogatory by the Central Authority of the State Party of destination and its judicial or administrative authorities shall be free of charge. However, this State Party may seek payment by parties requesting execution of letters rogatory for those services which, in accordance with its local law, are required to be paid for directly by those parties.

The party requesting the execution of a letter rogatory shall, at its election, either select and indicate in the letter rogatory the person who is responsible in the State of destination for the cost of such services or, alternatively, shall attach to the letter rogatory a check for the fixed amount that is specified in Article 6 of this Protocol for its processing by the State of destination and will cover the cost of such services or a document proving that such amount has been transferred by some other means to the Central Authority of the State of destination.

The fact that the cost of such services ultimately exceeds the fixed amount shall not delay or prevent the processing or execution of the letter rogatory by the Central Authority or the judicial or administrative authorities of the State of destination. Should the cost exceed that amount, the Central Authority of the State of destination may, when returning the executed letter rogatory, seek payment of the outstanding amount due from the party requesting execution of the letter rogatory.

Article 6

At the time of deposit of its instrument of ratification or accession to this Protocol with the General Secretariat of the Organization of American States, each State Party shall attach a schedule of the services and the costs and other expenses that, in accordance with its local law, shall be paid directly by the party requesting execution of the letter rogatory. In addition, each State Party shall specify in the above-mentioned schedule the single amount which it considers will reasonably cover the cost of such services, regardless of the number or nature thereof. This amount shall be paid when the person requesting execution of the letter rogatory has not designated a person responsible for the payment of such services in the State of destination but has decided to pay for them directly in the manner provided for in Article 5 of this Protocol.

The General Secretariat of the Organization of American States shall distribute the information received to the States Parties to this Protocol. A State Party may at any time notify the General Secretariat of the Organization of American States of changes in the above-mentioned schedules, which shall be communicated by the General Secretariat to the other States Parties to this Protocol.

Article 7

States Parties may declare in the schedules mentioned in the foregoing articles that, provided there is reciprocity, they will not charge parties requesting execution of letters rogatory for the services necessary for executing them, or will accept in complete satisfaction of the cost of such services either the single fixed amount specified in Article 6 or another specified amount.

Article 8

This Protocol shall be open for signature and subject to ratification or accession by those Member States of the Organization of American States that have signed, ratified, or acceded to the Inter-American Convention on Letters Rogatory signed in Panama on January 30, 1975.

This Protocol shall remain open for accession by any other State that accedes or has acceded to the Inter-American Convention on Letters Rogatory, under the conditions set forth in this article.

The instruments of ratification and accession shall be deposited with the General Secretariat of the Organization of American States.

Article 9

This Protocol shall enter into force on the thirtieth day following the date on which two States Parties to the Convention have deposited their instruments of ratification or accession to this Protocol.

For each State ratifying or acceding to the Protocol after its entry into force, the Protocol shall enter into force on the thirtieth day following deposit by such State of its instrument of ratification or accession, provided that such State is a Party to the Convention.

Article 10

If a State Party has two or more territorial units in which different systems of law apply in relation to matters dealt with in this Protocol, it may, at the time of signature, ratification or accession, declare that this Protocol shall extend to all its territorial units or only to one or more of them.

Such declaration may be modified by subsequent declarations that shall expressly indicate the territorial unit or units to which this Protocol applies. Such subsequent declarations shall be transmitted to the General Secretariat of the Organization of American States, and shall become effective thirty days after the date of their receipt.

Article 11

This Protocol shall remain in force indefinitely, but any of the States Parties may denounce it. The instrument of denunciation shall be deposited with the General Secretariat of the Organization of American States. After one year from the date of deposit of the instrument of denunciation, the Protocol shall no longer be in effect for the denouncing State, but shall remain in effect for the other States Parties.

Article 12

The original instrument of this Protocol and its Annex (Forms A, B and C), the English, French, Portuguese and Spanish texts of which are equally authentic, shall be deposited with the General Secretariat of the Organization of American States, which will forward an authenticated copy of the text to the Secretariat of the United Nations for registration and publication in accordance with Article 102 of its Charter. The General Secretariat of the Organization of American States shall notify the Member States of that Organization and the States that have acceded to the Protocol of the signatures, deposits of instruments of ratification, accession and denunciation, as well as of reservations, if any. It shall also transmit to them the information mentioned in Article 2, the last paragraph of Article 3, and Article 6 and the declarations referred to in Article 10 of this Protocol.

IN WITNESS WHEREOF the undersigned Plenipotentiaries, being duly authorized thereto by their respective Governments, have signed this Protocol.

DONE AT MONTEVIDEO, Republic of Uruguay, this eighth day of May, one thousand nine hundred and seventy-nine.

[Signatures omitted]

ANNEX TO THE ADDITIONAL PROTOCOL
TO THE INTER-AMERICAN CONVENTION ON LETTERS ROGATORY

FORM A
LETTER ROGATORY[1]

1 REQUESTING JUDICIAL OR OTHER ADJUDICATORY AUTHORITY Name Address	2 CASE: Docket No.:
3 CENTRAL AUTHORITY OF THE STATE OF ORIGIN Name Address	4 CENTRAL AUTHORITY OF THE STATE OF DESTINATION Name Address
5 REQUESTING PARTY Name Address	6 COUNSEL TO THE REQUESTING PARTY Name Address
PERSON DESIGNATED TO ACT IN CONNECTION WITH THE LETTER ROGATORY	
Name Address	Is this person responsible for costs and expenses? YES ☐ NO ☐ *If not, check in the amount of $_____ is attached *Or proof of payment is attached

---

[1] Complete the original and two copies of this form; if A(1) is applicable, attach the original and two copies of the translation of this item in the language of the State of destination.

The Central Authority signing this letter rogatory has the honor to transmit to you in triplicate the documents listed below and, in conformity with the Protocol to the Inter-American Convention on Letters Rogatory:

*A.   Requests their prompt service on:

The undersigned authority requests that service be carried out in the following manner:

    *(1).   In accordance with the special procedure or additional formalities that are described below, as provided for in the second paragraph of Article 10 of the above-mentioned Convention; or

    *(2).   By service personally on the identified addressee or, in the case of a legal entity, on its authorized agent; or

    *(3).   If the person or the authorized agent of the entity to be served is not found, service shall be made in accordance with the law of the State of destination.

*B.   Requests the delivery of the documents listed below to the following judicial or administrative authority:
Authority_____

_____

*C.   Requests the Central Authority of the State of destination to return to the Central Authority of the State of origin one copy of the documents listed below and attached to this letter rogatory, and an executed Certificate on the attached Form C.
    Done at _____ this _____ date of _____, 19___.

_____   _____
  Signature and stamp of the   Signature and stamp of the
  judicial or other adjudicatory   Central Authority of the
  authority of the State of origin   State of origin

Title or other identification of each document to be delivered:
_____

_____

(Attach additional pages, if necessary.)

ANNEX TO THE ADDITIONAL PROTOCOL TO THE
INTER-AMERICAN CONVENTION ON LETTERS ROGATORY

FORM B

ESSENTIAL INFORMATION FOR THE ADDRESSEE[1]

To   (Name and address of the person being served)_____

_____

You are hereby informed that (Brief statement of nature of service)_____

_____

_____

 *   Delete if inapplicable.

A copy of the letter rogatory that gives rise to the service or delivery of these documents is attached to this document. This copy also contains essential information for you. Also attached are copies of the complaint or pleading initiating the action in which the letter rogatory was issued, of the documents attached to the complaint or pleading, and of any rulings that ordered the issuance of the letter rogatory.

ADDITIONAL INFORMATION

I*

FOR SERVICE

A.   The document being served on you (original or copy) concerns the following:

_____

_____

B.   The remedies sought or the amount in dispute is as follows:

_____

_____

C.   By this service, you are requested:

_____

_____

D.   *   In case of service on you as a defendant you can answer the complaint before the judicial or other adjudicatory authority specified in Form A, Box 1 (State place, date and hour):

     *   You are being summoned to appear as:

     *   If some other action is being requested of the person served, please describe:

E.   If you fail to comply, the consequences might be: _____

_____

_____

_____

F.   You are hereby informed that a defense counsel appointed by the Court or the following legal aid societies are available to you at the place where the proceeding is pending.
Name:

Address:

The documents listed in Part III are being furnished to you so that you may better understand and defend your interests.

II*

FOR INFORMATION FROM JUDICIAL OR ADMINISTRATIVE AUTHORITY

To:

(Name and address of the judicial or administrative authority)

You are respectfully requested to furnish the undersigned authority with the following information:

The documents listed in Part III are being furnished to you to facilitate your reply.

III

LIST OF ATTACHED DOCUMENTS

(Attach additional pages if necessary.)

Done at _____ this _____ day of _____, 19___

Signature and stamp of the judicial or other adjudicatory authority of the State of origin	Signature and stamp of the Central Authority of the State of Origin

[1] Complete the original and two copies of this form in the language of the State of origin and two copies in the language of the State of destination.
* Delete if inapplicable.

ANNEX TO THE ADDITIONAL PROTOCOL
TO THE INTER-AMERICAN CONVENTION ON LETTERS ROGATORY

FORM C

CERTIFICATE OF EXECUTION[1]

To:

(Name and address of judicial or other adjudicatory authority that issued the letter rogatory)

In conformity with the Additional Protocol to the Inter-American Convention on Letters Rogatory, signed at Montevideo on May 8, 1979, and in accordance with the attached original letter rogatory, the undersigned Central Authority has the honor to certify the following:

*A.   That one copy of the documents attached to this Certificate has been served or delivered as follows:

Date:
At (Address)

By one of the following methods authorized by the Convention.

*(1)   In accordance with the special procedure or additional formalities that are described below, as provided for in the second paragraph of Article 10 of the above-mentioned Convention, or

*(2)   By service personally on the identified addressee or, in the case of a legal entity, on its authorized agent, or

*(3)   If the person or the authorized agent of the entity to be served was not found, in accordance with the law of the State of destination: (Specify method used)

*B.   That the documents referred to in the letter rogatory have been delivered to:

Identity of person

Relationship to the addressee
(Family, business or other)

*C.   That the documents attached to the Certificate have not been served or delivered for the following reason(s):

*D.   In conformity with the Protocol, the party requesting execution of the letter rogatory is requested to pay the outstanding balance of costs in the amount indicated in the attached statement.

Done at _____ the _____ day of _____ 19___

Signature and stamp of Central Authority of the State of destination

Where appropriate, attach originals or copies of any additional documents proving service or delivery, and identify them.

¹ Complete the original and one copy in the language of the State of destination.
* Delete if inapplicable.

Additional Protocol to the Inter-American Convention on Letters Rogatory, with Annex. Done at Montevideo May 8, 1979; entered into force for the United States August 27, 1988.

§ 1782.   Assistance to foreign and international tribunals and to litigants before such tribunals

(a)   The district court of the district in which a person resides or is found may order him to give his testimony or statement or to produce a document or other thing for use in a proceeding in a foreign or international tribunal, including criminal investigations conducted before formal accusation. The order may be made pursuant to a letter rogatory issued, or request made, by a foreign or international tribunal or upon the application of any interested person and may direct that the testimony or statement be given, or the document or other thing be produced, before a person appointed by the court. By virtue of his appointment, the person appointed has power to administer any necessary oath and take the testimony or statement. The order may prescribe the practice and procedure, which may be in whole or part the practice and procedure of the foreign country or the international tribunal, for taking the testimony or statement or producing the document or other thing. To the extent that the order does not prescribe otherwise, the testimony or statement shall be taken, and the document or other thing produced, in accordance with the Federal Rules of Civil Procedure.

A person may not be compelled to give his testimony or statement or to produce a document or other thing in violation of any legally applicable privilege.

(b)   This chapter does not preclude a person within the United States from voluntarily giving his testimony or statement, or producing a document or other thing, for use in a proceeding in a foreign or international tribunal before any person and in any manner acceptable to him.

(June 25, 1948, c. 646, 62 Stat. 949; May 24, 1949, c. 139, § 93, 63 Stat. 103; Oct. 3, 1964, Pub.L. 88–619, § 9(a), 78 Stat. 997; Feb. 10, 1996, Pub.L. 104–106, Div. A, Title XIII, § 1342(b), 110 Stat. 486.)

HISTORICAL AND STATUTORY NOTES

References in Text

The Federal Rules of Civil Procedure, referred to in subsec. (a), are set out in this title.

§ 1783.   Subpoena of person in foreign country

(a)   A court of the United States may order the issuance of a subpoena requiring the appearance as a witness before it, or before a person or body designated by it, of a national or resident of the United

States who is in a foreign country, or requiring the production of a specified document or other thing by him, if the court finds that particular testimony or the production of the document or other thing by him is necessary in the interest of justice, and, in other than a criminal action or proceeding, if the court finds, in addition, that it is not possible to obtain his testimony in admissible form without his personal appearance or to obtain the production of the document or other thing in any other manner.

(b) The subpoena shall designate the time and place for the appearance or for the production of the document or other thing. Service of the subpoena and any order to show cause, rule, judgment, or decree authorized by this section or by section 1784 of this title shall be effected in accordance with the provisions of the Federal Rules of Civil Procedure relating to service of process on a person in a foreign country. The person serving the subpoena shall tender to the person to whom the subpoena is addressed his estimated necessary travel and attendance expenses, the amount of which shall be determined by the court and stated in the order directing the issuance of the subpoena.

(June 25, 1948, c. 646, 62 Stat. 949; Oct. 3, 1964, Pub.L. 88–619, § 10(a), 78 Stat. 997.)

HISTORICAL AND STATUTORY NOTES

References in Text

The Federal Rules of Civil Procedure, referred to in subsec. (b), are set out in this title.

§ 1784. Contempt

(a) The court of the United States which has issued a subpoena served in a foreign country may order the person who has failed to appear or who has failed to produce a document or other thing as directed therein to show cause before it at a designated time why he should not be punished for contempt.

(b) The court, in the order to show cause, may direct that any of the person's property within the United States be levied upon or seized, in the manner provided by law or court rules governing levy or seizure under execution, and held to satisfy any judgment that may be rendered against him pursuant to subsection (d) of this section if adequate security, in such amount as the court may direct in the order, be given for any damage that he might suffer should he not be found in contempt. Security under this subsection may not be required of the United States.

(c) A copy of the order to show cause shall be served on the person in accordance with section 1783(b) of this title.

(d) On the return day of the order to show cause or any later day to which the hearing may be continued, proof shall be taken. If the person is found in contempt, the court, notwithstanding any limitation upon its power generally to punish for contempt, may fine him not more than $100,000 and direct that the fine and costs of the proceedings be satisfied by a sale of the property levied upon or seized, conducted upon the notice required and in the manner provided for sales upon execution.

(June 25, 1948, c. 646, 62 Stat. 949; Oct. 3, 1964, Pub.L. 88–619, § 11, 78 Stat. 998.)

§ 1785. Subpoenas in multiparty, multiforum actions

When the jurisdiction of the district court is based in whole or in part upon section 1369 of this title, a subpoena for attendance at a hearing or trial may, if authorized by the court upon motion for good cause shown, and upon such terms and conditions as the court may impose, be served at any place within the United States, or anywhere outside the United States if otherwise permitted by law.

(Added Pub.L. 107–273, Div. C, Title I, § 11020(b)(4)(B)(i), Nov. 2, 2002, 116 Stat. 1828.)

HISTORICAL AND STATUTORY NOTES

Effective and Applicability Provisions

2002 Acts. Amendments by section 11020(b) of Pub.L. 107–273 shall apply to a civil action if the accident giving rise to the cause of action occurred on or after the 90th day after Nov. 2, 2002, see section 11020(c) of Pub.L. 107–273, set out as a note under 28 U.S.C.A. § 1369.

Prior Provisions

A prior section 1785, Act June 25, 1948, c. 646, 62 Stat. 950, relating to the privilege against self-incrimination on examination under letters rogatory (see section 1782(a) of this title), was repealed by Pub.L. 88–619, § 12(a), Oct. 3, 1964, 78 Stat. 998.

CHAPTER 119—EVIDENCE; WITNESSES

§ 1821. Per diem and mileage generally; subsistence

(a)(1) Except as otherwise provided by law, a witness in attendance at any court of the United States, or before a United States Magistrate Judge, or before any person authorized to take his deposition pursuant to any rule or order of a court of the United States, shall be paid the fees and allowances provided by this section.

(2) As used in this section, the term "court of the United States" includes, in addition to the courts listed in section 451 of this title, any court created by Act of Congress in a territory which is invested with any jurisdiction of a district court of the United States.

(b) A witness shall be paid an attendance fee of $40 per day for each day's attendance. A witness shall also be paid the attendance fee for the time necessarily occupied in going to and returning from the place of attendance at the beginning and end of such attendance or at any time during such attendance.

(c)(1) A witness who travels by common carrier shall be paid for the actual expenses of travel on the basis of the means of transportation reasonably utilized and the distance necessarily traveled to and from such witness's residence by the shortest practical route in going to and returning from the place of attendance. Such a witness shall utilize a common carrier at the most economical rate reasonably available. A receipt or other evidence of actual cost shall be furnished.

(2) A travel allowance equal to the mileage allowance which the Administrator of General Services has prescribed, pursuant to section 5704 of title 5, for official travel of employees of the Federal Government shall be paid to each witness who travels by privately owned vehicle. Computation of mileage under this paragraph shall be made on the basis of a uniformed table of distances adopted by the Administrator of General Services.

(3) Toll charges for toll roads, bridges, tunnels, and ferries, taxicab fares between places of lodging and carrier terminals, and parking fees (upon presentation of a valid parking receipt), shall be paid in full to a witness incurring such expenses.

(4) All normal travel expenses within and outside the judicial district shall be taxable as costs pursuant to section 1920 of this title.

(d)(1)   A subsistence allowance shall be paid to a witness when an overnight stay is required at the place of attendance because such place is so far removed from the residence of such witness as to prohibit return thereto from day to day.

(2)   A subsistence allowance for a witness shall be paid in an amount not to exceed the maximum per diem allowance prescribed by the Administrator of General Services, pursuant to section 5702(a) of title 5, for official travel in the area of attendance by employees of the Federal Government.

(3)   A subsistence allowance for a witness attending in an area designated by the Administrator of General Services as a high-cost area shall be paid in an amount not to exceed the maximum actual subsistence allowance prescribed by the Administrator, pursuant to section 5702(c)(B)[1] of title 5, for official travel in such area by employees of the Federal Government.

(4)   When a witness is detained pursuant to section 3144 of title 18 for want of security for his appearance, he shall be entitled for each day of detention when not in attendance at court, in addition to his subsistence, to the daily attendance fee provided by subsection (b) of this section.

(e)   An alien who has been paroled into the United States for prosecution, pursuant to section 212(d)(5) of the Immigration and Nationality Act (8 U.S.C. 1182(d)(5)), or an alien who either has admitted belonging to a class of aliens who are deportable or has been determined pursuant to section 240 of such Act (8 U.S.C. 1252(b))[1] to be deportable, shall be ineligible to receive the fees or allowances provided by this section.

(f)   Any witness who is incarcerated at the time that his or her testimony is given (except for a witness to whom the provisions of section 3144 of title 18 apply) may not receive fees or allowances under this section, regardless of whether such a witness is incarcerated at the time he or she makes a claim for fees or allowances under this section.

(June 25, 1948, c. 646, 62 Stat. 950; May 10, 1949, c. 96, 63 Stat. 65; May 24, 1949, c. 139, § 94, 63 Stat. 103; Oct. 31, 1951, c. 655, § 51(a), 65 Stat. 727; Sept. 3, 1954, c. 1263, § 45, 68 Stat. 1242; Aug. 1, 1956, c. 826, 70 Stat. 798; Mar. 27, 1968, Pub.L. 90–274, § 102(b), 82 Stat. 62; Oct. 27, 1978, Pub.L. 95–535, § 1, 92 Stat. 2033; Dec. 1, 1990, Pub.L. 101–650, Title III, §§ 314(a), 321, 104 Stat. 5115, 5117; Oct. 14, 1992, Pub.L. 102–417, § 2(a)–(c), 106 Stat. 2138; Sept. 30, 1996, Pub.L. 104–208, Div. C, Title III, § 308(g)(5)(E), 110 Stat. 3009–623.)

HISTORICAL AND STATUTORY NOTES

References in Text

Subsection (c) of section 5702 of title 5, referred to in subsec. (d)(3), which related to conditions under which an employee could be reimbursed for actual and necessary expenses of official travel when the maximum per diem allowance was less than these expenses, was repealed, and subsec. (e) of section 5702 of title 5, was redesignated as subsec. (c), by Pub. L. 99–234, title I, § 102, Jan. 2, 1986, 99 Stat. 1756.

Section 240 of the Immigration and Nationality Act, referred to in subsec. (e), is classified to section 1229a of Title 8, Aliens and Nationality.

Change of Name

"United States magistrate judge" substituted for "United States magistrate" in text pursuant to section 321 of Pub.L. 101–650, set out as a note under 28 U.S.C.A. § 631.

Severability of Provisions

If any provision of Division C of Pub.L. 104–208 or the application of such provision to any person or circumstances is held to be unconstitutional, the remainder of Division C of Pub.L. 104–208 and the application of the provisions of Division C of Pub.L. 104–208 to any person or circumstance not to be affected thereby, see section 1(e) of Pub.L. 104–208, set out as a note under section 1101 of Title 8, Aliens and Nationality.

---

[1]   [Footnote to 28 U.S.C. § 1821(d)(3):] See References in Text note below.

Payment of Fact Witness Fee to Incarcerated Person Prohibited

Pub.L. 102–395, Title I, § 108, Oct. 6, 1992, 106 Stat. 1841, provided that: "Notwithstanding 28 U.S.C. 1821 [this section], no funds appropriated to the Department of Justice in fiscal year 1993 or any prior fiscal year, or any other funds available from the Treasury of the United States, shall be obligated or expended to pay a fact witness fee to a person who is incarcerated testifying as a fact witness in a court of the United States, as defined in 28 U.S.C. 1821(a)(2) [subsec. (a)(2) of this section]."

Similar provisions were contained in the following prior appropriations Acts:

Pub.L. 102–140, Title I, § 110, Oct. 28, 1991, 105 Stat. 795.

Pub.L. 102–27, Title II, § 102, Apr. 10, 1991, 105 Stat. 136.

§ 1822.   Competency of interested persons; share of penalties payable

Any person interested in a share of any fine, penalty or forfeiture incurred under any Act of Congress, may be examined as a witness in any proceeding for the recovery of such fine, penalty or forfeiture by any party thereto. Such examination shall not deprive the witness of his share.

(June 25, 1948, c. 646, 62 Stat. 950.)

[§ 1823.   Repealed. Pub.L. 91–563, § 5(a), Dec. 19, 1970, 84 Stat. 1478]

HISTORICAL AND STATUTORY NOTES

Section, Acts June 25, 1948, c. 646, 62 Stat. 950; May 24, 1949, c. 139, § 95, 63 Stat. 103; Oct. 5, 1949, c. 601, 63 Stat. 704; July 7, 1952, c. 581, 66 Stat. 439; July 28, 1955, c. 424, § 3, 69 Stat. 394, related to payment of witness fees to officers and employees of the United States, and is now covered by sections 5515, 5537, 5751, and 6322 of Title 5, Government Organization and Employees.

§ 1824.   Mileage fees under summons as both witness and juror

No constructive or double mileage fees shall be allowed by reason of any person being summoned both as a witness and a juror.

(June 25, 1948, c. 646, 62 Stat. 951.)

§ 1825.   Payment of fees

(a)   In any case in which the United States or an officer or agency of the United States is a party, the United States marshal for the district shall pay all fees of witnesses on the certificate of the United States attorney or assistant United States attorney, and in the proceedings before a United States magistrate judge, on the certificate of such magistrate judge, except that any fees of defense witnesses, other than experts, appearing pursuant to subpoenas issued upon approval of the court, shall be paid by the United States marshal for the district—

(1)   on the certificate of a Federal public defender or assistant Federal public defender, in a criminal case in which the defendant is represented by such Federal public defender or assistant Federal public defender, and

(2)   on the certificate of the clerk of the court upon the affidavit of such witnesses' attendance given by other counsel appointed pursuant to section 3006A of title 18, in a criminal case in which a defendant is represented by such other counsel.

(b)   In proceedings in forma pauperis for a writ of habeas corpus, and in proceedings in forma pauperis under section 2255 of this title, the United States marshal for the district shall pay, on the certificate of the district judge, all fees of witnesses for the party authorized to proceed in forma pauperis, except that any fees of witnesses for such party, other than experts, appearing pursuant to subpoenas issued upon approval of the court, shall be paid by the United States marshal for the district—

(1)　on the certificate of a Federal public defender or assistant Federal public defender, in any such proceedings in which a party is represented by such Federal public defender or assistant Federal public defender, and

(2)　on the certificate of the clerk of the court upon the affidavit of such witnesses' attendance given by other counsel appointed pursuant to section 3006A of title 18, in any such proceedings in which a party is represented by such other counsel.

(c)　Fees and mileage need not be tendered to a witness upon service of a subpoena issued on behalf of the United States or an officer or agency of the United States, upon service of a subpoena issued on behalf of a defendant represented by a Federal public defender, assistant Federal public defender, or other attorney appointed pursuant to section 3006A of title 18, or upon service of a subpoena issued on behalf of a party authorized to proceed in forma pauperis, if the payment of such fees and mileage is to be made by the United States marshal under this section.

(June 25, 1948, c. 646, 62 Stat. 951; Sept. 2, 1965, Pub.L. 89–162, 79 Stat. 618; Nov. 14, 1986, Pub.L. 99–651, Title I, § 104, 100 Stat. 3645; Dec. 1, 1990, Pub.L. 101–650, Title III, § 321, 104 Stat. 5117.)

HISTORICAL AND STATUTORY NOTES

Effective and Applicability Provisions

1986 Acts. Amendment to this section by section 104 of Pub.L. 99–651 to take effect one hundred and twenty days after Nov. 14, 1986, see section 105 of Pub.L. 99–651, set out as a note under section 3006A of Title 18, Crimes and Criminal Procedure.

Change of Name

"United States magistrate judge" substituted for "United States magistrate" in text pursuant to section 321 of Pub.L. 101–650, set out as a note under 28 U.S.C.A. § 631.

§ 1826.　Recalcitrant witnesses

(a)　Whenever a witness in any proceeding before or ancillary to any court or grand jury of the United States refuses without just cause shown to comply with an order of the court to testify or provide other information, including any book, paper, document, record, recording or other material, the court, upon such refusal, or when such refusal is duly brought to its attention, may summarily order his confinement at a suitable place until such time as the witness is willing to give such testimony or provide such information. No period of such confinement shall exceed the life of—

(1)　the court proceeding, or

(2)　the term of the grand jury, including extensions,

before which such refusal to comply with the court order occurred, but in no event shall such confinement exceed eighteen months.

(b)　No person confined pursuant to subsection (a) of this section shall be admitted to bail pending the determination of an appeal taken by him from the order for his confinement if it appears that the appeal is frivolous or taken for delay. Any appeal from an order of confinement under this section shall be disposed of as soon as practicable, but not later than thirty days from the filing of such appeal.

(c)　Whoever escapes or attempts to escape from the custody of any facility or from any place in which or to which he is confined pursuant to this section or section 4243 of title 18, or whoever rescues or attempts to rescue or instigates, aids, or assists the escape or attempt to escape of such a person, shall be subject to imprisonment for not more than three years, or a fine of not more than $10,000, or both.

(Added Pub.L. 91–452, Title III, § 301(a), Oct. 15, 1970, 84 Stat. 932; amended Pub.L. 98–473, Title II, § 1013, Oct. 12, 1984, 98 Stat. 2142.)

§ 1827.   Interpreters in courts of the United States

(a)   The Director of the Administrative Office of the United States Courts shall establish a program to facilitate the use of certified and otherwise qualified interpreters in judicial proceedings instituted by the United States.

(b)(1)   The Director shall prescribe, determine, and certify the qualifications of persons who may serve as certified interpreters, when the Director considers certification of interpreters to be merited, for the hearing impaired (whether or not also speech impaired) and persons who speak only or primarily a language other than the English language, in judicial proceedings instituted by the United States. The Director may certify interpreters for any language if the Director determines that there is a need for certified interpreters in that language. Upon the request of the Judicial Conference of the United States for certified interpreters in a language, the Director shall certify interpreters in that language. Upon such a request from the judicial council of a circuit and the approval of the Judicial Conference, the Director shall certify interpreters for that circuit in the language requested. The judicial council of a circuit shall identify and evaluate the needs of the districts within a circuit. The Director shall certify interpreters based on the results of criterion-referenced performance examinations. The Director shall issue regulations to carry out this paragraph within 1 year after the date of the enactment of the Judicial Improvements and Access to Justice Act.

(2)   Only in a case in which no certified interpreter is reasonably available as provided in subsection (d) of this section, including a case in which certification of interpreters is not provided under paragraph (1) in a particular language, may the services of otherwise qualified interpreters be used. The Director shall provide guidelines to the courts for the selection of otherwise qualified interpreters, in order to ensure that the highest standards of accuracy are maintained in all judicial proceedings subject to the provisions of this chapter.

(3)   The Director shall maintain a current master list of all certified interpreters and otherwise qualified interpreters and shall report periodically on the use and performance of both certified and otherwise qualified interpreters in judicial proceedings instituted by the United States and on the languages for which interpreters have been certified. The Director shall prescribe, subject to periodic review, a schedule of reasonable fees for services rendered by interpreters, certified or otherwise, used in proceedings instituted by the United States, and in doing so shall consider the prevailing rate of compensation for comparable service in other governmental entities.

(c)(1)   Each United States district court shall maintain on file in the office of the clerk, and each United States attorney shall maintain on file, a list of all persons who have been certified as interpreters by the Director in accordance with subsection (b) of this section. The clerk shall make the list of certified interpreters for judicial proceeding available upon request.

(2)   The clerk of the court, or other court employee designated by the chief judge, shall be responsible for securing the services of certified interpreters and otherwise qualified interpreters required for proceedings initiated by the United States, except that the United States attorney is responsible for securing the services of such interpreters for governmental witnesses.

(d)(1)   The presiding judicial officer, with the assistance of the Director of the Administrative Office of the United States Courts, shall utilize the services of the most available certified interpreter, or when no certified interpreter is reasonably available, as determined by the presiding judicial officer, the services of an otherwise qualified interpreter, in judicial proceedings instituted by the United States, if the presiding judicial officer determines on such officer's own motion or on the motion of a party that such party (including a defendant in a criminal case), or a witness who may present testimony in such judicial proceedings—

(A)   speaks only or primarily a language other than the English language; or

(B)   suffers from a hearing impairment (whether or not suffering also from a speech impairment)

so as to inhibit such party's comprehension of the proceedings or communication with counsel or the presiding judicial officer, or so as to inhibit such witness' comprehension of questions and the presentation of such testimony.

(2) Upon the motion of a party, the presiding judicial officer shall determine whether to require the electronic sound recording of a judicial proceeding in which an interpreter is used under this section. In making this determination, the presiding judicial officer shall consider, among other things, the qualifications of the interpreter and prior experience in interpretation of court proceedings; whether the language to be interpreted is not one of the languages for which the Director has certified interpreters, and the complexity or length of the proceeding. In a grand jury proceeding, upon the motion of the accused, the presiding judicial officer shall require the electronic sound recording of the portion of the proceeding in which an interpreter is used.

(e)(1) If any interpreter is unable to communicate effectively with the presiding judicial officer, the United States attorney, a party (including a defendant in a criminal case), or a witness, the presiding judicial officer shall dismiss such interpreter and obtain the services of another interpreter in accordance with this section.

(2) In any judicial proceedings instituted by the United States, if the presiding judicial officer does not appoint an interpreter under subsection (d) of this section, an individual requiring the services of an interpreter may seek assistance of the clerk of court or the Director of the Administrative Office of the United States Courts in obtaining the assistance of a certified interpreter.

(f)(1) Any individual other than a witness who is entitled to interpretation under subsection (d) of this section may waive such interpretation in whole or in part. Such a waiver shall be effective only if approved by the presiding judicial officer and made expressly by such individual on the record after opportunity to consult with counsel and after the presiding judicial officer has explained to such individual, utilizing the services of the most available certified interpreter, or when no certified interpreter is reasonably available, as determined by the presiding judicial officer, the services of an otherwise competent interpreter, the nature and effect of the waiver.

(2) An individual who waives under paragraph (1) of this subsection the right to an interpreter may utilize the services of a noncertified interpreter of such individual's choice whose fees, expenses, and costs shall be paid in the manner provided for the payment of such fees, expenses, and costs of an interpreter appointed under subsection (d) of this section.

(g)(1) There are authorized to be appropriated to the Federal judiciary, and to be paid by the Director of the Administrative Office of the United States Courts, such sums as may be necessary to establish a program to facilitate the use of certified and otherwise qualified interpreters, and otherwise fulfill the provisions of this section and the Judicial Improvements and Access to Justice Act, except as provided in paragraph (3).

(2) Implementation of the provisions of this section is contingent upon the availability of appropriated funds to carry out the purposes of this section.

(3) Such salaries, fees, expenses, and costs that are incurred with respect to Government witnesses (including for grand jury proceedings) shall, unless direction is made under paragraph (4), be paid by the Attorney General from sums appropriated to the Department of Justice.

(4) Upon the request of any person in any action for which interpreting services established pursuant to subsection (d) are not otherwise provided, the clerk of the court, or other court employee designated by the chief judge, upon the request of the presiding judicial officer, shall, where possible, make such services available to that person on a cost-reimbursable basis, but the judicial officer may also require the prepayment of the estimated expenses of providing such services.

(5) If the Director of the Administrative Office of the United States Courts finds it necessary to develop and administer criterion-referenced performance examinations for purposes of certification, or other examinations for the selection of otherwise qualified interpreters, the Director may prescribe for each examination a uniform fee for applicants to take such examination. In determining the rate of the fee for each examination, the Director shall consider the fees charged by other organizations for examinations that are similar in scope or nature. Notwithstanding section 3302(b) of title 31, the Director is authorized to provide in any contract or agreement for the development or administration of examinations and the collection of fees that the contractor may retain all or a portion of the fees in payment for the services. Notwithstanding paragraph (6) of this subsection, all fees collected after the effective date of this paragraph and not retained by a contractor shall be deposited in the fund established under section 1931 of this title and shall remain available until expended.

(6) Any moneys collected under this subsection may be used to reimburse the appropriations obligated and disbursed in payment for such services.

(h) The presiding judicial officer shall approve the compensation and expenses payable to interpreters, pursuant to the schedule of fees prescribed by the Director under subsection (b)(3).

(i) The term "presiding judicial officer" as used in this section refers to any judge of a United States district court, including a bankruptcy judge, a United States magistrate judge, and in the case of grand jury proceedings conducted under the auspices of the United States attorney, a United States attorney.

(j) The term "judicial proceedings instituted by the United States" as used in this section refers to all proceedings, whether criminal or civil, including pretrial and grand jury proceedings (as well as proceedings upon a petition for a writ of habeas corpus initiated in the name of the United States by a relator) conducted in, or pursuant to the lawful authority and jurisdiction of a United States district court. The term "United States district court" as used in this subsection includes any court which is created by an Act of Congress in a territory and is invested with any jurisdiction of a district court established by chapter 5 of this title.

(k) The interpretation provided by certified or otherwise qualified interpreters pursuant to this section shall be in the simultaneous mode for any party to a judicial proceeding instituted by the United States and in the consecutive mode for witnesses, except that the presiding judicial officer, sua sponte or on the motion of a party, may authorize a simultaneous, or consecutive interpretation when such officer determines after a hearing on the record that such interpretation will aid in the efficient administration of justice. The presiding judicial officer, on such officer's motion or on the motion of a party, may order that special interpretation services as authorized in section 1828 of this title be provided if such officer determines that the provision of such services will aid in the efficient administration of justice.

(l) Notwithstanding any other provision of this section or section 1828, the presiding judicial officer may appoint a certified or otherwise qualified sign language interpreter to provide services to a party, witness, or other participant in a judicial proceeding, whether or not the proceeding is instituted by the United States, if the presiding judicial officer determines, on such officer's own motion or on the motion of a party or other participant in the proceeding, that such individual suffers from a hearing impairment. The presiding judicial officer shall, subject to the availability of appropriated funds, approve the compensation and expenses payable to sign language interpreters appointed under this section in accordance with the schedule of fees prescribed by the Director under subsection (b)(3) of this section.

(Added Pub.L. 95–539, § 2(a), Oct. 28, 1978, 92 Stat. 2040; amended Pub.L. 100–702, Title VII, §§ 702–710, Nov. 19, 1988, 102 Stat. 4654–4657; Pub.L. 101–650, Title III, § 321, Dec. 1, 1990, 104 Stat. 5117; Pub.L. 104–317, Title III, § 306, Title IV, § 402(a), Oct. 19, 1996, 110 Stat. 3852, 3854.)

HISTORICAL AND STATUTORY NOTES

References in Text

The date of the enactment of the Judicial Improvements and Access to Justice Act, referred to in subsec. (b)(1), is the date of enactment of Pub.L. 100–702, which was approved Nov. 19, 1988.

The Judicial Improvements and Access to Justice Act, referred to in subsec. (g)(1), is Pub.L. 100–702, Nov. 19, 1988, 102 Stat. 4642. For complete classification of this Act to the Code, see Short Title note set out under section 1 of this title and Tables.

The effective date of this paragraph, referred to in subsec. (g)(5), probably means the date of enactment of Pub.L. 104–317, which was approved Oct. 19, 1996.

Change of Name

"United States magistrate judge" substituted for "United States magistrate" in text pursuant to section 321 of Pub.L. 101–650, set out as a note under 28 U.S.C.A. § 631.

Short Title

1978 Acts. For Short title of Pub.L. 95–539 as "Court Interpreters Act", see section 1 of Pub.L. 95–539, set out as a note under section 1 of this title.

Payment for Contractual Services

Section 402(b) of Pub.L. 104–317 provided that: "Notwithstanding sections 3302(b), 1341, and 1517 of title 31, United States Code [sections 3302(b), 1341, and 1517 of Title 31, Money and Finance], the Director of the Administrative Office of the United States Courts may include in any contract for the development or administration of examinations for interpreters (including such a contract entered into before the date of the enactment of this Act [Oct. 19, 1996]) a provision which permits the contractor to collect and retain fees in payment for contractual services in accordance with section 1827(g)(5) of title 28, United States Code [subsec. (g)(5) of this section]."

§ 1828.   Special interpretation services

(a) The Director of the Administrative Office of the United States Courts shall establish a program for the provision of special interpretation services in criminal actions and in civil actions initiated by the United States (including petitions for writs of habeas corpus initiated in the name of the United States by relators) in a United States district court. The program shall provide a capacity for simultaneous interpretation services in multidefendant criminal actions and multidefendant civil actions.

(b) Upon the request of any person in any action for which special interpretation services established pursuant to subsection (a) are not otherwise provided, the Director, with the approval of the presiding judicial officer, may make such services available to the person requesting the services on a reimbursable basis at rates established in conformity with section 9701 of title 31, but the Director may require the prepayment of the estimated expenses of providing the services by the person requesting them.

(c) Except as otherwise provided in this subsection, the expenses incident to providing services under subsection (a) of this section shall be paid by the Director from sums appropriated to the Federal judiciary. A presiding judicial officer, in such officer's discretion, may order that all or part of the expenses shall be apportioned between or among the parties or shall be taxed as costs in a civil action, and any moneys collected as a result of such order may be used to reimburse the appropriations obligated and disbursed in payment for such services.

(d) Appropriations available to the Director shall be available to provide services in accordance with subsection (b) of this section, and moneys collected by the Director under that subsection may be used to reimburse the appropriations charged for such services. A presiding judicial officer, in such officer's discretion, may order that all or part of the expenses shall be apportioned between or among the parties or shall be taxed as costs in the action.

(Added Pub.L. 95–539, § 2(a), Oct. 28, 1978, 92 Stat. 2042; amended Pub.L. 97–258, § 3(g), Sept. 13, 1982, 96 Stat. 1065.)

HISTORICAL AND STATUTORY NOTES

Effective and Applicability Provisions

1978 Acts. Section effective 90 days after Oct. 28, 1978, see section 10(b) of Pub.L. 95–539, set out as a note under section 602 of this title.

CHAPTER 121—JURIES; TRIAL BY JURY

§ 1861.   Declaration of policy

It is the policy of the United States that all litigants in Federal courts entitled to trial by jury shall have the right to grand and petit juries selected at random from a fair cross section of the community in the district or division wherein the court convenes. It is further the policy of the United States that all citizens shall have the opportunity to be considered for service on grand and petit juries in the district courts of the United States, and shall have an obligation to serve as jurors when summoned for that purpose.

(June 25, 1948, c. 646, 62 Stat. 951; Sept. 9, 1957, Pub.L. 85–315, Part V, § 152, 71 Stat. 638; Mar. 27, 1968, Pub.L. 90–274, § 101, 82 Stat. 54.)

HISTORICAL AND STATUTORY NOTES

Effective and Applicability Provisions

1968 Acts. Section 104 of Pub.L. 90–274 provided that: "This Act [amending this section and sections 1821, 1862–1869, and 1871 of this title, repealing section 867 of Title 48, Territories and Insular Possessions, and enacting provisions set out as notes under this section] shall become effective two hundred and seventy days after the date of enactment [Mar. 27, 1968]: *Provided* That this Act shall not apply in any case in which an indictment has been returned or petit jury empaneled prior to such effective date."

Short Title

1978 Acts. Pub.L. 95–572, § 1, Nov. 2, 1978, 92 Stat. 2453, provided that: "This Act [which enacted sections 1363 and 1875 of this title, renumbered as section 1364 prior section 1363 of this title, amended sections 1863, 1865, 1866, 1869, and 1871 of this title, and enacted provisions set out as a note under section 1363 of this title] may be cited as the 'Jury System Improvements Act of 1978'."

1968 Acts. Section 1 of Pub.L. 90–274 provided: "That this Act [amending this section and sections 1821, 1862–1869, and 1871 of this title, repealing section 867 of Title 48, Territories and Insular Possessions, and enacting material set out as notes under this section] may be cited as the 'Jury Selection and Service Act of 1968'."

§ 1862.   Discrimination prohibited

No citizen shall be excluded from service as a grand or petit juror in the district courts of the United States or in the Court of International Trade on account of race, color, religion, sex, national origin, or economic status.

(June 25, 1948, c. 646, 62 Stat. 952; Mar. 27, 1968, Pub.L. 90–274, § 101, 82 Stat. 54; Oct. 10, 1980, Pub.L. 96–417, Title III, § 302(c), 94 Stat. 1739.)

§ 1863.   Plan for random jury selection

(a)   Each United States district court shall devise and place into operation a written plan for random selection of grand and petit jurors that shall be designed to achieve the objectives of sections 1861 and 1862 of this title, and that shall otherwise comply with the provisions of this title. The plan shall be placed into operation after approval by a reviewing panel consisting of the members of the judicial council of the circuit and either the chief judge of the district whose plan is being reviewed or such other active district judge of that district as the chief judge of the district may designate. The panel shall examine the plan to ascertain that it complies with the provisions of this title. If the reviewing panel finds that the plan does not comply, the panel shall state the particulars in which the plan fails to comply and direct the district court to present within a reasonable time an alternative plan remedying the defect or defects. Separate plans may be adopted for each division or combination of divisions within a judicial district. The district court may modify a plan at any time and it shall modify the plan when so directed by the reviewing panel. The district court shall promptly notify the panel, the Administrative Office of the United States Courts, and the Attorney General of the United States, of the initial adoption and future modifications of the plan by filing copies therewith. Modifications of the plan made at the instance of the district court shall become effective after approval by the panel. Each district court shall submit a report on the jury selection process within its jurisdiction to the Administrative Office of the United States Courts in such form and at such times as the Judicial Conference of the United States may specify. The Judicial Conference of the United States may, from time to time, adopt rules and regulations governing the provisions and the operation of the plans formulated under this title.

(b)   Among other things, such plan shall—

(1)   either establish a jury commission, or authorize the clerk of the court, to manage the jury selection process. If the plan establishes a jury commission, the district court shall appoint one citizen to serve with the clerk of the court as the jury commission: *Provided, however*, That the plan for the District of Columbia may establish a jury commission consisting of three citizens. The citizen jury commissioner shall not belong to the same political party as the clerk serving with him. The clerk or the jury commission, as the case may be, shall act under the supervision and control of the chief judge of the district court or such other judge of the district court as the plan may provide. Each jury commissioner shall, during his tenure in office, reside in the judicial district or division for which he is appointed. Each citizen jury commissioner shall receive compensation to be fixed by the district court plan at a rate not to exceed $50 per day for each day necessarily employed in the performance of his duties, plus reimbursement for travel, subsistence, and other necessary expenses incurred by him in the performance of such duties. The Judicial Conference of the United States may establish standards for allowance of travel, subsistence, and other necessary expenses incurred by jury commissioners.

(2)   specify whether the names of prospective jurors shall be selected from the voter registration lists or the lists of actual voters of the political subdivisions within the district or division. The plan shall prescribe some other source or sources of names in addition to voter lists where necessary to foster the policy and protect the rights secured by sections 1861 and 1862 of this title. The plan for the District of Columbia may require the names of prospective jurors to be selected from the city directory rather than from voter lists. The plans for the districts of Puerto Rico and the Canal Zone may prescribe some other source or sources of names of prospective jurors in lieu of voter lists, the use of which shall be consistent with the policies declared and rights secured by sections 1861 and 1862 of this title. The plan for the district of Massachusetts may require the names of prospective jurors to be selected from the resident list provided for in chapter 234A, Massachusetts General Laws, or comparable authority, rather than from voter lists.

(3)   specify detailed procedures to be followed by the jury commission or clerk in selecting names from the sources specified in paragraph (2) of this subsection. These procedures shall be designed to ensure the random selection of a fair cross section of the persons residing in the community in the district or division wherein the court convenes. They shall ensure that names of persons residing in each of the counties, parishes, or similar political subdivisions within the judicial district or division are placed in a master jury wheel; and shall ensure that each county, parish, or similar political subdivision within the district or division is substantially proportionally represented in the master jury wheel for that judicial district, division, or combination of divisions. For the purposes of determining proportional representation in the master jury wheel, either the number of actual voters at the last general election in each county, parish, or similar political subdivision, or the number of registered voters if registration of voters is uniformly required throughout the district or division, may be used.

(4)   provide for a master jury wheel (or a device similar in purpose and function) into which the names of those randomly selected shall be placed. The plan shall fix a minimum number of names to be placed initially in the master jury wheel, which shall be at least one-half of 1 per centum of the total number of persons on the lists used as a source of names for the district or division; but if this number of names is believed to be cumbersome and unnecessary, the plan may fix a smaller number of names to be placed in the master wheel, but in no event less than one thousand. The chief judge of the district court, or such other district court judge as the plan may provide, may order additional names to be placed in the master jury wheel from time to time as necessary. The plan shall provide for periodic emptying and refilling of the master jury wheel at specified times, the interval for which shall not exceed four years.

(5)(A)   except as provided in subparagraph (B), specify those groups of persons or occupational classes whose members shall, on individual request therefor, be excused from jury service. Such groups or classes shall be excused only if the district court finds, and the plan states, that jury service by such class or group would entail undue hardship or extreme inconvenience to the members thereof, and excuse of members thereof would not be inconsistent with sections 1861 and 1862 of this title.

(B)   specify that volunteer safety personnel, upon individual request, shall be excused from jury service. For purposes of this subparagraph, the term "volunteer safety personnel" means individuals serving a public agency (as defined in section 1203(6) of title I of the Omnibus Crime Control and Safe Streets Act of 1968) in an official capacity, without compensation, as firefighters or members of a rescue squad or ambulance crew.

(6)   specify that the following persons are barred from jury service on the ground that they are exempt: (A) members in active service in the Armed Forces of the United States; (B) members of the fire or police departments of any State, the District of Columbia, any territory or possession of the United States, or any subdivision of a State, the District of Columbia, or such territory or possession; (C) public officers in the executive, legislative, or judicial branches of the Government of the United States, or of any State, the District of Columbia, any territory or possession of the

United States, or any subdivision of a State, the District of Columbia, or such territory or possession, who are actively engaged in the performance of official duties.

(7) fix the time when the names drawn from the qualified jury wheel shall be disclosed to parties and to the public. If the plan permits these names to be made public, it may nevertheless permit the chief judge of the district court, or such other district court judge as the plan may provide, to keep these names confidential in any case where the interests of justice so require.

(8) specify the procedures to be followed by the clerk or jury commission in assigning persons whose names have been drawn from the qualified jury wheel to grand and petit jury panels.

(c) The initial plan shall be devised by each district court and transmitted to the reviewing panel specified in subsection (a) of this section within one hundred and twenty days of the date of enactment of the Jury Selection and Service Act of 1968. The panel shall approve or direct the modification of each plan so submitted within sixty days thereafter. Each plan or modification made at the direction of the panel shall become effective after approval at such time thereafter as the panel directs, in no event to exceed ninety days from the date of approval. Modifications made at the instance of the district court under subsection (a) of this section shall be effective at such time thereafter as the panel directs, in no event to exceed ninety days from the date of modification.

(d) State, local, and Federal officials having custody, possession, or control of voter registration lists, lists of actual voters, or other appropriate records shall make such lists and records available to the jury commission or clerks for inspection, reproduction, and copying at all reasonable times as the commission or clerk may deem necessary and proper for the performance of duties under this title. The district courts shall have jurisdiction upon application by the Attorney General of the United States to compel compliance with this subsection by appropriate process.

(June 25, 1948, c. 646, 62 Stat. 952; Mar. 27, 1968, Pub.L. 90–274, § 101, 82 Stat. 54; Apr. 6, 1972, Pub.L. 92–269, § 2, 86 Stat. 117; Nov. 2, 1978, Pub.L. 95–572, § 2(a), 92 Stat. 2453; Nov. 19, 1988, Pub.L. 100–702, Title VIII, § 802(b), (c), 102 Stat. 4657, 4658; Oct. 29, 1992, Pub.L. 102–572, Title IV, § 401, 106 Stat. 4511.)

HISTORICAL AND STATUTORY NOTES

References in Text

Section 1203(6) of title I of the Omnibus Crime Control and Safe Streets Act of 1968, referred to in subsec. (b)(5)(B), was successively renumbered and redesignated as section 1204(8) of the Act which is classified to 42 U.S.C.A. § 3796b(8).

The date of enactment of the Jury Selection and Service Act of 1968, referred to in subsec. (c), is the date of enactment of Pub.L. 90–274, which was approved on Mar. 27, 1968.

Effective and Applicability Provisions

1992 Acts. Amendment by Pub.L. 102–572 effective Jan. 1, 1993, see section 1101(a) of Pub.L. 102–572, set out as a note under section 905 of Title 2, The Congress.

1978 Acts. Amendment by Pub.L. 95–572 applicable with respect to any grand or petit juror summoned for service or actually serving on or after Nov. 2, 1978, see section 7(a) of Pub.L. 95–572, set out as a note under section 1363 of this title.

1968 Acts. Amendment by Pub.L. 90–274 effective 270 days after Mar. 27, 1968, except as to cases in which an indictment has been returned or a petit jury empaneled prior to such effective date, see section 104 of Pub.L. 90–274, set out as a note under section 1861 of this title.

Refilling of Master Jury Wheel Not Later Than September 1, 1973; Refilling of Qualified Jury Wheel Not Later Than October 1, 1973; Retroactive Effect

Sections 3 and 4 of Pub.L. 92–269 provided that:

"**Sec. 3. (a)** Each judicial district and each division or combination of divisions within a judicial district, for which a separate plan for random selection of jurors has been adopted pursuant to section 1863 of title

28, United States Code [this section], other than the District of Columbia and the districts of Puerto Rico and the Canal Zone, shall not later than September 1, 1973, refill its master jury wheel with names obtained from the voter registration lists for, or the lists of actual voters in, the 1972 general election.

"**(b)** The District of Columbia and the judicial districts of Puerto Rico and the Canal Zone shall not later than September 1, 1973, refill their master jury wheels from sources which include the names of persons eighteen years of age or older.

"**(c)** The qualified jury wheel in each judicial district, and in each division or combination of divisions in a judicial district for which a separate plan for random selection of jurors has been adopted, shall be refilled from the master jury wheel not later than October 1, 1973.

"**Sec. 4. (a)** Nothing in this Act [amending this section and section 1865 of this title] shall affect the composition of any master jury wheel or qualified jury wheel prior to the date on which it is first refilled in compliance with the terms of section 3.

"**(b)** Nothing in this Act shall affect the composition or preclude the service of any jury empaneled on or before the date on which the qualified jury wheel from which the jurors' names were drawn is refilled in compliance with the provisions of section 3."

§ 1864.   Drawing of names from the master jury wheel; completion of juror qualification form

(a) From time to time as directed by the district court, the clerk or a district judge shall draw at random from the master jury wheel the names of as many persons as may be required for jury service. The clerk or jury commission shall post a general notice for public review in the clerk's office and on the court's website explaining the process by which names are periodically and randomly drawn. The clerk or jury commission may, upon order of the court, prepare an alphabetical list of the names drawn from the master jury wheel. Any list so prepared shall not be disclosed to any person except pursuant to the district court plan or pursuant to section 1867 or 1868 of this title. The clerk or jury commission shall mail to every person whose name is drawn from the master wheel a juror qualification form accompanied by instructions to fill out and return the form, duly signed and sworn, to the clerk or jury commission by mail within ten days. If the person is unable to fill out the form, another shall do it for him, and shall indicate that he has done so and the reason therefor. In any case in which it appears that there is an omission, ambiguity, or error in a form, the clerk or jury commission shall return the form with instructions to the person to make such additions or corrections as may be necessary and to return the form to the clerk or jury commission within ten days. Any person who fails to return a completed juror qualification form as instructed may be summoned by the clerk or jury commission forthwith to appear before the clerk or jury commission to fill out a juror qualification form. A person summoned to appear because of failure to return a juror qualification form as instructed who personally appears and executes a juror qualification form before the clerk or jury commission may, at the discretion of the district court, except where his prior failure to execute and mail such form was willful, be entitled to receive for such appearance the same fees and travel allowances paid to jurors under section 1871 of this title. At the time of his appearance for jury service, any person may be required to fill out another juror qualification form in the presence of the jury commission or the clerk or the court, at which time, in such cases as it appears warranted, the person may be questioned, but only with regard to his responses to questions contained on the form. Any information thus acquired by the clerk or jury commission may be noted on the juror qualification form and transmitted to the chief judge or such district court judge as the plan may provide.

(b) Any person summoned pursuant to subsection (a) of this section who fails to appear as directed shall be ordered by the district court forthwith to appear and show cause for his failure to comply with the summons. Any person who fails to appear pursuant to such order or who fails to show good cause for noncompliance with the summons may be fined not more than $1,000, imprisoned not more than three days, ordered to perform community service, or any combination thereof. Any person who willfully misrepresents a material fact on a juror qualification form for the purpose of avoiding or securing service as a juror may be fined not more than $1,000, imprisoned not more than three days, ordered to perform community service, or any combination thereof.

(June 25, 1948, c. 646, 62 Stat. 952; Mar. 27, 1968, Pub.L. 90–274, § 101, 82 Stat. 57; Nov. 19, 1988, Pub.L. 100–702, Title VIII, § 803(a), 102 Stat. 4658; Oct. 13, 2008, Pub.L. 110–406, §§ 5(a), 17(a), 122 Stat. 4292, 4295.)

§ 1865. Qualifications for jury service

(a) The chief judge of the district court, or such other district court judge as the plan may provide, on his initiative or upon recommendation of the clerk or jury commission, or the clerk under supervision of the court if the court's jury selection plan so authorizes, shall determine solely on the basis of information provided on the juror qualification form and other competent evidence whether a person is unqualified for, or exempt, or to be excused from jury service. The clerk shall enter such determination in the space provided on the juror qualification form and in any alphabetical list of names drawn from the master jury wheel. If a person did not appear in response to a summons, such fact shall be noted on said list.

(b) In making such determination the chief judge of the district court, or such other district court judge as the plan may provide, or the clerk if the court's jury selection plan so provides, shall deem any person qualified to serve on grand and petit juries in the district court unless he—

(1) is not a citizen of the United States eighteen years old who has resided for a period of one year within the judicial district;

(2) is unable to read, write, and understand the English language with a degree of proficiency sufficient to fill out satisfactorily the juror qualification form;

(3) is unable to speak the English language;

(4) is incapable, by reason of mental or physical infirmity, to render satisfactory jury service; or

(5) has a charge pending against him for the commission of, or has been convicted in a State or Federal court of record of, a crime punishable by imprisonment for more than one year and his civil rights have not been restored.

(June 25, 1948, c. 646, 62 Stat. 952; Mar. 27, 1968, Pub.L. 90–274, § 101, 82 Stat. 58; Apr. 6, 1972, Pub.L. 92–269, § 1, 86 Stat. 117; Nov. 2, 1978, Pub.L. 95–572, § 3(a), 92 Stat. 2453; Nov. 19, 1988, Pub.L. 100–702, Title VIII, § 803(b), 102 Stat. 4658; Nov. 13, 2000, Pub.L. 106–518, Title III, § 305, 114 Stat. 2418.)

§ 1866. Selection and summoning of jury panels

(a) The jury commission, or in the absence thereof the clerk, shall maintain a qualified jury wheel and shall place in such wheel names of all persons drawn from the master jury wheel who are determined to be qualified as jurors and not exempt or excused pursuant to the district court plan. From time to time, the jury commission or the clerk shall draw at random from the qualified jury wheel such number of names of persons as may be required for assignment to grand and petit jury panels. The clerk or jury commission shall post a general notice for public review in the clerk's office and on the court's website explaining the process by which names are periodically and randomly drawn. The jury commission or the clerk shall prepare a separate list of names of persons assigned to each grand and petit jury panel.

(b) When the court orders a grand or petit jury to be drawn, the clerk or jury commission or their duly designated deputies shall issue summonses for the required number of jurors.

Each person drawn for jury service may be served personally, or by registered, certified, or first-class mail addressed to such person at his usual residence or business address.

If such service is made personally, the summons shall be delivered by the clerk or the jury commission or their duly designated deputies to the marshal who shall make such service.

If such service is made by mail, the summons may be served by the marshal or by the clerk, the jury commission or their duly designated deputies, who shall make affidavit of service and shall attach thereto any receipt from the addressee for a registered or certified summons.

(c) Except as provided in section 1865 of this title or in any jury selection plan provision adopted pursuant to paragraph (5) or (6) of section 1863(b) of this title, no person or class of persons shall be disqualified, excluded, excused, or exempt from service as jurors: *Provided*, That any person summoned for jury service may be (1) excused by the court, or by the clerk under supervision of the court if the court's jury selection plan so authorizes, upon a showing of undue hardship or extreme inconvenience, for such period as the court deems necessary, at the conclusion of which such person either shall be summoned again for jury service under subsections (b) and (c) of this section or, if the court's jury selection plan so provides, the name of such person shall be reinserted into the qualified jury wheel for selection pursuant to subsection (a) of this section, or (2) excluded by the court on the ground that such person may be unable to render impartial jury service or that his service as a juror would be likely to disrupt the proceedings, or (3) excluded upon peremptory challenge as provided by law, or (4) excluded pursuant to the procedure specified by law upon a challenge by any party for good cause shown, or (5) excluded upon determination by the court that his service as a juror would be likely to threaten the secrecy of the proceedings, or otherwise adversely affect the integrity of jury deliberations. No person shall be excluded under clause (5) of this subsection unless the judge, in open court, determines that such is warranted and that exclusion of the person will not be inconsistent with sections 1861 and 1862 of this title. The number of persons excluded under clause (5) of this subsection shall not exceed one per centum of the number of persons who return executed jury qualification forms during the period, specified in the plan, between two consecutive fillings of the master jury wheel. The names of persons excluded under clause (5) of this subsection, together with detailed explanations for the exclusions, shall be forwarded immediately to the judicial council of the circuit, which shall have the power to make any appropriate order, prospective or retroactive, to redress any misapplication of clause (5) of this subsection, but otherwise exclusions effectuated under such clause shall not be subject to challenge under the provisions of this title. Any person excluded from a particular jury under clause (2), (3), or (4) of this subsection shall be eligible to sit on another jury if the basis for his initial exclusion would not be relevant to his ability to serve on such other jury.

(d) Whenever a person is disqualified, excused, exempt, or excluded from jury service, the jury commission or clerk shall note in the space provided on his juror qualification form or on the juror's card drawn from the qualified jury wheel the specific reason therefor.

(e) In any two-year period, no person shall be required to (1) serve or attend court for prospective service as a petit juror for a total of more than thirty days, except when necessary to complete service in a particular case, or (2) serve on more than one grand jury, or (3) serve as both a grand and petit juror.

(f) When there is an unanticipated shortage of available petit jurors drawn from the qualified jury wheel, the court may require the marshal to summon a sufficient number of petit jurors selected at random from the voter registration lists, lists of actual voters, or other lists specified in the plan, in a manner ordered by the court consistent with sections 1861 and 1862 of this title.

(g) Any person summoned for jury service who fails to appear as directed may be ordered by the district court to appear forthwith and show cause for failure to comply with the summons. Any person who fails to show good cause for noncompliance with a summons may be fined not more than $1,000, imprisoned not more than three days, ordered to perform community service, or any combination thereof.

(June 25, 1948, c. 646, 62 Stat. 952; May 24, 1949, c. 139, § 96, 63 Stat. 103; Mar. 27, 1968, Pub.L. 90–274, § 101, 82 Stat. 58; Dec. 11, 1970, Pub.L. 91–543, 84 Stat. 1408; Nov. 2, 1978, Pub.L. 95–572, § 2(b), 92 Stat. 2453; Jan. 12, 1983, Pub.L. 97–463, § 2, 96 Stat. 2531; Nov. 19, 1988, Pub.L. 100–702, Title VIII, § 801, 102 Stat. 4657; Oct. 13, 2008, Pub.L. 110–406, §§ 4, 5(b), 17(b), 122 Stat. 4292, 4295.)

§ 1867.   Challenging compliance with selection procedures

(a) In criminal cases, before the voir dire examination begins, or within seven days after the defendant discovered or could have discovered, by the exercise of diligence, the grounds therefor, whichever is earlier, the defendant may move to dismiss the indictment or stay the proceedings against him on the ground of substantial failure to comply with the provisions of this title in selecting the grand or petit jury.

(b) In criminal cases, before the voir dire examination begins, or within seven days after the Attorney General of the United States discovered or could have discovered, by the exercise of diligence, the grounds therefor, whichever is earlier, the Attorney General may move to dismiss the indictment or stay the proceedings on the ground of substantial failure to comply with the provisions of this title in selecting the grand or petit jury.

(c) In civil cases, before the voir dire examination begins, or within seven days after the party discovered or could have discovered, by the exercise of diligence, the grounds therefor, whichever is earlier, any party may move to stay the proceedings on the ground of substantial failure to comply with the provisions of this title in selecting the petit jury.

(d) Upon motion filed under subsection (a), (b), or (c) of this section, containing a sworn statement of facts which, if true, would constitute a substantial failure to comply with the provisions of this title, the moving party shall be entitled to present in support of such motion the testimony of the jury commission or clerk, if available, any relevant records and papers not public or otherwise available used by the jury commissioner or clerk, and any other relevant evidence. If the court determines that there has been a substantial failure to comply with the provisions of this title in selecting the grand jury, the court shall stay the proceedings pending the selection of a grand jury in conformity with this title or dismiss the indictment, whichever is appropriate. If the court determines that there has been a substantial failure to comply with the provisions of this title in selecting the petit jury, the court shall stay the proceedings pending the selection of a petit jury in conformity with this title.

(e) The procedures prescribed by this section shall be the exclusive means by which a person accused of a Federal crime, the Attorney General of the United States or a party in a civil case may challenge any jury on the ground that such jury was not selected in conformity with the provisions of this title. Nothing in this section shall preclude any person or the United States from pursuing any other remedy, civil or criminal, which may be available for the vindication or enforcement of any law prohibiting discrimination on account of race, color, religion, sex, national origin or economic status in the selection of persons for service on grand or petit juries.

(f) The contents of records or papers used by the jury commission or clerk in connection with the jury selection process shall not be disclosed, except pursuant to the district court plan or as may be necessary in the preparation or presentation of a motion under subsection (a), (b), or (c) of this section, until after the master jury wheel has been emptied and refilled pursuant to section 1863(b)(4) of this title and all persons selected to serve as jurors before the master wheel was emptied have completed such service. The parties in a case shall be allowed to inspect, reproduce, and copy such records or papers at all reasonable times during the preparation and pendency of such a motion. Any person who discloses the contents of any record or paper in violation of this subsection may be fined not more than $1,000 or imprisoned not more than one year, or both.

(June 25, 1948, c. 646, 62 Stat. 953; Sept. 2, 1957, Pub.L. 85–259, 71 Stat. 583; Mar. 27, 1968, Pub.L. 90–274, § 101, 82 Stat. 59.)

§ 1868.   Maintenance and inspection of records

After the master jury wheel is emptied and refilled pursuant to section 1863(b)(4) of this title, and after all persons selected to serve as jurors before the master wheel was emptied have completed such service, all records and papers compiled and maintained by the jury commission or clerk before the master wheel was emptied shall be preserved in the custody of the clerk for four years or for such longer period as may be ordered by a court, and shall be available for public inspection for the purpose of determining the validity of the selection of any jury.

(June 25, 1948, c. 646, 62 Stat. 953; Mar. 27, 1968, Pub.L. 90–274, § 101, 82 Stat. 60.)

§ 1869. Definitions

For purposes of this chapter—

(a) "clerk" and "clerk of the court" shall mean the clerk of the district court of the United States, any authorized deputy clerk, and any other person authorized by the court to assist the clerk in the performance of functions under this chapter;

(b) "chief judge" shall mean the chief judge of any district court of the United States;

(c) "voter registration lists" shall mean the official records maintained by State or local election officials of persons registered to vote in either the most recent State or the most recent Federal general election, or, in the case of a State or political subdivision thereof that does not require registration as a prerequisite to voting, other official lists of persons qualified to vote in such election. The term shall also include the list of eligible voters maintained by any Federal examiner pursuant to the Voting Rights Act of 1965 where the names on such list have not been included on the official registration lists or other official lists maintained by the appropriate State or local officials. With respect to the districts of Guam and the Virgin Islands, "voter registration lists" shall mean the official records maintained by territorial election officials of persons registered to vote in the most recent territorial general election;

(d) "lists of actual voters" shall mean the official lists of persons actually voting in either the most recent State or the most recent Federal general election;

(e) "division" shall mean: (1) one or more statutory divisions of a judicial district; or (2) in statutory divisions that contain more than one place of holding court, or in judicial districts where there are no statutory divisions, such counties, parishes, or similar political subdivisions surrounding the places where court is held as the district court plan shall determine: *Provided*, That each county, parish, or similar political subdivision shall be included in some such division;

(f) "district court of the United States", "district court", and "court" shall mean any district court established by chapter 5 of this title, and any court which is created by Act of Congress in a territory and is invested with any jurisdiction of a district court established by chapter 5 of this title;

(g) "jury wheel" shall include any device or system similar in purpose or function, such as a properly programed electronic data processing system or device;

(h) "juror qualification form" shall mean a form prescribed by the Administrative Office of the United States Courts and approved by the Judicial Conference of the United States, which shall elicit the name, address, age, race, occupation, education, length of residence within the judicial district, distance from residence to place of holding court, prior jury service, and citizenship of a potential juror, and whether he should be excused or exempted from jury service, has any physical or mental infirmity impairing his capacity to serve as juror, is able to read, write, speak, and understand the English language, has pending against him any charge for the commission of a State or Federal criminal offense punishable by imprisonment for more than one year, or has been convicted in any State or Federal court of record of a crime punishable by imprisonment for more than one year and has not had his civil rights restored. The form shall request, but not require, any other information not inconsistent with the provisions of this title and required by the district court plan in the interests of the sound administration of justice. The form shall also elicit the sworn statement that his responses are true to the best of his knowledge. Notarization shall not be required. The form shall contain words clearly informing the person that the furnishing of any information with respect to his religion, national origin, or economic status is not a prerequisite to his qualification for jury service, that such information need not be furnished if the person finds it objectionable to do so, and that information concerning race is required solely to enforce nondiscrimination in jury selection and has no bearing on an individual's qualification for jury service.

(i) "public officer" shall mean a person who is either elected to public office or who is directly appointed by a person elected to public office;

(j) "undue hardship or extreme inconvenience", as a basis for excuse from immediate jury service under section 1866(c)(1) of this chapter, shall mean great distance, either in miles or traveltime, from the place of holding court, grave illness in the family or any other emergency which outweighs in immediacy and urgency the obligation to serve as a juror when summoned, or any other factor which the court determines to constitute an undue hardship or to create an extreme inconvenience to the juror; and in addition, in situations where it is anticipated that a trial or grand jury proceeding may require more than thirty days of service, the court may consider, as a further basis for temporary excuse, severe economic hardship to an employer which would result from the absence of a key employee during the period of such service; and

(k) "jury summons" shall mean a summons issued by a clerk of court, jury commission, or their duly designated deputies, containing either a preprinted or stamped seal of court, and containing the name of the issuing clerk imprinted in preprinted, type, or facsimile manner on the summons or the envelopes transmitting the summons.

(June 25, 1948, c. 646, 62 Stat. 953; Oct. 16, 1963, Pub.L. 88–139, § 2, 77 Stat. 248; Mar. 27, 1968, Pub.L. 90–274, § 101, 82 Stat. 61; July 29, 1970, Pub.L. 91–358, Title I, § 172(b), 84 Stat. 590; Sept. 29, 1972, Pub.L. 92–437, § 1, 86 Stat. 740; Nov. 2, 1978, Pub.L. 95–572, §§ 3(b), (4), 92 Stat. 2453; Nov. 6, 1978, Pub.L. 95–598, Title II, § 243, 92 Stat. 2671; Nov. 14, 1986, Pub.L. 99–650, § 3, 100 Stat. 3641; Nov. 19, 1988, Pub.L. 100–702, Title VIII, §§ 802(a), 804, 102 Stat. 4657, 4658; Oct. 13, 2008, Pub.L. 110–406, § 5(c), 122 Stat. 4292.)

HISTORICAL AND STATUTORY NOTES

References in Text

The Voting Rights Act of 1965, referred to in subsec. (c), is Pub.L. 89–110, Aug. 6, 1965, 79 Stat. 437, as amended, which is classified generally to subchapters I-A (Section 1973 et seq.), I-B (Section 1973aa et seq.), and I-C (Section 1973bb et seq.) of chapter 20 of Title 42, The Public Health and Welfare, prior to editorial reclassification and renumbering in Title 52, Voting and Elections, and is now classified generally to chapters 103 (§ 10301 et seq.), 105 (§ 10501 et seq.), and 107 (§ 10701 et seq.) of Title 52. For complete classification of this Act to the Code, see Tables.

Termination of United States District Court for the District of the Canal Zone

For termination of the United States District Court for the District of the Canal Zone at end of the "transition period", being the 30-month period beginning Oct. 1, 1979, and ending midnight Mar. 31, 1982, see Paragraph 5 of Article XI of the Panama Canal Treaty of 1977 and Pub. L. 96–70, title II, §§ 2101, 2202–2203, Sept. 27, 1979, 93 Stat. 493, 494, formerly classified to sections 3831 and 3841 to 3843, respectively, of Title 22, Foreign Relations and Intercourse.

§ 1870.　　Challenges

In civil cases, each party shall be entitled to three peremptory challenges. Several defendants or several plaintiffs may be considered as a single party for the purposes of making challenges, or the court may allow additional peremptory challenges and permit them to be exercised separately or jointly.

All challenges for cause or favor, whether to the array or panel or to individual jurors, shall be determined by the court.

(June 25, 1948, c. 646, 62 Stat. 953; Sept. 16, 1959, Pub.L. 86–282, 73 Stat. 565.)

§ 1871.　　Fees

(a) Grand and petit jurors in district courts appearing pursuant to this chapter shall be paid the fees and allowances provided by this section. The requisite fees and allowances shall be disbursed on the certificate of the clerk of court in accordance with the procedure established by the Director of the Administrative Office of the United States Courts. Attendance fees for extended service under subsection (b) of this section shall be certified by the clerk only upon the order of a district judge.

(b)(1) A juror shall be paid an attendance fee of $50 per day for actual attendance at the place of trial or hearing. A juror shall also be paid the attendance fee for the time necessarily occupied in going to and returning from such place at the beginning and end of such service or at any time during such service.

(2) A petit juror required to attend more than ten days in hearing one case may be paid, in the discretion of the trial judge, an additional fee, not exceeding $10 more than the attendance fee, for each day in excess of ten days on which he is required to hear such case.

(3) A grand juror required to attend more than forty-five days of actual service may be paid, in the discretion of the district judge in charge of the particular grand jury, an additional fee, not exceeding $10 more than the attendance fee, for each day in excess of forty-five days of actual service.

(4) A grand or petit juror required to attend more than ten days of actual service may be paid, in the discretion of the judge, the appropriate fees at the end of the first ten days and at the end of every ten days of service thereafter.

(5) Certification of additional attendance fees may be ordered by the judge to be made effective commencing on the first day of extended service, without reference to the date of such certification.

(c)(1) A travel allowance not to exceed the maximum rate per mile that the Director of the Administrative Office of the United States Courts has prescribed pursuant to section 604(a)(7) of this title for payment to supporting court personnel in travel status using privately owned automobiles shall be paid to each juror, regardless of the mode of transportation actually employed. The prescribed rate shall be paid for the distance necessarily traveled to and from a juror's residence by the shortest practical route in going to and returning from the place of service. Actual mileage in full at the prescribed rate is payable at the beginning and at the end of a juror's term of service.

(2) The Director shall promulgate rules regulating interim travel allowances to jurors. Distances traveled to and from court should coincide with the shortest practical route.

(3) Toll charges for toll roads, bridges, tunnels, and ferries shall be paid in full to the juror incurring such charges. In the discretion of the court, reasonable parking fees may be paid to the juror incurring such fees upon presentation of a valid parking receipt. Parking fees shall not be included in any tabulation of mileage cost allowances.

(4) Any juror who travels to district court pursuant to summons in an area outside of the contiguous forty-eight States of the United States shall be paid the travel expenses provided under this section, or actual reasonable transportation expenses subject to the discretion of the district judge or clerk of court as circumstances indicate, exercising due regard for the mode of transportation, the availability of alternative modes, and the shortest practical route between residence and court.

(5) A grand juror who travels to district court pursuant to a summons may be paid the travel expenses provided under this section or, under guidelines established by the Judicial Conference, the actual reasonable costs of travel by aircraft when travel by other means is not feasible and when certified by the chief judge of the district court in which the grand juror serves.

(d)(1) A subsistence allowance covering meals and lodging of jurors shall be established from time to time by the Director of the Administrative Office of the United States Courts pursuant to section 604(a)(7) of this title, except that such allowance shall not exceed the allowance for supporting court personnel in travel status in the same geographical area. Claims for such allowance shall not require itemization.

(2) A subsistence allowance shall be paid to a juror when an overnight stay is required at the place of holding court, and for the time necessarily spent in traveling to and from the place of attendance if an overnight stay is required.

(3) A subsistence allowance for jurors serving in district courts outside of the contiguous forty-eight States of the United States shall be allowed at a rate not to exceed that per diem allowance which is paid to supporting court personnel in travel status in those areas where the Director of the Administrative Office of the United States Courts has prescribed an increased per diem fee pursuant to section 604(a)(7) of this title.

(e) During any period in which a jury is ordered to be kept together and not to separate, the actual cost of subsistence shall be paid upon the order of the court in lieu of the subsistence allowances payable under subsection (d) of this section. Such allowance for the jurors ordered to be kept separate or sequestered shall include the cost of meals, lodging, and other expenditures ordered in the discretion of the court for their convenience and comfort.

(f) A juror who must necessarily use public transportation in traveling to and from court, the full cost of which is not met by the transportation expenses allowable under subsection (c) of this section on account of the short distance traveled in miles, may be paid, in the discretion of the court, the actual reasonable expense of such public transportation, pursuant to the methods of payment provided by this section. Jurors who are required to remain at the court beyond the normal business closing hour for deliberation or for any other reason may be transported to their homes, or to temporary lodgings where such lodgings are ordered by the court, in a manner directed by the clerk and paid from funds authorized under this section.

(g) The Director of the Administrative Office of the United States Courts shall promulgate such regulations as may be necessary to carry out his authority under this section.

(June 25, 1948, c. 646, 62 Stat. 953; May 24, 1949, c. 139, § 97, 63 Stat. 103; July 14, 1949, c. 333, 63 Stat. 411; Sept. 7, 1957, Pub.L. 85–299, 71 Stat. 618; Sept. 2, 1965, Pub.L. 89–165, 79 Stat. 645; Mar. 27, 1968, Pub.L. 90–274, § 102(a), 82 Stat. 62; Nov. 2, 1978, Pub.L. 95–572, § 5, 92 Stat. 2454; Dec. 1, 1990, Pub.L. 101–650, Title III, § 314(b), 104 Stat. 5115; Oct. 29, 1992, Pub.L. 102–572, Title IV, § 402, 106 Stat. 4511; Oct. 13, 2008, Pub.L. 110–406, § 3(a), 122 Stat. 4292; Mar. 23, 2018, Pub.L. 115–141, 132 Stat. 348.)

HISTORICAL AND STATUTORY NOTES

Refreshment of Jurors

Pub.L. 101–162, Title IV, Nov. 21, 1989, 103 Stat. 1012, provided in part: "That for fiscal year 1990 and hereafter, funds appropriated under this heading [Courts of Appeals, District Courts and Other Judicial Services and Fees of Jurors and Commissioners] shall be available for refreshment of jurors."

§ 1872.   Issues of fact in Supreme Court

In all original actions at law in the Supreme Court against citizens of the United States, issues of fact shall be tried by a jury.

(June 25, 1948, c. 646, 62 Stat. 953.)

§ 1873.   Admiralty and maritime cases

In any case of admiralty and maritime jurisdiction relating to any matter of contract or tort arising upon or concerning any vessel of twenty tons or upward, enrolled and licensed for the coasting trade, and employed in the business of commerce and navigation between places in different states upon the lakes and navigable waters connecting said lakes, the trial of all issues of fact shall be by jury if either party demands it.

(June 25, 1948, c. 646, 62 Stat. 953.)

§ 1874.   Actions on bonds and specialties

In all actions to recover the forfeiture annexed to any articles of agreement, covenant, bond, or other specialty, wherein the forfeiture, breach, or nonperformance appears by default or confession of the defendant, the court shall render judgment for the plaintiff for such amount as is due. If the sum is uncertain, it shall, upon request of either party, be assessed by a jury.

(June 25, 1948, c. 646, 62 Stat. 953.)

§ 1875.   Protection of jurors' employment

(a)   No employer shall discharge, threaten to discharge, intimidate, or coerce any permanent employee by reason of such employee's jury service, or the attendance or scheduled attendance in connection with such service, in any court of the United States.

(b)   Any employer who violates the provisions of this section—

(1)   shall be liable for damages for any loss of wages or other benefits suffered by an employee by reason of such violation;

(2)   may be enjoined from further violations of this section and ordered to provide other appropriate relief, including but not limited to the reinstatement of any employee discharged by reason of his jury service; and

(3)   shall be subject to a civil penalty of not more than $5,000 for each violation as to each employee, and may be ordered to perform community service.

(c)   Any individual who is reinstated to a position of employment in accordance with the provisions of this section shall be considered as having been on furlough or leave of absence during his period of jury service, shall be reinstated to his position of employment without loss of seniority, and shall be entitled to participate in insurance or other benefits offered by the employer pursuant to established rules and practices relating to employees on furlough or leave of absence in effect with the employer at the time such individual entered upon jury service.

(d)(1)   An individual claiming that his employer has violated the provisions of this section may make application to the district court for the district in which such employer maintains a place of business and the court shall, upon finding probable merit in such claim, appoint counsel to represent such individual in any action in the district court necessary to the resolution of such claim. Such counsel shall be compensated and necessary expenses repaid to the extent provided by section 3006A of title 18, United States Code.

(2)   In any action or proceeding under this section, the court may award a prevailing employee who brings such action by retained counsel a reasonable attorney's fee as part of the costs. The court may tax a defendant employer, as costs payable to the court, the attorney fees and expenses incurred on behalf of a prevailing employee, where such costs were expended by the court pursuant to paragraph (1) of this subsection. The court may award a prevailing employer a reasonable attorney's fee as part of the costs only if the court finds that the action is frivolous, vexatious, or brought in bad faith.

(Added Pub.L. 95–572, § 6(a)(1), Nov. 2, 1978, 92 Stat. 2456; amended Pub.L. 97–463, § 1, Jan. 12, 1983, 96 Stat. 2531; Pub.L. 110–406, § 19, Oct. 13, 2008, 122 Stat. 4295.)

§ 1876.   Trial by jury in the Court of International Trade

(a)   In any civil action in the Court of International Trade which is to be tried before a jury, the jury shall be selected in accordance with the provisions of this chapter and under the procedures set forth in the jury selection plan of the district court for the judicial district in which the case is to be tried.

(b) Whenever the Court of International Trade conducts a jury trial—

(1) the clerk of the district court for the judicial district in which the Court of International Trade is sitting, or an authorized deputy clerk, shall act as clerk of the Court of International Trade for the purposes of selecting and summoning the jury;

(2) the qualifications for jurors shall be the same as those established by section 1865(b) of this title for jurors in the district courts of the United States;

(3) each party shall be entitled to challenge jurors in accordance with section 1870 of this title; and

(4) jurors shall be compensated in accordance with section 1871 of this title.

(Added Pub.L. 96–417, Title III, § 302(a), Oct. 10, 1980, 94 Stat. 1739.)

§ 1877.   Protection of jurors

(a) Subject to the provisions of this section and title 5 of the United States Code, subchapter 1 of chapter 81, title 5, United States Code, applies to a Federal grand or petit juror, except that entitlement to disability compensation payments does not commence until the day after the date of termination of service as a juror.

(b) In administering this section with respect to a juror covered by this section—

(1) a juror is deemed to receive monthly pay at the minimum rate for grade GS-2 of the General Schedule unless his actual pay as a Government employee while serving on court leave is higher, in which case monthly pay is determined in accordance with section 8114 of title 5, United States Code, and

(2) performance of duty as a juror includes that time when a juror is (A) in attendance at court pursuant to a summons, (B) in deliberation, (C) sequestered by order of a judge, or (D) at a site, by order of the court, for the taking of a view.

(Added Pub.L. 97–463, § 3(1), Jan. 12, 1983, 96 Stat. 2531.)

HISTORICAL AND STATUTORY NOTES

References in Text

The General Schedule, referred to in subsec. (b)(1), is set out under 5 U.S.C.A. § 5332.

§ 1878.   Optional use of a one-step summoning and qualification procedure

(a) At the option of each district court, jurors may be summoned and qualified in a single procedure, if the court's jury selection plan so authorizes, in lieu of the two separate procedures otherwise provided for by this chapter. Courts shall ensure that a one-step summoning and qualification procedure conducted under this section does not violate the policies and objectives set forth in sections 1861 and 1862 of this title.

(b) Jury selection conducted under this section shall be subject to challenge under section 1867 of this title for substantial failure to comply with the provisions of this title in selecting the jury. However, no challenge under section 1867 of this title shall lie solely on the basis that a jury was selected in accordance with a one-step summoning and qualification procedure authorized by this section.

(Added Pub.L. 100–702, Title VIII, § 805(a), Nov. 19, 1988, 102 Stat. 4658; amended Pub.L. 102–572, Title IV, § 403(a), Oct. 29, 1992, 106 Stat. 4512.)

HISTORICAL AND STATUTORY NOTES

Savings Provisions

Section 403(c) of Pub.L. 102–572 provided that: "For courts participating in the experiment authorized under section 1878 of title 28, United States Code [this section] (as in effect before the effective date of this section [see Effective and Applicability Provisions of 1992 Amendments note set out under this section]), the amendment made by subsection (a) of this section [amending this section] shall be effective on and after January 1, 1992."

CHAPTER 123—FEES AND COSTS

HISTORICAL AND STATUTORY NOTES

Change of Name

"United States magistrate judge" substituted for "United States magistrate" in text pursuant to section 321 of Pub.L. 101–650, set out as a note under 28 U.S.C.A. § 631. Previously, United States commissioners, referred to in text, were replaced by United States magistrates pursuant to Pub.L. 90–578, Oct. 17, 1968, 82 Stat. 1118. See chapter 43 of Title 28, 28 U.S.C.A. § 631 et seq.

§ 1911.   Supreme Court

The Supreme Court may fix the fees to be charged by its clerk.

The fees of the clerk, cost of serving process, and other necessary disbursements incidental to any case before the court, may be taxed against the litigants as the court directs.

(June 25, 1948, c. 646, 62 Stat. 954.)

---

[1]   [Footnote to 1932 entry in the Chapter 123 table:] So in original. Two sections 1932 have been enacted.

§ 1912.   Damages and costs on affirmance

Where a judgment is affirmed by the Supreme Court or a court of appeals, the court in its discretion may adjudge to the prevailing party just damages for his delay, and single or double costs.

(June 25, 1948, c. 646, 62 Stat. 954.)

§ 1913.   Courts of appeals

The fees and costs to be charged and collected in each court of appeals shall be prescribed from time to time by the Judicial Conference of the United States. Such fees and costs shall be reasonable and uniform in all the circuits.

(June 25, 1948, c. 646, 62 Stat. 954.)

JUDICIAL CONFERENCE SCHEDULE OF FEES

Court of Appeals Miscellaneous Fee Schedule

(Effective October 1, 2019)

The fees included in the Court of Appeals Miscellaneous Fee Schedule[1] are to be charged for services provided by the courts of appeals, including relevant services[2] provided by the bankruptcy appellate panels established under 28 U.S.C. § 158(b)(1).

- The United States should not be charged fees under this schedule, except as prescribed in Items 2, 4, and 5 when the information requested is available through remote electronic access.

- Federal agencies or programs that are funded from judiciary appropriations (agencies, organizations, and individuals providing services authorized by the Criminal Justice Act, 18 U.S.C. § 3006A, and bankruptcy administrators) should not be charged any fees under this schedule.

(1)   For docketing a case on appeal or review, or docketing any other proceeding, $500.

- Each party filing a notice of appeal pays a separate fee to the district court, but parties filing a joint notice of appeal pay only one fee.

- There is no docketing fee for an application for an interlocutory appeal under 28 U.S.C. § 1292(b) or other petition for permission to appeal under Fed. R. App. P. 5, unless the appeal is allowed.

- There is no docketing fee for a direct bankruptcy appeal or a direct bankruptcy cross appeal, when the fee has been collected by the bankruptcy court in accordance with item 14 of the Bankruptcy Court Miscellaneous Fee Schedule.

- This fee is collected in addition to the statutory fee of $5 that is collected under 28 U.S.C. § 1917.

(2)   For conducting a search of the court of appeals records, $31 per name or item searched. This fee applies to services rendered on behalf of the United States if the information requested is available through remote electronic access.

(3)   For certification of any document, $11. For issuance of an apostille,* $47.

---

[1]   Issued in accordance with 28 U.S.C. § 1913.

[2]   Item 13 does not apply to bankruptcy appellate panels.

*   [An apostille is an authentication of public documents so that they can be recognized in foreign countries that are members of the 1961 Hague Convention. Ed.]

(4)

    a.   For reproducing any document and providing a copy in paper form, $.50 per page. This fee applies to services rendered on behalf of the United States if the document requested is available through remote electronic access.

    b.   For or reproducing and transmitting in any manner a copy of an electronic record stored outside of the court's electronic case management system, including but not limited to, document files, audio and video recordings (other than a recording of a court proceeding), $31 per record provided.

(5)　For reproducing recordings of proceedings, regardless of the medium, $31, including the cost of materials. This fee applies to services rendered on behalf of the United States if the recording is available through remote electronic access.

(6)　For reproducing the record in any appeal in which the court of appeals does not require an appendix pursuant to Fed. R. App. P. 30(f), (or, in appeals before a bankruptcy appellate panel, pursuant to Fed. R. Bankr. P. 8018(e)), $86.

(7)　For retrieval of one box of records from a Federal Records Center, National Archives, or other storage location removed from the place of business of the court, $64. For retrievals involving multiple boxes, $39 for each additional box. For electronic retrievals, $10 plus any charges assessed by the Federal Records Center, National Archives, or other storage location removed from the place of business of the courts.

(8)　For any payment returned or denied for insufficient funds, $53.

(9)　For copies of opinions, a fee commensurate with the cost of printing, as fixed by each court.

(10)　For copies of the local rules of court, a fee commensurate with the cost of distributing the copies. The court may also distribute copies of the local rules without charge.

(11)　For filing:

    •   Any separate or joint notice of appeal or application for appeal from the bankruptcy appellate panel, $5;

    •   A notice of the allowance of an appeal from the bankruptcy appellate panel, $5.

(12)　For counsel's requested use of the court's videoconferencing equipment in connection with each oral argument, the court may charge and collect a fee of $200 per remote location.

(13)　For original admission of attorney to practice, including a certificate of admission, $181. For a duplicate certificate of admission or certificate of good standing, $19.

Electronic Public Access Fee Schedule (Eff. Jan. 1, 2020)

(Issued in Accordance with 28 U.S.C. §§ 1913, 1914, 1926, 1930, 1932)

    The fees included in the Electronic Public Access Fee Schedule are to be charged for providing electronic public access to court records.

Fees for Public Access to Court Electronic Records (PACER)

    (1)　Except as provided below, for electronic access to any case document, docket sheet, or case-specific report via PACER: $0.10 per page, not to exceed the fee for thirty pages.

    (2)　For electronic access to transcripts and non-case specific reports via PACER (such as reports obtained from the PACER Case Locator or docket activity reports): $0.10 per page.

    (3)　For electronic access to an audio file of a court hearing via PACER: $2.40 per audio file.

Fees for Courthouse Electronic Access

(4) For printing copies of any record or document accessed electronically at a public terminal in a courthouse: $0.10 per page.

PACER Service Center Fees

(5) For every search of court records conducted by the PACER Service Center, $30 per name or item searched.

(6) For the PACER Service Center to reproduce on paper any record pertaining to a PACER account, if this information is remotely available through electronic access: $0.50 per page.

(7) For any payment returned or denied for insufficient funds, $53.

Free Access and Exemptions

(8) Automatic Fee Exemptions:

- No fee is owed for electronic access to court data or audio files via PACER until an account holder accrues charges of more than $30.00 in a quarterly billing cycle.

- Parties in a case (including *pro se* litigants) and attorneys of record receive one free electronic copy, via the notice of electronic filing or notice of docket activity, of all documents filed electronically, if receipt is required by law or directed by the filer.

- No fee is charged for access to judicial opinions.

- No fee is charged for viewing case information or documents at courthouse public access terminals.

- No fee is charged for Chapter 13 bankruptcy trustees to download quarterly (i.e., once every 90 days) a list of the trustee's cases from the PACER Case Locator.

(9) Discretionary Fee Exemptions:

- Courts may exempt certain persons or classes of persons from payment of the user access fee. Examples of individuals and groups that a court may consider exempting include: indigents, bankruptcy case trustees, *pro bono* attorneys, *pro bono* alternative dispute resolution neutrals, Section 501(c)(3) not-for-profit organizations, and individual researchers associated with educational institutions. Courts should not, however, exempt individuals or groups that have the ability to pay the statutorily established access fee. Examples of individuals and groups that a court should not exempt include: local, state or federal government agencies, members of the media, privately paid attorneys or others who have the ability to pay the fee.

- In considering granting an exemption, courts must find:

  - that those seeking an exemption have demonstrated that an exemption is necessary in order to avoid unreasonable burdens and to promote public access to information;

  - that individual researchers requesting an exemption have shown that the defined research project is intended for scholarly research, that it is limited in scope, and that it is not intended for redistribution on the internet or for commercial purposes.

- If the court grants an exemption:

  - the user receiving the exemption must agree not to sell the data obtained as a result, and must not transfer any data obtained as the result of a fee exemption, unless expressly authorized by the court; and

- the exemption should be granted for a definite period of time, should be limited in scope, and may be revoked at the discretion of the court granting the exemption.

- Courts may provide local court information at no cost (e.g., local rules, court forms, news items, court calendars, and other information) to benefit the public.

Applicability to the United States and State and Local Governments

(10) Unless otherwise authorized by the Judicial Conference, these fees must be charged to the United States, except to federal agencies or programs that are funded from judiciary appropriations (including, but not limited to, agencies, organizations, and individuals providing services authorized by the Criminal Justice Act [18 U.S.C. § 3006A], and bankruptcy administrators).

(11) The fee for printing copies of any record or document accessed electronically at a public terminal ($0.10 per page) described in (4) above does not apply to services rendered on behalf of the United States if the record requested is not remotely available through electronic access.

(12) The fee for local, state, and federal government entities, shall be $0.08 per page until April 1, 2015, after which time, the fee shall be $0.10 per page.

Judicial Conference Policy Notes

The Electronic Public Access (EPA) fee and its exemptions are directly related to the requirement that the judiciary charge user-based fees for the development and maintenance of electronic public access services. The fee schedule provides examples of users that may not be able to afford reasonable user fees (such as indigents, bankruptcy case trustees, individual researchers associated with educational institutions, 501(c)(3) not-for-profit organizations, and court-appointed pro bono attorneys), but requires those seeking an exemption to demonstrate that an exemption is limited in scope and is necessary in order to avoid an unreasonable burden. In addition, the fee schedule includes examples of other entities that courts should not exempt from the fee (such as local, state or federal government agencies, members of the media, and attorneys). The goal is to provide courts with guidance in evaluating a requestor's ability to pay the fee.

Judicial Conference policy also limits exemptions in other ways. First, it requires exempted users to agree not to sell the data they receive through an exemption (unless expressly authorized by the court). This prohibition is not intended to bar a quote or reference to information received as a result of a fee exemption in a scholarly or other similar work. Second, it permits courts to grant exemptions for a definite period of time, to limit the scope of the exemptions, and to revoke exemptions. Third, it cautions that exemptions should be granted as the exception, not the rule, and prohibits courts from exempting all users from EPA fees.

HISTORICAL AND STATUTORY NOTES

Appeals Filed in Courts of Appeals

Pub.L. 109–171, Title X, § 10001(b), Feb. 8, 2006, 120 Stat. 183, provided that: "The $250 fee for docketing a case on appeal or review, or docketing any other proceeding, in a court of appeals, as prescribed by the Judicial Conference, effective as of January 1, 2005, under section 1913 of title 28, United States Code [this section], shall be increased to $450."

[This note effective 60 days after Feb. 8, 2006, see Pub.L. 109–171, § 10001(d), set out as a note under 28 U.S.C.A. § 1914]

Court Fees for Electronic Access to Information

Pub.L. 102–140, Title III, § 303, Oct. 28, 1991, 105 Stat. 810, as amended Pub.L. 104–317, Title IV, § 403(b), Oct. 19, 1996, 110 Stat. 3854; Pub.L. 107–347, Title II, § 205(e), Dec. 17, 2002, 116 Stat. 2915, provided that:

"**(a)** The Judicial Conference may, only to the extent necessary, prescribe reasonable fees, pursuant to sections 1913, 1914, 1926, 1930, and 1932 of title 28, United States Code [this section and sections 1914, 1926, 1930, and 1932 of this title], for collection by the courts under those sections for access to information available through automatic data processing equipment. These fees may distinguish between classes of persons, and shall provide for exempting persons or classes of persons from the fees, in order to avoid unreasonable burdens and to promote public access to such information. The Director of the Administrative Office of the United States Courts, under the direction of the Judicial Conference of the United States, shall prescribe a schedule of reasonable fees for electronic access to information which the Director is required to maintain and make available to the public.

"**(b)** The Judicial Conference and the Director shall transmit each schedule of fees prescribed under paragraph (a) to the Congress at least 30 days before the schedule becomes effective. All fees hereafter collected by the Judiciary under paragraph (a) as a charge for services rendered shall be deposited as offsetting collections to the Judiciary Automation Fund pursuant to 28 U.S.C. 612(c)(1)(A) [section 612(c)(1)(A) of this title] to reimburse expenses incurred in providing these services."

[Amendment by Pub.L. 107–347, § 205, effective 120 days after Dec. 17, 2002, see section 402(a) of Pub.L. 107–347, set out as a note under 44 U.S.C.A. § 3601.]

Similar provisions were contained in the following prior appropriation Act:

Pub.L. 101–515, Title IV, § 404, Nov. 5, 1990, 104 Stat. 2132.

§ 1914.   District court; filing and miscellaneous fees; rules of court

(a) The clerk of each district court shall require the parties instituting any civil action, suit or proceeding in such court, whether by original process, removal or otherwise, to pay a filing fee of $350, except that on application for a writ of habeas corpus the filing fee shall be $5.

(b) The clerk shall collect from the parties such additional fees only as are prescribed by the Judicial Conference of the United States.

(c) Each district court by rule or standing order may require advance payment of fees.

(June 25, 1948, c. 646, 62 Stat. 954; Nov. 6, 1978, Pub.L. 95–598, Title II, § 244, 92 Stat. 2671; June 19, 1986, Pub.L. 99–336, § 4(a), 100 Stat. 637; Oct. 18, 1986, Pub.L. 99–500, Title I, § 101(b) [Title IV, § 407(a)], 100 Stat. 1783–39, 1783–64, and Oct. 30, 1986, Pub.L. 99–591, Title I, § 101(b) [Title IV, § 407(a)], 100 Stat. 3341–39, 3341–64; Oct. 19, 1996, Pub.L. 104–317, Title IV, § 401(a), 110 Stat. 3853; Pub.L. 108–447, Div. B, Title III, § 307(a), Dec. 8, 2004, 118 Stat. 2895; Feb. 8, 2006, Pub.L. 109–171, Title X, § 10001(a), 120 Stat. 183.)

JUDICIAL CONFERENCE SCHEDULE OF FEES
District Court Miscellaneous Fee Schedule*
(Effective October 1, 2019)

The fees included in the District Court Miscellaneous Fee Schedule[1] are to be charged for services provided by the district courts.

- The United States should not be charged fees under this schedule, with the exception of those specifically prescribed in Items 2, 4 and 5, when the information requested is available through remote electronic access.

- Federal agencies or programs that are funded from judiciary appropriations (agencies, organizations, and individuals providing services authorized by the Criminal Justice Act, 18 U.S.C. § 3006 and bankruptcy administrators) should not be charged any fees under this schedule.

1. For filing any document that is not related to a pending case or proceeding, $47.

---

* [The Electronic Public Access Fee Schedule and Judicial Conference Policy Notes are set out in this volume, *supra*, in the notes following 28 U.S.C. § 1913. Ed.]

[1] Issued in accordance with 28 U.S.C. § 1914.

2. For conducting a search of the district court records, $31 per name or item searched. This fee applies to services rendered on behalf of the United States if the information requested is available through electronic access.

3. For certification of any document, $11. For exemplification of any document, $22. For the issuance of an apostille, $47.

4.

a. For reproducing any record or paper, $.50 per page. This fee shall apply to paper copies made from either: (1) original documents; or (2) microfiche or microfilm reproductions of the original records. This fee shall apply to services rendered on behalf of the United States if the record or paper requested is available through electronic access.

b. For reproducing and transmitting in any manner a copy of an electronic record stored outside of the court's electronic case management system, including but not limited to, document files, audio recordings, and video recordings, $31 per record provided. Audio recordings of court proceedings continue to be governed by a separate fee in item 5 of this schedule.

5. For reproduction of an audio recording of a court proceeding, $31. This fee applies to services rendered on behalf of the United States, if the recording is available electronically.

6. For each microfiche sheet of film or microfilm jacket copy of any court record, where available, $6.

7. For retrieval of one box of records from a Federal Records Center, National Archives, or other storage location removed from the place of business of the court, $64. For retrievals involving multiple boxes, $39 for each additional box. For electronic retrievals, $10 plus any charges assessed by the Federal Records Center, National Archives, or other storage location removed from the place of business of the courts.

8. For any payment returned or denied for insufficient funds, $53.

9. For an appeal to a district judge from a judgment of conviction by a magistrate judge in a misdemeanor case, $38.

10. For original admission of attorneys to practice, $181 each, including a certificate of admission. For a duplicate certificate of admission or certificate of good standing, $19.

11. The court may charge and collect fees commensurate with the cost of providing copies of the local rules of court. The court may also distribute copies of the local rules without charge.

12.

• For handling registry funds deposited with and held by the court, the clerk shall assess a charge from interest earnings, in accordance with the detailed fee schedule issued by the Director of the Administrative Office of the United States Courts.

• For management of registry funds invested through the Court Registry Investment System, a fee at an annual rate of 10 basis points of assets on deposit shall be assessed from interest earnings, excluding registry funds from disputed ownership interpleader cases deposited under 28 U.S.C. § 1335 and held in a Court Registry Investment System Disputed Ownership Fund.

• For management of funds deposited under 28 U.S.C. § 1335 and invested in a Disputed Ownership Fund through the Court Registry Investment System, a fee at an annual rate of 20 basis points of assets on deposit shall be assessed from interest earnings.

• The Director of the Administrative Office has the authority to waive these fees for cause.

13. For filing an action brought under Title III of the Cuban Liberty and Democratic Solidarity (LIBERTAD) Act of 1996, Pub. L. 104–114, 110 Stat. § 785 (1996), $6,548. (This fee is in addition to the filing fee prescribed in 28 U.S.C. § 1914(a) for instituting any civil action other than a writ of habeas corpus.)

14. Administrative fee for filing a civil action, suit, or proceeding in a district court, $50. This fee does not apply to applications for a writ of habeas corpus or to persons granted *in forma pauperis* status under 28 U.S.C. § 1915.

15. Processing fee for a petty offense charged on a federal violation notice, $30.

Registry Fund Fees—Item 13 (54 F.R 20407, May 11, 1989)

Effective June 12, 1989, a fee will be assessed for handling funds deposited in noncriminal proceedings with the court and held in interest bearing accounts or instruments pursuant to 28 U.S.C. § 2041 and Federal Rules of Civil Procedure rule 67. For new accounts, i.e., investments made on or after June 12, 1989, the fee will be equal to the first 45 days income earned on the deposit. Each subsequent deposit of new principal in the same case or proceeding will be subject to the fee. Reinvestment of prior deposits will not be subject to the fee. For existing accounts, i.e., investments held by the court prior to June 12, 1989, a fee will be assessed equal to the first 45 days of income earned beginning 30 days after June 12, 1989. Subsequent deposits of new principal in the same account will be subject to the fee. Subsequent reinvestment of existing deposits will not be subject to the fee.

The fee will apply only once to each sum deposited regardless of the length of time deposits are held and will not exceed income actually earned on the account.

The fee does not apply in the District Courts of Guam, Northern Mariana Islands, the Virgin Islands, the United States Claims Court, or other courts whose fees are not set under 28 U.S.C. § 1914.

Registry Fund Fees—Item 13 (55 F.R. 42867, October 24, 1990)

Effective December 1, 1990, the registry fee assessment provisions were revised and converted from a one-time charge equal to all income earned in the first 45 days of the investment to a charge of 10 percent of the income earned while funds are held in the court registry. Additionally, the fee was extended to any funds placed in the court's registry and invested regardless of the nature of the action underlying the deposit.

The new method will not be applied on investments in cases from which a fee has been exacted based on the prior method (interest earned in the first 45 days the funds were invested or the first 45 days following July 12, 1989). The new method will also not be applied in cases where the investment instrument has a maturity date greater than one year, but where a fee under the prior method applies but has not been deducted.

The fee does not apply in the District Courts of Guam, the Northern Mariana Islands, the Virgin Islands, the United States Claims Court, or any other federal court whose fees are not set under 28 U.S.C. §§ 1913, 1914, and 1930.

Registry Fund Fees—Item 13 (56 F.R. 56356, November 4, 1991)

Effective February 3, 1992, the registry fee assessment provisions are revised and converted from a charge equal to 10 percent of the income earned while funds are held in the court's registry to a variable rate based on the amount deposited with the court and, in certain cases, the length of time funds are held in the court's registry.

The revised fee will be a fee of 10 percent of the total income received during each income period from investments of less than $100,000,000 of registry funds in income-bearing accounts. On investments exceeding $100,000,000 the 10 percent fee shall be reduced by one percent for each increment of $50,000,000 over the initial $100,000,000. For those deposits where funds are placed in the registry by court order for a time certain, for example, by the terms of an adjudicated trust, the fee will be further reduced. This further reduction will amount to 2.5 percent for each five-year interval or part thereof. The total minimum fee to be charged will be no less than two percent of the income on investments.

The following table sets out the fee schedule promulgated by this notice:

REGISTRY—SCHEDULE OF FEES

[% of income earned]

Amount of deposit*	0–5 yrs.	>5–10 yrs.	>10–15 yrs.	<15 yrs.
less than 100M	10	7.5	5.0	2.5
100M–<150M	9	6.5	4.0	2.0
150M–<200M	8	5.5	3.0	2.0
200M–<250M	7	4.5	2.0	2.0
250M–<300M	6	3.5	2.0	2.0
300M–<350M	5	2.5	2.0	2.0
350M–<400M	4	2.0	2.0	2.0
400M–<450M	3	2.0	2.0	2.0
over 450M	2	2.0	2.0	2.0

* Except where otherwise authorized by the Director, each deposit into any account is treated separately in determining the fee.

The new fee applies to all earnings applied to investments on and after the effective date of this change, except for earnings on investments in cases being administered under the provisions of the May 11, 1989 notice [54 FR 20407], i.e., to which the fee equal to the first 45 days income is applicable.

The fee, as modified herein, will continue to apply to any case where the court has authorized the investment of funds placed in its custody or held by it in trust in its registry regardless of the nature of the underlying action.

The fee does not apply in the District Court of Guam, the Northern Mariana Islands, the Virgin Islands, the United States Claims Court, or any other Federal court whose fees are not set under 28 U.S.C. §§ 1913, 1914, and 1930.

HISTORICAL AND STATUTORY NOTES

Codifications

Pub.L. 99–591 is a corrected version of Pub.L. 99–500.

Court Fees for Electronic Access to Information

Judicial Conference to prescribe reasonable fees for collection by courts under this section for access to information available through automatic data processing equipment and fees to be deposited in Judiciary Automation Fund, see section 303 of Pub.L. 102–140, set out as a note under section 1913 of this title.

§ 1915.   Proceedings in forma pauperis

(a)(1) Subject to subsection (b), any court of the United States may authorize the commencement, prosecution or defense of any suit, action or proceeding, civil or criminal, or appeal therein, without prepayment of fees or security therefor, by a person who submits an affidavit that includes a statement of all assets such prisoner possesses that the person is unable to pay such fees or give security therefor. Such affidavit shall state the nature of the action, defense or appeal and affiant's belief that the person is entitled to redress.

(2) A prisoner seeking to bring a civil action or appeal a judgment in a civil action or proceeding without prepayment of fees or security therefor, in addition to filing the affidavit filed under paragraph (1), shall submit a certified copy of the trust fund account statement (or institutional equivalent) for the prisoner for the 6-month period immediately preceding the filing of the complaint or notice of appeal, obtained from the appropriate official of each prison at which the prisoner is or was confined.

(3) An appeal may not be taken in forma pauperis if the trial court certifies in writing that it is not taken in good faith.

(b)(1) Notwithstanding subsection (a), if a prisoner brings a civil action or files an appeal in forma pauperis, the prisoner shall be required to pay the full amount of a filing fee. The court shall assess and, when funds exist, collect, as a partial payment of any court fees required by law, an initial partial filing fee of 20 percent of the greater of—

    (A)   the average monthly deposits to the prisoner's account; or

    (B)   the average monthly balance in the prisoner's account for the 6-month period immediately preceding the filing of the complaint or notice of appeal.

    (2)   After payment of the initial partial filing fee, the prisoner shall be required to make monthly payments of 20 percent of the preceding month's income credited to the prisoner's account. The agency having custody of the prisoner shall forward payments from the prisoner's account to the clerk of the court each time the amount in the account exceeds $10 until the filing fees are paid.

    (3)   In no event shall the filing fee collected exceed the amount of fees permitted by statute for the commencement of a civil action or an appeal of a civil action or criminal judgment.

    (4)   In no event shall a prisoner be prohibited from bringing a civil action or appealing a civil or criminal judgment for the reason that the prisoner has no assets and no means by which to pay the initial partial filing fee.

    (c)   Upon the filing of an affidavit in accordance with subsections (a) and (b) and the prepayment of any partial filing fee as may be required under subsection (b), the court may direct payment by the United States of the expenses of (1) printing the record on appeal in any civil or criminal case, if such printing is required by the appellate court; (2) preparing a transcript of proceedings before a United States magistrate judge in any civil or criminal case, if such transcript is required by the district court, in the case of proceedings conducted under section 636(b) of this title or under section 3401(b) of title 18, United States Code; and (3) printing the record on appeal if such printing is required by the appellate court, in the case of proceedings conducted pursuant to section 636(c) of this title. Such expenses shall be paid when authorized by the Director of the Administrative Office of the United States Courts.

    (d)   The officers of the court shall issue and serve all process, and perform all duties in such cases. Witnesses shall attend as in other cases, and the same remedies shall be available as are provided for by law in other cases.

    (e)(1)   The court may request an attorney to represent any person unable to afford counsel.

    (2)   Notwithstanding any filing fee, or any portion thereof, that may have been paid, the court shall dismiss the case at any time if the court determines that—

    (A)   the allegation of poverty is untrue; or

    (B)   the action or appeal—

        (i)   is frivolous or malicious;

        (ii)   fails to state a claim on which relief may be granted; or

        (iii)   seeks monetary relief against a defendant who is immune from such relief.

    (f)(1)   Judgment may be rendered for costs at the conclusion of the suit or action as in other proceedings, but the United States shall not be liable for any of the costs thus incurred. If the United States has paid the cost of a stenographic transcript or printed record for the prevailing party, the same shall be taxed in favor of the United States.

    (2)(A)   If the judgment against a prisoner includes the payment of costs under this subsection, the prisoner shall be required to pay the full amount of the costs ordered.

    (B)   The prisoner shall be required to make payments for costs under this subsection in the same manner as is provided for filing fees under subsection (a)(2).

    (C) In no event shall the costs collected exceed the amount of the costs ordered by the court.

(g) In no event shall a prisoner bring a civil action or appeal a judgment in a civil action or proceeding under this section if the prisoner has, on 3 or more prior occasions, while incarcerated or detained in any facility, brought an action or appeal in a court of the United States that was dismissed on the grounds that it is frivolous, malicious, or fails to state a claim upon which relief may be granted, unless the prisoner is under imminent danger of serious physical injury.

(h) As used in this section, the term "prisoner" means any person incarcerated or detained in any facility who is accused of, convicted of, sentenced for, or adjudicated delinquent for, violations of criminal law or the terms and conditions of parole, probation, pretrial release, or diversionary program.

(June 25, 1948, c. 646, 62 Stat. 954; May 24, 1949, c. 139, § 98, 63 Stat. 104; Oct. 31, 1951, c. 655, § 51(b), (c), 65 Stat. 727; Sept. 21, 1959, Pub.L. 86–320, 73 Stat. 590; Oct. 10, 1979, Pub.L. 96–82, § 6, 93 Stat. 645; Dec. 1, 1990, Pub.L. 101–650, Title III, § 321, 104 Stat. 5117; Apr. 26, 1996, Pub.L. 104–134, Title I, § 101[(a)] [Title VIII, § 804(a), (c) to (e)], 110 Stat. 1321–73, 1321–74, 1321–75; renumbered Title I May 2, 1996, Pub.L. 104–140, § 1(a), 110 Stat. 1327.)

HISTORICAL AND STATUTORY NOTES

Change of Name

"United States magistrate judge" substituted for "United States magistrate" in text pursuant to section 321 of Pub.L. 101–650, set out as a note under 28 U.S.C.A. § 631.

Severability of Provisions

If any provision of section 101[a] [Title VIII] of Pub.L. 104–134, an amendment made by such Title, or the application of such provision or amendment to any person or circumstance is held to be unconstitutional, the remainder of such Title, the amendments made by such Title, and the application of the provisions of such Title to any person or circumstance not affected thereby, see section 101[a] [Title VIII, § 810] of Pub.L. 104–134, set out as a note under section 3626 of Title 18, Crimes and Criminal Procedure.

§ 1915A.   Screening

(a) Screening.—The court shall review, before docketing, if feasible or, in any event, as soon as practicable after docketing, a complaint in a civil action in which a prisoner seeks redress from a governmental entity or officer or employee of a governmental entity.

(b) Grounds for dismissal.—On review, the court shall identify cognizable claims or dismiss the complaint, or any portion of the complaint, if the complaint—

    (1) is frivolous, malicious, or fails to state a claim upon which relief may be granted; or

    (2) seeks monetary relief from a defendant who is immune from such relief.

(c) Definition.—As used in this section, the term "prisoner" means any person incarcerated or detained in any facility who is accused of, convicted of, sentenced for, or adjudicated delinquent for, violations of criminal law or the terms and conditions of parole, probation, pretrial release, or diversionary program.

(Added Pub.L. 104–134, Title I, § 101[(a)][Title VIII, § 805(a)], Apr. 26, 1996, 110 Stat. 1321–75; renumbered Title I Pub.L. 104–140, § 1(a), May 2, 1996, 110 Stat. 1327.)

HISTORICAL AND STATUTORY NOTES

Severability of Provisions

If any provision of section 101[a] [Title VIII] of Pub.L. 104–134, an amendment made by such Title, or the application of such provision or amendment to any person or circumstance is held to be unconstitutional, the remainder of such Title, the amendments made by such Title, and the application of the provisions of such Title to any person or circumstance not affected thereby, see section 101[a] [Title VIII, § 810] of Pub.L. 104–134, set out as a note under section 3626 of Title 18, Crimes and Criminal Procedure.

§ 1916.   Seamen's suits

In all courts of the United States, seamen may institute and prosecute suits and appeals in their own names and for their own benefit for wages or salvage or the enforcement of laws enacted for their health or safety without prepaying fees or costs or furnishing security therefor.

(June 25, 1948, c. 646, 62 Stat. 955.)

§ 1917.   District courts; fee on filing notice of or petition for appeal

Upon the filing of any separate or joint notice of appeal or application for appeal or upon the receipt of any order allowing, or notice of the allowance of, an appeal or of a writ of certiorari $5 shall be paid to the clerk of the district court, by the appellant or petitioner.

(June 25, 1948, c. 646, 62 Stat. 955.)

§ 1918.   District courts; fines, forfeitures and criminal proceedings

(a) Costs shall be included in any judgment, order, or decree rendered against any person for the violation of an Act of Congress in which a civil fine or forfeiture of property is provided for.

(b) Whenever any conviction for any offense not capital is obtained in a district court, the court may order that the defendant pay the costs of prosecution.

(June 25, 1948, c. 646, 62 Stat. 955.)

§ 1919.   Dismissal for lack of jurisdiction

Whenever any action or suit is dismissed in any district court, the Court of International Trade, or the Court of Federal Claims for want of jurisdiction, such court may order the payment of just costs.

(June 25, 1948, c. 646, 62 Stat. 955; Oct. 10, 1980, Pub.L. 96–417, Title V, § 510, 94 Stat. 1743; Oct. 29, 1992, Pub.L. 102–572, Title IX, § 908(a), (b)(1), 106 Stat. 4519.)

§ 1920.   Taxation of costs

A judge or clerk of any court of the United States may tax as costs the following:

    (1) Fees of the clerk and marshal;

    (2) Fees for printed or electronically recorded transcripts necessarily obtained for use in the case;

    (3) Fees and disbursements for printing and witnesses;

    (4) Fees for exemplification and the costs of making copies of any materials where the copies are necessarily obtained for use in the case;

    (5) Docket fees under section 1923 of this title;

    (6) Compensation of court appointed experts, compensation of interpreters, and salaries, fees, expenses, and costs of special interpretation services under section 1828 of this title.

A bill of costs shall be filed in the case and, upon allowance, included in the judgment or decree.

(June 25, 1948, c. 646, 62 Stat. 955; Oct. 28, 1978, Pub.L. 95–539, § 7, 92 Stat. 2044; Oct. 13, 2008, Pub.L. 110–406, § 6, 122 Stat. 4292.)

§ 1921.   United States marshal's fees

(a)(1) The United States marshals or deputy marshals shall routinely collect, and a court may tax as costs, fees for the following:

(A) Serving a writ of possession, partition, execution, attachment in rem, or libel in admiralty, warrant, attachment, summons, complaints, or any other writ, order or process in any case or proceeding.

(B) Serving a subpoena or summons for a witness or appraiser.

(C) Forwarding any writ, order, or process to another judicial district for service.

(D) The preparation of any notice of sale, proclamation in admiralty, or other public notice or bill of sale.

(E) The keeping of attached property (including boats, vessels, or other property attached or libeled), actual expenses incurred, such as storage, moving, boat hire, or other special transportation, watchmen's or keepers' fees, insurance, and an hourly rate, including overtime, for each deputy marshal required for special services, such as guarding, inventorying, and moving.

(F) Copies of writs or other papers furnished at the request of any party.

(G) Necessary travel in serving or endeavoring to serve any process, writ, or order, except in the District of Columbia, with mileage to be computed from the place where service is returnable to the place of service or endeavor.

(H) Overtime expenses incurred by deputy marshals in the course of serving or executing civil process.

(2) The marshals shall collect, in advance, a deposit to cover the initial expenses for special services required under paragraph (1)(E), and periodically thereafter such amounts as may be necessary to pay such expenses until the litigation is concluded. This paragraph applies to all private litigants, including seamen proceeding pursuant to section 1916 of this title.

(3) For purposes of paragraph (1)(G), if two or more services or endeavors, or if an endeavor and a service, are made in behalf of the same party in the same case on the same trip, mileage shall be computed to the place of service or endeavor which is most remote from the place where service is returnable, adding thereto any additional mileage traveled in serving or endeavoring to serve in behalf of the party. If two or more writs of any kind, required to be served in behalf of the same party on the same person in the same case or proceeding, may be served at the same time, mileage on only one such writ shall be collected.

(b) The Attorney General shall from time to time prescribe by regulation the fees to be taxed and collected under subsection (a). Such fees shall, to the extent practicable, reflect the actual and reasonable cost of the service provided.

(c)(1) The United States Marshals Service shall collect a commission of 3 percent of the first $1,000 collected and $1^{1}/_{2}$ percent on the excess of any sum over $1,000, for seizing or levying on property (including seizures in admiralty), disposing of such property by sale, setoff, or otherwise, and receiving and paying over money, except that the amount of commission shall be within the range set by the Attorney General. if[1] the property is not disposed of by marshal's sale, the commission shall be in such amount, within the range set by the Attorney General, as may be allowed by the court. In any case in which the vessel or other property is sold by a public auctioneer, or by some party other than a marshal or deputy marshal, the commission authorized under this subsection shall be reduced by the amount paid to such auctioneer or other party. This subsection applies to any judicially ordered sale or execution sale, without regard to whether the judicial order of sale constitutes a seizure or levy within the meaning of State law. This subsection shall not apply to any seizure, forfeiture, sale, or other disposition of property pursuant to the applicable provisions of law amended by the Comprehensive Forfeiture Act of 1984 (98 Stat. 2040).

---

[1]   [Footnote to 28 U.S.C. § 1921(c)(1):] So in original. Probably should be capitalized.

(2) The Attorney General shall prescribe from time to time regulations which establish a minimum and maximum amount for the commission collected under paragraph (1).

(d) The United States marshals may require a deposit to cover the fees and expenses prescribed under this section.

(e) Notwithstanding section 3302 of title 31, the United States Marshals Service is authorized, to the extent provided in advance in appropriations Acts—

(1) to credit to such Service's appropriation all fees, commissions, and expenses collected by such Service for—

(A) the service of civil process, including complaints, summonses, subpoenas, and similar process; and

(B) seizures, levies, and sales associated with judicial orders of execution; and

(2) to use such credited amounts for the purpose of carrying out such activities.

(June 25, 1948, c. 646, 62 Stat. 955; Sept. 9, 1950, c. 937, 64 Stat. 824; Aug. 31, 1962, Pub.L. 87–621, § 1, 76 Stat. 417; Nov. 10, 1986, Pub.L. 99–646, § 39(a), 100 Stat. 3600; Nov. 18, 1988, Pub.L. 100–690, Title VII, § 7608(c), 102 Stat. 4515; Nov. 29, 1990, Pub.L. 101–647, Title XII, § 1212, 104 Stat. 4833.)

HISTORICAL AND STATUTORY NOTES

References in Text

The Comprehensive Forfeiture Act of 1984, referred to in subsec. (c)(1), is chapter III (sections 301 to 322) of Title II of Pub.L. 98–473, Oct. 12, 1984, 98 Stat. 2040, as amended. For complete classification of this Act to the Code, see Short Title of 1984 Amendments note set out under section 1961 of Title 18, Crimes and Criminal Procedure, and Tables.

Collection and Disposition of Fees and Expenses for Services

Pub.L. 101–162, Title II, Nov. 21, 1989, 103 Stat. 997, provided in part: "That notwithstanding the provisions of title 31 U.S.C. 3302 [section 3302 of Title 31, Money and Finance], for fiscal year 1990 and hereafter the Director of the United States Marshals Service may collect fees and expenses for the services authorized by 28 U.S.C. 1921 as amended by Public Law 100–690 [this section], and credit such fees to this appropriation to be used for salaries and other expenses incurred in providing these services."

§ 1922.   Witness fees before United States magistrate judges

The fees of more than four witnesses shall not be taxed against the United States, in the examination of any criminal case before a United States magistrate judge, unless their materiality and importance are first approved and certified to by the United States attorney for the district in which the examination is had.

(June 25, 1948, c. 646, 62 Stat. 956; Oct. 17, 1968, Pub.L. 90–578, Title IV, § 402(b)(2), 82 Stat. 1118; Dec. 1, 1990, Pub.L. 101–650, Title III, § 321, 104 Stat. 5117.)

HISTORICAL AND STATUTORY NOTES

Change of Name

"United States magistrate judge" substituted for "United States magistrate" in text pursuant to section 321 of Pub.L. 101–650, set out as a note under 28 U.S.C.A. § 631. Previously, United States commissioners, referred to in text, were replaced by United States magistrates pursuant to Pub.L. 90–578, Oct. 17, 1968, 82 Stat. 1118. See chapter 43 of Title 28, 28 U.S.C.A. § 631 et seq.

§ 1923.   Docket fees and costs of briefs

(a) Attorney's and proctor's docket fees in courts of the United States may be taxed as costs as follows:

$20 on trial or final hearing (including a default judgment whether entered by the court or by the clerk) in civil, criminal, or admiralty cases, except that in cases of admiralty and maritime jurisdiction where the libellant recovers less than $50 the proctor's docket fee shall be $10;

$20 in admiralty appeals involving not over $1,000;

$50 in admiralty appeals involving not over $5,000;

$100 in admiralty appeals involving more than $5,000;

$5 on discontinuance of a civil action;

$5 on motion for judgment and other proceedings on recognizances;

$2.50 for each deposition admitted in evidence.

(b) The docket fees of United States attorneys and United States trustees shall be paid to the clerk of court and by him paid into the Treasury.

(c) In admiralty appeals the court may allow as costs for printing the briefs of the successful party not more than:

$25 where the amount involved is not over $1,000;

$50 where the amount involved is not over $5,000;

$75 where the amount involved is over $5,000.

(June 25, 1948, c. 646, 62 Stat. 956; June 18, 1954, c. 304, 68 Stat. 253; Nov. 6, 1978, Pub.L. 95–598, Title II, § 245, 92 Stat. 2671.)

HISTORICAL AND STATUTORY NOTES

Codifications

Section 408(c) of Pub.L. 95–598, Nov. 6, 1978, 92 Stat. 2687, as amended by Pub.L. 98–166, Title II, § 200, Nov. 28, 1983, 97 Stat. 1081; Pub.L. 98–353, Title III, § 323, July 10, 1984, 98 Stat. 358; Pub.L. 99–429, Sept. 30, 1986, 100 Stat. 985; Pub.L. 99–500, § 101(b) [title II, § 200], Oct. 18, 1986, 100 Stat. 1783–39, 1783–45, and Pub.L. 99–591, § 101(b) [Title II, § 200], Oct. 30, 1986, 100 Stat. 3341–39, 3341–45; Pub.L. 99–554, Title III, § 307(a), Oct. 27, 1986, 100 Stat. 3125, which provided for the deletion of any references to United States Trustees in this title at a prospective date, was repealed by Pub.L. 99–554, Title III, § 307(b), Oct. 27, 1986, 100 Stat. 3125.

[For effective date of repeal, see section 302 of Pub.L. 99–554, set out as a note under section 581 of Title 28.]

§ 1924.   Verification of bill of costs

Before any bill of costs is taxed, the party claiming any item of cost or disbursement shall attach thereto an affidavit, made by himself or by his duly authorized attorney or agent having knowledge of the facts, that such item is correct and has been necessarily incurred in the case and that the services for which fees have been charged were actually and necessarily performed.

(June 25, 1948, c. 646, 62 Stat. 957.)

§ 1925.   Admiralty and maritime cases

Except as otherwise provided by Act of Congress, the allowance and taxation of costs in admiralty and maritime cases shall be prescribed by rules promulgated by the Supreme Court.

(June 25, 1948, c. 646, 62 Stat. 957.)

§ 1926.   Court of Federal Claims

(a)   The Judicial Conference of the United States shall prescribe from time to time the fees and costs to be charged and collected in the United States Court of Federal Claims.

(b)   The court and its officers shall collect only such fees and costs as the Judicial Conference prescribes. The court may require advance payment of fees by rule.

(June 25, 1948, c. 646, 62 Stat. 957; Apr. 2, 1982, Pub.L. 97–164, Title I, § 139(p)(1), 96 Stat. 44; Oct. 29, 1992, Pub.L. 102–572, Title IX, § 902(b), 106 Stat. 4516.)

JUDICIAL CONFERENCE SCHEDULE OF FEES

United States Court of Federal Claims Fee Schedule[*]

(Effective October 1, 2019)

Following are fees to be charged for services provided by the United States Court of Federal Claims[1].

For checks, please make them payable to: Clerk, U.S. Court of Federal Claims. No fees are to be charged for services rendered on behalf of the United States, with the exception of those specifically prescribed in items (2), (8) and (9). No fees under this schedule shall be charged to federal agencies or programs which are funded from judiciary appropriations, including, but not limited to, agencies, organizations, and individuals providing services authorized by the Criminal Justice Act, 18 U.S.C. § 3006A, and Bankruptcy Administrator programs.

(1)   For filing a civil action or proceeding, $350.[2]

(2)

     a.   For reproducing any record or paper, $.50 per page. This fee shall apply to paper copies made from either: (a) original documents; or (b) microfiche or microfilm reproduction of the original records. This fee shall apply to services rendered on behalf of the United States if the record or paper requested is available through electronic access.

     b.   For reproducing and transmitting in any manner a copy of an electronic record stored outside of the court's electronic case management system, including but not limited to, document files, audio recordings, and video recordings, $31 per record provided. Audio recordings of court proceedings continue to be governed by a separate fee in item 9 of this schedule.

(3)   For certification of any document or paper, whether the certification is made directly on the document or by separate instrument, $11. For exemplification of any document or paper, twice the amount of the charge for certification.

(4)   For admission of attorneys to practice, $181 each, including a certificate of admission.[3] For a duplicate certificate of admission or certificate of good standing, $19.

(5)   For receipt of a monthly listing of court orders and opinions, $23 per year.

(6)   The court may charge and collect fees commensurate with the cost of providing copies of the local rules of court. The court may also distribute copies of the local rules without charge.

(7)   For any payment returned or denied for insufficient funds, $53.

(8)   For every search of the records of the Court of Federal Claims conducted by the clerk of the court or a deputy clerk, $31 per name or item searched. This fee shall apply to services rendered on behalf of the United States if the information requested is available through electronic access.

---

[*]   [The Electronic Public Access Fee Schedule is set out in this volume, *supra*, in the notes following 28 U.S.C. § 1913. Ed.]

[1]   Issued in accordance with 28 U.S.C. § 1926(a).

[2]   Filing fee increase effective January 1, 2010.

[3]   Admission of attorneys to practice fee increase effective September 18, 2005. [This fee has been raised since then. Ed.]

(9) For reproduction of an audio recording of a court proceeding, $31. This fee applies to services rendered on behalf of the United States, if the recording is available electronically.

(10) For filing or indexing any document not in a case or proceeding for which a filing fee has been paid, $47.

(11) For retrieval of one box of records from a Federal Records Center, National Archives, or other storage location removed from the place of business of the court, $64. For retrievals involving multiple boxes, $39 for each additional box. For electronic retrievals, $10 plus any charges assessed by the Federal Records Center, National Archives, or other storage location removed from the place of business of the courts.

(12) Administrative fee for filing a civil action, suit, or proceeding with the Court of Federal Claims, $50. This fee does not apply to petitioners granted *in forma pauperis* status under 28 U.S.C. § 1915.

HISTORICAL AND STATUTORY NOTES

Court Fees for Electronic Access to Information

Judicial Conference to prescribe reasonable fees for collection by courts under this section for access to information available through automatic data processing equipment and fees to be deposited in Judiciary Automation Fund, see section 303 of Pub.L. 102–140, set out as a note under section 1913 of this title.

§ 1927.   Counsel's liability for excessive costs

Any attorney or other person admitted to conduct cases in any court of the United States or any Territory thereof who so multiplies the proceedings in any case unreasonably and vexatiously may be required by the court to satisfy personally the excess costs, expenses, and attorneys' fees reasonably incurred because of such conduct.

(June 25, 1948, c. 646, 62 Stat. 957; Sept. 12, 1980, Pub.L. 96–349, § 3, 94 Stat. 1156.)

§ 1928.   Patent infringement action; disclaimer not filed

Whenever a judgment is rendered for the plaintiff in any patent infringement action involving a part of a patent and it appears that the patentee, in his specifications, claimed to be, but was not, the original and first inventor or discoverer of any material or substantial part of the thing patented, no costs shall be included in such judgment, unless the proper disclaimer has been filed in the United States Patent and Trademark Office prior to the commencement of the action.

(June 25, 1948, c. 646, 62 Stat. 957; Nov. 29, 1999, Pub.L. 106–113, Div. B, § 1000(a)(9) [Title IV, § 4732(b)(17)], 113 Stat. 1536, 1501A–585.)

HISTORICAL AND STATUTORY NOTES

Change of Name

Patent Office redesignated Patent and Trademark Office by section 3 of Pub.L. 93–596, Jan. 2, 1975, 88 Stat. 1949, set out as a note under section 1 of Title 35, Patents.

§ 1929.   Extraordinary expenses not expressly authorized

Where the ministerial officers of the United States incur extraordinary expense in executing Acts of Congress, the payment of which is not specifically provided for, the Attorney General may allow the payment thereof.

(June 25, 1948, c. 646, 62 Stat. 957.)

§ 1930.   Bankruptcy fees

(a) The parties commencing a case under title 11 shall pay to the clerk of the district court or the clerk of the bankruptcy court, if one has been certified pursuant to section 156(b) of this title, the following filing fees:

    (1) For a case commenced under—

(A) chapter 7 of title 11, $245, and

(B) chapter 13 of title 11, $235.

(2) For a case commenced under chapter 9 of title 11, equal to the fee specified in paragraph (3) for filing a case under chapter 11 of title 11. The amount by which the fee payable under this paragraph exceeds $300 shall be deposited in the fund established under section 1931 of this title.

(3) For a case commenced under chapter 11 of title 11 that does not concern a railroad, as defined in section 101 of title 11, $1,167.

(4) For a case commenced under chapter 11 of title 11 concerning a railroad, as so defined, $1,000.

(5) For a case commenced under chapter 12 of title 11, $200.

(6)(A) Except as provided in subparagraph (B), in addition to the filing fee paid to the clerk, a quarterly fee shall be paid to the United States trustee, for deposit in the Treasury, in each case under chapter 11 of title 11, other than under subchapter V, for each quarter (including any fraction thereof) until the case is converted or dismissed, whichever occurs first. The fee shall be $325 for each quarter in which disbursements total less than $15,000; $650 for each quarter in which disbursements total $15,000 or more but less than $75,000; $975 for each quarter in which disbursements total $75,000 or more but less than $150,000; $1,625 for each quarter in which disbursements total $150,000 or more but less than $225,000; $1,950 for each quarter in which disbursements total $225,000 or more but less than $300,000; $4,875 for each quarter in which disbursements total $300,000 or more but less than $1,000,000; $6,500 for each quarter in which disbursements total $1,000,000 or more but less than $2,000,000; $9,750 for each quarter in which disbursements total $2,000,000 or more but less than $3,000,000; $10,400 for each quarter in which disbursements total $3,000,000 or more but less than $5,000,000; $13,000 for each quarter in which disbursements total $5,000,000 or more but less than $15,000,000; $20,000 for each quarter in which disbursements total $15,000,000 or more but less than $30,000,000; $30,000 for each quarter in which disbursements total more than $30,000,000. The fee shall be payable on the last day of the calendar month following the calendar quarter for which the fee is owed.

(B) During each of fiscal years 2018 through 2022, if the balance in the United States Trustee System Fund as of September 30 of the most recent full fiscal year is less than $200,000,000, the quarterly fee payable for a quarter in which disbursements equal or exceed $1,000,000 shall be the lesser of 1 percent of such disbursements or $250,000.

(7) In districts that are not part of a United States trustee region as defined in section 581 of this title, the Judicial Conference of the United States may require the debtor in a case under chapter 11 of title 11 to pay fees equal to those imposed by paragraph (6) of this subsection. Such fees shall be deposited as offsetting receipts to the fund established under section 1931 of this title and shall remain available until expended.

An individual commencing a voluntary case or a joint case under title 11 may pay such fee in installments. For converting, on request of the debtor, a case under chapter 7, or 13 of title 11, to a case under chapter 11 of title 11, the debtor shall pay to the clerk of the district court or the clerk of the bankruptcy court, if one has been certified pursuant to section 156(b) of this title, a fee of the amount equal to the difference between the fee specified in paragraph (3) and the fee specified in paragraph (1).

(b) The Judicial Conference of the United States may prescribe additional fees in cases under title 11 of the same kind as the Judicial Conference prescribes under section 1914(b) of this title.

(c) Upon the filing of any separate or joint notice of appeal or application for appeal or upon the receipt of any order allowing, or notice of the allowance of, an appeal or a writ of certiorari $5 shall be paid to the clerk of the court, by the appellant or petitioner.

(d) Whenever any case or proceeding is dismissed in any bankruptcy court for want of jurisdiction, such court may order the payment of just costs.

(e) The clerk of the court may collect only the fees prescribed under this section.

(f)(1) Under the procedures prescribed by the Judicial Conference of the United States, the district court or the bankruptcy court may waive the filing fee in a case under chapter 7 of title 11 for an individual if the court determines that such individual has income less than 150 percent of the income official poverty line (as defined by the Office of Management and Budget, and revised annually in accordance with section 673(2) of the Omnibus Budget Reconciliation Act of 1981) applicable to a family of the size involved and is unable to pay that fee in installments. For purposes of this paragraph, the term "filing fee" means the filing fee required by subsection (a), or any other fee prescribed by the Judicial Conference under subsections (b) and (c) that is payable to the clerk upon the commencement of a case under chapter 7.

(2) The district court or the bankruptcy court may waive for such debtors other fees prescribed under subsections (b) and (c).

(3) This subsection does not restrict the district court or the bankruptcy court from waiving, in accordance with Judicial Conference policy, fees prescribed under this section for other debtors and creditors.

(Added Pub.L. 95–598, Title II, § 246(a), Nov. 6, 1978, 92 Stat. 2671; amended Pub.L. 98–353, Title I, § 111(a), (b), July 10, 1984, 98 Stat. 342; Pub.L. 99–500, Title I, § 101(b) [Title IV, § 407(b)], Oct. 18, 1986, 100 Stat. 1783–64; Pub.L. 99–554, Title I, §§ 117, 144(f), Oct. 27, 1986, 100 Stat. 3095, 3097; Pub.L. 99–591, Title I, § 101(b) [Title IV, § 407(b)], Oct. 30, 1986, 100 Stat. 3341–64; Pub.L. 101–162, Title IV, § 406(a), Nov. 21, 1989, 103 Stat. 1016; Pub.L. 102–140, Title I, § 111(a), Oct. 28, 1991, 105 Stat. 795; Pub.L. 103–121, Title I, § 111(a)(1), (b)(1), Oct. 27, 1993, 107 Stat. 1164; Pub.L. 104–91, Title I, § 101(a), Jan. 6, 1996, 110 Stat. 11; Pub.L. 104–99, Title II, § 211, Jan. 26, 1996, 110 Stat. 37; Pub.L. 104–208, Div. A, Title I, § 101(a) [Title I, § 109(a)], Sept. 30, 1996, 110 Stat. 3009–18; Pub.L. 106–113, Div. B, § 1000(a)(1) [Title I, § 113], Nov. 29, 1999, 113 Stat. 1535, 1501A–20; Pub.L. 106–518, Title I, §§ 103 to 105, Nov. 13, 2000, 114 Stat. 2411; Pub.L. 109–8, Title III, § 325(a), Title IV, § 418, Apr. 20, 2005, 119 Stat. 98, 108; Pub.L. 109–13, Div. A, Title VI, § 6058(a), May 11, 2005, 119 Stat. 297; Pub.L. 109–171, Title X, § 10101(a), Feb. 8, 2006, 120 Stat. 184; Pub.L. 110–161, Div. B, Title II, § 213(a), Dec. 26, 2007, 121 Stat. 1914; Pub.L. 112–121, § 3(a), May 25, 2012, 126 Stat. 348; Pub.L. 115–72, Div. B, § 1004(a), Oct. 26, 2017, 131 Stat. 1232; Pub.L. 116–54, § 4(b)(3), Aug. 23, 2019, 133 Stat. 1087.)

JUDICIAL CONFERENCE SCHEDULE OF FEES

Bankruptcy Court Miscellaneous Fee Schedule*

(Effective September 1, 2018)

The fees included in the Bankruptcy Court Miscellaneous Fee Schedule[1] are to be charged for services provided by the bankruptcy courts.

- The United States should not be charged fees under this schedule, with the exception of those specifically prescribed in Items 1, 3 and 5 when the information requested is available through remote electronic access.

- Federal agencies or programs that are funded from judiciary appropriations (agencies, organizations, and individuals providing services authorized by the Criminal Justice Act, 18 U.S.C. § 3006A, and bankruptcy administrators) should not be charged any fees under this schedule.

---

* [The Electronic Public Access Fee Schedule is set out in this volume, *supra*, in the notes following 28 U.S.C. § 1913. Ed.]

[1] Issued in accordance with 28 U.S.C. § 1930.

(1)

     a.   For reproducing any document, $.50 per page. This fee applies to services rendered on behalf of the United States if the document requested is available through electronic access.

     b.   For reproducing and transmitting in any manner a copy of an electronic record stored outside of the court's electronic case management system, including but not limited to, document files, audio recordings, and video recordings, $31 per record provided. Audio recordings of court proceedings continue to be governed by a separate fee under item 3 of this schedule.

(2)   For certification of any document, $11.

      For exemplification of any document, $22.

(3)   For reproduction of an audio recording of a court proceeding, $31. This fee applies to services rendered on behalf of the United States if the recording is available electronically.

(4)   For filing an amendment to the debtor's schedules of creditors, lists of creditors, or mailing list, $31, except:

- The bankruptcy judge may, for good cause, waive the charge in any case.

- This fee must not be charged if—

  - the amendment is to change the address of a creditor or an attorney for a creditor listed on the schedules; or

  - the amendment is to add the name and address of an attorney for a creditor listed on the schedules.

(5)   For conducting a search of the bankruptcy court records, $31 per name or item searched. This fee applies to services rendered on behalf of the United States if the information requested is available through electronic access.

(6)   For filing a complaint, $350, except:

- If the trustee or debtor-in-possession files the complaint, the fee must be paid only by the estate, to the extent there is an estate.

- This fee must not be charged if—

  - the debtor is the plaintiff; or

  - a child support creditor or representative files the complaint and submits the form required by § 304(g) of the Bankruptcy Reform Act of 1994.

(7)   For filing any document that is not related to a pending case or proceeding, $47.

(8)   Administrative fee:

- For filing a petition under Chapter 7, 12, or 13, $75.

- For filing a petition under Chapter 9, 11, or 15, $550.

- When a motion to divide a joint case under Chapter 7, 12, or 13 is filed, $75.

- When a motion to divide a joint case under Chapter 11 is filed, $550.

(9)   For payment to trustees pursuant to 11 U.S.C. § 330(b)(2), a $15 fee applies in the following circumstances:

- For filing a petition under Chapter 7.

- For filing a motion to reopen a Chapter 7 case.

- For filing a motion to divide a joint Chapter 7 case.

- For filing a motion to convert a case to a Chapter 7 case.

- For filing a notice of conversion to a Chapter 7 case.

(10) In addition to any fees imposed under Item 9, above, the following fees must be collected:

- For filing a motion to convert a Chapter 12 case to a Chapter 7 case or a notice of conversion pursuant to 11 U.S.C. § 1208(a), $45.

- For filing a motion to convert a Chapter 13 case to a Chapter 7 case or a notice of conversion pursuant to 11 U.S.C. § 1307(a), $10.

The fee amounts in this item are derived from the fees prescribed in 28 U.S.C. § 1930(a).

If the trustee files the motion to convert, the fee is payable only from the estate that exists prior to conversion.

If the filing fee for the chapter to which the case is requested to be converted is less than the fee paid at the commencement of the case, no refund may be provided.

(11) For filing a motion to reopen, the following fees apply:

- For filing a motion to reopen a Chapter 7 case, $245.

- For filing a motion to reopen a Chapter 9 case, $1167.

- For filing a motion to reopen a Chapter 11 case, $1167.

- For filing a motion to reopen a Chapter 12 case, $200.

- For filing a motion to reopen a Chapter 13 case, $235.

- For filing a motion to reopen a Chapter 15 case, $1167.

The fee amounts in this item are derived from the fees prescribed in 28 U.S.C. § 1930(a).

The reopening fee must be charged when a case has been closed without a discharge being entered.

The court may waive this fee under appropriate circumstances or may defer payment of the fee from trustees pending discovery of additional assets. If payment is deferred, the fee should be waived if no additional assets are discovered.

The reopening fee must not be charged in the following situations:

- to permit a party to file a complaint to obtain a determination under Rule 4007(b); or

- when a debtor files a motion to reopen a case based upon an alleged violation of the terms of the discharge under 11 U.S.C. § 524; or

- when the reopening is to correct an administrative error.

- to redact a record already filed in a case, pursuant to Fed. R. Bankr. P. 9037, if redaction is the only reason for reopening.

(12) For retrieval of one box of records from a Federal Records Center, National Archives, or other storage location removed from the place of business of the court, $64. For retrievals involving multiple boxes, $39 for each additional box. For electronic retrievals, $10 plus any charges assessed by the Federal Records Center, National Archives, or other storage location removed from the place of business of the courts.

(13) For any payment returned or denied for insufficient funds, $53.

(14) For filing an appeal or cross appeal from a judgment, order, or decree, $293.

This fee is collected in addition to the statutory fee of $5 that is collected under 28 U.S.C. § 1930(c) when a notice of appeal is filed.

Parties filing a joint notice of appeal should pay only one fee.

If a trustee or debtor-in-possession is the appellant, the fee must be paid only by the estate, to the extent there is an estate.

Upon notice from the court of appeals that a direct appeal or direct cross-appeal has been authorized, an additional fee of $207 must be collected.

(15) For filing a case under Chapter 15 of the Bankruptcy Code, $1167.

This fee is derived from and equal to the fee prescribed in 28 U.S.C. § 1930(a)(3) for filing a case commenced under Chapter 11 of Title 11.

(16) The court may charge and collect fees commensurate with the cost of providing copies of the local rules of court. The court may also distribute copies of the local rules without charge.

(17)

- For handling registry funds deposited with and held by the court, the clerk shall assess a charge from interest earnings, in accordance with the detailed fee schedule issued by the Director of the Administrative Office of the United States Courts.

- For management of registry funds invested through the Court Registry Investment System, a fee at a rate of 10 basis points of assets on deposit shall be assessed from interest earnings, excluding registry funds from disputed ownership interpleader cases deposited under 28 U.S.C. § 1335 and held in a Court Registry Investment System Disputed Ownership Fund.

- For management of funds deposited under 28 U.S.C. § 1335 and invested in a Disputed Ownership Fund through the Court Registry Investment System, a fee at an annual rate of 20 basis points of assets on deposit shall be assessed from interest earnings.

- The Director of the Administrative Office has the authority to waive these fees for cause.

(18) For a motion filed by the debtor to divide a joint case filed under 11 U.S.C. § 302, the following fees apply:

- For filing a motion to divide a joint Chapter 7 case, $245.

- For filing a motion to divide a joint Chapter 11 case, $1167.

- For filing a motion to divide a joint Chapter 12 case, $200.

- For filing a motion to divide a joint Chapter 13 case, $235.

These fees are derived from and equal to the filing fees prescribed in 28 U.S.C. § 1930(a).

(19) For filing the following motions, $181:

- To terminate, annul, modify or condition the automatic stay;

- To compel abandonment of property of the estate pursuant to Rule 6007(b) of the Federal Rules of Bankruptcy Procedure;

- To withdraw the reference of a case or proceeding under 28 U.S.C. § 157(d); or

- To sell property of the estate free and clear of liens under 11 U.S.C. § 363(f).

This fee must not be collected in the following situations:

- For a motion for relief from the co-debtor stay;

- For a stipulation for court approval of an agreement for relief from a stay; or

- For a motion filed by a child support creditor or its representative, if the form required by § 304(g) of the Bankruptcy Reform Act of 1994 is filed.

(20) For filing a transfer of claim, $25 per claim transferred.

(21) For filing a motion to redact a record, $25 per affected case. The court may waive this fee under appropriate circumstances.

STATEMENT RESPECTING 1988 AMENDMENTS FROM ADMINISTRATIVE OFFICE OF UNITED STATES COURTS

The Director of the Administrative Office of the United States Courts in a memorandum to the Chief Judges of the United States Courts of Appeals, United States District Courts, and United States Bankruptcy Courts, dated April 19, 1988, provided in part that: "The amendment establishing a fee for filing a petition ancillary to a foreign proceeding under § 304 of the Bankruptcy Code will become effective May 1, 1988. The amendment expanding the exemption for services rendered 'to the United States' to include services rendered to bankruptcy administrators simply expresses a policy which has been in effect since the creation of the bankruptcy administrator program by Congress in the Bankruptcy Judges, United States Trustees and Family Farmer Bankruptcy Act of 1986. [Pub.L. No. 99–554, § 302(d)(3)(I).]"

Statement from 1989 Meeting of Judicial Conference

The Judicial Conference, at the September 20, 1989 meeting, provided in part that Item 21 takes effect on December 21, 1989. The Conference further provided that: "The remaining fees, Items 20 and 22, take effect on January 11, 1990, pending approval of the Appropriations Committees."

Registry Fund Fees—Item 19 (54 F.R. 20407, May 11, 1989)

Effective June 12, 1989, a fee will be assessed for handling funds deposited in noncriminal proceedings with the court and held in interest bearing accounts or instruments pursuant to 28 U.S.C. § 2041 and Federal Rules of Civil Procedure rule 67. For new accounts, i.e., investments made on or after June 12, 1989, the fee will be equal to the first 45 days income earned on the deposit. Each subsequent deposit of new principal in the same case or proceeding will be subject to the fee. Reinvestment of prior deposits will not be subject to the fee. For existing accounts, i.e., investments held by the court prior to June 12, 1989, a fee will be assessed equal to the first 45 days of income earned beginning 30 days after June 12, 1989. Subsequent deposits of new principal in the same account will be subject to the fee. Subsequent reinvestment of existing deposits will not be subject to the fee.

The fee will apply only once to each sum deposited regardless of the length of time deposits are held and will not exceed income actually earned on the account.

The fee does not apply in the District Courts of Guam, Northern Mariana Islands, the Virgin Islands, the United States Claims Court, or other courts whose fees are not set under 28 U.S.C. § 1930.

Registry Fund Fees—Item 19 (55 F.R. 42867, October 24, 1990)

Effective December 1, 1990, the registry fee assessment provisions were revised and converted from a one-time charge equal to all income earned in the first 45 days of the investment to a charge of 10 percent of the income earned while funds are held in the court registry. Additionally, the fee was extended to any funds placed in the court's registry and invested regardless of the nature of the action underlying the deposit.

The new method will not be applied on investments in cases from which a fee has been exacted based on the prior method (interest earned in the first 45 days the funds were invested or the first 45 days following July 12, 1989). The new method will also not be applied in cases where the investment instrument has a maturity date greater than one year, but where a fee under the prior method applies but has not been deducted.

The fee does not apply in the District Courts of Guam, the Northern Mariana Islands, the Virgin Islands, the United States Claims Court, or any other federal court whose fees are not set under 28 U.S.C. §§ 1913, 1914, and 1930.

Registry Fund Fees—Item 19 (56 F.R. 56356, November 4, 1991)

Effective February 3, 1992, the registry fee assessment provisions are revised and converted from a charge equal to 10 percent of the income earned while funds are held in the court's registry to a variable rate based on the amount deposited with the court and, in certain cases, the length of time funds are held in the court's registry.

The revised fee will be a fee of 10 percent of the total income received during each income period from investments of less than $100,000,000 of registry funds in income-bearing accounts. On investments exceeding $100,000,000 the 10 percent fee shall be reduced by one percent for each increment of $50,000,000 over the initial $100,000,000. For those deposits where funds are placed in the registry by court order for a time certain, for example, by the terms of an adjudicated trust, the fee will be further reduced. This further reduction will amount to 2.5 percent for each five-year interval or part thereof. The total minimum fee to be charged will be no less than two percent of the income on investments.

The following table sets out the fee schedule promulgated by this notice:

REGISTRY—SCHEDULE OF FEES

[% of income earned]

Amount of deposit*	0–5 yrs.	>5–10 yrs.	>10–15 yrs.	>15 yrs.
less than 100M	10	7.5	5.0	2.5
100M–150M	9	6.5	4.0	2.0
150M–200M	8	5.5	3.0	2.0
200M–250M	7	4.5	2.0	2.0
250M–300M	6	3.5	2.0	2.0
300M–350M	5	2.5	2.0	2.0
350M–400M	4	2.0	2.0	2.0
400M–450M	3	2.0	2.0	2.0
over 450M	2	2.0	2.0	2.0

* Except where otherwise authorized by the Director, each deposit into any account is treated separately in determining the fee.

The new fee applies to all earnings applied to investments on and after the effective date of this change, except for earnings on investments in cases being administered under the provisions of the May 11, 1989 notice [54 FR 20407], i.e., to which the fee equal to the first 45 days income is applicable.

The fee, as modified herein, will continue to apply to any case where the court has authorized the investment of funds placed in its custody or held by it in trust in its registry regardless of the nature of the underlying action.

The fee does not apply in the District Court of Guam, the Northern Mariana Islands, the Virgin Islands, the United States Claims Court, or any other Federal court whose fees are not set under 28 U.S.C. §§ 1913, 1914, and 1930.

HISTORICAL AND STATUTORY NOTES

References in Text

Chapter 7, 11, 12, or 13 of title 11, referred to in text, is 11 U.S.C.A. § 701 et seq., 11 U.S.C.A. § 1101 et seq., 11 U.S.C.A. § 1201 et seq., or 11 U.S.C.A. § 1301 et seq., respectively.

Section 673(2) of the Omnibus Budget Reconciliation Act of 1981, referred to in subsec. (f)(1), is Pub.L. 97–35, Title VI, § 673(2), Aug. 13, 1981, as added Pub.L. 105–285, Title II, § 201, Oct. 27, 1998, 112 Stat. 2729, which is classified to 42 U.S.C.A. § 9902(2).

Codifications

Pub.L. 99–591 is a corrected version of Pub.L. 99–500.

The Chapter 11 filing fee will not change from its current amount of $1,000. It appears that Congress intended to increase chapter 11 filing fees from $1,000 to $2,750. However, there is a drafting error in the language of the Deficit Reduction Act of 2005 which references the incorrect statutory subsection [Pub.L. 109–171, Title X, § 10101(a)(2), Feb. 8, 2006, 120 Stat. 184]. Thus, the chapter 11 fee, at this time, is unaltered. See 2006 Amendments note set out under this section.

Section 101(a) of Pub.L. 104–91, as amended by section 211 of Pub.L. 104–99, provided in part that section 111(a) of the General Provisions for the Department of Justice in Title I of the Departments of Commerce, Justice, and State, the Judiciary, and Related Agencies Appropriations Act, 1996 (H.R. 2076) as passed by the House of Representatives on Dec. 6, 1995, was enacted into permanent law. Such section 111(a) of H.R. 2076 amended subsec. (a)(6) of this section. See 1996 Amendments note set out under this section.

Miscellaneous Fees

Section 406(a) of Pub.L. 101–162 provided in part that: "Pursuant to section 1930(b) of title 28 [subsec. (b) of this section] the Judicial Conference of the United States shall prescribe a fee of $60 on motions seeking relief from the automatic stay under 11 U.S.C. section 362(b) [section 362(b) of Title 11, Bankruptcy] and motions to compel abandonment of property of the estate. The fees established pursuant to the preceding two sentences shall take effect 30 days after the enactment of this Act [Nov. 21, 1989]."

Accrual and Payment of Quarterly Fees in Chapter 11 Cases After Jan. 27, 1996; Confirmation Status of Plans

Section 101(a) of Pub.L. 104–91, as amended Pub.L. 104–99, Title II, § 211, Jan. 26, 1996, 110 Stat. 37; Pub.L. 104–208, Div. A, Title I, § 101(a) [Title I, § 109(d)], Sept. 30, 1996, 110 Stat. 3009–19, provided, in part: "That, notwithstanding any other provision of law, the fees under 28 U.S.C. 1930(a)(6) [subsec. (a)(6) of this section] shall accrue and be payable from and after January 27, 1996, in all cases (including, without limitation, any cases pending as of that date), regardless of confirmation status of their plans."

Collection and Disposition of Fees in Bankruptcy Cases

Section 404(a) of Pub. L. 101–162 provided that: "For fiscal year 1990 and hereafter, such fees as shall be collected for the preparation and mailing of notices in bankruptcy cases as prescribed by the Judicial Conference of the United States pursuant to 28 U.S.C. 1930(b) [subsec. (b) of this section] shall be deposited to the 'Courts of Appeals, District Courts, and Other Judicial Services, Salaries and Expenses' appropriation to be used for salaries and other expenses incurred in providing these services."

Court Fees for Electronic Access to Information

Judicial Conference to prescribe reasonable fees for collection by courts under this section for access to information available through automatic data processing equipment and fees to be deposited in Judiciary Automation Fund, see section 303 of Pub.L. 102–140, set out as a note under section 1913 of this title.

Issuance of Notices to Creditors and Other Interested Parties

Section 403 of Pub.L. 101–162 provided that: "Notwithstanding any other provision of law, for fiscal year 1990 and hereafter, (a) The Administrative Office of the United States Courts, or any other agency or instrumentality of the United States, is prohibited from restricting solely to staff of the Clerks of the United States Bankruptcy Courts the issuance of notices to creditors and other interested parties. (b) The Administrative Office shall permit and encourage the preparation and mailing of such notices to be performed by or at the expense of the debtors, trustees or such other interested parties as the Court may direct and approve. (c) The Director of the Administrative Office of the United States Courts shall make appropriate provisions for the use of and accounting for any postage required pursuant to such directives."

Report on Bankruptcy Fees

Section 111(d) of Pub.L. 103–121 provided that:

"(1) **Report required.**—Not later than March 31, 1998, the Judicial Conference of the United States shall submit to the Committees on the Judiciary of the House of Representatives and the Senate, a report relating to the bankruptcy fee system and the impact of such system on various participants in bankruptcy cases.

"(2) **Contents of report.**—Such report shall include—

"(A)(i) an estimate of the costs and benefits that would result from waiving bankruptcy fees payable by debtors who are individuals, and

"(ii) recommendations regarding various revenue sources to offset the net cost of waiving such fees; and

"(B)(i) an evaluation of the effects that would result in cases under chapters 11 and 13 of title 11, United States Code [sections 1101 et seq. and 1301 et seq., respectively, of Title 11, Bankruptcy], from using a graduated bankruptcy fee system based on assets, liabilities, or both of the debtor, and

"(ii) recommendations regarding various methods to implement such a graduated bankruptcy fee system.

"(3) **Waiver of fees in selected districts.**—For purposes of carrying out paragraphs (1) and (2), the Judicial Conference of the United States shall carry out in not more than six judicial districts, throughout the 3-year period beginning on October 1, 1994, a program under which fees payable under section 1930 of title 28, United States Code [this section], may be waived in cases under chapter 7 of title 11, United States Code [section 701 et seq. of Title 11], for debtors who are individuals unable to pay such fees in installments.

"**(4) Study of graduated fee system.**—For purposes of carrying out paragraphs (1) and (2), the Judicial Conference of the United States shall carry out, in not fewer than six judicial districts, a study to estimate the results that would occur in cases under chapters 11 and 13 of title 11, United States Code [sections 1101 et seq. and 1301 et seq., respectively, of Title 11], if filing fees payable under section 1930 of title 28, United States Code [this section], were paid on a graduated scale based on assets, liabilities, or both of the debtor."

§ 1931.   Disposition of filing fees

(a) Of the amounts paid to the clerk of court as a fee under section 1914(a) or as part of a judgment for costs under section 2412(a)(2) of this title, $190 shall be deposited into a special fund of the Treasury to be available to offset funds appropriated for the operation and maintenance of the courts of the United States.

(b) If the court authorizes a fee under section 1914(a) or an amount included in a judgment for costs under section 2412(a)(2) of this title of less than $250, the entire fee or amount, up to $190, shall be deposited into the special fund provided in this section.

(Added Pub.L. 99–500, Title I, § 101(b) [Title IV, § 407(c)], Oct. 18, 1986, 100 Stat. 1783–64, and Pub.L. 99–591, Title I, § 101(b) [Title IV, § 407(c)], Oct. 30, 1986, 100 Stat. 3341–64; amended Pub.L. 101–162, Title IV, § 406(d), Nov. 21, 1989, 103 Stat. 1016; Pub.L. 102–572, Title III, § 301(b), Oct. 29, 1992, 106 Stat. 4511; Pub.L. 104–317, Title IV, § 401(b), Oct. 19, 1996, 110 Stat. 3853; Pub.L. 108–447, Div. B, Title III, § 307(b), Dec. 8, 2004, 118 Stat. 2895.)

HISTORICAL AND STATUTORY NOTES

Codifications

Pub.L. 99–591 is a corrected version of Pub.L. 99–500.

PayGo Offset Expenditure Limitation

Pub.L. 112–121, § 3(d), May 25, 2012, 126 Stat. 348, provided that: "$42 of the incremental amounts collected by reason of the enactment of subsection (a) [amending 28 U.S.C.A. § 1930(a)(3)] shall be deposited in a special fund in the Treasury to be established after the date of enactment of this Act [May 25, 2012]. Such amounts shall be available for the purposes specified in section 1931(a) of title 28, United States Code [subsec. (a) of this section], but only to the extent specifically appropriated by an Act of Congress enacted after the date of enactment of this Act [May 25, 2012]."

[Pub.L. 112–121, § 3, and amendments made by Pub.L. 112–121, § 3, shall take effect 180 days after May 25, 2012, see Pub.L. 112–121, § 3(e), set out as a note under 28 U.S.C.A. § 589a.]

Expenditure Limitation

Pub.L. 109–171, Title X, § 10001(c), Feb. 8, 2006, 120 Stat. 183, provided that: "Incremental amounts collected by reason of the enactment of this section [Pub.L. 109–171, Title X, § 10001, Feb. 8, 2006, 120 Stat. 183, which amended 28 U.S.C.A. § 1914 and enacted this note and provisions set out as notes under 28 U.S.C.A. §§ 1913 and 1914] shall be deposited in a special fund in the Treasury to be established after the enactment of this Act [Feb. 8, 2006]. Such amounts shall be available for the purposes specified in section 1931(a) of title 28, United States Code [subsec. (a) of this section], but only to the extent specifically appropriated by an Act of Congress enacted after the enactment of this Act [Feb. 8, 2006]."

[This note effective 60 days after Feb. 8, 2006, see Pub.L. 109–171, § 10001(d), set out as a note under 28 U.S.C.A. § 1914]

Pub.L. 109–171, Title X, § 10101(b), Feb. 8, 2006, 120 Stat. 184, provided that: "Incremental amounts collected by reason of the amendments made by subsection (a) [amending 28 U.S.C.A. § 1930] shall be deposited in a special fund in the Treasury to be established after the enactment of this Act [Feb. 8, 2006]. Such amounts shall be available for the purposes specified in section 1931(a) of title 28, United States Code [subsec. (a) of this section], but only to the extent specifically appropriated by an Act of Congress enacted after the enactment of this Act [Feb. 8, 2006]."

[This note effective 60 days after Feb. 8, 2006, see Pub.L. 109–171, § 10101(c), set out as a note under 28 U.S.C.A. § 1930]

Disposition of Miscellaneous Fees

Pub.L. 106–518, Title I, § 102, Nov. 13, 2000, 114 Stat. 2411, provided that: "For fiscal year 2001 and each fiscal year thereafter, any portion of miscellaneous fees collected as prescribed by the Judicial Conference of the United States under sections 1913 [this section], 1914(b), 1926(a), 1930(b), and 1932 of title 28, United States Code, exceeding the amount of such fees in effect on September 30, 2000, shall be deposited into the special fund of the Treasury established under section 1931 of title 28, United States Code [this section]."

Collection and Deposit of Miscellaneous Bankruptcy Fees

Section 406(b) of Pub.L. 101–162, as amended Pub.L. 103–121, Title I, § 111(a)(3), (b)(4), Oct. 27, 1993, 107 Stat. 1164; Pub.L. 106–113, Div. B, § 1000(a)(1) [Title I, § 113], Nov. 29, 1999, 113 Stat. 1535, 1501A–20; Pub.L. 106–518, Title II, § 209(a), Nov. 13, 2000, 114 Stat. 2415; Pub.L. 109–8, Title III, § 325(c), Apr. 20, 2005, 119 Stat. 99; Pub.L. 109–13, Div. A, Title VI, § 6058(a), May 11, 2005, 119 Stat. 297; Pub.L. 112–121, § 3(c), May 25, 2012, 126 Stat. 348, provided that: "All fees as shall be hereafter collected for any service not of a kind described in any of the items enumerated as items 1 through 7 and as items 9 through 18, as in effect on November 21, 1989, of the bankruptcy miscellaneous fee schedule prescribed by the Judicial Conference of the United States under section 1930(b) of title 28, United States Code [28 U.S.C.A. § 1930(b)], 28.87 percent of the fees collected under section 1930(a)(1)(A) of that title [28 U.S.C.A. § 1930(a)(1)(A)], 35.00 percent of the fees collected under section 1930(a)(1)(B) of that title [28 U.S.C.A. § 1930(a)(1)(B)], and 33.33 percent of the fees collected under section 1930(a)(3) of that title [28 U.S.C.A. § 1930(a)(3)] shall be deposited as offsetting receipts to the fund established under section 1931 of that title [this section] and shall remain available to the Judiciary until expended to reimburse any appropriation for the amount paid out of such appropriation for expenses of the Courts of Appeals, District Courts, and other Judicial Services and the Administrative Office of the United States Courts. The Judicial Conference shall report to the Committees on Appropriations of the House of Representatives and the Senate on a quarterly basis beginning on the first day of each fiscal year regarding the sums deposited in said fund."

[Pub.L. 112–121, § 3, and amendments made by Pub.L. 112–121, § 3, shall take effect 180 days after May 25, 2012, see Pub.L. 112–121, § 3(e), set out as a note under 28 U.S.C.A. § 589a.]

[Pub.L. 109–8, § 325(c), as amended by Pub.L. 109–13, § 6058(a), amended this note effective immediately after the enactment of the Bankruptcy Abuse Prevention and Consumer Protection Act of 2005 [Pub.L. 109–8, Apr. 20, 2005, 119 Stat. 23], see Pub.L. 109–13, § 6058(b), set out as an Effective and Applicability Provisions note under 28 U.S.C.A. § 589a.]

[Amendment of this note by Pub.L. 109–8, § 325(c), to become effective during the 2-year period beginning on Apr. 20, 2005, under the terms of Pub.L. 109–8, § 325(d), but was omitted in the amendment of Pub.L. 109–8, § 325 by Pub.L. 109–13, § 6058(a); see Pub.L. 109–8, § 325(d), as amended by Pub.L. 109–13, § 6058(a), set out as a Sunset Provisions note under 28 U.S.C.A. § 589a.]

[For termination, effective May 15, 2000, of provisions relating to a quarterly report to the Committees on Appropriations of the House of Representatives and the Senate in section 406(b) of Pub.L. 101–162, as amended, set out as a note above, see Pub.L. 104–66, § 3003, as amended, set out as a note under 31 U.S.C.A. § 1113 and page 12 of House Document No. 103–7.]

[Amendment of this note by Pub.L. 106–113, [§ 113], effective 30 days after Nov. 29, 1999, see Pub.L. 106–113, [§ 113], set out as a note under section 589a of this title.]

[Pub.L. 106–518, Title II, § 209(b), Nov. 13, 2000, 114 Stat. 2415, provided that: "The amendment made by subsection (a) [amending this note] shall not apply with respect to fees collected before the date of enactment of this Act [Nov. 13, 2000]."

[Section 111(a) of Pub.L. 103–121 provided in part that amendment of this note by section 111(a)(3) of Pub.L. 103–121 is effective 30 days after Oct. 27, 1993.]

[Section 111(b) of Pub.L. 103–121 provided in part that amendment of this note by section 111(b)(4) of Pub.L. 103–121 is effective 30 days after Oct. 27, 1993.]

Disposition of Fees

Section 404 of Pub.L. 104–317 provided that:

"**(a) Disposition of attorney admission fees.**—For each fee collected for admission of an attorney to practice, as prescribed by the Judicial Conference of the United States pursuant to section 1914 of title 28, United States Code [section 1914 of this title], $30 of that portion of the fee exceeding $20 shall be deposited into the special fund of the Treasury established under section 1931 of title 28, United States Code [this section]. Any portion exceeding $5 of the fee for a duplicate certificate of admission or certificate of good standing, as prescribed by the Judicial Conference of the United States pursuant to section 1914 of title 28, United States Code [section 1914 of this title], shall be deposited into the special fund of the Treasury established under section 1931 of title 28, United States Code [this section].

"**(b) Disposition of bankruptcy complaint filing fees.**—For each fee collected for filing an adversary complaint in a bankruptcy proceeding, as established in Item 6 of the Bankruptcy Court Miscellaneous Fee Schedule prescribed by the Judicial Conference of the United States [set out under section 1930 of this title] pursuant to section 1930(b) of title 28, United States Code [section 1930(b) of this title], the portion of the fee exceeding $120 shall be deposited into the special fund of the Treasury established under section 1931 of title 28, United States Code [this section].

"**(c) Effective date.**—This section shall take effect 60 days after the date of the enactment of this Act [Oct. 19, 1996]."

§ 1932.[1]   Judicial Panel on Multidistrict Litigation

The Judicial Conference of the United States shall prescribe from time to time the fees and costs to be charged and collected by the Judicial Panel on Multidistrict Litigation.

(Added Pub.L. 104–317, Title IV, § 403(a)(1), Oct. 19, 1996, 110 Stat. 3854.)

JUDICIAL CONFERENCE SCHEDULE OF FEES

Judicial Panel on Multidistrict Litigation Fee Schedule*

(Effective September 1, 2018)

Following are fees to be charged for services to be performed by the clerk of the Judicial Panel on Multidistrict Litigation[1].

No fees are to be charged for services rendered on behalf of the United States, with the exception of those specifically prescribed in items 1 and 3. No fees under this schedule shall be charged to federal agencies or programs which are funded from judiciary appropriations, including, but not limited to, agencies, organizations, and individuals providing services authorized by the Criminal Justice Act, 18 U.S.C. § 3006A.

(1)   For every search of the records of the court conducted by the clerk of the court or a deputy clerk, $31 per name or item searched. This fee shall apply to services rendered on behalf of the United States if the information requested is available through electronic access.

(2)   For certification of any document or paper, whether the certification is made directly on the document or by separate instrument, $11.

(3)

    a.   For reproducing any record or paper, $.50 per page. This fee shall apply to paper copies made from either: (1) original documents; or (2) microfiche or microfilm reproductions

---

[1]   Another section 1932 is set out after this section.

*   [The Electronic Public Access Fee Schedule is set out in this volume, *supra*, in the notes following 28 U.S.C. § 1913. Ed.]

[1]   [Footnote to text of Judicial Conference Schedule of Fees:] Issued in accordance with 28 U.S.C. § 1932.

of the original records. This fee shall apply to services rendered on behalf of the United States if the record or paper requested is available through electronic access.

b.   For reproducing and transmitting in any manner a copy of an electronic record stored outside of the court's electronic case management system, including but not limited to, document files, audio recordings, and video recordings, $31 per record provided.

(4)   For retrieval of one box of records from a Federal Records Center, National Archives, or other storage location removed from the place of business of the court, $64. For retrievals involving multiple boxes, $39 for each additional box. For electronic retrievals, $10 plus any charges assessed by the Federal Records Center, National Archives, or other storage location removed from the place of business of the courts.

(5)   For any payment returned or denied for insufficient funds, $53.

§ 1932.[1]   Revocation of earned release credit

In any civil action brought by an adult convicted of a crime and confined in a Federal correctional facility, the court may order the revocation of such earned good time credit under section 3624(b) of title 18, United States Code, that has not yet vested, if, on its own motion or the motion of any party, the court finds that—

(1)   the claim was filed for a malicious purpose;

(2)   the claim was filed solely to harass the party against which it was filed; or

(3)   the claimant testifies falsely or otherwise knowingly presents false evidence or information to the court.

(Added Pub.L. 104–134, Title I, § 101[(a)][Title VIII, § 809(a)], Apr. 26, 1996, 110 Stat. 1321–76; renumbered Title I Pub.L. 104–140, § 1(a), May 2, 1996, 110 Stat. 1327.)

HISTORICAL AND STATUTORY NOTES

Severability of Provisions

If any provision of section 101[a] [Title VIII] of Pub.L. 104–134, an amendment made by such Title, or the application of such provision or amendment to any person or circumstance is held to be unconstitutional, the remainder of such Title, the amendments made by such Title, and the application of the provisions of such Title to any person or circumstance not affected thereby, see section 101[a] [Title VIII, § 810] of Pub.L. 104–134, set out as a note under section 3626 of Title 18, Crimes and Criminal Procedure.

CHAPTER 125—PENDING ACTIONS AND JUDGMENTS

§ 1961.   Interest

(a)   Interest shall be allowed on any money judgment in a civil case recovered in a district court. Execution therefor may be levied by the marshal, in any case where, by the law of the State in which such court is held, execution may be levied for interest on judgments recovered in the courts of the State. Such interest shall be calculated from the date of the entry of the judgment, at a rate equal to the weekly average 1-year constant maturity Treasury yield, as published by the Board of Governors

---

[1]   [Footnote to Section 1932 heading:] Another section 1932 is set out preceding this section.

of the Federal Reserve System, for the calendar week preceding.[1] the date of the judgment. The Director of the Administrative Office of the United States Courts shall distribute notice of that rate and any changes in it to all Federal judges.

(b) Interest shall be computed daily to the date of payment except as provided in section 2516(b) of this title and section 1304(b) of title 31, and shall be compounded annually.

(c)(1) This section shall not apply in any judgment of any court with respect to any internal revenue tax case. Interest shall be allowed in such cases at the underpayment rate or overpayment rate (whichever is appropriate) established under section 6621 of the Internal Revenue Code of 1986.

(2) Except as otherwise provided in paragraph (1) of this subsection, interest shall be allowed on all final judgments against the United States in the United States Court of Appeals for the Federal circuit,[2] at the rate provided in subsection (a) and as provided in subsection (b).

(3) Interest shall be allowed, computed, and paid on judgments of the United States Court of Federal Claims only as provided in paragraph (1) of this subsection or in any other provision of law.

(4) This section shall not be construed to affect the interest on any judgment of any court not specified in this section.

(June 25, 1948, c. 646, 62 Stat. 957; Apr. 2, 1982, Pub.L. 97–164, Title III, § 302(a), 96 Stat. 55; Sept. 13, 1982, Pub.L. 97–258, § 2(m)(1), 96 Stat. 1062; Jan. 12, 1983, Pub.L. 97–452, § 2(d)(1), 96 Stat. 2478; Oct. 22, 1986, Pub.L. 99–514, § 2, Title XV, § 1511(c)(17), 100 Stat. 2095, 2745; Oct. 29, 1992, Pub.L. 102–572, Title IX, § 902(b)(1), 106 Stat. 4516; Dec. 21, 2000, Pub.L. 106–554, § 1(a)(7) [Title III, § 307(d)(1)], 114 Stat. 2763, 2763A–636.)

HISTORICAL AND STATUTORY NOTES

References in Text

Section 6621 of the Internal Revenue Code of 1986, referred to in subsec. (c)(1), is classified to section 6621 of Title 26, Internal Revenue Code.

Codifications

Amendment of subsec. (b) by Pub.L. 97–452, substituting "section 1304(b) of title 31" for "section 1302 of the Act of July 27, 1956 (31 U.S.C. 724a)" was executed without reference to the intervening amendment by Pub.L. 97–258, as the probable intent of Congress.

Calculation of Interest

The method of calculation of interest on money judgments in civil cases recovered in district courts changed as of December 21, 2000, the date of enactment of Pub.L. 106–554, § 1(a)(7) [Title III, § 307(d)(1)] which amended subsec. (a) of this section. It was formerly calculated at a rate equal to the coupon issue yield equivalent (as determined by the Secretary of the Treasury) of the average accepted auction price for the last auction of fifty-two week United States Treasury bills * * *. It is now calculated at a rate equal to the weekly average 1-year constant maturity Treasury yield, as published by the Board of Governors of the Federal Reserve System. For information regarding weekly releases, see *www.federalreserve.gov.*

§ 1962.   Lien

Every judgment rendered by a district court within a State shall be a lien on the property located in such State in the same manner, to the same extent and under the same conditions as a judgment of a court of general jurisdiction in such State, and shall cease to be a lien in the same manner and time. This section does not apply to judgments entered in favor of the United States. Whenever the law of any State requires a judgment of a State court to be registered, recorded, docketed or indexed, or any other act to be done, in a particular manner, or in a certain office or county or parish before

---

[1]   [Footnote to 28 U.S.C. § 1961(a):] So in original. The period probably should not appear.

[2]   [Footnote to 28 U.S.C. § 1961(c)(2):] So in original. Probably should be capitalized.

such lien attaches, such requirements shall apply only if the law of such State authorizes the judgment of a court of the United States to be registered, recorded, docketed, indexed or otherwise conformed to rules and requirements relating to judgments of the courts of the State.

(June 25, 1948, c. 646, 62 Stat. 958; Nov. 29, 1990, Pub.L. 101–647, Title XXXVI, § 3627, 104 Stat. 4965.)

§ 1963.   Registration of judgments for enforcement in other districts

A judgment in an action for the recovery of money or property entered in any court of appeals, district court, bankruptcy court, or in the Court of International Trade may be registered by filing a certified copy of the judgment in any other district or, with respect to the Court of International Trade, in any judicial district, when the judgment has become final by appeal or expiration of the time for appeal or when ordered by the court that entered the judgment for good cause shown. Such a judgment entered in favor of the United States may be so registered any time after judgment is entered. A judgment so registered shall have the same effect as a judgment of the district court of the district where registered and may be enforced in like manner.

A certified copy of the satisfaction of any judgment in whole or in part may be registered in like manner in any district in which the judgment is a lien.

The procedure prescribed under this section is in addition to other procedures provided by law for the enforcement of judgments.

(June 25, 1948, c. 646, 62 Stat. 958; Aug. 23, 1954, c. 837, 68 Stat. 772; July 7, 1958, Pub.L. 85–508, § 12(o), 72 Stat. 349; Nov. 19, 1988, Pub.L. 100–702, Title X, § 1002(a), (b)(1), 102 Stat. 4664; Nov. 29, 1990, Pub.L. 101–647, Title XXXVI, § 3628, 104 Stat. 4965; Oct. 19, 1996, Pub.L. 104–317, Title II, § 203(a), 110 Stat. 3849.)

[§ 1963A. Repealed. Pub.L. 100–702, Title X, § 1002(b)(2), Nov. 19, 1988, 102 Stat. 4664]

HISTORICAL AND STATUTORY NOTES

Section, added Pub.L. 96–417, Title V, § 511(a), Oct. 10, 1980, 94 Stat. 1743, provided for registration of judgments of the Court of International Trade. See section 1963 of this title.

Effective Date of Repeal

Section repealed 90 days after Nov. 19, 1988, see section 1002(c) of Pub.L. 100–702, set out as a note under section 1963 of this title.

§ 1964.   Constructive notice of pending actions

Where the law of a State requires a notice of an action concerning real property pending in a court of the State to be registered, recorded, docketed, or indexed in a particular manner, or in a certain office or county or parish in order to give constructive notice of the action as it relates to the real property, and such law authorizes a notice of an action concerning real property pending in a United States district court to be registered, recorded, docketed, or indexed in the same manner, or in the same place, those requirements of the State law must be complied with in order to give constructive notice of such an action pending in a United States district court as it relates to real property in such State.

(Added Pub.L. 85–689, § 1(a), Aug. 20, 1958, 72 Stat. 683.)

CHAPTER 127—EXECUTIONS AND JUDICIAL SALES

§ 2001.   Sale of realty generally

(a)   Any realty or interest therein sold under any order or decree of any court of the United States shall be sold as a whole or in separate parcels at public sale at the courthouse of the county, parish, or city in which the greater part of the property is located, or upon the premises or some parcel thereof located therein, as the court directs. Such sale shall be upon such terms and conditions as the court directs.

Property in the possession of a receiver or receivers appointed by one or more district courts shall be sold at public sale in the district wherein any such receiver was first appointed, at the courthouse of the county, parish, or city situated therein in which the greater part of the property in such district is located, or on the premises or some parcel thereof located in such county, parish, or city, as such court directs, unless the court orders the sale of the property or one or more parcels thereof in one or more ancillary districts.

(b)   After a hearing, of which notice to all interested parties shall be given by publication or otherwise as the court directs, the court may order the sale of such realty or interest or any part thereof at private sale for cash or other consideration and upon such terms and conditions as the court approves, if it finds that the best interests of the estate will be conserved thereby. Before confirmation of any private sale, the court shall appoint three disinterested persons to appraise such property or different groups of three appraisers each to appraise properties of different classes or situated in different localities. No private sale shall be confirmed at a price less than two-thirds of the appraised value. Before confirmation of any private sale, the terms thereof shall be published in such newspaper or newspapers of general circulation as the court directs at least ten days before confirmation. The private sale shall not be confirmed if a bona fide offer is made, under conditions prescribed by the court, which guarantees at least a 10 per centum increase over the price offered in the private sale.

(c)   This section shall not apply to sales and proceedings under Title 11 or by receivers or conservators of banks appointed by the Comptroller of the Currency.

(June 25, 1948, c. 646, 62 Stat. 958; May 24, 1949, c. 139, § 99, 63 Stat. 104.)

§ 2002.   Notice of sale of realty

A public sale of realty or interest therein under any order, judgment or decree of any court of the United States shall not be made without notice published once a week for at least four weeks prior to the sale in at least one newspaper regularly issued and of general circulation in the county, state, or judicial district of the United States wherein the realty is situated.

If such realty is situated in more than one county, state, district or circuit, such notice shall be published in one or more of the counties, states, or districts wherein it is situated, as the court directs. The notice shall be substantially in such form and contain such description of the property by reference or otherwise as the court approves. The court may direct that the publication be made in other newspapers.

This section shall not apply to sales and proceedings under Title 11 or by receivers or conservators of banks appointed by the Comptroller of the Currency.

(June 25, 1948, c. 646, 62 Stat. 959; May 24, 1949, c. 139, § 100, 63 Stat. 104.)

§ 2003.   Marshal's incapacity after levy on or sale of realty

Whenever a United States marshal dies, is removed from office, or the term of his commission expires, after levying on realty or any interest therein under a writ of execution issued by a court of the United States, and before sale or other final disposition thereof, like process shall issue to the succeeding marshal and the same proceedings shall be had as if such contingency had not occurred.

Whenever any such contingency arises after a marshal has sold any realty or interest therein and before a deed is executed, the court may, on application by the purchaser, or the plaintiff in whose action the sale was made, setting forth the facts of the case and the reason why the title was not perfected by such marshal, order the succeeding marshal to perfect the title and execute a deed to the purchaser, upon payment of the purchase money and unpaid costs.

(June 25, 1948, c. 646, 62 Stat. 959; May 24, 1949, c. 139, § 101, 63 Stat. 104.)

§ 2004.   Sale of personalty generally

Any personalty sold under any order or decree of any court of the United States shall be sold in accordance with section 2001 of this title, unless the court orders otherwise.

This section shall not apply to sales and proceedings under Title 11 or by receivers or conservators of banks appointed by the Comptroller of the Currency.

(June 25, 1948, c. 646, 62 Stat. 959.)

§ 2005.   Appraisal of goods taken on execution

Whenever State law requires that goods taken on execution be appraised before sale, goods taken under execution issued from a court of the United States shall be appraised in like manner.

The United States marshal shall summon the appraisers in the same manner as the sheriff is required to summon appraisers under State law.

If the appraisers fail to attend and perform their required duties, the marshal may sell the goods without an appraisal. Appraisers attending and performing their duties, shall receive the fees allowed for appraisals under State law.

(June 25, 1948, c. 646, 62 Stat. 959.)

§ 2006.   Execution against revenue officer

Execution shall not issue against a collector or other revenue officer on a final judgment in any proceeding against him for any of his acts, or for the recovery of any money exacted by or paid to him and subsequently paid into the Treasury, in performing his official duties, if the court certifies that:

    (1)   probable cause existed; or

    (2)   the officer acted under the directions of the Secretary of the Treasury, the Director, Bureau of Alcohol, Tobacco, Firearms, and Explosives, Department of Justice, or other proper Government officer.

When such certificate has been issued, the amount of the judgment shall be paid out of the proper appropriation by the Treasury.

(June 25, 1948, c. 646, 62 Stat. 960; Nov. 25, 2002, Pub.L. 107–296, Title XI, § 1112(*l*), 116 Stat. 2277.)

§ 2007.   Imprisonment for debt

    (a)   A person shall not be imprisoned for debt on a writ of execution or other process issued from a court of the United States in any State wherein imprisonment for debt has been abolished. All modifications, conditions, and restrictions upon such imprisonment provided by State law shall apply to any writ of execution or process issued from a court of the United States in accordance with the procedure applicable in such State.

(b) Any person arrested or imprisoned in any State on a writ of execution or other process issued from any court of the United States in a civil action shall have the same jail privileges and be governed by the same regulations as persons confined in like cases on process issued from the courts of such State. The same requirements governing discharge as are applicable in such State shall apply. Any proceedings for discharge shall be conducted before a United States magistrate judge for the judicial district wherein the defendant is held.

(June 25, 1948, c. 646, 62 Stat. 960; Oct. 17, 1968, Pub.L. 90–578, Title IV, § 402(b)(2), 82 Stat. 1118; Dec. 1, 1990, Pub.L. 101–650, Title III, § 321, 104 Stat. 5117.)

HISTORICAL AND STATUTORY NOTES

Change of Name

"United States magistrate judge" substituted for "United States magistrate" in text pursuant to section 321 of Pub.L. 101–650, set out as a note under 28 U.S.C.A. § 631. Previously, United States commissioners, referred to in text, were replaced by United States magistrates pursuant to Pub.L. 90–578, Oct. 17, 1968, 82 Stat. 1118. See chapter 43 of Title 28, 28 U.S.C.A. § 631 et seq.

CHAPTER 129—MONEYS PAID INTO COURT

§ 2041.   Deposit of moneys in pending or adjudicated cases

All moneys paid into any court of the United States, or received by the officers thereof, in any case pending or adjudicated in such court, shall be forthwith deposited with the Treasurer of the United States or a designated depositary, in the name and to the credit of such court.

This section shall not prevent the delivery of any such money to the rightful owners upon security, according to agreement of parties, under the direction of the court.

(June 25, 1948, c. 646, 62 Stat. 960; Sept. 13, 1982, Pub.L. 97–258, § 2(g)(4)(C), 96 Stat. 1061.)

HISTORICAL AND STATUTORY NOTES

Registry Administration Account

Pub.L. 100–459, Title IV, Oct. 1, 1988, 102 Stat. 2211, provided in part: "That any funds hereafter collected by the Judiciary as a charge for services rendered in administering accounts kept in a court's registry shall be deposited into a separate account entitled 'Registry Administration Account' in the Treasury of the United States. Such funds shall remain available to the Judiciary until expended to reimburse any appropriation for the amount paid out of such appropriation for expenses of the Courts of Appeals, District Courts and Other Judicial Services and the Administrative Office of the United States Courts."

§ 2042.   Withdrawal

No money deposited under section 2041 of this title shall be withdrawn except by order of court.

In every case in which the right to withdraw money deposited in court under section 2041 has been adjudicated or is not in dispute and such money has remained so deposited for at least five years unclaimed by the person entitled thereto, such court shall cause such money to be deposited in the Treasury in the name and to the credit of the United States. Any claimant entitled to any such money may, on petition to the court and upon notice to the United States attorney and full proof of the right thereto, obtain an order directing payment to him.

(June 25, 1948, c. 646, 62 Stat. 960; Sept. 13, 1982, Pub.L. 97–258, § 2(g)(4)(D), 96 Stat. 1061.)

§ 2043. Deposit of other moneys

Except for public moneys deposited under section 2041 of this title, each clerk of the United States courts shall deposit public moneys that the clerk collects into a checking account in the Treasury, subject to disbursement by the clerk. At the end of each accounting period, the earned part of public moneys accruing to the United States shall be deposited in the Treasury to the credit of the appropriate receipt accounts.

(Added Pub.L. 97–258, § 2(g)(4)(E), Sept. 13, 1982, 96 Stat. 1061.)

§ 2044. Payment of fine with bond money

On motion of the United States attorney, the court shall order any money belonging to and deposited by or on behalf of the defendant with the court for the purposes of a criminal appearance bail bond (trial or appeal) to be held and paid over to the United States attorney to be applied to the payment of any assessment, fine, restitution, or penalty imposed upon the defendant. The court shall not release any money deposited for bond purposes after a plea or a verdict of the defendant's guilt has been entered and before sentencing except upon a showing that an assessment, fine, restitution or penalty cannot be imposed for the offense the defendant committed or that the defendant would suffer an undue hardship. This section shall not apply to any third party surety.

(Added Pub.L. 101–647, Title XXXVI, § 3629(a), Nov. 29, 1990, 104 Stat. 4966.)

§ 2045. Investment of court registry funds

(a) The Director of the Administrative Office of the United States Courts, or the Director's designee under subsection (b), may request the Secretary of the Treasury to invest funds received under section 2041 in public debt securities with maturities suitable to the needs of the funds, as determined by the Director or the Director's designee, and bearing interest at a rate determined by the Secretary of the Treasury, taking into consideration current market yields on outstanding marketable obligations of the United States of comparable maturity.

(b) The Director may designate the clerk of a court described in section 610 to exercise the authority conferred by subsection (a).

(Added Pub.L. 110–406, § 8(a), Oct. 13, 2008, 122 Stat. 4293.)

CHAPTER 131—RULES OF COURTS

§ 2071. Rule-making power generally

(a) The Supreme Court and all courts established by Act of Congress may from time to time prescribe rules for the conduct of their business. Such rules shall be consistent with Acts of Congress and rules of practice and procedure prescribed under section 2072 of this title.

(b) Any rule prescribed by a court, other than the Supreme Court, under subsection (a) shall be prescribed only after giving appropriate public notice and an opportunity for comment. Such rule shall take effect upon the date specified by the prescribing court and shall have such effect on pending proceedings as the prescribing court may order.

(c)(1) A rule of a district court prescribed under subsection (a) shall remain in effect unless modified or abrogated by the judicial council of the relevant circuit.

(2) Any other rule prescribed by a court other than the Supreme Court under subsection (a) shall remain in effect unless modified or abrogated by the Judicial Conference.

(d) Copies of rules prescribed under subsection (a) by a district court shall be furnished to the judicial council, and copies of all rules prescribed by a court other than the Supreme Court under subsection (a) shall be furnished to the Director of the Administrative Office of the United States Courts and made available to the public.

(e) If the prescribing court determines that there is an immediate need for a rule, such court may proceed under this section without public notice and opportunity for comment, but such court shall promptly thereafter afford such notice and opportunity for comment.

(f) No rule may be prescribed by a district court other than under this section.

(June 25, 1948, c. 646, 62 Stat. 961; May 24, 1949, c. 139, § 102, 63 Stat. 104; Nov. 19, 1988, Pub.L. 100–702, Title IV, § 403(a)(1), 102 Stat. 4650.)

HISTORICAL AND STATUTORY NOTES

Effective and Applicability Provisions

1988 Acts. Section 407 of Title IV of Pub.L. 100–702 provided that: "This title [enacting sections 332(d)(4), 604(a)(19) [redesignated (a)(20)], 2071(b)–(f), and 2072–2074 of this title; amending sections 331, 332(d)(1), 372(c)(11), 636(d), 2071(a) [formerly designated 2071], and 2077(b) of this title and sections 460n–8 of Title 16, Conservation and 3402 of Title 18, Crimes and Criminal Procedure; redesignating as 604(a)(23) former section 604(a)(18) of this title; repealing former section 2072 and section 2076 of this title and sections 3771 and 3772 of Title 18; and enacting provisions set out as notes under this section] shall take effect on December 1, 1988."

1983 Acts. Pub.L. 97–462, § 4, Jan. 12, 1983, 96 Stat. 2530, provided: "The amendments made by this Act [which amended Rule 4 of the Federal Rules of Civil Procedure, added Form 18-A, Appendix of Forms, enacted provisions set out as notes under this section, and amended section 951 of Title 18, Crimes and Criminal Procedure] shall take effect 45 days after the enactment of this Act [Jan. 12, 1983]."

Savings Provisions

Section 406 of Title IV of Pub.L. 100–702 provided that: "The rules prescribed in accordance with law before the effective date of this title [Dec. 1, 1988] and in effect on the date of such effective date [Dec. 1, 1988] shall remain in force until changed pursuant to the law as amended by this title [see Effective and Applicability Provisions of 1988 Amendments note under this section]."

Short Title

1983 Acts. Pub.L. 97–462, § 1, Jan. 12, 1983, 96 Stat. 2527, provided: "That this Act [which amended Rule 4 of the Federal Rules of Civil Procedure, enacted Form 18-A, Appendix of Forms, enacted provisions set out as notes under this section, and amended section 951 of Title 18, Crimes and Criminal Procedure] may be cited as the 'Federal Rules of Civil Procedure Amendments Act of 1982'."

Rulemaking Authority of Supreme Court and Judicial Conference

Pub.L. 109–2, § 8, Feb. 18, 2005, 119 Stat. 14, provided that: "Nothing in this Act [the Class Action Fairness Act of 2005, which enacted this note and 28 U.S.C.A. §§ 1453 and 1711 to 1715, amended 28 U.S.C.A. §§ 1332, 1335, and 1603, and enacted provisions set out as notes under 28 U.S.C.A. §§ 1332, 1711, and 2074] shall restrict in any way the authority of the Judicial Conference and the Supreme Court to propose and prescribe general rules of practice and procedure under chapter 131 of title 28, United States Code [this chapter]."

[Enactment of this note by Class Action Fairness Act of 2005, Pub.L. 109–2, Feb. 18, 2005, 119 Stat. 4, applicable to any civil action commenced on or after Feb. 18, 2005, see Pub.L. 109–2, § 9, set out as a note under 28 U.S.C.A. § 1332.]

Admiralty Rules

The Rules of Practice in Admiralty and Maritime Cases, promulgated by the Supreme Court on Dec. 20, 1920, effective Mar. 7, 1921, as revised, amended, and supplemented, were rescinded, effective July 1, 1966, in accordance with the general unification of civil and admiralty procedure which became effective July 1, 1966. Provision for certain distinctively maritime remedies were preserved however in the Supplemental Rules for Certain Admiralty and Maritime Claims, Rules A to F, Federal Rules of Civil Procedure.

Tax Court Rulemaking Not Affected

Section 405 of Title IV of Pub.L. 100–702 provided that: "The amendments made by this title [see Effective and Applicability Provisions of 1988 Amendments note set out under this section] shall not affect the authority of the Tax Court to prescribe rules under section 7453 of the Internal Revenue Code of 1986 [section 7453 of Title 26, Internal Revenue Code]."

§ 2072.   Rules of procedure and evidence; power to prescribe

(a)   The Supreme Court shall have the power to prescribe general rules of practice and procedure and rules of evidence for cases in the United States district courts (including proceedings before magistrate judges thereof) and courts of appeals.

(b)   Such rules shall not abridge, enlarge or modify any substantive right. All laws in conflict with such rules shall be of no further force or effect after such rules have taken effect.

(c)   Such rules may define when a ruling of a district court is final for the purposes of appeal under section 1291 of this title.

(Added Pub.L. 100–702, Title IV, § 401(a), Nov. 19, 1988, 102 Stat. 4648; amended Pub.L. 101–650, Title III, §§ 315, 321, Dec. 1, 1990, 104 Stat. 5115, 5117.)

HISTORICAL AND STATUTORY NOTES

Effective and Applicability Provisions

1988 Acts. Section effective Dec. 1, 1988, see section 407 of Pub.L. 100–702, set out as a note under section 2071 of this title.

Change of Name

"United States magistrate judge" substituted for "United States magistrate" in text pursuant to section 321 of Pub.L. 101–650, set out as a note under 28 U.S.C.A. § 631.

Prior Provisions

A prior section 2072, Acts June 25, 1948, c. 646, 62 Stat. 961; May 24, 1949, c. 139, § 103, 63 Stat. 104; July 18, 1949, c. 343, § 2, 63 Stat. 446; May 10, 1950, c. 174, § 2, 64 Stat. 158; July 7, 1958, Pub.L. 85–508, § 12(m), 72 Stat. 348; Nov. 6, 1966, Pub.L. 89–773, § 1, 80 Stat. 1323, which authorized the Supreme Court to prescribe rules of civil procedure, was repealed by Pub.L. 100–702, Title IV, §§ 401(a), 407, Nov. 19, 1988, 102 Stat. 4648, 4652, effective Dec. 1, 1988.

Admiralty Rules

The Rules of Practice in Admiralty and Maritime Cases, promulgated by the Supreme Court on Dec. 20, 1920, effective Mar. 7, 1921, as revised, amended, and supplemented, were rescinded, effective July 1, 1966, in accordance with the general unification of civil and admiralty procedure which became effective July 1, 1966. Provision for certain distinctively maritime remedies were preserved however, in the Supplemental Rules for Certain Admiralty and Maritime Claims, Rules A to F, Federal Rules of Civil Procedure, this title.

Applicability to Virgin Islands

Rules of civil procedure promulgated under this section as applicable to the District Court of the Virgin Islands, see section 1614 of Title 48, Territories and Insular Possessions.

§ 2073.   Rules of procedure and evidence; method of prescribing

(a)(1)   The Judicial Conference shall prescribe and publish the procedures for the consideration of proposed rules under this section.

(2)   The Judicial Conference may authorize the appointment of committees to assist the Conference by recommending rules to be prescribed under sections 2072 and 2075 of this title. Each such committee shall consist of members of the bench and the professional bar, and trial and appellate judges.

(b)   The Judicial Conference shall authorize the appointment of a standing committee on rules of practice, procedure, and evidence under subsection (a) of this section. Such standing committee shall review each recommendation of any other committees so appointed and recommend to the Judicial Conference rules of practice, procedure, and evidence and such changes in rules proposed by a committee appointed under subsection (a)(2) of this section as may be necessary to maintain consistency and otherwise promote the interest of justice.

(c)(1)   Each meeting for the transaction of business under this chapter by any committee appointed under this section shall be open to the public, except when the committee so meeting, in open session and with a majority present, determines that it is in the public interest that all or part of the remainder of the meeting on that day shall be closed to the public, and states the reason for so closing the meeting. Minutes of each meeting for the transaction of business under this chapter shall be maintained by the committee and made available to the public, except that any portion of such minutes, relating to a closed meeting and made available to the public, may contain such deletions as may be necessary to avoid frustrating the purposes of closing the meeting.

(2)   Any meeting for the transaction of business under this chapter, by a committee appointed under this section, shall be preceded by sufficient notice to enable all interested persons to attend.

(d)   In making a recommendation under this section or under section 2072 or 2075, the body making that recommendation shall provide a proposed rule, an explanatory note on the rule, and a written report explaining the body's action, including any minority or other separate views.

(e)   Failure to comply with this section does not invalidate a rule prescribed under section 2072 or 2075 of this title.

(Added Pub.L. 100–702, Title IV, § 401(a), Nov. 19, 1988, 102 Stat. 4649; amended Pub.L. 103–394, Title I, § 104(e), Oct. 22, 1994, 108 Stat. 4110.)

HISTORICAL AND STATUTORY NOTES

Effective and Applicability Provisions

1994 Acts. Amendment by Pub.L. 103–394 effective on Oct. 22, 1994, and not to apply with respect to cases commenced under Title 11 of the United States Code before Oct. 22, 1994, see section 702 of Pub.L. 103–394, set out as a note under section 101 of Title 11, Bankruptcy.

1988 Acts. Section effective Dec. 1, 1988, see section 407 of Pub.L. 100–702, set out as a note under section 2071 of this title.

Separability of Provisions

If any provision of or amendment made by Pub.L. 103–394 or the application of such provision or amendment to any person or circumstance is held to be unconstitutional, the remaining provisions of and amendments made by Pub.L. 103–394 and the application of such provisions and amendments to any person or circumstance shall not be affected thereby, see section 701 of Pub.L. 103–394, set out as a note under section 101 of Title 11, Bankruptcy.

Prior Provisions

A prior section 2073, Acts June 25, 1948, c. 646, 62 Stat. 961; May 24, 1949, c. 139, § 104, 63 Stat. 104; May 10, 1950, c. 174, § 3, 64 Stat. 158, which empowered the Supreme Court to prescribe, by general rules, the practice and procedure in admiralty and maritime cases in the district courts, was repealed by Pub.L. 89–773, § 2, Nov. 6, 1966, 80 Stat. 1323, which provided in part that the repeal of section 2073 should not operate to invalidate or repeal rules adopted under the authority of such section prior to the enactment of Pub.L. 89–773, which rules should remain in effect until superseded by rules prescribed under the authority of former section 2072 of this title as amended by Pub.L. 89–773. See sections 2071 to 2074 of this title.

More Complete Information Regarding Assets of the Estate

Pub.L. 109–8, Title IV, § 419, Apr. 20, 2005, 119 Stat. 109, provided that:

"**(a) In general.**—

"**(1) Disclosure.**—The Judicial Conference of the United States, in accordance with section 2075 of title 28 of the United States Code and after consideration of the views of the Director of the Executive Office for United States Trustees, shall propose amended Federal Rules of Bankruptcy Procedure and in accordance with rule 9009 of the Federal Rules of Bankruptcy Procedure [set out in Title 11] shall prescribe official bankruptcy forms directing debtors under chapter 11 of title 11 of United States Code [11 U.S.C.A. § 1101 et seq.], to disclose the information described in paragraph (2) by filing and serving periodic financial and other reports designed to provide such information.

"**(2) Information.**—The information referred to in paragraph (1) is the value, operations, and profitability of any closely held corporation, partnership, or of any other entity in which the debtor holds a substantial or controlling interest.

"**(b) Purpose.**—The purpose of the rules and reports under subsection (a) [of this note] shall be to assist parties in interest taking steps to ensure that the debtor's interest in any entity referred to in subsection (a)(2) [of this note] is used for the payment of allowed claims against debtor."

[Except as otherwise provided, amendments by Pub.L. 109–8 effective 180 days after April 20, 2005, and inapplicable with respect to cases commenced under Title 11 before the effective date, see Pub.L. 109–8, § 1501, set out as a note under 11 U.S.C.A. § 101.]

Standard Form Disclosure Statement and Plan

Pub.L. 109–8, Title IV, § 433, Apr. 20, 2005, 119 Stat. 110, provided that: "Within a reasonable period of time after the date of enactment of this Act [Apr. 20,. 2005], the Judicial Conference of the United States shall prescribe in accordance with rule 9009 of the Federal Rules of Bankruptcy Procedure [set out in Title 11] official standard form disclosure statements and plans of reorganization for small business debtors (as defined in section 101 of title 11, United States Code, as amended by this Act), designed to achieve a practical balance between—

"**(1)** the reasonable needs of the courts, the United States trustee, creditors, and other parties in interest for reasonably complete information; and

"**(2)** economy and simplicity for debtors."

[Except as otherwise provided, amendments by Pub.L. 109–8 effective 180 days after April 20, 2005, and inapplicable with respect to cases commenced under Title 11 before the effective date, see Pub.L. 109–8, § 1501, set out as a note under 11 U.S.C.A. § 101.]

Uniform Reporting Rules and Forms for Small Business Cases

Pub.L. 109–8, Title IV, § 435, Apr. 20, 2005, 119 Stat. 111, provided that:

"**(a) Proposal of rules and forms.**—The Judicial Conference of the United States shall propose in accordance with section 2073 of title 28 of the United States Code [this section] amended Federal Rules of Bankruptcy Procedure, and shall prescribe in accordance with rule 9009 of the Federal Rules of Bankruptcy Procedure [set out in Title 11] official bankruptcy forms, directing small business debtors to file periodic financial and other reports containing information, including information relating to—

"**(1)** the debtor's profitability;

"**(2)** the debtor's cash receipts and disbursements; and

"**(3)** whether the debtor is timely filing tax returns and paying taxes and other administrative expenses when due.

"**(b)** **Purpose.**—The rules and forms proposed under subsection (a) [of this note] shall be designed to achieve a practical balance among—

"**(1)** the reasonable needs of the bankruptcy court, the United States trustee, creditors, and other parties in interest for reasonably complete information;

"**(2)** a small business debtor's interest that required reports be easy and inexpensive to complete; and

"**(3)** the interest of all parties that the required reports help such debtor to understand such debtor's financial condition and plan the [sic] such debtor's future."

[Except as otherwise provided, amendments by Pub.L. 109–8 effective 180 days after April 20, 2005, and inapplicable with respect to cases commenced under Title 11 before the effective date, see Pub.L. 109–8, § 1501, set out as a note under 11 U.S.C.A. § 101.]

§ 2074.   Rules of procedure and evidence; submission to Congress; effective date

(a) The Supreme Court shall transmit to the Congress not later than May 1 of the year in which a rule prescribed under section 2072 is to become effective a copy of the proposed rule. Such rule shall take effect no earlier than December 1 of the year in which such rule is so transmitted unless otherwise provided by law. The Supreme Court may fix the extent such rule shall apply to proceedings then pending, except that the Supreme Court shall not require the application of such rule to further proceedings then pending to the extent that, in the opinion of the court in which such proceedings are pending, the application of such rule in such proceedings would not be feasible or would work injustice, in which event the former rule applies.

(b) Any such rule creating, abolishing, or modifying an evidentiary privilege shall have no force or effect unless approved by Act of Congress.

(Added Pub.L. 100–702, Title IV, § 401(a), Nov. 19, 1988, 102 Stat. 4649.)

HISTORICAL AND STATUTORY NOTES

Prior Provisions

A prior section 2074, Act July 27, 1954, c. 583, § 1, 68 Stat. 567, empowered the Supreme Court to prescribe rules for review of decisions of the Tax Court of the United States, prior to repeal by Pub.L. 89–773, § 2, Nov. 6, 1966, 80 Stat. 1323.

Effective and Applicability Provisions

1988 Acts. Section effective Dec. 1, 1988, see section 407 of Pub.L. 100–702, set out as a note under section 2071 of this title.

Amendment to Rule 23 of Federal Rules of Civil Procedure; Effective Date

Pub.L. 109–2, § 7, Feb. 18, 2005, 119 Stat. 13, provided that: "Notwithstanding any other provision of law, the amendments to rule 23 of the Federal Rules of Civil Procedure, which are set forth in the order entered by the Supreme Court of the United States on March 27, 2003, shall take effect on the date of enactment of this Act [Feb. 18, 2005] or on December 1, 2003 (as specified in that order), whichever occurs first."

[Enactment of this note by Class Action Fairness Act of 2005, Pub.L. 109–2, Feb. 18, 2005, 119 Stat. 4, applicable to any civil action commenced on or after Feb. 18, 2005, see Pub.L. 109–2, § 9, set out as a note under 28 U.S.C.A. § 1332.]

Modification of Amendments to Federal Rules of Criminal Procedure Proposed April 29, 2002; Effective Date

Pub.L. 107–273, Div. C, Title I, § 11019(a), Nov. 2, 2002, 116 Stat. 1825, provided that: "The proposed amendments to the Federal Rules of Criminal Procedure that are embraced by an order entered by the

Supreme Court of the United States on April 29, 2002, shall take effect on December 1, 2002, as otherwise provided by law, but with the amendments made in subsection (b) [amending Rule 16 of the Federal Rules of Criminal Procedure]."

Modification of Amendments to Federal Rules of Evidence Proposed on April 29, 1994, Effective Date

Pub.L. 103–322, Title IV, § 40141, Sept. 13, 1994, 108 Stat. 1918, provided that:

"**(a) Modification of proposed amendment.**—The proposed amendments to the Federal Rules of Evidence that are embraced by an order entered by the Supreme Court of the United States on April 29, 1994, shall take effect on December 1, 1994, as otherwise provided by law, but with the amendment made by subsection (b).

"**(b) Rule.**—[Amended Rule 412 of the Federal Rules of Evidence.]

"**(c) Technical amendment.**—[Amended table of contents for the Federal Rules of Evidence .]"

Modification of Amendments to Federal Rules of Criminal Procedure Proposed April 29, 1994; Effective Date

Pub.L. 103–322, Title XXIII, § 230101, Sept. 13, 1994, 108 Stat. 2077, provided that:

"**(a) Modification of proposed amendments.**—The proposed amendments to the Federal Rules of Criminal Procedure which are embraced by an order entered by the Supreme Court of the United States on April 29, 1994, shall take effect on December 1, 1994, as otherwise provided by law, but with the following amendments:

"**(b) In general.**—[Amended Rule 32 of the Federal Rules of Criminal Procedure.]

"**(c) Effective date.**—The amendments made by subsection (b) shall become effective on December 1, 1994."

Amendments to Civil Rules Proposed April 30, 1991

Pub.L. 102–198, § 11, Dec. 9, 1991, 105 Stat. 1626, provided that:

"**(a) Technical amendment.**—Rule 15(c)(3) of the Federal Rules of Civil Procedure for the United States Courts, as transmitted to the Congress by the Supreme Court pursuant to section 2074 of title 28, United States Code [this section], to become effective on December 1, 1991, is amended by striking 'Rule 4(m)' and inserting 'Rule 4(j)'.

"**(b) Amendment to Forms.**—Form 1-A, Notice of Lawsuit and Request for Waiver of Service of Summons, and Form 1-B, Waiver of Service of Summons, included in the transmittal by the Supreme Court described in subsection (a), shall not be effective and Form 18-A, Notice and Acknowledgment for Service by Mail, abrogated by the Supreme Court in such transmittal, effective December 1, 1991, shall continue in effect on or after that date."

Amendments to Civil Rules Proposed April 28, 1982

Pub.L. 97–462, § 5, Jan. 12, 1983, 96 Stat. 2530, provided: "The amendments to the Federal Rules of Civil Procedure [Rule 4], the effective date [Aug. 1, 1982] of which was delayed [to Oct. 1, 1983] by the Act [Pub.L. 97–227] entitled 'An Act to delay the effective date of proposed amendments to rule 4 of the Federal Rules of Civil Procedure', [proposed by the Supreme Court of the United States and transmitted to the Congress by the Chief Justice on Apr. 28, 1982], approved August 2, 1982 (96 Stat. 246), shall not take effect."

Pub.L. 97–227, Aug. 2, 1982, 96 Stat. 246, provided: "That notwithstanding the provisions of section 2072 of title 28, United States Code, [section 2072 of this title] the amendments to rule 4 of the Federal Rules of Civil Procedure as proposed by the Supreme Court of the United States and transmitted to the Congress by the Chief Justice on April 28, 1982, shall take effect on October 1, 1983, unless previously approved, disapproved, or modified by Act of Congress.

"**Sec. 2.** This Act shall be effective as of August 1, 1982, but shall not apply to the service of process that takes place between August 1, 1982, and the date of enactment of this Act [Aug. 2, 1982]."

Amendments to Criminal Rules and Rules of Evidence Proposed April 30, 1979; Postponement of Effective Date

Pub.L. 96–42, July 31, 1979, 93 Stat. 326, provided: "That notwithstanding any provision of section 3771 or 3772 of title 18 of the United States Code [section 3771 or 3772 of Title 18, Crimes and Criminal Procedure] or of section 2072, 2075, or 2076 of title 28 of the United States Code [sections 2072, 2075 and 2076 of this title] to the contrary—

"(1) the amendments proposed by the United States Supreme Court and transmitted by the Chief Justice on April 30, 1979, to the Federal Rules of Criminal Procedure affecting rules 11(e)(6), 17(h), 32(f), and 44(c), and adding new rules 26.2 and 32.1, and the amendment so proposed and transmitted to the Federal Rules of Evidence affecting rule 410, shall not take effect until December 1, 1980, or until and then only to the extent approved by Act of Congress, whichever is earlier; and

"(2) the amendment proposed by the United States Supreme Court and transmitted by the Chief Justice on April 30, 1979, affecting rule 40 of the Federal Rules of Criminal Procedure shall take effect on August 1, 1979, with the following amendments:

"(A) In the matter designated as paragraph (1) of subdivision (d), strike out 'in accordance with Rule 32.1(a).'

"(B) In the matter designated as paragraph (2) of subdivision (d), strike out 'in accordance with Rule 32.1(a)(1)'."

Approval and Effective Date of Rules Governing Section 2254 Cases and Section 2255 Proceedings for United States District Courts

Pub.L. 94–426, § 1, Sept. 28, 1976, 90 Stat. 1334, provided: "That the rules governing section 2254 cases in the United States district courts and the rules governing section 2255 proceedings for the United States district courts, as proposed by the United States Supreme Court, which were delayed by the Act entitled 'An Act to delay the effective date of certain proposed amendments to the Federal Rules of Criminal Procedure and certain other rules promulgated by the United States Supreme Court' (Public Law 94–349), are approved with the amendments set forth in section 2 of this Act and shall take effect as so amended, with respect to petitions under section 2254 and motions under section 2255 of title 28 of the United States Code [sections 2254 and 2255 of this title] filed on or after February 1, 1977."

Approval and Effective Date of Amendments Proposed November 20, 1972 and December 18, 1972

Pub.L. 93–595, § 3, Jan. 2, 1975, 88 Stat. 1949, provided that: "The Congress expressly approves the amendments to the Federal Rules of Civil Procedure [Rules 30(c), 32(c), 43 and 44.1] and the amendments to the Federal Rules of Criminal Procedure [Rules 26, 26.1 and 28], which are embraced by the orders entered by the Supreme Court of the United States on November 20, 1972, and December 18, 1972, and such amendments shall take effect on the one hundred and eightieth day beginning after the date of the enactment of this Act [Jan. 2, 1975]."

Congressional Approval Requirement for Proposed Rules of Evidence for United States Courts and Amendments to Federal Rules of Civil Procedure and Criminal Procedure; Suspension of Effectiveness of Such Rules

Pub.L. 93–12, Mar. 30, 1973, 87 Stat. 9, provided: "That notwithstanding any other provisions of law, the Rules of Evidence for United States Courts and Magistrates, the Amendments to the Federal Rules of Civil Procedure, and the Amendments to the Federal Rules of Criminal Procedure, which are embraced by the orders entered by the Supreme Court of the United States on Monday, November 20, 1972, and Monday, December 18, 1972, shall have no force or effect except to the extent, and with such amendments, as they may be expressly approved by Act of Congress."

§ 2075.   Bankruptcy rules

The Supreme Court shall have the power to prescribe by general rules, the forms of process, writs, pleadings, and motions, and the practice and procedure in cases under title 11.

Such rules shall not abridge, enlarge, or modify any substantive right.

The Supreme Court shall transmit to Congress not later than May 1 of the year in which a rule prescribed under this section is to become effective a copy of the proposed rule. The rule shall take effect no earlier than December 1 of the year in which it is transmitted to Congress unless otherwise provided by law.

The bankruptcy rules promulgated under this section shall prescribe a form for the statement required under section 707(b)(2)(C) of title 11 and may provide general rules on the content of such statement.

(Added Pub.L. 88–623, § 1, Oct. 3, 1964, 78 Stat. 1001; amended Pub.L. 95–598, Title II, § 247, Nov. 6, 1978, 92 Stat. 2672; Pub.L. 103–394, Title I, § 104(f), Oct. 22, 1994, 108 Stat. 4110; Pub.L. 109–8, Title XII, § 1232, Apr. 20, 2005, 119 Stat. 202.)

HISTORICAL AND STATUTORY NOTES

Effective and Applicability Provisions

2005 Acts. Except as otherwise provided, amendments by Pub.L. 109–8 effective 180 days after April 20, 2005, and inapplicable with respect to cases commenced under Title 11 before the effective date, see Pub.L. 109–8, § 1501, set out as a note under 11 U.S.C.A. § 101.

1994 Acts. Amendment by Pub.L. 103–394 effective on Oct. 22, 1994, and not to apply with respect to cases commenced under Title 11 of the United States Code before Oct. 22, 1994, see section 702 of Pub.L. 103–394, set out as a note under section 101 of Title 11, Bankruptcy.

1978 Acts. Amendment by Pub.L. 95–598 effective Nov. 6, 1978, see section 402(d) of Pub.L. 95–598, set out as a note preceding section 101 of Title 11, Bankruptcy.

Separability of Provisions

If any provision of or amendment made by Pub.L. 103–394 or the application of such provision or amendment to any person or circumstance is held to be unconstitutional, the remaining provisions of and amendments made by Pub.L. 103–394 and the application of such provisions and amendments to any person or circumstance shall not be affected thereby, see section 701 of Pub.L. 103–394, set out as a note under section 101 of Title 11, Bankruptcy.

Additional Rulemaking Power

Pub.L. 95–598, Title IV, § 410, Nov. 6, 1978, 92 Stat. 2687, provided that: "The Supreme Court may issue such additional rules of procedure, consistent with Acts of Congress, as may be necessary for the orderly transfer of functions and records and the orderly transition to the new bankruptcy court system created by this Act [see Tables for complete classification of Pub.L. 95–598]."

Applicability of Rules to Cases Under Title 11

Pub.L. 95–598, Title IV, § 405(d), Nov. 6, 1978, 92 Stat. 2685, provided that: "The rules prescribed under section 2075 of title 28 of the United States Code and in effect on September 30, 1979, shall apply to cases under title 11, to the extent not inconsistent with the amendments made by this Act, or with this Act [see Tables for complete classification of Pub.L. 95–598], until such rules are repealed or superseded by rules prescribed and effective under such section, as amended by section 248 of this Act."

Rules Promulgated by Supreme Court

Pub.L. 98–353, Title III, § 320, July 10, 1984, 98 Stat. 357, provided that: "The Supreme Court shall prescribe general rules implementing the practice and procedure to be followed under section 707(b) of title 11, United States Code [section 707(b) of Title 11, Bankruptcy]. Section 2075 of title 28, United States Code [this section], shall apply with respect to the general rules prescribed under this section."

[§ 2076.   Repealed. Pub.L. 100–702, Title IV, § 401(c), Nov. 19, 1988, 102 Stat. 4650]

HISTORICAL AND STATUTORY NOTES

Section, added Pub.L. 93–595, § 2(a)(1), Jan. 2, 1975, 88 Stat. 1948, and amended Pub.L. 94–149, § 2, Dec. 12, 1975, 89 Stat. 806, related to Federal Rules of Evidence prescribed by the Supreme Court and amendment thereof. See sections 2072 to 2074 of this title.

Effective Date of Repeal

Section repealed effective Dec. 1, 1988, see section 407 of Pub.L. 100–702, set out as a note under section 2071 of this title.

§ 2077.   Publication of rules; advisory committees

(a) The rules for the conduct of the business of each court of appeals, including the operating procedures of such court, shall be published. Each court of appeals shall print or cause to be printed necessary copies of the rules. The Judicial Conference shall prescribe the fees for sales of copies under section 1913 of this title, but the Judicial Conference may provide for free distribution of copies to members of the bar of each court and to other interested persons.

(b) Each court, except the Supreme Court, that is authorized to prescribe rules of the conduct of such court's business under section 2071 of this title shall appoint an advisory committee for the study of the rules of practice and internal operating procedures of such court and, in the case of an advisory committee appointed by a court of appeals, of the rules of the judicial council of the circuit. The advisory committee shall make recommendations to the court concerning such rules and procedures. Members of the committee shall serve without compensation, but the Director may pay travel and transportation expenses in accordance with section 5703 of title 5.

(Added Pub.L. 97–164, Title II, § 208(a), Apr. 2, 1982, 96 Stat. 54; amended Pub.L. 100–702, Title IV, § 401(b), Nov. 19, 1988, 102 Stat. 4650; Pub.L. 101–650, Title IV, § 406, Dec. 1, 1990, 104 Stat. 5124.)

HISTORICAL AND STATUTORY NOTES

Effective and Applicability Provisions

1990 Acts. Amendment by section 406 of Pub.L. 101–650 effective 90 days after Dec. 1, 1990, see section 407 of Pub.L. 101–650, set out as a note under section 332 of this title.

1988 Acts. Amendment by Pub.L. 100–702 effective Dec. 1, 1988, see section 407 of Pub.L. 100–702, set out as a note under section 2071 of this title.

1982 Acts. Section effective Oct. 1, 1982, see section 402 of Pub.L. 97–164, set out as a note under section 171 of this title.

CHAPTER 133—REVIEW—MISCELLANEOUS PROVISIONS

§ 2101.   Supreme Court; time for appeal or certiorari; docketing; stay

(a) A direct appeal to the Supreme Court from any decision under section 1253 of this title, holding unconstitutional in whole or in part, any Act of Congress, shall be taken within thirty days after the entry of the interlocutory or final order, judgment or decree. The record shall be made up and the case docketed within sixty days from the time such appeal is taken under rules prescribed by the Supreme Court.

(b) Any other direct appeal to the Supreme Court which is authorized by law, from a decision of a district court in any civil action, suit or proceeding, shall be taken within thirty days from the judgment, order or decree, appealed from, if interlocutory, and within sixty days if final.

(c) Any other appeal or any writ of certiorari intended to bring any judgment or decree in a civil action, suit or proceeding before the Supreme Court for review shall be taken or applied for within ninety days after the entry of such judgment or decree. A justice of the Supreme Court, for good cause shown, may extend the time for applying for a writ of certiorari for a period not exceeding sixty days.

(d) The time for appeal or application for a writ of certiorari to review the judgment of a State court in a criminal case shall be as prescribed by rules of the Supreme Court.

(e) An application to the Supreme Court for a writ of certiorari to review a case before judgment has been rendered in the court of appeals may be made at any time before judgment.

(f) In any case in which the final judgment or decree of any court is subject to review by the Supreme Court on writ of certiorari, the execution and enforcement of such judgment or decree may be stayed for a reasonable time to enable the party aggrieved to obtain a writ of certiorari from the Supreme Court. The stay may be granted by a judge of the court rendering the judgment or decree or by a justice of the Supreme Court, and may be conditioned on the giving of security, approved by such judge or justice, that if the aggrieved party fails to make application for such writ within the period allotted therefor, or fails to obtain an order granting his application, or fails to make his plea good in the Supreme Court, he shall answer for all damages and costs which the other party may sustain by reason of the stay.

(g) The time for application for a writ of certiorari to review a decision of the United States Court of Appeals for the Armed Forces shall be as prescribed by rules of the Supreme Court.

(June 25, 1948, c. 646, 62 Stat. 961; May 24, 1949, c. 139, § 106, 63 Stat. 104; Dec. 6, 1983, Pub.L. 98–209, § 10(b), 97 Stat. 1406; June 27, 1988, Pub.L. 100–352, § 5(b), 102 Stat. 663; Oct. 5, 1994, Pub.L. 103–337, Div. A, Title IX, § 924(d)(1)(C), 108 Stat. 2832.)

HISTORICAL AND STATUTORY NOTES

Effective and Applicability Provisions

1988 Acts. Amendment by section 5(b) of Pub.L. 100–352, which substituted "section 1253" for "sections 1252, 1253 and 2282" in subsec. (a), effective ninety days after June 27, 1988, except that such amendment not to apply to cases pending in the Supreme Court on such effective date or affect the right to review or the manner of reviewing the judgment or decree of a court which was entered before such effective date, see section 7 of Pub.L. 100–352, set out as a note under section 1254 of this title.

1983 Acts. Amendment by Pub.L. 98–209 effective on the first day of the eighth calendar month beginning after Dec. 6, 1983, see section 12(a)(1) of Pub.L. 98–209, set out as a note under section 801 of Title 10, Armed Forces.

§ 2102.   Priority of criminal case on appeal from State court

Criminal cases on review from State courts shall have priority, on the docket of the Supreme Court, over all cases except cases to which the United States is a party and such other cases as the court may decide to be of public importance.

(June 25, 1948, c. 646, 62 Stat. 962.)

[§ 2103. Repealed. Pub.L. 100–352, § 5(c), June 27, 1988, 102 Stat. 663]

HISTORICAL AND STATUTORY NOTES

Section, Acts June 25, 1948, c. 646, 62 Stat. 962; Sept. 19, 1962, Pub.L. 87–669, § 1, 76 Stat. 556, provided that appeal from State court or from a United States court of appeals improvidently taken be regarded as petition for writ of certiorari.

Effective Date of Repeal

Repeal of section effective ninety days after June 27, 1988, except that such repeal not to apply to cases pending in the Supreme Court on such effective date or affect the right to review or the manner of reviewing the judgment or decree of a court which was entered before such effective date, see section 7 of Pub.L. 100–352, set out as a note under section 1254 of this title.

§ 2104. Reviews of State court decisions

A review by the Supreme Court of a judgment or decree of a State court shall be conducted in the same manner and under the same regulations, and shall have the same effect, as if the judgment or decree reviewed had been rendered in a court of the United States.

(June 25, 1948, c. 646, 62 Stat. 962; June 27, 1988, Pub.L. 100–352, § 5(d)(1), 102 Stat. 663.)

HISTORICAL AND STATUTORY NOTES

Effective and Applicability Provisions

1988 Acts. Amendment by section 5(d)(1) of Pub.L. 100–352 effective ninety days after June 27, 1988, except that such amendment not to apply to cases pending in the Supreme Court on such effective date or affect the right to review or the manner of reviewing the judgment or decree of a court which was entered before such effective date, see section 7 of Pub.L. 100–352, set out as a note under section 1254 of this title.

§ 2105. Scope of review; abatement

There shall be no reversal in the Supreme Court or a court of appeals for error in ruling upon matters in abatement which do not involve jurisdiction.

(June 25, 1948, c. 646, 62 Stat. 963.)

§ 2106. Determination

The Supreme Court or any other court of appellate jurisdiction may affirm, modify, vacate, set aside or reverse any judgment, decree, or order of a court lawfully brought before it for review, and may remand the cause and direct the entry of such appropriate judgment, decree, or order, or require such further proceedings to be had as may be just under the circumstances.

(June 25, 1948, c. 646, 62 Stat. 963.)

§ 2107. Time for appeal to court of appeals

(a) Except as otherwise provided in this section, no appeal shall bring any judgment, order or decree in an action, suit or proceeding of a civil nature before a court of appeals for review unless notice of appeal is filed, within thirty days after the entry of such judgment, order or decree.

(b) In any such action, suit, or proceeding, the time as to all parties shall be 60 days from such entry if one of the parties is—

    (1) the United States;

    (2) a United States agency;

    (3) a United States officer or employee sued in an official capacity; or

    (4) a current or former United States officer or employee sued in an individual capacity for an act or omission occurring in connection with duties performed on behalf of the United States, including all instances in which the United States represents that officer or employee when the judgment, order, or decree is entered or files the appeal for that officer or employee.

(c) The district court may, upon motion filed not later than 30 days after the expiration of the time otherwise set for bringing appeal, extend the time for appeal upon a showing of excusable neglect or good cause. In addition, if the district court finds—

(1) that a party entitled to notice of the entry of a judgment or order did not receive such notice from the clerk or any party within 21 days of its entry, and

(2) that no party would be prejudiced,

the district court may, upon motion filed within 180 days after entry of the judgment or order or within 14 days after receipt of such notice, whichever is earlier, reopen the time for appeal for a period of 14 days from the date of entry of the order reopening the time for appeal.

(d) This section shall not apply to bankruptcy matters or other proceedings under Title 11.

(June 25, 1948, c. 646, 62 Stat. 963; May 24, 1949, c. 139, §§ 107, 108, 63 Stat. 104; Nov. 6, 1978, Pub.L. 95–598, Title II, § 248, 92 Stat. 2672; Dec. 9, 1991, Pub.L. 102–198, § 12, 105 Stat. 1627; May 7, 2009, Pub.L. 111–16, § 6(3), 123 Stat. 1608; Pub.L. 112–62, § 3, Nov. 29, 2011, 125 Stat. 757.)

HISTORICAL AND STATUTORY NOTES

Codifications

This section was amended by Pub.L. 95–598, Title II, § 248, Nov. 6, 1978, 92 Stat. 2672, effective June 28, 1984, pursuant to Pub.L. 95–598, Title IV, § 402(b), Nov. 6, 1978, 92 Stat. 2682, as amended by Pub.L. 98–249, § 1(a), Mar. 31, 1984, 98 Stat. 116; Pub.L. 98–271, § 1(a), Apr. 30, 1984, 98 Stat. 163; Pub.L. 98–299, § 1(a), May 25, 1984, 98 Stat. 214; Pub.L. 98–325, § 1(a), June 20, 1984, 98 Stat. 268 [set out as an Effective and Applicability Provisions note preceding section 101 of Title 11, Bankruptcy], by adding "or the bankruptcy court" following "district court" and by striking out the final paragraph relating to nonapplicability to bankruptcy matters or other proceedings under Title 11.

Section 402(b) of Pub.L. 95–598 was amended by section 113 of Pub.L. 98–353, Title I, July 10, 1984, 98 Stat. 343, by substituting "shall not be effective" for "shall take effect on June 28, 1984", thereby eliminating the amendment by section 248 of Pub.L. 95–598, effective June 27, 1984, pursuant to section 122(c) of Pub.L. 98–353, set out as an Effective Date note under section 151 of this title.

Section 121(a) of Pub.L. 98–353 directed that section 402(b) of Pub.L. 95–598 be amended by substituting "the date of enactment of the Bankruptcy Amendments and Federal Judgeship Act of 1984 [i.e. July 10, 1984]" for "June 28, 1984". This amendment was not executed in view of the prior amendment to section 402(b) of Pub.L. 95–598 by section 113 of Pub.L. 98–353.

Effective and Applicability Provisions

2011 Acts. Pub.L. 112–62, § 4, Nov. 29, 2011, 125 Stat. 757, provided that: "The amendment made by this Act [Appeal Time Clarification Act of 2011, Pub.L. 112–62, which amended this section and enacted provisions set out as a note under this section] shall take effect on December 1, 2011."

2009 Acts. Amendments by Pub.L. 111–16 effective Dec. 1, 2009, see Pub.L. 111–16, § 7, set out as a note under 11 U.S.C.A. § 109.

Findings

Pub.L. 112–62, § 2, Nov. 29, 2011, 125 Stat. 756, provided that:

"Congress finds that—

"**(1)** section 2107 of title 28, United States Code [this section], and rule 4 of the Federal Rules of Appellate Procedure provide that the time to appeal for most civil actions is 30 days, but that the appeal time for all parties is 60 days when the parties in the civil action include the United States, a United States officer, or a United States agency;

"**(2)** the 60-day period should apply if one of the parties is—

"**(A)** the United States;

"**(B)** a United States agency;

"**(C)** a United States officer or employee sued in an official capacity; or

"**(D)** a current or former United States officer or employee sued in an individual capacity for an act or omission occurring in connection with duties performed on behalf of the United States;

"**(3)** section 2107 of title 28, United States Code, and rule 4 of the Federal Rules of Appellate Procedure (as amended to take effect on December 1, 2011, in accordance with section 2074 of that title) should uniformly apply the 60-day period to those civil actions relating to a Federal officer or employee sued in an individual capacity for an act or omission occurring in connection with Federal duties;

"**(4)** the civil actions to which the 60-day periods should apply include all civil actions in which a legal officer of the United States represents the relevant officer or employee when the judgment or order is entered or in which the United States files the appeal for that officer or employee; and

"**(5)** the application of the 60-day period in section 2107 of title 28, United States Code, and rule 4 of the Federal Rules of Appellate Procedure—

"**(A)** is not limited to civil actions in which representation of the United States is provided by the Department of Justice; and

"**(B)** includes all civil actions in which the representation of the United States is provided by a Federal legal officer acting in an official capacity, such as civil actions in which a Member, officer, or employee of the Senate or the House of Representatives is represented by the Office of Senate Legal Counsel or the Office of General Counsel of the House of Representatives."

§ 2108. Proof of amount in controversy

Where the power of any court of appeals to review a case depends upon the amount or value in controversy, such amount or value, if not otherwise satisfactorily disclosed upon the record, may be shown and ascertained by the oath of a party to the case or by other competent evidence.

(June 25, 1948, c. 646, 62 Stat. 963.)

§ 2109. Quorum of Supreme Court justices absent

If a case brought to the Supreme Court by direct appeal from a district court cannot be heard and determined because of the absence of a quorum of qualified justices, the Chief Justice of the United States may order it remitted to the court of appeals for the circuit including the district in which the case arose, to be heard and determined by that court either sitting in banc or specially constituted and composed of the three circuit judges senior in commission who are able to sit, as such order may direct. The decision of such court shall be final and conclusive. In the event of the disqualification or disability of one or more of such circuit judges, such court shall be filled as provided in chapter 15 of this title.

In any other case brought to the Supreme Court for review, which cannot be heard and determined because of the absence of a quorum of qualified justices, if a majority of the qualified justices shall be of opinion that the case cannot be heard and determined at the next ensuing term, the court shall enter its order affirming the judgment of the court from which the case was brought for review with the same effect as upon affirmance by an equally divided court.

(June 25, 1948, c. 646, 62 Stat. 963.)

[§ 2110.   Repealed. Pub.L. 97–164, Title I, § 136, Apr. 2, 1982, 96 Stat. 41]

HISTORICAL AND STATUTORY NOTES

Section, Act June 25, 1948, c. 646, 62 Stat. 964; May 24, 1949, c. 139, § 109, 63 Stat. 105, provided that appeals to the Court of Claims in tort claims cases, as provided in section 1504 of this title, be taken within 90 days after the entry of the final judgment of the district court.

Effective Date of Repeal

Repeal effective Oct. 1, 1982, see section 402 of Pub.L. 97–164, set out as a note under section 171 of this title.

§ 2111.   Harmless error

On the hearing of any appeal or writ of certiorari in any case, the court shall give judgment after an examination of the record without regard to errors or defects which do not affect the substantial rights of the parties.

(Added May 24, 1949, c. 139, § 110, 63 Stat. 105.)

§ 2112.   Record on review and enforcement of agency orders

(a)   The rules prescribed under the authority of section 2072 of this title may provide for the time and manner of filing and the contents of the record in all proceedings instituted in the courts of appeals to enjoin, set aside, suspend, modify, or otherwise review or enforce orders of administrative agencies, boards, commissions, and officers. Such rules may authorize the agency, board, commission, or officer to file in the court a certified list of the materials comprising the record and retain and hold for the court all such materials and transmit the same or any part thereof to the court, when and as required by it, at any time prior to the final determination of the proceeding, and such filing of such certified list of the materials comprising the record and such subsequent transmittal of any such materials when and as required shall be deemed full compliance with any provision of law requiring the filing of the record in the court. The record in such proceedings shall be certified and filed in or held for and transmitted to the court of appeals by the agency, board, commission, or officer concerned within the time and in the manner prescribed by such rules. If proceedings are instituted in two or more courts of appeals with respect to the same order, the following shall apply:

(1)   If within ten days after issuance of the order the agency, board, commission, or officer concerned receives, from the persons instituting the proceedings, the petition for review with respect to proceedings in at least two courts of appeals, the agency, board, commission, or officer shall proceed in accordance with paragraph (3) of this subsection. If within ten days after the issuance of the order the agency, board, commission, or officer concerned receives, from the persons instituting the proceedings, the petition for review with respect to proceedings in only one court of appeals, the agency, board, commission, or officer shall file the record in that court notwithstanding the institution in any other court of appeals of proceedings for review of that order. In all other cases in which proceedings have been instituted in two or more courts of appeals with respect to the same order, the agency, board, commission, or officer concerned shall file the record in the court in which proceedings with respect to the order were first instituted.

(2)   For purposes of paragraph (1) of this subsection, a copy of the petition or other pleading which institutes proceedings in a court of appeals and which is stamped by the court with the date of filing shall constitute the petition for review. Each agency, board, commission, or officer, as the case may be, shall designate by rule the office and the officer who must receive petitions for review under paragraph (1).

(3)   If an agency, board, commission, or officer receives two or more petitions for review of an order in accordance with the first sentence of paragraph (1) of this subsection, the agency, board, commission, or officer shall, promptly after the expiration of the ten-day period specified in that sentence, so notify the judicial panel on multidistrict litigation authorized by section 1407

of this title, in such form as that panel shall prescribe. The judicial panel on multidistrict litigation shall, by means of random selection, designate one court of appeals, from among the courts of appeals in which petitions for review have been filed and received within the ten-day period specified in the first sentence of paragraph (1), in which the record is to be filed, and shall issue an order consolidating the petitions for review in that court of appeals. The judicial panel on multidistrict litigation shall, after providing notice to the public and an opportunity for the submission of comments, prescribe rules with respect to the consolidation of proceedings under this paragraph. The agency, board, commission, or officer concerned shall file the record in the court of appeals designated pursuant to this paragraph.

(4) Any court of appeals in which proceedings with respect to an order of an agency, board, commission, or officer have been instituted may, to the extent authorized by law, stay the effective date of the order. Any such stay may thereafter be modified, revoked, or extended by a court of appeals designated pursuant to paragraph (3) with respect to that order or by any other court of appeals to which the proceedings are transferred.

(5) All courts in which proceedings are instituted with respect to the same order, other than the court in which the record is filed pursuant to this subsection, shall transfer those proceedings to the court in which the record is so filed. For the convenience of the parties in the interest of justice, the court in which the record is filed may thereafter transfer all the proceedings with respect to that order to any other court of appeals.

(b) The record to be filed in the court of appeals in such a proceeding shall consist of the order sought to be reviewed or enforced, the findings or report upon which it is based, and the pleadings, evidence, and proceedings before the agency, board, commission, or officer concerned, or such portions thereof (1) as the rules prescribed under the authority of section 2072 of this title may require to be included therein, or (2) as the agency, board, commission, or officer concerned, the petitioner for review or respondent in enforcement, as the case may be, and any intervenor in the court proceeding by written stipulation filed with the agency, board, commission, or officer concerned or in the court in any such proceeding may consistently with the rules prescribed under the authority of section 2072 of this title designate to be included therein, or (3) as the court upon motion of a party or, after a prehearing conference, upon its own motion may by order in any such proceeding designate to be included therein. Such a stipulation or order may provide in an appropriate case that no record need be filed in the court of appeals. If, however, the correctness of a finding of fact by the agency, board, commission, or officer is in question all of the evidence before the agency, board, commission, or officer shall be included in the record except such as the agency, board, commission, or officer concerned, the petitioner for review or respondent in enforcement, as the case may be, and any intervenor in the court proceeding by written stipulation filed with the agency, board, commission, or officer concerned or in the court agree to omit as wholly immaterial to the questioned finding. If there is omitted from the record any portion of the proceedings before the agency, board, commission, or officer which the court subsequently determines to be proper for it to consider to enable it to review or enforce the order in question the court may direct that such additional portion of the proceedings be filed as a supplement to the record. The agency, board, commission, or officer concerned may, at its option and without regard to the foregoing provisions of this subsection, and if so requested by the petitioner for review or respondent in enforcement shall, file in the court the entire record of the proceedings before it without abbreviation.

(c) The agency, board, commission, or officer concerned may transmit to the court of appeals the original papers comprising the whole or any part of the record or any supplemental record, otherwise true copies of such papers certified by an authorized officer or deputy of the agency, board, commission, or officer concerned shall be transmitted. Any original papers thus transmitted to the court of appeals shall be returned to the agency, board, commission, or officer concerned upon the final determination of the review or enforcement proceeding. Pending such final determination any such papers may be returned by the court temporarily to the custody of the agency, board, commission, or officer concerned if needed for the transaction of the public business. Certified copies of any papers included in the record or any supplemental record may also be returned to the agency, board, commission, or officer concerned upon the final determination of review or enforcement proceedings.

(d) The provisions of this section are not applicable to proceedings to review decisions of the Tax Court of the United States or to proceedings to review or enforce those orders of administrative agencies, boards, commissions, or officers which are by law reviewable or enforceable by the district courts.

(Added Pub.L. 85–791, § 2, Aug. 28, 1958, 72 Stat. 941; amended Pub.L. 89–773, § 5(a), (b), Nov. 6, 1966, 80 Stat. 1323; Pub.L. 100–236, § 1, Jan. 8, 1988, 101 Stat. 1731.)

HISTORICAL AND STATUTORY NOTES

Effective and Applicability Provisions

1988 Acts. Section 3 of Pub.L. 100–236 provided that: "The amendments made by this Act [amending subsec. (a) of this section and section 1369(b) of Title 33, Navigation and Navigable Waters] take effect 180 days after the date of the enactment of this Act [Jan. 8, 1988], except that the judicial panel on multidistrict litigation may issue rules pursuant to subsection (a)(3) of section 2112 of title 28, United States Code (as added by section 1) [subsec. (a)(3) of this section], on or after such date of enactment."

Savings Provisions

Section 5(c) of Pub.L. 89–773 provided that: "The amendments of section 2112 of title 28 of the United States Code [this section] made by this Act shall not operate to invalidate or repeal rules adopted under the authority of that section prior to the enactment of this Act [Nov. 6, 1966], which rules shall remain in effect until superseded by rules prescribed under the authority of section 2072 of title 28 of the United States Code [section 2072 of this title] as amended by this Act."

§ 2113.   Definition

For purposes of this chapter, the terms "State court", "State courts", and "highest court of a State" include the District of Columbia Court of Appeals.

(Added Pub.L. 91–358, Title I, § 172(a)(2)(A), July 29, 1970, 84 Stat. 590.)

PART VI—PARTICULAR PROCEEDINGS

Effective and Applicability Provisions

1996 Acts. Amendment of analysis by section 3(e) of Pub.L. 104–331, effective Oct. 1, 1997, see section 3(d) of Pub.L. 104–331, set out as a note under section 1296 of this title.

CHAPTER 151—DECLARATORY JUDGMENTS

Sec.
2201.   Creation of remedy.
2202.   Further relief.

§ 2201.   Creation of remedy

(a) In a case of actual controversy within its jurisdiction, except with respect to Federal taxes other than actions brought under section 7428 of the Internal Revenue Code of 1986, a proceeding under section 505 or 1146 of title 11, or in any civil action involving an antidumping or countervailing duty proceeding regarding a class or kind of merchandise of a free trade area country (as defined in section 516A(f)(9) of the Tariff Act of 1930), as determined by the administering authority, any court of the United States, upon the filing of an appropriate pleading, may declare the rights and other legal relations of any interested party seeking such declaration, whether or not further relief is or could be sought. Any such declaration shall have the force and effect of a final judgment or decree and shall be reviewable as such.

(b) For limitations on actions brought with respect to drug patents see section 505 or 512 of the Federal Food, Drug, and Cosmetic Act, or section 351 of the Public Health Service Act.

(June 25, 1948, c. 646, 62 Stat. 964; May 24, 1949, c. 139, § 111, 63 Stat. 105; Aug. 28, 1954, c. 1033, 68 Stat. 890; July 7, 1958, Pub.L. 85–508, § 12(p), 72 Stat. 349; Oct. 4, 1976, Pub.L. 94–455, Title XIII, § 1306(b)(8), 90 Stat. 1719; Nov. 6, 1978, Pub.L. 95–598, Title II, § 249, 92 Stat. 2672; Sept. 24, 1984, Pub.L. 98–417, Title I, § 106, 98 Stat. 1597; Sept. 28, 1988, Pub.L. 100–449, Title IV, § 402(c), 102 Stat. 1884; Nov. 16, 1988, Pub.L. 100–670, Title I, § 107(b), 102 Stat. 3984; Dec. 8, 1993, Pub.L. 103–182, Title IV, § 414(b), 107 Stat. 2147; Mar. 23, 2010, Pub.L. 111–148, Title VII, § 7002(c)(2), 124 Stat. 816; Pub. L. 116–113, Jan. 29, 2020, 134 Stat. 11.)

Termination of Amendment

For termination of amendment by section 501(c) of Pub.L. 100–449, see Sunset Provisions note set out under this section.

HISTORICAL AND STATUTORY NOTES

References in Text

Section 7428 of the Internal Revenue Code of 1986, referred to in subsec. (a), is classified to section 7428 of Title 26, Internal Revenue Code.

Section 516A(f)(10) of the Tariff Act of 1930, referred to in subsec. (a), is classified to section 1516a(f)(10) of Title 19, Customs Duties.

Sections 505 and 512 of the Federal Food, Drug, and Cosmetic Act, referred to in subsec. (b), are classified to sections 355 and 360b, respectively, of Title 21, Food and Drugs.

The Public Health Service Act, referred to in subsec. (b), is Act July 1, 1944, c. 373, 58 Stat. 682, as amended, which is classified principally to chapter 6A of Title 42, 42 U.S.C.A. § 201 et seq. Section 351 of the Act is classified to 42 U.S.C.A. § 262. For complete classification, see Short Title note set out under 42 U.S.C.A. § 201 and Tables.

Effective and Applicability Provisions

1993 Acts. Amendment of this section by section 414 of Pub.L. 103–182 to take effect on the date the North American Free Trade Agreement enters into force with respect to the United States, but not to apply to any final determination described in section 1516a(a)(1)(B) or (2)(B)(i), (ii), or (iii) of Title 19, Customs Duties, notice of which is published in the Federal Register before such date, or to a determination described in section 1516a(a)(2)(B)(vi) of Title 19 notice of which is received by the Government of Canada or Mexico before such date, or to any binational panel review under the United States-Canada Free-Trade Agreement, or to any extraordinary challenge arising out of any such review that was commenced before such date, see section 416 of Pub.L. 103–182, set out as a note under section 3431 of Title 19.

1988 Acts. Amendment by Pub.L. 100–449 effective on the date the United States-Canada Free-Trade Agreement enters into force (Jan. 1, 1989), and to cease to have effect on the date the Agreement ceases to be in force, see section 501(a), (c) of Pub.L. 100–449, set out in a note under section 2112 of Title 19, Customs Duties. [A Presidential Memorandum on the Canada-United States Free-Trade Agreement, dated Dec. 31, 1988, directing the Secretary of State to exchange notes with the Government of Canada to provide for the entry into force of the Agreement on Jan. 1, 1989, is set out in 24 Weekly Compilation of Presidential Documents 1688, Jan. 2, 1989.]

1978 Acts. Amendment by Pub.L. 95–598 effective Oct. 1, 1979, see section 402(c) of Pub.L. 95–598, set out as a note preceding section 101 of Title 11, Bankruptcy.

1976 Acts. Amendment by Pub.L. 94–455 applicable with respect to pleadings filed with the United States Tax Court, the District Court of the United States for the District of Columbia, or the United States Court of Claims more than 6 months after Oct. 4, 1976, but only with respect to determinations (or requests for determinations) made after Jan. 1, 1976, see section 1306(c) of Pub.L. 94–455, set out as a note under section 7428 of Title 26, Internal Revenue Code.

1958 Acts. Amendment by Pub.L. 85–508 effective Jan. 3, 1959, upon admission of Alaska into the Union pursuant to Proc. No. 3269, Jan. 3, 1959, 24 F.R. 81, 73 Stat. c. 16, as required by sections 1 and 8(c) of Pub.L. 85–508, see notes set out under section 81A of this title and preceding section 21 of Title 48, Territories and Insular Possessions.

Sunset Provisions

For provisions relating to the effect of termination of NAFTA country status on the provisions of Pub.L. 103–182, §§ 401 to 416, see 19 U.S.C.A. § 3451.

For provisions directing that the amendments made by Pub.L. 100–449, which amended this section, shall cease to have effect on the date on which the United States-Canada Free-Trade Agreement ceases to be in force, see Pub.L. 100–449, § 501(c), set out in the note under 19 U.S.C.A. § 2112.

§ 2202.   Further relief

Further necessary or proper relief based on a declaratory judgment or decree may be granted, after reasonable notice and hearing, against any adverse party whose rights have been determined by such judgment.

(June 25, 1948, c. 646, 62 Stat. 964.)

CHAPTER 153—HABEAS CORPUS

HISTORICAL AND STATUTORY NOTES

Codifications

The table of sections for chapter 153 was amended by Pub.L. 95–598, Title II, § 250(b), Nov. 6, 1978, 92 Stat. 2672, effective June 28, 1984, pursuant to Pub.L. 95–598, Title IV, § 402(b), Nov. 6, 1978, 92 Stat. 2682, as amended by Pub.L. 98–249, § 1(a), Mar. 31, 1984, 98 Stat. 116; Pub.L. 98–271, § 1(a), Apr. 30, 1984, 98 Stat. 163; Pub.L. 98–299, § 1(a), May 25, 1984, 98 Stat. 214; Pub.L. 98–325, § 1(a), June 20, 1984, 98 Stat. 268, set out as an Effective and Applicability Provisions note preceding section 101 of Title 11, Bankruptcy, by adding:

"2256. Habeas corpus from bankruptcy courts.".

Section 402(b) of Pub.L. 95–598 was amended by section 113 of Pub.L. 98–353, Title I, July 10, 1984, 98 Stat. 343, by substituting "shall not be effective" for "shall take effect on June 28, 1984", thereby eliminating the amendment by section 250(b) of Pub.L. 95–598, effective June 27, 1984, pursuant to section 122(c) of Pub.L. 98–353, set out as an Effective and Applicability Provisions note under section 151 of this title.

Section 121(a) of Pub.L. 98–353 directed that section 402(b) of Pub.L. 95–598 be amended by substituting "the date of enactment of the Bankruptcy Amendments and Federal Judgeship Act of 1984 [i.e. July 10, 1984]" for "June 28, 1984". This amendment was not executed in view of the prior amendment to section 402(b) of Pub.L. 95–598 by section 113 of Pub.L. 98–353.

§ 2241.   Power to grant writ

(a) Writs of habeas corpus may be granted by the Supreme Court, any justice thereof, the district courts and any circuit judge within their respective jurisdictions. The order of a circuit judge shall be entered in the records of the district court of the district wherein the restraint complained of is had.

(b) The Supreme Court, any justice thereof, and any circuit judge may decline to entertain an application for a writ of habeas corpus and may transfer the application for hearing and determination to the district court having jurisdiction to entertain it.

(c) The writ of habeas corpus shall not extend to a prisoner unless—

(1) He is in custody under or by color of the authority of the United States or is committed for trial before some court thereof; or

(2) He is in custody for an act done or omitted in pursuance of an Act of Congress, or an order, process, judgment or decree of a court or judge of the United States; or

(3) He is in custody in violation of the Constitution or laws or treaties of the United States; or

(4) He, being a citizen of a foreign state and domiciled therein is in custody for an act done or omitted under any alleged right, title, authority, privilege, protection, or exemption claimed under the commission, order or sanction of any foreign state, or under color thereof, the validity and effect of which depend upon the law of nations; or

(5) It is necessary to bring him into court to testify or for trial.

(d) Where an application for a writ of habeas corpus is made by a person in custody under the judgment and sentence of a State court of a State which contains two or more Federal judicial districts, the application may be filed in the district court for the district wherein such person is in custody or in the district court for the district within which the State court was held which convicted and sentenced him and each of such district courts shall have concurrent jurisdiction to entertain the application. The district court for the district wherein such an application is filed in the exercise of its discretion and in furtherance of justice may transfer the application to the other district court for hearing and determination.

(e)(1)   No court, justice, or judge shall have jurisdiction to hear or consider an application for a writ of habeas corpus filed by or on behalf of an alien detained by the United States who has been determined by the United States to have been properly detained as an enemy combatant or is awaiting such determination.

(2)   Except as provided in paragraphs (2) and (3) of section 1005(e) of the Detainee Treatment Act of 2005 (10 U.S.C. 801 note), no court, justice, or judge shall have jurisdiction to hear or consider any other action against the United States or its agents relating to any aspect of the detention, transfer, treatment, trial, or conditions of confinement of an alien who is or was detained by the United States and has been determined by the United States to have been properly detained as an enemy combatant or is awaiting such determination.

(June 25, 1948, c. 646, 62 Stat. 964; May 24, 1949, c. 139, § 112, 63 Stat. 105; Sept. 19, 1966, Pub.L. 89–590, 80 Stat. 811; Dec. 30, 2005, Pub.L. 109–148, Div. A, Title X, § 1005(e)(1), 119 Stat. 2741; Jan. 6, 2006, Pub.L. 109–163, Div. A, Title XIV, § 1405(e)(1), 119 Stat. 3477; Oct. 17, 2006, Pub.L. 109–366, § 7(a), 120 Stat. 2635; Jan. 28, 2008, Pub.L. 110–181, Div. A, Title X, § 1063(f), 122 Stat. 323.)

HISTORICAL AND STATUTORY NOTES

References in Text

Section 1005(e) of the Detainee Treatment Act of 2005, referred to in subsec. (e)(2), probably means Pub.L. 109–148, Div. A, Title X, § 1005, Dec. 30, 2005, 119 Stat. 2740, which is set out in a note under 10 U.S.C.A. § 801 note. Pub.L. 109–163, Div. A, Title XIV, Jan. 6, 2006, 119 Stat. 3474, also enacted a "Detainee Treatment Act of 2005", see Short Title note under 42 U.S.C.A. § 2000dd and Tables, but that Act contains no section 1005(e).

Constitutionality

For information regarding constitutionality of certain provisions of this section, as added and amended by section 1005(e)(1) of Pub. L. 109–148 and section 7(a) of Pub. L. 109–366 [28 U.S.C. § 2241(e)], see Congressional Research Service, The Constitution of the United States of America: Analysis and Interpretation, Appendix 1, Acts of Congress Held Unconstitutional in Whole or in Part by the Supreme Court of the United States.*

Effective and Applicability Provisions

2006 Acts. Pub.L. 109–366, § 7(b), Oct. 17, 2006, 120 Stat. 2635, provided that: "The amendment made by subsection (a) [amending this section] shall take effect on the date of the enactment of this Act [Oct. 17, 2006], and shall apply to all cases, without exception, pending on or after the date of the enactment of this Act which relate to any aspect of the detention, transfer, treatment, trial, or conditions of detention of an alien detained by the United States since September 11, 2001."

Treaty Obligations not Establishing Grounds for Certain Claims

Pub.L. 109–366, § 5, Oct. 17, 2006, 120 Stat. 2631, provided that:

"**(a) In general.**—No person may invoke the Geneva Conventions or any protocols thereto in any habeas corpus or other civil action or proceeding to which the United States, or a current or former officer,

---

*   [The United States Supreme Court has held invalid the referenced provisions of this section, finding that the process provided by the Detainee Treatment Act of 2005 for review of the status of aliens detained as enemy combatants at the United States Naval Station at Guantanamo Bay, Cuba, did not provide an adequate substitute for habeas corpus, given the lack of opportunity for detainees to present relevant exculpatory evidence not made part of the record in earlier proceedings; thus, section 7 of the Military Commissions Act of 2006, which denied federal courts jurisdiction to hear a habeas corpus action by an alien detained and determined to be an enemy combatant, or awaiting such determination, was an unconstitutional suspension of writ of habeas corpus under the Suspension Clause, Art. 1, § 9, clause 2. *Boumediene v. Bush*, 553 U.S. 723 (2008). Ed.]

employee, member of the Armed Forces, or other agent of the United States is a party as a source of rights in any court of the United States or its States or territories.

"**(b) Geneva conventions defined.**—In this section, the term 'Geneva Conventions' means—

"**(1)** the Convention for the Amelioration of the Condition of the Wounded and Sick in Armed Forces in the Field, done at Geneva August 12, 1949 (6 UST 3114);

"**(2)** the Convention for the Amelioration of the Condition of the Wounded, Sick, and Shipwrecked Members of the Armed Forces at Sea, done at Geneva August 12, 1949 (6 UST 3217);

"**(3)** the Convention Relative to the Treatment of Prisoners of War, done at Geneva August 12, 1949 (6 UST 3316); and

"**(4)** the Convention Relative to the Protection of Civilian Persons in Time of War, done at Geneva August 12, 1949 (6 UST 3516)."

§ 2242.　　Application

Application for a writ of habeas corpus shall be in writing signed and verified by the person for whose relief it is intended or by someone acting in his behalf.

It shall allege the facts concerning the applicant's commitment or detention, the name of the person who has custody over him and by virtue of what claim or authority, if known.

It may be amended or supplemented as provided in the rules of procedure applicable to civil actions.

If addressed to the Supreme Court, a justice thereof or a circuit judge it shall state the reasons for not making application to the district court of the district in which the applicant is held.

(June 25, 1948, c. 646, 62 Stat. 965.)

§ 2243.　　Issuance of writ; return; hearing; decision

A court, justice or judge entertaining an application for a writ of habeas corpus shall forthwith award the writ or issue an order directing the respondent to show cause why the writ should not be granted, unless it appears from the application that the applicant or person detained is not entitled thereto.

The writ, or order to show cause shall be directed to the person having custody of the person detained. It shall be returned within three days unless for good cause additional time, not exceeding twenty days, is allowed.

The person to whom the writ or order is directed shall make a return certifying the true cause of the detention.

When the writ or order is returned a day shall be set for hearing, not more than five days after the return unless for good cause additional time is allowed.

Unless the application for the writ and the return present only issues of law the person to whom the writ is directed shall be required to produce at the hearing the body of the person detained.

The applicant or the person detained may, under oath, deny any of the facts set forth in the return or allege any other material facts.

The return and all suggestions made against it may be amended, by leave of court, before or after being filed.

The court shall summarily hear and determine the facts, and dispose of the matter as law and justice require.

(June 25, 1948, c. 646, 62 Stat. 965.)

§ 2244.   Finality of determination

(a)   No circuit or district judge shall be required to entertain an application for a writ of habeas corpus to inquire into the detention of a person pursuant to a judgment of a court of the United States if it appears that the legality of such detention has been determined by a judge or court of the United States on a prior application for a writ of habeas corpus, except as provided in section 2255.

(b)(1)   A claim presented in a second or successive habeas corpus application under section 2254 that was presented in a prior application shall be dismissed.

(2)   A claim presented in a second or successive habeas corpus application under section 2254 that was not presented in a prior application shall be dismissed unless—

(A)   the applicant shows that the claim relies on a new rule of constitutional law, made retroactive to cases on collateral review by the Supreme Court, that was previously unavailable; or

(B)(i)   the factual predicate for the claim could not have been discovered previously through the exercise of due diligence; and

(ii)   the facts underlying the claim, if proven and viewed in light of the evidence as a whole, would be sufficient to establish by clear and convincing evidence that, but for constitutional error, no reasonable factfinder would have found the applicant guilty of the underlying offense.

(3)(A)   Before a second or successive application permitted by this section is filed in the district court, the applicant shall move in the appropriate court of appeals for an order authorizing the district court to consider the application.

(B)   A motion in the court of appeals for an order authorizing the district court to consider a second or successive application shall be determined by a three-judge panel of the court of appeals.

(C)   The court of appeals may authorize the filing of a second or successive application only if it determines that the application makes a prima facie showing that the application satisfies the requirements of this subsection.

(D)   The court of appeals shall grant or deny the authorization to file a second or successive application not later than 30 days after the filing of the motion.

(E)   The grant or denial of an authorization by a court of appeals to file a second or successive application shall not be appealable and shall not be the subject of a petition for rehearing or for a writ of certiorari.

(4)   A district court shall dismiss any claim presented in a second or successive application that the court of appeals has authorized to be filed unless the applicant shows that the claim satisfies the requirements of this section.

(c)   In a habeas corpus proceeding brought in behalf of a person in custody pursuant to the judgment of a State court, a prior judgment of the Supreme Court of the United States on an appeal or review by a writ of certiorari at the instance of the prisoner of the decision of such State court, shall be conclusive as to all issues of fact or law with respect to an asserted denial of a Federal right which constitutes ground for discharge in a habeas corpus proceeding, actually adjudicated by the Supreme Court therein, unless the applicant for the writ of habeas corpus shall plead and the court shall find the existence of a material and controlling fact which did not appear in the record of the proceeding in the Supreme Court and the court shall further find that the applicant for the writ of habeas corpus could not have caused such fact to appear in such record by the exercise of reasonable diligence.

(d)(1)   A 1-year period of limitation shall apply to an application for a writ of habeas corpus by a person in custody pursuant to the judgment of a State court. The limitation period shall run from the latest of—

(A) the date on which the judgment became final by the conclusion of direct review or the expiration of the time for seeking such review;

(B) the date on which the impediment to filing an application created by State action in violation of the Constitution or laws of the United States is removed, if the applicant was prevented from filing by such State action;

(C) the date on which the constitutional right asserted was initially recognized by the Supreme Court, if the right has been newly recognized by the Supreme Court and made retroactively applicable to cases on collateral review; or

(D) the date on which the factual predicate of the claim or claims presented could have been discovered through the exercise of due diligence.

(2) The time during which a properly filed application for State post-conviction or other collateral review with respect to the pertinent judgment or claim is pending shall not be counted toward any period of limitation under this subsection.

(June 25, 1948, c. 646, 62 Stat. 965; Nov. 2, 1966, Pub.L. 89–711, § 1, 80 Stat. 1104; Apr. 24, 1996, Pub.L. 104–132, Title I, §§ 101, 106, 110 Stat. 1217, 1220.)

§ 2245.   Certificate of trial judge admissible in evidence

On the hearing of an application for a writ of habeas corpus to inquire into the legality of the detention of a person pursuant to a judgment the certificate of the judge who presided at the trial resulting in the judgment, setting forth the facts occurring at the trial, shall be admissible in evidence. Copies of the certificate shall be filed with the court in which the application is pending and in the court in which the trial took place.

(June 25, 1948, c. 646, 62 Stat. 966.)

§ 2246.   Evidence; depositions; affidavits

On application for a writ of habeas corpus, evidence may be taken orally or by deposition, or, in the discretion of the judge, by affidavit. If affidavits are admitted any party shall have the right to propound written interrogatories to the affiants, or to file answering affidavits.

(June 25, 1948, c. 646, 62 Stat. 966.)

§ 2247.   Documentary evidence

On application for a writ of habeas corpus documentary evidence, transcripts of proceedings upon arraignment, plea and sentence and a transcript of the oral testimony introduced on any previous similar application by or in behalf of the same petitioner, shall be admissible in evidence.

(June 25, 1948, c. 646, 62 Stat. 966.)

§ 2248.   Return or answer; conclusiveness

The allegations of a return to the writ of habeas corpus or of an answer to an order to show cause in a habeas corpus proceeding, if not traversed, shall be accepted as true except to the extent that the judge finds from the evidence that they are not true.

(June 25, 1948, c. 646, 62 Stat. 966.)

§ 2249.   Certified copies of indictment, plea and judgment; duty of respondent

On application for a writ of habeas corpus to inquire into the detention of any person pursuant to a judgment of a court of the United States, the respondent shall promptly file with the court certified copies of the indictment, plea of petitioner and the judgment, or such of them as may be material to the questions raised, if the petitioner fails to attach them to his petition, and same shall be attached to the return to the writ, or to the answer to the order to show cause.

(June 25, 1948, c. 646, 62 Stat. 966.)

§ 2250.   Indigent petitioner entitled to documents without cost

If on any application for a writ of habeas corpus an order has been made permitting the petitioner to prosecute the application in forma pauperis, the clerk of any court of the United States shall furnish to the petitioner without cost certified copies of such documents or parts of the record on file in his office as may be required by order of the judge before whom the application is pending.

(June 25, 1948, c. 646, 62 Stat. 966.)

§ 2251.   Stay of State court proceedings

(a) In general.—

(1) Pending matters.—A justice or judge of the United States before whom a habeas corpus proceeding is pending, may, before final judgment or after final judgment of discharge, or pending appeal, stay any proceeding against the person detained in any State court or by or under the authority of any State for any matter involved in the habeas corpus proceeding.

(2) Matter not pending.—For purposes of this section, a habeas corpus proceeding is not pending until the application is filed.

(3) Application for appointment of counsel.—If a State prisoner sentenced to death applies for appointment of counsel pursuant to section 3599(a)(2) of title 18 in a court that would have jurisdiction to entertain a habeas corpus application regarding that sentence, that court may stay execution of the sentence of death, but such stay shall terminate not later than 90 days after counsel is appointed or the application for appointment of counsel is withdrawn or denied.

(b) No further proceedings.—After the granting of such a stay, any such proceeding in any State court or by or under the authority of any State shall be void. If no stay is granted, any such proceeding shall be as valid as if no habeas corpus proceedings or appeal were pending.

(June 25, 1948, c. 646, 62 Stat. 966; Mar. 9, 2006, Pub.L. 109–177, Title V, § 507(f), 120 Stat. 251.)

HISTORICAL AND STATUTORY NOTES

Application to Pending Cases

Pub.L. 109–177, Title V, § 507(d), Mar. 9, 2006, 120 Stat. 251, provided that:

"**(1) In general.**—This section and the amendments made by this section [enacting 28 U.S.C.A. § 2265, amending 28 U.S.C.A. §§ 2251, 2261, and 2266, and repealing 28 U.S.C.A. § 2265] shall apply to cases pending on or after the date of enactment of this Act [Mar. 9, 2006].

"**(2) Time limits.**—In a case pending on the date of enactment of this Act [Mar. 9, 2006], if the amendments made by this section [enacting 28 U.S.C.A. § 2265, amending 28 U.S.C.A. §§ 2251, 2261, and 2266, and repealing 28 U.S.C.A. § 2265] establish a time limit for taking certain action, the period of which began on the date of an event that occurred prior to the date of enactment of this Act [Mar. 9, 2006], the period of such time limit shall instead begin on the date of enactment of this Act [Mar. 9, 2006]."

§ 2252.   Notice

Prior to the hearing of a habeas corpus proceeding in behalf of a person in custody of State officers or by virtue of State laws notice shall be served on the attorney general or other appropriate officer of such State as the justice or judge at the time of issuing the writ shall direct.

(June 25, 1948, c. 646, 62 Stat. 967.)

§ 2253.   Appeal

(a)   In a habeas corpus proceeding or a proceeding under section 2255 before a district judge, the final order shall be subject to review, on appeal, by the court of appeals for the circuit in which the proceeding is held.

(b)   There shall be no right of appeal from a final order in a proceeding to test the validity of a warrant to remove to another district or place for commitment or trial a person charged with a criminal offense against the United States, or to test the validity of such person's detention pending removal proceedings.

(c)(1)   Unless a circuit justice or judge issues a certificate of appealability, an appeal may not be taken to the court of appeals from—

       (A)   the final order in a habeas corpus proceeding in which the detention complained of arises out of process issued by a State court; or

       (B)   the final order in a proceeding under section 2255.

       (2)   A certificate of appealability may issue under paragraph (1) only if the applicant has made a substantial showing of the denial of a constitutional right.

       (3)   The certificate of appealability under paragraph (1) shall indicate which specific issue or issues satisfy the showing required by paragraph (2).

(June 25, 1948, c. 646, 62 Stat. 967; May 24, 1949, c. 139, § 113, 63 Stat. 105; Oct. 31, 1951, c. 655, § 52, 65 Stat. 727; Apr. 24, 1996, Pub.L. 104–132, Title I, § 102, 110 Stat. 1217.)

§ 2254.   State custody; remedies in Federal courts*

(a)   The Supreme Court, a Justice thereof, a circuit judge, or a district court shall entertain an application for a writ of habeas corpus in behalf of a person in custody pursuant to the judgment of a State court only on the ground that he is in custody in violation of the Constitution or laws or treaties of the United States.

(b)(1)   An application for a writ of habeas corpus on behalf of a person in custody pursuant to the judgment of a State court shall not be granted unless it appears that—

       (A)   the applicant has exhausted the remedies available in the courts of the State; or

       (B)(i) there is an absence of available State corrective process; or

          (ii)   circumstances exist that render such process ineffective to protect the rights of the applicant.

       (2)   An application for a writ of habeas corpus may be denied on the merits, notwithstanding the failure of the applicant to exhaust the remedies available in the courts of the State.

       (3)   A State shall not be deemed to have waived the exhaustion requirement or be estopped from reliance upon the requirement unless the State, through counsel, expressly waives the requirement.

(c)   An applicant shall not be deemed to have exhausted the remedies available in the courts of the State, within the meaning of this section, if he has the right under the law of the State to raise, by any available procedure, the question presented.

(d)   An application for a writ of habeas corpus on behalf of a person in custody pursuant to the judgment of a State court shall not be granted with respect to any claim that was adjudicated on the merits in State court proceedings unless the adjudication of the claim—

---

*   [The Rules Governing Section 2254 Cases in the United States District Courts are set out in a separate section of this volume, *supra*. Ed.]

(1) resulted in a decision that was contrary to, or involved an unreasonable application of, clearly established Federal law, as determined by the Supreme Court of the United States; or

(2) resulted in a decision that was based on an unreasonable determination of the facts in light of the evidence presented in the State court proceeding.

(e)(1) In a proceeding instituted by an application for a writ of habeas corpus by a person in custody pursuant to the judgment of a State court, a determination of a factual issue made by a State court shall be presumed to be correct. The applicant shall have the burden of rebutting the presumption of correctness by clear and convincing evidence.

(2) If the applicant has failed to develop the factual basis of a claim in State court proceedings, the court shall not hold an evidentiary hearing on the claim unless the applicant shows that—

(A) the claim relies on—

(i) a new rule of constitutional law, made retroactive to cases on collateral review by the Supreme Court, that was previously unavailable; or

(ii) a factual predicate that could not have been previously discovered through the exercise of due diligence; and

(B) the facts underlying the claim would be sufficient to establish by clear and convincing evidence that but for constitutional error, no reasonable factfinder would have found the applicant guilty of the underlying offense.

(f) If the applicant challenges the sufficiency of the evidence adduced in such State court proceeding to support the State court's determination of a factual issue made therein, the applicant, if able, shall produce that part of the record pertinent to a determination of the sufficiency of the evidence to support such determination. If the applicant, because of indigency or other reason is unable to produce such part of the record, then the State shall produce such part of the record and the Federal court shall direct the State to do so by order directed to an appropriate State official. If the State cannot provide such pertinent part of the record, then the court shall determine under the existing facts and circumstances what weight shall be given to the State court's factual determination.

(g) A copy of the official records of the State court, duly certified by the clerk of such court to be a true and correct copy of a finding, judicial opinion, or other reliable written indicia showing such a factual determination by the State court shall be admissible in the Federal court proceeding.

(h) Except as provided in section 408 of the Controlled Substances Act, in all proceedings brought under this section, and any subsequent proceedings on review, the court may appoint counsel for an applicant who is or becomes financially unable to afford counsel, except as provided by a rule promulgated by the Supreme Court pursuant to statutory authority. Appointment of counsel under this section shall be governed by section 3006A of title 18.

(i) The ineffectiveness or incompetence of counsel during Federal or State collateral post-conviction proceedings shall not be a ground for relief in a proceeding arising under section 2254.

(June 25, 1948, c. 646, 62 Stat. 967; Nov. 2, 1966, Pub.L. 89–711, § 2, 80 Stat. 1105; Apr. 24, 1996, Pub.L. 104–132, Title I, § 104, 110 Stat. 1218.)

HISTORICAL AND STATUTORY NOTES

References in Text

Section 408 of the Controlled Substances Act, referred to in subsec. (h), is classified to section 848 of Title 21, Food and Drugs.

Approval and Effective Date of Rules Governing Section 2254 Cases and Section 2255 Proceedings for United States District Courts

Pub.L. 94–426, § 1, Sept. 28, 1976, 90 Stat. 1334, provided: "That the rules governing section 2254 cases in the United States district courts and the rules governing section 2255 proceedings for the United States district courts, as proposed by the United States Supreme Court, which were delayed by the Act entitled 'An Act to delay the effective date of certain proposed amendments to the Federal Rules of Criminal Procedure and certain other rules promulgated by the United States Supreme Court' (Public Law 94–349), are approved with the amendments set forth in section 2 of this Act and shall take effect as so amended, with respect to petitions under section 2254 and motions under section 2255 of title 28 of the United States Code filed on or after February 1, 1977."

Postponement of Effective Date of Proposed Rules Governing Proceedings Under Sections 2254 and 2255 of this Title

Rules and forms governing proceedings under sections 2254 and 2255 of this title proposed by Supreme Court order of Apr. 26, 1976, effective 30 days after adjournment sine die of 94th Congress, or until and to the extent approved by Act of Congress, whichever is earlier, see section 2 of Pub.L. 94–349, set out as a note under section 2074 of this title.

§ 2255.   Federal custody; remedies on motion attacking sentence*

   (a)   A prisoner in custody under sentence of a court established by Act of Congress claiming the right to be released upon the ground that the sentence was imposed in violation of the Constitution or laws of the United States, or that the court was without jurisdiction to impose such sentence, or that the sentence was in excess of the maximum authorized by law, or is otherwise subject to collateral attack, may move the court which imposed the sentence to vacate, set aside or correct the sentence.

   (b)   Unless the motion and the files and records of the case conclusively show that the prisoner is entitled to no relief, the court shall cause notice thereof to be served upon the United States attorney, grant a prompt hearing thereon, determine the issues and make findings of fact and conclusions of law with respect thereto. If the court finds that the judgment was rendered without jurisdiction, or that the sentence imposed was not authorized by law or otherwise open to collateral attack, or that there has been such a denial or infringement of the constitutional rights of the prisoner as to render the judgment vulnerable to collateral attack, the court shall vacate and set the judgment aside and shall discharge the prisoner or resentence him or grant a new trial or correct the sentence as may appear appropriate.

   (c)   A court may entertain and determine such motion without requiring the production of the prisoner at the hearing.

   (d)   An appeal may be taken to the court of appeals from the order entered on the motion as from a final judgment on application for a writ of habeas corpus.

   (e)   An application for a writ of habeas corpus in behalf of a prisoner who is authorized to apply for relief by motion pursuant to this section, shall not be entertained if it appears that the applicant has failed to apply for relief, by motion, to the court which sentenced him, or that such court has denied him relief, unless it also appears that the remedy by motion is inadequate or ineffective to test the legality of his detention.

   (f)   A 1-year period of limitation shall apply to a motion under this section. The limitation period shall run from the latest of—

      (1)   the date on which the judgment of conviction becomes final;

---

    *   [The Rules Governing Section 2255 Proceedings for the United States District Courts are set out in a separate section of this volume, *supra.* Ed.]

    (2) the date on which the impediment to making a motion created by governmental action in violation of the Constitution or laws of the United States is removed, if the movant was prevented from making a motion by such governmental action;

    (3) the date on which the right asserted was initially recognized by the Supreme Court, if that right has been newly recognized by the Supreme Court and made retroactively applicable to cases on collateral review; or

    (4) the date on which the facts supporting the claim or claims presented could have been discovered through the exercise of due diligence.

    (g) Except as provided in section 408 of the Controlled Substances Act, in all proceedings brought under this section, and any subsequent proceedings on review, the court may appoint counsel, except as provided by a rule promulgated by the Supreme Court pursuant to statutory authority. Appointment of counsel under this section shall be governed by section 3006A of title 18.

    (h) A second or successive motion must be certified as provided in section 2244 by a panel of the appropriate court of appeals to contain—

    (1) newly discovered evidence that, if proven and viewed in light of the evidence as a whole, would be sufficient to establish by clear and convincing evidence that no reasonable factfinder would have found the movant guilty of the offense; or

    (2) a new rule of constitutional law, made retroactive to cases on collateral review by the Supreme Court, that was previously unavailable.

(June 25, 1948, c. 646, 62 Stat. 967; May 24, 1949, c. 139, § 114, 63 Stat. 105; Apr. 24, 1996, Pub.L. 104–132, Title I, § 105, 110 Stat. 1220; Jan. 7, 2008, Pub.L. 110–177, Title V, § 511, 121 Stat. 2545.)

HISTORICAL AND STATUTORY NOTES

References in Text

    Section 408 of the Controlled Substances Act, referred to in text, is classified to section 848 of Title 21, Food and Drugs.

Approval and Effective Date of Rules Governing Section 2254 Cases and Section 2255 Proceedings For United States District Courts

    Pub.L. 94–426, § 1, Sept. 28, 1976, 90 Stat. 1334, provided: "That the rules governing section 2254 cases in the United States district courts and the rules governing section 2255 proceedings for the United States district courts, as proposed by the United States Supreme Court, which were delayed by the Act entitled 'An Act to delay the effective date of certain proposed amendments to the Federal Rules of Criminal Procedure and certain other rules promulgated by the United States Supreme Court' (Public Law 94–349), are approved with the amendments set forth in section 2 of this Act and shall take effect as so amended, with respect to petitions under section 2254 and motions [sections 2254 and 2255 of this title] under section 2255 of title 28 of the United States Code filed on or after February 1, 1977."

Postponement of Effective Date of Proposed Rules and Forms Governing Proceedings Under Sections 2254 and 2255 of this Title

    Rules and forms governing proceedings under this section and section 2254 of this title proposed by Supreme Court order of Apr. 26, 1976, effective 30 days after adjournment sine die of 94th Congress, or until and to the extent approved by Act of Congress, whichever is earlier, see section 2 of Pub.L. 94–349, set out as a note under section 2074 of this title.

[§ 2256.   Omitted]

HISTORICAL AND STATUTORY NOTES

Codification

    This section, added by Pub. L. 95–598, title II, § 250(a), Nov. 6, 1978, 92 Stat. 2672, did not become effective pursuant to section 402(b) of Pub. L. 95–598, as amended, set out as an Effective Date note preceding section 101 of Title 11, Bankruptcy. The section read as follows:

§ 2256. Habeas corpus from bankruptcy courts

A bankruptcy court may issue a writ of habeas corpus—

    (1) when appropriate to bring a person before the court—

        (A) for examination;

        (B) to testify; or

        (C) to perform a duty imposed on such person under this title; or

    (2) ordering the release of a debtor in a case under title 11 in custody under the judgment of a Federal or State court if—

        (A) such debtor was arrested or imprisoned on process in any civil action;

        (B) such process was issued for the collection of a debt—

            (i) dischargeable under title 11; or

            (ii) that is or will be provided for in a plan under chapter 11 or 13 of title 11; and

        (C) before the issuance of such writ, notice and a hearing have been afforded the adverse party of such debtor in custody to contest the issuance of such writ.

Prior Provisions

A prior section 2256, added by Pub. L. 95–144, § 3, Oct. 28, 1977, 91 Stat. 1220, which related to jurisdiction of proceedings relating to transferred offenders, was transferred to section 3244 of Title 18, Crimes and Criminal Procedure, by Pub. L. 95–598, Title III, § 314(j), Nov. 6, 1978, 92 Stat. 2677.

CHAPTER 154—SPECIAL HABEAS CORPUS PROCEDURES IN CAPITAL CASES

§ 2261. Prisoners in State custody subject to capital sentence; appointment of counsel; requirement of rule of court or statute; procedures for appointment

(a) This chapter shall apply to cases arising under section 2254 brought by prisoners in State custody who are subject to a capital sentence. It shall apply only if the provisions of subsections (b) and (c) are satisfied.

(b) Counsel.—This chapter is applicable if—

    (1) the Attorney General of the United States certifies that a State has established a mechanism for providing counsel in postconviction proceedings as provided in section 2265; and

    (2) counsel was appointed pursuant to that mechanism, petitioner validly waived counsel, petitioner retained counsel, or petitioner was found not to be indigent.

(c) Any mechanism for the appointment, compensation, and reimbursement of counsel as provided in subsection (b) must offer counsel to all State prisoners under capital sentence and must provide for the entry of an order by a court of record—

(1) appointing one or more counsels to represent the prisoner upon a finding that the prisoner is indigent and accepted the offer or is unable competently to decide whether to accept or reject the offer;

(2) finding, after a hearing if necessary, that the prisoner rejected the offer of counsel and made the decision with an understanding of its legal consequences; or

(3) denying the appointment of counsel upon a finding that the prisoner is not indigent.

(d) No counsel appointed pursuant to subsections (b) and (c) to represent a State prisoner under capital sentence shall have previously represented the prisoner at trial in the case for which the appointment is made unless the prisoner and counsel expressly request continued representation.

(e) The ineffectiveness or incompetence of counsel during State or Federal post-conviction proceedings in a capital case shall not be a ground for relief in a proceeding arising under section 2254. This limitation shall not preclude the appointment of different counsel, on the court's own motion or at the request of the prisoner, at any phase of State or Federal post-conviction proceedings on the basis of the ineffectiveness or incompetence of counsel in such proceedings.

(Added Pub.L. 104–132, Title I, § 107(a), Apr. 24, 1996, 110 Stat. 1221; amended Pub.L. 109–177, Title V, § 507(a), (b), Mar. 9, 2006, 120 Stat. 250.)

HISTORICAL AND STATUTORY NOTES

Effective and Applicability Provisions

1996 Acts. Section 107(c) of Pub.L. 104–132 provided that: "Chapter 154 of title 28, United States Code (as added by subsection (a)) [this chapter] shall apply to cases pending on or after the date of enactment of this Act [Apr. 24, 1996]."

§ 2262. Mandatory stay of execution; duration; limits on stays of execution; successive petitions

(a) Upon the entry in the appropriate State court of record of an order under section 2261(c), a warrant or order setting an execution date for a State prisoner shall be stayed upon application to any court that would have jurisdiction over any proceedings filed under section 2254. The application shall recite that the State has invoked the post-conviction review procedures of this chapter and that the scheduled execution is subject to stay.

(b) A stay of execution granted pursuant to subsection (a) shall expire if—

(1) a State prisoner fails to file a habeas corpus application under section 2254 within the time required in section 2263;

(2) before a court of competent jurisdiction, in the presence of counsel, unless the prisoner has competently and knowingly waived such counsel, and after having been advised of the consequences, a State prisoner under capital sentence waives the right to pursue habeas corpus review under section 2254; or

(3) a State prisoner files a habeas corpus petition under section 2254 within the time required by section 2263 and fails to make a substantial showing of the denial of a Federal right or is denied relief in the district court or at any subsequent stage of review.

(c) If one of the conditions in subsection (b) has occurred, no Federal court thereafter shall have the authority to enter a stay of execution in the case, unless the court of appeals approves the filing of a second or successive application under section 2244(b).

(Added Pub.L. 104–132, Title I, § 107(a), Apr. 24, 1996, 110 Stat. 1222.)

HISTORICAL AND STATUTORY NOTES

Effective and Applicability Provisions

1996 Acts. Section applicable to cases pending on or after Apr. 24, 1996, see section 107(c) of Pub.L. 104–132, set out as a note under section 2261 of this title.

§ 2263.   Filing of habeas corpus application; time requirements; tolling rules

(a) Any application under this chapter for habeas corpus relief under section 2254 must be filed in the appropriate district court not later than 180 days after final State court affirmance of the conviction and sentence on direct review or the expiration of the time for seeking such review.

(b) The time requirements established by subsection (a) shall be tolled—

(1) from the date that a petition for certiorari is filed in the Supreme Court until the date of final disposition of the petition if a State prisoner files the petition to secure review by the Supreme Court of the affirmance of a capital sentence on direct review by the court of last resort of the State or other final State court decision on direct review;

(2) from the date on which the first petition for post-conviction review or other collateral relief is filed until the final State court disposition of such petition; and

(3) during an additional period not to exceed 30 days, if—

(A) a motion for an extension of time is filed in the Federal district court that would have jurisdiction over the case upon the filing of a habeas corpus application under section 2254; and

(B) a showing of good cause is made for the failure to file the habeas corpus application within the time period established by this section.

(Added Pub.L. 104–132, Title I, § 107(a), Apr. 24, 1996, 110 Stat. 1223.)

HISTORICAL AND STATUTORY NOTES

Effective and Applicability Provisions

1996 Acts. Section applicable to cases pending on or after Apr. 24, 1996, see section 107(c) of Pub.L. 104–132, set out as a note under section 2261 of this title.

§ 2264.   Scope of Federal review; district court adjudications

(a) Whenever a State prisoner under capital sentence files a petition for habeas corpus relief to which this chapter applies, the district court shall only consider a claim or claims that have been raised and decided on the merits in the State courts, unless the failure to raise the claim properly is—

(1) the result of State action in violation of the Constitution or laws of the United States;

(2) the result of the Supreme Court's recognition of a new Federal right that is made retroactively applicable; or

(3) based on a factual predicate that could not have been discovered through the exercise of due diligence in time to present the claim for State or Federal post-conviction review.

(b) Following review subject to subsections (a), (d), and (e) of section 2254, the court shall rule on the claims properly before it.

(Added Pub.L. 104–132, Title I, § 107(a), Apr. 24, 1996, 110 Stat. 1223.)

§ 2265.   Certification and judicial review

(a) **Certification.**—

(1) **In general.**—If requested by an appropriate State official, the Attorney General of the United States shall determine—

    (A) whether the State has established a mechanism for the appointment, compensation, and payment of reasonable litigation expenses of competent counsel in State postconviction proceedings brought by indigent prisoners who have been sentenced to death;

    (B) the date on which the mechanism described in subparagraph (A) was established; and

    (C) whether the State provides standards of competency for the appointment of counsel in proceedings described in subparagraph (A).

  (2) Effective date.—The date the mechanism described in paragraph (1)(A) was established shall be the effective date of the certification under this subsection.

  (3) Only express requirements.—There are no requirements for certification or for application of this chapter other than those expressly stated in this chapter.

(b) Regulations.—The Attorney General shall promulgate regulations to implement the certification procedure under subsection (a).

(c) Review of certification.—

  (1) In general.—The determination by the Attorney General regarding whether to certify a State under this section is subject to review exclusively as provided under chapter 158 of this title.

  (2) Venue.—The Court of Appeals for the District of Columbia Circuit shall have exclusive jurisdiction over matters under paragraph (1), subject to review by the Supreme Court under section 2350 of this title.

  (3) Standard of review.—The determination by the Attorney General regarding whether to certify a State under this section shall be subject to de novo review.

(Added Pub.L. 109–177, Title V, § 507(c)(1), Mar. 9, 2006, 120 Stat. 250.)

HISTORICAL AND STATUTORY NOTES

References in Text

    Chapter 158 of this title, referred to in subsec. (c)(1), is Orders of Federal Agencies; Review, 28 U.S.C.A. § 2341 et seq.

Prior Provisions

    A prior section 2265, added Pub.L. 104–132, Title I, § 107(a), Apr. 24, 1996, 110 Stat. 1223, relating to application to State unitary review procedure, was repealed by Pub.L. 109–177, Title V, § 507(c)(1), Mar. 9, 2006, 120 Stat. 250.

§ 2266.   Limitation periods for determining applications and motions

  (a) The adjudication of any application under section 2254 that is subject to this chapter, and the adjudication of any motion under section 2255 by a person under sentence of death, shall be given priority by the district court and by the court of appeals over all noncapital matters.

  (b)(1)(A) A district court shall render a final determination and enter a final judgment on any application for a writ of habeas corpus brought under this chapter in a capital case not later than 450 days after the date on which the application is filed, or 60 days after the date on which the case is submitted for decision, whichever is earlier.

    (B) A district court shall afford the parties at least 120 days in which to complete all actions, including the preparation of all pleadings and briefs, and if necessary, a hearing, prior to the submission of the case for decision.

    (C)(i) A district court may delay for not more than one additional 30-day period beyond the period specified in subparagraph (A), the rendering of a determination of an application for a writ of habeas corpus if the court issues a written order making a finding, and stating the reasons for the finding, that the ends of justice that would be served by allowing the delay outweigh the best interests of the public and the applicant in a speedy disposition of the application.

    (ii) The factors, among others, that a court shall consider in determining whether a delay in the disposition of an application is warranted are as follows:

        (I) Whether the failure to allow the delay would be likely to result in a miscarriage of justice.

        (II) Whether the case is so unusual or so complex, due to the number of defendants, the nature of the prosecution, or the existence of novel questions of fact or law, that it is unreasonable to expect adequate briefing within the time limitations established by subparagraph (A).

        (III) Whether the failure to allow a delay in a case that, taken as a whole, is not so unusual or so complex as described in subclause (II), but would otherwise deny the applicant reasonable time to obtain counsel, would unreasonably deny the applicant or the government continuity of counsel, or would deny counsel for the applicant or the government the reasonable time necessary for effective preparation, taking into account the exercise of due diligence.

    (iii) No delay in disposition shall be permissible because of general congestion of the court's calendar.

    (iv) The court shall transmit a copy of any order issued under clause (i) to the Director of the Administrative Office of the United States Courts for inclusion in the report under paragraph (5).

(2) The time limitations under paragraph (1) shall apply to—

    (A) an initial application for a writ of habeas corpus;

    (B) any second or successive application for a writ of habeas corpus; and

    (C) any redetermination of an application for a writ of habeas corpus following a remand by the court of appeals or the Supreme Court for further proceedings, in which case the limitation period shall run from the date the remand is ordered.

(3)(A) The time limitations under this section shall not be construed to entitle an applicant to a stay of execution, to which the applicant would otherwise not be entitled, for the purpose of litigating any application or appeal.

    (B) No amendment to an application for a writ of habeas corpus under this chapter shall be permitted after the filing of the answer to the application, except on the grounds specified in section 2244(b).

(4)(A) The failure of a court to meet or comply with a time limitation under this section shall not be a ground for granting relief from a judgment of conviction or sentence.

    (B) The State may enforce a time limitation under this section by petitioning for a writ of mandamus to the court of appeals. The court of appeals shall act on the petition for a writ of mandamus not later than 30 days after the filing of the petition.

(5)(A) The Administrative Office of the United States Courts shall submit to Congress an annual report on the compliance by the district courts with the time limitations under this section.

    (B) The report described in subparagraph (A) shall include copies of the orders submitted by the district courts under paragraph (1)(B)(iv).

(c)(1)(A) A court of appeals shall hear and render a final determination of any appeal of an order granting or denying, in whole or in part, an application brought under this chapter in a capital case not later than 120 days after the date on which the reply brief is filed, or if no reply brief is filed, not later than 120 days after the date on which the answering brief is filed.

(B)(i) A court of appeals shall decide whether to grant a petition for rehearing or other request for rehearing en banc not later than 30 days after the date on which the petition for rehearing is filed unless a responsive pleading is required, in which case the court shall decide whether to grant the petition not later than 30 days after the date on which the responsive pleading is filed.

(ii) If a petition for rehearing or rehearing en banc is granted, the court of appeals shall hear and render a final determination of the appeal not later than 120 days after the date on which the order granting rehearing or rehearing en banc is entered.

(2) The time limitations under paragraph (1) shall apply to—

(A) an initial application for a writ of habeas corpus;

(B) any second or successive application for a writ of habeas corpus; and

(C) any redetermination of an application for a writ of habeas corpus or related appeal following a remand by the court of appeals en banc or the Supreme Court for further proceedings, in which case the limitation period shall run from the date the remand is ordered.

(3) The time limitations under this section shall not be construed to entitle an applicant to a stay of execution, to which the applicant would otherwise not be entitled, for the purpose of litigating any application or appeal.

(4)(A) The failure of a court to meet or comply with a time limitation under this section shall not be a ground for granting relief from a judgment of conviction or sentence.

(B) The State may enforce a time limitation under this section by applying for a writ of mandamus to the Supreme Court.

(5) The Administrative Office of the United States Courts shall submit to Congress an annual report on the compliance by the courts of appeals with the time limitations under this section.

(Added Pub.L. 104–132, Title I, § 107(a), Apr. 24, 1996, 110 Stat. 1224; amended Pub.L. 109–177, Title V, § 507(e), Mar. 9, 2006, 120 Stat. 251.)

CHAPTER 155—INJUNCTIONS; THREE-JUDGE COURTS

[§§ 2281, 2282. Repealed. Pub.L. 94–381, §§ 1, 2, Aug. 12, 1976, 90 Stat. 1119]

HISTORICAL AND STATUTORY NOTES

Section [2281], Act June 25, 1948, c. 646, 62 Stat. 968, provided that an interlocutory or permanent injunction restraining the enforcement, operation or execution of a State statute on grounds of unconstitutionality should not be granted unless the application has been heard and determined by a three-judge district court.

---

[1]   So in original. Does not conform to section catchline.

Section [2282], Act June 25, 1948, c. 646, 62 Stat. 968, provided that an interlocutory or permanent injunction restraining the enforcement, operation or execution of any Act of Congress on grounds of unconstitutionality should not be granted unless the application therefor has been heard and determined by a three-judge district court.

Effective Date of Repeal

Repeal by Pub.L. 94–381 not applicable to any action commenced on or before Aug. 12, 1976, see section 7 of Pub.L. 94–381, set out as an Effective and Applicability Provisions note under section 2284 of this title.

§ 2283.   Stay of State court proceedings

A court of the United States may not grant an injunction to stay proceedings in a State court except as expressly authorized by Act of Congress, or where necessary in aid of its jurisdiction, or to protect or effectuate its judgments.

(June 25, 1948, c. 646, 62 Stat. 968.)

§ 2284.   Three-judge court; when required; composition; procedure

(a) A district court of three judges shall be convened when otherwise required by Act of Congress, or when an action is filed challenging the constitutionality of the apportionment of congressional districts or the apportionment of any statewide legislative body.

(b) In any action required to be heard and determined by a district court of three judges under subsection (a) of this section, the composition and procedure of the court shall be as follows:

(1) Upon the filing of a request for three judges, the judge to whom the request is presented shall, unless he determines that three judges are not required, immediately notify the chief judge of the circuit, who shall designate two other judges, at least one of whom shall be a circuit judge. The judges so designated, and the judge to whom the request was presented, shall serve as members of the court to hear and determine the action or proceeding.

(2) If the action is against a State, or officer or agency thereof, at least five days' notice of hearing of the action shall be given by registered or certified mail to the Governor and attorney general of the State.

(3) A single judge may conduct all proceedings except the trial, and enter all orders permitted by the rules of civil procedure except as provided in this subsection. He may grant a temporary restraining order on a specific finding, based on evidence submitted, that specified irreparable damage will result if the order is not granted, which order, unless previously revoked by the district judge, shall remain in force only until the hearing and determination by the district court of three judges of an application for a preliminary injunction. A single judge shall not appoint a master, or order a reference, or hear and determine any application for a preliminary or permanent injunction or motion to vacate such an injunction, or enter judgment on the merits. Any action of a single judge may be reviewed by the full court at any time before final judgment.

(June 25, 1948, c. 646, 62 Stat. 968; June 11, 1960, Pub.L. 86–507, § 1(19), 74 Stat. 201; Aug. 12, 1976, Pub.L. 94–381, § 3, 90 Stat. 1119; Nov. 8, 1984, Pub.L. 98–620, Title IV, § 402(29)(E), 98 Stat. 3359.)

HISTORICAL AND STATUTORY NOTES

References in Text

The rules of civil procedure, referred to in subsec. (b)(3), are classified generally to this title.

Effective and Applicability Provisions

1984 Acts. Amendment by Pub.L. 98–620 not to apply to cases pending on Nov. 8, 1984, see section 403 of Pub.L. 98–620, set out as a note under section 1657 of this title.

1976 Acts. Section 7 of Pub.L. 94–381 provided that: "This Act [amending this section and section 2403 of this title and repealing sections 2281 and 2282 of this title] shall not apply to any action commenced on or before the date of enactment [Aug. 12, 1976]."

CHAPTER 159—INTERPLEADER

Sec.
2361.   Process and procedure.

§ 2361.   Process and procedure

In any civil action of interpleader or in the nature of interpleader under section 1335 of this title, a district court may issue its process for all claimants and enter its order restraining them from instituting or prosecuting any proceeding in any State or United States court affecting the property, instrument or obligation involved in the interpleader action until further order of the court. Such process and order shall be returnable at such time as the court or judge thereof directs, and shall be addressed to and served by the United States marshals for the respective districts where the claimants reside or may be found.

Such district court shall hear and determine the case, and may discharge the plaintiff from further liability, make the injunction permanent, and make all appropriate orders to enforce its judgment.

(June 25, 1948, c. 646, 62 Stat. 970; May 24, 1949, c. 139, § 117, 63 Stat. 105.)

CHAPTER 161—UNITED STATES AS PARTY GENERALLY

Sec.
2401.   Time for commencing action against United States.
2402.   Jury trial in actions against United States.
2403.   Intervention by United States or a State; constitutional question.
2404.   Death of defendant in damage action.
2405.   Garnishment.
2406.   Credits in actions by United States; prior disallowance.
2407.   Delinquents for public money; judgment at return term; continuance.
2408.   Security not required of United States.
2409.   Partition actions involving United States.
2409a.   Real property quiet title actions.
2410.   Actions affecting property on which United States has lien.
2411.   Interest.
2412.   Costs and fees.
2413.   Executions in favor of United States.
2414.   Payment of judgments and compromise settlements.
2415.   Time for commencing actions brought by the United States.
2416.   Time for commencing actions brought by the United States—Exclusions.

§ 2401.   Time for commencing action against United States

(a) Except as provided by chapter 71 of title 41, every civil action commenced against the United States shall be barred unless the complaint is filed within six years after the right of action first accrues. The action of any person under legal disability or beyond the seas at the time the claim accrues may be commenced within three years after the disability ceases.

(b) A tort claim against the United States shall be forever barred unless it is presented in writing to the appropriate Federal agency within two years after such claim accrues or unless action is begun within six months after the date of mailing, by certified or registered mail, of notice of final denial of the claim by the agency to which it was presented.

(June 25, 1948, c. 646, 62 Stat. 971; Apr. 25, 1949, c. 92, § 1, 63 Stat. 62; Sept. 8, 1959, Pub.L. 86–238, § 1(3), 73 Stat. 472; July 18, 1966, Pub.L. 89–506, § 7, 80 Stat. 307; Nov. 1, 1978, Pub.L. 95–563, § 14(b), 92 Stat. 2389; Jan. 4, 2011, Pub.L. 111–350, § 5(g)(8), 124 Stat. 3848.)

HISTORICAL AND STATUTORY NOTES

References in Text

Chapter 71 of title 41, referred to in subsec. (a), is classified to 41 U.S.C.A. § 7101 et seq.

§ 2402.   Jury trial in actions against United States

Subject to chapter 179 of this title, any action against the United States under section 1346 shall be tried by the court without a jury, except that any action against the United States under section 1346(a)(1) [civil action for recovery of any internal-revenue tax, penalty, or sum] shall, at the request of either party to such action, be tried by the court with a jury.

(June 25, 1948, c. 646, 62 Stat. 971; July 30, 1954, c. 648, § 2(a), 68 Stat. 589; Oct. 26, 1996, Pub.L. 104–331, § 3(b)(3), 110 Stat. 4069.)

§ 2403.   Intervention by United States or a State; constitutional question

(a) In any action, suit or proceeding in a court of the United States to which the United States or any agency, officer or employee thereof is not a party, wherein the constitutionality of any Act of Congress affecting the public interest is drawn in question, the court shall certify such fact to the Attorney General, and shall permit the United States to intervene for presentation of evidence, if evidence is otherwise admissible in the case, and for argument on the question of constitutionality. The United States shall, subject to the applicable provisions of law, have all the rights of a party and be subject to all liabilities of a party as to court costs to the extent necessary for a proper presentation of the facts and law relating to the question of constitutionality.

(b) In any action, suit, or proceeding in a court of the United States to which a State or any agency, officer, or employee thereof is not a party, wherein the constitutionality of any statute of that State affecting the public interest is drawn in question, the court shall certify such fact to the attorney general of the State, and shall permit the State to intervene for presentation of evidence, if evidence is otherwise admissible in the case, and for argument on the question of constitutionality. The State shall, subject to the applicable provisions of law, have all the rights of a party and be subject to all liabilities of a party as to court costs to the extent necessary for a proper presentation of the facts and law relating to the question of constitutionality.

(June 25, 1948, c. 646, 62 Stat. 971; Aug. 12, 1976, Pub.L. 94–381, § 5, 90 Stat. 1120.)

§ 2404.   Death of defendant in damage action

A civil action for damages commenced by or on behalf of the United States or in which it is interested shall not abate on the death of a defendant but shall survive and be enforceable against his estate as well as against surviving defendants.

(June 25, 1948, c. 646, 62 Stat. 971.)

§ 2405.   Garnishment

In any action or suit commenced by the United States against a corporation for the recovery of money upon a bill, note, or other security, the debtors of the corporation may be summoned as garnishees. Any person so summoned shall appear in open court and depose in writing to the amount of his indebtedness to the corporation at the time of the service of the summons and at the time of making the deposition, and judgment may be entered in favor of the United States for the sum admitted by the garnishee to be due the corporation as if it had been due the United States. A judgment shall not be entered against any garnishee until after judgment has been rendered against the corporation, nor until the sum in which the garnishee is indebted is actually due.

When any garnishee deposes in open court that he is not and was not at the time of the service of the summons indebted to the corporation, an issue may be tendered by the United States upon such deposition. If, upon the trial of that issue, a verdict is rendered against the garnishee, judgment shall be entered in favor of the United States, pursuant to such verdict, with costs.

Any garnishee who fails to appear at the term to which he is summoned shall be subject to attachment for contempt.

(June 25, 1948, c. 646, 62 Stat. 971.)

§ 2406.   Credits in actions by United States; prior disallowance

In an action by the United States against an individual, evidence supporting the defendant's claim for a credit shall not be admitted unless he first proves that such claim has been disallowed, in whole or in part, by the Government Accountability Office, or that he has, at the time of the trial, obtained possession of vouchers not previously procurable and has been prevented from presenting such claim to the Government Accountability Office by absence from the United States or unavoidable accident.

(June 25, 1948, c. 646, 62 Stat. 972; July 7, 2004, Pub.L. 108–271, § 8(b), 118 Stat. 814.)

§ 2407.   Delinquents for public money; judgment at return term; continuance

In an action by the United States against any person accountable for public money who fails to pay into the Treasury the sum reported due the United States, upon the adjustment of his account the court shall grant judgment upon motion unless a continuance is granted as specified in this section.

A continuance may be granted if the defendant, in open court and in the presence of the United States attorney, states under oath that he is equitably entitled to credits which have been disallowed by the Government Accountability Office prior to the commencement of the action, specifying each particular claim so rejected, and stating that he cannot safely come to trial.

A continuance may also be granted if such an action is commenced on a bond or other sealed instrument and the court requires the original instrument to be produced.

(June 25, 1948, c. 646, 62 Stat. 972; Pub.L. 108–271, § 8(b), July 7, 2004, 118 Stat. 814.)

§ 2408.   Security not required of United States

Security for damages or costs shall not be required of the United States, any department or agency thereof or any party acting under the direction of any such department or agency on the issuance of process or the institution or prosecution of any proceeding.

Costs taxable, under other Acts of Congress, against the United States or any such department, agency or party shall be paid out of the contingent fund of the department or agency which directed the proceedings to be instituted.

(June 25, 1948, c. 646, 62 Stat. 972.)

§ 2409.   Partition actions involving United States

Any civil action by any tenant in common or joint tenant owning an undivided interest in lands, where the United States is one of such tenants in common or joint tenants, against the United States alone or against the United States and any other of such owners, shall proceed, and be determined, in the same manner as would a similar action between private persons.

Whenever in such action the court orders a sale of the property or any part thereof the Attorney General may bid for the same in behalf of the United States. If the United States is the purchaser, the amount of the purchase money shall be paid from the Treasury upon a warrant drawn by the Secretary of the Treasury on the requisition of the Attorney General.

(June 25, 1948, c. 646, 62 Stat. 972.)

§ 2409a.   Real property quiet title actions

(a) The United States may be named as a party defendant in a civil action under this section to adjudicate a disputed title to real property in which the United States claims an interest, other than a security interest or water rights. This section does not apply to trust or restricted Indian lands, nor does it apply to or affect actions which may be or could have been brought under sections 1346, 1347, 1491, or 2410 of this title, sections 7424, 7425, or 7426 of the Internal Revenue Code of 1986, as amended (26 U.S.C. 7424, 7425, and 7426), or section 208 of the Act of July 10, 1952 (43 U.S.C. 666).

(b) The United States shall not be disturbed in possession or control of any real property involved in any action under this section pending a final judgment or decree, the conclusion of any appeal therefrom, and sixty days; and if the final determination shall be adverse to the United States, the United States nevertheless may retain such possession or control of the real property or of any part thereof as it may elect, upon payment to the person determined to be entitled thereto of an amount which upon such election the district court in the same action shall determine to be just compensation for such possession or control.

(c) No preliminary injunction shall issue in any action brought under this section.

(d) The complaint shall set forth with particularity the nature of the right, title, or interest which the plaintiff claims in the real property, the circumstances under which it was acquired, and the right, title, or interest claimed by the United States.

(e) If the United States disclaims all interest in the real property or interest therein adverse to the plaintiff at any time prior to the actual commencement of the trial, which disclaimer is confirmed by order of the court, the jurisdiction of the district court shall cease unless it has jurisdiction of the civil action or suit on ground other than and independent of the authority conferred by section 1346(f) of this title.

(f) A civil action against the United States under this section shall be tried by the court without a jury.

(g) Any civil action under this section, except for an action brought by a State, shall be barred unless it is commenced within twelve years of the date upon which it accrued. Such action shall be deemed to have accrued on the date the plaintiff or his predecessor in interest knew or should have known of the claim of the United States.

(h) No civil action may be maintained under this section by a State with respect to defense facilities (including land) of the United States so long as the lands at issue are being used or required by the United States for national defense purposes as determined by the head of the Federal agency with jurisdiction over the lands involved, if it is determined that the State action was brought more than twelve years after the State knew or should have known of the claims of the United States. Upon cessation of such use or requirement, the State may dispute title to such lands pursuant to the provisions of this section. The decision of the head of the Federal agency is not subject to judicial review.

(i) Any civil action brought by a State under this section with respect to lands, other than tide or submerged lands, on which the United States or its lessee or right-of-way or easement grantee has made substantial improvements or substantial investments or on which the United States has conducted substantial activities pursuant to a management plan such as range improvement, timber harvest, tree planting, mineral activities, farming, wildlife habitat improvement, or other similar activities, shall be barred unless the action is commenced within twelve years after the date the State received notice of the Federal claims to the lands.

(j) If a final determination in an action brought by a State under this section involving submerged or tide lands on which the United States or its lessee or right-of-way or easement grantee has made substantial improvements or substantial investments is adverse to the United States and it is determined that the State's action was brought more than twelve years after the State received notice of the Federal claim to the lands, the State shall take title to the lands subject to any existing lease, easement, or right-of-way. Any compensation due with respect to such lease, easement, or right-of-way shall be determined under existing law.

(k) Notice for the purposes of the accrual of an action brought by a State under this section shall be—

    (1) by public communications with respect to the claimed lands which are sufficiently specific as to be reasonably calculated to put the claimant on notice of the Federal claim to the lands, or

    (2) by the use, occupancy, or improvement of the claimed lands which, in the circumstances, is open and notorious.

(*l*) For purposes of this section, the term "tide or submerged lands" means "lands beneath navigable waters" as defined in section 2 of the Submerged Lands Act (43 U.S.C. 1301).

(m) Not less than one hundred and eighty days before bringing any action under this section, a State shall notify the head of the Federal agency with jurisdiction over the lands in question of the State's intention to file suit, the basis therefor, and a description of the lands included in the suit.

(n) Nothing in this section shall be construed to permit suits against the United States based upon adverse possession.

(Added Pub.L. 92–562, § 3(a), Oct. 25, 1972, 86 Stat. 1176; amended Pub.L. 99–514, § 2, Oct. 22, 1986, 100 Stat. 2095; Pub.L. 99–598, Nov. 4, 1986, 100 Stat. 3351.)

HISTORICAL AND STATUTORY NOTES

References in Text

    Section 208 of the Act July 10, 1952, referred to in subsec. (a), is section 208 (a) to (d) of Act July 10, 1952, c. 651, 66 Stat. 560. Section 208 (a) to (c) is classified to section 666 of Title 43, Public Lands. Section 208(d) is not classified to the Code.

§ 2410.   Actions affecting property on which United States has lien

(a) Under the conditions prescribed in this section and section 1444 of this title for the protection of the United States, the United States may be named a party in any civil action or suit in any district court, or in any State court having jurisdiction of the subject matter—

    (1) to quiet title to,

    (2) to foreclose a mortgage or other lien upon,

    (3) to partition,

    (4) to condemn, or

    (5) of interpleader or in the nature of interpleader with respect to,

real or personal property on which the United States has or claims a mortgage or other lien.

(b) The complaint or pleading shall set forth with particularity the nature of the interest or lien of the United States. In actions or suits involving liens arising under the internal revenue laws, the complaint or pleading shall include the name and address of the taxpayer whose liability created the lien and, if a notice of the tax lien was filed, the identity of the internal revenue office which filed the notice, and the date and place such notice of lien was filed. In actions in the State courts service upon the United States shall be made by serving the process of the court with a copy of the complaint upon the United States attorney for the district in which the action is brought or upon an assistant United States attorney or clerical employee designated by the United States attorney in writing filed with the clerk of the court in which the action is brought and by sending copies of the process and complaint, by registered mail, or by certified mail, to the Attorney General of the United States at Washington,

District of Columbia. In such actions the United States may appear and answer, plead or demur within sixty days after such service or such further time as the court may allow.

(c) A judgment or decree in such action or suit shall have the same effect respecting the discharge of the property from the mortgage or other lien held by the United States as may be provided with respect to such matters by the local law of the place where the court is situated. However, an action to foreclose a mortgage or other lien, naming the United States as a party under this section, must seek judicial sale. A sale to satisfy a lien inferior to one of the United States shall be made subject to and without disturbing the lien of the United States, unless the United States consents that the property may be sold free of its lien and the proceeds divided as the parties may be entitled. Where a sale of real estate is made to satisfy a lien prior to that of the United States, the United States shall have one year from the date of sale within which to redeem, except that with respect to a lien arising under the internal revenue laws the period shall be 120 days or the period allowable for redemption under State law, whichever is longer, and in any case in which, under the provisions of section 505 of the Housing Act of 1950, as amended (12 U.S.C. 1701k), and subsection (d) of section 3720 of title 38 of the United States Code, the right to redeem does not arise, there shall be no right of redemption. In any case where the debt owing the United States is due, the United States may ask, by way of affirmative relief, for the foreclosure of its own lien and where property is sold to satisfy a first lien held by the United States, the United States may bid at the sale such sum, not exceeding the amount of its claim with expenses of sale, as may be directed by the head (or his delegate) of the department or agency of the United States which has charge of the administration of the laws in respect to which the claim of the United States arises. In any case where the United States is a bidder at the judicial sale, it may credit the amount determined to be due it against the amount it bids at such sales.

(d) In any case in which the United States redeems real property under this section or section 7425 of the Internal Revenue Code of 1986, the amount to be paid for such property shall be the sum of—

(1) the actual amount paid by the purchaser at such sale (which, in the case of a purchaser who is the holder of the lien being foreclosed, shall include the amount of the obligation secured by such lien to the extent satisfied by reason of such sale),

(2) interest on the amount paid (as determined under paragraph (1)) at 6 percent per annum from the date of such sale, and

(3) the amount (if any) equal to the excess of (A) the expenses necessarily incurred in connection with such property, over (B) the income from such property plus (to the extent such property is used by the purchaser) a reasonable rental value of such property.

(e) Whenever any person has a lien upon any real or personal property, duly recorded in the jurisdiction in which the property is located, and a junior lien, other than a tax lien, in favor of the United States attaches to such property, such person may make a written request to the officer charged with the administration of the laws in respect of which the lien of the United States arises, to have the same extinguished. If after appropriate investigation, it appears to such officer that the proceeds from the sale of the property would be insufficient to wholly or partly satisfy the lien of the United States, or that the claim of the United States has been satisfied or by lapse of time or otherwise has become unenforceable, such officer may issue a certificate releasing the property from such lien.

(June 25, 1948, c. 646, 62 Stat. 972; May 24, 1949, c. 139, § 119, 63 Stat. 105; July 7, 1958, Pub.L. 85–508, § 12(h), 72 Stat. 348; June 11, 1960, Pub.L. 86–507, § 1(20), 74 Stat. 201; Nov. 2, 1966, Pub.L. 89–719, Title II, § 201, 80 Stat. 1147; Oct. 22, 1986, Pub.L. 99–514, § 2, 100 Stat. 2095; Nov. 29, 1990, Pub.L. 101–647, Title XXXVI, § 3630, 104 Stat. 4966; Aug. 6, 1991, Pub.L. 102–83, § 5(c)(2), 105 Stat. 406; Oct. 19, 1996, Pub.L. 104–316, Title I, § 114, 110 Stat. 3834.)

HISTORICAL AND STATUTORY NOTES

References in Text

The internal revenue laws, referred to in subsec. (b), are classified generally to Title 26, Internal Revenue Code.

Section 7425 of the Internal Revenue Code of 1986, referred to in subsec. (d), is classified to section 7425 of Title 26, Internal Revenue Code.

§ 2411.　　Interest

In any judgment of any court rendered (whether against the United States, a collector or deputy collector of internal revenue, a former collector or deputy collector, or the personal representative in case of death) for any overpayment in respect of any internal-revenue tax, interest shall be allowed at the overpayment rate established under section 6621 of the Internal Revenue Code of 1986 upon the amount of the overpayment, from the date of the payment or collection thereof to a date preceding the date of the refund check by not more than thirty days, such date to be determined by the Commissioner of Internal Revenue. The Commissioner is authorized to tender by check payment of any such judgment, with interest as herein provided, at any time after such judgment becomes final, whether or not a claim for such payment has been duly filed, and such tender shall stop the running of interest, whether or not such refund check is accepted by the judgment creditor.

(June 25, 1948, c. 646, 62 Stat. 973; May 24, 1949, c. 139, § 120, 63 Stat. 106; Jan. 3, 1975, Pub.L. 93–625, § 7(a)(2), 88 Stat. 2115; Apr. 2, 1982, Pub.L. 97–164, Title III, § 302(b), 96 Stat. 56; Oct. 22, 1986, Pub.L. 99–514, § 2, Title XV, § 1511(c)(18), 100 Stat. 2095, 2746.)

HISTORICAL AND STATUTORY NOTES

References in Text

Section 6621 of the Internal Revenue Code of 1986, referred to in text, is classified to section 6621 of Title 26, Internal Revenue Code.

§ 2412.　　Costs and fees

(a)(1) Except as otherwise specifically provided by statute, a judgment for costs, as enumerated in section 1920 of this title, but not including the fees and expenses of attorneys, may be awarded to the prevailing party in any civil action brought by or against the United States or any agency or any official of the United States acting in his or her official capacity in any court having jurisdiction of such action. A judgment for costs when taxed against the United States shall, in an amount established by statute, court rule, or order, be limited to reimbursing in whole or in part the prevailing party for the costs incurred by such party in the litigation.

(2) A judgment for costs, when awarded in favor of the United States in an action brought by the United States, may include an amount equal to the filing fee prescribed under section 1914(a) of this title. The preceding sentence shall not be construed as requiring the United States to pay any filing fee.

(b) Unless expressly prohibited by statute, a court may award reasonable fees and expenses of attorneys, in addition to the costs which may be awarded pursuant to subsection (a), to the prevailing party in any civil action brought by or against the United States or any agency or any official of the United States acting in his or her official capacity in any court having jurisdiction of such action. The United States shall be liable for such fees and expenses to the same extent that any other party would be liable under the common law or under the terms of any statute which specifically provides for such an award.

(c)(1) Any judgment against the United States or any agency and any official of the United States acting in his or her official capacity for costs pursuant to subsection (a) shall be paid as provided in sections 2414 and 2517 of this title and shall be in addition to any relief provided in the judgment.

(2) Any judgment against the United States or any agency and any official of the United States acting in his or her official capacity for fees and expenses of attorneys pursuant to subsection (b) shall be paid as provided in sections 2414 and 2517 of this title, except that if the basis for the award is a finding that the United States acted in bad faith, then the award shall be paid by any agency found to have acted in bad faith and shall be in addition to any relief provided in the judgment.

(d)(1)(A) Except as otherwise specifically provided by statute, a court shall award to a prevailing party other than the United States fees and other expenses, in addition to any costs awarded pursuant to subsection (a), incurred by that party in any civil action (other than cases sounding in tort), including proceedings for judicial review of agency action, brought by or against the United States in any court having jurisdiction of that action, unless the court finds that the position of the United States was substantially justified or that special circumstances make an award unjust.

(B) A party seeking an award of fees and other expenses shall, within thirty days of final judgment in the action, submit to the court an application for fees and other expenses which shows that the party is a prevailing party and is eligible to receive an award under this subsection, and the amount sought, including an itemized statement from any attorney or expert witness representing or appearing in behalf of the party stating the actual time expended and the rate at which fees and other expenses were computed. The party shall also allege that the position of the United States was not substantially justified. Whether or not the position of the United States was substantially justified shall be determined on the basis of the record (including the record with respect to the action or failure to act by the agency upon which the civil action is based) which is made in the civil action for which fees and other expenses are sought.

(C) The court, in its discretion, may reduce the amount to be awarded pursuant to this subsection, or deny an award, to the extent that the prevailing party during the course of the proceedings engaged in conduct which unduly and unreasonably protracted the final resolution of the matter in controversy.

(D) If, in a civil action brought by the United States or a proceeding for judicial review of an adversary adjudication described in section 504(a)(4) of title 5, the demand by the United States is substantially in excess of the judgment finally obtained by the United States and is unreasonable when compared with such judgment, under the facts and circumstances of the case, the court shall award to the party the fees and other expenses related to defending against the excessive demand, unless the party has committed a willful violation of law or otherwise acted in bad faith, or special circumstances make an award unjust. Fees and expenses awarded under this subparagraph shall be paid only as a consequence of appropriations provided in advance.

(2) For the purposes of this subsection—

(A) "fees and other expenses" includes the reasonable expenses of expert witnesses, the reasonable cost of any study, analysis, engineering report, test, or project which is found by the court to be necessary for the preparation of the party's case, and reasonable attorney fees (The amount of fees awarded under this subsection shall be based upon prevailing market rates for the kind and quality of the services furnished, except that (i) no expert witness shall be compensated at a rate in excess of the highest rate of compensation for expert witnesses paid by the United States; and (ii) attorney fees shall not be awarded in excess of $125 per hour unless the court determines that an increase in the cost of living or a special factor, such as the limited availability of qualified attorneys for the proceedings involved, justifies a higher fee.);

(B) "party" means (i) an individual whose net worth did not exceed $2,000,000 at the time the civil action was filed, or (ii) any owner of an unincorporated business, or any partnership, corporation, association, unit of local government, or organization, the net worth of which did not exceed $7,000,000 at the time the civil action was filed, and which had not more than 500 employees at the time the civil action was filed; except that an organization described in section 501(c)(3) of the Internal Revenue Code of 1986 (26 U.S.C. 501(c)(3)) exempt from taxation under section 501(a) of such Code, or a cooperative association as defined in section 15(a) of the Agricultural Marketing Act (12 U.S.C. 1141j(a)), may be a party regardless of the net worth of such organization or cooperative association or for purposes of subsection (d)(1)(D), a small entity as defined in section 601 of Title 5;

(C) "United States" includes any agency and any official of the United States acting in his or her official capacity;

(D) "position of the United States" means, in addition to the position taken by the United States in the civil action, the action or failure to act by the agency upon which the civil action is based; except that fees and expenses may not be awarded to a party for any portion of the litigation in which the party has unreasonably protracted the proceedings;

(E) "civil action brought by or against the United States" includes an appeal by a party, other than the United States, from a decision of a contracting officer rendered pursuant to a disputes clause in a contract with the Government or pursuant to chapter 71 of title 41;

(F) "court" includes the United States Court of Federal Claims and the United States Court of Appeals for Veterans Claims;

(G) "final judgment" means a judgment that is final and not appealable, and includes an order of settlement;

(H) "prevailing party", in the case of eminent domain proceedings, means a party who obtains a final judgment (other than by settlement), exclusive of interest, the amount of which is at least as close to the highest valuation of the property involved that is attested to at trial on behalf of the property owner as it is to the highest valuation of the property involved that is attested to at trial on behalf of the Government; and

(I) "demand" means the express demand of the United States which led to the adversary adjudication, but shall not include a recitation of the maximum statutory penalty (i) in the complaint, or (ii) elsewhere when accompanied by an express demand for a lesser amount.

(3) In awarding fees and other expenses under this subsection to a prevailing party in any action for judicial review of an adversary adjudication, as defined in subsection (b)(1)(C) of section 504 of title 5, or an adversary adjudication subject to chapter 71 of title 41, the court shall include in that award fees and other expenses to the same extent authorized in subsection (a) of such section, unless the court finds that during such adversary adjudication the position of the United States was substantially justified, or that special circumstances make an award unjust.

(4) Fees and other expenses awarded under this subsection to a party shall be paid by any agency over which the party prevails from any funds made available to the agency by appropriation or otherwise.

(5)(A) Not later than March 31 of the first fiscal year beginning after the date of enactment of the John D. Dingell, Jr. Conservation, Management, and Recreation Act, and every fiscal year thereafter, the Chairman of the Administrative Conference of the United States shall submit to Congress and make publicly available online a report on the amount of fees and other expenses awarded during the preceding fiscal year pursuant to this subsection.

(B) Each report under subparagraph (A) shall describe the number, nature, and amount of the awards, the claims involved in the controversy, and any other relevant information that may aid Congress in evaluating the scope and impact of such awards.

(C)(i) Each report under subparagraph (A) shall account for all payments of fees and other expenses awarded under this subsection that are made pursuant to a settlement agreement, regardless of whether the settlement agreement is sealed or otherwise subject to a nondisclosure provision.

(ii) The disclosure of fees and other expenses required under clause (i) shall not affect any other information that is subject to a nondisclosure provision in a settlement agreement.

(D) The Chairman of the Administrative Conference of the United States shall include and clearly identify in each annual report under subparagraph (A), for each case in which an award of fees and other expenses is included in the report—

(i) any amounts paid under section 1304 of title 31 for a judgment in the case;

(ii) the amount of the award of fees and other expenses; and

(iii) the statute under which the plaintiff filed suit.

(6) As soon as practicable, and in any event not later than the date on which the first report under paragraph (5)(A) is required to be submitted, the Chairman of the Administrative Conference of the United States shall create and maintain online a searchable database containing, with respect to each award of fees and other expenses under this subsection made on or after the date of enactment of the John D. Dingell, Jr. Conservation, Management, and Recreation Act, the following information:

(A) The case name and number, hyperlinked to the case, if available.

(B) The name of the agency involved in the case.

(C) The name of each party to whom the award was made as such party is identified in the order or other court document making the award.

(D) A description of the claims in the case.

(E) The amount of the award.

(F) The basis for the finding that the position of the agency concerned was not substantially justified.

(7) The online searchable database described in paragraph (6) may not reveal any information the disclosure of which is prohibited by law or a court order.

(8) The head of each agency (including the Attorney General of the United States) shall provide to the Chairman of the Administrative Conference of the United States in a timely manner all information requested by the Chairman to comply with the requirements of paragraphs (5), (6), and (7).

(e) The provisions of this section shall not apply to any costs, fees, and other expenses in connection with any proceeding to which section 7430 of the Internal Revenue Code of 1986 applies (determined without regard to subsections (b) and (f) of such section). Nothing in the preceding sentence shall prevent the awarding under subsection (a) of this section of costs enumerated in section 1920 of this title (as in effect on October 1, 1981).

(f) If the United States appeals an award of costs or fees and other expenses made against the United States under this section and the award is affirmed in whole or in part, interest shall be paid on the amount of the award as affirmed. Such interest shall be computed at the rate determined under section 1961(a) of this title, and shall run from the date of the award through the day before the date of the mandate of affirmance.

(June 25, 1948, c. 646, 62 Stat. 973; July 18, 1966, Pub.L. 89–507, § 1, 80 Stat. 308; Oct. 21, 1980, Pub. L. 96–481, Title II, § 204(a), (c), 94 Stat. 2327, 2329; Sept. 3, 1982, Pub. L. 97–248, Title II, § 292(c), 96 Stat. 574; Aug. 5, 1985, Pub. L. 99–80, §§ 2, 6(a), (b)(2), 99 Stat. 184, 186; Oct. 22, 1986, Pub.L. 99–514, § 2, 100

Stat. 2095; Oct. 29, 1992, Pub.L. 102–572, Title III, § 301(a), Title V, §§ 502(b), 506(a), Title IX, § 902(b)(1), 106 Stat. 4511–4513, 4516; Dec. 21, 1995, Pub.L. 104–66, Title I, § 1091(b), 109 Stat. 722; Mar. 29, 1996, Pub.L. 104–121, Title II, § 232, 110 Stat. 863; Pub.L. 105–368, Title V, § 512(b)(1)(B), Nov. 11, 1998, 112 Stat. 3342; Jan. 4, 2011, Pub.L. 111–350, § 5(g)(9), 124 Stat. 3848; Pub.L. 116–9, Title IV, § 4201(a)(2), (3), Mar. 12, 2019, 133 Stat. 763.)

HISTORICAL AND STATUTORY NOTES

References in Text

Chapter 71 of title 41, referred to in subsec. (d)(2)(E), (3), is classified to 41 U.S.C.A. § 7101 et seq.

Section 7430 of the Internal Revenue Code of 1986, referred to in subsec. (e), is classified to section 7430 of Title 26, Internal Revenue Code.

Effective and Applicability Provisions

1998 Acts. Amendment by Pub.L. 105–368 effective on the first day of the first month beginning more than 90 days after Nov. 11, 1998, see section 513 of Pub.L. 105–368, set out as a note under section 7251 of Title 38.

1996 Acts. Amendment by Pub.L. 104–121 applicable to civil actions and adversary adjudications commenced on or after March 29, 1996, see section 233 of Pub.L. 104–121, set out as a note under section 504 of Title 5, Government Organization and Employees.

1992 Acts. Section 506(b) of Pub.L. 102–572 provided that: "The amendment made by subsection (a) [amending subsec. (d)(2)(F) of this section] shall apply to any case pending before the United States Court of Veterans Appeals on the date of the enactment of this Act [Oct. 29, 1992], to any appeal filed in that court on or after such date, and to any appeal from that court that is pending on such date in the United States Court of Appeals for the Federal Circuit."

Section 506(d) of Pub.L. 102–572 provided that: "This section, and the amendment made by this section [amending subsec. (d)(2)(F) of this section and enacting provisions set out as notes under this section], shall take effect on the date of the enactment of this Act [Oct. 29, 1992]."

Amendment by section 902(b)(1) of Pub.L. 102–572 effective Oct. 29, 1992, see section 911 of Pub.L. 102–572, set out as a note under section 171 of this title.

Amendments by sections 301(a) and 502(b) of Pub.L. 102–572 effective Jan. 1, 1993, see section 1101(a) of Pub.L. 102–572, set out as a note under section 905 of Title 2, The Congress.

1985 Acts. Amendment by Pub. L. 99–80 applicable to cases pending on or commenced on or after Aug. 5, 1985, but with provision for additional applicability to certain prior cases and to prior board of contracts appeals cases, see section 7 of Pub. L. 99–80, set out as a note under section 504 of Title 5, Government Organization and Employees.

1982 Acts. Amendment by Pub.L. 97–248 applicable to civil actions or proceedings commenced after Feb. 28, 1983, see section 292(e)(1) of Pub.L. 97–248, as amended, set out as a note under section 7430 of Title 26, Internal Revenue Code.

1980 Acts. Amendment by section 204(a) of Pub.L. 96–481 to take effect on Oct. 1, 1981, and applicable to any adversary adjudication, as defined in section 504(b)(1)(C) of Title 5, and to civil actions and adversary adjudications described in this section, which are pending on, or commenced on or after, Oct. 1, 1981, see section 208 of Pub.L. 96–481, as amended, set out as a note under section 504 of Title 5, Government Organization and Employees.

Section 204(c) of Pub.L. 96–481 which provided in part that effective Oct. 1, 1984, subsec. (d) of this section is repealed, except that the provisions of subsec. (d) shall continue to apply through final disposition of any adversary adjudication initiated before the date of repeal, was repealed by Pub.L. 99–80, § 6(b)(2), Aug. 5, 1985, 99 Stat. 186.

1966 Acts. Section 3 of Pub.L. 89–507 provided that: "These amendments [to this section and section 2520 of this title] shall apply only to judgments entered in actions filed subsequent to the date of enactment of this Act [July 18, 1966]. These amendments [to this section and section 2520 of this title] shall not authorize the reopening or modification of judgments entered prior to the enactment of this Act [July 18, 1966]."

Savings Provisions

Section 206 of Pub.L. 96–481, as amended by Pub.L. 99–80, § 3, Aug. 5, 1985, 99 Stat. 186, provided that:

"**(a)** Except as provided in subsection (b), nothing in section 2412(d) of title 28, United States Code, as added by section 204(a) of this title [subsec. (d) of this section], alters, modifies, repeals, invalidates, or supersedes any other provision of Federal law which authorizes an award of such fees and other expenses to any party other than the United States that prevails in any civil action brought by or against the United States.

"**(b)** Section 206(b) of the Social Security Act (42 U.S.C. 406(b)(1)) [section 406(b) of Title 42, The Public Health and Welfare] shall not prevent an award of fees and other expenses under section 2412(d) of title 28, United States Code [subsec. (d) of this section]. Section 206(b)(2) of the Social Security Act [section 406(b)(2) of Title 42] shall not apply with respect to any such award but only if, where the claimant's attorney receives fees for the same work under both section 206(b) of that Act [section 406(b) of Title 42] and section 2412(d) of title 28, United States Code [subsec. (d) of this section], the claimant's attorney refunds to the claimant the amount of the smaller fee."

Congressional Findings and Purposes

For Congressional findings and purposes relating to 1980 amendment of this section, see section 202 of Pub.L. 96–481, set out as a note under section 504 of Title 5, Government Organization and Employees.

Fees Awarded to Non-attorney Practitioners

Pub.L. 107–330, Title IV, § 403, Dec. 6, 2002, 116 Stat. 2833, provided that: "The authority of the United States Court of Appeals for Veterans Claims to award reasonable fees and expenses of attorneys under section 2412(d) of title 28, United States Code [Subsec. (d) of this section], shall include authority to award fees and expenses, in an amount determined appropriate by the United States Court of Appeals for Veterans Claims, of individuals admitted to practice before the Court as non-attorney practitioners under subsection (b) or (c) of Rule 46 of the Rules of Practice and Procedure of the United States Court of Appeals for Veterans Claims."

Fee Agreements

Section 506(c) of Pub.L. 102–572 provided that: "Section 5904(d) of title 38, United States Code [section 5904(d) of Title 38, Veterans' Benefits], shall not prevent an award of fees and other expenses under section 2412(d) of title 28, United States Code [subsec. (d) of this section]. Section 5904(d) of title 38, United States Code, shall not apply with respect to any such award but only if, where the claimant's attorney receives fees for the same work under both section 5904 of title 38, United States Code, and section 2412(d) of title 28, United States Code, the claimant's attorney refunds to the claimant the amount of the smaller fee."

Nonliability of Judicial Officers for Costs

Pub.L. 104–317, Title III, § 309(a), Oct. 19, 1996, 110 Stat. 3853, provided that: "Notwithstanding any other provision of law, no judicial officer shall be held liable for any costs, including attorney's fees, in any action brought against such officer for an act or omission taken in such officer's judicial capacity, unless such action was clearly in excess of such officer's jurisdiction."

Revival of Previously Repealed Provisions

For revival of subsec. (d) of this section effective on or after Aug. 5, 1985, as if it had not been repealed by section 204(c) of Pub.L. 96–481, and repeal of section 204(c) of Pub.L. 96–481, see section 6 of Pub.L. 99–80, set out as a note under section 504 of Title 5, Government Organization and Employees.

§ 2413.   Executions in favor of United States

A writ of execution on a judgment obtained for the use of the United States in any court thereof shall be issued from and made returnable to the court which rendered the judgment, but may be executed in any other State, in any Territory, or in the District of Columbia.

(June 25, 1948, c. 646, 62 Stat. 974.)

§ 2414.   Payment of judgments and compromise settlements

Except as provided by chapter 71 of title 41, payment of final judgments rendered by a district court or the Court of International Trade against the United States shall be made on settlements by the Secretary of the Treasury. Payment of final judgments rendered by a State or foreign court or tribunal against the United States, or against its agencies or officials upon obligations or liabilities of the United States, shall be made on settlements by the Secretary of the Treasury after certification by the Attorney General that it is in the interest of the United States to pay the same.

Whenever the Attorney General determines that no appeal shall be taken from a judgment or that no further review will be sought from a decision affirming the same, he shall so certify and the judgment shall be deemed final.

Except as otherwise provided by law, compromise settlements of claims referred to the Attorney General for defense of imminent litigation or suits against the United States, or against its agencies or officials upon obligations or liabilities of the United States, made by the Attorney General or any person authorized by him, shall be settled and paid in a manner similar to judgments in like causes and appropriations or funds available for the payment of such judgments are hereby made available for the payment of such compromise settlements.

(June 25, 1948, c. 646, 62 Stat. 974; Aug. 30, 1961, Pub.L. 87–187, § 1, 75 Stat. 415; Nov. 1, 1978, Pub.L. 95–563, § 14(d), 92 Stat. 2390; Oct. 10, 1980, Pub.L. 96–417, Title V, § 512, 94 Stat. 1744; Oct. 19, 1996, Pub.L. 104–316, Title II, § 202(k), 110 Stat. 3843; Jan. 4, 2011, Pub.L. 111–350, § 5(g)(10), 124 Stat. 3878.)

HISTORICAL AND STATUTORY NOTES

References in Text

Chapter 71 of title 41, referred to in text, is classified to 41 U.S.C.A. § 7101 et seq.

Transfer of Functions

Effective June 30, 1996, the functions of the Comptroller General under this section to be transferred to the Director of the Office of Management and Budget, contingent upon the additional transfer to the Office of Management and Budget of such personnel, budget authority, records, and property of the General Accounting Office relating to such functions as the Comptroller General and the Director jointly determine to be necessary, see section 211 of Pub.L. 104–53, set out as a note under section 501 of Title 31, Money and Finance.

§ 2415.   Time for commencing actions brought by the United States

(a) Subject to the provisions of section 2416 of this title, and except as otherwise provided by Congress, every action for money damages brought by the United States or an officer or agency thereof which is founded upon any contract express or implied in law or fact, shall be barred unless the complaint is filed within six years after the right of action accrues or within one year after final decisions have been rendered in applicable administrative proceedings required by contract or by law, whichever is later: *Provided,* That in the event of later partial payment or written acknowledgment of debt, the right of action shall be deemed to accrue again at the time of each such payment or acknowledgment: *Provided further,* That an action for money damages brought by the United States for or on behalf of a recognized tribe, band or group of American Indians shall not be barred unless the complaint is filed more than six years and ninety days after the right of action accrued: *Provided further,* That an action for money damages which accrued on the date of enactment of this Act in accordance with subsection (g) brought by the United States for or on behalf of a recognized tribe, band, or group of American Indians, or on behalf of an individual Indian whose land is held in trust or restricted status, shall not be barred unless the complaint is filed sixty days after the date of publication of the list required by section 4(c) of the Indian Claims Limitation Act of 1982: *Provided,* That, for those claims that are on either of the two lists published pursuant to the Indian Claims Limitation Act of 1982, any right of action shall be barred unless the complaint is filed within (1) one year after the Secretary of the Interior has published in the Federal Register a notice rejecting such claim or (2) three years after the date the Secretary of the Interior has submitted legislation or legislative report to Congress to resolve such claim or more than two years after a final decision has been rendered in applicable administrative proceedings required by contract or by law, whichever is later.

(b) Subject to the provisions of section 2416 of this title, and except as otherwise provided by Congress, every action for money damages brought by the United States or an officer or agency thereof which is founded upon a tort shall be barred unless the complaint is filed within three years after the right of action first accrues: *Provided,* That an action to recover damages resulting from a trespass on lands of the United States; an action to recover damages resulting from fire to such lands; an action to recover for diversion of money paid under a grant program; and an action for conversion of property of the United States may be brought within six years after the right of action accrues, except that such actions for or on behalf of a recognized tribe, band or group of American Indians, including actions relating to allotted trust or restricted Indian lands, may be brought within six years and ninety days after the right of action accrues, except that such actions for or on behalf of a recognized tribe, band, or group of American Indians, including actions relating to allotted trust or restricted Indian lands, or on behalf of an individual Indian whose land is held in trust or restricted status which accrued on the date of enactment of this Act in accordance with subsection (g) may be brought on or before sixty days after the date of the publication of the list required by section 4(c) of the Indian Claims Limitation Act of 1982: *Provided,* That, for those claims that are on either of the two lists published pursuant to the Indian Claims Limitation Act of 1982, any right of action shall be barred unless the complaint is filed within (1) one year after the Secretary of the Interior has published in the Federal Register a notice rejecting such claim or (2) three years after the Secretary of the Interior has submitted legislation or legislative report to Congress to resolve such claim.

(c) Nothing herein shall be deemed to limit the time for bringing an action to establish the title to, or right of possession of, real or personal property.

(d) Subject to the provisions of section 2416 of this title and except as otherwise provided by Congress, every action for the recovery of money erroneously paid to or on behalf of any civilian employee of any agency of the United States or to or on behalf of any member or dependent of any member of the uniformed services of the United States, incident to the employment or services of such employee or member, shall be barred unless the complaint is filed within six years after the right of action accrues: *Provided,* That in the event of later partial payment or written acknowledgment of debt, the right of action shall be deemed to accrue again at the time of each such payment or acknowledgment.

(e) In the event that any action to which this section applies is timely brought and is thereafter dismissed without prejudice, the action may be recommenced within one year after such dismissal, regardless of whether the action would otherwise then be barred by this section. In any action so recommenced the defendant shall not be barred from interposing any claim which would not have been barred in the original action.

(f) The provisions of this section shall not prevent the assertion, in an action against the United States or an officer or agency thereof, of any claim of the United States or an officer or agency thereof against an opposing party, a co-party, or a third party that arises out of the transaction or occurrence that is the subject matter of the opposing party's claim. A claim of the United States or an officer or agency thereof that does not arise out of the transaction or occurrence that is the subject matter of the opposing party's claim may, if time-barred, be asserted only by way of offset and may be allowed in an amount not to exceed the amount of the opposing party's recovery.

(g) Any right of action subject to the provisions of this section which accrued prior to the date of enactment of this Act shall, for purposes of this section, be deemed to have accrued on the date of enactment of this Act.

(h) Nothing in this Act shall apply to actions brought under the Internal Revenue Code or incidental to the collection of taxes imposed by the United States.

(i) The provisions of this section shall not prevent the United States or an officer or agency thereof from collecting any claim of the United States by means of administrative offset, in accordance with section 3716 of title 31.

(Added Pub.L. 89–505, § 1, July 18, 1966, 80 Stat. 304; amended Pub.L. 92–353, July 18, 1972, 86 Stat. 499; Pub.L. 92–485, Oct. 13, 1972, 86 Stat. 803; Pub.L. 95–64, July 11, 1977, 91 Stat. 268; Pub.L. 95–103, Aug. 15, 1977, 91 Stat. 842; Pub.L. 96–217, § 1, Mar. 27, 1980, 94 Stat. 126; Pub.L. 97–365, § 9, Oct. 25, 1982, 96 Stat. 1754; Pub.L. 97–394, Title I, § 2, Dec. 30, 1982, 96 Stat. 1976; Pub.L. 97–452, § 2(d)(2), Jan. 12, 1983, 96 Stat. 2478; Pub.L. 98–250, § 4(a), Apr. 3, 1984, 98 Stat. 118.)

HISTORICAL AND STATUTORY NOTES

References in Text

The date of enactment of this Act, referred to in subsecs. (a), (b), and (g), means the date of enactment of Pub.L. 89–505, which was approved on July 18, 1966.

The Indian Claims Limitation Act of 1982, referred to in subsecs. (a) and (b), is Pub.L. 97–394, Title I, §§ 2–6, Dec. 30, 1982, 96 Stat. 1976–1978, which amended this section and enacted provisions set out as notes under this section. For complete classification of this Act to the Code, see Short Title of 1982 Amendments note set out under this section and Tables.

This Act, referred to in subsec. (h), means Pub.L. 89–505, July 18, 1966, 80 Stat. 304, which enacted this section and section 2416 of this title. For complete classification of this Act to the Code see Tables.

Short Title

1982 Amendments. Section 1 of Pub.L. 97–394, as amended by Pub.L. 98–250, § 4(b), Apr. 3, 1984, 98 Stat. 119, provided that: "Sections 2 through 6 of this Act [sections 2–6 of Pub.L. 97–394, which amended this section and enacted provisions set out as a note under this section] may be cited as the 'Indian Claims Limitation Act of 1982'."

Legislative Proposals Respecting Appropriateness of Resolution By Litigation of Unresolved Indian Claims

Section 2 of Pub.L. 96–217 provided that: "Not later than June 30, 1981, the Secretary of the Interior, after consultation with the Attorney General, shall submit to the Congress legislative proposals to resolve those Indian claims subject to the amendments made by the first section of this Act [amending this section] that the Secretary of the Interior or the Attorney General believes are not appropriate to resolve by litigation."

Publication of List of Indian Claims; Additional Claims; Time to Commence Action; Rejection of Claims; Claims Resolved By Legislation

Sections 3 to 6 of Pub.L. 97–394 provided that:

"**Sec. 3. (a)** Within ninety days after the enactment of this Act [Dec. 30, 1982], the Secretary of the Interior (hereinafter referred to as the 'Secretary') shall publish in the Federal Register a list of all claims accruing to any tribe, band or group of Indians or individual Indian on or before July 18, 1966, which have at any time been identified by or submitted to the Secretary under the 'Statute of Limitation Project' undertaken by the Department of the Interior and which, but for the provisions of this Act [sections 2–6 of Pub.L. 97–394; see Short Title of 1982 Amendments note set out under this section] would be barred by the provisions of section 2415 of title 28, United States Code [this section]: *Provided,* That the Secretary shall have the discretion to exclude from such list any matter which was erroneously identified as a claim and which has no legal merit whatsoever.

"**(b)** Such list shall group the claims on a reservation-by-reservation, tribe-by-tribe, or State-by-State basis, as appropriate, and shall state the nature and geographic location of each claim and only such other additional information as may be needed to identify specifically such claims.

"**(c)** Within thirty days after the publication of this list, the Secretary shall provide a copy of the Indian Claims Limitation Act of 1982 [sections 2–6 of Pub.L. 97–394; see short title of 1982 Amendments note under this section] and a copy of the Federal Register containing this list, or such parts as may be pertinent, to each Indian tribe, band or group whose rights or the rights of whose members could be affected by the provisions of section 2415 of title 28, United States Code [this section].

"**Sec. 4. (a)** Any tribe, band or group of Indians or any individual Indian shall have one hundred and eighty days after the date of the publication in the Federal Register of the list provided for in section 3 of this Act [section 3 of Pub.L. 97–394] to submit to the Secretary any additional specific claim or claims which such tribe, band or group of Indians or individual Indian believes may be affected by section 2415 of title 28, United States Code [this section], and desires to have considered for litigation or legislation by the United States.

"**(b)** Any such claim submitted to the Secretary shall be accompanied by a statement identifying the nature of the claim, the date when the right of action allegedly accrued, the names of the potential plaintiffs and defendants, if known, and such other information needed to identify and evaluate such claim.

"**(c)** Not more than thirty days after the expiration of the one hundred and eighty day period provided for in subsection (a) of this section, the Secretary shall publish in the Federal Register a list containing the additional claims submitted during such period: *Provided*, That the Secretary shall have the discretion to exclude from such list any matter which has not been sufficiently identified as a claim.

"**Sec. 5. (a)** Any right of action shall be barred sixty days after the date of the publication of the list required by section 4(c) of this Act [section 4(c) of Pub.L. 97–394] for those pre-1966 claims which, but for the provisions of this Act [sections 2–6 of Pub.L. 97–394; see Short Title of 1982 Amendments note set out under this section] would have been barred by section 2415 of title 28, United States Code [this section], unless such claims are included on either of the lists required by section 3 or 4(c) of this Act [section 3 or 4(c) of Pub.L. 97–394].

"**(b)** If the Secretary decides to reject for litigation any of the claims or groups or categories of claims contained on either of the lists required by section 3 or 4(c) of this Act [section 3 or 4(c) of Pub.L. 97–394], he shall send a report to the appropriate tribe, band, or group of Indians, whose rights or the rights of whose members could be affected by such rejection, advising them of his decision. The report shall identify the nature and geographic location of each rejected claim and the name of the potential plaintiffs and defendants if they are known or can be reasonably ascertained and shall, briefly, state the reasons why such claim or claims were rejected for litigation. Where the Secretary knows or can reasonably ascertain the identity of any of the potential individual Indian plaintiffs and their present addresses, he shall provide them with written notice of such rejection. Upon the request of any Indian claimant, the Secretary shall, without undue delay, provide to such claimant any nonprivileged research materials or evidence gathered by the United States in the documentation of such claim.

"**(c)** The Secretary, as soon as possible, after providing the report required by subsection (b) of this section, shall publish a notice in the Federal Register identifying the claims covered in such report. With respect to any claim covered by such report, any right of action shall be barred unless the complaint is filed within one year after the date of publication in the Federal Register.

"**Sec. 6. (a)** If the Secretary determines that any claim or claims contained in either of the lists as provided in sections 3 or 4(c) of this Act [sections 3 or 4(c) of Pub.L. 97–394] is not appropriate for litigation, but determines that such claims may be appropriately resolved by legislation, he shall submit to the Congress legislation to resolve such claims or shall submit to Congress a report setting out options for legislative resolution of such claims.

"**(b)** Any right of action on claims covered by such legislation or report shall be barred unless the complaint is filed within 3 years after the date of submission of such legislation or legislative report to Congress."

[For termination of reporting provisions pertaining to proposed legislation to resolve Indian claims, effective May 15, 2000, see Pub.L. 104–66, § 3003, as amended, set out as a note under 31 U.S.C.A. § 1113, and the last item on page 113 of House Document No. 103–7.]

§ 2416.   Time for commencing actions brought by the United States—Exclusions

For the purpose of computing the limitations periods established in section 2415, there shall be excluded all periods during which—

(a) the defendant or the res is outside the United States, its territories and possessions, the District of Columbia, or the Commonwealth of Puerto Rico; or

(b) the defendant is exempt from legal process because of infancy, mental incompetence, diplomatic immunity, or for any other reason; or

(c) facts material to the right of action are not known and reasonably could not be known by an official of the United States charged with the responsibility to act in the circumstances; or

(d) the United States is in a state of war declared pursuant to article I, section 8, of the Constitution of the United States.

(Added Pub.L. 89–505, § 1, July 18, 1966, 80 Stat. 305.)

CHAPTER 163—FINES, PENALTIES AND FORFEITURES

§ 2461.   Mode of recovery

(a) Whenever a civil fine, penalty or pecuniary forfeiture is prescribed for the violation of an Act of Congress without specifying the mode of recovery or enforcement thereof, it may be recovered in a civil action.

(b) Unless otherwise provided by Act of Congress, whenever a forfeiture of property is prescribed as a penalty for violation of an Act of Congress and the seizure takes place on the high seas or on navigable waters within the admiralty and maritime jurisdiction of the United States, such forfeiture may be enforced by libel in admiralty but in cases of seizures on land the forfeiture may be enforced by a proceeding by libel which shall conform as near as may be to proceedings in admiralty.

(c) If a person is charged in a criminal case with a violation of an Act of Congress for which the civil or criminal forfeiture of property is authorized, the Government may include notice of the forfeiture in the indictment or information pursuant to the Federal Rules of Criminal Procedure. If the defendant is convicted of the offense giving rise to the forfeiture, the court shall order the forfeiture of the property as part of the sentence in the criminal case pursuant to the Federal Rules of Criminal Procedure and section 3554 of title 18, United States Code. The procedures in section 413 of the Controlled Substances Act (21 U.S.C. 853) apply to all stages of a criminal forfeiture proceeding, except that subsection (d) of such section applies only in cases in which the defendant is convicted of a violation of such Act.

(June 25, 1948, c. 646, 62 Stat. 974; Apr. 25, 2000, Pub.L. 106–185, § 16, 114 Stat. 221; Mar. 9, 2006, Pub.L. 109–177, Title IV, § 410, 120 Stat. 246.)

HISTORICAL AND STATUTORY NOTES

References in Text

The Federal Rules of Criminal Procedure, referred to in subsec. (c), are set out in Title 18, Rules of Criminal Procedure, Fed.Rules Cr.Proc., Rule 1 et seq., 18 U.S.C.A.

Section 413 of the Controlled Substances Act, referred to in subsec. (c), is Pub.L. 91–513, Title II, § 413, as added Pub.L. 98–473, Title II, § 303, Oct. 12, 1984, 98 Stat. 2044, as amended, which is classified to 21 U.S.C.A. § 853. The Controlled Substances Act (CSA), is title II of Pub.L. 91–513, Oct. 27, 1970, 84 Stat. 1242, as amended, which is classified principally to subchapter I of chapter 13, of Title 21, 21 U.S.C.A. § 801 et seq. For complete classification of Title II to the Code, see Short Title note set out under 21 U.S.C.A. § 801 and Tables.

Effective and Applicability Provisions

2000 Acts. Amendments by Pub.L. 106–185, applicable to any forfeiture proceeding commenced on or after the date that is 120 days after April 25, 2000, see section 21 of Pub.L. 106–185, set out as a note under section 1324 of Title 8.

Federal Civil Penalties Inflation Adjustment

Pub.L. 101–410, Oct. 5, 1990, 104 Stat. 890, as amended Pub.L. 104–134, Title III, § 31001(s)(1), Apr. 26, 1996, 110 Stat. 1321–373; Pub.L. 105–362, Title XIII, § 1301(a), Nov. 10, 1998, 112 Stat. 3293; Pub.L. 114–74, Title VII, § 701, Nov. 2, 2015, 129 Stat. 599, provided that:

"SHORT TITLE

"**Section 1.** This Act may be cited as the 'Federal Civil Penalties Inflation Adjustment Act of 1990'.

"FINDINGS AND PURPOSE

"**Sec. 2. (a) Findings.**—The Congress finds that—

"**(1)** the power of Federal agencies to impose civil monetary penalties for violations of Federal law and regulations plays an important role in deterring violations and furthering the policy goals embodied in such laws and regulations;

"**(2)** the impact of many civil monetary penalties has been and is diminished due to the effect of inflation;

"**(3)** by reducing the impact of civil monetary penalties, inflation has weakened the deterrent effect of such penalties; and

"**(4)** the Federal Government does not maintain comprehensive, detailed accounting of the efforts of Federal agencies to assess and collect civil monetary penalties.

"**(b) Purpose.**—The purpose of this Act is to establish a mechanism that shall—

"**(1)** allow for regular adjustment for inflation of civil monetary penalties;

"**(2)** maintain the deterrent effect of civil monetary penalties and promote compliance with the law; and

"**(3)** improve the collection by the Federal Government of civil monetary penalties.

"DEFINITIONS

"**Sec. 3.** For purposes of this Act, the term—

"**(1)** 'agency' means an Executive agency as defined under section 105 of title 5, United States Code [5 U.S.C.A. § 105], and includes the United States Postal Service;

"**(2)** 'civil monetary penalty' means any penalty, fine, or other sanction that—

"**(A)(i)** is for a specific monetary amount as provided by Federal law; or

"**(ii)** has a maximum amount provided for by Federal law; and

"**(B)** is assessed or enforced by an agency pursuant to Federal law; and

"**(C)** is assessed or enforced pursuant to an administrative proceeding or a civil action in the Federal courts; and

"**(3)** 'Consumer Price Index' means the Consumer Price Index for all-urban consumers published by the Department of Labor.

"CIVIL MONETARY PENALTY INFLATION ADJUSTMENT REPORTS

"**Sec. 4. (a) In General**.—Not later than July 1, 2016, and not later than January 15 of every year thereafter, and subject to subsections (c) and (d), the head of each agency shall—

"**(1)** in accordance with subsection (b), adjust each civil monetary penalty provided by law within the jurisdiction of the Federal agency, except for any penalty (including any addition to tax and additional amount) under the Internal Revenue Code of 1986 [26 U.S.C.A. § 1 et seq.] or the Tariff Act of 1930 [19 U.S.C.A. § 1202 et seq.], by the inflation adjustment described under section 5 of this Act; and

"**(2)** publish each such adjustment in the Federal Register.

"**(b) Procedures for Adjustments**.—

"**(1) Catch up adjustment.**—For the first adjustment made under subsection (a) after the date of enactment of the Federal Civil Penalties Inflation Adjustment Act Improvements Act of 2015—

"**(A)** the head of an agency shall adjust civil monetary penalties through an interim final rulemaking; and

"**(B)** the adjustment shall take effect not later than August 1, 2016.

"**(2) Subsequent adjustments.**—For the second adjustment made under subsection (a) after the date of enactment of the Federal Civil Penalties Inflation Adjustment Act Improvements Act of 2015, and each adjustment thereafter, the head of an agency shall adjust civil monetary penalties and shall make the adjustment notwithstanding section 553 of title 5, United States Code.

"**(c) Exception.**—For the first adjustment made under subsection (a) after the date of enactment of the Federal Civil Penalties Inflation Adjustment Act Improvements Act of 2015, the head of an agency may adjust the amount of a civil monetary penalty by less than the otherwise required amount if—

"**(1)** the head of the agency, after publishing a notice of proposed rulemaking and providing an opportunity for comment, determines in a final rule that—

"**(A)** increasing the civil monetary penalty by the otherwise required amount will have a negative economic impact; or

"**(B)** the social costs of increasing the civil monetary penalty by the otherwise required amount outweigh the benefits; and

"**(2)** the Director of the Office of Management and Budget concurs with the determination of the head of the agency under paragraph (1).

"**(d) Other Adjustments Made.**—If a civil monetary penalty subject to a cost-of-living adjustment under this Act is, during the 12 months preceding a required cost-of-living adjustment, increased by an amount greater than the amount of the adjustment required under subsection (a), the head of the agency is not required to make the cost-of-living adjustment for that civil monetary penalty in that year.

"COST-OF-LIVING ADJUSTMENTS OF CIVIL MONETARY PENALTIES

"**Sec. 5. (a) Adjustment.**—The inflation adjustment under section 4 shall be determined by increasing the maximum civil monetary penalty or the range of minimum and maximum civil monetary penalties, as applicable, for each civil monetary penalty by the cost-of-living adjustment. Any increase determined under this subsection shall be rounded to the nearest to the nearest multiple of $1.

"**(b) Definition.**—

"**(1) In General.**—Except as provided in paragraph (2), for purposes of subsection (a), the term 'cost-of-living adjustment' means the percentage (if any) for each civil monetary penalty by which—

"**(A)** the Consumer Price Index for the month of October preceding the date of the adjustment, exceeds

"**(B)** the Consumer Price Index for the month of October 1 year before the month of October referred to in subparagraph (A)

"**(2) Initial Adjustment.**—

"**(A) In General.**—Subject to subparagraph (C), for the first inflation adjustment under section 4 made by an agency after the date of enactment of the Federal Civil Penalties Inflation Adjustment Act Improvements Act of 2015, the term 'cost-of-living adjustment' means the percentage (if any) for each civil monetary penalty by which the Consumer Price Index for the month of October, 2015 exceeds the Consumer Price Index for the month of October of the calendar year during which the amount of such civil monetary penalty was established or adjusted under a provision of law other than this Act [this note].

"**(B) Application of Adjustment.**—The cost-of-living adjustment described in subparagraph (A) shall be applied to the amount of the civil monetary penalty as it was most recently established or adjusted under a provision of law other than this Act [this note].

"**(C) Maximum Adjustment.**—The amount of the increase in a civil monetary penalty under subparagraph (A) shall not exceed 150 percent of the amount of that civil monetary penalty on the date of enactment of the Federal Civil Penalties Inflation Adjustment Act Improvements Act of 2015 [Nov. 2, 2015].

"ANNUAL REPORT

"**Sec. 6.** Any increase under this Act in a civil monetary penalty shall apply only to civil monetary penalties, including those whose associated violation predated such increase, which are assessed after the date the increase takes effect.

"IMPLEMENTATION AND OVERSIGHT ENHANCEMENTS

"**Sec. 7.**   **(a)**   **OMB Guidance.**—Not later than February 29, 2016, not later than December 15, 2016, and December 15 of every year thereafter, the Director of the Office of Management and Budget shall issue guidance to agencies on implementing the inflation adjustments required under this Act [Federal Civil Penalties Inflation Adjustment Act Improvements Act of 2015, Pub.L. 114–74, Title VII, § 701 et seq., Nov. 2, 2015, 129 Stat. 599, which enacted this note and provisions set out as a note under 28 U.S.C.A. § 1 and amended provisions set out as a note under this section].

"**(b) Agency Financial Reports.**—The head of each agency shall include in the Agency Financial Report submitted under OMB Circular A–136, or any successor thereto, information about the civil monetary penalties within the jurisdiction of the agency, including the adjustment of the civil monetary penalties by the head of the agency under this Act [Federal Civil Penalties Inflation Adjustment Act Improvements Act of 2015, Pub.L. 114–74, Title VII, § 701 et seq., Nov. 2, 2015, 129 Stat. 599, which enacted this note and provisions set out as a note under 28 U.S.C.A. § 1 and amended provisions set out as a note under this section].

"**(c) GAO Review.**—The Comptroller General of the United States shall annually submit to Congress a report assessing the compliance of agencies with the inflation adjustments required under this Act [Federal Civil Penalties Inflation Adjustment Act Improvements Act of 2015, Pub.L. 114–74, Title VII, § 701 et seq., Nov. 2, 2015, 129 Stat. 599, which enacted this note and provisions set out as a note under 28 U.S.C.A. § 1 and amended provisions set out as a note under this section], which may be included as part of another report submitted to Congress."

[Pub. L. 104–134, title III, § 31001(s)(2), Apr. 26, 1996, 110 Stat. 1321–373, which provided that the first adjustment of a civil monetary penalty made pursuant to the amendment by paragraph (1), which amend Pub.L. 101–410, set out as above note, may not exceed 10 percent of such penalty, was repealed by Pub. L. 114–74, title VII, § 701(c), Nov. 2, 2015, 129 Stat. 601.]

[For authority of the Director of the Office of Management and Budget to consolidate reports required under the Federal Civil Penalties Inflation Adjustment Act of 1990, Pub.L. 101–410, set out above, to be submitted between Jan. 1, 1995, and Sept. 30, 1997, or to adjust their frequency and due dates, see section 404 of Pub.L. 103–356, set out as a note under section 501 of Title 31, Money and Finance.]

§ 2462.   Time for commencing proceedings

Except as otherwise provided by Act of Congress, an action, suit or proceeding for the enforcement of any civil fine, penalty, or forfeiture, pecuniary or otherwise, shall not be entertained unless commenced within five years from the date when the claim first accrued if, within the same period, the offender or the property is found within the United States in order that proper service may be made thereon.

(June 25, 1948, c. 646, 62 Stat. 974.)

§ 2463.   Property taken under revenue law not repleviable

All property taken or detained under any revenue law of the United States shall not be repleviable, but shall be deemed to be in the custody of the law and subject only to the orders and decrees of the courts of the United States having jurisdiction thereof.

(June 25, 1948, c. 646, 62 Stat. 974.)

§ 2464.   Security; special bond

(a) Except in cases of seizures for forfeiture under any law of the United States, whenever a warrant of arrest or other process in rem is issued in any admiralty case, the United States marshal shall stay the execution of such process, or discharge the property arrested if the process has been levied, on receiving from the respondent or claimant of the property a bond or stipulation in double the amount claimed by the libellant, with sufficient surety, to be approved by the judge of the district court where the case is pending, or, in his absence, by the collector of the port, conditioned to answer the decree of the court in such case. Such bond or stipulation shall be returned to the court, and judgment or decree thereon, against both the principal and sureties, may be secured at the time of rendering the decree in the original case. The owner of any vessel may deliver to the marshal a bond or stipulation, with sufficient surety, to be approved by the judge of the district court, conditioned to answer the decree of such court in all or any cases that are brought thereafter in such court against the vessel. Thereupon the execution of all such process against such vessel shall be stayed so long as the amount secured by such bond or stipulation is at least double the aggregate amount claimed by libellants in such suits which are begun and pending against such vessel. Similar judgments or decrees and remedies may be had on such bond or stipulation as if a special bond or stipulation had been filed in each of such suits.

(b) The court may make necessary orders to carry this section into effect, particularly in giving proper notice of any such suit. Such bond or stipulation shall be indorsed by the clerk with a minute of the suits wherein process is so stayed. Further security may be required by the court at any time.

(c) If a special bond or stipulation in the particular case is given under this section, the liability as to said case on the general bond or stipulation shall cease. The parties may stipulate the amount of the bond or stipulation for the release of a vessel or other property to be not more than the amount claimed in the libel, with interest, plus an allowance for libellant's costs. In the event of the inability or refusal of the parties to so stipulate, the court shall fix the amount, but if not so fixed then a bond shall be required in the amount prescribed in this section.

(June 25, 1948, c. 646, 62 Stat. 974.)

HISTORICAL AND STATUTORY NOTES

Transfer of Functions

All offices of Collector of Customs, Comptroller of Customs, Surveyor of Customs, and Appraiser of Merchandise in the Bureau of Customs of the Department of the Treasury to which appointments were required to be made by the President with the advice and consent of the Senate were ordered abolished, with such offices to be terminated not later than December 31, 1966, by 1965 Reorg. Plan No. 1, eff. May 25, 1965, 30 F.R. 7035, 79 Stat. 1317, set out in Appendix 1 to Title 5, Government Organization and Employees.

All functions of the offices eliminated were already vested in the Secretary of the Treasury by 1950 Reorg. Plan No. 26, eff. July 31, 1950, 15 F.R. 4935, 64 Stat. 1280, set out in Appendix 1 to Title 5.

§ 2465.   Return of property to claimant; liability for wrongful seizure; attorney fees, costs, and interest

(a) Upon the entry of a judgment for the claimant in any proceeding to condemn or forfeit property seized or arrested under any provision of Federal law—

(1) such property shall be returned forthwith to the claimant or his agent; and

(2) if it appears that there was reasonable cause for the seizure or arrest, the court shall cause a proper certificate thereof to be entered and, in such case, neither the person who made the seizure or arrest nor the prosecutor shall be liable to suit or judgment on account of such suit or prosecution, nor shall the claimant be entitled to costs, except as provided in subsection (b).

(b)(1) Except as provided in paragraph (2), in any civil proceeding to forfeit property under any provision of Federal law in which the claimant substantially prevails, the United States shall be liable for—

(A) reasonable attorney fees and other litigation costs reasonably incurred by the claimant;

(B) post-judgment interest, as set forth in section 1961 of this title; and

(C) in cases involving currency, other negotiable instruments, or the proceeds of an interlocutory sale—

(i) interest actually paid to the United States from the date of seizure or arrest of the property that resulted from the investment of the property in an interest-bearing account or instrument; and

(ii) an imputed amount of interest that such currency, instruments, or proceeds would have earned at the rate applicable to the 30-day Treasury Bill, for any period during which no interest was paid (not including any period when the property reasonably was in use as evidence in an official proceeding or in conducting scientific tests for the purpose of collecting evidence), commencing 15 days after the property was seized by a Federal law enforcement agency, or was turned over to a Federal law enforcement agency by a State or local law enforcement agency.

(2)(A) The United States shall not be required to disgorge the value of any intangible benefits nor make any other payments to the claimant not specifically authorized by this subsection.

(B) The provisions of paragraph (1) shall not apply if the claimant is convicted of a crime for which the interest of the claimant in the property was subject to forfeiture under a Federal criminal forfeiture law.

(C) If there are multiple claims to the same property, the United States shall not be liable for costs and attorneys fees associated with any such claim if the United States—

(i) promptly recognizes such claim;

(ii) promptly returns the interest of the claimant in the property to the claimant, if the property can be divided without difficulty and there are no competing claims to that portion of the property;

(iii) does not cause the claimant to incur additional, reasonable costs or fees; and

(iv) prevails in obtaining forfeiture with respect to one or more of the other claims.

(D) If the court enters judgment in part for the claimant and in part for the Government, the court shall reduce the award of costs and attorney fees accordingly.

(June 25, 1948, c. 646, 62 Stat. 975; Apr. 25, 2000, Pub.L. 106–185, § 4(a), 114 Stat. 211.)

HISTORICAL AND STATUTORY NOTES

Effective and Applicability Provisions

2000 Acts. Amendments by Pub.L. 106–185, applicable to any forfeiture proceeding commenced on or after the date that is 120 days after April 25, 2000, see section 21 of Pub.L. 106–185, set out as a note under section 1324 of Title 8.

§ 2466.   Fugitive disentitlement

(a) A judicial officer may disallow a person from using the resources of the courts of the United States in furtherance of a claim in any related civil forfeiture action or a claim in third party proceedings in any related criminal forfeiture action upon a finding that such person—

(1) after notice or knowledge of the fact that a warrant or process has been issued for his apprehension, in order to avoid criminal prosecution—

(A) purposely leaves the jurisdiction of the United States;

(B) declines to enter or reenter the United States to submit to its jurisdiction; or

(C) otherwise evades the jurisdiction of the court in which a criminal case is pending against the person; and

(2) is not confined or held in custody in any other jurisdiction for commission of criminal conduct in that jurisdiction.

(b) Subsection (a) may be applied to a claim filed by a corporation if any majority shareholder, or individual filing the claim on behalf of the corporation is a person to whom subsection (a) applies.

(Added Pub.L. 106–185, § 14(a), Apr. 25, 2000, 114 Stat. 219; amended Pub.L. 107–56, Title III, § 322, Oct. 26, 2001, 115 Stat. 315; Pub.L. 109–162, Title XI, § 1171(c), Jan. 5, 2006, 119 Stat. 3123; Pub.L. 109–177, Title IV, § 406(a)(1), Mar. 9, 2006, 120 Stat. 244.)

HISTORICAL AND STATUTORY NOTES

Codifications

Pub.L. 109–177, § 406(a)(1), which directed the amendment of directory language of Pub.L. 107–56, § 322, was incapable of execution due to prior identical amendment by Pub.L. 109–162, 1171(c). See 2006 Amendments notes under this section.

Effective and Applicability Provisions

2006 Acts. Pub.L. 109–162, Title XI, § 1171(c), Jan. 5, 2006, 119 Stat. 3123, provided in part that the amendment of the directory language of Pub.L. 107–56, § 322 was "effective on the date of enactment of that section [Oct. 26, 2001]".

2000 Acts. Pub.L. 106–185, § 14(c), Apr. 25, 2000, 114 Stat. 219, provided that: "The amendments made by this section [adding this section] shall apply to any case pending on or after the date of the enactment of this Act [Apr. 25, 2000]."

4-year Congressional Review; Expedited Consideration

Effective on and after the first day of fiscal year 2005, amendments by Title III (§§ 301 to 377) of Pub.L. 107–56 shall terminate if Congress enacts a joint resolution, and such resolution shall be given expedited consideration, see Pub.L. 107–56, Title III, § 303, Oct. 26, 2001, 115 Stat. 298, set out as a note under 31 U.S.C.A. § 5311.

§ 2467.　　Enforcement of foreign judgment

(a)　Definitions.—In this section—

(1)　the term "foreign nation" means a country that has become a party to the United Nations Convention Against Illicit Traffic in Narcotic Drugs and Psychotropic Substances (referred to in this section as the "United Nations Convention") or a foreign jurisdiction with which the United States has a treaty or other formal international agreement in effect providing for mutual forfeiture assistance; and

(2)　the term "forfeiture or confiscation judgment" means a final order of a foreign nation compelling a person or entity—

(A)　to pay a sum of money representing the proceeds of an offense described in Article 3, Paragraph 1, of the United Nations Convention, any violation of foreign law that would constitute a violation or an offense for which property could be forfeited under Federal law if the offense were committed in the United States, or any foreign offense described in section 1956(c)(7)(B) of title 18, or property the value of which corresponds to such proceeds; or

(B)　to forfeit property involved in or traceable to the commission of such offense.

(b)　Review by attorney general.—

(1)　In general.—A foreign nation seeking to have a forfeiture or confiscation judgment registered and enforced by a district court of the United States under this section shall first submit a request to the Attorney General or the designee of the Attorney General, which request shall include—

(A)　a summary of the facts of the case and a description of the proceedings that resulted in the forfeiture or confiscation judgment;

(B)　certified[1] copy of the forfeiture or confiscation judgment;

(C)　an affidavit or sworn declaration establishing that the foreign nation took steps, in accordance with the principles of due process, to give notice of the proceedings to all persons with an interest in the property in sufficient time to enable such persons to defend against the charges and that the judgment rendered is in force and is not subject to appeal; and

(D)　such additional information and evidence as may be required by the Attorney General or the designee of the Attorney General.

(2)　Certification of request.—The Attorney General or the designee of the Attorney General shall determine whether, in the interest of justice, to certify the request, and such decision shall be final and not subject to either judicial review or review under subchapter II of chapter 5, or chapter 7, of title 5 (commonly known as the "Administrative Procedure Act").

(c)　Jurisdiction and venue.—

(1)　In general.—If the Attorney General or the designee of the Attorney General certifies a request under subsection (b), the United States may file an application on behalf of a foreign nation in district court of the United States seeking to enforce the foreign forfeiture or confiscation judgment as if the judgment had been entered by a court in the United States.

(2)　Proceedings.—In a proceeding filed under paragraph (1)—

(A)　the United States shall be the applicant and the defendant or another person or entity affected by the forfeiture or confiscation judgment shall be the respondent;

---

[1]　[Footnote to 28 U.S.C. § 2467(b)(1)(B):] So in original. Probably should be preceded by "a".

(B) venue shall lie in the district court for the District of Columbia or in any other district in which the defendant or the property that may be the basis for satisfaction of a judgment under this section may be found; and

(C) the district court shall have personal jurisdiction over a defendant residing outside of the United States if the defendant is served with process in accordance with rule 4 of the Federal Rules of Civil Procedure.

(d) Entry and enforcement of judgment.—

(1) In general.—The district court shall enter such orders as may be necessary to enforce the judgment on behalf of the foreign nation unless the court finds that—

(A) the judgment was rendered under a system that provides tribunals or procedures incompatible with the requirements of due process of law;

(B) the foreign court lacked personal jurisdiction over the defendant;

(C) the foreign court lacked jurisdiction over the subject matter;

(D) the foreign nation did not take steps, in accordance with the principles of due process, to give notice of the proceedings to a person with an interest in the property of the proceedings[2] in sufficient time to enable him or her to defend; or

(E) the judgment was obtained by fraud.

(2) Process.—Process to enforce a judgment under this section shall be in accordance with rule 69(a) of the Federal Rules of Civil Procedure.

(3) Preservation of property.—

(A) Restraining orders.—

(i) In general.—To preserve the availability of property subject to civil or criminal forfeiture under foreign law, the Government may apply for, and the court may issue, a restraining order at any time before or after the initiation of forfeiture proceedings by a foreign nation.

(ii) Procedures.—

(I) In general.—A restraining order under this subparagraph shall be issued in a manner consistent with subparagraphs (A), (C), and (E) of paragraph (1) and the procedural due process protections for a restraining order under section 983(j) of title 18.

(II) Application.—For purposes of applying such section 983(j)—

(aa) references in such section 983(j) to civil forfeiture or the filing of a complaint shall be deemed to refer to the applicable foreign criminal or forfeiture proceedings; and

(bb) the reference in paragraph (1)(B)(i) of such section 983(j) to the United States shall be deemed to refer to the foreign nation.

(B) Evidence.—The court, in issuing a restraining order under subparagraph (A)—

(i) may rely on information set forth in an affidavit describing the nature of the proceeding or investigation underway in the foreign country, and setting forth a reasonable basis to believe that the property to be restrained will be named in a judgment of forfeiture at the conclusion of such proceeding; or

---

[2] [Footnote to 28 U.S.C. § 2467(d)(1)(D):] So in original. The words "of the proceedings" probably should not appear.

        (ii) may register and enforce a restraining order that has been issued by a court of competent jurisdiction in the foreign country and certified by the Attorney General pursuant to subsection (b)(2).

        (C) Limit on grounds for objection.—No person may object to a restraining order under subparagraph (A) on any ground that is the subject of parallel litigation involving the same property that is pending in a foreign court.

    (e) Finality of foreign findings.—In entering orders to enforce the judgment, the court shall be bound by the findings of fact to the extent that they are stated in the foreign forfeiture or confiscation judgment.

    (f) Currency conversion.—The rate of exchange in effect at the time the suit to enforce is filed by the foreign nation shall be used in calculating the amount stated in any forfeiture or confiscation judgment requiring the payment of a sum of money submitted for registration.

(Added Pub.L. 106–185, § 15(a), Apr. 25, 2000, 114 Stat. 219; amended Pub.L. 107–56, Title III, § 323, Oct. 26, 2001, 115 Stat. 315; Pub.L. 111–342, § 2, Dec. 22, 2010, 124 Stat. 3607.)

HISTORICAL AND STATUTORY NOTES

References in Text

    Rule 4 of the Federal Rules of Civil Procedure, referred to in subsec. (c)(2)(C), is set out in this title.

Effective and Applicability Provisions

    2000 Acts. Enactment by Pub.L. 106–185, applicable to any forfeiture proceeding commenced on or after the date that is 120 days after April 25, 2000, see section 21 of Pub.L. 106–185, set out as a note under section 1324 of Title 8.

4-year Congressional Review; Expedited Consideration

    Effective on and after the first day of fiscal year 2005, amendments by Title III (§§ 301 to 377) of Pub.L. 107–56 shall terminate if Congress enacts a joint resolution to that effect; such resolution shall be given expedited consideration, see Pub.L. 107–56, Title III, § 303, Oct. 26, 2001, 115 Stat. 298, set out as a note under 31 U.S.C.A. § 5311.

CHAPTER 165—UNITED STATES COURT OF
FEDERAL CLAIMS PROCEDURE

---

    [1]   So in original. Does not conform to section catchline.

§ 2501.   Time for filing suit

Every claim of which the United States Court of Federal Claims has jurisdiction shall be barred unless the petition thereon is filed within six years after such claim first accrues.

Every claim under section 1497 of this title shall be barred unless the petition thereon is filed within two years after the termination of the river and harbor improvements operations on which the claim is based.

A petition on the claim of a person under legal disability or beyond the seas at the time the claim accrues may be filed within three years after the disability ceases.

A suit for the fees of an officer of the United States shall not be filed until his account for such fees has been finally acted upon, unless the Government Accountability Office fails to act within six months after receiving the account.

(June 25, 1948, c. 646, 62 Stat. 976; Sept. 3, 1954, c. 1263, § 52, 68 Stat. 1246; Apr. 2, 1982, Pub.L. 97–164, Title I, § 139(a), 96 Stat. 42; Oct. 29, 1992, Pub.L. 102–572, Title IX, § 902(a)(1), 106 Stat. 4516; July 7, 2004, Pub.L. 108–271, § 8(b), 118 Stat. 814.)

HISTORICAL AND STATUTORY NOTES

Effective and Applicability Provisions

1992 Acts. Amendment by Title IX of Pub.L. 102–572 effective Oct. 29, 1992, see section 911 of Pub.L. 102–572, set out as a note under section 171 of Title 28, Judiciary and Judicial Procedure.

1982 Acts. Amendment by Pub.L. 97–164 effective Oct. 1, 1982, see section 402 of Pub.L. 97–164, set out as a note under section 171 of this title.

§ 2502.   Aliens' privilege to sue

(a) Citizens or subjects of any foreign government which accords to citizens of the United States the right to prosecute claims against their government in its courts may sue the United States in the United States Court of Federal Claims if the subject matter of the suit is otherwise within such court's jurisdiction.

(b) See section 7422(f) of the Internal Revenue Code of 1986 for exception with respect to suits involving internal revenue taxes.

(June 25, 1948, c. 646, 62 Stat. 976; Nov. 2, 1966, Pub.L. 89–713, § 3(b), 80 Stat. 1108; Apr. 2, 1982, Pub.L. 97–164, Title I, § 139(a), 96 Stat. 42; Oct. 22, 1986, Pub.L. 99–514, § 2, 100 Stat. 2095; Oct. 29, 1992, Pub.L. 102–572, Title IX, § 902(a)(1), 106 Stat. 4516.)

HISTORICAL AND STATUTORY NOTES

References in Text

Section 7422(f) of the Internal Revenue Code of 1986, referred to in subsec. (b), is classified to section 7422(f) of Title 26, Internal Revenue Code.

Effective and Applicability Provisions

1992 Acts. Amendment by Title IX of Pub.L. 102–572 effective Oct. 29, 1992, see section 911 of Pub.L. 102–572, set out as a note under section 171 of Title 28, Judiciary and Judicial Procedure.

1982 Acts. Amendment by Pub.L. 97–164 effective Oct. 1, 1982, see section 402 of Pub.L. 97–164, set out as a note under section 171 of this title.

1966 Acts. Amendment by Pub.L. 89–713, which added subsec. (b) to this section, applicable to suits brought against officers, employees, or personal representatives instituted 90 days or more after Nov. 2, 1966, see section 3(d) of Pub.L. 89–713, set out as a note under section 7422 of Title 26, Internal Revenue Code.

§ 2503.   Proceedings generally

(a) Parties to any suit in the United States Court of Federal Claims may appear before a judge of that court in person or by attorney, produce evidence, and examine witnesses.

(b) The proceedings of the Court of Federal Claims shall be in accordance with such rules of practice and procedure (other than the rules of evidence) as the Court of Federal Claims may prescribe and in accordance with the Federal Rules of Evidence.

(c) The judges of the Court of Federal Claims shall fix times for trials, administer oaths or affirmations, examine witnesses, receive evidence, and enter dispositive judgments. Hearings shall, if convenient, be held in the counties where the witnesses reside.

(d) For the purpose of construing sections 1821, 1915, 1920, and 1927 of this title, the United States Court of Federal Claims shall be deemed to be a court of the United States.

(June 25, 1948, c. 646, 62 Stat. 976; Sept. 3, 1954, c. 1263, § 53, 68 Stat. 1246; Apr. 2, 1982, Pub.L. 97–164, Title I, § 139(b)(1), 96 Stat. 42; Oct. 29, 1992, Pub.L. 102–572, Title IX, §§ 902(a), 909, 106 Stat. 4516, 4519.)

HISTORICAL AND STATUTORY NOTES

References in Text

The Federal Rules of Evidence, referred to in subsec. (b), are set out in this title.

Effective and Applicability Provisions

1992 Acts. Amendment by Title IX of Pub.L. 102–572 effective Oct. 29, 1992, see section 911 of Pub.L. 102–572, set out as a note under section 171 of Title 28, Judiciary and Judicial Procedure.

1982 Acts. Amendment by Pub.L. 97–164 effective Oct. 1, 1982, see section 402 of Pub.L. 97–164, set out as a note under section 171 of this title.

§ 2504.   Plaintiff's testimony

The United States Court of Federal Claims may, at the instance of the Attorney General, order any plaintiff to appear, upon reasonable notice, before any judge of the court and be examined on oath as to all matters pertaining to his claim. Such examination shall be reduced to writing by the judge, and shall be returned to and filed in the court, and may, at the discretion of the attorneys for the United States, be read and used as evidence on the trial. If any plaintiff, after such order is made and due and reasonable notice thereof is given to him, fails to appear, or refuses to testify or answer fully as to all material matters within his knowledge, the court may order that the case shall not be tried until he fully complies with such order.

(June 25, 1948, c. 646, 62 Stat. 976; Apr. 2, 1982, Pub.L. 97–164, Title I, § 139(c), 96 Stat. 42; Oct. 29, 1992, Pub.L. 102–572, Title IX, § 902(a)(1), 106 Stat. 4516.)

§ 2505.   Trial before judges

Any judge of the United States Court of Federal Claims may sit at any place within the United States to take evidence and enter judgment.

(June 25, 1948, c. 646, 62 Stat. 976; Sept. 3, 1954, c. 1263, § 54(a), (b), 68 Stat. 1246; Apr. 2, 1982, Pub.L. 97–164, Title I, § 139(d), 96 Stat. 42; Oct. 29, 1992, Pub.L. 102–572, Title IX, § 902(a)(1), 106 Stat. 4516.)

§ 2506.   Interest of witness

A witness in a suit in the United States Court of Federal Claims shall not be exempt or disqualified because he is a party to or interested in such suit.

(June 25, 1948, c. 646, 62 Stat. 977; Apr. 2, 1982, Pub.L. 97–164, Title I, § 139(e), 96 Stat. 42; Oct. 29, 1992, Pub.L. 102–572, Title IX, § 902(a)(1), 106 Stat. 4516.)

§ 2507.   Calls and discovery

(a) The United States Court of Federal Claims may call upon any department or agency of the United States or upon any party for any information or papers, not privileged, for purposes of discovery or for use as evidence. The head of any department or agency may refuse to comply with a call issued pursuant to this subsection when, in his opinion, compliance will be injurious to the public interest.

(b) Without limitation on account of anything contained in subsection (a) of this section, the court may, in accordance with its rules, provide additional means for the discovery of any relevant facts, books, papers, documents or tangible things, not privileged.

(c) The Court of Federal Claims may use all recorded and printed reports made by the committees of the Senate or House of Representatives.

(June 25, 1948, c. 646, 62 Stat. 977; Sept. 3, 1954, c. 1263, § 55(a)–(c), 68 Stat. 1247; Apr. 2, 1982, Pub.L. 97–164, Title I, § 139(f), 96 Stat. 42; Oct. 29, 1992, Pub.L. 102–572, Title IX, § 902(a), 106 Stat. 4516.)

§ 2508.   Counterclaim or set-off; registration of judgment

Upon the trial of any suit in the United States Court of Federal Claims in which any setoff, counterclaim, claim for damages, or other demand is set up on the part of the United States against any plaintiff making claim against the United States in said court, the court shall hear and determine such claim or demand both for and against the United States and plaintiff.

If upon the whole case it finds that the plaintiff is indebted to the United States it shall render judgment to that effect, and such judgment shall be final and reviewable.

The transcript of such judgment, filed in the clerk's office of any district court, shall be entered upon the records and shall be enforceable as other judgments.

(June 25, 1948, c. 646, 62 Stat. 977; July 28, 1953, c. 253, § 10, 67 Stat. 227; Sept. 3, 1954, c. 1263, § 47(a), 68 Stat. 1243; Apr. 2, 1982, Pub.L. 97–164, Title I, § 139(g), 96 Stat. 42; Oct. 29, 1992, Pub.L. 102–572, Title IX, § 902(a)(1), 106 Stat. 4516.)

§ 2509.   Congressional reference cases

(a) Whenever a bill, except a bill for a pension, is referred by either House of Congress to the chief judge of the United States Court of Federal Claims pursuant to section 1492 of this title, the chief judge shall designate a judge as hearing officer for the case and a panel of three judges of the court to serve as a reviewing body. One member of the review panel shall be designated as presiding officer of the panel.

(b) Proceedings in a congressional reference case shall be under rules and regulations prescribed for the purpose by the chief judge who is hereby authorized and directed to require the application of the pertinent rules of practice of the Court of Federal Claims insofar as feasible. Each hearing officer and each review panel shall have authority to do and perform any acts which may be necessary or proper for the efficient performance of their duties, including the power of subpena and the power to administer oaths and affirmations. None of the rules, rulings, findings, or conclusions authorized by this section shall be subject to judicial review.

(c) The hearing officer to whom a congressional reference case is assigned by the chief judge shall proceed in accordance with the applicable rules to determine the facts, including facts relating to delay or laches, facts bearing upon the question whether the bar of any statute of limitation should be removed, or facts claimed to excuse the claimant for not having resorted to any established legal remedy. He shall append to his findings of fact conclusions sufficient to inform Congress whether the demand is a legal or equitable claim or a gratuity, and the amount, if any, legally or equitably due from the United States to the claimant.

(d) The findings and conclusions of the hearing officer shall be submitted by him, together with the record in the case, to the review panel for review by it pursuant to such rules as may be provided for the purpose, which shall include provision for submitting the report of the hearing officer to the parties for consideration, exception, and argument before the panel. The panel, by majority vote, shall adopt or modify the findings or the conclusions of the hearing officer.

(e) The panel shall submit its report to the chief judge for transmission to the appropriate House of Congress.

(f) Any act or failure to act or other conduct by a party, a witness, or an attorney which would call for the imposition of sanctions under the rules of practice of the Court of Federal Claims shall be noted by the panel or the hearing officer at the time of occurrence thereof and upon failure of the delinquent or offending party, witness, or attorney to make prompt compliance with the order of the panel or the hearing officer a full statement of the circumstances shall be incorporated in the report of the panel.

(g) The Court of Federal Claims is hereby authorized and directed, under such regulations as it may prescribe, to provide the facilities and services of the office of the clerk of the court for the filing, processing, hearing, and dispatch of congressional reference cases and to include within its annual appropriations the costs thereof and other costs of administration, including (but without limitation to the items herein listed) the salaries and traveling expenses of the judges serving as hearing officers and panel members, mailing and service of process, necessary physical facilities, equipment, and supplies, and personnel (including secretaries and law clerks).

(June 25, 1948, c. 646, 62 Stat. 977; Oct. 15, 1966, Pub.L. 89–681, § 2, 80 Stat. 958; Apr. 2, 1982, Pub.L. 97–164, Title I, § 139(h), 96 Stat. 42; Oct. 29, 1992, Pub.L. 102–572, Title IX, § 902(a), 106 Stat. 4516.)

HISTORICAL AND STATUTORY NOTES

Termination of Reporting Requirements

For termination of reporting provisions of this section, effective May 15, 2000, see Pub.L. 104–66, § 3003, as amended, set out as a note under 31 U.S.C.A. § 1113, and page 13 of House Document No. 103–7.

§ 2510.   Referral of cases by Comptroller General

(a) The Comptroller General may transmit to the United States Court of Federal Claims for trial and adjudication any claim or matter of which the Court of Federal Claims might take jurisdiction on the voluntary action of the claimant, together with all vouchers, papers, documents, and proofs pertaining thereto.

(b) The Court of Federal Claims shall proceed with the claims or matters so referred as in other cases pending in such Court and shall render judgment thereon.

(June 25, 1948, c. 646, 62 Stat. 977; July 28, 1953, c. 253, § 11, 67 Stat. 227; Sept. 3, 1954, c. 1263, § 47(b), 68 Stat. 1243; Nov. 1, 1978, Pub.L. 95–563, § 14(h)(1), (2)(A), 92 Stat. 2390; Apr. 2, 1982, Pub.L. 97–164, Title I, § 139(i)(1), 96 Stat. 43; Oct. 29, 1992, Pub.L. 102–572, Title IX, § 902(a), 106 Stat. 4516.)

§ 2511.   Accounts of officers, agents or contractors

Notice of suit under section 1494 of this title shall be given to the Attorney General, to the Comptroller General, and to the head of the department requested to settle the account in question.

The judgment of the United States Court of Federal Claims in such suit shall be conclusive upon the parties, and payment of the amount found due shall discharge the obligation.

The transcript of such judgment, filed in the clerk's office of any district court, shall be entered upon the records, and shall be enforceable as other judgments.

(June 25, 1948, c. 646, 62 Stat. 977; July 28, 1953, c. 253, § 12, 67 Stat. 227; Apr. 2, 1982, Pub.L. 97–164, Title I, § 139(j), 96 Stat. 43; Oct. 29, 1992, Pub.L. 102–572, Title IX, § 902(a)(1), 106 Stat. 4516.)

HISTORICAL AND STATUTORY NOTES

Termination of Reporting Requirements

For termination of reporting provisions of subsec. (i) of this section, effective May 15, 2000, see Pub.L. 104–66, § 3003, as amended, set out as a note under 31 U.S.C.A. § 1113, and the 1st provision on page 14 of House Document No. 103–7.

§ 2512.   Disbursing officers; relief

Whenever the United States Court of Federal Claims finds that any loss by a disbursing officer of the United States was without his fault or negligence, it shall render a judgment setting forth the amount thereof, and the Government Accountability Office shall allow the officer such amount as a credit in the settlement of his accounts.

(June 25, 1948, c. 646, 62 Stat. 978; Apr. 2, 1982, Pub.L. 97–164, Title I, § 139(j)(2), 96 Stat. 43; Oct. 29, 1992, Pub.L. 102–572, Title IX, § 902(a)(1), 106 Stat. 4516; Pub.L. 108–271, § 8(b), July 7, 2004, 118 Stat. 814.)

§ 2513.   Unjust conviction and imprisonment

(a)   Any person suing under section 1495 of this title must allege and prove that:

(1)   His conviction has been reversed or set aside on the ground that he is not guilty of the offense of which he was convicted, or on new trial or rehearing he was found not guilty of such offense, as appears from the record or certificate of the court setting aside or reversing such conviction, or that he has been pardoned upon the stated ground of innocence and unjust conviction and

(2)   He did not commit any of the acts charged or his acts, deeds, or omissions in connection with such charge constituted no offense against the United States, or any State, Territory or the District of Columbia, and he did not by misconduct or neglect cause or bring about his own prosecution.

(b)   Proof of the requisite facts shall be by a certificate of the court or pardon wherein such facts are alleged to appear, and other evidence thereof shall not be received.

(c)   No pardon or certified copy of a pardon shall be considered by the United States Court of Federal Claims unless it contains recitals that the pardon was granted after applicant had exhausted all recourse to the courts and that the time for any court to exercise its jurisdiction had expired.

(d)   The Court may permit the plaintiff to prosecute such action in forma pauperis.

(e)   The amount of damages awarded shall not exceed $100,000 for each 12-month period of incarceration for any plaintiff who was unjustly sentenced to death and $50,000 for each 12-month period of incarceration for any other plaintiff.

(June 25, 1948, c. 646, 62 Stat. 978; Sept. 3, 1954, c. 1263, § 56, 68 Stat. 1247; Apr. 2, 1982, Pub.L. 97–164, Title I, § 139(j)(2), 96 Stat. 43; Oct. 29, 1992, Pub.L. 102–572, Title IX, § 902(a)(1), 106 Stat. 4516; Oct. 30, 2004, Pub.L. 108–405, Title IV, § 431, 118 Stat. 2293.)

§ 2514.   Forfeiture of fraudulent claims

A claim against the United States shall be forfeited to the United States by any person who corruptly practices or attempts to practice any fraud against the United States in the proof, statement, establishment, or allowance thereof.

In such cases the United States Court of Federal Claims shall specifically find such fraud or attempt and render judgment of forfeiture.

(June 25, 1948, c. 646, 62 Stat. 978; Apr. 2, 1982, Pub.L. 97–164, Title I, § 139(j)(2), 96 Stat. 43; Oct. 29, 1992, Pub.L. 102–572, Title IX, § 902(a)(1), 106 Stat. 4516.)

§ 2515.   New trial; stay of judgment

(a) The United States Court of Federal Claims may grant a plaintiff a new trial on any ground established by rules of common law or equity applicable as between private parties.

(b) Such court, at any time while any suit is pending before it, or after proceedings for review have been instituted, or within two years after the final disposition of the suit, may grant the United States a new trial and stay the payment of any judgment upon satisfactory evidence, cumulative or otherwise, that any fraud, wrong, or injustice has been done the United States.

(June 25, 1948, c. 646, 62 Stat. 978; Apr. 2, 1982, Pub.L. 97–164, Title I, § 139(j)(2), 96 Stat. 43; Oct. 29, 1992, Pub.L. 102–572, Title IX, § 902(a)(1), 106 Stat. 4516.)

§ 2516.   Interest on claims and judgments

(a) Interest on a claim against the United States shall be allowed in a judgment of the United States Court of Federal Claims only under a contract or Act of Congress expressly providing for payment thereof.

(b) Interest on a judgment against the United States affirmed by the Supreme Court after review on petition of the United States is paid at a rate equal to the weekly average 1-year constant maturity Treasury yield, as published by the Board of Governors of the Federal Reserve System, for the calendar week preceding the date of the judgment.

(June 25, 1948, c. 646, 62 Stat. 978; Sept. 3, 1954, c. 1263, § 57, 68 Stat. 1248; Apr. 2, 1982, Pub.L. 97–164, Title I, § 139(j)(2), Title III, § 302(d), 96 Stat. 43, 56; Sept. 13, 1982, Pub.L. 97–258, § 2(g)(5), (m)(3), 96 Stat. 1061, 1062; Oct. 29, 1992, Pub.L. 102–572, Title IX, § 902(a)(1), 106 Stat. 4516; Dec. 21, 2000, Pub.L. 106–554, § 1(a)(7) [Title III, § 307(d)(2)], 114 Stat. 2763, 2763A–636.)

§ 2517.   Payment of judgments

(a) Except as provided by chapter 71 of title 41, every final judgment rendered by the United States Court of Federal Claims against the United States shall be paid out of any general appropriation therefor, on presentation to the Secretary of the Treasury of a certification of the judgment by the clerk and chief judge of the court.

(b) Payment of any such judgment and of interest thereon shall be a full discharge to the United States of all claims and demands arising out of the matters involved in the case or controversy, unless the judgment is designated a partial judgment, in which event only the matters described therein shall be discharged.

(June 25, 1948, c. 646, 62 Stat. 979; Nov. 1, 1978, Pub.L. 95–563, § 14(e), (f), 92 Stat. 2390; Apr. 2, 1982, Pub.L. 97–164, Title I, § 139(k), 96 Stat. 43; Oct. 29, 1992, Pub.L. 102–572, Title IX, § 902(a)(1), 106 Stat. 4516; Oct. 19, 1996, Pub.L. 104–316, Title II, § 202(*l*), 110 Stat. 3843; Jan. 4, 2011, Pub.L. 111–350, § 5(g)(11), 124 Stat. 3848.)

HISTORICAL AND STATUTORY NOTES

References in Text

Chapter 71 of title 41, referred to in subsec. (a), is classified to 41 U.S.C.A. § 7101 et seq.

Transfer of Functions

Effective June 30, 1996, the functions of the Comptroller General under this section to be transferred to the Director of the Office of Management and Budget, contingent upon the additional transfer to the Office of Management and Budget of such personnel, budget authority, records, and property of the General Accounting Office relating to such functions as the Comptroller General and the Director jointly determine to be necessary, see section 211 of Pub.L. 104–53, set out as a note under section 501 of Title 31, Money and Finance.

[§ 2518.   Repealed. Pub.L. 97–164, Title I, § 139(*l*), Apr. 2, 1982, 96 Stat. 43]

HISTORICAL AND STATUTORY NOTES

Section, Act June 25, 1948, c. 646, 62 Stat. 979, directed the Secretary of the Treasury to certify to Congress for appropriation only such judgments of the Court of Claims as were not to be reviewed or were entered upon the mandate of the Supreme Court.

Effective Date of Repeal

Repeal effective Oct. 1, 1982, see section 402 of Pub.L. 97–164, set out as an Effective Date of 1982 Amendment note under section 171 of this title.

§ 2519.   Conclusiveness of judgment

A final judgment of the United States Court of Federal Claims against any plaintiff shall forever bar any further claim, suit, or demand against the United States arising out of the matters involved in the case or controversy.

(June 25, 1948, c. 646, 62 Stat. 979; Apr. 2, 1982, Pub.L. 97–164, Title I, § 139(m), 96 Stat. 43; Oct. 29, 1992, Pub.L. 102–572, Title IX, § 902(a)(1), 106 Stat. 4516.)

[§ 2520.   Repealed. Pub.L. 106–518, Title II, § 207, Nov. 13, 2000, 114 Stat. 2414]

HISTORICAL AND STATUTORY NOTES

Section, Act June 25, 1948, c. 646, 62 Stat. 979; Sept. 3, 1954, c. 1263, § 58, 68 Stat. 1248; July 18, 1966, Pub.L. 89–507, § 2, 80 Stat. 308; Apr. 2, 1982, Pub.L. 97–164, Title I, § 139(n)(1)–(3), 96 Stat. 43, 44; Nov. 19, 1988, Pub.L. 100–702, Title X, § 1012(a)(1), 102 Stat. 4668; Oct. 29, 1992, Pub.L. 102–572, Title IX, § 902(a)(1), 106 Stat. 4516 related to fees for the filing of any petition.

Effective and Applicability Provisions

1988 Acts. Section 1012(a)(2) of Title X of Pub.L. 100–702 provided that: "The amendment made by this subsection [amending this section] shall take effect 30 days after the date of enactment of this title [Nov. 19, 1988]."

§ 2521.   Subpoenas and incidental powers

(a) Subpoenas requiring the attendance of parties or witnesses and subpoenas requiring the production of books, papers, documents or tangible things by any party or witness having custody or control thereof, may be issued for purposes of discovery or for use of the things produced as evidence in accordance with the rules and orders of the court. Such subpoenas shall be issued and served and compliance therewith shall be compelled as provided in the rules and orders of the court.

(b) The United States Court of Federal Claims shall have power to punish by fine or imprisonment, at its discretion, such contempt of its authority as—

    (1) misbehavior of any person in its presence or so near thereto as to obstruct the administration of justice;

    (2) misbehavior of any of its officers in their official transactions; or

    (3) disobedience or resistance to its lawful writ, process, order, rule, decree, or command.

(c) The United States Court of Federal Claims shall have such assistance in the carrying out of its lawful writ, process, order, rule, decree, or command as is available to a court of the United States. The United States marshal for any district in which the Court of Federal Claims is sitting shall, when requested by the chief judge of the Court of Federal Claims, attend any session of the Court of Federal Claims in such district.

(Added Sept. 3, 1954, c. 1263, § 59(a), 68 Stat. 1248; amended Oct. 29, 1992, Pub.L. 102–572, Title IX, § 910(a), 106 Stat. 4519.)

§ 2522.   Notice of appeal

Review of a decision of the United States Court of Federal Claims shall be obtained by filing a notice of appeal with the clerk of the Court of Federal Claims within the time and in the manner prescribed for appeals to United States courts of appeals from the United States district courts.

(Added Pub.L. 97–164, Title I, § 139(q)(1), Apr. 2, 1982, 96 Stat. 44; amended Pub.L. 102–572, Title IX, § 902(a), Oct. 29, 1992, 106 Stat. 4516.)

CHAPTER 171—TORT CLAIMS PROCEDURE

§ 2671.   Definitions

As used in this chapter and sections 1346(b) and 2401(b) of this title, the term "Federal agency" includes the executive departments, the judicial and legislative branches, the military departments, independent establishments of the United States, and corporations primarily acting as instrumentalities or agencies of the United States, but does not include any contractor with the United States.

"Employee of the government" includes (1) officers or employees of any federal agency, members of the military or naval forces of the United States, members of the National Guard while engaged in training or duty under section 115, 316, 502, 503, 504, or 505 of title 32, and persons acting on behalf of a federal agency in an official capacity, temporarily or permanently in the service of the United States, whether with or without compensation, and (2) any officer or employee of a Federal public defender organization, except when such officer or employee performs professional services in the course of providing representation under section 3006A of title 18.

"Acting within the scope of his office or employment", in the case of a member of the military or naval forces of the United States or a member of the National Guard as defined in section 101(3) of title 32, means acting in line of duty.

(June 25, 1948, c. 646, 62 Stat. 982; May 24, 1949, c. 139, § 124, 63 Stat. 106; July 18, 1966, Pub.L. 89–506, § 8, 80 Stat. 307; Dec. 29, 1981, Pub.L. 97–124, § 1, 95 Stat. 1666; Nov. 18, 1988, Pub.L. 100–694, § 3, 102 Stat. 4564; Oct. 30, 2000, Pub.L. 106–398, § 1 [Div. A, Title VI, § 665(b)], 114 Stat. 1654, 1654A–169; Nov. 13, 2000, Pub.L. 106–518, Title IV, § 401, 114 Stat. 2421.)

HISTORICAL AND STATUTORY NOTES

Severability of Provisions

Section 7 of Pub.L. 100–694 provided that: "If any provision of this Act or the amendments made by this Act [enacting section 831c–2 of Title 16, Conservation, amending sections 2671, 2674, and 2679 of this title, and enacting provisions set out as notes under sections 1, 2671, and 2679 of this title] or the application of the provision to any person or circumstance is held invalid, the remainder of this Act and such amendments and the application of the provision to any other person or circumstance shall not be affected by that invalidation."

Law Enforcement Officer Acting Within Scope of Office or Employment

Pub.L. 105–277, § 101(h) [Title VI, § 627], 112 Stat. 2681–519, as amended Pub.L. 106–58, Title VI, § 623, Sept. 29, 1999, 113 Stat. 471, provided that:

"**(a) Definitions.**—In this section—

"**(1)** the term 'crime of violence' has the meaning given that term in section 16 of title 18, United States Code; and

"**(2)** the term 'law enforcement officer' means any employee described in subparagraph (A), (B), or (C) of section 8401(17) of title 5, United States Code; and any special in the Diplomatic Security Service of the Department of State.

"**(b) Rules of construction.**—Effective on the date of enactment of this Act [Oct. 21, 1998] and thereafter, and notwithstanding any other provision of law, for purposes of chapter 171 of title 28, United States Code, or any other provision of law relating to tort liability, a law enforcement officer shall be construed to be acting within the scope of his or her office or employment, if the officer takes reasonable action, including the use of force, to—

"**(1)** protect an individual in the presence of the officer from a crime of violence;

"**(2)** provide immediate assistance to an individual who has suffered or who is threatened with bodily harm; or

"**(3)** prevent the escape of any individual who the officer reasonably believes to have committed in the presence of the officer a crime of violence."

Congressional Findings and Purposes

Section 2 of Pub.L. 100–694 provided that:

"**(a) Findings.**—the Congress finds and declares the following:

"**(1)** For more than 40 years the Federal Tort Claims Act [28 U.S.C.A. §§ 1346(b), 2671 et seq.] has been the legal mechanism for compensating persons injured by negligent or wrongful acts of Federal employees committed within the scope of their employment.

"**(2)** The United States, through the Federal Tort Claims Act, is responsible to injured persons for the common law torts of its employees in the same manner in which the common law historically has recognized the responsibility of an employer for torts committed by its employees within the scope of their employment.

"**(3)** Because Federal employees for many years have been protected from personal common law tort liability by a broad based immunity, the Federal Tort Claims Act has served as the sole means for compensating persons injured by the tortious conduct of Federal employees.

"**(4)** Recent judicial decisions, and particularly the decision of the United States Supreme Court in Westfall v. Erwin [1988, 108 S.Ct. 580], have seriously eroded the common law tort immunity previously available to Federal employees.

"**(5)** This erosion of immunity of Federal employees from common law tort liability has created an immediate crisis involving the prospect of personal liability and the threat of protracted personal tort litigation for the entire Federal workforce.

"**(6)** The prospect of such liability will seriously undermine the morale and well being of Federal employees, impede the ability of agencies to carry out their missions, and diminish the vitality of the Federal Tort Claims Act as the proper remedy for Federal employee torts.

"**(7)** In its opinion in Westfall v. Erwin [1988, 108 S.Ct. 580], the Supreme Court indicated that the Congress is in the best position to determine the extent to which Federal employees should be personally liable for common law torts, and that legislative consideration of this matter would be useful.

"**(b) Purpose.**—It is the purpose of this Act [enacting section 831c–2 of Title 16, Conservation, amending sections 2671, 2674, and 2679 of this title, and enacting provisions set out as notes under sections 1, 2671, and 2679 of this title] to protect Federal employees from personal liability for common law torts committed within the scope of their employment, while providing persons injured by the common law torts of Federal employees with an appropriate remedy against the United States."

§ 2672. Administrative adjustment of claims

The head of each Federal agency or his designee, in accordance with regulations prescribed by the Attorney General, may consider, ascertain, adjust, determine, compromise, and settle any claim for money damages against the United States for injury or loss of property or personal injury or death caused by the negligent or wrongful act or omission of any employee of the agency while acting within the scope of his office or employment, under circumstances where the United States, if a private person, would be liable to the claimant in accordance with the law of the place where the act or omission occurred: *Provided*, That any award, compromise, or settlement in excess of $25,000 shall be effected only with the prior written approval of the Attorney General or his designee. Notwithstanding the proviso contained in the preceding sentence, any award, compromise, or settlement may be effected without the prior written approval of the Attorney General or his or her designee, to the extent that the Attorney General delegates to the head of the agency the authority to make such award, compromise, or settlement. Such delegations may not exceed the authority delegated by the Attorney General to the United States attorneys to settle claims for money damages against the United States. Each Federal agency may use arbitration, or other alternative means of dispute resolution under the provisions of subchapter IV of chapter 5 of title 5, to settle any tort claim against the United States, to the extent of the agency's authority to award, compromise, or settle such claim without the prior written approval of the Attorney General or his or her designee.

Subject to the provisions of this title relating to civil actions on tort claims against the United States, any such award, compromise, settlement, or determination shall be final and conclusive on all officers of the Government, except when procured by means of fraud.

Any award, compromise, or settlement in an amount of $2,500 or less made pursuant to this section shall be paid by the head of the Federal agency concerned out of appropriations available to that agency. Payment of any award, compromise, or settlement in an amount in excess of $2,500 made pursuant to this section or made by the Attorney General in any amount pursuant to section 2677 of this title shall be paid in a manner similar to judgments and compromises in like causes and appropriations or funds available for the payment of such judgments and compromises are hereby made available for the payment of awards, compromises, or settlements under this chapter.

The acceptance by the claimant of any such award, compromise, or settlement shall be final and conclusive on the claimant, and shall constitute a complete release of any claim against the United States and against the employee of the government whose act or omission gave rise to the claim, by reason of the same subject matter.

(June 25, 1948, c. 646, 62 Stat. 983; Apr. 25, 1949, c. 92, § 2(b), 63 Stat. 62; May 24, 1949, c. 139, § 125, 63 Stat. 106; Sept. 23, 1950, c. 1010, § 9, 64 Stat. 987; Sept. 8, 1959, Pub.L. 86–238, § 1(1), 73 Stat. 471; July 18, 1966, Pub.L. 89–506, §§ 1, 9(a), 80 Stat. 306, 308; Nov. 15, 1990, Pub.L. 101–552, § 8(a), 104 Stat. 2746.)

HISTORICAL AND STATUTORY NOTES

Effective and Applicability Provisions

1990 Acts. The termination of amendments by Pub.L. 101–552 and authority to use dispute resolution proceedings on Oct. 1, 1995, provided by section 11 of Pub.L. 101–552, set out as a note under section 571 of Title 5, Government Organization and Employees, was repealed by section 9 of Pub.L. 104–320.

1966 Acts. Section 10 of Pub.L. 89–506 provided that: "This Act [amending this section and sections 2401(b), 2671, 2675, 2677, 2678, and 2679(b) of this title, section 724a of former Title 31, Money and Finance, and section 4116(a) of Title 38, Veteran's Benefits (see Section 7316 of Title 38)] shall apply to claims accruing six months or more after the date of its enactment [July 18, 1966]."

Laws Unaffected

Section 424(b) of Act Aug. 2, 1946, c. 753, Title IV, 60 Stat. 847, provided that: "Nothing contained herein shall be deemed to repeal any provision of law authorizing any Federal agency to consider, ascertain, adjust, settle, determine, or pay any claim on account of damage to or loss of property or on account of personal injury or death, in cases in which such damage, loss, injury, or death was not caused by any negligent or wrongful act or omission of an employee of the Government while acting within the scope of his office or employment, or any other claim not cognizable under part 2 of this title."

§ 2673. Reports to Congress

The head of each federal agency shall report annually to Congress all claims paid by it under section 2672 of this title, stating the name of each claimant, the amount claimed, the amount awarded, and a brief description of the claim.

(June 25, 1948, c. 646, 62 Stat. 983.)

Repeal

Section 1(1) of Pub.L. 89–348, Nov. 8, 1965, 79 Stat. 1310, repealed the requirement that an annual report to Congress be made of the administrative adjustment of tort claims of $2,500 or less, stating the name of each claimant, the amount claimed, the amount awarded, and a brief description of the claim.

§ 2674. Liability of United States

The United States shall be liable, respecting the provisions of this title relating to tort claims, in the same manner and to the same extent as a private individual under like circumstances, but shall not be liable for interest prior to judgment or for punitive damages.

If, however, in any case wherein death was caused, the law of the place where the act or omission complained of occurred provides, or has been construed to provide, for damages only punitive in nature, the United States shall be liable for actual or compensatory damages, measured by the pecuniary injuries resulting from such death to the persons respectively, for whose benefit the action was brought, in lieu thereof.

With respect to any claim under this chapter, the United States shall be entitled to assert any defense based upon judicial or legislative immunity which otherwise would have been available to the employee of the United States whose act or omission gave rise to the claim, as well as any other defenses to which the United States is entitled.

With respect to any claim to which this section applies, the Tennessee Valley Authority shall be entitled to assert any defense which otherwise would have been available to the employee based upon judicial or legislative immunity, which otherwise would have been available to the employee of the Tennessee Valley Authority whose act or omission gave rise to the claim as well as any other defenses to which the Tennessee Valley Authority is entitled under this chapter.

(June 25, 1948, c. 646, 62 Stat. 983; Nov. 18, 1988, Pub.L. 100–694, §§ 4, 9(c), 102 Stat. 4564, 4567.)

§ 2675. Disposition by federal agency as prerequisite; evidence

(a) An action shall not be instituted upon a claim against the United States for money damages for injury or loss of property or personal injury or death caused by the negligent or wrongful act or omission of any employee of the Government while acting within the scope of his office or employment, unless the claimant shall have first presented the claim to the appropriate Federal agency and his claim shall have been finally denied by the agency in writing and sent by certified or registered mail. The failure of an agency to make final disposition of a claim within six months after it is filed shall, at the option of the claimant any time thereafter, be deemed a final denial of the claim for purposes of this section. The provisions of this subsection shall not apply to such claims as may be asserted under the Federal Rules of Civil Procedure by third party complaint, cross-claim, or counterclaim.

(b) Action under this section shall not be instituted for any sum in excess of the amount of the claim presented to the federal agency, except where the increased amount is based upon newly discovered evidence not reasonably discoverable at the time of presenting the claim to the federal agency, or upon allegation and proof of intervening facts, relating to the amount of the claim.

(c) Disposition of any claim by the Attorney General or other head of a federal agency shall not be competent evidence of liability or amount of damages.

(June 25, 1948, c. 646, 62 Stat. 983; May 24, 1949, c. 139, § 126, 63 Stat. 107; July 18, 1966, Pub.L. 89–506, § 2, 80 Stat. 306.)

§ 2676.   Judgment as bar

The judgment in an action under section 1346(b) of this title shall constitute a complete bar to any action by the claimant, by reason of the same subject matter, against the employee of the government whose act or omission gave rise to the claim.

(June 25, 1948, c. 646, 62 Stat. 984.)

§ 2677.   Compromise

The Attorney General or his designee may arbitrate, compromise, or settle any claim cognizable under section 1346(b) of this title, after the commencement of an action thereon.

(June 25, 1948, c. 646, 62 Stat. 984; July 18, 1966, Pub.L. 89–506, § 3, 80 Stat. 307.)

§ 2678.   Attorney fees; penalty

No attorney shall charge, demand, receive, or collect for services rendered, fees in excess of 25 per centum of any judgment rendered pursuant to section 1346(b) of this title or any settlement made pursuant to section 2677 of this title, or in excess of 20 per centum of any award, compromise, or settlement made pursuant to section 2672 of this title.

Any attorney who charges, demands, receives, or collects for services rendered in connection with such claim any amount in excess of that allowed under this section, if recovery be had, shall be fined not more than $2,000 or imprisoned not more than one year, or both.

(June 25, 1948, c. 646, 62 Stat. 984; July 18, 1966, Pub.L. 89–506, § 4, 80 Stat. 307.)

§ 2679.   Exclusiveness of remedy

(a) The authority of any federal agency to sue and be sued in its own name shall not be construed to authorize suits against such federal agency on claims which are cognizable under section 1346(b) of this title, and the remedies provided by this title in such cases shall be exclusive.

(b)(1) The remedy against the United States provided by sections 1346(b) and 2672 of this title for injury or loss of property, or personal injury or death arising or resulting from the negligent or wrongful act or omission of any employee of the Government while acting within the scope of his office or employment is exclusive of any other civil action or proceeding for money damages by reason of the same subject matter against the employee whose act or omission gave rise to the claim or against the estate of such employee. Any other civil action or proceeding for money damages arising out of or relating to the same subject matter against the employee or the employee's estate is precluded without regard to when the act or omission occurred.

(2) Paragraph (1) does not extend or apply to a civil action against an employee of the Government—

    (A) which is brought for a violation of the Constitution of the United States, or

    (B) which is brought for a violation of a statute of the United States under which such action against an individual is otherwise authorized.

(c) The Attorney General shall defend any civil action or proceeding brought in any court against any employee of the Government or his estate for any such damage or injury. The employee against whom such civil action or proceeding is brought shall deliver within such time after date of service or knowledge of service as determined by the Attorney General, all process served upon him or an attested true copy thereof to his immediate superior or to whomever was designated by the head of his department to receive such papers and such person shall promptly furnish copies of the pleadings and process therein to the United States attorney for the district embracing the place wherein the proceeding is brought, to the Attorney General, and to the head of his employing Federal agency.

(d)(1) Upon certification by the Attorney General that the defendant employee was acting within the scope of his office or employment at the time of the incident out of which the claim arose, any civil action or proceeding commenced upon such claim in a United States district court shall be deemed an action against the United States under the provisions of this title and all references thereto, and the United States shall be substituted as the party defendant.

(2) Upon certification by the Attorney General that the defendant employee was acting within the scope of his office or employment at the time of the incident out of which the claim arose, any civil action or proceeding commenced upon such claim in a State court shall be removed without bond at any time before trial by the Attorney General to the district court of the United States for the district and division embracing the place in which the action or proceeding is pending. Such action or proceeding shall be deemed to be an action or proceeding brought against the United States under the provisions of this title and all references thereto, and the United States shall be substituted as the party defendant. This certification of the Attorney General shall conclusively establish scope of office or employment for purposes of removal.

(3) In the event that the Attorney General has refused to certify scope of office or employment under this section, the employee may at any time before trial petition the court to find and certify that the employee was acting within the scope of his office or employment. Upon such certification by the court, such action or proceeding shall be deemed to be an action or proceeding brought against the United States under the provisions of this title and all references thereto, and the United States shall be substituted as the party defendant. A copy of the petition shall be served upon the United States in accordance with the provisions of Rule 4(d)(4)[1] of the Federal Rules of Civil Procedure. In the event the petition is filed in a civil action or proceeding pending in a State court, the action or proceeding may be removed without bond by the Attorney General to the district court of the United States for the district and division embracing the place in which it is pending. If, in considering the petition, the district court determines that the employee was not acting within the scope of his office or employment, the action or proceeding shall be remanded to the State court.

(4) Upon certification, any action or proceeding subject to paragraph (1), (2), or (3) shall proceed in the same manner as any action against the United States filed pursuant to section 1346(b) of this title and shall be subject to the limitations and exceptions applicable to those actions.

(5) Whenever an action or proceeding in which the United States is substituted as the party defendant under this subsection is dismissed for failure first to present a claim pursuant to section 2675(a) of this title, such a claim shall be deemed to be timely presented under section 2401(b) of this title if—

(A) the claim would have been timely had it been filed on the date the underlying civil action was commenced, and

---

[1] [Footnote to 28 U.S.C. § 2679(d)(3):] So in original. Probably should be a reference to Rule (4)(i). [At the time this provision was enacted, service on the United States was governed by Rule 4(d)(4) of the Federal Rules of Civil Procedure. Today, such service is governed by Rule 4(i). Ed.]

(B) the claim is presented to the appropriate Federal agency within 60 days after dismissal of the civil action.

(e) The Attorney General may compromise or settle any claim asserted in such civil action or proceeding in the manner provided in section 2677, and with the same effect.

(June 25, 1948, c. 646, 62 Stat. 984; Sept. 21, 1961, Pub.L. 87–258, § 1, 75 Stat. 539; July 18, 1966, Pub.L. 89–506, § 5(a), 80 Stat. 307; Nov. 18, 1988, Pub.L. 100–694, §§ 5, 6, 102 Stat. 4564.)

HISTORICAL AND STATUTORY NOTES

Effective and Applicability Provisions

1988 Acts. Section 8 of Pub.L. 100–694 provided that:

"**(a) General rule.**—This Act and the amendments made by this Act [enacting section 831c–2 of Title 16, Conservation; amending sections 2671, 2674, and 2679(b), (d) of this title, and enacting provisions set out as notes under this section and sections 1 and 2671 of this title] shall take effect on the date of the enactment of this Act [Nov. 18, 1988].

"**(b) Applicability to proceedings.**—The amendments made by this Act [amending sections 2671, 2674, and 2679 of this title] shall apply to all claims, civil actions, and proceedings pending on, or filed on or after, the date of the enactment of this Act [Nov. 18, 1988].

"**(c) Pending State proceedings.**—With respect to any civil action or proceeding pending in a State court to which the amendments made by this Act apply, and as to which the period for removal under section 2679(d) of title 28, United States Code [subsec. (d) of this section] (as amended by section 6 of this Act), has expired, the Attorney General shall have 60 days after the date of the enactment of this Act [Nov. 18, 1988] during which to seek removal under such section 2679(d) [subsec. (d) of this section].

"**(d) Claims accruing before enactment.**—With respect to any civil action or proceeding to which the amendments made by this Act apply in which the claim accrued before the date of the enactment of this Act [Nov. 18, 1988], the period during which the claim shall be deemed to be timely presented under section 2679(d)(5) of title 28, United States Code [subsec. (d)(5) of this section] (as amended by section 6 of this Act) shall be that period within which the claim could have been timely filed under applicable State law, but in no event shall such period exceed two years from the date of the enactment of this Act [Nov. 18, 1988]."

1966 Acts. Amendment of section by Pub.L. 89–506 applicable to claims accruing six months or more after July 18, 1966, see section 10 of Pub.L. 89–506, set out as a note under section 2672 of this title.

1961 Acts. Section 2 of Pub.L. 87–258 provided that: "The amendments made by this Act [adding subsecs. (b)–(e) of this section] shall be deemed to be in effect six months after the enactment hereof [Sept. 21, 1961] but any rights or liabilities then existing shall not be affected."

§ 2680.   Exceptions

The provisions of this chapter and section 1346(b) of this title shall not apply to—

(a) Any claim based upon an act or omission of an employee of the Government, exercising due care, in the execution of a statute or regulation, whether or not such statute or regulation be valid, or based upon the exercise or performance or the failure to exercise or perform a discretionary function or duty on the part of a federal agency or an employee of the Government, whether or not the discretion involved be abused.

(b) Any claim arising out of the loss, miscarriage, or negligent transmission of letters or postal matter.

(c) Any claim arising in respect of the assessment or collection of any tax or customs duty, or the detention of any goods, merchandise, or other property by any officer of customs or excise or any other law enforcement officer, except that the provisions of this chapter and section 1346(b) of this title apply to any claim based on injury or loss of goods, merchandise, or other property, while in the possession of any officer of customs or excise or any other law enforcement officer, if—

(1) the property was seized for the purpose of forfeiture under any provision of Federal law providing for the forfeiture of property other than as a sentence imposed upon conviction of a criminal offense;

(2) the interest of the claimant was not forfeited;

(3) the interest of the claimant was not remitted or mitigated (if the property was subject to forfeiture); and

(4) the claimant was not convicted of a crime for which the interest of the claimant in the property was subject to forfeiture under a Federal criminal forfeiture law.

(d) Any claim for which a remedy is provided by chapter 309 or 311 of title 46 relating to claims or suits in admiralty against the United States.

(e) Any claim arising out of an act or omission of any employee of the Government in administering the provisions of sections 1–31 of Title 50, Appendix.

(f) Any claim for damages caused by the imposition or establishment of a quarantine by the United States.

[(g) Repealed. Sept. 26, 1950, c. 1049, § 13(5), 64 Stat. 1043.]

(h) Any claim arising out of assault, battery, false imprisonment, false arrest, malicious prosecution, abuse of process, libel, slander, misrepresentation, deceit, or interference with contract rights: *Provided*, That, with regard to acts or omissions of investigative or law enforcement officers of the United States Government, the provisions of this chapter and section 1346(b) of this title shall apply to any claim arising, on or after the date of the enactment of this proviso, out of assault, battery, false imprisonment, false arrest, abuse of process, or malicious prosecution. For the purpose of this subsection, "investigative or law enforcement officer" means any officer of the United States who is empowered by law to execute searches, to seize evidence, or to make arrests for violations of Federal law.

(i) Any claim for damages caused by the fiscal operations of the Treasury or by the regulation of the monetary system.

(j) Any claim arising out of the combatant activities of the military or naval forces, or the Coast Guard, during time of war.

(k) Any claim arising in a foreign country.

(*l*) Any claim arising from the activities of the Tennessee Valley Authority.

(m) Any claim arising from the activities of the Panama Canal Company.

(n) Any claim arising from the activities of a Federal land bank, a Federal intermediate credit bank, or a bank for cooperatives.

(June 25, 1948, c. 646, 62 Stat. 984; July 16, 1949, c. 340, 63 Stat. 444; Sept. 26, 1950, c. 1049, §§ 2(a)(2), 13(5), 64 Stat. 1038, 1043; Aug. 18, 1959, Pub.L. 86–168, Title II, § 202(b), 73 Stat. 389; Mar. 16, 1974, Pub.L. 93–253, § 2, 88 Stat. 50; Apr. 25, 2000, Pub.L. 106–185, § 3(a), 114 Stat. 211; Oct. 6, 2006, Pub.L. 109–304, § 17(f)(4), 120 Stat. 1708.)

HISTORICAL AND STATUTORY NOTES

References in Text

Chapter 309 or 311 of title 46, referred to in subsec. (d), are Suits in Admiralty Against the United States, 46 U.S.C.A. § 30901 et seq., and Commercial Instruments and Maritime Liens, 46 U.S.C.A. § 31101 et seq.

Sections 1–31 of Title 50, Appendix, referred to in subsec. (e), was in the original source of this section (section 943 [of Title 28, which was section 421] of Act Aug. 2, 1946) a reference to the Trading with the

Enemy Act, as amended. The Trading with the Enemy Act is now comprised of sections 1 to 43, which are classified to sections 1 to 6, 7 to 39, and 41 to 44 of Title 50, Appendix, War and National Defense.

Date of the enactment of this proviso, referred to in subsec. (h), means Mar. 16, 1974, the date on which Pub.L. 93–253, enacting the proviso, was approved.

Panama Canal Company, referred to in subsec. (m), deemed to refer to Panama Canal Commission, see section 3602(b)(5) of Title 22, Foreign Relations and Intercourse.

Effective and Applicability Provisions

2000 Acts. Amendments by Pub.L. 106–185, applicable to any forfeiture proceeding commenced on or after the date that is 120 days after April 25, 2000, see section 21 of Pub.L. 106–185, set out as a note under section 1324 of Title 8.

1959 Acts. Amendment by Pub.L. 86–168 effective Jan. 1, 1960, pursuant to section 203(c) of Pub.L. 86–168.

1950 Acts. Section 14 of Act Sept. 26, 1950, provided that the repeal of subsec. (g) and amendment of subsec. (m) of this section by such Act shall take effect upon the effective date of the transfer to the Panama Canal Company, pursuant to the provisions of section 256 of the Canal Zone Code, as added by section 10 of such Act, of the Panama Canal together with the facilities and appurtenances related thereto.

Transfer of Functions

The Coast Guard was transferred to the Department of Transportation and all functions, powers, and duties, relating to the Coast Guard, of the Secretary of the Treasury and of all other offices and officers of the Department of the Treasury were transferred to the Secretary of Transportation by Pub.L. 89–670, § 6(b)(1), Oct. 15, 1966, 80 Stat. 938. Section 6(b)(2) of Pub.L. 89–670, however, provided that notwithstanding such transfer of functions, the Coast Guard shall operate as part of the Navy in time of war or when the President directs as provided in section 3 of Title 14, Coast Guard. See section 108 of Title 49, Transportation.

For transfer of certain functions relating to claims and litigation, insofar as they pertain to the Air Force, from the Secretary of the Army to the Secretary of the Air Force, see Secretary of Defense Transfer Order No. 34 [§ 1a(2)(4)], eff. July 1, 1949.

Applicability of Subsec. (j)

Section 1(a)(32) of Joint Res. July 3, 1952, c. 570, 66 Stat. 333, as amended by Joint Res. Mar. 31, 1953, c. 13, § 1, 67 Stat. 18 and Joint Res. June 30, 1953, c. 172, 67 Stat. 132, provided that subsec. (j) of this section should continue in force until six months after the termination of the national emergency proclaimed by the President on Dec. 16, 1950, by 1950 Proc. No. 2914, 15 F.R. 9029, set out as a note preceding section 1 of the Appendix to Title 50, War and National Defense, or such earlier date or dates as may be provided for by Congress, but in no event beyond Aug. 1, 1953. Section 7 of Joint Res. July 3, 1952, provided that it should become effective June 16, 1952.

Section 6 of Joint Res. July 3, 1952, c. 570, § 6, 66 Stat. 334, repealed Joint Res. Apr. 14, 1952, c. 204, 66 Stat. 54 as amended by Joint Res. May 28, 1952, c. 339, 66 Stat. 96; Joint Res. June 14, 1952, c. 437, 66 Stat. 137; Joint Res. June 30, 1952, c. 526, 66 Stat. 296, which continued provisions of subsection (j) of this section (see note above) until July 3, 1952. This repeal was made effective June 16, 1952, by section 7 of Joint Res. July 3, 1952.

Northern Mariana Islands as Foreign Country With Respect to Claims Accruing No More than Two Years Prior to Oct. 19, 1982

Pub.L. 97–357, Title II, § 204, Oct. 19, 1982, 96 Stat. 1708, provided: "That the Northern Mariana Islands shall not be considered a foreign country for purposes of subsection (k) of section 2680 of Title 28, United States Code [subsec. (k) of this section], with respect to claims which accrued no more than two years prior to the effective date of this Act [Oct. 19, 1982]."

Termination of National Emergency

    Declaration of national emergency in effect on Sept. 14, 1976, was terminated two years from that date by Section 1601 of Title 50, War and National Defense.

CHAPTER 173—ATTACHMENT IN POSTAL SUITS [Omitted]

CHAPTER 176—FEDERAL DEBT COLLECTION PROCEDURE

SUBCHAPTER A—DEFINITIONS AND GENERAL PROVISIONS

§ 3001.   Applicability of chapter

    (a) In general.—Except as provided in subsection (b), the[1] chapter provides the exclusive civil procedures for the United States—

        (1) to recover a judgment on a debt; or

        (2) to obtain, before judgment on a claim for a debt, a remedy in connection with such claim.

    (b) Limitation.—To the extent that another Federal law specifies procedures for recovering on a claim or a judgment for a debt arising under such law, those procedures shall apply to such claim or judgment to the extent those procedures are inconsistent with this chapter.

    (c) Amounts owing other than debts.—This chapter shall not apply with respect to an amount owing that is not a debt or to a claim for an amount owing that is not a debt.

(Added Pub.L. 101–647, Title XXXVI, § 3611, Nov. 29, 1990, 104 Stat. 4933.)

---

   [1]   [Footnote to Chapter 176 table:] Editorially supplied.

   [2]   So in original. Does not conform to subchapter heading.

   [1]   [Footnote to 28 U.S.C. § 3001(a):] So in original. Probably should be "this".

HISTORICAL AND STATUTORY NOTES

Effective and Applicability Provisions

1990 Acts. Section 3631 of Title XXXVI of Pub.L. 101–647 provided that:

"**(a)** Except as provided in subsection (b), this Act and the amendments made by this Act [Pub.L. 101–647, Title XXXVI, Nov. 29, 1990, 104 Stat. 4933, popularly known as the Federal Debt Collection Procedures Act of 1990. For distribution of this Act to the Code, see Short Title note set out under section 1 of this title and Tables] shall take effect 180 days after the date of the enactment of this Act [Nov. 29, 1990].

"**(b)(1)** The amendments made by title I of this Act [probably means subtitle A of Title XXXVI of Pub.L. 101–647, which enacted this chapter] shall apply with respect to actions pending on the effective date of this Act [180 days after Nov. 29, 1990] in any court on—

"**(A)** a claim for a debt; or

"**(B)** a judgment for a debt.

"**(2)** All notices, writs, orders, and judgments in effect in such actions shall continue in effect until superseded or modified in an action under chapter 176 of title 28 of the United States Code, as added by title I of this Act [this chapter].

"**(3)** For purposes of this subsection—

"**(A)** the term 'court' means a Federal, State, or local court, and

"**(B)** the term 'debt' has the meaning given such term in section and 3002(3) of such chapter [probably means section 3002(3) of this title]."

§ 3002.   Definitions

As used in this chapter:

(1) "Counsel for the United States" means—

(A) a United States attorney, an assistant United States attorney designated to act on behalf of the United States attorney, or an attorney with the United States Department of Justice or with a Federal agency who has litigation authority; and

(B) any private attorney authorized by contract made in accordance with section 3718 of title 31 to conduct litigation for collection of debts on behalf of the United States.

(2) "Court" means any court created by the Congress of the United States, excluding the United States Tax Court.

(3) "Debt" means—

(A) an amount that is owing to the United States on account of a direct loan, or loan insured or guaranteed, by the United States; or

(B) an amount that is owing to the United States on account of a fee, duty, lease, rent, service, sale of real or personal property, overpayment, fine, assessment, penalty, restitution, damages, interest, tax, bail bond forfeiture, reimbursement, recovery of a cost incurred by the United States, or other source of indebtedness to the United States, but that is not owing under the terms of a contract originally entered into by only persons other than the United States;

and includes any amount owing to the United States for the benefit of an Indian tribe or individual Indian, but excludes any amount to which the United States is entitled under section 3011(a).

(4) "Debtor" means a person who is liable for a debt or against whom there is a claim for a debt.

(5) "Disposable earnings" means that part of earnings remaining after all deductions required by law have been withheld.

(6) "Earnings" means compensation paid or payable for personal services, whether denominated as wages, salary, commission, bonus, or otherwise, and includes periodic payments pursuant to a pension or retirement program.

(7) "Garnishee" means a person (other than the debtor) who has, or is reasonably thought to have, possession, custody, or control of any property in which the debtor has a substantial nonexempt interest, including any obligation due the debtor or to become due the debtor, and against whom a garnishment under section 3104 or 3205 is issued by a court.

(8) "Judgment" means a judgment, order, or decree entered in favor of the United States in a court and arising from a civil or criminal proceeding regarding a debt.

(9) "Nonexempt disposable earnings" means 25 percent of disposable earnings, subject to section 303 of the Consumer Credit Protection Act.

(10) "Person" includes a natural person (including an individual Indian), a corporation, a partnership, an unincorporated association, a trust, or an estate, or any other public or private entity, including a State or local government or an Indian tribe.

(11) "Prejudgment remedy" means the remedy of attachment, receivership, garnishment, or sequestration authorized by this chapter to be granted before judgment on the merits of a claim for a debt.

(12) "Property" includes any present or future interest, whether legal or equitable, in real, personal (including choses in action), or mixed property, tangible or intangible, vested or contingent, wherever located and however held (including community property and property held in trust (including spendthrift and pension trusts)), but excludes—

    (A) property held in trust by the United States for the benefit of an Indian tribe or individual Indian; and

    (B) Indian lands subject to restrictions against alienation imposed by the United States.

(13) "Security agreement" means an agreement that creates or provides for a lien.

(14) "State" means any of the several States, the District of Columbia, the Commonwealth of Puerto Rico, the Commonwealth of the Northern Marianas, or any territory or possession of the United States.

(15) "United States" means—

    (A) a Federal corporation;

    (B) an agency, department, commission, board, or other entity of the United States; or

    (C) an instrumentality of the United States.

(16) "United States marshal" means a United States marshal, a deputy marshal, or an official of the United States Marshals Service designated under section 564.

(Added Pub.L. 101–647, Title XXXVI, § 3611, Nov. 29, 1990, 104 Stat. 4933.)

HISTORICAL AND STATUTORY NOTES

References in Text

Section 303 of the Consumer Credit Protection Act, referred to in par. (9), is classified to section 1673 of Title 15, Commerce and Trade.

§ 3003.   Rules of construction

    (a) Terms.—For purposes of this chapter—

        (1) the terms "includes" and "including" are not limiting;

        (2) the term "or" is not exclusive; and

        (3) the singular includes the plural.

    (b) Effect on rights of the United States.—This chapter shall not be construed to curtail or limit the right of the United States under any other Federal law or any State law—

        (1) to collect taxes or to collect any other amount collectible in the same manner as a tax;

        (2) to collect any fine, penalty, assessment, restitution, or forfeiture arising in a criminal case;

        (3) to appoint or seek the appointment of a receiver; or

        (4) to enforce a security agreement.

    (c) Effect on other laws.—This chapter shall not be construed to supersede or modify the operation of—

        (1) title 11;

        (2) admiralty law;

        (3) section 3713 of title 31;

        (4) section 303 of the Consumer Credit Protection Act (15 U.S.C. 1673);

        (5) a statute of limitation applicable to a criminal proceeding;

        (6) the common law or statutory rights to set-off or recoupment;

        (7) any Federal law authorizing, or any inherent authority of a court to provide, injunctive relief;

        (8) the authority of a court—

            (A) to impose a sanction under the Federal Rules of Civil Procedure;

            (B) to appoint a receiver to effectuate its order; or

            (C) to exercise the power of contempt under any Federal law;

        (9) any law authorizing the United States to obtain partition, or to recover possession, of property in which the United States holds title; or

        (10) any provision of any other chapter of this title, except to the extent such provision is inconsistent with this chapter.

    (d) Preemption.—This chapter shall preempt State law to the extent such law is inconsistent with a provision of this chapter.

    (e) Effect on rights of the United States under foreign and international law.—This chapter shall not be construed to curtail or limit the rights of the United States under foreign law, under a treaty or an international agreement, or otherwise under international law.

    (f) Applicability of Federal Rules of Civil Procedure.—Except as provided otherwise in this chapter, the Federal Rules of Civil Procedure shall apply with respect to actions and proceedings under this chapter.

(Added Pub.L. 101–647, Title XXXVI, § 3611, Nov. 29, 1990, 104 Stat. 4935.)

§ 3004.   Service of process; enforcement; notice

(a) **Manner of service.**—A complaint, notice, writ, or other process required to be served in an action or proceeding under this chapter shall be served in accordance with the Federal Rules of Civil Procedure unless otherwise provided in this chapter.

(b) **Nationwide enforcement.**—

(1) Except as provided in paragraph (2)—

(A) any writ, order, judgment, or other process, including a summons and complaint, filed under this chapter may be served in any State; and

(B) such writ, order, or judgment may be enforced by the court issuing the writ, order, or process, regardless of where the person is served with the writ, order, or process.

(2) If the debtor so requests, within 20 days after receiving the notice described in section 3101(d) or 3202(b), the action or proceeding in which the writ, order, or judgment was issued shall be transferred to the district court for the district in which the debtor resides.

(c) **Notice and other process.**—At such time as counsel for the United States considers appropriate, but not later than the time a prejudgment or postjudgment remedy is put into effect under this chapter, counsel for the United States shall exercise reasonable diligence to serve on the debtor and any person who the United States believes, after exercising due diligence, has possession, custody, or control of the property, a copy of the application for such remedy, the order granting such remedy, and the notice required by section 3101(d) or 3202(b).

(Added Pub.L. 101–647, Title XXXVI, § 3611, Nov. 29, 1990, 104 Stat. 4936.)

§ 3005.   Application of chapter to judgments

This chapter shall not apply with respect to a judgment on a debt if such judgment is entered more than 10 years before the effective date of this chapter.

(Added Pub.L. 101–647, Title XXXVI, § 3611, Nov. 29, 1990, 104 Stat. 4936.)

§ 3006.   Affidavit requirements

Any affidavit required of the United States by this chapter may be made on information and belief, if reliable and reasonably necessary, establishing with particularity, to the court's satisfaction, facts supporting the claim of the United States.

(Added Pub.L. 101–647, Title XXXVI, § 3611, Nov. 29, 1990, 104 Stat. 4936.)

§ 3007.   Perishable personal property

(a) **Authority to sell.**—If at any time during any action or proceeding under this chapter the court determines on its own initiative or upon motion of any party, that any seized or detained personal property is likely to perish, waste, or be destroyed, or otherwise substantially depreciate in value during the pendency of the proceeding, the court shall order a commercially reasonable sale of such property.

(b) **Deposit of sale proceeds.**—Within 5 days after such sale, the proceeds shall be deposited with the clerk of the court, accompanied by a statement in writing and signed by the United States marshal, to be filed in the action or proceeding, stating the time and place of sale, the name of the purchaser, the amount received, and an itemized account of expenses.

(c) **Presumption.**—For purposes of liability on the part of the United States, there shall be a presumption that the price paid at a sale under subsection (a) is the fair market value of the property or portion.

(Added Pub.L. 101–647, Title XXXVI, § 3611, Nov. 29, 1990, 104 Stat. 4937.)

§ 3008.   Proceedings before United States magistrate judges

A district court of the United States may assign its duties in proceedings under this chapter to a United States magistrate judge to the extent not inconsistent with the Constitution and laws of the United States.

(Added Pub.L. 101–647, Title XXXVI, § 3611, Nov. 29, 1990, 104 Stat. 4937; amended Pub.L. 101–650, Title III, § 321, Dec. 1, 1990, 104 Stat. 5117.)

HISTORICAL AND STATUTORY NOTES

Change of Name

"United States magistrate judges" substituted for "United States magistrates" in the catchline and "United States magistrate judge" substituted for "United States magistrate" in text pursuant to section 321 of Pub.L. 101–650, set out as a note under 28 U.S.C.A. § 631.

§ 3009.   United States marshals' authority to designate keeper

Whenever a United States marshal is authorized to seize property pursuant to this chapter, the United States marshal may designate another person or Federal agency to hold for safekeeping such property seized.

(Added Pub.L. 101–647, Title XXXVI, § 3611, Nov. 29, 1990, 104 Stat. 4937.)

§ 3010.   Co-owned property

(a) **Limitation.**—The remedies available to the United States under this chapter may be enforced against property which is co-owned by a debtor and any other person only to the extent allowed by the law of the State where the property is located. This section shall not be construed to limit any right or interest of a debtor or co-owner in a retirement system for Federal military or civilian personnel established by the United States or any agency thereof or in a qualified retirement arrangement.

(b) **Definitions.**—For purposes of subsection (a)—

(1) the term "retirement system for Federal military or civilian personnel" means a pension or annuity system for Federal military or civilian personnel of more than one agency, or for some or all of such personnel of a single agency, established by statute or by regulation pursuant to statutory authority; and

(2) the term "qualified retirement arrangement" means a plan qualified under section 401(a), 403(a), or 409 of the Internal Revenue Code of 1986 or a plan that is subject to the requirements of section 205 of the Employee Retirement Income Security Act of 1974.

(Added Pub.L. 101–647, Title XXXVI, § 3611, Nov. 29, 1990, 104 Stat. 4937.)

HISTORICAL AND STATUTORY NOTES

References in Text

Sections 401(a), 403(a) and 409 of the Internal Revenue Code of 1986, referred to in subsec. (b)(2), are set out in sections 401(a), 403(a) and 409, respectively, of Title 26, Internal Revenue Code.

Section 205 of the Employee Retirement Income Security Act of 1974, referred to in subsec. (b)(2), is classified to section 1055 of Title 29, Labor.

§ 3011.   Assessment of surcharge on a debt

(a) **Surcharge authorized.**—In an action or proceeding under subchapter B or C, and subject to subsection (b), the United States is entitled to recover a surcharge of 10 percent of the amount of the debt in connection with the recovery of the debt, to cover the cost of processing and handling the litigation and enforcement under this chapter of the claim for such debt.

(b) Limitation.—Subsection (a) shall not apply if—

(1) the United States receives an attorney's fee in connection with the enforcement of the claim; or

(2) the law pursuant to which the action on the claim is based provides any other amount to cover such costs.

(Added Pub.L. 101–647, Title XXXVI, § 3611, Nov. 29, 1990, 104 Stat. 4937.)

§ 3012.   Joinder of additional defendant

The United States or the debtor may join as an additional defendant in an action or proceeding under this chapter any person reasonably believed to owe money (including money owed on account of a requirement to provide goods or services pursuant to a loan or loan guarantee extended under Federal law) to the debtor arising out of the transaction or occurrence giving rise to a debt.

(Added Pub.L. 101–647, Title XXXVI, § 3611, Nov. 29, 1990, 104 Stat. 4938.)

§ 3013.   Modification or protective order; supervision of enforcement

The court may at any time on its own initiative or the motion of any interested person, and after such notice as it may require, make an order denying, limiting, conditioning, regulating, extending, or modifying the use of any enforcement procedure under this chapter.

(Added Pub.L. 101–647, Title XXXVI, § 3611, Nov. 29, 1990, 104 Stat. 4938.)

§ 3014.   Exempt property

(a) Election to exempt property.—An individual debtor may, in an action or proceeding under this chapter, elect to exempt property listed in either paragraph (1) or, in the alternative, paragraph (2). If such action or proceeding is against debtors who are husband and wife, one debtor may not elect to exempt property listed in paragraph (1) and the other debtor elect to exempt property listed in paragraph (2). If the debtors cannot agree on the alternative to be elected, they shall be deemed to elect paragraph (1). Such property is either—

(1) property that is specified in section 522(d) of title 11, as amended from time to time; or

(2)(A) any property that is exempt under Federal law, other than paragraph (1), or State or local law that is applicable on the date of the filing of the application for a remedy under this chapter at the place in which the debtor's domicile has been located for the 180 days immediately preceding the date of the filing of such application, or for a longer portion of such 180-day period than in any other place; and

(B) any interest in property in which the debtor had, immediately before the filing of such application, an interest as a tenant by the entirety or joint tenant, or an interest in a community estate, to the extent that such interest is exempt from process under applicable nonbankruptcy law.

(b) Effect on assertion and manner of determination.—

(1) **Statement.**—A court may order the debtor to file a statement with regard to any claimed exemption. A copy of such statement shall be served on counsel for the United States. Such statement shall be under oath and shall describe each item of property for which exemption is claimed, the value and the basis for such valuation, and the nature of the debtor's ownership interest.

(2) **Hearing.**—The United States or the debtor, by application to the court in which an action or proceeding under this chapter is pending, may request a hearing on the applicability of any exemption claimed by the debtor. The court shall determine the extent (if any) to which the exemption applies. Unless it is reasonably evident that the exemption applies, the debtor shall bear the burden of persuasion.

(3) **Stay of disposition.**—Assertion of an exemption shall prevent the United States from selling or otherwise disposing of the property for which such exemption is claimed until the court determines whether the debtor has a substantial nonexempt interest in such property. The United States may not take possession of, dispose of, sell, or otherwise interfere with the debtor's normal use and enjoyment of an interest in property the United States knows or has reason to know is exempt.

(c) **Debtors in joint cases.**—Subject to the limitation in subsection (a), this section shall apply separately with respect to each debtor in a joint case.

(Added Pub.L. 101–647, Title XXXVI, § 3611, Nov. 29, 1990, 104 Stat. 4938.)

§ 3015.   Discovery as to debtor's financial condition

(a) **In general.**—Except as provided in subsection (b), in an action or proceeding under subchapter B or C, the United States may have discovery regarding the financial condition of the debtor in the manner in which discovery is authorized by the Federal Rules of Civil Procedure in an action on a claim for a debt.

(b) **Limitation.**—Subsection (a) shall not apply with respect to an action or proceeding under subchapter B unless there is a reasonable likelihood that the debt involved exceeds $50,000.

(Added Pub.L. 101–647, Title XXXVI, § 3611, Nov. 29, 1990, 104 Stat. 4939.)

SUBCHAPTER B—PREJUDGMENT REMEDIES

§ 3101.   Prejudgment remedies

(a) **Application.**—**(1)** The United States may, in a proceeding in conjunction with the complaint or at any time after the filing of a civil action on a claim for a debt, make application under oath to a court to issue any prejudgment remedy.

(2) Such application shall be filed with the court and shall set forth the factual and legal basis for each prejudgment remedy sought.

(3) Such application shall—

(A) state that the debtor against whom the prejudgment remedy is sought shall be afforded an opportunity for a hearing; and

(B) set forth with particularity that all statutory requirements under this chapter for the issuance of the prejudgment remedy sought have been satisfied.

(b) **Grounds.**—Subject to section 3102, 3103, 3104, or 3105, a prejudgment remedy may be granted by any court if the United States shows reasonable cause to believe that—

(1) the debtor—

(A) is about to leave the jurisdiction of the United States with the effect of hindering, delaying, or defrauding the United States in its effort to recover a debt;

(B) has or is about to assign, dispose, remove, conceal, ill treat, waste, or destroy property with the effect of hindering, delaying, or defrauding the United States;

(C) has or is about to convert the debtor's property into money, securities, or evidence of debt in a manner prejudicial to the United States with the effect of hindering, delaying, or defrauding the United States; or

(D) has evaded service of process by concealing himself or has temporarily withdrawn from the jurisdiction of the United States with the effect of hindering, delaying, or defrauding the United States; or

(2) a prejudgment remedy is required to obtain jurisdiction within the United States and the prejudgment remedy sought will result in obtaining such jurisdiction.

(c) Affidavit.—(1) The application under subsection (a) shall include an affidavit establishing with particularity to the court's satisfaction facts supporting the probable validity of the claim for a debt and the right of the United States to recover what is demanded in the application.

(2) The affidavit shall state—

(A) specifically the amount of the debt claimed by the United States and any interest or costs attributable to such debt;

(B) one or more of the grounds specified in subsection (b); and

(C) the requirements of section 3102(b), 3103(a), 3104(a), or 3105(b), as the case may be.

(3) No bond is required of the United States.

(d) Notice and hearing.—(1) On filing an application by the United States as provided in this section, the counsel for the United States shall prepare, and the clerk shall issue, a notice for service on the debtor against whom the prejudgment remedy is sought and on any other person whom the United States reasonably believes, after exercising due diligence, has possession, custody, or control of property affected by such remedy. Three copies of the notice shall be served on each such person. The form and content of such notice shall be approved jointly by a majority of the chief judges of the Federal districts in the State in which the court is located and shall be in substantially the following form:

"NOTICE

"You are hereby notified that this [property] is being taken by the United States Government ('the Government'), which says that [name of debtor] owes it a debt of $ [amount] for [reason for debt] and has filed a lawsuit to collect this debt. The Government says it must take this property at this time because [recite the pertinent ground or grounds from section 3101(b)]. The Government wants to make sure [name of debtor] will pay if the court determines that this money is owed.

"In addition, you are hereby notified that there are exemptions under the law which may protect some of this property from being taken by the Government if [name of debtor] can show that the exemptions apply. Below is a summary of the major exemptions which apply in most situations in the State of [State where property is located]:

"[A statement summarizing in plain and understandable English the election available with respect to such State under section 3014 and the types of property that may be exempted under each of the alternatives specified in paragraphs (1) and (2) of section 3014(a), and a statement that different property may be so exempted with respect to the State in which the debtor resides.]

"If you are [name of debtor] and you disagree with the reason the Government gives for taking your property now, or if you think you do not owe the money to the Government that it says you do, or if you think the property the Government is taking qualifies under one of the above exemptions, you have a right to ask the court to return your property to you.

"If you want a hearing, you must promptly notify the court. You must make your request in writing, and either mail it or deliver it in person to the clerk of the court at [address]. If you wish, you may use this notice to request the hearing by checking the box below and mailing this notice to the court clerk. You must also send a copy of your request to the Government at [address], so the Government will know you want a hearing. The hearing will take place within 5 days after the clerk receives your request, if you ask for it to take place that quickly, or as soon after that as possible.

"At the hearing you may explain to the judge why you think you do not owe the money to the Government, why you disagree with the reason the Government says it must take your property at this time, or why you believe the property the Government has taken is exempt or belongs to someone else. You may make any or all of these explanations as you see fit.

"If you think you live outside the Federal judicial district in which the court is located, you may request, not later than 20 days after you receive this notice, that this proceeding to take your property be transferred by the court to the Federal judicial district in which you reside. You must make your request in writing, and either mail it or deliver it in person to the clerk of the court at [address]. You must also send a copy of your request to the Government at [address], so the Government will know you want the proceeding to be transferred.

"Be sure to keep a copy of this notice for your own records. If you have any questions about your rights or about this procedure, you should contact a lawyer, an office of public legal assistance, or the clerk of the court. The clerk is not permitted to give legal advice, but can refer you to other sources of information."

    (2) By requesting, at any time before judgment on the claim for a debt, the court to hold a hearing, the debtor may move to quash the order granting such remedy. The court shall hold a hearing on such motion as soon as practicable, or, if requested by the debtor, within 5 days after receiving the request for a hearing or as soon thereafter as possible. The issues at such hearing shall be limited to—

        (A) the probable validity of the claim for the debt for which such remedy was granted and of any defense or claim of exemption asserted by such person;

        (B) compliance with any statutory requirement for the issuance of the prejudgment remedy granted;

        (C) the existence of any ground set forth in subsection (b); and

        (D) the inadequacy of alternative remedies (if any) to protect the interests of the United States.

    (e) **Issuance of writ.**—On the court's determination that the requirements of subsections (a), (b), and (c) have been met, the court shall issue all process sufficient to put into effect the prejudgment remedy sought.

(Added Pub.L. 101–647, Title XXXVI, § 3611, Nov. 29, 1990, 104 Stat. 4939.)

§ 3102.   Attachment

    (a) **Property subject to attachment.**—**(1)** Any property in the possession, custody, or control of the debtor and in which the debtor has a substantial nonexempt interest, except earnings, may be attached pursuant to a writ of attachment in an action or proceeding against a debtor on a claim for a debt and may be held as security to satisfy such judgment, and interest and costs, as the United States may recover on such claim.

    (2) The value of property attached shall not exceed the amount by which the sum of the amount of the debt claimed by the United States and the amount of interest and costs reasonably likely to be assessed against the debtor by the court exceeds the aggregate value of the nonexempt interest of the debtor in any—

        (A) property securing the debt; and

        (B) property garnished or in receivership, or income sequestered, under this subchapter.

(b) Availability of attachment.—If the requirements of section 3101 are satisfied, a court shall issue a writ authorizing the United States to attach property in which the debtor has a substantial nonexempt interest, as security for such judgment (and interest and costs) as the United States may recover on a claim for a debt—

(1)   in an action on a contract, express or implied, against the debtor for payment of money, only if the United States shows reasonable cause to believe that—

(A)   the contract is not fully secured by real or personal property; or

(B)   the value of the original security is substantially diminished, without any act of the United States or the person to whom the security was given, below the amount of the debt;

(2)   in an action against the debtor for damages in tort;

(3)   if the debtor resides outside the jurisdiction of the United States; or

(4)   in an action to recover a fine, penalty, or tax.

(c) Issuance of writ; contents.—(1) Subject to subsections (a) and (b), a writ of attachment shall be issued by the court directing the United States marshal of the district where property described in subsection (a) is located to attach the property.

(2)   Several writs of attachment may be issued at the same time, or in succession, and sent to different judicial districts until sufficient property is attached.

(3)   The writ of attachment shall contain—

(A)   the date of the issuance of the writ;

(B)   the identity of the court, the docket number of the action, and the identity of the cause of action;

(C)   the name and last known address of the debtor;

(D)   the amount to be secured by the attachment; and

(E)   a reasonable description of the property to be attached.

(d) Levy of attachment.—(1) The United States marshal receiving the writ shall proceed without delay to levy upon the property specified for attachment if found within the district. The marshal may not sell property unless ordered by the court.

(2)   In performing the levy, the United States marshal may enter any property owned, occupied, or controlled by the debtor, except that the marshal may not enter a residence or other building unless the writ expressly authorizes the marshal to do so or upon specific order of the court.

(3)   Levy on real property is made by entering the property and posting the writ and notice of levy in a conspicuous place upon the property.

(4)   Levy on personal property is made by taking possession of it. Levy on personal property not easily taken into possession or which cannot be taken into possession without great inconvenience or expense may be made by affixing a copy of the writ and notice of levy on it or in a conspicuous place in the vicinity of it describing in the notice of levy the property by quantity and with sufficient detail to identify the property levied on.

(5)   The United States marshal shall file a copy of the notice of levy in the same manner as provided for judgments in section 3201(a)(1). The United States marshal shall serve a copy of the writ and notice of levy on—

(A)   the debtor against whom the writ is issued; and

(B)   the person who has possession of the property subject to the writ;

in the same manner that a summons is served in a civil action and make the return thereof.

(e) Return of writ; duties of marshal; further return.—**(1)** A United States marshal executing a writ of attachment shall return the writ with the marshal's action endorsed thereon or attached thereto and signed by the marshal, to the court from which it was issued, within 5 days after the date of the levy.

(2) The return shall describe the property attached with sufficient certainty to identify it and shall state the location where it was attached, the date and time it was attached, and the disposition made of the property. If no property was attached, the return shall so state.

(3) If the property levied on is claimed, replevied under subsection (j)(2), or sold under section 3007 after the return, the United States marshal shall immediately make a further return to the clerk of the court showing the disposition of the property.

(4) If personal property is replevied, the United States marshal shall deliver the replevin bond to the clerk of the court to be filed in the action.

(f) Levy of attachment as lien on property; satisfaction of lien.—**(1)** A levy on property under a writ of attachment under this section creates a lien in favor of the United States on the property or, in the case of perishable property sold under section 3007, on the proceeds of the sale.

(2) Such lien shall be ranked ahead of any other security interests perfected after the later of the time of levy and the time a copy of the notice of levy is filed under subsection (d)(5).

(3) Such lien shall arise from the time of levy and shall continue until a judgment in the action is obtained or denied, or the action is otherwise dismissed. The death of the debtor whose property is attached does not terminate the attachment lien. Upon issuance of a judgment in the action and registration under this chapter, the judgment lien so created relates back to the time of levy.

(g) Reduction or dissolution of attachment.—**(1)** If an excessive or unreasonable attachment is made, the debtor may submit a motion to the court for a reduction of the amount of the attachment or its dissolution. Notice of such motion shall be served on the United States.

(2) The court shall order a part of the property to be released, if after a hearing the court finds that the amount of the attachment is excessive or unreasonable or if the attachment is for an amount larger than the sum of the liquidated or ascertainable amount of the debt and the amount of interest and costs likely to be taxed.

(3) The court shall dissolve the attachment if the amount of the debt is unliquidated and unascertainable by calculation.

(4) If any property claimed to be exempt is levied on, the debtor may, at any time after such levy, request that the court vacate such levy. If it appears to the court that the property so levied upon is exempt, the court shall order the levy vacated and the property returned to the debtor.

(h) Replevin of attached property by debtor; bond.—If attached property is not sold before judgment, the debtor may replevy such property or any part thereof by giving a bond approved by counsel for the United States or the court and payable to the United States in double the reasonable value of the property to be replevied or double the value of the claim, whichever is less.

(i) Preservation of personal property under attachment.—If personal property in custody of the United States marshal under a writ of attachment is not replevied, claimed, or sold, the court may make such order for its preservation or use as appears to be in the interest of the parties.

(j) Judgment and disposition of attached property.—

(1) Judgment for the United States.—On entry of judgment for the United States, the court shall order the proceeds of personal property sold pursuant to section 3007 to be applied to the satisfaction of the judgment, and shall order the sale of any remaining personal property and any real property levied on to the extent necessary to satisfy the judgment.

(2) **Judgment for the United States when personal property replevied.**—With respect to personal property under attachment that is replevied, the judgment which may be entered shall be against the debtor against whom the writ of attachment is issued and also against the sureties on the debtor's replevin bond for the value of the property.

(3) **Restoration of property and exoneration of replevin bond.**—If the attachment is vacated or if the judgment on the claim for the debt is for the person against whom the writ attachment is issued, the court shall order the property, or proceeds of perishable property sold under section 3007, restored to the debtor and shall exonerate any replevin bond.

(Added Pub.L. 101–647, Title XXXVI, § 3611, Nov. 29, 1990, 104 Stat. 4942.)

§ 3103.   Receivership

(a) **Appointment of a receiver.**—If the requirements of section 3101 are satisfied, a court may appoint a receiver for property in which the debtor has a substantial nonexempt interest if the United States shows reasonable cause to believe that there is a substantial danger that the property will be removed from the jurisdiction of the court, lost, concealed, materially injured or damaged, or mismanaged.

(b) **Powers of receiver.**—

(1) The appointing court may authorize a receiver—

(A) to take possession of real and personal property and sue for, collect, and sell obligations upon such conditions and for such purposes as the court shall direct; and

(B) to administer, collect, improve, lease, repair or sell pursuant to section 3007 such real and personal property as the court shall direct.

A receiver appointed to manage residential or commercial property shall have demonstrable expertise in the management of these types of property.

(2) Unless expressly authorized by order of the court, a receiver shall have no power to employ attorneys, accountants, appraisers, auctioneers, or other professional persons.

(c) **Duration of receivership.**—A receivership shall not continue past the entry of judgment, or the conclusion of an appeal of such judgment, unless the court orders it continued under section 3203(e) or unless the court otherwise directs its continuation.

(d) **Accounts; requirement to report.**—A receiver shall keep written accounts itemizing receipts and expenditures, describing the property and naming the depository of receivership funds. The receiver's accounts shall be open to inspection by any person having an apparent interest in the property. The receiver shall file reports at regular intervals as directed by the court and shall serve the debtor and the United States with a copy thereof.

(e) **Modification of powers; removal.**—On motion of the receiver or on its own initiative, the court which appointed the receiver may remove the receiver or modify the receiver's powers at any time.

(f) **Priority.**—If more than one court appoints a receiver for particular property, the receiver first qualifying under law shall be entitled to take possession, control, or custody of the property.

(g) **Compensation of receivers.**—

(1) A receiver is entitled to such commissions, not exceeding 5 percent of the sums received and disbursed by him, as the court allows unless the court otherwise directs.

(2) If, at the termination of a receivership, there are no funds in the hands of a receiver, the court may fix the compensation of the receiver in accordance with the services rendered and

may direct the party who moved for the appointment of the receiver to pay such compensation in addition to the necessary expenditures incurred by the receiver which remain unpaid.

(3) At the termination of a receivership, the receiver shall file a final accounting of the receipts and disbursements and apply for compensation setting forth the amount sought and the services rendered by the receiver.

(Added Pub.L. 101–647, Title XXXVI, § 3611, Nov. 29, 1990, 104 Stat. 4944.)

§ 3104.   Garnishment

(a) In general.—If the requirements of section 3101 are satisfied, a court may issue a writ of garnishment against property (excluding earnings) in which the debtor has a substantial nonexempt interest and which is in the possession, custody, or control of a person other than the debtor in order to satisfy a claim for a debt. Co-owned property shall be subject to garnishment to the same extent as co-owned property is subject to garnishment under the law of the State in which such property is located. A court may issue simultaneous separate writs of garnishment to several garnishees. A writ of garnishment issued under this subsection shall be continuing and shall terminate only as provided in section 3205(c)(10).

(b) Writ.—

(1) Subsections (b)(2) and (c) of section 3205 shall apply with respect to garnishment under this section, except that for purposes of this section—

    (A) earnings of the debtor shall not be subject to garnishment; and

    (B) a reference in such subsections to a judgment debtor shall be deemed to be a reference to a debtor.

(2) The United States shall include in its application for a writ of garnishment—

    (A) the amount of the claim asserted by the United States for a debt; and

    (B) the date the writ is issued.

(c) Limitation.—The value of property garnished shall not exceed the amount by which the sum of the amount of the debt claimed by the United States and the amount of interest and costs reasonably likely to be assessed against the debtor by the court exceeds the aggregate value of the nonexempt interest of the debtor in any—

    (1) property securing the debt; and

    (2) property attached or in receivership, or income sequestered, under this subchapter.

(Added Pub.L. 101–647, Title XXXVI, § 3611, Nov. 29, 1990, 104 Stat. 4945.)

§ 3105.   Sequestration

(a) Property subject to sequestration.—**(1)** Any income from property in which the debtor has a substantial nonexempt interest may be sequestered pursuant to a writ of sequestration in an action or proceeding against a debtor on a claim for a debt and may be held as security to satisfy such judgment, and interest and costs, as the United States may recover on such claim.

(2) The amount of income sequestered shall not exceed the amount by which the sum of the amount of the debt claimed by the United States and the amount of interest and costs reasonably likely to be assessed against the debtor by the court exceeds the aggregate value of the nonexempt interest of the debtor in any

    (A) property securing the debt; and

    (B) property attached, garnished, or in receivership under this subchapter.

(b) Availability of sequestration.—If the requirements of section 3101 are satisfied, a court shall issue a writ authorizing the United States to sequester income from property in which the debtor has a substantial nonexempt interest, as security for such judgment (and interest and costs) as the United States may recover on a claim for a debt—

(1) in an action on a contract, express or implied, against the debtor for payment of money, only if the United States shows reasonable cause to believe that—

(A) the contract is not fully secured by real or personal property; or

(B) the value of the original security is substantially diminished, without any act of the United States or the person to whom the security was given, below the amount of the debt;

(2) in an action against the debtor for damages in tort;

(3) if the debtor resides outside the jurisdiction of the United States; or

(4) in an action to recover a fine, penalty, or tax.

(c) Issuance of writ; contents.—

(1) Subject to subsections (a) and (b), a writ of sequestration shall be issued by the court directing the United States marshal of the district where income described in subsection (a) is located to sequester the income.

(2) Several writs of sequestration may be issued at the same time, or in succession, and sent to different judicial districts until sufficient income is sequestered.

(3) The writ of sequestration shall contain—

(A) the date of the issuance of the writ;

(B) the identity of the court, the docket number of the action, and the identity of the cause of action;

(C) the name and last known address of the debtor;

(D) the amount to be secured by the sequestration; and

(E) a reasonable description of the income to be sequestered.

(d) Execution of writ.—(1) The United States marshal receiving the writ shall proceed without delay to execute the writ.

(2) The United States marshal shall file a copy of the notice of sequestration in the same manner as provided for judgments in section 3201(a)(1). The United States marshal shall serve a copy of the writ and notice of sequestration on—

(A) the debtor against whom the writ is issued; and

(B) the person who has possession of the income subject to the writ;

in the same manner that a summons is served in a civil action and make the return thereof.

(e) Deposit of sequestered income.—A person who has possession of the income subject to a writ of sequestration shall deposit such income with the clerk of the court, accompanied by a statement in writing stating the person's name, the name of the debtor, the amount of such income, the property from which such income is produced, and the period during which such income is produced.

(f) Return of writ; duties of marshal; further return.—

(1) A United States marshal executing a writ of sequestration shall return the writ with the marshal's action endorsed thereon or attached thereto and signed by the marshal, to the court from which it was issued, within 5 days after the date of the execution.

(2) The return shall describe the income sequestered with sufficient certainty to identify it and shall state the location where it was sequestered, and the date and time it was sequestered. If no income was sequestered, the return shall so state.

(3) If sequestered income is claimed after the return, the United States marshal shall immediately make a further return to the clerk of the court showing the disposition of the income.

(g) Reduction or dissolution of sequestration.—

(1) If an excessive or unreasonable sequestration is made, the debtor may submit a motion to the court for a reduction of the amount of the sequestration or its dissolution. Notice of such motion shall be served on the United States.

(2) The court shall order a part of the income to be released, if after a hearing the court finds that the amount of the sequestration is excessive or unreasonable or if the sequestration is for an amount larger than the sum of the liquidated or ascertainable amount of the debt and the amount of interest and costs likely to be taxed.

(3) The court shall dissolve the sequestration if the amount of the debt is unliquidated and unascertainable by calculation.

(h) Preservation of income under sequester.—If personal property in custody of the United States marshal under a writ of sequestration is not claimed, the court may make such order for its preservation or use as appears to be in the interest of the parties.

(i) Judgment and disposition of sequestered income.—

(1) **Judgment for the United States.**—On entry of judgment for the United States, the court shall order the sequestered income to be applied to the satisfaction of the judgment.

(2) **Restoration of income.**—If the sequestration is vacated or if the judgment on the claim for the debt is for the person against whom the writ of sequestration is issued, the court shall order the income restored to the debtor.

(Added Pub.L. 101–647, Title XXXVI, § 3611, Nov. 29, 1990, 104 Stat. 4946.)

SUBCHAPTER C—POSTJUDGMENT REMEDIES

§ 3201. Judgment liens

(a) Creation.—A judgment in a civil action shall create a lien on all real property of a judgment debtor on filing a certified copy of the abstract of the judgment in the manner in which a notice of tax lien would be filed under paragraphs (1) and (2) of section 6323(f) of the Internal Revenue Code of 1986. A lien created under this paragraph is for the amount necessary to satisfy the judgment, including costs and interest.

(b) Priority of lien.—A lien created under subsection (a) shall have priority over any other lien or encumbrance which is perfected later in time.

(c) Duration of lien; renewal.—

(1) Except as provided in paragraph (2), a lien created under subsection (a) is effective, unless satisfied, for a period of 20 years.

(2) Such lien may be renewed for one additional period of 20 years upon filing a notice of renewal in the same manner as the judgment is filed and shall relate back to the date the judgment is filed if—

    (A) the notice of renewal is filed before the expiration of the 20-year period to prevent the expiration of the lien; and

    (B) the court approves the renewal of such lien under this paragraph.

(d) Release of judgment lien.—A judgment lien shall be released on the filing of a satisfaction of judgment or release of lien in the same manner as the judgment is filed to obtain the lien.

(e) Effect of lien on eligibility for Federal grants, loans or programs.—A debtor who has a judgment lien against the debtor's property for a debt to the United States shall not be eligible to receive any grant or loan which is made, insured, guaranteed, or financed directly or indirectly by the United States or to receive funds directly from the Federal Government in any program, except funds to which the debtor is entitled as beneficiary, until the judgment is paid in full or otherwise satisfied. The agency of the United States that is responsible for such grants and loans may promulgate regulations to allow for waiver of this restriction on eligibility for such grants, loans, and funds.

(f) Sale of property subject to judgment lien.—

(1) On proper application to a court, the court may order the United States to sell, in accordance with sections 2001 and 2002, any real property subject to a judgment lien in effect under this section.

(2) This subsection shall not preclude the United States from using an execution sale pursuant to section 3203(g) to sell real property subject to a judgment lien.

(Added Pub.L. 101–647, Title XXXVI, § 3611, Nov. 29, 1990, 104 Stat. 4948.)

HISTORICAL AND STATUTORY NOTES

References in Text

Section 6323(f) of the Internal Revenue Code of 1986, referred to in subsec. (a), is classified to section 6323(f) of Title 26, Internal Revenue Code.

Effective and Applicability Provisions

1990 Acts. Section to take effect 180 days after Nov. 29, 1990, except as otherwise provided, see section 3631 of Pub.L. 101–647, set out as a note under section 3001 of this title.

§ 3202. Enforcement of judgments

(a) Enforcement remedies.—A judgment may be enforced by any of the remedies set forth in this subchapter. A court may issue other writs pursuant to section 1651 of title 28, United States Code, as necessary to support such remedies, subject to rule 81(b) of the Federal Rules of Civil Procedure.

(b) Notice.—On the commencement by the United States of an action or proceeding under this subchapter to obtain a remedy, the counsel for the United States shall prepare, and clerk of the court shall issue, a notice in substantially the following form:

"NOTICE

"You are hereby notified that this [property] is being taken by the United States Government, which has a court judgment in [case docket number and jurisdiction of court] of $[amount] for [reason of debt].

"In addition, you are hereby notified that there are exemptions under the law which may protect some of this property from being taken by the United States Government if [name of judgment debtor] can show that the exemptions apply. Below is a summary of the major exemptions which apply in most situations in the State of [State where property is located]:

"[A statement summarizing in plain and understandable English the election available with respect to such State under section 3014 and the types of property that may be exempted under each of the alternatives specified in paragraphs (1) and (2) of section 3014(a) and a statement that different property may be so exempted with respect to the State in which the debtor resides.]

"If you are [name of judgment debtor], you have a right to ask the court to return your property to you if you think the property the Government is taking qualifies under one of the above exemptions [For a default judgment:] or if you think you do not owe the money to the United States Government that it says you do.

"If you want a hearing, you must notify the court within 20 days after you receive this notice. You must make your request in writing, and either mail it or deliver it in person to the clerk of the court at [address]. If you wish, you may use this notice to request the hearing by checking the box below and mailing this notice to the court clerk. You must also send a copy of your request to the Government at [address], so the Government will know you want a hearing. The hearing will take place within 5 days after the clerk receives your request, if you ask for it to take place that quickly, or as soon after that as possible.

"At the hearing you may explain to the judge why you believe the property the Government has taken is exempt [For a default judgment:] or why you think you do not owe the money to the Government. [For a writ of execution:] If you do not request a hearing within 20 days of receiving this notice, your [property] may be sold at public auction and the payment used toward the money you owe the Government.

"If you think you live outside the Federal judicial district in which the court is located, you may request, not later than 20 days after your[1] receive this notice, that this proceeding to take your property be transferred by the court to the Federal judicial district in which you reside. You must make your request in writing, and either mail it or deliver it in person to the clerk of the court at [address]. You must also send a copy of your request to the Government at [address], so the Government will know you want the proceeding to be transferred.

"Be sure to keep a copy of this notice for your own records. If you have any questions about your rights or about this procedure, you should contact a lawyer, an office of public legal assistance, or the clerk of the court. The clerk is not permitted to give legal advice, but can refer you to other sources of information."

(c) Service.—A copy of the notice and a copy of the application for granting a remedy under this subchapter shall be served by counsel for the United States on the judgment debtor against whom such remedy is sought and on each person whom the United States, after diligent inquiry, has reasonable cause to believe has an interest in property to which the remedy is directed.

(d) Hearing.—By requesting, within 20 days after receiving the notice described in section 3202(b), the court to hold a hearing, the judgment debtor may move to quash the order granting such remedy. The court that issued such order shall hold a hearing on such motion as soon as practicable, or, if so requested by the judgment debtor, within 5 days after receiving the request or as soon thereafter as possible. The issues at such hearing shall be limited—

    (1) to the probable validity of any claim of exemption by the judgment debtor;

    (2) to compliance with any statutory requirement for the issuance of the postjudgment remedy granted; and

    (3) if the judgment is by default and only to the extent that the Constitution or another law of the United States provides a right to a hearing on the issue, to—

        (A) the probable validity of the claim for the debt which is merged in the judgment; and

---

[1]   [Footnote to 28 U.S.C. § 3202(b):] So in original. Probably should be "you".

(B) the existence of good cause for setting aside such judgment.

This subparagraph shall not be construed to afford the judgment debtor the right to more than one such hearing except to the extent that the Constitution or another law of the United States provides a right to more than one such hearing.

(e) Sale of property.—The property of a judgment debtor which is subject to sale to satisfy the judgment may be sold by judicial sale, pursuant to sections 2001, 2002, and 2004 or by execution sale pursuant to section 3203(g). If a hearing is requested pursuant to subsection (d), property with respect to which the request relates shall not be sold before such hearing.

(Added Pub.L. 101–647, Title XXXVI, § 3611, Nov. 29, 1990, 104 Stat. 4949.)

§ 3203.   Execution

(a) Property subject to execution.—All property in which the judgment debtor has a substantial nonexempt interest shall be subject to levy pursuant to a writ of execution. The debtor's earnings shall not be subject to execution while in the possession, custody, or control of the debtor's employer. Co-owned property shall be subject to execution to the extent such property is subject to execution under the law of the State in which it is located.

(b) Creation of execution lien.—A lien shall be created in favor of the United States on all property levied on under a writ of execution and shall date from the time of the levy. Such lien shall have priority over all subsequent liens and shall be for the aggregate amount of the judgment, costs, and interest. The execution lien on any real property as to which the United States has a judgment lien shall relate back to the judgment lien date.

(c) Writ of execution.—

(1) Issuance.—On written application of counsel for the United States, the court may issue a writ of execution. Multiple writs may issue simultaneously, and successive writs may issue before the return date of a writ previously issued.

(2) Form of writ.—

(A) General contents.—A writ of execution shall specify the date that the judgment is entered, the court in which it is entered, the amount of the judgment if for money, the amount of the costs, the amount of interest due, the sum due as of the date the writ is issued, the rate of postjudgment interest, the name of the judgment debtor, and the judgment debtor's last known address.

(B) Additional contents.—

(i) Except as provided in clauses (ii) and (iii), the writ shall direct the United States marshal to satisfy the judgment by levying on and selling property in which the judgment debtor has a substantial nonexempt interest, but not to exceed property reasonably equivalent in value to the aggregate amount of the judgment, costs, and interest.

(ii) A writ of execution issued on a judgment for the delivery to the United States of the possession of personal property, or for the delivery of the possession of real property, shall particularly describe the property, and shall require the marshal to deliver the possession of the property to the United States.

(iii) A writ of execution on a judgment for the recovery of personal property or its value shall direct the marshal, in case a delivery of the specific property cannot be had, to levy and collect such value out of any property in which the judgment debtor has a substantial nonexempt interest.

(d) Levy of execution.—

(1) In general.—Levy on property pursuant to a writ of execution issued under this section shall be made in the same manner as levy on property is made pursuant to a writ of attachment issued under section 3102(d).

(2) Death of judgment debtor.—The death of the judgment debtor after a writ of execution is issued stays the execution proceedings, but any lien acquired by levy of the writ shall be recognized and enforced by the court for the district in which the estate of the deceased is located. The execution lien may be enforced—

    (A) against the executor, administrator, or personal representative of the estate of the deceased; or

    (B) if there be none, against the deceased's property coming to the heirs or devisees or at their option against cash in their possession, but only to the extent of the value of the property coming to them.

(3) Records of United States marshal.—

    (A) A United States marshal receiving a writ of execution shall endorse thereon the exact hour and date of receipt.

    (B) The United States marshal shall make a written record of every levy, specify the property on which levy is made, the date on which levy is made, and the marshal's costs, expenses, and fees.

    (C) The United States marshal shall make a written return to the court on each writ of execution stating concisely what is done pursuant to the writ and shall deliver a copy to counsel for the United States who requests the writ. The writ shall be returned not more than—

        (i) 90 days after the date of issuance if levy is not made; or

        (ii) 10 days after the date of sale of property on which levy is made.

(e) Appointment of receiver.—Pending the levy of execution, the court may appoint a receiver to manage property described in such writ if there is a substantial danger that the property will be removed from the jurisdiction of the court, lost, materially injured or damaged, or mismanaged.

(f) Replevy; redemption.—

(1) Before execution sale.—

    (A) Before execution sale, the United States marshal may return property[1] to the judgment debtor any personal property taken in execution, on—

        (i) satisfaction of the judgment, interest, and costs, and any costs incurred in connection with scheduling the sale; or

        (ii) receipt from the judgment debtor of a bond—

            (I) payable to the United States, with 2 or more good and sufficient sureties to be approved by the marshal, conditioned on the delivery of the property to the marshal at the time and place named in the bond to be sold under subsection (g); or

            (II) for the payment to the marshal of a fair value thereof which shall be stated in the bond.

    (B) A judgment debtor who sells or disposes of property replevied under subparagraph (A) shall pay the United States marshal the stipulated value of such property.

---

[1]   [Footnote to 28 U.S.C. § 3203(f)(1)(A):] So in original. The word "property" probably should not appear.

(C) If the judgment debtor fails to deliver such property to the United States marshal pursuant to the terms of the delivery described in subparagraph (A)(ii)(I) and fails to pay the United States marshal the stipulated value of such property, the United States marshal shall endorse the bond "forfeited" and return it to the court from which the writ of execution issued. If the judgment is not fully satisfied, the court shall issue a writ of execution against the judgment debtor and the sureties on the bond for the amount due, not exceeding the stipulated value of the property, on which execution no delivery bond shall be taken, which instruction shall be endorsed on the writ.

(2) After execution sale.—The judgment debtor shall not be entitled to redeem the property after the execution sale.

(g) Execution sale.—

(1) General procedures.—An execution sale under this section shall be conducted in a commercially reasonable manner—

(A) Sale of real property.—

(i) In general.—

(I) Except as provided in clause (ii), real property, or any interest therein, shall be sold, after the expiration of the 90-day period beginning on the date of levy under subsection (d), for cash at public auction at the courthouse of the county, parish, or city in which the greater part of the property is located or on the premises or some parcel thereof.

(II) The court may order the sale of any real property after the expiration of the 30-day period beginning on the date of levy under subsection (d) if the court determines that such property is likely to perish, waste, be destroyed, or otherwise substantially depreciate in value during the 90-day period beginning on the date of levy.

(III) The time and place of sale of real property, or any interest therein, under execution shall be advertised by the United States marshal, by publication of notice, once a week for at least 3 weeks prior to the sale, in at least one newspaper of general circulation in the county or parish where the property is located. The first publication shall appear not less than 25 days preceding the day of sale. The notice shall contain a statement of the authority by which the sale is to be made, the time of levy, the time and place of sale, and a brief description of the property to be sold, sufficient to identify the property (such as a street address for urban property and the survey identification and location for rural property), but it shall not be necessary for the notice to contain field notes. Such property shall be open for inspection and appraisal, subject to the judgment debtor's reasonable objections, for a reasonable period before the day of sale.

(IV) The United States marshal shall serve written notice of public sale by personal delivery, or certified or registered mail, to each person whom the marshal has reasonable cause to believe, after a title search is conducted by the United States, has an interest in property under execution, including lienholders, co-owners, and tenants, at least 25 days before the day of sale, to the last known address of each such person.

(ii) Sale of city lots.—If the real property consists of several lots, tracts, or parcels in a city or town, each lot, tract, or parcel shall be offered for sale separately, unless not susceptible to separate sale because of the character of improvements.

(iii) Sale of rural property.—If the real property is not located in a city or town, the judgment debtor may—

(I)   divide the property into lots of not less than 50 acres or in such greater or lesser amounts as ordered by the court;

(II)   furnish a survey of such prepared by a registered surveyor; and

(III) designate the order in which those lots shall be sold.

When a sufficient number of lots are sold to satisfy the amount of the execution and costs of sale, the marshal shall stop the sale.

(B)   Sale of personal property.—**(i)** Personal property levied on shall be offered for sale on the premises where it is located at the time of levy, at the courthouse of the county, parish or city wherein it is located, or at another location if ordered by the court. Personal property susceptible of being exhibited shall not be sold unless it is present and subject to the view of those attending the sale unless—

(I)   the property consists of shares of stock in corporations;

(II)   by reason of the nature of the property, it is impractical to exhibit it; or

(III) the debtor's interest in the property does not include the right to the exclusive possession.

(ii)(I)   Except as provided in subclause (II), personal property, or any interest therein, shall be sold after the expiration of the 30-day period beginning on the date of levy under subsection (d).

(II)   The court may order the sale of any personal property before the expiration of such 30-day period if the court determines that such property is likely to perish, waste, be destroyed, or otherwise substantially depreciate in value during such 30-day period.

(iii) Notice of the time and place of the sale of personal property shall be given by the United States marshal by posting notice thereof for not less than 10 days successively immediately before the day of sale at the courthouse of any county, parish, or city, and at the place where the sale is to be made.

(iv) The United States marshal shall serve written notice of public sale by personal delivery, or registered or certified mail at their last known addresses, on the judgment debtor and other persons who the marshal has reasonable cause to believe, after diligent inquiry, have a substantial interest in the property.

(2)   Postponement of sale.—The United States marshal may postpone an execution sale from time to time by continuing the required posting or publication of notice until the date to which the sale is postponed, and appending, at the foot of each such notice of a current copy of the following:

"The above sale is postponed until the _____ day of _____, 19____, at ____ o'clock ____.M., _____, United States Marshal for the District of _____, by _____, Deputy, dated _____."

(3)   Sale procedures.—

(A)   Bidding requirements.—A bidder at an execution sale of property, may be required by the United States marshal to make a cash deposit of as much as 20 percent of the sale price proposed before the bid is accepted.

(B)   Resale of property.—If the terms of the sale are not complied with by the successful bidder, the United States marshal shall proceed to sell the property again on the same day if there is sufficient time. If there is insufficient time, the marshal shall schedule and notice a subsequent sale of the property as provided in paragraphs (1) and (2).

(4) Rights and liabilities of purchasers.—

(A) Transfer of title after sale.—

(i) If property is sold under this subsection and the successful bidder complies with the terms of the sale, the United States marshal shall execute and deliver all documents necessary to transfer to the successful bidder, without warranty, all the rights, titles, interests, and claims of the judgment debtor in the property.

(ii) If the successful bidder dies before execution and delivery of the documents needed to transfer ownership, the United States marshal shall execute and deliver them to the successful bidder's estate. Such delivery to the estate shall have the same effect as if accomplished during the lifetime of the purchaser.

(B) Purchaser considered innocent purchaser without notice.—The purchaser of property sold under execution shall be deemed to be an innocent purchaser without notice if the purchaser would have been considered an innocent purchaser without notice had the sale been made voluntarily and in person by the judgment debtor.

(C) Liability of successful bidder who fails to comply.—A successful bidder at an execution sale who fails to comply with the terms of the sale shall forfeit to the United States the cash deposit or, at the election of the United States, shall be liable to the United States, on a subsequent sale of the property, for all net losses incurred by the United States as a result of such failure.

(h) Disposition of proceeds; further levy.—

(1) Distribution of sale proceeds.—

(A) The United States marshal shall first deliver to the judgment debtor such amounts to which the judgment debtor is entitled from the sale of partially exempt property.

(B) The United States marshal shall next deduct from the proceeds of an execution sale of property an amount equal to the reasonable expenses incurred in making the levy of execution and in keeping and maintaining the property.

(C) Except as provided in subparagraph (D), the United States marshal shall deliver the balance of the proceeds to the counsel for the United States as soon as practicable.

(D) If more proceeds are received from the execution sale than is necessary to satisfy the executions held by the United States marshal, the marshal shall pay the surplus to the judgment debtor.

(2) Further levy if execution not satisfied.—If the proceeds of the execution sale of the property levied on are insufficient to satisfy the execution, the United States marshal shall proceed on the same writ of execution to levy other property of the judgment debtor.

(Added Pub.L. 101–647, Title XXXVI, § 3611, Nov. 29, 1990, 104 Stat. 4950.)

§ 3204.   Installment payment order

(a) Authority to issue order.—Subject to subsection (c), if it is shown that the judgment debtor—

(1) is receiving or will receive substantial nonexempt disposable earnings from self employment that are not subject to garnishment; or

(2) is diverting or concealing substantial earnings from any source, or property received in lieu of earnings;

then upon motion of the United States and notice to the judgment debtor, the court may, if appropriate, order that the judgment debtor make specified installment payments to the United States. Notice of the motion shall be served on the judgment debtor in the same manner as a summons or by registered or certified mail, return receipt requested. In fixing the amount of the payments, the court shall take into consideration after a hearing, the income, resources, and reasonable requirements of the judgment debtor and the judgment debtor's dependents, any other payments to be made in satisfaction of judgments against the judgment debtor, and the amount due on the judgment in favor of the United States.

(b) Modification of order.—On motion of the United States or the judgment debtor, and upon a showing that the judgment debtor's financial circumstances have changed or that assets not previously disclosed by the judgment debtor have been discovered, the court may modify the amount of payments, alter their frequency, or require full payment.

(c) Limitation.—

(1) An order may not be issued under subsection (a), and if so issued shall have no force or effect, against a judgment debtor with respect to whom there is in effect a writ of garnishment of earnings issued under this chapter and based on the same debt.

(2) An order may not be issued under subsection (a) with respect to any earnings of the debtor except nonexempt disposable earnings.

(Added Pub.L. 101–647, Title XXXVI, § 3611, Nov. 29, 1990, 104 Stat. 4955.)

§ 3205.   Garnishment

(a) In general.—A court may issue a writ of garnishment against property (including nonexempt disposable earnings) in which the debtor has a substantial nonexempt interest and which is in the possession, custody, or control of a person other than the debtor, in order to satisfy the judgment against the debtor. Co-owned property shall be subject to garnishment to the same extent as co-owned property is subject to garnishment under the law of the State in which such property is located. A court may issue simultaneous separate writs of garnishment to several garnishees. A writ of garnishment issued under this subsection shall be continuing and shall terminate only as provided in subsection (c)(10).

(b) Writ.—

(1) General requirements.—The United States shall include in its application for a writ of garnishment—

(A) the judgment debtor's name, social security number (if known), and last known address;

(B) the nature and amount of the debt owed and the facts that not less than 30 days has elapsed since demand on the debtor for payment of the debt was made and the judgment debtor has not paid the amount due; and

(C) that the garnishee is believed to have possession of property (including nonexempt disposable earnings) in which the debtor has a substantial nonexempt interest.

(2) Proper garnishee for particular property.—

(A) If the property consists of a right to or share in the stock of an association or corporation, or interests or profits therein, for which a certificate of stock or other negotiable instrument is not outstanding, the corporation, or the president or treasurer of the association shall be the garnishee.

(B) If the property consists of an interest in a partnership interest, any partner other than the debtor shall be the garnishee on behalf of the partnership.

(C) If the property or a debt is evidenced by a negotiable instrument for the payment of money, a negotiable document of title or a certificate of stock of an association or corporation, the instrument, document, or certificate shall be treated as property capable of delivery and the person holding it shall be the garnishee, except that—

      (i)   subject to clause (ii), in the case of a security which is transferable in the manner set forth in State law, the entity that carries on its books an account in the name of the debtor in which is reflected such security shall be the garnishee; and

      (ii)   notwithstanding clause (i), the pledgee shall be the garnishee if such security is pledged.

(c)   **Procedures applicable to writ.—**

    (1)   **Court determination.—**If the court determines that the requirements of this section are satisfied, the court shall issue an appropriate writ of garnishment.

    (2)   **Form of writ.—**The writ shall state—

      (A)   The nature and amount of the debt, and any cost and interest owed with respect to the debt.

      (B)   The name and address of the garnishee.

      (C)   The name and address of counsel for the United States.

      (D)   The last known address of the judgment debtor.

      (E)   That the garnishee shall answer the writ within 10 days of service of the writ.

      (F)   That the garnishee shall withhold and retain any property in which the debtor has a substantial nonexempt interest and for which the garnishee is or may become indebted to the judgment debtor pending further order of the court.

    (3)   **Service of writ.—**The United States shall serve the garnishee and the judgment debtor with a copy of the writ of garnishment and shall certify to the court that this service was made. The writ shall be accompanied by—

      (A)   an instruction explaining the requirement that the garnishee submit a written answer to the writ; and

      (B)   instructions to the judgment debtor for objecting to the answer of the garnishee and for obtaining a hearing on the objections.

    (4)   **Answer of the garnishee.—**In its written answer to the writ of garnishment, the garnishee shall state under oath—

      (A)   whether the garnishee has custody, control or possession of such property;

      (B)   a description of such property and the value of such interest;

      (C)   a description of any previous garnishments to which such property is subject and the extent to which any remaining property is not exempt; and

      (D)   The amount of the debt the garnishee anticipates owing to the judgment debtor in the future and whether the period for payment will be weekly or another specified period.

The garnishee shall file the original answer with the court issuing the writ and serve a copy on the debtor and counsel for the United States.

    (5)   **Objections to answer.—**Within 20 days after receipt of the answer, the judgment debtor or the United States may file a written objection to the answer and request a hearing. The party objecting shall state the grounds for the objection and bear the burden of proving such grounds. A copy of the objection and request for a hearing shall be served on the garnishee and all other parties. The court shall hold a hearing within 10 days after the date the request is received by the court, or as soon thereafter as is practicable, and give notice of the hearing date to all the parties.

    (6)   **Garnishee's failure to answer or pay.—**If a garnishee fails to answer the writ of garnishment or to withhold property in accordance with the writ, the United States may petition the court for an order requiring the garnishee to appear before the court to answer the writ and to so withhold property before the appearance date. If the garnishee fails to appear, or appears and fails to show good cause why the garnishee failed to comply with the writ, the court shall enter judgment against the garnishee for the value of the judgment debtor's nonexempt interest in such property (including nonexempt disposable earnings). The court may award a reasonable attorney's fee to the United States and against the garnishee if the writ is not answered within the time specified therein and a petition requiring the garnishee to appear is filed as provided in this section.

(7) **Disposition order.**—After the garnishee files an answer and if no hearing is requested within the required time period, the court shall promptly enter an order directing the garnishee as to the disposition of the judgment debtor's nonexempt interest in such property. If a hearing is timely requested, the order shall be entered within 5 days after the hearing, or as soon thereafter as is practicable.

(8) **Priorities.**—Judicial orders and garnishments for the support of a person shall have priority over a writ of garnishment issued under this section. As to any other writ of garnishment or levy, a garnishment issued under this section shall have priority over writs which are issued later in time.

(9) **Accounting.**—(A) While a writ of garnishment is in effect under this section, the United States shall give an annual accounting on the garnishment to the judgment debtor and the garnishee.

(B) Within 10 days after the garnishment terminates, the United States shall give a cumulative written accounting to the judgment debtor and garnishee of all property it receives under a writ of garnishment. Within 10 days after such accounting is received, the judgment debtor or garnishee may file a written objection to the accounting and a request for hearing. The party objecting shall state grounds for the objection. The court shall hold a hearing on the objection within 10 days after the court receives the request for a hearing, or as soon thereafter as is practicable.

(10) **Termination of garnishment.**—A garnishment under this chapter is terminated only by—

(A) a court order quashing the writ of garnishment;

(B) exhaustion of property in the possesion,[1] custody, or control of the garnishee in which the debtor has a substantial nonexempt interest (including nonexempt disposable earnings), unless the garnishee reinstates or reemploys the judgment debtor within 90 days after the judgment debtor's dismissal or resignation; or

(C) satisfaction of the debt with respect to which the writ is issued.

(Added Pub.L. 101–647, Title XXXVI, § 3611, Nov. 29, 1990, 104 Stat. 4956.)

§ 3206. Discharge

A person who pursuant to an execution or order issued under this chapter by a court pays or delivers to the United States, a United States marshal, or a receiver, money or other personal property in which a judgment debtor has or will have an interest, or so pays a debt such person owes the judgment debtor, is discharged from such debt to the judgment debtor to the extent of the payment or delivery.

(Added Pub.L. 101–647, Title XXXVI, § 3611, Nov. 29, 1990, 104 Stat. 4959.)

---

[1] [Footnote to 28 U.S.C. § 3205(c)(10)(B):] So in original. Probably should be "possession,".

SUBCHAPTER D—FRAUDULENT TRANSFERS INVOLVING DEBTS

§ 3301.   Definitions

As used in this subchapter:

(1) "Affiliate" means—

(A) a person who directly or indirectly owns, controls, or holds with power to vote, 20 percent or more of the outstanding voting securities of the debtor, other than a person who holds the securities—

(i) as a fiduciary or agent without sole discretionary power to vote the securities; or

(ii) solely to secure a debt, if the person has not exercised the power to vote;

(B) a corporation 20 percent or more of whose outstanding voting securities are directly or indirectly owned, controlled, or held with power to vote, by the debtor or a person who directly or indirectly owns, controls, or holds with power to vote, 20 percent or more of the outstanding voting securities of the debtor, other than the person who holds securities—

(i) as a fiduciary or agent without sole power to vote the securities; or

(ii) solely to secure a debt, if the person has not in fact exercised the power to vote;

(C) a person whose business is operated by the debtor under a lease or other agreement, or a person substantially all of whose assets are controlled by the debtor; or

(D) a person who operates the debtor's business under a lease or other agreement or controls substantially all of the debtor's assets.

(2) "Asset" means property of a debtor, but does not include—

(A) property to the extent it is encumbered by a valid lien;

(B) property to the extent it is generally exempt under nonbankruptcy law; or

(C) an interest in real property held in tenancy by the entirety, or as part of a community estate, to extent such interest is not subject to process by the United States holding a claim against only one tenant or co-owner.

(3) "Claim" means a right to payment, whether or not the right is reduced to judgment, liquidated, unliquidated, fixed, contingent, matured, unmatured, disputed, undisputed, legal, equitable, secured, or unsecured.

(4) "Creditor" means a person who has a claim.

(5) "Insider" includes—

---

[1] [Footnote to subchapter D table:] So in original. Does not conform to section catchline.

  (A) if the debtor is an individual—

    (i) a relative of the debtor or of a general partner of the debtor;

    (ii) a partnership in which the debtor is a general partner;

    (iii) a general partner in a partnership described in clause (ii); or

    (iv) a corporation of which the debtor is a director, officer, or person in control;

  (B) if the debtor is a corporation—

    (i) a director of the debtor;

    (ii) an officer of the debtor;

    (iii) a person in control of the debtor;

    (iv) a partnership in which the debtor is a general partner;

    (v) a general partner in a partnership described in clause (iv); or

    (vi) a relative of a general partner, director, officer, or person in control of the debtor;

  (C) if the debtor is a partnership—

    (i) a general partner in the debtor;

    (ii) a relative of a general partner in, a general partner of, or a person in control of the debtor;

    (iii) another partnership in which the debtor is a general partner;

    (iv) a general partner in a partnership described in clause (iii); or

    (v) a person in control of the debtor.[1]

  (D) an affiliate, or an insider of an affiliate as if the affiliate were the debtor; and

  (E) a managing agent of the debtor.

  (4)[2] "Lien" means a charge against or an interest in property to secure payment of a debt and includes a security interest created by agreement, a judicial lien obtained by legal or equitable process or proceedings, a common law lien, or a statutory lien.

  (5)[3] "Relative" means an individual related, by consanguinity or adoption, within the third degree as determined by the common law, a spouse, or an individual so related to a spouse within the third degree as so determined.

  (6)[4] "Transfer" means every mode, direct or indirect, absolute or conditional, voluntary or involuntary, of disposing of or parting with an asset or an interest in an asset, and includes payment of money, release, lease, and creation of a lien or other encumbrance.

  (7)[5] "Valid lien" means a lien that is effective against the holder of a judicial lien subsequently obtained in legal or equitable proceeding.

(Added Pub.L. 101–647, Title XXXVI, § 3611, Nov. 29, 1990, 104 Stat. 4959.)

---

[1]   So in original. The period should probably be a semicolon.

[2]   So in original. Probably should be "(6)".

[3]   So in original. Probably should be "(7)".

[4]   So in original. Probably should be "(8)".

[5]   So in original. Probably should be "(9)".

§ 3302.   Insolvency

(a) **In general.**—Except as provided in subsection (c), a debtor is insolvent if the sum of the debtor's debts is greater than all of the debtor's assets at a fair valuation.

(b) **Presumption.**—A debtor who is generally not paying debts as they become due is presumed to be insolvent.

(c) **Calculation.**—A partnership is insolvent under subsection (a) if the sum of the partnership's debts is greater than the aggregate, at a fair valuation, of—

     (1)   all of the partnership's assets; and

     (2)   the sum of the excess of the value of each general partner's non-partnership assets over the partner's non-partnership debts.

(d) **Assets.**—For purposes of this section, assets do not include property that is transferred, concealed, or removed with intent to hinder, delay, or defraud creditors or that has been transferred in a manner making the transfer voidable under this subchapter.

(e) **Debts.**—For purposes of this section, debts do not include an obligation to the extent such obligation is secured by a valid lien on property of the debtor not included as an asset.

(Added Pub.L. 101–647, Title XXXVI, § 3611, Nov. 29, 1990, 104 Stat. 4961.)

§ 3303.   Value for transfer or obligation

(a) **Transaction.**—Value is given for a transfer or an obligation if, in exchange for the transfer or obligation, property is transferred or an antecedent debt is secured or satisfied, but value does not include an unperformed promise made otherwise than in the ordinary course of the promisor's business to furnish support to the debtor or another person.

(b) **Reasonably equivalent value.**—For the purposes of sections 3304 and 3307, a person gives a reasonably equivalent value if the person acquires an interest of the debtor in an asset pursuant to a regularly conducted, noncollusive foreclosure sale or execution of a power of sale for the acquisition or disposition of such interest upon default under a mortgage, deed of trust, or security agreement.

(c) **Present value.**—A transfer is made for present value if the exchange between the debtor and the transferee is intended by them to be contemporaneous and is in fact substantially contemporaneous.

(Added Pub.L. 101–647, Title XXXVI, § 3611, Nov. 29, 1990, 104 Stat. 4961.)

§ 3304.   Transfer fraudulent as to a debt to the United States

(a) **Debt arising before transfer.**—Except as provided in section 3307, a transfer made or obligation incurred by a debtor is fraudulent as to a debt to the United States which arises before the transfer is made or the obligation is incurred if—

     (1)(A)   the debtor makes the transfer or incurs the obligation without receiving a reasonably equivalent value in exchange for the transfer or obligation; and

     (B)   the debtor is insolvent at that time or the debtor becomes insolvent as a result of the transfer or obligation; or

     (2)(A)   the transfer was made to an insider for an antecedent debt, the debtor was insolvent at the time; and

     (B)   the insider had reasonable cause to believe that the debtor was insolvent.

(b) **Transfers without regard to date of judgment.**—(1) Except as provided in section 3307, a transfer made or obligation incurred by a debtor is fraudulent as to a debt to the United States, whether such debt arises before or after the transfer is made or the obligation is incurred, if the debtor makes the transfer or incurs the obligation—

   (A) with actual intent to hinder, delay, or defraud a creditor; or

   (B) without receiving a reasonably equivalent value in exchange for the transfer or obligation if the debtor—

      (i) was engaged or was about to engage in a business or a transaction for which the remaining assets of the debtor were unreasonably small in relation to the business or transaction; or

      (ii) intended to incur, or believed or reasonably should have believed that he would incur, debts beyond his ability to pay as they became due.

   (2) In determining actual intent under paragraph (1), consideration may be given, among other factors, to whether—

   (A) the transfer or obligation was to an insider;

   (B) the debtor retained possession or control of the property transferred after the transfer;

   (C) the transfer or obligation was disclosed or concealed;

   (D) before the transfer was made or obligation was incurred, the debtor had been sued or threatened with suit;

   (E) the transfer was of substantially all the debtor's assets;

   (F) the debtor absconded;

   (G) the debtor removed or concealed assets;

   (H) the value of the consideration received by the debtor was reasonably equivalent to the value of the asset transferred or the amount of the obligation incurred;

   (I) the debtor was insolvent or became insolvent shortly after the transfer was made or the obligation was incurred;

   (J) the transfer occurred shortly before or shortly after a substantial debt was incurred; and

   (K) the debtor transferred the essential assets of the business to a lienor who transferred the assets to an insider of the debtor.

(Added Pub.L. 101–647, Title XXXVI, § 3611, Nov. 29, 1990, 104 Stat. 4961.)

§ 3305.   When transfer is made or obligation is incurred

For the purposes of this subchapter:

   (1) A transfer is made—

   (A) with respect to an asset that is real property (other than a fixture, but including the interest of a seller or purchaser under a contract for the sale of the asset), when the transfer is so far perfected that a good-faith purchaser of the asset from the debtor against whom applicable law permits the transfer to be perfected cannot acquire an interest in the asset that is superior to the interest of the transferee; and

   (B) with respect to an asset that is not real property or that is a fixture, when the transfer is so far perfected that a creditor on a simple contract cannot acquire, otherwise than under this subchapter, a judicial lien that is superior to the interest of the transferee.

   (2) If applicable law permits the transfer to be perfected as approved in paragraph (1) and the transfer is not so perfected before the commencement of an action or proceeding for relief under this subchapter, the transfer is deemed made immediately before the commencement of the action or proceeding.

(3) If applicable law does not permit the transfer to be perfected as provided in paragraph (1), the transfer is made when it becomes effective between the debtor and the transferee.

(4) A transfer is not made until the debtor has acquired rights in the asset transferred.

(5) An obligation is incurred—

(A) if oral, when it becomes effective between the parties; or

(B) if evidenced by a writing executed by the obligor, when such writing is delivered to or for the benefit of the obligee.

(Added Pub.L. 101–647, Title XXXVI, § 3611, Nov. 29, 1990, 104 Stat. 4962.)

§ 3306.   Remedies of the United States

(a) **In general.**—In an action or proceeding under this subchapter for relief against a transfer or obligation, the United States, subject to section 3307 and to applicable principles of equity and in accordance with the Federal Rules of Civil Procedure, may obtain—

(1) avoidance of the transfer or obligation to the extent necessary to satisfy the debt to the United States;

(2) a remedy under this chapter against the asset transferred or other property of the transferee; or

(3) any other relief the circumstances may require.

(b) **Limitation.**—A claim for relief with respect to a fraudulent transfer or obligation under this subchapter is extinguished unless action is brought—

(1) under section 3304(b)(1)(A) within 6 years after the transfer was made or the obligation was incurred or, if later, within 2 years after the transfer or obligation was or could reasonably have been discovered by the claimant;

(2) under subsection (a)(1) or (b)(1)(B) of section 3304 within 6 years after the transfer was made or the obligation was incurred; or

(3) under section 3304(a)(2) within 2 years after the transfer was made or the obligation was incurred.

(Added Pub.L. 101–647, Title XXXVI, § 3611, Nov. 29, 1990, 104 Stat. 4963.)

§ 3307.   Defenses, liability, and protection of transferee

(a) **Good faith transfer.**—A transfer or obligation is not voidable under section 3304(b) with respect to a person who took in good faith and for a reasonably equivalent value or against any transferee or obligee subsequent to such person.

(b) **Limitation.**—Except as provided in subsection (d), to the extent a transfer is voidable in an action or proceeding by the United States under section 3306(a)(1), the United States may recover judgment for the value of the asset transferred, but not to exceed the judgment on a debt. The judgment may be entered against—

(1) the first transferee of the asset or the person for whose benefit the transfer was made; or

(2) any subsequent transferee, other than a good faith transferee who took for value or any subsequent transferee of such good-faith transferee.

(c) **Value of asset.**—For purposes of subsection (b), the value of the asset is the value of the asset at the time of the transfer, subject to adjustment as the equities may require.

(d) Rights of good faith transferees and obligees.—Notwithstanding voidability of a transfer or an obligation under this subchapter, a good-faith transferee or obligee is entitled, to the extent of the value given the debtor for the transfer or obligation, to—

(1) a lien on or a right to retain any interest in the asset transferred;

(2) enforcement of any obligation incurred; or

(3) a reduction in the amount of the liability on the judgment.

(e) Exceptions.—A transfer is not voidable under section 3304(a) or section 3304(b)(2) if the transfer results from—

(1) termination of a lease upon default by the debtor when the termination is pursuant to the lease and applicable law; or

(2) enforcement of a security interest in compliance with article 9 of the Uniform Commercial Code or its equivalent in effect in the State where the property is located.

(f) Limitation of voidability.—A transfer is not voidable under section 3304(a)(2)—

(1) to the extent the insider gives new value to or for the benefit of the debtor after the transfer is made unless the new value is secured by a valid lien;

(2) if made in the ordinary course of business or financial affairs of the debtor and the insider; or

(3) if made pursuant to a good-faith effort to rehabilitate the debtor and the transfer secured both present value given for that purpose and an antecedent debt of the debtor.

(Added Pub.L. 101–647, Title XXXVI, § 3611, Nov. 29, 1990, 104 Stat. 4963.)

§ 3308.   Supplementary provision

Except as provided in this subchapter, the principles of law and equity, including the law merchant and the law relating to principal and agent, estoppel, laches, fraud, misrepresentation, duress, coercion, mistake, insolvency, or other validating or invalidating cause shall apply to actions and proceedings under this subchapter.

(Added Pub.L. 101–647, Title XXXVI, § 3611, Nov. 29, 1990, 104 Stat. 4964.)

CHAPTER 179—JUDICIAL REVIEW OF CERTAIN ACTIONS BY PRESIDENTIAL OFFICES

§ 3901.   Civil actions

(a) Parties.—In an action under section 1346(g) of this title, the defendant shall be the employing office alleged to have committed the violation involved.

(b) Jury trial.—In an action described in subsection (a), any party may demand a jury trial where a jury trial would be available in an action against a private defendant under the relevant law made applicable by chapter 5 of title 3. In any case in which a violation of section 411 of title 3 is alleged, the court shall not inform the jury of the maximum amount of compensatory damages available under section 411(b)(1) or 411(b)(3) of title 3.

(Added Pub.L. 104–331, § 3(c), Oct. 26, 1996, 110 Stat. 4070.)

§ 3902.   Judicial review of regulations

In any proceeding under section 1296 or 1346(g) of this title in which the application of a regulation issued under chapter 5 of title 3 is at issue, the court may review the validity of the regulation in accordance with the provisions of subparagraphs (A) through (D) of section 706(2) of title 5. If the court determines that the regulation is invalid, the court shall apply, to the extent necessary and appropriate, the most relevant substantive executive agency regulation promulgated to implement the statutory provisions with respect to which the invalid regulation was issued. Except as provided in this section, the validity of regulations issued under this chapter is not subject to judicial review.

(Added Pub.L. 104–331, § 3(c), Oct. 26, 1996, 110 Stat. 4070.)

§ 3903.   Effect of failure to issue regulations

In any proceeding under section 1296 or 1346(g) of this title, if the President, the designee of the President, or the Federal Labor Relations Authority has not issued a regulation on a matter for which chapter 5 of title 3 requires a regulation to be issued, the court shall apply, to the extent necessary and appropriate, the most relevant substantive executive agency regulation promulgated to implement the statutory provision at issue in the proceeding.

(Added Pub.L. 104–331, § 3(c), Oct. 26, 1996, 110 Stat. 4070.)

§ 3904.   Expedited review of certain appeals

(a) **In general.**—An appeal may be taken directly to the Supreme Court of the United States from any interlocutory or final judgment, decree, or order of a court upon the constitutionality of any provision of chapter 5 of title 3.

(b) **Jurisdiction.**—The Supreme Court shall, if it has not previously ruled on the question, accept jurisdiction over the appeal referred to in subsection (a), advance the appeal on the docket, and expedite the appeal to the greatest extent possible.

(Added Pub.L. 104–331, § 3(c), Oct. 26, 1996, 110 Stat. 4070.)

§ 3905.   Attorney's fees and interest

(a) **Attorney's fees.**—If a covered employee, with respect to any claim under chapter 5 of title 3, or a qualified person with a disability, with respect to any claim under section 421 of title 3, is a prevailing party in any proceeding under section 1296 or section 1346(g), the court may award attorney's fees, expert fees, and any other costs as would be appropriate if awarded under section 706(k) of the Civil Rights Act of 1964.

(b) **Interest.**—In any proceeding under section 1296 or section 1346(g), the same interest to compensate for delay in payment shall be made available as would be appropriate if awarded under section 717(d) of the Civil Rights Act of 1964.

(c) **Punitive damages.**—Except as otherwise provided in chapter 5 of title 3, no punitive damages may be awarded with respect to any claim under chapter 5 of title 3.

(Added Pub.L. 104–331, § 3(c), Oct. 26, 1996, 110 Stat. 4070.)

HISTORICAL AND STATUTORY NOTES

References in Text

The Civil Rights Act of 1964, referred to in subsecs. (a) and (b), is Pub.L. 88–352, July 2, 1964, 78 Stat. 252, as amended. Title VII of such Act is classified generally to subchapter VI (section 2000e et seq.) of chapter 21 of Title 42, The Public Health and Welfare. Sections 706 and 717 of such Act are classified to sections 2000e–5 and 2000e–16, respectively, of Title 42. For complete classification of this Act to the Code, see Short Title note set out under section 2000a of Title 42 and Tables.

§ 3906.   Payments

A judgment, award, or compromise settlement against the United States under this chapter (including any interest and costs) shall be paid—

    (1) under section 1304 of title 31, if it arises out of an action commenced in a district court of the United States (or any appeal therefrom); or

    (2) out of amounts otherwise appropriated or available to the office involved, if it arises out of an appeal from an administrative proceeding under chapter 5 of title 3.

(Added Pub.L. 104–331, § 3(c), Oct. 26, 1996, 110 Stat. 4071.)

§ 3907.   Other judicial review prohibited

Except as expressly authorized by this chapter and chapter 5 of title 3, the compliance or noncompliance with the provisions of chapter 5 of title 3, and any action taken pursuant to chapter 5 of title 3, shall not be subject to judicial review.

(Added Pub.L. 104–331, § 3(c), Oct. 26, 1996, 110 Stat. 4071.)

§ 3908.   Definitions

For purposes of applying this chapter, the terms "employing office" and "covered employee" have the meanings given those terms in section 401 of title 3.

(Added Pub.L. 104–331, § 3(c), Oct. 26, 1996, 110 Stat. 4071.)

CHAPTER 180—ASSUMPTION OF CERTAIN CONTRACTUAL OBLIGATIONS

§ 4001.   Assumption of contractual obligations related to transfers of rights in motion pictures

    (a) Assumption of obligations.—

    (1) In the case of a transfer of copyright ownership under United States law in a motion picture (as the terms "transfer of copyright ownership" and "motion picture" are defined in section 101 of title 17) that is produced subject to 1 or more collective bargaining agreements negotiated under the laws of the United States, if the transfer is executed on or after the effective date of this chapter and is not limited to public performance rights, the transfer instrument shall be deemed to incorporate the assumption agreements applicable to the copyright ownership being transferred that are required by the applicable collective bargaining agreement, and the transferee shall be subject to the obligations under each such assumption agreement to make residual payments and provide related notices, accruing after the effective date of the transfer and applicable to the exploitation of the rights transferred, and any remedies under each such assumption agreement for breach of those obligations, as those obligations and remedies are set forth in the applicable collective bargaining agreement, if—

    (A) the transferee knows or has reason to know at the time of the transfer that such collective bargaining agreement was or will be applicable to the motion picture; or

    (B) in the event of a court order confirming an arbitration award against the transferor under the collective bargaining agreement, the transferor does not have the financial ability to satisfy the award within 90 days after the order is issued.

  (2) For purposes of paragraph (1)(A), "knows or has reason to know" means any of the following:

    (A) Actual knowledge that the collective bargaining agreement was or will be applicable to the motion picture.

    (B)(i) Constructive knowledge that the collective bargaining agreement was or will be applicable to the motion picture, arising from recordation of a document pertaining to copyright in the motion picture under section 205 of title 17 or from publication, at a site available to the public on-line that is operated by the relevant union, of information that identifies the motion picture as subject to a collective bargaining agreement with that union, if the site permits commercially reasonable verification of the date on which the information was available for access.

    (ii) Clause (i) applies only if the transfer referred to in subsection (a)(1) occurs—

      (I) after the motion picture is completed, or

      (II) before the motion picture is completed and—

        (aa) within 18 months before the filing of an application for copyright registration for the motion picture under section 408 of title 17, or

        (bb) if no such application is filed, within 18 months before the first publication of the motion picture in the United States.

    (C) Awareness of other facts and circumstances pertaining to a particular transfer from which it is apparent that the collective bargaining agreement was or will be applicable to the motion picture.

  (b) **Scope of exclusion of transfers of public performance rights.**—For purposes of this section, the exclusion under subsection (a) of transfers of copyright ownership in a motion picture that are limited to public performance rights includes transfers to a terrestrial broadcast station, cable system, or programmer to the extent that the station, system, or programmer is functioning as an exhibitor of the motion picture, either by exhibiting the motion picture on its own network, system, service, or station, or by initiating the transmission of an exhibition that is carried on another network, system, service, or station. When a terrestrial broadcast station, cable system, or programmer, or other transferee, is also functioning otherwise as a distributor or as a producer of the motion picture, the public performance exclusion does not affect any obligations imposed on the transferee to the extent that it is engaging in such functions.

  (c) **Exclusion for grants of security interests.**—Subsection (a) shall not apply to—

  (1) a transfer of copyright ownership consisting solely of a mortgage, hypothecation, or other security interest; or

  (2) a subsequent transfer of the copyright ownership secured by the security interest described in paragraph (1) by or under the authority of the secured party, including a transfer through the exercise of the secured party's rights or remedies as a secured party, or by a subsequent transferee.

The exclusion under this subsection shall not affect any rights or remedies under law or contract

  (d) **Deferral pending resolution of bona fide dispute.**—A transferee on which obligations are imposed under subsection (a) by virtue of paragraph (1) of that subsection may elect to defer performance of such obligations that are subject to a bona fide dispute between a union and a prior transferor until that dispute is resolved, except that such deferral shall not stay accrual of any union claims due under an applicable collective bargaining agreement.

(e) Scope of obligations determined by private agreement.—Nothing in this section shall expand or diminish the rights, obligations, or remedies of any person under the collective bargaining agreements or assumption agreements referred to in this section.

(f) Failure to notify.—If the transferor under subsection (a) fails to notify the transferee under subsection (a) of applicable collective bargaining obligations before the execution of the transfer instrument, and subsection (a) is made applicable to the transferee solely by virtue of subsection (a)(1)(B), the transferor shall be liable to the transferee for any damages suffered by the transferee as a result of the failure to notify.

(g) Determination of disputes and claims.—Any dispute concerning the application of subsections (a) through (f) shall be determined by an action in United States district court, and the court in its discretion may allow the recovery of full costs by or against any party and may also award a reasonable attorney's fee to the prevailing party as part of the costs.

(h) Study.—The Comptroller General, in consultation with the Register of Copyrights, shall conduct a study of the conditions in the motion picture industry that gave rise to this section, and the impact of this section on the motion picture industry. The Comptroller General shall report the findings of the study to the Congress within 2 years after the effective date of this chapter.

(Added Pub.L. 105–304, Title IV, § 406(a), Oct. 28, 1998, 112 Stat. 2902.)

CHAPTER 181—FOREIGN JUDGMENTS

§ 4101.　　Definitions

In this chapter:

(1) Defamation.—The term "defamation" means any action or other proceeding for defamation, libel, slander, or similar claim alleging that forms of speech are false, have caused damage to reputation or emotional distress, have presented any person in a false light, or have resulted in criticism, dishonor, or condemnation of any person.

(2) Domestic court.—The term "domestic court" means a Federal court or a court of any State.

(3) Foreign court.—The term "foreign court" means a court, administrative body, or other tribunal of a foreign country.

(4) Foreign judgment.—The term "foreign judgment" means a final judgment rendered by a foreign court.

(5) State.—The term "State" means each of the several States, the District of Columbia, and any commonwealth, territory, or possession of the United States.

(6) United States person.—The term "United States person" means—

---

[1]　[Footnote to Chapter 181 table:] So in original. Does not conform to section catchline.

(A) a United States citizen;

(B) an alien lawfully admitted for permanent residence to the United States;

(C) an alien lawfully residing in the United States at the time that the speech that is the subject of the foreign defamation action was researched, prepared, or disseminated; or

(D) a business entity incorporated in, or with its primary location or place of operation in, the United States.

(Added Pub. L. 111–223, § 3(a), Aug. 10, 2010, 124 Stat. 2381.)

§ 4102.   Recognition of foreign defamation judgments

(a) First amendment considerations.—

(1) In general.—Notwithstanding any other provision of Federal or State law, a domestic court shall not recognize or enforce a foreign judgment for defamation unless the domestic court determines that—

(A) the defamation law applied in the foreign court's adjudication provided at least as much protection for freedom of speech and press in that case as would be provided by the first amendment to the Constitution of the United States and by the constitution and law of the State in which the domestic court is located; or

(B) even if the defamation law applied in the foreign court's adjudication did not provide as much protection for freedom of speech and press as the first amendment to the Constitution of the United States and the constitution and law of the State, the party opposing recognition or enforcement of that foreign judgment would have been found liable for defamation by a domestic court applying the first amendment to the Constitution of the United States and the constitution and law of the State in which the domestic court is located.

(2) Burden of establishing application of defamation laws.—The party seeking recognition or enforcement of the foreign judgment shall bear the burden of making the showings required under subparagraph (A) or (B).

(b) Jurisdictional considerations.—

(1) In general.—Notwithstanding any other provision of Federal or State law, a domestic court shall not recognize or enforce a foreign judgment for defamation unless the domestic court determines that the exercise of personal jurisdiction by the foreign court comported with the due process requirements that are imposed on domestic courts by the Constitution of the United States.

(2) Burden of establishing exercise of jurisdiction.—The party seeking recognition or enforcement of the foreign judgment shall bear the burden of making the showing that the foreign court's exercise of personal jurisdiction comported with the due process requirements that are imposed on domestic courts by the Constitution of the United States.

(c) Judgment against provider of interactive computer service.—

(1) In general.—Notwithstanding any other provision of Federal or State law, a domestic court shall not recognize or enforce a foreign judgment for defamation against the provider of an interactive computer service, as defined in section 230 of the Communications Act of 1934 (47 U.S.C. 230) unless the domestic court determines that the judgment would be consistent with section 230 if the information that is the subject of such judgment had been provided in the United States.

(2) Burden of establishing consistency of judgment.—The party seeking recognition or enforcement of the foreign judgment shall bear the burden of establishing that the judgment is consistent with section 230.

(d) Appearances not a bar.—An appearance by a party in a foreign court rendering a foreign judgment to which this section applies shall not deprive such party of the right to oppose the recognition or enforcement of the judgment under this section, or represent a waiver of any jurisdictional claims.

(e) Rule of construction.—Nothing in this section shall be construed to—

(1) affect the enforceability of any foreign judgment other than a foreign judgment for defamation; or

(2) limit the applicability of section 230 of the Communications Act of 1934 (47 U.S.C. 230) to causes of action for defamation.

(Added Pub. L. 111–223, § 3(a), Aug. 10, 2010, 124 Stat. 2381.)

§ 4103.   Removal

In addition to removal allowed under section 1441, any action brought in a State domestic court to enforce a foreign judgment for defamation in which—

(1) any plaintiff is a citizen of a State different from any defendant;

(2) any plaintiff is a foreign state or a citizen or subject of a foreign state and any defendant is a citizen of a State; or

(3) any plaintiff is a citizen of a State and any defendant is a foreign state or citizen or subject of a foreign state,

may be removed by any defendant to the district court of the United States for the district and division embracing the place where such action is pending without regard to the amount in controversy between the parties.

(Added Pub. L. 111–223, § 3(a), Aug. 10, 2010, 124 Stat. 2383.)

§ 4104.   Declaratory judgments

(a) Cause of action.—

(1) In general.—Any United States person against whom a foreign judgment is entered on the basis of the content of any writing, utterance, or other speech by that person that has been published, may bring an action in district court, under section 2201(a), for a declaration that the foreign judgment is repugnant to the Constitution or laws of the United States. For the purposes of this paragraph, a judgment is repugnant to the Constitution or laws of the United States if it would not be enforceable under section 4102(a), (b), or (c).

(2) Burden of establishing unenforceability of judgment.—The party bringing an action under paragraph (1) shall bear the burden of establishing that the foreign judgment would not be enforceable under section 4102(a), (b), or (c).

(b) Nationwide service of process.—Where an action under this section is brought in a district court of the United States, process may be served in the judicial district where the case is brought or any other judicial district of the United States where the defendant may be found, resides, has an agent, or transacts business.

(Added Pub. L. 111–223, § 3(a), Aug. 10, 2010, 124 Stat. 2383.)

§ 4105.   Attorneys' fees

In any action brought in a domestic court to enforce a foreign judgment for defamation, including any such action removed from State court to Federal court, the domestic court shall, absent exceptional circumstances, allow the party opposing recognition or enforcement of the judgment a reasonable attorney's fee if such party prevails in the action on a ground specified in section 4102(a), (b), or (c).

(Added Pub. L. 111–223, § 3(a), Aug. 10, 2010, 124 Stat. 2383.)

CHAPTER 190—MISCELLANEOUS

Sec.

§ 5001.   Civil action for death or personal injury in a place subject to exclusive jurisdiction of United States

(a) Death.—In the case of the death of an individual by the neglect or wrongful act of another in a place subject to the exclusive jurisdiction of the United States within a State, a right of action shall exist as though the place were under the jurisdiction of the State in which the place is located.

(b) Personal injury.—In a civil action brought to recover on account of an injury sustained in a place described in subsection (a), the rights of the parties shall be governed by the law of the State in which the place is located.

(Added Pub.L. 113–287, § 4(b)(1), Dec. 19, 2014, 128 Stat. 3261.)

APPENDIX A
SELECTED STATE PROVISIONS

Analysis

Uniform Law Commissioner's Model Class Action [Act] [Rule].
Uniform Certification of Questions of Law [Act] [Rule] (1995).
Revised Uniform Enforcement of Foreign Judgments Act.
Uniform Interstate Depositions and Discovery Act.

INTRODUCTION

The following pages contain the text of several Uniform Acts relating to civil procedural laws. These Acts were drafted by the National Conference of Commissioners on Uniform State Laws and are recommended for adoption in all states.

These Acts have been variously adopted among the states. The legislative deliberations of numerous others have been greatly informed by the content of the Uniform provisions.

The Uniform Acts are attended by Official Comments prepared by the drafters. These comments are a valuable insight into the text and its underlying influences (much like the Advisory Committee Notes pertaining to the Federal Rules).

UNIFORM LAW COMMISSIONERS'
MODEL CLASS ACTION [ACT] [RULE]*

1976 ACT

Historical Note

The Uniform Class Actions Act was approved by the National Conference of Commissioners on Uniform State Laws in 1976 and officially changed to a Model Act in 1987.

PREFATORY NOTE

A class action is an equitable concept which originated as an exception to the general rule in equity that all persons (however numerous) materially interested in the subject matter of a suit were to be made parties to it. The class suit was an invention of equity to allow a suit to proceed when the parties interested in the subject were so numerous that it would have been impracticable to join them without long delays and inconveniences which would obstruct the purposes of justice. Under these conditions representatives of a class conduct litigation on behalf of themselves and all others similarly situated and the judgment binds all members.

The first state statute on class suits was the 1849 Amendment to the Field Code of New York which attempted to codify the pre-existing equity law on representative suits. Two types of representative suits which could be maintained under the rules of equity were specially adopted as allowable under the Field Code. The first type of suit involved actions where the question was one of a common or general interest and one or more class members sued for the benefit of the entire class. The second type involved cases in which the parties were very numerous and it was impracticable to bring them all before the court. A common interest or right was present among the members and the representatives sought to establish or enforce this right in order to benefit all the members of the class in common and injure none. Other states have adopted statutes modeled on these concepts.

In 1938 the Supreme Court adopted the Federal Rules of Civil Procedure including Rule 23 which governed class actions for federal courts. Many states have adopted a version of this rule. The 1938 Rule 23 created three separate categories of class actions based on the substantive character of the right asserted by the class and the *res judicata* effect of the class action judgments on nonappearing members. The first category, the "true" class suit, requires a common or joint cause of action that exists for all parties and the issues determined in the suit are preclusive to all class members. The second type is the "hybrid" suit requiring each member to have an interest in a specific fund or property which is in controversy and the judgment binds the rights of the class with respect to the property involved. The third type, "spurious," requires that a common question of law or fact affect the several rights involved and a common relief must be sought. The decree in such actions had no binding effect on nonappearing members. Class actions of the latter sort were merely invitations to join.

In 1966 Federal Rule 23 was amended. The new Rule 23 is divided into five subsections dealing with different procedural requirements for bringing into five suit. After satisfying the four prerequisites of subsection (a), a class suit must fit in one of the three categories of subsection (b) which describe appropriate occasions for maintaining a class action: 23(b)(1) where difficulties would be likely to arise if separate actions were brought by class members; 23(b)(2) where the party opposing the class has improperly acted on grounds generally applicable to the class so as to create a need for injunctive relief; or 23(b)(3) where common questions predominate over any questions affecting only individual class members and a class action is superior to other adjudicatory methods. A judgment under the amended rule binds all those whom the court finds to be members of the class. Several states have a version of this rule for their class action statute.

Presently three types of class action statutes predominate in the United States; (1) the Field Code provision, (2) state statutes modeled on Rule 23 of the Federal Rules of Civil Procedure as it existed prior to July, 1966, and (3) statutes modeled on the new Federal Rule 23. Some states still do not have a class action statute. State rules based on the Field Code and the earlier Federal Rule pose distinct problems and disadvantages in maintaining class suits. Recent Supreme Court decisions have severely limited the

---

* [This model act has been enacted in two states: Iowa and North Dakota. *See* www.uniformlaws.org for the most recent enactment status. Ed.]

APPENDIX A

availability of the present Rule 23 as a group remedy. In Zahn v. International Paper Co., 414 U.S. 291 (1973) the Court held that each of the class members in a diversity action under Rule 23 must satisfy the jurisdictional amount of more than $10,000 and any members who do not must be dismissed from the case. In Eisen v. Carlisle & Jacquelin, 417 U.S. 136 (1974) the Supreme Court interpreted Rule 23(b)(3) and (c)(2) to require personal notice of the action to all identifiable class members with service costs to be borne by the plaintiffs.

More classes with claims will be seeking redress in state courts because the federal courts have severely restricted the availability of class actions in their forum. Presently state states vary in their treatment of class actions. A strong need exists for states to adopt a uniform class action act. Many activities have impact on large numbers of persons often from several states. Adoption of a uniform act will assist states in handling multistate class actions, thereby reducing multiplicity of litigation and the change of inconsistent judgments. The Act provides supervision of the adequacy of representation by the representative parties to insure that the interests of the class will be protected. Subsections to cover special problems of the class action are provided: notice techniques, discovery of the members of the class, effect of the judgment on the members of the class, methods of fashioning relief, and liability for costs and expenses.

This Act applies whenever an action involving a class is commenced. When a final order refusing to certify a class action is entered, the application of this Act will terminate. The scope of this Act is similar to that of F.R.C.P. 23 and does not cover derivative actions by shareholders or suits by unincorporated associations.

Within the limits of practicality, due process requires that all individuals be afforded a meaningful opportunity to be heard, Boddie v. Connecticut, 401 U.S. 371 (1971). A class action is a procedure by which people with small claims or limited means can exercise their rights and thereby make our system of justice more responsive to their needs.

UNIFORM LAW COMMISSIONERS'
MODEL CLASS ACTIONS [ACT] [RULE]
1976 ACT

Section

1. [Commencement of a Class Action].
2. [Certification of Class Action].
3. [Criteria Considered].
4. [Order on Certification].
5. [Amendment of Certification Order].
6. [Jurisdiction over Multi-State Classes (Reserved)].
7. [Notice of Action].
8. [Exclusion].
9. [Conduct of Action].
10. [Discovery by or against Class Members].
11. [Counterclaims].
12. [Dismissal or Compromise].
13. [Effect of Judgment on Class].
14. [Costs].
15. [Relief Afforded].
16. [Attorney's Fees].
17. [Arrangements for Attorney's Fees and Expenses].
18. [Statute of Limitations].
19. [Short Title].
20. [Repeal].
21. [Time of Taking Effect].

§ 1. [Commencement of a Class Action].

One or more members of a class may sue or be sued as representative parties on behalf of all in a class action if:

(1) the class is so numerous or so constituted that joinder of all members, whether or not otherwise required or permitted, is impracticable; and

(2) there is a question of law or fact common to the class.

Comment

This section sets forth the requirements that must be satisfied if a class action is to be brought. Section 2 authorizes the certification of a class action.

§ 2. [Certification of Class Action].

(a) Unless deferred by the court, as soon as practicable after the commencement of a class action the court shall hold a hearing and determine whether or not the action is to be maintained as a class action and by order certify or refuse to certify it as a class action.

(b) The court may certify an action as a class action, if it finds that (1) the requirements of Section 1 have been satisfied, (2) a class action should be permitted for the fair and efficient adjudication of the controversy, and (3) the representative parties fairly and adequately will protect the interests of the class.

(c) If appropriate, the court may (1) certify an action as a class action with respect to a particular claim or issue, (2) certify an action as a class action to obtain one or more forms of relief, equitable, declaratory, or monetary, or (3) divide a class into subclasses and treat each subclass as a class.

Comment

The standard established under 2(b)(2) is elaborated in Section 3(a) and that established under 2(b)(3) is elaborated in Section 3(b).

§ 3. [Criteria Considered].

(a) In determining whether the class action should be permitted for the fair and efficient adjudication of the controversy, as appropriately limited under Section 2(c), the court shall consider, and give appropriate weight to, the following and other relevant factors:

(1) whether a joint or common interest exists among members of the class;

(2) whether the prosecution of separate actions by or against individual members of the class would create a risk of inconsistent or varying adjudications with respect to individual members of the class that would establish incompatible standards of conduct for a party opposing the class;

(3) whether adjudications with respect to individual members of the class as a practical matter would be dispositive of the interests of other members not parties to the adjudication or substantially impair or impede their ability to protect their interests;

(4) whether a party opposing the class has acted or refused to act on grounds generally applicable to the class, thereby making final injunctive relief or corresponding declaratory relief appropriate with respect to the class as a whole;

(5) whether common questions of law or fact predominate over any questions affecting only individual members;

(6) whether other means of adjudicating the claims and defenses are impracticable or inefficient;

(7) whether a class action offers the most appropriate means of adjudicating the claims and defenses;

(8) whether members not representative parties have a substantial interest in individually controlling the prosecution or defense of separate actions;

(9) whether the class action involves a claim that is or has been the subject of a class action, a government action, or other proceeding;

(10) whether it is desirable to bring the class action in another forum;

(11) whether management of the class action poses unusual difficulties;

(12) whether any conflict of laws issues involved pose unusual difficulties; and

(13) whether the claims of individual class members are insufficient in the amounts or interests involved, in view of the complexities of the issues and the expenses of the litigation, to afford significant relief to the members of the class.

(b) In determining under Section 2(b) that the representative parties fairly and adequately will protect the interests of the class, the court must find that:

(1) the attorney for the representative parties will adequately represent the interests of the class;

(2) the representative parties do not have a conflict of interest in the maintenance of the class action; and

(3) the representative parties have or can acquire adequate financial resources, considering Section 17, to assure that the interests of the class will not be harmed.

Comment

The factors listed in Section 3(a)(1) to (13), possibly along with other factors, are to be considered by the court in determining whether or certify the action as a class action. The factors may be given different weight by the court.

After an action has been brought as a class action, if the court determines that there is pending in another court an action which encompasses the action pending both as to general class and claim, it may refuse under Subsection 3(a)(9) and (10) to certify the action against or on behalf of the class if it concludes that this forum is not the most appropriate one. The court in making this decision should consider the sequence of the suits, the residence of the members of the class, where the transaction or occurrence involved took place, where the relevant evidence is available, and other pertinent facts.

§ 4. [Order on Certification].

(a) The order of certification shall describe the class and state: (1) the relief sought, (2) whether the action is maintained with respect to particular claims or issues, and (3) whether subclasses have been created.

(b) The order certifying or refusing to certify a class action shall state the reasons for the court's ruling and its findings on the facts listed in Section 3(a).

(c) An order certifying or refusing to certify an action as a class action is appealable.

(d) Refusal of certification does not terminate the action, but does preclude it from being maintained as a class action.

Comment

If class certification is denied, subsection (d) presupposes the existence of rules of civil procedure which will allow the action to continue with the representative parties as properly joined parties.

Denial of certification and the allowance of a personal action under subsection (d) does not affect any possible intervention or joinder of class members who are not representative parties under the applicable state laws.

§ 5.   [Amendment of Certification Order].

(a)   The court may amend the certification order at any time before entry of judgment on the merits. The amendment may (1) establish subclasses, (2) eliminate from the class any class member who was included in the class as certified, (3) provide for an adjudication limited to certain claims or issues, (4) change the relief sought, or (5) make any other appropriate change in the order.

(b)   If notice of certification has been given pursuant to Section 7, the court may order notice of the amendment of the certification order to be given in terms and to any members of the class the court directs.

(c)   The reasons for the court's ruling shall be set forth in the amendment of the certification order.

(d)   An order amending the certification order is appealable. An order denying the motion of a member of a defendant class, not a representative party, to amend the certification order is appealable if the court certifies it for immediate appeal.

Comment

An order amending an order of certification is an appealable order as is an order certifying or refusing to certify an action as a class action.

A member of a defendant class can attempt to get out of a class action by seeking an amendment of the order of certification. If a member of a defendant class seeks an amendment which would delete him or her from the class and the court refused to make such an order, an appeal can be taken if the court certifies it for appeal.

Under Section 5(b) the court may order notice given of an amendment if it deems it desirable in light of the nature of the amendments and the notice previously given.

§ 6.   [Jurisdiction over Multi-State Classes (Reserved)].

Comment

The Section is reserved for provisions that may be added to govern jurisdiction of the person over class members who are non-residents or lack traditional minimum contacts with the state. See Phillips Petroleum Company v. Shutts, 472 U.S. 797, 86 L.Ed.2d 628 (1985), rendering obsolete the jurisdictional limitations of this Section as contained in the 1976 version.

§ 7.   [Notice of Action].

(a)   Following certification, the court by order, after hearing, shall direct the giving of notice to the class.

(b)   The notice, based on the certification order and any amendment of the order, shall include:

(1)   a general description of the action, including the relief sought, and the names and addresses of the representative parties;

(2)   a statement of the right of a member of the class under Section 8 to be excluded from the action by filing an election to be excluded, in the manner specified, by a certain date;

(3)   a description of possible financial consequences on the class;

(4)   a general description of any counterclaim being asserted by or against the class, including the relief sought;

(5)   a statement that the judgment, whether favorable or not, will bind all members of the class who are not excluded from the action;

(6)   a statement that any member of the class may enter an appearance either personally or through counsel;

(7)   an address to which inquiries may be directed; and

(8)   other information the court deems appropriate.

(c)   The order shall prescribe the manner of notification to be used and specify the members of the class to be notified. In determining the manner and form of the notice to be given, the court shall consider the interests of the class, the relief requested, the cost of notifying the members of the class, and the possible prejudice to members who do not receive notice.

(d)   Each member of the class, not a representative party, whose potential monetary recovery or liability is estimated to exceed $100 shall be given personal or mailed notice if his identity and whereabouts can be ascertained by the exercise of reasonable diligence.

(e)   For members of the class not given personal or mailed notice under subsection (d), the court shall provide, as a minimum, a means of notice reasonably calculated to apprise the members of the class of the pendency of the action. Techniques calculated to assure effective communication of information concerning commencement of the action shall be used. The techniques may include personal or mailed notice, notification by means of newspaper, television, radio, posting in public or other places, and distribution through trade, union, public interest, or other appropriate groups.

(f)   The plaintiff shall advance the expense of notice under this section if there is no counterclaim asserted. If a counterclaim is asserted the expense of notice shall be allocated as the court orders in the interest of justice.

(g)   The court may order that steps be taken to minimize the expense of notice.

Comment

The hearing required by subsection (a) can be combined with the hearing required by Section 2(a).

Personal mailed notice to all members of the class is not required by this Act. For consideration of the notice required by the U.S. Constitution, see Gant v. City of Lincoln, 225 N.W.2d 549 (Neb.1975), and Cartt v. Superior Court in and for County of Los Angeles, 50 Cal.App.3d 960, 124 Cal.Rptr. 376 (Ct.App.1975).

The notice to be given may vary as to the persons to be notified and the form of notice and, to some extent, the content. Subsection (c) indicates that the court must consider a number of factors in deciding what type of notice to give.

Subsection (g) allows the court to order a defendant who has a mailing list of class members to co-operate with the representative parties in notifying the class members. Use of a computer or enclosing notice in a regular mailing would be possibilities.

§ 8.   [Exclusion].

(a)   A member of a plaintiff class may elect to be excluded from the action unless (1) he is a representative party, (2) the certification order contains an affirmative finding under paragraph (1), (2), or (3) of Section 3(a), or (3) a counterclaim under Section 11 is pending against the member or his class or subclass.

(b)   Any member of a plaintiff class entitled to be excluded under subsection (a) who files an election to be excluded, in the manner and in the time specified in the notice, is excluded from and not bound by the judgment in the class action.

(c)   The elections shall be [docketed] [made a part of the record] in the action.

(d)   A member of a defendant class may not elect to be excluded.

Comment

Under some circumstances members of a plaintiff class cannot elect to be excluded because they are indispensable parties. This would be determined by the court in ruling on certification considering the criteria of Section 3(a). Such situations might arise in actions comparable to those under Federal Rule 23(b)(1); see 3B, Moore's Federal Practice, ¶ 23.35. In most situations members of a plaintiff class will be permitted to elect to be excluded.

A class member aggrieved by an affirmative finding under Section 3(a)(1), (2) or (3) might seek relief through one of the extraordinary writs or through an interlocutory appeal if authorized by the state practice.

§ 9.   [Conduct of Action].

(a)   The court on motion of a party or its own motion may make or amend any appropriate order dealing with the conduct of the action including, but not limited to, the following: (1) determining the course of proceedings or prescribing measures to prevent undue repetition or complication in the presentation of evidence or argument; (2) requiring, for the protection of the members of the class or otherwise for the fair conduct of the action, that notice be given as the court directs, of (i) any step in the action, (ii) the proposed extent of the judgment, or (iii) the opportunity of members to signify whether they consider the representation fair and adequate, to enter an appearance and present claims or defenses, or otherwise participate in the action; (3) imposing conditions on the representative parties or on intervenors; (4) inviting the attorney general to participate with respect to the question of adequacy of class representation; (5) making any other order to assure that the class action proceeds only with adequate class representation; and (6) making any order to assure that the class action proceeds only with competent representation by the attorney for the class.

(b)   A class member not a representative party may appear and be represented by separate counsel.

Comment

The rules governing civil procedure in the courts of the state normally will govern procedures in class actions. Section 9 covers certain matters which deserve special consideration. Section 9(a)(4) does not limit the power of the attorney general to participate in litigation under other applicable provisions.

§ 10.   [Discovery by or against Class Members].

(a)   Discovery under [applicable discovery rules] may be used only on order of the court against a member of the class who is not a representative party or who has not appeared. In deciding whether discovery should be allowed the court shall consider, among other relevant factors, the timing of the request, the subject matter to be covered, whether representatives of the class are seeking discovery on the subject to be covered, and whether the discovery will result in annoyance, oppression, or undue burden or expense for the member of the class.

(b)   Discovery by or against representative parties or those appearing is governed by the rules dealing with discovery by or against a party to a civil action.

Comment

Under Section 10 members of the class not representative parties and not appearing are not treated as parties to the litigation for discovery purposes. Discovery can be obtained of these members only on order of court.

Discovery against representative parties may include the representative parties' fee arrangement with counsel. Disclosure of this arrangement is required under Section 17.

§ 11.   [Counterclaims].

(a)   A defendant in an action brought by a class may plead as a counterclaim any claim the court certifies as a class action against the plaintiff class. On leave of court, the defendant may plead as a counterclaim a claim against a member of the class or a claim the court certifies as a class action against a subclass.

(b)   Any counterclaim in an action brought by a plaintiff class must be asserted before notice is given under Section 7.

(c)   If a judgment for money is recovered against a party on behalf of a class, the court rendering judgment may stay distribution of any award or execution of any portion of a judgment allocated to a member of the class against whom the losing party has pending an action in or out of state for a judgment for money, and continue the stay so long as the losing party in the class action pursues the pending action with reasonable diligence.

(d) A defendant class may plead as a counterclaim any claim on behalf of the class that the court certifies as a class action against the plaintiff. The court may certify as a class action a counterclaim against the plaintiff on behalf of a subclass or permit a counterclaim by a member of the class. The court shall order that notice of the counterclaim by the class, subclass, or member of the class be given to the members of the class as the court directs, in the interest of justice.

(e) A member of a class or subclass asserting a counterclaim shall be treated as a member of a plaintiff class for the purpose of exclusion under Section 8.

(f) The court's refusal to allow, or the defendant's failure to plead, a claim as a counterclaim in a class action does not bar the defendant from asserting the claim in a subsequent action.

Comment

Nothing in this Act precludes a party opposing the class from bringing an action against a member of the class concurrently with the class action or in the future. Subsection (f) makes the ordinary rules concerning compulsory counterclaims inapplicable in a class action under this Act.

The expense of notification of actions involving counterclaims is to be determined as provided in Section 7(f).

§ 12. [Dismissal or Compromise].

(a) Unless certification has been refused under Section 2, a class action, without the approval of the court after hearing, may not be (1) dismissed voluntarily, (2) dismissed involuntarily without an adjudication on the merits, or (3) compromised.

(b) If the court has certified the action under Section 2, notice of hearing on the proposed dismissal or compromise shall be given to all members of the class in a manner the court directs. If the court has not ruled on certification, notice of hearing on the proposed dismissal or compromise may be ordered by the court which shall specify the persons to be notified and the manner in which notice is to be given.

(c) Notice given under subsection (b) shall include a full disclosure of the reasons for the dismissal or compromise including, but not limited to, (1) any payments made or to be made in connection with the dismissal or compromise, (2) the anticipated effect of the dismissal or compromise on the class members, (3) any agreement made in connection with the dismissal or compromise, (4) a description and evaluation of alternatives considered by the representative parties and (5) an explanation of any other circumstances giving rise to the proposal. The notice also shall include a description of the procedure available for modification of the dismissal or compromise.

(d) On the hearing of the dismissal or compromise, the court may:

(1) as to the representative parties or a class certified under Section 2, permit dismissal with or without prejudice or approve the compromise;

(2) as to a class not certified, permit dismissal without prejudice;

(3) deny the dismissal;

(4) disapprove the compromise; or

(5) take other appropriate action for the protection of the class and in the interest of justice.

(e) The cost of notice given under subsection (b) shall be paid by the party seeking dismissal, or as agreed in case of a compromise, unless the court after hearing orders otherwise.

Comment

This section covers class actions brought under Section 1 until certification has been refused under Section 2, as well as class actions certified under Section 2.

§ 13.   [Effect of Judgment on Class].

In a class action certified under Section 2 in which notice has been given under Section 7 or 12, a judgment as to the claim or particular claim or issue certified is binding, according to its terms, on any member of the class who has not filed an election of exclusion under Section 8. The judgment shall name or describe the members of the class who are bound by its terms.

Comment

Section 13 deals with the application of a class action judgment to the members of the class. This Act does not deal with the preclusive effect of a class action upon a member of the class who has requested exclusion. This is a matter which is governed by the normal rules of res judicata/preclusion.

§ 14.   [Costs].

(a)   Only the representative parties and those members of the class who have appeared individually are liable for costs assessed against a plaintiff class.

(b)   The court shall apportion the liability for costs assessed against a defendant class.

(c)   Expenses of notice advanced under Section 7 are taxable as costs in favor of the prevailing party.

Comment

Section 14 specifies the liability of class members when costs are assessed against the class and provides for assessment of the expenses of notification under Section 7.

The nature of other costs and assessments against parties in a class action is left to the law generally applicable in the state.

§ 15.   [Relief Afforded].

(a)   The court may award any form of relief consistent with the certification order to which the party in whose favor it is rendered is entitled including equitable, declaratory, monetary, or other relief to individual members of the class or the class in a lump sum or installments.

(b)   Damages fixed by a minimum measure of recovery provided by any statute may not be recovered in a class action.

(c)   If a class is awarded a judgment for money, the distribution shall be determined as follows:

(1)   The parties shall list as expeditiously as possible all members of the class whose identity can be determined without expending a disproportionate share of the recovery.

(2)   The reasonable expense of identification and distribution shall be paid, with the court's approval, from the funds to be distributed.

(3)   The court may order steps taken to minimize the expense of identification.

(4)   The court shall supervise, and may grant or stay the whole or any portion of, the execution of the judgment and the collection and distribution of funds to the members of the class as their interests warrant.

(5)   The court shall determine what amount of the funds available for the payment of the judgment cannot be distributed to members of the class individually because they could not be identified or located or because they did not claim or prove the right to money apportioned to them. The court after hearing shall distribute that amount, in whole or in part, to one or more states as unclaimed property or to the defendant.

(6)   In determining the amount, if any, to be distributed to a state or to the defendant, the court shall consider the following criteria: (i) any unjust enrichment of the defendant; (ii) the willfulness or lack of willfulness on the part of the defendant; (iii) the impact on the defendant of the relief granted; (iv) the pendency of other claims against the defendant; (v) any criminal sanction imposed on the defendant; and (vi) the loss suffered by the plaintiff class.

(7)   The court, in order to remedy or alleviate any harm done, may impose conditions on the defendant respecting the use of the money distributed to him.

(8)   Any amount to be distributed to a state shall be distributed as unclaimed property to any state in which are located the last known addresses of the members of the class to whom distribution could not be made. If the last known addresses cannot be ascertained with reasonable diligence, the court may determine by other means what portion of the unidentified or unlocated members of the class were residents of a state. A state shall receive that portion of the distribution that its residents would have received had they been identified and located. Before entering an order distributing any part of the amount to a state, the court shall give written notice of its intention to make distribution to the attorney general of the state of the residence of any person given notice under Section 7 or 12 and shall afford the attorney general an opportunity to move for an order requiring payment to the state.

Comment

Subsection (c)(3) is similar to subsection 7(g) in its purpose and scope and should be construed similarly.

Subsection 15(c)(5) provides for the possibility of escheat of funds available for the payment of the judgment if the court, applying the relevant criteria, so orders. The escheat provision is similar to that found in the Model Escheat of Postal Savings System Accounts Act.

If the court decides that undistributed funds available for the payment of the judgment should be distributed to the defendant, the court under subsection 15(c)(7), "in order to remedy or alleviate any harm done, may impose conditions on the defendant respecting the use of the money distributed to him." For example, if the plaintiff class sued for damage done because of the discharge of pollutants by the defendant and the class won a money judgment, the court might distribute to the defendant funds undistributed to the plaintiff class on condition that the defendant use the funds to install pollution-control devices.

§ 16.   [Attorney's Fees].

(a)   Attorney's fees for representing a class are subject to control of the court.

(b)   If under an applicable provision of law a defendant or defendant class is entitled to attorney's fees from a plaintiff class, only representative parties and those members of the class who have appeared individually are liable for those fees. If a plaintiff is entitled to attorney's fees from a defendant class, the court may apportion the fees among the members of the class.

(c)   If a prevailing class recovers a judgment for money or other award that can be divided for the purpose, the court may order reasonable attorney's fees and litigation expenses of the class to be paid from the recovery.

(d)   If the prevailing class is entitled to declaratory or equitable relief, the court may order the adverse party to pay to the class its reasonable attorney's fees and litigation expenses if permitted by law in similar cases not involving a class or the court finds that the judgment has vindicated an important public interest. However, if any monetary award is also recovered, the court may allow reasonable attorney's fees and litigation expenses only to the extent that a reasonable proportion of that award is insufficient to defray the fees and expenses.

(e)   In determining the amount of attorney's fees for a prevailing class the court shall consider the following factors:

(1)   the time and effort expended by the attorney in the litigation, including the nature, extent, and quality of the services rendered;

(2)   results achieved and benefits conferred upon the class;

(3)   the magnitude, complexity, and uniqueness of the litigation;

(4)   the contingent nature of success;

(5)   in cases awarding attorney's fees and litigation expenses under subsection (d) because of the vindication of an important public interest, the economic impact on the party against whom the award is made; and

(6)   appropriate criteria in the [state's Code of Professional Responsibility].

Comment

Most of the factors listed in subsection (e) are taken from Lindy Bros. v. American Radiator & Standard Sanitary Corp., 487 F.2d 161 (3rd Cir. 1973).

§ 17.   [Arrangements for Attorney's Fees and Expenses].

(a)   Before a hearing under Section 2(a) or at any other time the court directs, the representative parties and the attorney for the representative parties shall file with the court, jointly or separately: (1) a statement showing any amount paid or promised them by any person for the services rendered or to be rendered in connection with the action or for the costs and expenses of the litigation and the source of all of the amounts; (2) a copy of any written agreement, or a summary of any oral agreement, between the representative parties and their attorney concerning financial arrangements or fees and (3) a copy of any written agreement, or a summary of any oral agreement, by the representative parties or the attorney to share these amounts with any person other than a member, regular associate, or an attorney regularly of counsel with his law firm. This statement shall be supplemented promptly if additional arrangements are made.

(b)   Upon a determination that the costs and litigation expenses of the action cannot reasonably and fairly be defrayed by the representative parties or by other available sources, the court by order may authorize and control the solicitation and expenditure of voluntary contributions for this purpose from members of the class, advances by the attorneys or others, or both, subject to reimbursement from any recovery obtained for the class. The court may order any available funds so contributed or advanced to be applied to the payment of any costs taxed in favor of a party opposing the class.

Comment

Section 17 requires this information to be disclosed in order to assist the court in making determinations concerning (1) adequacy of representation by the representative parties and by the attorney for the class, (2) any possible collusion between the representative parties and the attorney for the class, and (3) any possible conflict of interests among the representative parties and the class members.

This section is grounded on the idea that representative parties are fiduciaries for the class and that class actions are unique and require treatment different from ordinary actions.

If the information available under this section shows that an action has been improvidently brought, action can then be taken under Section 9(a)(5) or (6).

§ 18.   [Statute of Limitations].

The statute of limitations is tolled for all class members upon the commencement of an action asserting a class action. The statute of limitations resumes running against a member of a class:

(1)   upon his filing an election of exclusion;

(2)   upon entry of an order of certification, or of an amendment thereof, eliminating him from the class;

(3)   except as to representative parties, upon entry of an order under Section 2 refusing to certify the action as a class action; and

(4)   upon dismissal of the action without an adjudication on the merits.

Comment

Section 18 adopts the principles of American Pipe and Construction Co. v. Utah, 415 U.S. 952, 94 S.Ct. 756, 38 L.Ed.2d 713 (1974), which held that the commencement of a class action under Federal Rule 23 suspends the applicable statute of limitation to all members of the class pending a determination of class action status.

§ 19.   [Short Title].

This [Act] [Rule] may be cited as the "Uniform Law Commissioners' Model Class Actions [Act] [Rule]."

Comment

With the deletion of the jurisdictional and reciprocal provisions of former Section 6, the need for uniformity is diminished, and the Act or Rule is therefore re-titled as "Model."

§ 20.   [Repeal].

The following acts and parts of acts are repealed:

§ 21.   [Time of Taking Effect].

This [Act] [Rule] shall take effect

UNIFORM CERTIFICATION OF QUESTIONS OF LAW [ACT] [RULE] (1995)*

1995 ACT

PREFATORY NOTE

The Problem Addressed by The Uniform Act/Rule

Since the announcement in Erie R. Co. v. Tompkins, 304 U.S. 64 (1938) that federal courts in nonfederal matters would be required to follow state law rather than some general common law, the federal courts have often been faced with the difficult problem of ascertaining state law when there is no controlling state constitutional provision, state statute or definitive state appellate judicial decision on the matter. In such circumstances, the federal courts have been forced to guess what the state court might rule if the precise issue of law were presented to it. Such speculation invited divergent answers to unsettled questions of state law from the federal courts and worked to undermine the two major purposes of the Erie doctrine; that is, the "discouragement of forum-shopping and the avoidance of inequitable administration of the laws." Hanna v. Plumer, 380 U.S. 460, 468 (1965). Essentially the same problem confronts a state appellate court when it determines that the law of another State should control the resolution of a key issue of law in a case pending before it, but where there is no controlling constitutional provision, statute or appellate decision in that other State on that issue of law.

The federal courts sought to try to avoid the problem by developing an abstention doctrine whereby the federal courts refrained from acting while the litigants attempted to obtain from the state court a definitive statement of the state law. This proved to be quite unsatisfactory. See 1A Moore's Federal Practice ¶ 0.203.

The History of the Use of Certification

Dissatisfaction with the use of the abstention doctrine led to efforts to find an alternative solution to the problem that also served the interests of cooperative judicial federalism. As a result, federal courts confronting issues of unsettled state law began to explore ways by which such issues could be submitted to, and answered by, the appropriate state court.[1] This process, known as "certification," has worked well to the extent it has been used. Among the various jurisdictions that have attempted to utilize certification, however, there are substantial differences in the procedures developed to accomplish the certification process. Where the procedures for certification have been relatively simple, and the appropriate state court has cooperated by agreeing to answer the question, certification has proven to be a more rapid and orderly method for handling the problem than the use of the abstention doctrine by the federal courts.

Over 35 years ago, the United States Supreme Court urged the use of the certified question by the Court of Appeals for the 5th Circuit, Clay v. Sun Insurance Office, 363 U.S. 207, 212 (1960). Three years later, the 5th Circuit expressed its approval of certification in Green v. American Tobacco Co., 325 F2d 673 (5th Cir.1963). In Lehman Brothers v. Schein, 416 U.S. 386 (1974), the United States Supreme Court again endorsed the use of certification by the federal courts in cases involving doubt as to issues of state law. While the Court noted that it did not mean to suggest that certification was obligatory in such cases, it made clear its strong approval of the use of certification, stating: "It [certification] does, of course, in the long run save time, energy, and resources and helps build a cooperative judicial federalism." Lehman Brothers, 416 U.S. at 391 (footnote omitted).

---

* [This model act has been enacted in eight states (Connecticut, Maryland, Minnesota, Montana, New Mexico, Oklahoma, Vermont, and West Virginia) and the District of Columbia. *See* www.uniformlaws.org for the most recent enactment status. Ed.]

[1] The certified question of law has a long history in the United States and the English speaking world. The British Law Ascertainment Act of 1859 provided for certification of questions of law within the British Empire, while the Foreign Law Ascertainment Act of 1861 made provision for certification of questions to foreign states. 9 Halsbury's Statutes of England (2d ed.) 58206. Within the federal court system, the Courts of Appeals and the Court of Claims have by statute been permitted to certify questions to the United States Supreme Court pursuant to 28 U.S.C. Secs. 1254–1255. See Moore and Vestal, Present and Potential Role of Certification in Federal Appellate Procedure, 35 Va. L. Rev. 1 (1940). In addition, a great number of states have provided for certified questions within their court systems. At least two state supreme courts have held that they need no express grant of jurisdiction to answer certified questions form the federal court. Shebester v. Triple Crown Insurers, 826 P2d 603 (Okla.1992); Scott v. Bank One Trust Co., 577 NE2d 1077 (Ohio 1991).

APPENDIX A

When, prior to the 1991, federal district courts took it upon themselves to decide issues of unsettled state law, a majority of the federal Courts of Appeals gave deference to those decisions when reviewing such issues on appeal. This "rule of deference" was ended by the decision of the United States Supreme Court in Salve Regina v. Russell, 499 U.S. 225, 111 S.Ct. 1217 (1991), 113 L.Ed.2d 190. Holding that the federal Courts of Appeals are required to independently review such state law issues, the Court expressly rejected the notion upon which the "rule of deference" was based; that is, that federal District Courts were better able to "intuit" answers to unsettled questions of state law than the federal Courts of Appeals. Salve Regina College, 499 U.S. 225, 111 S.Ct. at 1217, 1225, 113 L.Ed. 2d 190. Thus, the Court further encouraged the federal trial courts to use certification when confronted with issues of unsettled state law.

The federal District Courts and federal Courts of Appeals have been increasingly relying upon certification to ascertain uncertain state law. A 1994 American Judicature Society study of all federal circuit court appellate decisions published since 1990 showed the importance of the certification process to the federal circuit appellate courts.[2] For example, the study revealed that the federal Court of Appeals for the 11th Circuit granted 90% of the certification applications it received. By comparison, the federal Court of Appeals for the 10th Circuit, which granted the lowest percentage of such applications, nevertheless granted more than a third of the certification applications submitted to it (34%).

Need for Uniformity

Since the certification of a question of law involves more than one jurisdiction, the development of procedures for certification raises important issues of sovereignty, comity, and efficiency in the relationships between individual States and between the state and federal courts.

As of 1994, 44 state supreme courts and the Court of Appeals for the District of Columbia were authorized by constitutional provision, statute or court rule to answer certified questions of law from other courts. Of these, 19 States and the District of Columbia adopted the earlier versions of the Uniform Certification of Question of Law Act or amended versions of them. Nevertheless, the certification process is not utilized as frequently as it could and should be. One of the main reasons for this is that there is still widespread lack of uniformity in the laws of the various jurisdictions which authorize their courts to send and answer certified questions of law to and from other courts. A leading commentator argues that inconsistency of statutory language among the States has significantly impeded the use of certification.[3]

The Uniform Act/Rule provides a relatively simple and efficient means by which federal courts and state appellate courts can efficiently obtain answers to questions of law from the highest court of the controlling State.[4] Where adopted, it would allow a federal court or state appellate court, having determined that the law of another State controls a controversy, to avoid guessing what that law is when there is no definitive answer in the law of the controlling State. Instead, the court would simply certify the question of law to the highest court of the controlling State.

A combined Erie and state conflicts problem can also be handled under the Uniform Act/Rule. For example, a federal court sitting in State A might decide that the Erie doctrine applies so it should look to the law of State A on a problem. The federal court might then decide that the court in State A, under its conflicts of law rules, would look to the law of State B for the solution of the legal problem. Under the Uniform Act/Rule, the federal court in State A can ask the court in State B to answer the unsettled issue of its law on the point.

It is reasonable to expect that the goal of encouraging courts to certify questions of law in appropriate cases will be advanced as judges and lawyers become more aware of and familiar with the certification process.

---

[2] J. Goldschmidt, "Results of A National Survey of Federal Judges and State Supreme Court Justices Regarding Certification of Questions of Law," American Judicature Society (Nov. 1994).

[3] Ira P. Robbins, The Uniform Certification of Questions of Law Act: A Proposal for Reform, 18 JOURNAL OF LEGISLATION 127, 183 (1992). See also, Ira P. Robbins, Interstate Certification of Questions of Law: A Valuable Process in Need of Reform, 76 JUDICATURE 125 (1992); John B. Corr & Ira P. Robbins, Interjurisdictional Certification and Choice of Law, 41 VANDERBILT LAW REVIEW 411 (1988).

[4] The inclusion of certain bracketed language in sections 1,2, and 3 of the Uniform Act/Rule would also authorize the state appellate court to certify questions of law to a tribal court or answer questions of law from a tribal court. In addition, bracketed language in Sections 2 and 3 would, if included in the Act or Rule, authorize certifications to, and answers to questions from, appropriate courts in jurisdictions of Mexico and Canada.

To this end, uniformity of law in this area is highly desirable in that it is likely to result in the greater use of certification.

Adopted by Legislature or Court

The Conference has promulgated the Uniform Act/Rule for certified questions in a form which can be enacted by a legislature or adopted by a court as a rule. In some jurisdictions, action by the highest court will suffice with no legislative action required.

UNIFORM CERTIFICATION OF QUESTIONS OF LAW [ACT] [RULE] (1995)

1995 ACT

Section

1. Definition[s].
2. Power to Certify.
3. Power to Answer.
4. Power to Reformulate Question.
5. Certification Order; Record.
6. Contents of Certification Order.
7. Notice; Response.
8. Procedures.
9. Opinion.
10. Cost of Certification.
11. Severability.
12. Uniformity of Application and Construction.
13. Short Title.
14. Effective Date.

---

§ 1.   Definition[s].

In this [Act] [Rule]:

(1) "State means a State of the United States, the District of Columbia, the Commonwealth of Puerto Rico, or any territory or insular possession subject to the jurisdiction of the United States.

[(2) "Tribe" means a tribe, band, or village of native Americans which is recognized by federal law or formally acknowledged by a State.]

Comment

A section containing definitions was not part of the 1967 Act. The definition of "State" is consistent with that used in other Uniform Acts.

The section affords States the option of authorizing a state court to certify questions to a tribal court or answer questions from a tribal court. However, it does not purport to authorize tribal courts to certify or answer questions. Tribal law determines whether the tribal court may certify question to a state court or answer a question from a state court. A Tribe can adopt this Act as enabling legislation by simply replacing references to "this State" with "this Tribe" and by substituting the name of its highest court for the "Supreme Court" in Sections 2 and 3.

The definition of "Tribe" is broad and is intended to include both Native American tribes in the technical sense of that term and other Native American governmental units that perform functions similar to a tribe. The option of limiting the definition of "tribes" to those listed in 25 C.F.R. Part 2 was rejected because that list does not include certain Native American governmental units that have existing court systems.

§ 2.   Power to Certify.

The [Supreme Court] [or an intermediate appellate court] of this State, on the motion of a party to pending litigation or its own motion, may certify a question of law to the highest court of another State [or of a tribe] [or of Canada, a Canadian province or territory, Mexico, or a Mexican state] if:

(1)   the pending litigation involves a question to be decided under the law of the other jurisdiction;

(2)   the answer to the question may be determinative of an issue in the pending litigation; and

(3)   the question is one for which an answer is not provided by a controlling appellate decision, constitutional provision, or statute of the other jurisdiction.

Comment

This section replaces Section 8 of the 1967 Act. This revision organizes the Act so that the Power to Certify is set forth prior to the Power to Answer which makes the order of the Act easier to follow. Although limiting the power to certify to the highest court of a State would reduce the number of courts that could certify and correspondingly reduce the number of certified questions, the bracketed language from the 1967 Act authorizing certification by intermediate appellate courts is retained. The receiving court has the discretion to accept or reject a certified question and can use this power to avoid being burdened by an excessive number of certified questions.

As noted in the Comment to Section 1, this section affords States the option of permitting certification of a question of tribal law to a tribal court having the power to answer such questions.

Also included as an option is the bracketed language in this section and in Section 3 permitting certification to and from Canada, a Canadian province or territory, Mexico or a Mexican state. Because the concept of certification to and from international tribunals and courts of other nations still presents numerous uncertainties, this section does not include such other tribunals and courts at this time. Obviously, the enacting State is free to include any other courts it may choose.

The provisions of Section 8 of the 1967 Act have been revised to make it clear that certification is appropriate only when there is no "controlling constitutional provision, statute or appellate decision" in the receiving State. This language replaces the term "controlling precedents" as used in the 1967 Act.

The 1967 Act's standard that a question may be certified if it "may be determinative of the cause" was revised to require that it "may be determinative of an issue in the pending litigation." A stricter standard requiring that the question "must be" or "is" determinative of the issue or the cause was rejected due to concerns that a "must be" or "is" standard would spawn satellite controversies over whether the question was properly certified in light of the ultimate outcome of the underlying litigation.

§ 3.   Power to Answer.

The [Supreme Court] of this State may answer a question of law certified to it by a court of the United States or by [an appellate] [the highest] court of another State [or of a tribe] [or of Canada, a Canadian province or territory, Mexico, or a Mexican state], if the answer may be determinative of an issue in pending litigation in the certifying court and there is no controlling appellate decision, constitutional provision, or statute of this State.

Comment

This section replaces Section 1 of the 1967 Act. Revisions were made to this section to make it consistent with the "Power to Certify" section. The existence of a controlling constitutional provision, statute or appellate decision in the receiving State is a barrier to answering a certified question.

This section has been revised to replace the previous list of federal courts with the term "a court of the United States." This is intended to permit a court in a State adopting the section to answer questions certified by any United States court including bankruptcy courts. Ultimately, the receiving court retains the power to accept or reject a certified question so that it can control its docket even though the number of courts from whom it may receive a certified question has been expanded.

In dealing with the phrase "[an appellate] [the highest] court of another State . . ." appearing in this section, an adopting jurisdiction should select one or the other of the bracketed alternatives. This Act seeks to promote the widest possible use of the certification process in order to promote judicial economy and the proper application of a particular jurisdiction's law in a foreign forum. For this reason, it is suggested that the first alternative be adopted. The term "appellate court" here contemplates any appellate court that has the ability to issue an officially published opinion with precedential effect in a jurisdiction; the term would not include, for example, a general trial court that has appellate jurisdiction from a limited trial court but whose rulings are not officially reported as precedent.

In view of the discretion vested by the Act in the receiving court to accept or reject questions, a reciprocity requirement is not included in the Act. However, in determining whether to accept a certified question, the receiving court may consider among other factors, whether the highest appellate court of the State from which the certification order is issued has authority to answer a certified question of law from an appellate court of the receiving State under essentially similar provisions.

§ 4.   Power to Reformulate Question.

The [Supreme Court] of this State may reformulate a question of law certified to it.

Comment

This section is new and authorizes the receiving court to "reformulate" the certified question. Requiring a question to be answered precisely as it is certified imposes a counterproductive rigidity that could decrease the utility of the answer received. Permitting the receiving court to amend the certified question freely may also adversely affect the utility of the answer and result in the issuance of an advisory opinion. The term "reformulate" is intended to connote a retention of the specific terms and concepts of the question while allowing some flexibility in restating the question in light of the justiciable controversy pending before the certifying court.

§ 5.   Certification Order; Record.

The court certifying a question of law to the [Supreme Court] of this State shall issue a certification order and forward it to the [Supreme Court] of this State. Before responding to a certified question, the [Supreme Court] of this State may require the certifying court to deliver all or part of its record to the [Supreme Court] of this State.

Comment

This section replaces Section 4 of the 1967 Act. The title of the section has been amended to indicate that the section deals not only with the issuance of the order but also with the handling of the record. The first sentence is deliberately less specific so as to accommodate different procedures that may exist in the courts of the various States.

§ 6.   Contents of Certification Order.

(a)   A certification order must contain:

(1)   the question of law to be answered;

(2)   the facts relevant to the question, showing fully the nature of the controversy out of which the question arose;

(3)   a statement acknowledging that the [Supreme Court] of this State, acting as the receiving court, may reformulate the question; and

(4)   the names and addresses of counsel of record and parties appearing without counsel.

(b)   If the parties cannot agree upon a statement of facts, the certifying court shall determine the relevant facts and state them as a part of its certification order.

Comment

This section replaces Section 3 of the 1967 Act. It makes three changes. First, it provides that the order must expressly permit the receiving court to reformulate the question certified to it. Second, the new section requires that the certification order state the names and addresses of counsel of record and of unrepresented parties. This is intended for the convenience of the receiving court. Third, it requires the parties to attempt to agree on a statement of facts to be included in the certification order and requires the certifying court to determine the relevant facts and state them if the parties cannot agree.

This section applies to certification orders being issued to an adopting jurisdiction. Under the second sentence of Section 8 of this Act, the contents required in a certification order being sent by an adopting jurisdiction to another jurisdiction are governed by the rules and statutes of that receiving forum.

§ 7.   Notice; Response.

The [Supreme Court] of this State, acting as a receiving court, shall notify the certifying court of acceptance or rejection of the question and, in accordance with notions of comity and fairness, respond to an accepted certified question as soon as practicable.

Comment

This section is new and is intended to promote communication between the receiving and certifying court and to urge the receiving court to afford priority to answering certified questions of law consistent with notions of comity and fairness. The receiving court, may, but is not obligated to, advise the certifying court of the reasons for a rejection.

§ 8.   Procedures.

After the [Supreme Court] of this State has accepted a certified question, proceedings are governed by [the rules and statutes governing briefs, arguments, and other appellate procedures]. Procedures for certification from this State to a receiving court are those provided in the rules and statutes of the receiving forum.

Comment

This section replaces Sections 6 and 9 of the 1967 Act.

§ 9.   Opinion.

The [Supreme Court] of this State shall state in a written opinion the law answering the certified question and send a copy of the opinion to the certifying court, counsel of record, and parties appearing without counsel.

Comment

This section is substantively the same as Section 7 of the 1967 Act. The Act contemplates an officially published opinion which will have precedential effect in the receiving State.

§ 10.   Cost of Certification.

Fees and costs are the same as in [civil appeals] docketed before the [Supreme Court] of this State and must be equally divided between the parties unless otherwise ordered by the certifying court.

Comment

This section is substantively unchanged from Section 5 of the 1967 Act.

§ 11.   Severability.

If any provision of this [Act] [Rule] or its application to any person or circumstance is held invalid, the invalidity does not affect other provisions or applications of this [Act] [Rule] which can be given effect without the invalid provision or application, and to this end the provisions of this [Act] [Rule] are severable.

Comment

This section is substantively the same as Section 10 of the 1967 Act.

§ 12. Uniformity of Application and Construction.

This [Act] [Rule] shall be applied and construed to effectuate its general purpose to make uniform law with respect to the subject of the [Act] [Rule] among States [enacting] [adopting] it.

Comment

This section is substantively the same as Section 11 of the 1967 Act.

§ 13. Short Title.

This [Act] [Rule] may be cited as the Uniform Certification of Questions of Law [Act] [Rule] (1995).

Comment

This section is substantively the same as Section 12 of the 1967 Act.

§ 14. Effective Date.

This [Act] [Rule] takes effect on _____.

Comment

This section is substantively the same as Section 13 of the 1967 Act.

REVISED UNIFORM ENFORCEMENT OF FOREIGN JUDGMENTS ACT*
1964 REVISED ACT

Historical Note

The Revised Uniform Enforcement of Foreign Judgments Act was approved by the National Conference of commissioners on Uniform State Laws, and the American Bar Association, in 1964. The original Act, as adopted in 1948, is set out following this Revised Act.

PREFATORY NOTE

Court congestion is a problem common to all states. Overcrowded dockets, overworked judges and court officials, with attendant delays, inevitably tend to lower standards for the administration of justice. One of the things that contributes to calendar congestion is the Federal necessity of giving full faith and credit to the judgments of courts of other states. U.S. Const. art. IV, § 1. While there is no constitutional requirement that a debtor who has had a full due process trial in one state need be given a second full scale trial on the judgment in another state, this is the only course generally available to creditors. The usual practice requires that an action be commenced on the foreign judgment. The full procedural requirements apply to the second action.

In 1948 the National Conference of Commissioners on Uniform State Laws approved the original Uniform Enforcement of Foreign Judgments Act. This act was a distinct advance over the usual method. It provided a summary judgment procedure for actions on foreign judgments. Even this advance, however, fell far short of the method provided by Congress in 1948 for the inter-district enforcement of the judgments of the Federal District Courts. 28 U.S.C., § 1963. Further, widespread adoption by the states of some form of the Federal Rules of Civil Procedure which include regular summary judgment practice made special summary judgment acts superfluous.

This 1964 revision of the Uniform Enforcement of Foreign Judgments Act adopts the practice which, in substance, is used in Federal courts. It provides the enacting state with a speedy and economical method of doing that which it is required to do by the Constitution of the United States. It also relieves creditors and debtors of the additional cost and harassment of further litigation which would otherwise be incident to the enforcement of the foreign judgment. This act offers the states a chance to achieve uniformity in a field where uniformity is highly desirable. Its enactment by the states should forestall Federal legislation in this field.

---

§ 1.   [Definition.]

In this Act "foreign judgment" means any judgment, decree, or order of a court of the United States or of any other court which is entitled to full faith and credit in this state.

---

* [This model act has been enacted every state except California and Vermont. The District of Columbia and the U.S. Virgin Islands have enacted this model act as well. *See* www.uniformlaws.org for the most recent enactment status. Ed.]

§ 2.   [Filing and Status of Foreign Judgments.]

A copy of any foreign judgment authenticated in accordance with the act of Congress or the statutes of this state may be filed in the office of the Clerk of any [District Court of any city or county] of this state. The Clerk shall treat the foreign judgment in the same manner as a judgment of the [District Court of any city or county] of this state. A judgment so filed has the same effect and is subject to the same procedures, defenses and proceedings for reopening, vacating, or staying as a judgment of a [District Court of any city or county] of this state and may be enforced or satisfied in like manner.

§ 3.   [Notice of Filing.]

(a)   At the time of the filing of the foreign judgment, the judgment creditor or his lawyer shall make and file with the Clerk of Court an affidavit setting forth the name and last known post office address of the judgment debtor, and the judgment creditor.

(b)   Promptly upon the filing of the foreign judgment and the affidavit, the Clerk shall mail notice of the filing of the foreign judgment to the judgment debtor at the address given and shall make a note of the mailing in the docket. The notice shall include the name and post office address of the judgment creditor and the judgment creditor's lawyer, if any, in this state. In addition, the judgment creditor may mail a notice of the filing of the judgment to the judgment debtor and may file proof of mailing with the Clerk. Lack of mailing notice of filing by the Clerk shall not affect the enforcement proceedings if proof of mailing by the judgment creditor has been filed.

[(c)   No execution or other process for enforcement of a foreign judgment filed hereunder shall issue until [ ] days after the date the judgment is filed.]

§ 4.   [Stay.]

(a)   If the judgment debtor shows the [District Court of any city or county] that an appeal from the foreign judgment is pending or will be taken, or that a stay of execution has been granted, the court shall stay enforcement of the foreign judgment until the appeal is concluded, the time for appeal expires, or the stay of execution expires or is vacated, upon proof that the judgment debtor has furnished the security for the satisfaction of the judgment required by the state in which it was rendered.

(b)   If the judgment debtor shows the [District Court of any city or county] any ground upon which enforcement of a judgment of any [District Court of any city or county] of this state would be stayed, the court shall stay enforcement of the foreign judgment for an appropriate period, upon requiring the same security for satisfaction of the judgment which is required in this state.

§ 5.   [Fees.]

Any person filing a foreign judgment shall pay to the Clerk of Court _____ dollars. Fees for docketing, transcription or other enforcement proceedings shall be as provided for judgments of the [District Court of any city or county of this state].

§ 6.   [Optional Procedure.]

The right of a judgment creditor to bring an action to enforce his judgment instead of proceeding under this Act remains unimpaired.

§ 7.   [Uniformity of Interpretation.]

This Act shall be so interpreted and construed as to effectuate its general purpose to make uniform the law of those states which enact it.

§ 8.   [Short Title.]

This Act may be cited as the Uniform Enforcement of Foreign Judgments Act.

§ 9.   [Repeal.]

The following Acts and parts of Acts are repealed:

(1)

(2)

(3)

§ 10.   [Taking Effect.]

This Act takes effect on _____.

UNIFORM INTERSTATE DEPOSITIONS AND DISCOVERY ACT*

2007 ACT

Prefatory Note

1.   History of Uniform Acts

The National Conference of Commissioners on Uniform State Laws has twice promulgated acts dealing with interstate discovery procedures.

In 1920, the Uniform Foreign Depositions Act was adopted by NCCUSL. The pertinent section of that act provides:

> *Whenever any mandate, writ or commission is issued from any court of record in any foreign jurisdiction, or whenever upon notice or agreement it is required to take the testimony of a witness in this state, the witness may be compelled to appear and testify in the same manner and by the same process as employed for taking testimony in matters pending in the courts of this state.*

The UFDA was originally adopted in 13 states. The states and territories which currently have the act include Florida, Georgia, Louisiana, Maryland, Nevada, New Hampshire, Ohio, Oklahoma, South Dakota, Tennessee, Virginia, Wyoming, and the Virgin Islands.

In 1962, the Uniform Interstate and International Procedure Act was adopted by NCCUSL. The act was designed to supercede any previous interstate jurisdiction acts, including the UFDA, and was more extensive than the UFDA, having provisions on personal jurisdiction, service methods, deposition methods, and other topics. Section 3.02(a) of the act provides:

> *[A court][The _____ court] of this state may order a person who is domiciled or is found within this state to give his testimony or statement or to produce documents or other things for use in a proceeding in a tribunal outside this state. The order may be made upon the application of any interested person or in response to a letter rogatory and may prescribe the practice and procedure, which may be wholly or in part the practice and procedure of the tribunal outside this state, for taking the testimony or statement or producing the documents or other things. To the extent that the order does not prescribe otherwise, the practice and procedure shall be in accordance with that of the court of this state issuing the order. The order may direct that the testimony or statement be given, or document or other thing produced, before a person appointed by the court. The person appointed shall have power to administer any necessary oath.*

The UIIPA was originally adopted by 6 states. The states, districts, and territories which currently have the act include Arkansas, District of Columbia, Louisiana, Massachusetts, Pennsylvania, and the Virgin Islands.

In 1977 the National Conference of Commissioners on Uniform State Laws withdrew the UIIPA from recommendation "due to its being obsolete." Until now, no other uniform act for interstate depositions has been proposed.

2.   Common issues

While every state has a rule governing foreign depositions, those rules are hardly uniform. These differences are extensively detailed in *Interstate Deposition Statutes: Survey and Analysis*, 11 U. Balt. L. Rev 1, 1981. Some of the more important differences among the various states are the following:

a.   In what kind of proceeding may depositions be taken?

Many states restrict depositions to those that will be used in the "courts" or "judicial proceedings" of the other state. Some states allow depositions for any "proceeding." The UFDA and UIIPA take a similar approach.

---

*   [This model act has been enacted every state except Connecticut, Massachusetts, Missouri, Nebraska, New Hampshire, Oklahoma, Texas, and Wyoming. In 2020, it was introduced for enactment in Missouri. The District of Columbia and the U.S. Virgin Islands have enacted this model act as well. *See* www.uniformlaws.org for the most recent enactment status. Ed.]

APPENDIX A

b.   Who may seek depositions?

A few states limit discovery to only the parties in the action or proceeding. Other states simply use the term "party" without any further qualifier, which may be interpreted broadly to include any interested party. Still other states expressly allow any person who would have the power to take a deposition in the trial state to take a deposition in the discovery state. The UIIPA allows any "interested party" to seek discovery. The UFDA does not state who may seek discovery.

c.   What matters can be covered in a subpoena?

The UFDA expressly applies only to the "testimony" of witnesses. The UIIPA expressly applies to "testimony or documents or other things." Several states follow the UIIPA approach, while others seem to limit production to documents but not physical things, and still others are silent on the subject, although some of those states recognize that the power to produce documents is implicit. Rule 45 of the FRCP is more explicit, and provides that a subpoena may be issued to a witness "to attend and give testimony or to produce and permit inspection and copying of designated books, documents or tangible things in the possession, custody or control of that person, or to permit inspection of premises . . . "

d.   What is the procedure for obtaining a deposition subpoena?

Under the UFDA, a party must file the same notice of deposition that would be used in the trial state and then serve the witness with a subpoena under the law of the trial state. If a motion to compel is necessary, it must be filed in the discovery state (the deponent's home court). Other states require that a notice of deposition be shown to a clerk or judge in the discovery state, after which a subpoena will automatically issue. Still other states require a letter rogatory requesting the trial state to issue a subpoena. Under the UIIPA, either an application or letter rogatory is required. About 20 states require an attorney in the discovery state to file a miscellaneous action to establish jurisdiction over the witness so that the witness can then be subpoenaed.

e.   What is the procedure for serving a deposition subpoena?

The UFDA provides that the witness "may be compelled to appear and testify in the same manner and by the same process and proceeding as may be employed for the purpose of taking testimony in proceedings pending in this state." The UIIPA provides that methods of service includes service "in the manner prescribed by the law of the place in which the service is made for service in that place in an action in any of its courts of general jurisdiction." State rules usually follow the procedure of the UFDA and UIIPA.

f.   Which jurisdiction has power to enforce or quash a subpoena?

Most states give the discovery state power to issue, refuse to issue, or quash a subpoena.

g.   Where can the deponent be deposed?

Some states limit the place where a deposition can be taken to the discovery state, and some limit it to the deponent's home county. The UFDA and UIIPA are silent on this issue.

h.   What witness fees are required?

A few states require the payment of witness fees. While most states are silent on the issue, it is probably assumed that the witness fee rules generally existing in the discovery state apply. These usually include fees and mileage, and are usually required to be paid at the time the witness testifies.

i.   Which jurisdiction's discovery procedure applies?

A significant issue is whether the trial state's or discovery state's discovery procedure controls, and on what issues. The general Restatement rule is that the forum state's (the discovery state's) procedure applies. The UIIPA, as well as many states, provides that the discovery state can use the procedure of either the trial or discovery state, with a presumption for the procedure of the discovery state. Some states reverse this presumption, while others are unclear, and still others are silent on the issue.

Another significant issue is whether the trial state's or discovery state's courts can issue protective orders. Both states have interests: the trial state's courts have an interest in protecting witnesses and litigants from improper practices, and the discovery state's courts have an obvious interest in protecting its residents from unreasonable and overly burdensome discovery requests. Most states expressly or implicitly allow the discovery state's courts to issue protective orders.

     j.   Which jurisdiction's evidence law applies?

Evidentiary disputes usually center on relevance and privilege issues. Most states indicate that the discovery state should rule on all relevance issues. Other states indicate that relevance issues should be resolved before a subpoena issues, which would necessarily mean that such issues be decided by the trial state. If the discovery state makes such determinations, it is unclear which state's evidence law should apply (if there is a difference).

Perhaps the most difficult issues are whether the trial state or discovery state should determine issues of privilege, and which state's privilege law will apply. Here both jurisdictions have important interests: the trial state has an interest in obtaining all information relevant to the lawsuit consistent with its laws, while the discovery state has an interest in protecting its residents from intrusive foreign laws. The Restatement (Second) Conflict of Laws provides that the state which has the "most significant relationship" to the communication at issue applies its laws. The issue is further compounded by the general rule that once the privilege is waived, it is generally waived. If the deponent does not object at the deposition and testifies about privileged communications, the privilege will usually be waived.

3.   This act

A uniform act needs to set forth a procedure that can be easily and efficiently followed, that has a minimum of judicial oversight and intervention, that is cost-effective for the litigants, and is fair to the deponents. And it should be patterned after Rule 45 of the FRCP, which appears to be universally admired by civil litigators for its simplicity and efficiency.

The Drafting Committee believes that the proposed uniform act meets these requirements, should be supported by the various constituencies that have an interest in how interstate discovery is conducted in state courts, and should be adopted by most of the states. The act is simple and efficient: it establishes a simple clerical procedure under which a trial state subpoena can be used to issue a discovery state subpoena. The act has minimal judicial oversight: it eliminates the need for obtaining a commission, letters rogatory, filing a miscellaneous action, or other preliminary steps before obtaining a subpoena in the discovery state. The act is cost effective: it eliminates the need to obtain local counsel in the discovery state to obtain an enforceable subpoena. And the act is fair to deponents: it provides that motions brought to enforce, quash, or modify a subpoena, or for protective orders, shall be brought in the discovery state and will be governed by the discovery state's laws.

UNIFORM INTERSTATE DEPOSITIONS AND DISCOVERY ACT

Section
1.   Short Title.
2.   Definitions.
3.   Issuance of Subpoena.
4.   Service of Subpoena.
5.   Deposition, Production, and Inspection.
6.   Application to Court.
7.   Uniformity of Application and Construction.
8.   Application to Pending Actions.
9.   Effective Date.

---

§ 1.   Short Title.

This [act] may be cited as the Uniform Interstate Depositions and Discovery Act.

§ 2.   Definitions.

In this [act]:

(1)   "Foreign jurisdiction" means a state other than this state.

(2)   "Foreign subpoena" means a subpoena issued under authority of a court of record of a foreign jurisdiction.

(3)   "Person" means an individual, corporation, business trust, estate, trust, partnership, limited liability company, association, joint venture, public corporation, government, or governmental subdivision, agency or instrumentality, or any other legal or commercial entity.

(4)   "State" means a state of the United States, the District of Columbia, Puerto Rico, the United States Virgin Islands, [a federally recognized Indian tribe], or any territory or insular possession subject to the jurisdiction of the United States.

(5)   "Subpoena" means a document, however denominated, issued under authority of a court of record requiring a person to:

(A)   attend and give testimony at a deposition;

(B)   produce and permit inspection and copying of designated books, documents, records, electronically stored information, or tangible things in the possession, custody, or control of the person; or

(C)   permit inspection of premises under the control of the person.

Comment

This Act is limited to discovery in state courts, the District of Columbia, Puerto Rico, the United States Virgin Islands, and the territories of the United States. The committee decided not to extend this Act to include foreign countries including the Canadian provinces. The committee felt that international litigation is sufficiently different and is governed by different principles, so that discovery issues in that arena should be governed by a separate act.

The term "Subpoena" includes a subpoena duces tecum. The description of a subpoena in the Act is based on the language of Rule 45 of the FRCP.

The term "Subpoena" does not include a subpoena for the inspection of a person (subsection (3)(C) is limited to inspection of premises). Medical examinations in a personal injury case, for example, are separately controlled by state discovery rules (the corresponding federal rule is Rule 35 of the FRCP). Since the plaintiff is already subject to the jurisdiction of the trial state, a subpoena is never necessary.

§ 3.   Issuance of Subpoena.

(a)   To request issuance of a subpoena under this section, a party must submit a foreign subpoena to a court of court in the [county, district, circuit, or parish] in which discovery is sought to be conducted in this state. A request for the issuance of a subpoena under this act does not constitute an appearance in the courts of this state.

(b)   When a party submits a foreign subpoena to a clerk of court in this state, the clerk, in accordance with that court's procedure, shall promptly issue a subpoena for service upon the person to which the foreign subpoena is directed.

(c)   A subpoena under subsection (b) must:

(A)   incorporate the terms used in the foreign subpoena; and

(B)   contain or be accompanied by the names, addresses, and telephone numbers of all counsel of record in the proceeding to which the subpoena relates and of any party not represented by counsel.

Comment

The term "Court of Record" was chosen to exclude non-court of record proceedings from the ambit of the Act. The committee concluded that extending the Act to such proceedings as arbitrations would be a significant expansion that might generate resistance to the Act. A "Court of Record" includes anyone who is authorized to issue a subpoena under the laws of that state, which usually includes an attorney of record for a party in the proceeding.

The term "Presented" to a clerk of court includes delivering to or filing. Presenting a subpoena to the clerk of court in the discovery state, so that a subpoena is then issued in the name of the discovery state, is the necessary act that invokes the jurisdiction of the discovery state, which in turn makes the newly issued subpoena both enforceable and challengeable in the discovery state.

The committee envisions the standard procedure under this section will become as follows, using as an example a case filed in Kansas (the trial state) where the witness to be deposed lives in Florida (the discovery state): A lawyer of record for a party in the action pending in Kansas will issue a subpoena in Kansas (the same way lawyers in Kansas routinely issue subpoenas in pending actions). That lawyer will then check with the clerk's office, in the Florida county or district in which the witness to be deposed lives, to obtain a copy of its subpoena form (the clerk's office will usually have a Web page explaining its forms and procedures). The lawyer will then prepare a Florida subpoena so that it has the same terms as the Kansas subpoena. The lawyer will then hire a process server (or local counsel) in Florida, who will take the completed and executed Kansas subpoena and the completed but not yet executed Florida subpoena to the clerk's office in Florida. In addition, the lawyer might prepare a short transmittal letter to accompany the Kansas subpoena, advising the clerk that the Florida subpoena is being sought pursuant to Florida statute ___ (citing the appropriate statute or rule and quoting Sec. 3). The clerk of court, upon being given the Kansas subpoena, will then issue the identical Florida subpoena ("issue" includes signing, stamping, and assigning a case or docket number). The process server (or other agent of the party) will pay any necessary filing fees, and then serve the Florida subpoena on the deponent in accordance with Florida law (which includes any applicable local rules).

The advantages of this process are readily apparent. The act of the clerk of court is ministerial, yet is sufficient to invoke the jurisdiction of the discovery state over the deponent. The only documents that need to be presented to the clerk of court in the discovery state are the subpoena issued in the trial state and the draft subpoena of the discovery state. There is no need to hire local counsel to have the subpoena issued in the discovery state, and there is no need to present the matter to a judge in the discovery state before the subpoena can be issued. In effect, the clerk of court in the discovery state simply reissues the subpoena of the trial state, and the new subpoena is then served on the deponent in accordance with the laws of the discovery state. The process is simple and efficient, costs are kept to a minimum, and local counsel and judicial participation are unnecessary to have the subpoena issued and served in the discovery state.

This Act will not change or repeal the law in those states that still require a commission or letters rogatory to take a deposition in a foreign jurisdiction. The Act does, however, repeal the law in those discovery states that still require a commission or letter rogatory from a trial state before a deposition can be taken in those states. It is the hope of the Conference that this Act will encourage states that still require the use of commissions or letters rogatory to repeal those laws.

The Act requires that, when the subpoena is served, it contain or be accompanied by the names, addresses, and telephone numbers of all counsel of record and of any party not represented by counsel. The committee believes that this requirement imposes no significant burden on the lawyer issuing the subpoena, given that the lawyer already has the obligation to send a notice of deposition to every counsel of record and any unrepresented parties. The benefits in the discovery state, by contrast, are significant. This requirement makes it easy for the deponent (or, as will frequently be the case, the deponent's lawyer) to learn the names of and contact the other lawyers in the case. This requirement can easily be met, since the subpoena will contain or be accompanied by the names, addresses, and telephone numbers of all counsel of record and of any party not represented by counsel (which is the same information that will ordinarily be contained on a notice of deposition and proof of service).

§ 4.   Service of Subpoena.

A subpoena issued by a clerk of court under Section 3 must be served in compliance with [cite applicable rules or statutes of this state for service of subpoena].

§ 5.   Deposition, Production, and Inspection.

[Cite rules or statutes of this state applicable to compliance with subpoenas to attend and give testimony, produce designated books, documents, records, electronically stored information, or tangible things, or permit inspection of premises] apply to subpoenas issued under Section 3.

Comment

The Act requires that the discovery permitted by this section must comply with the laws of the discovery state. The discovery state has a significant interest in these cases in protecting its residents who become non-party witnesses in an action pending in a foreign jurisdiction from any unreasonable or unduly burdensome discovery request. Therefore, the committee believes that the discovery procedure must be the same as it would be if the case had originally been filed in the discovery state.

The committee believes that the fee, if any, for issuing a subpoena should be sufficient to cover only the actual transaction costs, or should be the same as the fee for local deposition subpoenas.

§ 6.   Application to Court.

An application to the court for a protective order or to enforce, quash, or modify a subpoena issued by a clerk of court under Section 3 must comply with the rules or statutes of this state and be submitted to the court in the [county, district, circuit, or parish] in which discovery is to be conducted.

Comment

The act requires that any application to the court for a protective order, or to enforce, quash, or modify a subpoena, or for any other dispute relating to discovery under this Act, must comply with the law of the discovery state. Those laws include the discovery state's procedural, evidentiary, and conflict of laws rules. Again, the discovery state has a significant interest in protecting its residents who become non-party witnesses in an action pending in a foreign jurisdiction from any unreasonable or unduly burdensome discovery requests, and this is easily accomplished by requiring that any discovery motions must be decided under the laws of the discovery state. This protects the deponent by requiring that all applications to the court that directly affect the deponent must be made in the discovery state.

The term "modify" a subpoena means to alter the terms of a subpoena, such as the date, time, or location of a deposition.

Evidentiary issues that may arise, such as objections based on grounds such as relevance or privilege, are best decided in the discovery state under the laws of the discovery state (including its conflict of laws principles).

Nothing in this act limits any party from applying for appropriate relief in the trial state. Applications to the court that affect only the parties to the action can be made in the trial state. For example, any party can apply for an order in the trial state to bar the deposition of the out-of-state deponent on grounds of relevance, and that motion would be made and ruled on before the deposition subpoena is ever presented to the clerk of court in the discovery state.

If a party makes or responds to an application to enforce, quash, or modify a subpoena in the discovery state, the lawyer making or responding to the application must comply with the discovery state's rules governing lawyers appearing in its courts. This act does not change existing state rules governing out-of-state lawyers appearing in its courts. (See Model Rule 5.5 and state rules governing the unauthorized practice of law.)

§ 7. Uniformity of Application and Construction.

In applying and construing this uniform act, consideration must be given to the need to promote uniformity of the law with respect to its subject matter among states that enact it

§ 8. Application to Pending Actions.

This [act] applies to requests for discovery in cases pending on [the effective date of this [act]].

§ 9. Effective Date.

This [act] takes effect _____.

APPENDIX B
CONSTITUTION OF THE UNITED STATES

UNANNOTATED

PREAMBLE

WE THE PEOPLE of the United States, in Order to form a more perfect Union, establish Justice, insure domestic Tranquility, provide for the common defence, promote the general Welfare, and secure the Blessings of Liberty to ourselves and our Posterity, do ordain and establish this CONSTITUTION for the United States of America.

ARTICLE I

§ 1. All legislative Powers herein granted shall be vested in a Congress of the United States, which shall consist of a Senate and House of Representatives.

§ 2. The House of Representatives shall be composed of Members chosen every second Year by the People of the several States, and the Electors in each State shall have the Qualifications requisite for Electors of the most numerous Branch of the State Legislature. No Person shall be a Representative who shall not have attained to the Age of twenty five Years, and been seven Years a Citizen of the United States, and who shall not, when elected, be an Inhabitant of that State in which he shall be chosen. [Representatives and direct Taxes shall be apportioned among the several States which may be included within this Union, according to their respective Numbers, which shall be determined by adding to the whole Number of free Persons, including those bound to Service for a Term of Years, and excluding Indians not taxed, three fifths of all other Persons.][1] The actual Enumeration shall be made within three Years after the first Meeting of the Congress of the United States, and within every subsequent Term of ten Years, in such Manner as they shall by Law direct. The Number of Representatives shall not exceed one for every thirty Thousand, but each State shall have at Least one Representative; and until such enumeration shall be made, the State of New Hampshire shall be entitled to chuse three, Massachusetts eight, Rhode-Island and Providence Plantations one, Connecticut five, New-York six, New Jersey four, Pennsylvania eight, Delaware one, Maryland six, Virginia ten, North Carolina five, South Carolina five, and Georgia three.

When vacancies happen in the Representation from any State, the Executive Authority thereof shall issue Writs of Election to fill such Vacancies.

The House of Representatives shall chuse their Speaker and other Officers; and shall have the sole Power of Impeachment.

§ 3. [The Senate of the United States shall be composed of two Senators from each State, chosen by the Legislature thereof, for six Years; and each Senator shall have one Vote.][2]

Immediately after they shall be assembled in Consequence of the first Election, they shall be divided as equally as may be into three Classes. The Seats of the Senators of the first Class shall be vacated at the Expiration of the second Year, of the second Class at the Expiration of the fourth Year, and of the third Class at the Expiration of the sixth Year, so that one third may be chosen every second Year; [and if Vacancies happen by Resignation, or otherwise, during the Recess of the Legislature of

---

[1] The clause of this paragraph inclosed in brackets was amended, as to the mode of apportionment of representatives among the several states, by the Fourteenth Amendment, § 2, and as to taxes on incomes without apportionment, by the Sixteenth Amendment.

[2] This paragraph, inclosed in brackets, was superseded by the Seventeenth Amendment.

any State, the Executive thereof may make temporary Appointments until the next Meeting of the Legislature, which shall then fill such Vacancies.][3]

No Person shall be a Senator who shall not have attained to the Age of thirty Years, and been nine Years a Citizen of the United States, and who shall not, when elected, be an Inhabitant of that State for which he shall be chosen.

The Vice President of the United States shall be President of the Senate, but shall have no Vote, unless they be equally divided.

The Senate shall chuse their other Officers, and also a President pro tempore, in the Absence of the Vice President, or when he shall exercise the Office of President of the United States.

The Senate shall have the sole Power to try all Impeachments. When sitting for that Purpose, they shall be on Oath or Affirmation. When the President of the United States is tried, the Chief Justice shall preside: And no Person shall be convicted without the Concurrence of two thirds of the Members present.

Judgment in Cases of Impeachment shall not extend further than to removal from Office, and disqualification to hold and enjoy any Office of honor, Trust or Profit under the United States: but the Party convicted shall nevertheless be liable and subject to Indictment, Trial, Judgment and Punishment, according to Law.

§ 4. The Times, Places and Manner of holding Elections for Senators and Representatives, shall be prescribed in each State by the Legislature thereof; but the Congress may at any time by Law make or alter such Regulations, except as to the Places of chusing Senators.

The Congress shall assemble at least once in every Year, and such Meeting shall be on the [first Monday in December],[4] unless they shall by Law appoint a different Day.

§ 5. Each House shall be the Judge of the Elections, Returns and Qualifications of its own Members, and a Majority of each shall constitute a Quorum to do Business; but a smaller Number may adjourn from day to day, and may be authorized to compel the Attendance of absent Members, in such Manner, and under such Penalties as each House may provide.

Each House may determine the Rules of its Proceedings, punish its Members for disorderly Behaviour, and, with the Concurrence of two thirds, expel a Member.

Each House shall keep a Journal of its Proceedings, and from time to time publish the same, excepting such Parts as may in their Judgment require Secrecy; and the Yeas and Nays of the Members of either House on any question shall, at the Desire of one fifth of those Present, be entered on the Journal.

Neither House, during the Session of Congress, shall, without the Consent of the other, adjourn for more than three days, nor to any other Place than that in which the two Houses shall be sitting.

§ 6. The Senators and Representatives shall receive a Compensation for their Services, to be ascertained by Law, and paid out of the Treasury of the United States. They shall in all Cases, except Treason, Felony and Breach of the Peace, be privileged from Arrest during their Attendance at the Session of their respective Houses, and in going to and returning from the same; and for any Speech or Debate in either House, they shall not be questioned in any other Place.

No Senator or Representative shall, during the Time for which he was elected, be appointed to any civil Office under the Authority of the United States, which shall have been created, or the Emoluments whereof shall have been encreased during such time; and no Person holding any Office under the United States, shall be a Member of either House during his Continuance in Office.

---

[3]   The clause of this paragraph inclosed in brackets was superseded by the Seventeenth Amendment.

[4]   The clause of this paragraph inclosed in brackets was superseded by the Twentieth Amendment.

§ 7. All Bills for raising Revenue shall originate in the House of Representatives; but the Senate may propose or concur with Amendments as on other Bills.

Every Bill which shall have passed the House of Representatives and the Senate, shall, before it becomes a Law, be presented to the President of the United States; If he approve he shall sign it, but if not he shall return it, with his Objections to that House in which it shall have originated, who shall enter the Objections at large on their Journal, and proceed to reconsider it. If after such Reconsideration two thirds of that House shall agree to pass the Bill, it shall be sent, together with the Objections, to the other House, by which it shall likewise be reconsidered, and if approved by two thirds of that House, it shall become a Law. But in all such Cases the Votes of both Houses shall be determined by Yeas and Nays, and the Names of the Persons voting for and against the Bill shall be entered on the Journal of each House respectively. If any Bill shall not be returned by the President within ten Days (Sundays excepted) after it shall have been presented to him, the Same shall be a Law, in like Manner as if he had signed it, unless the Congress by their Adjournment prevent its Return, in which Case it shall not be a Law.

Every Order, Resolution, or Vote to which the Concurrence of the Senate and House of Representatives may be necessary (except on a question of Adjournment) shall be presented to the President of the United States; and before the Same shall take Effect, shall be approved by him, or being disapproved by him, shall be repassed by two thirds of the Senate and House of Representatives, according to the Rules and Limitations prescribed in the Case of a Bill.

§ 8. The Congress shall have Power To lay and collect Taxes, Duties, Imposts and Excises, to pay the Debts and provide for the common Defence and general Welfare of the United States; but all Duties, Imposts and Excises shall be uniform throughout the United States;

To borrow Money on the credit of the United States;

To regulate Commerce with foreign Nations, and among the several States, and with the Indian Tribes;

To establish an uniform Rule of Naturalization, and uniform Laws on the subject of Bankruptcies throughout the United States;

To coin Money, regulate the Value thereof, and of foreign Coin, and fix the Standard of Weights and Measures;

To provide for the Punishment of counterfeiting the Securities and current Coin of the United States;

To establish Post Offices and post Roads;

To promote the Progress of Science and useful Arts, by securing for limited Times to Authors and Inventors the exclusive Right to their respective Writings and Discoveries;

To constitute Tribunals inferior to the supreme Court;

To define and punish Piracies and Felonies committed on the high Seas, and Offences against the Law of Nations;

To declare War, grant Letters of Marque and Reprisal, and make Rules concerning Captures on Land and Water;

To raise and support Armies, but no Appropriation of Money to that Use shall be for a longer Term than two Years;

To provide and maintain a Navy;

To make Rules for the Government and Regulation of the land and naval Forces;

To provide for calling forth the Militia to execute the Laws of the Union, suppress Insurrections and repel Invasions;

To provide for organizing, arming, and disciplining, the Militia, and for governing such Part of them as may be employed in the Service of the United States, reserving to the States respectively, the Appointment of the Officers, and the Authority of training the Militia according to the discipline prescribed by Congress;

To exercise exclusive Legislation in all Cases whatsoever, over such District (not exceeding ten Miles square) as may, by Cession of particular States, and the Acceptance of Congress, become the Seat of the Government of the United States, and to exercise like Authority over all Places purchased by the Consent of the Legislature of the State in which the Same shall be, for the Erection of Forts, Magazines, Arsenals, dock-Yards, and other needful Buildings;—And

To make all Laws which shall be necessary and proper for carrying into Execution the foregoing Powers, and all other Powers vested by this Constitution in the Government of the United States, or in any Department or Officer thereof.

§ 9. The Migration or Importation of such Persons as any of the States now existing shall think proper to admit, shall not be prohibited by the Congress prior to the Year one thousand eight hundred and eight, but a Tax or duty may be imposed on such Importation, not exceeding ten dollars for each Person.

The Privilege of the Writ of Habeas Corpus shall not be suspended, unless when in Cases of Rebellion or Invasion the public Safety may require it.

No Bill of Attainder or ex post facto Law shall be passed.

No Capitation, or other direct, Tax shall be laid, unless in Proportion to the Census or Enumeration herein before directed to be taken.[5]

No Tax or Duty shall be laid on Articles exported from any State.

No Preference shall be given by any Regulation of Commerce or Revenue to the Ports of one State over those of another; nor shall Vessels bound to, or from, one State, be obliged to enter, clear, or pay Duties in another.

No Money shall be drawn from the Treasury, but in Consequence of Appropriations made by Law; and a regular Statement and Account of the Receipts and Expenditures of all public Money shall be published from time to time.

No Title of Nobility shall be granted by the United States: And no Person holding any Office of Profit or Trust under them, shall, without the Consent of the Congress, accept of any present, Emolument, Office, or Title, of any kind whatever, from any King, Prince, or foreign State.

§ 10. No State shall enter into any Treaty, Alliance, or Confederation; grant Letters of Marque and Reprisal; coin Money; emit Bills of Credit; make any Thing but gold and silver Coin a Tender in Payment of Debts; pass any Bill of Attainder, ex post facto Law, or Law impairing the Obligation of Contracts, or grant any Title of Nobility.

No State shall, without the Consent of the Congress, lay any Imposts or Duties on Imports or Exports, except what may be absolutely necessary for executing it's inspection Laws: and the net Produce of all Duties and Imposts, laid by any State on Imports or Exports, shall be for the Use of the Treasury of the United States; and all such Laws shall be subject to the Revision and Controul of the Congress.

No State shall, without the Consent of Congress, lay any Duty of Tonnage, keep Troops, or Ships of War in time of Peace, enter into any Agreement or Compact with another State, or with a foreign Power, or engage in War, unless actually invaded, or in such imminent Danger as will not admit of delay.

---

[5]   This paragraph has been affected by the Sixteenth Amendment.

ARTICLE II

§ 1. The executive Power shall be vested in a President of the United States of America. He shall hold his Office during the Term of four Years, and, together with the Vice President, chosen for the same Term, be elected, as follows:

Each State shall appoint, in such Manner as the Legislature thereof may direct, a Number of Electors, equal to the whole Number of Senators and Representatives to which the State may be entitled in the Congress: but no Senator or Representative, or Person holding an Office of Trust or Profit under the United States, shall be appointed an Elector.

[The Electors shall meet in their respective States, and vote by Ballot for two Persons, of whom one at least shall not be an Inhabitant of the same State with themselves. And they shall make a List of all the Persons voted for, and of the Number of Votes for each; which List they shall sign and certify, and transmit sealed to the Seat of the Government of the United States, directed to the President of the Senate. The President of the Senate shall, in the Presence of the Senate and House of Representatives, open all the Certificates, and the Votes shall then be counted. The Person having the greatest Number of Votes shall be the President, if such Number be a Majority of the whole Number of Electors appointed; and if there be more than one who have such Majority, and have an equal Number of Votes, then the House of Representatives shall immediately chuse by Ballot one of them for President; and if no Person have a Majority, then from the five highest on the List the said House shall in like Manner chuse the President. But in chusing the President, the Votes shall be taken by States, the Representation from each State having one Vote; A quorum for this Purpose shall consist of a Member or Members from two thirds of the States, and a Majority of all the States shall be necessary to a Choice. In every Case, after the Choice of the President, the Person having the greatest Number of Votes of the Electors shall be the Vice President. But if there should remain two or more who have equal Votes, the Senate shall chuse from them by Ballot the Vice President.][6]

The Congress may determine the Time of chusing the Electors, and the Day on which they shall give their Votes; which Day shall be the same throughout the United States.

No Person except a natural born Citizen, or a Citizen of the United States, at the time of the Adoption of this Constitution, shall be eligible to the Office of President; neither shall any Person be eligible to that Office who shall not have attained to the Age of thirty five Years, and been fourteen Years a Resident within the United States.

In Case of the Removal of the President from Office, or of his Death, Resignation, or Inability to discharge the Powers and Duties of the said Office, the Same shall devolve on the Vice President, and the Congress may by Law provide for the Case of Removal, Death, Resignation or Inability, both of the President and Vice President, declaring what Officer shall then act as President, and such Officer shall act accordingly, until the Disability be removed, or a President shall be elected.

The President shall, at stated Times, receive for his Services, a Compensation, which shall neither be increased nor diminished during the Period for which he shall have been elected, and he shall not receive within that Period any other Emolument from the United States, or any of them.

Before he enter on the Execution of his Office, he shall take the following Oath or Affirmation:—"I do solemnly swear (or affirm) that I will faithfully execute the Office of President of the United States, and will to the best of my Ability, preserve, protect and defend the Constitution of the United States."

§ 2. The President shall be Commander in Chief of the Army and Navy of the United States, and of the Militia of the several States, when called into the actual Service of the United States; he may require the Opinion, in writing, of the principal Officer in each of the executive Departments, upon any Subject relating to the Duties of their respective Offices, and he shall have Power to grant Reprieves and Pardons for Offences against the United States, except in Cases of Impeachment.

---

[6]   This paragraph, inclosed in brackets, was superseded by the Twelfth Amendment, post.

He shall have Power, by and with the Advice and Consent of the Senate, to make Treaties, provided two thirds of the Senators present concur; and he shall nominate, and by and with the Advice and Consent of the Senate, shall appoint Ambassadors, other public Ministers and Consuls, Judges of the supreme Court, and all other Officers of the United States, whose Appointments are not herein otherwise provided for, and which shall be established by Law: but the Congress may by Law vest the Appointment of such inferior Officers, as they think proper, in the President alone, in the Courts of Law, or in the Heads of Departments.

The President shall have Power to fill up all Vacancies that may happen during the Recess of the Senate, by granting Commissions which shall expire at the End of their next Session.

§ 3. He shall from time to time give to the Congress Information of the State of the Union, and recommend to their Consideration such Measures as he shall judge necessary and expedient; he may, on extraordinary Occasions, convene both Houses, or either of them, and in Case of Disagreement between them, with Respect to the Time of Adjournment, he may adjourn them to such Time as he shall think proper; he shall receive Ambassadors and other public Ministers; he shall take Care that the Laws be faithfully executed, and shall Commission all the Officers of the United States.

§ 4. The President, Vice President and all civil Officers of the United States, shall be removed from Office on Impeachment for, and Conviction of, Treason, Bribery, or other high Crimes and Misdemeanors.

ARTICLE III

§ 1. The judicial Power of the United States, shall be vested in one supreme Court, and in such inferior Courts as the Congress may from time to time ordain and establish. The Judges, both of the supreme and inferior Courts, shall hold their Offices during good Behaviour, and shall, at stated Times, receive for their Services, a Compensation, which shall not be diminished during their Continuance in Office.

§ 2. The judicial Power shall extend to all Cases, in Law and Equity, arising under this Constitution, the Laws of the United States, and Treaties made, or which shall be made, under their Authority;—to all Cases affecting Ambassadors, other public Ministers and Consuls;—to all Cases of admiralty and maritime Jurisdiction;—to Controversies to which the United States shall be a Party;—to Controversies between two or more States;—between a State and Citizens of another State;—between citizens of different States;—between Citizens of the same State claiming Lands under Grants of different States, and between a State, or the Citizens thereof, and foreign States, Citizens or Subjects.[7]

In all Cases affecting Ambassadors, other public Ministers and Consuls, and those in which a State shall be Party, the supreme Court shall have original Jurisdiction. In all the other Cases before mentioned, the supreme Court shall have appellate Jurisdiction, both as to Law and Fact, with such Exceptions, and under such Regulations as the Congress shall make.

The Trial of all Crimes, except in Cases of Impeachment, shall be by Jury; and such Trial shall be held in the State where the said Crimes shall have been committed; but when not committed within any State, the Trial shall be at such Place or Places as the Congress may by Law have directed.

§ 3. Treason against the United States, shall consist only in levying War against them, or in adhering to their Enemies, giving them Aid and Comfort. No Person shall be convicted of Treason unless on the Testimony of two Witnesses to the same overt Act, or on Confession in open Court.

The Congress shall have Power to declare the Punishment of Treason, but no Attainder of Treason shall work Corruption of Blood, or Forfeiture except during the Life of the Person attainted.

---

[7] This section has been affected by the Eleventh Amendment.

ARTICLE IV

§ 1. Full Faith and Credit shall be given in each State to the public Acts, Records, and judicial Proceedings of every other State. And the Congress may by general Laws prescribe the Manner in which such Acts, Records and Proceedings shall be proved, and the Effect thereof.

§ 2. The Citizens of each State shall be entitled to all Privileges and Immunities of Citizens in the several States.

A Person charged in any State with Treason, Felony, or other Crime, who shall flee from Justice, and be found in another State, shall on Demand of the executive Authority of the State from which he fled, be delivered up, to be removed to the State having Jurisdiction of the Crime.

No Person held to Service or Labour in one State, under the Laws thereof, escaping into another, shall, in Consequence of any Law or Regulation therein, be discharged from such Service or Labour, but shall be delivered up on Claim of the Party to whom such Service or Labour may be due.[8]

§ 3. New States may be admitted by the Congress into this Union; but no new State shall be formed or erected within the Jurisdiction of any other State; nor any State be formed by the Junction of two or more States, or Parts of States, without the Consent of the Legislatures of the States concerned as well as of the Congress.

The Congress shall have Power to dispose of and make all needful Rules and Regulations respecting the Territory or other Property belonging to the United States; and nothing in this Constitution shall be so construed as to Prejudice any Claims of the United States, or of any particular State.

§ 4. The United States shall guarantee to every State in this Union a Republican Form of Government, and shall protect each of them against Invasion; and on Application of the Legislature, or of the Executive (when the Legislature cannot be convened) against domestic Violence.

ARTICLE V

The Congress, whenever two thirds of both Houses shall deem it necessary, shall propose Amendments to this Constitution, or, on the Application of the Legislatures of two thirds of the several States, shall call a Convention for proposing Amendments, which, in either Case, shall be valid to all Intents and Purposes, as Part of this Constitution, when ratified by the Legislatures of three fourths of the several States, or by Conventions in three fourths thereof, as the one or the other Mode of Ratification may be proposed by the Congress; Provided that no Amendment which may be made prior to the Year One thousand eight hundred and eight shall in any Manner affect the first and fourth Clauses in the Ninth Section of the first Article; and that no State, without its Consent, shall be deprived of its equal Suffrage in the Senate.

ARTICLE VI

All Debts contracted and Engagements entered into, before the Adoption of this Constitution, shall be as valid against the United States under this Constitution, as under the Confederation.

This Constitution, and the Laws of the United States which shall be made in Pursuance thereof; and all Treaties made, or which shall be made, under the Authority of the United States, shall be the supreme Law of the Land; and the Judges in every State shall be bound thereby, any Thing in the Constitution or Laws of any State to the Contrary notwithstanding.

The Senators and Representatives before mentioned, and the Members of the several State Legislatures, and all executive and judicial Officers, both of the United States and of the several States, shall be bound by Oath or Affirmation, to support this Constitution; but no religious Test shall ever be required as a Qualification to any Office or public Trust under the United States.

---

[8]   This section has been affected by the Thirteenth Amendment.

APPENDIX B

ARTICLE VII

The Ratification of the Conventions of nine States, shall be sufficient for the Establishment of this Constitution between the States so ratifying the Same.

DONE in Convention by the Unanimous Consent of the States present the Seventeenth Day of September in the Year of Our Lord one thousand seven hundred and Eighty seven and of the Independence of the United States of America the Twelfth. IN WITNESS whereof We have hereunto subscribed our Names.

Go. WASHINGTON—Presidt.
and deputy from Virginia

Attest WILLIAM JACKSON *Secretary*

Delaware

GEO: READ   RICHARD BASSETT

GUNNING BEDFORD jun   JACO: BROOM

JOHN DICKINSON

Maryland

JAMES MCHENRY   DANL CARROLL

DAN OF ST THOS. JENIFER

Virginia

JOHN BLAIR—   JAMES MADISON JR.

North Carolina

WM. BLOUNT   HU WILLIAMSON

RICHD. DOBBS SPAIGHT

South Carolina

J. RUTLEDGE   CHARLES PINCKNEY

CHARLES COTESWORTH PINCKNEY   PIERCE BUTLER

Georgia

WILLIAM FEW   ABR BALDWIN

New Hampshire

JOHN LANGDON   NICHOLAS GILMAN

Massachusetts

NATHANIEL GORHAM   RUFUS KING

Connecticut

WM. SAML. JOHNSON   ROGER SHERMAN

New York

ALEXANDER HAMILTON

New Jersey

WIL: LIVINGSTON   WM. PATERSON

DAVID BREARLEY   JONA: DAYTON

Pennsylvania

B Franklin	Thos. FitzSimons
Thomas Mifflin	Jared Ingersoll
Robt Morris	James Wilson
Geo. Clymer	Gouv Morris

Articles in Addition to, and Amendment of, the Constitution of the United States of America, Proposed by Congress, and Ratified by the Legislatures of the Several States Pursuant to the Fifth Article of the Original Constitution

AMENDMENT I

Congress shall make no law respecting an establishment of religion, or prohibiting the free exercise thereof; or abridging the freedom of speech, or of the press; or the right of the people peaceably to assemble, and to petition the Government for a redress of grievances.

AMENDMENT II

A well regulated Militia, being necessary to the security of a free State, the right of the people to keep and bear Arms, shall not be infringed.

AMENDMENT III

No Soldier shall, in time of peace be quartered in any house, without the consent of the Owner, nor in time of war, but in a manner to be prescribed by law.

AMENDMENT IV

The right of the people to be secure in their persons, houses, papers, and effects, against unreasonable searches and seizures, shall not be violated, and no Warrants shall issue, but upon probable cause, supported by Oath or affirmation, and particularly describing the place to be searched, and the persons or things to be seized.

AMENDMENT V

No person shall be held to answer for a capital, or otherwise infamous crime, unless on a presentment or indictment of a Grand Jury, except in cases arising in the land or naval forces, or in the Militia, when in actual service in time of War or public danger; nor shall any person be subject for the same offence to be twice put in jeopardy of life or limb; nor shall be compelled in any criminal case to be a witness against himself, nor be deprived of life, liberty, or property, without due process of law; nor shall private property be taken for public use, without just compensation.

AMENDMENT VI

In all criminal prosecutions, the accused shall enjoy the right to a speedy and public trial, by an impartial jury of the State and district wherein the crime shall have been committed, which district shall have been previously ascertained by law, and to be informed of the nature and cause of the accusation; to be confronted with the witnesses against him; to have compulsory process for obtaining witnesses in his favor, and to have the Assistance of Counsel for his defence.

APPENDIX B

AMENDMENT VII

In Suits at common law, where the value in controversy shall exceed twenty dollars, the right of trial by jury shall be preserved, and no fact tried by a jury, shall be otherwise reexamined in any Court of the United States, than according to the rules of the common law.

AMENDMENT VIII

Excessive bail shall not be required, nor excessive fines imposed, nor cruel and unusual punishments inflicted.

AMENDMENT IX

The enumeration in the Constitution, of certain rights, shall not be construed to deny or disparage others retained by the people.

AMENDMENT X

The powers not delegated to the United States by the Constitution, nor prohibited by it to the States, are reserved to the States respectively, or to the people.

AMENDMENT XI

The Judicial power of the United States shall not be construed to extend to any suit in law or equity, commenced or prosecuted against one of the United States by Citizens of another State, or by Citizens or Subjects of any Foreign State.

AMENDMENT XII

The Electors shall meet in their respective states, and vote by ballot for President and Vice-President, one of whom, at least, shall not be an inhabitant of the same state with themselves; they shall name in their ballots the person voted for as President, and in distinct ballots the person voted for as Vice-President, and they shall make distinct lists of all persons voted for as President, and of all persons voted for as Vice-President, and of the number of votes for each, which lists they shall sign and certify, and transmit sealed to the seat of the government of the United States, directed to the President of the Senate;—The President of the Senate shall, in the presence of the Senate and House of Representatives, open all the certificates and the votes shall then be counted;—The person having the greatest number of votes for President, shall be the President, if such number be a majority of the whole number of Electors appointed; and if no person have such majority, then from the persons having the highest numbers not exceeding three on the list of those voted for as President, the House of Representatives shall choose immediately, by ballot, the President. But in choosing the President, the votes shall be taken by states, the representation from each state having one vote; a quorum for this purpose shall consist of a member or members from two-thirds of the states, and a majority of all the states shall be necessary to a choice. And if the House of Representatives shall not choose a President whenever the right of choice shall devolve upon them, before the fourth day of March next following, then the Vice-President shall act as President, as in the case of the death or other constitutional disability of the President.—The person having the greatest number of votes as Vice-President, shall be the Vice-President, if such number be a majority of the whole number of Electors appointed, and if no person have a majority, then from the two highest numbers on the list, the Senate shall choose the Vice-President; a quorum for the purpose shall consist of two-thirds of the whole number of Senators, and a majority of the whole number shall be necessary to a choice. But no person constitutionally ineligible to the office of President shall be eligible to that of Vice-President of the United States.[9]

---

[9] This Amendment was affected by the Twentieth Amendment.

AMENDMENT XIII

§ 1. Neither slavery nor involuntary servitude, except as a punishment for crime whereof the party shall have been duly convicted, shall exist within the United States, or any place subject to their jurisdiction.

§ 2. Congress shall have power to enforce this article by appropriate legislation.

AMENDMENT XIV

§ 1. All persons born or naturalized in the United States, and subject to the jurisdiction thereof, are citizens of the United States and of the State wherein they reside. No State shall make or enforce any law which shall abridge the privileges or immunities of citizens of the United States; nor shall any State deprive any person of life, liberty, or property, without due process of law; nor deny to any person within its jurisdiction the equal protection of the laws.

§ 2. Representatives shall be apportioned among the several States according to their respective numbers, counting the whole number of persons in each State, excluding Indians not taxed. But when the right to vote at any election for the choice of electors for President and Vice President of the United States, Representatives in Congress, the Executive and Judicial officers of a State, or the members of the Legislature thereof, is denied to any of the male inhabitants of such State, being twenty-one years of age, and citizens of the United States, or in any way abridged, except for participation in rebellion, or other crime, the basis of representation therein shall be reduced in the proportion which the number of such male citizens shall bear to the whole number of male citizens twenty-one years of age in such State.

§ 3. No person shall be a Senator or Representative in Congress, or elector of President and Vice President, or hold any office, civil or military, under the United States, or under any State, who, having previously taken an oath, as a member of Congress, or as an officer of the United States, or as a member of any State legislature, or as an executive or judicial officer of any State, to support the Constitution of the United States, shall have engaged in insurrection or rebellion against the same, or given aid or comfort to the enemies thereof. But Congress may by a vote of two-thirds of each House, remove such disability.

§ 4. The validity of the public debt of the United States, authorized by law, including debts incurred for payment of pensions and bounties for services in suppressing insurrection or rebellion, shall not be questioned. But neither the United States nor any State shall assume or pay any debt or obligation incurred in aid of insurrection or rebellion against the United States, or any claim for the loss or emancipation of any slave; but all such debts, obligations and claims shall be held illegal and void.

§ 5. The Congress shall have power to enforce, by appropriate legislation, the provisions of this article.

AMENDMENT XV

§ 1. The right of citizens of the United States to vote shall not be denied or abridged by the United States or by any State on account of race, color, or previous condition of servitude.

§ 2. The Congress shall have power to enforce this article by appropriate legislation.

AMENDMENT XVI

The Congress shall have power to lay and collect taxes on incomes, from whatever source derived, without apportionment among the several States, and without regard to any census or enumeration.

AMENDMENT XVII

The Senate of the United States shall be composed of two Senators from each state, elected by the people thereof, for six years; and each Senator shall have one vote. The electors in each State shall have the qualifications requisite for electors of the most numerous branch of the State legislatures.

When vacancies happen in the representation of any State in the Senate, the executive authority of such State shall issue writs of election to fill such vacancies: *Provided,* That the legislature of any State may empower the executive thereof to make temporary appointments until the people fill the vacancies by election as the legislature may direct.

This amendment shall not be so construed as to affect the election or term of any Senator chosen before it becomes valid as part of the Constitution.

AMENDMENT XVIII [Repealed. See Article XXI]

§ 1. After one year from the ratification of this article the manufacture, sale, or transportation of intoxicating liquors within, the importation thereof into, or the exportation thereof from the United States and all territory subject to the jurisdiction thereof for beverage purposes is hereby prohibited.

§ 2. The Congress and the several States shall have concurrent power to enforce this article by appropriate legislation.

§ 3. This article shall be inoperative unless it shall have been ratified as an amendment to the Constitution by the legislatures of the several States, as provided in the Constitution, within seven years from the date of the submission hereof to the States by the Congress.

AMENDMENT XIX

The right of citizens of the United States to vote shall not be denied or abridged by the United States or by any State on account of sex.

Congress shall have power to enforce this article by appropriate legislation.

AMENDMENT XX

§ 1. The terms of the President and Vice President shall end at noon on the 20th day of January, and the terms of Senators and Representatives at noon on the 3d day of January, of the years in which such terms would have ended if this article had not been ratified; and the terms of their successors shall then begin.

§ 2. The Congress shall assemble at least once in every year, and such meeting shall begin at noon on the 3d day of January, unless they shall by law appoint a different day.

§ 3. If, at the time fixed for the beginning of the term of the President, the President elect shall have died, the Vice President elect shall become President. If a President shall not have been chosen before the time fixed for the beginning of his term, or if the President elect shall have failed to qualify, then the Vice President elect shall act as President until a President shall have qualified; and the Congress may by law provide for the case wherein neither a President elect nor a Vice President elect shall have qualified, declaring who shall then act as President, or the manner in which one who is to act shall be selected, and such person shall act accordingly until a President or Vice President shall have qualified.

§ 4. The Congress may by law provide for the case of the death of any of the persons from whom the House of Representatives may choose a President whenever the right of choice shall have devolved upon them, and for the case of the death of any of the persons from whom the Senate may choose a Vice President whenever the right of choice shall have devolved upon them.

§ 5. Sections 1 and 2 shall take effect on the 15th day of October following the ratification of this article.

§ 6. This article shall be inoperative unless it shall have been ratified as an amendment to the Constitution by the legislatures of three-fourths of the several States within seven years from the date of its submission.

AMENDMENT XXI

§ 1. The eighteenth article of amendment to the Constitution of the United States is hereby repealed.

§ 2. The transportation or importation into any State, Territory, or possession of the United States for delivery or use therein of intoxicating liquors, in violation of the laws thereof, is hereby prohibited.

§ 3. This article shall be inoperative unless it shall have been ratified as an amendment to the Constitution by conventions in the several States, as provided in the Constitution, within seven years from the date of the submission hereof to the States by the Congress.

AMENDMENT XXII

§ 1. No person shall be elected to the office of the President more than twice, and no person who has held the office of President, or acted as President, for more than two years of a term to which some other person was elected President shall be elected to the office of the President more than once. But this Article shall not apply to any person holding the office of President when this Article was proposed by the Congress, and shall not prevent any person who may be holding the office of President, or acting as President, during the term within which this Article becomes operative from holding the office of President or acting as President during the remainder of such term.

§ 2. This Article shall be inoperative unless it shall have been ratified as an amendment to the Constitution by the legislatures of three-fourths of the several States within seven years from the date of its submission to the States by the Congress.

AMENDMENT XXIII

§ 1. The District constituting the seat of Government of the United States shall appoint in such manner as the Congress may direct:

A number of electors of President and Vice President equal to the whole number of Senators and Representatives in Congress to which the District would be entitled if it were a State, but in no event more than the least populous State; they shall be in addition to those appointed by the States, but they shall be considered, for the purposes of the election of President and Vice President, to be electors appointed by a State; and they shall meet in the District and perform such duties as provided by the twelfth article of amendment.

§ 2. The Congress shall have power to enforce this article by appropriate legislation.

AMENDMENT XXIV

§ 1. The right of citizens of the United States to vote in any primary or other election for President or Vice President, for electors for President or Vice President, or for Senator or Representative in Congress, shall not be denied or abridged by the United States or any State by reason of failure to pay any poll tax or other tax.

§ 2. The Congress shall have power to enforce this article by appropriate legislation.

AMENDMENT XXV

§ 1. In case of the removal of the President from office or of his death or resignation, the Vice President shall become President.

§ 2. Whenever there is a vacancy in the office of the Vice President, the President shall nominate a Vice President who shall take office upon confirmation by a majority vote of both Houses of Congress.

§ 3. Whenever the President transmits to the President pro tempore of the Senate and the Speaker of the House of Representatives his written declaration that he is unable to discharge the powers and duties of his office, and until he transmits to them a written declaration to the contrary, such powers and duties shall be discharged by the Vice President as Acting President.

§ 4. Whenever the Vice President and a majority of either the principal officers of the executive departments or of such other body as Congress may by law provide, transmit to the President pro tempore of the Senate and the Speaker of the House of Representatives their written declaration that the President is unable to discharge the powers and duties of his office, the Vice President shall immediately assume the powers and duties of the office as Acting President.

Thereafter, when the President transmits to the President pro tempore of the Senate and the Speaker of the House of Representatives his written declaration that no inability exists, he shall resume the powers and duties of his office unless the Vice President and a majority of either the principal officers of the executive department or of such other body as Congress may by law provide, transmit within four days to the President pro tempore of the Senate and the Speaker of the House of Representatives their written declaration that the President is unable to discharge the powers and duties of his office. Thereupon Congress shall decide the issue, assembling within forty-eight hours for that purpose if not in session. If the Congress, within twenty-one days after receipt of the latter written declaration, or, if Congress is not in session, within twenty-one days after Congress is required to assemble, determines by two-thirds vote of both Houses that the President is unable to discharge the powers and duties of his office, the Vice President shall continue to discharge the same as Acting President; otherwise, the President shall resume the powers and duties of his office.

AMENDMENT XXVI

§ 1. The right of citizens of the United States, who are eighteen years of age or older, to vote shall not be denied or abridged by the United States or by any State on account of age.

§ 2. The Congress shall have power to enforce this article by appropriate legislation.

AMENDMENT XXVII

No law, varying the compensation for the services of the Senators and Representatives, shall take effect, until an election of Representatives shall have intervened.

APPENDIX C
FEDERAL RULES OF EVIDENCE

Amendments received to June 15, 2020*

ARTICLE I. GENERAL PROVISIONS

Rule 101.   Scope; Definitions

(a) Scope. These rules apply to proceedings in United States courts. The specific courts and proceedings to which the rules apply, along with exceptions, are set out in Rule 1101.

(b) Definitions. In these rules:

(1) "civil case" means a civil action or proceeding;

(2) "criminal case" includes a criminal proceeding;

(3) "public office" includes a public agency;

(4) "record" includes a memorandum, report, or data compilation;

(5) a "rule prescribed by the Supreme Court" means a rule adopted by the Supreme Court under statutory authority; and

(6) a reference to any kind of written material or any other medium includes electronically stored information.

(Pub.L. 93–595, § 1, Jan. 2, 1975, 88 Stat. 1929; Mar. 2, 1987, eff. Oct. 1, 1987; Apr. 25, 1988, eff. Nov. 1, 1988; Apr. 22, 1993, eff. Dec. 1, 1993; Apr. 26, 2011, eff. Dec. 1, 2011.)

Rule 102.   Purpose

These rules should be construed so as to administer every proceeding fairly, eliminate unjustifiable expense and delay, and promote the development of evidence law, to the end of ascertaining the truth and securing a just determination.

(Pub.L. 93–595, § 1, Jan. 2, 1975, 88 Stat.1929; Apr. 26, 2011, eff. Dec. 1, 2011.)

Rule 103.   Rulings on Evidence

(a) Preserving a Claim of Error. A party may claim error in a ruling to admit or exclude evidence only if the error affects a substantial right of the party and:

(1) if the ruling admits evidence, a party, on the record:

(A) timely objects or moves to strike; and

(B) states the specific ground, unless it was apparent from the context; or

(2) if the ruling excludes evidence, a party informs the court of its substance by an offer of proof, unless the substance was apparent from the context.

(b) Not Needing to Renew an Objection or Offer of Proof. Once the court rules definitively on the record—either before or at trial—a party need not renew an objection or offer of proof to preserve a claim of error for appeal.

---

*   [The Federal Rules of Evidence as reproduced herein include an amendment to Rule 404 that has been approved by the U.S. Supreme Court. New language is indicated by <u>underlined</u> type and matter to be omitted is ~~stricken through~~. These amendments will become effective on December 1, 2020 absent contrary congressional action. Ed.]

(c) Court's Statement About the Ruling; Directing an Offer of Proof. The court may make any statement about the character or form of the evidence, the objection made, and the ruling. The court may direct that an offer of proof be made in question-and-answer form.

(d) Preventing the Jury from Hearing Inadmissible Evidence. To the extent practicable, the court must conduct a jury trial so that inadmissible evidence is not suggested to the jury by any means.

(e) Taking Notice of Plain Error. A court may take notice of a plain error affecting a substantial right, even if the claim of error was not properly preserved.

(Pub.L. 93–595, § 1, Jan. 2, 1975, 88 Stat. 1929; Apr. 17, 2000, eff. Dec. 1, 2000; Apr. 26, 2011, eff. Dec. 1, 2011.)

Rule 104.   Preliminary Questions

(a) In General. The court must decide any preliminary question about whether a witness is qualified, a privilege exists, or evidence is admissible. In so deciding, the court is not bound by evidence rules, except those on privilege.

(b) Relevance That Depends on a Fact. When the relevance of evidence depends on whether a fact exists, proof must be introduced sufficient to support a finding that the fact does exist. The court may admit the proposed evidence on the condition that the proof be introduced later.

(c) Conducting a Hearing So That the Jury Cannot Hear It. The court must conduct any hearing on a preliminary question so that the jury cannot hear it if:

　　(1) the hearing involves the admissibility of a confession;

　　(2) a defendant in a criminal case is a witness and so requests; or

　　(3) justice so requires.

(d) Cross-Examining a Defendant in a Criminal Case. By testifying on a preliminary question, a defendant in a criminal case does not become subject to cross-examination on other issues in the case.

(e) Evidence Relevant to Weight and Credibility. This rule does not limit a party's right to introduce before the jury evidence that is relevant to the weight or credibility of other evidence.

(Pub.L. 93–595, § 1, Jan. 2, 1975, 88 Stat.1930; Mar. 2, 1987, eff. Oct. 1, 1987; Apr. 26, 2011, eff. Dec. 1, 2011.)

Rule 105.   Limiting Evidence That Is Not Admissible Against Other Parties or for Other Purposes

If the court admits evidence that is admissible against a party or for a purpose—but not against another party or for another purpose—the court, on timely request, must restrict the evidence to its proper scope and instruct the jury accordingly.

(Pub.L. 93–595, § 1, Jan. 2, 1975, 88 Stat. 1930; Apr. 26, 2011, eff. Dec. 1, 2011.)

Rule 106.   Remainder of or Related Writings or Recorded Statements

If a party introduces all or part of a writing or recorded statement, an adverse party may require the introduction, at that time, of any other part—or any other writing or recorded statement—that in fairness ought to be considered at the same time.

(Pub.L. 93–595, § 1, Jan. 2, 1975, 88 Stat. 1930; Mar. 2, 1987, eff. Oct. 1, 1987; Apr. 26, 2011, eff. Dec. 1, 2011.)

ARTICLE II.   JUDICIAL NOTICE

Rule 201.   Judicial Notice of Adjudicative Facts

(a) **Scope.** This rule governs judicial notice of an adjudicative fact only, not a legislative fact.

(b) **Kinds of Facts That May Be Judicially Noticed.** The court may judicially notice a fact that is not subject to reasonable dispute because it:

    (1) is generally known within the trial court's territorial jurisdiction; or

    (2) can be accurately and readily determined from sources whose accuracy cannot reasonably be questioned.

(c) **Taking Notice.** The court:

    (1) may take judicial notice on its own; or

    (2) must take judicial notice if a party requests it and the court is supplied with the necessary information.

(d) **Timing.** The court may take judicial notice at any stage of the proceeding.

(e) **Opportunity to Be Heard.** On timely request, a party is entitled to be heard on the propriety of taking judicial notice and the nature of the fact to be noticed. If the court takes judicial notice before notifying a party, the party, on request, is still entitled to be heard.

(f) **Instructing the Jury.** In a civil case, the court must instruct the jury to accept the noticed fact as conclusive. In a criminal case, the court must instruct the jury that it may or may not accept the noticed fact as conclusive.

(Pub.L. 93–595, § 1, Jan. 2, 1975, 88 Stat. 1930; Apr. 26, 2011, eff. Dec. 1, 2011.)

ARTICLE III.   PRESUMPTIONS IN CIVIL CASES

Rule 301.   Presumptions in Civil Cases Generally

In a civil case, unless a federal statute or these rules provide otherwise, the party against whom a presumption is directed has the burden of producing evidence to rebut the presumption. But this rule does not shift the burden of persuasion, which remains on the party who had it originally.

(Pub.L. 93–595, § 1, Jan. 2, 1975, 88 Stat. 1931; Apr. 26, 2011, eff. Dec. 1, 2011.)

Rule 302.   Applying State Law to Presumptions in Civil Cases

In a civil case, state law governs the effect of a presumption regarding a claim or defense for which state law supplies the rule of decision.

(Pub.L. 93–595, § 1, Jan. 2, 1975, 88 Stat. 1931; Apr. 26, 2011, eff. Dec. 1, 2011.)

ARTICLE IV.   RELEVANCE AND ITS LIMITS

Rule 401.   Test for Relevant Evidence

Evidence is relevant if:

(a) it has any tendency to make a fact more or less probable than it would be without the evidence; and

(b) the fact is of consequence in determining the action.

(Pub.L. 93–595, § 1, Jan. 2, 1975, 88 Stat.1931; Apr. 26, 2011, eff. Dec. 1, 2011.)

Rule 402. General Admissibility of Relevant Evidence

Relevant evidence is admissible unless any of the following provides otherwise:

- the United States Constitution;
- a federal statute;
- these rules; or
- other rules prescribed by the Supreme Court.

Irrelevant evidence is not admissible.

(Pub.L. 93–595, § 1, Jan. 2, 1975, 88 Stat. 1931; Apr. 26, 2011, eff. Dec. 1, 2011.)

Rule 403. Excluding Relevant Evidence for Prejudice, Confusion, Waste of Time, or Other Reasons

The court may exclude relevant evidence if its probative value is substantially outweighed by a danger of one or more of the following: unfair prejudice, confusing the issues, misleading the jury, undue delay, wasting time, or needlessly presenting cumulative evidence.

(Pub.L. 93–595, § 1, Jan. 2, 1975, 88 Stat. 1932; Apr. 26, 2011, eff. Dec. 1, 2011.)

Rule 404. Character Evidence; Other Crimes, Wrongs, or Other Acts

(a) Character Evidence.

(1) Prohibited Uses. Evidence of a person's character or character trait is not admissible to prove that on a particular occasion the person acted in accordance with the character or trait.

(2) Exceptions for a Defendant or Victim in a Criminal Case. The following exceptions apply in a criminal case:

(A) a defendant may offer evidence of the defendant's pertinent trait, and if the evidence is admitted, the prosecutor may offer evidence to rebut it;

(B) subject to the limitations in Rule 412, a defendant may offer evidence of an alleged victim's pertinent trait, and if the evidence is admitted, the prosecutor may:

(i) offer evidence to rebut it; and

(ii) offer evidence of the defendant's same trait; and

(C) in a homicide case, the prosecutor may offer evidence of the alleged victim's trait of peacefulness to rebut evidence that the victim was the first aggressor.

(3) Exceptions for a Witness. Evidence of a witness's character may be admitted under Rules 607, 608, and 609.

(b) Other Crimes, Wrongs, or Other Acts.

(1) Prohibited Uses. Evidence of a~~ any other~~ crime, wrong, or ~~other~~ act is not admissible to prove a person's character in order to show that on a particular occasion the person acted in accordance with the character.

(2) Permitted Uses; ~~Notice in a Criminal Case.~~ This evidence may be admissible for another purpose, such as proving motive, opportunity, intent, preparation, plan, knowledge, identity, absence of mistake, or lack of accident. ~~On request by a defendant in a criminal case, the prosecutor must:~~

(3) Notice in a Criminal Case. In a criminal case, the prosecutor must:

(A) provide reasonable notice ~~of the general nature~~ of any such evidence that the prosecutor intends to offer at trial, so that the defendant has a fair opportunity to meet it; ~~and~~

(B) articulate in the notice the permitted purpose for which the prosecutor intends to offer the evidence and the reasoning that supports the purpose; and

(C) do so in writing before trial—or in any form during trial if the court, for good cause, excuses lack of pretrial notice.

(Pub.L. 93–595, § 1, Jan. 2, 1975, 88 Stat. 1932; Mar. 2, 1987, eff. Oct. 1, 1987; Apr. 30, 1991, eff. Dec. 1, 1991; Apr. 17, 2000, eff. Dec. 1, 2000; Apr. 12, 2006, eff. Dec. 1, 2006; Apr. 26, 2011, eff. Dec. 1, 2011; Apr. 27, 2020, eff. Dec. 1, 2020 absent contrary congressional action.)

Rule 405.   Methods of Proving Character

(a) **By Reputation or Opinion.** When evidence of a person's character or character trait is admissible, it may be proved by testimony about the person's reputation or by testimony in the form of an opinion. On cross-examination of the character witness, the court may allow an inquiry into relevant specific instances of the person's conduct.

(b) **By Specific Instances of Conduct.** When a person's character or character trait is an essential element of a charge, claim, or defense, the character or trait may also be proved by relevant specific instances of the person's conduct.

(Pub.L. 93–595, § 1, Jan. 2, 1975, 88 Stat. 1932; Mar. 2, 1987, eff. Oct. 1, 1987; Apr. 26, 2011, eff. Dec. 1, 2011.)

Rule 406.   Habit; Routine Practice

Evidence of a person's habit or an organization's routine practice may be admitted to prove that on a particular occasion the person or organization acted in accordance with the habit or routine practice. The court may admit this evidence regardless of whether it is corroborated or whether there was an eyewitness.

(Pub.L. 93–595, § 1, Jan. 2, 1975, 88 Stat. 1932; Apr. 26, 2011, eff. Dec. 1, 2011.)

Rule 407.   Subsequent Remedial Measures

When measures are taken that would have made an earlier injury or harm less likely to occur, evidence of the subsequent measures is not admissible to prove:

- negligence;

- culpable conduct;

- a defect in a product or its design; or

- a need for a warning or instruction.

But the court may admit this evidence for another purpose, such as impeachment or—if disputed—proving ownership, control, or the feasibility of precautionary measures.

(Pub.L. 93–595, § 1, Jan. 2, 1975, 88 Stat. 1932; Apr. 11, 1997, eff. Dec. 1, 1997; Apr. 26, 2011, eff. Dec. 1, 2011.)

Rule 408.   Compromise Offers and Negotiations

(a) **Prohibited Uses.** Evidence of the following is not admissible—on behalf of any party— either to prove or disprove the validity or amount of a disputed claim or to impeach by a prior inconsistent statement or a contradiction:

(1) furnishing, promising, or offering—or accepting, promising to accept, or offering to accept—a valuable consideration in compromising or attempting to compromise the claim; and

(2) conduct or a statement made during compromise negotiations about the claim—except when offered in a criminal case and when the negotiations related to a claim by a public office in the exercise of its regulatory, investigative, or enforcement authority.

(b) **Exceptions.** The court may admit this evidence for another purpose, such as proving a witness's bias or prejudice, negating a contention of undue delay, or proving an effort to obstruct a criminal investigation or prosecution.

(Pub.L. 93–595, § 1, Jan. 2, 1975, 88 Stat. 1933; Apr. 12, 2006, eff. Dec. 1, 2006; Apr. 26, 2011, eff. Dec. 1, 2011.)

Rule 409.   Offers to Pay Medical and Similar Expenses

Evidence of furnishing, promising to pay, or offering to pay medical, hospital, or similar expenses resulting from an injury is not admissible to prove liability for the injury.

(Pub.L. 93–595, § 1, Jan. 2, 1975, 88 Stat.1933; Apr. 26, 2011, eff. Dec. 1, 2011.)

Rule 410.   Pleas, Plea Discussions, and Related Statements

(a) **Prohibited Uses.** In a civil or criminal case, evidence of the following is not admissible against the defendant who made the plea or participated in the plea discussions:

(1) a guilty plea that was later withdrawn;

(2) a nolo contendere plea;

(3) a statement made during a proceeding on either of those pleas under Federal Rule of Criminal Procedure 11 or a comparable state procedure; or

(4) a statement made during plea discussions with an attorney for the prosecuting authority if the discussions did not result in a guilty plea or they resulted in a later-withdrawn guilty plea.

(b) **Exceptions.** The court may admit a statement described in Rule 410(a)(3) or (4):

(1) in any proceeding in which another statement made during the same plea or plea discussions has been introduced, if in fairness the statements ought to be considered together; or

(2) in a criminal proceeding for perjury or false statement, if the defendant made the statement under oath, on the record, and with counsel present.

(Pub.L. 93–595, § 1, Jan. 2, 1975, 88 Stat. 1933; Pub.L. 94–149, § 1(9), Dec. 12, 1975, 89 Stat. 805; Apr. 30, 1979, eff. Dec. 1, 1980; Apr. 26, 2011, eff. Dec. 1, 2011.)

Rule 411.   Liability Insurance

Evidence that a person was or was not insured against liability is not admissible to prove whether the person acted negligently or otherwise wrongfully. But the court may admit this evidence for another purpose, such as proving a witness's bias or prejudice or proving agency, ownership, or control.

(Pub.L. 93–595, § 1, Jan. 2, 1975, 88 Stat.1933; Mar. 2, 1987, eff. Oct. 1, 1987; Apr. 26, 2011, eff. Dec. 1, 2011.)

Rule 412.   Sex-Offense Cases: The Victim's Sexual Behavior or Predisposition

(a) **Prohibited Uses.** The following evidence is not admissible in a civil or criminal proceeding involving alleged sexual misconduct:

(1) evidence offered to prove that a victim engaged in other sexual behavior; or

(2) evidence offered to prove a victim's sexual predisposition.

(b) Exceptions.

(1) Criminal Cases. The court may admit the following evidence in a criminal case:

(A) evidence of specific instances of a victim's sexual behavior, if offered to prove that someone other than the defendant was the source of semen, injury, or other physical evidence;

(B) evidence of specific instances of a victim's sexual behavior with respect to the person accused of the sexual misconduct, if offered by the defendant to prove consent or if offered by the prosecutor; and

(C) evidence whose exclusion would violate the defendant's constitutional rights.

(2) Civil Cases. In a civil case, the court may admit evidence offered to prove a victim's sexual behavior or sexual predisposition if its probative value substantially outweighs the danger of harm to any victim and of unfair prejudice to any party. The court may admit evidence of a victim's reputation only if the victim has placed it in controversy.

(c) Procedure to Determine Admissibility.

(1) Motion. If a party intends to offer evidence under Rule 412(b), the party must:

(A) file a motion that specifically describes the evidence and states the purpose for which it is to be offered;

(B) do so at least 14 days before trial unless the court, for good cause, sets a different time;

(C) serve the motion on all parties; and

(D) notify the victim or, when appropriate, the victim's guardian or representative.

(2) Hearing. Before admitting evidence under this rule, the court must conduct an in camera hearing and give the victim and parties a right to attend and be heard. Unless the court orders otherwise, the motion, related materials, and the record of the hearing must be and remain sealed.

(d) Definition of "Victim." In this rule, "victim" includes an alleged victim.

(Added Pub.L. 95–540, § 2(a), Oct. 28, 1978, 92 Stat. 2046; amended Pub.L. 100–690, Title VII, § 7046(a), Nov. 18, 1988, 102 Stat. 4400; Apr. 29, 1994, eff. Dec. 1, 1994; Pub.L. 103–322, Title IV, § 40141(b), Sept. 13, 1994, 108 Stat. 1919; Apr. 26, 2011, eff. Dec. 1, 2011.)

Rule 413.   Similar Crimes in Sexual-Assault Cases

(a) Permitted Uses. In a criminal case in which a defendant is accused of a sexual assault, the court may admit evidence that the defendant committed any other sexual assault. The evidence may be considered on any matter to which it is relevant.

(b) Disclosure to the Defendant. If the prosecutor intends to offer this evidence, the prosecutor must disclose it to the defendant, including witnesses' statements or a summary of the expected testimony. The prosecutor must do so at least 15 days before trial or at a later time that the court allows for good cause.

(c) Effect on Other Rules. This rule does not limit the admission or consideration of evidence under any other rule.

(d) Definition of "Sexual Assault." In this rule and Rule 415, " sexual assault" means a crime under federal law or under state law (as " state" is defined in 18 U.S.C. § 513) involving:

(1) any conduct prohibited by 18 U.S.C. chapter 109A;

(2) contact, without consent, between any part of the defendant's body—or an object—and another person's genitals or anus;

(3) contact, without consent, between the defendant's genitals or anus and any part of another person's body;

(4) deriving sexual pleasure or gratification from inflicting death, bodily injury, or physical pain on another person; or

(5) an attempt or conspiracy to engage in conduct described in subparagraphs (1)–(4).

(Added Pub.L. 103–322, Title XXXII, § 320935(a), Sept. 13, 1994, 108 Stat. 2136; amended Apr. 26, 2011, eff. Dec. 1, 2011.)

Rule 414.   Similar Crimes in Child-Molestation Cases

(a) **Permitted Uses.** In a criminal case in which a defendant is accused of child molestation, the court may admit evidence that the defendant committed any other child molestation. The evidence may be considered on any matter to which it is relevant.

(b) **Disclosure to the Defendant.** If the prosecutor intends to offer this evidence, the prosecutor must disclose it to the defendant, including witnesses' statements or a summary of the expected testimony. The prosecutor must do so at least 15 days before trial or at a later time that the court allows for good cause.

(c) **Effect on Other Rules.** This rule does not limit the admission or consideration of evidence under any other rule.

(d) **Definition of "Child" and "Child Molestation."** In this rule and Rule 415:

(1) "child" means a person below the age of 14; and

(2) "child molestation" means a crime under federal law or under state law (as "state" is defined in 18 U.S.C. § 513) involving:

(A) any conduct prohibited by 18 U.S.C. chapter 109A and committed with a child;

(B) any conduct prohibited by 18 U.S.C. chapter 110;

(C) contact between any part of the defendant's body—or an object—and a child's genitals or anus;

(D) contact between the defendant's genitals or anus and any part of a child's body;

(E) deriving sexual pleasure or gratification from inflicting death, bodily injury, or physical pain on a child; or

(F) an attempt or conspiracy to engage in conduct described in subparagraphs (A)–(E).

(Added Pub.L. 103–322, Title XXXII, § 320935(a), Sept. 13, 1994, 108 Stat. 2135; amended Apr. 26, 2011, eff. Dec. 1, 2011.)

Rule 415.   Similar Acts in Civil Cases Involving Sexual Assault or Child Molestation

(a) **Permitted Uses.** In a civil case involving a claim for relief based on a party's alleged sexual assault or child molestation, the court may admit evidence that the party committed any other sexual assault or child molestation. The evidence may be considered as provided in Rules 413 and 414.

(b) **Disclosure to the Opponent.** If a party intends to offer this evidence, the party must disclose it to the party against whom it will be offered, including witnesses' statements or a summary of the expected testimony. The party must do so at least 15 days before trial or at a later time that the court allows for good cause.

(c) **Effect on Other Rules.** This rule does not limit the admission or consideration of evidence under any other rule.

(Added Pub.L. 103–322, Title XXXII, § 320935(a), Sept. 13, 1994, 108 Stat. 2137; amended Apr. 26, 2011, eff. Dec. 1, 2011.)

ARTICLE V.   PRIVILEGES

Rule 501.   Privilege in General

The common law—as interpreted by United States courts in the light of reason and experience—governs a claim of privilege unless any of the following provides otherwise:

- the United States Constitution;

- a federal statute; or

- rules prescribed by the Supreme Court.

But in a civil case, state law governs privilege regarding a claim or defense for which state law supplies the rule of decision.

(Pub.L. 93–595, § 1, Jan. 2, 1975, 88 Stat. 1933; Apr. 26, 2011, eff. Dec. 1, 2011.)

Rule 502.   Attorney-Client Privilege and Work Product; Limitations on Waiver

The following provisions apply, in the circumstances set out, to disclosure of a communication or information covered by the attorney-client privilege or work-product protection.

(a)   Disclosure Made in a Federal Proceeding or to a Federal Office or Agency; Scope of a Waiver. When the disclosure is made in a federal proceeding or to a federal office or agency and waives the attorney-client privilege or work-product protection, the waiver extends to an undisclosed communication or information in a federal or state proceeding only if:

(1)   the waiver is intentional;

(2)   the disclosed and undisclosed communications or information concern the same subject matter; and

(3)   they ought in fairness to be considered together.

(b)   Inadvertent Disclosure. When made in a federal proceeding or to a federal office or agency, the disclosure does not operate as a waiver in a federal or state proceeding if:

(1)   the disclosure is inadvertent;

(2)   the holder of the privilege or protection took reasonable steps to prevent disclosure; and

(3)   the holder promptly took reasonable steps to rectify the error, including (if applicable) following Federal Rule of Civil Procedure 26(b)(5)(B).

(c)   Disclosure Made in a State Proceeding. When the disclosure is made in a state proceeding and is not the subject of a state-court order concerning waiver, the disclosure does not operate as a waiver in a federal proceeding if the disclosure:

(1)   would not be a waiver under this rule if it had been made in a federal proceeding; or

(2)   is not a waiver under the law of the state where the disclosure occurred.

(d)   Controlling Effect of a Court Order. A federal court may order that the privilege or protection is not waived by disclosure connected with the litigation pending before the court—in which event the disclosure is also not a waiver in any other federal or state proceeding.

(e)   Controlling Effect of a Party Agreement. An agreement on the effect of disclosure in a federal proceeding is binding only on the parties to the agreement, unless it is incorporated into a court order.

(f)   Controlling Effect of This Rule. Notwithstanding Rules 101 and 1101, this rule applies to state proceedings and to federal court-annexed and federal court-mandated arbitration proceedings, in the circumstances set out in the rule. And notwithstanding Rule 501, this rule applies even if state law provides the rule of decision.

(g) Definitions. In this rule:

(1) "attorney-client privilege" means the protection that applicable law provides for confidential attorney-client communications; and

(2) "work-product protection" means the protection that applicable law provides for tangible material (or its intangible equivalent) prepared in anticipation of litigation or for trial.

(Pub.L. 110–322, § 1(a), Sept. 19, 2008, 122 Stat. 3537; Apr. 26, 2011, eff. Dec. 1, 2011.)

ARTICLE VI. WITNESSES

Rule 601.   Competency to Testify in General

Every person is competent to be a witness unless these rules provide otherwise. But in a civil case, state law governs the witness's competency regarding a claim or defense for which state law supplies the rule of decision.

(Pub.L. 93–595, § 1, Jan. 2, 1975, 88 Stat.1934; Apr. 26, 2011, eff. Dec. 1, 2011.)

Rule 602.   Need for Personal Knowledge

A witness may testify to a matter only if evidence is introduced sufficient to support a finding that the witness has personal knowledge of the matter. Evidence to prove personal knowledge may consist of the witness's own testimony. This rule does not apply to a witness's expert testimony under Rule 703.

(Pub.L. 93–595, § 1, Jan. 2, 1975, 88 Stat. 1934; Mar. 2, 1987, eff. Oct. 1, 1987; Apr. 25, 1988, eff. Nov. 1, 1988; Apr. 26, 2011, eff. Dec. 1, 2011.)

Rule 603.   Oath or Affirmation to Testify Truthfully

Before testifying, a witness must give an oath or affirmation to testify truthfully. It must be in a form designed to impress that duty on the witness's conscience.

(Pub.L. 93–595, § 1, Jan. 2, 1975, 88 Stat. 1934; Mar. 2, 1987, eff. Oct. 1, 1987; Apr. 26, 2011, eff. Dec. 1, 2011.)

Rule 604.   Interpreter

An interpreter must be qualified and must give an oath or affirmation to make a true translation.

(Pub.L. 93–595, § 1, Jan. 2, 1975, 88 Stat. 1934; Mar. 2, 1987, eff. Oct. 1, 1987; Apr. 26, 2011, eff. Dec. 1, 2011.)

Rule 605.   Judge's Competency as a Witness

The presiding judge may not testify as a witness at the trial. A party need not object to preserve the issue.

(Pub.L. 93–595, § 1, Jan. 2, 1975, 88 Stat. 1934; Apr. 26, 2011, eff. Dec. 1, 2011.)

Rule 606.   Juror's Competency as a Witness

(a) At the Trial. A juror may not testify as a witness before the other jurors at the trial. If a juror is called to testify, the court must give a party an opportunity to object outside the jury's presence.

(b) During an Inquiry Into the Validity of a Verdict or Indictment.

(1) Prohibited Testimony or Other Evidence. During an inquiry into the validity of a verdict or indictment, a juror may not testify about any statement made or incident that occurred during the jury's deliberations; the effect of anything on that juror's or another juror's vote; or any juror's mental processes concerning the verdict or indictment. The court may not receive a juror's affidavit or evidence of a juror's statement on these matters.

    (2) Exceptions. A juror may testify about whether:

        (A) extraneous prejudicial information was improperly brought to the jury's attention;

        (B) an outside influence was improperly brought to bear on any juror; or

        (C) a mistake was made in entering the verdict on the verdict form.

(Pub.L. 93–595, § 1, Jan. 2, 1975, 88 Stat. 1934; Pub.L. 94–149, § 1(10), Dec. 12, 1975, 89 Stat. 805; Mar. 2, 1987, eff. Oct. 1, 1987; Apr. 12, 2006, eff. Dec. 1, 2006; Apr. 26, 2011, eff. Dec. 1, 2011.)

Rule 607.   Who May Impeach a Witness

Any party, including the party that called the witness, may attack the witness's credibility.

(Pub.L. 93–595, § 1, Jan. 2, 1975, 88 Stat.1934; Mar. 2, 1987, eff. Oct. 1, 1987; Apr. 26, 2011, eff. Dec. 1, 2011.)

Rule 608.   A Witness's Character for Truthfulness or Untruthfulness

    (a) Reputation or Opinion Evidence. A witness's credibility may be attacked or supported by testimony about the witness's reputation for having a character for truthfulness or untruthfulness, or by testimony in the form of an opinion about that character. But evidence of truthful character is admissible only after the witness's character for truthfulness has been attacked.

    (b) Specific Instances of Conduct. Except for a criminal conviction under Rule 609, extrinsic evidence is not admissible to prove specific instances of a witness's conduct in order to attack or support the witness's character for truthfulness. But the court may, on cross-examination, allow them to be inquired into if they are probative of the character for truthfulness or untruthfulness of:

        (1) the witness; or

        (2) another witness whose character the witness being cross-examined has testified about.

By testifying on another matter, a witness does not waive any privilege against self-incrimination for testimony that relates only to the witness's character for truthfulness.

(Pub.L. 93–595, § 1, Jan. 2, 1975, 88 Stat.1935; Mar. 2, 1987, eff. Oct. 1, 1987; Apr. 25, 1988, eff. Nov. 1, 1988; Mar. 27, 2003, eff. Dec. 1, 2003; Apr. 26, 2011, eff. Dec. 1, 2011.)

Rule 609.   Impeachment by Evidence of a Criminal Conviction

    (a) In General. The following rules apply to attacking a witness's character for truthfulness by evidence of a criminal conviction:

        (1) for a crime that, in the convicting jurisdiction, was punishable by death or by imprisonment for more than one year, the evidence:

            (A) must be admitted, subject to Rule 403, in a civil case or in a criminal case in which the witness is not a defendant; and

            (B) must be admitted in a criminal case in which the witness is a defendant, if the probative value of the evidence outweighs its prejudicial effect to that defendant; and

        (2) for any crime regardless of the punishment, the evidence must be admitted if the court can readily determine that establishing the elements of the crime required proving—or the witness's admitting—a dishonest act or false statement.

    (b) Limit on Using the Evidence After 10 Years. This subdivision (b) applies if more than 10 years have passed since the witness's conviction or release from confinement for it, whichever is later. Evidence of the conviction is admissible only if:

(1) its probative value, supported by specific facts and circumstances, substantially outweighs its prejudicial effect; and

(2) the proponent gives an adverse party reasonable written notice of the intent to use it so that the party has a fair opportunity to contest its use.

(c) Effect of a Pardon, Annulment, or Certificate of Rehabilitation. Evidence of a conviction is not admissible if:

(1) the conviction has been the subject of a pardon, annulment, certificate of rehabilitation, or other equivalent procedure based on a finding that the person has been rehabilitated, and the person has not been convicted of a later crime punishable by death or by imprisonment for more than one year; or

(2) the conviction has been the subject of a pardon, annulment, or other equivalent procedure based on a finding of innocence.

(d) Juvenile Adjudications. Evidence of a juvenile adjudication is admissible under this rule only if:

(1) it is offered in a criminal case;

(2) the adjudication was of a witness other than the defendant;

(3) an adult's conviction for that offense would be admissible to attack the adult's credibility; and

(4) admitting the evidence is necessary to fairly determine guilt or innocence.

(e) Pendency of an Appeal. A conviction that satisfies this rule is admissible even if an appeal is pending. Evidence of the pendency is also admissible.

(Pub.L. 93–595, § 1, Jan. 2, 1975, 88 Stat.1935; Mar. 2, 1987, eff. Oct. 1, 1987; Jan. 26, 1990, eff. Dec. 1, 1990; Apr. 12, 2006, eff. Dec. 1, 2006; Apr. 26, 2011, eff. Dec. 1, 2011.)

Rule 610. Religious Beliefs or Opinions

Evidence of a witness's religious beliefs or opinions is not admissible to attack or support the witness's credibility.

(Pub.L. 93–595, § 1, Jan. 2, 1975, 88 Stat.1936; Mar. 2, 1987, eff. Oct. 1, 1987; Apr. 26, 2011, eff. Dec. 1, 2011.)

Rule 611. Mode and Order of Examining Witnesses and Presenting Evidence

(a) Control by the Court; Purposes. The court should exercise reasonable control over the mode and order of examining witnesses and presenting evidence so as to:

(1) make those procedures effective for determining the truth;

(2) avoid wasting time; and

(3) protect witnesses from harassment or undue embarrassment.

(b) Scope of Cross-Examination. Cross-examination should not go beyond the subject matter of the direct examination and matters affecting the witness's credibility. The court may allow inquiry into additional matters as if on direct examination.

(c) Leading Questions. Leading questions should not be used on direct examination except as necessary to develop the witness's testimony. Ordinarily, the court should allow leading questions:

(1) on cross-examination; and

(2) when a party calls a hostile witness, an adverse party, or a witness identified with an adverse party.

(Pub.L. 93–595, § 1, Jan. 2, 1975, 88 Stat. 1936; Mar. 2, 1987, eff. Oct. 1, 1987; Apr. 26, 2011, eff. Dec. 1, 2011.)

Rule 612.   Writing Used to Refresh a Witness's Memory

(a) **Scope.** This rule gives an adverse party certain options when a witness uses a writing to refresh memory:

　　(1) while testifying; or

　　(2) before testifying, if the court decides that justice requires the party to have those options.

(b) **Adverse Party's Options; Deleting Unrelated Matter.** Unless 18 U.S.C. § 3500 provides otherwise in a criminal case, an adverse party is entitled to have the writing produced at the hearing, to inspect it, to cross-examine the witness about it, and to introduce in evidence any portion that relates to the witness's testimony. If the producing party claims that the writing includes unrelated matter, the court must examine the writing in camera, delete any unrelated portion, and order that the rest be delivered to the adverse party. Any portion deleted over objection must be preserved for the record.

(c) **Failure to Produce or Deliver the Writing.** If a writing is not produced or is not delivered as ordered, the court may issue any appropriate order. But if the prosecution does not comply in a criminal case, the court must strike the witness's testimony or—if justice so requires—declare a mistrial.

(Pub.L. 93–595, § 1, Jan. 2, 1975, 88 Stat. 1936; Mar. 2, 1987, eff. Oct. 1, 1987; Apr. 26, 2011, eff. Dec. 1, 2011.)

Rule 613.   Witness's Prior Statement

(a) **Showing or Disclosing the Statement During Examination.** When examining a witness about the witness's prior statement, a party need not show it or disclose its contents to the witness. But the party must, on request, show it or disclose its contents to an adverse party's attorney.

(b) **Extrinsic Evidence of a Prior Inconsistent Statement.** Extrinsic evidence of a witness's prior inconsistent statement is admissible only if the witness is given an opportunity to explain or deny the statement and an adverse party is given an opportunity to examine the witness about it, or if justice so requires. This subdivision (b) does not apply to an opposing party's statement under Rule 801(d)(2).

(Pub.L. 93–595, § 1, Jan. 2, 1975, 88 Stat.1936; Mar. 2, 1987, eff. Oct. 1, 1987; Apr. 25, 1988, eff. Nov. 1, 1988; Apr. 26, 2011, eff. Dec. 1, 2011.)

Rule 614.   Court's Calling or Examining a Witness

(a) **Calling.** The court may call a witness on its own or at a party's request. Each party is entitled to cross-examine the witness.

(b) **Examining.** The court may examine a witness regardless of who calls the witness.

(c) **Objections.** A party may object to the court's calling or examining a witness either at that time or at the next opportunity when the jury is not present.

(Pub.L. 93–595, § 1, Jan. 2, 1975, 88 Stat.1937; Apr. 26, 2011, eff. Dec. 1, 2011.)

Rule 615.   Excluding Witnesses

At a party's request, the court must order witnesses excluded so that they cannot hear other witnesses' testimony. Or the court may do so on its own. But this rule does not authorize excluding:

(a) a party who is a natural person;

(b) an officer or employee of a party that is not a natural person, after being designated as the party's representative by its attorney;

(c) a person whose presence a party shows to be essential to presenting the party's claim or defense; or

(d) a person authorized by statute to be present.

(Pub.L. 93–595, § 1, Jan. 2, 1975, 88 Stat.1937; Mar. 2, 1987, eff. Oct. 1, 1987; Apr. 25, 1988, eff. Nov. 1, 1988; Pub.L. 100–690, Nov. 18, 1988, Title VII, § 7075(a), 102 Stat. 4405; Apr. 24, 1998, eff. Dec. 1, 1998; Apr. 26, 2011, eff. Dec. 1, 2011.)

ARTICLE VII. OPINIONS AND EXPERT TESTIMONY

Rule 701.   Opinion Testimony by Lay Witnesses

If a witness is not testifying as an expert, testimony in the form of an opinion is limited to one that is:

(a) rationally based on the witness's perception;

(b) helpful to clearly understanding the witness's testimony or to determining a fact in issue; and

(c) not based on scientific, technical, or other specialized knowledge within the scope of Rule 702.

(Pub.L. 93–595, § 1, Jan. 2, 1975, 88 Stat.1937; Mar. 2, 1987, eff. Oct. 1, 1987; Apr. 17, 2000, eff. Dec. 1, 2000; Apr. 26, 2011, eff. Dec. 1, 2011.)

Rule 702.   Testimony by Expert Witnesses

A witness who is qualified as an expert by knowledge, skill, experience, training, or education may testify in the form of an opinion or otherwise if:

(a) the expert's scientific, technical, or other specialized knowledge will help the trier of fact to understand the evidence or to determine a fact in issue;

(b) the testimony is based on sufficient facts or data;

(c) the testimony is the product of reliable principles and methods; and

(d) the expert has reliably applied the principles and methods to the facts of the case.

(Pub.L. 93–595, § 1, Jan. 2, 1975, 88 Stat. 1937; Apr. 17, 2000, eff. Dec. 1, 2000; Apr. 26, 2011, eff. Dec. 1, 2011.)

Rule 703.   Bases of an Expert's Opinion Testimony

An expert may base an opinion on facts or data in the case that the expert has been made aware of or personally observed. If experts in the particular field would reasonably rely on those kinds of facts or data in forming an opinion on the subject, they need not be admissible for the opinion to be admitted. But if the facts or data would otherwise be inadmissible, the proponent of the opinion may disclose them to the jury only if their probative value in helping the jury evaluate the opinion substantially outweighs their prejudicial effect.

(Pub.L. 93–595, § 1, Jan. 2, 1975, 88 Stat.1937; Mar. 2, 1987, eff. Oct. 1, 1987; Apr. 17, 2000, eff. Dec. 1, 2000; Apr. 26, 2011, eff. Dec. 1, 2011.)

Rule 704.   Opinion on an Ultimate Issue

(a) In General—Not Automatically Objectionable. An opinion is not objectionable just because it embraces an ultimate issue.

(b) Exception. In a criminal case, an expert witness must not state an opinion about whether the defendant did or did not have a mental state or condition that constitutes an element of the crime charged or of a defense. Those matters are for the trier of fact alone.

(Pub.L. 93–595, § 1, Jan. 2, 1975, 88 Stat. 1937; Pub.L. 98–473, Title IV, § 406, Oct. 12, 1984, 98 Stat. 2067; Apr. 26, 2011, eff. Dec. 1, 2011.)

Rule 705.   Disclosing the Facts or Data Underlying an Expert's Opinion

Unless the court orders otherwise, an expert may state an opinion—and give the reasons for it—without first testifying to the underlying facts or data. But the expert may be required to disclose those facts or data on cross-examination.

(Pub.L. 93–595, § 1, Jan. 2, 1975, 88 Stat. 1938; Mar. 2, 1987, eff. Oct. 1, 1987; Apr. 22, 1993, eff. Dec. 1, 1993; Apr. 26, 2011, eff. Dec. 1, 2011.)

Rule 706.   Court-Appointed Expert Witnesses

(a) Appointment Process. On a party's motion or on its own, the court may order the parties to show cause why expert witnesses should not be appointed and may ask the parties to submit nominations. The court may appoint any expert that the parties agree on and any of its own choosing. But the court may only appoint someone who consents to act.

(b) Expert's Role. The court must inform the expert of the expert's duties. The court may do so in writing and have a copy filed with the clerk or may do so orally at a conference in which the parties have an opportunity to participate. The expert:

(1)   must advise the parties of any findings the expert makes;

(2)   may be deposed by any party;

(3)   may be called to testify by the court or any party; and

(4)   may be cross-examined by any party, including the party that called the expert.

(c) Compensation. The expert is entitled to a reasonable compensation, as set by the court. The compensation is payable as follows:

(1)   in a criminal case or in a civil case involving just compensation under the Fifth Amendment, from any funds that are provided by law; and

(2)   in any other civil case, by the parties in the proportion and at the time that the court directs—and the compensation is then charged like other costs.

(d) Disclosing the Appointment to the Jury. The court may authorize disclosure to the jury that the court appointed the expert.

(e) Parties' Choice of Their Own Experts. This rule does not limit a party in calling its own experts.

(Pub.L. 93–595, § 1, Jan. 2, 1975, 88 Stat.1938; Mar. 2, 1987, eff. Oct. 1, 1987; Apr. 26, 2011, eff. Dec. 1, 2011.)

ARTICLE VIII. HEARSAY

Rule 801.   Definitions That Apply to This Article; Exclusions From Hearsay

(a) Statement. "Statement" means a person's oral assertion, written assertion, or nonverbal conduct, if the person intended it as an assertion.

(b) Declarant. "Declarant" means the person who made the statement.

(c) Hearsay. "Hearsay" means a statement that:

(1) the declarant does not make while testifying at the current trial or hearing; and

(2) a party offers in evidence to prove the truth of the matter asserted in the statement.

(d) Statements That Are Not Hearsay. A statement that meets the following conditions is not hearsay:

(1) A Declarant-Witness's Prior Statement. The declarant testifies and is subject to cross-examination about a prior statement, and the statement:

(A) is inconsistent with the declarant's testimony and was given under penalty of perjury at a trial, hearing, or other proceeding or in a deposition;

(B) is consistent with the declarant's testimony and is offered:

(i) to rebut an express or implied charge that the declarant recently fabricated it or acted from a recent improper influence or motive in so testifying; or

(ii) to rehabilitate the declarant's credibility as a witness when attacked on another ground; or

(C) identifies a person as someone the declarant perceived earlier.

(2) An Opposing Party's Statement. The statement is offered against an opposing party and:

(A) was made by the party in an individual or representative capacity;

(B) is one the party manifested that it adopted or believed to be true;

(C) was made by a person whom the party authorized to make a statement on the subject;

(D) was made by the party's agent or employee on a matter within the scope of that relationship and while it existed; or

(E) was made by the party's coconspirator during and in furtherance of the conspiracy.

The statement must be considered but does not by itself establish the declarant's authority under (C); the existence or scope of the relationship under (D); or the existence of the conspiracy or participation in it under (E).

(Pub.L. 93–595, § 1, Jan. 2, 1975, 88 Stat.1938; Pub.L. 94–113, § 1, Oct. 16, 1975, 89 Stat. 576; Mar. 2, 1987, eff. Oct. 1, 1987; Apr. 11, 1997, eff. Dec. 1, 1997; Apr. 26, 2011, eff. Dec. 1, 2011; Apr. 25, 2014, eff. Dec. 1, 2014.)

Rule 802.   The Rule Against Hearsay

Hearsay is not admissible unless any of the following provides otherwise:

- a federal statute;
- these rules; or
- other rules prescribed by the Supreme Court.

(Pub.L. 93–595, § 1, Jan. 2, 1975, 88 Stat. 1939; Apr. 26, 2011, eff. Dec. 1, 2011.)

Rule 803.   Exceptions to the Rule Against Hearsay—Regardless of Whether the Declarant Is Available as a Witness

The following are not excluded by the rule against hearsay, regardless of whether the declarant is available as a witness:

(1) Present Sense Impression. A statement describing or explaining an event or condition, made while or immediately after the declarant perceived it.

(2) Excited Utterance. A statement relating to a startling event or condition, made while the declarant was under the stress of excitement that it caused.

(3) Then-Existing Mental, Emotional, or Physical Condition. A statement of the declarant's then-existing state of mind (such as motive, intent, or plan) or emotional, sensory, or physical condition (such as mental feeling, pain, or bodily health), but not including a statement of memory or belief to prove the fact remembered or believed unless it relates to the validity or terms of the declarant's will.

(4) Statement Made for Medical Diagnosis or Treatment. A statement that:

(A) is made for—and is reasonably pertinent to—medical diagnosis or treatment; and

(B) describes medical history; past or present symptoms or sensations; their inception; or their general cause.

(5) Recorded Recollection. A record that:

(A) is on a matter the witness once knew about but now cannot recall well enough to testify fully and accurately;

(B) was made or adopted by the witness when the matter was fresh in the witness's memory; and

(C) accurately reflects the witness's knowledge.

If admitted, the record may be read into evidence but may be received as an exhibit only if offered by an adverse party.

(6) Records of a Regularly Conducted Activity. A record of an act, event, condition, opinion, or diagnosis if:

(A) the record was made at or near the time by—or from information transmitted by— someone with knowledge;

(B) the record was kept in the course of a regularly conducted activity of a business, organization, occupation, or calling, whether or not for profit;

(C) making the record was a regular practice of that activity;

(D) All these conditions are shown by the testimony of the custodian or another qualified witness, or by a certification that complies with Rule 902(11) or (12) or with a statute permitting certification; and

(E) the opponent does not show that the source of information or the method or circumstances of preparation indicate a lack of trustworthiness.

(7) Absence of a Record of a Regularly Conducted Activity. Evidence that a matter is not included in a record described in paragraph (6) if:

(A) the evidence is admitted to prove that the matter did not occur or exist;

(B) a record was regularly kept for a matter of that kind; and

(C) the opponent does not show that the possible source of the information or other circumstances indicate a lack of trustworthiness.

(8) Public Records. A record or statement of a public office if:

(A) it sets out:

(i) the office's activities;

(ii) a matter observed while under a legal duty to report, but not including, in a criminal case, a matter observed by law-enforcement personnel; or

(iii) in a civil case or against the government in a criminal case, factual findings from a legally authorized investigation; and

(B) the opponent does not show that the source of information or other circumstances indicate a lack of trustworthiness.

(9)   **Public Records of Vital Statistics.** A record of a birth, death, or marriage, if reported to a public office in accordance with a legal duty.

(10) Absence of a Public Record. Testimony—or a certification under Rule 902—that a diligent search failed to disclose a public record or statement if:

(A) the testimony or certification is admitted to prove that

(i) the record or statement does not exist; or

(ii) a matter did not occur or exist, if a public office regularly kept a record or statement for a matter of that kind; and

(B) in a criminal case, a prosecutor who intends to offer a certification provides written notice of that intent at least 14 days before trial, and the defendant does not object in writing within 7 days of receiving the notice—unless the court sets a different time for the notice or the objection.

(11) Records of Religious Organizations Concerning Personal or Family History. A statement of birth, legitimacy, ancestry, marriage, divorce, death, relationship by blood or marriage, or similar facts of personal or family history, contained in a regularly kept record of a religious organization.

(12) Certificates of Marriage, Baptism, and Similar Ceremonies. A statement of fact contained in a certificate:

(A) made by a person who is authorized by a religious organization or by law to perform the act certified;

(B) attesting that the person performed a marriage or similar ceremony or administered a sacrament; and

(C) purporting to have been issued at the time of the act or within a reasonable time after it.

(13) Family Records. A statement of fact about personal or family history contained in a family record, such as a Bible, genealogy, chart, engraving on a ring, inscription on a portrait, or engraving on an urn or burial marker.

(14) Records of Documents That Affect an Interest in Property. The record of a document that purports to establish or affect an interest in property if:

(A) the record is admitted to prove the content of the original recorded document, along with its signing and its delivery by each person who purports to have signed it;

(B) the record is kept in a public office; and

(C) a statute authorizes recording documents of that kind in that office.

(15) Statements in Documents That Affect an Interest in Property. A statement contained in a document that purports to establish or affect an interest in property if the matter stated was relevant to the document's purpose—unless later dealings with the property are inconsistent with the truth of the statement or the purport of the document.

(16) Statements in Ancient Documents. A statement in a document that was prepared before January 1, 1998, and whose authenticity is established.

(17) Market Reports and Similar Commercial Publications. Market quotations, lists, directories, or other compilations that are generally relied on by the public or by persons in particular occupations.

(18) Statements in Learned Treatises, Periodicals, or Pamphlets. A statement contained in a treatise, periodical, or pamphlet if:

(A) the statement is called to the attention of an expert witness on cross-examination or relied on by the expert on direct examination; and

(B) the publication is established as a reliable authority by the expert's admission or testimony, by another expert's testimony, or by judicial notice.

If admitted, the statement may be read into evidence but not received as an exhibit.

(19) Reputation Concerning Personal or Family History. A reputation among a person's family by blood, adoption, or marriage—or among a person's associates or in the community—concerning the person's birth, adoption, legitimacy, ancestry, marriage, divorce, death, relationship by blood, adoption, or marriage, or similar facts of personal or family history.

(20) Reputation Concerning Boundaries or General History. A reputation in a community—arising before the controversy—concerning boundaries of land in the community or customs that affect the land, or concerning general historical events important to that community, state, or nation.

(21) Reputation Concerning Character. A reputation among a person's associates or in the community concerning the person's character.

(22) Judgment of a Previous Conviction. Evidence of a final judgment of conviction if:

(A) the judgment was entered after a trial or guilty plea, but not a nolo contendere plea;

(B) the conviction was for a crime punishable by death or by imprisonment for more than a year;

(C) the evidence is admitted to prove any fact essential to the judgment; and

(D) when offered by the prosecutor in a criminal case for a purpose other than impeachment, the judgment was against the defendant.

The pendency of an appeal may be shown but does not affect admissibility.

(23) Judgments Involving Personal, Family, or General History, or a Boundary. A judgment that is admitted to prove a matter of personal, family, or general history, or boundaries, if the matter:

(A) was essential to the judgment; and

(B) could be proved by evidence of reputation.

(24) [Other Exceptions.] [Transferred to Rule 807.]

(Pub.L. 93–595, § 1, Jan. 2, 1975, 88 Stat. 1939; Pub.L. 94–149, § 1(11), Dec. 12, 1975, 89 Stat. 805; Mar. 2, 1987, eff. Oct. 1, 1987; Apr. 11, 1997, eff. Dec. 1, 1997; Apr. 17, 2000, eff. Dec. 1, 2000; Apr. 26, 2011, eff. Dec. 1, 2011; Apr. 16, 2013, eff. Dec. 1, 2013; Apr. 25, 2014, eff. Dec. 1, 2014; Apr. 27, 2017, eff. Dec. 1, 2017.)

Rule 804. Exceptions to the Rule Against Hearsay—When the Declarant Is Unavailable as a Witness

(a) Criteria for Being Unavailable. A declarant is considered to be unavailable as a witness if the declarant:

(1) is exempted from testifying about the subject matter of the declarant's statement because the court rules that a privilege applies;

(2) refuses to testify about the subject matter despite a court order to do so;

(3) testifies to not remembering the subject matter;

(4) cannot be present or testify at the trial or hearing because of death or a then-existing infirmity, physical illness, or mental illness; or

(5) is absent from the trial or hearing and the statement's proponent has not been able, by process or other reasonable means, to procure:

(A) the declarant's attendance, in the case of a hearsay exception under Rule 804(b)(1) or (6); or

(B) the declarant's attendance or testimony, in the case of a hearsay exception under Rule 804(b)(2), (3), or (4).

But this subdivision (a) does not apply if the statement's proponent procured or wrongfully caused the declarant's unavailability as a witness in order to prevent the declarant from attending or testifying.

(b) The Exceptions. The following are not excluded by the rule against hearsay if the declarant is unavailable as a witness:

(1) Former Testimony. Testimony that:

(A) was given as a witness at a trial, hearing, or lawful deposition, whether given during the current proceeding or a different one; and

(B) is now offered against a party who had—or, in a civil case, whose predecessor in interest had—an opportunity and similar motive to develop it by direct, cross-, or redirect examination.

(2) Statement Under the Belief of Imminent Death. In a prosecution for homicide or in a civil case, a statement that the declarant, while believing the declarant's death to be imminent, made about its cause or circumstances.

(3) Statement Against Interest. A statement that:

(A) a reasonable person in the declarant's position would have made only if the person believed it to be true because, when made, it was so contrary to the declarant's proprietary or pecuniary interest or had so great a tendency to invalidate the declarant's claim against someone else or to expose the declarant to civil or criminal liability; and

(B) is supported by corroborating circumstances that clearly indicate its trustworthiness, if it is offered in a criminal case as one that tends to expose the declarant to criminal liability.

(4) Statement of Personal or Family History. A statement about:

(A) the declarant's own birth, adoption, legitimacy, ancestry, marriage, divorce, relationship by blood, adoption, or marriage, or similar facts of personal or family history, even though the declarant had no way of acquiring personal knowledge about that fact; or

(B) another person concerning any of these facts, as well as death, if the declarant was related to the person by blood, adoption, or marriage or was so intimately associated with the person's family that the declarant's information is likely to be accurate.

(5) [Other Exceptions.] [Transferred to Rule 807.]

(6) Statement Offered Against a Party That Wrongfully Caused the Declarant's Unavailability. A statement offered against a party that wrongfully caused—or acquiesced in wrongfully causing—the declarant's unavailability as a witness, and did so intending that result.

(Pub.L. 93–595, § 1, Jan. 2, 1975, 88 Stat. 1942; Pub.L. 94–149, § 1(12), (13), Dec. 12, 1975, 89 Stat. 806; Mar. 2, 1987, eff. Oct. 1, 1987; Pub.L. 100–690, Title VII, § 7075(b), Nov. 18, 1988, 102 Stat. 4405; Apr. 11, 1997, eff. Dec. 1, 1997; Apr. 28, 2010, eff. Dec. 1, 2010; Apr. 26, 2011, eff. Dec. 1, 2011.)

Rule 805. Hearsay Within Hearsay

Hearsay within hearsay is not excluded by the rule against hearsay if each part of the combined statements conforms with an exception to the rule.

(Pub.L. 93–595, § 1, Jan. 2, 1975, 88 Stat. 1943; Apr. 26, 2011, eff. Dec. 1, 2011.)

Rule 806. Attacking and Supporting the Declarant's Credibility

When a hearsay statement—or a statement described in Rule 801(d)(2)(C), (D), or (E)—has been admitted in evidence, the declarant's credibility may be attacked, and then supported, by any evidence that would be admissible for those purposes if the declarant had testified as a witness. The court may admit evidence of the declarant's inconsistent statement or conduct, regardless of when it occurred or whether the declarant had an opportunity to explain or deny it. If the party against whom the statement was admitted calls the declarant as a witness, the party may examine the declarant on the statement as if on cross-examination.

(Pub.L. 93–595, § 1, Jan. 2, 1975, 88 Stat. 1943; Mar. 2, 1987, eff. Oct. 1, 1987; Apr. 11, 1997, eff. Dec. 1, 1997; Apr. 26, 2011, eff. Dec. 1, 2011.)

Rule 807. Residual Exception

(a) In General. Under the following conditions, a hearsay statement is not excluded by the rule against hearsay even if the statement is not admissible under a hearsay exception in Rule 803 or 804:

(1) the statement is supported by sufficient guarantees of trustworthiness—after considering the totality of circumstances under which it was made and evidence, if any, corroborating the statement; and

(2) it is more probative on the point for which it is offered than any other evidence that the proponent can obtain through reasonable efforts.

(b) Notice. The statement is admissible only if the proponent gives an adverse party reasonable notice of the intent to offer the statement—including its substance and the declarant's name—so that the party has a fair opportunity to meet it. The notice must be provided in writing before the trial or hearing—or in any form during the trial or hearing if the court, for good cause, excuses a lack of earlier notice.

(Added Apr. 11, 1997, eff. Dec. 1, 1997; Apr. 26, 2011, eff. Dec. 1, 2011; Apr. 25, 2019, eff. Dec. 1, 2019.)

ARTICLE IX. AUTHENTICATION AND IDENTIFICATION

Rule 901. Authenticating or Identifying Evidence

(a) In General. To satisfy the requirement of authenticating or identifying an item of evidence, the proponent must produce evidence sufficient to support a finding that the item is what the proponent claims it is.

(b) Examples. The following are examples only—not a complete list—of evidence that satisfies the requirement:

(1) Testimony of a Witness with Knowledge. Testimony that an item is what it is claimed to be.

(2) Nonexpert Opinion About Handwriting. A nonexpert's opinion that handwriting is genuine, based on a familiarity with it that was not acquired for the current litigation.

(3) Comparison by an Expert Witness or the Trier of Fact. A comparison with an authenticated specimen by an expert witness or the trier of fact.

(4) Distinctive Characteristics and the Like. The appearance, contents, substance, internal patterns, or other distinctive characteristics of the item, taken together with all the circumstances.

(5) Opinion About a Voice. An opinion identifying a person's voice—whether heard firsthand or through mechanical or electronic transmission or recording—based on hearing the voice at any time under circumstances that connect it with the alleged speaker.

(6) Evidence About a Telephone Conversation. For a telephone conversation, evidence that a call was made to the number assigned at the time to:

(A) a particular person, if circumstances, including self-identification, show that the person answering was the one called; or

(B) a particular business, if the call was made to a business and the call related to business reasonably transacted over the telephone.

(7) Evidence About Public Records. Evidence that:

(A) a document was recorded or filed in a public office as authorized by law; or

(B) a purported public record or statement is from the office where items of this kind are kept.

(8) Evidence About Ancient Documents or Data Compilations. For a document or data compilation, evidence that it:

(A) is in a condition that creates no suspicion about its authenticity;

(B) was in a place where, if authentic, it would likely be; and

(C) is at least 20 years old when offered.

(9) Evidence About a Process or System. Evidence describing a process or system and showing that it produces an accurate result.

(10) Methods Provided by a Statute or Rule. Any method of authentication or identification allowed by a federal statute or a rule prescribed by the Supreme Court.

(Pub.L. 93–595, § 1, Jan. 2, 1975, 88 Stat.1943; Apr. 26, 2011, eff. Dec. 1, 2011.)

Rule 902.   Evidence That Is Self-Authenticating

The following items of evidence are self-authenticating; they require no extrinsic evidence of authenticity in order to be admitted:

(1) Domestic Public Documents That Are Sealed and Signed. A document that bears:

(A) a seal purporting to be that of the United States; any state, district, commonwealth, territory, or insular possession of the United States; the former Panama Canal Zone; the Trust Territory of the Pacific Islands; a political subdivision of any of these entities; or a department, agency, or officer of any entity named above; and

(B) a signature purporting to be an execution or attestation.

(2) Domestic Public Documents That Are Not Sealed but Are Signed and Certified. A document that bears no seal if:

(A) it bears the signature of an officer or employee of an entity named in Rule 902(1)(A); and

(B) another public officer who has a seal and official duties within that same entity certifies under seal—or its equivalent—that the signer has the official capacity and that the signature is genuine.

(3) Foreign Public Documents. A document that purports to be signed or attested by a person who is authorized by a foreign country's law to do so. The document must be accompanied by a final certification that certifies the genuineness of the signature and official position of the signer or attester—or of any foreign official whose certificate of genuineness relates to the signature or attestation or is in a chain of certificates of genuineness relating to the signature or attestation. The certification may be made by a secretary of a United States embassy or legation; by a consul general, vice consul, or consular agent of the United States; or by a diplomatic or consular official of the foreign country assigned or accredited to the United States. If all parties have been given a reasonable opportunity to investigate the document's authenticity and accuracy, the court may, for good cause, either:

(A) order that it be treated as presumptively authentic without final certification; or

(B) allow it to be evidenced by an attested summary with or without final certification.

(4) Certified Copies of Public Records. A copy of an official record—or a copy of a document that was recorded or filed in a public office as authorized by law—if the copy is certified as correct by:

(A) the custodian or another person authorized to make the certification; or

(B) a certificate that complies with Rule 902(1), (2), or (3), a federal statute, or a rule prescribed by the Supreme Court.

(5) Official Publications. A book, pamphlet, or other publication purporting to be issued by a public authority.

(6) Newspapers and Periodicals. Printed material purporting to be a newspaper or periodical.

(7) Trade Inscriptions and the Like. An inscription, sign, tag, or label purporting to have been affixed in the course of business and indicating origin, ownership, or control.

(8) Acknowledged Documents. A document accompanied by a certificate of acknowledgment that is lawfully executed by a notary public or another officer who is authorized to take acknowledgments.

(9) Commercial Paper and Related Documents. Commercial paper, a signature on it, and related documents, to the extent allowed by general commercial law.

(10) Presumptions Under a Federal Statute. A signature, document, or anything else that a federal statute declares to be presumptively or prima facie genuine or authentic.

(11) Certified Domestic Records of a Regularly Conducted Activity. The original or a copy of a domestic record that meets the requirements of Rule 803(6)(A)–(C), as shown by a certification of the custodian or another qualified person that complies with a federal statute or a rule prescribed by the Supreme Court. Before the trial or hearing, the proponent must give an adverse party reasonable written notice of the intent to offer the record—and must make the record and certification available for inspection—so that the party has a fair opportunity to challenge them.

(12) Certified Foreign Records of a Regularly Conducted Activity. In a civil case, the original or a copy of a foreign record that meets the requirements of Rule 902(11), modified as follows: the certification, rather than complying with a federal statute or Supreme Court rule, must be signed in a manner that, if falsely made, would subject the maker to a criminal penalty in the country where the certification is signed. The proponent must also meet the notice requirements of Rule 902(11).

(13) Certified Records Generated by an Electronic Process or System. A record generated by an electronic process or system that produces an accurate result, as shown by a certification of a qualified person that complies with the certification requirements of Rule 902(11) or (12). The proponent must also meet the notice requirements of Rule 902(11).

(14) Certified Data Copied from an Electronic Device, Storage Medium, or File. Data copied from an electronic device, storage medium, or file, if authenticated by a process of digital identification, as shown by a certification of a qualified person that complies with the certification requirements of Rule 902(11) or (12). The proponent also must meet the notice requirements of Rule 902(11).

(Pub.L. 93–595, § 1, Jan. 2, 1975, 88 Stat. 1944; Mar. 2, 1987, eff. Oct. 1, 1987; Apr. 25, 1988, eff. Nov. 1, 1988; Apr. 17, 2000, eff. Dec. 1, 2000; Apr. 26, 2011, eff. Dec. 1, 2011; Apr. 27, 2017, eff. Dec. 1, 2017.)

Rule 903.   Subscribing Witness's Testimony

A subscribing witness's testimony is necessary to authenticate a writing only if required by the law of the jurisdiction that governs its validity.

(Pub.L. 93–595, § 1, Jan. 2, 1975, 88 Stat.1945; Apr. 26, 2011, eff. Dec. 1, 2011.)

ARTICLE X. CONTENTS OF WRITINGS, RECORDINGS, AND PHOTOGRAPHS

Rule 1001.   Definitions That Apply to This Article

In this article:

(a) A "writing" consists of letters, words, numbers, or their equivalent set down in any form.

(b) A "recording" consists of letters, words, numbers, or their equivalent recorded in any manner.

(c) A "photograph" means a photographic image or its equivalent stored in any form.

(d) An "original" of a writing or recording means the writing or recording itself or any counterpart intended to have the same effect by the person who executed or issued it. For electronically stored information, "original" means any printout—or other output readable by sight—if it accurately reflects the information. An "original" of a photograph includes the negative or a print from it.

(e) A "duplicate" means a counterpart produced by a mechanical, photographic, chemical, electronic, or other equivalent process or technique that accurately reproduces the original.

(Pub.L. 93–595, § 1, Jan. 2, 1975, 88 Stat. 1945; Apr. 26, 2011, eff. Dec. 1, 2011.)

Rule 1002.   Requirement of the Original

An original writing, recording, or photograph is required in order to prove its content unless these rules or a federal statute provides otherwise.

(Pub.L. 93–595, § 1, Jan. 2, 1975, 88 Stat. 1946; Apr. 26, 2011, eff. Dec. 1, 2011.)

Rule 1003.   Admissibility of Duplicates

A duplicate is admissible to the same extent as the original unless a genuine question is raised about the original's authenticity or the circumstances make it unfair to admit the duplicate.

(Pub.L. 93–595, § 1, Jan. 2, 1975, 88 Stat. 1946; Apr. 26, 2011, eff. Dec. 1, 2011.)

Rule 1004.   Admissibility of Other Evidence of Content

An original is not required and other evidence of the content of a writing, recording, or photograph is admissible if:

(a) all the originals are lost or destroyed, and not by the proponent acting in bad faith;

(b) an original cannot be obtained by any available judicial process;

(c) the party against whom the original would be offered had control of the original; was at that time put on notice, by pleadings or otherwise, that the original would be a subject of proof at the trial or hearing; and fails to produce it at the trial or hearing; or

(d) the writing, recording, or photograph is not closely related to a controlling issue.

(Pub.L. 93–595, § 1, Jan. 2, 1975, 88 Stat. 1946; Mar. 2, 1987, eff. Oct. 1, 1987; Apr. 26, 2011, eff. Dec. 1, 2011.)

Rule 1005.   Copies of Public Records to Prove Content

The proponent may use a copy to prove the content of an official record—or of a document that was recorded or filed in a public office as authorized by law—if these conditions are met: the record or document is otherwise admissible; and the copy is certified as correct in accordance with Rule 902(4) or is testified to be correct by a witness who has compared it with the original. If no such copy can be obtained by reasonable diligence, then the proponent may use other evidence to prove the content.

(Pub.L. 93–595, § 1, Jan. 2, 1975, 88 Stat. 1946; Apr. 26, 2011, eff. Dec. 1, 2011.)

Rule 1006.   Summaries to Prove Content

The proponent may use a summary, chart, or calculation to prove the content of voluminous writings, recordings, or photographs that cannot be conveniently examined in court. The proponent must make the originals or duplicates available for examination or copying, or both, by other parties at a reasonable time and place. And the court may order the proponent to produce them in court.

(Pub.L. 93–595, § 1, Jan. 2, 1975, 88 Stat. 1946; Apr. 26, 2011, eff. Dec. 1, 2011.)

Rule 1007.   Testimony or Statement of a Party to Prove Content

The proponent may prove the content of a writing, recording, or photograph by the testimony, deposition, or written statement of the party against whom the evidence is offered. The proponent need not account for the original.

(Pub.L. 93–595, § 1, Jan. 2, 1975, 88 Stat. 1947; Mar. 2, 1987, eff. Oct. 1, 1987; Apr. 26, 2011, eff. Dec. 1, 2011.)

Rule 1008.   Functions of the Court and Jury

Ordinarily, the court determines whether the proponent has fulfilled the factual conditions for admitting other evidence of the content of a writing, recording, or photograph under Rule 1004 or 1005. But in a jury trial, the jury determines—in accordance with Rule 104(b)—any issue about whether:

(a) an asserted writing, recording, or photograph ever existed;

(b) another one produced at the trial or hearing is the original; or

(c) other evidence of content accurately reflects the content.

(Pub.L. 93–595, § 1, Jan. 2, 1975, 88 Stat. 1947; Apr. 26, 2011, eff. Dec. 1, 2011.)

ARTICLE XI. MISCELLANEOUS RULES

Rule 1101.   Applicability of the Rules

(a) To Courts and Judges. These rules apply to proceedings before:

- United States district courts;

- United States bankruptcy and magistrate judges;

- United States courts of appeals;
- the United States Court of Federal Claims; and
- the district courts of Guam, the Virgin Islands, and the Northern Mariana Islands.

(b) To Cases and Proceedings. These rules apply in:

- civil cases and proceedings, including bankruptcy, admiralty, and maritime cases;
- criminal cases and proceedings; and
- contempt proceedings, except those in which the court may act summarily.

(c) Rules on Privilege. The rules on privilege apply to all stages of a case or proceeding.

(d) Exceptions. These rules—except for those on privilege—do not apply to the following:

(1) the court's determination, under Rule 104(a), on a preliminary question of fact governing admissibility;

(2) grand-jury proceedings; and

(3) miscellaneous proceedings such as:

- extradition or rendition;
- issuing an arrest warrant, criminal summons, or search warrant;
- a preliminary examination in a criminal case
- sentencing;
- granting or revoking probation or supervised release; and
- considering whether to release on bail or otherwise.

(e) Other Statutes and Rules. A federal statute or a rule prescribed by the Supreme Court may provide for admitting or excluding evidence independently from these rules.

(Pub.L. 93–595, § 1, Jan. 2, 1975, 88 Stat. 1947; Pub.L. 94–149, § 1(14), Dec. 12, 1975, 89 Stat. 806; Pub.L. 95–598, Title II, § 251, Nov. 6, 1978, 92 Stat. 2673; Pub.L. 97–164, Title I, § 142, Apr. 2, 1982, 96 Stat. 45; Mar. 2, 1987, eff. Oct. 1, 1987; Apr. 25, 1988, eff. Nov. 1, 1988; Pub.L. 100–690, Title VII, § 7075(c), Nov. 18, 1988, 102 Stat. 4405; Apr. 22, 1993, eff. Dec. 1, 1993; Apr. 26, 2011, eff. Dec. 1, 2011.)

Rule 1102.　　Amendments

These rules may be amended as provided in 28 U.S.C. § 2072.

(Pub.L. 93–595, § 1, Jan. 2, 1975, 88 Stat.1948; Apr. 30, 1991, eff. Dec. 1, 1991; Apr. 26, 2011, eff. Dec. 1, 2011.)

Rule 1103.　　Title

These rules may be cited as the Federal Rules of Evidence.

(Pub.L. 93–595, § 1, Jan. 2, 1975, 88 Stat.1948; Apr. 26, 2011, eff. Dec. 1, 2011.)